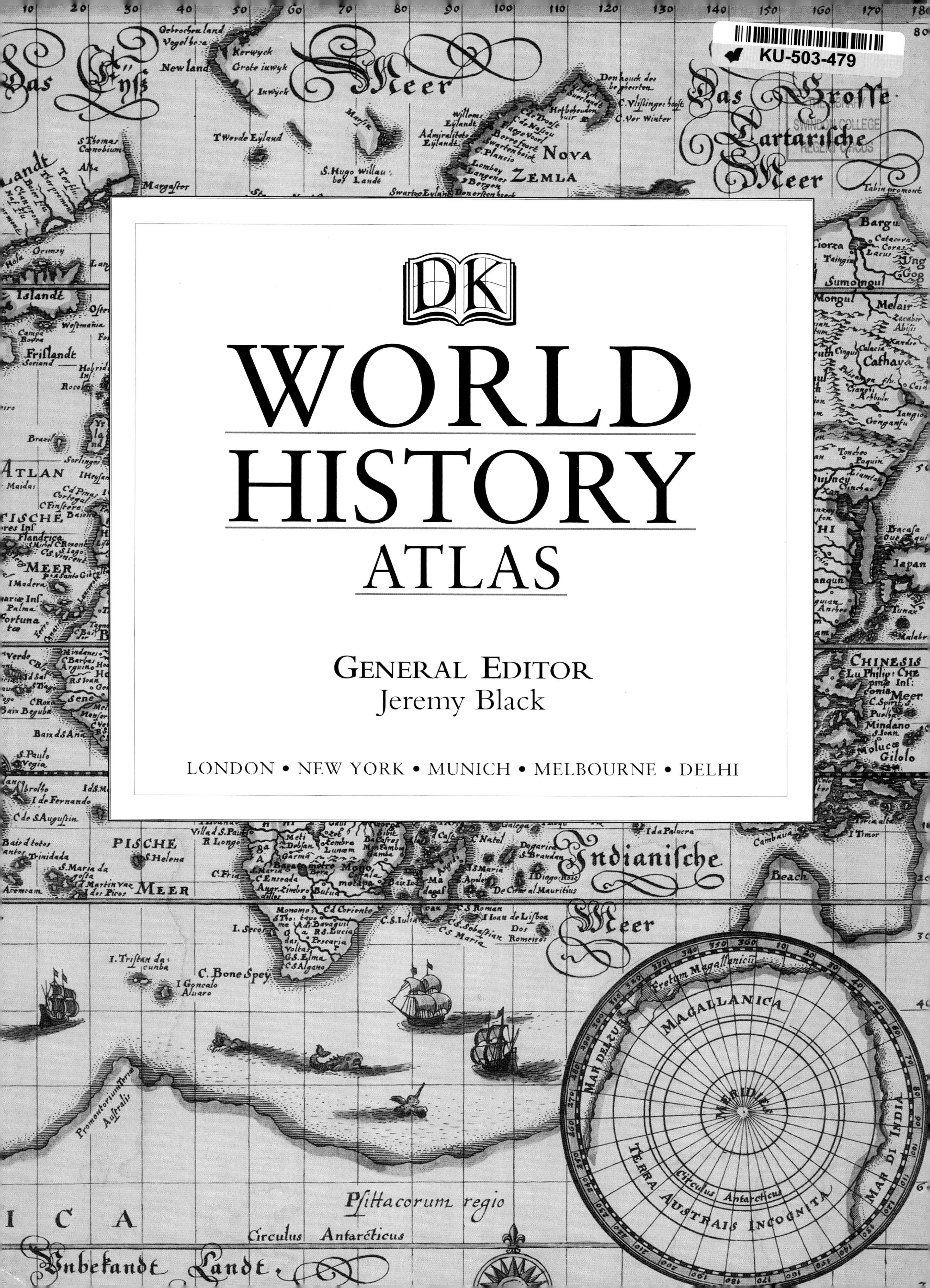

DK

WORLD HISTORY ATLAS

General Editor
Jeremy Black

LONDON • NEW YORK • MUNICH • MELBOURNE • DELHI

A DORLING KINDERSLEY BOOK

www.dk.com

CONSULTANTS

General Editor Professor Jeremy Black, Department of History, University of Exeter, UK

World History
Professor Jerry Bentley, Department of History, University of Hawaii, USA
Professor James Chambers, Department of History, Texas Christian University, USA
Dr John France, Department of History, University of Swansea, UK
Dr Guy Halsall, Department of History, Birkbeck College, London, UK
Dr Chris Scarre, Department of Archaeology, Cambridge University, UK
H. P. Willmott, Royal Military Academy, Sandhurst, UK

North America
Professor Donald S. Frazier, Department of History, McMurray University, Texas, USA
Professor Ross Hassig, Department of Anthropology, Oklahoma State University, USA
Dr Kendrick Oliver, Department of History, University of Southampton, UK
Professor George Raudzens, Department of History, Macquarie University, Sydney, Australia
Dr Brian Ward, Department of History, University of Florida, USA

South America
Dr Edwin F. Early, Department of Economics, University of Plymouth, UK
Dr Anthony McFarlane, Department of History, University of Warwick, UK
Dr Nicholas James, Cambridge, UK
Professor Neil Whitehead, Department of Anthropology, University of Wisconsin, USA

Africa
Professor John Thornton, Department of History, Millersville University, USA

Europe
Professor Richard Britnell, Department of History, University of Durham, UK
Dr Michael Broers, School of History, University of Leeds, UK
Professor Brian Davies, Department of History, University of Texas, San Antonio USA

Europe (continued)
Professor Michael Jones, Department of History, University of Nottingham, UK
Dr Don McRaild, Department of History, University of Sunderland
Dr Susan Rose, Department of History, Roehampton Institute, London, UK
Professor Peter Waldron, Department of History, University of Sunderland, UK
Dr Peter Wilson, Department of History, University of Sunderland, UK
Professor Spencer Tucker, Department of History, Virginia Military Institute, USA
Professor Edward M. Yates, Department of Geography, King's College, London, UK

West Asia
Dr Ahron Bregman, Webster University, Regent's College, London, UK
Professor Ian Netton, School of Arabic Studies, University of Leeds, UK
Sajjid Rizvi, Department of Oriental Studies, Cambridge University, UK

South and Southeast Asia
Professor Joseph E. Schwartzberg, Department of Geography, University of Minnesota, USA
Dr Sunil Kumar, Department of Medieval History, University of New Delhi, India

North and East Asia
Professor Gina Barnes, Department of East Asian Studies, University of Durham, UK

Australasia and Oceania
Dr Steven Roger Fischer, Institute of Polynesian Languages and Literatures, Auckland, New Zealand

The publishers would like to acknowledge additional contributions and advice from the following people: Professor Richard Overy, Professor Geoffrey Parker, Gordon Marsden, Professor Kenneth Kiple, Paul Keeler.

FOR THE SECOND EDITION

Editorial Direction Ailsa Heritage

Dr Paul Cornish, Centre for Defence Studies. King's College, London, UK
Dr Jane McIntosh
CIRCA Research and Reference Information, Cambridge, UK
Calum Macleod, Director, Great Britain - China Centre, London, UK

DORLING KINDERSLEY CARTOGRAPHY

Editor-in-Chief Andrew Heritage

Managing Editor Lisa Thomas

Senior Editor Ferdie McDonald

Project Editors Margaret Hynes, Elizabeth Wyse, Ailsa Heritage, Caroline Chapman, Debra Clapson, Wim Jenkins

Additional Editorial Assistance Louise Keane, Adele Rackley

Senior Managing Art Editor Philip Lord

Principal Designer Nicola Liddiard

Project Art Editors Rhonda Fisher, Carol Ann Davis, Karen Gregory

Cartographic Manager David Roberts

Senior Cartographic Editor Roger Bullen

Cartographic Design John Plumer

Digital Maps Created by Rob Stokes

Project Cartographers Pamela Alford, James Anderson, Dale Buckton, Tony Chambers, Jan Clark, Tom Coulson, Martin Darlison, Jeremy Hepworth, Chris Jackson, Julia Lunn, John Plumer, Alka Ranger, Ann Stephenson, Julie Turner, Peter Winfield

Additional Cartography Advanced Illustration Ltd., Arcadia Ltd., Lovell Johns Ltd.

Historical Cartographic Consultant András Bereznay

Picture Research Deborah Pownall, Louise Thomas, Anna Bedewell

Jacket Designer Bob Warner

Jacket Copywriter Adam Powley

Jacket Editor Mariza O'Keeffe

Indexing Julia Lynch, Janet Smy, Jo Russ, Sophie Park, Ruth Duxbury, Zoë Ellinson

Database Consultant Simon Lewis

Systems Manager Philip Rowles

Production Stuart Masheter

First published as the DK Atlas of World History in 1999 by Dorling Kindersley Limited, 80 Strand, London, WC2R 0RL

A Penguin Company

 A CIP catalogue record for this book is available from the British Library ISBN: 1-4053-0267-4

Printed and bound by Star Standard, Singapore.

Picture information: *p.1* Andreas Cellarius, rector of the Latin school at Hoorn in northern Holland, produced this map of the eastern hemisphere in 1708 as part of his exquisite atlas of the heavens, *Atlas Coelestis; seu Harmonia Macrocosmica*. The map illustrates the seasons of the year and the various climate zones from pole to pole. *pp.2–3* Produced in 1646, by Matthaüs Merian, a Swiss engraver. The geography in the map is based on world maps using the influential Mercator projection, produced by the Dutch Blaeu family, a dynasty of master cartographers. *p.5* This 1598 Dutch engraving shows a cartographer at work, probably Rogerius Bullenius.

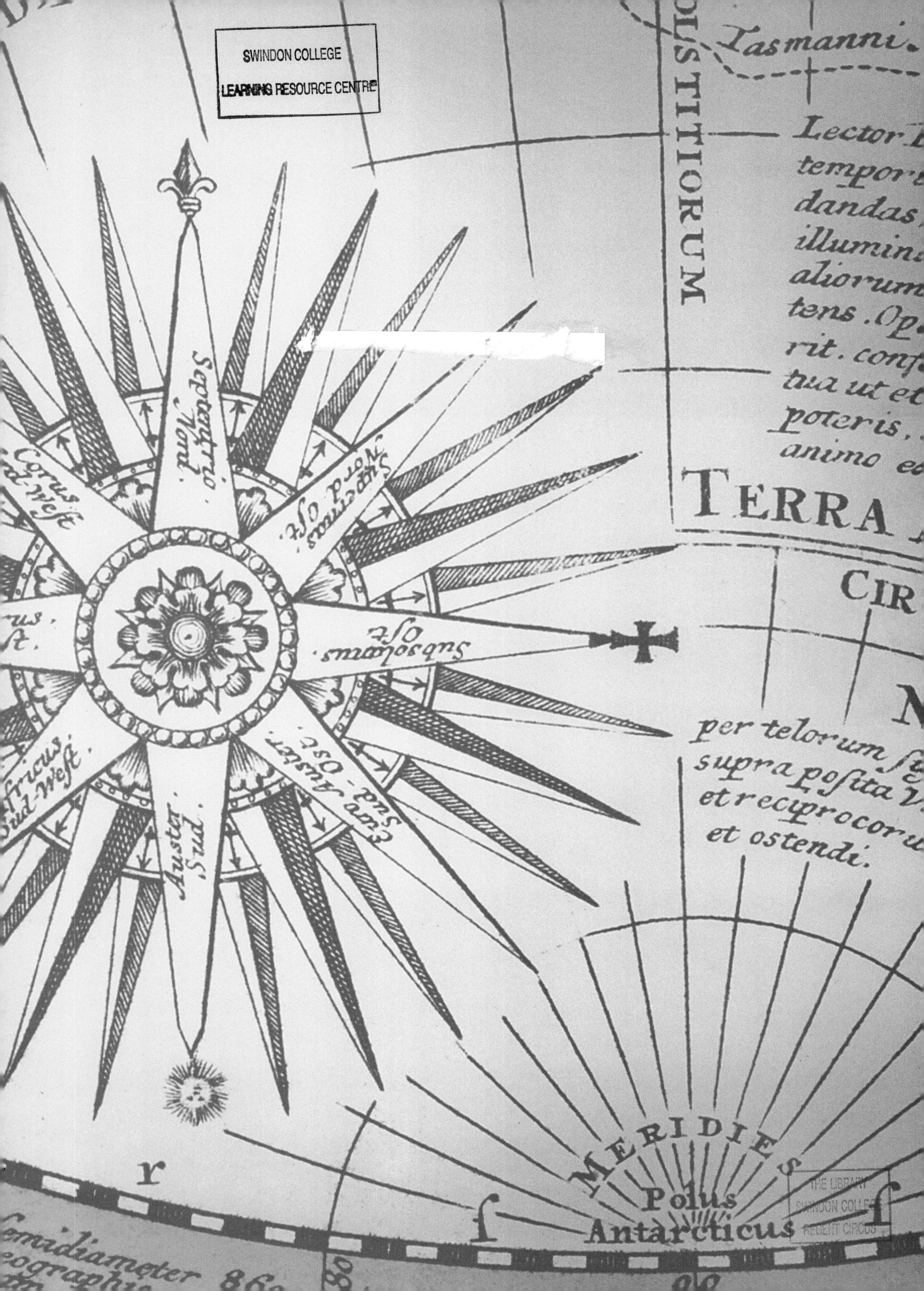
Tasmanni.
TERRA
CIR
per telorum
et ostendi.
Septentrio Nord
Subsolanus Ost
Auster Sud
MERIDIES
Polus
Antarcticus

WORLD HISTORY ATLAS

Das Eüsserste Mitternächtische
Theil Americæ Welches noch zur Zeit
Unbekandt.
AMERICA Von Christophoro
Columbo In Nahmen des Königs
In Castilien Erstlich Erfündē im
Jahr 1492, Und von Americo
Vesputio den Nahmen emp
fangen A°. 1499.
Mitternachtische
AMERICA
Circulus Arcticus
Anian Regnum
Quiuira Regnum
Fretum Davis
Canada
Terra de Labrador
Terra Corterealis
Totuna gay
Chilaga
Avanares
Albardos
Auacal
Capalschi
Calicuas
Apalchen
Norumbega
Nova Francia
Ter Noua
Sierra Nevada
California
Florida
Bermuda
Nort
Sinus Mexicanus
Nova His
Tropicus Cancri
Spaniola
See
Ladronen Insul
Mar del
Circulus Æquinoctialis
Zur
Insulæ Salomonis
Noua Guinea
Galapagos
Guiana
Amazones
Peru
Brasilia
Tropicus Capricorni
Chili
Rica
Rio de Plata
Das Stille Meer
Patagonum
Fretum Magalanicum
Terra del Fuego
Fretum le Marie
Staten landt
Magallan
Terra Australis Incognita
America Septentrionalis
Circulus Arcticus
Catha
Tartaria
Nova Zemla
Moscou
Europa
Groenlande
Frislant
Anglia
Terra Noua

INTRODUCTION

SINCE THIS ATLAS was first published in 1999, the world has become a very different place. The process of globalization, already well under way by the end of the last century, has met with violent reaction and resistance, which has changed the international geo-political landscape in an unprecedented manner.

This new edition of the DK *World History Atlas* offers a history of the world relevant to the new Millennium, as we look back to see where we have come from and how we have created our world. Unlike other works of this type, we have produced an atlas that will make sense for all parts of the world. To achieve this, we have combined a comprehensive global overview of world history in Part One, with more detailed narratives of the development of each of the world's regions in Part Two.

This is not the only unique feature of this atlas. Again, unlike most historical atlases, this is a work that puts maps first, not simply a book with maps. The maps have been created using the most modern techniques and accurate digital data, drawing on the established state-of-the-art skills of DK as innovative map publishers. In addition, the atlas includes numerous examples of historical maps, setting past views on the world in contrast with modern knowledge.

The atlas is structured so that readers can look at history from a number of different angles: global, thematic, regional, and chronological. This offers a rich variety of approaches which allows the reader to form a comprehensive picture of the past.

The inclusion of past maps, both European and non-European, is valuable, as it reminds us that there are, and have been, many different ways of describing the world. Ours is not the only way to consider space, place, and the world.

A range of devices has been used to relate the past world to our own: the distribution of sites and cultures, political borders and structures, areas of cultural influence and political control, with arrows indicating the movements of peoples and the spread of technologies and ideas. Frequently, explanatory annotations have been added to the maps. Beyond the maps themselves, each page offers texts, chronological timelines, and carefully chosen pictures to build up as complete an impression of each period or historical episode as possible.

Change through time is multi-faceted: political and economic, demographic and social, cultural and ecological. The DK *World History Atlas* attempts to cover all these features and, benefiting from a wide range of talent, it pushes forward the geography of the past as never before. It includes maps of familiar episodes from history and many more never previously described in cartographic form.

Mapping episodes through time demands dynamic narrative tools. The digital mapmaking techniques used in this atlas make it possible to offer exciting and informative perspectives and projections. The Earth can be seen from any viewpoint, creating explanatory yet accurate formats for the visualization of historical stories. The rigid orthodoxy of the north-oriented map is, after all, a relatively recent – and European – invention.

This atlas is produced with an awareness of the relationship between geography and history. It is up-to-date and of its time, not an atlas for all time, but the best possible for the new Millennium.

Since its first publication, foreign language editions of this atlas have appeared in Germany, Italy, Norway, Iceland, and Japan, and more are in preparation, significantly in many east and southeast European countries. We have received countless suggestions for adjustments and improvements from our co-publishers and from members of the public; all of these have been considered and, where possible, incorporated in this second edition. The publishers would like to thank all those responsible for such suggestions and contributions.

Jeremy Black, November 2004

CONTENTS

5 **Introduction**

6 **Contents**

10–113 PART ONE: ERAS OF WORLD HISTORY

12 **The Early History of Humanity to 30,000 BCE**
Map 1: Hominid ancestors
Map 2: The emergence of modern humans

14 **From Prehistory to 10,000 BCE**
Map: The World in 10,000 BCE

16 **The Settling of the Globe to 10,000 BCE**
Map 1: Different ways of life c.10,000 BCE
Map 2: Palaeolithic art
Map 3: Painted caves and rock art
Map 4: Venus figurines in Europe
Map 5: Australian rock art

18 **The World 10,000–5000 BCE**
Map: The World in 5000 BCE

20 **The Advent of Agriculture 10,500–4000 BCE**
Map 1: The development of pottery
Map 2: The spread of agriculture

22 **The World 5000–2500 BCE**
Map: The World in 2500 BCE

24 **Trade and the First Cities 5000–2500 BCE**
Map 1: Ur
Map 2: Urban centres and trade routes 3500–2000 BCE

26 **The World 2500–1250 BCE**
Map: The World in 1250 BCE

28 **The Growth of the City 3500–1250 BCE**
Map 1: Urbanism 1250 BCE
Map 2: Nippur
Map 3: Hattushash
Map 4: Zhengzhou
Map 5: El-Amarna

30 **The World 1250–750 BCE**
Map: The World in 750 BCE

32 **Writing, Counting, and Calendars 3400 BCE–1 CE**
Map 1: The evolution and spread of major scripts
Map 2: The evolution of numerical systems
Map 3: The evolution and spread of calendrical systems

34 **The World 750–500 BCE**
Map: The World in 500 BCE

36 **The Origins of Organized Religion 1500–500 BCE**
Map 1: The emergence of organized religion
Map 2: Religions of South Asia
Map 3: The Mediterranean cults
Map 4: Taoism and Confucianism

38 **The World 500–250 BCE**
Map: The World in 250 BCE

40 **The Empire of Alexander 336–200 BCE**
Map 1: The Empire of Alexander
Map 2: Hellenistic kingdoms 240 BCE
Cultural exchange between Greece and the Orient

42 **The World 250 BCE–1 CE**
Map: The World in 1 CE

44 **Trade in the Classical World 150 BCE–400 CE**
Map 1: Eurasian and African trade c.1 CE
Map 2: Reconstruction of Ptolemy's map of Classical Eurasia

46 **The World 1–250 CE**
Map: The World in 250 CE

48 **The Emergence of Global Religions 1–800 CE**
Map 1: The spread of Mithraism, Judaism, and Christianity by 600 CE
Map 2: The spread of Hinduism
Map 3: The spread of Buddhism to 400 CE
Map 4: Religions of the Old World after 400 CE

50 **The World 250–500**
Map: The World in 500

52 **Migrations and Invasions c.350–500**
Map 1: Migrations of peoples 300–500 CE
Map 2: Europe in 526

54 **The World 500–750**
Map: The World in 750

56 **The Impact of Islam c.622–1200 CE**
Map 1: The growth of the Islamic world
Map 2: The Islamic imprint c.800–1200
Map 3: Samarra

58 **The World 750–1000**
Map: The World in 1000

60 **Explorers of the Oceans c.200 BCE–1000 CE**
Map 1: The Viking world c.1000 CE
Map 2: Polynesian migrations
Map 3: The Indian Ocean c.1000 CE

62 **The World 1000–1200**
Map: The World in 1200

64 **The Age of the Crusades 1095–1300**
Map 1: Islam and Christianity c.1090
Map 2: The Crusades 1096–1270
Map 3: The Latin states in the Holy Land 1099–1229

66 **The World 1200–1300**
Map: The World in 1300

68 **The Age of the Mongols 1200–1350**
Map 1: Mongol campaigns 1206–94
Map 2: Eurasia and Africa c.1300
Mongol warfare

70 **The World 1300–1400**
Map: The World in 1400

72 **Trade and Biological Diffusion 700–1500**
Map 1: The spread of the Black Death
Map 2: Distribution of world population c.1400
Map 3: The diffusion of staple crops to c.1500

74 **The World 1400–1500**
Map: The World in 1500

76 **Global Knowledge c.1500**
Map 1: Global economies and technologies c.1500
Maps 2–7: Regional knowledge of the world c.1500
Maps 8–10: The emergence of the modern globe

78 **The World 1500–1600**
Map: The World in 1600

80 **The Age of European Expansion 1492–1600**
Map 1: Voyages of European expansion 1492–1597
Map 2: Biological exchanges
Map 3: The Spanish Empire in 1600
East meets West

82 **The World 1600–1700**
Map: The World in 1700

84 **Trading in Human Lives c.1400–1865**
Map 1: The world slave trade 1400–1860
Map 2: Piracy in the Caribbean in the 16th and 17th centuries

86 **The World 1700–1800**
Map: The World in 1800

88 **Empire and Revolution 1750–1868**
Map 1: The European empires and the first world wars
Map 2: Revolutions and rebellions 1768–1868
Map 3: The revolution in Haiti

90 **The World 1800–1850**
Map: The World in 1850

92 **The World's Economic Revolution 1848–1914**
Map 1: The impact of technology on the world trading system 1870–1914
Map 2: Major mineral finds of the late 19th century
Map 3: The Yukon and Klondike gold rushes
Map 4: The cotton towns of Yorkshire and Lancashire
Map 5: The politics of cotton

94 **The World 1850–1900**
Map: The World in 1900

96 **The Era of Western Imperialism 1879–1920**
Map 1: Imperialism in Africa 1880–1920
Map 2: The struggle for South Africa 1854–1910
Map 3: Imperialism in Southeast Asia
Map 4: Movements against colonial rule 1880–1920

98 **The World 1900–1925**
Map: The World in 1925

100 **Global Migration 1800–1920**
Map 1: World migration c.1860–1920
Map 2: The great Jewish migration 1880–1914
Map 3: The movement of indentured labour

102 **The World 1925–1950**
Map: The World in 1950

104 **The Second World War 1939–45**
Map 1: The Second World War, Sep 1939–Dec 1941
Map 2: The Second World War, Dec 1941–Jul 1943
Map 3: The Second World War, Jul 1943–Aug 1945
Map 4: Global warfare
Table of casualty figures

106 **The World 1950–1975**
Map: The World in 1975

108 **The Cold War 1945–1989**
Map 1: The alliances of the Cold War
Map 2: The Cuban missile crisis 1961–62
Map 3: The Cold War in Europe
Map 4: The Korean War 1950–53
Map 5: The Angolan Civil War from 1975
The arms race

110 **The Modern Age from 1975**
Map: The Modern World

112 **Hidden Worlds of Today**
Map 1: The greater African nation
Map 2: Devolution and statehood in Europe
Map 3: The pan-Islamic world
Map 4: The world of organized crime

114–287 PART TWO: REGIONAL HISTORY

116 **NORTH AMERICA**
Map: North America: 18,000 years ago

118 **North America: Exploration and Mapping**
Map 1: The first European explorers of North America
Map 2: Journeys into the North American interior 1600–1775
Map 3: 19th-century exploration and surveys of the US and Canada

120 **Early Peoples of North America to 400 CE**
Map 1: Subsistence and agriculture in early North America
Map 2: Early civilizations of Central America
Map 3: The heartland of the Olmecs
Map 4: Moundbuilders of eastern North America c.700 BCE–c.400 CE

122 **Cities and Empires 1–1500 CE**
Map 1: Major civilizations of Mexico
Map 2: The civilization of the Maya
Map 3: Peoples of the far North to 1500
Map 4: Cultures of the Southwest 600–1500
Map 5: Mississippian cultures of eastern North America

124 **Competing Empires 1200–1600**
Map 1: The expansion of the Aztec Empire in post-Classic Central America
Map 2: Aztec rule in the Valley of Mexico
Map 3: Tenochtitlan and satellite towns
Map 4: Spanish exploration and colonization in the New World 1492–c.1600
Map 5: Cortés' invasion and conquest of Mexico 1519–21

126 **From Colonization to Independence 1600–1783**
Map 1: The colonization of North America to 1750
Map 2: Anglo-French conflict 1754–1760
Map 3: The American Revolutionary War

128 **Building New Nations 1783–1890**
Map 1: The growth of the US 1783–1896
Map 2: North America 1783–1900: struggles for nationhood and the seizing of the West

130 **The American Civil War 1861–1865**
Map 1: 1820: the Missouri Compromise
Map 2: 1850: a new compromise
Map 3: 1854: the Kansas-Nebraska Act
Map 4: 1857: the Dred Scott decision
Map 5: North versus South: the state of the Union in 1861
Map 6: The Civil War to the fall of Vicksburg, Apr 1861–Jul 1863
Map 7: Grant's War: the Civil War Jul 1863–Apr 1865

132 **North America 1865–1920**
Map 1: Industrialization, urbanization, and immigration in the US and Canada 1860–1920
Map 2: Ethnic neighbourhoods in Manhattan c.1920
Map 3: The Mexican Revolution 1910–17
Map 4: US territorial expansion and imperialism 1860–1920
Map 5: US intervention in Cuba

134 **An Era of Boom and Bust 1914–1941**
Map 1: Major US industries c.1925
Map 2: The impact of the Great Depression 1933–34
Map 3: People on the move 1914–41
Map 4: The major Hollywood studios in 1919
Map 5: Presidential elections 1928–40 (5 maps)
Map 6: Racial intolerance 1914–41

136 **Societies in Transition 1941–1998**
Map 1: Average family income by region, 1949
Map 2: Postwar North America
Map 3: High-tech industry in Silicon Valley 1980
Map 4: Chicago: 1850–1969
Map 5: Ethnic distribution in South Central Los Angeles 1960–90 (4 maps)
Map 6: Protest movements and urban unrest of the 1960s

138 **The USA: Growth of a Superpower 1941–1998**
Map 1: Strategic alliances 1948–89
Map 2: US investment overseas
Map 3: The collapse of cotton-growing (2 maps)
Map 4: Presidential elections 1948, 1968, 2000 (3 maps)
Map 5: US intervention in Central America and the Caribbean

140 **SOUTH AMERICA**
Map: South America: 18,000 years ago

142 **South America: Exploration and Mapping**
Map 1: The first European explorers of South America
Map 2: South America 1750
Map 3: Scientific explorers

144 **Early Cultures of South America 12,000 BCE–10 CE**
Map 1: Settlement and agriculture in early South America
Map 2: Early settlement of Amazonia and eastern South America
Map 3: Chavín culture
Map 4: Coastal Peru c.600 BCE–600 CE

146 **The Empires of South America 250–1500**
Map 1: Empires of the Andean coast
Map 2: South America c.1500
Map 3: The Inca Empire 1525
The vertical economy of the Andes

148 **Colonial South America 1500–1800**
Map 1: Pizarro's conquest of the Inca Empire
Map 2: Spanish South America
Map 3: Portuguese South America
Map 4: Brazil and the Guianas c.1640
The search for El Dorado

150 **The Age of Independence c.1800–1930**
Map 1: The independence of South America 1810–30
Map 2: The dissolution of Great Colombia
Map 3: Political and economic development in South America 1830–1930
Map 4: The War of the Pacific

152 **Modern South America from 1930**
Map 1: Political change in South America from 1930
Map 2: The disputed territory of the Chaco 1887–1938
Map 3: Industry and resources
Map 4: Development and deforestation in Amazonia
Map 5: The narcotics trade

154 **AFRICA**
Map: Africa: 18,000 years ago

156 **Africa: Exploration and Mapping**
Map 1: Arabic views of the Niger basin
Map 2: Portuguese views of the Niger basin
Map 3: 14th- and 15th-century exploration
Map 4: 19th-century exploration
Map 5: Tracking the Nile

158 **The Early History of Africa 15,000–500 BCE**
Map 1: The development of agriculture and technology 10,000–500 BCE
Map 2: Pre-Dynastic Egypt c.5000–3000 BCE
Map 3: Old Kingdom Egypt c.2795–2180 BCE
Map 4: Middle Kingdom Egypt c.2134–1640 BCE
Map 5: New Kingdom Egypt c.1530–1070 BCE

160 **The Development of Complex Societies 500 BCE–500 CE**
Map 1: The development of complex societies
Map 2: States of North Africa
Map 3: Northeast Africa 100–600 CE (3 maps)

162 **The Impact of Islam in Africa 500–1600**
Map 1: African trade and the spread of Islam 500–1500
Map 2: Political entities and types of economic activity c.1350
Map 3: The ruins of Great Zimbabwe
Maps 4–7: Western Sudan c.1068–1530

164 **Early Modern Africa 1500–1800**
Map 1: Southern and East Africa c.1700
Map 2: States of West and Central Africa 1625
Map 3: The Horn of Africa 1500–1700
Map 4: The African slave trade c.1750

166 **The Colonization of Africa 1800–1910**
Map 1: Commercial and political Africa c.1830
Map 2: The Afrikaner treks and the Mfecane wars
Map 3: 19th-century West African *jihads*
Map 4: European penetration of Africa

168 **Post-Colonial Africa from 1955**
Map 1: The decolonization of Africa
Map 2: Industry in Africa 2004
Map 3: Debt as a percentage of GNP 2004
Map 4: Post-independence conflict and crisis
Map 5: Crisis in Central Africa

170 **EUROPE**
Map: Europe: 18,000 years ago

172 **Europe: Exploration and Mapping**
Map 1: Defining the boundaries of ancient Europe
Map 2: The Viking discovery of Iceland
Medieval mapping of Europe
The beginnings of modern cartography

174 **Prehistoric Europe 7000–1000 BCE**
Map 1: The introduction of farming 7000–5000 BCE
Map 2: Europe in the Copper Age 4500–2500 BCE
Map 3: Europe in the Bronze Age 2300–1500 BCE
Map 4: Mycenaean Greece c.1550–1150 BCE

176 The Mediterranean World 700–300 BCE
Map 1: The Mediterranean world 700–300 BCE
Map 2: The Athenian Empire 454–428 BCE
Map 3: The Peloponnesian War 431–404 BCE
Map 4: The city of Athens

178 The Rise of Rome 500–100 BCE
Map 1: Italy in 240 BCE
Map 2: The peoples of Italy in 500 BCE
Map 3: The First and Second Punic Wars 264–201 BCE
Map 4: Greece in 200 BCE
Map 5: Roman conquests to 120 BCE

180 The Roman Empire 1–400 CE
Map 1: The Roman Empire under Hadrian c.120 BCE
Map 2: Imperial Rome c.300 CE
Map 3: Supply routes to Rome
Map 4: The Roman Empire 240–395 CE

182 Europe After the Fall of Rome 400–775
Map 1: The inheritors of the Roman Empire at 500
Map 2: The new kingdoms at 600
Map 3: Britain c.750
Map 4: The struggle for Italy 565–750
Map 5: The kingdom of the Franks 486–537
Map 6: Division of the Frankish kingdoms 561

184 The Holy Roman Empire c.750–1000
Map 1: The advance of Islam to 750
Map 2: The empire of Charlemagne
Map 3: Europe c.800–1000

186 Europe in the Age of the Crusades c.1200–1400
Map 1: The crusading ideal in Europe 1100–1300
Map 2: The Norman conquest of England 1066–1095
Map 3: The 12th-century renaissance in Europe
Map 4: The possessions of Henry II, 1180
Map 5: The eastern Mediterranean c.1214

188 Europe in Crisis 1200–1400
Map 1: The Empire of Frederick II
Map 2: The British Isles 1200–1400
Map 3: The Baltic states 1100–1400
Map 4: Central and Southeast Europe 1200–1400

190 Trade in Medieval Europe c.1200–1400
Map 1: Trade in Europe c.1300 (inset of Italy)
Map 2: Paris c.1400
Map 3: Venice in the 14th century
Money and banking

192 The Emergence of Modern States 1400–1500
Map 1: The Hundred Years' War to 1400
Map 2: The Hundred Years' War after 1400
Map 3: The *Reconquista*
Map 4: Central Europe 1400–1500
Map 5: The growth of the Swiss Confederation

194 The Age of the Reformation 1500–1600
Map 1: The struggle for supremacy in Europe 1493–1551
Map 2: The religious map of Europe 1590
Map 3: The Baltic in the 16th century
Map 4: The Ottoman frontier in the 16th century
Map 5: The Dutch Revolt 1565–1609

196 Early Modern Europe 1600–1700
Map 1: The Treaty of Westphalia 1648
Map 2: Political consolidation and resistance in 17th-century Europe
Map 3: The Swedish Empire 1560–1721
Map 4: The Ottoman frontier 1683–1739
Map 5: France 1648–1715

198 The Age of Enlightenment 1700–1800
Map 1: Cities and economic life c.1750
Map 2: The partitions of Poland 1722–95
Map 3: The rise of Brandenburg Prussia
Map 4: The French Revolution 1789–95
The Enlightenment

200 Napoleonic Europe 1796–1815
Map 1: The campaigns of Napoleon 1794–1815
Map 2: The Empire of Napoleon by 1812
Map 3: Alliances in opposition to France 1792–1815

202 The Growth of Nationalism 1814–1913
Map 1: Europe after the Congress of Vienna 1815–52
Map 2: The independence of Belgium
Map 3: The unification of Germany
Map 4: Italy 1815–70
Map 5: The Balkans and the Black Sea to 1913

204 The Industrial Revolution 1750–1920
Map 1: The industrial revolution in Britain 1770–1870
Map 2: The growth of Manchester 1840–1900
Map 3: The Newcastle cholera epidemic of 1854
Map 4: The industrialization of Europe by 1914
Urbanization and public health

206 The First World War 1914–1918
Map 1: The balance of power in Europe 1879–1918
Map 2: The Western Front 1914–17
Map 3: The Western Front 1916–18
Map 4: The Eastern Front 1914–17
Map 5: The war in Southeast Europe and the Balkans
Map 6: The Italian Front 1915–18
Casualties of war

208 Europe Between the Wars 1917–1939
Map 1: Europe after the First World War
Map 2: The Russian Revolution, the Russian Civil War, and the formation of the Soviet Union 1917–24
Map 3: The Great Depression in Europe and the growth of political extremism
Map 4: The Spanish Civil War 1936–39
Map 5: Territorial expansion in Central Europe 1936–39

210 The Second World War in Europe 1939–1945
Map 1: Blitzkrieg in Europe 1939–42
Map 2: The Greater German Reich 1942
Map 3: The organization of persecution
Map 4: The Allied invasion of Europe 1942–45

212 The Division of Postwar Europe 1945–1960
Map 1: The partition of Germany and Austria
Map 2: The division of Berlin
Map 3: Displaced peoples in East and Central Europe
Map 4: Soviet expansionism 1949–59
Map 5: Marshal Aid and military alliances in Europe 1948–55

214 Modern Europe from 1957
Map 1: The growth of the European Union
Map 2: The collapse of Communism in Eastern Europe
Map 3: Conflict in former Yugoslavia 1990–99
Map 4: The legacy of the Soviet Union

216 WEST ASIA
Map: West Asia: 18,000 years ago

218 West Asia: Exploration and Mapping
Map 1: Greek and Roman expeditions
Map 2: The journeys of Ibn Battuta
Map 3: Medieval and Renaissance travellers
Map 4: European travellers in Arabia 1500–1950

220 From Village to Empire 10,000–1000 BCE
Map 1: Early farming in southwest Asia 8000–5000 BCE
Map 2: The first cities c.4300–2300 BCE
Map 3: Uruk
Map 4: The first empires c.2300–1750 BCE
Map 5: Southwest Asia 1650–1200 BCE

222 Early Empires of West Asia c.1000–500 BCE
Map 1: Palestine in the time of David c.1006–966 BCE
Map 2: The Assyrian and Babylonian empires c.950–539 BCE
Map 3: The spread of writing
Map 4: The Achaemenid Empire c.550–331 BCE
The history and legends of Mesopotamia

224 Greek and Roman Expansion 323 BCE–642 CE
Map 1: Alexander's successors from 301 BCE
Map 2: Wars between Parthia and Rome 53 BCE–217 CE
Map 3: Red Sea trade in the 1st century CE
Map 4: Jewish revolts 66–74 CE
Map 5: The Jewish world c.150 CE
Map 6: Sassanian Persia c.224–642 CE

226 The Advent of Islam c.600–1000
Map 1: The religions of West Asia c.600
Map 2: The Hegira 622
Map 3: The diffusion of Islam to 661
Map 4: The Abbasid Caliphate c.850
Map 5: The inner city of Baghdad c.800
Map 6: The fragmentation of the Caliphate c.900–1030
The Koran

228 Turkish and Mongol Invaders c.1000–1405
Map 1: The Seljuk Turks and the Byzantine Empire from c.1025
Map 2: Saladin and the Ayyubid Sultanate 1169–93
Map 3: The rise of the Mamluks and the Il-Khanate 1250–1300
Map 4: The dominions of Timur

230 The Ottoman Empire c.1300–1650
Map 1: The rise of the Ottoman Empire c.1300–1500
Map 2: Trade in the Indian Ocean in the 15th and 16th centuries
Map 3: The height of Ottoman power 1512–1639
Map 4: Safavid Persia 1501–1736

232 The Decline of the Ottomans 1800–1930
Map 1: The Ottoman Empire 1800–1913
Map 2: The First World War in Southwest Asia
Map 3: Southwest Asia after the First World War
Map 4: The formation of Saudi Arabia (2 maps)

234 Modern West Asia from 1945
Map 1: Oil production
Map 2: The Arab-Israeli wars 1947–82
Map 3: Migration 1947–96
Map 4: Islam in the modern world
Map 5: Conflict in the Gulf

236 SOUTH AND SOUTHEAST ASIA
Map: South and Southeast Asia: 18,000 years ago

238 **South and Southeast Asia: Exploration and Mapping**
Map 1: Travellers and explorers in South and Southeast Asia
Map 2: The scientific journeys of Alfred Wallace in Southeast Asia
The cosmographic tradition
Indigenous mapping of South and Southeast Asia
The Survey of India

240 **Early Civilizations of South Asia 5000 BCE–650 CE**
Map 1: The citadel at Mohenjo-Daro
Map 2: The development of Harappan culture, late 4th–early 2nd millennium BCE
Map 3: Bronze Age Southeast Asia from c.1500 BCE
Map 4: The Nanda and Mauryan Empires c.365–181 BCE
Map 5: Opposing forces in the Mahabharata War
Map 6: Areas influenced by India in Southeast Asia to 650 CE

242 **The Religions of Southern Asia c.900 BCE–c.1980 CE**
Map 1: The India of the Vedas
Map 2: The India of the Puranas
Map 3: The hearth of Buddhism and Jainism
Map 4: Religious change 8th–12th centuries
Map 5: The spread of Buddhism 5th–12th centuries
Map 6: The spread of Islam in Southeast Asia

244 **States and Empires 300–1525**
Map 1: Imperial Guptas and contemporary powers 300–550
Map 2: The medieval states of South Asia
Map 3: The Delhi Sultanate
Map 4: Vijayanagara, the Bahmani Kingdom, and successor states
Map 5: Southeast Asia 650–1250
Map 6: Southeast Asia 1250–1550

246 **Mughals, Marathas, Europeans 1526–1800**
Map 1: The Mughal Empire 1526–1707
Map 2: Maratha expansion 1708–1800
Map 3: European commerce with South Asia 16th–18th centuries
Map 4: Southeast Asian contacts with Europe c.1550–1800

248 **The Age of Colonial Expansion 1757–1914**
Map 1: South and Southeast Asia 1765
Map 2: British territorial expansion 1757–1914
Map 3: The Revolt of 1857–59
Map 4: The economy of India and Ceylon 1857

250 **The Colonial Apogee and Demise 1879–1989**
Map 1: The independence struggle 1879–1947
Map 2: The partition and reunification of Bengal 1905–12 (2 maps)
Map 3: The impact of the Second World War
Map 4: The decolonization of South and Southeast Asia
Map 5: The Vietnam War

252 **Modern South and Southeast Asia from 1947**
Map 1: The formation of contemporary South Asia 1947–2000
Map 2: Jammu and Kashmir
Map 3: The birth of Bangladesh
Map 4: Secessionist movements and regional cooperation
Map: 5 The urbanization of South and Southeast Asia

254 NORTH AND EAST ASIA
Map: North and East Asia: 18,000 years ago

256 **North and East Asia: Exploration and Mapping**
Map 1: Travellers in Central Asia 140 BCE–1295 CE
Map 2: European exploration of North and East Asia
Map 3: Exploring Asia's great mountains 1873–1929

258 **The First East Asian Civilizations to 200 BCE**
Map 1: The agricultural revolution 6000–2000 BCE
Map 2: Neolithic China c.4000–200 BCE
Map 3: Shang China 1800–1027 BCE
Map 4: Zhou China 1027–403 BCE
Map 5: Qin China 221–206 BCE

260 **The Han and the Great Migrations 21 BCE–c.600 CE**
Map 1: The Han Empire 140 BCE–220 CE
Map 2: The Three Kingdoms c.250 CE
Map 3: The later Sixteen Kingdoms period c.400 CE
Map 4: The Toba Wei c.440–500 CE
Map 5: China c.560 CE
Map 6: The steppe kingdoms of Central Asia

262 **Early Medieval East Asia 618–c.1300**
Map 1: Tang China and its neighbours c.750
Map 2: Chang'an
Map 3: The Five Dynasties 881–979
Map 4: Song China 960–1127
Map 5: The Southern Song 1127–1234
Map 6: The Mongol (Yuan) period c.1300

264 **The First States in Japan and Korea 300 BCE–1333 CE**
Map 1: State formation in Korea and Japan 100 BCE–650 CE
Map 2: The first empires c.300–900 CE
Map 3: Japan under the Nara Ritsuryo state
Map 4: The rise of Taira and the Bushi
Map 5: The age of the Shoguns

266 **East Asia and the Ming 1368–1600**
Map 1: China under the Ming c.1600
Map 2: Revolts under the Ming
Map 3: The Ming and the outside world
Map 4: The reunification of Japan
Map 5: The rise of Edo Japan

268 **The Era of the Qing Empire 1644–1914**
Map 1: Qing China 1644–1911
Map 2: Revolts under the Qing Empire
Map 3: Russian expansion in Asia 1600–1914
Map 4: Foreign imperialism in East Asia 1840–1910

270 **The Modernization of East Asia 1860–1936**
Map 1: Japanese modernization 1868–1918
Map 2: Japanese expansion 1868–1936
Map 3: The Sino-Japanese War 1894–95
Map 4: The Russo-Japanese War 1904–05
Map 5: The Chinese Revolution 1911
Map 6: The Chinese Civil War 1920–26 (3 maps)
Map 7: Nationalist China
Map 8: The Red Flag over Asia 1917–30

272 **The War in the Pacific 1937–1945**
Map 1: The Japanese offensive 1941–42
Map 2: The Allied counter-offensive 1942–45
Map 3: The bombardment of Japan 1945

274 **Communism and Capitalism in East Asia from 1945**
Map 1: The Communist Revolution in China
Map 2: Chinese economic development from 1950
Map 3: Chinese expansion from 1949
Map 4: The 'Tiger' economies from 1960
Map 5: Islam and nationalism in Central Asia

276 AUSTRALASIA AND OCEANIA
Map: Australasia and Oceania: 18,000 years ago

278 **Australasia and Oceania: Exploration and Mapping**
Map 1: Oceania: the major European voyages
Map 2: The exploration of Australia and New Guinea 1798–1928
Map 3: Europeans and Americans in the Pacific 1800–1850
Stick charts of the Marshall Islands

280 **Prehistoric Oceania 60,000 BCE–1000 CE**
Map 1: The settlement of Australia, Tasmania, and New Guinea
Map 2: Prehistoric New Guinea
Map 3: Austronesian and Polynesian migrations
Map 4: Rapa Nui (Easter Island)
The Dreamtime

282 **The Colonization of Australia from 1788**
Map 1: Early European impact in Australia
Map 2: Australian goldfields 1850–90
Map 3: Federal Australia from 1901
Map 4: New Zealand 1800–40
Map 5: The colonization of New Zealand 1830–75
The First Fleet and Botany Bay

284 **The Colonization of the Pacific from 1780**
Map 1: Imperialism in the Pacific
Map 2: The use and abuse of Pacific resources
Map 3: Decolonization and nationhood
Missionaries in the South Seas

286 **The Arctic and Antarctica: Exploration and Mapping**
Map 1: The search for new routes to Asia: explorers of the far north 1550–1820
Map 2: Charting the Arctic coast and the race to the North Pole
Map 3: Exploring the Antarctic

288 Key to the Maps

289 Subject Index and Glossary

319 Index-Gazetteer

350 Bibliography

352 Acknowledgments

CAVRVS·CHORVS·VEL·IAPIX·SIVE·ARGESTES
CIRCTVS
VEL·TRESIIAS
SEPTENTRIO
FAVONIVS·ZEPHIRVS
mare glaciale
EVROPA
DATIA
Pontus euxinus
Getulia
Deserta
libia
Armenia
LIBIA·INTERIOR
AFFRICA
ARABIA FELIX
Rubeu mare
Sinus hesperius
Circulus equinoctialis
Ethiopia
ETHIOPIA·INTERIOR
Terra incognita scdm ptholomeum
Sinus Barbaricus
Tropicus
9 10 15 20 25 30 35 40 45 50 55 60 65 70 75 80 85 90
AFRICVS·VEL·LIBS
LIBONOTVS·EVROAV·STER
AVSTER

PART ONE

ERAS OF WORLD HISTORY

GLOBAL CITIZENS at the beginning of the 3rd millennium are uniquely able to regard their world both as a totality and as a sum of its constituent parts. The first section of this Atlas presents history on a global basis, comprising a series of chronological overviews of the world across the last twenty millennia. These maps portray the changing map of the world and its cultures from ancient times down to the present day, accompanied by summaries of regional developments. Features highlighting the main technological advances of the period are complemented by maps or views of the world produced at the time. Each overview is followed by pages which examine aspects of the changing global scene – political, economic, religious, or demographic – which had a global impact during that period.

The Greek polymath, Ptolemy wrote his famous *Guide to Geography* in the 2nd century CE, and his conclusions about the map of the world held sway until the 16th century. This woodcut map of the Ptolemaic world – incorporating Africa, Europe, and Asia – was published in 1486.

THE EARLY HISTORY OF HUMANITY

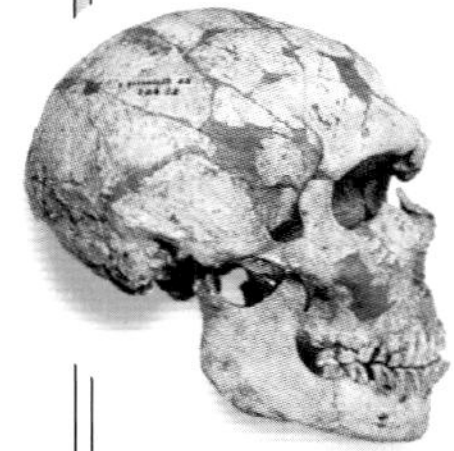

This skull comes from the Neanderthal burial site at La Ferrassie, southwest France.

THE AUSTRALOPITHECINES, OR SOUTHERN APES, which emerged in Africa c.4.5 million years ago, possessed many ape-like characteristics, but crucially had evolved the ability to walk upright. The best known of these species, *Australopithecus afarensis*, which is represented by the find of a skeleton of a small adult female, known as 'Lucy', from the Hadar region of Ethiopia, may be ancestral to the earliest species of *Homo* (man), which emerged some 2.5 million years ago. The increased brain capacity of *Homo* was matched by the ability to make tools and control fire, vital cultural developments which enabled human ancestors to exploit a wide range of foods and colonize marginal environments. Fully modern humans, distinguished by their refined tool-making skills, resourcefulness, and ingenuity, were able to withstand the fluctuating and harsh climates of the last Ice Age and reach the most remote corners of the globe.

Human ancestors

The genus *Australopithecus* inhabited eastern and southern Africa between 4.5 and 1.7 million years ago. Australopithecines were small and sturdy, with apelike bodies, but they had mastered bipedalism, as finds of fossilized footprints, 3.6 million years old, from Laetolil in Tanzania testify. Four major Australopithecine species, classified by variations in their skulls and teeth, have been identified. The earliest known fossils of the *Homo* genus date to 2.5 million years ago. They are distinguished by larger brain size, rounded skulls and a distinctively human formation to the hips and pelvis.

The virtually complete skeleton of a fully mature adult female, known as 'Lucy', found at Hadar in Ethiopia, is c.3.4 million years old and belongs to the *Australopithecus afarensis* species.

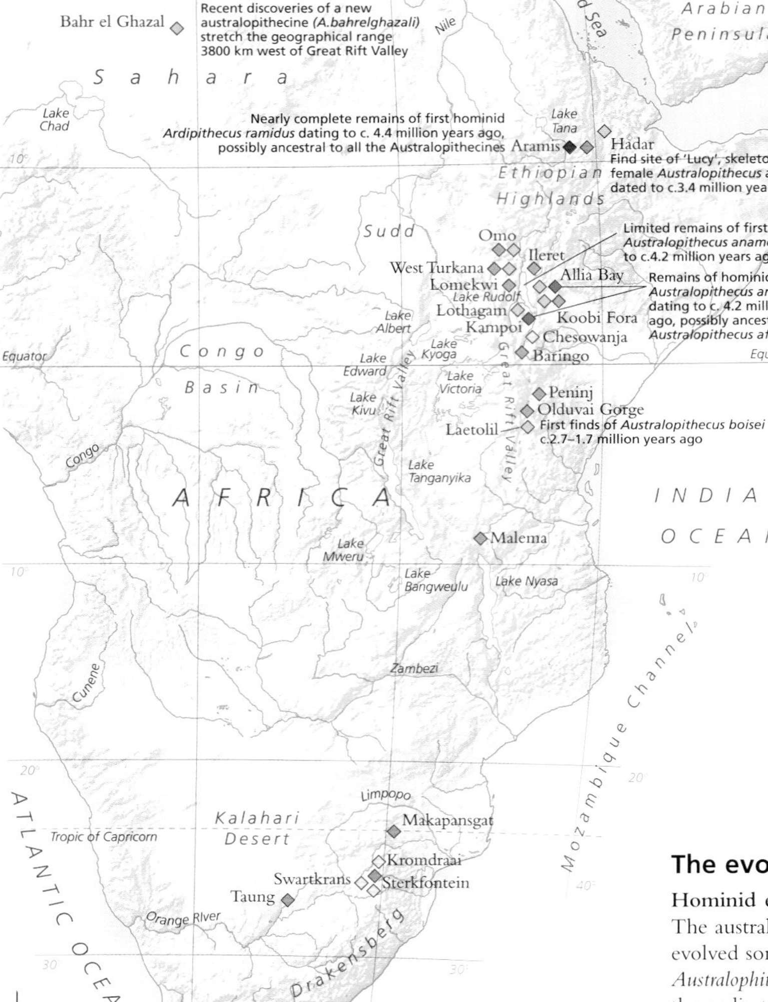
Bahr el Ghazal
Recent discoveries of a new australopithecine (A.bahrelghazali) stretch the geographical range 3800 km west of Great Rift Valley
Nile
Red Sea
Arabian Peninsula
Sahara
Lake Chad
Nearly complete remains of first hominid Ardipithecus ramidus dating to c. 4.4 million years ago, possibly ancestral to all the Australopithecines
Lake Tana
Aramis
Hadar
Find site of 'Lucy', skeleton of an adult female Australopithecus afarensis, dated to c.3.4 million years ago
Ethiopian Highlands
Sudd
Omo
Ileret
Limited remains of first hominid Australopithecus anamensis dating to c.4.2 million years ago
West Turkana
Allia Bay
Lomekwi
Lake Rudolf
Remains of hominid Australopithecus anamensis dating to c. 4.2 million years ago, possibly ancestral to Australopithecus afarensis
Lothagam
Kanapoi
Koobi Fora
Lake Albert
Chesowanja
Lake Kyoga
Baringo
Equator
Congo Basin
Lake Edward
Lake Victoria
Lake Kivu
Great Rift Valley
Peninj
Olduvai Gorge
Laetolil
First finds of Australopithecus boisei c.2.7–1.7 million years ago
Congo
Lake Tanganyika
AFRICA
INDIAN OCEAN
Malema
Lake Mweru
Lake Bangweulu
Lake Nyasa
Mozambique Channel
Zambezi
Cunene
Limpopo
Kalahari Desert
Makapansgat
Tropic of Capricorn
Kromdraai
Swartkrans
Sterkfontein
Taung
Orange River
Drakensberg
ATLANTIC OCEAN
500 km
500 miles
1 Hominid ancestors
Ardipithecus ramidus
Australopithecus remains
anamensis
afarensis
africanus
boisei
robustus
other

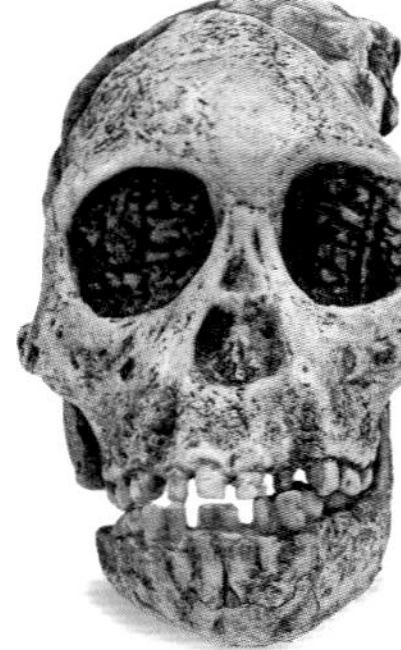

The skull of the 'Taung child', is c.2.5 million years old. It was discovered in 1924 and revolutionized theories about human evolution.

The evolution of hominids

Hominid evolution is still a matter of dispute. The australopithecines, the earliest hominids, evolved some 4.5 million years ago. *Australophithecus anamensis* may be ancestral to the earliest species of *Homo*, the precursors of modern humans, which evolved some 2.5 million years ago. Alternatively, *Homo* may have evolved separately.

Neanderthals

The Neanderthals, a separate and distinct branch of the *Homo* genus, evolved in Europe and West Asia about 120,000 years ago, surviving until up to 28,000 years ago. They had powerful heavy skeletons, with a projecting jaw, and broad nose and brow ridge, and their brains were the same size as those of fully modern humans. They adapted to a wide range of habitats and harsh climates. Neanderthal burials are clear evidence that they had developed cultural rituals.

The Neanderthal burial at Kebara in Israel is c.60,000 years old. The discovery of burials, often with items intended to equip the deceased for the afterlife, led to a revision of the view that Neanderthals were both brutal and primitive.

Prehistoric technology

A crucial development in the history of early technology was the appearance, about 1.3 million years ago, of stone handaxes, used for butchering hides, cutting wood, and preparing plant foods. Around 100,000 years ago, stone tools, shaped by striking flakes from the core, started to be made. Composite tools, where points, blades and scrapers were mounted in wooden or bone hafts, developed c.45,000 years ago.

Stone handaxes, such as these examples from Hoxne in eastern England dating to at least 100,000 years ago, were made by chipping away flakes to create a sharp, bifacial cutting edge. They became standard implements throughout Africa, Asia, and Europe.

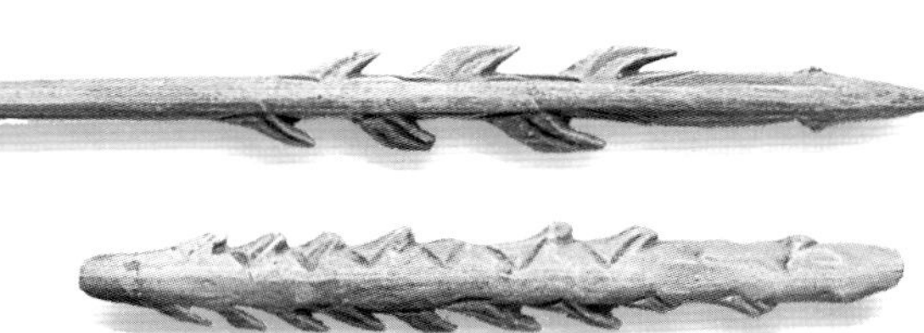

By around 30,000 years ago, tools and weapons had become infinitely more sophisticated, adapted both to the environment and methods of hunting, as demonstrated by the detailed carving and attention to function on these bone spearheads.

Human evolution

- **c.4.4 million years ago:** *Ardipithecus ramidus:* nearly complete skeleton found at Aramis, Ethiopia
- **c.4.2 million years ago:** *Australopithecus anamensis*: limited remains of bipedal hominid found on shores of Lake Rudolf
- **4,000,000 BP**
- **c.3.8 million years ago:** *Australopithecus afarensis*: based on find of "Lucy" skeleton at Hadar, Ethiopia. Average male height, 1.5 m
- **c.3 million years ago:** *Australopithecus africanus*: notable for powerful build of upper body
- **3,000,000 BP**
- **c.2.6 million years ago:** *Australopithecus boisei* with massive chewing muscles
- **c.2.5 million years ago:** *Homo habilis*: large brain in relation to body size; thought to be maker of first stone tools; average male height, 1.32 m
- **2,000,000 BP**
- **c.1.8 million years ago:** *Homo ergaster*: distinguished by long limbs; average male height, 1.77 m
- **c.1.6 million years ago:** Earliest evidence of hominids in Asia
- **c.1.3 million years ago:** First stone handaxes made
- **1,000,000 BP**
- **c.850,000 years ago:** Hominids reach Europe from Africa
- **c.800,000 years ago:** Archaic *Homo sapiens*; average male height, 1.75 m
- **c.500,000 years ago:** Earliest well-attested evidence of use of fire
- **c.150,000 years ago:** *Homo sapiens* (anatomically modern humans): earliest evidence in Africa
- **c.120,000 years ago:** Neanderthals: short-limbed, thick-bodied; average male height, 1.65 m. They disappear from Europe c.28,000 years ago
- **c.45,000 years ago:** First fully modern humans in Europe
- **present**

The emergence and spread of early humans

The first representative of the *Homo* genus, *Homo habilis* ('handy man'), emerged about 2.5 million years ago and was distinguished by the ability to make and use tools. *Homo ergaster*, which appeared about 1.8 million years ago, had a still larger brain capacity, tall, long-legged physique and ability to walk fully upright, and adapted successfully to a wide range of environments, rapidly spreading as far as East Asia, where it evolved into *Homo erectus*. The earliest fossil remains of fully modern humans, *Homo sapiens sapiens*, found in Africa, date to c.150,000 years ago. Resourceful and inventive, modern humans colonized the most marginal regions, and became the sole surviving human species.

Fossils of *Homo habilis* were discovered in the Olduvai Gorge in the 1960s, and are dated to 2.5 million years ago.

The fossils found at Koobi Fora in Kenya, dating to 1.7 million years ago, are amongst the earliest finds of *Homo ergaster*, and clearly demonstrate a marked increase in brain size.

Modern humans reached Europe from Africa c.45,000 years ago, and replaced the Neanderthal population by 28,000 years ago. This skull was found at the site of Predmostí in eastern Europe.

SEE ALSO:

North America: pp.120–121

South America: pp.142–143

Africa: pp.160–161

Europe: pp.174–175

West Asia: pp.220–221

South and Southeast Asia: pp.240–241

North and East Asia: pp.258–259

Australasia and Oceania: pp.278–279

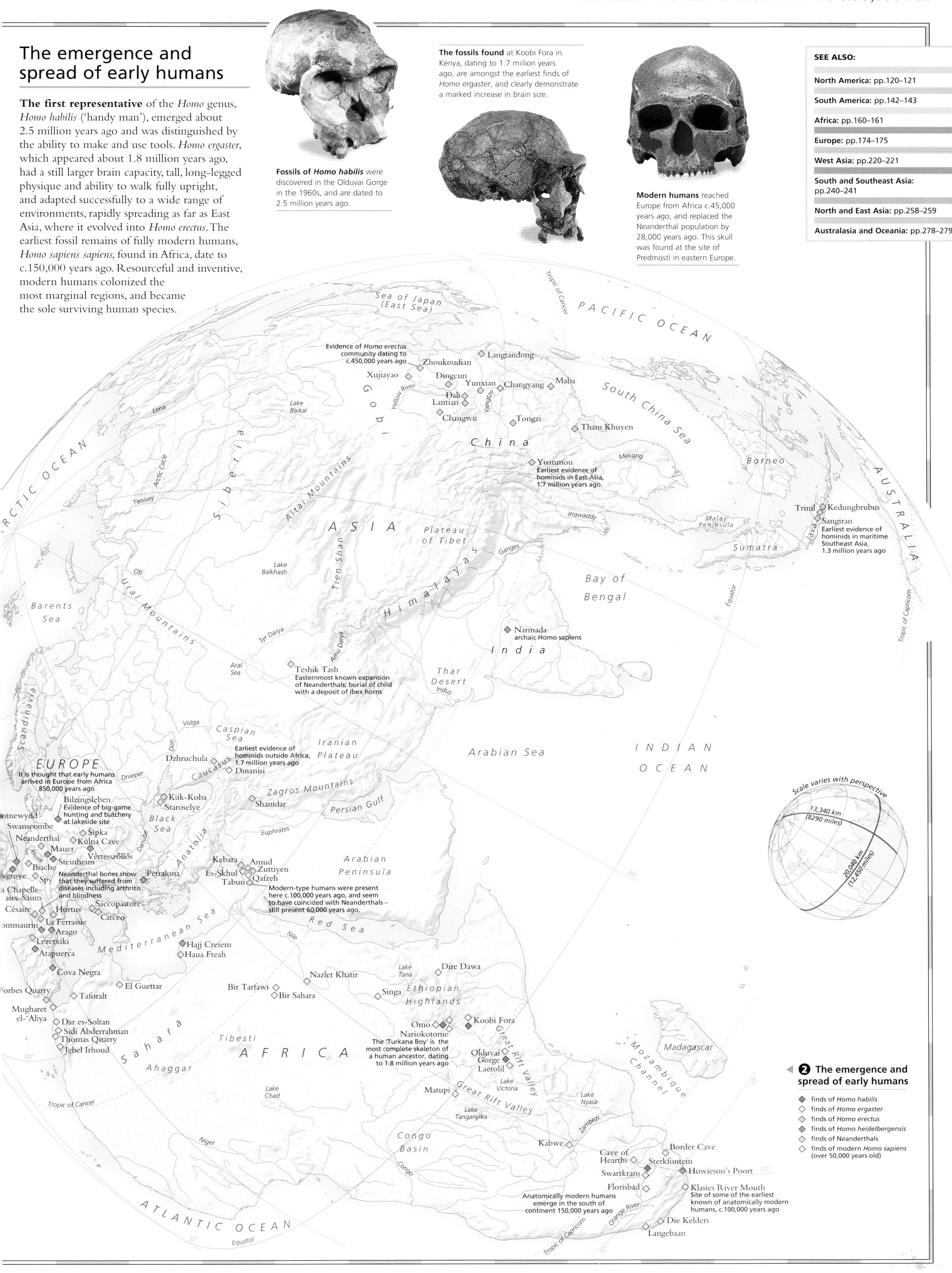

THE WORLD FROM PREHISTORY TO 10,000 BCE

FULLY MODERN HUMANS evolved in Africa between 200,000 and 100,000 years ago. With their tool-making skills and abilities to communicate and organize themselves into groups, these early hunter-gatherers were uniquely well-equipped to explore and settle new environments. By 30,000 years ago, they had colonized much of the globe. When the last Ice Age reached its peak, 20,000 years ago, they were able to adapt; they refined their tool technology, enabling them to fully exploit the depleted resources, and used sturdy shelters and warm clothing to survive the harsh conditions. As the temperatures rose and the ice sheets retreated, plants and animals became more abundant and new areas were settled. By 9000 BCE larger populations and intense hunting had contributed to the near-extinction of large mammals, such as mastodons and mammoths. By 8000 BCE in the Near East, groups of hunter-gatherers were living in permanent settlements, harvesting wild cereals and experimenting with the domestication of local animals and the transition to agriculture was under way.

HUNTER-GATHERERS AND THE ENVIRONMENT

Hunter-gatherers, whether semi-settled in one location or constantly on the move in search of food, would have carried a detailed mental map of important local landmarks. Precious water or food sources may have become centres of cultic activity, as in the rock painting below. Though its meaning is far from clear, the wavy vertical lines seem to represent cascades of water. The painting may even be a representation of a specific sacred site.

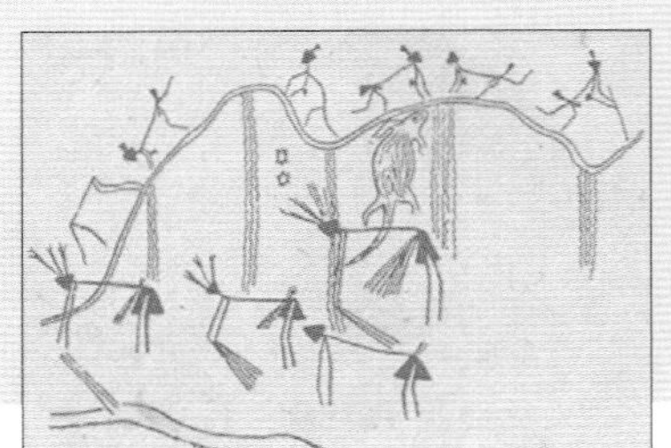

This painting, discovered at Kalhotia in central India, seems to show a lizard or crocodile, cascades, a stream, and people carrying bundles of stone-tipped arrows.

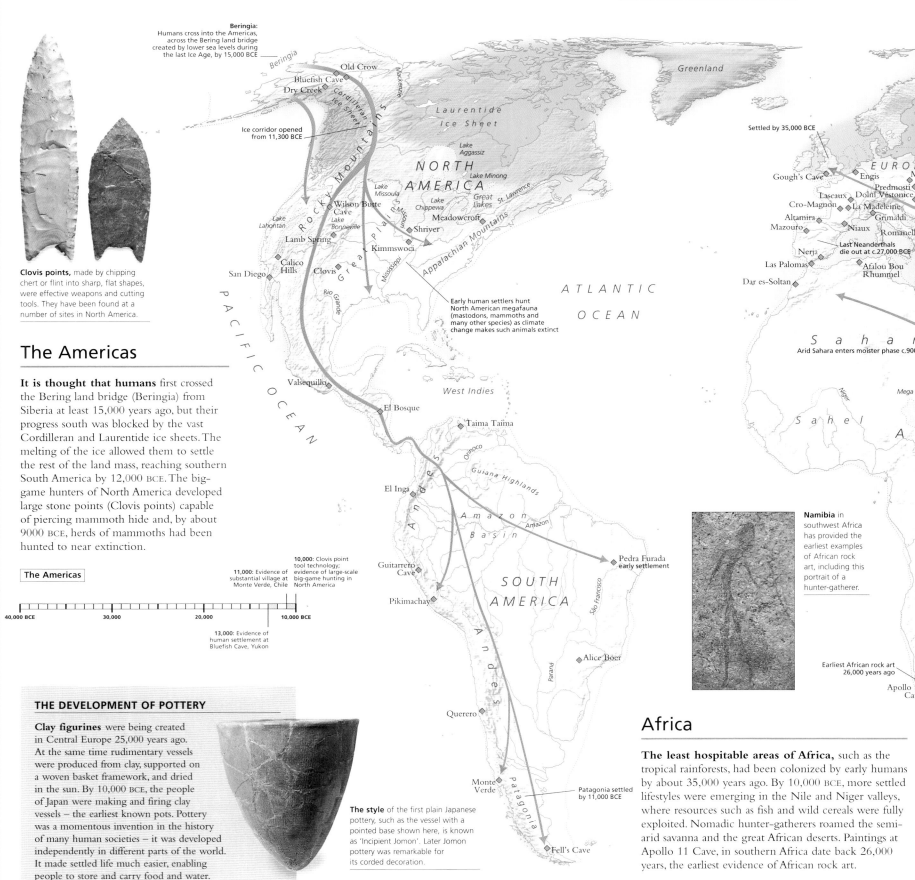

Clovis points, made by chipping chert or flint into sharp, flat shapes, were effective weapons and cutting tools. They have been found at a number of sites in North America.

Beringia: Humans cross into the Americas, across the Bering land bridge created by lower sea levels during the last Ice Age, by 15,000 BCE

Ice corridor opened from 11,300 BCE

Early human settlers hunt North American megafauna (mastodons, mammoths and many other species) as climate change makes such animals extinct

Settled by 35,000 BCE

Last Neanderthals die out at c.27,000 BCE

Arid Sahara enters moister phase c.9000

Patagonia settled by 11,000 BCE

Pedra Furada early settlement

Earliest African rock art 26,000 years ago

The Americas

It is thought that humans first crossed the Bering land bridge (Beringia) from Siberia at least 15,000 years ago, but their progress south was blocked by the vast Cordilleran and Laurentide ice sheets. The melting of the ice allowed them to settle the rest of the land mass, reaching southern South America by 12,000 BCE. The big-game hunters of North America developed large stone points (Clovis points) capable of piercing mammoth hide and, by about 9000 BCE, herds of mammoths had been hunted to near extinction.

The Americas

40,000 BCE — 30,000 — 20,000 — 10,000 BCE

13,000: Evidence of human settlement at Bluefish Cave, Yukon

11,000: Evidence of substantial village at Monte Verde, Chile

10,000: Clovis point tool technology; evidence of large-scale big-game hunting in North America

Namibia in southwest Africa has provided the earliest examples of African rock art, including this portrait of a hunter-gatherer.

THE DEVELOPMENT OF POTTERY

Clay figurines were being created in Central Europe 25,000 years ago. At the same time rudimentary vessels were produced from clay, supported on a woven basket framework, and dried in the sun. By 10,000 BCE, the people of Japan were making and firing clay vessels – the earliest known pots. Pottery was a momentous invention in the history of many human societies – it was developed independently in different parts of the world. It made settled life much easier, enabling people to store and carry food and water.

The style of the first plain Japanese pottery, such as the vessel with a pointed base shown here, is known as 'Incipient Jomon'. Later Jomon pottery was remarkable for its corded decoration.

Africa

The least hospitable areas of Africa, such as the tropical rainforests, had been colonized by early humans by about 35,000 years ago. By 10,000 BCE, more settled lifestyles were emerging in the Nile and Niger valleys, where resources such as fish and wild cereals were fully exploited. Nomadic hunter-gatherers roamed the semi-arid savanna and the great African deserts. Paintings at Apollo 11 Cave, in southern Africa date back 26,000 years, the earliest evidence of African rock art.

Portable art objects – sculptures and engravings of animals, like these chamois, on bone and antler, or small stone slabs or plaques – were being produced in Europe by 25,000 years ago.

Europe

Settled by modern humans by about 45,000 BCE, Ice Age conditions over much of Europe tested their ingenuity; wood, bone, hide, and antler were all used to build a range of shelters, and new tools – bows and arrows, spear-throwers, and harpoons – were used to hunt big game. As the climate stabilized, some sites were occupied year round, while others were used by seasonal hunters.

West Asia

The world's earliest known burial, at Qafzeh Cave in Israel, dates back 100,000 years and is evidence of human self-awareness and ritual activity. By 13,000 BCE people from Wadi en-Natuf, also in Israel, were intensively harvesting, grinding, and storing the abundant wild grains which grew there. The same people also hunted gazelle herds, using drive lanes leading to traps.

This bone and shell necklace was one of the personal items found at a burial in Mugharet el-Kebara in Israel.

SEE ALSO:

North America: pp.118–119

South America: pp.144–145

Africa: pp.158–159

Europe: pp.174–175

West Asia: pp.220–221

South and Southeast Asia: pp.240–241

North and East Asia: pp.258–259

Australasia and Oceania: pp.280–281

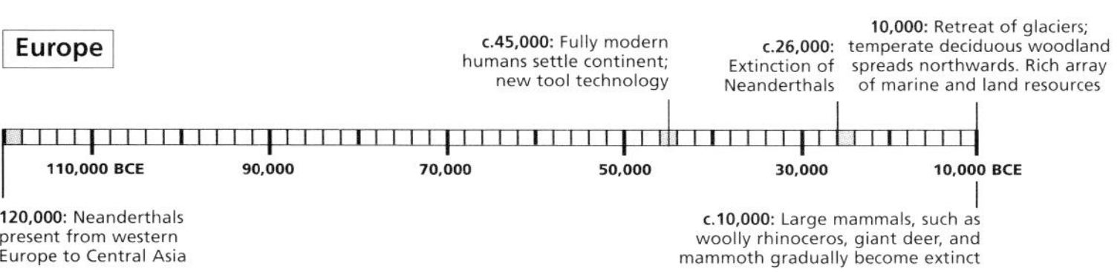

Europe
120,000: Neanderthals present from western Europe to Central Asia
c.45,000: Fully modern humans settle continent; new tool technology
c.26,000: Extinction of Neanderthals
10,000: Retreat of glaciers; temperate deciduous woodland spreads northwards. Rich array of marine and land resources
c.10,000: Large mammals, such as woolly rhinoceros, giant deer, and mammoth gradually become extinct
110,000 BCE
90,000
70,000
50,000
30,000
10,000 BCE

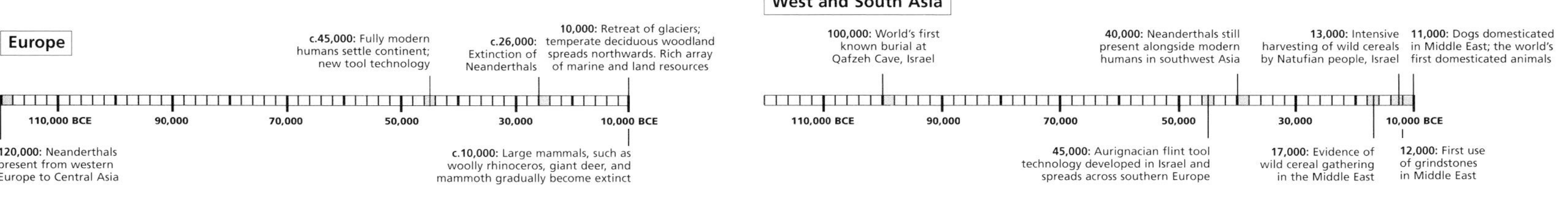

West and South Asia
100,000: World's first known burial at Qafzeh Cave, Israel
40,000: Neanderthals still present alongside modern humans in southwest Asia
13,000: Intensive harvesting of wild cereals by Natufian people, Israel
11,000: Dogs domesticated in Middle East; the world's first domesticated animals
45,000: Aurignacian flint tool technology developed in Israel and spreads across southern Europe
17,000: Evidence of wild cereal gathering in the Middle East
12,000: First use of grindstones in Middle East
110,000 BCE
90,000
70,000
50,000
30,000
10,000 BCE

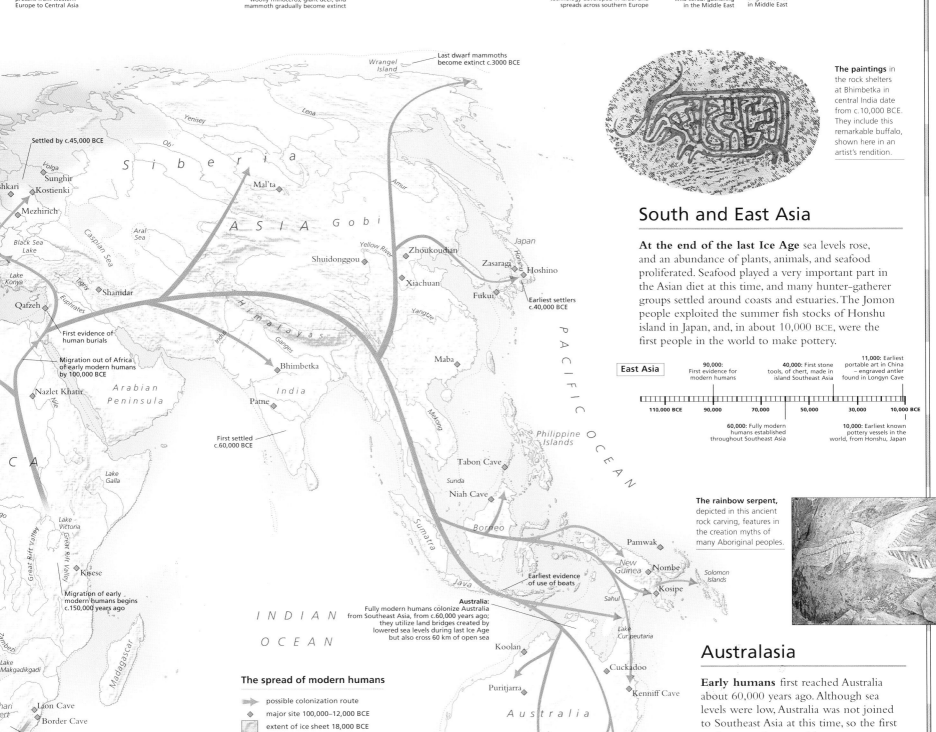

Wrangel Island — Last dwarf mammoths become extinct c.3000 BCE

Settled by c.45,000 BCE

First evidence of human burials

Migration out of Africa of early modern humans by 100,000 BCE

First settled c.60,000 BCE

Earliest settlers c.40,000 BCE

Migration of early modern humans begins c.150,000 years ago

Earliest evidence of use of boats

Australia: Fully modern humans colonize Australia from Southeast Asia, from c.60,000 years ago; they utilize land bridges created by lowered sea levels during last Ice Age but also cross 60 km of open sea

Southern Africa: From c.120,000 years ago, early hominids colonize more marginal areas of Africa

Earliest evidence of human cremation c.26,000 BCE

The spread of modern humans

- possible colonization route
- major site 100,000–12,000 BCE
- extent of ice sheet 18,000 BCE
- extent of ice sheet 10,000 BCE
- coastline 18,000 BCE
- ancient river
- ancient lake

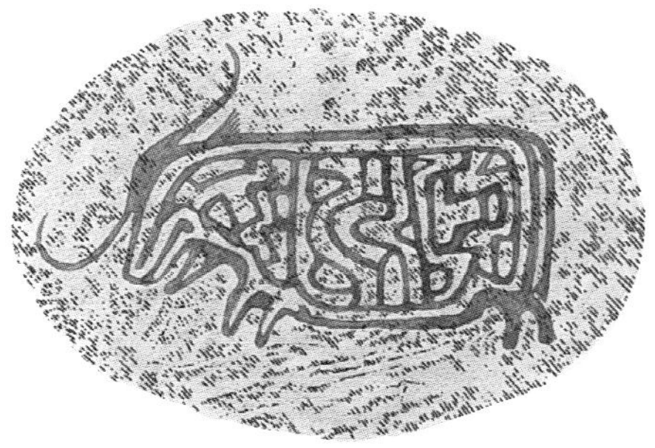

The paintings in the rock shelters at Bhimbetka in central India date from c.10,000 BCE. They include this remarkable buffalo, shown here in an artist's rendition.

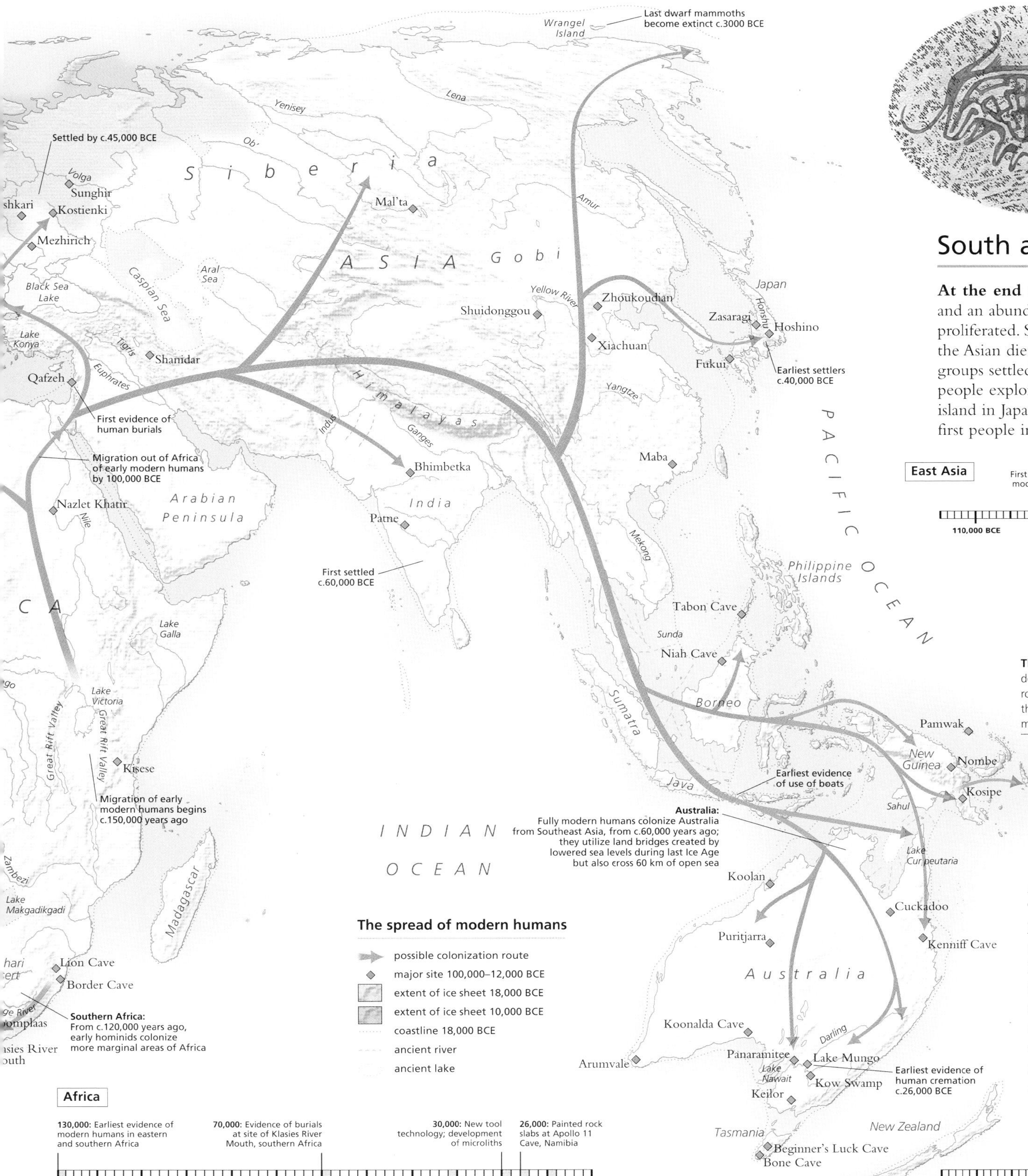

South and East Asia

At the end of the last Ice Age sea levels rose, and an abundance of plants, animals, and seafood proliferated. Seafood played a very important part in the Asian diet at this time, and many hunter-gatherer groups settled around coasts and estuaries. The Jomon people exploited the summer fish stocks of Honshu island in Japan, and, in about 10,000 BCE, were the first people in the world to make pottery.

East Asia

- **90,000:** First evidence for modern humans
- **60,000:** Fully modern humans established throughout Southeast Asia
- **40,000:** First stone tools, of chert, made in island Southeast Asia
- **11,000:** Earliest portable art in China – engraved antler found in Longyin Cave
- **10,000:** Earliest known pottery vessels in the world, from Honshu, Japan

The rainbow serpent, depicted in this ancient rock carving, features in the creation myths of many Aboriginal peoples.

Australasia

Early humans first reached Australia about 60,000 years ago. Although sea levels were low, Australia was not joined to Southeast Asia at this time, so the first settlers must have used boats to cross 60 km of open sea. Early sites were clustered along the coasts and rivers but rising sea levels at the end of the last Ice Age forced settlers inland.

Africa

- **130,000:** Earliest evidence of modern humans in eastern and southern Africa
- **70,000:** Evidence of burials at site of Klasies River Mouth, southern Africa
- **42,000:** Red ochre being mined from Lion Cave, southern Africa; probably used for body decoration
- **30,000:** New tool technology; development of microliths
- **26,000:** Painted rock slabs at Apollo 11 Cave, Namibia
- **20,000:** Terracotta figurines from Algeria. Engraved objects from Border Cave, South Africa

Australasia

- **60,000:** Settlement of Australia by groups from Southeast Asia
- **45,000:** World's first known rock art, from Panaramitee, South Australia
- **20,000:** Settlement extends to southern coast of Tasmania
- **16,000:** Extinction of giant marsupials caused by changing climate

THE SETTLING OF THE GLOBE

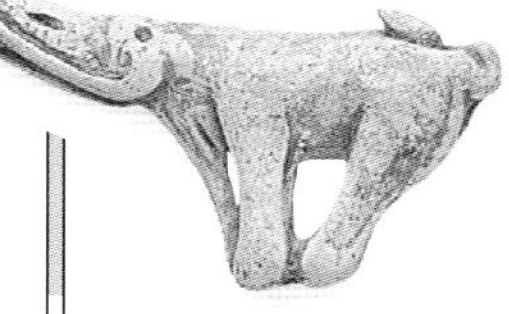

This figure of a mammoth, carved from an animal's shoulder bone, dates from the last Ice Age.

MANY INNOVATIONS, such as sewn clothing, efficient housing, and a range of well-designed tools enabled modern humans to adapt to a diversity of environments and colonize new areas. The melting of the glaciers at the end of the last Ice Age radically transformed the global environment; as the climate changed, with warmer temperatures and increased rainfall, food sources became more abundant and diverse, and populations increased. In many regions, people began to live together in larger, more sedentary communities, working co-operatively and evolving more specialized roles within the group. Rituals and symbols were used to reinforce group identity – the beginnings of truly modern behaviour.

Survival strategies

The challenging environments of the Ice Age and the rapidly changing conditions of the early postglacial world required a wide range of adaptations. In some regions, such as eastern Europe and North America, plentiful supplies of big game meant that hunters could depend on a specialized diet of mammoth, mastodon, or bison. In other regions, such as the fertile river valleys of the Middle East and East Asia, wild cereals – the ancestors of cultivated grains – were harvested. In Europe, a varied diet encompassed game, edible plants, and fish and shellfish, evidenced by deposits of discarded shells, or middens. The building of shelters was influenced by climate and local resources. Some shelters were portable, used by hunters following migrating herds; in other areas plentiful food supplies allowed year-round occupation.

Early peoples

40,000 BP – 30,000 – 20,000 – 10,000 BP

- **35,000:** Microliths developed as weapons in Africa
- **27,000:** Coldest phase of last Ice Age begins
- **26,000:** First known cremation, at Lake Mungo, Australia
- **20,000:** Peak of last Ice Age
- **19,000:** Wild cereals harvested from shores of Lake Galilee
- **16,000:** Climate starts to improve
- **12,000:** Grindstones in Fertile Crescent, to crush harvested seeds for flour
- **12,000:** Mammoth and woolly rhinoceros extinct in Eurasia

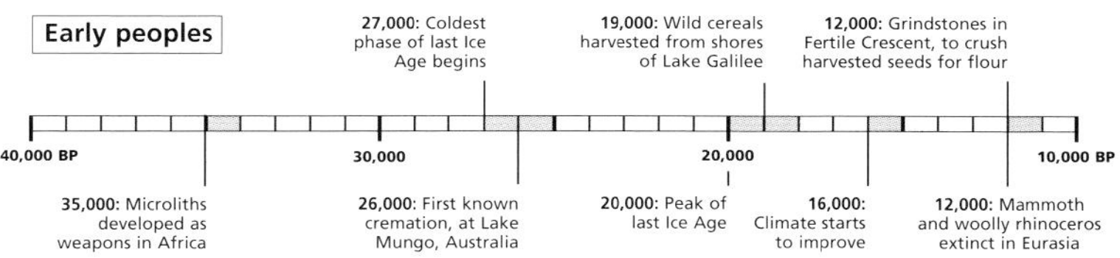

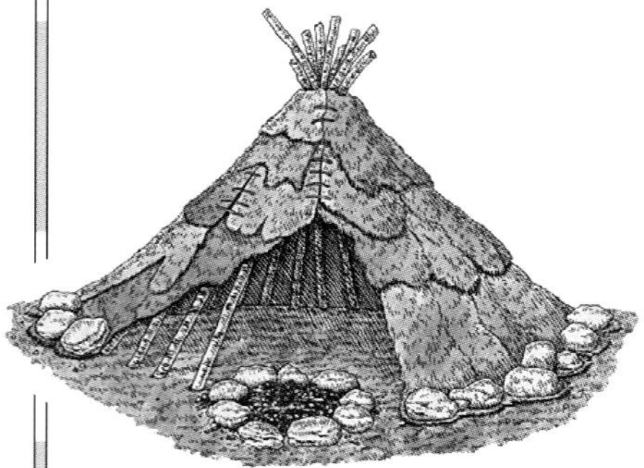

France

At Pincevent, in the Seine valley, hunters following migrating reindeer herds around 14,000 BCE camped from midsummer to midwinter in portable tents, made of wooden poles covered by animal skins.

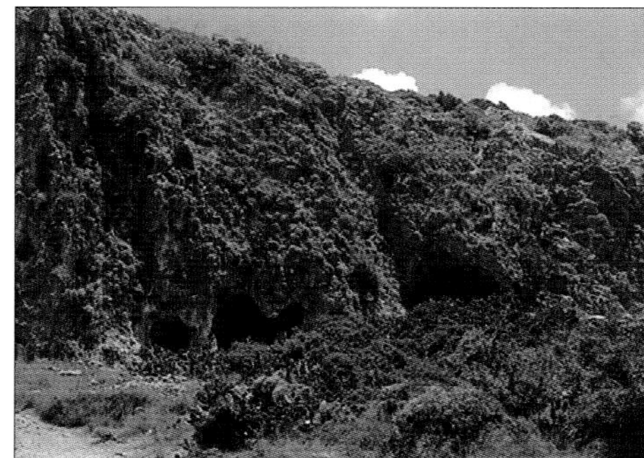

Israel

The El Wad cave on the eastern Mediterranean coast was used as a shelter by hunters stalking fallow deer in the nearby hills. The site may have been used during the summer months. The cave has been occupied many times in the past 100,000 years.

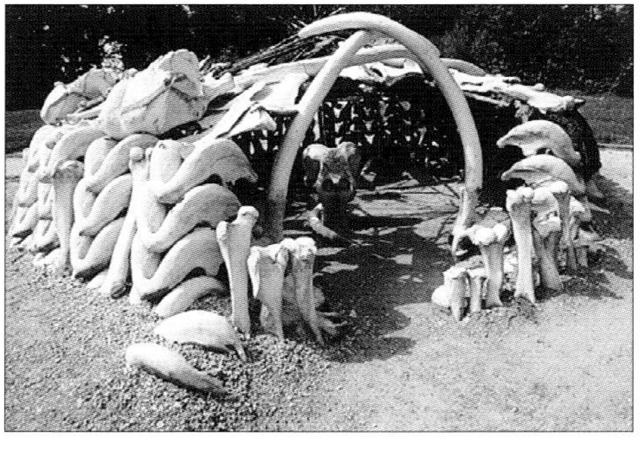

Ukraine

On the treeless, windswept steppes of the Ukraine, Ice Age mammoth-hunters, lacking wood, used the remains of their prey to build shelters. They constructed the walls from mammoth bones, which were then covered with animal hides, anchored down in high winds by heavy mammoth jawbones.

1 Different ways of life c.10,000 BCE

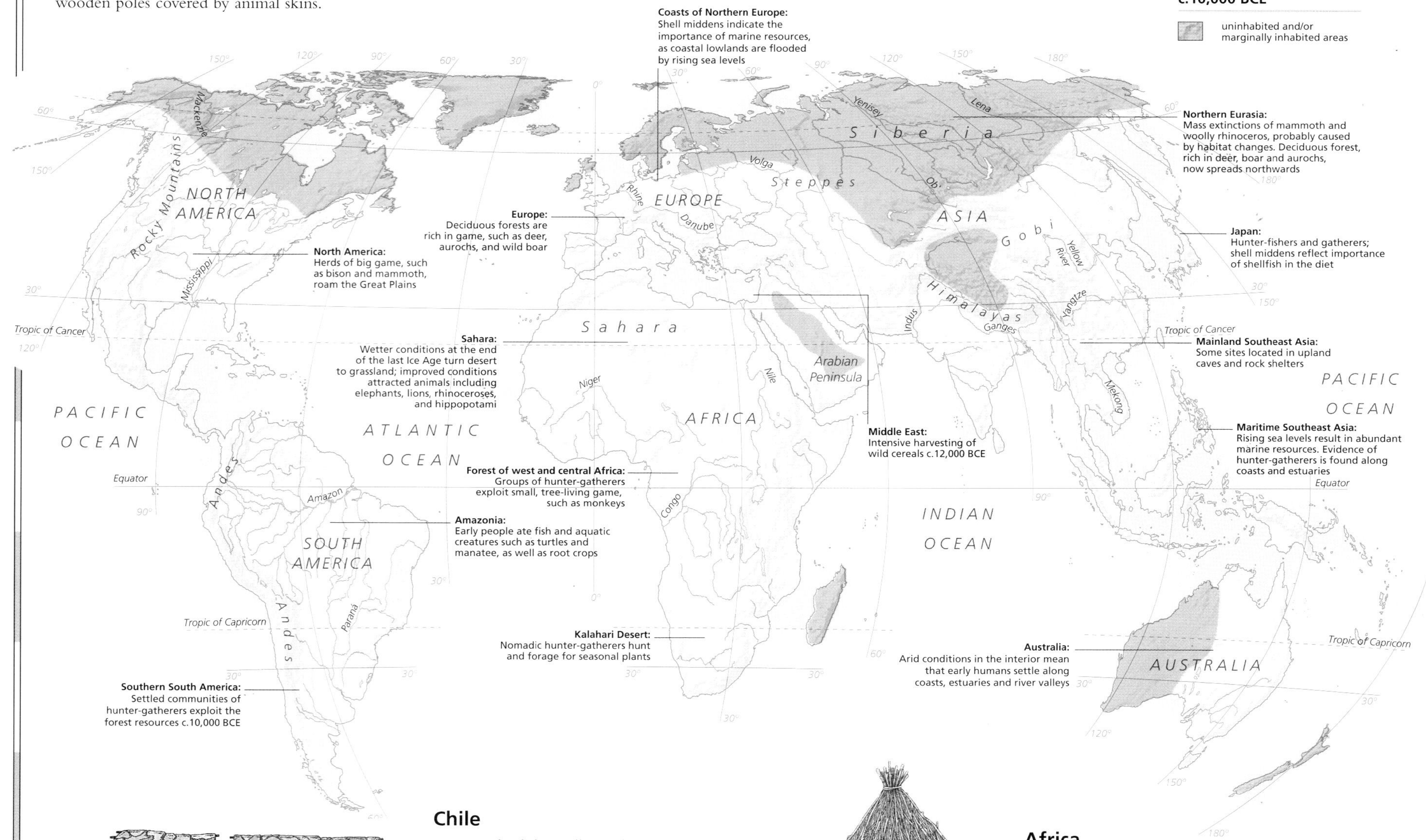

uninhabited and/or marginally inhabited areas
Coasts of Northern Europe: Shell middens indicate the importance of marine resources, as coastal lowlands are flooded by rising sea levels
Northern Eurasia: Mass extinctions of mammoth and woolly rhinoceros, probably caused by habitat changes. Deciduous forest, rich in deer, boar and aurochs, now spreads northwards
Europe: Deciduous forests are rich in game, such as deer, aurochs, and wild boar
North America: Herds of big game, such as bison and mammoth, roam the Great Plains
Japan: Hunter-fishers and gatherers; shell middens reflect importance of shellfish in the diet
Sahara: Wetter conditions at the end of the last Ice Age turn desert to grassland; improved conditions attracted animals including elephants, lions, rhinoceroses, and hippopotami
Mainland Southeast Asia: Some sites located in upland caves and rock shelters
Middle East: Intensive harvesting of wild cereals c.12,000 BCE
Maritime Southeast Asia: Rising sea levels result in abundant marine resources. Evidence of hunter-gatherers is found along coasts and estuaries
Forest of west and central Africa: Groups of hunter-gatherers exploit small, tree-living game, such as monkeys
Amazonia: Early people ate fish and aquatic creatures such as turtles and manatee, as well as root crops
Kalahari Desert: Nomadic hunter-gatherers hunt and forage for seasonal plants
Australia: Arid conditions in the interior mean that early humans settle along coasts, estuaries and river valleys
Southern South America: Settled communities of hunter-gatherers exploit the forest resources c.10,000 BCE
NORTH AMERICA
Rocky Mountains
Mackenzie
Mississippi
EUROPE
Rhine
Danube
Volga
Steppes
Siberia
Yenisey
Lena
Ob
ASIA
Gobi
Yellow River
Himalayas
Indus
Ganges
Yangtze
Mekong
Sahara
Niger
Nile
Arabian Peninsula
AFRICA
Congo
PACIFIC OCEAN
ATLANTIC OCEAN
INDIAN OCEAN
SOUTH AMERICA
Andes
Amazon
Paraná
AUSTRALIA
Tropic of Cancer
Equator
Tropic of Capricorn

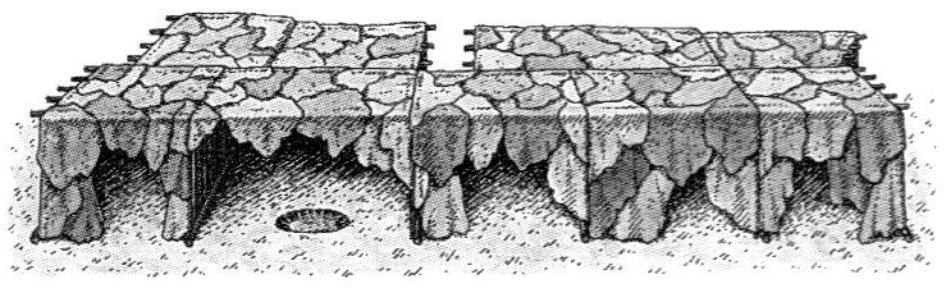

Chile

In central Chile a village of timber buildings, roofed with animal hides, was built by early settlers at Monte Verde around 10,000 BCE. A small hearth was used to heat each hut; communal hearths were used for cooking.

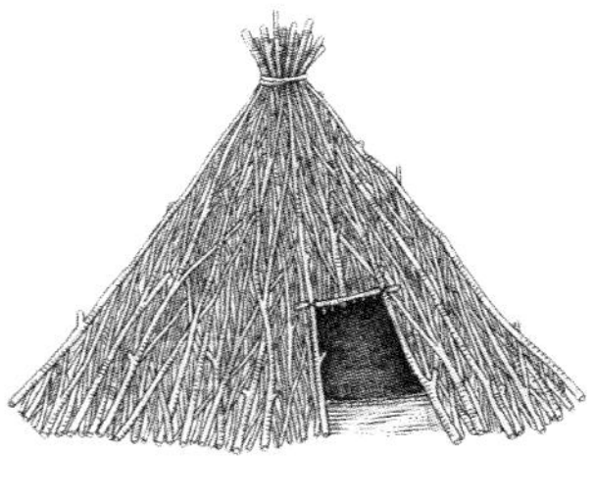

Africa

In the more fertile conditions of the period, hunters foraging for seasonal plants in the Kalahari Desert built temporary shelters from brushwood branches.

Palaeolithic art

The art of the last Ice Age and its aftermath, ranging from painted caves to engraved and finely carved objects and clay sculptures, is found in many parts of the world. Since much of this art is probably associated with religious rituals concerned with hunting, fertility, and the initiation of the young, it is a testament to the increasing complexity and sophistication of human society. One of the greatest flowerings of palaeolithic art is undoubtedly the extraordinary painted caves of southwestern Europe, but there is evidence of a wide range of different regional artistic traditions, from the ochre-decorated rock shelters of Kisesse in East Africa to the rock art of Bhimbetka in South Asia, which dates to the coldest phase of the last Ice Age.

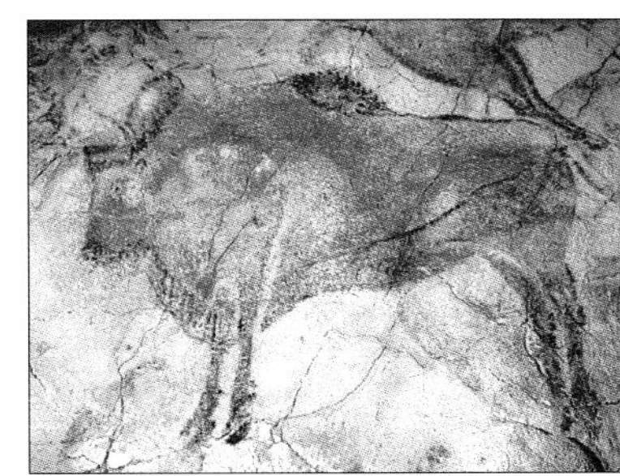

In the caves of southwest Europe, animals such as bison are depicted with grace and fluidity.

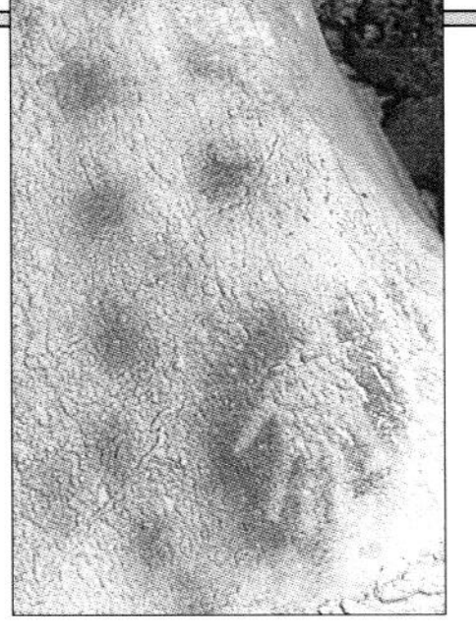

Hand stencils often dominate the part of the cave in which they are found. The red pigments could be made from either iron oxide or red ochre.

Hand paintings

Stencils of hands, made by blowing a spray of powdered pigment over the outstretched hand, are found on cave walls in both western Europe and Australia. The stencils may be associated with initiation rites – children's footprints have also been found in the European caves.

SEE ALSO:

North America: pp.116–117

South America: pp.140–141

Africa: pp.154–155

Europe: pp.170–171

West Asia: pp.216–217

South and Southeast Asia: pp.236–237

North and East Asia: pp.254–255

Australasia and Oceania: pp.276–277

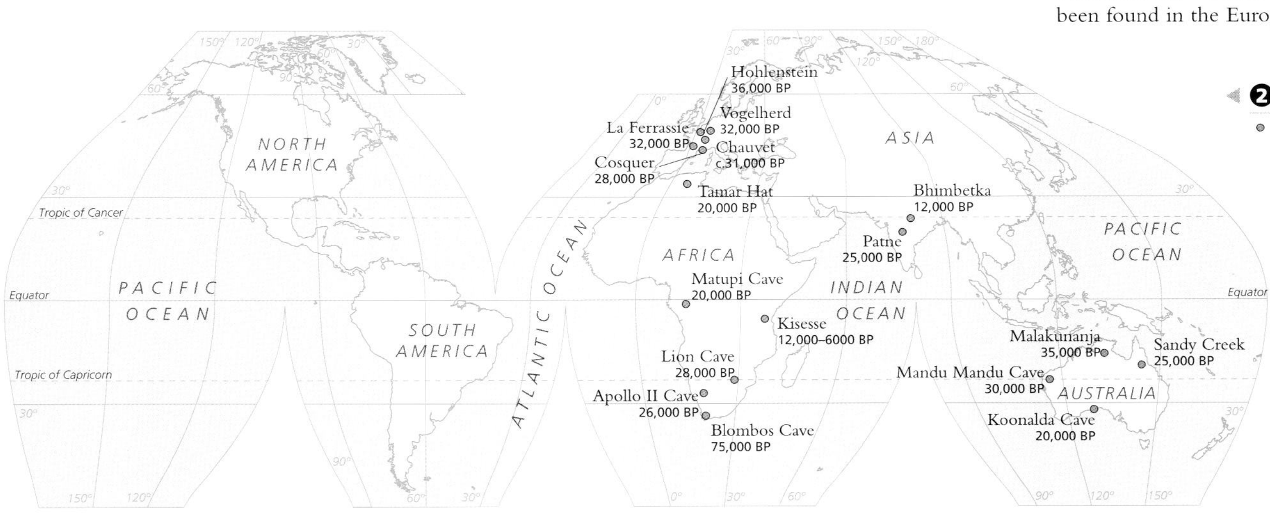

2 Palaeolithic art

early art site

European cave paintings

The caves of southwestern Europe, with their vibrant paintings and engravings of bison, deer, oxen, and horses, are unique. These images, often found in the darkest and most inaccessible parts of the caves, may have acted as forms of hunting magic or illustrated myths and traditions.

3 Painted caves and rock art

important rock art site

200 km
200 miles
ATLANTIC OCEAN
Arcy-sur-Cure
Angles-sur-l'Anglin
France
Loire
Roc-de-Sers
Montgaudier
Candamo
Le Gabillou
Lascaux
Laugerie Basse
Les Combarelles
Ebbou
Dordogne
Font-de-Gaume
Cantabrian Mountains
Herrerias
Altamira
El Castillo
Cullalvera
Ekain
Lot
Altxerri
Garonne
Pech-Merle
Massif Central
Rhône
La Baume-Latrone
Duero
Ebro
Montespan
Gargas
Le Mas d'Azil
Le Tuc d'Audoubert
Niaux
Pyrenees
Les Trois Frères
Alps
Iberian Peninsula
Tagus
Mediterranean Sea

Portable art

Small plaques of engraved antler and bone, decorated ornaments of amber and ivory – including pendants and beads – and carved figurines of both animals and humans are found throughout Europe. Highly stylized female figurines *(right)* are possibly representations of the mother goddess, and may have been associated with fertility rituals.

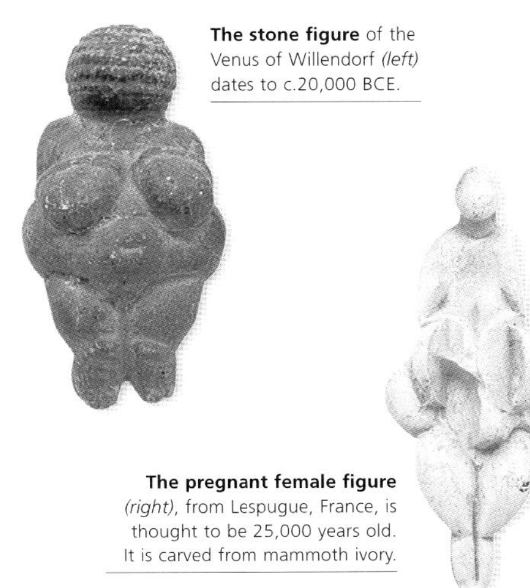

The stone figure of the Venus of Willendorf *(left)* dates to c.20,000 BCE.

The pregnant female figure *(right)*, from Lespugue, France, is thought to be 25,000 years old. It is carved from mammoth ivory.

4 Venus figurines in Europe

important find of Venus figurines

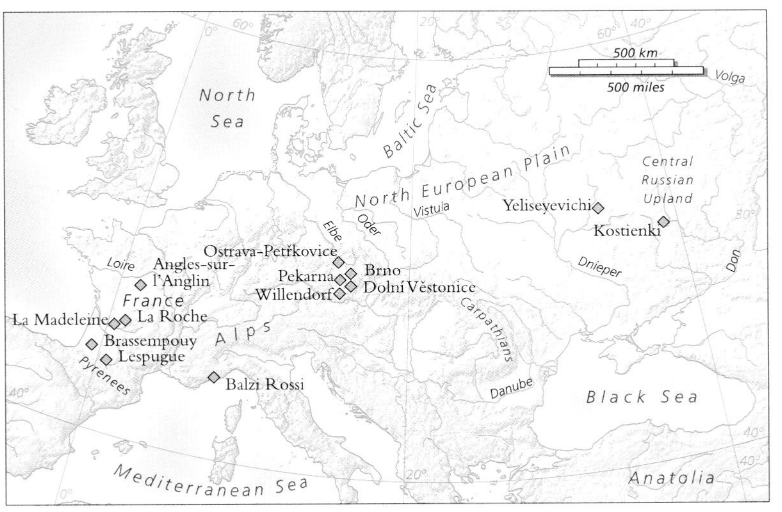

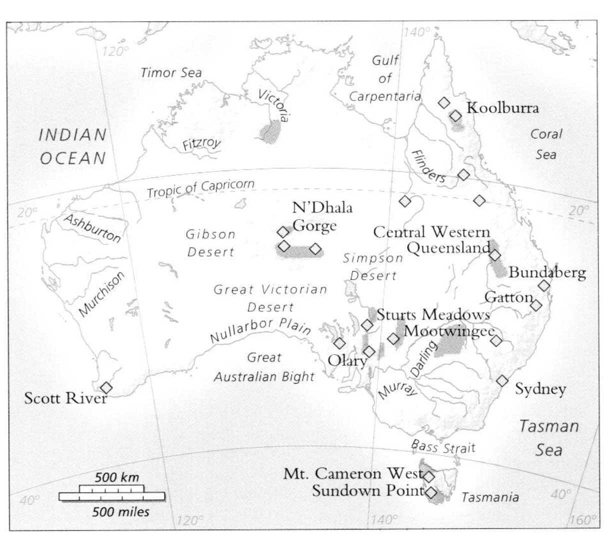

5 Australian rock art

Panaramittee style rock engraving

major rock art region

Australia

The oldest rock engravings in the world, from Panaramittee, date to 45,000 BCE. Australian rock paintings and engravings are widespread; most designs are abstract, using lines, dots, crescents, and spirals. Some are thought to represent kangaroo and bird tracks.

Some of the earliest examples of Aboriginal rock carvings or petroglyphs – here in the form of circles and stars – are found at Wilpena Sacred Canyon in southern Australia.

Early examples of human art

- **75,000:** Geometric designs engraved on prepared pieces of ochre at Blombos Cave, South Africa
- **45,000:** Oldest rock engravings from Panaramittee, South Australia
- **40,000:** Ostrich eggshells, engraved with abstract patterns, from central India
- **32,000:** Carved ivory statuette from Hohlenstein-Stadel Cave, Germany, is one of world's earliest figurines
- **29,000:** Caves at Kisesse, East Africa decorated with ochre-stained palettes
- **26,000:** Oldest rock paintings in Africa, from Apollo II Cave, Namibia
- **25,000:** Stylized female figurines found throughout Europe
- **20,000:** Limestone pebble with human head from Aq Kupruk in central Asia
- **17,000:** Cave paintings produced at Lascaux
- **15,000:** Hand stencils found in Wargata Mina Cave, Tasmania

75,000 BP | 65,000 BP | 55,000 BP | 45,000 BP | 35,000 BP | 25,000 BP | 15,000 BP

THE WORLD 10,000–5000 BCE

IN THE MORE HOSPITABLE CLIMATE and terrain of the post-glacial world, groups of hunter-gatherers began to experiment with the domestication of wild cereals and animals. By 7000 BCE, farming was the main means of subsistence in West Asia, although hunter-gathering remained the most common form of subsistence elsewhere. Over the next 5000 years farming became established independently in other areas. The impact of the agricultural revolution on early societies was immense. Farming could support much larger populations, so settlement sizes increased significantly. Larger communities generated new demands and possibilities, and a class of specialized craftsmen evolved. Trade in raw materials and manufactured goods increased contact between farming communities. Communal ventures, such as irrigation, encouraged co-operation. All these developments paved the way for the much larger cities and states which were soon to follow.

THE FIRST USE OF METAL

The discovery that metals can be isolated from ore-bearing rocks by heating appears to have been made independently in West Asia and southeastern Europe between 7000–5000 BCE. Copper, gold, and lead, all soft metals that melt at relatively low temperatures, were the first metals in use. In early copper-using societies, most copper objects were decorative items that denoted the status of the owner: tools made from the new material could not compete with those of flint and stone.

This horned bull, fashioned from sheet gold is one of a pair from a rich set of grave goods unearthed at a cemetery in Varna, southeast Europe.

The community that settled at Lepenski Vir on the banks of the Danube c.6000 BCE placed fish sculptures, which may depict a local river god, inside their homes.

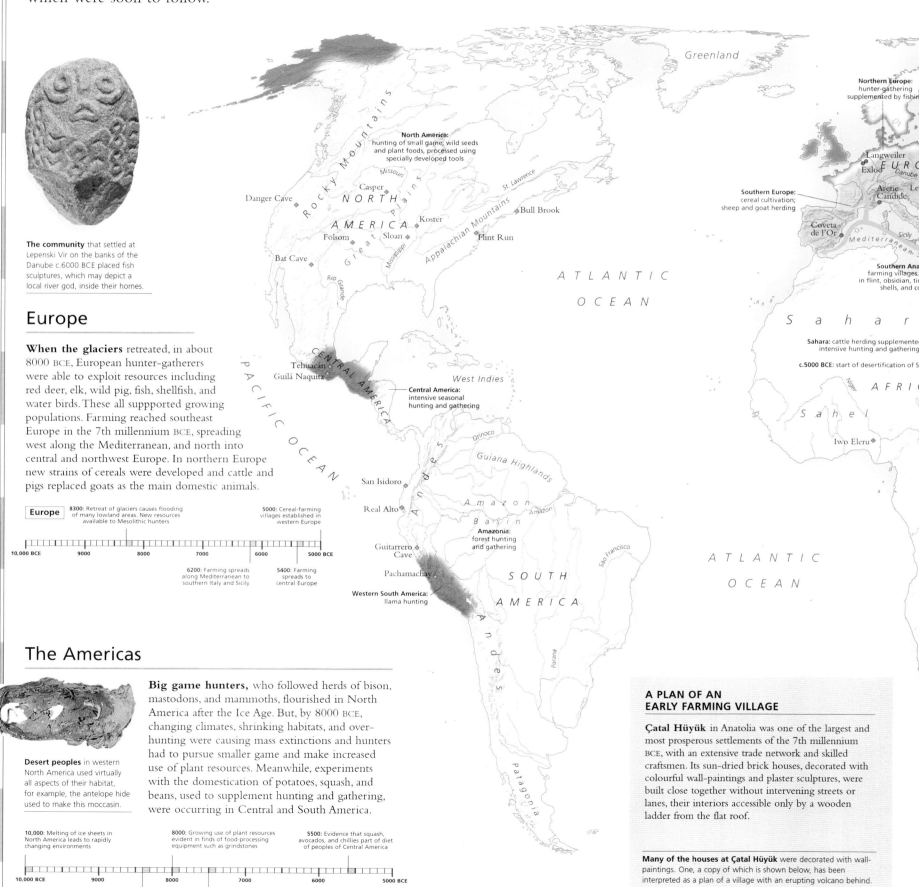

North America: hunting of small game; wild seeds and plant foods, processed using specially developed tools

Central America: intensive seasonal hunting and gathering

Amazonia: forest hunting and gathering

Western South America: llama hunting

Northern Europe: hunter-gathering supplemented by fishing

Southern Europe: cereal cultivation; sheep and goat herding

Southern Anatolia: farming villages trade in flint, obsidian, timber shells, and coppe

Sahara: cattle herding supplemented by intensive hunting and gathering

c.5000 BCE: start of desertification of Sahar

Europe

When the glaciers retreated, in about 8000 BCE, European hunter-gatherers were able to exploit resources including red deer, elk, wild pig, fish, shellfish, and water birds. These all suppported growing populations. Farming reached southeast Europe in the 7th millennium BCE, spreading west along the Mediterranean, and north into central and northwest Europe. In northern Europe new strains of cereals were developed and cattle and pigs replaced goats as the main domestic animals.

Europe (timeline 10,000 BCE – 5000 BCE)

- **8300:** Retreat of glaciers causes flooding of many lowland areas. New resources available to Mesolithic hunters
- **6200:** Farming spreads along Mediterranean to southern Italy and Sicily
- **5400:** Farming spreads to central Europe
- **5000:** Cereal-farming villages established in western Europe

The Americas

Desert peoples in western North America used virtually all aspects of their habitat, for example, the antelope hide used to make this moccasin.

Big game hunters, who followed herds of bison, mastodons, and mammoths, flourished in North America after the Ice Age. But, by 8000 BCE, changing climates, shrinking habitats, and over-hunting were causing mass extinctions and hunters had to pursue smaller game and make increased use of plant resources. Meanwhile, experiments with the domestication of potatoes, squash, and beans, used to supplement hunting and gathering, were occurring in Central and South America.

The Americas (timeline 10,000 BCE – 5000 BCE)

- **10,000:** Melting of ice sheets in North America leads to rapidly changing environments
- **8500:** Evidence of grasses, squash, beans, peppers, and potatoes in use in Andes
- **8000:** Growing use of plant resources evident in finds of food-processing equipment such as grindstones
- **7500:** Earliest known cemetery in North America: Sloan burial site
- **5500:** Evidence that squash, avocados, and chillies part of diet of peoples of Central America

A PLAN OF AN EARLY FARMING VILLAGE

Çatal Hüyük in Anatolia was one of the largest and most prosperous settlements of the 7th millennium BCE, with an extensive trade network and skilled craftsmen. Its sun-dried brick houses, decorated with colourful wall-paintings and plaster sculptures, were built close together without intervening streets or lanes, their interiors accessible only by a wooden ladder from the flat roof.

Many of the houses at Çatal Hüyük were decorated with wall-paintings. One, a copy of which is shown below, has been interpreted as a plan of a village with an erupting volcano behind.

West Asia

The world's earliest farmers settled in the fertile arc of land stretching from the Persian Gulf to the eastern Mediterranean. Large-seeded grains were domesticated in Jericho by 8000 BCE. Villages of mud-brick houses appeared in Anatolia, and in central Mesopotamia by the 7th millennium BCE and craftsmen were smelting copper and lead by 6000 BCE. By 5500 BCE the farmers of southern Mesopotamia were irrigating arid land to improve crop yields.

Terracotta figurines of goddesses with swollen abdomens were found at Çatal Hüyük, suggesting a fertility cult.

West Asia

- **9000:** Wheat (einkorn) harvested in Mesopotamia
- **8000:** First fully domesticated cereals harvested in Jericho
- **7000:** Goat becomes main domesticated animal throughout region. Foundation of settlement of Çatal Hüyük, Anatolia
- **6500:** Earliest known Old World textiles (linen) from Çatal Hüyük
- **6000:** At Hassuna in northern Mesopotamia; painted pottery and copper and lead smelting
- **5500:** Ubaid culture of southern Mesopotamia harnesses spring floods of Euphrates for irrigation

East Asia

In northern China, agriculture dates back to c.7000 BCE. At farming villages such as Banpo, millet was cultivated and kept in grain storage pits, and there is evidence that pigs and dogs were domesticated. In a separate development, rice cultivation was initiated in the lowlands of the Yangtze delta, probably by 6000 BCE. In Japan, the Jomon people lived by hunting, fishing, and gathering in the well-stocked mountains and coastal waters. Although the Japanese were making pottery by 10,500 BCE, their way of life would remain based on hunting and gathering for several thousand years.

The people of Banpo were producing and firing pottery such as this cord-scored amphora by the 5th millennium BCE.

East Asia

- **9000:** Limestone caves in central China give evidence of hunting, fishing, and gathering way of life
- **6500:** 'Jomon' pottery spreads throughout southern Japanese archipelago
- **c.6000:** Hunting and fishing villages in Yangtze river delta begin cultivating rice
- **5000:** Jade imported into northern Manchuria from Central Asia or Siberia

SEE ALSO:

North America: pp.120–121

South America: pp.144–145

Africa: pp.158–159

Europe: pp.174–175

West Asia: pp.220–221

South and Southeast Asia: pp.240–241

North and East Asia: pp.258–259

Australasia and Oceania: pp.280–281

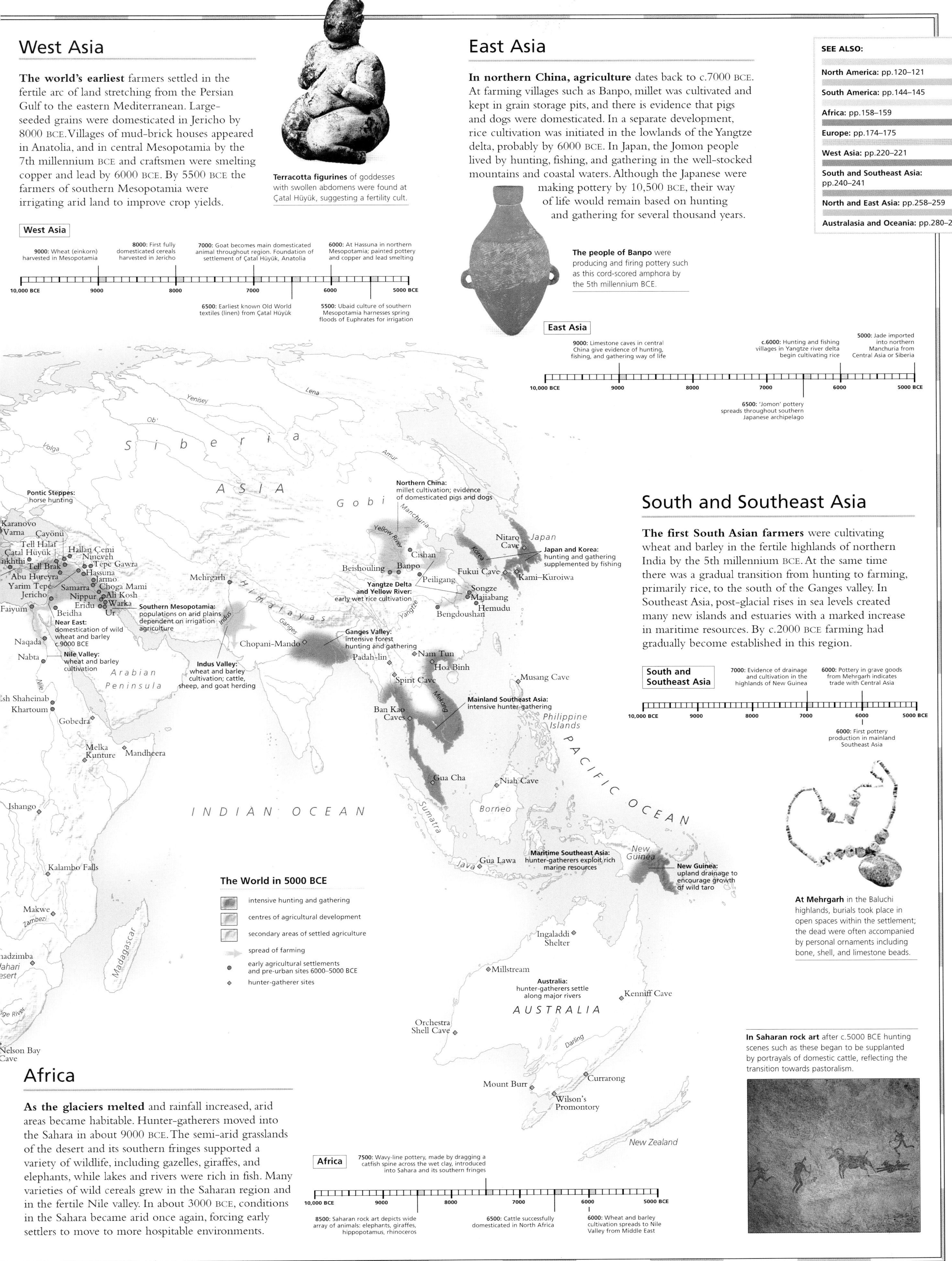

South and Southeast Asia

The first South Asian farmers were cultivating wheat and barley in the fertile highlands of northern India by the 5th millennium BCE. At the same time there was a gradual transition from hunting to farming, primarily rice, to the south of the Ganges valley. In Southeast Asia, post-glacial rises in sea levels created many new islands and estuaries with a marked increase in maritime resources. By c.2000 BCE farming had gradually become established in this region.

South and Southeast Asia

- **7000:** Evidence of drainage and cultivation in the highlands of New Guinea
- **6000:** Pottery in grave goods from Mehrgarh indicates trade with Central Asia
- **6000:** First pottery production in mainland Southeast Asia

At Mehrgarh in the Baluchi highlands, burials took place in open spaces within the settlement; the dead were often accompanied by personal ornaments including bone, shell, and limestone beads.

Africa

As the glaciers melted and rainfall increased, arid areas became habitable. Hunter-gatherers moved into the Sahara in about 9000 BCE. The semi-arid grasslands of the desert and its southern fringes supported a variety of wildlife, including gazelles, giraffes, and elephants, while lakes and rivers were rich in fish. Many varieties of wild cereals grew in the Saharan region and in the fertile Nile valley. In about 3000 BCE, conditions in the Sahara became arid once again, forcing early settlers to move to more hospitable environments.

Africa

- **8500:** Saharan rock art depicts wide array of animals: elephants, giraffes, hippopotamus, rhinoceros
- **7500:** Wavy-line pottery, made by dragging a catfish spine across the wet clay, introduced into Sahara and its southern fringes
- **6500:** Cattle successfully domesticated in North Africa
- **6000:** Wheat and barley cultivation spreads to Nile Valley from Middle East

In Saharan rock art after c.5000 BCE hunting scenes such as these began to be supplanted by portrayals of domestic cattle, reflecting the transition towards pastoralism.

THE ADVENT OF AGRICULTURE

Fragments of Egyptian wavy-line pottery, decorated with a fish spine from c.7000 BCE

THE APPEARANCE OF FARMING transformed the face of the Earth. It was not merely a change in subsistence – perhaps in some regions a necessity caused by over-hunting, limited natural resources and population growth – it also transformed the way in which our ancestors lived. Agriculture, and the vastly greater crop yields it produced, enabled large groups of people to live in permanent villages, surrounded by material goods and equipment. Specialized craftsmen produced these goods, supported by the community as a whole – the beginnings of social differentiation. These developments led ultimately to the emergence of the first cities, but in 5000 BCE only a limited number of regions were fully dependent on agriculture. In many parts of the globe, small-scale farming was being used to supplement hunting and gathering – the first steps in the gradual transition to the sedentary agricultural way of life.

The agricultural revolution

The advent of farming brought large groups of people together into settled communities. Not only could food production be made more efficient, but animals could be tended communally, and food surpluses used to support villagers through the winter months. Some members of the community were therefore able to develop craft skills, engage in long-distance trade, and experiment with technology, such as pottery kilns, gold, and copper metallurgy and, by c.5500 BCE, irrigation. But sedentary co-existence also exposed people to infectious disease; the settlement of Çatal Hüyük, for example, was plagued by malaria.

Stone querns, dating to about 6000 years ago, were used by farmers for grinding grain into flour, which could then be kept in storage pits.

Ways of life

The exceptional productivity of the major cultivated species, in particular cereals, was vital to the viability of early farming villages. Cereals can be kept as a year-round resource, providing a staple supplement to more seasonal foods, thus creating a total dependence on farming. An inevitable, and necessary, by-product of this settled way of life was pottery – pottery containers could be used for both storing and cooking the harvested food. The technique of hand-modelling and firing clay pots evolved independently in many regions. Moulds, wheels and kilns were later innovations, and became the province of specialized craftsmen.

The earliest pottery had a round-based shape *(right)*, and was sometimes decorated with incisions or impressions. A characteristic later vessel from western Europe was the flat-based beaker *(left)*, again decorated with incisions. In other regions of Europe, notably the southeast, painted decoration was also used.

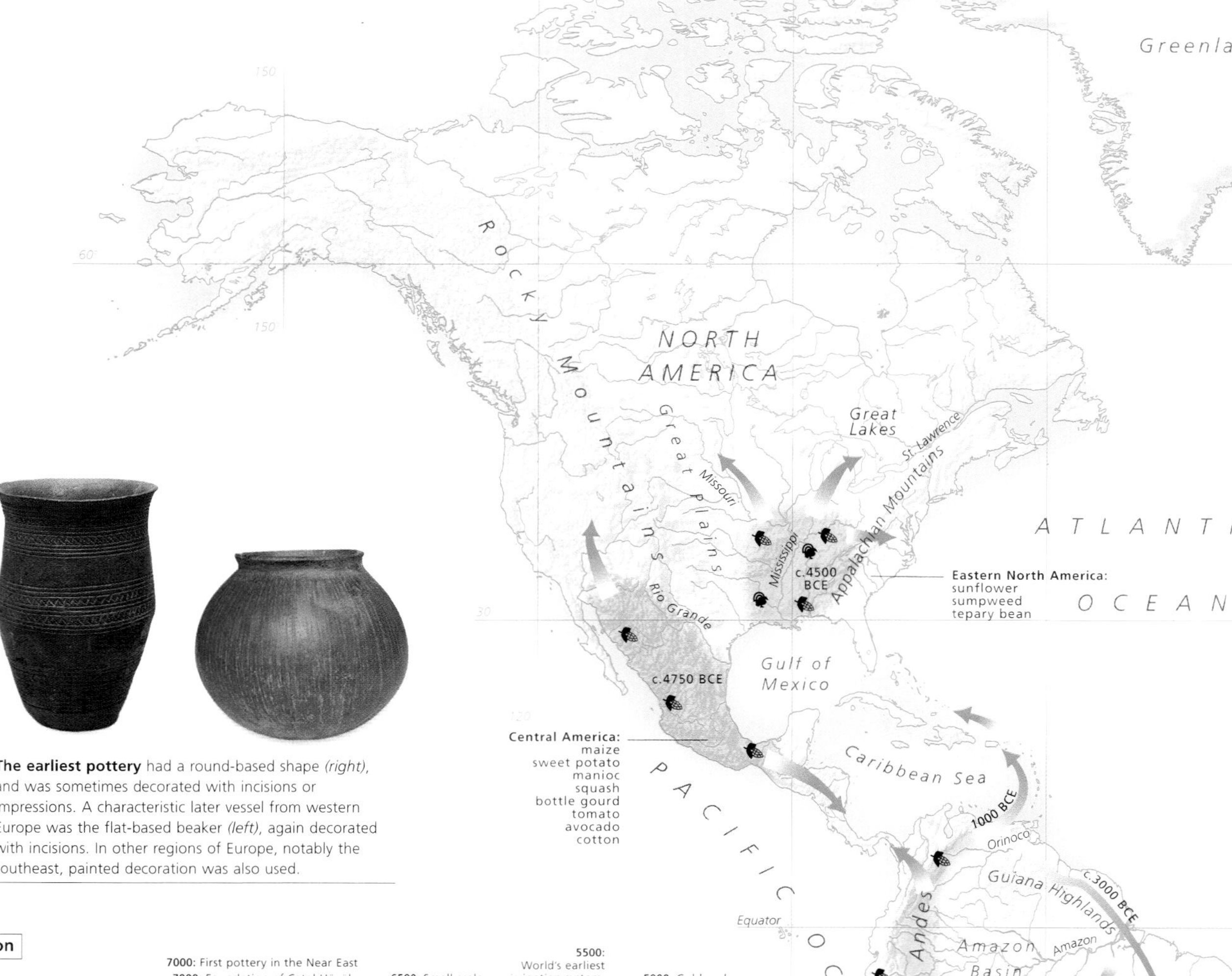

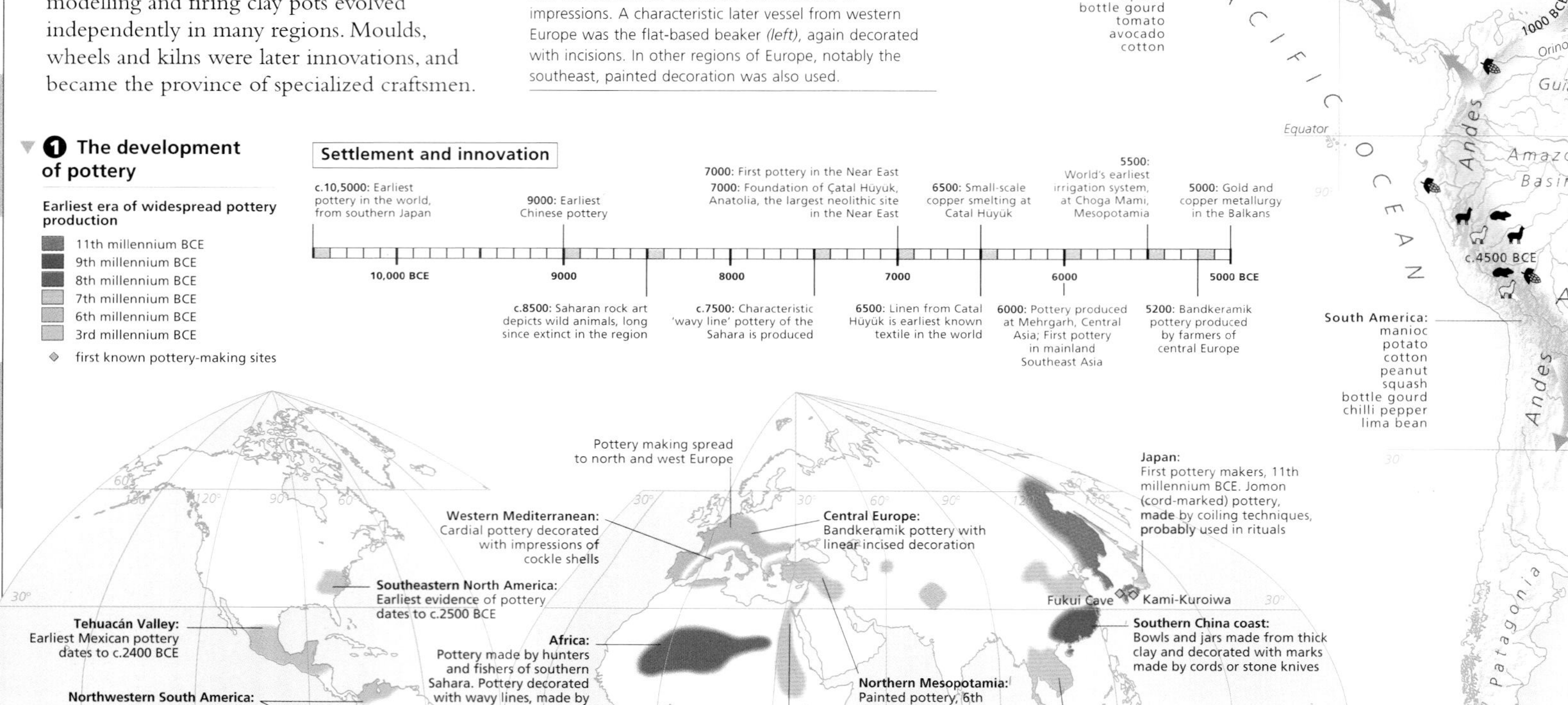

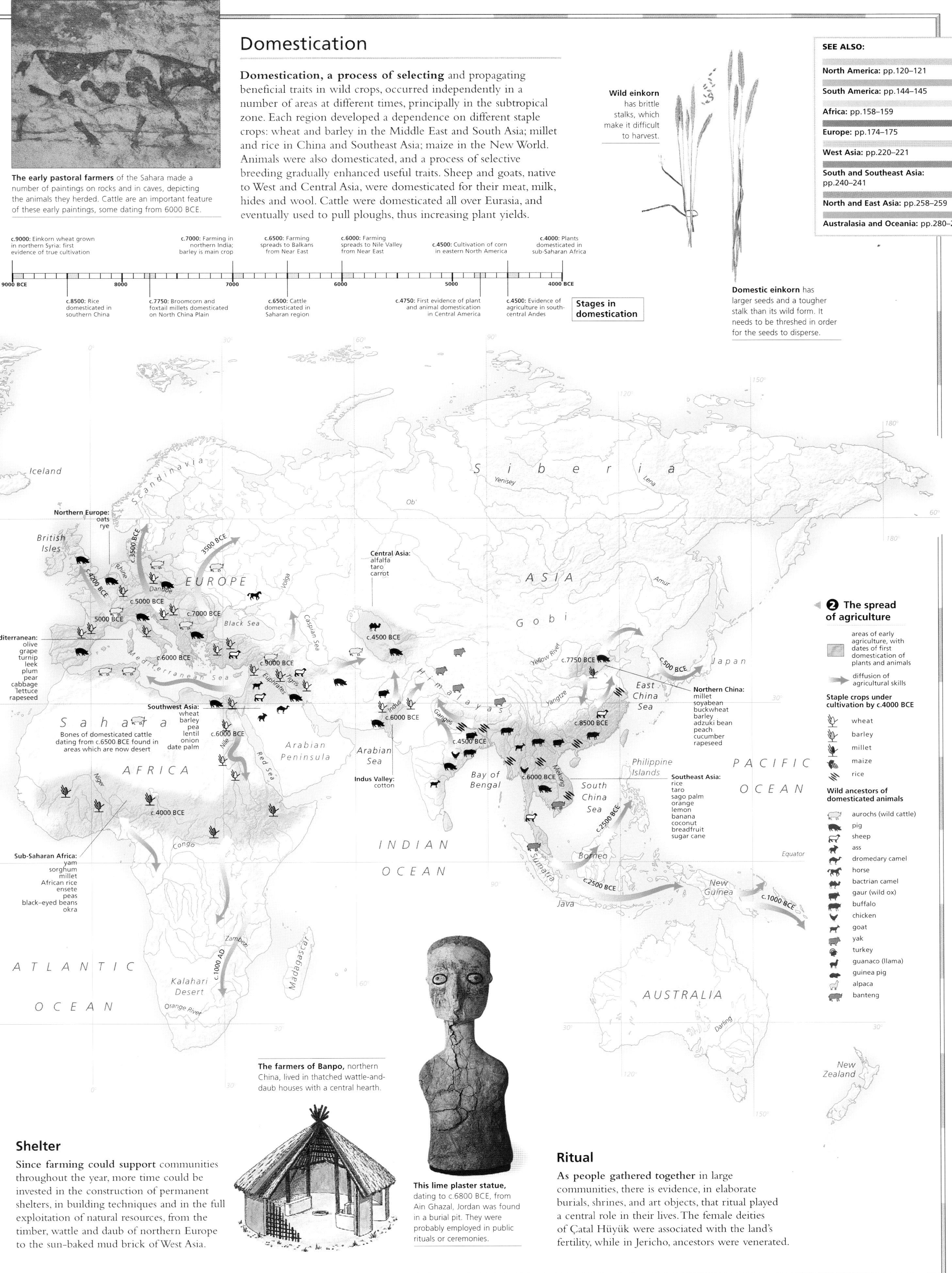
Stages in domestication
9000 BCE
8000
7000
6000
5000
4000 BCE
c.9000: Einkorn wheat grown in northern Syria: first evidence of true cultivation
c.8500: Rice domesticated in southern China
c.7750: Broomcorn and foxtail millets domesticated on North China Plain
c.7000: Farming in northern India; barley is main crop
c.6500: Farming spreads to Balkans from Near East
c.6500: Cattle domesticated in Saharan region
c.6000: Farming spreads to Nile Valley from Near East
c.4750: First evidence of plant and animal domestication in Central America
c.4500: Cultivation of corn in eastern North America
c.4500: Evidence of agriculture in south-central Andes
c.4000: Plants domesticated in sub-Saharan Africa
2 The spread of agriculture
areas of early agriculture, with dates of first domestication of plants and animals
diffusion of agricultural skills
Staple crops under cultivation by c.4000 BCE
wheat
barley
millet
maize
rice
Wild ancestors of domesticated animals
aurochs (wild cattle)
pig
sheep
ass
dromedary camel
horse
bactrian camel
gaur (wild ox)
buffalo
chicken
goat
yak
turkey
guanaco (llama)
guinea pig
alpaca
banteng
Northern Europe: oats rye
Mediterranean: olive grape turnip leek plum pear cabbage lettuce rapeseed
Southwest Asia: wheat barley pea lentil onion date palm
Central Asia: alfalfa taro carrot
Indus Valley: cotton
Northern China: millet soyabean buckwheat barley adzuki bean peach cucumber rapeseed
Southeast Asia: rice taro sago palm orange lemon banana coconut breadfruit sugar cane
Sub-Saharan Africa: yam sorghum millet African rice ensete peas black-eyed beans okra
Bones of domesticated cattle dating from c.6500 BCE found in areas which are now desert
Iceland
Scandinavia
British Isles
Rhine
Danube
EUROPE
Volga
Black Sea
Caspian Sea
Mediterranean Sea
Euphrates
Tigris
Nile
Red Sea
Sahara
AFRICA
Niger
Congo
Zambezi
Kalahari Desert
Orange River
Madagascar
Arabian Peninsula
Arabian Sea
Indus
Ganges
Himalayas
Bay of Bengal
INDIAN OCEAN
Siberia
Yenisey
Ob'
Lena
Amur
ASIA
Gobi
Yellow River
Yangtze
Mekong
East China Sea
Japan
Philippine Islands
South China Sea
Borneo
Sumatra
Java
New Guinea
PACIFIC OCEAN
Equator
AUSTRALIA
Darling
New Zealand
ATLANTIC OCEAN
c.3500 BCE
c.4200 BCE
3500 BCE
c.5000 BCE
5000 BCE
c.7000 BCE
c.6000 BCE
c.9000 BCE
c.6000 BCE
c.4000 BCE
c.4500 BCE
c.6000 BCE
c.4500 BCE
c.6000 BCE
c.7750 BCE
c.8500 BCE
c.500 BCE
c.2500 BCE
c.2500 BCE
c.1000 BCE
c.1000 AD

The early pastoral farmers of the Sahara made a number of paintings on rocks and in caves, depicting the animals they herded. Cattle are an important feature of these early paintings, some dating from 6000 BCE.

Domestication

Domestication, a process of selecting and propagating beneficial traits in wild crops, occurred independently in a number of areas at different times, principally in the subtropical zone. Each region developed a dependence on different staple crops: wheat and barley in the Middle East and South Asia; millet and rice in China and Southeast Asia; maize in the New World. Animals were also domesticated, and a process of selective breeding gradually enhanced useful traits. Sheep and goats, native to West and Central Asia, were domesticated for their meat, milk, hides and wool. Cattle were domesticated all over Eurasia, and eventually used to pull ploughs, thus increasing plant yields.

Wild einkorn has brittle stalks, which make it difficult to harvest.

Domestic einkorn has larger seeds and a tougher stalk than its wild form. It needs to be threshed in order for the seeds to disperse.

SEE ALSO:

North America: pp.120–121

South America: pp.144–145

Africa: pp.158–159

Europe: pp.174–175

West Asia: pp.220–221

South and Southeast Asia: pp.240–241

North and East Asia: pp.258–259

Australasia and Oceania: pp.280–281

The farmers of Banpo, northern China, lived in thatched wattle-and-daub houses with a central hearth.

This lime plaster statue, dating to c.6800 BCE, from Ain Ghazal, Jordan was found in a burial pit. They were probably employed in public rituals or ceremonies.

Shelter

Since farming could support communities throughout the year, more time could be invested in the construction of permanent shelters, in building techniques and in the full exploitation of natural resources, from the timber, wattle and daub of northern Europe to the sun-baked mud brick of West Asia.

Ritual

As people gathered together in large communities, there is evidence, in elaborate burials, shrines, and art objects, that ritual played a central role in their lives. The female deities of Çatal Hüyük were associated with the land's fertility, while in Jericho, ancestors were venerated.

THE WORLD 5000 – 2500 BCE

THE FERTILE RIVER VALLEYS of the Nile, Tigris, Euphrates, Indus, and Yellow River were able to support very large populations, and it was here that the great urban civilizations of the ancient world emerged. Although cities developed independently in several regions, they shared certain characteristics. Urban societies were hierarchical, with complex labour divisions. They were administered, economically and spiritually, by an elite literate class, and in some cases, were subject to a divine monarch. Monuments came to symbolize and represent the powers of the ruling elite. Elsewhere, farming communities came together to create ritual centres or burial sites, while craftsmen experimented with new materials and techniques, such as copper and bronze casting, and glazed pottery. All these developments indicate that urban and non-urban societies were attaining a high degree of social organization.

EARLY PERCEPTIONS OF THE COSMOS

The stone circles and alignments of northwestern Europe are extraordinary prehistoric monuments which have mystified successive generations. Astronomical observations are central to the ritual purpose of these structures; some have chambers or stone settings arranged to be illuminated by the Sun only on certain days, such as the winter solstice or midsummer's day.

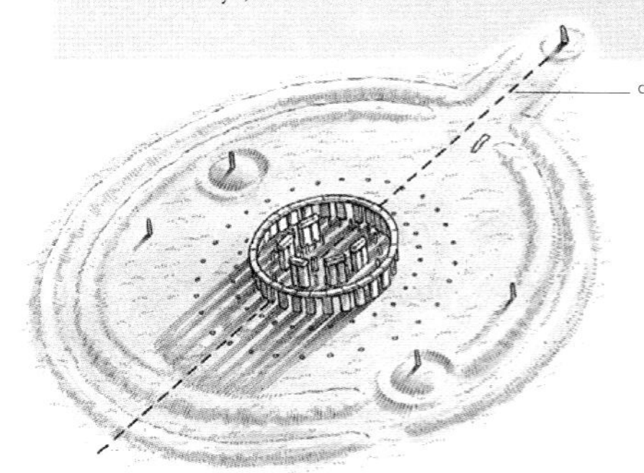

Stonehenge became the preeminent ritual centre of southern Britain c.2500 BCE. The rising sun on midsummer's day shines along the central axis of the site, but little is known of the ritual enacted there.

WHEELED VEHICLES

The origin of the wheel is uncertain; humans probably first made use of rotary motion in log rollers, and then in the potter's wheel. Wheeled vehicles were known in southwest Asia by 3500 BCE – a Sumerian pictograph from this period depicts a sledge equipped with wheels – and their use had spread to Europe and India by 3000 BCE. Early vehicles were probably ox-drawn, two-wheeled carts, on wheels formed from planks of wood secured with crosspieces.

This ceramic model of a two-wheeled bullock cart is from a grave at Harappa in the Indus Valley.

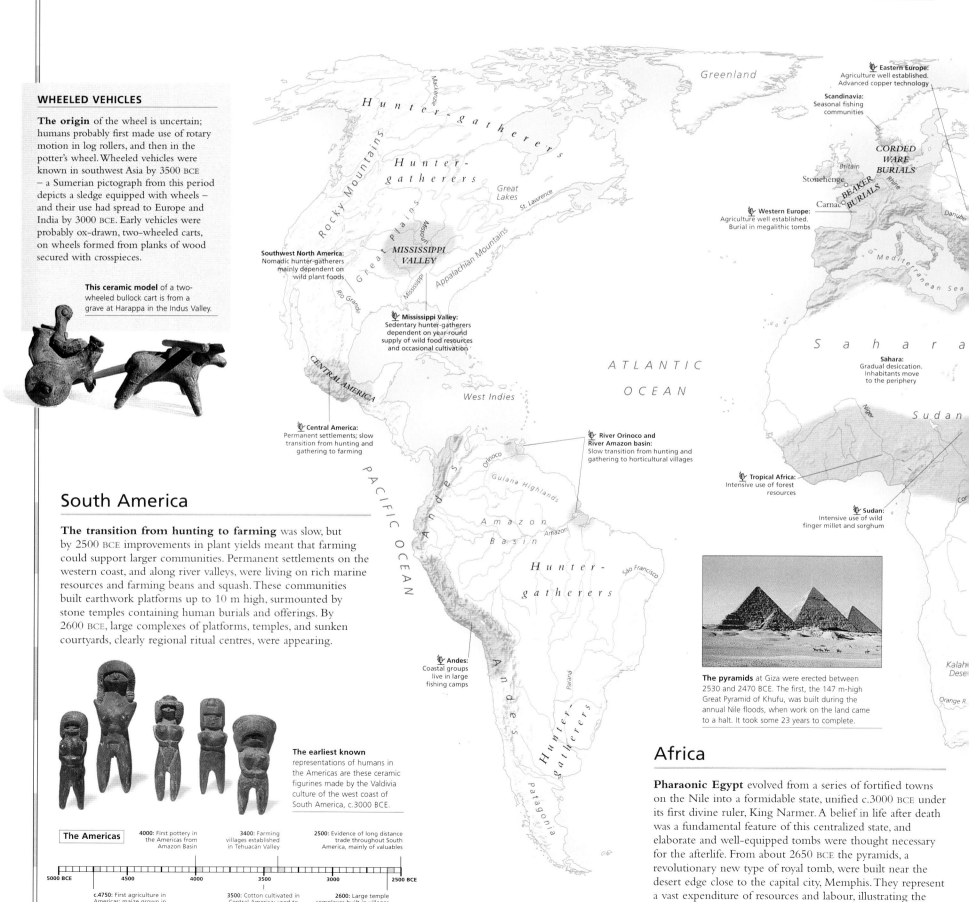

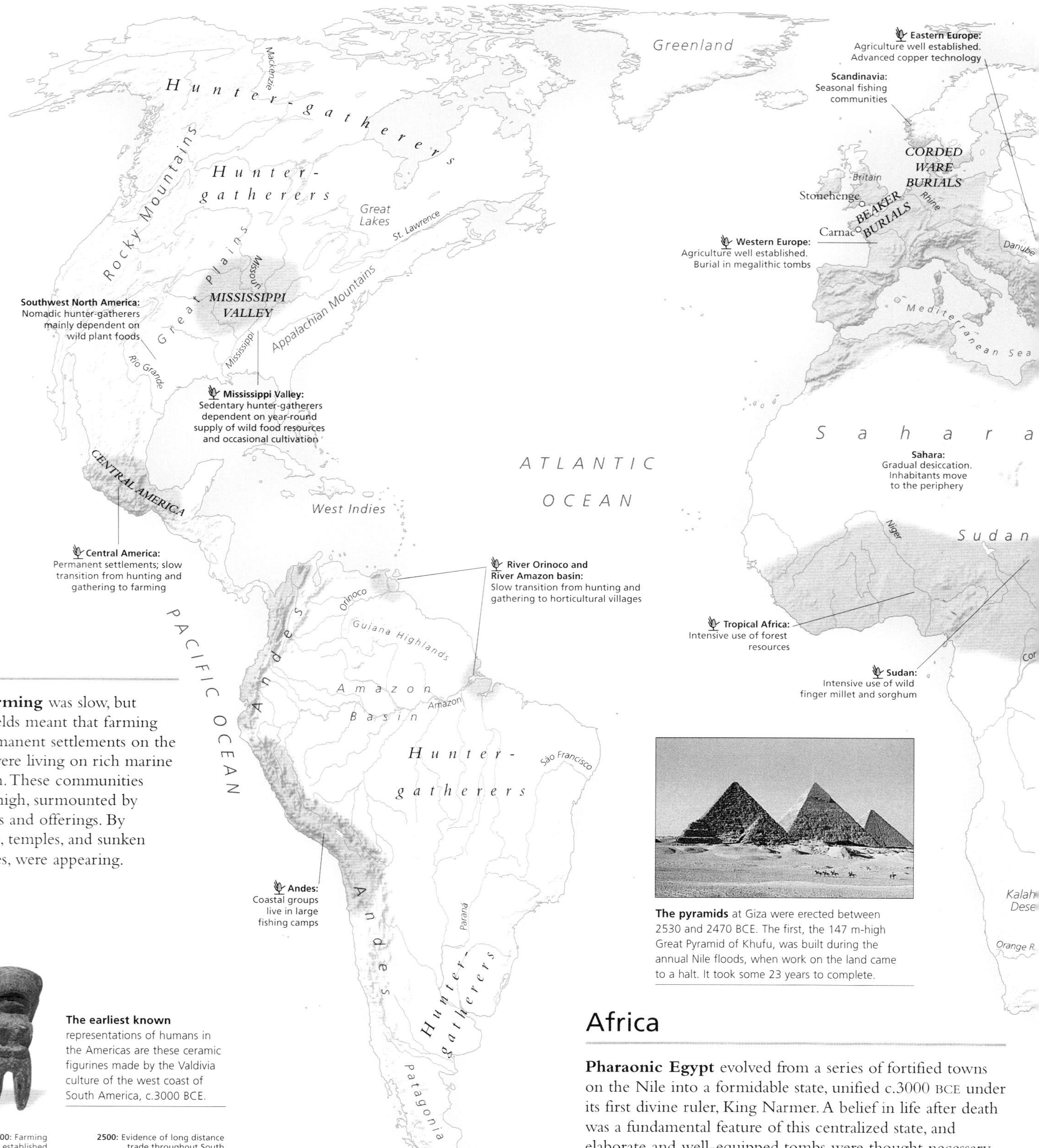

Greenland
Hunter-gatherers
Hunter-gatherers
Rocky Mountains
Great Plains
MISSISSIPPI VALLEY
Appalachian Mountains
Great Lakes
St. Lawrence
Mackenzie
Missouri
Mississippi
Rio Grande

Southwest North America: Nomadic hunter-gatherers mainly dependent on wild plant foods

Mississippi Valley: Sedentary hunter-gatherers dependent on year-round supply of wild food resources and occasional cultivation

CENTRAL AMERICA

Central America: Permanent settlements; slow transition from hunting and gathering to farming

West Indies
ATLANTIC OCEAN
PACIFIC OCEAN

River Orinoco and River Amazon basin: Slow transition from hunting and gathering to horticultural villages

Orinoco
Guiana Highlands
Amazon Basin
Amazon
Andes
Hunter-gatherers
São Francisco
Paraná
Patagonia

Andes: Coastal groups live in large fishing camps

Eastern Europe: Agriculture well established. Advanced copper technology

Scandinavia: Seasonal fishing communities

CORDED WARE BURIALS
BEAKER BURIALS
Britain
Stonehenge
Carnac
Rhine
Danube
Mediterranean Sea

Western Europe: Agriculture well established. Burial in megalithic tombs

Sahara

Sahara: Gradual desiccation. Inhabitants move to the periphery

Sudan
Niger

Tropical Africa: Intensive use of forest resources

Sudan: Intensive use of wild finger millet and sorghum

Kalahari Desert
Orange R.

South America

The transition from hunting to farming was slow, but by 2500 BCE improvements in plant yields meant that farming could support larger communities. Permanent settlements on the western coast, and along river valleys, were living on rich marine resources and farming beans and squash. These communities built earthwork platforms up to 10 m high, surmounted by stone temples containing human burials and offerings. By 2600 BCE, large complexes of platforms, temples, and sunken courtyards, clearly regional ritual centres, were appearing.

The earliest known representations of humans in the Americas are these ceramic figurines made by the Valdivia culture of the west coast of South America, c.3000 BCE.

The Americas

5000 BCE – 4500 – 4000 – 3500 – 3000 – 2500 BCE

c.4750: First agriculture in Americas: maize grown in Central America's Tehuacán valley

4000: First pottery in the Americas from Amazon Basin

3500: Cotton cultivated in Central America; used to make fishing nets and textiles

3400: Farming villages established in Tehuacán Valley

2600: Large temple complexes built in villages along the Andean coast

2500: Evidence of long distance trade throughout South America, mainly of valuables

The pyramids at Giza were erected between 2530 and 2470 BCE. The first, the 147 m-high Great Pyramid of Khufu, was built during the annual Nile floods, when work on the land came to a halt. It took some 23 years to complete.

Africa

Pharaonic Egypt evolved from a series of fortified towns on the Nile into a formidable state, unified c.3000 BCE under its first divine ruler, King Narmer. A belief in life after death was a fundamental feature of this centralized state, and elaborate and well-equipped tombs were thought necessary for the afterlife. From about 2650 BCE the pyramids, a revolutionary new type of royal tomb, were built near the desert edge close to the capital city, Memphis. They represent a vast expenditure of resources and labour, illustrating the control the pharaoh exercised over his subjects.

Europe

Skara Brae is a magnificently preserved prehistoric village on the Orkneys. The village consists of one-room houses of undressed stone, with paved walkways between them and a drainage system.

Elaborate burials, from the megalithic tombs of northern Europe to the large cemeteries of central and eastern Europe, indicate an increasing level of social organization among the scattered farming communities of the European continent. By the 3rd millennium BCE small farming communities were gathering to build defensive enclosures and to create regional centres. Stone circles, such as Stonehenge, or stone avenues, such as Carnac, were major communal undertakings which acted as social, economic, and ritual centres.

Europe

4500: Large cemeteries, for example on the western coast of the Black Sea, contain rich burials with elaborate gold jewellery

3800: Ditched enclosures around settlements in central Europe create defended villages

3200: Stone circles and rows of standing stones built throughout northern and western Europe

5000 BCE | 4500 | 4000 | 3500 | 3000 | 2500 BCE

c.5000: Metallurgy discovered in south-eastern Europe

c.4500: In western Europe, megalithic (large stone) chamber tombs, built as communal burial places

2900: Earliest burials containing Corded Ware pottery in northern and central Europe

East Asia

As the early farming villages of China became more prosperous, new skills emerged. Farmers of the Longshan culture of eastern China invented the potter's wheel and were making eggshell-thin vessels by 3000 BCE; 250 years later they were raising silkworms and weaving silk. By 3000 BCE there was a marked difference between rich and poor burials, and walled settlements were appearing. The more complex social organization that these developments indicate was soon to lead to China's first urban civilization, the Shang.

This Kui (a pitcher with three hollow legs) is typical of Longshan pottery from the late 3rd millennium BCE.

SEE ALSO:

North America: pp.120–121

South America: pp.144–145

Africa: pp.158–159

Europe: pp.174–175

West Asia: pp.220–221

South and Southeast Asia: pp.240–241

North and East Asia: pp.258–259

Australasia and Oceania: pp.280–281

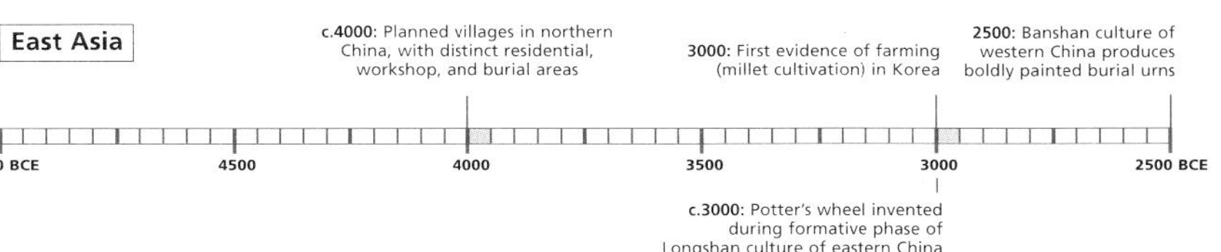

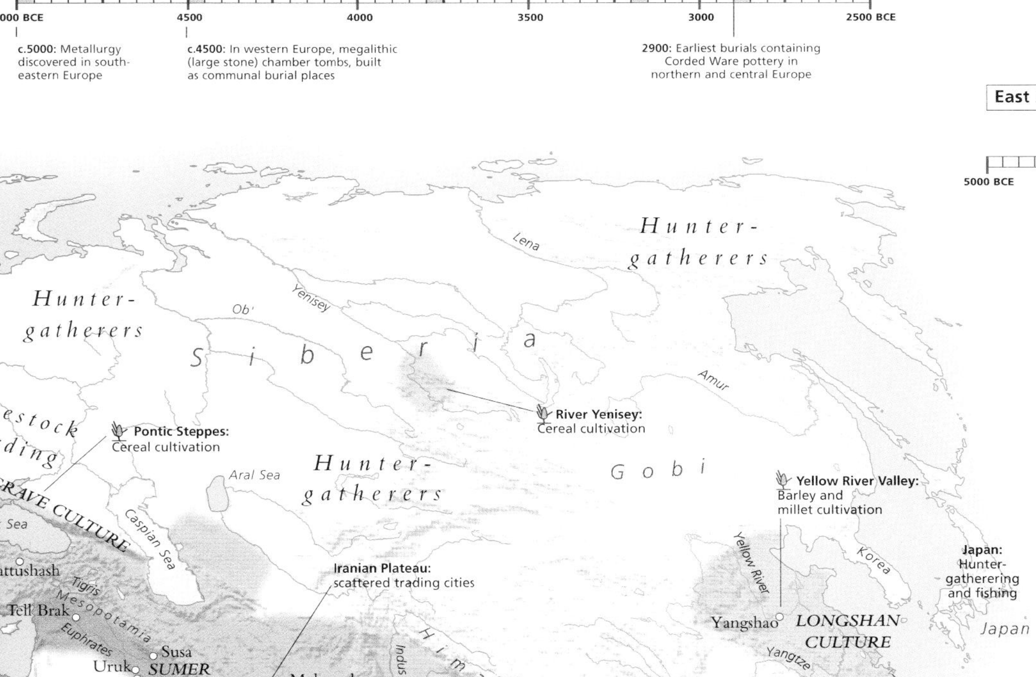

The Harappans developed a pictographic form of writing which they used mainly on sealstones.

South Asia

By 2500 BCE, an urban civilization had developed in the Indus Valley, dominated by Harappa and Mohenjo-Daro. At its height, the latter had a population of about 40,000. A network of residential streets, houses made with standardized bricks and sophisticated drains running into main sewers, overlooked by the 'citadel', the religious and ceremonial focus of the city. Merchandise was traded as far afield as Mesopotamia.

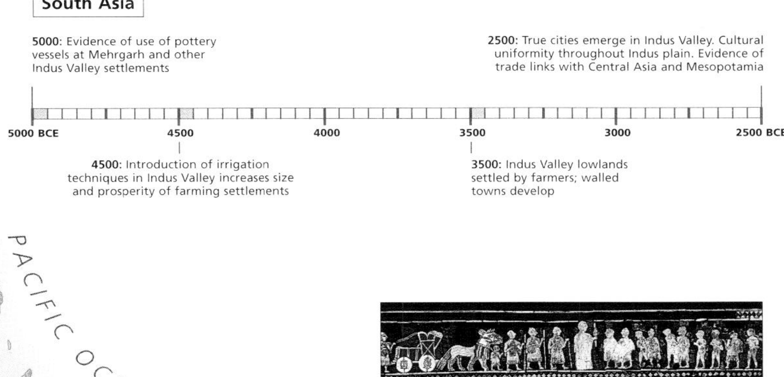

Arabian Peninsula

Nile

Kachhi: Wheat and barley cultivation

Deccan: Cattle pastoralists

Mekong

Coastal Vietnam: Rice-farming villages, domesticated animals, bronze tools and ornaments

Philippine Islands

PACIFIC OCEAN

Upper Nile Valley: Wheat and barley cultivation

Sumatra

Borneo

Maritime Southeast Asia: Slow transition from hunting and gathering to farming

Java

New Guinea

Hunter-gatherers

INDIAN OCEAN

Madagascar

Zambezi

The world in 2500 BCE

transition from hunting and gathering to agriculture

agricultural areas

urban areas

urban hinterland

Hunter-gatherers

Australia

Darling

New Zealand

The royal standard of Ur depicts the Sumerian ruler at war and in peacetime. The panels are crafted in lapis lazuli and shell from as far away as Afghanistan.

West Asia

Mesopotamia's fertile floodplains were the crucible of the urban revolution. Uruk, one of the first city-states, developed c.3500 BCE. The early cities of Mesopotamia were built around the raised mud-brick temple complex. The temple administered much of the city's land and livestock and a priestly elite was responsible for recording and storing produce. The temple accounting system led to pictographic writing by c.3250 BCE.

Africa

3400: First walled towns appear in Egypt

3000: Narmer unifies Upper and Lower Egypt, and becomes first pharaoh. City of Memphis founded

2530: Construction of Great Pyramid of Khufu, the largest of the Eyptian pyramids, at Giza

5000 BCE | 4500 | 4000 | 3500 | 3000 | 2500 BCE

3200: Earliest evidence of hieroglyphic writing system in Egypt

2650: The step pyramid of Zoser, the first Egyptian pyramid, is built at Saqqara

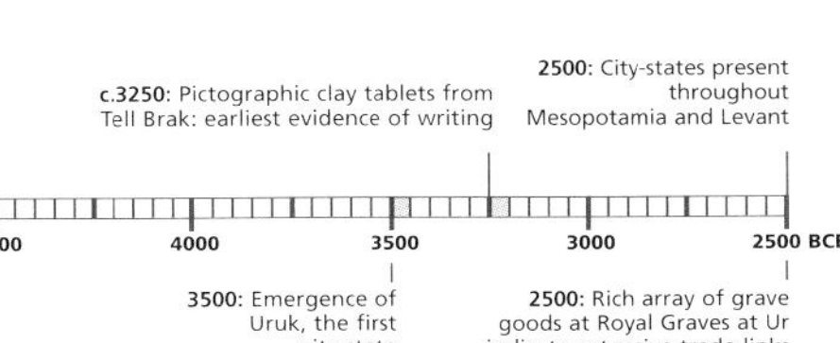

TRADE AND THE FIRST CITIES

This Egyptian ivory label is inscribed with the name of King Djet (c.3000 BCE).

BY 2500 BCE, CITIES WERE ESTABLISHED in three major centres: the Nile Valley, Mesopotamia, and the Indus valley, with a scattering of other cities across the intervening terrain. The culmination of a long process of settlement and expansion – some early cities had populations tens of thousands strong – the first urban civilizations all relied on rich agricultural lands to support their growth. In each case, lack of the most important natural resources – timber, metal, and stone – forced these urban civilizations to establish trading networks which ultimately extended from the Hindu Kush to the Mediterranean. They imported a diverse range of goods: metals and precious stones, such as lapis lazuli, gold, and turquoise, met the demands of the growing social elites for luxury goods; diorite, limestone, and timber were needed for the monumental construction programmes which were an integral part of urban life. Where trading contacts led, cultural influence followed, and cities soon began to develop in the trading hinterlands of the Iranian Plateau and Anatolia.

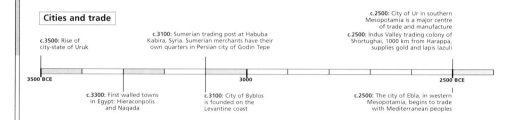

Cities and trade

- **c.3500:** Rise of city-state of Uruk
- **c.3300:** First walled towns in Egypt: Hieraconpolis and Naqada
- **c.3100:** Sumerian trading post at Habuba Kabira, Syria. Sumerian merchants have their own quarters in Persian city of Godin Tepe
- **c.3100:** City of Byblos is founded on the Levantine coast
- **c.2500:** City of Ur in southern Mesopotamia is a major centre of trade and manufacture
- **c.2500:** Indus Valley trading colony of Shortughai, 1000 km from Harappa, supplies gold and lapis lazuli
- **c.2500:** The city of Ebla, in western Mesopotamia, begins to trade with Mediterranean peoples

3500 BCE — 3000 — 2500 BCE

Ur: a trading city

The ancient city of Ur, was the capital of a south Mesopotamian empire towards the end of the 3rd millennium. It was a major economic centre, with extensive trade links extending as far as Dilmun (Bahrain) and the cities of the Indus. Ships, laden with gold, copper, timber, ivory, and precious stones, had access to the Persian Gulf via canals which linked the city to the Euphrates. Archives of clay tablets record, in minute detail, transactions and ships' cargoes. The wealth this trade generated is reflected in the grandiose buildings which adorned the city, most notably the ziggurat dedicated to the city's deity, Ur-Nammu, and in the lavishly furnished burials of Ur's so-called 'Royal Graves'.

1 Ur

- sacred enclosure
- royal palace
- other building
- inner walls
- outer walls

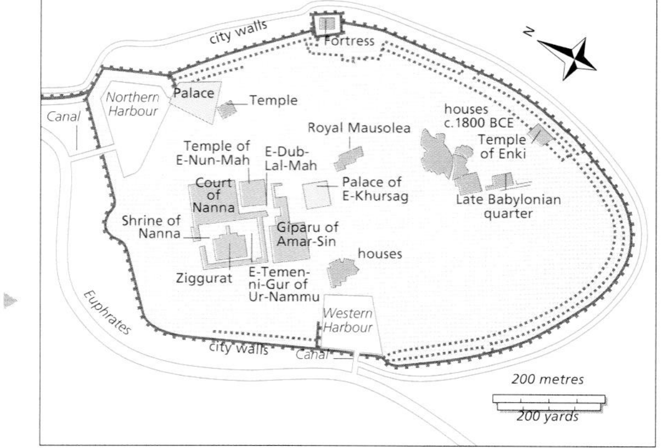

Transport

The long-distance trading networks of the ancient world required revolutionary developments in transport. Much of the trade was maritime; the cities of Mesopotamia all had access, via rivers and canals, to the Persian Gulf and Indus Valley, and there is ample evidence for trade along the Gulf coast and Arabian Sea to the mouth of the Indus. The timber boats of the Nile, depicted carrying great columns of granite and alabaster, are known from tomb reliefs, models and burials. Overland trade was dependent on newly-domesticated beasts of burden, such as asses and camels. Wheeled carts, pulled by oxen and bullocks, were also used.

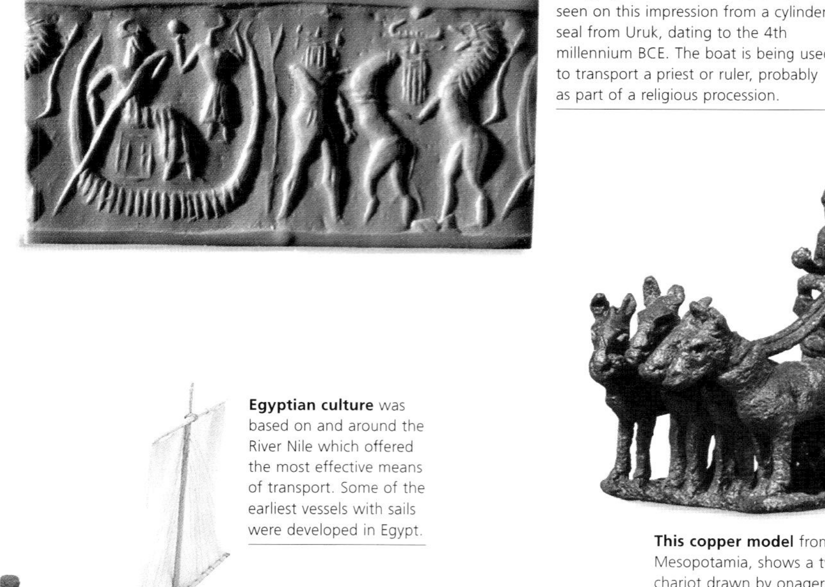

A high-prowed reed boat can be seen on this impression from a cylinder seal from Uruk, dating to the 4th millennium BCE. The boat is being used to transport a priest or ruler, probably as part of a religious procession.

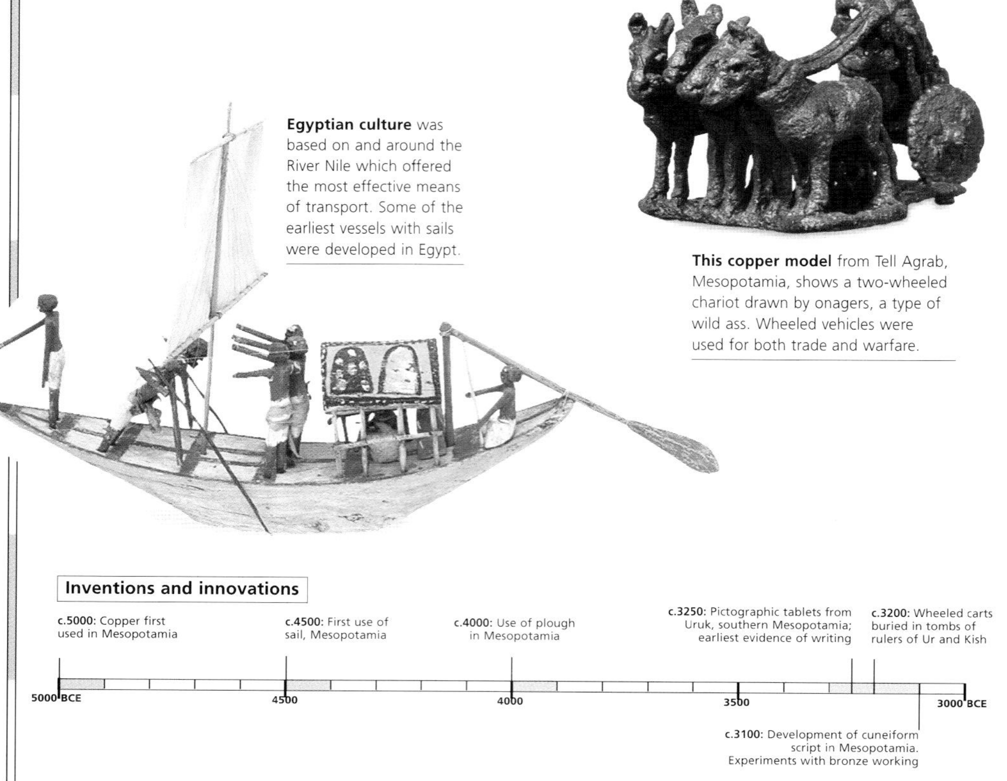

Egyptian culture was based on and around the River Nile which offered the most effective means of transport. Some of the earliest vessels with sails were developed in Egypt.

This copper model from Tell Agrab, Mesopotamia, shows a two-wheeled chariot drawn by onagers, a type of wild ass. Wheeled vehicles were used for both trade and warfare.

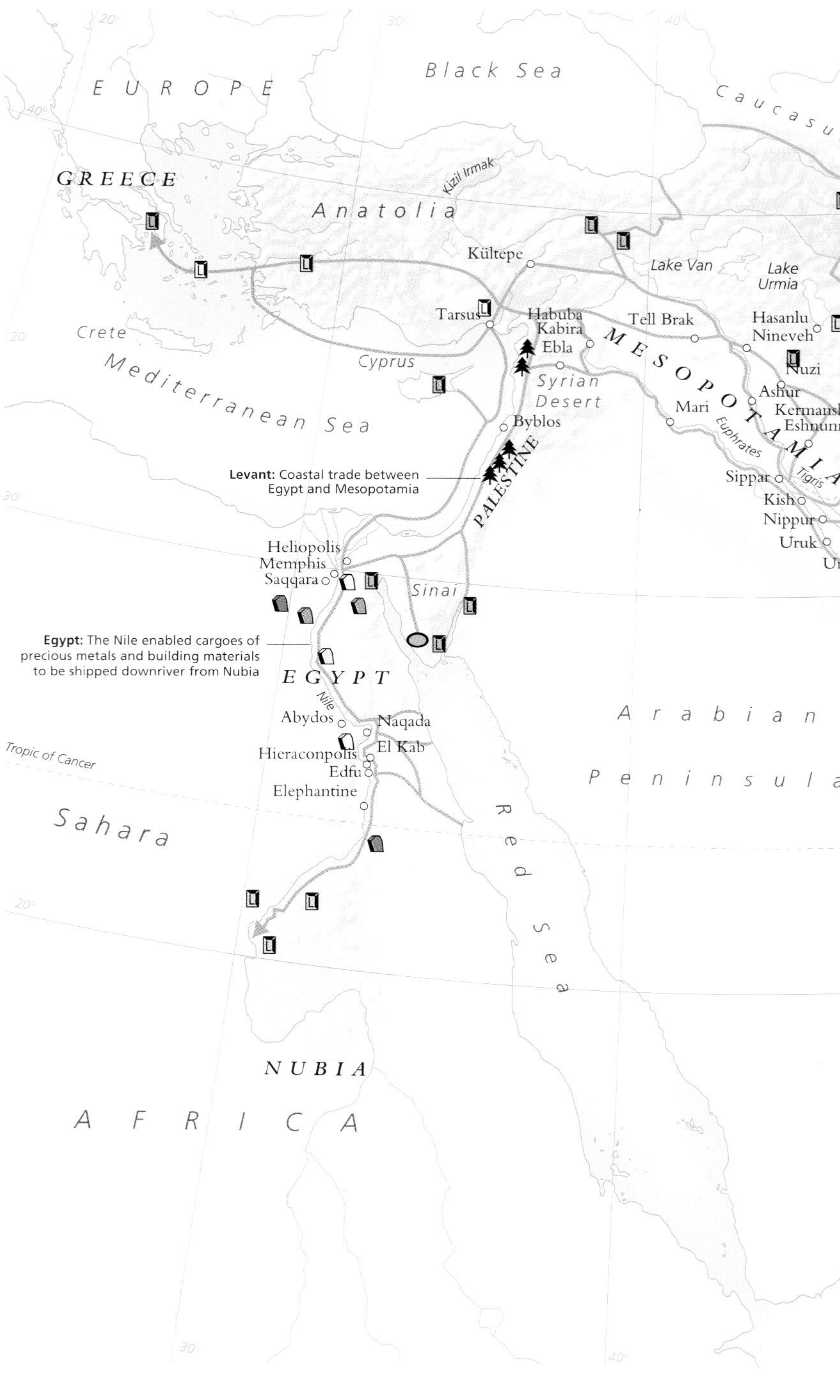

Inventions and innovations

- **c.5000:** Copper first used in Mesopotamia
- **c.4500:** First use of sail, Mesopotamia
- **c.4000:** Use of plough in Mesopotamia
- **c.3250:** Pictographic tablets from Uruk, southern Mesopotamia; earliest evidence of writing
- **c.3200:** Wheeled carts buried in tombs of rulers of Ur and Kish
- **c.3100:** Development of cuneiform script in Mesopotamia. Experiments with bronze working

5000 BCE — 4500 — 4000 — 3500 — 3000 BCE

SEE ALSO:

Africa: pp.158–159

West Asia: pp.174–175

South and Southeast Asia: pp.240–241

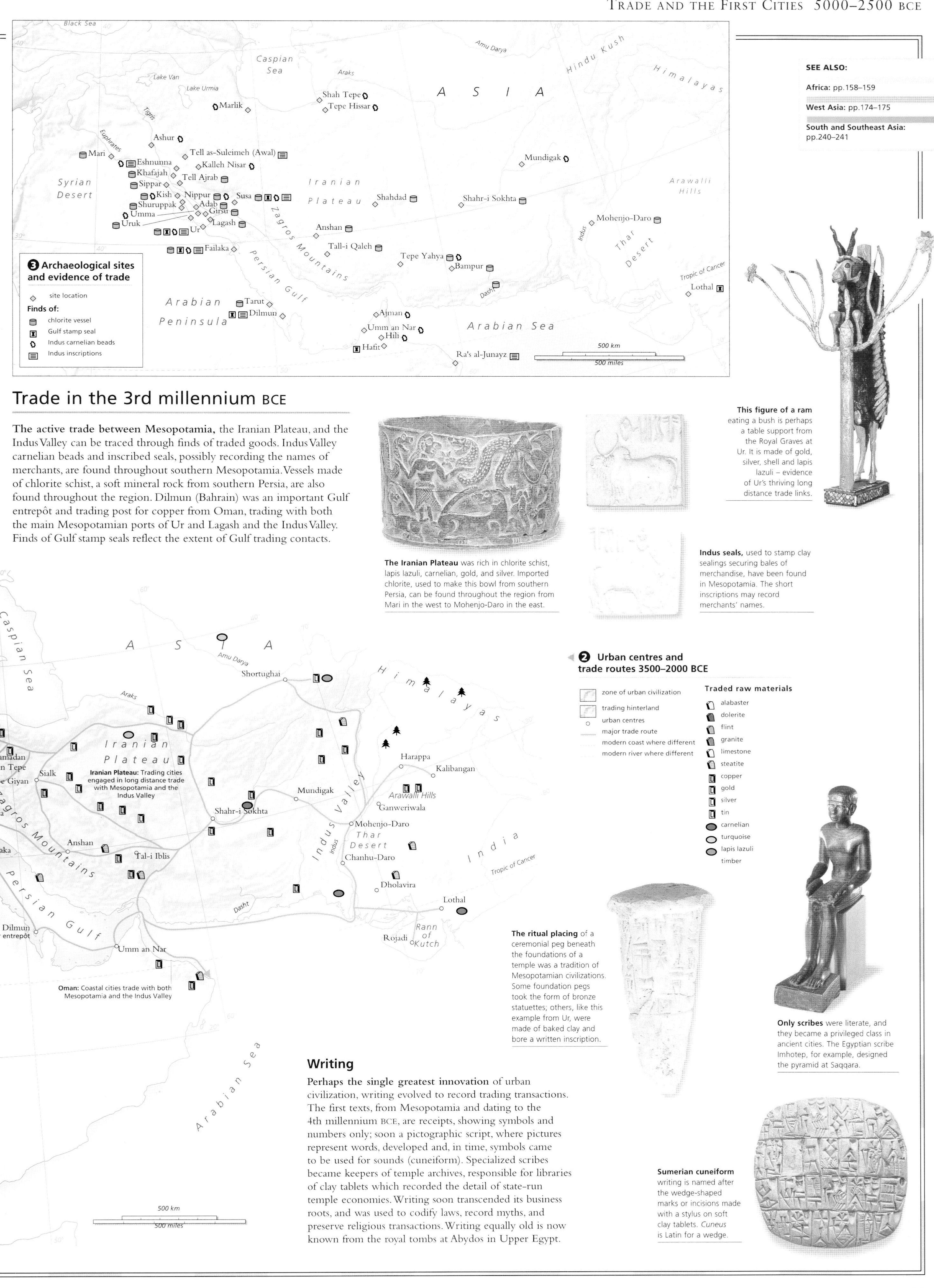

Trade in the 3rd millennium BCE

The active trade between Mesopotamia, the Iranian Plateau, and the Indus Valley can be traced through finds of traded goods. Indus Valley carnelian beads and inscribed seals, possibly recording the names of merchants, are found throughout southern Mesopotamia. Vessels made of chlorite schist, a soft mineral rock from southern Persia, are also found throughout the region. Dilmun (Bahrain) was an important Gulf entrepôt and trading post for copper from Oman, trading with both the main Mesopotamian ports of Ur and Lagash and the Indus Valley. Finds of Gulf stamp seals reflect the extent of Gulf trading contacts.

The Iranian Plateau was rich in chlorite schist, lapis lazuli, carnelian, gold, and silver. Imported chlorite, used to make this bowl from southern Persia, can be found throughout the region from Mari in the west to Mohenjo-Daro in the east.

Indus seals, used to stamp clay sealings securing bales of merchandise, have been found in Mesopotamia. The short inscriptions may record merchants' names.

This figure of a ram eating a bush is perhaps a table support from the Royal Graves at Ur. It is made of gold, silver, shell and lapis lazuli – evidence of Ur's thriving long distance trade links.

The ritual placing of a ceremonial peg beneath the foundations of a temple was a tradition of Mesopotamian civilizations. Some foundation pegs took the form of bronze statuettes; others, like this example from Ur, were made of baked clay and bore a written inscription.

Only scribes were literate, and they became a privileged class in ancient cities. The Egyptian scribe Imhotep, for example, designed the pyramid at Saqqara.

Writing

Perhaps the single greatest innovation of urban civilization, writing evolved to record trading transactions. The first texts, from Mesopotamia and dating to the 4th millennium BCE, are receipts, showing symbols and numbers only; soon a pictographic script, where pictures represent words, developed and, in time, symbols came to be used for sounds (cuneiform). Specialized scribes became keepers of temple archives, responsible for libraries of clay tablets which recorded the detail of state-run temple economies. Writing soon transcended its business roots, and was used to codify laws, record myths, and preserve religious transactions. Writing equally old is now known from the royal tombs at Abydos in Upper Egypt.

Sumerian cuneiform writing is named after the wedge-shaped marks or incisions made with a stylus on soft clay tablets. *Cuneus* is Latin for a wedge.

THE WORLD 2500–1250 BCE

AS THE FIRST CITIES expanded and proliferated, states developed, populations grew, and economic pressures increased. Rivalry for territory and power made the early states increasingly militaristic, and warfare, weapons, and diplomacy are conspicuous in the archaeology of this period. As these early societies became more stratified, distinct classes – warriors, priests, scribes, craftspeople, labourers – began to emerge. The great wealth of rulers and the social elite is reflected in the rich array of grave goods found in their burials. Urban civilizations still covered only a tiny fraction of the Earth's surface; in Europe, scattered agricultural communities were becoming more sophisticated, developing metallurgy and trade, and beginning to compete for land and resources. Hunter-gatherer groups still thrived in many areas, and many islands in the Pacific were yet to be settled at this time.

SUN SYMBOLISM

Symbolic representations of the Sun, suggestive of life, fertility, and creation, are found in almost all cultures. During this period in Egypt, the sun god Ra was the dominant figure among the high gods, his enhanced status culminating in the brief solar monotheism under Pharaoh Akhenaten c.1350 BCE. In Scandinavia, ritual finds such as the sun chariot found in a bog at Trundholm (*below*) attest to monotheistic sun worship and fertility rites in the region during the Bronze Age.

This bronze wheeled model of a horse drawing a disc, which dates to c.1650 BCE, may depict the sun's progress across the heavens.

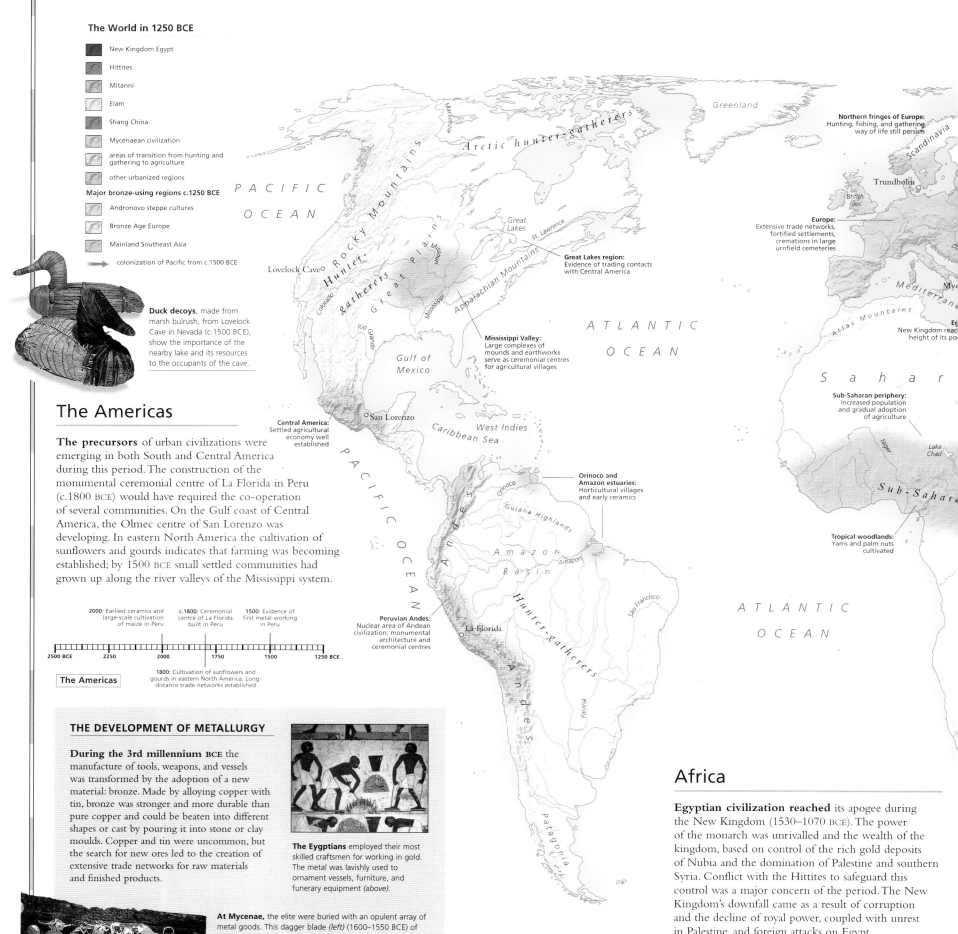

The World in 1250 BCE

- New Kingdom Egypt
- Hittites
- Mitanni
- Elam
- Shang China
- Mycenaean civilization
- areas of transition from hunting and gathering to agriculture
- other urbanized regions

Major bronze-using regions c.1250 BCE

- Andronovo steppe cultures
- Bronze Age Europe
- Mainland Southeast Asia
- colonization of Pacific from c.1500 BCE

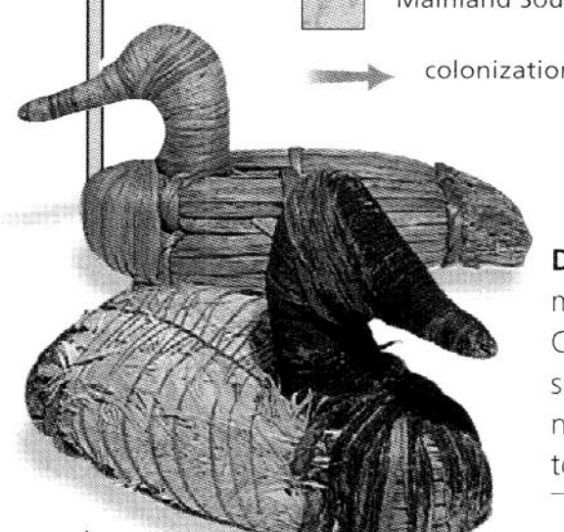

Duck decoys, made from marsh bulrush, from Lovelock Cave in Nevada (c.1500 BCE), show the importance of the nearby lake and its resources to the occupants of the cave.

Greenland

Arctic hunter-gatherers

Mackenzie

Rocky Mountains

PACIFIC OCEAN

Lovelock Cave

Hunter-gatherers

Great Plains

Colorado

Missouri

Great Lakes

St. Lawrence

Appalachian Mountains

Mississippi

Rio Grande

Gulf of Mexico

Great Lakes region: Evidence of trading contacts with Central America

Mississippi Valley: Large complexes of mounds and earthworks serve as ceremonial centres for agricultural villages

ATLANTIC OCEAN

Northern fringes of Europe: Hunting, fishing, and gathering way of life still persists

Scandinavia

Trundholm

British Isles

Europe: Extensive trade networks, fortified settlements, cremations in large urnfield cemeteries

Mediterranean

Atlas Mountains

New Kingdom reac[hes] height of its po[wer]

Sahara

Sub-Saharan periphery: Increased population and gradual adoption of agriculture

Niger

Lake Chad

Sub-Sahara

Tropical woodlands: Yams and palm nuts cultivated

San Lorenzo

Central America: Settled agricultural economy well established

West Indies

Caribbean Sea

Orinoco and Amazon estuaries: Horticultural villages and early ceramics

Orinoco

Guiana Highlands

Amazon Basin

Amazon

São Francisco

Andes

PACIFIC OCEAN

Peruvian Andes: Nuclear area of Andean civilization; monumental architecture and ceremonial centres

La Florida

Hunter-gatherers

Paraná

Patagonia

ATLANTIC OCEAN

The Americas

The precursors of urban civilizations were emerging in both South and Central America during this period. The construction of the monumental ceremonial centre of La Florida in Peru (c.1800 BCE) would have required the co-operation of several communities. On the Gulf coast of Central America, the Olmec centre of San Lorenzo was developing. In eastern North America the cultivation of sunflowers and gourds indicates that farming was becoming established; by 1500 BCE small settled communities had grown up along the river valleys of the Mississippi system.

2000: Earliest ceramics and large-scale cultivation of maize in Peru

c.1800: Ceremonial centre of La Florida built in Peru

1500: Evidence of first metal-working in Peru

2500 BCE – 2250 – 2000 – 1750 – 1500 – 1250 BCE

The Americas

1800: Cultivation of sunflowers and gourds in eastern North America. Long-distance trade networks established

THE DEVELOPMENT OF METALLURGY

During the 3rd millennium BCE the manufacture of tools, weapons, and vessels was transformed by the adoption of a new material: bronze. Made by alloying copper with tin, bronze was stronger and more durable than pure copper and could be beaten into different shapes or cast by pouring it into stone or clay moulds. Copper and tin were uncommon, but the search for new ores led to the creation of extensive trade networks for raw materials and finished products.

The Eygptians employed their most skilled craftsmen for working in gold. The metal was lavishly used to ornament vessels, furniture, and funerary equipment *(above)*.

At Mycenae, the elite were buried with an opulent array of metal goods. This dagger blade *(left)* (1600–1550 BCE) of bronze inlaid with silver portrays a lion hunt.

Africa

Egyptian civilization reached its apogee during the New Kingdom (1530–1070 BCE). The power of the monarch was unrivalled and the wealth of the kingdom, based on control of the rich gold deposits of Nubia and the domination of Palestine and southern Syria. Conflict with the Hittites to safeguard this control was a major concern of the period. The New Kingdom's downfall came as a result of corruption and the decline of royal power, coupled with unrest in Palestine, and foreign attacks on Egypt.

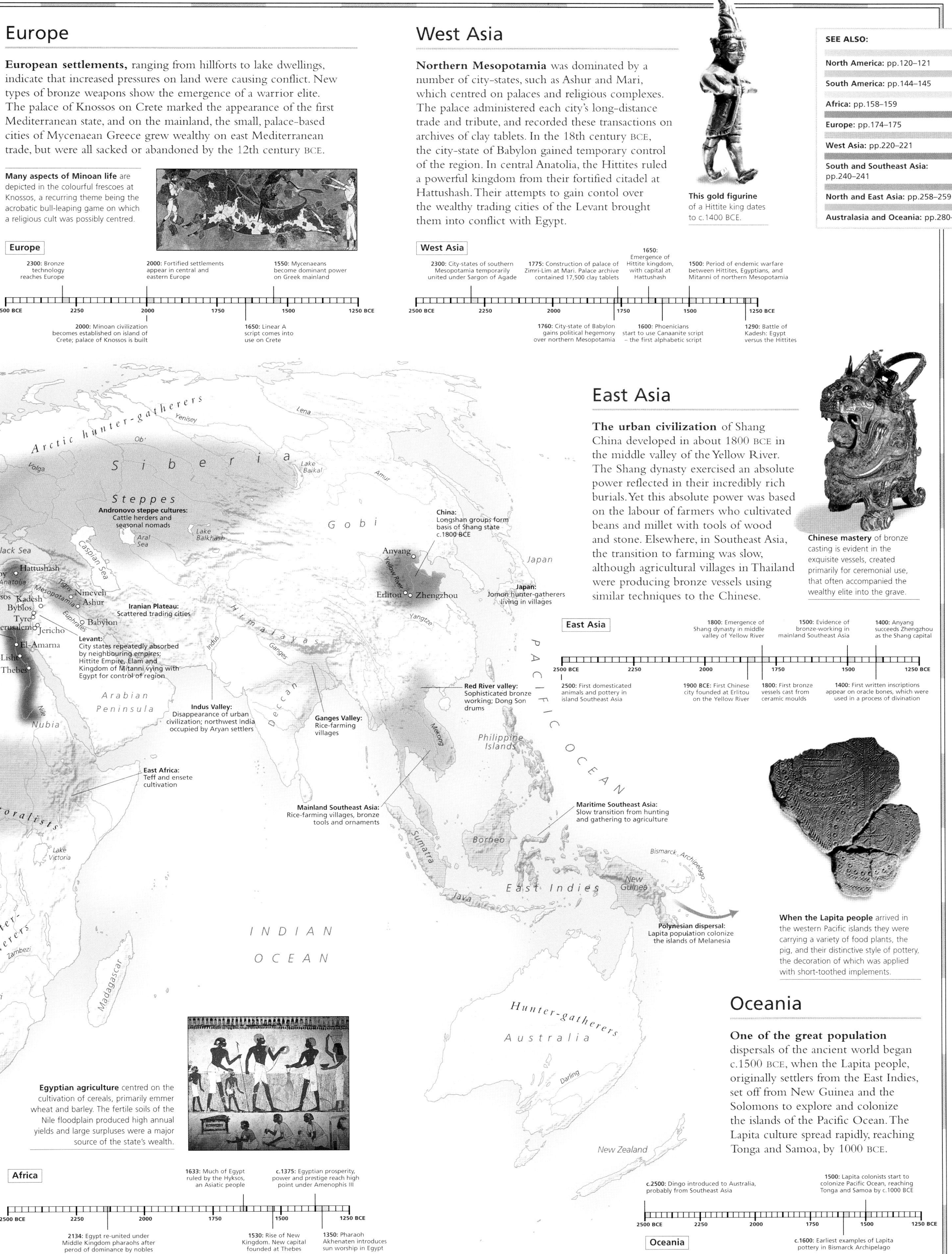

Europe

European settlements, ranging from hillforts to lake dwellings, indicate that increased pressures on land were causing conflict. New types of bronze weapons show the emergence of a warrior elite. The palace of Knossos on Crete marked the appearance of the first Mediterranean state, and on the mainland, the small, palace-based cities of Mycenaean Greece grew wealthy on east Mediterranean trade, but were all sacked or abandoned by the 12th century BCE.

Many aspects of Minoan life are depicted in the colourful frescoes at Knossos, a recurring theme being the acrobatic bull-leaping game on which a religious cult was possibly centred.

Europe
2300: Bronze technology reaches Europe
2000: Fortified settlements appear in central and eastern Europe
1550: Mycenaeans become dominant power on Greek mainland
2500 BCE
2250
2000
1750
1500
1250 BCE
2000: Minoan civilization becomes established on island of Crete; palace of Knossos is built
1650: Linear A script comes into use on Crete

West Asia

Northern Mesopotamia was dominated by a number of city-states, such as Ashur and Mari, which centred on palaces and religious complexes. The palace administered each city's long-distance trade and tribute, and recorded these transactions on archives of clay tablets. In the 18th century BCE, the city-state of Babylon gained temporary control of the region. In central Anatolia, the Hittites ruled a powerful kingdom from their fortified citadel at Hattushash. Their attempts to gain contol over the wealthy trading cities of the Levant brought them into conflict with Egypt.

This gold figurine of a Hittite king dates to c.1400 BCE.

SEE ALSO:

North America: pp.120–121

South America: pp.144–145

Africa: pp.158–159

Europe: pp.174–175

West Asia: pp.220–221

South and Southeast Asia: pp.240–241

North and East Asia: pp.258–259

Australasia and Oceania: pp.280–281

West Asia
2300: City-states of southern Mesopotamia temporarily united under Sargon of Agade
1775: Construction of palace of Zimri-Lim at Mari. Palace archive contained 17,500 clay tablets
1650: Emergence of Hittite kingdom, with capital at Hattushash
1500: Period of endemic warfare between Hittites, Egyptians, and Mitanni of northern Mesopotamia
2500 BCE
2250
2000
1750
1500
1250 BCE
1760: City-state of Babylon gains political hegemony over northern Mesopotamia
1600: Phoenicians start to use Canaanite script – the first alphabetic script
1290: Battle of Kadesh: Egypt versus the Hittites

East Asia

The urban civilization of Shang China developed in about 1800 BCE in the middle valley of the Yellow River. The Shang dynasty exercised an absolute power reflected in their incredibly rich burials. Yet this absolute power was based on the labour of farmers who cultivated beans and millet with tools of wood and stone. Elsewhere, in Southeast Asia, the transition to farming was slow, although agricultural villages in Thailand were producing bronze vessels using similar techniques to the Chinese.

Chinese mastery of bronze casting is evident in the exquisite vessels, created primarily for ceremonial use, that often accompanied the wealthy elite into the grave.

East Asia
1800: Emergence of Shang dynasty in middle valley of Yellow River
1500: Evidence of bronze-working in mainland Southeast Asia
1400: Anyang succeeds Zhengzhou as the Shang capital
2500 BCE
2250
2000
1750
1500
1250 BCE
2500: First domesticated animals and pottery in island Southeast Asia
1900 BCE: First Chinese city founded at Erlitou on the Yellow River
1800: First bronze vessels cast from ceramic moulds
1400: First written inscriptions appear on oracle bones, which were used in a process of divination

Arctic hunter-gatherers
Yenisey
Lena
Ob'
Siberia
Lake Baikal
Amur
Volga
Steppes
Andronovo steppe cultures: Cattle herders and seasonal nomads
Aral Sea
Lake Balkhash
Gobi
China: Longshan groups form basis of Shang state c.1800 BCE
Anyang
Yellow River
Erlitou
Zhengzhou
Japan
Japan: Jomon hunter-gatherers living in villages
Black Sea
Caspian Sea
Troy
Hattushash
Anatolia
Knossos
Kadesh
Mesopotamia
Tigris
Nineveh
Ashur
Byblos
Euphrates
Tyre
Babylon
Jerusalem
Jericho
El-Amarna
El-Lisht
Thebes
Iranian Plateau: Scattered trading cities
Levant: City states repeatedly absorbed by neighbouring empires; Hittite Empire, Elam and Kingdom of Mitanni vying with Egypt for control of region
Himalayas
Indus
Ganges
Yangtze
Arabian Peninsula
Nile
Nubia
Indus Valley: Disappearance of urban civilization; northwest India occupied by Aryan settlers
Deccan
Ganges Valley: Rice-farming villages
Red River valley: Sophisticated bronze working; Dong Son drums
Mekong
Philippine Islands
PACIFIC OCEAN
East Africa: Teff and ensete cultivation
pastoralists
Mainland Southeast Asia: Rice-farming villages, bronze tools and ornaments
Maritime Southeast Asia: Slow transition from hunting and gathering to agriculture
Borneo
Sumatra
Bismarck Archipelago
New Guinea
East Indies
Java
Lake Victoria
Polynesian dispersal: Lapita population colonize the islands of Melanesia
INDIAN OCEAN
Zambezi
Madagascar
Hunter-gatherers
Australia
Darling
New Zealand

When the Lapita people arrived in the western Pacific islands they were carrying a variety of food plants, the pig, and their distinctive style of pottery, the decoration of which was applied with short-toothed implements.

Oceania

One of the great population dispersals of the ancient world began c.1500 BCE, when the Lapita people, originally settlers from the East Indies, set off from New Guinea and the Solomons to explore and colonize the islands of the Pacific Ocean. The Lapita culture spread rapidly, reaching Tonga and Samoa, by 1000 BCE.

Oceania
c.2500: Dingo introduced to Australia, probably from Southeast Asia
1500: Lapita colonists start to colonize Pacific Ocean, reaching Tonga and Samoa by c.1000 BCE
2500 BCE
2250
2000
1750
1500
1250 BCE
c.1600: Earliest examples of Lapita pottery in Bismarck Archipelago

Egyptian agriculture centred on the cultivation of cereals, primarily emmer wheat and barley. The fertile soils of the Nile floodplain produced high annual yields and large surpluses were a major source of the state's wealth.

Africa
1633: Much of Egypt ruled by the Hyksos, an Asiatic people
c.1375: Egyptian prosperity, power and prestige reach high point under Amenophis III
2500 BCE
2250
2000
1750
1500
1250 BCE
2134: Egypt re-united under Middle Kingdom pharaohs after perod of dominance by nobles
1530: Rise of New Kingdom. New capital founded at Thebes
1350: Pharaoh Akhenaten introduces sun worship in Egypt

THE GROWTH OF THE CITY

Pharaoh Akhenaten (1353–1336 BCE) was the founder of the new city of El-Amarna.

OVER THE COURSE OF 2000 YEARS from c.3500 BCE, cities evolved in many different ways, reflecting the culture from which they emerged, outside pressures, and the preoccupations of their rulers. Yet, in a period of increasing social stratification, all cities represented the gulf between the ruler and the ruled, the sacred and the secular. They were physically, and symbolically, dominated by the palaces of the ruling elite, and by temples and religious precincts. The elaborate monuments of these early centres, clearly segregated from the houses and workshops of the labouring classes, symbolized the absolute power wielded by royal dynasties, priests, and the aristocracy. But the *status quo* was underpinned by a relentless quest for new territory and greater wealth; ultimately, this urge to expand was to evolve into imperialism.

The urban heartland

By 1250 BCE, zones of urbanism extended from the Mediterranean to China. The early expansion of urban civilization in southern Mesopotamia had created a swathe of cities, from Ur to Mycenae, which thrived on trade and contact, supplemented by the levying of taxes, tolls, and tribute. Rivalry for control of key cities, especially in the Levant, was endemic. While Egypt was also vying for political and economic control of the Levant, the cities of the Nile were stately religious and dynastic centres, adorned by magnificent temples, palaces, and cities of the dead. The distant cities of Shang China were strictly segregated – symbolic of a stratified society where the great wealth and luxury of the few rested on a simple farming base.

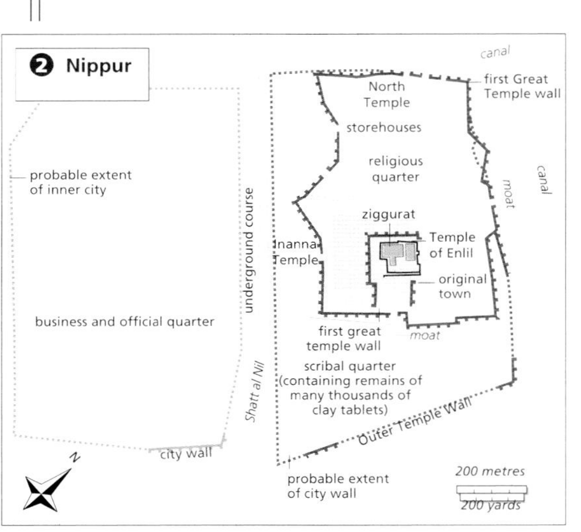

A ruler's power was legitimized by the foundation of cities and temples, as this sculpture of a Babylonian king carrying building materials shows.

Nippur

Centre of the worship of Enlil, the chief deity of the Sumerian pantheon, Nippur retained its importance over three millennia. Located on the Shatt al Nil, an ancient course of the Euphrates, the city was first occupied in c.4000 BCE. In c.2100 BCE, Ur-Nammu, ruler of the city-state of Ur, legitimized his role as Enlil's earthly representative by building the first temple and ziggurat to the deity. The temple was subsequently destroyed and rebuilt at least three times. The remains of the extensive religious quarter encompass a large scribal district as well as a temple to Inanna, queen of heaven.

A map of the city of Nippur – probably the oldest plan in the world – was found on a clay tablet from the site dating to c.1500 BCE. The two lines on the far left denote the River Euphrates; adjoining lines show one wall of the city.

Sculpted lions flank the 'Lion Gate', a major entrance into the city of Hattushash. In the 14th century BCE the fortifications of Hattushash were extended and strengthened, as befitted its status as an important imperial capital.

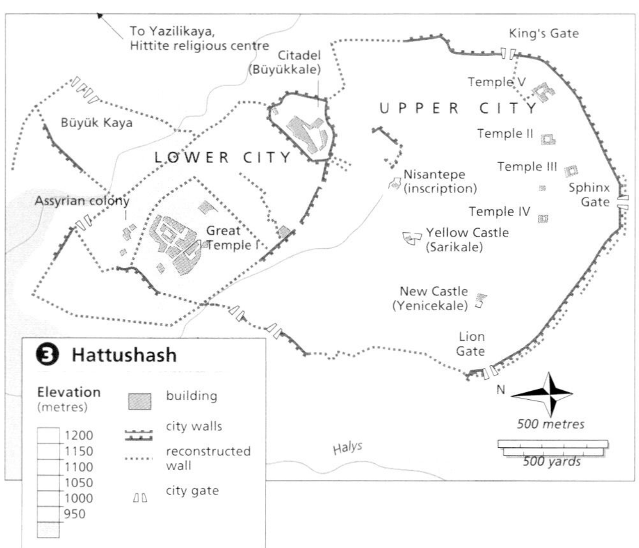

Hattushash

The Hittite kingdom, which emerged from the conquest of a number of Anatolian city states in the 17th century BCE, adopted the site of Hattushash (Boğazköy) as its capital. Situated at the head of a fertile river valley, the citadel, Büyükkale, was the core of the old city. By c.1400 BCE the walls had been extended to encompass the 'Upper City', and Hattushash had been adorned with a series of grandiose monuments – five temples and a palace within the citadel with a large pillared audience hall and a royal archive of 3000 clay tablets. The city walls, which stood on stone-faced ramparts, with projecting towers and twin-towered gateways, made Hattushash one of the most strongly fortified cities in the Middle East.

The development of cities

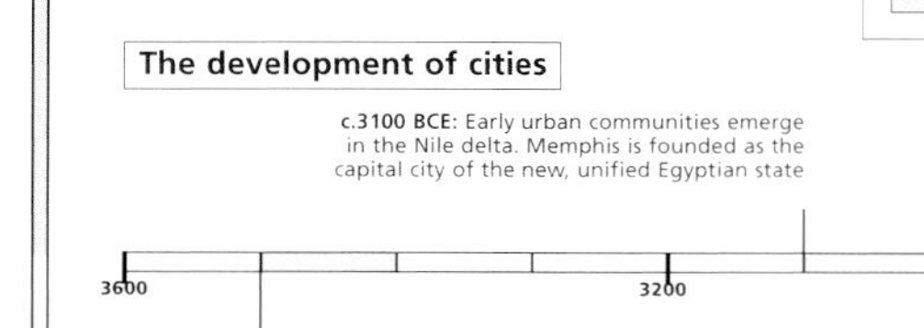
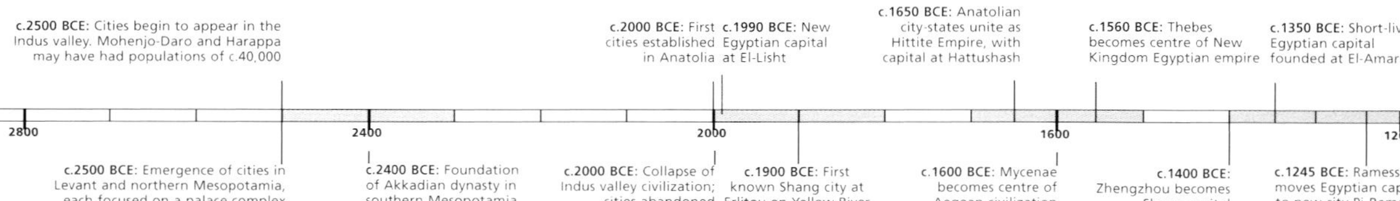

c.3500 BCE: Uruk period; emergence of first city-states in southern Mesopotamia. Uruk may have been the first city in the world

c.3100 BCE: Early urban communities emerge in the Nile delta. Memphis is founded as the capital city of the new, unified Egyptian state

c.2500 BCE: Cities begin to appear in the Indus valley. Mohenjo-Daro and Harappa may have had populations of c.40,000

c.2500 BCE: Emergence of cities in Levant and northern Mesopotamia, each focused on a palace complex

c.2400 BCE: Foundation of Akkadian dynasty in southern Mesopotamia

c.2000 BCE: First cities established in Anatolia

c.2000 BCE: Collapse of Indus valley civilization; cities abandoned

c.1990 BCE: New Egyptian capital at El-Lisht

c.1900 BCE: First known Shang city at Erlitou on Yellow River

c.1650 BCE: Anatolian city-states unite as Hittite Empire, with capital at Hattushash

c.1600 BCE: Mycenae becomes centre of Aegean civilization

c.1560 BCE: Thebes becomes centre of New Kingdom Egyptian empire

c.1400 BCE: Zhengzhou becomes Shang capital

c.1350 BCE: Short-lived Egyptian capital founded at El-Amarna

c.1245 BCE: Ramesses II moves Egyptian capital to new city Pi-Ramesse

Zhengzhou

The Shang dynasty ruled in the middle valley of the Yellow River from c.1800 BCE. Remains of Shang cities, rich tombs and luxury artefacts all indicate the presence of a highly sophisticated urban elite. Zhengzhou, one of successive Shang capitals, was founded c.1700 BCE. It consists of a roughly square enclosure, surrounded by 7 km-long, 10 m-high rammed earth walls. Within these walls stood the palace and ritual altar, dwelling places, storage pits for grain, pottery, and oracle bones (a means of divination, used by the Shang to consult their ancestors) and pits for human sacrifices. Outside the walls stood the residential areas, and specialist workshops producing fine artefacts in bone, bronze, and pottery.

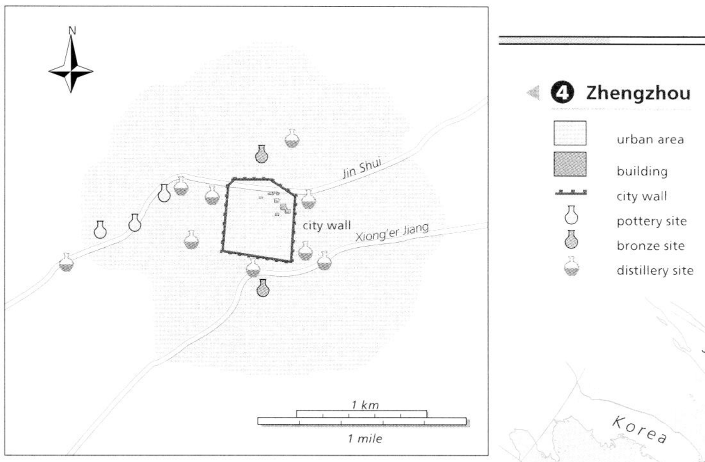

N
Jin Shui
city wall
Xiong'er Jiang
1 km
1 mile

4 Zhengzhou

- urban area
- building
- city wall
- pottery site
- bronze site
- distillery site

SEE ALSO:

Africa: pp.158–159

Europe: pp.174–175

West Asia: pp.220–221

South and Southeast Asia: pp.240–241

North and East Asia: pp.258–259

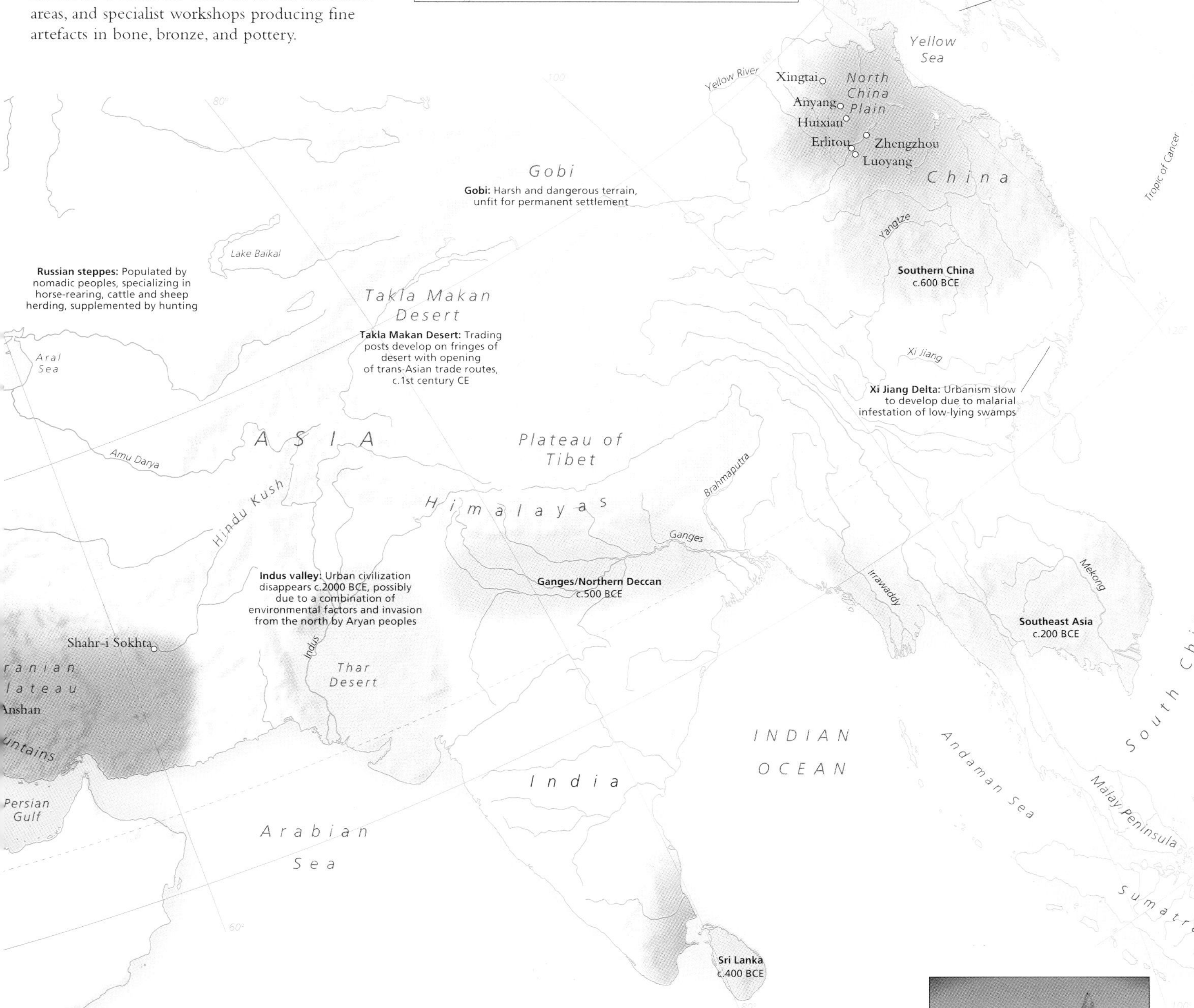

Japan
Korea
Japan and Korea: Cities do not appear until 1st millennium CE
Yellow Sea
Yellow River
Xingtai
North China Plain
Anyang
Huixian
Erlitou
Zhengzhou
Luoyang
China
Tropic of Cancer
Gobi
Gobi: Harsh and dangerous terrain, unfit for permanent settlement
Lake Baikal
Russian steppes: Populated by nomadic peoples, specializing in horse-rearing, cattle and sheep herding, supplemented by hunting
Yangtze
Southern China c.600 BCE
Takla Makan Desert
Takla Makan Desert: Trading posts develop on fringes of desert with opening of trans-Asian trade routes, c.1st century CE
Aral Sea
Xi Jiang
Xi Jiang Delta: Urbanism slow to develop due to malarial infestation of low-lying swamps
Amu Darya
ASIA
Plateau of Tibet
Hindu Kush
Himalayas
Brahmaputra
Ganges
Indus valley: Urban civilization disappears c.2000 BCE, possibly due to a combination of environmental factors and invasion from the north by Aryan peoples
Ganges/Northern Deccan c.500 BCE
Irrawaddy
Mekong
Southeast Asia c.200 BCE
South China Sea
Shahr-i Sokhta
Iranian Plateau
Anshan
Indus
Thar Desert
Mountains
INDIAN OCEAN
Andaman Sea
Borneo
Malay Peninsula
India
Persian Gulf
Arabian Sea
Equator
Maritime Southeast Asia: Cities do not appear until 1st millennium CE
Sumatra
Sri Lanka c.400 BCE
Java

The major cities of Shang China lay on the edge of the North China Plain. This fertile area, rich in alluvium deposited by the Yellow River, provided the agricultural base for Shang civilization.

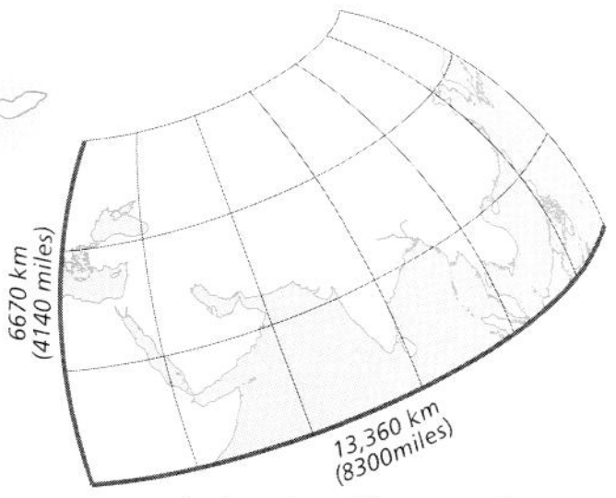

6670 km (4140 miles)
13,360 km (8300miles)
Scale varies with perspective

El-Amarna

El-Amarna was built by the Egyptian pharaoh Akhenaten to honour his god, Aten, in the 14th century BCE, and was abandoned shortly after his death. The city stood on a cliff-encircled plain on the east bank of the Nile. The Great Temple of Aten dominated the city, while immediately to the south lay the palace, bisected by the Royal Road, running parallel to the Nile, which divided it into private and official quarters. Outlying residential areas contained many fine private houses, with gardens and pools, probably the homes of prominent courtiers, interspersed with the tightly-packed dwellings of the poor.

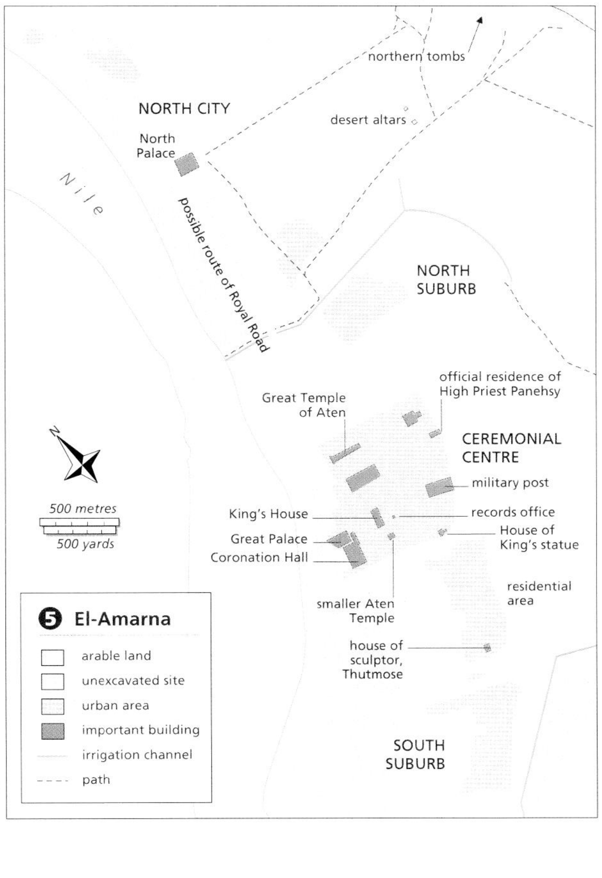

northern tombs
NORTH CITY
desert altars
North Palace
Nile
possible route of Royal Road
NORTH SUBURB
official residence of High Priest Panehsy
Great Temple of Aten
CEREMONIAL CENTRE
military post
King's House
records office
Great Palace
House of King's statue
Coronation Hall
residential area
smaller Aten Temple
house of sculptor, Thutmose
SOUTH SUBURB
500 metres
500 yards

5 El-Amarna

- arable land
- unexcavated site
- urban area
- important building
- irrigation channel
- path

Akhenaten built El-Amarna to symbolize his rejection of Egyptian tradition. His successor, Tutankhamun, returned to Thebes *(left)* and re-opened the temples of the old gods.

This plaster fragment decorated the walls of Akhenaten's Great Palace. It shows two of the king's daughters; their distorted features are typical of the art of the period.

THE WORLD 1250–750 BCE

THE INEXORABLE RIVALRIES between the cities and states of the Old World and incursions by nomadic tribes created a shifting pattern of allegiance and control within West Asia. The Assyrians formed the world's first large empire, and ruled their territory with ruthless efficiency, utilizing cavalry and new iron technology to fashion more effective weapons and armour. In both Europe and Asia iron revolutionized weapons, tools, and agricultural implements. More efficient farming produced higher crop yields and supported larger populations. Long-distance trade networks disseminated political and cultural influences across Europe and along the Mediterranean shores, but many areas remained unaffected. The first major centres of the Americas, the Chavín in Peru and the Olmec in Central America, developed in isolation, evolving the art styles, religious motifs, and ceremonies which were to imbue the civilizations that succeeded them.

North America

The first great Mexican civilization, the Olmec, emerged in the coastal lowlands southwest of Yucatán in about 1200 BCE. The Olmec founded a number of ceremonial centres, notably at San Lorenzo and La Venta. They also established trade networks in commodities such as obsidian, jade, and basalt which extended far to the north and west. To the northeast, the peoples of the Adena culture, based along the Ohio River from about 1000–300 BCE, constructed burial chambers beneath earthen mounds.

At San Lorenzo, the Olmec sculpted remarkable stone monuments, including colossal basalt heads with characteristic flat faces, thickened lips, and protective helmets.

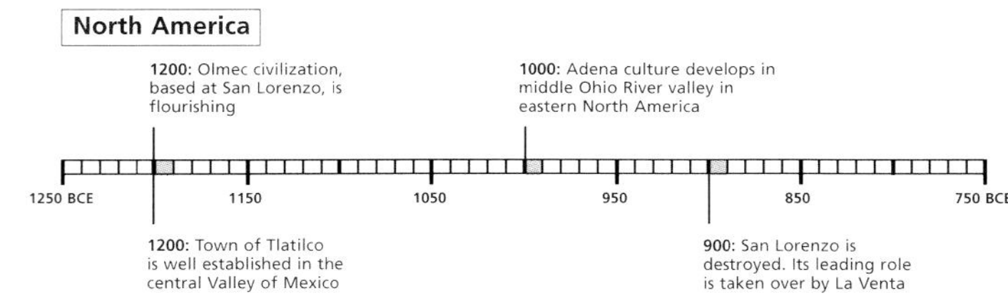

The World in 750 BCE

- Greek cities and territories
- Phoenician cities and territories
- small Chinese states under the Eastern Zhou dynasty

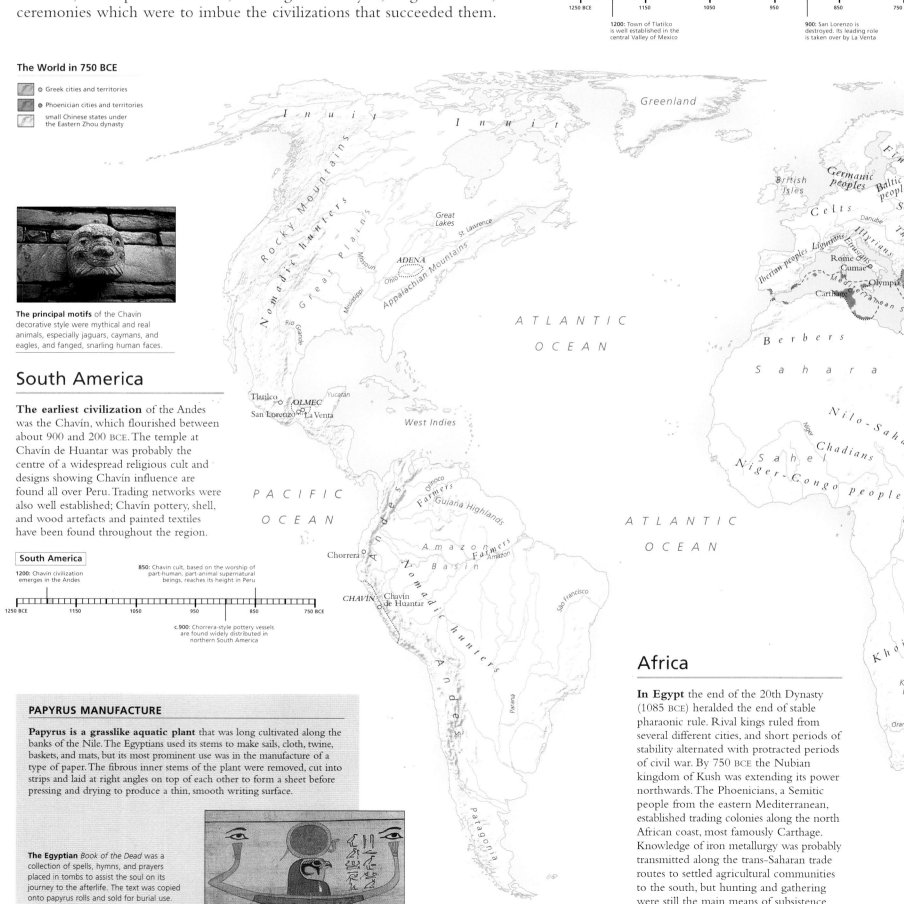

The principal motifs of the Chavin decorative style were mythical and real animals, especially jaguars, caymans, and eagles, and fanged, snarling human faces.

South America

The earliest civilization of the Andes was the Chavín, which flourished between about 900 and 200 BCE. The temple at Chavín de Huantar was probably the centre of a widespread religious cult and designs showing Chavín influence are found all over Peru. Trading networks were also well established; Chavín pottery, shell, and wood artefacts and painted textiles have been found throughout the region.

South America

1200: Chavin civilization emerges in the Andes

850: Chavin cult, based on the worship of part-human, part-animal supernatural beings, reaches its height in Peru

1250 BCE – 1150 – 1050 – 950 – 850 – 750 BCE

c.900: Chorrera-style pottery vessels are found widely distributed in northern South America

PAPYRUS MANUFACTURE

Papyrus is a grasslike aquatic plant that was long cultivated along the banks of the Nile. The Egyptians used its stems to make sails, cloth, twine, baskets, and mats, but its most prominent use was in the manufacture of a type of paper. The fibrous inner stems of the plant were removed, cut into strips and laid at right angles on top of each other to form a sheet before pressing and drying to produce a thin, smooth writing surface.

The Egyptian *Book of the Dead* was a collection of spells, hymns, and prayers placed in tombs to assist the soul on its journey to the afterlife. The text was copied onto papyrus rolls and sold for burial use.

Africa

In Egypt the end of the 20th Dynasty (1085 BCE) heralded the end of stable pharaonic rule. Rival kings ruled from several different cities, and short periods of stability alternated with protracted periods of civil war. By 750 BCE the Nubian kingdom of Kush was extending its power northwards. The Phoenicians, a Semitic people from the eastern Mediterranean, established trading colonies along the north African coast, most famously Carthage. Knowledge of iron metallurgy was probably transmitted along the trans-Saharan trade routes to settled agricultural communities to the south, but hunting and gathering were still the main means of subsistence for large areas of sub-Saharan Africa.

Europe

Independent city-states were founded throughout Greece and western Asia Minor. The establishment of trade links with Italy and the Levant increased prosperity and population and colonists began to build Greek trading cities along the shores of the Mediterranean. In Italy, the Etruscans built fortified hilltop cities and established trade links with Africa and Europe. Iron metallurgy, established in Central Europe by 1000 BCE, had reached Britain and Ireland by the 8th century. Iron was used to make sophisticated weapons and tools.

Mastery of the seas was vitally important to the Greeks as they began to establish overseas colonies. By 700 BCE advances in shipbuilding technology had produced swift, manoeuvrable galleys driven by three banks of oarsmen (triremes), as depicted on this pot.

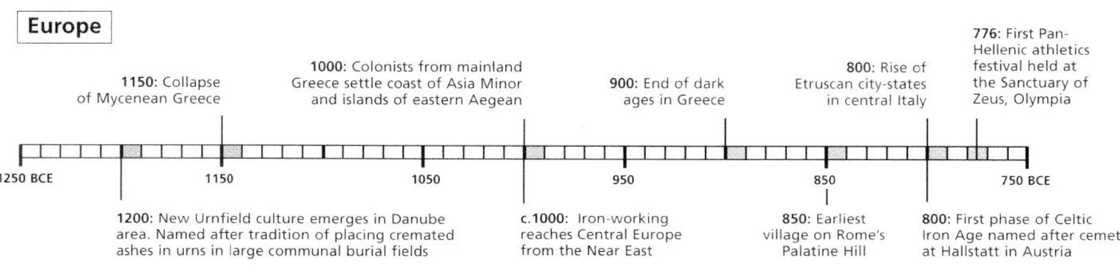

Europe
1150: Collapse of Mycenean Greece
1000: Colonists from mainland Greece settle coast of Asia Minor and islands of eastern Aegean
900: End of dark ages in Greece
800: Rise of Etruscan city-states in central Italy
776: First Pan-Hellenic athletics festival held at the Sanctuary of Zeus, Olympia
1250 BCE
1150
1050
950
850
750 BCE
1200: New Urnfield culture emerges in Danube area. Named after tradition of placing cremated ashes in urns in large communal burial fields
c.1000: Iron-working reaches Central Europe from the Near East
850: Earliest village on Rome's Palatine Hill
800: First phase of Celtic Iron Age named after cemetery at Hallstatt in Austria

BABYLONIAN ASTRONOMY

The Babylonians were one of the earliest peoples to make a systematic, scientific study of the skies. Their records go back to c.1800 BCE and accumulated over centuries. By 1000 BCE they were able to predict lunar eclipses and within two or three hundred years, the path of the Sun and some of the planets had been plotted with considerable accuracy. These astronomical records contributed to the later flowering of western astronomy.

This bronze model of the solar system is from Lake Sevan in Armenia. It dates from 10th–9th century BCE.

SEE ALSO:

North America: pp.120–121

South America: pp.144–145

Africa: pp.160–161

Europe: pp.176–177

West Asia: pp.222–223

South and Southeast Asia: pp.240–243

North and East Asia: pp.258–259

Australasia and Oceania: pp.280–281

West Asia

Power struggles between the established empires of West Asia created opportunities for infiltration by barbarian tribes, such as the Medes, Chaldeans, Philistines, Hebrews, and Phrygians, who attempted to seize power. In the 9th century BCE Ahab, son of Omri, founder of the Kingdom of Israel, consolidated the power of his state by marrying Jezebel, princess of Sidon. However, from the 9th century BCE, the dominant power in the region was Assyria, originally based in the Tigris valley. By the 8th century BCE the Assyrian Empire extended from the Levant to the Persian Gulf. Subject peoples were ruled by provincial governors and resistance was ruthlessly suppressed. Only the Armenian kingdom of Urartu remained beyond Assyrian control.

Assyrian kings ploughed the proceeds of their military conquests into the building of vast temples and palaces at Nimrud and Nineveh. Booty acquired during the campaigns, like this ivory panel of a sphinx, enriched many palace furnishings.

West Asia

- **1200:** Collapse of the Hittite Empire
- **c.1100:** Syria and Palestine settled by nomadic tribes
- **900:** Kingdom of Urartu established in Armenia resists Assyrian expansion
- **c.1200:** Jewish exodus from Egypt and settlement in Palestine
- **c.1000:** Phoenicians dominate trade of Levant and develop an alphabetic script
- **950:** Foundation of the Assyrian Empire
- **c.882:** Omri founds the Kingdom of Israel

Zhou rulers maintained Shang cultural traditions, including ancestor worship. Food and drink were offered in bronze ritual vessels, often shaped into bizarre combinations of animal forms.

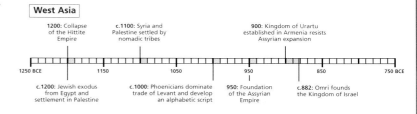

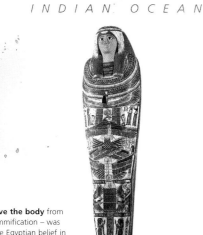

The need to preserve the body from decay – through mummification – was an integral part of the Egyptian belief in a life after death. This anthropomorphic case belonged to Shepenmut, Priestess of Thebes, who was buried around 800 BCE.

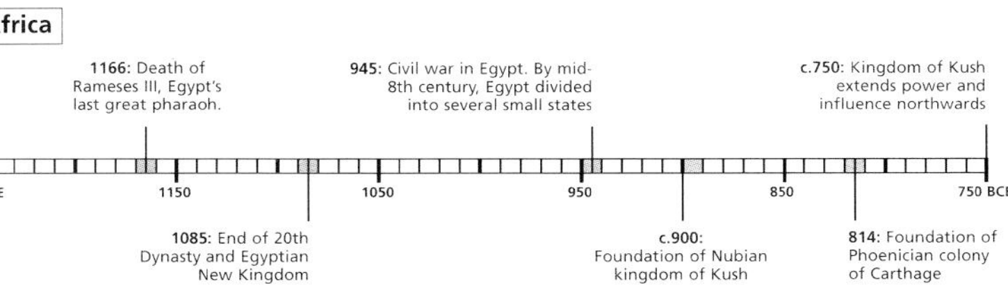

Africa
1166: Death of Rameses III, Egypt's last great pharaoh.
945: Civil war in Egypt. By mid-8th century, Egypt divided into several small states
c.750: Kingdom of Kush extends power and influence northwards
1250 BCE
1150
1050
950
850
750 BCE
1085: End of 20th Dynasty and Egyptian New Kingdom
c.900: Foundation of Nubian kingdom of Kush
814: Foundation of Phoenician colony of Carthage

East Asia

In China the Zhou dynasty succeeded the Shang in the 11th century BCE, heralding a period of stability until the 8th century when central authority collapsed, former fiefs rose up against the Zhou, and China split into separate kingdoms. Bronze technology for weapons and ornaments reached the Korean peninsula from Manchuria in about 1000 BCE.

East Asia

- **1027:** Zhou dynasty replaces Shang in China
- **1000:** Chinese bronze casting reaches level of craftsmanship unrivalled elsewhere at this period
- **c.1000:** Wet rice cultivation introduced to Korea from China
- **c.770:** Western Zhou period ends with collapse of centralized power

WRITING, COUNTING, AND CALENDARS

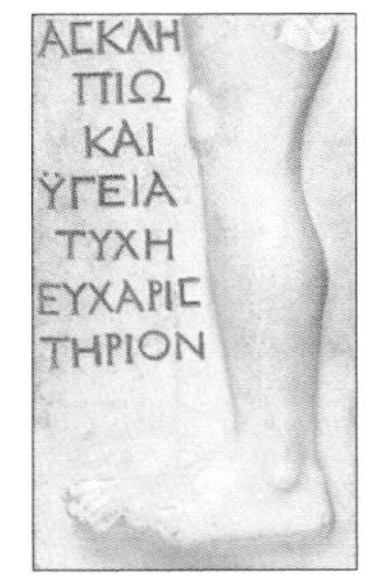

The Greek inscription *(above)* is an offering of thanks to Asclepius, the god of healing.

THE INTERTWINED DEVELOPMENT of writing and counting was closely related to the advent of agriculture and the need to record and tally stored goods, livestock, and commercial transactions. The precursors of the first known writing and numerical systems were clay counting tokens, used in Sumer from c.3400 BCE to record quantities of stored goods. They were eventually sealed in clay envelopes, and marked on the outside with signs indicating their contents – the first written symbols. Within a thousand years, writing and numerical systems had spread throughout West Asia (they evolved separately in China and Central America), bringing a revolutionary change in human consciousness. The ability to count in abstract enabled humans to measure, assess, record, and evaluate their world – calendrical systems, weights and measures, coinage, astronomical calculations, and geometry all followed. Writing became a powerful tool of government, a means of communicating over increasing distances, codifying laws, and recording myths and history.

The evolution and spread of major scripts

The earliest symbolic records, of economic transactions, were used in Sumer from c.3400 BCE, and gradually evolved into a pictographic script, where pictures represented words. Cuneiform writing was used to record a variety of languages, and spread throughout West Asia. The system eventually became more complex, and written symbols also came to stand for concepts or sounds. Egyptian hieroglyphics probably developed under Sumerian influence, though the system was unique. Chinese pictographic writing developed independently, as did the Zapotec and Maya systems in Central America. The Proto-Canaanite alphabet, based on a selection of Egyptian hieroglyphs (developed by 1200 BCE), was the probable precursor of the Phoenician alphabet, adapted by the Greeks in the 8th century BCE.

This inscription in Egyptian hieratic is a record of a trading transaction. Hieratic was a form of cursive script, written with ink and a reed brush.

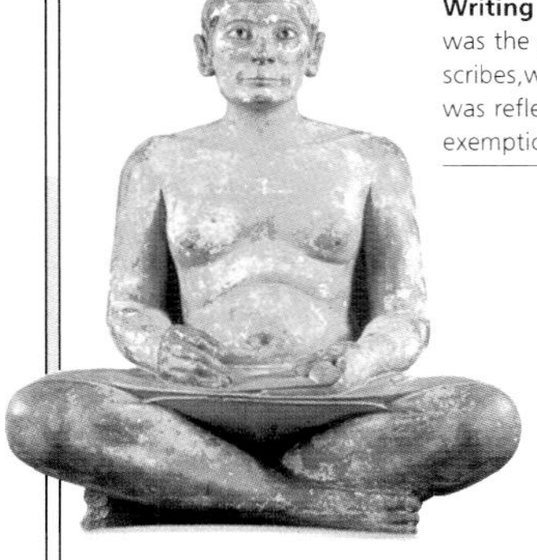

Writing in Ancient Egypt was the preserve of trained scribes, whose high status was reflected in their exemption from taxes.

This glyph from Central America, represents the word 'grass'.

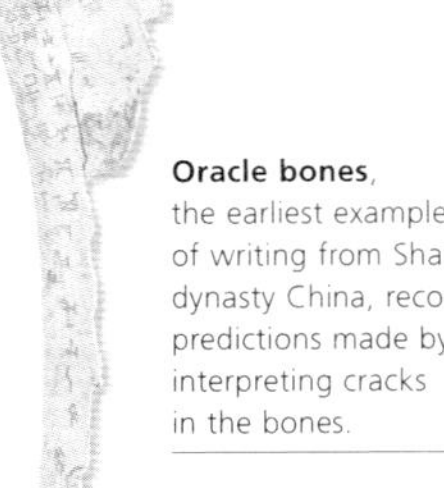

Oracle bones, the earliest examples of writing from Shang dynasty China, record predictions made by interpreting cracks in the bones.

The inscriptions on this black basalt pillar are the most complete example of the lawcode of Hammurabi, king of Babylonia (c.1790–1750 BCE), who is depicted on the top of the pillar.

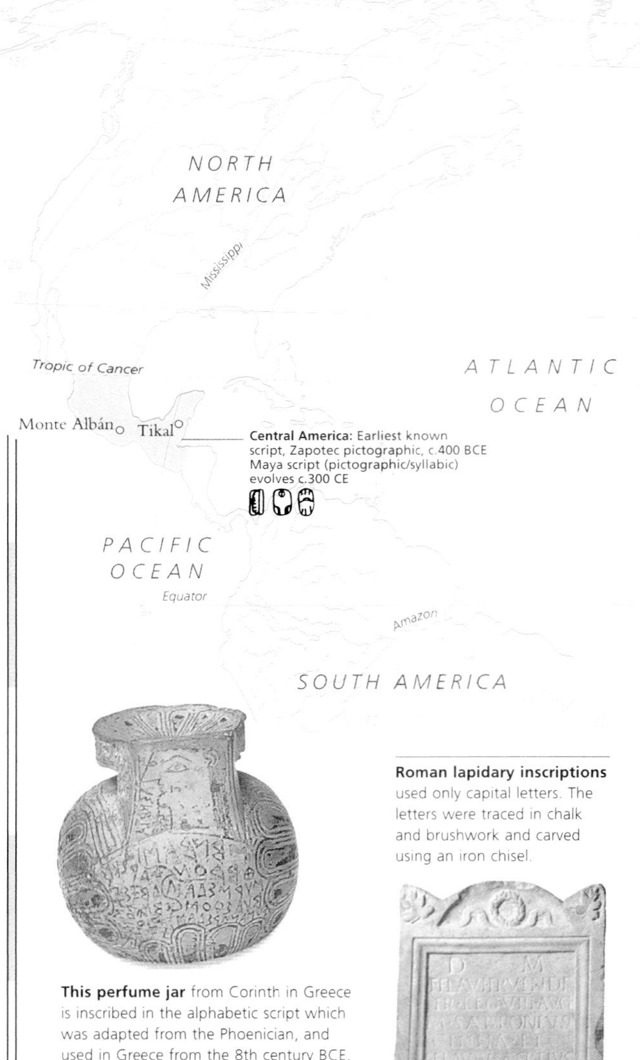

This perfume jar from Corinth in Greece is inscribed in the alphabetic script which was adapted from the Phoenician, and used in Greece from the 8th century BCE.

Roman lapidary inscriptions used only capital letters. The letters were traced in chalk and brushwork and carved using an iron chisel.

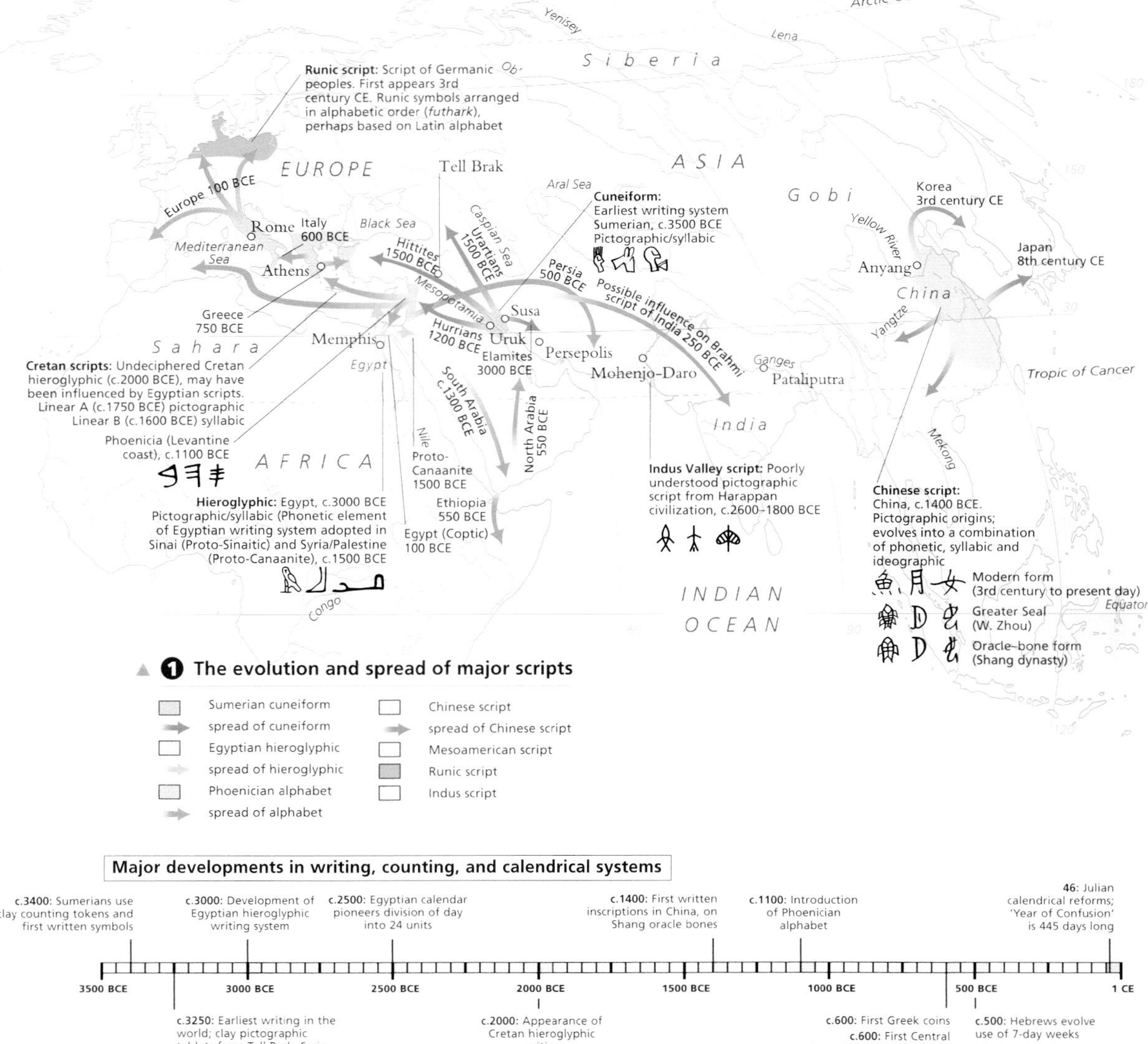

1 The evolution and spread of major scripts

Sumerian cuneiform	Chinese script
spread of cuneiform	spread of Chinese script
Egyptian hieroglyphic	Mesoamerican script
spread of hieroglyphic	Runic script
Phoenician alphabet	Indus script
spread of alphabet	

Major developments in writing, counting, and calendrical systems

- **c.3400**: Sumerians use clay counting tokens and first written symbols
- **c.3250**: Earliest writing in the world; clay pictographic tablets from Tell Brak, Syria
- **c.3000**: Development of Egyptian hieroglyphic writing system
- **c.2500**: Egyptian calendar pioneers division of day into 24 units
- **c.2000**: Appearance of Cretan hieroglyphic writing
- **c.1400**: First written inscriptions in China, on Shang oracle bones
- **c.1100**: Introduction of Phoenician alphabet
- **c.600**: First Greek coins
- **c.600**: First Central American script (Zapotec)
- **c.500**: Hebrews evolve use of 7-day weeks
- **c.500**: First coins used in China
- **46**: Julian calendrical reforms; 'Year of Confusion' is 445 days long

3500 BCE – 3000 BCE – 2500 BCE – 2000 BCE – 1500 BCE – 1000 BCE – 500 BCE – 1 CE

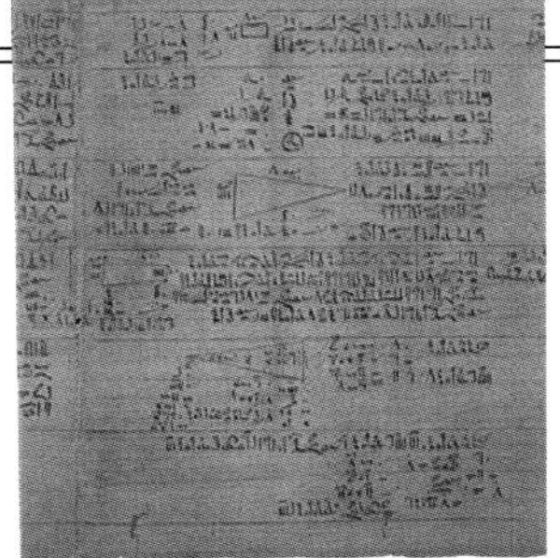

The Rhind mathematical papyrus dates to c.1575 BCE. It demonstrates that the Egyptians had some understanding of the properties of right-angled triangles.

The evolution of numerical systems

Wooden tally sticks were used over 30,000 years ago, probably to record numbers of animals killed. From c.3400 BCE the Sumerians used clay counting tokens to represent order of magnitude, and evolved the first written numbering system. As humans count using their fingers and toes, most systems used base 10, while the Maya, Aztecs, and Celts chose base 20. The Sumerian and Babylonian use of base 60 (still evident in our use of 60 minutes and seconds, and 360 degrees) remains mysterious. Alphabetic counting systems, used by Greeks, Hebrews, and Arabs, wrote numbers by using letters. The concept of zero and the positional numbering system were independent Maya and Indian inventions.

This Babylonian mathematical text with cuneiform numbers dates to c.500 BCE. The use of the sexagesimal system was an important factor in the development of Babylonian astronomy.

SEE ALSO:

North America: pp.122–123

South America: pp.146–147

West Asia: pp.222–223

North and East Asia: pp.258–259

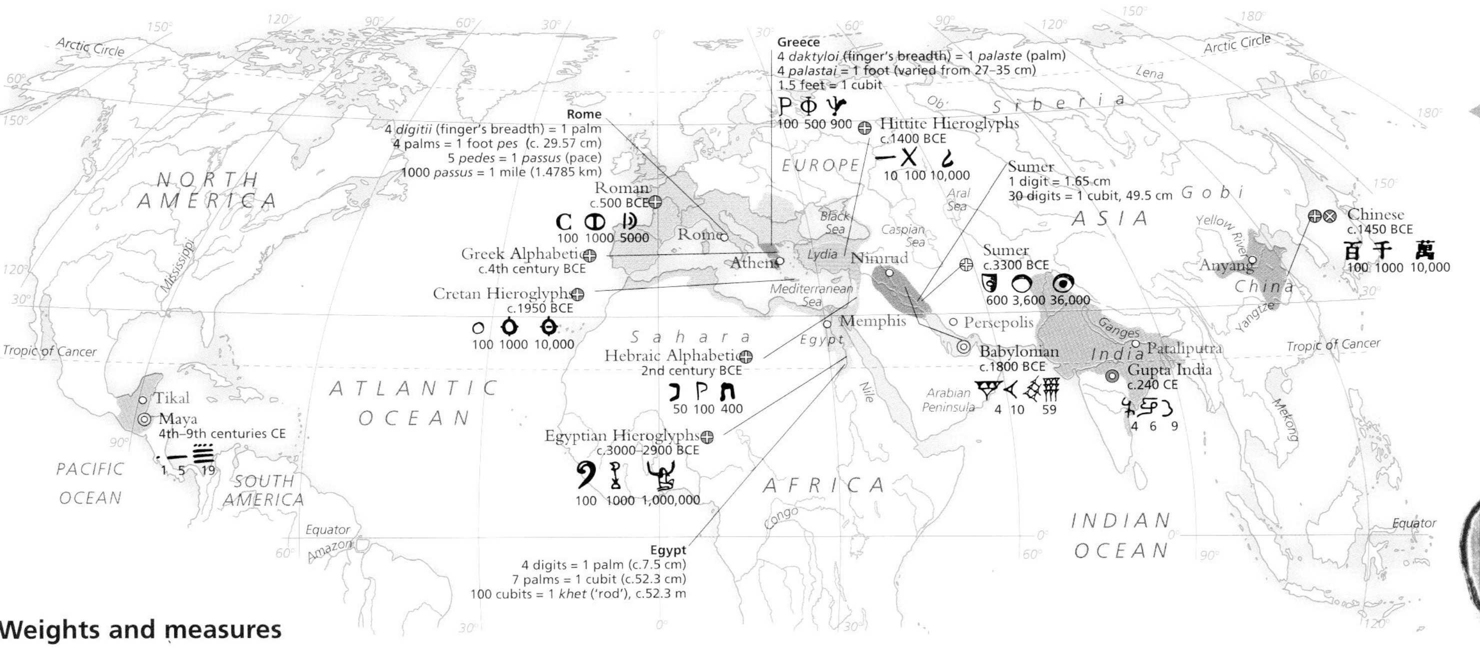

2 The evolution of numerical systems

Earliest known date of counting system

Numerical system	Regions
additive	Mesopotamian
multiplicative	Maya
positional	Roman
Base	Hittite
Base 10	Egyptian
Base 20	Greek
Base 60	Hebraic
	Gupta India
	Chinese

Heracles is shown stringing a bow on this Theban coin (c.446–426 BCE).

Weights and measures

The parts of the body, such as the fingers, palms, and toes, were used by all ancient civilizations for shorter units of measurement. Greater distances reflect the nature of the civilization; the Roman *passus* (1.6 m) reflects the Romans' road system and marching armies, the Greek stadion originates in the length of an athletic race track.

Bronze scales, using a simple balance system, were used extensively in Ancient Rome. Weights were verified by officials.

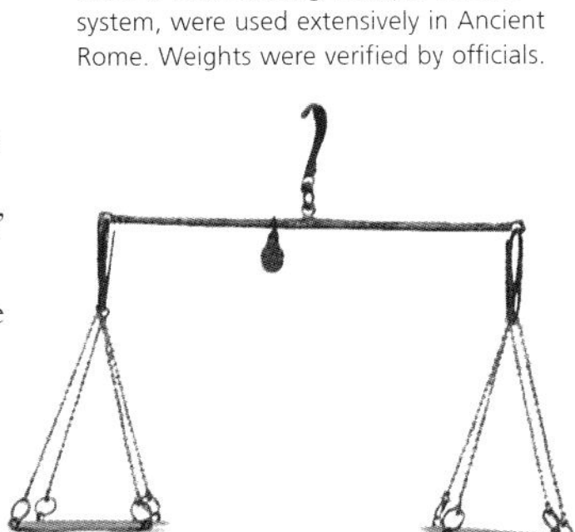

Mesopotamian weights were calculated according to the sexagesimal system. This 1st-millennium relief from Nimrud, Iraq, shows tribute being weighed.

Coinage

As trade networks expanded, barter, which depended on long negotiations, became increasingly inconvenient. The need for an agreed system of equivalences of value led to the invention of coins, metal objects with a constant weight, marked with the official stamp of a public authority. The Greeks of Lydia developed the system in the 7th century BCE, and it was rapidly adopted elsewhere.

This Athenian coin is known as a tetradrachm (479 BCE). The owl was a symbol of Athena.

This early Egyptian counting stick was found with pieces of metal, used as money.

Fragments of a bronze Celtic lunisolar calendar have been found at Coligny, France. Pegs may have been inserted into holes to mark the passage of the days.

The evolution of calendrical systems

The development of calendars was linked to religion and the need to predict days of ritual significance, such as the summer solstice. Calendrical systems developed through astronomical observation and record-keeping, and were dependent on both writing and numeracy. All calendars had to resolve the incommensurate cycles of days, lunations and solar years, usually by intercalating extra days or months at regular intervals. Eras were assessed by different means, most commonly from the regnal years of monarchy, or from the year of birth of significant individuals, such as Buddha or Christ.

Light penetrates the neolithic tomb at Newgrange in Ireland at sunrise on 21 December, an example of the astronomical significance of many stone settings.

The Babylonians made systematic observations of the setting and rising of the planet Venus at the city of Kish, recorded on the Venus tablet (c.1700 BCE).

3 The evolution and spread of calendrical systems

- lunar (months are kept in step with lunar cycle by intercalating days)
- solar (lunar cycle is ignored; years are kept in step with the Sun by intercalating days)
- lunisolar (month are geared to lunar cycle; extra months are intercalated to key year synchronized with sun)
- wandering year (fixed number of days; lunar and solar cycles abandoned)
- extent of Roman Empire in 2nd century CE

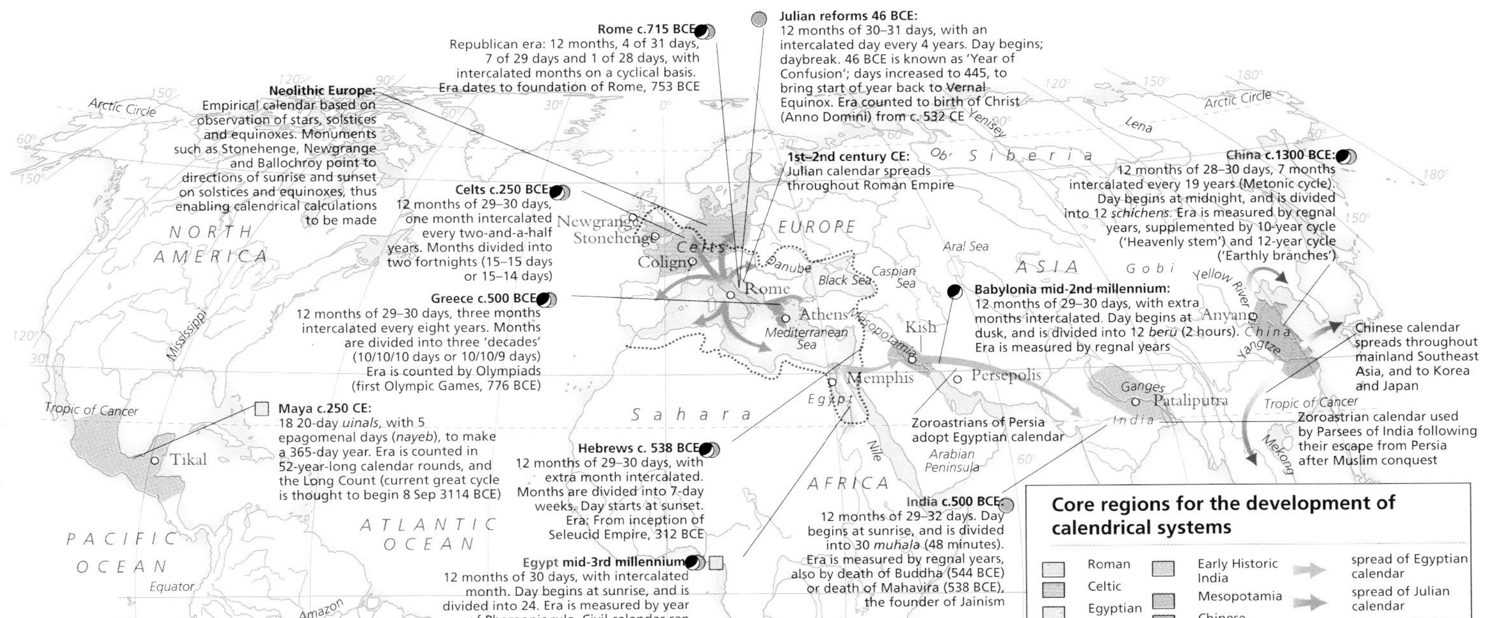

THE WORLD 750 – 500 BCE

THE CIVILIZATIONS OF EURASIA, although they only occupied a small portion of the Earth's surface, now lay in a more or less continuous belt from the Mediterranean to China. Both trade and cultural contact were well-established; understanding of iron metallurgy had spread from the Middle East as far as China, and by the 6th century BCE Chinese silk was beginning to appear in Europe, marking the beginning of 1,500 years of trans-Asian trade. All these civilizations, however, were increasingly subjected to incursions by tribes of nomadic pastoralists who were rapidly spreading across Central Asia, eastern Europe, and Siberia – a result of the invention of horse-riding. By 500 BCE, the Classical Age in Greece – a high point in the history of western civilization – was beginning. It was to have a profound impact on European political institutions, art, architecture, drama, and philosophy. In 505 BCE, the *polis* of Athens initiated radical political reforms and became the birthplace of democracy.

Europe

As the city-states of Greece became more prosperous, their civic pride was expressed through magnificent buildings. Greek colonies, which stretched from the Black Sea to the Iberian Peninsula, were major trading centres, importing raw materials and food supplies in exchange for manufactures, such as pottery. The expanding European population moved into more marginal areas, using iron tools for land clearance and agriculture. Northern Europe was occupied by Celtic and Germanic peoples, whose tribal societies centred on princely graves and hill-top fortresses.

Revelry is a common theme in the tomb frescoes of the Etruscans, whose urban civilization reached its height in 6th-century BCE Italy.

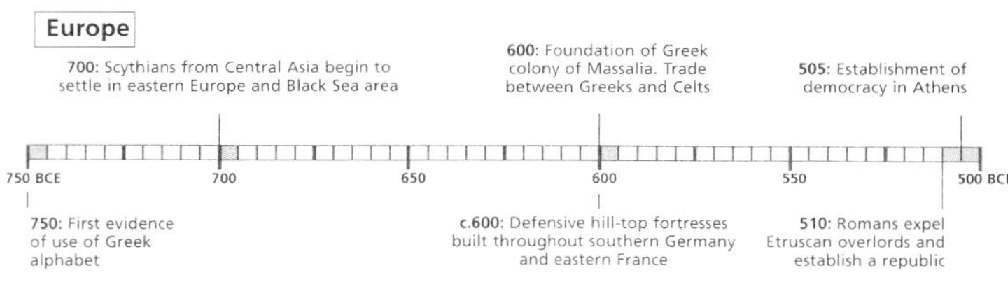
Europe
700: Scythians from Central Asia begin to settle in eastern Europe and Black Sea area
600: Foundation of Greek colony of Massalia. Trade between Greeks and Celts
505: Establishment of democracy in Athens
750 BCE
700
650
600
550
500 BCE
750: First evidence of use of Greek alphabet
c.600: Defensive hill-top fortresses built throughout southern Germany and eastern France
510: Romans expel Etruscan overlords and establish a republic

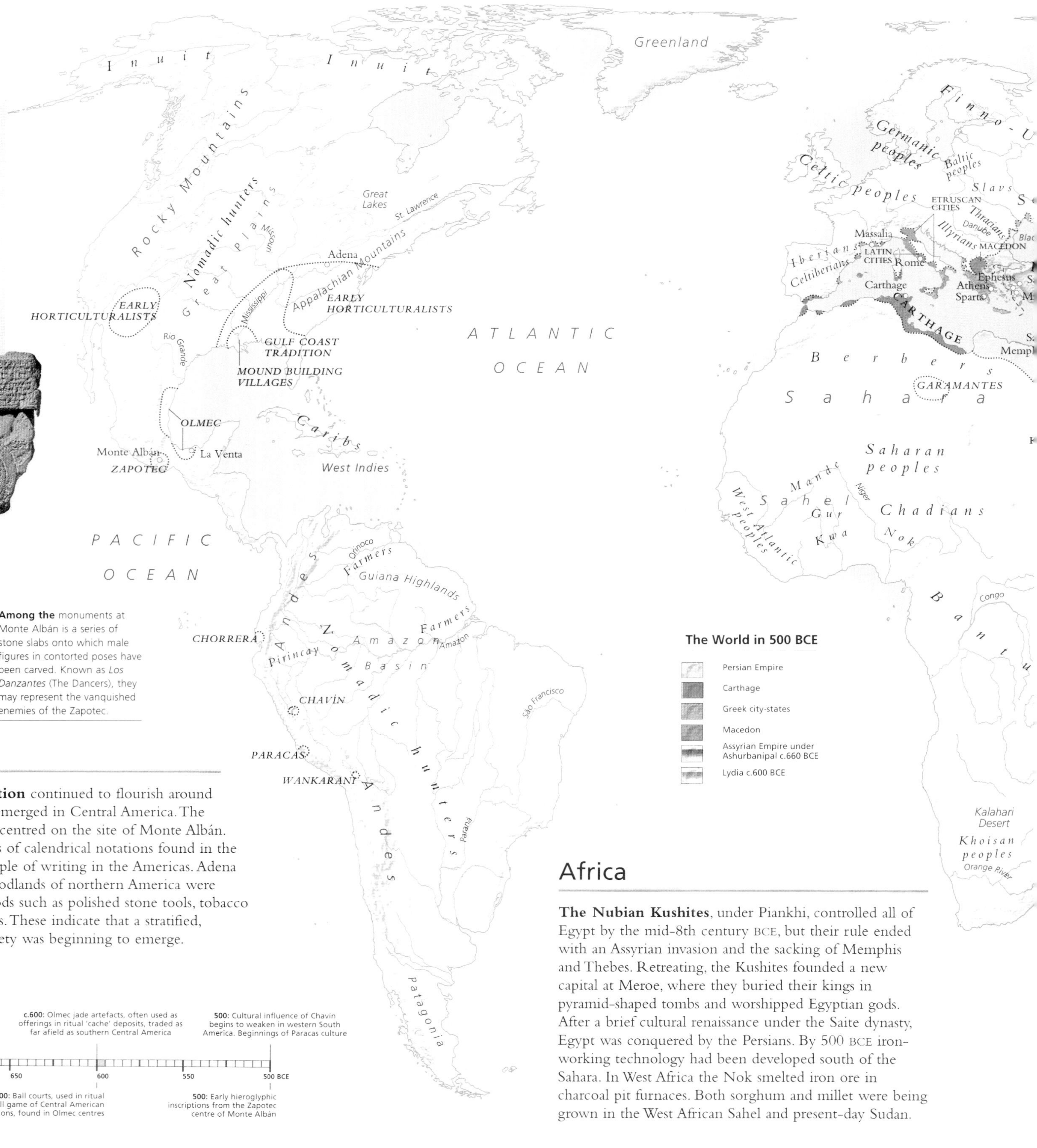

BABYLONIAN MAP

The earliest known graphic representations of parts of the Earth are the maps engraved by the Babylonians on clay tablets. On this tablet from around 600 BCE the Earth is depicted as a disc surrounded by water. The Euphrates River is shown as two curved lines and small circles carry the names of cities and adjacent countries in cuneiform script.

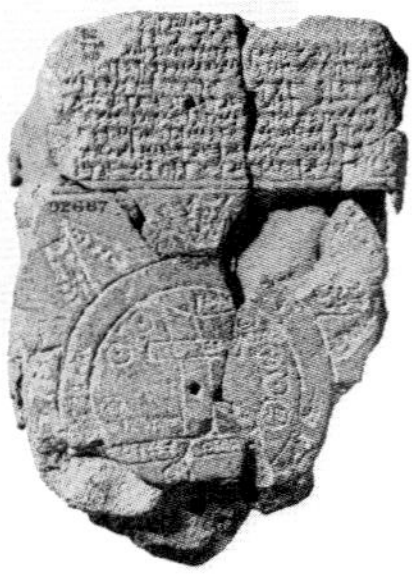

The Babylonians oriented their maps with Babylon at the centre.

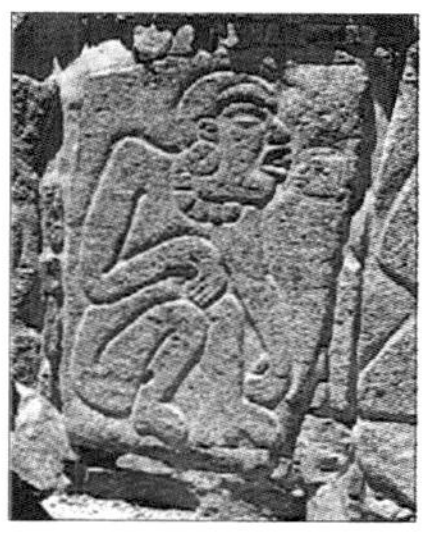

Among the monuments at Monte Albán is a series of stone slabs onto which male figures in contorted poses have been carved. Known as *Los Danzantes* (The Dancers), they may represent the vanquished enemies of the Zapotec.

The World in 500 BCE

- Persian Empire
- Carthage
- Greek city-states
- Macedon
- Assyrian Empire under Ashurbanipal c.660 BCE
- Lydia c.600 BCE

The Americas

As the Olmec civilization continued to flourish around La Venta, other cultures emerged in Central America. The Zapotec civilization was centred on the site of Monte Albán. Hieroglyphic inscriptions of calendrical notations found in the city are the earliest example of writing in the Americas. Adena burials in the eastern woodlands of northern America were furnished with grave goods such as polished stone tools, tobacco pipes, beads, and bracelets. These indicate that a stratified, politically organized society was beginning to emerge.

The Americas

- **c.700**: Growth of permanent horticulture villages in southeastern North America
- **c.600**: Olmec jade artefacts, often used as offerings in ritual 'cache' deposits, traded as far afield as southern Central America
- **c.600**: Ball courts, used in ritual ball game of Central American civilizations, found in Olmec centres
- **500**: Cultural influence of Chavín begins to weaken in western South America. Beginnings of Paracas culture
- **500**: Early hieroglyphic inscriptions from the Zapotec centre of Monte Albán

750 BCE · 700 · 650 · 600 · 550 · 500 BCE

Africa

The Nubian Kushites, under Piankhi, controlled all of Egypt by the mid-8th century BCE, but their rule ended with an Assyrian invasion and the sacking of Memphis and Thebes. Retreating, the Kushites founded a new capital at Meroe, where they buried their kings in pyramid-shaped tombs and worshipped Egyptian gods. After a brief cultural renaissance under the Saite dynasty, Egypt was conquered by the Persians. By 500 BCE iron-working technology had been developed south of the Sahara. In West Africa the Nok smelted iron ore in charcoal pit furnaces. Both sorghum and millet were being grown in the West African Sahel and present-day Sudan.

THE FIRST COINS

The use of metals to make payments can be traced back more than 4000 years, but standardization and certification in the form of coinage did not arrive until the 7th century BCE. The first coins were issued by the Lydians of western Anatolia. They consisted of bean-sized pieces of electrum – a natural alloy of gold and silver – with punchmarks testifying to their weight and therefore their value in payments. By 570 BCE coinage had spread west to Greece and east to Persia. It was invented independently in China and India c.500 BCE.

The first Chinese coins, introduced c.500 BCE, were miniature bronze hoes or spades (*left*), copies of the tools that previously had been used for barter. Early Greek coins carried stamped designs, many derived from the animal world (*right*).

West Asia

Assyria's enemies united to overthrow the empire in 612 BCE, and for a brief period Babylon again enjoyed ascendancy in Mesopotamia. This changed with the arrival of the Medes and Persians, Indo-Europeans from Central Asia. In 550 BCE the Persian king, Cyrus the Great, defeated the Medes and united the two peoples, founding the Achaemenid Empire, which became the largest state the world had yet seen, stretching from the Nile to the Indus. A later Persian ruler, Darius I, consolidated imperial rule: subject peoples were divided into provinces, or satrapies; taxes were levied and the construction of the Royal Road from Sardis to Susa facilitated fast, efficient communications.

The king is the focus of the decoration of the palace at Persepolis, ceremonial capital of the Achaemenid Persians. Reliefs depict his court and processions of tribute-bearers from his empire.

SEE ALSO:

North America: pp.120–121

South America: pp.144–145

Africa: pp.158–159

Europe: pp.176–179

West Asia: pp.222–223

South and Southeast Asia: pp.240–243

North and East Asia: pp.258–259

Australasia and Oceania: pp.280–281

West Asia

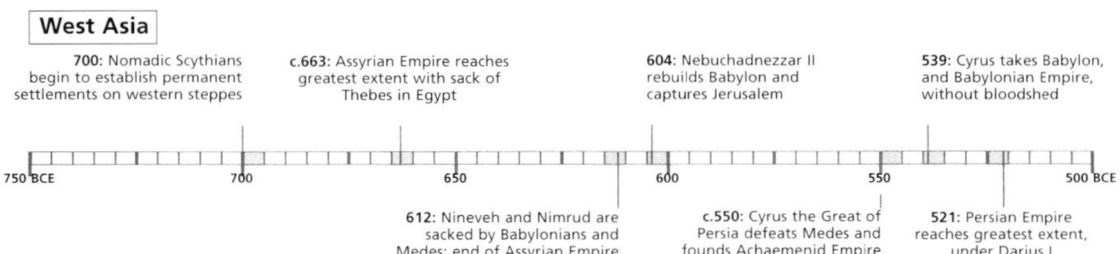

700: Nomadic Scythians begin to establish permanent settlements on western steppes
c.663: Assyrian Empire reaches greatest extent with sack of Thebes in Egypt
604: Nebuchadnezzar II rebuilds Babylon and captures Jerusalem
539: Cyrus takes Babylon, and Babylonian Empire, without bloodshed
750 BCE
700
650
600
550
500 BCE
612: Nineveh and Nimrud are sacked by Babylonians and Medes; end of Assyrian Empire
c.550: Cyrus the Great of Persia defeats Medes and founds Achaemenid Empire
521: Persian Empire reaches greatest extent, under Darius I

East Asia

With the beginning of the Eastern Zhou period in 770 BCE, China experienced several centuries of conflict as many former vassals of the Zhou competed for supremacy. This was a period of technological and cultural change. The widespread use of iron tools improved the productivity of the land and led to a marked population increase. At the same time new ideas stimulated feverish intellectual debate. The teaching of Confucius was a practical, ethical guide to good government and social behaviour, whereas Taoism was a philosophy based on a mystical faith in natural forces.

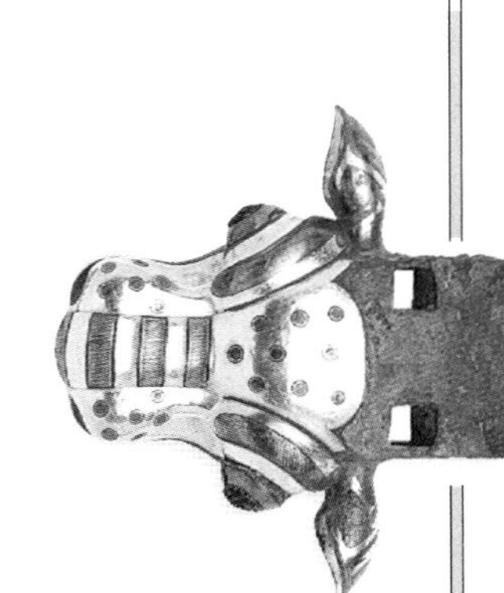

During this period Chinese chariots were elaborately decorated to enhance their appearance in battle. This bronze bull's head chariot fitting is inlaid with gold.

East Asia

c.650: Introduction of iron technology to China. Silk painting, lacquerwork, and ceramics become highly skilled

605: Birth of Lao-tzu, founder of Taoism

551: Birth of Confucius

c.500: Bronze coinage introduced in China

750 BCE – 700 – 650 – 600 – 550 – 500 BCE

c.500: Iron-casting used to manufacture huge quantities of tools and weapons in China

Paleosiberians · Samoyeds · Turks · Tungus · Mongols · Gobi · Scythians · Tochari · Koreans · Ainu · Japan · Japanese · Zhengzhou · ZHOU CHINA · Wu · Yangtze · Sinitic peoples · YUE · Tibetans · GANDHARA · Bactra · Taxila · Himalayas · INDIAN STATES · KOSALA · VAJJI CONFEDERATION · VATSA · Kapilavastu · Pataliputra · AVANTI · MAGADHA · INDIAN STATES · Dravidians · Mon-Khmer peoples · Chams · Mekong · Philippine Islands · PACIFIC OCEAN · Malays · Borneo · Sumatra · Java · Papuans · New Guinea · INDIAN OCEAN · Madagascar · Australian Aborigines · Darling · New Zealand · Arabian Peninsula · SABA · DAAMAT · Cushites · Ecbatana · Susa · Babylon · Persepolis · Tigris · Indus · Ganges · Yellow River · Amur · Lena · Yenisey · Ob' · Caspian Sea · Red Sea

In India, early traditions, dating back before 2000 BCE, evolved into Hinduism. This stone statue portrays an early deity, Surya, the sun god.

South Asia

From about 1500 BCE the peoples of central north India began to adopt a sedentary life and expanded eastwards to settle the Ganges plain. By the 7th century BCE, a patchwork of small states had emerged in northern India. Some were tribal republics, others absolute monarchies, but their common roots – apparent in the Hindu religion and the caste system – underpinned their religious and social organization. The Afghan region of Gandhara and the Indus Valley were absorbed into the Persian Empire in the late 6th century BCE.

From Meroe, the Cushites were able to maintain their rule over the middle Nile until the 4th century CE, while Egypt suffered a series of invasions. This stone ram lies among the ruins of a Meroitic temple at Naqa.

Africa

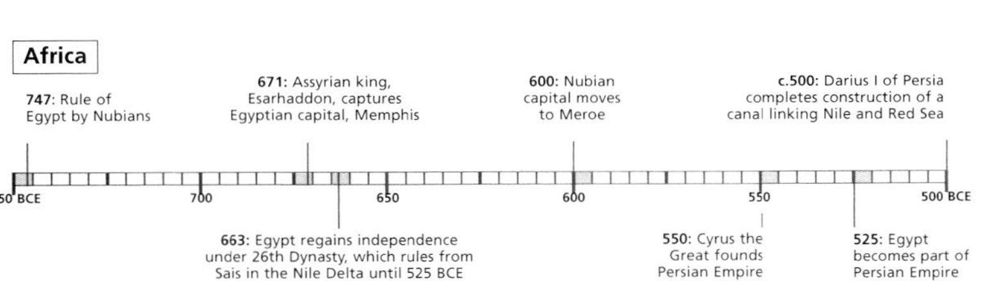

747: Rule of Egypt by Nubians
671: Assyrian king, Esarhaddon, captures Egyptian capital, Memphis
600: Nubian capital moves to Meroe
c.500: Darius I of Persia completes construction of a canal linking Nile and Red Sea
750 BCE
700
650
600
550
500 BCE
663: Egypt regains independence under 26th Dynasty, which rules from Sais in the Nile Delta until 525 BCE
550: Cyrus the Great founds Persian Empire
525: Egypt becomes part of Persian Empire

South Asia

c.600: 16 Aryan kingdoms are spread across northern India

c.540: Birth of Mahavira, founder of Jain religion

750 BCE – 700 – 650 – 600 – 550 – 500 BCE

c.566: Birth of Buddha, who forsakes life of a nobleman to seek enlightenment through asceticism and good conduct

533: Kingdom of Gandhara becomes satrapy of Persia

THE ORIGINS OF ORGANIZED RELIGION

The development of a priestly class, as here at Sumer, was central in the organization of religious practice as a core social activity.

THE 6TH CENTURY BCE has been called the 'axial age' in the development of religion. Judaism, Hinduism, and Taoism were well established. Reformers such as Deutero-Isaiah, Mahavira, Siddhartha Gautama, and Confucius were at work. Around the Mediterranean, a melting-pot of local cults was forming the roots of European Classical civilization, while in the Americas the first urban cultures brought with them organized religion. And frequently, it was the adoption by political rulers of a particular religion which would ensure its longevity and evolution – as in Buddhism, Confucianism, and, later, Christianity – into a world religion.

The development of organized religion

Zoroastrian worship focused on a supreme being, Ahura Mazda, who was widely worshipped at fire altars.

The development of organized religions was linked to the emergence of urban civilization. The earliest known state religion was that of Sumer in the 3rd millennium BCE, and the oldest coherent written mythology was that of Egypt, from the 2nd millennium BCE. By the 1st millennium a range of common characteristics and practices had emerged from local cults to acquire the trappings of organized religion: shamans became priests; myth became doctrine; sacrifice became ceremony; ancestor worship was celebrated in increasingly rich and elaborate burial practices and grandiose monumental architecture.

NORTH AMERICA

Widespread animistic cults and ancestor worship

Adena before 1000 BCE–c.100 CE: Earth temple mounds; burials with grave goods

Mississippian c.1000–1500 CE: Earthwork ceremonial centres; rich grave goods

Olmec c.1200–300 BCE: Monumental sculpture; ceremonial centres; votive burials

Oaxaca c.500–150 BCE: Zapotec temples

Maya c.300 BCE–900 CE: Ceremonial centres with pyramids

Hopewell, Adena, Serpent Mound, Cahokia, Marksville, Mandeville, Monte Albán, San Lorenzo, La Venta, Chichén Itzá

CENTRAL AMERICA

PACIFIC OCEAN

ATLANTIC OCEAN

SOUTH AMERICA

Chavin c.850–200 BCE: Temple complex; anthropomorphic pantheon

Chavín de Huantar

Northwest Europe: Bog bodies reveal human sacrifice

Northern Europe: Celtic ceremonial centres; burials with rich grave goods

Etruscans c.800–400 BCE: Rich burials and sarcophagi

Rome c.550 BCE–410 CE: 510 BCE: Dedication of temple of Jupiter Optimus Maximus; increasing adoption of Greek pantheon

Phoenician colonies c.800–146 BCE: Cult centre at Carthage

Stonehenge, Caere, Rome, Delphi, Athens, Mt. Olympus, Carthage

EUROPE

Mediterranean Sea

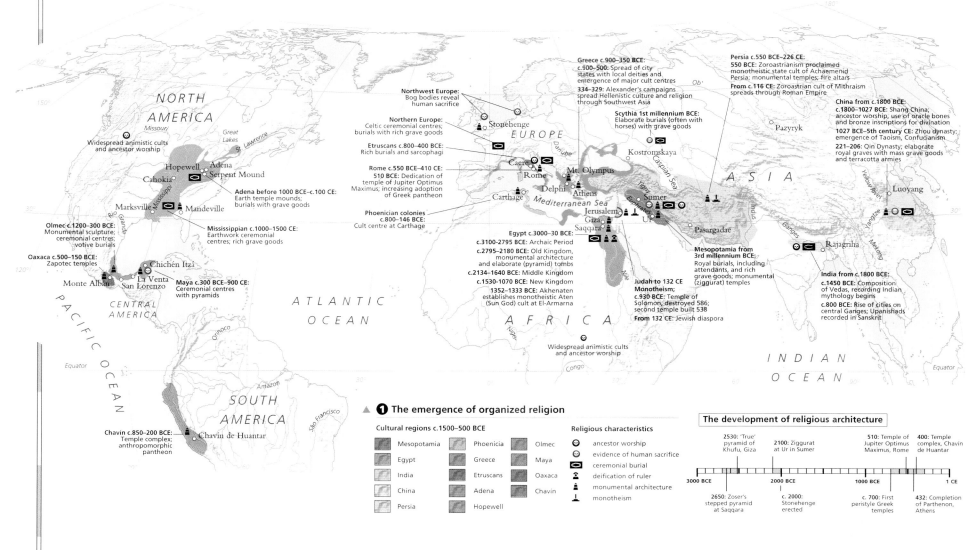

Greece c.900–350 BCE: c.900–500: Spread of city states with local deities and emergence of major cult centres

334–329: Alexander's campaigns spread Hellenistic culture and religion through Southwest Asia

Scythia 1st millennium BCE: Elaborate burials (often with horses) with grave goods

Kostromskaya

Egypt c.3000–30 BCE: c.3100–2795 BCE: Archaic Period; c.2795–2180 BCE: Old Kingdom, monumental architecture and elaborate (pyramid) tombs; c.2134–1640 BCE: Middle Kingdom; c.1530–1070 BCE: New Kingdom; 1352–1333 BCE: Akhenaten establishes monotheistic Aten (Sun God) cult at El-Armarna

Giza, Saqqara, Jerusalem, Sumer, Ur

Judah to 132 CE Monotheism; c.930 BCE: Temple of Solomon, destroyed 586; second temple built 538; From 132 CE: Jewish diaspora

Mesopotamia from 3rd millennium BCE: Royal burials, including attendants, and rich grave goods; monumental (ziggurat) temples

AFRICA

Widespread animistic cults and ancestor worship

Persia c.550 BCE–226 CE: 550 BCE: Zoroastrianism proclaimed monotheistic state cult of Achaemenid Persia; monumental temples; fire altars. From c.116 CE: Zoroastrian cult of Mithraism spreads through Roman Empire

Pazyryk, Pasargadae

ASIA

China from c.1800 BCE: c.1800–1027 BCE: Shang China; ancestor worship, use of oracle bones and bronze inscriptions for divination. 1027 BCE–5th century CE: Zhou dynasty; emergence of Taoism, Confucianism. 221–206: Qin Dynasty; elaborate royal graves with mass grave goods and terracotta armies

Luoyang

India from c.1800 BCE: c.1450 BCE: Composition of Vedas, recording Indian mythology begins. c.800 BCE: Rise of cities on central Ganges; Upanishads recorded in Sanskrit

Rajagriha

INDIAN OCEAN

1 The emergence of organized religion

Cultural regions c.1500–500 BCE

Mesopotamia, Egypt, India, China, Persia, Phoenicia, Greece, Etruscans, Adena, Hopewell, Olmec, Maya, Oaxaca, Chavin

Religious characteristics

- ancestor worship
- evidence of human sacrifice
- ceremonial burial
- deification of ruler
- monumental architecture
- monotheism

The development of religious architecture

3000 BCE – 2000 BCE – 1000 BCE – 1 CE

- 2650: Zoser's stepped pyramid at Saqqara
- 2530: 'True' pyramid of Khufu, Giza
- c. 2000: Stonehenge erected
- 2100: Ziggurat at Ur in Sumer
- c. 700: First peristyle Greek temples
- 510: Temple of Jupiter Optimus Maximus, Rome
- 432: Completion of Parthenon, Athens
- 400: Temple complex, Chavin de Huantar

Early religion in South Asia

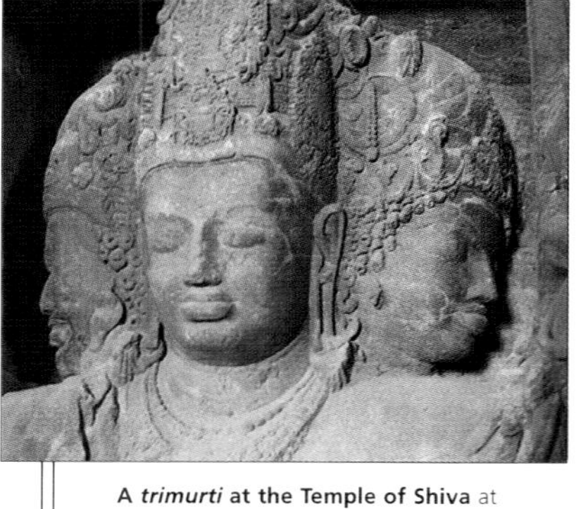

A *trimurti* at the Temple of Shiva at Elephanta depicts the three principal Hindu divinities, Shiva, Vishnu, and Brahma.

The religion of the ancient Aryan tribes is known largely from the hymns of the *Rig Veda*, and the *Vedas*, *Brahmanas*, and *Upanishads*. It focused on sacrifices to a pantheon of deities and semigods. Vedic Hinduism spread over much of India before the rise of Buddhism and Jainism, which developed in reaction to the excesses of Aryan religious practices. These faiths emphasized *ahimsa* (non-violence), meditation, and the suppression of desire for worldly possessions: these and other elements of Hinduism may derive from the religion of the Indus civilization (c.2600–1800 BCE).

2 Religions of South Asia

- UDICHYA broad cultural region recognised by ancient Aryans
- MAGADHA other regions
- *Yamuna* sacred river
- core area of Buddhism and Jainism
- Ashokan rock and pillar edicts

Early religion in South Asia

1400 BCE – 1000 – 600 – 200 BCE

- c.1550: Aryans settle northern India
- c.800: Rise of urban culture in Ganges valley
- 6th century: Life of Mahavira, founder of Jainism
- c.600: Rise to dominance of Magadha
- 566: Birth of Siddhartha Gautama, founder of Buddhism
- 322: Chandragupta founds Mauryan dynasty
- 272–232: Reign of Ashoka, who promulgates Buddhism as state religion

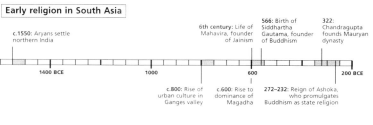

Legendary descent of the Buddha from heaven

566: Birthplace

537: Great Renunciation

483: Attainment of Nirvana

528: Attainment of Enlightenment

528: Sermon in the Deer Park

Kampilya, Samkashya, Kanauj, Lumbini, Shravasti, Kapilavatthu, Ayodhya, Kusinagara, KOSHALA, Vaishali, Prayaga, Sarnath, Kaushambi, Benares, Pataliputra, Champa, MAGADHA, Nalanda, Rajgir, Bodh Gaya, Gaya, ANGA

200 km / 200 miles

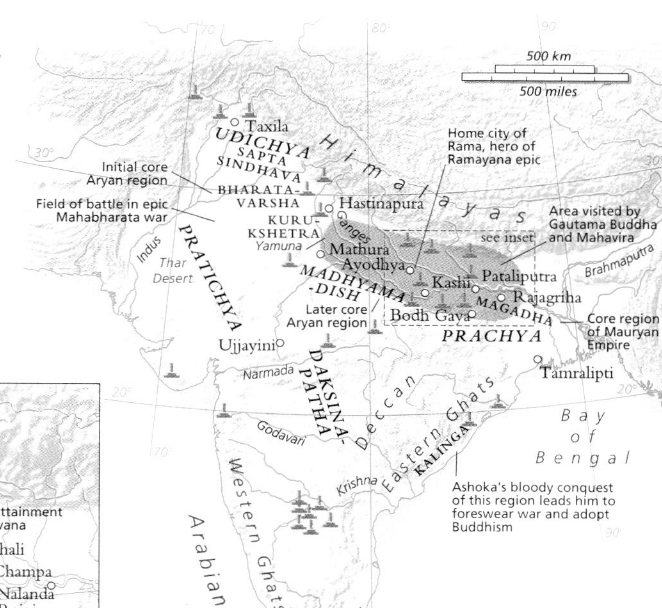

Religions of the Mediterranean

The Mediterranean world in the 1st millennium BCE was the home of a range of discrete cultures, each supporting its own religious beliefs. However, many of these shared striking similarities in mythology, in the character and nature of their pantheons and in religious practice and observance. Rivalry, warfare, and trade created an interaction of influences and cross-fertilizations, and with the rise of Classical Greece, Hellenistic culture and then Rome, certain local beliefs and practices became widespread.

Zeus (Jupiter for the Romans) was the supreme Greek deity.

Greece

The Greek mythological pantheon, developed during the Mycenaean period, was described by writers such as Homer and became, during the Classic Greek period, a central force in Greek life. Each city-state practised favoured cults, but the emergence of oracles and other cult centres (such as Mount Olympus) codified a pan-Hellenic religious tradition which was spread widely by colonization and the campaigns of Alexander the Great *(see pp. 40–41).*

SEE ALSO:

Africa: pp.160–161

Europe: pp.174–179

West Asia: pp.220–221

South and Southeast Asia: pp.242–243

North and East Asia: pp.258–259

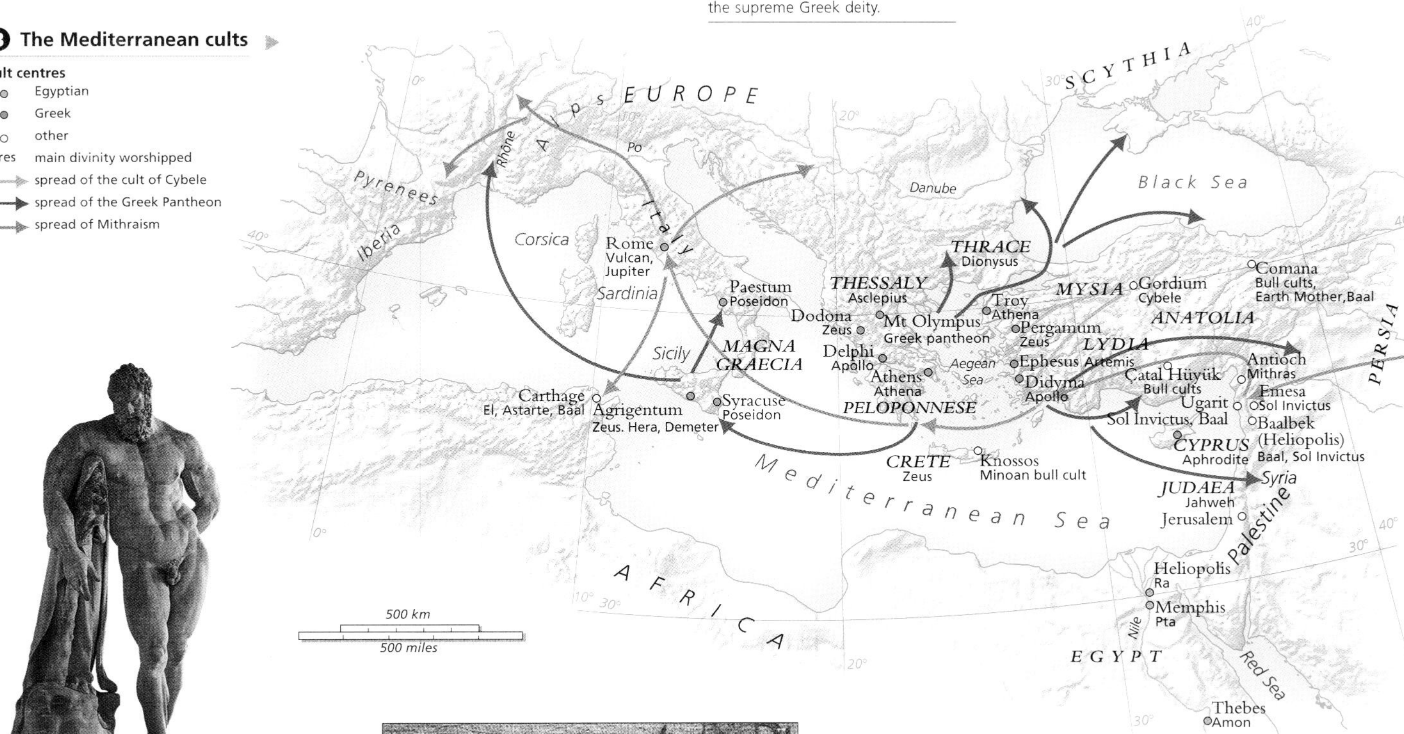

Judaism

The traditional religion of Israel and Judah was unusual in having a single deity, Jahweh. The Babylonian exile (587–538 BCE) strengthened Judaism and encouraged the crystallization of its core beliefs by Deutero-Isaiah and other prophets. The religion survived persecution to become the seedbed of Christianity.

The Jewish candelabra *(menorah)* symbolizes the eternal light *(ner tamid)* which burned in the first Temple of Solomon.

The demi-god Heracles (Hercules in Latin) formed part of the Greek mythological pantheon adopted by the Romans.

Rome

Rome's pantheon was largely adopted from that of Greece, although certain local cults gained popularity as the empire grew. One of the most widespread was that of Mithras, which spread from Persia to Syria, then throughout the empire; eventually the most influential was Christianity.

A dead man kneels before Anubis, god of mummification. Life after death was central to Egyptian theology, celebrated through a series of elaborate rituals.

Egypt

A detailed mythology and pantheon permeated Ancient Egyptian life and thought, and is recorded abundantly in votive statuary and hieroglyphic tomb paintings. The hierarchy and character of Egyptian cosmology probably influenced the development of the Mycenaean and Greek pantheon.

This Mycenaean ritual sprinkler takes the form of a bull's head.

Bull cults

Bull worshipping was widespread in the Mediterranean region, from Çatal Hüyük (c.7000 BCE) to the famous Minotaur cult in Crete (from c.2000 BCE); bulls also played a significant role in Egyptian, Mesopotamian and Greek mythology.

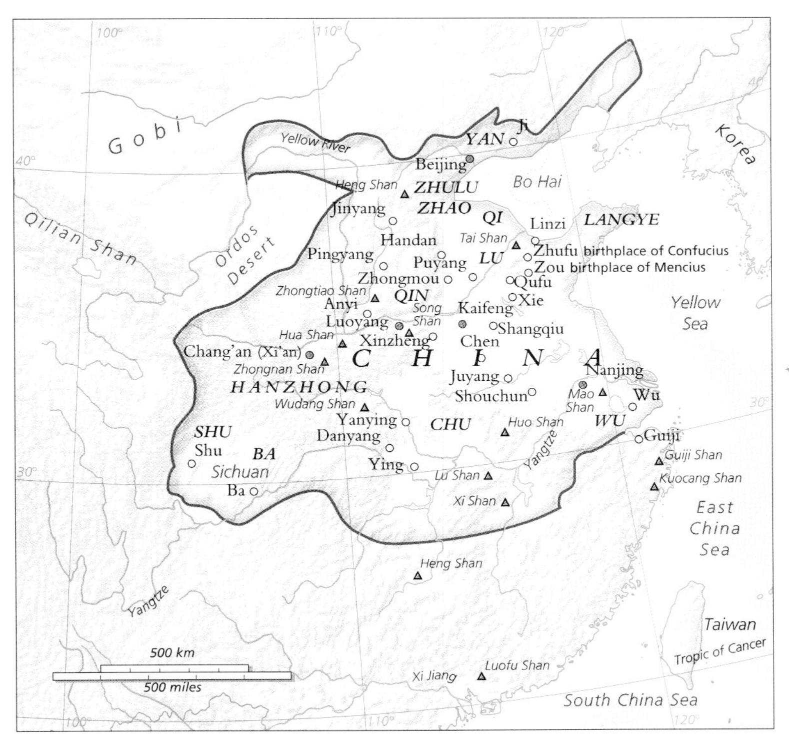

Taoism and Confucianism

Taoism developed during the Zhou dynasty as the most widespread of Chinese religions. Based on the worship of ancestors, nature spirits, and sacred places, it was codified by Lao-tzu (605–520 BCE). The philosopher Confucius (551–479 BCE) promulgated a system of filial observance, learning, obedience, and selflessness which became central to Chinese imperial policy and governance. Followers such as Mencius (c.370–300 BCE) ensured that his teachings survived the Warring States period (403–221 BCE).

The teachings of Confucius ensured that even the most lowly could, by ability, correct behaviour, and hard work, aspire to high office.

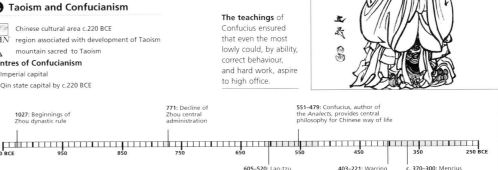

Taoism and Confucianism in China

1050 BCE – 950 – 850 – 750 – 650 – 550 – 450 – 350 – 250 BCE

- **1027:** Beginnings of Zhou dynastic rule
- **771:** Decline of Zhou central administration
- **605–520:** Lao-tzu, traditional founder of Taoism
- **551–479:** Confucius, author of the *Analects*, provides central philosophy for Chinese way of life
- **403–221:** Warring States period
- **c. 370–300:** Mencius continues Confucian teaching

THE WORLD 500–250 BCE

THE 5TH CENTURY BCE was an age of enlightened and innovative thought. It was the climax of the Classical Age in Greece, a period that was remarkable for its art, philosophy, drama, architecture, and political theory. At the same time the Buddhist religion, based on the precepts of renouncing all material desires as practised by Siddhartha Gautama (c.566–486 BCE), was spreading throughout the Indian subcontinent. In China, the teachings of Confucius (551–479 BCE) were concerned with ethical conduct and propriety in human relations. Yet the ensuing centuries were a time of conflict and conquest. From 331–323 BCE Alexander the Great's military conquests created an empire which stretched from Macedon to the Indus. From c.272 BCE the emperor Ashoka absorbed most of the Indian subcontinent into his empire, while in China the Warring States period was a time of violent turmoil.

The shrine of Delphi was the site of the Pythian Games, one of four great athletic festivals that brought Greeks together at set intervals of years.

Europe

In the 5th century BCE, Greece reached the pinnacle of the Classical Age. Athens' conflict with Sparta in the Peloponnesian Wars weakened the Greek city-states, which in the 4th century fell to Philip of Macedon. Under his son, Alexander the Great, who conquered the Persian Empire, Macedon became a great imperial power. In Italy, by 264 BCE, Rome was poised to become a world power.

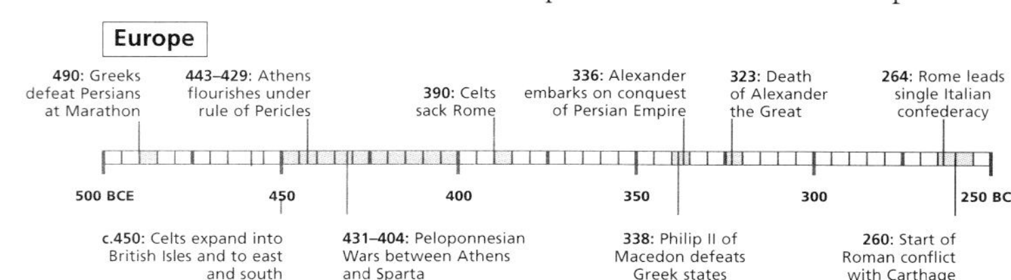
Europe
490: Greeks defeat Persians at Marathon
443–429: Athens flourishes under rule of Pericles
390: Celts sack Rome
336: Alexander embarks on conquest of Persian Empire
323: Death of Alexander the Great
264: Rome leads single Italian confederacy
500 BCE
450
400
350
300
250 BCE
c.450: Celts expand into British Isles and to east and south
431–404: Peloponnesian Wars between Athens and Sparta
338: Philip II of Macedon defeats Greek states
260: Start of Roman conflict with Carthage

THE ARCHIMEDEAN SCREW

Named after Archimedes, the Greek mathematician (287–212 BCE), the Archimedean screw is one of the earliest devices for raising water. It was probably invented in the 7th or 8th century BCE in Mesopotamia. Consisting of a spiral screw revolving inside a close-fitting cylinder, it has been widely used over the centuries for irrigation and land drainage.

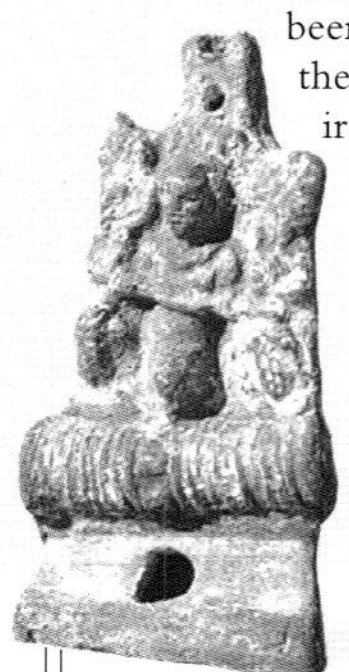

This Egyptian terracotta figurine from c.30 BCE shows a slave driving an Archimedean screw by means of a treadmill.

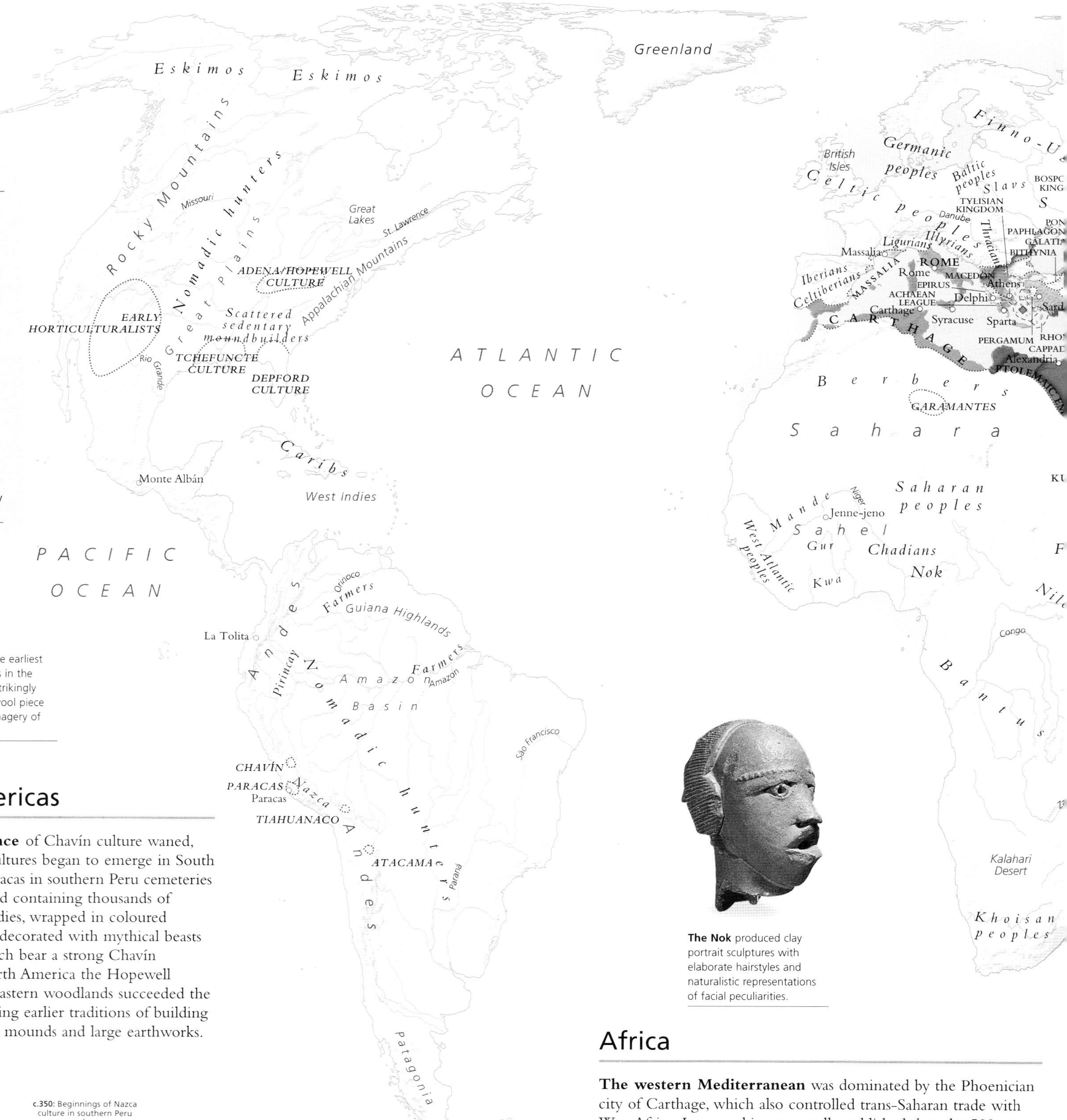

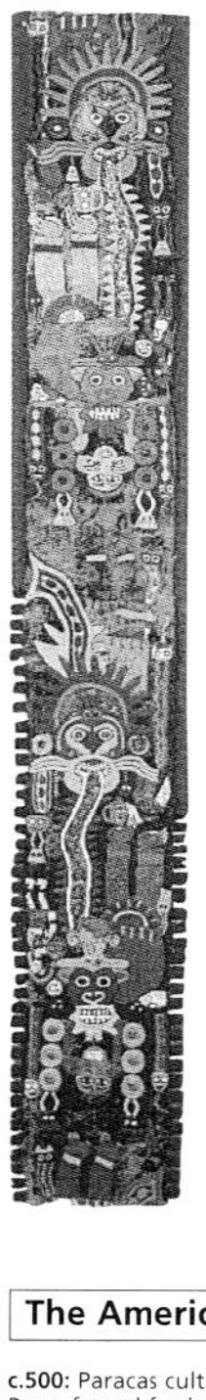

Textiles are one of the earliest and greatest art forms in the Andean region. This strikingly embroidered alpaca-wool piece shows the complex imagery of the Paracas culture.

The Americas

As the influence of Chavín culture waned, distinct local cultures began to emerge in South America. At Paracas in southern Peru cemeteries have been found containing thousands of mummified bodies, wrapped in coloured woven textiles, decorated with mythical beasts and deities which bear a strong Chavín imprint. In North America the Hopewell culture of the eastern woodlands succeeded the Adena, continuing earlier traditions of building elaborate burial mounds and large earthworks.

The Americas

c.500: Paracas culture of southern Peru, famed for brightly coloured textiles, emerges

c.350: Beginnings of Nazca culture in southern Peru

500 BCE — 450 — 400 — 350 — 300 — 250 BCE

c.400: Early Zapotec culture flourishing around city of Monte Albán

c.300: Hopewell culture in eastern North America develops traditions of earlier Adena culture

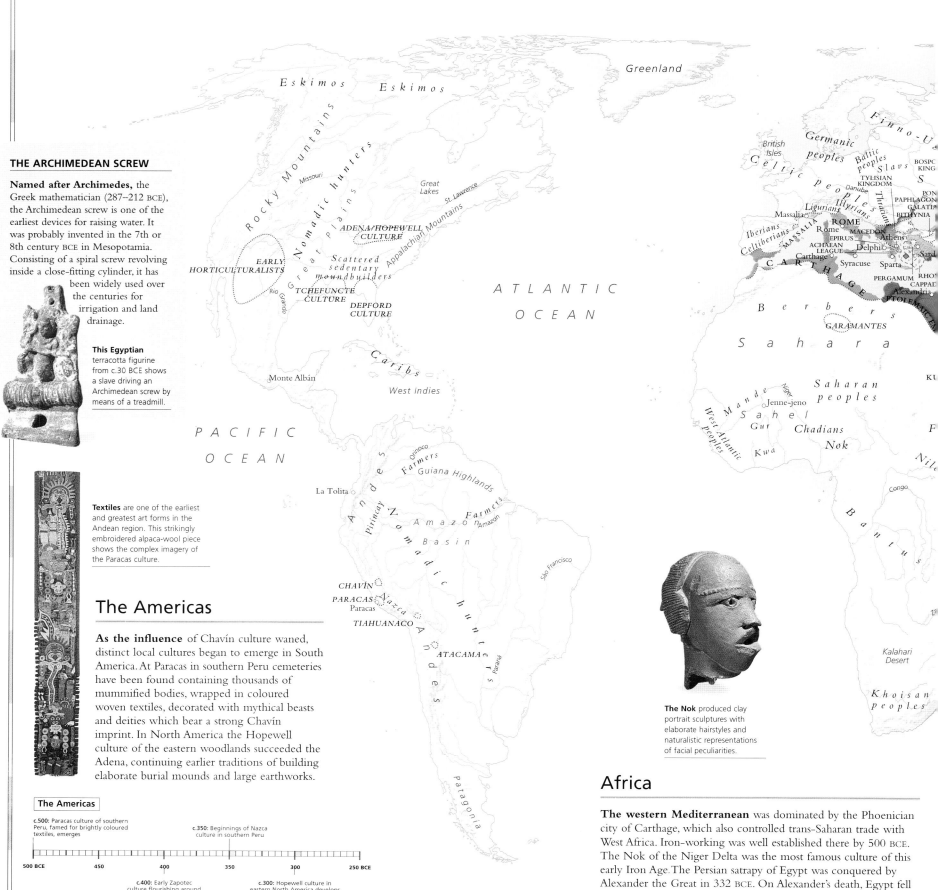

The Nok produced clay portrait sculptures with elaborate hairstyles and naturalistic representations of facial peculiarities.

Africa

The western Mediterranean was dominated by the Phoenician city of Carthage, which also controlled trans-Saharan trade with West Africa. Iron-working was well established there by 500 BCE. The Nok of the Niger Delta was the most famous culture of this early Iron Age. The Persian satrapy of Egypt was conquered by Alexander the Great in 332 BCE. On Alexander's death, Egypt fell to his successor, Ptolemy, who founded the Ptolemaic dynasty.

MAPPING THE FIXED STARS

Ancient astronomers had noticed that the Sun, Moon, and planets did not remain stationary relative to the 'fixed' stars. Instead, over the course of a year, they seemed to pass through a region in the sky occupied by twelve specific constellations that we now call the zodiac, from a Greek term meaning 'circle of animals'. The zodiacal signs appear to have been a Babylonian invention: their first appearance is on a cuneiform horoscope from c.410 BCE.

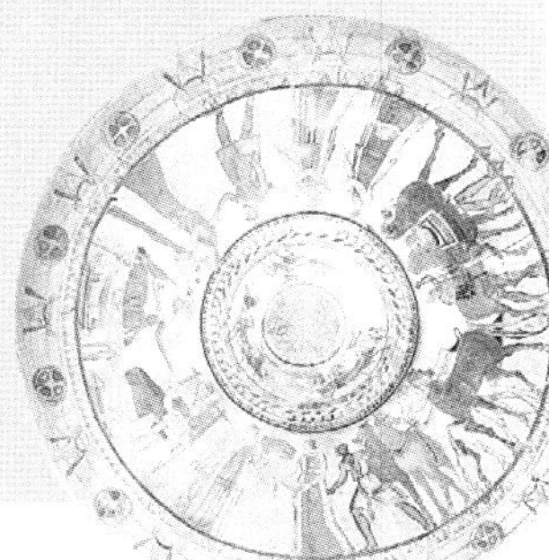

The twelve signs of the zodiac border a procession of horses and musicians on this 4th-century BCE fresco from a Thracian tomb.

West Asia

In 490 BCE Darius I of Persia sent a punitive expedition against Athens and other cities that had helped Greek cities in Asia Minor to rebel, but it was defeated at Marathon. Over the next century, the Persian empire was weakened by strife and rebellion. In 331 BCE Alexander the Great of Macedon defeated Darius III and brought the Persian Empire to an end. In 323 BCE, Alexander's vast empire was divided among three successors. Most of West Asia became part of the Seleucid Empire. Small local kingdoms were ruled by ethnic or mixed Greek dynasties.

Following his untimely death at the age of 32, Alexander the Great remained a legendary figure in the ancient world. This detail of a 1st-century BCE mosaic from Pompeii shows the young king in battle against the Persians at Issus in 333 BCE.

SEE ALSO:

North America: pp.120–121

South America: pp.144–147

Africa: pp.158–161

Europe: pp.176–179

West Asia: pp.222–223

South and Southeast Asia: pp.240–243

North and East Asia: pp.258–259

Australasia and Oceania: pp.280–281

West Asia

500 BCE – 450 – 400 – 350 – 300 – 250 BCE

- **490:** Persian expedition to Greece is defeated at Marathon
- **480:** Darius I is succeeded by his son Xerxes who invades Greece, and is defeated at Salamis, Plataea, and Mycale
- **331:** Alexander the Great's victory at the battle of Gaugamela brings Achaemenid Persian Empire to an end
- **312:** Seleucus gains control of Persia, Syria, and much of Asia Minor; founds the Seleucid dynasty
- **276–272:** Ptolemaic Empire expands into Syria during war with Seleucids

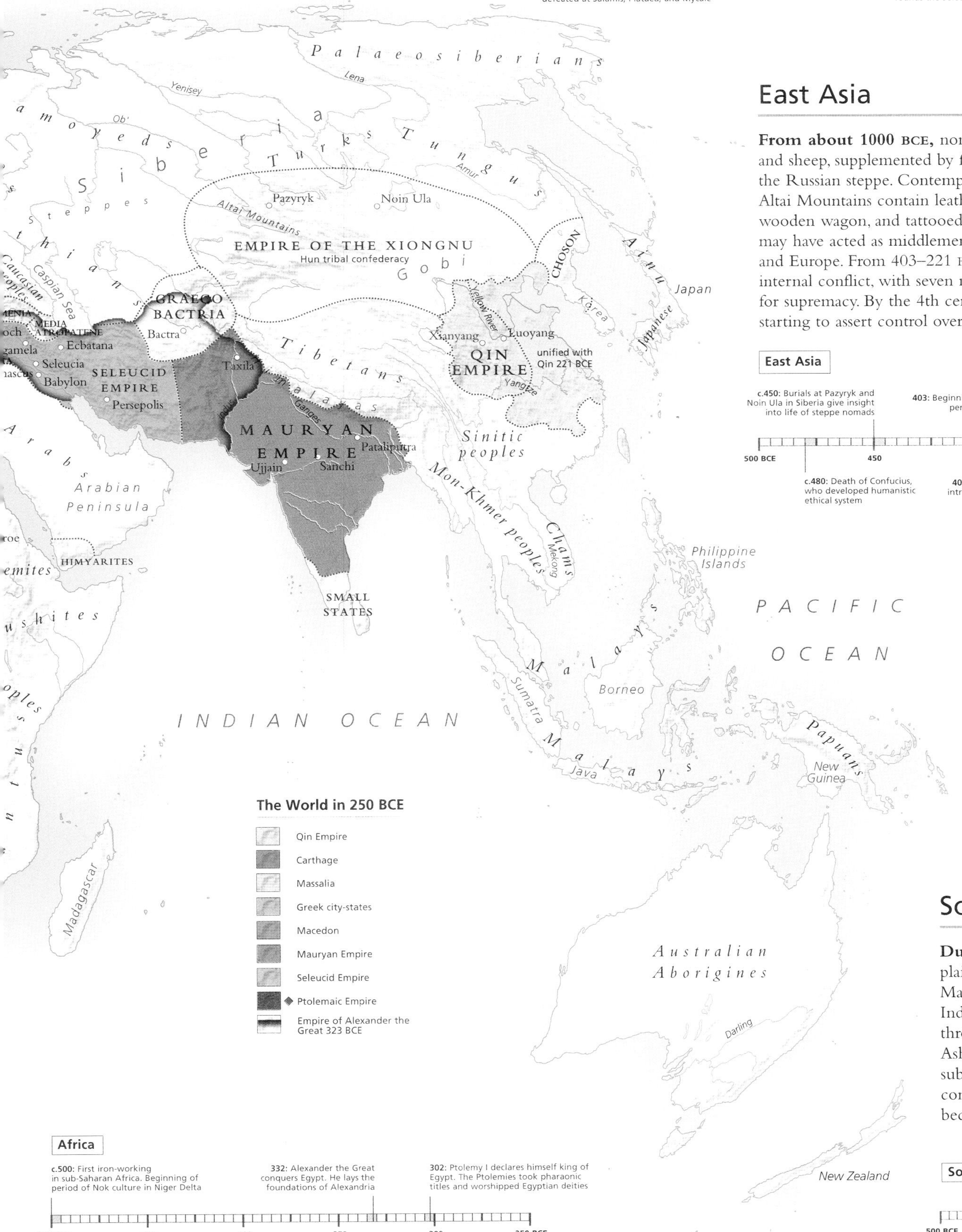

East Asia

From about 1000 BCE, nomads reared cattle, goats, and sheep, supplemented by farming and hunting, on the Russian steppe. Contemporary burial sites in the Altai Mountains contain leather, wood, fur, textiles, a wooden wagon, and tattooed bodies. Steppe chieftains may have acted as middlemen in trade between China and Europe. From 403–221 BCE, China was locked in internal conflict, with seven major states competing for supremacy. By the 4th century BCE the Qin were starting to assert control over the whole region.

Mythical combat was a favoured theme in the art of the hunting and herding peoples of the Altai region. On this wooden carving, a stag is gripped in the jaws of a griffin.

East Asia

500 BCE – 450 – 400 – 350 – 300 – 250 BCE

- **c.450:** Burials at Pazyryk and Noin Ula in Siberia give insight into life of steppe nomads
- **c.480:** Death of Confucius, who developed humanistic ethical system
- **403:** Beginning of Warring States period in China
- **400:** Iron-working introduced to Korea
- **c.350:** The crossbow invented in China
- **c.350:** Qin state develops new political and economic system based on strict system of rewards and punishments
- **256:** Qin takes Luoyang area

The World in 250 BCE

- Qin Empire
- Carthage
- Massalia
- Greek city-states
- Macedon
- Mauryan Empire
- Seleucid Empire
- ◆ Ptolemaic Empire
- Empire of Alexander the Great 323 BCE

Ashoka recorded his understanding of the moral teachings of Buddhism by inscribing edicts on pillars and stones at suitable sites throughout India. One pillar is crowned with four beautifully carved lions. These were chosen as the emblem of the modern state of India.

South Asia

During the 5th century BCE the states of the Ganges plain were eventually absorbed into the kingdom of Magadha. Shortly after Alexander's invasion of northwest India in 327 BCE, Chandragupta Maurya seized the throne and began to expand the empire. By the time of Ashoka (297–232 BCE), the Mauryans ruled most of the subcontinent. Ashoka became repelled by warfare and converted to Buddhism, which, under his patronage, became a major force in India, and beyond.

Africa

500 BCE – 450 – 400 – 350 – 300 – 250 BCE

- **c.500:** First iron-working in sub-Saharan Africa. Beginning of period of Nok culture in Niger Delta
- **c.500:** Iron-using Bantu begin to spread from Niger to East African lakes region and down west coast of Africa
- **332:** Alexander the Great conquers Egypt. He lays the foundations of Alexandria
- **302:** Ptolemy I declares himself king of Egypt. The Ptolemies took pharaonic titles and worshipped Egyptian deities
- **c.250:** Settlement of Jenne-jeno is founded on inland Niger Delta

South Asia

500 BCE – 450 – 400 – 350 – 300 – 250 BCE

- **327:** Alexander the Great occupies northwest India
- **320:** Chandragupta Maurya controls Magadha kingdom and advances towards Indus and central India
- **272:** Ashoka seizes throne and embarks on further imperial conquests
- **260:** Ashoka converts to Buddhism

THE EMPIRE OF ALEXANDER

Alexander the Great, (356–323 BCE), was king of Macedonia and conqueror of a great Afro-Eurasian empire.

THE CONQUESTS OF ALEXANDER took Greek armies to Egypt, Mesopotamia, the Hindu Kush, and India's western borders, and forced Achaemenid Persia, the most powerful empire in the world, into submission. This extraordinary and audacious military feat, accomplished in just ten years, was to create a truly cosmopolitan civilization. Hellenism permeated the cultures of West Asia: some Hellenistic kingdoms survived into the 1st century CE, while Greek remained the official language in many parts of West Asia until the 8th and 9th centuries CE; cities founded in the aftermath of Alexander's conquests, perpetuated the ideals of Greek civilization – some, such as Alexandria, Kandahar, and Tashkent, survive to this day. Ultimately, Alexander opened up new horizons; his followers encountered different peoples and cultures and established trade routes which linked the Mediterranean with East Africa, India, and Asia.

The battle between the Greeks and Persians is depicted with vigorous, high-relief realism on this sarcophagus, found at Sidon.

The conquests of Alexander

Alexander succeeded to the Macedonian throne after the assassination of his father, Philip, in 336 BCE. He crossed into Asia in 334 BCE, defeated the Persian provincial army at Granicus and liberated the old Greek cities of Asia Minor. After a brief sojourn in Egypt, he won a spectacular victory over the Persian emperor, Darius III, at Issus and pursued him into Persia, taking the cities of Babylon, Susa, and Persepolis. He pressed on to Bactria and Sogdiana, the eastern outposts of the Persian Empire, and crossed the Hindu Kush. At the River Hyphasis (Beas) his army refused to go further. He died in Babylon in 323 BCE, aged 32.

This 1st-century Roman mosaic (based possibly on a Macedonian original) shows Darius III, the Persian emperor, at the battle of Issus (333 BCE). His crushing defeat allowed Alexander to conquer the western half of the Persian Empire.

Hellenistic cities of West Asia

The most magnificent West Asian Hellenistic foundation was Pergamum, capital of the Attalid dynasty (282 to 133 BCE). Adorned by a new school of baroque architecture, characterized by its ornate and heavy style, the city had a spectacular theatre and an impressive library, second only to Alexandria.

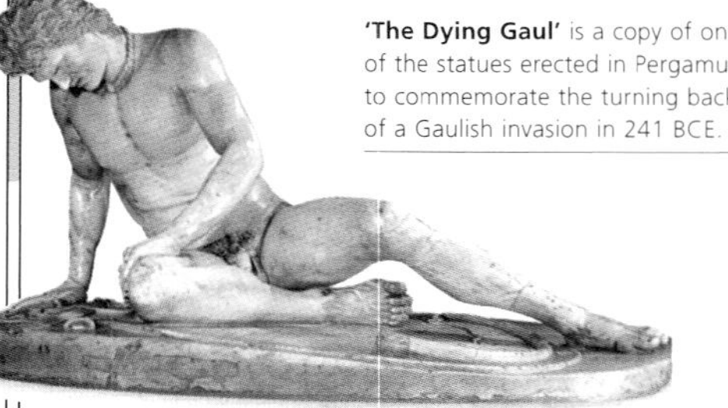

'The Dying Gaul' is a copy of one of the statues erected in Pergamum to commemorate the turning back of a Gaulish invasion in 241 BCE.

1 The Empire of Alexander
Empire of Alexander
dependent regions
independent states
route of Alexander the Great
route of Nearchus
return route of Craterus
major battle
Persian Royal Road
Scale varies with perspective
3330 km (2070 miles)
8900 km (5530 miles)
Spring 333 BCE: Over 30 cities in Lycia surrender to Alexander; he reaches Gordium, where he cuts Gordian Knot, said to be sign he will rule all Asia
May 334 BCE: Alexander visits Troy, where he appropriates so-called sword of Achilles
1 Oct 331 BCE: Alexander's second battle with Darius III, whose army includes elephants and sycthe-wheeled chariots. Victory for Alexander signals effective end of Persian Empire
Nov 333 BCE: Alexander's first meeting in battle with Darius III. Persian army taken by surprise, suffer heavy losses, and Darius flees
Sep–Nov 332 BCE: Siege of key Persian fortress of Gaza. Alexander wounded by catapult bolt
Nov 331 BCE: Following surrender of Babylon, Alexander enters city in triumph
10 Jun 323 BCE: Alexander dies in Babylon
Midwinter 331 BCE: Alexander visits oracle of Ammon at Siwa; kinship with Ammon-Zeus proclaimed
SCYTHIA
Black Sea
Sea of Azov
Caucasus
COLCHIS
ARMENIA
PAPHLAGONIA
CAPPADOCIA
THRACE
BITHYNIA
GALATIA
Asia Minor
PHRYGIA
MYSIA
LYCAONIA
PISIDIA
CILICIA
LYDIA
CARIA
LYCIA
ISAURIA
MACEDONIA
ILLYRIA
EPIRUS
AETOLIA
HELLAS
ITALY
Adriatic Sea
Aegean Sea
CRETE
Mediterranean Sea
MESOPOTAMIA
SYRIA
PHOENICIA
PALESTINE
Syrian Desert
EGYPT
Sahara
Sinai
Red Sea
Steppes
Caspian Sea
Babylon
Alexandria
Memphis
Sanctuary of Ammon (Siwa Oasis)
Gaugamela
Issus
Tyre
Granicus

The growth of Macedonian power

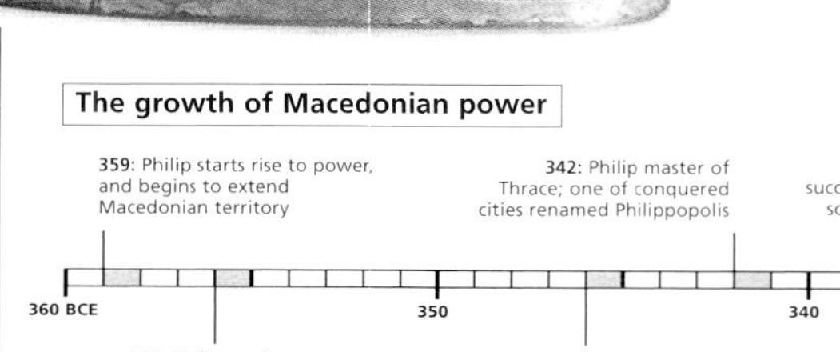

359: Philip starts rise to power, and begins to extend Macedonian territory
356: Philip II takes title of king; birth of his son Alexander
346: War in central Greece ends in uneasy peace between Philip and Athens
342: Philip master of Thrace; one of conquered cities renamed Philippopolis
338: Battle of Chaeronea; Philip II defeats Greek states
336: Philip is succeeded by his son Alexander
333: Persian king Darius III is defeated at Issus
332: Alexander founds the city of Alexandria in northern Egypt
331: Decisive defeat of the Persians at battle of Gaugamela
326: Alexander reaches Taxila; prevented from advancing into India by revolt of his troops
323: Death of Alexander
360 BCE
350
340
330
320 BCE

SEE ALSO:

Africa: pp.160–161

Europe: pp.176–179

West Asia pp.222–225

South and Southeast Asia: pp.240–241

CULTURAL EXCHANGE BETWEEN GREECE AND THE ORIENT

The diffusion of Greek civilization resulted in a rich interplay of influences. The impact of Greek culture was extensive. Greek was spoken over a vast area; in Egypt it started to replace the native language, and inscriptions in Greek are found as far east as northern India. Greek styles of portraiture can be traced in the coins from the remote Graeco-Bactrian kingdom of Central Asia, and in the massive sculptured heads of Nemrut Dag in Asia Minor. But Greek culture also absorbed oriental influences, most notably in the appropriation of Egyptian deities into the Ptolemaic pantheon.

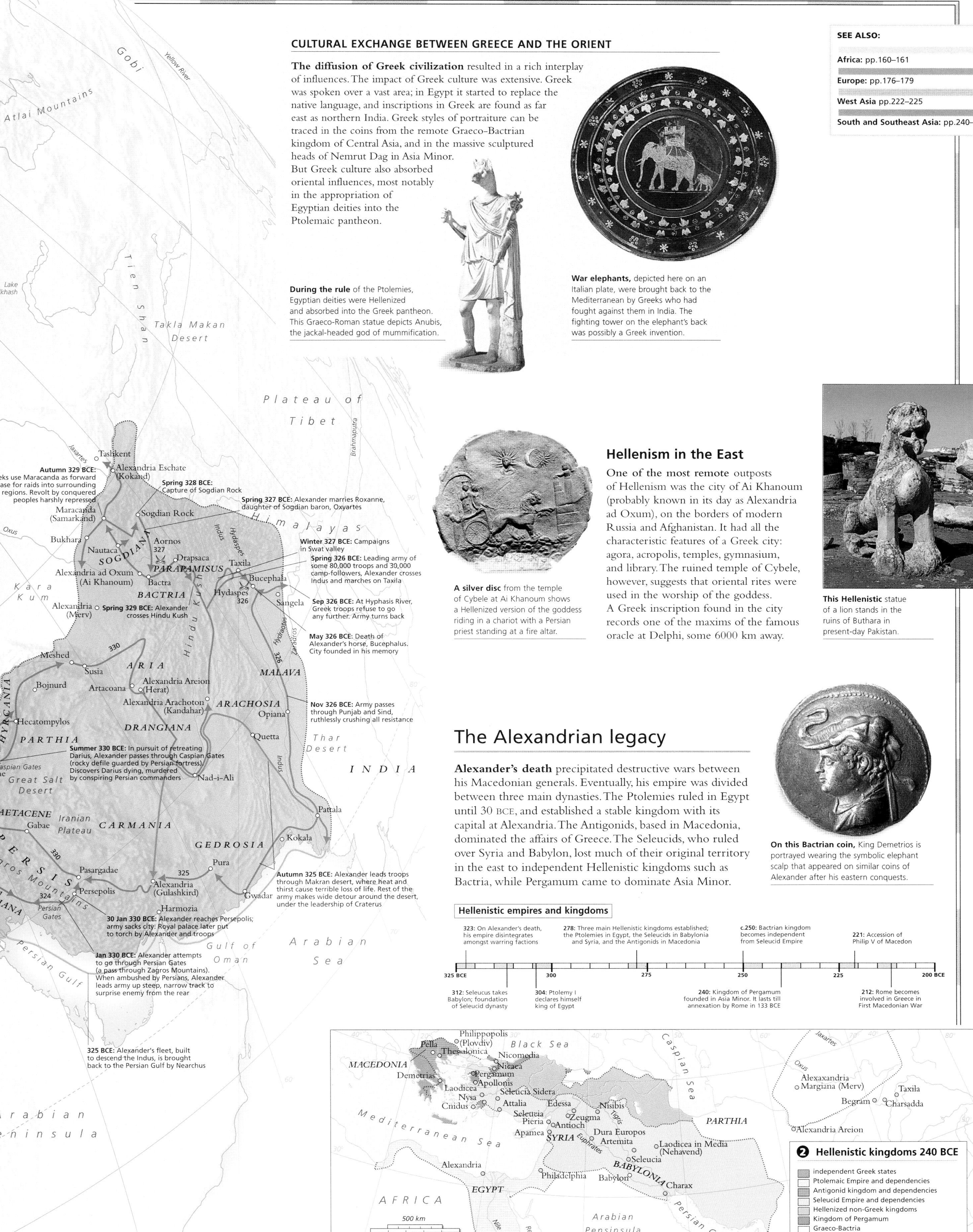

During the rule of the Ptolemies, Egyptian deities were Hellenized and absorbed into the Greek pantheon. This Graeco-Roman statue depicts Anubis, the jackal-headed god of mummification.

War elephants, depicted here on an Italian plate, were brought back to the Mediterranean by Greeks who had fought against them in India. The fighting tower on the elephant's back was possibly a Greek invention.

A silver disc from the temple of Cybele at Ai Khanoum shows a Hellenized version of the goddess riding in a chariot with a Persian priest standing at a fire altar.

Hellenism in the East

One of the most remote outposts of Hellenism was the city of Ai Khanoum (probably known in its day as Alexandria ad Oxum), on the borders of modern Russia and Afghanistan. It had all the characteristic features of a Greek city: agora, acropolis, temples, gymnasium, and library. The ruined temple of Cybele, however, suggests that oriental rites were used in the worship of the goddess. A Greek inscription found in the city records one of the maxims of the famous oracle at Delphi, some 6000 km away.

This Hellenistic statue of a lion stands in the ruins of Buthara in present-day Pakistan.

The Alexandrian legacy

Alexander's death precipitated destructive wars between his Macedonian generals. Eventually, his empire was divided between three main dynasties. The Ptolemies ruled in Egypt until 30 BCE, and established a stable kingdom with its capital at Alexandria. The Antigonids, based in Macedonia, dominated the affairs of Greece. The Seleucids, who ruled over Syria and Babylon, lost much of their original territory in the east to independent Hellenistic kingdoms such as Bactria, while Pergamum came to dominate Asia Minor.

On this Bactrian coin, King Demetrios is portrayed wearing the symbolic elephant scalp that appeared on similar coins of Alexander after his eastern conquests.

Hellenistic empires and kingdoms

2 Hellenistic kingdoms 240 BCE

- independent Greek states
- Ptolemaic Empire and dependencies
- Antigonid kingdom and dependencies
- Seleucid Empire and dependencies
- Hellenized non-Greek kingdoms
- Kingdom of Pergamum
- Graeco-Bactria
- Hellenistic cities (founded 350–100 BCE)

THE WORLD 250 BCE – 1 CE

BY 1 CE HALF THE GLOBAL population, which had reached about 250 million, lived within three major empires, Rome, Parthia, and Han China. With the addition of the developing kingdoms of northern India and Southeast Asia, urban civilization now existed in a wide swathe across the Old World, from the Iberian Peninsula in the west to Korea in the east, surrounded by nomadic pastoralists, farmers, and increasingly marginalized hunter-gatherers. The opening up of the Silk Road in the 1st century BCE and the discovery of monsoon trade routes across the Indian Ocean led to an unprecedented degree of contact between empires, disseminating both religious and cultural influences. In the New World the increasingly sophisticated Nazca and Moche cultures were developing in Peru, while Teotihuacán in Mexico was poised to become one of the world's most populous cities.

Europe

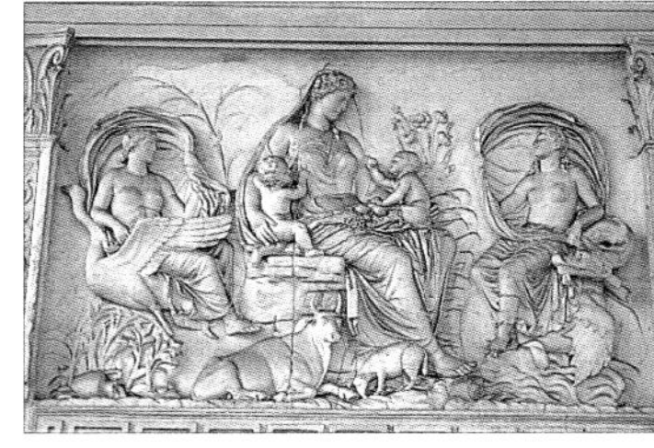

The Ara Pacis (Altar of Peace) was set up in Rome in 9 BCE to commemorate the pacification of Gaul and Iberia by the Emperor Augustus.

Following the defeat of Carthage in the 2nd century BCE, Rome embarked on a programme of expansion, which extended control to Greek territories in the east and Gaul to the north. In the 1st century BCE, a period of civil wars and rule by military dictators threatened the unity of the growing empire.

In 27 BCE Octavian assumed imperial power (and the title Augustus), reuniting the Roman world and ushering in two centuries of stability and prosperity.

Europe

218–201: Second Punic War. Hannibal crosses Alps and invades Italy

146: With the sack of Corinth, Greece comes under Roman rule. Third Punic War ends with sack of Carthage by Rome

58–51: Gallic conquests of Julius Caesar

46: Julius Caesar appointed dictator. He is assassinated two years later

250 BCE | 200 | 150 | 100 | 50 | 1 CE

241: End of First Punic War between Rome and Carthage

168: Roman expansion into eastern Mediterranean begins

89: Roman citizenship extended to all Italians

31: Octavian defeats Antony and Cleopatra at Actium

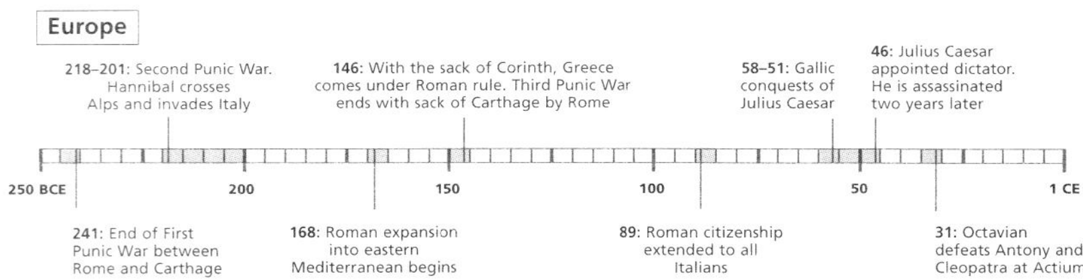

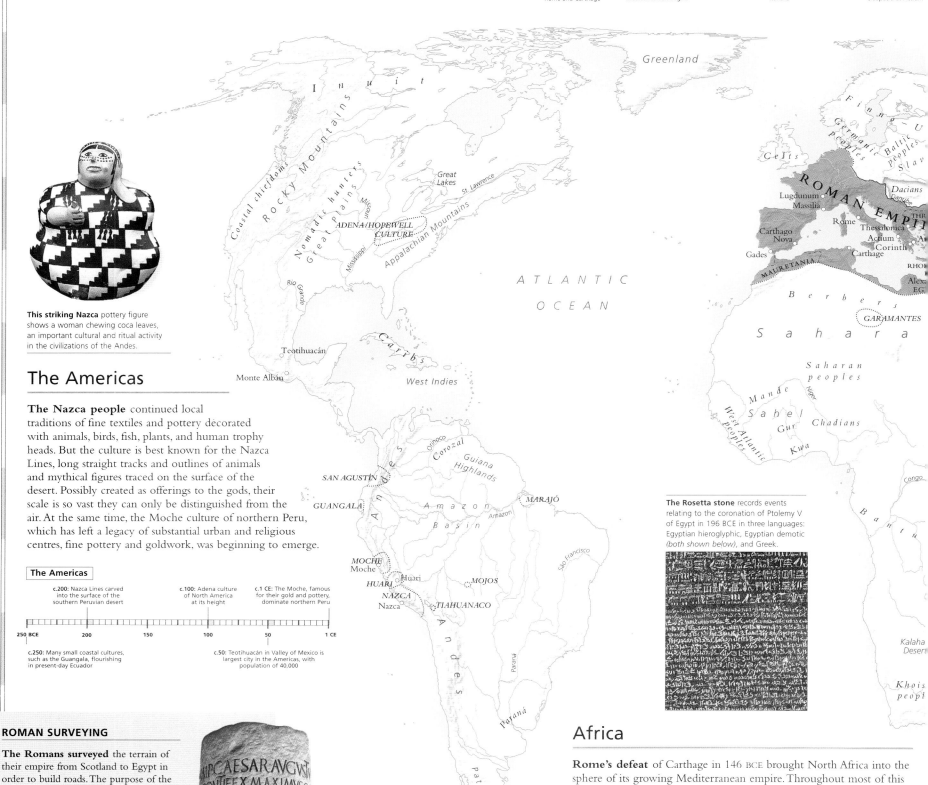

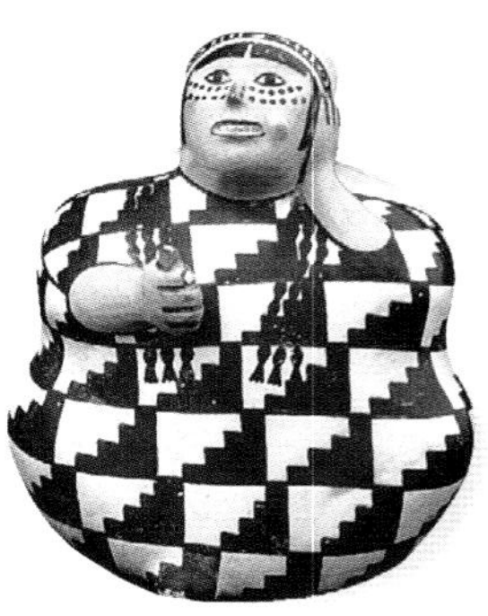

This **striking Nazca** pottery figure shows a woman chewing coca leaves, an important cultural and ritual activity in the civilizations of the Andes.

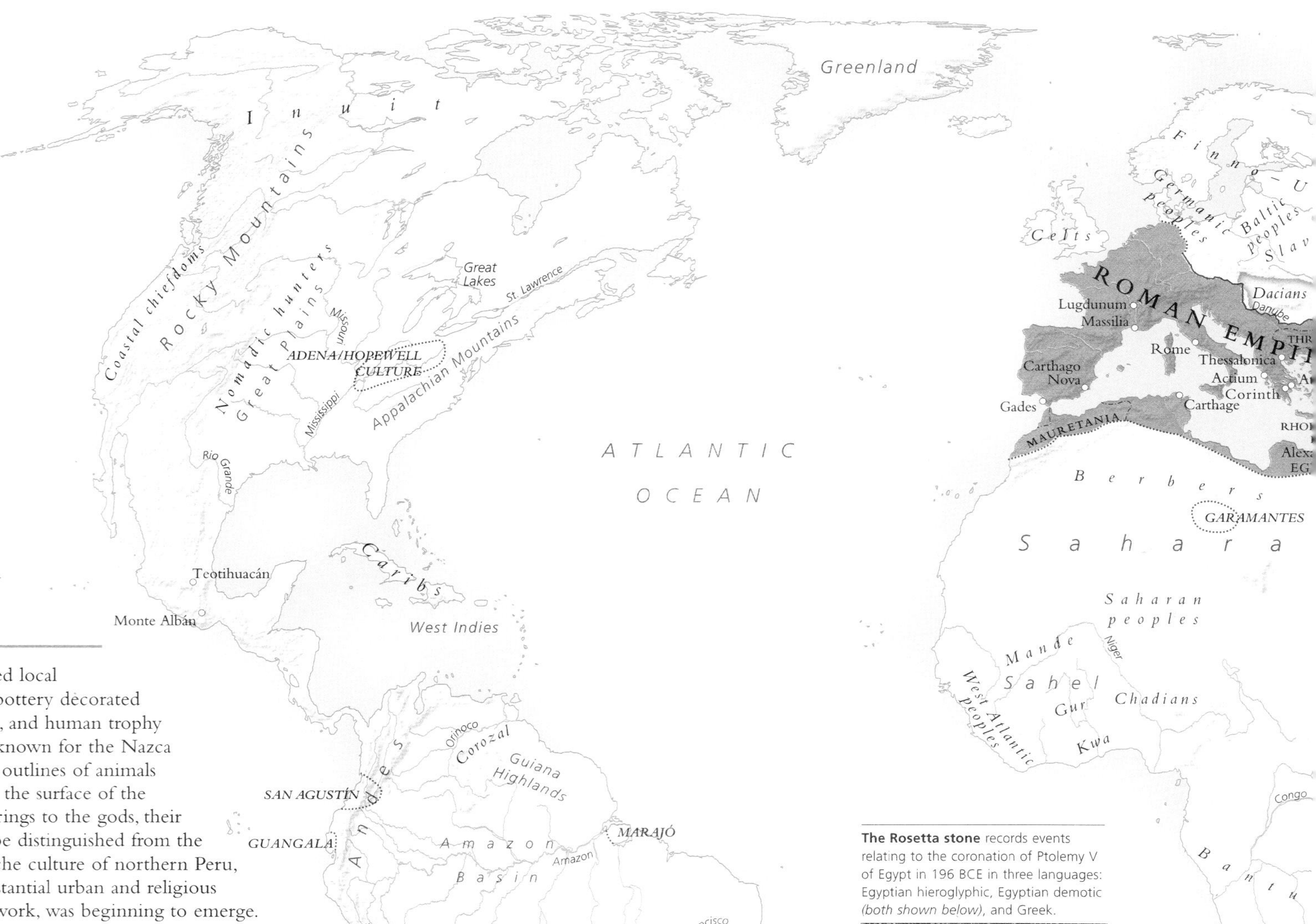

The Americas

The Nazca people continued local traditions of fine textiles and pottery decorated with animals, birds, fish, plants, and human trophy heads. But the culture is best known for the Nazca Lines, long straight tracks and outlines of animals and mythical figures traced on the surface of the desert. Possibly created as offerings to the gods, their scale is so vast they can only be distinguished from the air. At the same time, the Moche culture of northern Peru, which has left a legacy of substantial urban and religious centres, fine pottery and goldwork, was beginning to emerge.

The Americas

c.200: Nazca Lines carved into the surface of the southern Peruvian desert

c.100: Adena culture of North America at its height

c.1 CE: The Moche, famous for their gold and pottery, dominate northern Peru

250 BCE | 200 | 150 | 100 | 50 | 1 CE

c.250: Many small coastal cultures, such as the Guangala, flourishing in present-day Ecuador

c.50: Teotihuacán in Valley of Mexico is largest city in the Americas, with population of 40,000

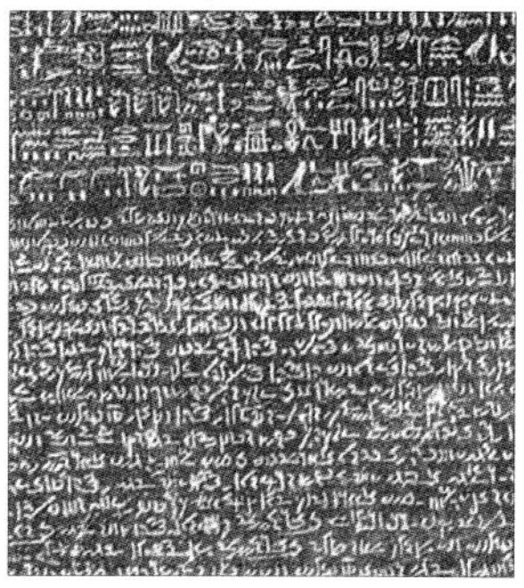

The Rosetta stone records events relating to the coronation of Ptolemy V of Egypt in 196 BCE in three languages: Egyptian hieroglyphic, Egyptian demotic *(both shown below)*, and Greek.

Africa

Rome's defeat of Carthage in 146 BCE brought North Africa into the sphere of its growing Mediterranean empire. Throughout most of this period, Egypt was ruled by the Ptolemies, whose introduction of Greek language and writing hastened the decline of Egyptian civilization. In 31 BCE, when Octavian defeated Antony and Cleopatra at the battle of Actium, Egypt became a Roman province destined to serve as Rome's granary. To the south the kingdom of Meroe prospered, exporting frankincense to Rome along the Red Sea. The Bantu continued their progress into southern Africa, introducing agriculture and iron-working.

ROMAN SURVEYING

The Romans surveyed the terrain of their empire from Scotland to Egypt in order to build roads. The purpose of the roads was primarily military – to enable Roman legions to move quickly to troublespots within the empire – but they also carried local commercial traffic. Distances were measured in thousands of paces *(milia passuum)* – hence the word mile – and milestones were placed at regular intervals. The Roman mile was about 1540 metres (1680 yards).

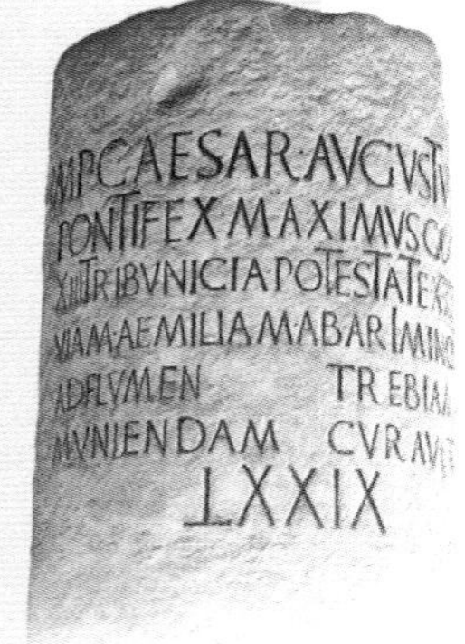

This Roman milestone stood on the Via Aemilia, which ran in a straight line across northern Italy. The inscription records road repairs undertaken in the reign of Augustus (27 BCE–14 CE).

West Asia

This ivory rhyton (horn-shaped drinking cup) was found at Nisa, the early capital of the Parthians after they expanded south from their homelands east of the Caspian Sea.

Following the secession of Bactria, Sogdiana, and Parthia from Seleucid rule in the mid-3rd century BCE, the nomadic Parthians took advantage of the upheaval to extend their territory. By the early 1st century BCE, their empire included Mesopotamia and stretched from Syria to Bactria. With their light, manoeuvrable mounted bowmen, the Parthians withstood the might of Rome at the battle of Carrhae (53 BCE), halting Rome's eastern expansion. The Parthian Empire lasted 500 years, growing wealthy from its control of the Silk Road linking China and Rome.

West Asia

- **247:** Arsaces founds the Arsacid, or Parthian, dynasty
- **171:** Mithradates II founds Parthian Empire
- **141:** Parthians control Mesopotamia following capture of the old Seleucid capital, Seleucia-on-the-Tigris
- **124:** Accession of Mithradates II. Parthian Empire reaches greatest extent
- **90:** Ctesiphon established as Parthian capital
- **53:** Defeat of Roman infantry at the battle of Carrhae in northern Syria
- **40:** Rome recognizes Herod the Great as ruler of Judaea

250 BCE · 200 · 150 · 100 · 50 · 1 CE

East Asia

The Qin unified China in 221 BCE, their leader taking the title 'First Emperor' and introducing a harsh, centralized, bureaucratic regime. His death in 210 was followed by widespread revolts. By 206 the Han dynasty under Gao Zu had taken power. The Han too presided over a highly centralized bureaucracy, their state monopoly on iron and salt, combined with the opening up of the Silk Road to Central Asia, ensuring their prosperity.

Shi Huangdi, the Qin First Emperor, imposed his autocratic rule through military force. A symbolic army of thousands of life-sized, terracotta soldiers was assembled to guard his tomb.

East Asia

- **221:** Great Wall built as protection against northern nomadic incursions
- **210:** Death of Shi Huangdi leads to revolts throughout Qin Empire
- **206:** Han dynasty, under Gao Zu, assumes control
- **136:** Confucianism becomes state religion of China
- **119:** State monopoly on iron-working established
- **c.112:** Opening up of Silk Road across Central Asia
- **108:** Chinese take military control of Korea
- **55:** Xiongnu confederacy breaks up; southern group becomes tributary of Han China

250 BCE · 200 · 150 · 100 · 50 · 1 CE

SEE ALSO:

North America: pp.120–121

South America: pp.144–145

Africa: pp.160–161

Europe: pp.178–179

West Asia: pp.224–225

South and Southeast Asia: pp.240–243

North and East Asia: pp.258–261

Australasia and Oceania: pp.280–281

ROMAN BUILDINGS

Architecturally, the Romans borrowed freely from the Greeks and other earlier civilizations. The most distinctive feature of their buildings, the arch, was inherited from the Etruscans. One of the Romans' major innovations was the use of *pozzolana,* concrete made of sand mixed with slaked lime and volcanic ash. This enabled them to build temples, bath houses, aqueducts, and amphitheatres on a prodigious scale.

The coffered dome of the Pantheon in Rome is made of *pozzolana*. It was still the largest in the world even when the dome of St Peter's was completed in the 16th century.

The great complex of rock-carved temples and monasteries at Ajanta in central India became an important Buddhist centre in the 1st century BCE. It is famous for its many fine ceiling paintings of the Buddha.

South and Southeast Asia

On the death of Ashoka in 232 BCE, the Mauryan Empire disintegrated and, in 185 BCE, was supplanted by the Shunga dynasty. The Greek colony of Bactria became independent and, in the Indus valley region, Bactrians established kingdoms where Hellenic and Indian influences mingled. Much of Southeast Asia fell under Indian cultural influence as Hinduism and Buddhism spread eastwards. Chinese contact was political and military; Annam fell under Han control in the 1st century BCE.

South and Southeast Asia

- **232:** Start of disintegration of Mauryan Empire
- **c.200:** Bactrian Greeks establish small kingdoms
- **185:** Pusyamitra founds Shunga dynasty
- **111:** Annam falls to Han Empire
- **c.100:** Indian influences spread to Southeast Asia via maritime trade routes
- **90:** Bactrian kingdom of Gandhara falls to Scythians (Shakas)
- **c.30:** Shakas overrun Indo-Greek kingdoms of Indus valley

250 BCE · 200 · 150 · 100 · 50 · 1 CE

Africa

- **146:** Destruction of Carthage; Rome creates province of Africa from former Carthaginian possessions
- **105:** Jugurtha, king of Numidia defeated by Roman general Gaius Marius
- **c.100:** Camel introduced into Sahara by the Romans
- **46:** Foundation of Roman colony of Carthage
- **31:** Cleopatra's death marks end of Ptolemaic dynasty in Egypt

250 BCE · 200 · 150 · 100 · 50 · 1 CE

TRADE IN THE CLASSICAL WORLD

Fine Chinese silks from this period, lightweight and of high value, have been found throughout Eurasia, as far west as Egypt and Greece.

BY THE BEGINNING of the 1st millennium CE, a series of commercial and political networks had evolved which combined to form a nexus of trade which linked the eastern shores of the Atlantic Ocean, the Indian Ocean, and the western shores of the Pacific. At its extremes this network linked the Roman Empire, centred on the Mediterranean, and the land-based Han Empire of China. As the commercial and territorial influences of these two power bases spread beyond their political domains, so outlying regions were drawn into the web, from sub-Saharan Africa to the East Indies. However, the most important link to emerge was the Silk Road which spanned Asia, threading through the mountain ranges and deserts of the central Asian landmass, and along which a chain of powerful trading cities and states came into being.

Han China and the wider world

The Han Dynasty, which emerged to take over the territorial extent of the Qin Empire from 206 BCE, was largely self-sufficient. Trade was not regarded as an imperial concern, although desirable goods were drawn into Han markets by successive middlemen on the empire's fringes – spices from South and Southeast Asia, trepang and mother-of-pearl from the East Indies and, with the extension of the empire into Central Asia, the swift cavalry horses of Ferghana became highly prized. Conversely, Chinese products such as silk and lacquerware commanded high prices across Asia.

Decorated Han votive mirrors were used as diplomatic gifts by the Chinese, and have been found as far away as Siberia, the Caucasus, and southern Russia.

The nimble 'Horses of Heaven' from Ferghana provided the Chinese with the style of cavalry needed to keep the Xiongnu at bay.

Han trade
(in approximate order of value)

Exports	Imports
silk	horses
lacquerware	spices
	precious stones

The Classical world

141: Wudi expands Han power into Central Asia
60: Establishment of Kushan Empire
c.150: Ptolemy publishes first World Atlas
200: Han dynasty collapses
396: Roman Empire divided into eastern and western halves

200 BCE — 100 BCE — 1 CE — 100 — 200 — 300 — 400

31: Roman victory at Actium consolidates control of eastern Mediterranean
117: Roman Empire at greatest extent
224: Beginning of Sassanian control in Persia
238: First Germanic incursions into Roman Empire
370: Huns enter Europe

Roman trade

Rome, in contrast to Han China, was an empire largely dependent on trade. Rome's imports were prodigious. A single currency, common citizenship, low customs barriers, and the development of a broadly secure network of roads, inland waterways, harbours, and sea-routes provided a hub of commerce which drew in produce from far beyond the imperial boundaries.

The popular Roman taste for combat with exotic wild animals in the arena saw bears, bulls, and boars being imported from northern Europe, lions and tigers from Asia, crocodiles from Egypt, and rhinoceros, hippopotami, and a variety of large cats from sub-Saharan Africa.

Roman trade
(in approximate order of value)

Exports	Imports
gold	food
silver	slaves
wine	animals
olive oil	spices
glassware	silk
	incense
	ivory
	cotton

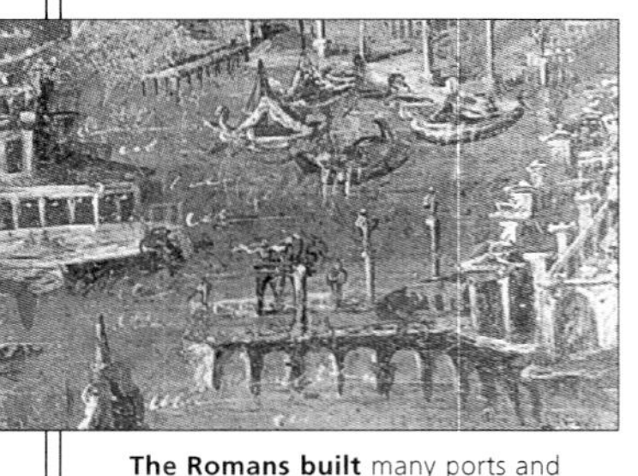
The Romans built many ports and harbours around the Mediterranean, elaborate complexes with lighthouses and quays, which serviced the Roman maritime trading network.

Knowledge of Classical Eurasia

There is some evidence of direct contact between Rome and the Han Empire and Europeans clearly had extensive knowledge of the general shape of Classical Eurasia. The Greek geographer Strabo gave a detailed description of the known world in his 17-volume *Geography* (c.20 CE) and by 150 CE the Alexandrian Ptolemy's *Geography* formally laid out the topography of Eurasia. His world view (*below*) names Sinae (China), Taprobane (Sri Lanka), and Sera Metropolis (Chang'an).

Reconstruction of Ptolemy's map of Classical Eurasia

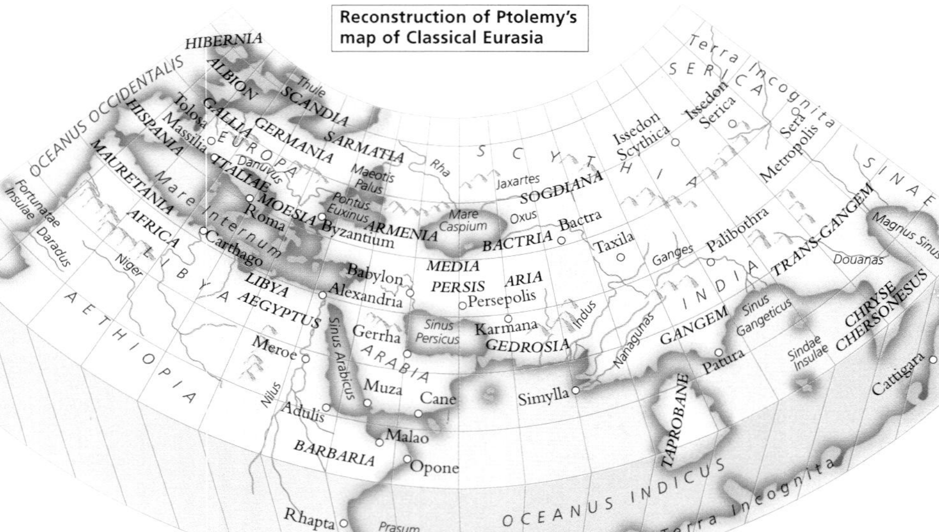

Central Asian trade

The development of the Silk Road saw the growth of a string of powerful cities and states which thrived, controlling the trade which passed through them. The greatest of these was the Parthian Empire of Persia (247 BCE–244 CE), while to the north Transoxiana, Bactria, and the Kushan Empire of modern Uzbekistan straddled the region in which the Silk Road converged and intersected with routes travelling north from India through the Hindu Kush, and on to the Caspian Sea and the river routes of Scythia.

The Silk Road

The campaigns by the Qin First Emperor, Shi Huangdi, and his Han successor Wudi against the nomadic Xiongnu opened a series of routes which traversed Central Asia, remaining the principal east-west trade route for centuries. The Silk Road linked Samarkand in the west with Anxi in the east; a summer route went north of the Tien Shan range, while the main route split to skirt the Takla Makan.

SEE ALSO:
Africa: pp.160–161
Europe: pp.180–181
West Asia: pp.224–225
South and Southeast Asia: pp.240–241
North and East Asia: pp.260–261

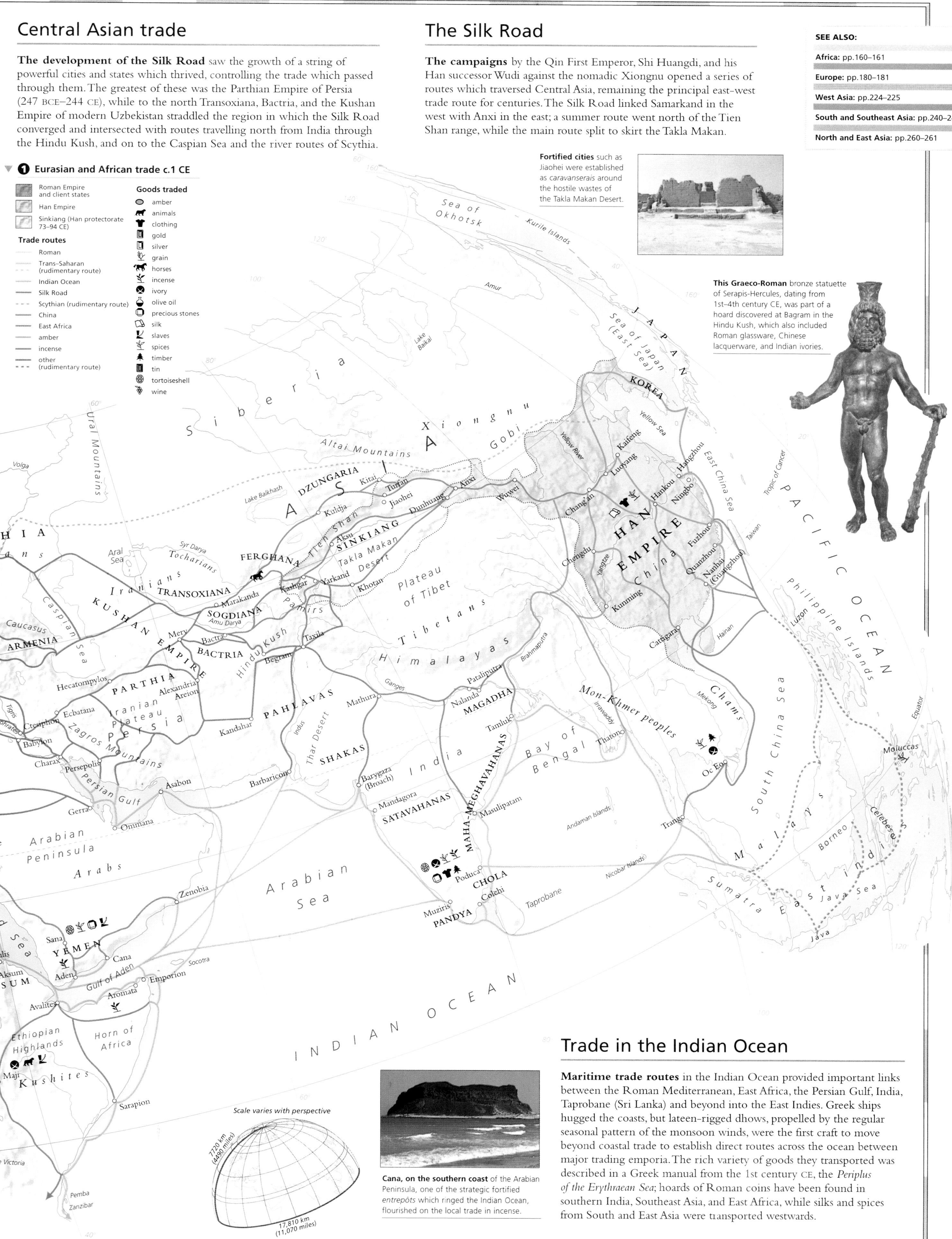

Fortified cities such as Jiaohei were established as *caravanserais* around the hostile wastes of the Takla Makan Desert.

This Graeco-Roman bronze statuette of Serapis-Hercules, dating from 1st–4th century CE, was part of a hoard discovered at Bagram in the Hindu Kush, which also included Roman glassware, Chinese lacquerware, and Indian ivories.

Cana, on the southern coast of the Arabian Peninsula, one of the strategic fortified *entrepôts* which ringed the Indian Ocean, flourished on the local trade in incense.

Trade in the Indian Ocean

Maritime trade routes in the Indian Ocean provided important links between the Roman Mediterranean, East Africa, the Persian Gulf, India, Taprobane (Sri Lanka) and beyond into the East Indies. Greek ships hugged the coasts, but lateen-rigged dhows, propelled by the regular seasonal pattern of the monsoon winds, were the first craft to move beyond coastal trade to establish direct routes across the ocean between major trading emporia. The rich variety of goods they transported was described in a Greek manual from the 1st century CE, the *Periplus of the Erythraean Sea*; hoards of Roman coins have been found in southern India, Southeast Asia, and East Africa, while silks and spices from South and East Asia were tıansported westwards.

THE WORLD 1–250 CE

AS THE EMPIRES OF THE OLD WORLD expanded, the protection of their borders and far-flung imperial outposts became an urgent priority. Increasing threats from the mounted nomadic pastoralists of Asia, the Germanic tribes of eastern Europe and the Berbers of northern Africa stretched resources to the limit, weakening Roman control, and leading to economic and social chaos. The empire of Han China collapsed in 220 CE, a victim of famine, floods, insurgency, and the growing power of regional warlords. By the early 3rd century CE, pressures on Rome's eastern borders precipitated a stormy century of civil wars, dynastic disputes, and army revolts. Against this troubled backdrop a new religion, Christianity, was beginning to spread throughout the Roman world. Originating with the teachings of Jesus of Nazareth in Palestine, the new religion proved remarkably resistant to Roman persecution.

Marcus Aurelius was one of the most conscientious Roman emperors: a Stoic philosopher and tireless campaigner on the German frontier.

Europe

In the 2nd century CE the Roman Empire stretched from West Asia to the Atlantic, united by one language, one coinage, and a system of well-paved roads, and protected by fortified frontiers. The empire prospered under strong emperors, but stresses began to appear. Conflict over the imperial succession undermined central authority, leading to civil wars between rivals, economic breakdown, and revolts by the army. Pressure on imperial frontiers, especially from the Germanic tribes to the east of the Rhine, stretched the empire's resources, leading to inflation, famine, disease, and lawlessness.

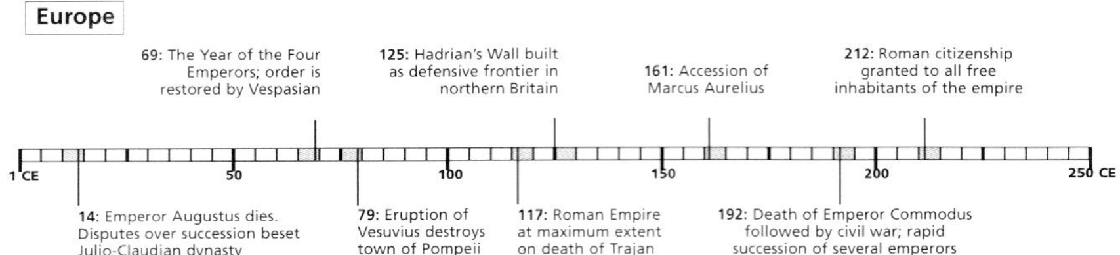
Europe
69: The Year of the Four Emperors; order is restored by Vespasian
125: Hadrian's Wall built as defensive frontier in northern Britain
161: Accession of Marcus Aurelius
212: Roman citizenship granted to all free inhabitants of the empire
1 CE
50
100
150
200
250 CE
14: Emperor Augustus dies. Disputes over succession beset Julio-Claudian dynasty
79: Eruption of Vesuvius destroys town of Pompeii
117: Roman Empire at maximum extent on death of Trajan
192: Death of Emperor Commodus followed by civil war; rapid succession of several emperors

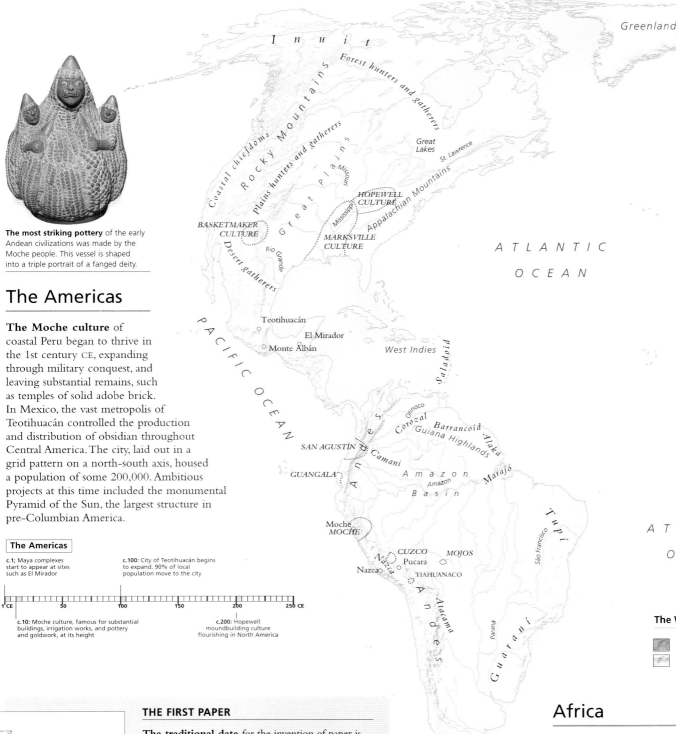

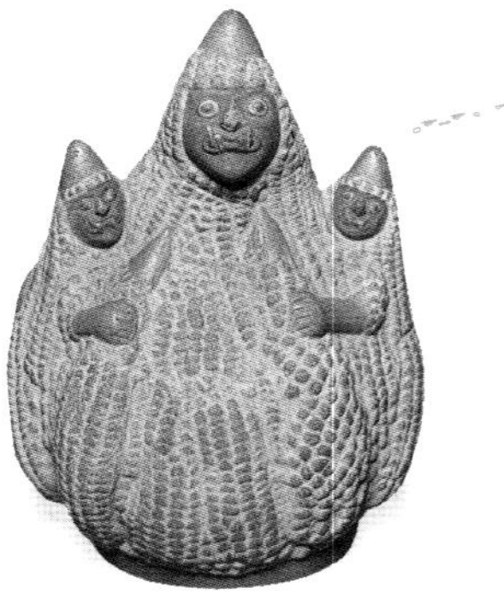

The most striking pottery of the early Andean civilizations was made by the Moche people. This vessel is shaped into a triple portrait of a fanged deity.

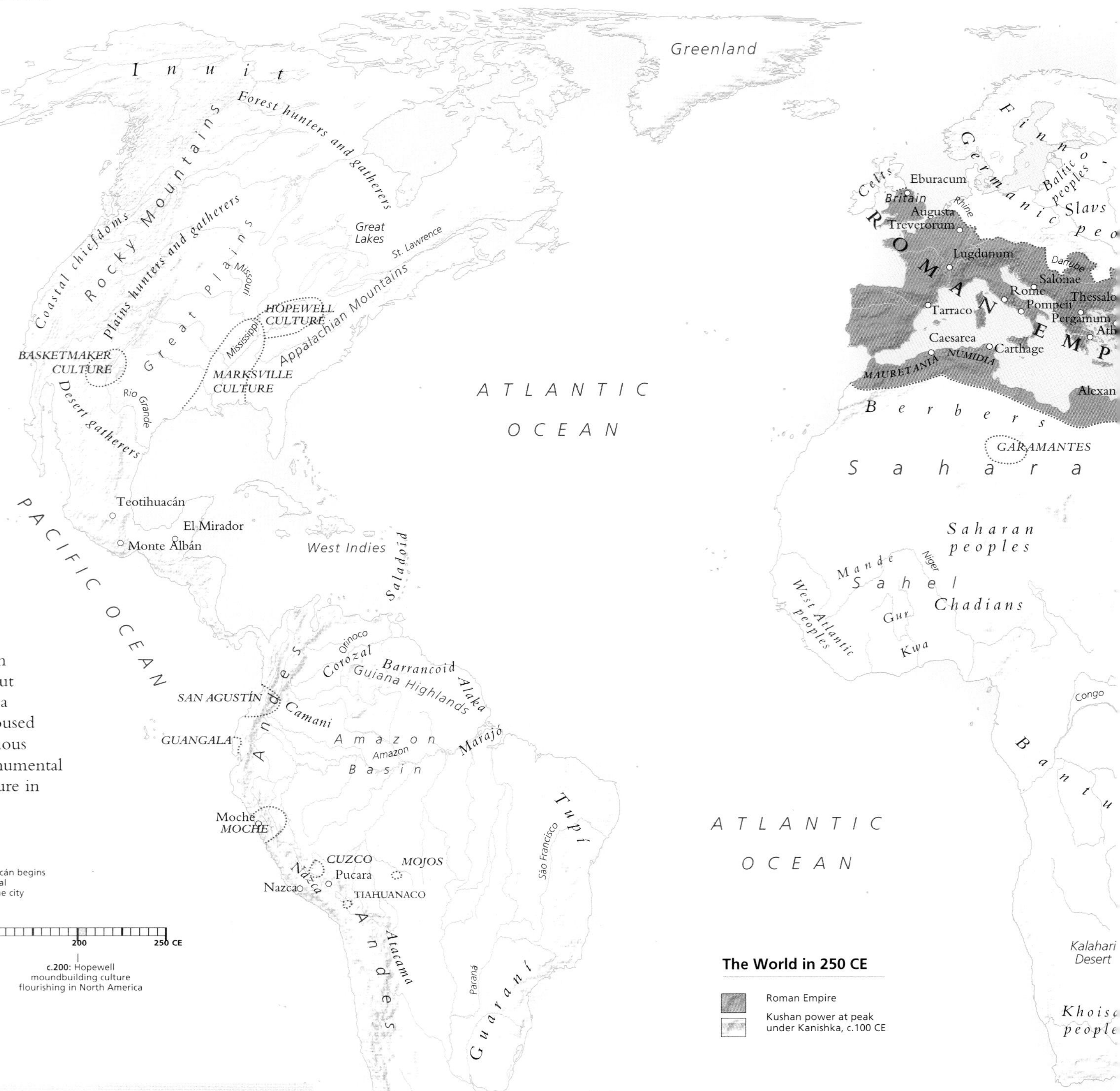

The Americas

The Moche culture of coastal Peru began to thrive in the 1st century CE, expanding through military conquest, and leaving substantial remains, such as temples of solid adobe brick. In Mexico, the vast metropolis of Teotihuacán controlled the production and distribution of obsidian throughout Central America. The city, laid out in a grid pattern on a north-south axis, housed a population of some 200,000. Ambitious projects at this time included the monumental Pyramid of the Sun, the largest structure in pre-Columbian America.

The Americas

c.1: Maya complexes start to appear at sites such as El Mirador

c.100: City of Teotihuacán begins to expand. 90% of local population move to the city

1 CE — 50 — 100 — 150 — 200 — 250 CE

c.10: Moche culture, famous for substantial buildings, irrigation works, and pottery and goldwork, at its height

c.200: Hopewell moundbuilding culture flourishing in North America

The World in 250 CE

Roman Empire

Kushan power at peak under Kanishka, c.100 CE

THE FIRST PAPER

The traditional date for the invention of paper is 105 CE, but lightweight felted material for writing had been made in China for some time before then. The pulp was made of scraps of bark, bamboo, and hemp, finely chopped and boiled with wood ash. As techniques improved, paper replaced expensive silk and cumbersome wooden tablets.

A Chinese worker lifts a mesh screen covered with a thin layer of pulp that will drain and dry to form a sheet of paper.

Africa

Under Roman rule, Egypt experienced a remarkable economic recovery. As ancient Egyptian cults and traditions declined, Christianity found converts amongst the Egyptians. To the west, the Romans extended their control to the Berber kingdoms of Numidia and Mauretania. The fertile coastal plains were fully exploited, but the southern borders of Roman territory were under constant threat of Berber invasion. By 100 CE the Red Sea kingdom of Axum, its wealth based on control of the incense trade, had become a major power.

The ruined city of Petra contains remarkable rock-cut tombs. It was annexed by Rome in 106 as capital of the province of Arabia.

West Asia

In the 1st century CE the Parthian Empire was torn by internal dissent and dynastic struggles. Between 114 and 198, the Romans invaded three times, sacking the cities of Seleucia and Ctesiphon. In 224 Ardashir Papakan defeated his Parthian overlords and founded the Sassanian dynasty. He introduced a centralized administration, and transformed vassal kingdoms into provinces, ruled by Sassanian princes. His son Shapur repelled the Romans and made Sassanian Persia the most stable power of late antiquity.

West Asia (timeline, 1 CE–250 CE)

- **70**: Romans suppress Jewish revolt and destroy temple in Jerusalem
- **c.114**: Trajan annexes Armenia, takes Seleucia and reaches Persian Gulf
- **c.132**: Second Jewish revolt precipitates diaspora
- **c.150**: Petra, a major trading post for incense, at height of prosperity
- **165**: Avidius Cassius sacks Seleucia and Ctesiphon
- **197**: Septimus Severus sails down Euphrates to invade Parthian Empire
- **224**: Sassanians take over Parthian Empire

East Asia

In 25 CE, after a brief interregnum, Han emperors regained control of China, but their rule depended on the support of powerful landowners. The capital moved to Luoyang, and eastern and southern China exerted greater political influence. In the early 3rd century the empire, beset by rebellions and feuds, collapsed. Regional warlords carved out three new kingdoms and China remained fragmented for over 300 years. With the decline of the Han, small local states, notably Koguryo and Silla, took control of Korea.

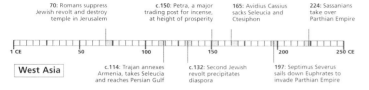

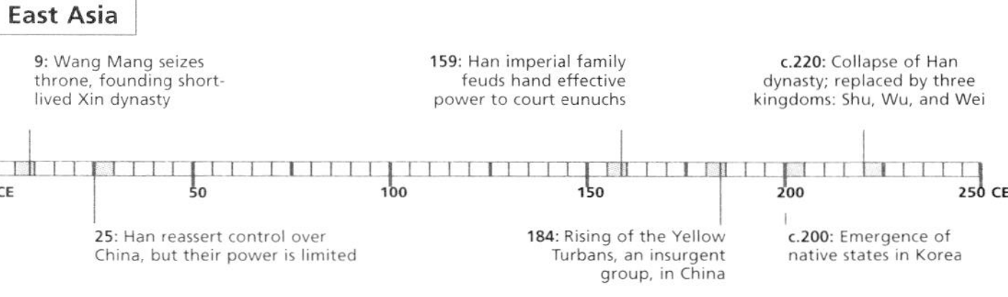
This model horse and trap was found among the goods in the grave of a high-ranking officer of the Han period.

East Asia (timeline, 1 CE–250 CE)

- **9**: Wang Mang seizes throne, founding short-lived Xin dynasty
- **25**: Han reassert control over China, but their power is limited
- **159**: Han imperial family feuds hand effective power to court eunuchs
- **184**: Rising of the Yellow Turbans, an insurgent group, in China
- **c.200**: Emergence of native states in Korea
- **c.220**: Collapse of Han dynasty; replaced by three kingdoms: Shu, Wu, and Wei

SEE ALSO:

North America: pp.120–121

South America: pp.144–145

Africa: pp.160–161

Europe: pp.180–181

West Asia: pp.224–225

South and Southeast Asia: pp.240–243

North and East Asia: pp.260–261

Australasia and Oceania: pp.280–281

Palaeosiberians
Lena
Yenisey
Ob'
Samoyeds
Siberia
Tungus
Amur
Turks
Mongols
Huns
Gobi
Xianbi (Tungus)
Ainu
BOSPORAN KINGDOM
Iranians
Caucasian peoples
Caspian Sea
ARMENIA
Bactra
BACTRIA
Begram
KUSHANA
Peshawar
Taxila
SASSANIAN EMPIRE
Tigris
Euphrates
Ctesiphon
Seleucia
Jerusalem
Petra
Persian Gulf
Tibetans
Himalayas
Indus
Ganges
Pataliputra
Ujjain
INDIAN STATES
Deccan
Satavahanas
Tamils
LAMBAKANNAS
Arabs
Arabian Peninsula
Red Sea
Meroe
AKSUM
Aksum
HIMYARITES
Semites
Fur
Kushites
Madagascar
KOGURYO
Yellow River
WEI
Chang'an
Luoyang
PAEKCHE
SILLA
KAYA
JAPAN
Jianye
Yangtze
Chengdu
SHU HAN
WU
Mon-Khmer peoples
CHAMPA
Mekong
FUNAN
Vyadhapura
MON AND MALAY STATES
Philippine Islands
PACIFIC OCEAN
Malays
Borneo
Sumatra
Java
Papuans
New Guinea
Australian Aborigines
Darling
New Zealand

MOSAIC OF THE NILE IN FLOOD

The Romans drew maps, but unfortunately only a few fragments carved on stone survive. Some others have come down to us through medieval copies. One highly imaginative representation of the contemporary world that has been preserved is this mosaic of a panoramic view of *The Nile in Flood* found at Praeneste, near Rome.

The River Nile was of great importance to Rome: its fertile floodplain was a major source of grain for feeding the city.

South Asia

In the 1st century CE the nomadic Yuezhi were pushed westwards from the borders of China. One of the tribes, the Kushans, united the others, moved into Bactria, and from there expanded into northern India, founding their capital at Peshawar. The Kingdom of Kushana crumbled at the end of the 2nd century, when native peoples – the Tamils of southern India and the Satavahanas of the Deccan – were beginning to assert their power.

The Kushans' wealth came from their control of east–west trade routes. This ivory plaque was part of a famous hoard found at Begram, which contained artefacts from Rome, Africa, India, and China.

Egyptian mummy cases took on a curious hybrid appearance under Roman rule. The portrait on this 2nd-century example shows the Egyptians' Hellenistic taste in art.

Africa (timeline, 1 CE–250 CE)

- **44**: Mauretania annexed by Rome
- **c.50**: Kingdom of Axum starts to emerge
- **69**: Romans defeat powerful Saharan kingdom of Garamantes, but do not absorb it into empire
- **c.100**: Alexandria emerges as a centre of Christian scholarship, seat of one of the earliest Christian bishoprics
- **c.150**: Christianity starts to spread westwards to Roman provinces of Numidia and Mauretania

South Asia (timeline, 1 CE–250 CE)

- **c.60**: Kushans, under Kadphises I, unite Yuezhi tribes and advance into northern India
- **99**: Indian embassy to court of Trajan in Rome, probably to announce Kushan conquests
- **c.102**: Death of Kushans' greatest ruler, Kanishka
- **c.150**: Kushans become Persian vassals
- **c.200**: Cities appear for first time on Deccan plateau

THE EMERGENCE OF GLOBAL RELIGIONS

This 7th-century silver plaque from Hexham, England is thought to depict a Christian saint.

BY 250 CE SOME OLD WORLD religions *(see pp.36–37)* had spread far beyond their areas of origin to become substantial bodies of faith. In the west, the Roman taste for monotheistic Mithraism, derived from Persian Zoroastrianism, spread throughout the empire, although it was always a minority cult. But in its wake the cult of Christianity was becoming firmly established. Further, the Roman suppression of the Jewish revolt in 132 CE had caused a diaspora through much of the empire. In South Asia, Hinduism became deeply rooted throughout the subcontinent as Dravidians and tribal peoples adopted the practices of their Aryan conquerors; meanwhile Buddhism was spread overland to Central Asia and China and beyond by missionaries of various sectarian schools.

Mithraism, Judaism, and Christianity

The worship of Mithras was arduous and limited to males; it was popular among the Roman legions, spreading to the corners of the empire. Its monotheism paved the way for Christianity which, in parallel to the Jewish diaspora, spread to centres throughout the empire. This was inaugurated by the missionary journeys of St. Paul, in the 1st century CE. By the time of Diocletian's persecutions (304 CE) centres had been established in Asia Minor, Mesopotamia, and around the Mediterranean. The fusion of Christian theology with the ethical concerns of Greek philosophy gave it intellectual respectability, and when Constantine (306–337) adopted the faith, Christianity became the official religion of the empire.

This 5th-century pottery amphora is decorated with two versions of the Christian cross, which became the most widely used symbol of the religion.

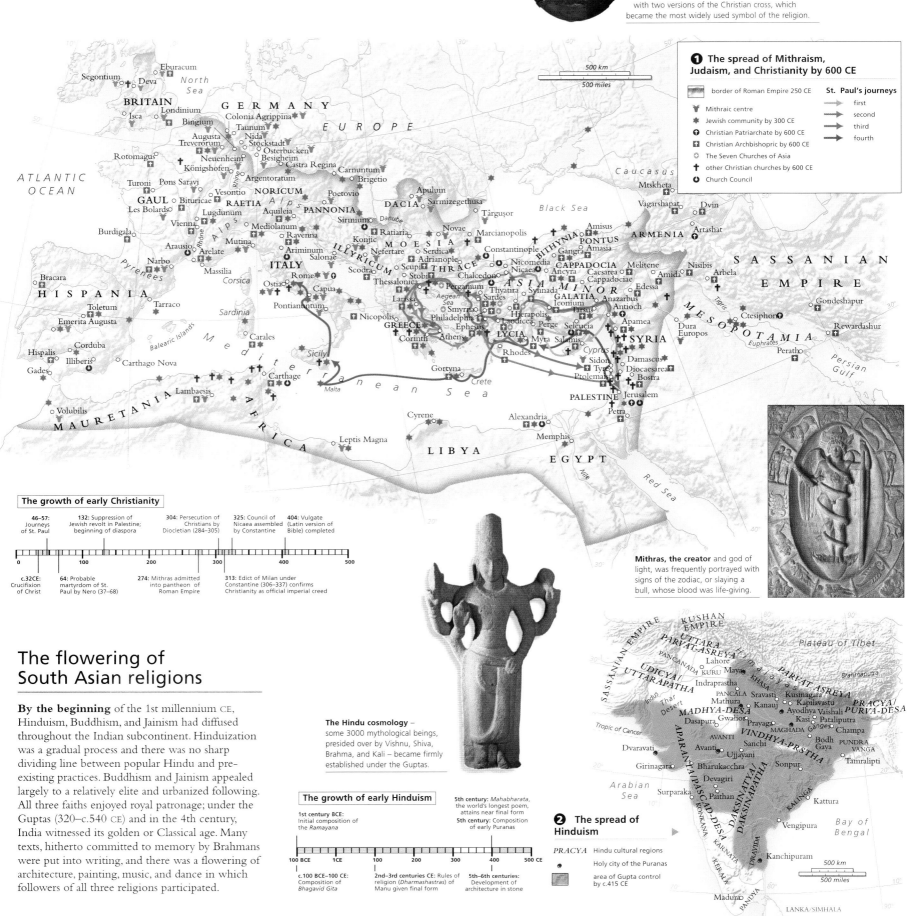

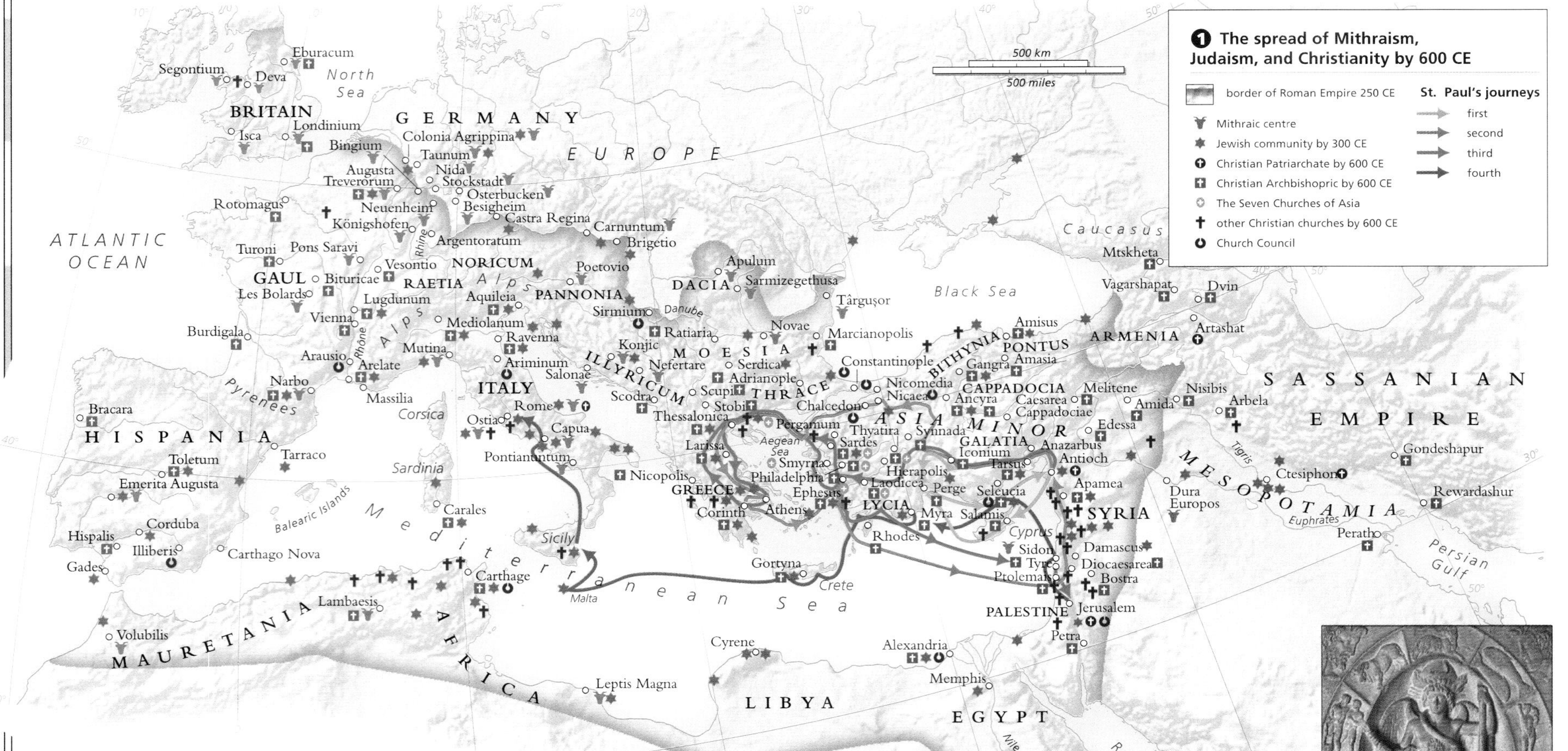

1 The spread of Mithraism, Judaism, and Christianity by 600 CE

- border of Roman Empire 250 CE
- Mithraic centre
- Jewish community by 300 CE
- Christian Patriarchate by 600 CE
- Christian Archbishopric by 600 CE
- The Seven Churches of Asia
- other Christian churches by 600 CE
- Church Council

St. Paul's journeys: first, second, third, fourth

The growth of early Christianity

- **c.32CE:** Crucifixion of Christ
- **46–57:** Journeys of St. Paul
- **64:** Probable martyrdom of St. Paul by Nero (37–68)
- **132:** Suppression of Jewish revolt in Palestine; beginning of diaspora
- **274:** Mithras admitted into pantheon of Roman Empire
- **304:** Persecution of Christians by Diocletian (284–305)
- **313:** Edict of Milan under Constantine (306–337) confirms Christianity as official imperial creed
- **325:** Council of Nicaea assembled by Constantine
- **404:** Vulgate (Latin version of Bible) completed

Mithras, the creator and god of light, was frequently portrayed with signs of the zodiac, or slaying a bull, whose blood was life-giving.

The flowering of South Asian religions

By the beginning of the 1st millennium CE, Hinduism, Buddhism, and Jainism had diffused throughout the Indian subcontinent. Hinduization was a gradual process and there was no sharp dividing line between popular Hindu and pre-existing practices. Buddhism and Jainism appealed largely to a relatively elite and urbanized following. All three faiths enjoyed royal patronage; under the Guptas (320–c.540 CE) and in the 4th century, India witnessed its golden or Classical age. Many texts, hitherto committed to memory by Brahmans were put into writing, and there was a flowering of architecture, painting, music, and dance in which followers of all three religions participated.

The Hindu cosmology – some 3000 mythological beings, presided over by Vishnu, Shiva, Brahma, and Kali – became firmly established under the Guptas.

The growth of early Hinduism

- **1st century BCE:** Initial composition of the *Ramayana*
- **c.100 BCE–100 CE:** Composition of *Bhagavid Gita*
- **2nd–3rd centuries CE:** Rules of religion (*Dharmashastras*) of Manu given final form
- **5th century:** *Mahabharata*, the world's longest poem, attains near final form
- **5th century:** Composition of early Puranas
- **5th–6th centuries:** Development of architecture in stone

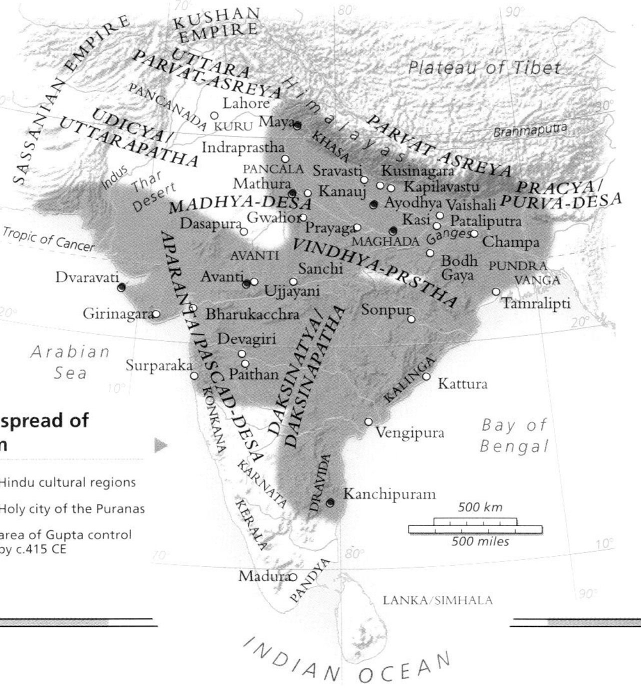

2 The spread of Hinduism

- *PRACYA* Hindu cultural regions
- Holy city of the Puranas
- area of Gupta control by c.415 CE

SEE ALSO:
Africa: pp.160–161
Europe: pp.180–183
West Asia: pp.224–225
South and Southeast Asia: pp.242–245
North and East Asia: pp.260–265

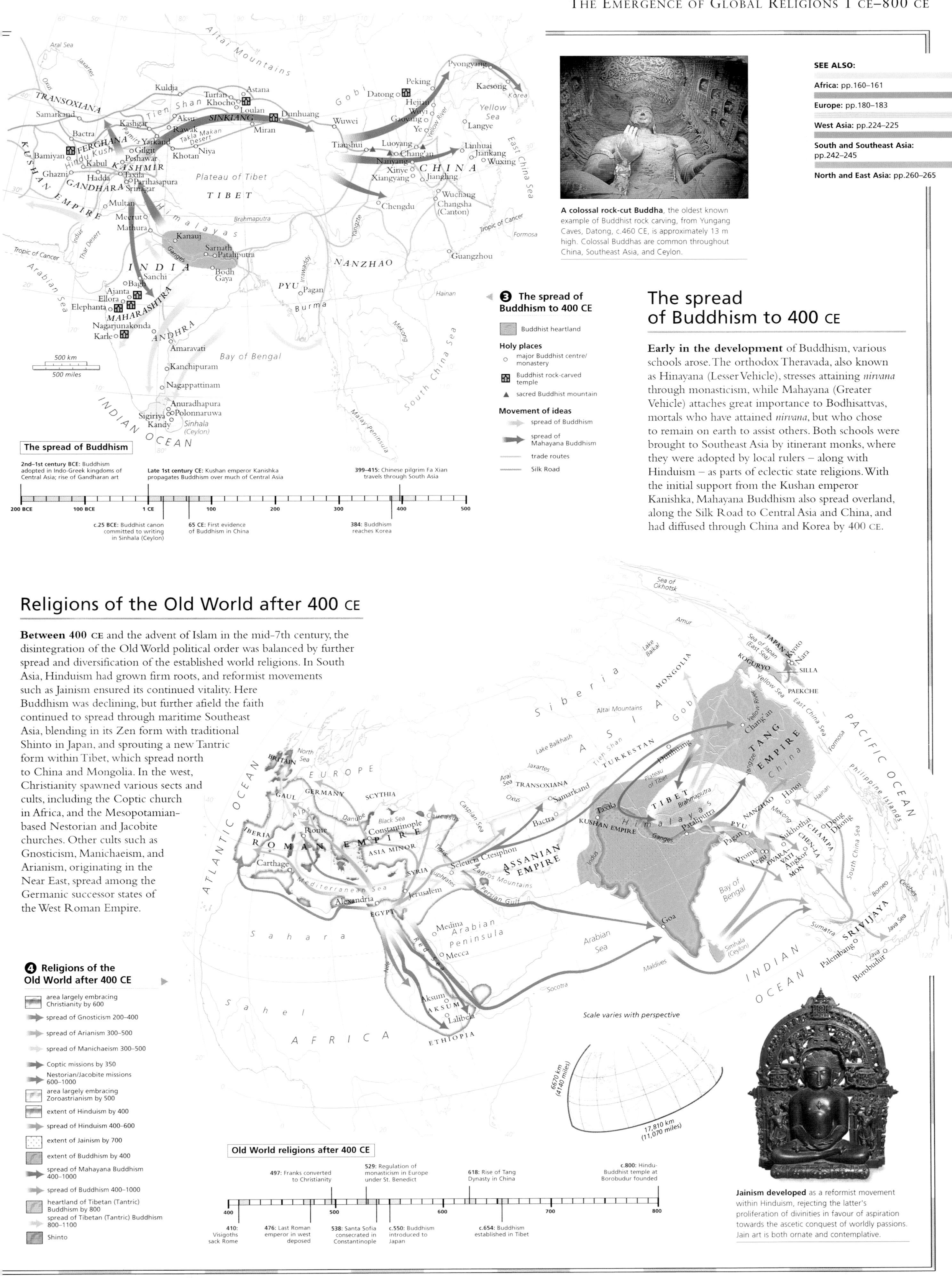

A colossal rock-cut Buddha, the oldest known example of Buddhist rock carving, from Yungang Caves, Datong, c.460 CE, is approximately 13 m high. Colossal Buddhas are common throughout China, Southeast Asia, and Ceylon.

The spread of Buddhism to 400 CE

Early in the development of Buddhism, various schools arose. The orthodox Theravada, also known as Hinayana (Lesser Vehicle), stresses attaining *nirvana* through monasticism, while Mahayana (Greater Vehicle) attaches great importance to Bodhisattvas, mortals who have attained *nirvana*, but who chose to remain on earth to assist others. Both schools were brought to Southeast Asia by itinerant monks, where they were adopted by local rulers – along with Hinduism – as parts of eclectic state religions. With the initial support from the Kushan emperor Kanishka, Mahayana Buddhism also spread overland, along the Silk Road to Central Asia and China, and had diffused through China and Korea by 400 CE.

Religions of the Old World after 400 CE

Between 400 CE and the advent of Islam in the mid-7th century, the disintegration of the Old World political order was balanced by further spread and diversification of the established world religions. In South Asia, Hinduism had grown firm roots, and reformist movements such as Jainism ensured its continued vitality. Here Buddhism was declining, but further afield the faith continued to spread through maritime Southeast Asia, blending in its Zen form with traditional Shinto in Japan, and sprouting a new Tantric form within Tibet, which spread north to China and Mongolia. In the west, Christianity spawned various sects and cults, including the Coptic church in Africa, and the Mesopotamian-based Nestorian and Jacobite churches. Other cults such as Gnosticism, Manichaeism, and Arianism, originating in the Near East, spread among the Germanic successor states of the West Roman Empire.

Jainism developed as a reformist movement within Hinduism, rejecting the latter's proliferation of divinities in favour of aspiration towards the ascetic conquest of worldly passions. Jain art is both ornate and contemplative.

THE WORLD 250–500

BY 500, MIGRATIONS IN ASIA AND EUROPE had so weakened the civilizations of the Old World that only the East Roman Empire and Sassanian Persia survived. Asian nomads broke the power of the Chinese and destroyed India's Gupta Empire. The Huns even invaded Europe, where the Romans repulsed them, but only with the aid of their Gothic allies. Rome relied increasingly on the aid of the Goths and other Germanic peoples, who settled within the empire and, as central authority waned, carved out new kingdoms for themselves. In contrast to the collapsing empires of the Old World, the great urban civilizations of Central America, Teotihuacán, the Maya, and the Zapotecs, were beginning to flourish.

Much of the best late Roman sculpture is found in the carving of Christian scenes on sarcophagi.

Europe

In 284, Diocletian divided the Roman Empire into eastern and western halves. With the advent of Christianity and the establishment of Constantinople as a new capital in 330, the empire's centre of gravity shifted eastward. Meanwhile, Germanic and Slav peoples, living on Rome's northern borders, infiltrated imperial territory, at times peacefully, often by force. The Western Empire collapsed in 476 to be replaced by a series of Germanic kingdoms and the mantle of empire passed to Constantinople in the east.

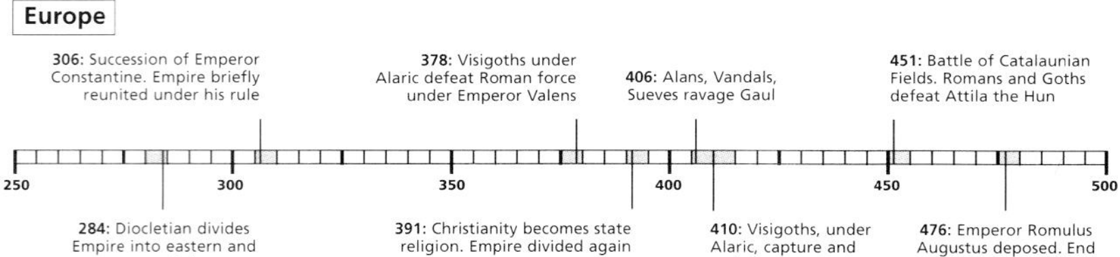
Europe
306: Succession of Emperor Constantine. Empire briefly reunited under his rule
378: Visigoths under Alaric defeat Roman force under Emperor Valens
406: Alans, Vandals, Sueves ravage Gaul
451: Battle of Catalaunian Fields. Romans and Goths defeat Attila the Hun
250
300
350
400
450
500
284: Diocletian divides Empire into eastern and western halves
391: Christianity becomes state religion. Empire divided again
410: Visigoths, under Alaric, capture and sack Rome
476: Emperor Romulus Augustus deposed. End of Western Empire

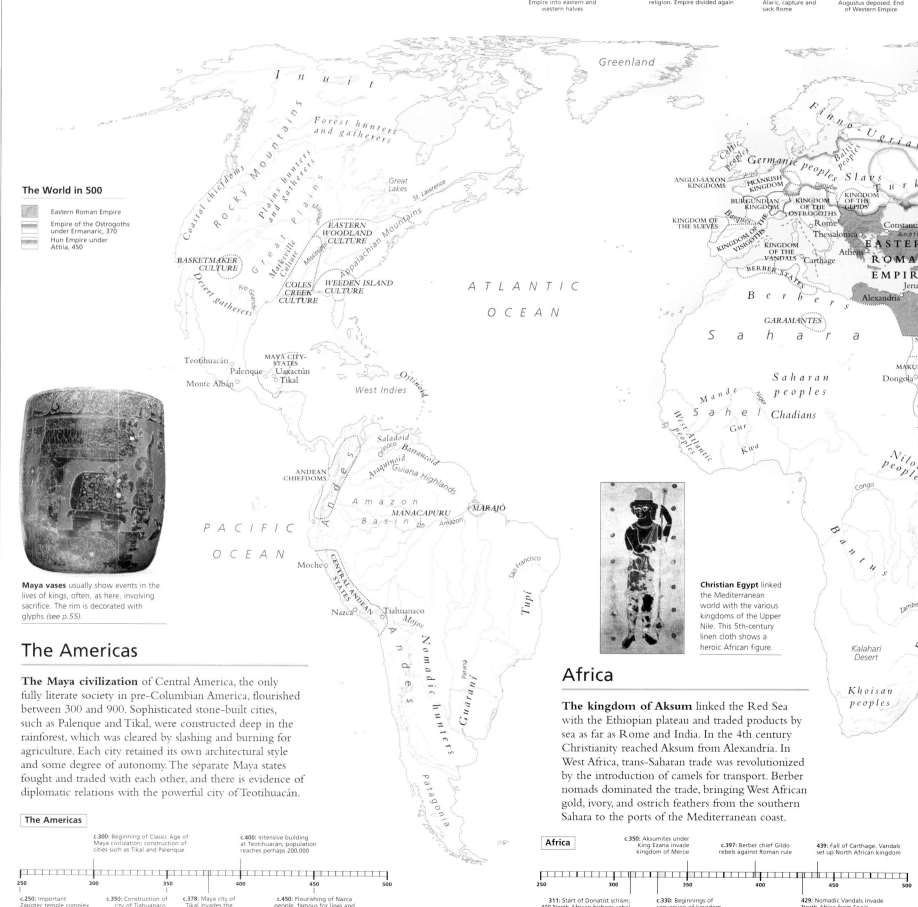

The World in 500

- Eastern Roman Empire
- Empire of the Ostrogoths under Ermanaric, 370
- Hun Empire under Attila, 450

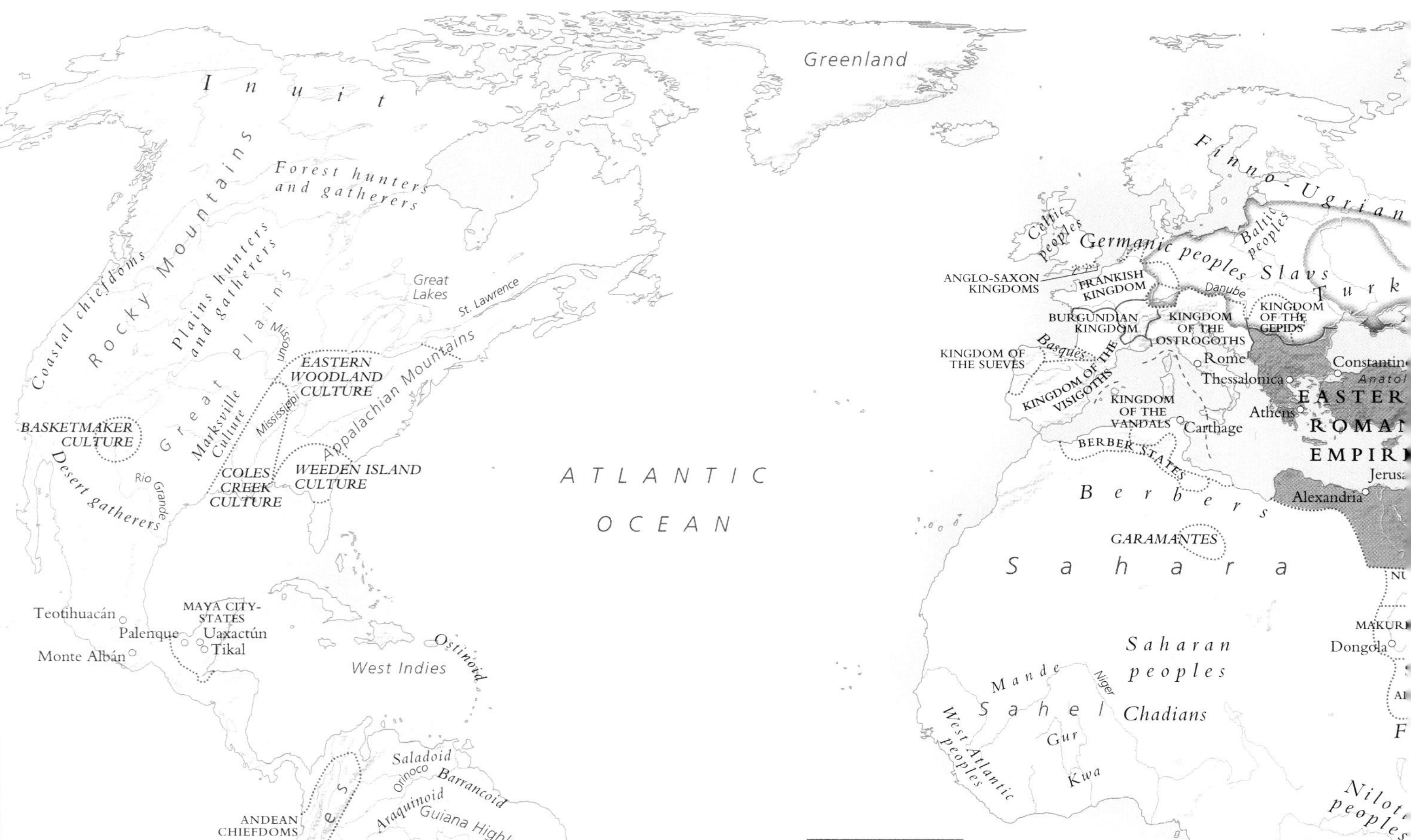

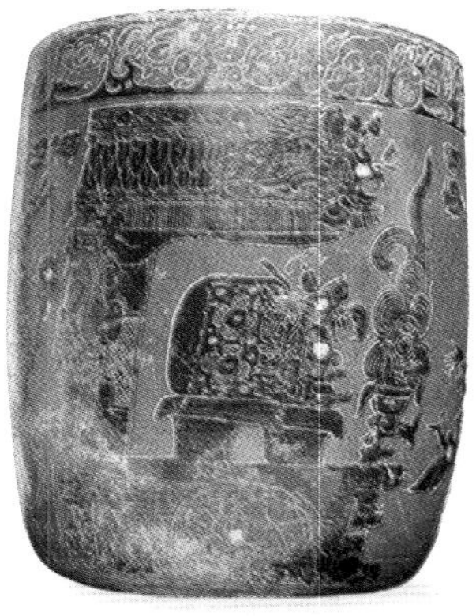

Maya vases usually show events in the lives of kings, often, as here, involving sacrifice. The rim is decorated with glyphs *(see p.55)*.

The Americas

The Maya civilization of Central America, the only fully literate society in pre-Columbian America, flourished between 300 and 900. Sophisticated stone-built cities, such as Palenque and Tikal, were constructed deep in the rainforest, which was cleared by slashing and burning for agriculture. Each city retained its own architectural style and some degree of autonomy. The separate Maya states fought and traded with each other, and there is evidence of diplomatic relations with the powerful city of Teotihuacán.

The Americas

- c.300: Beginning of Classic Age of Maya civilization; construction of cities such as Tikal and Palenque
- c.400: Intensive building at Teotihuacán; population reaches perhaps 200,000
- c.250: Important Zapotec temple complex built at Monte Albán
- c.350: Construction of city of Tiahuanaco, near Lake Titicaca
- c.378: Maya city of Tikal invades the city of Uaxactún
- c.450: Flourishing of Nazca people, famous for lines and giant figures drawn in desert

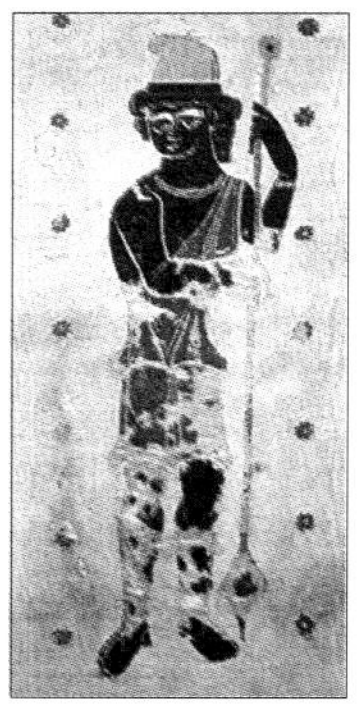

Christian Egypt linked the Mediterranean world with the various kingdoms of the Upper Nile. This 5th-century linen cloth shows a heroic African figure.

Africa

The kingdom of Aksum linked the Red Sea with the Ethiopian plateau and traded products by sea as far as Rome and India. In the 4th century Christianity reached Aksum from Alexandria. In West Africa, trans-Saharan trade was revolutionized by the introduction of camels for transport. Berber nomads dominated the trade, bringing West African gold, ivory, and ostrich feathers from the southern Sahara to the ports of the Mediterranean coast.

Africa

- 311: Start of Donatist schism; 400 North African bishops rebel against Roman Christian church
- c.330: Beginnings of conversion of kingdom of Aksum to Christianity
- c.350: Aksumites under King Ezana invade kingdom of Meroe
- c.397: Berber chief Gildo rebels against Roman rule
- 429: Nomadic Vandals invade North Africa from Spain
- 439: Fall of Carthage. Vandals set up North African kingdom

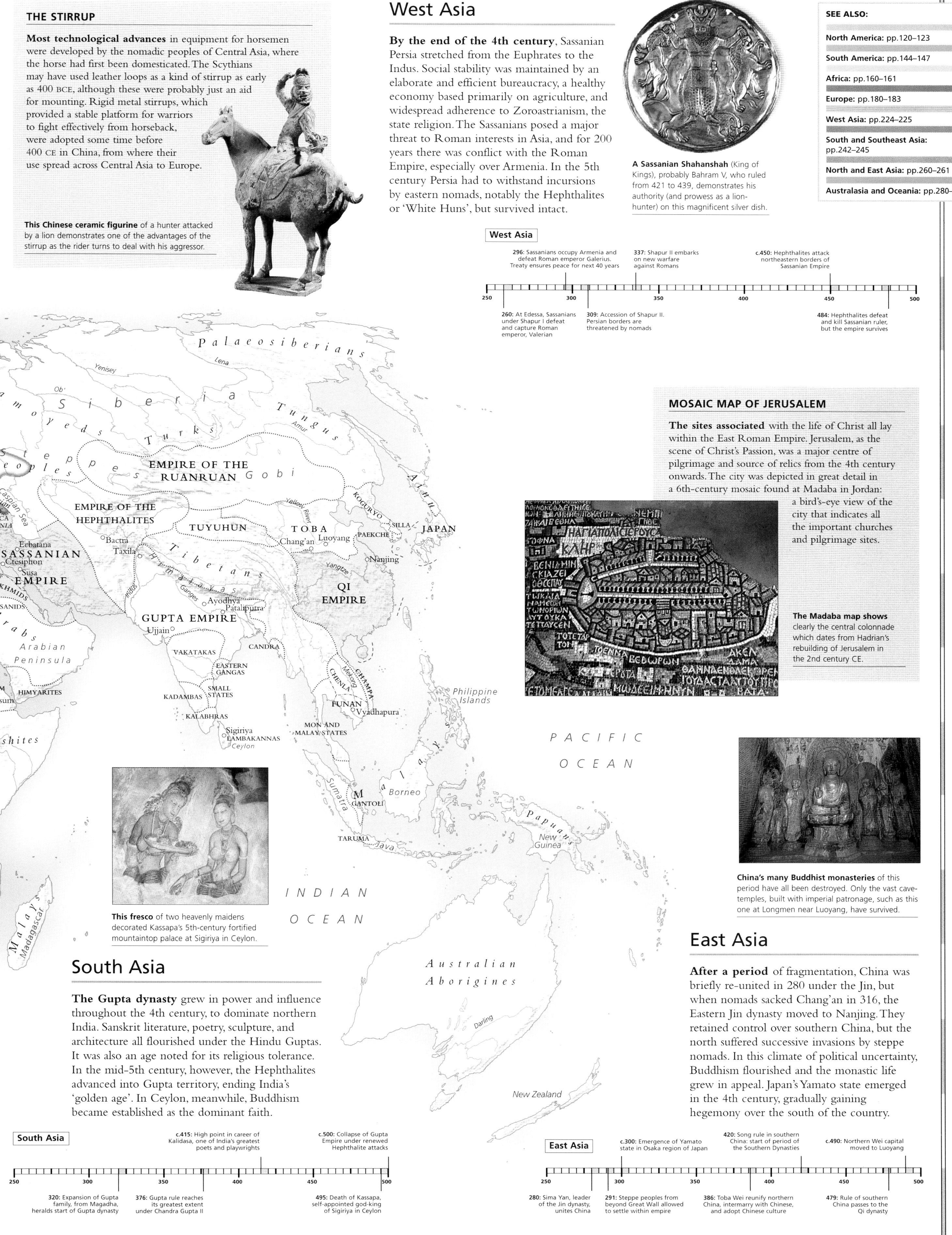

THE STIRRUP

Most technological advances in equipment for horsemen were developed by the nomadic peoples of Central Asia, where the horse had first been domesticated. The Scythians may have used leather loops as a kind of stirrup as early as 400 BCE, although these were probably just an aid for mounting. Rigid metal stirrups, which provided a stable platform for warriors to fight effectively from horseback, were adopted some time before 400 CE in China, from where their use spread across Central Asia to Europe.

This Chinese ceramic figurine of a hunter attacked by a lion demonstrates one of the advantages of the stirrup as the rider turns to deal with his aggressor.

West Asia

By the end of the 4th century, Sassanian Persia stretched from the Euphrates to the Indus. Social stability was maintained by an elaborate and efficient bureaucracy, a healthy economy based primarily on agriculture, and widespread adherence to Zoroastrianism, the state religion. The Sassanians posed a major threat to Roman interests in Asia, and for 200 years there was conflict with the Roman Empire, especially over Armenia. In the 5th century Persia had to withstand incursions by eastern nomads, notably the Hephthalites or 'White Huns', but survived intact.

A Sassanian Shahanshah (King of Kings), probably Bahram V, who ruled from 421 to 439, demonstrates his authority (and prowess as a lion-hunter) on this magnificent silver dish.

SEE ALSO:

North America: pp.120–123
South America: pp.144–147
Africa: pp.160–161
Europe: pp.180–183
West Asia: pp.224–225
South and Southeast Asia: pp.242–245
North and East Asia: pp.260–261
Australasia and Oceania: pp.280–281

West Asia

250 — 300 — 350 — 400 — 450 — 500

260: At Edessa, Sassanians under Shapur I defeat and capture Roman emperor, Valerian

296: Sassanians occupy Armenia and defeat Roman emperor Galerius. Treaty ensures peace for next 40 years

309: Accession of Shapur II. Persian borders are threatened by nomads

337: Shapur II embarks on new warfare against Romans

c.450: Hephthalites attack northeastern borders of Sassanian Empire

484: Hephthalites defeat and kill Sassanian ruler, but the empire survives

MOSAIC MAP OF JERUSALEM

The sites associated with the life of Christ all lay within the East Roman Empire. Jerusalem, as the scene of Christ's Passion, was a major centre of pilgrimage and source of relics from the 4th century onwards. The city was depicted in great detail in a 6th-century mosaic found at Madaba in Jordan: a bird's-eye view of the city that indicates all the important churches and pilgrimage sites.

The Madaba map shows clearly the central colonnade which dates from Hadrian's rebuilding of Jerusalem in the 2nd century CE.

China's many Buddhist monasteries of this period have all been destroyed. Only the vast cave-temples, built with imperial patronage, such as this one at Longmen near Luoyang, have survived.

This fresco of two heavenly maidens decorated Kassapa's 5th-century fortified mountaintop palace at Sigiriya in Ceylon.

South Asia

The Gupta dynasty grew in power and influence throughout the 4th century, to dominate northern India. Sanskrit literature, poetry, sculpture, and architecture all flourished under the Hindu Guptas. It was also an age noted for its religious tolerance. In the mid-5th century, however, the Hephthalites advanced into Gupta territory, ending India's 'golden age'. In Ceylon, meanwhile, Buddhism became established as the dominant faith.

South Asia

250 — 300 — 350 — 400 — 450 — 500

320: Expansion of Gupta family, from Magadha, heralds start of Gupta dynasty

376: Gupta rule reaches its greatest extent under Chandra Gupta II

c.415: High point in career of Kalidasa, one of India's greatest poets and playwrights

495: Death of Kassapa, self-appointed god-king of Sigiriya in Ceylon

c.500: Collapse of Gupta Empire under renewed Hephthalite attacks

East Asia

After a period of fragmentation, China was briefly re-united in 280 under the Jin, but when nomads sacked Chang'an in 316, the Eastern Jin dynasty moved to Nanjing. They retained control over southern China, but the north suffered successive invasions by steppe nomads. In this climate of political uncertainty, Buddhism flourished and the monastic life grew in appeal. Japan's Yamato state emerged in the 4th century, gradually gaining hegemony over the south of the country.

East Asia

250 — 300 — 350 — 400 — 450 — 500

280: Sima Yan, leader of the Jin dynasty, unites China

291: Steppe peoples from beyond Great Wall allowed to settle within empire

c.300: Emergence of Yamato state in Osaka region of Japan

386: Toba Wei reunify northern China, intermarry with Chinese, and adopt Chinese culture

420: Song rule in southern China: start of period of the Southern Dynasties

479: Rule of southern China passes to the Qi dynasty

c.490: Northern Wei capital moved to Luoyang

MIGRATIONS AND INVASIONS

The half-Vandal general Stilicho was regent during the reign of the child emperor Honorius.

THE GERMANIC PEOPLES who migrated into the Roman Empire during the 5th century were seeking to share in the fruits of empire, not to destroy it. They were spurred to move west in search of land by a combination of factors: famine, population pressure, and the prospects of a better standard of living. Rome initially accepted 'barbarian' recruits into its depleted army as *foederati* (federates), and allowed them to retain their own leaders and laws. But when the Romans opposed the settlement of large groups or refused to reward them for their services, the results could be disastrous: campaigns of plunder, sacked cities, and the breakdown of imperial control.

Honorius succeeded his father, Theodosius, as western emperor in 395 while still a child. He lived in comfortable seclusion while senior ministers governed.

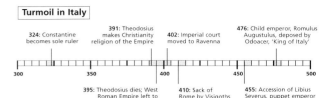

Turmoil in Italy

From the late 4th century, the Western Roman Empire was plagued by disputes over the imperial succession, which led to factionalism and civil wars. These were very destructive of Roman manpower and led to the recruitment of large numbers of barbarians under their own leaders. Emperors were often pawns in the power struggles of generals. Many of these, such as the half-Vandal Stilicho and the Suevian Ricimer, were of Germanic origin.

Turmoil in Italy (timeline 300–500)

- **324:** Constantine becomes sole ruler
- **391:** Theodosius makes Christianity religion of the Empire
- **395:** Theodosius dies; West Roman Empire left to child emperor Honorius
- **402:** Imperial court moved to Ravenna
- **410:** Sack of Rome by Visigoths
- **455:** Accession of Libius Severus, puppet emperor controlled by Ricimer
- **476:** Child emperor, Romulus Augustulus, deposed by Odoacer, 'King of Italy'

The aims of the migrations

The peoples who invaded the Roman Empire in the 4th and 5th centuries were driven by a variety of motives. Some, like Alaric's Visigoths, sought official acceptance by the Roman authorities, others, such as the peoples of the Great Migration of 406, were intent on finding land anywhere and by any means. The only invaders bent purely on destruction and plunder were the Huns. As steppe nomads, the Huns' strength lay in their mobility and their skill with bow, lance, and sabre. They were able to smash the overstretched imperial defences, but were repulsed when Goths and Roman joined forces against them. The Romans relied more and more on Gothic military support and it was the Goths who emerged as the first inheritors of the Empire's western territories.

c.410: Romans abandon Britain

453: On death of Attila, Empire of the Huns collapses

452: Attila persuaded to leave Roman Empire

402: Capital of West Roman Empire moved to Ravenna

410: Visigoths sack Rome
455: Vandals sack Rome

410: Death of Alaric; Visigoths abandon plan to invade Africa

414: Athaulf, leader of the Visigoths, marries Galla Placidia, daughter of late Emperor Theodosius. She had been captured during sack of Rome

430: City of Hippo taken by Vandals. St. Augustine, church father and bishop of the city, dies during siege

429: Gaiseric leads Vandals into North Africa

Vandal nobles in North Africa led the same privileged life as their Roman predecessors, as this mosaic of a Vandal landowner shows.

The Great Migration

At Christmas 406, vast hordes of Vandals, Sueves, and Alans crossed the frozen River Rhine and poured into Gaul, where they greatly disrupted settled life. They then moved in a southwesterly direction and eventually reached the Iberian Peninsula. The Vandals pressed on to North Africa, crossing the Strait of Gibraltar in 429, while the Sueves and Alans set up kingdoms in Iberia.

The Great Migration (timeline 400–500)

- **406:** Vandals, Sueves, and Alans cross Rhine
- **409:** Vandals, Sueves, and Alans cross the Pyrenees
- **c.411:** Sueves establish kingdom in northwestern Iberia
- **429:** Vandals cross Strait of Gibraltar
- **439:** Vandals reach city of Carthage
- **455:** Sack of Rome by Vandal king, Gaiseric
- **474:** Rome recognizes Vandal kingdom

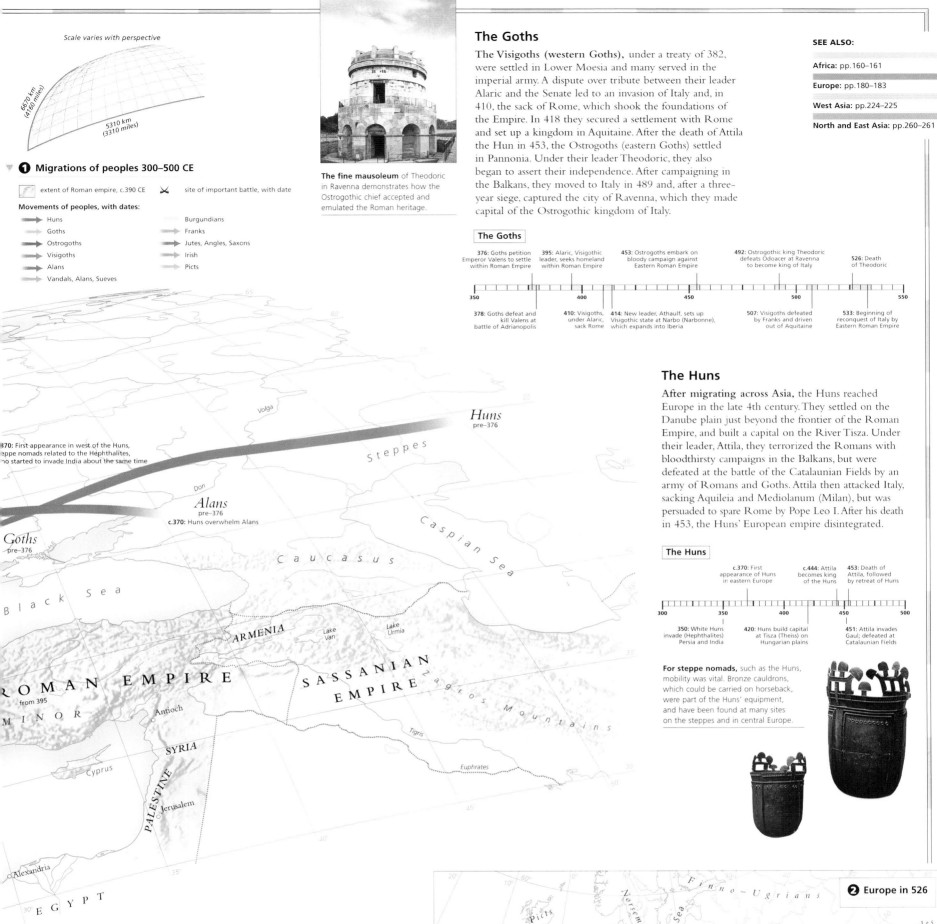

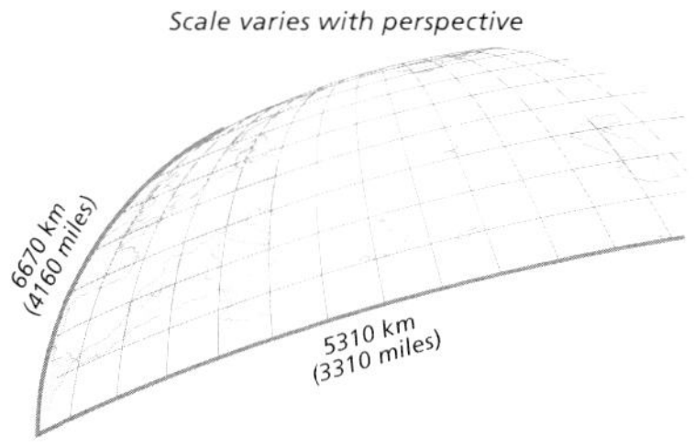

Scale varies with perspective

6670 km (4160 miles)

5310 km (3310 miles)

1 Migrations of peoples 300–500 CE

extent of Roman empire, c.390 CE

site of important battle, with date

Movements of peoples, with dates:

- Huns
- Goths
- Ostrogoths
- Visigoths
- Alans
- Vandals, Alans, Sueves
- Burgundians
- Franks
- Jutes, Angles, Saxons
- Irish
- Picts

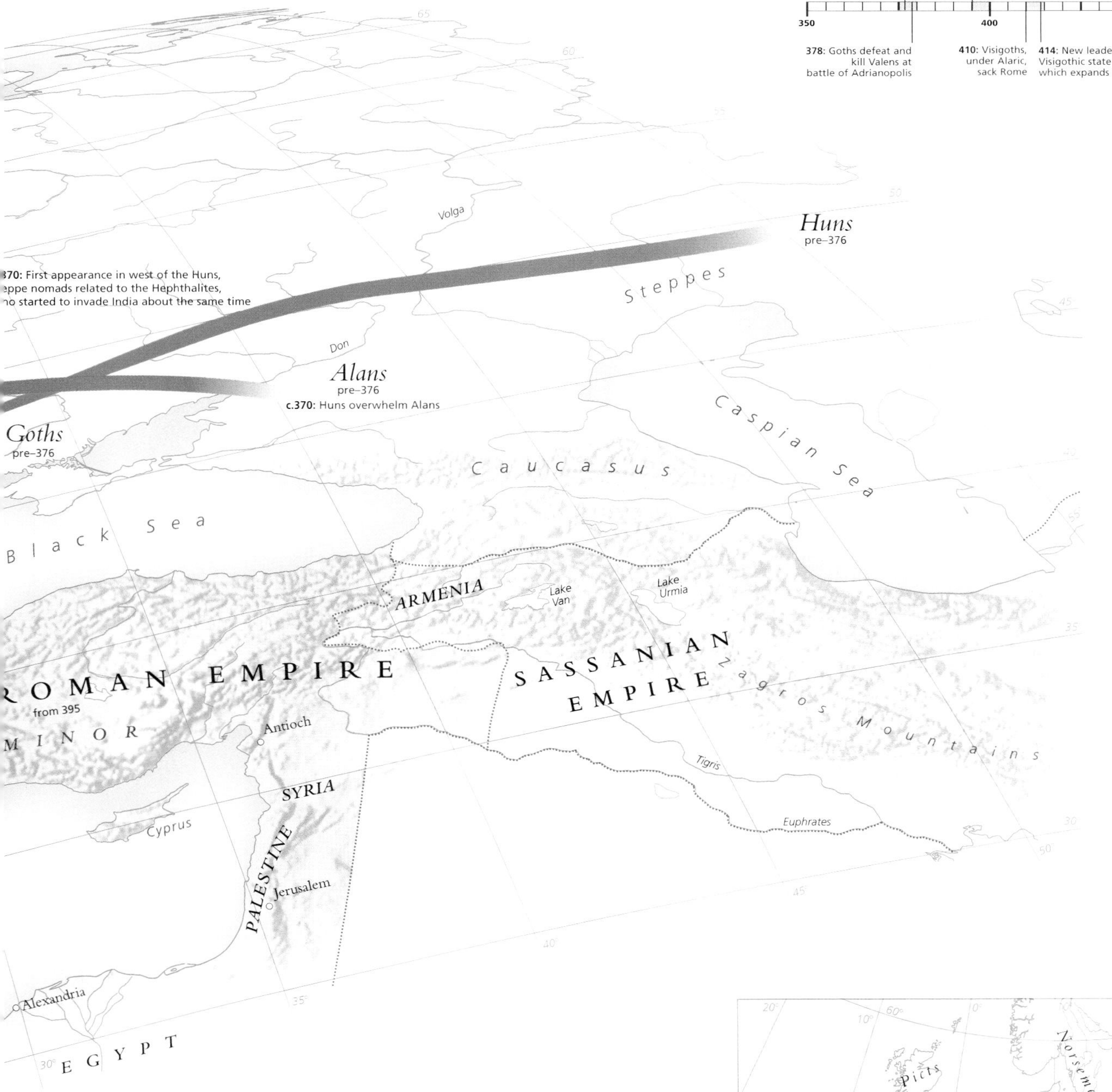

Huns pre–376

370: First appearance in west of the Huns, steppe nomads related to the Hephthalites, who started to invade India about the same time

Alans pre–376

c.370: Huns overwhelm Alans

Goths pre–376

Volga

Don

Steppes

Caucasus

Caspian Sea

Black Sea

ARMENIA

Lake Van

Lake Urmia

SASSANIAN EMPIRE

Zagros Mountains

ROMAN EMPIRE from 395

MINOR

Antioch

SYRIA

Tigris

Euphrates

Cyprus

PALESTINE

Jerusalem

Alexandria

EGYPT

The fine mausoleum of Theodoric in Ravenna demonstrates how the Ostrogothic chief accepted and emulated the Roman heritage.

The Goths

The Visigoths (western Goths), under a treaty of 382, were settled in Lower Moesia and many served in the imperial army. A dispute over tribute between their leader Alaric and the Senate led to an invasion of Italy and, in 410, the sack of Rome, which shook the foundations of the Empire. In 418 they secured a settlement with Rome and set up a kingdom in Aquitaine. After the death of Attila the Hun in 453, the Ostrogoths (eastern Goths) settled in Pannonia. Under their leader Theodoric, they also began to assert their independence. After campaigning in the Balkans, they moved to Italy in 489 and, after a three-year siege, captured the city of Ravenna, which they made capital of the Ostrogothic kingdom of Italy.

SEE ALSO:

Africa: pp.160–161

Europe: pp.180–183

West Asia: pp.224–225

North and East Asia: pp.260–261

The Goths

350 – 400 – 450 – 500 – 550

- **376:** Goths petition Emperor Valens to settle within Roman Empire
- **378:** Goths defeat and kill Valens at battle of Adrianopolis
- **395:** Alaric, Visigothic leader, seeks homeland within Roman Empire
- **410:** Visigoths, under Alaric, sack Rome
- **414:** New leader, Athaulf, sets up Visigothic state at Narbo (Narbonne), which expands into Iberia
- **453:** Ostrogoths embark on bloody campaign against Eastern Roman Empire
- **492:** Ostrogothic king Theodoric defeats Odoacer at Ravenna to become king of Italy
- **507:** Visigoths defeated by Franks and driven out of Aquitaine
- **526:** Death of Theodoric
- **533:** Beginning of reconquest of Italy by Eastern Roman Empire

The Huns

After migrating across Asia, the Huns reached Europe in the late 4th century. They settled on the Danube plain just beyond the frontier of the Roman Empire, and built a capital on the River Tisza. Under their leader, Attila, they terrorized the Romans with bloodthirsty campaigns in the Balkans, but were defeated at the battle of the Catalaunian Fields by an army of Romans and Goths. Attila then attacked Italy, sacking Aquileia and Mediolanum (Milan), but was persuaded to spare Rome by Pope Leo I. After his death in 453, the Huns' European empire disintegrated.

The Huns

300 – 350 – 400 – 450 – 500

- **350:** White Huns invade (Hephthalites) Persia and India
- **c.370:** First appearance of Huns in eastern Europe
- **420:** Huns build capital at Tisza (Theiss) on Hungarian plains
- **c.444:** Attila becomes king of the Huns
- **451:** Attila invades Gaul; defeated at Catalaunian Fields
- **453:** Death of Attila, followed by retreat of Huns

For steppe nomads, such as the Huns, mobility was vital. Bronze cauldrons, which could be carried on horseback, were part of the Huns' equipment, and have been found at many sites on the steppes and in central Europe.

The inheritors of western Europe

By 526, the waves of migrations had redrawn the map of western Europe. The Ostrogoths, under their charismatic leader Theodoric, controlled Italy, while the Visigoths had captured most of the Iberian Peninsula. The Vandals were established in North Africa, the Sueves in Galicia, and the Burgundians, who crossed the Rhine c.400, had settled in southeast France. The most enduring of the many Germanic kingdoms, however, would prove to be that of the Franks, founded in 456 by Clovis, which laid the foundations of modern France and Germany.

The magnificent votive crown of the 7th-century king Reccesuinth illustrates the importance of Christianity in Iberia under the Visigoths. Their rule lasted from the 5th century to the Arab conquest of 711.

THE WORLD 500–750

THE RAPID RECOVERY of the ancient world from the onslaught of invading nomads is evident in the rise of two great empires in West Asia and China. The new religion of Islam was based on the teachings of Muhammad, an Arabian merchant from Mecca. Fired by a zeal for conquest and conversion, Islamic armies overran West Asia and North Africa, and by 750, had created an empire that stretched from the Indus to Spain. Under the Tang dynasty, Chinese civilization reached new heights; Tang control penetrated deep into Central Asia and Chinese cultural influence was widespread. In the Americas, the Maya remained the most advanced civilization, though their small city-states did not have the far-reaching influence of the great city of Teotihuacán.

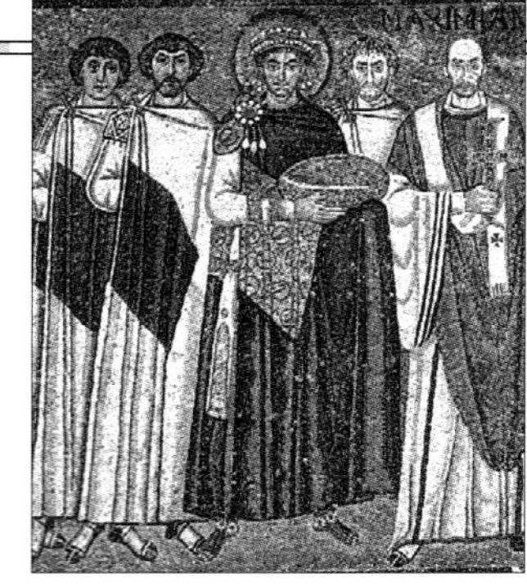

The Byzantines were the champions of Christianity. This mosaic shows Emperor Justinian as God's representative on Earth.

Europe

The Franks became the most powerful of all Rome's Germanic successors. United under Clovis I, their overlordship was extended to the south of France and east of the Rhine. Constantinople was the Christian capital of the Byzantine Empire. The Emperor Justinian (527–65) reconquered North Africa and much of Italy, briefly creating an empire stretching from Spain to Persia. Over the next two centuries much of this territory was lost to Islam and, in the Balkans, to Slavic invaders.

Europe

500 – 550 – 600 – 650 – 700 – 750

- **511:** Death of Frankish king Clovis
- **527:** Justinian becomes Byzantine emperor
- **531:** Frankish kingdom absorbs Burgundy
- **c.590:** The Avars, nomads from the steppes, establish state on Hungarian plains
- **597:** Papal missionary Augustine converts the king of Kent to Christianity
- **674–78:** Arabs besiege Constantinople, but fail to take it
- **680:** Bulgars invade Balkans
- **711:** Muslim invasion of Spain
- **732:** Frankish leader Charles Martel defeats Arab armies at battle of Poitiers

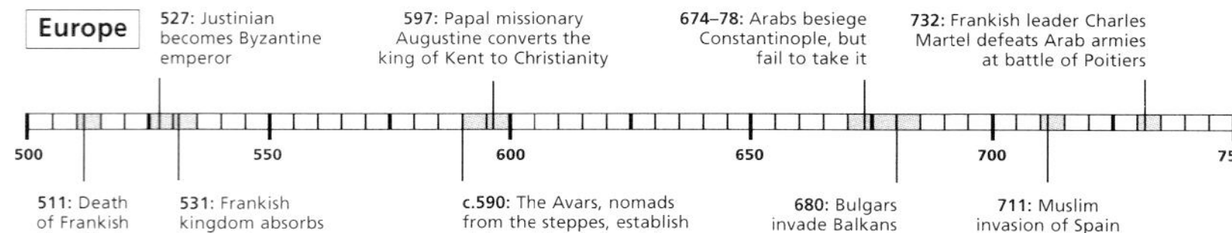

The World in 750

- Tang Empire
- Byzantine Empire
- Umayyad Caliphate
- Kök Türk Empire 551–572
- East Roman Empire 554–565
- Horsha's Empire c.640
- Avar Empire c.595

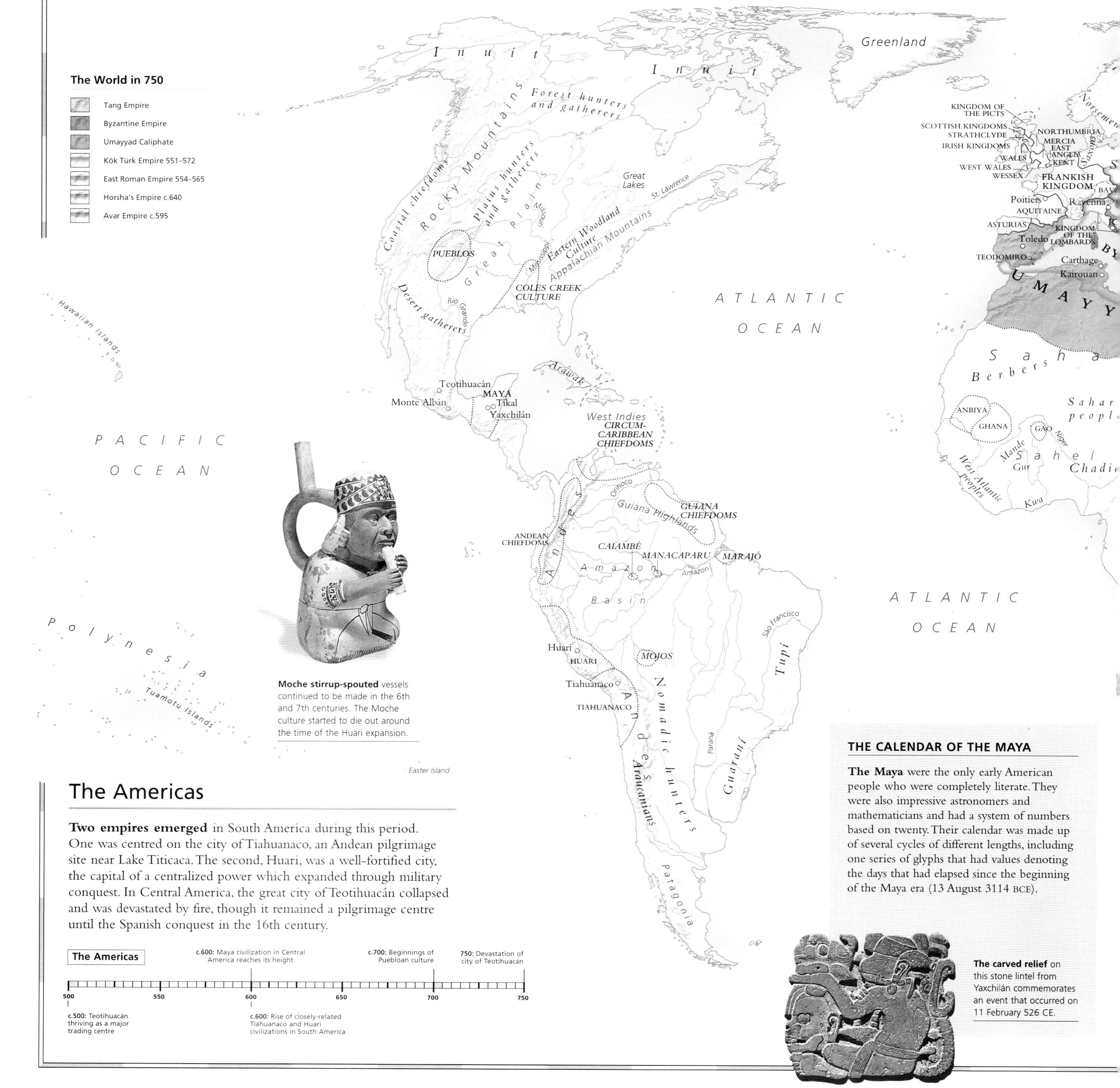

Moche stirrup-spouted vessels continued to be made in the 6th and 7th centuries. The Moche culture started to die out around the time of the Huari expansion.

The Americas

Two empires emerged in South America during this period. One was centred on the city of Tiahuanaco, an Andean pilgrimage site near Lake Titicaca. The second, Huari, was a well-fortified city, the capital of a centralized power which expanded through military conquest. In Central America, the great city of Teotihuacán collapsed and was devastated by fire, though it remained a pilgrimage centre until the Spanish conquest in the 16th century.

The Americas

500 – 550 – 600 – 650 – 700 – 750

- **c.500:** Teotihuacán thriving as a major trading centre
- **c.600:** Maya civilization in Central America reaches its height
- **c.600:** Rise of closely-related Tiahuanaco and Huari civilizations in South America
- **c.700:** Beginnings of Puebloan culture
- **750:** Devastation of city of Teotihuacán

THE CALENDAR OF THE MAYA

The Maya were the only early American people who were completely literate. They were also impressive astronomers and mathematicians and had a system of numbers based on twenty. Their calendar was made up of several cycles of different lengths, including one series of glyphs that had values denoting the days that had elapsed since the beginning of the Maya era (13 August 3114 BCE).

The carved relief on this stone lintel from Yaxchilán commemorates an event that occurred on 11 February 526 CE.

The Dome of the Rock in Jerusalem was built in 692 over the ruins of the Jewish Temple. It is sacred to Islam as the site of Muhammad's journey to heaven.

West Asia

In the 7th century the whole of West Asia was overrun by Arabian armies, soldiers of Islam, inspired to conquer and convert by the new religion founded by Muhammad. They were able to exploit the weaknesses of the two great powers in the region, the Sassanians and the Byzantines. Sassanian Persia had reached its peak under Khosrau I (531–79), who invaded Byzantine Syria and captured Antioch. But continuing conflict with the Byzantines led to a crushing defeat at Nineveh in 628.

CLASSICAL ARAB WORLD MAPS

When the Arabs took over much of the Greek-speaking eastern Mediterranean, they seized on the Classical scholarship of Alexandria, including the famous *Geography* of Ptolemy *(see p.44)*. Though no maps from this period survive, it seems that, while the map-making tradition died out in the west, it was kept alive by Arab scholars, albeit in the academic style of this later world map.

Al-Istakhri's world map, from the 10th century, uses a Ptolemaic projection, but with south at the top.

SEE ALSO:

North America: pp.122–123

South America: pp.142–145

Africa: pp.162–163

Europe: pp.182–185

West Asia: pp.226–227

South and Southeast Asia: pp.242–245

North and East Asia: pp.262–265

Australasia and Oceania: pp.280–281

West Asia

- **531:** Beginning of reign of Sassanian ruler, Khosrau I Anohshirvanh
- **570:** Prophet Muhammad born in Mecca
- **622:** The Hegira: Muhammad and his followers move to Medina; start of Islamic era
- **628:** Defeat of Sassanians by Byzantine emperor Heraclius
- **637:** Arabian armies capture Sassanian capital, Ctesiphon
- **656:** Arabians overrun Persia
- **661:** Start of Umayyad dynasty. Damascus is centre of Islamic empire
- **674–78:** Arabian siege of Constantinople
- **698:** Arabs capture Carthage
- **711:** Islamic armies cross the Strait of Gibraltar and conquer Spain

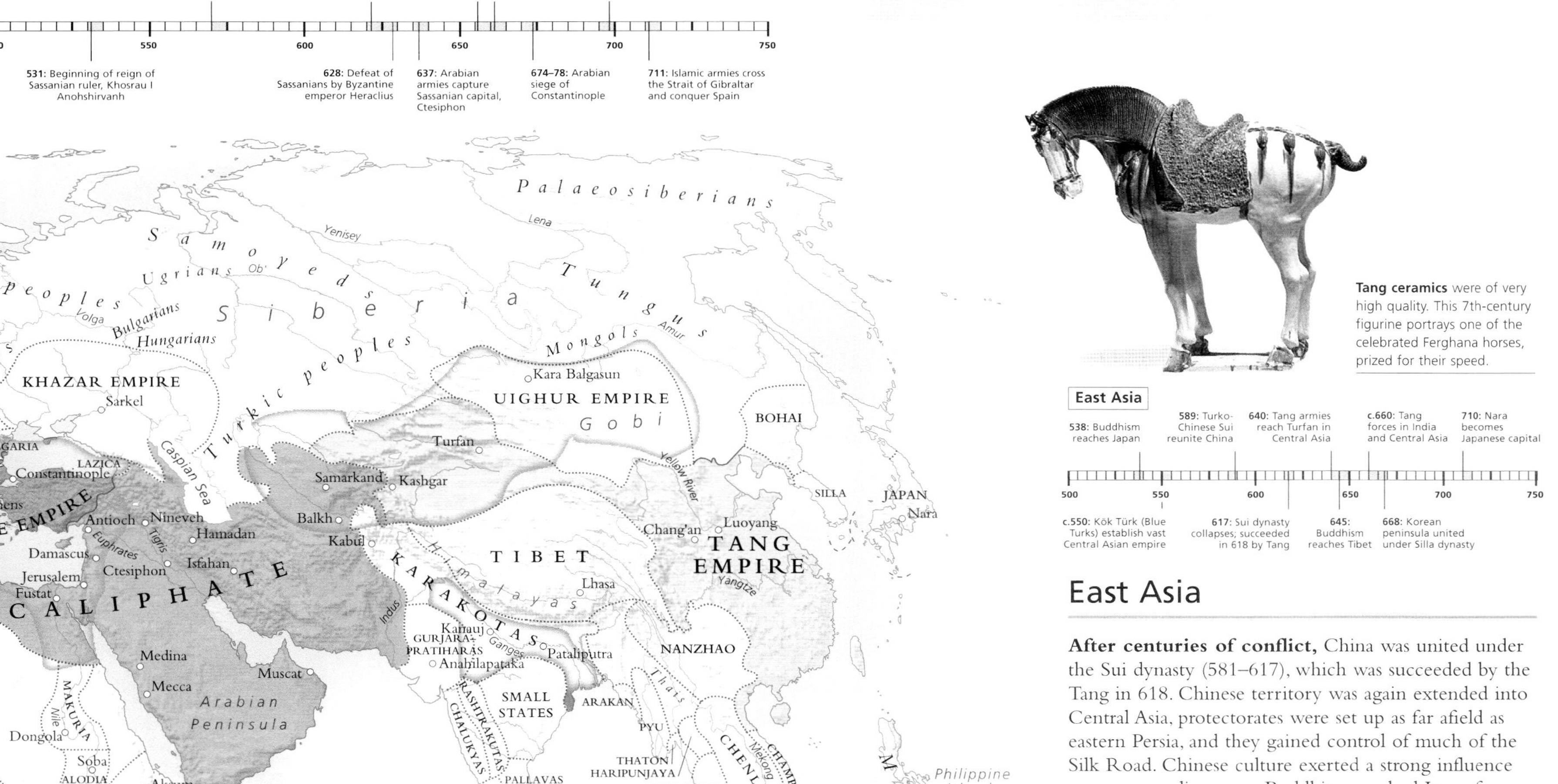

Tang ceramics were of very high quality. This 7th-century figurine portrays one of the celebrated Ferghana horses, prized for their speed.

East Asia

- **538:** Buddhism reaches Japan
- **c.550:** Kök Türk (Blue Turks) establish vast Central Asian empire
- **589:** Turko-Chinese Sui reunite China
- **617:** Sui dynasty collapses; succeeded in 618 by Tang
- **640:** Tang armies reach Turfan in Central Asia
- **645:** Buddhism reaches Tibet
- **c.660:** Tang forces in India and Central Asia
- **668:** Korean peninsula united under Silla dynasty
- **710:** Nara becomes Japanese capital

East Asia

After centuries of conflict, China was united under the Sui dynasty (581–617), which was succeeded by the Tang in 618. Chinese territory was again extended into Central Asia, protectorates were set up as far afield as eastern Persia, and they gained control of much of the Silk Road. Chinese culture exerted a strong influence over surrounding areas; Buddhism reached Japan from China in about 538. Under Chinese influence, Japan underwent a series of social and political reforms: the abolition of slavery, the creation of a civil service, and the adoption of a modified form of written Chinese.

Oceania

The island of Fiji was first settled around 1500 BCE and it was there and in nearby islands that Polynesian culture developed. Descendants of these first settlers would eventually colonize the whole Pacific Ocean. The Polynesians sailed across the open ocean in twin-hulled outrigger canoes, using sails and paddles, with only their knowledge of the skies, winds, and ocean currents to guide them. By 400 CE they had reached Easter Island and the Hawaiian Islands, but did not colonize New Zealand until about 1200.

Oceania

- **c.600:** Polynesian colonists settle the Tuamotu Islands
- **c.650:** Easter Islanders start to build *ahus*, sacred stone platforms

Many deities with a clear common ancestry appear in slightly different forms throughout Polynesia. This wooden carving of the war-god Ku was made in Hawaii in the early 19th century.

THE IMPACT OF ISLAM

This richly-decorated copy of the Koran dates from 704.

THE RAPID SPREAD OF ISLAM was one of the most decisive developments of the medieval period. The Arabian Peninsula was conquered for Islam within ten years, and following the death of Muhammad in 632, the expansion of Islam continued unabated. By the early 8th century, Arab armies fired by the concept of *jihad* (holy war) had reached the borders of India in the east and were invading Spain in the west. With the establishment of the Abbasid Caliphate, by 750 the Muslim realm was second only to that of China in extent and cultural sophistication. The Caliphate controlled Eurasian trade on land and by sea – trade which would spread the faith further afield, deep into Africa, across the Indian Ocean and north into Central Asia, over the subsequent centuries.

The spread of Islam 623–751

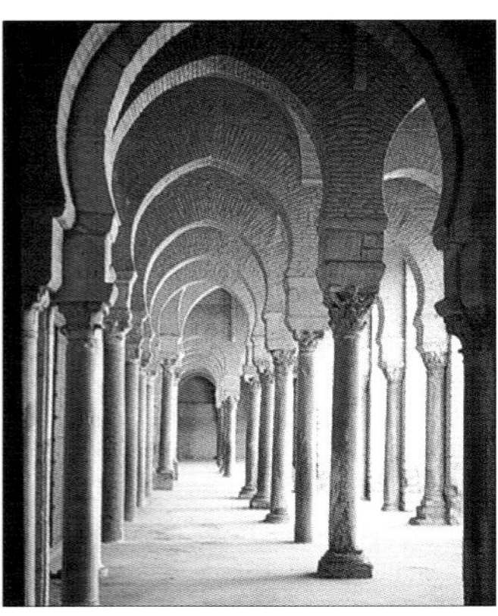

The Great Mosque at Kairouan is one of the oldest surviving Islamic buildings. It was begun in 670, shortly after Arab armies had swept through the Byzantine possessions along the North African coast.

Muhammad's vision of the Archangel Gabriel in about 610 began a process of revelation, enshrined in the Koran, the Holy Book which lies at the heart of Islam. His opposition to polytheism and adherence to a strict code of observance and conduct led to hostility in Mecca, and his withdrawal to Medina (the Hegira) in 622. Here the first Muslim state was established. By 630, with an army of 10,000 followers, he re-entered Mecca, and began the conquest of Arabia. Conversion swelled the Muslim ranks, and Muhammad's work was continued after his death in 632 by his disciples. Within a century the heartland of Eurasia was dominated by Islam. Although Muslim warriors believed it their duty to conquer in the name of Islam, conquered peoples, especially Christians and Jews, were treated with tolerance.

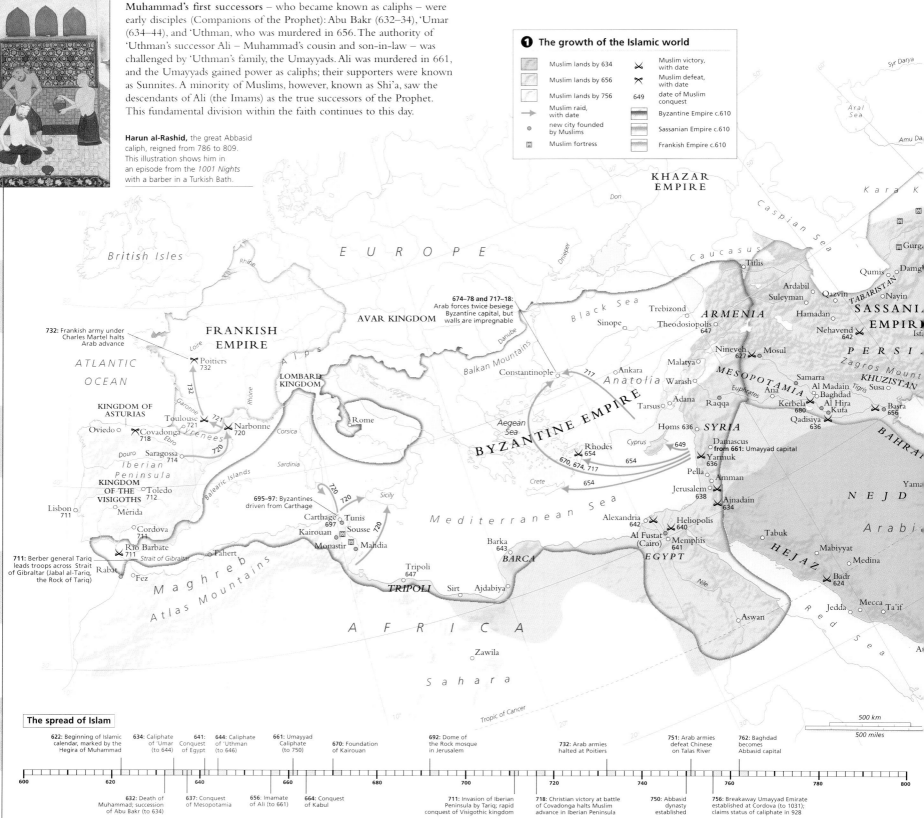

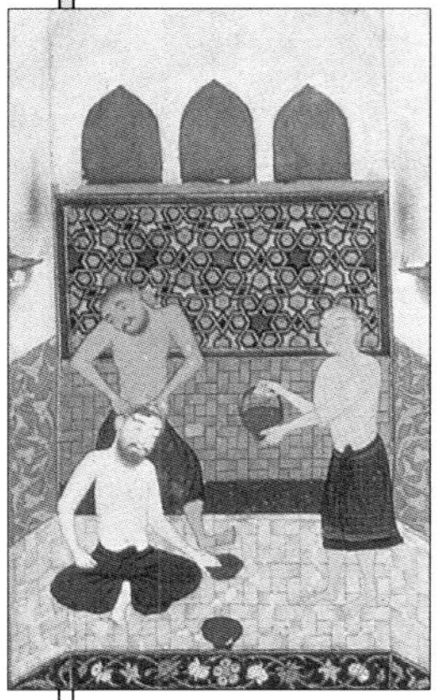

The early history of the Caliphate

Muhammad's first successors – who became known as caliphs – were early disciples (Companions of the Prophet): Abu Bakr (632–34), 'Umar (634–44), and 'Uthman, who was murdered in 656. The authority of 'Uthman's successor Ali – Muhammad's cousin and son-in-law – was challenged by 'Uthman's family, the Umayyads. Ali was murdered in 661, and the Umayyads gained power as caliphs; their supporters were known as Sunnites. A minority of Muslims, however, known as Shi'a, saw the descendants of Ali (the Imams) as the true successors of the Prophet. This fundamental division within the faith continues to this day.

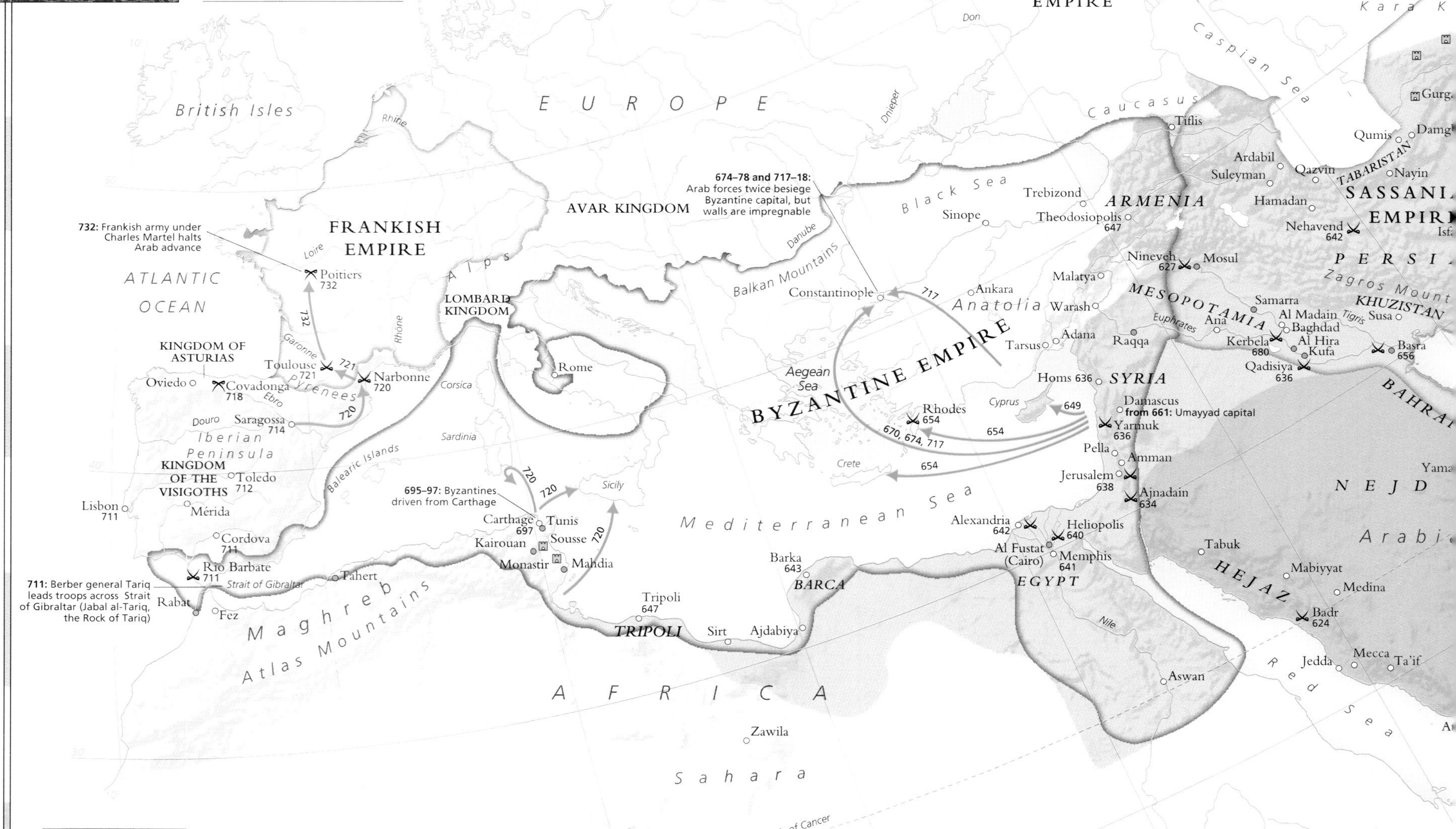

Harun al-Rashid, the great Abbasid caliph, reigned from 786 to 809. This illustration shows him in an episode from the *1001 Nights* with a barber in a Turkish Bath.

1 The growth of the Islamic world

Muslim lands by 634		Muslim victory, with date	
Muslim lands by 656		Muslim defeat, with date	
Muslim lands by 756		649	date of Muslim conquest
Muslim raid, with date		Byzantine Empire c.610	
new city founded by Muslims		Sassanian Empire c.610	
Muslim fortress		Frankish Empire c.610	

732: Frankish army under Charles Martel halts Arab advance

674–78 and 717–18: Arab forces twice besiege Byzantine capital, but walls are impregnable

695–97: Byzantines driven from Carthage

711: Berber general Tariq leads troops across Strait of Gibraltar (Jabal al-Tariq, the Rock of Tariq)

Damascus from 661: Umayyad capital

KHAZAR EMPIRE · EUROPE · FRANKISH EMPIRE · AVAR KINGDOM · LOMBARD KINGDOM · KINGDOM OF ASTURIAS · KINGDOM OF THE VISIGOTHS · BYZANTINE EMPIRE · ARMENIA · MESOPOTAMIA · SYRIA · EGYPT · SASSANIAN EMPIRE · PERSIA · KHUZISTAN · TABARISTAN · HEJAZ · NEJD · BARCA · TRIPOLI · AFRICA · ATLANTIC OCEAN · Mediterranean Sea · Black Sea · Caspian Sea · Aral Sea · Red Sea · Sahara · British Isles · Iberian Peninsula · Anatolia · Maghreb · Atlas Mountains · Arabia

Poitiers 732 · Toulouse 721 · Narbonne 720 · Covadonga 718 · Saragossa 714 · Toledo 712 · Lisbon 711 · Cordova 711 · Rio Barbate 711 · Carthage 697 · Kairouan · Tripoli 647 · Barka 643 · Alexandria 642 · Heliopolis 640 · Memphis 641 · Al Fustat (Cairo) · Jerusalem 638 · Ajnadain 634 · Yarmuk 636 · Homs 636 · Rhodes 654 · Theodosiopolis 647 · Nineveh 627 · Nehavend 642 · Kerbela 680 · Qadisiya 636 · Basra 656 · Badr 624 · Mecca · Medina

The spread of Islam

622: Beginning of Islamic calendar, marked by the Hegira of Muhammad

632: Death of Muhammad; succession of Abu Bakr (to 634)

634: Caliphate of 'Umar (to 644)

637: Conquest of Mesopotamia

641: Conquest of Egypt

644: Caliphate of 'Uthman (to 656)

656: Imamate of Ali (to 661)

661: Umayyad Caliphate (to 750)

664: Conquest of Kabul

670: Foundation of Kairouan

692: Dome of the Rock mosque in Jerusalem

711: Invasion of Iberian Peninsula by Tariq; rapid conquest of Visigothic kingdom

718: Christian victory at battle of Covadonga halts Muslim advance in Iberian Peninsula

732: Arab armies halted at Poitiers

750: Abbasid dynasty established

751: Arab armies defeat Chinese on Talas River

756: Breakaway Umayyad Emirate established at Cordova (to 1031); claims status of caliphate in 928

762: Baghdad becomes Abbasid capital

Preaching and teaching spread the Arabic language throughout the Islamic world. This 13th-century Persian illustration shows a preacher in the mosque at Samarkand.

Water-wheels for irrigation were introduced wherever the Arabs settled. This example stands at Hamah in Syria. The Arabs also introduced Asian fruits, such as peaches and apricots.

The Islamic imprint 1000–1200

By 1000, the Islamic world had become broadly divided into two caliphates: the Abbasids, based at Baghdad, and, in the west, the Umayyads (a branch of the Abbasids' predecessors), who ruled the Iberian Peninsula. So extensive were the Abbasid domains that many subsidiary rulers wielded local power in varying degrees and were able to found autonomous dynasties. Further, the movement of peoples into the Islamic world caused further decentralization of power. In the west, the Berbers gradually established a string of local dynasties along the Maghreb coast. The Shi'ite Fatimids emerged in North Africa, conquered Egypt, and claimed caliphate status, but the most significant blow to the Abbasid Caliphate was the invasion of the Seljuk Turks from Central Asia, who moved across southwest Asia, conquered Baghdad and drove back the frontiers of the Byzantine Empire, eventually occupying Anatolia.

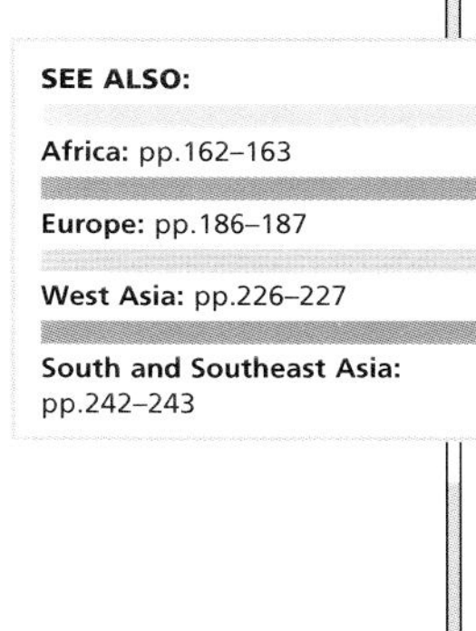

SEE ALSO:

Africa: pp.162–163

Europe: pp.186–187

West Asia: pp.226–227

South and Southeast Asia: pp.242–243

The impact of the Islamic advance

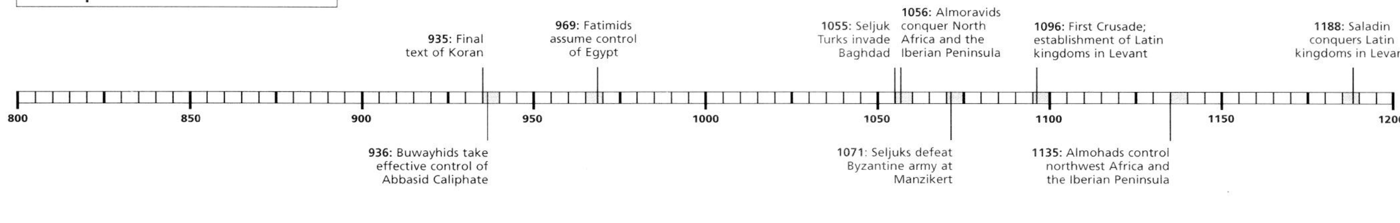

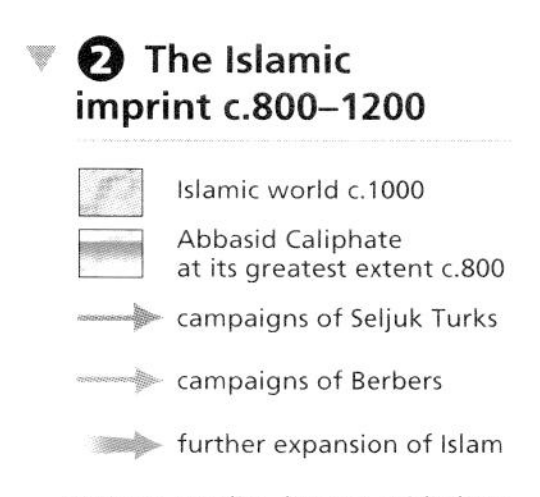

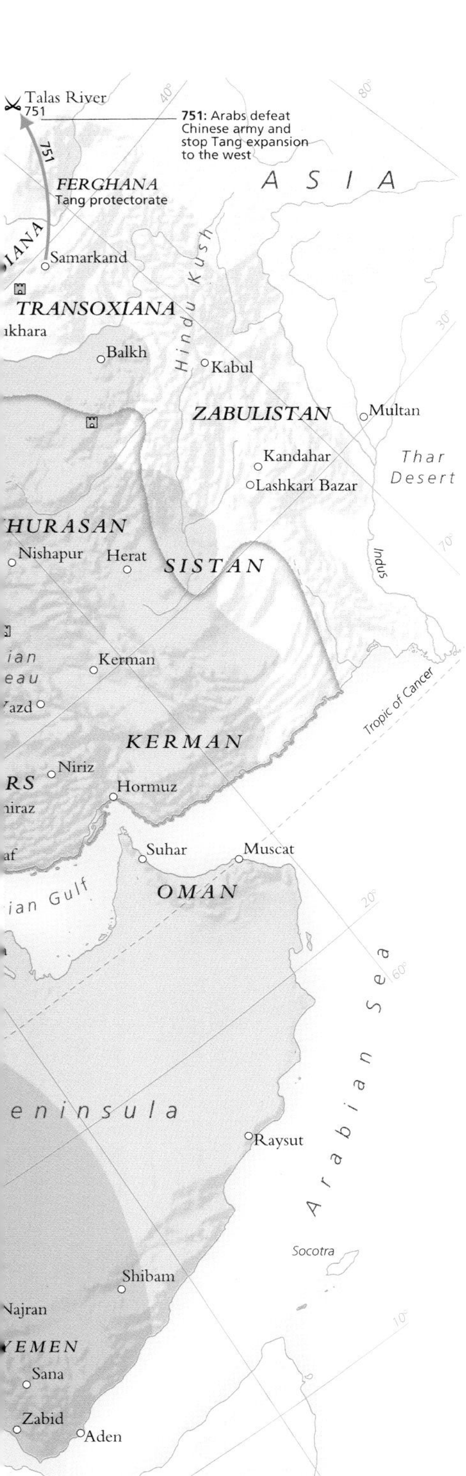

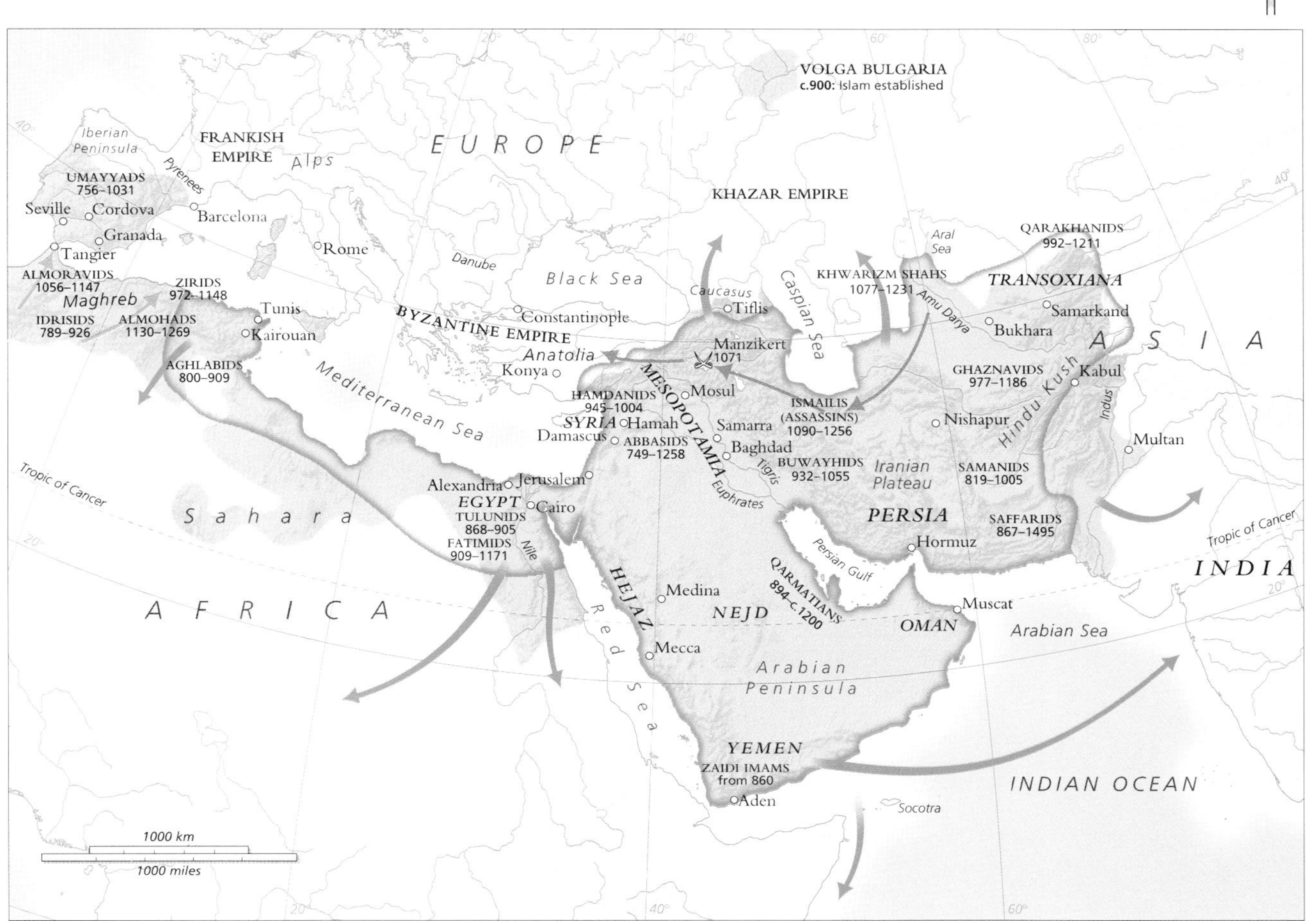

Samarra: an Islamic city

Founded by the Abbasid caliph al-Mu'tasim, Samarra was the Abbasid capital from 836–892, and grew to sprawl some 40 km (25 miles) along the east bank of the Tigris. The new city was based around earlier settlements; it was not walled, and was organized into residential cantonments arranged around central features such as palaces and mosques, and included luxurious facilities such as racetracks and a gigantic 30 sq km game reserve. Later caliphs added substantial areas, notably al-Mu'tasim's successor al-Mutawakkil, who built a new centre to the north, Ja'fariyya. The Abbasid court returned to its original capital at Baghdad after the death of the eighth caliph, al-Mu'tamid.

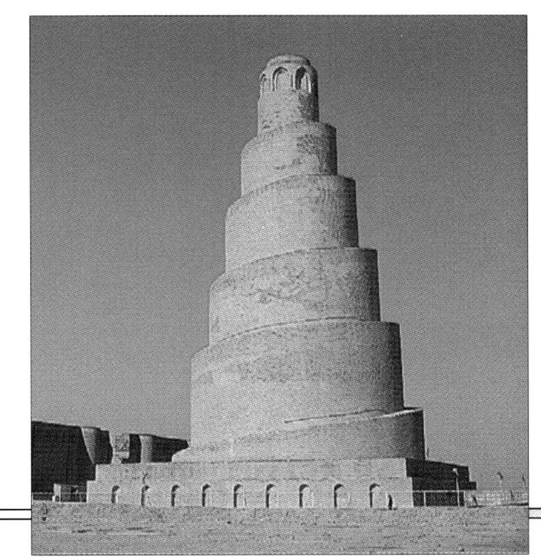

The spiral minaret of the Great Mosque of al-Mutawakkil at Samarra is one of the few standing remains of the city.

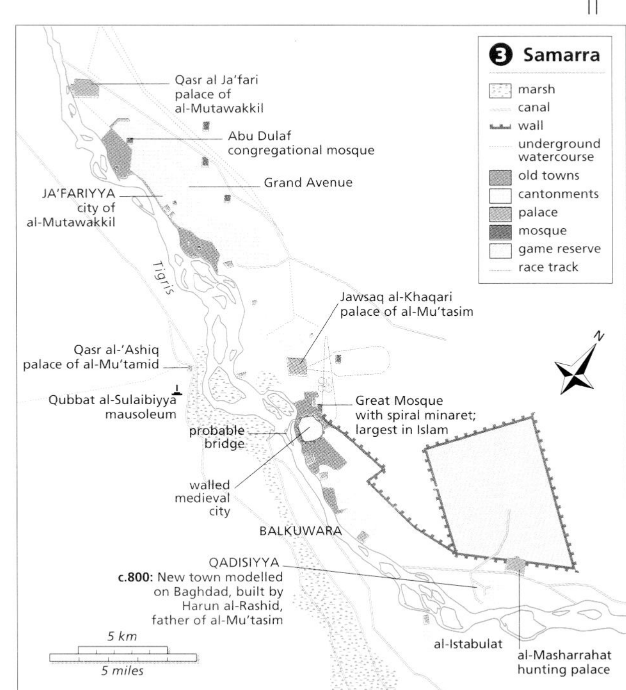

THE WORLD 750–1000

THE DISINTEGRATION OF GREAT EMPIRES and conflicts between warring dynasties were widespread throughout the 9th and 10th centuries. In Europe, Charlemagne was crowned western Emperor in 800, but his Frankish Empire was broken apart by disputes over inheritance. The Abbasid Caliphate, based in Baghdad, could not maintain central control over the vast Islamic world. New Islamic dynasties, such as the Fatimids of northern Africa, broke away from Baghdad's authority. In China, the mighty Tang Empire split into small warring states while in Central America, the Maya were in decline. In contrast to this political fragmentation, powerful new states developed in many parts of the world: the Khmers in Southeast Asia, Koryo in Korea, the Toltecs in Mexico, Ghana and Kanem-Bornu in Africa, and Kievan Rus in eastern Europe.

Ireland suffered badly from Viking raids in the 9th and 10th centuries, so monasteries built distinctive round towers, such as these at Glendalough, as lookouts and refuges.

Europe

Charlemagne, king of the Franks, incorporated most of western Europe into a single dominion. After disputes over his inheritance, the kingdom was divided into three parts. Henry I, the Saxon successor, extended his influence over the German duchies, and conquered Italy. His son, Otto I, defeated the Magyars and was crowned Holy Roman Emperor. In the west, the Carolingian Empire and the British Isles fell prey to Viking raiders.

The World in 1000

- Song Empire
- Byzantine Empire
- Denmark and possessions
- Toltec Empire
- Kievan Rus and possessions
- Abbasid Caliphate under Harun al-Rashid, 786
- Tibet c.800
- Empire of the Franks under Charlemagne, 814
- Holy Roman Empire

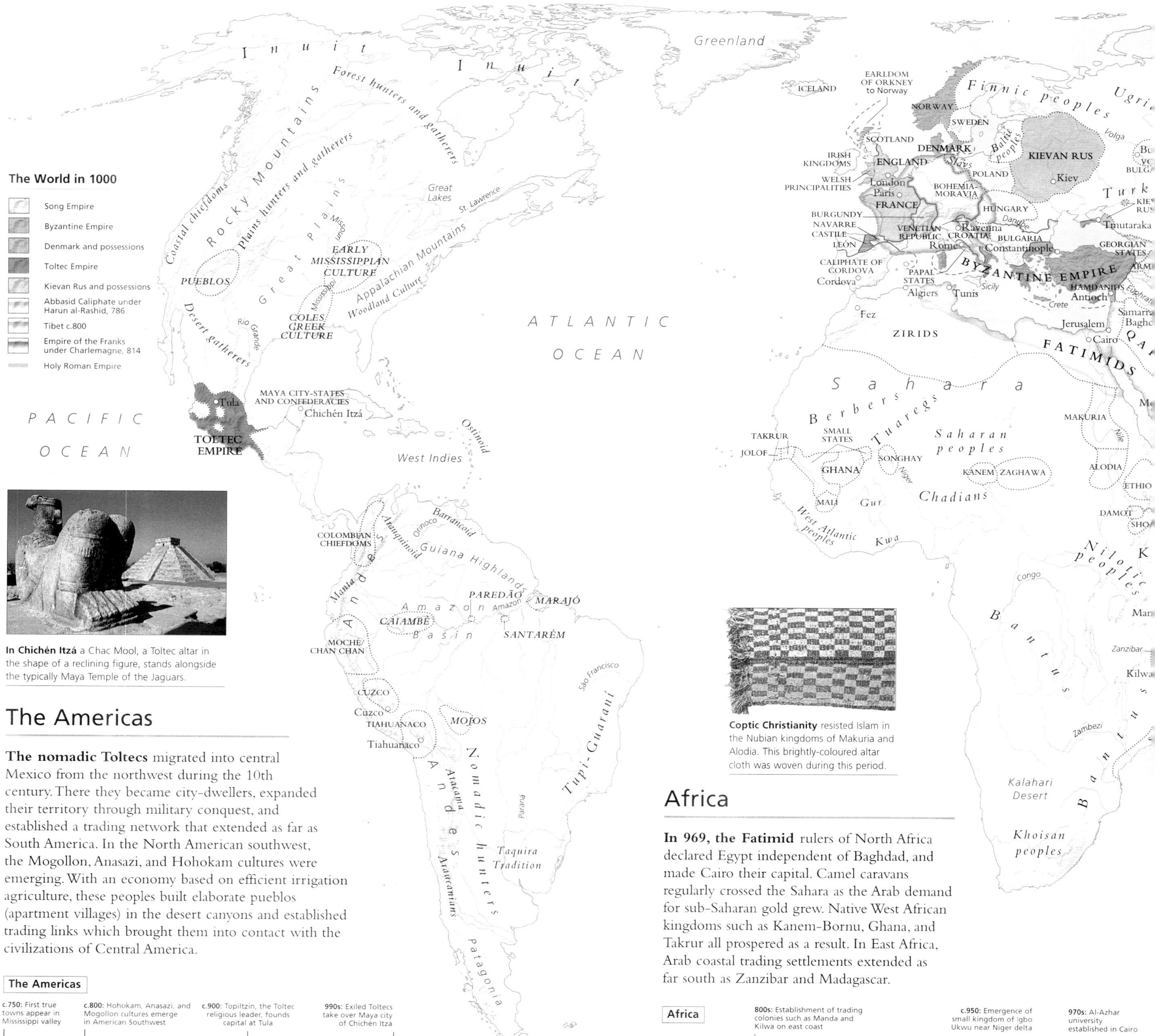

In Chichén Itzá a Chac Mool, a Toltec altar in the shape of a reclining figure, stands alongside the typically Maya Temple of the Jaguars.

The Americas

The nomadic Toltecs migrated into central Mexico from the northwest during the 10th century. There they became city-dwellers, expanded their territory through military conquest, and established a trading network that extended as far as South America. In the North American southwest, the Mogollon, Anasazi, and Hohokam cultures were emerging. With an economy based on efficient irrigation agriculture, these peoples built elaborate pueblos (apartment villages) in the desert canyons and established trading links which brought them into contact with the civilizations of Central America.

The Americas

c.750: First true towns appear in Mississippi valley

c.800: Hohokam, Anasazi, and Mogollon cultures emerge in American Southwest

c.850: Collapse of Maya civilization in Mexico's southern lowlands

c.900: Topiltzin, the Toltec religious leader, founds capital at Tula

c.900: Advanced Thule culture among Inuit of Alaska

987: High priest and followers expelled from Tula by rival cult that favours human sacrifice

990s: Exiled Toltecs take over Maya city of Chichén Itzá

Coptic Christianity resisted Islam in the Nubian kingdoms of Makuria and Alodia. This brightly-coloured altar cloth was woven during this period.

Africa

In 969, the Fatimid rulers of North Africa declared Egypt independent of Baghdad, and made Cairo their capital. Camel caravans regularly crossed the Sahara as the Arab demand for sub-Saharan gold grew. Native West African kingdoms such as Kanem-Bornu, Ghana, and Takrur all prospered as a result. In East Africa, Arab coastal trading settlements extended as far south as Zanzibar and Madagascar.

Africa

800: Start of Aghlabid dynasty in Tunis

800s: Establishment of trading colonies such as Manda and Kilwa on east coast

868: Ahmad ibn-Tulun founds the Tulunid dynasty in Egypt

909: Shi'ite Fatimids expel Aghlabids from Tunis

c.950: Emergence of small kingdom of Igbo Ukwu near Niger delta

969: Fatimids seize control of Egypt

970s: Al-Azhar university established in Cairo

PRINTING IN CHINA

The Chinese had been experimenting with ways of reproducing writing and illustrations for centuries, before they made their greatest breakthrough under the Tang in the 8th century. Carving characters and pictures in reverse onto wooden blocks was a time-consuming process, but it allowed many hundreds of copies to made before the wood's surface became too worn. All kinds of documents – from religious texts to tax receipts – were printed by this method.

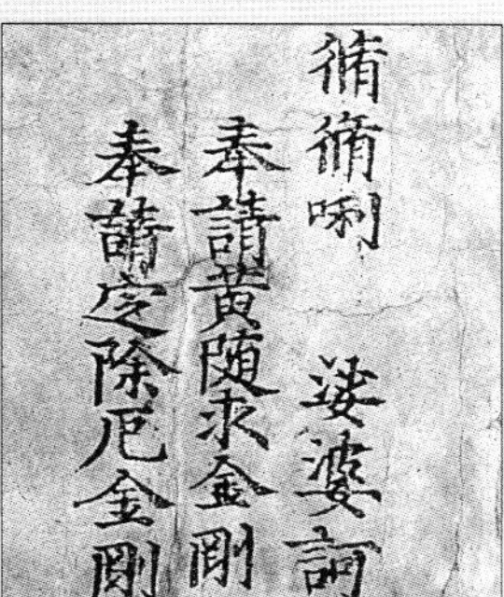

The earliest printed document that can be dated with certainty is *The Diamond Sutra*, a work of Buddhist doctrine printed on a scroll, produced in 868.

After the fervour of the 7th-century *jihads*, many Arab tribes subsequently turned against one another as they competed to rule the various parts of the Islamic world.

West Asia

The Abbasid dynasty came to power in 750. Though the arts, culture, and trade flourished under their rule, disagreements over the succession meant that their authority was not universally recognized. Even in Baghdad the caliphs became figureheads, real power being in the hands of Turkish mercenary or slave troops and Persian administrators. Under a new dynasty of Macedonian rulers (867–1081) the Byzantine Empire reached its apogee, and came into conflict with the Arabs to the east. Byzantine troops regained control of most of Anatolia and, in 969, reconquered Antioch.

SEE ALSO:

North America: pp.122–123
South America: pp.144–145
Africa: pp.162–163
Europe: pp.184–185
West Asia: pp.226–227
South and Southeast Asia: pp.244–245
North and East Asia: pp.262–265
Australasia and Oceania: pp.280–281

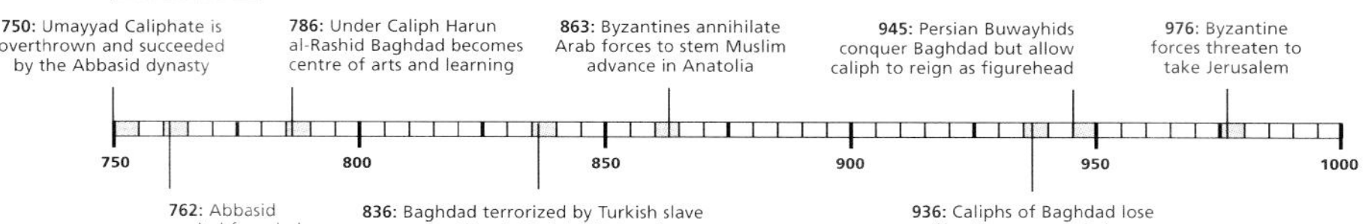

West Asia
750: Umayyad Caliphate is overthrown and succeeded by the Abbasid dynasty
786: Under Caliph Harun al-Rashid Baghdad becomes centre of arts and learning
863: Byzantines annihilate Arab forces to stem Muslim advance in Anatolia
945: Persian Buwayhids conquer Baghdad but allow caliph to reign as figurehead
976: Byzantine forces threaten to take Jerusalem
750
800
850
900
950
1000
762: Abbasid capital founded at Baghdad
836: Baghdad terrorized by Turkish slave troops; Abbasid Caliph al-Mutasim builds new capital at Samarra
936: Caliphs of Baghdad lose effective power; caliphate under control of Turkish troops

Palaeosiberians
Tungus
Mongols
KHITAN EMPIRE
Gobi
Linhuang
Ainu
Kaesong
KORYO
JAPAN
Kyoto
Kaifeng
Chang'an
Yellow River
Yangtze
SONG EMPIRE
TIBET
Tanguts
Uighurs
Dunhuang
QARAKHANIDS
Samarkand
Oxus
GHAZNAVIDS
Ghazni
KASHMIR
HINDU SHAHIS
QARMATIS
Himalayas
GURJARA-PRATIHARAS
CHAHAMANAS
SMALL STATES
PARAMARAS
CHANDELLAS
KALACURIS
BHAUMAS
PALAS
NANZHAO
CHAULUKYAS
ABHIRAS
SMALL STATES
ARAKAN
PAGAN
EASTERN GANGAS
Thais
ANNAM
Kalyani
Godavari
Krishna
EASTERN CHALUKYAS
HARIPUNJAYA
PEGU
THATON
DVARAVATI
KHMER
Angkor
CHAMPA
CHALUKYAS
SMALL STATES
CHOLAS
Ceylon
LAMBAKANNAS
Philippine Islands
Malays
PACIFIC OCEAN
INDIAN OCEAN
SRIVIJAYA
Borneo
Malay Peninsula
Palembang
EAST JAVA KINGDOM
Borobudur
Java
Papuans
New Guinea
Australian Aborigines
Darling
New Zealand

ARAB STAR MAPS

Arab scientists and mathematicians were the finest in the world and their astronomers added greatly to our knowledge of the heavens during this period. As well as using the night sky to set a course at sea and help them cross the desert, the Arabs continued to name stars and map constellations in the tradition of Ptolemy and other Greek astronomers. Many stars, such as Aldebaran, Rigel, and Rasalgethi, are still known by their Arab names.

The constellation of Andromeda is one of many attractive illustrations in *The Book of the Fixed Stars* compiled by Abd al-Rahman ibn Umar al-Sufi in the 10th century. The individual stars forming the constellation are shown in red.

Buddhism affected all aspects of life in Tang China, the Buddha assuming Chinese features, as in this wall painting from Dunhuang.

This bronze of the god Shiva was made under the Chola dynasty. In this period cults of individual Hindu deities grew in popularity.

South and Southeast Asia

In the north, the Islamic kingdom of the Afghan ruler Mahmud of Ghazni stretched from the Oxus to the Indus, while states such as Gurjara-Pratiharas and the Buddhist Palas vied for the Ganges plain. To the south, the Tamil Cholas and the Chalukyas fought over the Godavari and Krishna rivers. Chola conquests expanded to include Ceylon and parts of the Malay Peninsula.

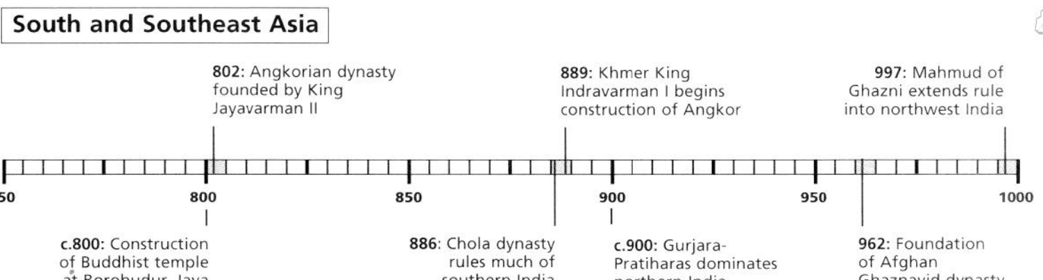

South and Southeast Asia
802: Angkorian dynasty founded by King Jayavarman II
889: Khmer King Indravarman I begins construction of Angkor
997: Mahmud of Ghazni extends rule into northwest India
750
800
850
900
950
1000
c.800: Construction of Buddhist temple at Borobudur, Java
886: Chola dynasty rules much of southern India
c.900: Gurjara-Pratiharas dominates northern India
962: Foundation of Afghan Ghaznavid dynasty

East Asia

Threats of internal rebellion in the middle of the 8th century weakened the Tang dynasty's control of China. As a result the empire became more inward looking and the political and economic centre of gravity began to shift south to the Yangtze valley. The Tang dynasty eventually collapsed after massive peasant uprisings in the 9th century, and China split into ten separate states until 960–79, when it was reunified under the Song. Both Korea and Japan were governed by strong, centralized Buddhist dynasties.

East Asia

751: Defeat of Chinese by Muslim forces at battle of Talas River
794: Kyoto becomes capital of Japan
868: *The Diamond Sutra*, world's oldest surviving printed work
935: Foundation of kingdom of Koryo in Korea
979: Song establish power in China

750 800 850 900 950 1000

756: Rebel general An Lushan captures Chang'an
763: Tang China is invaded by Tibetans
870s: Peasant uprisings throughout Tang China
907: End of the Tang dynasty
970: Paper money introduced by Chinese government

EXPLORERS OF THE OCEANS

The stylized image of a ship decorates this early Viking coin, which was minted at Hedeby in the 9th century.

IN THE 1ST MILLENNIUM CE, three peoples excelled all others as navigators of the world's oceans: the Vikings, the Arabs, and the Polynesians. The traders and raiders of Scandinavia created the fast, efficient Viking longship, which took them along the rivers of Russia to the Black Sea, and across the Atlantic Ocean to Iceland and North America. The Arabs were already accomplished seafarers; the discovery, in the 8th century, of the sea route to China via the Strait of Malacca heralded a new era of long-distance trade, and Arab ships sailed to the East Indies, East Africa, and China. Perhaps the most extraordinary seafarers of all were the Polynesians, who by 1200 CE had completed the colonization of all the islands of the Pacific.

These 12th-century walrus ivory chesspieces are from Lewis in the Outer Hebrides. The islands were settled by Norwegians in the 9th and 10th centuries.

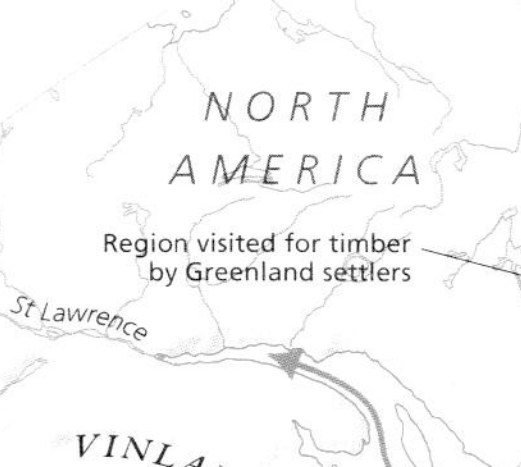

The Viking world

Ocean-going ships allowed the Vikings to sail in search of new lands and trading opportunities. At first they dominated their Baltic neighbours, taking tribute in the form of amber, wax, fish, ivory, and furs. Norwegians and Danes exploited weaknesses in France, England, and Ireland, using their fast, manoeuvrable longships to conduct lightning raids, exacting tribute, conquering, and colonizing. Eventually, in a quest for land, they crossed the Atlantic, reaching Iceland in 860 and Newfoundland c.1000. Swedish traders penetrated the navigable rivers of Russia to dominate the lucrative trade with Constantinople and the Arab world. Varangians (as these eastern Vikings were called) founded Kievan Rus, the first Russian state, and their fighting qualities were recognized by the Byzantine emperors, who employed them as their elite mercenary guard.

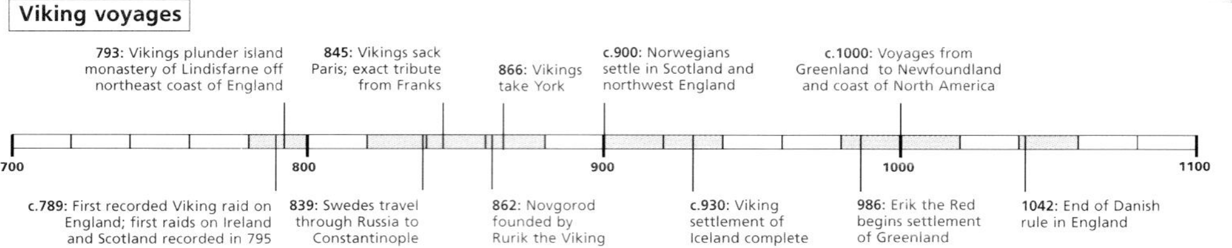

Viking longships were oar-powered, ranging from 16–30 m in length. Their light, flexible hulls 'rode' the waves and made them ideal for raiding in shallow, coastal waters.

The Polynesians

The first wave of colonization of the Pacific, between 2000 and 1500 BCE, took settlers from New Guinea and neighbouring islands as far as the Fiji Islands. From there, they sailed on to the Tonga and Samoa groups. In about 200 BCE, the Polynesians embarked on a series of far longer voyages, crossing vast tracts of empty ocean to settle the Marquesas, the Society Islands, Hawaii, Rapa Nui (Easter Island), and New Zealand. By about 1200 CE they had discovered almost every island in the Pacific. They sailed in double-hulled canoes, laden with seed plants, chickens, and pigs. The canoes could tack into the wind, and they probably navigated by observing the sun and the stars, the direction of prevailing winds, and the flight patterns of homing birds.

On their epic ocean voyages, the Polynesians used twin-hulled canoes, similar to the one in this 19th-century engraving, up to 30 m long. Canoes with an outrigger, attached to the hull and kept to windward for balance, were probably for inshore sailing and shorter voyages. Both types of vessel could be powered by oars or sails.

Polynesian voyages 1500 BCE–1000 CE

c.1500 BCE: Earliest evidence of colonization of Fiji – by makers of incised Lapita pottery

c.1300 BCE: Colonization of Tonga

c.1000 BCE: Distinct Polynesian culture starts to emerge in Fiji, Tonga, and Samoa

c.500 BCE: On Samoa, Lapita style of pottery is replaced by plain, undecorated bowls

c.200 BCE: Polynesians reach Marquesas Islands from Samoa

c.300 CE: Settlement of Rapa Nui (Easter Island)

c.400 CE: Polynesians reach Hawaiian Islands

c.400 CE: Colonization of Society Islands

c.700 CE: Earliest temple platforms (*ahu*) built on Rapa Nui (Easter Island)

1500 BCE · 1000 BCE · 500 BCE · 1 CE · 500 CE · 1000 CE

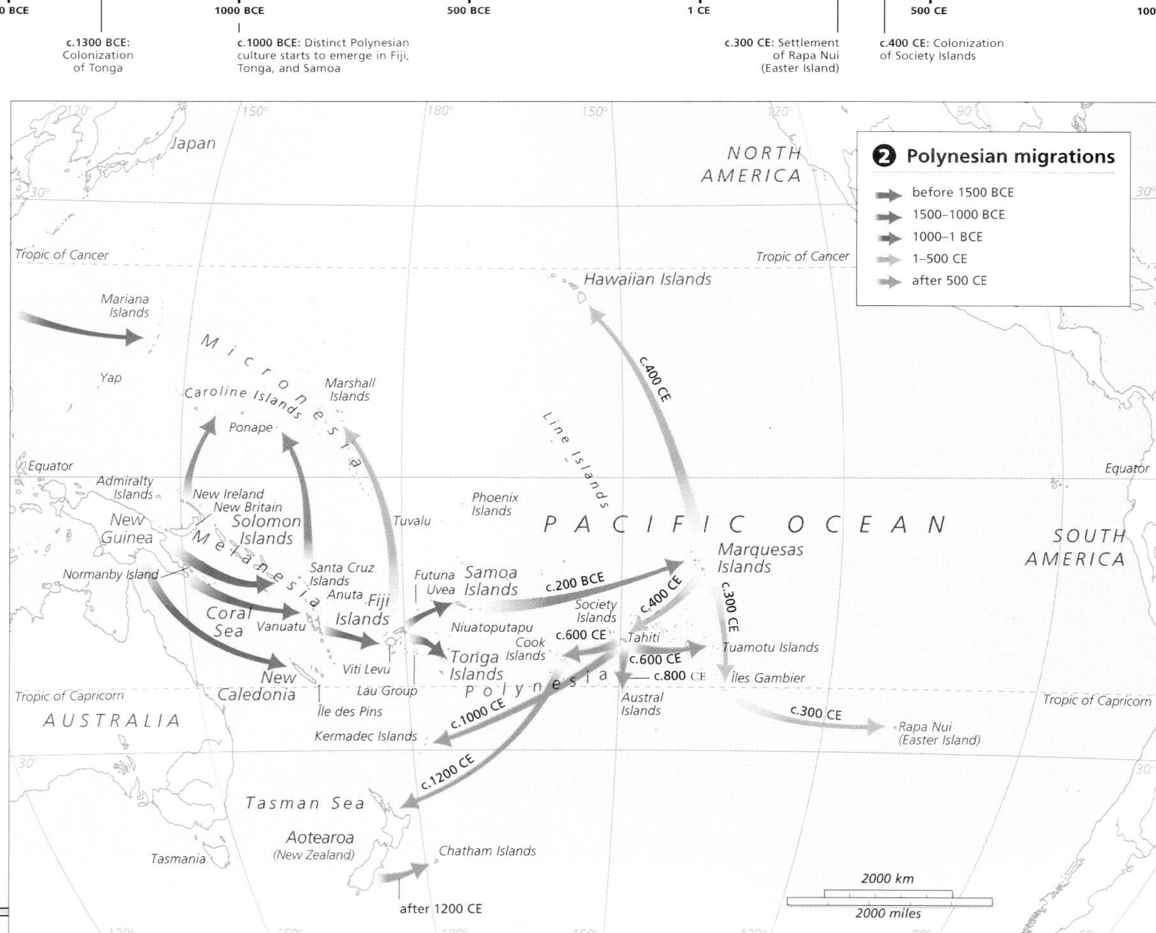

SEE ALSO:
North America: pp.122–123
Europe: pp.184–185
West Asia: pp.226–227
South and Southeast Asia: pp.244–245
Australasia and Oceania: pp.280–281

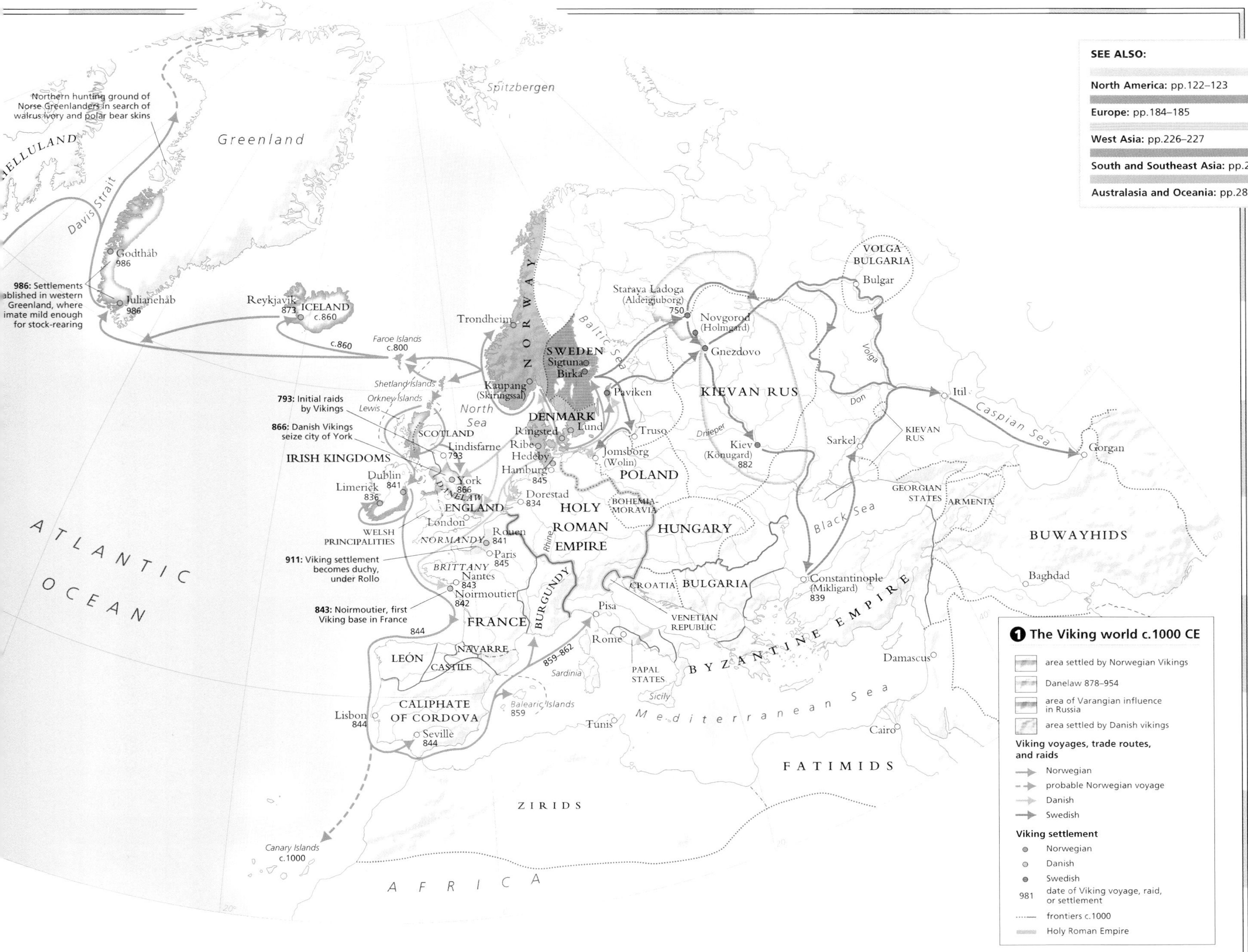

Northern hunting ground of Norse Greenlanders in search of walrus ivory and polar bear skins

986: Settlements established in western Greenland, where climate mild enough for stock-rearing

793: Initial raids by Vikings

866: Danish Vikings seize city of York

911: Viking settlement becomes duchy, under Rollo

843: Noirmoutier, first Viking base in France

1 The Viking world c.1000 CE

- area settled by Norwegian Vikings
- Danelaw 878–954
- area of Varangian influence in Russia
- area settled by Danish vikings

Viking voyages, trade routes, and raids

- Norwegian
- probable Norwegian voyage
- Danish
- Swedish

Viking settlement

- Norwegian
- Danish
- Swedish
- 981 date of Viking voyage, raid, or settlement
- frontiers c.1000
- Holy Roman Empire

Arab traders in the Indian Ocean

The Arabs used the wind systems of the monsoon to propel their ships eastward from the Persian Gulf in November and to return them westward in the summer. In the 8th century, Arab traders discovered the sea-route to Guangzhou (Canton) by way of the Malabar Coast, the Strait of Malacca, and Hanoi, a journey of 120 days, which nevertheless could take between 18 months and three years. The Arabs exported iron, wool, incense, and bullion in return for silk and spices. When the fall of the Tang Empire disrupted trade with China c.1000 CE, the Arabs turned to the East Indies, and Islam consequently became well established in the the islands of Southeast Asia. They also navigated the East African coast to Zanzibar and Madagascar, where they met the Malays who had colonized the island some 300 years earlier.

An Indian ship is depicted in an Arab manuscript of 1238. It has a square-rigged sail, suitable for running with the strong monsoonal winds, well known from the 1st century CE. The capacious hold could carry both passengers and cargo, essential for thriving Indian Ocean trade routes from the 8th century CE.

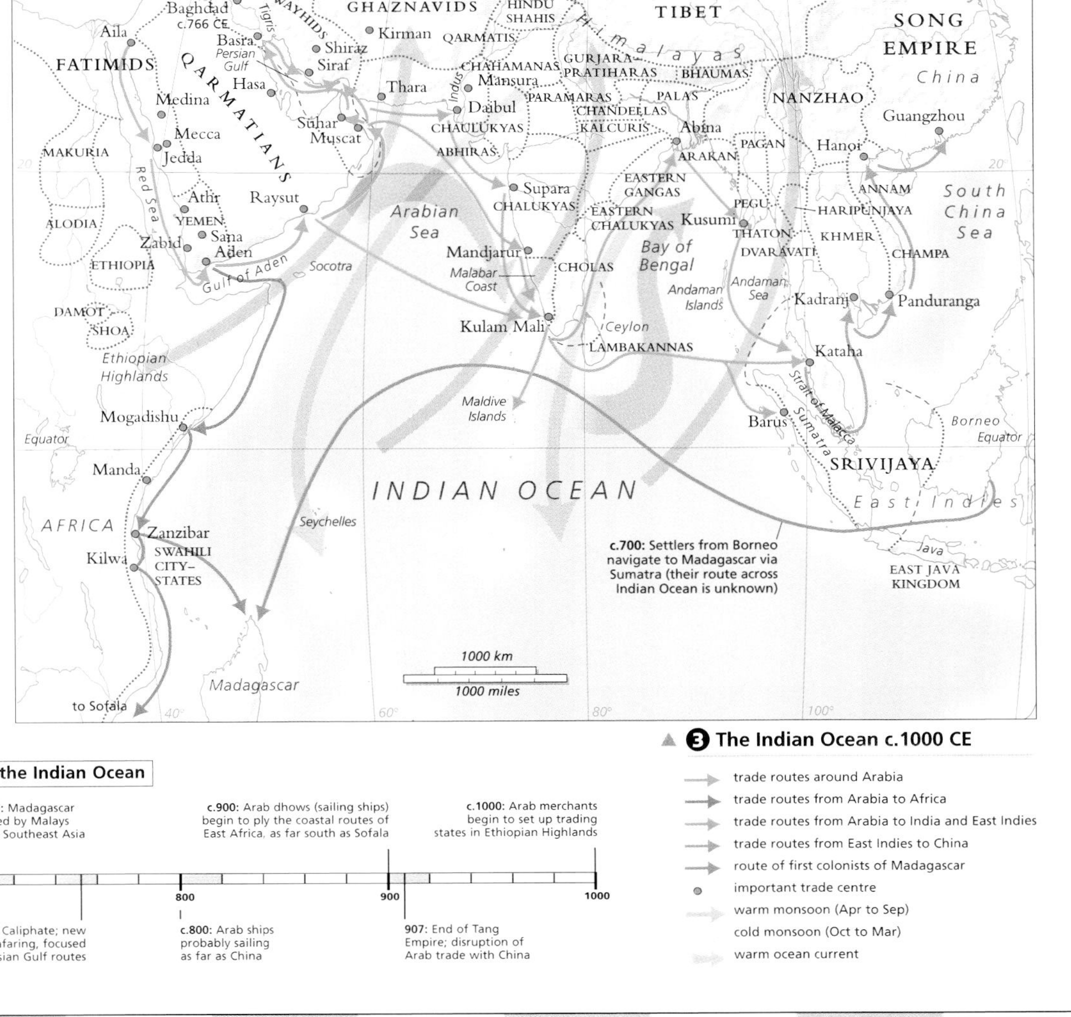

3 The Indian Ocean c.1000 CE

- trade routes around Arabia
- trade routes from Arabia to Africa
- trade routes from Arabia to India and East Indies
- trade routes from East Indies to China
- route of first colonists of Madagascar
- important trade centre
- warm monsoon (Apr to Sep)
- cold monsoon (Oct to Mar)
- warm ocean current

THE WORLD 1000–1200

IN MANY PARTS OF THE WORLD conflict over territory and religion was intense. This was a time when the Christian west was recovering from the tumult that followed the fall of Rome. As marginal land was cleared for agriculture, the population expanded. Trade routes crossed Europe and a mercantile economy developed and prospered. Yet the resurgence of Christian Europe brought it into direct confrontation with Islam when it launched the Crusades to conquer the Holy Land. This ultimately proved a failure, but in Spain and Portugal the Christian reconquest made intermittent progress. To the east, the states of northern India fell to Muslim invaders, and Buddhism was finally driven from the sub-continent. In China the Song Empire shrank under pressure from powerful nomadic peoples to the north, such as the Xixia and the Jin.

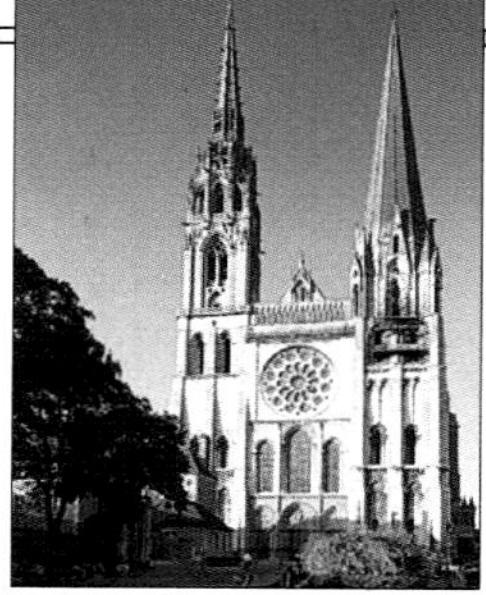

The power of the Church was expressed in new cathedrals built first in the Romanesque and then in the Gothic style, typified by the soaring facade of Chartres.

Europe

The assimilation in the 11th century of Poland, Hungary, and the Scandinavian kingdoms into the realm of western Christianity brought it to a new peak of power and influence. As western Europeans began to wrest control of the Mediterranean from the Arabs and Byzantines, a new era of prosperity based on trade began. Italian merchants became middlemen in Byzantine trade, and north Italian towns, such as Venice, Genoa, and Pisa, prospered. Elsewhere, forests and marginal land were cleared for agriculture, populations grew, and new towns were founded.

Europe

- **1000:** Hungary officially becomes a Christian state
- **1016:** Accession of Canute unites England, Denmark, and Norway
- **1031:** Beginning of Christian reconquest of Spain
- **1054:** Final schism between Roman and Orthodox churches
- **1066:** Battle of Hastings; Norman conquest of England
- **1077:** German king, Henry IV, forced to seek absolution from Pope Gregory VII
- **1091:** Completion of Norman conquest of Sicily
- **1119:** Bologna University founded in Italy
- **1136:** Independence of Russian state of Novgorod
- **1147:** Second Crusade; Lisbon taken from Moors
- **1154:** Building of Chartres cathedral

1000 1050 1100 1150 1200

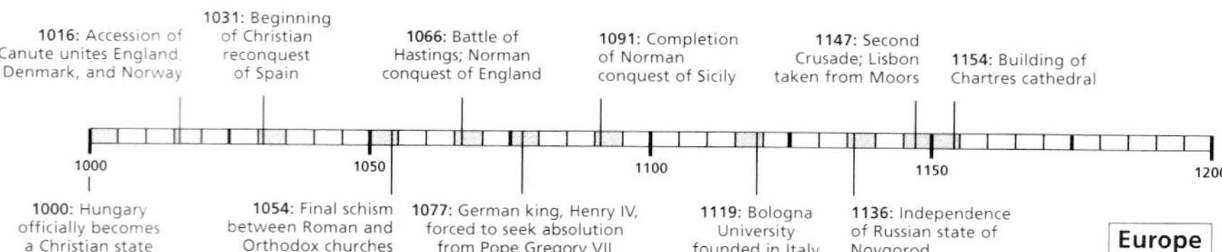

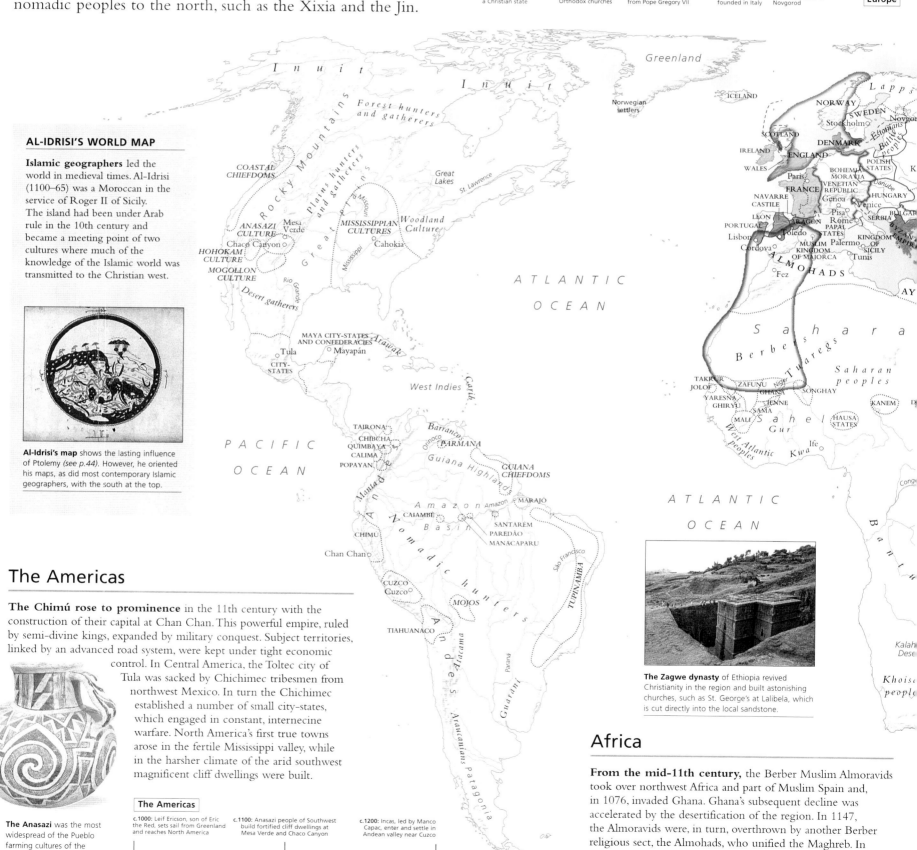

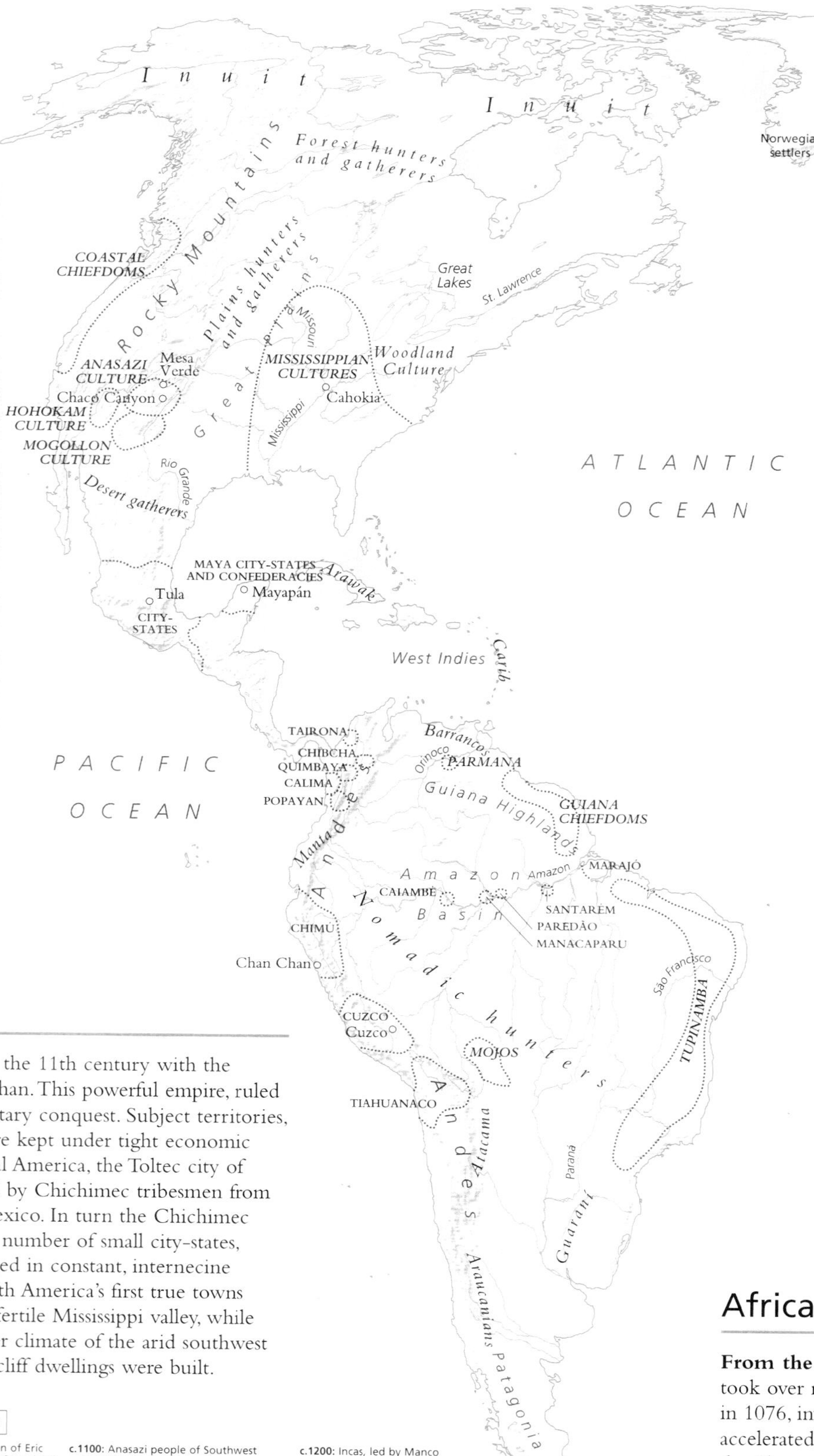

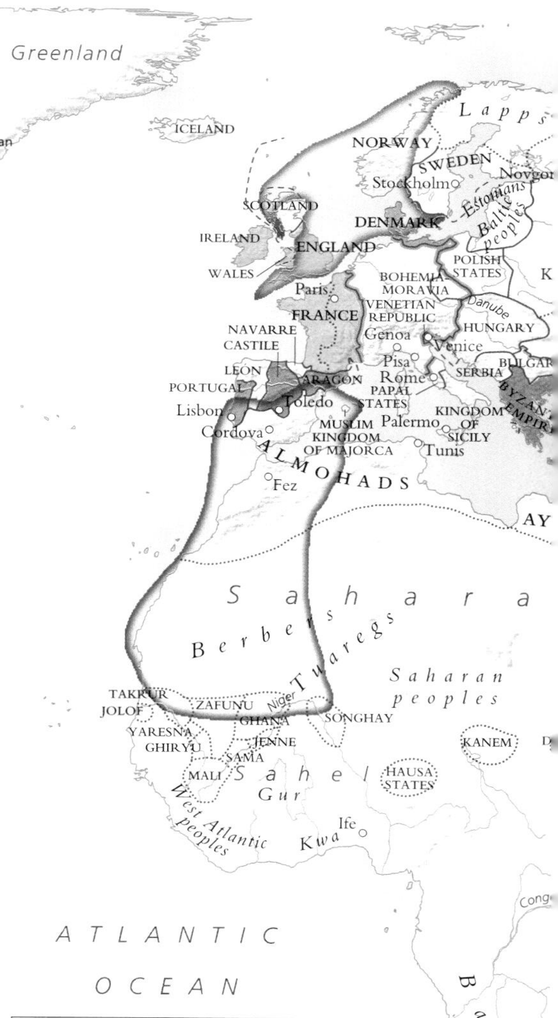

AL-IDRISI'S WORLD MAP

Islamic geographers led the world in medieval times. Al-Idrisi (1100–65) was a Moroccan in the service of Roger II of Sicily. The island had been under Arab rule in the 10th century and became a meeting point of two cultures where much of the knowledge of the Islamic world was transmitted to the Christian west.

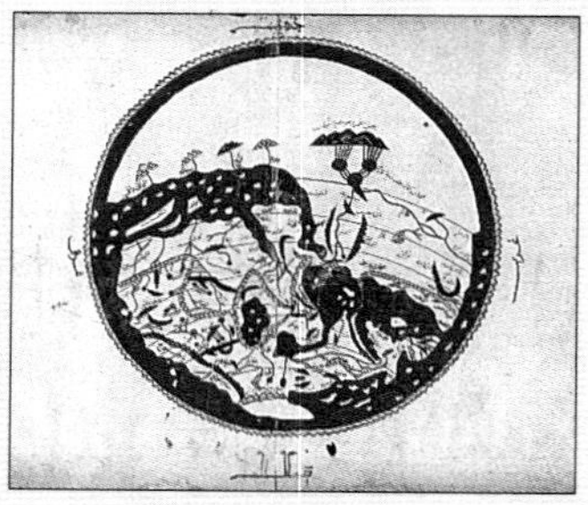

Al-Idrisi's map shows the lasting influence of Ptolemy *(see p.44)*. However, he oriented his maps, as did most contemporary Islamic geographers, with the south at the top.

The Zagwe dynasty of Ethiopia revived Christianity in the region and built astonishing churches, such as St. George's at Lalibela, which is cut directly into the local sandstone.

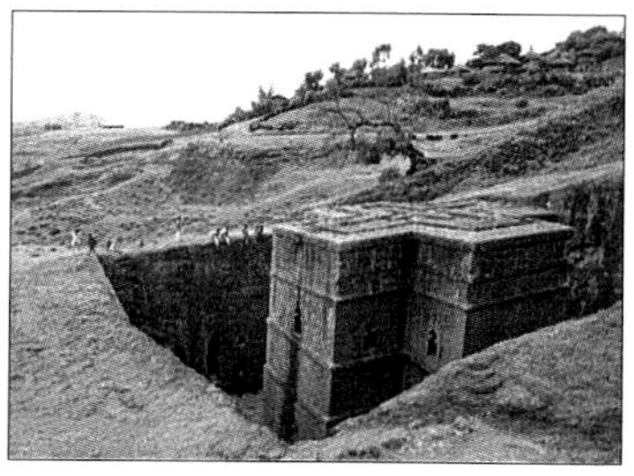

The Americas

The Chimú rose to prominence in the 11th century with the construction of their capital at Chan Chan. This powerful empire, ruled by semi-divine kings, expanded by military conquest. Subject territories, linked by an advanced road system, were kept under tight economic control. In Central America, the Toltec city of Tula was sacked by Chichimec tribesmen from northwest Mexico. In turn the Chichimec established a number of small city-states, which engaged in constant, internecine warfare. North America's first true towns arose in the fertile Mississippi valley, while in the harsher climate of the arid southwest magnificent cliff dwellings were built.

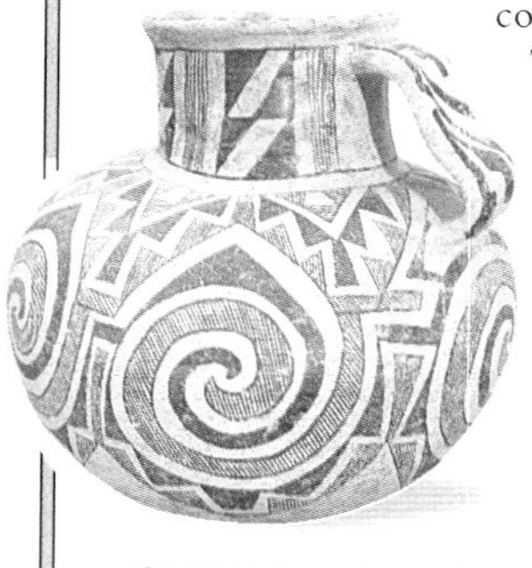

The Anasazi was the most widespread of the Pueblo farming cultures of the American Southwest. Roads linked their impressive canyon villages, where they produced fine black and white pottery.

The Americas

- **c.1000:** Leif Ericson, son of Eric the Red, sets sail from Greenland and reaches North America
- **c.1050:** Settlements of mound-builders of Mississippi valley expand to become true towns
- **c.1100:** Anasazi people of Southwest build fortified cliff dwellings at Mesa Verde and Chaco Canyon
- **1121:** Bishop Eirik visits North America from Greenland
- **c.1175:** Toltec capital, Tula, is sacked by Chichimec
- **c.1200:** Incas, led by Manco Capac, enter and settle in Andean valley near Cuzco

1000 1050 1100 1150 1200

Africa

From the mid-11th century, the Berber Muslim Almoravids took over northwest Africa and part of Muslim Spain and, in 1076, invaded Ghana. Ghana's subsequent decline was accelerated by the desertification of the region. In 1147, the Almoravids were, in turn, overthrown by another Berber religious sect, the Almohads, who unified the Maghreb. In Ethiopia, a revival of Red Sea trade and the emergence of the Zagwe dynasty in 1150, led to a more expansionist, prosperous era. In Egypt, the military leader Saladin became ruler in 1174, ending the Fatimid dynasty and founding that of the Ayyubids.

WINDMILLS

Wind power had been harnessed in various different ways, notably in Persia and China, for grinding corn and raising water, but it was not until the 12th century that the windmill started to take on its familiar European form. The mills of northern Europe differed from earlier versions in that the shaft turned horizontally rather than vertically and the sails were turned so that they kept facing the wind. The first northern European mills were simple post-mills. These evolved gradually into bulkier tower mills with rotating caps.

In Europe windmills were used only for grinding corn up until the 15th century, as illustrated in this English woodcut from c.1340. Their power was then adapted for tasks such as land drainage, particularly in Holland.

West Asia

Byzantium's resurgence under Basil II did not last and in the 11th century most of the empire's Asian lands fell to the Seljuk Turks. The Islamic Turks, originally from Central Asia, established themselves in Baghdad in 1055. As 'men of the sword', they formed a partnership with the Persians and Arabs, the 'men of the law'. Tens of thousands of Europeans answered Pope Urban II's call in 1095 to recapture Jerusalem for Christendom. In 1099 the holy city was taken and the Crusaders set up states in Antioch, Edessa, Tripoli, and Jerusalem. In the following century, Muslim leaders, notably Saladin, founder of the Ayyubid dynasty in Egypt, embarked on a campaign of reconquest.

The capture of Antioch in 1098 was one of the first Christian successes on the First Crusade. The strongly fortified city held out for seven months.

West Asia

- **1025**: Death of great Byzantine emperor, Basil II
- **1055**: Seljuk Turks capture Baghdad
- **1071**: Seljuk Turks defeat Byzantines at Manzikert
- **1099**: Jerusalem captured by Crusaders
- **1144**: Fall of Edessa to Muslims
- **1174**: Founding of Ayyubid Sultanate in Egypt
- **1187**: Saladin recaptures Jerusalem
- **1188**: Crusader states reduced to coastal enclaves by Saladin

SEE ALSO:

North America: pp.122–123

South America: pp.146–147

Africa: pp.162–163

Europe: pp.186–187

West Asia: pp.228–229

South and Southeast Asia: pp.244–245

North and East Asia: pp.262–265

East Asia

By 1110, Song China was the most advanced, prosperous, and populous state in the world. However the Song alliance with the Manchurian Jin to dislodge the hostile Liao from their northern border, fatally weakened the Song Empire. The Jin overran northern China and the Song were forced to regroup in the southeast, defensive and hostile to outside influences. In Japan, the emperors lost power to the Fujiwara family in the mid-12th century. A period of violent inter-clan warfare followed, ending with the victory of the Minamoto clan.

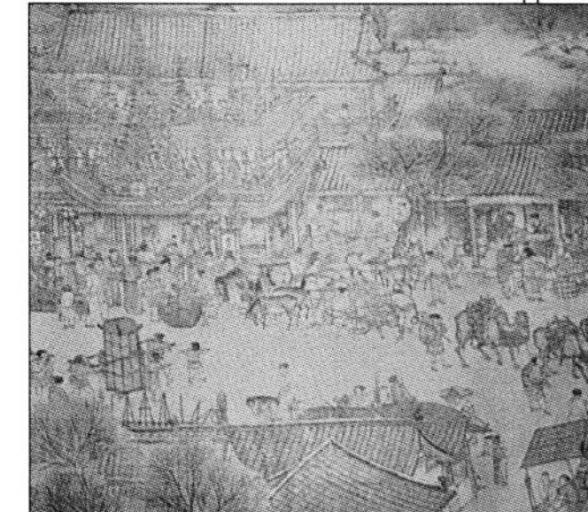

This Song scroll gives a vivid depiction of the bustling street life and prosperity of Kaifeng in the 12th century. In 1105 the city's population had risen to 260,000.

East Asia

- **1005**: Song China becomes subject state of northern Liao kingdom, with capital at Beijing
- **c.1045**: Movable type printing invented in China
- **1125**: Liao defeated by Jin from Manchuria
- **1130**: Song capital moves to Hangzhou
- **1191**: Zen Buddhist order founded in Japan
- **1192**: Minamoto Yoritomo becomes Shogun and forms military government in Japan

Palaeosiberians · Samoyeds · Ugrians · Siberia peoples · Tungus · Yenisey · Lena · Ob' · Amur · Volga · VOLGA BULGARIA · RUSSIAN PRINCIPALITIES · Gobi · Mongols · Liao · Manchuria · KARA KHITAI EMPIRE · UIGHUR CITY-STATES · XIXIA · Yanjing · Beijing · KORYO · JAPAN · Kyoto · Yellow River · JIN EMPIRE · Kaifeng · Caspian Sea · DAGHESTAN · GEORGIA · Manzikert · Edessa · LITTLE ARMENIA · EMPIRE OF THE KHWARIZM SHAH · Bukhara · KASHMIR · Kabul · TIBET · GHURID EMPIRE · Baghdad · ABBASIDS · TRIPOLI · JERUSALEM · Cairo · SULTANATE · SALGHURIDS · Euphrates · Tigris · Himalayas · Yangtze · Hangzhou · SOUTHERN SONG EMPIRE · Delhi · Indus · PARAMARAS · Ganges · SMALL DYNASTIES · NANZHAO · Bedouins · OMAN · CAULUKYAS · EASTERN GANGAS · PAGAN · Thais · ANNAM · Mecca · Red Sea · Arabian Peninsula · YADAVAS · SILAHARAS · KAKATIYAS · ARAKAN · HARIPUNJAYA · Nile · MAKURIA · YEMEN · ALWA · ETHIOPIA · Lalibela · KADAMBAS · HOYSALAS · TELUGUCODAS · KHMER · Angkor · Mekong · CHAMPA · Philippine Islands · GOJJAM · DAMOT · IFAT · SHOA · HARAR · DAWARO · FETEGAR · CERAS · PANDYAS · CHOLAS · Ceylon · SIMHALA · Nilotic peoples · Kushites · PACIFIC OCEAN · Malays · SRIVIJAYA · Borneo · INDIAN OCEAN · Sumatra · SWAHILI CITY-STATES · Papuans · New Guinea · Java · KEDIRI · Malays · Madagascar · MAPUNGUBWE · Australian Aborigines · Darling · New Zealand · Maoris

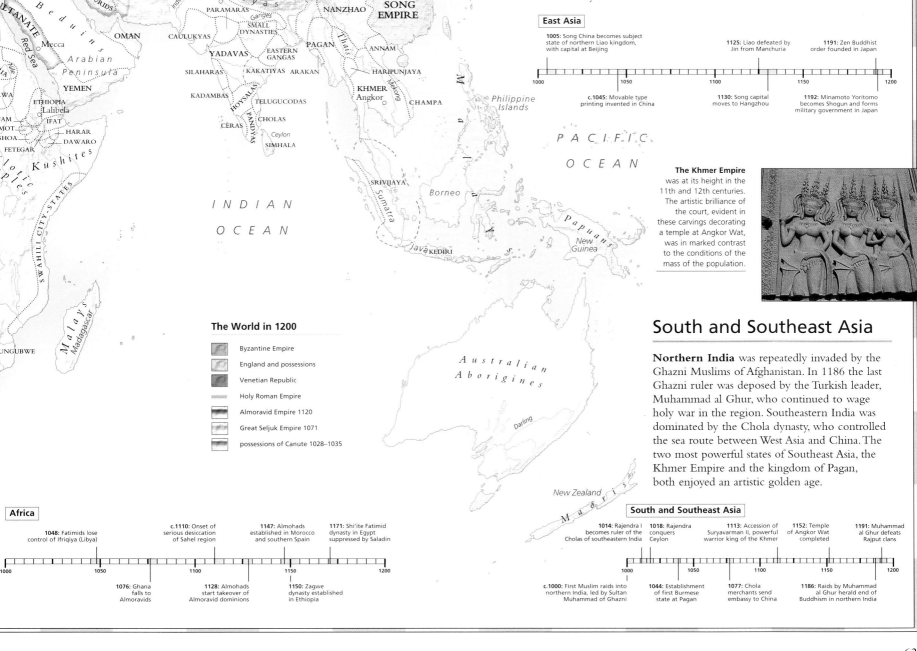

The World in 1200

- Byzantine Empire
- England and possessions
- Venetian Republic
- Holy Roman Empire
- Almoravid Empire 1120
- Great Seljuk Empire 1071
- possessions of Canute 1028–1035

The Khmer Empire was at its height in the 11th and 12th centuries. The artistic brilliance of the court, evident in these carvings decorating a temple at Angkor Wat, was in marked contrast to the conditions of the mass of the population.

South and Southeast Asia

Northern India was repeatedly invaded by the Ghazni Muslims of Afghanistan. In 1186 the last Ghazni ruler was deposed by the Turkish leader, Muhammad al Ghur, who continued to wage holy war in the region. Southeastern India was dominated by the Chola dynasty, who controlled the sea route between West Asia and China. The two most powerful states of Southeast Asia, the Khmer Empire and the kingdom of Pagan, both enjoyed an artistic golden age.

Africa

- **1048**: Fatimids lose control of Ifriqiya (Libya)
- **1076**: Ghana falls to Almoravids
- **c.1110**: Onset of serious desiccation of Sahel region
- **1128**: Almohads start takeover of Almoravid dominions
- **1147**: Almohads established in Morocco and southern Spain
- **1150**: Zagwe dynasty established in Ethiopia
- **1171**: Shi'ite Fatimid dynasty in Egypt suppressed by Saladin

South and Southeast Asia

- **c.1000**: First Muslim raids into northern India, led by Sultan Muhammad of Ghazni
- **1014**: Rajendra I becomes ruler of the Cholas of southeastern India
- **1018**: Rajendra conquers Ceylon
- **1044**: Establishment of first Burmese state at Pagan
- **1077**: Chola merchants send embassy to China
- **1113**: Accession of Suryavarman II, powerful warrior king of the Khmer
- **1152**: Temple of Angkor Wat completed
- **1186**: Raids by Muhammad al Ghur herald end of Buddhism in northern India
- **1191**: Muhammad al Ghur defeats Rajput clans

THE AGE OF THE CRUSADES

The idealism of a devout Crusader is captured in this 13th-century drawing.

THE IDEA OF A HOLY WAR was never part of the doctrine of the early Christian church. This changed in 1095, when Pope Urban II made an impassioned speech at Clermont, urging French barons and knights to go to the aid of the beleaguered Christians of the Byzantine Empire. In return, they were promised indulgences. When they got to the Holy Land and captured Jerusalem in 1099, the aims of the Crusaders became rather less spiritual. Those rewarded with land tried to recreate the society of feudal Europe, but there was always a shortage of manpower to maintain the Crusader states in their precarious two centuries of existence. Nevertheless, the crusading ideal became firmly established in European consciousness and there were many subsequent expeditions to defend or recapture Jerusalem, but none was as successful as the first.

The most devout and determined of all the crusading kings of Europe was Louis IX of France (St. Louis). He sailed on two Crusades, once to invade Egypt, the second time to convert the King of Tunis. Both ended in disaster. In 1270, Louis and his men were struck down by disease as they camped before Tunis. Louis himself died. Here his coffin is being loaded on a ship to be carried back to France.

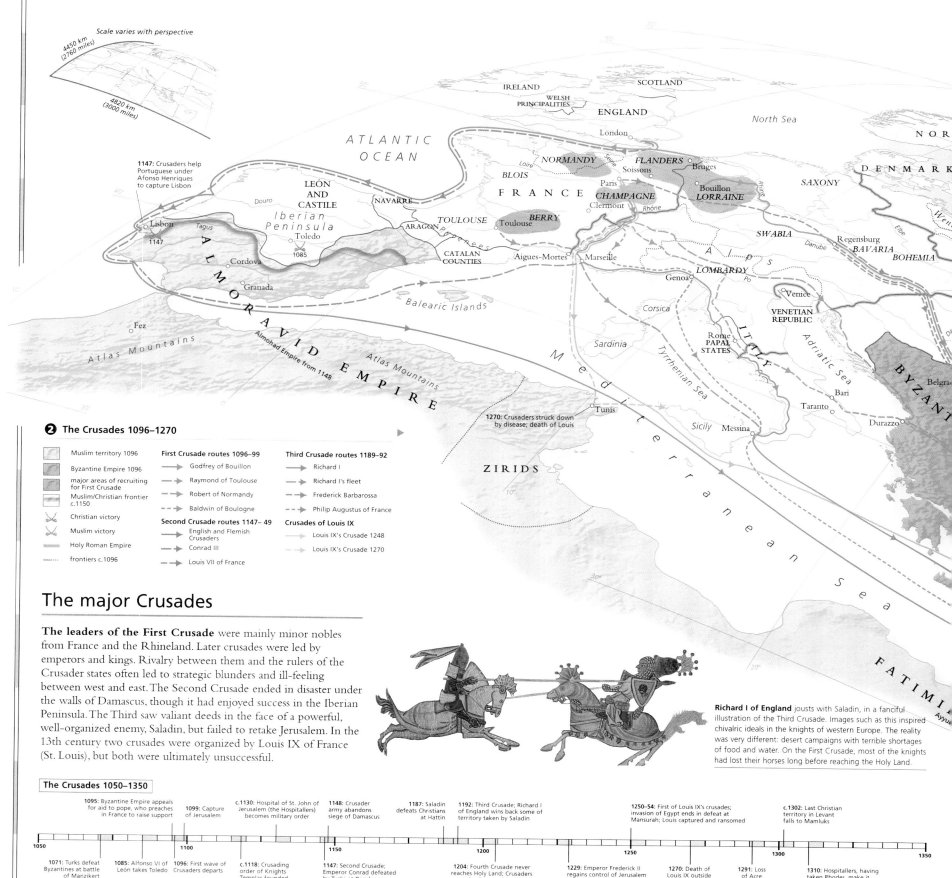

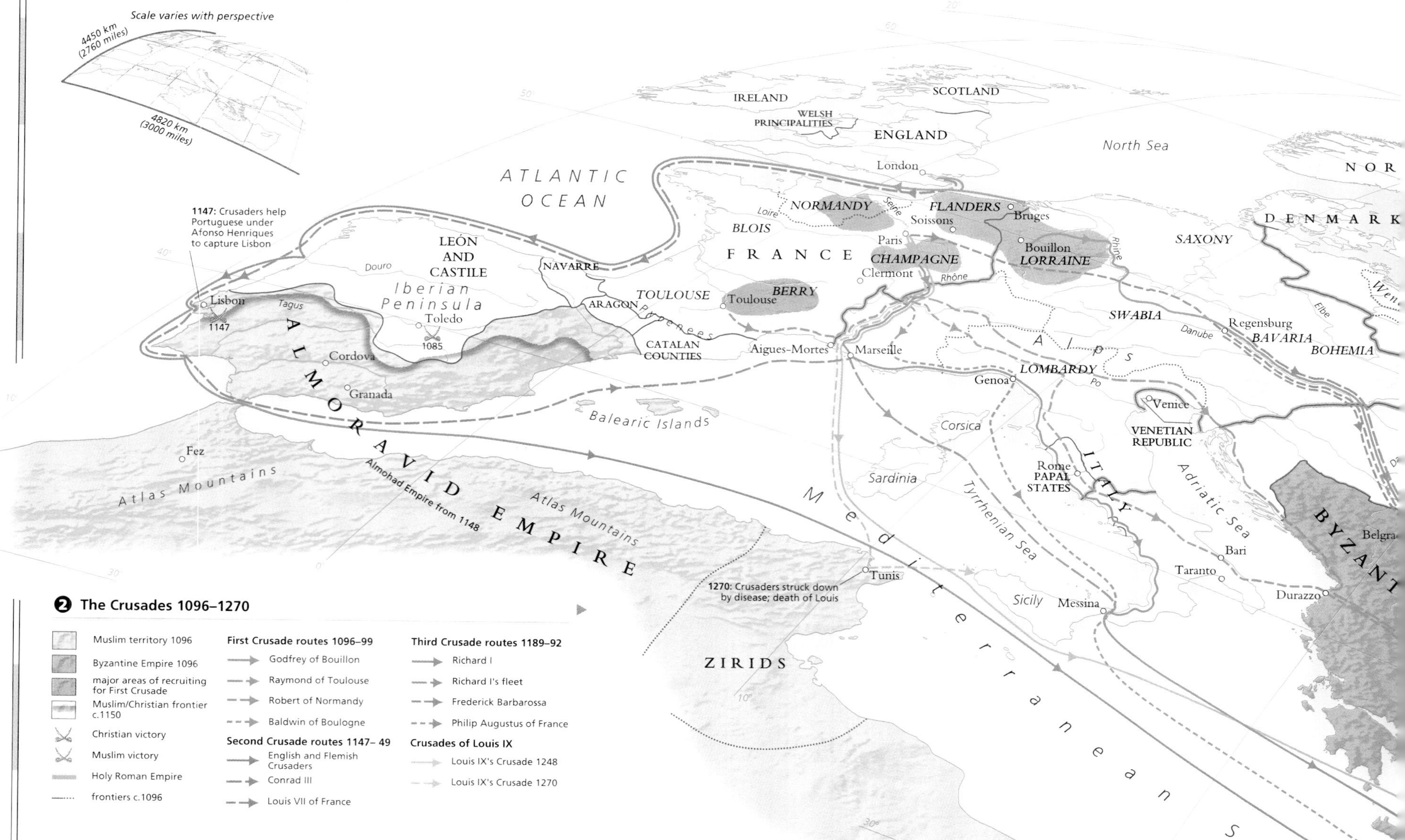

Scale varies with perspective

4450 km (2760 miles)

4820 km (3000 miles)

ATLANTIC OCEAN

IRELAND · WELSH PRINCIPALITIES · SCOTLAND · ENGLAND · London · North Sea · NORMANDY · FLANDERS · Bruges · Soissons · BLOIS · Paris · Bouillon · LORRAINE · FRANCE · CHAMPAGNE · Clermont · TOULOUSE · Toulouse · BERRY · SAXONY · DENMARK · SWABIA · Regensburg · BAVARIA · BOHEMIA · LEÓN AND CASTILE · NAVARRE · ARAGON · Iberian Peninsula · Toledo · Lisbon · Cordova · Granada · CATALAN COUNTIES · Aigues-Mortes · Marseille · Alps · LOMBARDY · Genoa · Venice · VENETIAN REPUBLIC · Balearic Islands · Corsica · Sardinia · Rome · PAPAL STATES · ITALY · Adriatic Sea · Tyrrhenian Sea · Bari · Taranto · Durazzo · BYZANT[INE] · Sicily · Messina · Tunis · ZIRIDS · Fez · Atlas Mountains · ALMORAVID EMPIRE · Almohad Empire from 1148 · Mediterranean Sea · FATIMI[D]

1147: Crusaders help Portuguese under Afonso Henriques to capture Lisbon

1270: Crusaders struck down by disease; death of Louis

❷ The Crusades 1096–1270

- Muslim territory 1096
- Byzantine Empire 1096
- major areas of recruiting for First Crusade
- Muslim/Christian frontier c.1150
- Christian victory
- Muslim victory
- Holy Roman Empire
- frontiers c.1096

First Crusade routes 1096–99
- Godfrey of Bouillon
- Raymond of Toulouse
- Robert of Normandy
- Baldwin of Boulogne

Second Crusade routes 1147–49
- English and Flemish Crusaders
- Conrad III
- Louis VII of France

Third Crusade routes 1189–92
- Richard I
- Richard I's fleet
- Frederick Barbarossa
- Philip Augustus of France

Crusades of Louis IX
- Louis IX's Crusade 1248
- Louis IX's Crusade 1270

The major Crusades

The leaders of the First Crusade were mainly minor nobles from France and the Rhineland. Later crusades were led by emperors and kings. Rivalry between them and the rulers of the Crusader states often led to strategic blunders and ill-feeling between west and east. The Second Crusade ended in disaster under the walls of Damascus, though it had enjoyed success in the Iberian Peninsula. The Third saw valiant deeds in the face of a powerful, well-organized enemy, Saladin, but failed to retake Jerusalem. In the 13th century two crusades were organized by Louis IX of France (St. Louis), but both were ultimately unsuccessful.

Richard I of England jousts with Saladin, in a fanciful illustration of the Third Crusade. Images such as this inspired chivalric ideals in the knights of western Europe. The reality was very different: desert campaigns with terrible shortages of food and water. On the First Crusade, most of the knights had lost their horses long before reaching the Holy Land.

The Crusades 1050–1350

- **1071:** Turks defeat Byzantines at battle of Manzikert
- **1085:** Alfonso VI of León takes Toledo
- **1095:** Byzantine Empire appeals for aid to pope, who preaches in France to raise support
- **1096:** First wave of Crusaders departs
- **1099:** Capture of Jerusalem
- **c.1118:** Crusading order of Knights Templar founded
- **c.1130:** Hospital of St. John of Jerusalem (the Hospitallers) becomes military order
- **1147:** Second Crusade; Emperor Conrad defeated by Turks at Dorylaeum
- **1148:** Crusader army abandons siege of Damascus
- **1187:** Saladin defeats Christians at Hattin
- **1192:** Third Crusade; Richard I of England wins back some of territory taken by Saladin
- **1204:** Fourth Crusade never reaches Holy Land; Crusaders take Constantinople
- **1229:** Emperor Frederick II regains control of Jerusalem through diplomacy
- **1250–54:** First of Louis IX's crusades; invasion of Egypt ends in defeat at Mansurah; Louis captured and ransomed
- **1270:** Death of Louis IX outside walls of Tunis
- **1291:** Loss of Acre
- **c.1302:** Last Christian territory in Levant falls to Mamluks
- **1310:** Hospitallers, having taken Rhodes, make it their headquarters

The boundaries of Christianity and Islam

In the 9th and 10th centuries, the boundaries between the Islamic and Christian worlds shifted very little. A new threat to Christianity came in the mid-11th century with the advance of the Seljuk Turks, newly converted to Islam, and effective rulers of the Abbasid Caliphate after reaching Baghdad in 1055. Following their victory over the Byzantines in 1071 at Manzikert, they won control of almost all Asia Minor, home to former Christian subjects of the Byzantine Empire. In the Iberian Peninsula, however, the Christian kingdoms won back land from the Muslims in the course of the 11th century.

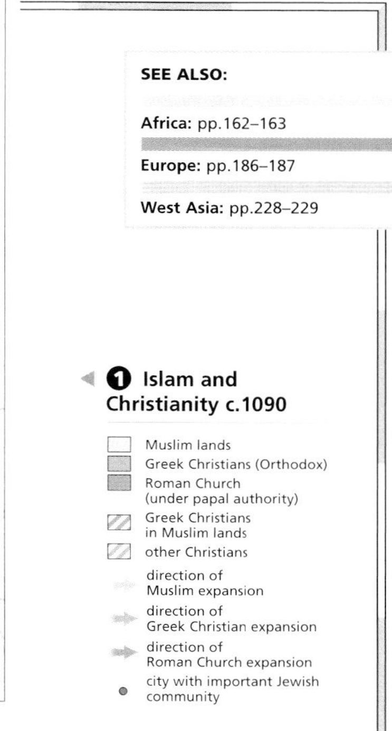

1 Islam and Christianity c.1090

Godfrey of Bouillon leads the attack on Jerusalem in 1099. After all the hardship and the long journey there, the capture of the Holy City was hailed as a miracle. It was followed by the murder or brutal eviction of many of the city's Muslims and Jews.

Crusader states in the Levant

How the Crusaders' conquests should be ruled was not considered until after Jerusalem had fallen. The solution – a feudal kingdom of Jerusalem buttressed by the counties of Edessa, Tripoli, and Antioch – alienated the Byzantines, who had hoped to regain their former territories. Jerusalem was always a weak state with a small population, heavily dependent on supplies and recruits from western Christendom. When a strong Islamic ruler such as Saladin emerged, the colonists had little hope against a determined Muslim onslaught. They held on to the coast through the 13th century, but in 1291, Acre, the last major city in Christian hands, fell to the Mamluks of Egypt.

Krak des Chevaliers was one of many heavily fortified Crusader castles. Manned by the Hospitallers, it held out against Saladin's forces, but fell to the Mamluks in 1271 after a month's siege.

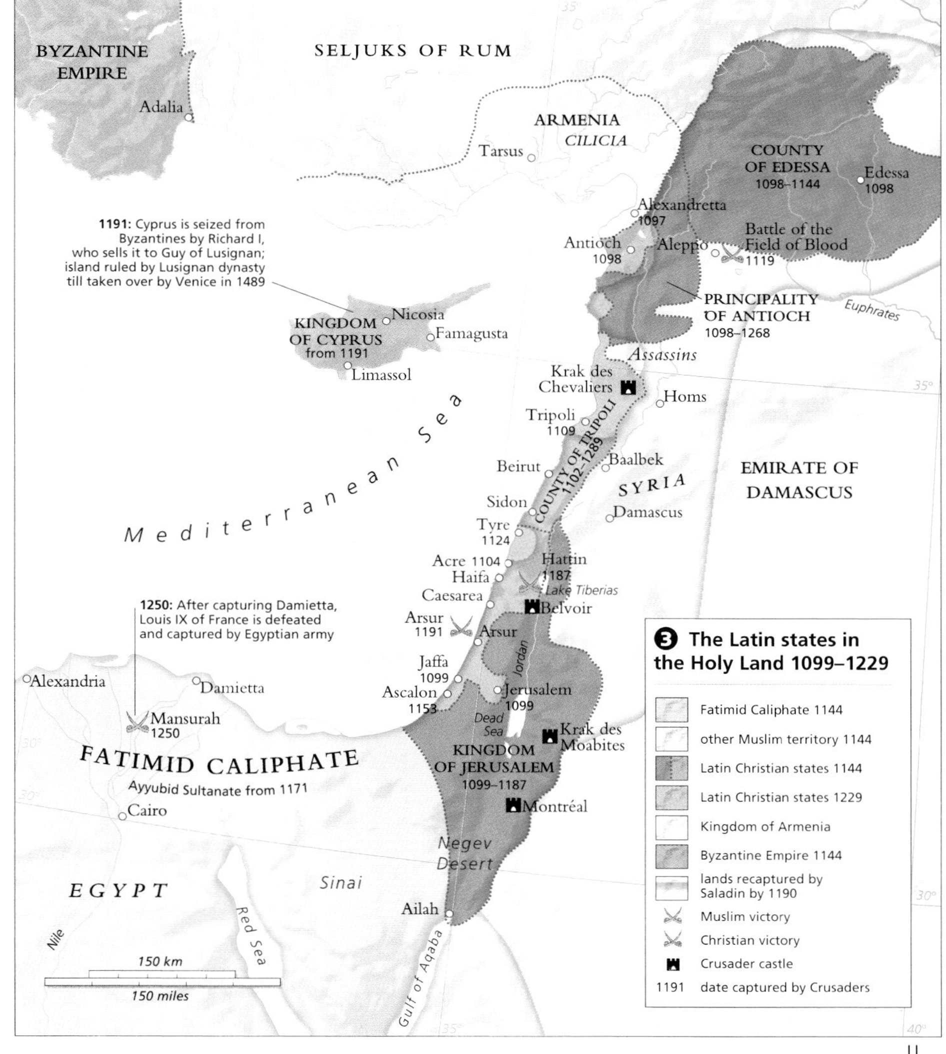

The Crusader states 1099–1250

- 1098: Crusaders take Antioch
- 1099: Godfrey of Bouillon elected King of Jerusalem
- 1124: Capture of important port of Tyre
- 1144: Edessa lost to Zangi, governor of Mosul
- 1151: Last Christian stronghold in County of Edessa falls to Nur al-Din
- 1187–88: Crusaders states ravaged by Saladin's armies
- 1191–92: Richard I wins back Jaffa, but fails to reach Jerusalem
- 1225: Emperor Frederick II inherits Kingdom of Jerusalem
- 1229: Frederick negotiates agreement which wins back control over Jerusalem

(1090 · 1120 · 1150 · 1180 · 1210 · 1240)

THE WORLD 1200–1300

IN THE 13TH CENTURY Mongol horsemen burst out of their central Asian homeland and conquered a vast swathe of the Eurasian landmass. By 1300, they had divided their conquests into four large empires that stretched from China to eastern Europe. Mongol campaigns brought devastation, particularly to China and the Islamic states of southwest Asia but, once all resistance had been crushed, merchants, ambassadors, and other travellers were able to move safely through the Mongol realms. Though the old political order of the Islamic world, centred on the Abbasid Caliphate and Baghdad, was swept away, the influence of Islam continued to spread as many Mongols adopted the religion. Powerful new Muslim states also emerged in Mamluk Egypt and the Sultanate of Delhi. Europe remained on the defensive in the face of the Mongols and Islam, but city-states such as Venice and Genoa prospered through increased trading links with the East.

The port of Venice was the richest city in western Europe. This illustration shows Marco Polo with his father and uncle setting off in 1271 on the first stage of their incredible journey to the court of the Great Khan.

Europe

The feudal monarchies of England and France consolidated large regional states, but conflict between popes and emperors prevented any similar process in Italy and Germany. In Spain, Christian forces took Córdoba and Seville, leaving only the small kingdom of Granada in Moorish control. In eastern Europe, the Mongols of the Golden Horde collected tribute from the Russian principalities. Western Europe, in contrast, prospered economically as Italian merchants linked northern lands to the commerce of the Mediterranean basin.

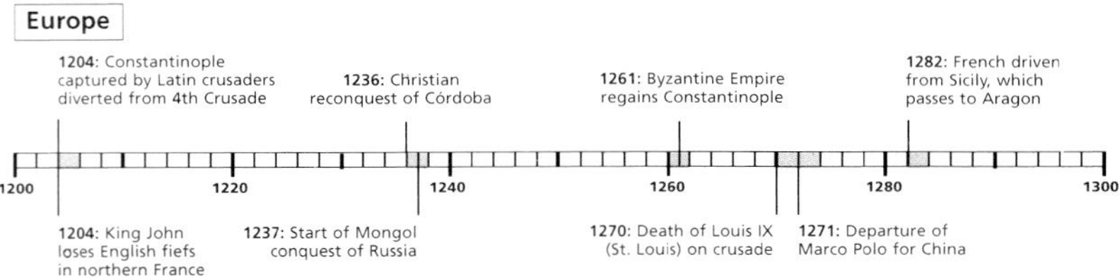
Europe
1204: Constantinople captured by Latin crusaders diverted from 4th Crusade
1236: Christian reconquest of Córdoba
1261: Byzantine Empire regains Constantinople
1282: French driven from Sicily, which passes to Aragon
1200
1220
1240
1260
1280
1300
1204: King John loses English fiefs in northern France
1237: Start of Mongol conquest of Russia
1270: Death of Louis IX (St. Louis) on crusade
1271: Departure of Marco Polo for China

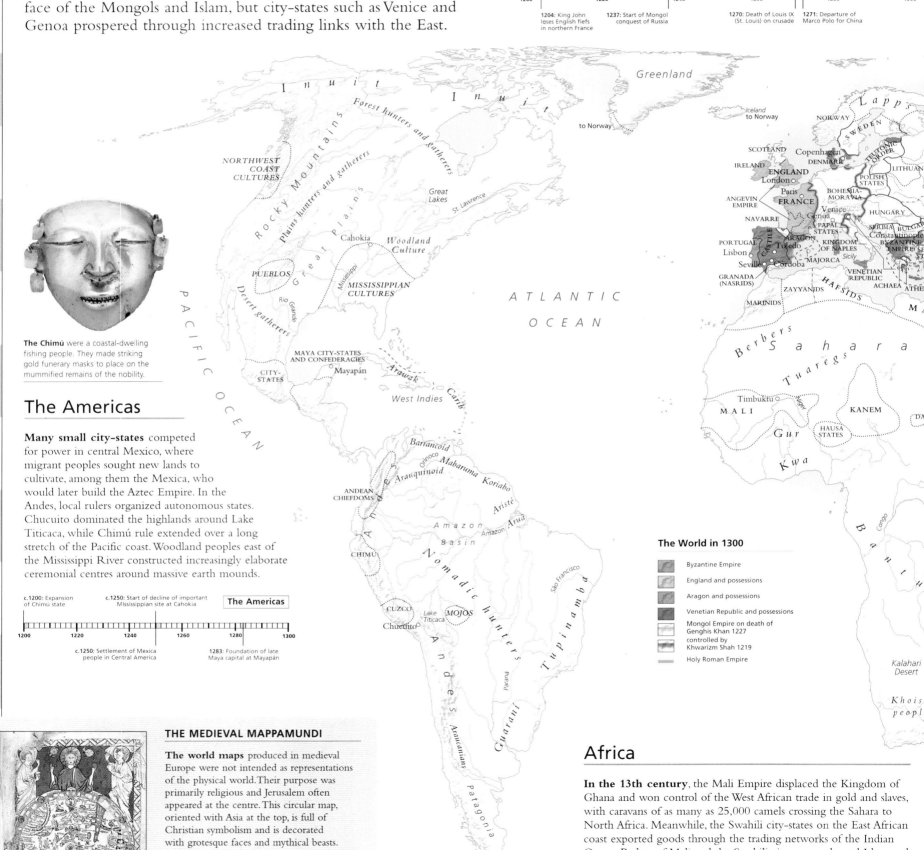

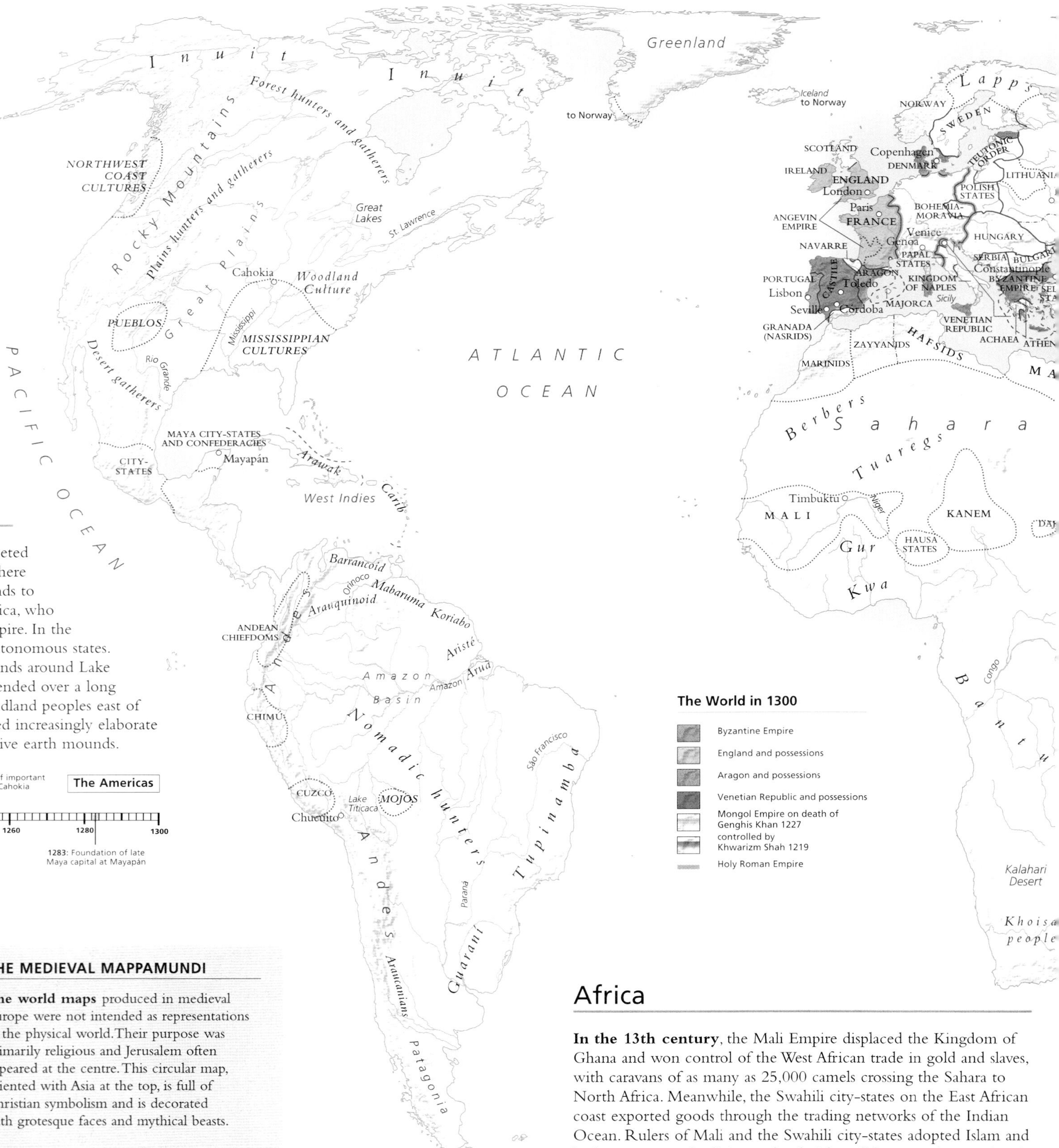

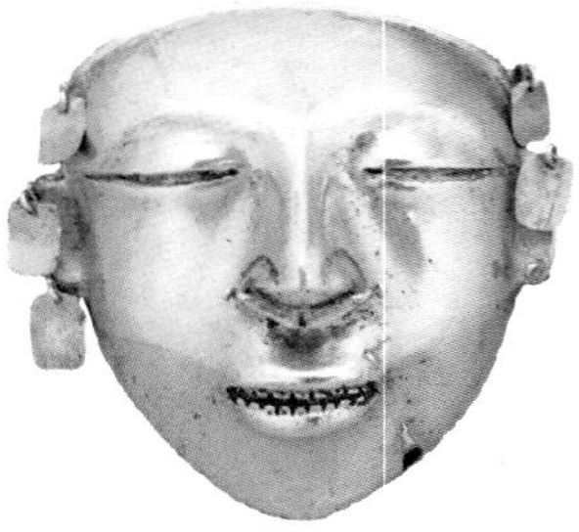

The Chimú were a coastal-dwelling fishing people. They made striking gold funerary masks to place on the mummified remains of the nobility.

The Americas

Many small city-states competed for power in central Mexico, where migrant peoples sought new lands to cultivate, among them the Mexica, who would later build the Aztec Empire. In the Andes, local rulers organized autonomous states. Chucuito dominated the highlands around Lake Titicaca, while Chimú rule extended over a long stretch of the Pacific coast. Woodland peoples east of the Mississippi River constructed increasingly elaborate ceremonial centres around massive earth mounds.

The Americas

c.1200: Expansion of Chimú state
c.1250: Start of decline of important Mississippian site at Cahokia
1200 – 1220 – 1240 – 1260 – 1280 – 1300
c.1250: Settlement of Mexica people in Central America
1283: Foundation of late Maya capital at Mayapán

The World in 1300

- Byzantine Empire
- England and possessions
- Aragon and possessions
- Venetian Republic and possessions
- Mongol Empire on death of Genghis Khan 1227
- controlled by Khwarizm Shah 1219
- Holy Roman Empire

THE MEDIEVAL MAPPAMUNDI

The world maps produced in medieval Europe were not intended as representations of the physical world. Their purpose was primarily religious and Jerusalem often appeared at the centre. This circular map, oriented with Asia at the top, is full of Christian symbolism and is decorated with grotesque faces and mythical beasts.

A 13th-century English psalter contains this tiny world map or *mappamundi*, which measures just 10 cm across.

Africa

In the 13th century, the Mali Empire displaced the Kingdom of Ghana and won control of the West African trade in gold and slaves, with caravans of as many as 25,000 camels crossing the Sahara to North Africa. Meanwhile, the Swahili city-states on the East African coast exported goods through the trading networks of the Indian Ocean. Rulers of Mali and the Swahili city-states adopted Islam and built mosques and religious schools. Islam did not reach central and southern Africa, but the trade it generated led to the establishment of wealthy inland states such as the Kingdom of Great Zimbabwe.

West Asia

In 1258 the Mongols sacked Baghdad and overthrew the Abbasid Caliphate. Their leaders established themselves as Il-Khans, nominally subordinate to the Great Khan in China. Their empire extended almost to the Mediterranean, where their westward expansion was halted by the Mamluks of Egypt. By 1300 most Mongols of the Il-Khanate had embraced Islam, as had many of their fellow Mongols of the Golden Horde. Meanwhile, the Seljuks and other Turkic peoples consolidated their position in formerly Byzantine territory by establishing regional states.

This lustre tile from 13th-century Persia is decorated with a verse from the Koran. The Mongols were too few to impose their beliefs on the peoples they conquered. Instead, many of them became Muslims.

THE MAGNETIC COMPASS

The Chinese had long known that a floating magnetized needle always points in the same direction. Their sailors started to make regular use of this fact in about 1100. By the 13th century, the magnetic compass was probably in widespread use among the Arab navigators of the Indian Ocean. In Europe, a written account of its principles appeared as early as 1190.

In the 13th century the Chinese simply floated a magnetized needle on water. This boxed compass is an early example.

SEE ALSO:

North America: pp.122–123

South America: pp.146–147

Africa: pp.162–163

Europe: pp.186–191

West Asia: pp.228–229

South and Southeast Asia: pp.244–245

North and East Asia: pp.262–265

West Asia

- **1219:** Mongol invasion of Khwarizm Empire
- **1231:** Mongols reconquer resurgent Empire of the Khwarizm Shah
- **1258:** Sack of Baghdad and fall of Abbasid Caliphate; Hülegü founds Il-Khanate
- **1260:** Battle of Ain Jalut; Mamluks defeat Mongol army north of Jerusalem
- **1265:** Death of Hülegü
- **1295:** Conversion of the Il-Khan Ghazan to Islam
- **1299:** Osman founds Ottoman state among the small Seljuk states in western Turkey

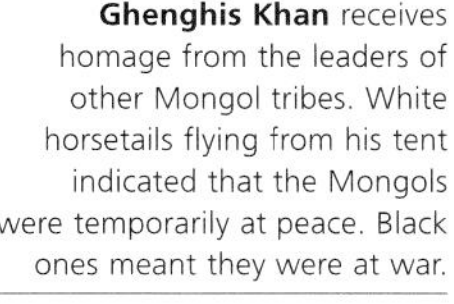

North and East Asia

Genghis Khan invaded northern China in 1211, but the Southern Song Empire fell only after a long campaign (1260–79) directed by Kublai Khan. China was the richest of all the Mongol conquests. Kublai became emperor and founded the Yuan dynasty. He appointed many foreigners to govern the empire and fostered both maritime and overland trade with other lands throughout East Asia. From Korea (Koryo) the Mongols made two failed attempts to invade Japan.

Ghenghis Khan receives homage from the leaders of other Mongol tribes. White horsetails flying from his tent indicated that the Mongols were temporarily at peace. Black ones meant they were at war.

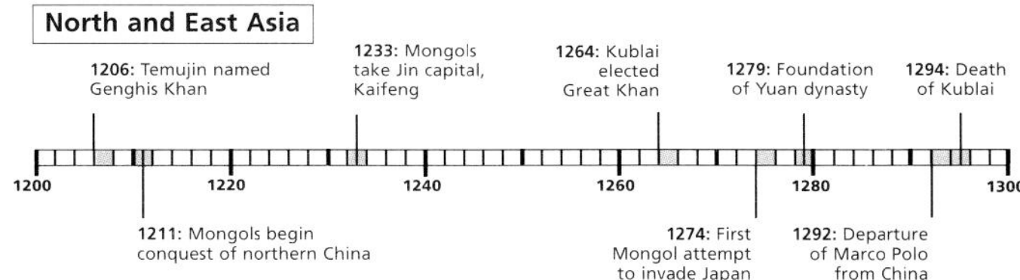

North and East Asia

- **1206:** Temujin named Genghis Khan
- **1211:** Mongols begin conquest of northern China
- **1233:** Mongols take Jin capital, Kaifeng
- **1264:** Kublai elected Great Khan
- **1274:** First Mongol attempt to invade Japan
- **1279:** Foundation of Yuan dynasty
- **1292:** Departure of Marco Polo from China
- **1294:** Death of Kublai

South and Southeast Asia

In 1206 Qutb al-din, leader of the Islamic raiders who had terrorized northern India for the past 30 years, fixed the capital of a new sultanate at Delhi. The Sultanate suffered occasional Mongol raids, whereas the Mongols made repeated forays from China into Annam and Pagan, without ever gaining secure control of the region. They also launched a massive seaborne attack on Java, but their tactics were ineffective in the island's tropical jungles.

The spectacular royal enclosure of Great Zimbabwe was rebuilt many times between the 11th and the 15th century. The kings owed their wealth to trade in cattle, gold, and copper.

The Qutb Minar minaret rises beside the Quwwat-al-Islam mosque in Delhi. Begun in 1199, it became a powerful symbol of Islamic rule in northern India.

Africa

- **1228:** Start of collapse of Almohad Empire in North Africa
- **1230:** Establishment of the Mali Empire by Sundiata
- **c.1250:** Building of stone mosques in Swahili city-states
- **1250:** Mamluk military caste takes over Egypt
- **1255:** Death of Sundiata
- **1269:** Marinids inflict final defeat on Almohads in Morocco
- **1270:** Expansion of Christian Kingdom of Ethiopia

South and Southeast Asia

- **1206:** Foundation of Sultanate of Delhi
- **1258:** First Mongol expedition to Annam
- **1288:** Kublai Khan gives up attempt to subdue Annam and Champa
- **1293:** Failed Mongol invasion of Java

THE AGE OF THE MONGOLS

Genghis Khan – the title means 'universal ruler' – was born Temujin, son of a minor Mongol chief.

THE NOMADIC HERDSMEN of the Mongolian steppe traded livestock, horses, and hides with the settled agricultural civilization of China to the south, but relations between the two were usually marked by hostility and suspicion. By the 13th century, the Chinese empire had become weak and fragmented. Into this power vacuum burst the Mongols, a fierce race of skilled horsemen, their normally warring tribes united under the inspired leadership of Genghis Khan. Genghis did not seek war at all costs; he first gave his enemies a chance to submit – on his terms. If they refused, he unleashed a campaign of terror, sacking cities and massacring entire populations. Although at first the Mongols numbered no more than a million, their ranks were swelled by Turks, Arabs, and other subject peoples. Genghis's successors extended his conquests across Asia and deep into Europe, but his empire then split into four khanates. By 1400, the Mongols were a divided and weakened force and most of their conquests had been lost.

Genghis Khan, preceded by Jebe, one of his most trusted commanders, leads a cavalry charge. Jebe and another great general, Sübedei, made the astonishing raid into Russia in 1222 that first made Europe aware of the Mongols' existence.

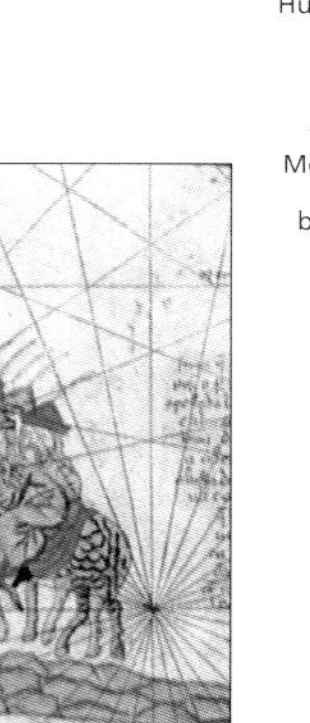

Caravan routes across Central Asia thrived in the climate of law and order imposed by Mongol rule. This illustration from the Catalan Atlas of 1375 shows a group of European merchants riding along the Silk Road.

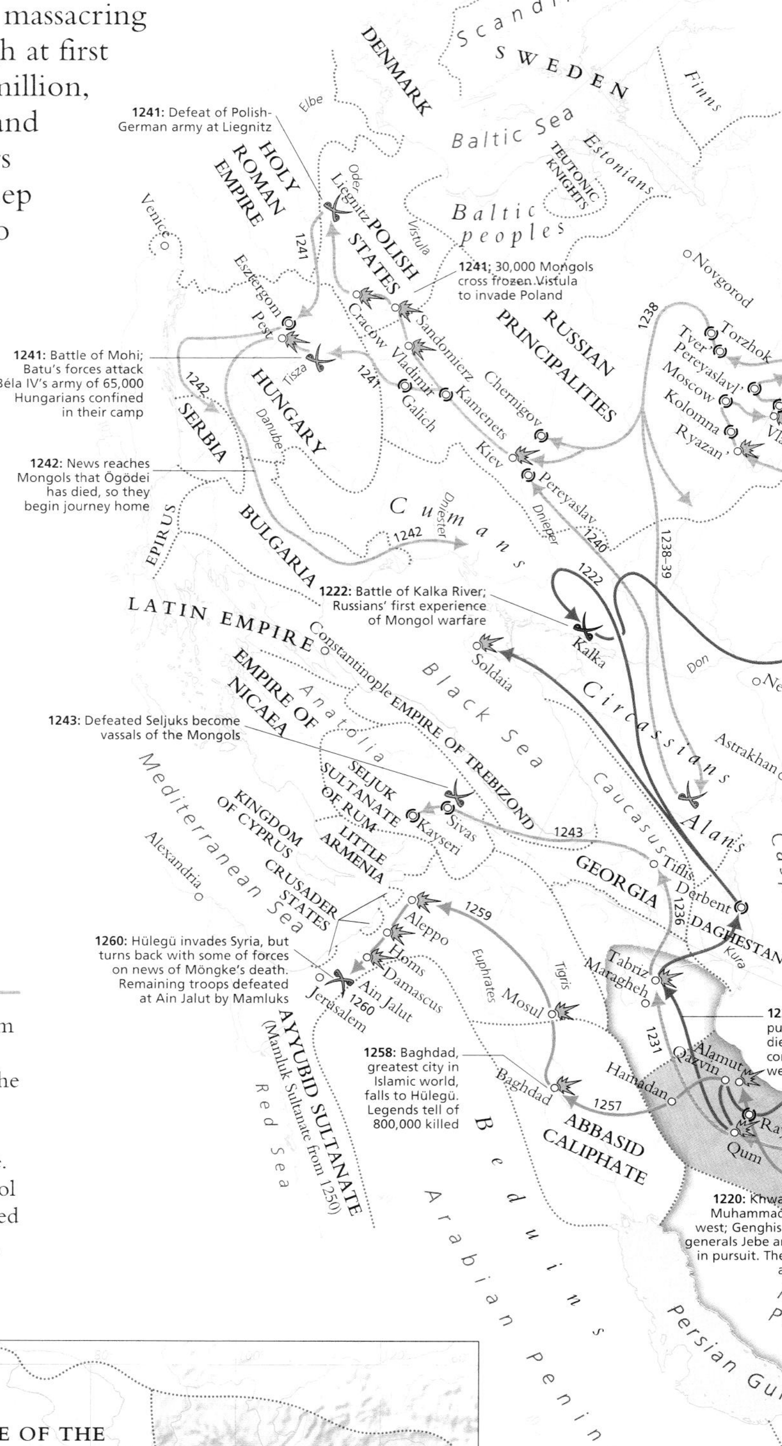

The Mongol peace

The Mongols' chief aim was always to exact tribute from conquered peoples, but they also brought long periods of peace; travellers were able to cross Eurasia in safety along the old Silk Road. In the reign of Genghis Khan's grandson Möngke (1251–59) it was said that a virgin with a pot of gold on her head could walk unmolested across his empire. The two most famous travellers to benefit from the Mongol peace were the Venetian merchant Marco Polo, who claimed to have spent 17 years in the employment of Kublai Khan, and Ibn Battuta, a Muslim legal scholar from Tangier in Morocco, who also travelled as far as China.

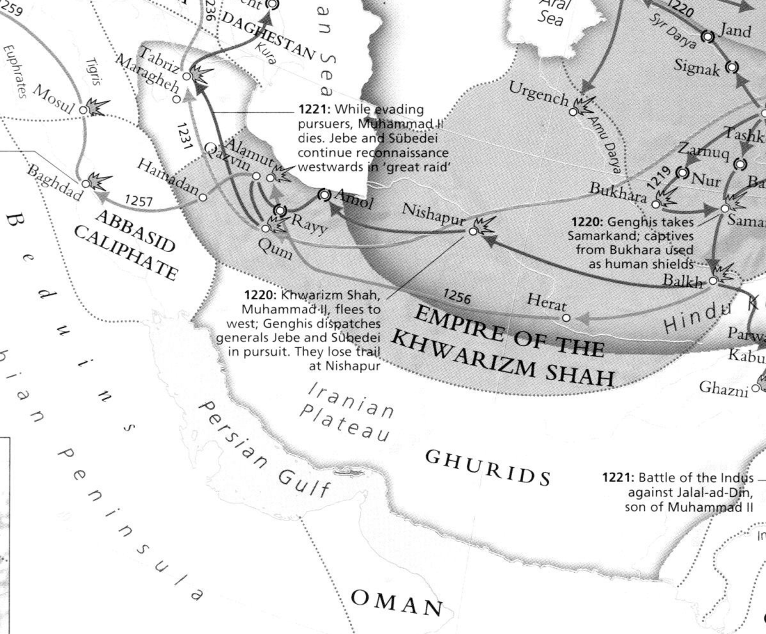

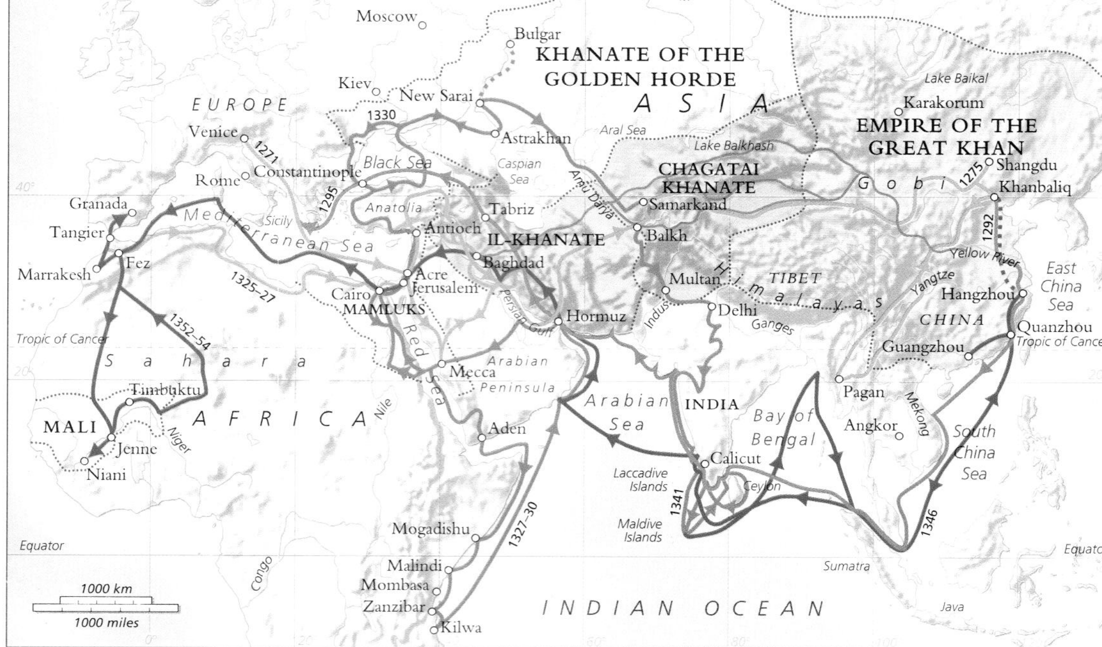

2 Eurasia and Africa c.1300

route of Marco Polo 1271–1295

route of Ibn Battuta 1325–1345

disputed journeys of Ibn Battuta

Silk Road

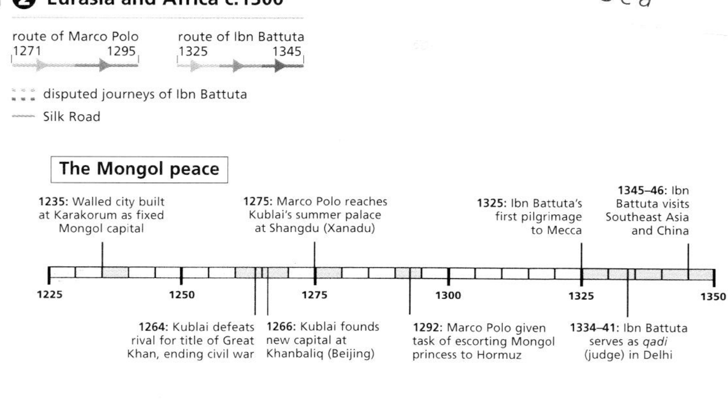

The Mongol peace

1235: Walled city built at Karakorum as fixed Mongol capital

1264: Kublai defeats rival for title of Great Khan, ending civil war

1266: Kublai founds new capital at Khanbaliq (Beijing)

1275: Marco Polo reaches Kublai's summer palace at Shangdu (Xanadu)

1292: Marco Polo given task of escorting Mongol princess to Hormuz

1325: Ibn Battuta's first pilgrimage to Mecca

1334–41: Ibn Battuta serves as *qadi* (judge) in Delhi

1345–46: Ibn Battuta visits Southeast Asia and China

The Mongol conquests

In less than 20 years, in a series of conquests without parallel in history, Genghis Khan shattered the Muslim states of Central Asia, overran northern China, and sent troops on a lightning raid into Russia. Genghis's immediate successor was his third son Ögödei, whose reign as Great Khan saw the destruction of the Jin and Khwarizm empires, continued fighting with Song China, and an invasion of Europe that reached Hungary and Poland. The conquest of the Song was completed by Kublai Khan, a grandson of Genghis, who became emperor of China, while Kublai's brother, Hülegü, founder of the Il-Khanate, destroyed the Abbasid Caliphate, sacking the great Islamic city of Baghdad. The first setback to Mongol expansion came at the hands of the Mamluks, who, in 1260, prevented their advance into Egypt at Ain Jalut.

Mongol conquests of the 13th century

- **1206:** Mongols united by Genghis Khan
- **1211:** First invasion of Jin Empire
- **1219:** Genghis attacks Khwarizm
- **1227:** Death of Genghis
- **1229:** Ögödei elected Great Khan
- **1242:** Batu founds Golden Horde
- **1258:** Sack of Baghdad
- **1260:** Hülegü invades Syria; Mongols suffer first major defeat at Ain Jalut
- **1279:** Last Song resistance crushed
- **1281:** Second failed invasion of Japan
- **1294:** Death of Kublai

SEE ALSO:

Europe: pp.188–189

West Asia: pp.228–229

South and Southeast Asia: pp.244–245

North and East Asia: pp.262–265

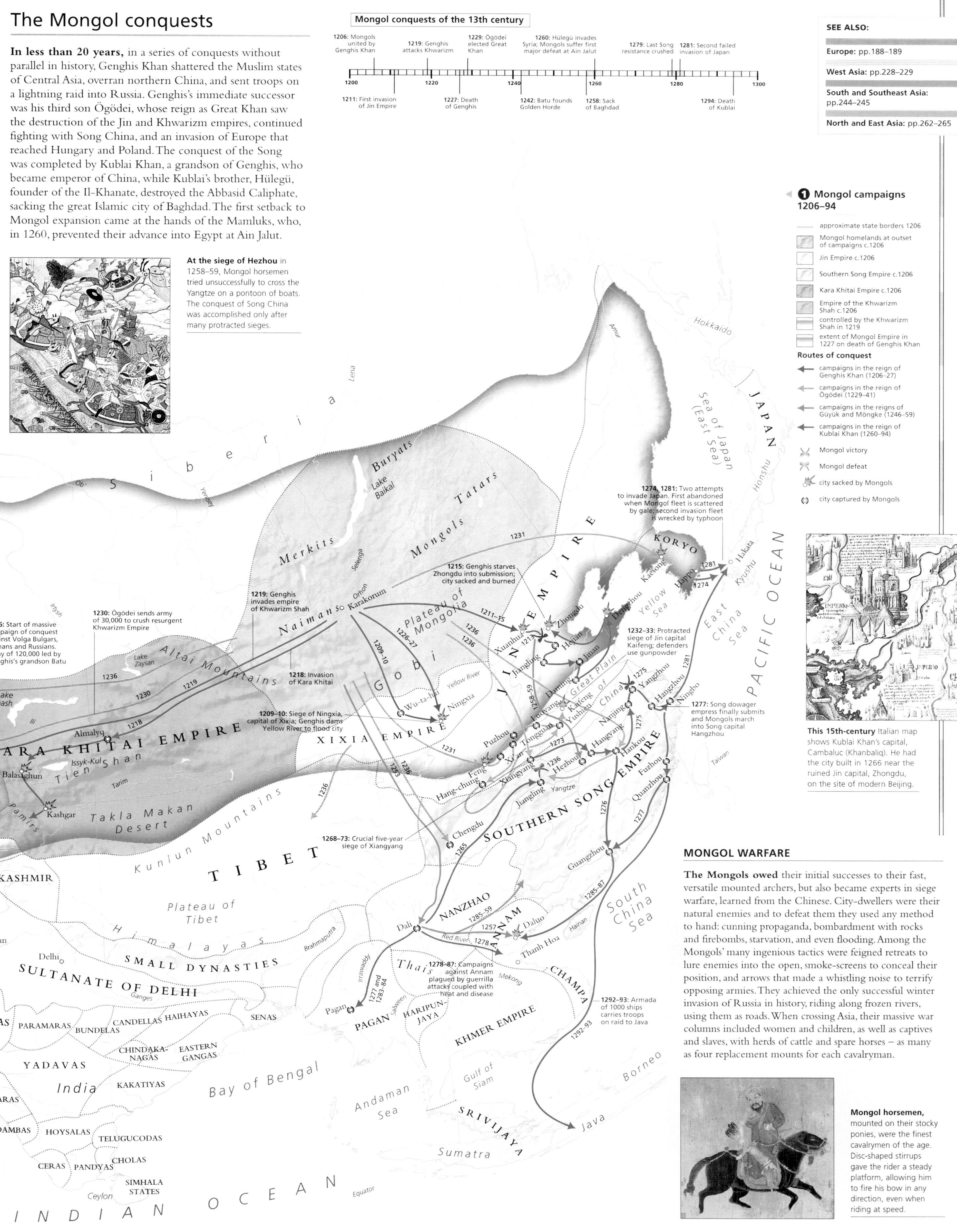

At the siege of Hezhou in 1258–59, Mongol horsemen tried unsuccessfully to cross the Yangtze on a pontoon of boats. The conquest of Song China was accomplished only after many protracted sieges.

This 15th-century Italian map shows Kublai Khan's capital, Cambaluc (Khanbaliq). He had the city built in 1266 near the ruined Jin capital, Zhongdu, on the site of modern Beijing.

MONGOL WARFARE

The Mongols owed their initial successes to their fast, versatile mounted archers, but also became experts in siege warfare, learned from the Chinese. City-dwellers were their natural enemies and to defeat them they used any method to hand: cunning propaganda, bombardment with rocks and firebombs, starvation, and even flooding. Among the Mongols' many ingenious tactics were feigned retreats to lure enemies into the open, smoke-screens to conceal their position, and arrows that made a whistling noise to terrify opposing armies. They achieved the only successful winter invasion of Russia in history, riding along frozen rivers, using them as roads. When crossing Asia, their massive war columns included women and children, as well as captives and slaves, with herds of cattle and spare horses – as many as four replacement mounts for each cavalryman.

Mongol horsemen, mounted on their stocky ponies, were the finest cavalrymen of the age. Disc-shaped stirrups gave the rider a steady platform, allowing him to fire his bow in any direction, even when riding at speed.

THE WORLD 1300–1400

DURING THE 14TH CENTURY epidemics of bubonic plague swept across the Old World from China and Korea to the west coast of Europe. Dramatic demographic decline led to economic and social disruption that weakened states throughout Eurasia and North Africa. In addition, the onset of the so-called 'Little Ice Age', which would last till the 19th century, brought bad weather and poor harvests to many of the regions affected by plague. The Mongol empires, which had dominated Eurasia since the conquests of Genghis Khan in the 13th century, began to disintegrate, though the Khanate of the Golden Horde maintained its hegemony in southern Russia into the 15th century. In both China and Persia the Mongols were assimilated into the local population, but in China, a new dynasty, the Ming, introduced a Han Chinese aristocratic regime.

The Black Death reached Europe from Asia in 1347. In three years it probably killed one third of the population. The fear it generated is captured in this image of Death strangling a plague victim.

Europe

Europe struggled to recover from the social and economic disruption caused by the Black Death. Scarcity of labour led peasants and workers to seek improved conditions and higher wages, but landlords and employers resisted their demands, provoking many revolts in western Europe. France suffered too from the military campaigns of the Hundred Years' War, fuelled by the dynastic ambitions of English kings. Religious differences also brought disorder. Rival popes residing in Rome and Avignon both claimed authority over the Catholic church, while in England the Lollards challenged the authority and doctrine of the church itself.

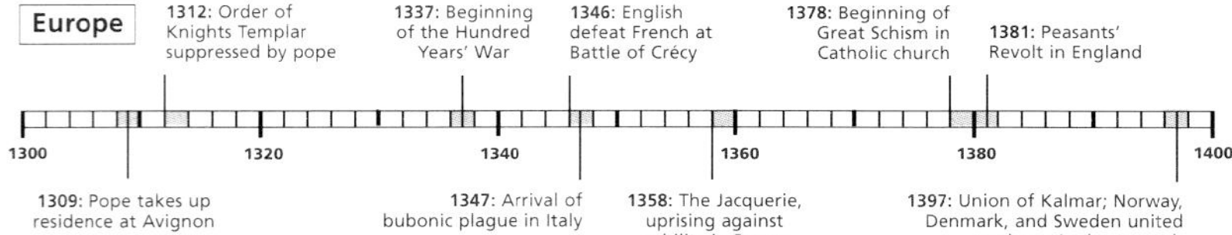
Europe
1312: Order of Knights Templar suppressed by pope
1337: Beginning of the Hundred Years' War
1346: English defeat French at Battle of Crécy
1378: Beginning of Great Schism in Catholic church
1381: Peasants' Revolt in England
1300
1320
1340
1360
1380
1400
1309: Pope takes up residence at Avignon
1347: Arrival of bubonic plague in Italy
1358: The Jacquerie, uprising against nobility in France
1397: Union of Kalmar; Norway, Denmark, and Sweden united under a single monarch

The World in 1400

- Ming Empire
- Byzantine Empire
- Ottoman Empire
- England and possessions
- Union of Kalmar
- Aragon and possessions
- Muscovy
- Genoa and possessions
- Burgundy and possessions
- Venetian Republic and possessions
- Habsburg possessions
- Luxembourg possessions
- Holy Roman Empire
- Tughluq's Empire 1335

THE CATALAN ATLAS

The Catalans were fine seamen who sailed regularly as far as the Black Sea and the Baltic. The Catalan Atlas of 1375 is a large world map on wooden panels, probably the work of the king of Aragon's mapmaker, Abraham Cresques, a Majorcan Jew. Most of the information for Europe is derived from the mariners' charts known as portolans that were used by Italian and Catalan ships' captains. The main source for China and the Far East, which are far less accurately mapped, is Marco Polo's account of his journeys *(see p.68)*.

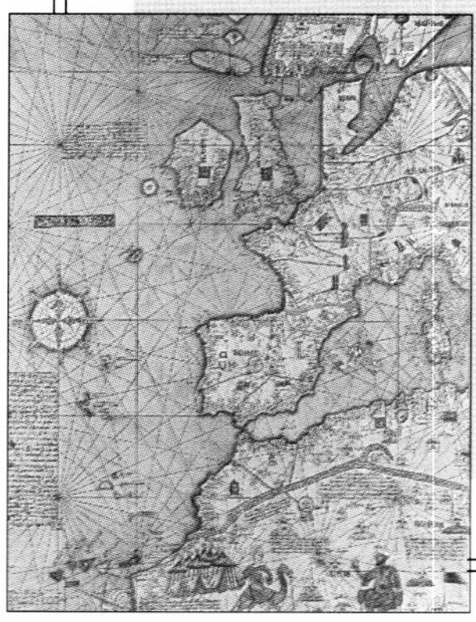

The Catalan map gives a comprehensive and accurate picture of the coastline and ports of Europe and North Africa.

Africa

The Islamic Mali Empire controlled the trans-Saharan caravan trade, using the profits to maintain a powerful army and dominate West Africa. Gold and slaves went north in exchange for salt, textiles, horses, and manufactured goods. Tales of the wealth of Mali spread to Europe and West Asia, especially after the ostentatious pilgrimage to Mecca made by one of the country's most powerful rulers, Mansa Musa. Many smaller states emerged in the region as rulers sought to ensure a regular supply of trade goods. The Swahili cities of East Africa were not hit by plague, but commercial traffic declined as their trading partners in Asia experienced social and economic disruption.

THE CANNON

The Chinese had a long tradition of using gunpowder weapons, including bamboo tubes that fired arrows and bullets. The English word 'cannon' comes from the Italian *cannone*, meaning a large bamboo cane. Metal cannon were probably first used in China, but by the early 14th century were in action across Asia and in most of Europe. The earliest metal cannons in Europe were forged, but these were superseded by much larger ones cast using the technology initially developed for making church bells.

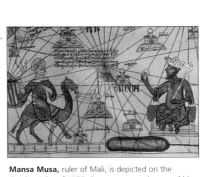

The cannon was primarily used as a siege weapon. Its effectiveness had a major influence on castle design.

West Asia

During the late 14th century the Turkish warrior chieftain Timur (Tamerlane), who claimed descent from Genghis Khan, carved out a vast central Asian empire, and built himself a magnificent capital at Samarkand. Timur invaded India and sacked the city of Delhi, and he was planning an invasion of China when he died in 1405. One other empire expanded during this period – that of the Ottoman Turks, who seized Anatolia and encroached on Byzantine holdings in southeastern Europe. By 1400 the once-mighty Byzantine Empire consisted of Constantinople and a few coastal regions in Greece and western Anatolia that maintained maritime links with the capital.

Timur's ambition and cruelty revived memories of Genghis Khan. He instilled fear into conquered peoples and opponents of his rule by building towers studded with the severed heads of his victims.

SEE ALSO:

North America: pp.122–123

South America: pp.146–147

Africa: pp.162–163

Europe: pp.188–191

West Asia: pp.228–231

South and Southeast Asia: pp.242–243

North and East Asia: pp.262–267

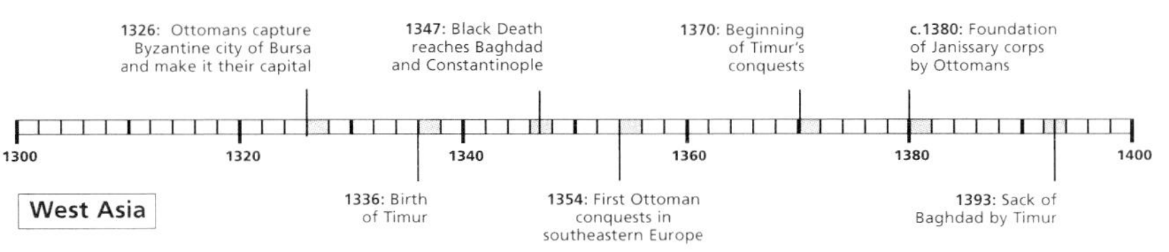

West Asia

- **1326:** Ottomans capture Byzantine city of Bursa and make it their capital
- **1336:** Birth of Timur
- **1347:** Black Death reaches Baghdad and Constantinople
- **1354:** First Ottoman conquests in southeastern Europe
- **1370:** Beginning of Timur's conquests
- **c.1380:** Foundation of Janissary corps by Ottomans
- **1393:** Sack of Baghdad by Timur

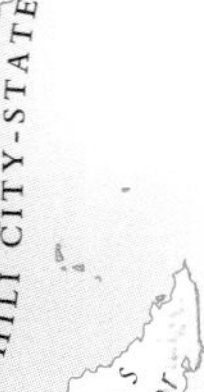

East Asia

Plague, floods, and famine all contributed to the build-up of Chinese resentment at Mongol rule. Local uprisings became increasingly frequent, culminating in 1356 in a rebellion in southeastern China, which carried Zhu Yuanzhang, founder of the Ming dynasty, to power. War with the Mongols continued for some years, but the Chinese drove them back to their original homelands in the north. Japan had successfully resisted Mongol attempts at invasion, but their own Kamakura shogunate collapsed in 1333. The new shoguns of the Ashikaga family never succeeded in exercising the same degree of control over the country.

The Ming emperors restored Chinese values after a century of Mongol rule. This statue portrays a guardian of the spirit world.

East Asia

- **1335:** Rebellions against Mongol rule in China
- **1336:** Foundation of Ashikaga shogunate in Japan
- **1351:** Massive flooding of Yellow River
- **1368:** Establishment of the Ming dynasty
- **1392:** Foundation of Yi dynasty in Korea

South and Southeast Asia

In India, the Sultanate of Delhi reached its greatest extent in the reign of Tughluq, but by the end of the century had lost control of most of the peninsula. The small kingdoms of mainland Southeast Asia all maintained diplomatic and commercial links with Ming China. The new Thai kingdom of Siam proved especially skilful in its dealings with its powerful neighbour to the north. During the 14th century island Southeast Asia fell increasingly under the influence of the Majapahit empire based in Java. A Javanese navy, financed by taxes levied on the lucrative trade in spices, patrolled the waters of the archipelago and controlled maritime trade.

Mansa Musa, ruler of Mali, is depicted on the Catalan Atlas of 1375. Europeans were in awe of his reported wealth and the splendour of his court.

The marble dome of Tughluq's mausoleum rises above the ramparts of the fortified city he built at Delhi in 1321.

Africa

- **1324:** Pilgrimage to Mecca by Mansa Musa of Mali
- **1331:** Ibn Battuta's voyage to the Swahili cities of East Africa
- **1344:** Ethiopia at its height at death of ruler Amde Sion
- **1347:** Marinids take Tunis
- **1352:** Ibn Battuta's travels to the Mali Empire
- **c.1390:** Formation of the kingdom of Kongo

South and Southeast Asia

- **1320:** Muhammad ibn Tughluq succeeds to Sultanate of Delhi
- **1343:** Majapahit Empire completes conquest of Bali
- **c.1350:** Founding of Ayutthaya, capital of new kingdom of Siam
- **1378:** Sukhothai becomes vassal of Siam and is gradually absorbed
- **1398:** Delhi sacked by Timur

TRADE AND BIOLOGICAL DIFFUSION

CAMPAIGNS OF IMPERIAL EXPANSION, mass migration, cross-cultural trade, and long-distance travel all facilitated the spread of agricultural crops, domesticated animals, and diseases throughout much of the Old World. From 500 to 1500 CE, an array of historical processes helped introduce biological species to new regions and peoples. Chinese rulers extended their authority south of the Yangtze river; Muslim armies pushed into India, Persia, and North Africa; Bantu-speaking peoples migrated throughout most of sub-Saharan Africa; Muslim merchants pursued commercial opportunities throughout the Indian Ocean basin and across the Sahara; and missionaries, pilgrims, diplomats, administrators, and other travellers ventured throughout Eurasia and North Africa. Biological exchanges resulting from these changes profoundly influenced the development of societies throughout the eastern hemisphere.

The peripatetic black rat, at home in a wide range of human environments, was the host for plague-carrying fleas.

Skulls, crossbones, and other images of death were frequently represented in both religious and secular art during the period of the so-called 'Black Death'.

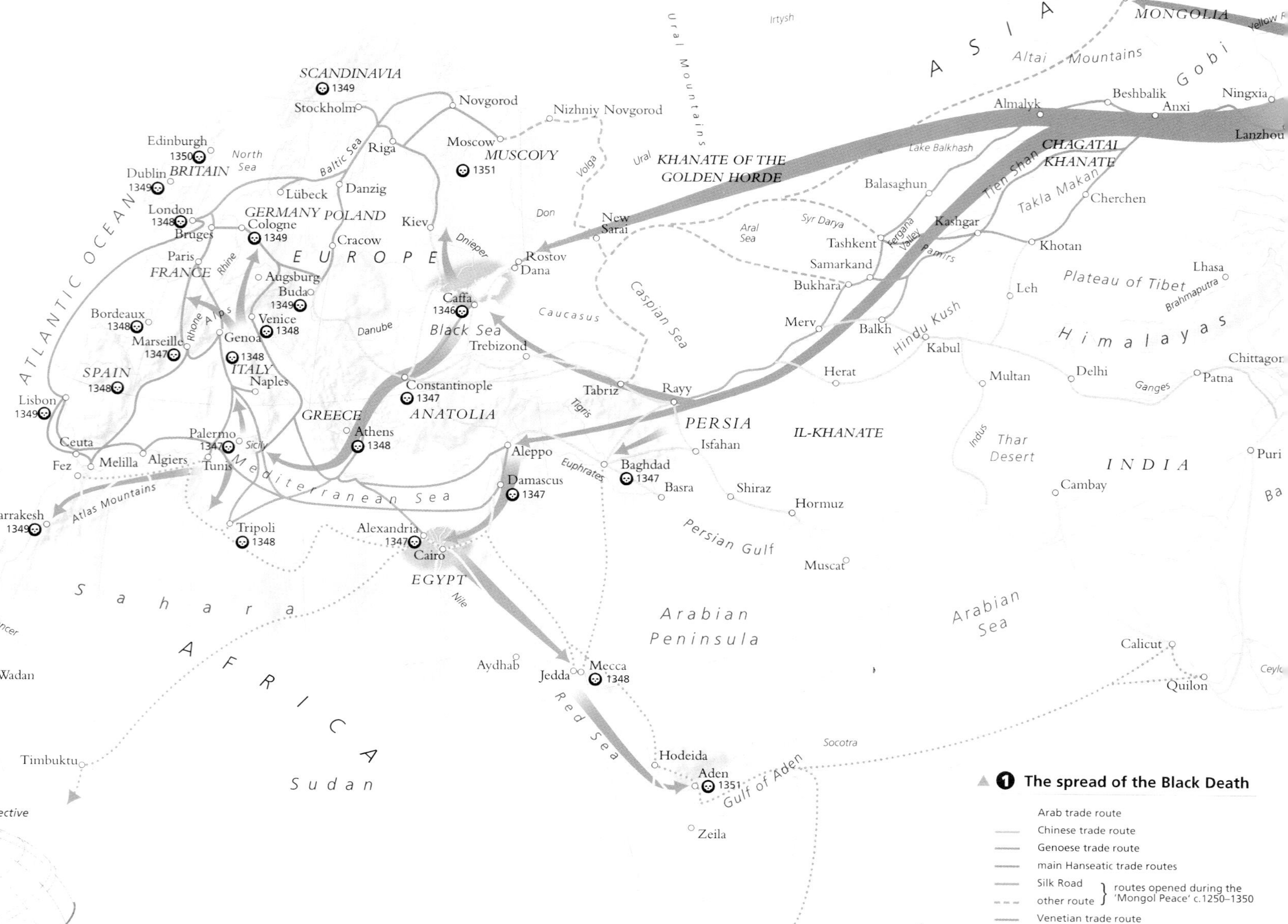

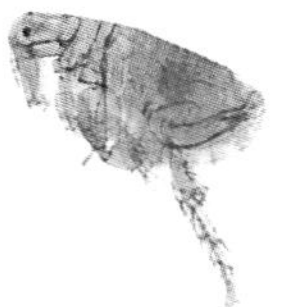

The flea is the agent of transmission of bubonic plague between rats and humans.

1 The spread of the Black Death

- Arab trade route
- Chinese trade route
- Genoese trade route
- main Hanseatic trade routes
- Silk Road } routes opened during the 'Mongol Peace' c.1250–1350
- other route } routes opened during the 'Mongol Peace' c.1250–1350
- Venetian trade route
- other trade route
- principal route of Hajj pilgrimage to Mecca
- progress of bubonic plague
- area of earliest outbreak of bubonic plague
- area of outbreak of bubonic plague
- recorded outbreak of bubonic plague

Scale varies with perspective

Come fu una morìa in molti luoghi e morìono migliaia di persone ... Essendo il mondo tanto mal disposto per i peccati delli uomini, Adiutorio ...

At the height of the Black Death in Europe, so many people died daily that it was impossible to bury them all separately. The bodies were buried together in mass graves, usually outside the settlement walls. This manuscript illustration shows plague victims carried off by agents of Death.

The spread of plague during the 14th century

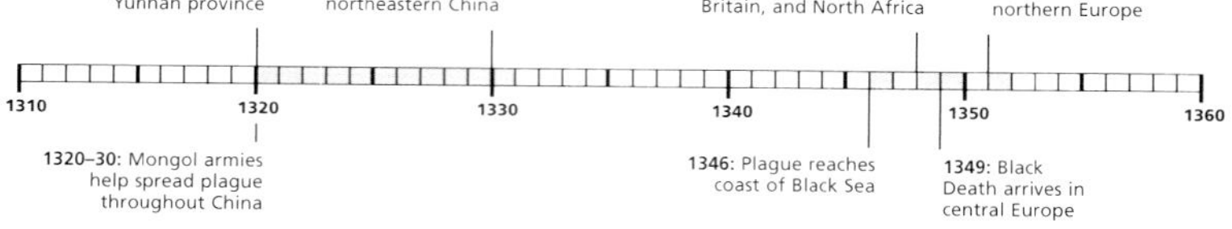

- **1320:** Outbreak of plague in Yunnan province
- **1320–30:** Mongol armies help spread plague throughout China
- **1330:** Plague reaches northeastern China
- **1346:** Plague reaches coast of Black Sea
- **1348:** Black Death hits Greece, Italy, France, Spain, Britain, and North Africa
- **1349:** Black Death arrives in central Europe
- **1351:** Black Death reaches much of northern Europe

The plague made no concessions to status, infecting rich and poor alike. This 14th-century painting shows the deathbed of Queen Anne of Bohemia, wife of King Richard II of England.

The spread of bubonic plague

Bubonic plague has long maintained an endemic presence in rodent communities in both Yunnan in southwest China and the Great Lakes region of East Africa. In the early 14th century, Mongol armies helped infected fleas spread from Yunnan to the rest of China. In 1331 an outbreak of plague reportedly carried away 90% of the population in parts of northeast China, and by the 1350s there were widely scattered epidemics throughout China. From China, bubonic plague spread rapidly west along the Silk Roads of Central Asia. By 1346 it had reached the Black Sea. Muslim merchants carried it south and west to southwest Asia, Egypt, and North Africa, while Italian merchants carried it west to Italy and then to northern and western Europe, where it became known as the Black Death. Up to one-third of Europe's population is thought to have died in this one episode.

The changing balance of world population

The spread of diseases and agricultural crops decisively influenced population levels throughout the Old World. In sub-Saharan Africa, for example, bananas grew well in forested regions that did not favour yams and millet, the earliest staples of Bantu cultivators. In 500 CE the population of sub-Saharan Africa was about 12 million, but following the spread of bananas it rose to 20 million by 1000 and 35.5 million by 1500. The spread of fast-ripening rice in China fuelled an even more dramatic demographic surge: from 60 million in 1000, when fast-ripening rice went north from Vietnam to the Yangtze river valley, the Chinese population climbed to 100 million in 1100 and 115 million in 1200. However, beginning in the 14th century, bubonic plague raced through densely-populated lands from China to Morocco, thinning human numbers with drastic effect. By 1400, China's population had fallen to about 70 million.

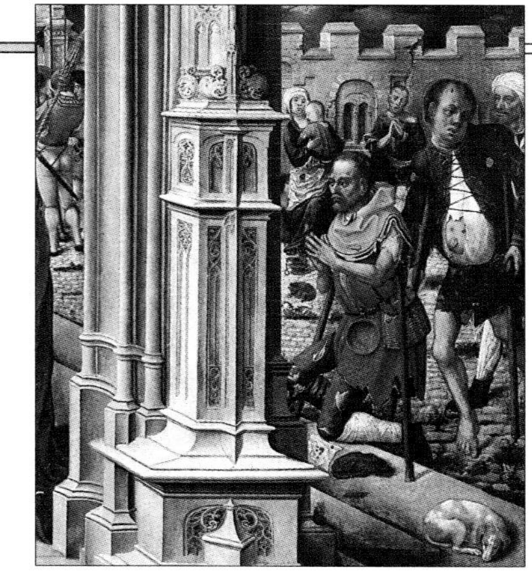

SEE ALSO:
Africa: pp.162–163
Europe: pp.188–193
West Asia: pp.228–229
North and East Asia: pp.262–263

Many people were displaced by the depopulation of the Black Death and the societal changes that it wrought. Those reduced to begging often sought alms at the doors of churches or other religious foundations.

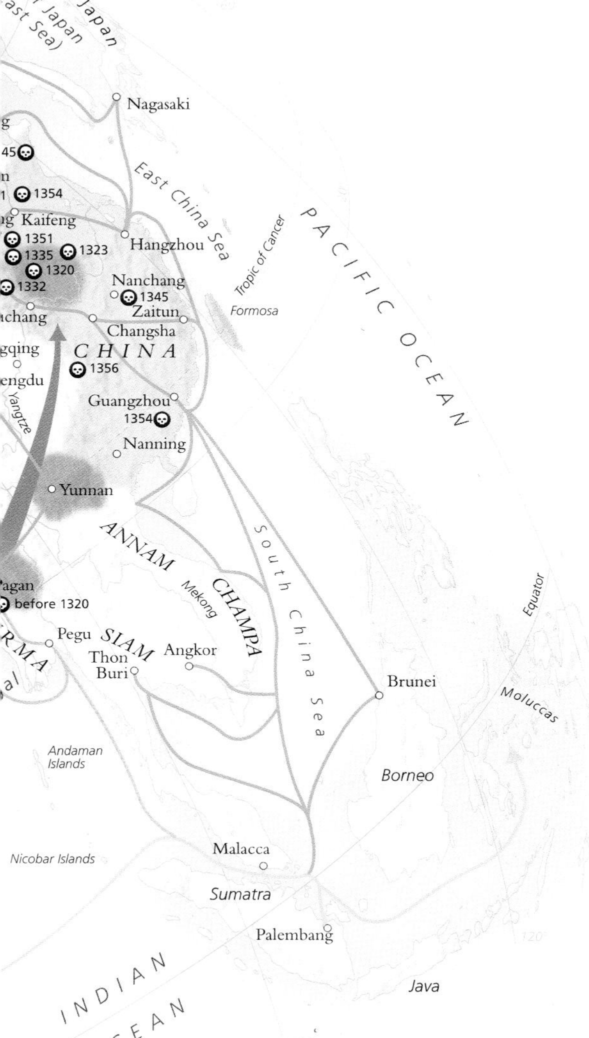

Some towns and villages suffered such depradations in population during the Black Death that they were abandoned by those who were left. The ruined church *(left)* is one of few remnants of the former village of Calceby, in the fenlands of eastern England.

2 Distribution of world population c.1400

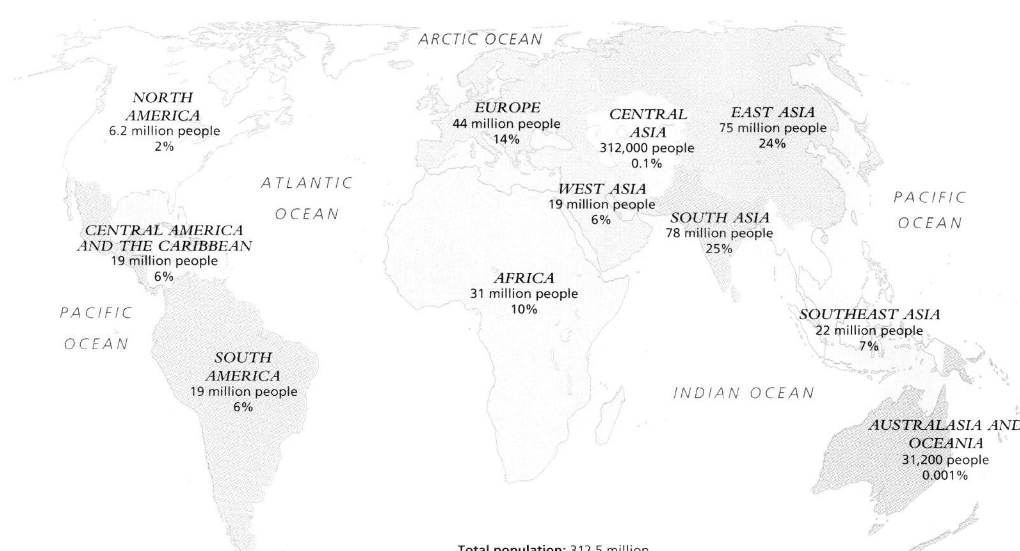

3 The diffusion of staple crops to c.1500

Original source areas (pre-700)
- bananas
- sugar cane
- cotton
- sorghum

Spread of crops c.700–1500
- spread of bananas
- spread of sugar cane
- spread of cotton
- spread of sorghum

Areas to which crops had spread by 1500
- bananas
- sugar cane
- cotton
- sorghum

Sugar cane was taken westward to Europe from India from c.600 CE. This 16th-century engraving of a Sicilian sugar mill shows raw sugar being transformed into sugar loaves.

The diffusion of staple crops

A massive diffusion of agricultural crops took place between about 700 and 1400 CE. Most crops spread from tropical or subtropical lands in South and Southeast Asia to the more temperate regions of the eastern hemisphere. Many crops moved with the aid of Muslim merchants, administrators, diplomats, soldiers, missionaries, pilgrims, and other travellers who visited lands from Morocco and Spain to Java and southern China. Sugar cane, native to New Guinea, arrived in the Mediterranean basin as a result of this biological diffusion, along with hard wheat, aubergines, spinach, artichokes, lemons, and limes. Other crops that dispersed widely during this era included rice, sorghum, bananas, coconuts, watermelons, oranges, mangoes, cotton, indigo, and henna.

THE WORLD 1400–1500

BY 1500 MOST OF THE EASTERN HEMISPHERE had recovered from the depopulation caused by the Black Death in the 14th century. China began the 15th century by sponsoring naval expeditions in the Indian Ocean, but in the 1430s the Ming rulers ended these voyages and concentrated on their land empire. In southwest Asia, two Turkish peoples established strong empires – the Ottomans in Anatolia and the Safavids in Persia. European states, meanwhile, were starting to build central governments with standing armies and gunpowder weapons. In the course of the 15th century Portuguese mariners settled the Atlantic islands, explored the west coast of Africa, and completed a sea voyage to India. It was, however, a Spanish expedition under the Genoese Columbus that crossed the Atlantic to make contact with the Americas, where the Aztec and Inca empires ruled over complex organized agricultural societies.

North America

The Aztec Empire reached its height in the late 1400s, exacting heavy tribute from the small city-states it had conquered. Through trade, Aztec influence reached far beyond the borders of the empire, extending across most of Central America as far as the Pueblo farmers north of the Rio Grande. In the woodlands around the Mississippi River, mound-building peoples maintained sizeable communities based on the cultivation of maize.

Human sacrifice to the sun god Huitzilopochtli was the core of the Aztec religion. Thousands of prisoners might be killed in a single ceremony.

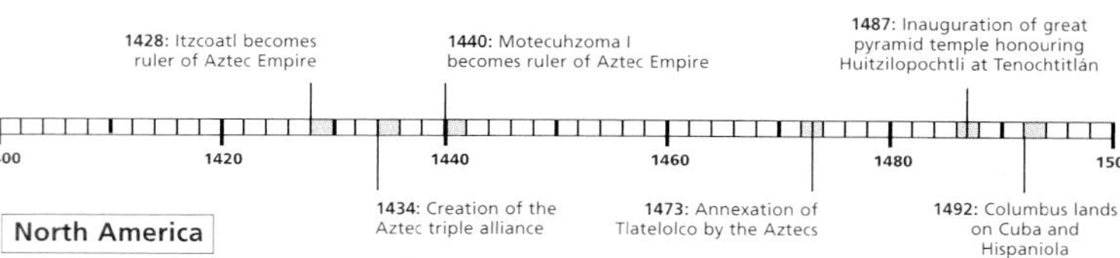
1428: Itzcoatl becomes ruler of Aztec Empire
1440: Motecuhzoma I becomes ruler of Aztec Empire
1487: Inauguration of great pyramid temple honouring Huitzilopochtli at Tenochtitlan
1400
1420
1440
1460
1480
1500
North America
1434: Creation of the Aztec triple alliance
1473: Annexation of Tlatelolco by the Aztecs
1492: Columbus lands on Cuba and Hispaniola

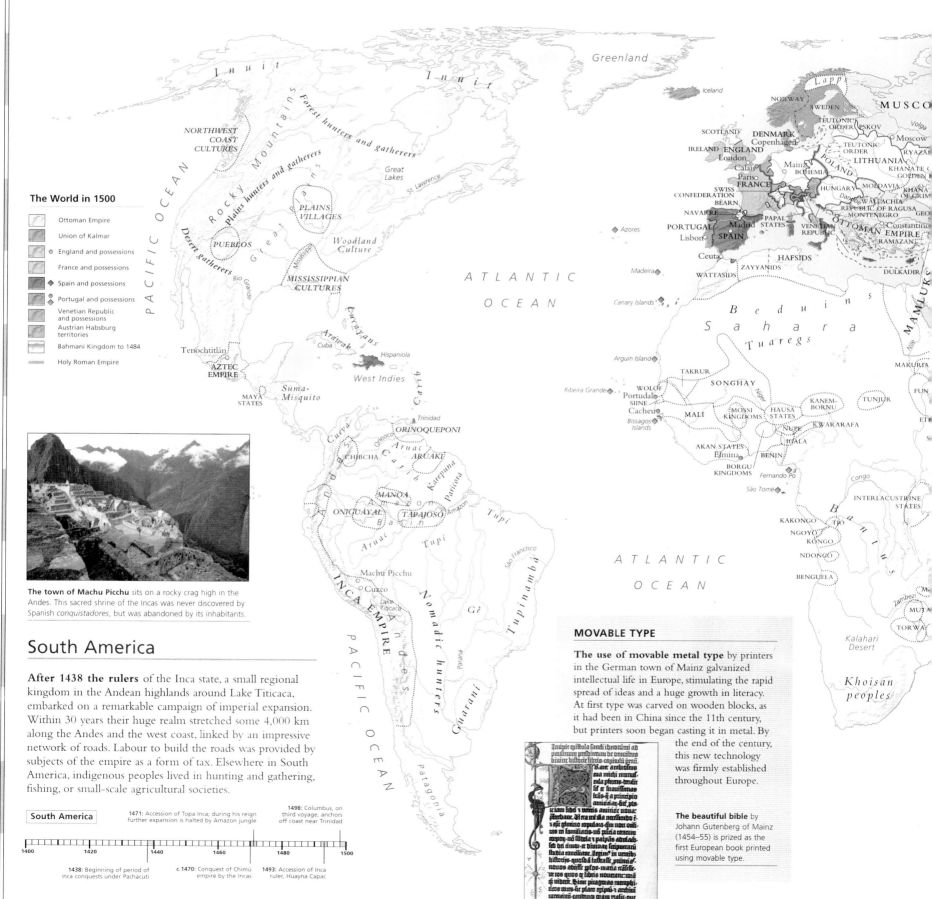

The World in 1500

- Ottoman Empire
- Union of Kalmar
- England and possessions
- France and possessions
- Spain and possessions
- Portugal and possessions
- Venetian Republic and possessions
- Austrian Habsburg territories
- Bahmani Kingdom to 1484
- Holy Roman Empire

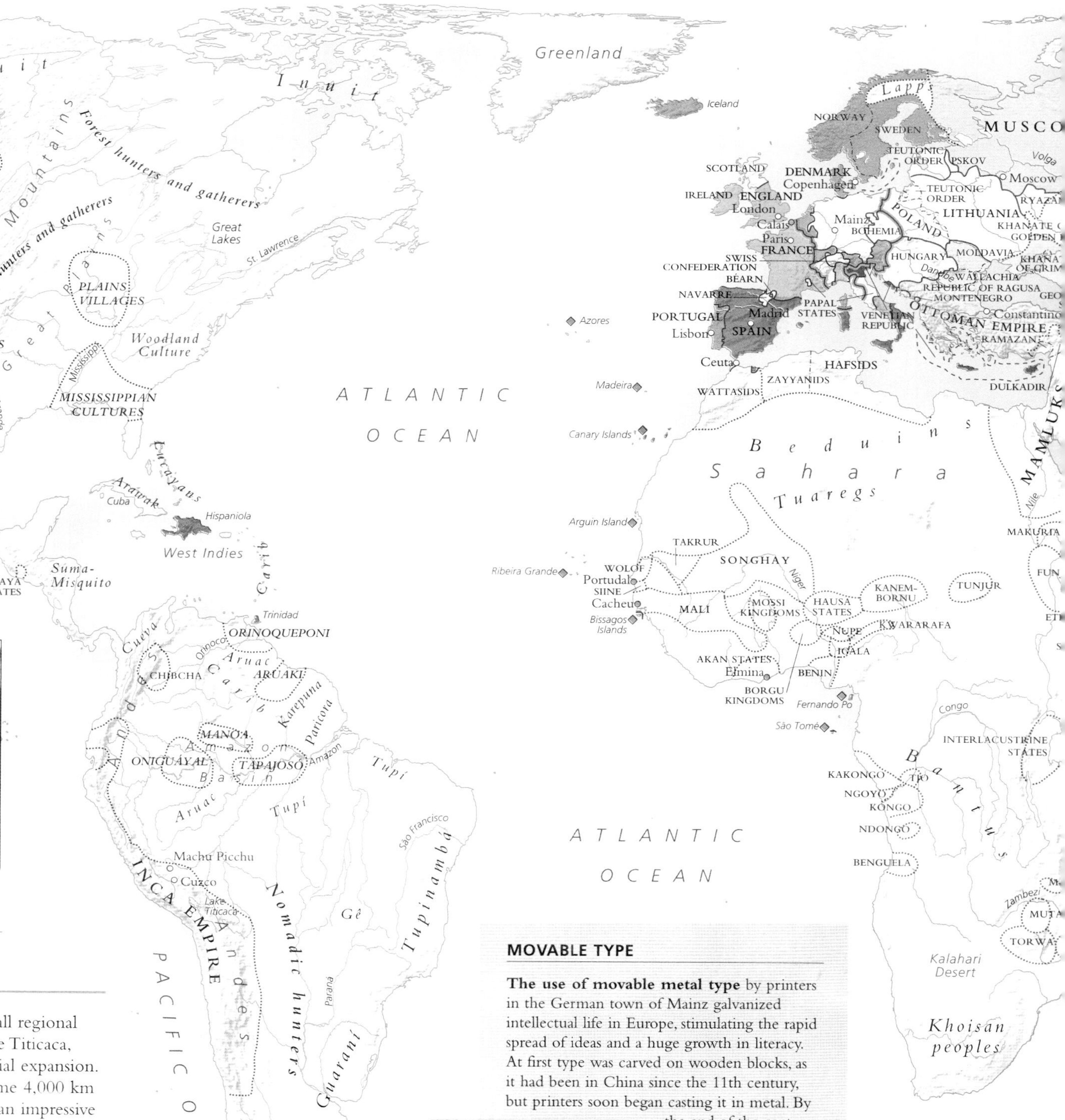

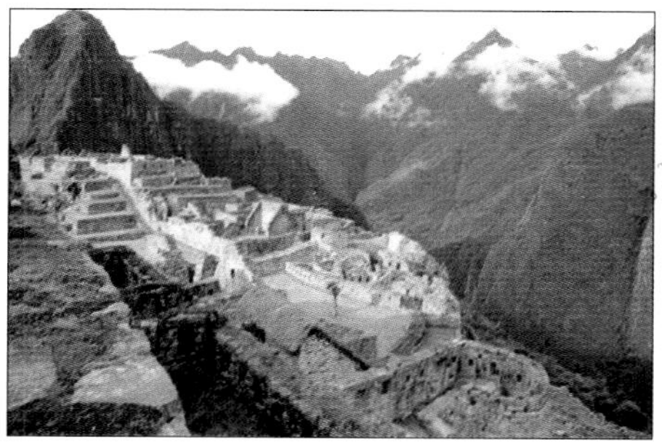

The town of Machu Picchu sits on a rocky crag high in the Andes. This sacred shrine of the Incas was never discovered by Spanish *conquistadores*, but was abandoned by its inhabitants.

South America

After 1438 the rulers of the Inca state, a small regional kingdom in the Andean highlands around Lake Titicaca, embarked on a remarkable campaign of imperial expansion. Within 30 years their huge realm stretched some 4,000 km along the Andes and the west coast, linked by an impressive network of roads. Labour to build the roads was provided by subjects of the empire as a form of tax. Elsewhere in South America, indigenous peoples lived in hunting and gathering, fishing, or small-scale agricultural societies.

South America

1471: Accession of Topa Inca; during his reign further expansion is halted by Amazon jungle

1498: Columbus, on third voyage, anchors off coast near Trinidad

1400 1420 1440 1460 1480 1500

1438: Beginning of period of Inca conquests under Pachacuti

c.1470: Conquest of Chimú empire by the Incas

1493: Accession of Inca ruler, Huayna Capac

MOVABLE TYPE

The use of movable metal type by printers in the German town of Mainz galvanized intellectual life in Europe, stimulating the rapid spread of ideas and a huge growth in literacy. At first type was carved on wooden blocks, as it had been in China since the 11th century, but printers soon began casting it in metal. By the end of the century, this new technology was firmly established throughout Europe.

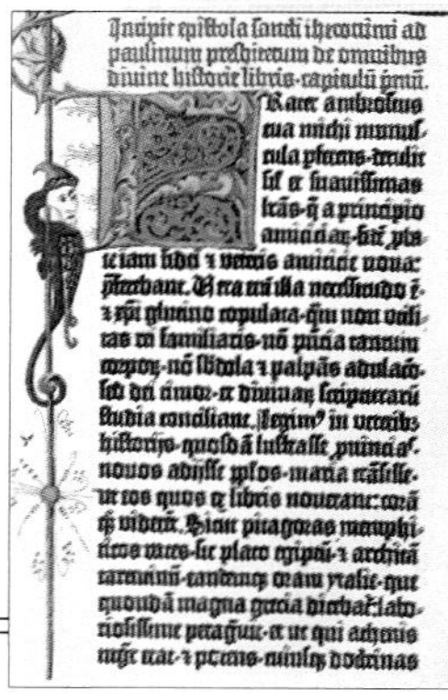

The beautiful bible by Johann Gutenberg of Mainz (1454–55) is prized as the first European book printed using movable type.

Sixtus IV, elected in 1471, was typical of the popes of the Renaissance. A worldly, nepotistic prince, he commissioned great works of art and architecture, including the Sistine Chapel.

Europe

The 15th century saw the start of the Renaissance, a flowering of architecture, art, and humanist idealism inspired by Classical models. The city-states of Italy were the cultural leaders of Europe, but political power was shifting towards the 'new monarchs', who created strong, centralized kingdoms in England, France, and Spain. Poland dominated eastern Europe, but here the future lay with Muscovy, where Ivan III launched Russian expansion to the east and south and in 1472 assumed the title of 'tsar'.

MARTIN BEHAIM'S GLOBE

Martin Behaim was a geographer of Nuremberg who visited Portugal and sailed down the west coast of Africa with Portuguese mariners in the 1480s. His globe, produced in 1490–92, is the oldest surviving globe in the world. Since he knew nothing of the existence of America, he depicted the island of 'Cipangu' (Japan) and the east Asian mainland directly across the Atlantic from western Europe.

Martin Behaim's globe gives a very good picture of how Columbus must have imagined the world before he set sail across the Atlantic Ocean.

SEE ALSO:
North America: pp.122–123
South America: pp.146–147
Africa: pp.162–163
Europe: pp.192–193
West Asia: pp.228–231
South and Southeast Asia: pp.244–245
North and East Asia: pp.264–267

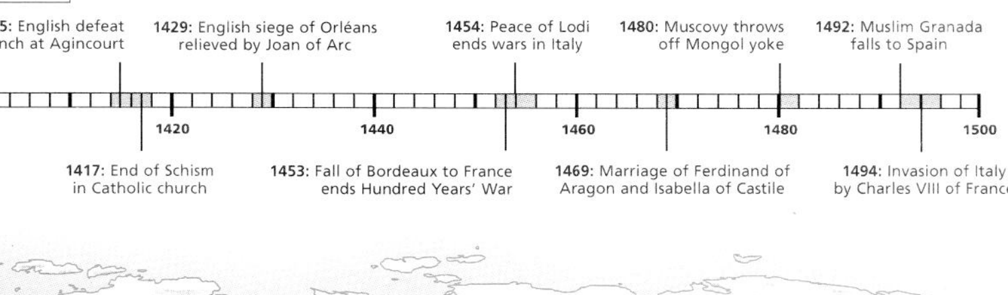
Europe
1415: English defeat French at Agincourt
1429: English siege of Orléans relieved by Joan of Arc
1454: Peace of Lodi ends wars in Italy
1480: Muscovy throws off Mongol yoke
1492: Muslim Granada falls to Spain
1400
1420
1440
1460
1480
1500
1417: End of Schism in Catholic church
1453: Fall of Bordeaux to France ends Hundred Years' War
1469: Marriage of Ferdinand of Aragon and Isabella of Castile
1494: Invasion of Italy by Charles VIII of France

Samoyeds
Palaeosiberians
Ugrians
Yenisei
Lena
KHANATE OF SIBIR
Ob'
Siberia
Tungus
Turkic peoples
Buryats
Amur
KHANATE OF THE OIRATS
Gobi
KHANATE OF ASTRAKHAN
Syr Darya
CHAGATAI KHANATE
SHAYBANIDS
Beijing
KOREA
JAPAN
Yellow River
TIMURIDS
KASHMIR
SMALL RAJPUT STATES
TIBET
NEPALESE PRINCIPALITIES
ASSAMESE STATES
MING EMPIRE
Nanjing
Yangtze
MULTAN
LODI SULTANATE OF DELHI
RAJPUT STATES
Ganges
SIND
BENGAL
SHAN STATES
OMAN
GUJARAT
MALWA
GONDWANA
AVA
Arabian Peninsula
KHANDESH
BERAR
ARAKAN
TOUNGOO
CHIENGMAI
ANNAM
AHMADNAGAR
GAJAPATIS
LAOS
FARTAK
BIJAPUR
PEGU
SIAM
BAHMANI KINGDOM
CAMBODIA
Mekong
Philippine Islands
CHAMPA
VIJAYANAGAR
CEYLON
PACIFIC OCEAN
ATJEH
SULTANATE OF MALACCA
BRUNEI
Malacca
INDIAN OCEAN
Malays
MALAY STATES
SULTANATE OF TERNATE
Papuans
New Guinea
MAJAPAHIT
Madagascar
Australian Aborigines
Darling
Maoris
New Zealand

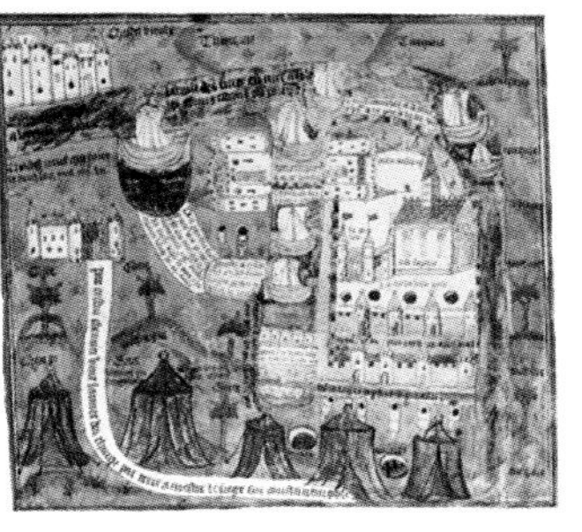

The fall of Constantinople removed the major Christian stronghold barring Islam's spread to the west. The small defending force of Byzantines and Italians was no match for the besieging army of 100,000.

West Asia

When Timur died in 1405, his empire was divided among his four sons. After a series of quarrels, Shah Rukh, who inherited the eastern part, presided over an era of peace, in which the arts and architecture flourished. The Shaybanids, who expanded south across the Syr Darya, were descendants of Genghis Khan. However, a new power was rising that would eclipse the Mongol dynasties that vied to control Persia – the Shi'ite Safavids. In the west, the Ottoman Turks, led by Sultan Mehmed II ('the Conqueror') and aided by powerful cannons, took Constantinople in 1453 and put an end to the Byzantine Empire.

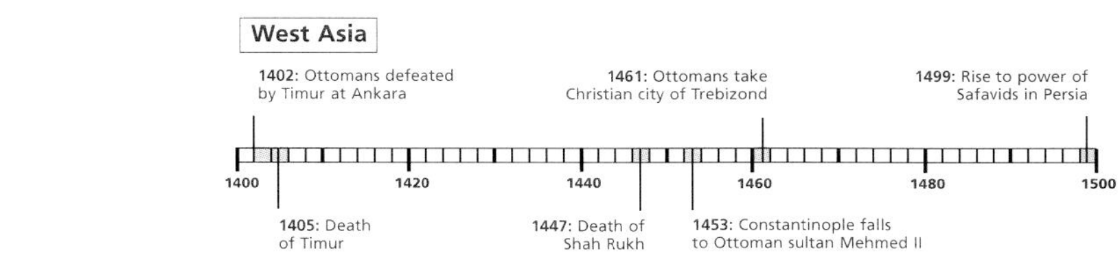
West Asia
1402: Ottomans defeated by Timur at Ankara
1461: Ottomans take Christian city of Trebizond
1499: Rise to power of Safavids in Persia
1400
1420
1440
1460
1480
1500
1405: Death of Timur
1447: Death of Shah Rukh
1453: Constantinople falls to Ottoman sultan Mehmed II

This painting on silk shows the courtyards of the Forbidden City, the compound of the imperial palace at the centre of Beijing. The Ming capital was moved north from Nanjing to Beijing in 1421 during Yung Luo's campaign against the Mongols.

This bronze statue of a Portuguese soldier was made in Benin, one of Portugal's West African trading partners.

Africa

Between the 1460s and 1490s the Songhay ruler Sunni Ali conquered Mali and took over the Saharan caravan trade. Meanwhile, the Portuguese explored the west coast, where African rulers, seeing opportunities for trade, laid the foundations for the small kingdoms of Akan and Benin. Sailors from the Swahili city-states in East Africa helped Vasco da Gama understand the local monsoon winds and complete his voyage to India.

Africa

1441: First shipment of African slaves to Portugal
1464: Beginning of Songhay expansion under Sunni Ali
1400 · 1420 · 1440 · 1460 · 1480 · 1500
1415: Portuguese capture Ceuta in Morocco
c.1450: Eclipse of Great Zimbabwe by Mutapa empire
1482: Fort of Elmina founded by Portuguese

East and Southeast Asia

The Ming dynasty consolidated its hold on China, rebuilding the Great Wall to prevent raids by Mongol Oirats to the north. After Zheng He's epic, but costly, voyages in the Indian Ocean, the Ming rulers adopted a policy of self-sufficiency, discouraging travel and trade. In contrast to this defensive, inward-looking attitude, Southeast Asia thrived on trade. The most important entrepôt was Malacca. By 1500 its population was about 50,000, and it was reported that 84 languages could be heard in the city's streets.

East and Southeast Asia

c.1400: Foundation of Malacca
1424: End of long Ming campaign against Mongols
1445: Conversion of Malacca to Islam
1472: Birth of Neoconfucian philosopher Wang Yangming
1400 · 1420 · 1440 · 1460 · 1480 · 1500
1405: Beginning of Zheng He's voyages in Indian Ocean
1449: Mongols defeat Chinese and capture emperor
1471: Annamites expand to south by invading Champa

GLOBAL KNOWLEDGE

Knowledge of the world and its peoples was coloured by hearsay and travellers' tales.

THE GLOBAL WORLD VIEW is a relatively modern concept. The Americas were unknown to Old World Eurasia until 500 years ago, and each of the major cultural regions had discrete world views of varying extents. Each region had developed its own means of subsistence, and technologies which were direct responses to their immediate environment. In Eurasia, ideas, faiths, and technical achievements were spread by trade, migration, and cultural or political expansion; thus the imprint of Buddhism, Christianity, and Islam was widespread, and technical ideas as diverse as printing and gunpowder, originating in East Asia, had reached Europe. Mapping in one form or another was used by all cultures as a means of recording geographical information and knowledge, although pathfinding and navigation was usually a matter of handed-down knowledge, experience, and word of mouth.

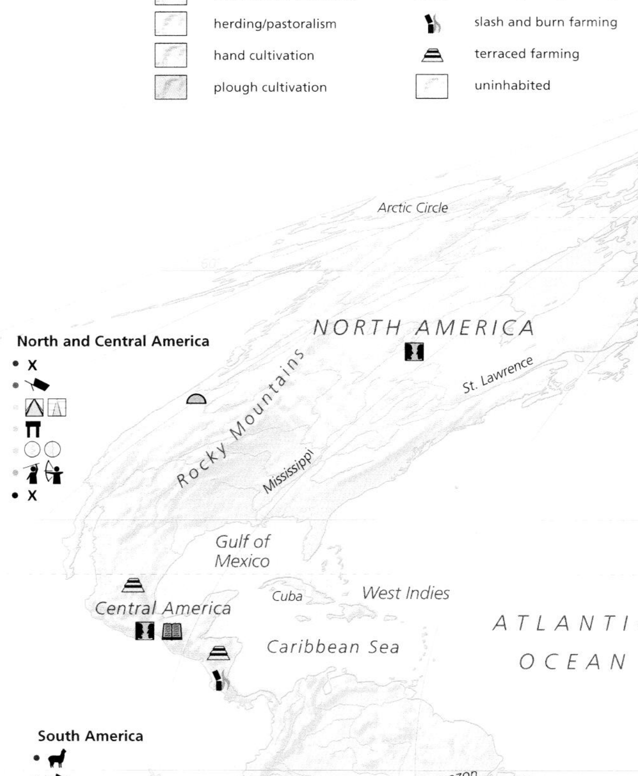

The Americas

Both the Aztecs of Central America and the Incas of the Andes were still in the process of consolidating their young empires when the first Europeans arrived. Although there is evidence in both regions of extensive trading contacts, geographical obstacles (deserts, jungle) and relative immaturity meant their worlds were closely defined.

2 The Americas

The size of the globe

The rediscovery of Classical texts was an important stimulus to the development of technology, science, and the arts, which flowered in the European Renaissance. European cartographers began to build a more detailed world map, using the works of Classical geographers such as Strabo and Ptolemy. The voyage of Bartolomeu Dias (1487–88) around the Cape of Good Hope established the limits of Africa; but in 1492, when Columbus made landfall in the Caribbean four weeks after leaving the Canary Islands, he assumed he had reached China (Cathay) rather than the West Indies. Although the circumnavigation by Magellan and del Cano some 30 years later (1519–22) dispelled many uncertainties, the accurate charting of the world's oceans and coasts would not be completed until the 20th century.

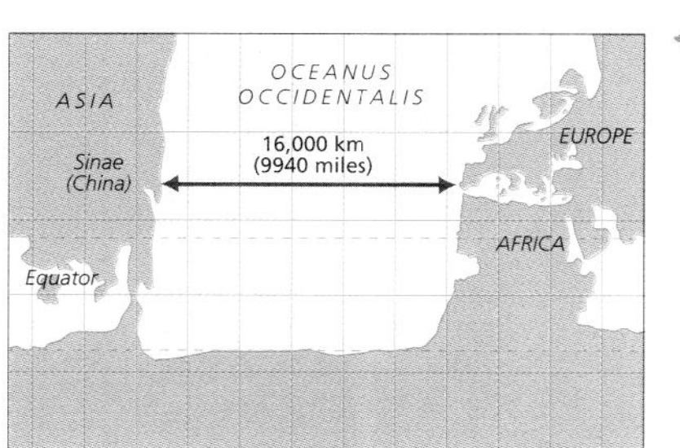

8 The Ptolemaic map of the world

9 The Behaim map of the world 1492

Marco Polo 1271-75
Marco Polo assumed he had travelled 16,000 miles instead of 7000 miles

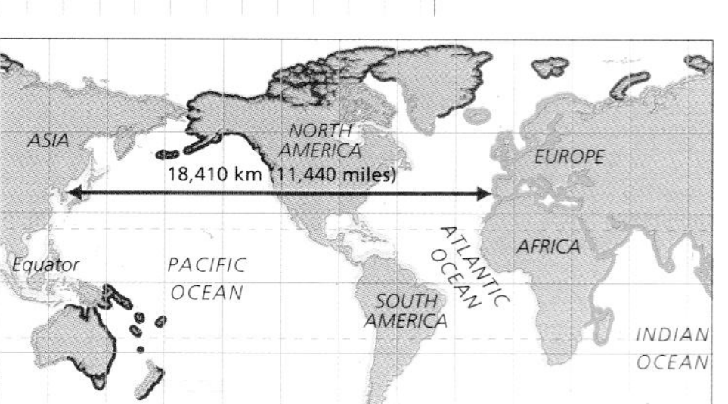

10 The modern map of the world

Coasts charted by
1500
1600
1700
1800
1900

1 Global economies and technologies c.1500

Significant technologies

- draft animals: buffalo; oxen; horse/mule; camel; elephant; llama/alpaca
- transport: wheeled vehicles; dragged vehicles
- hydraulics: canals; aqueducts; irrigation
- architecture: temporary shelters; post and lintel; barrel vaulting; groyne vaulting
- navigation: riverine; coastal; oceanic; lodestone/compass
- warfare: thrown missiles; archery; gunpowder
- power: windmills; watermills
- X technology not developed
- recording of knowledge: knowledge recorded in writing; knowledge preserved orally; empirical cartographic tradition

The Muslim World

The most extensive and cosmopolitan of the Old World cultures, by 1500 Islam straddled large extents of three continents, stretching from the islands of the southwest Pacific to the shores of the Atlantic. Knowledge acquired from trade and travel underpinned much Muslim cultural hegemony and scholarship.

3 The Muslim world

Muslim heartland
known world 1500

6 South Asia

South Asian states
known world 1500

South Asia

In 1500, India was about to become subject to Muslim (Mughal) rule. Nevertheless its position on the crossroads of trade across the Indian Ocean, and overland routes from East and Southeast Asia, dated back many centuries, and its exports were known in Europe. Although essentially inward-looking, South Asian rulers and scholars had an extensive knowledge of the Old World.

Europe

By the end of the 15th century, Europe was poised on the brink of rapid territorial expansion. Technically sophisticated and resourceful, the Europeans had built up through trade and travel, a fairly detailed knowledge of much of the Old World, from coastal Africa, through Arabia and southern Asia, to China and the many islands of the East Indies.

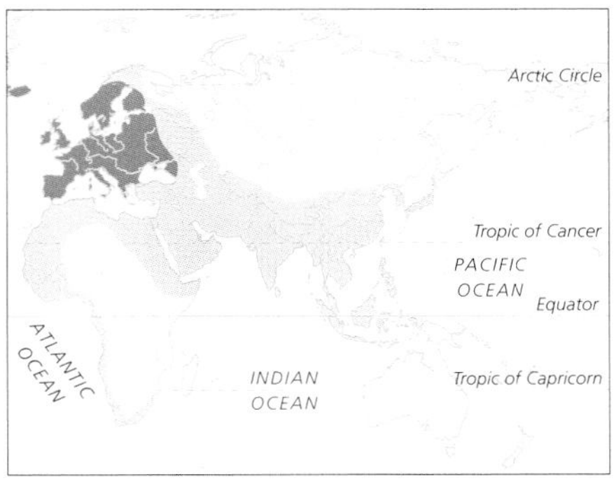

5 Europe

Western Christendom
known world 1492

East Asia

China, Korea, and Japan, although frequently isolationist – the Chinese 'Middle Kingdom' regarded itself, with some justification, as the most powerful in the world – had nevertheless acquired considerable knowledge of the Old World, illustrated by the ambassadorial voyages of the Ming admiral Zheng He throughout the Indian Ocean (1405–33).

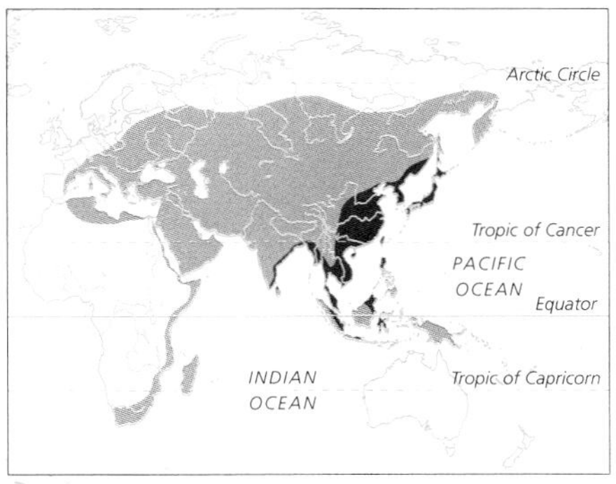

4 East Asia

charted by Chinese c.1500
known world c.1500

SEE ALSO:

North America: pp.118–119

South America: pp.142–143

Africa: pp.156–157

Europe: pp.172–173

West Asia: pp.218–219

South and Southeast Asia: pp.238–239

North and East Asia: 256–257

Australasia and Oceania: pp.278–279

Oceania

Some of the great early oceanic voyages were made between the scattered islands of the southwest Pacific by Polynesian sailors. By 1500, they had knowledge of most of the islands in the region, including New Zealand – settled some 800 years earlier.

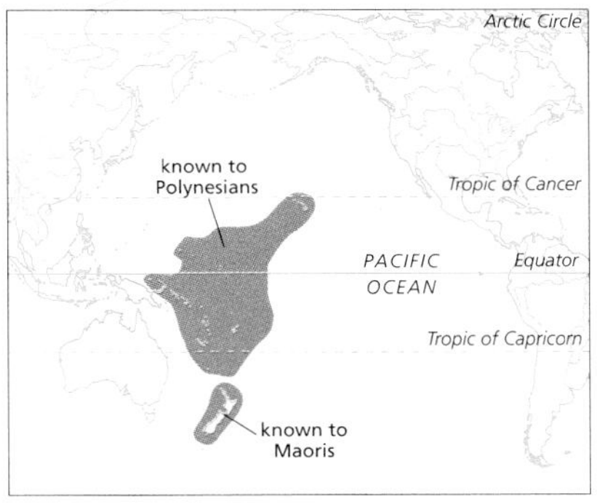

7 Oceania

known worlds c.1500

known to Polynesians

known to Maoris

Islamic knowledge of astronomy and weather patterns was essential to their ability to navigate. Here, celestial observations are undertaken with a variety of instruments.

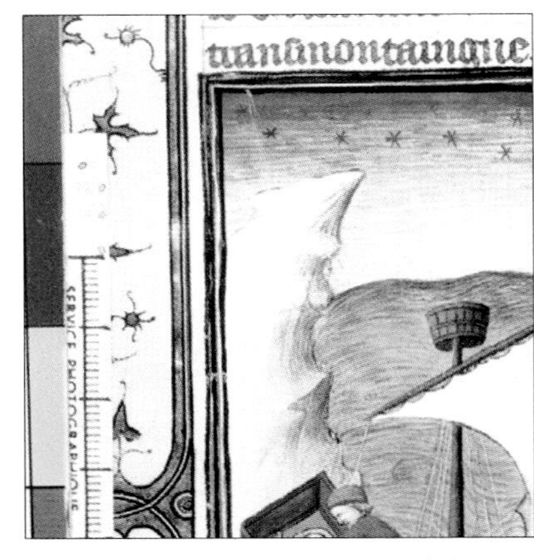

European navigators used an astrolabe, which gave an approximate postion in relation to the position of the stars. For lunar and solar measures, an almanac was also necessary.

Chinese cartographers produced detailed and very accurate maps as a navigational aid. This example showing the Philippines, Taiwan, and the East Indies is from Zhu Siben's 14th-century world atlas.

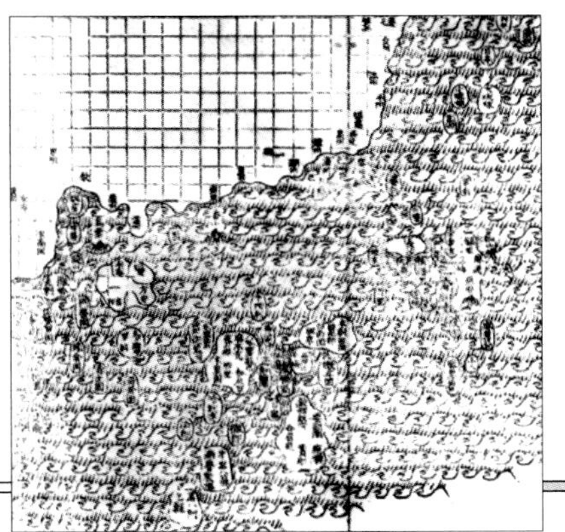

Mariners and technology

In 1500 the principal seafaring cultures were those of the Atlantic nations of western Europe – Spain, Portugal, England, and the Netherlands – the Islamic traders of the Indian Ocean, and the Chinese. Although Norsemen had crossed the North Atlantic to reach Greenland and the Americas 400 years previously, it was the navigators from Atlantic Europe who, in the 15th century, began the systematic exploration of Atlantic island groups and the African coastline. When they sailed east into the Indian Ocean, they benefited from the superior local knowledge of Arab, and later, Chinese navigators.

THE WORLD 1500–1600

IN THE 16TH CENTURY Spain seized a vast land empire that encompassed much of South and Central America, the West Indies, and the Philippine Islands. Meanwhile, the Portuguese acquired a largely maritime empire stretching from Brazil to Malacca and Macao. Ferdinand Magellan, a Portuguese in the service of Spain, demonstrated that all the world's oceans were linked and sea lanes were established through the Indian, Atlantic, and Pacific oceans, creating for the first time a genuinely global trading network. Although the Portuguese traded with the Ming Empire and Japan, cultural contact between Europeans and East Asia was limited. In Africa, too, European impact barely extended beyond the coast. Missionaries took the Catholic faith to distant parts of the Spanish and Portuguese empires, but in Europe the church of Rome faced the threat of the Reformation, while Catholic kingdoms fought to stem Ottoman expansion in the Mediterranean and into the Habsburg lands of central Europe.

Europe

The Protestant Reformation dominated 16th-century Europe. Rulers in Scandinavia, England, Scotland, and many German states abandoned the Roman church and took over monasteries and the running of church affairs. In France Protestants fought Catholics in a debilitating round of civil wars (1562–98) and religion was a major factor in the Dutch revolt against Spanish rule in 1565. The kings of Spain championed Catholicism and promoted missions worldwide. In the east, Russia's tsars extended their empire to the Caspian Sea and western Siberia.

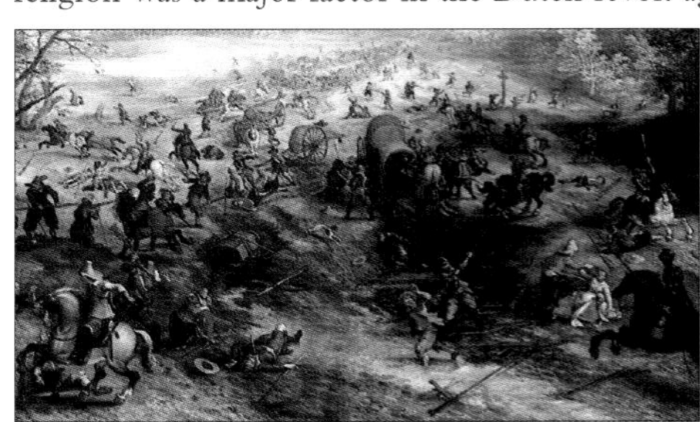

Spanish troops raid a convoy in a scene typical of the atrocities of the Dutch Wars of Independence.

Europe

- **1517:** Martin Luther's *95 Theses* attack abuses of Catholic church
- **1519:** Charles V elected Holy Roman Emperor
- **1534:** Act of Supremacy; Henry VIII of England breaks with Rome
- **1545:** Council of Trent called to counter threat of Protestantism
- **1565:** Dutch Revolt starts long series of wars to gain independence from Spain
- **1580:** Philip II of Spain seizes Portuguese crown
- **1588:** English defeat Spanish Armada
- **1598:** Edict of Nantes ends over 30 years of religious wars in France

1500 1520 1540 1560 1580 1600

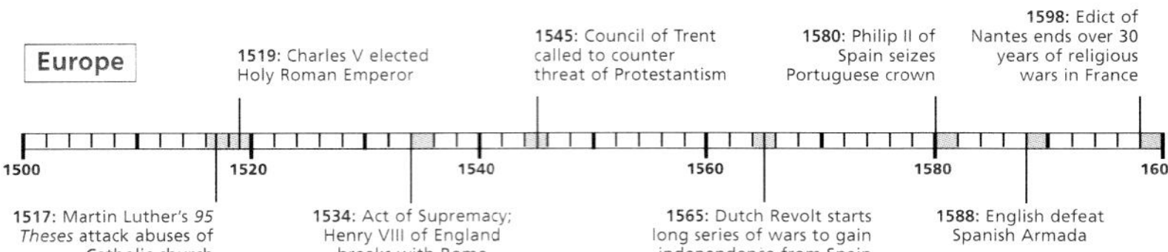

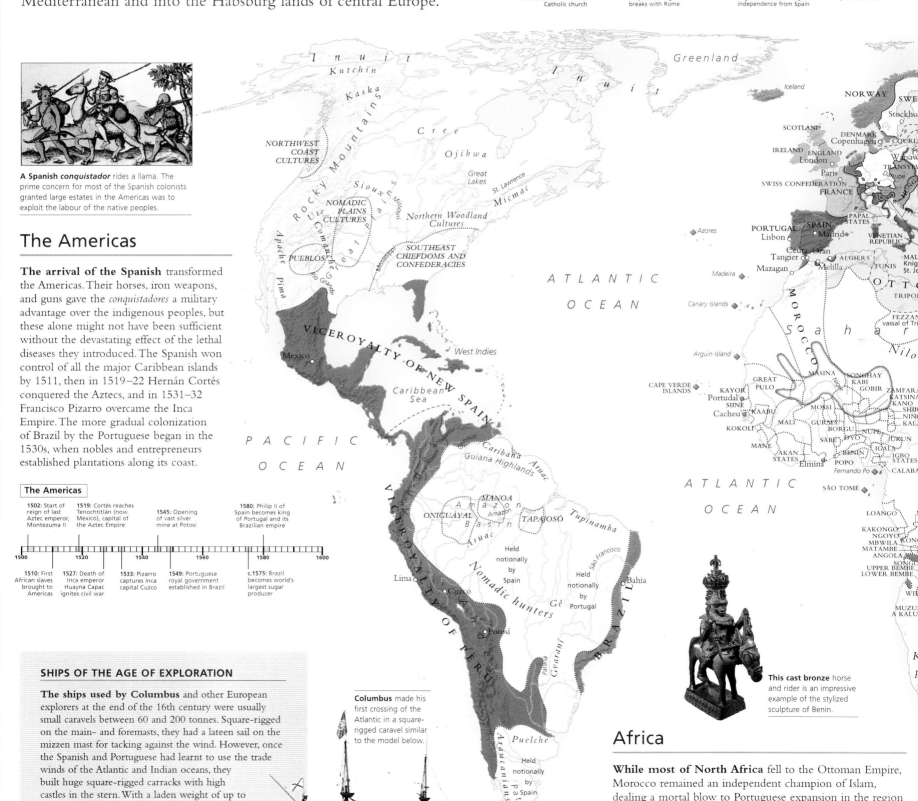

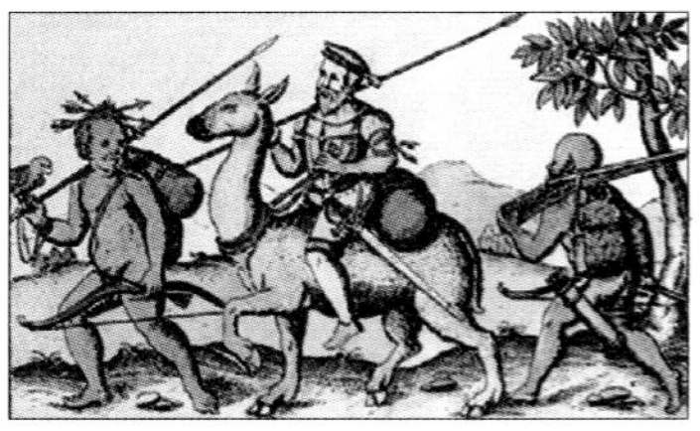

A Spanish ***conquistador*** rides a llama. The prime concern for most of the Spanish colonists granted large estates in the Americas was to exploit the labour of the native peoples.

The Americas

The arrival of the Spanish transformed the Americas. Their horses, iron weapons, and guns gave the *conquistadores* a military advantage over the indigenous peoples, but these alone might not have been sufficient without the devastating effect of the lethal diseases they introduced. The Spanish won control of all the major Caribbean islands by 1511, then in 1519–22 Hernán Cortés conquered the Aztecs, and in 1531–32 Francisco Pizarro overcame the Inca Empire. The more gradual colonization of Brazil by the Portuguese began in the 1530s, when nobles and entrepreneurs established plantations along its coast.

The Americas

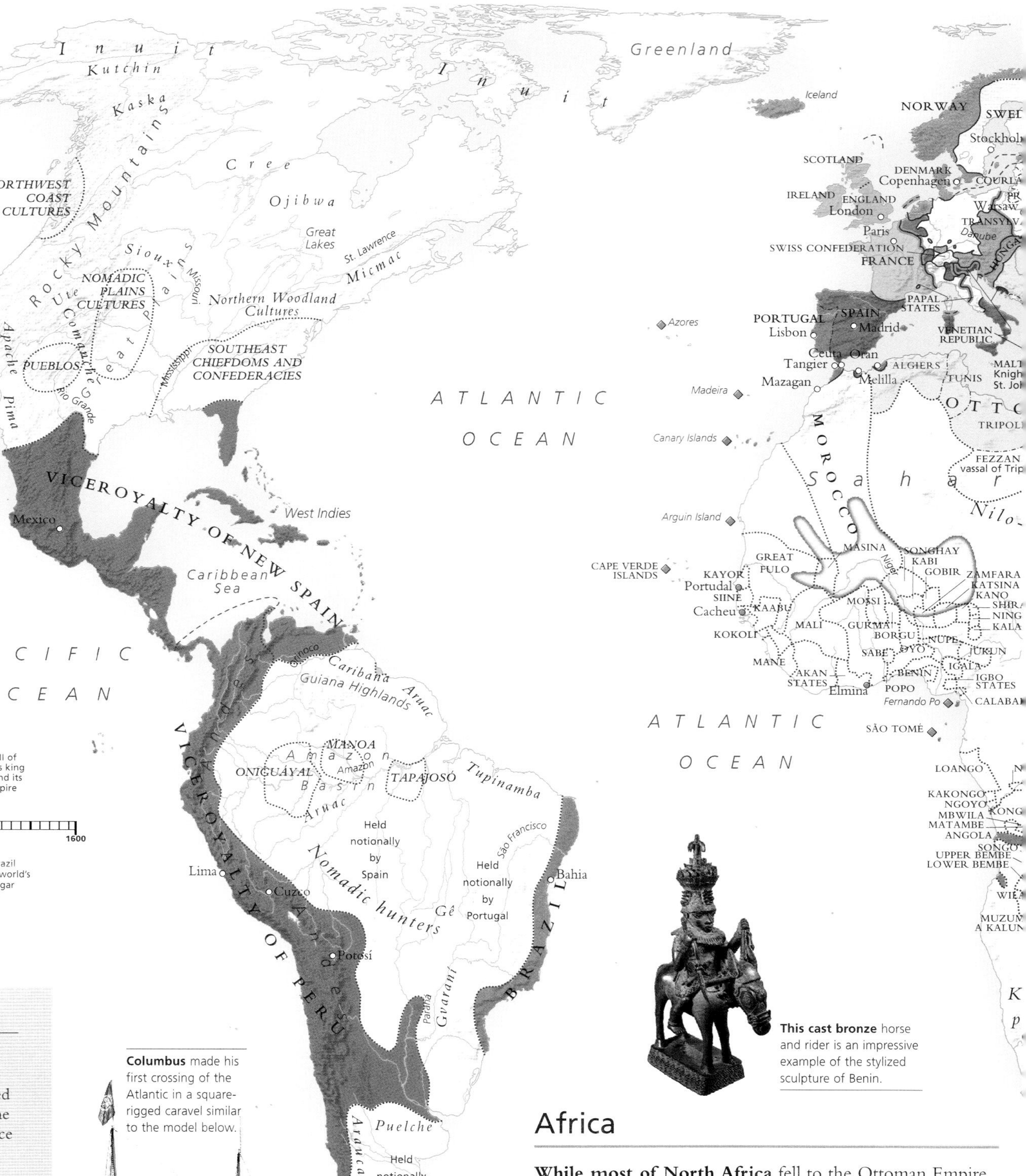

- **1502:** Start of reign of last Aztec emperor, Montezuma II
- **1510:** First African slaves brought to Americas
- **1519:** Cortés reaches Tenochtitlán (now Mexico), capital of the Aztec Empire
- **1527:** Death of Inca emperor Huayna Capac ignites civil war
- **1533:** Pizarro captures Inca capital Cuzco
- **1545:** Opening of vast silver mine at Potosí
- **1549:** Portuguese royal government established in Brazil
- **c.1575:** Brazil becomes world's largest sugar producer
- **1580:** Philip II of Spain becomes king of Portugal and its Brazilian empire

1500 1520 1540 1560 1580 1600

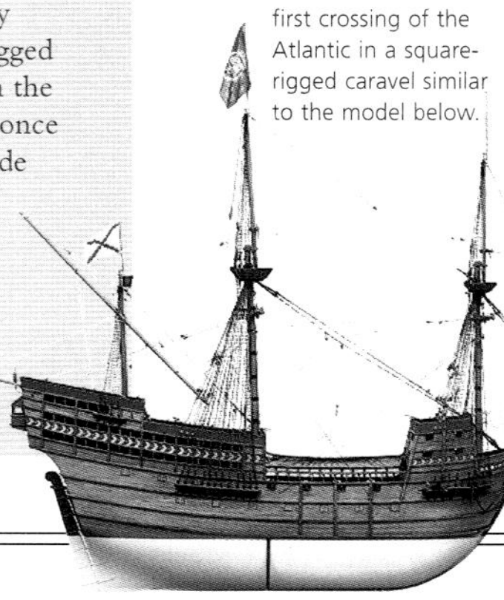

This cast bronze horse and rider is an impressive example of the stylized sculpture of Benin.

Africa

While most of North Africa fell to the Ottoman Empire, Morocco remained an independent champion of Islam, dealing a mortal blow to Portuguese expansion in the region and conquering Songhay to gain control of the valuable trans-Saharan caravan trade. Many of the small West African states had trade links both with Morocco and the Portuguese, who established a fortified trading post at Elmina.

SHIPS OF THE AGE OF EXPLORATION

The ships used by Columbus and other European explorers at the end of the 16th century were usually small caravels between 60 and 200 tonnes. Square-rigged on the main- and foremasts, they had a lateen sail on the mizzen mast for tacking against the wind. However, once the Spanish and Portuguese had learnt to use the trade winds of the Atlantic and Indian oceans, they built huge square-rigged carracks with high castles in the stern. With a laden weight of up to 1,600 tonnes, they were designed to maximize the cargoes of spices and precious metals shipped back from the East Indies and the Americas.

Columbus made his first crossing of the Atlantic in a square-rigged caravel similar to the model below.

Suleiman the Magnificent extended Ottoman rule far into southeastern Europe. In this miniature, he is seen receiving homage from his many Christian vassals.

West Asia

In the 16th century the Ottoman Empire expanded into southwest Asia, North Africa, and southeastern Europe. The Ottoman navy was the pre-eminent power in the Mediterranean until its defeat by a Christian fleet at Lepanto in 1571 and Muslim vessels dominated the region's shipping. Ottoman rulers clashed constantly with the Safavids in Persia, and in the late 16th and early 17th centuries the two empires fought for control of Mesopotamia and the Caucasus. Many earlier Ottoman gains were reversed during the reign of Shah Abbas the Great, the Safavid ruler from 1588 to 1629.

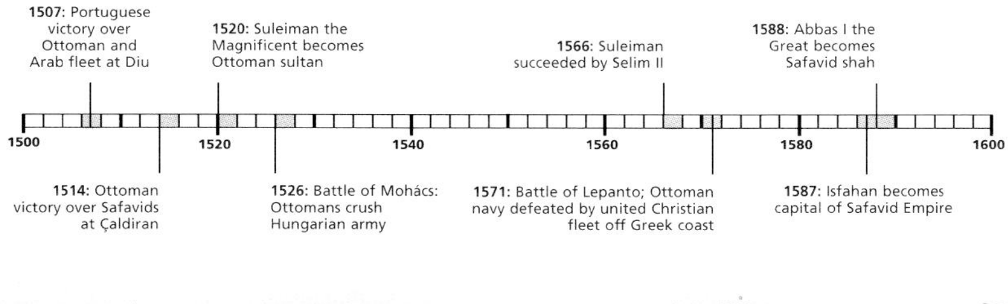
West Asia
1507: Portuguese victory over Ottoman and Arab fleet at Diu
1520: Suleiman the Magnificent becomes Ottoman sultan
1566: Suleiman succeeded by Selim II
1588: Abbas I the Great becomes Safavid shah
1500
1520
1540
1560
1580
1600
1514: Ottoman victory over Safavids at Çaldiran
1526: Battle of Mohács: Ottomans crush Hungarian army
1571: Battle of Lepanto; Ottoman navy defeated by united Christian fleet off Greek coast
1587: Isfahan becomes capital of Safavid Empire

THE NEW WORLD BY ABRAHAM ORTELIUS

Abraham Ortelius was a mapseller from Antwerp whose *Theatrum Orbis Terrarum* of 1570 is considered the first modern atlas. He was not an original cartographer, but he travelled widely in search of reliable sources and his atlas sold well throughout Europe for over 40 years. His map of the New World was a fairly accurate summary of European explorers' knowledge of the Americas and the Pacific. The vast southern continent, *Terra Australis*, a relic of the Classical geography of Claudius Ptolemy, was a feature of most maps of the period. It includes Tierra del Fuego and part of the coast of New Guinea, but the rest is pure conjecture. Ortelius was a contemporary of Gerardus Mercator. Between them, the two great mapmakers did much to shift the centre of European cartography from Italy to the Low Countries.

The map gives a fairly accurate picture of Central America and the Caribbean; however many parts of America had still not been explored by Europeans at all.

SEE ALSO:

North America: pp.124–125

South America: pp.146–149

Africa: pp.162–163

Europe: pp.194–195

West Asia: pp.230–231

South and Southeast Asia: pp.244–247

North and East Asia: pp.264–267

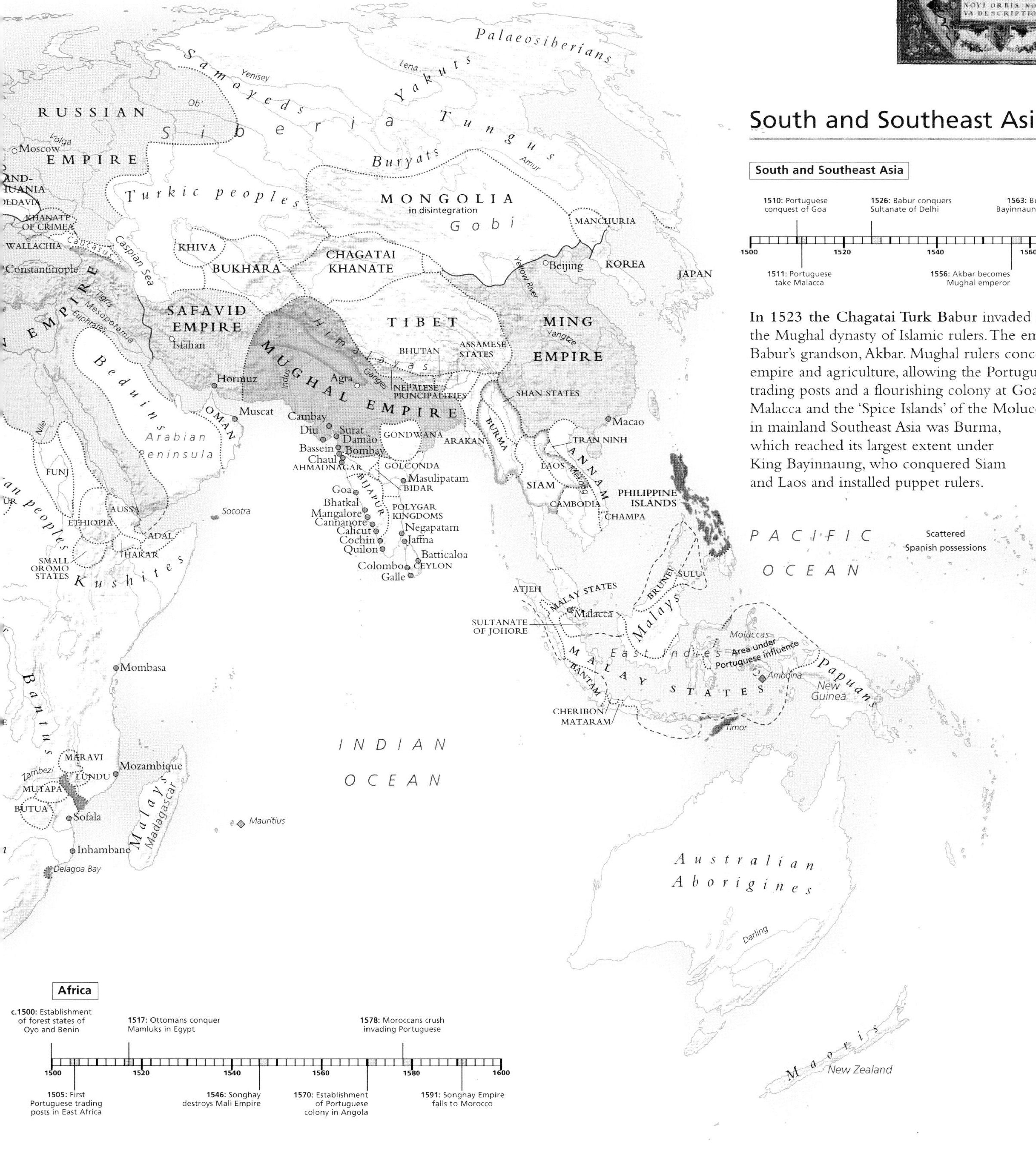

South and Southeast Asia

South and Southeast Asia

1510: Portuguese conquest of Goa
1526: Babur conquers Sultanate of Delhi
1563: Burmese King Bayinnaung invades Siam
1600: English East India Company founded

1500 · 1520 · 1540 · 1560 · 1580 · 1600

1511: Portuguese take Malacca
1556: Akbar becomes Mughal emperor
1565: Spanish fleet claims Philippines in name of King Philip II

In 1523 the Chagatai Turk Babur invaded northern India, founding the Mughal dynasty of Islamic rulers. The empire was consolidated by Babur's grandson, Akbar. Mughal rulers concentrated on their land empire and agriculture, allowing the Portuguese to maintain coastal trading posts and a flourishing colony at Goa. Portugal also conquered Malacca and the 'Spice Islands' of the Moluccas. The dominant power in mainland Southeast Asia was Burma, which reached its largest extent under King Bayinnaung, who conquered Siam and Laos and installed puppet rulers.

The richest prize for European merchants in South and Southeast Asia was control of the valuable spice trade. This French illustration shows the pepper harvest in southern India.

The World in 1600
Ming Empire
Ottoman Empire
Spain and possessions
Portugal and possessions (ruled by Kings of Spain 1580–1640)
England and possessions
Austrian Habsburg territories
France
Denmark and possessions
Venetian Republic and possessions
United Provinces (fighting for independence from Spain)
Dutch (United Provinces) possessions
Mughal Empire at Akbar's accession, 1556
under Burmese control, 1575
Songhay to 1590
Holy Roman Empire

Africa

c.1500: Establishment of forest states of Oyo and Benin
1517: Ottomans conquer Mamluks in Egypt
1578: Moroccans crush invading Portuguese

1500 · 1520 · 1540 · 1560 · 1580 · 1600

1505: First Portuguese trading posts in East Africa
1546: Songhay destroys Mali Empire
1570: Establishment of Portuguese colony in Angola
1591: Songhay Empire falls to Morocco

THE AGE OF EUROPEAN EXPANSION

The Portuguese, Vasco da Gama was the first European navigator to reach India by sea.

THE 16TH CENTURY saw the expansion of several of the great European nations far beyond their continental limits. Explorers searching for new sources of luxury goods and precious metals began to open up new territories which monarchs such as Philip II of Spain quickly built up into great empires in the 'New World'. The Spanish and Portuguese, inspired by the voyages of Columbus and da Gama, led the way, closely followed by the Dutch and the English. The explorers were aided by technological advances in shipbuilding, navigational equipment, and cartography. At the start of the 16th century, the Americas were virtually unknown to Europeans; by 1700, outposts of a greater European empire had been established almost everywhere the explorers landed.

European voyages of expansion and discovery

Spain and Portugal were the leaders of world exploration in the 16th century. In search of maritime trade routes to Asia, the Portuguese found sea lanes through the Atlantic and Indian oceans to India. By 1512, fortified trading posts were in place at Goa and Malacca, and they had reached the 'Spice Islands' of the Moluccas in eastern Indonesia. The Spanish, taking a westward route, found the Caribbean islands and the Americas instead. Magellan's three-year global circumnavigation revealed a western route through the Strait of Magellan and across the Pacific Ocean. English and French mariners sought northern passages to Asian markets and their voyages paved the way for the establishment of European settlements in North America.

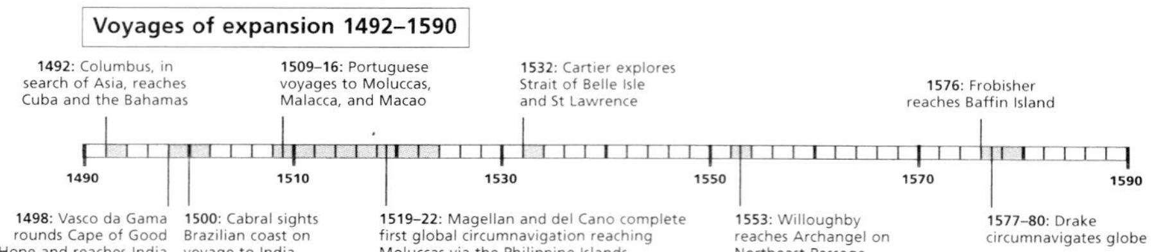

1 Voyages of European expansion 1492–1597

Spanish expeditions
Portuguese expeditions
English expeditions
French expeditions
Dutch expeditions

ARCTIC OCEAN
Limit of summer pack ice
Arctic Circle
Greenland
Baffin Island
Spitsbergen
Limit of winter pack ice
Barents 1596–97
Novaya Zemlya
Willoughby 1553
Iceland
Archangel
Frobisher 1576
ENGLAND
Labrador
Cabot 1497
NETHERLANDS
EUROPE
FRANCE
Cartier 1534–36
NORTH AMERICA
St. Lawrence
Hochelaga (Montreal)
Corte-Real 1500
PORTUGAL
SPAIN
Azores
ASIA
JAPAN
Nagasaki
MING CHINA
ATLANTIC OCEAN
Canary Islands
Bahamas
Tropic of Cancer
INDIA
Goa
Calicut
ANNAM
Macao
Hainan
Philippine Islands
Loaisa 1526
Drake 1577–80
Acapulco
Cuba
Columbus 1492
Caribbean Sea
Columbus 1502–04
AFRICA
Pires 1515–16
Panama
Cape Tiburón
Cape Sierra Leone
Equator
Malacca
Borneo
Moluccas
PACIFIC OCEAN
Mogadishu
Cabral 1500
Sumatra
New Guinea
Malindi
da Gama 1497–98
INDIAN OCEAN
de Abreu 1511
Java
Magellan 1519–21
Lima
SOUTH AMERICA
Kilwa
Drake 1577–80
Loaisa 1526
Sofala
Tropic of Capricorn
del Cano (after death of Magellan) 1521–22
AUSTRALIA
Cabral 1500
Madagascar
Isla de Chiloé
River Plate
Cape of Good Hope
Puerto San Julián
SOUTHERN
Strait of Magellan
Cape Horn
Limit of winter pack ice

Magellan's global circumnavigation was so extraordinary that contemporary artists portrayed him abetted on his voyage by both the latest navigational technology and weaponry, and by mythical creatures such as monsters and mermaids. He was killed by hostile local people in the Philippine Islands in 1521.

EAST MEETS WEST

Europeans and the peoples they encountered in the East had much to learn from one another. Jesuit missionaries were particularly successful at establishing links between China and Japan and the West. During the 1580s, the Jesuit Matteo Ricci informed the Chinese emperor and his court about many European inventions. He presented them with elaborate clocks and taught them about astronomical equipment and weapons such as cannon. His primary purpose was to convert the Chinese to Christianity, using European scientific advances to demonstrate the superiority of European religion. Despite his efforts to accommodate Chinese culture – including the celebration of the mass in Chinese – large-scale conversion eluded him. But much future scientific endeavour was due to these cultural contacts: the revival of Chinese mathematics, the development of the suspension bridge, and early Western experiments in electrostatics and magnetism.

The arrival of Portuguese merchants in Japan is shown below by a Japanese artist. From the mid-16th century, Portuguese traders provided a link between a hostile China and Japan and St. Francis Xavier began a mission to gain new Christian converts. They were soon perceived as a threat to Japanese security and ships which landed were ordered to be confiscated and their crews executed.

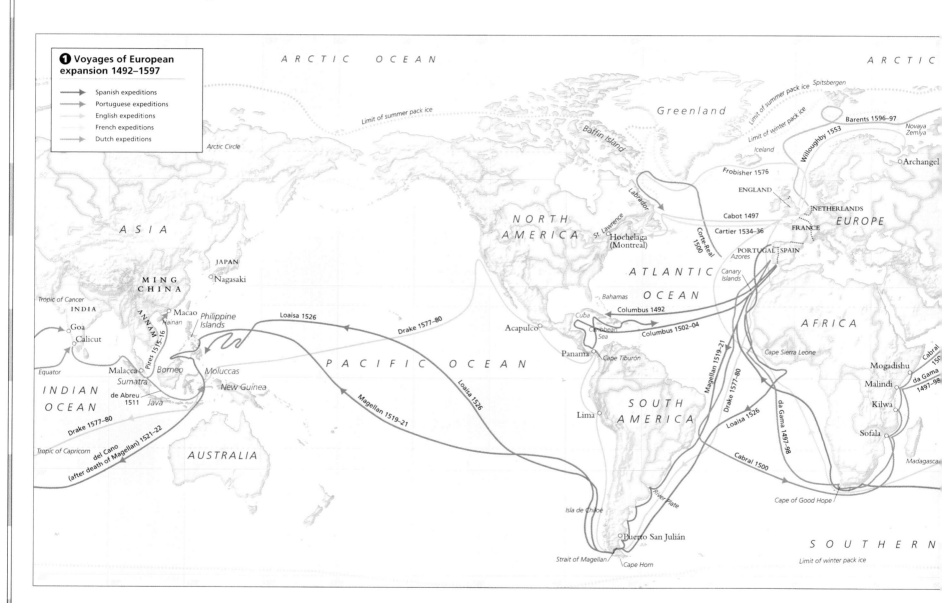

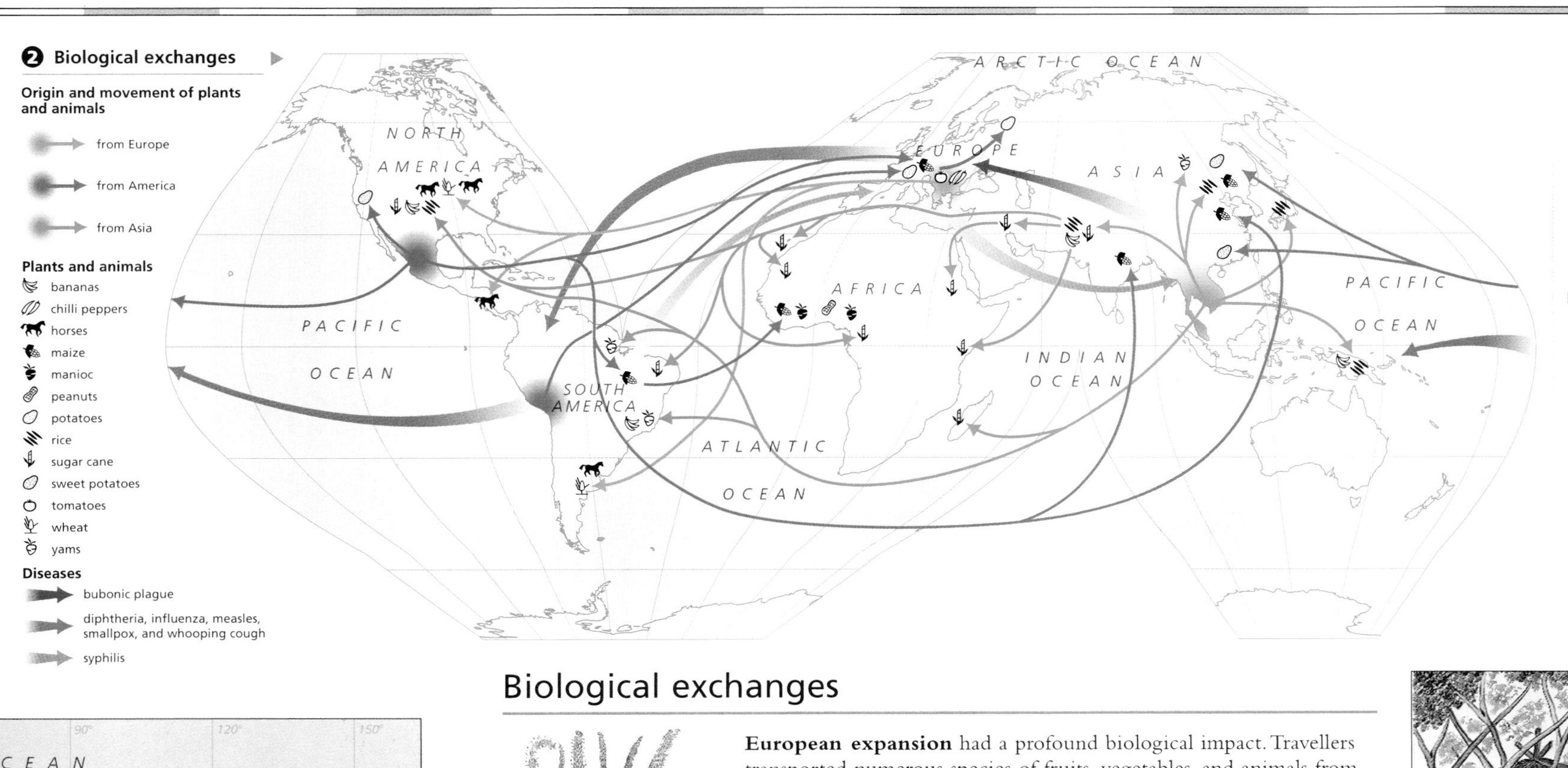

SEE ALSO:

North America: pp.118–119, 122–123

South America: pp.142–143, 148–149

Africa: pp.156–157, 162–163

South and Southeast Asia: pp.238–239, 246–247

North and East Asia: pp.256–257

Australasia and Oceania: pp.278–279

Biological exchanges

The plantain, a herb with medicinal properties, was known as 'Englishman's foot' by native North Americans who believed it would grow only where the English had trodden.

European expansion had a profound biological impact. Travellers transported numerous species of fruits, vegetables, and animals from the Americas to Europe. At the same time, settlers introduced European species to the Americas and Oceania. Horses, pigs, and cattle were transported to the western hemisphere where, without natural predators, their numbers increased spectacularly. The settlers consciously introduced food crops, such as wheat, grapes, apples, peaches, and citrus fruits. Some plants, such as nettles, dandelions, and other weeds were inadvertently dispersed by the winds or on the coats of animals. European expansion also led to a spread of European diseases. Vast numbers of indigenous American peoples died from measles and smallpox, which broke out in massive epidemics among populations with no natural or acquired immunity. During the 16th century, syphilis – thought now to be the result of the fusion of two similar diseases from Europe and the New World – killed a million Europeans.

Many more indigenous Americans were killed by smallpox and measles than were slaughtered by the colonizers. Up to 90% of the total population may have perished from European diseases.

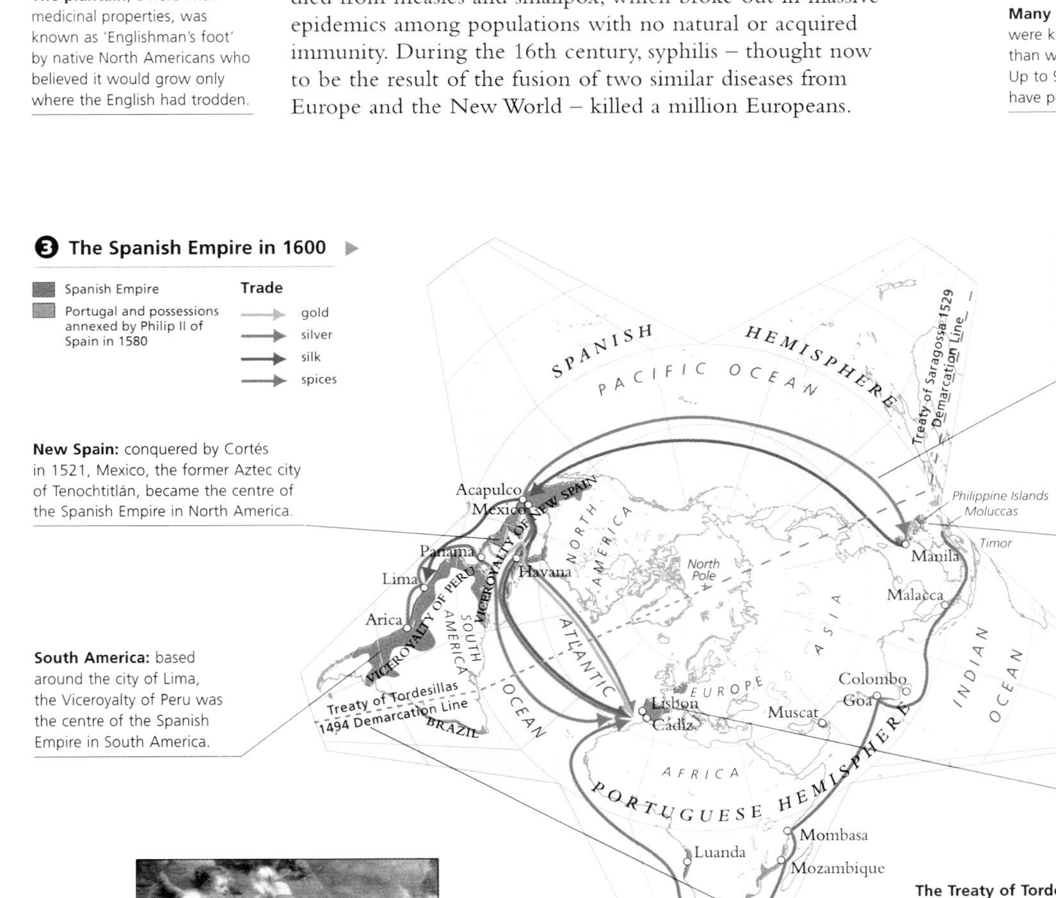

New Spain: conquered by Cortés in 1521, Mexico, the former Aztec city of Tenochtitlán, became the centre of the Spanish Empire in North America.

South America: based around the city of Lima, the Viceroyalty of Peru was the centre of the Spanish Empire in South America.

The Manila galleon: brought silver once a year from Acapulco in New Spain to Manila. The silver was used to buy silk, porcelain, and lacquerware which were transported back to New Spain and then to Spain.

The Philippine Islands: first discovered in 1521 by Magellan and claimed for Spain. A governorship and Spanish settlement of the Philippines began in 1565.

Europe: by 1600, the Spanish Empire in Europe included Portugal, Flanders, Naples, and Sicily.

The Treaty of Tordesillas (1494)

Under this treaty between Spain and Portugal, the yet-to-be-discovered world was divided, with Spain taking the western portion and Portugal the east. In 1529 a further treaty divided the eastern hemisphere.

The Spanish Empire

By the end of the 16th century the Spanish Empire included Central America, the West Indies, western South America, and most of the Philippine Islands. The need to safeguard the new lands, their precious natural resources and the new trading networks which evolved, led to the development of a colonial administration of unparalleled scope. Royal authority was vested in the twin institutions of *audiencias*, with political, administrative, and judicial functions, and a series of viceroys, who acted primarily as powerful governors, though they possessed no judicial powers. All information relating to government in the Spanish territories was controlled by specially created councils, the Council of Castile and the Council of the Indies, which met regularly to ensure communication between Spain and the distant possessions of the Spanish Empire.

The New World empire Philip II inherited from his father, Charles V, was greatly expanded after 1580 following the annexation of Portugal which added Brazil and the East Indies.

The Expansion of the Spanish Empire

- **1493:** Columbus establishes first Spanish settlement in western hemisphere
- **1494:** Treaty of Tordesillas divides western hemisphere between Spain and Portugal
- **1509:** Spanish settlement of mainland Central America begins
- **1519–21:** Cortés conquers Aztec Empire
- **1532–40:** Pizarro conquers Inca Empire
- **1540s:** Potosí becomes greatest single source of silver in the world
- **1564:** System of Atlantic convoys established
- **1565–75:** Spanish conquest of Philippine Islands
- **1571:** Foundation of Manila
- **1580:** Union of Spanish and Portuguese crowns
- **1590:** Silver shipped to Manila almost equal in value to Atlantic trade

THE WORLD 1600–1700

DURING THE 17TH CENTURY Dutch, British, and French mariners followed Iberians into the world's seas. All three lands established colonies in North America, and all entered the trade networks of the Indian Ocean. British and French mariners searched for a northeast and a northwest passage from Europe to Asia and, although unsuccessful, their efforts expanded their understanding of the world's geography. Dutch incursions into the East Indies began to erode the dominance of the Portuguese empire in this region. Trade between Europe, Africa, North America, and South America pushed the Atlantic Ocean basin toward economic integration, while European trade in the Indian Ocean linked European and Asian markets.

Many European rulers believed that they governed by divine right. Louis XIV of France is here portrayed in a classical fashion which reflects both his supreme power and his belief in his godlike status.

Europe

The ramifications of the Protestant Reformation complicated political affairs in western and central Europe. The Thirty Years' War (1618–48) ravaged much of Germany, but the Peace of Westphalia that ended the war established a system of states based on a balance of power. This system did not eliminate conflict but maintained relative stability until the French Revolution. The Russian Empire expanded to reach the Pacific Ocean by the mid-17th century as Cossacks and other adventurers established forts throughout Siberia while searching for furs.

Europe (timeline, 1600–1700)

- 1611: Accession of Gustavus Adolphus signals Swedish expansion
- 1618: Start of Thirty Years' War
- 1643: Louis XIV becomes King of France
- 1648: Thirty Years' War ended by Peace of Westphalia
- 1649: Execution of Charles I of England
- 1682: Peter the Great becomes tsar of Russia
- 1683: Siege of Vienna ends in Ottoman defeat

The World in 1700

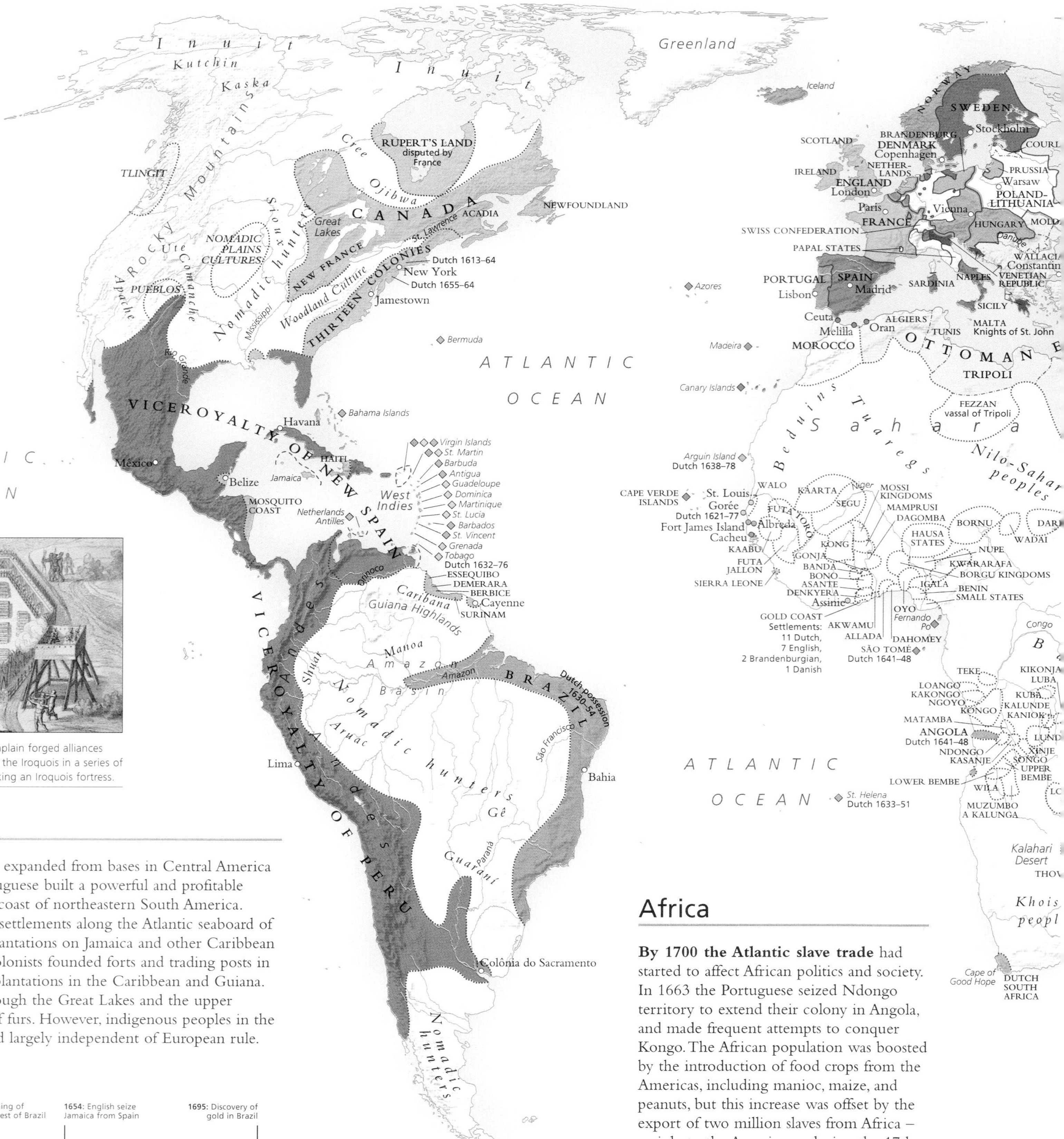

- Ottoman Empire
- England and possessions
- France and possessions
- Denmark and possessions
- Spain and possessions
- Portugal and possessions
- Netherlands and possessions
- Hohenzollern possessions
- Sweden and possessions
- Venetian Republic and possessions
- Austrian Habsburg territories
- held temporarily by Netherlands during 17th century
- Holy Roman Empire

The French explorer Samuel de Champlain forged alliances with other Indian peoples as he fought the Iroquois in a series of violent struggles. He is seen here attacking an Iroquois fortress.

The Americas

The Spanish land empire expanded from bases in Central America and the Andes, and the Portuguese built a powerful and profitable plantation society along the coast of northeastern South America. English colonists established settlements along the Atlantic seaboard of North America, and sugar plantations on Jamaica and other Caribbean islands. French and Dutch colonists founded forts and trading posts in North America, with sugar plantations in the Caribbean and Guiana. French hunters travelled through the Great Lakes and the upper Mississippi valley in search of furs. However, indigenous peoples in the continental interior remained largely independent of European rule.

The Americas (timeline, 1600–1700)

- 1604–08: Foundation of French colony of Acadia
- 1607: Foundation of English colony at Jamestown
- 1630: Beginning of Dutch conquest of Brazil
- 1630: Foundation of English Massachusetts Bay colony
- 1654: English seize Jamaica from Spain
- 1664: English seizure of Dutch colony of New Amsterdam; renamed New York
- 1695: Discovery of gold in Brazil

Africa

By 1700 the Atlantic slave trade had started to affect African politics and society. In 1663 the Portuguese seized Ndongo territory to extend their colony in Angola, and made frequent attempts to conquer Kongo. The African population was boosted by the introduction of food crops from the Americas, including manioc, maize, and peanuts, but this increase was offset by the export of two million slaves from Africa – mainly to the Americas – during the 17th century. States such as Asante, Dahomey, and Oyo raided their neighbours in search of slaves to exchange for European guns.

OPTICAL INSTRUMENTS

The development of telescopes and microscopes geatly advanced human knowledge of both distant objects and those too small to see with the naked eye during the 17th century. The refracting telescope, using a combination of lenses, was first used for observation of the Moon and distant universe by Galileo in 1609. Newton's reflecting telescope, using lenses and mirrors, gave a still clearer picture of the stars and planets. In 1683, Anton van Leeuwenhoek made the first high-powered precision microscope.

A model of Newton's reflecting telescope, made in 1668.

The Qing dynasty began their rule with great energy, encouraging many projects for the improvement of their new lands. These workers are building a new dyke constructed from timber and brushwood.

East Asia

In 1644 a Manchu army toppled the Ming dynasty, entered Beijing, and established the Qing dynasty (1644–1911). By the 1680s they had consolidated their hold on southern China, conquered the island of Formosa, and extended Chinese influence far into North and Central Asia. The Qing adapted to Chinese ways and largely preserved the Ming administrative structure. In Japan, the Tokugawa dynasty imposed a central government for the first time. Foreign trade was strictly controlled by both the Chinese and Japanese, confined mainly to Macao in China and Nagasaki in Japan.

SEE ALSO:

North America: pp.126–127

South America: pp.148–149

Africa: pp.164–165

Europe: pp.196–197

West Asia: pp.230–231

South and Southeast Asia: pp.244–245

North and East Asia: pp.268–269

Australasia and Oceania: pp.278–279

East Asia

- **1603:** Establishment of Tokugawa dynasty in Japan
- **1633:** Closure of Japan by Tokugawa shoguns
- **1644:** Manchu forces topple the Ming and establish the Qing dynasty
- **1661:** Kangxi becomes Qing emperor
- **1683:** Conquest of Formosa by Kangxi
- **1689:** Treaty of Nerchinsk between Russia and China; Russians withdraw from Amur basin

JOAN BLAEU'S EASTERN HEMISPHERE

During the 17th century, Dutch mariners and merchants pushed forward the boundaries of the world known to Europeans. Willem Blaeu and his son Joan were official cartographers to the Dutch East India Company (VOC), publishing maps and charts based on the most up-to-date and accurate information provided by explorers, as well as a series of world atlases.

The eastern hemisphere of Joan Blaeu's *Nova et accuratissima totius terrarum orbis tabula*, was first published in his *Atlas Major* in 1662. The map presents a familiar view of Africa, Europe, and most of Asia, although Australia is shown only sketchily.

The Taj Mahal was built by the Mughal emperor Shah Jahan as a mausoleum for his beloved wife, Mumtaz. Exquisitely conceived on a massive scale, it also reflects the great power and wealth of the Mughals.

South and Southeast Asia

Mughal territory was extended by Shah Jahan during the mid-17th century but the empire was increasingly riven by religious intolerance, leading to instability. English and Dutch trading companies consolidated their possessions in the Indian Ocean. The English East India Company built forts and trading posts along the coasts of India, while the Dutch East India Company established headquarters on Java to control the production and distribution of spices from the Moluccas, increasingly taking over territory held by the expansionist sultanate of Mataram.

Fort Jesus near Mombasa was built by the Portuguese in 1593. It was lost in 1698 following persistent raids by Omani Arabs on Portuguese possessions in East Africa.

Africa

- **1619:** African slaves taken to the English colony at Jamestown
- **1641:** Dutch capture Portuguese possessions in Angola
- **1652:** Establishment of Dutch colony at the Cape of Good Hope
- **1665:** Portuguese defeat Kongo at Battle of Mbwila. Death of king
- **1670:** Angola gives up attempt to conquer Kongo after defeat of Portuguese army
- **1698:** Omani Arabs capture Mombasa

South and Southeast Asia

- **1619:** Dutch found Batavia as centre of trading empire in Southeast Asia
- **1627:** Shah Jahan becomes Mughal emperor
- **1641:** Dutch conquest of Malacca
- **1658:** Aurangzeb becomes Mughal emperor
- **1663:** Dutch complete expulsion of Portuguese from Ceylon
- **1679:** Fleeing Manchus settle in Mekong Delta
- **1691:** South Cambodia organized into two provinces of Annam

TRADING IN HUMAN LIVES

Hugh Crow was a Liverpool trader who made a fortune from slaves in the early 19th century.

THE USE OF SLAVES seems to have been endemic in most human societies. Normally taken as prisoners of war, slaves were also acquired as a form of tribute. The establishment of European colonies and overseas empires between the 16th and 19th centuries saw the creation of a slave trade on an industrial scale, a commerce which laid the foundations for pan-global trading networks. Trading concerns such as the English and Dutch East India companies developed trade on a larger scale than ever before; but it was the need to supply labour for the plantations of the Americas which led to the greatest movement of peoples across the face of the earth.

The Atlantic slave trade

From the late 15th to the early 19th century, European merchants – especially the British and Portuguese – carried on a massive trade in African slaves across the Atlantic. As well as utilizing the established sources of slaves from the central and West African kingdoms, they also raided coastal areas of West Africa for additional supplies of slaves. European manufactured goods, especially guns, were exchanged for slaves destined to work as agricultural labourers on plantations in the Caribbean and the tropical Americas. Slaves transported to the western hemisphere may have numbered 12 million or more.

Conditions on the terrible 'Middle Passage' from the slave ports of West Africa to the New World improved little over the centuries, although the death rate declined because journey times decreased significantly. Between four and five million people are thought to have perished before reaching the Americas.

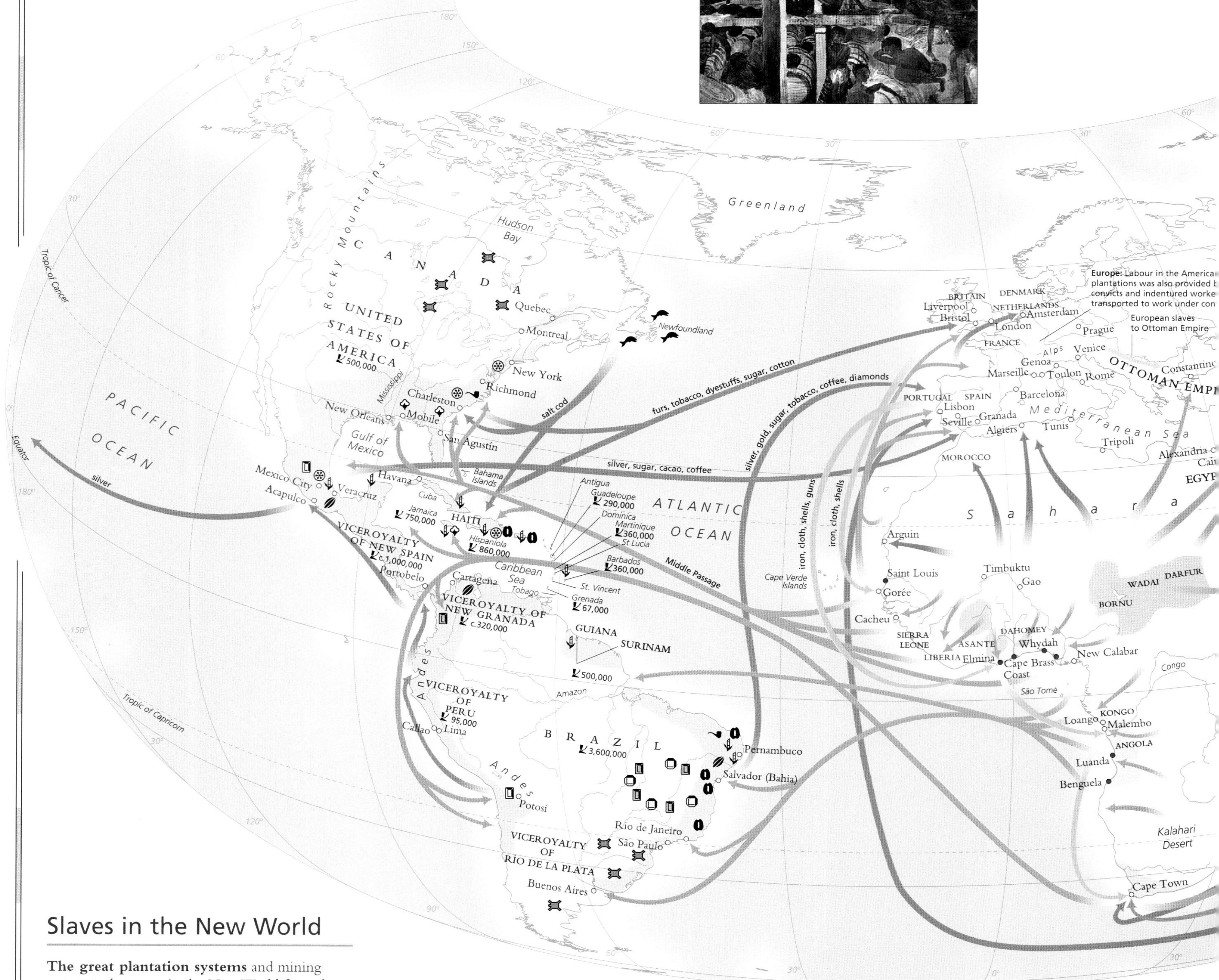

Greenland
Hudson Bay
Rocky Mountains
CANADA
Quebec
Montreal
Newfoundland
UNITED STATES OF AMERICA 500,000
New York
Richmond
Charleston
Mobile
New Orleans
Mississippi
San Agustín
Gulf of Mexico
PACIFIC OCEAN
silver
Mexico City
Veracruz
Acapulco
Havana
Cuba
Bahama Islands
Jamaica 750,000
HAITI
Hispaniola 860,000
Antigua
Guadeloupe 290,000
Dominica
Martinique 360,000
St Lucia
Barbados 360,000
St. Vincent
Grenada 67,000
Tobago
Caribbean Sea
VICEROYALTY OF NEW SPAIN c.1,000,000
Portobelo
Cartagena
VICEROYALTY OF NEW GRANADA c.320,000
GUIANA
SURINAM 500,000
Amazon
Andes
VICEROYALTY OF PERU 95,000
Callao
Lima
BRAZIL 3,600,000
Pernambuco
Salvador (Bahia)
Potosí
Rio de Janeiro
São Paulo
VICEROYALTY OF RÍO DE LA PLATA
Buenos Aires
salt cod
furs, tobacco, dyestuffs, sugar, cotton
sugar, tobacco, coffee, diamonds
silver, sugar, cacao, coffee
silver, gold, sugar, tobacco, coffee, diamonds
iron, cloth, shells, guns
iron, cloth, shells
ATLANTIC OCEAN
Middle Passage
Cape Verde Islands
Tropic of Cancer
Equator
Tropic of Capricorn
BRITAIN
Liverpool
Bristol
DENMARK
NETHERLANDS
Amsterdam
London
FRANCE
Prague
Alps
Venice
Genoa
Marseille
Toulon
Rome
OTTOMAN EMPI[RE]
Constantino[ple]
PORTUGAL
SPAIN
Lisbon
Seville
Granada
Barcelona
Algiers
Tunis
Tripoli
Mediterranean Sea
Alexandria
Cai[ro]
EGYP[T]
MOROCCO
Sahara
Arguin
Saint Louis
Gorée
Cacheu
Timbuktu
Gao
WADAI
DARFUR
BORNU
SIERRA LEONE
LIBERIA
ASANTE
Elmina
DAHOMEY
Whydah
Cape Brass
Coast
New Calabar
São Tome
Congo
KONGO
Loango
Malembo
ANGOLA
Luanda
Benguela
Kalahari Desert
Cape Town

Europe: Labour in the America[s] plantations was also provided b[y] convicts and indentured worke[rs] transported to work under con[…]

European slaves to Ottoman Empire

Slaves in the New World

The great plantation systems and mining concerns that arose in the New World from the 16th century onward demanded large reservoirs of labour. Though the Spanish and Portuguese initially used enslaved indigenous people, they soon required a more reliable source of labour. The Portuguese began bringing African slaves to the Caribbean and Brazil in the early 16th century. The cotton plantations of the southern US which boomed in the early 19th century were a key factor in sustaining the Atlantic trade.

Slaves planting sugar cane cuttings in specially-prepared plots on an Antiguan plantation in 1823 illustrate the labour-intensiveness of plantation agriculture. As European colonies, the Caribbean islands concentrated on cash crops such as sugar, coffee, and spices.

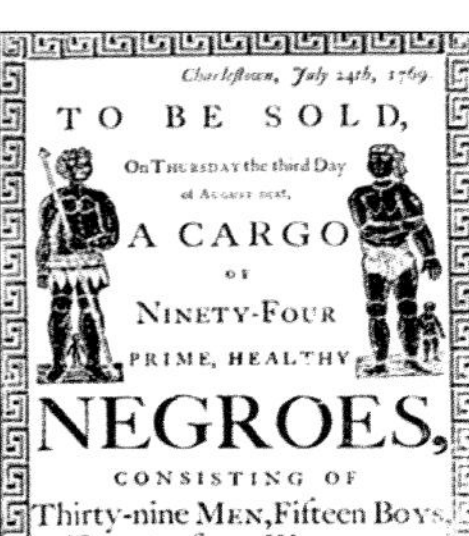
Charlestown, July 24th, 1769.
TO BE SOLD,
On THURSDAY the third Day of AUGUST next,
A CARGO
OF
NINETY-FOUR
PRIME, HEALTHY
NEGROES,
CONSISTING OF
Thirty-nine MEN, Fifteen BOYS,
Twenty-four WOMEN, and
Sixteen GIRLS.
JUST ARRIVED,
In the Brigantine DEMBIA, Francis Bare, Master, from SIERRA-LEON, by
DAVID & JOHN DEAS.

Slaves were sold at auction at ports such as Charleston. They swelled the population of southern North America: in the early 18th century, they comprised more than half of South Carolina's population

Other slave trades

By the 9th and 10th centuries, a number of complex slave-trading routes were in existence in Europe and the Near East. Viking and Russian merchants traded in slaves from the Balkans who were often sold to harems in southern Spain and North Africa. The Baghdad Caliphate drew slaves from western Europe via the ports of Venice, Prague, and Marseille, and Slavic and Turkic slaves from eastern Europe and Central Asia. In the 13th century, the Mongols sold slaves at Karakorum and in the Volga region. There was long-standing commerce in African slaves – primarily from East Africa before European mariners entered the slave trade. Between the 9th and 19th centuries Muslim merchants may have transported as many as 14 million across the Sahara by camel caravan and through East African ports, principally to destinations in the Indian Ocean basin.

This illustration from a 13th-century Arabic manuscript shows Africans and Europeans for sale at a slave market. Arab slave traders drew slaves from much of mainland Europe, Central Asia, and Africa.

SEE ALSO:
North America: pp.126–127, 130–131
South America: pp.148–149
Africa: pp.162–165

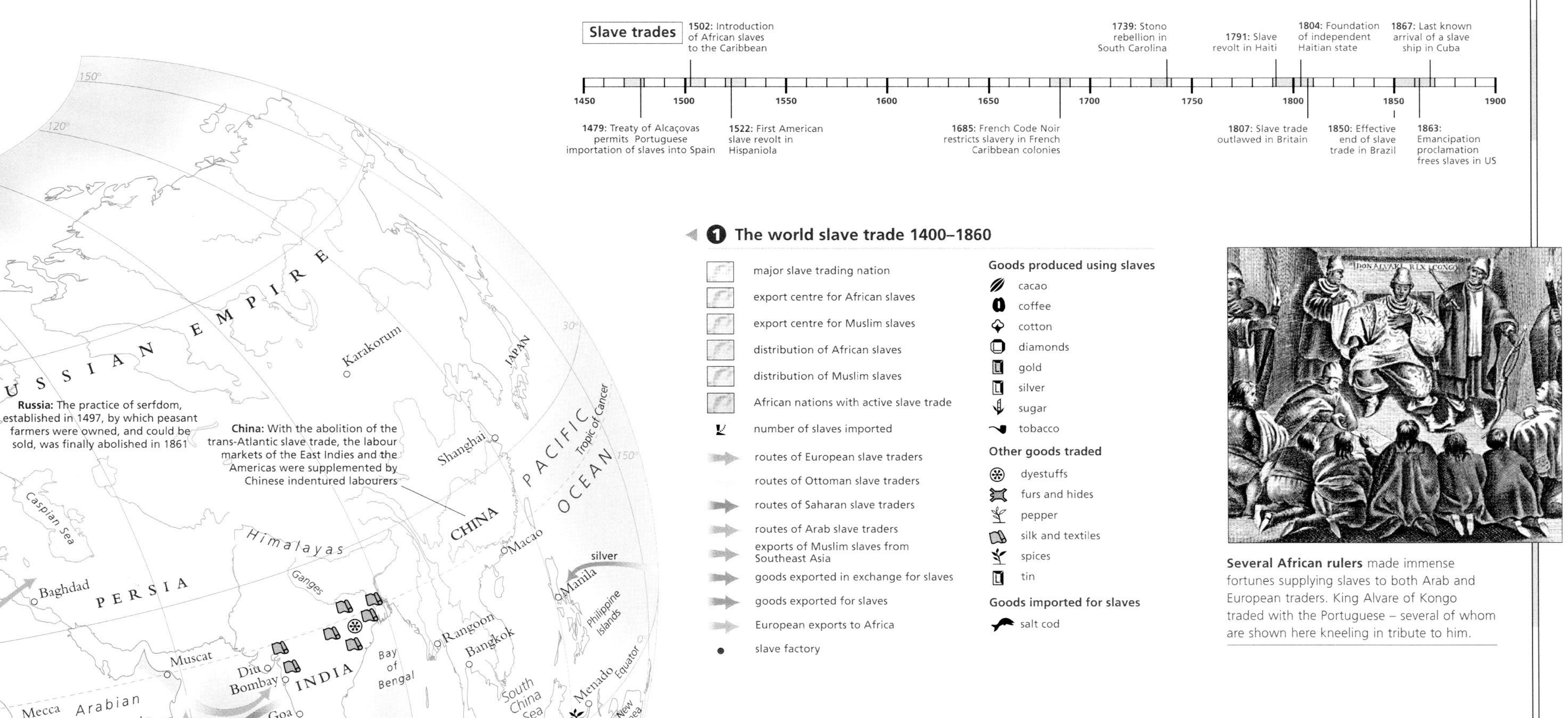
Slave trades
1502: Introduction of African slaves to the Caribbean
1739: Stono rebellion in South Carolina
1791: Slave revolt in Haiti
1804: Foundation of independent Haitian state
1867: Last known arrival of a slave ship in Cuba
1450
1500
1550
1600
1650
1700
1750
1800
1850
1900
1479: Treaty of Alcaçovas permits Portuguese importation of slaves into Spain
1522: First American slave revolt in Hispaniola
1685: French Code Noir restricts slavery in French Caribbean colonies
1807: Slave trade outlawed in Britain
1850: Effective end of slave trade in Brazil
1863: Emancipation proclamation frees slaves in US
1 The world slave trade 1400–1860
major slave trading nation
export centre for African slaves
export centre for Muslim slaves
distribution of African slaves
distribution of Muslim slaves
African nations with active slave trade
number of slaves imported
routes of European slave traders
routes of Ottoman slave traders
routes of Saharan slave traders
routes of Arab slave traders
exports of Muslim slaves from Southeast Asia
goods exported in exchange for slaves
goods exported for slaves
European exports to Africa
slave factory
Goods produced using slaves
cacao
coffee
cotton
diamonds
gold
silver
sugar
tobacco
Other goods traded
dyestuffs
furs and hides
pepper
silk and textiles
spices
tin
Goods imported for slaves
salt cod
RUSSIAN EMPIRE
Russia: The practice of serfdom, established in 1497, by which peasant farmers were owned, and could be sold, was finally abolished in 1861
China: With the abolition of the trans-Atlantic slave trade, the labour markets of the East Indies and the Americas were supplemented by Chinese indentured labourers
Karakorum
JAPAN
Shanghai
CHINA
PACIFIC OCEAN
Tropic of Cancer
Caspian Sea
Himalayas
Macao
silver
Manila
Philippine Islands
Baghdad
PERSIA
Ganges
Rangoon
Bangkok
Muscat
Diu
Bombay
INDIA
Bay of Bengal
Mecca
Arabian Peninsula
Goa
South China Sea
Menado
Equator
New Guinea
Cochin
Ceylon
Borneo
Shihr
Aden
Zeila
Horn of Africa
Sumatra
Java
Bali
Timor
Tambora
AUSTRALIA
Mogadishu
cotton, pepper, spices
INDIAN OCEAN
Tropic of Capricorn
Mozambique
Madagascar
Mauritius
Réunion
Quelimane
pepper, tin, spices

Several African rulers made immense fortunes supplying slaves to both Arab and European traders. King Alvare of Kongo traded with the Portuguese – several of whom are shown here kneeling in tribute to him.

Henry Morgan was a Welsh buccaneer who made a number of successful raids on Spanish ships and territory in the late 17th century – the most devastating being the destruction of Panamá in 1671.

Piracy and smuggling

High volumes of trade in lucrative commodities created abundant opportunities for piracy, privateering, and smuggling. Predators were most active in relatively unpoliced Caribbean and American waters. The numerous tiny islands, hidden harbours and dense, tropical vegetation – and the access it provided to valuable cargoes of sugar, rum, silver, and slaves – made the Caribbean a notorious hotspot for piracy and smuggling. Some predators were privateers who worked with the blessing of their home governments, such as Sir Francis Drake, but most maritime predators were freelance pirates, who selected their victims without discrimination.

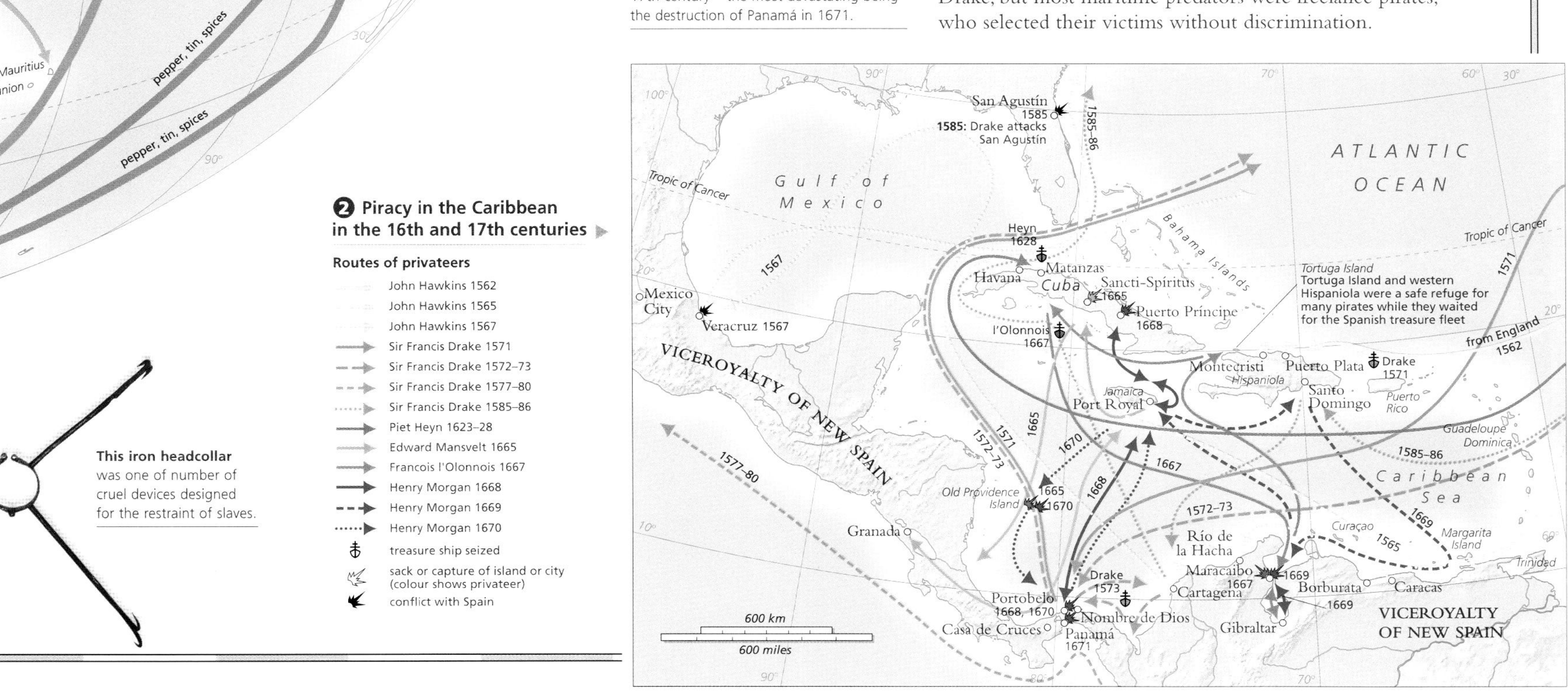
2 Piracy in the Caribbean in the 16th and 17th centuries
Routes of privateers
John Hawkins 1562
John Hawkins 1565
John Hawkins 1567
Sir Francis Drake 1571
Sir Francis Drake 1572–73
Sir Francis Drake 1577–80
Sir Francis Drake 1585–86
Piet Heyn 1623–28
Edward Mansvelt 1665
Francois l'Olonnois 1667
Henry Morgan 1668
Henry Morgan 1669
Henry Morgan 1670
treasure ship seized
sack or capture of island or city (colour shows privateer)
conflict with Spain
San Agustín 1585
1585: Drake attacks San Agustín
ATLANTIC OCEAN
Gulf of Mexico
Tropic of Cancer
Bahama Islands
Heyn 1628
Matanzas
Havana
Cuba
Sancti-Spiritus 1665
Puerto Príncipe 1668
Mexico City
Veracruz 1567
l'Olonnois 1667
Tortuga Island
Tortuga Island and western Hispaniola were a safe refuge for many pirates while they waited for the Spanish treasure fleet
from England 1562
VICEROYALTY OF NEW SPAIN
Montecristi
Puerto Plata
Drake 1571
Hispaniola
Jamaica
Port Royal
Santo Domingo
Puerto Rico
Guadeloupe
Dominica
1585–86
Caribbean Sea
Old Providence Island
1665
1670
Granada
1572–73
Río de la Hacha
Curaçao
Margarita Island
Trinidad
Drake 1573
Maracaibo
1669
1667
Cartagena
Borburata
Caracas
Portobelo 1668, 1670
Nombre de Dios
Gibraltar
Casa de Cruces
Panamá 1671
VICEROYALTY OF NEW SPAIN
600 km
600 miles

This iron headcollar was one of number of cruel devices designed for the restraint of slaves.

THE WORLD 1700–1800

FROM THE BEGINNING of the 18th century, new ideas in science, philosophy, and political organization fuelled change throughout the world. Popular reaction against the *ancien régime* in both France and North America led to the overthrow of the ruling governments. Improvements in agricultural techniques and land reform increased food production, and the population – especially in Europe – began to expand rapidly. Technological innovations in Europe led to the beginning of the Industrial Revolution and consequent urban growth. The expansion of European influence and territorial possessions throughout the world continued apace, with explorers charting the scattered islands of the Pacific and Britain establishing her power in India and Australia.

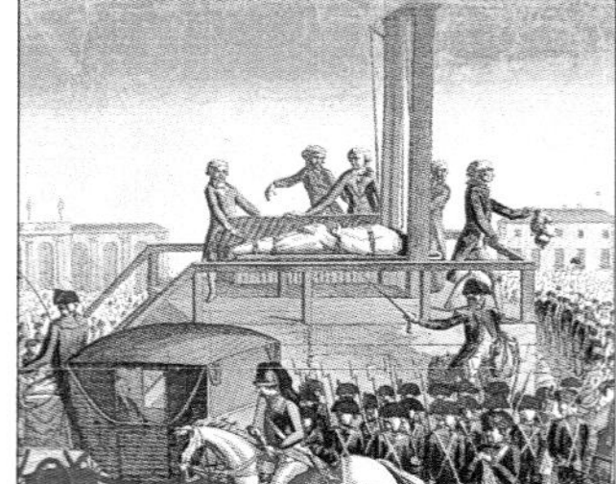

On 21 January 1793 the French king, Louis XVI was guillotined in front of a huge Parisian crowd. His wife, Marie Antoinette was executed later in the year.

Europe

Throughout Europe, government became more powerful, especially in the Russia of Peter the Great, and the Prussia of Frederick the Great. In France, Bourbon monarchy had reached its peak during the reign of Louis XIV (1643–1715). Revolutionary ideas unleashed by the 'enlightenment', combined with political relaxation, created an incendiary situation, leading in 1789 to the French Revolution whose effects reverberated throughout Europe.

Europe

- **1703:** Foundation of St. Petersburg by Peter the Great
- **1715:** Death of Louis XIV
- **1740:** Prussia launches War of Austrian Succession and becomes major European power
- **1756–63:** Seven Years' War in Europe
- **1768:** War between Russia and the Ottomans
- **1774:** Ottoman decline follows Treaty of Kuchuk Kainarji
- **1783:** Russia conquers and annexes Crimea
- **1789:** French Revolution begins
- **1799:** Coup brings Napoleon to power in France

1700 1720 1740 1760 1780 1800

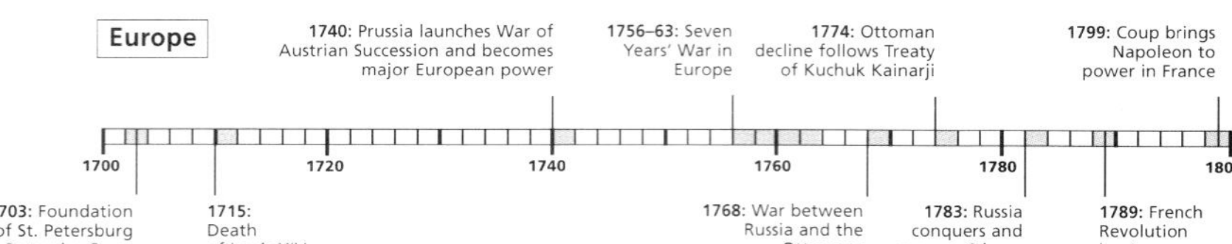

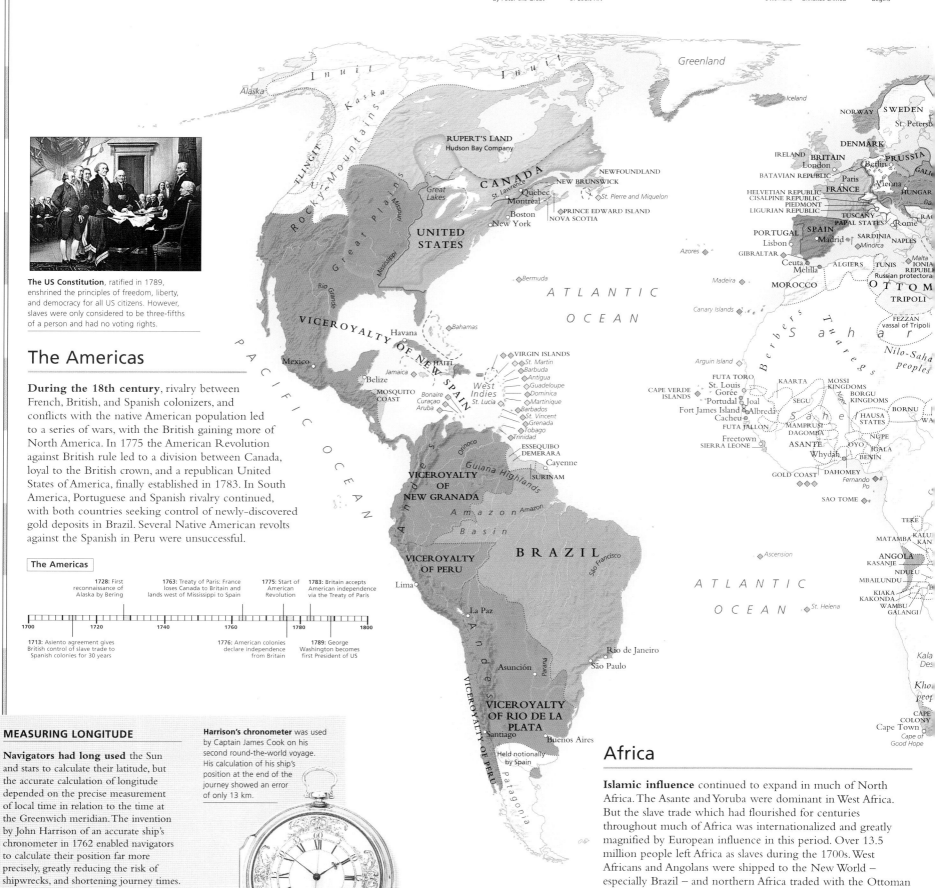

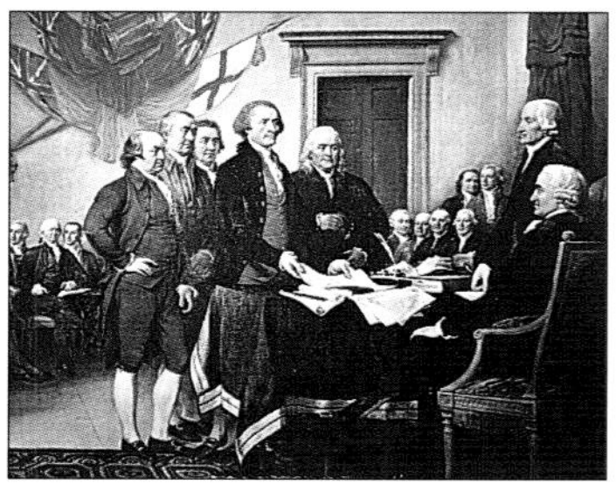

The US Constitution, ratified in 1789, enshrined the principles of freedom, liberty, and democracy for all US citizens. However, slaves were only considered to be three-fifths of a person and had no voting rights.

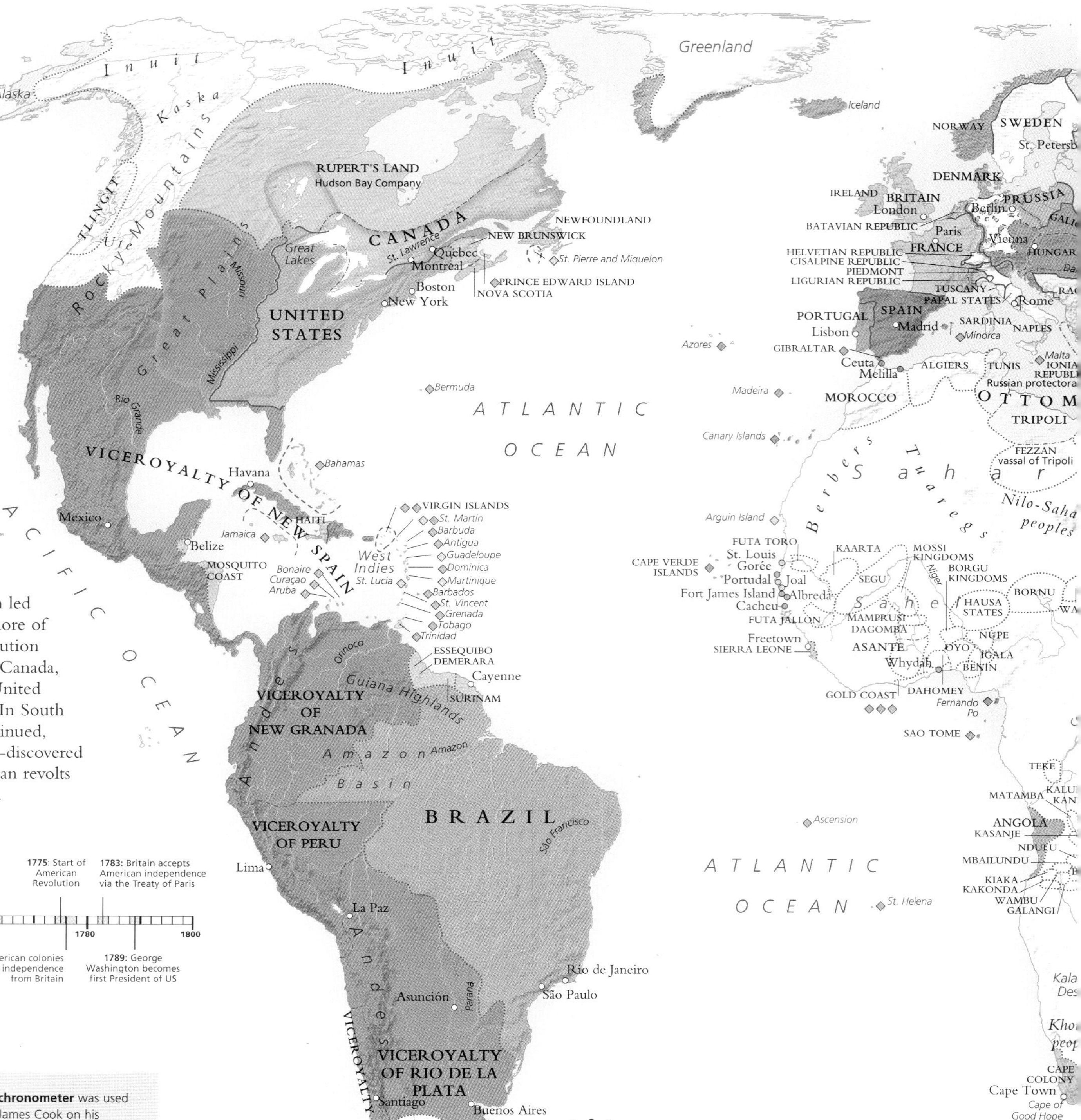

The Americas

During the 18th century, rivalry between French, British, and Spanish colonizers, and conflicts with the native American population led to a series of wars, with the British gaining more of North America. In 1775 the American Revolution against British rule led to a division between Canada, loyal to the British crown, and a republican United States of America, finally established in 1783. In South America, Portuguese and Spanish rivalry continued, with both countries seeking control of newly-discovered gold deposits in Brazil. Several Native American revolts against the Spanish in Peru were unsuccessful.

The Americas

- **1713:** Asiento agreement gives British control of slave trade to Spanish colonies for 30 years
- **1728:** First reconnaissance of Alaska by Bering
- **1763:** Treaty of Paris: France loses Canada to Britain and lands west of Mississippi to Spain
- **1775:** Start of American Revolution
- **1776:** American colonies declare independence from Britain
- **1783:** Britain accepts American independence via the Treaty of Paris
- **1789:** George Washington becomes first President of US

1700 1720 1740 1760 1780 1800

MEASURING LONGITUDE

Navigators had long used the Sun and stars to calculate their latitude, but the accurate calculation of longitude depended on the precise measurement of local time in relation to the time at the Greenwich meridian. The invention by John Harrison of an accurate ship's chronometer in 1762 enabled navigators to calculate their position far more precisely, greatly reducing the risk of shipwrecks, and shortening journey times.

Harrison's chronometer was used by Captain James Cook on his second round-the-world voyage. His calculation of his ship's position at the end of the journey showed an error of only 13 km.

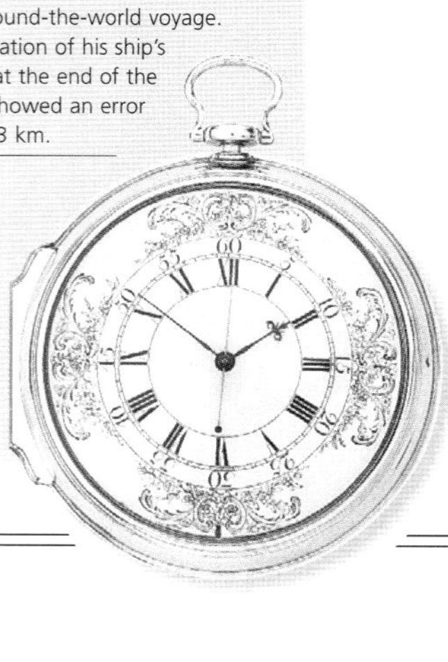

Africa

Islamic influence continued to expand in much of North Africa. The Asante and Yoruba were dominant in West Africa. But the slave trade which had flourished for centuries throughout much of Africa was internationalized and greatly magnified by European influence in this period. Over 13.5 million people left Africa as slaves during the 1700s. West Africans and Angolans were shipped to the New World – especially Brazil – and northern Africa traded with the Ottoman Empire. In southern Africa, Dutch and British colonists struggled for supremacy against organized Xhosa resistance.

CAPTAIN COOK'S MAP OF NEW ZEALAND

Until the 18th century Oceania and the South Seas remained a mystery to most navigators. The English sailor, Captain James Cook made three exploratory voyages to the South Pacific between 1768 and 1779. This map of New Zealand was made on Cook's first voyage. His ship, the *Endeavour*, traced the coast to make this remarkably accurate map.

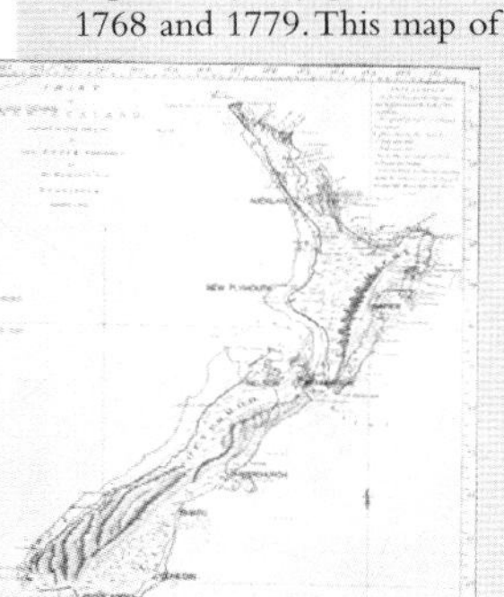

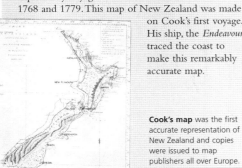

Cook's map was the first accurate representation of New Zealand and copies were issued to map publishers all over Europe.

By the late 18th century, many Indian rulers such as the Nawab of Bengal had assigned administrative powers to the British.

South and West Asia

The Persians under Nadir Shah began to challenge the Ottomans and pushed eastward into Mughal India, even sacking the city of Delhi in 1739. By the middle of the 18th century, the Marathas were emerging as successors to the Mughals, but they were comprehensively defeated by an Afghan army at Panipat in 1761. By the end of the century, the British East India Company had established firm control over much of India via a series of effective military campaigns.

SEE ALSO:

North America: pp.126–129

South America: pp.148–149

Africa: pp.164–165

Europe: pp.198–201

West Asia: pp.230–231

South and Southeast Asia: pp.246–249

North and East Asia: pp.268–269

Australasia and Oceania: pp.282–283

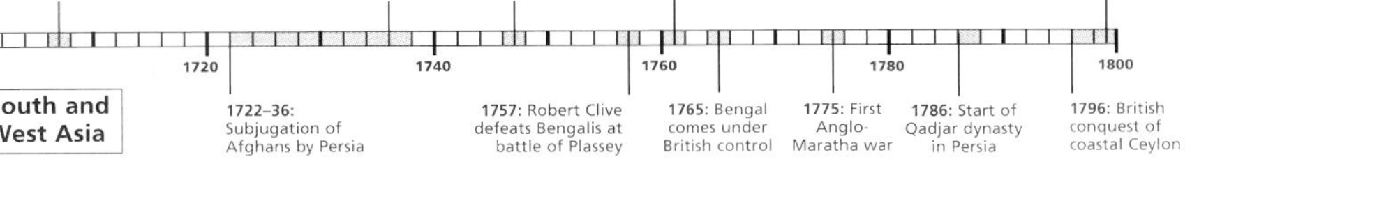

East Asia, Southeast Asia, and Oceania

The Qing dynasty extended its empire to include a protectorate over Tibet and the conquest of Xiankiang (Dzungaria) by 1760. By 1790, the Chinese population had virtually tripled to 300 million. Trade in tea, porcelain, and silk with Russia and the West boosted the economy and Manchu China was able to resist European incursion. The kingdoms of Southeast Asia were frequently at war, and subject to invasion by the Chinese, as with Burma in 1765–69. Though the Portuguese and Dutch had set up trading ports, much of the East Indies had yet to be formally colonized.

East Asia, Southeast Asia, and Oceania

1716	Start of Kyoho era in Japan
1751	Tibet, Dzungaria, and the Tarim Basin overrun by the Chinese
1752	Start of Konbaung dynasty in Burma
1755	Alaungpaya founds Rangoon and reunites Burma
1765–69	Manchus invade Burma
1768	Captain James Cook starts exploration of Pacific
1774	Nguyen Anh becomes emperor of Vietnam
1788	First British settlement at Botany Bay in Australia

Skilled Qing artists rendered images such as this vivid portrayal of an archery contest on silk. Silk and porcelain produced to a quality unknown in the West were prized by European traders.

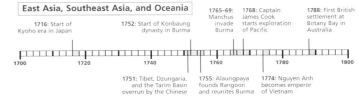

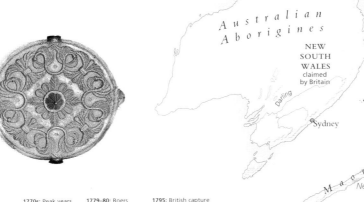

RUSSIAN EMPIRE
Siberia
Kazakhs
Gobi
QING EMPIRE
PERSIA
AFGHANISTAN
MARATHA CONFEDERACY
BURMA
SIAM
JAPAN
KOREA
PHILIPPINE ISLANDS
PACIFIC OCEAN
INDIAN OCEAN
Dutch possessions
Spanish possessions
Australian Aborigines
NEW SOUTH WALES claimed by Britain
New Zealand

Finely chased gold ornaments like this were worn as insignia by officials of the Asante court.

Africa

1705	Foundation of Husaynid dynasty in Tunis, which rules until 1957
1720	Dutch settlers reach Orange River from Cape
1730	Revival of ancient empire of Bornu in central Africa
1747	Oyo become main power in Niger Delta after defeat of Dahomey
1757	Muhammad III becomes Sultan of Morocco
1770s	Peak years of European slave trade with Africa
1779–80	Boers and Bantu at war in southern Africa
1787	Settlement of first freed slaves from Britain at Freetown
1795	British capture Cape of Good Hope from the Dutch
1798	Occupation of Egypt by Napoleon Bonaparte

The World in 1800

- Qing Empire
- Persia and possessions
- Ottoman Empire
- Britain and possessions
- France and possessions
- Denmark and possessions
- Spain and possessions
- Portugal and possessions
- Netherlands and possessions
- Prussia and possessions
- Russian Empire
- Austrian Habsburg territories
- Holy Roman Empire
- Persia on death of Nadir Shah 1747
- French possessions lost during 18th century

EMPIRE AND REVOLUTION

João V, king of Portugal from 1706–50, used most of the gold imported from his colonies in Brazil to finance his own grandiose building schemes.

RAPID POPULATION GROWTH, the creation of the first industrial societies, the maturing of Europe's American colonies, and new ideas about statehood and freedom of the individual, combined to create an overwhelming demand for political change in the late 18th century. Royal tax demands to finance expensive wars, and their often harsh attempts to control imperial subjects, became major focuses of discontent. The success of the Americans in their rebellion against British rule, and the total rejection of royal authority in favour of representative government during the French Revolution, had profound repercussions throughout Europe, with the revolutionary flame lit on numerous occasions from the 1790s onwards.

War on a global scale

With the acquisition of new territories overseas during the 18th century, the major European powers often transferred their local conflicts to a far wider arena. The Seven Years' War (1756–63) was fought in the colonies as well as in Europe, with Britain able to take control of the Atlantic and defeat the French in North America. A few years later, however, French support for the American rebels and the resurgence of French naval power thwarted Britain's attempts to hold on to its American colonies. The position was reversed in India, where British victory at Plassey in 1757 gave her vital control of the state of Bengal, and enabled the rapid expansion of British India.

The signing of the Treaty of Paris in 1763 ended seven years of bitter fighting between Britain and France in North America. Great celebrations were held in London's Green Park to mark the agreement.

The export of European conflict

- **1743:** King George's War between Britain and France in North America lasts until 1748
- **1744:** Britain and France join Carnatic War in India
- **1754:** French-Indian War between France and Indian allies and Britain
- **1756:** Start of Seven Years' War in Europe parallels conflict in North America
- **1757:** British victory at battle of Plassey in northern India
- **1758:** British take Senegal in West Africa from French
- **1758–61:** British victorious over French at Fort St. David and Pondicherry in India
- **1760:** End of French resistance in North America; Britain gains control of much of French America
- **1763:** Treaty of Paris ends Seven Years' War

1740 1750 1760 1770

❶ The European empires and the first world wars

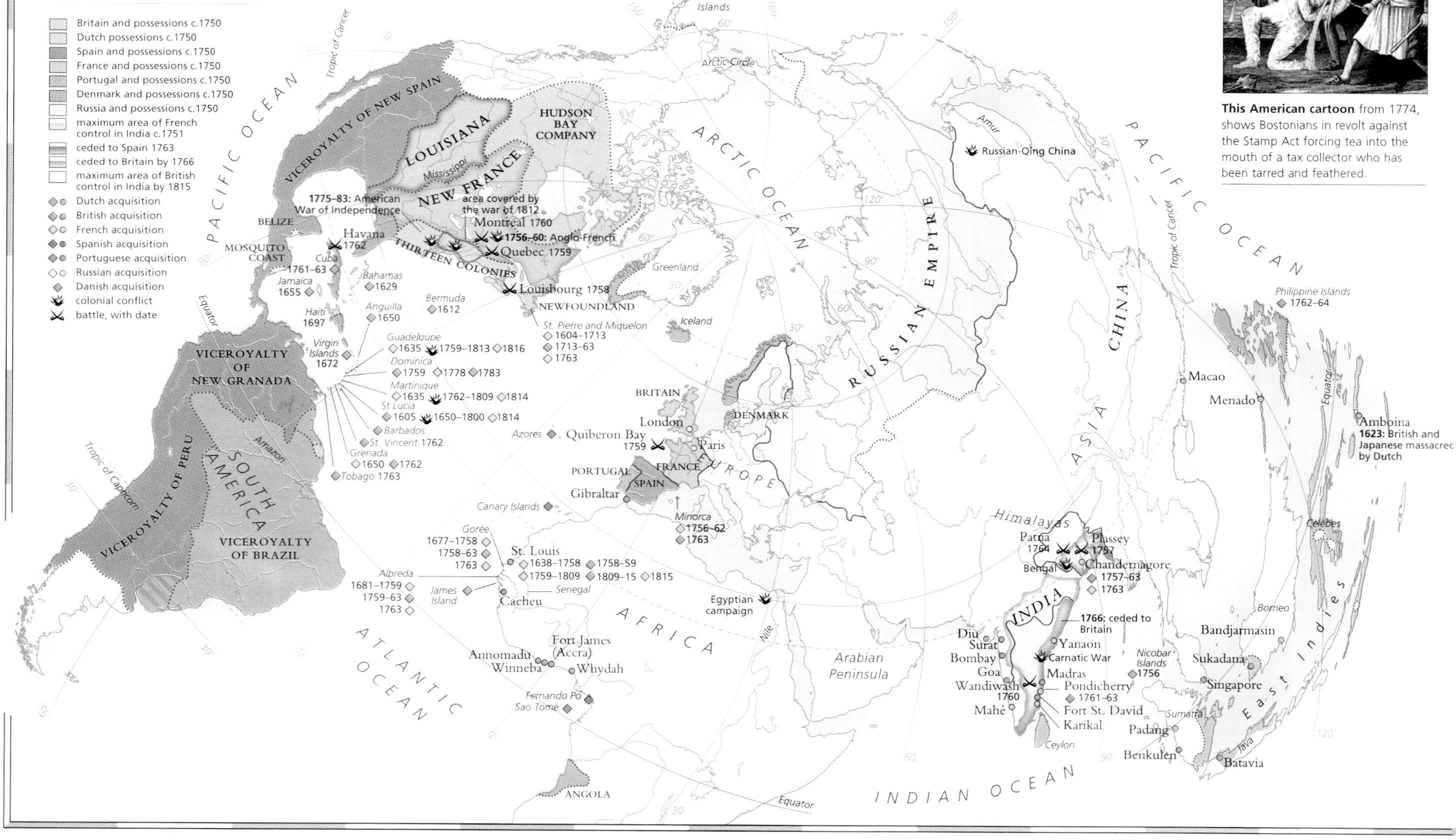

- Britain and possessions c.1750
- Dutch possessions c.1750
- Spain and possessions c.1750
- France and possessions c.1750
- Portugal and possessions c.1750
- Denmark and possessions c.1750
- Russia and possessions c.1750
- maximum area of French control in India c.1751
- ceded to Spain 1763
- ceded to Britain by 1766
- maximum area of British control in India by 1815
- Dutch acquisition
- British acquisition
- French acquisition
- Spanish acquisition
- Portuguese acquisition
- Russian acquisition
- Danish acquisition
- colonial conflict
- battle, with date

VICEROYALTY OF NEW SPAIN
LOUISIANA
HUDSON BAY COMPANY
NEW FRANCE
area covered by the war of 1812
1775–83: American War of Independence
THIRTEEN COLONIES
Montreal 1760
1756–60: Anglo-French
Quebec 1759
Louisbourg 1758
NEWFOUNDLAND
Havana 1762
BELIZE
MOSQUITO COAST
Cuba 1761–63
Jamaica 1655
Bahamas 1629
Bermuda 1612
Haiti 1697
Anguilla 1650
Virgin Islands 1672
Guadeloupe 1635 1759–1813 1816
Dominica 1759 1778 1783
Martinique 1635 1762–1809 1814
St Lucia 1605 1650–1800 1814
Barbados
St. Vincent 1762
Grenada 1650 1762
Tobago 1763
St. Pierre and Miquelon 1604–1713 1713–63 1763
VICEROYALTY OF NEW GRANADA
VICEROYALTY OF PERU
SOUTH AMERICA
VICEROYALTY OF BRAZIL
Greenland
Iceland
BRITAIN
London
Paris
Quiberon Bay 1759
Azores
PORTUGAL
SPAIN
FRANCE
DENMARK
EUROPE
Gibraltar
Minorca 1756–62 1763
Canary Islands
Gorée 1677–1758 1758–63 1763
St. Louis 1638–1758 1758–59 1759–1809 1809–15 1815
Senegal
Albreda 1681–1759 1759–63 1763
James Island
Cacheu
AFRICA
Egyptian campaign
Annomadu
Winneba
Fort James (Accra)
Whydah
Fernando Po
Sao Tome
ANGOLA
ATLANTIC OCEAN
PACIFIC OCEAN
ARCTIC OCEAN
Aleutian Islands
Arctic Circle
RUSSIAN EMPIRE
Russian-Qing China
CHINA
ASIA
Arabian Peninsula
Himalayas
Patna 1764
Plassey 1757
Bengal
Chandernagore 1757–63 1763
INDIA
1766: ceded to Britain
Diu
Surat
Bombay
Goa
Wandiwash 1760
Mahé
Yanaon
Carnatic War
Madras
Pondicherry 1761–63
Fort St. David
Karikal
Ceylon
Nicobar Islands 1756
Macao
Menado
Philippine Islands 1762–64
Amboina
1623: British and Japanese massacred by Dutch
Celebes
Borneo
Bandjarmasin
Sukadana
Singapore
Sumatra
Padang
Benkulen
Java
Batavia
East Indies
INDIAN OCEAN

❷ An era of revolution 1768–1868

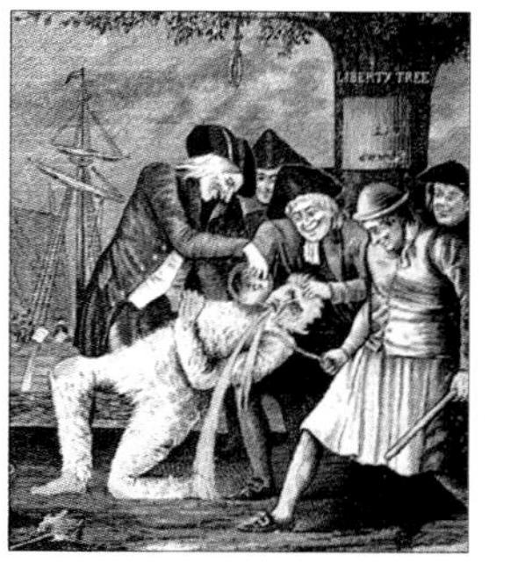

- area gaining independence from imperial control c.1750–1850
- area resisting imperial control or expansion c.1750–1850
- Britain and possessions
- Netherlands and possessions
- Spain and possessions
- France and possessions
- Portugal and possessions
- Denmark and possessions
- Russia and possessions
- independence achieved following war or revolution with date of independence
- European revolution or uprising 1750–1830 with date
- European revolution or uprising after 1830 with date
- area affected by 1848 revolutions
- important non-European uprising with date

MEXICO 1821 including United Provinces of Central America
Gulf of Mexico
UNITED PROVINCES OF CENTRAL AMERICA 1823
REPUBLIC OF HAITI 1804
GREAT COLOMBIA 1822
PERU 1821
BOLIVIA 1825
CHILE 1818
UNITED PROVINCES OF LA PLATA 1816
PARAGUAY 1813
URUGUAY 1828
BRAZIL 1822 including Uruguay at date of independence
Amazon
Patagonia
PACIFIC OCEAN

This American cartoon from 1774, shows Bostonians in revolt against the Stamp Act forcing tea into the mouth of a tax collector who has been tarred and feathered.

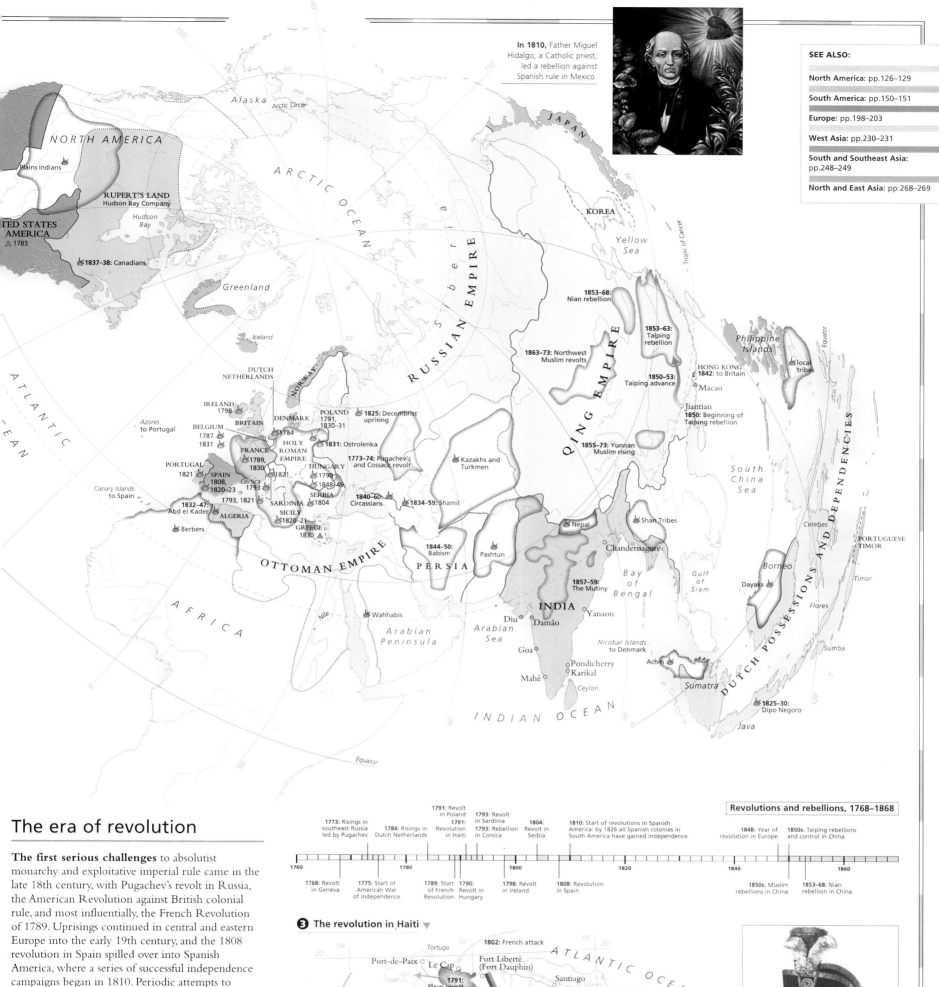

In 1810, Father Miguel Hidalgo, a Catholic priest, led a rebellion against Spanish rule in Mexico.

SEE ALSO:

North America: pp.126–129

South America: pp.150–151

Europe: pp.198–203

West Asia: pp.230–231

South and Southeast Asia: pp.248–249

North and East Asia: pp.268–269

Revolutions and rebellions, 1768–1868

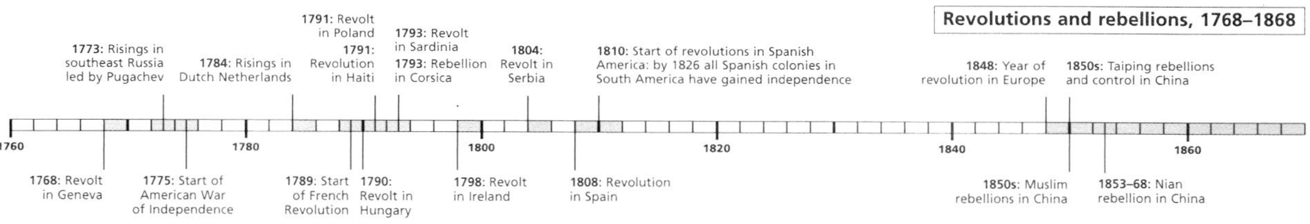

- **1768:** Revolt in Geneva
- **1773:** Risings in southeast Russia led by Pugachev
- **1775:** Start of American War of Independence
- **1784:** Risings in Dutch Netherlands
- **1789:** Start of French Revolution
- **1790:** Revolt in Hungary
- **1791:** Revolt in Poland
- **1791:** Revolution in Haiti
- **1793:** Revolt in Sardinia
- **1793:** Rebellion in Corsica
- **1798:** Revolt in Ireland
- **1804:** Revolt in Serbia
- **1808:** Revolution in Spain
- **1810:** Start of revolutions in Spanish America: by 1826 all Spanish colonies in South America have gained independence
- **1848:** Year of revolution in Europe
- **1850s:** Muslim rebellions in China
- **1850s:** Taiping rebellions and control in China
- **1853–68:** Nian rebellion in China

The era of revolution

The first serious challenges to absolutist monarchy and exploitative imperial rule came in the late 18th century, with Pugachev's revolt in Russia, the American Revolution against British colonial rule, and most influentially, the French Revolution of 1789. Uprisings continued in central and eastern Europe into the early 19th century, and the 1808 revolution in Spain spilled over into Spanish America, where a series of successful independence campaigns began in 1810. Periodic attempts to reastablish the old regime were continually met by risings, culminating in the 'year of revolutions' in 1848, when the fall of Louis Philippe in France inspired uprisings across most of Europe.

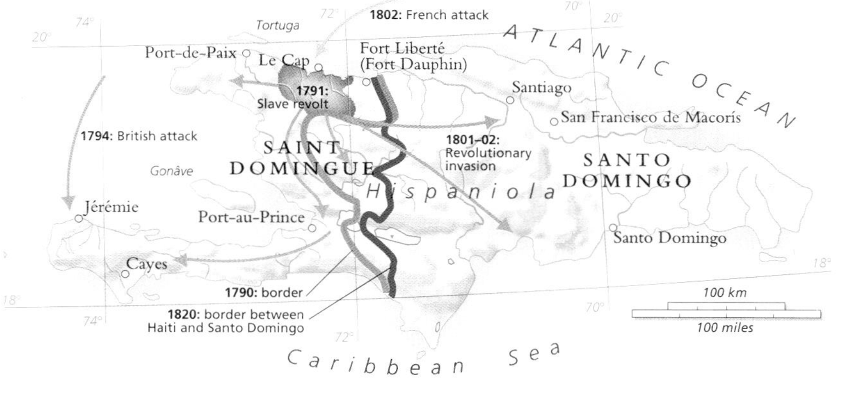

Delacroix's famous painting *Liberty on the Barricades*, became a banner of inspiration to French (and other European) revolutionary movements during the 19th century.

3 The revolution in Haiti

Haiti: a post-revolutionary state

In 1791, **fired by the French Revolution,** slaves in the prosperous French colony of Saint-Domingue rebelled, and by 1794, slavery was abolished. In 1801, rebel forces entered Spanish Santo Domingo, briefly uniting the whole island. Intervention by British and French forces failed to stop Haiti declaring its independence in 1804.

Toussaint l'Ouverture, a former slave, led the revolt of 1791, but did not declare Haiti fully independent. As a concession, he was appointed governor-general by the French in 1801. When French troops were sent to the island in 1802, Toussaint was forced to make terms with the commander of the invasion force. Subsequently betrayed, he died in prison in France in 1803.

THE WORLD 1800–1850

THE AFTERMATH OF THE FRENCH and American revolutions and the Napoleonic wars, led to a new nationalism and demands for democracy and freedom. The colonial regimes of South America were overthrown, and in Europe, Belgium and Greece gained independence. The US and northern Europe were transformed by the Industrial Revolution, as mass production and transportation led to an economic boom. There were mass movements of peoples to the expanding cities or to new lives abroad. Hunger for raw materials to feed industry and the desire to dominate world markets was soon to lead to unprecedented colonial expansion. In the US, Australia, and New Zealand, indigenous peoples were fighting a futile battle for lost territory.

A series of major innovations put Britain at the forefront of industrial development. The Nielsen hot blast process, invented in 1824, made iron smelting more efficient.

Europe

The Napoleonic Empire convulsed the established European order, abolishing states and national institutions. While liberals preached democracy, the ruling class responded with repressive measures to restrict freedom of speech and political expression. By the late 1840s civil unrest in the growing cities, bad harvests, and economic crisis, led to open rebellion. In 1848, Louis Philippe of France was forced to abdicate and revolution broke out throughout Europe.

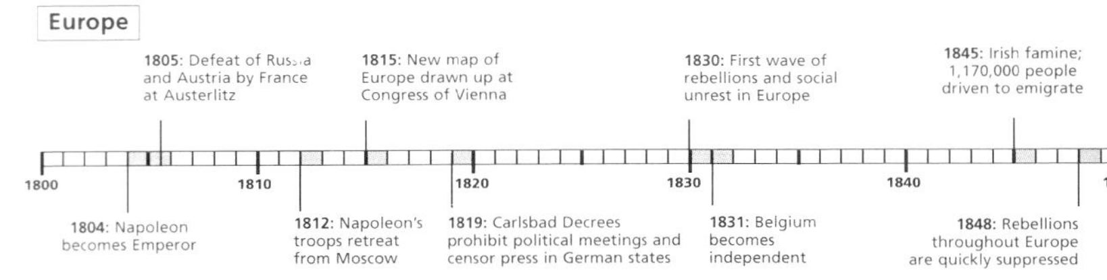

Europe
1805: Defeat of Russia and Austria by France at Austerlitz
1815: New map of Europe drawn up at Congress of Vienna
1830: First wave of rebellions and social unrest in Europe
1845: Irish famine; 1,170,000 people driven to emigrate
1800
1810
1820
1830
1840
1804: Napoleon becomes Emperor
1812: Napoleon's troops retreat from Moscow
1819: Carlsbad Decrees prohibit political meetings and censor press in German states
1831: Belgium becomes independent
1848: Rebellions throughout Europe are quickly suppressed

North America

The acquisition of new territories opened up the vast interior of North America to new settlement. Settlers pushing across the plains in search of fertile land and new wealth came into bloody conflict with native Americans who, equipped with both horses and guns, proved to be formidable foes. The mechanization of agriculture increased exports of wheat, tobacco, and cotton and as the economy prospered, cities expanded and immigrants arrived in great numbers.

The intensive plantation economy of the southern US was dependent on slave labour to pick cotton and harvest tobacco.

North America

1819: Parts of Spanish Florida conquered by US
1836: Texans rebel against Mexican rule and declare Republic of Texas
1849: Californian Gold Rush

1800 1810 1820 1830 1840 1850

1803: France sells territory between Mississippi and Rockies in Louisiana Purchase
1821: Mexico gains independence from Spanish colonists
1846–48: US victory in war with Mexico which cedes New Mexico and California to US

South America

When Spain was cut off from her colonies by the Napoleonic wars, nationalist forces took advantage of the resulting disorder and weakness of the colonial regimes. Argentina's struggle for independence was led by José de San Martín who marched an army across the Andes to liberate Chile and Peru from royalist control. Simón Bolívar led Venezuela and New Granada to independence, and helped found the new republic of Bolivia in 1825.

The Venezuelan Simón Bolívar (1783–1830) was known as the 'liberator of South America'.

South America

1810: Argentina declares independence from Spain
1821: Bolívar secures Venezuelan independence

1800 1810 1820 1830 1840 1850

1817: San Martín wins a decisive victory over the Spanish and liberates Chile
1822: Empire of Brazil becomes independent from Portugal

RAILWAYS

The steam locomotive was first developed in Britain in the early 19th century to haul heavy industrial loads. By 1830, engines were being used to pull carriages on iron rails and the first steam railway – the Stockton to Darlington – had opened. By 1850, railways had been built throughout Britain and were being introduced throughout its empire.

The steam engine, *Locomotion*, built by Robert Stephenson and Co. hauled the first train at the opening of the Stockton to Darlington railway in 1825.

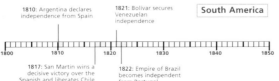

Africa

In sub-Saharan west Africa several Islamic leaders waged *jihad* against neighbouring states. Under the Ottoman leader, Muhammad Ali, the viceroyalty of Egypt extended south to incorporate Sudan. The French invasion of Algeria in 1830 led to a war of resistance, led by Abd al-Qadir. In southeastern Africa, conflict broke out between different tribal groups (the *mfecane*) as natural resources became scarce. Shaka, the Zulu leader, established a united kingdom in southern Africa. In the late 1830s the 'Great Trek' of the Boers from Cape Colony extended European influence into the African interior.

East and Southeast Asia

Superior firepower such as that displayed by the merchant steamer *Nemesis* enabled the British to overwhelm the wooden junks used by the Chinese in the first Opium War.

In the early 19th century, British merchants began to exploit the Chinese desire for Indian opium. As the trade flourished and the problem of opium addiction grew, the Chinese authorities attempted to stamp out the trade. The British objected and the first Opium War ensued. Japan, ruled by the inward-looking, Tokugawa shogunate for the last two centuries, remained closed to all foreigners, except a small Dutch trading community.

GEOLOGICAL MAPS

In the 19th century newly-discovered fossil remains were used to classify rocks and determine the sequence of geological strata. Geographical names were often used in the naming of rock types; for example, the Jura Mountains gave their name to the dinosaur-bearing Jurassic rocks.

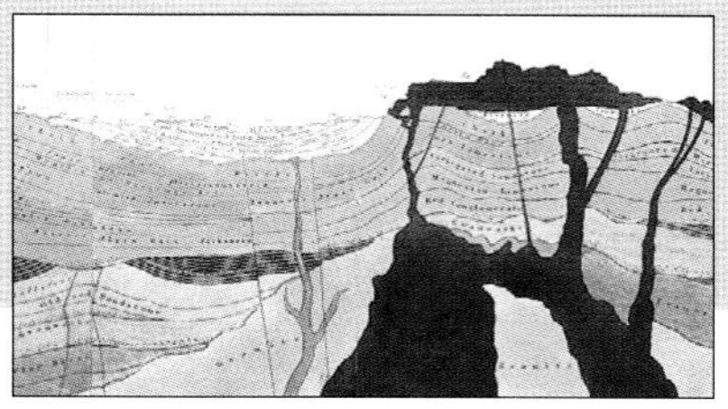

Geologists used cross-sections to map the age of rocks. This one is taken from the Reverend William Buckland's *Bridgewater Treatise on Mineralogy and Geology.*

SEE ALSO:

North America: pp.128–131

South America: pp.150–151

Africa: pp.166–167

Europe: pp.200–205

West Asia: pp.232–233

South and Southeast Asia: pp.248–249

North and East Asia: pp.268–271

Australasia and Oceania: pp.282–285

East and Southeast Asia

- **1802:** Gia-Long proclaimed emperor of united Annam (Vietnam)
- **1804:** Russian envoy fails to agree commercial treaty with Japan
- **1819:** Stamford Raffles, of the British East India company, founds Singapore
- **1834:** Monopoly of China trade by East India Company abolished
- **1837:** Tokugawa Ieyoshi succeeds Ienari as Japanese shogun
- **1839–42:** First Opium War in China
- ***1842:*** Treaty of Nanjing. Hong Kong ceded to British and five ports opened to foreign trade

Australasia and Oceania

New Zealand and Australia became British colonies in the first half of the 19th century. In Australia settlement spread from the penal colony at Port Jackson, now part of Sydney. As settlers founded towns at Adelaide, Melbourne, and Perth, they expropriated Aboriginal lands, and infected the people with fatal diseases, destroying local Aboriginal communities.

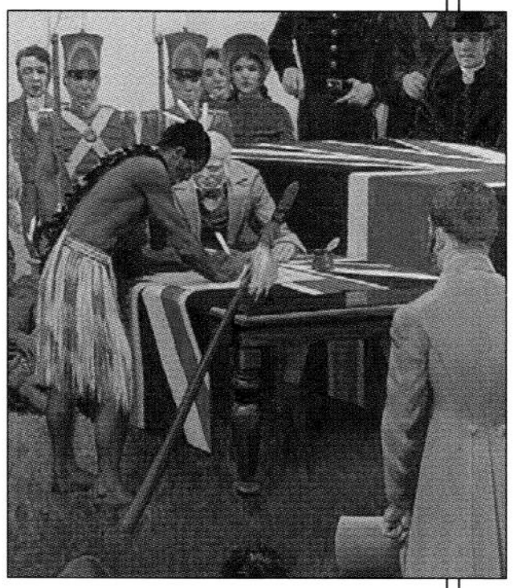

The Treaty of Waitangi allowed the Maori to maintain control over their lands while ceding the sovereignty of New Zealand to Britain, an unequal exchange which soon led to resentment and further wars.

Australasia and Oceania

- **1810:** Kamehameha I unites Hawaiian islands
- **1825:** Dutch annex western New Guinea
- **1829:** Britain annexes the whole continent of Australia
- **1835–36:** British found Melbourne and Adelaide
- **1840:** British takeover of New Zealand under Treaty of Waitangi

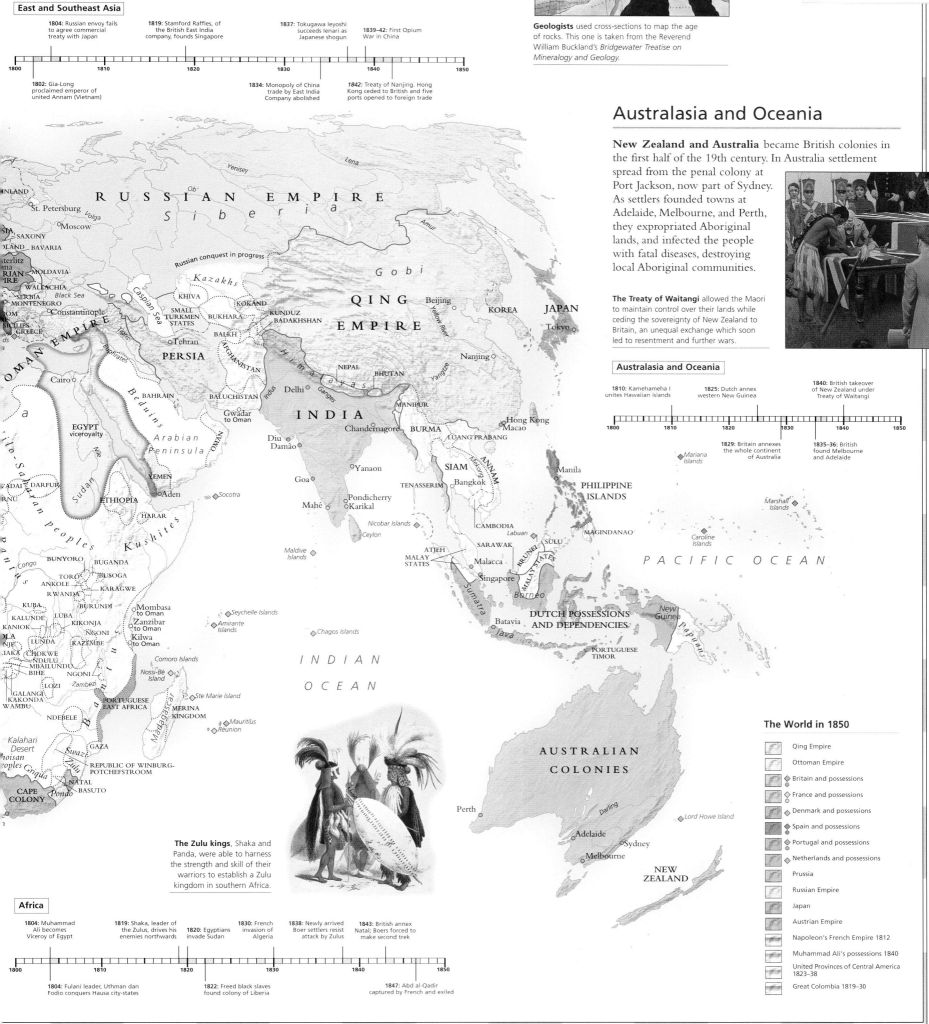

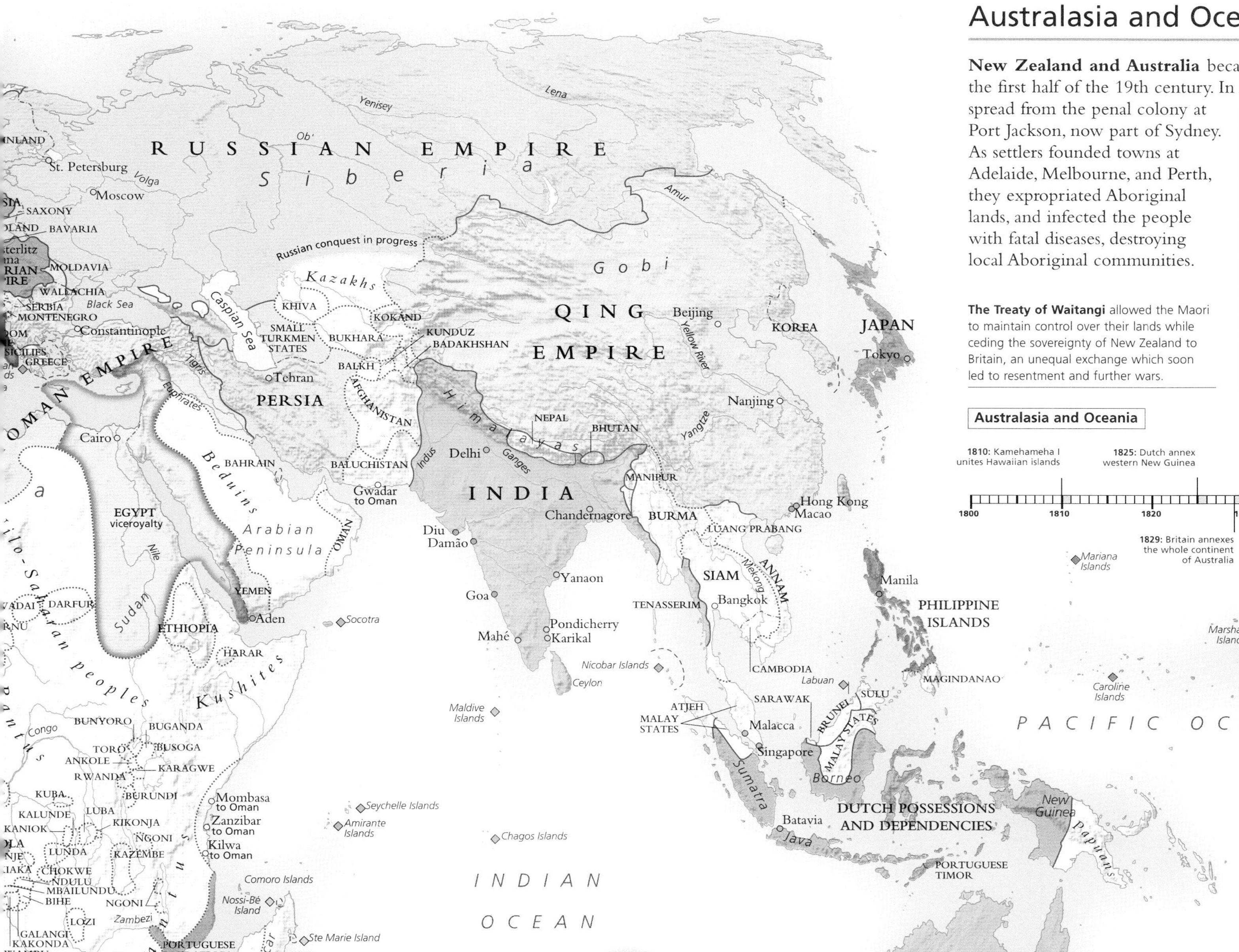

The Zulu kings, Shaka and Panda, were able to harness the strength and skill of their warriors to establish a Zulu kingdom in southern Africa.

The World in 1850

- Qing Empire
- Ottoman Empire
- Britain and possessions
- France and possessions
- Denmark and possessions
- Spain and possessions
- Portugal and possessions
- Netherlands and possessions
- Prussia
- Russian Empire
- Japan
- Austrian Empire
- Napoleon's French Empire 1812
- Muhammad Ali's possessions 1840
- United Provinces of Central America 1823–38
- Great Colombia 1819–30

Africa

- **1804:** Muhammad Ali becomes Viceroy of Egypt
- **1804:** Fulani leader, Uthman dan Fodio conquers Hausa city-states
- **1819:** Shaka, leader of the Zulus, drives his enemies northwards
- **1820:** Egyptians invade Sudan
- **1822:** Freed black slaves found colony of Liberia
- **1830:** French invasion of Algeria
- **1838:** Newly arrived Boer settlers resist attack by Zulus
- **1843:** British annex Natal; Boers forced to make second trek
- **1847:** Abd al-Qadir captured by French and exiled

THE WORLD'S ECONOMIC REVOLUTION

Innovative new constructions of the late-19th century included the Eiffel Tower, built in 1889.

IN THE FIRST HALF of the 19th century, world trade and industry was dominated by Britain; by the 1870s the industrial balance was shifting in favour other nations, especially Germany, France, Russia, and the US, with rapid industrialization occurring throughout most of Europe by the end of the century. A stable currency, a standard (i.e. the price of gold) against which the currency's value could be measured, and an effective private banking system were seen as essential to the growth and success of every industrializing nation. The major industrial nations also began to invest heavily overseas. Their aims were the discovery and exploitation of cheaper raw materials, balanced by the development of overseas markets for their products.

The impact of the Industrial Revolution

The introduction of steam to ocean-going ships decreased journey times, and increased reliability because ships were no longer reliant on the wind.

World industrial output from 1870–1914 increased at an extraordinary rate: coal production by as much as 650%; steel by 2500%; steam engine capacity by over 350%. Technology revolutionized the world economy: the invention of refrigerated ships meant that meat, fruit, and other perishables could be shipped to Europe from as far away as New Zealand; sewing machines and power looms allowed the mass production of textiles and clothing; telephones, telegraphs, and railroads made communications faster.

The opening of the Suez Canal in 1869, linking the Red Sea to the Mediterranean, reduced the journey time from Europe to India by 50%.

By the 1880s almost all of the US was connected by long-distance rail networks including the Illinois Central Railroad *(below)*.

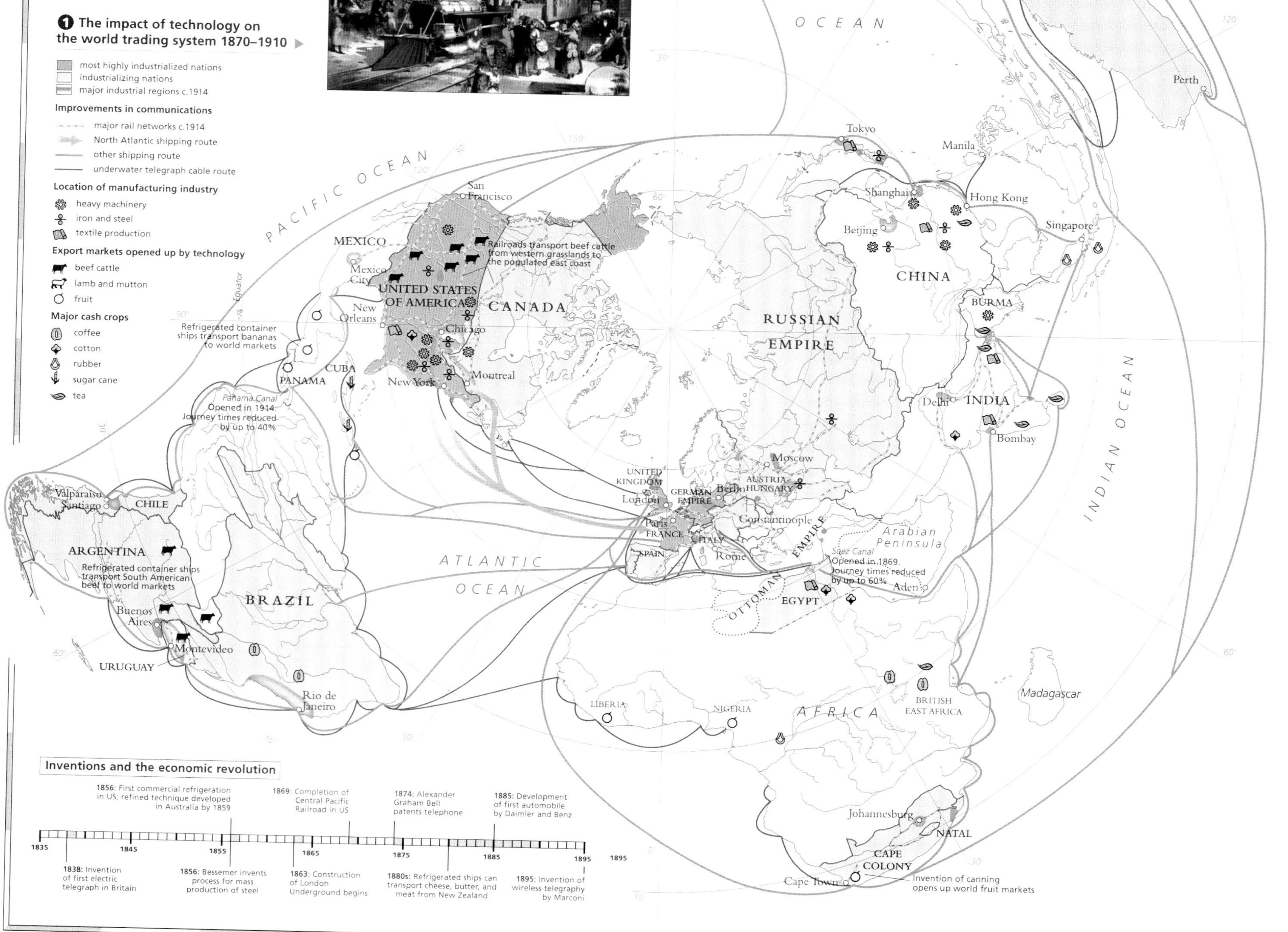

1 The impact of technology on the world trading system 1870–1910

most highly industrialized nations
industrializing nations
major industrial regions c.1914

Improvements in communications

major rail networks c.1914
North Atlantic shipping route
other shipping route
underwater telegraph cable route

Location of manufacturing industry

heavy machinery
iron and steel
textile production

Export markets opened up by technology

beef cattle
lamb and mutton
fruit

Major cash crops

coffee
cotton
rubber
sugar cane
tea

1859: Refrigerated container ships transport lamb and mutton to world markets

Railroads transport beef cattle from western grasslands to the populated east coast

Refrigerated container ships transport bananas to world markets

Panama Canal Opened in 1914 Journey times reduced by up to 40%

Refrigerated container ships transport South American beef to world markets

Suez Canal Opened in 1869 Journey times reduced by up to 60%

Invention of canning opens up world fruit markets

NEW ZEALAND, Sydney, Melbourne, Adelaide, AUSTRALIA, Perth, PACIFIC OCEAN, Tokyo, Manila, Shanghai, Hong Kong, Beijing, Singapore, CHINA, BURMA, INDIA, Delhi, Bombay, INDIAN OCEAN, RUSSIAN EMPIRE, Moscow, AUSTRIA-HUNGARY, Berlin, GERMAN EMPIRE, UNITED KINGDOM, London, Paris, FRANCE, SPAIN, ITALY, Rome, Constantinople, OTTOMAN EMPIRE, Arabian Peninsula, Aden, EGYPT, AFRICA, LIBERIA, NIGERIA, BRITISH EAST AFRICA, Madagascar, Johannesburg, NATAL, CAPE COLONY, Cape Town, ATLANTIC OCEAN, San Francisco, MEXICO, Mexico City, UNITED STATES OF AMERICA, CANADA, New Orleans, Chicago, New York, Montreal, CUBA, PANAMA, Valparaiso, Santiago, CHILE, ARGENTINA, Buenos Aires, Montevideo, URUGUAY, BRAZIL, Rio de Janeiro

Inventions and the economic revolution

1835 · 1845 · 1855 · 1865 · 1875 · 1885 · 1895

1838: Invention of first electric telegraph in Britain

1856: First commercial refrigeration in US; refined technique developed in Australia by 1859

1856: Bessemer invents process for mass production of steel

1863: Construction of London Underground begins

1869: Completion of Central Pacific Railroad in US

1874: Alexander Graham Bell patents telephone

1880s: Refrigerated ships can transport cheese, butter, and meat from New Zealand

1885: Development of first automobile by Daimler and Benz

1895: Invention of wireless telegraphy by Marconi

The great mineral rush

The search for new sources of minerals, both precious and functional, reached new heights of intensity in the industrial 19th century. New finds of gold and diamonds in the US, Canada, Australia, and South Africa fuelled the so-called gold and diamond rushes of the later 19th century. Though individuals could pan for gold in the Australian and North American rushes, the depth of gold and diamond deposits in South Africa meant that they could only be fully exploited with mechanical diggers owned by mining companies.

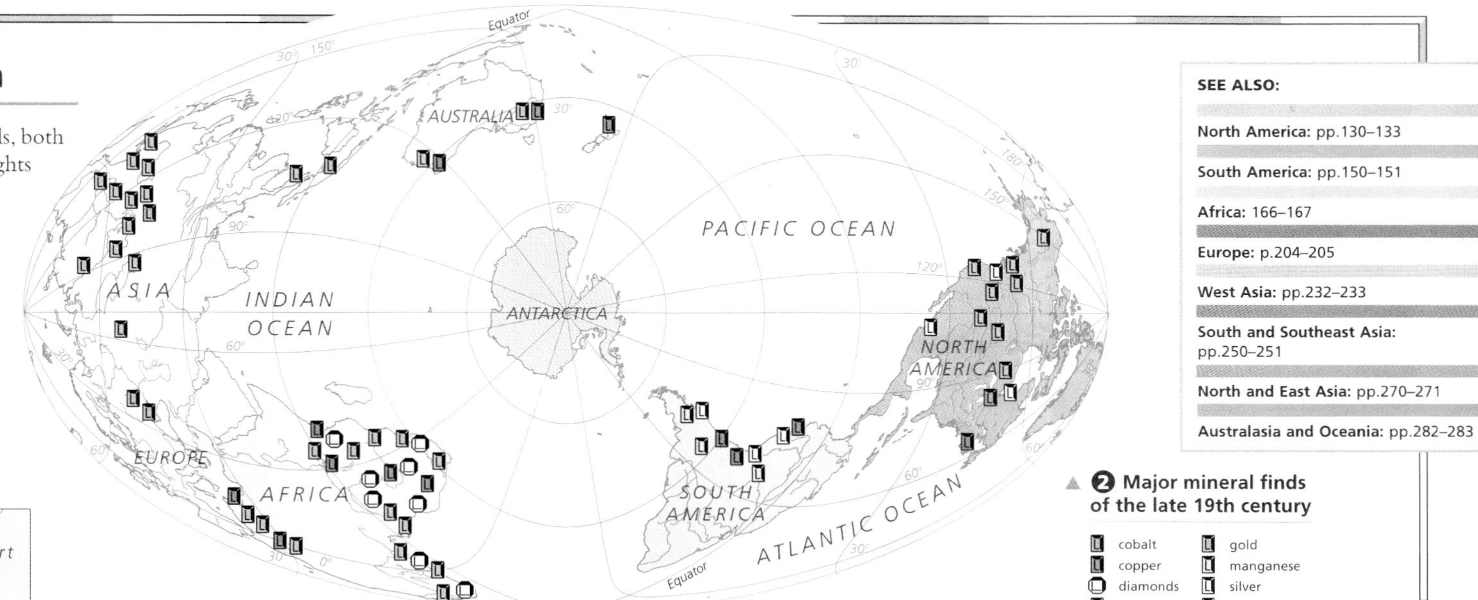

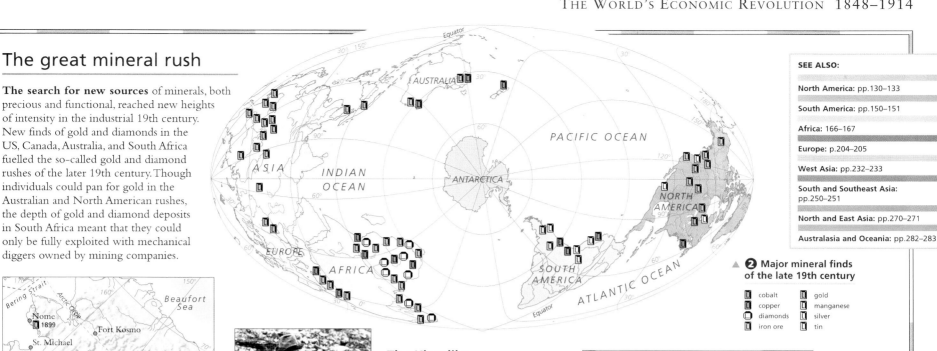

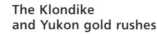

SEE ALSO:

North America: pp.130–133

South America: pp.150–151

Africa: 166–167

Europe: p.204–205

West Asia: pp.232–233

South and Southeast Asia: pp.250–251

North and East Asia: pp.270–271

Australasia and Oceania: pp.282–283

2 Major mineral finds of the late 19th century

cobalt, copper, diamonds, iron ore, gold, manganese, silver, tin

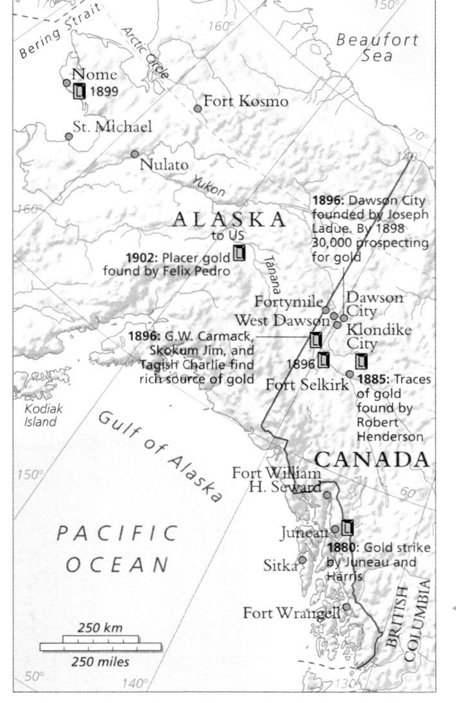

In the rush for instant riches miners such as this man, panning for gold in British Columbia in 1900, were prepared to undergo extreme hardship.

3 The Yukon and Klondike gold rushes

major gold strike
settlement or fort

The Klondike and Yukon gold rushes

Gold was first discovered near the Pacific coast of Alaska in 1880 by the explorers Juneau and Harris. The mid-1890s saw frenzied activity along the Yukon river and its tributaries, with an influx of many thousands of prospectors into one of the world's most desolate regions. Though Dawson City and other settlements grew up to supply the miners, the boom had receded by 1899.

Boom towns sprang up rapidly during the Yukon gold rush. Such was the passion for gold that even the city streets were dug up by eager prospectors.

Gold and diamond rushes

- **1848:** California Gold Rush starts near Sutter's Mill on the Sacramento River
- **1849–50:** Comstock Lode found near Virginia City, Nevada, USA
- **1851:** Rich gold deposits found in southern Australia
- **1858:** Gold discovered on Fraser River, northwest Canada
- **1867:** Diamonds found at Kimberley, north of Cape Colony, South Africa
- **1869:** Discovery of 'Star of South Africa' diamond sets off diamond rush
- **1876–78:** Gold found near Black Hills of Dakota
- **1886:** Deep seams of gold discovered on the Witwatersrand, South Africa
- **1896–98:** Yukon and Klondike gold rushes

The politics of cotton

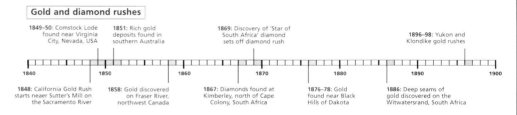

In the 1870s woven cotton in India was still produced on a local scale, by individuals, rather than factories, and traded at local markets *(above)*.

Cotton production was an early beneficiary of the Industrial Revolution. Eli Whitney's invention of the cotton gin led to a huge increase in the volume of cotton that could be processed; the invention of the power loom industrialized the weaving of cotton textiles. Britain's colonies in India and America supplied raw cotton for the cotton towns of Lancashire and Yorkshire; even with American independence, the Southern states continued to provide much of Britain's cotton. The economic and political importance of cotton to the US was reflected in the Confederate states' decision to use it as a bargaining tool during their struggle for international recognition following secession in 1861. The ploy failed as a strategy; during the Civil War, Britain turned to India for its raw cotton supplies. British cloth woven with Indian cotton was then exported back to India, a policy which benefited British producers, while keeping the Indian textile industry at a local level until the end of the 19th century.

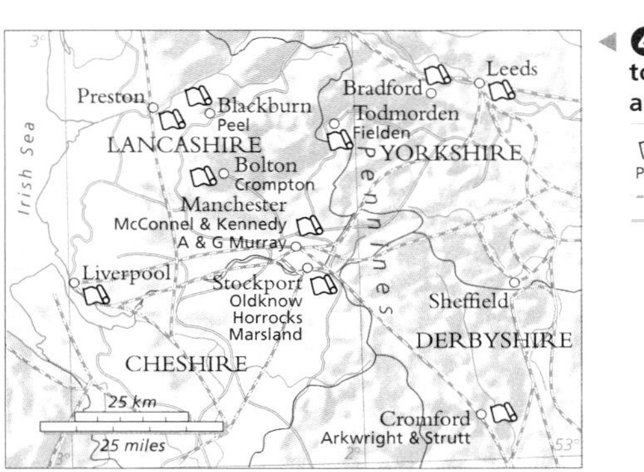

4 The cotton towns of Lancashire and Yorkshire

cotton town
Peel textile firm
major railway c.1850
major canal

Cotton production in Lancashire

With plentiful water to power new machinery, Lancashire had developed as a major cotton-weaving centre by the late 18th century. Textile towns such as Stockport, Blackburn, and Cromford, often containing several firms, grew up in the area around Manchester, which acted as a major market for finished cloth.

5 The politics of cotton

raw cotton from US to Britain
cotton textiles to India
raw cotton from India to Britain
cotton producing region
textile town
major cotton-producing states

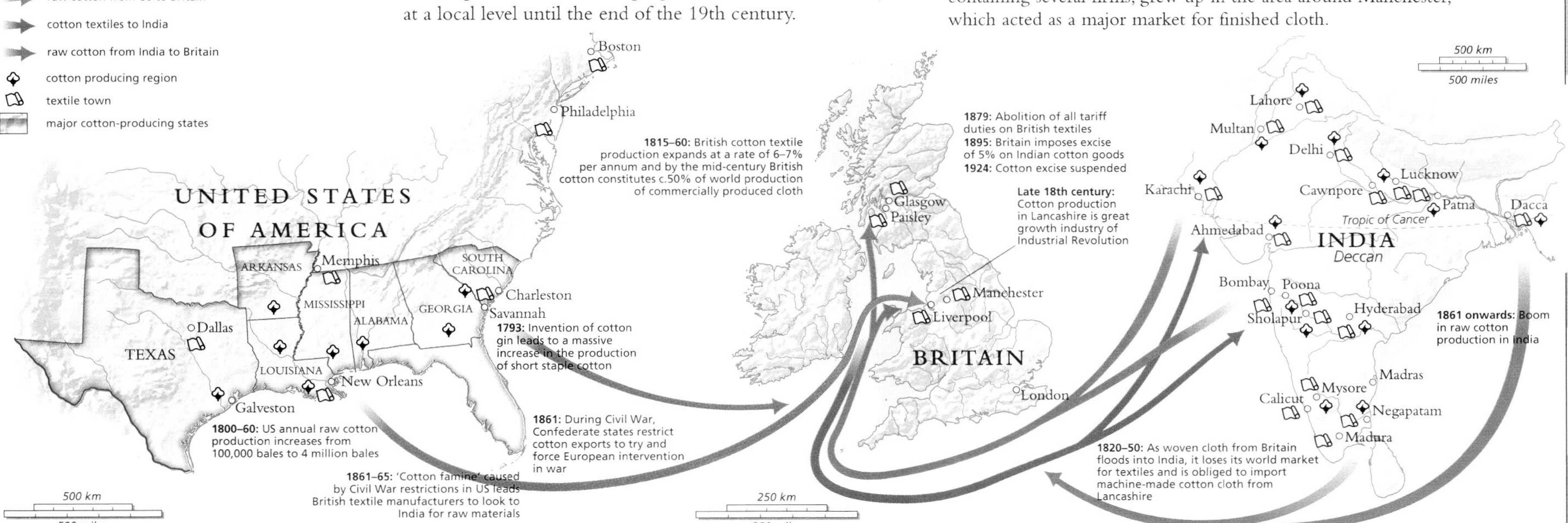

THE WORLD 1850–1900

BY 1900 THE EUROPEAN POPULATION had more than doubled to 420 million, while the population of the US had reached 90 million. Industry and commerce were booming, and both Europe and the US were traversed by railway networks. The major European powers were extending their economic and political influence to the very ends of the globe, while fierce rivalries and competition were being enacted on the international as well as the domestic scene. Within two decades the European powers had colonized virtually the whole of the African continent, the British had claimed India for the Crown, and the western powers had exploited the fatal weaknesses of China's crumbling Qing dynasty to penetrate deep into the heart of Asia.

Kaiser Wilhelm II was determined to establish Germany as Europe's leading military power.

Europe

The emergence of new states, the rise of nationalism, and growing economic and political power led to rivalry and conflict. Expansionist Russia's activities in the Balkans led in 1854 to the Crimean War, between a Franco-British-Turkish alliance and Russia. In 1870 Bismarck, prime minister of Prussia, goaded the French into war; the French defeat led to the collapse of the Second Empire, providing the final impetus to the creation of the new German and Italian nations.

Europe
1854–56: Franco-British-Turkish alliance victorious against Russians in Crimea
1862: Otto von Bismarck prime minister of Prussia
1870: Franco-Prussian war; Prussian victory leads to collapse of Second Empire
1887: Bulgaria, independent of Ottoman empire, becomes leading Balkan state
1850
1860
1870
1880
1890
1900
1861: Abolition of serfdom in Russia
1867: Dual monarchy of Austria-Hungary established
1871: Rome becomes capital of united Italy; King Wilhelm I of Prussia declared German emperor
1896: Revival of Olympic Games at Athens, Greece

CAMPAIGN MAPS

During the American Civil War, new printing technology, combined with up-to-date information from correspondents on the battlefields allowed US newspapers to produce simplified campaign maps to explain the stages of the war to a fascinated public.

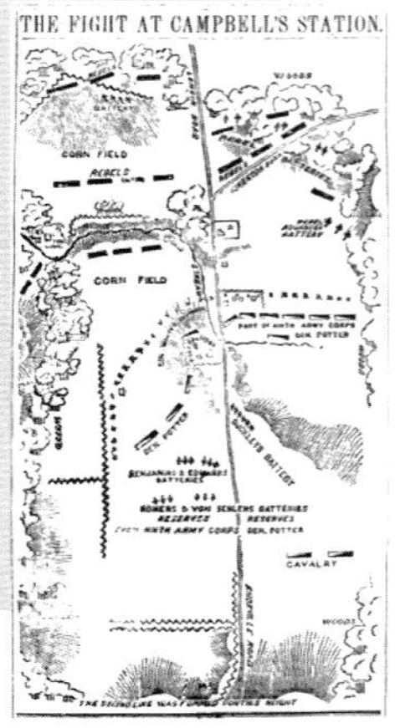

THE FIGHT AT CAMPBELL'S STATION.

This map shows the battle of Campbell's Station, Tennessee, as witnessed from the Union position by the *New York Tribune's* correspondent, Elias Smith.

The final push to populate the western US occurred in the latter half of the 19th century. Settlers and their wagon trains braved sometimes horrific conditions to claim new lands in the west.

The World in 1900

- Ottoman Empire
- Britain and possessions
- France and possessions
- Denmark and possessions
- Spain and possessions
- Portugal and possessions
- Netherlands and possessions
- German Empire and possessions
- Russian Empire and possessions
- Japan and possessions
- Italy and possessions
- US and possessions
- Confederate States 1861–65

The Americas

In 1861 seven southern states, fearful that the north was about to abolish slavery, left the Union and formed the Confederacy, beginning the Civil War, in which over 600,000 soldiers lost their lives. Following the Civil War the US became the fastest growing economy in the world, its population swollen by waves of immigrants. In South America, economic prosperity, especially from the export of meat and rubber, was enjoyed by the ruling elite, while border disputes bedevilled the new republics.

The Americas

- 1861–65: US Civil War
- 1864–70: Paraguayan War: Brazil, Argentina, and Uruguay defeat Paraguay
- 1879–83: War of Pacific; Chile, Peru, and Bolivia fight for control of Atacama Desert
- 1858: Mexican Civil War between conservatives and liberals
- 1867: Canada becomes a British dominion
- 1876: Battle of Little Bighorn; Sioux warriors kill 250 US soldiers
- 1898: Spanish-American War. US occupies Cuba, and gains control of Philippines

From the late 19th century, the newly-modernized Japan reopened its doors to foreign trade.

East Asia

Agrarian unrest in China in the 1850s led to rebellion and famine. Western powers were quick to exploit internal dissent, carving out spheres of influence and annexing territory. A wave of xenophobia led to the Boxer Rebellion of 1900. Western troops were sent to China and concessions were extracted from the weak government. In Japan, the overthrow of the Tokugawa shogunate in 1868 was followed by industrial and economic modernization.

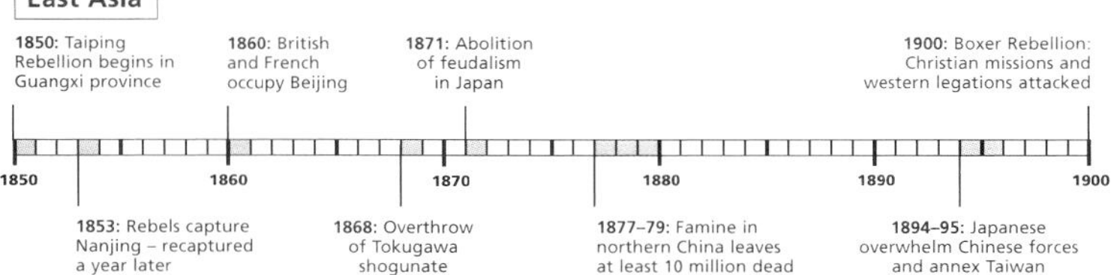

East Asia
1850: Taiping Rebellion begins in Guangxi province
1860: British and French occupy Beijing
1871: Abolition of feudalism in Japan
1900: Boxer Rebellion: Christian missions and western legations attacked
1850
1860
1870
1880
1890
1900
1853: Rebels capture Nanjing – recaptured a year later
1868: Overthrow of Tokugawa shogunate
1877–79: Famine in northern China leaves at least 10 million dead
1894–95: Japanese overwhelm Chinese forces and annex Taiwan

South Asia

The railway station in Bombay was opened in 1887. The style and scale of the building reflected the great self-confidence of India's British rulers.

By 1850 the British East India Company emerged as the major power on the sub-continent. Hostility to the British, combined with suspicions about their attitude to India's traditional faiths, led to the Mutiny of 1857–59. Following the Mutiny, the British took administrative control of India, developed an extensive railway network, and began to industrialize the Indian economy.

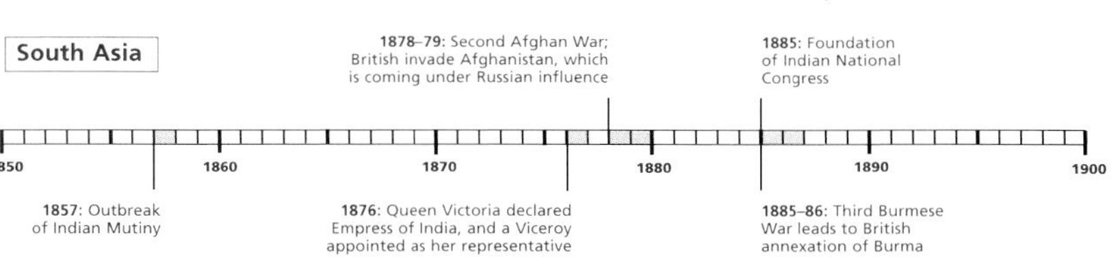

South Asia
1878–79: Second Afghan War; British invade Afghanistan, which is coming under Russian influence
1885: Foundation of Indian National Congress
1850
1860
1870
1880
1890
1900
1857: Outbreak of Indian Mutiny
1876: Queen Victoria declared Empress of India, and a Viceroy appointed as her representative
1885–86: Third Burmese War leads to British annexation of Burma

SEE ALSO:

North America: pp.128–133

South America: pp.150–151

Africa: pp.166–167

Europe: pp.202–207

West Asia: pp.232–233

South and Southeast Asia: pp.248–251

North and East Asia: pp.268–270

Australasia and Oceania: pp.282–285

THE TELEPHONE

The telephone was invented in 1876 by the Scottish-born inventor and speech therapist, Alexander Graham Bell. His device used a thin diaphragm to convert vibrations from the human voice into electrical signals. These were then reconverted into sound waves. Within a few years of its invention, the telephone had been installed in many city homes in Europe and the USA.

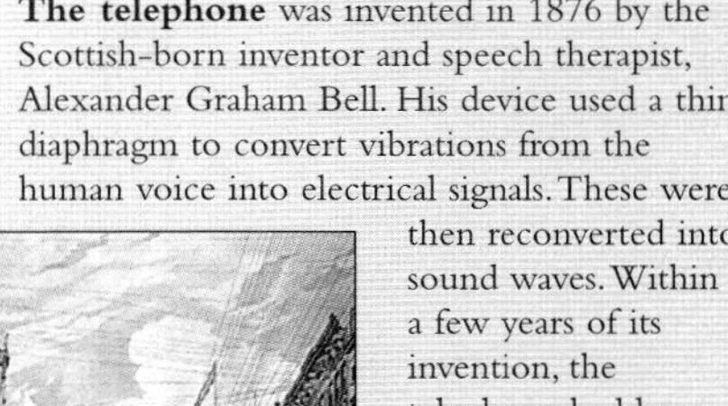

This view of Broadway in 1880 shows its skyline criss-crossed by telegraph and telephone wires.

ALGERIA
TUNIS
EGYPT
Cairo
Ottoman dominions under British control
FRENCH WEST AFRICA
French in terms of 1899 Franco-British agreement. French control in part notional
NIGERIA
KAMERUN
ANGLO-EGYPTIAN SUDAN
ERITREA
ABYSSINIA
Addis Ababa
FRENCH SOMALILAND
BRITISH SOMALILAND
ITALIAN SOMALILAND
BRITISH EAST AFRICA
LADO
CONGO FREE STATE
nominally independent under Belgian control
FRENCH CONGO
RIO MUNI
GERMAN EAST AFRICA
Zanzibar
ANGOLA
NORTHEASTERN RHODESIA
BAROTSELAND-NORTHWESTERN RHODESIA
BRITISH CENTRAL AFRICA
SOUTHERN RHODESIA
PORTUGUESE EAST AFRICA
GERMAN SOUTHWEST AFRICA
WALVIS BAY to Cape Colony
BECHUANALAND
SOUTH AFRICAN REPUBLIC
ORANGE FREE STATE
NATAL
BASUTOLAND
CAPE COLONY
Cape Town
MADAGASCAR
Comoro Islands

RUSSIAN EMPIRE
Siberia
OTTOMAN EMPIRE
PERSIA
Tehran
AFGHANISTAN
BUKHARA
KHIVA
INDIA
Delhi
Bombay
Goa
Madras
Pondicherry
CEYLON
MALDIVE ISLANDS
Chagos Islands
Seychelles
INDIAN OCEAN

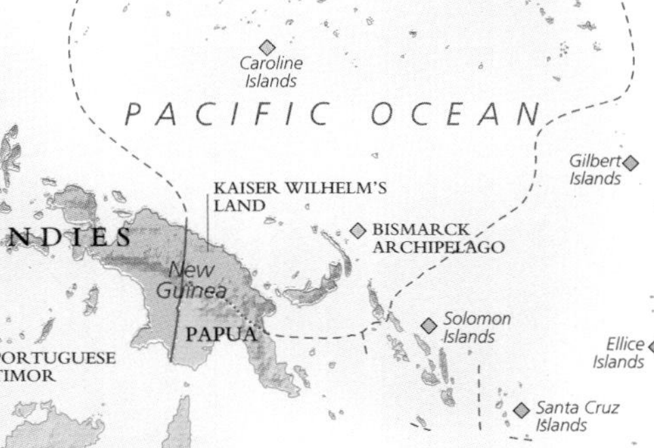

QING EMPIRE
Beijing
KOREA
JAPAN
Tokyo
Shanghai
Hong Kong
SIAM
FRENCH INDOCHINA
PHILIPPINE ISLANDS
DUTCH EAST INDIES
PACIFIC OCEAN

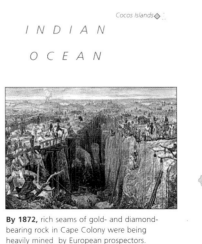

By 1872, rich seams of gold- and diamond-bearing rock in Cape Colony were being heavily mined by European prospectors.

AUSTRALIAN COLONIES
Sydney
NEW ZEALAND

Africa

In 1850 Africa was a patchwork of kingdoms and states, mostly unknown to Europeans. But, by 1900, the major European powers had seized virtually the entire continent. Rivalries between European nations were played out in Africa as colonizing countries raced for territory, raw materials, and new markets. In 1898, open war between France and the British in the White Nile region was only just averted. In 1899, the Boer War, a bitter struggle between the British and Afrikaaners, began.

Africa

1869: Opening of Suez Canal
1880: White Boers have appropriated most habitable land in Cape Colony
1896: Abyssinia defeats Italians at Adowa
1899: Boer War begins

1850 · 1860 · 1870 · 1880 · 1890 · 1900

1863: Al-Hajj 'Umar clashes with French in Senegal valley and creates a Muslim empire
1879: Zulu War with British; Zulus defeated
1882: British invade and occupy Egypt
1893: French conquer Dahomey
1898: British and French clash at Fashoda

THE ERA OF WESTERN IMPERIALISM

This *Punch* cartoon from 1890 depicts Germany as an eagle, with Africa as her prey. The caption reads, 'On the Swoop'.

THE LAST TWENTY YEARS of the 19th century saw unprecedented competition by the major European nations for control of territory overseas. The balance of imperial power was changing: having lost their American empires, Spain and Portugal were no longer pre-eminent. From the 1830s, France began to build a new empire, and Britain continued to acquire new lands throughout the century. Newly-unified Italy and Germany sought to bolster their nation status from the 1880s with their own empires. Africa was the most fiercely contested prize in this race to absorb the non-industrialized world, but much of Southeast Asia and Oceania was also appropriated in this period. Even the US, historically the champion of anti-colonial movements began to expand across the Pacific.

Other nations were frequently critical of the behaviour of European imperialists in Africa. This German cartoon *(left)* has the caption: 'Even the lions weep at the way the native Africans are treated by the French'.

Many British officials in India maintained rituals of extreme formality *(below)*, rather than adapting to native patterns of behaviour.

The scramble for Africa

The race for European political control in Africa began in the early 1880s. The Berlin Conference of 1884–85, convened to discuss rival European claims to Africa, was the starting point for the 'scramble'. Some governments worked through commercial companies; elsewhere, land was independently annexed by these companies; sometimes Africans actually invited Europeans in. In most cases, however, European political control was directly imposed by conquest. By 1914, Africa was fully partitioned, along lines that bore little relation to cultural or linguistic traditions.

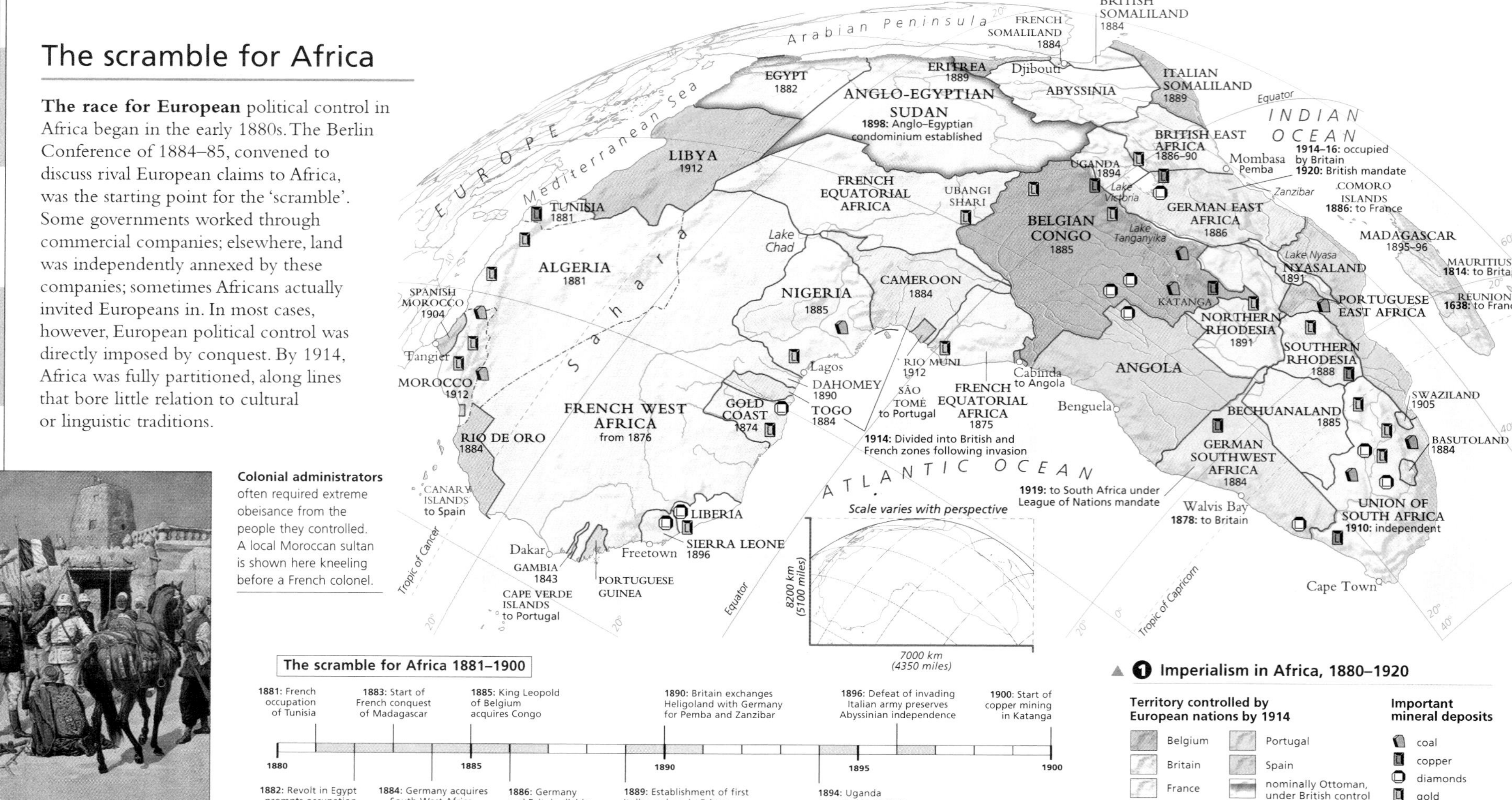

Colonial administrators often required extreme obeisance from the people they controlled. A local Moroccan sultan is shown here kneeling before a French colonel.

▲ ❶ Imperialism in Africa, 1880–1920

The struggle for South Africa

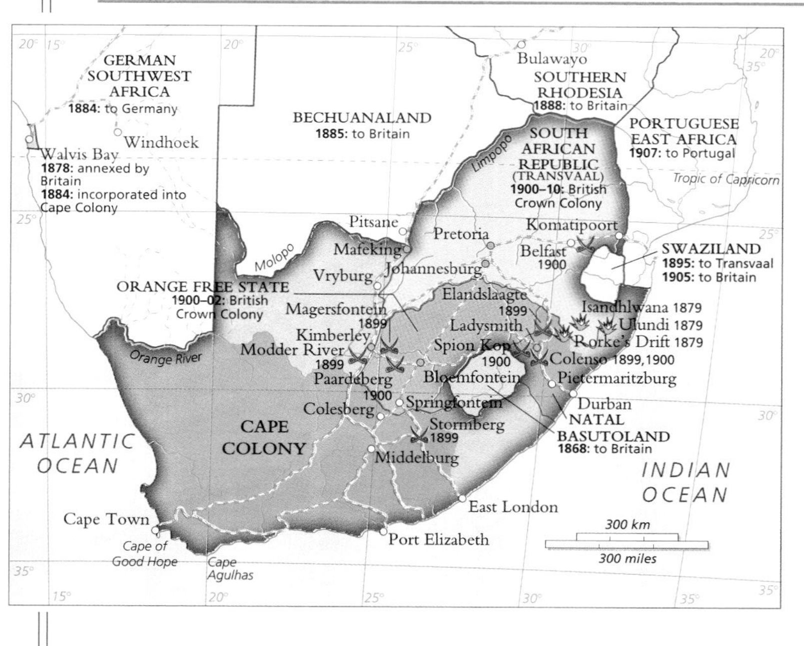

The British, with political control, the Afrikaners (Boers) – the first European settlers – and the Zulus all fought for control of South Africa in the 19th century. Seeking political autonomy, the Boers moved to found their own republics. The success of Transvaal, which grew rich from gold, led to annexation by Britain in 1877. British invasion of Zulu territory led to the First Zulu War, and British defeat, although this was swiftly reversed. In 1881, Boers in Transvaal rebelled against British rule, to set up the South African Republic. In 1899, the second Anglo-Boer war, broke out, lasting until 1902. The former Boer Republics became part of the British Empire as part of the Peace of Vereeniging.

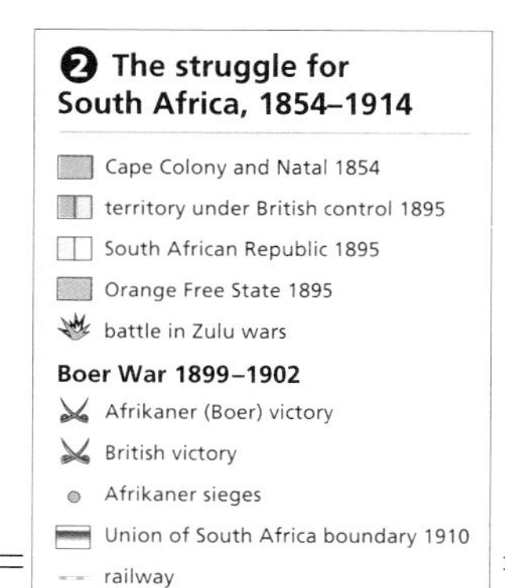

It took more than 300,000 British soldiers five years to subdue 75,000 heavily-armed Boers, skilled in guerrilla and siege tactics, and with intimate knowledge of the terrain.

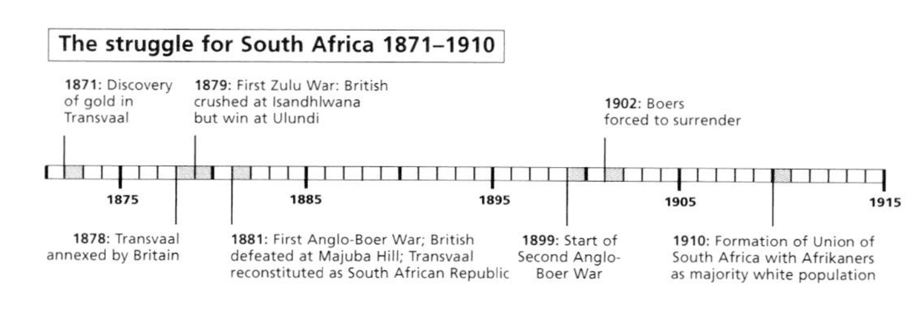

Imperialism in Southeast Asia

Though the Dutch East Indian Empire had existed since the early 17th century, much of Southeast Asia was not colonized until the mid-19th century. Moving east from India, British ambitions concentrated on Burma, the Malay Peninsula, and north Borneo. Renewed French interest in empire-building began in earnest with the capture of Saigon in 1858 following a concerted naval effort. By 1893, France controlled Tongking, Laos, Annam, and Cambodia, collectively known as Indo-China.

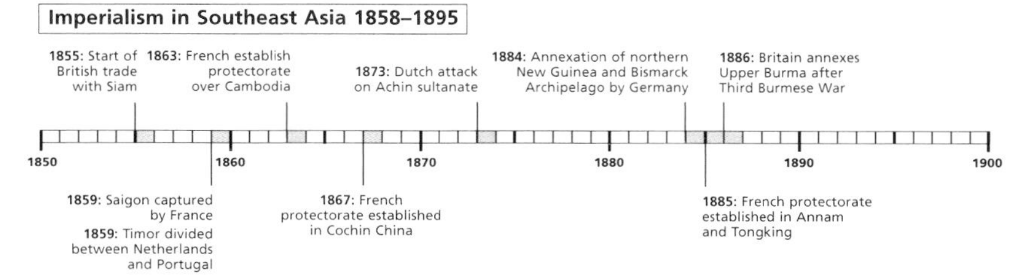

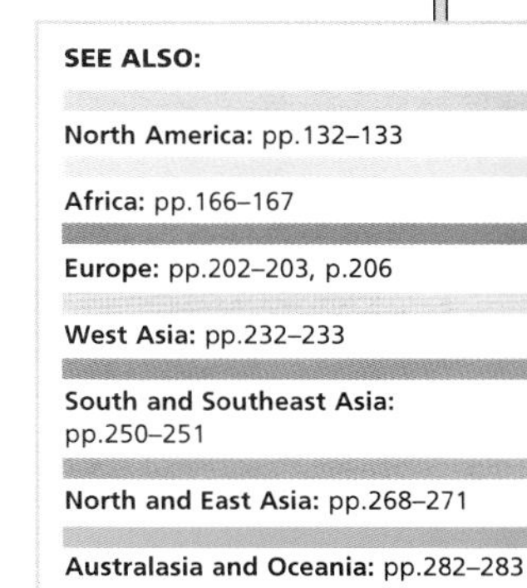

SEE ALSO:
North America: pp.132–133
Africa: pp.166–167
Europe: pp.202–203, p.206
West Asia: pp.232–233
South and Southeast Asia: pp.250–251
North and East Asia: pp.268–271
Australasia and Oceania: pp.282–283

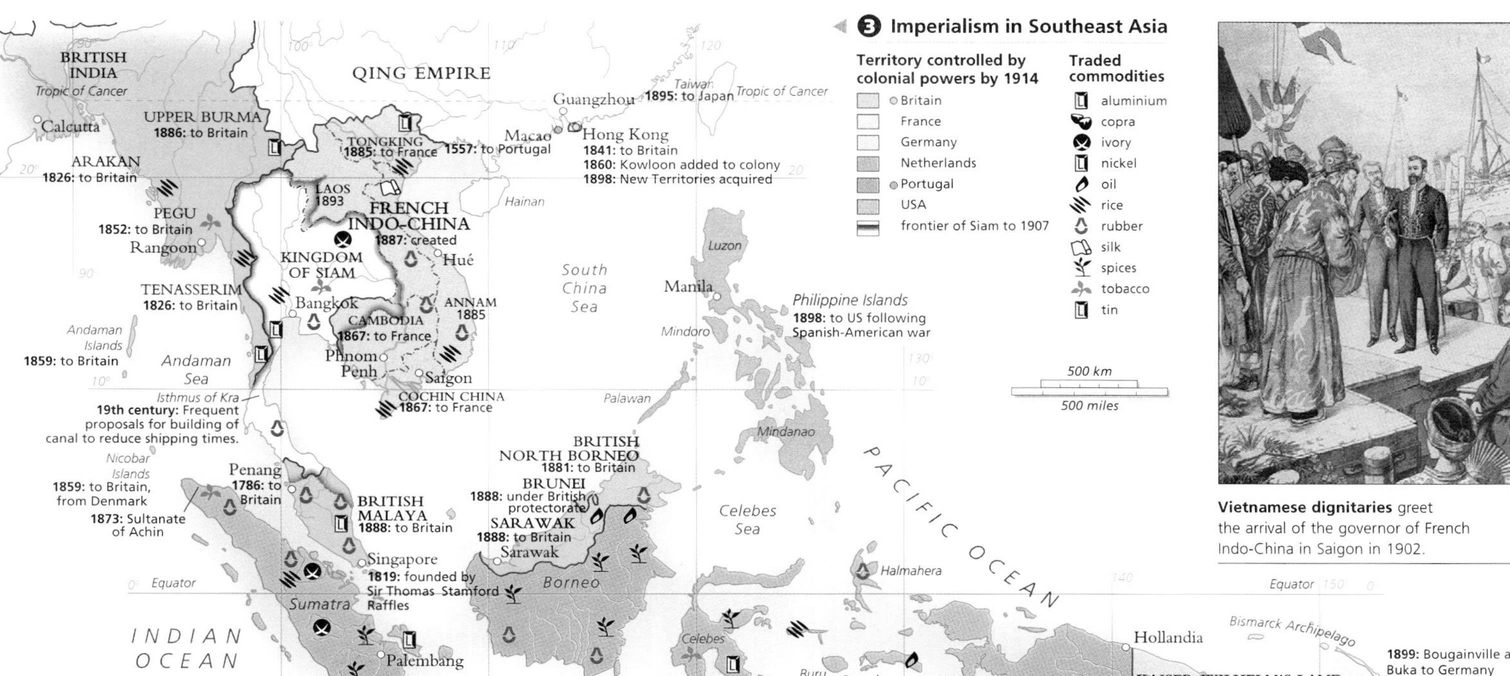

Vietnamese dignitaries greet the arrival of the governor of French Indo-China in Saigon in 1902.

The Malay Peninsula became a British possession in 1888. Vast rubber plantations provided a firm economic basis for imperial control.

Reactions to imperialism

The aggressive scramble for empire provoked determined armed resistance across Africa and Asia. Local peoples rose up to repel the European intruders – for example against the British in Sudan, the Italians in Libya, and the Dutch in Sumatra – but in most cases they had to submit when faced by superior fire-power. One exception was the defeat of the Italians at Adowa in Abyssinia in 1896. Imperialist meddling in countries such as China and Persia led to rebellions against the governments of the day, and the tottering Russian Empire faced a major revolt in Central Asia in 1916.

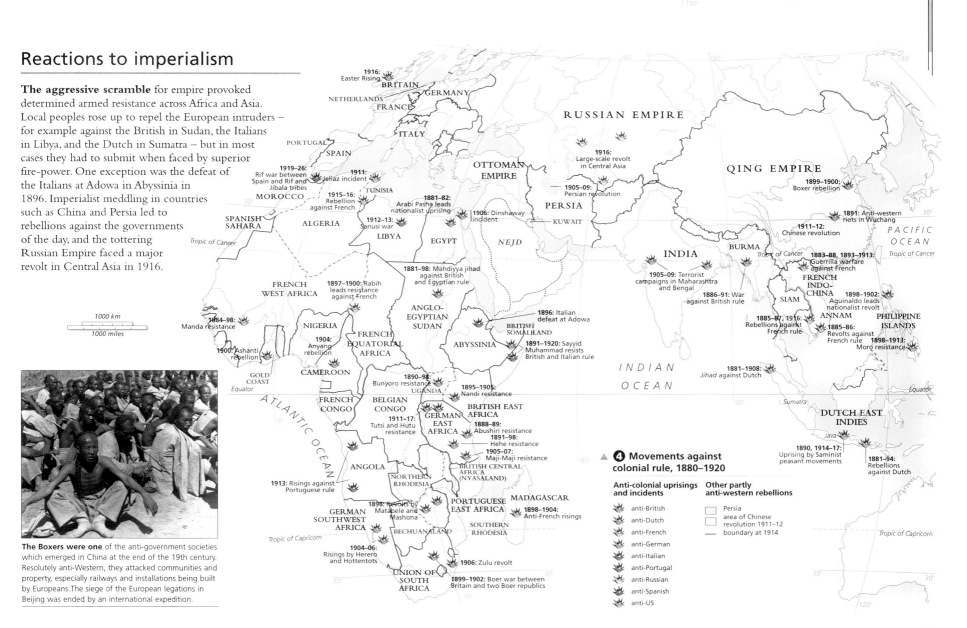

The Boxers were one of the anti-government societies which emerged in China at the end of the 19th century. Resolutely anti-Western, they attacked communities and property, especially railways and installations being built by Europeans. The siege of the European legations in Beijing was ended by an international expedition.

THE WORLD 1900–1925

THE IMPERIAL AND MILITARY RIVALRY between Britain and France, and Germany and Austria-Hungary led, in 1914, to the First World War, which left millions dead and re-drew the map of Europe. The Habsburg and Ottoman empires broke up, leading to the emergence of a number of smaller nation states, while the end of the Ottoman Empire also created a territorial crisis in the Middle East. In 1917, the Russian Empire collapsed in revolution and civil war, to be transformed by the victorious Bolsheviks into the world's first Communist empire. US participation in the war confirmed its status as a world power, cemented by the central role played by President Wilson in the Versailles Settlement, and by the nation's increasing economic dominance.

German soldiers wearing gas masks emerge from a dug out. Troops on both sides endured terrible conditions in the trench warfare which dominated the war in France.

Europe

Most countries in Europe and their colonies took part in the First World War, which was fought on a scale unimagined in the 19th century. Years of rivalry between the major European powers, France, Britain and Germany had created an incendiary situation, finally touched off by a crisis in the Balkans. The Versailles Settlement of 1919 altered the balance of power in Europe irrevocably, setting up the conditions for a second European war 20 years later.

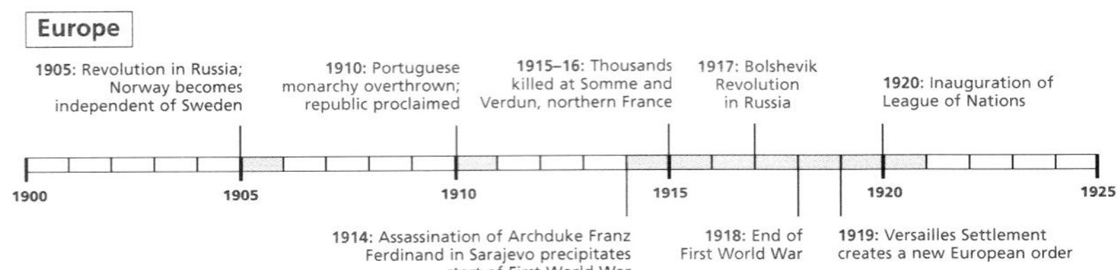
Europe
1905: Revolution in Russia; Norway becomes independent of Sweden
1910: Portuguese monarchy overthrown; republic proclaimed
1915–16: Thousands killed at Somme and Verdun, northern France
1917: Bolshevik Revolution in Russia
1920: Inauguration of League of Nations
1900
1905
1910
1915
1920
1925
1914: Assassination of Archduke Franz Ferdinand in Sarajevo precipitates start of First World War
1918: End of First World War
1919: Versailles Settlement creates a new European order

RADIO

Radio technology was first invented by Guglielmo Marconi in 1894. In 1901 he was able to send Morse Code messages across the Atlantic and by 1920 the first commercial radio station was set up in Pittsburgh, US. By the mid-1920s, radio was established as an immensely effective means of mass communication.

This radio, advertised using the famous fox terrier listening to 'His Master's Voice', dates from the 1920s.

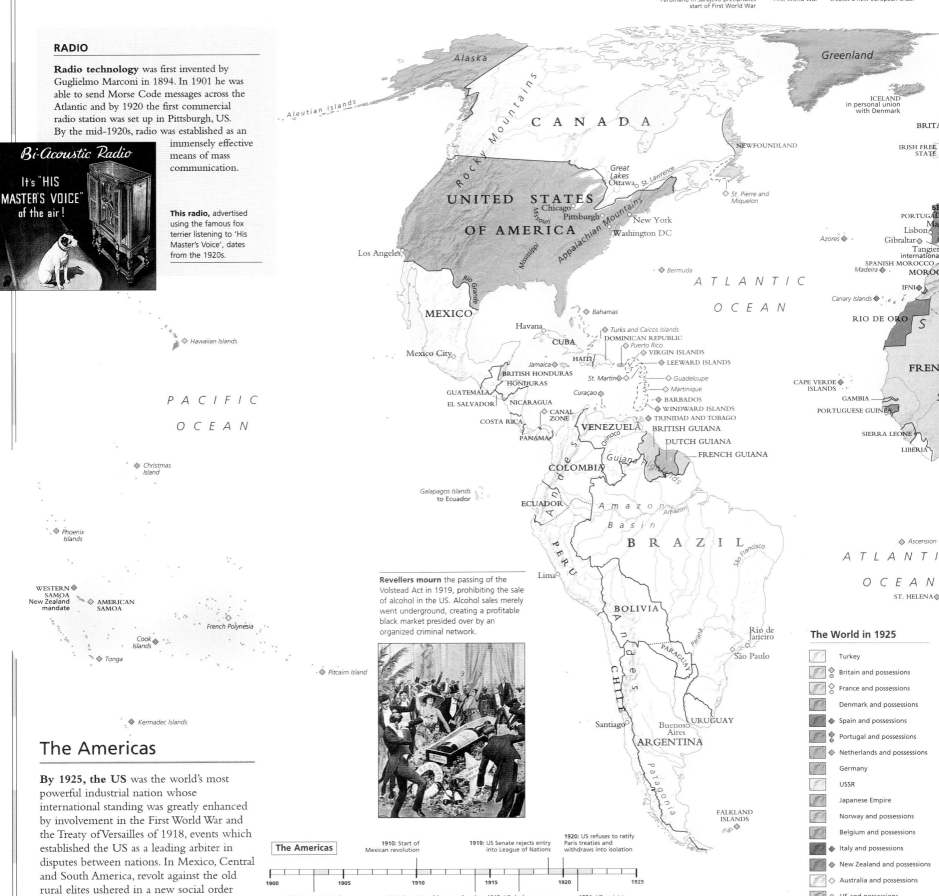

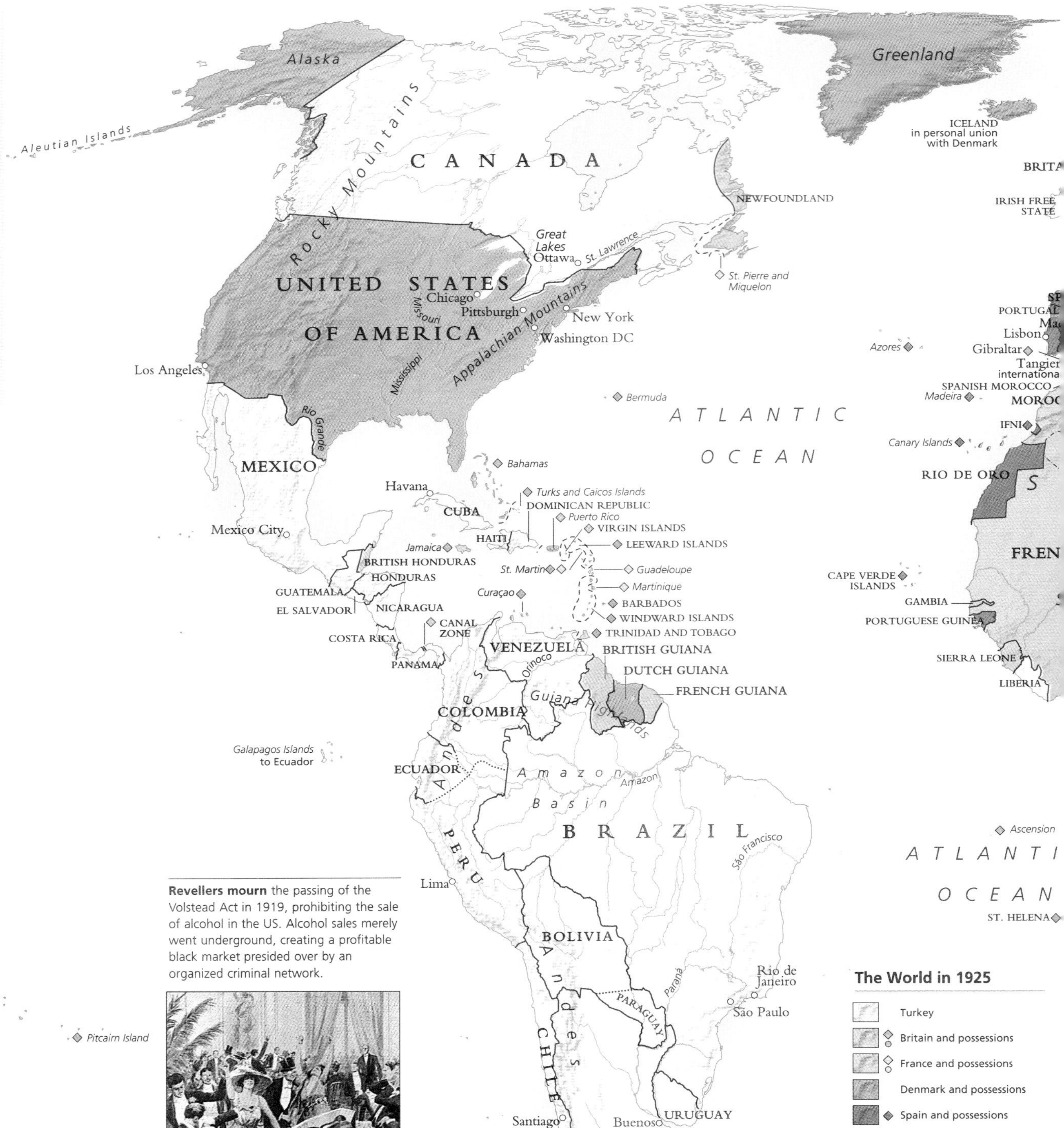

Revellers mourn the passing of the Volstead Act in 1919, prohibiting the sale of alcohol in the US. Alcohol sales merely went underground, creating a profitable black market presided over by an organized criminal network.

The World in 1925

- Turkey
- Britain and possessions
- France and possessions
- Denmark and possessions
- Spain and possessions
- Portugal and possessions
- Netherlands and possessions
- Germany
- USSR
- Japanese Empire
- Norway and possessions
- Belgium and possessions
- Italy and possessions
- New Zealand and possessions
- Australia and possessions
- US and possessions

The Americas

By 1925, the US was the world's most powerful industrial nation whose international standing was greatly enhanced by involvement in the First World War and the Treaty of Versailles of 1918, events which established the US as a leading arbiter in disputes between nations. In Mexico, Central and South America, revolt against the old rural elites ushered in a new social order and an increasingly urban society.

The Americas

- 1903: Panama Canal Zone ceded to US
- 1910: Start of Mexican revolution
- 1914: Opening of Panama Canal joins Atlantic and Pacific oceans
- 1917: US declares war on Germany and her allies
- 1919: US Senate rejects entry into League of Nations
- 1920: US refuses to ratify Paris treaties and withdraws into isolation
- 1921: US restricts immigration

Kemal Atatürk was the first leader of the new Turkish republic. From 1923–38 he radically overhauled Ottoman institutions to bring Turkey into the modern age.

West Asia

In 1918, the Ottoman Empire collapsed after more than 400 years. A new Turkish republic was inaugurated in 1923. In the post-war period much of the former Ottoman Empire, including Transjordan, Syria, and Iraq was controlled by Britain and France. A new Arab nationalism was becoming more strident, resulting in numerous political disturbances.

West Asia

- 1908: Ottoman sultan deposed in Young Turk Revolution
- 1912–13: Ottomans lose most of their European lands in Balkan Wars
- 1914: Ottomans ally with Germany and Austria after Britan, France and Russia declare war
- 1915: Allied attack on Gallipoli
- 1917: Balfour Declaration commits to creation of Jewish state in Palestine
- 1918: Collapse of Ottoman Empire
- 1923: Foundation of modern Turkey by Kemal Atatürk

A Soviet propaganda poster encourages peasants to invest their savings in state projects. Much policy at this time was aimed at exerting control over the peasants.

Northeast Asia

Much of North and East Asia was destabilized by the collapse of the Chinese Empire into civil war in 1911, and the Russian Revolution of 1917. The victorious Bolsheviks hoped for the spread of revolution in other countries. Meanwhile, Japanese expansionism was rewarded by territorial gains in Siberia, China, and the Pacific islands.

Northeast Asia
1904–05: Russo-Japanese War; series of Russian defeats
1910: Japanese annexation of Korea
1911: Qing dynasty overthrown by Sun Yat Sen's nationalists and Republic of China declared
1914: Japan takes over many German colonies in the Pacific
1918–20: Japan occupies part of Manchuria and Siberia
1922: Washington Naval Agreement limits Japanese naval power in the Pacific
1900
1905
1910
1915
1920
1925

SEE ALSO:

North America: pp.132–133

South America: pp.152–153

Africa: pp.166–167

Europe: pp.206–207

West Asia: pp.232–233

South and Southeast Asia: pp.250–251

North and East Asia: pp.270–271

Australasia and Oceania: pp.284–285

ROAD MAPS

The growth in automobile use, a burgeoning road network and an increasingly mobile population, necessitated the creation of a new type of road map, more detailed than any made previously.

The cover of this 1920s road map emphasizes the link between car usage and leisure pursuits.

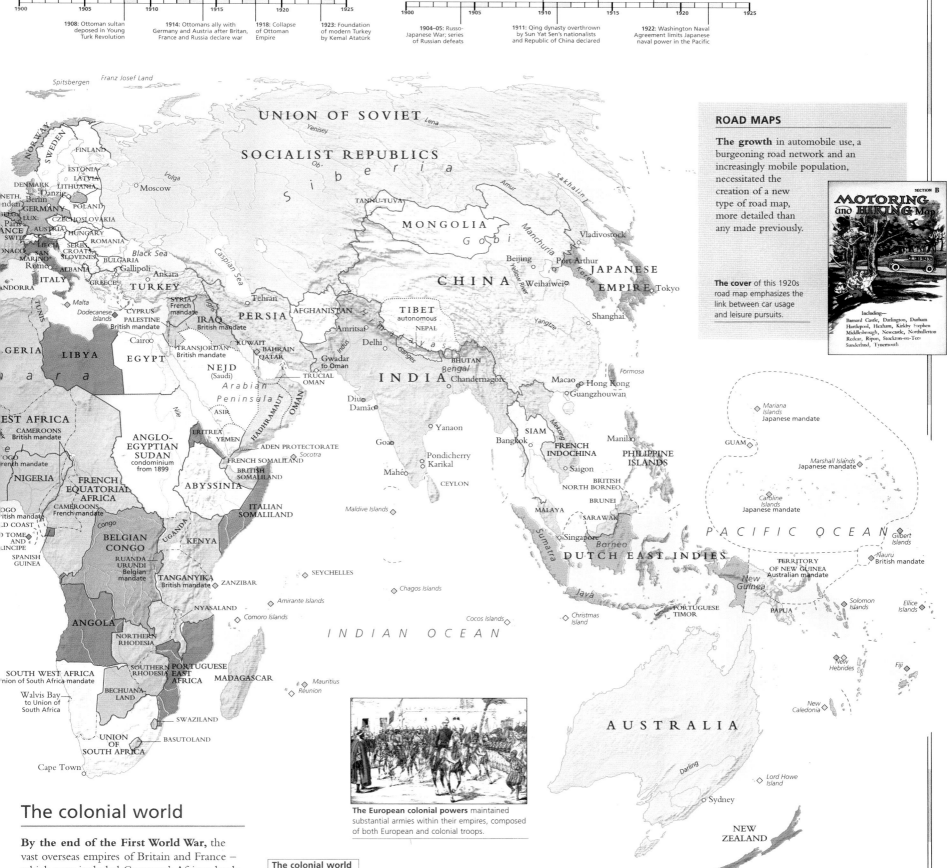

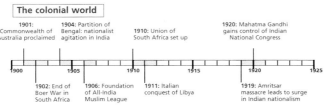

The European colonial powers maintained substantial armies within their empires, composed of both European and colonial troops.

The colonial world

By the end of the First World War, the vast overseas empires of Britain and France – which now included Germany's African lands – were becoming increasingly expensive and difficult to maintain. Colonialism was criticized by the US and the USSR, and independence movements developed in India and a number of African territories, alongside a growing nationalism in Southeast Asia.

The colonial world

- 1901: Commonwealth of Australia proclaimed
- 1902: End of Boer War in South Africa
- 1904: Partition of Bengal: nationalist agitation in India
- 1906: Foundation of All-India Muslim League
- 1910: Union of South Africa set up
- 1911: Italian conquest of Libya
- 1919: Amritsar massacre leads to surge in Indian nationalism
- 1920: Mahatma Gandhi gains control of Indian National Congress

GLOBAL MIGRATION

The Japanese shipping line *Osaka Shoshen Kaisha* carried thousands of immigrants to the US.

THE TECHNICAL INNOVATIONS of the Industrial Revolution made the 19th-century world seem a much smaller place. Railroads could quickly transport large human cargoes across continents, the Suez and Panama canals reduced travel times – sometimes by as much as 50%, and ships became larger, faster, and more seaworthy. The mechanization and centralization of industry required the concentration of labour on a scale never seen before. At the same time, the European imperial powers were exploiting their tropical possessions for economic benefit. Cash crops, grown on large plantations, needed a plentiful supply of labour as well. Political upheaval, wars, and economic hardship provided the most dramatic impetus to emigration – especially in the Russian Empire and Central Europe, and in southeastern China.

Migration in the 19th century

More than 80 million people emigrated from their country of origin during the 19th and early 20th centuries. Over half of them moved across the Atlantic to North and South America. The end of the American Civil War in 1865, and the opening up of Indian land to settlers saw the greatest period of immigration to the US and Canada. In the Russian Empire, movement was eastward from European Russia into Siberia and the Caspian region. Europeans moved south and east to take up employment in the colonies, while indentured labourers travelled to the Americas, Africa, and Southeast Asia.

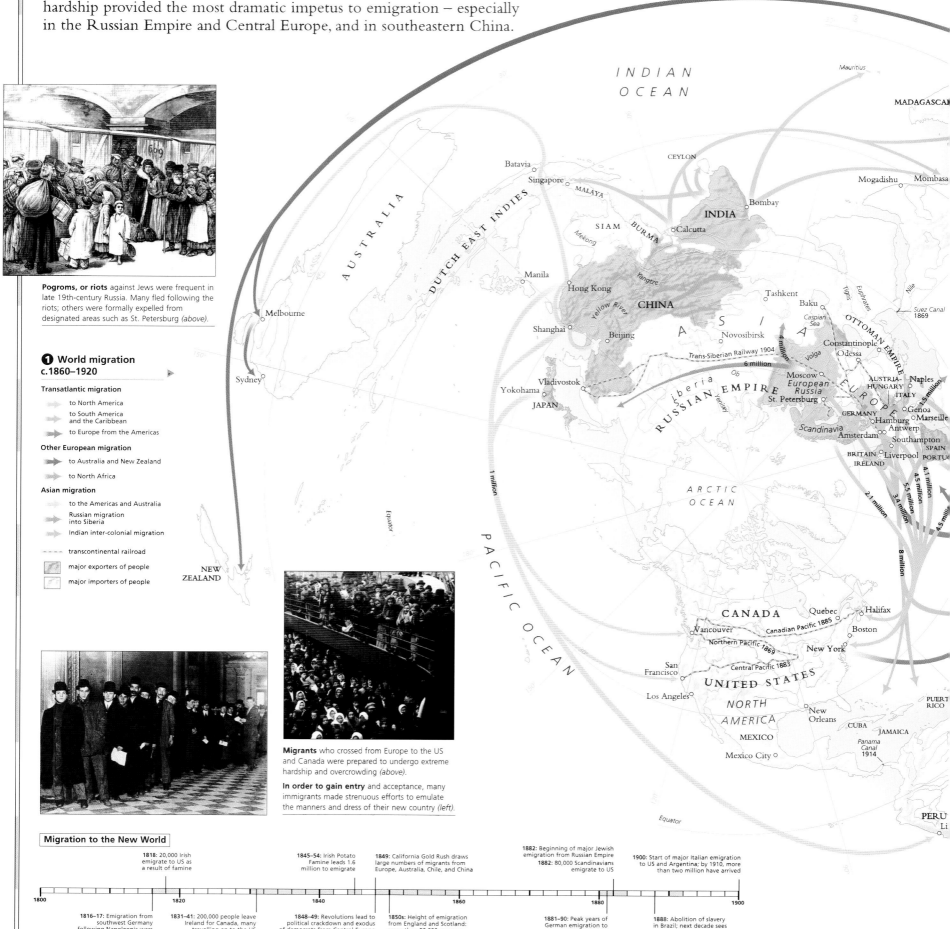

Pogroms, or riots against Jews were frequent in late 19th-century Russia. Many fled following the riots; others were formally expelled from designated areas such as St. Petersburg *(above)*.

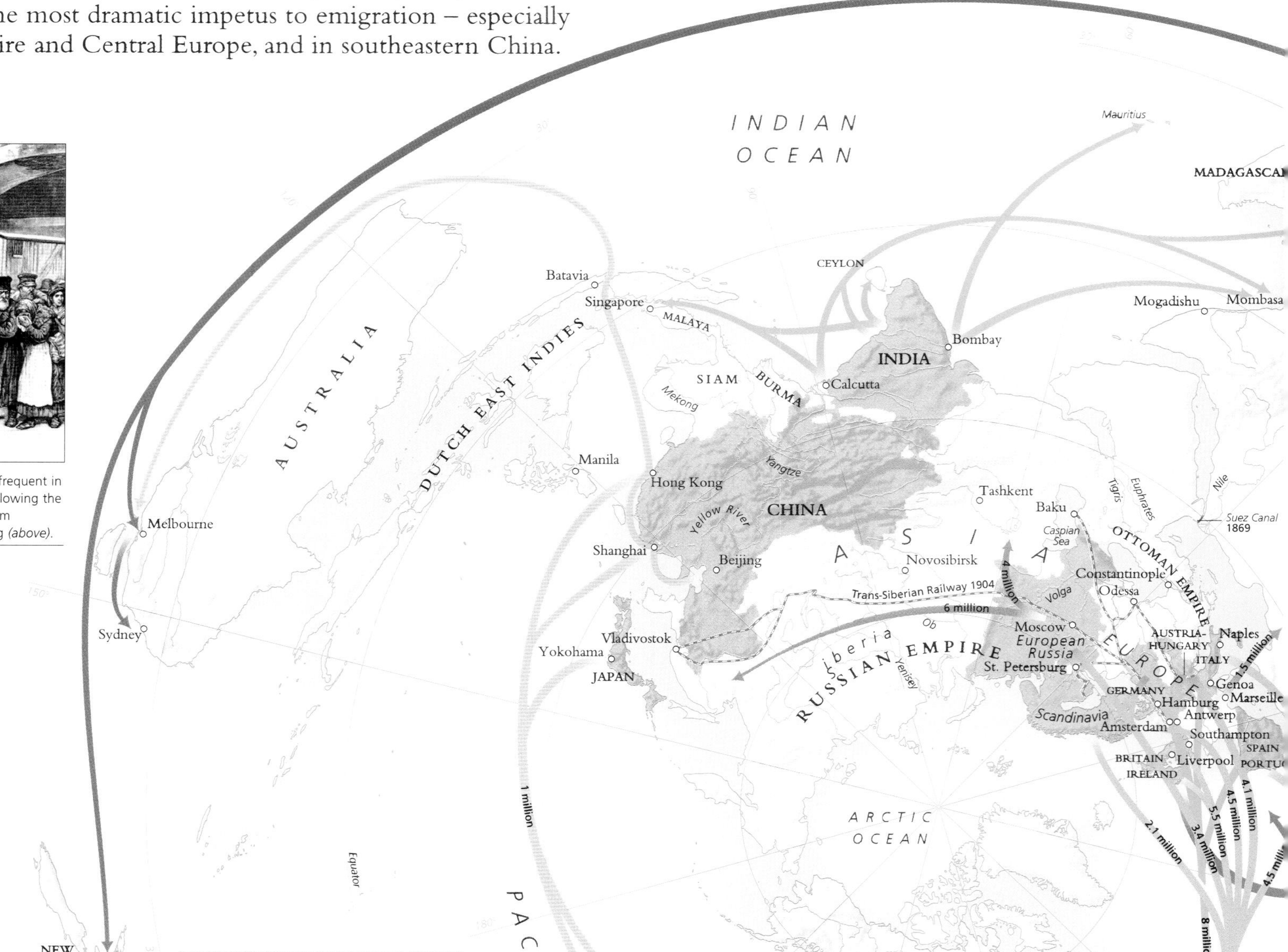

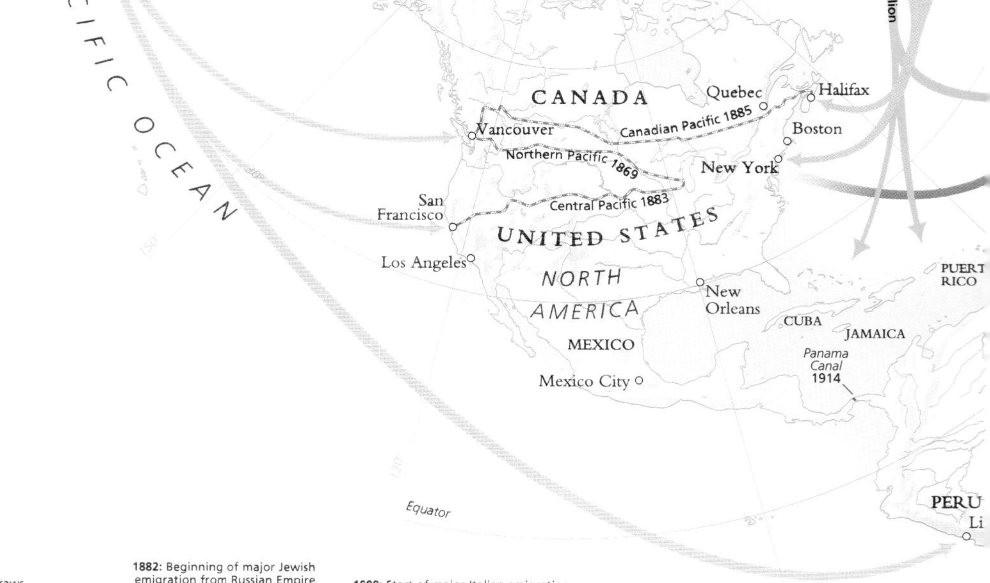

1 World migration c.1860–1920

Transatlantic migration
- to North America
- to South America and the Caribbean
- to Europe from the Americas

Other European migration
- to Australia and New Zealand
- to North Africa

Asian migration
- to the Americas and Australia
- Russian migration into Siberia
- Indian inter-colonial migration

- transcontinental railroad
- major exporters of people
- major importers of people

Migrants who crossed from Europe to the US and Canada were prepared to undergo extreme hardship and overcrowding *(above)*.

In order to gain entry and acceptance, many immigrants made strenuous efforts to emulate the manners and dress of their new country *(left)*.

Migration to the New World

- **1816–17:** Emigration from southwest Germany following Napoleonic wars
- **1818:** 20,000 Irish emigrate to US as a result of famine
- **1831–41:** 200,000 people leave Ireland for Canada, many travelling on to the US
- **1845–54:** Irish Potato Famine leads 1.6 million to emigrate
- **1848–49:** Revolutions lead to political crackdown and exodus of democrats from Central Europe
- **1849:** California Gold Rush draws large numbers of migrants from Europe, Australia, Chile, and China
- **1850s:** Height of emigration from England and Scotland: more than 50,000 per year
- **1881–90:** Peak years of German emigration to US (1,300,000)
- **1882:** Beginning of major Jewish emigration from Russian Empire
- **1882:** 80,000 Scandinavians emigrate to US
- **1888:** Abolition of slavery in Brazil; next decade sees over a million immigrants
- **1900:** Start of major Italian emigration to US and Argentina; by 1910, more than two million have arrived

1800 · 1820 · 1840 · 1860 · 1880 · 1900

SEE ALSO:

North America: pp.132–133

South America: pp.150–151

Africa: pp.166–167

Europe: pp.202–205

West Asia: pp.232–233

South and Southeast Asia: pp.250–251

North and East Asia: pp.270–271

Australasia and Oceania: pp.282–283

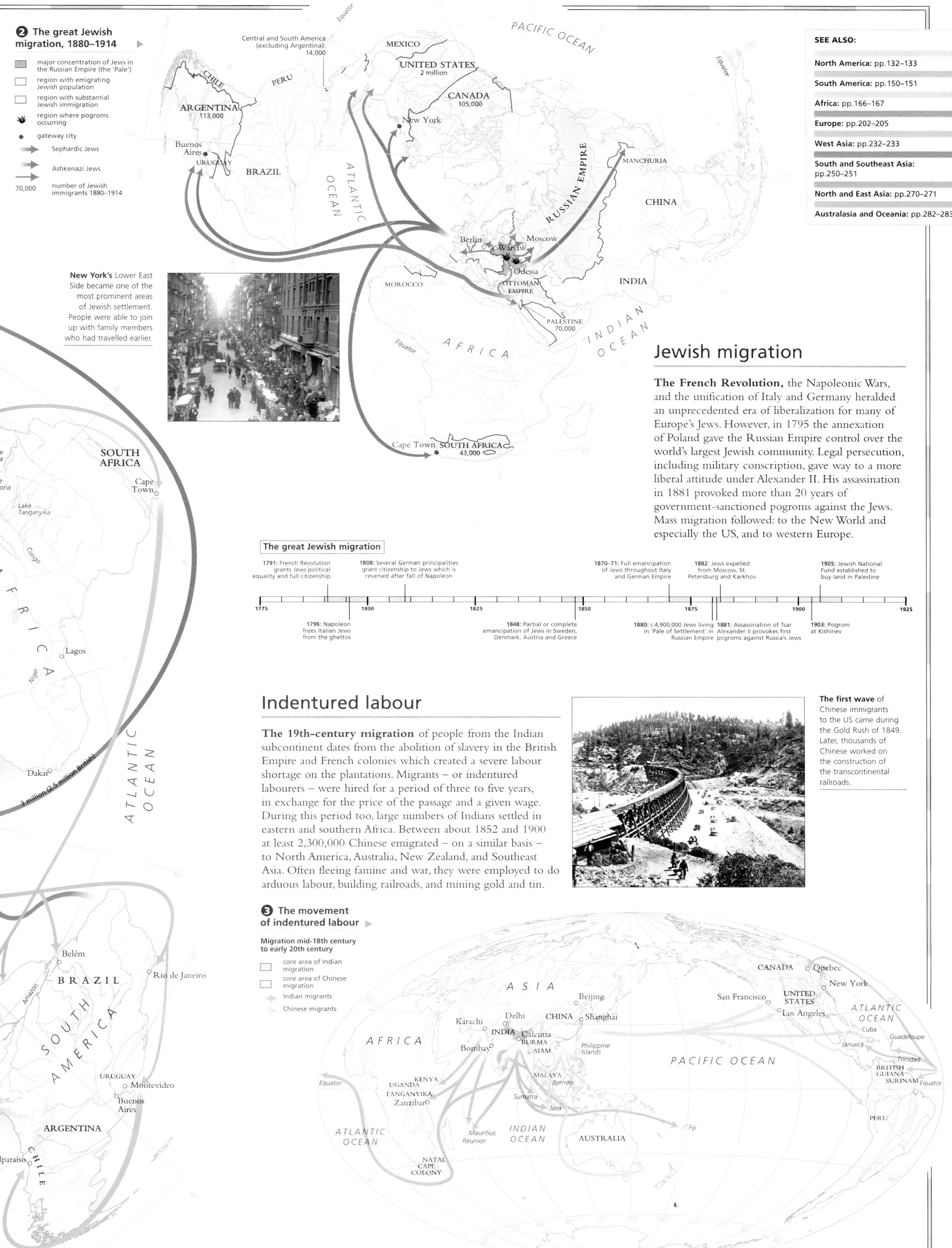

New York's Lower East Side became one of the most prominent areas of Jewish settlement. People were able to join up with family members who had travelled earlier.

Jewish migration

The French Revolution, the Napoleonic Wars, and the unification of Italy and Germany heralded an unprecedented era of liberalization for many of Europe's Jews. However, in 1795 the annexation of Poland gave the Russian Empire control over the world's largest Jewish community. Legal persecution, including military conscription, gave way to a more liberal attitude under Alexander II. His assassination in 1881 provoked more than 20 years of government-sanctioned pogroms against the Jews. Mass migration followed: to the New World and especially the US, and to western Europe.

The great Jewish migration

- **1791:** French Revolution grants Jews political equality and full citizenship
- **1796:** Napoleon frees Italian Jews from the ghettos
- **1808:** Several German principalities grant citizenship to Jews which is reversed after fall of Napoleon
- **1848:** Partial or complete emancipation of Jews in Sweden, Denmark, Austria and Greece
- **1870–71:** Full emancipation of Jews throughout Italy and German Empire
- **1880:** c.4,900,000 Jews living in 'Pale of Settlement' in Russian Empire
- **1881:** Assassination of Tsar Alexander II provokes first pogroms against Russia's Jews
- **1882:** Jews expelled from Moscow, St. Petersburg and Karkhov
- **1903:** Pogrom at Kishinev
- **1905:** Jewish National Fund established to buy land in Palestine

Indentured labour

The 19th-century migration of people from the Indian subcontinent dates from the abolition of slavery in the British Empire and French colonies which created a severe labour shortage on the plantations. Migrants – or indentured labourers – were hired for a period of three to five years, in exchange for the price of the passage and a given wage. During this period too, large numbers of Indians settled in eastern and southern Africa. Between about 1852 and 1900 at least 2,300,000 Chinese emigrated – on a similar basis – to North America, Australia, New Zealand, and Southeast Asia. Often fleeing famine and war, they were employed to do arduous labour, building railroads, and mining gold and tin.

The first wave of Chinese immigrants to the US came during the Gold Rush of 1849. Later, thousands of Chinese worked on the construction of the transcontinental railroads.

THE WORLD 1925–1950

THOUGH THE PARTIES to the Versailles Treaty of 1919, which followed the First World War hoped for stability, the League of Nations, set up in 1920, proved ineffective. By 1939 expansionist nationalism in Germany, Italy, and Japan led once more to war on a massive scale. The Second World War devastated Europe, Asia, and the USSR, killing more than 50 million people – among them perhaps 21 million Soviet citizens and more than six million Jewish civilians. The real victors of the war were the US and the USSR, who emerged as the world's most powerful nations. The great empires of Britain and France began to fragment under the financial strain of war and the rise of independence movements in their territories, beginning with India in 1947.

Adolf Hitler used vast rallies such as this at Nuremberg to muster his followers and show the world the strength of his popular support.

Europe

Germany's humiliation at Versailles, alongside economic depression, created the conditions for a revival of aggressive German nationalism. In its efforts to create a greater Germany, Hitler's Nazi party seized much of continental Europe and launched a policy of genocide of European Jews. Only with US intervention and a resurgent Soviet Union was their advance finally halted.

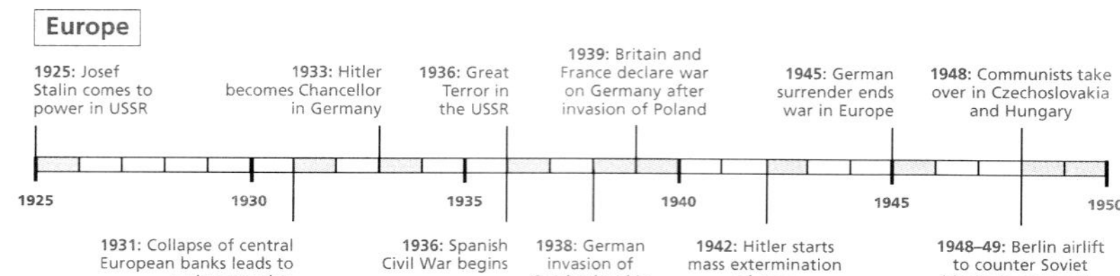

SCHEMATIC MAPS

The subway and metro maps produced in the 1930s are some of the simplest, yet most sophisticated maps ever produced. Using bold, clearly differentiated coloured lines for routes, and clear symbols to represent stations, they made no attempt to reproduce distances accurately, and showed direction only roughly. This schematic approach helped travellers to identify their destination and the quickest way to reach it.

The London Underground map devised by Harry Beck in 1931 and printed in 1933 is one of the most famous topological maps. Its design is based on electrical circuit diagrams.

Eva Perón was the charismatic wife of the Argentinian president Juan Perón. Her immense popularity helped to mask the ruthlessness of his regime.

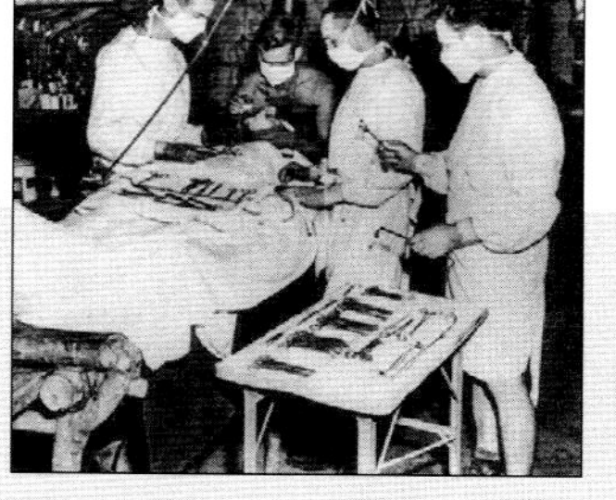

Among the first to benefit from antibiotics were US troops wounded in the Pacific theatre of the Second World War.

The Americas

The Wall Street Crash of 1929 plunged the US into a severe depression. Only with the war effort was the economy rejuvenated: the mobilization of industry established the US as the world's leading military and industrial power. In South and Central America, a number of states sought to diversify their economies and gain control over valuable mineral reserves in neighbouring countries. The Chaco War between Bolivia and Paraguay was the most serious of these conflicts prior to the Second World War.

The Americas

1930: Military revolution in Brazil
1933: Roosevelt's New Deal begins
1945: United Nations established in New York
1946: Juan Perón comes to power in Argentina

1925 | 1930 | 1935 | 1940 | 1945 | 1950

1929: Wall Street Crash starts Great Depression
1932–35: Paraguay defeats Bolivia in Chaco War
1941: US enters war following Japanese air attack on Pearl Harbor
1947: Marshall Plan drawn up to aid recovery in western Europe

ANTIBIOTICS

The discovery of penicillin in 1928 led to the creation of antibiotics, powerful drugs which were able to combat epidemic diseases such as tuberculosis. Over-prescription has led to many bacteria developing antibiotic immunity, prompting a search for new agents to combat disease.

Gandhi's strategy against British rule in India was based on non-violent civil disobedience.

South and East Asia

Japanese expansionism during the 1930s led to war with China in 1937 and in 1941 Japan's bombing of Pearl Harbor forced US entry into the Second World War. Chinese Communist and Nationalist forces held the Japanese at bay; after the war the Communists overwhelmed their former allies. In India the move to independence became irresistible following the war. In 1947 the British withdrew and the separate nations of India and Pakistan were created.

South and East Asia

- **1925:** Civil war in China
- **1926:** Chiang Kai-shek begins Chinese reunification
- **1934:** Start of the Chinese Communists' 'Long March' to Yan'an
- **1936:** Japan signs anti-Comintern pact with Germany
- **1937:** War between China and Japan
- **1941:** Russo-Japanese neutrality pact
- **1942:** Japanese control much of South and East Asia; arrest of Congress leaders in India
- **1945:** Atomic bombs at Hiroshima and Nagasaki force Japanese surrender
- **1947:** India and Pakistan gain independence
- **1949:** Mao Zedong and Chinese Communists win Chinese Civil War

Southeast Asia and Oceania

In 1941–42 Japanese forces rapidly overran European troops throughout Southeast Asia, in a campaign of 'liberation'. Their eventual defeat by Allied forces nevertheless precipitated a widespread reluctance to return to colonial rule among the peoples of the region.

The mighty Japanese fleet was eventually destroyed by US planes launched from aircraft carriers.

Southeast Asia and Oceania

- **1926–27:** Rebellion against Dutch rule in Java and Sumatra
- **1932:** End of absolute monarchy in Siam (renamed Thailand in 1939)
- **1942:** Indonesia, Indo-China, Malaya, the Philippines, New Guinea and Singapore seized by Japan
- **1942:** US navy halts Japanese expansion at battle of Midway in the Pacific
- **1945:** Ho Chi Minh proclaims independent Vietnam
- **1946:** Philippines become independent
- **1949:** Indonesia gains independence from the Dutch

SEE ALSO:

North America: pp.134–137

South America: pp.152–153

Africa: pp.168–169

Europe: pp.208–209

West Asia: pp.232–235

South and Southeast Asia: pp.250–251

North and East Asia: pp.272–273

Australasia and Oceania: pp.282–285

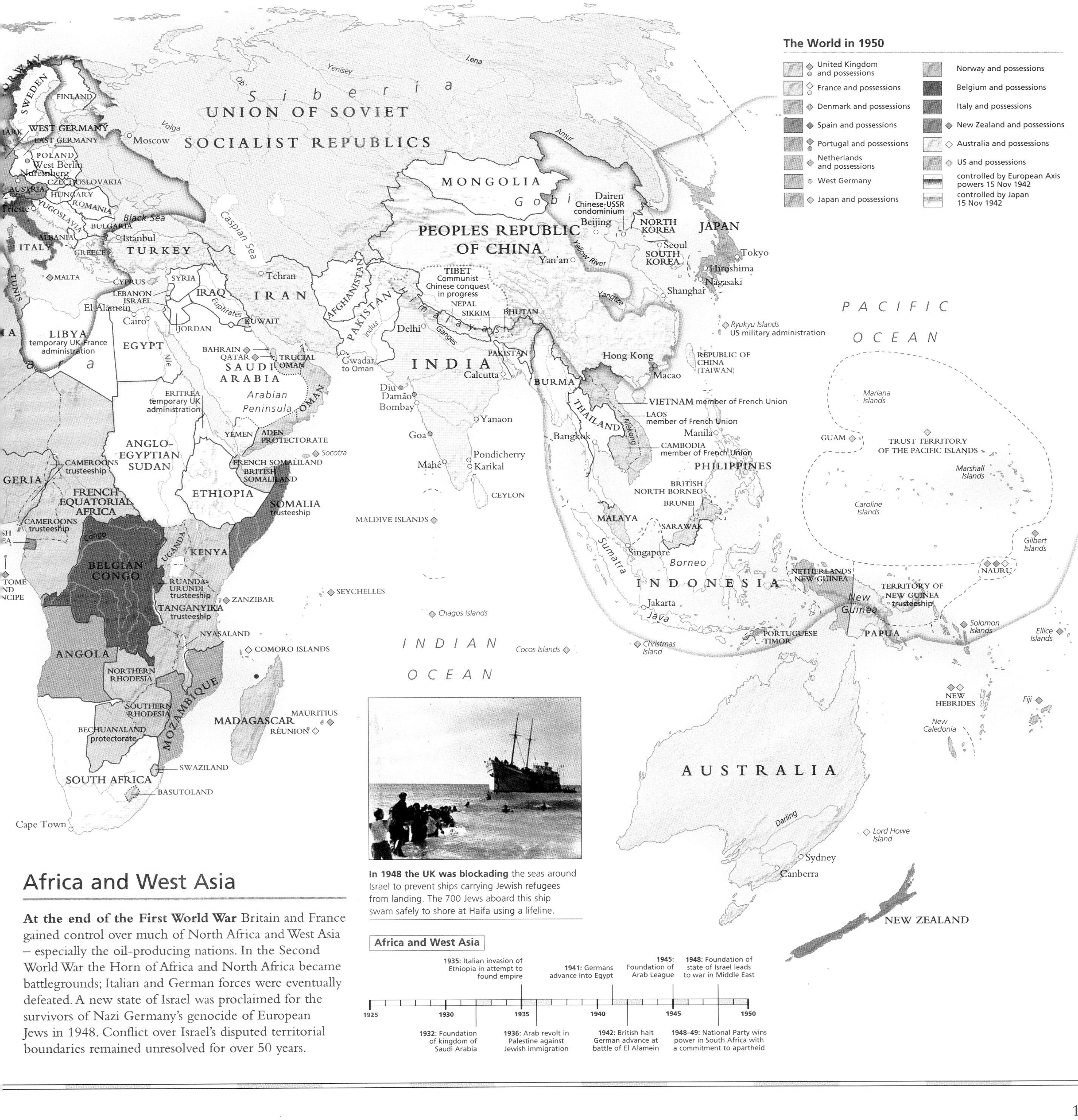

The World in 1950

- United Kingdom and possessions
- France and possessions
- Denmark and possessions
- Spain and possessions
- Portugal and possessions
- Netherlands and possessions
- West Germany
- Japan and possessions
- Norway and possessions
- Belgium and possessions
- Italy and possessions
- New Zealand and possessions
- Australia and possessions
- US and possessions
- controlled by European Axis powers 15 Nov 1942
- controlled by Japan 15 Nov 1942

In 1948 the UK was blockading the seas around Israel to prevent ships carrying Jewish refugees from landing. The 700 Jews aboard this ship swam safely to shore at Haifa using a lifeline.

Africa and West Asia

At the end of the First World War Britain and France gained control over much of North Africa and West Asia – especially the oil-producing nations. In the Second World War the Horn of Africa and North Africa became battlegrounds; Italian and German forces were eventually defeated. A new state of Israel was proclaimed for the survivors of Nazi Germany's genocide of European Jews in 1948. Conflict over Israel's disputed territorial boundaries remained unresolved for over 50 years.

Africa and West Asia

- **1932:** Foundation of kingdom of Saudi Arabia
- **1935:** Italian invasion of Ethiopia in attempt to found empire
- **1936:** Arab revolt in Palestine against Jewish immigration
- **1941:** Germans advance into Egypt
- **1942:** British halt German advance at battle of El Alamein
- **1945:** Foundation of Arab League
- **1948:** Foundation of state of Israel leads to war in Middle East
- **1948–49:** National Party wins power in South Africa with a commitment to apartheid

THE SECOND WORLD WAR

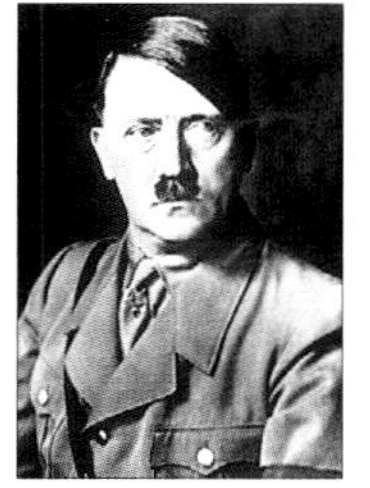

Adolf Hitler's National Socialist (NAZI) party was underpinned by extreme nationalism and racism, enforced though a police state.

THE SECOND WORLD WAR was a protracted struggle by a host of Allied nations to contain, and eventually destroy, the political, economic, social, and territorial ambitions of the Axis, a small group of extreme right-wing nationalist states led by Germany and Japan. The struggle led to the mobilization of manpower and economic might on an unprecedented scale, a deployment of forces on land, sea, and air globally, and the prosecution of war far beyond the front line, deep into the civilian hinterland in all theatres. For these reasons it has been called a 'Total War'. Its human costs were enormous, variously estimated at between 50 and 60 million dead, and its conclusion – with the detonation of two atomic bombs over Japan – heralded the Nuclear Age.

The Second World War, 1939–41

Until May 1941 Japan and Germany fought and won localized conflicts: in a series of campaigns they conquered and denied isolated enemies the opportunity to gather support and mobilize potentially far superior resources. In summer 1941, with Britain isolated but for its empire, the German invasion of the Soviet Union and the Japanese move into Southeast Asia marked the point at which their separate conflicts changed and came together. Japan's provocation of the US and Germany's failure in Russia marked the end of Axis successes and the advent of global warfare.

The war to December 1941

Sep 1939: Invasion of Poland by Germany and Soviet Union
Sep 1939: Britain and France declare war on Germany
Jan 1940
Jun 1940: Italy declares war on Britain and France
Jun 1940: German troops enter Paris; fall of France
Jul–Oct 1940: Battle of Britain waged in air over southern England
Jan 1941
Jun 1941: Germany invades the Soviet Union (Operation Barbarossa)
Jul 1941: Soviet Union and Britain sign pact of mutual assistance
Dec 1941: Japan attacks Pearl Harbor; US enters the war
Dec 1941: Germany declares war on US
Jan 1942

1 The Second World War, Sep 1939–Dec 1941

- political boundaries in 1939
- Axis and its allies in Mar 1940
- Allies in May 1940
- Allies by Dec 1941
- Axis territorial expansion by Jun 1940
- Axis territorial expansion by Dec 1941
- Axis satellites following the German invasion of France, May 1940
- neutral state

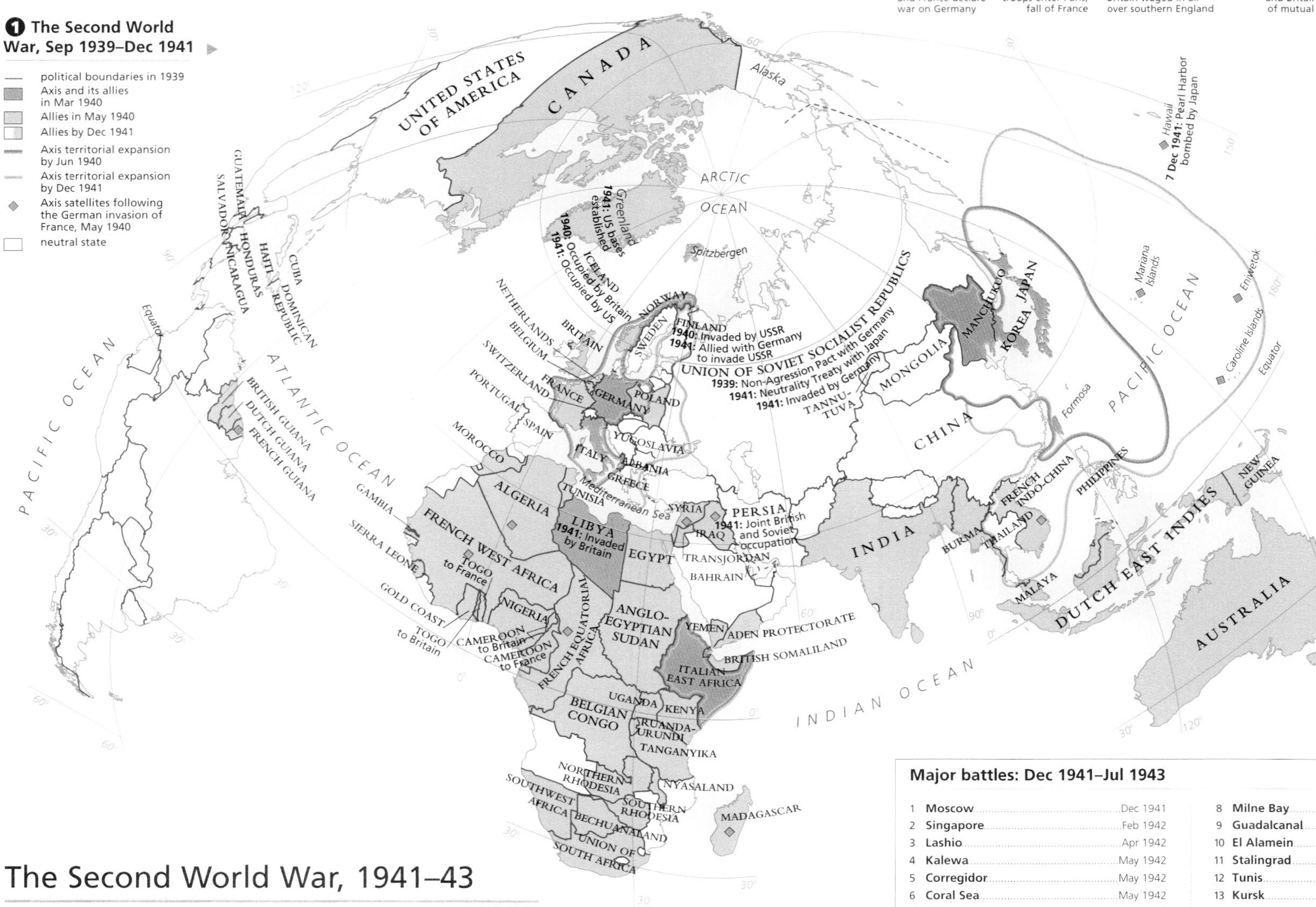

Japan's campaigns in Asia aimed to destroy British, US, and Dutch influence and create a 'Greater East Asian Co-Prosperity Sphere' in the region.

Major battles: Dec 1941–Jul 1943

1	Moscow	Dec 1941	8	Milne Bay	Aug 1942
2	Singapore	Feb 1942	9	Guadalcanal	Aug 1942–Feb 1943
3	Lashio	Apr 1942	10	El Alamein	Oct–Nov 1942
4	Kalewa	May 1942	11	Stalingrad	Oct 1942–Feb 1943
5	Corregidor	May 1942	12	Tunis	Apr–May 1943
6	Coral Sea	May 1942	13	Kursk	Jun–Aug 1943
7	Midway	Jun 1942	14	Minsk	Jun–Aug 1943

The Second World War, 1941–43

By late 1942 Germany and Japan were isolated and besieged; they had to win the wars they had initiated or suffer defeat by the the massive forces ranged against them. Despite initial successes, their undoing was ensured by November 1942 with Anglo-American success in North Africa, the Soviet counter-offensive at Stalingrad, and US victories off Guadalcanal. By summer 1943 Allied consolidation in the Mediterranean, Soviet victory at Kursk and Japanese reverses at Guadalcanal and Milne Bay fatally compromised the Axis positions.

2 The Second World War, Dec 1941–Jul 1943

- extent of Axis powers Dec 1942
- Allies Jul 1943
- Axis powers Jul 1943
- neutral state
- Allied base
- Axis base
- major battle

The war to July 1943

Feb 1942: Surrender of British forces to Japan in Singapore
Mar 1942: Dutch surrender East Indies to Japan
Aug 1942: US bombing raids over Europe begin
Sep 1942: Start of German siege of Stalingrad (ends Jan 1943)
Oct–Nov 1942: British defeat Germans at El Alamein
Jan 1943: Roosevelt and Churchill meet at Casablanca
Apr 1943

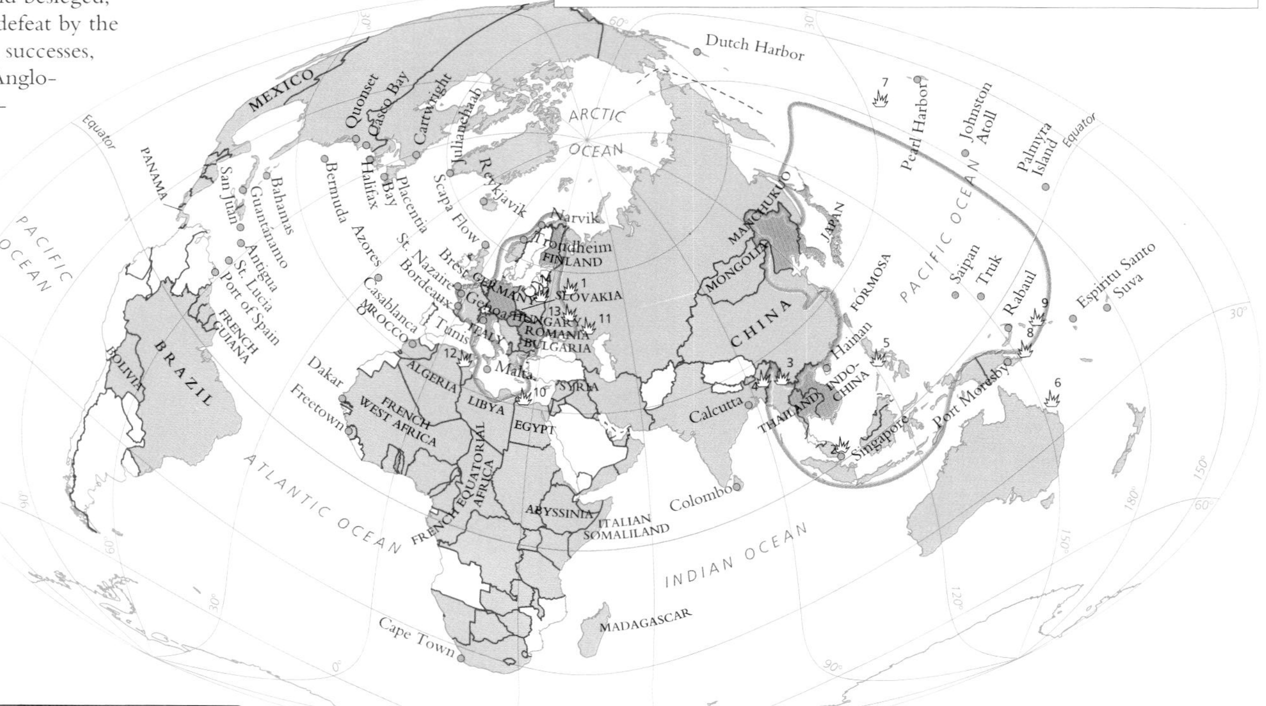

The Second World War, 1943–45

In 1943 Allied success was piecemeal and attritional; after June 1944 they achieved increasing depth of penetration and permanency of conquest. The Axis suffered escalating losses on the front line and in their heartlands. By August 1944 Germany's 'Fortress Europe' was breached by the Soviets in Central Europe, and by Anglo-American forces in Italy and Normandy, while US victory in the Philippine Sea fatally split Japan's 'Greater East Asian Co-Prosperity Sphere'. However, Axis tenacity and the Allied insistence upon unconditional surrender, meant that peace would only be achieved with the devastation of Europe and Japan.

July 1943 to the end of the war

- **Jul 1943:** Allied forces land in Sicily
- **Sep 1943:** Italy surrenders to Allies; German forces occupy Milan and Rome
- **Oct 1943:** Italy declares war on Germany
- **Nov 1943:** Roosevelt, Stalin, and Churchill meet at Tehran
- **Jun 1944:** D-Day: Allied landings in Normandy
- **Aug 1944:** Allied forces liberate Paris
- **Oct 1944:** Battle of Leyte Gulf against Japan
- **Nov 1944:** US begins direct aerial bombing of Japan
- **May 1945:** Germany surrenders
- **May 1945:** Berlin surrenders to the Red Army
- **Aug 1945:** Atomic bombs exploded over Hiroshima and Nagasaki
- **Sep 1945:** Formal Japanese surrender

Jul 1943 · Jan 1944 · Jan 1945 · Oct 1945

SEE ALSO:

Europe: pp.210–211

West Asia: pp.234–235

South and Southeast Asia: pp.250–251

North and East Asia: pp.272–273

Heavily armoured B17 or 'Flying Fortress' bombers were used by US forces for high-level daylight bombing over Europe – leading to the devastation of many parts of Germany.

3 The Second World War, Jul 1943–Aug 1945

- under Tripartite Pact powers control Jul 1943
- countries liberated by Allied forces by Feb 1945
- extent of Axis powers Jan 1945
- Allies in May 1945
- Axis powers in May 1945
- neutral state
- major battle

Major battles: Jul 1943–Aug 1945

1	**Kiev**	Sep–Oct 1943
2	**Anzio**	Jan–Mar 1944
3	**Monte Cassino**	Jan–May 1944
4	**Mariana Islands**	Jun–Aug 1944
5	**Normandy**	Jun–Jul 1944
6	**Arnhem**	Sep 1944
7	**Leyte Gulf**	Oct 1944
8	**Ardennes**	Dec 1944–Feb 1945
9	**Iwo Jima**	Feb–Mar 1945
10	**Königsberg**	Feb–Apr 1945
11	**Okinawa**	Mar–Jun 1945
12	**Vienna**	Apr 1945
13	**Prague**	May 1945
14	**Berlin**	May 1945

Global warfare

The spherical shape of the operational theatre meant that the Allies could isolate the Axis on all fronts. Global warfare involved troops fighting far from their home nations. South Asians and Australasians fought in Africa and Europe, Europeans and Americans in Southeast Asia, and Siberians in Europe. Major shifts of population occurred in the US and USSR, producing enormous changes in patterns of trade and drawing in the economic involvement of neutrals. The powerhouse of the Allied cause was the US, which alone raised a hundred military divisions, as well as supplying aid to her allies with a cash value equivalent to 2000 infantry divisions. At peak production, US industry built an aircraft every 294 seconds and 130 merchantmen in a single month.

The 'Big Three' Allied leaders, Stalin, Churchill, and Roosevelt, met at Yalta in February 1945 to discuss the postwar division of the fatally weakened Nazi Empire.

4 Global warfare

- maximum extent of Axis powers in Europe/Russia
- maximum extent of Japanese expansion in Asia/Pacific

Movement of troops

Axis
- German
- Japanese

Allies
- British
- British Commonwealth
- American
- Soviet

Women such as these aviation engineers were enormously important to the booming US defence industry.

The human cost of global war

More than 80 million troops were mobilized by the Allied and Axis powers during the war. Nearly one-third of them were killed or injured. The civilian cost was equally high, particularly in the Soviet Union and among Europe's Jews and other minorities, who were systematically exterminated by both the Nazis and the Soviets. The scale of Japanese atrocities in China remains unknown.

The Second World War: mobilization and casualty figures

Country	Troops mobilized	Military casualities	Civilian casualties
US	11,490,000	292,100	–
Canada	780,000	39,319	–
New Zealand	150,000	12,162	–
Australia	680,000	29,395	–
South Africa	140,000	8681	–
Norway	25,000	4780	–
Finland	250,000	79,047	–
Soviet Union	20,000,000	14,500,000	c.7,000,000
Poland	1,000,000	850,000	5,778,000
Czechoslovakia	180,000	6683	310,000
Hungary	350,000	750,000 military and civilian	
Romania	600,000	519,822	465,000
Bulgaria	450,000	18,500	1500
Greece	150,000	16,357	155,300
Yugoslavia	3,740,000	1,700,000 military and civilian	
Italy	4,500,000	279,820	93,000
France	5,600,000	210,671	173,260
Belgium	800,000	9561	75,000
Netherlands	500,000	13,700	236,300
Great Britain	4,600,000	271,311	60,595
Germany	10,800,000	2,850,000	2,300,000
Japan	7,400,000	1,506,000	300,000
India	2,400,000	36,092	–
China (Nationalist)	3,800,000	1,324,000	c.10,000,000
China (Communist)	1,200,000	Not known	Not known
Denmark	Not known	4339	–
Spain	Not known	23,000 military and civilian	

THE WORLD 1950–1975

WORLD POLITICS IN THE ERA following the close of the Second World War were defined by the tense relationship between the US and the USSR. The 'Cold War' between liberal-capitalism and Communism saw each side constantly attempting to contain and subvert the other. The Korean War (1950–55), the Cuban Missile Crisis of 1962, and the Vietnam War (1954–75), as well as many smaller conflicts – particularly in Central America and Africa – were all manifestations of the Cold War. Though no nuclear weapons were ever used in anger, both sides built up huge nuclear arsenals whose potential for mass destruction acted as a deterrent to conflict on a global scale.

Europe

During the Soviet era the May Day parade in Moscow's Red Square became the focus for the USSR's display of her military might. Weapons such as these ballistic rockets were wheeled through the streets.

The 1950s and 1960s were a period of widespread prosperity and political stability in Western Europe, faltering only in the early 1970s. West Germany, banned from keeping an army, rebuilt its shattered economy and infrastructure with stunning success. Eastern Europe was overshadowed by Soviet Communism, which restricted both economic development and the personal freedom of its citizens.

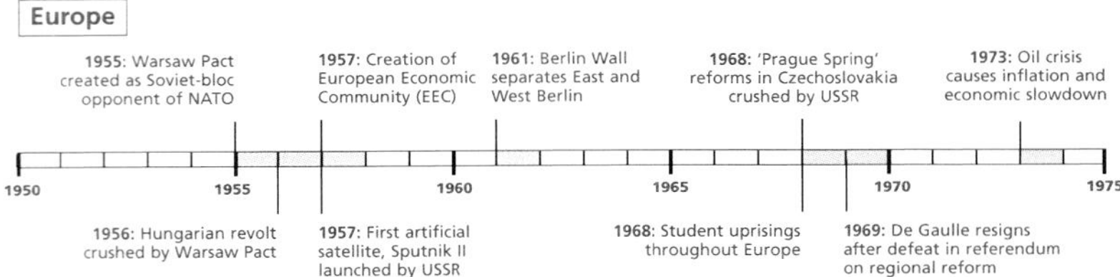
Europe
1955: Warsaw Pact created as Soviet-bloc opponent of NATO
1957: Creation of European Economic Community (EEC)
1961: Berlin Wall separates East and West Berlin
1968: 'Prague Spring' reforms in Czechoslovakia crushed by USSR
1973: Oil crisis causes inflation and economic slowdown
1950
1955
1960
1965
1970
1975
1956: Hungarian revolt crushed by Warsaw Pact
1957: First artificial satellite, Sputnik II launched by USSR
1968: Student uprisings throughout Europe
1969: De Gaulle resigns after defeat in referendum on regional reform

SATELLITE IMAGERY

With space technology came the ability to keep artificial satellites in permanent orbit round the Earth. They are used to carry transmitters for telecommunications, as aids to navigation and as bases for space exploration. The data picked up by sensors can be digitally combined to create images of the Earth.

This satellite image of North and South America shows both vegetation cover and weather conditions at the time at which it was taken.

ALASKA
CANADA
Greenland
Rocky Mountains
Great Lakes
St. Lawrence
UNITED STATES OF AMERICA
Chicago
Missouri
Mississippi
Appalachian Mountains
New York
Washington
Los Angeles
Rio Grande
ST. PIERRE AND MIQUELON
BERMUDA
ATLANTIC OCEAN
Azores
Madeira
Canary Islands
GIBRALTAR
SPANISH SAHARA
MAURITANIA
CAPE VERDE
SENEGAL
GAMBIA
GUINEA-BISSAU
GUINEA
SIERRA LEONE
LIBERIA
MEXICO
Mexico City
HAWAII
PACIFIC OCEAN
CAYMAN ISLANDS
BAHAMAS
CUBA
JAMAICA
HAITI
TURKS AND CAICOS ISLANDS
DOMINICAN REPUBLIC
PUERTO RICO
VIRGIN ISLANDS
BRITISH VIRGIN ISLANDS
ANTIGUA AND BARBUDA
ST. KITTS AND NEVIS
MONTSERRAT
GUADELOUPE
DOMINICA
MARTINIQUE
ST. LUCIA
BARBADOS
ST. VINCENT AND THE GRENADINES
GRENADA
TRINIDAD AND TOBAGO
NETHERLANDS ANTILLES
BRITISH HONDURAS
HONDURAS
GUATEMALA
EL SALVADOR
NICARAGUA
COSTA RICA
PANAMA
CANAL ZONE
CLIPPERTON ISLAND
VENEZUELA
GUYANA
SURINAM
FRENCH GUIANA
Orinoco
Guiana Highlands
COLOMBIA
ECUADOR
Galapagos Islands to Ecuador
Amazon Basin
Amazon
BRAZIL
São Francisco
PERU
Lima
Andes
BOLIVIA
PARAGUAY
Paraná
Asunción
Rio de Janeiro
São Paulo
CHILE
Santiago
URUGUAY
Buenos Aires
ARGENTINA
Patagonia
FALKLAND ISLANDS
ASCENSION
ST. HELENA
GILBERT AND ELLICE ISLANDS
TOKELAU
WESTERN SAMOA
WALLIS AND FUTUNA
AMERICAN SAMOA
TONGA
NIUE
FIJI
COOK ISLANDS
FRENCH POLYNESIA
PITCAIRN ISLANDS
Kermadec Islands

South America's great cities grew massively in this period as landless people from rural areas moved to urban areas in search of work. Many informal shanty towns grew up on the edges of cities like São Paulo in Brazil.

The World in 1975

- United Kingdom and possessions
- France and possessions
- Denmark and possessions
- Spain and possessions
- Portugal and possessions
- Netherlands and possessions
- West Germany
- Norway and possessions
- Belgium
- Italy
- New Zealand and possessions
- Australia and possessions
- US and possessions
- Biafra 1967–70
- Katanga 1960–63
- South Vietnam 1954–75

The Americas

Using its economic and military strength, the US became a global superpower, providing a bulwark against the perceived Communist threat and ensuring the world dominance of American popular culture. Many of the nations of Central and South America were ruled by military dictatorships which severely restricted the freedom of their citizens. Economic instability, high population growth – especially in urban areas – and high inflation were still major problems.

The Americas

1955: Argentinian leader Perón ousted by military coup. Remains out of power until 1973
1964: US Congress approves war with Vietnam
1969: NASA puts first humans on the Moon
1974: Resignation of Nixon following Watergate scandal
1950
1955
1960
1965
1970
1975
1959: Fidel Castro becomes Cuban leader; reorganizes economy along Soviet lines
1962: Cuban Missile Crisis
1967: Widespread protests against US involvement in Vietnam
1973: US backs coup against elected Marxist government in Chile

West and South Asia

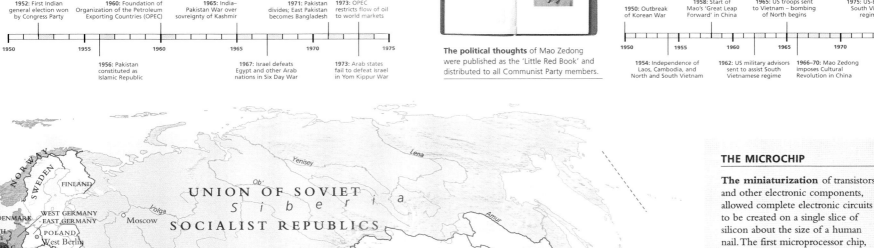

Israel, supported by Western powers, fought a series of wars with its Arab neighbours to define its boundaries. The exploitation of extensive oil reserves brought immense wealth to the undeveloped Arabian Peninsula. Relations between India and Pakistan were strained by territorial disputes, and in 1971, the geographical separation of Pakistan proved unsustainable with East Pakistan becoming Bangladesh.

Intense rivalry between Israel and Egypt led in June 1967 to the Six Day War. Superior Israeli air power routed the Egyptian air force and the ground forces of Egypt, Jordan, Iraq, and Syria.

East and Southeast Asia

In China and mainland Southeast Asia, power passed to native Communist movements. Mao Zedong's Communist China became a superpower to rival the USSR, while the US intervened in Korea and Vietnam in response to the perceived threat of Communism. Japan began rebuilding its economy with American aid to become, by the mid-1970s, one of the world's richest nations. From 1950 onwards, mainland Southeast Asia was destabilized by Cold War-inspired conflict: in Laos, Vietnam, and Cambodia.

The political thoughts of Mao Zedong were published as the 'Little Red Book' and distributed to all Communist Party members.

SEE ALSO:

North America: pp.136–137

South America: pp.152–153

Africa: pp.168–169

Europe: pp.212–213

West Asia: pp.234–235

South and Southeast Asia: pp.250–253

North and East Asia: pp.274–275

Australasia and Oceania: pp.284–285

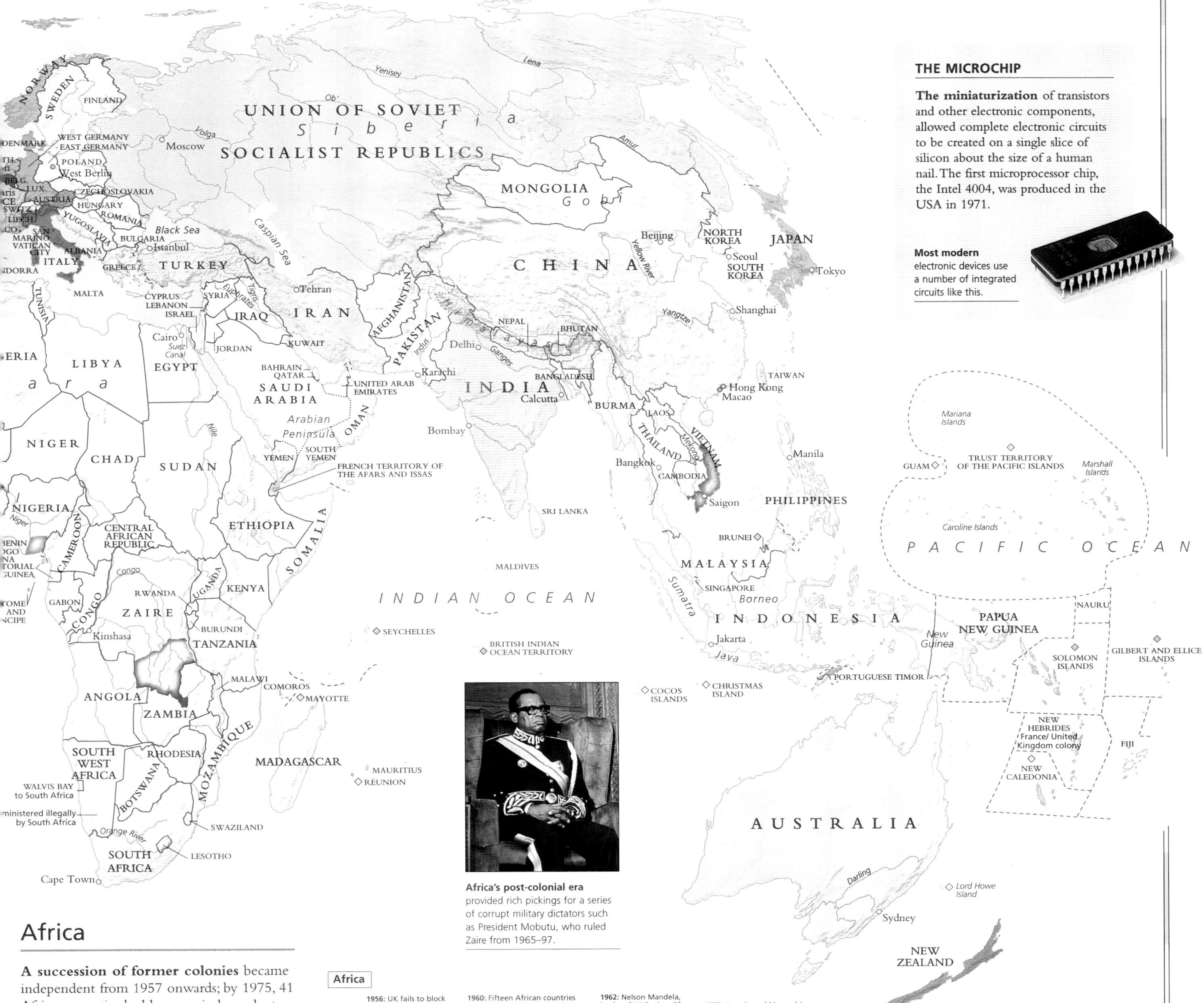

West and South Asia

- **1952:** First Indian general election won by Congress Party
- **1956:** Pakistan constituted as Islamic Republic
- **1960:** Foundation of Organization of the Petroleum Exporting Countries (OPEC)
- **1965:** India–Pakistan War over sovereignty of Kashmir
- **1967:** Israel defeats Egypt and other Arab nations in Six Day War
- **1971:** Pakistan divides; East Pakistan becomes Bangladesh
- **1973:** OPEC restricts flow of oil to world markets
- **1973:** Arab states fail to defeat Israel in Yom Kippur War

East and Southeast Asia

- **1950:** Outbreak of Korean War
- **1954:** Independence of Laos, Cambodia, and North and South Vietnam
- **1958:** Start of Mao's 'Great Leap Forward' in China
- **1962:** US military advisors sent to assist South Vietnamese regime
- **1965:** US troops sent to Vietnam – bombing of North begins
- **1966–70:** Mao Zedong imposes Cultural Revolution in China
- **1975:** US-backed South Vietnam regime falls

THE MICROCHIP

The miniaturization of transistors and other electronic components, allowed complete electronic circuits to be created on a single slice of silicon about the size of a human nail. The first microprocessor chip, the Intel 4004, was produced in the USA in 1971.

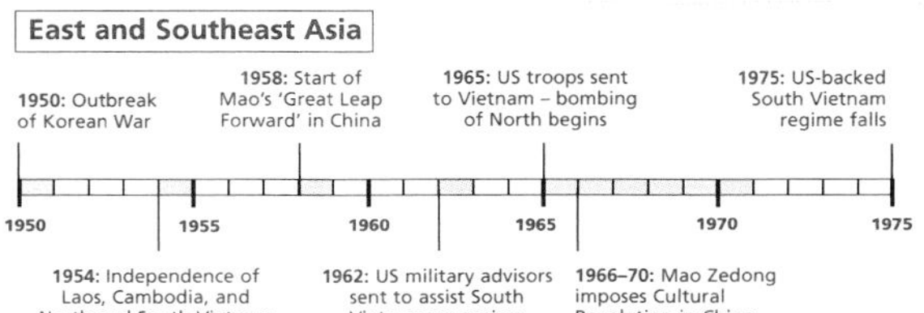

Most modern electronic devices use a number of integrated circuits like this.

Africa's post-colonial era provided rich pickings for a series of corrupt military dictators such as President Mobutu, who ruled Zaire from 1965–97.

Africa

A succession of former colonies became independent from 1957 onwards; by 1975, 41 African counties had become independent. Few were fully prepared for the demands of independence and many countries remained pawns in the Cold War, armed by the opposing powers, and fighting wars on behalf of their conflicting ideologies.

Africa

- **1954:** Algerian uprising against French rule
- **1956:** UK fails to block Egypt's nationalization of Suez Canal
- **1957:** Ghana becomes first British colony to achieve independence
- **1960:** Fifteen African countries gain independence; South Africa leaves Commonwealth
- **1960:** Katanga province secedes from Republic of Congo (Zaire); UN intervention follows
- **1962:** Nelson Mandela, leader of ANC, given life sentence in South Africa
- **1967–70:** Civil war in Nigeria over secession of oil-rich east (Biafra). Over one million die
- **1975:** Angola and Mozambique gain independence from Portugal

THE COLD WAR

Spies, such as the Rosenbergs, executed in 1953 for passing US nuclear secrets to the USSR, were endemic during the Cold War.

FROM THE MEETING OF US AND SOVIET FORCES on the Elbe in April 1945 came a division of Europe and a confrontation between the former allies which would last for almost five decades. Defensive needs – for the US the security of Western Europe, for the USSR a buffer zone in Eastern Europe – appeared to each other offensive intents, overlaid by ideological, political, and economic rivalries. Thus the Cold War took shape, with the US committed to a policy of containment and attrition by all means just short of open conflict, and the USSR intent on supporting anti-Western revolutionary movements throughout the world. Strategic and armed stalemate gave rise to détente in the 1970s, but only the collapse of Soviet system in 1989–91 ended the Cold War.

The Cuban missile crisis 1961–62

The Cold War's most dangerous single episode arose from the Castro Revolution (1956–59) and subsequent US–Cuban estrangement. Castro's alignment with the Eastern bloc provided the USSR with an opportunity to offset its strategic inferiority by the creation of Cuban bases from which missiles could strike at the heart of continental USA. This was forestalled by a US blockade, and a stand-off following which the Soviets were forced to withdraw their missiles.

Cold warriors J. F. Kennedy and Nikita Khrushchev underestimated each other's strength and determination when they met in Vienna in 1961. By 1962 they had taken the world to the verge of nuclear conflict during the Cuban missile crisis.

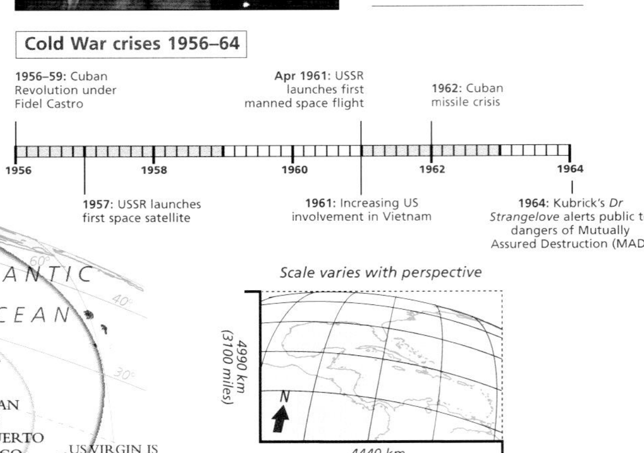

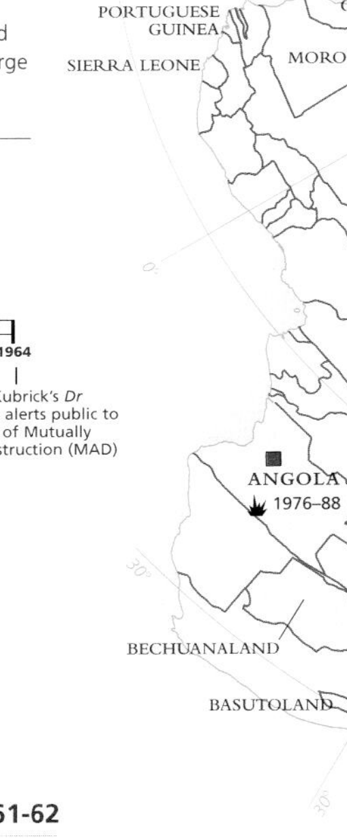

★Apr 1961: CIA-backed invasion force of Cuban exiles aborted

2 The Cuban missile crisis 1961-62

- potential range of Soviet missiles (1100 miles)
- US blockade zone
- Soviet missile and jet base
- US air base
- US naval base

NATO and the Warsaw Pact

On 23 June 1948, the Soviet army blockaded the Western-controlled sectors of Berlin, forcing the Allied powers to mount a massive airlift to supply the beleaguered enclave.

Deepening US-Soviet hostility, plus Western Europe's patent inability to defend itself, led to the creation of the North Atlantic Treaty Organization (NATO) in April 1949; in effect, the US provided guarantee of Western Europe's security. The latter's continuing war-weariness saw a build-up of US forces in Europe, and contributed to the decision to permit West Germany to have armed forces, admitting the nation to NATO in 1955. This in turn prompted the USSR and its satellite countries in Eastern Europe to form the Warsaw Pact. The building of the Berlin Wall in 1961 consolidated the 'Iron Curtain' which divided Europe into two zones – East and West – until 1989.

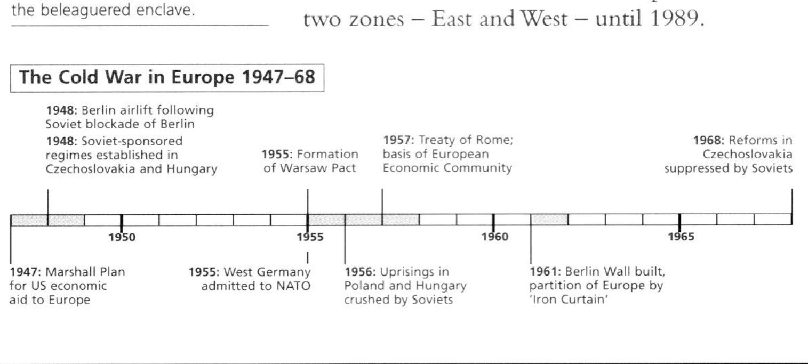

3 The Cold War in Europe

- original NATO members in 1949
- later NATO members (with dates)
- Warsaw Pact members in 1955
- neutral states

From the early 1960s the Western allies depended increasingly on long-range nuclear-powered submarines to deliver missiles in the event of war. With the development of Trident submarines in the 1980s the range extended to 7400 km, a key factor in the Strategic Arms Reduction (START) negotiations of 1982–91.

SEE ALSO:

North America: pp.138–139

South America: pp.152–153

Africa: pp.168–169

Europe: pp.212–215

West Asia: pp.234–235

South and Southeast Asia: pp.252–253

North and East Asia: pp.274–275

Australasia and Oceania: pp.284–285

Strategic manoeuvres in the Cold War

- **1945:** Yalta Conference; division between Allies; origins of Cold War
- **1947:** Truman Doctrine seeks 'containment' of USSR
- **1949:** Formation of NATO
- **1955:** Formation of Warsaw Pact
- **1972:** SALT I strategic arms limitation talks
- **1979:** SALT II arms limitation agreement signed
- **1989–90:** Collapse of Communism in Europe
- **1990:** NATO and Warsaw Pact agree on conventional arms limitation in Europe
- **1991:** US and USSR sign START arms reduction treaty

The strategic balance

In the Cold War's first decade the US sought to contain the threat of global Communism by a series of regional treaties and alliances backed by economic and military strength. But by 1960, with a rift in Sino-Soviet relations splitting the Communist bloc, and as the simultaneous process of decolonization (endorsed by the US) deprived its European NATO allies of their global outreach, so the theatre of the Cold War shifted from Europe to the developing world. Here a series of conflicts from Cuba to Vietnam saw both the US and the Communist world frequently fighting a war by proxy.

THE ARMS RACE

As the Cold War arms race began, the US held technological, numerical and positional advantages over the Soviet Union. In the 1960s, as US vulnerability increased, deterrence shifted from bombers to a triad built around submarine- and land-based intercontinental missiles (ICBMs). With the USSR acquiring ICBM capability by the late 1960s, both superpowers faced the future with secure second-strikes: MAD (Mutually Assured Destruction). This situation, and the development of multiple-warhead (MRV, MIRV) technology threatened a new round in the arms race. The 1970s saw ceilings on missile and warhead numbers, and anti-missile defences (ABM) were limited (SALT I in 1972, and SALT II in 1979). The brief period of détente gave way to perhaps the most dangerous phase of the Cold War, one that witnessed ABM revival with the Strategic Defence Initiative (SDI, Star Wars) which only ended with the collapse of the USSR in 1991.

The Korean War 1950–53

Reluctantly sanctioned by the USSR, North Korea's invasion of the south in June 1950 was immediately seen as a test of US global credibility. The challenge was initially countered by a US-led UN force, which was met in turn by Chinese intervention. Thereafter the front stabilized around the pre-war border. The US, confronted by the need to garrison Europe, and by a reluctance to carry the war beyond Korea's borders, accepted a policy of defensive self-restraint, which formed the basis of the Western Allies' Limited War doctrine.

The Korean War effectively ended in stalemate in July 1953, with the partition of Korea into a Communist North and a nominally democratic South along an armistice line, straddling the 38th parallel. This border has remained a heavily armed military frontier ever since. These South Korean troops were photographed in 1996.

Ideological indoctrination by both East and West during the Cold War conflicts in the developing world was enforced irrespective of sex or age. The image of the child soldier is an enduring legacy of these conflicts in Africa.

The Angolan Civil War 1975–88

By the 1970s Soviet naval and airlift capacity enabled it to give active support to anti-Western revolution globally. However, its major efforts in Africa, in Angola (1976–88) and Ethiopia (1977–89), were conducted by proxy via Cuba. In Angola, the three main organizations which had fought to end Portuguese rule were bitterly hostile to each other, and by 1975 there was a three-way civil war, the Marxist MPLA initially clearing the FNLA and UNITA from the north. The Soviets sustained the MPLA with Cuban troops, while the Western powers, through South Africa, secured southern borders in support of UNITA. The conflict lasted until 1988, the Cubans, MPLA and South Africa concluding an uneasy ceasefire. Throughout the struggle, UNITA dominated most of Angola through guerrilla warfare, but 50,000 Cuban troops ensured the survival of the MPLA.

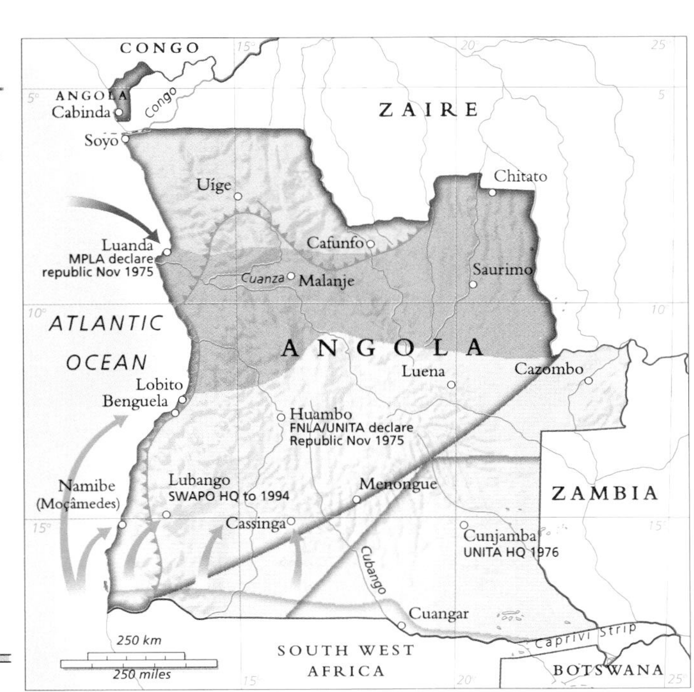

THE WORLD

THE MODERN AGE

WITH THE CLOSE OF THE COLD WAR IN 1989, rivalry between the US and the USSR ended. The USSR collapsed in 1991, and the former Eastern bloc was opened up to Western political influence and free-market forces. But hopes for a 'new world order' were premature. Russia suffered crises of confidence over democracy and capitalism. In the Middle East, disputes between Israel and her neighbours continued, while Islamic fundamentalism took hold in several countries. Saddam Hussein's regime in Iraq kept much of the region on constant standby for war. In Southeast Asia, massive investment during the 1980s fed an unsustainable economic boom, leading to depression in the late 1990s. South Africa's elections of 1994 were a triumph for democracy in Africa, but the following decade saw ethnic and resource-based conflict in many parts of the continent. After the atrocities of 11 September 2001, the US embarked on a so-called 'war on terror' with military operations in Afghanistan and Iraq.

The Berlin Wall, hated symbol of division between East and West was torn down in 1989, and Germany's two halves were reunited the following year.

Europe

While Western Europe progressed towards economic and political unity under the European Union (EU), eastern Europe was still economically constrained by Soviet Communism. But in 1989 popular movements rejected Communism, fracturing first the Eastern bloc and in 1991, the USSR itself. The fragmentation boiled over into civil war, notably in Yugoslavia and Georgia, where conflicts were fuelled by ethnic nationalism.

Europe

- 1975: General Franco dies in Spain. He is replaced by King Juan Carlos
- **1985:** Mikhail Gorbachev becomes Soviet leader; moves to end Cold War
- **1989:** End of Communism in Poland, Hungary, Czechoslovakia, Romania, East Germany, and Bulgaria
- **1990:** East and West Germany reunited
- **1991:** Breakup of USSR; Start of civil war in Yugoslavia
- **1995:** Ceasefire agreed in Bosnia and Herzegovina; UN troops remain
- **1999:** Kosovo crisis; Yugoslavia bombed
- **2004:** Islamic extremist outrages in Madrid and North Ossetia, Russia

REMOTE-SENSED MAPPING

The detailed data collected by sensor-bearing satellites can be used to map changing geographic patterns. Examples include climatic conditions, soils, vegetation, pollution, and levels of urbanization.

An infrared satellite image of Buenos Aires taken from a French SPOT satellite shows densely populated urban areas in blue, vegetation in red and water – including the River Plate – in black.

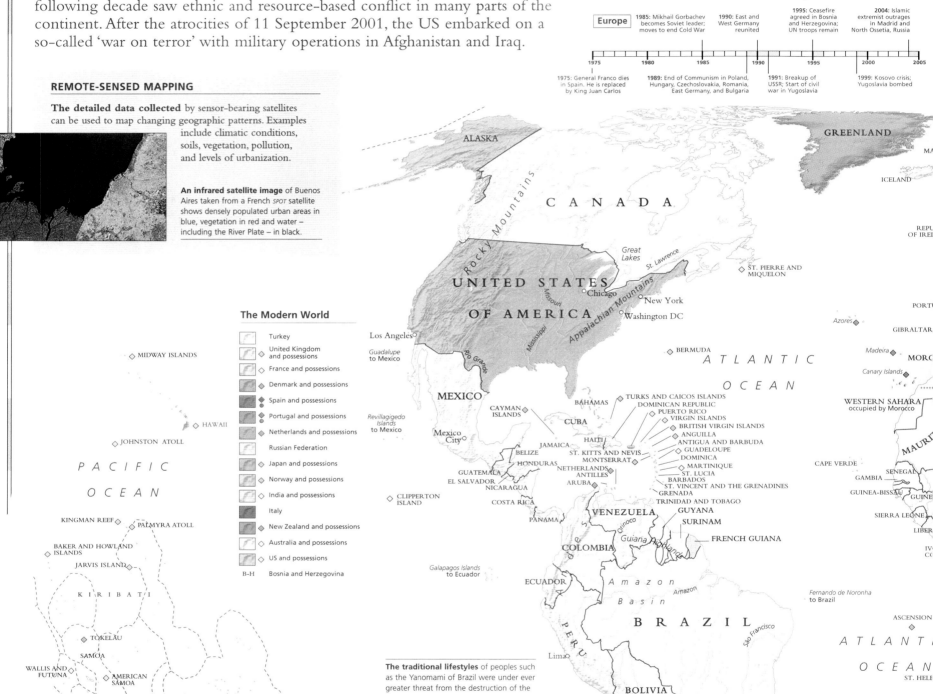

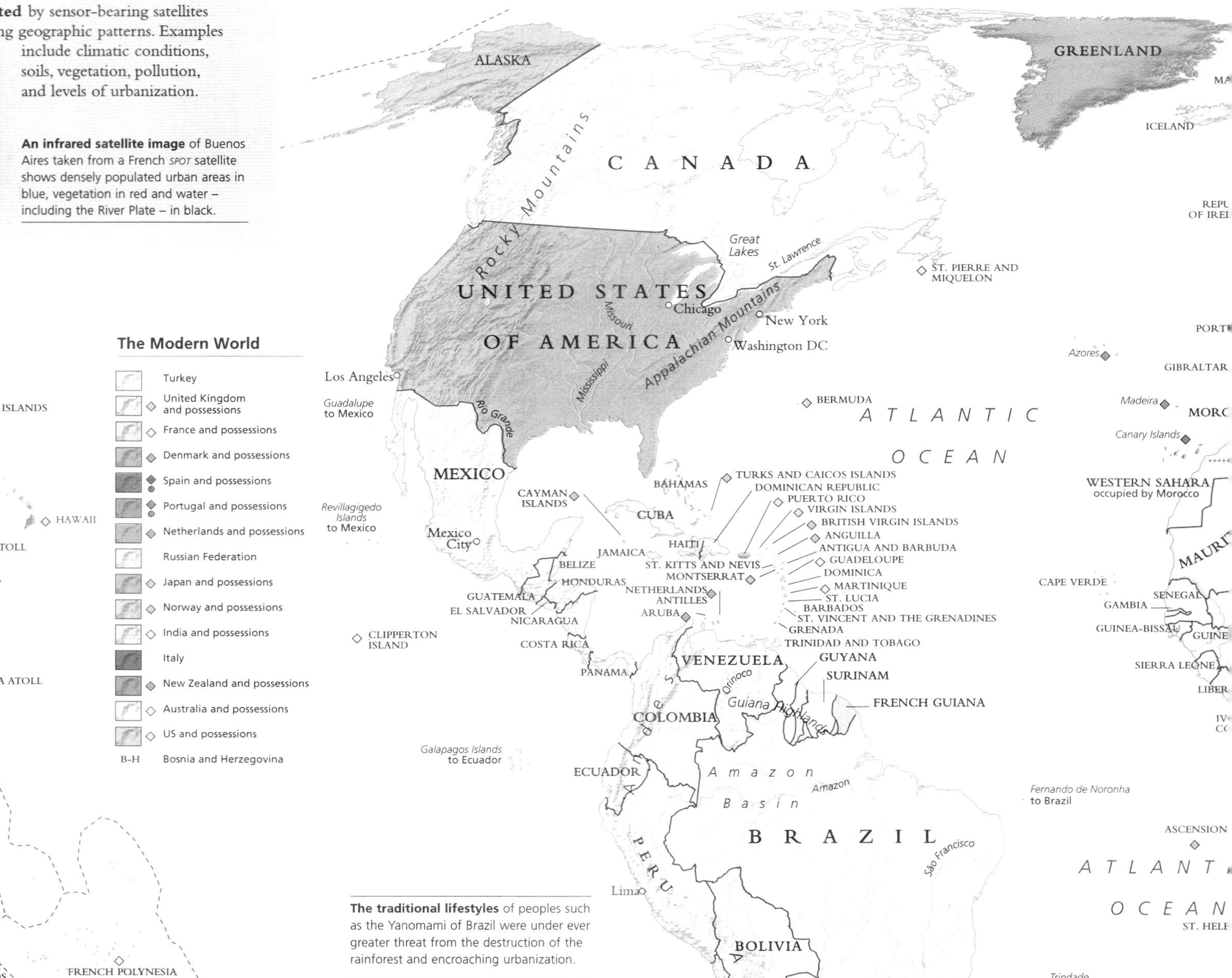

The Modern World

- Turkey
- United Kingdom and possessions
- France and possessions
- Denmark and possessions
- Spain and possessions
- Portugal and possessions
- Netherlands and possessions
- Russian Federation
- Japan and possessions
- Norway and possessions
- India and possessions
- Italy
- New Zealand and possessions
- Australia and possessions
- US and possessions
- B-H Bosnia and Herzegovina

ALASKA
GREENLAND
ICELAND
CANADA
UNITED STATES OF AMERICA
Rocky Mountains
Appalachian Mountains
Great Lakes
Chicago
New York
Washington DC
Los Angeles
ST. PIERRE AND MIQUELON
BERMUDA
ATLANTIC OCEAN
PACIFIC OCEAN
MEXICO
Mexico City
CUBA
BAHAMAS
JAMAICA
HAITI
BELIZE
HONDURAS
GUATEMALA
EL SALVADOR
NICARAGUA
COSTA RICA
PANAMA
VENEZUELA
GUYANA
SURINAM
FRENCH GUIANA
COLOMBIA
ECUADOR
PERU
Lima
BRAZIL
Amazon Basin
BOLIVIA
PARAGUAY
CHILE
Santiago
URUGUAY
Buenos Aires
ARGENTINA
Rio de Janeiro
São Paulo
FALKLAND ISLANDS
SOUTH GEORGIA AND THE SOUTH SANDWICH ISLANDS
HAWAII
FRENCH POLYNESIA
PITCAIRN ISLANDS
Galapagos Islands to Ecuador

The traditional lifestyles of peoples such as the Yanomami of Brazil were under ever greater threat from the destruction of the rainforest and encroaching urbanization.

The Americas

From the end of the 1970s Central and South America began to move towards democracy, but economic instability and chronic inflation remained major problems. After the collapse of the USSR, the US maintained its economic dominance, but was less self-confident politically. All that changed after 11 September 2001, as the US embarked on a 'war on terror' and a campaign against the 'axis of evil' (Iran, Iraq and North Korea).

The Americas

- **1979:** Start of civil war in Nicaragua between Sandinistas and US-backed Contras
- **1982:** Falklands War between UK and Argentina
- **1987:** US and USSR agree to limit intermediate nuclear weapons
- **1989:** Democracy restored in Chile as Pinochet steps down
- **1991:** UN-brokered peace ends 10-year civil war in El Salvador
- **1991–92:** USSR ends preferential trade agreement with Cuba
- **1996:** Guatemalan civil war ends after 36 years
- **2001:** Terrorist attacks kill almost 3000 in US

In 1979, an Islamic revolution led by the Ayatollah Khomeini overthrew the corrupt regime of the Shah of Iran. Iran became an Islamic state, vilifying the West, governed by religious laws and ruthlessly suppressing political opposition.

West and South Asia

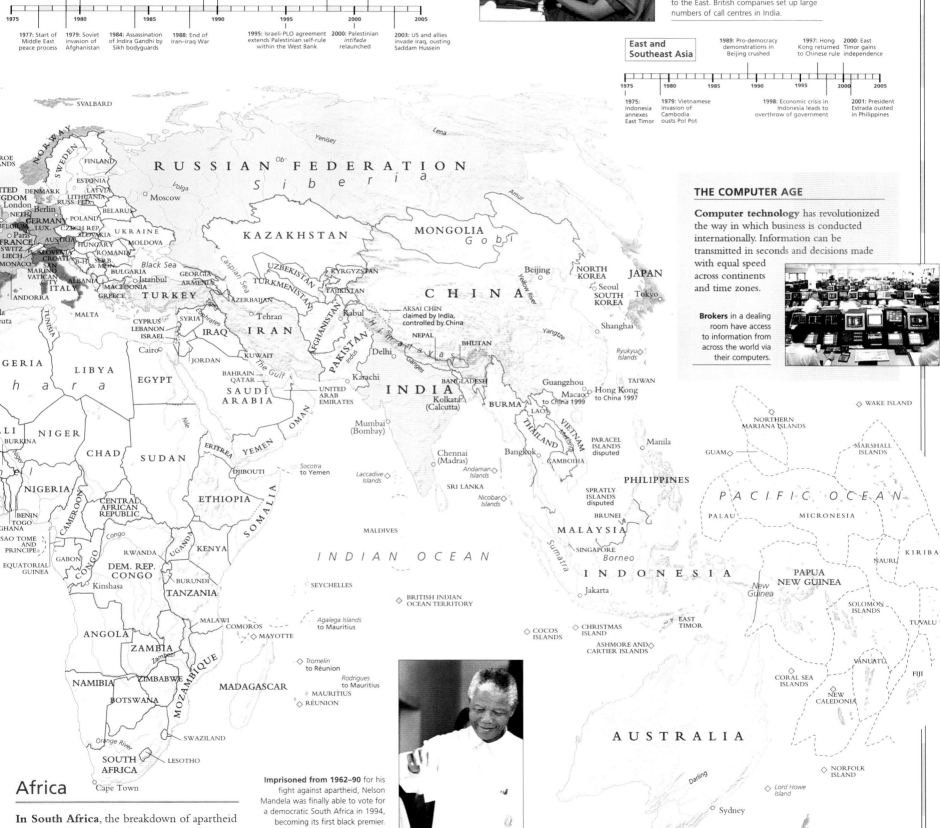

Violence continued throughout the Middle East, often accompanied by the rise of fundamentalist Islam. Instability and open conflict affected much of the western region, particularly Lebanon, Iraq, Syria, Kuwait, and Saudi Arabia. The issue of Palestinian self-government proved as difficult as ever to resolve. In 2003 the EU, Russia, the UN and the US launched the 'Road Map' to peace and a Palestinian state by 2005.

East and Southeast Asia

From the late 1970s, China sought closer links with the West and began a programme of industrial expansion and econonomic liberalization. As a result, China's economy grew rapidly, but calls for greater democracy were halted in 1989 following the massacre of students in Tiananmen Square. Elsewhere, the 'tiger economies' of South Korea, Taiwan, and Singapore enjoyed a spectacular boom until the depression of the late 1990s.

SEE ALSO:

North America: pp.136–137

South America: pp.152–153

Africa: pp.168–169

Europe: pp.214–215

West Asia: pp.234–235

South and Southeast Asia: pp.252–253

North and East Asia: pp.274–275

Australasia and Oceania: pp.284–285

Cheaper labour costs led many Western firms to relocate their production to Asia during the 1980s. In the 1990s service industries also began to outsource work to the East. British companies set up large numbers of call centres in India.

West and South Asia

- 1977: Start of Middle East peace process
- 1979: Islamic revolution in Iran
- 1979: Soviet invasion of Afghanistan
- 1980: Start of Iran–Iraq War
- 1984: Assassination of Indira Gandhi by Sikh bodyguards
- 1988: End of Iran–Iraq War
- 1989: USSR withdraws from Afghanistan
- 1990: Iraqi invasion of Kuwait sparks Gulf War
- 1995: Israeli-PLO agreement extends Palestinian self-rule within the West Bank
- 1998: Indian and Pakistani nuclear tests
- 2000: Palestinian *intifada* relaunched
- 2001: US and allies oust Taliban from Afghanistan
- 2003: US and allies invade Iraq, ousting Saddam Hussein

East and Southeast Asia

- 1975: Indonesia annexes East Timor
- 1979: Vietnamese invasion of Cambodia ousts Pol Pot
- 1989: Pro-democracy demonstrations in Beijing crushed
- 1997: Hong Kong returned to Chinese rule
- 1998: Economic crisis in Indonesia leads to overthrow of government
- 2000: East Timor gains independence
- 2001: President Estrada ousted in Philippines

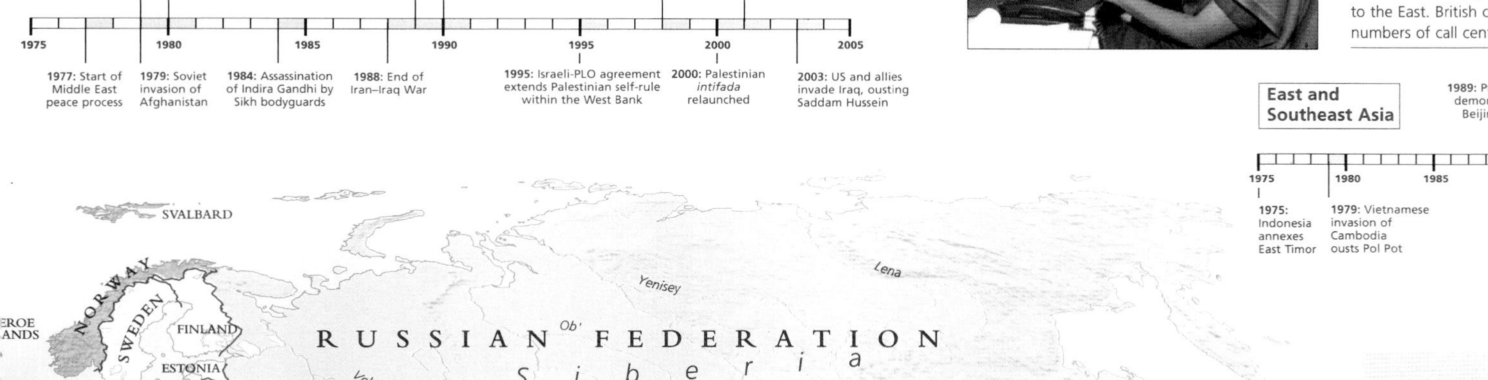

THE COMPUTER AGE

Computer technology has revolutionized the way in which business is conducted internationally. Information can be transmitted in seconds and decisions made with equal speed across continents and time zones.

Brokers in a dealing room have access to information from across the world via their computers.

Africa

In South Africa, the breakdown of apartheid led to the first completely democratic elections, held in 1994. In East, Central, and West Africa, however, ongoing conflicts affected the lives of millions of people. In 2001 the Organization of African Unity launched NEPAD, the New Partnership for Africa's Development, intended to eradicate poverty and foster sustainable development and good governance.

Imprisoned from 1962–90 for his fight against apartheid, Nelson Mandela was finally able to vote for a democratic South Africa in 1994, becoming its first black premier.

Africa

- 1975: Independence in Angola and Mozambique followed by civil wars
- 1986: US bombs Libya
- 1987: Famine in Ethiopia
- 1994: Nelson Mandela wins presidency of South Africa
- 1994: Massacre of 500,000 Tutsis by Hutu in Rwanda
- 1997: President Mobutu overthrown in Zaire
- 2001: End of civil war in Sierra Leone
- 2003: EU intervention in Democratic Republic of Congo; peace accord signed
- 2004: Ethnic conflict and humanitarian crisis in W Sudan

HIDDEN WORLDS OF TODAY

The production of illegal drugs occurs globally. These examples of 'kif' and opium were made in Morocco.

THE WORLD ECONOMY at the end of the 20th century was shaped increasingly by the investment practices and preferences of huge global businesses. The World Trade Organization (WTO), formed in 1995 and enshrining liberal free trade principles, found itself managing disputes between trade blocs as much as between individual countries. The phenomenon of globalization grew out of the rapid growth of digital processing technology and the expansion of telecommunications. But local communities continued to matter: ethnic origin, cultural affinity, shared history and religious identity connected communities across national boundaries. International terrorism, often driven by deep animosity towards the US and the Western world, together with the activities of international criminal networks, dominated the news media and public debate in the first years of the 21st century.

The Greater African Nation

The African diaspora in the Americas, originating with the slave trade in the 16th–18th centuries, is today over 80 million strong. Only the Caribbean states have majority black populations, but African Americans in the US are the world's fourth largest black community and Brazil's population is also in the world top ten. The UK's black minority is a more recent result of post-war immigration, as is Portugal's. The black community has few political ties internationally, but a shared sense of identity and awareness of their African roots.

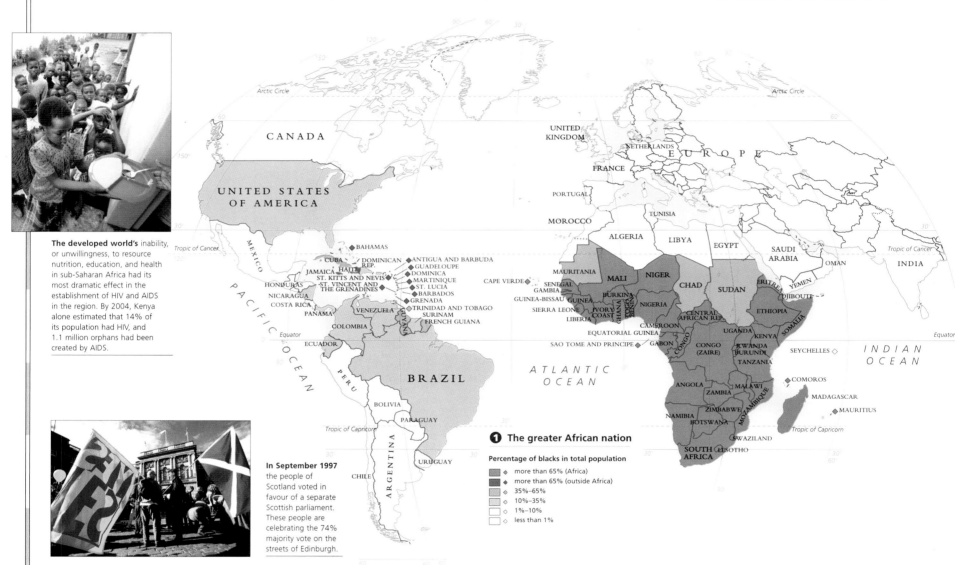

The developed world's inability, or unwillingness, to resource nutrition, education, and health in sub-Saharan Africa had its most dramatic effect in the establishment of HIV and AIDS in the region. By 2004, Kenya alone estimated that 14% of its population had HIV, and 1.1 million orphans had been created by AIDS.

In September 1997 the people of Scotland voted in favour of a separate Scottish parliament. These people are celebrating the 74% majority vote on the streets of Edinburgh.

1 The greater African nation

Percentage of blacks in total population

- more than 65% (Africa)
- more than 65% (outside Africa)
- 35%–65%
- 10%–35%
- 1%–10%
- less than 1%

Devolution in Europe

Europe's new nation states of the 1990s emerged from the demise of the Soviet Union, the 'velvet divorce' of Czechs from Slovaks, and the break-up of the former Yugoslavia. Eight of these countries – the Czech Republic, Estonia, Hungary, Latvia, Lithuania, Poland, Slovakia, and Slovenia – joined the EU in 2004, together with Malta and Cyprus. The Central and Eastern European countries formed a counterbalance to the supranational, federalizing inclinations of some 'old Europe' members of the EU. Elsewhere, unresolved separatist aspirations and ethnic divisions resulted in armed conflict and, eventually, in uneasy peace agreements. Bosnia and Herzegovina now barely exists beyond its separate Serb and Muslim-Croat 'entities', while even after the conflict of 1999 the future remained uncertain for ethnic Albanians nominally under Serbian rule in Kosovo.

2 Devolution and statehood in Europe

- new state since 1990
- a degree of devolution acknowledged
- substantial ethnic groups without their own state
- pressure for greater self-determination

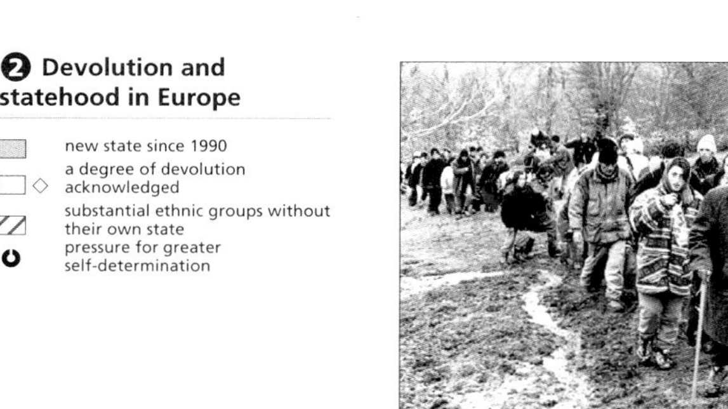

Serbian persecution of ethnic Albanians in the Kosovo region of the rump state of Yugoslavia led, in early 1999 to air strikes against Serbia by NATO and the murder or exodus of hundreds of thousands of refugees, 'ethnically cleansed' from their former homes.

The pan-Islamic world

Sunni Islam is the dominant tradition in the Islamic world, encompassing some 90% of the world's one billion Muslims. The revivalist Salafi interpretation of the Sunni tradition – often known as 'Wahhabism' – developed in Saudi Arabia and has taken hold in several parts of the Islamic world. In some cases, notably the activities of Osama bin Laden and the al-Qaeda movement, it has been associated with anti-Western terrorism. Shi'a Islam, with its reputation for religious zeal and martyrdom, is the majority religion in Iran.

The unity of the Muslim world is maintained by the annual pilgrimage to Mecca – the Haj. As many as two million pilgrims from all over the world congregate at the birthplace of Muhammad to perform a series of rituals at Islam's holiest shrines.

SEE ALSO:

North America: pp.138–139

South America: p152–153

Africa: pp.168–169

Europe: pp.214–215

West Asia: pp.234–235

South and Southeast Asia: pp.252–253

North and East Asia: pp.274–275

THE WORLD WIDE WEB

Wide-area computer networking, developed originally for sharing information between academic institutions, expanded to become a worldwide Internet whose user numbers exploded in the 1990s. The big stimulus to its popular success was the creation of a graphical interface for 'surfing' hyperlinked sites on what became known as the World Wide Web. The opportunities for anonymity, the use of encrypted communications, and the problems of authentication and copyright protection posed great difficulties for policing and control.

This 'Internet Cafe' in Taiwan, offers diners access to the Internet while they eat.

The subterranean world of organized crime

Ease of travel and speed of communication encouraged the spread of organized crime syndicates far beyond national borders. As business became globalized, so too was corruption in business and finance; traditional criminal industries such as narcotics, prostitution, gambling, extortion, and money-laundering were transformed into global industries. Law enforcement had some successes in curtailing the Italian and US mafia, but the collapse of Communism in the Soviet Union created conditions in which a Russian mafia grew rapidly, becoming established across Eurasia and America. The big drug cartels, dealing in cocaine or heroin, fought for control of the production and distribution channels to the rich markets of North America and Europe. Profits, 'laundered' through other businesses and exploiting the confidentiality of banking systems, were used to acquire increasing political influence and protection.

❹ The world of organized crime

Narcotics production and trafficking
- cannabis production
- cocaine production
- heroin production
- heroin and cannabis production
- heroin trafficking
- cocaine trafficking
- cannabis trafficking

Major centres for criminal organizations
- Mafia
- Triads
- major centre for drug-related crime
- drug transit centres
- 'Golden Triangle'
- major centre for money laundering
- murder rate greater than 20 per 100,000, with figure

Extent of international organized crime
- Italian Mafia
- Triads
- Jamaican Posses
- Russian Mafia
- Colombian cartels
- Japanese Yakuzas
- United States Cosa Nostra
- Turkish Mafia

Human trafficking was, by the end of the 20th century, the single most lucrative and globalized activity for organized criminals. Slavery, the sex industry, debt bondage, economic migration, and the developed world's increasing reliance on cheap labour, fed a multi-billion dollar trade based on the recruitment, transportation, and exploitation of humans as mere commodities.

DIVERSI
GLOBI TERR-AQVEI
STATIONE VARIANTE
ET VISU INTERCEDENTE,
PER COLUROS TROPICORUM,
PER AMBOS POLOS
ET PARTICUL. SPHÆRÆ ZENITH
IN PLANUM DELINEATI
ORTHOGRAPHICI
PROSPECTUS;
ZONA FRIGIDA (SEPTENTRIO) SEPTENTRIONALIS
ZONA TEMPERATA SEPTENTRIONALIS
AMERICA SEPTENTRIONALIS
AMERICA MERIDIONALIS
MAR DEL ZUR
MARE PACIFICUM
TROPICUS CANCRI Sive ÆSTATIS
TROPICUS CAPRICORNI Sive
ÆQUATOR sive LINEA ÆQUIDIALIS Vulgo ÆQUINOCTIALIS
REGIONES AUSTRALES NONDUM COGNITÆ
ZONA FRIGI-(MERIDIES)-DA AUSTRALIS
Polus Arcticus
Polus Antarcticus

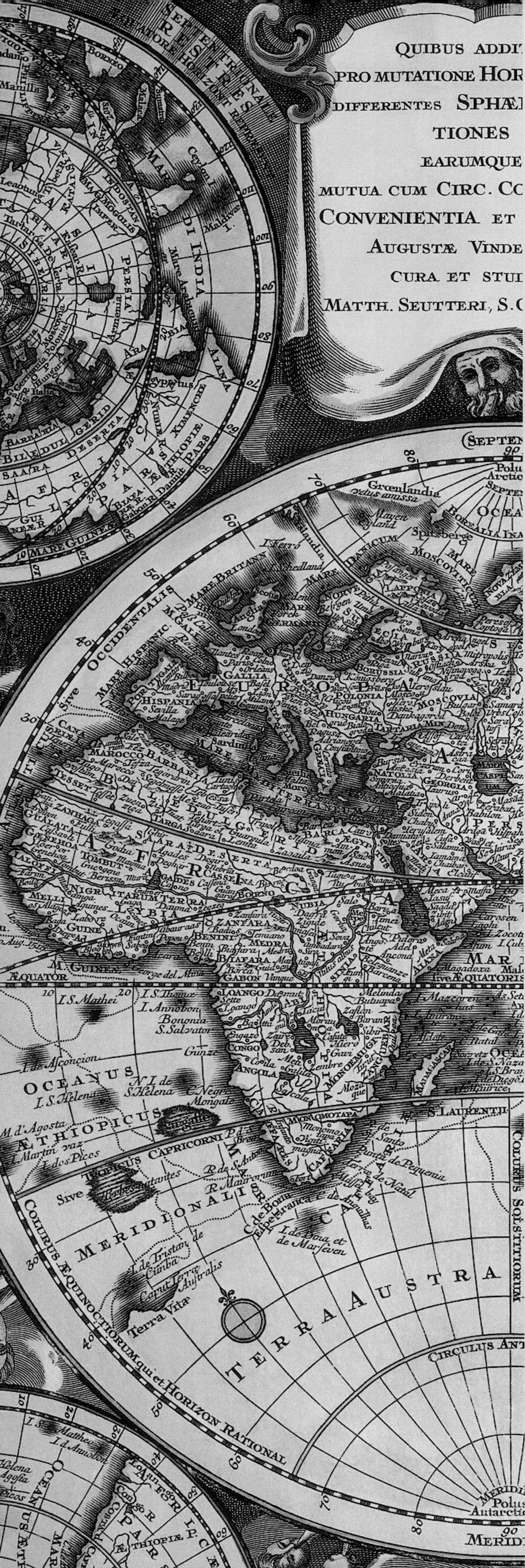

PART TWO

REGIONAL HISTORY

INHABITANTS OF EACH PART of the globe view the history of the world through the lens of their regional heritage. The second section of this atlas presents the chronological story of eight principal geographic regions: North America, South America, Africa, Europe, West Asia, South and Southeast Asia, North and East Asia and, finally, Australasia and Oceania. Each regional narrative is prefaced by a map which examines its historical geography. This is followed by pages covering the exploration and mapping of the area, showing how it came to be known in its present form. Thereafter, the maps are organized to present the continuous historical development of each region through time.

By the 18th century, the modern world map was clearly emerging. This map, produced by the Dutch cartographer, Matthias Seutter in 1730, combines a series of detailed projections of the various hemispheres, with compass points depicted as a variety of different windheads.

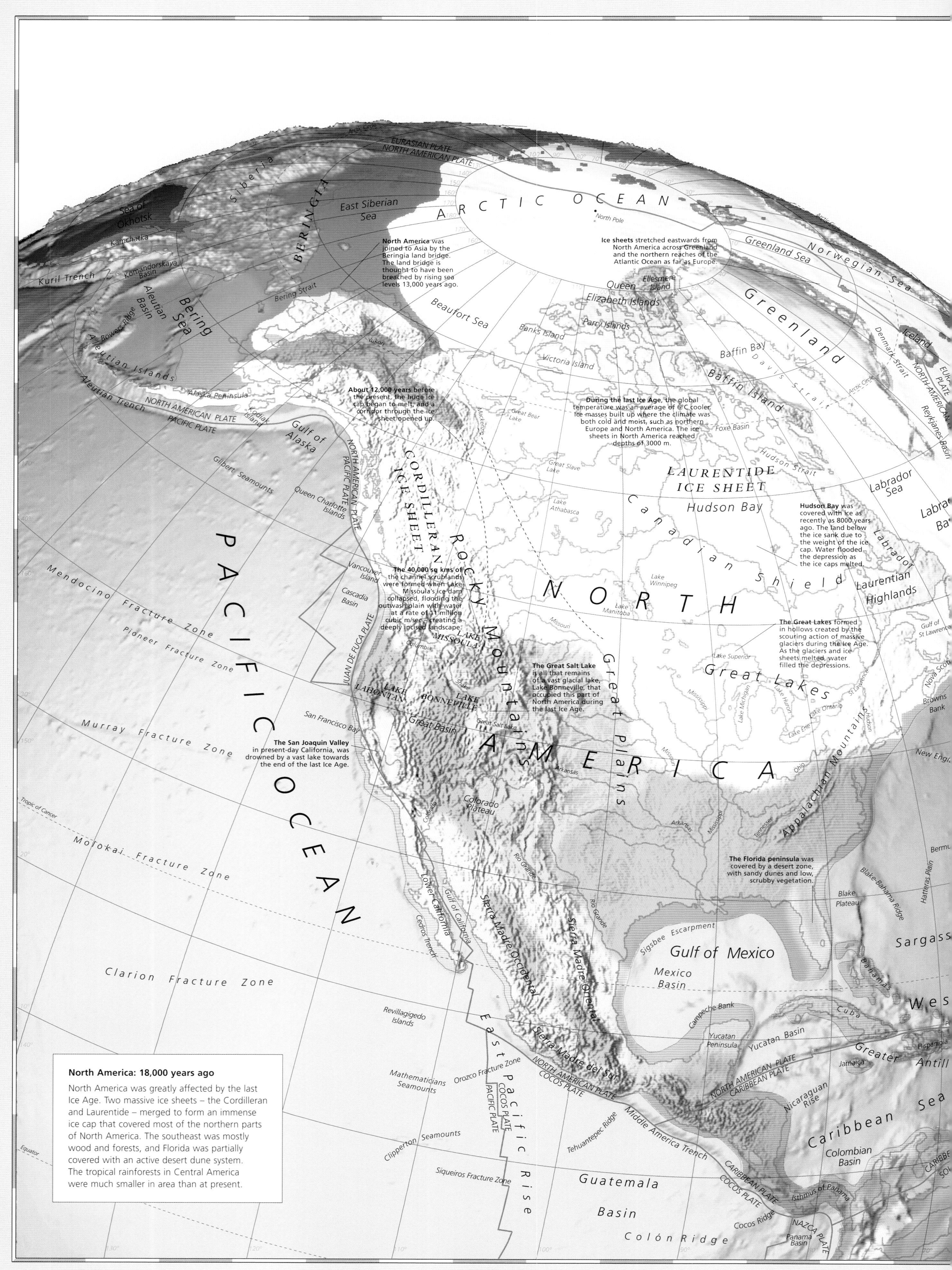

North America: 18,000 years ago

North America was greatly affected by the last Ice Age. Two massive ice sheets – the Cordilleran and Laurentide – merged to form an immense ice cap that covered most of the northern parts of North America. The southeast was mostly wood and forests, and Florida was partially covered with an active desert dune system. The tropical rainforests in Central America were much smaller in area than at present.

Vegetation type

- ice cap and glacier
- tundra
- polar and alpine desert
- semi-desert or sparsely vegetated
- grassland
- forest or open woodland
- tropical rainforest
- temperate desert
- tropical desert
- coastline (present-day)
- coastline (18,000 years ago)

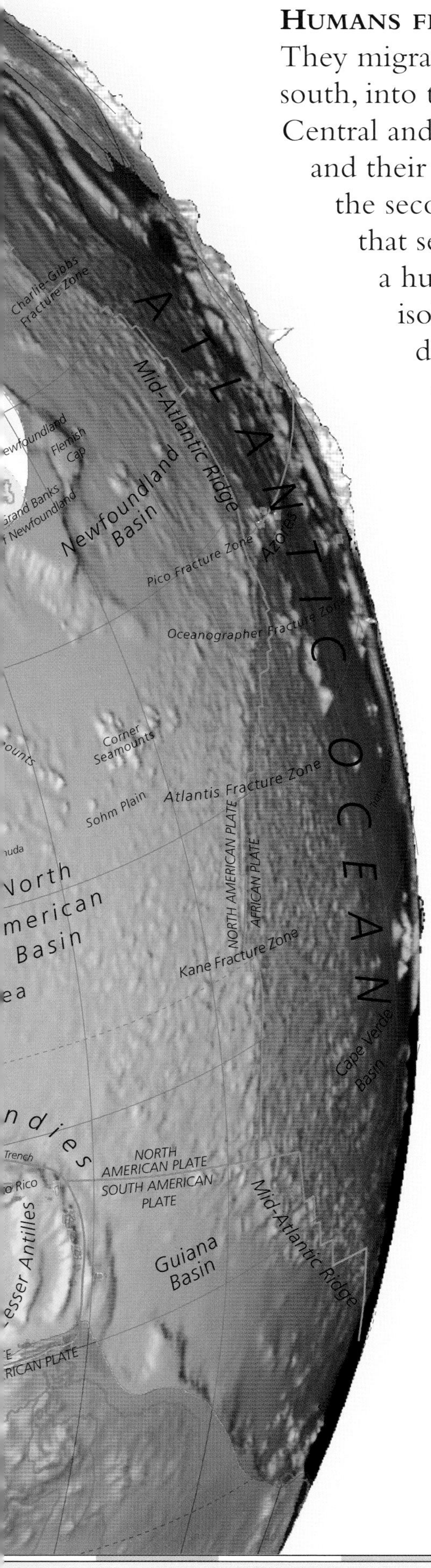

NORTH AMERICA

REGIONAL HISTORY

THE HISTORICAL LANDSCAPE

HUMANS FIRST ENTERED NORTH AMERICA FROM SIBERIA some 15,000 years ago. They migrated over the land bridge across the Bering Strait and, as the ice receded, moved south, into the rich gamelands of the Great Plains and onwards to eventually populate Central and South America. As the ice melted and sea levels rose, these early settlers and their new homeland became isolated from Eurasia, and would remain so until the second millennium CE. The low population level and abundance of foods meant that sedentary agricultural life evolved only sporadically, some groups sustaining a hunting and gathering way of life to the present day. During this period of isolation, unique ecological, genetic, and social patterns emerged which proved disastrously fragile when challenged by the first European colonists in the 15th century CE. Within 500 years the indigenous cultures of North America had been destroyed or marginalized by waves of migrants from the Old World who, with astonishing energy and ferocity, transformed the continent into the World's foremost economic, industrial, and political power.

At the heart of the continent, it was the plains which provided homelands for Native North Americans, displaced and driven west by European immigrants.

The gigantic basin drained by the Mississippi, spanning the entire tract between the Appalachians and the Rockies, provided a suitable environment for some of the first agricultural communities.

The Central American mountain plateaux and uplands were where some of the earliest complex civilizations in the Americas developed. A combination of favourable climate and fertile land allowed plants to be cultivated and early agriculture to develop.

NORTH AMERICA

EXPLORATION AND MAPPING

Lewis *(above)* and Clark led an epic expedition to explore the west in 1805–06.

FOR MANY CENTURIES North America was untouched by contact with other continents. Viking seafarers en route from Iceland and Greenland made landfall at Newfoundland over 1000 years ago, but their settlements were short-lived and their area of operation quite limited. Not until the early 16th century was the presence of a vast continent across the Atlantic fully accepted, and knowledge about it remained fragmentary. Once Europeans began to investigate North America, they were able to draw heavily on information from indigenous peoples, and use their pre-existing trails to explore the continent.

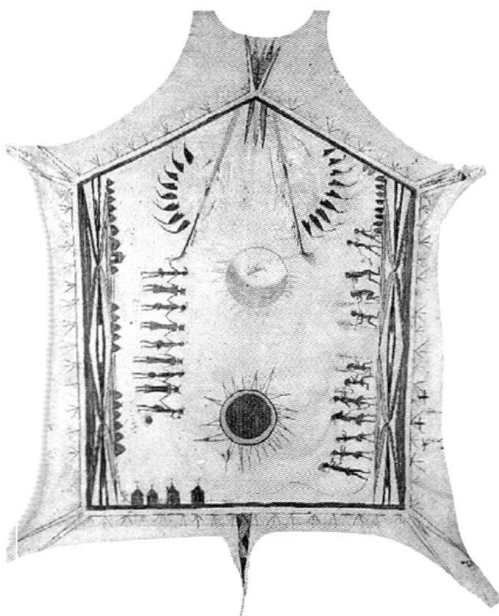

This map of three Indian villages showing their positions relative to the Sun and Moon was painted on a cured buffalo skin by members of the Qapaw tribe.

Native American maps

The indigenous peoples of North and Central America had detailed knowledge of the continent long before the first European expeditions. Much knowledge was undoubtedly passed on orally. But the location of early petroglyph maps carved on rocks suggests that they may have been produced as guides for travelling hunters, and to define territorial boundaries. Later maps – sometimes produced at the request of Europeans – reveal an intimate knowledge of the landscape and principles of space and distance. Several tribes used maps to show the long history of their tenure of the land when they were fighting for territory during the Indian removals of the 19th century.

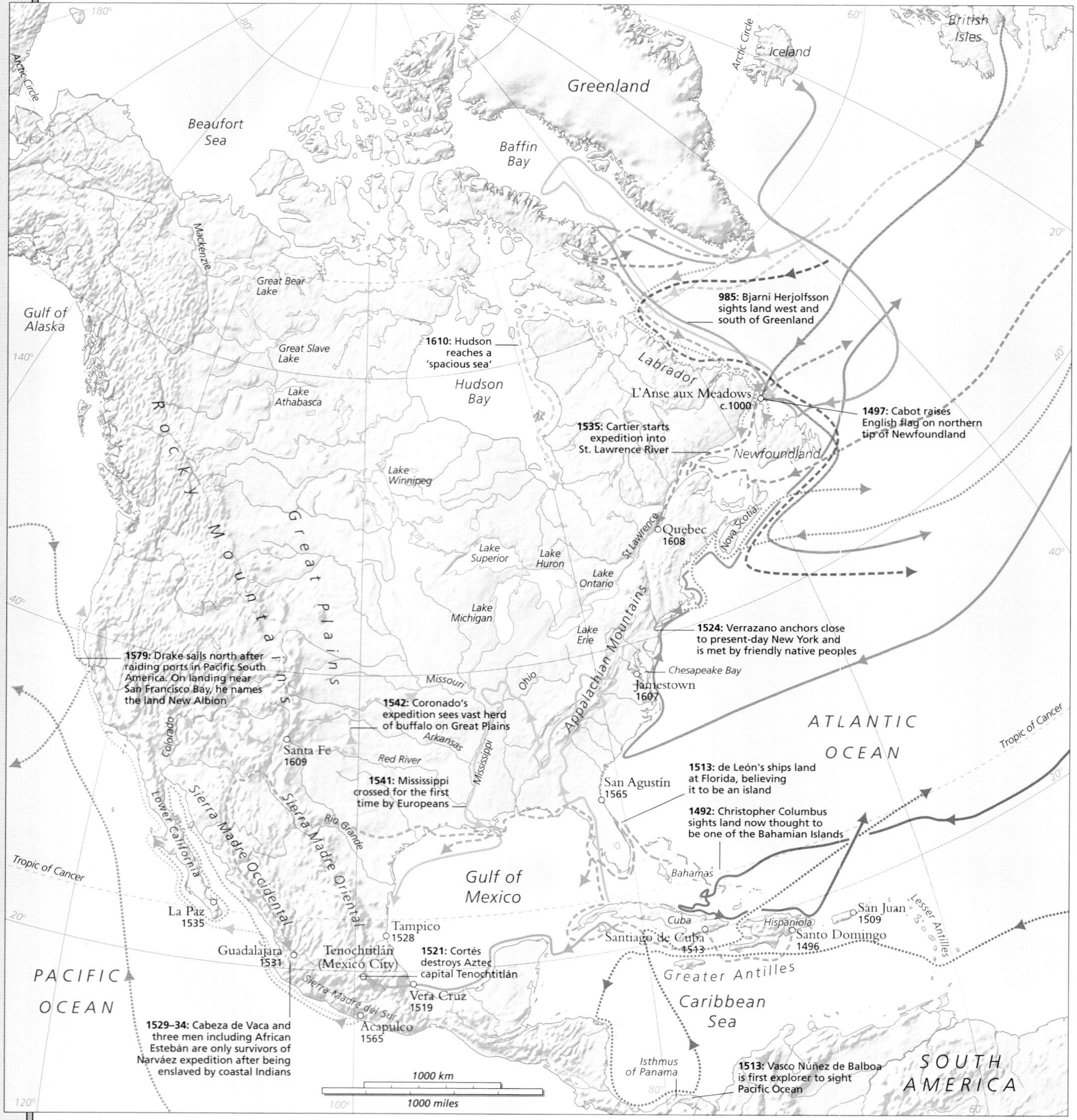

985: Bjarni Herjolfsson sights land west and south of Greenland

1610: Hudson reaches a 'spacious sea'

1535: Cartier starts expedition into St. Lawrence River

1497: Cabot raises English flag on northern tip of Newfoundland

L'Anse aux Meadows c.1000

Quebec 1608

1524: Verrazano anchors close to present-day New York and is met by friendly native peoples

Jamestown 1607

1579: Drake sails north after raiding ports in Pacific South America. On landing near San Francisco Bay, he names the land New Albion

1542: Coronado's expedition sees vast herd of buffalo on Great Plains

Santa Fe 1609

1541: Mississippi crossed for the first time by Europeans

San Agustín 1565

1513: de León's ships land at Florida, believing it to be an island

1492: Christopher Columbus sights land now thought to be one of the Bahamian Islands

La Paz 1535

Tampico 1528

Guadalajara 1531

Tenochtitlán (Mexico City)

1521: Cortés destroys Aztec capital Tenochtitlán

Vera Cruz 1519

Acapulco 1565

Santiago de Cuba 1513

Santo Domingo 1496

San Juan 1509

1529–34: Cabeza de Vaca and three men including African Estebán are only survivors of Narváez expedition after being enslaved by coastal Indians

1513: Vasco Núñez de Balboa is first explorer to sight Pacific Ocean

1000 km

1000 miles

Early European explorers

Though the first Europeans to visit North America were 10th-century Norsemen, European exploration began in earnest in the late 15th century when improvements in shipping made the longer exploratory voyages of Columbus and Cabot viable. By the mid-16th century Spanish-sponsored expeditions in search of gold and territory founded settlements in Florida, Central America, and the Caribbean, and explored the lands of the southeast and southwest. Meanwhile, English and French expeditions traced the Atlantic coast in detail, moving north in search of new routes to Asia.

1 The first European explorers of North America

Norse expeditions
- Bjarni Herjolfsson 985–86
- Leif Eriksson 1003
- Thorvald Eriksson 1005–12

Spanish and Portuguese expeditions
- Christopher Columbus 1492–93
- Miguel Corte-Real 1501,1502
- Christopher Columbus 1502–04
- Hernán Cortés 1519–21
- Juan Ponce de León 1513
- Panfilo de Narváez and Álvar Núñez Cabeza de Vaca 1528–36
- Francisco de Ulloa 1539–40
- Hernando de Soto 1539–43
- Francisco Vázquez de Coronado and García Lopez de Cardeñas 1540–42
- Sebastián Vizcaino 1602–03

English expeditions
- John Cabot 1497
- Martin Frobisher 1576–77
- Francis Drake 1579
- John Davis 1585–87
- Henry Hudson 1610–11

French expeditions
- Giovanni da Verrazano 1524
- Jacques Cartier 1535–36
- Samuel de Champlain 1604–07

○ European settlement
1608 and date of foundation

15th- and 16th-century European expeditions

- 1492: Columbus lands in the Bahamas thinking he has reached Asia
- 1497: Cabot lands on Newfoundland
- 1501: Miguel Corte-Real enslaves 50 Indians from Beothuk
- 1513: Ponce de León traces coast of Florida
- 1524: Verrazano sails up Atlantic coast as far as Nova Scotia
- 1528: Cabeza de Vaca explores Gulf of Mexico and southwest
- 1534: Cartier begins exploration of St. Lawrence
- 1539–43: De Soto explores southeastern North America

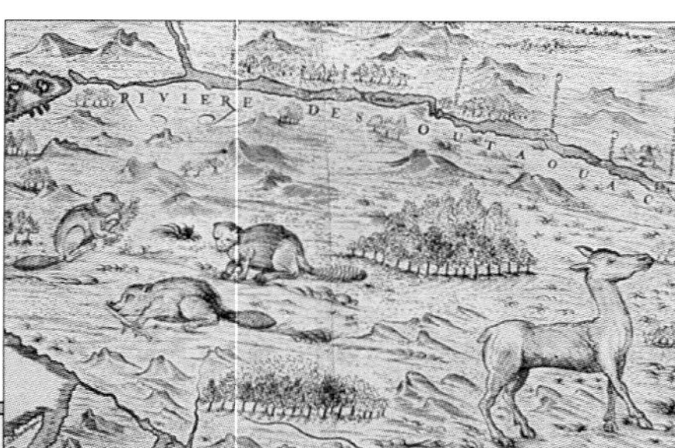

This map of Florida and Chesapeake Bay *(above)* was painted in the late 16th century. The spatial relationships are very inaccurate, with the Caribbean islands depicted much too far to the north.

European explorers were astonished by the quantity of wildlife they encountered in North America *(left)*. Fur-bearing animals such as beavers were quickly exploited for their pelts.

Exploring the eastern interior

The rich Atlantic fisheries and the bounteous wildlife of the northeast were magnets for European hunters and fishermen, and many of the earliest settlements were fur-trading posts. Samuel de Champlain, aided by Iroquois and Montagnais, explored the St. Lawrence and the Great Lakes, while Hudson and Davis ventured further west into Canada's great bays. Other expeditions were undertaken for missionary purposes, including Jolliet's Mississippian journey, where he was accompanied by Father Marquette. During the late 17th and early 18th centuries, several expeditions sought routes through the Appalachians, which would open up the Midwest to settlers.

One of America's great frontiersmen, Daniel Boone, is shown here leading a group of settlers through the Cumberland Gap, a pass through the Appalachian system which provided a route to the West.

❷ Journeys into the North American interior 1600–1775

British expeditions
- John Smith 1608
- Thomas Batts and Robert Fallam 1671
- James Needham and Gabriel Arthur 1673
- Dr Henry Woodward 1674, 1685

French expeditions
- Samuel de Champlain 1609–16
- Medart Chouart des Groseillers and Pierre-Esprit Radisson 1659–1660
- Father Claude Allouez 1665–67
- Father Charles Albanel 1671–72
- Louis Jolliet and Jacques Marquette 1672–73
- René-Robert Cavelier Sieur de La Salle 1684–87
- Louis Hennepin 1680
- Chaussegros de Léry 1729

Dutch expeditions
- Arnout Viele 1682–84
- Johannes Rosebloom 1685–87

American expeditions
- Christopher Gist 1750–51
- Thomas Walker 1750
- Daniel Boone 1769–71

1671: Guided by Indians, Batts and Fallam become first Europeans to cross Appalachians and reach Mississippi watershed

1750: Walker reaches Cumberland Gap, the gateway to Kentucky

1607: Settlement founded by 120 colonists from England

By the late 17th century knowledge of the east coast of North America had improved significantly. This plate from Visscher's *Atlas Contractus* of 1671 shows the Atlantic coast from New England south as far as Chesapeake Bay. Detail of the lands further west and the Great Lakes remained limited.

17th- and 18th-century expeditions in eastern North America

- **1607–08:** John Smith leads colonizing expeditions in Virginia
- **1609–13:** Champlain explores St. Lawrence and eastern Great Lakes
- **1665–67:** Father Allouez explores Great Lakes
- **1673:** Needham and Arthur follow Occaneechee Path across Appalachians
- **1673:** Jolliet and Marquette explore Mississippi and Illinois Rivers
- **1682:** La Salle follows Mississippi to its mouth
- **1729:** de Léry makes first proper survey of Allegheny and upper Ohio Rivers
- **1752:** John Finley realizes that Cumberland Gap is gateway to Kentucky lowlands

Charting the West

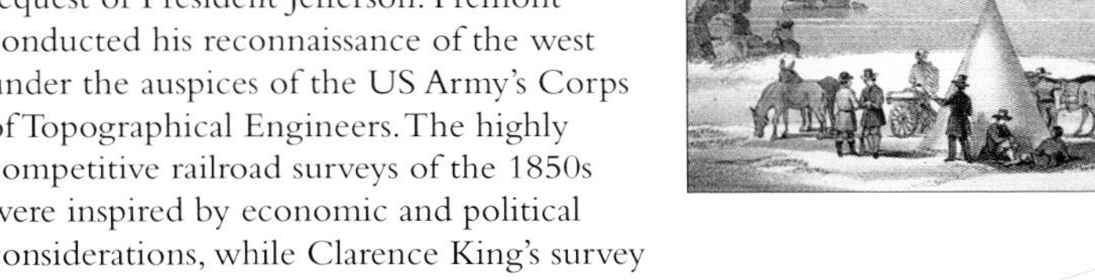

The rapid expansion of the US created the need to survey and quantify the vast territories of the new nation. Lewis and Clark's famous cross-continental expedition was funded by Congress at the express request of President Jefferson. Fremont conducted his reconnaissance of the west under the auspices of the US Army's Corps of Topographical Engineers. The highly competitive railroad surveys of the 1850s were inspired by economic and political considerations, while Clarence King's survey of the western deserts was motivated primarily by scientific curiosity.

An illustration from Lieutenant Fremont's *Memoirs* shows members of his Great Basin survey team camped on the shores of the Pyramid Lake. The lake was later surveyed in detail by Clarence King.

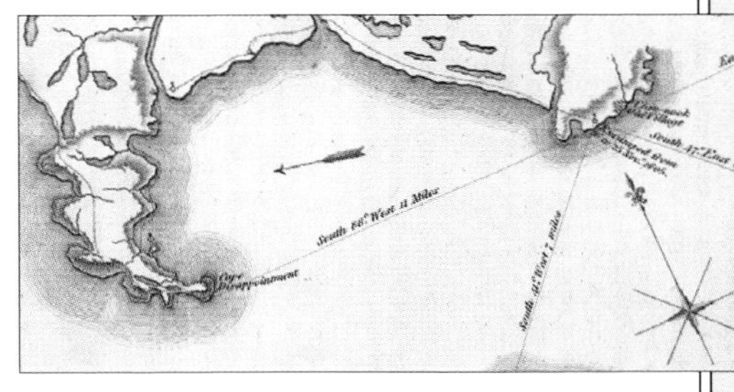

Lewis and Clark kept a series of illustrated notebooks on their westward journey. This map shows the mouth of the Columbia River.

❸ 19th-century exploration and surveys of the US and Canada

Individual expeditions
- Meriwether Lewis and William Clark 1804–06
- Lt. Zebulon M. Pike 1806–07
- Major Stephen Long 1819–20
- Lt. John Franklin 1820–21
- Lt. John Franklin 1825–27
- Lt. John C. Fremont 1842–44
- Lt. William Emory 1846
- Lt. James Simpson and Capt. Lorenzo Sitgreaves 1849–51
- Lt. John Palliser 1857–59

Other expeditions and surveys
- Russian expeditions to Alaska 1816–65
- Western Railroad surveys 1853–55
- Western Union Telegraph survey 1865–67
- Canadian Yukon Exploring expedition 1887–89

Survey areas
- Henry Hind 1857–58
- George Wheeler 1867–72
- Clarence King 1867–73

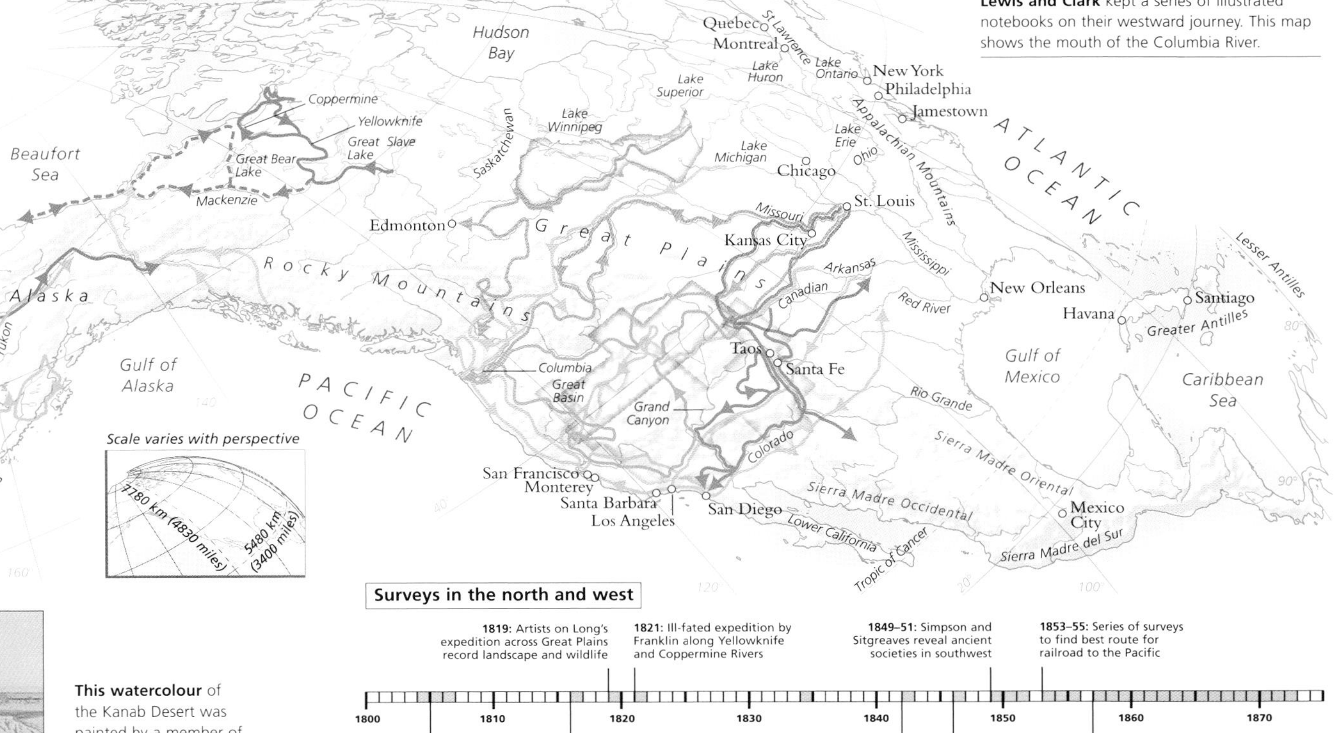

This watercolour of the Kanab Desert was painted by a member of the US Geological Survey team in 1880.

Surveys in the north and west

- **1804–06:** Lewis and Clark explore new land acquired in the Louisiana Purchase and reach Pacific coast
- **1816:** Start of Russian exploration of Alaska
- **1819:** Artists on Long's expedition across Great Plains record landscape and wildlife
- **1821:** Ill-fated expedition by Franklin along Yellowknife and Coppermine Rivers
- **1842:** Fremont begins series of expeditions to map American west and encourage settlement
- **1846:** Emory surveys Spanish territory during Mexican War
- **1849–51:** Simpson and Sitgreaves reveal ancient societies in southwest
- **1853–55:** Series of surveys to find best route for railroad to the Pacific
- **1857–72:** Wheeler produces first contour maps of southwest

EARLY PEOPLES OF NORTH AMERICA

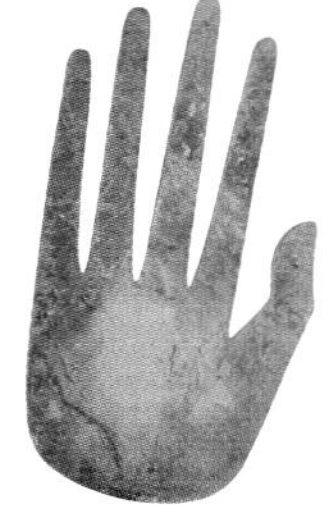

The Hopewell produced beautifully-made grave offerings for burial with their dead, such as this hand, carved from a flat sheet of mica.

THE FIRST PEOPLE to settle North America are thought to have crossed over from Asia during the last Ice Age – possibly 15,000 years ago. They moved south through the corridor between the ice sheets to settle the prairies. By 11,000 BCE they had reached the southern tip of South America. By this time significant hunting activities were taking place in North America and many large mammals, such as the woolly mammoth, may have become extinct as a result of hunting and climate change. Once humans were established in Central America, they quickly became more sedentary, simple village structures evolving within a small time frame into far more complex societies. The archaeological evidence left by the Olmec and Zapotec in Central America, and the burial mounds of the Adena and Hopewell of the American southeast reveal sophisticated societies.

The hunter-gatherers

Hunter-gatherers recorded events in their lives on the walls of caves. This series of images from Cueva Flecha in Lower California, shows humans and animals pierced by spears – perhaps as a result of conflict with other groups in the area.

The first peoples of North and Central America banded together in egalitarian, extended-family groups, living by hunting and gathering. They eventually become specialized and adapted to the continent's various ecological niches: plains, mountains, deserts, woodlands, river valleys, and coastal areas. Specially-adapted spear points and other weaponry reveal the major prey species in different culture areas. The fine 'Clovis' spearheads were used by plains hunters to kill bison, barbed harpoon heads were developed by coastal peoples for spearing marine creatures; and stone-tipped darts were thrown by the basin and mountain dwellers at the wildfowl which provided them with the bulk of their diet.

1 Subsistence and agriculture in early North America

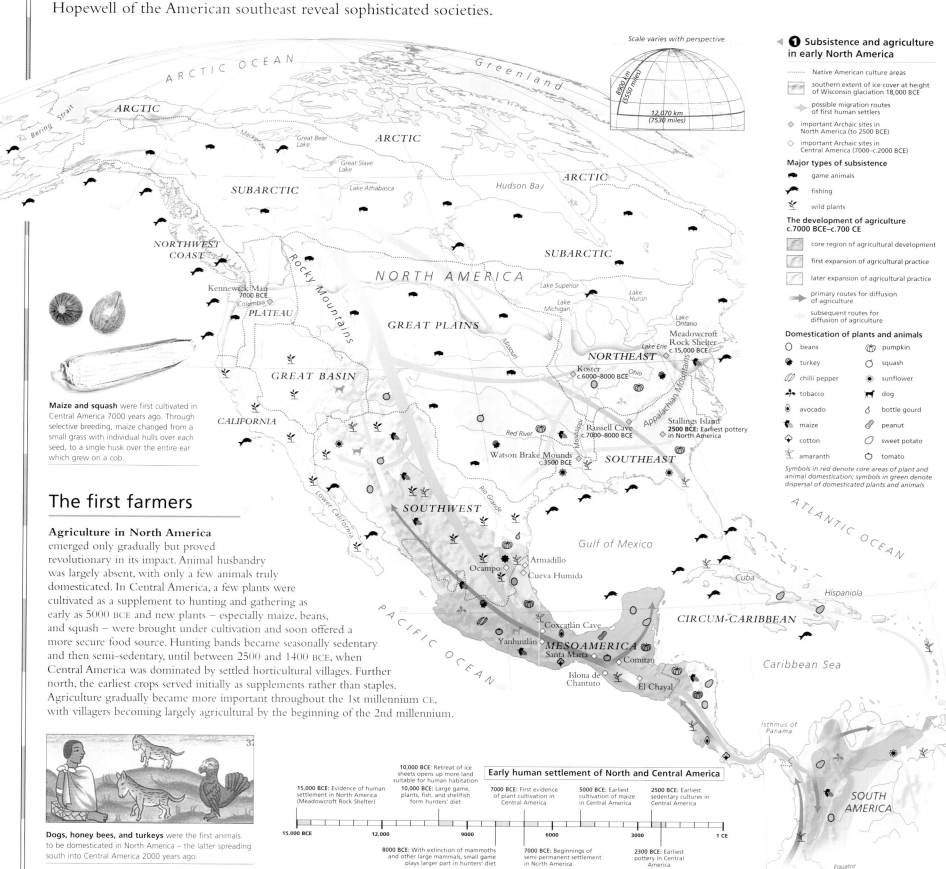

Scale varies with perspective

- Native American culture areas
- southern extent of ice cover at height of Wisconsin glaciation 18,000 BCE
- possible migration routes of first human settlers
- important Archaic sites in North America (to 2500 BCE)
- important Archaic sites in Central America (7000–c.2000 BCE)

Major types of subsistence
- game animals
- fishing
- wild plants

The development of agriculture c.7000 BCE–c.700 CE
- core region of agricultural development
- first expansion of agricultural practice
- later expansion of agricultural practice
- primary routes for diffusion of agriculture
- subsequent routes for diffusion of agriculture

Domestication of plants and animals
beans, pumpkin, turkey, squash, chilli pepper, sunflower, tobacco, dog, avocado, bottle gourd, maize, peanut, cotton, sweet potato, amaranth, tomato

Symbols in red denote core areas of plant and animal domestication; symbols in green denote dispersal of domesticated plants and animals

Maize and squash were first cultivated in Central America 7000 years ago. Through selective breeding, maize changed from a small grass with individual hulls over each seed, to a single husk over the entire ear which grew on a cob.

The first farmers

Agriculture in North America emerged only gradually but proved revolutionary in its impact. Animal husbandry was largely absent, with only a few animals truly domesticated. In Central America, a few plants were cultivated as a supplement to hunting and gathering as early as 5000 BCE and new plants – especially maize, beans, and squash – were brought under cultivation and soon offered a more secure food source. Hunting bands became seasonally sedentary and then semi-sedentary, until between 2500 and 1400 BCE, when Central America was dominated by settled horticultural villages. Further north, the earliest crops served initially as supplements rather than staples. Agriculture gradually became more important throughout the 1st millennium CE, with villagers becoming largely agricultural by the beginning of the 2nd millennium.

Dogs, honey bees, and turkeys were the first animals to be domesticated in North America – the latter spreading south into Central America 2000 years ago.

Early human settlement of North and Central America

- 15,000 BCE: Evidence of human settlement in North America (Meadowcroft Rock Shelter)
- 10,000 BCE: Retreat of ice sheets opens up more land suitable for human habitation
- 10,000 BCE: Large game, plants, fish, and shellfish form hunters' diet
- 8000 BCE: With extinction of mammoths and other large mammals, small game plays larger part in hunters' diet
- 7000 BCE: First evidence of plant cultivation in Central America
- 7000 BCE: Beginnings of semi-permanent settlement in North America
- 5000 BCE: Earliest cultivation of maize in Central America
- 2500 BCE: Earliest sedentary cultures in Central America
- 2300 BCE: Earliest pottery in Central America

15,000 BCE | 12,000 | 9000 | 6000 | 3000 | 1 CE

Early civilizations of Central America

With the establishment of village life, the earliest complex settlements occurred in the tropical lowlands from the Gulf of Mexico across the Isthmus of Tehuantepec to the Pacific coast of present-day Guatemala. Increasingly sophisticated societies were made possible by new crops and productive soils. The Olmec civilization – widely regarded as the mother culture of Central America – emerged on the Gulf Coast c.1500 BCE and persisted as an important culture until 400 BCE. Slightly later than the Olmecs, the Valley of Oaxaca witnessed the development of a sophisticated society, and by 500 BCE, complex chiefdoms or early states dominated the three interconnected valleys of central Oaxaca. At their juncture, the Zapotecs built the hilltop city of Monte Albán which would dominate the region for over 1000 years. Further south, Kaminaljuyú emerged by c.500 BCE, but a nearby volcanic eruption c.250–200 BCE, and consequent mass migration, deprived the site of much of the population in the southern part of its trading area. In the highlands south of Yucatan, the Maya civilization was starting to emerge as early as 1000 BCE.

This Olmec ceremonial adze from La Venta is carved from the pale green jade typical of the site.

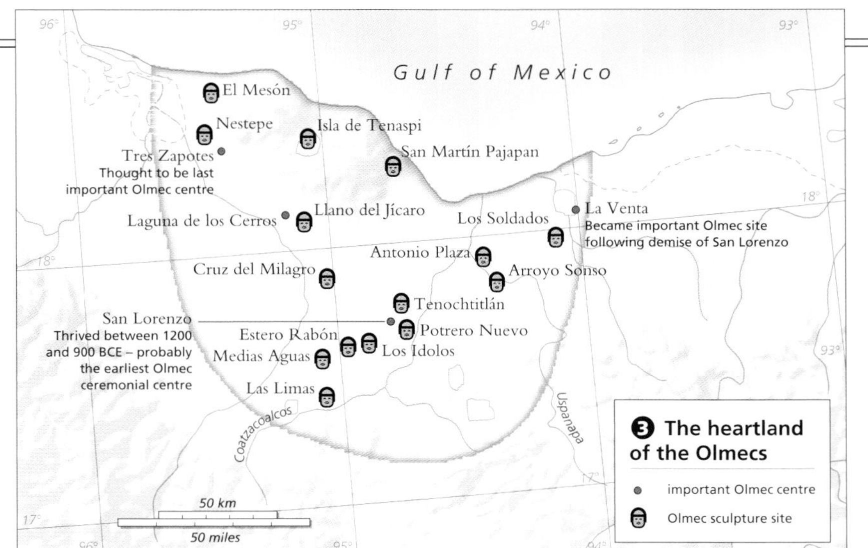

The Olmecs

The earliest civilization in Central America, the Olmecs initiated the Mesoamerican pantheon of gods, gave rise to kings and classes, and fought wars, as well as trading over vast distances and heavily influencing other cultures. They built elaborate platforms and mounds, made fine ceramics, worked precious stone, engaged in complex and sophisticated stone sculpture, established the Mesoamerican calendar, and invented the syllabary writing system. By 500–400 BCE, the Olmecs, although remaining an intellectually vibrant culture throughout the 1st millennium BCE, ceased to influence groups elsewhere directly.

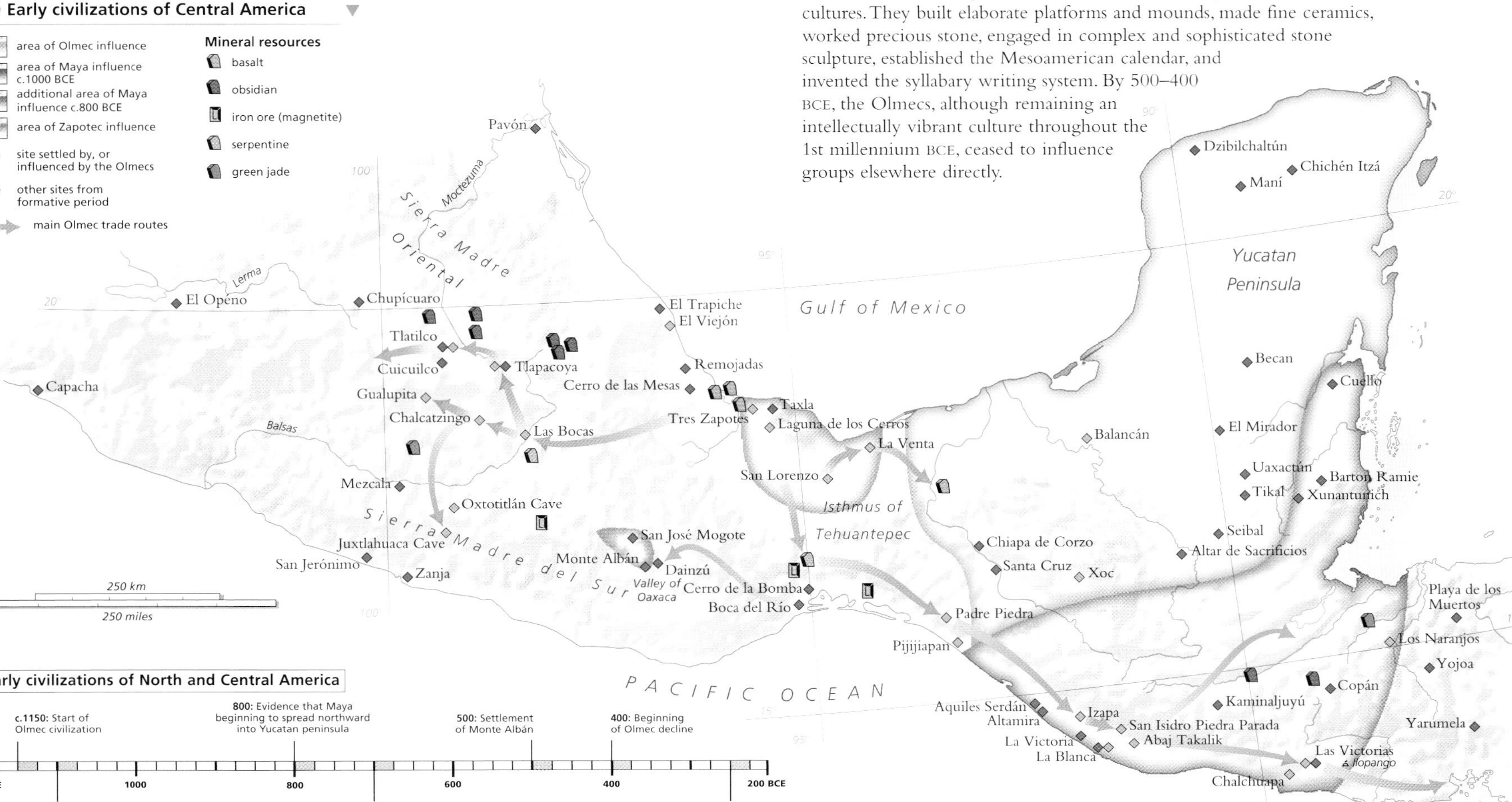

Early civilizations of North and Central America

c.1150	Start of Olmec civilization
1100	Establishment of Poverty Point in present-day Louisiana, an early non-agrarian settlement
800	Evidence that Maya beginning to spread northward into Yucatan peninsula
700	Start of Adena culture
500	Settlement of Monte Albán
400	Beginning of Olmec decline
c.250	El Mirador, the largest early Maya city flourishing. Sites, such as Becan, fortified

1200 BCE – 1000 – 800 – 600 – 400 – 200 BCE

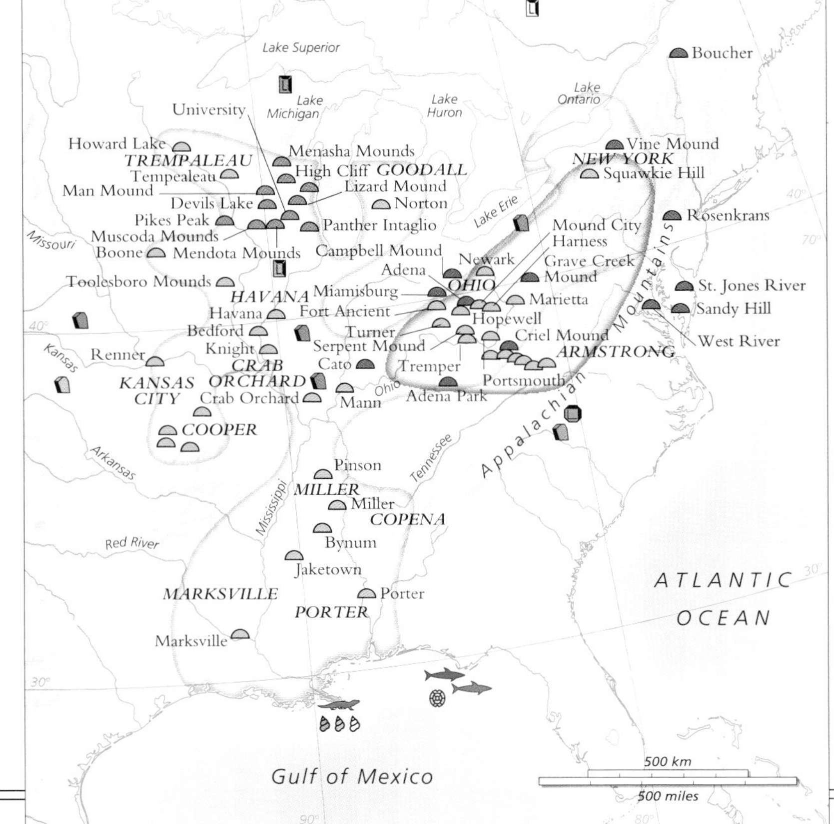

4 Moundbuilders of eastern North America c.700 BCE–c.400 CE

- Adena heartland
- Adena site
- Hopewell area of influence
- *OHIO* Hopewell cultural area
- Hopewell burial mound site
- effigy mound site

Resources traded by the Hopewell

- chert
- chlorite
- obsidian
- silver
- copper
- galena
- mica crystals
- olive shell
- tulip shell
- whelks
- turtle
- alligator
- barracuda
- shark

The moundbuilders of the eastern river valleys

The Adena culture was found in the upper Ohio valley as early as 1000 BCE. Settlements were centred on burial mounds and extensive earthworks. Their grave goods included jewellery made from imported copper, carved tablets, and tubular pipes – which provide evidence of the early cultivation of tobacco *(see Map 1)*. The Hopewell culture had emerged by c.100 CE, and spread throughout the Mississippi Valley, sustained by small-scale agriculture. They created a complex and far-reaching trade network to source the many raw materials – including obsidian, mica sheets, quartz, shells, teeth, and copper – used in their characteristic animal and bird sculptures. Elements of Hopewell culture appear to have been adopted by many other Indian groups.

The Hopewell produced many objects in the shape of animals including birds, beavers, and bears. The frog adorns a platform effigy pipe; tobacco was placed in a bowl in its back and inhaled through the hole in the front of the pipe.

CITIES AND EMPIRES

Hollow pottery dogs, typical of the highly realistic ceramics of western Mexico, are common grave offerings.

CENTRAL AMERICA was split into the Highland Mexican and the Lowland Maya areas, between which there were some major differences, including languages, writing systems, and art and architectural styles. City-states dominated both areas: in the Maya area these tended to be small, multi-city regional polities or autonomous cities, while Highland Mexico was dominated by a series of empires. The peoples of southern North America were turning to agriculture and establishing settled communities. Several overlapping cultures settled the desert southwest, including the Hohokam, Anasazi, and Mogollon. In the southeast, larger settlements in the Mississippi valley replaced the Hopewell by 800 CE.

Central American civilizations 400–1400

Teotihuacan emerged as the capital of the first major empire in the 1st century CE and influenced cities throughout Mexico and Guatemala, spreading ideas and innovations. The multi-ethnic city reached a population of 125,000–200,000 by 500, exporting goods to the rest of Central America. By 550, Teotihuacán was in decline, and by 750, the city was largely abandoned. The resulting political vacuum encouraged the rise of several independent, fortified hilltop cities from about 650, including Cacaxtla and Xochicalco. All had extensive trade links and varying degrees of contact with other cultures. Centred at Tula, the Toltec Empire emerged in the 10th century. The Toltecs were traders, trading as far south as Costa Rica and north into the desert. Drought undermined Tula's agriculture and by 1200, it was abandoned.

Teotihuacán was centrally planned, laid out in a grid, and dominated by huge pyramids which would have held temples on their summits. It traded over much of Central America, dealing in obsidian products, ceramics, stone carvings, and featherwork.

These massive basalt figures stand on top of the central pyramid at Tula, the Toltec capital. The city reached a peak population of 60,000 inhabitants, with an equal number in the immediate hinterland.

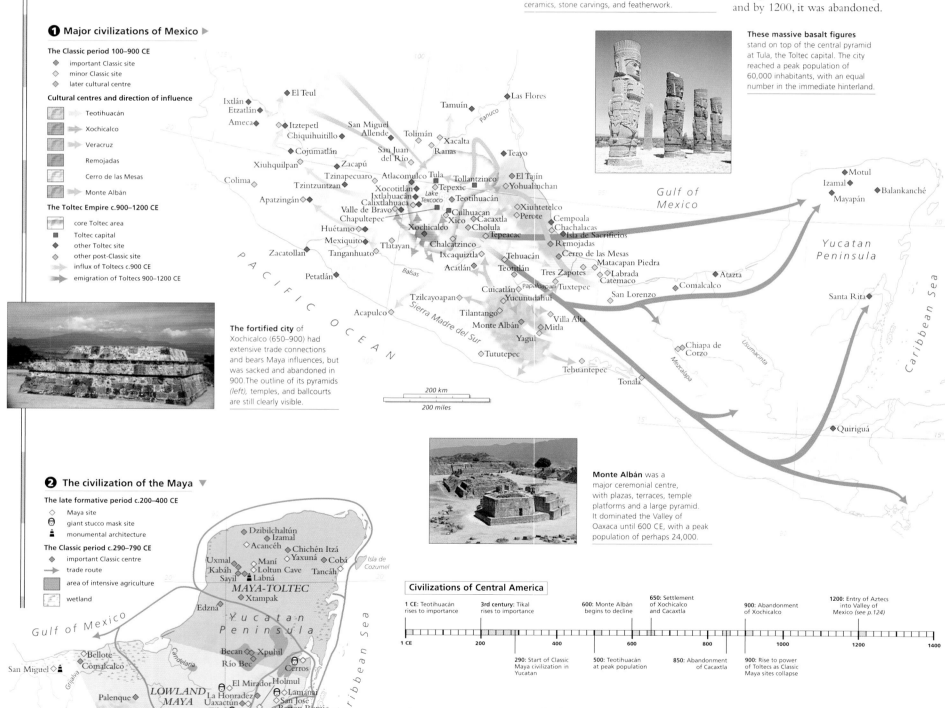

1 Major civilizations of Mexico

The Classic period 100–900 CE
- important Classic site
- minor Classic site
- later cultural centre

Cultural centres and direction of influence
- Teotihuacán
- Xochicalco
- Veracruz
- Remojadas
- Cerro de las Mesas
- Monte Albán

The Toltec Empire c.900–1200 CE
- core Toltec area
- Toltec capital
- other Toltec site
- other post-Classic site
- influx of Toltecs c.900 CE
- emigration of Toltecs 900–1200 CE

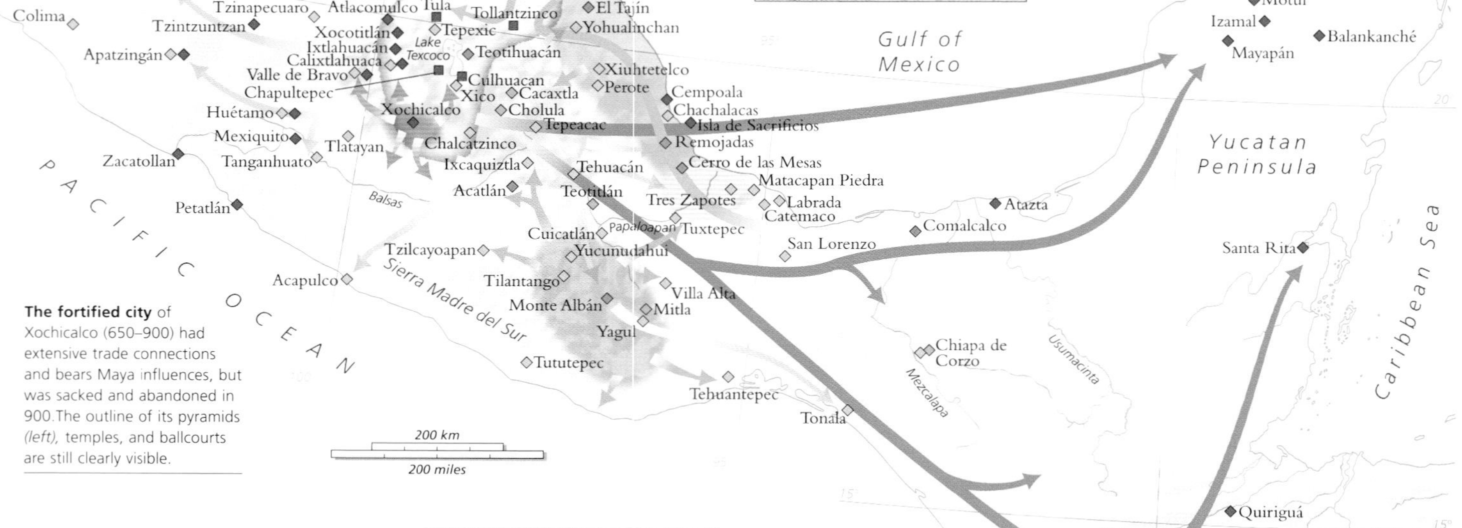

The fortified city of Xochicalco (650–900) had extensive trade connections and bears Maya influences, but was sacked and abandoned in 900. The outline of its pyramids *(left)*, temples, and ballcourts are still clearly visible.

Monte Albán was a major ceremonial centre, with plazas, terraces, temple platforms and a large pyramid. It dominated the Valley of Oaxaca until 600 CE, with a peak population of perhaps 24,000.

2 The civilization of the Maya

The late formative period c.200–400 CE
- Maya site
- giant stucco mask site
- monumental architecture

The Classic period c.290–790 CE
- important Classic centre
- trade route
- area of intensive agriculture
- wetland

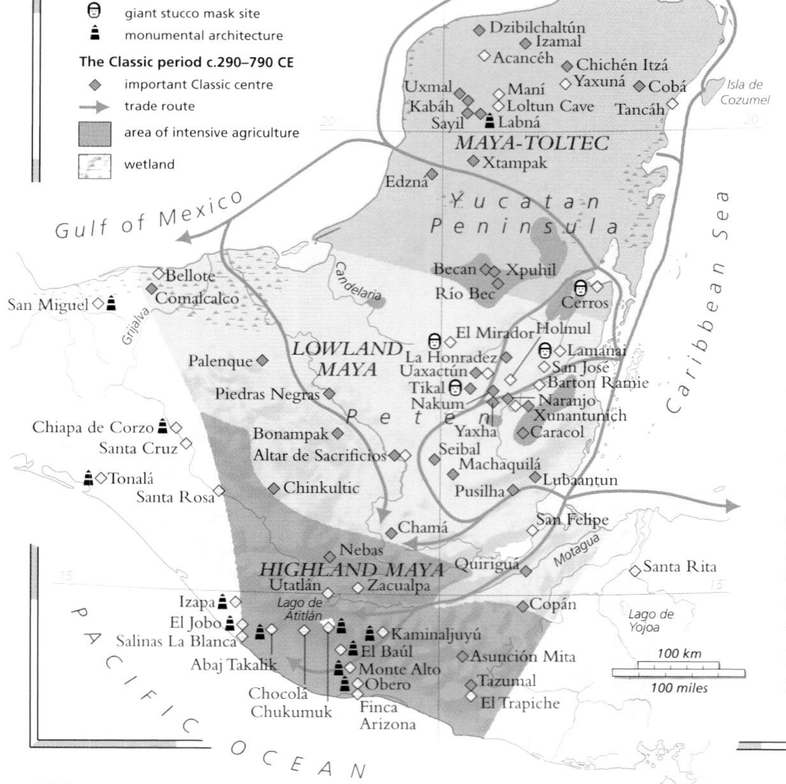

Civilizations of Central America

- 1 CE: Teotihuacán rises to importance
- 3rd century: Tikal rises to importance
- 290: Start of Classic Maya civilization in Yucatan
- 500: Teotihuacán at peak population
- 600: Monte Albán begins to decline
- 650: Settlement of Xochicalco and Cacaxtla
- 850: Abandonment of Cacaxtla
- 900: Abandonment of Xochicalco
- 900: Rise to power of Toltecs as Classic Maya sites collapse
- 1200: Entry of Aztecs into Valley of Mexico *(see p.124)*

The city-states of the Maya

The jungle of Guatemala and Yucatan became the centre for the florescence of Maya civilization. Many city-states emerged, sometimes linked by elite marriages and sometimes by descent, but political ties were few and fleeting. The Classic Maya civilization is thought to be the first fully literate culture of the Americas, developing a hieroglyphic writing system. Classic Maya cities were characterized by their massive size and structural complexity. From 800, the major cities were progressively abandoned and the focus of Maya civilization shifted to the northern lowlands.

The corbelled Arch of Labna in northern Yucatan dates from the late Classic period. Its intricate reliefs and massive size typify Maya archtecture during this period.

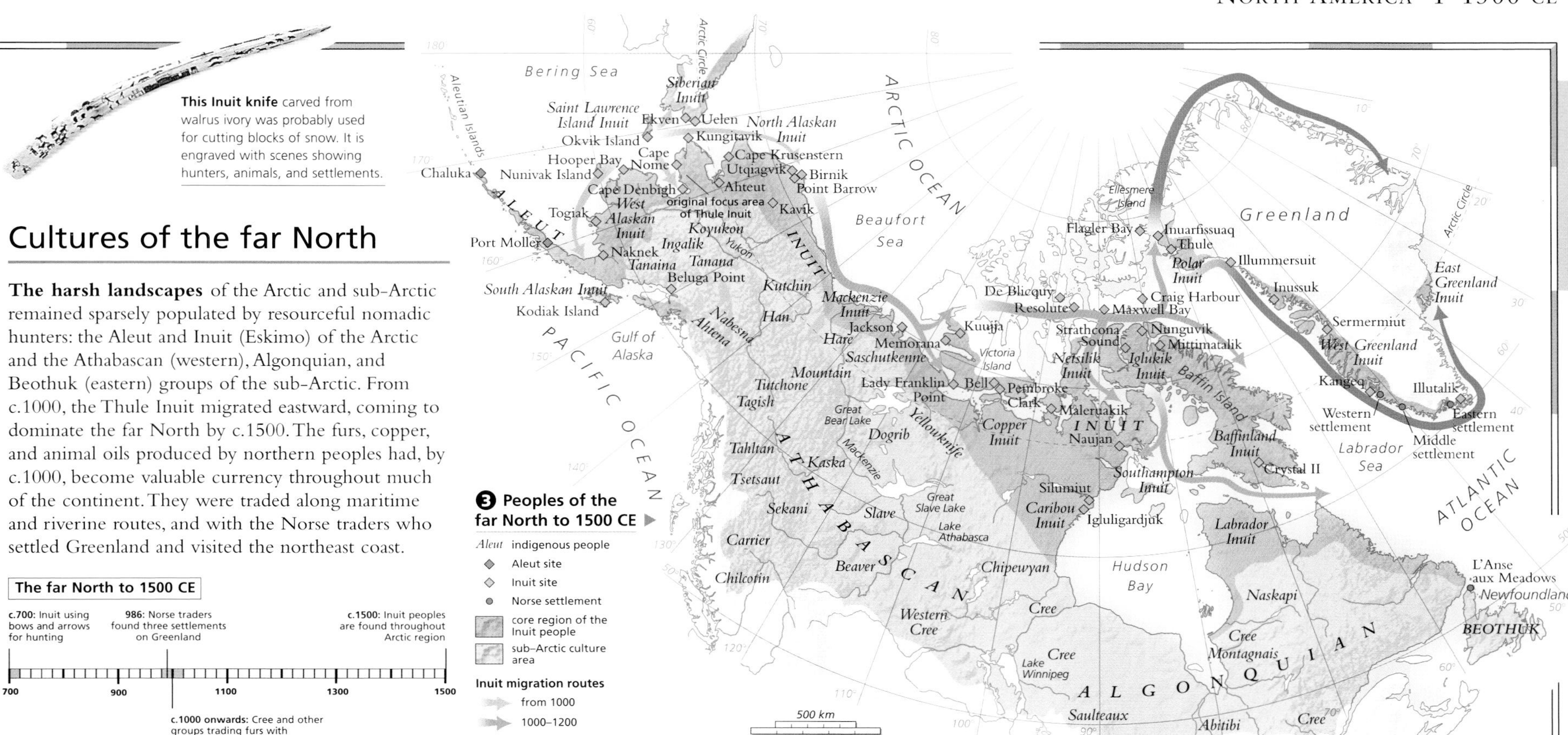

This Inuit knife carved from walrus ivory was probably used for cutting blocks of snow. It is engraved with scenes showing hunters, animals, and settlements.

Cultures of the far North

The harsh landscapes of the Arctic and sub-Arctic remained sparsely populated by resourceful nomadic hunters: the Aleut and Inuit (Eskimo) of the Arctic and the Athabascan (western), Algonquian, and Beothuk (eastern) groups of the sub-Arctic. From c.1000, the Thule Inuit migrated eastward, coming to dominate the far North by c.1500. The furs, copper, and animal oils produced by northern peoples had, by c.1000, become valuable currency throughout much of the continent. They were traded along maritime and riverine routes, and with the Norse traders who settled Greenland and visited the northeast coast.

The far North to 1500 CE

- **c.700:** Inuit using bows and arrows for hunting
- **986:** Norse traders found three settlements on Greenland
- **c.1000 onwards:** Cree and other groups trading furs with southern peoples for grain
- **c.1500:** Inuit peoples are found throughout Arctic region

The American Southwest

In the Southwest, sedentary ways of life spread throughout the 1st millennium CE, producing villages and cliff dwellings, such those of the Hohokam in Arizona, after 1000, and regional polities such as Chaco Canyon and Casas Grandes. The Hohokam developed irrigation systems to allow them to grow maize in the arid semi-desert and built multi-storey pueblos: storehouses and dwellings of stone or adobe sometimes with ball courts and low platform mounds. The Anasazi and Mogollon peoples left evidence of pueblos constructed for defensive purposes – probably to counter other hostile groups who entered the area from c.1300. Increasing aridity caused a decline in the southwest after 1250 leaving only dispersed puebloan groups.

The Mimbres branch of the Mogollon culture produced spectacular pottery, usually for burial purposes. The pots, adorned with geometric designs, were often ritually 'killed' by having a hole drilled through their base.

Settlement in the Southwest to 1500

- **100:** Emergence of Hohokam and Mogollon cultures
- **800:** Mimbres pottery starts to be made by Mogollon
- **c.950:** Flourishing pueblo culture in Southwest
- **1050:** Pueblos built for defensive purposes by Anasazi
- **1100:** Construction of the Cliff Palace at Mesa Verde
- **1200:** Peak of importance of Chaco Canyon
- **1350:** Most Anasazi pueblos abandoned – probably due to drought

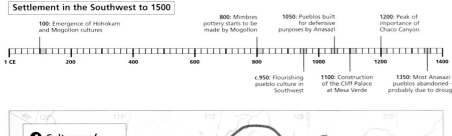

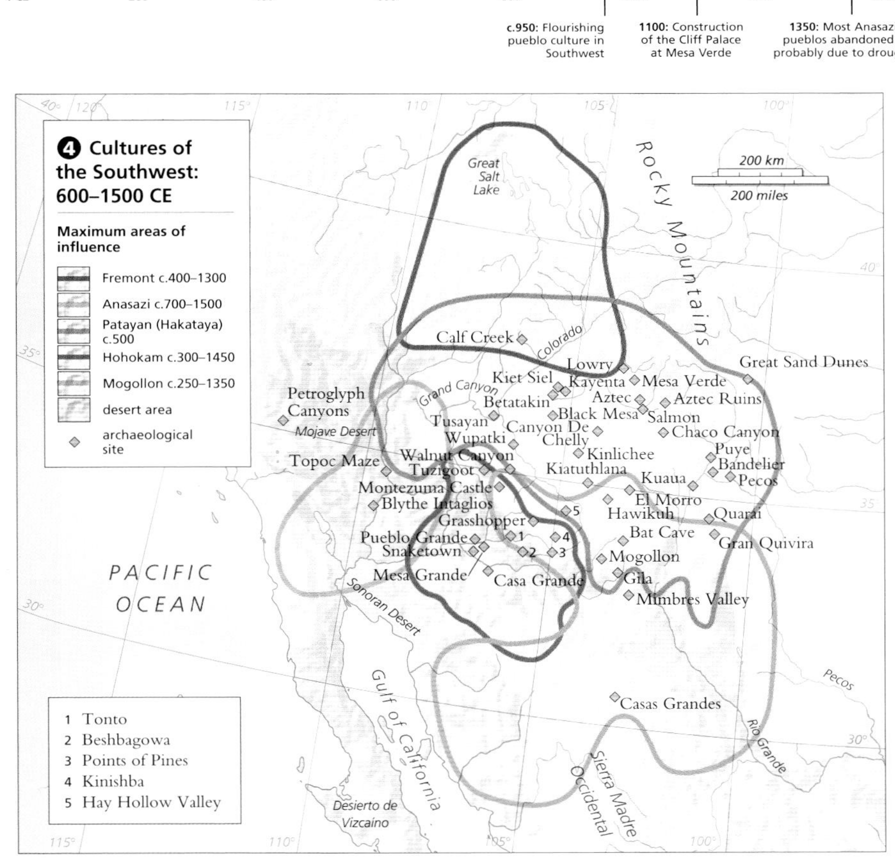

The American South and Mississippi Valley

In eastern North America there were improvements in agricultural technology, and crops such as beans and new varieties of maize were imported from Mexico. There was a developmental hiatus for about 400 years following the decline of the Hopewell interaction sphere but from c.800, settlements grew larger until, in around 1000, the Mississippian chiefdoms emerged, leading to more regional integration and significantly greater social differentiation. Many centres including sites such as Etowah and Moundville, became regional foci, with the largest being Cahokia, with a peak population of 15,000.

This sculpted soapstone pipe from the Spiro mound site is thought to depict a warrior beheading his victim.

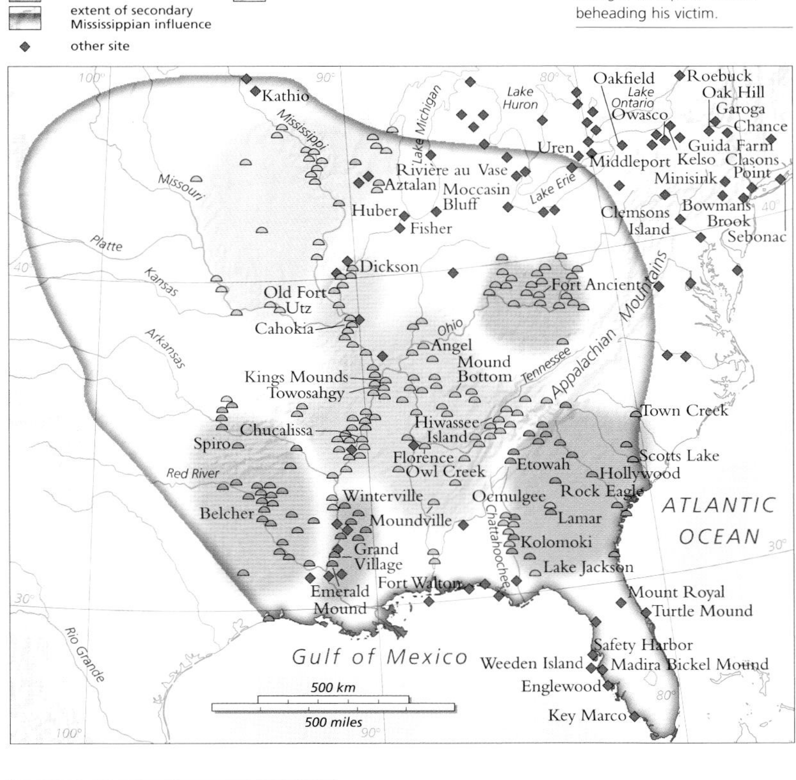

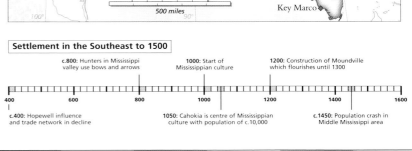

Settlement in the Southeast to 1500

- **c.400:** Hopewell influence and trade network in decline
- **c.800:** Hunters in Mississippi valley use bows and arrows
- **1000:** Start of Mississippian culture
- **1050:** Cahokia is centre of Mississippian culture with population of c.10,000
- **1200:** Construction of Moundville which flourishes until 1300
- **c.1450:** Population crash in Middle Mississippi area

COMPETING EMPIRES

Quetzalcoatl, the god of wind, was one of a pantheon of gods worshipped by the Aztecs.

UNTIL THE EUROPEAN INCURSIONS of the late 15th century, North and Central America remained largely untouched by contacts with other continents. Spanish explorers and traders, seeking new routes and markets, first reconnoitred the Caribbean islands and Central America, returning later to claim Mexico, the Caribbean and much of the southern half of America as new territory for the Spanish crown. One of their most significant conquests was the Aztec Empire that dominated central Mexico. Elsewhere European impact was slight during the 16th century; they passed through, leaving little of their own cultures behind, save for animals, such as horses, that transformed native lives, and diseases that decimated populations.

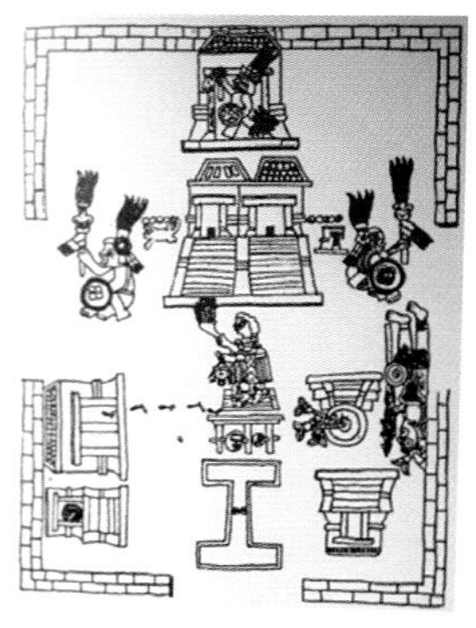

The Great Temple dominated the central plaza of Tenochtitlan. The northern temple *(left)* was dedicated to Tlaloc, god of rain and the southern temple *(right)* to the Aztec patron god of war, Huitzilopochtli.

The Aztec Empire

The Aztecs entered the already highly urbanized Valley of Mexico around 1200, establishing their island capital of Tenochtitlan on Lake Texcoco in 1325, and overthrowing their imperial masters, the Tepanecs, in 1428 to begin their own empire. By 1519, the Aztec Empire controlled most of central Mexico as well as the Maya areas of further east. The Aztecs presided over a collection of city-states which remained autonomous except for their tributary obligations to the Aztecs. The Aztec Empire maintained a state of constant military activity which served to provide a flow of tributes from neighbouring states.

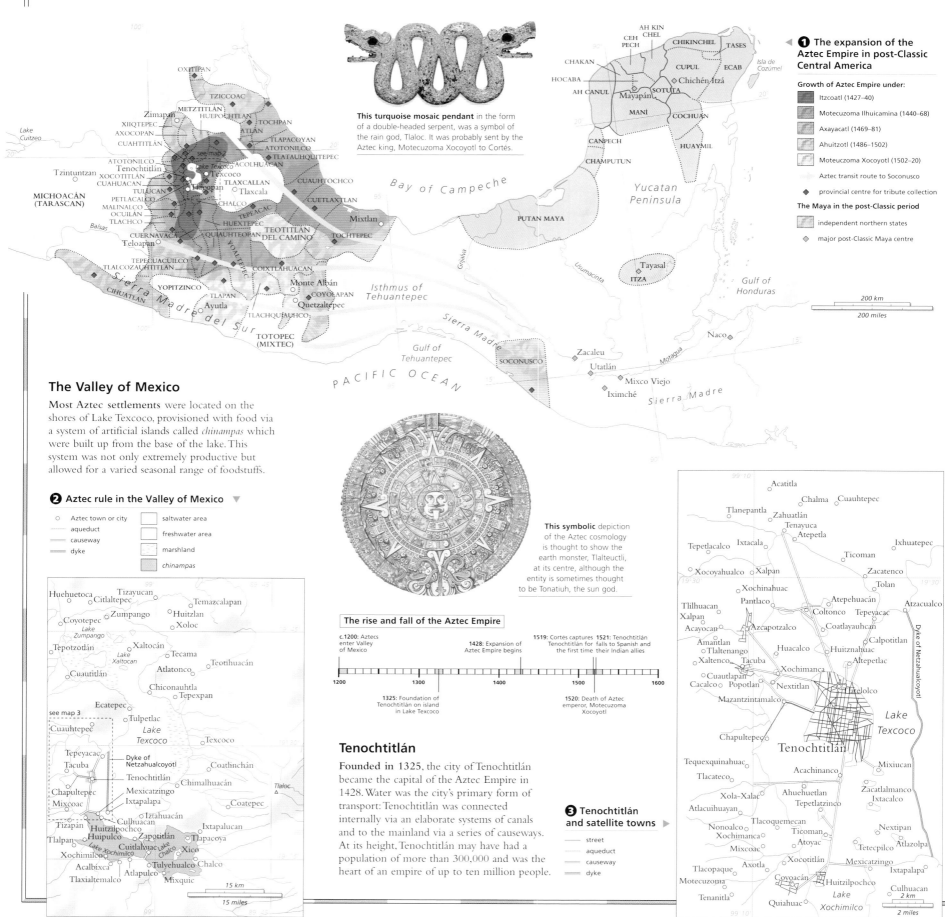

This turquoise mosaic pendant in the form of a double-headed serpent, was a symbol of the rain god, Tlaloc. It was probably sent by the Aztec king, Motecuzoma Xocoyotl to Cortés.

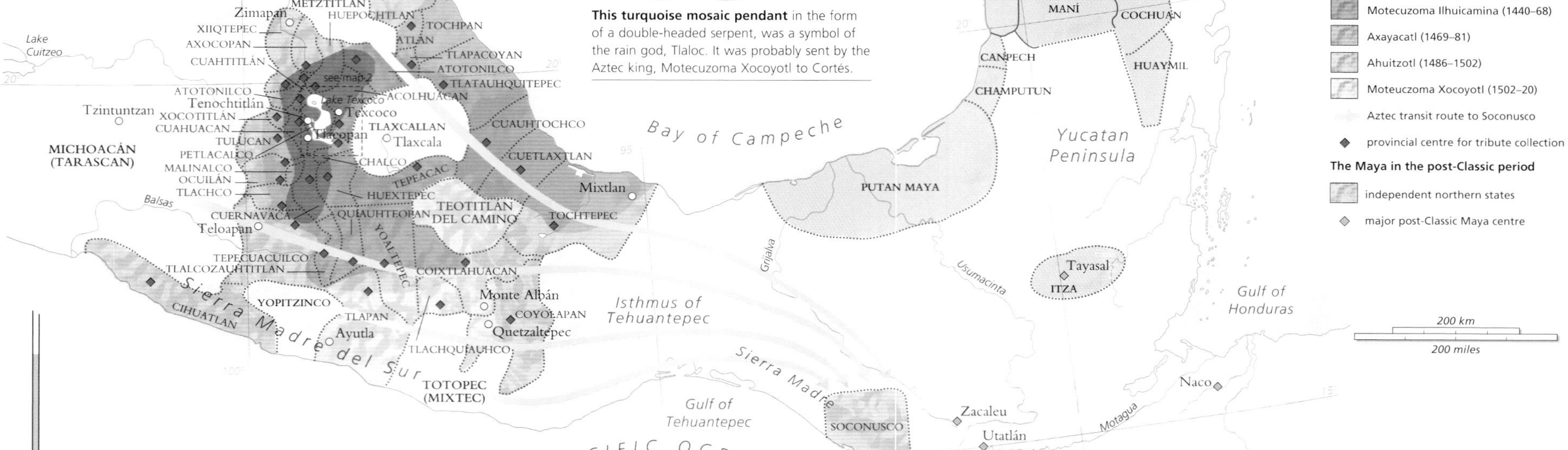

1 The expansion of the Aztec Empire in post-Classic Central America

Growth of Aztec Empire under:
- Itzcoatl (1427–40)
- Motecuzoma Ilhuicamina (1440–68)
- Axayacatl (1469–81)
- Ahuitzotl (1486–1502)
- Motecuzoma Xocoyotl (1502–20)
- Aztec transit route to Soconusco
- provincial centre for tribute collection

The Maya in the post-Classic period
- independent northern states
- major post-Classic Maya centre

200 km / 200 miles

The Valley of Mexico

Most Aztec settlements were located on the shores of Lake Texcoco, provisioned with food via a system of artificial islands called *chinampas* which were built up from the base of the lake. This system was not only extremely productive but allowed for a varied seasonal range of foodstuffs.

2 Aztec rule in the Valley of Mexico

- Aztec town or city
- aqueduct
- causeway
- dyke
- saltwater area
- freshwater area
- marshland
- *chinampas*

15 km / 15 miles

This symbolic depiction of the Aztec cosmology is thought to show the earth monster, Tlalteuctli, at its centre, although the entity is sometimes thought to be Tonatiuh, the sun god.

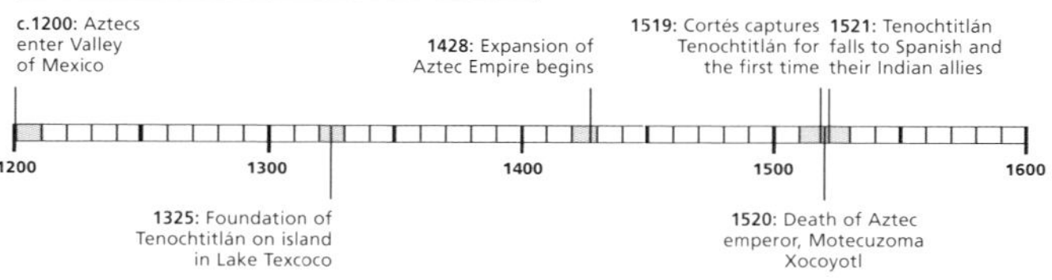

The rise and fall of the Aztec Empire

c.1200: Aztecs enter Valley of Mexico
1325: Foundation of Tenochtitlán on island in Lake Texcoco
1428: Expansion of Aztec Empire begins
1519: Cortés captures Tenochtitlán for the first time
1520: Death of Aztec emperor, Motecuzoma Xocoyotl
1521: Tenochtitlán falls to Spanish and their Indian allies

1200 1300 1400 1500 1600

Tenochtitlán

Founded in 1325, the city of Tenochtitlán became the capital of the Aztec Empire in 1428. Water was the city's primary form of transport: Tenochtitlán was connected internally via an elaborate systems of canals and to the mainland via a series of causeways. At its height, Tenochtitlán may have had a population of more than 300,000 and was the heart of an empire of up to ten million people.

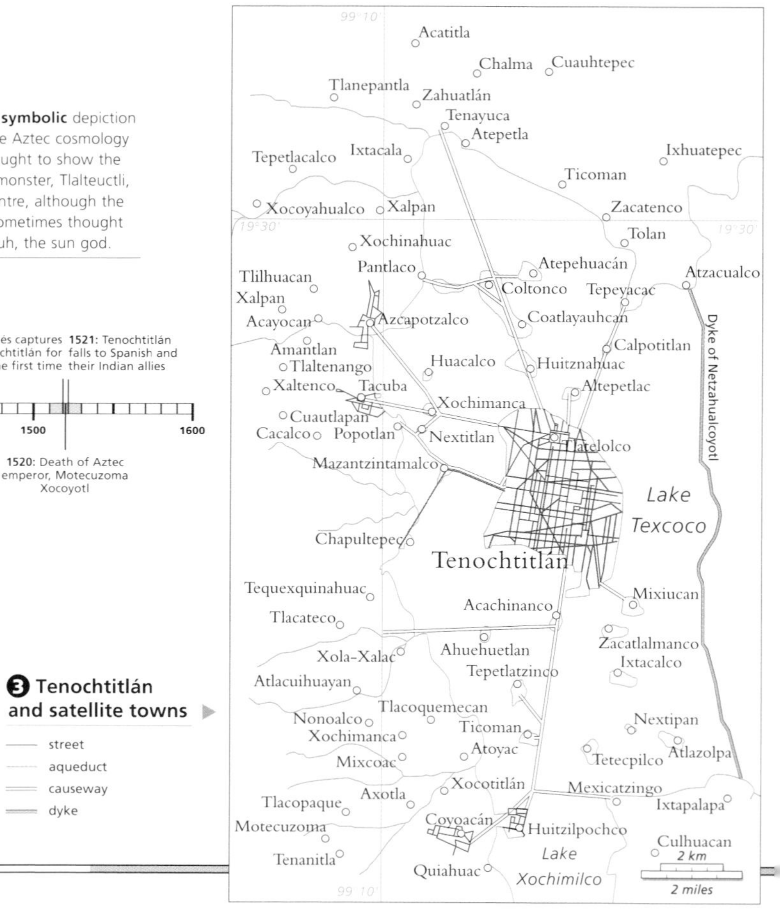

3 Tenochtitlán and satellite towns

- street
- aqueduct
- causeway
- dyke

2 km / 2 miles

Some of the earliest evidence of Spanish incursions into Mexico and North America is in the form of religious buildings. The church of St. Francis at Tlaxcala dates from 1521.

European exploration and conquest

The Spanish first visited the Gulf of Mexico and the Caribbean in the late 1400s and early 1500s, quickly conquering the West Indies whose people were enslaved or impressed into forced labour and devastated by European diseases such as smallpox. The first formal expedition to Mexico, led by Córdoba, reached the Yucatán Peninsula in 1517. In 1518, Grijalva landed on the Vera Cruz coast, trading with the natives and giving Aztec emissaries their first glimpse of Europeans. The rest of the 16th century saw the replacement of Indian leaders with Spanish, the substitution of Christianity for Indian religions, and the imposition of Spanish rule in Central America. Major entries were made into North America – in the southeast by expeditions, such as de Soto's in 1539–42, and in the southwest by Coronado in 1540, leading to the initial conquest of New Mexico and the founding of Santa Fe in 1609.

Spanish colonizing expeditions in the New World

1	Sebastian de Ocampo	1508	18	Pedro de Alvarado	1523–24
2	Juan Ponce de León	1508 and 1512	19	Cristóbal de Olid	1524
3	Juan de Esquival	1509	20	Francisco Hernández de Córdoba	1524
4	Diego Velasquez	1511	21	Estaban Gomez	1524–25
5	Vasco Núñez de Balboa	1513–14	22	Lucas Vázquez de Ayllón	1526
6	Pedrarias Dávila	1514–19	23	The Montejos	1527
7	Hernández de Córdoba, Juan de Grijalva, Alonso Álvarez de Peneda and Francisco de Garay	1517–23	24	Pánfilo de Narváez and Álvar Núñez Cabeza de Vaca	1528
8	Pedrarias Dávila	1519	25	Nuño de Guzmán and Cristóbal de Oñate	1529
9	Hernán Cortés	1519	26	Hurtado de Mendoza, Becerra, Grijalva, Cortés, Tapia, Ulloa, Alárcon	1532–42
10	Gonzalo de Sandoval	1521	27	Hernando de Soto	1539–42
11	Luis Marin	1521–24	28	Francisco Vásquez de Coronado	1540
12	Francisco Orozco	1521	29	The Montejos	1545
13	Francisco Gordillo and Pedro de Quexos	1521	30	Francisco de Ibarra	1554
14	Pedro de Alvarado	1522	31	Pedro Menéndez de Avilés	1565
15	Hernán Cortés	1522	32	Juan de Oñate	1595
16	Cristóbal de Olid	1522	33	Sebastián Vizcaino	1596
17	Gil González Dávila and Andrés Niño	1522–23			

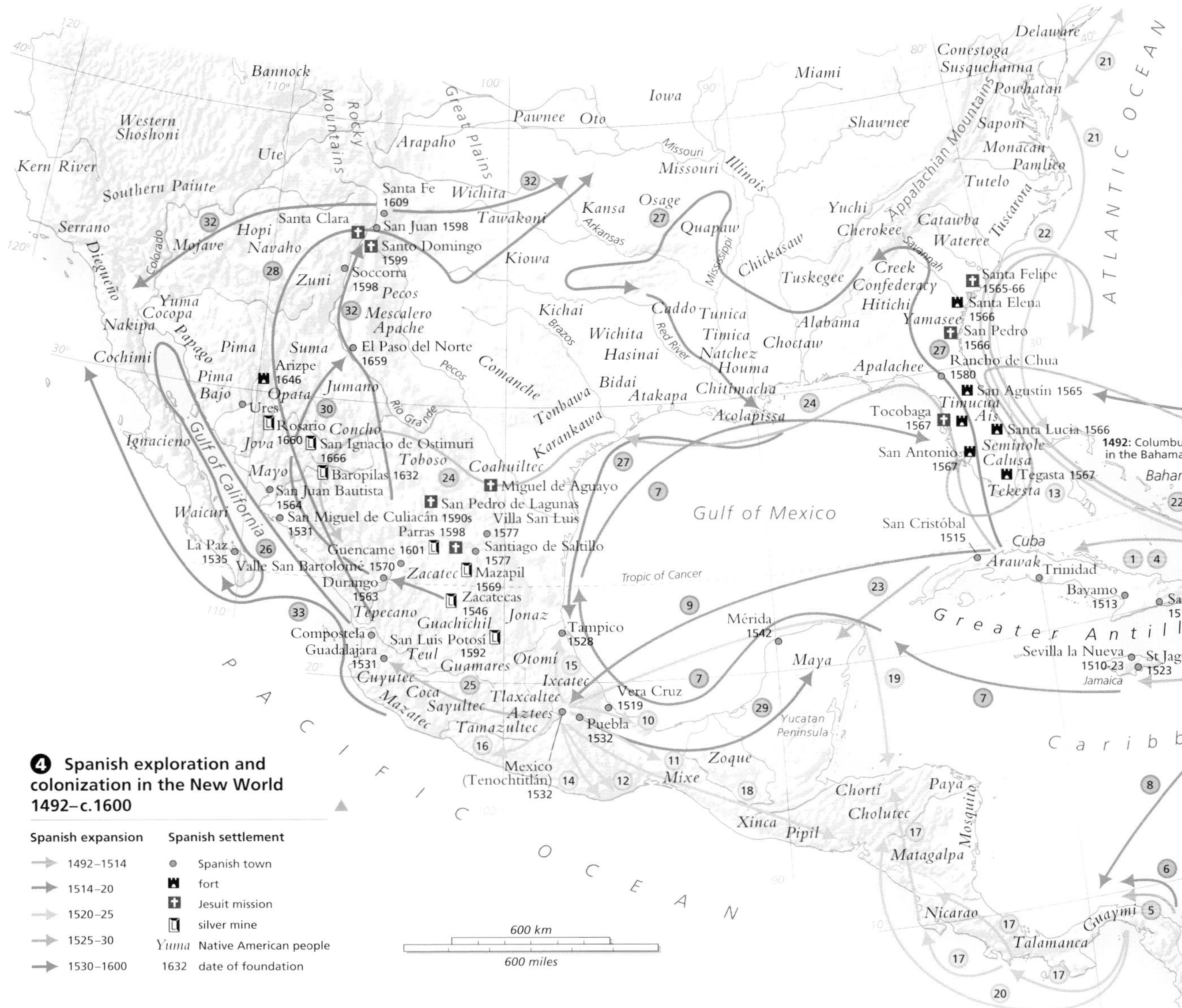

San Agustín was founded by Pedro Menéndez de Avilés in 1565. Its massive coastal fort, the Castillo de San Marcos was a classic example of 16th-century military technology.

4 Spanish exploration and colonization in the New World 1492–c.1600

Spanish expansion: 1492–1514; 1514–20; 1520–25; 1525–30; 1530–1600

Spanish settlement: Spanish town; fort; Jesuit mission; silver mine; *Yuma* Native American people; 1632 date of foundation

600 km / 600 miles

The Spanish colonization of Mexico and North America

1490 – 1510 – 1530 – 1550 – 1570

1492: Columbus' first expedition lands in the Bahamas

1496: Foundation of Santo Domingo on Hispaniola

1509: Foundation of San Juan on Puerto Rico

1517: Córdoba leads expedition to Mexico

1518: Grijalva lands on Vera Cruz coast

1519–21: Cortés' expedition into Mexico leads to collapse of Aztec Empire

1539: De Soto leads expedition into south-eastern North America

1540: Coronado leads expedition into south-western North America

1560s: Jesuit missions established in the southeast (Florida) and in the southwest

1565–67: Spanish found San Agustin and build other fortified towns on east and Gulf coasts of Mexico

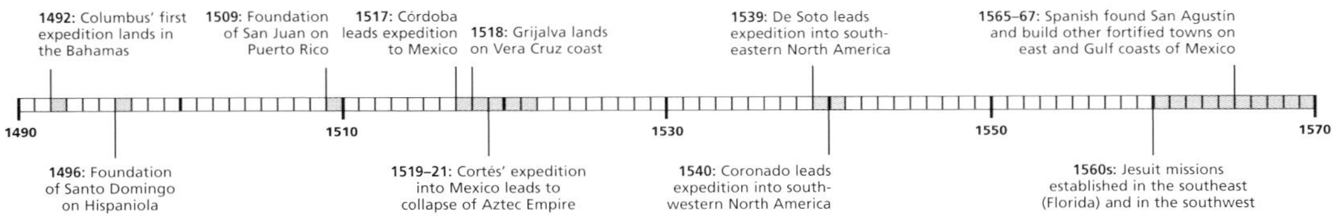

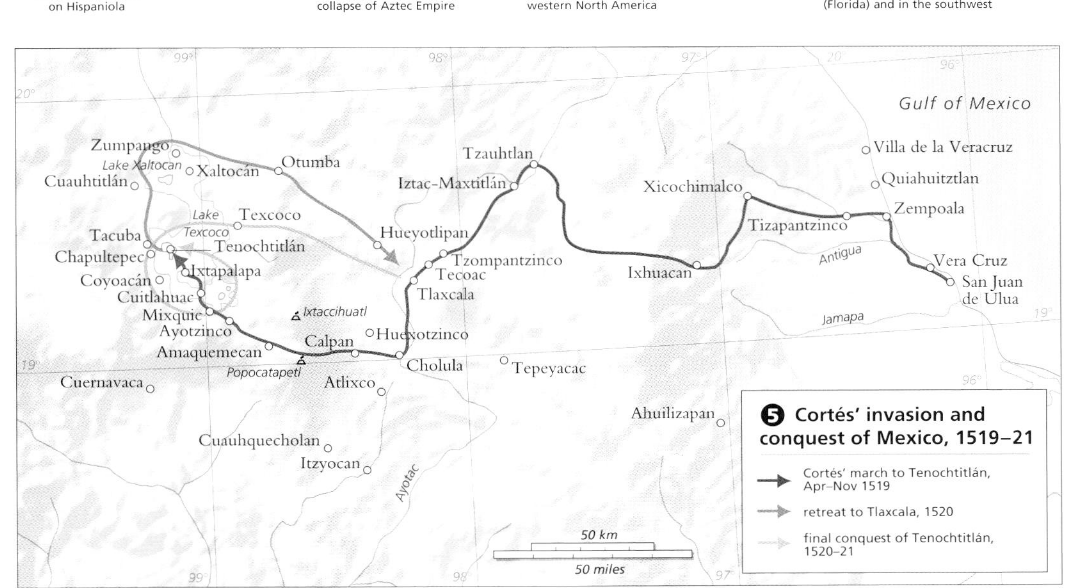

The conquest of the Aztecs

In 1519, Hernán Cortés, sponsored by the Governor of Cuba, landed on the Vera Cruz coast with about 450 soldiers. Forging alliances with the Totonacs and the Tlaxcaltecs he was able to seize the Aztec capital, Tenochtitlán in November 1519. Governor Velasquez then attempted to punish Cortés for disobeying his orders, sending a force to retrieve him which ultimately led to his being forced out of Tenochtitlan. But he was able to maintain his alliances with groups, such as the Chalcas and the Acolhua. In 1520 Cortés again led expeditions around the Valley of Mexico and beseiged Tenochtitlan, defeating the Aztecs in August 1521.

While Cortés claimed victory for Spain, the battles against the Aztecs were actually won by his tens of thousands of Indian allies. With several major allied groups, no one group was able to take power and Cortés reaped the benefits of what was in fact an Indian victory over Indians.

FROM COLONIZATION TO INDEPENDENCE

George Washington, the first US president, came to prominence in the Anglo-French conflicts of the 1750s.

FROM THE EARLY 17TH CENTURY, British, French, and Dutch migrants settled along the Atlantic seaboard and in the Gulf of St. Lawrence. As they grew in numbers, they displaced native Indian peoples from their lands. Though the French were able to form mutually beneficial alliances with Indian peoples, relationships elsewhere were characterized by conflict, and by 1759, most of the surviving Indians had been driven westward. By the second half of the 18th century, the British emerged as the major political power in North America. By 1775, and with the elimination of French power in Canada, the American desire for self determination led to revolution, and the creation of an independent United States of America by 1783.

European colonial settlement 1600–1750

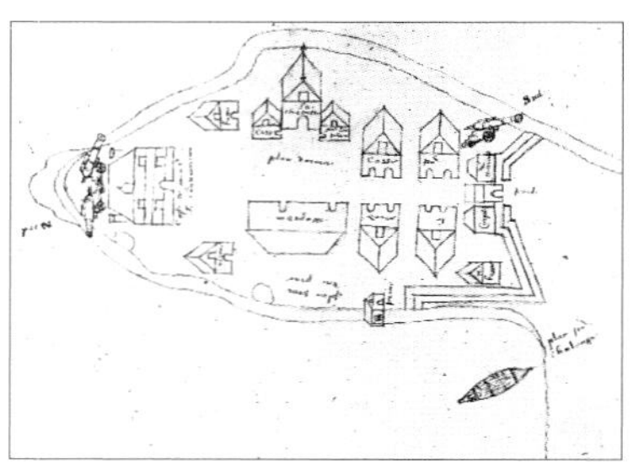

The site of Montreal was first visited by Jacques Cartier in 1535. In 1642, when this map was drawn, the first French settlement was set up.

During the 17th century, the British established a string of Atlantic colonies with a population that grew to about a million settlers, including African slaves. They produced export tobacco, timber, fish, and food, and ran a thriving colonial merchant fleet that dominated Atlantic trade, along with sugar colonies in the West Indies. To the north and west, a small number of French settlers forged strong alliances with native peoples, traded in fur, and established an arc of territories designed to stop further British expansion.

Settlement and conflict in 17th-century North America

- **1607:** Foundation of Jamestown
- **1608:** Champlain colonizes Quebec for France
- **1609:** Champlain allies with Algonquin and initiates war with Iroquois
- **1609–14:** War between English and Powhatan
- **1620:** Settlement of New England begins
- **1637:** Local Indians defeated in Pequot War
- **1648–51:** Iroquois destroy French allies, the Huron
- **1653–60:** Temporary French-Iroquois peace
- **1661:** French-Iroquois war resumes
- **1675:** Indian forces under 'King Philip' wiped out by British
- **1690:** Iroquois neutrality is followed by alliance to British

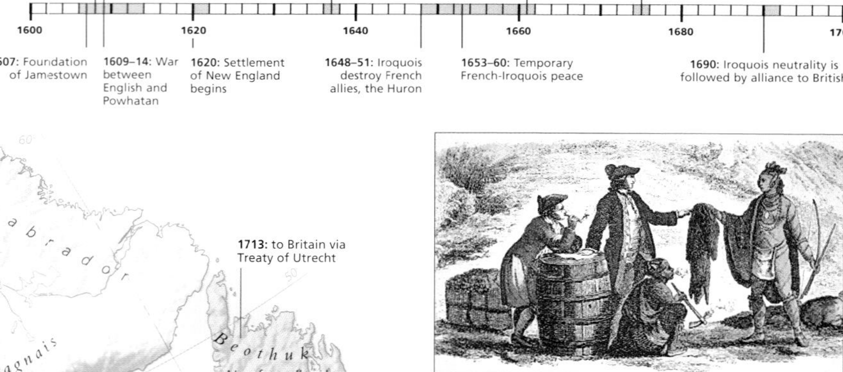

European traders made use of the fur trade routes established by native peoples. In 1670, the Hudson's Bay Company established fur 'factories' to tap the fur trade of the far interior.

Changing populations

The population composition of North America changed radically with the European incursion. Indigenous peoples succumbed to European diseases such as plague and measles, and to the settlers' superior firepower and ability to organize themselves quickly. Only small numbers of Africans were brought to North America as slaves in the 17th century, but the growth of labour-intensive plantation agriculture in the south and the West Indies led to the burgeoning of the Atlantic slave trade.

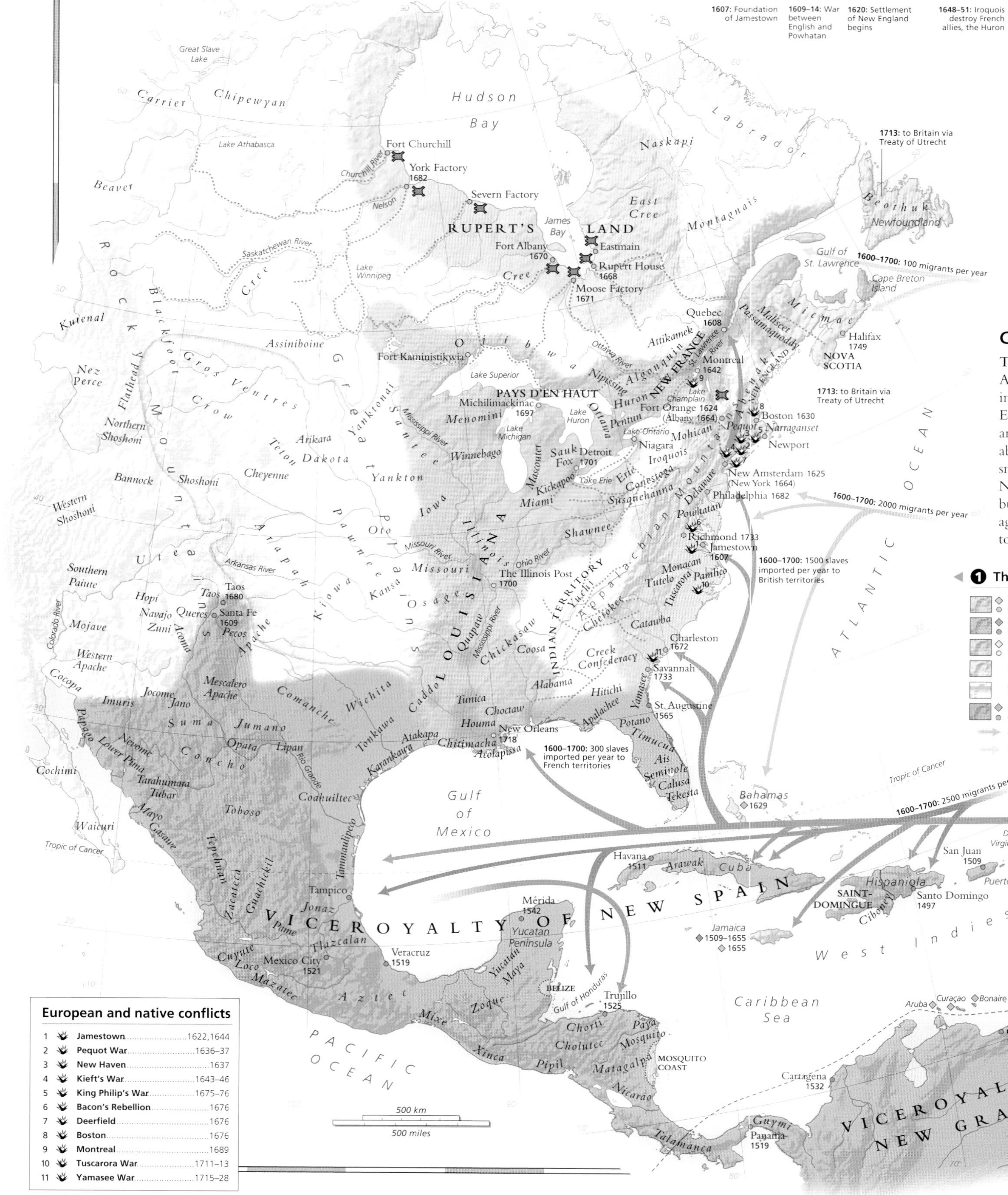

1 The colonization of North America to 1750

- British control and settlement
- Spanish control and settlement
- French control and settlement
- French influence
- approximate western limit of French claim
- Dutch control and settlement
- migration from Britain
- migration from France
- migration from Spain
- movement of slaves
- fur trade routes
- 1682 date of foundation
- conflict with native Americans
- fur trading post
- *Houma* indigenous people

1713: to Britain via Treaty of Utrecht

1600–1700: 100 migrants per year

1600–1700: 2000 migrants per year

1600–1700: 1500 slaves imported per year to British territories

1600–1700: 300 slaves imported per year to French territories

1600–1700: 2500 migrants per year

1600–1700: 100,000 slaves imported per year to Spanish territories

European and native conflicts

	Conflict	Date
1	Jamestown	1622, 1644
2	Pequot War	1636–37
3	New Haven	1637
4	Kieft's War	1643–46
5	King Philip's War	1675–76
6	Bacon's Rebellion	1676
7	Deerfield	1676
8	Boston	1676
9	Montreal	1689
10	Tuscarora War	1711–13
11	Yamasee War	1715–28

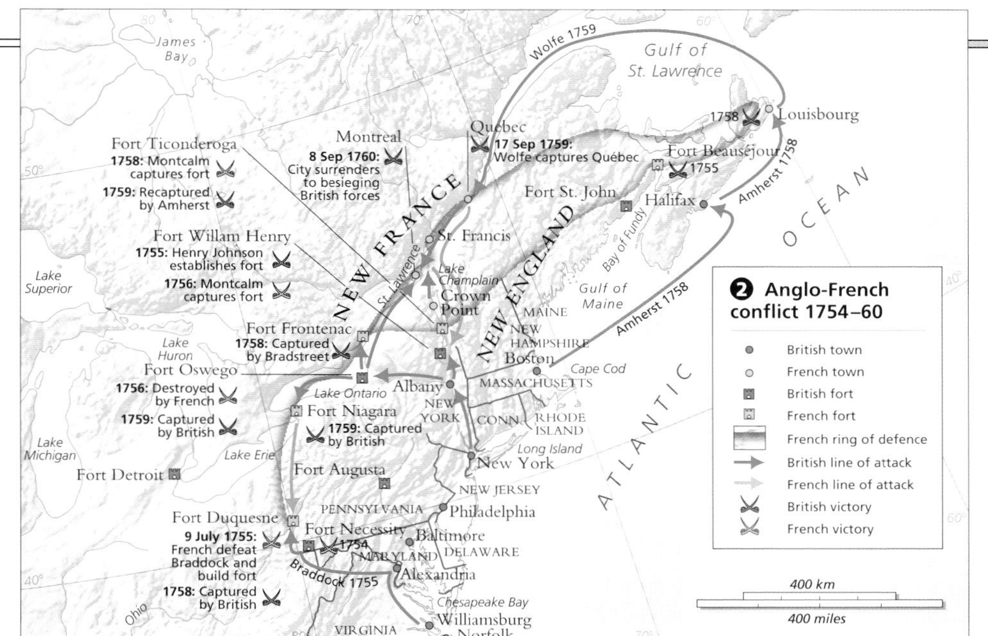

Competition for North America 1690–1761

Conflict between France and Britain in North America at first mirrored the wars of Louis XIV in Europe in the 1690s. In the late 1730s Britain and Spain clashed in the Spanish colonies. Serious fighting between the British and French resumed in 1744–48, but the decisive struggle for the continent occurred between 1754–61. In July 1755, General Braddock, aided by provincial troops including George Washington, marched on Fort Duquesne but was repelled by the French. It took the full weight of the British army until 1759 to gain ascendancy over the French and their Indian allies. General Wolfe's capture of Quebec in September 1759 was followed by the surrender of Montreal. With peace agreed at the Treaty of Paris in 1763, Britain became the dominant colonial power in the New World.

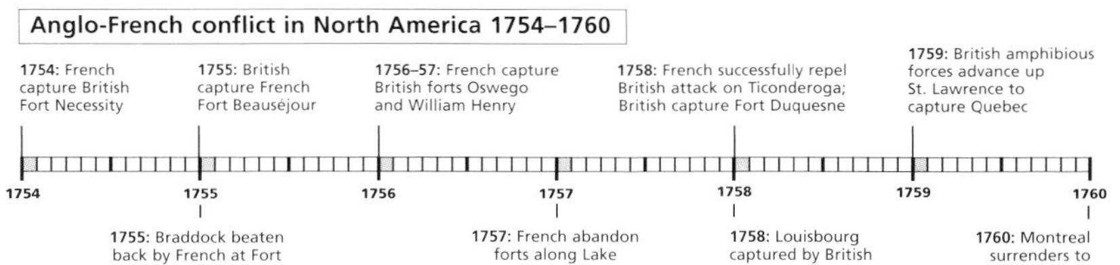

The brief but fierce battle for Quebec in September 1759, claimed the lives of the commanders of both sides: the British General Wolfe (*left*), and the French Marquis de Montcalm the following day. Final victory belonged to the British who had been advancing up the Gulf of St. Lawrence for over a year.

The Revolutionary War 1775–1783

By the 1760s, the inhabitants of the British colonies had grown rapidly in population, wealth, and self-confidence and were increasingly resistant to conventional methods of colonial control, such as taxation. In addition, the British government was perceived to be keeping all the fruits of victory against the French for itself, including the Canadian fur trade and the western lands. In 1775, the first shots of the Revolutionary War were fired in Boston. Almost all of the early campaigns ended in stalemate: British forces were superior in numbers and weaponry, but the patriots gained support with every campaign as the struggle moved south. The American victory at Saratoga in 1777 convinced the French government to support the Americans with troops and ships. Later the Dutch and Spanish also joined against Britain. In 1781 George Washington forced General Cornwallis to surrender at Yorktown and the new nation was secure.

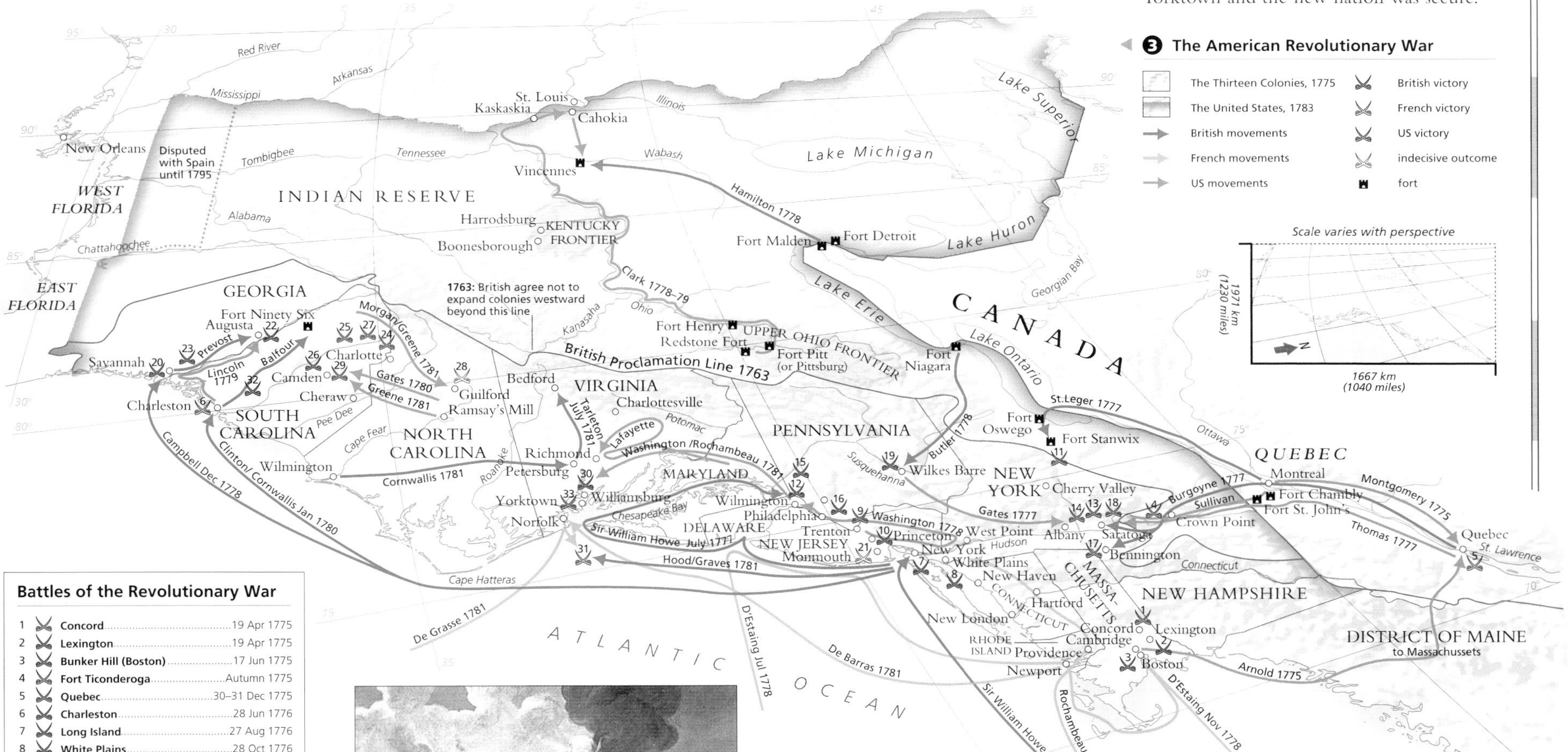

3 The American Revolutionary War

- The Thirteen Colonies, 1775
- The United States, 1783
- British movements
- French movements
- US movements
- British victory
- French victory
- US victory
- indecisive outcome
- fort

Scale varies with perspective

1971 km (1230 miles)

1667 km (1040 miles)

1763: British agree not to expand colonies westward beyond this line

British Proclamation Line 1763

Disputed with Spain until 1795

DISTRICT OF MAINE to Massachussets

Battles of the Revolutionary War

1	Concord	19 Apr 1775
2	Lexington	19 Apr 1775
3	Bunker Hill (Boston)	17 Jun 1775
4	Fort Ticonderoga	Autumn 1775
5	Quebec	30–31 Dec 1775
6	Charleston	28 Jun 1776
7	Long Island	27 Aug 1776
8	White Plains	28 Oct 1776
9	Trenton	25 Dec 1776
10	Princeton	3 Jan 1777
11	Oriskany	6 Aug 1777
12	Brandywine	11 Sep 1777
13	Freeman's Farm	19 Sep 1777
14	Bemis Heights	19 Sep, 7 Oct 1777
15	Paoli	20 Sep 1777
16	Germantown	4 Oct 1777
17	Bennington	15 Oct 1777
18	Saratoga	17 Oct 1777
19	Wyoming Massacre	Autumn 1778
20	Savannah	29 Dec 1778
21	Monmouth Court House	28 Jun 1778
22	Augusta	29 Jan 1779
23	Briar Creek	3 Mar 1779
24	King's Mountain	7 Oct 1780
25	Blackstock	20 Nov 1780
26	Camden	16 Jan 1781
27	Cowpens	17 Jan 1781
28	Guilford Court House	5 Mar 1781
29	Hobkirk's Hill	25 Apr 1781
30	Jamestown	6 Jul 1781
31	Virginia Capes	5 Sep 1781
32	Eutaw Springs	8 Sep 1781
33	Yorktown	19 Oct 1781

At the battle of Bunker Hill on 17 June 1775 British forces attempted to loosen the American encirclement of Boston. The British eventually gained the position, but their heavy losses and the ability of the colonists to stand firm under fire was an important boost to American morale.

The road to independence

- **1764:** Sugar Act imposes tax on molasses brought from non-British colonies
- **1765:** Stamp Act inspires the slogan 'taxation without representation is tyranny'
- **1767:** Townshend Acts tax tea, paper, and other imports
- **1770:** Soldiers shoot five colonists in 'Boston Massacre'
- **1772:** Committees of Correspondence promote American identity
- **1773:** Militants destroy shipments of tea in 'Boston Tea Party'
- **1775:** Start of Revolutionary War
- **4 Jul 1776:** Adoption of Declaration of Independence
- **1778:** France enters war as American ally
- **1781:** Washington defeats British at Yorktown
- **1783:** End of Revolutionary War. Treaty of Paris creates new United States

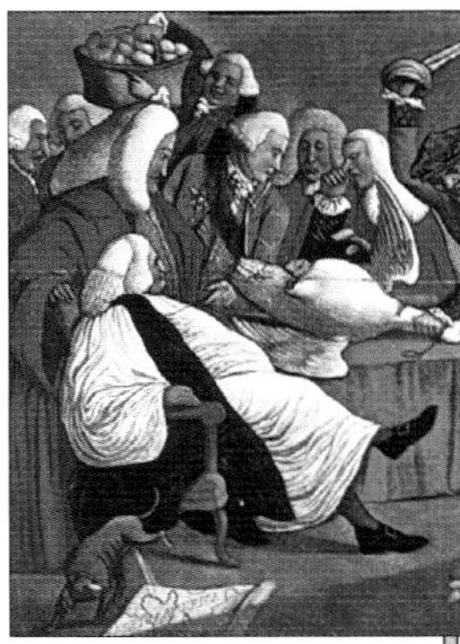

This cartoon, published in 1776, shows the British government killing their 'golden goose' – the American colonies. Unpopular taxes combined with the harsh suppression of opposition alienated many colonists and hardened American resistance to the British government.

BUILDING NEW NATIONS

Thomas Jefferson was the principal author of the Declaration of Independence and the third US president.

BY 1783, THE NEWLY-FORMED United States of America had a draft constitution and a border which soon extended as far as the Mississippi, causing considerable alarm among its Indian, Spanish, and Canadian neighbours. In the War of 1812, Canada successfully fended off invasion by the United States, but remained fearful of the growing power to its south. In Mexico and Central America, Creole dissenters launched a disastrous war for independence from Spain starting in 1810. Mexico plunged into a bloody race war that killed hundreds of thousands and wrecked the colonial infrastructure. The nations of Central America and Mexico emerged independent during the 1820s, though greatly weakened from their former colonial status.

The growth of the US

The Louisiana Purchase of 1803 added to the US a huge swathe of western lands formerly controlled by France. After the War of 1812, all hope of annexing Canada was abandoned, and the US began the great push westward. Settlers poured into the Great Plains, Oregon, and eventually the northern periphery of the Republic of Mexico, including Texas and California. The Santa Fe trail, open for trade by 1823, brought New Mexico under US influence. By mid-century, the US boasted an extensive communications network. Steamboat traffic dominated the riverine highway system, augmented by canals and railroads running cross-country.

The consolidation of western lands encouraged millions of pioneers to forge new lives in the West. The spirit of aggressive progress which drove settlers westward soon became known as 'manifest destiny'.

2 North America 1783–1905: struggles for nationhood and the seizing of the West

European settlement in the US and Canada
- by c.1860
- extent of Russian claim 1821–24
- northern frontier of Mexico 1821
- Mexican territory 1821–23, United Provinces of Central America 1823–38
- Mexico after 1854
- Alaska Purchase 1867
- Canada at the creation of the Dominion, 1867
- Canadian territory 1880 with dates of provincial incorporation
- Canadian territory added in 1905

Conflicts between Indians and settlers
- 'Trail of Tears' removal of the southern tribes
- flight of the Nez Percé
- Indian wars 1783–1850
- Creek War 1813–14
- Seminole Wars 1816–58
- battles for the West 1850–1890

International conflicts
- War of 1812
- Texas Revolution 1835–36
- US victory: US-Mexican War 1846–48
- Mexican victory: US-Mexican War 1846–48
- Riel rebellions 1869–1885

Texas Revolution 1835–36
- routes of Santa Ana

The US-Mexican War 1846–48
- movement of US forces
- movement of Mexican forces

Wagon trails
- Oregon Trail
- Mormon Trail
- Central Overland Trail
- Southern Overland Trail
- Santa Fe Trail
- Old Spanish Trail
- California Trail
- Chisholm Trail
- Bozeman Trail

- country capital
- state/province capital
- 1804 date of independence
- railroad
- Pony Express route
- range of buffalo

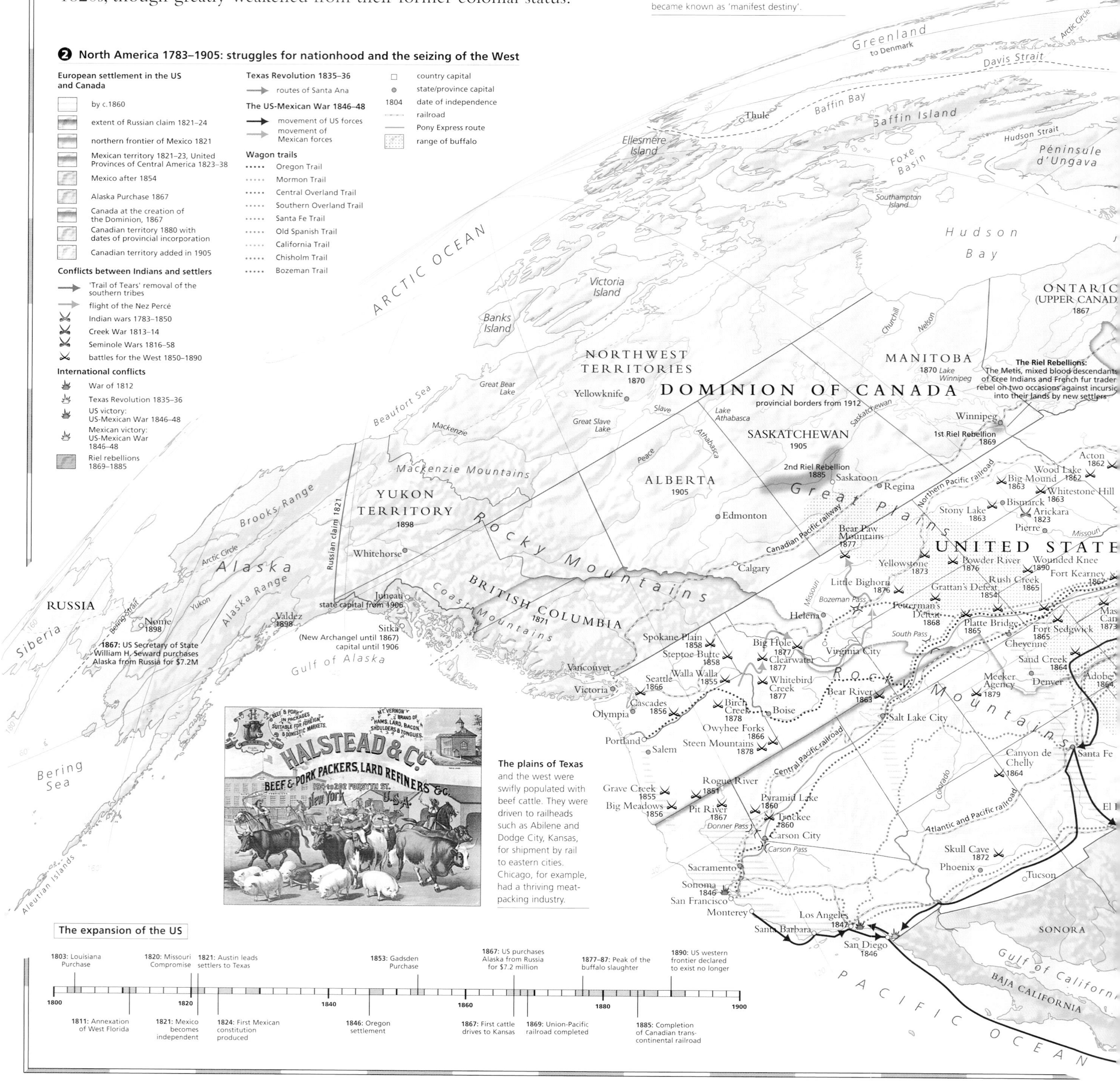

The Riel Rebellions: The Metis, mixed blood descendants of Cree Indians and French fur trader rebel on two occasions against incursic into their lands by new settlers

1867: US Secretary of State William H. Seward purchases Alaska from Russia for $7.2M

The plains of Texas and the west were swiftly populated with beef cattle. They were driven to railheads such as Abilene and Dodge City, Kansas, for shipment by rail to eastern cities. Chicago, for example, had a thriving meat-packing industry.

The expansion of the US

- **1803:** Louisiana Purchase
- **1811:** Annexation of West Florida
- **1820:** Missouri Compromise
- **1821:** Mexico becomes independent
- **1821:** Austin leads settlers to Texas
- **1824:** First Mexican constitution produced
- **1846:** Oregon settlement
- **1853:** Gadsden Purchase
- **1867:** US purchases Alaska from Russia for $7.2 million
- **1867:** First cattle drives to Kansas
- **1869:** Union-Pacific railroad completed
- **1877–87:** Peak of the buffalo slaughter
- **1885:** Completion of Canadian trans-continental railroad
- **1890:** US western frontier declared to exist no longer

Territorial conflict and US expansion

Although involved in conflicts with Britain over the boundary with Canada, the US managed to solve these issues peacefully. A weak, divided Mexico however, feared US territorial demands, especially after President Andrew Jackson offered to purchase Texas. By 1835 the Texans had seceded. Suspicion between the US and Mexico turned quickly to crisis, and in 1846, to war. In 1848 Mexico yielded nearly half its territory to the US as terms of peace, and descended into civil war. The cession of the northern Oregon Country by Britain in 1846, and James Gadsden's 1853 purchase of 30,000 square miles south of the Gila river, from Mexico, completed the westward expansion of the US. The last piece of land added to the US was the northwestern territory of Alaska in 1867.

The destruction of the Indians

From the 1790s, Indians were removed westward in a migration forever afterwards known as the 'Trail of Tears' although some, like the Seminole in Florida, resisted stoutly. The settlement of the West from the 1860s was met with serious armed resistance from the Indians. With the final loss of their lands, Indian society was reorganized so as to eliminate native culture, and pave the way for their integration into the national population.

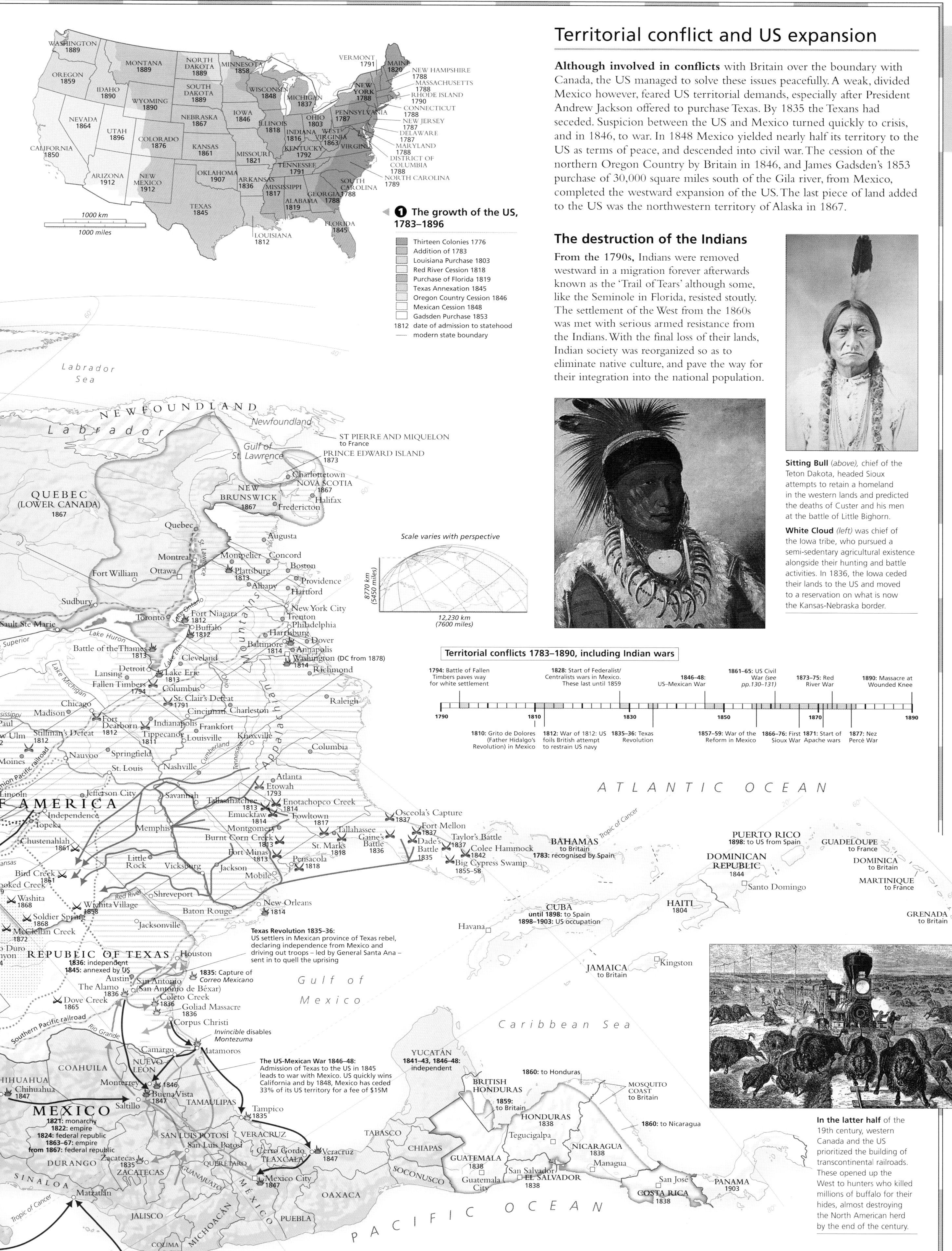

Sitting Bull *(above)*, chief of the Teton Dakota, headed Sioux attempts to retain a homeland in the western lands and predicted the deaths of Custer and his men at the battle of Little Bighorn.

White Cloud *(left)* was chief of the Iowa tribe, who pursued a semi-sedentary agricultural existence alongside their hunting and battle activities. In 1836, the Iowa ceded their lands to the US and moved to a reservation on what is now the Kansas-Nebraska border.

In the latter half of the 19th century, western Canada and the US prioritized the building of transcontinental railroads. These opened up the West to hunters who killed millions of buffalo for their hides, almost destroying the North American herd by the end of the century.

THE AMERICAN CIVIL WAR

Abraham Lincoln's 1863 Emancipation Proclamation freed the slaves of the south.

BETWEEN INDEPENDENCE in 1783 and 1860 there developed within the United States two very different, regional societies. In the North there emerged an industrialized society, committed to liberal banking and credit systems, and protective tariffs. The south was a less populous agrarian society opposed to the sale of public land in the Midwest, high duties, and restrictions upon the institution of slavery. Moreover, the libertarian North increasingly resented Southern political and judicial over-representation. The Democratic Party held the two parts together until 1859; its split, and the election of a president committed to opposing the spread of slavery, provoked the Union's collapse – even before Lincoln's inauguration, seven Southern states had seceded, and war became inevitable.

The cotton gin invented by Eli Whitney in 1793 enabled the swift processing of short-staple cotton. Cotton production increased massively in the Southern states with a resultant rise in the number of slaves required to work the burgeoning plantations.

6 The Civil War to the fall of Vicksburg Apr 1861–Jul 1863 ▶

Union states 1861
Confederate states 1861
Union front line to Dec 1861
Union front line to Dec 1862
Union movement
Confederate movement
Union fort
Confederate fort
Union naval blockade
Union victory
Confederate victory
12 Apr 1865 date of battle or attack

FLORIDA

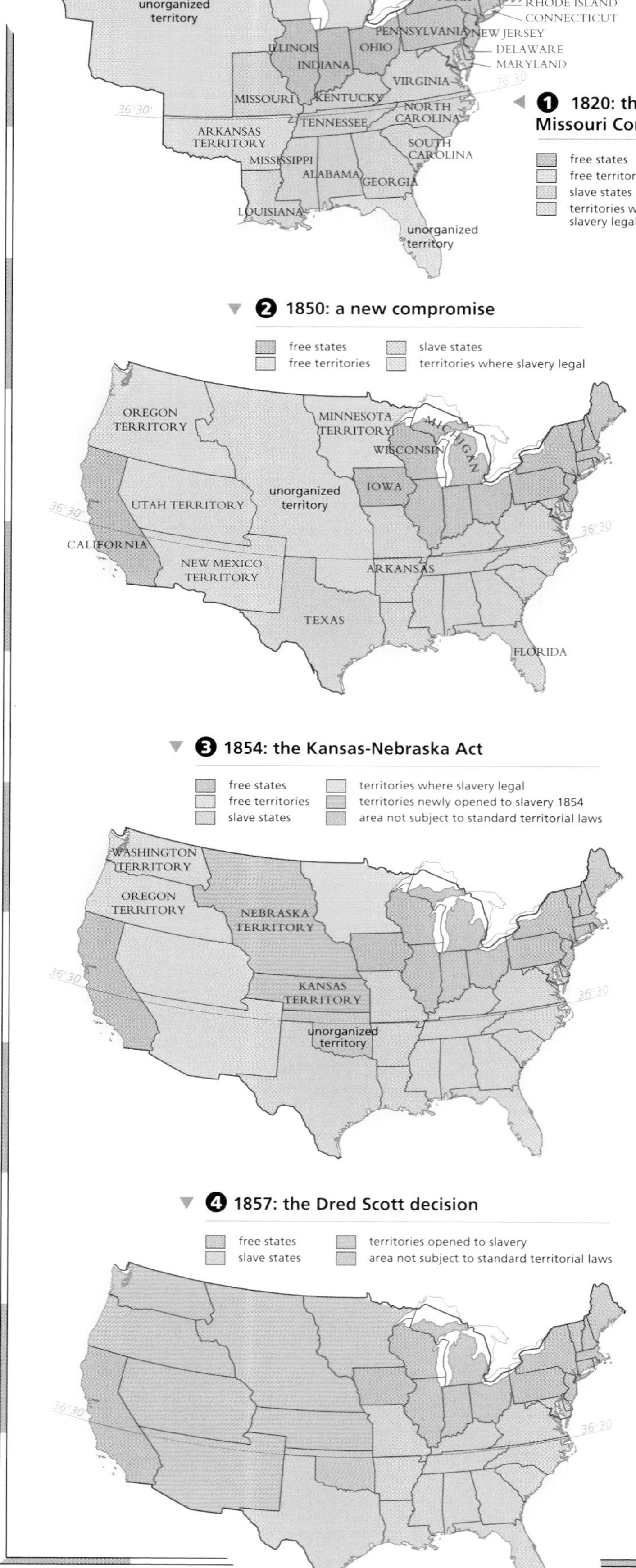

1 1820: the Missouri Compromise

free states
free territories
slave states
territories where slavery legal

2 1850: a new compromise

free states
free territories
slave states
territories where slavery legal

3 1854: the Kansas-Nebraska Act

free states
free territories
slave states
territories where slavery legal
territories newly opened to slavery 1854
area not subject to standard territorial laws

4 1857: the Dred Scott decision

free states
slave states
territories opened to slavery
area not subject to standard territorial laws

An unequal nation

By 1860 the US was composed of 18 'free' states – mainly in the North, and 15 'slave' states – mainly in the South. On the issue of slavery, as well as economics, the expanding nation was divided. Industry and finance dominated the North which also had 71% of the population, 81% of bank deposits, 72% of railroad mileage and 85% of the country's factories. The South concentrated on farming, in particular on the production of cotton, tobacco, and sugar for export to Europe. In 1850 347,000 Southern families out of a total population of 6,000,000 were slave-owners. The West was developing an agricultural economy, but produced a greater variety of crops, and sold most of its produce to the northeast.

Industrial production fuelled the growth of Northern cities such as Chicago, seen here in the 1860s. The Southern states, largely dependent on agriculture, remained far less economically developed.

Compromises on the road to civil war

The addition of Missouri in 1820 was the first extension of Union territory west of the Mississippi. The question of whether slavery should be allowed in the new state was settled by the so-called Missouri Compromise, with an artificial limit of 36° 30' marking the boundary between slave and free territory. In 1854 the Kansas-Nebraska Act established two new territories and proposed to allow territorial legislatures to decide the issue of slavery. The Dred Scott decision of 1857 – whereby a slave who had been taken west by his master claimed that he was free because slavery was not legal in the new territory – led to the ruling that slavery could not be excluded from new territories.

5 North versus South: the state of the Union in 1861

Union states
Confederate states
slavery legal
major slave trade routes
Jan 1861 date of secession from the Union

Resources and industry
southern cotton belt
northern corn belt
coal
iron ore
precious metal
textile production
manufacturing city

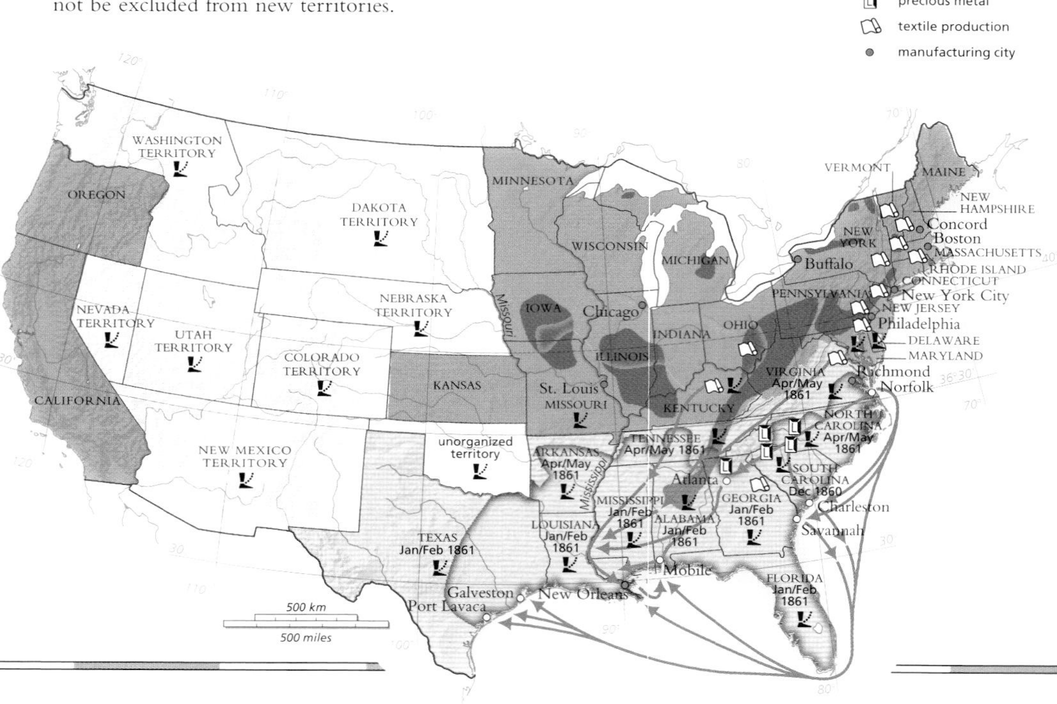

The Civil War 1861–65

In 1860, seven Southern states, fearing restrictions on slavery, seceded from the US. By 1861, they had been joined by four more and became known as the Confederacy. The remaining 23 so-called Union states remained loyal to the US. In April 1861, an attack on Fort Sumter in Charleston harbour started a war for which neither side was prepared. The Civil War became a war of exhaustion. The superior demographic, industrial, and positional resources of the North, combined with sea power that ensured the Confederacy's isolation, slowly destroyed the capacity and will of the Confederacy to wage war. The Confederacy rarely tried to carry the war to the North, meeting crushing defeat at Gettysburg in July 1863. For the most part it waged a defensive war in order to sap the will of the Union. Certainly by 1864 war-weariness had set in in the North, but the successes of the 1864 campaign ensured Lincoln's re-election and sealed the South's defeat.

The Civil War was the first war to be recorded using photography. Field photographers such as Matthew Brady were able to record the true horrors of battles such as Gettysburg, the dead from which are seen above.

The Civil War to the fall of Vicksburg

During 1861–62 Union forces lost a series of battles to an enemy with superior military skills. However, the Northern naval blockade began to cut off both Southern exports and essential supplies. With no Confederate offensive in the upper Ohio which might have split the Union, the North was able to undertake offensives against the Confederate capital, Richmond, and along the Tennessee and Mississippi. Repulsed before Richmond and obliged thereafter to move directly against the city, Union forces secured Memphis and New Orleans, capturing Vicksburg on 4 July 1863, to divide the Confederacy.

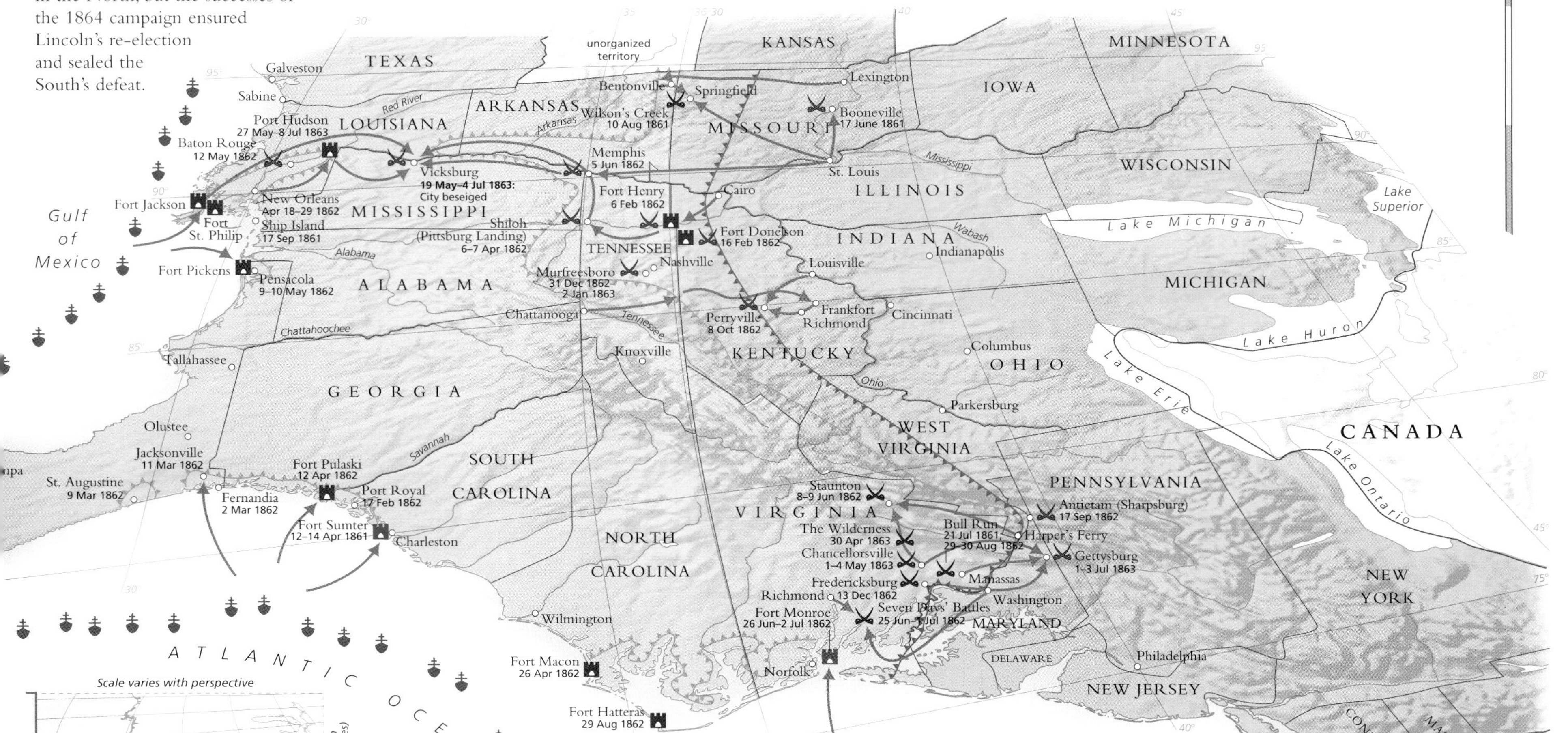

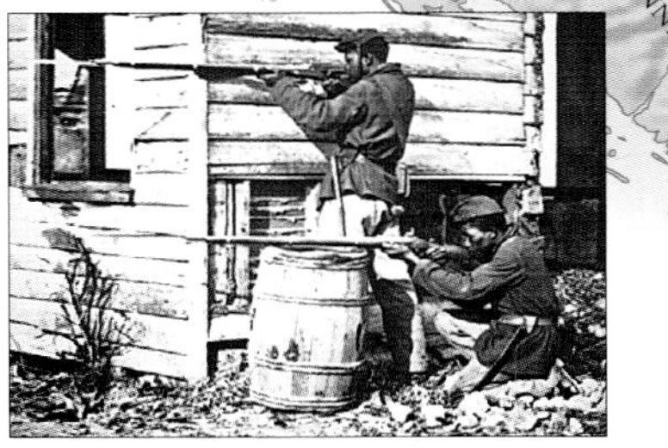

Scale varies with perspective

2070 km (1290 miles)

1890 km (1170 miles)

Black fighting troops were not used by the Union army until 1863. The passage of the Militia Act in 1862 allowed them to enlist as soldiers. By the end of the war, more than 180,000 blacks had fought for the Union, although only about 100 had been able to achieve officer rank.

From Gettysburg to Petersburg

After victories at Fredericksburg and The Wilderness, the Confederate offensive into Pennsylvania was defeated at Gettysburg, on the same day as Vicksburg fell. Thereafter on the defensive, Confederate armies were increasingly outnumbered: with Grant's appointment as commander, they were also increasingly outfought. Grant undertook an offensive against Richmond that broke the Confederate freedom of action in a series of battles and the siege of Petersburg: at the same time Sherman's army broke into Georgia and South Carolina. With defeat in front of Petersburg, Confederate resistance collapsed in April 1865.

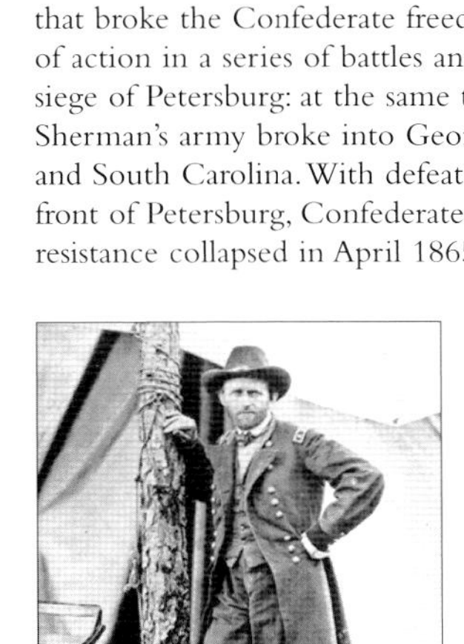

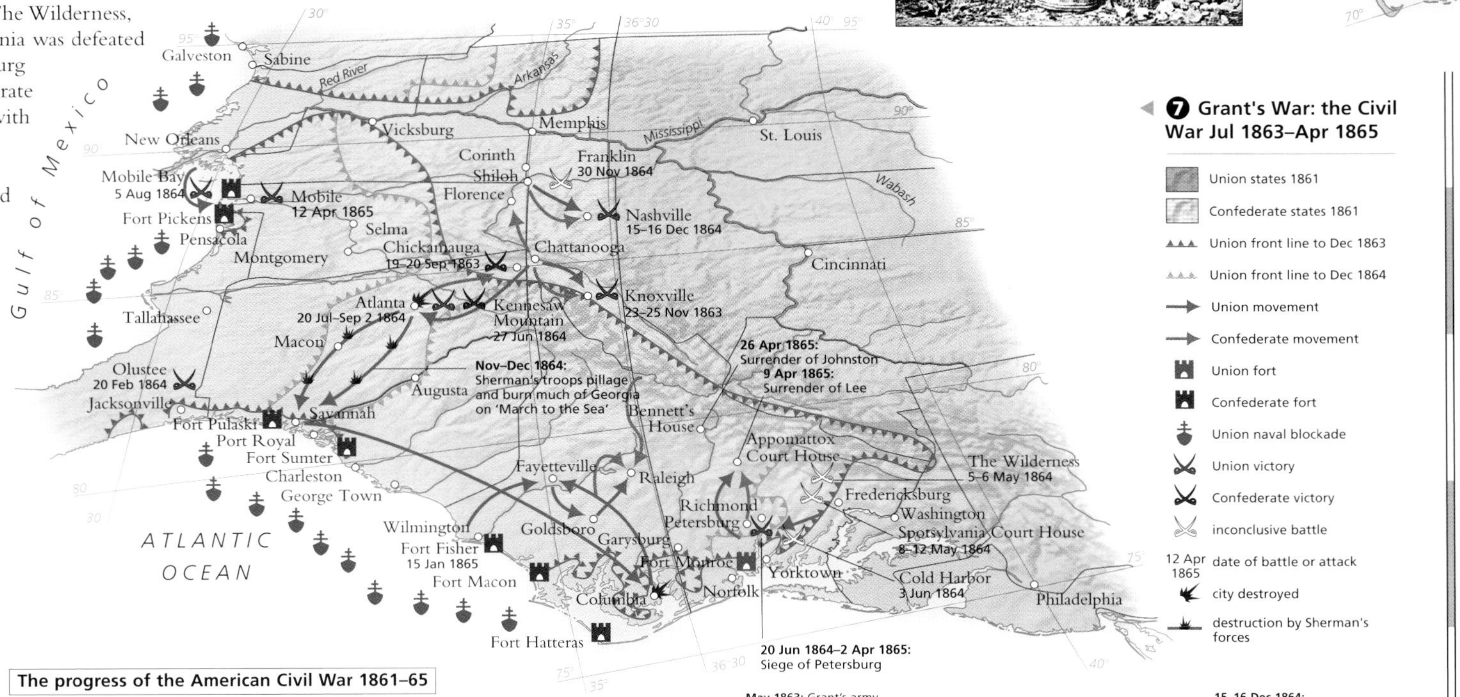

Ulysses S. Grant was appointed supreme commander of the Union forces in 1864.

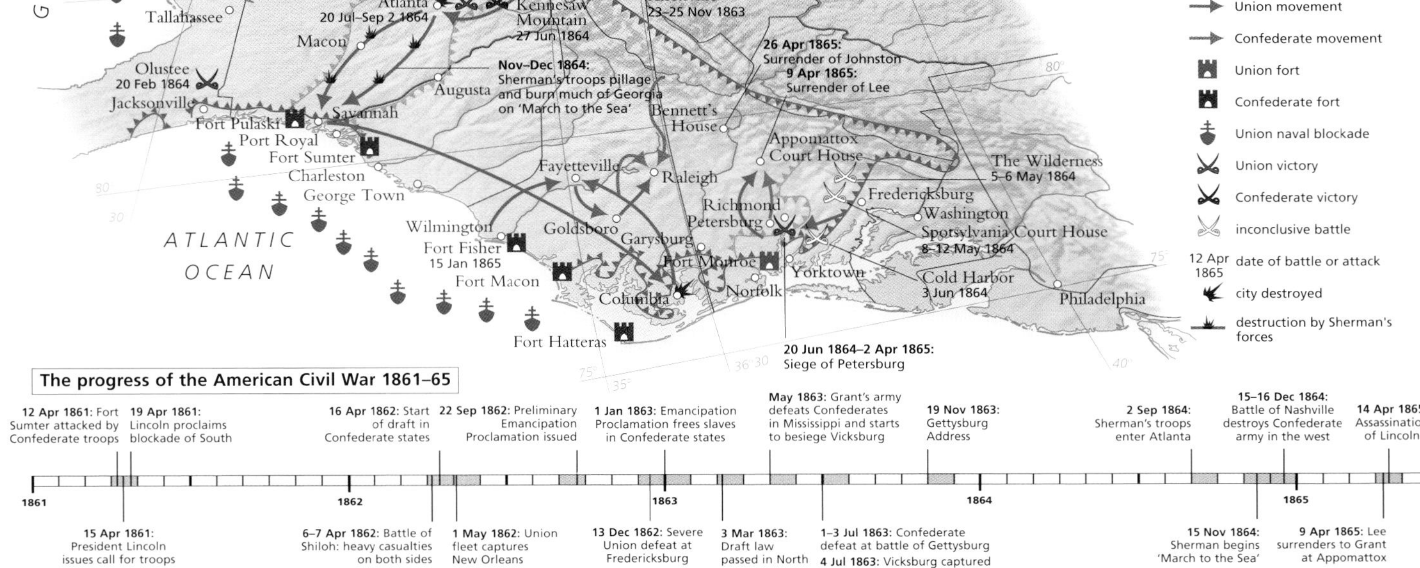

7 Grant's War: the Civil War Jul 1863–Apr 1865
Union states 1861
Confederate states 1861
Union front line to Dec 1863
Union front line to Dec 1864
Union movement
Confederate movement
Union fort
Confederate fort
Union naval blockade
Union victory
Confederate victory
inconclusive battle
12 Apr 1865 date of battle or attack
city destroyed
destruction by Sherman's forces
20 Jun 1864–2 Apr 1865: Siege of Petersburg
Nov–Dec 1864: Sherman's troops pillage and burn much of Georgia on 'March to the Sea'
26 Apr 1865: Surrender of Johnston
9 Apr 1865: Surrender of Lee
The progress of the American Civil War 1861–65
12 Apr 1861: Fort Sumter attacked by Confederate troops
19 Apr 1861: Lincoln proclaims blockade of South
15 Apr 1861: President Lincoln issues call for troops
16 Apr 1862: Start of draft in Confederate states
22 Sep 1862: Preliminary Emancipation Proclamation issued
6–7 Apr 1862: Battle of Shiloh: heavy casualties on both sides
1 May 1862: Union fleet captures New Orleans
1 Jan 1863: Emancipation Proclamation frees slaves in Confederate states
13 Dec 1862: Severe Union defeat at Fredericksburg
3 Mar 1863: Draft law passed in North
May 1863: Grant's army defeats Confederates in Mississippi and starts to besiege Vicksburg
1–3 Jul 1863: Confederate defeat at battle of Gettysburg
4 Jul 1863: Vicksburg captured by Union troops
19 Nov 1863: Gettysburg Address
2 Sep 1864: Sherman's troops enter Atlanta
15 Nov 1864: Sherman begins 'March to the Sea'
15–16 Dec 1864: Battle of Nashville destroys Confederate army in the west
14 Apr 1865: Assassination of Lincoln
9 Apr 1865: Lee surrenders to Grant at Appomattox
1861
1862
1863
1864
1865

NORTH AMERICA 1865–1920

The Statue of Liberty came to symbolize the hope and freedom offered by the US.

THE NATIONS OF NORTH AMERICA focused on the development of their own resources after 1865. The US worked to reconstruct itself after the Civil War and like Canada, concentrated on the completion of transcontinental railroads to further exploit the continent's immense resources. Abroad, the US extended its influence in Central America and west across the Pacific, gaining new territory and economic advantage. In Mexico, Benito Juárez and his Republican forces felled the regime of Maximilian, ushering in a period of relative calm. Under Porfirio Díaz, Mexico attracted foreign investment and immigration, but its population remained brutally suppressed.

Industrialization and urbanization

US manufacturing techniques and machinery were refined throughout the second half of the 19th century.

The growth of the railroads and industrialization transformed the North American landscape. The economic boom turned the continent into a magnet for immigration: thousands came to its shores seeking a better life. Inventions and innovations abounded; cities arose across the continent, supporting factories that had expanded rapidly because of the demands of the American Civil War. The new industrial cities became pressure cookers of societal and political discontent, with often bloody confrontations between organized labour, police, and even the military.

Theodore Roosevelt, president 1901–09, presided over the economic boom of the early 20th century.

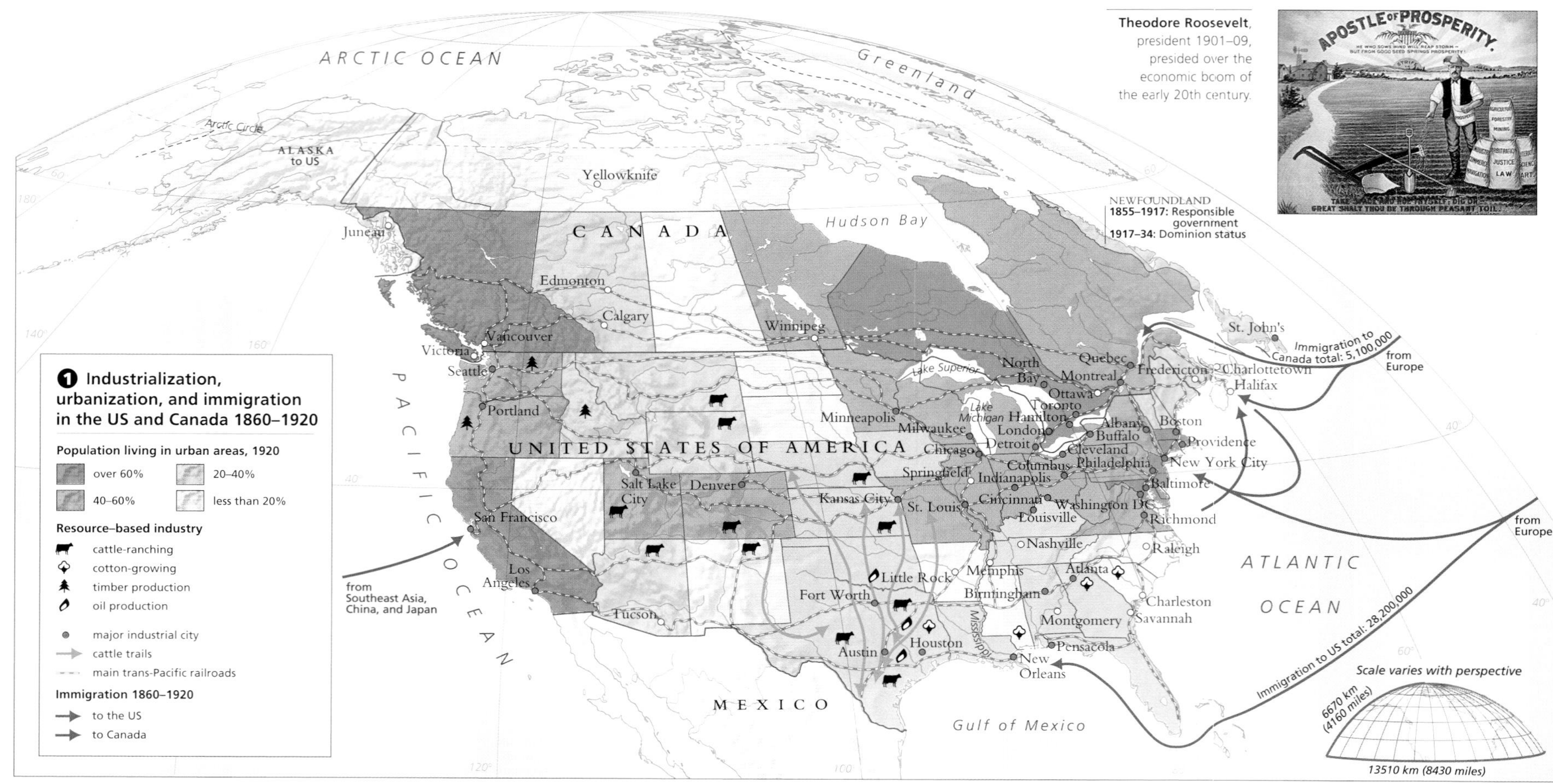

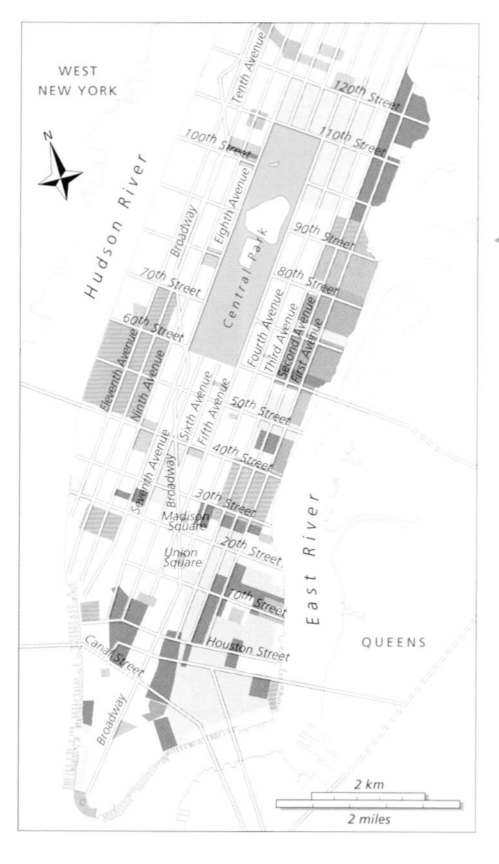

❷ Ethnic neighbourhoods in Manhattan c.1920

- African-American
- Chinese
- Czech, Hungarian
- French
- German
- Irish
- Italian
- Jewish
- Scandinavian, Finnish
- Syrian, Turkish, Armenian, Greek

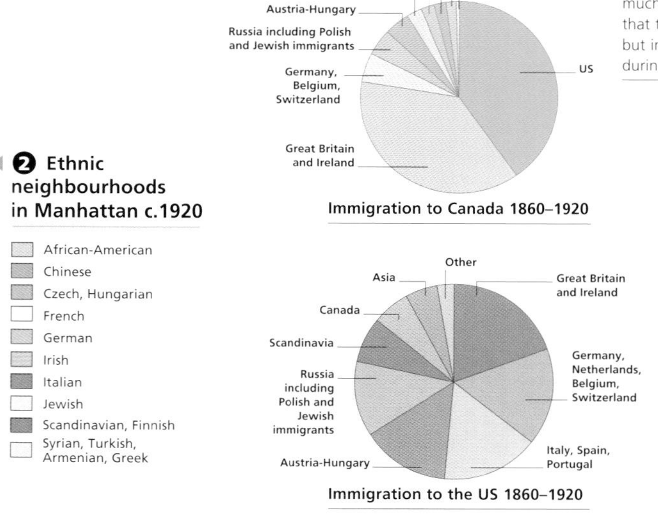

Canadian immigration was much lower than that to the US, but increased during the 1890s.

The era of mass migration

During the 19th century nearly 50 million immigrants swelled the populations of Canada and the US. Immigration was initially from northern Europe: Germany, Scandinavia, Britain, and Ireland, but from the 1880s, the bulk of migrants came from eastern and southern Europe. Most settlers were lured by the economic opportunities offered by the Americas but others sought freedom from religious persecution and political uncertainty. After the First World War, immigration was severely curtailed.

The majority of new arrivals to the Americas were able to gain entry. Only about 2% were refused leave to stay.

New York

New York's Ellis Island was the point of entry for millions of immigrants between 1892 and 1920. Many people remained within the city, finding comfort and support in ethnic neighbourhoods which had grown up there. By the 1920s, the diversity of nationalities on Manhattan was a reflection of the diverse strains that made up the population of the US.

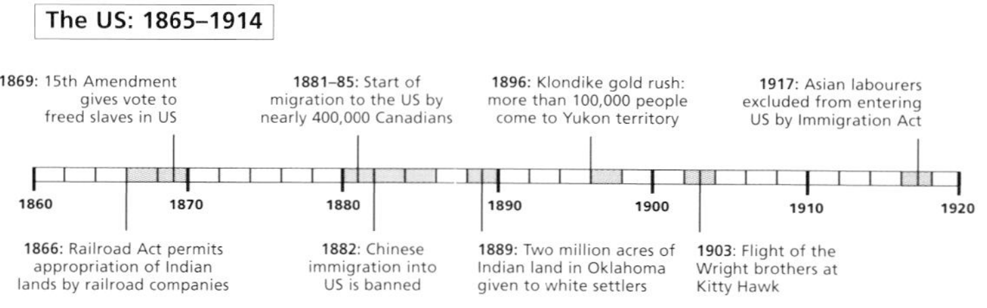

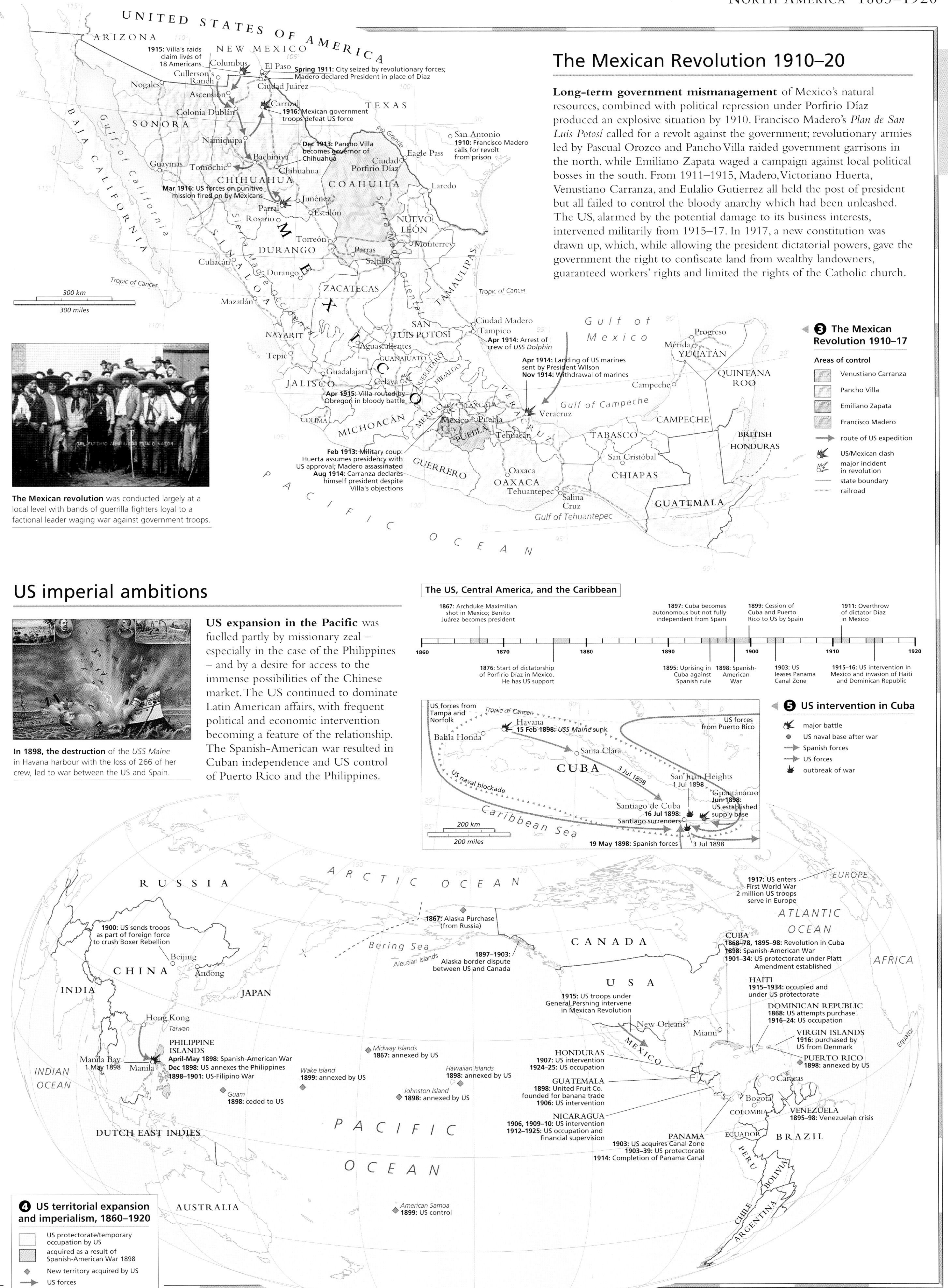

UNITED STATES OF AMERICA
ARIZONA
NEW MEXICO
TEXAS
1915: Villa's raids claim lives of 18 Americans
Spring 1911: City seized by revolutionary forces; Madero declared President in place of Diaz
1916: Mexican government troops defeat US force
Dec 1913: Pancho Villa becomes governor of Chihuahua
1910: Francisco Madero calls for revolt from prison
Mar 1916: US forces on punitive mission fired on by Mexicans
Apr 1914: Arrest of crew of USS Dolphin
Apr 1914: Landing of US marines sent by President Wilson
Nov 1914: Withdrawal of marines
Apr 1915: Villa routed by Obregon in bloody battle
Feb 1913: Military coup: Huerta assumes presidency with US approval; Madero assassinated
Aug 1914: Carranza declares himself president despite Villa's objections
SONORA
CHIHUAHUA
COAHUILA
NUEVO LEÓN
DURANGO
SINALOA
ZACATECAS
TAMAULIPAS
SAN LUIS POTOSÍ
NAYARIT
JALISCO
MICHOACÁN
GUERRERO
OAXACA
VERACRUZ
PUEBLA
TABASCO
CHIAPAS
CAMPECHE
YUCATÁN
QUINTANA ROO
BRITISH HONDURAS
GUATEMALA
BAJA CALIFORNIA
Gulf of California
Gulf of Mexico
Gulf of Campeche
Gulf of Tehuantepec
PACIFIC OCEAN
Tropic of Cancer
300 km
300 miles
3 The Mexican Revolution 1910–17
Areas of control
Venustiano Carranza
Pancho Villa
Emiliano Zapata
Francisco Madero
route of US expedition
US/Mexican clash
major incident in revolution
state boundary
railroad
The US, Central America, and the Caribbean
1867: Archduke Maximilian shot in Mexico; Benito Juárez becomes president
1876: Start of dictatorship of Porfirio Diaz in Mexico. He has US support
1895: Uprising in Cuba against Spanish rule
1897: Cuba becomes autonomous but not fully independent from Spain
1898: Spanish-American War
1899: Cession of Cuba and Puerto Rico to US by Spain
1903: US leases Panama Canal Zone
1911: Overthrow of dictator Diaz in Mexico
1915–16: US intervention in Mexico and invasion of Haiti and Dominican Republic
5 US intervention in Cuba
major battle
US naval base after war
Spanish forces
US forces
outbreak of war
US forces from Tampa and Norfolk
15 Feb 1898: USS Maine sunk
US forces from Puerto Rico
CUBA
US naval blockade
San Juan Heights 1 Jul 1898
Guantánamo Jun 1898: US established supply base
16 Jul 1898: Santiago surrenders
19 May 1898: Spanish forces
3 Jul 1898
Caribbean Sea
200 km
200 miles
4 US territorial expansion and imperialism, 1860–1920
US protectorate/temporary occupation by US
acquired as a result of Spanish-American War 1898
New territory acquired by US
US forces
major battle
RUSSIA
CHINA
INDIA
JAPAN
CANADA
USA
ARCTIC OCEAN
ATLANTIC OCEAN
PACIFIC OCEAN
INDIAN OCEAN
AFRICA
EUROPE
AUSTRALIA
DUTCH EAST INDIES
1900: US sends troops as part of foreign force to crush Boxer Rebellion
1867: Alaska Purchase (from Russia)
1897–1903: Alaska border dispute between US and Canada
1917: US enters First World War 2 million US troops serve in Europe
CUBA 1868–78, 1895–98: Revolution in Cuba 1898: Spanish-American War 1901–34: US protectorate under Platt Amendment established
HAITI 1915–1934: occupied and under US protectorate
DOMINICAN REPUBLIC 1868: US attempts purchase 1916–24: US occupation
VIRGIN ISLANDS 1916: purchased by US from Denmark
PUERTO RICO 1898: annexed by US
1915: US troops under General Pershing intervene in Mexican Revolution
HONDURAS 1907: US intervention 1924–25: US occupation
GUATEMALA 1898: United Fruit Co. founded for banana trade 1906: US intervention
NICARAGUA 1906, 1909–10: US intervention 1912–1925: US occupation and financial supervision
PANAMA 1903: US acquires Canal Zone 1903–39: US protectorate 1914: Completion of Panama Canal
VENEZUELA 1895–98: Venezuelan crisis
PHILIPPINE ISLANDS April–May 1898: Spanish-American War Dec 1898: US annexes the Philippines 1898–1901: US-Filipino War
Manila Bay 1 May 1898
Guam 1898: ceded to US
Midway Islands 1867: annexed by US
Wake Island 1899: annexed by US
Hawaiian Islands 1898: annexed by US
Johnston Island 1898: annexed by US
American Samoa 1899: US control

The Mexican Revolution 1910–20

Long-term government mismanagement of Mexico's natural resources, combined with political repression under Porfirio Díaz produced an explosive situation by 1910. Francisco Madero's *Plan de San Luis Potosí* called for a revolt against the government; revolutionary armies led by Pascual Orozco and Pancho Villa raided government garrisons in the north, while Emiliano Zapata waged a campaign against local political bosses in the south. From 1911–1915, Madero, Victoriano Huerta, Venustiano Carranza, and Eulalio Gutierrez all held the post of president but all failed to control the bloody anarchy which had been unleashed. The US, alarmed by the potential damage to its business interests, intervened militarily from 1915–17. In 1917, a new constitution was drawn up, which, while allowing the president dictatorial powers, gave the government the right to confiscate land from wealthy landowners, guaranteed workers' rights and limited the rights of the Catholic church.

The Mexican revolution was conducted largely at a local level with bands of guerrilla fighters loyal to a factional leader waging war against government troops.

US imperial ambitions

US expansion in the Pacific was fuelled partly by missionary zeal – especially in the case of the Philippines – and by a desire for access to the immense possibilities of the Chinese market. The US continued to dominate Latin American affairs, with frequent political and economic intervention becoming a feature of the relationship. The Spanish-American war resulted in Cuban independence and US control of Puerto Rico and the Philippines.

In 1898, the destruction of the *USS Maine* in Havana harbour with the loss of 266 of her crew, led to war between the US and Spain.

AN ERA OF BOOM AND BUST

The NRA, set up in 1933, was the first New Deal recovery programme.

INVOLVEMENT IN THE FIRST WORLD WAR confirmed the US's position as a world power in the first quarter of the century. Immigration greatly magnified the population, but during the 1920s, laws were enacted to control the tide of European settlers. The economy grew quickly, but the boom proved vulnerable and in 1929 the stock market collapsed. Between 1930 and 1932, the number of unemployed rose from 4 million to between 12 and 15 million – 25% of the total workforce. The Republican government, which had promoted the boom and was blamed for the crash, was rejected by the electorate, leading to the political dominance of a Democrat, Franklin Delano Roosevelt for 13 years.

The depression and the New Deal

The stock market crash of 1929 shattered millions of dreams and left many Americans destitute. Farmers were particularly hard hit, as banks withdrew funding, as were black people in both cities and rural areas. The Roosevelt administration devised a series of relief programmes known as the 'New Deal' to restart the economy and provide new jobs. Though millions of dollars of federal funding were spent on relief, 20% of Americans were still unemployed in 1939. Not until the Second World War did the economy recover.

The Works Progress Administration (WPA) provided work relief for 8.5 million unemployed. Projects included the building and repair of roads, bridges, schools, and hospitals.

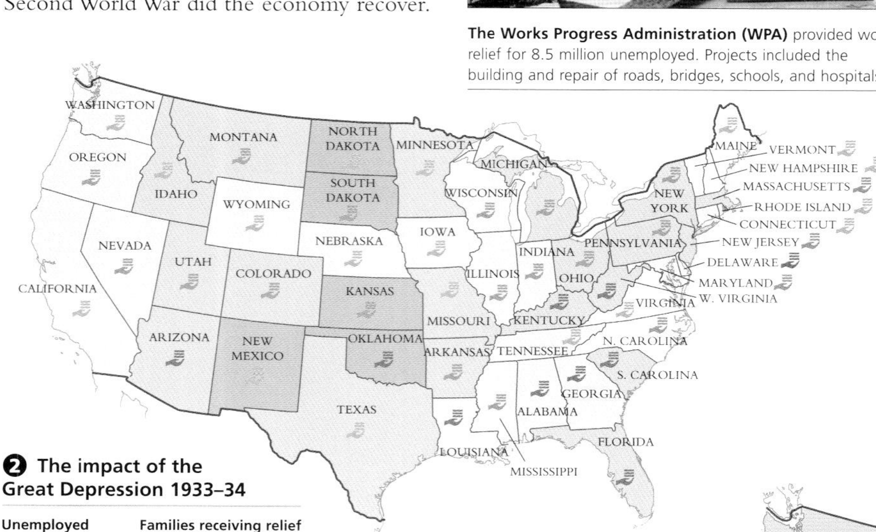

2 The impact of the Great Depression 1933–34

Unemployed: less than 10%; 11–15%; 16–25%; over 25%

Families receiving relief: less than 10%; 10–15%; over 15%

The industrial boom

The Model-T Ford was the first car to be built using production line techniques and initially produced only in black. By the 1930s, Henry Ford achieved his dream of 'a car so low in price that no man making a good salary will be unable to afford one'.

The early 1920s saw a massive growth in US production. Traditional industries such as iron and steel were in relative decline, but automobiles, petro-chemicals, construction, and the service industries grew rapidly, as did speculation on the stock market. But the boom was built on shaky foundations. High rates of small business failure in the 1920s gave the first signs of fragility and it was clear that production was outstripping consumption. Paper fortunes that had accrued in stocks and shares were wiped out by the Wall Street Crash of 1929.

1 Major US industries c.1925

iron and steel; meat processing; oil and gas; textile production; timber; vehicle manufacture; coalfield; major industrial city

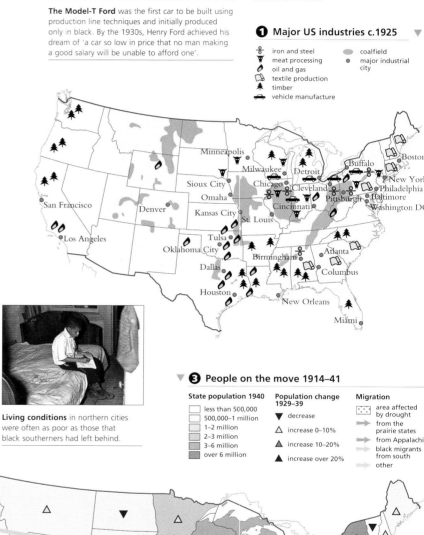

Living conditions in northern cities were often as poor as those that black southerners had left behind.

Migration in the US, 1914–41

Refugees from the Dust Bowl carry only the bare essentials as they walk towards Los Angeles in search of work (1939).

By the 1920s, more than 50% of Americans lived in urban areas. From 1917–20, more than 400,000 rural black southerners moved to northern cities and 600,000 more went in the 1920s. In the mid-1930s, farmers from the drought-affected prairie states abandoned their farms by the thousands and moved west – primarily to California's cities and valleys. Appalachia also saw a mass transference of people north to Indiana and Ohio and west to California.

3 People on the move 1914–41

State population 1940: less than 500,000; 500,000–1 million; 1–2 million; 2–3 million; 3–6 million; over 6 million

Population change 1929–39: decrease; increase 0–10%; increase 10–20%; increase over 20%

Migration: area affected by drought; from the prairie states; from Appalachia; black migrants from south; other

The US 1914–1941

- 1917–20: Start of migration of southern blacks to northern cities
- 1917: US enters First World War
- 1918: Armistice ends First World War
- 1919: Influenza kills 500,000 Americans
- 1920: American women granted the vote
- 1923: More than 13 million cars on US roads
- 1923: Republican Calvin Coolidge becomes president after death of Warren Harding
- 1928: Republican Herbert Hoover elected president
- 1929: Wall Street Crash: collapse of US stock market leads to prolonged depression
- 1930–31: Over 3000 bank failures
- 1930: Introduction of Smoot-Hawley tariff leads to worsening of depression worldwide
- 1932: Democrat Franklin Roosevelt elected President
- 1933: NRA (National Recovery Administration) set up to regulate wage levels and child labour
- 1934–36: Mass migration of farmers from the Great Plains to California
- 1937: Roosevelt attempts to 'pack' Supreme Court to ensure passage of New Deal legislation
- 1941: Bombing of Pearl Harbor; US enters Second World War

Popular culture in the US

Developments in technology during the First World War improved communications throughout the US. By the 1920s virtually all of the nation was connected to the Bell Telephone network. Radio sets enabled news and information to reach even isolated areas. The cinema became the first mass entertainment industry. From small beginnings in the early 1900s, by the 1930s, the film industry in Hollywood was exporting its glamorous products worldwide. During the Depression, cheap cinema tickets kept audience numbers buoyant despite an initial downturn. Professional sports such as football, baseball, and boxing became of national interest for the first time, with huge attendances and highly-paid celebrities.

4 The major Hollywood studios in 1919

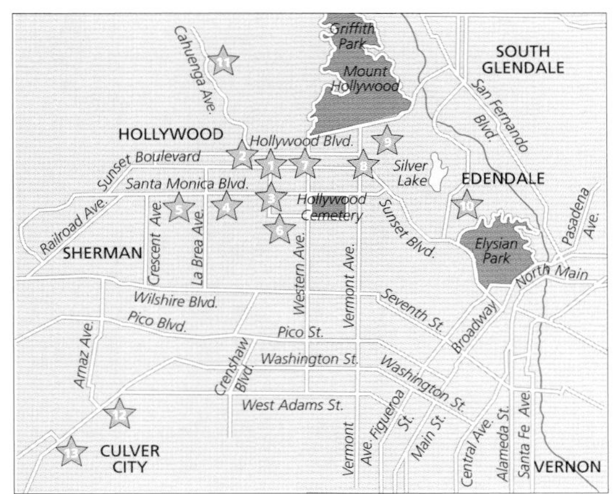

By 1919, most of the major film studios had established themselves to the north of Los Angeles. Hollywood became the heart of the world motion picture industry and a magnet for all aspiring film-makers.

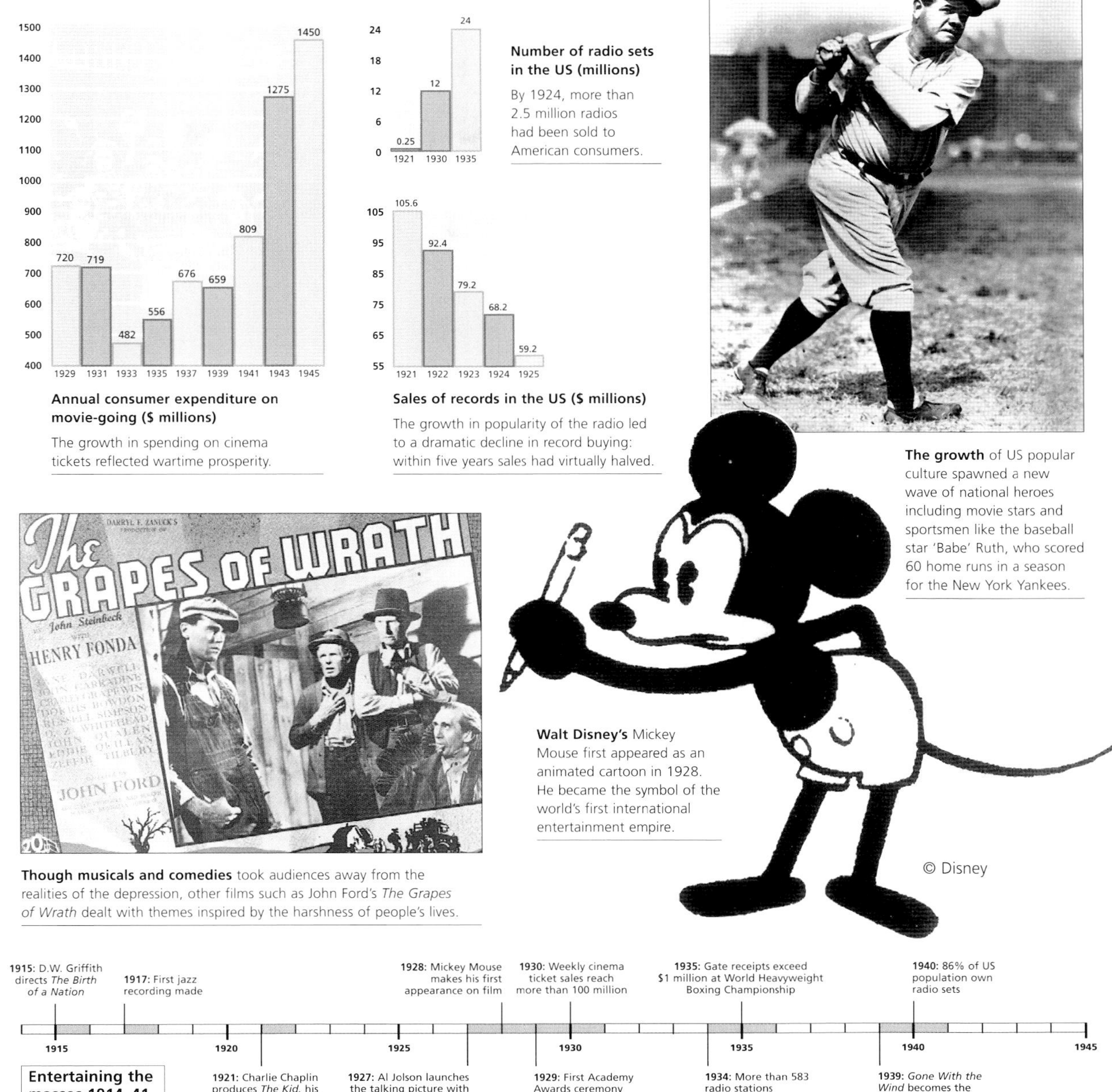

Annual consumer expenditure on movie-going ($ millions)

The growth in spending on cinema tickets reflected wartime prosperity.

Number of radio sets in the US (millions)

By 1924, more than 2.5 million radios had been sold to American consumers.

Sales of records in the US ($ millions)

The growth in popularity of the radio led to a dramatic decline in record buying: within five years sales had virtually halved.

The growth of US popular culture spawned a new wave of national heroes including movie stars and sportsmen like the baseball star 'Babe' Ruth, who scored 60 home runs in a season for the New York Yankees.

Walt Disney's Mickey Mouse first appeared as an animated cartoon in 1928. He became the symbol of the world's first international entertainment empire.

Though musicals and comedies took audiences away from the realities of the depression, other films such as John Ford's *The Grapes of Wrath* dealt with themes inspired by the harshness of people's lives.

Entertaining the masses 1914–41

- **1915:** D.W. Griffith directs *The Birth of a Nation*
- **1917:** First jazz recording made
- **1921:** Charlie Chaplin produces *The Kid*, his first full-length film
- **1927:** Al Jolson launches the talking picture with *The Jazz Singer*
- **1928:** Mickey Mouse makes his first appearance on film
- **1929:** First Academy Awards ceremony introduces the 'Oscar'
- **1930:** Weekly cinema ticket sales reach more than 100 million
- **1934:** More than 583 radio stations established nationwide
- **1935:** Gate receipts exceed $1 million at World Heavyweight Boxing Championship
- **1939:** *Gone With the Wind* becomes the highest-grossing film yet
- **1940:** 86% of US population own radio sets

1915 1920 1925 1930 1935 1940 1945

THE FDR EFFECT

The political complexion of the US altered radically during the 1930s. Hoover's Republican party, so dominant at the height of the '20s boom, was routed by the Democrats in 1932. The patrician Franklin Delano Roosevelt attracted a 'New Deal coalition' of Blacks, women, labour groups, and southern whites which dominated American politics for over 30 years.

Roosevelt spoke regularly to the American people via his 'fireside chats' which were broadcast on national radio.

5 Presidential elections

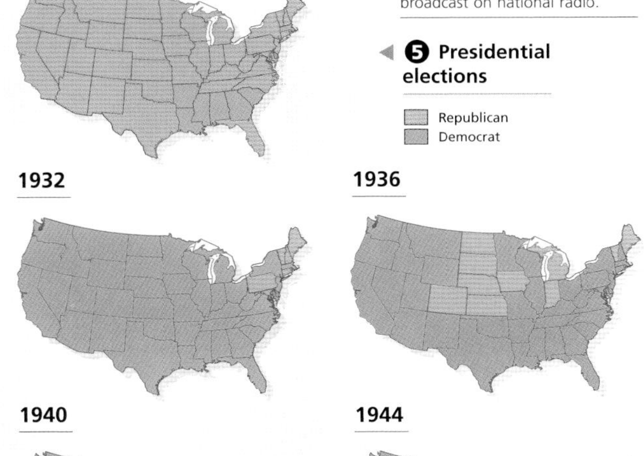

Intolerance

This period, particularly the 1920s, was marked by diverse displays of intolerance against perceived threats to the 'American Way of Life'. 'New' immigrants, black migration, the increased freedom of women, and economic instability all fuelled anxieties. The prohibition of alcohol, immigration 'Quota Acts', and the formation of the FBI in response to the 'Red Scare' of 1919–20 and the fear of Communism, were official responses to this new intolerance. Other – unofficial – reactions included race riots in the southern states and Midwest and the revival of the white supremacist Ku Klux Klan whose membership increased to more than two million in the 1920s.

The growth of the Ku Klux Klan in this period was largely an expression of insecurity among small-town White Anglo-Saxon Protestants towards a multitude of apparent threats to their power and influence.

6 Racial intolerance 1914–41

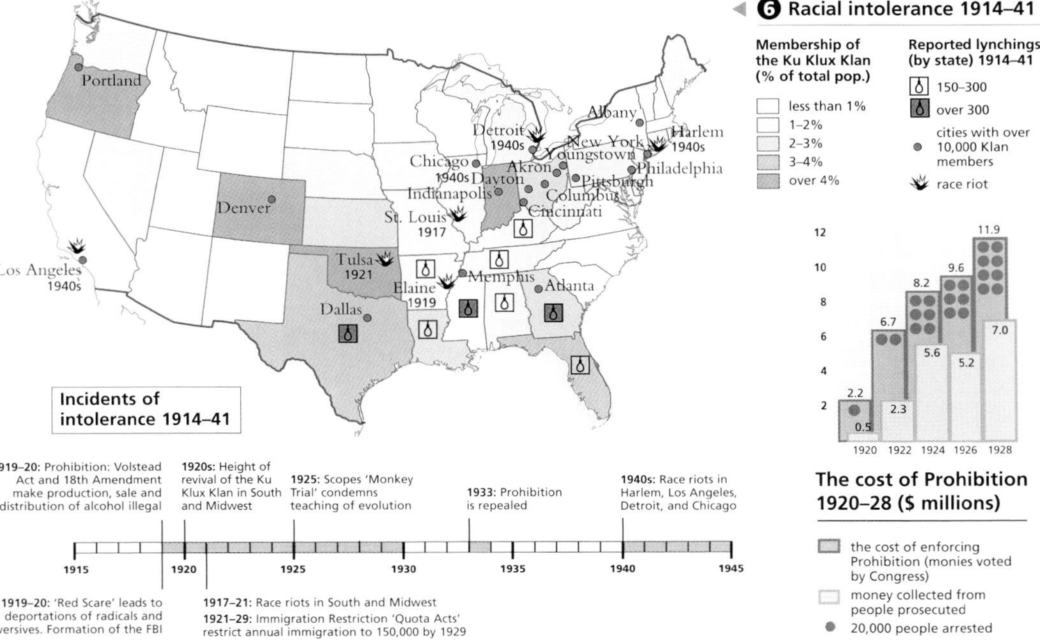

The cost of Prohibition 1920–28 ($ millions)

- the cost of enforcing Prohibition (monies voted by Congress)
- money collected from people prosecuted
- 20,000 people arrested

Incidents of intolerance 1914–41

- **1917–21:** Race riots in South and Midwest
- **1919–20:** Prohibition: Volstead Act and 18th Amendment make production, sale and distribution of alcohol illegal
- **1919–20:** 'Red Scare' leads to deportations of radicals and subversives. Formation of the FBI
- **1920s:** Height of revival of the Ku Klux Klan in South and Midwest
- **1921–29:** Immigration Restriction 'Quota Acts' restrict annual immigration to 150,000 by 1929
- **1925:** Scopes 'Monkey Trial' condemns teaching of evolution
- **1933:** Prohibition is repealed
- **1940s:** Race riots in Harlem, Los Angeles, Detroit, and Chicago

1915 1920 1925 1930 1935 1940 1945

SOCIETIES IN TRANSITION

Martin Luther King harnessed the spontaneous protests of the 1950s to create a massive anti-racial movement.

IN THE 1950S, THE UNITED STATES was labelled 'the affluent society'. This phrase reflected the experience of unprecedented economic prosperity and social progress in the years since the Second World War ended the Great Depression. Most Americans enjoyed rising incomes on the back of the postwar boom. The quality of life was further enhanced by the availability of new consumer goods, new leisure opportunities, and suburban housing. The people of Mexico, Central America, and the Caribbean continued to have a much lower standard of living than the US and Canada. And within the US, itself, not all regions and social groups experienced equal advances in affluence and status.

Postwar prosperity in the US

The idealized family unit, headed by a male breadwinner, became a favourite image for advertisers and politicians during the 1950s.

The economic stimulus provided by the war and, later, the arms race with the Soviet Union were key factors in creating the affluence of the immediate postwar decades. As manufacturing switched to a peacetime mode, consumer durables flowed into the domestic marketplace. Consumerism generated a flourishing service sector. America's position at the hub of the international trading system gave her access to foreign markets and raw materials crucial to economic success. The boom ended in the early 1970s, with the Vietnam War and the energy crisis producing prolonged inflation and recession. Europe and Japan were also challenging American economic dominance.

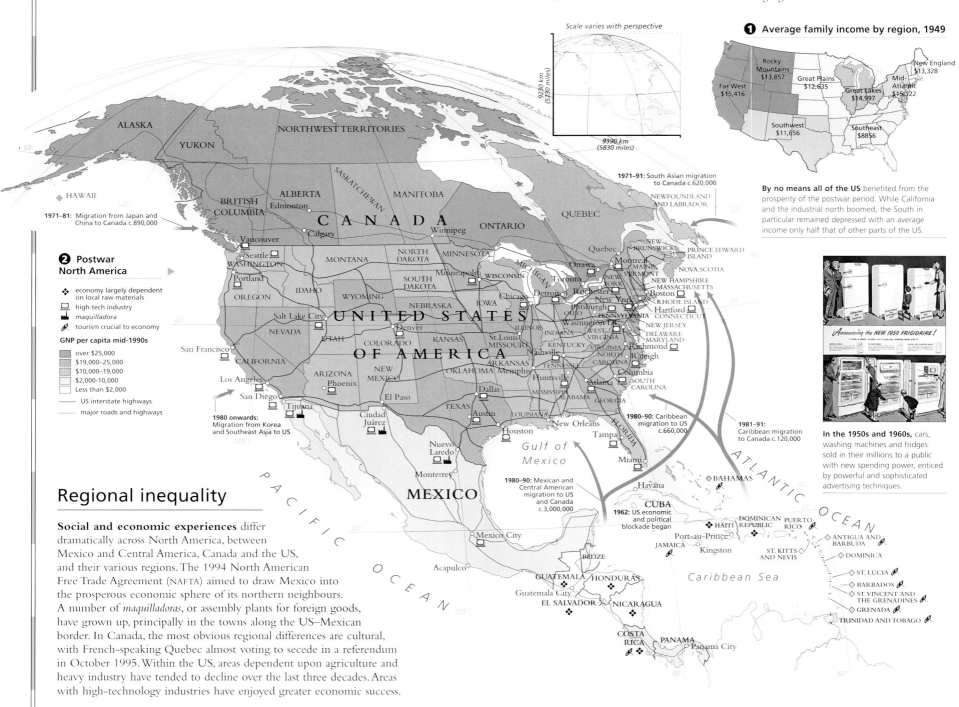

Scale varies with perspective

9230 km (5730 miles)

9390 km (5830 miles)

1 Average family income by region, 1949

Rocky Mountains $13,857
Far West $15,416
Great Plains $12,635
Great Lakes $14,997
Mid-Atlantic $15,122
New England $13,328
Southwest $11,656
Southeast $8856

By no means all of the US benefited from the prosperity of the postwar period. While California and the industrial north boomed, the South in particular remained depressed with an average income only half that of other parts of the US.

2 Postwar North America

- economy largely dependent on local raw materials
- high-tech industry
- *maquilladora*
- tourism crucial to economy

GNP per capita mid-1990s

- over $25,000
- $19,000–25,000
- $10,000–19,000
- $2,000–10,000
- Less than $2,000
- US interstate highways
- major roads and highways

1971–81: Migration from Japan and China to Canada c.890,000

1971–91: South Asian migration to Canada c.620,000

1980 onwards: Migration from Korea and Southeast Asia to US

1980–90: Caribbean migration to US c.660,000

1981–91: Caribbean migration to Canada c.120,000

1980–90: Mexican and Central American migration to US and Canada c.3,000,000

1962: US economic and political blockade began

Announcing the NEW 1950 FRIGIDAIRE!

In the 1950s and 1960s, cars, washing machines and fridges sold in their millions to a public with new spending power, enticed by powerful and sophisticated advertising techniques.

Regional inequality

Social and economic experiences differ dramatically across North America, between Mexico and Central America, Canada and the US, and their various regions. The 1994 North American Free Trade Agreement (NAFTA) aimed to draw Mexico into the prosperous economic sphere of its northern neighbours. A number of *maquilladoras*, or assembly plants for foreign goods, have grown up, principally in the towns along the US–Mexican border. In Canada, the most obvious regional differences are cultural, with French-speaking Quebec almost voting to secede in a referendum in October 1995. Within the US, areas dependent upon agriculture and heavy industry have tended to decline over the last three decades. Areas with high-technology industries have enjoyed greater economic success.

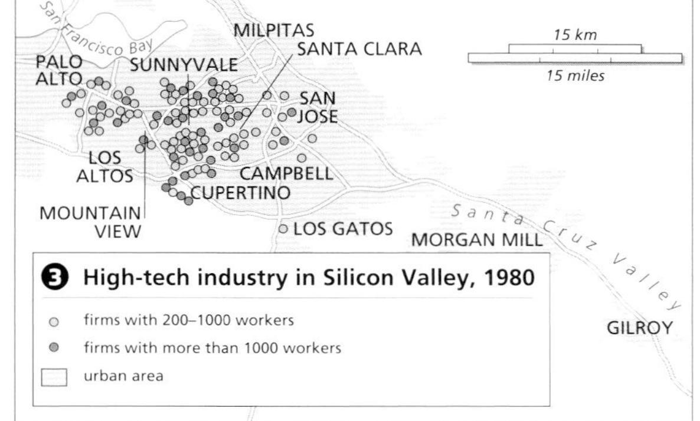

SILICON VALLEY

Without specific locational needs, many high-tech firms were able to site their businesses in non-urban areas in the South and West, helping to revitalize the economy of these regions. Silicon Valley near San Francisco, California, contains one of the world's highest concentrations of computing and electronic industries. Initially, many high-tech manufacturers relied upon contracts from the US military, but the age of the personal computer has allowed these manufacturers to play a key role in sustaining American exports and growth.

New high-tech industries including aerospace and electronics, as at Silicon Valley *(right)*, grew up in the late 1970s to fill the gaps left by the decline of traditional US heavy industries.

Changes in urban life

As black Americans migrated from the rural South to urban centres in the 1940s and 1950s, many whites abandoned city life for the suburbs. These areas became increasingly detached from the cities; instead of petitioning for access to the cities' municipal facilities, postwar suburban residents fought fiercely against annexation proposals. The tax dollars of prosperous whites were no longer available to maintain the city infrastructure. The financial crisis was made worse by the decline of traditional US industries, and many of America's cities sank into crisis during the 1960s and 1970s. Housing stock deteriorated, roads were not repaired, and poverty, crime, and racial tension were common features of many urban areas in the US. Poverty was not confined to the inner cities: people in rural areas in the deep South, and the Appalachians were some of the most deprived in the US.

The centres of many of America's great cities declined physically as people move to the suburbs. Old housing stock was torn down but not replaced, and the infrastructure declined through lack of funding.

The new suburbs provided a safe haven away from the cities. Mortgage assistance was readily available to those wishing to move to suburban areas. Until the 1960s, money was siphoned into the suburbs by federal housing officials, who simultaneously denied loans to people still living in urban areas.

The growth of the suburbs

The 1950s saw the growth of suburban America. New construction techniques lowered the cost of new homes, and expressways improved access to and from urban centres. In the postwar era, cities like Chicago absorbed ever more of their surrounding areas.

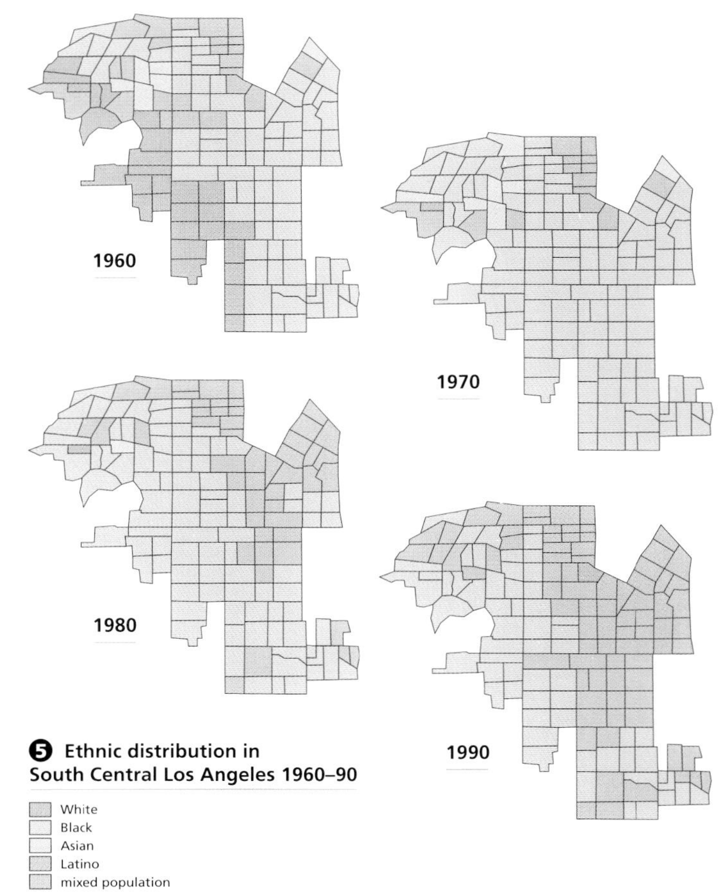

Poverty and ethnic balance in inner city Los Angeles

Los Angeles demonstrates how wealth and poverty live separate lives in postwar urban America. The central neighbourhoods in an otherwise prosperous city have a massively disproportionate number of poor residents, with an ethnic mix in constant flux. In 1960, a substantial white population remained in South Central Los Angeles. By 1970, whites had largely left the area, which had a now predominantly black population. Twenty years later, Latinos formed a majority in many South Central neighbourhoods.

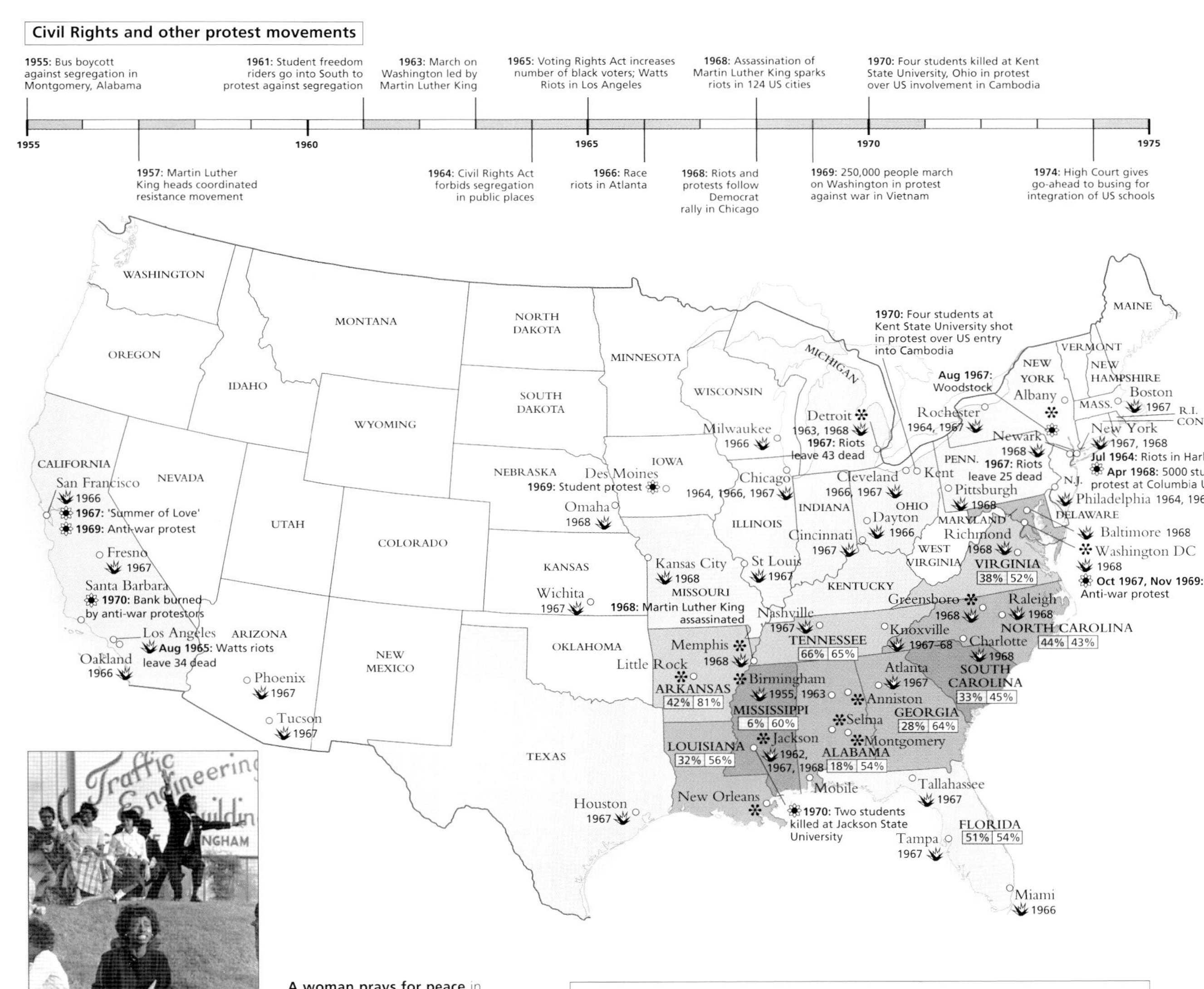

A woman prays for peace in Birmingham, Alabama, during a Civil Rights protest in May 1963, as fellow demonstrators dance and sing behind her.

In August 1969, 400,000 people gathered at a farm near Bethel in upper New York state to form the 'Woodstock Nation', a music festival which was also a celebration of peaceful, anti-establishment co-existence.

Moves for freedom

The opportunities presented by postwar America were denied to many black Americans, particularly in the still-segregated South, where they were prevented by whites from voting. Inspired by decolonization movements abroad, and aided by a 1954 Supreme Court judgement that segregation was unconstitutional, black Americans began to challenge discrimination. In 1955, a bus boycott in Montgomery, Alabama forced the bus company to end segregation. The success inspired similar protests throughout the South. In 1964 and 1965, the US Congress passed legislation banning racial discrimination and protecting the democratic rights of all Americans. The 1960s also saw a rise in political consciousness among other groups; protests against the Vietnam War grew in number throughout the late 1960s, as did the movement for women's rights.

THE USA: GROWTH OF A SUPERPOWER

John F. Kennedy, a charismatic and popular US president, was assassinated in 1963.

THE JAPANESE ATTACK on Pearl Harbor in December 1941 and the subsequent US entry into the Second World War caused a shift in the US view of the world. Thereafter, through alliances, military interventions, and trade, the United States dominated world affairs. Although challenged by the Cuban Revolution in 1959, the US maintained its position in the Americas, a secure base from which to fight the Cold War. The collapse of the Soviet Union in 1991 left the US as the world's only superpower. After the atrocities of 11 September 2001, the US embarked on a new phase of unilateralist interventionism, determined to stamp out terrorist and other threats to US security.

America and the world

During the Second World War, the US established military bases around the world, which remained important throughout the Cold War with the Soviet Union. The Cold War also encouraged the US to form alliances, such as the North Atlantic Treaty Organization (NATO) of 1949. After the Vietnam War, the US retreated from international politics, but the Soviet invasion of Afghanistan in 1979 revived the Cold War for another decade. With the collapse of the Soviet Union in 1991, the US was left as the sole superpower. After 11 September 2001, the United States took on a more assertive and unilateralist role in international affairs.

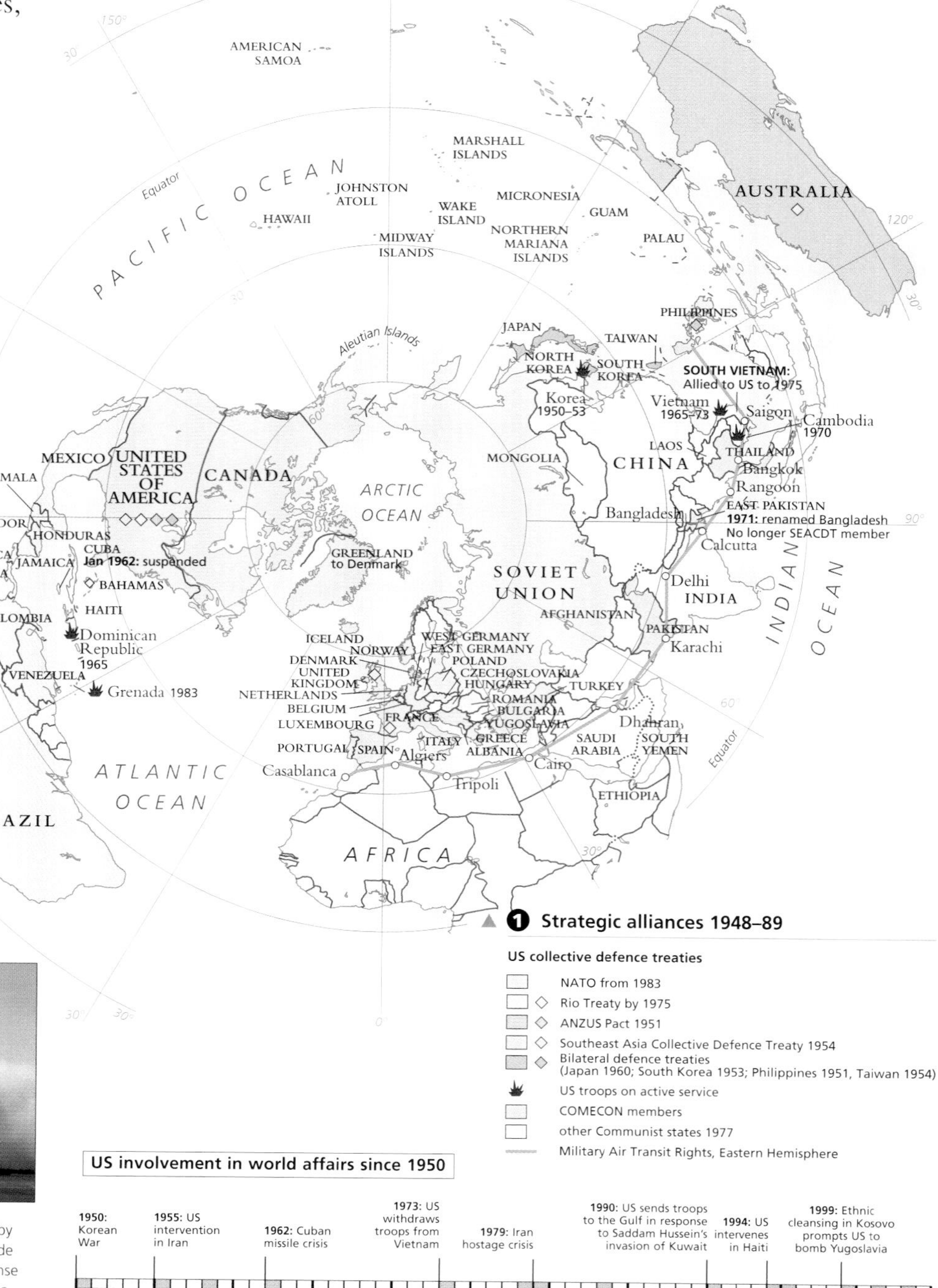

1 Strategic alliances 1948–89

US collective defence treaties
- NATO from 1983
- Rio Treaty by 1975
- ANZUS Pact 1951
- Southeast Asia Collective Defence Treaty 1954
- Bilateral defence treaties (Japan 1960; South Korea 1953; Philippines 1951, Taiwan 1954)
- US troops on active service
- COMECON members
- other Communist states 1977
- Military Air Transit Rights, Eastern Hemisphere

US soldiers with a Viet Cong suspect during the Vietnam War (1950–73), the longest and most costly of US attempts to contain the perceived Communist threat during the Cold War.

On 11 September 2001, two aircraft hijacked by Muslim terrorists were flown into the World Trade Center, New York, killing over 2,700. The response of US President George W. Bush was to declare a 'War on Terror', stepping up security at home and invading Afghanistan (2001) and Iraq (2003).

US involvement in world affairs since 1950

- **1950:** Korean War
- **1950:** Start of US involvement in Vietnam
- **1955:** US intervention in Iran
- **1958:** Eisenhower Doctrine commits US to prevent spread of Communism in Middle East
- **1962:** Cuban missile crisis
- **1973:** US withdraws troops from Vietnam
- **1973:** US assists in right-wing coup in Chile
- **1978:** US-brokered peace deal between Egypt and Israel
- **1979:** Iran hostage crisis
- **1983:** US intervention in Grenada
- **1990:** US sends troops to the Gulf in response to Saddam Hussein's invasion of Kuwait
- **1994:** US intervenes in Haiti
- **1995:** US troops withdraw from Somalia after failing to restore democracy
- **1999:** Ethnic cleansing in Kosovo prompts US to bomb Yugoslavia
- **2001:** Taliban ousted in Afghanistan by US-led forces
- **2003:** US leads invasion of Iraq

US investment overseas

During the Cold War, investment overseas was seen as a way to bind other nations to the capitalist sphere. The Marshall Plan of 1948 aimed both to aid the postwar recovery of Western Europe and reduce the chances of Communist subversion. American firms also tried to secure access to valuable raw materials, most importantly oil in the Middle East. Since the end of the Cold War, US investment in Western Europe has grown significantly, as American companies have sought industrial partnerships and a share of the growing European economy.

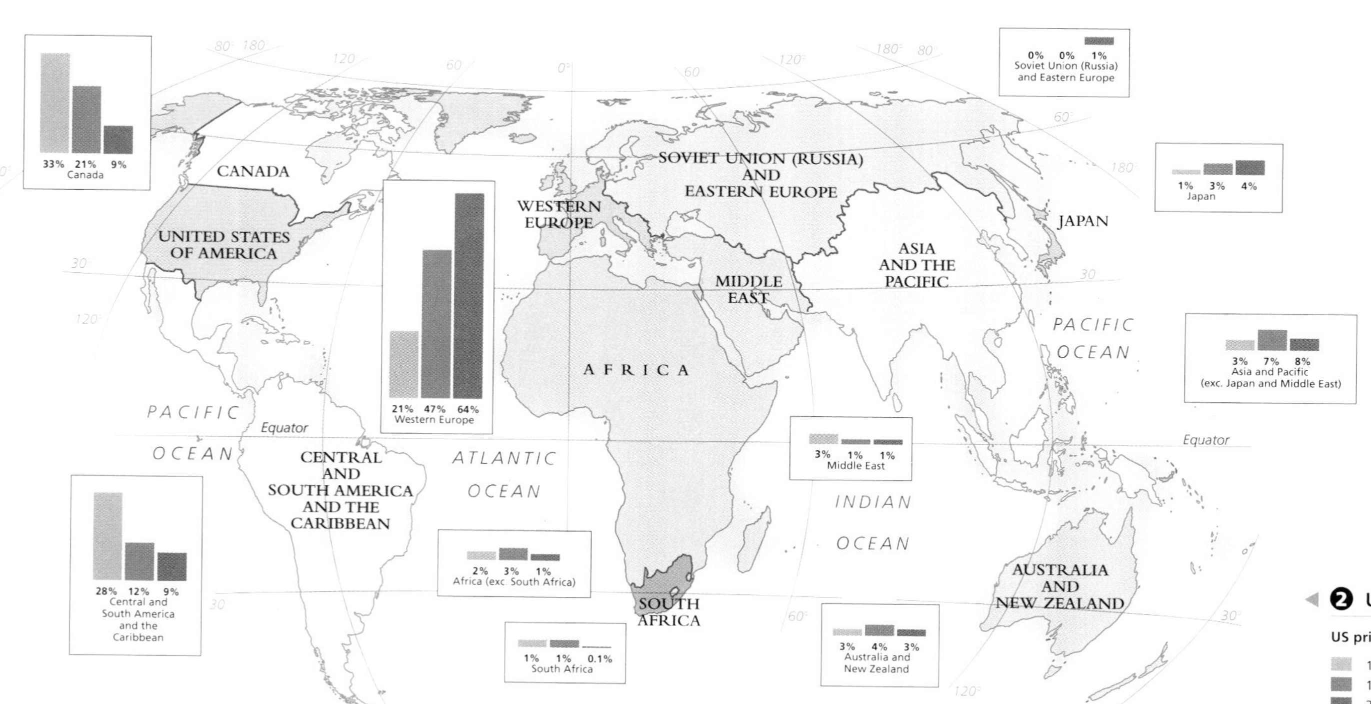

2 US investment overseas

US private direct investment abroad
- 1960
- 1984
- 2003

The decline of the Democratic South

The migration of Southern blacks to northern cities in the 1940s and 1950s killed off most of the remaining cotton plantations in the South, which had depended on their cheap labour, leading to a decline in the Southern economy. In the North, black Americans became an important political constituency. The Democratic Party tried to reconcile its desire for their votes with its desire for the continued support of white Southerners who traditionally voted Democrat. By the late 1960s, after the Civil Rights legislation of President Lyndon Johnson, many Southerners abandoned their traditional commitment to the Democratic Party.

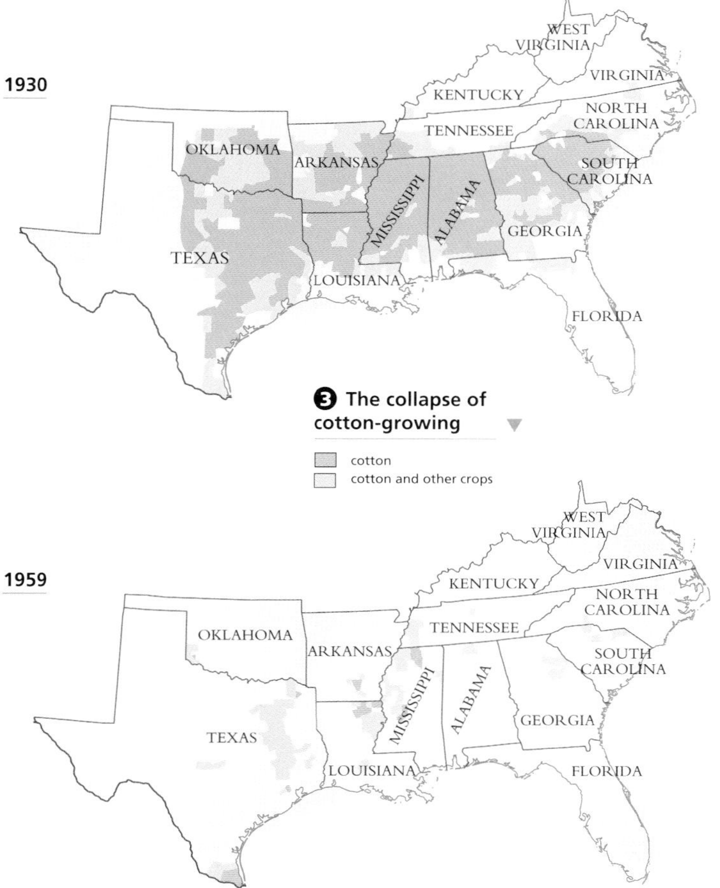

3 The collapse of cotton-growing

cotton
cotton and other crops

KEY ELECTIONS 1948–2000

In 1948 Democrat President Harry Truman won a shock victory over the Republican Thomas Dewey. However, the success of the pro-segregationist States Rights Party indicated that the Democrats might have problems maintaining the support of both blacks and Southerners, and in 1968 the Democrats lost every Southern state except Texas. Though Republicans held the Presidency throughout the 1980s, the elections of 1992 and 1996 proved that the Democrats could still win despite a largely Republican South. The 2000 election was the most controversial for over a century. Republican George W. Bush secured a smaller share of the popular vote (49.8 million) than his Democrat rival, Al Gore (50.2 million). Only when the bitterly disputed result for Florida finally went his way did Bush win the Presidency on the votes of the states in the electoral college (271 votes to 267).

The Chicago Daily Tribune was so confident of the outcome of the 1948 US Presidential elections that the paper was printed without confirmation of the results, leaving the victorious Democratic candidate Harry Truman to revel in the premature headline.

George W. Bush had to wait five weeks after the election in 2000 before his opponent, Al Gore, conceded. All depended on the extremely close result in Florida, where, amid a flurry of legal actions, votes were counted and recounted manually until the US Supreme Court stepped in to call a halt.

1948

1968

Alaska
Hawaii

2000

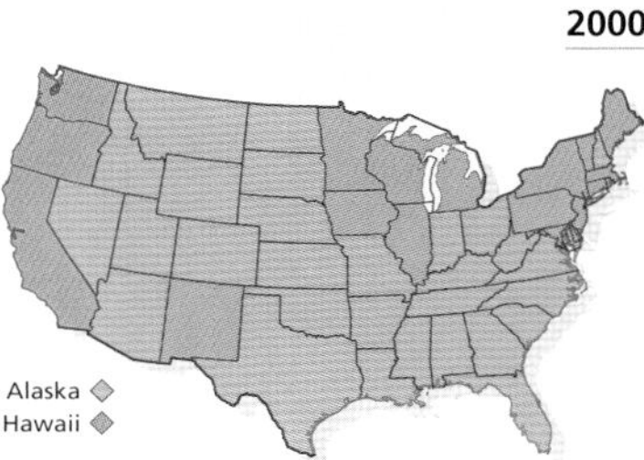

Alaska
Hawaii

4 Presidential elections

States won by each party

Republicans
Democrats
States Rights
American Independent

US election results 1944–2000

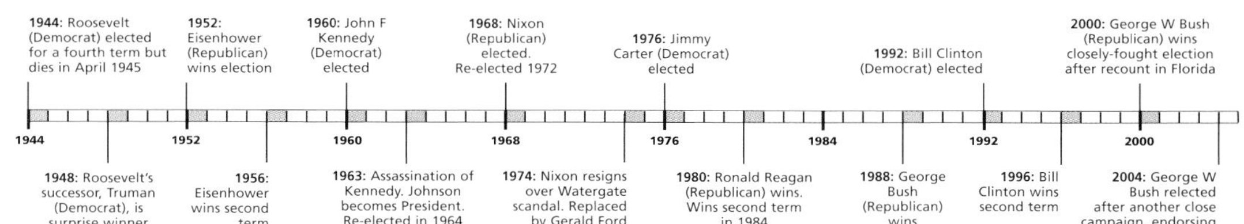

US intervention in Central America

Historically the US has acted under the 'Monroe Doctrine' to ensure stability and protect its business interests in Central America. During the Cold War, the US feared Communist subversion in its own backyard. In 1954, US agents organized the downfall of a left-wing government in Guatemala. In 1962, a crisis over Soviet nuclear arms in Cuba *(see p.108)* almost caused nuclear war. During the 1980s, President Reagan acted against leftists in Grenada and Nicaragua. After the Cold War, the US became more constructively engaged in combating the drugs trade in the region.

The Sandinista revolution of 1978 put an end to more than 40 years of military dictatorship in Nicaragua. The left-wing Sandinistas were distrusted by the US which sponsored Contra guerrillas based in Honduras *(left)* against the government.

US military advisors have been active, often working with the Drug Enforcement Administration (DEA), in training local troups in many Central and South American countries since its invasion of Panama in 1989.

5 US intervention in Central America and the Caribbean

Cuban-sponsored guerrilla activities 1959–68
US intervention

UNITED STATES OF AMERICA
US exploitation of cheap Mexican labour in free trade zone (see p.136)
Gulf of Mexico
ATLANTIC OCEAN
Tropic of Cancer
MEXICO
1980s: Serious economic difficulties
1993–94: NAFTA creates free-trade community of US, Mexico, and Canada
1999: Agreement with US to counter drugs-trafficking
BELIZE
1978–90: Staging area for anti-Sandinista rebel army (Contras) organized and financed by US
GUATEMALA
1954: Military, with US backing topples democratic government pledged to land and social reforms
1961: Appearance of revolutionaries
1968–70: US ambassador and military advisors killed by rebels
1980s–90s: Ongoing guerrilla activity
HONDURAS
EL SALVADOR
1960s: The 'model' of the Alliance for Progress
1970: First revolutionaries appear
1991: Right-wing government and opposition leaders sign unbrokered peace treaty
1990s: Continued reliance on US aid; heavy influence of US ambassador
2001: Adopts US $ as official currency
NICARAGUA
1961: FSLN (Sandinista) rebels appear
1978: Sandinista revolution
1982–83: US finances guerrilla army fighting leftist Sandinista government
1990: Anti-Sandinista coalition wins election
2002: US agrees to resume military aid to Nicaraguan armed forces in their campaign against smuggling and terrorism
COSTA RICA
PANAMA
1959, 1964: Anti-US riots
1978: Panama Canal Treaties
Dec 1989: US invades Panama to capture General Noriega
1999: US returns control of Panama Canal to government of Panama
PACIFIC OCEAN
Equator
CUBA
1961: Attempted invasion at Bay of Pigs by US-supported forces
1962: Cuban Missile Crisis
Apr–Sep 1980: Migration of thousands of Cubans to US
1990: Severe economic distress following withdrawal of Soviet aid
2001: First US-Cuba trade agreement since 1962
2003: US government launches Commission for Assistance to a Free Cuba
BAHAMAS
Guantanamo Bay to US
JAMAICA
HAITI
1991: Ongoing unrest; military coup ousts elected government
2004: US troops assist in the removal of President Jean-Bertrand Aristide
DOMINICAN REPUBLIC
1961: Assassination of President Trujillo
1965: US President Johnson intervenes with 22,000 troops
PUERTO RICO to US
Caribbean Sea
ST. KITTS AND NEVIS
ANTIGUA AND BARBUDA
DOMINICA
ST. VINCENT AND THE GRENADINES
ST. LUCIA
BARBADOS
GRENADA
Oct 1983: Radical left-wing government overthrown by US intervention
TRINIDAD AND TOBAGO
Caracas
COLOMBIA
1980s/1990s: Flow of drugs to US causes serious crime
2000: US launches 'Plan Colombia' to tackle drugs and violence
VENEZUELA
GUYANA
ECUADOR

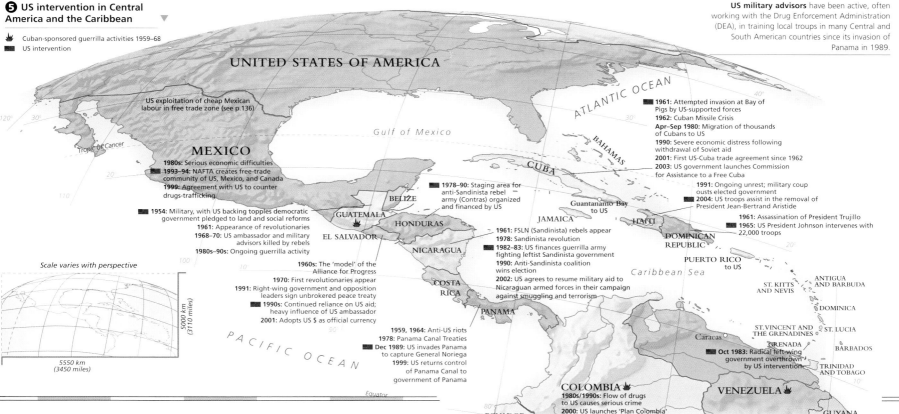

Scale varies with perspective
5550 km (3450 miles)
5000 km (3110 miles)

SOUTH AMERICA
REGIONAL HISTORY

THE HISTORICAL LANDSCAPE

THE LAST CONTINENT – APART FROM ANTARCTICA – to be colonized by humans, (the first settlers arrived from North America no more than 13,000 years ago), South America remains a realm of harsh extremes of climate, environment, and human society. The cordillera spine of the Andes was the heartland of the first complex societies and civilizations. Early settlers spread through the fertile tracts of the Amazon Basin, but few ventured to the sterile salt pans of the Atacama Desert – one of the driest places on Earth – or Patagonia – one of the least hospitable. European contact in the 16th century brought, as elsewhere in the Americas, the decline of indigenous cultures, although here widespread intermarriage and the enforced importation of African slaves to work on plantations created an extraordinarily varied genetic, linguistic, and cultural pool. The continent struggled free of European colonialism in the 19th century only to be confronted by the challenge of economic, social, and political modernization, which was met with varying success. This process brought wealth for some, marginalization for many – especially in the continent's burgeoning but scattered centres of population – and a threat to the global ecosystem, as the resources of the Amazonian wilderness were increasingly placed under pressure.

The Andes were one of the sites of the earliest agricultural civilizations in South America, perhaps as much as 10,000 years ago. The mountains and temperate climate provided a wide range of habitats for wild plants. Tubers – such as potatoes and sweet potatoes – grew naturally and were simple to cultivate.

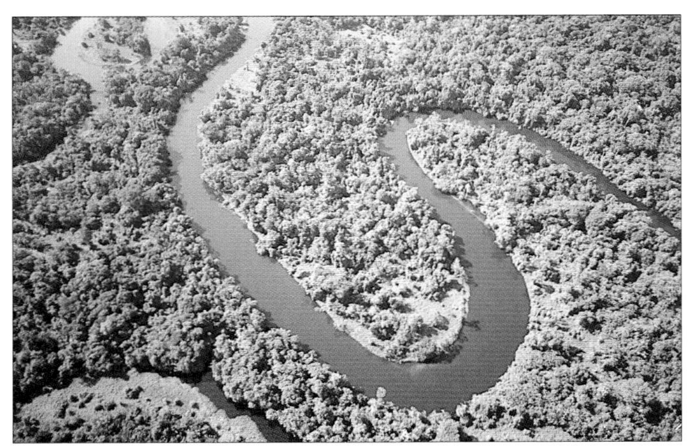

The Amazon rainforests now cover about 5,300,000 sq km of South America. At the height of the last Ice Age around 18,000 years ago, the cool arid climate, unsuitable for rainforest plants, had reduced the forest to only about 10% of its present area. Over the past 10,000 years, wetter climates have enabled the forest to grow in size.

The flat grassland plains of the pampas of southeastern South America were mainly desert during the era covered by the map *(opposite)*. Higher levels of rainfall have allowed grasslands to develop, but the area remains dry, and has always been a region of low human population.

Vegetation type

- ice cap and glacier
- tundra
- polar and alpine desert
- semi-desert or sparsely vegetate
- grassland
- forest or open woodland
- tropical rainforest
- temperate desert
- tropical desert
- coastline (present-day)
- coastline (18,000 years ago)

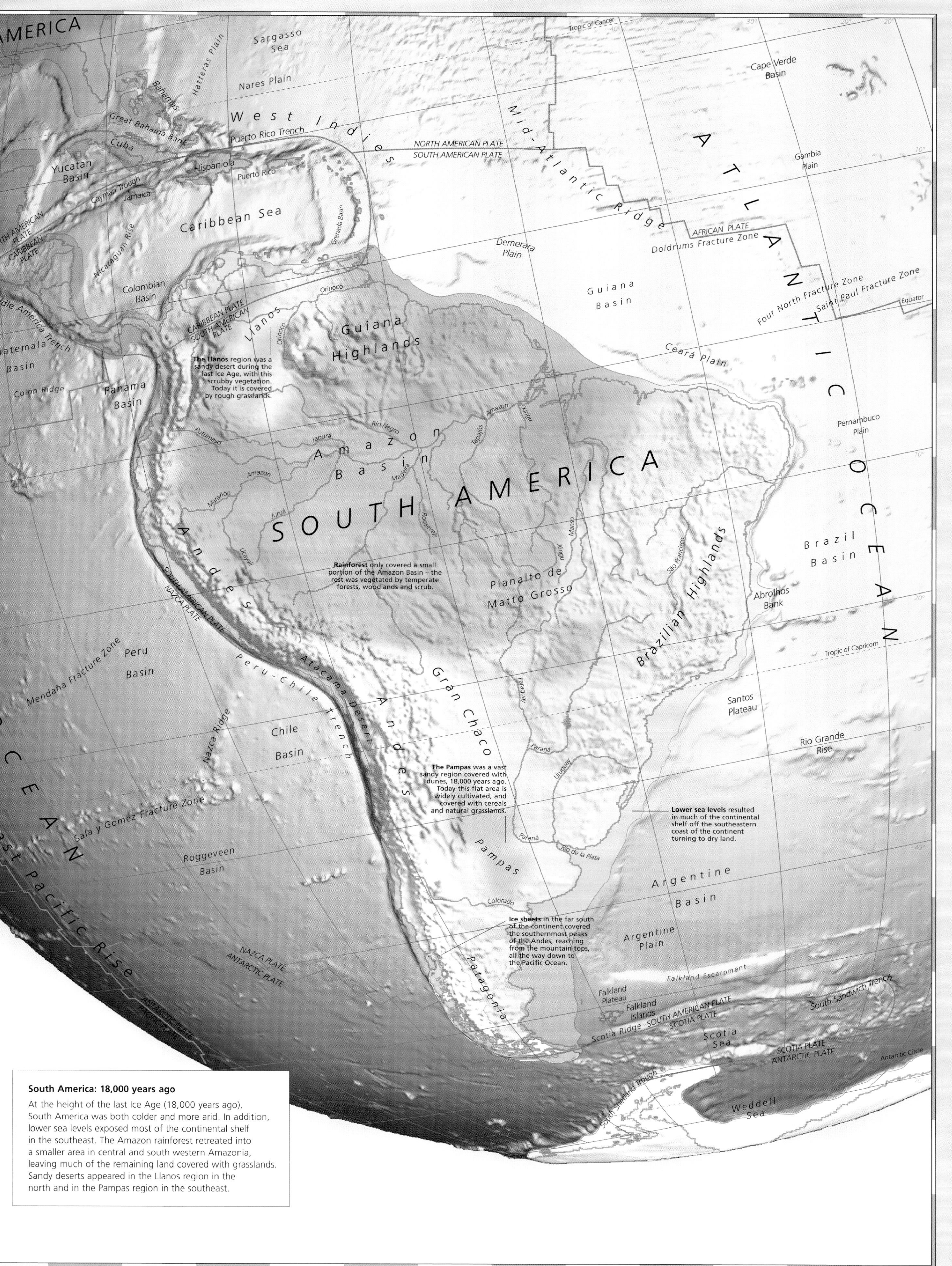

South America: 18,000 years ago

At the height of the last Ice Age (18,000 years ago), South America was both colder and more arid. In addition, lower sea levels exposed most of the continental shelf in the southeast. The Amazon rainforest retreated into a smaller area in central and south western Amazonia, leaving much of the remaining land covered with grasslands. Sandy deserts appeared in the Llanos region in the north and in the Pampas region in the southeast.

SOUTH AMERICA

EXPLORATION AND MAPPING

The name America was coined to honor Amerigo Vespucci, an Italian explorer in the service of Portugal.

THOUGH THE INCAS left no maps, their Andean empire's extensive road system was testimony to their topographical skills. It was a long time before any Europeans had a similar understanding of the continent. When Columbus first sighted the South American coast in 1498, he realized he had found a continental landmass, but thought it was part of Asia. This was disproved by the voyages of Vespucci and others along the Atlantic coast, culminating in Ferdinand Magellan's reaching the Pacific in 1520. In the wake of Pizarro's conquest of Peru and theft of the Incas' gold, many explorers were fired by dreams of instant riches. The net products of most expeditions, however, were the alienation of native tribes and the spread of European killer diseases. From the mid-17th century to the late 18th century, when serious scientific surveys began, exploration was largely the preserve of intrepid missionaries, notably the Jesuits, and slave-raiders from Brazil.

European conquerors and explorers

Throughout the first two decades of the 16th century Portuguese and Spanish explorers of the Atlantic coast sailed into every wide estuary in the hope that it would prove to be a passage to the Indies. Magellan eventually demonstrated that such a route existed, but it proved impracticable for the purpose of trade with the East. As a result, the Atlantic coastal regions of the continent were soon well understood and mapped, further information coming from Portuguese traders who sailed there in search of brazil wood, a tree that produced a valuable red dye and gave its name to the region. In the Andes, Pizarro, Benalcázar, and their fellow *conquistadores* were able to follow the well-maintained roads of the Inca Empire; but in most other parts of the continent, expeditions were forced back by hostile indigenous peoples, trackless swamps and forests, or impassable rapids.

This detail from a map of South America produced by John Rotz in 1542 shows Native Americans carrying logs of brazil wood for trade with Europeans.

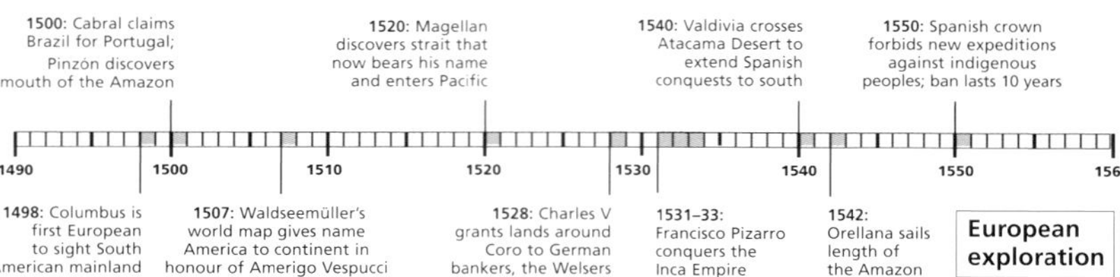

1500: Cabral claims Brazil for Portugal; Pinzón discovers mouth of the Amazon
1520: Magellan discovers strait that now bears his name and enters Pacific
1540: Valdivia crosses Atacama Desert to extend Spanish conquests to south
1550: Spanish crown forbids new expeditions against indigenous peoples; ban lasts 10 years
1490
1500
1510
1520
1530
1540
1550
1560
1498: Columbus is first European to sight South American mainland
1507: Waldseemüller's world map gives name America to continent in honour of Amerigo Vespucci
1528: Charles V grants lands around Coro to German bankers, the Welsers
1531–33: Francisco Pizarro conquers the Inca Empire
1542: Orellana sails length of the Amazon
European exploration

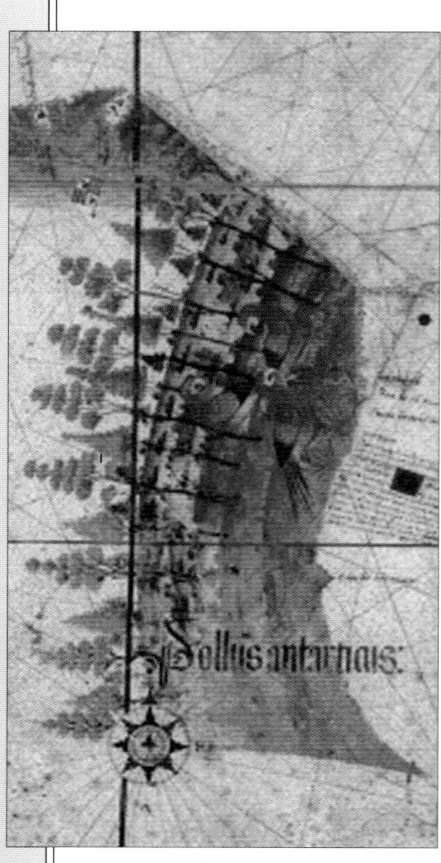

The Cantino planisphere, the earliest known map showing South America, was produced in Lisbon in 1502. It shows part of Brazil and the line agreed by the Treaty of Tordesillas in 1494, dividing the world between Portugal and Spain.

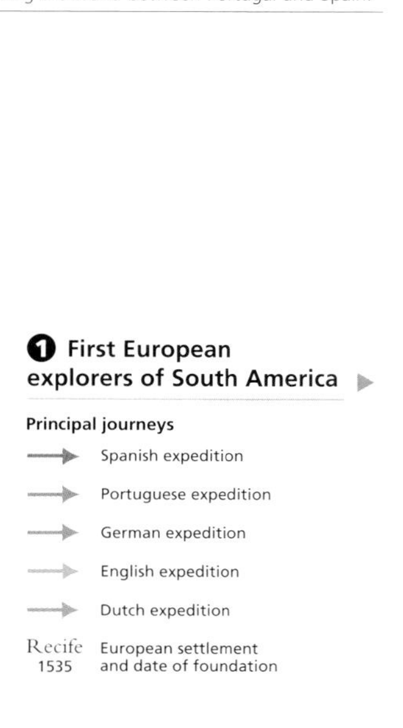

1 First European explorers of South America
Principal journeys
Spanish expedition
Portuguese expedition
German expedition
English expedition
Dutch expedition
Recife 1535 European settlement and date of foundation

ATLANTIC OCEAN
Caribbean Sea
Hispaniola
PACIFIC OCEAN
1498: Columbus anchors in Gulf of Paria
Christopher Columbus 3rd voyage 1498
Jiménez de Quesada 1536–37
Santa Marta 1525
Coro 1527
Panama 1519
Nikolaus Federmann 1537–39
Diego de Ordás 1531–32
Santa Fé de Bogotá 1539
Vicente Yáñez Pinzón 1499–1500
Guiana Highlands
1542: Orellana, detached from expedition led by Gonzalo de Pizarro, decides to sail down Amazon
Francisco de Orellana 1541–42
Quito 1534
Sebastián Benalcázar 1533–39
Galapagos Islands
Tomás de Berlanga 1535
1535: Berlanga, Bishop of Panama, sights Galapagos
Cajamarca
Francisco Pizarro 1531–33
1533: Pizarro captures Inca Capital, Cuzco
Lima 1535
Cuzco
Recife 1535
Bahia 1549
1543: Irala's party first to cross southern half of continent
Planalto de Mato Grosso
Brazilian Highlands
La Plata 1538
Potosí 1545
Pedro de Valdivia 1540–53
Diego de Almagro 1535–37
Francis Drake 1577–80
Domingo Martinez de Irala 1543–48
Álvar Núñez Cabeza de Vaca 1541–42
Gran Chaco
Willem Schouten and Jacob le Maire 1615–16
1500: Cabral makes accidental landfall on journey to India
Pedro Álvares Cabral 1500
Juan Díaz de Solís 1515–16
Amerigo Vespucci 3rd voyage 1501–02
Pedro Álvares Cabral 1500
Francis Drake 1577–80
Ferdinand Magellan 1519–21
Cape Verde Islands
Equator
Tropic of Capricorn
Ferdinand Magellan 1519–21
Francisco de Aguirre 1553–65
Sebastian Cabot 1528
1520: Magellan crosses Pacific in first circumnavigation of the world
Santiago 1541
1502: Vespucci reaches point that he calls San Julian; exact location is uncertain
River Plate
Buenos Aires 1536
Pampas
1553: Valdivia killed in battle with Araucanians
Amerigo Vespucci 3rd voyage 1501–02
1516: Diaz de Solís is first to reach mouth of River Plate, where he is killed by native Americans
Patagonia
Andes
1000 km
1000 miles
Falkland Islands
Strait of Magellan
1520: Magellan reaches Pacific after perilous 7-week journey through strait
Tierra del Fuego
South Georgia
1578: Drake, blown south by gales, is first to sight Cape Horn
Cape Horn
1616: Schouten names cape after his home town of Horn

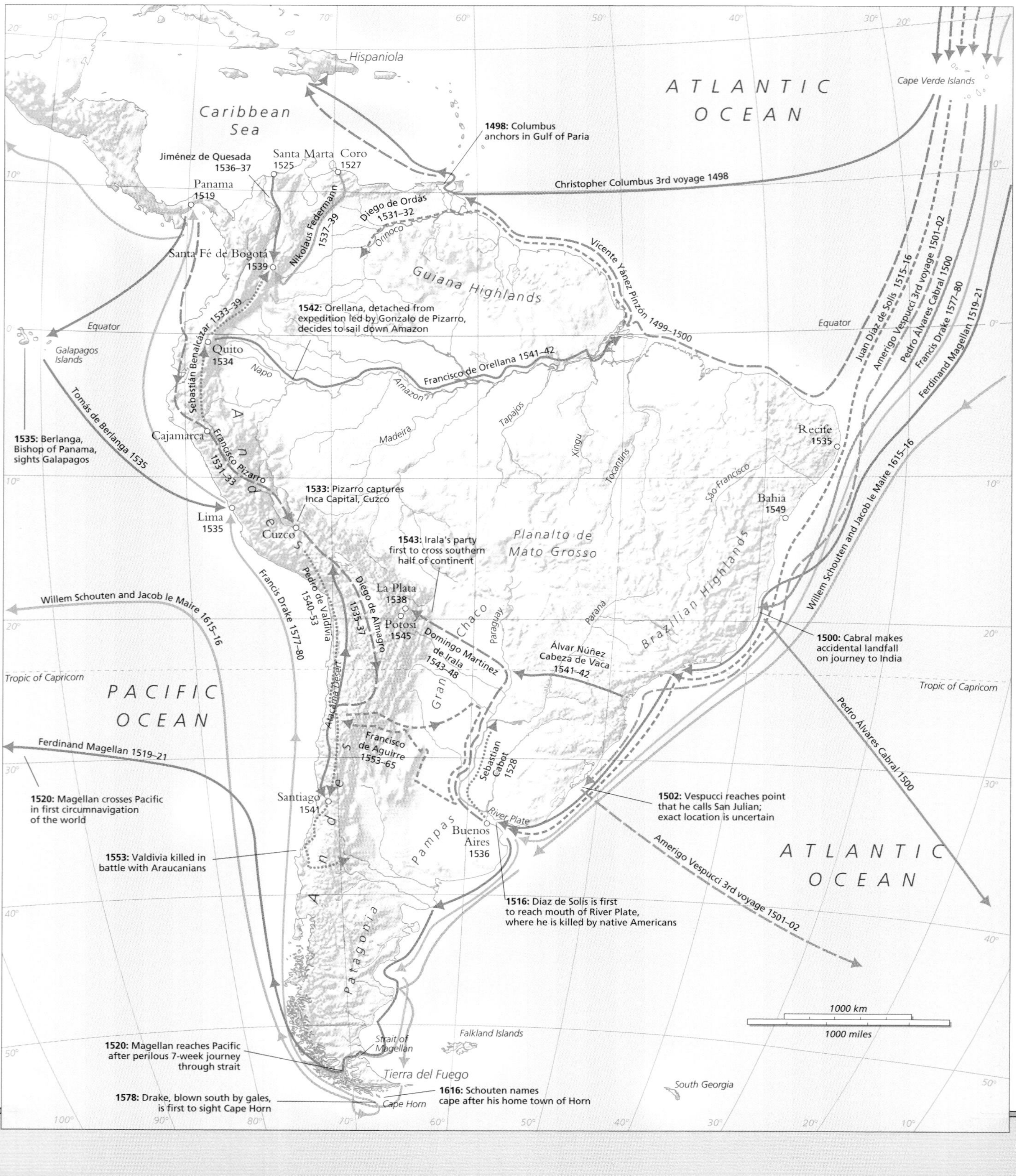

Jesuit missions in the interior

Spanish Jesuits created frontier settlements – often of three or four thousand people – known as *reducciones*. These had their own churches, workshops, foundries, even armories, and lands where the Native Americans grew crops and raised herds of cattle. Money was not used, but the Jesuits traded with local Spanish settlers, who envied their success, especially among the Guaraní tribes. For the authorities, however, the *reducciones* formed a defense against Portuguese encroachment on Spanish lands; Native Americans fought many battles with the slave-raiders from São Paulo known as Paulistas or *mamelucos*.

From the 17th century, most serious exploration and mapping of the interior of South America was the work of missionaries. This detail is from a map of the Amazon compiled by Samuel Fritz, a Bohemian-born Jesuit, and published in 1707. Note the Jesuits' IHS monogram above the Equator.

The Jesuits in South America

- **1550:** First Jesuits reach Brazil
- **1573:** Rules drawn up for planning Jesuit towns
- **1607:** Jesuits found province of Paraguay around Asunción
- **1631:** Father Ruiz de Montoya descends Paraná River with 12,000 Indians to escape slave-raiders
- **1641:** Indians and Jesuits defeat slave-raiders from São Paulo on Uruguay River
- **1640s:** Long-running quarrel between Jesuits and governor of Asunción
- **1649:** Viceroy grants *reducciones* virtual independence
- **1690:** Foundation of first Chiquito *reduccion*
- **1711:** Jesuits banned from entering Minas Gerais region
- **1750:** Treaty of Madrid: territory of seven Guarani *reducciones* ceded to Portugal
- **1754–55:** Guarani War in protest at terms of treaty
- **1759:** Expulsion of Jesuits from Brazil
- **1767:** Expulsion of Jesuits from all Spanish colonies

2 South America 1750

Areas colonized
- Spanish by 1650
- Spanish by 1750
- Portuguese by 1650
- Portuguese by 1750
- Dutch
- French

Missionary activity
- principal areas of Jesuit *reducciones*
- other major Jesuit missions
- major Franciscan missions
- *CHACO* 1732 *reduccion* with date of foundation
- 1630–32 active between these dates

Exploration of the interior
- Jesuits
- Franciscans
- Paulista raids

The area covered by the detail from Father Fritz's map *(shown left)*.

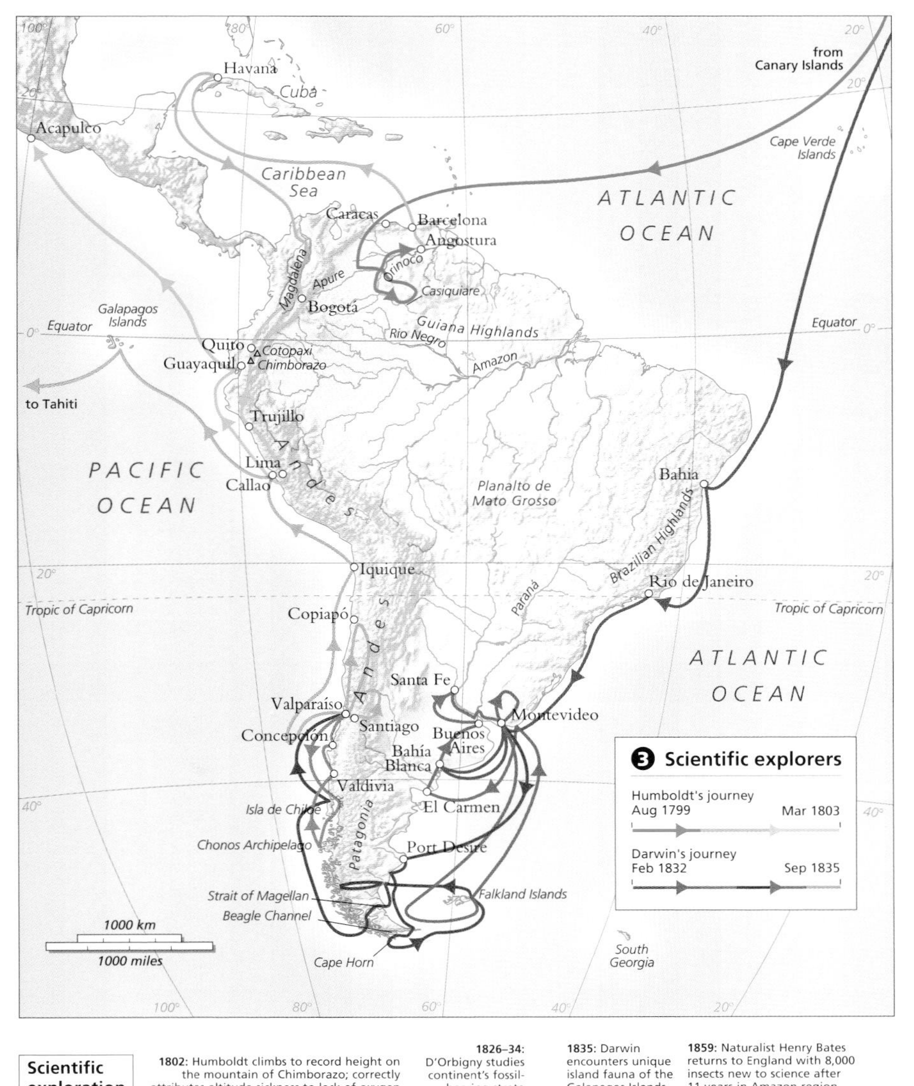

Scientific exploration

- **1735:** Expedition to Quito led by French scientist La Condamine to test sphericity of the Earth
- **1783:** Spanish crown sponsors botanical expedition to South American colonies
- **1802:** Humboldt climbs to record height on the mountain of Chimborazo; correctly attributes altitude sickness to lack of oxygen
- **1826–34:** D'Orbigny studies continent's fossil-bearing strata
- **1832:** Darwin discovers fossils of giant mammals near Bahia Blanca, including *Megatherium*
- **1835:** Darwin encounters unique island fauna of the Galapagos Islands
- **1835–44:** Guiana region explored by Sir Robert Schomburgk, who fixes boundary of British colony
- **1859:** Naturalist Henry Bates returns to England with 8,000 insects new to science after 11 years in Amazon region
- **1872:** German Wilhelm Reiss scales Cotopaxi, which Humboldt had pronounced unclimbable

Later scientific exploration

Humboldt endured far greater hardship than this studio portrait suggests, as he traveled with French botanist, Aimé Bonpland, by canoe and on foot through the rainforests of the Orinoco.

For three centuries, the colonial authorities in South America did little to encourage scientific exploration. In the 19th century, however, scientists of all kinds began to explore the peaks of the Andes, the Amazon Basin, and even the wilds of Patagonia. The Prussian Alexander von Humboldt amassed unparalleled data on the geography, geology, meteorology, and natural history of South America. He mapped the course of the Casiquiare, a most unusual river in that it links the Amazon and Orinoco drainage basins. Of later travelers, the most famous was Charles Darwin, whose observations as a young naturalist aboard *HMS Beagle* in 1831–36 would inspire his theory of evolution expounded in *On the Origin of Species*. The French paleontologist Alcide d'Orbigny, who spent eight years studying the continent's microfossils, published the first detailed physical map of South America in 1842.

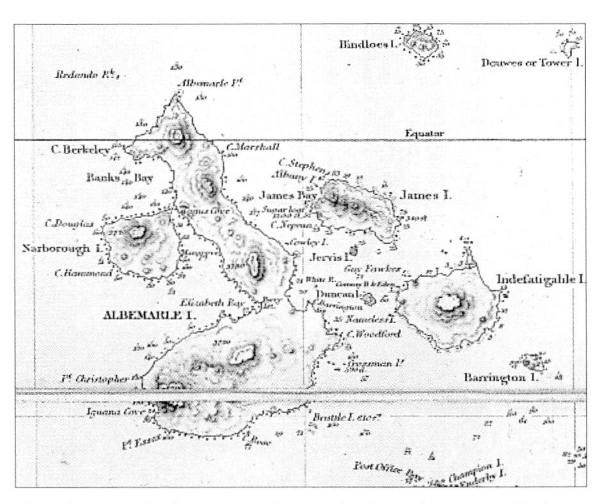

The Galapagos Islands are a volcanic group that lies on the equator. This chart was drawn by the officers of the *Beagle*, who were surveying the coast of South America for the British Navy. Darwin's interest was aroused by the peculiarities of the islands' fauna, such as the giant tortoises, which had evolved slightly different forms on each of the main islands, and the curious marine iguanas.

Large-billed seed-eating finch

Insectivorous warbler finch

The finches Darwin collected on the Galapagos Islands later provided powerful evidence for his theory of natural selection. Several closely related species had diverged from a common ancestor to occupy the various ecological niches on the islands.

EARLY CULTURES OF SOUTH AMERICA

The Bahia people of coastal Ecuador made clay sculptures such as this figure holding a swaddled child.

SOUTH AMERICA WAS COLONIZED by settlers from the north possibly more than 13,000 years ago. By 10,000 BCE, hunter-gatherers had reached its southern tip and, by 5000 BCE, communities were beginning to exploit local resources, such as maize, manioc, and potatoes. Successful agriculture led to growing populations and increasingly stratified societies. The distinctive temple mounds of Peru appeared by c.2500 BCE, and characteristic elements of South American religious iconography were disseminated all over Peru from the site of Chavín de Huantar, from c.1200 BCE. By 300 CE, Peru was dominated by two major civilizations: the Nazca, and the more expansionist Moche.

The earliest settlements

The first South American settlers were hunter-gatherers, exploiting the big game which flourished following the last Ice Age. Spearheads and arrowheads found at Fell's Cave indicate that this way of life had reached the far south of the continent by 10,000 BCE. In Chile, the site of Monte Verde (c.11,000 BCE) is a village of timber huts draped with animal hides. Finds of medicinal plants, potato peelings, digging sticks, wooden bowls, and mortars, reveal an intimate knowledge of plant resources which supplemented a diet of small game and mastodon.

Monte Verde, the earliest known settlement in the southern half of the continent, is thought to have existed by at least 11,000 BCE. Stone tools found there include devices for chopping, scraping, and pounding *(left)*.

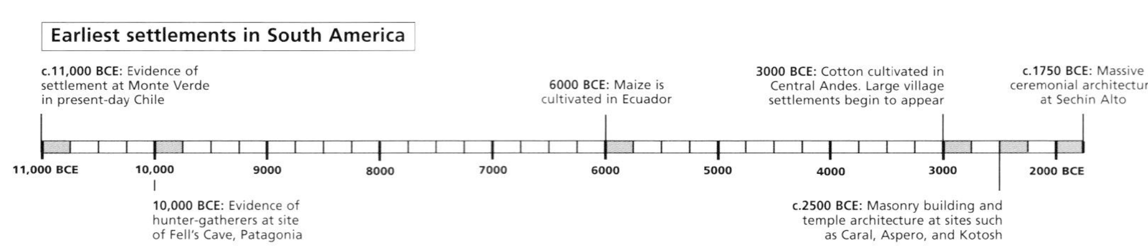

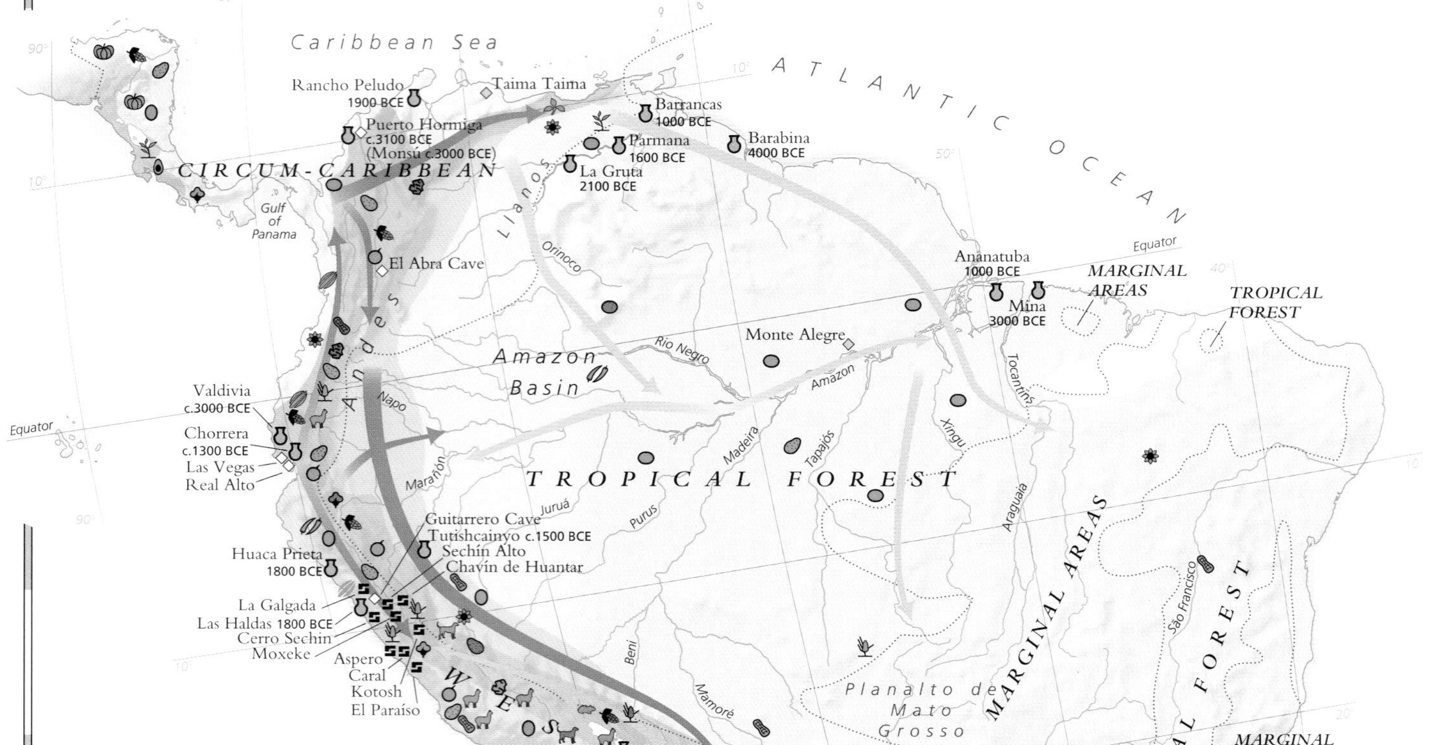

Monumental centres

Spectacular improvements in plant yields sustained growing populations; villages grew into small towns and the large temple mounds which appeared on the coast of central Peru from c.2500 BCE are evidence of organized, stratified societies. Major sites of this kind include Huaricoto, La Galgada, Caral and Aspero, and the later El Paraíso.

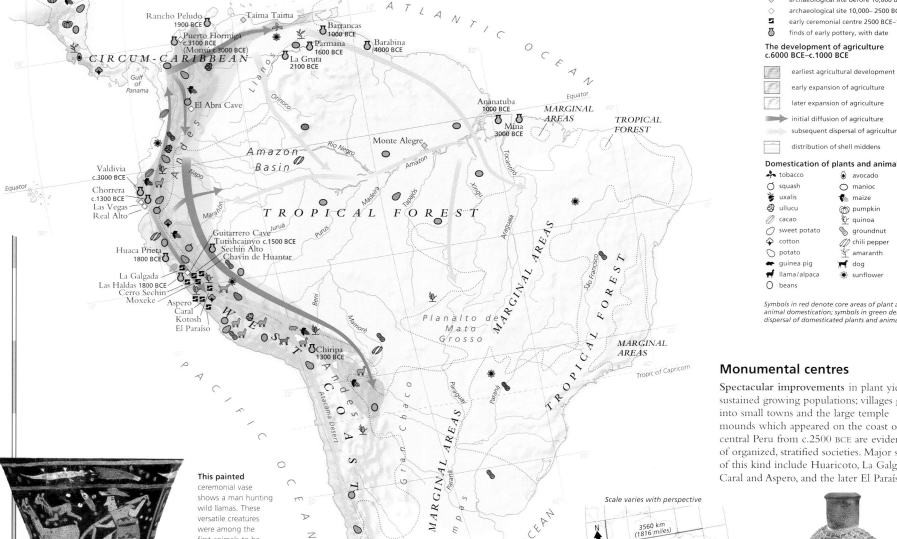

This painted ceremonial vase shows a man hunting wild llamas. These versatile creatures were among the first animals to be fully domesticated by the early farmers of the Andes.

Agriculture

The first farmers of South America were located on the northern Pacific coast. Maize, the staple crop of the Americas, was cultivated in Ecuador c.6000 BCE, and the major high-altitude crop in the Andes, the potato, may have been grown by 4000 BCE. Llamas and alpaca, domesticated for their wool, were used as Andean pack animals. Manioc, which became a staple of tropical forest farmers, was cultivated in the Amazon Basin by 3000 BCE.

This water vessel, dating from 900–200 BCE, was found near Cupisnique in the north of the Chavín region.

The peoples of the Amazon Basin and the Atlantic coast

Rock shelters and flaked stone tools, dating to c.10,000 BCE provide the earliest evidence of settlement east of the Andes. The transition from hunting and gathering to agriculture – principally the cultivation of manioc – probably began c.3000 BCE. Large shell middens at the mouths of the Amazon and Orinoco rivers contain remains of pottery dating to c.5000 BCE – far earlier than the first pottery of Peru. When maize was introduced into the river flood plains in the 1st millennium BCE, populations expanded and hierarchical societies (chiefdoms) developed. Drainage earthworks on the Llanos de Mojos suggest that large populations were cooperating to farm the landscape.

2 Early settlement of Amazonia and eastern South America

- early archaeological site 12,000–6000 BCE
- early ceramic site 5000–1000 BCE
- early lithic site
- earthworks and hydrological systems
- shell midden

The cultures of Peru 1300 BCE–600 CE

The most influential culture of the middle Andes was that of the Chavín which flourished at and around the major religious centre of Chavín de Huantar between 850 BCE and 200 BCE. The Chavín were distinguished by the sophistication of their architecture and sculptural style and by technological developments including the building of canals. As Chavín influence waned, from c.200 BCE, many distinctive regional cultures developed in the Andean highlands. Coastal Peru, however, was dominated by two major civilizations, Nazca in the south, and Moche in the north. As these cultures developed a strong identity, military rivalries intensified, paving the way for the appearance of other major states from 500 CE including Tiahuanaco and Huari.

Large cemeteries in the Paracas region contained thousands of mummified bodies wrapped in colourful wool. The motif of a large-eyed deity, the Oculate Being, on these textiles shows a strong affinity with the Chavín deity, known as the Smiling God.

4 Coastal Peru c.600 BCE–600 CE

- Paracas cultural region c. 600–350 BCE
- major Paracas sites
- Ecuadorian cultural region c.500 BCE–500 CE
- Lima cultural region c.400 BCE–500 CE
- Nazca cultural region c.350 BCE–450 CE
- earliest Moche sites c.1 CE
- Moche cultural region c.1–600 CE
- Recuay cultural region c.500 CE
- irrigated river valley

Moche

Moche culture was centred on the capital of Moche, dominated by the famous Temple of the Sun, a massive structure of solid adobe, 40 m high. The Moche state was powerful, well-organized and expanded by military conquest. Mass labour was organized to participate in major public works and civil engineering projects and the construction of 'royal' tombs.

The stirrup-spout on this drinking vessel is a typical feature of Moche pottery, as is the marvellously realistic and sensitive modelling of the facial features.

3 Chavín culture

- Chavín heartland
- early Chavín sites, 2000–850 BCE
- Chavín sites, 850–200 BCE
- trade route

The Chavín

Chavín de Huantar (c.1200–200 BCE), with its large stone sculptures and grand temples, became a cult centre. Chavín motifs, in architecture, textiles, pottery, and goldwork, are found throughout Peru.

Nazca

Based on the south coast of Peru, Nazca culture is famous for its superb and graphic pottery, textiles, and above all, the enigmatic 'Nazca lines', straight, geometric, or figurative designs etched onto the surface of the desert, possibly as offerings to the gods.

Cultures of Peru 1300 BCE–1 CE

- **1300 BCE:** Cerro Sechin is earliest central Andean site with Chavín-style iconography
- **850 BCE:** Florescence of Chavín de Huantar; Chavín style widely disseminated
- **500 BCE:** Paracas culture in southern Peru produces textiles woven with Chavín-style images
- **200 BCE:** Regional cultures begin to appear in central Andes
- **c.1 CE:** Emergence of Moche culture of coastal Peru

This aerial view shows Nazca lines etched into the shape of a hummingbird. Some of these images can be over 100 m across.

THE EMPIRES OF SOUTH AMERICA

This gold knife in the form of a Chimú (or Sicán) sun god dates from c.1100 CE. The body is decorated with turquoises.

THE EMPIRES WHICH DOMINATED the Andes between 500 and 1450, Tiahuanaco, Huari, and Chimú, were important precursors of the Inca, laying down the religious and social foundations, and the authoritarian government which were to serve the Inca so well. The Inca Empire (1438–1532) was the greatest state in South America, exercising stringent control over its subjects, through taxation, forced labour, compulsory migration, and military service. With its unyielding hierarchy and ill-defined line of succession, the Empire was fatally weakened by a leadership crisis at the very point when Pizarro arrived in 1532, and was unable to prevent its own destruction at the hands of the Spanish *conquistadores*.

Empires of the Andean coast 250–1375

The empires of Tiahuanaco and Huari, which together dominated the Andes from 500 CE, shared a similar art style, and probably the same religion. The city of Tiahuanaco, on the windswept Altiplano of modern Bolivia, was a major pilgrimage centre, and its cultural influence diffused throughout the south-central Andes from 500–1000. The contemporary Huari Empire, which controlled the coast around present-day Lima, was, by contrast, centralized and militaristic, expanding its influence through conquest. The Inca owed most to their direct predecessor, the Chimú Empire of the northern Andes, with its efficient administration, colonial expansionism, irrigation projects, and stress on an effective communication system.

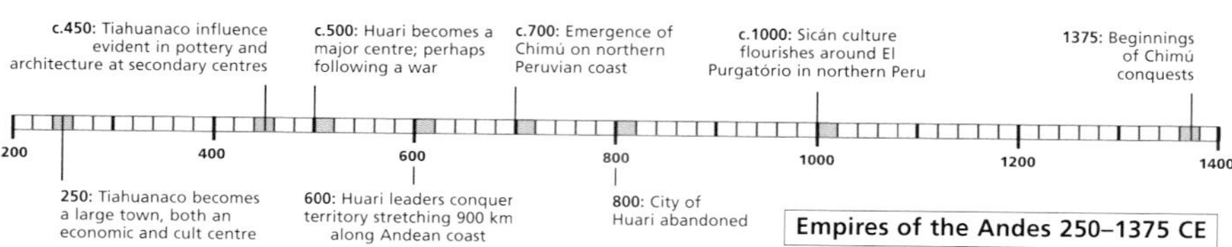

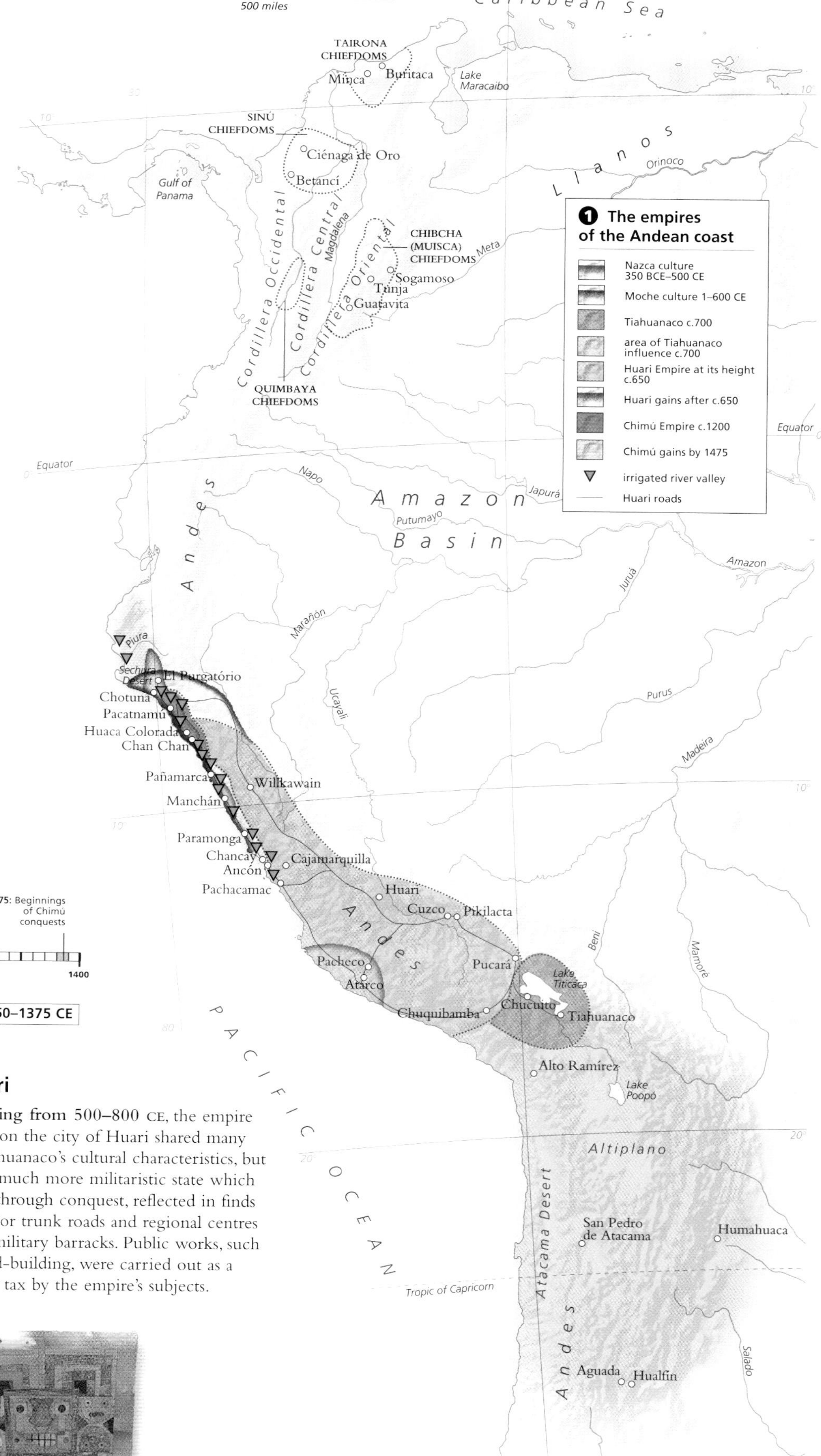

Tiahuanaco

By 500 CE the city of Tiahuanaco on Lake Titicaca's southeastern shore had become a major population centre, housing up to 40,000 people, and a focus of pilgrimage for the entire Andean region. It was dominated by palaces and a cult centre, consisting of temples, monumental gateways, and large monolithic sculptures. The city's iconography, with its symbolism of water, sun, and weather, spread throughout the south-central Andes.

Carved from a single slab of andesite, the Gateway of the Sun at Tiahuanaco is a representation of the cosmos, with the creator god at the centre of the frieze.

Huari

Thriving from 500–800 CE, the empire based on the city of Huari shared many of Tiahuanaco's cultural characteristics, but was a much more militaristic state which grew through conquest, reflected in finds of major trunk roads and regional centres with military barracks. Public works, such as road-building, were carried out as a labour tax by the empire's subjects.

The back of this Huari hand mirror contains a central face, with small heads at each side. The reflecting surface is of pyrite and the mosaic back of a variety of stones of contrasting texture and colour.

Chimú

The Chimú Empire which ruled over the coast of northern Peru (c.700–1476) was centred on the capital of Chan Chan. A series of great royal compounds within the city served as both the palaces and mausolea of ten successive monarchs. The empire stretched for 1000 km along the Peruvian coast, administered by a series of regional centres.

The Chimú people were skilled metalworkers, producing a wide variety of ceremonial objects such as this gold dove with turquoise eyes.

This small figure reflects the intricate casting and polishing typical of the goldsmiths of the Quimbaya chiefdoms. They also produced masks, spear tips, pendants, and helmets

Chiefdoms of the northern Andes

By the 15th century, many peoples of the northern Andes were organized into chiefdoms, based on large villages, supported by wetland farming, and capable of mobilizing sizeable armies. Their gold-working skills gave rise to myths of 'El Dorado' *(see p.149)*. Gold and copper resources were exploited by efficient mining operations – an indication of their impressive organizational ability.

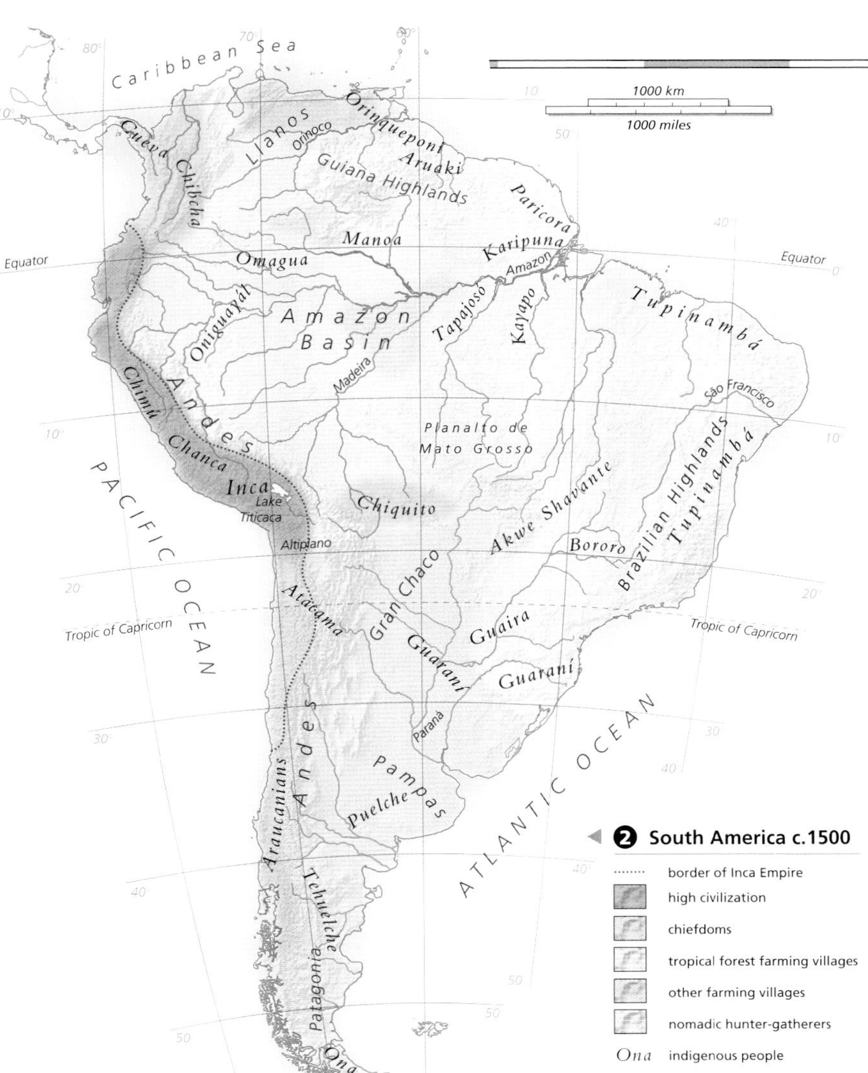

The Inca Empire

The Inca *quipumayoc*, or grand treasurer, is shown holding a *quipu*, a device made of knotted strings, used to record administrative matters and sacred histories. Information was encoded in the colours of the strings and the style of the knots.

The Inca emerged, in less than a century, as the preeminent state in South America; from 1470 they ruled vast territories from their capital, Cuzco. Their hierarchical society, ruled by the Sapa Inca (believed to be descended from the sun), depended on the mass organization of labour. Adult men were liable for forced labour, and worked in the fields, on public works (terracing, building, mining), and served in the army. An extensive road network, interspersed with way stations and regional centres, bound the empire together. Yet this complex bureaucracy had no form of writing, although arithmetic records were used for administration, tribute, and taxation.

The peoples of South America c.1500

The golden raft, bearing a god-like figure surrounded by attendants, is a detailed example of a *tunjo* or offering piece, produced by the Muisca (Chibcha) people of the northeastern Andes.

A great diversity of indigenous cultures existed in South America by the start of the 16th century, ranging from the high civilization of the Incas to the hunter-gatherers of Patagonia. Large populations lived along the Amazon, the upper river dominated by the Omagua people, its lower reaches controlled by the warlike Tapajosó. Many chiefdoms held sway over huge areas, some extracting forced labour from subject peoples, who were often engaged on extensive building projects. Ancestor cults, based on the mummified bodies of chiefs, were widespread.

This stylized carving in the shape of a tree is etched on a hillside in the coastal desert above present-day Paracas.

THE VERTICAL ECONOMY OF THE ANDES

The rugged terrain of the Andes provided a series of contiguous, but contrasting environments, fully exploited by the Incas and their predecessors. High, treeless, grassy plains (the *puna*) were used for grazing llamas. Below this, at heights up to 4000 m above sea level, lay the *suni*, where potatoes and tubers could be cultivated. Maize, squash, fruits, and cocoa grew in lower, frost-free valleys (the *quechua*), while the lower slopes of the mountains (the *yunga*) were planted with peppers, coca plants, and other fruits. Sources of shellfish and fish from the ocean were periodically disrupted by El Niño, an irregular climatic disturbance which warmed the ocean, leading to torrential rains and disastrous flooding.

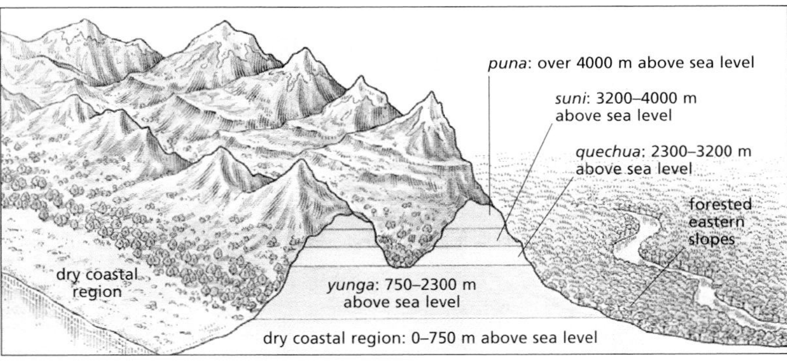

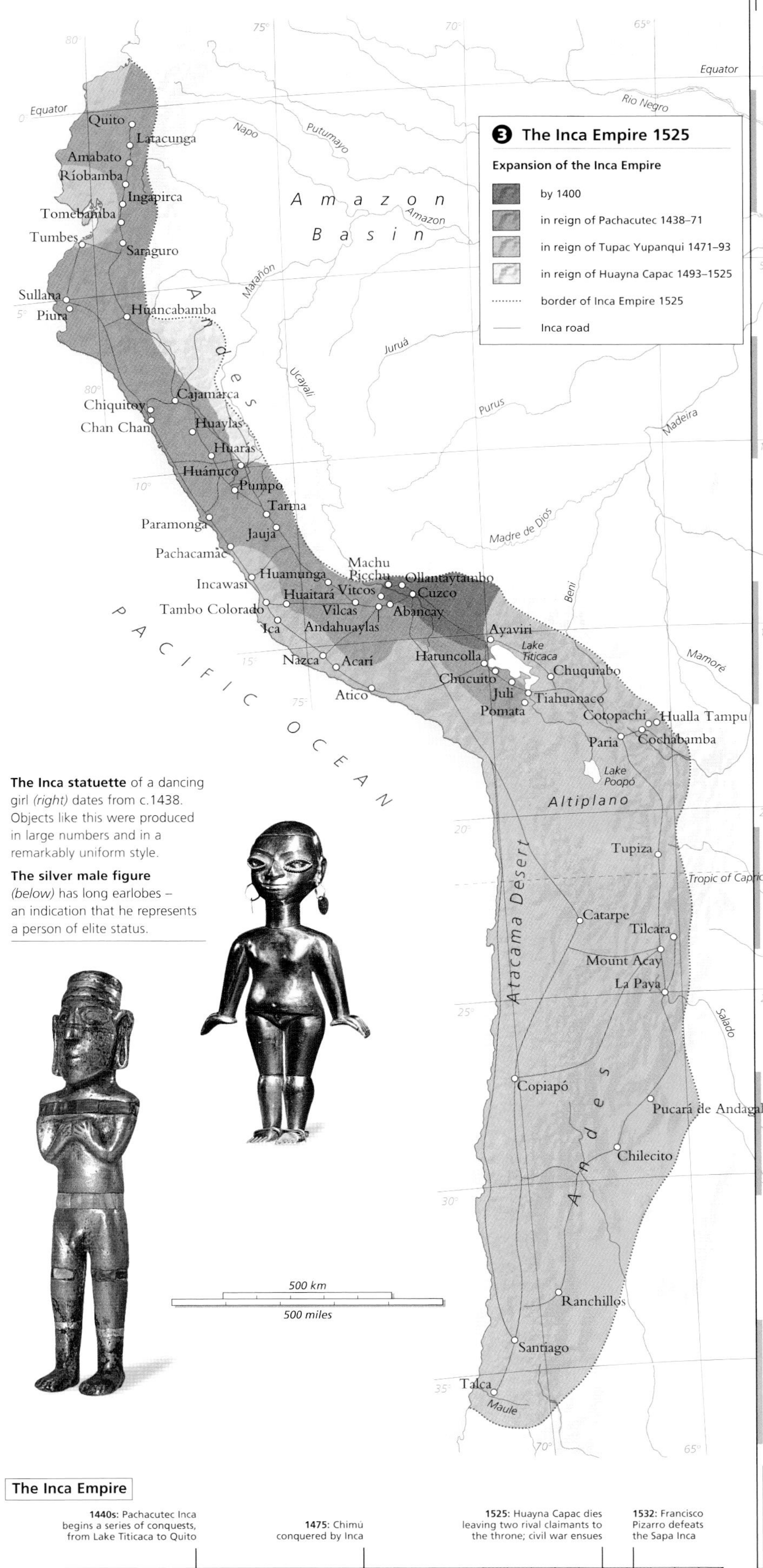

The Inca statuette of a dancing girl *(right)* dates from c.1438. Objects like this were produced in large numbers and in a remarkably uniform style.

The silver male figure *(below)* has long earlobes – an indication that he represents a person of elite status.

The Inca Empire

1400 | 1425 | 1450 | 1475 | 1500 | 1525 | 1550

1440s: Pachacutec Inca begins a series of conquests, from Lake Titicaca to Quito

1438: Incas rise to power; attack Lake Titicaca basin, and establish upland empire

1475: Chimú conquered by Inca

1500: Protracted military campaigns at northern and southern extremes of empire lead to establishment of second capital at Tomebamba

1525: Huayna Capac dies leaving two rival claimants to the throne; civil war ensues

1532: Francisco Pizarro defeats the Sapa Inca

COLONIAL SOUTH AMERICA

Christianity in South America blended with local traditions to produce colourful spectacles such as this 18th-century Corpus Christi procession in Cuzco.

IN THEIR CONQUEST of South America the Spanish were so driven by the quest for gold and silver, that it took the *conquistadores* less than ten years to take over the rich, organized states of the Andes. The Portuguese were slower to settle Brazil, first trading with the Indians, then turning to sugar production. Wherever Europeans settled, the native population declined rapidly, mainly through lack of resistance to alien diseases. There were also periodic wars against the colonists. Large cattle stations that destroyed native arable smallholdings were a further factor in their decline. Emigration to South America from both Spain and Portugal was light; settlers mixed with the natives, creating a mixed-race *mestizo* population. To make up for shortages in labour, they imported African slaves. Catholic missionaries, notably the Jesuits, were active throughout the colonial era, often defending the rights of the Indians against the settlers. Both colonial empires collapsed in the 19th century, but the religion and languages of the conquerors survived.

The silver mine at Potosí was the prime source of revenue to the Spanish crown between 1550 and 1650. At first the native population supplied all the labour and technology. The silver was extracted using mercury, mined at Huancavelica.

The conquest of Peru

In 1531 Francisco Pizarro sailed from Panama to conquer Peru. By the time the expedition had penetrated inland to Cajamarca, where the reigning Inca, Atahualpa, and 40,000 men were camped, Pizarro had only 180 men. Yet he succeeded in capturing Atahualpa, whom he held for ransom. When this was paid, Atahualpa was executed, and the *conquistadores* moved on to capture the Inca capital, Cuzco. The Incas were in awe of the Spanish horses and guns, but this astonishing feat of conquest would have been impossible, had the Inca Empire not been weakened by a smallpox epidemic and civil war.

SOMQVISTA CORTALE·LACAVESA·A ATAGVALPA·INGA·VMATACVCHV

Atahualpa was given a summary trial by Pizarro and then garrotted, or – as this contemporary Inca illustration shows – beheaded.

1 Pizarro's conquest of the Inca Empire

- 1524 expedition
- 1526 expedition
- 1531–33 expedition
- extent of Inca Empire
- 1526 date of foundation

Inca ornaments, such as this gold llama, are very rare, because most were melted down and shipped to Spain.

2 Spanish South America

- Spanish territory before 1650
- Spanish territory after 1650
- region disputed by Spain and Portugal up to 1777
- Jesuit mission states, with dates
- border with Brazil by Treaty of Madrid 1750
- border with Brazil where modified by Treaty of San Ildefonso 1777
- Portuguese settlement
- gold, silver, copper, mercury, drugs, hides, cocoa

Caribbean Sea
Santa Marta 1525
Cartagena 1532
Maracaibo 1529
Caracas 1567
Cumaná 1521
Panama 1519
Gulf of Darien
Gulf of Panama
CAPTAINCY-GENERAL AND PRESIDENCIA OF CARACAS 1742–86
AUDIENCIA OF SANTA FE 1548
CASANARE AND LOS LLANOS 1659–1767
Santa Fé de Bogotá 1538
Guiana Highlands
VICEROYALTY OF NEW GRANADA 1739
Quito 1534
PRESIDENCIA OF QUITO 1563
Tumbes 1526
Cuenca 1557
Paita 1532
MAYNAS 1638–1767
Cajamarca 1532
Trujillo 1525
AUDIENCIA OF LIMA 1543
Lima 1535
Callao 1537
Huancavelica
Cuzco 1533
PACIFIC OCEAN
MOJOS 1659–1767
La Paz 1548
Arequipa 1540
Arica 1537
La Plata 1538
Potosí 1545
CHIQUITOS 1691
Corumbá 1788
VICEROYALTY OF PERU 1543
PRESIDENCIA OF CHARCAS 1559
ITATÍN 1609–60
GUAIRÁ c.1630–32
Tropic of Capricorn
Gran Chaco
VICEROYALTY OF RÍO DE LA PLATA 1776
Asunción 1537
Ciudad Real 1630
CHACO 1732–67

Spanish South America

Spain ruled her American colonies through two great viceroyalties, New Spain (centred on Mexico) and Peru. The viceroys' principal duty was to guarantee a steady flow of bullion for the Spanish Crown. When booty from the native empires was exhausted, the colonists turned to the region's mineral resources, using forced native labour *(mita)* to extract precious metals, in particular silver. Smaller administrative units called *audiencias* were presided over by a judge who enacted the complex laws devised in Spain for the running of the colonies. Attempts to expand the empire were thwarted in the south by the fierce Araucanian people, elsewhere by the inhospitable nature of the terrain.

The founder of Spain's South American empire, Pizarro was an ageing soldier of fortune. Some of his own lieutenants rebelled against him and he was killed in a riot in Lima in 1541.

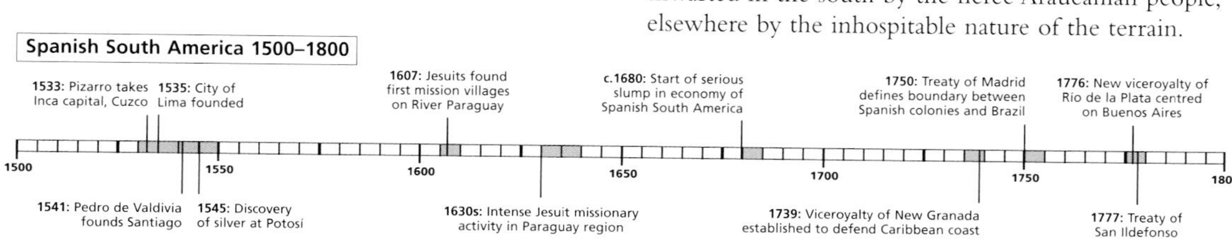

Portuguese South America

Brazil was formally claimed by Portugal in 1500. There were no conspicuous mineral resources, so colonization depended on agriculture. In the 1530s, in an attempt to encourage settlement, João III made grants of land to 12 hereditary 'captains', each captaincy consisting of 50 leagues of coastline. Some failed completely and little of the coastal plain was settled before 1549 when a royal governor-general was sent to Bahia. The captaincy system continued, but the colonists' fortunes changed with the success of sugar. The native population living near the coast had been almost wiped out by disease and wars. The few that remained had no wish to labour on sugar plantations, so slaves were imported from Africa. In the 18th century, a gold boom opened up the Minas Gerais region, but apart from slave-raiders hunting for Indians and prospectors searching for gold and diamonds, penetration of the interior was limited.

Between 1550 and 1800, some 2.5 million African slaves were taken to Brazil, more than 70% of them to work for the sugar plantations and mills which were the backbone of the economy.

Slaves were also employed at the gold and diamond mines of the interior. This early 19th-century print shows slaves washing diamond-bearing rock.

3 Portuguese South America

- Portuguese territory by 1600
- Portuguese territory by 1750
- Portuguese frontier territory
- region disputed by Spain and Portugal up to 1777
- PARÁ 1616 captaincy and date of foundation
- capital city
- gold
- diamonds
- dyes
- hides
- sugar

Brazil 1500–1800

- **1502:** First expedition sent from Lisbon to exploit new-found coastline
- **1532:** First captaincies granted for purposes of settlement
- **1549:** Direct royal rule imposed from new capital at Bahia
- **1562–63:** War and disease kill much of Indian population
- **1580:** Portugal and her empire come under rule of Spanish kings
- **1621:** Formation of separate Estado do Maranhão with its own governor-general
- **1663:** Brazil becomes viceroyalty
- **1674:** Foundation of Manaus, 1,600 km from mouth of Amazon
- **1680s:** Portuguese found Colônia do Sacramento
- **1695:** Gold discovered in Minas Gerais region
- **1750:** Portugal renounces claim to Colônia do Sacramento
- **1763:** Rio de Janeiro becomes Brazilian capital

THE SEARCH FOR EL DORADO

From the 1530s until well into the 17th century, fantastic tales of the kingdom of El Dorado (the gilded man) inspired many foolhardy expeditions through the Andes, the Orinoco basin, and the Guiana Highlands. The English sea captain Walter Raleigh twice sailed to the Orinoco, but both his voyages ended in failure and on the second in 1617 his teenaged son was killed by the Spanish.

The legend of El Dorado took many forms. The most persistent was of a chieftain so rich that he was regularly painted in gold by his subjects.

Other colonial powers

For 150 years Portugal's hold on Brazil was far from secure. The French, who traded along the coast with the Indians, made several attempts to found colonies. In the first half of the 17th century, the defence of Portuguese colonies was neglected by the ruling Spanish kings. This allowed the Dutch to capture a long stretch of the northeast coast. They were finally expelled in 1654 and had to be content, like the English and French, with a small colony in the Guianas.

Dutch Brazil thrived under the governorship of Prince Maurits of Nassau (1636–44), when many new towns were built. The artist Franz Post painted idealized views of the colony during this period. This detail shows the slave quarters on a plantation.

4 Brazil and the Guianas c.1640

- Portuguese possession and settlement
- Dutch possession and settlement
- French possession and settlement
- temporary French colonies in Brazil

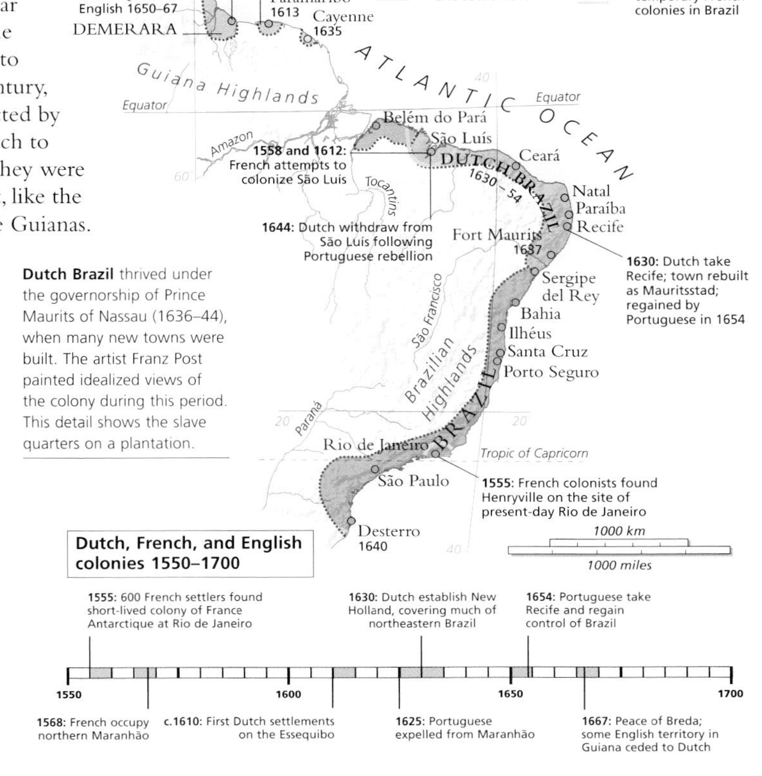

Dutch, French, and English colonies 1550–1700

- **1555:** 600 French settlers found short-lived colony of France Antarctique at Rio de Janeiro
- **1568:** French occupy northern Maranhão
- **c.1610:** First Dutch settlements on the Essequibo
- **1625:** Portuguese expelled from Maranhão
- **1630:** Dutch establish New Holland, covering much of northeastern Brazil
- **1654:** Portuguese take Recife and regain control of Brazil
- **1667:** Peace of Breda; some English territory in Guiana ceded to Dutch

THE AGE OF INDEPENDENCE

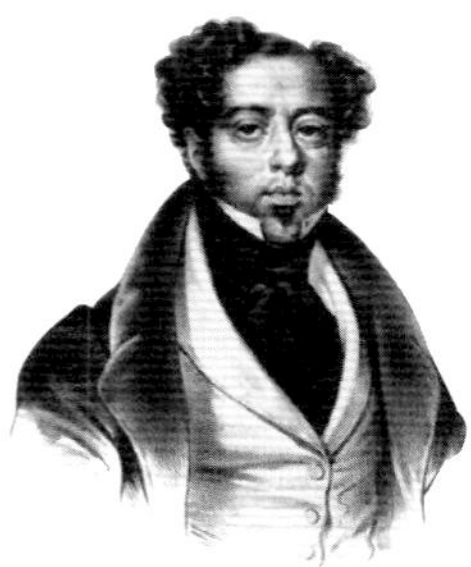

Pedro I became the emperor of an independent Brazil in 1822, when his father and the royal family returned from exile to Portugal.

AFTER THREE CENTURIES of rule by Spain, the colonial families of South America began to demand more autonomy. When Spain was invaded by Napoleon in 1808, it was cut off from its empire, and in 1810 several colonies established independent ruling juntas. The struggle for independence lasted until 1826, when the last Spanish troops departed. The heroic deeds of the Liberators, Simón Bolívar, José de San Martín, and others passed into legend, but the task of forming new republics proved harder. Liberals and Conservatives fought numerous civil wars and military dictators ran countries as their personal fiefs. The economies of the new states were dominated by foreign trading powers, especially Britain. Brazil gained its independence from Portugal more peacefully, a result of the royal family's flight to Brazil in 1807. The two states separated when they returned to Portugal in 1822.

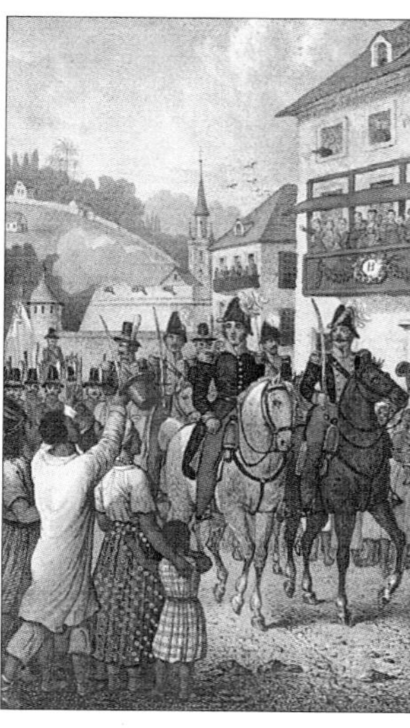

Bolívar enters Caracas in triumph in 1829 after putting down the uprising of his former lieutenant Antonio Páez. But it was Páez who became dictator of the new republic of Venezuela on Bolívar's death in 1830.

The break-up of Great Colombia

The personality of Simón Bolívar and the need for military unity in confronting the Spanish created the republic of Great Colombia. It proved an unwieldy state with a very remote capital at Bogotá. Commercial links and communications between the three former Spanish colonies of New Granada, Venezuela, and Quito (Ecuador) were very limited, and in 1830, the year of Bolívar's death, they became separate states under the leadership of generals Santander, Páez, and Flores respectively.

Dec 1830: Death of Bolívar
Santa Marta
Cartagena
Puerto Cabello
Caracas
Cumaná
Maracaibo
Colón
Puerto Bello
Panamá
San Fernando de Apure
Orinoco
Angostura
1846: renamed Ciudad Bolívar
Cúcuta
San Cristóbal
Llanos
Antioquia
Medellín
Bogotá
VENEZUELA
Magdalena
Cali
Popayán
NEW GRANADA (COLOMBIA)
1861
Pasto
Equator
Quito
Caquetá
ECUADOR
Putumayo
Napo
Guayaquil
BRAZIL
Amazon
Iquitos
Tumbes
Andes
PERU
500 km
500 miles

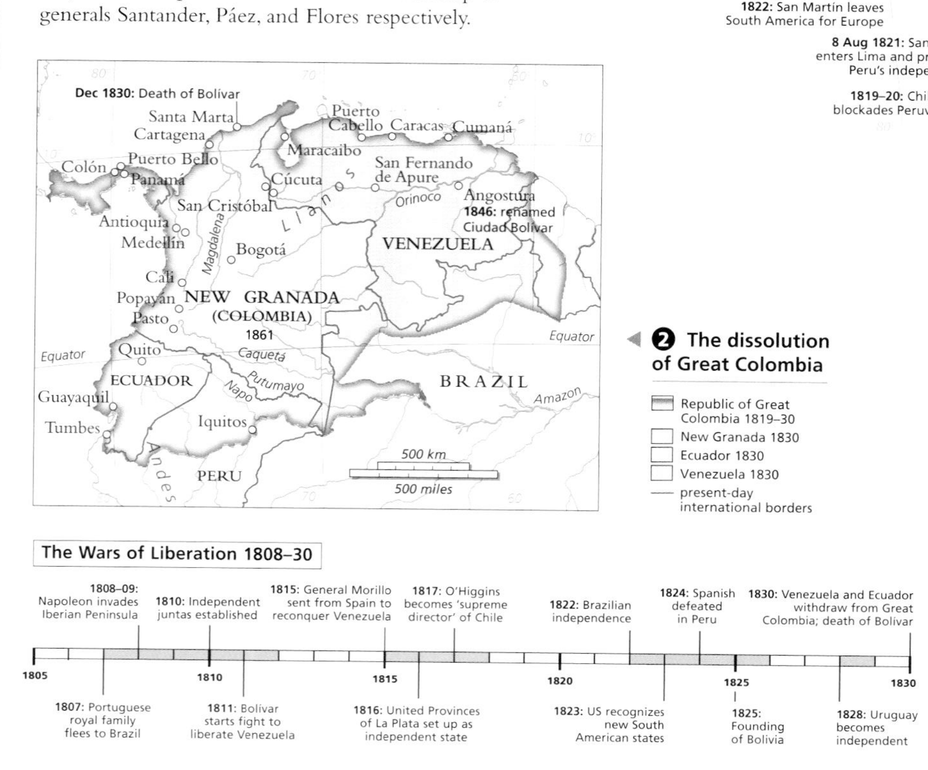

2 The dissolution of Great Colombia

- Republic of Great Colombia 1819–30
- New Granada 1830
- Ecuador 1830
- Venezuela 1830
- present-day international borders

The Wars of Liberation 1808–30

- 1805
- 1807: Portuguese royal family flees to Brazil
- 1808–09: Napoleon invades Iberian Peninsula
- 1810: Independent juntas established
- 1811: Bolívar starts fight to liberate Venezuela
- 1815: General Morillo sent from Spain to reconquer Venezuela
- 1816: United Provinces of La Plata set up as independent state
- 1817: O'Higgins becomes 'supreme director' of Chile
- 1822: Brazilian independence
- 1823: US recognizes new South American states
- 1824: Spanish defeated in Peru
- 1825: Founding of Bolivia
- 1828: Uruguay becomes independent
- 1830: Venezuela and Ecuador withdraw from Great Colombia; death of Bolívar

The liberation of Spanish South America

The wars of liberation were fought between patriots and those who remained loyal to the Spanish crown. The longest struggle was that of Simón Bolívar in his native Venezuela and neighbouring Colombia. The first states to achieve independence were Paraguay and Argentina, from where in 1817 José de San Martín led an army over the Andes to help liberate Chile. Bolívar's campaigns regained momentum in 1818–22 in a triumphal progress from Venezuela to Ecuador. The armies of liberation from north and south then joined forces for the liberation of Peru and, in honour of Bolívar, Upper Peru was renamed Bolivia.

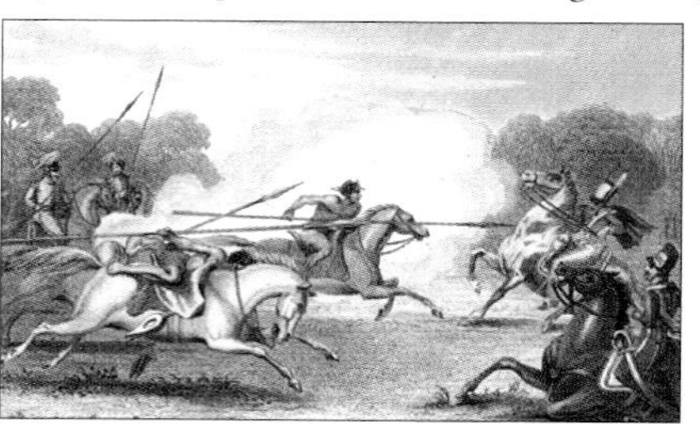

The *llanero* lancers, from the plains of Venezuela, were praised by Bolívar as his 'cossacks'. They continually harrassed the army sent from Spain in 1815 to oppose the liberation movement.

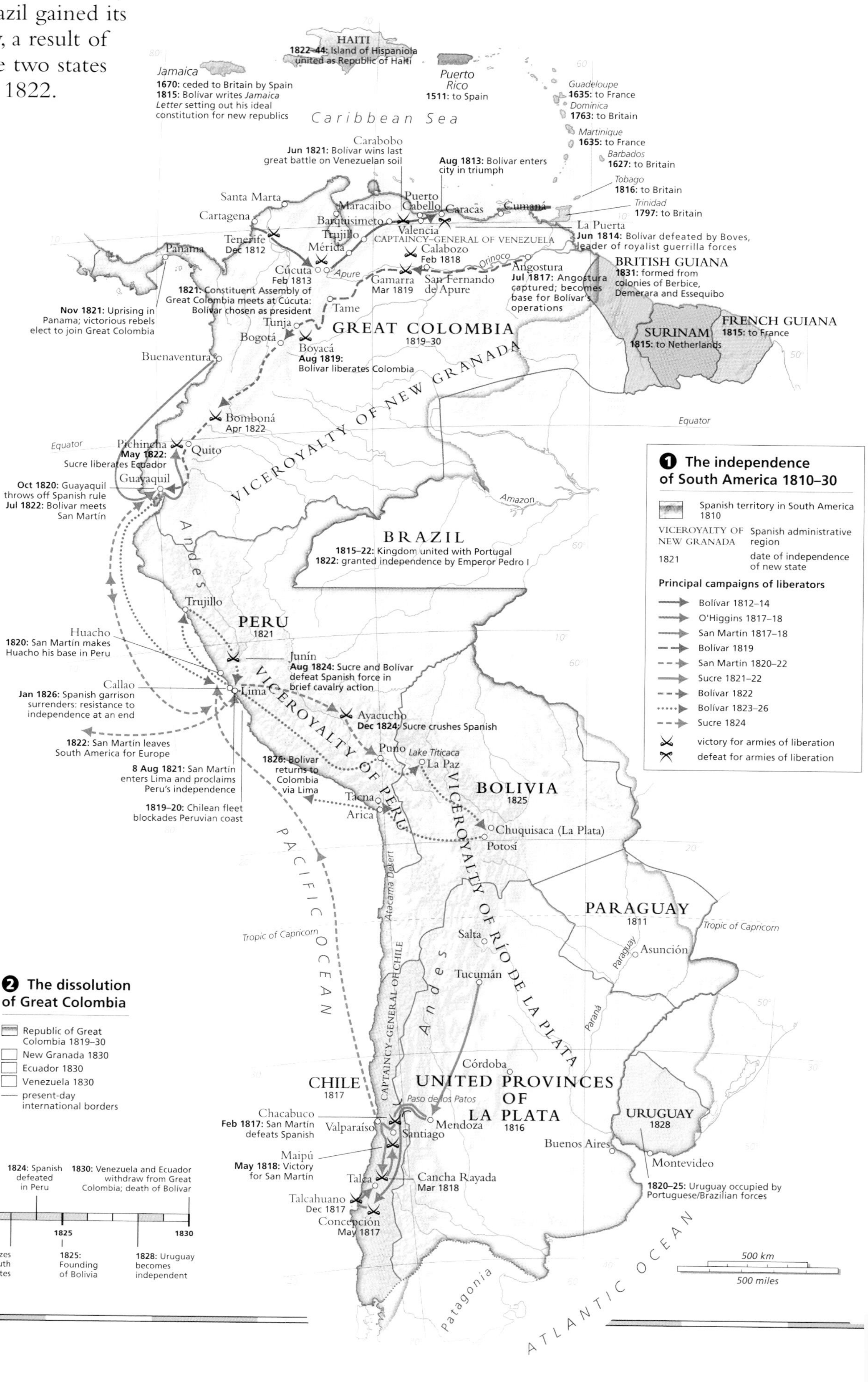

HAITI
1822–44: Island of Hispaniola united as Republic of Haiti
Jamaica
1670: ceded to Britain by Spain
1815: Bolívar writes Jamaica Letter setting out his ideal constitution for new republics
Puerto Rico
1511: to Spain
Guadeloupe
1635: to France
Dominica
1763: to Britain
Martinique
1635: to France
Barbados
1627: to Britain
Tobago
1816: to Britain
Trinidad
1797: to Britain
Caribbean Sea
Carabobo
Jun 1821: Bolívar wins last great battle on Venezuelan soil
Aug 1813: Bolívar enters city in triumph
Santa Marta
Cartagena
Maracaibo
Puerto Cabello
Caracas
Cumaná
Barquisimeto
Trujillo
Valencia
La Puerta
Jun 1814: Bolívar defeated by Boves, leader of royalist guerrilla forces
Tenerife
Dec 1812
Mérida
CAPTAINCY-GENERAL OF VENEZUELA
Calabozo
Feb 1818
Panamá
Cúcuta
Feb 1813
Apure
Orinoco
Angostura
Jul 1817: Angostura captured; becomes base for Bolívar's operations
BRITISH GUIANA
1831: formed from colonies of Berbice, Demerara and Essequibo
Gamarra
Mar 1819
San Fernando de Apure
1821: Constituent Assembly of Great Colombia meets at Cúcuta: Bolívar chosen as president
Nov 1821: Uprising in Panamá; victorious rebels elect to join Great Colombia
Tame
Tunja
Bogotá
GREAT COLOMBIA
1819–30
SURINAM
1815: to Netherlands
FRENCH GUIANA
1815: to France
Boyacá
Aug 1819: Bolívar liberates Colombia
Buenaventura
VICEROYALTY OF NEW GRANADA
Bomboná
Apr 1822
Equator
Pichincha
May 1822: Sucre liberates Ecuador
Quito
Guayaquil
Oct 1820: Guayaquil throws off Spanish rule
Jul 1822: Bolívar meets San Martín
Amazon
BRAZIL
1815–22: Kingdom united with Portugal
1822: granted independence by Emperor Pedro I
Andes
Trujillo
PERU
1821
Huacho
1820: San Martín makes Huacho his base in Peru
Junín
Aug 1824: Sucre and Bolívar defeat Spanish force in brief cavalry action
Callao
Jan 1826: Spanish garrison surrenders: resistance to independence at an end
Lima
VICEROYALTY OF PERU
Ayacucho
Dec 1824: Sucre crushes Spanish
1822: San Martín leaves South America for Europe
Puno
Lake Titicaca
La Paz
8 Aug 1821: San Martín enters Lima and proclaims Peru's independence
1826: Bolívar returns to Colombia via Lima
BOLIVIA
1825
Tacna
Arica
1819–20: Chilean fleet blockades Peruvian coast
Chuquisaca (La Plata)
Potosí
PACIFIC OCEAN
Atacama Desert
VICEROYALTY OF RÍO DE LA PLATA
PARAGUAY
1811
Tropic of Capricorn
Salta
Asunción
Paraguay
CAPTAINCY-GENERAL OF CHILE
Tucumán
Paraná
Córdoba
CHILE
1817
UNITED PROVINCES OF LA PLATA
1816
Paso de los Patos
Chacabuco
Feb 1817: San Martín defeats Spanish
Valparaíso
Santiago
Mendoza
URUGUAY
1828
Buenos Aires
Maipú
May 1818: Victory for San Martín
Montevideo
Talca
Cancha Rayada
Mar 1818
1820–25: Uruguay occupied by Portuguese/Brazilian forces
Talcahuano
Dec 1817
Concepción
May 1817
Patagonia
ATLANTIC OCEAN
500 km
500 miles
1 The independence of South America 1810–30
Spanish territory in South America 1810
VICEROYALTY OF NEW GRANADA Spanish administrative region
1821 date of independence of new state
Principal campaigns of liberators
Bolívar 1812–14
O'Higgins 1817–18
San Martín 1817–18
Bolívar 1819
San Martín 1820–22
Sucre 1821–22
Bolívar 1822
Bolívar 1823–26
Sucre 1824
victory for armies of liberation
defeat for armies of liberation

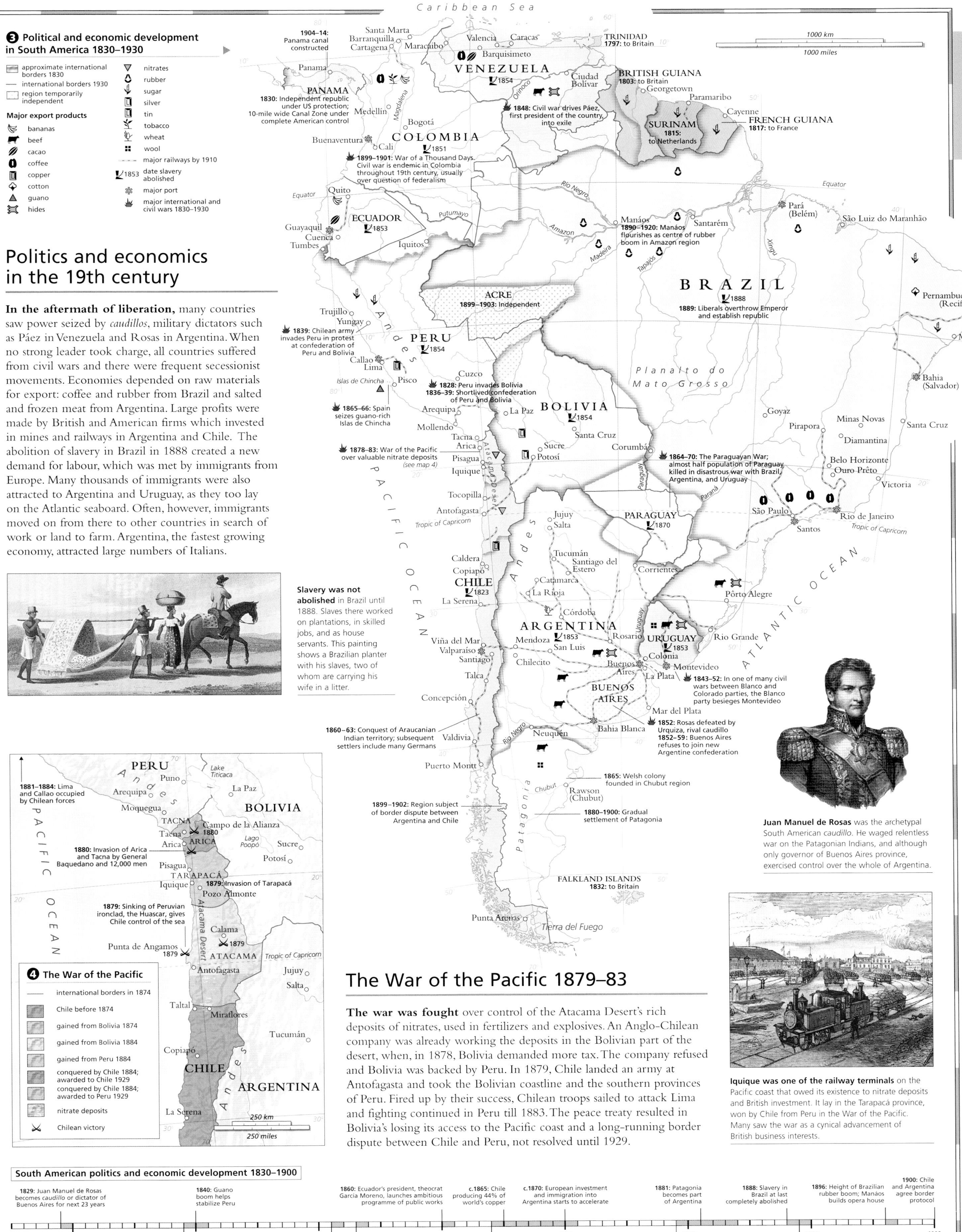

Politics and economics in the 19th century

In the aftermath of liberation, many countries saw power seized by *caudillos*, military dictators such as Páez in Venezuela and Rosas in Argentina. When no strong leader took charge, all countries suffered from civil wars and there were frequent secessionist movements. Economies depended on raw materials for export: coffee and rubber from Brazil and salted and frozen meat from Argentina. Large profits were made by British and American firms which invested in mines and railways in Argentina and Chile. The abolition of slavery in Brazil in 1888 created a new demand for labour, which was met by immigrants from Europe. Many thousands of immigrants were also attracted to Argentina and Uruguay, as they too lay on the Atlantic seaboard. Often, however, immigrants moved on from there to other countries in search of work or land to farm. Argentina, the fastest growing economy, attracted large numbers of Italians.

Slavery was not abolished in Brazil until 1888. Slaves there worked on plantations, in skilled jobs, and as house servants. This painting shows a Brazilian planter with his slaves, two of whom are carrying his wife in a litter.

Juan Manuel de Rosas was the archetypal South American *caudillo*. He waged relentless war on the Patagonian Indians, and although only governor of Buenos Aires province, exercised control over the whole of Argentina.

The War of the Pacific 1879–83

The war was fought over control of the Atacama Desert's rich deposits of nitrates, used in fertilizers and explosives. An Anglo-Chilean company was already working the deposits in the Bolivian part of the desert, when, in 1878, Bolivia demanded more tax. The company refused and Bolivia was backed by Peru. In 1879, Chile landed an army at Antofagasta and took the Bolivian coastline and the southern provinces of Peru. Fired up by their success, Chilean troops sailed to attack Lima and fighting continued in Peru till 1883. The peace treaty resulted in Bolivia's losing its access to the Pacific coast and a long-running border dispute between Chile and Peru, not resolved until 1929.

Iquique was one of the railway terminals on the Pacific coast that owed its existence to nitrate deposits and British investment. It lay in the Tarapacá province, won by Chile from Peru in the War of the Pacific. Many saw the war as a cynical advancement of British business interests.

South American politics and economic development 1830–1900

- **1829:** Juan Manuel de Rosas becomes *caudillo* or dictator of Buenos Aires for next 23 years
- **1839:** Confederation of Bolivia and Peru shattered at battle of Yungay by Chileans and Peruvian nationalists
- **1840:** Guano boom helps stabilize Peru
- **1851:** Railway track completed from Copiapó to port of Caldera in Chile
- **1853:** Slave traffic to Brazil ceases
- **1860:** Ecuador's president, theocrat Garcia Moreno, launches ambitious programme of public works
- **1864–70:** Paraguayan War; catastrophic defeat of Paraguay by Brazil, Argentina, and Uruguay
- **c.1865:** Chile producing 44% of world's copper
- **c.1870:** European investment and immigration into Argentina starts to accelerate
- **1879–83:** War of the Pacific
- **1881:** Patagonia becomes part of Argentina
- **1888:** Slavery in Brazil at last completely abolished
- **1889:** Brazil gains republican status as Emperor is forced to leave
- **1896:** Height of Brazilian rubber boom; Manáos builds opera house
- **1900:** Chile and Argentina agree border protocol
- **1900:** Brazil produces 66% of the world's coffee; tin supersedes silver as Bolivia's chief export.

MODERN SOUTH AMERICA

Augusto Pinochet headed Chile's military government from 1974 to 1990.

POLITICAL AND ECONOMIC instability arose in South America as a result of the great depression of the 1930s. Border disputes persisted, although few flared up like the Chaco War of 1932–35. In most states, a sharp rise in population, together with rapid urbanization and industrialization, exerted great pressures on weak democratic institutions. Opposition to the conservative status quo was pronounced among intellectuals and trade unionists. In the late 1960s, social conflicts and ideological battles shook governments and set many countries on a new course of repressive, conservative authoritarianism. In the 1980s, South America began to turn towards democracy, free markets and international trade. By the start of the 21st century, most countries were benefiting from improved levels of social, political and economic stability.

South America: from instability to democracy

After killing some 35,000 people in the 1980s and 1990s, the Maoist Sendero Luminoso (Shining Path) terrorist movement was largely defeated by the Peruvian government. However, drug-trafficking and kidnapping enabled a resurgence of terrorism in the early 2000s.

In response to the global recession of the 1930s, populist governments promoted economic nationalism and industrial development. By the late 1950s economic and social progress had led to greater democracy, but the Communist-inspired Cuban Revolution threatened the status quo. Fearing the spread of Communism, the US pledged $10 billion in aid, but massive population growth soon absorbed this. As conflict mounted between ruling elites and leftist guerrillas, military regimes, backed by the US, took control. The tide of military rule began to recede in the 1980s. By the end of the 20th century, most states were functioning multi-party democracies, although in some cases authoritarian tendencies remained.

Political development from 1935

- **1937:** 'New State' in Brazil launched by Vargas
- **1946:** Peron comes to power in Argentina
- **1968:** Tupamaros urban guerrilla group founded in Uruguay. Military junta takes over in Peru
- **1974:** Brutal dictatorship of Pinochet in Chile
- **1976:** 15,000 political subversives killed during 'Dirty War', by military and right-wing death squads in Argentina
- **1982:** Argentina occupies Falkland Islands; troops surrender to UK forces
- **1989:** Free elections in Brazil; democracy restored in Chile
- **1995:** Fujimori re-elected in Peru after 'self-coup'
- **1998:** Left-wing Hugo Chávez wins election in Venezuela
- **2001:** Economic crisis in Argentina
- **2003:** Peru elects first female prime minister

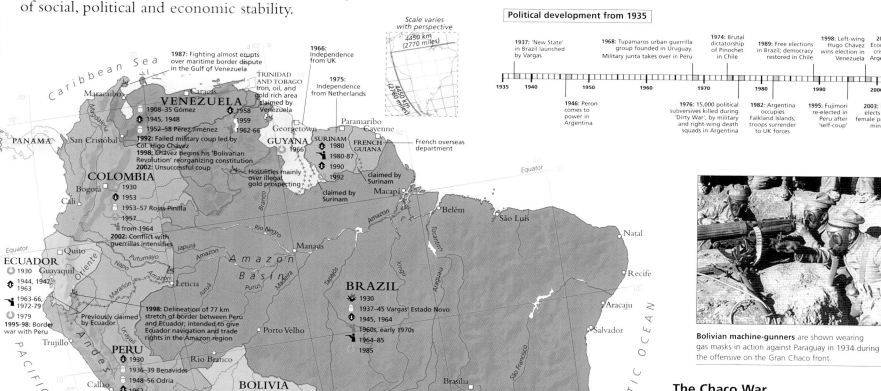

1 Political change in South America from 1930

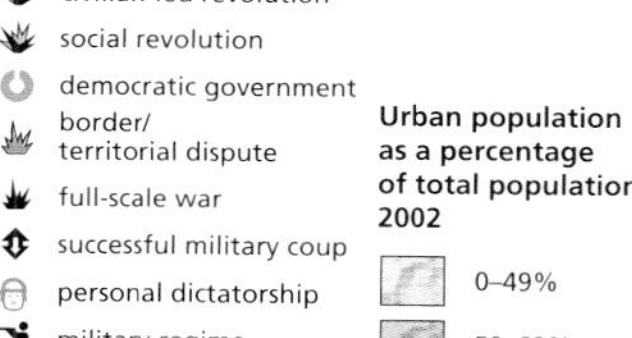

The urban explosion

After 1930, the large cities of Latin America which had been predominantly commercial and administrative centres became increasingly industrialized. Rapid population growth, coupled with worker migration, led to the growth of slum areas in most cities.

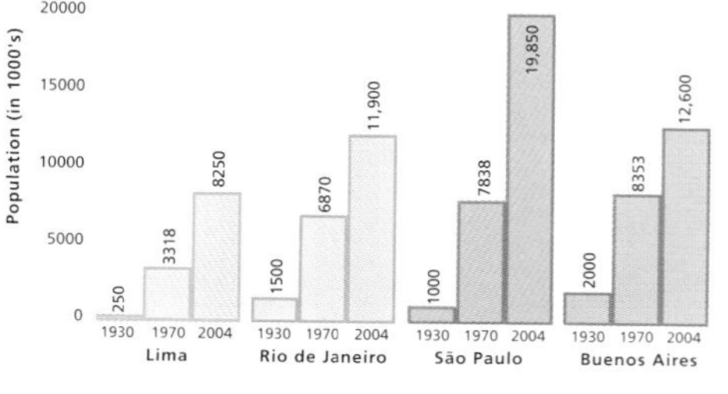

Bolivian machine-gunners are shown wearing gas masks in action against Paraguay in 1934 during the offensive on the Gran Chaco front.

The Chaco War

Bolivian claims to the Chaco territory, north of the Pilcomayo river, led to a three-year war with Paraguay from 1932. The conflict grew out of Bolivia's desire to gain access to the Atlantic coast via the river system which ran across the region to the River Plate, and Paraguay's interest in potential oil deposits. At the end of the war, Paraguay, the supposedly weaker militarily of the two countries, had gained more territory than its pre-war claims.

2 The disputed territory of the Chaco 1887–1938

BOLIVIA · Santa Cruz · Altiplano · BRAZIL · Bahía Negra · Camiri · Villa Montes · Sanandita · Mar–Nov 1934 · Fortín Ballivián · Jun–Sep 1932 · Fortín Boquerón · Fortín Nanawa · Puerto Casado · Gran Chaco · Pilcomayo · Tropic of Capricorn · PARAGUAY · Asunción · ARGENTINA · Paraguay · Paraná · Iguaçu · Uruguay · 250 km · 250 miles

- Bolivia's claim
- Paraguay's claim
- Tamayo-Aceval Treaty 1887
- Quijarro-Decoud Treaty 1879
- Ichazo-Benites Treaty 1894
- Pinilla-Soler Treaty 1907
- frontiers 1932
- ceasefire front line
- peace conference boundary award 1938 and final frontier
- major battle
- fort
- oilfield
- railway

The Chaco War

- **Jun 1932:** Chaco War begins; Bolivians seize Paraguayan positions; they successfuly attack Fortin Boqueron
- **Aug 1932:** Paraguayans mobilized in major offensive against Boquerón
- **Sep 1932:** Fortin Boquerón falls to Paraguay
- **May 1933:** Paraguay formally declares war
- **Oct 1933:** Paraguay makes spectacular gains along the war front
- **Mar–Jul 1934:** Heaviest fighting of the war occurs near Fortin Ballivián
- **Nov 1934:** Fortin Balliván falls to Paraguayans
- **Jun 1935:** Truce arranged; peace treaty signed in 1938

Economic development

After 1930, many South American nations adopted industrial development policies in an attempt to restructure their economies. Trade tariffs were imposed from the 1940s to accelerate industrialization while high inflation was tolerated in the hope of maintaining a strong demand for goods and services. Manufacturing industries became concentrated in a number of locations, yet income distribution remained unequal. From the 1980s, more open economies attracted investment. Economic reforms in the 1990s, aimed at defeating spiralling inflation, saw the privatization of many state-run enterprises. However, a number of states still suffer from underdevelopment, as well as debt and inflation. The Argentine economy collapsed in 2001, though recovery is underway.

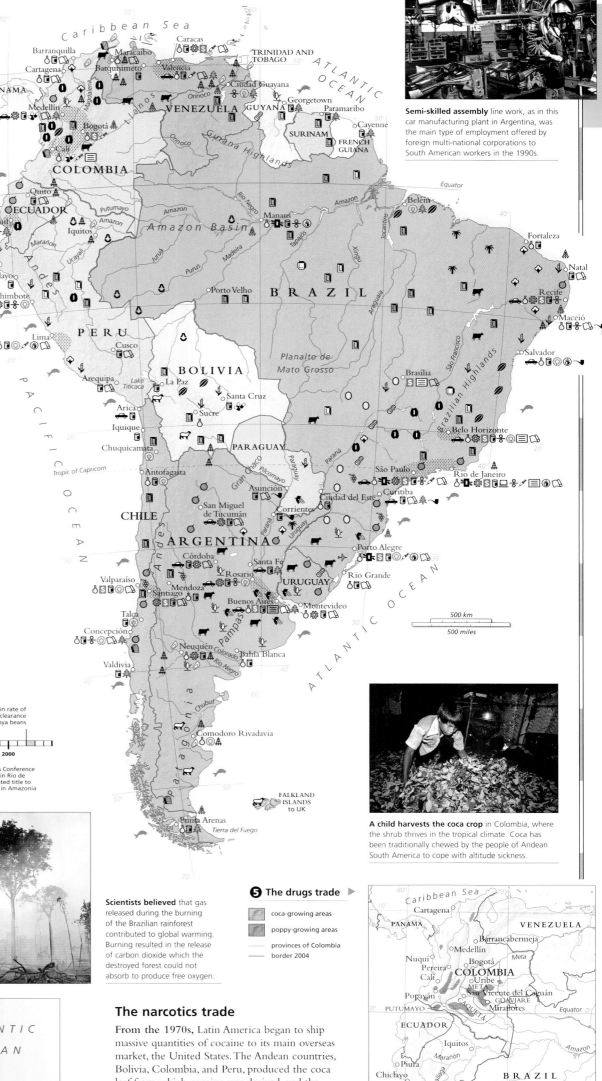

Semi-skilled assembly line work, as in this car manufacturing plant in Argentina, was the main type of employment offered by foreign multi-national corporations to South American workers in the 1990s.

❸ Industry and resources in modern South America

Industry
- aerospace
- car/vehicle manufacture
- chemicals
- electronics
- engineering
- finance
- food processing (includes brewing, fish processing, meat processing, and sugar processing)
- gas
- hi-tech industry
- iron and steel
- metal refining
- narcotics
- oil
- pharmaceuticals
- printing and publishing
- shipbuilidng
- textiles
- timber processing
- tobacco processing
- main industrial areas

Agricultural resources
- cattle
- cocoa
- corn (maize)
- cotton
- coffee
- fishing
- fruit
- oil palms
- peanuts
- rubber
- sheep
- shellfish
- soya beans
- sugar cane
- vineyards
- wheat

Mineral resources
- bauxite (aluminium)
- copper
- diamonds
- gold
- iron ore
- lead
- manganese
- nickel
- silver
- tin
- coal field
- gasfield
- oilfield

Gross national product per capita, 2002
- no data available
- less than $1000
- $1000–$2500
- $2501–$4500

A child harvests the coca crop in Colombia, where the shrub thrives in the tropical climate. Coca has been traditionally chewed by the people of Andean South America to cope with altitude sickness.

Development and deforestation in Amazonia

In the 1950s, the Brazilian government attempted to alleviate poverty amongst landless rural populations by granting resettlement plots along new roads in the Amazonian rainforest. From the 1960s, the government pursued vigorous economic policies which encouraged the development of the region. Subsidies and tax incentives made the clearing of Amazonia especially profitable for large land-holders involved in cattle ranching, and these farms were responsible for 80% of the destruction of the forest. By 2004, 16% of Brazil's rainforest had been cleared.

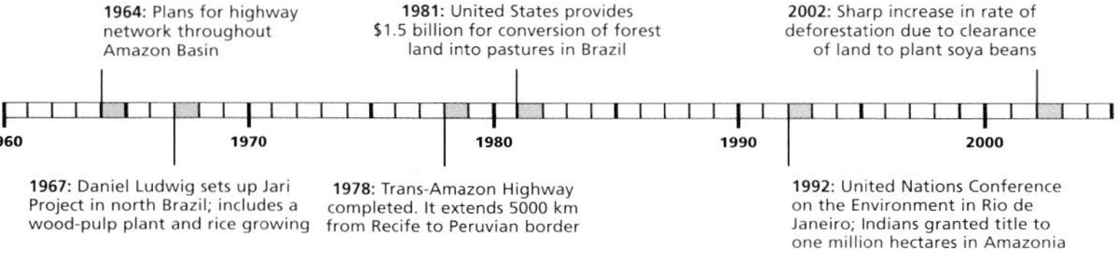
1964: Plans for highway network throughout Amazon Basin
1981: United States provides $1.5 billion for conversion of forest land into pastures in Brazil
2002: Sharp increase in rate of deforestation due to clearance of land to plant soya beans
1960
1970
1980
1990
2000
1967: Daniel Ludwig sets up Jari Project in north Brazil; includes a wood-pulp plant and rice growing
1978: Trans-Amazon Highway completed. It extends 5000 km from Recife to Peruvian border
1992: United Nations Conference on the Environment in Rio de Janeiro; Indians granted title to one million hectares in Amazonia

Economic development of the Brazilian rainforest from 1960

❹ Development and deforestation in Amazonia

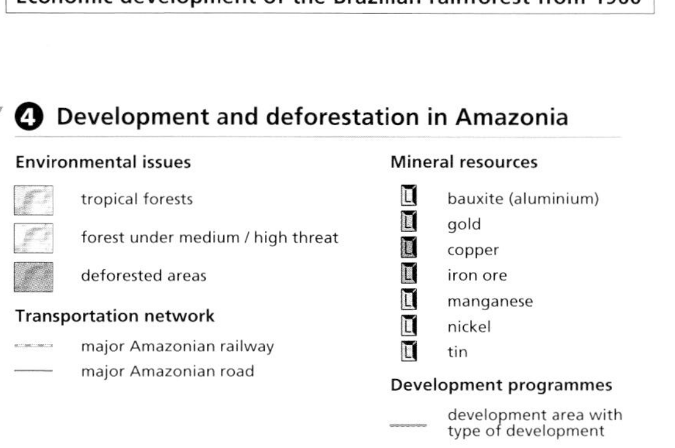
Environmental issues
tropical forests
forest under medium / high threat
deforested areas
Transportation network
major Amazonian railway
major Amazonian road
Mineral resources
bauxite (aluminium)
gold
copper
iron ore
manganese
nickel
tin
Development programmes
development area with type of development

Caribbean Sea
ATLANTIC OCEAN
PACIFIC OCEAN
PANAMA
VENEZUELA
GUYANA
SURINAM
FRENCH GUIANA
COLOMBIA
ECUADOR
PERU
BOLIVIA
BRAZIL
gold (originally an agriculture and livestock zone)
bauxite mining
agriculture and livestock
manganese mining
livestock
timber
Boa Vista
Macapá
Belém
São Luís
Manaus
Santarém
Carajás
iron ore and gold
livestock
Recife
Trans-Amazon Highway
Porto Velho
Cruzeiro do Sul
agriculture and livestock
livestock and meat processing
Cuiabá
Brasília
gold mining
Equator
500 km
500 miles

Scientists believed that gas released during the burning of the Brazilian rainforest contributed to global warming. Burning resulted in the release of carbon dioxide which the destroyed forest could not absorb to produce free oxygen.

❺ The drugs trade

- coca-growing areas
- poppy-growing areas
- provinces of Colombia
- border 2004

Caribbean Sea
Cartagena
PANAMA
VENEZUELA
Barrancabermeja
Medellín
Nuquí
Pereira
Bogotá
Meta
Cali
COLOMBIA
Uribe
META
San Vicente del Caguán
GUAVIARE
Miraflores
Popayán
PUTUMAYO
Equator
ECUADOR
Iquitos
Amazon
Piura
Chiclayo
BRAZIL
Tingo María
PERU
Huancayo
Lima
Ayacucho
PACIFIC OCEAN
Ica
Cusco
BOLIVIA
Lake Titicaca
La Paz
Santa Cruz
500 km
500 miles

The narcotics trade

From the 1970s, Latin America began to ship massive quantities of cocaine to its main overseas market, the United States. The Andean countries, Bolivia, Colombia, and Peru, produced the coca leaf from which cocaine was derived, and the trade was organized and directed by the Medellín and Cali drugs cartels in Colombia. International intervention did little to depress the profits of drug barons, who later diversified into poppy growing in Colombia, for the production of heroin. By 1995, some 90% of the world's cocaine was being produced in Bolivia and Peru. South America also became the main source for the US heroin market.

AFRICA
REGIONAL HISTORY

THE HISTORICAL LANDSCAPE

THE GEOGRAPHY AND CLIMATE OF AFRICA has, to possibly a greater extent than in any other continent, determined its role in world history. The earliest human remains have been found here, in the arid geological block faults of the Great Rift Valley and southern Africa. Although unaffected by the glaciation of the last Ice Age, attendant climatic changes witnessed a transformation of the Sahara from a desert during the Ice Age, into a belt of temperate grassland, inhabited by herds of game and groups of hunter-gatherers by 8000 years ago. By around 4000 BCE, the process of desiccation began which continues today, effectively isolating sub-Saharan Africa from the Mediterranean. Only the Nile valley provided a link, and here one of the world's oldest civilizations emerged. South of the Sahara, a wide range of isolated cultures developed, their nature determined largely by their environment, linked by rich non-literate oral traditions. The plateau nature of much of Africa, and the desert and jungle which dominate much of the landscape, meant that Africa was one of the last continents to be colonized by Europeans, and their brief and callous century of tenancy left a legacy of underdevelopment and political strife.

The Great Rift Valley was home to one of the earliest known human ancestors, *Australopithecus afarensis,* 3.8 million years ago. Modern humans *(Homo sapiens)* evolved here about 100,000 years ago, before migrating to Asia and Australasia, Europe, and finally the Americas.

The Sahara covers much of northern Africa, although sand dunes account for only a quarter of the desert's area. The rest is made up of barren, rock-strewn surfaces. Desert has existed in this part of Africa for almost five million years, and the harsh climate and inhospitable landscape have prevented the establishment of permanent settlements.

The River Nile winds its way across the hostile Sahara to the Mediterranean Sea, flanked by fertile floodplains. Humans have inhabited the Nile region since the early Stone Age, making use of the fertile soils that have built up as a result of the annual flooding of the river.

Vegetation type

- semi-desert or sparsely vegetated
- grassland
- forest or open woodland
- tropical rainforest
- tropical desert (18,000 years ago)
- desert (8000 years ago)
- coastline (present-day)
- coastline (18,000 years ago)

EUROPE
ASIA
Mediterranean Sea
Ionian Basin
EURASIAN PLATE
AFRICAN PLATE
ANATOLIAN PLATE
AFRICAN PLATE
Anatolia
Tigris
Euphrates
Dead Sea
IRANIAN PLATE
ARABIAN PLATE
Tropic of Cancer
Atlas Mountains
Sea levels at the Strait of Gibraltar, between Africa and Europe, were lower, but the two continents were not joined. It is thought that seawater breached this narrow gap about 5.5 million years ago, flooding the deep basins of the Mediterranean.
Nile
DESERT MARGIN 8000 YEARS AGO
Arabian Peninsula
Ahaggar
Sahara
Tibesti
Lower sea levels meant that the Red Sea was narrower and shallower than it is today.
Red Sea
East Sheba Ridge
Owen Fracture Zone
Alula-Fartak Trench
Socotra
ARABIAN PLATE
AFRICAN PLATE
The swampy inland delta of the Niger River is all that remains of this lake today.
MEGA CHAD (8000 YEARS AGO)
ARAOUANE LAKE (8000 YEARS AGO)
Much of the Chad Basin was filled by the huge lake Mega Chad, as the climate warmed at the end of the last Ice Age. The deserts receded about 8000 years ago, allowing nomads and pastoralists to inhabit the Sahara.
Blue Nile
White Nile
Horn of Africa
Niger
Lake Chad
Ethiopian Highlands
Ogaden
Chain Ridge
Lake Volta
AFRICA
Somali Basin
Equator
Lake Rudolf
Juba
Shebeli
Somali Plain
During the last Ice Age, the Congo Basin was not covered by dense rainforests as it is today. The colder, dryer climate meant that most of the basin was covered by grassland and scrub.
Uele
Bioko
Guinea Basin
Congo
Lake Albert
INDIAN OCEAN
São Tomé
Congo Basin
Lake Victoria
Ogooué
Lomami
Great Rift Valley
Zanzibar
Amirante Trench
Lake Tanganyika
Lake Rukwa
Chain Fracture Zone
Congo Canyon
Lake Mweru
Comoro Islands
Comoro Basin
Lake Nyasa
Luangwa
Angola Basin
18,000 years ago Madagascar was covered with great temperate forests in place of the lush tropical forests that exist today.
Deserts extended from southern Africa, as far north as the Congo River.
Lake Cabora Bassa
Zambezi
Cuando
Cubango
Mascarene Plain
Wilshaw Ridge
Madagascar
Tropic of Capricorn
Sabi
Kalahari Desert
LAKE MAKGADIKGADI
Runde
Limpopo
Madagascar Basin
ATLANTIC OCEAN
Mid-Atlantic Ridge
SOUTH AMERICAN PLATE
AFRICAN PLATE
Walvis Ridge
The area once covered by this vast lake is now occupied by the Okavango Delta.
Olifants
Madagascar Plateau
Vaal
Natal Basin
Mozambique Plateau
Orange River
Natal Valley
Southwest Indian Ridge
Drakensberg
Discovery II Fracture Zone
Indomed Fracture Zone
Cape Basin
Agulhas Plateau
Cape Rise
Agulhas Basin
AFRICAN PLATE
ANTARCTICA PLATE
Du Toit Fracture Zone
Prince Edward Fracture
Atlantic-Indian Ridge
Crozet Plateau

Africa: 18,000 years ago

Africa was both colder and drier during the Ice Age. These two factors produced a marked change in the vegetation of the continent. The Sahara expanded southwards, and rainforests shrank to a fraction of their present size, surviving in small strips next to rivers in the Congo Basin, and replaced for the most part by open grasslands and scrub. Deserts also spread in southwestern Africa, advancing northwards and inland from the dry coastal zone.

AFRICA

EXPLORATION AND MAPPING

To stake a territorial claim, Portuguese sailors would place a stone cross (*padrão*) on the African shore.

IN THE ABSENCE OF A WRITTEN historical record, little is known of early local knowledge of Africa south of the Sahara. Writing in the 5th century BCE, the Greek historian Herodotus reported an attempt by a Phoenician crew to circumnavigate the continent in 600 BCE. By 150 CE, the Greek geographer Ptolemy had mapped the area north of the line between Mombasa and the Canary Islands (*see p.44*). From 600 CE Arab merchants criss-crossed the Sahara establishing Muslim settlements. Several trading nations of Europe had secured coastal toeholds by 1600; however, by 1800, the African land mass remained relatively uncharted. The great 19th-century explorers of the interior meticulously recorded those features they encountered.

MEDIEVAL ACCOUNTS OF THE INTERIOR OF WEST AFRICA

Though the West Africans did not have maps, travellers in the region built up a considerable store of topographic information. It was this knowledge that Arabs and later the Portuguese tapped as their source for maps of the interior. Al-Idrisi, in 1154 reported a single river in West Africa. The Egyptian geographer al-'Umari had an account of a Nile of the Blacks which divided into two rivers, one flowing to the ocean, the other to the East African Nile via Lake Chad. Writing in 1456, a Portuguese squire called Diogo Gomes recounted the testimony of Buquer, an African merchant, who talked of a great river called Emin. The reports of Mandinka merchants in 1585 agreed with Buquer's account and gave additional detail.

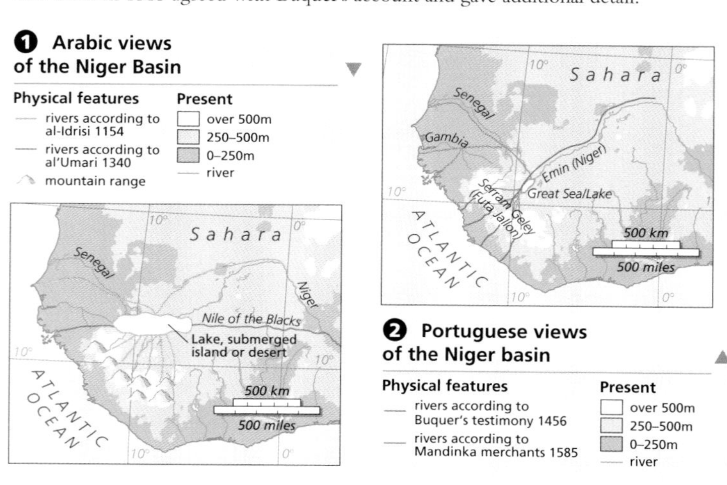

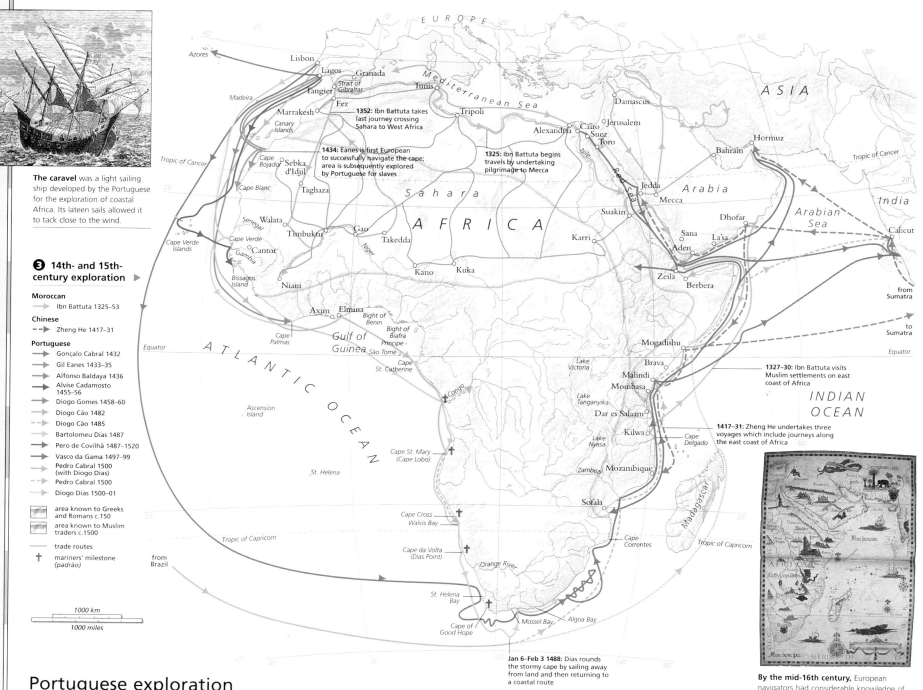

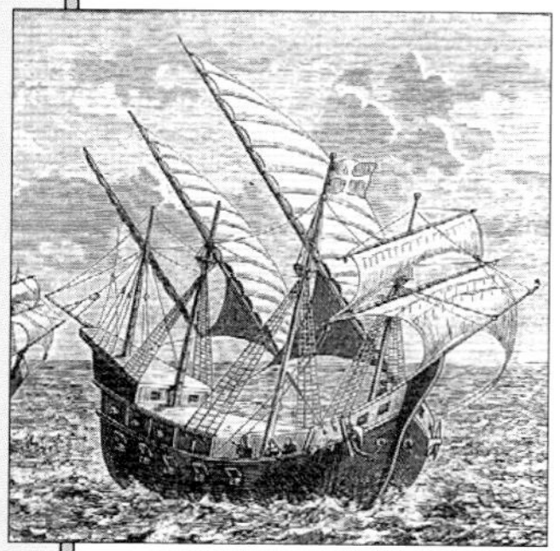

The caravel was a light sailing ship developed by the Portuguese for the exploration of coastal Africa. Its lateen sails allowed it to tack close to the wind.

3 14th- and 15th-century exploration

Moroccan
- Ibn Battuta 1325–53

Chinese
- Zheng He 1417–31

Portuguese
- Gonçalo Cabral 1432
- Gil Eanes 1433–35
- Alfonso Baldaya 1436
- Alvise Cadamosto 1455–56
- Diogo Gomes 1458–60
- Diogo Cão 1482
- Diogo Cão 1485
- Bartolomeu Dias 1487
- Pero de Covilhã 1487–1520
- Vasco da Gama 1497–99
- Pedro Cabral 1500 (with Diogo Dias)
- Pedro Cabral 1500
- Diogo Dias 1500–01

- area known to Greeks and Romans c.150
- area known to Muslim traders c.1500
- trade routes
- mariners' milestone (*padrão*)

1352: Ibn Battuta takes last journey crossing Sahara to West Africa

1434: Eanes is first European to successfully navigate the cape; area is subsequently explored by Portuguese for slaves

1325: Ibn Battuta begins travels by undertaking pilgrimage to Mecca

1327–30: Ibn Battuta visits Muslim settlements on east coast of Africa

1417–31: Zheng He undertakes three voyages which include journeys along the east coast of Africa

Jan 6–Feb 3 1488: Dias rounds the stormy cape by sailing away from land and then returning to a coastal route

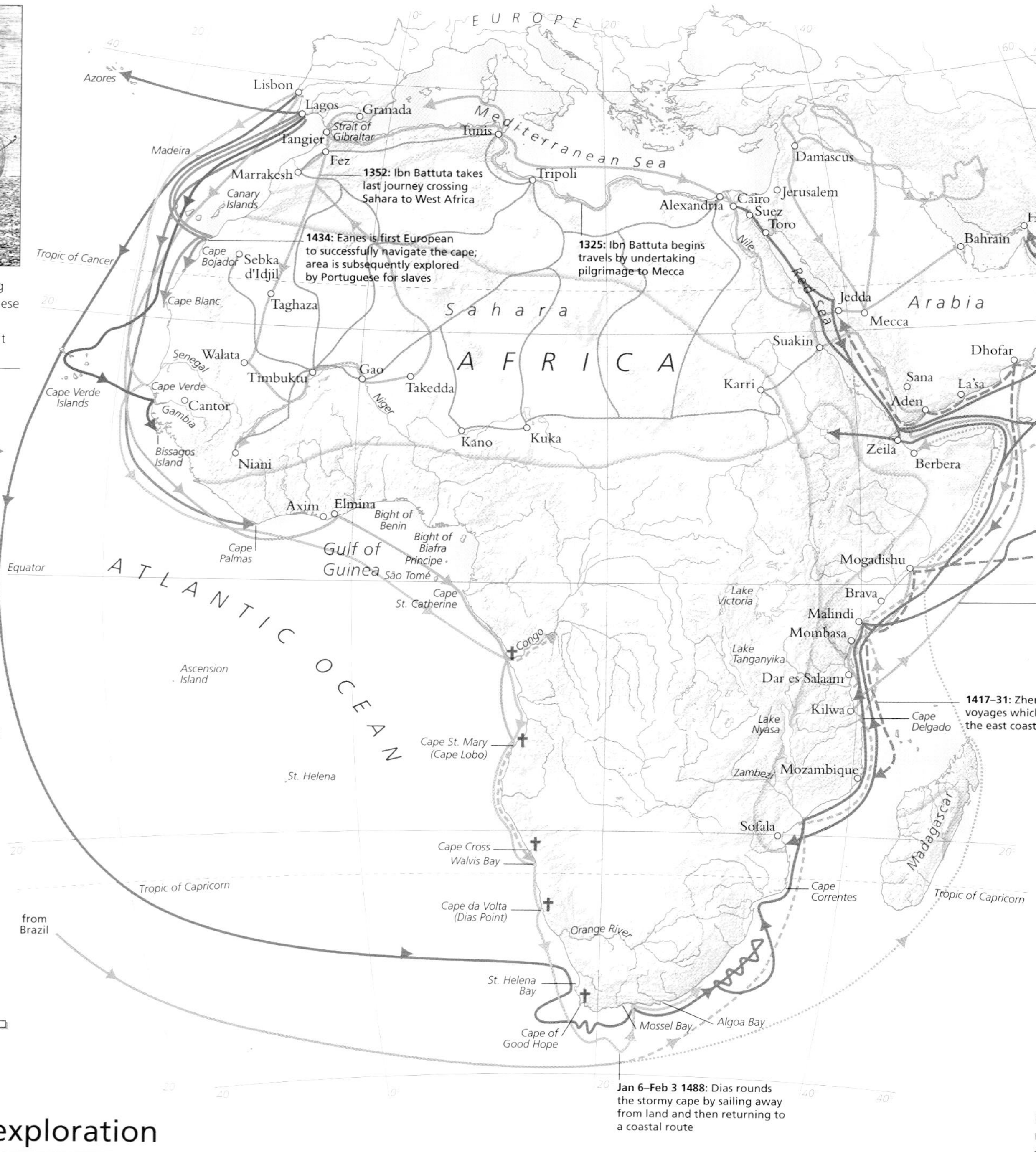

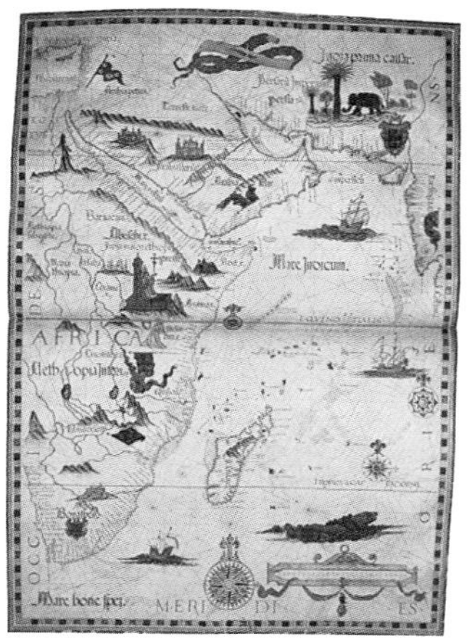

By the mid-16th century, European navigators had considerable knowledge of the coasts of Madagascar and East Africa, as depicted in this Portuguese map of 1558.

Portuguese exploration

Systematic voyages of discovery were undertaken by the Portuguese along the western coast of Africa. These and later expeditions were made in the hope both of making contact with the gold-producing centres known to exist in West Africa, and of establishing a trade route to India around the tip of the continent. In consequence, the lower reaches of the rivers Gambia and Senegal were explored, contact was made with the Empire of Mali, and the Cape Verde Islands were discovered.

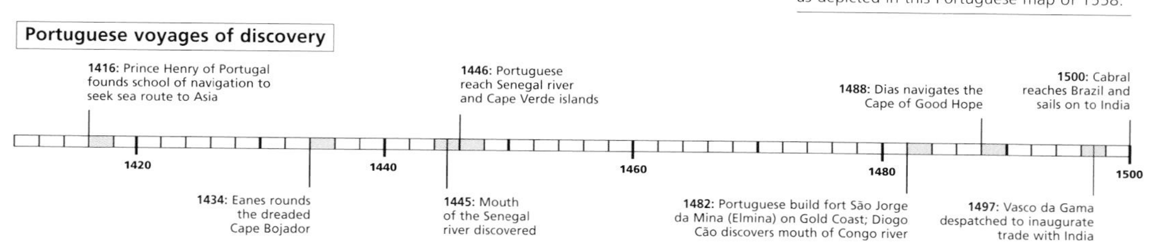

Exploration of the African interior

The European exploration of the African interior is largely the story of the search for the sources of some of the world's greatest rivers. The Scottish explorer, James Bruce toured Ethiopia between 1768 and 1773, discovering the source of the Blue Nile in 1772. Systematic exploration may be said to have begun in 1788, under the auspices of the African Association, a group of English scientists and scholars. In 1795 the Association sponsored Mungo Park's first journey to West Africa; he investigated the Gambia river and reached the Niger, showing that it flowed eastward. British exploration intensified in the first half of the 19th century culminating in John Hanning Speke's triumphant discovery of the source of the Nile at Ripon Falls, Lake Victoria in 1862. In anticipation of the scramble for territorial control, a number of continental Europeans also embarked on investigative expeditions.

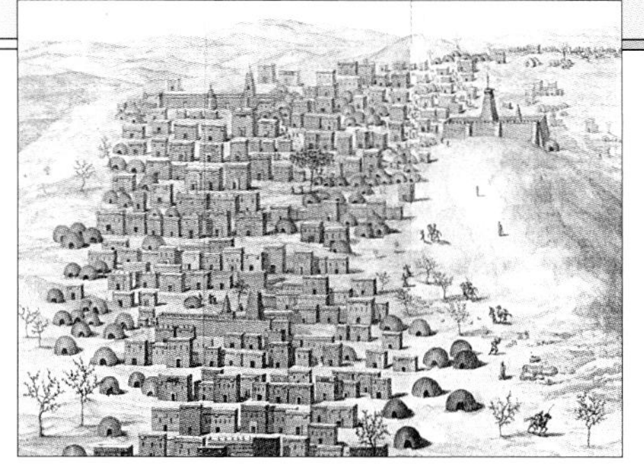

French explorer René Caillié made this sketch of Timbuktu in 1828, when he fulfilled his great ambition to visit the Saharan city, and secured a 10,000 francs prize for his efforts. The sum had been offered by the Société Géographique to the first European to return from the city.

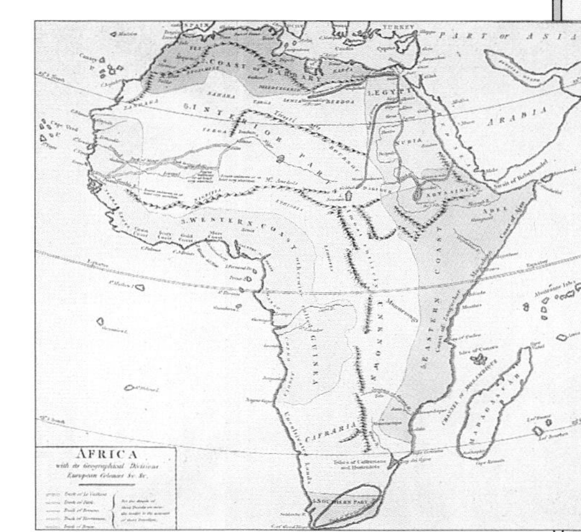

The 19th century saw the systematic and scientific exploration ot the African interior. As a result, cartographers were reluctant to represent uncertain data. Published in 1808, this map of Africa shows less information than its more speculative predecessors.

❹ 19th-century exploration

British
- James Bruce 1768–73
- Mungo Park 1795–96
- Mungo Park 1805–06
- Hugh Clapperton, Dixon Denham, and Walter Oudney 1821–25
- Hugh Clapperton and Richard Lander 1825–27
- David Livingstone 1841–53
- David Livingstone 1849
- David Livingstone 1853–56
- David Livingstone 1866–73
- Samuel and Florence Baker 1861–65
- Henry Stanley 1871–89
- Mary Kingsley 1895

French
- René Caillié 1827–28
- Pierre Savorgnan de Brazza 1875–78
- Jean-Baptiste Marchand 1897–98

German
- Heinrich Barth 1850–55

Italian
- Vittorio Bottego 1892–97

Portuguese
- Alexandre Serpa Pinto 1877–79

Swedish
- Charles Andersson 1853–59

1000 km
1000 miles

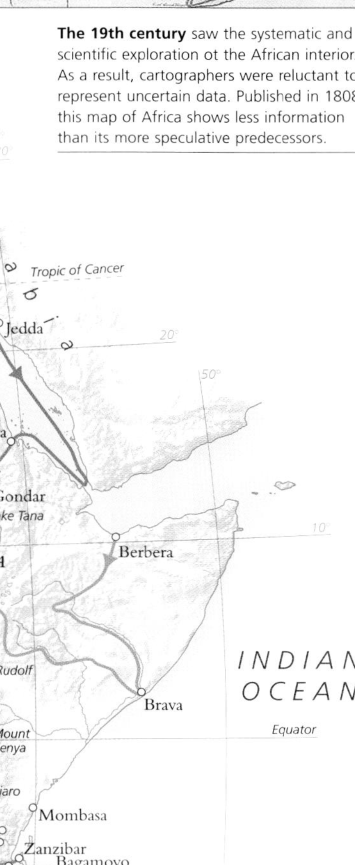

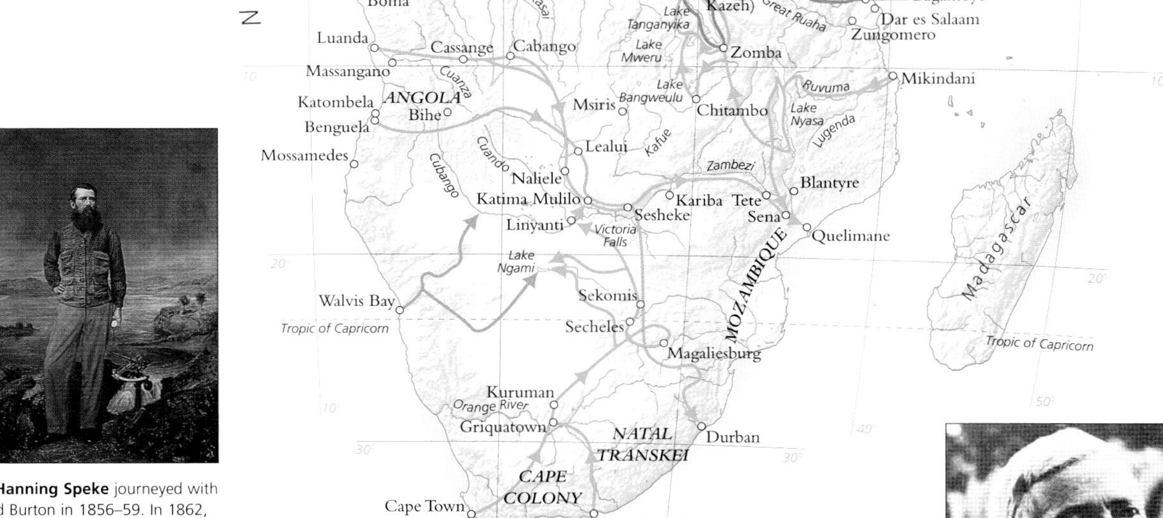

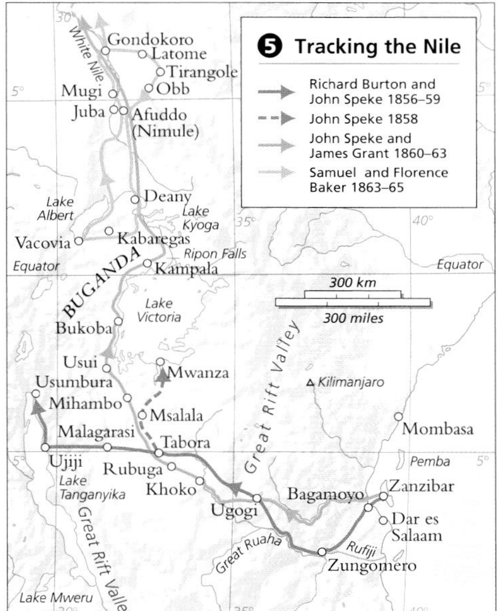

John Hanning Speke journeyed with Richard Burton in 1856–59. In 1862, James Grant and he came across the source of the Nile at Lake Victoria.

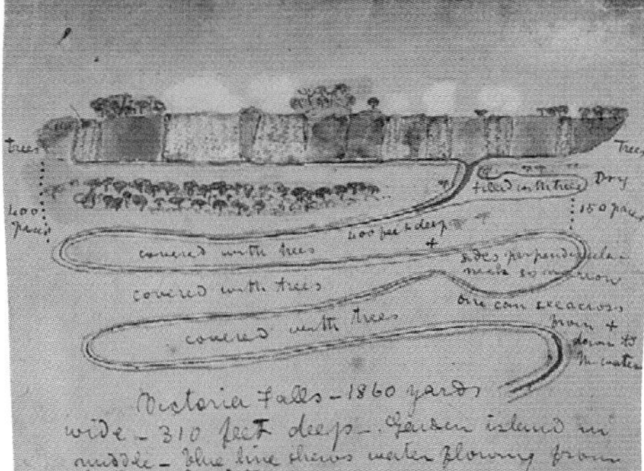

Livingstone carefully noted the dimensions of those physical features he encountered. He annotated this map of Victoria Falls with precise measurements and descriptive detail.

The source of the Nile

The quest for the source of the Nile captured the imagination of 19th-century Europe. The adventure stimulated intellectual debate and provoked fierce personal jealousies. After Speke had identified the source as Ripon Falls, Lake Victoria, persistent attempts were made to discredit his discovery. The political and economic importance of the region made it the objective of rival imperialists.

Sir Henry Morton Stanley, the British-American journalist, was sent to Africa by the New York Herald in 1871 to find David Livingstone, of whom nothing had been heard for several months. In the 1880s he helped create Léopold's Congo Free State.

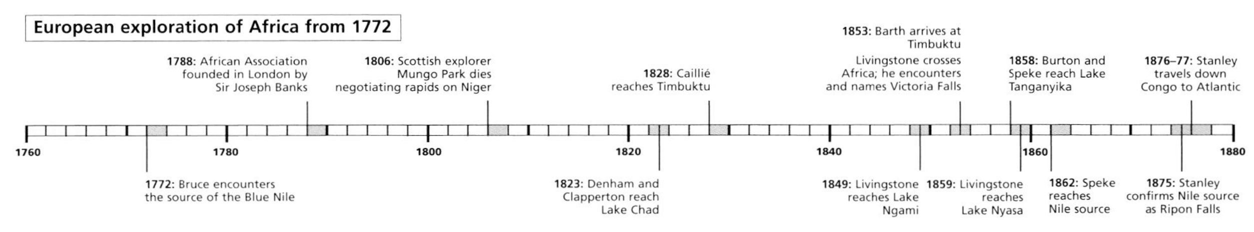

THE EARLY HISTORY OF AFRICA

Hatshepsut seized the throne in Egypt from her stepson and reigned from 1472 to 1458 BCE.

THREE EVENTS contributed to the growth and spread of farming in Africa: the spread of cattle pastoralism in the Sahara, the domestication of indigenous crops further south, and the introduction of cereals to Egypt. Asian wheat and barley spread along the Mediterranean coast, up the Nile valley to the Sudan and the Ethiopian Highlands. Drier conditions from 3000 BCE forced Saharan pastoralists to migrate to the Nile valley where from 5000 BCE, crops had thrived in fertile soil deposited by annual floods. Egypt thereafter emerged as a powerful state, organized conventionally into 30 'Dynasties', broken down into three 'Kingdoms' separated by two 'Intermediate Periods' of disunity and instability.

The development of agriculture

From 4000 BCE bulrush millet was cultivated alongside sorghum in southern Sudan.

Both the herding of wild cattle in the Sahara and the cultivation of indigenous plants further south began c.6000 BCE. From 5000 BCE, Asian wheat and barley were grown in Egypt. By 2000 BCE pastoralism was widespread north of the Equator. Farming and herding south of the Equator however, were impeded by dense forests and the presence of the parasitic tsetse fly. As a result pastoralism progressed only slowly down the east coast reaching southern Africa by 1000 CE.

Saharan rock art provide vivid pictures of what life was like in the region. This example from the Tassili n'Ajjer plateau, dates from c.6000 BCE. It depicts the hunting of giraffes, now only found south of the Sahara.

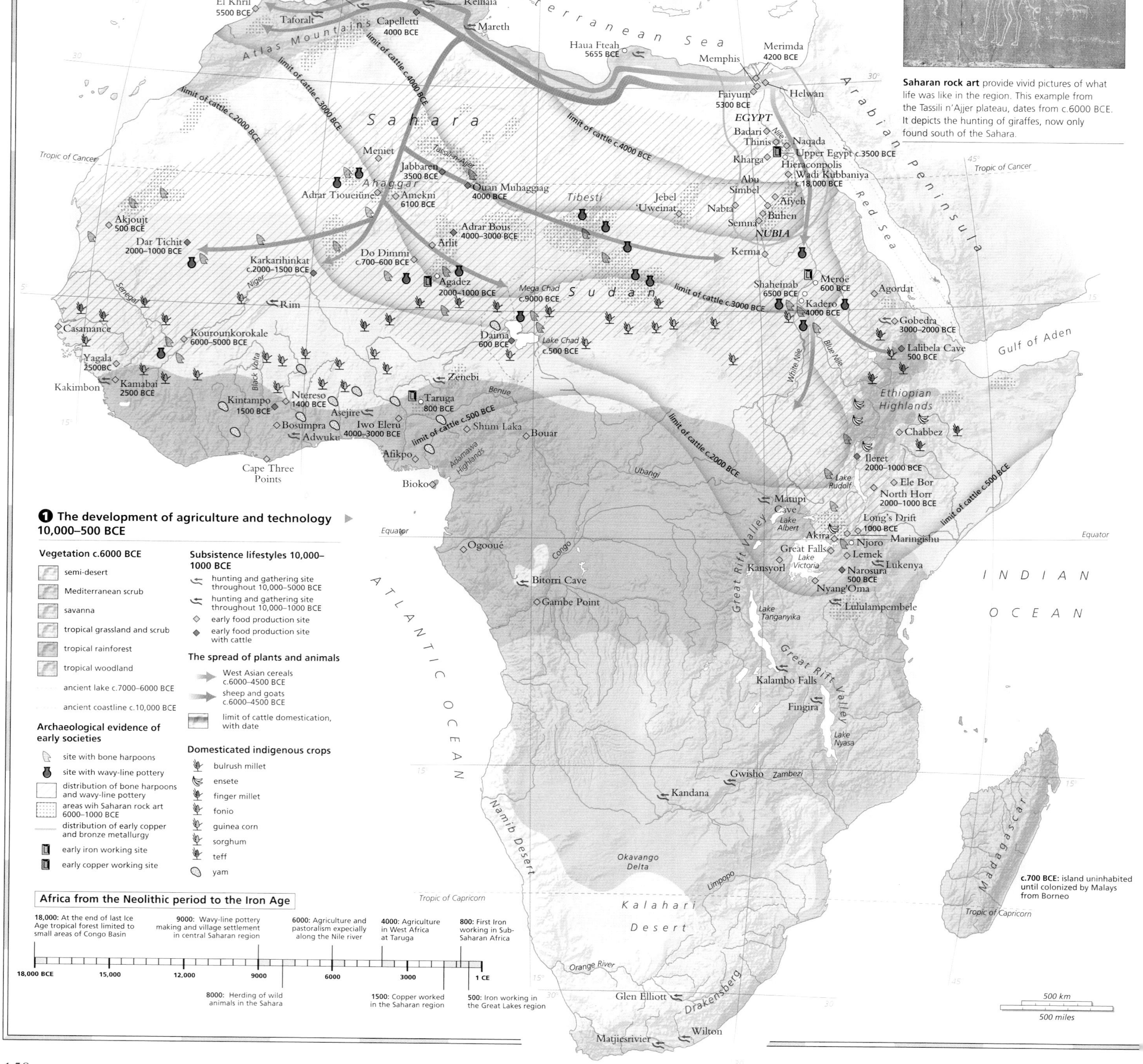

1 The development of agriculture and technology 10,000–500 BCE

Vegetation c.6000 BCE

- semi-desert
- Mediterranean scrub
- savanna
- tropical grassland and scrub
- tropical rainforest
- tropical woodland
- ancient lake c.7000–6000 BCE
- ancient coastline c.10,000 BCE

Archaeological evidence of early societies

- site with bone harpoons
- site with wavy-line pottery
- distribution of bone harpoons and wavy-line pottery
- areas wih Saharan rock art 6000–1000 BCE
- distribution of early copper and bronze metallurgy
- early iron working site
- early copper working site

Subsistence lifestyles 10,000–1000 BCE

- hunting and gathering site throughout 10,000–5000 BCE
- hunting and gathering site throughout 10,000–1000 BCE
- early food production site
- early food production site with cattle

The spread of plants and animals

- West Asian cereals c.6000–4500 BCE
- sheep and goats c.6000–4500 BCE
- limit of cattle domestication, with date

Domesticated indigenous crops

- bulrush millet
- ensete
- finger millet
- fonio
- guinea corn
- sorghum
- teff
- yam

c.700 BCE: island uninhabited until colonized by Malays from Borneo

Africa from the Neolithic period to the Iron Age

- **18,000:** At the end of last Ice Age tropical forest limited to small areas of Congo Basin
- **9000:** Wavy-line pottery making and village settlement in central Saharan region
- **8000:** Herding of wild animals in the Sahara
- **6000:** Agriculture and pastoralism expecially along the Nile river
- **4000:** Agriculture in West Africa at Taruga
- **1500:** Copper worked in the Saharan region
- **800:** First Iron working in Sub-Saharan Africa
- **500:** Iron working in the Great Lakes region

18,000 BCE · 15,000 · 12,000 · 9000 · 6000 · 3000 · 1 CE

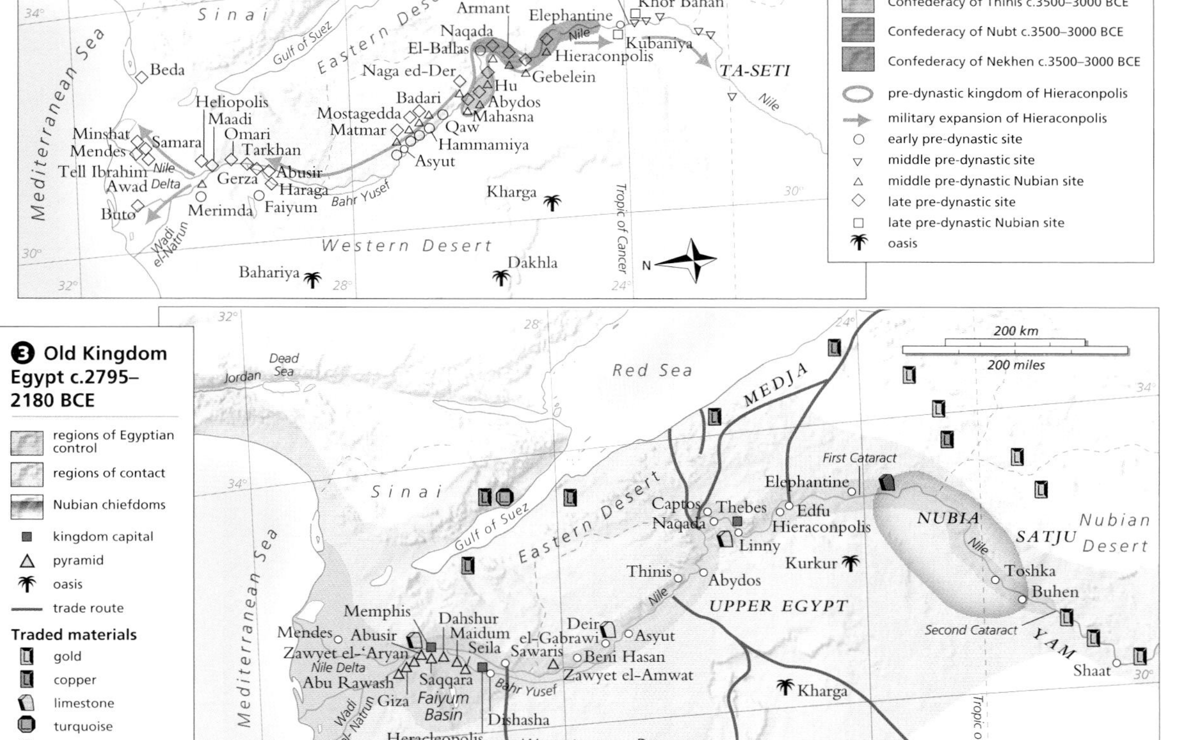

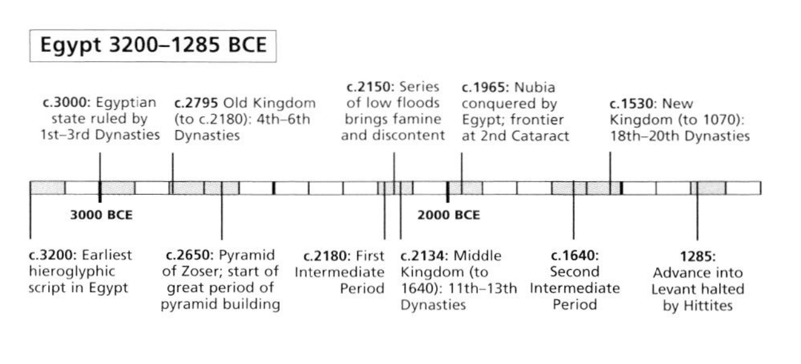

The growth of Egypt 3500–2180 BCE

From 5000 BCE settled communites of farmers in the Nile valley gradually coalesced into urban centres under local rulers who developed efficient administrations. Narmer of the 1st Dynasty established the Egyptian state c.3000 BCE. From this time the use of hieroglyphic writing spread and Memphis was founded. With greater centralization of power the Old Kingdom emerged and the building of the great pyramids which served as royal burial places began. From 2400 BCE royal power began to decline and by 2180 BCE the Old Kingdom was divided between two rival dynasties in Upper and Lower Egypt. The years of political instability that followed became known as the First Intermediate Period.

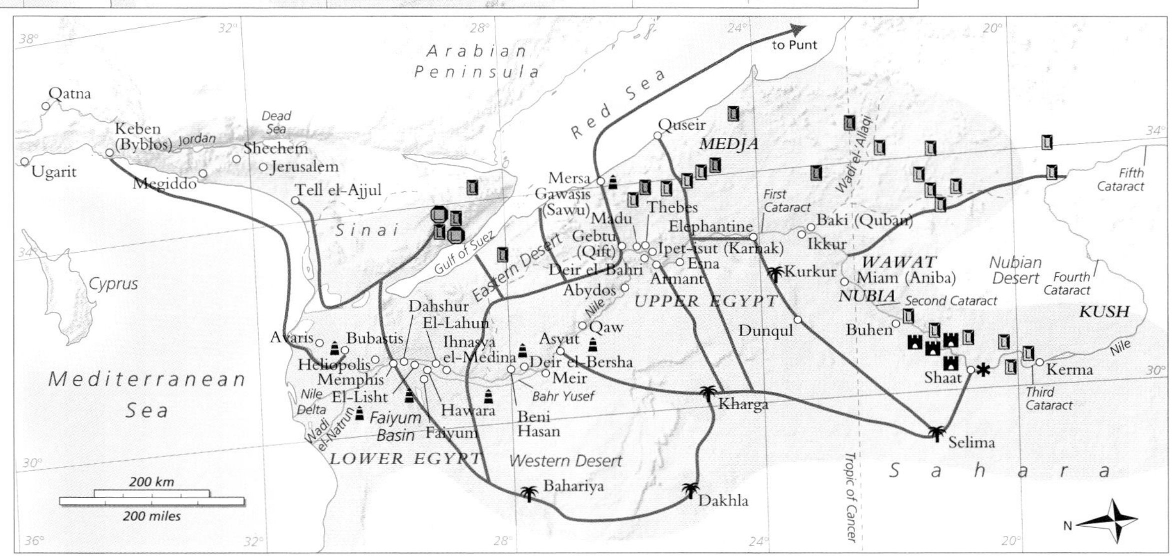

4 Middle Kingdom Egypt c.2134–1640 BCE

regions of Egyptian control
regions of contact
trading centre
Nubian fort
Middle Kingdom temple
oasis
trade route

Traded materials
gold
copper
turquoise

The step-pyramid of Zoser dating from c.2650 BCE was the earliest pyramid built in Egypt. Its construction required the large-scale mobilization of thousands of workers

Hatshepsut's temple at Deir el-Bahri was built c.1473 BCE. A fine example of architecture from the 18th Dynasty, the building has a series of colonnades and courts on three levels.

Expansion and division in Egypt

The governors of Thebes emerged from the First Intermediate Period as rulers of Upper Egypt. They later successfully challenged Lower Egypt for control of the entire region, and the Middle Kingdom was established by c.2134 BCE. Its army and administration systematically enriched Egypt's economy by dominating, and eventually annexing, Wawat and northern Kush. The Second Intermediate saw Nubia lost from Egyptian control, and the division of the Nile Delta region into several kingdoms. From 1640 BCE much of Egypt was ruled by the Hyksos from the Levant. They were later expelled by Ahmose, king of Thebes, who became the first ruler of the New Kingdom. During the New Kingdom Egypt embarked on a policy of expansion both north and south which made it the major commercial power in the ancient world. By 1000 BCE, however, the New Kingdom was in decline.

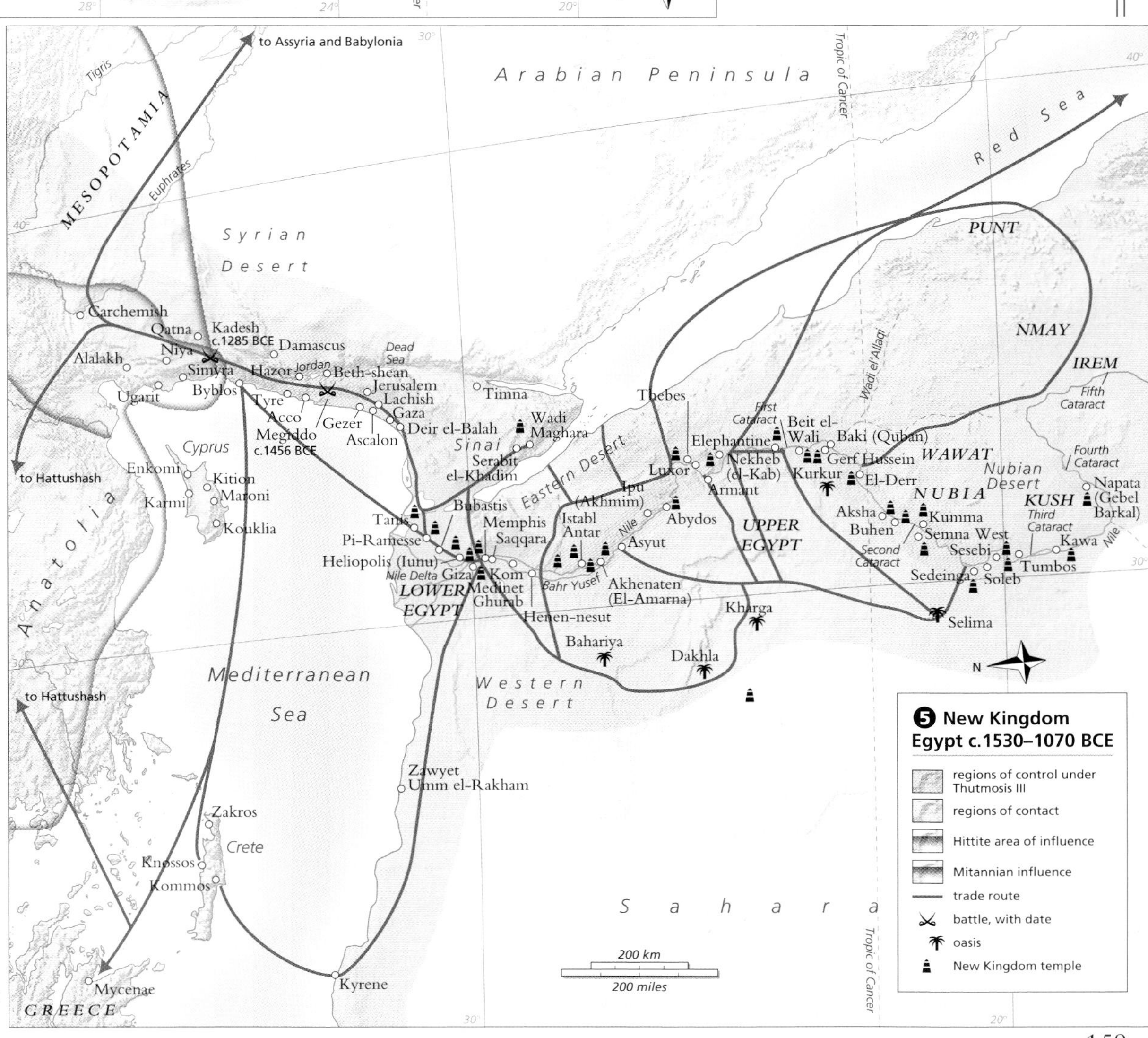

THE SPREAD OF COMPLEX SOCIETIES

The Nok culture of West Africa was noted for its terracotta sculptures.

ALTHOUGH TRADE ROUTES connected sub-Saharan Africa to the Mediterranean civilizations of the north, the two regions developed very much in isolation. The southward migrations of Bantu-speakers from 2000 BCE, may have contributed to the diffusion of settled agriculture in sub-Saharan Africa. Sheep-herding and iron-working spread south at a later date. The Nok of West Africa were smelting iron by 600 BCE. In North Africa, the rich lands of the Mediterranean coast and Egypt attracted foreign invaders, including the Greeks and Romans. However, from 300 BCE, powerful native states also emerged, notably Aksum, which dominated the Red Sea, and the Berber states which competed with Rome for the lands of northwest Africa.

The Bantu influence

From their homeland in modern-day Nigeria on Africa's west coast, the Bantu-speaking peoples dispersed along eastern and western routes into the equatorial rainforests and then on to southern Africa during the 1st millennium BCE. The migrating Bantu cleared forests and engaged in mixed farming. From the late 1st century BCE, their knowledge of iron-working gave them a distinct advantage over hunter-gatherers such as the Khoisan people. They established an economic basis for new societies which could sustain greater populations than those based on hunting and gathering. Thus the period from 500 BCE to 1000 CE saw the transfer of Bantu traditions to much of sub-Saharan Africa.

During the first millennium BCE the Bantu settled in villages on the edge of the rainforest in central Africa, engaging in mixed farming.

The spread of iron-working

The earliest evidence for iron-working south of the Sahara is found at the settlements of the Nok culture in West Africa, including Taruga and Samun Dukiya and dates from c.600 BCE. By 300 BCE, iron-working had spread as far south as the Congo river. From 1 CE, dates from sites on the sub-equatorial west coast correspond with those in East Africa. It is possible therefore, that iron smelting diffused southward along two separate routes: one along the eastern part of the continent and the other along the west. In addition to its use for tools such as hoes, axes, knives, and spears, iron was also a luxury trade item, and helped to sustain inter-community relations in the sub-Saharan region.

Paintings of chariots are found along ancient trans-Saharan routes. They may provide evidence for the transport of iron-working to sub-Saharan Africa.

The development of iron technology and social organization

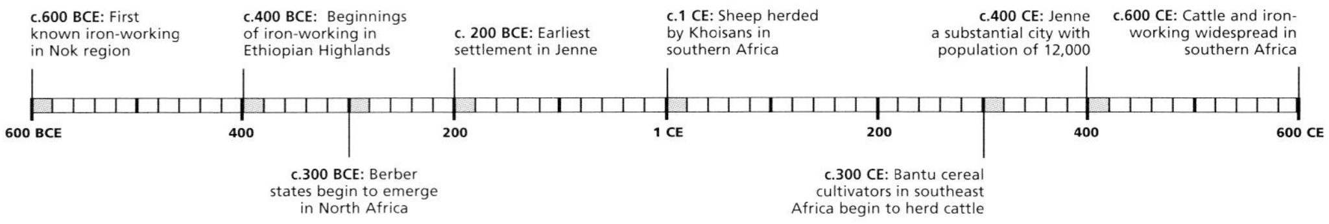

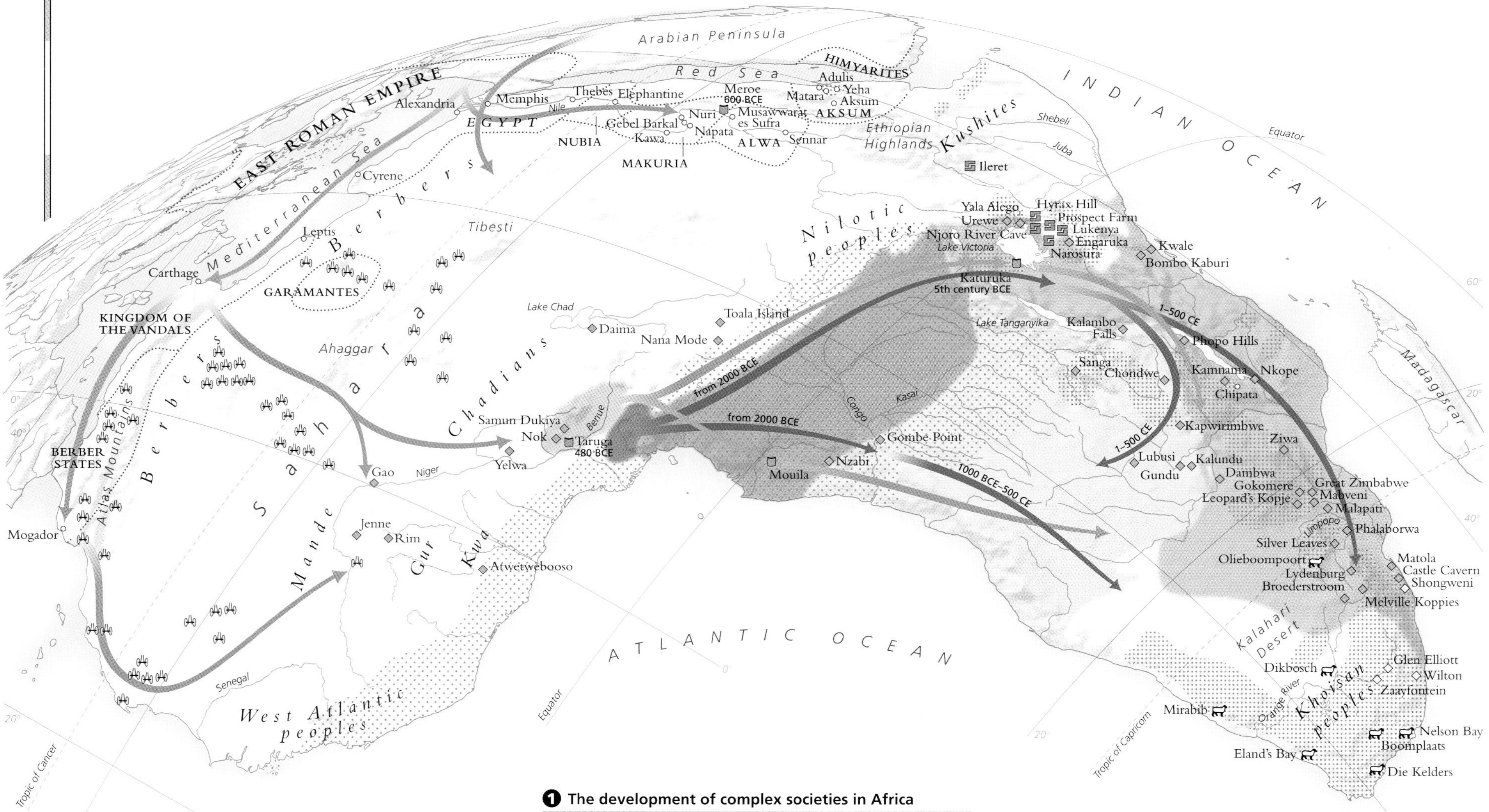

- **c.600 BCE:** First known iron-working in Nok region
- **c.400 BCE:** Beginnings of iron-working in Ethiopian Highlands
- **c.300 BCE:** Berber states begin to emerge in North Africa
- **c. 200 BCE:** Earliest settlement in Jenne
- **c.1 CE:** Sheep herded by Khoisans in southern Africa
- **c.300 CE:** Bantu cereal cultivators in southeast Africa begin to herd cattle
- **c.400 CE:** Jenne a substantial city with population of 12,000
- **c.600 CE:** Cattle and iron-working widespread in southern Africa

600 BCE | 400 | 200 | 1 CE | 200 | 400 | 600 CE

Arabian Peninsula · Red Sea · HIMYARITES · Adulis · Yeha · Aksum · Matara · AKSUM · Meroe 600 BCE · Musawwarat es Sufra · Nuri · Napata · Gebel Barkal · Kawa · ALWA · Sennar · NUBIA · MAKURIA · Thebes · Elephantine · Nile · Memphis · EGYPT · Alexandria · EAST ROMAN EMPIRE · Mediterranean Sea · Cyrene · Berbers · Leptis · GARAMANTES · Carthage · KINGDOM OF THE VANDALS · BERBER STATES · Atlas Mountains · Mogador · Tibesti · Ahaggar · Sahara · Gao · Niger · Jenne · Rim · Mande · Gur · Kwa · Atwetwebooso · Senegal · West Atlantic peoples · Tropic of Cancer · Lake Chad · Daima · Chadians · Samun Dukiya · Nok · Taruga 480 BCE · Benue · Yelwa · Toala Island · Nana Mode · Ethiopian Highlands · Kushites · Shebeli · Juba · Ileret · Nilotic peoples · Yala Alego · Urewe · Hyrax Hill · Prospect Farm · Lukenya · Njoro River Cave · Engaruka · Narosura · Lake Victoria · Kwale · Bombo Kaburi · Katuruka 5th century BCE · from 2000 BCE · Lake Tanganyika · Kalambo Falls · Sanga · Chondwe · 1–500 CE · Phopo Hills · Kamnama · Nkope · Chipata · Kapwirimbwe · Congo · Kasai · Gombe Point · Nzabi · Mouila · 1000 BCE–500 CE · Lubusi · Kalundu · Gundu · Dambwa · Gokomere · Zıwa · Great Zimbabwe · Mabveni · Leopard's Kopje · Malapati · Limpopo · Phalaborwa · Silver Leaves · Olieboompoort · Lydenburg · Broederstroom · Matola · Castle Cavern · Shongweni · Melville Koppies · Kalahari Desert · Dikbosch · Orange River · Khoisan peoples · Glen Elliott · Wilton · Zaayfontein · Mirabib · Nelson Bay · Boomplaats · Eland's Bay · Die Kelders · Tropic of Capricorn · Madagascar · INDIAN OCEAN · ATLANTIC OCEAN · Equator

1 The development of complex societies in Africa

- Bantu homeland 2000 BCE
- Northwestern Bantu by 500 CE
- Eastern Bantu by 500 CE
- Western Bantu by 500 CE
- spread of Bantu, with date
- Nok early Iron Age culture, 6th century BCE–5th century BCE
- possible route of spread of iron-working c.600 BCE–400 CE
- area of sub-Saharan rock art from 1000 BCE
- East African pastoral Neolithic site
- early Iron Age settlement 600 BCE–600 CE
- early iron-working site with date
- Late Stone Age settlement, c.3000–600 BCE
- evidence of sheep domestication of the late Stone Age
- chariot rock art 1200 BCE
- frontiers at 500 CE
- equatorial rain forest

Scale varies with perspective

6280 km (3920 miles)

4450 km (2780 miles)

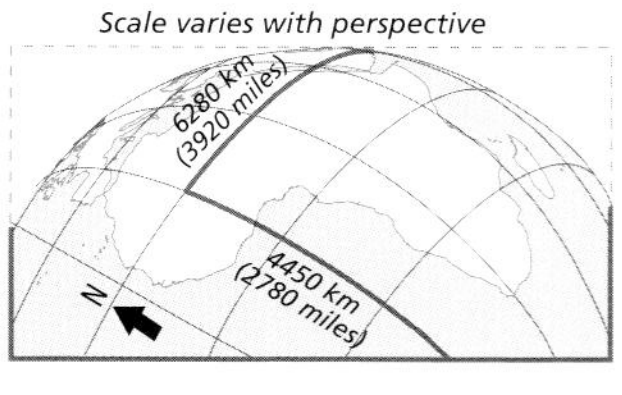

Berber states in North Africa

From 300 BCE, the Berber inhabitants of North Africa, including the Mauri, Masaesyli, and Massyli, began to form states, building cities and developing administrative structures. In alliance with Rome the kingdoms were largely united to form Numidia by Masinissa of the Massyli in 201 BCE. Masinissa's grandson, Jugurtha later incited war with Rome and was defeated in 104 BCE. His territory was subsequently absorbed into the Roman Empire as a client state. In 33 BCE King Boccus II of Mauretania willed his kingdom to the empire thus completing the annexation of the region. The entire North African coast supplied Rome with agricultural products, primarily wheat and olives; cities on the coast, such as Carthage, were centres of exchange.

The Berber states issued their own coinage. This coin dating from the 2nd century BCE depicts Jugurtha, ruler of Numidia from 118 BCE until his defeat at the hands of the Romans in 104 BCE.

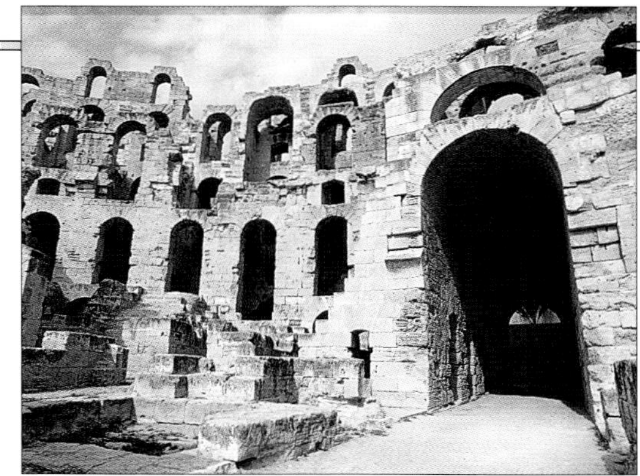

An enduring consequence of the Roman Empire was the spread of the Latin language and Roman architecture. As towns sprang up in North Africa, they acquired characteristic features of Roman cities and architecture such as this Roman amphitheatre at Thysdrus (El Djem) in present-day Tunisia. Built in 225 CE, the building could seat 50,000 people.

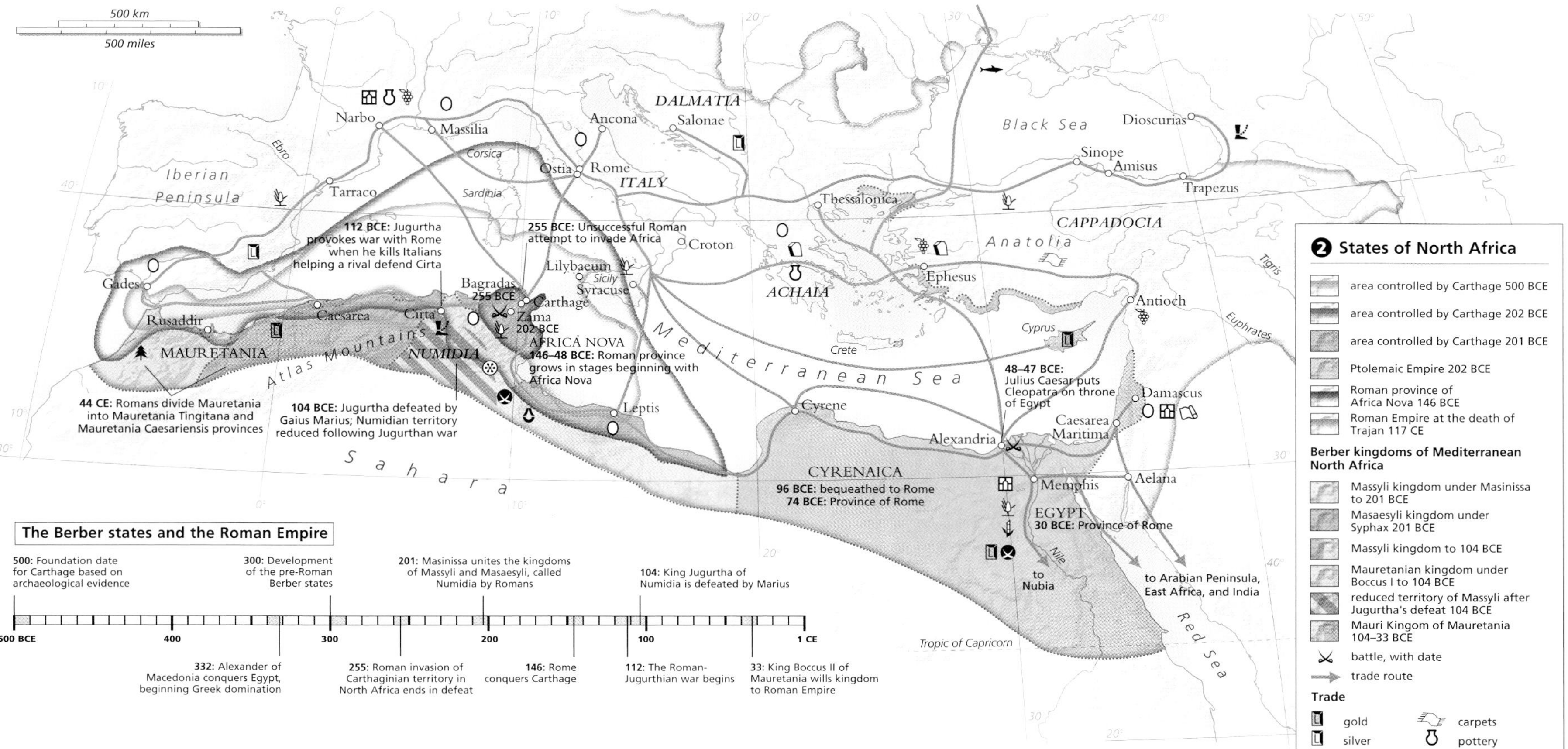

2 States of North Africa

- area controlled by Carthage 500 BCE
- area controlled by Carthage 202 BCE
- area controlled by Carthage 201 BCE
- Ptolemaic Empire 202 BCE
- Roman province of Africa Nova 146 BCE
- Roman Empire at the death of Trajan 117 CE

Berber kingdoms of Mediterranean North Africa

- Massyli kingdom under Masinissa to 201 BCE
- Masaesyli kingdom under Syphax 201 BCE
- Massyli kingdom to 104 BCE
- Mauretanian kingdom under Boccus I to 104 BCE
- reduced territory of Massyli after Jugurtha's defeat 104 BCE
- Mauri Kingom of Mauretania 104–33 BCE
- battle, with date
- trade route

Trade: gold, silver, copper, timber, salt, marble, glass, slaves, ivory, carpets, pottery, cloth, wine, olives, incense, wheat, fish, papyrus

112 BCE: Jugurtha provokes war with Rome when he kills Italians helping a rival defend Cirta

255 BCE: Unsuccessful Roman attempt to invade Africa

146–48 BCE: Roman province grows in stages beginning with Africa Nova

44 CE: Romans divide Mauretania into Mauretania Tingitana and Mauretania Caesariensis provinces

104 BCE: Jugurtha defeated by Gaius Marius; Numidian territory reduced following Jugurthan war

96 BCE: bequeathed to Rome
74 BCE: Province of Rome

48–47 BCE: Julius Caesar puts Cleopatra on throne of Egypt

30 BCE: Province of Rome

to Nubia

to Arabian Peninsula, East Africa, and India

The Berber states and the Roman Empire

500: Foundation date for Carthage based on archaeological evidence

332: Alexander of Macedonia conquers Egypt, beginning Greek domination

300: Development of the pre-Roman Berber states

255: Roman invasion of Carthaginian territory in North Africa ends in defeat

201: Masinissa unites the kingdoms of Massyli and Masaesyli, called Numidia by Romans

146: Rome conquers Carthage

112: The Roman-Jugurthian war begins

104: King Jugurtha of Numidia is defeated by Marius

33: King Boccus II of Mauretania wills kingdom to Roman Empire

The rise of Aksum 100 BCE–600 CE

Aksum, the centre of the Ethiopian state, began its rise around 100 BCE, becoming a major trading power by the end of the first century CE. The kingdom grew wealthy through its control of the incense-trading port of Adulis on the Red Sea *(see p.225)*. Aksum provided Egypt, India, Persia, and Arabia with tortoiseshell, ivory, and rhinoceros horn. The kingdom reached its peak during the reign of King Ezana who converted to Christianity c.350 CE. By 500 CE most of the country had adopted the new religion. In 525 CE Kaleb, one of Ezana's successors, conquered the southern part of the Arabian Peninsula, and Aksum occupied this territory until 574 CE. With the spread of Islam in the 7th century, Aksum lost its monopoly of the Red Sea to Muslim traders, and began to decline.

Aksum's rulers commemorated their victories with stone stelae, sometimes up to 30 m high, which were built above subterranean royal tombs.

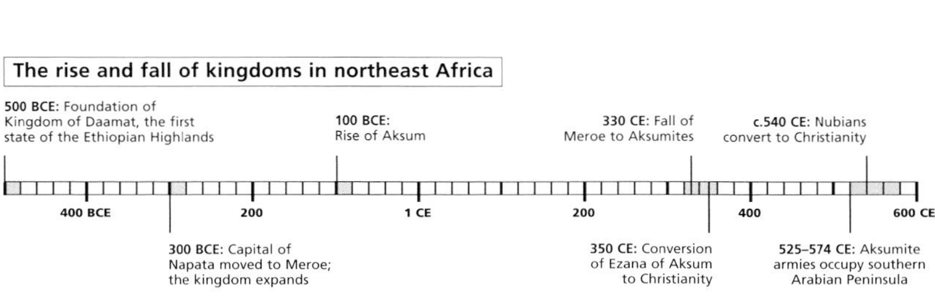

3 Northeast Africa 100 CE

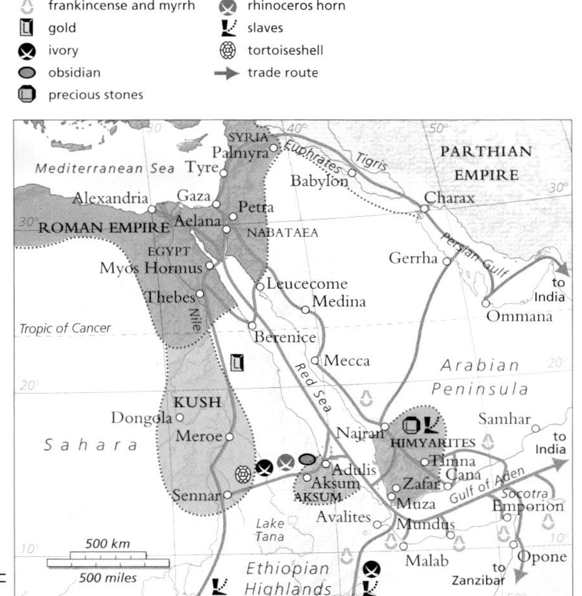

4 Northeast Africa 350 CE

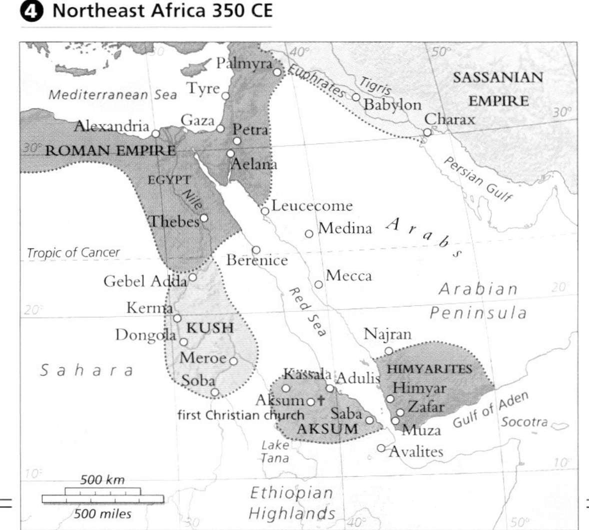

5 Northeast Africa 500 CE

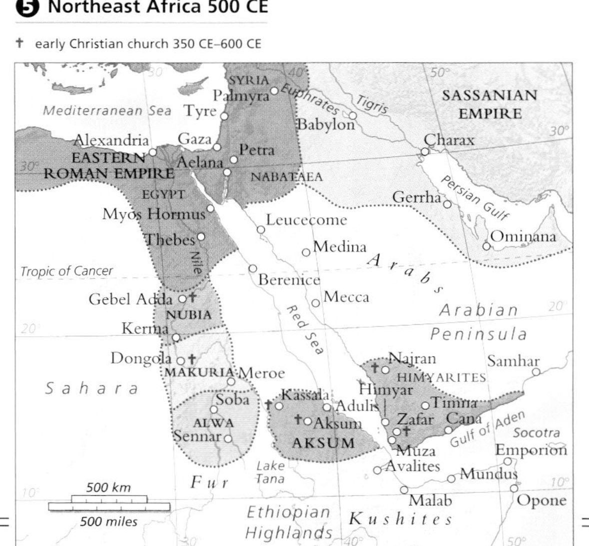

ISLAM AND NEW STATES IN AFRICA

Unearthed on the island of Pemba, these North African gold coins testify to Swahili trade with the Arab world.

FROM THE 10TH CENTURY, A SERIES of empires arose in the sub-Saharan savannah. They attracted Muslim Arab traders who travelled south in search of salt, gold, and slaves. Through frequent contact, Islam gradually infiltrated the region by means of peaceful conversion. When the Muslim Berber Almoravids captured the capital of Ghana in 1076, causing the collapse of the empire, their conquest did little to advance the spread of Islam. Christian Ethiopia also withstood Muslim advances. However, Ghana's successors, Mali and Songhay, owed much of their wealth and civilization to the advent and adoption of Islam, as did the Kanem-Bornu Empire around Lake Chad, and, after the 15th century, the Hausa city-states. From the late 10th century, Arab merchant colonies were established in the coastal towns of East Africa, stimulating African trade with Arabia and India, and accelerating the southward spread of Islam.

African trade and the spread of Islam

Built in the 14th century, the great mosque at Jenne in Mali was constructed with sun-dried mud bricks.

Islamic expansion out of Arabia began in earnest following the death of the Prophet Muhammad in 632. By 640 Egypt had fallen into the hands of Muslim soldiers and settlers. From the 8th century, traders and clerics were the agents of Islam, spreading the religion along the commercial arteries of the Sahara which extended into West Africa; and up the Nile. By the 13th century the Saifawa kings of Kanem had adopted the faith. Islam had also travelled down the east coast of Africa, taken by seafaring Arabs who set up coastal trading centres. Trade between Arabs and Bantu necessitated a new language, therefore Swahili became the *lingua franca* of the east coast.

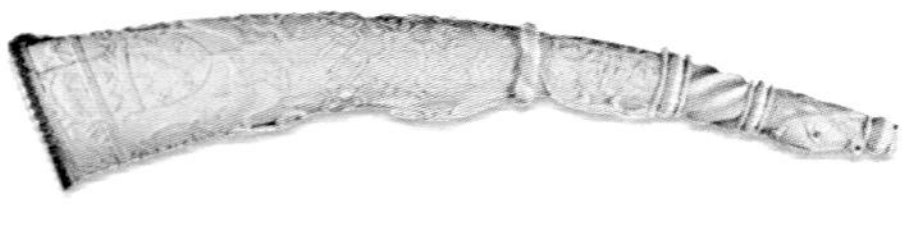

Carved by West African craftsmen, this 16th-century ivory horn *(above)* was produced for the European market. This is confirmed by its Portuguese-style inscriptions.

Dating from the 16th century, this blue and white Ming dynasty bowl *(left)* was found on the east coast of Africa, and provides evidence of trade with China.

Islamic expansion in Africa from 600

- **625:** First Islamic Arab invasion of Makuria
- **632:** Death of Muhammad
- **635–40:** Conquest of Egypt by Arabs
- **680:** Arab armies reach Atlantic at Morocco
- **c.800:** Emergence of trading towns on East African coast.
- **909:** Fatimid dynasty founded by Ubaydullah
- **1050:** King of Takrur converts to Islam
- **1076:** King of Ghana converts to Islam
- **1270:** Beginning of Solomid dynasty in Ethiopia

600 700 800 900 1000 1100 1200 1300

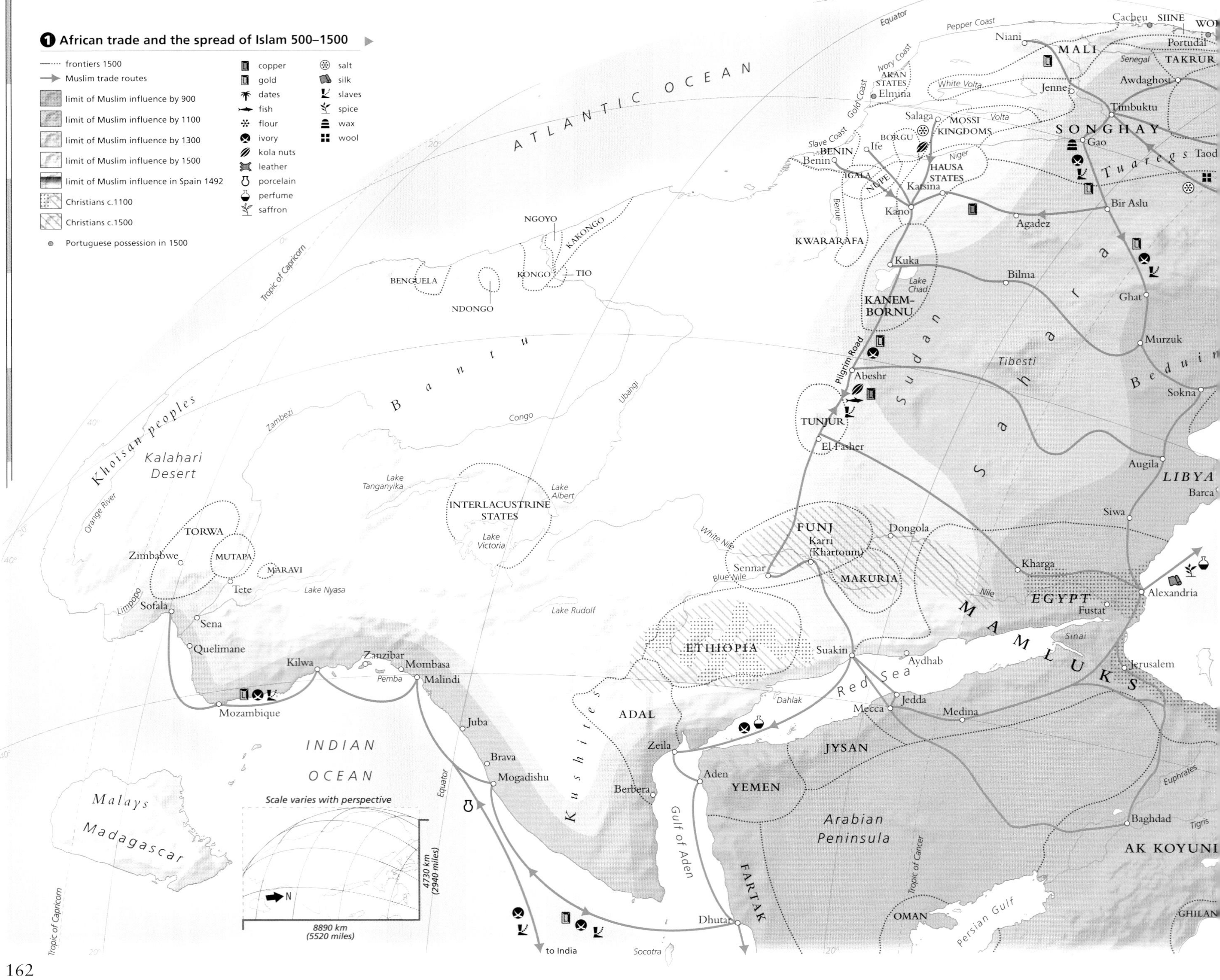

1 African trade and the spread of Islam 500–1500

frontiers 1500
Muslim trade routes
limit of Muslim influence by 900
limit of Muslim influence by 1100
limit of Muslim influence by 1300
limit of Muslim influence by 1500
limit of Muslim influence in Spain 1492
Christians c.1100
Christians c.1500
Portuguese possession in 1500

copper, gold, dates, fish, flour, ivory, kola nuts, leather, porcelain, perfume, saffron, salt, silk, slaves, spice, wax, wool

Scale varies with perspective
4730 km (2940 miles)
8890 km (5520 miles)

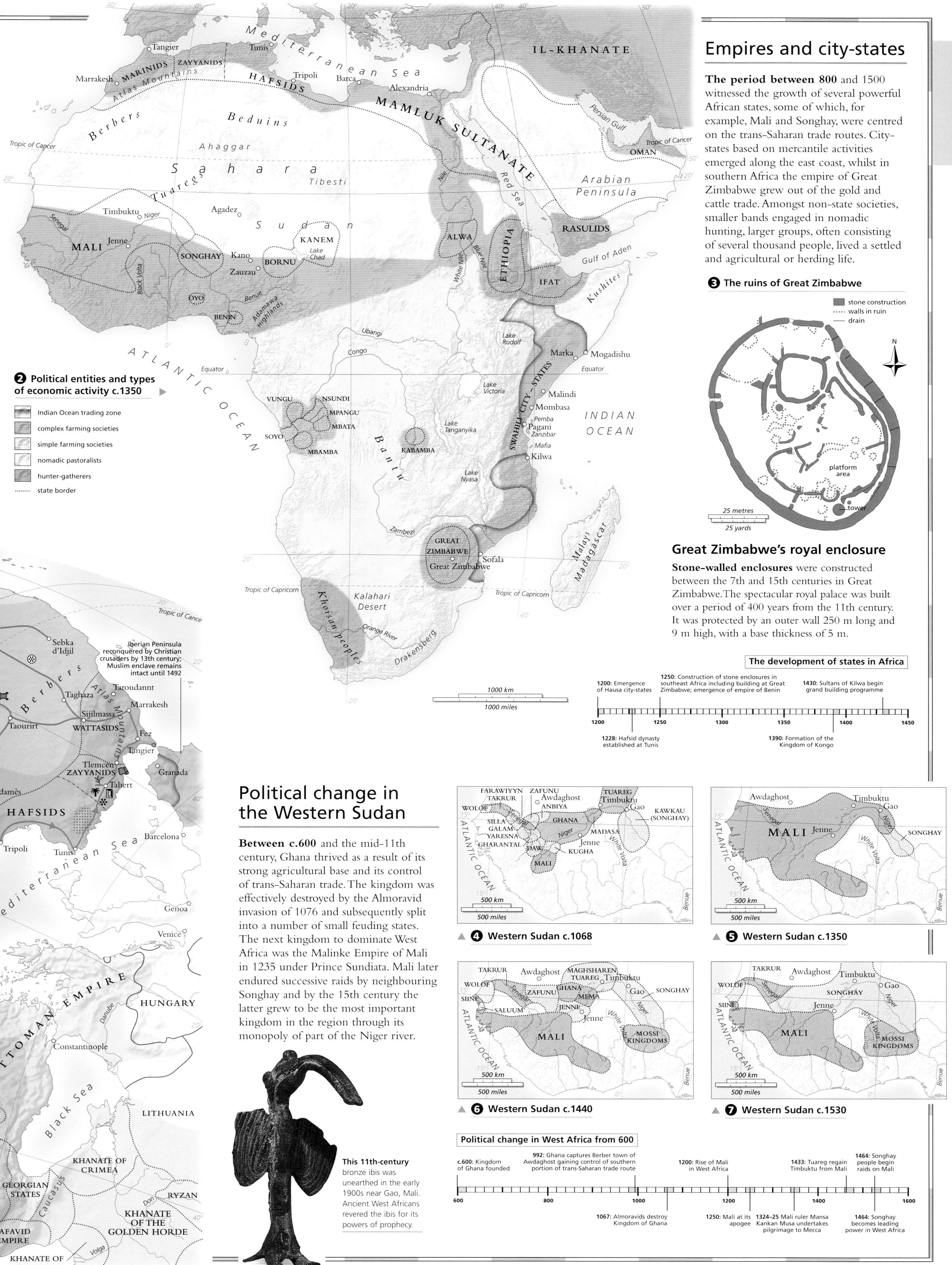

2 Political entities and types of economic activity c.1350

- Indian Ocean trading zone
- complex farming societies
- simple farming societies
- nomadic pastoralists
- hunter-gatherers
- state border

Empires and city-states

The period between 800 and 1500 witnessed the growth of several powerful African states, some of which, for example, Mali and Songhay, were centred on the trans-Saharan trade routes. City-states based on mercantile activities emerged along the east coast, whilst in southern Africa the empire of Great Zimbabwe grew out of the gold and cattle trade. Amongst non-state societies, smaller bands engaged in nomadic hunting, larger groups, often consisting of several thousand people, lived a settled and agricultural or herding life.

3 The ruins of Great Zimbabwe

Great Zimbabwe's royal enclosure

Stone-walled enclosures were constructed between the 7th and 15th centuries in Great Zimbabwe. The spectacular royal palace was built over a period of 400 years from the 11th century. It was protected by an outer wall 250 m long and 9 m high, with a base thickness of 5 m.

The development of states in Africa

- **1200:** Emergence of Hausa city-states
- **1228:** Hafsid dynasty established at Tunis
- **1250:** Construction of stone enclosures in southeast Africa including building at Great Zimbabwe; emergence of empire of Benin
- **1390:** Formation of the Kingdom of Kongo
- **1430:** Sultans of Kilwa begin grand building programme

Political change in the Western Sudan

Between c.600 and the mid-11th century, Ghana thrived as a result of its strong agricultural base and its control of trans-Saharan trade. The kingdom was effectively destroyed by the Almoravid invasion of 1076 and subsequently split into a number of small feuding states. The next kingdom to dominate West Africa was the Malinke Empire of Mali in 1235 under Prince Sundiata. Mali later endured successive raids by neighbouring Songhay and by the 15th century the latter grew to be the most important kingdom in the region through its monopoly of part of the Niger river.

4 Western Sudan c.1068

5 Western Sudan c.1350

6 Western Sudan c.1440

7 Western Sudan c.1530

This 11th-century bronze ibis was unearthed in the early 1900s near Gao, Mali. Ancient West Africans revered the ibis for its powers of prophecy.

Political change in West Africa from 600

- **c.600:** Kingdom of Ghana founded
- **992:** Ghana captures Berber town of Awdaghost gaining control of southern portion of trans-Saharan trade route
- **1067:** Almoravids destroy Kingdom of Ghana
- **1200:** Rise of Mali in West Africa
- **1250:** Mali at its apogee
- **1324–25** Mali ruler Mansa Kankan Musa undertakes pilgrimage to Mecca
- **1433:** Tuareg regain Timbuktu from Mali
- **1464:** Songhay people begin raids on Mali
- **1464:** Songhay becomes leading power in West Africa

EARLY MODERN AFRICA

Asante's well-armed warriors made it the most powerful state on the Gold Coast.

AFTER THE PORTUGUESE had led European expansion into Africa in the 15th century, a few colonies were established – in Angola, along the Zambezi valley, and in the region of the Cape of Good Hope – but for the most part, African rulers contained and controlled the activities of the newcomers. In parts of West Africa they allowed Europeans to establish coastal forts and trading posts. With this new presence came increased opportunities for external trade, principally in gold, ivory, and slaves. After 1700, however, the importance of all other goods was totally eclipsed by the value of the Atlantic slave trade.

The 16th century saw the Ottoman Empire advance across North Africa as far as the Atlas Mountains. To the south, the great empire of Songhay yielded to Moroccan invaders in 1591, though the cycle of empires continued in West Africa with Great Fulo. In the early 18th century powerful coastal kingdoms arose in Asante and Dahomey, while Rozwi replaced Mwenemutapa in southeast Africa.

Southern and East Africa

The Portuguese presence in the region was challenged in the 17th century by the Rozwi empire, which drove them from the highlands of Zimbabwe, while Omani fleets captured many of their coastal forts in East Africa. Portugal was left with the semi-independent *prazos* (estates) of the Zambezi valley and the coastal towns of Sofala, Mozambique, and Inhambane. In 1652 the Dutch East India Company founded its colony at Cape Town. Rapid expansion in the 18th century brought Dutch settlers into conflict with the many small states of the Nguni region.

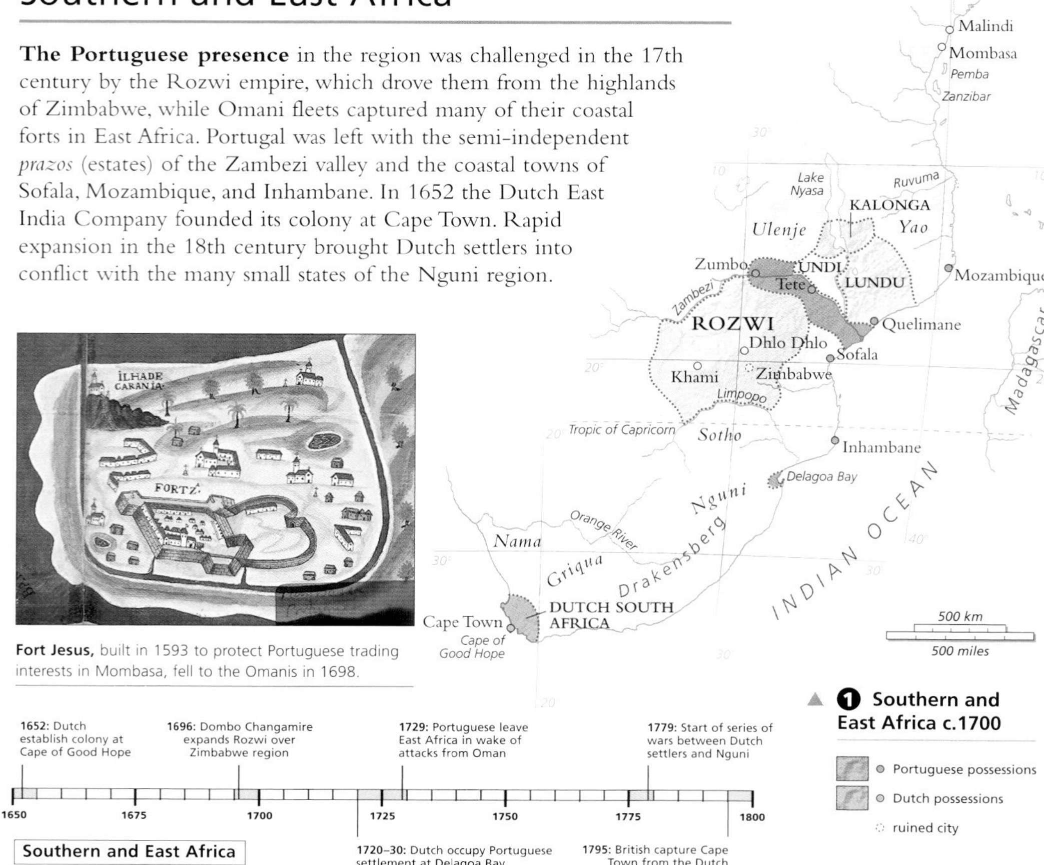

Fort Jesus, built in 1593 to protect Portuguese trading interests in Mombasa, fell to the Omanis in 1698.

The Fulbe, who lived by raising cattle for their neighbours, were found throughout much of West Africa. This 1730 engraving shows a Fulbe town on the River Gambia with a plantation and a corral for livestock.

2 States of West and Central Africa 1625

- Portuguese possessions
- Dutch settlement

African political development

In the 17th century, much of sub-Saharan Africa consisted of many small, self-governing units, typically about 50 km across. In West Africa some 70% of the population probably lived in these 'mini-states'. Boundaries remained stable for long periods, the people choosing their leaders on the basis of heredity, election or other local customs. There were extensive empires, such as Songhay and Mali, but these lay in the sparsely populated region now known as the Sahel. These and the other larger states, which ruled the remainder of the population, usually grew by incorporating smaller units, although they continued to use the local polities to enforce the law and raise tribute. Taxation took the form of a head or house tax. There was no concept of land ownership; it could not be bought or sold. Land was regarded as belonging to whoever farmed it. Slave ownership, on the other hand, was an important measure of personal wealth.

The formidable Queen Njinga ruled the kingdom of Ndongo from 1624 to 1663. She fought the Portuguese to a standstill.

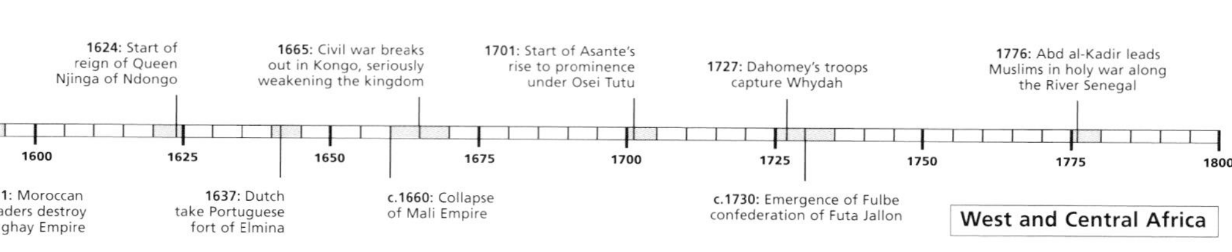

The struggle for the Horn of Africa

Ethiopia's domination of the region came to an end in the 16th century. The Christian empire's expansion into Muslim lands to the south had often involved forced conversion and the destruction of Islamic literature and places of worship. In 1529 a dynamic imam from Adal, Ahmad Grañ, proclaimed a holy war against Ethiopia, winning many striking victories. In 1540 the Ethiopians sought aid from Portugal and Grañ was killed in battle in 1543. This ultimately inconclusive war laid waste the region, which allowed the Oromo to invade from the south. Organized in many independent mobile bands, they took over both Christian and Muslim lands and founded new kingdoms of their own. Many Oromo embraced Islam and some fought as mercenaries in civil wars in Ethiopia. The fortunes of the Ethiopian empire revived somewhat in the Gondar period in the 17th century, but its lands were much reduced.

The decline of Ethiopia

- **1529:** Ahmad Grañ leads *jihad* against Ethiopia
- **1540:** Portuguese come to the aid of Ethiopia
- **1543:** Death of Ahmad Grañ, shot by a Portuguese musketeer
- **1590:** Oromo bands begin occupation of southern Ethiopia
- **1597:** Start of period of civil war
- **1632:** End of civil wars. Jesuit missionaries expelled from Ethiopia
- **1636:** King Fasiladas founds permanent capital at Gondar
- **1682:** Accession of Iyasu I, last great king of Gondar period

1500 1550 1600 1650 1700

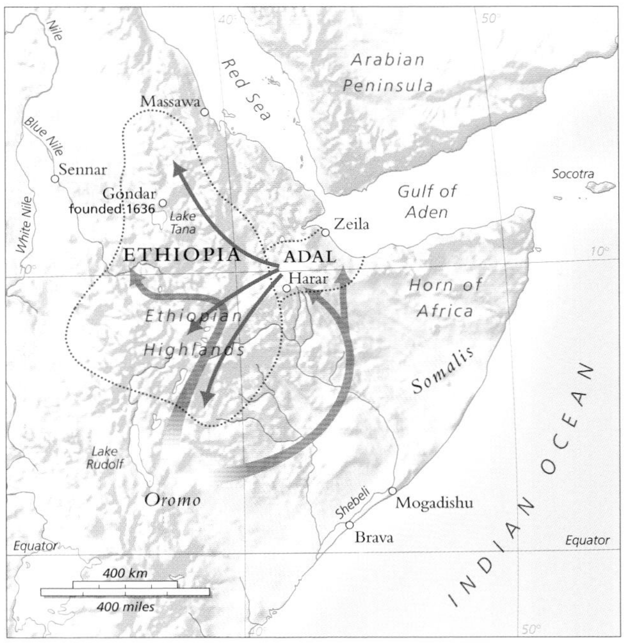

3 Horn of Africa 1500–1700

Jihad of Ahmad Grañ 1529–43
Oromo expansion 1550–1700
approximate state border 1500

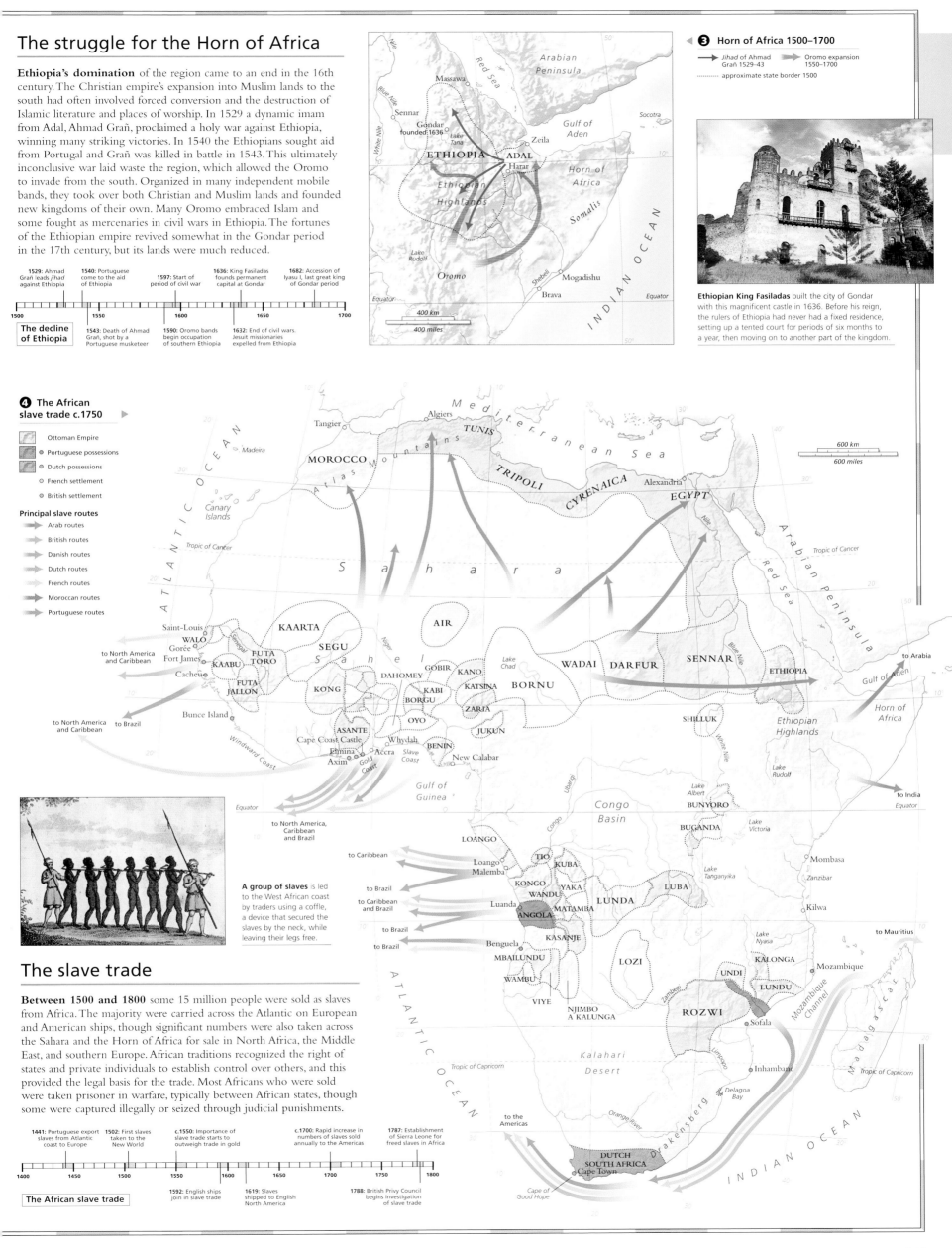

Ethiopian King Fasiladas built the city of Gondar with this magnificent castle in 1636. Before his reign, the rulers of Ethiopia had never had a fixed residence, setting up a tented court for periods of six months to a year, then moving on to another part of the kingdom.

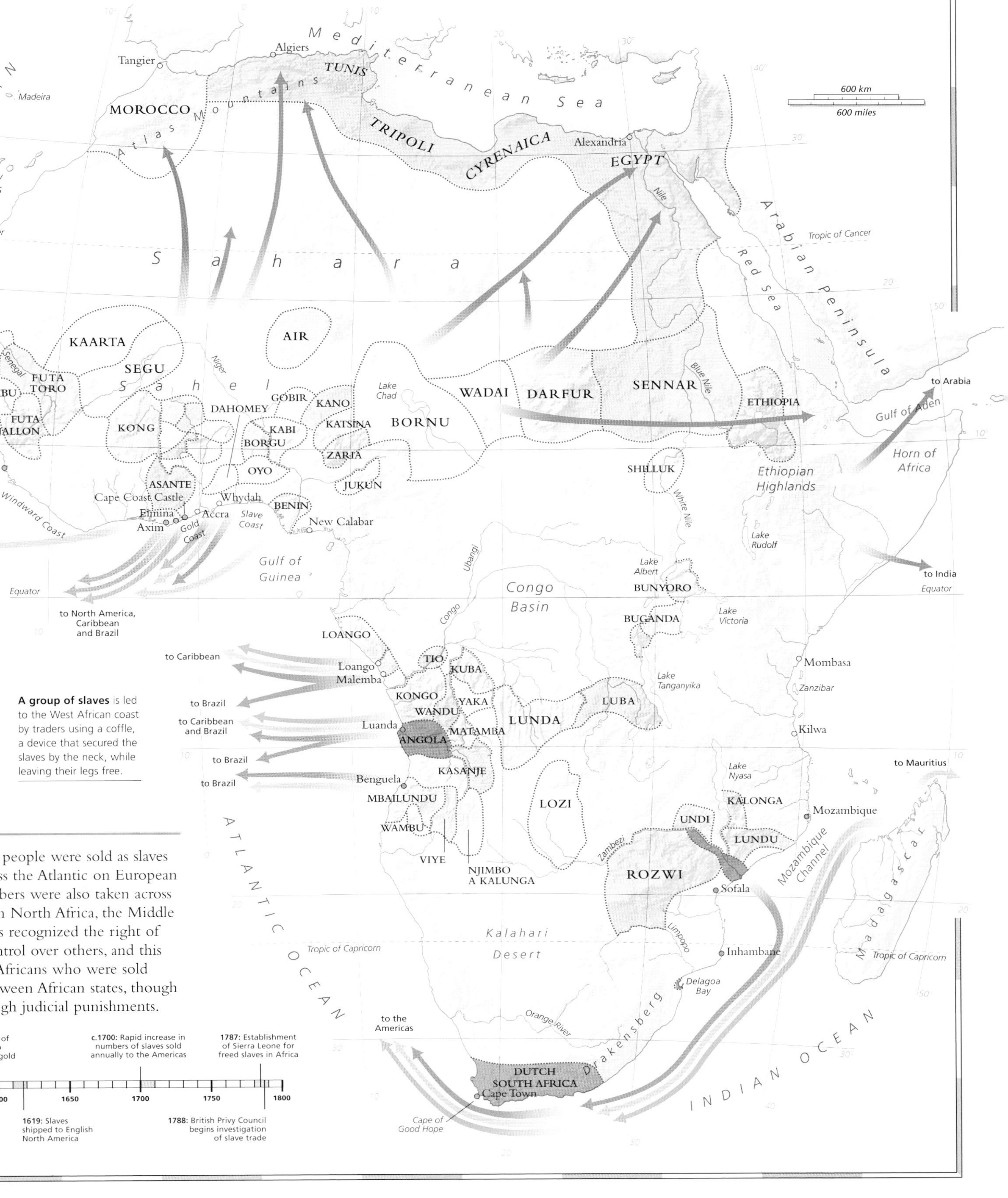

4 The African slave trade c.1750

Ottoman Empire
Portuguese possessions
Dutch possessions
French settlement
British settlement

Principal slave routes
Arab routes
British routes
Danish routes
Dutch routes
French routes
Moroccan routes
Portuguese routes

A group of slaves is led to the West African coast by traders using a coffle, a device that secured the slaves by the neck, while leaving their legs free.

The slave trade

Between 1500 and 1800 some 15 million people were sold as slaves from Africa. The majority were carried across the Atlantic on European and American ships, though significant numbers were also taken across the Sahara and the Horn of Africa for sale in North Africa, the Middle East, and southern Europe. African traditions recognized the right of states and private individuals to establish control over others, and this provided the legal basis for the trade. Most Africans who were sold were taken prisoner in warfare, typically between African states, though some were captured illegally or seized through judicial punishments.

The African slave trade

- **1441:** Portuguese export slaves from Atlantic coast to Europe
- **1502:** First slaves taken to the New World
- **c.1550:** Importance of slave trade starts to outweigh trade in gold
- **1592:** English ships join in slave trade
- **1619:** Slaves shipped to English North America
- **c.1700:** Rapid increase in numbers of slaves sold annually to the Americas
- **1787:** Establishment of Sierra Leone for freed slaves in Africa
- **1788:** British Privy Council begins investigation of slave trade

1400 1450 1500 1550 1600 1650 1700 1750 1800

THE COLONIZATION OF AFRICA

Cecil Rhodes, the embodiment of colonialism, planned to extend British rule in Africa from Cairo to Cape Town.

THE 19TH CENTURY was a period of revolutionary change in Africa. The states of West Africa were convulsed by a series of reformist Islamic *jihads*, while in the south the rise of Zulu militarism had catastrophic consequences for neighbouring peoples. By the mid-19th century Africa was also undergoing a commercial revolution. Europeans could now offer high-quality machined goods in large quantities. As a result Africa was condemned to the role of producer of primary goods. By the end of the century, many African kingdoms and clan-based communities were being replaced by states organized along indigenous lines. However, this process was forestalled by the decision of the major European powers to carve up the continent between them.

Commerce in the 19th century

The Arab slave trader, Tibbu Tib organized his own state and security system in 1875 with the help of armed followers.

The development of new export goods in Europe had social implications for Africa. Reduced shipping costs brought about by the introduction of the steamship meant that European textile and metal goods arrived in force. The resultant decline in local industries was accompanied by a growth in the internal slave trade. The substantial carrying trade, especially the porterage trade of east and central Africa, was run by small-scale entrepreneurs. While such ventures did not bring large profit, those involved enjoyed new and elevated social positions. Often the carrying trade was organized from a particular region, giving it an ethnic character. Enterprising African traders took advantage of the expanding economy to gain political power, for example, the copper trader Msiri won himself a kingdom.

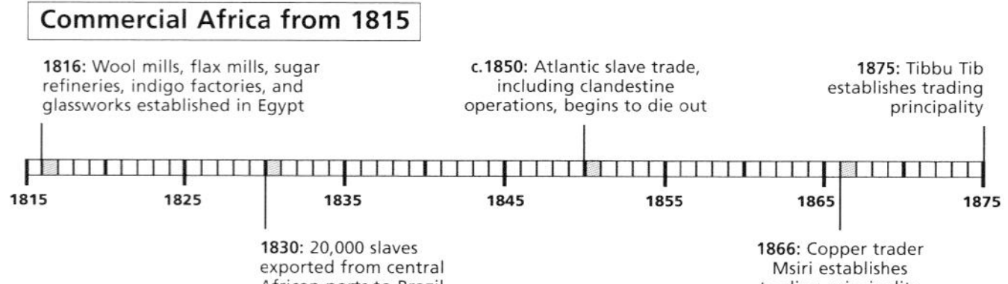

Commercial Africa from 1815
1816: Wool mills, flax mills, sugar refineries, indigo factories, and glassworks established in Egypt
c.1850: Atlantic slave trade, including clandestine operations, begins to die out
1875: Tibbu Tib establishes trading principality
1815
1825
1835
1845
1855
1865
1875
1830: 20,000 slaves exported from central African ports to Brazil
1866: Copper trader Msiri establishes trading principality

1 Commercial and political Africa c.1830

- cloves
- cocoa
- coffee
- copper
- cotton
- diamonds
- gold
- gum arabic
- honey and wax
- ivory
- olives
- palm products
- peanuts
- rubber
- slaves/migrant workers
- wheat
- wine
- trade route
- British possession
- French possession
- Ottoman territory
- Portuguese possession
- Spanish possession
- commercial group

to Europe · MOROCCO · ALGIERS · TUNIS · TRIPOLI · Mediterranean Sea · EGY · Sanussi · Tropic of Cancer · Sahara · Senegal · KAARTA · FUTA TORO · WAALO · Gambia · to western Europe · SEGU · HAMDULLAHI · Niger · SOKOTO · Sudan · Lake Chad · BORNU · WADAI · DARFUR · Egyptians · Rabeh · BAGIRMI · FUTA JALLON · KONG · YATENGA · WAGADUGU · SIERRA LEONE · to Central America · LIBERIA · ASANTE · OYO · IGALA · DAHOMEY · GOLD COAST · FANTE · BENIN · to Central America · Equator · ATLANTIC OCEAN · ZANDE · MANGB · Congo · Tibbu Tib · LOANGO · TIO · Bobangi · Kongo · KUBA · YAKA · KONGO · LUNDA · LUBA · Msiri · to the Americas; slaves to Brazil · ANGOLA · Chokwe · Kasanje · KAZEMBE · VIYE · Ovimbundu · WAMBU · MBAILUNDU · LOZI · Tropic of Capricorn · Kalahari Desert · SWAZILAND · GRIQUAS · CAPE COLONY · to East Indies, Europe, the Americas

Zulu and Afrikaner expansion

Under the leadership of Shaka, the Zulu were organized into a highly militarized kingdom. They conquered neighbouring Nguni tribes and set off a series of wars which depopulated large parts of the southern interior, leaving it vulnerable to Afrikaner expansion. Afrikaners left Cape Colony between 1835 and the 1840s in search of pastureland, and to escape from unwelcome British rule. They successfully defeated powerful military kingdoms as they progressed northwards.

British reforms, such as the abolition of slavery, caused the exodus of many Boers from Cape Colony. They undertook the 'Great Trek' in ox wagons.

2 The Afrikaner treks and the Mfecane wars

- the nuclear Zulu chiefdom
- Shaka's Zulu kingdom 1817
- Sobhuza's Swazi kingdom 1820
- Moshoeshoe's Lesotho kingdom 1824
- Mzilikazi's Ndebele kingdom 1826
- Nguni victory
- British victory
- Boer victory
- main Boer trek route 1836–54
- Nguni migrations
- borders 1895

Kalahari Desert · Tropic of Capricorn · Kololo · Limpopo · Pietersburg · Ndebele 1823 · Ngoni · Mariqua · 1837: Boers defeat Ndebele · Nylstroom 1852 · Pretoria · TRANSVAAL 1852 · 1877–88: annexed by British · Soshangane · Lourenço Marques · Rustenburg 1852 · Mosega · 1837: Boers defeat Zulus · Johannesburg 1837 · Potchefstroom 1837 · Vaal · Vegkop · ORANGE FREE STATE 1854 · 1836: Boers defeat Zulus · Winburg 1836 · Isandhlwana · 1879: Zulus defeat British · Tugela · INDIAN OCEAN · Thaba Nchu · Orange River · Bloemfontein · Sotho refugees · Thaba Bosiu · BASUTOLAND British Protectorate · Weenen · Pietermaritzburg · Boomplaats · 1848: Boers under Andries Pretorius defeated by British · Drakensberg · Ngwane · Mfengu · Durban (Port Natal) · CAPE COLONY · Colesberg · NATAL 1838 · 1843: annexed by British · 200 km · 200 miles · Graaff-Reinet 1786 · Fish · Tarka · Kei · Slagtersnek · Uitenhage · Grahamstown · Port Elizabeth

Zulu and Afrikaner expansion

- 1816: Shaka becomes leader of the Zulu, a clan of the Nguni
- 1820: Nguni clans disperse to avoid Mfecane wars brought about by rise of Zulu Empire
- 1835: Zwangendaba crosses the Limpopo taking the Mfecane northward
- 1836: Start of the Great Trek
- 1843: Short-lived Boer republic of Natal annexed by Britain
- 1852: Independence granted by British to Voortrekkers in Transvaal
- 1854: Boers found the Orange Free State

1820 · 1830 · 1840 · 1850 · 1860

Shaka armed the Zulu with long-bladed, stabbing *assegais*, which forced them to fight at close quarters. Shield markings and headdress distinguished different regiments.

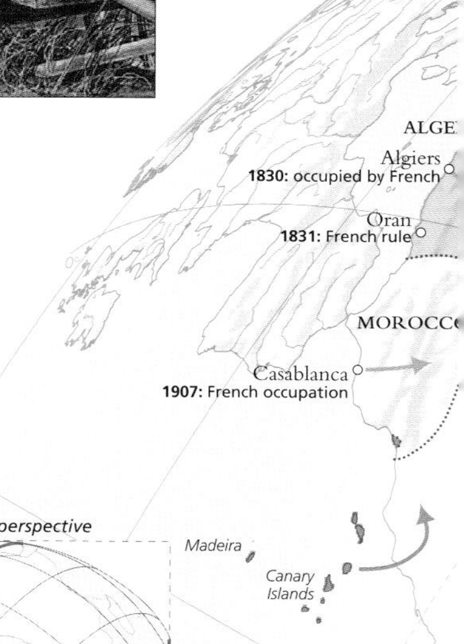

ALGE
Algiers
1830: occupied by French
Oran
1831: French rule
MOROCCO
Casablanca
1907: French occupation
Scale varies with perspective
6280 km (3920 miles)
4450 km (2780 miles)
Madeira
Canary Islands
Tropic of Cancer

Islamic wars in western Africa

- **1804:** *Jihad* of Usuman dan Fodio
- **1807:** Hausa kings replaced by Fulani emirs
- **1816:** Inspired by Usuman dan Fodio, Amadu Lobbo launches *jihad* in Masina
- **1820:** Usuman dan Fodio establishes Sokoto Fulani Kingdom
- **1852:** 'Umar Tal conquers the Senegal valley
- **1861:** 'Umar Tal's forces conquer Segu
- **1863:** Timbuktu falls to 'Umar Tal; he founds Tukulor Empire
- **1864:** 'Umar Tal is killed attemping to suppress Fulani rebellion

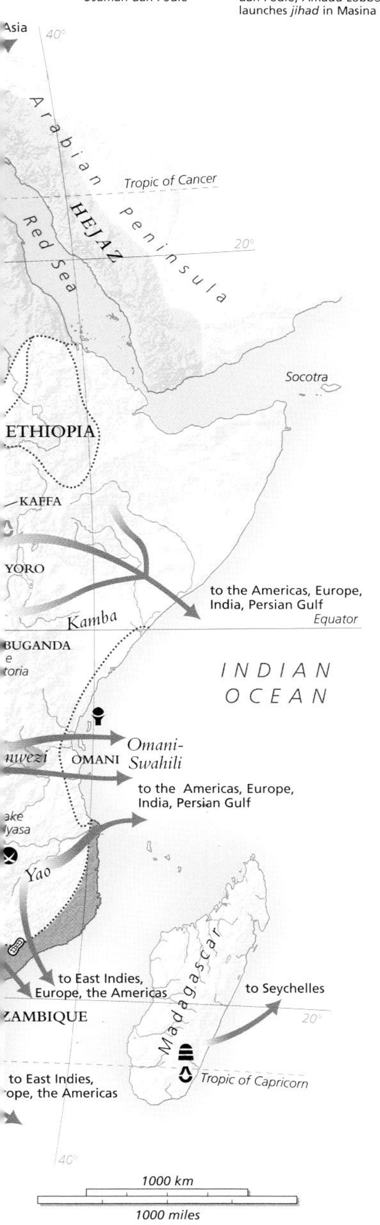

The text of this richly decorated19th-century Koran is written in West African Sudani script. The large rectangular design marks the end of a chapter.

Islamic reform in West Africa

The *jihads* of West Africa were a source of major turmoil in the 19th century. The idea that reformers could overthrow governments they thought were unjust was deeply rooted in the region, and dated back to the 11th century Almoravid movement. Holy men challenged rulers, often because of their tyranny and corruption, and demanded change. Social problems also promoted reform, for example, Fula herdsmen often backed reformers against those who taxed and mistreated them. In other cases, it was humble peasants or slaves who converted to Islam. Tukulor cleric Usuman dan Fodio's *jihad* in Hausaland in 1804 led to the establishment of the Islamic Sokoto Fulani Kingdom in 1820. Fulani cleric al-Hajj 'Umar Tal set about reforming the Segu region in 1851 and by 1863 had founded the Tukulor Empire.

3 19th-century West African *jihads*

- Sokoto Fulani Kingdom c.1820
- Tukulor Empire c.1864
- British possession
- French possession
- Portuguese posssession
- *jihad* route of al-Hajj 'Umar Tal
- borders c.1850
- conflict

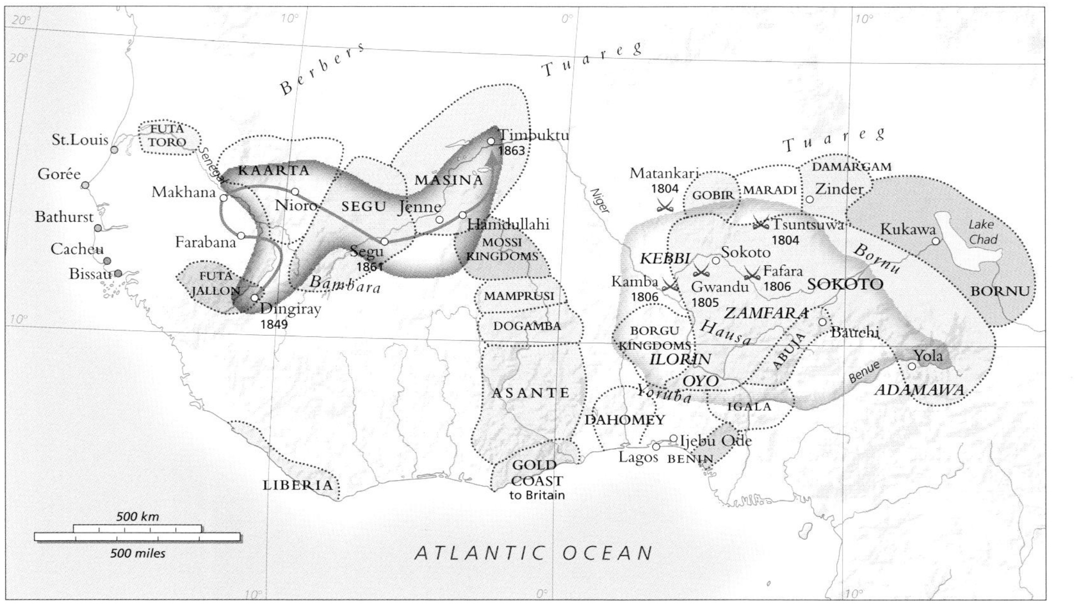

The conquest of the interior

The years after 1885 saw a race to complete the conquest of the African interior *(see p.96)*. International rivalries between European powers, coupled with local merchant competition and the popularity of African conquest in the home arena ensured European governmental interest in the continent. In many cases, initial conquests were funded by commercial interests, such as Cecil Rhodes' De Beers Consolidated Mines company. Most of the fighting personnel were Africans, hired mercenaries, or militarily trained slaves. The use of commercial contacts with African traders and the exploitation of local rivalries were as effective as brute force and the Maxim gun.

The conquest of Africa from 1880

- **1882:** Britain occupies Egypt; Congo Free State formed by King Leopold of Belgium
- **1883:** France begins its conquest of Madagascar
- **1884:** Berlin Conference on Africa; Samore Touré proclaims his Islamic theocracy
- **1889:** Italy establishes its first colony in Eritrea
- **1892:** France destroys the Tukulor Empire
- **1894:** Britain occupies Buganda
- **1896:** France takes Madagascar
- **1900-01:** Britain annexes Asante
- **1904:** French create federation of French West Africa
- **1908:** Belgium takes over Congo Free State

4 European penetration of Africa

Colonial territory c.1880

- Ottoman suzerainty
- British
- Portuguese
- French
- Spanish
- Boer Republics
- frontier of Christian missionary activities c.1880

European routes of expansion

- Belgian
- British
- French
- German
- Italian
- Portuguese
- Spanish
- main lines of missionary advance
- 1888 foundation date of colonial settlement

Colonial settlements

- Belgian
- Boer
- British
- French
- German
- Italian
- Portuguese
- other settlement

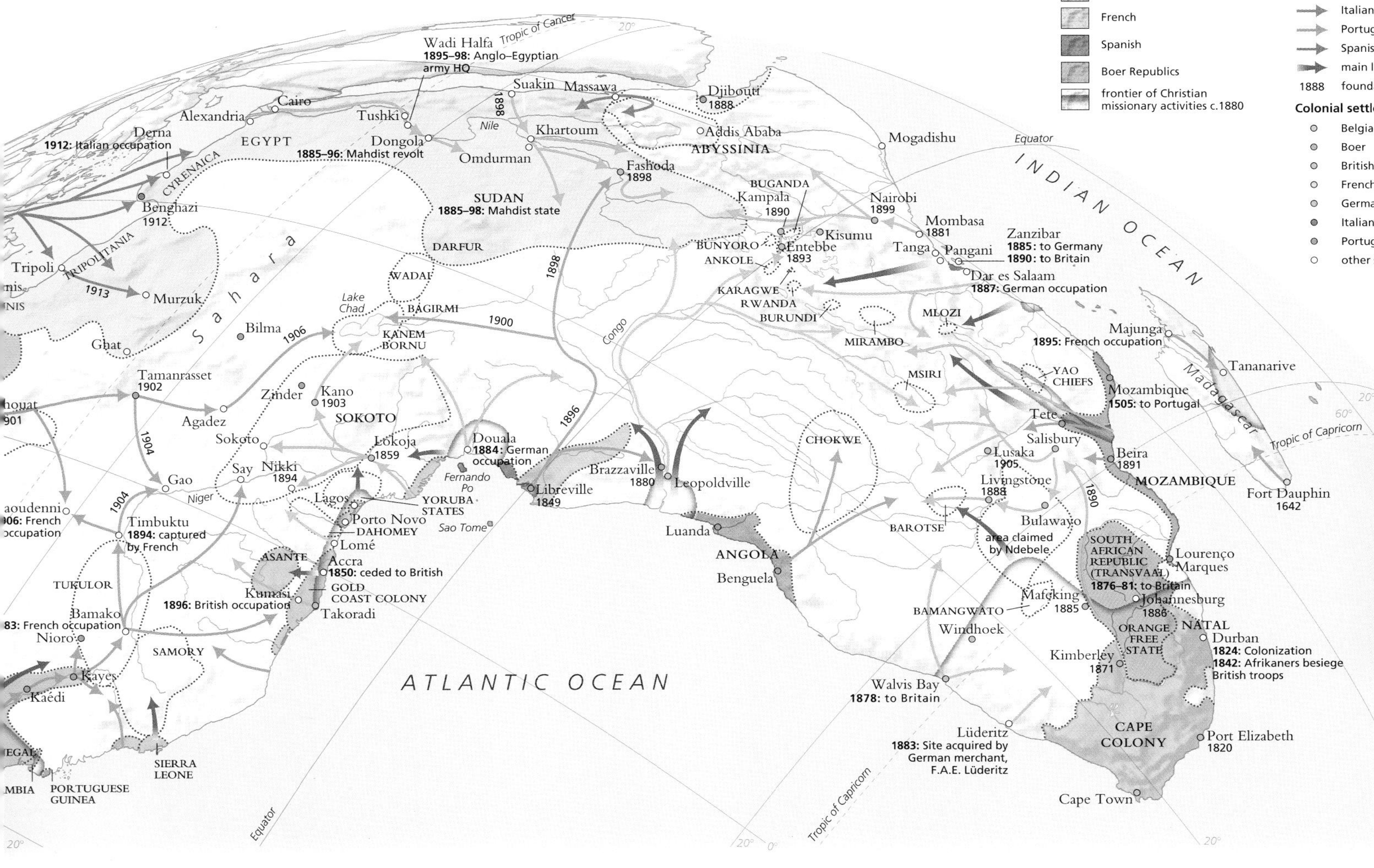

Armed and trained by France, these African soldiers, known as the Senegalese Rifles, helped France win territory in Africa.

POST-COLONIAL AFRICA

Julius Nyerere led the fight for independence in Tanganyika.

MOST AFRICAN COUNTRIES gained independence between 1956 and 1968. The new states, with few exceptions, were territorially identical to the European colonies they replaced. Following independence, leaders often became dictators, or the army seized power; many governments were corrupt and a number of countries were devastated by war. Moves were made towards multiparty democracy, most notably in South Africa where apartheid was dismantled in 1990. During the 1990s and 2000s, many western and central African states were gripped by bitter conflicts, stemming from ethnic rivalries and disputes over natural resources, such as timber and diamonds.

African independence

After the Second World War the colonial powers in Africa faced demands for self-determination and most countries gained independence around 1960. In the face of widespread opposition, Portugal clung on to its territories through the 1960s. This resulted in long and bloody wars in Angola, Guinea-Bissau, and Mozambique. There were also protracted struggles for majority rule in the former British colonies of Zimbabwe and South Africa. The presidential election victory of Nelson Mandela in 1994 marked the end of white minority rule in South Africa.

The national flag is raised in Ghana during an independence ceremony. The country was declared a republic on 1 July 1960 with Dr Kwame Nkrumah as the first president.

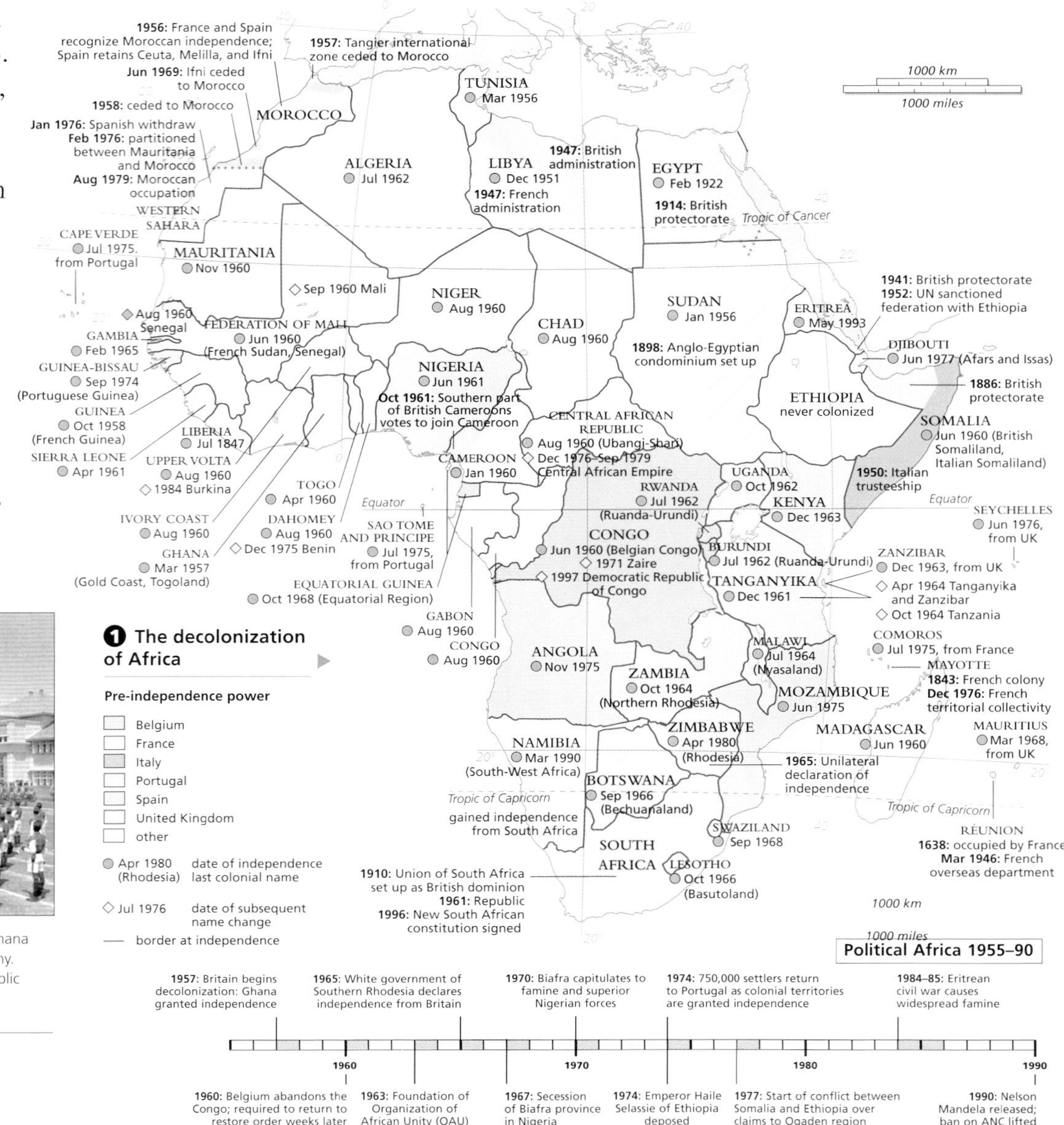

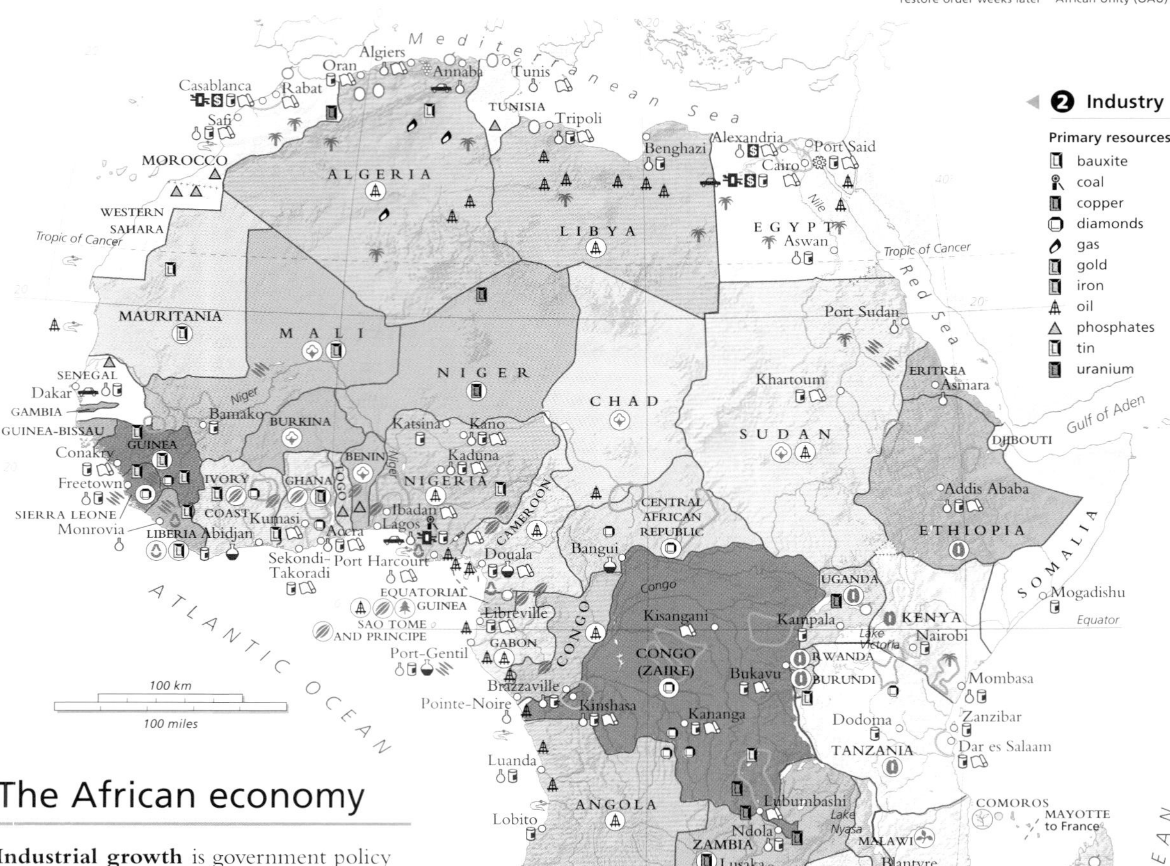

2 Industry in Africa, 2004

Primary resources: bauxite, coal, copper, diamonds, gas, gold, iron, oil, phosphates, tin, uranium

Secondary industry: car/vehicle manufacture, chemicals, electronics, engineering, finance, food processing, palm oil processing, pharmaceuticals, textiles, major industrial areas

Major cash crops: cocoa, coffee, cotton, dates, fruit, olives, rice, rubber, shellfish, spices, timber, tobacco, vineyards

Ecological tourism: national parks

Percentages of total export earnings: 40–59, 60–80, more than 80

agriculture and fishing

crude oil and petroleum products

metals and minerals

Main export product

The African economy

Industrial growth is government policy in a number of countries in Africa, and is seen as the way to progress economically. Countries with large manufacturing sectors include South Africa and oil-rich states such as Nigeria, Algeria, and Libya. Many other states rely on a single resource or cash crop for export income, leaving them vulnerable to market fluctuations.

The burden of debt

The HIPC (Highly Indebted Poor Countries) initiative was proposed by the World Bank and IMF in 1996. It aims to lessen the debt burden of the poorest countries, with the promise to erase $100 billion of debt. Forty-two countries were deemed eligible, 27 of which (23 of them African) have joined the scheme so far. There was significant early progress, but the fairness and effectiveness of the initiative are vigorously debated.

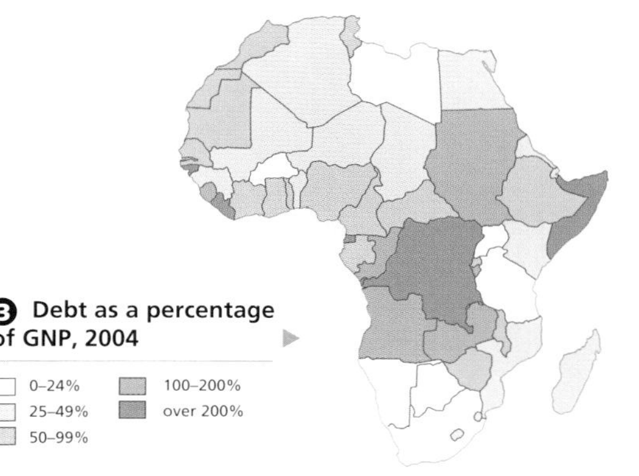

3 Debt as a percentage of GNP, 2004

0–24%
25–49%
50–99%
100–200%
over 200%

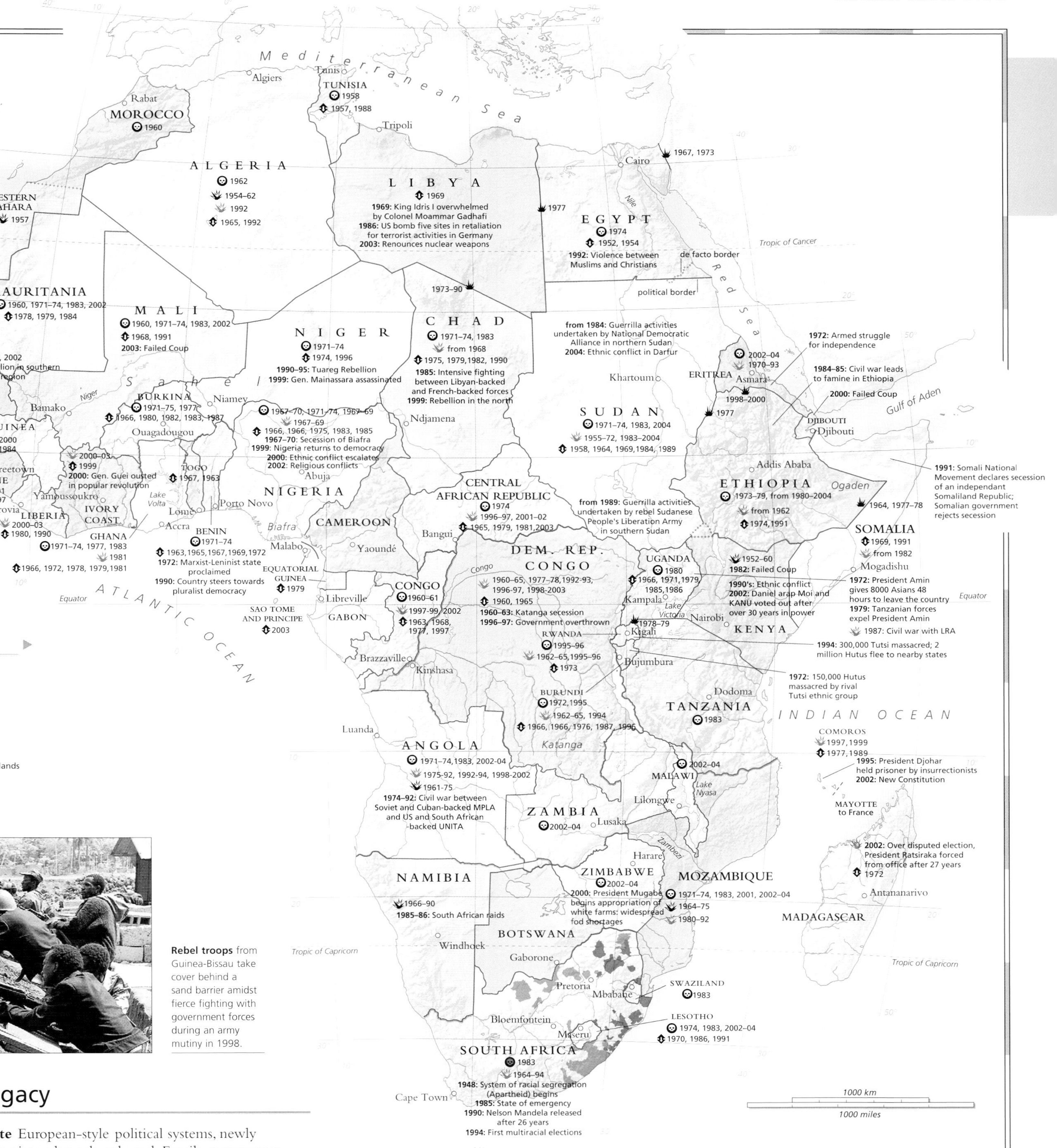

Mediterranean Sea
Algiers
Tunis
TUNISIA
1958
1957, 1988
Rabat
MOROCCO
1960
Tripoli
ALGERIA
1962
1954–62
1992
1965, 1992
LIBYA
1969
1969: King Idris I overwhelmed by Colonel Moammar Gadhafi
1986: US bomb five sites in retaliation for terrorist activities in Germany
2003: Renounces nuclear weapons
Cairo
1967, 1973
1977
EGYPT
1974
1952, 1954
1992: Violence between Muslims and Christians
de facto border
political border
Nile
Red Sea
WESTERN SAHARA
1957
Tropic of Cancer
MAURITANIA
1960, 1971–74, 1983, 2002
1978, 1979, 1984
Nouakchott
MALI
1960, 1971–74, 1983, 2002
1968, 1991
2003: Failed Coup
NIGER
1971–74
1974, 1996
1990–95: Tuareg Rebellion
1999: Gen. Mainassara assassinated
CHAD
1971–74, 1983
from 1968
1975, 1979, 1982, 1990
1985: Intensive fighting between Libyan-backed and French-backed forces
1999: Rebellion in the north
1973–90
from 1984: Guerrilla activities undertaken by National Democratic Alliance in northern Sudan
2004: Ethnic conflict in Darfur
1972: Armed struggle for independence
1984–85: Civil war leads to famine in Ethiopia
2000: Failed Coup
CAPE VERDE
SENEGAL
Dakar
1971–74, 2002
1982: Rebellion in southern Casamance region
2000: Failed Coup
GAMBIA
Banjul
1973
1994
Bissau
GUINEA-BISSAU
1998
1959–74
1980, 1999
GUINEA
2000
1984
Conakry
2000: Failed Coup
SIERRA LEONE
Freetown
1991–2001
1967, 1968, 1992, 1997
Monrovia
LIBERIA
2003: President Taylor flees into exile
2000–03
1980, 1990
Sahel
Niger
Bamako
BURKINA
1971–75, 1977
1966, 1980, 1982, 1983, 1987
Ouagadougou
Niamey
2000–03
1999
2000: Gen. Guei ousted in popular revolution
Yamoussoukro
IVORY COAST
GHANA
1971–74, 1977, 1983
1981
1966, 1972, 1978, 1979, 1981
Lake Volta
Accra
TOGO
1967, 1963
Lomé
Porto Novo
BENIN
1971–74
1963, 1965, 1967, 1969, 1972
1972: Marxist-Leninist state proclaimed
1990: Country steers towards pluralist democracy
1967–70, 1971–74, 1967–69
1967–69
1966, 1966, 1975, 1983, 1985
1967–70: Secession of Biafra
1999: Nigeria returns to democracy
2000: Ethnic conflict escalates
2002: Religious conflicts
Abuja
NIGERIA
Biafra
Malabo
CAMEROON
Yaoundé
EQUATORIAL GUINEA
1979
Libreville
GABON
SAO TOME AND PRINCIPE
2003
ATLANTIC OCEAN
Equator
Ndjamena
CENTRAL AFRICAN REPUBLIC
1974
1996–97, 2001–02
1965, 1979, 1981, 2003
Bangui
CONGO
1960–61
1997–99, 2002
1963, 1968, 1977, 1997
Brazzaville
Kinshasa
DEM. REP. CONGO
Congo
1960–65, 1977–78, 1992–93, 1996–97, 1998–2003
1960, 1965
1960–63: Katanga secession
1996–97: Government overthrown
Khartoum
SUDAN
1971–74, 1983, 2004
1955–72, 1983–2004
1958, 1964, 1969, 1984, 1989
from 1989: Guerrilla activities undertaken by rebel Sudanese People's Liberation Army in southern Sudan
ERITREA
2002–04
1970–93
Asmara
1998–2000
1977
DJIBOUTI
Djibouti
Gulf of Aden
Addis Ababa
ETHIOPIA
1973–79, from 1980–2004
from 1962
1974, 1991
Ogaden
1964, 1977–78
1991: Somali National Movement declares secession of an independant Somaliland Republic; Somalian government rejects secession
SOMALIA
1969, 1991
from 1982
Mogadishu
UGANDA
1980
1966, 1971, 1979, 1985, 1986
Kampala
1952–60
1982: Failed Coup
1990's: Ethnic conflict
2002: Daniel arap Moi and KANU voted out after over 30 years in power
1972: President Amin gives 8000 Asians 48 hours to leave the country
1979: Tanzanian forces expel President Amin
1987: Civil war with LRA
Lake Victoria
Nairobi
KENYA
1978–79
Kigali
RWANDA
1995–96
1962–65, 1995–96
1973
1994: 300,000 Tutsi massacred; 2 million Hutus flee to nearby states
Bujumbura
1972: 150,000 Hutus massacred by rival Tutsi ethnic group
BURUNDI
1972, 1995
1962–65, 1994
1966, 1966, 1976, 1987, 1996
Dodoma
TANZANIA
1983
INDIAN OCEAN
COMOROS
1997, 1999
1977, 1989
1995: President Djohar held prisoner by insurrectionists
2002: New Constitution
MAYOTTE to France
Luanda
ANGOLA
1971–74, 1983, 2002–04
1975–92, 1992–94, 1998–2002
1961–75
1974–92: Civil war between Soviet and Cuban-backed MPLA and US and South African -backed UNITA
Katanga
2002–04
MALAWI
Lake Nyasa
Lilongwe
ZAMBIA
2002–04
Lusaka
Zambezi
Harare
ZIMBABWE
2002–04
2000: President Mugabe begins appropriation of white farms: widespread fod shortages
MOZAMBIQUE
1971–74, 1983, 2001, 2002–04
1964–75
1980–92
2002: Over disputed election, President Ratsiraka forced from office after 27 years
1972
Antananarivo
MADAGASCAR
NAMIBIA
1966–90
1985–86: South African raids
Windhoek
BOTSWANA
Gaborone
Tropic of Capricorn
Pretoria
Mbabane
SWAZILAND
1983
LESOTHO
1974, 1983, 2002–04
1970, 1986, 1991
Bloemfontein
Maseru
SOUTH AFRICA
1983
1964–94
1948: System of racial segregation (Apartheid) begins
1985: State of emergency
1990: Nelson Mandela released after 26 years
1994: First multiracial elections
Cape Town
1000 km
1000 miles
4 Post-independence conflict and crisis
famine
anti-colonial war
civil war
interstate war
successful coup d'état
South African tribal homelands
independent South African homelands

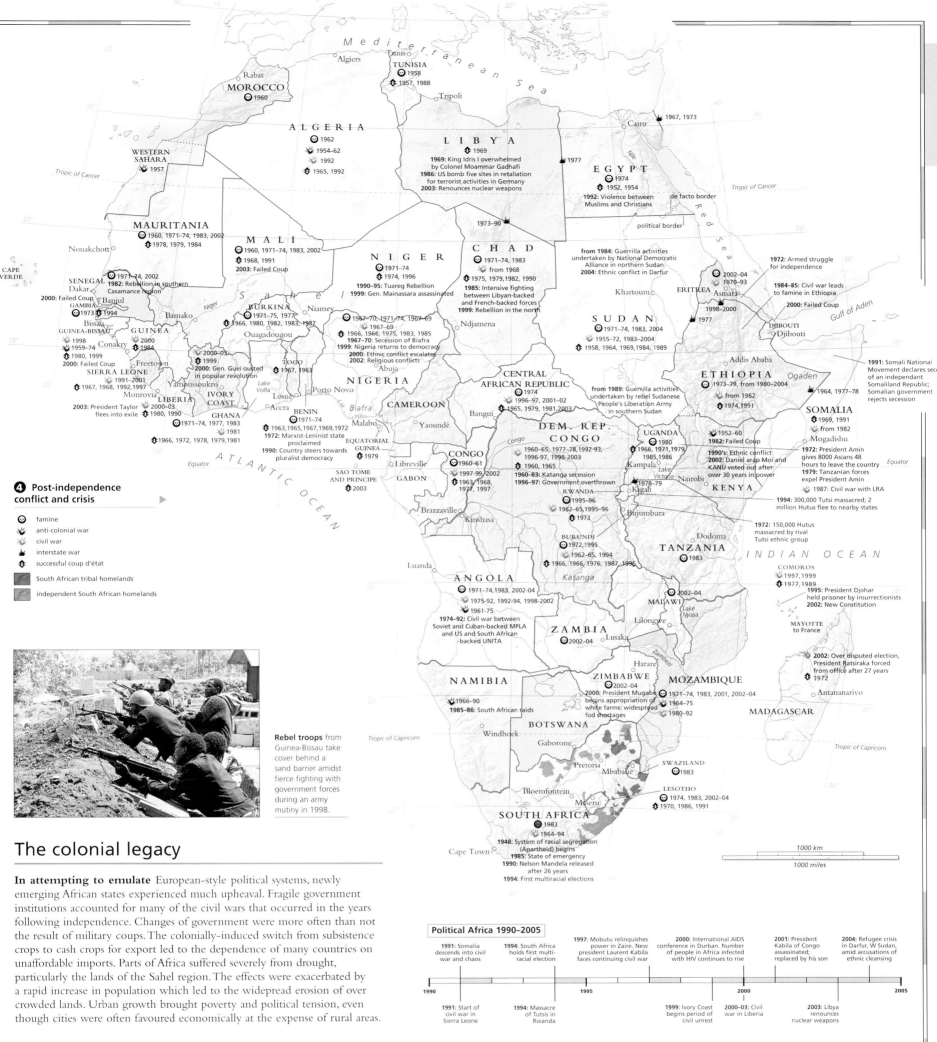

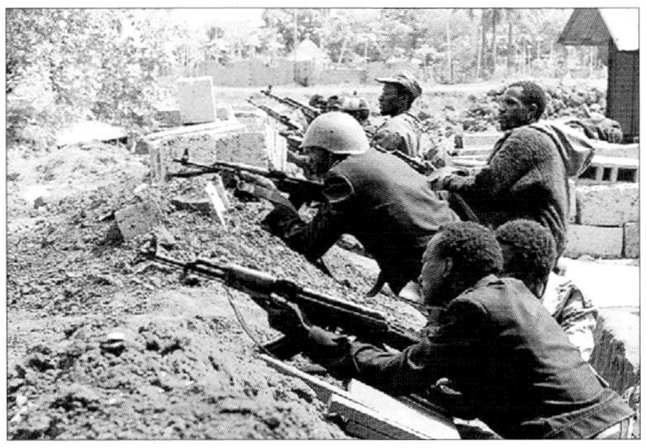

Rebel troops from Guinea-Bissau take cover behind a sand barrier amidst fierce fighting with government forces during an army mutiny in 1998.

The colonial legacy

In attempting to emulate European-style political systems, newly emerging African states experienced much upheaval. Fragile government institutions accounted for many of the civil wars that occurred in the years following independence. Changes of government were more often than not the result of military coups. The colonially-induced switch from subsistence crops to cash crops for export led to the dependence of many countries on unaffordable imports. Parts of Africa suffered severely from drought, particularly the lands of the Sahel region. The effects were exacerbated by a rapid increase in population which led to the widepread erosion of over crowded lands. Urban growth brought poverty and political tension, even though cities were often favoured economically at the expense of rural areas.

Political Africa 1990–2005

- **1990**
- **1991:** Somalia descends into civil war and chaos
- **1991:** Start of civil war in Sierra Leone
- **1994:** South Africa holds first multi-racial election
- **1994:** Massacre of Tutsis in Rwanda
- **1995**
- **1997:** Mobutu relinquishes power in Zaire. New president Laurent Kabila faces continuing civil war
- **1999:** Ivory Coast begins period of civil unrest
- **2000**
- **2000:** International AIDS conference in Durban. Number of people in Africa infected with HIV continues to rise
- **2000–03:** Civil war in Liberia
- **2001:** President Kabila of Congo assassinated; replaced by his son
- **2003:** Libya renounces nuclear weapons
- **2004:** Refugee crisis in Darfur, W Sudan, amid accusations of ethnic cleansing
- **2005**

The Rwandan crisis

Following a violent revolt in 1959 the Hutu ethnic group in Rwanda grasped political power from the Tutsi minority. In 1990, the Tutsi Rwandan Patriotic Front (RPF) mounted an invasion from Uganda. Genocidal violence broke out in 1994 and an estimated 500,000 Tutsi were massacred. Two million Hutus subsequently fled the country. An international criminal tribunal, set up to investigate the genocide, has indicted only a handful of those responsible.

UGANDA
Katale
Apr 1994: RPF begin advance on Kigali
CONGO (ZAIRE)
Byumba
Goma
Kigali
Aug 1994: RPF take control of Rwanda
RWANDA
Lake Kivu
Gitarama
TANZANIA
Bukavu
Ngara
Ngozi
Muyinga
BURUNDI
Uriva
Lake Tanganyika
Bujumbura
Ruyigi
50 km
50 miles

5 Crisis in Central Africa

- advancing RPF (Tutsi) forces
- migrating Hutu refugees
- refugee camp

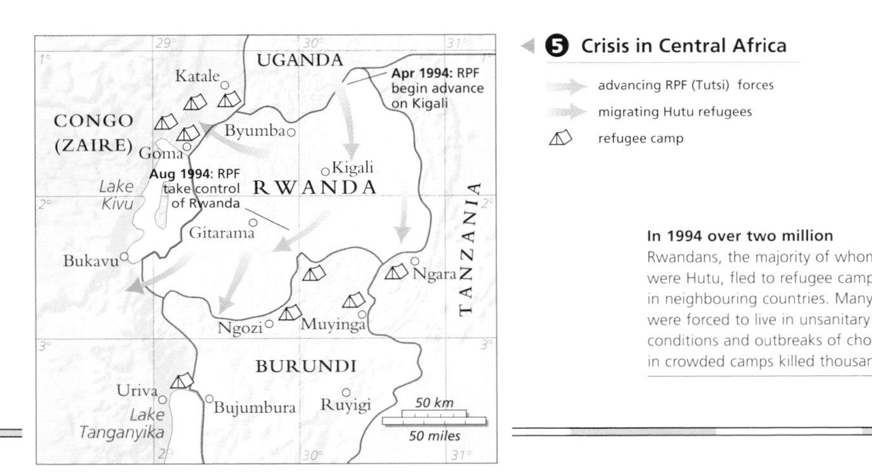

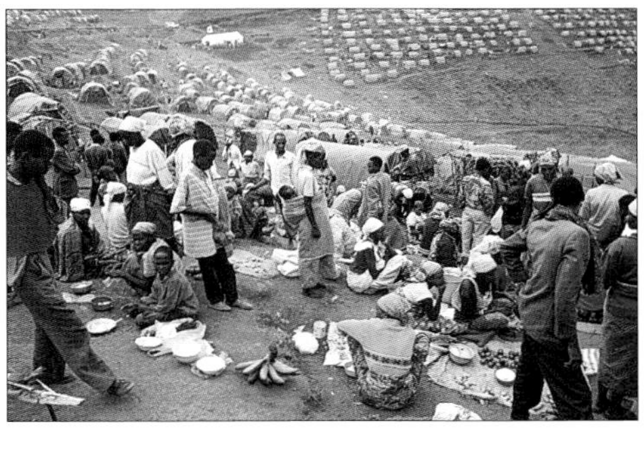

In 1994 over two million Rwandans, the majority of whom were Hutu, fled to refugee camps in neighbouring countries. Many were forced to live in unsanitary conditions and outbreaks of cholera in crowded camps killed thousands.

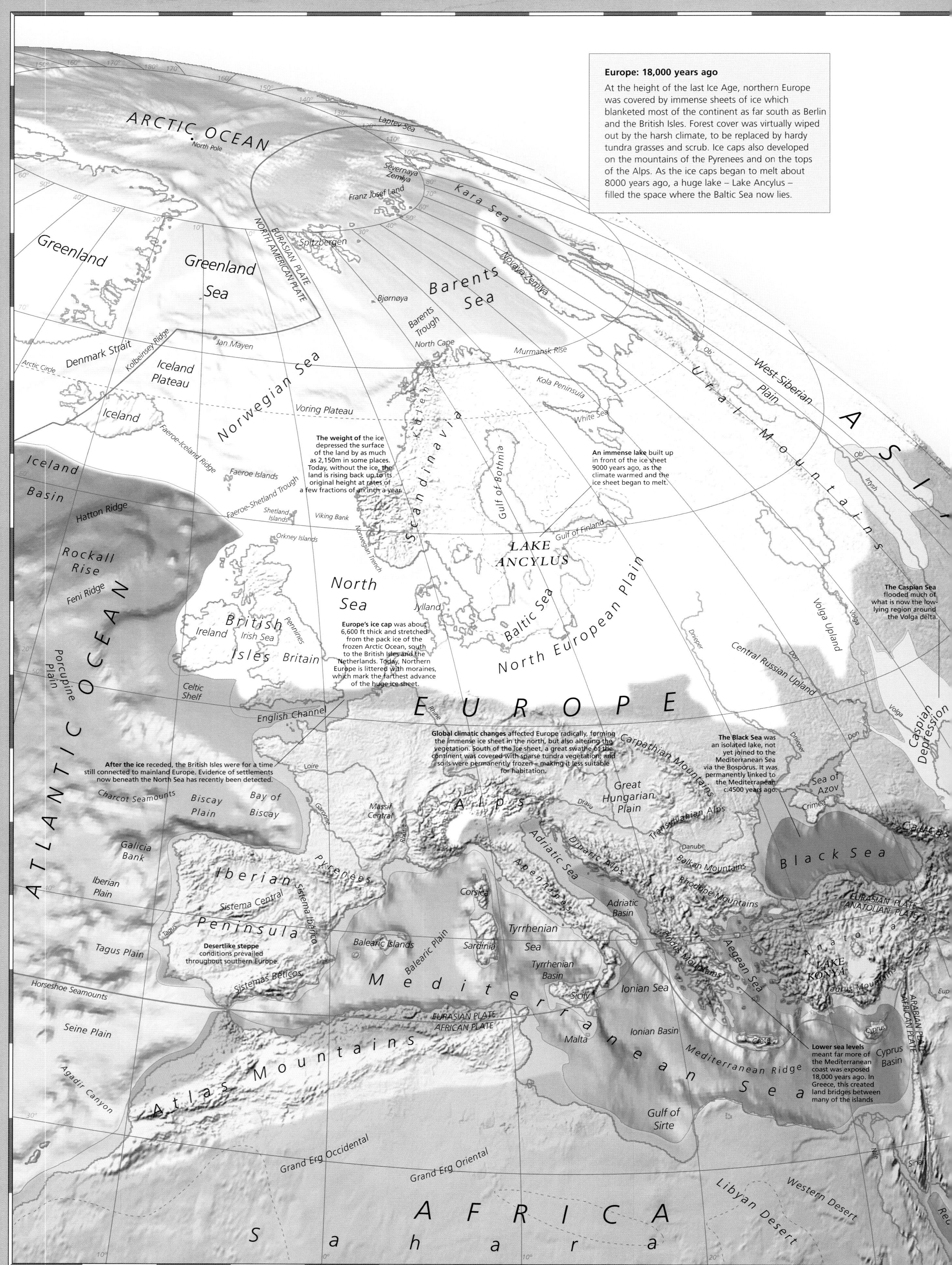

Europe: 18,000 years ago
At the height of the last Ice Age, northern Europe was covered by immense sheets of ice which blanketed most of the continent as far south as Berlin and the British Isles. Forest cover was virtually wiped out by the harsh climate, to be replaced by hardy tundra grasses and scrub. Ice caps also developed on the mountains of the Pyrenees and on the tops of the Alps. As the ice caps began to melt about 8000 years ago, a huge lake – Lake Ancylus – filled the space where the Baltic Sea now lies.
ARCTIC OCEAN
North Pole
Laptev Sea
Severnaya Zemlya
Franz Josef Land
Kara Sea
Spitzbergen
EURASIAN PLATE
NORTH AMERICAN PLATE
Greenland
Greenland Sea
Barents Sea
Novaya Zemlya
Bjørnøya
Barents Trough
North Cape
Jan Mayen
Denmark Strait
Kolbeinsey Ridge
Arctic Circle
Iceland Plateau
Norwegian Sea
Murmansk Rise
Kola Peninsula
White Sea
Ob'
West Siberian Plain
Ural Mountains
ASIA
Iceland
Voring Plateau
Kölen
Scandinavia
Faeroe-Iceland Ridge
Faeroe Islands
The weight of the ice depressed the surface of the land by as much as 2,150m in some places. Today, without the ice, the land is rising back up to its original height at rates of a few fractions of an inch a year.
Gulf of Bothnia
An immense lake built up in front of the ice sheet 9000 years ago, as the climate warmed and the ice sheet began to melt.
Irtysh
Iceland Basin
Hatton Ridge
Faeroe-Shetland Trough
Shetland Islands
Viking Bank
Orkney Islands
Norwegian Trench
Gulf of Finland
LAKE ANCYLUS
Rockall Rise
Feni Ridge
North Sea
Jylland
Baltic Sea
North European Plain
The Caspian Sea flooded much of what is now the low-lying region around the Volga delta.
Volga
Volga Upland
British Isles
Ireland
Irish Sea
Pennines
Britain
Europe's ice cap was about 6,600 ft thick and stretched from the pack ice of the frozen Arctic Ocean, south to the British Isles and the Netherlands. Today, Northern Europe is littered with moraines, which mark the farthest advance of the huge ice sheet.
Dnieper
Central Russian Upland
Don
Porcupine Plain
ATLANTIC OCEAN
Celtic Shelf
EUROPE
Rhine
Caspian Depression
English Channel
Global climatic changes affected Europe radically, forming the immense ice sheet in the north, but also altering the vegetation. South of the ice sheet, a great swathe of the continent was covered with sparse tundra vegetation, and soils were permanently frozen – making it less suitable for habitation.
Carpathian Mountains
The Black Sea was an isolated lake, not yet joined to the Mediterranean Sea via the Bosporus. It was permanently linked to the Mediterranean c.4500 years ago.
After the ice receded, the British Isles were for a time still connected to mainland Europe. Evidence of settlements now beneath the North Sea has recently been detected.
Loire
Sea of Azov
Charcot Seamounts
Biscay Plain
Bay of Biscay
Garonne
Massif Central
Alps
Drava
Great Hungarian Plain
Crimea
Transylvanian Alps
Galicia Bank
Rhône
Adriatic Sea
Dinaric Alps
Danube
Balkan Mountains
Black Sea
Caucasus
Iberian Plain
Pyrenees
Iberian Peninsula
Sistema Central
Sistema Ibérico
Corsica
Apennines
Adriatic Basin
Rhodope Mountains
EURASIAN PLATE
ANATOLIAN PLATE
Tagus
Balearic Islands
Balearic Plain
Sardinia
Tyrrhenian Sea
Pindus Mountains
Aegean Sea
Anatolia
Tagus Plain
Desertlike steppe conditions prevailed throughout southern Europe.
Tyrrhenian Basin
LAKE KONYA
Taurus Mountains
Sistemas Béticos
Mediterranean Sea
Horseshoe Seamounts
Sicily
Ionian Sea
ARABIAN PLATE
AFRICAN PLATE
EURASIAN PLATE
AFRICAN PLATE
Cyprus
Seine Plain
Malta
Ionian Basin
Crete
Lower sea levels meant far more of the Mediterranean coast was exposed 18,000 years ago. In Greece, this created land bridges between many of the islands
Cyprus Basin
Atlas Mountains
Mediterranean Ridge
Agadir Canyon
Gulf of Sirte
Grand Erg Occidental
Grand Erg Oriental
Nile
Sinai
Libyan Desert
Western Desert
AFRICA
Sahara

Vegetation type

- ice cap and glacier
- polar or alpine desert
- tundra
- semidesert or sparsely vegetated
- forest or open woodland
- temperate desert
- tropical desert
- desert
- coastline (present-day)
- coastline (18,000 years ago)

Mountains
Aral Sea
Tien Shan
Caspian Sea
EURASIAN PLATE
IRANIAN PLATE
Iranian Plateau
Dasht-e Lut
IRANIAN PLATE
INDO-AUSTRALIAN PLATE
Tigris
Zagros Mountains
IRANIAN PLATE
ARABIAN PLATE
rian
esert
The Gulf
Arabian
Peninsula
Ar Rub' al Khali
Arabian Sea
Tropic of Cancer
40°
50°

EUROPE
REGIONAL HISTORY

THE HISTORICAL LANDSCAPE

EUROPE, THE SECOND SMALLEST OF THE WORLD'S CONTINENTS, has a great diversity of topography, climate, and ecology, a rich pattern which contributed greatly to its inordinate influence on global history. Extensive oceanic and inland shorelines, abundantly fertile soils, and broadly temperate conditions provided innumerable heartlands for a wide array of cultures. Internecine rivalries created shifting patterns, themselves frequently overlaid by successive waves of migration and incursion. The shores of the Mediterranean provided a cradle for many powerful cultural groups, which formed myriad states and several empires until the 15th century, when the power base shifted to the emergent nations of the Atlantic coast. It was these aggressive, mercantile and pioneering maritime powers who vaulted Europe to a globally dominant position, through trade and colonialism, during the closing centuries of the 2nd millennium. As they collapsed, a seemingly ineradicable linguistic, economic, technological, and cultural imprint remained, which in the 20th century was widely adopted and adapted, creating an almost universal global culture.

During the Ice Ages, the Alps were covered with extensive glacier systems, vestiges of which remain today. After the ice had receded, the mountains provided a barrier between the cultures of the Mediterranean and those of Northern Europe.

The fertile plains of rivers such as the Danube provided the setting for early agricultural settlements, which spread north from the shores of the Aegean Sea from around 7000 BCE.

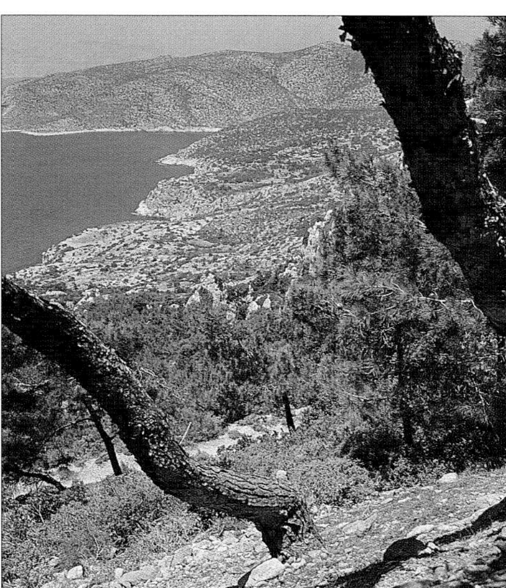

Europe's first cultures spread westward from Anatolia, reaching the fertile, often isolated coastal valleys around the Aegean between 7000 and 6000 BCE.

EUROPE

EXPLORATION AND MAPPING

The theodolite was first used in the 17th century. This model, dating from 1765 could measure both altitude and azimuth.

EUROPEANS LEARNED TO KNOW their lands by practical experience and scientific study. Trade and the acquisition of new land provided an impetus for travel and exploration. Phoenician traders moving west in the 9th century BCE, and the Greeks from the 8th century BCE explored the Mediterranean. They were followed by the Romans, whose road system eventually covered much of southern and western Europe. Long-range travel was next developed by the wide-ranging Scandinavians of the 9th and 10th centuries. The emphasis was on sea and river, not road transport. The Greeks were the earliest people to begin to codify their knowledge of Europe, and the sailors of the Mediterranean produced the most sophisticated charts and maps of Europe until the flowering of Dutch cartography in the 16th century, which laid the foundations for modern mapmaking.

Mapping in the Classical era

This map reconstructs the Europe known to Pytheas. His journey was the first scientific exploration of northern Europe by Greeks. The map is based on Eratosthenes' three-continent (Europe, Africa, and Asia) world view. The Mediterranean familiar to the Greeks is accurately plotted; the northern topography is far more speculative.

The peoples of the Mediterranean made the earliest attempts at a survey of Europe. In 340 BCE, the Greek Pytheas travelled from Massalia to Britain, visiting the Orkneys and Shetlands; he later visited Norway and north Germany. The first attempts at scientific mapping were made in the Mediterranean: Eratosthenes successfully measured the diameter of the earth; Hipparchus suggested lines of latitude and longitude as reference points, and Ptolemy tried to show the surface of the earth using two conical projections, and provided points of reference for more than 8000 places.

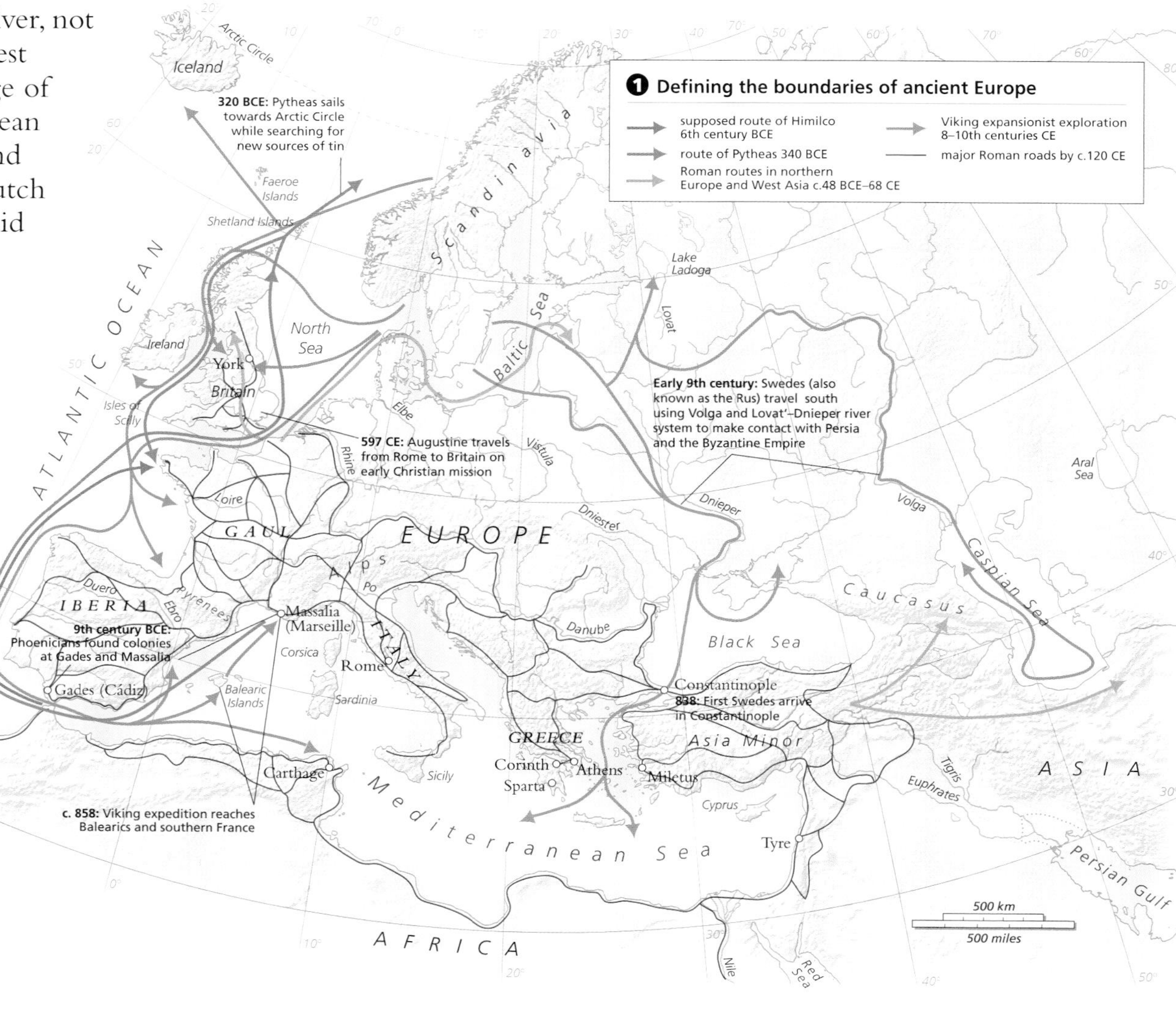

The Vikings in the North Atlantic

The extraordinary Viking voyages of the 9th and 10th centuries were primarily for booty – trade and the acquisition of new land came later. Sailing west from Norway into treacherous northern waters, the Vikings settled the Shetland islands and the Faeroes. Iceland was discovered in the mid-9th century, and despite the ice-logged winters, further travellers returned to colonize the island, founding settlements c.873, and establishing bases for voyages to Greenland and Labrador.

Viking ships were built with great care and attention to detail. The tiller *(left)* is carved in the shape of a snake, while the weather vane *(below)*, made from polished bronze, is topped with a figure of a dog.

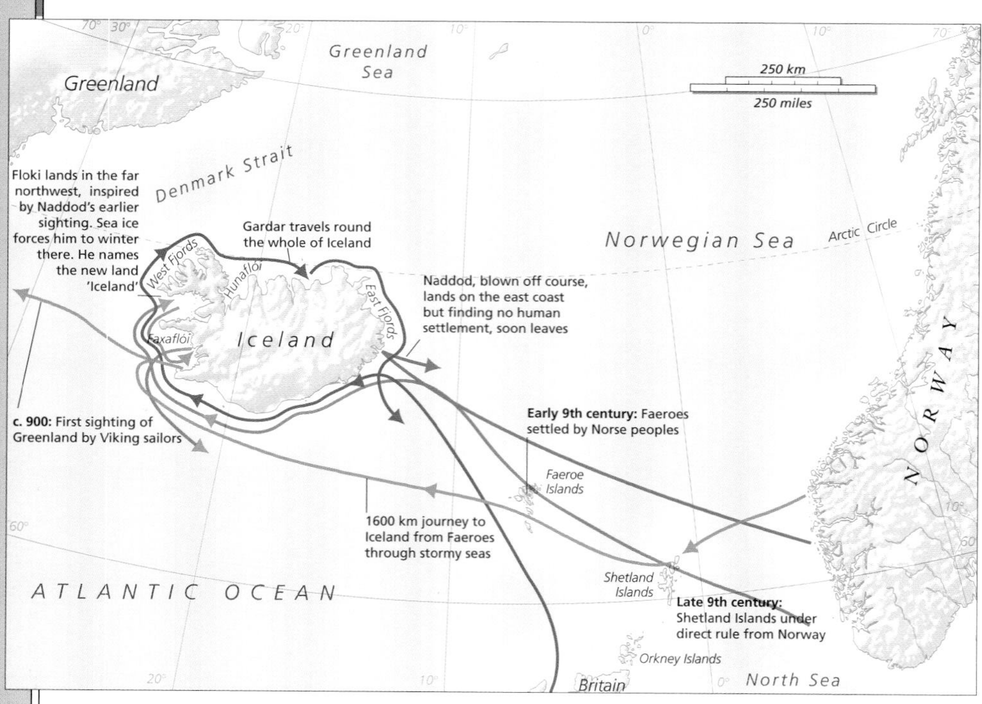

2 The Viking discovery of Iceland

- Gardar Svavarsson c. 860
- Naddod c. 870
- Floki Vilgerdarsson
- other Viking explorers

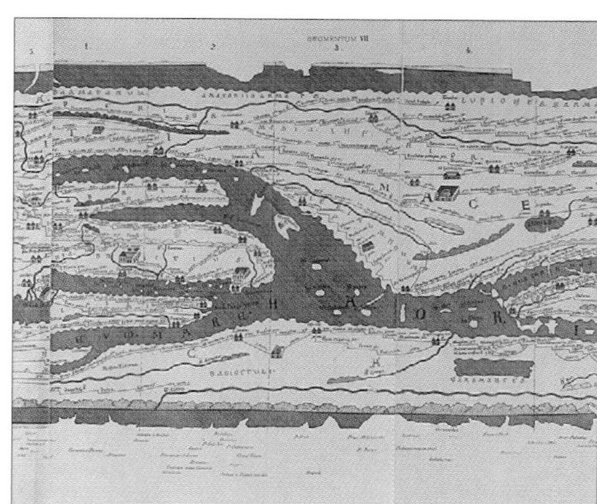

The Peutinger Table, a strip map 7 m long and 32 cm wide, showed roads in the Roman Empire – such as the Via Appia – with little reference to the surrounding countryside. It was probably first drawn in the 3rd century CE and was a useful tool for actually planning journeys. Some 5000 places are recorded, mostly in Europe.

The Vikings in the North Atlantic

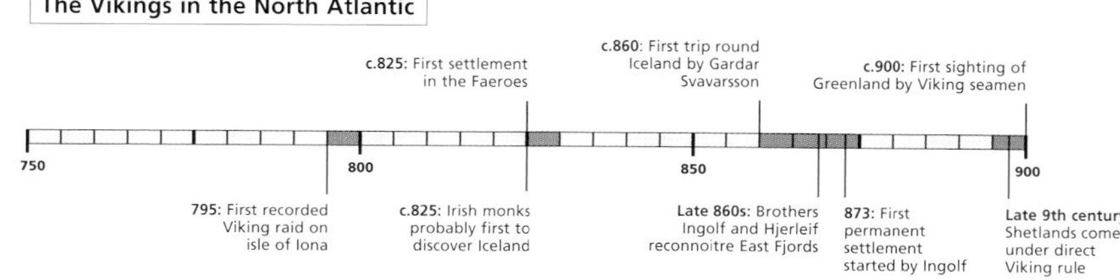

Medieval mapping of Europe

Most of Europe was well known to travellers by the 11th century, but the accuracy with which it was mapped was extremely variable. The literate sailors of the Mediterranean were able to draw on the relatively sophisticated Portolan charts, which were made chiefly by Italian and Catalan navigators, but nothing comparable existed for the sailors of the north. Inland, largely imaginary wall maps represented Christian beliefs and the known world, with Jerusalem at the centre of the earth, Europe at left, and Africa on the right. A second type of map was based on accumulated knowledge, and gave a recognizable if distorted picture of Europe. Examples include Gough's map, and the maps of Matthew Paris (1200–1259 CE). From the 15th century, Ptolemy's map of Europe *(see p.44)* was once again available and it was added to, and corrected in the light of new knowledge and re-published in the *Tabulae Modernae*. In 1425, Clavus, a Dane who had visited Iceland and Southern Greenland, added these, plus Norway, to the Ptolemaic base map.

The Hereford wall map *(left)* is perhaps the best known of the 600 or so 'T-in-O maps' which are known to have survived. The T-shape of the Mediterranean Sea which divides the world into Europe, Africa and Asia is contained within a circle – the O.

Portolan charts *(above)* were available to Mediterranean sailors from early Medieval times. They recorded the ports of the Mediterranean and Black Sea, giving landmarks, bearings, and distances, based on the Roman mile of 1000 paces.

Medieval mapping

1200 — 1300 — 1400 — 1500 — 1600

- **1276:** Hereford wall map designed by Richard of Haldingham and Lafford
- **1276:** Publication of *Il Compasso da Navigare*, a collection of verbal descriptions of key routes
- **1321:** Pietro Vesconte's *Mappamundi* incorporates some features of portolan charts
- **1472:** First publication of the *Etymologiae* by Archbishop Isidore of Seville, devisor of the concept of the T-in-O map in 7th century
- **1475:** Publication of Ptolemy's *Geography*
- **1485:** Bartolommeo dalli Sonetti's *Isolario* based on observation by navigators is published
- **16th century:** Latitude scales added to portolan charts
- **1539:** First printed portolan chart made in Venice by Giovanni Andrea di Vavasore

The beginnings of modern cartography

In early modern Europe, increasing trade and a growing gentry class, interested in their surroundings, encouraged a new phase of map making. Overseas territories, and the possessions of the rich, were mapped using surveying instruments such as the theodolite. Dutch cartographers made some of the most important innovations. Gerardus Mercator was the first to break from the Ptolemaic model. Mercator's projection rejected Ptolemy's conical model to show bearings with a scale identical in all directions. This made it particularly useful for navigators, and it is still widely used today. Another Dutchman, Willebrord Snell (Snellius), was the first to use triangulation to survey a large area. After carefully measuring a base line, he then employed trigonometry to calculate the distances to far-off landmarks.

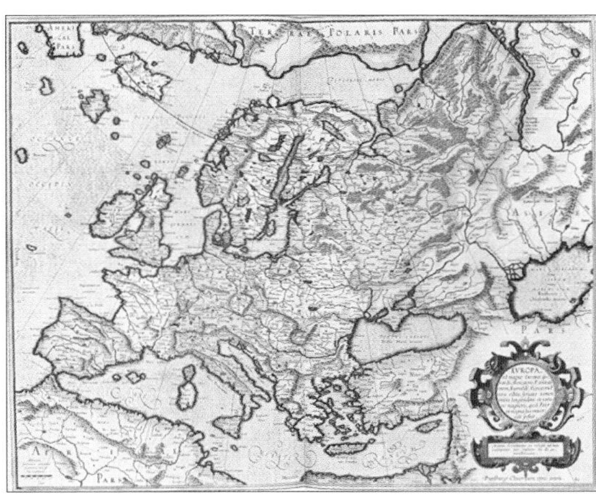

This map of Europe was produced by Mercator in 1554. It gives a detailed picture of settlement patterns, river networks, forest cover, and country boundaries, but some of the surrounding details, for example the proportions of Scandinavia, are far from accurate.

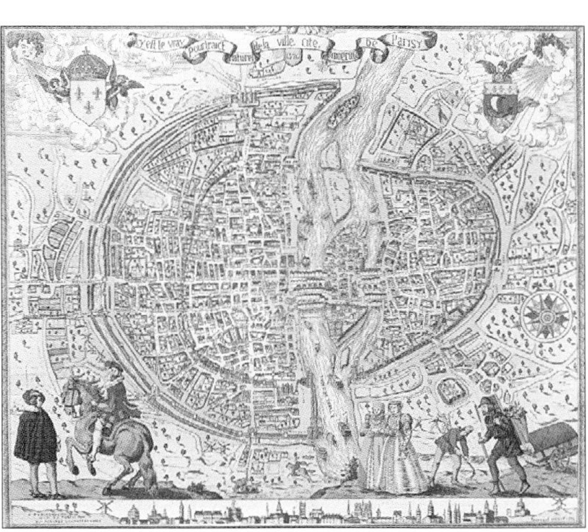

This detailed aerial view of Paris dates from 1576. It shows the original city wall, as well as building on the outskirts, agricultural areas – including windmills – and rough pasture on the edge of the city.

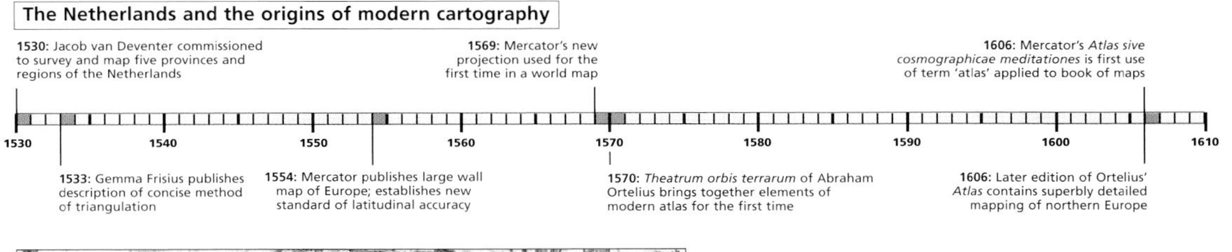
The Netherlands and the origins of modern cartography
1530: Jacob van Deventer commissioned to survey and map five provinces and regions of the Netherlands
1569: Mercator's new projection used for the first time in a world map
1606: Mercator's Atlas sive cosmographicae meditationes is first use of term 'atlas' applied to book of maps
1530
1540
1550
1560
1570
1580
1590
1600
1610
1533: Gemma Frisius publishes description of concise method of triangulation
1554: Mercator publishes large wall map of Europe; establishes new standard of latitudinal accuracy
1570: Theatrum orbis terrarum of Abraham Ortelius brings together elements of modern atlas for the first time
1606: Later edition of Ortelius' Atlas contains superbly detailed mapping of northern Europe

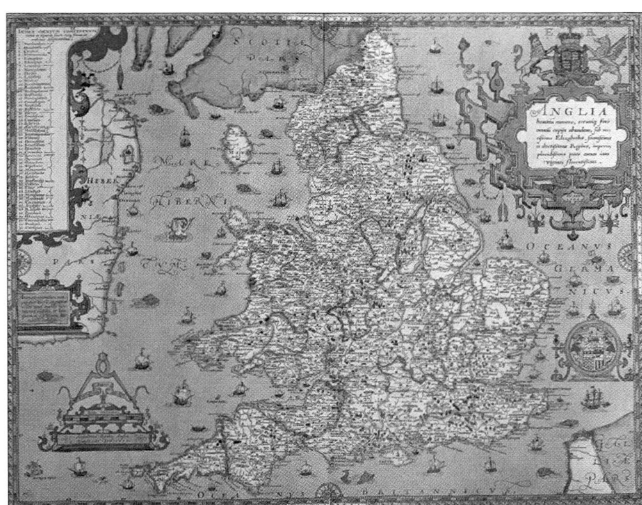

Saxton's county map of England and Wales, published in 1579, shows the detail and accuracy which was being achieved by the 16th century. Other similar examples include Norden's county maps of 1593, and Ogilvie's road map published in *Britannia*.

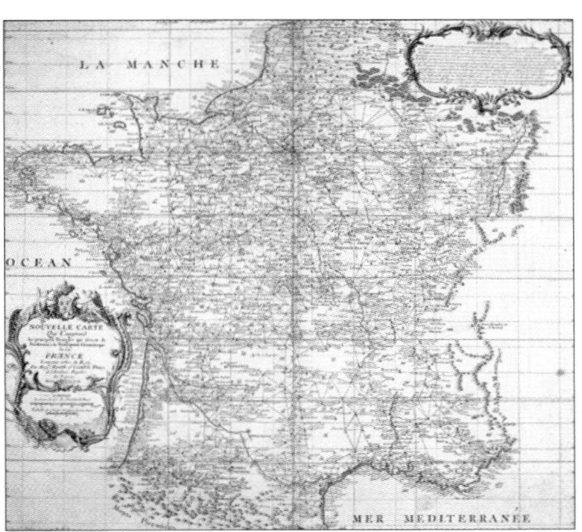
LA MANCHE
OCEAN
MER MEDITERRANEE

J.D. and C.F. Cassini continued Snellius' triangulation surveys in France. By 1744 all of France was covered by some 2000 triangles. The first sheets of a map of France on a scale of 1:86,400 were produced in 1756, but it was not until the Revolution that the last of the 182 sheets was published.

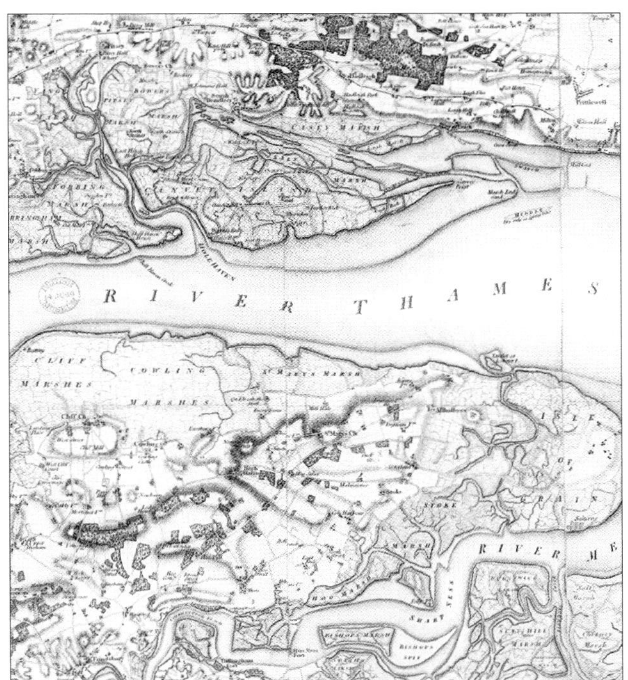
RIVER THAMES

In England, fear of Napoleonic invasion and a need for detailed information about the land, led to a survey on a scale of two inches to the mile and publication on a scale of one inch to the mile. The first map of this series was sold as four sheets in 1801.

Surveyors from the Royal Engineers were responsible for making accurate maps of Britain and its Empire during the 19th century. Here they are shown undertaking a triangulation.

PREHISTORIC EUROPE

Mycenaean pottery, such as this goblet from Rhodes (c.1300 BCE), was traded throughout the eastern Mediterranean.

IN 7000 BCE, postglacial Europe, with its deciduous forests and increasingly temperate climate, was rich in natural resources and thinly populated by hunter-gatherers. By 1000 BCE, villages stretched from the Balkans to Scandinavia, and agriculture had reached even the marginal regions of the continent; there was a flourishing trans-continental traffic in salt, metals, and amber; and the first palace-based states had emerged on Crete and the Greek mainland. Although remains of settlements are rarely well preserved, a wide range of burials reveal, through grave goods as varied as woven textiles, ceramic vessels, and bronze axe-heads, an increasingly stratified society, in which individual possessions were a reflection of status.

The introduction of farming 7000–5000 BCE

The first potters of Central Europe used fired clay to make stylized human figures.

As agriculture spread from Anatolia into the Balkans and beyond, farming practices were adapted to more northerly latitudes, with an increased reliance on cattle and pigs and new, hardy strains of cereal. The mud-brick hill villages (tells) of the Middle East were replaced, in the thickly forested river valleys of Central Europe, by clusters of timber longhouses. The location of early farming communities can be charted by different pottery styles; incised Bandkeramik pottery is found from Hungary to the North Sea, while Cardial pottery, decorated with shell impressions, is found along the Mediterranean.

The spread of farming 7000–5000 BCE

7000 BCE – 6500 – 6000 – 5500 – 5000 BCE

c.7000: Farming spreads from Anatolia to southeastern Europe

c.6500: Rising postglacial sea levels separate British Isles from the rest of the European continent

c.6000: Farming starts to spread along the western coast of Mediterranean

c.6000: First farming villages appear in southern Italy and Sicily

c.5600: Farming communities using Bandkeramik pottery in Central Europe

c.5000: Agriculture well established in southern France and in the Netherlands

Timber longhouses, such as this example from Bylany, in the Czech Republic, were built by the earliest farmers of Central Europe. The basic framework, made from plentiful timber supplies, was covered with wattle and daub. The buildings could be up to 45 m long, and housed one or more families, as well as livestock and stores of food.

1 The introduction of farming 7000–5000 BCE

- spread of farming
- cultivated land by c.7000 BCE
- cultivated land by c.6000 BCE
- cultivated land by c.5000 BCE
- concentrations of Mesolithic settlements c.5000 BCE
- early farming settlement
- Balkan painted ware site
- Bandkeramik pottery site
- Cardial and incised pottery site

500 km
500 miles

Scandinavia
Ural Mountains
British Isles
Ireland
Britain
Thames
North Sea
Baltic Sea
North European Plain
Steppes
Köln
Lindenthal
Langweiler
Elsloo
Westeregeln
Efurt
ATLANTIC OCEAN
Cuiry-lès-Chaudardes
La Tranche
Bylany
Olszanica
Těšetice-Kyjovice
Mohelnice
Carpathian Mountains
Florești
Alps
Grotte Gazel
Fontbrégoua
Arene Candide
Iberian Peninsula
Gomolava
Vinča
Divostin
Chevdar
Karanovo
Black Sea
Caucasus
Caspian Sea
Coveta de l'Or
Cueva de Nerja
Corsica
Sardinia
Passo di Corvo
Adriatic Sea
Balkan Mountains
Sitagroi
Nea Nikomedeia
Argissa
Aegean Sea
Grotta dell'Uzzo
Sicily
Stentinello
Franchthi
Hacilar
Beycesultan
Anatolia
Mersin
Canhasan
FERTILE CRESCENT
Euphrates
Tigris
Crete
Knossos
Mediterranean Sea
Atlas Mountains

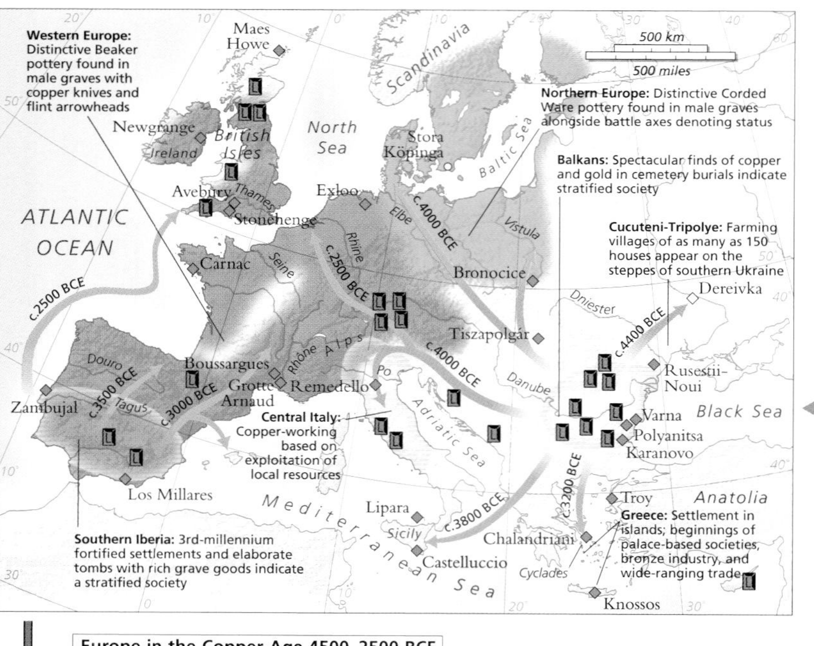

Western Europe: Distinctive Beaker pottery found in male graves with copper knives and flint arrowheads
Northern Europe: Distinctive Corded Ware pottery found in male graves alongside battle axes denoting status
Balkans: Spectacular finds of copper and gold in cemetery burials indicate stratified society
Cucuteni-Tripolye: Farming villages of as many as 150 houses appear on the steppes of southern Ukraine
Central Italy: Copper-working based on exploitation of local resources
Southern Iberia: 3rd-millennium fortified settlements and elaborate tombs with rich grave goods indicate a stratified society
Greece: Settlement in islands; beginnings of palace-based societies, bronze industry, and wide-ranging trade
Maes Howe
Newgrange
Avebury
Stonehenge
Carnac
Exloo
Stora Köpinge
Bronocice
Dereivka
Tiszapolgár
Rusesti-Noui
Varna
Polyanitsa
Karanovo
Boussargues
Grotte Arnaud
Remedello
Zambujal
Los Millares
Lipara
Castelluccio
Chalandriani
Troy
Knossos
Anatolia
ATLANTIC OCEAN
North Sea
Black Sea
Mediterranean Sea
c.2500 BCE
c.3500 BCE
c.3000 BCE
c.2500 BCE
c.4000 BCE
c.4400 BCE
c.3800 BCE
c.3200 BCE
500 km
500 miles

Europe in the Copper Age 4500–2500 BCE

This was an era of technological innovation and contact between communities. Both horses and wheeled vehicles spread westward from the steppes, reaching western Europe by c.2500 BCE, while the introduction of the scratch plough increased productivity. Copper technology, which was developed in eastern Europe c.5000 BCE, spread throughout Europe over the next millennium. Finds of high prestige metalwork in some individual burials indicate that society was becoming more hierarchical, while distinctive pottery styles, known as Beaker Ware and Corded Ware, became widespread in Central and western European burials, indicating the existence of a network of contact and exchange.

Marble figurines, made in the Cycladic Islands of Greece from c.2600 BCE, were placed in burials.

2 Europe in the Copper Age 4500–2500 BCE

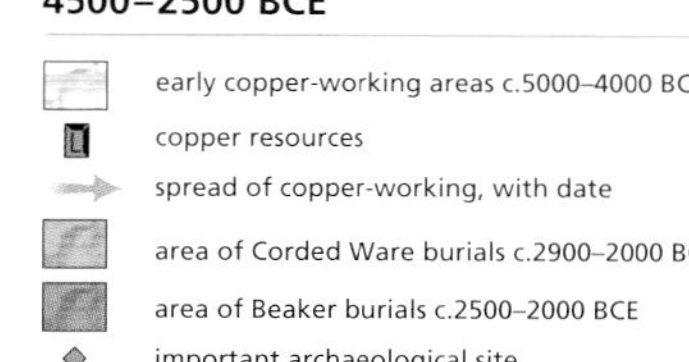

early copper-working areas c.5000–4000 BCE
copper resources
spread of copper-working, with date
area of Corded Ware burials c.2900–2000 BCE
area of Beaker burials c.2500–2000 BCE
important archaeological site

Europe in the Copper Age 4500–2500 BCE

4000 BCE – 3500 – 3000 – 2500 BCE

c.4000: Farming villages of the Cucuteni-Tripolye group appear in southern Ukraine

c.4000: Copper mines being exploited in Bulgaria and Yugoslavia

c.3500: Stone circles and alignments, henges, and menhirs appear throughout northwestern Europe

c.3500: First wheeled vehicles in central Europe

c.3000: Copper-working begins in southern France

c.2900: Appearance of Corded Ware pottery and stone battle-axes in burials in northern Europe

c.2500: Copper-working reaches British Isles. Bell beaker pottery found in individual burials in western Europe

The stone alignments at Kermario in northwestern France date to c.3000 BCE. They were probably associated with processions and seasonal rituals.

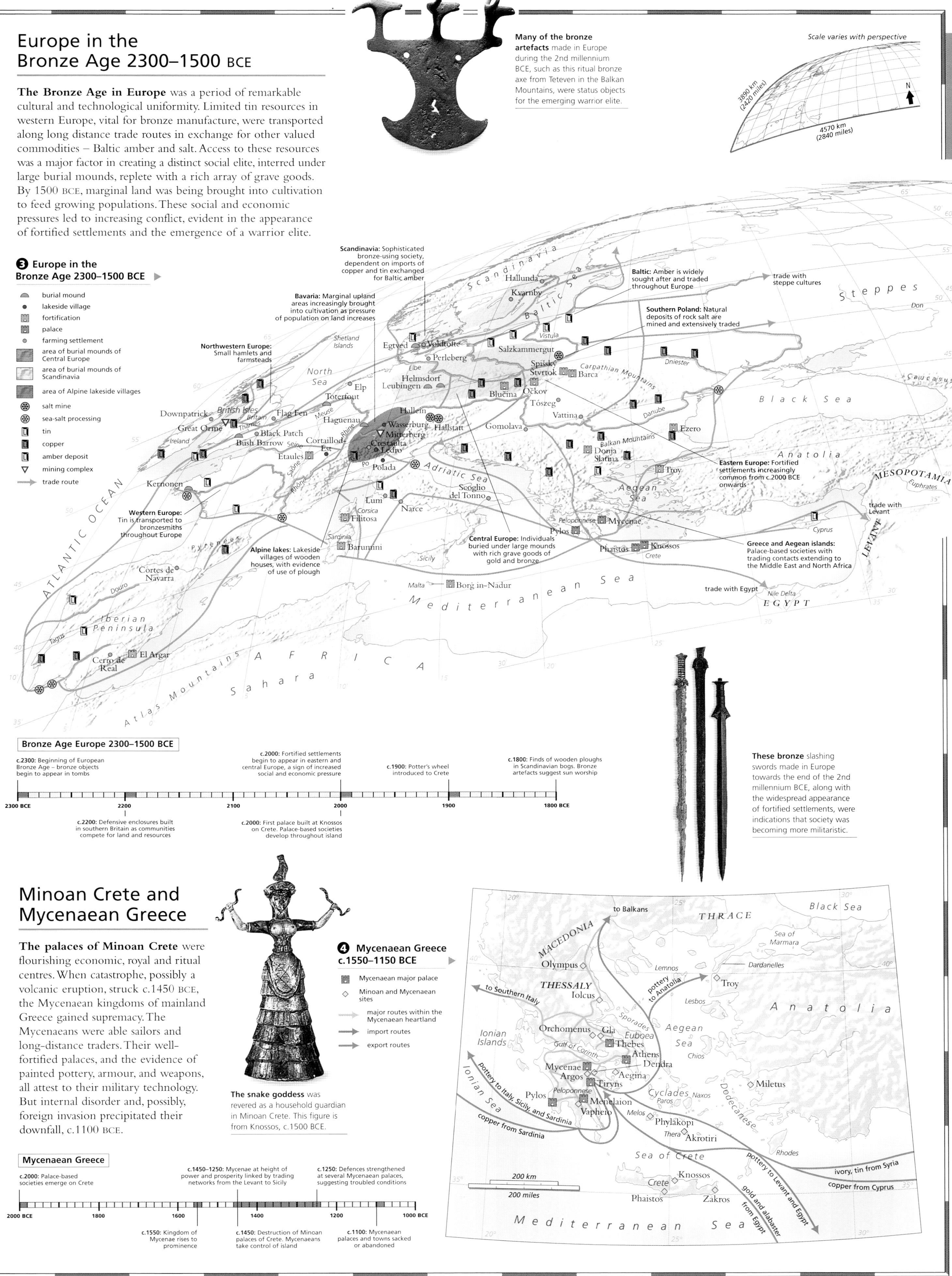

Europe in the Bronze Age 2300–1500 BCE

The Bronze Age in Europe was a period of remarkable cultural and technological uniformity. Limited tin resources in western Europe, vital for bronze manufacture, were transported along long distance trade routes in exchange for other valued commodities – Baltic amber and salt. Access to these resources was a major factor in creating a distinct social elite, interred under large burial mounds, replete with a rich array of grave goods. By 1500 BCE, marginal land was being brought into cultivation to feed growing populations. These social and economic pressures led to increasing conflict, evident in the appearance of fortified settlements and the emergence of a warrior elite.

Many of the bronze artefacts made in Europe during the 2nd millennium BCE, such as this ritual bronze axe from Teteven in the Balkan Mountains, were status objects for the emerging warrior elite.

Scale varies with perspective
3890 km (2420 miles)
4570 km (2840 miles)
N
❸ Europe in the Bronze Age 2300–1500 BCE
burial mound
lakeside village
fortification
palace
farming settlement
area of burial mounds of Central Europe
area of burial mounds of Scandinavia
area of Alpine lakeside villages
salt mine
sea-salt processing
tin
copper
amber deposit
mining complex
trade route
Scandinavia: Sophisticated bronze-using society, dependent on imports of copper and tin exchanged for Baltic amber
Bavaria: Marginal upland areas increasingly brought into cultivation as pressure of population on land increases
Baltic: Amber is widely sought after and traded throughout Europe
Southern Poland: Natural deposits of rock salt are mined and extensively traded
Northwestern Europe: Small hamlets and farmsteads
Western Europe: Tin is transported to bronzesmiths throughout Europe
Alpine lakes: Lakeside villages of wooden houses, with evidence of use of plough
Central Europe: Individuals buried under large mounds with rich grave goods of gold and bronze
Eastern Europe: Fortified settlements increasingly common from c.2000 BCE onwards
Greece and Aegean islands: Palace-based societies with trading contacts extending to the Middle East and North Africa
trade with steppe cultures
trade with Levant
trade with Egypt
Scandinavia
Baltic Sea
Steppes
Black Sea
Anatolia
MESOPOTAMIA
LEVANT
EGYPT
Mediterranean Sea
ATLANTIC OCEAN
North Sea
Iberian Peninsula
AFRICA
Sahara
Atlas Mountains

Bronze Age Europe 2300–1500 BCE

- c.2300: Beginning of European Bronze Age – bronze objects begin to appear in tombs
- c.2200: Defensive enclosures built in southern Britain as communities compete for land and resources
- c.2000: Fortified settlements begin to appear in eastern and central Europe, a sign of increased social and economic pressure
- c.2000: First palace built at Knossos on Crete. Palace-based societies develop throughout island
- c.1900: Potter's wheel introduced to Crete
- c.1800: Finds of wooden ploughs in Scandinavian bogs. Bronze artefacts suggest sun worship

These bronze slashing swords made in Europe towards the end of the 2nd millennium BCE, along with the widespread appearance of fortified settlements, were indications that society was becoming more militaristic.

Minoan Crete and Mycenaean Greece

The palaces of Minoan Crete were flourishing economic, royal and ritual centres. When catastrophe, possibly a volcanic eruption, struck c.1450 BCE, the Mycenaean kingdoms of mainland Greece gained supremacy. The Mycenaeans were able sailors and long-distance traders. Their well-fortified palaces, and the evidence of painted pottery, armour, and weapons, all attest to their military technology. But internal disorder and, possibly, foreign invasion precipitated their downfall, c.1100 BCE.

The snake goddess was revered as a household guardian in Minoan Crete. This figure is from Knossos, c.1500 BCE.

❹ Mycenaean Greece c.1550–1150 BCE
Mycenaean major palace
Minoan and Mycenaean sites
major routes within the Mycenaean heartland
import routes
export routes
to Balkans
to Southern Italy
pottery to Anatolia
pottery to Italy, Sicily, and Sardinia
copper from Sardinia
pottery to Levant and Egypt
gold and alabaster from Egypt
ivory, tin from Syria
copper from Cyprus
THRACE
MACEDONIA
THESSALY
Black Sea
Sea of Marmara
Aegean Sea
Ionian Sea
Sea of Crete
Mediterranean Sea
Anatolia
200 km
200 miles

Mycenaean Greece

- c.2000: Palace-based societies emerge on Crete
- c.1550: Kingdom of Mycenae rises to prominence
- c.1450–1250: Mycenae at height of power and prosperity linked by trading networks from the Levant to Sicily
- c.1450: Destruction of Minoan palaces of Crete. Mycenaeans take control of island
- c.1250: Defences strengthened at several Mycenaean palaces, suggesting troubled conditions
- c.1100: Mycenaean palaces and towns sacked or abandoned

THE MEDITERRANEAN WORLD

This Phoenician carved ivory plaque was found at the Assyrian city of Nimrud.

BETWEEN 700 AND 300 BCE, the Mediterranean world shaped western civilization. The impact of Classical Greek ideas on art, architecture, literature, philosophy, science, and, through the revolutionary innovation of democratic government, on political institutions was profound and wide ranging. The conquests of Philip of Macedon and his son Alexander the Great *(see pp. 40–41)* took the fundamental features of Greek culture as far as the borders of India. Of other major civilizations, the Etruscans were undoubtedly influenced by the Greeks, both in the layout of their grid-plan cities and in their lifesize terracotta statues. The Phoenicians, an energetic, maritime people based in city-states in the Levant, took their culture, through trade and colonization, to the western shores of the Mediterranean.

The colonization of the Mediterranean

This magnificent Attic red-figure vase, which illustrates the Homeric myth of Odysseus and the Sirens, dates from c.490 BCE.

Both the Phoenicians and the Greeks founded colonies during the 1st millennium BCE. The limited fertile terrain of the Greek homelands could not support the growing population, and many Greek cities sent colonists to western Anatolia, the Black Sea shores, Sicily and southern Italy, and even southern France, where Massalia (Marseille) was founded. The city of Miletus alone was responsible for establishing over 80 colonies. The Phoenicians set out in search of metals, initially setting up a colony in Cyprus to mine copper, and eventually founding Gades (Cadiz) because of nearby silver deposits. Their greatest colony was Carthage, which became a major power in its own right.

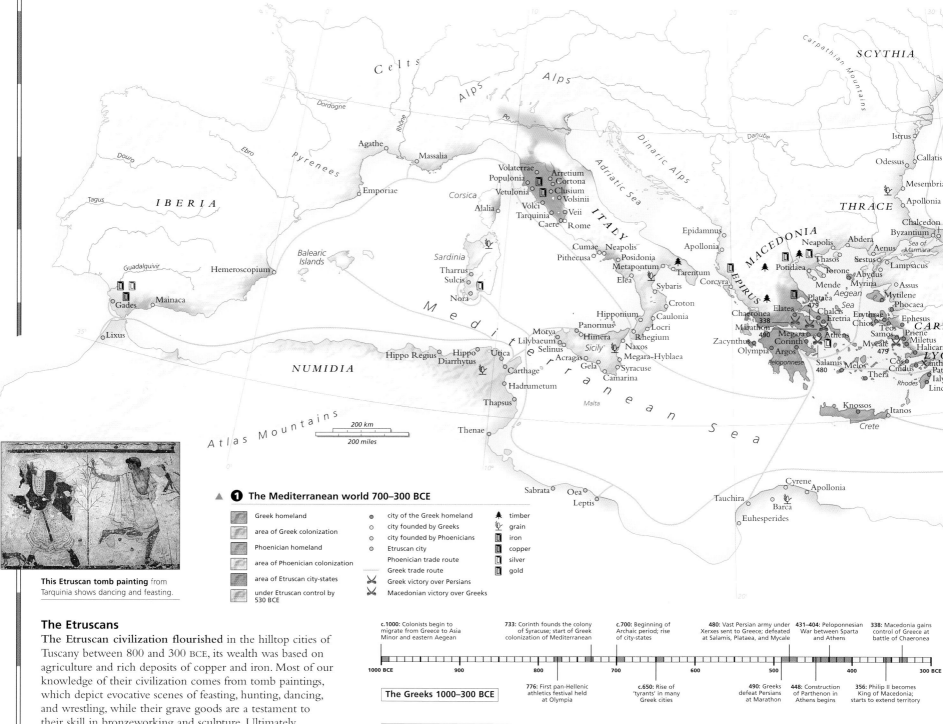

1 The Mediterranean world 700–300 BCE

- Greek homeland
- area of Greek colonization
- Phoenician homeland
- area of Phoenician colonization
- area of Etruscan city-states
- under Etruscan control by 530 BCE
- city of the Greek homeland
- city founded by Greeks
- city founded by Phoenicians
- Etruscan city
- Phoenician trade route
- Greek trade route
- Greek victory over Persians
- Macedonian victory over Greeks
- timber
- grain
- iron
- copper
- silver
- gold

This Etruscan tomb painting from Tarquinia shows dancing and feasting.

The Etruscans

The Etruscan civilization flourished in the hilltop cities of Tuscany between 800 and 300 BCE, its wealth was based on agriculture and rich deposits of copper and iron. Most of our knowledge of their civilization comes from tomb paintings, which depict evocative scenes of feasting, hunting, dancing, and wrestling, while their grave goods are a testament to their skill in bronzeworking and sculpture. Ultimately, however, they succumbed to the growing power of Rome.

The Etruscans 1000 BCE–1 CE

- **c.800:** Emergence of Etruscan city states
- **c.690:** Etruscan script developed from Greek
- **c.616:** Etruscan king Tarquin I rules Rome
- **509:** Romans expel Etruscan king Tarquin II
- **c.530:** Etruscan expansion into Po valley
- **396:** Etruscan city of Veii taken by Rome
- **250:** Whole Italian peninsula under control of Rome
- **c.100:** Language and culture of Etruscans in terminal decline

The Greeks 1000–300 BCE

- **c.1000:** Colonists begin to migrate from Greece to Asia Minor and eastern Aegean
- **776:** First pan-Hellenic athletics festival held at Olympia
- **733:** Corinth founds the colony of Syracuse; start of Greek colonization of Mediterranean
- **c.700:** Beginning of Archaic period; rise of city-states
- **c.650:** Rise of 'tyrants' in many Greek cities
- **490:** Greeks defeat Persians at Marathon
- **480:** Vast Persian army under Xerxes sent to Greece; defeated at Salamis, Plataea, and Mycale
- **448:** Construction of Parthenon in Athens begins
- **431–404:** Peloponnesian War between Sparta and Athens
- **356:** Philip II becomes King of Macedonia; starts to extend territory
- **338:** Macedonia gains control of Greece at battle of Chaeronea

The Greek colonies in Sicily were large, populous cities. When Selinus was captured in 409 BCE during the Peloponnesian War, 30,000 prisoners taken. Its impressive ruins include six temples like this one, all dating from the 6th and 5th centuries BCE.

The Greeks

The cornerstone of Greek civilization was the *polis*, or city-state. These independent, self-governing communities, frequently isolated by Greece's rugged terrain, were based on walled cities, with outlying villages and farmland. Yet, despite the multiplicity of city-states, Greece was united by language, religion, and culture, reflected in harmonious architecture, sculpture, philosophy, and drama. Politically, the city-states swung between the extremes of oligarchy and democracy. While Athens was the birthplace of democracy, in Sparta a militaristic society was ruled by kings, supported by an underclass of serfs (*helots*).

The limestone bust of 'the Lady of Elche', from southern Iberia, shows the artistic influence of the Phoenician city of Carthage, which had close links with cities throughout the western Mediterranean.

The Phoenicians

A Semitic people, whose home cities lay along a narrow strip of the eastern Mediterranean coast, the Phoenicians were the foremost traders and craftsmen of the Mediterranean, renowned for their skill in ivory carving, metalworking and glass manufacture. Perhaps their greatest legacy was their alphabetic writing system, which formed the basis of both the Greek and Roman scripts. The city of Carthage, founded as a colony, became a great power in its own right, leading a confederation of Phoenician cities which controlled southern Iberia, the western Mediterranean islands, and North Africa.

The Phoenicians and the Carthaginians 1000–200 BCE

- c. 1600: The Phoenicians begin to use the Canaanite script, the first alphabetic script
- c. 1000: Phoenicians become main maritime power in Levant region
- c. 900: Phoenician ships sail westwards in search of metals, and found colonies near rich metal deposits
- 814: Traditional date for foundation of Carthage
- 264–241: First Punic War; Rome gains control of Carthaginian Sicily
- 218–201: Second Punic War; Carthaginians invade Italy, but Rome eventually wins war to become regional superpower

1600 BCE 1400 1200 1000 800 600 400 200 BCE

❷ The Athenian Empire 454–428 BCE

Areas paying tribute to Athens: (number of tribute-paying states in brackets)

- Islands (29)
- Thrace (62)
- Hellespont (45)
- Ionia (35)
- Caria (81)
- Athenian homeland
- non-tribute paying areas belonging to Delian League
- states with tribute assessment of over 5 silver talents per annum (454–428 BCE)
- states with tribute assessment of 1–5 silver talents per annum (454–428 BCE)
- overseas dependencies of Athens
- states in revolt against Athens

The city of Athens claimed a special affinity with its patroness Athene, goddess of wisdom, war, and arts and crafts.

The Athenian Empire

The city-states of Greece were united in their bid to repulse the Persians, which culminated in famous victories at Marathon (490) and Salamis (480). In 478, Athens emerged as the leader of a loose maritime confederation of eastern Aegean states, based on the tiny island of Delos. Membership of the Delian League involved participating in a common military policy, and contributing to a common treasury. Athens came increasingly to dominate the League, transferring the treasury to the city in 454, and ruthlessly crushing any attempts at revolt. Greatly enriched by League funds, Athens now entered its greatest period of power and prosperity. The League had, in effect, become an Athenian empire, much resented in many Greek cities.

The Peloponnesian War

Athens' high-handed imperialism made war with Sparta inevitable, and a system of alliances embroiled much of Greece in the conflict. The Athenians withstood Sparta's attacks on Attica by withdrawing to the safety of the city, preferring to do battle at sea. A truce was reached in 421 BCE, but when Athens unwisely sent an expedition to attack Syracuse, the Spartans captured the Athenian navy, presaging the end of the conflict. Greece was plunged into disarray until it was forcibly united by Philip of Macedon in 338 BCE.

❸ The Peloponnesian War 431–404 BCE

- Athenian Empire
- Athenian ally
- Sparta and allied states
- neutral territory
- Athenian victory
- Spartan victory

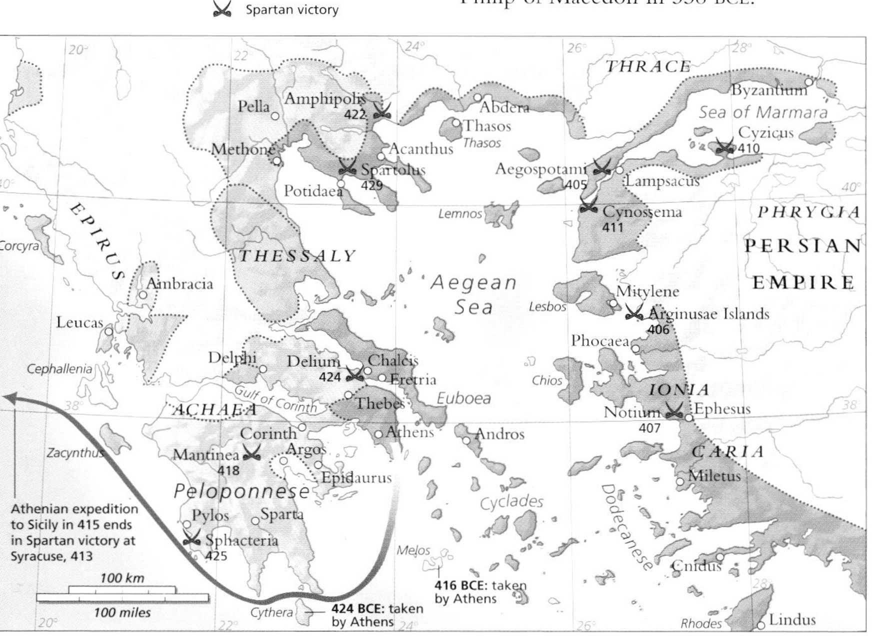

The fiercely patriotic, militaristic culture of Sparta is embodied in this small bronze of a soldier.

❹ The city of Athens

- remains from 6th–5th century BCE
- remains from 4th century BCE–2nd century CE
- road
- aqueduct
- city wall

Athens

The mid-5th century was Athens' golden age. Governed by the eminent statesman, Pericles, and the home of such great intellectuals such as Plato, Sophocles, and Euripides, the city was dominated by the Parthenon temple, built of local marble by the sculptor Phidias, and approached by the monumental Propylea Gate. The Acropolis was the military and religious centre of the city, while commercial and municipal life dominated the agora, or town square.

THE RISE OF ROME

The legionaries of Rome's citizen army were unmatched in discipline and skill.

ROME BEGAN THE 5TH CENTURY BCE as the most powerful city of the regional alliance known as the Latin League. By conquering the Etruscan city-state of Veii in 396 BCE, the Romans doubled their territory, and after the breakup of the Latin League in 338, they incorporated the whole Latin region. This gave them the manpower to defeat a coalition of Samnites, Etruscans, and Gauls in 295. When they faced the army of the Greek general Pyrrhus, they were able to sustain two crushing defeats before achieving victory in 275 BCE. With Italy now under its control, Rome turned its attention to foreign rivals. Following victory over Carthage in 202, it took less than a century to add North Africa, most of Iberia, southern Gaul, Macedon, Greece, and Asia Minor to its empire.

Rome and the Italian confederacy

Traditionally, this bronze bust of a stern Roman aristocrat has been identified as Lucius Junius Brutus, one of the founders of the Roman Republic in 509.

From the 5th to the 3rd century BCE, the city of Rome extended its area of domination to create a confederacy that united all Italy. Some cities were simply annexed and their inhabitants enjoyed the status of full Roman citizens, while others were granted a halfway form of citizenship that did not include the right to vote or hold office in Rome. Other peoples were considered 'allies' and united to Rome by individual treaties. New towns known as 'Latin colonies' extended the Roman presence throughout Italy, while 'Roman colonies', where the inhabitants were full citizens, were established for defensive purposes, primarily along the Tyrrhenian coast. Beginning with the Via Appia in the 4th century BCE, the Romans built a road network that linked the whole peninsula.

Rome and her Latin allies c.495 BCE

Rome was the most powerful of the Latin city-states when the Republic was established in 509, though it controlled just 800 sq km of territory.

1 Italy in 240 BCE

Territory under Roman control 240 BCE
- full Roman citizens
- Roman citizens without right to vote
- Latin colonies
- Allies (*Socii*) of Rome
- Roman colony
- other settlement
- 295 date of foundation
- administrative boundary
- Roman territory (*Ager Romanus*) 495 BCE
- Rome and allies c.300 BCE
- Roman road
- modern coastline

The peoples of Italy in 500 BCE

Latin, the language Rome would spread throughout western Europe, was just one of many closely related Italic languages spoken by the tribes of central Italy. The most powerful peoples in the peninsula were the Greek colonists and the Etruscans, a sophisticated city-state people whose language suggests eastern Mediterranean origins. It had been the Etruscans' arrival in Rome in the 7th century BCE that transformed a cluster of small villages into a city.

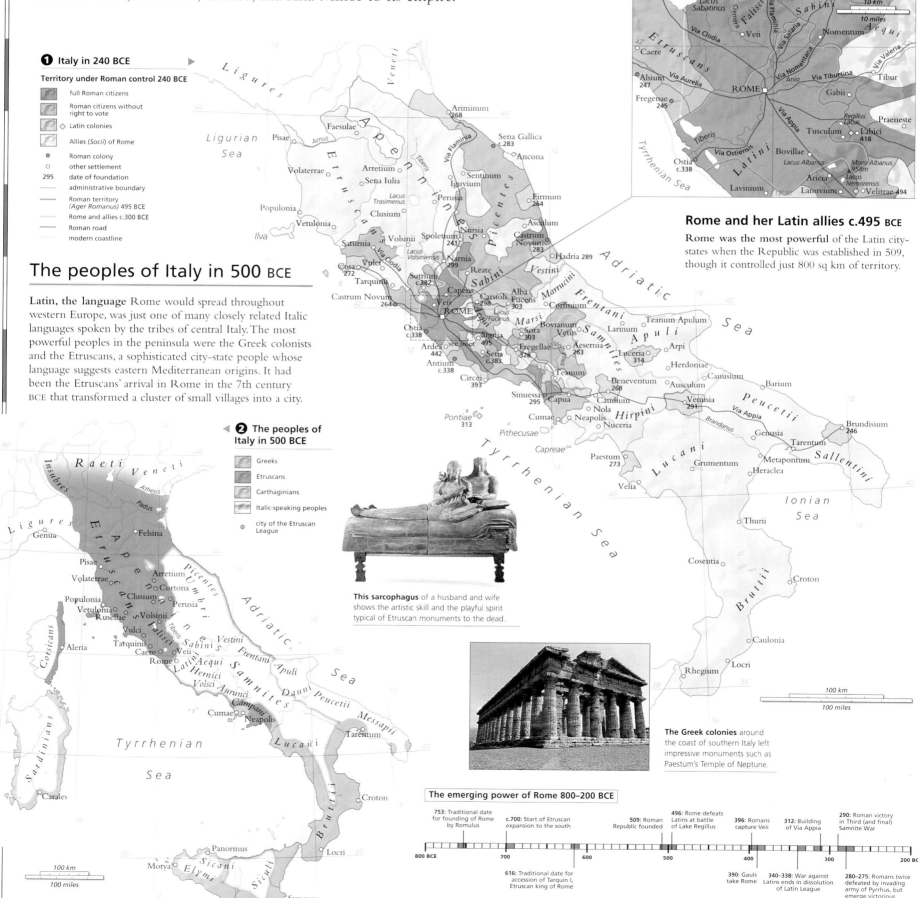

2 The peoples of Italy in 500 BCE

- Greeks
- Etruscans
- Carthaginians
- Italic-speaking peoples
- city of the Etruscan League

This sarcophagus of a husband and wife shows the artistic skill and the playful spirit typical of Etruscan monuments to the dead.

The Greek colonies around the coast of southern Italy left impressive monuments such as Paestum's Temple of Neptune.

The emerging power of Rome 800–200 BCE

- 753: Traditional date for founding of Rome by Romulus
- c.700: Start of Etruscan expansion to the south
- 616: Traditional date for accession of Tarquin I, Etruscan king of Rome
- 509: Roman Republic founded
- 496: Rome defeats Latins at battle of Lake Regillus
- 396: Romans capture Veii
- 390: Gauls take Rome
- 340–338: War against Latins ends in dissolution of Latin League
- 312: Building of Via Appia
- 290: Roman victory in Third (and final) Samnite War
- 280–275: Romans twice defeated by invading army of Pyrrhus, but emerge victorious

Rome and Carthage: the Punic Wars

Founded by Phoenicians *(Punici)* in 814 BCE, Carthage grew to be the pre-eminent naval power in the western Mediterranean. Rome came into conflict with the Carthaginians in 264, the start of a series of three wars. In the first, the Romans pushed their enemies out of Sicily. Then, in 218, Rome forced a second war by opposing Carthaginian actions in Iberia. Despite many defeats at the hands of Hannibal, the Romans won this war and stripped Carthage of its navy. The final war (149–146) ended in the destruction of Carthage and the enslavement of its people.

The Carthaginian general Hannibal *(left)* fought the Romans for 15 years in Italy. The smaller coin *(right)* shows an African elephant, used by the Carthaginians to strike terror into opposing armies.

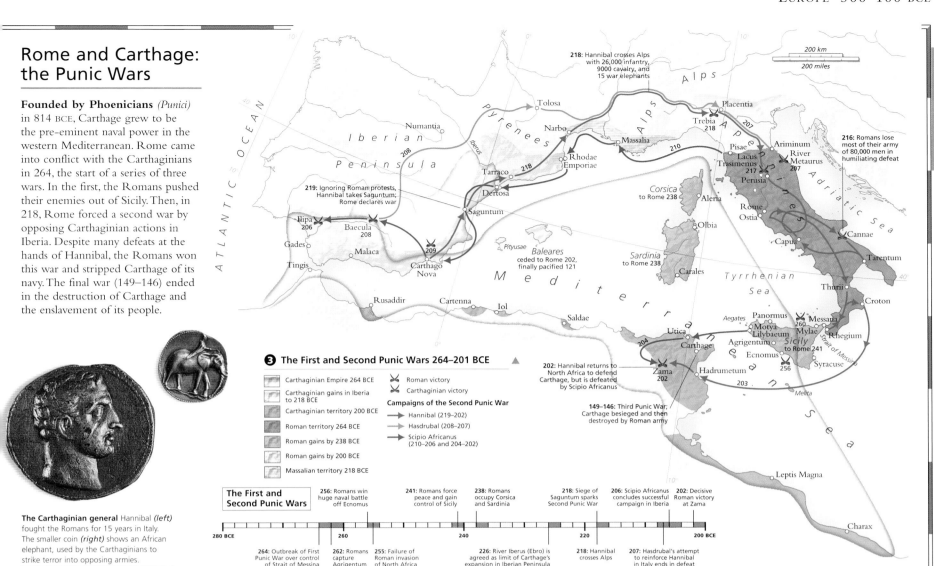

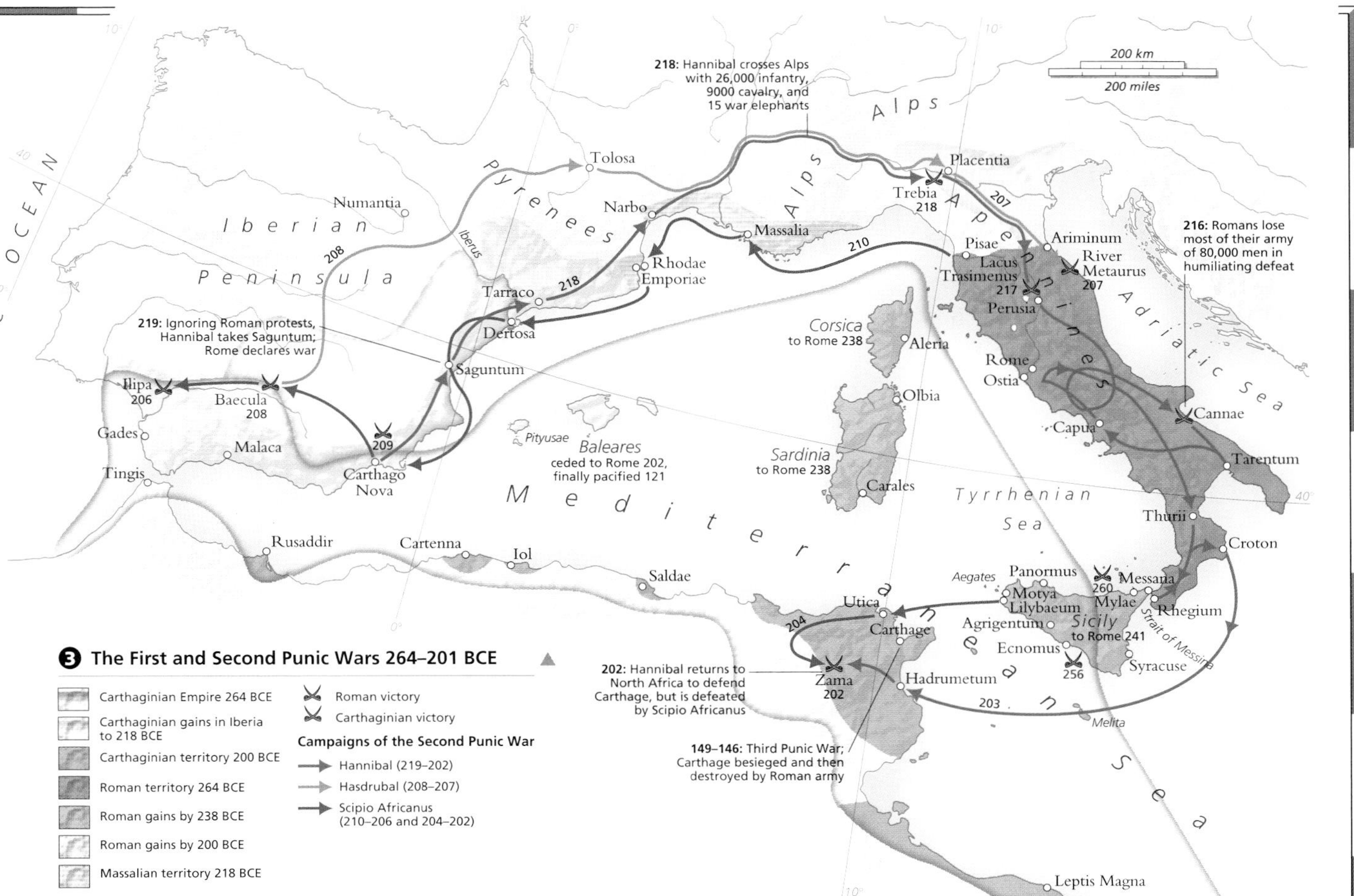

3 The First and Second Punic Wars 264–201 BCE

Carthaginian Empire 264 BCE
Carthaginian gains in Iberia to 218 BCE
Carthaginian territory 200 BCE
Roman territory 264 BCE
Roman gains by 238 BCE
Roman gains by 200 BCE
Massalian territory 218 BCE
Roman victory
Carthaginian victory
Campaigns of the Second Punic War
Hannibal (219–202)
Hasdrubal (208–207)
Scipio Africanus (210–206 and 204–202)

218: Hannibal crosses Alps with 26,000 infantry, 9000 cavalry, and 15 war elephants
219: Ignoring Roman protests, Hannibal takes Saguntum; Rome declares war
216: Romans lose most of their army of 80,000 men in humiliating defeat
202: Hannibal returns to North Africa to defend Carthage, but is defeated by Scipio Africanus
149–146: Third Punic War; Carthage besieged and then destroyed by Roman army

The First and Second Punic Wars

256: Romans win huge naval battle off Ecnomus
241: Romans force peace and gain control of Sicily
238: Romans occupy Corsica and Sardinia
218: Siege of Saguntum sparks Second Punic War
206: Scipio Africanus concludes successful campaign in Iberia
202: Decisive Roman victory at Zama
264: Outbreak of First Punic War over control of Strait of Messina
262: Romans capture Agrigentum
255: Failure of Roman invasion of North Africa
226: River Iberus (Ebro) is agreed as limit of Carthage's expansion in Iberian Peninsula
218: Hannibal crosses Alps
207: Hasdrubal's attempt to reinforce Hannibal in Italy ends in defeat

The subjugation of Greece by Rome

In 200 BCE the major powers of the Greek world were Macedon and the Seleucid Empire. Two Greek federations had also emerged: the Aetolian League and the Achaean League, which included Corinth, largest of the mainland Greek cities. Other city-states, such as Athens and Sparta, manoeuvred to maintain their independence, as did the Asian kingdom of Pergamum. Political tensions and appeals to Rome for help gave the Romans excuses for five major military interventions in the 2nd century. Macedon became a Roman province in 148; Greece succumbed in 146 after the Achaean War.

Corinth was first an ally of Rome, then an enemy. It was razed to the ground in 146 by the Roman general Mummius. The ruined temple *(left)* dates from the 6th century BCE.

This fine mosaic of a lion hunt decorated the royal palace in the Macedonian capital of Pella. Even before annexing Macedon and Greece, Rome eagerly embraced Hellenistic culture and customs.

Rome's overseas provinces in 120 BCE

Following the defeat of Carthage in 202 BCE, Rome's empire expanded rapidly. Greece and the Greek states of Asia Minor were won through a combination of diplomacy and war, but long, costly campaigns were needed to subdue the tribes of the Iberian Peninsula. Carthage itself was added to the empire in 146. As the Romans extended their rule beyond Italy, they largely abandoned the principles of incorporation that they had applied in Italy and instead set up provinces. These were ruled by governors, who served short one- or two-year terms, maintained order, and oversaw the collection of taxes. Corruption and plundering by governors were common enough for a special permanent court to be set up to try such cases in 149.

Roman expansion 200–120 BCE

200–196: Second Macedonian War
172–167: Third Macedonian War
148: Roman victory in Fourth Macedonian War
139: Defeat of Lusitani
133: Romans take Iberian city of Numantia
192–189: War with Seleucid king Antiochus; Roman victories at Thermopylae and Magnesia
168: Romans crush Macedonians at Pydna
146: Roman armies destroy conquered cities of Corinth and Carthage
133: Rome bequeathed province of Asia by king of Pergamum

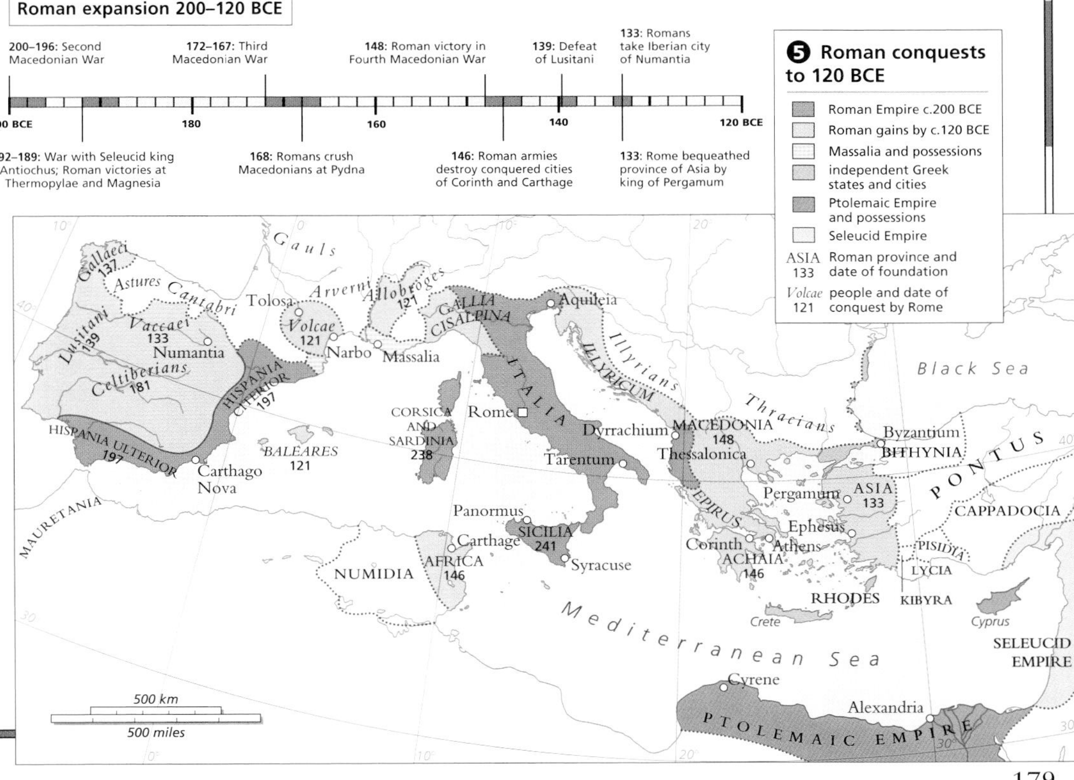

THE ROMAN EMPIRE

Constantine sealed the Empire's fate by moving the centre of power to the east.

REPUBLICAN ROME asserted military control over most of the Mediterranean, but a century of internal political conflict and civil war prevented the development of an orderly imperial system. The first emperor, Augustus (27 BCE–14 CE), ended this period of disorder with his defeat of Mark Antony in 31 BCE and established the Principate – the military and political system that defended and governed the empire until the reforms of Diocletian and Constantine at the end of the 3rd century. At the height of its power in the 2nd century Rome ruled over some 50 million people scattered in over 5000 administrative units. For the most part, subjects of the Empire accepted Roman rule, and, at least in the west, many adopted Roman culture and the Latin language. After 212 CE all free inhabitants of the Empire had the status of Roman citizens.

The Empire under Hadrian

The Empire reached its greatest extent early in the 2nd century under Trajan, who conquered Dacia, Arabia, Armenia, Assyria, and Mesopotamia. However, when Hadrian succeeded in 117 CE, he abandoned the last three provinces and adopted a defensive frontier strategy that would be followed by most of his successors. A professional army – under Hadrian it numbered just 300,000 – defended the frontiers and suppressed rebellions in trouble spots such as Britain and Judaea, while the navy kept the Mediterranean free of pirates. Fleets were also based on the Rhine and the Danube on the northeastern frontier.

The Pont du Gard, part of the aqueduct that supplied Nemausus (Nîmes) in the south of France, is a fine example of the Romans' skill in civil engineering.

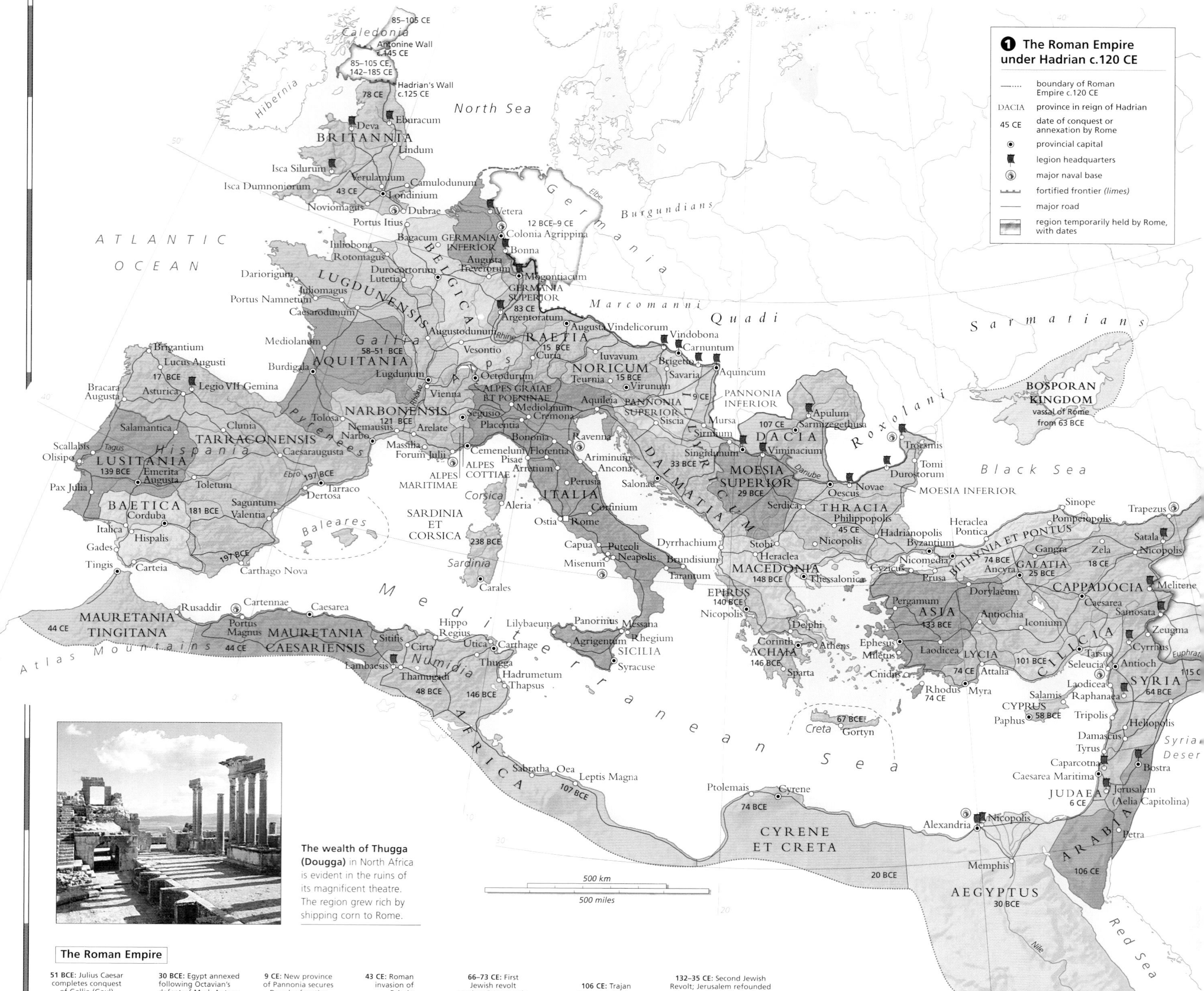

1 The Roman Empire under Hadrian c.120 CE

- boundary of Roman Empire c.120 CE
- DACIA province in reign of Hadrian
- 45 CE date of conquest or annexation by Rome
- provincial capital
- legion headquarters
- major naval base
- fortified frontier (limes)
- major road
- region temporarily held by Rome, with dates

The wealth of Thugga (Dougga) in North Africa is evident in the ruins of its magnificent theatre. The region grew rich by shipping corn to Rome.

The Roman Empire

- 51 BCE: Julius Caesar completes conquest of Gallia (Gaul)
- 30 BCE: Egypt annexed following Octavian's defeat of Mark Antony
- 27 BCE: Assuming the title Augustus, Octavian becomes first Roman emperor
- 9 CE: New province of Pannonia secures Danube frontier
- 9 CE: After defeat by Germans, Romans retreat to Rhine frontier
- 14 CE: Death of Augustus
- 43 CE: Roman invasion of Britain
- 44 CE: Client kingdom of Mauretania absorbed into empire
- 66–73 CE: First Jewish revolt against Roman rule
- 70 CE: Destruction of Jerusalem by Titus
- 106 CE: Trajan conquers Dacia
- 115–17 CE: In war against Parthia, Trajan extends Roman rule to Persian Gulf
- 132–35 CE: Second Jewish Revolt; Jerusalem refounded as Roman city, Aelia Capitolina
- 138 CE: Death of Hadrian

The city of Rome

As the empire grew, so did Rome, reaching a population of about one million in the 2nd century CE. The city was sustained by food shipped up the Tiber from Ostia and aqueducts that delivered 400 litres of water per head per day. Many Romans did not work, but were eligible for the *annona*, a free handout of grain. Following the example of Augustus, every emperor aimed to leave his mark on the city by building magnificent forums, theatres, arenas, and temples.

The Colosseum, completed in 80 CE, vied with the Circus Maximus race track as Rome's most popular stadium. It regularly attracted a full house of 50,000 to its gladiatorial and wild animal combats.

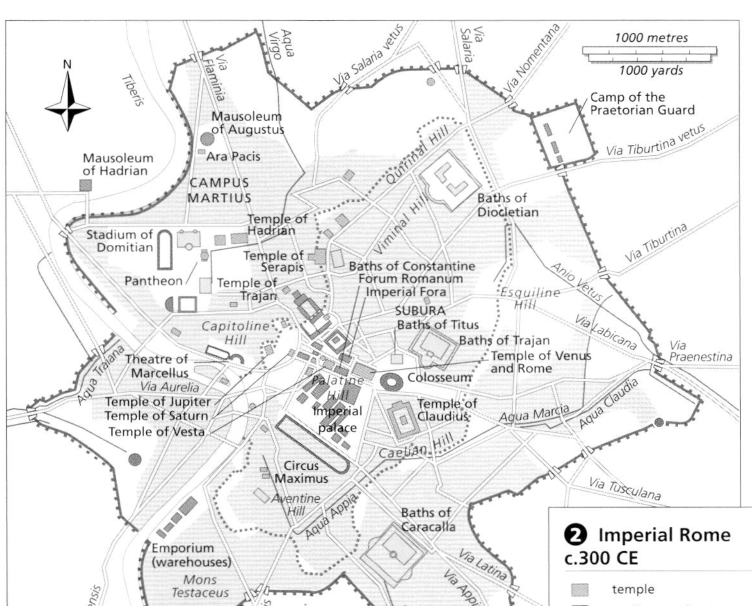

Earthenware amphorae were used to transport and store wine, olive oil, and fish sauce.

Supplying the city of Rome

Feeding the citizens of Rome required regular shipments of grain from Egypt and North Africa. These were landed at Ostia and Portus, a new port built by Trajan at the mouth of the Tiber, from where they were shipped on smaller galleys up river to the capital. Goods were carried by ship wherever possible, as this was much cheaper and faster than road transport. Rome imported food and raw materials from all over its empire. Marble for the pillars and statues that graced the city's temples and palaces often came from as far afield as Greece and Africa. Unusual imports included *garum*, a fermented fish sauce which the Romans used, rather like ketchup, to add flavour to a wide variety of dishes, and murex, a shellfish that produced the purple dye used for imperial togas. To give an idea of the volume of goods imported to the city, Mons Testaceus, a large hill, 50 m in height, was created in imperial times from the shards of broken amphorae from the rows of warehouses that lined the banks of the Tiber in the southwest of the city.

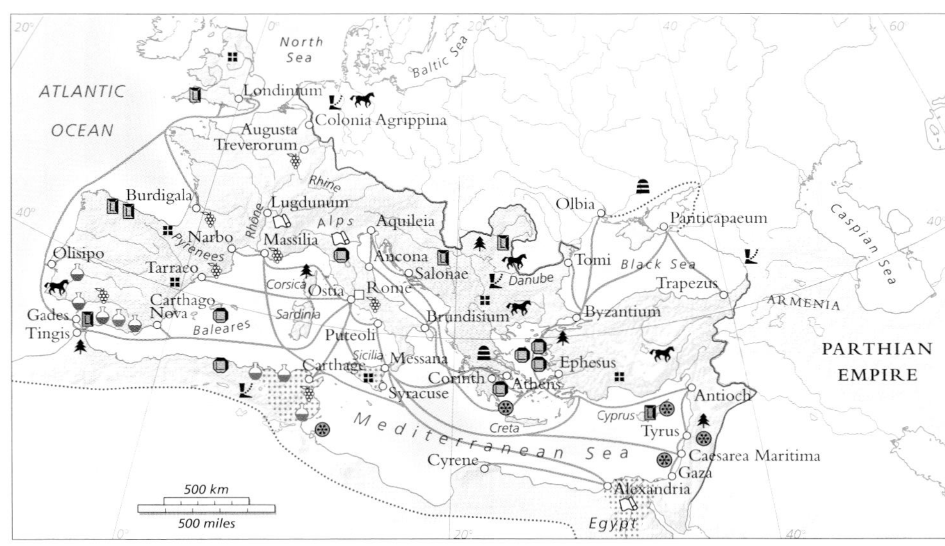

The Tetrarchy of Diocletian and the final division of the Empire

In the 3rd century CE, the Empire was threatened by invasions by the Persians and Germanic peoples and by breakaway states, such as the Kingdom of Palmyra. To counter this, Diocletian (284–305) and Constantine (307–337) reorganized the imperial administration. The existing provinces were divided into 100 smaller units, grouped in twelve larger regions called dioceses, each governed by a vicar. To share responsibility for defending the empire and to provide for an orderly succession, Diocletian established the Tetrarchy: two emperors with the title Augustus, one in the east, one in the west, each assisted by a junior emperor with the title of Caesar.

The later Roman Empire 250–400 CE

- **c.250:** Period of civil wars and runaway inflation
- **260:** Gallic empire established by Postumus
- **270:** Palmyra extends rule to Egypt
- **273:** Empire reunited by Aurelian
- **293:** Diocletian establishes Tetrarchy and twelve dioceses
- **305:** Abdication of Diocletian
- **312:** Battle of Milvian Bridge, just north of Rome; Constantine defeats rival Maxentius
- **324:** Constantine sole ruler
- **337:** Constantine's death leads to fresh struggles over succession
- **364:** Rome loses war for control of Armenia to Sassanian Empire
- **378:** Battle of Adrianople. Visigoths defeat Romans
- **395:** Definitive division of empire into east and west on death of Theodosius

250 CE — 300 — 350 — 400 CE

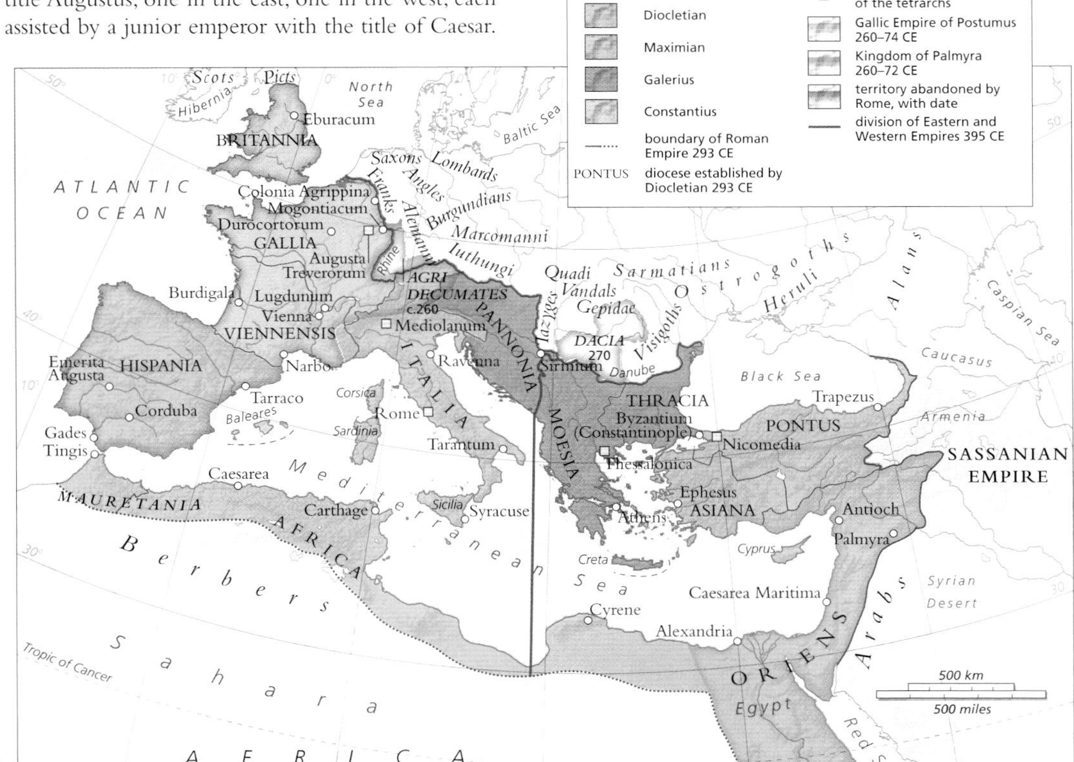

This floor mosaic of Orpheus decorated a villa in Daphne, a wealthy suburb of Antioch, capital of the province of Syria.

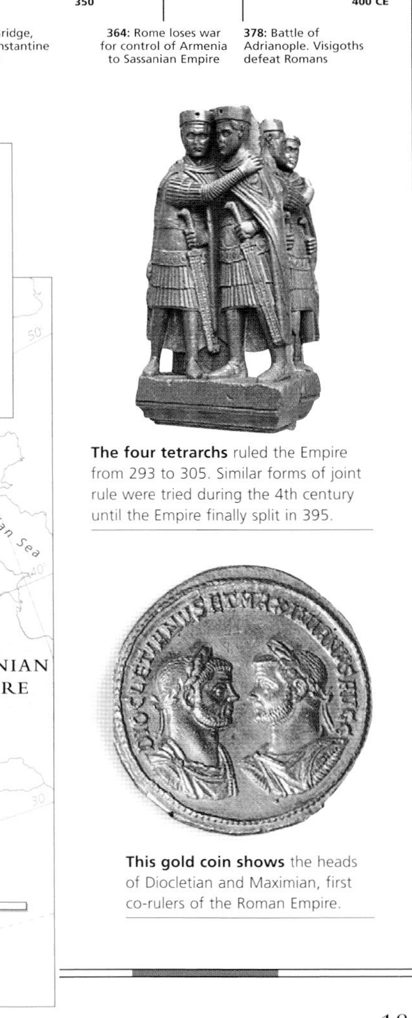

The four tetrarchs ruled the Empire from 293 to 305. Similar forms of joint rule were tried during the 4th century until the Empire finally split in 395.

This gold coin shows the heads of Diocletian and Maximian, first co-rulers of the Roman Empire.

EUROPE AFTER THE FALL OF ROME

This glass drinking horn would have been used at feasts of the Lombard rulers of Italy.

THE END OF THE WESTERN ROMAN EMPIRE in 476 did not signal an immediate descent into barbarism. The rulers of the new kingdoms maintained relations with the eastern emperor in Constantinople, and most pretended to govern on his behalf. In much of western Europe, Roman laws and institutions were retained and, sooner or later, the so-called 'barbarians' all converted to Christianity. The Eastern Roman (Byzantine) Empire continued to exert influence in the west. In the 6th century, Justinian, the most powerful emperor of the period, won back some of the Western Roman Empire. But, after failing to halt the Lombard invasion of Italy in 568, the Byzantines were unable to reassert their authority. The eventual successors to the Romans in the west were the Franks and the papacy.

The kingdoms of the new order

On the death of the emperor Theodosius in 395, the Roman Empire was divided definitively in two. The 5th century saw the transfer of power in western Europe from the emperors to Germanic immigrants, for the most part groups recruited by the Romans to help them defend their lands *(see pp.52–53)*. Chief beneficiaries were the Goths. By 480 the Visigoths had established a large kingdom in Aquitaine and Iberia, with its capital at Toulouse. In 492 the Ostrogoths took Italy and the Dalmatian coast.

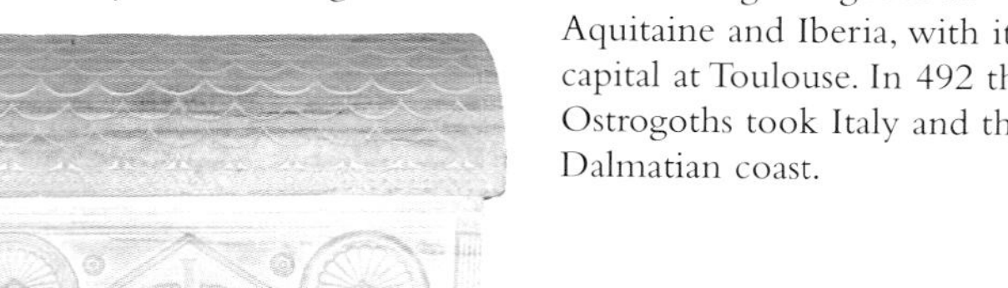

Christianity maintained a sense of continuity between the Western Roman Empire and the kingdoms that replaced it. This late Roman sarcophagus is from Ravenna, capital of the Ostrogoths, successors to the Romans in Italy.

Classis was the port of Ravenna, capital of Ostrogothic and Byzantine Italy. This detail from a 6th-century mosaic shows the castle and ships riding at anchor in the harbour.

Europe in 500

One of the most powerful of the new kingdoms established in western Europe in 500 was that of Theodoric the Great, leader of the Ostrogoths. Though he ruled from Ravenna, the Senate still sat in Rome and relations between Romans and Goths were largely amicable. Royal marriages helped forge alliances with the Vandal and Visigothic kings in North Africa and Iberia. Theodoric hoped to create a power bloc to counter the might of the Eastern Roman Empire, but after his death in 526 he was succeeded by his infant grandson, who died young, and the dynasty collapsed.

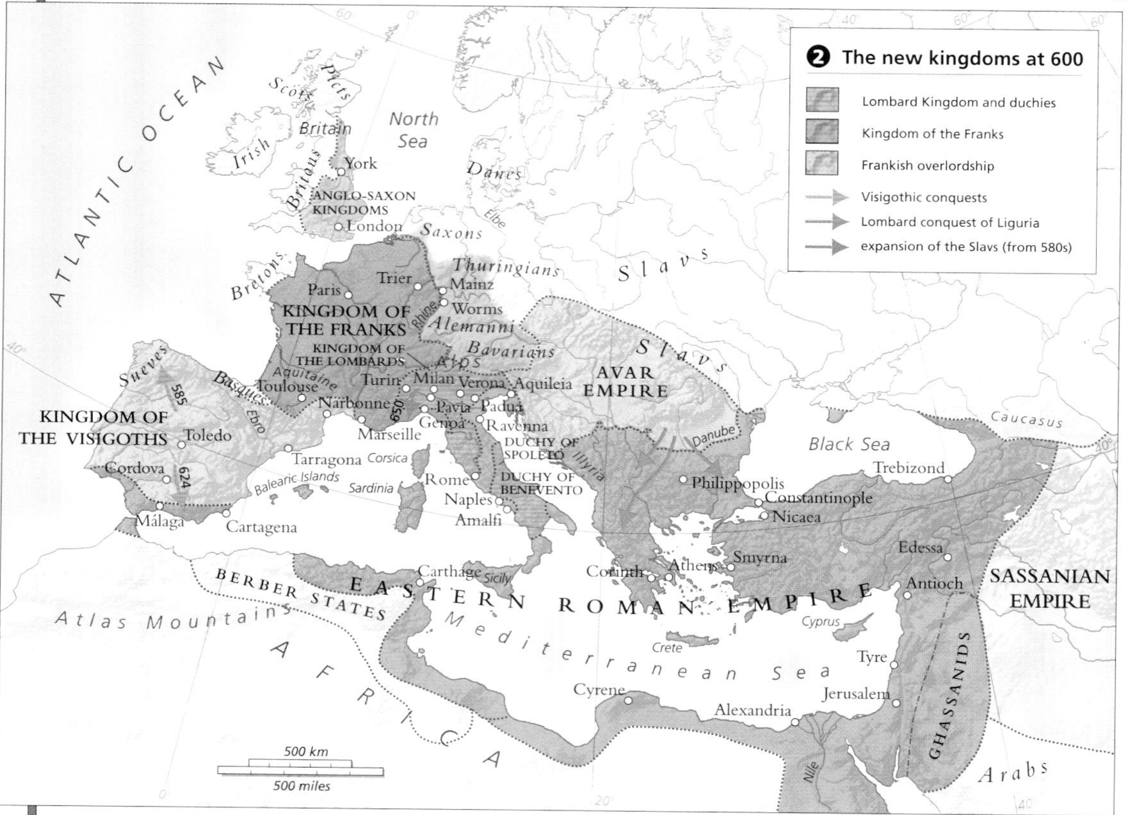

This Visigothic cross dates from the 6th century. Although Christian, the Visigoths were Arians (they denied the Trinity). This changed in 589, when King Reccared converted to the orthodox Catholicism of his Hispano-Roman subjects.

Europe in 600

The political map of Europe changed dramatically in the 6th century. In 600 the Visigoths still controlled the Iberian peninsula, but the Franks now ruled most of modern France. The Eastern Roman Empire had reconquered North Africa, Italy, Illyria, and even part of southern Iberia. The destruction of the Roman heritage was far greater during the long war waged by the Byzantines against the Goths than during the previous century. Italy then fell prey to the Lombards (Langobardi), Germanic invaders from the northeast.

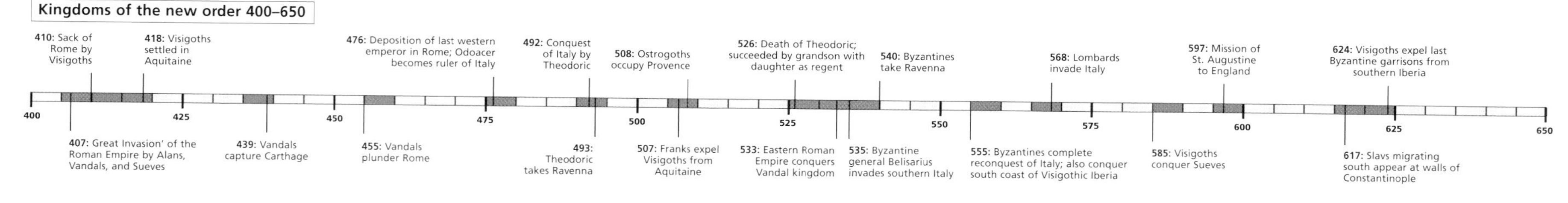

3 Britain c.750

Anglo-Saxon kingdoms
Mercia and dependencies
Celtic kingdoms
Pictish kingdoms
battle
important monastery

Excavation of a burial site at Sutton Hoo unearthed the treasure of a 7th-century Anglo-Saxon king or chieftain, including this striking gilt bronze helmet.

This gem-studded gold buckle is typical of the jewellery worn by the Lombard nobles who ruled Italy for two centuries.

Byzantine and Lombard Italy

After the expulsion of the Goths, control of Italy was contested by the Byzantines and the Lombards, the latter gradually winning more and more territory after their invasion of 568. Only rarely did the Lombard kings, based at Pavia, exercise authority over the southern dukedoms of Benevento and Spoleto. Similarly, representatives of Byzantium, including the pope, often acted independently according to their own interests. The Byzantines were ousted from Ravenna in 751, but Lombard rule there lasted only until 756. At the pope's request, Pepin, king of the Franks, invaded northern Italy and crushed the Lombards.

Following Lombard invasion of Italy in 568, their former territories are occupied by Avars and Slavs
c.700: conquered by Lombards
4 The struggle for Italy 565–750
East Roman Empire 565
Lombard territories 565
under Lombard rule 590
Lombard gains by 650
Lombard gains by 744
East Roman territory 744
External threats to Italy in the 7th century
Franks
Avars and Slavs

Early Anglo-Saxon kingdoms

597: St. Augustine begins conversion of Anglo-Saxon kings to Roman Christianity

603: Northumbrians defeat Scots at Degsastan

616: Northumbrians defeat Britons at Chester

655: Northumbrians defeat Mercians at Winwaed

663: Synod of Whitby. 'Roman' Christianity adopted instead of 'Celtic'

679: Mercians conquer Lindsey from Northumbrians

685: Last great king of Northumbria killed by Picts at Nechtansmere

716: Ethelbald fights way to crown of Mercia; kingdom dominates all England south of Humber

757: Accession of Offa, most powerful of Mercian Kings; treated as equal by Charlemagne

Anglo-Saxon Britain 600–800

For the two centuries that followed the Roman withdrawal in 410, there are no reliable accounts of events in Britain. The Celtic Britons fought each other, as well as Scottish invaders (from Ireland) and Angles, Saxons, and Jutes, who invaded across the North Sea from Denmark and north Germany. Around 600, following St Augustine's mission from Rome to convert the Anglo-Saxons, records appear of a number of kingdoms ruled by Anglo-Saxon kings (though some of these have British names). The west, notably Wales and West Wales (Dumnonia), remained in the hands of Celts. For most of the 7th century, the most powerful kingdom was Northumbria, whose kings briefly controlled much of Scotland. By 700, however, supremacy had passed to the midland kingdom of Mercia.

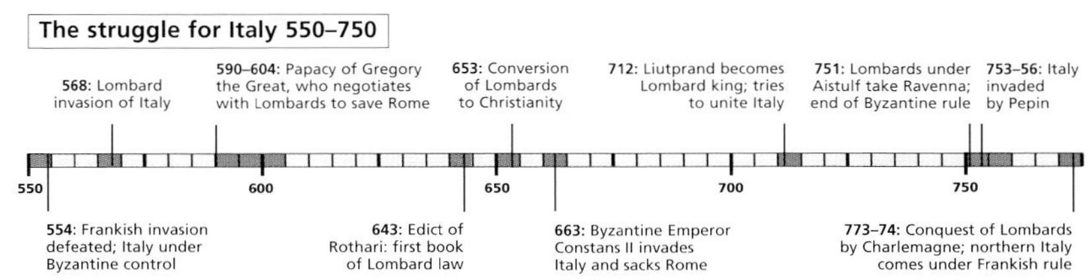

The struggle for Italy 550–750
568: Lombard invasion of Italy
554: Frankish invasion defeated; Italy under Byzantine control
590–604: Papacy of Gregory the Great, who negotiates with Lombards to save Rome
643: Edict of Rothari: first book of Lombard law
653: Conversion of Lombards to Christianity
663: Byzantine Emperor Constans II invades Italy and sacks Rome
712: Liutprand becomes Lombard king; tries to unite Italy
751: Lombards under Aistulf take Ravenna; end of Byzantine rule
753–56: Italy invaded by Pepin
773–74: Conquest of Lombards by Charlemagne; northern Italy comes under Frankish rule

The early Frankish kingdoms 481–650

The only Germanic kingdom of any permanence established in this period was the Kingdom of the Franks, foundation of modern France. The first Frankish dynasty, the Merovingians, expanded from lands around Tournai under Clovis, who pushed southwest to the Loire, then defeated the Visigoths in Aquitaine. Clovis's sons destroyed the Burgundians and exercised control over several Germanic tribes to the east. When a powerful king such as Clovis died, his territories were divided between his heirs, provoking dynastic civil wars. The three major kingdoms were Neustria and Austrasia (together referred to as Francia), and Burgundy.

Dagobert I's throne is a powerful emblem of the continuity of the French kingdom, which lasted till the Revolution in 1790.

5 The Kingdom of the Franks 486–537
Frankish lands 486
conquered by Clovis by 507
conquered by 511
Kingdom of Franks at the death of Clovis 511
conquered by Clovis's sons 534
conquered by Clovis's sons 537
battle

6 Division of the Frankish kingdoms 561
Charibert
Sigebert
Guntram
Chilperic
territory of Frankish overlordship
royal residence

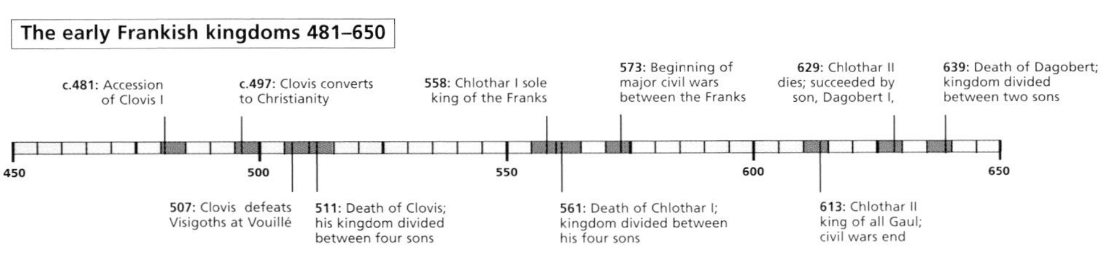

The early Frankish kingdoms 481–650
c.481: Accession of Clovis I
c.497: Clovis converts to Christianity
507: Clovis defeats Visigoths at Vouillé
511: Death of Clovis; his kingdom divided between four sons
558: Chlothar I sole king of the Franks
561: Death of Chlothar I; kingdom divided between his four sons
573: Beginning of major civil wars between the Franks
613: Chlothar II king of all Gaul; civil wars end
629: Chlothar II dies; succeeded by son, Dagobert I,
639: Death of Dagobert; kingdom divided between two sons

THE HOLY ROMAN EMPIRE

This bronze statue of Charlemagne is an idealized 9th-century portrait, created after the Emperor's death.

THE FRANKISH KINGS Pepin and Charlemagne crushed the Lombards in Italy, granted lands to the pope, and extended the frontiers of Christian Europe. The coronation of Charlemagne as Holy Roman Emperor in 800 was an ambitious attempt by the papacy to recreate the central authority of imperial Rome. Yet by 843, the empire was divided. In the 10th century, a smaller Holy Roman Empire was established under the Saxon Ottonian dynasty. Otto I, who, like Charlemagne, was crowned in Rome, helped convert the Bohemians, Danes, and Poles to Christianity and stopped the advancing Magyars. Meanwhile, Viking raiders terrorized much of western Europe and in Russia, Swedish Vikings helped establish the new state of Kievan Rus.

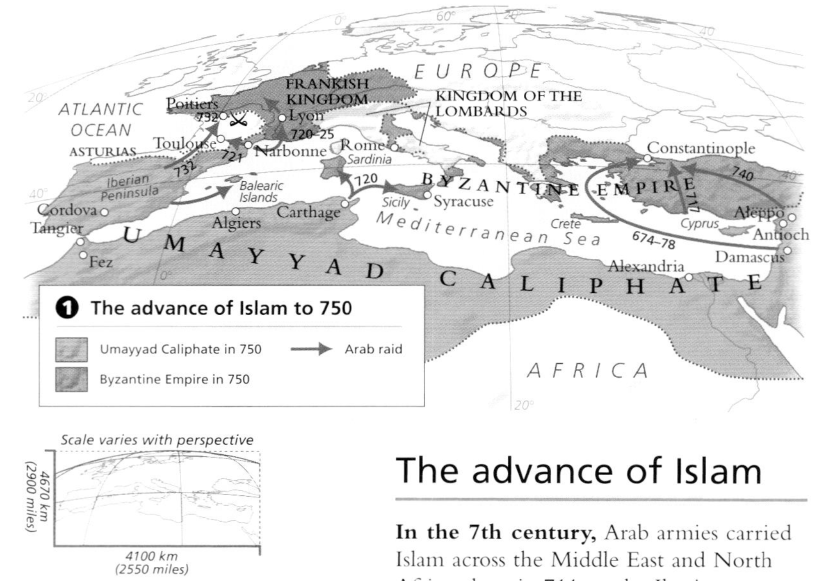

1 The advance of Islam to 750

Umayyad Caliphate in 750
Byzantine Empire in 750
Arab raid

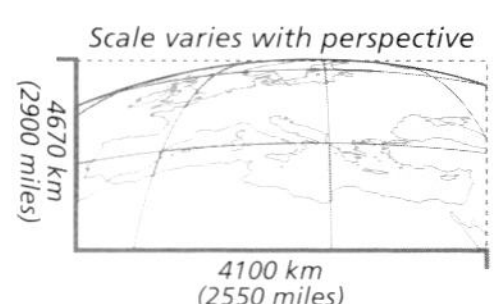

The advance of Islam

In the 7th century, Arab armies carried Islam across the Middle East and North Africa, then, in 711, to the Iberian Peninsula. The Byzantine Empire suffered severe losses and Constantinople had to withstand determined sieges in 674 and 717. In the west, an Islamic invasion of France was turned back in 732 at Poitiers by Charles Martel, the grandfather of Charlemagne. This stemmed the Muslim advance, but Arab raids on all the Christian states of the Mediterranean continued.

The empire of Charlemagne

Charlemagne was both a warrior and a reformer. By 800, he had established Christian hegemony over much of western Europe, his conquest and conversion of Saxony and defeat of the Avars taking the eastern borders of his empire to the Slav world. 'Marches', or buffer zones, protected the empire from the Slavs and from the Moorish Emirate of Cordova. The unity of western Christendom did not last: after the death of Louis the Pious in 840, the empire was divided between his three sons, and by 900 it had fragmented into smaller kingdoms. Local dukedoms and counties, the precursors of feudal domains, started to gain power at the expense of central authority.

Charlemagne's throne still stands in a vaulted chapel at Aachen (Aix-la-Chapelle), the most important of the emperor's many royal residences.

Pope Leo III crowned Charlemagne emperor in 800. This confirmed the Carolingians' right to their lands. When Charlemagne was born c.744, his father Pepin was not even king of the Franks, but mayor of the palace. He was elected king in 751.

2 The empire of Charlemagne

Frankish kingdom in 751
conquest of Pepin
conquest of Charlemagne
regions recognizing Charlemagne as overlord, at least nominally
states of the Church, part of Charlemagne's empire
marches
Byzantine possessions
SAXONY 804 division of Charlemagne's empire, with date of final conquest

Major campaigns
in reign of Pepin 751–68
in reign of Charlemagne 768–814
royal palace

The empire of Charlemagne

751: Pepin the Short crowned king, the founder of Carolingian dynasty
771: Charlemagne becomes sole king of Franks
772: Charlemagne embarks on conquest of Saxony (complete 802)
774: Charlemagne conquers Lombardy
800: Imperial coronation of Charlemagne by Pope Leo III in Rome
814: Accession of Charlemagne's son, Louis the Pious
840: Death of Louis the Pious; war between his sons
843: Treaty of Verdun divides Empire into three. Eastern and western parts roughly correspond to Germany and France

200 km
200 miles

Europe 800–1000

The fragmentation of the Carolingian Empire led, by 900, to its division into eastern and western parts. In 919, the East Frankish crown passed to Henry I of Saxony, who established the Ottonian dynasty, which was to dominate Europe for the next two centuries. The decisive Ottonian defeat of the Magyars earned the respect of rival noblemen, and Otto I's conquest of Italy, and coronation as Holy Roman Emperor (962), legitimized his rule. Otto's successors reinforced their power in Germany by constant movement around their empire. They controlled bishoprics and churches, encouraged learning and literature, and presided over the formation of Christian states in Poland, Hungary, and Bohemia.

Carvings of Viking ships appear on a picture stone in Gotland, dating from the 8th century, just before the raids began. This scene shows the spirits of dead heroes.

The Vikings of Scandinavia

The Vikings earned a fearsome reputation when they began their raids on Europe in the late 8th century. Their leaders were probably warlords who had been displaced by more powerful kings. They targeted the wealth of towns, monasteries, and churches in England, Ireland, and France. By the late 9th century, they ruled kingdoms in England and Ireland, and the Duchy of Normandy in France. Once settled, they adopted Christianity and established commercial towns. The Swedish Vikings raided and traded along the rivers of Russia, making contact with the Byzantine Empire and the Islamic world, a rich source of silver. They founded a merchant town at Novgorod and won control of Kiev, which became capital of the extensive state of Kievan Rus.

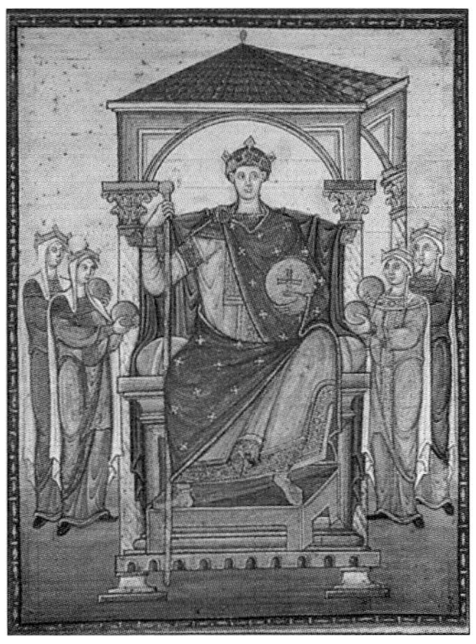

Otto II, who reigned from 973 to 983, receives homage from the subject nations of his empire. Portraits of Holy Roman Emperors emulated those of the Byzantine emperors, who were portrayed as God's representatives on earth.

3 Europe c.800–1000

- frontiers c.1000
- Muslim lands
- Hungary
- Denmark
- Sweden
- Norway (under Danish rule)
- Byzantine Empire (under direct Byzantine rule)
- Byzantine dependencies (effectively independent)
- Holy Roman Empire

Viking settlement

- Danish
- Swedish
- Norwegian
- Danelaw 878–954

Expeditions and raids

- Danish
- Swedish
- Norwegian
- Magyar migration
- Magyar raid
- Muslim raid

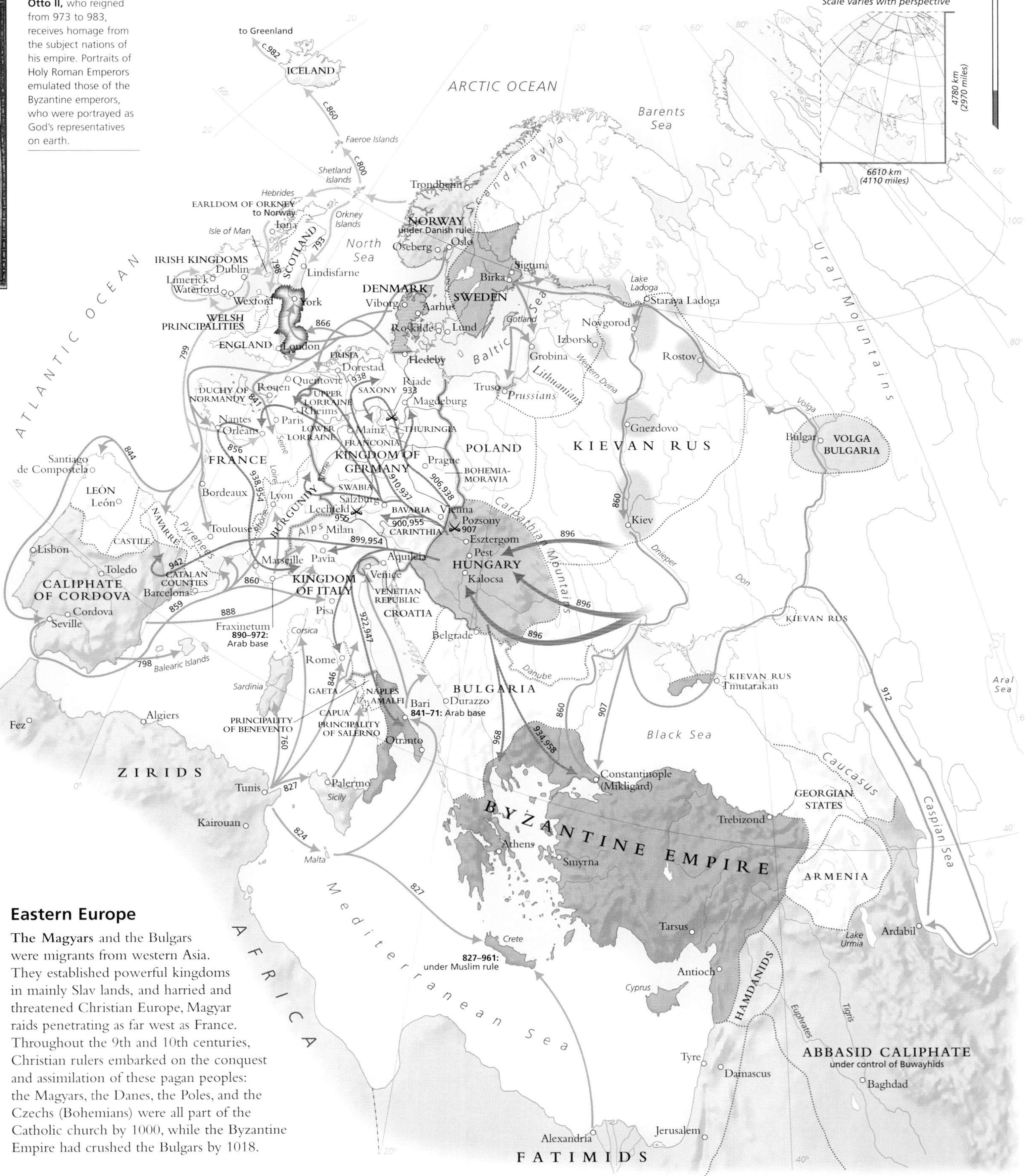

Scale varies with perspective

Eastern Europe

The Magyars and the Bulgars were migrants from western Asia. They established powerful kingdoms in mainly Slav lands, and harried and threatened Christian Europe, Magyar raids penetrating as far west as France. Throughout the 9th and 10th centuries, Christian rulers embarked on the conquest and assimilation of these pagan peoples: the Magyars, the Danes, the Poles, and the Czechs (Bohemians) were all part of the Catholic church by 1000, while the Byzantine Empire had crushed the Bulgars by 1018.

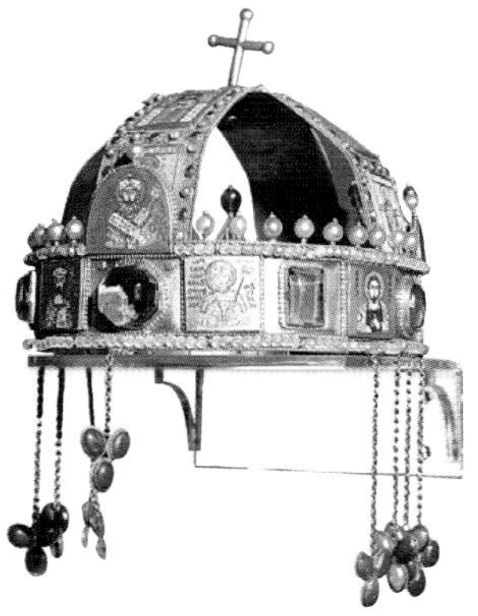

Stephen I of Hungary favoured the Roman church over the Orthodox and in 1001 was recognized as king by the pope who sent him a crown *(above)*.

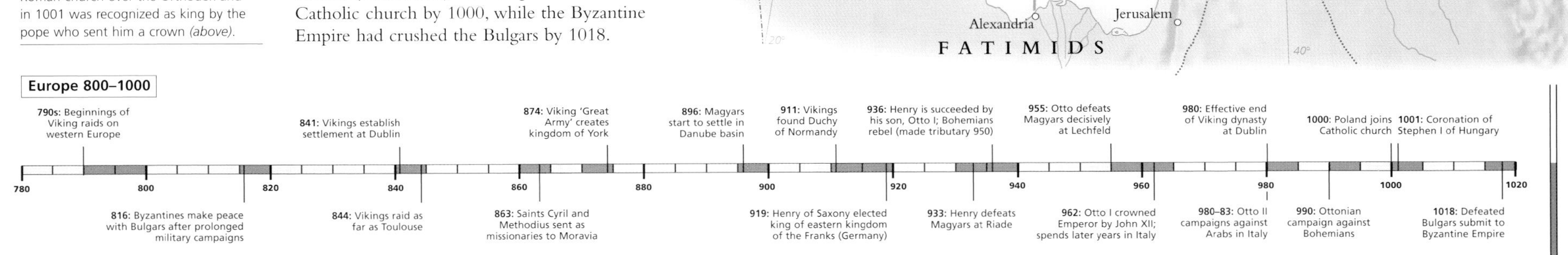
Europe 800–1000
790s: Beginnings of Viking raids on western Europe
816: Byzantines make peace with Bulgars after prolonged military campaigns
841: Vikings establish settlement at Dublin
844: Vikings raid as far as Toulouse
863: Saints Cyril and Methodius sent as missionaries to Moravia
874: Viking 'Great Army' creates kingdom of York
896: Magyars start to settle in Danube basin
911: Vikings found Duchy of Normandy
919: Henry of Saxony elected king of eastern kingdom of the Franks (Germany)
933: Henry defeats Magyars at Riade
936: Henry is succeeded by his son, Otto I; Bohemians rebel (made tributary 950)
955: Otto defeats Magyars decisively at Lechfeld
962: Otto I crowned Emperor by John XII; spends later years in Italy
980: Effective end of Viking dynasty at Dublin
980–83: Otto II campaigns against Arabs in Italy
990: Ottonian campaign against Bohemians
1000: Poland joins Catholic church
1001: Coronation of Stephen I of Hungary
1018: Defeated Bulgars submit to Byzantine Empire
780
800
820
840
860
880
900
920
940
960
980
1000
1020

EUROPE IN THE AGE OF THE CRUSADES

Emperor Frederick Barbarossa is shown in Crusader dress. He drowned in 1190 on his way to the Third Crusade.

FOLLOWING THE SUCCESS of the First Crusade *(see pp.64–65)*, the spirit of the venture captured the imagination of Christian Europe. Expeditions to subdue the pagans of the Baltic and campaigns against the Muslims in Iberia were undertaken with papal blessing. Ideals of chivalry inspired the new religious orders of warrior clerics established to protect pilgrims to the Holy Land, such as the Templars and Hospitallers. These organizations became immensely wealthy with hundreds of priories and estates in Europe. At the same time, it was a period of great intellectual excitement. The rediscovery of Classical texts inspired an interest in philosophy; universities were founded and new religious orders gave renewed energy to the Catholic Church.

The crusading ideal in Europe

The Knights Templar were so well rewarded for their services in the Levant that they became a powerful political force throughout Europe.

The ideal of Holy War which inspired the Crusaders to fight in the Iberian Peninsula and the Holy Land was used to justify other wars, conflicts, and even racist atrocities. In 1096, German mobs attacked and massacred as 'unbelievers' the Jews in their own communities. Missionary efforts to convert the pagan peoples of Livonia, Lithuania, and Prussia became a crusade, preached by Pope Innocent III. One crusade was mounted against 'heretics' within Christian Europe – the Cathars (Albigensians) of southern France. In 1212 a French shepherd boy even set out to lead a children's crusade to Jerusalem. Most of his followers got no further than Genoa and Marseille.

The crusading ideal

- **1096:** Attacks on Jewish communities by Crusaders and their supporters
- **1118:** Founder of Knights Templar granted site close to Solomon's temple in Jerusalem
- **1126:** Hospitallers of St. John adopt a military role
- **1197:** Order of Teutonic Knights established in the Holy Land
- **1208:** Crusade against Cathars, or Albigensians, in southern France
- **1233:** Inquisition established in Toulouse
- **1283:** Conquest of Prussia completed by Teutonic Knights
- **1306–10:** Hospitallers conquer Rhodes, which becomes their base
- **1312:** Order of Temple, accused of heresy and suppressed by Pope

1050 | 1100 | 1150 | 1200 | 1250 | 1300 | 1350

The Norman conquest of England

The Duchy of Normandy was established in northern France by 911. In 1066, William, Duke of Normandy led an expedition to win the English throne from Harold, the last Anglo-Saxon king. Harold had seen off the threat of another claimant, Harald Hardrada of Norway, but, after a long march south, he was defeated by William at Hastings. Once England had been conquered, it was parcelled out in fiefs amongst William's Norman knights.

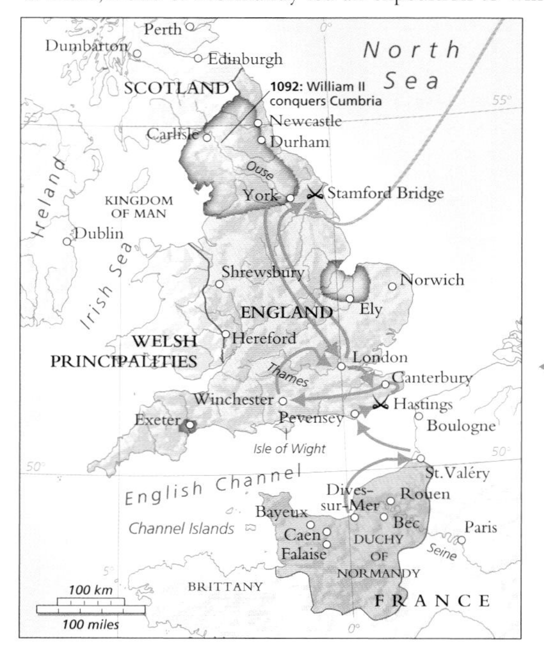

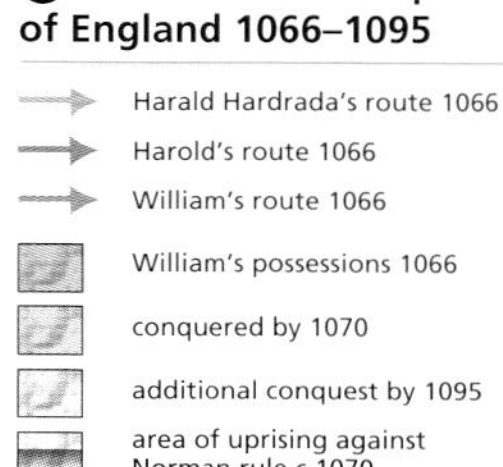

The Norman conquest of England 1066

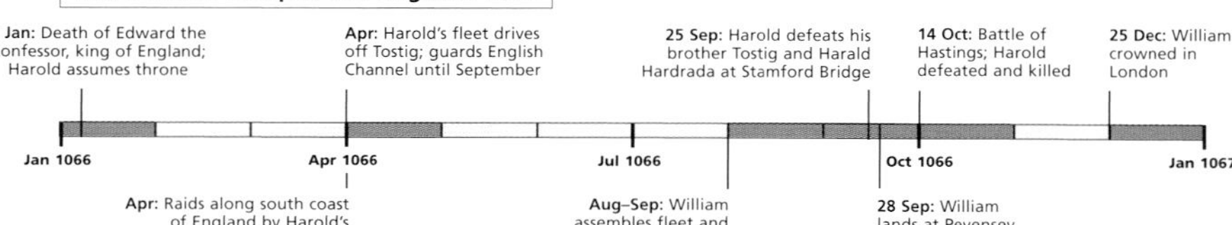

William's success depended on a large fleet to ship men and horses across the English Channel, but the Normans had long abandoned the seagoing life of their Viking forebears. Yet they managed to build a fleet, depicted here in a scene from the Bayeux Tapestry, large enough to transport an army of perhaps 7000 men to England.

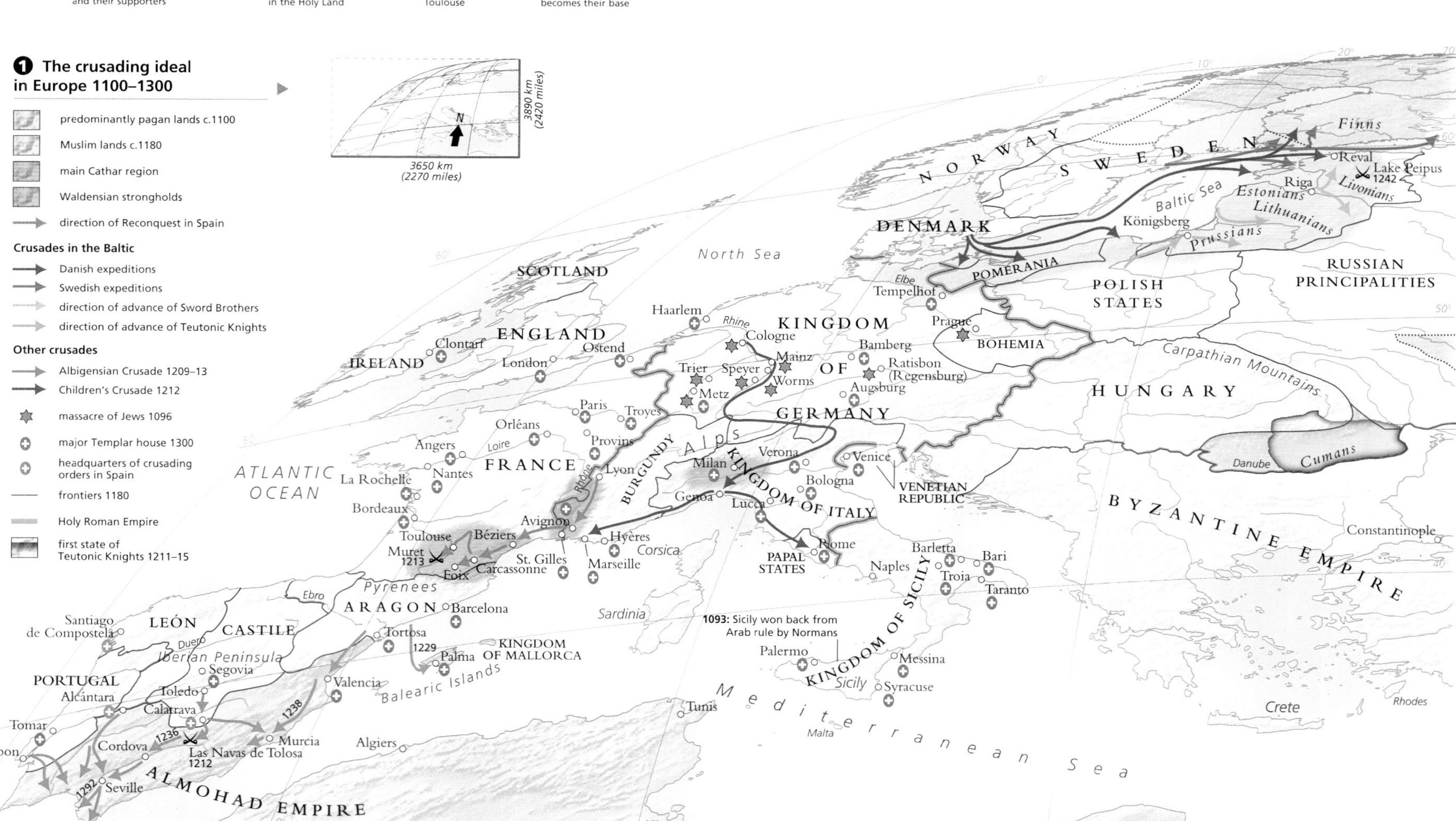

3 The 12th-century renaissance in Europe

- university with date of foundation
- other important theological school
- Muslim lands reconquered by Christians 1030–1200
- Muslim lands reconquered by Christians 1200–1300
- centre of contact with Arab scholarship
- major Cistercian house with date of foundation
- frontiers 1200
- Holy Roman Empire

c.1200: University of Paris has colleges for students from all over western Europe

1308: University of Lisbon transferred to Coimbra

Oxford early 12th century

Montpellier (medicine) 12th century

Salerno (medicine) since 9th century

Padua (law) 1222

Bologna (law) 1088

500 km
500 miles

The 12th-century renaissance

Christian idealism in this period was reflected in the growth of new monastic and teaching orders. The Cistercians, founded at Citeaux in 1098, spread throughout Europe under the charismatic leadership of St. Bernard of Clairvaux. The early 13th century saw the even more rapid expansion of the orders founded by St. Francis of Assisi and St. Dominic. At the same time a renewed interest in scholarship led to the founding of new universities. The increased availability of the seminal texts of the ancient world, obtained through the medium of Arabic translations, was critically important for medieval scholars. By reconciling the science of Aristotle with Christian faith, St. Thomas Aquinas (d. 1274) gave Catholic theology an intellectual basis that lasted for centuries.

The Cistercians were founded in reaction to the idle life of monasteries financed by tithes. They worked their own land and were self-supporting, though they accepted gifts of marginal or recently conquered land. Their graceful architecture was plain and unadorned, as seen here in the refectory of Fountains Abbey in northern England.

The 12th-century renaissance

- **1098:** Foundation of new monastery at Citeaux
- **1115:** Bernard founds Cistercian daughter house at Clairvaux
- **1126:** Birth of Muslim philosopher, Averroes, in Cordova
- **1158:** Frederick Barbarossa grants imperial protection to University of Bologna
- **1210:** St. Francis of Assisi gains papal recognition of his Order of friars dedicated to poverty
- **1220:** First chapter of the Dominican order of Friars
- **1249:** Foundation of Merton College, Oxford

The Angevin Empire

The laws of inheritance of feudal Europe enabled Henry II, Count of Anjou and King of England, to acquire lands that included England, Ireland, and most of western France. His marriage to Eleanor of Aquitaine meant that he ruled more of France than the French king, even though he was nominally the latter's vassal. He spent much of his reign defending his empire against Louis VII of France and the ambitions of his children. After his death in 1189, the Angevin empire soon disintegrated. In 1214, Philip II of France defeated Henry's son, John, ending English rule in Normandy. England, however, did keep western Aquitaine, and, in the 14th century, would renew its claims to France in the Hundred Years' War.

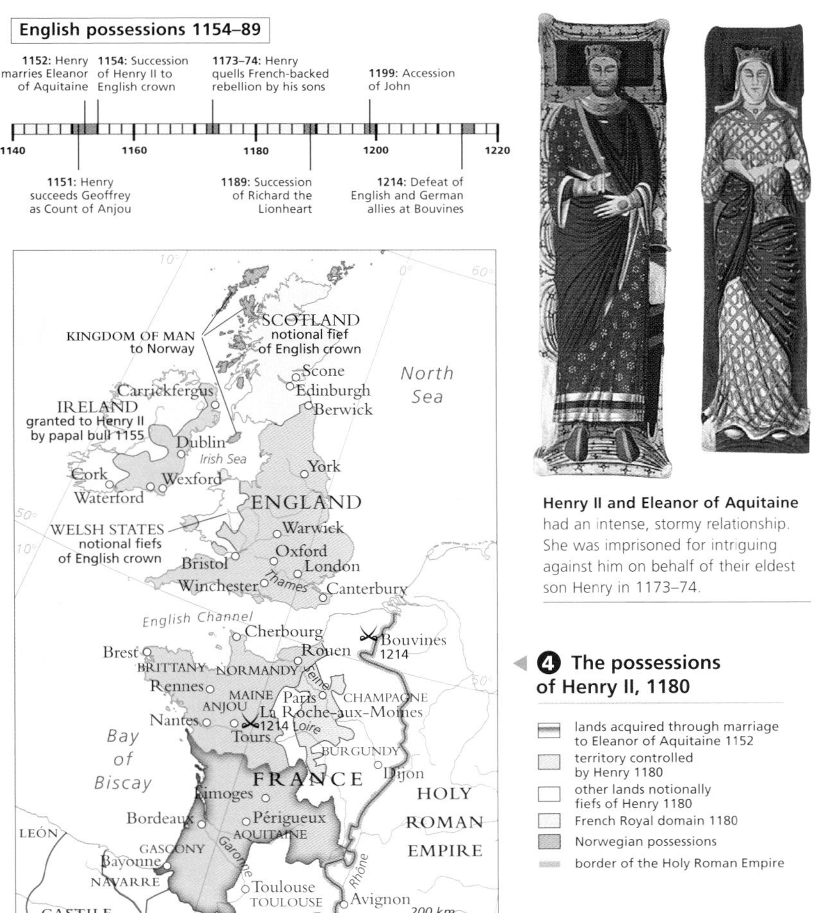

Henry II and Eleanor of Aquitaine had an intense, stormy relationship. She was imprisoned for intriguing against him on behalf of their eldest son Henry in 1173–74.

4 The possessions of Henry II, 1180

- lands acquired through marriage to Eleanor of Aquitaine 1152
- territory controlled by Henry 1180
- other lands notionally fiefs of Henry 1180
- French Royal domain 1180
- Norwegian possessions
- border of the Holy Roman Empire

Venice and the Latin Empire

The Crusaders' motive for attacking Constantinople in 1203 was financial reward for restoring Alexius IV (son of deposed emperor Isaac Angelus) to the imperial throne. When the population rebelled and killed Alexius in 1204, the Crusaders took over the city for themselves.

As well as being the principal emporium for east-west trade, Venice also made money shipping Crusaders to the Levant. When the Fourth Crusade gathered in Venice in 1203, the leaders did not have enough money to pay. The Venetians diverted the fleet first to capture the Adriatic port of Zara, long coveted by Venice, then to Constantinople, where in 1204, the Crusaders sacked the city and installed their own emperor. The Empire was divided into Venetian colonies and Latin fiefs. There were now two empires in the east; the 'Latin' empire, ruled from Constantinople, and a rump Byzantine Empire, ruled from Nicaea.

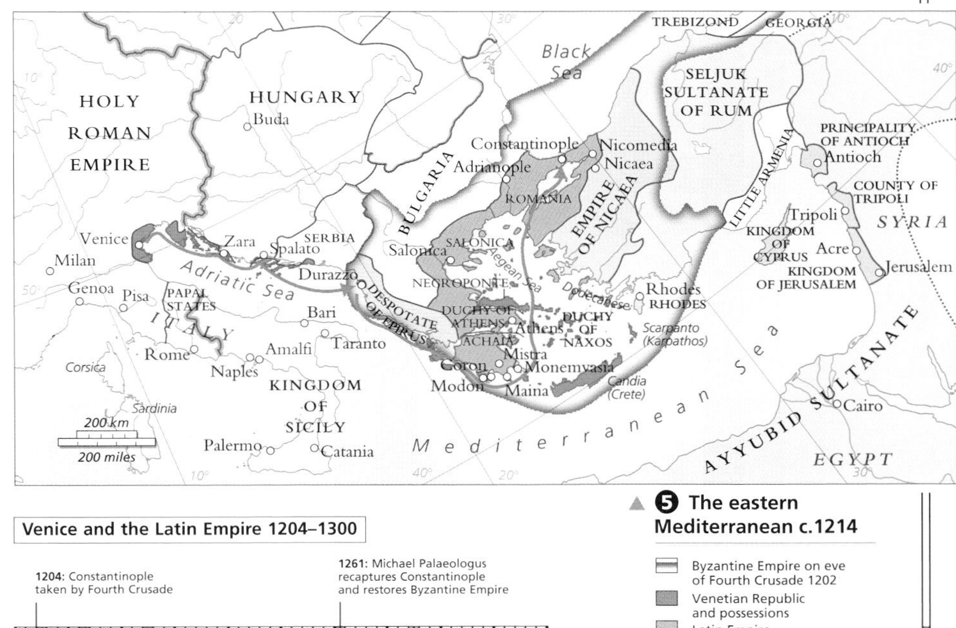

Venice and the Latin Empire 1204–1300

- **1204:** Constantinople taken by Fourth Crusade
- **1212:** Venetians occupy Crete
- **1224:** Latin kingdom of Salonica conquered by Despotate of Epirus
- **1261:** Michael Palaeologus recaptures Constantinople and restores Byzantine Empire
- **1275:** Principality of Achaia inherited by Philip of Anjou; ruled from Naples

5 The eastern Mediterranean c.1214

- Byzantine Empire on eve of Fourth Crusade 1202
- Venetian Republic and possessions
- Latin Empire
- Crusader states
- Byzantine states
- Muslim states
- route of Fourth Crusade
- border of Holy Roman Empire

EUROPE IN CRISIS

This silver pfennig shows the Emperor Frederick II, whose claim to rule Italy alienated the popes.

THE CONSOLIDATION of nation states on the eastern and western edges of Europe was matched, in the 13th century, by the decline of the Holy Roman Empire, its power depleted by long struggles with the papacy and the Italian city-states. In the east, raids by Mongols destroyed Kiev in 1240, and Russia, subject to Mongol overlords, developed in isolation until the 15th century. In the northeast, German colonization brought political and economic change, with a new trading axis around the Baltic Sea. During the 14th century, however, social unrest swept through Europe, compounded by famines, economic decline, dynastic wars, and the Black Death of 1347 *(see pp. 72–73)*, which wiped out a third of Europe's population in just two years.

The Empire and the papacy

Under the Hohenstaufen dynasty, the aspirations of the Holy Roman Emperors to universal authority were blocked by the papacy in central Italy, and the city-based communes of northern Italy. Emperor Frederick II (1211–50) clashed with Rome at a time when popes exercised great political power. After his death, the papacy gave the Kingdom of Sicily to Charles of Anjou, and Frederick's heirs were eliminated. Confronted with the growing power of France and England, the Empire lost any pretence to political supremacy in Europe; in Germany, a mosaic of clerical states, principalities, and free cities continued to undermine imperial authority.

Under Innocent III (1198–1216) the medieval papacy was at the height of its spiritual authority and temporal power.

The Scottish king, Robert Bruce, pictured here with his second wife, was a noble of Norman descent like his English enemies.

England, Scotland, and Wales

After a century of peace along the Anglo-Scottish border, Edward I (1272–1307) set out to assert his overlordship over all the British Isles. In 1284 he annexed Wales, bestowing the title of Prince of Wales on his son, but Scotland proved more intractable; Edward's attempts to subdue the Scots were met with resistance led by Robert Bruce, the victor at Bannockburn (1314). Hoping to extend his domains, Bruce sent an expedition to Ireland in 1315. His brother Edward continued fighting there until his death in 1318. In 1328, after a devastating period of guerrilla warfare and border raiding, England acknowledged Scottish independence.

England, Scotland, and Wales 1284–1337

- **1284:** Edward I invades Wales
- **1296:** Edward I invades Scotland
- **1305:** Execution of William Wallace, Scottish nationalist leader
- **1314:** English defeated at Bannockburn
- **1318:** Edward Bruce killed in Ireland
- **1322:** Scottish barons assert independence in Declaration of Arbroath
- **1328:** Scottish independence confirmed by Treaty of Northampton
- **1329:** Death of Robert Bruce
- **1337:** Start of Hundred Years' War; Scots ally with French against England

The Hohenstaufens and the papacy

- **1167:** Lombard League formed to oppose Emperor Frederick I Barbarossa in northern Italy
- **1194:** Emperor Henry VI crowned King of Sicily
- **1198:** Accession of Pope Innocent III
- **1211:** Frederick II becomes Emperor
- **1237:** Frederick II defeats Italian communes at Cortenuova
- **1245:** Innocent IV excommunicates Frederick
- **1250:** Death of Frederick
- **1268:** Charles of Anjou defeats Conradin, Frederick's grandson, at Tagliacozzo
- **1282:** Sicilian Vespers; Charles of Anjou defeated by Aragonese
- **1305:** Pope Clement V takes up residency at Avignon, under French supervision

Eastward expansion in the Baltic

A German-led wave of migration, from 1100–1350, transformed eastern and Baltic Europe. As peasants moved east in search of land and resources, German language and law became predominant; New towns were bound together in the Hanseatic League, a trading association with links from Muscovy to London. Crusades in the east were spearheaded by the Knights of the Teutonic Order, who began to wage war on the pagans of Prussia and Lithuania in 1226. They also took over the Sword Brothers' lands in Livonia. The Livonians and Prussians were subdued, but Lithuania expanded to the southeast to become a powerful state. It was united with Poland in 1386.

Marienburg was the headquarters of the Teutonic Knights from 1309. Part abbey, part fortress, it was built of brick like many of the castles erected by the crusading order in Prussia and Livonia.

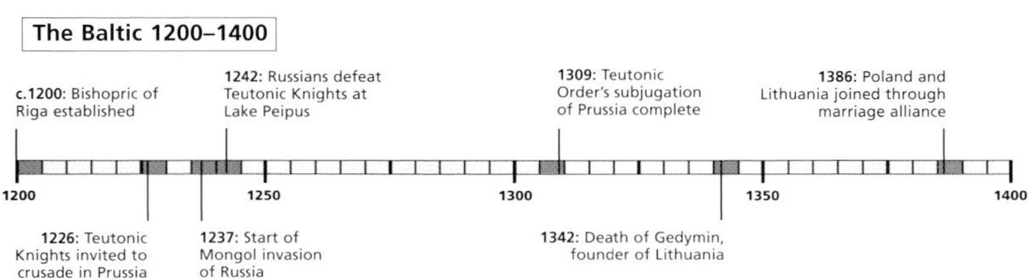

▲ **3 The Baltic states 1100–1400**

◄ **4 Central and Southeast Europe 1200–1400**

- Byzantine Empire
- Habsburg possessions
- Latin states
- Polish states
- Russian principalities, vassals of the Golden Horde
- Venetian Republic and possessions
- Bulgaria 1230
- Mongol-Tartar campaigns 1240–42
- possessions of Ottokar II of Bohemia at his death, 1278
- frontiers 1320
- Serbian Empire of Stefan Dušan at his death, 1355
- possessions of Casimir the Great of Poland at his death, 1370
- possessions of Louis the Great of Hungary at his death, 1382
- frontier of Ottoman Empire and dependencies 1400
- frontier of Lithuania 1400
- frontier of Holy Roman Empire

Central and southeastern Europe

After the setbacks of the early 13th century, when eastern Europe was devastated by Mongol invasions, the consolidation of powerful new states began. In Bohemia, the imperial ambitions of Ottakar II (1253–78) briefly expanded his domain from Silesia to the Adriatic, but he came into conflict with Bohemian and German princes, and the Habsburgs were able to seize power in Austria on his death. Powerful monarchies were established in Lithuania under Gedymin (c.1315–42), in Poland under Casimir the Great (1333–70), and in Hungary under Louis the Great (1342–82). Bohemia under the Luxembourg dynasty remained an influential state, especially when the king was elected as the Emperor Charles IV. In the Balkans, Stefan Dušan (1331–55) forged for himself a substantial Serbian Empire, but it fell to the Ottomans in 1389.

The Emperor Charles IV is shown with his Electors. His Golden Bull of 1356 set out clear rules for electing the emperor.

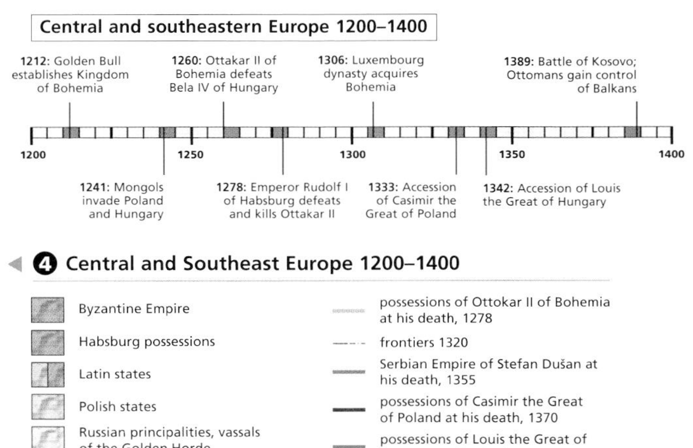

TRADE IN MEDIEVAL EUROPE

The seal of Lübeck shows a cog, the ship used for large cargoes in northern Europe.

THE EXPLOSION IN EUROPE'S POPULATION, which nearly doubled between the 10th and 14th centuries, was caused by greatly increased agricultural productivity, enhanced by technological innovations, in particular the use of the iron plough, and large land clearance projects, which brought marginal land, such as marshes and forests, under cultivation. This demographic surge inevitably led to increased trading activity; merchants traversed the continent, using the trans-Alpine passes which provided arterial routes between Italy and the north and, from c.1300, new maritime routes which opened up the North and Baltic Seas. Trade and commerce went hand in hand with urban development. Commercial wealth had a cultural impact; cities were enhanced with magnificent buildings and churches and, from c.1200, universities. As cities prospered, a new class, the bourgeoisie, emerged.

Medieval trade

From the 11th century the Alpine passes had linked the textile towns of Lombardy and manufacturing centres of the Po valley with northern Europe, rich in natural resources, such as timber, grain, wool, and metals. Merchants converged from all over Europe to trade at vast seasonal fairs. International bankers, such as the Florentine Peruzzi, facilitated payments and promoted business. Around 1300, the Genoese opened a new sea route to the North Sea, through the Strait of Gibraltar; Bruges, at the end of the route, became a major city. In the Mediterranean, Genoa competed with Venice for the carrying trade. Venice controlled the valuable eastern routes, profiting from trade in silks, sugar, spices, and gemstones from India and East Asia. In northern Germany, an association of trading cities centred on Lübeck, the Hanseatic League, promoted monopolies and sought exclusive trading rights with towns in England, Scandinavia, and Flanders.

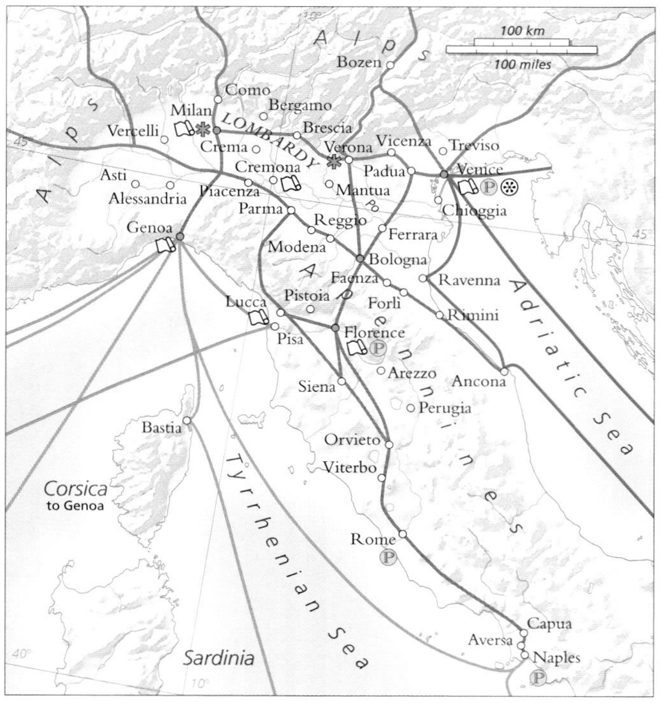

Italian towns

Northern Italy was well-endowed with populous, wealthy cities, such as Milan and Florence. The Italian cities did not develop under the direct rule of kings, emperors, or the nobility, and took advantage of this to assert their municipal rights, evolving their own constitutions, codes of law, and military forces, the 'communal movement'.

The textile industry flourished in Flanders and northern Italy. The horizontal loom *(above)* was introduced to Europe in the 11th century.

Medieval trade 1100–1400

- **1143:** Foundation of Lübeck
- **1167:** Lombard League opposes Frederick Barbarossa's attempt to abolish liberties of Italian communes
- **c.1200:** Silver coins, notably the grosso, introduced in northern Italy
- **1237:** Opening of St. Gotthard pass through Alps
- **1245:** Italian merchants granted own courts to settle trading disputes at Champagne fairs
- **1275:** Establishment of Peruzzi trading company in Florence
- **1291:** Genoese open sea route through Strait of Gibraltar to Bruges
- **c.1300:** Venetians improve Brenner Pass, so suitable for vehicles
- **1320:** Flanders loses wool monopoly to Brabant; start of decline of Champagne fairs
- **1340s:** Bankruptcy of Peruzzis; economic chaos compounded by arrival of Black Death in 1347

MONEY AND BANKING

Many gold and silver currencies circulated freely in Medieval Europe, irrespective of where they were minted, so money changing was inevitably an important profession. Travelling merchants left currency on deposit with money changers, in exchange for a receipt, the first stage in the evolution of banking. By the 14th century the use of the bill of exchange, where one person instructs another to pay a sum of money to a third party, was widespread. The organization of bills of exchange was lucrative, and banking families, such as the Peruzzi and Bardi of Florence, became rich and powerful.

Medieval Italy gave the world the word 'bank' from the *banco* (counter) where bankers transacted their business, as shown in this 14th-century illustration.

Venetian coinage included the silver grosso and the widely circulated gold ducat.

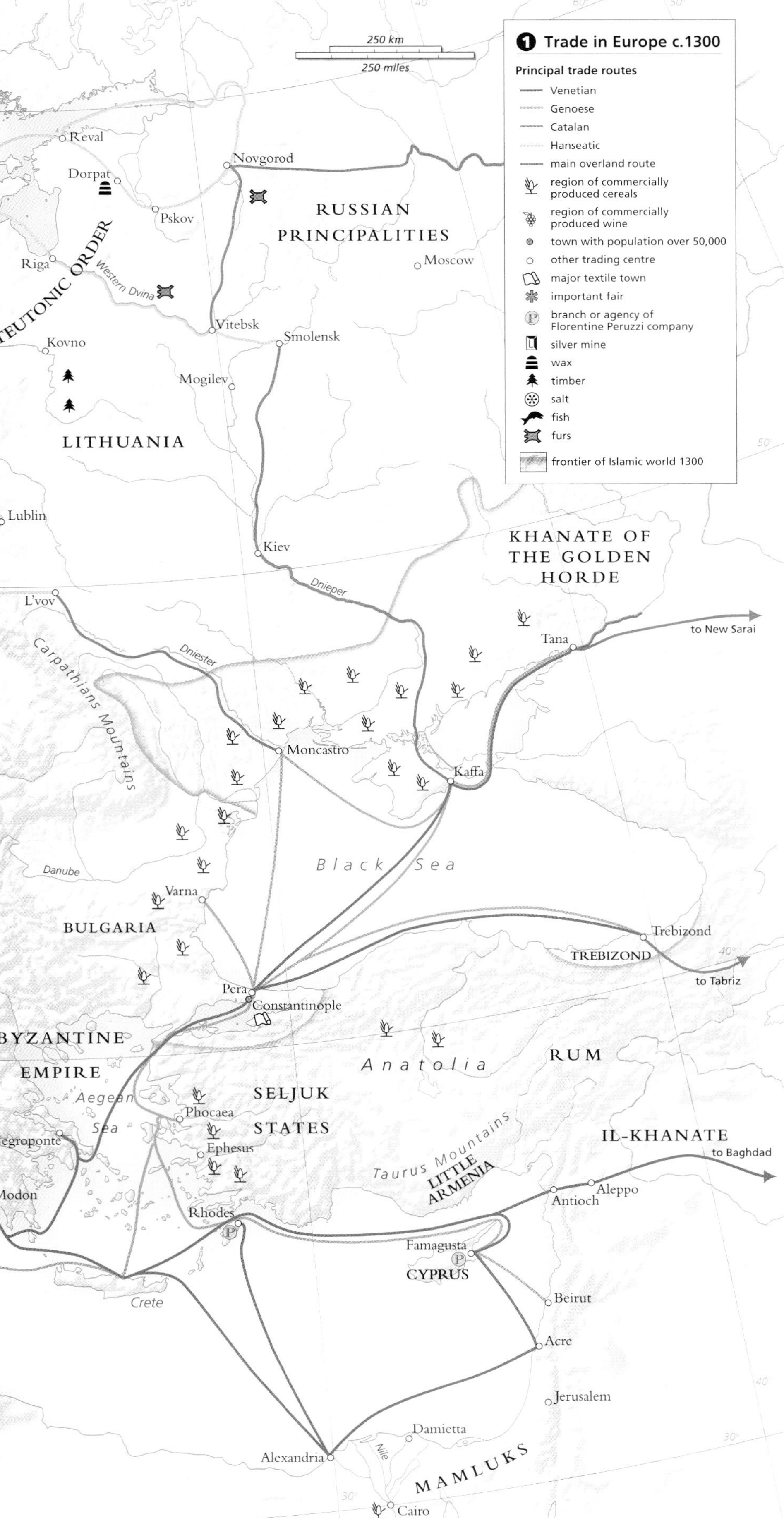

Medieval cities

Many of the cities of Medieval Europe owed their development to trade and commerce. The cities of northern Italy emerged from the 10th century onwards, as entrepôts in the trade between Europe, Byzantium, and the Islamic world. In the 13th century, the demand for manufactured goods, such as glassware, textiles, and metalwork, led to the emergence of industrial centres, notably the Lombard textile towns and the wool centres of Flanders, such as Ghent, Bruges, and Ypres. By the mid-13th century, German expansion eastward had led to the growth of a thriving network of Baltic trading cities, including Lübeck, Hamburg, Danzig, and Riga.

The Seine was vital to the economy of Paris. Boats of all sizes delivered goods along the river and the fortified bridges carried a constant flow of traders.

Medieval Paris

From the 11th century, Paris benefited from the return of order and stability under the Capetian kings. Streets were paved, city walls enlarged and three 'divisions' of the city emerged; the merchants were based on the right bank of the Seine, the university (recognized in 1200) on the left bank, with civic and religious institutions on the Île de la Cité. In the 14th century, however, the city stagnated under the dual blows of the Black Death (*see pp. 72–73*) and the Hundred Years' War; repeatedly fought over by the contending forces, it was beset by riots and civil disorder.

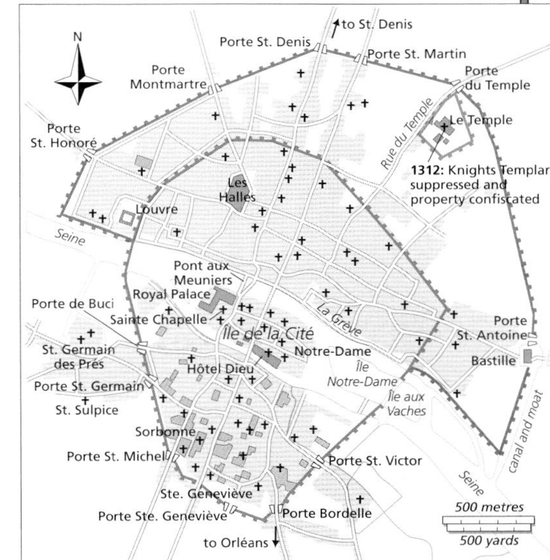

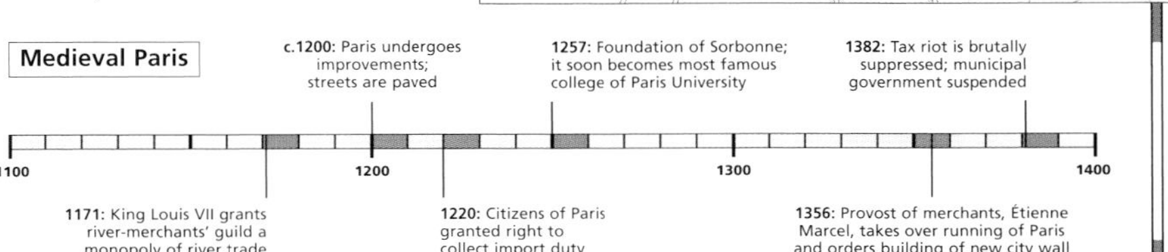

Medieval Venice

Venice was perceived as the symbolic centre of a liberal government and divinely ordered religious, civic, and commercial life. Its political focus was the Doge's Palace, residence of the elected Doge and centre of government. Since the city's wealth depended on maritime trade, the government maintained a vast shipyard – the Darsena – to build galleys for war and for merchant ventures.

A 13th-century mosaic in St. Mark's Basilica shows the Doge in a procession led by a bishop.

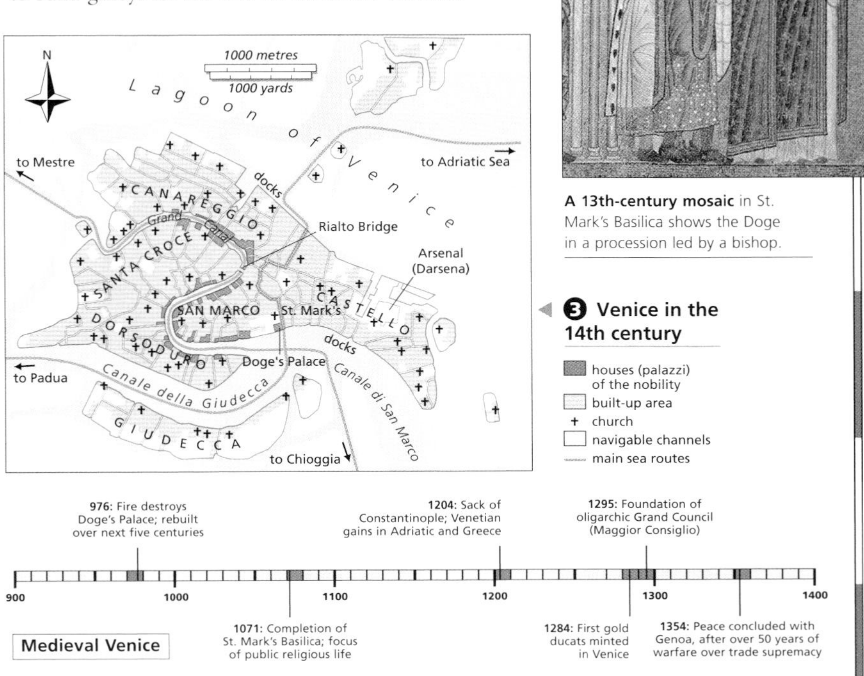

THE EMERGENCE OF MODERN STATES

Joan of Arc (1412–31) led the French to a famous victory against the English at Orléans in 1429 during the Hundred Years' War.

THE MAP OF EUROPE was redrawn throughout the 15th century, as new nation states appeared. France emerged, bruised but victorious, from the Hundred Years' War, soon to become the model of a modern nation state. Newly-unified Spain vanquished the last Iberian outpost of Islam in 1492, emerging as a formidable power. The vast realm of Poland-Lithuania dominated Eastern Europe, while the Bohemians threw off imperial control. Feudal models of government were disappearing everywhere and monarchies increasingly relied on the endorsement of the 'estates', representative bodies of nobility, clergy, and the newly-emerging bourgeoisie. Commercial centres such as the Netherlands and Italy saw a flowering of humanist philosophy, science, literature, and art, known as the Renaissance.

The Hundred Years' War

Over a century of intermittent conflict between France and England (1337–1453) was precipitated by the English kings' possessions in France and their claims to the French throne. Six major royal expeditions to France, starting with Edward III's landing in Antwerp in 1338 and ending with the death of Henry V in 1422, were interspersed with skirmishes and provincial campaigns led by independent war parties. After many setbacks, the triumphs of Joan of Arc (1429–30) led to a resurgence of French confidence and ultimately to English defeat.

The skill of 10,000 English longbowmen proved the deciding factor against the French cavalry at the battle of Crécy in 1346.

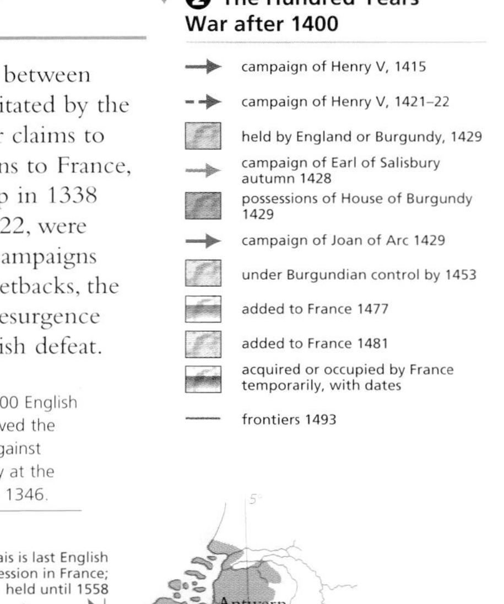

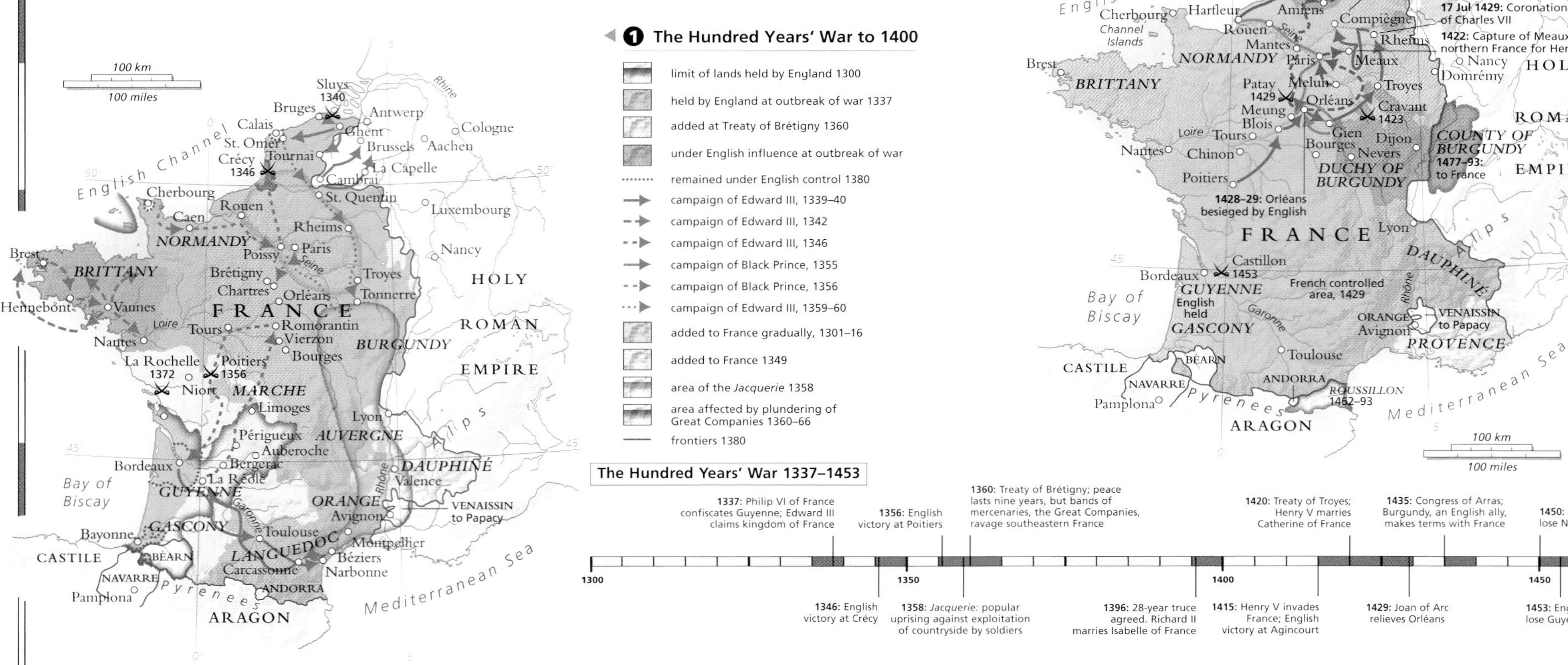

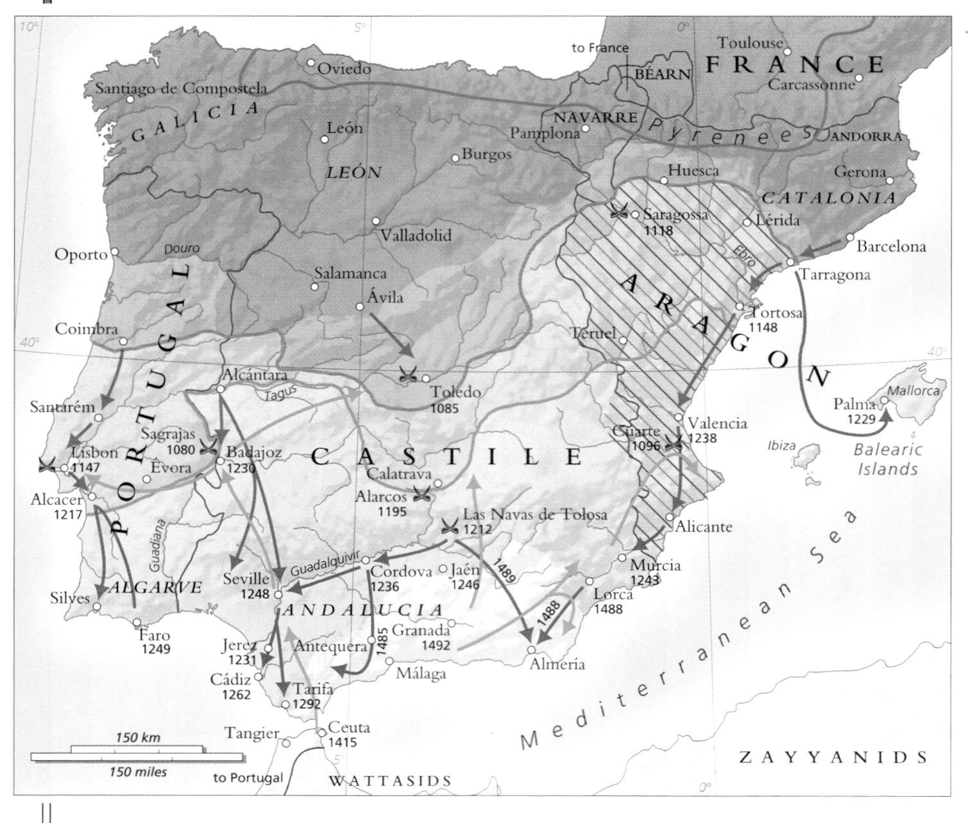

The *Reconquista*

The Christian reconquest of Moorish Spain began in earnest in the 11th century, led by the kingdoms of Navarre, Aragon, León-Castile, and Portugal. Despite strong Muslim counter-attacks, the Christians had reconquered all but the small kingdom of Granada by 1260. León-Castile now dominated Iberia, and Aragon acquired extensive possessions in the western Mediterranean. These kingdoms, united by the marriage of Ferdinand II of Aragon and Isabella of Castile, embarked on a final crusade, and Granada fell in 1492.

The Alhambra at Granada was built as a palace and fortress by the Moorish kings who ruled there until 1492. Following the expulsion of the Moors, much of the magnificent decoration was effaced or destroyed.

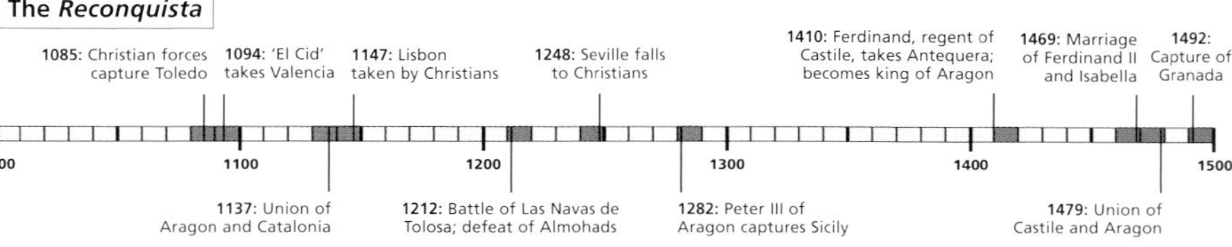

Central Europe in the 15th century

In Bohemia, the preachings of Jan Hus, which railed against the abuses of the clergy, were taken up by the Hussites, who called for a free Bohemia, and established a national Czech church. A new state in Bohemia was forged by Czech resistance to a series of bitter crusades launched by the Holy Roman Empire. The union of Poland and Lithuania in 1386 had created the largest realm in Christendom, its future secured by the defeat of the Teutonic Order in 1410. In the Holy Roman Empire, the Habsburgs sowed the seeds of future domination, acquiring, by treaty, marriage, and conquest, domains stretching from Austria and Styria to the Netherlands, and encompassing, from 1477, the lands of the Valois dukes of Burgundy.

The civil war initiated by the Hussites led to the deposing of Sigismund, king of Bohemia, who was forced to wage war on the Hussites on an almost annual basis until 1436. The picture *(left)* shows Hussite battle wagons drawn up in a defensive circle.

This coin was minted to honour Jan Hus, who was burnt at the stake for heresy in 1415.

Union of Kalmar 1397–1523: Denmark, Norway, and Sweden united under one ruler

PRUSSIA 1466: to Poland

MOLDAVIA 15th century: Intermittently Polish and Hungarian vassal

HUNGARY in personal union with Lands of the Bohemian Crown

WALLACHIA 15th century: Intermittently Ottoman and Hungarian vassal

PROVENCE 1481: to France

KINGDOM OF NAPLES to Spain

Calais to England

250 km

250 miles

4 Central Europe 1400–1500

- lost by Habsburgs during 14th and 15th centuries
- approximate extent of core Hussite area
- limit of area affected by Hussite campaigns 1425–34
- campaign of János Hunyadi, 1443
- limit of direct Ottoman control, 1451
- Burgundian control 1477
- possessions of Matthias Corvinus of Hungary at his death 1490
- Jagiello possessions 1500
- Habsburg possessions 1500
- Papal States and notional dependencies 1500
- Venetian Republic 1500
- frontiers 1500
- notional frontier of Holy Roman Empire 1500

Central and Eastern Europe 1400–1500

1410: Battle of Tannenberg Grunwald; Polish defeat of Teutonic Order

1415: Jan Hus burnt for heresy at Constance

1419: Defenestration of Prague; German bürgermeister thrown from window by Czech crowds

1434: Battle of Lipany; victory of moderate Hussites over extremists

1454: Beginning of Thirteen Years' War between Poland and Teutonic Order

1456: Death of János Hunyadi, leader of Hungarians

1466: Second Treaty of Toruń; Prussia becomes a fief of Poland

1477: Death of Charles the Bold. Habsburgs acquire former Burgundian lands including the Netherlands and Franche Comté

1490: Polish Jagiello dynasty controls Poland, Bohemia, and Hungary

The formation of Switzerland

The forest cantons of Switzerland were strategically placed to control vital Alpine passes, the route for pilgrims and merchants travelling between Italy and northern Europe. Increasingly, they resented attempts by their powerful neighbours to exert political control. In 1291, a union was formed by Uri, Schwyz, and Unterwalden, later joined by other cantons and cities, to defend a growing autonomy. The Swiss, in their conflicts with the Habsburgs and Burgundy, gained a formidable military reputation. Victory in the Swabian War by 1499 brought *de facto* independence from the Empire. Membership of the Union continued to expand until the 16th century.

At the battle of Morgarten in 1315, a Swiss peasant army was able to defeat a Habsburg attack led by Leopold I of Austria and an army of knights.

NEUCHÂTEL until 1857: to Prussia

5 The growth of the Swiss Confederation

- first three cantons 1291
- added to Swiss Confederation by 1501
- added further by 1579
- frontier of Switzerland 1579
- frontiers 1815

The formation of Switzerland

1291: Union of Uri, Schwyz, and Unterwalden

1315: Battle of Morgarten; defeat of Habsburgs

1332: Luzern joins Union

1352: Berne joins Union

1386: Habsburg emperor, Leopold III defeated and killed at Sempach

1476: Battles of Grandson and Morat against Charles the Bold of Burgundy

1477: Battle of Nancy: Charles the Bold killed

1499: Swiss victory in Swabian War

The growth of Hungary

Following the ravages of the Mongol campaigns of 1241, which reduced the population in some areas by up to 60%, a succession of Angevin and German princes were elected to the Hungarian throne. The growing threat from the Ottomans, who had taken Constantinople in 1453, precipitated a revolt led by János Hunyadi. In 1458 he secured the throne for his son, Matthias Corvinus (1458–90), who subsequently achieved many notable military successes against the Ottoman Turks.

Matthias Corvinus brought many of the ideas of the Renaissance to the business of government, simplifying the administration and laws. However, his subjects bore a heavy tax burden, partly to finance his huge standing army which was kept in readiness for campaigns against the Ottomans and other foreign adversaries.

THE AGE OF THE REFORMATION

Martin Luther's questioning of the doctrine and practice of Christianity led to the creation of the Protestant faith.

A SERIES OF PROFOUND CHANGES in theological doctrine and practice were to have violent political consequences in 16th-century Europe. The religious reformation, spearheaded by Martin Luther in 1517, divided much of the continent along religious lines, precipitating a series of wars which permanently sapped the strength of the Catholic Habsburg Empire. In northern Europe, new nations came to prominence; Sweden, Russia, and Denmark struggled for control of the Baltic, while in the Netherlands, a rising against the Catholic rule of Spain led to the independence of the Calvinist north. In the east, the expansion of the Ottoman Empire brought Christian Europe into conflict with Islam; the Turks exploited European disunity, penetrating as far as Vienna.

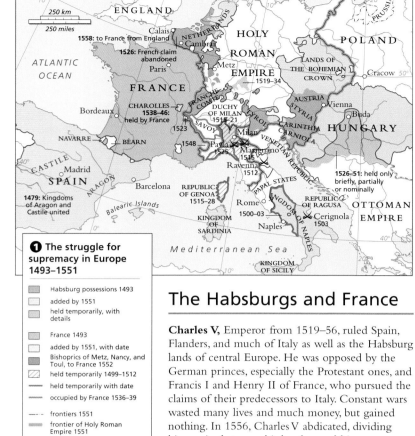

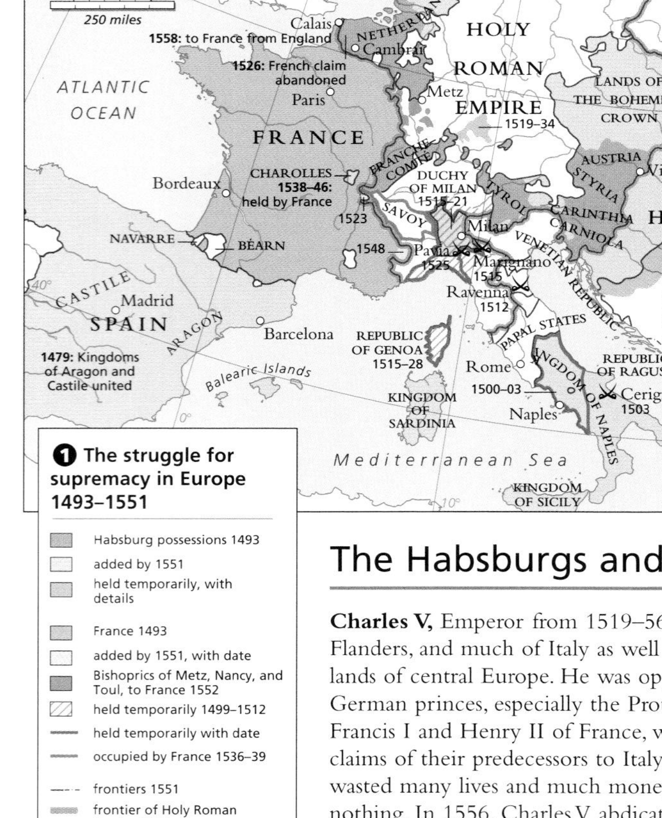

1 The struggle for supremacy in Europe 1493–1551

- Habsburg possessions 1493
- added by 1551
- held temporarily, with details
- France 1493
- added by 1551, with date
- Bishoprics of Metz, Nancy, and Toul, to France 1552
- held temporarily 1499–1512
- held temporarily with date
- occupied by France 1536–39
- frontiers 1551
- frontier of Holy Roman Empire 1551

The Reformation

The spiritual complacency, material wealth, and abuses of power of the Roman Catholic church provoked a revolution in Christianity, inspired by the teachings of Martin Luther (1483–1546). His reformed theology, with its emphasis on study of the Bible, spread rapidly through northern Europe. Some opportunistic rulers, such as Henry VIII of England, embraced 'Protestant' forms of religion in order to seize church lands. By 1570, Protestantism prevailed over much of central and northern Europe. In 1545, the Catholic Church summoned the Council of Trent, which reaffirmed fundamental doctrine, but condemned the worst clerical abuses.

The Habsburg defeat of France at the battle of Pavia in 1525 is here commemorated in a contemporary tapestry. Even though Francis I of France was captured by the Spanish, the French finally abandoned their claim to Italy at the Treaty of Cateau-Cambrésis in 1559.

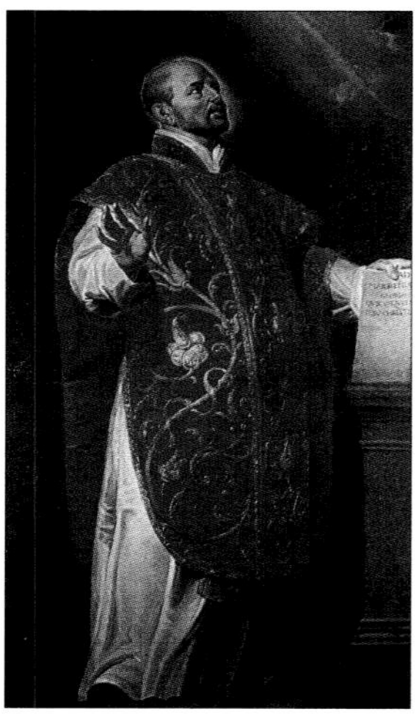

St. Ignatius Loyola founded the Society of Jesus in 1534 to champion the Catholic Counter-Reformation. Highly-educated and assertively evangelical, the Jesuits took Catholic teachings to territory throughout the rapidly expanding Spanish Empire.

The Habsburgs and France

Charles V, Emperor from 1519–56, ruled Spain, Flanders, and much of Italy as well as the Habsburg lands of central Europe. He was opposed by the German princes, especially the Protestant ones, and Francis I and Henry II of France, who pursued the claims of their predecessors to Italy. Constant wars wasted many lives and much money, but gained nothing. In 1556, Charles V abdicated, dividing his empire between his brother and his son.

French-Habsburg rivalry 1515-59

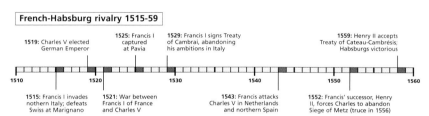

1510 · 1520 · 1530 · 1540 · 1550 · 1560

- **1515:** Francis I invades nothern Italy; defeats Swiss at Marignano
- **1519:** Charles V elected German Emperor
- **1521:** War between Francis I of France and Charles V
- **1525:** Francis I captured at Pavia
- **1529:** Francis I signs Treaty of Cambrai, abandoning his ambitions in Italy
- **1543:** Francis attacks Charles V in Netherlands and northern Spain
- **1552:** Francis' successor, Henry II, forces Charles to abandon Siege of Metz (truce in 1556)
- **1559:** Henry II accepts Treaty of Cateau-Cambrésis; Habsburgs victorious

The Reformation in Europe 1517–55

1510 · 1520 · 1530 · 1540 · 1550 · 1560

- **1517:** Martin Luther posts 95 Theses condemning abuses of Catholic church at Wittenberg
- **1529:** At Diet of Speyer, Charles V attempts to reach compromise with Lutheran princes
- **1532:** Henry VIII of England declares himself head of Church of England
- **1535:** John Calvin formulates doctrine of predestination in Geneva
- **1545:** Start of Council of Trent, which defines modern Catholicism
- **1555:** At Peace of Augsburg; Lutheran princes win right to choose their religion

2 The religious map of Europe 1590 ▶

- almost exclusively Catholic, with just minimal Protestant presence in northern areas
- overwhelmingly Catholic, with appreciable Protestant minority
- Catholic majority, but with very strong Protestant minority
- exclusively or overwhelmingly Protestant, with only slight Catholic presence in places
- Protestant majority, with some Catholic presence
- mainly Catholic, with strong Greek Orthodox presence
- Greek Orthodox, with significant Muslim presence in some areas of the Balkans
- Muslim majority
- frontiers 1590
- frontier of Holy Roman Empire 1590
- *Calvinist* locally dominant Protestant denomination

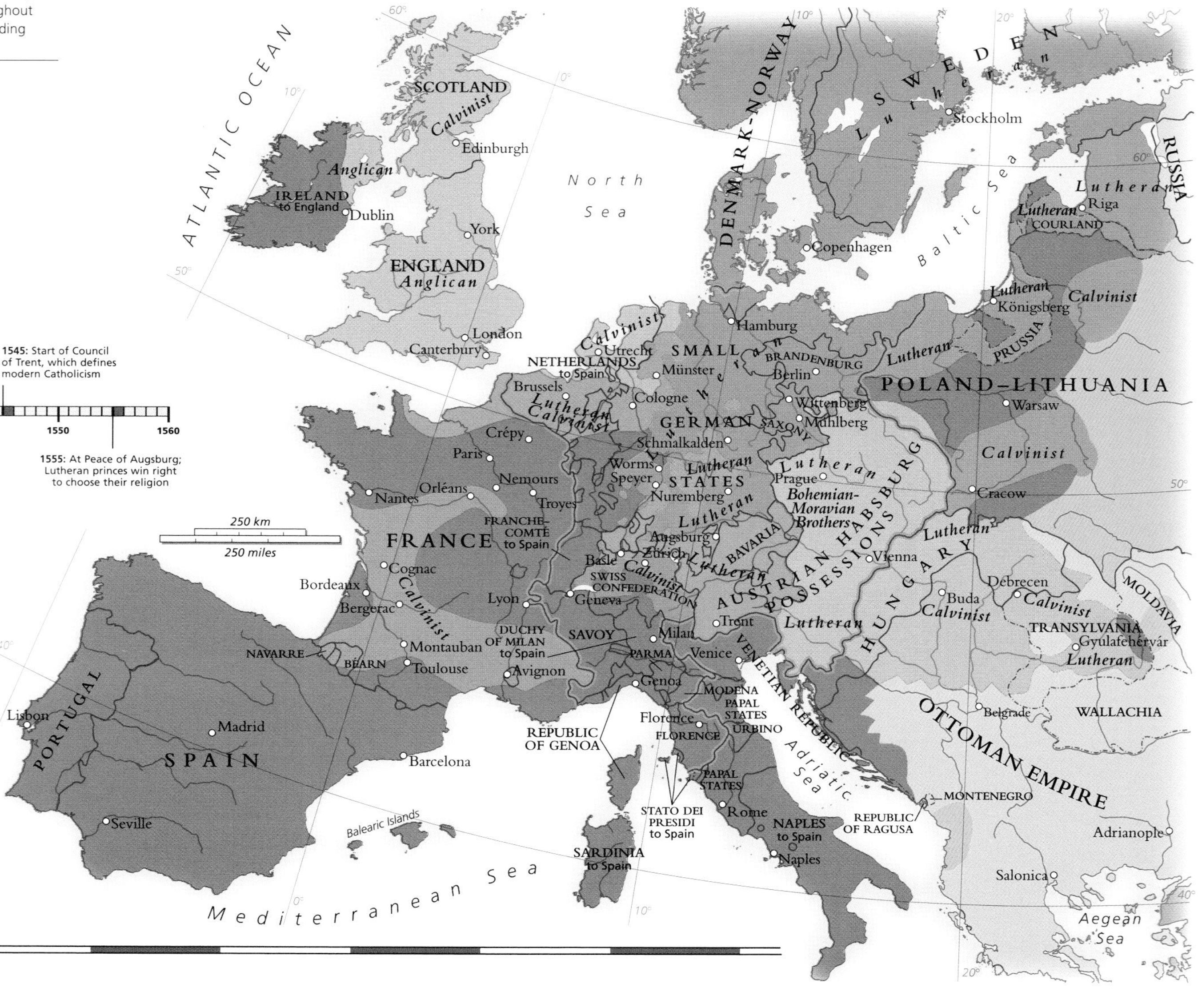

Conflict in the Baltic 1500–1595

The collapse of the Union of Kalmar, which bound Sweden, Denmark, and Norway together, in 1523, precipitated a century of warfare around the Baltic Sea, bringing the growing power of Sweden into conflict with Russia and Denmark, which controlled the narrow outlet to the North Sea, vital for Swedish trade interests. The Reformation had led to the collapse of crusading orders, such as the Teutonic Knights, opening up Livonia to the ambitions of Russia, Sweden, and Poland-Lithuania.

Ivan Vasilievich, Tsar of Russia from 1547 to 1584, was known as 'the Terrible' for his drastic reforming of the hereditary aristocracy. Although his wars with Sweden and Poland were largely unsuccessful, he was able to expand the Russian Empire to include non-Slav states.

The expansion of Ottoman power

By 1500, the Ottomans controlled the lands to the south and west of the Black Sea. With the accession of Suleyman I – 'the Magnificent' – (1520–66), they turned their attention to Europe, increasing naval pressure on the eastern Mediterranean, and pushing northward into Moldavia, the Danube valley, and Hungary. In 1529, they were turned back after their unsuccessful siege of Vienna, but continued to maintain their pressure on the frontier of the Habsburg Empire, exploiting conflict in Europe by forming alliances with France against the Habsburgs, and gaining control of Transylvania in 1562.

This detail from an Italian manuscript records the victory of Habsburg forces over the Ottomans at the siege of Vienna in 1529. The illumination is one of a series entitled 'Triumphs of Charles V'.

The Dutch Revolt

Philip II of Spain, a fierce champion of the Roman Catholic cause, was determined to suppress Calvinism in the Netherlands. He reacted harshly to demands by Dutch nobles for autonomy and religious freedom, and his reprisals, combined with onerous taxes, led to a general revolt under the leadership of William of Nassau, which the Spanish could not quell. In 1579, ten southern Catholic provinces were promised liberty; in reply, seven Calvinist northern provinces formed the Union of Utrecht. In a 1609 truce, their independence was conceded by Spain.

The Sea Beggars were Dutch rebels who took to the sea to combat the Spanish from foreign ports. In 1572, they mounted a successful attack on the fortress of Brill in southern Holland *(above)*, encouraging Holland and Zeeland to join the revolt.

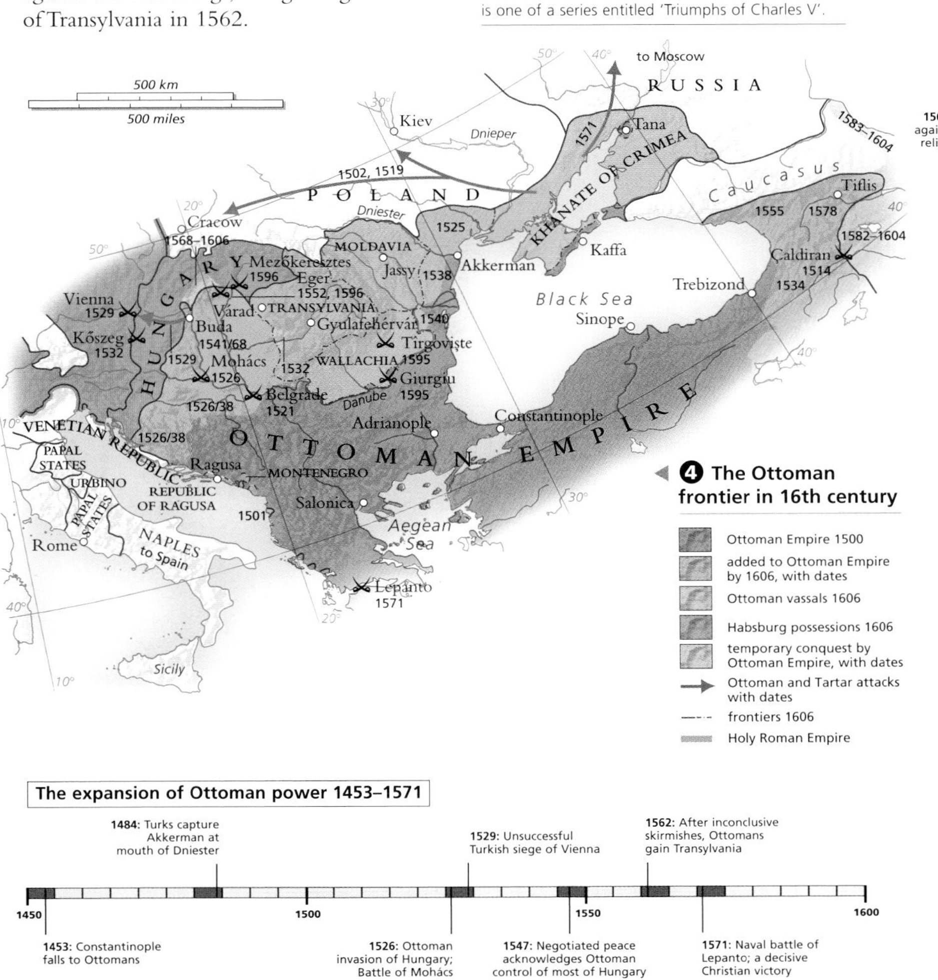

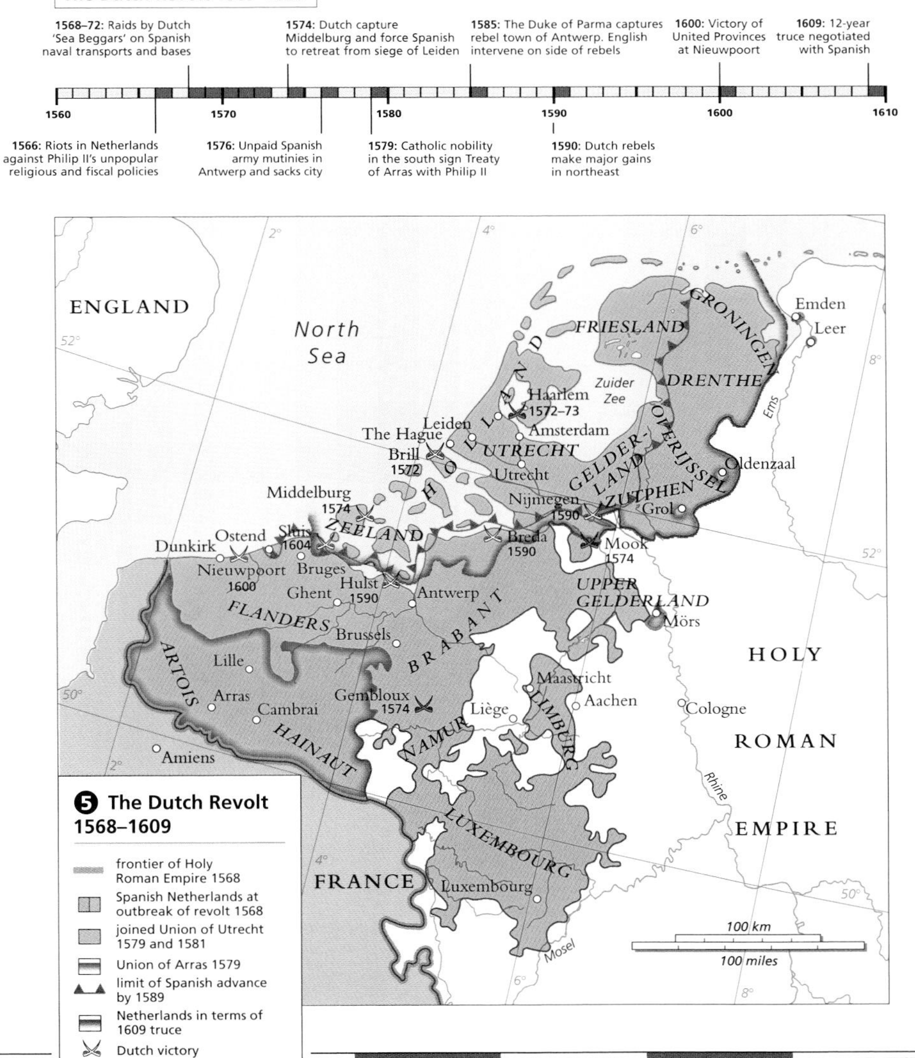

EARLY MODERN EUROPE

Cardinal Richelieu, was Louis XIII's chief minister and the architect of royal absolutism in France.

IN THE 17TH CENTURY, following years of destructive warfare, the modern European state system began to evolve. States were ruled centrally by autocratic (or absolutist) monarchs and bounded by clear, militarily secure frontiers. The Thirty Years' War laid waste large parts of central Europe, causing a decline in population from some 21 million in 1618 to 13 million in 1648. Under Louis XIV, France was involved in four costly wars, but emerged as the leading nation in Europe, eclipsing Spain which entered a long period of decline. After a period of expansion under the Vasa kings, Sweden lost much of its Baltic empire by 1721. The Ottoman Turks struck once again at the heart of Europe, but were met by an increasingly powerful Austria, whose main rival in the region was Russia.

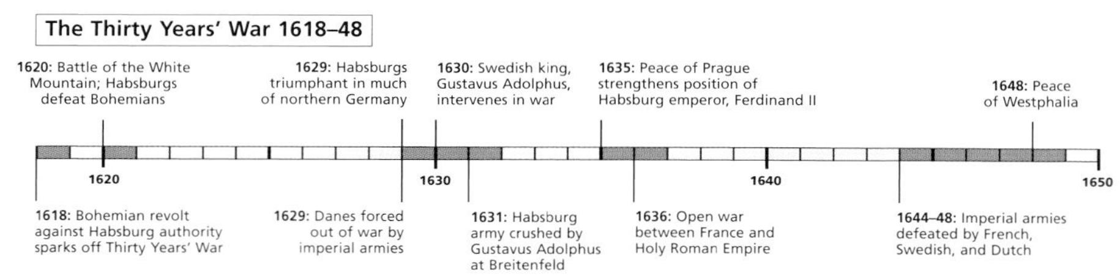

The Thirty Years' War

The Thirty Years' War provoked great advances in methods of mass destruction, and involved an unprecedented number of soldiers, over a million of whom died before it ceased. Much of Germany was devastated, towns were sacked, and their inhabitants raped and murdered.

The Thirty Years' War saw Protestant-Catholic rivalry and German constitutional issues subsumed in a wider European struggle. Habsburg attempts to control Bohemia and crush Protestantism coincided with the breakdown of constitutional mechanisms for resolving conflict in the Holy Roman Empire. Spain intervened to secure supply lines to the Netherlands; Danish and Swedish involvement followed as they competed for control of the Baltic. Fear of imperial absolutism, prompted by Austrian Habsburg victories in 1621 and 1634–35, led France to intervene in 1635 in support of Sweden. Prolonged negotiations from 1643 culminated in the Treaty of Westphalia which fused attempts to secure peace in Europe with curbs on the emperor's authority in Germany.

Civil wars and revolts 1625–65

1628–29	Siege of Protestant stronghold of La Rochelle
1640	Portugal declares independence from Spain
1640	Catalan Revolt
1640	Civil War breaks out in England
1648–53	The Fronde: resistance to royal authority throughout France
1649	Execution of Charles I of England
1660	Restoration of English monarchy

1625 1635 1645 1655 1665

Political consolidation and resistance

European states were transformed in a process of internal political centralization and external consolidation. The legitimacy of these developments was often questioned, leading to civil wars and popular resistance. Foreign intervention turned local disputes into international conflicts, as in the Thirty Years' War. In western Europe, Spain's dominant position was broken by Portuguese and Dutch independence. The two rising powers in the region, France and England, developed in very different ways. In France, Louis XIV assumed absolute power, whereas in England, Charles I was arrested and executed for disregarding parliament, and although the English monarchy was restored, its powers were drastically curbed.

The union of Spain and Portugal was ended in 1640 when the native House of Braganza led a nationalist revolt. The relief of the siege of the frontier town of Elvas during the War of Independence is depicted in a Portuguese tile painting *(above)*.

As one of the leading generals of the parliamentary army, Oliver Cromwell *(left)* played a decisive role in the English Civil War. After the execution of Charles I, he quelled the Royalists in Scotland and Ireland. Dissolving the 'Rump' Parliament, he became Lord Protector of the Commonwealth.

Sweden, Russia, and the Baltic

The 17th century witnessed the phenomenal growth of Sweden as an imperial power: by defeating regional rivals Denmark, Poland and Russia, it had, by 1648 established a Baltic empire, the high point of which was reached during the reign of Charles X (1654–60). Lacking indigenous resources, however, Sweden's strength rested on its control of strategic harbours and customs points along the Baltic shore. Defence of these positions forced Sweden into a series of costly wars from 1655. After the Great Northern War, much of the empire was lost to the rising powers of Russia, Prussia and Hanover.

Founded in 1703 by Peter the Great, St. Petersburg was modelled on European cities, its classical architecture and orderly street grid symbolizing the Tsar's westernizing policies.

Habsburg–Ottoman conflict 1663–1718

In 1683 the Ottomans began their greatest onslaught on the Habsburg Empire by besieging Vienna with a huge army. Poland and the Papacy joined the German princes in an international relief effort which ended in Ottoman defeat.

In the mid-17th century, the Ottoman Empire resumed its expansion into southeastern Europe. Austrian attempts to challenge the Ottomans' control of Transylvania led to full-scale war in 1663. The Turkish advance on Vienna in 1664 was halted, but in 1683 the Turks besieged the city. The siege failed, and by 1687 the war had become a Habsburg war of conquest. The acquisition of Transylvania and Turkish Hungary transformed Austria into a great European power and loosened its traditional ties to the Holy Roman Empire.

The French state under Louis XIV, 1660–1715

Under Louis XIV, France pursued an expansionist, anti-Spanish policy. The expense of maintaining a large army and building a ring of frontier fortresses was met by administrative reforms, and tax-collection in the provinces was overseen by royal officials *(intendants)*. In 1667–68 Louis' armies secured parts of the Spanish Netherlands. Although this provoked international opposition to French aggression, further gains were made in the Dutch War (1672–79). The occupation of various territories in 1679–84 (known as the *Réunions*) rationalized France's eastern frontier, but after defeat in the Nine Years' War (1688–97), most of these had to be given up. The War of the Spanish Succession (1701–14) brought France no further gains.

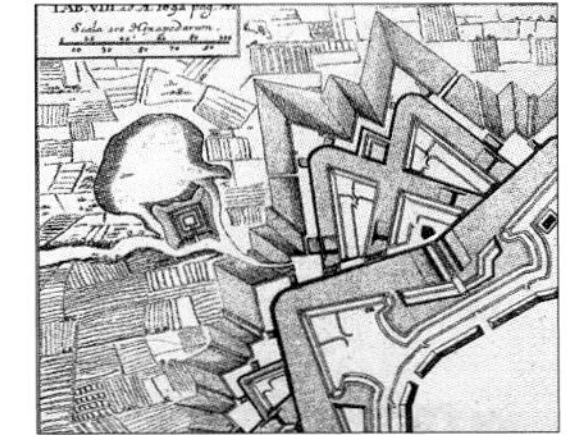

A ring of defensive fortresses was built by Vauban, a great military engineer, to secure French territory.

During his long reign, Louis XIV *(left)* established France as cultural and political leader of Europe.

The growth of France under Louis XIV

1667–68: France acquires parts of Flanders from Spain

1679–84: *Réunions*: annexation of territory west of the Rhine

1701–14: War of the Spanish Succession

1660 · 1680 · 1700 · 1720

1661: Louis XIV assumes personal rule

1672–79: Dutch War brings significant territorial gains

1688–97: Nine Years' War: Peace of Ryswick (Rijswijk) partially reverses the *Réunions*

1715: Death of Louis XIV

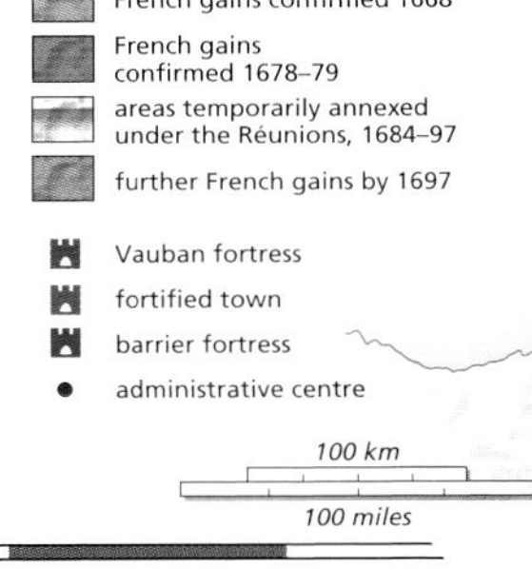

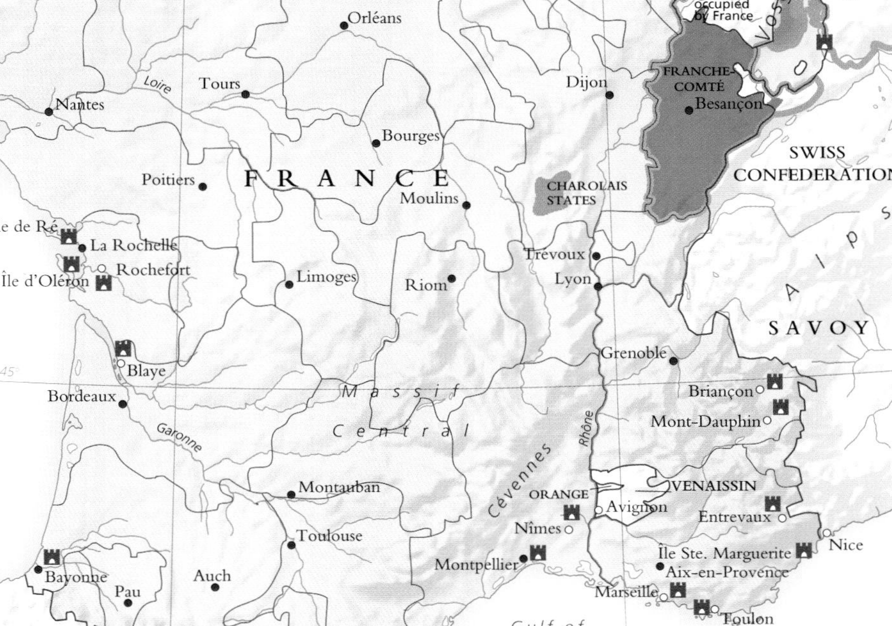

THE AGE OF ENLIGHTENMENT

Catherine the Great ruled the Russian Empire as an enlightened despot from 1762 to 1796.

THE 18TH CENTURY was a period of relative stability, when well-established monarchies ruled most of Europe and almost all the land was controlled by the nobility or the state. The Russian Empire and Prussia became leading powers. The rest of Germany remained a jigsaw of small states, as did Italy, while Poland was swallowed up by its powerful neighbours. Improved methods of cultivation fed Europe's escalating populations; towns and cities increased in size and number; trade and industry expanded to reach global markets; philosophy, science, and the arts flourished. Intellectual curiosity encouraged the radical political theories of the 'Enlightenment', but alarmed reaction set in when the flag of liberty was raised in France in the last decade of the century. Though ultimately unsuccessful, the French Revolution would inspire many social and political reforms in the 19th century.

Cities and economic life 1700–1800

Despite the beginnings of industrialization in the 18th century, principally in textile production, in 1800 four out of five Europeans still depended on agriculture for their livelihood. The growing population – largely due to a fall in the death rate as a result of better health and hygiene – led to a rapid increase in the size of cities; in 1700 Europe had ten cities with over 100,000 inhabitants; by 1800 there were 17. At the same time, farmers adopted a more scientific approach to agriculture, introducing new, more productive crops and livestock. A general improvement in transport by sea, road, river, and canal greatly stimulated trade throughout Europe and, as colonialism developed, with the rest of the world.

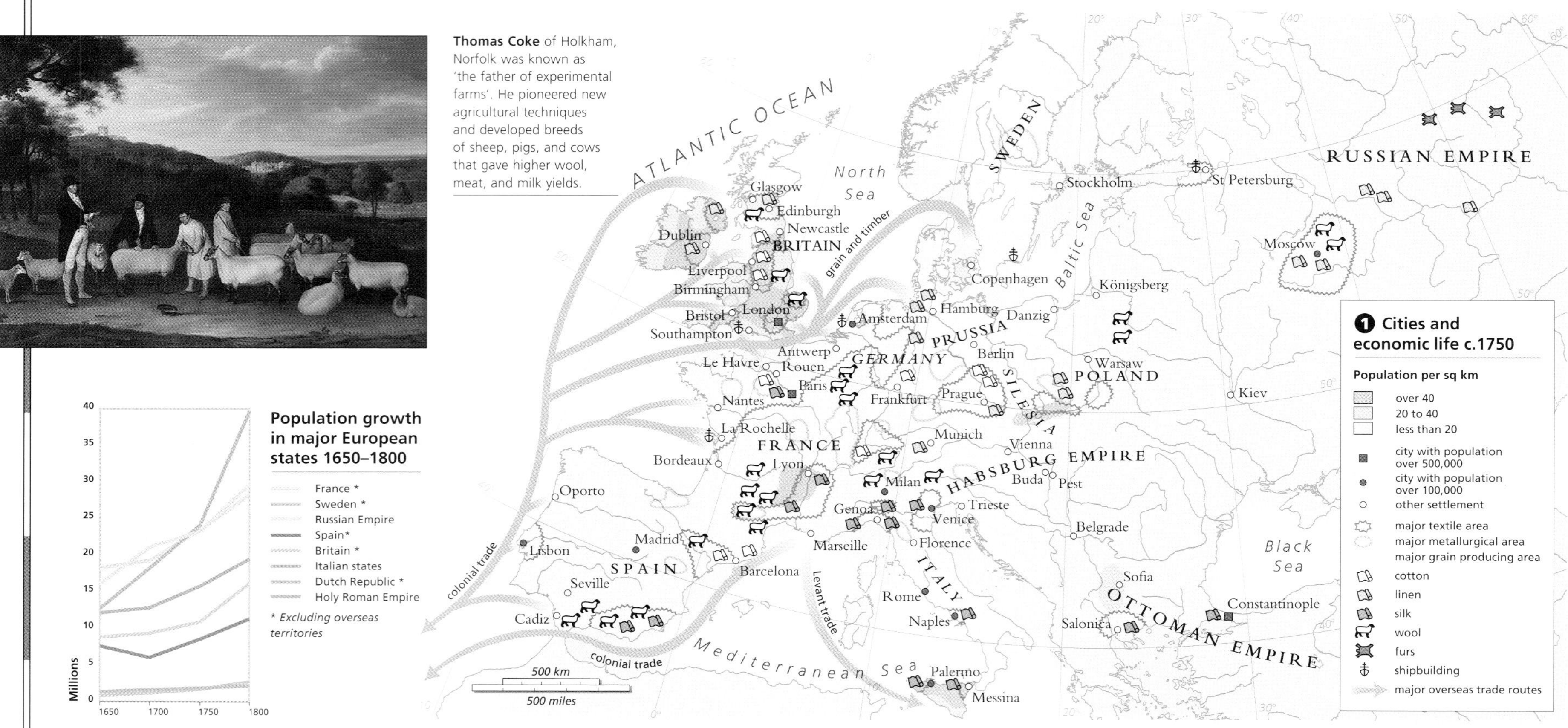

Thomas Coke of Holkham, Norfolk was known as 'the father of experimental farms'. He pioneered new agricultural techniques and developed breeds of sheep, pigs, and cows that gave higher wool, meat, and milk yields.

The partitions of Poland

17th-century Poland was one of Europe's largest states, but suffered frequent territorial losses to its neighbours, especially Russia. The elective monarchy allowed foreign powers to interfere in Polish affairs, and in the late 18th century the Russians, the Habsburgs, and Prussia settled their differences at Poland's expense in three partitions which removed the country from the map.

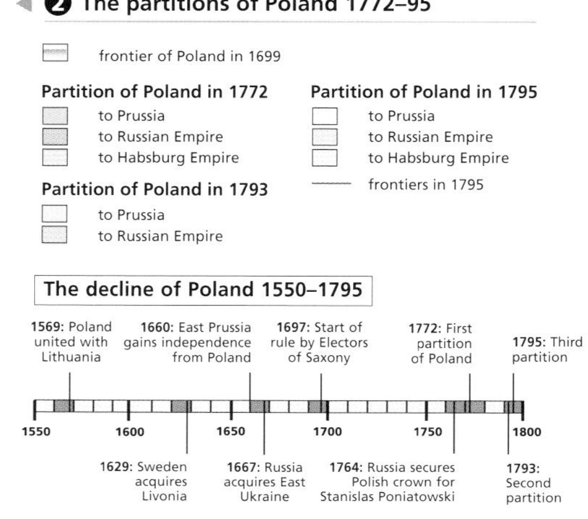

THE ENLIGHTENMENT

The 18th-century 'enlightened' writers, or *philosophes*, such as Voltaire and Diderot, appealed to human reason to challenge traditional assumptions about the Church, state, monarchy, education, and social institutions. 'Man is born free, but everywhere he is in chains', wrote Jean-Jacques Rousseau in his *Social Contract* (1762), in which he sought to show how a democratic society could work.

Voltaire (1694–1778) used poetry, drama, and satire to express his political views, including his opposition to the Catholic church. His radicalism often led to periods of exile from his native France.

Published in 28 volumes from 1751–72, the *Encyclopédie* spread the philosophic and scientific ideas of the Enlightenment. It gave a comprehensive account of contemporary institutions and technologies, while fine engravings illustrated the work of all kinds of craftsmen, such as the instrument makers above.

The rise of Brandenburg Prussia

After the Peace of Westphalia in 1648, Germany consisted of some 300 small principalities, some Catholic, some Protestant. By the end of the 17th century Brandenburg was the dominant Protestant state. Frederick William (the 'Great Elector') gained full sovereignty in Prussia and created a powerful state with a huge standing army. With the accession of Frederick II (the 'Great') in 1740, expansion continued, including the acquisition of Silesia from the Habsburg Empire. With additional territory from the partitions of Poland, by the end of the century Prussia had become one of Europe's Great Powers.

3 The rise of Brandenburg Prussia 1648–1795

- Brandenburg in 1648
- acquisitions 1648–1707
- area held 1713–42
- acquisitions 1715–20
- acquisitions by Frederick the Great 1740–86
- temporary acquisitions by Frederick the Great 1740–86
- acquisitions from Poland 1793
- acquisitions from Poland 1795
- Habsburg possessions in 1795
- frontier of Holy Roman Empire, 1789

These splendidly uniformed cavalry officers are representative of the highly-disciplined and efficient army which, by 1763, enabled Prussia to emerge as the dominant military force in 18th-century Europe.

The growth of Prussia in the 18th century

- **1713:** Accession of Frederick William I, King of Prussia
- **1713:** Treaty of Utrecht: Prussia gains Upper Gelderland and Neuchâtel
- **1715:** Prussia takes Stralsund in Great Northern War against Sweden
- **1720:** Treaty of Stockholm gives part of Western Pomerania to Prussia
- **1740:** Accession of Frederick II (the 'Great')
- **1740–48:** War of the Austrian Succession
- **1742:** Frederick completes rapid conquest of Silesia
- **1756–63:** Seven Years' War: Prussia faces coalition of Austria, Russia, and France
- **1760:** Austrian and Russian troops occupy Berlin, but Prussia survives
- **1763:** Treaty of Hubertusburg allows Prussia to keep Silesia
- **1772:** First partition of Poland; Prussian lands in the east now linked to Brandenburg
- **1786:** Death of Frederick the Great
- **1793:** Second partition of Poland
- **1795:** Third partition of Poland

The French Revolution 1789–95

In May 1789, a political crisis forced Louis XVI to summon the Estates-General, a parliament of nobles, clergy, and commoners. The third estate (the commoners) demanded reform and declared itself a National Assembly. Noble and clerical privileges were abolished; provincial uprisings were directed against landowners, many of whom fled into exile. In 1792 the Revolution gathered momentum: Louis was imprisoned, the monarchy abolished, and France declared a republic. Mass conscription was introduced to meet the threat of invasion by Austria and Prussia and the king was executed. Power shifted to the radical Jacobins, who ruled by means of 'the Terror', executing all 'enemies of the people'. Many regions opposed these excesses, notably the Vendée in the west, but resistance was crushed. In 1794 the Jacobins shared the fate of their victims. France, however, had been saved from invasion and there followed a period of moderate rule – the Directory.

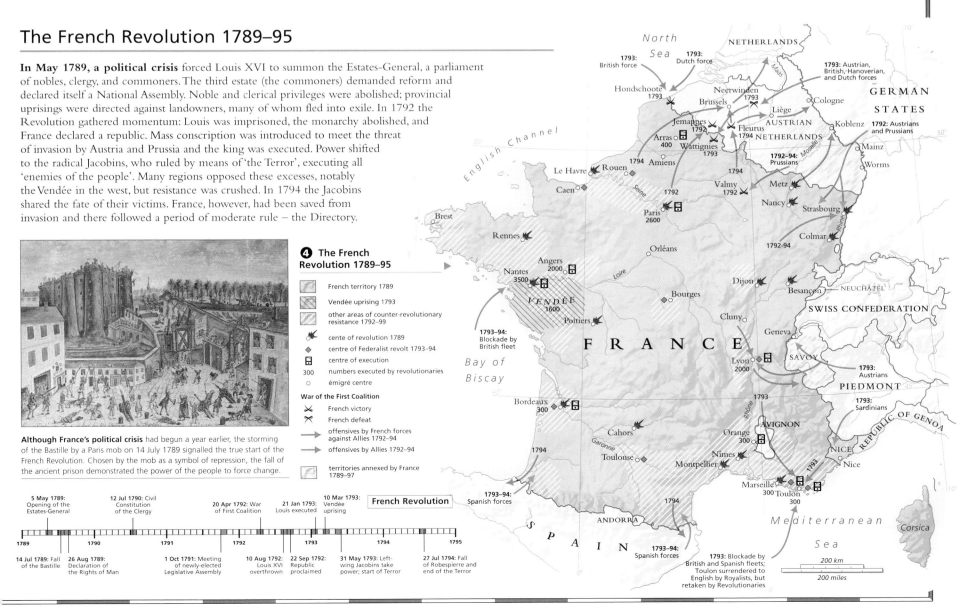

Although France's political crisis had begun a year earlier, the storming of the Bastille by a Paris mob on 14 July 1789 signalled the true start of the French Revolution. Chosen by the mob as a symbol of repression, the fall of the ancient prison demonstrated the power of the people to force change.

4 The French Revolution 1789–95

- French territory 1789
- Vendée uprising 1793
- other areas of counter-revolutionary resistance 1792–99
- cente of revolution 1789
- centre of Federalist revolt 1793–94
- centre of execution
- 300 numbers executed by revolutionaries
- émigré centre

War of the First Coalition

- French victory
- French defeat
- offensives by French forces against Allies 1792–94
- offensives by Allies 1792–94
- territories annexed by France 1789–97

French Revolution

- **5 May 1789:** Opening of the Estates-General
- **14 Jul 1789:** Fall of the Bastille
- **26 Aug 1789:** Declaration of the Rights of Man
- **12 Jul 1790:** Civil Constitution of the Clergy
- **1 Oct 1791:** Meeting of newly-elected Legislative Assembly
- **20 Apr 1792:** War of First Coalition
- **10 Aug 1792:** Louis XVI overthrown
- **22 Sep 1792:** Republic proclaimed
- **21 Jan 1793:** Louis executed
- **10 Mar 1793:** Vendée uprising
- **31 May 1793:** Left-wing Jacobins take power; start of Terror
- **27 Jul 1794:** Fall of Robespierre and end of the Terror

NAPOLEONIC EUROPE

THE BRILLIANT REVOLUTIONARY GENERAL, Napoleon Bonaparte, returned from his Egyptian campaign in 1799 to stage a *coup d'état* which made him ruler of France as First Consul. During the Consulate he began reforms of the administration, the legal system, the Church, and education. In 1804, just over ten years after revolutionaries had executed Louis XVI, Napoleon took the title of emperor and began to create a dynasty, members of his family being given the crowns of conquered states. His imperial ambitions were ultimately thwarted by Britain: its navy was used to blockade France and overrun French colonies, while a series of alliances completed an encirclement that contained and gradually reduced Napoleon's empire.

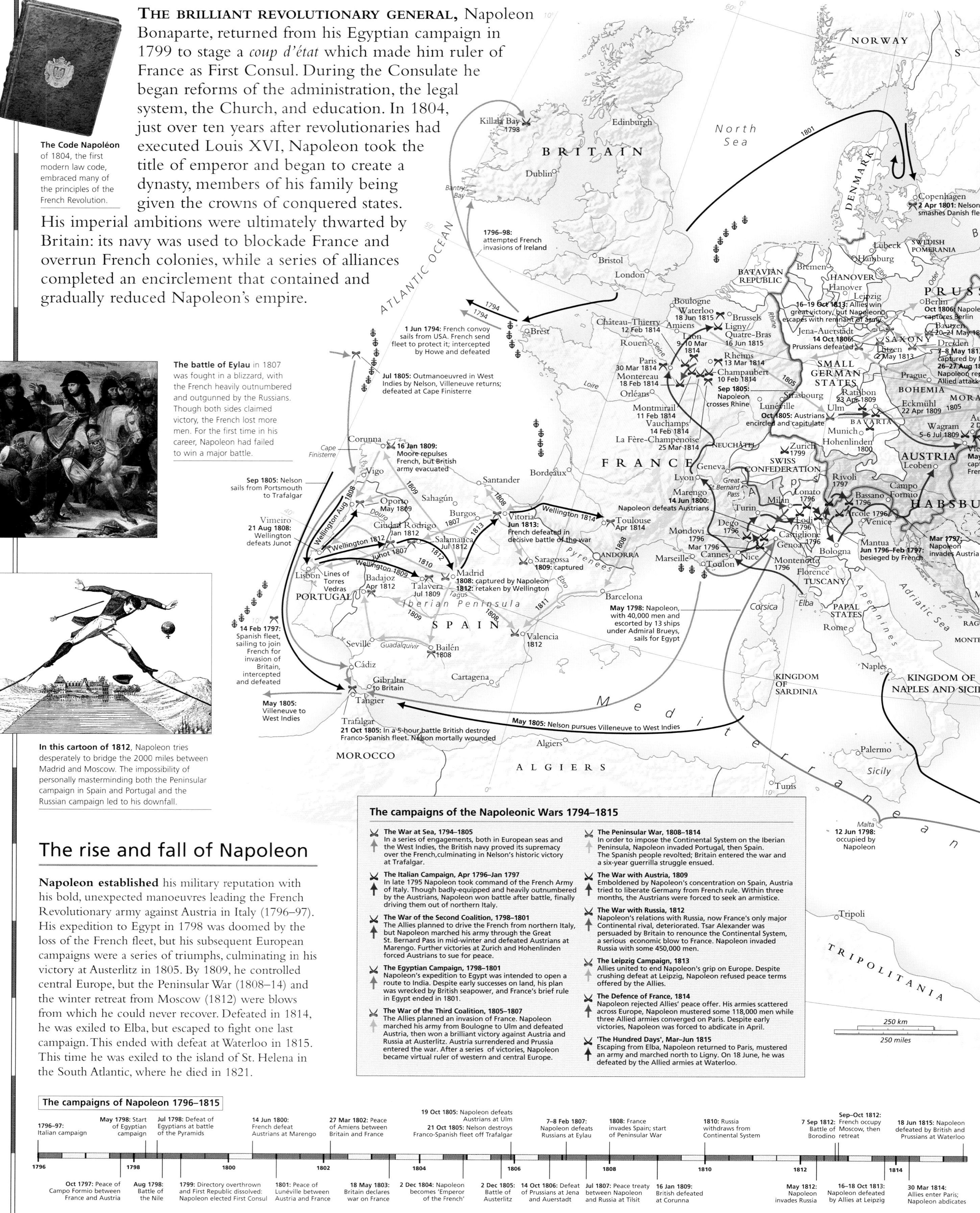

The Code Napoléon of 1804, the first modern law code, embraced many of the principles of the French Revolution.

The battle of Eylau in 1807 was fought in a blizzard, with the French heavily outnumbered and outgunned by the Russians. Though both sides claimed victory, the French lost more men. For the first time in his career, Napoleon had failed to win a major battle.

In this cartoon of 1812, Napoleon tries desperately to bridge the 2000 miles between Madrid and Moscow. The impossibility of personally masterminding both the Peninsular campaign in Spain and Portugal and the Russian campaign led to his downfall.

The campaigns of the Napoleonic Wars 1794–1815

The War at Sea, 1794–1805
In a series of engagements, both in European seas and the West Indies, the British navy proved its supremacy over the French, culminating in Nelson's historic victory at Trafalgar.

The Italian Campaign, Apr 1796–Jan 1797
In late 1795 Napoleon took command of the French Army of Italy. Though badly-equipped and heavily outnumbered by the Austrians, Napoleon won battle after battle, finally driving them out of northern Italy.

The War of the Second Coalition, 1798–1801
The Allies planned to drive the French from northern Italy, but Napoleon marched his army through the Great St. Bernard Pass in mid-winter and defeated Austrians at Marengo. Further victories at Zurich and Hohenlinden forced Austrians to sue for peace.

The Egyptian Campaign, 1798–1801
Napoleon's expedition to Egypt was intended to open a route to India. Despite early successes on land, his plan was wrecked by British seapower, and France's brief rule in Egypt ended in 1801.

The War of the Third Coalition, 1805–1807
The Allies planned an invasion of France. Napoleon marched his army from Boulogne to Ulm and defeated Austria, then won a brilliant victory against Austria and Russia at Austerlitz. Austria surrendered and Prussia entered the war. After a series of victories, Napoleon became virtual ruler of western and central Europe.

The Peninsular War, 1808–1814
In order to impose the Continental System on the Iberian Peninsula, Napoleon invaded Portugal, then Spain. The Spanish people revolted; Britain entered the war and a six-year guerrilla struggle ensued.

The War with Austria, 1809
Emboldened by Napoleon's concentration on Spain, Austria tried to liberate Germany from French rule. Within three months, the Austrians were forced to seek an armistice.

The War with Russia, 1812
Napoleon's relations with Russia, now France's only major Continental rival, deteriorated. Tsar Alexander was persuaded by Britain to renounce the Continental System, a serious economic blow to France. Napoleon invaded Russia with some 450,000 men.

The Leipzig Campaign, 1813
Allies united to end Napoleon's grip on Europe. Despite crushing defeat at Leipzig, Napoleon refused peace terms offered by the Allies.

The Defence of France, 1814
Napoleon rejected Allies' peace offer. His armies scattered across Europe, Napoleon mustered some 118,000 men while three Allied armies converged on Paris. Despite early victories, Napoleon was forced to abdicate in April.

'The Hundred Days', Mar–Jun 1815
Escaping from Elba, Napoleon returned to Paris, mustered an army and marched north to Ligny. On 18 June, he was defeated by the Allied armies at Waterloo.

The rise and fall of Napoleon

Napoleon established his military reputation with his bold, unexpected manoeuvres leading the French Revolutionary army against Austria in Italy (1796–97). His expedition to Egypt in 1798 was doomed by the loss of the French fleet, but his subsequent European campaigns were a series of triumphs, culminating in his victory at Austerlitz in 1805. By 1809, he controlled central Europe, but the Peninsular War (1808–14) and the winter retreat from Moscow (1812) were blows from which he could never recover. Defeated in 1814, he was exiled to Elba, but escaped to fight one last campaign. This ended with defeat at Waterloo in 1815. This time he was exiled to the island of St. Helena in the South Atlantic, where he died in 1821.

The campaigns of Napoleon 1796–1815

- **1796–97:** Italian campaign
- **Oct 1797:** Peace of Campo Formio between France and Austria
- **May 1798:** Start of Egyptian campaign
- **Jul 1798:** Defeat of Egyptians at battle of the Pyramids
- **Aug 1798:** Battle of the Nile
- **1799:** Directory overthrown and First Republic dissolved: Napoleon elected First Consul
- **14 Jun 1800:** French defeat Austrians at Marengo
- **1801:** Peace of Lunéville between Austria and France
- **27 Mar 1802:** Peace of Amiens between Britain and France
- **18 May 1803:** Britain declares war on France
- **2 Dec 1804:** Napoleon becomes 'Emperor of the French'
- **19 Oct 1805:** Napoleon defeats Austrians at Ulm
- **21 Oct 1805:** Nelson destroys Franco-Spanish fleet off Trafalgar
- **2 Dec 1805:** Battle of Austerlitz
- **14 Oct 1806:** Defeat of Prussians at Jena and Auerstadt
- **7–8 Feb 1807:** Napoleon defeats Russians at Eylau
- **Jul 1807:** Peace treaty between Napoleon and Russia at Tilsit
- **1808:** France invades Spain; start of Peninsular War
- **16 Jan 1809:** British defeated at Corunna
- **1810:** Russia withdraws from Continental System
- **May 1812:** Napoleon invades Russia
- **7 Sep 1812:** Battle of Borodino
- **Sep–Oct 1812:** French occupy Moscow, then retreat
- **16–18 Oct 1813:** Napoleon defeated by Allies at Leipzig
- **30 Mar 1814:** Allies enter Paris; Napoleon abdicates
- **18 Jun 1815:** Napoleon defeated by British and Prussians at Waterloo

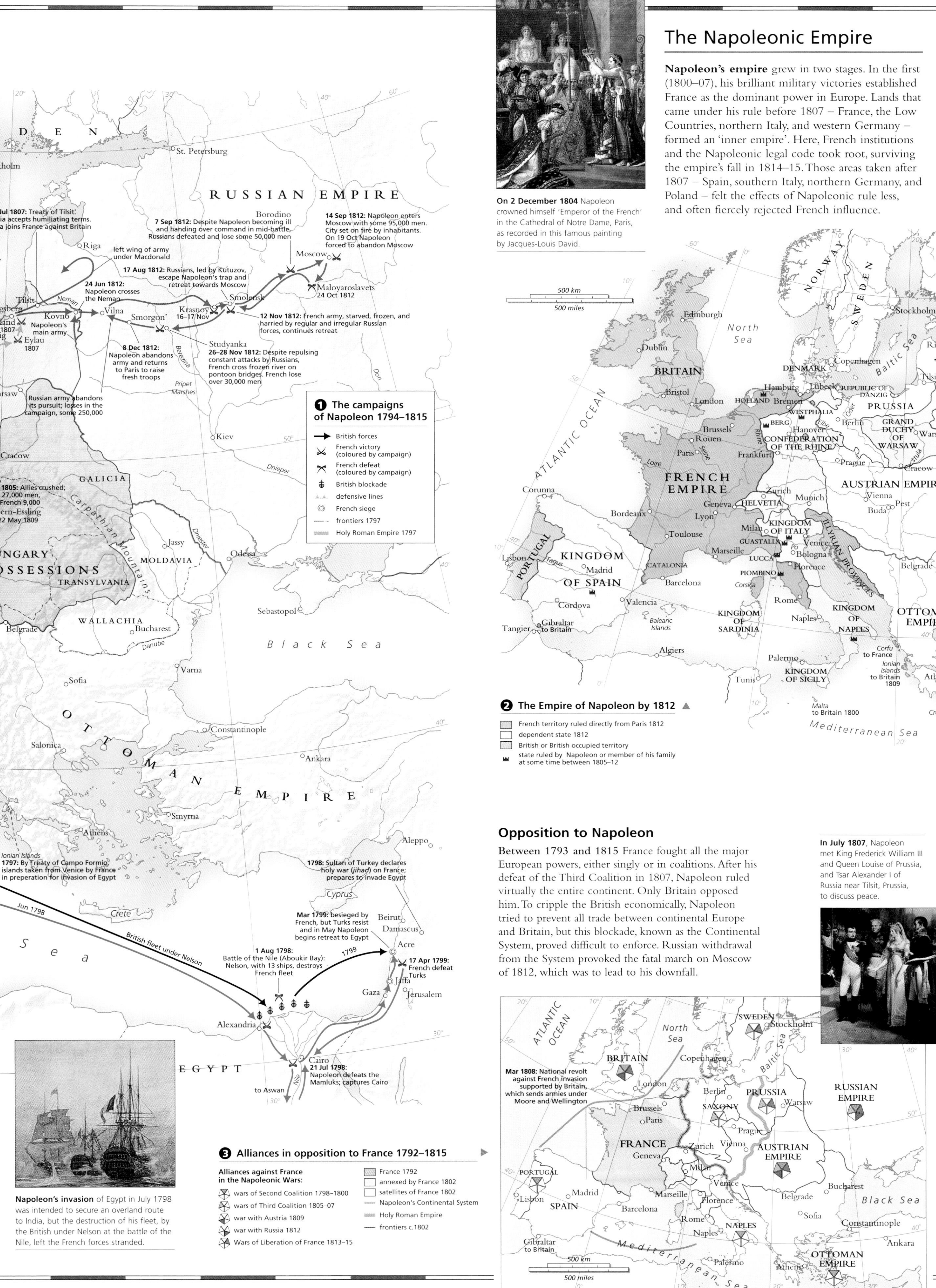
RUSSIAN EMPIRE
St. Petersburg
Riga
Moscow
Borodino
Smolensk
Krasnoy 16–17 Nov
Smorgon'
Vilna
Kovno
Tilsit
Eylau 1807
Studyanka
Maloyaroslavets 24 Oct 1812
Jul 1807: Treaty of Tilsit: ...sia accepts humiliating terms. ...sia joins France against Britain
7 Sep 1812: Despite Napoleon becoming ill and handing over command in mid-battle, Russians defeated and lose some 50,000 men
14 Sep 1812: Napoleon enters Moscow with some 95,000 men. City set on fire by inhabitants. On 19 Oct Napoleon forced to abandon Moscow
left wing of army under Macdonald
17 Aug 1812: Russians, led by Kutuzov, escape Napoleon's trap and retreat towards Moscow
24 Jun 1812: Napoleon crosses the Neman
Napoleon's main army
12 Nov 1812: French army, starved, frozen, and harried by regular and irregular Russian forces, continues retreat
8 Dec 1812: Napoleon abandons army and returns to Paris to raise fresh troops
26–28 Nov 1812: Despite repulsing constant attacks by Russians, French cross frozen river on pontoon bridges. French lose over 30,000 men
Russian army abandons its pursuit; losses in the campaign, some 250,000
Pripet Marshes
Kiev
Cracow
GALICIA
Carpathian Mountains
TRANSYLVANIA
MOLDAVIA
WALLACHIA
Jassy
Odessa
Bucharest
Belgrade
Sebastopol
Black Sea
Varna
Sofia
Constantinople
Salonica
Ankara
Smyrna
Athens
OTTOMAN EMPIRE
1797: By Treaty of Campo Formio, islands taken from Venice by France in preperation for invasion of Egypt
1798: Sultan of Turkey declares holy war (jihad) on France; prepares to invade Egypt
Aleppo
Cyprus
Crete
Mar 1799: besieged by French, but Turks resist and in May Napoleon begins retreat to Egypt
Beirut
Damascus
Acre
17 Apr 1799: French defeat Turks
Jaffa
Jerusalem
Gaza
1 Aug 1798: Battle of the Nile (Aboukir Bay): Nelson, with 13 ships, destroys French fleet
Jun 1798
British fleet under Nelson
Alexandria
Cairo
21 Jul 1798: Napoleon defeats the Mamluks; captures Cairo
to Aswan
EGYPT
Sea

1 The campaigns of Napoleon 1794–1815

- British forces
- French victory (coloured by campaign)
- French defeat (coloured by campaign)
- British blockade
- defensive lines
- French siege
- frontiers 1797
- Holy Roman Empire 1797

The Napoleonic Empire

Napoleon's empire grew in two stages. In the first (1800–07), his brilliant military victories established France as the dominant power in Europe. Lands that came under his rule before 1807 – France, the Low Countries, northern Italy, and western Germany – formed an 'inner empire'. Here, French institutions and the Napoleonic legal code took root, surviving the empire's fall in 1814–15. Those areas taken after 1807 – Spain, southern Italy, northern Germany, and Poland – felt the effects of Napoleonic rule less, and often fiercely rejected French influence.

On 2 December 1804 Napoleon crowned himself 'Emperor of the French' in the Cathedral of Notre Dame, Paris, as recorded in this famous painting by Jacques-Louis David.

FRENCH EMPIRE
BRITAIN
North Sea
ATLANTIC OCEAN
NORWAY
SWEDEN
DENMARK
HOLLAND
WESTPHALIA
BERG
CONFEDERATION OF THE RHINE
REPUBLIC OF DANZIG
PRUSSIA
GRAND DUCHY OF WARSAW
RUSSIAN EMPIRE
AUSTRIAN EMPIRE
HELVETIA
KINGDOM OF ITALY
GUASTALLA
LUCCA
PIOMBINO
ILLYRIAN PROVINCES
KINGDOM OF SPAIN
PORTUGAL
CATALONIA
KINGDOM OF SARDINIA
KINGDOM OF NAPLES
KINGDOM OF SICILY
OTTOMAN EMPIRE
Gibraltar to Britain
Corfu to France
Ionian Islands to Britain 1809
Malta to Britain 1800
Mediterranean Sea

2 The Empire of Napoleon by 1812

- French territory ruled directly from Paris 1812
- dependent state 1812
- British or British occupied territory
- state ruled by Napoleon or member of his family at some time between 1805–12

Opposition to Napoleon

Between 1793 and 1815 France fought all the major European powers, either singly or in coalitions. After his defeat of the Third Coalition in 1807, Napoleon ruled virtually the entire continent. Only Britain opposed him. To cripple the British economically, Napoleon tried to prevent all trade between continental Europe and Britain, but this blockade, known as the Continental System, proved difficult to enforce. Russian withdrawal from the System provoked the fatal march on Moscow of 1812, which was to lead to his downfall.

In July 1807, Napoleon met King Frederick William III and Queen Louise of Prussia, and Tsar Alexander I of Russia near Tilsit, Prussia, to discuss peace.

Napoleon's invasion of Egypt in July 1798 was intended to secure an overland route to India, but the destruction of his fleet, by the British under Nelson at the battle of the Nile, left the French forces stranded.

Mar 1808: National revolt against French invasion supported by Britain, which sends armies under Moore and Wellington
SWEDEN
BRITAIN
PRUSSIA
SAXONY
RUSSIAN EMPIRE
FRANCE
AUSTRIAN EMPIRE
PORTUGAL
SPAIN
NAPLES
OTTOMAN EMPIRE
Black Sea
Mediterranean Sea

3 Alliances in opposition to France 1792–1815

Alliances against France in the Napoleonic Wars:

- wars of Second Coalition 1798–1800
- wars of Third Coalition 1805–07
- war with Austria 1809
- war with Russia 1812
- Wars of Liberation of France 1813–15

- France 1792
- annexed by France 1802
- satellites of France 1802
- Napoleon's Continental System
- Holy Roman Empire
- frontiers c.1802

THE GROWTH OF NATIONALISM

Otto von Bismarck, prime minister of Prussia 1862–1890, was chief architect of the unification of Germany.

TO RESTORE PEACE and stability after the turmoil of the Napoleonic Wars, the Congress of Vienna was convened in 1814. Attended by all the major European powers, but dominated by Austria, Britain, Russia, and Prussia, the Congress redrew the political map of Europe and restored many former ruling houses. The result was three decades of reactionary rule, during which nationalist and republican movements, inspired by the American and French models, challenged the status quo. In eastern Europe, Greece and the Balkan states took advantage of the weakness of the Ottoman Empire to gain independence. In the west, Italy and Germany finally achieved their dreams of unification. But traditional rivalry between royal houses was now replaced by rivalry between industrialized nation states – a rivalry which led, ultimately, to the First World War.

Europe under the Vienna system

The Congress of Vienna met to share out the spoils of victory over Napoleon, though painful compromise was required to achieve a workable balance of power in Europe. Political stability was re-established by restoring the hereditary monarchs overthrown by Napoleon. France, though deprived of all her conquests, once more had a Bourbon on the throne. But the restored monarchs ruled with too heavy a hand: liberal, republican, and nationalist revolts began to break out, reaching a crescendo in 1848 when the governments of France, Italy, and Austria were all shaken by insurrection.

The Congress of Vienna was attended by five monarchs and the heads of 216 princely families. It was dominated by the Austrian chancellor, Prince Metternich, seen here standing on the left at the signing of the final settlement.

Threats to the Vienna system 1814–50

- **1806:** Abolition of Holy Roman Empire
- **1814:** Napoleon abdicates; opening of Congress of Vienna
- **1815:** Napoleon escapes from exile, but is defeated at Waterloo; restoration of French monarchy
- **1820–23:** Revolts in Spain, Portugal, Naples, Sicily, Piedmont, and the Balkans
- **1821:** Start of Greek War of Independence which lasts until 1833
- **1830:** Revolution in Paris
- **1830–31:** Belgian War of Independence
- **1833–39:** First Carlist War in Spain
- **1848:** Second Republic in France with Louis-Napoleon as president
- **1848:** Revolutions throughout Europe

1800 1810 1820 1830 1840 1850

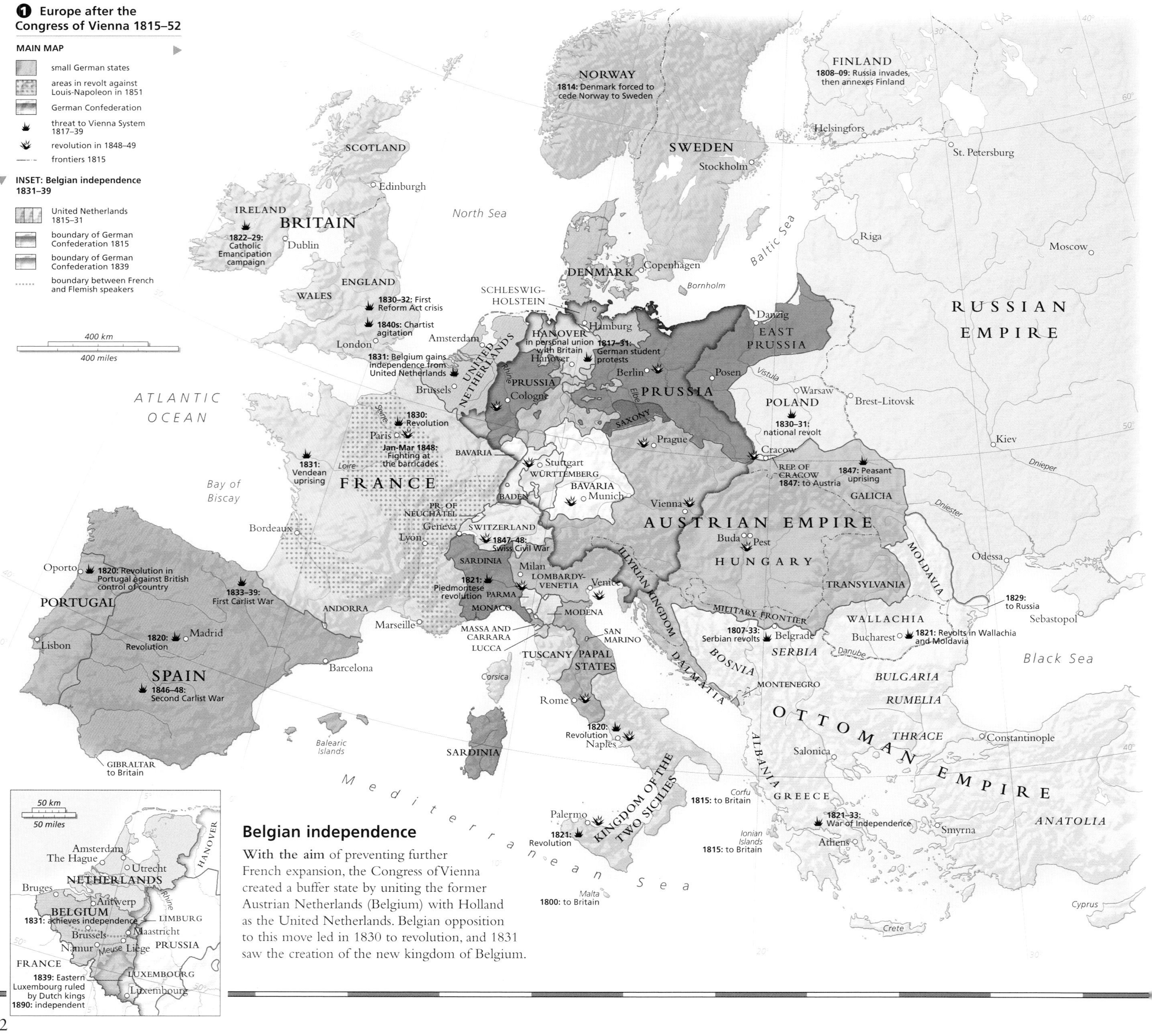

1 Europe after the Congress of Vienna 1815–52

MAIN MAP
- small German states
- areas in revolt against Louis-Napoleon in 1851
- German Confederation
- threat to Vienna System 1817–39
- revolution in 1848–49
- frontiers 1815

INSET: Belgian independence 1831–39
- United Netherlands 1815–31
- boundary of German Confederation 1815
- boundary of German Confederation 1839
- boundary between French and Flemish speakers

400 km / 400 miles

NORWAY
1814: Denmark forced to cede Norway to Sweden
FINLAND
1808–09: Russia invades, then annexes Finland
SWEDEN
IRELAND
1822–29: Catholic Emancipation campaign
BRITAIN
1830–32: First Reform Act crisis
1840s: Chartist agitation
1831: Belgium gains independence from United Netherlands
HANOVER in personal union with Britain
1817–31: German student protests
POLAND
1830–31: national revolt
1830: Revolution
Jan–Mar 1848: Fighting at the barricades
1831: Vendean uprising
FRANCE
REP. OF CRACOW 1847: to Austria
1847: Peasant uprising
AUSTRIAN EMPIRE
RUSSIAN EMPIRE
1847–48: Swiss Civil War
1821: Piedmontese revolution
1820: Revolution in Portugal against British control of country
1833–39: First Carlist War
1820: Revolution
SPAIN
1846–48: Second Carlist War
GIBRALTAR to Britain
1829: to Russia
1821: Revolts in Wallachia and Moldavia
1807–33: Serbian revolts
1820: Revolution
1821: Revolution
1815: to Britain
1821–33: War of Independence
1815: to Britain
1800: to Britain
OTTOMAN EMPIRE

50 km / 50 miles
NETHERLANDS
BELGIUM
1831: achieves independence
FRANCE
PRUSSIA
LUXEMBOURG
1839: Eastern Luxembourg ruled by Dutch kings
1890: independent

Belgian independence

With the aim of preventing further French expansion, the Congress of Vienna created a buffer state by uniting the former Austrian Netherlands (Belgium) with Holland as the United Netherlands. Belgian opposition to this move led in 1830 to revolution, and 1831 saw the creation of the new kingdom of Belgium.

The unification of Germany

In 1815 Germany's states were reduced to a Confederation of 39, under Austrian leadership. These states were further united in 1834 by the formation of a customs union (Zollverein). In 1866 Bismarck, prime minister of Prussia, proposed a German Confederation which would exclude Austria. When Austria refused, Bismarck – bent on German unification – declared war on Austria. Following Austria's defeat, Bismarck established the North German Confederation. The German Empire, including Bavaria and other south German states, was created after Prussia's victory in the Franco-Prussian War in 1870.

Spiked helmets such as this one worn by a dragoon officer became emblems of German militarism.

In 1870, alarmed at the intentions of Prussia, Napoleon III declared war, but the French were defeated. Here, Napoleon surrenders to the Prussian king, Wilhelm I.

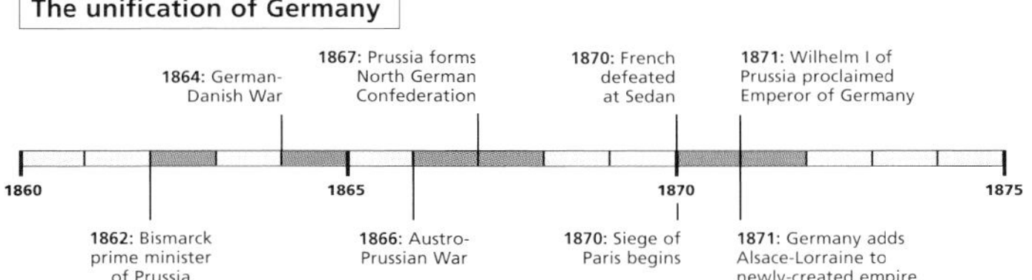

200 km
200 miles
SWEDEN
DENMARK
Baltic Sea
Copenhagen
SCHLESWIG-HOLSTEIN
Königsberg
Rostock
Hamburg
Bremen
MECKLENBURG
Elbe
POMERANIA
Danzig
EAST PRUSSIA
Amsterdam
The Hague
NETHERLANDS
HANOVER
WEST PRUSSIA
PRUSSIA
Berlin
BRANDENBURG
POSEN
Posen
Oder
RUSSIA
Warsaw
Vistula
BELGIUM
Brussels
Meuse
WESTPHALIA
Cologne
Rhine
THURINGIAN STATES
Leipzig
SAXONY
Breslau
POLAND
Moselle
Sedan 1870
Luxembourg
SILESIA
1871: Prussians besiege and occupy Paris
Prague
BOHEMIA
Sadowa 1866
Nuremberg
Karlsruhe
Stuttgart
Strassburg
BAVARIA
WÜRTTEMBERG
BADEN
HOHENZOLLERN
Munich
HUNGARY
FRANCE
Basle
ALSACE-LORRAINE
1871: Imperial territory
Danube
Vienna
SWITZERLAND
AUSTRIA
ITALY

2 The unification of Germany
- boundary of German Confederation of 1815
- Prussia in 1815
- Prussian gains by 1866
- other states in North German Confederation 1867
- other German states 1866
- Austro-Hungarian Empire 1867
- frontiers in 1866
- attack on Denmark by Austro-Prussian forces 1864
- Prussian armies in war with Austria 1866
- Prussian invasion of France in Franco-Prussian War 1870–71
- boundary of German Empire 1871

The unification of Italy

The restoration of the old order in 1815 provoked a movement to liberate and unite Italy. In 1859 Cavour, prime minister of Sardinia-Piedmont, enlisted the help of French emperor Napoleon III to drive the Austrians out of Lombardy. In 1860 Sicily and Naples were conquered by Garibaldi and his 1000 'Redshirts', then handed over to Victor Emmanuel II of Sardinia, who became king of a united Italy in 1861. Rome was finally added to the new kingdom in 1870.

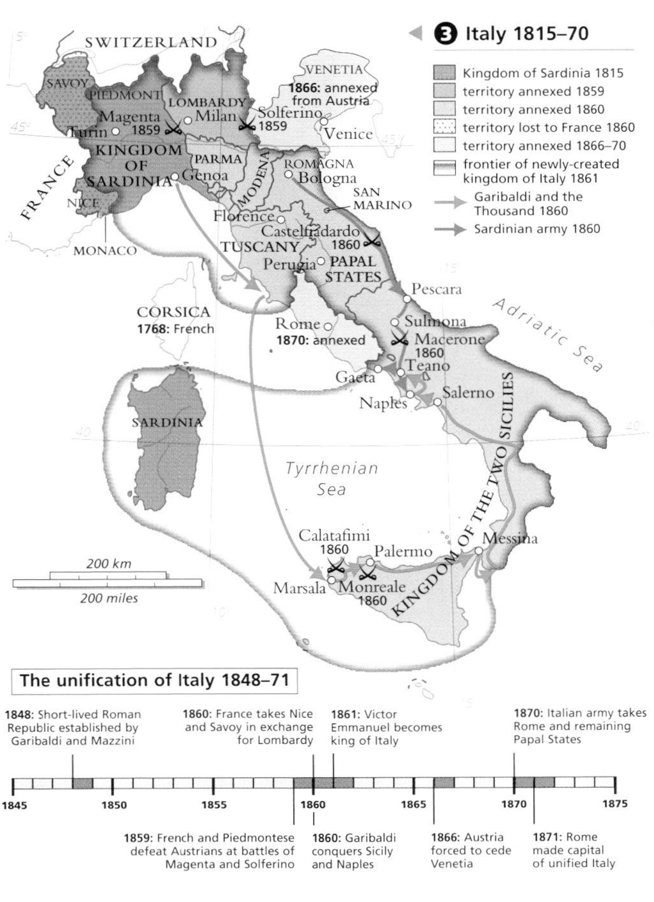

At the meeting in 1860 between Victor Emmanuel II and Garibaldi at Teano, Garibaldi – a lifelong Republican – effectively presented the king with half of Italy.

In this cartoon of 1908, Ottoman sultan, Abdul Hamid II, sulks as more Balkan territory is whipped from under his feet by Austria and Bulgaria.

Nationalism in the Balkans

Nationalism proved most volatile in the Balkans, where many subject peoples aspired to independence from the Ottomans. Initially only the Greeks were successful. Meanwhile Austria and Russia vied to replace the Turks as the dominant power in the region. Russian expansionism provoked the Crimean War in 1854, when Russia was defeated by Britain, France, Austria, and Turkey, and the Russo-Turkish War of 1877–78. At the Congress of Berlin in 1878, Turkey was forced to abandon all claims to Montenegro, Romania, and Serbia. In 1912, intent on seizing the Ottomans' last remaining European territories, Serbia, Bulgaria, and Greece were victorious in the First Balkan War. Resentment over the division of the spoils sparked a new war, from which Serbia emerged triumphant, but the precarious situation would be a major cause of the First World War.

THE INDUSTRIAL REVOLUTION

Matthew Boulton's metal works in Birmingham developed the steam engine for industrial use.

IN THE LATTER HALF of the 18th century, rapid technological, social, and economic changes began to transform Britain from an agrarian into a largely urban, industrial society. This process, which became known as the Industrial Revolution, spread to Europe in the course of the 19th century. The population of the continent doubled in this period and was fed by a similar growth in agricultural production. Changes included the use of new power sources such as coal and steam; new building materials, chiefly iron and steel; and technical innovations and improved systems of transport. These developments led to large-scale production and the growth of the factory system.

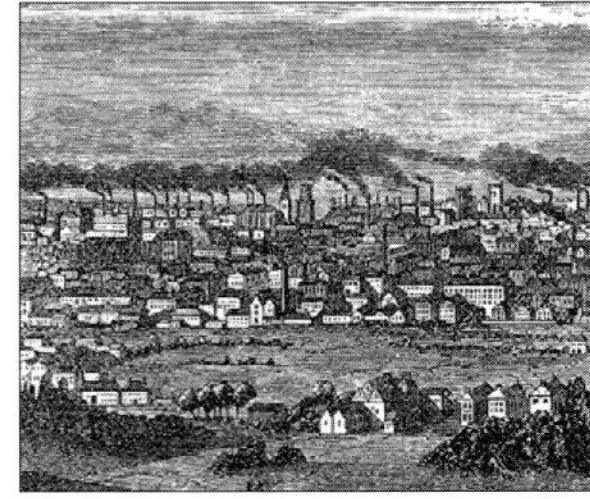

Industrial chimneys dominate the Manchester skyline in this 19th-century engraving. Industry in Britain concentrated in cities where rich coal and iron deposits were in close proximity.

The move to the towns

Urban development was inextricably linked to the process of industrialization. The most marked 19th-century urban growth occurred in areas where labour-intensive, mechanized, and often factory-based industries were emerging. Rapid urbanization first occurred in Britain, where the urban population grew from 20% of the total population in 1800, to 41% in 1850. By the 1850s, many other European countries experienced urban growth at a rate comparable with that of Britain in the first half of the century.

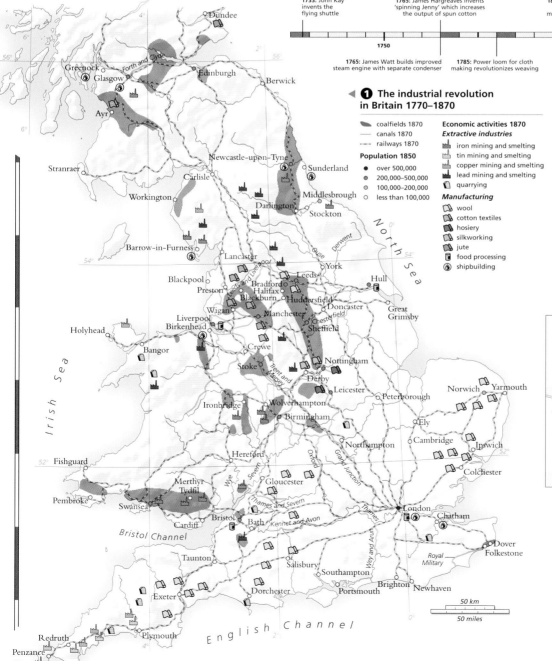

The replacement of water power with steam power greatly increased efficiency. Huge fly wheels could drive machinery, such as that used here to make cable, at greater speeds.

The Industrial Revolution in Britain

A combination of geographical, political, and social factors ensured that Britain became the first industrial nation. The country possessed a number of natural ports facing the Atlantic, an established shipping trade, and a network of internal navigable waterways. It was richly endowed with coal and iron ore and could draw on a large market both at home and overseas. British colonies supplied raw materials and custom and an expanding population ensured buoyant demand at home. The textile industry in Britain was the first to benefit from new technical innovations which brought about greater production efficiency and output.

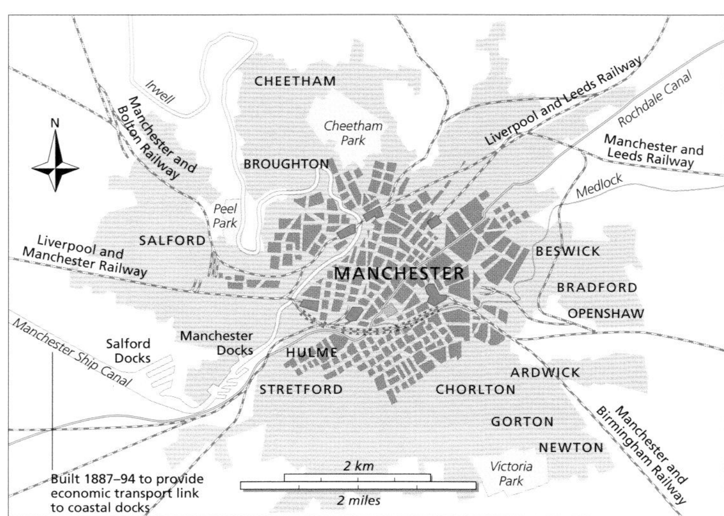

2 The growth of Manchester 1840–1900

- railway
- railway station
- Manchester South junction viaduct
- park
- built-up area 1840
- growth of city 1840–1900

The advance of British technology from 1733

- **1733:** John Kay invents the flying shuttle
- **1765:** James Hargreaves invents 'spinning Jenny' which increases the output of spun cotton
- **1765:** James Watt builds improved steam engine with separate condenser
- **1785:** Power loom for cloth making revolutionizes weaving
- **1811–12:** Luddite rioters wreck new textile machinery in Derbyshire
- **1825:** First passenger steam railway from Stockton to Darlington
- **1832:** Outbreak of cholera kills 31,000 people in Britain
- **1837:** First practical electric telegraph system produced by Cooke and Wheatstone
- **1838:** Launch of I.K. Brunel's *Great Western* steamship
- **1840:** Cheap postal system introduced; one penny per letter to anywhere in Britain
- **1842:** Lord Shaftesbury's Mines Act; underground employment of women and children prohibited

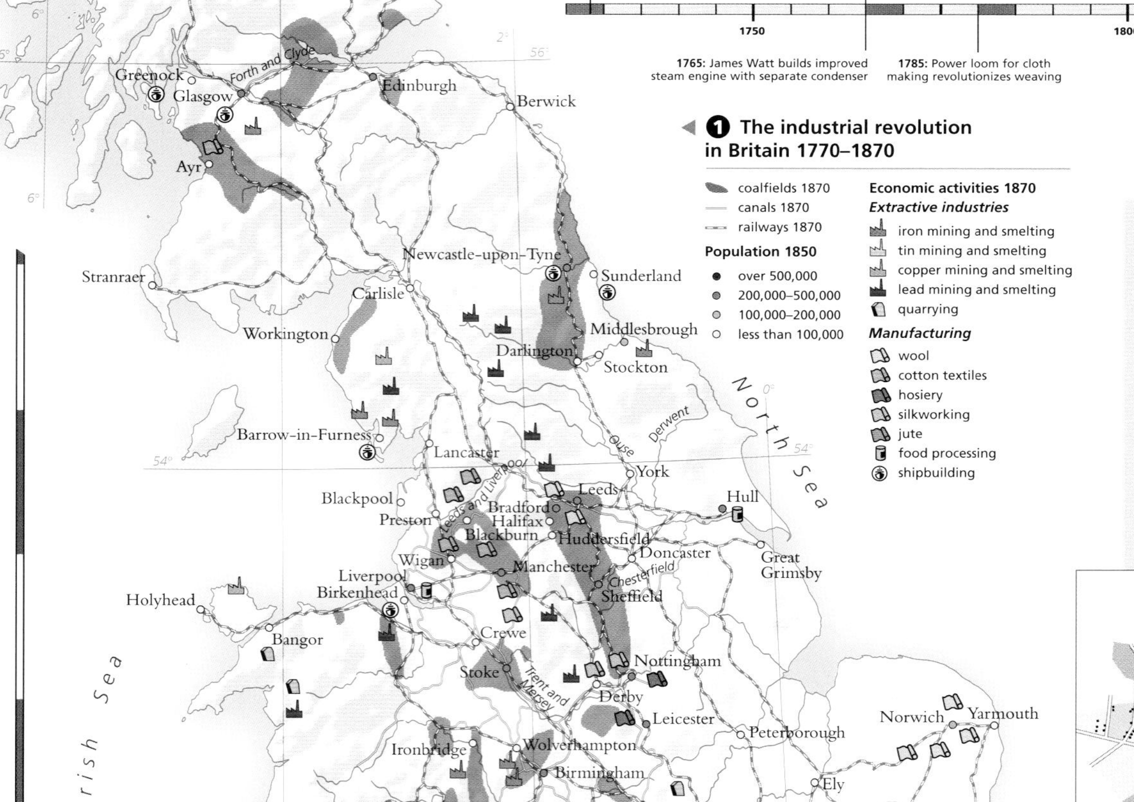

1 The industrial revolution in Britain 1770–1870

- coalfields 1870
- canals 1870
- railways 1870

Population 1850

- over 500,000
- 200,000–500,000
- 100,000–200,000
- less than 100,000

Economic activities 1870

Extractive industries

- iron mining and smelting
- tin mining and smelting
- copper mining and smelting
- lead mining and smelting
- quarrying

Manufacturing

- wool
- cotton textiles
- hosiery
- silkworking
- jute
- food processing
- shipbuilding

URBANIZATION AND PUBLIC HEALTH

From the 1850s, industrial cities in Britain began to grow faster than the infrastructure needed to support the growing populations. Poorly built workers' tenement housing became severely over-crowded, and people drank water contaminated by sewage and industrial effluent. These poor standards of living resulted in the proliferation of diseases such as cholera, smallpox, dysentery, tuberculosis, and rickets. In 1854 and 1855, cholera broke out in Newcastle, where steep banks produced a concentration of settlement in the commercial areas along the river. Families lived five to a room, without sanitation or ready access to clean water, and of the 9453 houses in the city in 1854, 8032 were without toilets. During the cholera epidemic of 1854, 1500 of the 90,000 population died of the disease in a period of five weeks.

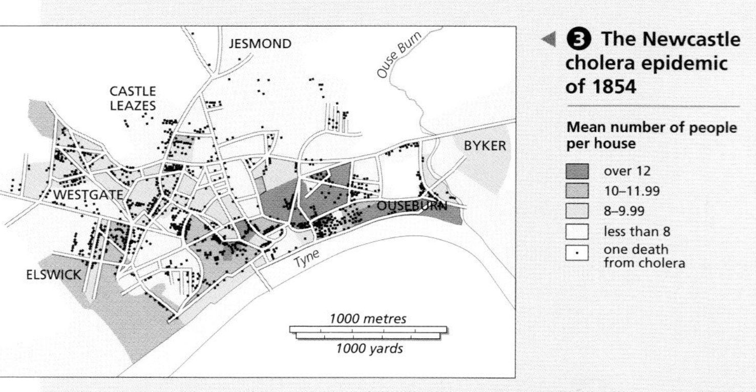

3 The Newcastle cholera epidemic of 1854

Mean number of people per house

- over 12
- 10–11.99
- 8–9.99
- less than 8
- one death from cholera

The Public Health Act of 1848 was a turning point for public health in Britain. It allowed for the formation of local Boards of Health and the appointment of medical officers. This public health poster entitled *Cholera Tramples the Victor and the Vanquish'd Both,* warned people that no class was immune from the disease.

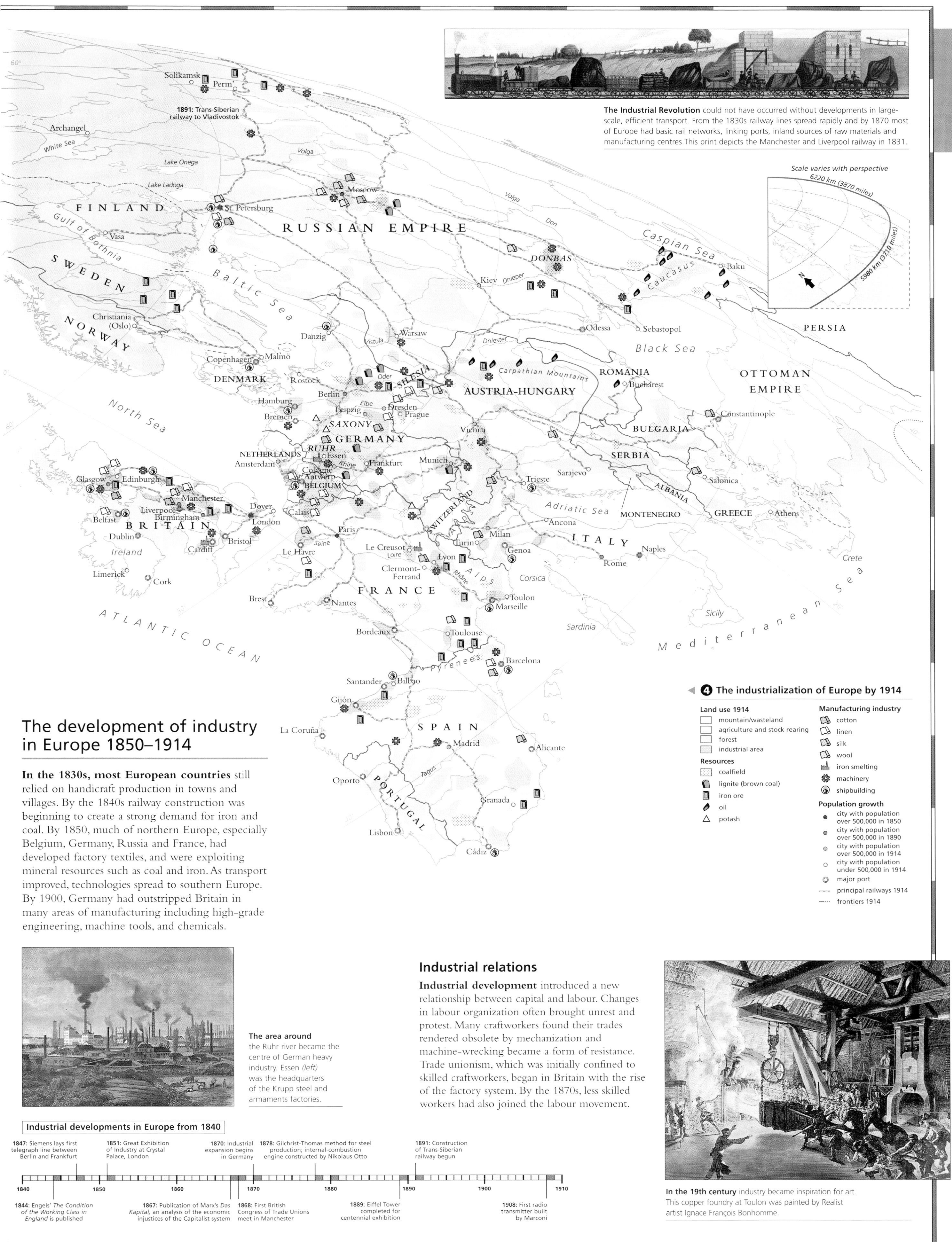

The Industrial Revolution could not have occurred without developments in large-scale, efficient transport. From the 1830s railway lines spread rapidly and by 1870 most of Europe had basic rail networks, linking ports, inland sources of raw materials and manufacturing centres. This print depicts the Manchester and Liverpool railway in 1831.

The development of industry in Europe 1850–1914

In the 1830s, most European countries still relied on handicraft production in towns and villages. By the 1840s railway construction was beginning to create a strong demand for iron and coal. By 1850, much of northern Europe, especially Belgium, Germany, Russia and France, had developed factory textiles, and were exploiting mineral resources such as coal and iron. As transport improved, technologies spread to southern Europe. By 1900, Germany had outstripped Britain in many areas of manufacturing including high-grade engineering, machine tools, and chemicals.

The area around the Ruhr river became the centre of German heavy industry. Essen *(left)* was the headquarters of the Krupp steel and armaments factories.

Industrial relations

Industrial development introduced a new relationship between capital and labour. Changes in labour organization often brought unrest and protest. Many craftworkers found their trades rendered obsolete by mechanization and machine-wrecking became a form of resistance. Trade unionism, which was initially confined to skilled craftworkers, began in Britain with the rise of the factory system. By the 1870s, less skilled workers had also joined the labour movement.

In the 19th century industry became inspiration for art. This copper foundry at Toulon was painted by Realist artist Ignace François Bonhomme.

Industrial developments in Europe from 1840

- **1844:** Engels' *The Condition of the Working Class in England* is published
- **1847:** Siemens lays first telegraph line between Berlin and Frankfurt
- **1851:** Great Exhibition of Industry at Crystal Palace, London
- **1867:** Publication of Marx's *Das Kapital*, an analysis of the economic injustices of the Capitalist system
- **1868:** First British Congress of Trade Unions meet in Manchester
- **1870:** Industrial expansion begins in Germany
- **1878:** Gilchrist-Thomas method for steel production; internal-combustion engine constructed by Nikolaus Otto
- **1889:** Eiffel Tower completed for centennial exhibition
- **1891:** Construction of Trans-Siberian railway begun
- **1908:** First radio transmitter built by Marconi

1840 · 1850 · 1860 · 1870 · 1880 · 1890 · 1900 · 1910

THE FIRST WORLD WAR

Dynamic recruiting posters appealed directly to the patriotism of Europe's young men.

THE FIRST WORLD WAR is one of history's watersheds. Austria-Hungary's attempt to assert its power developed into a protracted struggle that swept up most of Europe and the rest of the world in its train. The conflict mobilized 65 million troops, of whom nine million died and over one-third were wounded. Civilians also died – as a result of military action, starvation, and disease. The war was won by the Allied Powers, but at great cost. The German, Austro-Hungarian, Ottoman, and Russian empires were destroyed; European political and financial supremacy ended; and by 1918 the US had emerged as the greatest power in the world. The debt and disillusionment that followed paved the way for the revolutionary forces of the left and right that emerged in the 1930s in the wake of the Great Depression.

The start of the First World War

The First World War began in Europe in August 1914. A decade of increasingly severe political crises, combined with military and naval arms races among Europe's major powers created an incendiary situation. The murder of Austrian Archduke Franz Ferdinand in Sarajevo, in June 1914 proved the catalyst. Serbia, Montenegro, Russia, France, Belgium, and Britain (the Allied Powers) found themselves opposed to Austria-Hungary, Germany, and Turkey (the Central Powers). The Central powers were joined by Bulgaria in 1915, while the Allied powers gathered Italy by 1915, Romania in 1916, and the US in 1917.

War on the Western Front

By November 1914 the war on the Western Front had become largely static. A German offensive against Paris via Belgium was rapidly met by French and British forces, who forced them back to Flanders. For three years, the British and French armies, and the Germans at Verdun, undertook a series of futile and exceptionally costly offensives in which gains were generally no more than a few kilometres. The front was marked by long lines of trenches, from which the two sides sought to defend their positions. It was impossible for them to achieve any measure of surprise, or, with no room for manoeuvre, to shift their position at all.

For several years, the war in Western Europe was fought along a barely shifting frontline, marked by a series of trenches. These British troops, from the Border Regiment, are squatting in 'funk holes' near Thiepval Wood, during the battle of the Somme in 1916.

Tanks were first used at the end of the 1916 battle of the Somme, and later during the Allied advance in the summer and autumn of 1918. Though they could cope with difficult terrain, the trench system provided considerable obstacles *(left)*.

The Western Front

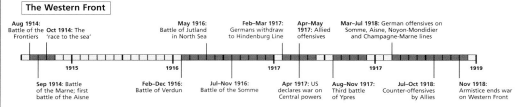

- Aug 1914: Battle of the Frontiers
- Oct 1914: The 'race to the sea'
- Sep 1914: Battle of the Marne; first battle of the Aisne
- 1915
- May 1916: Battle of Jutland in North Sea
- Feb–Dec 1916: Battle of Verdun
- Jul–Nov 1916: Battle of the Somme
- 1916
- Feb–Mar 1917: Germans withdraw to Hindenburg Line
- Apr 1917: US declares war on Central powers
- Apr–May 1917: Allied offensives
- 1917
- Aug–Nov 1917: Third battle of Ypres
- 1917
- Mar–Jul 1918: German offensives on Somme, Aisne, Noyon-Mondidier and Champagne-Marne lines
- Jul–Oct 1918: Counter-offensives by Allies
- Nov 1918: Armistice ends war on Western Front
- 1919

The German offensive leads to stalemate

Facing a war on two fronts against enemies with larger armies, Germany sought to defeat France before Russia could fully mobilize. They planned to outflank the main French defences by moving through Belgium and then through northern France to encircle France within six weeks. However, supply lines proved inadequate, and communications to, and between, the two main armies no better. The plan ignored British intervention, relying on the likelihood of French immobilization as the offensive progressed. French success at the battle of the Marne ended German hopes of a quick victory, and paved the way for the trench warfare that lasted until spring 1918.

Aircraft were used initially for reconnaissance and artillery spotting; later, in 1917–18 Germany and Britain used heavy bombers to destroy industrial and civilian targets.

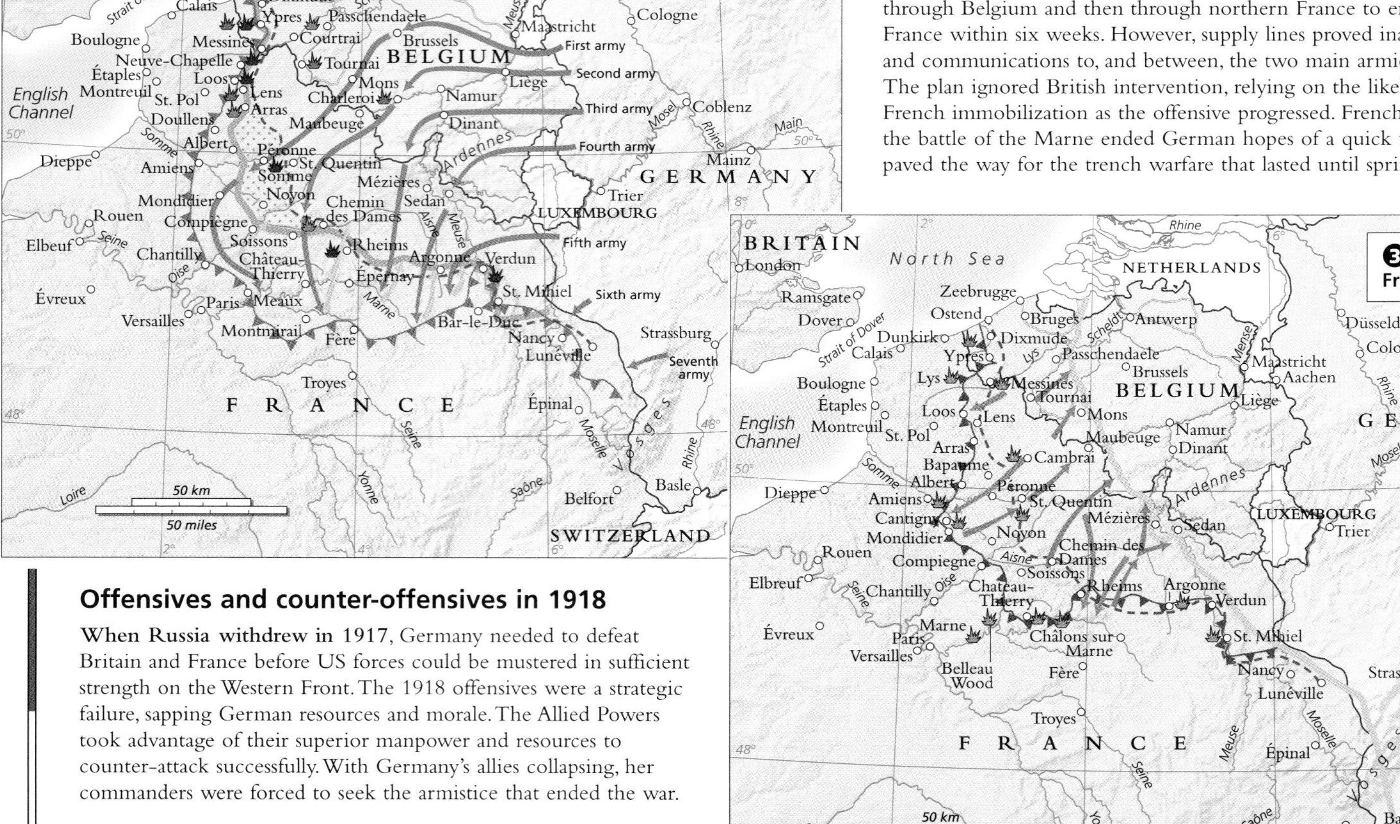

Offensives and counter-offensives in 1918

When Russia withdrew in 1917, Germany needed to defeat Britain and France before US forces could be mustered in sufficient strength on the Western Front. The 1918 offensives were a strategic failure, sapping German resources and morale. The Allied Powers took advantage of their superior manpower and resources to counter-attack successfully. With Germany's allies collapsing, her commanders were forced to seek the armistice that ended the war.

The Western Front 1914–1918

- German invasion of France and Belgium, 1914
- furthest extent of German advance, 1914
- German retreat
- line from end of 1914–Jul 1916
- Hindenburg line
- gains by Allied powers 1916–17
- Kaiserschlacht (the Kaiser's battles') 1918
- German offensive Mar–Jul 1918
- Allied counter-attacks, 1918
- line at the Armistice 11 Nov 1918

Major battles

- 1914
- 1915
- 1916
- 1917
- 1918

The Eastern Front

Sep–Oct 1914: German operations in southwestern Poland
Feb 1915: Second battle of Masurian Lakes
Jul–Sep 1915: Russian withdrawal
Aug–Sep 1916: Romanian offensive
Mar 1917: Russian Revolution
Jul 1917: Second Brusilov offensive
Dec 1917: Russian armistice

1914 – 1915 – 1916 – 1917 – 1918

Aug 1914: Battle of Tannenberg
Sep 1914: First battle of Masurian Lakes
Nov 1914: Battle of Lodz
May 1915: German breakthrough at Gorlice-Tarnow
Jun–Aug 1916: Brusilov offensive by Russia
Sep–Dec 1916: Elimination of Romania
Mar 1918: Treaty of Brest-Litovsk allows Germany to occupy Ukraine and gain access to food supplies

War on the Eastern Front

There was far more movement on the Eastern Front than in the West, partly because of the much greater distances involved. Though the Russian army was generally superior to Austria-Hungary militarily, they were invariably defeated by the force of German arms. By the end of 1915, Russia had lost most of Poland, with more than two million troops taken prisoner. Inadequate military supplies and poor leadership produced a consequently high casualty rate: war weariness and mutiny were key factors in bringing the Bolsheviks to power in 1917.

During the first German onslaught on the Eastern Front, casualty numbers were such that even churches were converted into makeshift field hospitals. The priest is giving a blessing to sick and injured troops.

CASUALTIES OF WAR

The toll of military dead and wounded was appalling; of the millions mobilized on the Allied side, fewer than half escaped death or injury. The Central Powers' losses were even higher, particularly in Austria-Hungary. In total, nearly nine million men died in four years, with 23 million left physically or psychologically scarred. Civilians died too, from bombing raids, malnutrition, and disease.

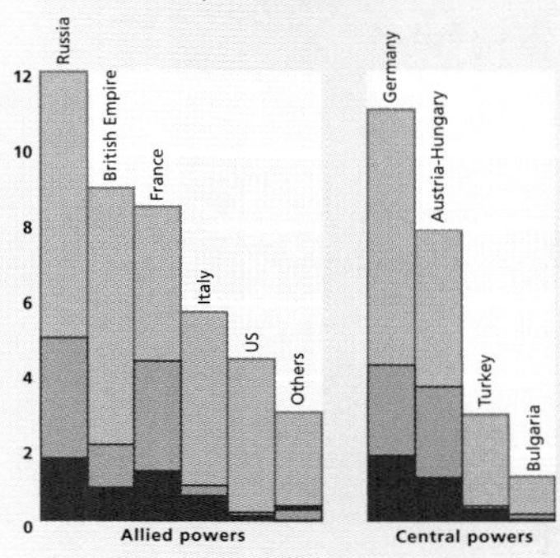

Military casualties (millions)

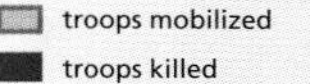

The Italian Front

Italy entered the war in 1915 in an opportunistic arrangement engineered by its leaders with the Allies to secure territory at the expense of Austria-Hungary. Fighting on the Italian Front was some of the most bitter of the war, with much of the fighting occurring in a series of battles close to the river Isonzo. The great battle of Caporetto in 1917 almost led to Italian defeat. Italy was more successful in subsequent fighting, but the terrible disillusionment after the war over the price paid for Italy's gains contributed heavily to the rise to power of Benito Mussolini and the Fascists.

▲ 5 The Italian Front 1915–1918

Italian offensives on the River Isonzo, 1915–17
Austro-German campaigns, 1917
front line in Sep 1917
front line Dec 1917–Oct 1918
Allied offensive, Oct 1918
Armistice line 4 Nov 1918

Major battles
1915
1917
1918

Italian civilians suffered great privations during the years of warfare in the north of the country. Here, women – wheeling handcarts – and children flee following the 6th battle of the Isonzo.

The war in Italy

Jun–Sep 1915: 1st and 2nd battle of the Isonzo
Mar 1916: 5th battle of the Isonzo
Aug–Sep 1916: 6th and 7th battles of the Isonzo
May–Jun 1917: 10th battle of the Isonzo
Oct–Nov 1917: Battle of Caporetto
Jun 1918: Battle of the Piave

1915 – 1916 – 1917 – 1918 – 1919

Oct–Nov 1915: 3rd and 4th battles of the Isonzo
May–Jun 1916: Asiago offensive by Austria
Oct–Nov 1916: 8th and 9th battles of the Isonzo
Aug–Sep 1917: 11th battle of the Isonzo
Nov 1918: Battle of Vittorio Veneto

Lying in a key position at the head of the Gulf of Salonica, the port city of Salonica was a major focus for Allied operations in the Balkans during the First World War.

War in the Balkans

Serbia survived three invasion attempts in 1914, but succumbed in 1915 to an Austro-German offensive supported by Bulgaria, which checked an Anglo-French attempt to support the Serbian army from Salonica. In 1916, having successfully contained Allied forces at Salonica and invaded Romania, Bulgarian armies were joined by Austro-German forces that captured Bucharest in December. The Bulgarians were able to defeat several Allied offensives in front of Salonica until September 1918 when a major offensive broke the Bulgarian front and morale. Forced to sue for an armistice, the Bulgarians saw their capital occupied by British forces, while French and Serbian forces liberated Belgrade on 1 November.

The war in the Balkans

Aug 1914: First invasion of Serbia
Nov–Dec 1914: Third invasion of Serbia
Oct–Dec 1915: Establishment of Salonican front
Aug 1916: Bulgarian surprise attack forces Allied counter-offensive
Dec 1917–Sep 1918: Advance to Greek frontier and limited offensive operations
Sep 1918: Allied offensive against weakened Bulgarian army

1915 – 1916 – 1917 – 1918 – 1919

Sep 1914: Second invasion of Serbia
Oct–Nov 1915: Final invasion and elimination of Serbia
Aug 1916: Entry of Romania into war
Nov 1917: Fall of Monastir to Allied forces
Sep 1918: Bulgarian armistice

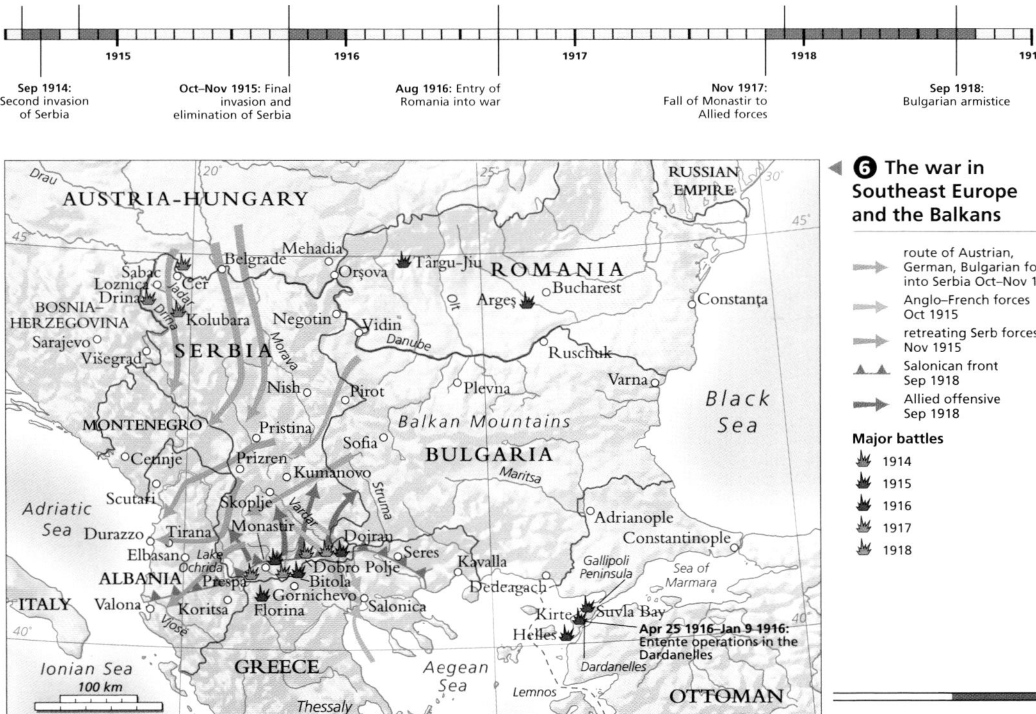

◀ 6 The war in Southeast Europe and the Balkans

route of Austrian, German, Bulgarian forces into Serbia Oct–Nov 1915
Anglo-French forces Oct 1915
retreating Serb forces Nov 1915
Salonican front Sep 1918
Allied offensive Sep 1918

Major battles
1914
1915
1916
1917
1918

EUROPE BETWEEN THE WARS

Vladimir Illich Lenin was the architect of the Bolshevik revolution.

AS THE FIRST WORLD WAR drew to its close, the three great conservative empires of Europe – Russia, Austria-Hungary, and Germany – suffered cataclysmic change. Revolution in 1917 in Russia led to the seizure of power by Lenin and the Bolsheviks. After the end of the war, the victorious allies imposed peace treaties which dismembered Austria-Hungary and sliced territory from Germany – as well as imposing punitive financial penalties. New states sprang up right across Europe as nationalist aspirations coincided with the collapse of multi-national empires.

Europe after the First World War

Following the end of the First World War, Finland, Estonia, Latvia, and Lithuania gained independence from Russia; Czechoslovakia and Yugoslavia emerged from the wreckage of Austria-Hungary, while Poland re-appeared as an independent state for the first time since its partition in 1794. In western Europe too, long-frustrated national discontent finally brought about the establishment of an independent Irish Free State in 1921. The birth of new states and changes in regime did not happen easily, and Finland and the new Irish state were both engulfed by civil war.

The immense reparations imposed on Germany by the Treaty of Versailles proved an impossible burden to a nation already crippled by the costs of the war. Hyperinflation during the 1920s so devalued the national currency that it became totally worthless. These children are using Deutschmarks as building blocks.

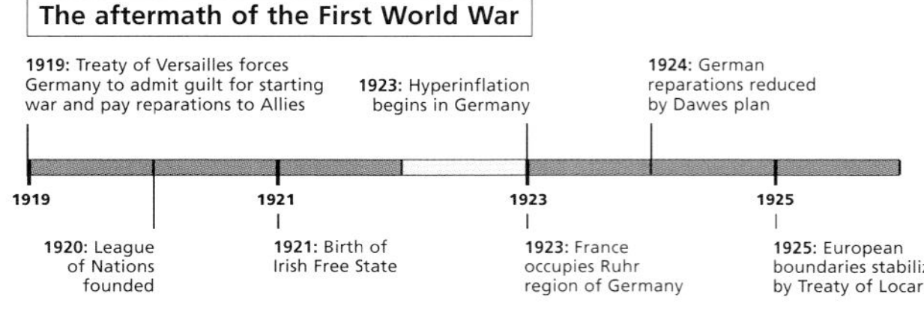

Revolution and civil war in Russia

In 1917, Russia's Tsarist regime, ravaged by war and a failing economy, collapsed. The provisional government which replaced it failed to improve the economy, and in October 1917, the socialist Bolsheviks seized key installations in Petrograd, and took control of a number of important towns. Civil war broke out as anti-Bolsheviks and pro-monarchists, aided by troops from other European nations (the Entente powers), tried to overthrow them. However the well-organized Bolsheviks (the 'Reds') held the heartland of Russia and by 1921 had defeated their weak, disunited opponents. Meanwhile, national groups on the periphery of Russia strove for independence. Finland, Estonia, Latvia, Lithuania, and Poland broke free and were able to remain so, but the independence of Armenia, Azerbaijan, and Georgia was short-lived. By 1924 the Bolsheviks were firmly in control and the Soviet Union came into being.

Scale varies with perspective

10,250 km (6370 miles)

6450 km (4010 miles)

1918–19: Kolchak

1918–20: Ural Cossack army

1917–19: Don Cossacks

1918: Denikin

1919 and 1920: Campaigns from the Caucasus

1920: Wrangel

Entente fleet via Murmansk and the Barents Sea

Japanese forces

Route of Czech forces

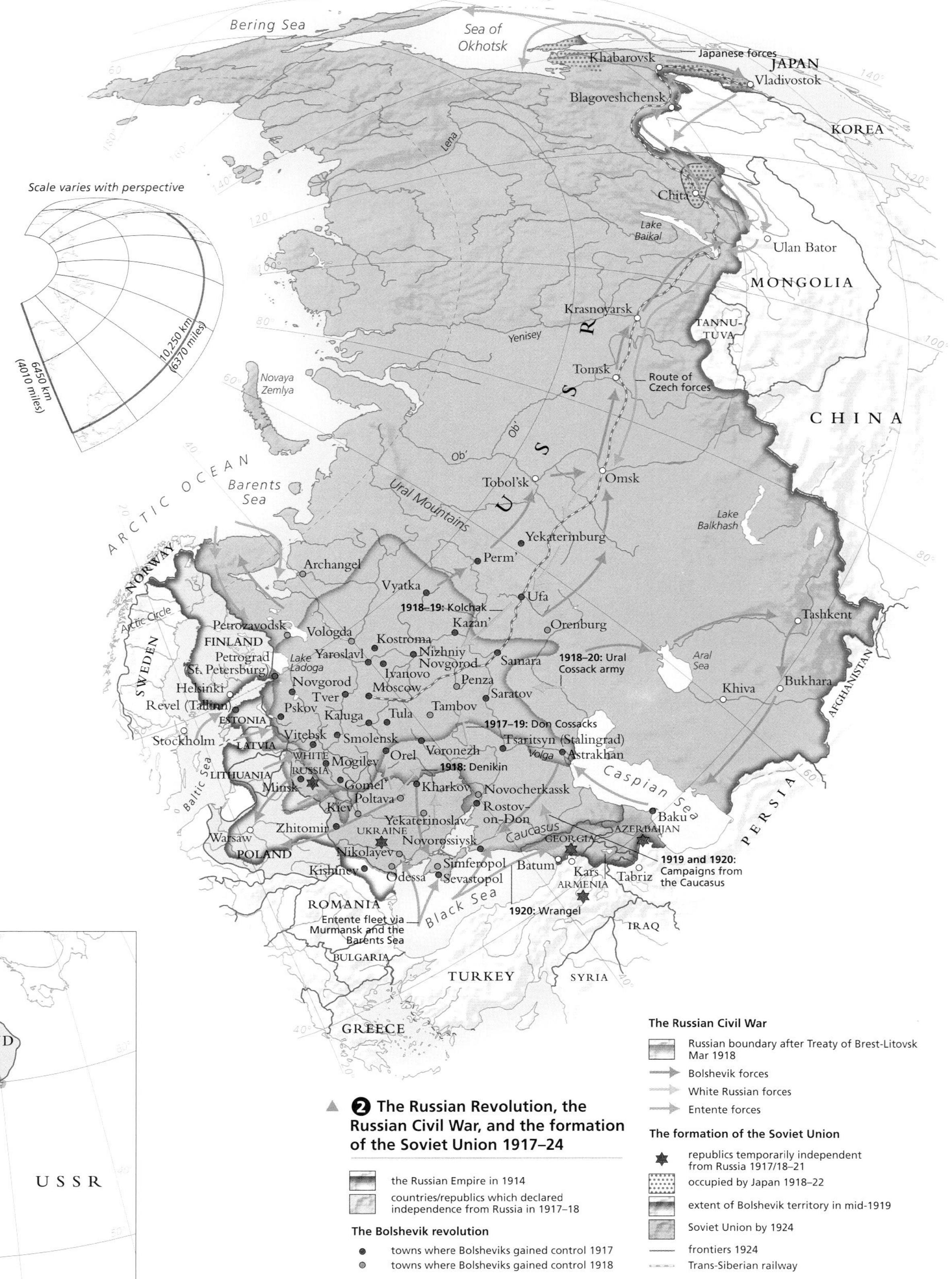

▲ **2 The Russian Revolution, the Russian Civil War, and the formation of the Soviet Union 1917–24**

- the Russian Empire in 1914
- countries/republics which declared independence from Russia in 1917–18

The Bolshevik revolution

- towns where Bolsheviks gained control 1917
- towns where Bolsheviks gained control 1918

The Russian Civil War

- Russian boundary after Treaty of Brest-Litovsk Mar 1918
- Bolshevik forces
- White Russian forces
- Entente forces

The formation of the Soviet Union

- republics temporarily independent from Russia 1917/18–21
- occupied by Japan 1918–22
- extent of Bolshevik territory in mid-1919
- Soviet Union by 1924
- frontiers 1924
- Trans-Siberian railway

Revolution and civil war in Russia 1917–24

- Mar 1917: Abdication of Tsar Nicholas II
- Nov 1917: Bolsheviks begin to take control of European Russia
- 1918: Start of civil war between Bolsheviks and White Russians
- 1918: Treaty of Brest-Litovsk ends First World War in the east
- 1920: Start of peasant revolts throughout Russia
- 1920: White Russia, Ukraine, and Caucasus Republics return to Russian control
- 1921: Russian civil war ends with Bolshevik victory. New economic policy encourages peasants to produce more food while modernization is taking place
- 1922: USSR (Union of Soviet Socialist Republics) is formed
- 1924: Lenin dies and is succeeded by Josef Stalin

Economic crisis and political extremism

The US economic crisis of 1929 hit a Europe suffering from the aftermath of wartime dislocation. Industrial output and agricultural production fell sharply across the world, but the industrial nations were hardest hit. Farmers survived by retreating to subsistence production, but the collapse in industrial output brought unemployment on a massive scale. Without proper systems of social security to support the unemployed, poverty became widespread. The economic and social problems of the 1930s encouraged the growth of extreme political movements on both Left and Right, especially in Germany and Italy, where Fascism under Hitler and Mussolini became the defining political force.

In 1936 more than 200 men marched from Jarrow in northern England to London to draw attention to the plight of their town – formerly a centre for shipbuilding – where male unemployment had reached more than 70%.

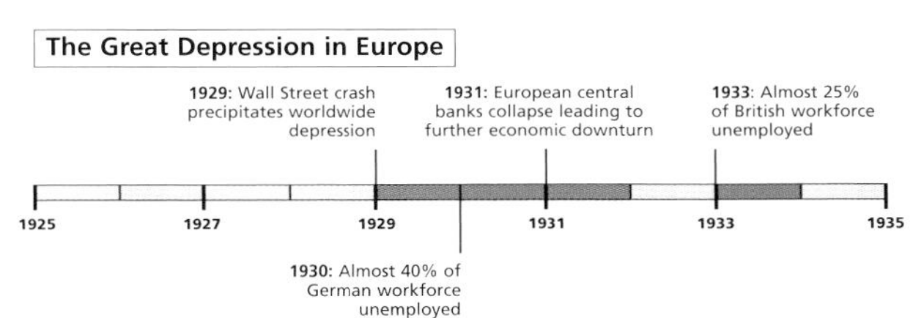

Revolution and nationalism in Europe

In March 1939 Nazi troops took control of the Czech lands and a puppet state was established in Slovakia. This photograph shows the entry of German troops into Prague, watched by wary Czech civilians.

On achieving power in 1933, Hitler began a campaign to restore Germany to its position as a great international power. In 1936, German troops marched back into the Rhineland. The response from the western powers was weak, and in March 1938, Nazi Germany annexed Austria in the *Anschluss*. At Munich six months later, Britain and France allowed Germany to annex the Czech Sudetenland, signalling the break-up of the Czechoslovak state. Fascist Italy aped Hitler, conquering Ethiopia in 1935–36 and occupying Albania in 1939. Finally, bolstered by the Nazi–Soviet Pact Hitler ignored British and French protests to invade Poland in September 1939.

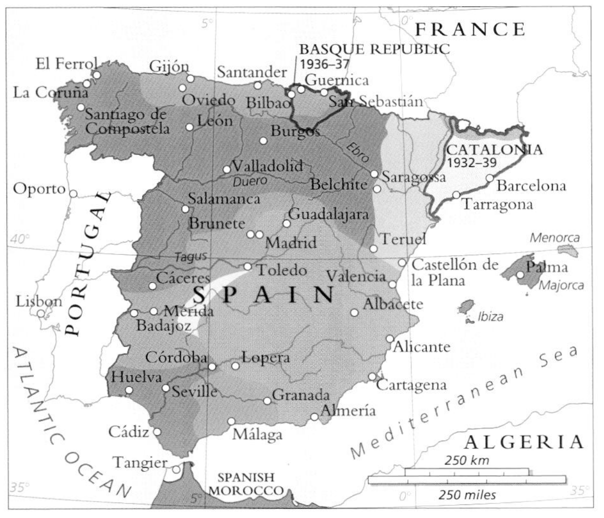

4 The Spanish Civil War 1936–39

Land held by Nationalist forces
- Jul 1936
- Oct 1937
- Jul 1938
- Feb 1939

Land held by Republican forces
- Feb 1939
- temporary independence, with dates

The Spanish Civil War

The Spanish elections of 1936 brought in the left-wing Popular Front government, precipitating a military revolt by conservative groups. A brutal civil war followed, with the right-wing Nationalists, led by General Franco and supported by Germany and Italy, triumphant against Republican groups.

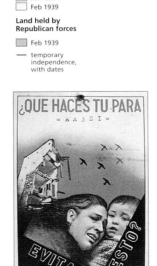

Many Spanish civilians were killed during the Civil War. This 1937 post card calls for aid for victims of air raids.

The growth of nationalism in Europe

- 1931: Republican success in Spanish elections leads to flight of king
- 1933: Hitler becomes Chancellor of Germany
- 1934: Murder of Austrian Chancellor, Dollfuss by Nazi supporters
- 1936: Germany reoccupies Rhineland
- 1936: Start of Spanish Civil War
- 1938: Break-up of Czechoslovakia
- 1938: Germany occupies Austria (*Anschluss*)
- 1938: Munich Agreement allows Germany to occupy Czech Sudetenland
- 1939: Signing of Nazi-Soviet pact
- 1939: German invasion of Poland

THE SECOND WORLD WAR IN EUROPE

Women were encouraged to join the war effort both as civilians and in the armed forces.

THE GREATEST WAR in Europe's history was initiated by a series of aggressive annexations and conquests by Hitler's Nazi Germany between 1939 and 1941. When the conflict ceased to be a series of campaigns and became a war, however, Germany was checked and then stripped of the initiative by an Allied force headed by two nations on the lateral extremes of Europe – Britain and the USSR – and from December 1941, a non-European nation, the US. Each of the latter proved more than Germany's equal in military and economic resources. The eventual Allied victory, following concerted assaults from the west, south, east, and the air, saved Europe from the scourge of Nazism but also completed Europe's devastation, bringing to an end 400 years of European global domination.

Following the Blitz (September 1940–May 1941) London became the first city in history to undergo ballistic missile attack from V1 flying bombs and V2 rockets (1944–45).

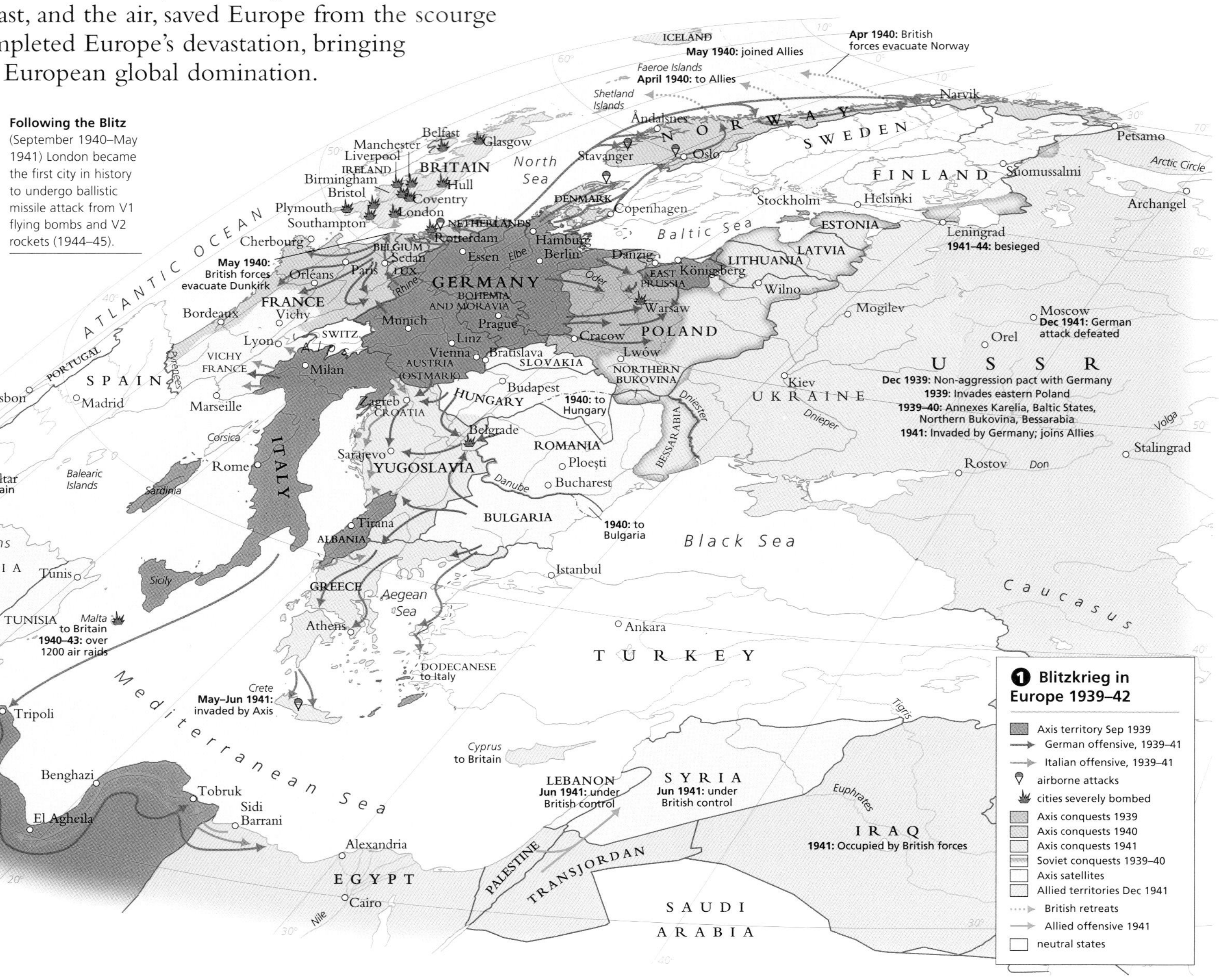

Blitzkrieg in Europe 1939–42

Between 1939 and 1941, lightning campaigns on land and in the air enabled Nazi Germany to conquer many of its weaker neighbours. In temporary alliance with the USSR, Germany annihilated Poland in the autumn of 1939. Denmark, Norway, Belgium, France, and the Netherlands were overrun in April–June 1940. Yugoslavia and Greece were occupied in April–May 1941, Britain was isolated, and Bulgaria, Romania, and Hungary brought under Nazi domination. Although a large contingent of German forces was committed to support Italy in North Africa, in June 1941 Hitler ordered a surprise attack on the USSR, hoping to destroy it in a single campaign. The attempt ended in failure because of the distances involved and unexpected Soviet resistance. In mid-winter 1941, the Nazi invasion forces were halted outside Moscow.

ICELAND
May 1940: joined Allies
Apr 1940: British forces evacuate Norway
Faeroe Islands
April 1940: to Allies
May 1940: British forces evacuate Dunkirk
Leningrad
1941–44: besieged
Moscow
Dec 1941: German attack defeated
Dec 1939: Non-aggression pact with Germany
1939: Invades eastern Poland
1939–40: Annexes Karelia, Baltic States, Northern Bukovina, Bessarabia
1941: Invaded by Germany; joins Allies
1940: to Hungary
1940: to Bulgaria
Gibraltar to Britain
1940–42: Controlled by Vichy France
Malta to Britain
1940–43: over 1200 air raids
DODECANESE to Italy
Crete
May–Jun 1941: invaded by Axis
Feb 1941: German Afrika Korps
Cyprus to Britain
LEBANON
Jun 1941: under British control
SYRIA
Jun 1941: under British control
IRAQ
1941: Occupied by British forces

1 Blitzkrieg in Europe 1939–42

- Axis territory Sep 1939
- German offensive, 1939–41
- Italian offensive, 1939–41
- airborne attacks
- cities severely bombed
- Axis conquests 1939
- Axis conquests 1940
- Axis conquests 1941
- Soviet conquests 1939–40
- Axis satellites
- Allied territories Dec 1941
- British retreats
- Allied offensive 1941
- neutral states

The Second World War 1939–42

- Aug 1939: Germany and USSR sign non-aggression pact
- Sep 1939: Germany and USSR invade Poland; France and Britain declare war on Germany
- Apr 1940: German invasion of Denmark and Norway
- May–Jun 1940: Germany invades France, Netherlands, and Belgium
- Jul–Oct 1940: Battle of Britain in skies over southern England
- Oct 1940: Italy invades Albania and Greece
- Apr 1941: German invasion of Yugoslavia and Greece
- Jun 1941: Operation Barbarossa: German invasion of USSR
- Nov 1941: USSR counter-attacks against Germany
- Dec 1941: Germany declares war on US
- Sep 1942: Start of German siege of Stalingrad
- Oct–Nov 1942: UK defeats Germany at El Alamein
- Nov 1942: Germans occupy Vichy France

The battle of the Atlantic

The battle over the supply of Europe was fought in the Atlantic. British destruction or containment of German surface warship raiders, following the sinking of the *Bismarck* in May 1941 and the blockade of supplies to 'Fortress Europe', was followed by a German submarine (U-Boat) campaign against British shipping in western waters. Once the US entered the war in December 1941, U-boat attacks spread across the Atlantic. By summer 1943, US mass production of 'Liberty' merchantmen, the use of the convoy system, increasing air cover, and the Allied interception of German radio traffic critically inhibited the effectiveness of the U-Boat 'wolf-packs'.

This Enigma encoding machine is being used by German naval troops. By summer 1940, British counter-intelligence experts had managed to crack the Enigma code, enabling them to interpret German radio traffic, and disperse the intercepted messages (codenamed Ultra) throughout Allied High Command.

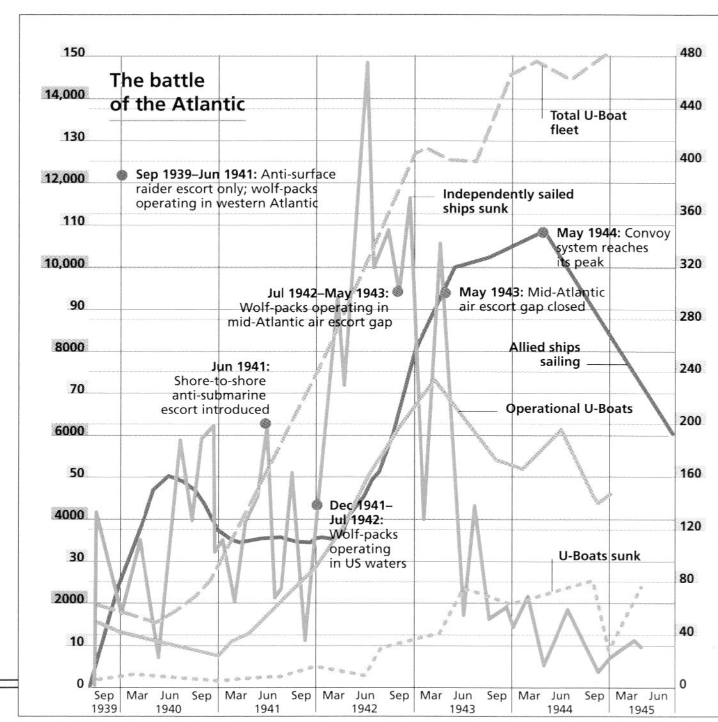

The Greater German Reich 1939–1943

The creation by the Nazis of a Greater German Reich encompassing their conquered and allied territories was based on five basic principles: pure 'Aryan' regions were annexed or occupied and integrated into Germany, under the aegis of the Gestapo secret police; non-incorporated areas were placed under military control; puppet and satellite states were strictly controlled and exploited by coercion; the conquered areas of the East were ravaged and cleared for German settlement; and underlying all these policies a principle of ethnic cleansing, targeting Jews, Gypsies, political dissidents, and 'social deviants', began with imprisonment, concentration camps or enslaved labour, but escalated by 1943 into a policy of systematic extermination.

The Nazi impact on Europe

- **Nov 1938:** *Kristallnacht*: coordinated Nazi attacks on Jews in Germany
- **Sep–Oct 1939:** Invasion of Poland; mass murder of Jews; establishment of ghettoes
- **Jun 1941:** Invasion of Russia; *Einsatzgruppen* murder squads active in Eastern Europe
- **Jul 1941:** Hitler orders Final Solution (extermination of Europe's Jews)
- **Dec 1941:** First death camp opened at Chelmno
- **Jan 1942:** Plans for Final Solution agreed at Wannsee Conference
- **mid-1942:** Auschwitz death camp opened
- **Apr 1943:** Jewish uprising at Warsaw
- **Jul 1944:** Majdanek camp liberated by Soviet Army
- **Jan 1945:** Auschwitz liberated by Soviet Army

The Allied invasion of Europe 1943–45

A final German attempt to conquer the USSR brought their forces to Stalingrad by August 1942. The following winter saw their defeat there which, with Anglo-US victories in North Africa, brought the strategic initiative to the Allies. July 1943 witnessed Soviet victory at Kursk and Anglo-US landings in Sicily, initiating a Soviet onslaught in the east, and the collapse of Italy. A sustained Anglo-US bombing offensive (from January 1943) and landings in southern France and Normandy meant, by summer 1944, that Germany was in retreat on all fronts. With its infrastructure, industry, capital, and leadership effectively destroyed, by May 1945 Germany was powerless to stop Soviet and Anglo-US forces finally meeting on the Elbe, and enforcing an unconditional surrender.

The Second World War 1942–45

- **Jan 1943:** Germans surrender at Stalingrad
- **Jun–Aug 1943:** USSR defeats Germans in tank battle at Kursk
- **Jul 1943:** Allied forces land in Sicily
- **Sep–Oct 1943:** Italian surrender to Allies; Germany occupies Rome and Milan. Italy declares war on Germany
- **Jan 1944:** End of 900-day siege of Leningrad
- **Jun 1944:** D-Day: Allied forces land in Normandy
- **Jul 1944:** USSR enters Poland
- **Oct–Nov 1944:** Allies liberate Greece
- **Jan 1945:** Soviet troops enter Budapest, Warsaw, and Auschwitz
- **Mar 1945:** Allied forces cross Rhine
- **May 1945:** Germany surrenders
- **May 1945:** Berlin surrenders to Soviet troops

The Allied invasion of northern Europe began with Operation Overlord, the largest combined operation and successful shore-to-shore invasion in history; eight seaborne and airborne divisions established a beachhead in Normandy, on D-Day (6 June 1944) supported by 6500 ships and 12,000 aircraft.

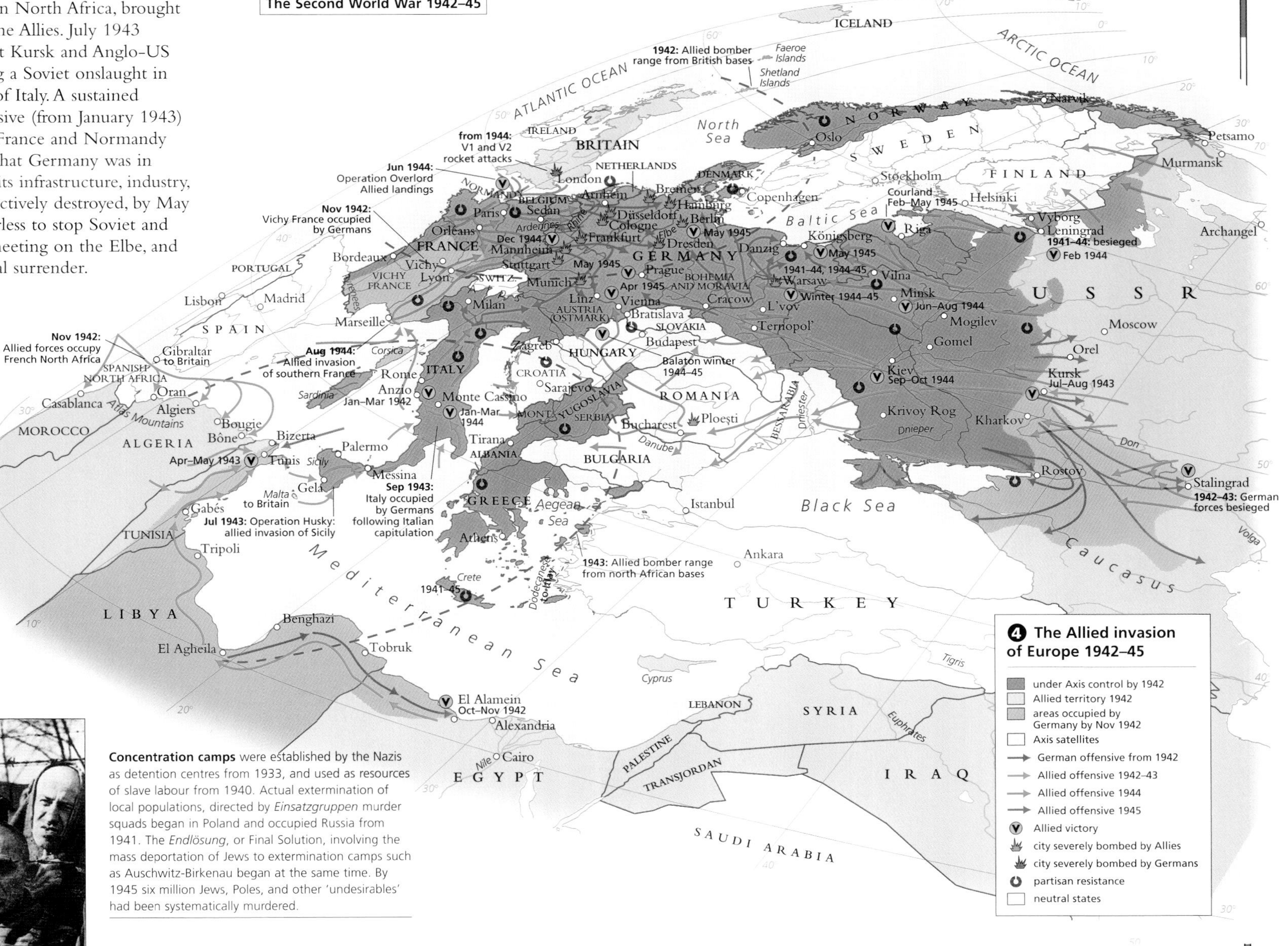

4 The Allied invasion of Europe 1942–45

- under Axis control by 1942
- Allied territory 1942
- areas occupied by Germany by Nov 1942
- Axis satellites
- German offensive from 1942
- Allied offensive 1942–43
- Allied offensive 1944
- Allied offensive 1945
- Allied victory
- city severely bombed by Allies
- city severely bombed by Germans
- partisan resistance
- neutral states

Concentration camps were established by the Nazis as detention centres from 1933, and used as resources of slave labour from 1940. Actual extermination of local populations, directed by *Einsatzgruppen* murder squads began in Poland and occupied Russia from 1941. The *Endlösung*, or Final Solution, involving the mass deportation of Jews to extermination camps such as Auschwitz-Birkenau began at the same time. By 1945 six million Jews, Poles, and other 'undesirables' had been systematically murdered.

THE DIVISION OF POSTWAR EUROPE

Joseph Stalin, leader of the Soviet Union 1929–53, headed a regime of terror and totalitarian rule.

AFTER THE SECOND WORLD WAR, Europe was divided into the capitalist West and Soviet-dominated Communist East. Germany, which by 1947 was partitioned along the same lines, played a pivotal role in the tensions between the two blocs. From 1945–52, millions of people were forcibly resettled while many others fled persecution. The US, fearing that Communism would be an attractive alternative to postwar poverty and dislocation, financed the 'Marshall Plan', an economic recovery programme for Europe. By 1948 a pro-Soviet bloc, bound by economic and military agreements, had been established in Eastern Europe. Attempts to challenge Soviet dominance in the Soviet bloc in the 1950s and 1960s were brutally suppressed.

The Allied occupation of postwar Germany

Following Germany's surrender in May 1945, the occupying powers, America, Britain, France and the USSR, divided Germany into four zones. Berlin, which lay within the Soviet zone, was similarly divided. In March 1948 the Western powers decided to unite their zones into a single economic unit. The USSR responded by launching a land blockade of Berlin in protest against the unification. The Western nations frustrated the blockade by airlifting essential supplies to their sectors of Berlin. The blockade was abandoned in 1949.

1 The partition of Germany and Austria

Occupation zones
- American
- British
- French
- Soviet
- Soviet allies
- checkpoint between East and West
- air corridor
- four sector city

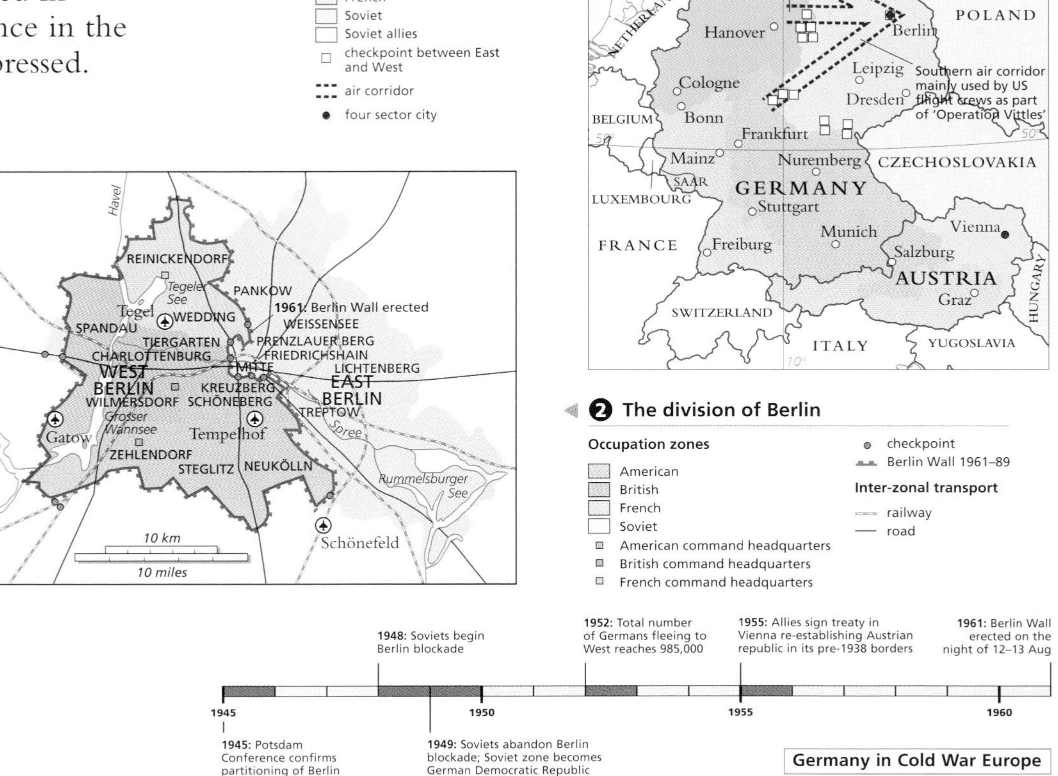

The occupation of Berlin

In accordance with agreements made at the Potsdam Conference in 1945, Berlin was partitioned in a similar way to Germany. Between 1949 and 1961, around 2.5 million East Germans fled from East to West Germany, including skilled workers and professionals. Their loss threatened to destroy the economic viability of the East German state. In response, East Germany built the Berlin Wall in 1961 to prevent migrations and possible economic catastrophe.

Straßensperrung verursacht durch die Schandmauer

With Soviet consent, the East German authorities constructed the Berlin Wall in 1961. For 28 years the wall served to segregate East Germans from West Germany becoming a potent symbol of the Cold War.

2 The division of Berlin

Occupation zones
- American
- British
- French
- Soviet
- American command headquarters
- British command headquarters
- French command headquarters

- checkpoint
- Berlin Wall 1961–89

Inter-zonal transport
- railway
- road

Germany in Cold War Europe

- **1945:** Potsdam Conference confirms partitioning of Berlin
- **1948:** Soviets begin Berlin blockade
- **1949:** Soviets abandon Berlin blockade; Soviet zone becomes German Democratic Republic
- **1952:** Total number of Germans fleeing to West reaches 985,000
- **1955:** Allies sign treaty in Vienna re-establishing Austrian republic in its pre-1938 borders
- **1961:** Berlin Wall erected on the night of 12–13 Aug

1945 1950 1955 1960

Refugees and resettlement 1945–52

The Second World War left millions of Europeans displaced. In an attempt to re-establish ethnic and linguistic uniformity within political boundaries, more than 31 million people were resettled between 1945 and 1952. Under the Potsdam agreement, Cossacks and Russian prisoners of war were forcibly repatriated, often to death or imprisonment. Millions of Germans fled Eastern Europe ahead of the Red Army. Mutual transfers of peoples were organized to coincide with shifts in boundaries, for example between Poland and the Baltic republics; and Hungary and Yugoslavia. Finns were displaced by the Soviet occupation of Karelia, and many Jewish Holocaust survivors fled to Palestine and the US.

These children were amongst millions forced to live in refugee camps while they waited to learn whether they could return to their former homes.

3 Displaced peoples in East and Central Europe

- USSR 1945
- Communist states by 1948
- pre-war boundary
- post-war boundary
- 'Iron Curtain' 1948

Movement of peoples 1945–52
- number of refugees in thousands (with colour of peoples)
- Baltic peoples
- Czechs
- Finns
- Germans
- Greeks
- Hungarians
- Italians
- Poles
- Romanians
- Russians
- Russians forcibly repatriated
- Turks
- Jewish emigration to Israel 1945–50 in thousands

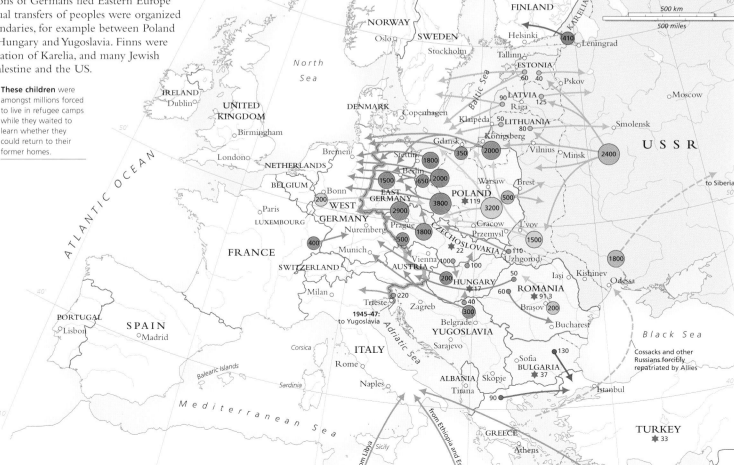

1945–47: to Yugoslavia

Cossacks and other Russians forcibly repatriated by Allies

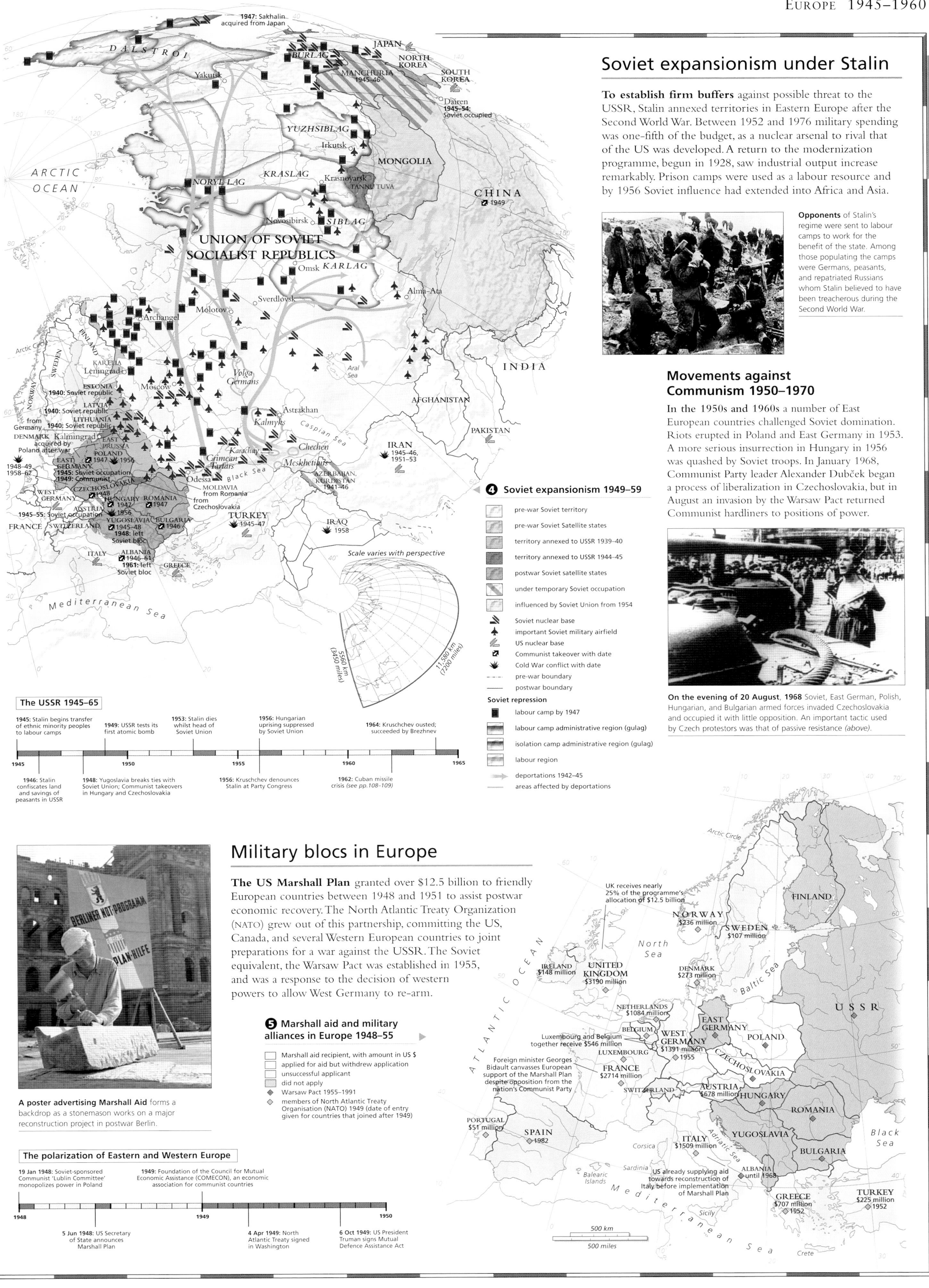

Soviet expansionism under Stalin

To establish firm buffers against possible threat to the USSR, Stalin annexed territories in Eastern Europe after the Second World War. Between 1952 and 1976 military spending was one-fifth of the budget, as a nuclear arsenal to rival that of the US was developed. A return to the modernization programme, begun in 1928, saw industrial output increase remarkably. Prison camps were used as a labour resource and by 1956 Soviet influence had extended into Africa and Asia.

Opponents of Stalin's regime were sent to labour camps to work for the benefit of the state. Among those populating the camps were Germans, peasants, and repatriated Russians whom Stalin believed to have been treacherous during the Second World War.

Movements against Communism 1950–1970

In the 1950s and 1960s a number of East European countries challenged Soviet domination. Riots erupted in Poland and East Germany in 1953. A more serious insurrection in Hungary in 1956 was quashed by Soviet troops. In January 1968, Communist Party leader Alexander Dubček began a process of liberalization in Czechoslovakia, but in August an invasion by the Warsaw Pact returned Communist hardliners to positions of power.

On the evening of 20 August, 1968 Soviet, East German, Polish, Hungarian, and Bulgarian armed forces invaded Czechoslovakia and occupied it with little opposition. An important tactic used by Czech protestors was that of passive resistance *(above)*.

4 Soviet expansionism 1949–59

- pre-war Soviet territory
- pre-war Soviet Satellite states
- territory annexed to USSR 1939–40
- territory annexed to USSR 1944–45
- postwar Soviet satellite states
- under temporary Soviet occupation
- influenced by Soviet Union from 1954
- Soviet nuclear base
- important Soviet military airfield
- US nuclear base
- Communist takeover with date
- Cold War conflict with date
- pre-war boundary
- postwar boundary

Soviet repression

- labour camp by 1947
- labour camp administrative region (gulag)
- isolation camp administrative region (gulag)
- labour region
- deportations 1942–45
- areas affected by deportations

Scale varies with perspective

The USSR 1945–65

- **1945:** Stalin begins transfer of ethnic minority peoples to labour camps
- **1946:** Stalin confiscates land and savings of peasants in USSR
- **1948:** Yugoslavia breaks ties with Soviet Union; Communist takeovers in Hungary and Czechoslovakia
- **1949:** USSR tests its first atomic bomb
- **1953:** Stalin dies whilst head of Soviet Union
- **1956:** Kruschchev denounces Stalin at Party Congress
- **1956:** Hungarian uprising suppressed by Soviet Union
- **1962:** Cuban missile crisis *(see pp.108–109)*
- **1964:** Kruschchev ousted; succeeded by Brezhnev

Military blocs in Europe

The US Marshall Plan granted over $12.5 billion to friendly European countries between 1948 and 1951 to assist postwar economic recovery. The North Atlantic Treaty Organization (NATO) grew out of this partnership, committing the US, Canada, and several Western European countries to joint preparations for a war against the USSR. The Soviet equivalent, the Warsaw Pact was established in 1955, and was a response to the decision of western powers to allow West Germany to re-arm.

A poster advertising Marshall Aid forms a backdrop as a stonemason works on a major reconstruction project in postwar Berlin.

5 Marshall aid and military alliances in Europe 1948–55

- Marshall aid recipient, with amount in US $
- applied for aid but withdrew application
- unsuccessful applicant
- did not apply
- Warsaw Pact 1955–1991
- members of North Atlantic Treaty Organisation (NATO) 1949 (date of entry given for countries that joined after 1949)

The polarization of Eastern and Western Europe

- **19 Jan 1948:** Soviet-sponsored Communist 'Lublin Committee' monopolizes power in Poland
- **5 Jun 1948:** US Secretary of State announces Marshall Plan
- **1949:** Foundation of the Council for Mutual Economic Assistance (COMECON), an economic association for communist countries
- **4 Apr 1949:** North Atlantic Treaty signed in Washington
- **6 Oct 1949:** US President Truman signs Mutual Defence Assistance Act

MODERN EUROPE

In January 1999, the Euro was formally adopted as currency of the European Union.

BETWEEN 1948 AND 1989, the ideological divide between Communist Eastern Europe and the West stood firm. Divisions within Europe were compounded by economic growth in the West and stagnation in the East. In November 1989, the fall of the Berlin Wall signalled the end of the Cold War, and a rise of nationalism in Eastern Europe brought about the collapse of Communism and the Soviet bloc. A range of newly-independent states moved toward free elections, but political freedom had other consequences. In 1991, historical ethnic tension fractured Yugoslavia. Conflict escalated into war in Bosnia in 1992, and atrocities in the Serbian province of Kosovo prompted NATO intervention in 1999. In 2004 both NATO and the EU accepted new members from Central and Eastern Europe.

FINLAND 1961-85: associate member

TURKEY 1987: applied for EC membership; 1996: Customs union with EU

The European Union

The European Economic Community (EEC) was established in 1957 to guarantee the economic success of its members, and to develop a union of states in an attempt to lessen the risk of another war. The success of the EEC's liberalized trade policies encouraged further integration. In December 1991, the Maastricht Treaty created the European Union (EU) and expanded the focus of the community to issues such as justice, citizens' rights, security, and the environment. From an initial six members in 1957, the EU now has 25, twelve of which have adopted the European single currency, the Euro. The EU aims to produce a constitution to help define and reaffirm its role.

The flags of the ten new members the European Union are unfurled, ready to be hoisted to join those of the 15 existing members at a ceremony in Brussels on 1 May 2004.

1 The growth of the European Union

- members of European Coal and Steel Community (ECSC), European Atomic Energy Community (EAEC) and European Economic Community (EEC) 1957
- EU original members 1957
- EU members by 1973
- EU members by 1986
- EU members by 1995
- EU members by 2004
- applicants to EU (with date of application)
- members of Council for Mutual Economic Assistance (COMECON) 1949
- € countries using the EURO
- members of NATO

KAZAKHSTAN 1991: President Nazarbayev runs in election unopposed 1995: Nationwide referendum extends his term to 2000

1992: Tensions between Russia and Ukraine over whether Black Sea Fleet is part of strategic forces controlled by CIS

1993: Joins the CIS to secure Russian military support against ousted President Gamsakhurdia

2 The collapse of Communism in Eastern Europe

- Soviet Union to 1991
- Soviet-dominated Eastern Europe to 1989
- German Democratic Republic (GDR), united with Federal Republic of Germany 1990
- Czechoslovakia to Dec 1992
- Yugoslavia to 1991
- other Communist state before 1991
- 1990 date of first free election

The disintegration of the Communist bloc

By the 1970s it became clear that Communist economic policies were failing the nations of Eastern Europe. Economic instability throughout the 1970s and 1980s brought much of the Eastern bloc to the point of bankruptcy. The Soviet President, Gorbachev abandoned the satellite states in an effort to save the economy of the USSR. Beginning with protests in East Germany in 1989 which brought down the Communist government, nation after nation asserted their independence in a series of massive popular demonstrations which swiftly ended more than 50 years of Soviet control in Eastern Europe.

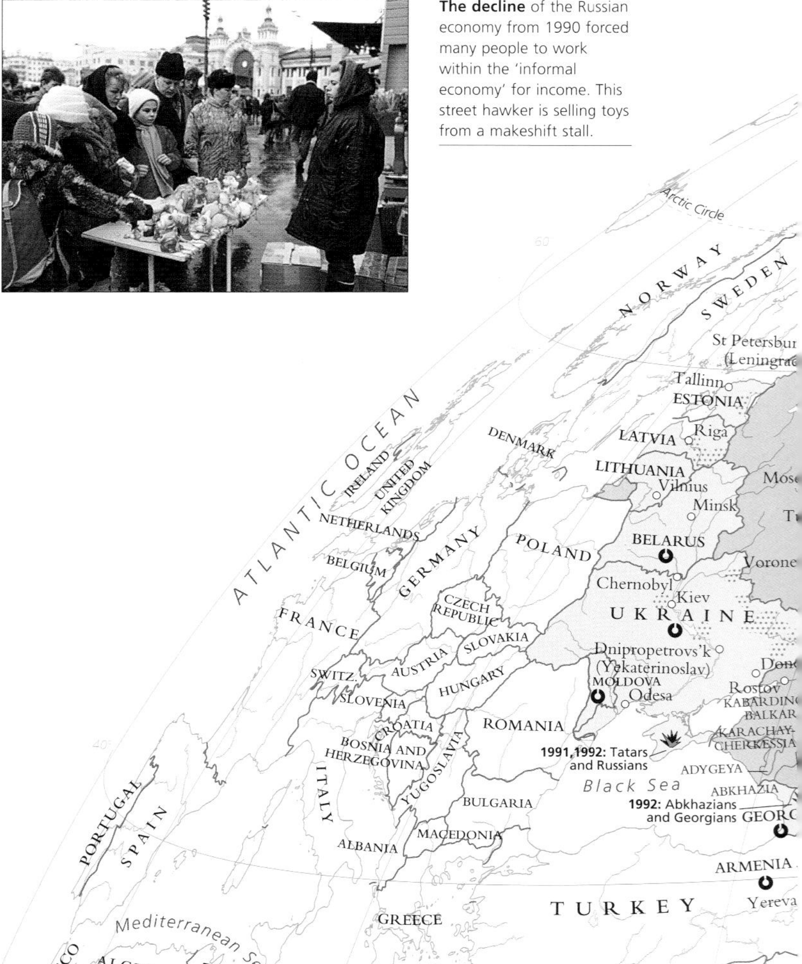

The decline of the Russian economy from 1990 forced many people to work within the 'informal economy' for income. This street hawker is selling toys from a makeshift stall.

In November 1989, these peaceful demonstrators in Prague united with other cities across Czechoslovakia in their protest against Communist rule to bring about the so-called 'Velvet Revolution'.

The rise of nationalism

The wave of nationalism which began in the German Democratic Republic was repeated throughout Eastern Europe. The reunification of Germany in 1990 was followed by the collapse of the USSR, and its division into 15 independent states. In 1993, Czechoslovakia split into two new republics: Slovakia and the Czech Republic. New governments were forced to implement strict economic measures to stem decline, and moderate socialism replaced Communism as the main political force in Eastern Europe. Nationalism continued to create tension in the Balkans, where internal ethnic conflict eventually led to the break-up of the state of Yugoslavia.

Conflict in Yugoslavia from 1991

Following the death of Communist premier Josip Broz (Tito) in 1980, the fragility of the multinational Federal People's Republic of Yugoslavia quickly became apparent. The election of Serbian leader Slobodan Milošević in 1987 brought an upsurge of Serb nationalism which struck fear in the multi-ethnic republics. In 1991, the provinces of Slovenia, Croatia and Bosnia declared their independence. Serbian forces attacked both republics in an effort to compel their return to the federation. In January 1992, Serbs in Bosnia and Herzegovina began the persecution, or 'ethnic cleansing', of Bosnia's Muslims. Bitter fighting between Serbs, Muslims, and Croats ensued, until foreign intervention brought the war to an end in 1995. In 1999, the persecution of ethnic Albanians in Kosovo provoked military intervention by NATO. The state of 'Yugoslavia' officially ceased to exist in 2003.

Bosnian Muslim refugees take up temporary residence on a basketball court as they flee Serbian forces at the height of the 'ethnic cleansing' campaign in 1993.

❸ Conflict in former Yugoslavia 1990–99

The ethnic composition of Yugoslavia, 1991

- Albanian
- Bulgarian
- Croat
- Hungarian
- Macedonian
- Muslim
- Romanian
- Serb and Montenegrin
- Slovene
- Yugoslav regions
- (Nov 1992) date of secession from Federal Republic of Yugoslavia

The Croatian conflict

- Serb advances by Dec 1991
- Serb controlled regions 1991–95/96
- Croat advances, autumn 1995

The Bosnian War

- secured by Yugoslav army and Bosnian Serb forces by Dec 1992
- area controlled by Bosnian Croat forces, Dec 1992
- attacking Serbs 1993
- attacking Bosnian Muslims 1993
- Autonomous Province of Western Bosnia Sep 1993–Aug 1994
- area remaining under control of breakaway Serbian forces, Oct 1995
- areas of combat between Croats and Bosnian Muslims
- Muslim secure zone

The Kosovan crisis

- Kosovo Liberation Army (KLA) stronghold
- Serb forces attacking KLA, 1999

The collapse of the Soviet Union

From 1985, Mikhail Gorbachev, leader of the Soviet Union, launched a series of political and economic reforms under the banner of *perestroika* (restructuring). The Supreme Soviet Council was replaced with a Congress of People's deputies and a parliament was elected in 1989. Russian president Boris Yeltsin quashed an attempted coup by hard-line Communists in 1991, which accelerated the end of the USSR. Russia and 14 other Soviet republics became independent in 1991, although 12 of them maintained a loose federation as the CIS (Commonwealth of Independent States). Russia and other states, such as Georgia, are beset by problems with separatist movements. There has been a bitter conflict between Russia and Chechnya since 1991.

War and ethnic tension in Yugoslavia from 1980

- **1980:** Death of Tito
- **1987:** Slobodan Milošević rises to power in Yugoslavia
- **1989:** Milošević strips Kosovo of autonomy it has enjoyed since 1974; tension between Serbs and ethnic Albanians escalates
- **1991:** Croatia, Slovenia, and Bosnia declare independence from Yugoslavia
- **1992:** All out war in Bosnia
- **1995:** Peace agreement ends the Bosnian war
- **1998:** Milošević sends troops into areas controlled by Kosovo Liberation Army (KLA)
- **1999:** Peace talks collapse; NATO begins bombing campaign
- **2000:** Milošević surrenders power
- **2001:** Milošević extradited to The Hague to stand trial for war crimes
- **2003:** Rump state of Yugoslavia renamed Serbia and Montenegro

Scale varies with perspective

❹ The legacy of the Soviet Union

- territory controlled by USSR in 1945
- Russian federation from 1991
- autonomous regions
- major concentration of minority Russians
- Commomwealth of Independent States 1991
- interstate conflict
- civil war
- ethnic conflict (with date)
- Islamic separatist attack
- autonomous district

1994: Chechen declaration of independence provokes war with Russia

1989: Kazakhs and Lezgians

1989–90: Uzbeks and Meskhetians

1990: Kirghiz and Uzbeks

1989: Kirghiz and Tajiks

1988: Armenians and Azerbaijanis

The decline of Soviet influence

- **1985:** Gorbachev initiates *perestroika* and *glasnost*
- **1987:** Washington arms control treaty decommissions one-fifth of Soviet arms
- **1989:** Anti-Communist protests across Eastern Europe
- **1990:** Germany reunified
- **1990–91:** Baltic republics declare independence
- **1991:** Unsuccessful coup attempt in USSR; disintegration of Soviet Union
- **1992:** Civil war in Georgia
- **1993:** Czech Republic and Slovakia become separate states
- **1994:** Russian troops march on Chechnya
- **1996:** Peace accord in Chechnya
- **1999:** New Russian offensive in Chechnya. Separatist violence in Dagestan
- **2000:** Russia starts to withdraw troops from Georgia
- **2002:** Chechen fighters occupy Moscow theatre
- **2004:** Chechen rebels occupy school in Beslan, N Ossetia; over 350 killed
- **2004:** Chechen president assassinated

West Asia
Regional History

The Historical Landscape

A seemingly inhospitable realm, arid, largely desert or mountainous plateau, West Asia lays claim to a panoply of grand names – the Garden of Eden, the Fertile Crescent, the Promised Land, the Cradle of Civilization, the Crossroads of History. Lying at the meeting point of the three Old World continents, Africa, Europe, and Asia, the region was blessed with the fertile soils, beneficent climate and diverse demography to earn these titles. As such it remained a pivotal point of Old World, or Afro-Eurasian, urbanization, culture, communications, trade, and – inevitably – warfare, until relatively recent times. In addition, possibly as a consequence of these factors, the region was also the birthplace of Judaism, Christianity, and Islam, which became three of the most widely observed world religions. Despite the attentions of European colonial powers, West Asia has upheld its inherent qualities and traditions; rivalries and divisions persist alongside ways of life and artistic traditions now centuries old, a cultural longevity sustained by religion on the one hand and, in the 20th century, the region's control of the world's most valuable commodity – oil.

West Asia, apart from its fertile riverine lowlands, is a combination of dry sandy deserts and mountainous plateaux that remain sparsely populated, or totally uninhabited even today.

The mountainous Iranian Plateau is cut off from the moist ocean air, and temperatures fluctuate greatly between winter and summer and night and day. Humans lived in the mountain fringes, but did not settle in the plateau's interior because of the cold, dry climate.

The banks of the Euphrates and Tigris rivers were where the world's first towns and cities were established.

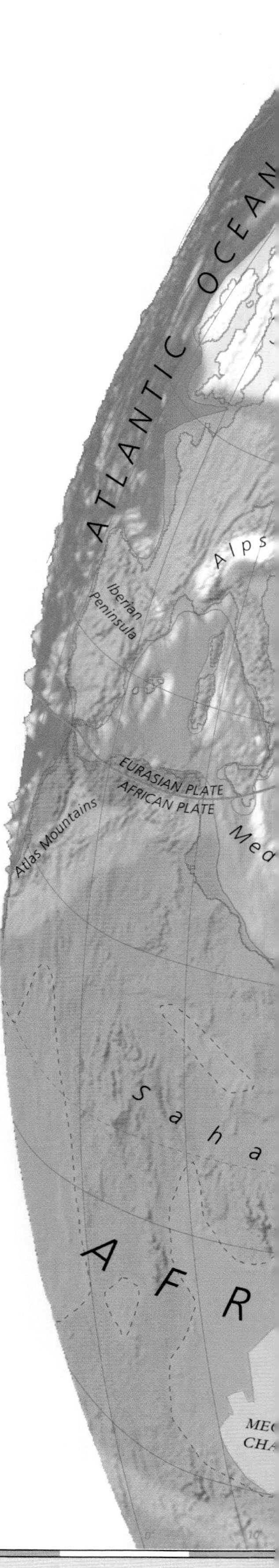

Vegetation type

- ice cap and glacier
- polar or alpine desert
- tundra
- semi-desert or sparsely vegetated
- grassland
- forest or open woodland
- temperate desert
- tropical desert
- desert
- coastline (present-day)
- coastline (18,000 years ago)

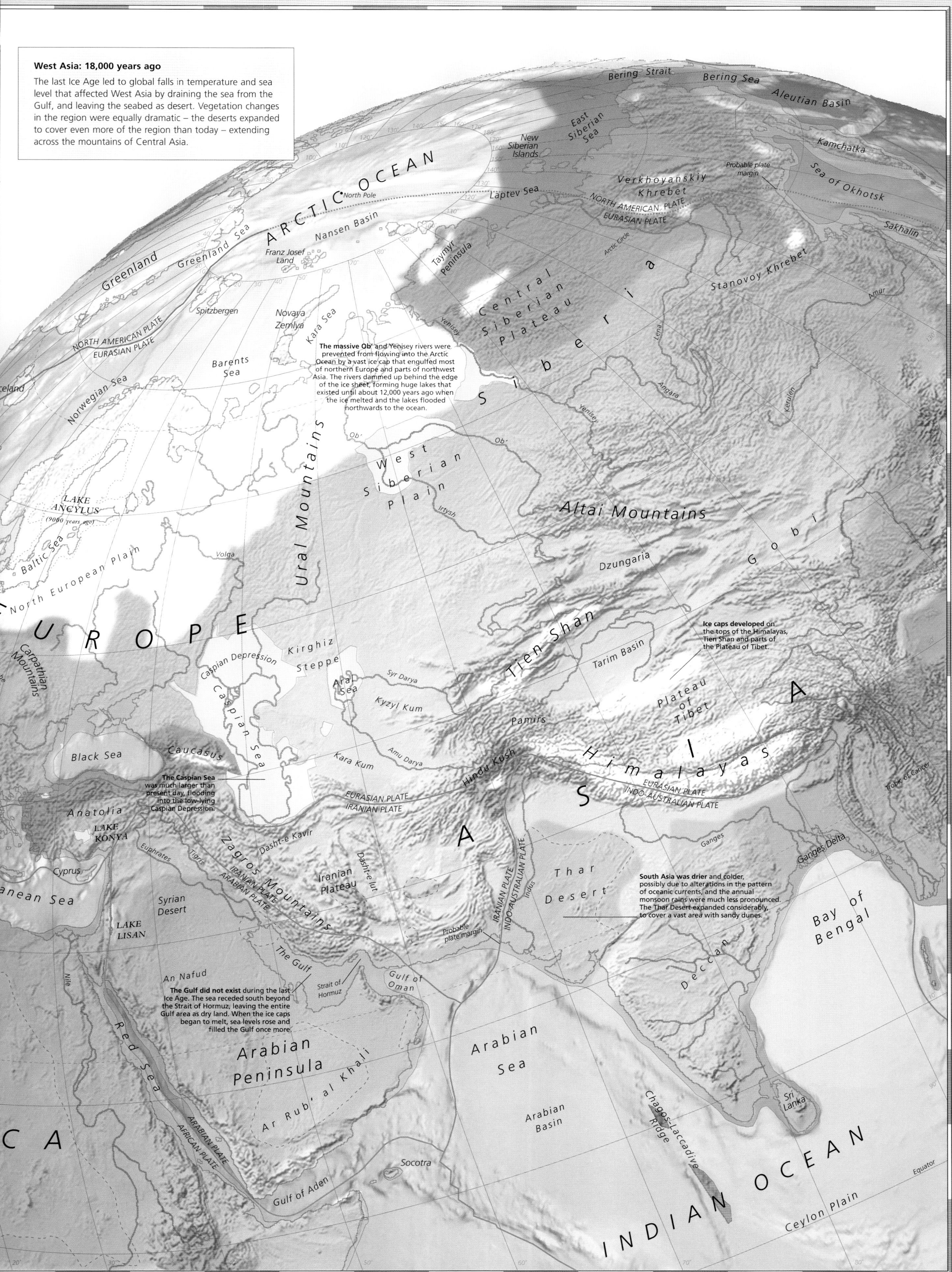

West Asia: 18,000 years ago
The last Ice Age led to global falls in temperature and sea level that affected West Asia by draining the sea from the Gulf, and leaving the seabed as desert. Vegetation changes in the region were equally dramatic – the deserts expanded to cover even more of the region than today – extending across the mountains of Central Asia.
The massive Ob' and Yenisey rivers were prevented from flowing into the Arctic Ocean by a vast ice cap that engulfed most of northern Europe and parts of northwest Asia. The rivers dammed up behind the edge of the ice sheet, forming huge lakes that existed until about 12,000 years ago when the ice melted and the lakes flooded northwards to the ocean.
Ice caps developed on the tops of the Himalayas, Tien Shan and parts of the Plateau of Tibet.
The Caspian Sea was much larger than present day, flooding into the low-lying Caspian Depression.
South Asia was drier and colder, possibly due to alterations in the pattern of oceanic currents, and the annual monsoon rains were much less pronounced. The Thar Desert expanded considerably, to cover a vast area with sandy dunes.
The Gulf did not exist during the last Ice Age. The sea receded south beyond the Strait of Hormuz, leaving the entire Gulf area as dry land. When the ice caps began to melt, sea levels rose and filled the Gulf once more.
ARCTIC OCEAN
North Pole
Bering Strait
Bering Sea
Aleutian Basin
East Siberian Sea
New Siberian Islands
Kamchatka
Probable plate margin
Sea of Okhotsk
Verkhoyanskiy Khrebet
Laptev Sea
NORTH AMERICAN PLATE
EURASIAN PLATE
Sakhalin
Nansen Basin
Greenland
Greenland Sea
Franz Josef Land
Taymyr Peninsula
Arctic Circle
Stanovoy Khrebet
Central Siberian Plateau
Siberia
Amur
Spitzbergen
Novaya Zemlya
Kara Sea
Yenisey
Lena
Barents Sea
Angara
Kerulen
Iceland
Norwegian Sea
Ob'
Ural Mountains
West Siberian Plain
Irtysh
Altai Mountains
LAKE ANCYLUS
(9000 years ago)
Baltic Sea
North European Plain
Volga
Dzungaria
Gobi
EUROPE
Carpathian Mountains
Caspian Depression
Kirghiz Steppe
Tien Shan
Tarim Basin
Aral Sea
Syr Darya
Caspian Sea
Kyzyl Kum
Plateau of Tibet
Pamirs
Black Sea
Caucasus
Kara Kum
Amu Darya
Hindu Kush
Himalayas
ASIA
Tropic of Cancer
EURASIAN PLATE
IRANIAN PLATE
INDO-AUSTRALIAN PLATE
Anatolia
LAKE KONYA
Dasht-e Kavir
Ganges
Ganges Delta
Euphrates
Tigris
Zagros Mountains
Cyprus
ARABIAN PLATE
Iranian Plateau
Dasht-e Lut
Thar Desert
Indus
Mediterranean Sea
Syrian Desert
Bay of Bengal
LAKE LISAN
Probable plate margin
The Gulf
Deccan
An Nafud
Strait of Hormuz
Gulf of Oman
Nile
Red Sea
Arabian Sea
Arabian Peninsula
Ar Rub' al Khali
Sri Lanka
Arabian Basin
Chagos-Laccadive Ridge
AFRICA
AFRICAN PLATE
Socotra
INDIAN OCEAN
Gulf of Aden
Equator
Ceylon Plain

WEST ASIA

EXPLORATION AND MAPPING

Invented by the Greeks, the astrolabe was developed by the Arabs into an indispensable tool of navigation.

SINCE THE EMERGENCE of city-states and trade, West Asia has formed the crossroads between Europe, Africa, and Asia. The Sumerians and Babylonians accumulated local geographical knowledge, but it was the Greeks, following the conquests of Alexander the Great, who began a systematic recording of the region's geography. The Romans built on the knowledge of the Greeks, as did the Arabs when, in the 7th century, Islam spread throughout West Asia. In the 13th century, when the Mongols controlled Central Asia, traffic between China and the West flourished, leaving the way open for the great journeys of Marco Polo and William of Rubruck. The region least well-known to outsiders, though its geography was well understood by its desert tribes, was Arabia, finally mapped in the 19th and 20th centuries.

The Graeco-Roman view

Many merchants from Greek colonies in Asia Minor traded eastwards to the Caspian Sea. Then, in the 4th century BCE, Alexander the Great led his army into West Asia, accompanied by a team of surveyors who recorded the route. Though none survive today, these records were a major source for subsequent geographers. Extending his quest for knowledge to the ocean, Alexander sent his admiral, Nearchus, to explore a route from the Indus to the Persian Gulf. The Greek merchant Hippalus was the first European sailor to recognize the regularity of the monsoon winds, harnessing them for his voyage to India. Arabia remained largely unknown, despite an exploratory expedition led by the Roman general Aelius Gallus.

This reconstructed map shows the world known to the Greeks in 5th century BCE. It is based on descriptions in the *History* of Herodotus, who travelled in Europe, Egypt, and West Asia, and gathered additional information from people he met en route.

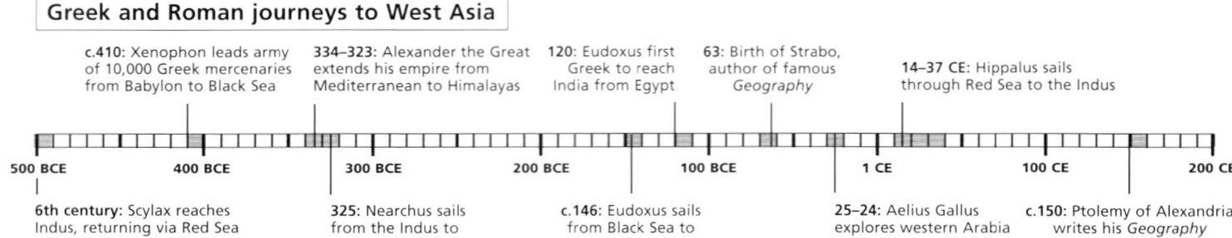

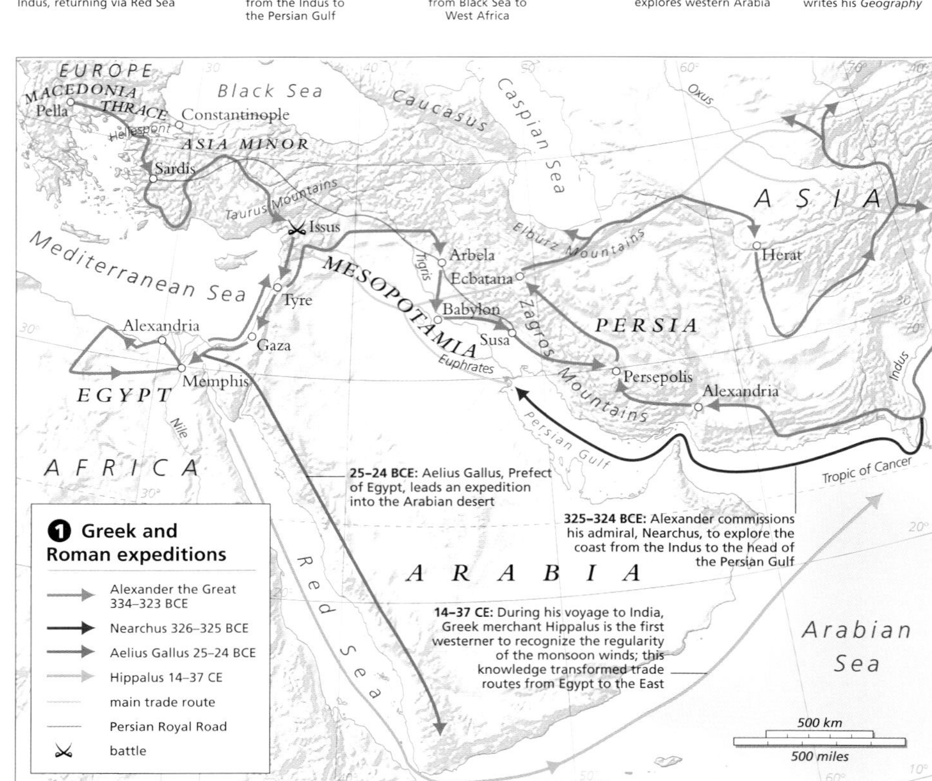

Islamic travellers

Within a century of the death of Muhammad in 632, the Muslim world stretched from the Iberian Peninsula to the borders of Tang China. Building on knowledge acquired by earlier civilizations, in particular the Greeks, and incorporating information gathered by merchants, sailors, and other travellers, Arab geographers were able to create maps of the vast Islamic realms. By the 12th century they had an excellent understanding of West Asia, Europe, and North Africa. In 1325 Ibn Battuta *(see p.68)* began the first of the great journeys which were to take him to all corners of the Islamic world.

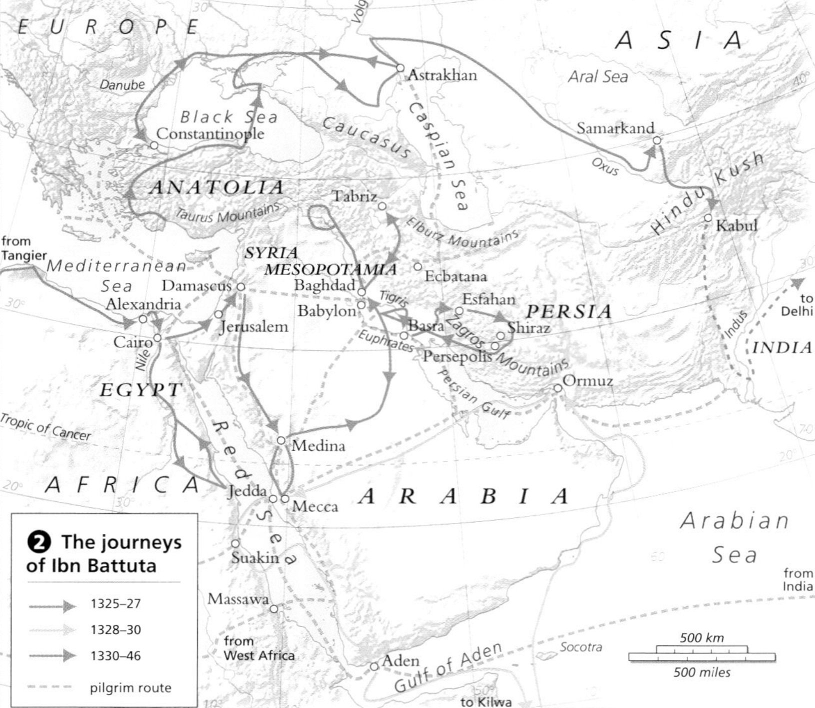

To a fanfare of trumpets, Muslims set out across the Arabian desert to make their annual pilgrimage to Mecca.

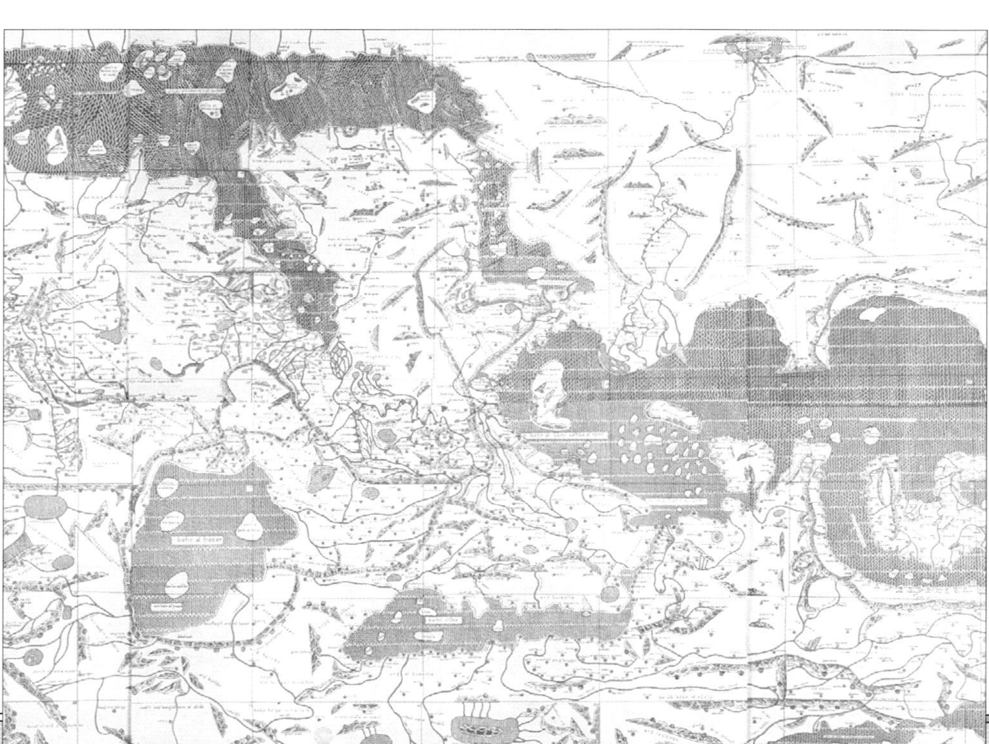

The Moroccan al-Idrisi was one of the most famous geographers of his day. The map shown here is a facsimile of the West Asian section of the beautiful world map he produced for Roger of Sicily c.1154. South is at the top, so the Mediterranean is on the right.

3 Medieval and Renaissance travellers

- William of Rubruck 1253–55
- possible route of Marco Polo 1271–95
- Anthony Jenkinson 1557–64
- John Newbery 1581–82
- Robert Sherley 1598–1600
- Thomas Herbert 1627–29

EUROPE · ASIA · ANATOLIA · MESOPOTAMIA · PERSIA · EGYPT · AFRICA · ARABIA · Mediterranean Sea · Black Sea · Caspian Sea · Aral Sea · Red Sea · Persian Gulf · Gulf of Aden · Arabian Sea · to Danzig · to Arctic Ocean · from Arctic Ocean · from Karakorum · to Karakorum · to Bukhara · to China · from China · to Venice · from Venice · Constantinople · Trebizond · Astrakhan · Tabriz · Mosul · Qazvin · Herat · Aleppo · Laias · Acre · Jerusalem · Baghdad · Shiraz · Persepolis · Kirman · Ormuz · Crimea · Caucasus · Taurus Mountains · Elburz Mountains · Zagros Mountains · Volga · Don · Oxus · Tigris · Euphrates · Nile · Tropic of Cancer · 500 km · 500 miles

European travellers in West Asia 1200–1700

- 1253–55: William of Rubruck crosses Asia to Karakorum
- 1271–95: Marco Polo travels throughout Asia, returning by ship through Persian Gulf
- 1487–89: Portuguese Pero de Covilhã sails through Red Sea to India
- 1502: Italian Lodovico di Varthema visits Arabia disguised as an Arab
- 1557–64: Jenkinson travels through Russia to Caspian Sea
- 1581–82: Newbery visits Mesopotamia and Persia
- 1598: Anthony and Robert Sherley travel to Persia, where they meet Shah Abbas
- 1627: Herbert's travels in Persia

Medieval and Renaissance travellers from Europe

In the late 13th century, in the lull following the first Mongol invasions, Europeans began to venture east across Asia. Both William of Rubruck's mission to the Mongol Khan for Louis IX of France and Marco Polo's epic journeys yielded a wealth of geographical information. But with the rise to power of the Ottoman Turks, Central Asia's trade routes were once more closed to Europeans. Later explorers, such as Sir Robert Sherley, focused their attention on Persia, sworn enemy of the Turks.

European pilgrims visit the Holy Sepulchre in Jerusalem in this illustration from an illuminated manuscript of the travels of Marco Polo.

Juan de la Cosa's early 16th-century world map demonstrates how little Europeans of the period knew of West Asia to the east of the Holy Land. Inland from the coast of the Levant, the cartographer compensated for lack of detail with an attractive illustration of the Three Kings on their journey to Bethlehem.

MAPS FOR PILGRIMS

The Holy Land has possibly been the subject of more maps than any other part of the world. To medieval Christians, the holy city of Jerusalem was the centre of their world, a concept depicted by many medieval maps which show a circular walled city, instead of a rectangular one, to symbolize the perfection of the Heavenly Jerusalem. Pilgrims and crusaders travelling to the Holy Land carried with them maps which were little more than illustrated itineraries of the towns they would pass through on their journey through Europe.

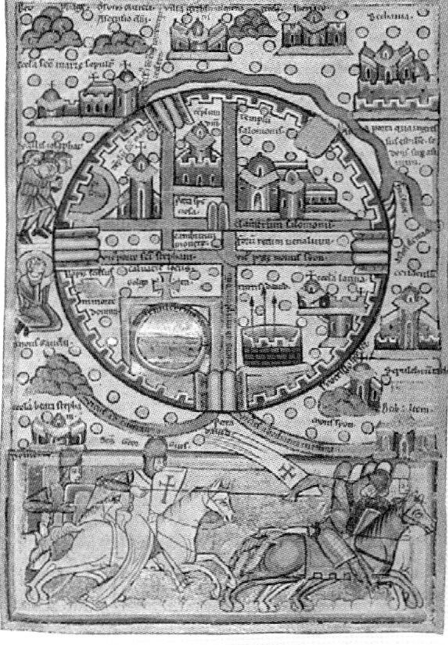

A 13th-century French map depicts the walled city of Jerusalem schematically, showing just the city's most important features, including the Holy Sepulchre and the Tower of David. Below, a crusader puts mounted Saracens to flight.

European travellers in Arabia

Although criss-crossed by Muslim pilgrim routes, maps of the interior of Arabia were rare until the 19th century. The region's hostile terrain and reputation for religious fanaticism remained considerable barriers to exploration by Europeans, despite the peninsula's wealth of valuable raw materials. Those that successfully penetrated Arabia did so armed with fluent Arabic and disguised as Muslims, particularly those who entered Islam's holy cities. The 19th century brought a rush of European explorers, especially the British, to Arabia. The last area to be explored was the Rub' al Khali (Empty Quarter), crossed first by Bertram Thomas in 1930–31 and explored more thoroughly by Wilfred Thesiger. The most detailed maps of the peninsula were made from the late 1920s following surveys by oil companies.

Europeans in the Arabian Peninsula 1800–1950

- 1812: Burckhardt discovers Petra, ancient capital of Nabataea
- 1814: Burckhardt visits Mecca
- 1818: Sadleir makes first east-west crossing
- 1853: Richard Burton visits Mecca and Medina in Arab disguise
- 1862–63: Palgrave makes first west-east crossing through the Nafud
- 1864: Guarmani travels through northern Nejd
- 1876–78: Doughty's Arabian journeys
- 1879: Wilfrid Scawen Blunt and his wife, Anne, travel to Nejd to buy horses
- 1888: Publication of Doughty's classic *Travels in Arabia Deserta*
- 1930: Thomas first European to cross Empty Quarter
- 1932: Philby crosses Empty Quarter
- 1946–48: Thesiger's double crossing of Empty Quarter

In 1762 a Danish surveyor, Carsten Niebuhr, took part in the first scientific expedition to the Arabian Peninsula. A team of Scandinavian and German experts recorded the flora and fauna of the Yemen and studied its peoples. Most of the party died, but Niebuhr survived and published an account of the expedition, *Descriptions of Arabia*, with several detailed maps of the region.

Non-Muslims entered Islam's holy cities at their peril. Richard Burton, seen here convincingly disguised as a Muslim pilgrim, visited both Mecca and Medina.

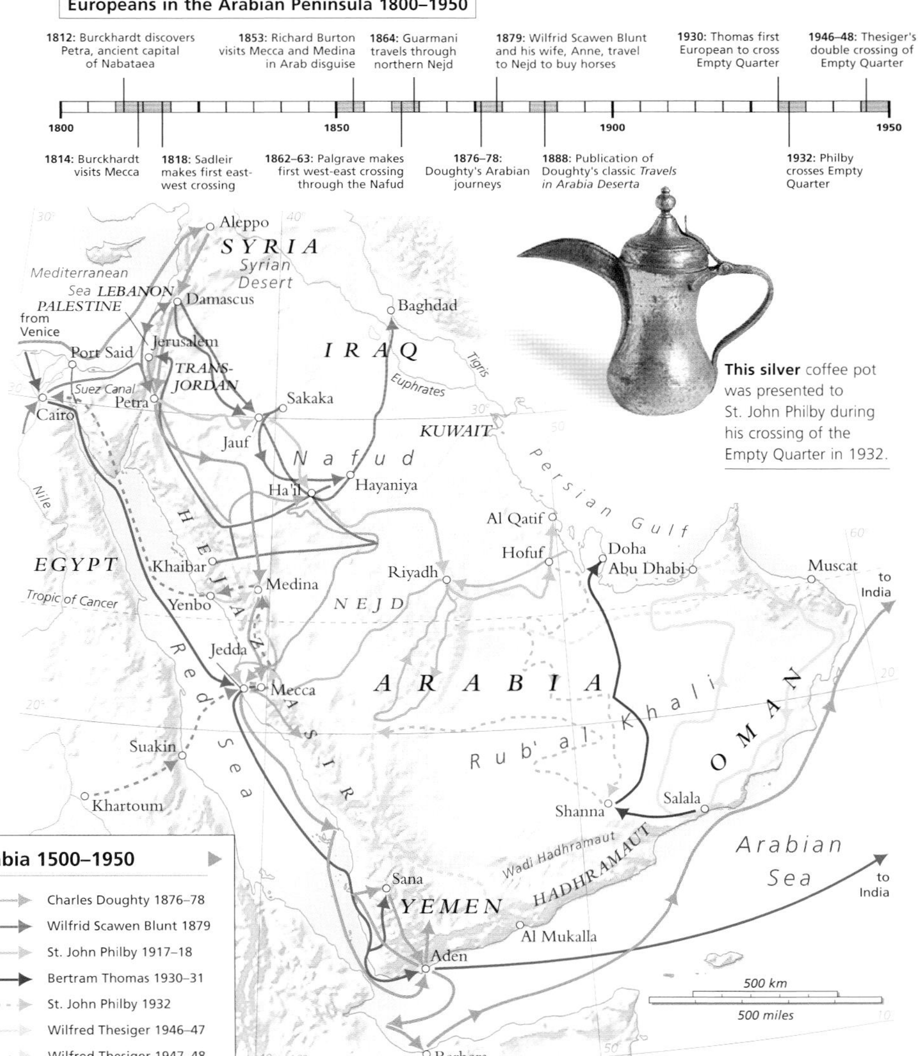

This silver coffee pot was presented to St. John Philby during his crossing of the Empty Quarter in 1932.

FROM VILLAGE TO EMPIRE

This inlaid chlorite vessel is decorated with a cat fighting a serpent Made in southern Persia, it was found at Nippur in Mesopotamia.

THE 'FERTILE CRESCENT' extends from the Persian Gulf along the flanks of the Zagros Mountains, swings west across northern Mesopotamia and down the Levant coast to Egypt. It was in this region that the first farming settlements were established, expanding into fortified walled towns. By 3500 BCE the first city-states, centres of production and trade *(see pp.24–25)*, had grown up in Mesopotamia. In 2300 BCE, a number of these were united by Sargon of Akkad to form the first empire. Other empires followed: the empire of Ur, the first Assyrian Empire, the first Babylonian Empire. In the 2nd millennium BCE, a new centre of power developed in Anatolia: the Hittite Empire, which battled with Egypt for control of the Levant.

The development of agriculture in the Fertile Crescent

Bounded by mountains to the north and east, and desert to the south, the Fertile Crescent is relatively well-watered. Wild grains, such as einkorn wheat and barley, grew on the moist mountain uplands, also home to the ancestors of domestic sheep and goats. By 10,000 BCE, this combination of resources enabled local groups to establish the first settled agricultural communities; cereals were cultivated and stored, and animals domesticated. Larger settlements, such as Jericho (8000 BCE) in the Jordan valley and Çatal Hüyük (7000 BCE) in Anatolia, became regional centres, surrounded by cultivable land and showing evidence of crafts and long-distance trade.

A number of skulls, with features modelled in gypsum and cowrie shells for eyes, were found beneath the floors of houses at Jericho.

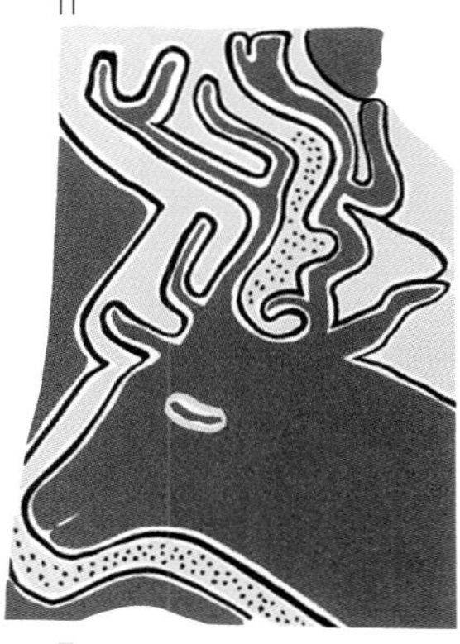

The wall of a shrine at Çatal Hüyük was decorated with this painting of a stag's head, seen here in an artist's reconstruction. One of the oldest towns in the world, Çatal Hüyük had tightly-packed houses built of mud bricks with flat roofs.

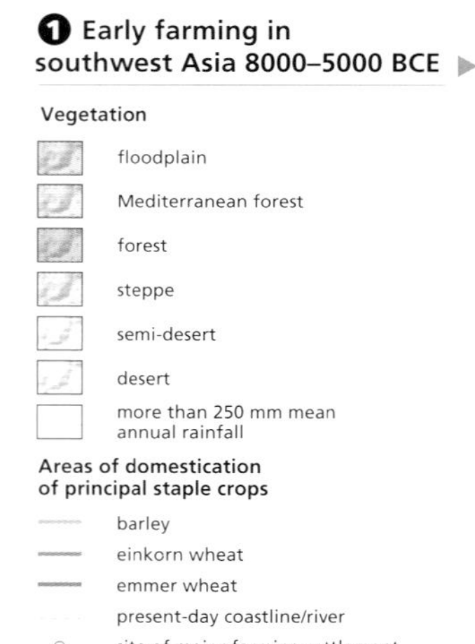

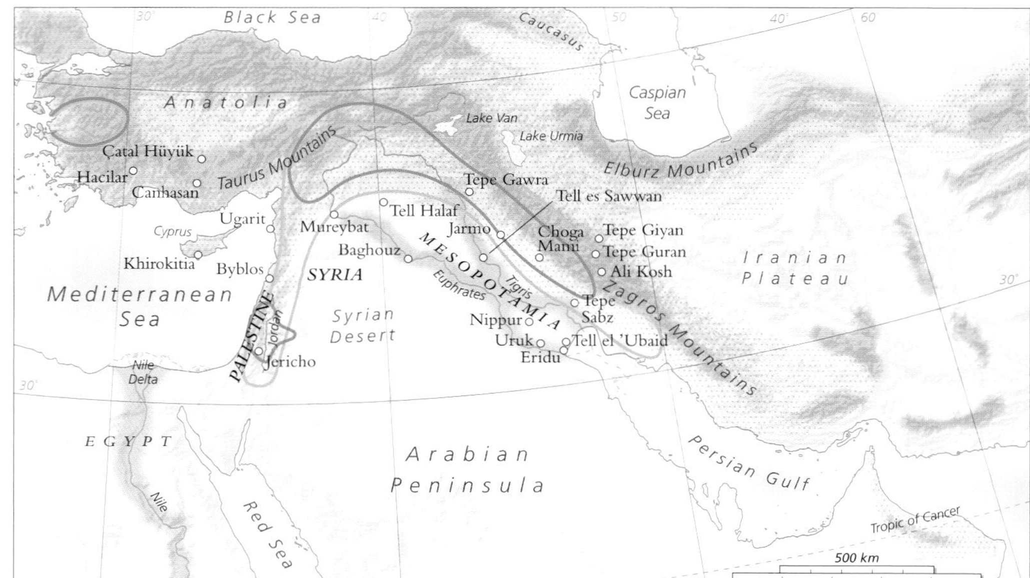

The first cities of West Asia

Farmers from northern and central Mesopotamia began to settle the alluvial plain of the Tigris and Euphrates around 6000 BCE. Irrigation enabled enough food to be produced to support large settled communities. In time, some settlements developed into cities. Each had at its heart a mud-brick temple raised on a high platform. These structures later became ziggurats like the one at Ur *(see pp.24–25)*, one of the great Sumerian cities of the 3rd millennium BCE. While sharing a common culture, each city remained an independent city-state.

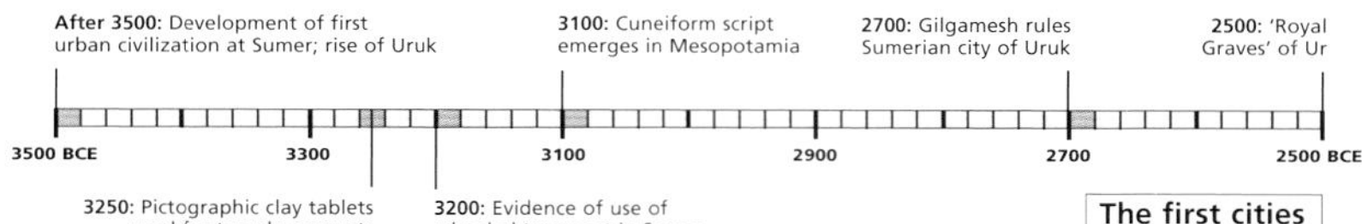

This Sumerian gaming-board (c.2500 BCE), made of wood and inlaid with shell, bone, and lapis lazuli, was found in the 'Royal Graves' at Ur. Players cast dice or threw sticks before moving their counters, which were kept in a drawer set into the board.

The growth of Uruk

From 4000 BCE, Uruk expanded into one of the leading Sumerian cities. Its closely-packed mud-brick houses were enclosed by a 9.5 km wall. Beyond the wall, crops such as barley, sesame, and onions grew in fields irrigated by a network of canals from the Euphrates. Two ceremonial complexes dominated the city; the Anu ziggurat, and the Sanctuary of Eanna. The latter contained a columned hall 30 m wide, the columns decorated with mosaics of coloured stone cones set in mud plaster. Many of the works of art found at Uruk, Ur, and other Sumerian cities used materials such as alabaster, gemstones, and lapis lazuli, from as far afield as Central Asia and the Indus Valley.

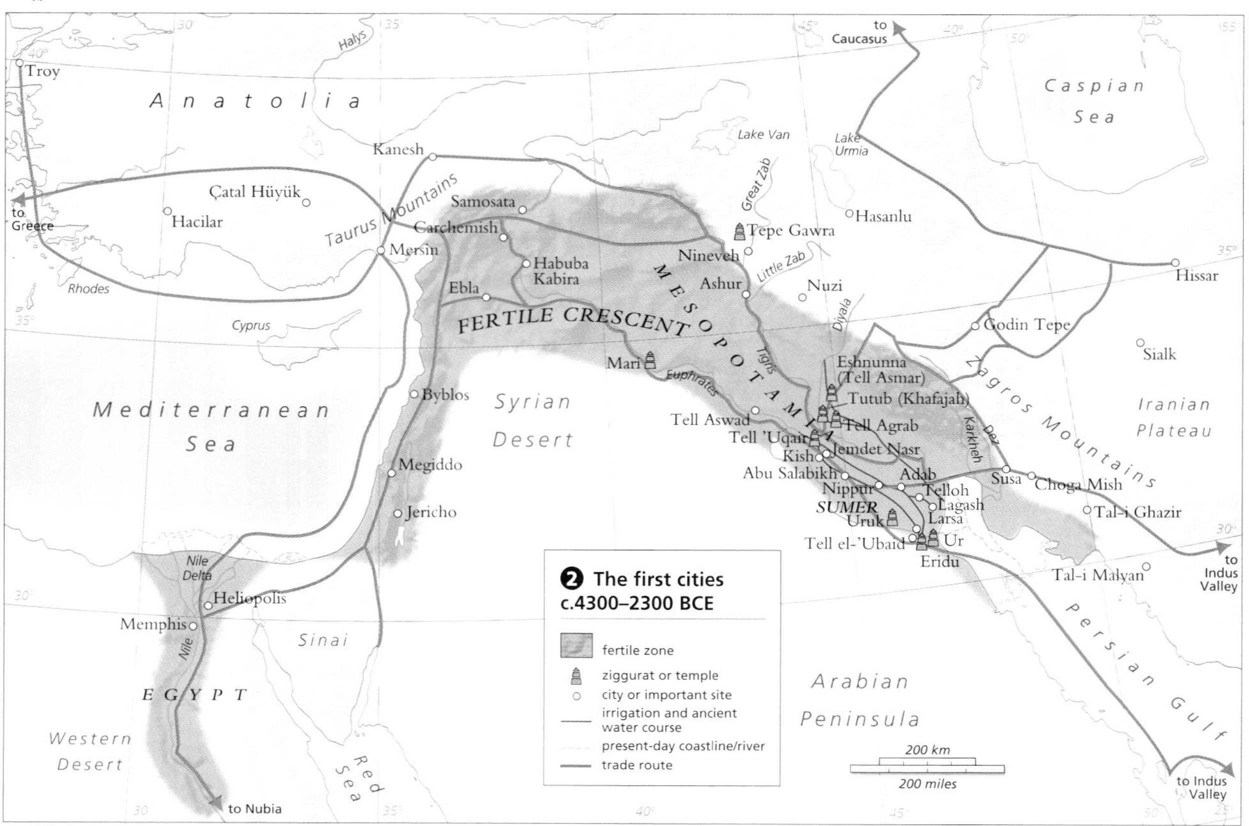

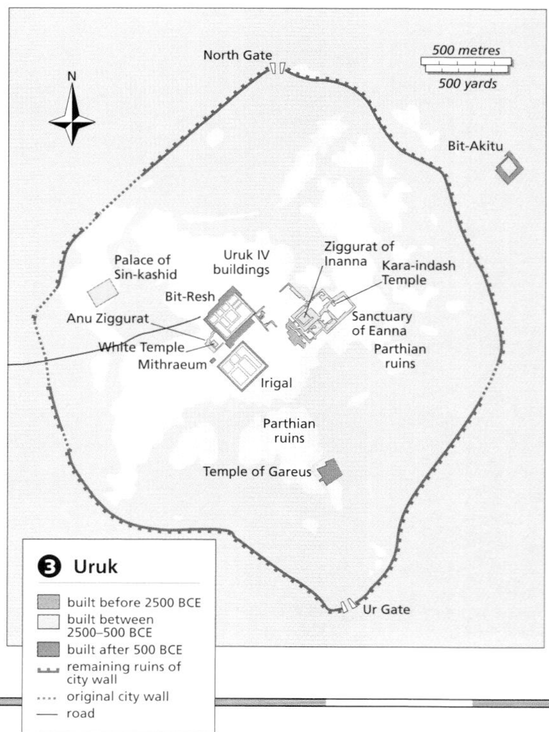

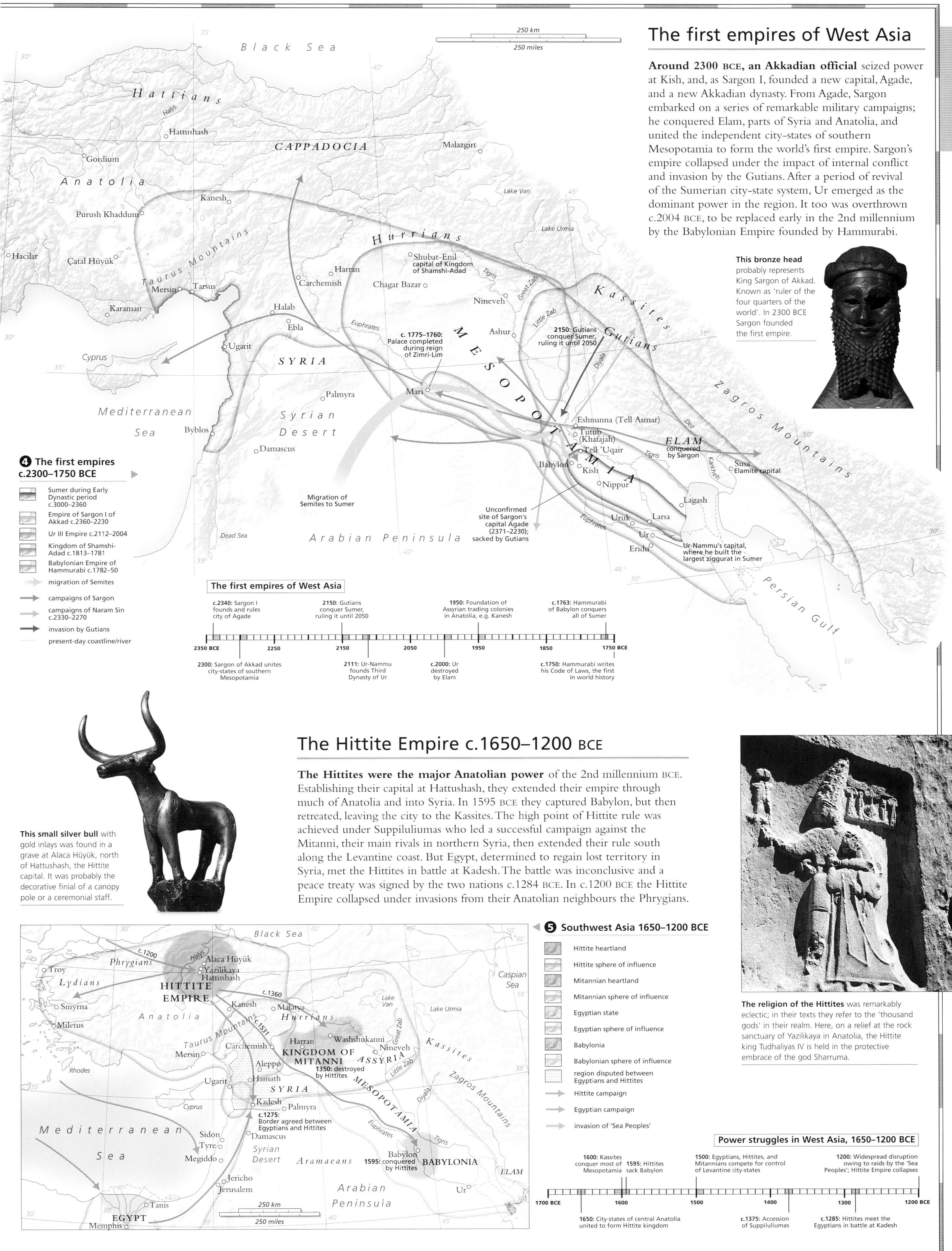

The first empires of West Asia

Around 2300 BCE, an Akkadian official seized power at Kish, and, as Sargon I, founded a new capital, Agade, and a new Akkadian dynasty. From Agade, Sargon embarked on a series of remarkable military campaigns; he conquered Elam, parts of Syria and Anatolia, and united the independent city-states of southern Mesopotamia to form the world's first empire. Sargon's empire collapsed under the impact of internal conflict and invasion by the Gutians. After a period of revival of the Sumerian city-state system, Ur emerged as the dominant power in the region. It too was overthrown c.2004 BCE, to be replaced early in the 2nd millennium by the Babylonian Empire founded by Hammurabi.

This bronze head probably represents King Sargon of Akkad. Known as 'ruler of the four quarters of the world'. In 2300 BCE Sargon founded the first empire.

4 The first empires c.2300–1750 BCE

- Sumer during Early Dynastic period c.3000–2360
- Empire of Sargon I of Akkad c.2360–2230
- Ur III Empire c.2112–2004
- Kingdom of Shamshi-Adad c.1813–1781
- Babylonian Empire of Hammurabi c.1782–50
- migration of Semites
- campaigns of Sargon
- campaigns of Naram Sin c.2330–2270
- invasion by Gutians
- present-day coastline/river

The first empires of West Asia

- c.2340: Sargon I founds and rules city of Agade
- 2300: Sargon of Akkad unites city-states of southern Mesopotamia
- 2150: Gutians conquer Sumer, ruling it until 2050
- 2111: Ur-Nammu founds Third Dynasty of Ur
- c.2000: Ur destroyed by Elam
- 1950: Foundation of Assyrian trading colonies in Anatolia, e.g. Kanesh
- c.1763: Hammurabi of Babylon conquers all of Sumer
- c.1750: Hammurabi writes his Code of Laws, the first in world history

The Hittite Empire c.1650–1200 BCE

The Hittites were the major Anatolian power of the 2nd millennium BCE. Establishing their capital at Hattushash, they extended their empire through much of Anatolia and into Syria. In 1595 BCE they captured Babylon, but then retreated, leaving the city to the Kassites. The high point of Hittite rule was achieved under Suppiluliumas who led a successful campaign against the Mitanni, their main rivals in northern Syria, then extended their rule south along the Levantine coast. But Egypt, determined to regain lost territory in Syria, met the Hittites in battle at Kadesh. The battle was inconclusive and a peace treaty was signed by the two nations c.1284 BCE. In c.1200 BCE the Hittite Empire collapsed under invasions from their Anatolian neighbours the Phrygians.

This small silver bull with gold inlays was found in a grave at Alaca Hüyük, north of Hattushash, the Hittite capital. It was probably the decorative finial of a canopy pole or a ceremonial staff.

The religion of the Hittites was remarkably eclectic; in their texts they refer to the 'thousand gods' in their realm. Here, on a relief at the rock sanctuary of Yazilikaya in Anatolia, the Hittite king Tudhaliyas IV is held in the protective embrace of the god Sharruma.

5 Southwest Asia 1650–1200 BCE

- Hittite heartland
- Hittite sphere of influence
- Mitannian heartland
- Mitannian sphere of influence
- Egyptian state
- Egyptian sphere of influence
- Babylonia
- Babylonian sphere of influence
- region disputed between Egyptians and Hittites
- Hittite campaign
- Egyptian campaign
- invasion of 'Sea Peoples'

Power struggles in West Asia, 1650–1200 BCE

- 1650: City-states of central Anatolia united to form Hittite kingdom
- 1600: Kassites conquer most of Mesopotamia
- 1595: Hittites sack Babylon
- 1500: Egyptians, Hittites, and Mitannians compete for control of Levantine city-states
- c.1375: Accession of Suppiluliumas
- c.1285: Hittites meet the Egyptians in battle at Kadesh
- 1200: Widespread disruption owing to raids by the 'Sea Peoples'; Hittite Empire collapses

EARLY EMPIRES OF WEST ASIA

The Ishtar Gate, the entrance to the great city of Babylon, was built by King Nebuchadnezzar II.

THE FIRST MILLENNIUM BCE saw a succession of powerful empires in West Asia. The first, established in the 10th century, was the Assyrian Empire. The Assyrians built their empire on the prowess of their armies and their administrative efficiency. After their overthrow by a Babylonian-Mede coalition in 612 BCE, Babylon became the dominant regional power, until it was overthrown in turn by the Persians. Founded by Cyrus the Great, the Persian Empire expanded to become the largest the world had yet seen, stretching from the Aegean to the Indus. While its empires rose and fell, West Asia was responsible for an invention of lasting value to the wider world. From its early beginnings in Mesopotamia, writing was developed into an alphabet by the Phoenicians, who carried it into the Mediterranean world, where it was adopted by the Greeks.

THE HISTORY AND LEGENDS OF MESOPOTAMIA

Much modern knowledge of the early history of West Asia is based on the libraries of clay tablets found at the palaces of the great rulers of Mesopotamia. The Royal Library of the Assyrian king Ashurbanipal at Nineveh yielded a spectacular find of some 20,000 clay tablets dealing with almost every aspect of life. One of the great literary compositions is the story of Gilgamesh, a legendary Sumerian king, based on an epic that dates back to the early 2nd millennium BCE. There is also an account of the creation, and another of a great deluge that covers the face of the earth with water. There are clear similarities between the account of the flood and the Old Testament account of Noah's Flood in Genesis.

Gilgamesh was the legendary king of the Sumerian city-state of Uruk, and the hero of an epic in which he recounts his exploits during his search for immortality.

This ivory plaque was found at Megiddo, a small, but important palace/fortress in northern Israel. It shows that Egyptian influence was still strong in the Levant.

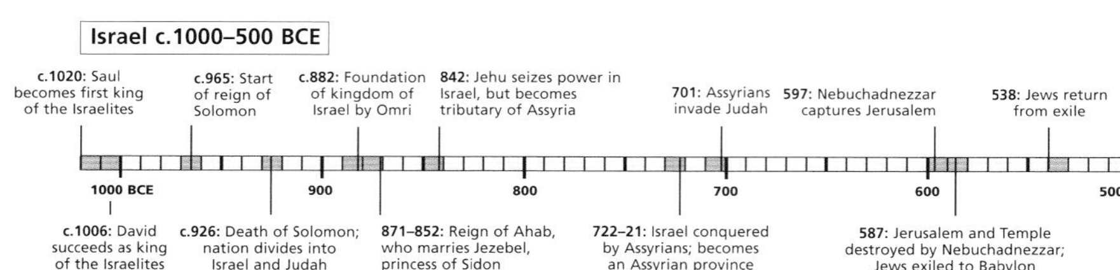
Israel c.1000–500 BCE
c.1020: Saul becomes first king of the Israelites
c.965: Start of reign of Solomon
c.882: Foundation of kingdom of Israel by Omri
842: Jehu seizes power in Israel, but becomes tributary of Assyria
701: Assyrians invade Judah
597: Nebuchadnezzar captures Jerusalem
538: Jews return from exile
1000 BCE
900
800
700
600
500 BCE
c.1006: David succeeds as king of the Israelites
c.926: Death of Solomon; nation divides into Israel and Judah
871–852: Reign of Ahab, who marries Jezebel, princess of Sidon
722–21: Israel conquered by Assyrians; becomes an Assyrian province
587: Jerusalem and Temple destroyed by Nebuchadnezzar; Jews exiled to Babylon

Israel in the time of David

According to the Bible, when David became king of Israel, he moved the capital from Hebron to Jerusalem, making it the political and religious centre of the Israelites. By defeating the Philistines, David extended Israelite rule in the region. Under his successor, Solomon – traditional builder of the Temple at Jerusalem – the nation prospered, but subsequently divided into two kingdoms, Judah and the larger kingdom of Israel under Omri and his son Ahab. In 721 BCE Israel was absorbed into the Assyrian Empire; Judah, having resisted repeated invasions, fell to Nebuchadnezzar of Babylon in 597 BCE. Jerusalem was destroyed and the Jews forced into exile in Babylon for almost 50 years.

1 Biblical Palestine at the time of David

- Judah and Israel
- conquered kingdom
- vassal
- boundary of David's empire
- boundary between kingdoms of Judah and Israel from 926

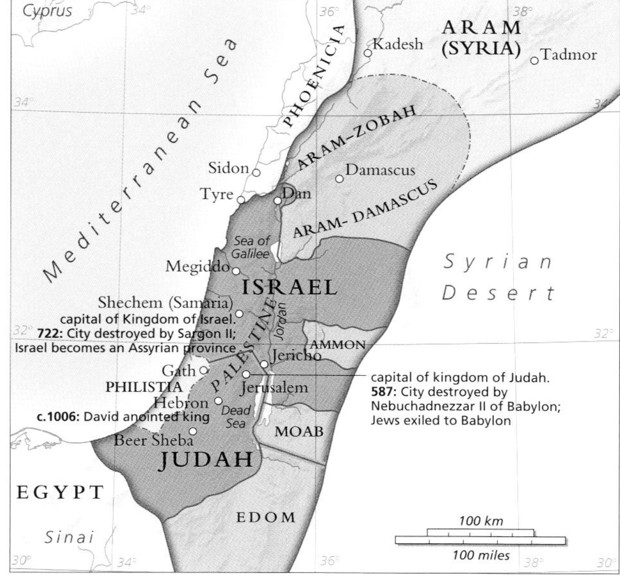
Cyprus
Mediterranean Sea
PHOENICIA
Kadesh
ARAM (SYRIA)
Tadmor
ARAM-ZOBAH
Sidon
Damascus
Tyre
Dan
ARAM-DAMASCUS
Sea of Galilee
Megiddo
ISRAEL
Syrian Desert
Shechem (Samaria)
capital of Kingdom of Israel.
722: City destroyed by Sargon II; Israel becomes an Assyrian province
PALESTINE
AMMON
Jericho
Jordan
Gath
PHILISTIA
Jerusalem
capital of kingdom of Judah.
587: City destroyed by Nebuchadnezzar II of Babylon; Jews exiled to Babylon
Hebron
c.1006: David anointed king
Dead Sea
Beer Sheba
MOAB
JUDAH
EGYPT
EDOM
Sinai
100 km
100 miles

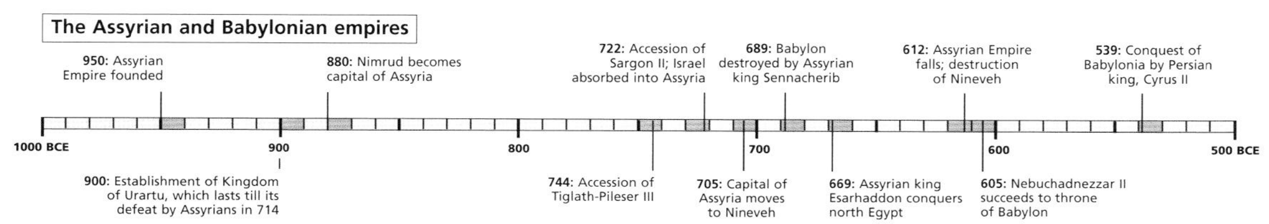
The Assyrian and Babylonian empires
950: Assyrian Empire founded
880: Nimrud becomes capital of Assyria
722: Accession of Sargon II; Israel absorbed into Assyria
689: Babylon destroyed by Assyrian king Sennacherib
612: Assyrian Empire falls; destruction of Nineveh
539: Conquest of Babylonia by Persian king, Cyrus II
1000 BCE
900
800
700
600
500 BCE
900: Establishment of Kingdom of Urartu, which lasts till its defeat by Assyrians in 714
744: Accession of Tiglath-Pileser III
705: Capital of Assyria moves to Nineveh
669: Assyrian king Esarhaddon conquers north Egypt
605: Nebuchadnezzar II succeeds to throne of Babylon

The Assyrian and Babylonian empires c.950–600 BCE

The first Assyrian Empire was established early in the 2nd millennium BCE, but collapsed under attacks from Babylon and the Mitanni. Under a series of powerful and ruthless kings it was revived, reaching its apogee during the reigns of Tiglath-Pileser III, Sargon II, and Ashurbanipal. Babylon was reconquered, the Kingdom of Urartu defeated, and the empire extended to the Mediterranean and, briefly, into northern Egypt. These conquests were achieved by a well-equipped, well-disciplined army that made skilful use of cavalry. But in the mid-7th century BCE, attacks by Medes and Scythians, combined with a revolt in Babylonia, sent the empire into a terminal decline. In 625 BCE the Chaldaeans took control of Babylon, and under Nebuchadnezzar II, the Babylonian Empire took over most of the former provinces of Assyria, including Syria and Palestine.

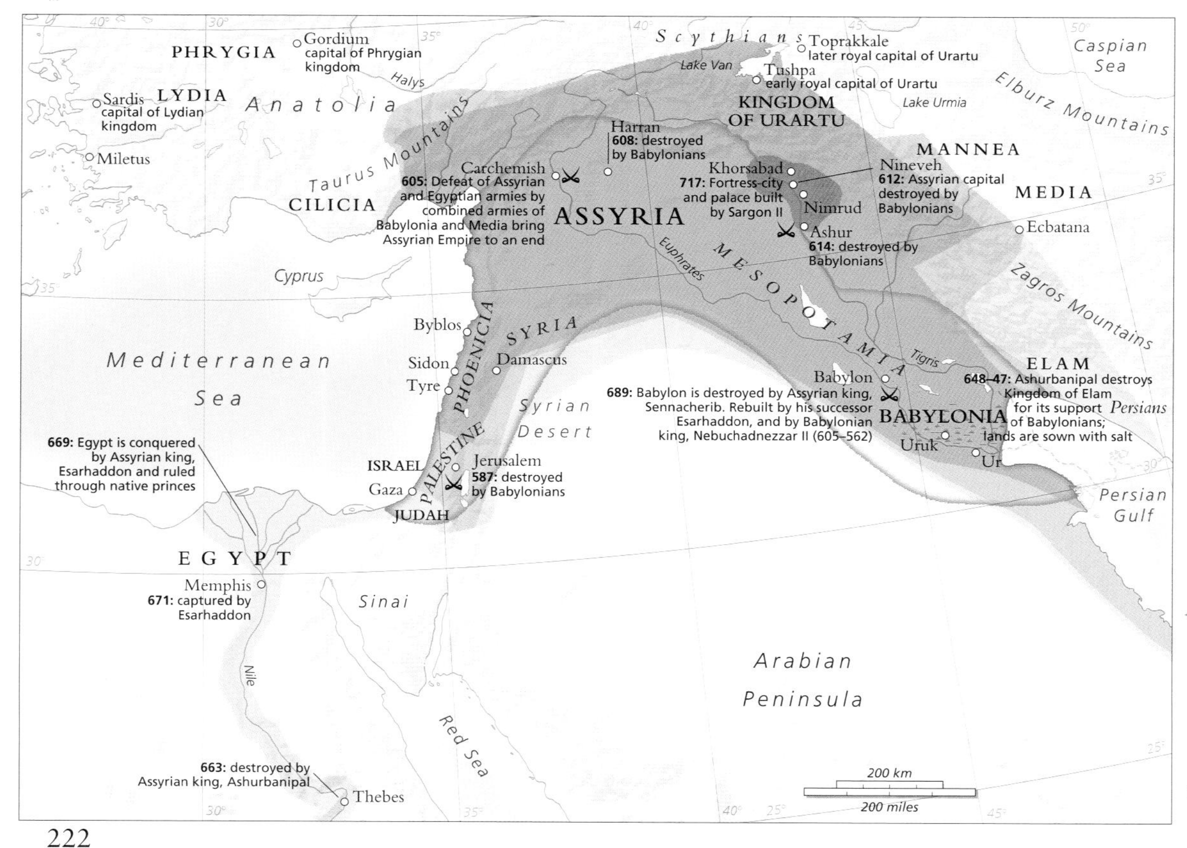
PHRYGIA
Gordium
capital of Phrygian kingdom
Scythians
Toprakkale
later royal capital of Urartu
Caspian Sea
Lake Van
Tushpa
early royal capital of Urartu
Sardis
LYDIA
capital of Lydian kingdom
Anatolia
Halys
KINGDOM OF URARTU
Lake Urmia
Elburz Mountains
Miletus
Taurus Mountains
Harran
608: destroyed by Babylonians
MANNEA
Carchemish
605: Defeat of Assyrian and Egyptian armies by combined armies of Babylonia and Media bring Assyrian Empire to an end
Khorsabad
717: Fortress-city and palace built by Sargon II
Nineveh
612: Assyrian capital destroyed by Babylonians
MEDIA
CILICIA
ASSYRIA
Nimrud
Ecbatana
Ashur
614: destroyed by Babylonians
Euphrates
MESOPOTAMIA
Cyprus
Zagros Mountains
Byblos
SYRIA
Mediterranean Sea
Sidon
Damascus
Tigris
Tyre
PHOENICIA
Babylon
648–47: Ashurbanipal destroys Kingdom of Elam for its support of Babylonians; lands are sown with salt
ELAM
689: Babylon is destroyed by Assyrian king, Sennacherib. Rebuilt by his successor Esarhaddon, and by Babylonian king, Nebuchadnezzar II (605–562)
Syrian Desert
BABYLONIA
Persians
669: Egypt is conquered by Assyrian king, Esarhaddon and ruled through native princes
ISRAEL
Jerusalem
587: destroyed by Babylonians
Uruk
Ur
Gaza
PALESTINE
JUDAH
Persian Gulf
EGYPT
Memphis
671: captured by Esarhaddon
Sinai
Nile
Arabian Peninsula
Red Sea
663: destroyed by Assyrian king, Ashurbanipal
Thebes
200 km
200 miles

A relief from the Assyrian capital at Nineveh shows Assyrian soldiers using scaling ladders during King Ashurbanipal's siege of an Elamite city.

2 The Assyrian and Babylonian Empires 950–539 BCE

- under Ashur-dan II (934–912)
- added by death of Shalmaneser III (858–824)
- added by death of Sargon II (745–705)
- added by death of Ashurbanipal (668–626)
- New Babylonian Empire (625–539)
- present-day coastline/river

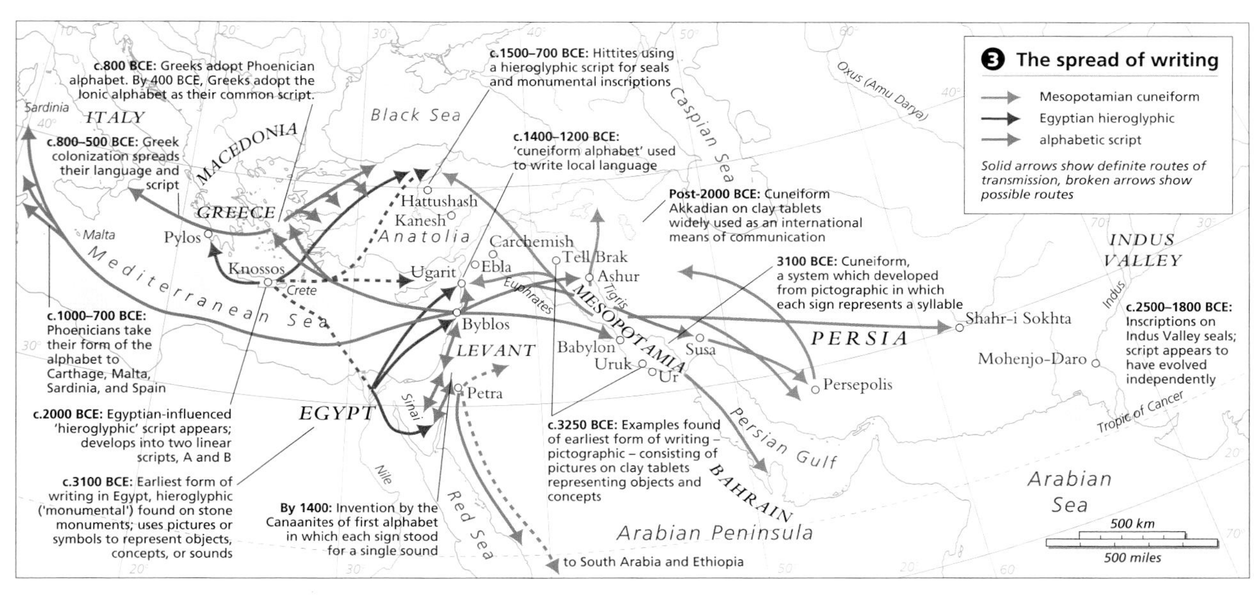

3 The spread of writing
Mesopotamian cuneiform
Egyptian hieroglyphic
alphabetic script
Solid arrows show definite routes of transmission, broken arrows show possible routes
c.800 BCE: Greeks adopt Phoenician alphabet. By 400 BCE, Greeks adopt the Ionic alphabet as their common script.
c.800–500 BCE: Greek colonization spreads their language and script
c.1500–700 BCE: Hittites using a hieroglyphic script for seals and monumental inscriptions
c.1400–1200 BCE: 'cuneiform alphabet' used to write local language
Post-2000 BCE: Cuneiform Akkadian on clay tablets widely used as an international means of communication
3100 BCE: Cuneiform, a system which developed from pictographic in which each sign represents a syllable
c.2500–1800 BCE: Inscriptions on Indus Valley seals; script appears to have evolved independently
c.1000–700 BCE: Phoenicians take their form of the alphabet to Carthage, Malta, Sardinia, and Spain
c.2000 BCE: Egyptian-influenced 'hieroglyphic' script appears; develops into two linear scripts, A and B
c.3100 BCE: Earliest form of writing in Egypt, hieroglyphic ('monumental') found on stone monuments; uses pictures or symbols to represent objects, concepts, or sounds
By 1400: Invention by the Canaanites of first alphabet in which each sign stood for a single sound
c.3250 BCE: Examples found of earliest form of writing – pictographic – consisting of pictures on clay tablets representing objects and concepts
to South Arabia and Ethiopia
Sardinia
ITALY
MACEDONIA
GREECE
Malta
Pylos
Knossos
Crete
Mediterranean Sea
Black Sea
Hattushash
Kanesh
Anatolia
Carchemish
Ebla
Ugarit
Tell Brak
Ashur
Byblos
LEVANT
EGYPT
Petra
Sinai
Nile
Red Sea
Babylon
Uruk
Ur
Susa
MESOPOTAMIA
Tigris
Euphrates
Caspian Sea
Oxus (Amu Darya)
PERSIA
Persepolis
Shahr-i Sokhta
Mohenjo-Daro
INDUS VALLEY
Indus
Tropic of Cancer
Persian Gulf
BAHRAIN
Arabian Peninsula
Arabian Sea
500 km
500 miles

The development of writing in West Asia

Pictographs, pictures representing words, were the earliest form of writing, emerging in Mesopotamia in the 4th millennium BCE. In time, pictographs developed into the cuneiform script, which was used to record several languages. The next step was taken by the Canaanites and developed by the Phoenicians: instead of using pictographs to represent words or ideas, they simplified writing into 22 different signs to represent the sounds of their speech. This alphabet is especially significant since it passed to the Greeks, then to the Romans, whose modified alphabet is still in use today.

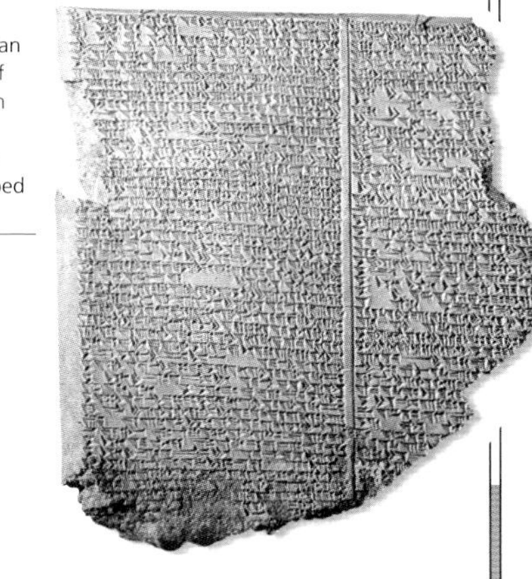

The 7th-century BCE tablet *(right)* is an Assyrian account of the legend of the flood. The cuneiform (from the Latin, *cuneus*, a wedge) characters are made up of wedge-shaped impressions in soft clay.

The development of writing in West Asia

3500 BCE – 3000 – 2500 – 2000 – 1500 – 1000 – 500 BCE

- **c.3250:** First pictographic writing from Tell Brak, Mesopotamia
- **c.3100:** Cuneiform writing emerges in Mesopotamia; hieroglyphic writing appears on Egyptian stone monuments
- **c.2500:** Earliest syllabic script used in Sumerian literature
- **c.2500:** Indus Valley civilization marks seals with inscriptions
- **c.2000:** Egyptian-influenced 'hieroglyphic' script in Crete; develops into two linear scripts, A and B
- **c.1400:** Development of first alphabets in Sinai and Levant
- **c.1000–700:** Phoenicians take alphabet to Carthage, Malta, Sardinia, and Spain
- **c.800:** Greeks adopt Phoenician alphabet

The language on the 5th-century BCE cylinder seal *(left)* is Aramaic, which used the Phoenician-Hebrew alphabet. Aramaic became the administrative language of the Persian Empire and was thus in use from Anatolia to the Indus.

The first Persian Empire

Babylonian rule in Mesopotamia was ended by Cyrus the Great. Uniting the Medes and Persians, he founded the Persian Empire, naming it the Achaemenid Empire after an ancestor. Once in power, Cyrus defeated the Lydians, then unseated Nabonidas, King of Babylon. A tolerant ruler and magnanimous victor, Cyrus released the Jews from captivity in Babylon and authorized the rebuilding of the Temple in Jerusalem. Under Darius I ('the Great') and Xerxes I, the empire was extended, organized into 20 provinces ruled by satraps (governors), and a major road network constructed. But both rulers failed in their attempts to conquer Greece. Weakened from without by raiding nomads, and from within by ambitious satraps, the empire was defeated at Issus in 333 by Alexander the Great.

The simple but imposing tomb of Cyrus the Great at Pasargadae, where Cyrus built himself a permanent residence, commemorates an outstanding leader and founder of the Achaemenid Persian Empire.

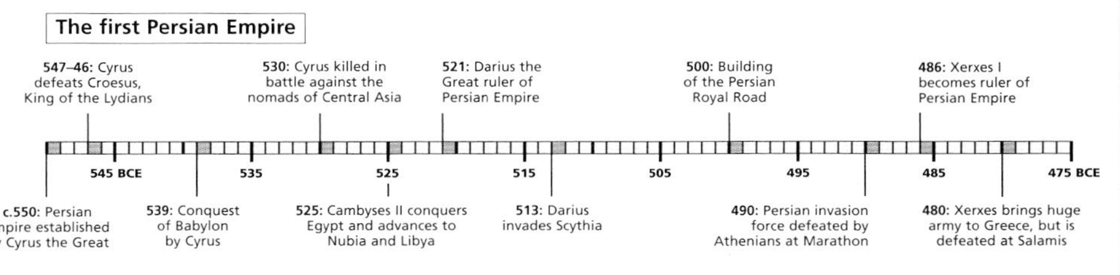

The first Persian Empire
545 BCE
535
525
515
505
495
485
475 BCE
547–46: Cyrus defeats Croesus, King of the Lydians
530: Cyrus killed in battle against the nomads of Central Asia
521: Darius the Great ruler of Persian Empire
500: Building of the Persian Royal Road
486: Xerxes I becomes ruler of Persian Empire
c.550: Persian Empire established by Cyrus the Great
539: Conquest of Babylon by Cyrus
525: Cambyses II conquers Egypt and advances to Nubia and Libya
513: Darius invades Scythia
490: Persian invasion force defeated by Athenians at Marathon
480: Xerxes brings huge army to Greece, but is defeated at Salamis

The great palace in Persepolis was begun in 518 BCE by Darius, but built mainly under Xerxes I. The wide staircase leading to the audience hall, or *apadana*, was decorated with carved reliefs of subject peoples bearing tribute.

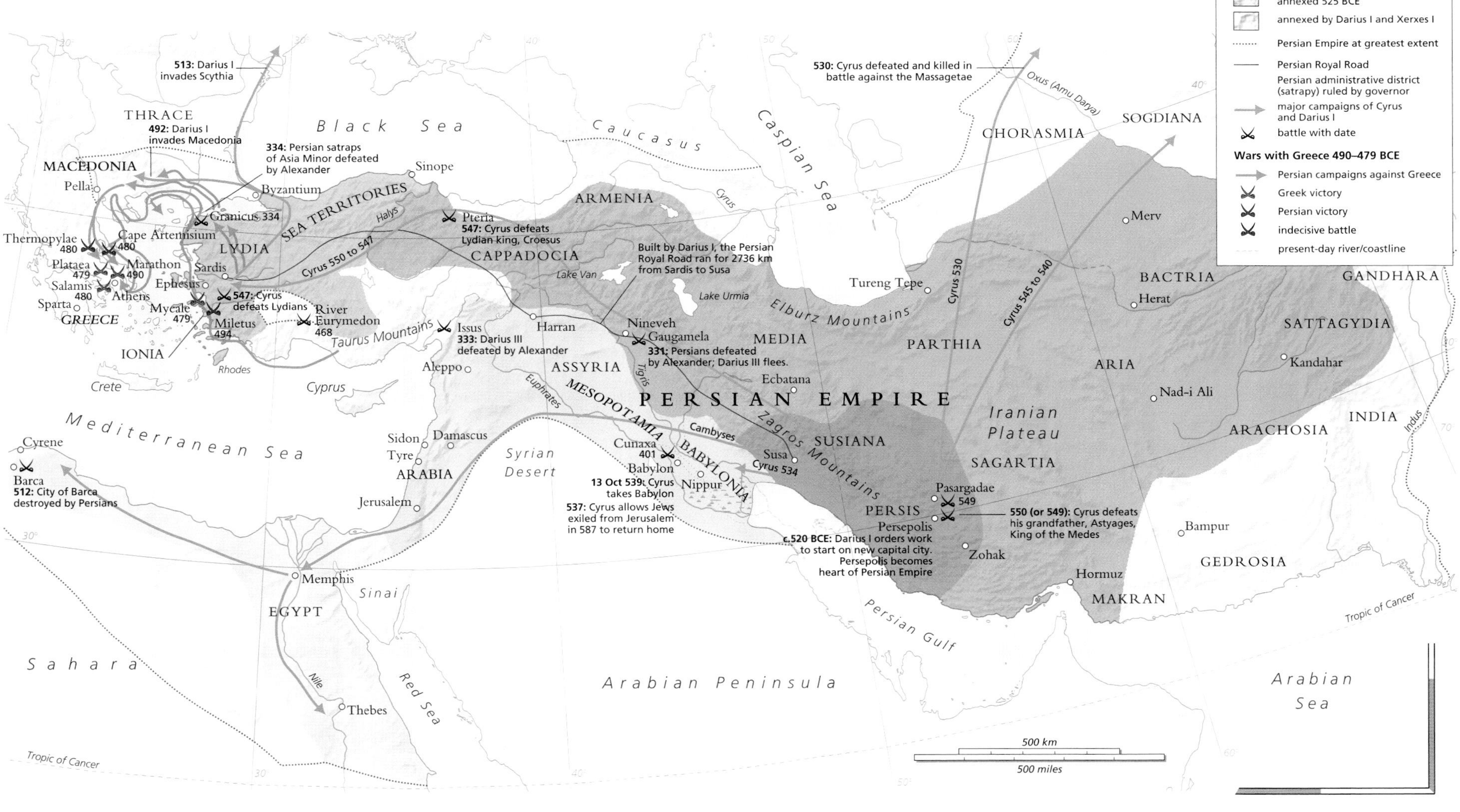

4 The Achaemenid Empire c.550–331 BCE

Persian homeland under Cyrus before 550 BCE
Kingdom of Medes, annexed 550 BCE
Kingdom of Lydians, annexed c.547 BCE
Kingdom of Babylonians, annexed 539 BCE
Kingdom of Egyptians, annexed 525 BCE
annexed by Darius I and Xerxes I

- Persian Empire at greatest extent
- Persian Royal Road
- Persian administrative district (satrapy) ruled by governor
- major campaigns of Cyrus and Darius I
- battle with date

Wars with Greece 490–479 BCE

- Persian campaigns against Greece
- Greek victory
- Persian victory
- indecisive battle
- present-day river/coastline

513: Darius I invades Scythia
492: Darius I invades Macedonia
334: Persian satraps of Asia Minor defeated by Alexander
530: Cyrus defeated and killed in battle against the Massagetae
547: Cyrus defeats Lydian king, Croesus
547: Cyrus defeats Lydians
Built by Darius I, the Persian Royal Road ran for 2736 km from Sardis to Susa
333: Darius III defeated by Alexander
331: Persians defeated by Alexander; Darius III flees.
512: City of Barca destroyed by Persians
13 Oct 539: Cyrus takes Babylon
537: Cyrus allows Jews exiled from Jerusalem in 587 to return home
c.520 BCE: Darius I orders work to start on new capital city. Persepolis becomes heart of Persian Empire
550 (or 549): Cyrus defeats his grandfather, Astyages, King of the Medes

GREEK AND ROMAN EXPANSION

This opalescent vase of moulded glass was produced in Roman Syria in the 1st century CE.

ALEXANDER THE GREAT'S CONQUESTS *(see pp.40–41)* briefly united a vast tract of West Asia. Subsequently, empires competed and dynasties fell, but a widespread Hellenistic culture survived. In Persia and Mesopotamia, the Seleucids were ousted by the Parthians, who then clashed with an expansionist Rome. By 1 CE, Rome's empire formed a single vast trading area; its West Asian Greek-speaking provinces were the richest of all. A particularly valuable trade was in incense from southern Arabia. Unrest in the Roman Empire was often religious. Rome suppressed two Jewish revolts, provoking a diaspora, but it was a new offshoot of Judaism, Christianity, that spread most effectively through the region *(see pp.48–49)*. In the east, c.226 CE, the Sassanians succeeded the Parthians, establishing a new capital at Ctesiphon.

Alexander's successors

Seleucus I took the largest portion of Alexander's empire. His dynasty lasted until 129 BCE, most of his lands falling to Rome and the Parthians.

The death of Alexander was followed by a long struggle for his empire between his generals. With the elimination of three principal contenders – Antigonus at the battle of Ipsus, Lysimachus at Corupedium, Cassander through disease – three great monarchies were established: Macedonia under the Antigonids; Egypt under the Ptolemies; Mesopotamia and Persia under Seleucus I. During the reign of Antiochus III, the greatest of the Seleucids, the Seleucid Empire was extended, but his invasion of Greece in 192 BCE led to conflict with Rome and he was forced to make peace. Thereafter the Seleucid Empire declined.

Alexander's successors in the 3rd century BCE

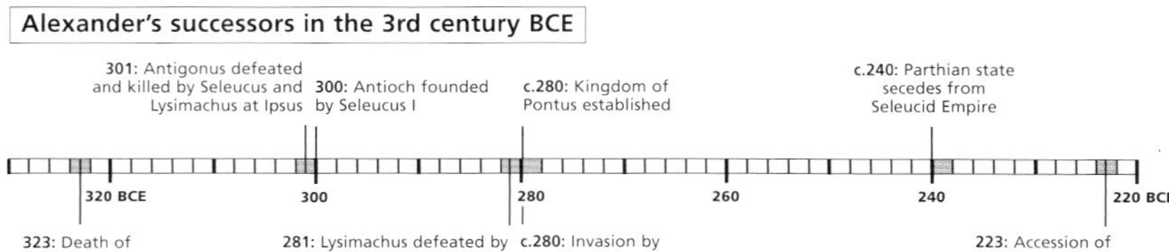

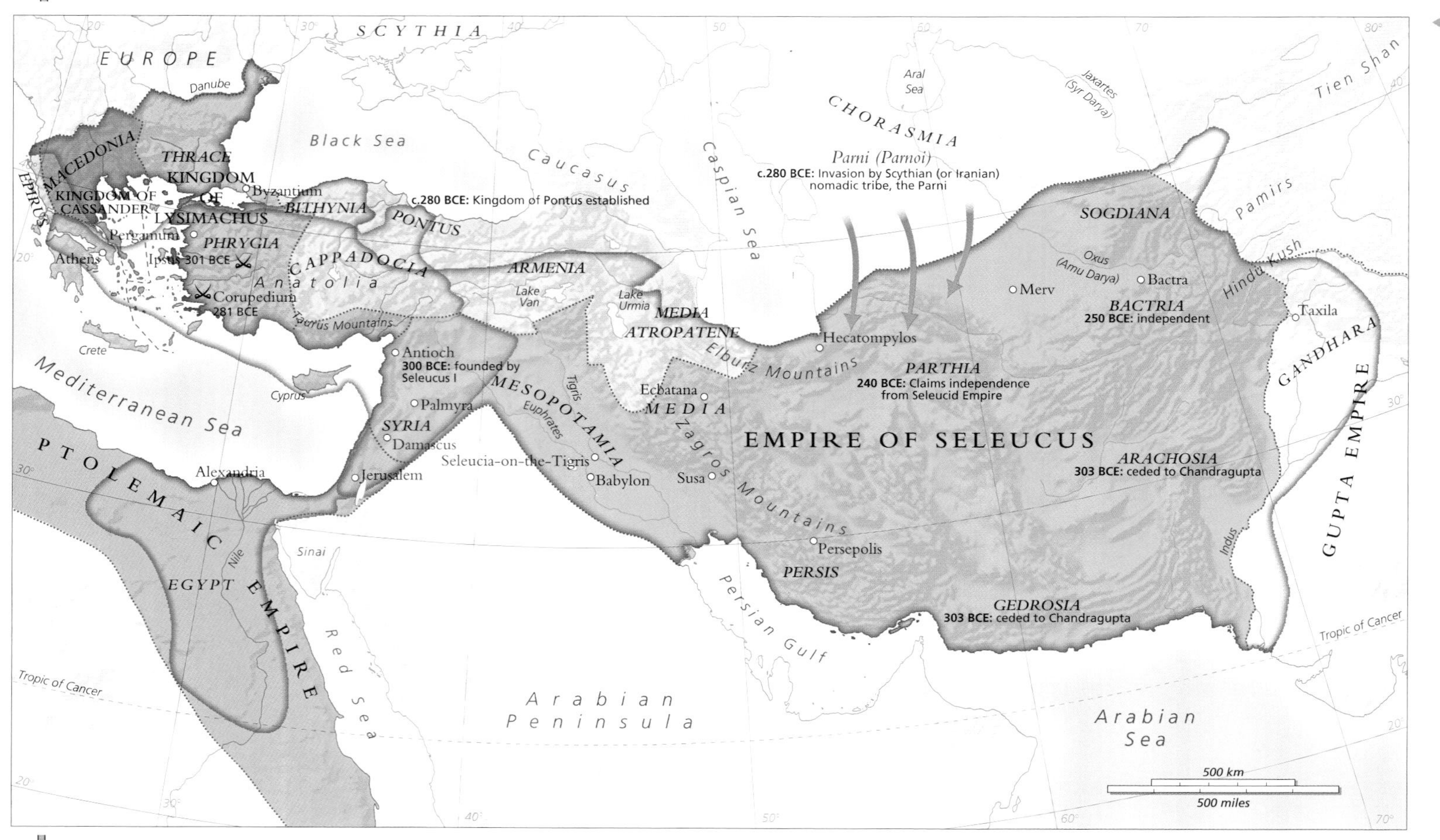

Parthia and Rome

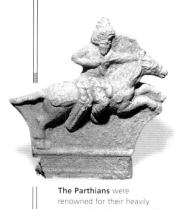

The Parthians were renowned for their heavily armoured cavalry and the skill of their mounted bowmen.

In about 240 BCE a Scythian people from the steppes of Turkmenistan broke away from Seleucid rule and established the Parthian state. A century later, under Mithridates I, they took Mesopotamia and founded a new capital at Ctesiphon. Roman expansion in the 1st century BCE brought conflict with Parthia; in 53 CE the Parthians defeated them at Carrhae. In the 2nd century CE, a weakened Parthia was invaded by Rome. Finally, 400 years of Parthian rule was ended by Ardashir, the first Sassanian ruler.

The Parthian Wars

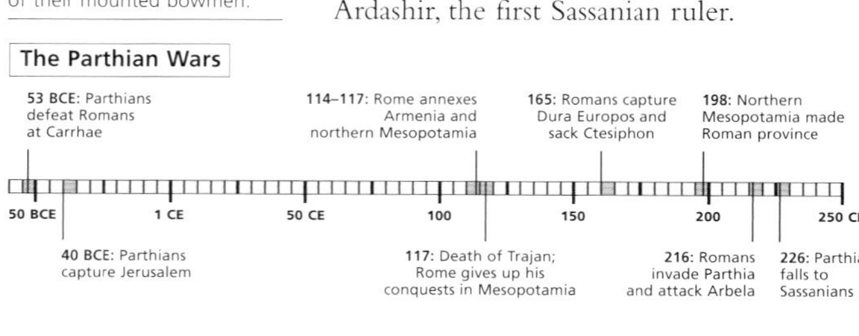

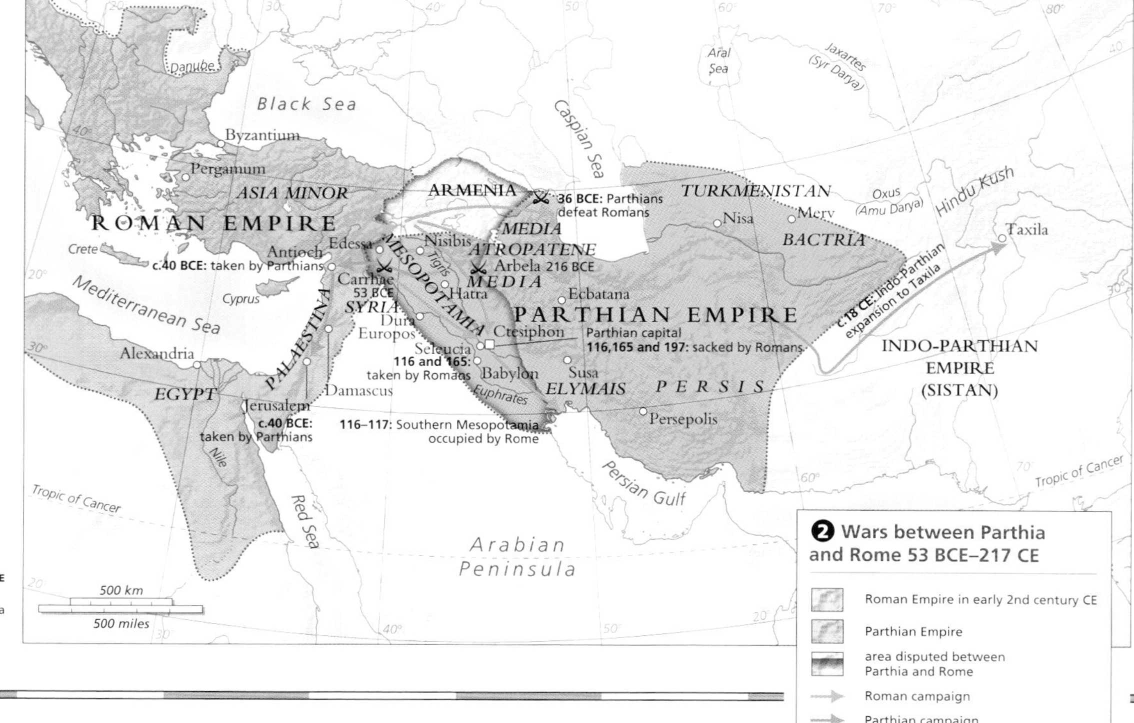

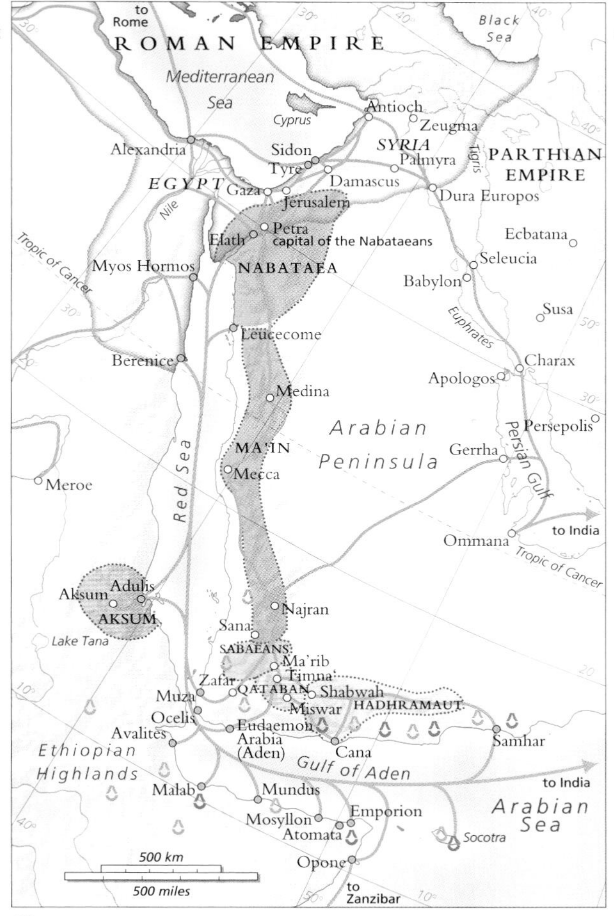

3 Red Sea trade in the 1st century CE

limit of Roman Empire 117 CE
major port
myrrh
trade route
frankincense

Arabia's Red Sea trade

The aromatic gums, frankincense and myrrh, were prized commodities in the early civilizations of Egypt and West Asia. Both were widely used to make incense, perfumes, and cosmetics, while myrrh was also used for embalming. Mainly cultivated in southern Arabia, Ethiopia, and the island of Socotra, frankincense and myrrh were carried north by camel caravan to the cities of the eastern Mediterranean. Occupying a key point on this overland route, Petra, capital of the Nabataeans, became a wealthy city. As navigational skills improved and sailors learnt to harness the monsoon winds, frankincense and myrrh were increasingly transported by sea, thus benefiting those Arab states with major ports around the Gulf of Aden, such as Cana, Muza, and Eudaemon Arabia.

Incense consists of a mixture of gums and spices. The fragrant odour of burning incense was associated with religious rites and prayer throughout West Asia and the eastern Mediterranean, hence its great value. It was burnt on small stone altars, such as this example from southern Arabia.

Roman Palestine

In 63 BCE Judaea was conquered by Rome and it was in an atmosphere of anti-Roman protest by Jewish Zealots that Christianity developed in the 1st century CE. In 66 CE, discontent flared into open revolt, suppressed by a force of 60,000 men under Vespasian, and then by his son, Titus, who destroyed and looted the Jewish Temple in Jerusalem. Diehard Zealots took refuge on the rock fortress at Masada and, rather than submit to Rome, committed mass suicide. In 132 CE Bar Cochba led another revolt, which ended with the Roman destruction of Jerusalem.

After Christianity won acceptance under Constantine, many Roman artists turned from secular to sacred themes, such as the biblical scene depicted on this early Christian sarcophagus.

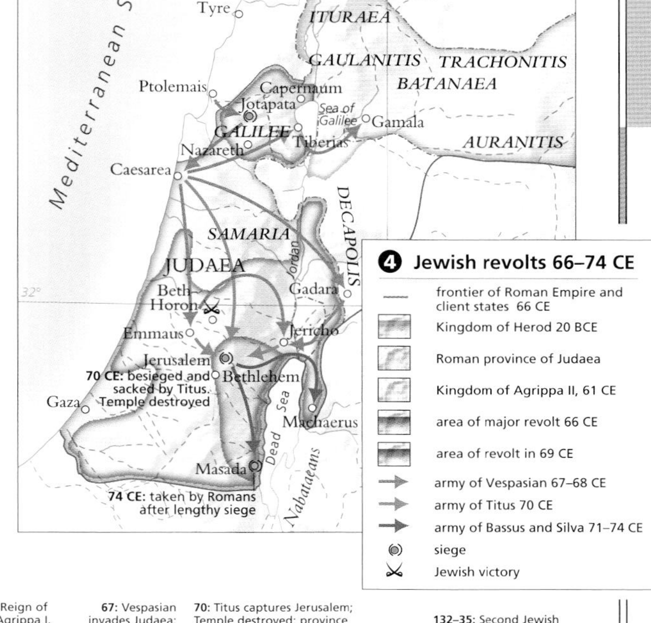

Rome and Palestine 63 BCE–135 CE

40 BCE: Herod the Great becomes king of Judaea, which remains loyal client kingdom of Rome
4 BCE: Generally accepted date of birth of Christ in Bethlehem
39–44: Reign of Herod Agrippa I, Ethnarch of Judaea
67: Vespasian invades Judaea; recovers Galilee
70: Titus captures Jerusalem; Temple destroyed; province of Judaea established
132–35: Second Jewish revolt, led by Bar Cochba

75 BCE | 45 | 1 CE | 45 | 75 | 105 | 135 CE

63 BCE: Pompey brings Judaea under Roman control
4 BCE: Death of Herod; kingdom divided between his three sons
6 CE: Judaea placed under Roman military procurator
66: Start of First Jewish Revolt
74: Romans take Masada after lengthy siege
135: Hadrian proceeds with building of Aelia Capitolina on ruins of Jerusalem

The Jewish diaspora 66–135 CE

The failed revolts of 66 and 132 CE precipitated a diaspora (Greek for 'dispersion') of Jews from Palestine. Vast numbers were sold into slavery, became refugees in Galilee or fled abroad, many to long-established centres in Babylonia and Mesopotamia. Jews were banished from Jerusalem, which was refounded as a Roman city (Aelia Capitolina). By the 2nd century CE Jews may have made up some 5–10% of the population of the Roman Empire; in some eastern cities, perhaps a quarter. Remaining loyal to their faith, the exiled Jews continued to regard Judaea as their homeland.

A detail from the triumphal arch of Titus shows the great candlestick *(menorah)* and other treasures being looted from the Temple at Jerusalem by Roman soldiers.

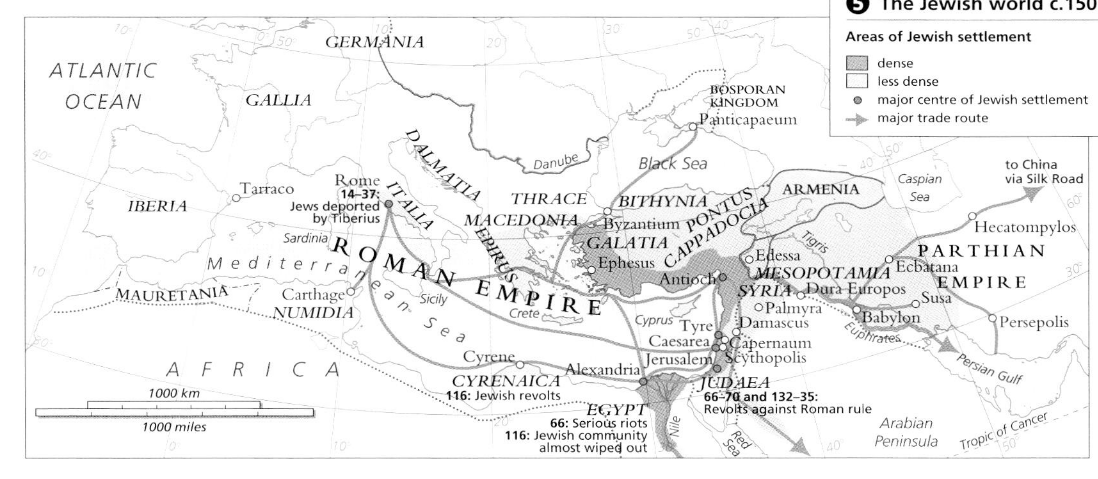

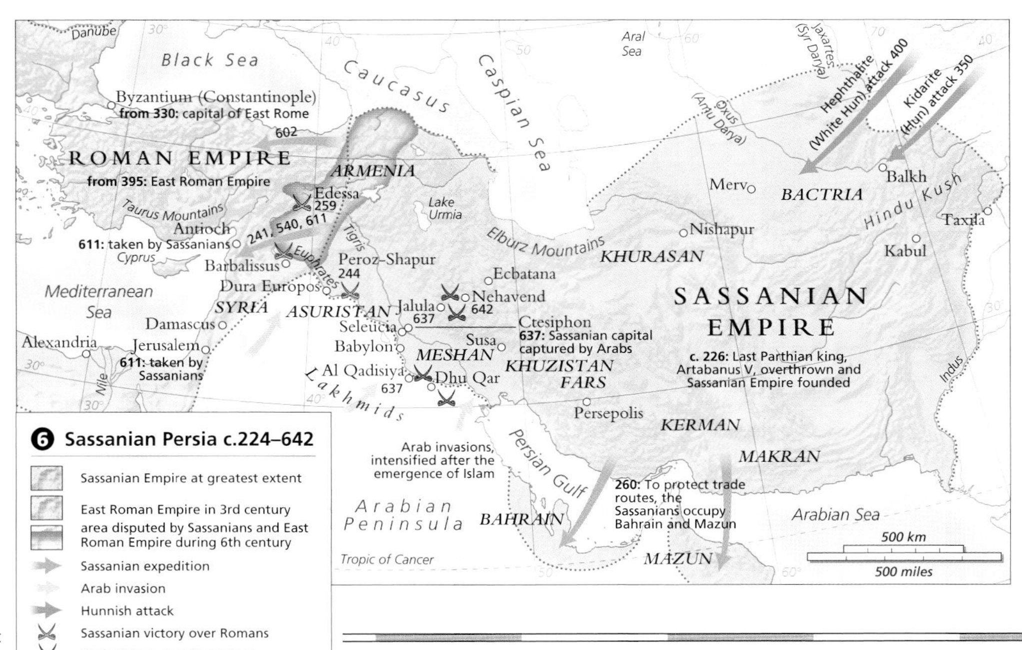

Sassanian Persia

Ardashir I rebelled against the Parthian king, Artabanus V, c.226 CE, and founded the Sassanian Empire He kept Ctesiphon as his capital and reintroduced Zoroastrianism as the state religion. The empire reached its peak of prosperity under Khosrau I. In the 7th century, his son, Khosrau II, invaded the Byzantine Empire, but was met by a successful counter-offensive. The weakened empire then fell to the Muslim Arabs.

A cameo depicts the capture of the Emperor Valerian by Shapur I, following the great Persian victory against the Romans near Edessa in 259 CE.

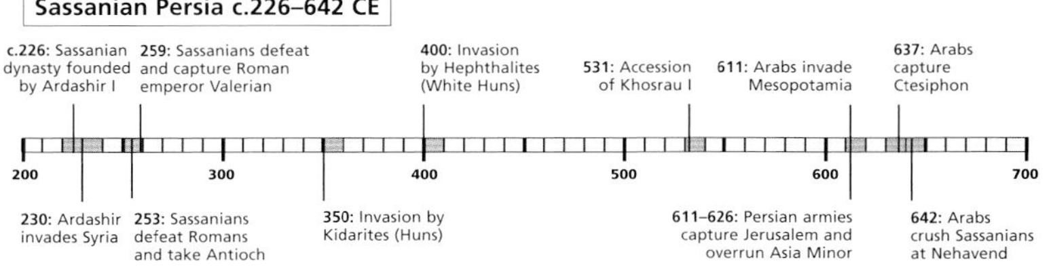

THE ADVENT OF ISLAM

This gold dinar shows Abd al-Malik, caliph from 685 to 705. He reorganized the army and the Islamic state.

IN 610, IN A CAVE south of Mecca, the Prophet Muhammad received the first of the messages from God which led him to found the Islamic faith. The clear, monotheistic message of Islam appealed to the Arabs, and within 30 years they had carried it to Persia and Palestine. The early Islamic empire was a single political entity, ruled by the caliph, or 'successor' of Muhammad *(see pp.56–57)*. By 750 CE, Arab armies had carried Islam west to the Iberian Peninsula and east to Central Asia. The Abbasid Caliphate, with its capital usually at Baghdad, was founded in 750. It was an era of great prosperity, especially in the reign of Harun al-Rashid, but later caliphs lost all political power, ruling in name only over a steadily diminishing Caliphate.

Fine textiles decorated with the Cross and other Christian imagery were woven by Egypt's Copts under Byzantine and Islamic rule.

Religions in West Asia c.600

By 600 CE three major religions were firmly rooted in West Asia: Christianity, Judaism, and Zoroastrianism. Orthodox Christianity was the state religion of the Byzantine Empire; other Christian sects, such as the Nestorians, had strong followings in Mesopotamia and Persia. Jewish communities were scattered throughout the region. The most populous was probably in Babylonia, which was also the leading cultural centre of the Jewish world. The Sassanian rulers of Persia tolerated Christians and Jews, although Zoroastrianism was the state religion. The Islamic invasion led to the emigration of many Zoroastrians, mainly to India.

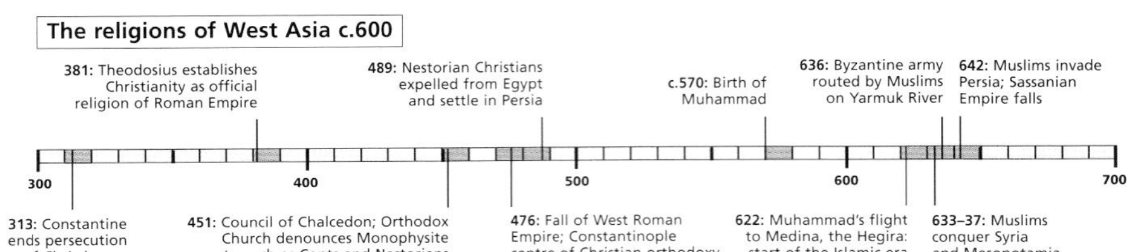

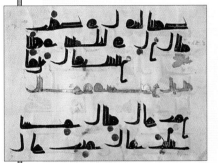

A fragment from a copy of the Koran (c.900) shows the beauty of Arabic calligraphy, regarded as the supreme art in the Islamic world. It is written in Kufic script, with the vowels indicated in red.

THE KORAN

The Koran (Qur'an) is the name given to the collected revelations transmitted to the Prophet Muhammad by the Archangel Gabriel, believed by Muslims to be the infallible word of Allah (God). Together, the revelations form the basis of Islam, the authority Muslims consult not only on questions of theological doctrine and ethics, but also on practical legal, political and social matters. The Koranic revelations were committed to memory by the first disciples of the Prophet, and in 651 CE the first authorized Arabic text was prepared. The Koran is about the length of the New Testament of the Bible, and is divided into 114 *suras* or chapters as revealed to the Prophet at Mecca or Medina.

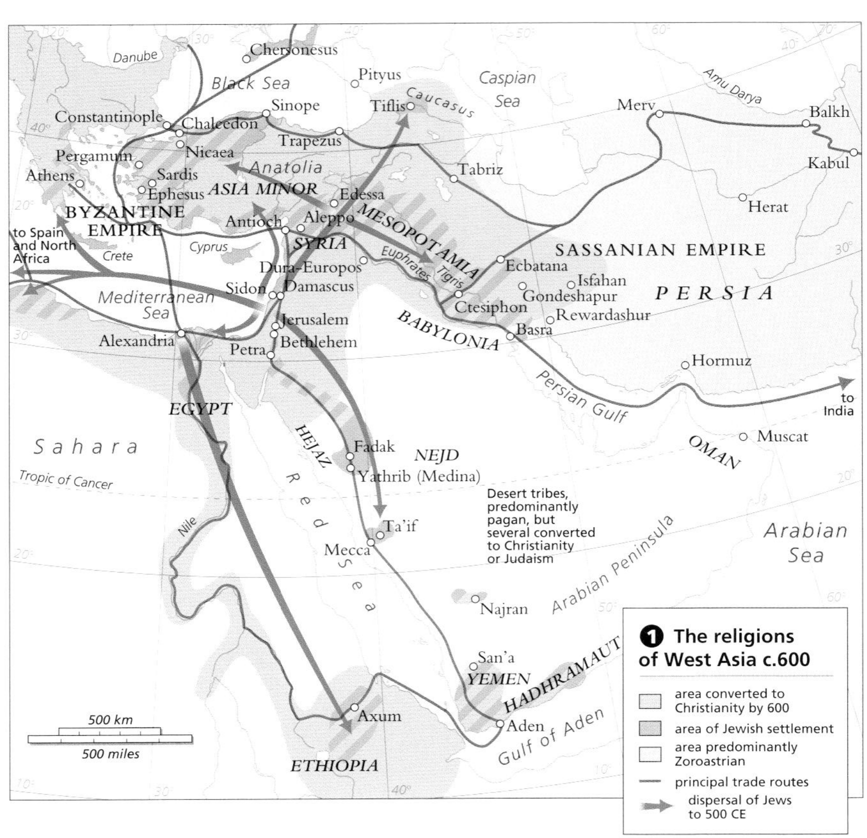

The spread of Islam

In 622 Muhammad and his followers, faced with hostility in Mecca, fled to Medina. In 630 he returned to Mecca with an army and took the city, thenceforth the religious centre of Islam. At his death, he ruled almost half the Arabian Peninsula. His successors, who took the title 'caliph' (successor or deputy), continued to spread his message through conquest: Syria, Mesopotamia, Persia, and Egypt were overrun by armies fired by the spirit of *jihad* (holy war). In 661 control of the Caliphate was gained by the Umayyad dynasty, who set up a new political capital at Damascus and extended the empire west to the Atlantic and east to the Indus.

Pilgrims in the ritual costume of two pieces of white cloth gather around the Ka' ba in the Great Mosque at Mecca.

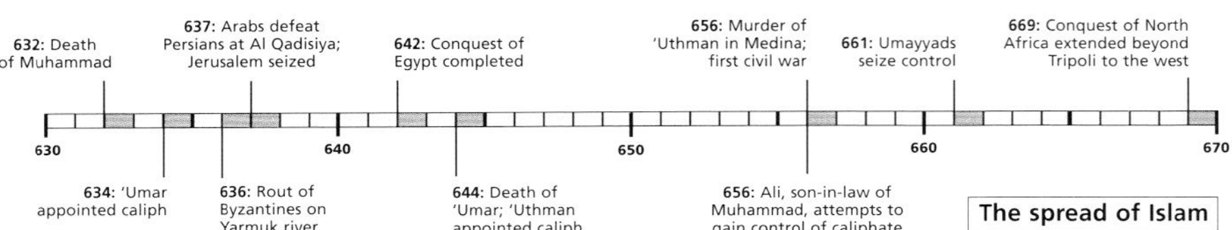

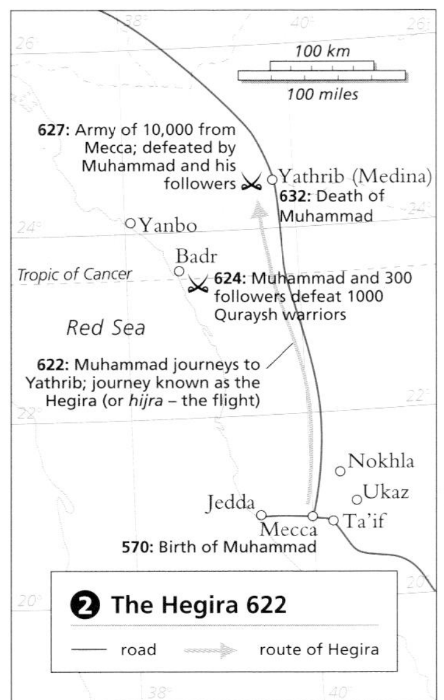

The Hegira *(hijra)*

Muhammad's flight from Mecca to Medina in 622 marks the start of the Islamic calendar. It was from Medina that Muhammad started to preach with success and spread the message of Islam. In recognition of this, the city's name was changed from Yathrib to Medina (the City), and it became the first political capital of the Islamic world. Mecca, however, had long been a holy city among the pagan tribes of the Arabian Peninsula and an important place of pilgrimage. Since it was also the birthplace of Muhammad and the site of his first revelations, it became the holiest city of Islam.

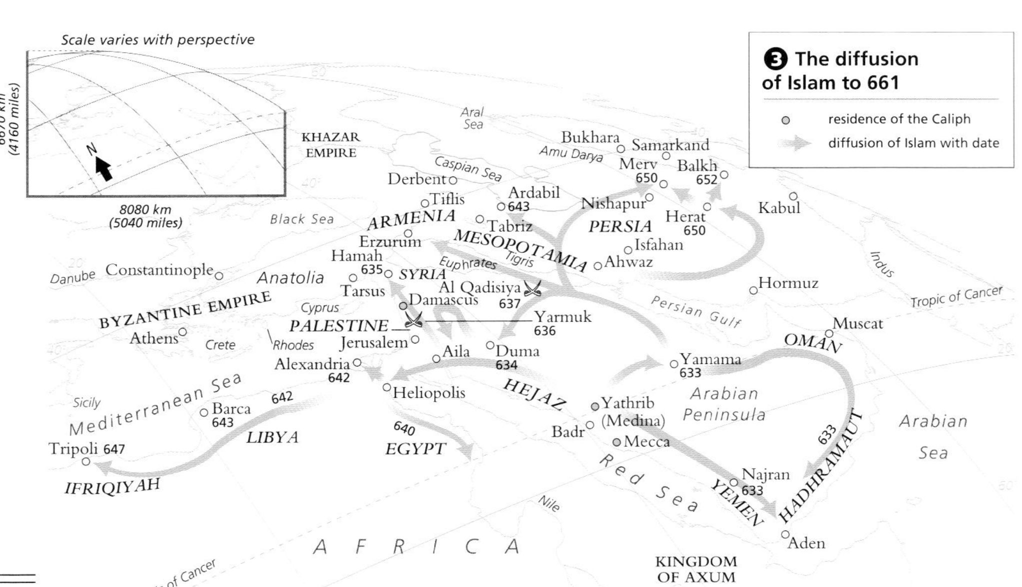

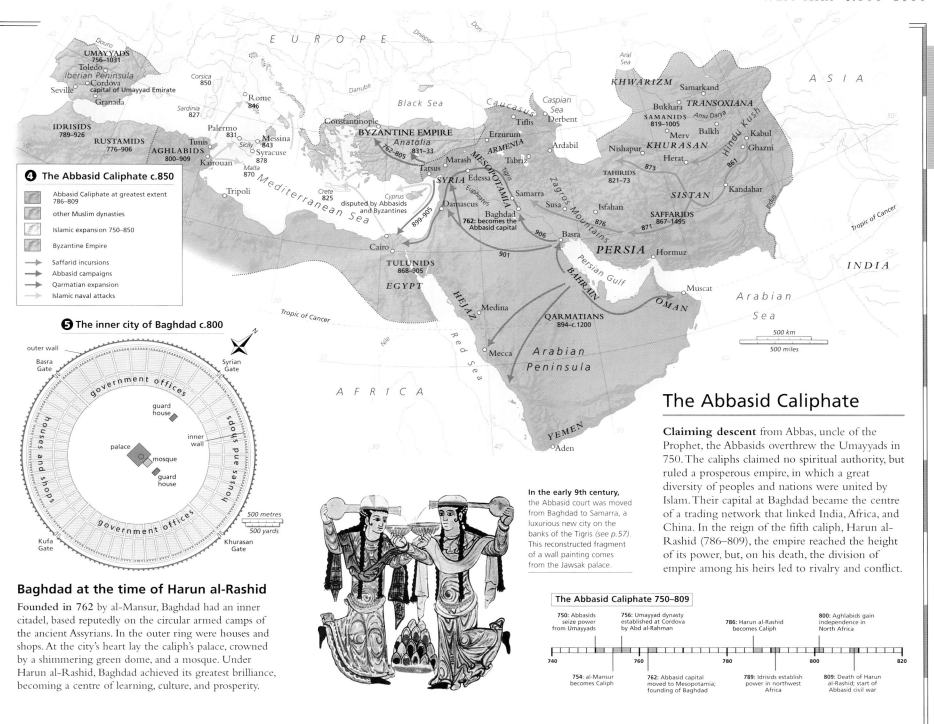

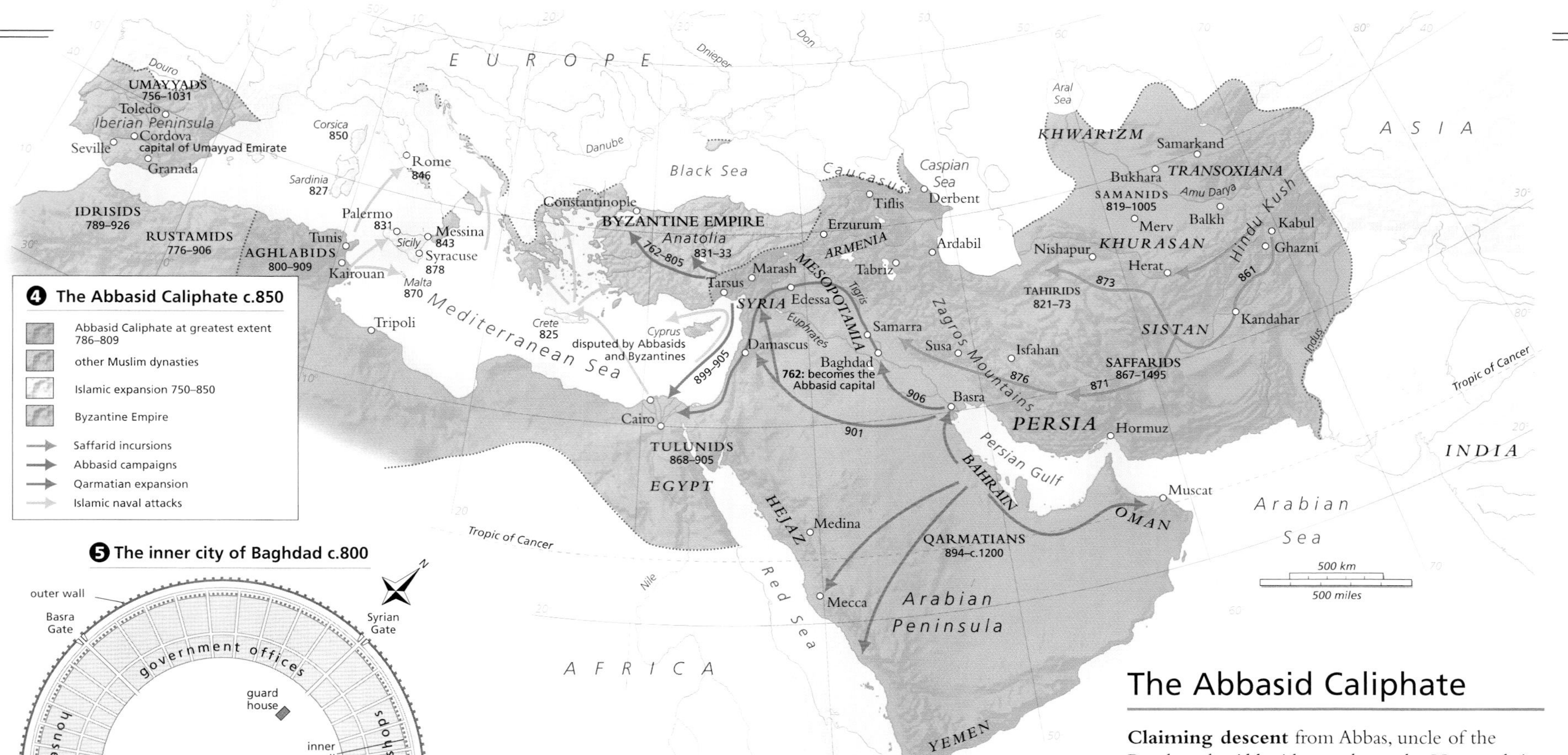

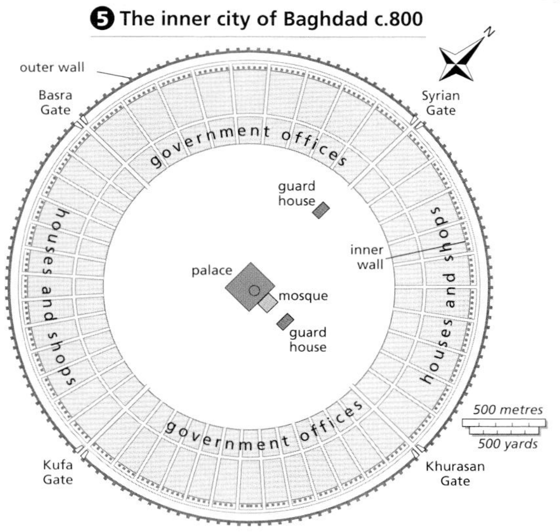

❹ The Abbasid Caliphate c.850

- Abbasid Caliphate at greatest extent 786–809
- other Muslim dynasties
- Islamic expansion 750–850
- Byzantine Empire
- Saffarid incursions
- Abbasid campaigns
- Qarmatian expansion
- Islamic naval attacks

EUROPE · ASIA · AFRICA · Iberian Peninsula · UMAYYADS 756–1031 · Toledo · Cordova capital of Umayyad Emirate · Seville · Granada · Douro · IDRISIDS 789–926 · RUSTAMIDS 776–906 · AGHLABIDS 800–909 · Tunis · Kairouan · Corsica 850 · Sardinia 827 · Rome 846 · Palermo 831 · Sicily · Messina 843 · Syracuse 878 · Malta 870 · Tripoli · Crete 825 · Cyprus disputed by Abbasids and Byzantines · Mediterranean Sea · Danube · Dnieper · Don · Black Sea · Constantinople · BYZANTINE EMPIRE · Anatolia · 762–805 · 831–33 · Tarsus · Marash · Caucasus · Tiflis · Erzurum · ARMENIA · Caspian Sea · Derbent · Ardabil · Tabriz · MESOPOTAMIA · Tigris · Euphrates · SYRIA · Edessa · Damascus · Samarra · Baghdad 762: becomes the Abbasid capital · Susa · Zagros Mountains · Isfahan · Basra · 899–905 · 906 · 901 · 876 · 871 · 873 · 861 · Cairo · TULUNIDS 868–905 · EGYPT · Aral Sea · KHWARIZM · Samarkand · Bukhara · TRANSOXIANA · SAMANIDS 819–1005 · Amu Darya · Merv · Balkh · Hindu Kush · Kabul · Ghazni · Nishapur · KHURASAN · Herat · TAHIRIDS 821–73 · SISTAN · Kandahar · Indus · SAFFARIDS 867–1495 · PERSIA · Hormuz · Persian Gulf · BAHRAIN · OMAN · Muscat · Tropic of Cancer · INDIA · Arabian Sea · HEJAZ · Medina · Mecca · QARMATIANS 894–c.1200 · Arabian Peninsula · Nile · Red Sea · YEMEN · Aden · 500 km · 500 miles

❺ The inner city of Baghdad c.800

outer wall · Basra Gate · Syrian Gate · government offices · houses and shops · guard house · inner wall · palace · mosque · guard house · houses and shops · government offices · Kufa Gate · Khurasan Gate · 500 metres · 500 yards

Baghdad at the time of Harun al-Rashid

Founded in 762 by al-Mansur, Baghdad had an inner citadel, based reputedly on the circular armed camps of the ancient Assyrians. In the outer ring were houses and shops. At the city's heart lay the caliph's palace, crowned by a shimmering green dome, and a mosque. Under Harun al-Rashid, Baghdad achieved its greatest brilliance, becoming a centre of learning, culture, and prosperity.

In the early 9th century, the Abbasid court was moved from Baghdad to Samarra, a luxurious new city on the banks of the Tigris (see p.57). This reconstructed fragment of a wall painting comes from the Jawsak palace.

The Abbasid Caliphate

Claiming descent from Abbas, uncle of the Prophet, the Abbasids overthrew the Umayyads in 750. The caliphs claimed no spiritual authority, but ruled a prosperous empire, in which a great diversity of peoples and nations were united by Islam. Their capital at Baghdad became the centre of a trading network that linked India, Africa, and China. In the reign of the fifth caliph, Harun al-Rashid (786–809), the empire reached the height of its power, but, on his death, the division of empire among his heirs led to rivalry and conflict.

The Abbasid Caliphate 750–809

- **750:** Abbasids seize power from Umayyads
- **754:** al-Mansur becomes Caliph
- **756:** Umayyad dynasty established at Cordova by Abd al-Rahman
- **762:** Abbasid capital moved to Mesopotamia; founding of Baghdad
- **786:** Harun al-Rashid becomes Caliph
- **789:** Idrisids establish power in northwest Africa
- **800:** Aghlabids gain independence in North Africa
- **809:** Death of Harun al-Rashid; start of Abbasid civil war

740 · 760 · 780 · 800 · 820

The fragmentation of the Caliphate

Civil war on the death of Harun al-Rashid accelerated the Abbasids' loss of power, though they ruled in name until 1258. The lands of Islam, once ruled by a single caliph, fragmented into semi-autonomous dynasties. Among these were the Fatimids of Egypt, the Samanids of Transoxiana, and the Ghaznavids of Afghanistan, who played a major role in the introduction of Islam to India. In 946, a Persian dynasty, the Buwayhids, invaded and occupied Baghdad. They became protectors of the Caliphate, an event that inspired a revival of Persian national identity.

All mosques share certain features, modelled on Muhammad's house at Medina. These include the *kibla*, the wall facing Mecca, the *minbar*, or pulpit, and the minaret – the tower from which the faithful are called to prayer. The minaret shown here is from the 9th-century mosque of Ibn Tulun at Cairo.

❻ The fragmentation of the Caliphate c.900–1030

- Abbasid Caliphate c.900
- residence of the Caliph c.900
- Byzantine Empire c.900
- Samanid expansion in early 10th century
- Ghaznavid expansion

Areas controlled in 1028 by

- Ghaznavids
- Fatimids
- Buwayhids

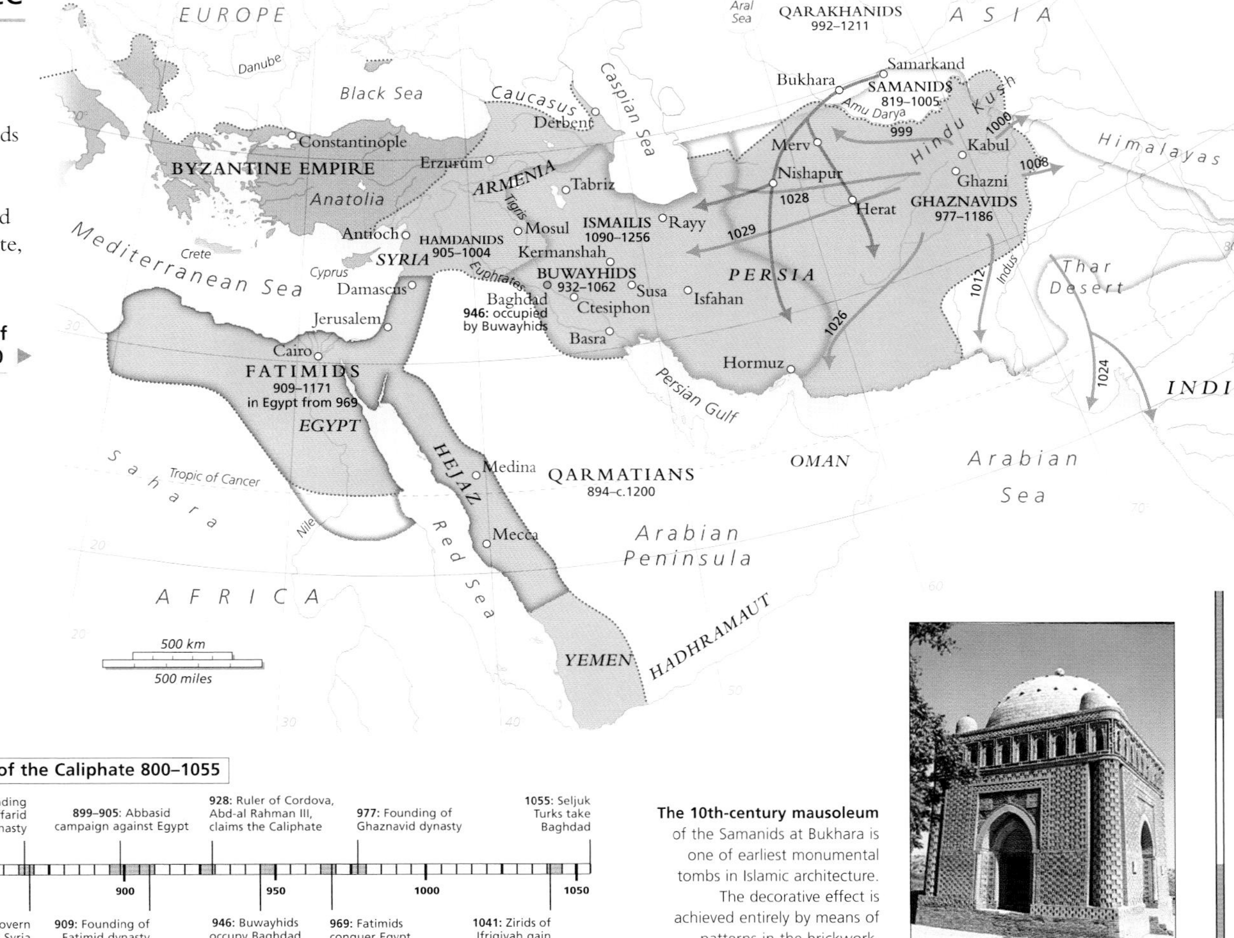

The fragmentation of the Caliphate 800–1055

- **819:** Founding of Samanid dynasty
- **867:** Founding of Saffarid dynasty
- **868:** Tulunids govern Egypt and Syria
- **899–905:** Abbasid campaign against Egypt
- **909:** Founding of Fatimid dynasty
- **928:** Ruler of Cordova, Abd-al Rahman III, claims the Caliphate
- **946:** Buwayhids occupy Baghdad
- **969:** Fatimids conquer Egypt
- **977:** Founding of Ghaznavid dynasty
- **1041:** Zirids of Ifriqiyah gain independence
- **1055:** Seljuk Turks take Baghdad

800 · 850 · 900 · 950 · 1000 · 1050

The 10th-century mausoleum of the Samanids at Bukhara is one of earliest monumental tombs in Islamic architecture. The decorative effect is achieved entirely by means of patterns in the brickwork.

TURKISH AND MONGOL INVADERS

The Islamic warrior was armed with a long curved sword, often of highly-tempered steel and finely engraved.

IN THE 11TH CENTURY West Asia was invaded by the Seljuk Turks, nomads from Central Asia. Reuniting the central Abbasid lands, they emerged as the dominant power in Mesopotamia, Persia, and Anatolia. Their crushing victory at Manzikert in 1071 drove the Byzantines out of Asia Minor and provoked the Crusades. The Crusaders set out to regain the lands lost to Islam, but their capture of Jerusalem in 1099 was countered a century later by Saladin, who had become ruler of Egypt. In the mid-13th century, a new threat was presented by the Mongols, who conquered much of the region, but were halted by the Mamluks, who now ruled Egypt. In the late 14th century, Timur, the last Mongol conqueror, launched a series of campaigns which took him from Ankara to Delhi.

The Seljuk Turks and the Byzantines

The Seljuks were great builders. Their architectural forms and intricate abstract designs had a lasting influence on Islamic art. This glazed tilework in Isfahan's Friday Mosque dates from the late 11th century.

In about 1040, a group of Turkish tribes swept out of the lands north of the Oxus. The Seljuks were the dominant clan. By 1055 they reached Baghdad, where they ruled in the name of the Abbasid caliph. Recent converts to Sunni Islam, the Seljuks planned to subdue all Shi'ites and infidels. Conquering Armenia, they then struck at the Byzantines in Asia Minor, defeating them at Manzikert in 1071. The seizure of Syria and much of Palestine from the Fatimids followed. After a period of civil war, the Seljuk Empire was split in two by the establishment in Anatolia of the independent Sultanate of Rum, with its capital at Konya. The Seljuks' control over their empire waned and they were crushed by the Mongols at Köse Dagh in 1243.

The growth of the Great Seljuk Empire

c.1040: Seljuks conquer Afghanistan and eastern Persia
1055: Seljuks established in Baghdad, ruling in the name of the Abbasid Caliph
1069: Seljuks take Konya (Iconium)
1071: Alp Arslan, Seljuk leader defeats Byzantines at Manzikert
1077: Province established in Anatolia with capital first at Nicaea and then Konya; dynasty comes to be known as the Seljuks of Rum (Rome)
1084: Fall of Antioch to Seljuks
1092: Vizier Nizam al-Mulk murdered by Ismaili Assassin
1094: Seljuk dynasty of Syria founded with capital at Aleppo
1098: Crusaders recover Antioch
1099: Crusaders recover Jerusalem

1040 1050 1060 1070 1080 1090 1100

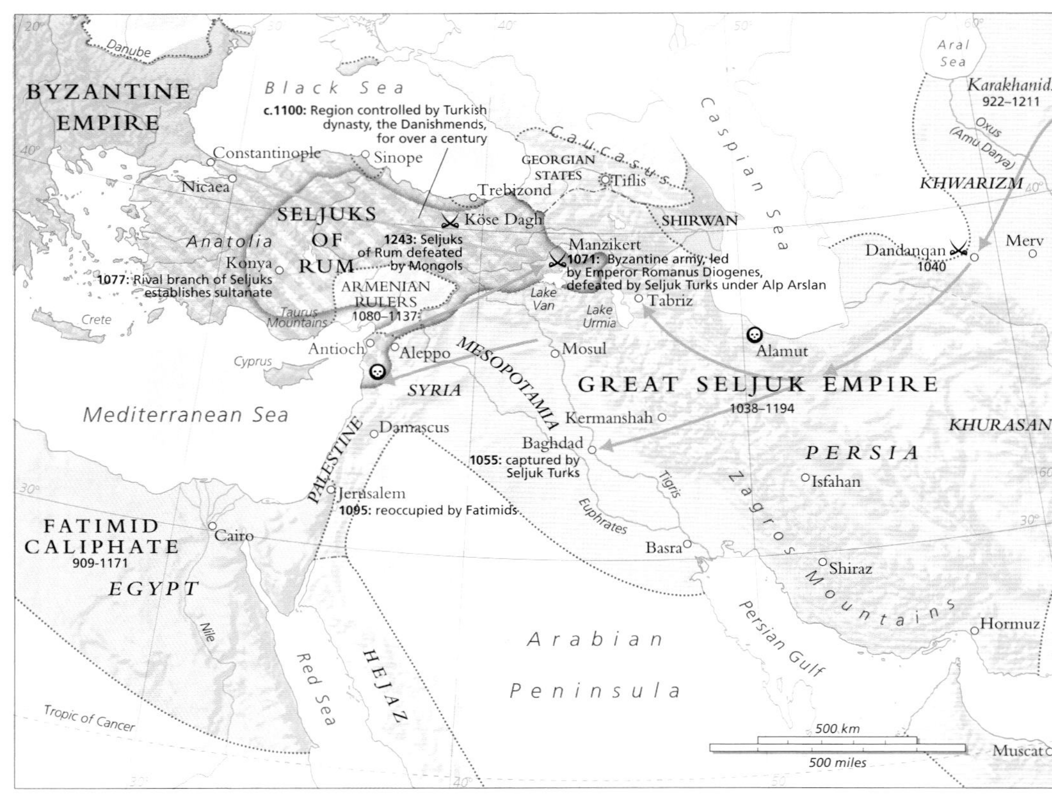

1 The Seljuk Turks and the Byzantine Empire from c.1025

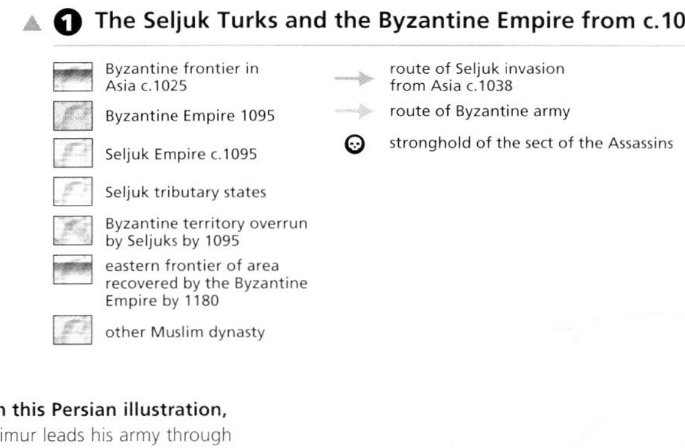

Saladin and the Ayyubid Sultanate

Saladin was a Kurdish general in the army of Nur al-Din, Zangid ruler of Mosul, who fought successfully against the Crusaders *(see pp.64–65)* and his Muslim neighbours. Ousting the Fatimids from Egypt, he united Egypt and Syria under his rule. Hostilities with the Crusader states led in 1187 to Saladin's annihilation of Christian forces at Hattin and the capture of Jerusalem and Acre. This provoked the Third Crusade, in which the Crusaders recaptured most of the coastal plain of Palestine. The dynasty founded by Saladin, the Ayyubids, dominated the region until it fell to the Mamluks in 1250.

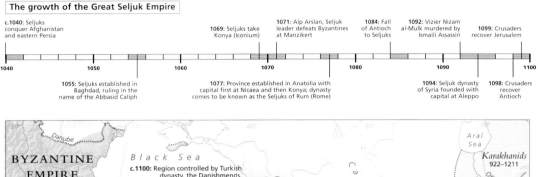

Saladin and the reconquest of Jerusalem

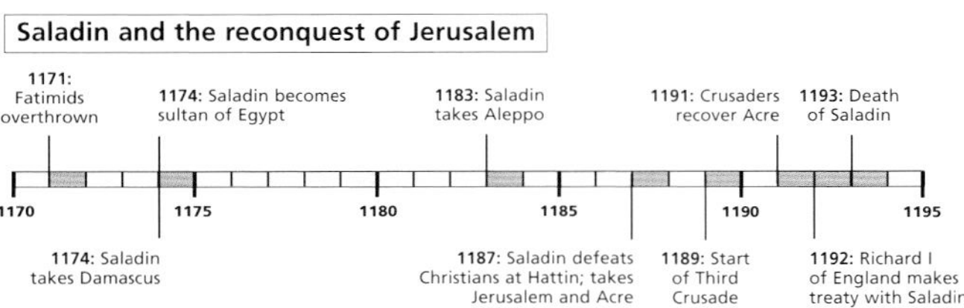

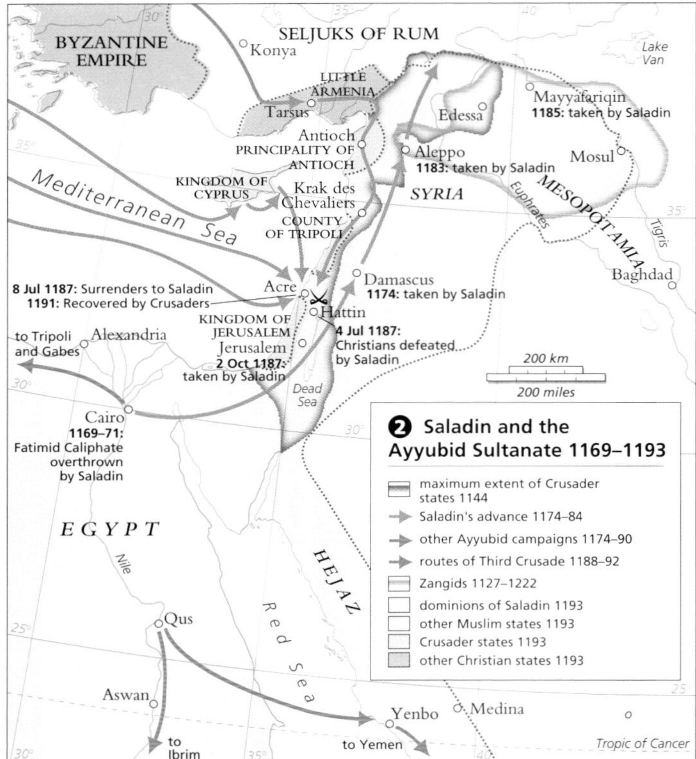

At the head of an army from Egypt, the Muslim leader Saladin (1138–1193) drove the Crusaders out of most of Palestine and Syria and recaptured Jerusalem, restoring the Dome of the Rock, one of Islam's oldest surviving shrines, to Muslim worship. Though a formidable leader, Saladin was recognized, even by the Crusaders, as a chivalrous opponent.

In this Persian illustration, Timur leads his army through the Hindu Kush in 1398, before falling upon the cities of the Punjab and sacking Delhi. This, like most of his conquests, was carried out in the name of Islam.

INDIAN OCEAN

INDIA

Bay of Bengal

Tropic of Cancer

Ganges

Equator

Mamluks and Mongols

The Mamluks, who seized power in Egypt in 1250,were chiefly Circassians from the Caucasus, captured in childhood and trained as slave bodyguards. Once in power, they extended their rule into Syria, and built up a trading network in Africa and the Indian Ocean. Within five years of the Mamluks' rise to power, the Mongol Hülegü *(see pp.68–69)* led a powerful army into West Asia. After destroying Alamut, the stronghold of the Assassins (an Ismaili Shi'ite sect), Hülegü sacked Baghdad. The Mongol threat was averted by the death of the Mongol khan, Möngke which required Hülegü to withdraw his main army. Seizing their advantage, in 1260 the Mamluks marched north in the defence of Islam, and crushed the Mongol army at Ain Jalut.

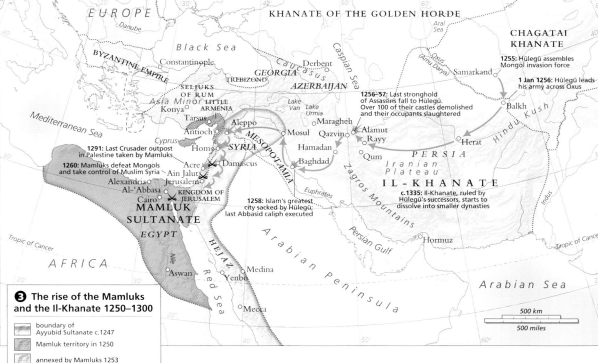

EUROPE
KHANATE OF THE GOLDEN HORDE
CHAGATAI KHANATE
Black Sea
BYZANTINE EMPIRE
Constantinople
SELJUKS OF RUM
Asia Minor
LITTLE ARMENIA
Konya
TREBIZOND
GEORGIA
Caucasus
Derbent
AZERBAIJAN
Caspian Sea
Aral Sea
Oxus (Amu Darya)
Samarkand
Balkh
Hindu Kush
Herat
Mediterranean Sea
Tarsus
Antioch
Aleppo
Cyprus
Homs
SYRIA
MESOPOTAMIA
Mosul
Maragheh
Alamut
Qazvin
Rayy
Hamadan
Qum
Baghdad
Damascus
Acre
Ain Jalut
Jerusalem
Alexandria
Al-'Abbasa
Cairo
KINGDOM OF JERUSALEM
MAMLUK SULTANATE
EGYPT
PERSIA
Iranian Plateau
IL-KHANATE
Zagros Mountains
Euphrates
Persian Gulf
Hormuz
Arabian Peninsula
Arabian Sea
HEJAZ
Red Sea
Medina
Yenbo
Mecca
Aswan
Nile
AFRICA
Tropic of Cancer
1255: Hülegü assembles Mongol invasion force
1 Jan 1256: Hülegü leads his army across Oxus
1256–57: Last stronghold of Assassins fall to Hülegü. Over 100 of their castles demolished and their occupants slaughtered
1291: Last Crusader outpost in Palestine taken by Mamluks
1260: Mamluks defeat Mongols and take control of Muslim Syria
1258: Islam's greatest city sacked by Hülegü; last Abbasid caliph executed
c.1335: Il-Khanate, ruled by Hülegü's successors, starts to dissolve into smaller dynasties
500 km
500 miles

3 The rise of the Mamluks and the Il-Khanate 1250–1300

- boundary of Ayyubid Sultanate c.1247
- Mamluk territory in 1250
- annexed by Mamluks 1253
- annexed by Mamluks 1260
- Christian territory in the Levant conquered by Mamluks 1263–1291
- Christian territory after 1291
- Il-Khanate and vassals c.1259
- route of Mongol invasion under Hülegü
- sacked by Mongols

The Mamluk warrior was superbly trained, studying both the theory and practice of combat in military manuals, such as this one which shows four cavalrymen exercising around a pool.

The Mongols and Mamluks in West Asia

- 1250: Mamluks seize power from Ayyubids
- 1251: Mamluks defeat Syrians at al-'Abbasa
- 1256: Hülegü crosses Oxus (Amu Darya)
- 1256–57: Assassins' stronghold at Alamut falls to Hülegü
- 1258: Hülegü sacks Baghdad; last Abbasid caliph executed
- 1259: Great Khan Möngke dies
- 1260: Mamluks defeat Mongols at Ain Jalut; take Aleppo and Damascus
- 1265: Death of Hülegü
- 1268: Mamluks capture Antioch from Crusaders

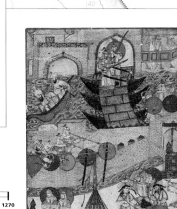

1250 1255 1260 1265 1270

The Il-Khanate c.1260–1353

The first Il-Khan, Hülegü, entered a period of conflict with Berke, Khan of the Golden Horde. Berke, who had converted to Islam and allied himself with the Mamluks, resented Hülegü's new empire. By 1262 the situation had stabilized, and Hülegü settled on the well-watered plains of Azerbaijan and built a capital at Maragheh, from where he ruled the lands he had gained in Persia, Mesopotamia, Asia Minor, and the Caucasus. The Mongol dynasty established by Hülegü – the Il-Khanate – ruled Persia until 1353.

In 1258 the Mongols under Hülegü sacked the great city of Baghdad, the very heart of Arab civilization, and reputedly murdered 800,000 of its inhabitants. The last Abbasid caliph was captured, rolled in a carpet, and then trampled to death by galloping horses.

The dominions of Timur

Claiming descent from Genghis Khan, Timur the Lame became master of Transoxiana in 1369. Making Samarkand his capital, he embarked on a series of campaigns against Persia, the Golden Horde, the Sultanate of Delhi, the Mamluks, and the Ottomans. At Ankara in 1402, he defeated and captured the Ottoman Sultan Bayezid. In 35 years Timur created a vast empire; plans for invading China ceased with his death. Though his conquests struck fear into Muslim Asia, Timur's empire proved short-lived.

Timur is buried beneath a slab of jade in the Gur-i Mir, Samarkand.

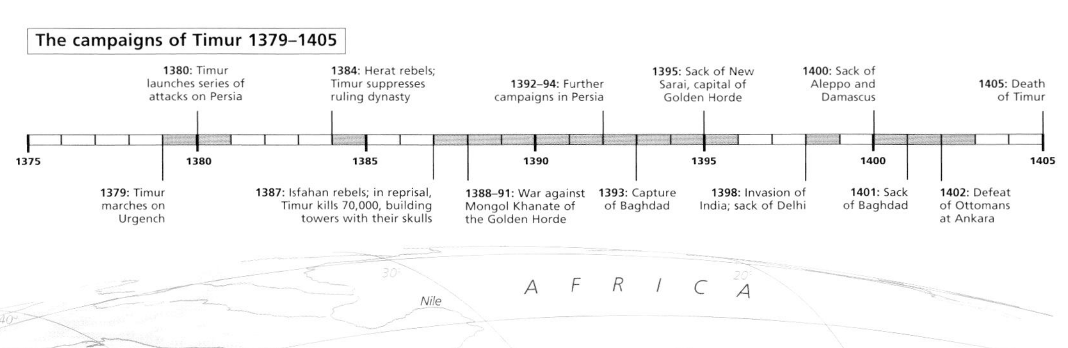

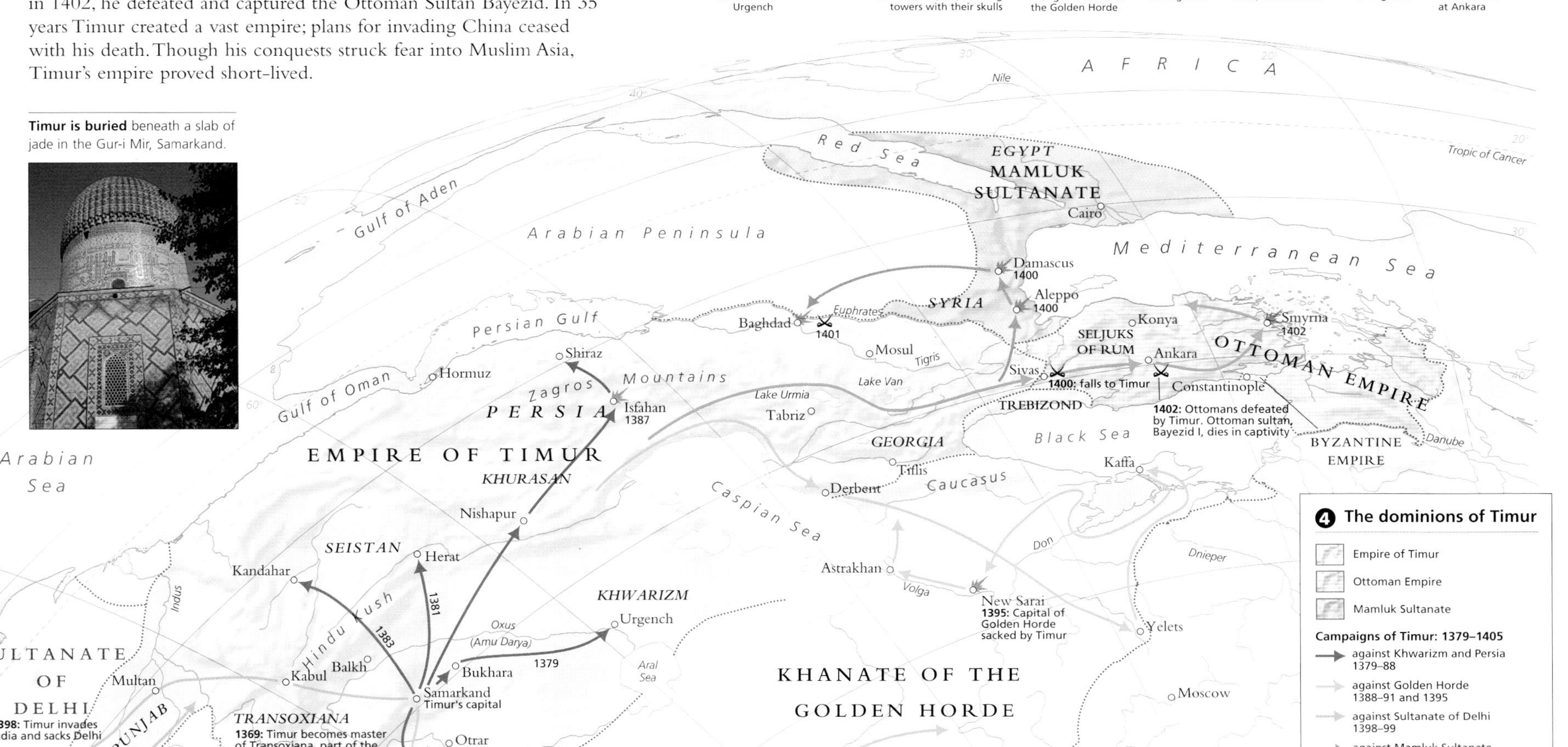

4 The dominions of Timur

- Empire of Timur
- Ottoman Empire
- Mamluk Sultanate

Campaigns of Timur: 1379–1405

- against Khwarizm and Persia 1379–88
- against Golden Horde 1388–91 and 1395
- against Sultanate of Delhi 1398–99
- against Mamluk Sultanate and Baghdad 1399–1401
- against Ottomans 1402
- planned invasion of China 1404–05
- city sacked by Timur

THE OTTOMAN EMPIRE

The conquests of Osman I (1299–1326) formed the nucleus of the Ottoman Empire.

THE OTTOMAN EMPIRE was one of the great world powers of the early modern age. At its height, the empire stretched from the Indian Ocean to Algiers, Hungary, and the Crimea. Constantinople, captured from the Byzantines in 1453 was a key centre of power that had resisted non-Christian attack for 1000 years. Turkish expansion in the Balkans led to shifts in religious, ethnic, linguistic, and economic frontiers, which still have serious consequences in the modern world. The conquest of Egypt and Syria established a powerful presence in Africa and West Asia, although, in the east, the Ottomans faced powerful opposition from Safavid Persia, which flourished in the 16th and 17th centuries.

The rise of the Ottomans

The Ottoman state started as a small frontier principality dedicated to raids on Christian Byzantium. In the 14th century, led by a succession of warrior sultans, Osman I, Orkhan, and Murad I, the Ottomans began a series of rapid conquests. Sultans often waged war to obtain more land and money to reward their loyal troops. In an attempt to halt their progress, the threatened Christian states of the Balkans amassed an army, but were defeated at Kosovo in 1389. Sultan Bayezid I exploited this victory by annexing Bulgaria and invading Hungary, but expansion eastwards was temporarily halted by Timur in 1402. Constantinople was finally taken by Mehmed II (the 'Conqueror') in 1453.

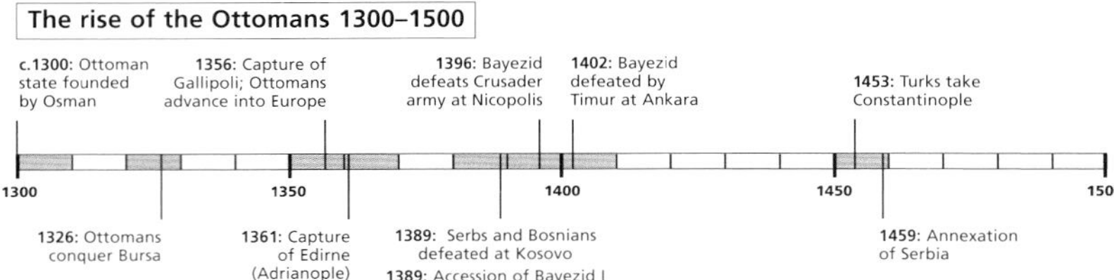

The Ottomans' rise to become a world power was based on their highly-trained army, seen here besieging Belgrade in 1456. The most feared troops were the janissaries, drawn from young slaves given in tribute and trained from childhood.

1517: Selim I orders construction of Ottoman fleet at Suez; Portuguese attack on Jedda repulsed
1538: Ottomans subjugate Yemen and Aden and take occupy port of Basra on Persian Gulf
1546: Ottomans retake Basra after revolt
1551–52: Ottomans fail to oust Portuguese from Hormuz
1510 1520 1530 1540 1550 1560
1516–17: Ottomans conquer Syria, Egypt, the Hejaz, and Yemen
1525: Ottomans again defeat Portuguese fleet in Red Sea
1538: Failure of Ottoman blockade of Portuguese at Diu

Ottoman attempts to control trade in the Indian Ocean

Trade in the Indian Ocean

With their conquest in the early 16th century of Egypt, Mesopotamia, the Hejaz, and Yemen, the Ottomans gained control of trade through the Persian Gulf and the Red Sea. Ships carrying goods such as spices from India and the Moluccas, and slaves from East Africa, docked at Aden and Jedda; from there they were transported overland to the markets of Cairo, Aleppo, Damascus, and north into Anatolia. Responding to persistent threats to their trade from the Portuguese, the Ottomans assembled fleets at Suez and Basra and made several attempts to oust the Portuguese from the region, but without lasting success.

2 Trade in the Indian Ocean in the 15th and 16th centuries

main trade route
Ottoman naval campaigns in the Indian Ocean in 16th century

Commodities and raw materials exported

ambergris	horses	silk
aromatic woods	incense	silver
carpets	indigo	slaves
porcelain	iron/steel	spices
coconuts	ivory	sugar
copper	manufactured goods	tea
cotton	metalware	textiles
gems	pearls	timber
gold	perfumes	tin
grain	rice	wine

ASIA · PERSIA · OTTOMAN EMPIRE · MAMLUKS · EGYPT · HEJAZ · YEMEN · ETHIOPIA · AFRICA · Arabian Peninsula · OMAN · INDIA · MING CHINA · Himalayas · Arabian Sea · Bay of Bengal · INDIAN OCEAN · South China Sea · Cairo · Suez · Mecca · Jedda · Suakin · Aden · Aleppo · Damascus · Basra · Bahrain · Isfahan · Bushire · Hormuz · Gwadar · Muscat · Qalhat · Diu · Surat · Daman · Bombay · Dabul · Goa · Calicut · Cochin · Colombo · Ceylon · Chittagong · Akyab · Martaban · Tawahi · Tanasari · Bangkok · Saigon · Finanj · Malacca · Sumatra · Borneo · Jakarta · Java · Tuban · Moluccas · Mogadishu · Malindi · Mombasa · Pemba · Zanzibar · Kilwa · Madagascar · Socotra · Maldive Islands · Seychelles · Andaman Islands · Nicobar Islands

Scale varies with perspective
7440 km (4630 miles)
11,600 km (7210 miles)

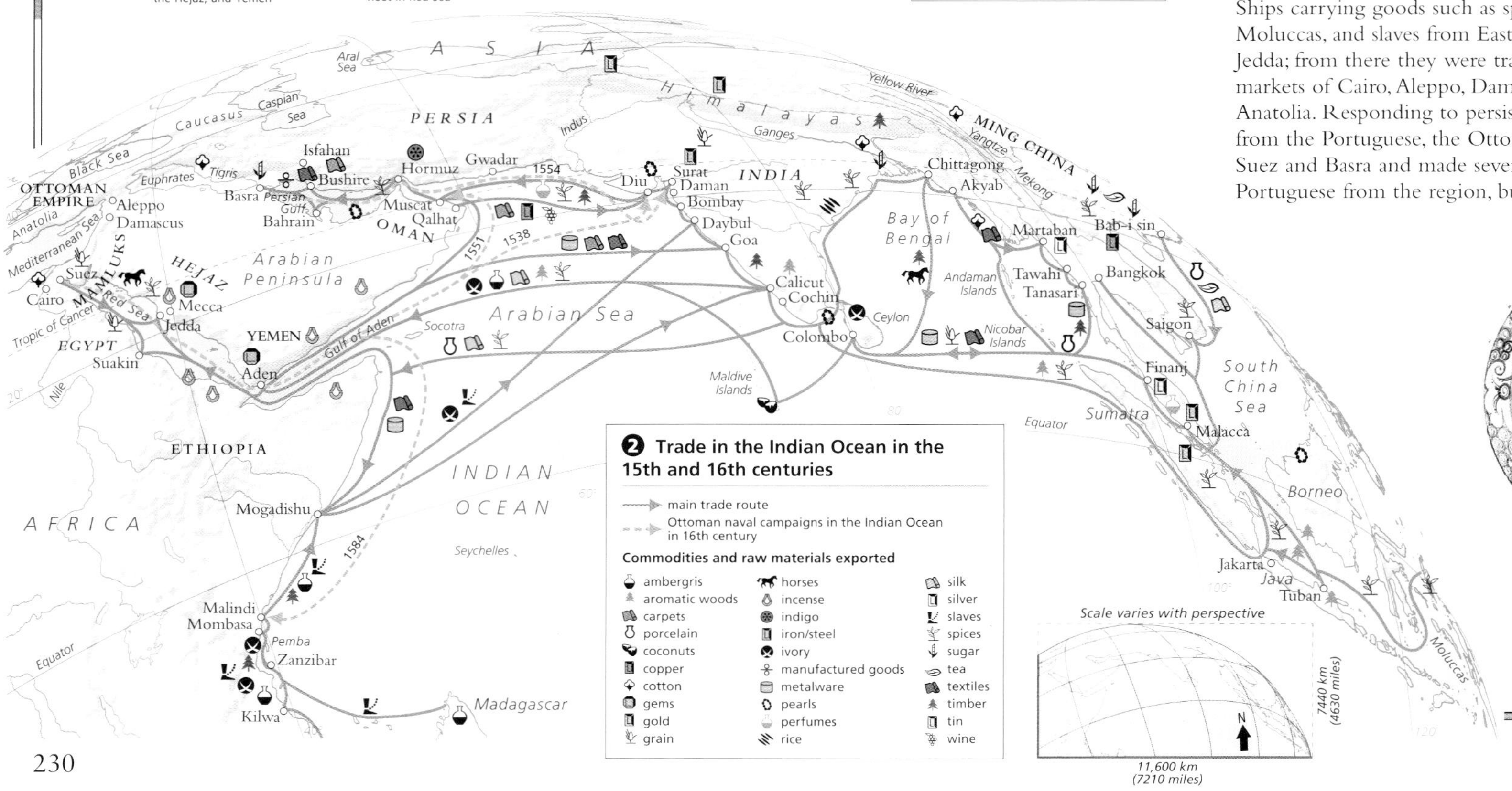

Iznik pottery, developed in the late 15th century, was among the finest made by the Ottomans. Designs were largely figurative, such as this Portuguese ship.

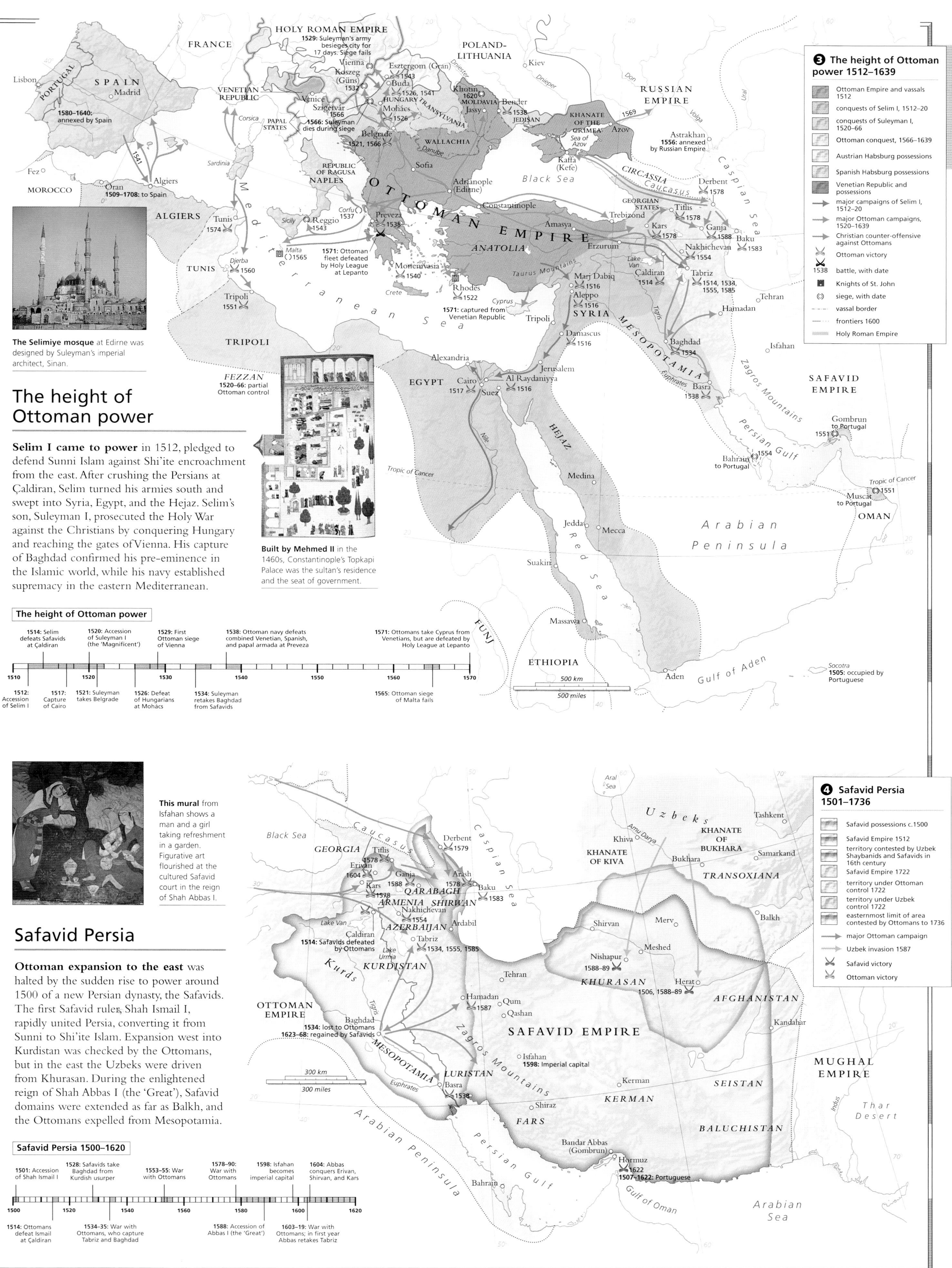

The Selimiye mosque at Edirne was designed by Suleyman's imperial architect, Sinan.

Built by Mehmed II in the 1460s, Constantinople's Topkapi Palace was the sultan's residence and the seat of government.

The height of Ottoman power

Selim I came to power in 1512, pledged to defend Sunni Islam against Shi'ite encroachment from the east. After crushing the Persians at Çaldiran, Selim turned his armies south and swept into Syria, Egypt, and the Hejaz. Selim's son, Suleyman I, prosecuted the Holy War against the Christians by conquering Hungary and reaching the gates of Vienna. His capture of Baghdad confirmed his pre-eminence in the Islamic world, while his navy established supremacy in the eastern Mediterranean.

The height of Ottoman power

1510: **1512:** Accession of Selim I
1514: Selim defeats Safavids at Çaldiran
1517: Capture of Cairo
1520: Accession of Suleyman I (the 'Magnificent')
1521: Suleyman takes Belgrade
1526: Defeat of Hungarians at Mohács
1529: First Ottoman siege of Vienna
1534: Suleyman retakes Baghdad from Safavids
1538: Ottoman navy defeats combined Venetian, Spanish, and papal armada at Preveza
1565: Ottoman siege of Malta fails
1571: Ottomans take Cyprus from Venetians, but are defeated by Holy League at Lepanto

This mural from Isfahan shows a man and a girl taking refreshment in a garden. Figurative art flourished at the cultured Safavid court in the reign of Shah Abbas I.

Safavid Persia

Ottoman expansion to the east was halted by the sudden rise to power around 1500 of a new Persian dynasty, the Safavids. The first Safavid ruler, Shah Ismail I, rapidly united Persia, converting it from Sunni to Shi'ite Islam. Expansion west into Kurdistan was checked by the Ottomans, but in the east the Uzbeks were driven from Khurasan. During the enlightened reign of Shah Abbas I (the 'Great'), Safavid domains were extended as far as Balkh, and the Ottomans expelled from Mesopotamia.

Safavid Persia 1500–1620

1501: Accession of Shah Ismail I
1514: Ottomans defeat Ismail at Çaldiran
1528: Safavids take Baghdad from Kurdish usurper
1534–35: War with Ottomans, who capture Tabriz and Baghdad
1553–55: War with Ottomans
1578–90: War with Ottomans
1588: Accession of Abbas I (the 'Great')
1598: Isfahan becomes imperial capital
1603–19: War with Ottomans; in first year Abbas retakes Tabriz
1604: Abbas conquers Erivan, Shirvan, and Kars

THE DECLINE OF THE OTTOMANS

Abdul Hamid II failed to modernize his empire and was deposed by the Young Turks in 1908.

AT THE HEIGHT OF ITS POWER, in the 16th century, the Ottoman Empire stretched from the gates of Vienna to the Indian Ocean, and from the Crimea to Algiers. By the end of the 18th century the empire was shrinking, its power eroded by a loss of internal authority and by the ambitions of the major European powers. Attempts to westernize and strengthen the Empire foundered, and when the Turks entered the First World War *(see pp.206–207)*, on the side of the Central Powers, they had lost all their territories in Africa, and most of them in Europe. Defeat in the war brought the empire to an end: British and French mandates were imposed in Mesopotamia and the Levant, and Saudi Arabia became independent. The Turks, however, established a new national identity for themselves by driving the Greeks from Anatolia and creating the modern republic of Turkey in 1923.

The empire in decline 1800–1913

By 1900 Turkey was attracting European tourists, seen here against the backdrop of Constantinople's domes and minarets. Many Turks now wore Western dress and had adopted Western habits.

Under pressure from the West, attempts were made to modernize the empire, notably in the period 1839–76. In 1908 a movement for more liberal government, led by the Young Turks, succeeded in deposing the sultan, Abdul Hamid II. The Ottomans' hold over the Balkans was broken by Greece gaining independence in 1830, followed by Serbia, Montenegro, and Romania in 1878, while Russia challenged Turkish control of the Black Sea. In Africa, the French seized Algeria and Tunisia, Britain occupied Egypt, and the Italians conquered Libya.

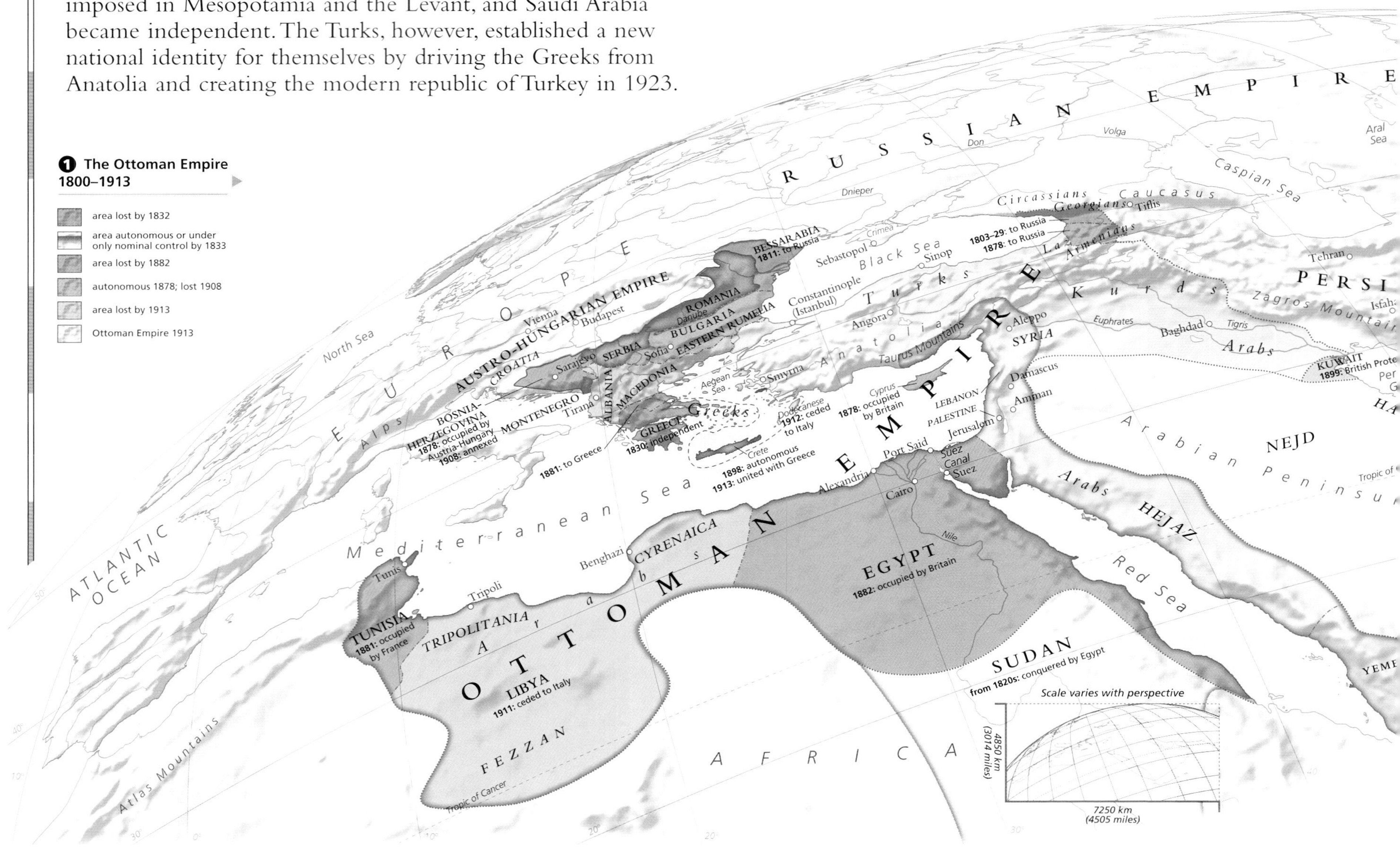

1 The Ottoman Empire 1800–1913

- area lost by 1832
- area autonomous or under only nominal control by 1833
- area lost by 1882
- autonomous 1878; lost 1908
- area lost by 1913
- Ottoman Empire 1913

BESSARABIA 1811: to Russia
1803–29: to Russia
1878: to Russia
BOSNIA-HERZEGOVINA 1878: occupied by Austria-Hungary 1908: annexed
GREECE 1830: independent
1881: to Greece
Crete 1898: autonomous 1913: united with Greece
Dodecanese 1912: ceded to Italy
Cyprus 1878: occupied by Britain
TUNISIA 1881: occupied by France
LIBYA 1911: ceded to Italy
EGYPT 1882: occupied by Britain
SUDAN from 1820s: conquered by Egypt
KUWAIT 1899: British protectorate

Scale varies with perspective
4850 km (3014 miles)
7250 km (4505 miles)

The Ottoman Empire 1815–1913

- **1821–30:** Greek War of Independence
- **1830:** Algiers occupied by France
- **1839–61:** Sultan Abdul Majid I makes series of liberal *Tanzimat* decrees
- **1840:** Empire under threat from Egypt; saved by British and Austrian intervention
- **1853:** Russians defeat Turkish navy at Sinop
- **1854–56:** Crimean War; French and British come to aid of Turks against Russia
- **1878:** Independence of Serbia, Montenegro, and Romania recognized at Berlin Congress
- **1878:** Cyprus occupied by British
- **1881:** Tunisia occupied by French
- **1882:** Egypt occupied by British
- **1908:** Bulgaria declares independence
- **1908:** Bosnia-Herzegovina annexed by Austro-Hungarian Empire
- **1911:** Libya occupied by Italy
- **1912–13:** Balkan Wars

1815 1825 1835 1845 1855 1865 1875 1885 1895 1905 1915

EGYPT AND THE SUEZ CANAL

An early sign of Ottoman decline was Muhammad Ali's establishment of a virtually independent Egypt after 1805. He and his successors encouraged European investment and in 1859 Egypt became the site of one of the century's greatest feats of engineering. The brainchild of a French diplomat, Ferdinand de Lesseps, who supervised its construction, the 170-km Suez Canal linked the Mediterranean to the Red Sea. Cutting the sea journey from Britain to India by 9,700 km, the canal opened in 1869 and became one of the world's most heavily used waterways. In 1875 Britain paid the bankrupt Khedive of Egypt four million pounds for a controlling interest in the canal, thus securing a lifeline to its empire in the east.

On the day after the opening ceremony in Port Said, 68 ships, headed by the *Aigle* with Empress Eugénie of France on board, sailed the length of the Suez Canal. This painting is from Eugénie's souvenir album of the event.

Emir Faisal, seen here with his bodyguard, united the Arabs and in 1916, together with Colonel T. E. Lawrence, led a successful revolt against the Turks. After the war Faisal became king of Iraq under the British mandate.

The First World War

- **Oct 1914:** Turkey closes Dardanelles
- **Feb 1915:** First Turkish attempt to capture Suez
- **Feb 1915:** Gallipoli landings
- **1915:** About one million Armenians massacred or deported by Turks
- **Feb 1916:** Russians take Erzurum
- **Apr 1916:** British surrender at Kut al Amara
- **Jun 1916:** Arab Revolt
- **Mar 1917:** British take Baghdad
- **Dec 1917:** British take Jerusalem
- **Sep 1918:** Battle of Megiddo
- **Oct 1918:** Turks surrender

1914 1915 1916 1917 1918 1919

The partition of the Ottoman Empire 1918–23

Following the Turkish surrender in 1918, Syria became a French mandate while Palestine, Iraq, and Transjordan became British mandates. By the Treaty of Sèvres (1920), Turkey was forced to give up all her non-Turkish lands; eastern Thrace and Smyrna were given to Greece. The Turkish sultan accepted the Treaty's conditions, but the Allies had underestimated the fervour of the Turkish Nationalists; led by Kemal Pasha, they launched an attack on the Greek invaders, driving them out of Anatolia. The present frontiers of Turkey were recognized by the Treaty of Lausanne in 1923. In the same year the last Ottoman sultan, Mehmed VI, was overthrown and Turkey became a republic.

▲ **3 Southwest Asia after the First World War**

- British mandate
- French mandate
- Turkey after Treaty of Sèvres (1920)
- area annexed by Turkey 1921
- area restored to Turkey by Treaty of Lausanne (1923)
- international border 1926

In an attempt to cover the retreat of their own troops, a Greek cavalry detachment charges a Turkish force near Smyrna in 1922. Under the inspired leadership of Mustafa Kemal Pasha, Turkish Nationalists fought a fierce three-year campaign, eventually regaining eastern Thrace and Smyrna.

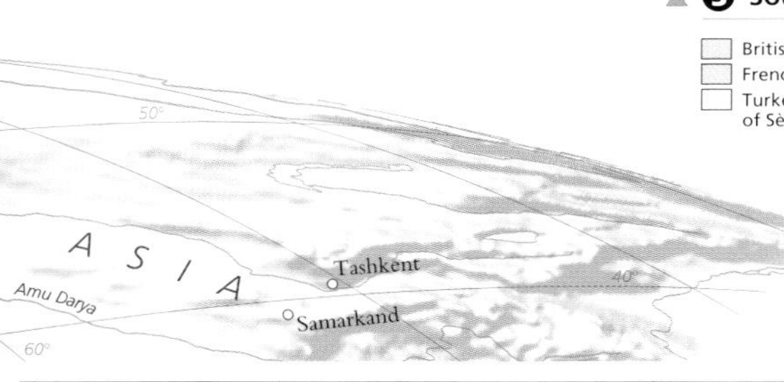

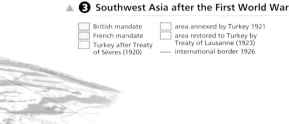

▲ **2 The First World War in Southwest Asia**

- Ottoman Empire 1914
- British Empire 1914
- Russian Empire 1914
- area of Arab revolt (1916–18)
- Russian/Turkish front 1917
- Turkish lines at surrender, 1918
- Turkish forces
- Allied forces
- Allied forces under Col T.E. Lawrence
- French forces
- Russian forces
- railway line

British and Australian troops *(left)* land on the Gallipoli peninsula. They abandoned the offensive in January 1916, having lost over 250,000 men.

French General d'Esperey lands in Istanbul in 1919 to be greeted by British General Wilson *(below)*. Behind Wilson stands Kemal Pasha (later known as Atatürk), who was to lead Turkey in its struggle to become a modern state.

The First World War 1914–18

The Turks began the war well, pinning down an Allied force on the Gallipoli peninsula for nine months and halting the British in Mesopotamia. But they twice failed to take Suez and in 1916 their Third Army was virtually destroyed by the Russians at Erzurum. The end came in 1918 when British forces, supported by Arab irregulars, drove north in a two-pronged attack, capturing Baghdad and Jerusalem, and eventually reaching Damascus.

The emergence of Saudi Arabia 1800–1932

The modern Saudi state has its origins in the 18th century when the Wahhabis – an orthodox sect attempting to preserve the 'purity of Islam'– united the previously divided Arab tribes. Led by the Saud family, the Wahhabis raided into Mesopotamia, the Hejaz, and Syria, capturing Mecca in 1806. But in a series of campaigns (1812–18), the Wahhabis were crushed by armies from Egypt and Ottoman forces from the north. In 1902, Abd al-Aziz Ibn Saud led a Saudi resurgence. The Saud family gradually consolidated its power within the peninsula and, in 1932, the kingdom of Saudi Arabia was proclaimed.

Abd al-Aziz Ibn Saud regained his family's homelands around Riyadh, then founded a kingdom that he ruled until his death in 1953.

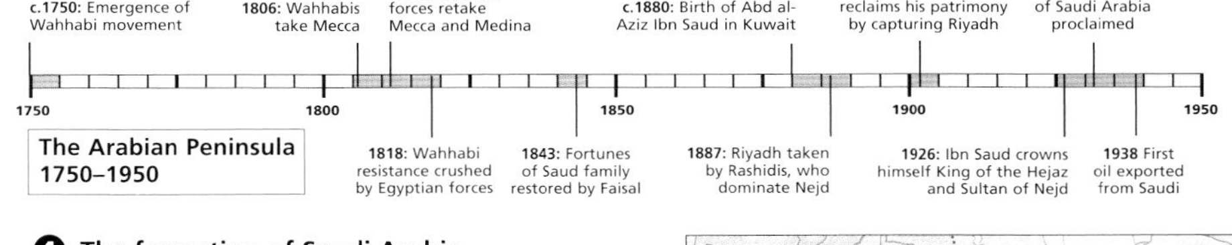

4 The formation of Saudi Arabia

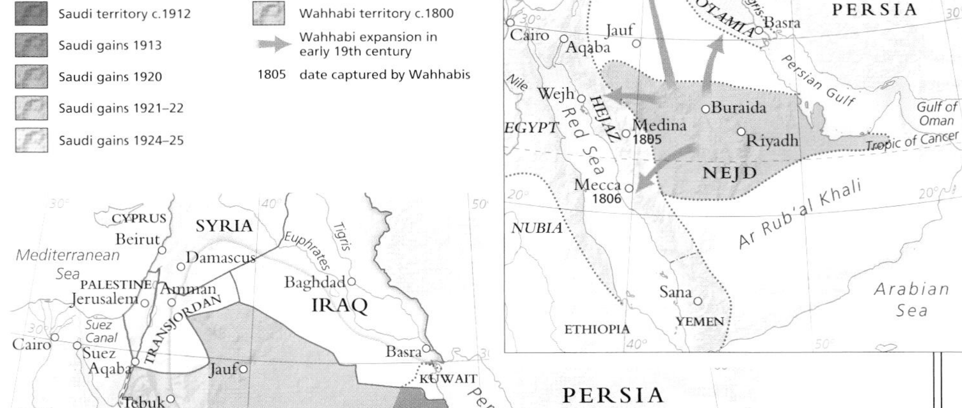

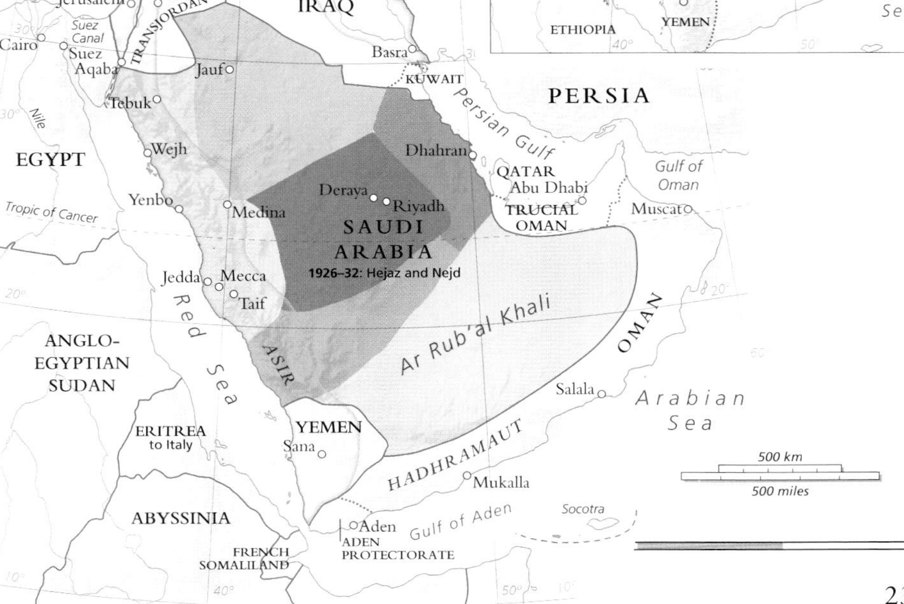

MODERN WEST ASIA

Yasser Arafat, the chairman of the PLO from 1969, led the fight for recognition of Palestinian rights.

THE HISTORY OF WEST ASIA after the Second World War was dominated by two things: oil, and the creation of the state of Israel. The discovery of huge oil reserves in the Gulf region influenced the economics and politics of all the states concerned. The UN decision of 1947 to partition Palestine and form the Jewish homeland of Israel sparked off Arab-Israeli wars in 1948, 1967, and 1973. Israel remains technically at war with all its Arab neighbours except Egypt and Jordan. The emergence of Islamic fundamentalism in the region, with the Iranian revolution (1979), the Palestinian *intifada* (from 1987) in Israel, and the international anti-Western campaign by al-Qaeda (from the 1990s), led to a seemingly intractable confrontation between Islamic and Western values. This provoked the invasion, without UN approval, of Saddam Hussein's Iraq by the US and its allies in 2003.

Oil production in the Gulf

The Gulf is the world's most valuable region of oil and natural gas, producing some 35% of the world's requirements. The Gulf states exert a powerful influence: increases in the price of crude oil, such as that imposed by OPEC in 1973–74, had worldwide repercussions. Regional conflicts that disrupt oil supplies, such as Iraq's invasion of Kuwait (1990) and the US-led intervention in 1991, and the toppling of Saddam Hussein's regime in 2003, seriously affected global confidence in the security of oil supplies. This was further undermined in the early 2000s by uncertainty over the durability of Saudi Arabia's ruling family.

The vulnerability of supplies in the Middle East in the current political climate can lead to huge rises in oil prices on the world market. Here Iraqi firemen put out the blaze after a bomb attack on an oil pipeline, just one of many such attacks in 2004.

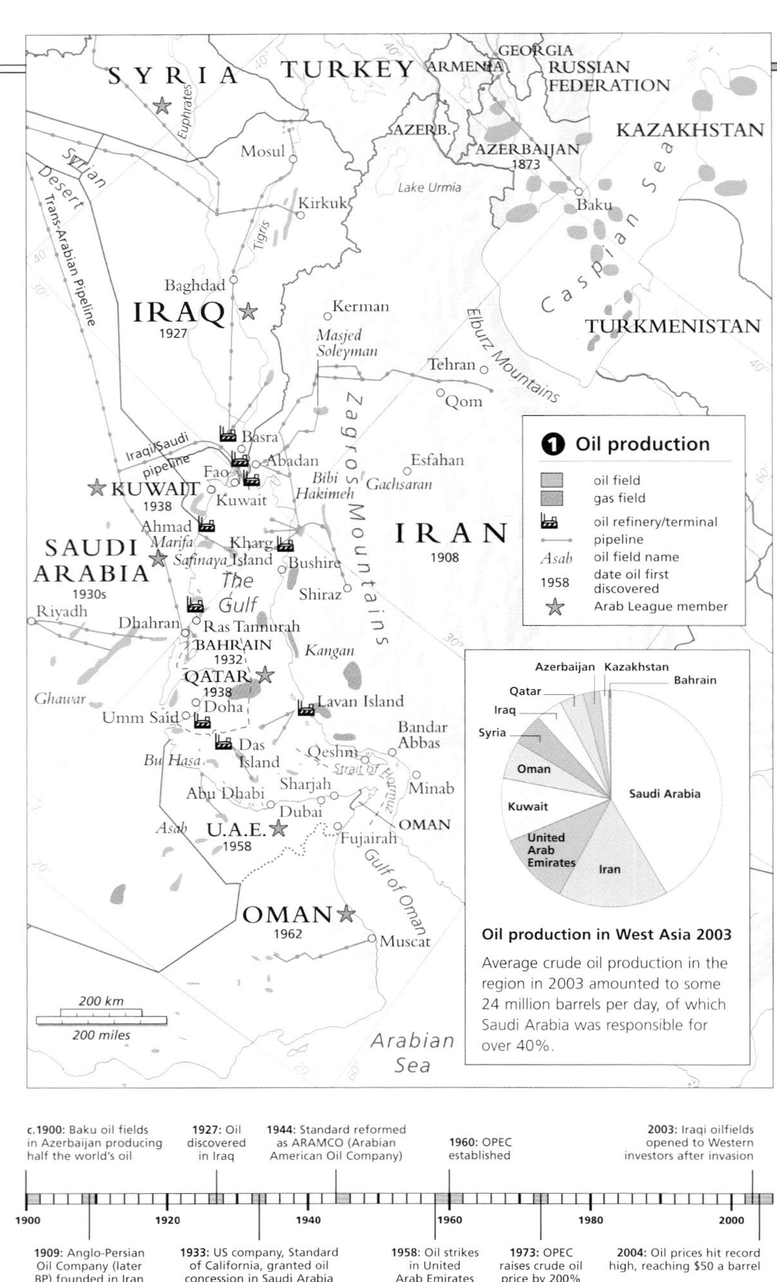

Oil production in West Asia 2003

Average crude oil production in the region in 2003 amounted to some 24 million barrels per day, of which Saudi Arabia was responsible for over 40%.

Oil in West Asia

- **c.1900:** Baku oil fields in Azerbaijan producing half the world's oil
- **1909:** Anglo-Persian Oil Company (later BP) founded in Iran
- **1927:** Oil discovered in Iraq
- **1933:** US company, Standard of California, granted oil concession in Saudi Arabia
- **1944:** Standard reformed as ARAMCO (Arabian American Oil Company)
- **1958:** Oil strikes in United Arab Emirates
- **1960:** OPEC established
- **1973:** OPEC raises crude oil price by 200%
- **2003:** Iraqi oilfields opened to Western investors after invasion
- **2004:** Oil prices hit record high, reaching $50 a barrel

Arab-Israeli wars

The state of Israel was established in May 1948. The next day, five Arab armies invaded; Israel survived, but its refusal to acknowledge Palestinian claims, and the refusal of Arab states to recognize Israel, led to a succession of wars in which the Arabs were defeated and Israel occupied more territories. A succession of initiatives, such as the Oslo Accords of 1993 and the 'Road Map' of 2003, tried to find a viable arrangement between Israel and the Palestinians. However, the Israeli settlements in the West Bank and Palestinian suicide bombing campaigns remain obstacles to any peace agreement.

In 2001, Israel's prime minister, Ariel Sharon, proposed a plan to withdraw troops from Palestinian-administered areas and authorized the construction of a 500-km security wall in the West Bank. This provoked an intensification of the *intifada*, characterized by a renewed suicide bombing campaign, and harsh Israeli reprisals.

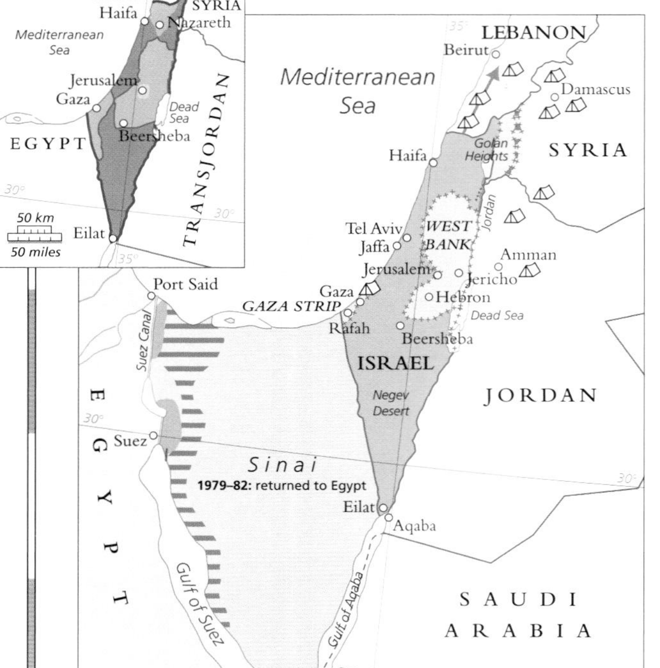

2 Arab-Israeli Wars 1947–82

MAIN MAP: Arab-Israeli Wars
- Israel in 1949
- occupied by Israel after 1967 war
- occupied by Israel after 1973 war
- occupied by Israel after 1967 war reoccupied by Egypt after 1973 war
- demilitarized zone held by UN after Israel-Syria agreement, 1974, and 2nd Sinai agreement, 1975
- route of Israel's invasion of Lebanon 1982
- Palestinian refugee camps 1982
- disputed border

INSET: UN Partition plan 1947
- border of British mandate 1923
- proposed Arab State
- proposed Jewish State
- proposed international zone

Arab-Israeli wars

- **1947:** UN partition of Palestine
- **1948:** Invading Arab armies repulsed; 725,000 Arabs flee Palestine
- **1956:** Suez crisis; Israel, France, and Britain invade Egypt
- **1967:** Six Day War; Israel takes Sinai, Gaza, Golan Heights, West Bank, and Jerusalem
- **1973:** Yom Kippur War
- **1979:** Egypt and Israel sign peace treaty based on Camp David accords
- **1982:** Israel invades Lebanon
- **1991:** Israel subjected to Iraqi missile attack
- **1993:** Oslo peace accords
- **2000:** Israeli withdrawal from Lebanon
- **2002:** Work starts on West Bank barrier

Jewish and Palestinian Migrations

Jewish immigration to Palestine from Europe increased sharply in the 1930s and 1940s as a result of persecution and the Holocaust. While the Jews accepted the UN partition plan, the Arabs declined it; in the subsequent civil war and Israel's 1948–49 war against the invading Arab states, tens of thousands of Palestinians fled their homes and became refugees (*left*). Since 1948 Israel has absorbed even greater numbers of Jewish immigrants (*below*).

3 Migration 1947–96

SMALL MAP: Palestinian emigration
- 1947–48

LARGE MAP: Jewish migration to Israel
- 1948–71
- 1972–96

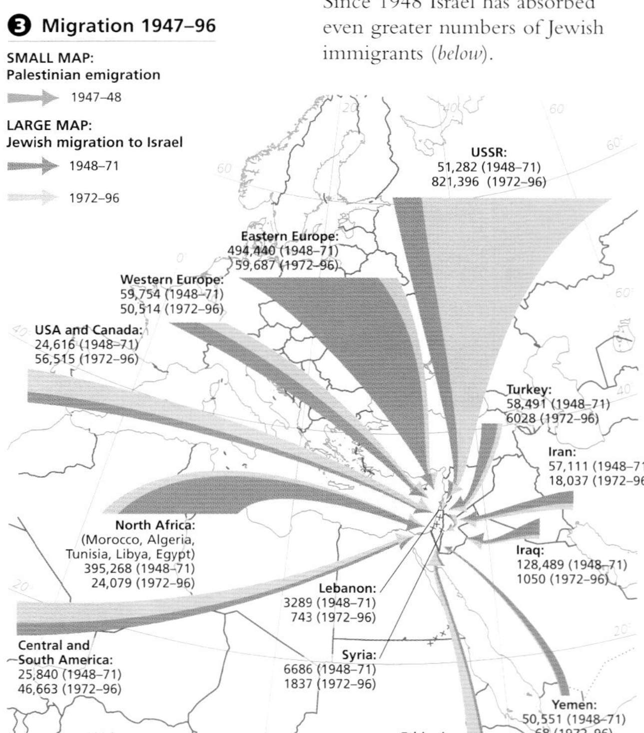

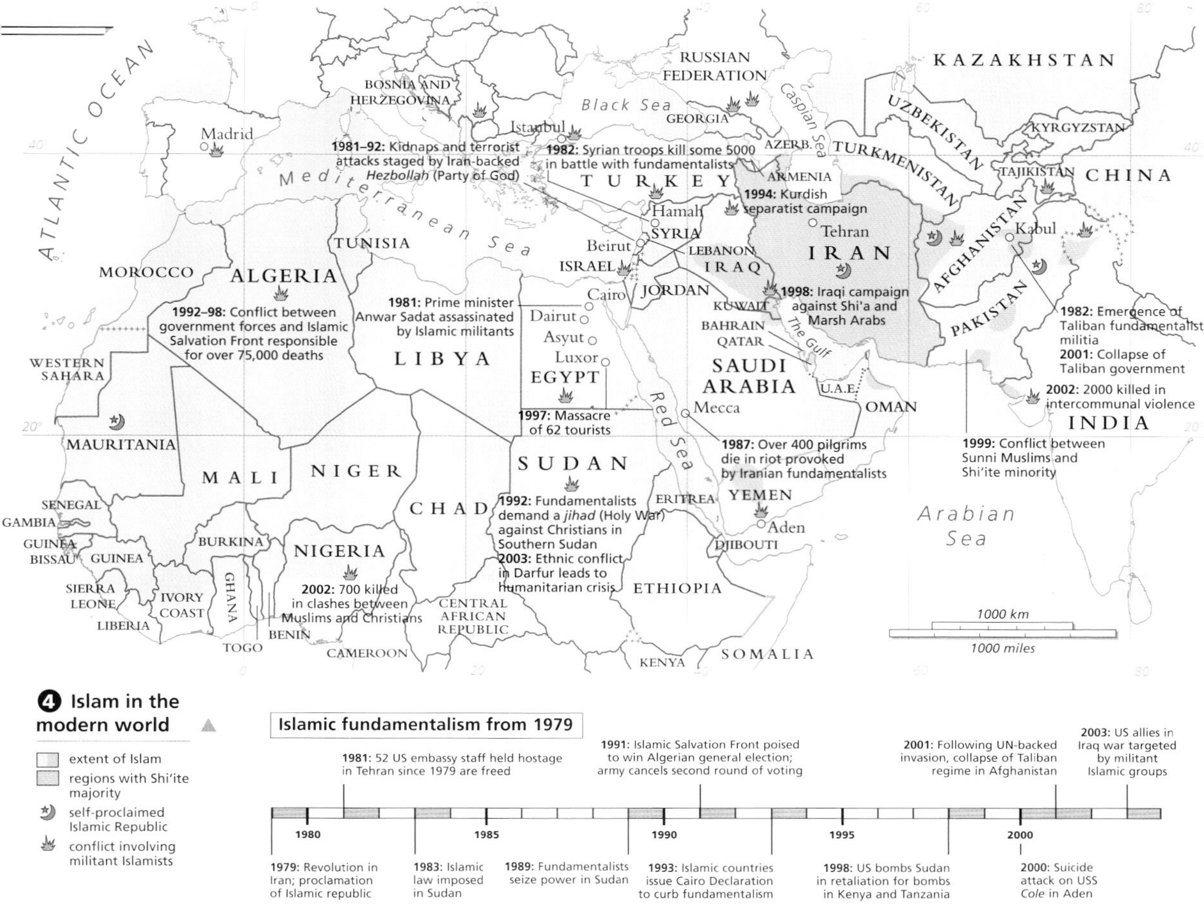

Islamic revivalism

Shi'a Islam was the driving force behind the Iranian Revolution of 1978–79. Under the leadership of Ayatollah Khomeini, political, social, educational, and cultural life in the Islamic Republic of Iran, were to be governed by the basic elements ('fundamentals') of the Sharia or Islamic law. The revivalist Salafi interpretation of the Sunni tradition – often known as 'Wahhabism' – developed in Saudi Arabia. In one form or the other, revivalist Islam has been associated with terrorism and conflict. 'Wahhabism', for example, has been linked to anti-Western terrorism, especially the activities of Osama bin Laden and the al-Qaeda movement.

Amid scenes of uncontrollable grief, Ayatollah Khomeini, Iran's leader and symbol of the Iranian revolution, is escorted to his grave by mourners in June 1989.

Al-Qaeda

Founded in the late 1980s by Osama bin Laden and his associates, al-Qaeda soon became the most notorious international terrorist network. Al-Qaeda organized a number of high-profile attacks, including the bombing of US embassies in Kenya and Tanzania in 1998, the suicide attack on the USS *Cole* in Aden in 2000, and the destruction of the World Trade Center in New York on 11 September 2001. Meaning 'the base' in Arabic, al-Qaeda latterly became more like a movement or ideology, inspiring terrorist groups and individuals around the world.

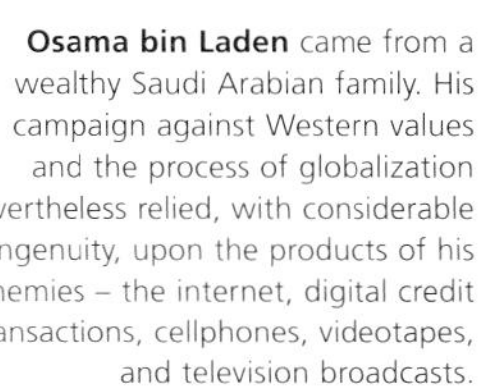

Osama bin Laden came from a wealthy Saudi Arabian family. His campaign against Western values and the process of globalization nevertheless relied, with considerable ingenuity, upon the products of his enemies – the internet, digital credit transactions, cellphones, videotapes, and television broadcasts.

Conflict in the Gulf

In September 1980, Iraq launched a massive attack against Iran. The war lasted until 1988, left over one million dead or injured, and wrecked the economies of both countries. The reasons for Iraq's aggression were complex: border disputes with Iran, long-standing rivalry in the region, and the opposition of Saddam Hussein's Arab nationalist regime to the revolutionary Islamic theocracy in Iran. In 1990, Saddam invaded Kuwait, aiming to gain control of its oil reserves to rebuild his war machine. With UN approval, a US-led coalition of 29 states liberated Kuwait in 2001. In 2003, US-Iraqi hostility culminated in the invasion of Iraq by US-led forces, ostensibly to destroy Iraqi weapons of mass destruction. The collapse of Saddam's regime left a power vacuum.

Saddam Hussein's Ba'athist regime controlled Iraq through a ministry of fear and the cult of the leader. His continued defiance of the West after the first Gulf War (1990–91) led to the US invasion of 2003.

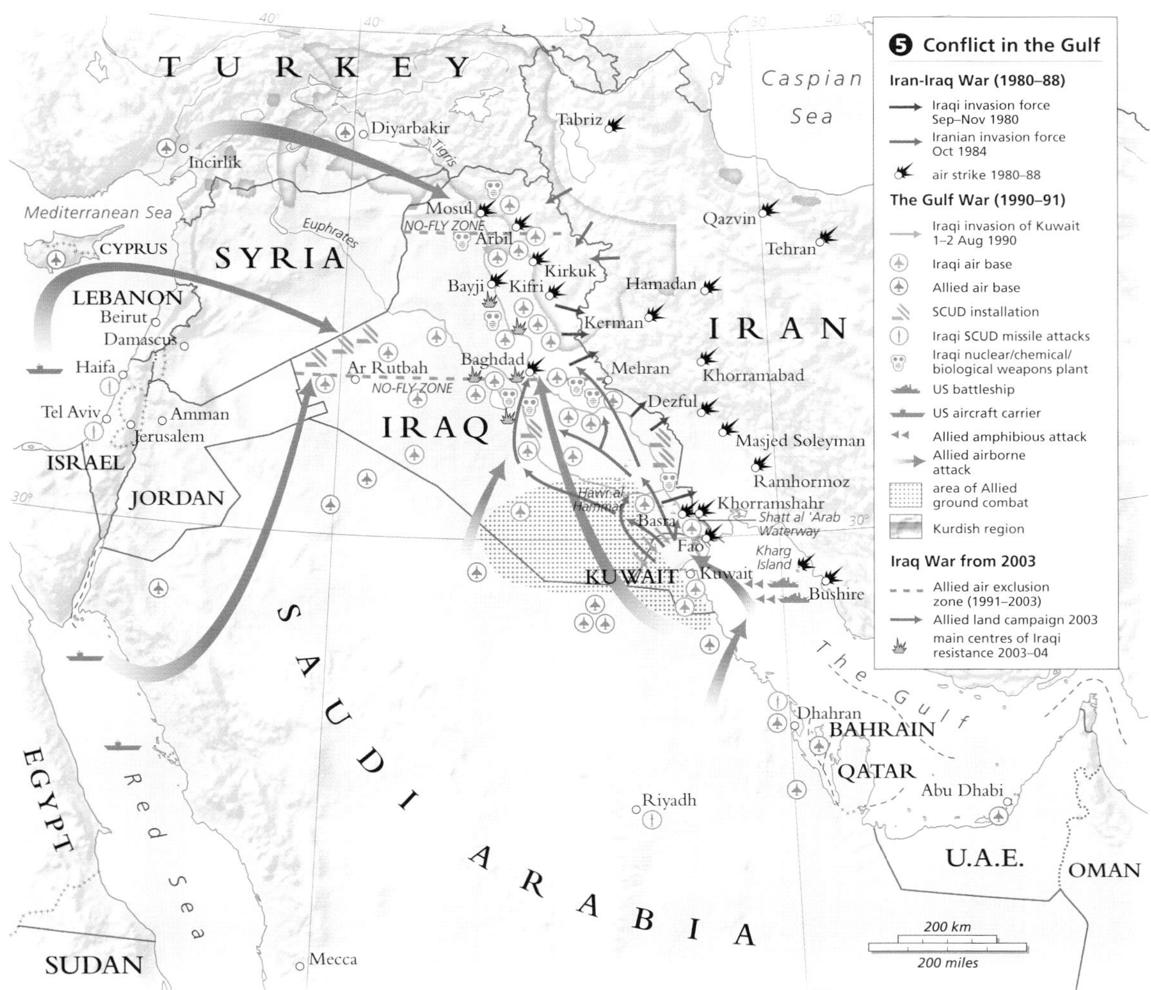

The plight of the Kurds

Numbering over 20 million, the Kurds inhabit large areas of Turkey, Iran, and Iraq, and some of Syria. But 'Kurdistan' is not officially recognized and Kurds have long experienced persecution over their aspirations for independence. From 1987 Saddam Hussein unleashed the 'al-Anfal' pacification/extermination campaign against the Iraqi Kurds, in which chemical weapons were used. After the 1990–91 Gulf War, they had some protection under a 'no fly zone' imposed by the US and its allies. The destruction of Saddam Hussein's regime in 2003 prompted debate on the place of the Kurds in the new Iraq.

Kurdish refugees flee across the mountains to Turkey in 1991 in the wake of Saddam Hussein's chemical attacks on their communities in northern Iraq. Over one million Kurds fled into Turkey and Iran. In May 1992 the Iraqi Kurds elected their own government and became a semi-independent political entity.

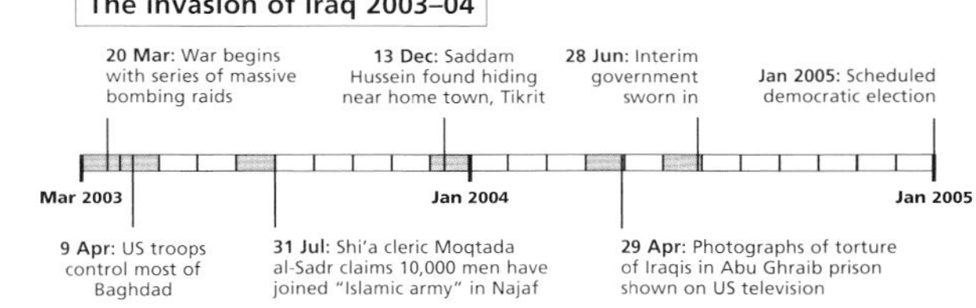

SOUTH AND SOUTHEAST ASIA

REGIONAL HISTORY

Vegetation type

- ice cap and glacier
- polar or alpine desert
- tundra
- semi-desert or sparsely vegetated
- grassland
- forest or open woodland
- tropical rainforest
- temperate desert
- tropical desert
- desert
- coastline (present-day)
- coastline (18,000 years ago)

THE HISTORICAL LANDSCAPE

LYING LARGELY BETWEEN THE TROPICS, this region enjoys a complex geography incorporating the world's greatest mountains, some of the world's largest river systems and tropical rainforests, and the globe's most extensive archipelago. During the last Ice Age, lower sea levels rendered the shallow seas surrounding Southeast Asia into dry land, allowing humans to migrate from the Asian mainland, through the islands of Southeast Asia. From 3000 BCE, the Indian subcontinent was home to some of the world's earliest civilizations, founded on the banks of the Indus and Ganges rivers. Historically, the sheer size of the Indian subcontinent and variety of its peoples have attracted and resisted political unity in equal parts, and Hinduism, Buddhism, and Islam have provided the inspiration for remarkable eras of cultural, economic, and political efflorescence. The region is well-endowed with valuable natural resources and has attracted and fostered trade since the earliest times. Only in the recent centuries of colonial rivalry have concerns about self-determination been overtaken by the need to meet the demands of soaring population growth.

The Mekong is one of many great rivers which radiate south and east from the Plateau of Tibet. The alluvial soils that accumulate around the lower reaches of these rivers are exceptionally fertile, and have long been utilized by humans for agriculture – especially the cultivation of rice.

The Himalayas have always provided a barrier to human migration between South and East Asia. The first settlers entered southern Asia by passes that still provide the only means of traversing the mountains.

The Indus river flows from the Himalayas, through mountain meadows and down across fertile plains to the sea. The Indus valley civilizations were the most sophisticated early societies in southern Asia.

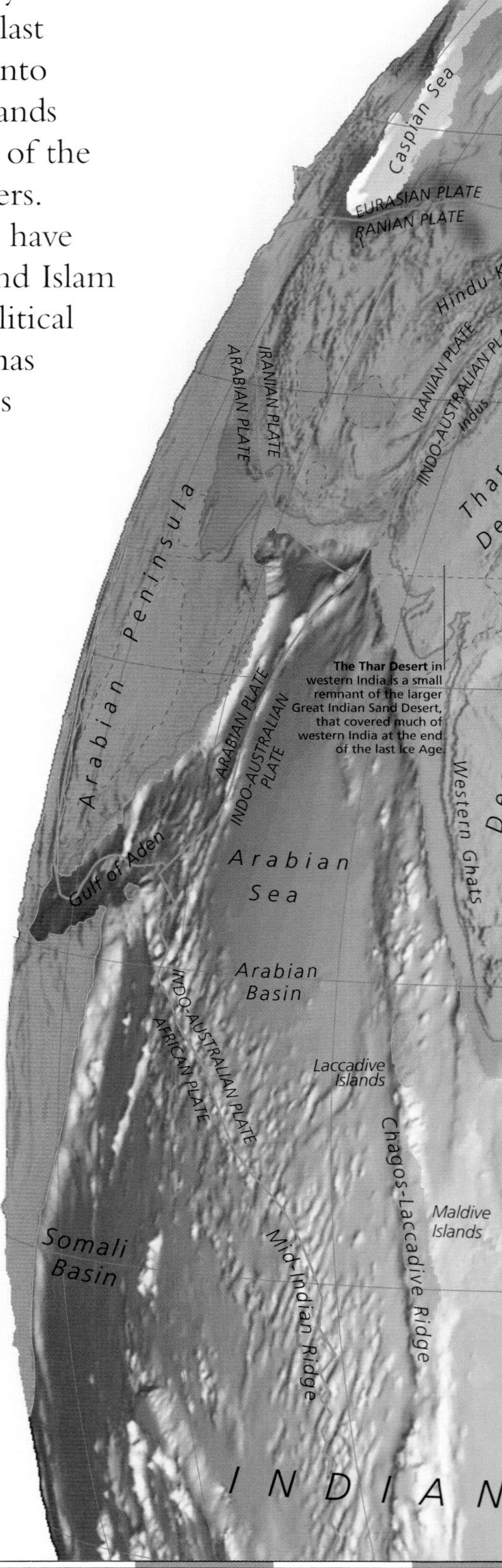

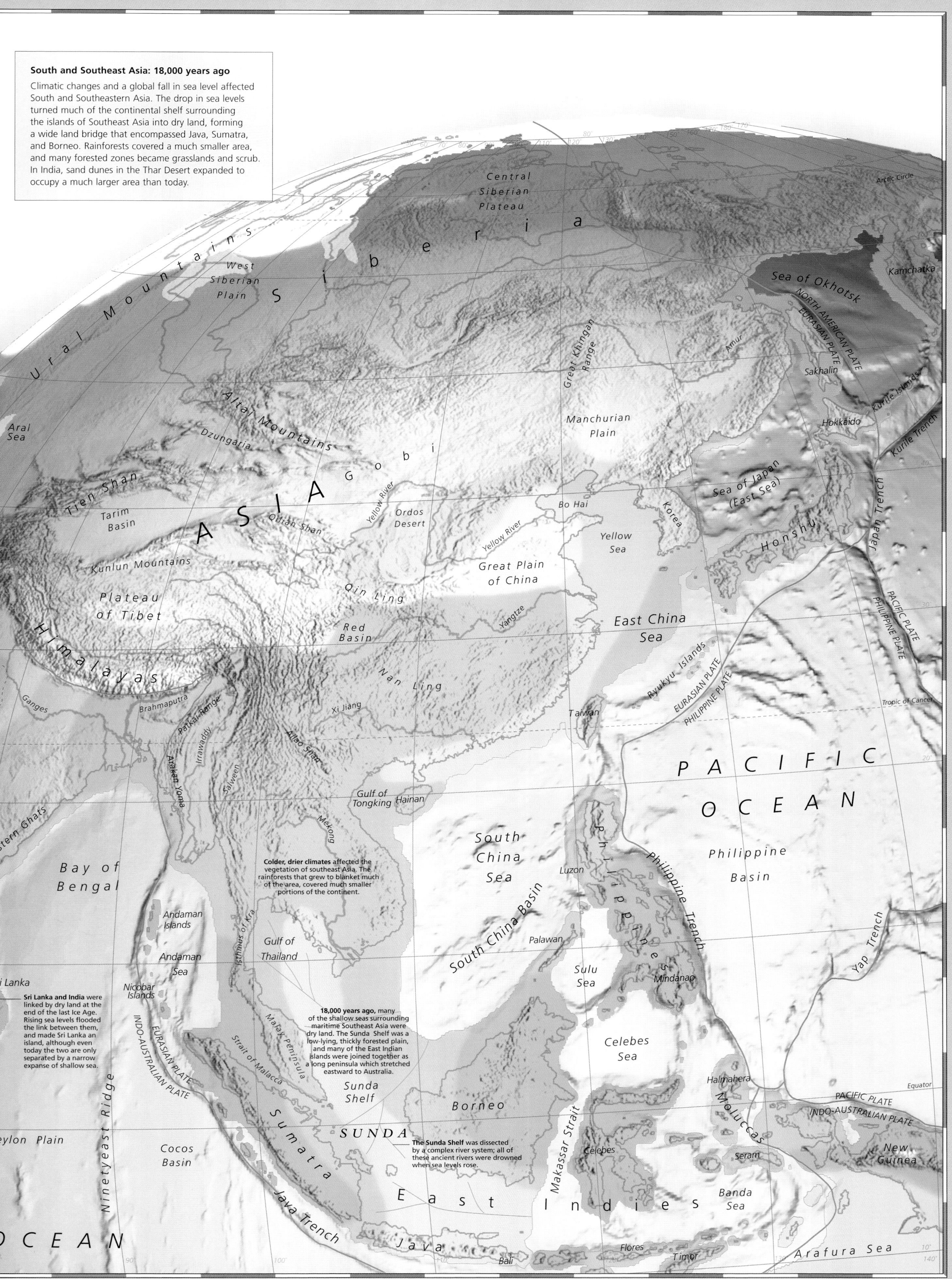

South and Southeast Asia: 18,000 years ago
Climatic changes and a global fall in sea level affected South and Southeastern Asia. The drop in sea levels turned much of the continental shelf surrounding the islands of Southeast Asia into dry land, forming a wide land bridge that encompassed Java, Sumatra, and Borneo. Rainforests covered a much smaller area, and many forested zones became grasslands and scrub. In India, sand dunes in the Thar Desert expanded to occupy a much larger area than today.
Central Siberian Plateau
S i b e r i a
West Siberian Plain
Ural Mountains
Arctic Circle
Kamchatka
Sea of Okhotsk
NORTH AMERICAN PLATE
EURASIAN PLATE
Amur
Sakhalin
Kurile Islands
Kurile Trench
Hokkaido
Great Khingan Range
Manchurian Plain
Aral Sea
Altai Mountains
Dzungaria
G o b i
A S I A
Tien Shan
Tarim Basin
Qilian Shan
Yellow River
Ordos Desert
Bo Hai
Korea
Sea of Japan (East Sea)
Honshu
Japan Trench
Yellow Sea
Great Plain of China
Kunlun Mountains
Plateau of Tibet
Qin Ling
Yangtze
East China Sea
PACIFIC PLATE
PHILIPPINE PLATE
Red Basin
Himalayas
Nan Ling
Ryukyu Islands
EURASIAN PLATE
PHILIPPINE PLATE
Tropic of Cancer
Ganges
Brahmaputra
Patkai Range
Xi Jiang
Taiwan
Irrawaddy
Arakan Yoma
Salween
Ailao Shan
PACIFIC OCEAN
Gulf of Tongking
Hainan
Mekong
…stern Ghats
Bay of Bengal
Colder, drier climates affected the vegetation of southeast Asia. The rainforests that grew to blanket much of the area, covered much smaller portions of the continent.
South China Sea
Luzon
Philippines
Philippine Trench
Philippine Basin
Andaman Islands
Isthmus of Kra
Gulf of Thailand
South China Basin
Palawan
Yap Trench
Andaman Sea
Sulu Sea
Mindanao
…ri Lanka
Nicobar Islands
Sri Lanka and India were linked by dry land at the end of the last Ice Age. Rising sea levels flooded the link between them, and made Sri Lanka an island, although even today the two are only separated by a narrow expanse of shallow sea.
INDO-AUSTRALIAN PLATE
EURASIAN PLATE
Malay Peninsula
Strait of Malacca
18,000 years ago, many of the shallow seas surrounding maritime Southeast Asia were dry land. The Sunda Shelf was a low-lying, thickly forested plain, and many of the East Indian islands were joined together as a long peninsula which stretched eastward to Australia.
Celebes Sea
Halmahera
Equator
Sunda Shelf
Borneo
Moluccas
PACIFIC PLATE
INDO-AUSTRALIAN PLATE
Ninetyeast Ridge
…eylon Plain
Sumatra
SUNDA
The Sunda Shelf was dissected by a complex river system; all of these ancient rivers were drowned when sea levels rose.
Makassar Strait
Celebes
Seram
New Guinea
Cocos Basin
E a s t I n d i e s
Banda Sea
Java Trench
…OCEAN
Java
Bali
Flores
Timor
Arafura Sea

SOUTH AND SOUTHEAST ASIA

EXPLORATION AND MAPPING

This 18th-century Hindu globe shows the heavens *(in the top half)* and the earthly realm *(below)*.

THE RELIGIONS OF SOUTH ASIA all have a long tradition of cosmography, though surviving maps are of relatively recent date. While some early maps may have related to secular themes, most would have been associated with religion and the place of humankind in a greater universe, reflecting the sacred geography of the Hindu, Jain, and Buddhist traditions. Despite the sophistication of Indian science and the great distances travelled by Indian – especially Buddhist – missionaries and merchants, there is little evidence of conventional geographical mapping until well after the establishment of Islam in the region. Following the establishment of the Portuguese in western India after 1498, European colonists, with competing territorial claims, spurred on the Western mapping of South and Southeast Asia. Commercial, economic, and military motives, combined with a zeal for knowledge, led to the British Survey of India from 1767, an epic project to map and define their eastern empire.

The cosmographic tradition

A Jain diagram of the universe shows Mount Meru surrounded by concentric circles representing different continents and oceans.

The cosmographic conceptions of Hinduism, Buddhism, and Jainism, which attempted to locate the sacred places of this world in an imagined universe, were remarkably complex. Within each of them, Jambudvipa – the world inhabited by humans – formed only a very small part. In all cultures of Asia there is a strong belief that the fortunes of humans are affected by extra-terrestrial forces whose influence can be foretold, in part, through astrology, with which astronomy was closely associated. Thus, mapping the heavens (on an astrolabe or other astronomical instruments) was a much more important concern than the geographic mapping of topography.

The lotus flower, redrawn here by Francis Wilford in 1805, was for Buddhists a symbol of the universe.

The astronomical observatory at Jaipur was one of five built by the Rajput king Sawai Jai Singh between 1722 and 1739. It contained remarkably accurate masonry instruments.

Indigenous mapping of South and Southeast Asia

Scarcely any surviving indigenous maps of the region are earlier than the 16th century. Maps were drawn for a variety of reasons: to provide information for the military; to illustrate itineraries or journeys; to legitimize territorial possessions. Maritime navigation charts from Gujarat date to the 17th century. Yet few surviving maps are strictly geographical, and virtually none are drawn to a fixed scale. Cosmographic views were sometimes combined with geographical knowledge of the known world.

Indigenous South and Southeast Asian mapping

1600 – 1650 – 1700 – 1750 – 1800

- **c.1647:** Completion of Atlas of India by Sadiq Isfahani
- **c.1660:** Gujaratis make earliest known Indian nautical charts
- **c.1700:** Probable commencement of Mughal military mapping
- **1776:** Trai Phum (Story of Three Worlds), Thai manuscript containing world's longest map (52 m)
- **c.1800:** Extensive military and administrative mapping by Marathas and Burmese

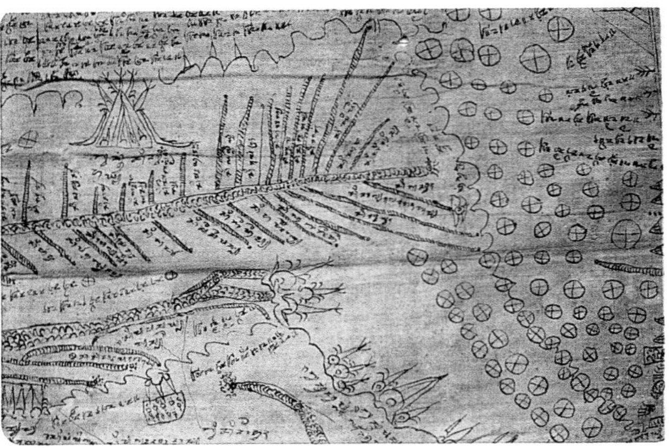

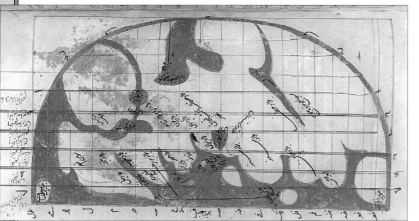

The sacred map of the Sundanese chiefdom of Timbanganten in western Java *(left)* was drawn in the late 16th century. It is still venerated by local villagers for its protective powers against the volcano clearly depicted on the left of the map.

The Mughal Emperor Jahangir is shown embracing Shah Abbas of Persia on a geographic globe, based on an Elizabethan model brought to the court by the first English ambassador in 1615 *(right)*.

An encyclopedic work in Persian by Sadiq Isfahani of Jaunpur in northern India was finished in 1647. The section on travel contains a map *(left)* of the 'inhabited quarter' (Africa and Eurasia), drawn in the traditional style of Islamic cosmography.

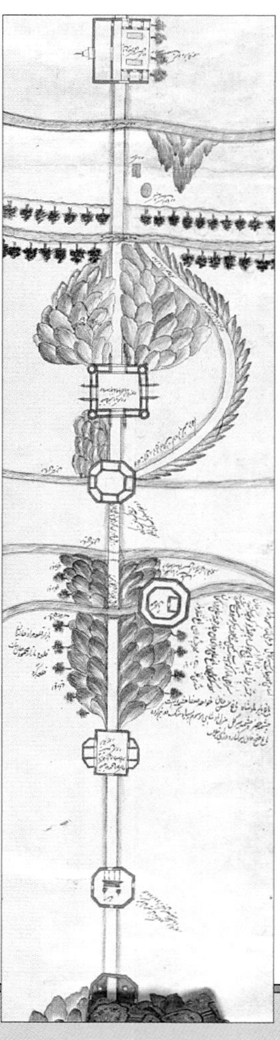

The detail *(right)* is from a Mughal map showing the route from Delhi to Kandahar by means of a system of straight lines and nodal points.

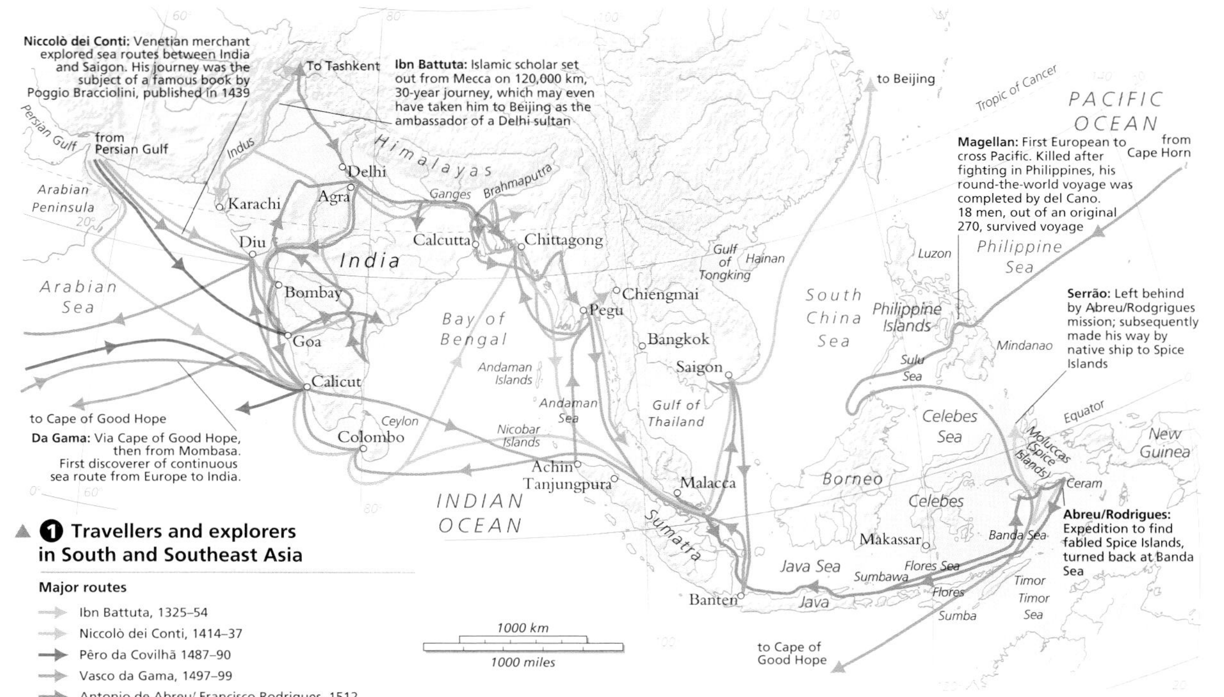

Niccolò dei Conti: Venetian merchant explored sea routes between India and Saigon. His journey was the subject of a famous book by Poggio Bracciolini, published in 1439
To Tashkent
Ibn Battuta: Islamic scholar set out from Mecca on 120,000 km, 30-year journey, which may even have taken him to Beijing as the ambassador of a Delhi sultan
to Beijing
Tropic of Cancer
PACIFIC OCEAN
Magellan: First European to cross Pacific. Killed after fighting in Philippines, his round-the-world voyage was completed by del Cano. 18 men, out of an original 270, survived voyage
from Cape Horn
Persian Gulf
from Persian Gulf
Indus
Himalayas
Delhi
Arabian Peninsula
Karachi
Agra
Ganges
Brahmaputra
Diu
Calcutta
Chittagong
India
Gulf of Tongking
Hainan
Luzon
Philippine Sea
Arabian Sea
Bombay
Chiengmai
South China Sea
Philippine Islands
Pegu
Bay of Bengal
Bangkok
Serrão: Left behind by Abreu/Rodrigues mission; subsequently made his way by native ship to Spice Islands
Goa
Andaman Islands
Saigon
Sulu Sea
Mindanao
Calicut
Andaman Sea
Gulf of Thailand
Celebes Sea
Equator
to Cape of Good Hope
Ceylon
Nicobar Islands
New Guinea
Da Gama: Via Cape of Good Hope, then from Mombasa. First discoverer of continuous sea route from Europe to India.
Colombo
Moluccas (Spice Islands)
Achin
Malacca
Borneo
Ceram
Tanjungpura
INDIAN OCEAN
Celebes
Abreu/Rodrigues: Expedition to find fabled Spice Islands, turned back at Banda Sea
Sumatra
Makassar
Banda Sea
Java Sea
Sumbawa
Flores Sea
Flores
Timor
Timor Sea
Banten
Java
Sumba
1000 km
1000 miles
to Cape of Good Hope

▲ ❶ **Travellers and explorers in South and Southeast Asia**

Major routes

- Ibn Battuta, 1325–54
- Niccolò dei Conti, 1414–37
- Pêro da Covilhã 1487–90
- Vasco da Gama, 1497–99
- Antonio de Abreu/ Francisco Rodrigues, 1512
- Francisco Serrão, 1512
- Ferdinand Magellan/Juan Sebastian del Cano, 1519–22
- Ralph Fitch 1583–91
- Jean Baptiste Tavernier 1639–67 (five visits)

Travellers in South and Southeast Asia
1498: Vasco da Gama's voyage to Calicut; secret Portuguese mapping follows
1535: Waldseemüller's map improves on shape of India
1596: J.H. Van Linschoten's Itinerario includes numerous large– and small–scale maps
1400
1450
1500
1550
1600
1439: Poggio Bracciolini records Asian journeys of Niccolò dei Conti
1502: First published map to show correct general shape of India, by Alberto Cantino
1512: Francisco Serrão (Portuguese) makes his way to Moluccas
1619: William Baffin's map of Mughal Empire, the first by an English cartographer

Travellers in South and Southeast Asia

The most celebrated medieval traveller in the region was Ibn Battuta of Tangier in the 14th century, even if his claim to have journeyed as far China may not be true. A century later Vasco da Gama was piloted across the Indian Ocean by a Gujarati Muslim. A yet more southerly route opened up the richest prize of Southeast Asia – the fabled Spice Islands, subject of a Portuguese monopoly from 1512. In the 1590s the Dutch began to probe the southern Indian Ocean, using Mauritius as a staging post.

This map of India and Ceylon dating from 1596 appears in Jan Huygen van Linschoten's *Itinerario*, a work instrumental in encouraging Dutch and English trade with India.

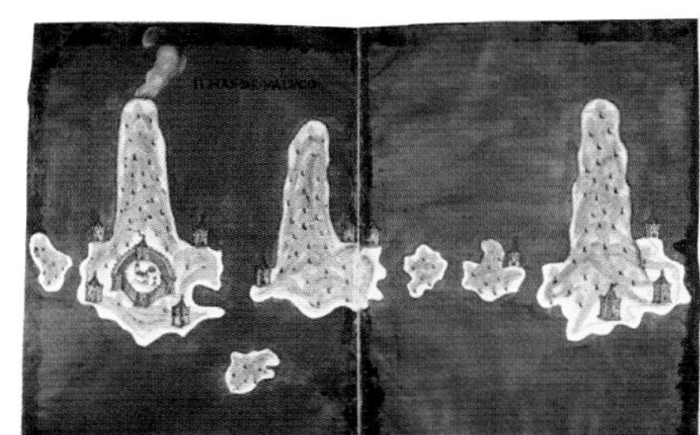

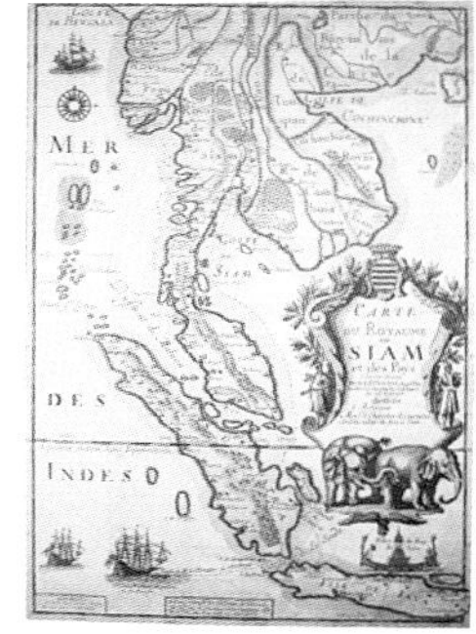

A Portuguese map of the Moluccas (1646) shows major settlements, volcanoes, and types of vegetation on the islands *(left)*.

This 17th-century French map shows the Kingdom of Siam, the Malay Peninsula, Sumatra, and Java, including political boundaries and areas of influence *(right)*.

The Survey of India

Although European mapping of India began in the wake of Vasco da Gama's 1498 landfall, it was not until after James Rennell's 1767 appointment as the first Surveyor General of the newly acquired province of Bengal that the British began to survey and map the country systematically. Initially, maps were based on observation, reports, and intelligence. From the late 18th century, British Army officers, such as Colin Mackenzie and William Lambton, began formal trigonometrical surveys. Sir George Everest, Lambton's successor, planned a vast network of triangulations, operated by a huge staff. He was careful to placate local princes, who feared that land surveys would infringe on their already eroded sovereignty.

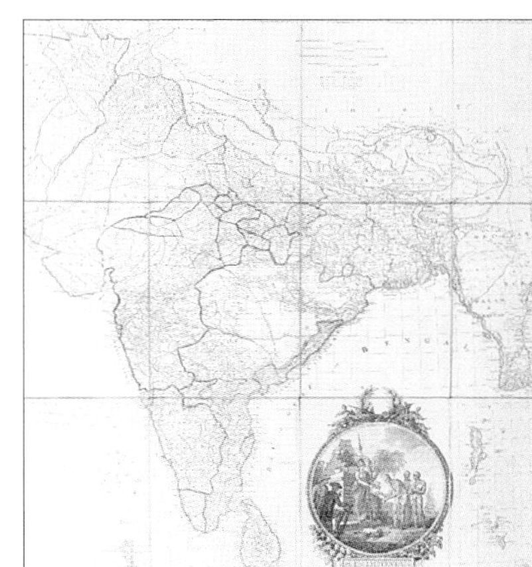

James Rennell, surveyor of Bengal and Bihar, published this map in 1782, four years after his return to England. The cartouche depicts Britannia receiving the sacred scriptures of India from a Brahmin.

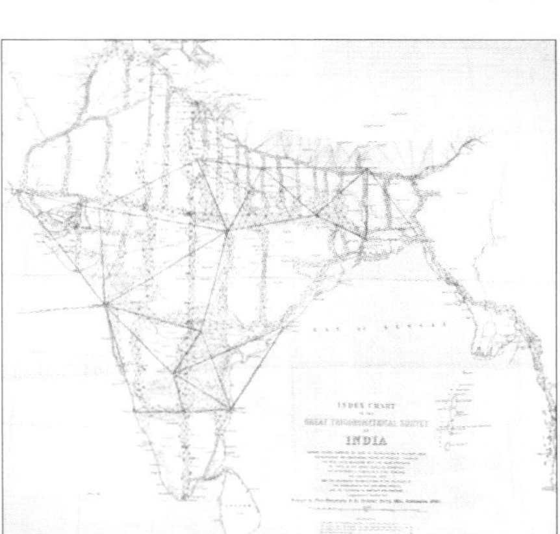

George Everest planned his trigonometrical triangulations on a grid overlying the entire subcontinent. His predecessor, William Lambton laid down the central north-south axis.

The Indian Atlas of J. & C. Walker was commissioned by the East India Company in 1823. It was produced at a scale of four miles to one inch.

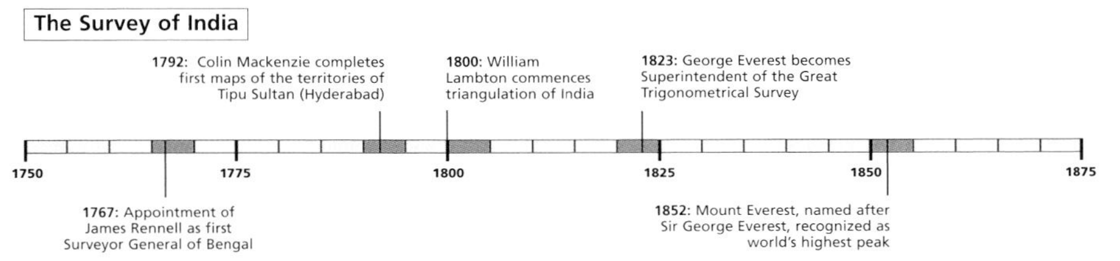

The Survey of India
1792: Colin Mackenzie completes first maps of the territories of Tipu Sultan (Hyderabad)
1800: William Lambton commences triangulation of India
1823: George Everest becomes Superintendent of the Great Trigonometrical Survey
1750
1775
1800
1825
1850
1875
1767: Appointment of James Rennell as first Surveyor General of Bengal
1852: Mount Everest, named after Sir George Everest, recognized as world's highest peak

The scientific exploration of Southeast Asia

In 1854, the British naturalist Alfred Wallace set out for Singapore, and spent the next eight years travelling around the islands of the East Indies and New Guinea. He observed and collected a vast number of animal species, many previously unknown to western science. Most importantly, he observed a dramatic change in fauna at the centre of the region; the eastern species are distinctly Australian, the western, Asian. He argued that the eastern part of the archipelago was therefore once part of a Pacific continent. The boundary between the two faunal regions came to be called the Wallace Line.

Alfred Wallace's account of his Southeast Asian travels, published in 1869, contains many fine illustrations of the species encountered on his journey such as this black cockatoo from the Aru Islands.

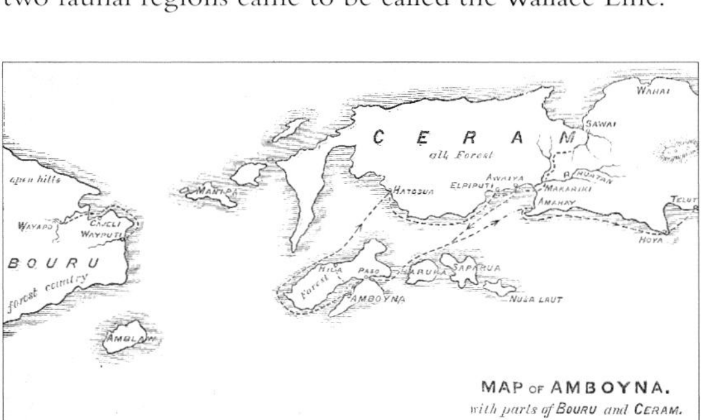

CERAM
BOURU
MAP OF AMBOYNA.

The series of maps published in Alfred Wallace's account of his journey to Southeast Asia show, in great detail, the terrain which he explored. This map, of Ceram in the Moluccas, shows the region where he encountered and carefully observed many different types of birds of paradise, and first began to devise his theories about species evolution.

▼ ❷ **The scientific journeys of Alfred Wallace in Southeast Asia**

- journeys of Alfred Wallace, 1854–62
- Wallace 'line'
- inferred ancient coastline
- eastern limit of transitional faunal zone

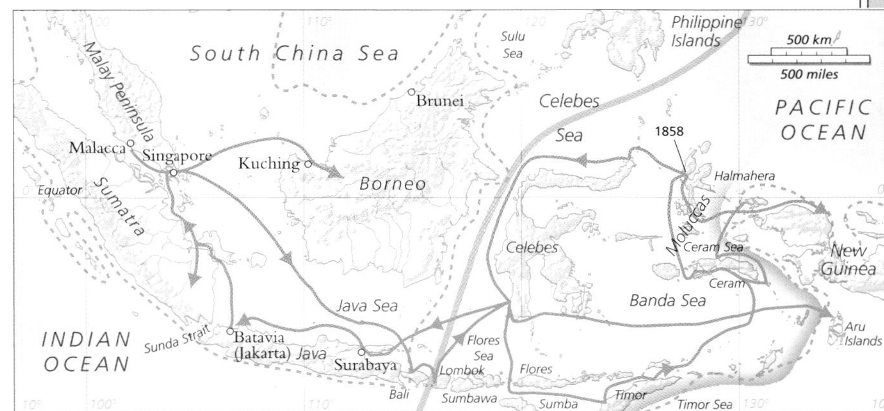

South China Sea
Sulu Sea
Philippine Islands
500 km
500 miles
Malay Peninsula
Brunei
Celebes Sea
PACIFIC OCEAN
Malacca
Singapore
Kuching
1858
Halmahera
Equator
Borneo
Sumatra
Moluccas
Celebes
Ceram Sea
New Guinea
Ceram
Java Sea
Banda Sea
INDIAN OCEAN
Sunda Strait
Batavia (Jakarta)
Java
Surabaya
Lombok
Flores Sea
Flores
Aru Islands
Bali
Sumbawa
Sumba
Timor
Timor Sea

EARLY CIVILIZATIONS OF SOUTH ASIA

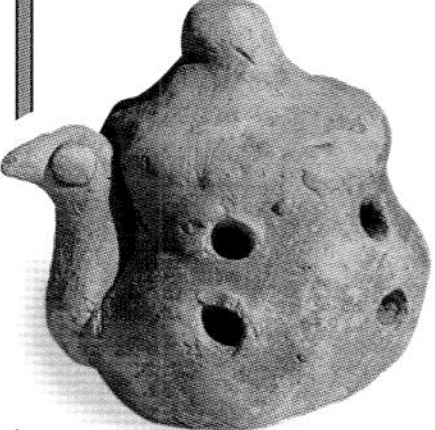

This perforated pot from Mohenjo-Daro was used for carrying perfume.

THE DEVELOPMENT of copper and bronze technology in South and Southeast Asia during the 5th to 3rd millennia BCE, preceded the emergence of urban civilizations in these regions. The cities of the Indus established trade networks which extended to Mesopotamia. Some time after the collapse of the Indus civilization c.1800 BCE, Sanskrit-speaking Aryans settled in the region and their influence spread across northern India over the next thousand years. In the 6th century BCE, the region of Magadha gained ascendancy over the small states of the Ganges plain. Chandragupta Maurya established a vigorous new dynasty with its capital at Pataliputra in 321 BCE, which reached its apogee in the following century in the reign of Ashoka. In Southeast Asia, Sanskrit inscriptions from c.400 BCE are evidence of early Indian influence in the region.

The development of Harappan culture

This bust of a bearded man from Mohenjo-Daro c.2100 BCE, may represent a priest-king.

Harappan (Indus) culture arose from agricultural and pastoral cultures in the hills of nearby Baluchistan during the late 4th millennium BCE and expanded from its core area on the Indus valley as far east as the Ganges river and south to present-day Maharashtra. Indus civilization is marked by regularly laid-out cities, built of baked brick, and dominated by imposing citadels, which contained religious, ceremonial and administrative buildings. Many of the streets of the residential areas had brick-roofed drains with regular inspection holes. Weights, measures, and bricks were all standardized, indicating a high level of cultural uniformity. The demise of the Indus civilization may have been caused by environmental change which disrupted the delicate balance between the cities and their agricultural base.

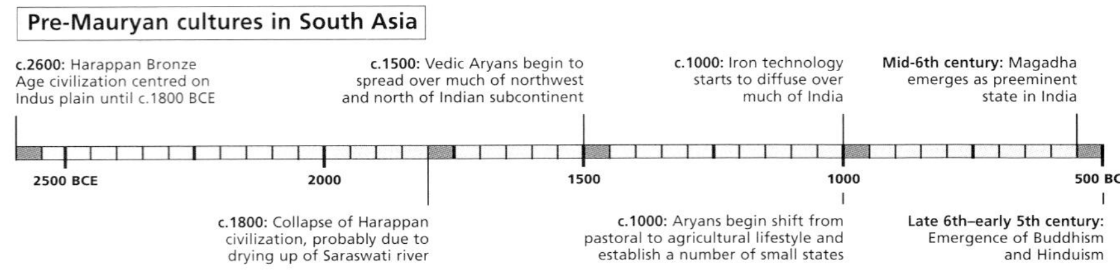

1 The citadel at Mohenjo-Daro

'college'

Great Bath

'granary'

N

200 metres

200 yards

2 The development of Harappan culture, late 4th–early 2nd millennium BCE

Baluchistan hill cultures

- hill cultures of Baluchistan, late 4th–late 3rd millennium BCE
- major site
- other site (selected)

Harappan cultures

- area of early Harappan culture, c.3000-2600 BCE
- limit of mature Harappan culture, c.1800 BCE
- principal cities
- other settlements
- major clusters of urban sites
- other important contemporary site

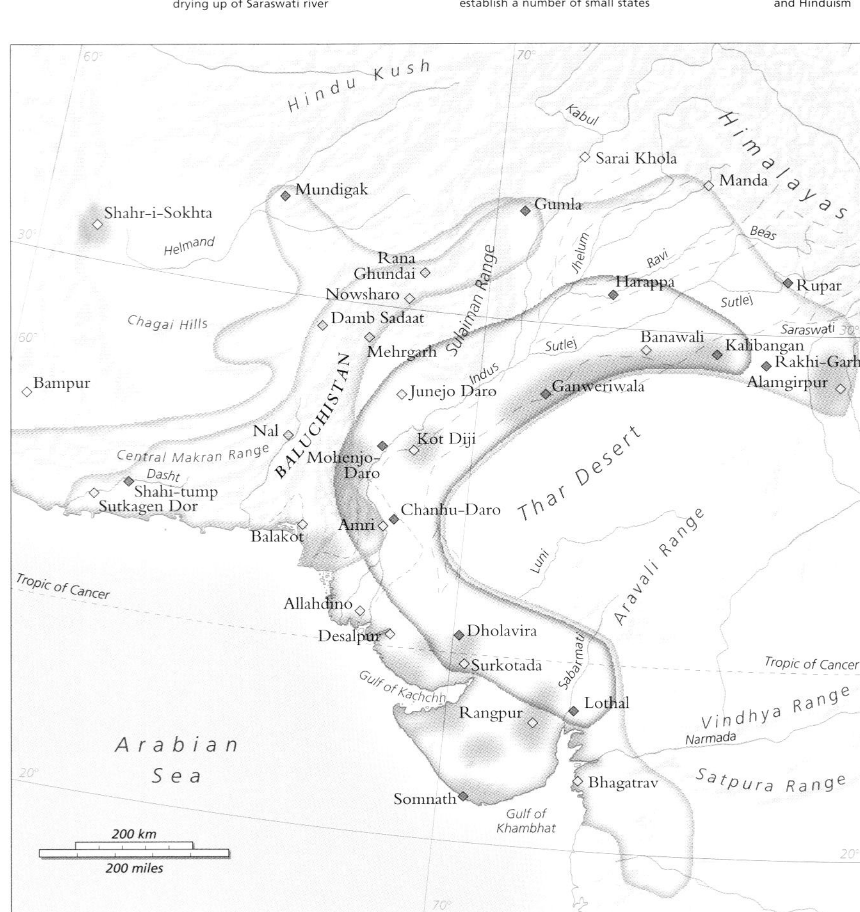

Bronze tools and weapons from Mohenjo-Daro reveal the city's high level of technological sophistication.

Mohenjo-Daro

This ancient city, along with Harappa, was one of the two greatest urban centres of Harappan civilization. With an area of more than 200 hectares, the city's population may have been as high as 50,000. The houses of the lower town were divided into blocks by regular streets. The city was a major centre of both trade and manufacture.

Stylish Harappan bronzes include this elegant dancer.

The Bronze Age in Southeast Asia to 1000 BCE

Archaeologists have unearthed numerous and diverse bronzes from Southeast Asia, some possibly dating as far back as 2000 BCE. The presence of bronze artefacts in some burials of the period, notably at Non Nok Tha and Ban Chiang in Thailand, indicates that society was becoming increasingly stratified. The background to this development, however, coming before the region was influenced by the civilized societies of India and China, is poorly understood. Sophisticated techniques, such as lost-wax casting and closed moulds, were used, and earthenware crucibles found near the burials indicate local mastery of complex bronze technology.

This pottery urn mounted on four supporting legs was made in Thailand c.3000–2000 BCE.

3 Bronze Age Southeast Asia from c.1500 BCE

- major Bronze Age site
- find of Dong Son-type drum

Bronze Dong Son drums, such as this one from Vietnam, c.500 BCE have been found throughout the region.

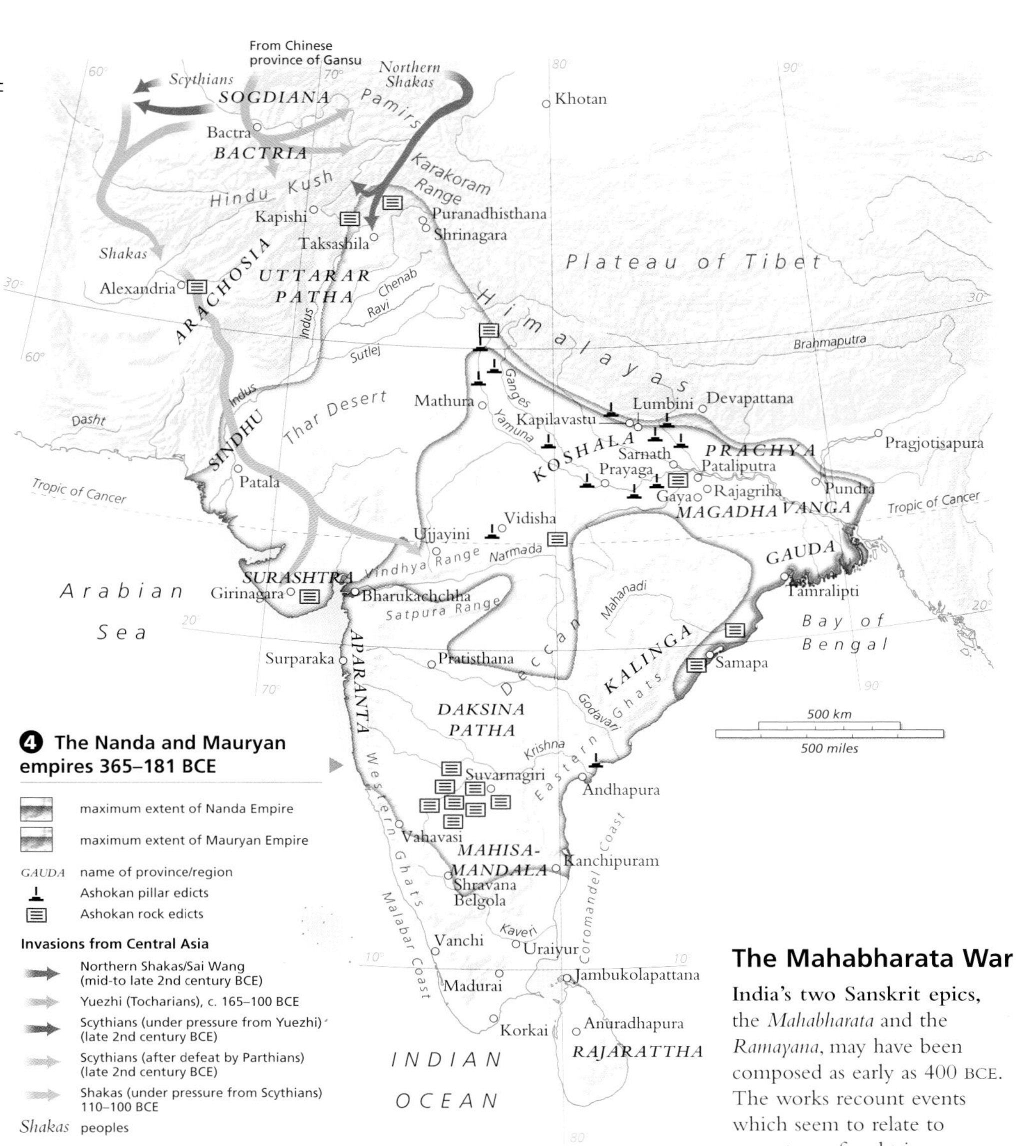

The central narrative of the *Mahabharata* tells the story of the struggle for supremacy between two groups of cousins – the Kauravas and the Pandavas. This manuscript illustration shows a chariot battle between the two forces.

The Nanda and Mauryan empires c.365–181 BCE

By c.600 BCE, the Ganges plain was dominated by 16 distinct political units which, over the next century, all came under the control of the state of Magadha. By the time of the Nanda dynasty (c.365–321 BCE) the extent of the Magadhan Empire was already substantial. The succeeding Mauryan Empire (321–181 BCE), however, was the first to achieve pan-Indian status and its political and cultural influence extended well beyond the subcontinent. When the Mauryan leader Ashoka converted to Buddhism (c.260 BCE), he foreswore war. Following the decline of the empire, northwest India suffered a series of invasions by peoples from northeast Asia, propelled into migration by the expansion of Han China.

A Buddhist stupa still stands at Sarnath, a Mauryan city on the northern Ganges plain.

The Mauryan Empire and successor states in South Asia

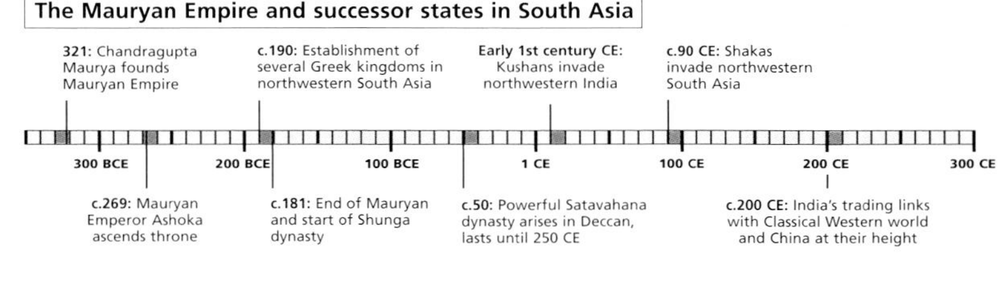

The Mahabharata War

India's two Sanskrit epics, the *Mahabharata* and the *Ramayana*, may have been composed as early as 400 BCE. The works recount events which seem to relate to a great war fought in northwestern India several centuries earlier. The later magnification of this conflict into a pan-Indian struggle is probably the result of post-Mauryan mythology. The peoples identified in this map are among those who came within the ambit of expanding Mauryan power.

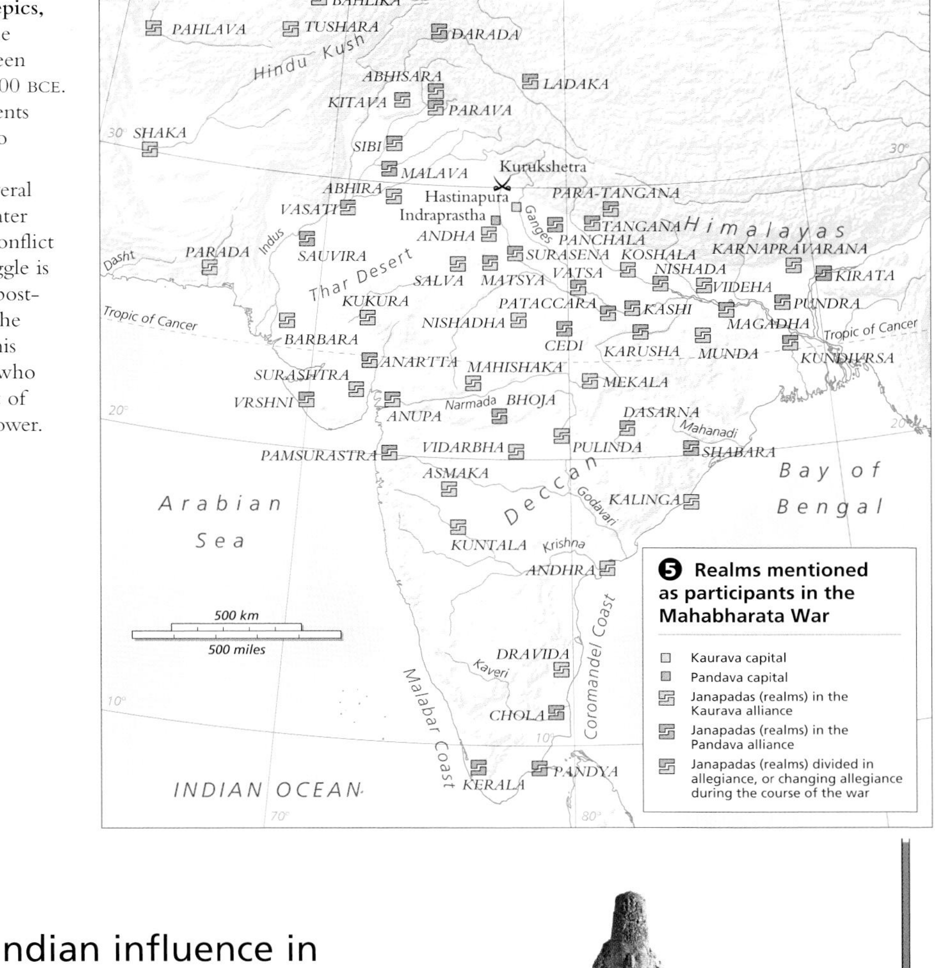

Indian influence in Southeast Asia to 650 CE

To ancient Indians Southeast Asia was known as *Suvarnadvipa*, the continent of gold. The number of Indians who traded and migrated there was not great, but their influence was profound. Brahmins, the high-caste priests of Hindu India, acted as ritual specialists, while other advisers attended numerous royal courts. Although indigenous cultures revered Indian traditions, art, and music, they also marked Hinduism and Buddhism with a distinctive local character.

A bronze statue of the Hindu deity Vishnu from Thailand (7th century CE) reflects the impact of Indian civilization on Southeast Asia.

Early Southeast Asian civilizations

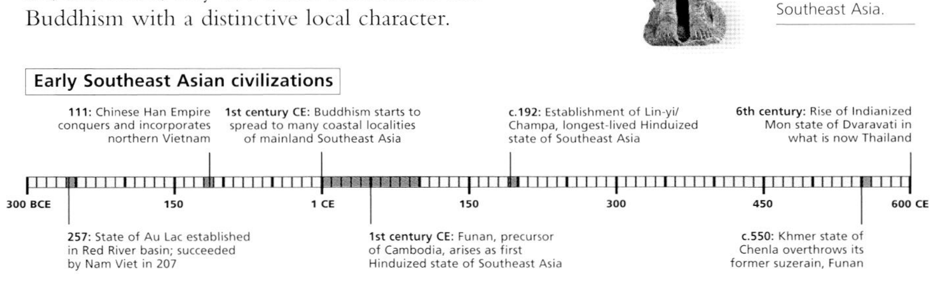

THE RELIGIONS OF SOUTHERN ASIA

This relief of the Buddha is in the Gandhara style, inspired by Graeco-Roman sculpture.

THE HISTORY OF SOUTH AND SOUTHEAST ASIA is inextricably linked to the diffusion and development of religions, and the interaction between different systems of belief. Indeed, the identity of most of the region's populations has long been defined by religion. India was the cultural birthplace of both Hinduism and Buddhism, as well as other, less widespread, faiths, such as Jainism and Sikhism. Buddhism once enjoyed substantial political patronage from Indian rulers, but ultimately failed to become established among the population at large. The resurgence of Hinduism in the course of the 1st millennium CE and the spread of Islam in the 8th–13th centuries also contributed to the demise of Buddhism in the land of its birth. Many imported faiths, including Buddhism, Hinduism, Islam, and, most recently, Christianity, have planted roots in the receptive soil of various parts of Southeast Asia.

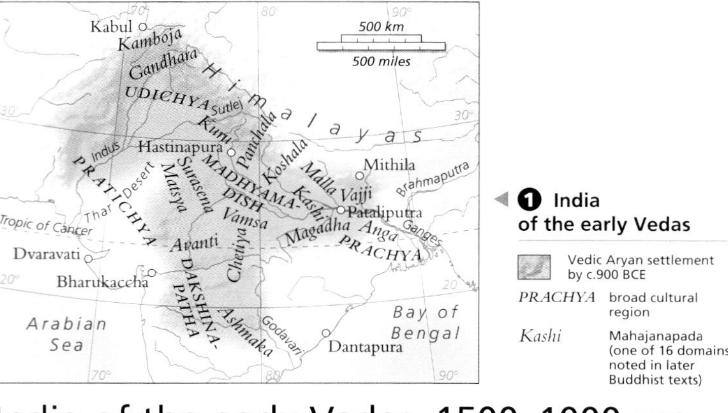

India of the early Vedas, 1500–1000 BCE

The *Rig Veda* (completed c.900 BCE) is the great literary monument left by the early Aryan settlers of northern India. This collection of sacred hymns traces the development of religious ideas as they were passed down orally from generation to generation. They depict the Aryans as chariot-driving warriors, formerly nomadic pastoralists, gradually adapting to a settled way of life. Later Buddhist texts abound in geographic references and mention the 16 great domains of north and central India – the *Mahajanapadas*.

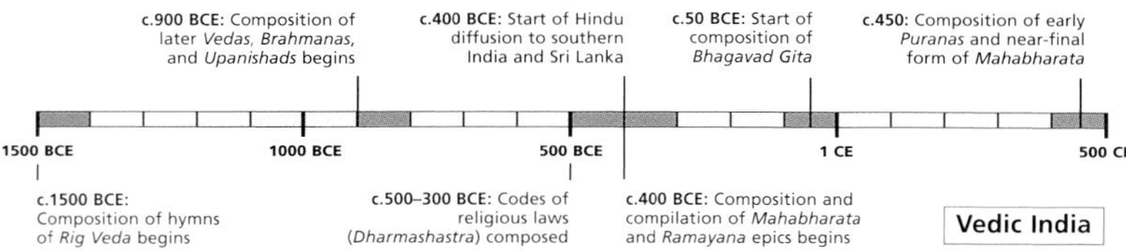

India of the Puranas

During the 1st millennium BCE, as the Aryan tribes coalesced into small kingdoms and republics, their religion became more comparable to the current form of Hinduism. As non-Aryan peoples were conquered and absorbed, a caste-based social order dominated by a Brahman priesthood, who oversaw increasingly elaborate rituals, and by a warrior caste (*Kshatriyas*) emerged. At first conquered peoples formed the lower strata of society. The expansion of Hindu culture can be traced through sacred texts; the collection of encyclopedic works – known as the *Puranas* – are rich in geographic content. They divide India up into a series of states or realms known as *janapadas*.

This bronze figure of Shiva, dating from the 11th century CE, depicts him as Lord of the Dance. He is surrounded by a circle of fire, which symbolizes both death and rebirth.

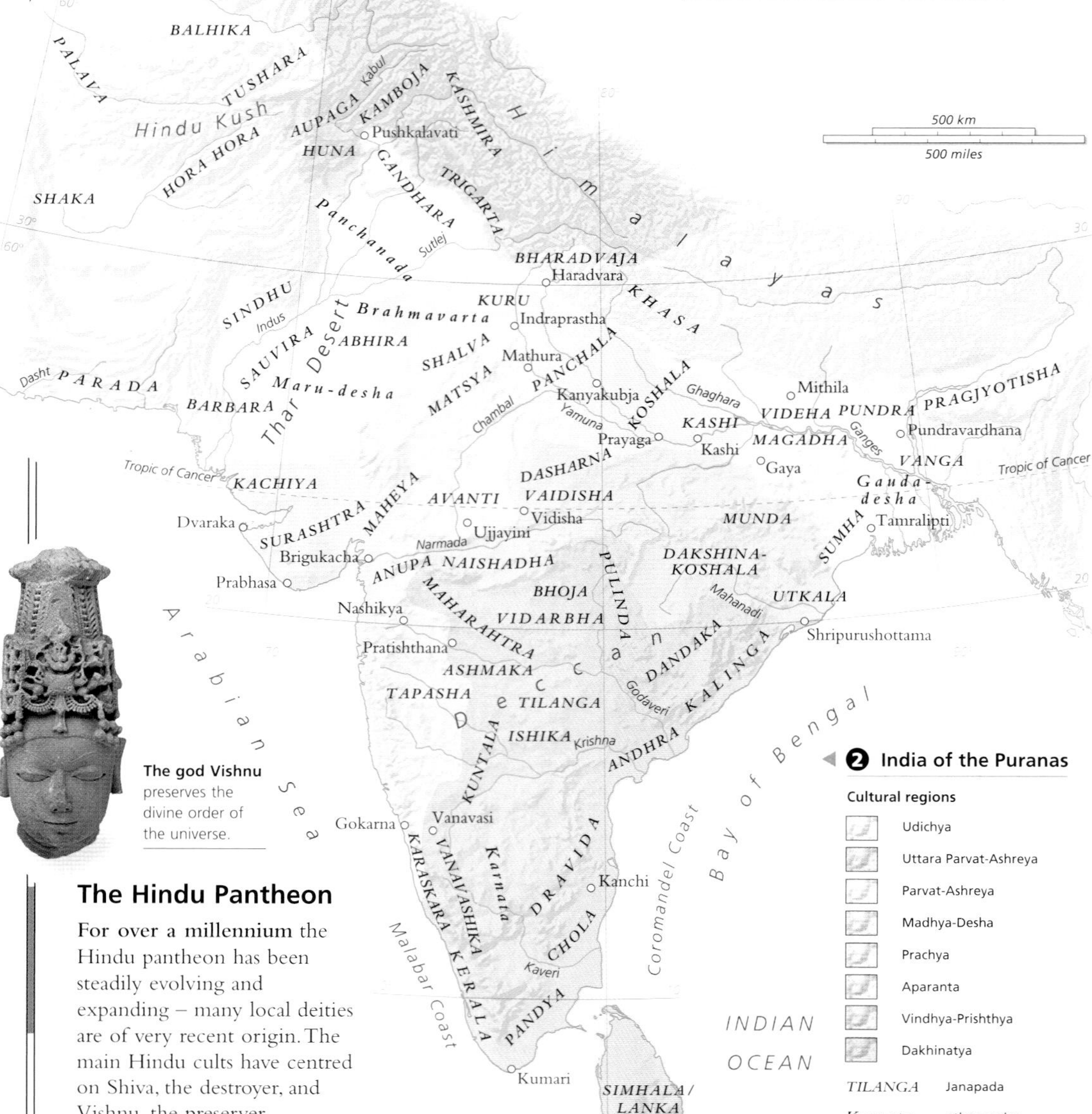

The god Vishnu preserves the divine order of the universe.

The Hindu Pantheon

For over a millennium the Hindu pantheon has been steadily evolving and expanding – many local deities are of very recent origin. The main Hindu cults have centred on Shiva, the destroyer, and Vishnu, the preserver.

The hearth of Buddhism and Jainism

Buddhism and Jainism arose in the Gangetic Plain during the 6th century BCE, partly in reaction to the ritual excesses and social inequalities within Brahmanism. Both faiths stress *ahisma* (non-violence), detachment from worldly possessions, and religious meditation. Both diffused widely and enjoyed the patronage of numerous political rulers before the advent of Islam in northern India, although the number of followers, especially of Jainism, may not have been great.

India's largest collection of Buddhist monuments is found at Sanchi in central India. They were built from the 3rd century BCE to the 11th century CE.

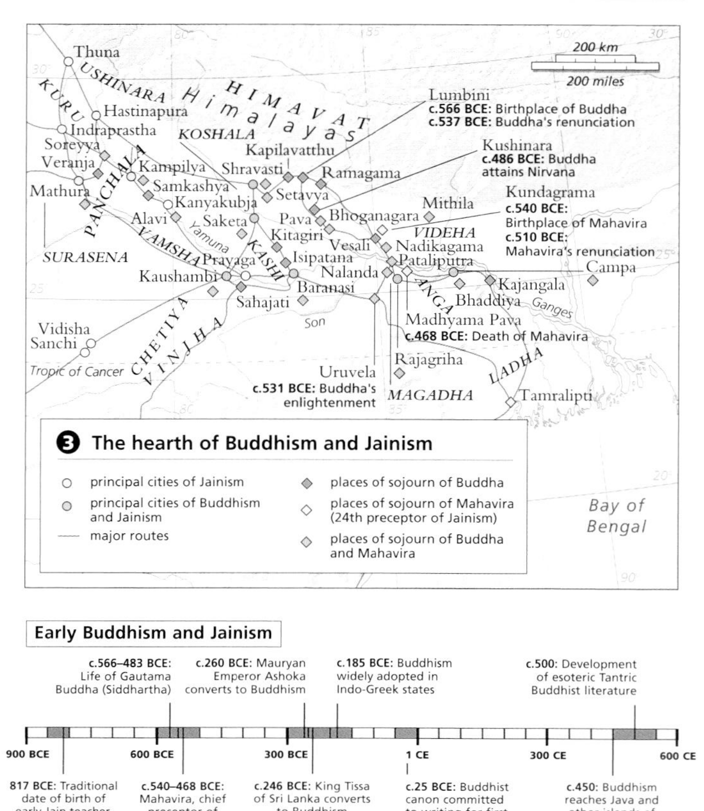

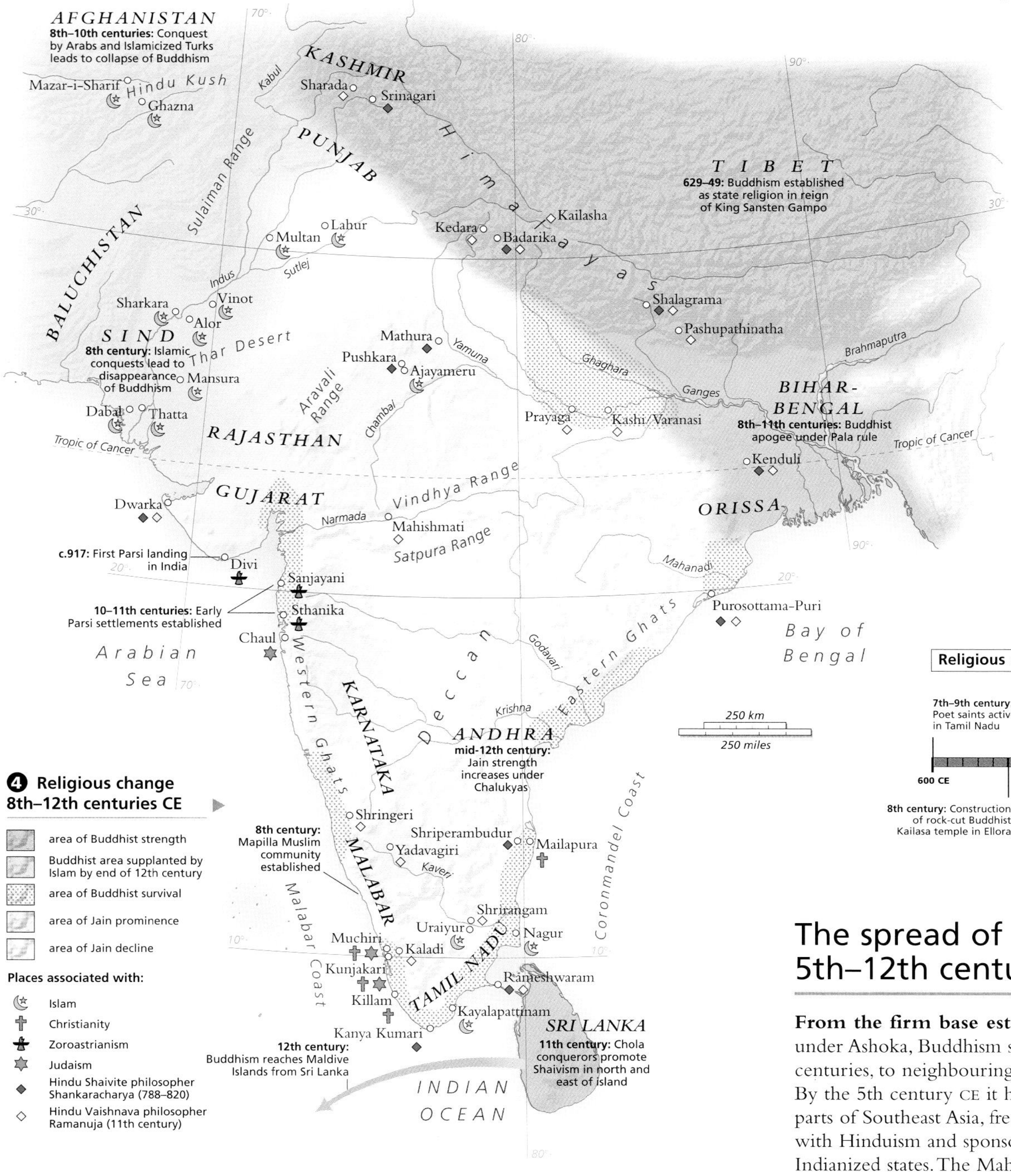

Religious movements in South Asia, 8th–12th centuries

With the Arab conquest of Sind in 711–13, Islam established its first toehold in South Asia, and by the end of the 12th century there was a strong Muslim presence in northwestern India. Meanwhile, religious ferment characterized India's other religions. Buddhism, though remaining the dominant faith in Ceylon (Sri Lanka), was entering a long period of decline in India. Among the many causes were the increasingly esoteric practices of the clergy and the destruction of Buddhist monasteries and libraries by conquering Muslims. Meanwhile, Hinduism, which had undergone a process of renewal in the first half of the millennium, continued to gain ground through the activities of philosophers such as the Shaivite Shankaracharya and the Vaishnavite Ramanuja.

A votive painting depicting one of the 24 *Tirthankaras* (saints) also known as *Jinas* (conquerors) revered as the founders of the Jain religion.

4 Religious change 8th–12th centuries CE

- area of Buddhist strength
- Buddhist area supplanted by Islam by end of 12th century
- area of Buddhist survival
- area of Jain prominence
- area of Jain decline

Places associated with:

- Islam
- Christianity
- Zoroastrianism
- Judaism
- Hindu Shaivite philosopher Shankaracharya (788–820)
- Hindu Vaishnava philosopher Ramanuja (11th century)

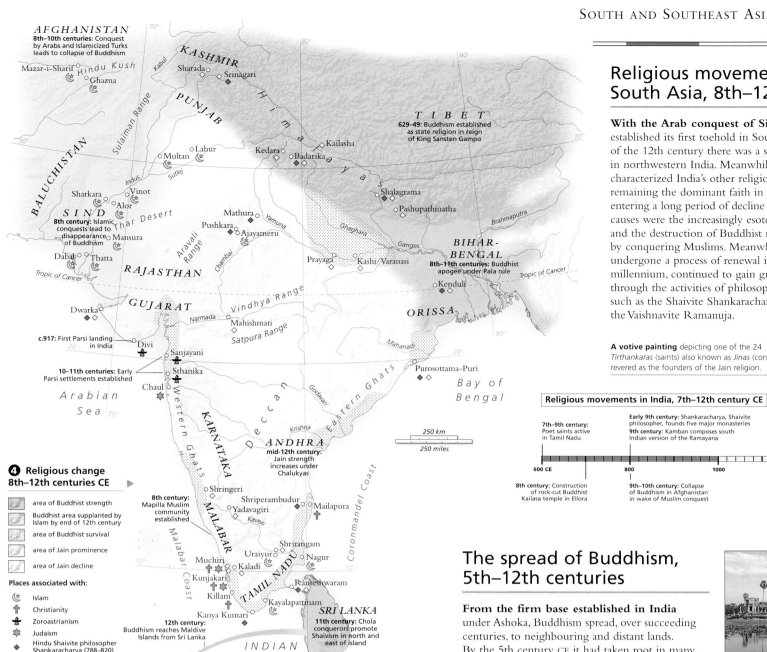

AFGHANISTAN 8th–10th centuries: Conquest by Arabs and Islamicized Turks leads to collapse of Buddhism

TIBET 629–49: Buddhism established as state religion in reign of King Sansten Gampo

SIND 8th century: Islamic conquests lead to disappearance of Buddhism

BIHAR-BENGAL 8th–11th centuries: Buddhist apogee under Pala rule

c.917: First Parsi landing in India

10–11th centuries: Early Parsi settlements established

ANDHRA mid-12th century: Jain strength increases under Chalukyas

8th century: Mapilla Muslim community established

12th century: Buddhism reaches Maldive Islands from Sri Lanka

SRI LANKA 11th century: Chola conquerors promote Shaivism in north and east of island

Religious movements in India, 7th–12th century CE

- 7th–9th century: Poet saints active in Tamil Nadu
- 8th century: Construction of rock-cut Buddhist Kailasa temple in Ellora
- Early 9th century: Shankaracharya, Shaivite philosopher, founds five major monasteries
- 9th century: Kamban composes south Indian version of the Ramayana
- 9th–10th century: Collapse of Buddhism in Afghanistan in wake of Muslim conquest
- Late 11th century–early 12th century: Career of Ramanuja, Vaishnava philosopher
- Mid-12th century: Rise of anti-caste Virashaiva (Lingayat) sect in southern India

600 CE · 800 · 1000 · 1200 · 1300 CE

The spread of Buddhism, 5th–12th centuries

From the firm base established in India under Ashoka, Buddhism spread, over succeeding centuries, to neighbouring and distant lands. By the 5th century CE it had taken root in many parts of Southeast Asia, frequently in conjunction with Hinduism and sponsored by increasingly Indianized states. The Mahayana and Theravada schools were both initially well represented; new contacts coming from Ceylon in the 12th century led to the increasing dominance of the latter.

The great temple complex of Angkor Wat in Cambodia was built by the Khmer ruler, Suryavarman II (1113–50) as a monument to his own divinity as the embodiment of Lord Vishnu.

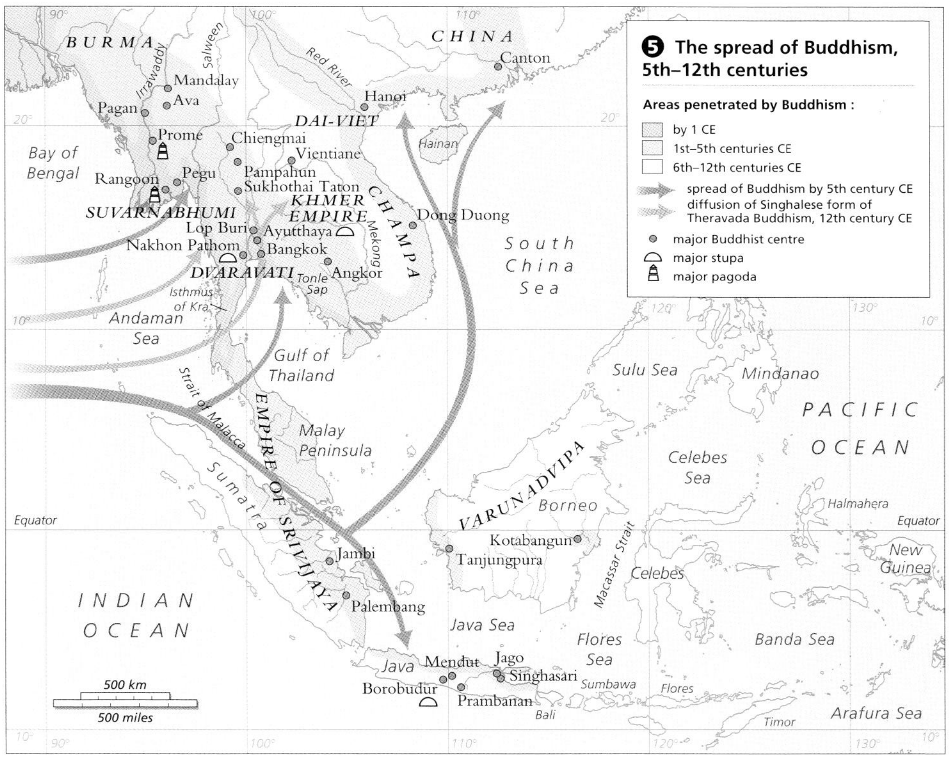

5 The spread of Buddhism, 5th–12th centuries

Areas penetrated by Buddhism:

- by 1 CE
- 1st–5th centuries CE
- 6th–12th centuries CE
- spread of Buddhism by 5th century CE
- diffusion of Singhalese form of Theravada Buddhism, 12th century CE
- major Buddhist centre
- major stupa
- major pagoda

The spread of Islam in Southeast Asia

Indian Muslim traders settled in the mercantile centres of Southeast Asia as early as the 10th century, but it was only after the conversion to Islam of the ruler of the powerful Sumatran state of Achin that the mainly peaceful process of Islamization began in earnest. In rapid succession, the princes of other small trading states also embraced the new faith. From their coastal capitals, Islam gradually penetrated inland, a process still underway in parts of present-day Indonesia.

A Dutch engraving of 1596 shows an envoy from Mecca meeting the governor of Bantam in west Java, an example of the East Indies' strong links with the Muslim world.

The diffusion of Islam in South and Southeast Asia

- 711–12: Arab conquest of Sind introduces Islam to South Asia
- c.750: Muslim merchants establish Islam in Kerala, southwest India
- c.1000: Mahmud of Ghazni conquers northwest India
- c.1200: Muslim Sufi saint, Mu'in al-Din Chishti, founds first Sufi order in subcontinent
- 1295: Conversion of Sultan of Achin to Islam, which spreads over much of the East Indies

700 CE · 800 · 900 · 1000 · 1100 · 1200 · 1300 CE

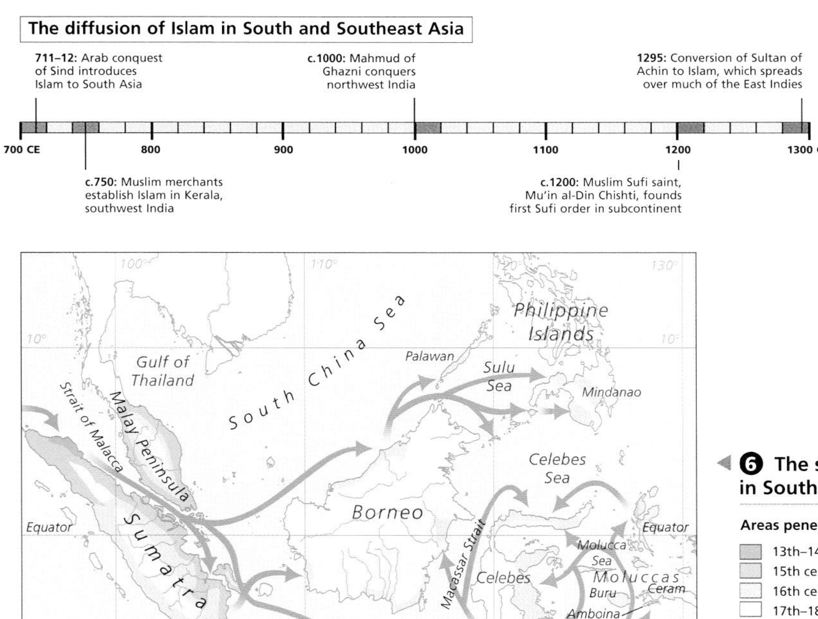

6 The spread of Islam in Southeast Asia

Areas penetrated by Islam:

- 13th–14th centuries
- 15th century
- 16th century
- 17th–18th centuries
- 19th–20th centuries
- spread of Islam

The Buddhist stupa at Borobudur, Java, symbolizes via its structure, the Buddhist transition from reality at its base – for example in this panel showing sailing vessels – to the achievement of spiritual enlightment at the summit.

STATES AND EMPIRES 300–1525

Bajang Ratu was the capital of the Majapahit kingdom in central Java.

SOUTH ASIA WAS ruled by a great diversity of regional powers for much of this period. However, in the 4th century CE, the Gupta dynasty succeeded in uniting much of the Indian subcontinent. The next 200 years are often described as a 'golden age' of Indian civilization. It was not until the 13th century that so much of India again came under the control of a single state, the Delhi Sultanate. The Turkish dynasties that ruled the Sultanate were unable to maintain effective control over so vast an area, and its power declined in the 14th century. Southeast Asia also witnessed the rise and fall of numerous states. Kambujadesha, with its magnificent capital at Angkor, dominated the mainland, while the two greatest states of the Indonesian archipelago were Srivijaya and, later, Majapahit.

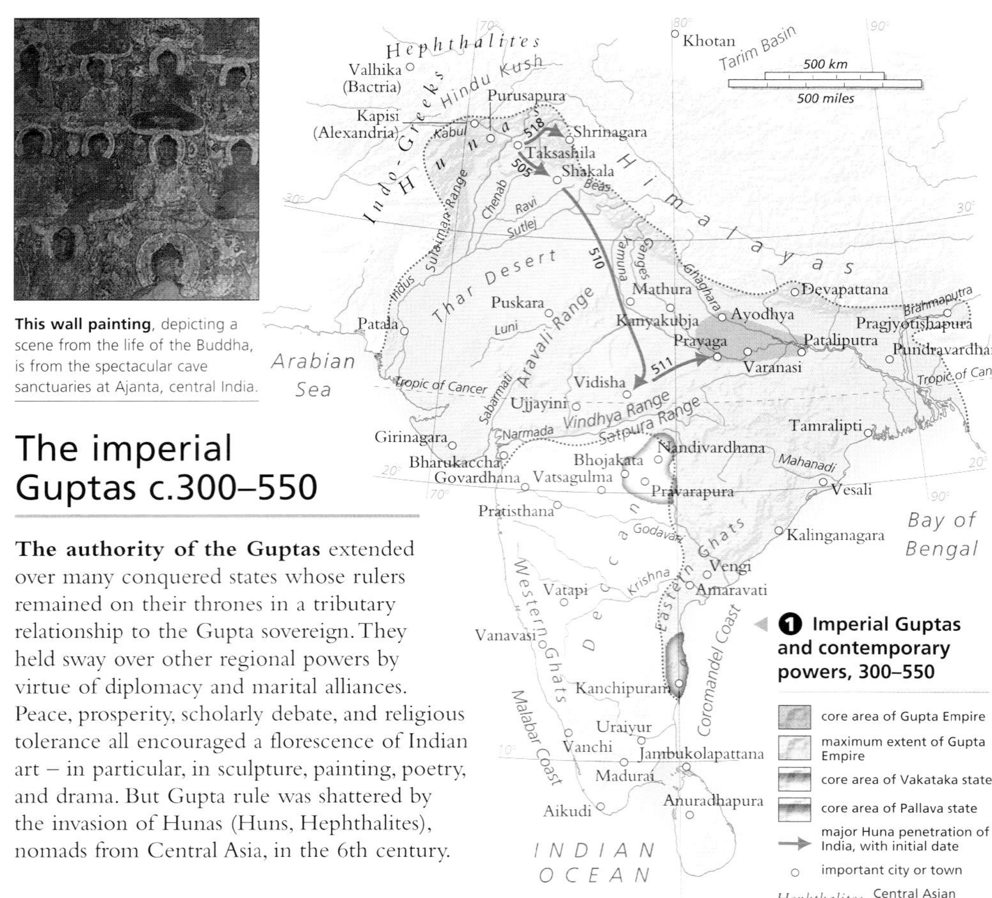

This wall painting, depicting a scene from the life of the Buddha, is from the spectacular cave sanctuaries at Ajanta, central India.

The imperial Guptas c.300–550

The authority of the Guptas extended over many conquered states whose rulers remained on their thrones in a tributary relationship to the Gupta sovereign. They held sway over other regional powers by virtue of diplomacy and marital alliances. Peace, prosperity, scholarly debate, and religious tolerance all encouraged a florescence of Indian art – in particular, in sculpture, painting, poetry, and drama. But Gupta rule was shattered by the invasion of Hunas (Huns, Hephthalites), nomads from Central Asia, in the 6th century.

1 Imperial Guptas and contemporary powers, 300–550

- core area of Gupta Empire
- maximum extent of Gupta Empire
- core area of Vakataka state
- core area of Pallava state
- major Huna penetration of India, with initial date
- important city or town
- *Hephthalites* Central Asian people

Medieval states 550–1206

This rock carving depicts a scene from the epic poem *Mahabharata*.

The multiplicity of regional powers that dominated India during this period all developed distinctive cultural styles, whose legacy survives in architecture, literature, and tradition. Some of them achieved, for brief periods, quasi-imperial status. The struggle for control of the Ganges plain was dominated by three major states: the Gurjara-Pratiharas, the Palas, and the Rashtrakutas. In the south, two major powers emerged; the Chalukyas in the west, and the Tamil Cholas in the east. Under Rajaraja (985–1014), the Cholas conquered much of southern India and Ceylon (Sri Lanka), their rule extending to the Malay Peninsula.

The Brihadeshwana temple at Thanjavur (Tanjore) is one of several fine Dravidian temples in the city, dating from the 11th century when it was the capital of the Chola kingdom.

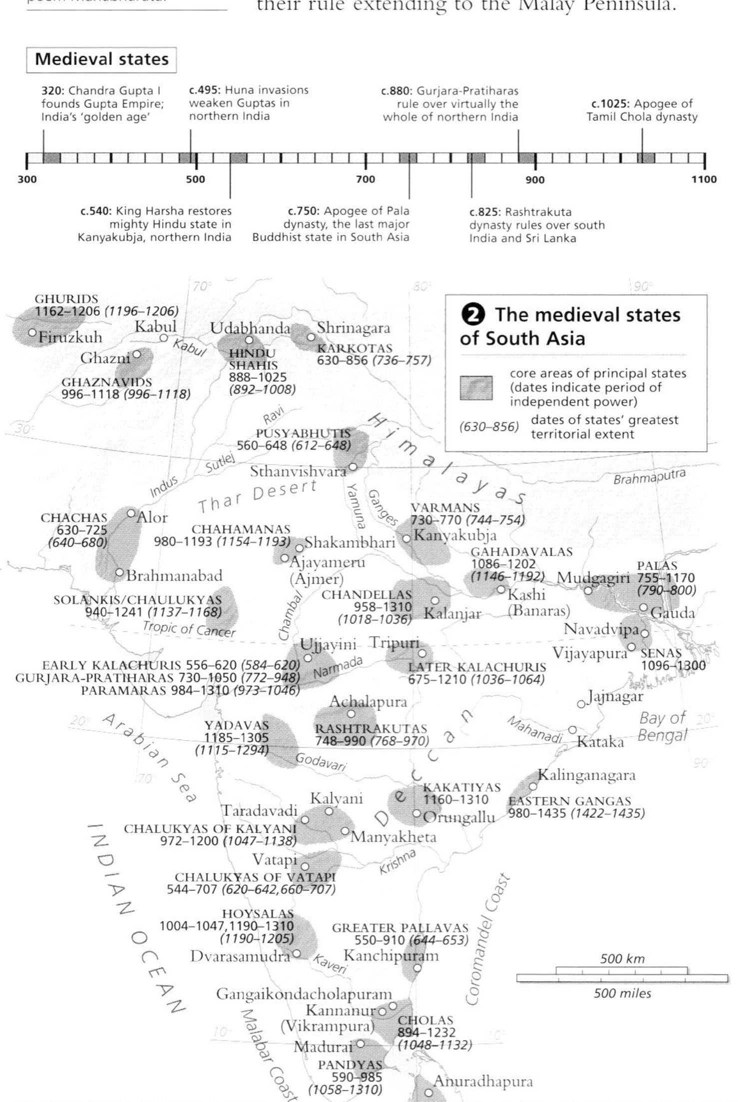

2 The medieval states of South Asia

- core areas of principal states (dates indicate period of independent power)
- (630–856) dates of states' greatest territorial extent

The Delhi Sultanate 1206–1526

The invasion of Mahmud of Ghazni in the 11th century, highlighted India's political and military vulnerability, and subsequent invasions by Turkish peoples from Central Asia led to the establishment of the Mamluk dynasty of the Delhi Sultanate in 1206. The territory controlled by the five successive dynasties that ruled the Sultanate fluctuated greatly, reaching its greatest extent under the Tughluqs. Administrative inefficiency and an ill-advised attempt to move the capital south to Daulatabad hastened the Sultanate's decline and much of India fragmented once again into warring kingdoms.

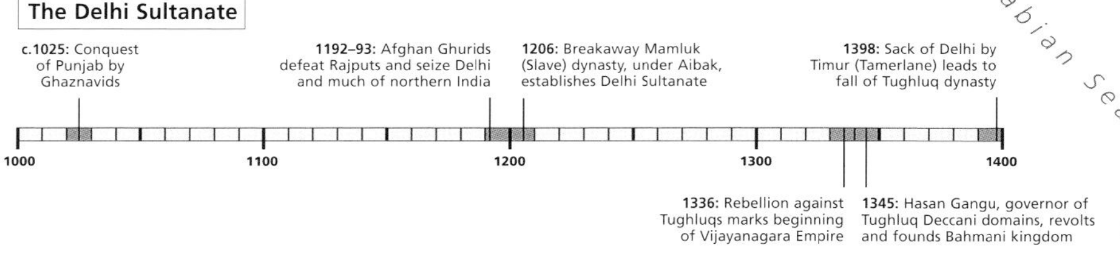

The Delhi Sultanate
c.1025: Conquest of Punjab by Ghaznavids
1192–93: Afghan Ghurids defeat Rajputs and seize Delhi and much of northern India
1206: Breakaway Mamluk (Slave) dynasty, under Aibak, establishes Delhi Sultanate
1398: Sack of Delhi by Timur (Tamerlane) leads to fall of Tughluq dynasty
1000
1100
1200
1300
1400
1336: Rebellion against Tughluqs marks beginning of Vijayanagara Empire
1345: Hasan Gangu, governor of Tughluq Deccani domains, revolts and founds Bahmani kingdom

Delhi's first congregational mosque, known today as the Quwwat al-Islam mosque was built by Qutb ud-Din Aibak, after the capture of Delhi in 1192.

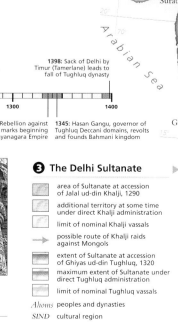

The ornate sandstone pillar of Delhi's Qutb Minar, built c.1200, is adorned with Arabic calligraphy.

3 The Delhi Sultanate

- area of Sultanate at accession of Jalal ud-din Khalji, 1290
- additional territory at some time under direct Khalji administration
- limit of nominal Khalji vassals
- possible route of Khalji raids against Mongols
- extent of Sultanate at accession of Ghiyas ud-din Tughluq, 1320
- maximum extent of Sultanate under direct Tughluq administration
- limit of nominal Tughluq vassals
- *Ahoms* peoples and dynasties
- *SIND* cultural region

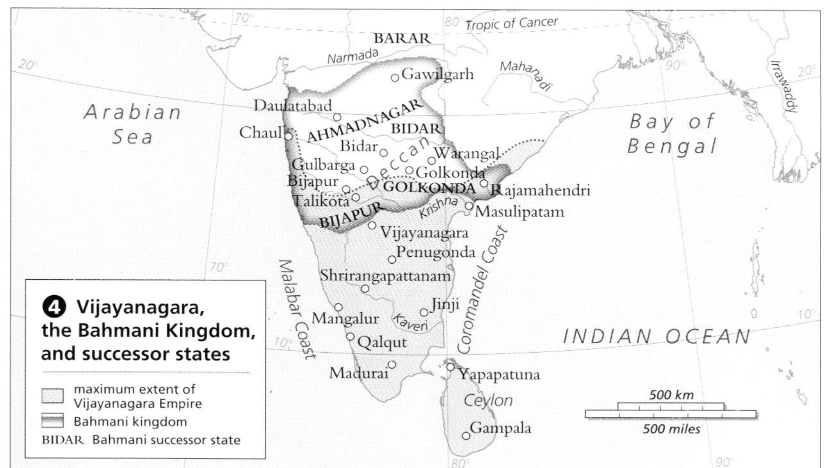

Principal states of Southeast Asia 650–1250

The major states of mainland Southeast Asia, although extensive, were loosely controlled and included substantial tribal populations. Their civilizations frequently displayed a strong Indian influence, most obviously in Hindu-Buddhist centres such as Borobudur. The Khmer state of Kambujadesha, with its impressive capital at Angkor, dominated the mainland. In the East Indies, the leading states were bound together largely by commercial ties. The maritime empire of Srivijaya, with its capital at Palembang in Sumatra, controlled international trade through the straits of Malacca and Sunda.

This carved relief from the 13th-century temple complex at Angkor Thom, part of the Khmer capital of Angkor, shows mounted soldiers accompanying a war elephant being transported in a cart pulled by asses.

The Vijayanagara Empire 1335–1570

The decline of the Delhi Sultanate led to the breakaway of the Muslim-controlled areas of the Deccan and the creation, in 1347, of the Bahmani Kingdom. To the south, in the Krishna valley, the powerful new Hindu kingdom of Vijayanagara was firmly established by 1345. Its splendid capital, Vijayanagara (modern Hampi), was a magnificent temple city, with massive fortifications and a royal palace. Vijayanagara successfully withstood repeated attempts by the Bahmani Kingdom to expand southward. The Bahmani Kingdom divided into five sultanates in 1518, and Vijayanagara finally succumbed in 1570, after a disastrous defeat at Talikota in 1565.

The royal capital of Vijayanagara ('city of victory'), founded in the mid-14th century, was destroyed by invaders from the Deccan sultanates in 1565.

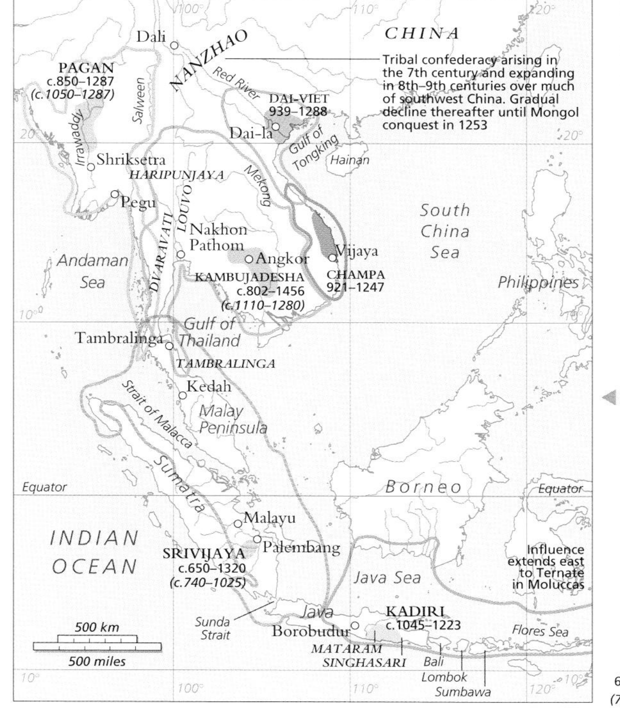

5 Southeast Asia, 650–1250

- core area of Pagan
- outermost limit of Pagan
- core area of Dai-Viet
- outermost limit of Dai-Viet
- core area of Champa
- outermost limit of Champa
- core area of Kambujadesha
- outermost limit of Kambujadesha
- core area of Srivijaya
- outermost limit of Srivijaya
- core area of Kadiri
- outermost limit of Kadiri
- 650–1320 period of state's duration
- (740–1025) period of state's apogee

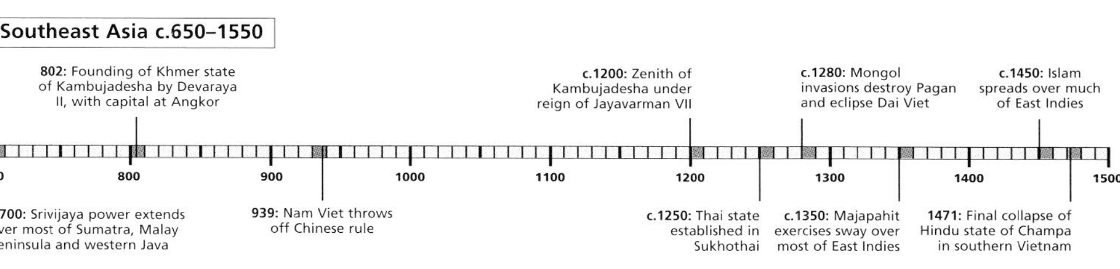

Principal states of Southeast Asia 1250–1550

During this period there was a marked increase in the number of medium-sized contenders for power throughout the region. The decline of Kambujadesha was matched by the rise of several ethnically Thai states and the destruction of the long-lived state of Champa by the sinicized kingdom of Dai-Viet. In the East Indies, dominance passed from Srivijaya to Majapahit which, in the 14th century, established the most extensive commercial empire that the area was to see in pre-colonial times.

6 Southeast Asia, 1250–1550

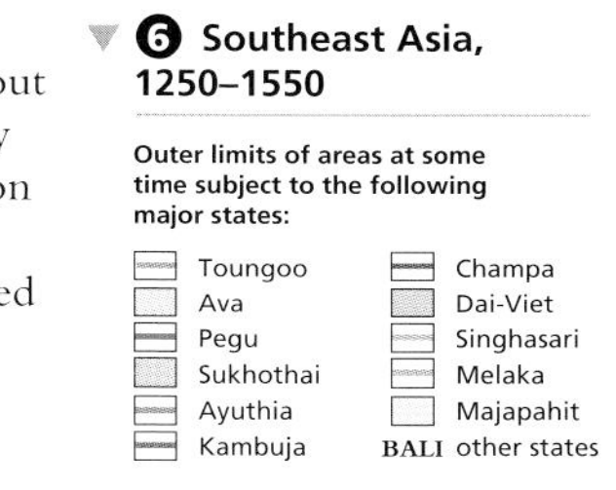

A bronze water vessel in the shape of a duck, from Thailand, demonstrates the technological sophistication of the metal-workers of Southeast Asia.

The Garai Cham tower from the city of Phan Rang, in the Hindu-Buddhist kingdom of Champa, which flourished in southern Vietnam (7th–12th centuries), but was absorbed by Dai-Viet in 1471.

MUGHALS, MARATHAS, EUROPEANS

Shah Jahan (1627–58) was one of the greatest of the Mughal emperors.

THE CONQUEST OF NORTHERN INDIA in 1526 by the Muslim Mughal chief, Babur, was to usher in a new era, marked by orderly government, economic prosperity, and great achievements in the arts, notably architecture, miniature painting, and literature. When, after the stern rule of Aurangzeb, the empire fell into disarray, the Hindu Marathas expanded rapidly from their Deccan base and dominated Indian affairs until their defeat by the British early in the 19th century. Vasco da Gama's voyage to India in 1498 opened up new trade routes, enabling European powers to establish commercial toeholds; spices, textiles, and jewels were soon being exported to western markets.

The Mughals, 1526–1857

This miniature shows Shah Jahan with his four sons. His third son, Aurangzeb, deposed him in 1658.

In 1526 the Mughals, led by Babur, a descendant of Timur *(see p.229)*, swept across much of northern India. His successor, Humayun, expelled by the governor of Bihar in 1539, returned in 1555 to establish a long-lived dynasty and an expansionist empire. The reign of Akbar (1556–1605) was a time of cultural florescence and religious tolerance. Later in the 17th century, Aurangzeb's long and harsh rule led to revolt. Many provinces seceded, and the rise of the Maratha confederacy from 1646 eventually reduced the Mughals to puppet rulers.

The tomb of Sheikh Salim lies in the Great Mosque at Fatehpur Sikri. Construction of the spectacular red limestone city began in the 1570s in the reign of Akbar.

Emperor Shah Jahan built the Taj Mahal c.1654 as a mausoleum for his beloved wife, Mumtaz. This exquisite structure of white marble is one of the masterpieces of Mughal architecture.

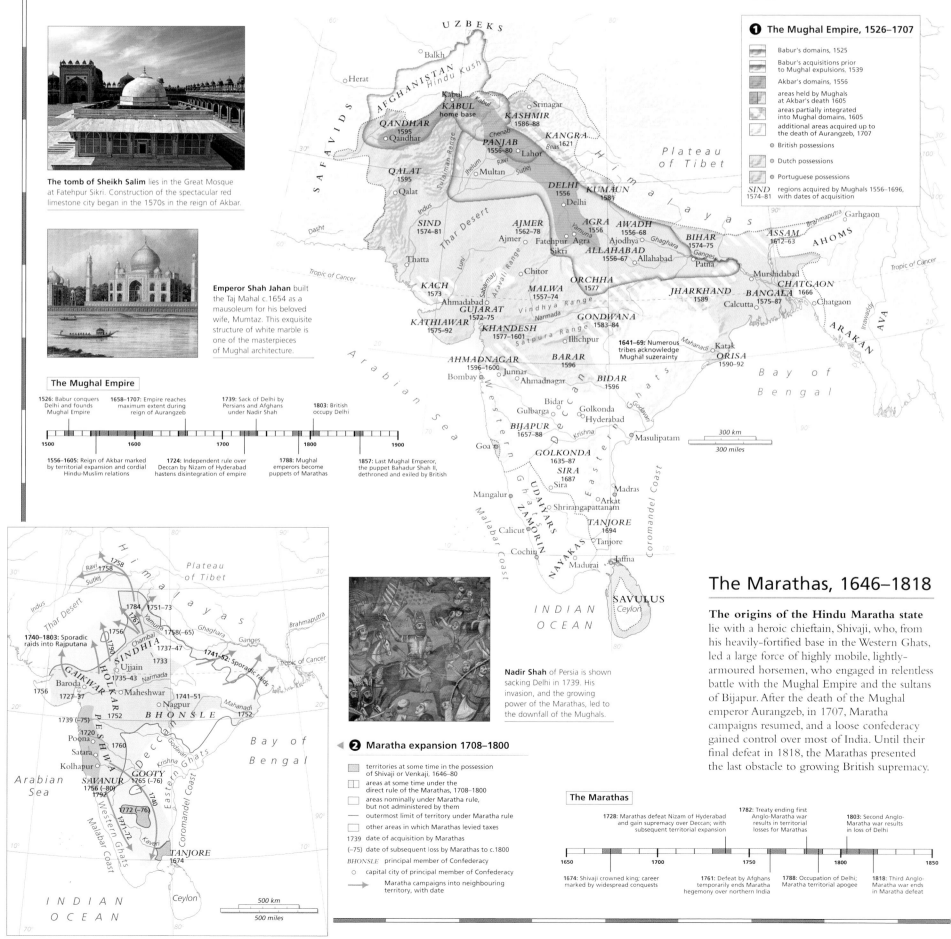

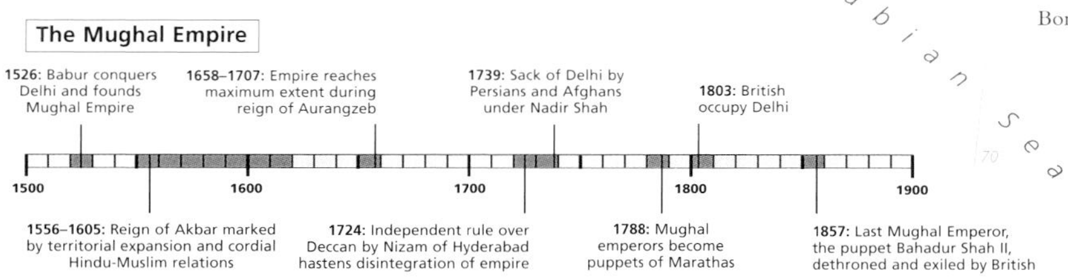

1 The Mughal Empire, 1526–1707

- Babur's domains, 1525
- Babur's acquisitions prior to Mughal expulsions, 1539
- Akbar's domains, 1556
- areas held by Mughals at Akbar's death 1605
- areas partially integrated into Mughal domains, 1605
- additional areas acquired up to the death of Aurangzeb, 1707
- British possessions
- Dutch possessions
- Portuguese possessions
- *SIND* 1574–81 regions acquired by Mughals 1556–1696, with dates of acquisition

1641–69: Numerous tribes acknowledge Mughal suzerainty

The Mughal Empire

- **1526:** Babur conquers Delhi and founds Mughal Empire
- **1556–1605:** Reign of Akbar marked by territorial expansion and cordial Hindu-Muslim relations
- **1658–1707:** Empire reaches maximum extent during reign of Aurangzeb
- **1724:** Independent rule over Deccan by Nizam of Hyderabad hastens disintegration of empire
- **1739:** Sack of Delhi by Persians and Afghans under Nadir Shah
- **1788:** Mughal emperors become puppets of Marathas
- **1803:** British occupy Delhi
- **1857:** Last Mughal Emperor, the puppet Bahadur Shah II, dethroned and exiled by British

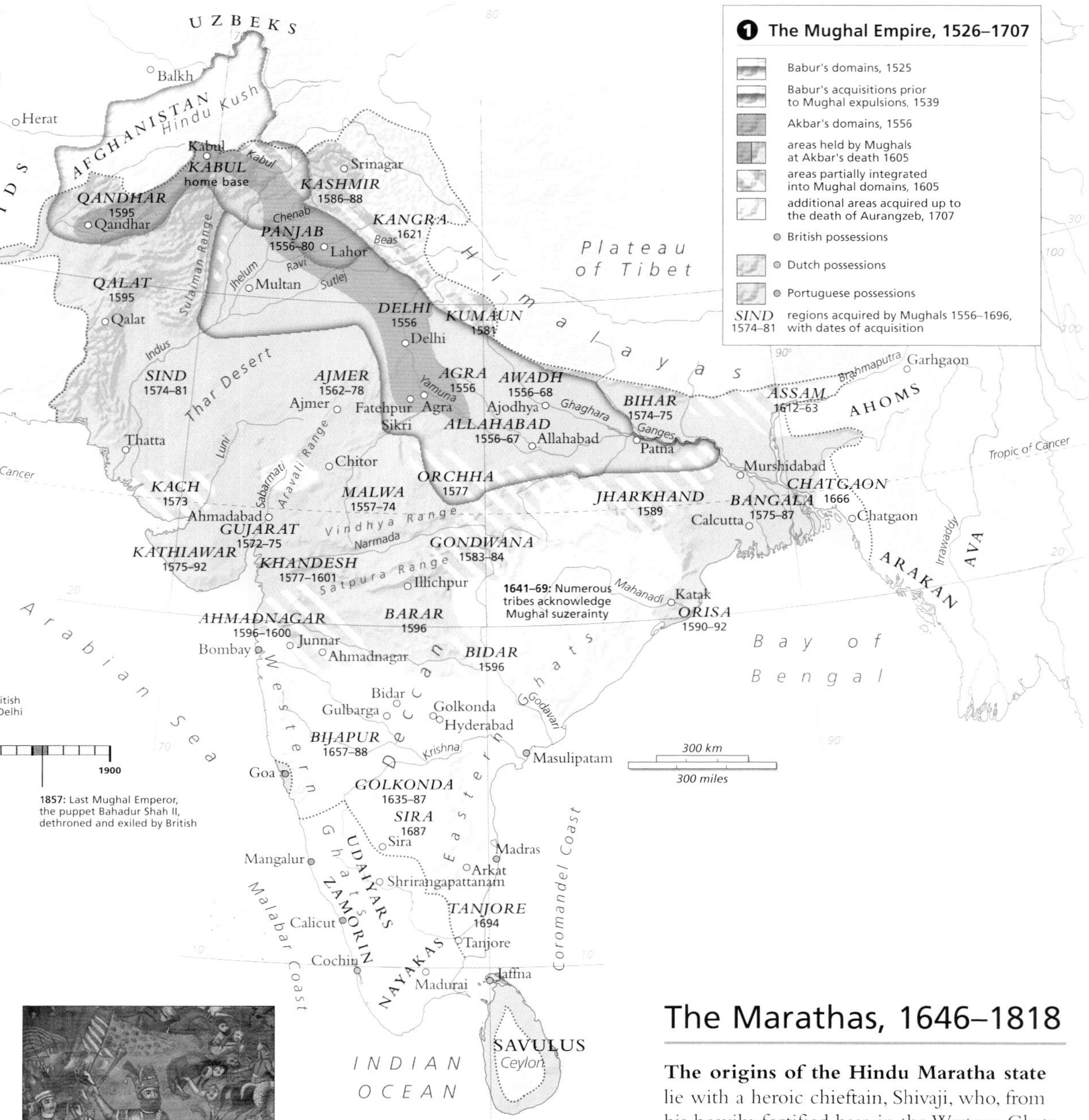

The Marathas, 1646–1818

The origins of the Hindu Maratha state lie with a heroic chieftain, Shivaji, who, from his heavily-fortified base in the Western Ghats, led a large force of highly mobile, lightly-armoured horsemen, who engaged in relentless battle with the Mughal Empire and the sultans of Bijapur. After the death of the Mughal emperor Aurangzeb, in 1707, Maratha campaigns resumed, and a loose confederacy gained control over most of India. Until their final defeat in 1818, the Marathas presented the last obstacle to growing British supremacy.

Nadir Shah of Persia is shown sacking Delhi in 1739. His invasion, and the growing power of the Marathas, led to the downfall of the Mughals.

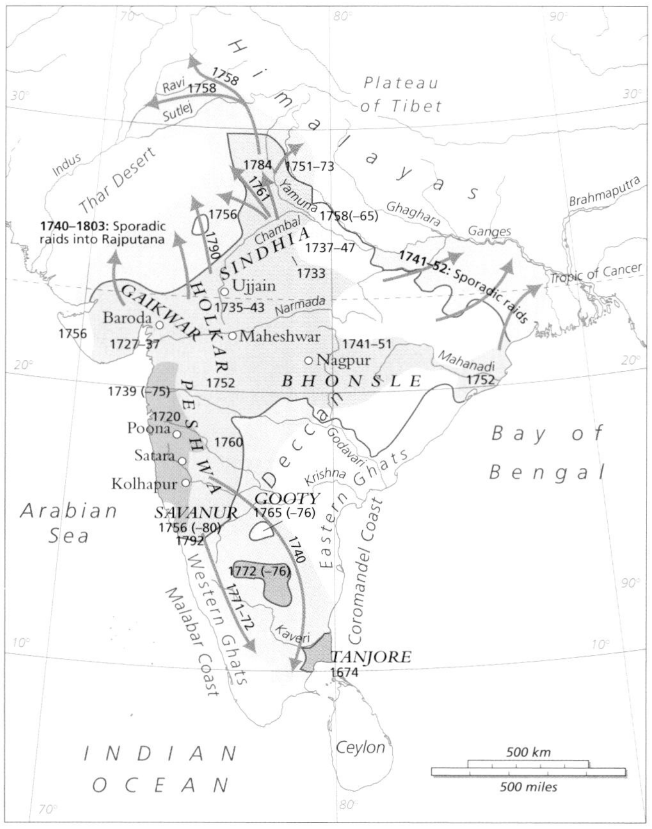

2 Maratha expansion 1708–1800

- territories at some time in the possession of Shivaji or Venkaji, 1646–80
- areas at some time under the direct rule of the Marathas, 1708–1800
- areas nominally under Maratha rule, but not administered by them
- outermost limit of territory under Maratha rule
- other areas in which Marathas levied taxes
- 1739 date of acquisition by Marathas
- (–75) date of subsequent loss by Marathas to c.1800
- *BHONSLE* principal member of Confederacy
- capital city of principal member of Confederacy
- Maratha campaigns into neighbouring territory, with date

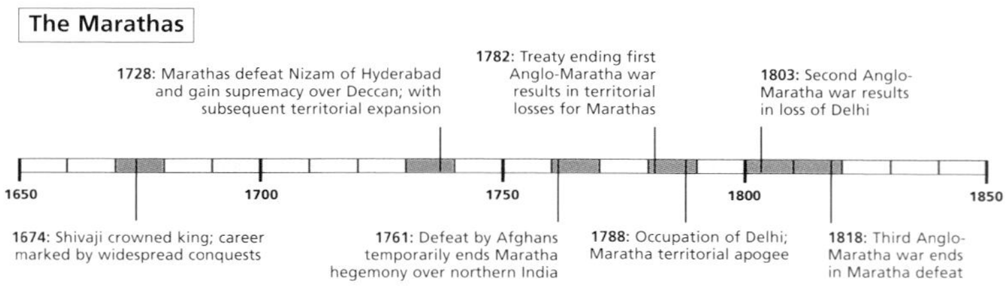

1740–1803: Sporadic raids into Rajputana

1741–52: Sporadic raids

The Marathas

- **1674:** Shivaji crowned king; career marked by widespread conquests
- **1728:** Marathas defeat Nizam of Hyderabad and gain supremacy over Deccan; with subsequent territorial expansion
- **1761:** Defeat by Afghans temporarily ends Maratha hegemony over northern India
- **1782:** Treaty ending first Anglo-Maratha war results in territorial losses for Marathas
- **1788:** Occupation of Delhi; Maratha territorial apogee
- **1803:** Second Anglo-Maratha war results in loss of Delhi
- **1818:** Third Anglo-Maratha war ends in Maratha defeat

3 European commerce with South Asia 16th–18th centuries

1505 date of first European trading contact
● important manufacturing centre

Colonial holdings

- ◇ Portuguese
- ◇ Dutch*
- ◇ British
- ◇ French*
- ◇ Austrian
- ◇ Danish*

on the map, diamonds reflect the chronological order in which European powers asserted control

**All French, Dutch, and Danish holdings in India were seized by the British during various wars between 1765–1815 and subsequently restored. Dutch and Danish possessions were ceded to Britain in 1825 and 1846 respectively.*

Main commodities manufactured and traded

embroidery, arms, carpets, woodwork, perfume, ghee, oils, paper, cotton, silk, other textiles, yarn, glass, leather goods, coconuts, tobacco, brassware, gold, and silver inlay wares, pottery, indigo, jute, rice, ships, opium, saltpetre, sugar, wheat, pepper, cinnamon, cardamom, coir, ginger, iron, precious stones, quilts and blankets

Plateau of Tibet · Himalayas · NEPAL · PUNJAB · ROHILKHAND · OUDH · RAJPUTANA · Thar Desert · MALWA · GUJARAT · GONDWANA · BENGAL · DECCAN · KONKAN · KANARA · CARNATIC · Arabian Sea · Bay of Bengal · INDIAN OCEAN · Ceylon

1 Vembar 1538 (Patmadoer)
2 Tuticorin 1535
3 Kayalpatnam 1535 (Punneikayal)

The Dutch were the main commercial power in Asia in the mid-17th century. They built trading posts in India – such as Cranganur near Cochin *(right)* – and in the East Indies.

European commerce with South Asia 1500–1800

In 1510, the Portuguese chose Goa to be capital of all their Indian possessions, and throughout the 16th century they were the sole European power to conduct significant trade with India. During the 17th century, Dutch, English, French, and Danish companies also established coastal trading centres, and Indian exports soon found their way onto world markets. During the multi-sided and sometimes lucrative commercial rivalry that ensued, control over large territorial holdings was long seen as neither necessary nor economically feasible. This view, however, was to change by the mid-18th century.

Fort St. George, founded in 1639 by Francis Day of the British East India Company, became the city of Madras (now Chennai).

The Portuguese seized Goa in 1510, making it the capital of their oriental trading empire. This map of the city was engraved c.1600.

Early European commercial contacts with South and Southeast Asia

- **1510:** Goa made capital of all Portuguese possessions in Asia
- **1511–12:** Portuguese establish base in Malacca and reach Moluccas
- **1585:** Spain establishes first permanent European settlement at Cebu, in Philippines
- **1600:** Founding of British East India Company
- **1650–90:** Dutch seize many Portuguese posts and become dominant mercantile power
- **1744–63:** Anglo-French wars eclipse French power in Asia
- **1811–15:** During Napoleonic Wars, British take over French and Dutch possessions
- **1819:** Sir Stamford Raffles obtains cession of Singapore for British East India Company

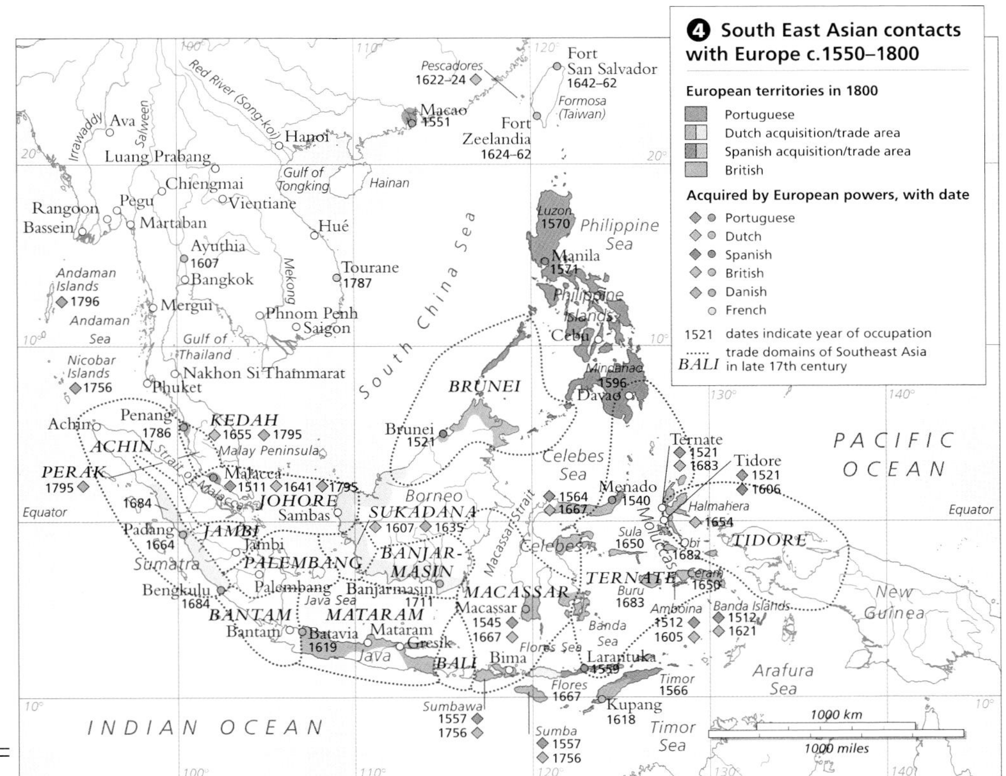

European and Southeast Asian contacts 1500–1800

The commercial penetration of Southeast Asia by Europeans began shortly after the Portuguese arrival in India. The Spanish established links with the Philippines after Magellan's discovery of the islands in 1521 during the first circumnavigation of the globe. Dutch and British trade in the region did not begin until the 17th century. As in India, the European powers established 'factories', often fortified, at many points along the coast. They cooperated with local magnates, both indigenous and Chinese, who had already carved out trading domains.

The Moluccan island of Ambon *(right)* was reached by the Portuguese in 1512. They were ousted by the Dutch in 1605. This 17th-century engraving shows Dutch East India Company ships sailing near the island.

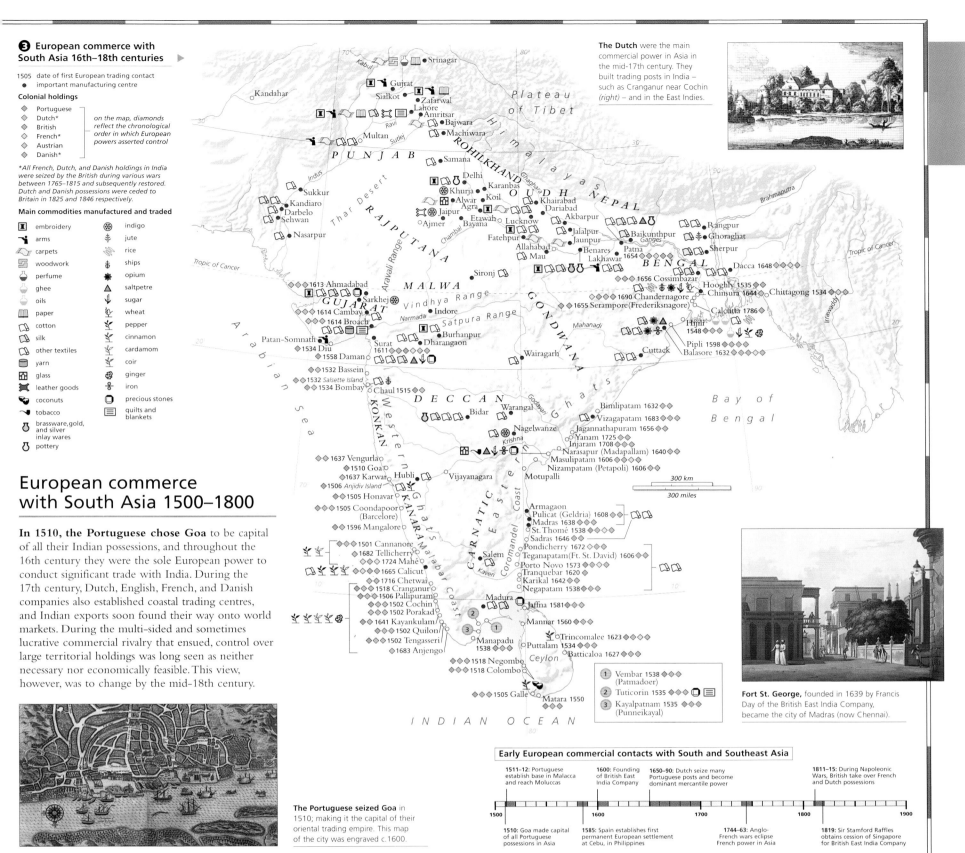

THE AGE OF COLONIAL EXPANSION

Sir Stamford Raffles re-founded the port city of Singapore in 1819.

BETWEEN 1765 AND 1914 the European powers completed their conquest and annexation of most of South and Southeast Asia. Nepal and Afghanistan were greatly reduced in size and made protectorates of Britain, while Siam, though shorn of most of its outer territories, maintained its independence, acting as a buffer between the British and the French. There were many reasons for European conquest, including commercial disputes, the desire to control resources, diplomatic entanglements, and strategic considerations. All were the inevitable result of interaction between nations with vastly differing military and naval resources in an age of imperial expansion.

Major indigenous powers confronting British and French colonizers

- **c.1720:** Marathas start to expand over most of India
- **1749:** Mysore starts to become major power in southern India
- **1754:** Powerful Burmese dynasty established on capture of Ava by Alaungpaya
- **1757:** Expansion of Gurkha (Nepali) domains over much of Himalayas
- **1782:** Siam reaches territorial apogee under Rama I
- **1785:** Burmese invasion of Siam and counter-invasion by Siam of Burma
- **1802:** With French aid, Nguyen Anh unites and becomes emperor of Vietnam
- **1839–42:** Afghans under Dost Mohammed defeat Britain in First Afghan War
- **1857–59:** Revolt ('Mutiny') attempts to oust British from India

Warren Hastings, the first British governor-general of India (1774–85), is shown here dining with Indian princes. He was forced to confront both the Marathas and Mysore, during the first phase of British expansion in India.

Indigenous powers and colonization

Even after the collapse of the Mughal Empire in 1761, significant states stood in the path of Western colonial expansion in both India and Southeast Asia. In India, the foremost power was the Maratha Confederacy, while in Southeast Asia, Burma, Siam, and Vietnam expanded in size and strength. At the dawn of the 19th century no large states remained over most of the East Indies, but Dutch commercial dominance was not yet reflected in territorial holdings.

1 South and southeast Asia 1765

- area under British control and possessions 1765
- Danish possessions
- area under Dutch control and possessions 1765
- French possessions
- area under Portuguese control and possessions 1765
- petty tribal polities
- other states
- frontiers c.1765

TIBET 1720: Chinese suzerainty 1751: Chinese protectorate

Macao 1557: to Portugal

Singapore 1819: re-founded by Sir Stamford Raffles

British control in South Asia 1757–1914

Britain's imperial ventures in India began with the commercial activities of the East India Company. In 1757, the victory of Robert Clive at Plassey over a French and Mughal force and the acquisition of the right to collect taxes in Bengal began an era of territorial expansion which ended with British claims to the Northeast Frontier Agency in 1914. With a pivotal role in the British Empire, India became enmeshed in European rivalries; from 1848, colonial acquisitions along the periphery of the subcontinent had greater strategic than economic impact.

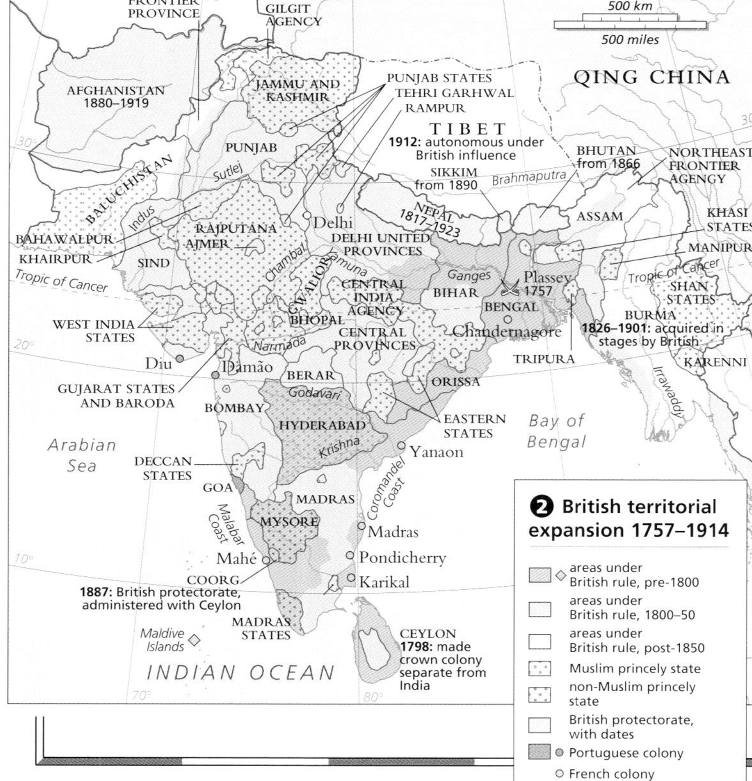

This miniature of 1830 shows an Englishman tiger-hunting, an activity greatly enjoyed by the British ruling class.

Native bearers are shown carrying a British officer in a palanquin, c.1828.

Territorial expansion of British in South Asia and Burma

- **1757:** Battle of Plassey; British victory over combined French and Mughal force
- **1799:** British-led coalition defeats and partitions Mysore; British obtain the Carnatic coast
- **1803:** Second Anglo-Maratha war leads to British acquisition of Delhi
- **1815:** Victory in Anglo-Gurkha war extends British possessions into the Himalayas
- **1815:** British annex Ceylonese kingdom of Kandy
- **1826:** First Anglo-Burmese War; British acquire coastal areas
- **1849:** British annex Punjab after two Sikh wars
- **1852:** Second Anglo-Burmese War; British occupy Lower Burma
- **1885:** Third Anglo-Burmese War; British annex Upper Burma

The Revolt of 1857–59

Much more than a mutiny, the revolt of 1857–59 involved not merely the defection of large sections of the British Indian army, but also a series of peasant insurrections, led either by local rulers or *zamindars* (great landlords), aimed at throwing off the imperial yoke. The revolt failed because of its lack of a coordinated command structure and British superiority in military intelligence, organization, and logistics.

British troops are shown rushing to quell the revolt at Umballa in 1859. The reforms made after the Revolt helped secure the British presence in India for another 90 years.

3 The Revolt of 1857–59

- princely states in rebellion
- states in which princes were loyal to British, but troops were in rebellion
- neutral princely states
- states actively aiding British
- British India
- areas in which British administration was disputed
- post at which Indian Sepoy troops mutinied
- site of major revolt, 29 Mar 1857–31 Aug 1858
- site of significant British victory, 16 Aug 1857–21 May 1859

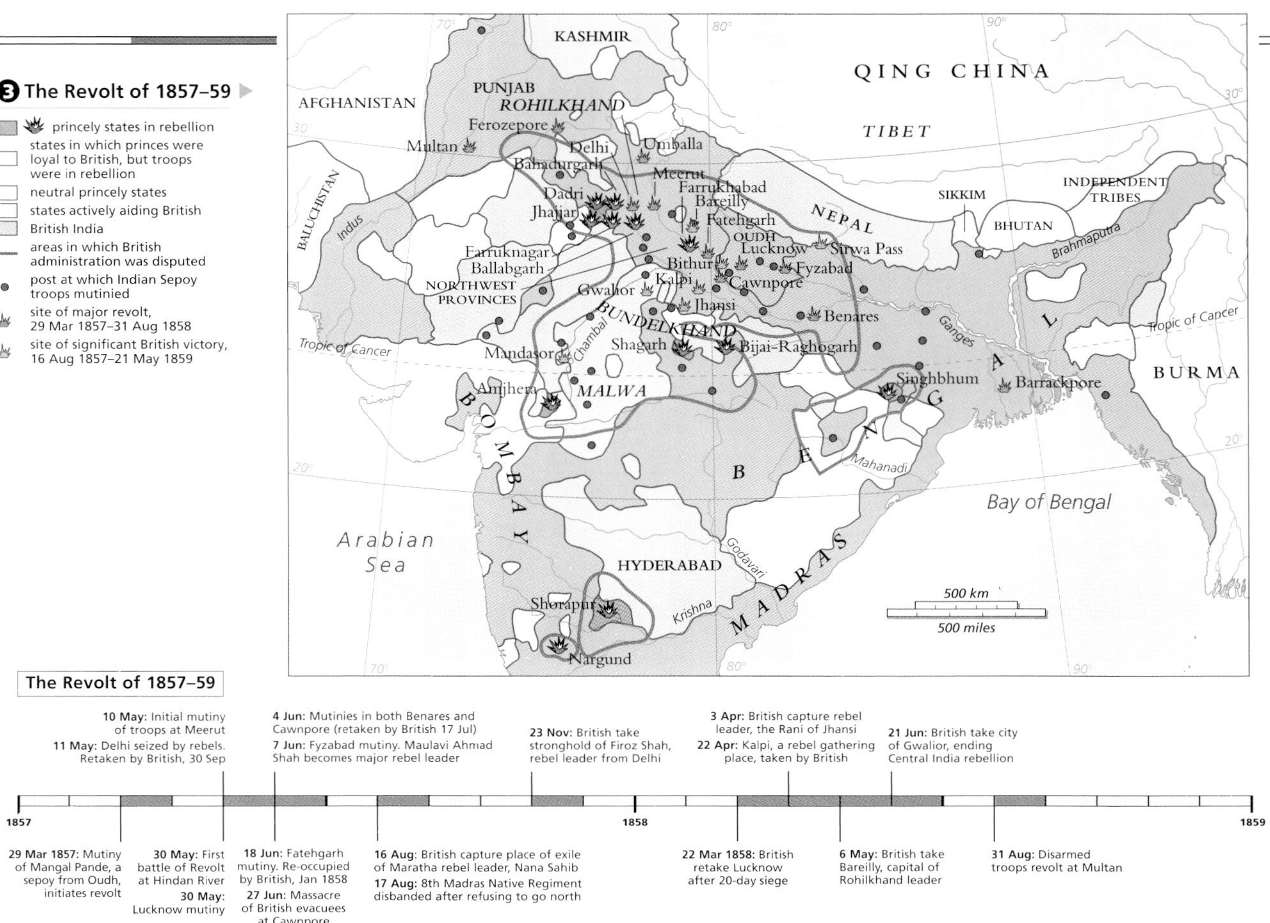

The Revolt of 1857–59

29 Mar 1857	Mutiny of Mangal Pande, a sepoy from Oudh, initiates revolt
10 May	Initial mutiny of troops at Meerut
11 May	Delhi seized by rebels. Retaken by British, 30 Sep
30 May	First battle of Revolt at Hindan River
30 May	Lucknow mutiny
4 Jun	Mutinies in both Benares and Cawnpore (retaken by British 17 Jul)
7 Jun	Fyzabad mutiny. Maulavi Ahmad Shah becomes major rebel leader
18 Jun	Fatehgarh mutiny. Re-occupied by British, Jan 1858
27 Jun	Massacre of British evacuees at Cawnpore
16 Aug	British capture place of exile of Maratha rebel leader, Nana Sahib
17 Aug	8th Madras Native Regiment disbanded after refusing to go north
23 Nov	British take stronghold of Firoz Shah, rebel leader from Delhi
22 Mar 1858	British retake Lucknow after 20-day siege
3 Apr	British capture rebel leader, the Rani of Jhansi
22 Apr	Kalpi, a rebel gathering place, taken by British
6 May	British take Bareilly, capital of Rohilkhand leader
21 Jun	British take city of Gwalior, ending Central India rebellion
31 Aug	Disarmed troops revolt at Multan

1857 — 1858 — 1859

4 The economy of India and Ceylon, 1857

Agriculture
- mainly peasant agriculture
- scattered cultivation, hunting and gathering, and limited pastoralism
- predominantly pastoralism, with scattered pockets of agriculture
- forested areas

Industry
- coal-mining areas
- sites of extraction of other minerals

Manufacturing centres
- metalworking
- arms
- ship building
- textiles
- glazed pottery, tiles, and ceramics
- woodworking and furniture making
- jewellery
- ivory carving

Transport
- important road
- railway
- railway under construction

Population
- city with population of over 500,000
- city with population of 100,000–500,000
- city with population of 50,000–100,000
- important city with population, of less than 50,000

Principal types of agricultural produce
- areca
- cacao
- cinnamon
- coconuts
- coffee
- cotton
- dates
- fruits
- indigo
- jute
- mustard
- opium
- palm sugar
- pepper
- potato
- rape
- salt
- sandalwood
- sesame
- spices
- sugar
- sunflower
- tea
- teak
- tobacco

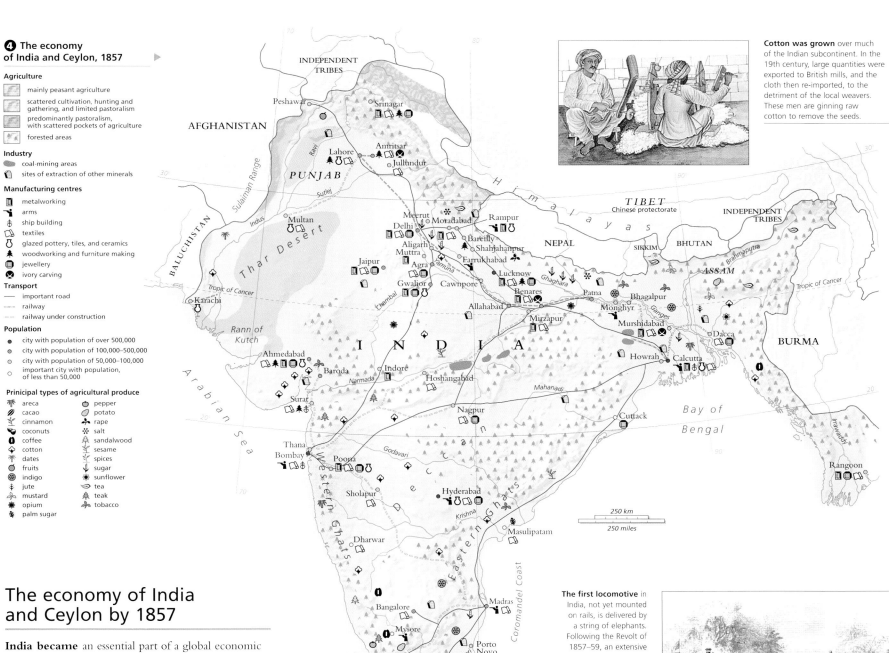

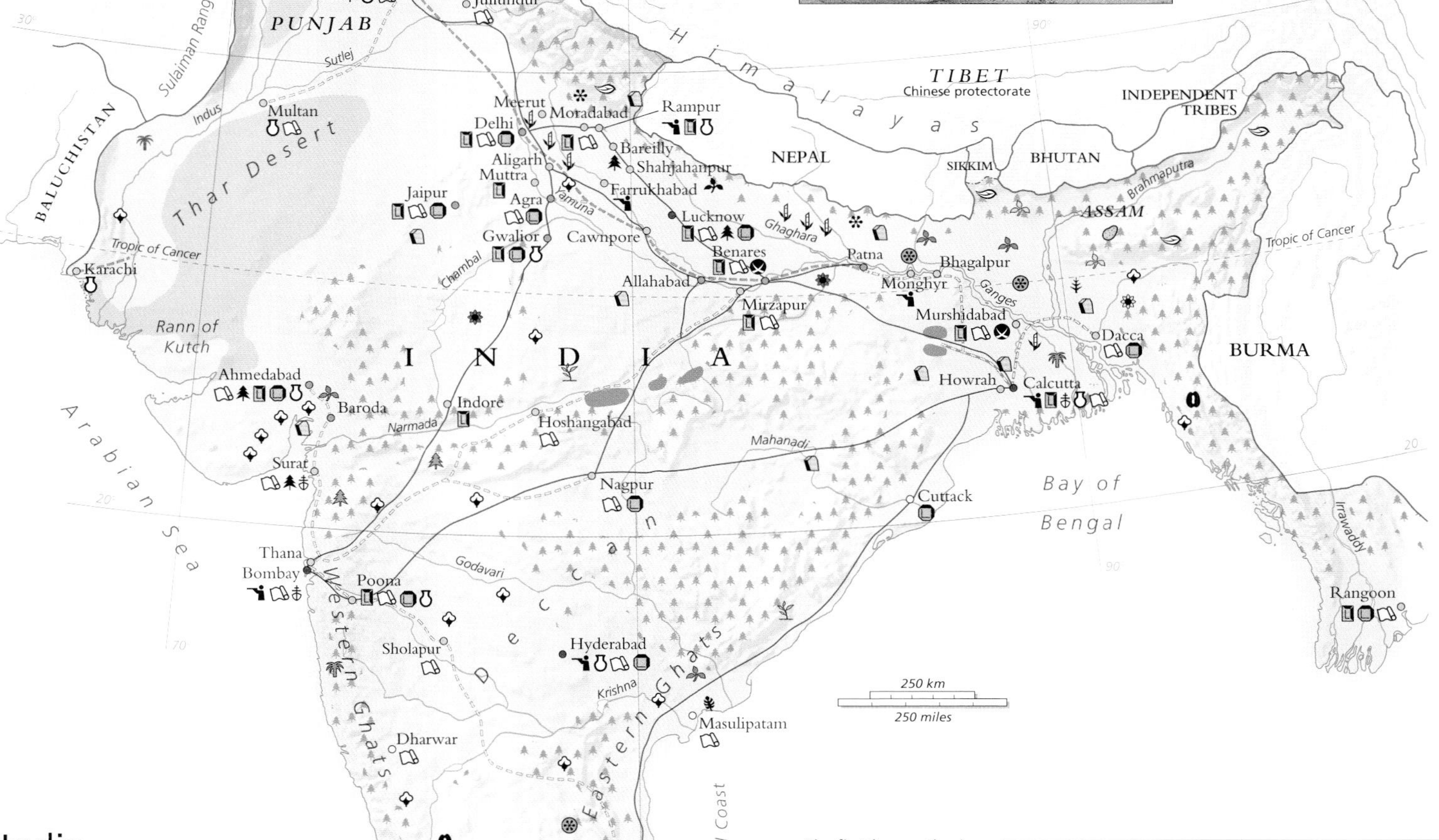

Cotton was grown over much of the Indian subcontinent. In the 19th century, large quantities were exported to British mills, and the cloth then re-imported, to the detriment of the local weavers. These men are ginning raw cotton to remove the seeds.

The economy of India and Ceylon by 1857

India became an essential part of a global economic network created by Britain during the 18th and 19th centuries. In some cases, British imports wiped out Indian industry – India was obliged to import woven cotton from Lancashire by 1853. India was an overwhelmingly peasant society in 1857, but railways, canals, plantations, mines, small-scale factories, and the growth of busy port cities and administrative centres were transforming its economic landscape.

The first locomotive in India, not yet mounted on rails, is delivered by a string of elephants. Following the Revolt of 1857–59, an extensive programme of railway-building helped secure Britain's military and economic hold on India.

THE COLONIAL APOGEE AND DEMISE

M.K. Gandhi (1869–1948) was the hero of India's independence movement.

TWO NEW COLONIAL POWERS, the US and Japan, entered Southeast Asia at the beginning of the 20th century. The Philippines were annexed by the US following the Spanish-American War of 1898; the Japanese took over the German Pacific island colonies north of the equator in 1919 and acquired virtually the whole of Southeast Asia by force in the Second World War. Though the early 20th century can be seen as the apogee of colonialism in the region, especially in British India, there was already strong opposition to foreign rule. The Indian National Congress, founded in 1885, initially sought reforms, but by the 1930s demanded complete independence. In the Philippines, a revolutionary independence movement was well established when the Americans took over. But whereas India's freedom struggle was, on the whole, peaceful, the struggle in most of Southeast Asia was bloody, nowhere more so than in Vietnam.

The partition and reunification of Bengal 1905–12

Lord Curzon's 1905 partition of India's most populous province, Bengal, was fiercely opposed on many grounds by both Hindus and Muslims. Some upper-class Hindus, for example, feared that the creation of East Bengal and Assam, a Muslim-majority province, would restrict their access to government employment. The Muslim League, formed in 1906, urged that legislation should provide for separate electorates for Muslim minorities, to guarantee their representation in Hindu-majority areas. In 1912, the Bengali-speaking areas of the old province were reunited.

2 The partition and reunification of Bengal, 1905–12

- national border
- provincial boundary
- provincial boundary prior to 1905
- line of 1905 partition
- Muslim majority area
- British districts
- native states and protectorates
- frontier area

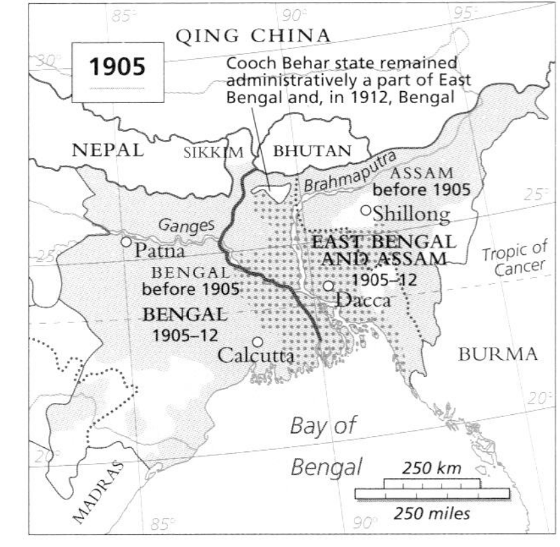

The independence struggle 1879–1947

Indian nationalist movements took many forms in the course of the long struggle for independence. The Indian National Congress, originally an organization of the Western-educated elite, became a mass, popular movement after the return to India in 1915 of the charismatic Mohandas K. Gandhi. By the 1930s, cautious calls for self-rule had become unequivocal demands for independence.

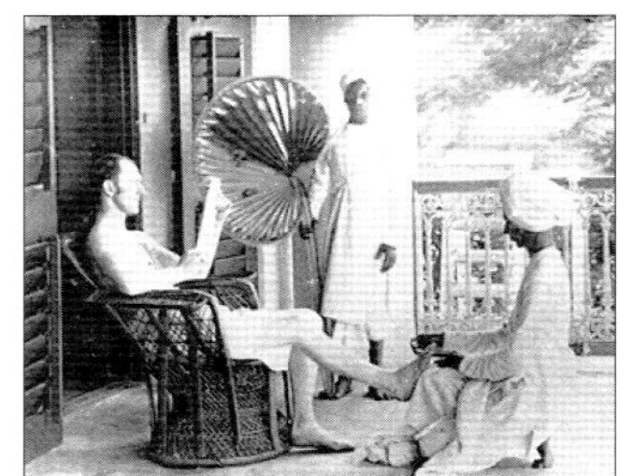

British officers serving in India led lives of conspicuous ease, their lifestyles supported by domestic staff, as this photograph of a servant giving a pedicure shows.

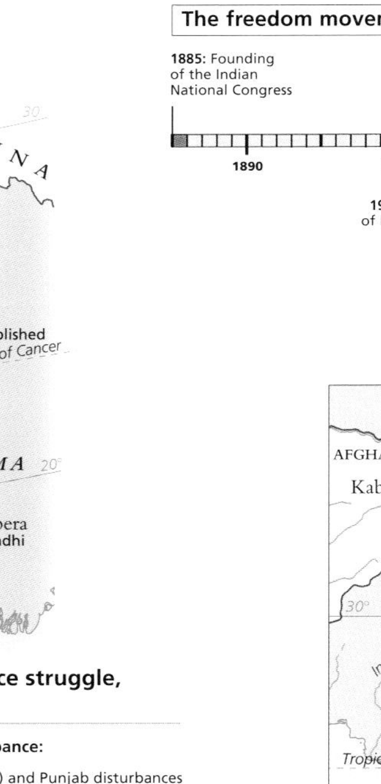

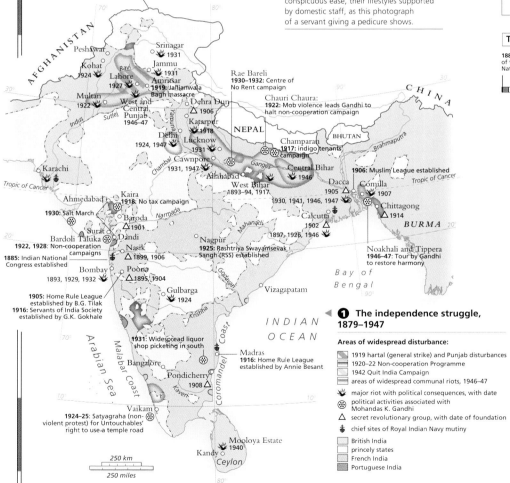

1 The independence struggle, 1879–1947

Areas of widespread disturbance:

- 1919 hartal (general strike) and Punjab disturbances
- 1920–22 Non-cooperation Programme
- 1942 Quit India Campaign
- areas of widespread communal riots, 1946–47
- major riot with political consequences, with date
- political activities associated with Mohandas K. Gandhi
- secret revolutionary group, with date of foundation
- chief sites of Royal Indian Navy mutiny
- British India
- princely states
- French India
- Portuguese India

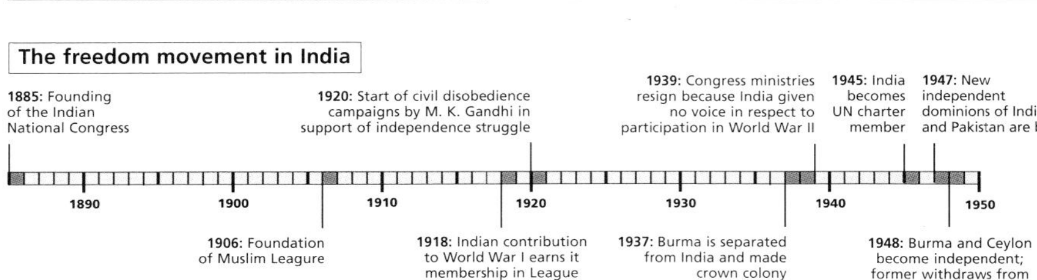

The Second World War in South and Southeast Asia

The Japanese swiftly overran Southeast Asia, occupying the whole region by March 1942. The Allied counter-offensive comprised US advances across the western Pacific from 1943, and the advance of British and Indian troops through Burma from 1944. But Japanese occupation had unleashed a tide of nationalism which was to have a grave impact on the postwar maintenance of the status quo, leading to the creation of new nations and the end of the European empires.

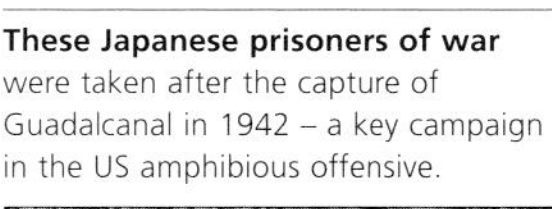

These Japanese prisoners of war were taken after the capture of Guadalcanal in 1942 – a key campaign in the US amphibious offensive.

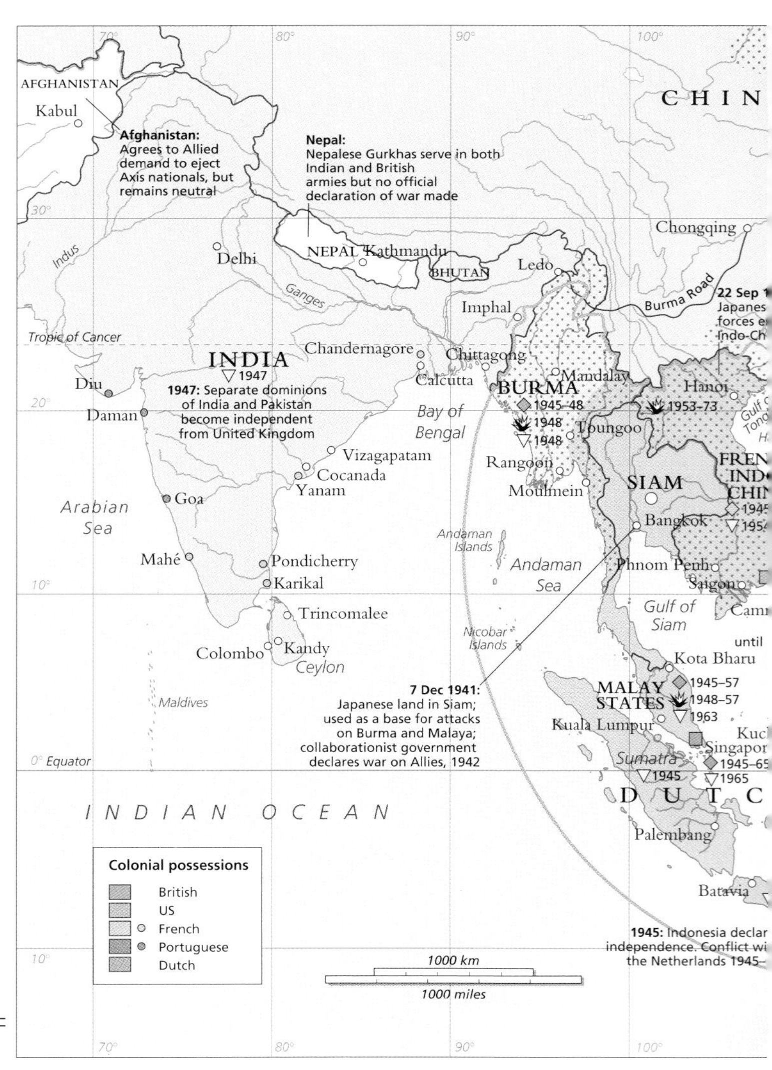

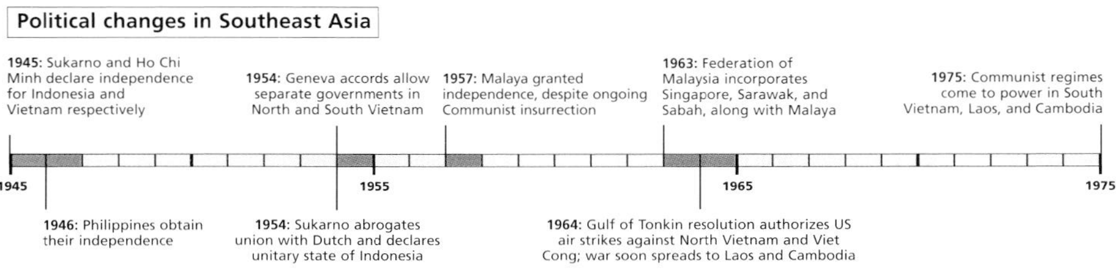

Political changes in Southeast Asia

1945: Sukarno and Ho Chi Minh declare independence for Indonesia and Vietnam respectively

1946: Philippines obtain their independence

1954: Geneva accords allow separate governments in North and South Vietnam

1954: Sukarno abrogates union with Dutch and declares unitary state of Indonesia

1957: Malaya granted independence, despite ongoing Communist insurrection

1963: Federation of Malaysia incorporates Singapore, Sarawak, and Sabah, along with Malaya

1964: Gulf of Tonkin resolution authorizes US air strikes against North Vietnam and Viet Cong; war soon spreads to Laos and Cambodia

1975: Communist regimes come to power in South Vietnam, Laos, and Cambodia

US troops are landed from a helicopter in Vietnam in 1967. Media coverage hardened public opposition to the war.

The decolonization of South and Southeast Asia

The global wave of decolonization swept over the region with remarkable speed. In 1946, the Philippines became the first country to be granted independence; India and Pakistan followed in 1947; and by 1948 all of South Asia was free. The last colonial territory in Southeast Asia, East Timor, was evacuated by Portugal in 1975. Grants of independence, however, did not always mean freedom from a foreign military presence, as Britain, France, and the US all sought to retain involvement in the region both commercially and through the maintenance of military bases.

4 The decolonization of South and Southeast Asia

Former colonial powers: United Kingdom; France; Netherlands; US; Portugal; Australia

1948 end of colonial/dependent status

member of British Commonwealth 1971

Kashmir: 1949: Status disputed by India and Pakistan leading to military conflict; 1949: Ceasefire agreed

Pakistan (West Pakistan) 1947: 1972: left British Commonwealth; 1989: readmitted

1971: independence from Pakistan and renamed Bangladesh

1949–71: Indian administration

Philippines: 1935: Commonwealth of Philippines established as transitional step to independence; 1941–45: occupied by Japanese

1941–45: occupied by Japanese; 1945–63: reverts to status of British protectorate

Malaya: 1942–45: Japanese occupation; 1948: State of emergency protracted period of anti-British insurgency. 1963: Federation of Malaysia (incorporating Singapore, Sarawak, Sabah). 1965: Singapore leaves

Netherlands cede colony to Indonesia

1973: Granted self-government as transitional step to independence

Indonesia: 1942–45: occupied by Japanese; 1945–49: Nationalist guerrilla war with Dutch

East Timor: 1975: occupied by Indonesia

British troops bring Communist insurgents out of the jungle during the Malaysian rebellion of 1947–48.

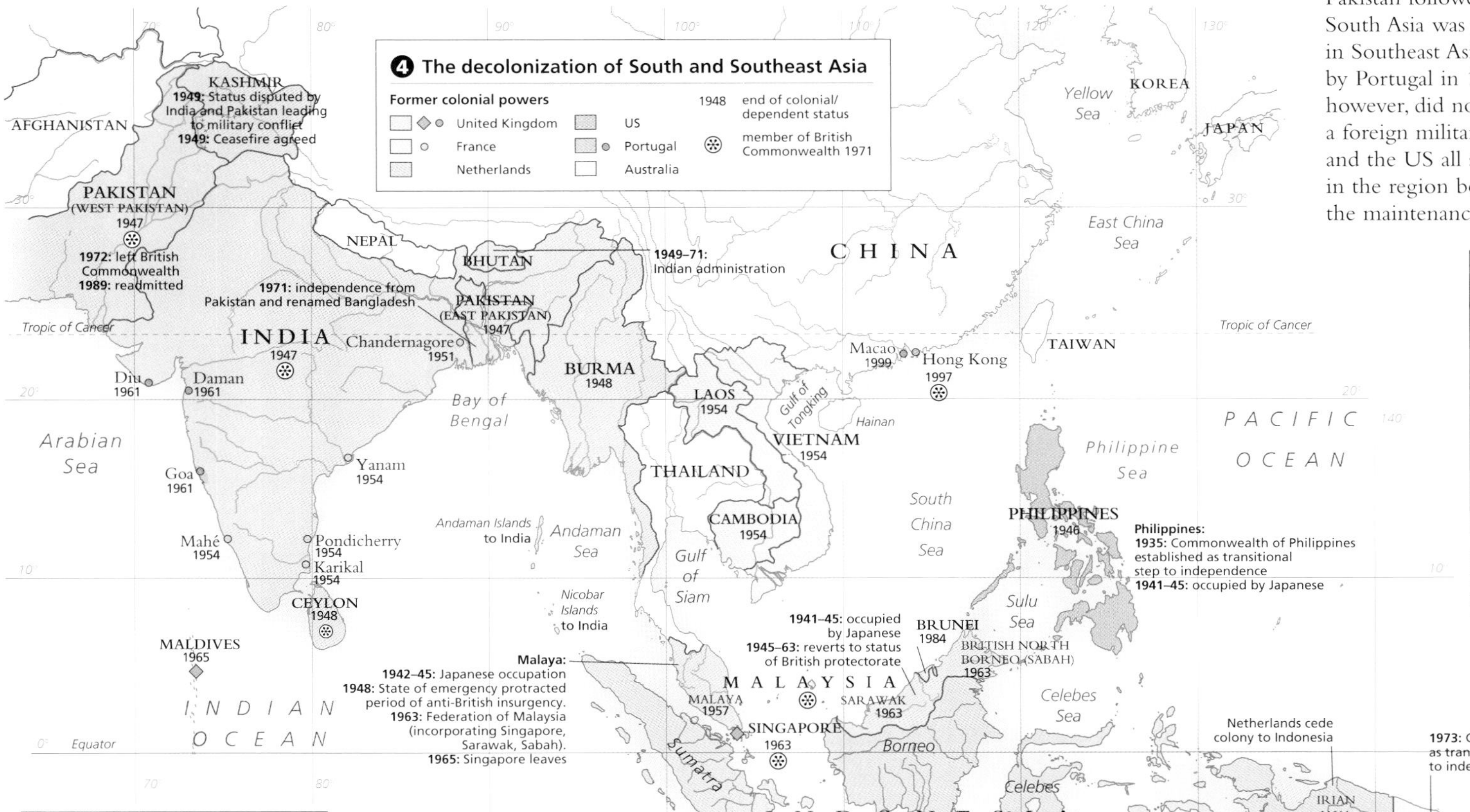

Jubilant citizens swarm through the streets of Calcutta, climbing over lorries and trams to celebrate Independence Day.

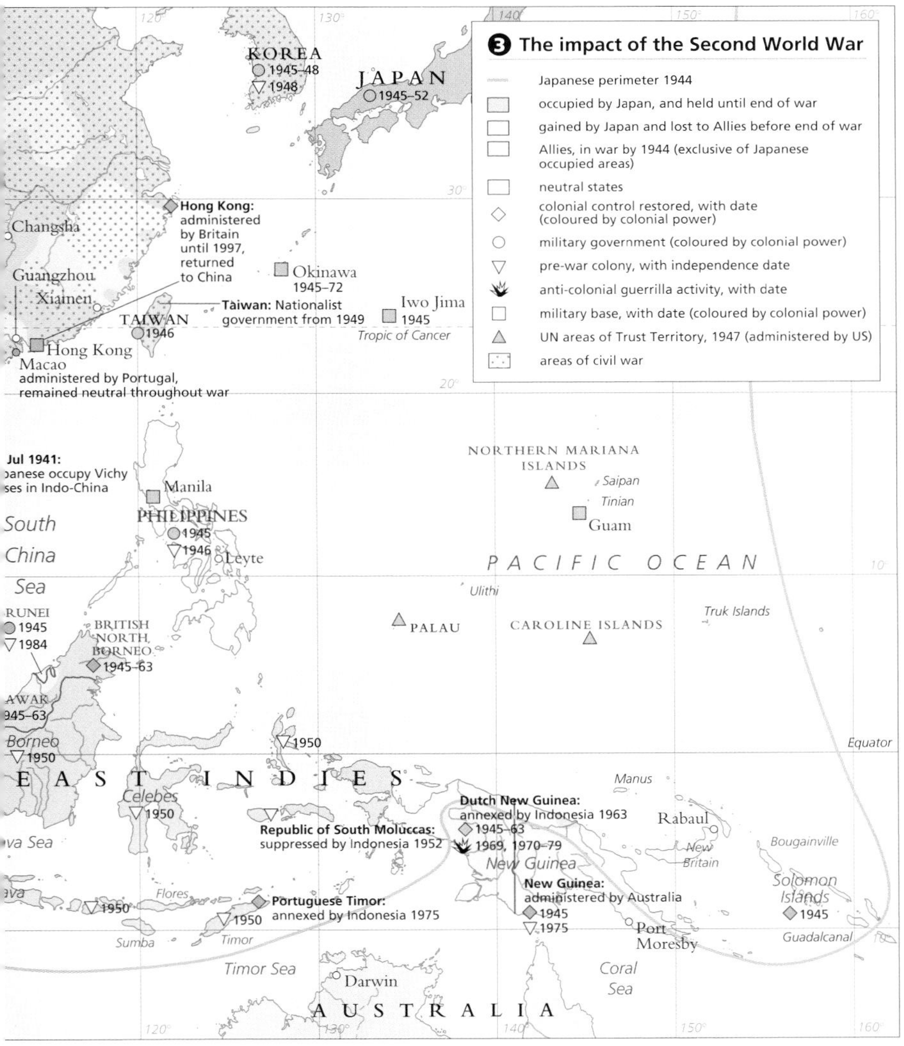

3 The impact of the Second World War

Japanese perimeter 1944; occupied by Japan, and held until end of war; gained by Japan and lost to Allies before end of war; Allies, in war by 1944 (exclusive of Japanese occupied areas); neutral states; colonial control restored, with date (coloured by colonial power); military government (coloured by colonial power); pre-war colony, with independence date; anti-colonial guerrilla activity, with date; military base, with date (coloured by colonial power); UN areas of Trust Territory, 1947 (administered by US); areas of civil war

Hong Kong: administered by Britain until 1997, returned to China

Taiwan: Nationalist government from 1949

Macao administered by Portugal, remained neutral throughout war

Republic of South Moluccas: suppressed by Indonesia 1952

Dutch New Guinea: annexed by Indonesia 1963

New Guinea: administered by Australia

Portuguese Timor: annexed by Indonesia 1975

The impact of the Cold War 1946–89

The Vietnam War, the most violent and protracted conflict in Southeast Asia in the 20th century, was, in many ways, a proxy struggle for the US, China, and the USSR within the global context of the Cold War. Although Vietnam's independence was proclaimed at the end of the Second World War, it took three decades of bloody struggle – affecting both Vietnam and the neighbouring states of Laos and Cambodia – before the French, and then the Americans who replaced them, were evicted from French Indochina.

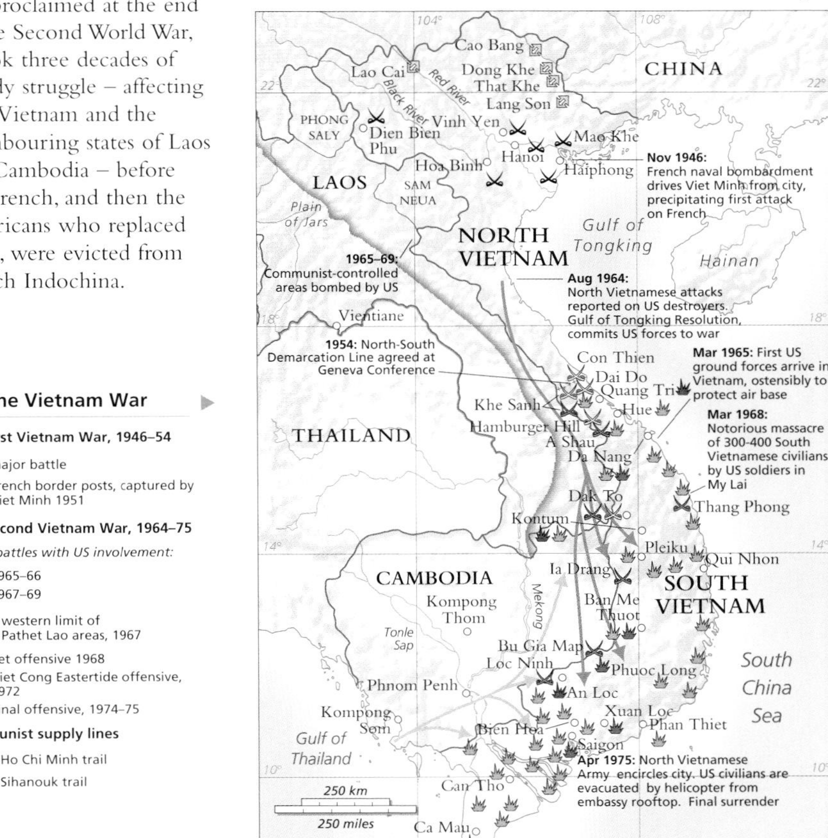

MODERN SOUTH AND SOUTHEAST ASIA

Jawaharlal Nehru, his daughter Indira Gandhi, and grandson Rajiv Gandhi *(above)* all served as Indian prime ministers.

IN MOST OF THE COUNTRIES of the region, securing independence failed to usher in an era of political peace and stability. The ethnic, religious, and linguistic heterogeneity of their populations quickly led to demands for readjustment of the political map and, in many instances, to secessionist movements and wars for independence. Notwithstanding all these internal and external stresses, most of the countries in South and Southeast Asia took great strides on the path of economic, social, and cultural development under a variety of political systems and economic philosophies. Life expectancy, levels of literacy, and per capita material consumption, especially for the growing middle and upper classes, were far higher than during the colonial era and the economic infrastructure greatly expanded, with the development of a varied commercial base. In 1998 both India and Pakistan successfully tested nuclear weapons, bringing a new level of risk to the subcontinent.

Territorial changes since 1947

The urgent task of integrating more than 600 largely autonomous princely states into the new Indian union was accomplished by 1950. But demands for more linguistically homogeneous states soon surfaced. The partition of the multi-lingual state of Madras in 1954 was the first in a long series of changes, including the creation of a number of tribal states, that have altered India's political map.

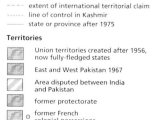

In 1984 the Indian army attacked Sikh militants who were occupying the Golden Temple of Amritsar, the Sikhs' holiest shrine.

South Asia from 1948

In creating Pakistan, the 1947 partition of India established a political entity which could not withstand the many subsequent stresses between its two distant wings. In 1971 Pakistan was split between its eastern and western halves, and the new state of Bangladesh was formed. There were also a series of international disputes over areas whose borders were not adequately defined during the colonial era or, in the still-unresolved case of Kashmir, over an area whose future was left undecided when the British left India.

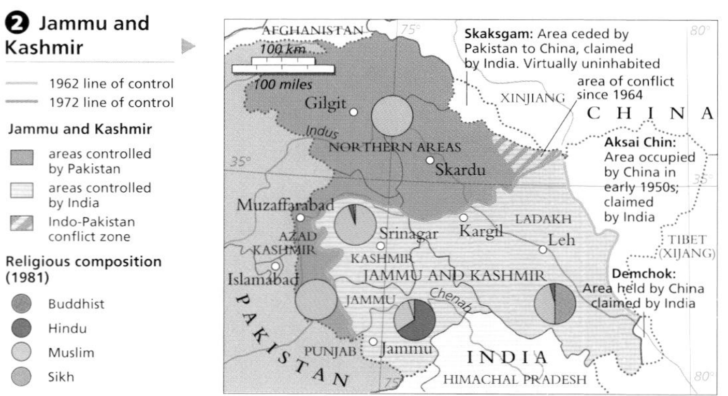

Conflict over Jammu and Kashmir

India and Pakistan have contested possession of the Muslim-majority state of Kashmir since 1947 and fought wars over the territory in 1947–48 and 1965. Since 1989, there has been an independence movement in the Indian-held portion of the state, although India insists this is the handiwork of terrorists aided by Pakistan. The Kashmir conflict continues, with tension heightened by the fact that both India and Pakistan now have nuclear capabilities.

The birth of Bangladesh

The two sectors of Pakistan had little in common apart from their Muslim faith, and the stresses on federalism and parliamentary democracy in the union caused its rupture. The Bangladeshi independence struggle was led by the Awami League, with active military support from India.

In 1949 refugees were driven from their homes by Indo-Pakistani border clashes in Kashmir.

Secessionist movements and regional cooperation

The post-independence era in South and Southeast Asia has been characterized by a multitude of internal movements among sub-national groups who have called for greater recognition, autonomy, and even independence. These have been treated with varying degrees of tolerance by the national governments. At the same time, the nations of South and Southeast Asia have embarked upon endeavours to bring about greater supranational and extra-regional cooperation. The latter efforts have been, in varying degrees, military, political, and economic in nature.

The Communist Khmer Rouge operated from a rural power base.

Cambodia

From 1975, Pol Pot's Communist Khmer Rouge conducted a social programme in Cambodia which led to the deaths of two million people, and the 're-education' of millions more. Parliamentary elections are now held in Cambodia. The UN is to set up a tribunal for the 'killing fields' genocide of the Pol Pot years.

Indonesian army troops are seen looting rice from paddy fields in East Timor, where repression of pro-secessionists was particularly brutal.

East Timor

Originally a Portuguese colony, East Timor was invaded by Indonesia in 1975. Resistance by the East Timor Revolutionary Liberation Front (FRETILIN) eventually led to independence in 2002, but a quarter of the population is thought to have died during the Indonesian occupation.

The Tamil Tigers fought for Tamil independence from the rest of Sri Lanka through the 1980s and 1990s. They remain the most feared militant group, notorious for suicide bombings.

Sri Lanka

Since Sri Lanka gained independence in 1948, relations have deteriorated between the Sinhalese majority and the Tamil minority. A bloody civil war was fought from 1984 until a fragile cease-fire agreement was reached in 2002.

CHINA
AFGHANISTAN
PAKISTAN
INDIA
NEPAL
BHUTAN
BANGLADESH
BURMA
THAILAND
LAOS
CAMBODIA
VIETNAM
MALAYSIA
SINGAPORE
BRUNEI
PHILIPPINES
INDONESIA
SRI LANKA
MALDIVES
EAST TIMOR

Afghanistan: Complete civil war since 1992; ethnic divisons between majority Pathans and minority tribes lie behind much of the conflict

Afghanistan: 2001 Taliban government falls after US-led strikes

Pakistan: Non-Punjabi minority secessionist movements

India: Internal riots and uprisings since the 1950s have been directed at reorganizing state boundaries mainly on linguistic grounds. Most civil disorder is confined to the larger cities. Tribal conflict in the northeast and secessionist movements in Kashmir are ongoing

Bhutan: Ethnic tension between indigenous Drupka people and Nepali immigrants in the south

Bangladesh: Tribes are demanding autonomy in the Chittagong Hills

Burma: Numerous dissident minorities in rebellion. Ethnic rebel groups (Karens) have joined forces with political groups to end military rule and bring in the democratic government which was legally elected in 1990.

Laos: Small pockets of resistance by Hmong (mountain tribes) to Communist government since 1975

Vietnam: Mountain minorities (Montagnards) and Chinese ethnic groups regarded with suspicion by Communist government

Cambodia: Following withdrawal of Vietnamese troops in 1989, Khmer Rouge resumed armed struggle in central and western Cambodia, provoking government counter-offensives

Thailand: Secessionist movement amongst Muslim Malays

Andaman Islands to India

Nicobar Islands to India

Sri Lanka: Ongoing conflict between majority Sinhalese government and Tamil minority who are fighting for an independent state, Tamil Eelam

Aceh: Aceh people of northern Sumatra in conflict with Indonesian governement

Malaysia: Malay/Chinese immigrant tension stimulated by positive discrimination laws introduced in 1970

Singapore: Multiparty democracy in name only; opposition faces severe restrictions

Indonesia: Java-dominated government suppresses local culture and politics, leading to secessionist movements Conflict with ethnic Chinese

Philippines: Communist and Muslim separatists have been fighting government for over 25 years

Brunei: Ruled by Sultan's decree following a failed rebellion in 1962

Irian Jaya: Free Papua movement seeking autonomy from Indonesia. Outbreaks of violence in 1977, 1978 and 1981

East Timor: Repression and persecution by Indonesian government from declaration of independence in 1985. Independent 2002

1000 km
1000 miles

4 Secessionist movements and regional cooperation

- secessionist movements
- violent protests against existing borders on linguistic grounds
- tribal/ethnic minority conflict with ruling power
- conflict between indigenous groups
- other violent uprisings

Membership of Asian Regional Movements:

ADB	Asian Development Bank, est. 1966
APEC	Asia-Pacific Economic Cooperation, est. 1989
ASEAN	Association for Southeast Asian Nations, est. 1967
CP	Colombo Plan, est. 1951
ESCAP	Economic and Social Commission for Asia and Pacific, est. 1947
SAARC	South Asian Association for Regional Cooperation, est. 1985

Secessionist movements and political coups

- **1955:** Naga uprising in northeastern India, the first of numerous tribal insurrections
- **1958:** Abortive secessionist uprisings in Baluchistan, Pakistan
- **1962:** Military take over rule of Burma
- **1965:** Failed Marxist coup and military countercoup in Indonesia ends Sukarno regime
- **1972:** Ferdinand Marcos declares martial law in Philippines
- **1975:** Khmer Rouge take over Cambodia; impose regime of extreme terror
- **1979:** Deposition of monarchy in Afghanistan; Soviet invasion and civil war
- **1981:** Start of struggle for independent Sikh state of Khalistan in Indian Punjab
- **1982:** Start of struggle in Sri Lanka for independent state of Tamil Eelam
- **1986:** 'People power' uprising ousts President Marcos of Philippines
- **1988:** Military seizes power in Burma; renames country Myanmar
- **1991:** Indian prime minister Rajiv Ghandi assassinated
- **1996:** Islamist Taliban take control of most of Afghanistan
- **1999:** General Musharraf overthrows the government of Pakistan
- **2001:** Crown Prince Dipendra murders most of royal family in Nepal
- **2002:** East Timor gains independence. Cease-fire agreed in Sri Lanka
- **2003:** Major offensive against Aceh separatists in Indonesia

The urbanization of South and Southeast Asia

The development of South and Southeast Asia is reflected dramatically in its burgeoning cities, some of which, notably Bombay (Mumbai), are among the largest in the world. Of the roughly 1.8 billion people now inhabiting the region about 500 million live in urban areas. However, growing populations, the majority still dependent on agriculture and living in densely settled areas such as the great river valleys of the Ganges, Indus, and Mekong, place an increasing burden on fragile ecosystems, with potentially disastrous consequences for the environment.

Poverty drives many of India's rural poor to the increasingly overcrowded cities.

The modern financial centre of Singapore towers over the harbour, a reminder of the island state's origins as a strategic trading settlement.

NORTH AND EAST ASIA

REGIONAL HISTORY

THE HISTORICAL LANDSCAPE

THE FRAGMENTED GEOGRAPHY of this, the world's largest uninterrupted land mass, has produced a wide variety of historical scenarios. The mountainous massifs at its heart – the Plateau of Tibet, the Altai, Tien Shan, and Pamir ranges – enclose the arid Takla Makan, Gobi, and Ordos deserts, which together comprise a hostile and sparsely inhabited realm. Stretching in a wide arc around this region are the massive steppes, long home to pastoral nomads whose turbulent history was punctuated by sorties against their sedentary neighbours and, occasionally, violent irruptions which impelled their skilled and fast-moving horsemen across Eurasia. Broad rivers flow north across Siberia to the Arctic, and west to inland deltas and landlocked seas such as the Aral and Caspian. To the east, the fertile floodplains of the Yellow River and the Yangtze were the focus of one of the world's oldest civilizations, that of China, an enormous demographic and cultural fulcrum which dominates East Asia, and whose influence has been cast far across the peninsulas and archipelagos of the Pacific Rim.

Japan was settled by hunter-gatherers by about 30,000 years ago. At the the time of the last Ice Age, most of the Japanese islands were densely forested with settlement only in the coastal regions.

The Yellow River flows down to the plains of eastern China across a plateau of fertile *loess* – fine silty soils laid down along the edges of glaciers. The river cuts down through the soft sediments, washing them downstream and depositing them on the Great Plain of China, resulting in exceptionally fertile soils, suitable for a wide range of crops.

Siberia was a cold, frozen region at the time of the last Ice Age, sparsely inhabited by hunter-gatherers. Unlike northern Europe and North America, Siberia was not covered by an ice cap because of the lack of moisture across the region. The extreme cold preserved the remains of creatures such as mammoths, along with evidence of the shelters built by the people who hunted them.

North and East Asia: 18,000 years ago
North Asia was relatively ice-free during the last Ice Age, except for the extension of the European ice sheet to the east of the Ural Mountains, covering only a small part of the West Siberian Plain. The climate, however, was still bitterly cold, far colder than it is today. Extreme temperatures in southern Siberia limited vegetation to scrubby tundra plants across most of North Asia. Along the Ob' and Yenisey rivers, two large lakes were formed where the rivers dammed up behind the edge of the European ice sheet.
The Ob' and Yenisey rivers were dammed by an ice cap, forming huge lakes.
The extent of the ice cap over northern Asia is still unclear. Many scientists believe that the ice sheet terminated near the Yenisey river, but other hypotheses suggest the ice sheet was much more extensive, stretching much further eastwards across the Central Siberian Plateau.
Siberia was a vast, windswept polar desert – temperatures and conditions were similar to those found in the dry valleys of Antarctica today. Tree cover was virtually non-existent, afforestation of this barren region only began around 9000 years ago, when global climate became warmer.
Central Asia was much drier, with a belt of desert lying just to the north of the main mountain ranges, stretching well into southern Siberia. Here, deposits of sand and loess were piled into dunes by high winds, and rocks and stones were eroded and sculpted by wind-borne sediments, to form extraordinary structures.
Northern China and the Manchurian Plain were mainly dry, covered by sparse, scrubby vegetation and tundra.
The Sea of Japan (East Sea) was almost totally enclosed, forming a huge lake that drained into the sea via a narrow channel between Japan and Korea.
China was much drier than at present, suggesting that monsoon conditions then did not reach as far north as they do today.
A scattering of ice caps existed on the Himalayas and the Plateau of Tibet, but there was insufficient moisture for full-scale glaciation. Some scientists however, have suggested that the glaciation may have been far more extensive, and ice caps may have covered most of the plateau.
As sea levels fell at the height of the Ice Age, broad plains were exposed on the Chinese continental shelf.
The Japanese islands were joined together, and linked to mainland Asia by a peninsula of land that today forms the island of Sakhalin.
ARCTIC OCEAN
North Pole
NORTH AMERICAN PLATE
EURASIAN PLATE
Norwegian Sea
Scandinavia
North Sea
Gulf of Bothnia
Barents Sea
Franz Josef Land
North Cape
Kola Peninsula
White Sea
Novaya Zemlya
Severnaya Zemlya
Kara Sea
Baltic Sea
Gulf of Finland
Lake Ladoga
Pechora
Poluostrov Yamal
Poluostrov Taymyr
Laptev Sea
New Siberian Islands
East Siberian Sea
BERINGIA
Arctic Circle
Bering Strait
Chukot Range
Bering Sea
Koryak Range
Rhine
Vistula
Dnieper
Central Russian Upland
Don
Volga
North European Plain
EUROPE
Ural Mountains
Ob'
Putorana Mountains
North Siberian Lowland
Lower Tunguska
Yenisey
Central Siberian Plateau
Siberia
Lena
Khrebet Cherskogo
Verkhoyanskiy Khrebet
Kolyma Range
Kamchatka
Aleutian Basin
Sea of Okhotsk
West Siberian Plain
Black Sea
Caucasus
Caspian Depression
Caspian Sea
Ustyurt Plateau
Aral Sea
Irtysh
Kirghiz Steppe
Lake Balkhash
Turan Lowland
Kara Kum
Elburz Mountains
Great Salt Desert
EURASIAN PLATE
IRANIAN PLATE
Zagros Mountains
Iranian Plateau
Strait of Hormuz
Gulf of Oman
Central Makran Range
Oman Basin
ARABIAN PLATE
INDO-AUSTRALIAN PLATE
Gulf of Kachchh
Gulf of Khambhat
Arabian Sea
Arabian Basin
ASIA
Altai Mountains
Sayanskiy Khrebet
Lake Baikal
Yablonovyy Khrebet
Stanovoy Khrebet
Amur
Sakhalin
Kurile Islands
Kurile Trench
Dzungaria
Tien Shan
Pamirs
Hindu Kush
Karakoram Range
Tarim Basin
Takla Makan Desert
Altun Shan
Kunlun Mountains
Nan Shan
Qilian Shan
Plateau of Mongolia
Gobi
Great Khingan Range
Manchurian Plain
Khrebet Sikhote Alin
Hokkaido
Sea of Japan (East Sea)
Japan Trench
PACIFIC PLATE
PHILIPPINE PLATE
Yellow River
Ordos Desert
Taihang Shan
Korea
Korea Strait
Honshu
Shikoku
Kyushu
Shikoku Basin
Japan
Sulaiman Range
Indus
Punjab Plains
Thar Desert
Plateau of Tibet
Himalayas
Xiqing Shan
Bayan Har Shan
Yellow Sea
Great Plain of China
East China Sea
Ryukyu Islands
Brahmaputra
Ganges
Khasi Hills
Patkai Range
Shaluli Shan
Yangtze
Ailao Shan
Wuyi Shan
Satpura Range
Ajanta Range
Deccan
Mouths of the Ganges
Arakan Yoma
Irrawaddy
Salween
Dongnan Qiuling
Taiwan
Tropic of Cancer
Luzon Strait
Philippine Sea
Kyushu-Palau Ridge
PACIFIC OCEAN
Western Ghats
Eastern Ghats
Malabar Coast
Coromandel Coast
Laccadive Islands
Bay of Bengal
Gulf of Martaban
Gulf of Tongking
Hainan
Mekong
Truong Phan
South China Sea
Luzon
Philippines
Philippine Basin
Philippine Trench
Andaman Islands
Andaman Sea
Nicobar Islands
Sri Lanka
Maldive Islands
Chagos-Laccadive Ridge
Isthmus of Kra
Gulf of Thailand
Mouths of the Mekong
South China Basin
Palawan
Sulu Sea
Mindanao
CAROLINE PLATE
Eauripik Rise
INDIAN OCEAN
INDO-AUSTRALIAN PLATE
AFRICAN PLATE
Ceylon Plain
Chagos Bank
Ninetyeast Ridge
Malay Peninsula
Strait of Malacca
Sunda Shelf
SUNDA
Borneo
Celebes Sea
Halmahera
Equator
Greater Sunda Islands
New Guinea Trench
Molucca Sea
Moluccas
Makassar Strait
Celebes
Pulau Bangka
Sumatra
Buru
Seram
New Guinea
Mid-Indian Ridge
Mid-Indian Basin
Cocos Basin
Mentawai Ridge
Sunda Strait
East Indies
Java Sea
Banda Sea
SAHUL
Investigator Ridge
Java
Bali
Flores Sea
Lesser Sunda Islands
Flores
Timor
Arafura Sea
Torres Strait
Sunda Trough
Java Trench
Sumba
Timor Trough
LAKE CARPENTARIA
Cocos Islands
AUSTRALIA
Tropic of Capricorn

NORTH AND EAST ASIA

EXPLORATION AND MAPPING

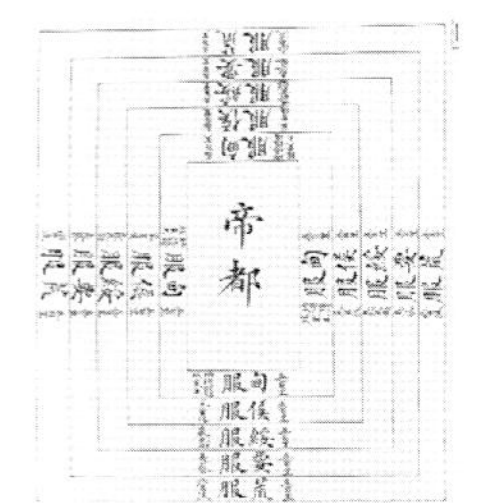

This 3rd-century Chinese view of the world placed the imperial capital at the centre of a grid, with outlying areas organized in a regular, diminishing hierarchy.

THE GROWTH OF KNOWLEDGE of Central Asia was very gradual. Mountain barriers, extensive deserts, and climatic extremes hemmed in and defined the cultures of the region. The rulers of both China and India rarely looked beyond their frontiers, while remote states such as Tibet and Japan actively shunned external contact. In the Classical and Medieval eras perilous trade routes provided limited passage for missionaries and entrepreneurs, supplanted in the 16th century by the growth of maritime trade and European colonialists. In the 19th-century imperial European powers vied for control of Asia's land and wealth, a struggle echoed today as rich mineral resources attract increasing attention.

The early mapping of Japan

Following the introduction of Chinese administrative ideas during the 7th century CE, the southern Japanese islands were divided into 68 provinces. The limited size of Japan made it possible to conduct surveys of land and population in order to raise taxes; the first maps were of individual estates, but with the creation of centralized government in 710, the Buddhist priest Gyogi began to draw up national diagrams featuring the provinces. Gyogi-style maps typically show south at the top, and often include fantastical lands.

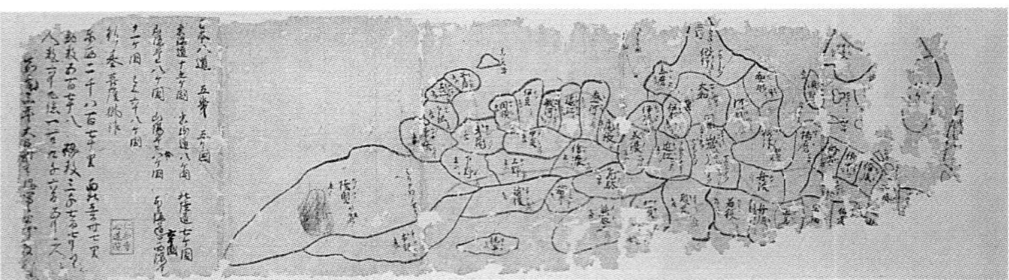

A Gyogi-style map of Honshu from 1305, orientated with south at the top, naming and listing the 68 Japanese provinces.

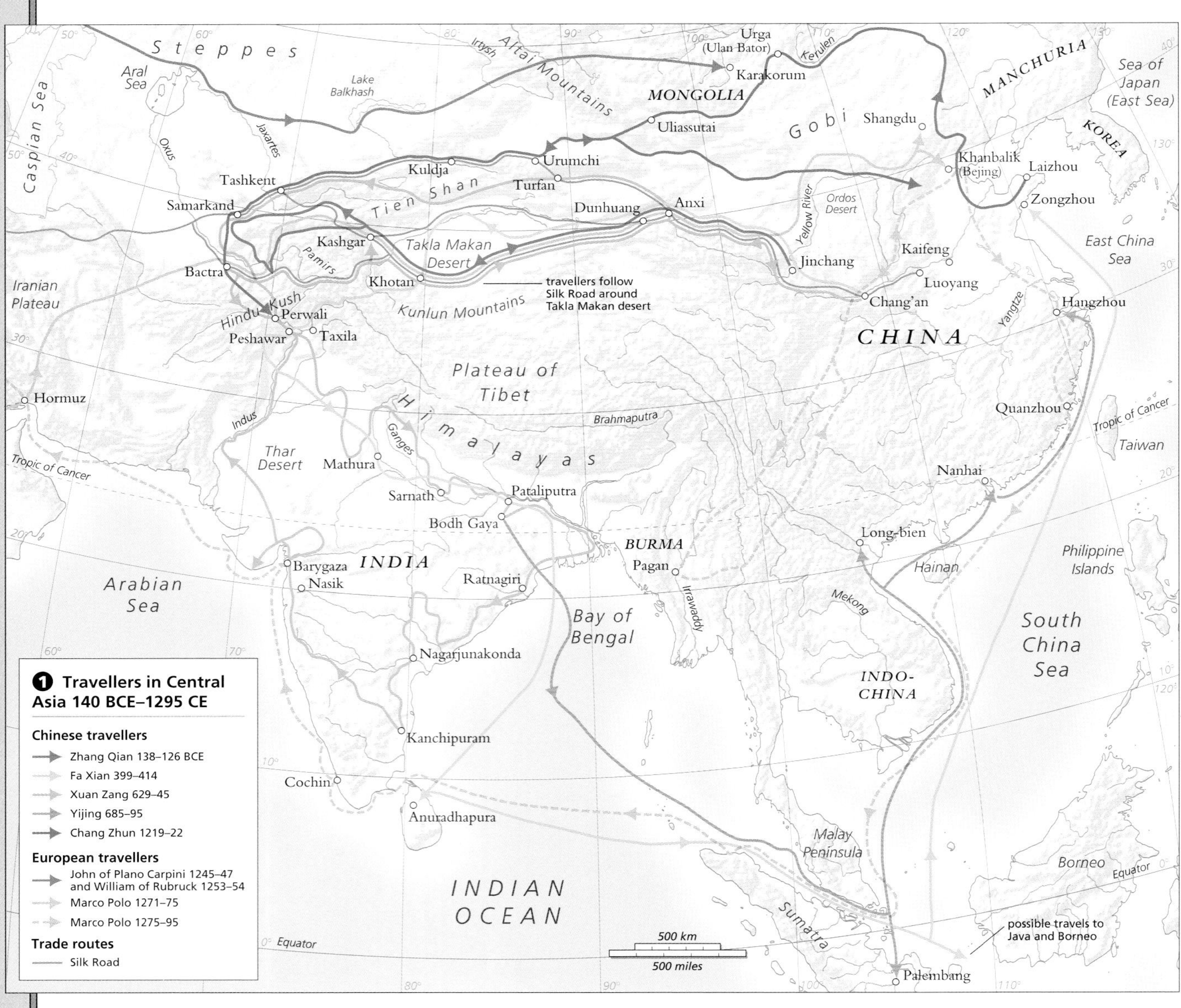

Mapping was an essential tool in administering the vast Chinese empire. Here a cartographer presents a Tang emperor with a map of his domains.

The conquest of Central Asia by the Mongols in the 13th century re-opened the Silk Road for trans-Asian trade. This Persian painting shows some Chinese merchant traders.

Travellers in Central Asia

The first recorded travellers in Central Asia were diplomatic missions, such as Zhang Qian, or Chinese Buddhist priests on pilgrimage to India, such as Fa Xian and Xuan Zang. Over 1000 years later the 'Mongol Peace' encouraged further missions (Chang Zhun), while the secure trading routes drew Christian missionaries and traders such as Marco Polo to the east. Their extensive accounts contributed greatly to knowledge of the region.

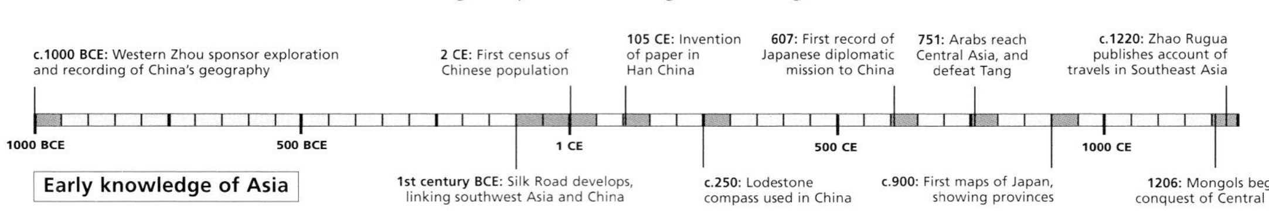

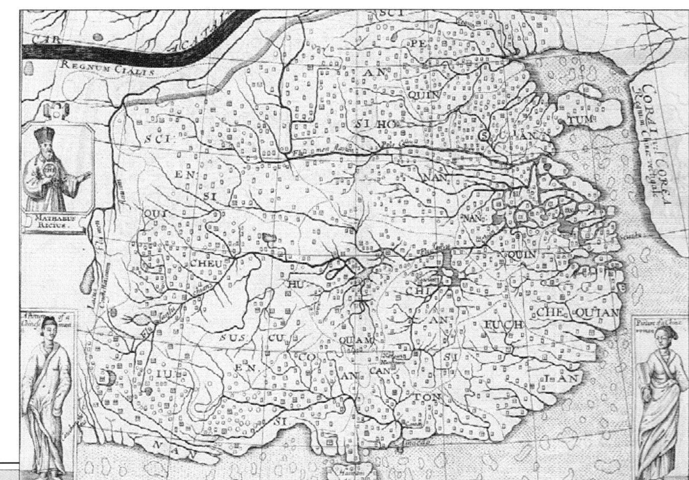

A 17th-century European copy of a Chinese map by Zhu Siben, a leading 14th-century Chinese cartographer. It is notable for the details of coastline and drainage – knowledge of river systems was regarded as a vital means of controlling China; the use of a grid to establish a projection was a Chinese invention.

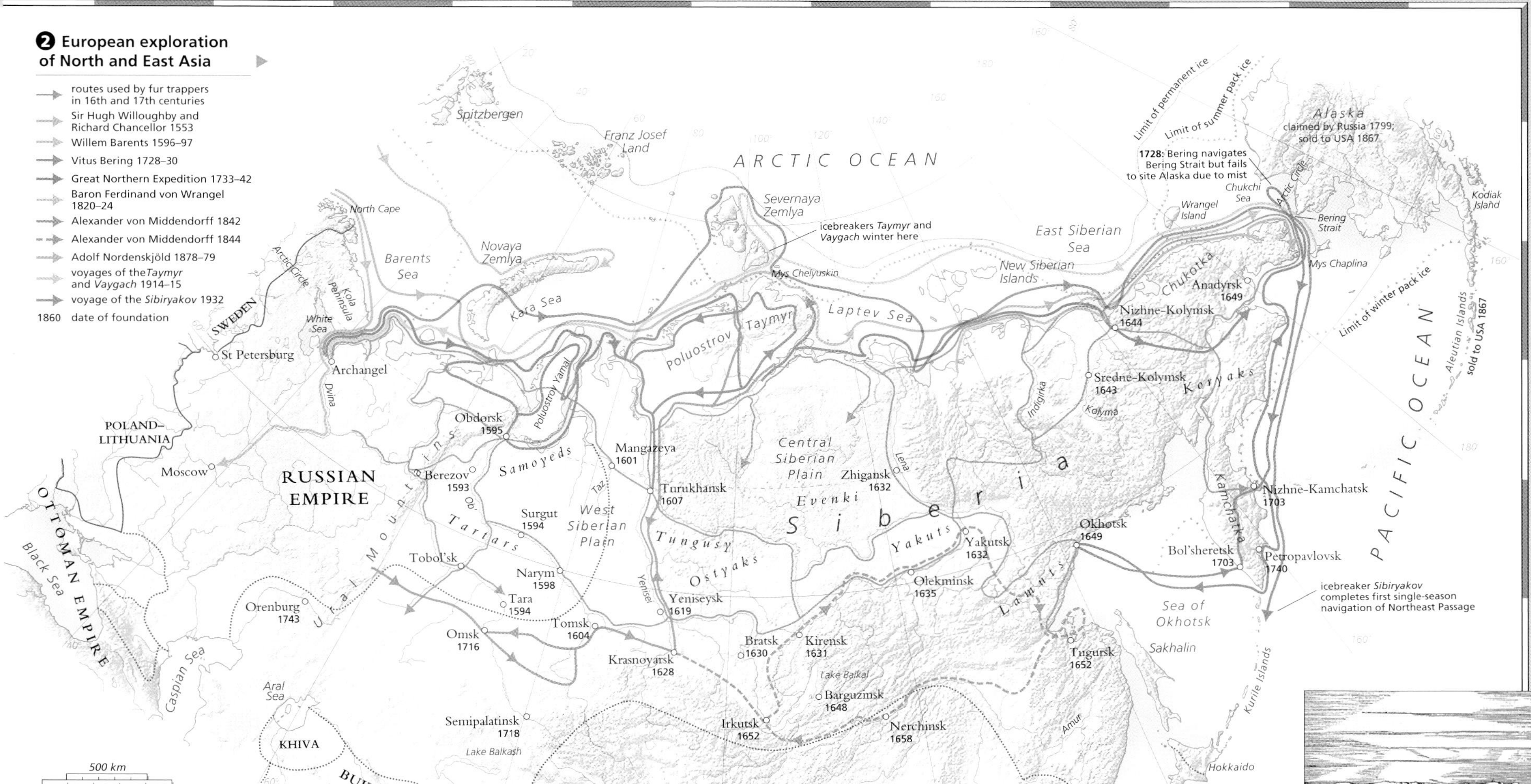

2 European exploration of North and East Asia

- routes used by fur trappers in 16th and 17th centuries
- Sir Hugh Willoughby and Richard Chancellor 1553
- Willem Barents 1596–97
- Vitus Bering 1728–30
- Great Northern Expedition 1733–42
- Baron Ferdinand von Wrangel 1820–24
- Alexander von Middendorff 1842
- Alexander von Middendorff 1844
- Adolf Nordenskjöld 1878–79
- voyages of the *Taymyr* and *Vaygach* 1914–15
- voyage of the *Sibiryakov* 1932
- 1860 date of foundation

1728: Bering navigates Bering Strait but fails to site Alaska due to mist

Alaska claimed by Russia 1799; sold to USA 1867

icebreakers *Taymyr* and *Vaygach* winter here

icebreaker *Sibiryakov* completes first single-season navigation of Northeast Passage

Aleutian Islands sold to USA 1867

The Northeast Passage and Siberia

The repeated failure to find a Northeast passage to Asia, and the abundance of furs and minerals beyond the Urals, led to a sudden and rapid expansion of the Russian Empire across Siberia. Military forays such as the great Northern Expedition followed fur traders' routes, subdued local tribes, and paved the way for colonists. Between the 1580s and 1650 Russians gained the largest land empire yet seen, crossed the Bering Strait and claimed Alaska. Only in the 20th century did icebreakers open the maritime route across the Arctic Ocean.

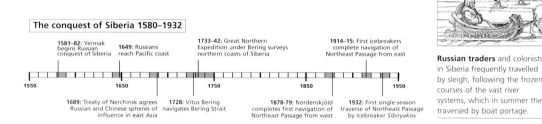

The conquest of Siberia 1580–1932

- 1581–82: Yermak begins Russian conquest of Siberia
- 1649: Russians reach Pacific coast
- 1689: Treaty of Nerchinsk agrees Russian and Chinese spheres of influence in east Asia
- 1728: Vitus Bering navigates Bering Strait
- 1733–42: Great Northern Expedition under Bering surveys northern coasts of Siberia
- 1878–79: Nordenskjöld completes first navigation of Northeast Passage from west
- 1914–15: First icebreakers complete navigation of Northeast Passage from east
- 1932: First single-season traverse of Northeast Passage by icebreaker *Sibiryakov*

Russian traders and colonists in Siberia frequently travelled by sleigh, following the frozen courses of the vast river systems, which in summer they traversed by boat portage.

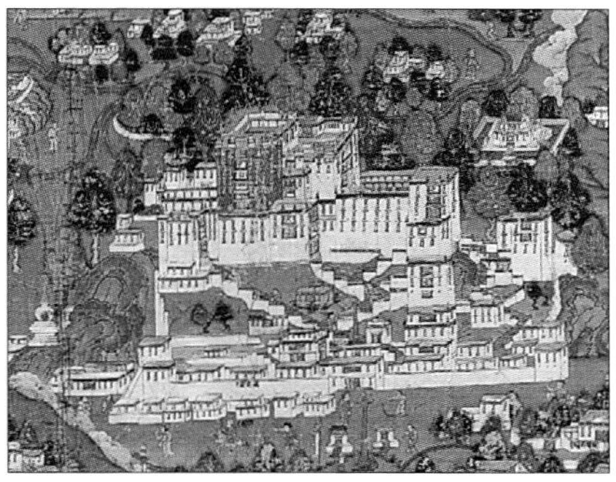

On the roof of the world

As the imperial world map was filled in during the 19th century, so the most remote regions of Central Asia began to be explored and claimed. Jesuit missionaries and diplomatic missions (frequently backed by force) had limited success in penetrating the fastnesses of Tibet. In India, the British recruited local guides as secret agents (pundits) to conduct clandestine surveys. Only during the last century did scientists (often Russian) such as Przhevalsky and Roerich explore the plateaux and mountains in any detail.

Nominally under Chinese control during the 19th century, in effect Tibet remained independent, closed to the outside world. This 18th-century Tibetan painting maps the splendour of the Dalai Lama's Potala palace in Lhasa.

Both Russia and Britain regarded accurate mapping *(below)* as essential to imperial control. The maps of Nepal and Tibet produced covertly by native 'pundits', provided essential intelligence for Anglo-Indian imperialists.

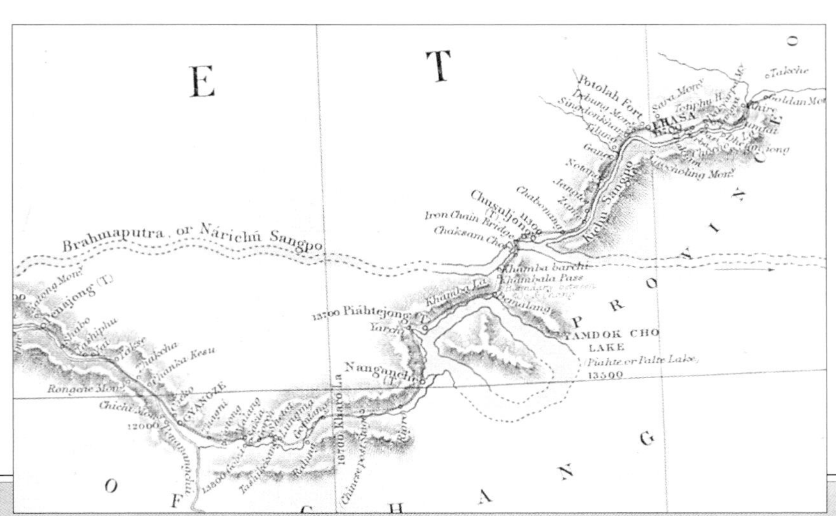

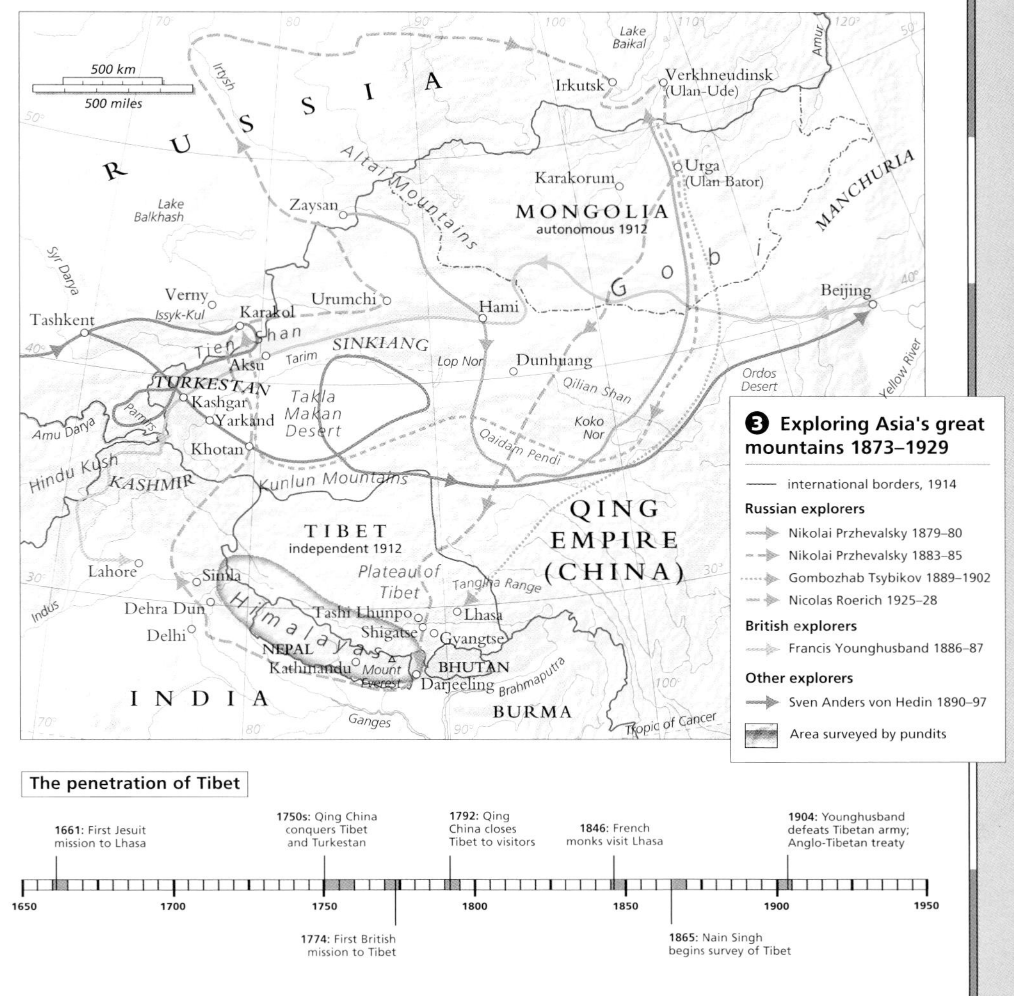

THE FIRST EAST ASIAN CIVILIZATIONS

Some of the earliest Chinese script is preserved on Shang period oracle bones (c.1400 BCE).

THE EMERGENCE OF ORGANIZED CULTURES in East Asia took a variety of forms. The fertile soils of the Yellow River basin and Yangtze valley provided the potential for the region's first agricultural communities 8000 years ago. Pottery working with kilns and bronze technology developed, accompanied by the first Chinese states and empires; the region remains to this day the heartland of China's culture and population. In Japan, the abundance of natural resources, especially fish and seafood, meant that hunter-gathering persisted, alongside features normally associated with sedentary agriculture – the world's earliest pottery is found here. Across the steppe grasslands of Central Asia, dominated by seasonal migration in search of pasture, communities developed a mobile culture now revealed through elaborate burials and decorated grave goods.

The agricultural revolution in Central and East Asia from c.10,000 BCE

The hardy yak provided abundant meat, furs for clothing and tents, and dairy products for the nomadic pastoralists of Central Asia.

A wide range of crops and plants was domesticated across East Asia from c.10,000 BCE. The pig was the most widely domesticated animal, and varieties of cattle such as oxen, yak, and banteng supported migratory herders. It was the domestication of staple crops such as millet and rice that provided the basis for population growth and, later the first Chinese cities and states. Rice was cultivated in the Yangtze valley around 6000 BCE, reaching Korea some 4000 years later and Japan in the 1st millennium BCE. In the Yellow River valley of northern China, millet was domesticated.

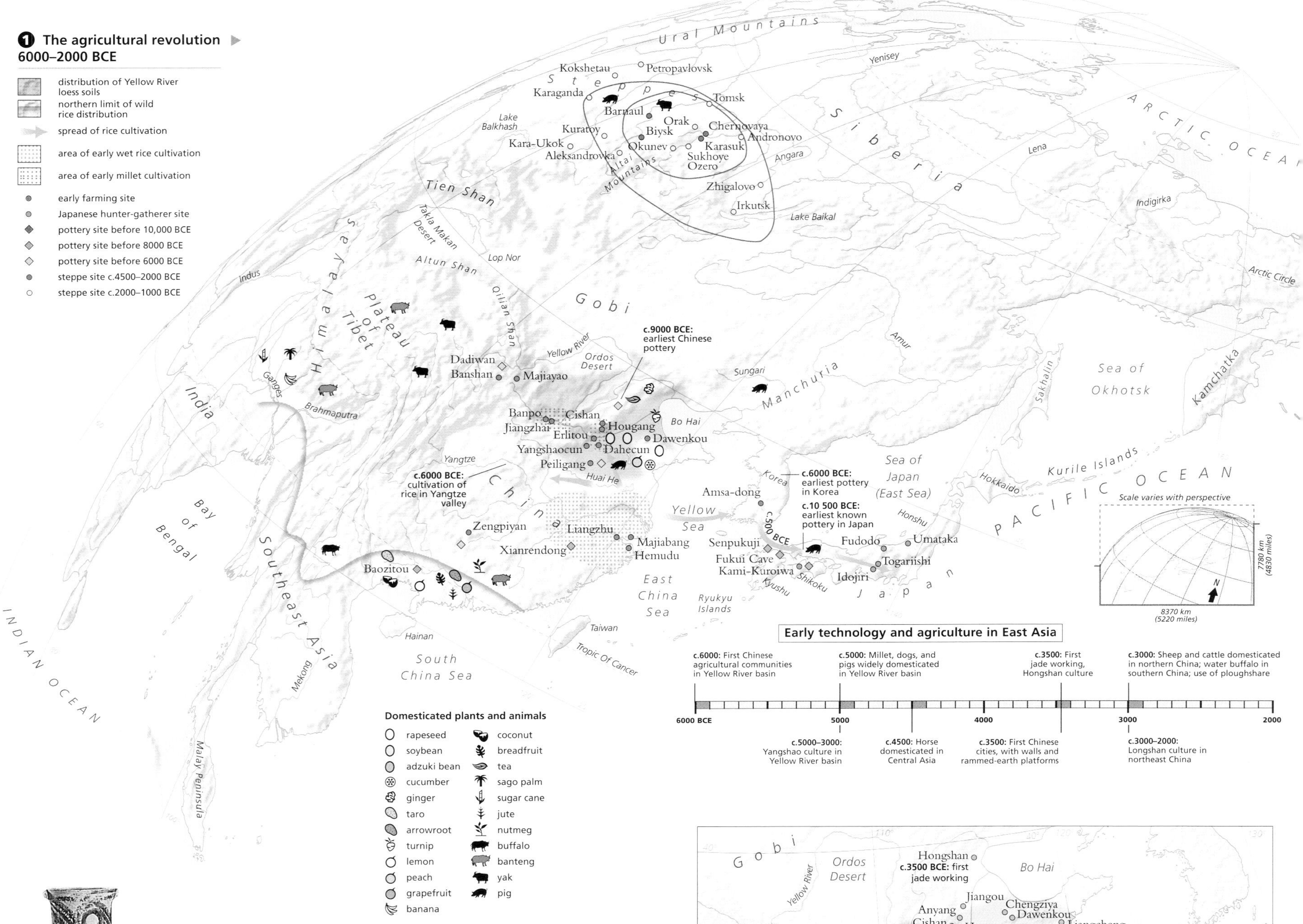

1 The agricultural revolution 6000–2000 BCE

- distribution of Yellow River loess soils
- northern limit of wild rice distribution
- spread of rice cultivation
- area of early wet rice cultivation
- area of early millet cultivation
- early farming site
- Japanese hunter-gatherer site
- pottery site before 10,000 BCE
- pottery site before 8000 BCE
- pottery site before 6000 BCE
- steppe site c.4500–2000 BCE
- steppe site c.2000–1000 BCE

c.9000 BCE: earliest Chinese pottery

c.6000 BCE: cultivation of rice in Yangtze valley

c.6000 BCE: earliest pottery in Korea

c.10 500 BCE: earliest known pottery in Japan

c.500 BCE

Scale varies with perspective

Domesticated plants and animals

- rapeseed
- soybean
- adzuki bean
- cucumber
- ginger
- taro
- arrowroot
- turnip
- lemon
- peach
- grapefruit
- banana
- coconut
- breadfruit
- tea
- sago palm
- sugar cane
- jute
- nutmeg
- buffalo
- banteng
- yak
- pig

Early technology and agriculture in East Asia

- c.6000: First Chinese agricultural communities in Yellow River basin
- c.5000–3000: Yangshao culture in Yellow River basin
- c.5000: Millet, dogs, and pigs widely domesticated in Yellow River basin
- c.4500: Horse domesticated in Central Asia
- c.3500: First Chinese cities, with walls and rammed-earth platforms
- c.3500: First jade working, Hongshan culture
- c.3000: Sheep and cattle domesticated in northern China; water buffalo in southern China; use of ploughshare
- c.3000–2000: Longshan culture in northeast China

6000 BCE · 5000 · 4000 · 3000 · 2000

Neolithic China c.4000–2000 BCE

The early agricultural communities in the Yellow River basin developed common cultural characteristics known to us through settlement patterns, burial practices and pottery. The Yangshao regional grouping was one of the earliest to be identified. By about 3000 BCE this was replaced by the more prosperous and sophisticated Longshan culture, which spread throughout the basin and the coastal plain. Technological advances occurred in pottery, copper-working was introduced, the ploughshare was in use, and by 2000 BCE silk weaving had begun.

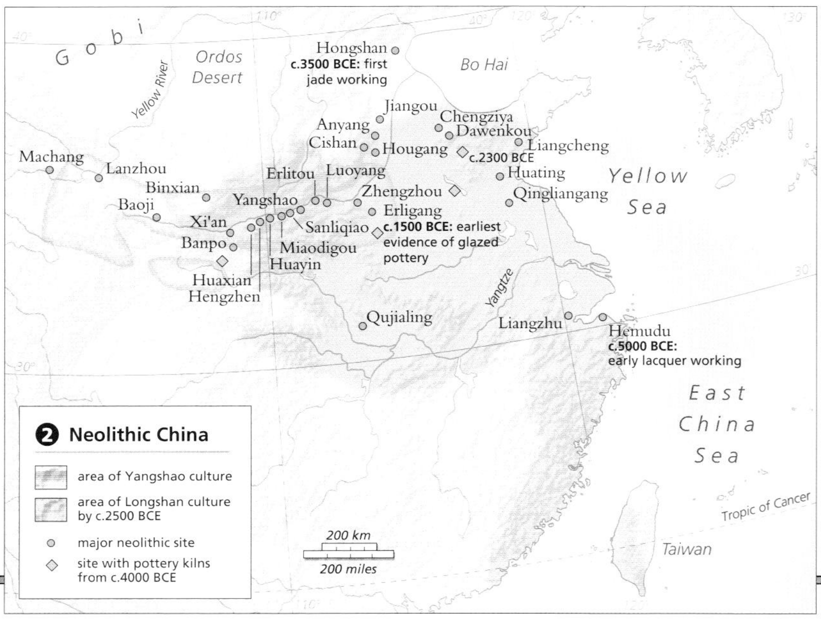

The geometric decoration of Yangshao pottery probably had a ritualistic significance.

2 Neolithic China

- area of Yangshao culture
- area of Longshan culture by c.2500 BCE
- major neolithic site
- site with pottery kilns from c.4000 BCE

c.3500 BCE: first jade working

c.2300 BCE

c.1500 BCE: earliest evidence of glazed pottery

c.5000 BCE: early lacquer working

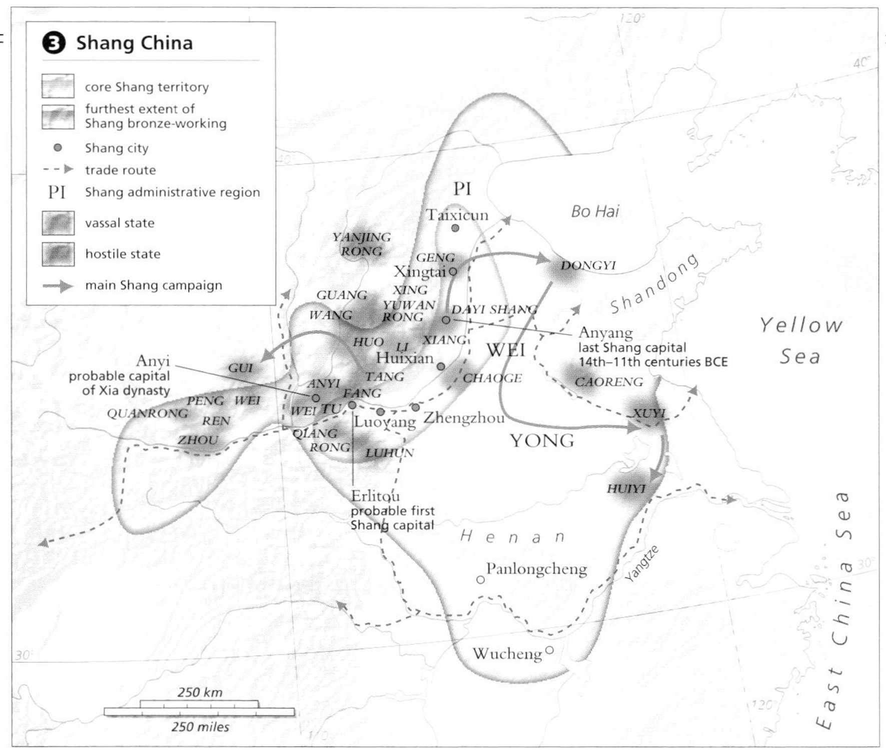

Shang China 1800–1027 BCE

In about 1800 BCE, the nucleus of the first Chinese state emerged in the Yellow River valley of northern China. The Shang state was feudal, with its core territory under the direct control of the kings, but outlying areas less securely attached. The Shang kings used ancestor worship and divination to confirm their dynastic status. Their successive capitals were mainly ritual centres with palace complexes and elaborate royal burial places. The Shang were skilled in writing, and were exponents of martial conquest, divination, and human sacrifice. Bronze-working (often for military purposes), stone carving, and pottery making were harnessed to religion and the state.

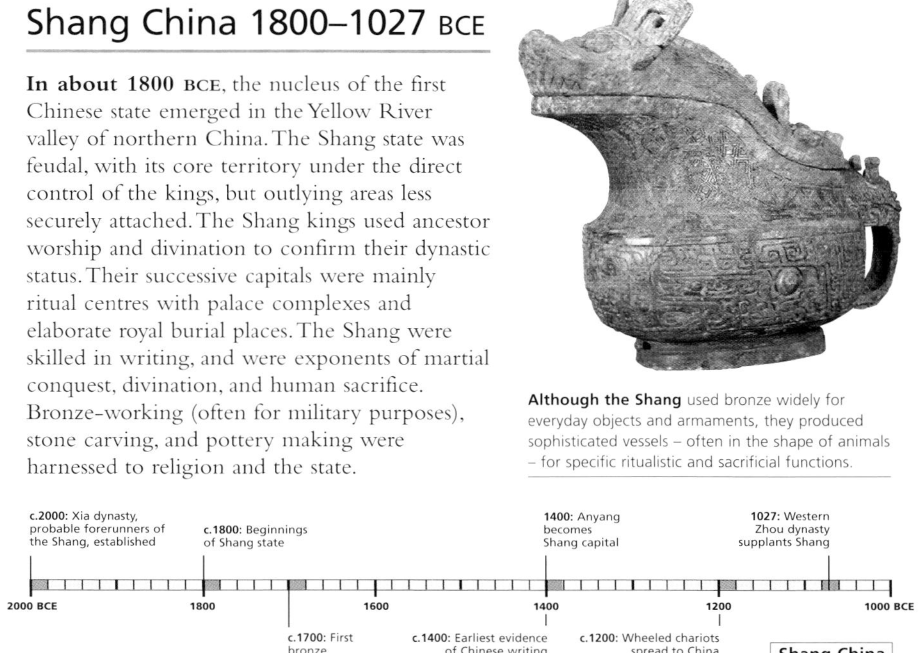

Although the Shang used bronze widely for everyday objects and armaments, they produced sophisticated vessels – often in the shape of animals – for specific ritualistic and sacrificial functions.

Shang China

- **c.2000:** Xia dynasty, probable forerunners of the Shang, established
- **c.1800:** Beginnings of Shang state
- **c.1700:** First bronze vessels cast
- **c.1400:** Earliest evidence of Chinese writing on oracle bones
- **1400:** Anyang becomes Shang capital
- **c.1200:** Wheeled chariots spread to China from Central Asia
- **1027:** Western Zhou dynasty supplants Shang

2000 BCE · 1800 · 1600 · 1400 · 1200 · 1000 BCE

Zhou China 1027–403 BCE

The 11th century BCE saw political control wrested from the Shang by the Zhou (Chou), based west of the Shang capital. Under the Western Zhou greater political unity developed, the royal family assigning territories to their vassals to create a proto-feudal state. Human sacrifice declined, defensive walls began to be built and the first literary records of Chinese history emerged. Constant rivalry and dissent gradually eroded centralized power, and from 770 BCE a new capital was established at Luoyang under the Eastern Zhou. A looser political federation came about, bound together by the need for defence against hostile neighbours, and by common cultural values reflected in the use of coinage, in richly decorated tombs, and in the writings of Confucius.

The first Chinese coins came into use around 500 BCE, and were normally cast in bronze in the form of tools.

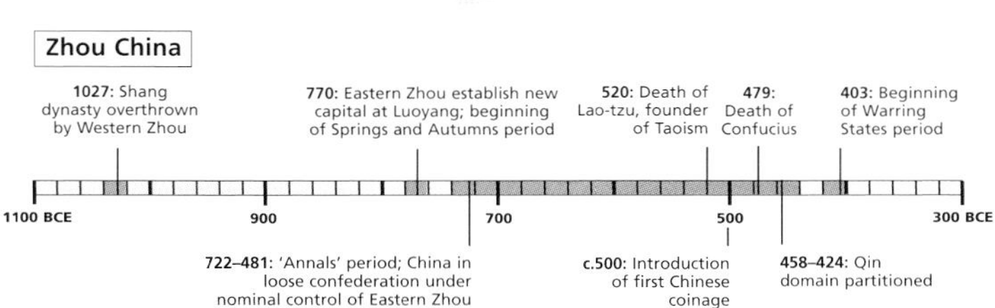

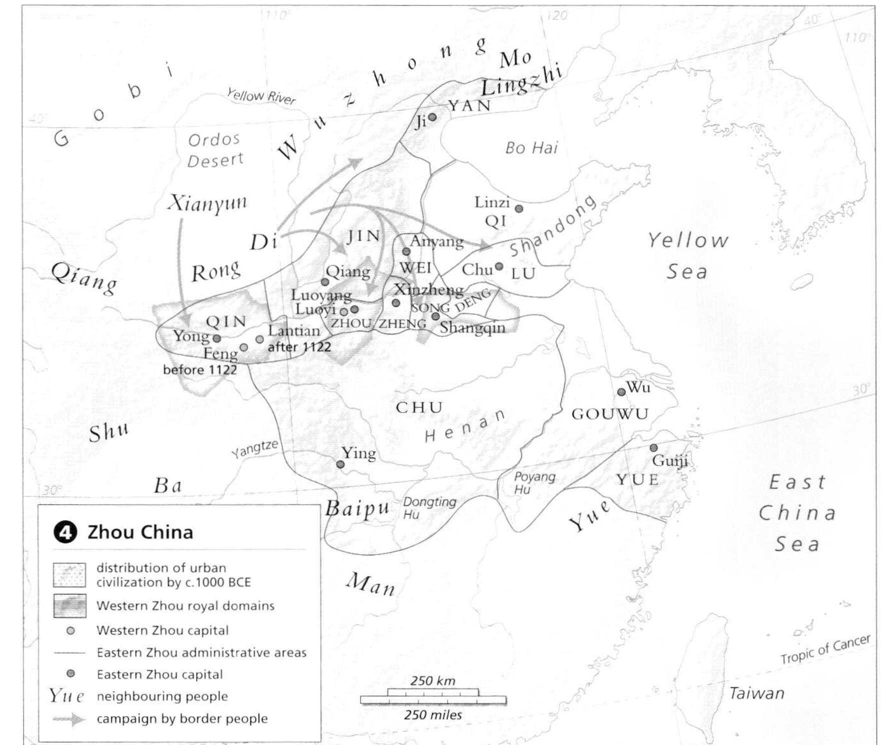

Qin China 221–206 BCE

The Zhou confederation eventually collapsed into bitter civil war. The Warring States period (403–221 BCE) was gradually brought to an end by the Qin dynasty, who created by alliance, diplomacy, and conquest, the first unified Chinese empire. A series of ruthless campaigns by Shi Huangdi (the First Emperor) extended Qin domains far to the north and to the south beyond the Yangtze valley to the borders of modern Vietnam; in their wake, a process of centralization and standardization was introduced to minimize regional differences and tribal dissent. The area of the Qin state was effectively tripled in 16 years, while the constant threat to the northern borders by nomadic steppe peoples such as the Xiongnu led to the construction of the first Great Wall.

Thousands of life-size terracotta soldiers and horses were buried near Shi Huangdi's tomb outside Xianyang, a testament to his military might and concern for his destiny in the afterlife.

Qin China

- **247:** King Zheng (later Shi Huangdi) becomes ruler of Qin domain
- **230:** Campaigns of Shi Huangdi begin
- **221–207:** General disarmament, standardization of weights, measures, and axle widths to facilitate commerce
- **221:** Qin Empire established, organized into 36 commanderies
- **214:** Slave labour used to link ramparts to form Great Wall
- **213:** Proscription of non-scientific books; standardization and simplification of Chinese script
- **210:** Death of Shi Huangdi, entombed with vast terracotta army
- **206:** Beginning of Han dynasty

250 BCE · 240 · 230 · 220 · 210 · 200 BCE

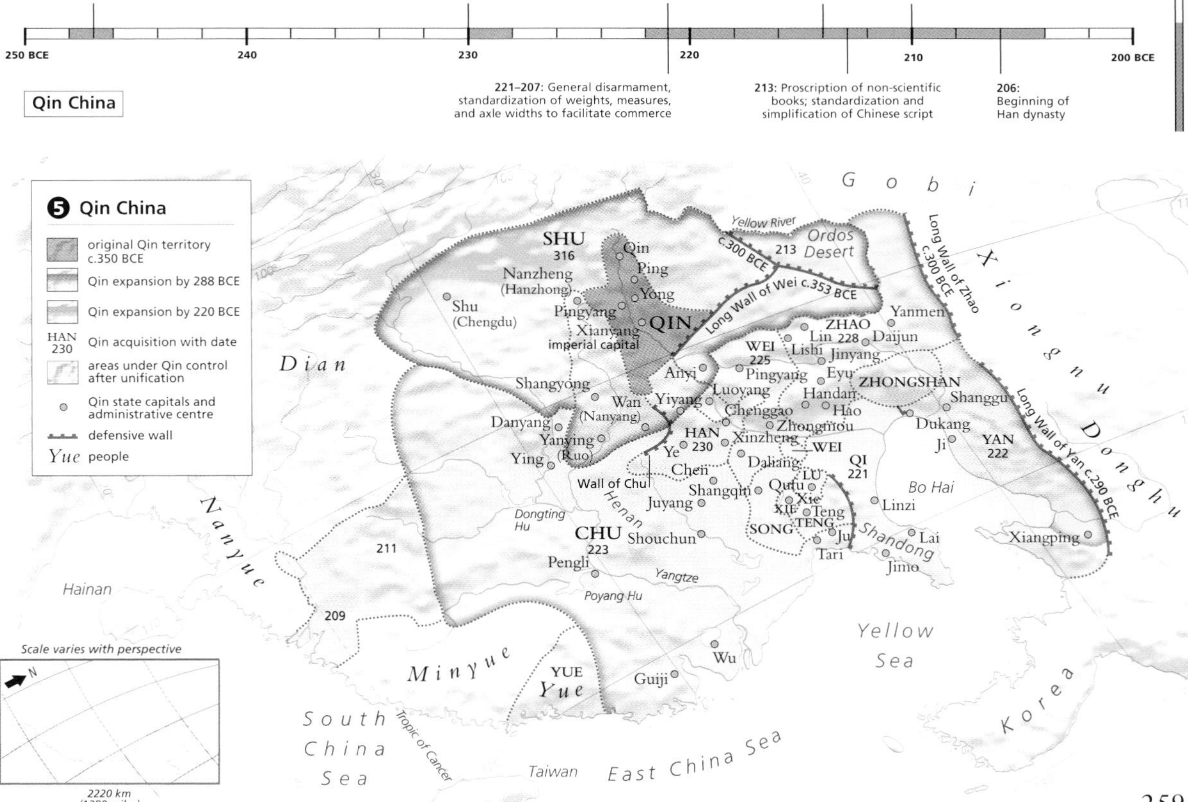

THE HAN AND THE GREAT MIGRATIONS

A ceremonial bronze bridle from the Han period reflects the importance of their cavalry skills.

THE UNIFICATION OF CHINA under an authoritarian, centralized regime by the Qin in 221 BCE paved the way for the Han, who assumed control in 206 BCE. The Han consolidated Chinese control of the south, pushing indigenous populations into more marginal areas, as well as expanding far into Central Asia along the Silk Road. In doing so, the Han established a domain by far the greatest the world had ever seen, and provided a template for Chinese territorial aspirations for the next two millennia. The Han benefited from trans-Asian trade *(see pp.44–45)*, but were constantly troubled by the steppe peoples, especially the Xiongnu, mounted pastoralists who harassed their northern borders.

Han China 206 BCE–220 CE

Tomb pottery from the Han period often celebrates daily life, as in this model of a farm building, complete with sheep and ass.

The Han, who ruled China for over 400 years (apart from a brief interregnum under Wang Mang from 9–25 CE), established China as the most dominant cultural, political, and economic force in Asia. They constructed a new Great Wall to protect their northern borders, and established military garrisons from Korea in the east to Champa (Vietnam) in the south and Ferghana in the west to protect their expanding empire. Trade – along the great trans-Eurasian land routes and by sea – flourished; Buddhism entered China during this period (although the Han bureaucracy was structured on Confucian principles); and by 2 CE the first imperial census revealed a Chinese population of over 57 million, living mainly in the river valleys of the north.

The Han dynasty

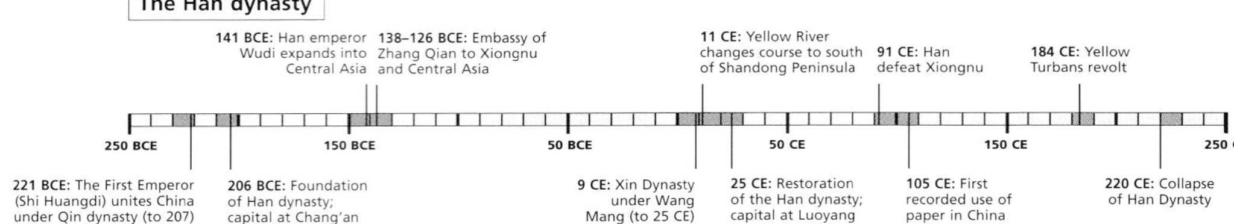

141 BCE: Han emperor Wudi expands into Central Asia
138–126 BCE: Embassy of Zhang Qian to Xiongnu and Central Asia
11 CE: Yellow River changes course to south of Shandong Peninsula
91 CE: Han defeat Xiongnu
184 CE: Yellow Turbans revolt
250 BCE
150 BCE
50 BCE
50 CE
150 CE
250 CE
221 BCE: The First Emperor (Shi Huangdi) unites China under Qin dynasty (to 207)
206 BCE: Foundation of Han dynasty; capital at Chang'an
9 CE: Xin Dynasty under Wang Mang (to 25 CE)
25 CE: Restoration of the Han dynasty; capital at Luoyang
105 CE: First recorded use of paper in China
220 CE: Collapse of Han Dynasty

Han Commanderies (administrative districts)

1 JINGZHAOYIN	6 HENEI	11 HEJIAN	16 YUNZHONG	21 GUANGYANG	26 JINAN	31 GAOMI	36 DONG	41 CHENLIU
2 YOUFUFENG	7 WEI	12 JULU	17 DINGXIANG	22 YUYANG	27 QIANCHENG	32 JIAODONG	37 DONGPING	42 HUAIYANG
3 ZUO PINGYI	8 GUANPING ZHAO	13 ZHONGSHAN	18 YANMEN	23 YOUBEIPING	28 QI	33 LANGYA	38 JIYIN	43 YINGCHUAN
4 HEDONG	9 QINGHE	14 CHANGSHAN	19 DAIZHUO	24 BOHAI	29 ZICHUAN	34 CHENGYANG	39 SHANYANG	44 HENAN
5 SHANGDANG	10 XINDU	15 WUYAN	20 SHANGGU	25 PINGYUAN	30 PEIHAN	35 TAISHAN	40 LIANG	45 HONGNONG

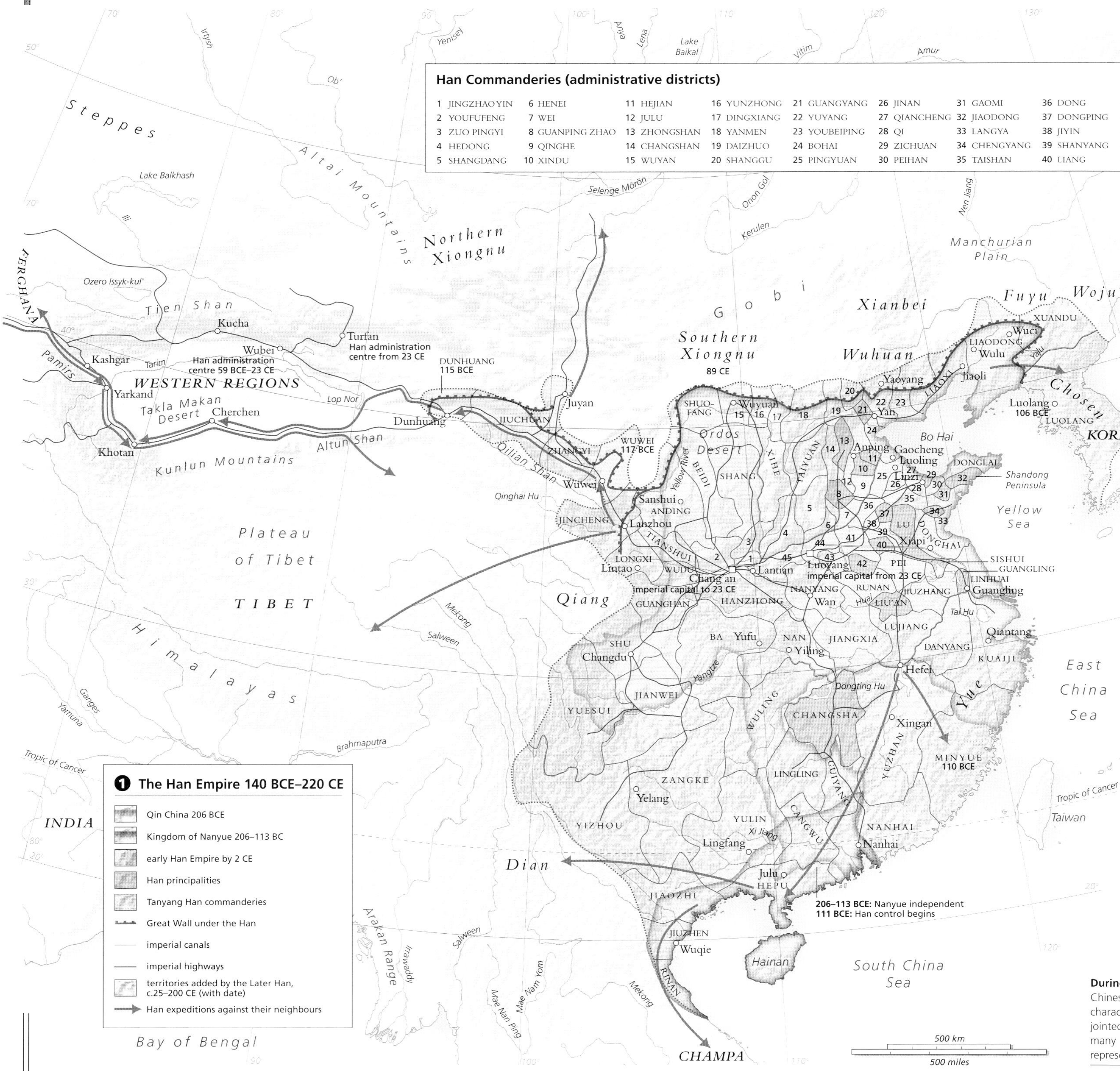

1 The Han Empire 140 BCE–220 CE

- Qin China 206 BCE
- Kingdom of Nanyue 206–113 BC
- early Han Empire by 2 CE
- Han principalities
- Tanyang Han commanderies
- Great Wall under the Han
- imperial canals
- imperial highways
- territories added by the Later Han, c.25–200 CE (with date)
- Han expeditions against their neighbours

Han administration centre 59 BCE–23 CE

Turfan Han administration centre from 23 CE

DUNHUANG 115 BCE

Southern Xiongnu 89 CE

Luolang 106 BCE

WUWEI 117 BCE

Luoyang imperial capital from 23 CE

Chang'an imperial capital to 23 CE

MINYUE 110 BCE

206–113 BCE: Nanyue independent
111 BCE: Han control begins

500 km
500 miles

During the Han period Chinese architecture acquired its characteristic qualities of finely jointed wooden structures supporting many broad-eaved storeys, here represented in a clay tomb model.

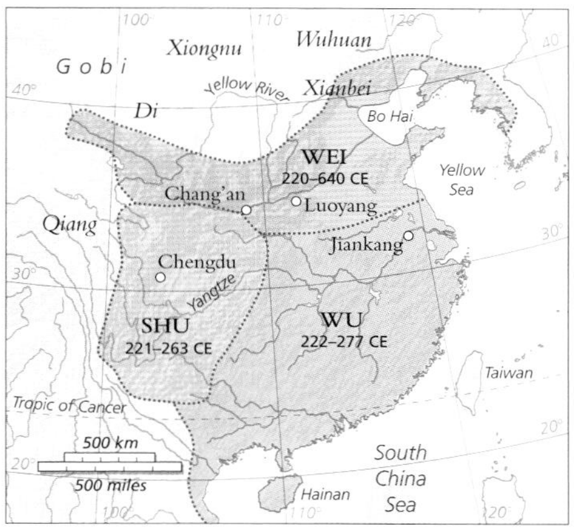

The fragmentation of China 220–589 CE

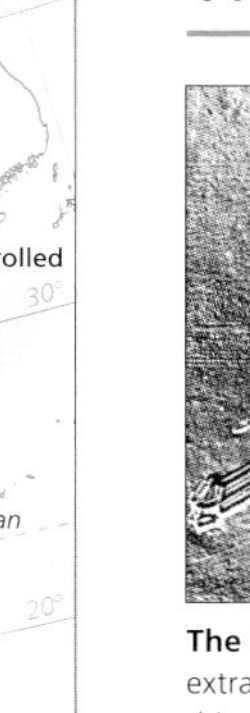

The threat posed by the steppe warriors' extraordinary horsemanship is illustrated in this relief tile from Sichuan. The mounted archer is performing a 'Parthian' shot at full gallop, in full control of both his weapon and his speeding horse.

A series of revolts, the inability to collect taxes from northern vassals, and an increasing reliance on mercenaries recruited from steppe tribes, led to the collapse of the Han dynasty and a prolonged period of turmoil in China. The north fell prey to a succession of non-Chinese peoples, the most notable being the Turkic Toba (or Northern) Wei, while the Chinese aristocracy withdrew to the south. During this period the collapse of Chinese institutions saw a decline in respect for Confucian values and the growth of Taoist cults and Buddhism.

❷ The Three Kingdoms c.250 CE

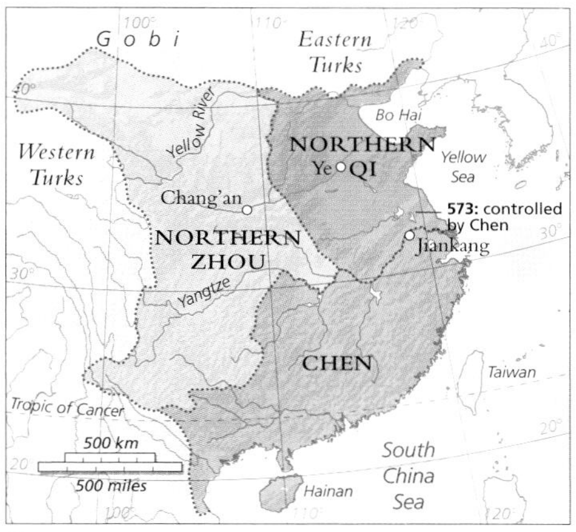

❺ China c.560 CE

❸ The later Sixteen Kingdoms period c.400 CE

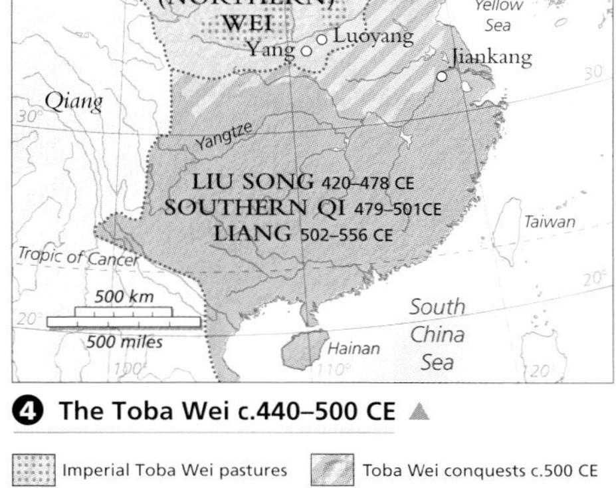

❹ The Toba Wei c.440–500 CE

Imperial Toba Wei pastures
Toba Wei conquests c.500 CE

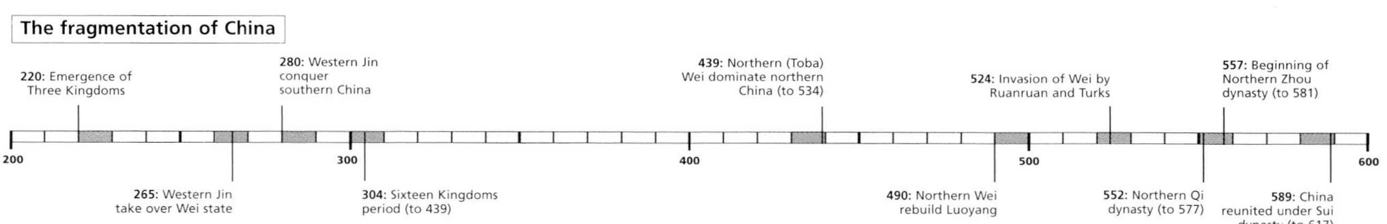

The fragmentation of China

220: Emergence of Three Kingdoms
265: Western Jin take over Wei state
280: Western Jin conquer southern China
304: Sixteen Kingdoms period (to 439)
439: Northern (Toba) Wei dominate northern China (to 534)
490: Northern Wei rebuild Luoyang
524: Invasion of Wei by Ruanruan and Turks
552: Northern Qi dynasty (to 577)
557: Beginning of Northern Zhou dynasty (to 581)
589: China reunited under Sui dynasty (to 617)

The steppe kingdoms of Central Asia

The collapse of Han China was only one product of the emergence of organized, militaristic confederations among the steppe peoples of northern and Central Asia. Between the 3rd and 6th centuries, jostling for territory and opportunistic campaigns against the more sedentary states to their south – the most serious being those of the Xiongnu – caused a domino pattern of migratory movements south and west, the effects of this irruption being felt across all Eurasia.

The Xiongnu owed much of their military success to their understanding of cavalry tactics. In addition to the fast, lightly armoured skirmishers associated with steppe peoples, they maintained a heavy cavalry capable of breaking through massed infantry. This figurine of an armoured horseman dates from the 5th century CE when the Toba Wei competed with other steppe peoples for control of northern China.

❻ The steppe kingdoms of Central Asia

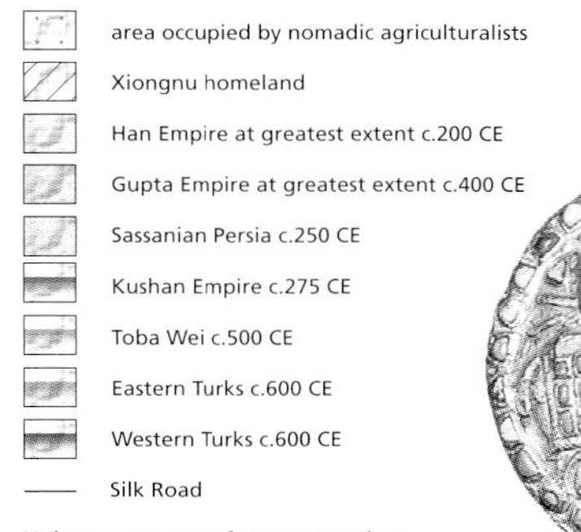

area occupied by nomadic agriculturalists
Xiongnu homeland
Han Empire at greatest extent c.200 CE
Gupta Empire at greatest extent c.400 CE
Sassanian Persia c.250 CE
Kushan Empire c.275 CE
Toba Wei c.500 CE
Eastern Turks c.600 CE
Western Turks c.600 CE
Silk Road

Major movements of steppe peoples:
1st–3rd century CE
300–350
350–500
after 500

This iron Bactrian plaque plated in sheet gold with turquoise gems, and depicting a horseman, is typical of the intricate but very portable art of the steppe peoples.

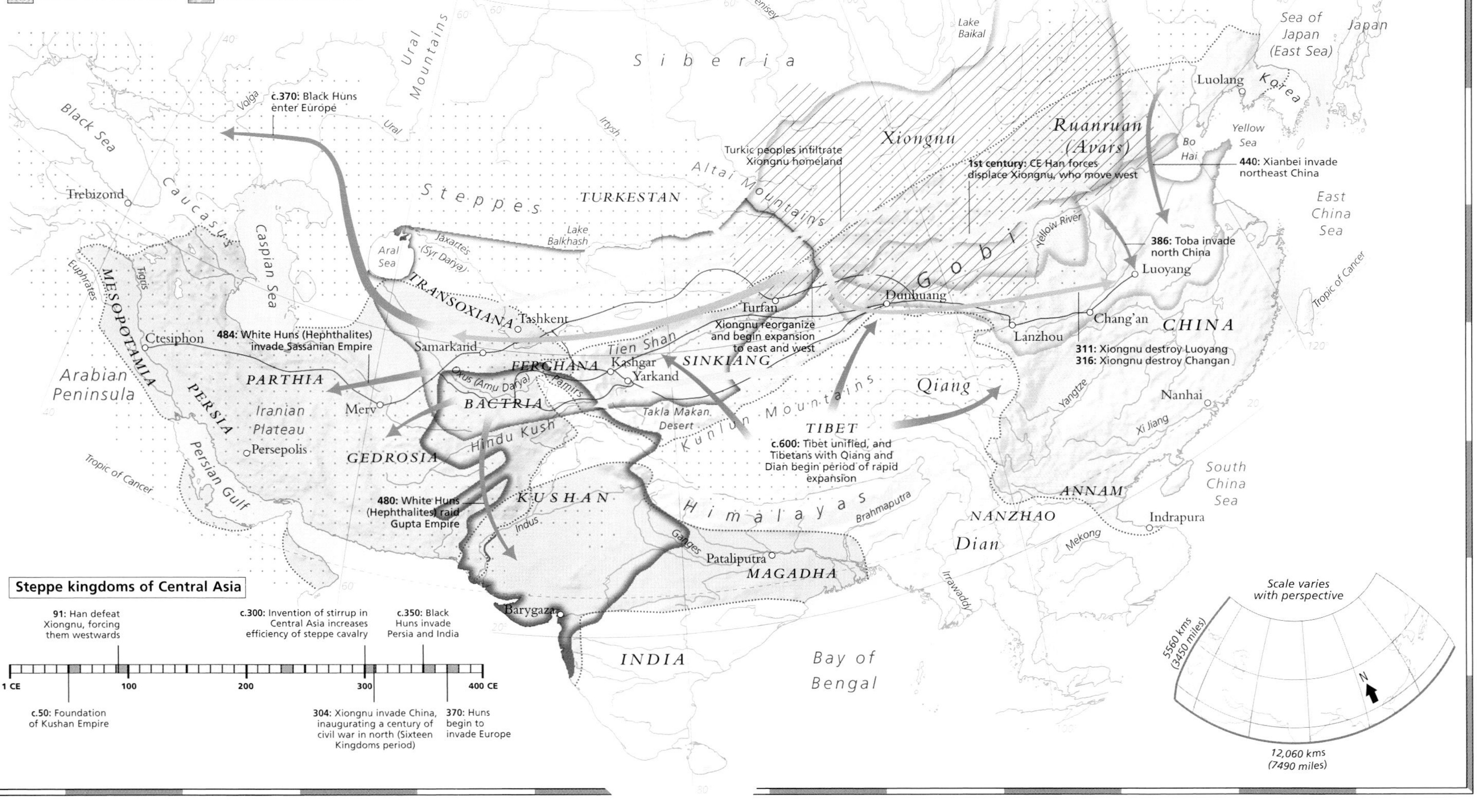

c.370: Black Huns enter Europe
Turkic peoples infiltrate Xiongnu homeland
1st century: CE Han forces displace Xiongnu, who move west
440: Xianbei invade northeast China
386: Toba invade north China
484: White Huns (Hephthalites) invade Sassanian Empire
Xiongnu reorganize and begin expansion to east and west
311: Xiongnu destroy Luoyang
316: Xiongnu destroy Changan
c.600: Tibet unified, and Tibetans with Qiang and Dian begin period of rapid expansion
480: White Huns (Hephthalites) raid Gupta Empire

Steppe kingdoms of Central Asia

c.50: Foundation of Kushan Empire
91: Han defeat Xiongnu, forcing them westwards
c.300: Invention of stirrup in Central Asia increases efficiency of steppe cavalry
304: Xiongnu invade China, inaugurating a century of civil war in north (Sixteen Kingdoms period)
c.350: Black Huns invade Persia and India
370: Huns begin to invade Europe

Scale varies with perspective

EARLY MEDIEVAL EAST ASIA

This porcelain incense burner in the shape of a duck dates from the Song period. Song pottery was widely traded.

THE TANG BROUGHT CHINA under a unified administration in 618, and rapidly extended its domains far into Central Asia, briefly achieving by 742 a territorial extent and era of stable growth comparable to that of their Han forebears. The influence of Chinese culture also spread during this period, which in turn saw the establishment of similarly organized states around their frontiers on all sides. Chinese forces were defeated in 751 by Arab armies on the Talas River, which inaugurated a process of Islamicization in Central Asia and loosened Tang control in the region. But China's greatest threats continued to lie to the north, where coalitions of steppe peoples began to establish expansionist regimes, eager to control the Chinese heartland.

Tang China

Tang China was unified under a centralized government, political and commercial integration established by a network of highways and canals, centred on the capital Chang'an. The Yangtze valley became an increasingly important economic region, while commerce focused on the coastal plain. The stability and prosperity of Tang China attracted both emulation and envy among its neighbours. But the Tang dynasty was fatally weakened by peasant revolts from the 870s and the empire eventually fragmented into local regimes which vied for power for over a century.

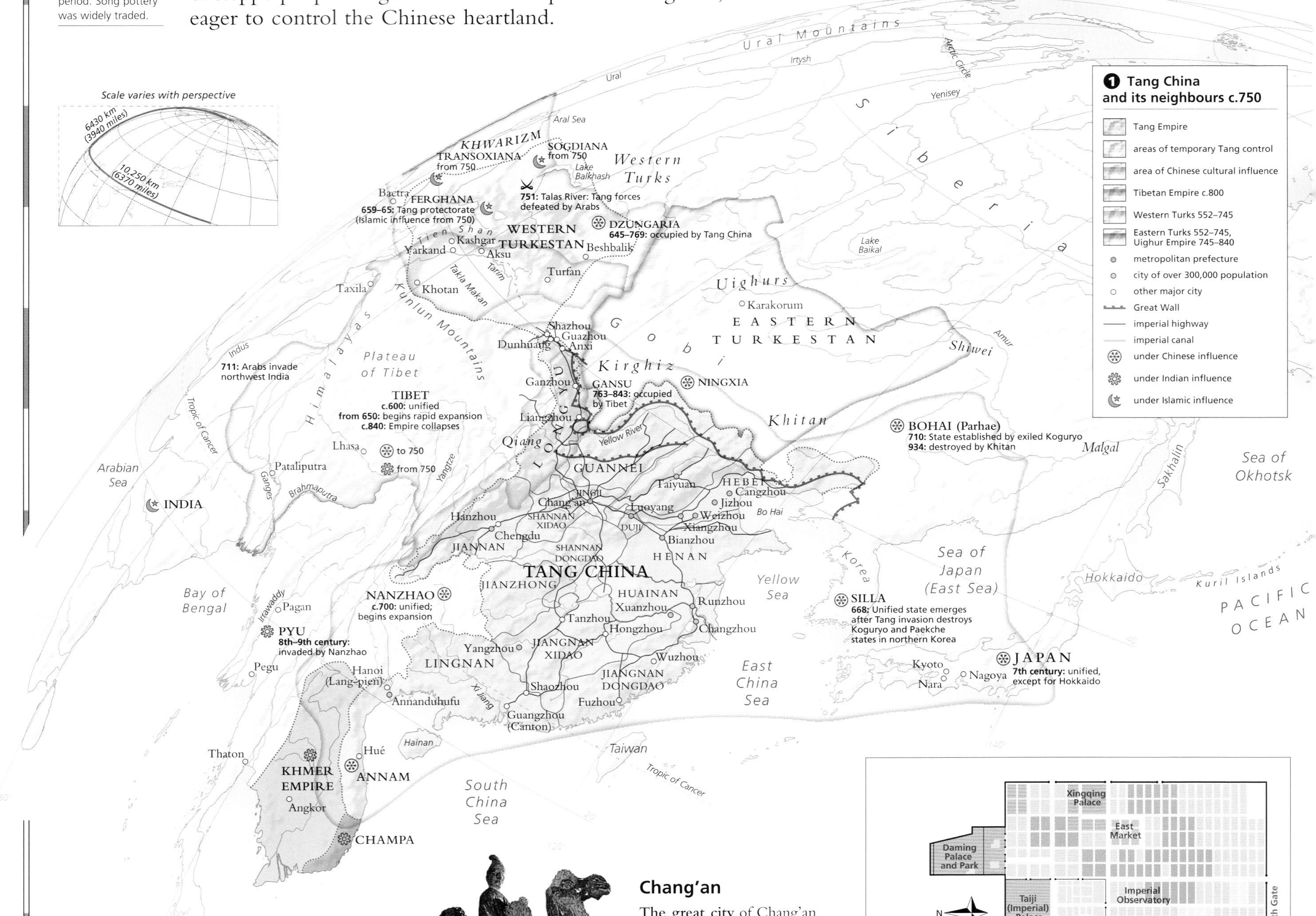

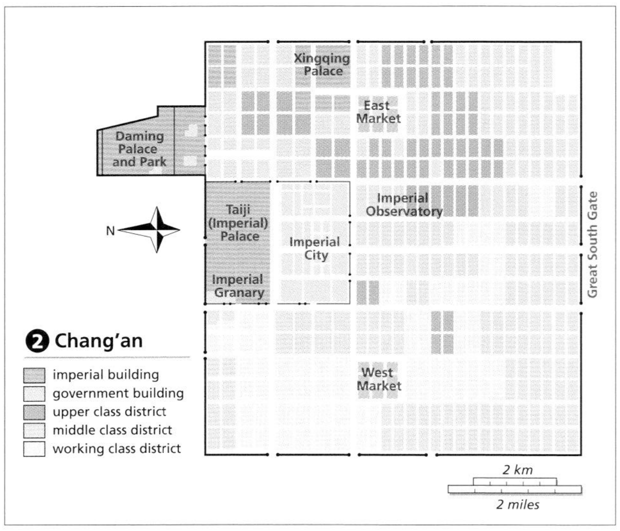

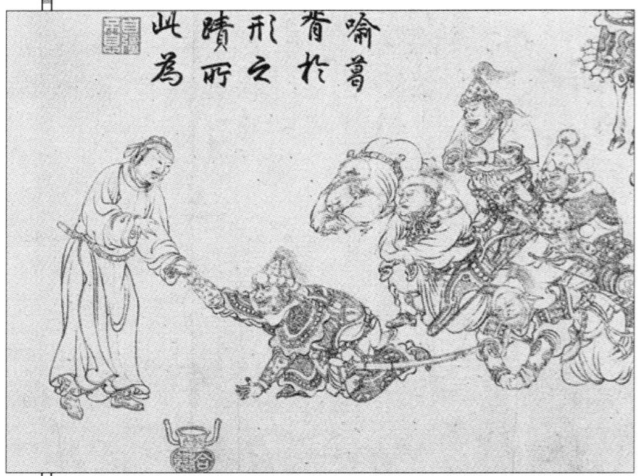

1 Tang China and its neighbours c.750

- Tang Empire
- areas of temporary Tang control
- area of Chinese cultural influence
- Tibetan Empire c.800
- Western Turks 552–745
- Eastern Turks 552–745, Uighur Empire 745–840
- metropolitan prefecture
- city of over 300,000 population
- other major city
- Great Wall
- imperial highway
- imperial canal
- under Chinese influence
- under Indian influence
- under Islamic influence

Scale varies with perspective

The stability of the Tang period saw a revival of trans-Asian trade. Bactrian camels with exotic traders, who entered China via the Silk Road, provided a common motif in Tang art *(above)*.

Tang domination of their neighbours is recorded here as caricatured Uighurs pay homage to an unarmed Tang general *(left)*.

Chang'an

The great city of Chang'an had been a Chinese capital since the Han period. By the 8th century there were around a million people within the city walls, with the same number close by outside, making it the largest city in the world at the time. The rigorous grid structure accommodated a variety of districts, each with its own function.

2 Chang'an

- imperial building
- government building
- upper class district
- middle class district
- working class district

Tang China and its neighbours

- **607:** Tibet unified (to 842)
- **618:** Tang begin to unite China
- **645:** Introduction of Chinese institutions to Japan
- **745:** Foundation of Uighur Empire (to 840)
- **751:** Battle of Talas River; Arabs defeat Tang
- **868:** The *Diamond Sutra*, world's oldest surviving printed work
- **870:** Series of peasant revolts in China

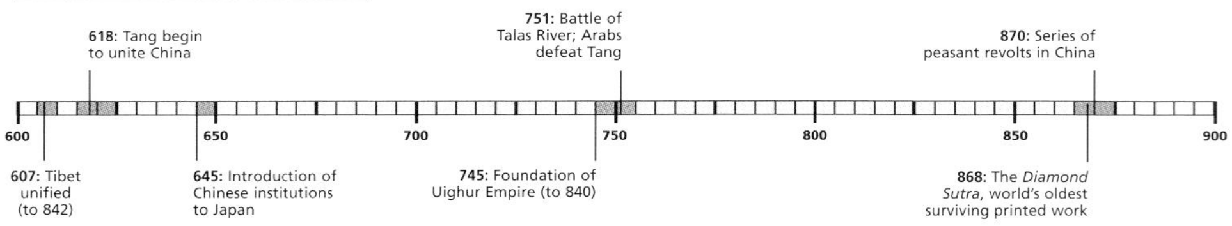

Song China

The anarchy which followed the fragmentation of the Tang Empire ushered in the period known as the Five Dynasties and Ten Kingdoms, when China was broken up into as many as ten states. The Song arose in northern China in 960, expanding to form a Chinese empire by 979, although they lost control of the north to the Khitans, who established the Liao Empire in Manchuria, balanced to the west by another steppe empire, the Tangut Xixia Empire. The Jurchen, vassals of the Liao, established the Jin state, which seized the Song capital of Kaifeng, restricting Song rule to the south. The Song period was nevertheless one of great prosperity.

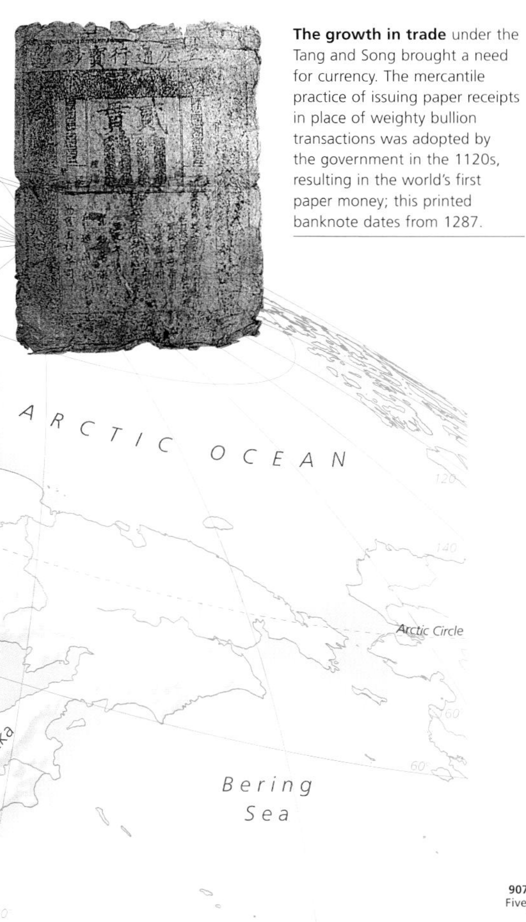

The growth in trade under the Tang and Song brought a need for currency. The mercantile practice of issuing paper receipts in place of weighty bullion transactions was adopted by the government in the 1120s, resulting in the world's first paper money; this printed banknote dates from 1287.

3 The Five Dynasties 881–979

Chinese states
states occupied by non-Chinese peoples

5 The Southern Song 1127–1234

capital city
Song empire
other states/empires

LIAO EMPIRE
Dading
Central capital
Gobi
Datong
XIXIA EMPIRE
Western capital
Southern capital
Bo Hai
GAOLI
Xingqingfu
Taiyuan
Zhending
Daming
Danzhou
Yingtian
Henan
Jingzhou
Kaifeng
Yangzhou
TIBET
Xingyuan
Xiangyang
Jiangning
Tongchuan
Kuizhou
Chengdu
Jiangling
Plateau of Tibet
Longxing
Yangtze
Fuzhou
NANZHAO
Qingzhou
Taiwan
Tropic of Cancer
Xi Jiang
Guangzhou
ANNAM
South China Sea
500 km
500 miles
Hainan

4 Song China 960–1127

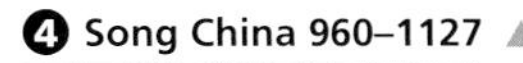
imperial canal
imperial highway
national capital
provincial capital

Fine porcelain and stoneware was produced in a range of regional centres in Song China, where mass production techniques developed to meet international demands.

POPULATION CHANGE IN CHINA

A shift in population distribution had occurred by the Song period: the Yellow River remained heavily populated, while the area south of the Yangtze became more intensively agricultural.

6 Chinese population

high density
low density

742

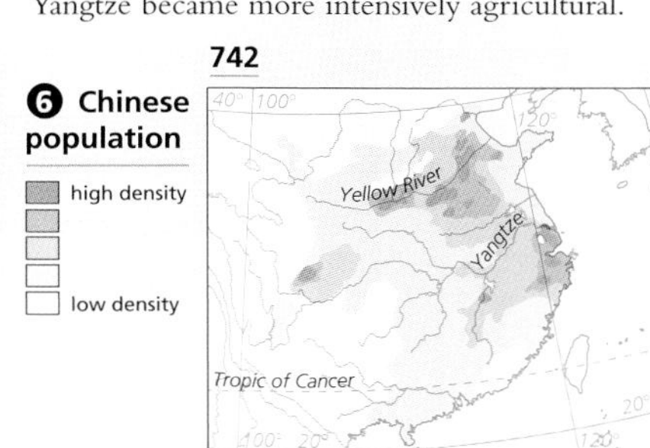

1102

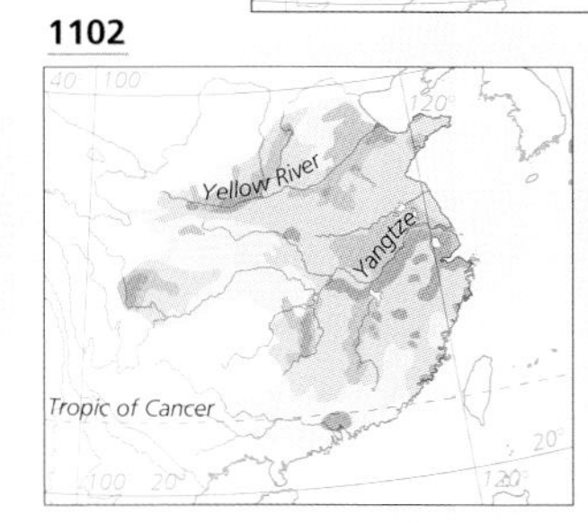

Song China

- **907:** Beginning of Five Dynasties and Ten Kingdoms period (to 960)
- **916:** Foundation of Khitan Empire
- **939:** Annam independent
- **947:** Khitans invade northern China, establishing Liao Dynasty at Beijing
- **979:** Song dynasty unites China
- **1038:** Foundation of Xixia Empire
- **1126:** Jin take control of northern China

900 950 1000 1050 1100 1150 1200

Lake Baikal
Sakhalin
Hokkaido
MONGOLIA (LINGBEI)
Karakorum
LIAOYANG
Amur
Gobi
Shangdu imperial capital
Sea of Japan (East Sea)
Daning
Liaoyang
JAPAN
Dunhuang
ZHONGSHU
Kamakura
Suzhou
GANSU
Yellow River
Dadu imperial capital
Bo Hai
Kaekyong
KORYO 1231–1364: dependent
Kyoto
Ganzhou
Ningxia
Zhending
Qingjiang
Yellow Sea
TIBET (TUFAN)
SHAANXI
Kaifeng
Bianliang
Fengyuan
Plateau of Tibet
HENAN
Changzhou
Lhasa
Luzhou
Chengdu
SICHUAN
Zhongxing
Wuchang
Hangzhou
East China Sea
Changde
Longxing
Tianlin
JIANGZHE
Ji'an
Hengzhou
Tropic of Cancer
Dingzhou
Chongqing
HUGUANG
JIANGXI
Taiwan
Dengchong
Jingjiang
PACIFIC OCEAN
YUNNAN
Xi Jiang
BURMA
Irrawaddy
Guangzhou
MIAN
Pagan
Hanoi
ANNAM
PEGU
Pegu
SHAN STATES
Hainan
Sukhothai
KHMER EMPIRE
CHAMPA
Mekong
South China Sea
500 km
500 miles

7 The Mongol (Yuan) period c.1300

southern extent of Mongol conquest to 1279
Mongol conquest 1280–1368
imperial capital
provincial capital
GANSU Yuan province
area of loose or temporary Mongol control

The Yuan (Mongol) invasion

The Mongol conquest of Jin in 1234 occasioned enormous violence and destruction. But the Mongols rapidly adopted Chinese customs and institutions *(see pp.68–69)*, and the eventual conquest of the Song south in 1278 was less brutal. Subsequent campaigns brought outlying areas under temporary Mongol control, and expanded Chinese administration far to the southwest, but the Mongols exercised only temporary control over Tibet and Southeast Asia and never conquered Japan.

This illustration from an early military manual shows a portable scaling ladder, used in siege warfare. Other innovations of this period included the catapult.

The Japanese defeat of Kublai's armies in 1274 (30,000 troops) and 1281 (140,000 troops), the largest amphibious invasion forces of pre-modern times, were recorded in an illustrated scroll in the 1290s *(left)*.

The Yuan Dynasty

- **1234:** Mongols invade Jin Empire
- **1264:** Foundation of Yuan dynasty by Kublai Khan
- **1274:** First attempted invasion of Japan
- **1279:** Yuan take over Southern Song
- **1281:** Second attempted invasion of Japan
- **1283:** Expeditions against Annam and Champa
- **1287:** Expedition to Pagan
- **1292:** Expedition to Java

1230 1250 1270 1290 1310

THE FIRST STATES IN JAPAN AND KOREA

Dotaku ceremonial bells, c.100 BCE, are typical of early Japanese bronze casting.

DURING THE FIRST CENTURIES CE a group of powerful states developed to the east of China. Yamato, centred on what was to became the traditional heartland of Japan, grew to dominate the southern Japanese islands, while Korea saw the development of three states, Paekche, Silla, and Koguryo. Both areas came under the influence of Buddhism and of Chinese culture and politics during the 5th and 6th centuries. The various states of Korea would continue to be regarded by the Chinese as vassals, but Japan affirmed its independent status, maintaining an imperial court, albeit dominated by a succession of warrior lords.

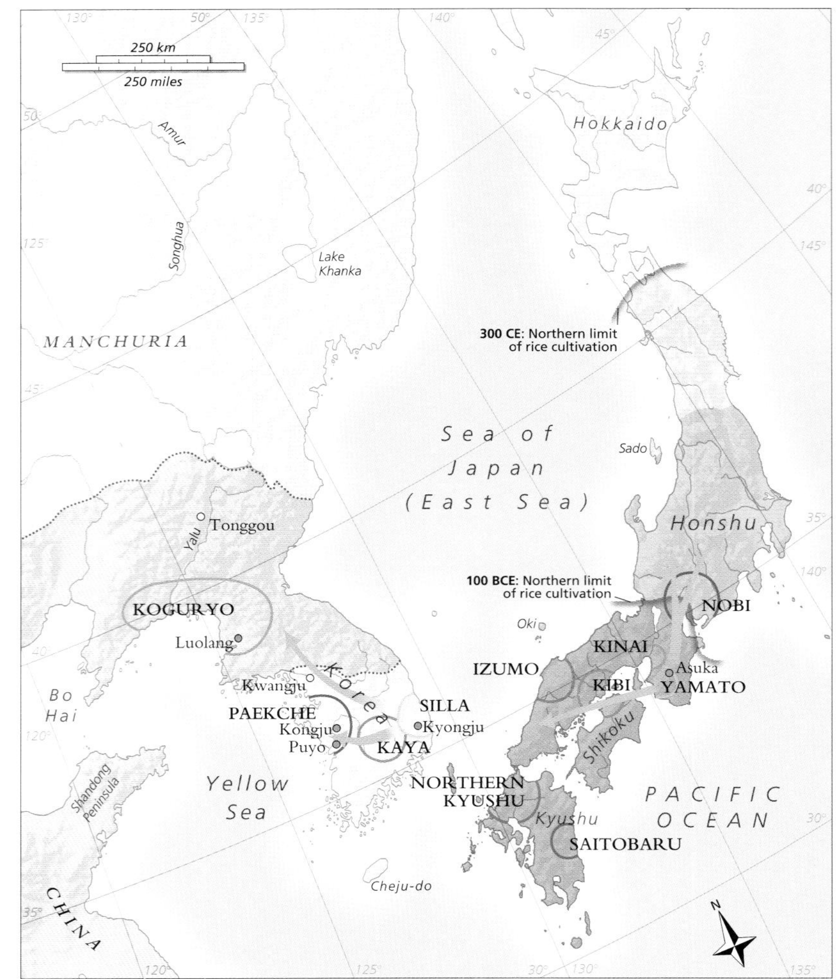

▲ **1** State formation in Korea and Japan 100 BCE–650 CE

- spread of Yayoi culture to 100 BCE
- 100 BCE–100 CE
- after 100 CE
- Han Empire c.108 BCE
- SILLA early states emerging c.100–650 CE
- expansion of Yamato state
- expansion of Silla state
- state capital

State formation in Japan and Korea

Japanese *haniwa* warrior figures, placed on tombs, reflect the martial qualities of Japan in the 5th and 6th centuries CE.

The basis for state formation in East Asia was the agricultural surplus provided by the spread of rice cultivation, associated with Yayoi culture in Japan. In southeast Japan, the Yamato state began to expand from about 500 CE, and in doing so provoked neighbouring cultures such as Kibi and Izumo, to become more politically organized in defence of their territory. In Korea, partly occupied by Han China in the 1st century BCE, the states of Koguryo, Paekche, and Silla emerged, Silla growing to dominate the peninsula by the end of the 7th century. Yamato came under increasing Chinese influence and the introduction of Buddhism in the mid-6th century began a transformation of Japanese society.

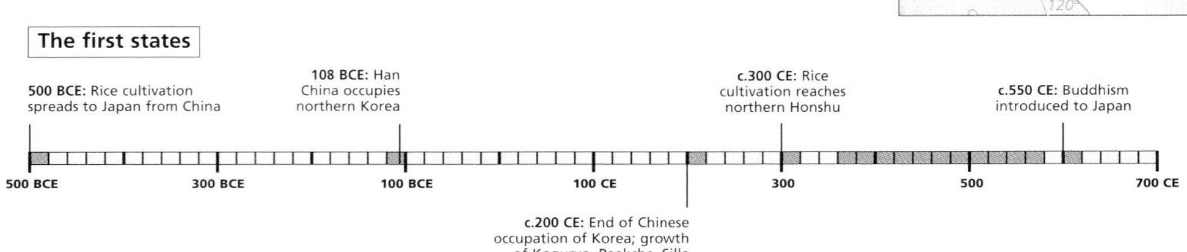

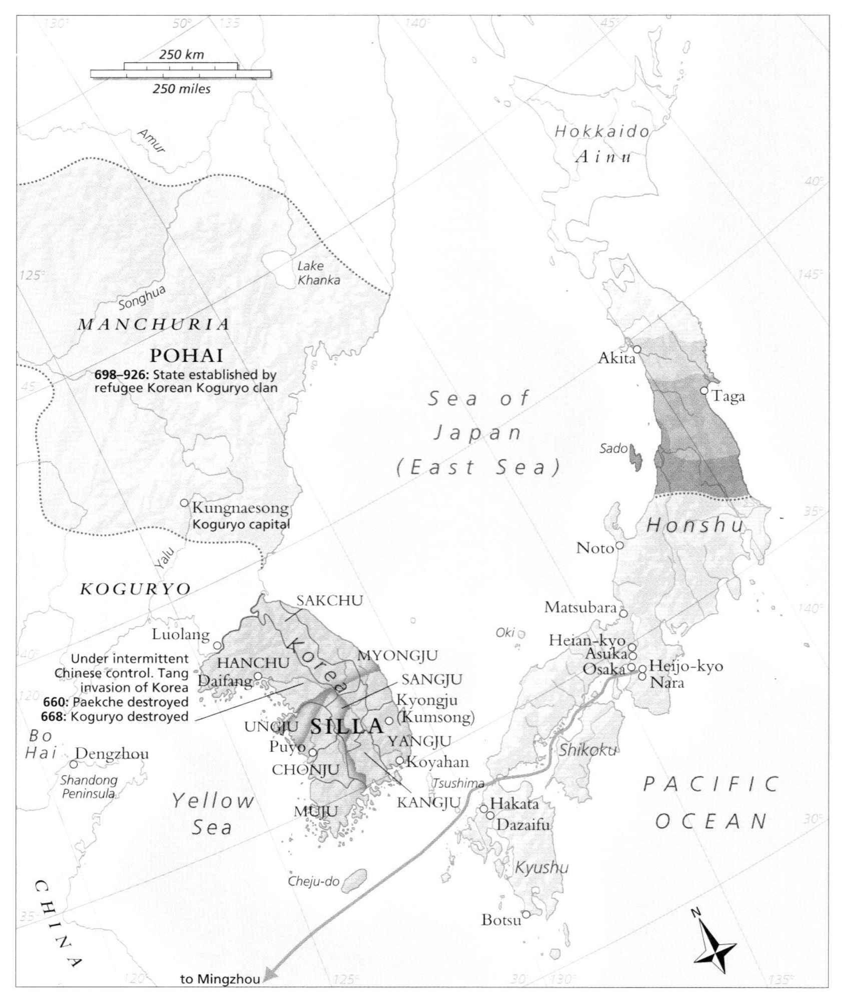

◀ **2** The first empires c.300–900 CE

- YANGJU administrative divisions of Silla
- extent of Paekche to 660
- furthest southern extent of Chinese (Han and Wei) control in Korea
- extent of Silla power 670–935
- extent of Nara state by 600
- trade route

Phases of Japanese settlement and expansion

- by mid-8th century
- by late 8th century
- by early 9th century
- by mid-9th century

The first empires c.600–900 CE

Early imperial ambitions from about 500 CE focused on the Korean peninsula. The Japanese Yamato state had exercised some influence in the south, and formed an alliance with Paekche against Silla. Tang China, which regarded all these states as effectively vassals, provided Silla with forces to overwhelm Paekche and the northern mountain state of Koguryo in the 660s. Thereafter, Japan withdrew and began to establish formal diplomatic relations with China, while the defeated Koguryo retreated north to establish an empire in Manchuria – Pohai which was similarly based on the Chinese model.

This Shinto shrine at Hakata in Kyushu is typical of traditional Japanese religion. Shinto observes the *kami*, the combined forces of nature and ancestral spirits. Shrines are often located on rocks, islands, and waterfalls, and include a *torii* or sacred gateway, significant features being linked by a straw rope, replaced each year.

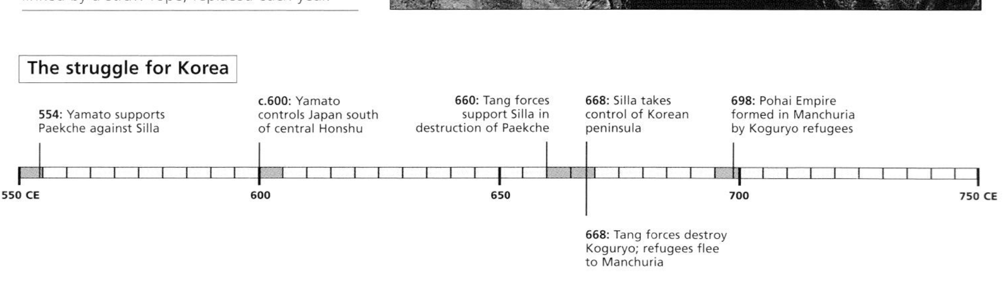

The Taika Reform and the Ritsuryo state

From the 6th century, the increasing influence of Chinese institutions and of Buddhism began to transform Japan from a clan-based society into an imperial state. Under Prince Shotoku a new imperial structure was introduced (based on Chinese criminal *(ritsu)* and civil *(ryu)* law). Provinces were linked by highways and there was a centralized tax system. New capitals were built at Fujiwara then Heijo-kyo, and Buddhism formalized as a state religion alongside traditional Shinto. By the 10th century the provincial governors, tasked with quelling regional rebellion, were also involved in internecine warfare, conflict which also drew in other groups such as the substantial armies of warrior priests maintained by Buddhist temples.

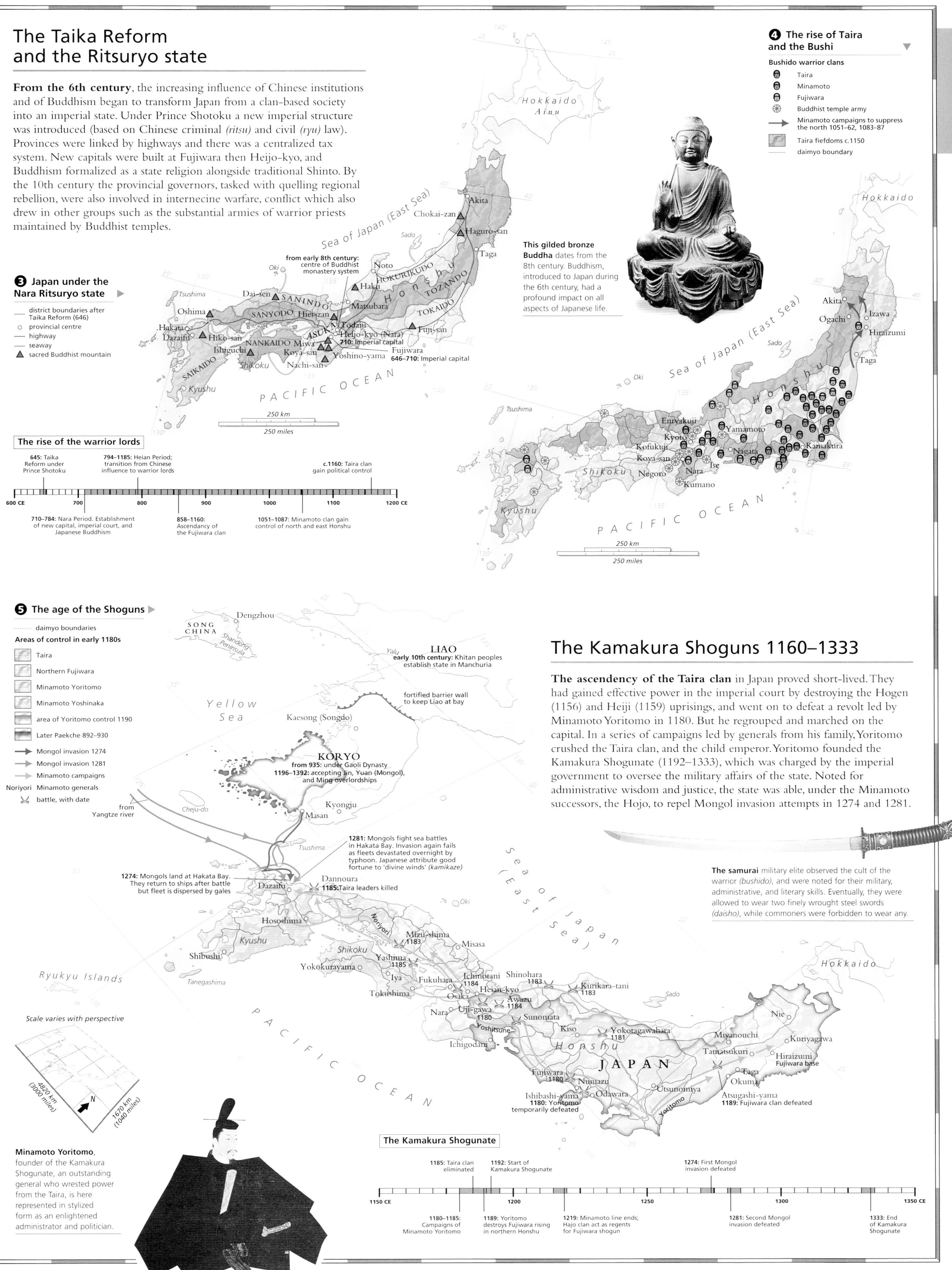

This gilded bronze Buddha dates from the 8th century. Buddhism, introduced to Japan during the 6th century, had a profound impact on all aspects of Japanese life.

The Kamakura Shoguns 1160–1333

The ascendancy of the Taira clan in Japan proved short-lived. They had gained effective power in the imperial court by destroying the Hogen (1156) and Heiji (1159) uprisings, and went on to defeat a revolt led by Minamoto Yoritomo in 1180. But he regrouped and marched on the capital. In a series of campaigns led by generals from his family, Yoritomo crushed the Taira clan, and the child emperor. Yoritomo founded the Kamakura Shogunate (1192–1333), which was charged by the imperial government to oversee the military affairs of the state. Noted for administrative wisdom and justice, the state was able, under the Minamoto successors, the Hojo, to repel Mongol invasion attempts in 1274 and 1281.

The samurai military elite observed the cult of the warrior *(bushido)*, and were noted for their military, administrative, and literary skills. Eventually, they were allowed to wear two finely wrought steel swords *(daisho)*, while commoners were forbidden to wear any.

Minamoto Yoritomo, founder of the Kamakura Shogunate, an outstanding general who wrested power from the Taira, is here represented in stylized form as an enlightened administrator and politician.

EAST ASIA AND THE MING

Zhu Yuanzhang, founder of the Ming Dynasty, ousted the Mongols to become emperor.

WITH THE ESTABLISHMENT of the Ming by Zhu Yuanzhang in 1368, China came under the unified control of a native dynasty for the first time in over 400 years. After an initial phase of expansionism and international diplomacy, most notably the missions of the great admiral Zheng He, the haughty and aristocratic Ming rulers became passive, inward-looking, and dominated by eunuch bureaucrats. Nevertheless, Ming China prospered greatly from the creation (largely by Europeans) of a global trading network, and the population boomed to some 150 million by 1600. Ming consolidation was emulated by their neighbours, with the growth of wealthy trading states across Central Asia, and the reunification of Japan under the Ashikaga Shogunate and their successors.

China under the Ming dynasty

The Great Wall had its origins in the Qin dynasty (221 BCE) but it was the Ming who, after ejecting the Mongol (Yuan) dynasty, rebuilt it and extended it in its current form.

The Ming arose from the increasing chaos which attended the decline of the Mongol Yuan dynasty. One rebel leader, Zhu Yuanzhang (or Taizu), eventually overcame his rivals and established a capital at Nanjing in 1356, and within 12 years had ousted the remaining Mongols. An initially aggressive foreign policy led to the reincorporation of the southwest and campaigns in Annam and Mongolia, but by the mid-15th century the empire became increasingly defensive and factionalized. However, the Chinese infrastructure grew under imperial patronage, and the impact of trade led to the growth of great industrial centres – including Yangzhou and Nanjing – at the mouth of the Yangtze, linked to Beijing by the Grand Canal. The unwieldy Ming bureaucracy was to prove incapable of responding swiftly to change.

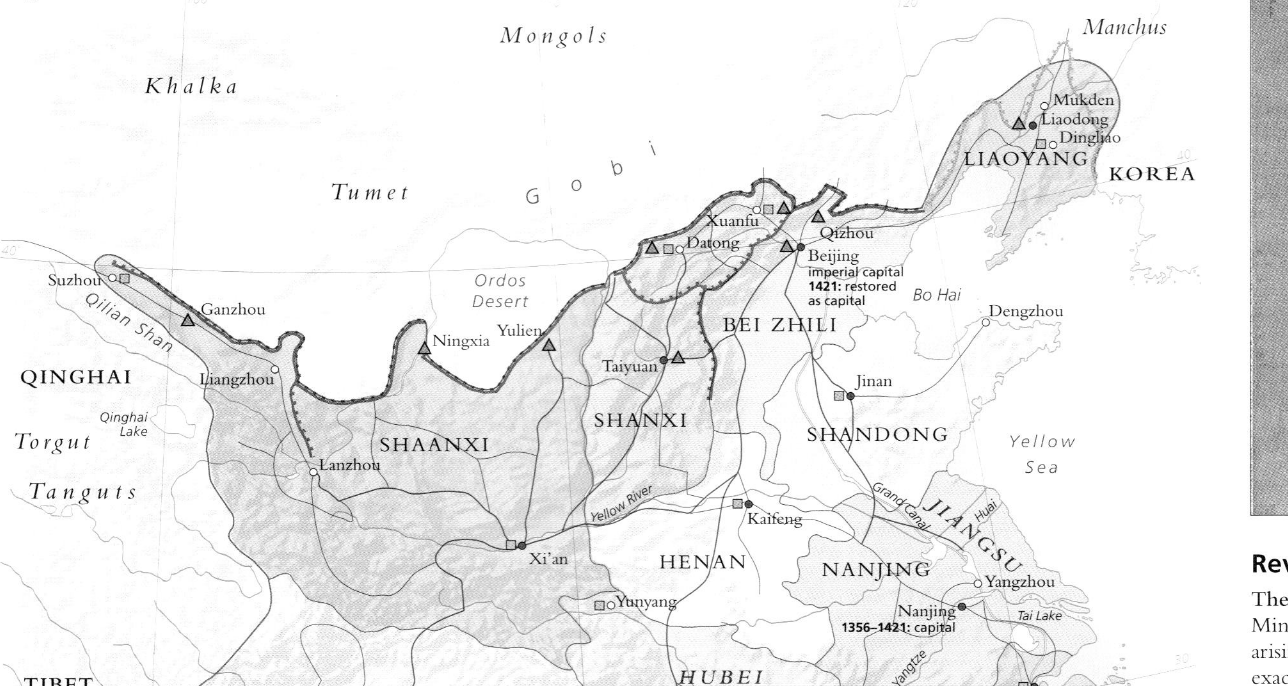

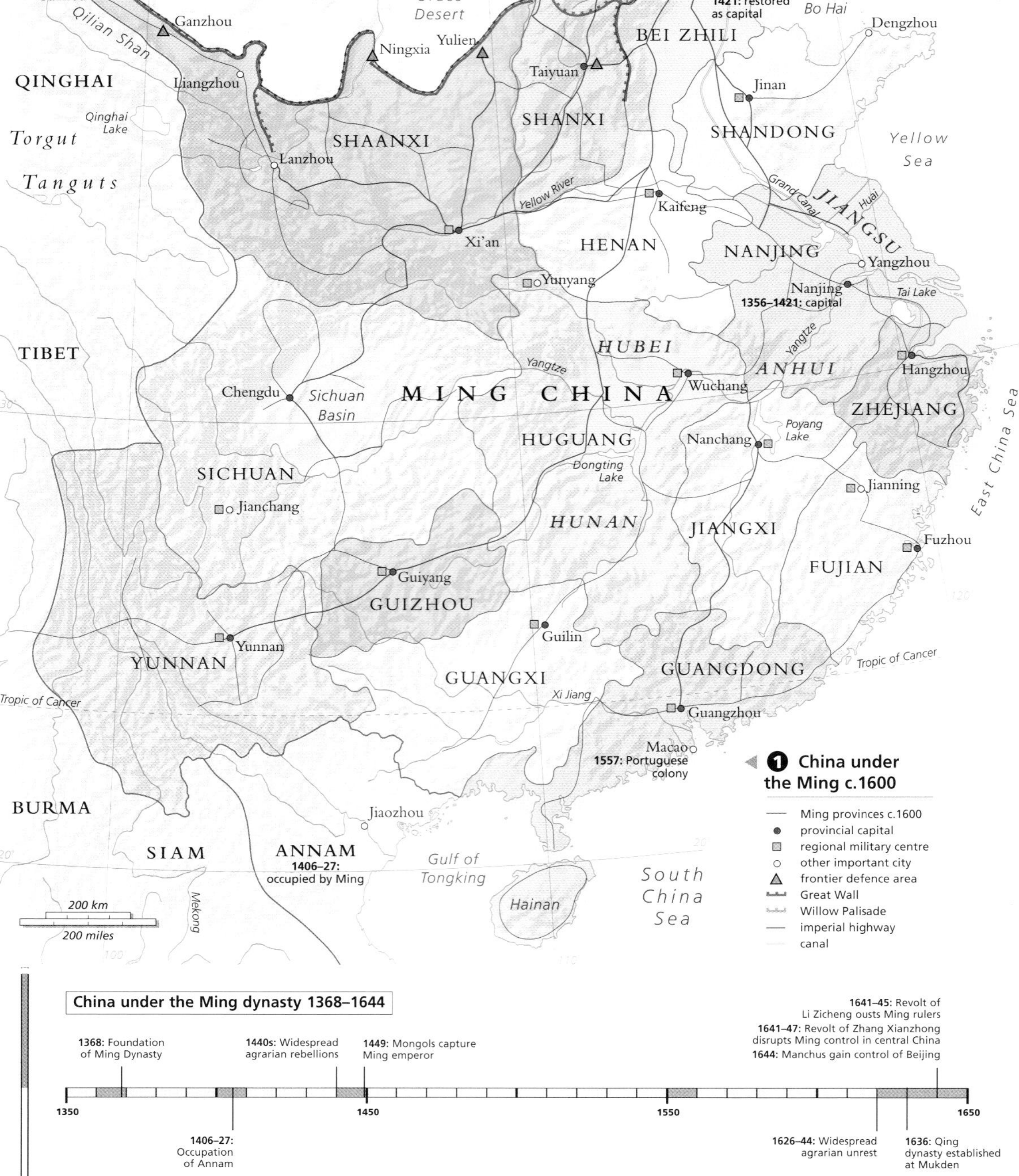

China under the Ming dynasty 1368–1644

- 1368: Foundation of Ming Dynasty
- 1406–27: Occupation of Annam
- 1440s: Widespread agrarian rebellions
- 1449: Mongols capture Ming emperor
- 1626–44: Widespread agrarian unrest
- 1636: Qing dynasty established at Mukden
- 1641–45: Revolt of Li Zicheng ousts Ming rulers
- 1641–47: Revolt of Zhang Xianzhong disrupts Ming control in central China
- 1644: Manchus gain control of Beijing

1350 · 1450 · 1550 · 1650

Under Taizu's son, Chengzu, Ming expansionism reached its apogee with the voyages of Zheng He to Southeast Asia and the Indian Ocean. Conceived on a grand scale (the fourth voyage, 1413–15, involved over 60 large vessels and 28,000 men), these missions were designed to exact tribute to the Ming court. This silk painting records a giraffe brought back from Africa on the seventh voyage (1431–33).

Revolts under the Ming

The ineffective government of the Ming was beset by internal dissent, often arising from crop failures and floods, exacerbated by resistance to taxation and the pressures of rapid urban growth and inflation. Rebellions in the 1440s led to over a million deaths, but two major revolts in the 1640s directly challenged Ming authority. When Li Zicheng's rebel forces took Beijing in 1644, the last Ming emperor committed suicide.

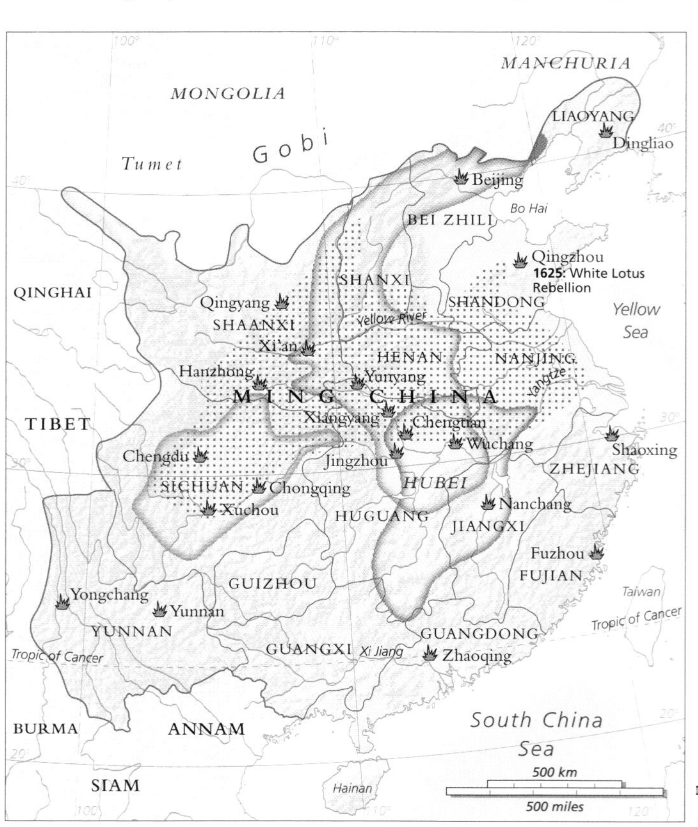

The states of Central Asia

By the mid-16th century, a range of largely Islamic states had evolved across Central Asia, thriving on control of the revitalized east-west trade that had emerged under the so-called 'Mongol Peace'. Some of these were devolved successor states to the brief era of Mongol dominance but others, such as the Uzbek Empire, were of Turkic origin. Although rulers constantly vied for territorial control, the region enjoyed an era of cultural wealth and continuity, thriving on the periphery of, and exhange between, older and more stable civilizations.

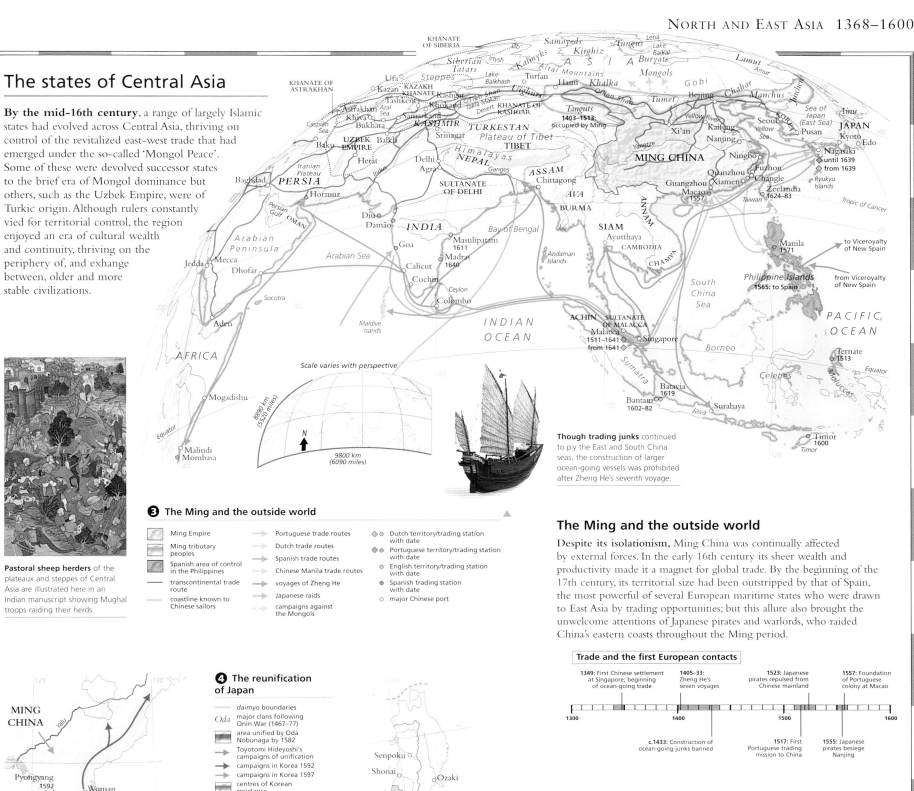

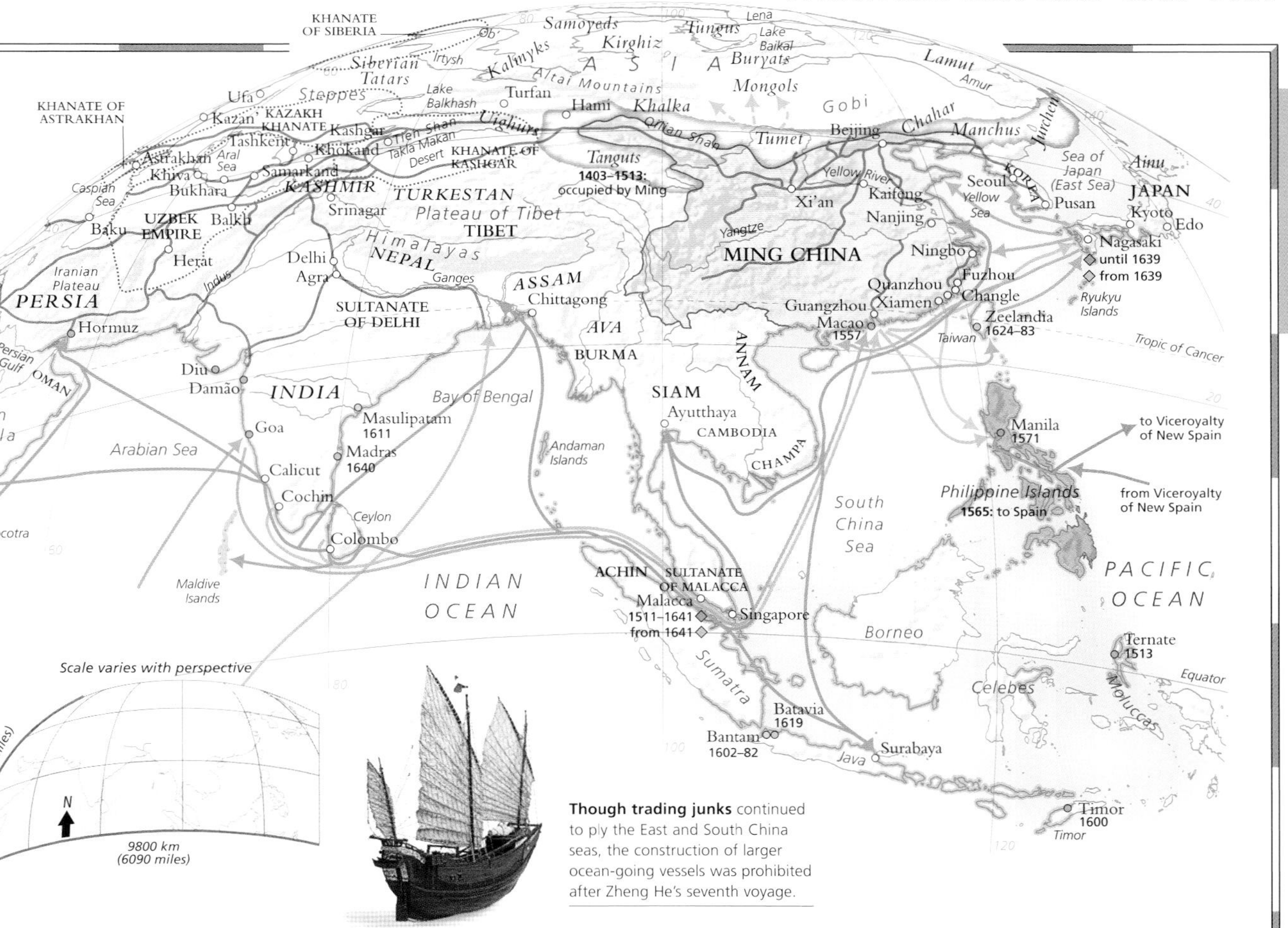

Pastoral sheep herders of the plateaux and steppes of Central Asia are illustrated here in an Indian manuscript showing Mughal troops raiding their herds.

Scale varies with perspective

8890 km (5520 miles)

9800 km (6090 miles)

Though trading junks continued to ply the East and South China seas, the construction of larger ocean-going vessels was prohibited after Zheng He's seventh voyage.

❸ The Ming and the outside world

- Ming Empire
- Ming tributary peoples
- Spanish area of control in the Philippines
- transcontinental trade route
- coastline known to Chinese sailors
- Portuguese trade routes
- Dutch trade routes
- Spanish trade routes
- Chinese Manila trade routes
- voyages of Zheng He
- Japanese raids
- campaigns against the Mongols
- Dutch territory/trading station with date
- Portuguese territory/trading station with date
- English territory/trading station with date
- Spanish trading station with date
- major Chinese port

The Ming and the outside world

Despite its isolationism, Ming China was continually affected by external forces. In the early 16th century its sheer wealth and productivity made it a magnet for global trade. By the beginning of the 17th century, its territorial size had been outstripped by that of Spain, the most powerful of several European maritime states who were drawn to East Asia by trading opportunities; but this allure also brought the unwelcome attentions of Japanese pirates and warlords, who raided China's eastern coasts throughout the Ming period.

Trade and the first European contacts

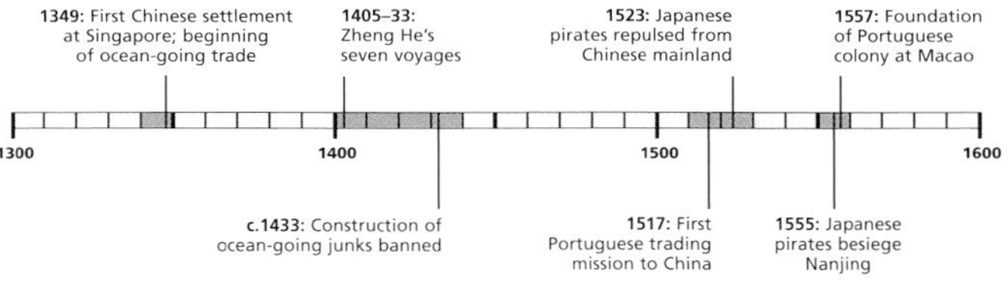

- **1349:** First Chinese settlement at Singapore; beginning of ocean-going trade
- **1405–33:** Zheng He's seven voyages
- **c.1433:** Construction of ocean-going junks banned
- **1517:** First Portuguese trading mission to China
- **1523:** Japanese pirates repulsed from Chinese mainland
- **1555:** Japanese pirates besiege Nanjing
- **1557:** Foundation of Portuguese colony at Macao

1300 1400 1500 1600

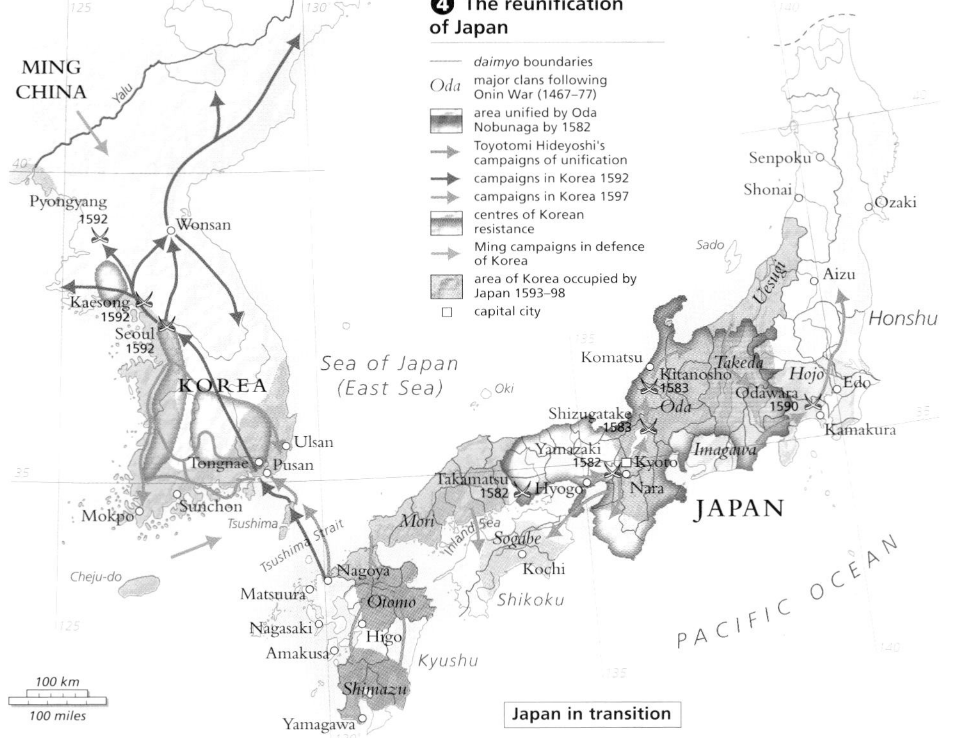

Pre-Edo Japan

The militaristic hegemony imposed by the Kamakura Shogunate and then by the Ashikaga was undermined by almost constant internecine warfare between *bushido* warlords, which culminated in the Onin War of 1467–77. This struggle for supremacy led to the emergence in the next century of two shoguns: Oda Nobunaga, who enforced national unification under a virtual dictatorship, and his successor Toyotomi Hideyoshi, whose imperial ambitions led to repeated campaigns in Korea. This period was accompanied by the first contacts with European trade and Christian missions.

Ieyasu (r.1603–05), founder of the Tokugawa Shogunate, (1603–1868), benefited from the centralizing policies of his predecessors, Oda Nobunaga and Toyotomi Hideyoshi.

Japan in transition

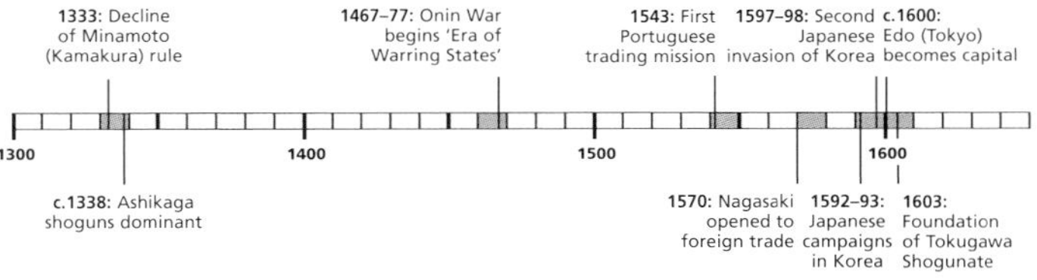

- **1333:** Decline of Minamoto (Kamakura) rule
- **c.1338:** Ashikaga shoguns dominant
- **1467–77:** Onin War begins 'Era of Warring States'
- **1543:** First Portuguese trading mission
- **1570:** Nagasaki opened to foreign trade
- **1592–93:** Japanese campaigns in Korea
- **1597–98:** Second invasion of Korea
- **c.1600:** Edo (Tokyo) becomes capital
- **1603:** Foundation of Tokugawa Shogunate

1300 1400 1500 1600

Himeji castle, Hyogo, was one of over 200 heavily fortified castles built between 1570 and 1630 to enforce imperial authority, and designed in response to the challenge of gunpowder.

The Edo period

The death of Hideyoshi in 1598 ignited a brief power struggle which was settled at the battle of Sekigahara (1600) by the victory of Tokugawa Ieyasu. Under the Tokugawa the imperial capital was established at Edo (Tokyo), European missions were violently suppressed, and Japan entered a 250-year period of isolationism.

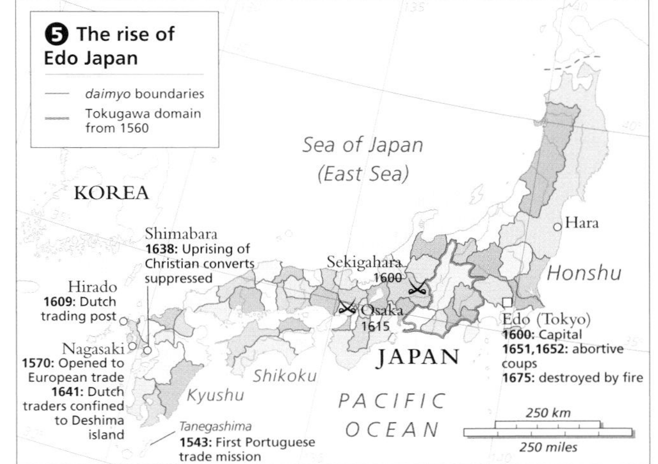

THE ERA OF THE QING EMPIRE

Qing China produced porcelain, jade, intaglio, carpets, and silk goods specifically for Western markets.

THE MANCHUS had already built a state along Chinese lines in southern Manchuria, based at Mukden, and were poised to take advantage of the Ming collapse in 1644. They swiftly suppressed the rebels and by the end of the 17th century had reduced Ming resistance in the south. The 18th century was a stable period of expansion and prosperity, as the Manchu, or Qing dynasty, adopted Chinese ways. Successive campaigns established an enormous empire and an array of tributary states, while regional uprisings were ruthlessly crushed. But by the 19th century the pressures of European imperial expansion and internal dissent on an unprecedented scale brought regression, isolationism, resistance to reform, and political decay.

The Manchu rulers of the Qing Dynasty rapidly adopted the courtly manners, customs, and aristocratic aloofness of their Ming forebears. Here Kangxi (r.1662–1722) is portrayed in formal imperial splendour.

China under the Qing

The military expansion of the Qing Empire continued throughout the 17th and 18th centuries, provoked in part by the threat of Russian, British, and French moves into Asia. Only part of the vast Qing realms were directly governed by the Manchus or settled by the Chinese, but were secured through military garrisons. The cost of this expansion was huge, and was funded by trade, largely paid for in bullion. In the 19th century, as the Qing economy faltered under pressure from European manipulation, so did the Manchu ability to administer their domains.

The expansion of Qing China

1600 — 1700 — 1800

- **1636:** Manchus establish Qing imperial rule at Mukden
- **1644:** Qing forces enter Beijing
- **1683:** Conquest of Taiwan
- **1689:** Treaty of Nerchinsk; acquisition of Amur and Ussuri regions from Russia
- **1696–97:** Suppression of Mongolia
- **1720:** Formal control of Xinjiang established
- **1751:** Invasion of Tibet
- **1758–59:** Campaigns against Kalmyks
- **1765–69:** Attempted invasion of Burma; establishment of suzerainty
- **1788:** Attempted invasion of Annam
- **1792:** Invasion of Nepal

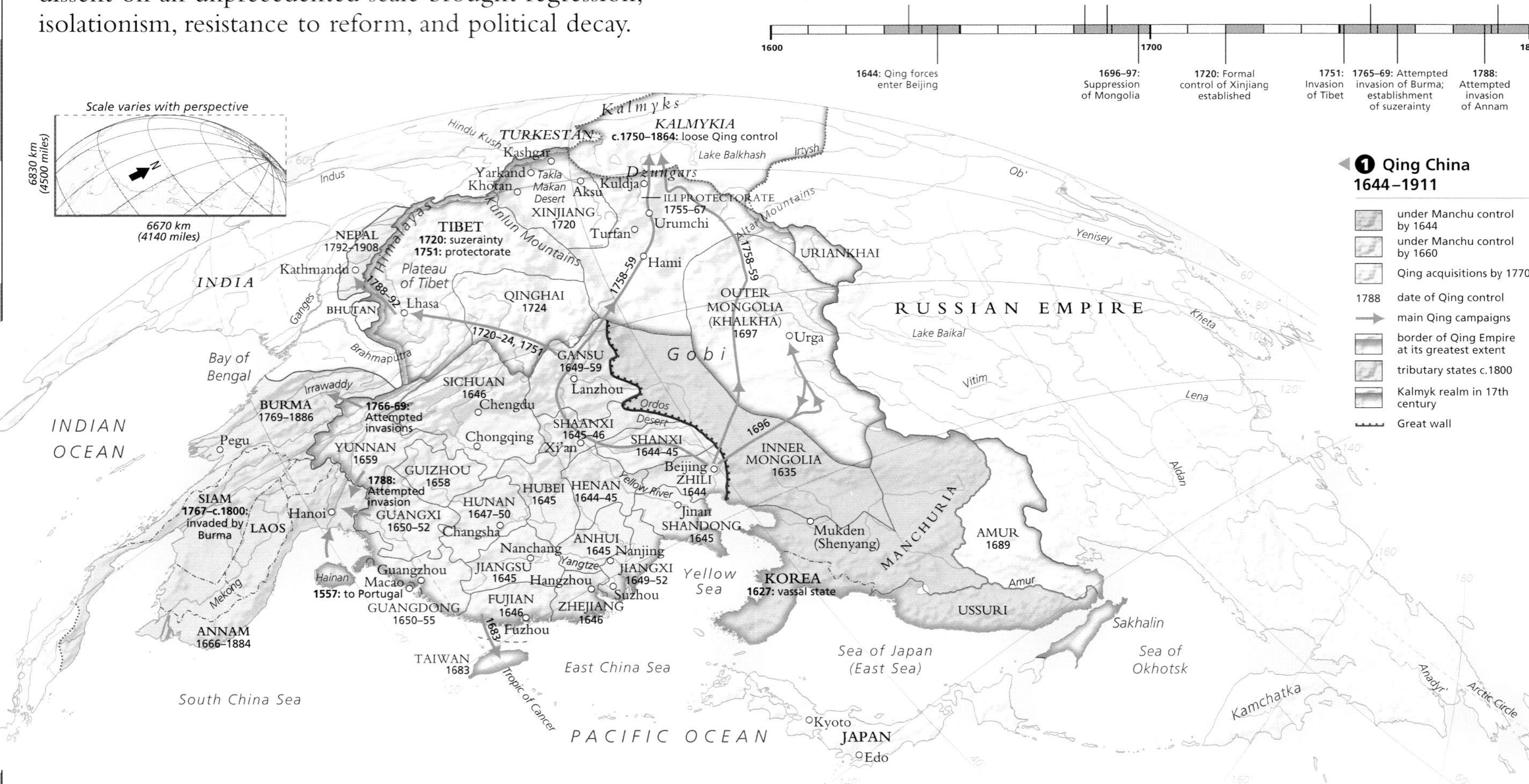

The decline of the Qing

The Manchus successfully suppressed a major rebellion by Ming supporters in southern China, largely by reduction and coercion, early in their reign. Subsequent revolts took a variety of forms: tribal uprisings, Muslim *jihads,* and millenarian sects. In most instances these were provoked by population pressures and economic distress. The great Taiping and Nian peasant rebellions in the mid-19th century left some 25 million dead and although they vitally threatened Qing stability they were ultimately unsuccessful. The former, led by a Christian visionary, invoked tacit support among the hawkish European powers. In contrast, the populist Boxer rebellion was explicitly anti-European and enjoyed covert support from the Qing rulers.

The Taiping rebellion began in southern China in 1850; by 1853 the rebel armies had moved north to establish a base at Nanjing *(above).* From here they courted foreign powers based at Shanghai, to threaten the Qing in Beijing.

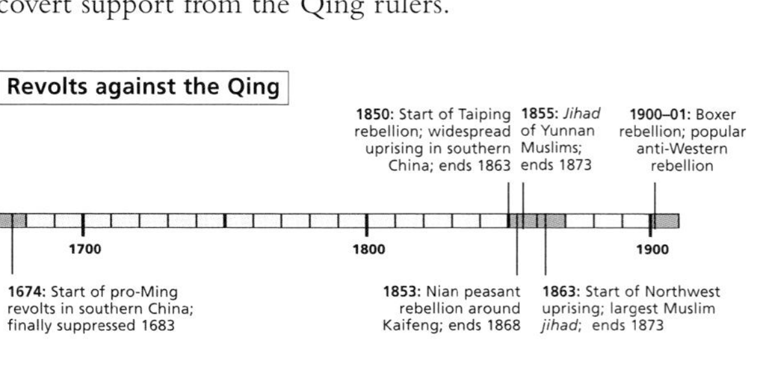

Revolts against the Qing

1700 — 1800 — 1900

- **1674:** Start of pro-Ming revolts in southern China; finally suppressed 1683
- **1850:** Start of Taiping rebellion; widespread uprising in southern China; ends 1863
- **1853:** Nian peasant rebellion around Kaifeng; ends 1868
- **1855:** *Jihad* of Yunnan Muslims; ends 1873
- **1863:** Start of Northwest uprising; largest Muslim *jihad;* ends 1873
- **1900–01:** Boxer rebellion; popular anti-Western rebellion

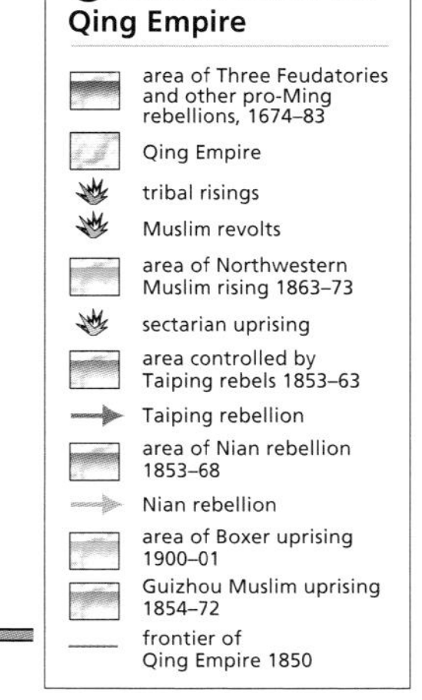

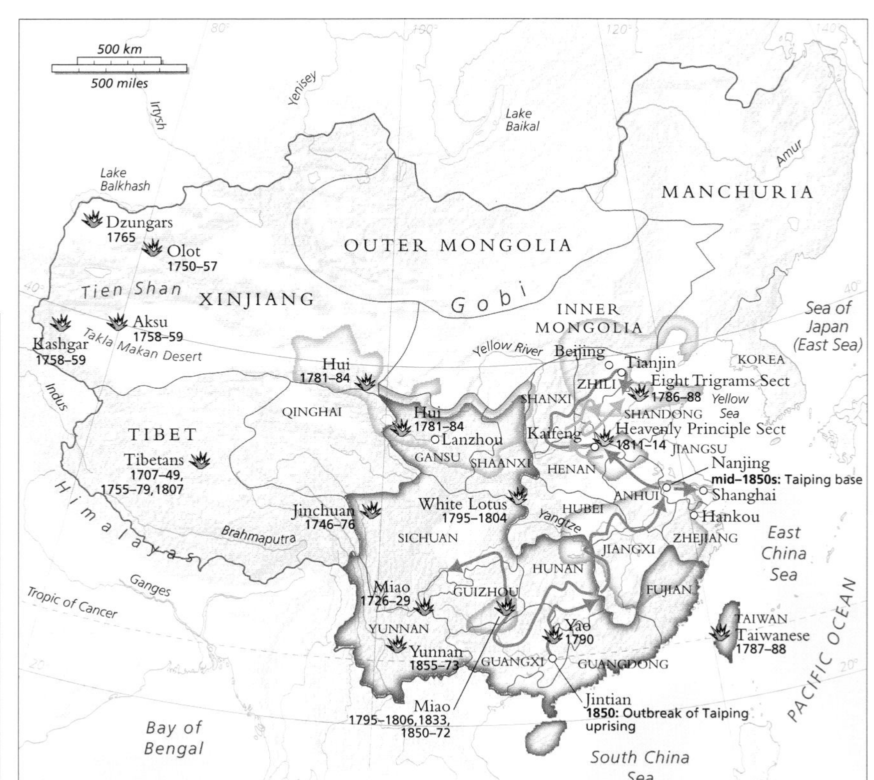

Russian expansion in North Asia 1600–1914

The Russian march across Siberia, in the wake of fur trappers, involved physical hardship but provoked little resistance from native peoples. The expansion to the south and east was more hard fought, against the Kazakhs and Turkic peoples of Central Asia, but western military techniques prevailed. Further east, the conquest of the Amur and Ussuri regions from Qing China gave Russia access to the Pacific. With the abolition of serfdom in 1861, a wave of Russian migrants swept east. Russian progress resulted in an Anglo-Japanese alliance (1902), and was only finally halted by the Russo-Japanese War of 1904–05 *(see page 270)*.

The Trans-Siberian Railway, covering 7360 km between Moscow and Vladivostok, was designed to bind Russia's Asian provinces together and to reinforce its presence in the Pacific.

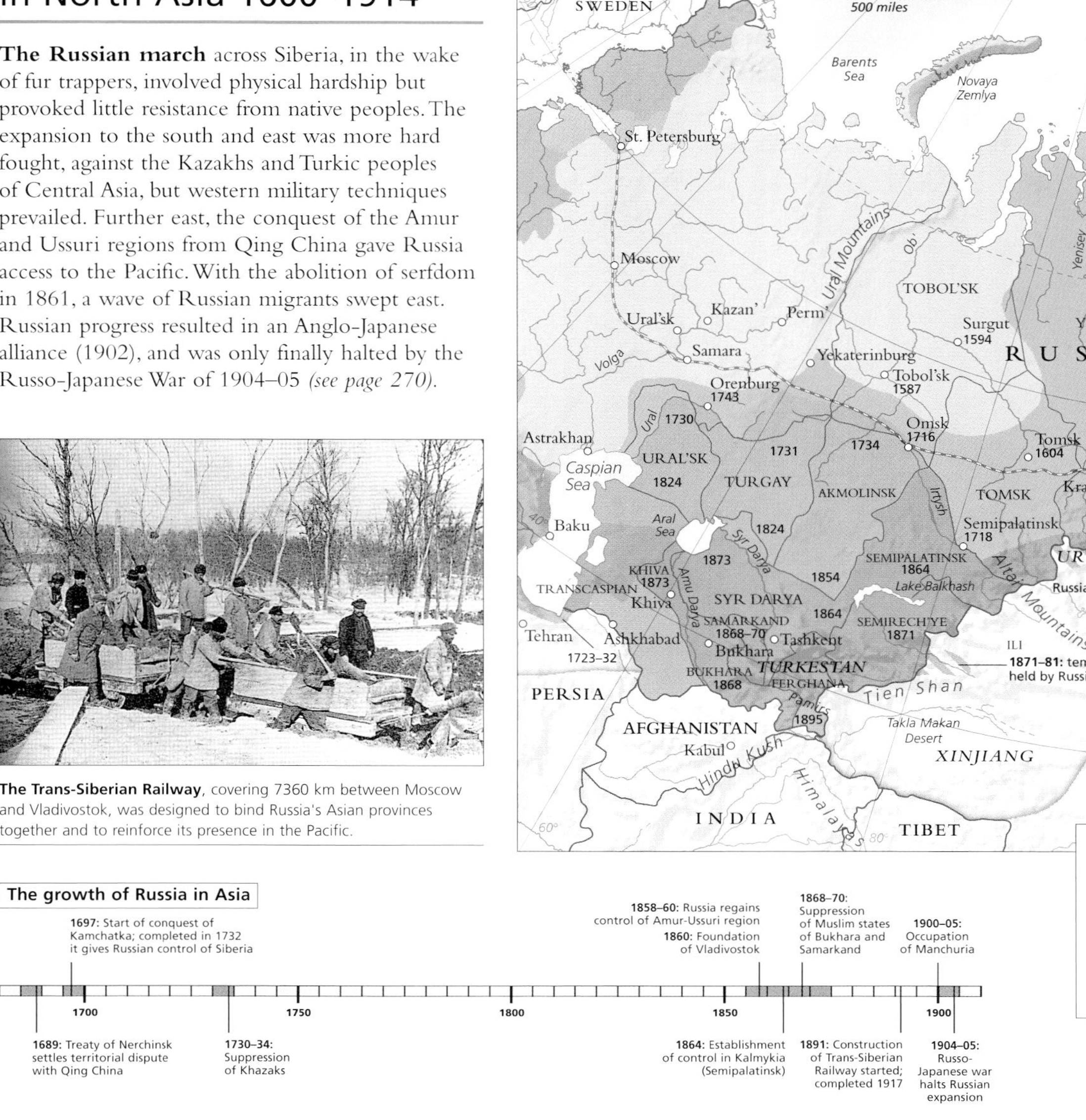

3 Russian expansion in Asia 1600–1914

- Russian Empire c.1600
- acquisitions 1600–1725
- acquisitions 1726–1855
- acquisitions 1856–76
- acquisitions 1877–1914
- temporary acquisition, with dates
- Russian sphere of influence, 1914
- 1788 date of foundation or acquisition
- Trans-Siberian Railway, built 1891–1917
- borders 1914

The growth of Russia in Asia

- **1689:** Treaty of Nerchinsk settles territorial dispute with Qing China
- **1697:** Start of conquest of Kamchatka; completed in 1732 it gives Russian control of Siberia
- **1730–34:** Suppression of Khazaks
- **1858–60:** Russia regains control of Amur-Ussuri region
- **1860:** Foundation of Vladivostok
- **1864:** Establishment of control in Kalmykia (Semipalatinsk)
- **1868–70:** Suppression of Muslim states of Bukhara and Samarkand
- **1891:** Construction of Trans-Siberian Railway started; completed 1917
- **1900–05:** Occupation of Manchuria
- **1904–05:** Russo-Japanese war halts Russian expansion

1700 | 1750 | 1800 | 1850 | 1900

Foreign imperialism in East Asia

The rapidly expanded Qing economy of the 18th century made it prey to foreign ambitions. The dynasty's failure to halt the highly profitable illegal British trade in opium in 1839–42 revealed its weaknesses. Hong Kong was the first of many territorial and trading concessions which gave not only the Europeans but the Russians and Japanese valuable toeholds in the Middle Kingdom. Qing complacency, resistance to modernization, and their inability to counter growing internal dissent played into their adversaries' hands. By the end of the 19th century, despite belated attempts to reform, the Qing were a power in name only.

Foreign incursions into China

- **1840–42:** Opium War; British attacks force trading concessions
- **1841:** Foundation of British colony at Hong Kong
- **1858–60:** Loss of Amur-Ussuri region to Russia
- **1860:** Anglo-French forces occupy Beijing forcing further cessions
- **1898–1905:** Port Arthur leased to Russia
- **1900–05:** Russian occupation of Manchuria
- **1904–05:** Russo-Japanese war; Russian occupied territories taken over by Japan

1840 | 1850 | 1860 | 1870 | 1880 | 1890 | 1900

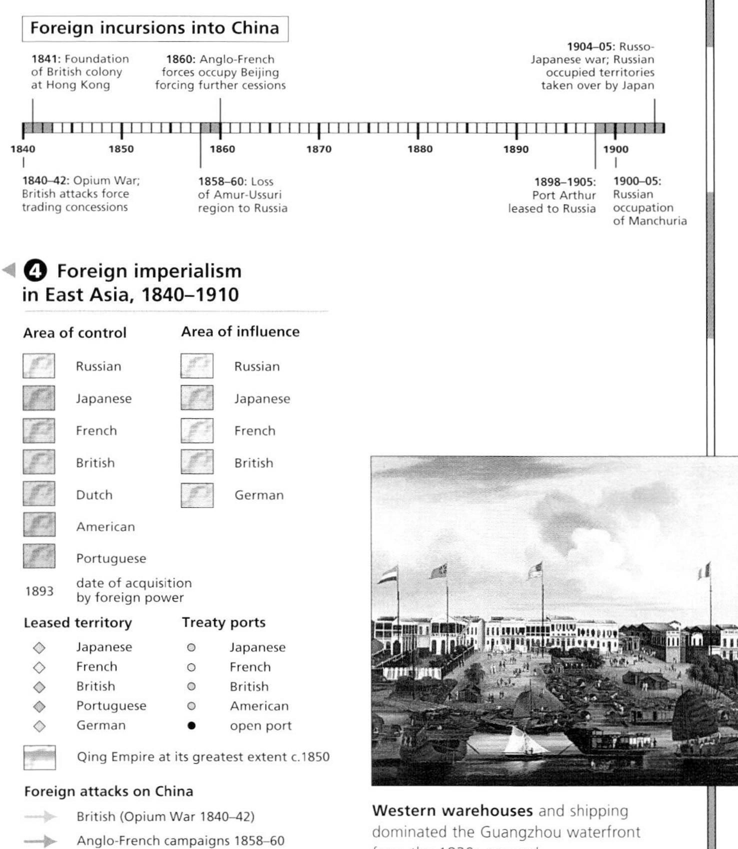

4 Foreign imperialism in East Asia, 1840–1910

Area of control: Russian; Japanese; French; British; Dutch; American; Portuguese

Area of influence: Russian; Japanese; French; British; German

1893 date of acquisition by foreign power

Leased territory: Japanese; French; British; Portuguese; German

Treaty ports: Japanese; French; British; American; open port

Qing Empire at its greatest extent c.1850

Foreign attacks on China:
- British (Opium War 1840–42)
- Anglo-French campaigns 1858–60
- French 1883–85

Western warehouses and shipping dominated the Guangzhou waterfront from the 1830s onward.

THE MODERNIZATION OF EAST ASIA

Jiang Jieshi (Chiang Kai-shek) assumed control of the Chinese Nationalist Party in 1925.

BOTH JAPAN AND CHINA entered the 19th century under feudal, courtly, isolationist, and reactionary regimes which had held power since the 17th century. By 1900 their development stood in stark contrast. Japan under the Tokugawa Shogunate was a prosperous, sophisticated society, socially developed, universally literate, and ready for modernization. When this came – through international trade pressure – Japan adopted the role of a progressive industrialized state, keen to dominate East Asian affairs. It was aided by the Qing dynasty's rejection of external pressures and internal demands for reform in China. The end of the Qing dynasty coincided with Japanese territorial aspirations, widespread factionalism among reforming groups in China itself, and the rise of Communism in its largest neighbour, Russia.

The modernization of Japan

1854: First foreign trade treaties

1868–69: Boshin War; Tokugawa Bakufu defeated by modernizing imperialists

1877: Satsuma rebellion, led by reformer Saigo Takamori, in defence of traditional values

1889: New constitution balances imperial authority with parliamentary government

1894–95: Sino-Japanese War; increases sphere of influence on mainland

1904–05: Russo-Japanese War consolidates influence in Korea and Manchuria

1918: Japan occupies areas of Russia during civil war

1919: League of Nations accords German Pacific territories under mandate to Japan

1840 1860 1880 1900 1920

Visitors to Japan were confined to Nagasaki for almost 400 years. In 1853, when Commodore Perry took warships into Tokyo Bay to enforce US trading treaties with Japan, the confrontation between Japan and the West reached crisis point.

Japanese modernization 1868–1919

When US Commodore Perry's fleet entered Tokyo Bay in 1853 to demand international trading rights with Japan, the 200-year policy of isolationism under the Tokugawa Shogunate (Bakufu) effectively ended. Reformist forces based in the south conducted a campaign (the Boshin War 1868–69) which restored the Meiji ('enlightened rule') emperor, and inaugurated political, social, and economic reform. The nation was divided into prefectures, and a centralized bureaucracy introduced a new constitution, the construction of a railway system, and the creation of modern industries, such as shipbuilding.

1 Japanese modernization 1868–1918

Boshin War 1868–69
- imperial (anti-Bakufu) alliance
- route of imperial army
- battle, with date

Modernization under the Meiji
- KOCHI prefectures established 1871
- main industrial areas by 1918
- railways built 1868–1918

Traditional industries
- ceramics
- textiles
- silk

Industries developed after 1868
- manufacturing
- machine-building
- shipbuilding
- chemicals
- city of over 500,000 in 1918
- city of over 100,000 in 1918
- other major city

Goryokaku 27 Jun 1869
Oct 1868–May 1869: besieged by imperial forces
1864,1865: Bakufu forces repulsed
1853: US Commodore Perry forces trade agreements
Jan 1868: renamed Tokyo
Fushimi 27 Jan 1868

Japanese expansion 1868–1936

The entry of Japan onto the world's stage in 1868 was accompanied by an active policy of territorial expansion to support its rapidly expanding economy. Supported by the US (its principal trading partner by 1918), Japan claimed neighbouring islands and gained territory as a result of wars against China (1894–95) and Russia (1904–05) – leading to the annexation of Formosa and Korea. Japan's firm commitment to the Allies during the First World War (1914–18) gave her lands in the Pacific, and she rapidly gained other substantial footholds on mainland Asia.

After the Meiji revolution Japanese transport modernized rapidly; steamships, railways, and automobiles were introduced.

3 The Sino-Japanese War 1894–95

- Japanese victory
- area leased to Japan 1895

The Sino-Japanese War 1894–95

Upon the outbreak of a populist, quasi-religious nationalist rebellion, the Tonghak Revolt (1894), the Korean court appealed to both Qing China and Japan for support. The Japanese forces compromised the Korean royal family, and open conflict with China erupted; the modern equipment and tactics employed by the Japanese forced Qing forces back to the Liaodong Peninsula, which with Taiwan was ceded to the victors, and Korea entered the Japanese sphere of influence.

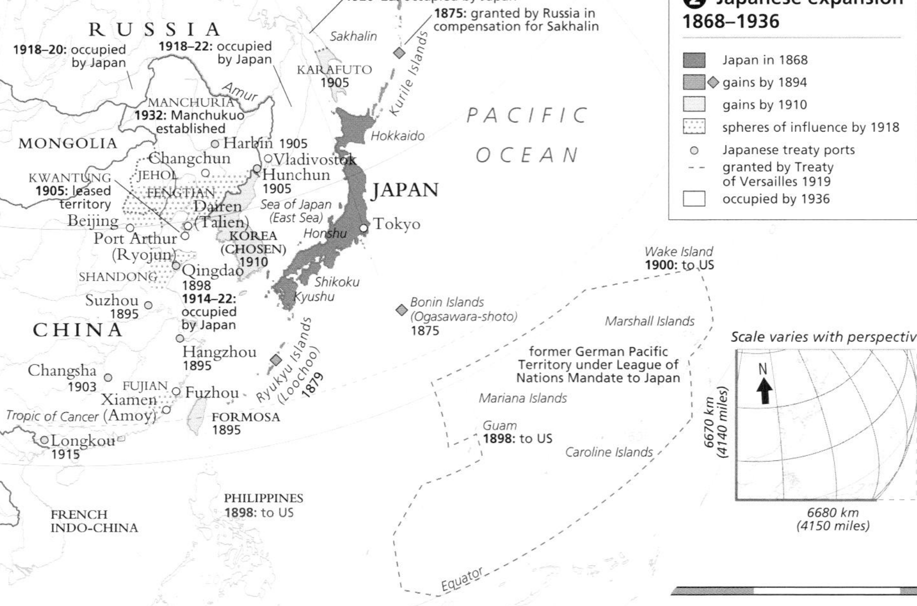

2 Japanese expansion 1868–1936

- Japan in 1868
- gains by 1894
- gains by 1910
- spheres of influence by 1918
- Japanese treaty ports
- granted by Treaty of Versailles 1919
- occupied by 1936

The Russo-Japanese War 1904–05

Territorial rivalry and mutual animosity between Russia and Japan, already overheated by Russia's adventurist occupation of Manchuria in 1897, came to a head when Japanese vessels bombarded Russian ships at Port Arthur in 1904. The Japanese moved rapidly to secure a series of successes in southern Manchuria, exploiting their effective control of Korea, and victory was sealed when the Russian Baltic Fleet was savaged by Japanese ships in the Tsushima Strait (1905).

National victories against China and Russia in the 1890s were celebrated in a dynamic manner by Japanese artists whose style influenced the development of 20th-century graphic art.

4 The Russo-Japanese War 1904–05

- Qing China
- to Russia 1897, to Japan 1905
- area leased to Japan 1895
- Japanese advances 1904–05
- route of Russian Baltic fleet
- Japanese victory, with date

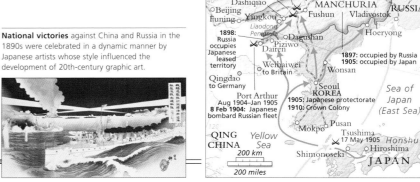

Mukden 1–10 Mar 1905
Liaoyang Aug–Sep 1904
1898: Russia occupies Japanese leased territory
1897: occupied by Russia 1905: occupied by Japan
Port Arthur Aug 1904–Jan 1905
8 Feb 1904: Japanese bombard Russian fleet
1905: Japanese protectorate 1910: Crown Colony
Weihaiwei to Britain
Qingdao to Germany
Tsushima 17 May 1905

The Chinese Revolution of 1911

After a century of almost continual internal dissent, and some ten attempted revolutions since 1890, the Qing dynasty finally recognized the need for reform in 1911. An almost spontaneous eruption of revolt across China (orchestrated by telegraph) led within five months to the abdication of the boy emperor in favour of a reformist Qing general, Yuan Shikai. Meanwhile, the leader of the Nationalist uprising, Sun Zhongshan, proclaimed a republican constitution in Nanjing. The fragile situation, with Yuan rapidly adopting dictatorial measures, began to collapse into bitter regional strife.

The Dowager Empress Cixi was photographed in regal splendour as the Qing dynasty drew to its close. Her regency between 1861 and 1908 represented the last bastion of Qing conservatism in the face of reform and modernization.

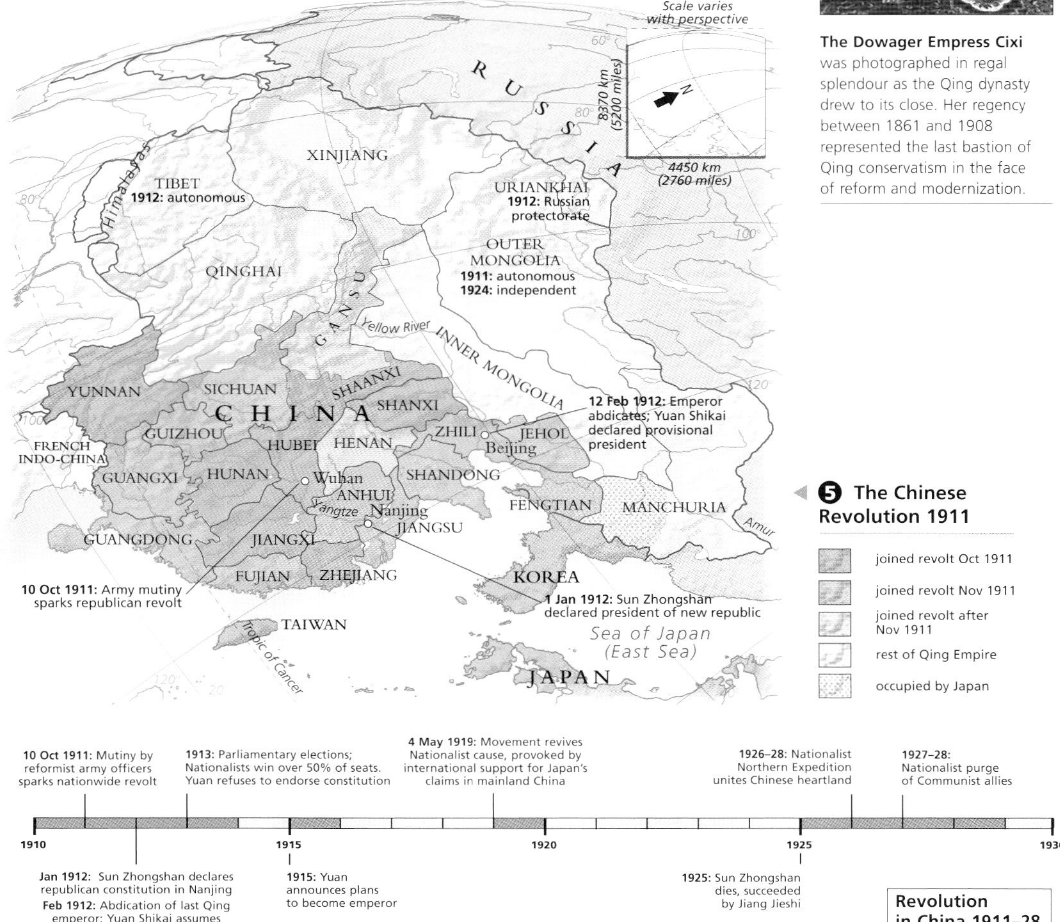

5 The Chinese Revolution 1911

- joined revolt Oct 1911
- joined revolt Nov 1911
- joined revolt after Nov 1911
- rest of Qing Empire
- occupied by Japan

Revolution in China 1911–28

1910 · 1915 · 1920 · 1925 · 1930

- **10 Oct 1911:** Mutiny by reformist army officers sparks nationwide revolt
- **Jan 1912:** Sun Zhongshan declares republican constitution in Nanjing
- **Feb 1912:** Abdication of last Qing emperor; Yuan Shikai assumes power as president
- **1913:** Parliamentary elections; Nationalists win over 50% of seats. Yuan refuses to endorse constitution
- **1915:** Yuan announces plans to become emperor
- **4 May 1919:** Movement revives Nationalist cause, provoked by international support for Japan's claims in mainland China
- **1925:** Sun Zhongshan dies, succeeded by Jiang Jieshi
- **1926–28:** Nationalist Northern Expedition unites Chinese heartland
- **1927–28:** Nationalist purge of Communist allies

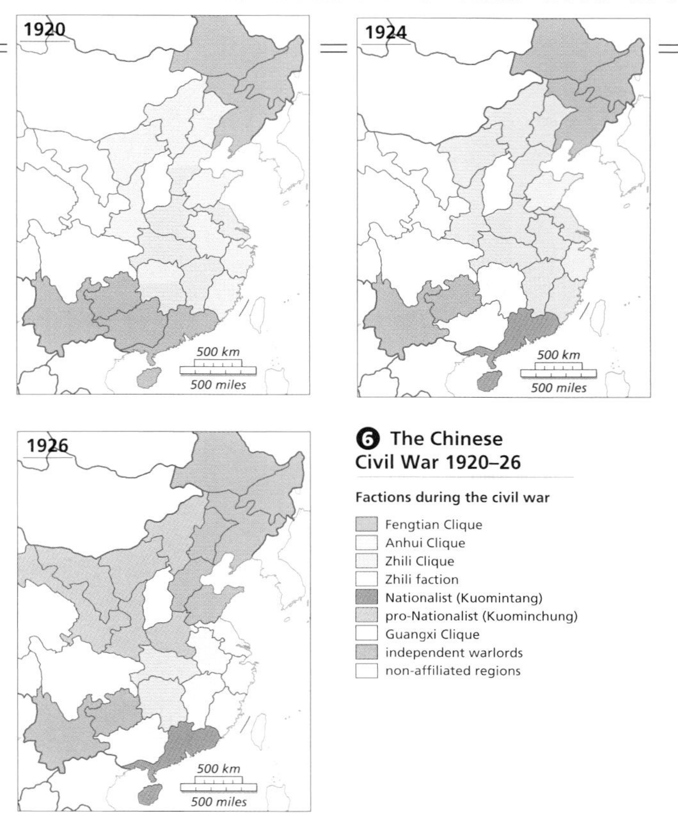

6 The Chinese Civil War 1920–26

Factions during the civil war

- Fengtian Clique
- Anhui Clique
- Zhili Clique
- Zhili faction
- Nationalist (Kuomintang)
- pro-Nationalist (Kuominchung)
- Guangxi Clique
- independent warlords
- non-affiliated regions

The Chinese Civil War 1920–26

Following the death of Yuan Shikai in 1916, the Chinese republic faltered. The nation fragmented further into regional power groups, often dominated by local warlords. Over the next 12 years a constantly shifting pattern of factionalism and alliance dominated the map of China. The 4 May Movement of 1919 in Shanghai provoked an upsurge of nationalist fervour, in the wake of which the Chinese Communist Party was formed (1921); Sun Zhongshan's Nationalists (Kuomintang) formed an alliance with the Communists, and began a campaign of unification which culminated in the Northern Expedition of 1926–28. This was led by Sun's successor, Moscow-trained Jiang Jieshi (Chiang Kai-shek), who then inaugurated a bloody purge of the Communists.

Bolshevik 'Agitation-Instruction' trains decorated with revolutionary themes travelled to every corner of the USSR to spread the gospel of Communism.

The Red Flag over Asia

In the wake of the Civil War (1918–21), the Russian Bolsheviks moved swiftly to consolidate their control of Asian areas of Russia. They harnessed technology and modernism with propaganda techniques to achieve the socialist revolution. Communist republics had been set up in the Far East, at Tannu-Tuva, and in Central Asia. These were gradually coerced into merging with the Soviet Union, while military support was provided to oust Chinese troops from Mongolia. The active export of Bolshevik Communism (Comintern) continued in various forms, notably in China and India.

7 Nationalist China

- under direct control of Nationalist government at Nanjing 1928
- Nanjing control 1929–34
- Nanjing control 1935–37
- Japanese sphere of influence by 1935
- route of Northern Expedition
- pro-Nationalist forces

The spread of Communism in Asia

1915 · 1920 · 1925 · 1930

- **1917:** Bolshevik revolution in Russia
- **1918–22:** Civil war and foreign intervention in Russia
- **4 May 1919:** Movement in China, resurgence of Nationalism
- **1919:** Third International (Comintern); Bolsheviks commit to international revolution
- **1921:** Chinese Communist Party founded
- **1924:** Death of Lenin
- **1925:** Asiatic borders of USSR consolidated
- **1926:** Jiang Jieshi leads Nationalist campaign to unify China
- **1927–28:** Chinese Nationalists purge Communists

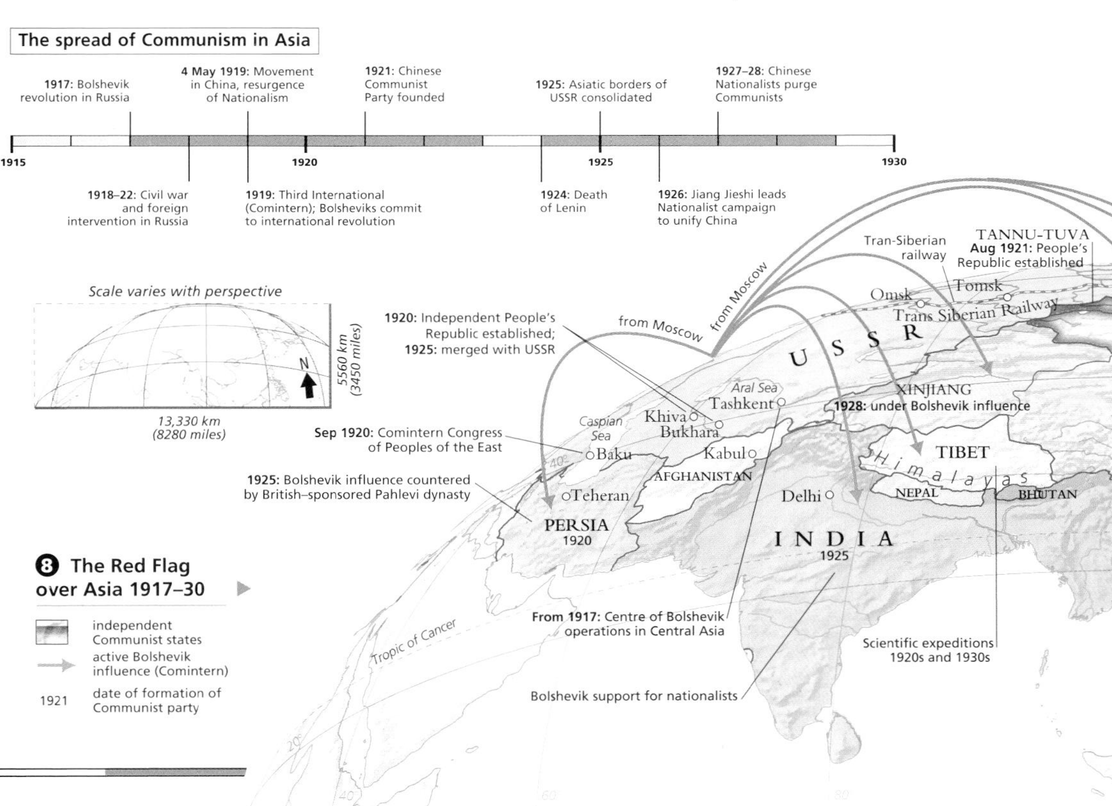
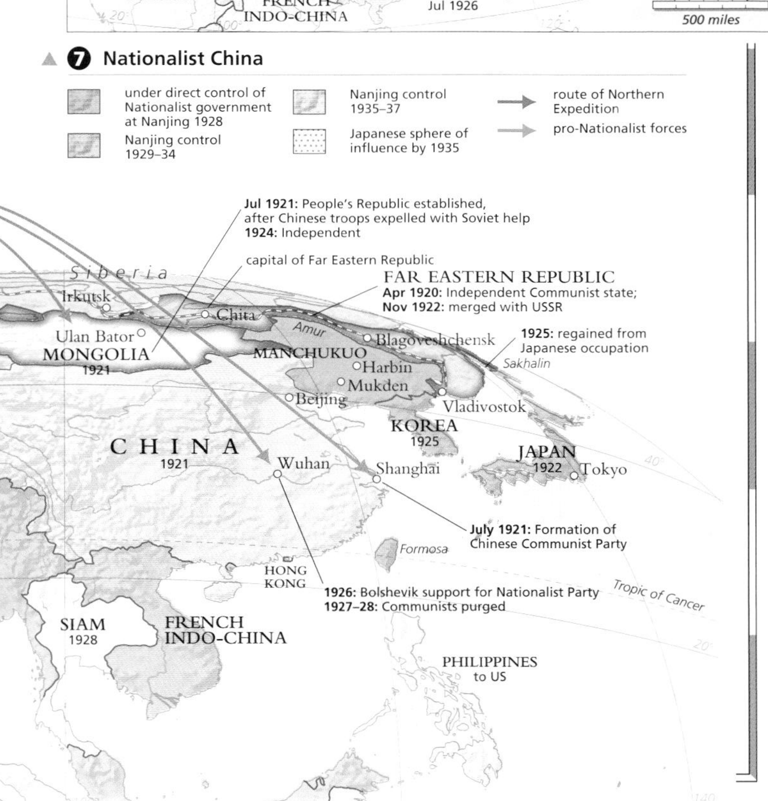

8 The Red Flag over Asia 1917–30

- independent Communist states
- active Bolshevik influence (Comintern)
- 1921 date of formation of Communist party

THE WAR IN THE PACIFIC

Japanese expansionism in Manchuria and Jehol accelerated in 1937 with a full-scale invasion of China.

FOLLOWING THE FIRST WORLD WAR, Japan was accorded an extended sphere of territorial control in the Pacific. The Chinese civil war enabled Japan to extend its territorial ambitions on the East Asian mainland, culminating in outright warfare in China by 1937. But international sanctions, designed to limit Japan's aspirations resulted, by 1940, in a political stand-off. Next year, Japan went to war, calculating its chances on the basis of its rapid industrial development, the colonial powers' involvement in Hitler's war in Europe, and the bounty which would accrue from the establishment of an anti-Western 'Greater East Asia Co-Prosperity Sphere'. By June 1942 Japan was trying to maintain a front line over 35,000 km in extent – inevitably, it proved indefensible.

The Japanese offensive 1941–42

Almost simultaneous pre-emptive strikes in December 1941 against the US naval base at Pearl Harbor, Hawaii, the US-controlled Philippines, the Dutch East Indies, and the British Malayan states created, at a stroke, for a brief historical moment, the largest contiguous empire the world has ever seen. Campaigns in New Guinea, the Solomons, and Burma extended it even further. The combination of surprise (Japan attacked before declaring war), detailed strategic planning, the use of innovative aggressive methods (amphibious landings, aircraft carriers, tactical bombing, jungle tactics), and a disregard for the 'acceptable' rules of warfare proved initially irresistible.

The Japanese army's comprehensive training in military techniques such as jungle warfare and amphibious assaults proved an essential element in their initial successes in China and tropical Southeast Asia.

The surprise Japanese bombing raid on the US naval base at Pearl Harbor on 7 December 1941 was designed, at least temporarily, to destroy US sea power in the Pacific. Only 18 of the 94 warships at anchor were actually put out of action, but as a result, the US was drawn into war against Japan and its Axis allies.

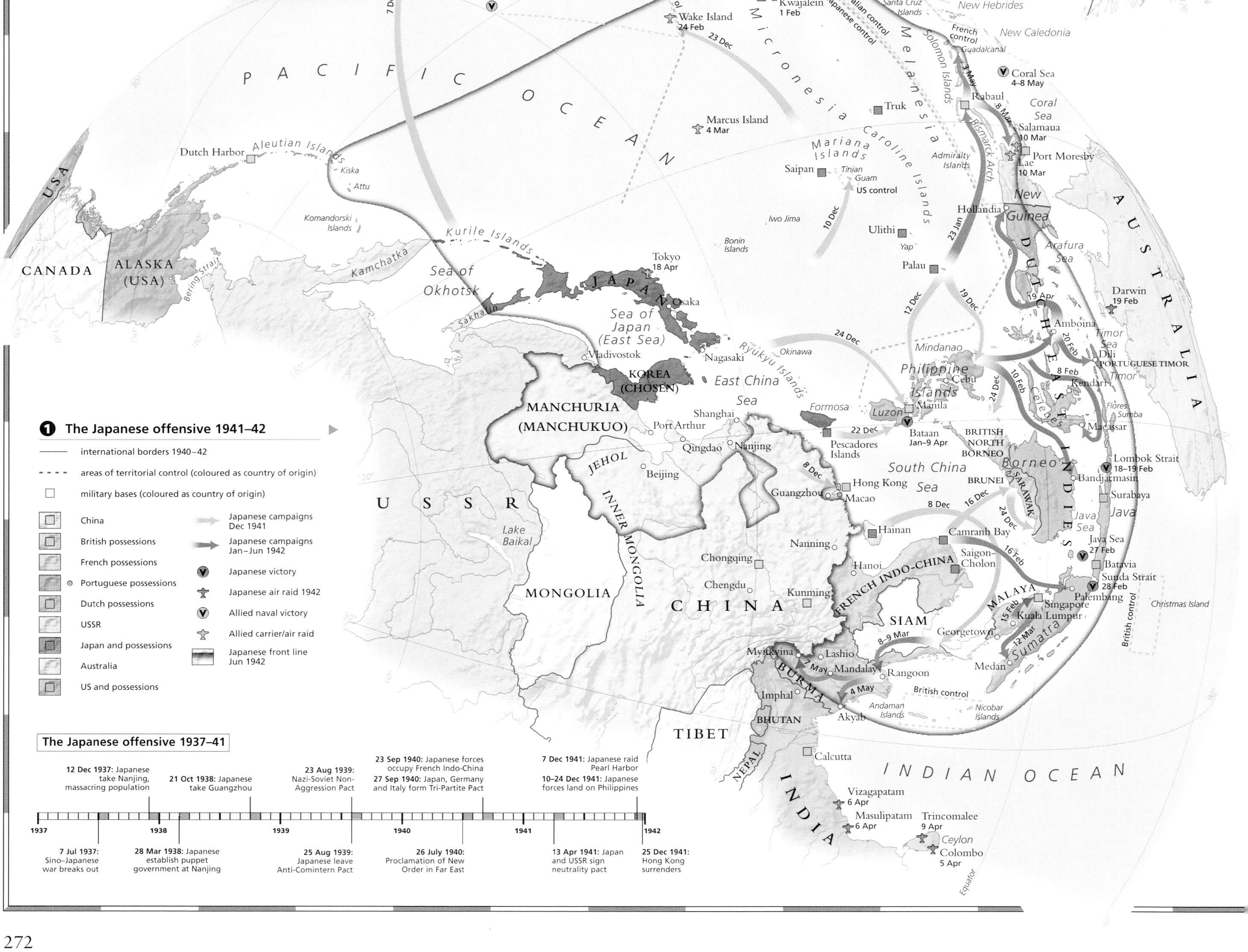

Scale varies with perspective

11,770 km (7310 miles)

10,000 km (6220 miles)

1 The Japanese offensive 1941–42

- international borders 1940–42
- areas of territorial control (coloured as country of origin)
- military bases (coloured as country of origin)
- China
- British possessions
- French possessions
- Portuguese possessions
- Dutch possessions
- USSR
- Japan and possessions
- Australia
- US and possessions
- Japanese campaigns Dec 1941
- Japanese campaigns Jan–Jun 1942
- Japanese victory
- Japanese air raid 1942
- Allied naval victory
- Allied carrier/air raid
- Japanese front line Jun 1942

The Japanese offensive 1937–41

- **7 Jul 1937:** Sino-Japanese war breaks out
- **12 Dec 1937:** Japanese take Nanjing, massacring population
- **28 Mar 1938:** Japanese establish puppet government at Nanjing
- **21 Oct 1938:** Japanese take Guangzhou
- **23 Aug 1939:** Nazi-Soviet Non-Aggression Pact
- **25 Aug 1939:** Japanese leave Anti-Comintern Pact
- **26 July 1940:** Proclamation of New Order in Far East
- **23 Sep 1940:** Japanese forces occupy French Indo-China
- **27 Sep 1940:** Japan, Germany and Italy form Tri-Partite Pact
- **13 Apr 1941:** Japan and USSR sign neutrality pact
- **7 Dec 1941:** Japanese raid Pearl Harbor
- **10–24 Dec 1941:** Japanese forces land on Philippines
- **25 Dec 1941:** Hong Kong surrenders

The Allied counter-offensive 1942–45

In mid-1942 the Allied defeat of naval forces in the Coral Sea and at Midway halted the Japanese advance. Over the next year, bitter campaigns on and around Guadalcanal in the Solomons proved a turning point. American industrial mobilization on a massive scale fed a selective island-hopping campaign designed to disrupt the internal communications of the Japanese empire and to bring air power within striking distance of the Japanese home islands. Japanese resistance was so fierce that it took the US explosion of two newly-developed atomic bombs over Japan, which was followed by a Soviet land campaign in Manchuria, to force a surrender.

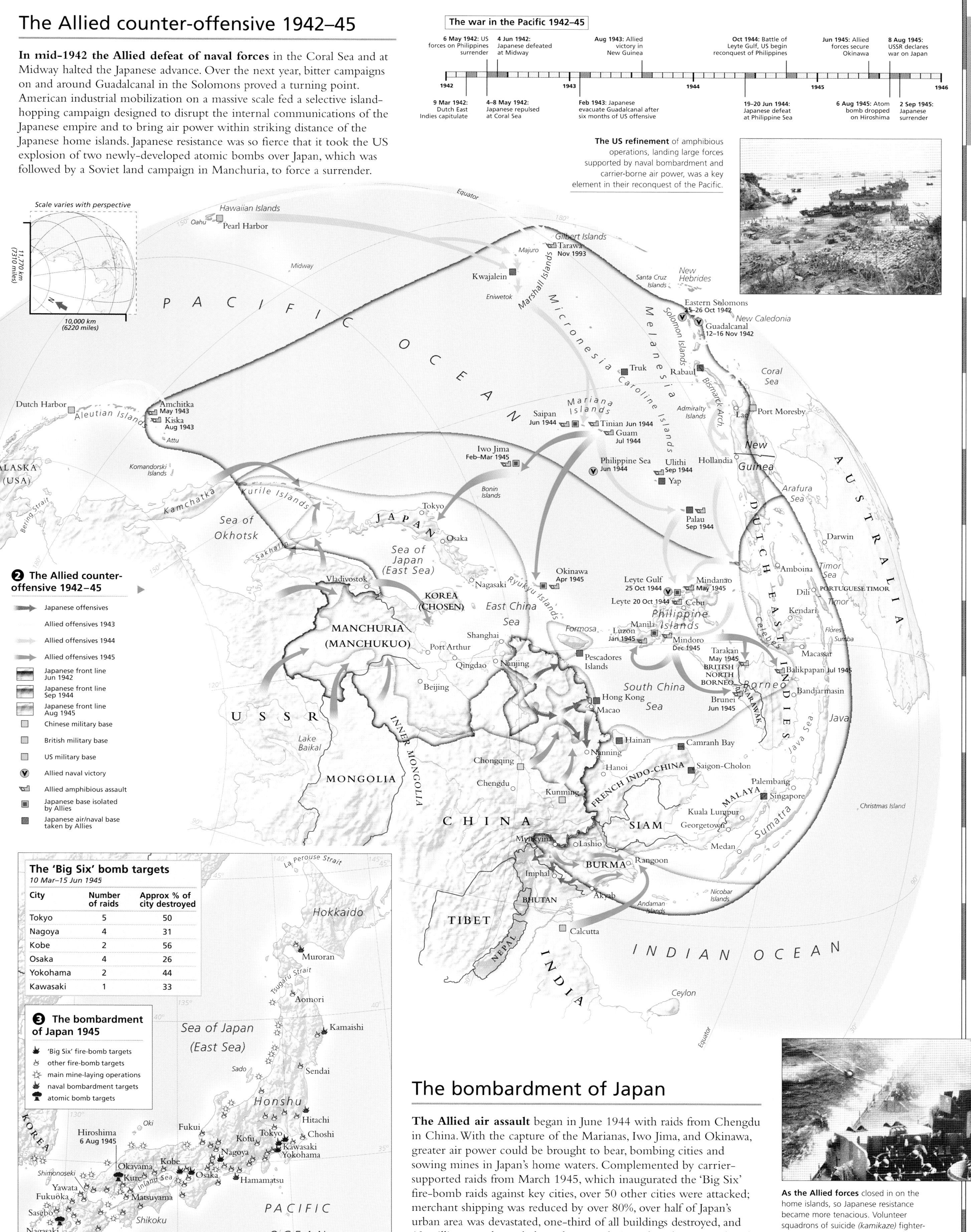

The US refinement of amphibious operations, landing large forces supported by naval bombardment and carrier-borne air power, was a key element in their reconquest of the Pacific.

The 'Big Six' bomb targets
10 Mar–15 Jun 1945

City	Number of raids	Approx % of city destroyed
Tokyo	5	50
Nagoya	4	31
Kobe	2	56
Osaka	4	26
Yokohama	2	44
Kawasaki	1	33

The bombardment of Japan

The Allied air assault began in June 1944 with raids from Chengdu in China. With the capture of the Marianas, Iwo Jima, and Okinawa, greater air power could be brought to bear, bombing cities and sowing mines in Japan's home waters. Complemented by carrier-supported raids from March 1945, which inaugurated the 'Big Six' fire-bomb raids against key cities, over 50 other cities were attacked; merchant shipping was reduced by over 80%, over half of Japan's urban area was devastated, one-third of all buildings destroyed, and 13 million people made homeless. It culminated in the atomic bomb attacks against Hiroshima and Nagasaki, killing over 150,000 people.

As the Allied forces closed in on the home islands, so Japanese resistance became more tenacious. Volunteer squadrons of suicide *(kamikaze)* fighter-bomber pilots were recruited to attack the Allied fleet.

COMMUNISM AND CAPITALISM

A high-speed train passing Mount Fuji exemplifies Japan's rapid development as one of the world's leading economies

FROM 1945, EAST ASIA was dominated by the conflicting ideologies of Communism and capitalism, which brought international war in Korea (1950–53) and Vietnam (1946–75). In China, Mao Zedong and his successors sought social revolution through centralization, collectivization, and the ruthless elimination of dissent, while attempting to manage phenomenal population growth. Meanwhile, spurred by the example of post-war Japan, and supported by the US in an attempt to contain Communism, capitalist economic growth spread around the Pacific Rim. By 2000, only North Korea remained isolated as China embraced market economics with dramatic results. In Central Asia, the collapse of the USSR in 1991 saw a resurgence of ethnic rivalries and Islamic revitalization, sparking another international conflict in Afghanistan.

Mao Zedong's vision of a Communist revolution in China was underpinned by the mobilization of the masses down to a family level, spread by his writings, mass education, and by propaganda *(above)*.

The Communist revolution in China 1927–49

Following the schism with the Guomindang Nationalists in 1927, the Communists fled to remote mountain bases. Harried by the Nationalists under Chiang Kai-shek (Jiang Jieshi), Mao Zedong and fellow Communists retreated north in 1934 to Yenan (the Long March). The war against Japan saved them, allowing Mao to rebuild the Party, hone its ideology and extend its influence, while the Nationalists withdrew to Chongqing in the southwest. Upon the Japanese surrender, Soviet forces occupied Manchuria. This gave the Communists an advantage, allowing them to gain control of China's northeast heartland. By 1948, open warfare had erupted, but, with the collapse of their forces north of the Yangtze, the Nationalists withdrew to Taiwan. The People's Republic of China was established in 1949.

The Great Leap Forward (1958–60) redirected peasant labour to massive public works projects, to transform China from an agricultural to an industrial economy. Yet the nation's agricultural capacity was drastically reduced, causing widespread famine in the 1960s.

China under the Communists

The victorious Chinese Communists moved from moderation to a radical agenda of socialist reform, creating a centralized, Party-led, political and economic infrastructure, and modernizing industry, after almost 40 years of turmoil. Mao Zedong used propaganda and coercion to mobilize the peasants through collectivization of agriculture and mass labour projects. The Great Leap Forward (1958–60) resulted in famine and 30 million deaths. Ideological purges continued, notably during the Cultural Revolution (1966). After Mao's death in 1976, China steadily reversed many economic and social policies, although the Communists brutally guarded their monopoly on power, massacring pro-democracy protestors in 1989. By 2000, China's 'open door' trading policy had led to a second industrial revolution, making it the fastest-growing economy in the world.

1 The Communist Revolution in China ▶

- Communist centres 1934
- Long March Oct 1934–Oct 1935
- area under Japanese control 1944
- area under Communist (PLA) control 1946
- area under Communist (PLA) control by mid-1949
- area of Communist guerrilla operations 1944–49
- battle
- principal Communist campaigns
- city with date of Communist control

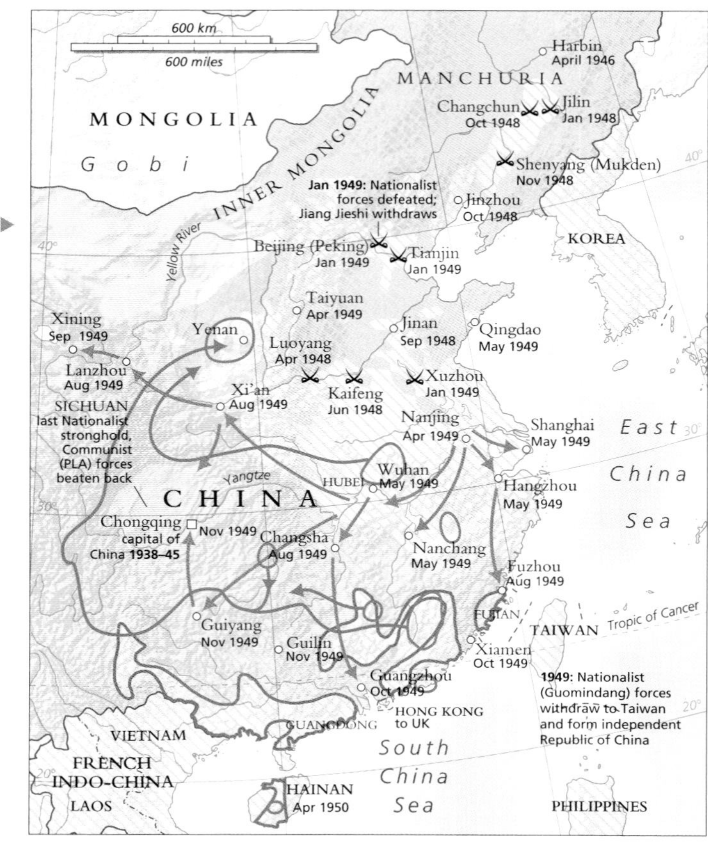

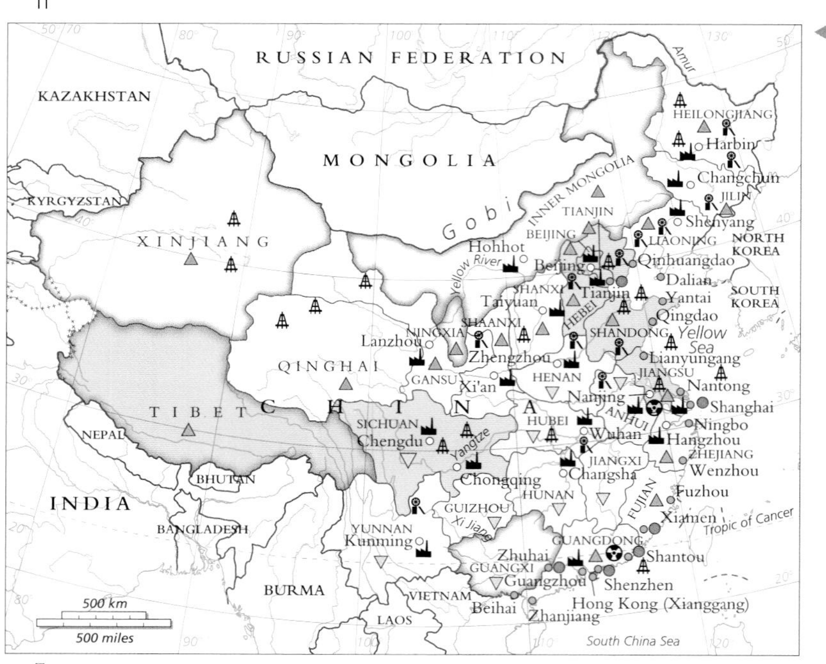

◀ **2 Chinese economic development from 1950**

- boundary of Autonomous Regions

Percentage population growth 1950–90

- over 100%
- 75–100%
- 55–75%
- less than 55%

Economic development under Mao Zedong

- oilfield
- coalfield
- nuclear plant
- industrial centre

Economic development since 1980

- Special Economic Zone
- open port
- average income more than 80% of national average, 1990s
- average income less than 80% of national average, 1990s

The Communist Revolution

- **1921:** Chinese Communist Party founded
- **1923:** First United Front: Guomindang and Communists unite against warlords
- **1927:** Split between Nationalists and Communists
- **Oct 1934–Oct 1935:** Long March unites Communists
- **1937:** Sino-Japanese war breaks out
- **1937–45:** Second United Front: Guomindang and Communists unite against Japanese
- **1945:** Japanese surrender in Second World War
- **1946–49:** Civil war between Nationalists and Communists
- **1949:** Republic of China set up in Taiwan
- **1949:** People's Republic of China established

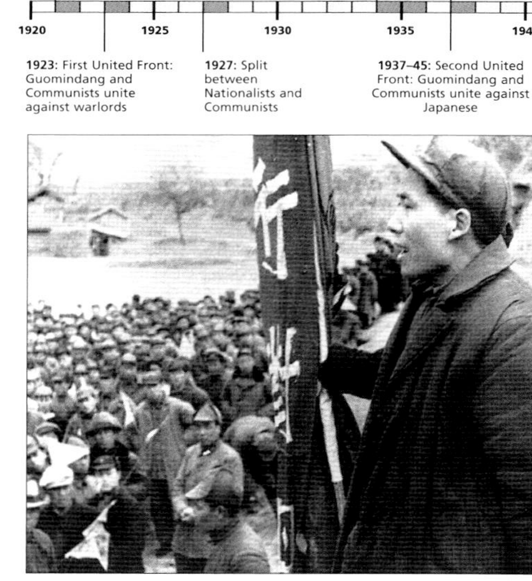

The Long March of 1934–35 was a scramble for survival that succeeded in strategically relocating and uniting the Communist forces. The 8000 or so survivors (of 100,000 who set out) later became the core of the Party. Mao Zedong, seen here addressing his troops, only became supreme leader after a power struggle en route.

China under Communist rule

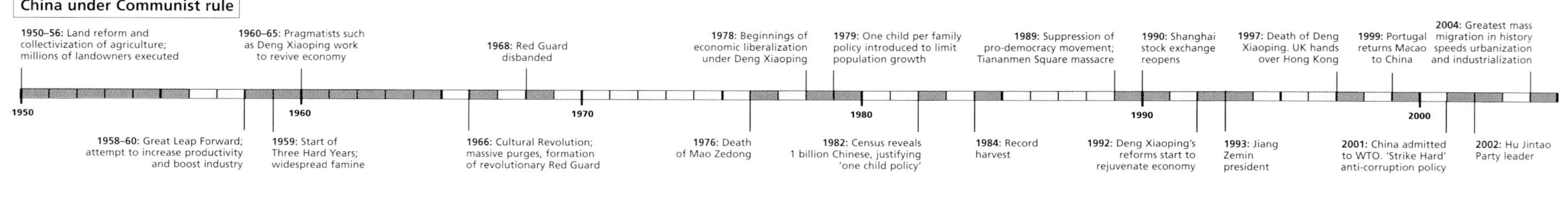

Chinese expansionism from 1949

The cooling of relations between the West and the Communist bloc was further chilled by China's involvement in the Korean War, its covert support for Communist guerrillas elsewhere, and by its ideological split with the Soviet Union in 1960, sparked off by the Amur-Ussuri border dispute. Chinese isolationism was balanced by an aggressive foreign policy. Tibet was invaded and occupied, and the divine ruler, the Dalai Lama, exiled in 1959. It was formally absorbed as an Autonomous Region of China in 1965. Border disputes brought a brief war with India in 1962, the highest in the history of warfare, and a temporary invasion of North Vietnam in 1979. Taiwan has remained a thorn in China's side, while the need to control potential oil and gas deposits has seen China defending remote claims in the South China Sea.

The invasion of Tibet in 1950 was the most significant incident of Chinese expansionism since the Communist Revolution. Traditional ways of life and beliefs were suppressed and, following a revolt in 1959, Tibet's spiritual and political leader, the Dalai Lama, was forced into exile.

3 Chinese expansion from 1949

- Chinese provinces
- Autonomous Regions (Zizhiqu)
- territorial/border dispute
- Chinese invasion
- Chinese support for Communist insurgents
- Soviet support for Communists after 1960
- suppression of anti-Communist movements

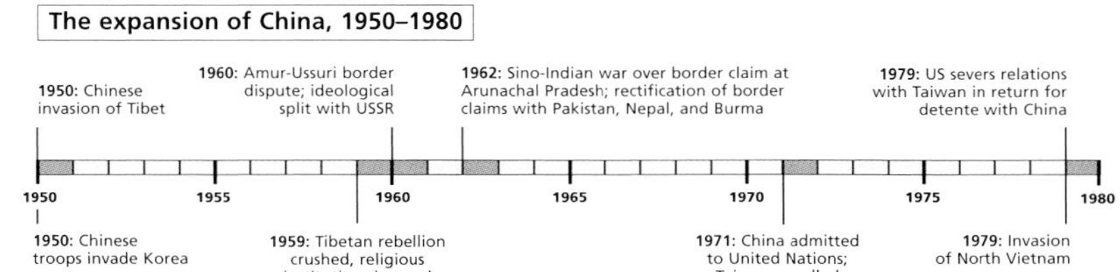
The expansion of China, 1950–1980
1950: Chinese invasion of Tibet
1960: Amur-Ussuri border dispute; ideological split with USSR
1962: Sino-Indian war over border claim at Arunachal Pradesh; rectification of border claims with Pakistan, Nepal, and Burma
1979: US severs relations with Taiwan in return for detente with China
1950
1955
1960
1965
1970
1975
1980
1950: Chinese troops invade Korea
1959: Tibetan rebellion crushed, religious institutions banned
1971: China admitted to United Nations; Taiwan expelled
1979: Invasion of North Vietnam

The 'Tiger' economies from 1960

During the US occupation of Japan (1945–52) a new conservative pro-capitalist constitution was created, along with the conditions for rapid economic growth. As a standing army was banned, greater investment could be made in industry. Japan's phenomenal growth focused on shipbuilding, electronic goods, cameras, and cars. By the 1970s Japan, the world's third largest industrial nation, had launched a global outward investment programme. The Japanese example encouraged the development of a string of economic successes around the Pacific Rim over the next 20 years, but China's spectacular growth in the early 21st century threatened to overshadow them all.

4 The 'Tiger' economies from 1960

- Communist states 1976
- ASEAN membership
- over 50% of workforce employed in primary industries by mid-1980s
- average GDP growth rate of over 8% in 1970s
- major industrial city

Economic growth in East Asia

- 1951: Treaty of San Francisco; Japan regains independence
- 1965: Singapore independent; rapid growth in service and electronics sector
- 1967: ASEAN created to promote economic cooperation
- 1973: Global oil crisis leads Japan to focus on high-tech industries
- 1975: End of Vietnam War
- 1980s: Rapid growth of South Korean economy
- 1986: Collapse of pro-US Marcos regime in Philippines
- 1989: Tokyo stock market crash ends period of exponential economic growth
- 1997: Domino effect of Japanese crash throughout Pacific Rim
- 1997: Hong Kong returned to China; end of boom

Growth of 'Tiger' economies of the Pacific Rim 1980–2002

GDP in $US billion: 1980, 1996, 2002 (China, Hong Kong, Indonesia, Japan, Malaysia, Philippines, Singapore, South Korea, Thailand)

Japan emerged in the 1960s as a beacon of modernization, dominating many of the world's industries. The economy faltered in the 1990s, but remains the second strongest in the world.

The Islamic states of Central Asia inherited widespread environmental damage, especially in Kazakhstan, where the Soviet nuclear testing and space centre at Baykonur *(above)* was based.

Islam and nationalism in Central Asia

Islam in Central Asia survived suppression and political change, to re-emerge as a vital force in the region's politics. Signalled by the *mujahedin* rebellion in Afghanistan (from 1973), and the establishment of an Islamic Republic in Iran in 1979, the revival progressed with the *mujahedin* defeat of a Soviet invasion (1979–89). Following the collapse of the USSR in 1991, ethnic and religious rivalry flared up across the new republics. The fundamentalist Taliban conquered Afghanistan in 1995–98, but were ousted by the US in 2001 for harbouring Islamic terrorists.

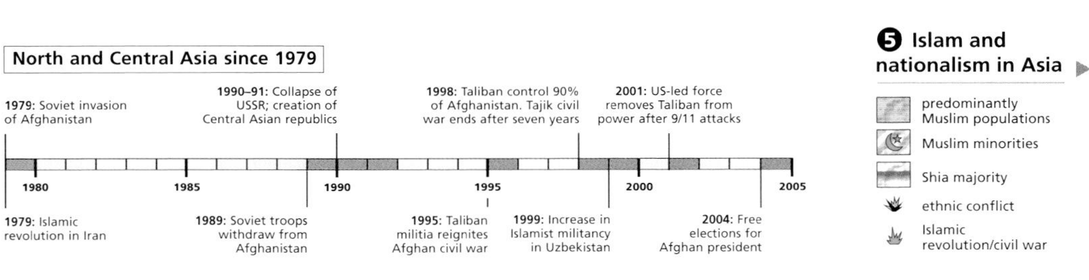
North and Central Asia since 1979
1979: Soviet invasion of Afghanistan
1990–91: Collapse of USSR; creation of Central Asian republics
1998: Taliban control 90% of Afghanistan. Tajik civil war ends after seven years
2001: US-led force removes Taliban from power after 9/11 attacks
1980
1985
1990
1995
2000
2005
1979: Islamic revolution in Iran
1989: Soviet troops withdraw from Afghanistan
1995: Taliban militia reignites Afghan civil war
1999: Increase in Islamist militancy in Uzbekistan
2004: Free elections for Afghan president

5 Islam and nationalism in Asia

- predominantly Muslim populations
- Muslim minorities
- Shia majority
- ethnic conflict
- Islamic revolution/civil war

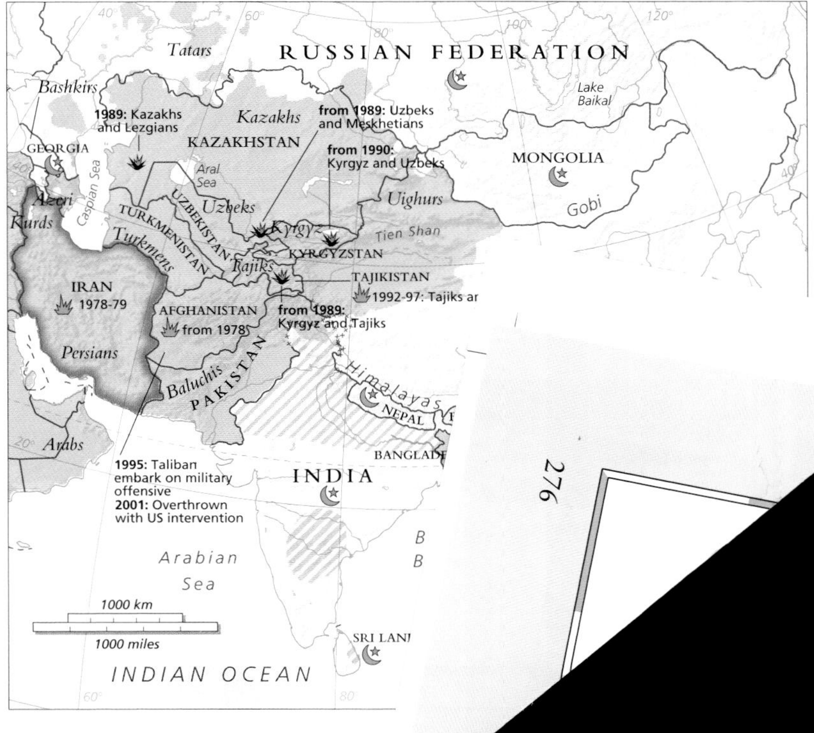
RUSSIAN FEDERATION
Tatars
Bashkirs
1989: Kazakhs and Lezgians
Kazakhs
from 1989: Uzbeks and Meskhetians
KAZAKHSTAN
from 1990: Kyrgyz and Uzbeks
MONGOLIA
GEORGIA
Uighurs
Gobi
Uzbeks
TURKMENISTAN
KYRGYZSTAN
Tien Shan
TAJIKISTAN
1992-97: Tajiks ar
IRAN
1978-79
AFGHANISTAN
from 1978
from 1989: Kyrgyz and Tajiks
Persians
PAKISTAN
NEPAL
Arabs
1995: Taliban embark on military offensive
2001: Overthrown with US intervention
INDIA
Arabian Sea
1000 km
1000 miles
INDIAN OCEAN
SRI LANKA

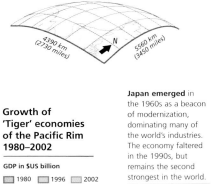

AUSTRALASIA AND OCEANIA

REGIONAL HISTORY

THE HISTORICAL LANDSCAPE

THE INSULAR CONTINENT OF AUSTRALIA and the myriad island groups of Melanesia, Micronesia, and Polynesia, strewn across the Pacific Ocean, share the most unlikely chapter in world history. Australia and New Guinea were first colonized some 60,000 years ago by migrants crossing the Southeast Asian landbridge, who completed their journey by boat – the world's first navigators. As sea levels rose after the last Ice Age, they became divided and isolated, maintaining simple, sustainable lifestyles in remote communities until European contact in the 18th century when their vulnerability was fatally exposed. The settlement of the Pacific islands, beginning some 30,000 years ago, again depended on navigational skills, and developed from about 1500 BCE into a process of active colonization. By 1200 CE, Polynesians were the most widely distributed ethnic group on the face of the earth, with settlements from New Zealand to Hawaii. The region was the penultimate target of European imperialists, leaving only the barren tracts of the Arctic ice cap and continental Antarctica as the final, ephemeral prizes in Europe's race for global domination – a race of heroic futility played out across the opening years of the 20th century.

Lower sea levels turned the Arafura Shelf into dry land, forming a substantial land bridge between Australia and New Guinea.

Drier climates encouraged the spread of desert conditions, and dunes across more than three-quarters of Australia.

Initially settlements were concentrated around the coasts; then, as the population grew, people moved inland to colonize the flat glacial plains of the interior.

Australia's deserts were more extensive during the last Ice Age. As the land bridge between Australia and New Guinea was flooded, settlers retreated south into the desert margins of Australia.

Most Pacific islands are volcanic, formed by eruptions on the sea floor which accumulate a cone of volcanic material, eventually rising above the ocean surface. As the volcano becomes extinct, coral reefs grow around the island's fringes. Humans first sailed to the Pacific islands from New Guinea and the Solomon Islands, reaching Fiji by 1500 BCE.

Vegetation type

- ice cap and glacier
- tundra
- semi desert or sparsely vegetated
- grassland
- forest or open woodland
- tropical rainforest
- tropical desert
- desert
- coastline (present-day)
- coastline (18,000 years ago)

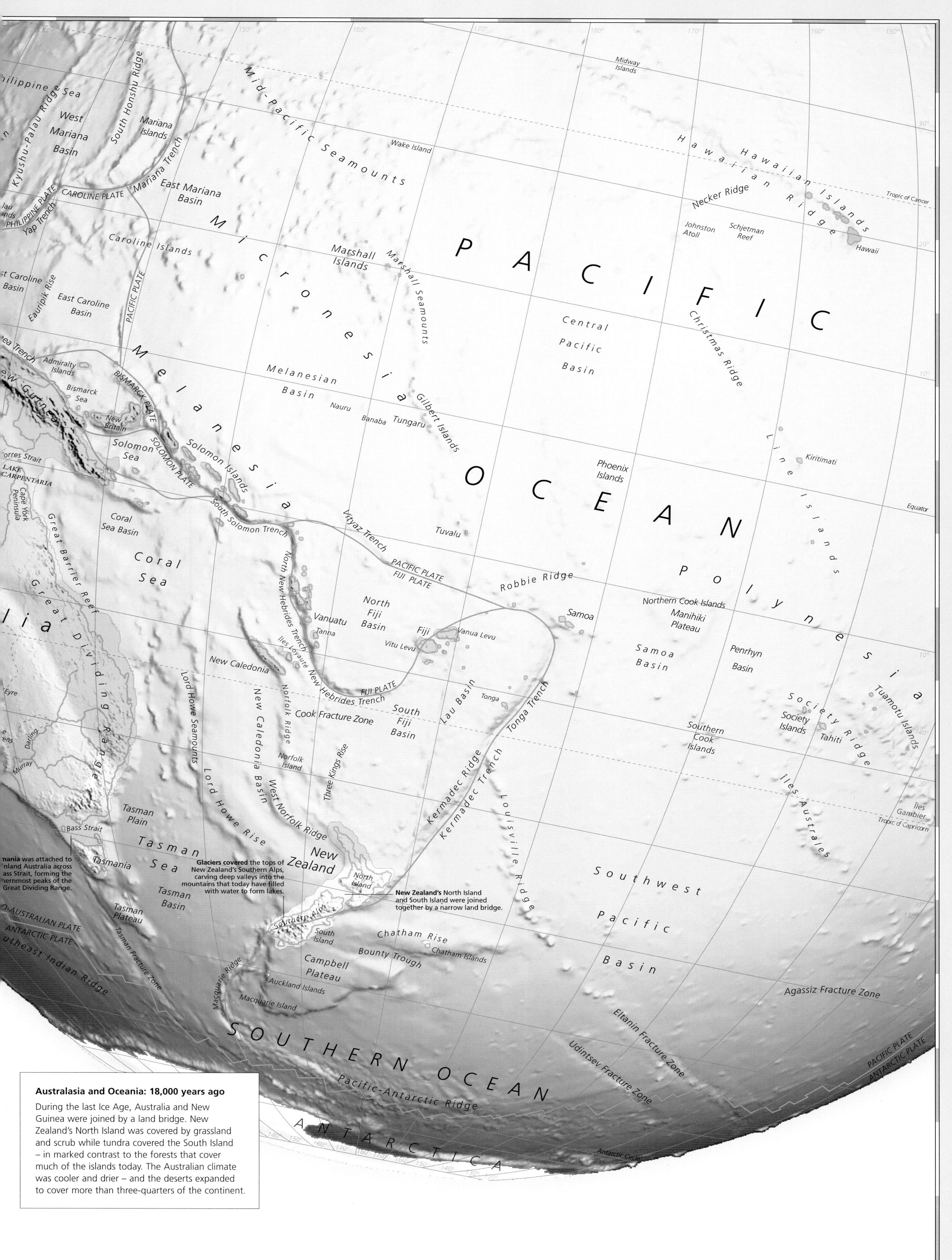

Australasia and Oceania: 18,000 years ago

During the last Ice Age, Australia and New Guinea were joined by a land bridge. New Zealand's North Island was covered by grassland and scrub while tundra covered the South Island – in marked contrast to the forests that cover much of the islands today. The Australian climate was cooler and drier – and the deserts expanded to cover more than three-quarters of the continent.

AUSTRALASIA AND OCEANIA

EXPLORATION AND MAPPING

Abel Tasman reached Tasmania and New Zealand in 1642 in his search for a great southern continent.

ALMOST ALL THE PACIFIC ISLANDS had been discovered and, when habitable, settled by Polynesian voyagers, some 500 years before European explorers ventured into the ocean. After Magellan's pioneering crossing of 1521, it took three centuries to chart the whole Pacific. The continent of Australia presented even greater problems. Ever since Classical times, European world maps had included a vast southern continent, *Terra Australis Incognita*. It was not until James Cook's voyages in the 18th century that the true extent of Australia was established. New Guinea's mountainous interior was not explored by Europeans until the 20th century.

STICK CHARTS OF THE MARSHALL ISLANDS

The Melanesian and Polynesian peoples who have been sailing the Pacific for four millennia have built up a vast store of knowledge of its islands, winds, and currents. The inhabitants of the Marshall Islands make charts of sticks and shells. Some are actual maps of surrounding islands and are carried aboard their canoes. Others are teaching aids. The *mattang*, for example, is not a map as such; it demonstrates the way islands affect patterns in the ocean's swell, an invaluable means of detecting the presence of low-lying atolls.

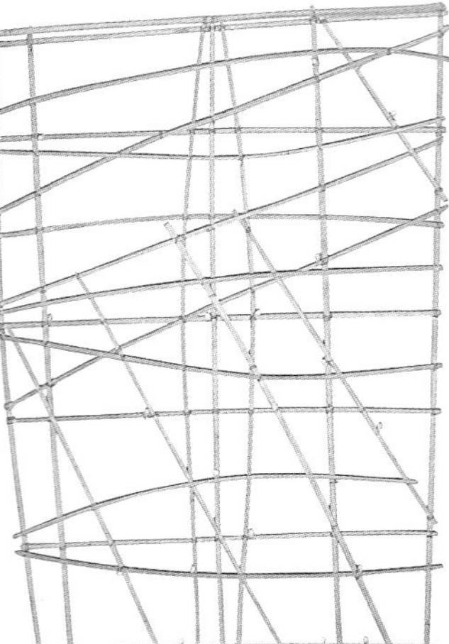

This typical *mattang* chart is made of the midribs of coconut fronds. Shells mark the location of islands and the sticks show variations in ocean swell.

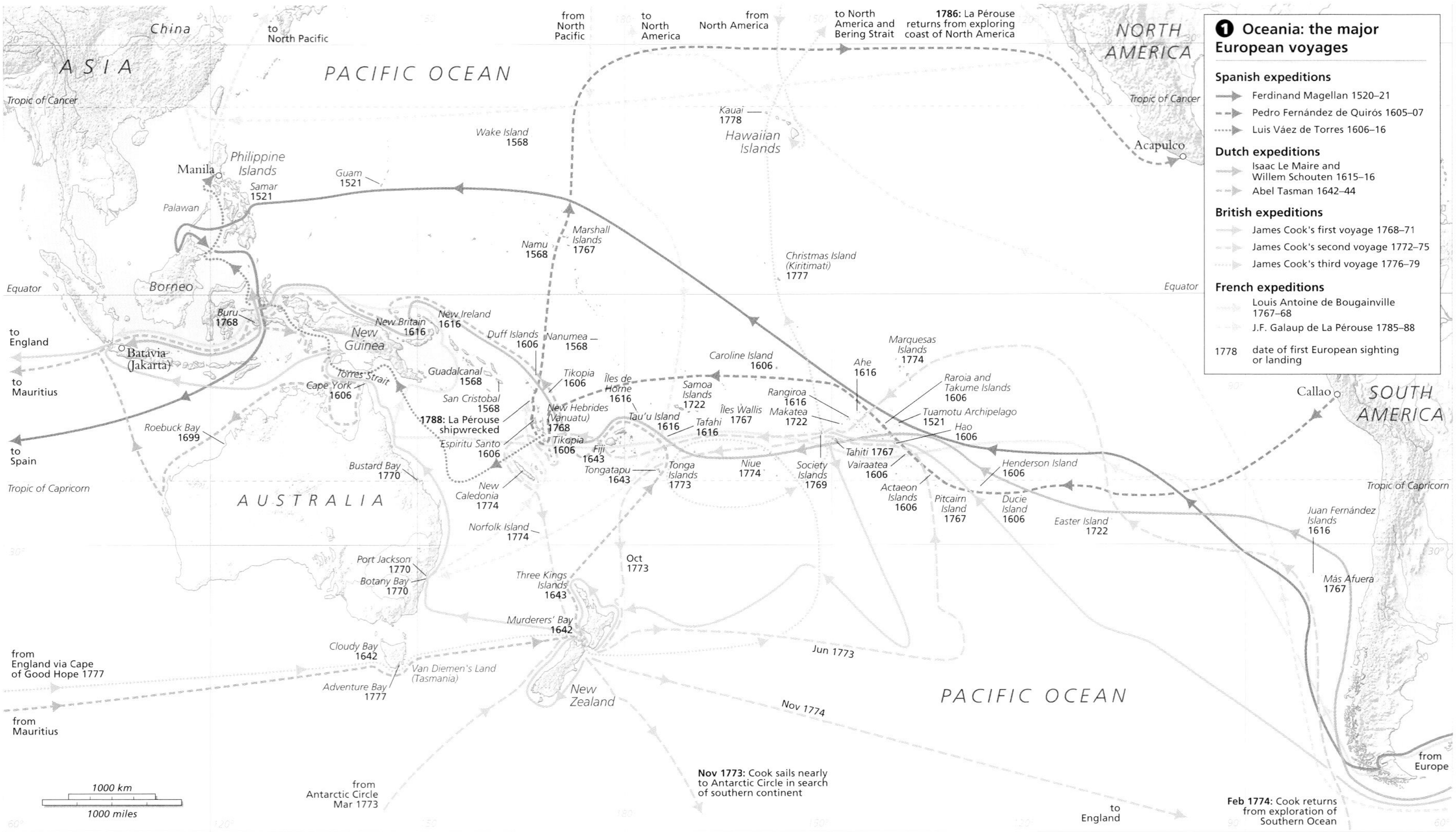

1 Oceania: the major European voyages

Spanish expeditions
- Ferdinand Magellan 1520–21
- Pedro Fernández de Quirós 1605–07
- Luis Váez de Torres 1606–16

Dutch expeditions
- Isaac Le Maire and Willem Schouten 1615–16
- Abel Tasman 1642–44

British expeditions
- James Cook's first voyage 1768–71
- James Cook's second voyage 1772–75
- James Cook's third voyage 1776–79

French expeditions
- Louis Antoine de Bougainville 1767–68
- J.F. Galaup de La Pérouse 1785–88

1778 date of first European sighting or landing

China
ASIA
PACIFIC OCEAN
NORTH AMERICA
SOUTH AMERICA
AUSTRALIA
Tropic of Cancer
Equator
Tropic of Capricorn
to North Pacific
from North Pacific
to North America
from North America
to North America and Bering Strait
1786: La Pérouse returns from exploring coast of North America
Kauai 1778
Hawaiian Islands
Acapulco
Wake Island 1568
Philippine Islands
Manila
Guam 1521
Samar 1521
Palawan
Marshall Islands 1767
Namu 1568
Christmas Island (Kiritimati) 1777
Borneo
Buru 1768
New Ireland 1616
New Britain 1616
New Guinea
Duff Islands 1606
Nanumea 1568
to England
Batavia (Jakarta)
to Mauritius
Torres Strait
Cape York 1606
Guadalcanal 1568
San Cristobal 1568
1788: La Pérouse shipwrecked
Espiritu Santo 1606
Tikopia 1606
Îles de Horne 1616
New Hebrides (Vanuatu) 1768
Tikopia 1606
Fiji 1643
Tongatapu 1643
Samoa Islands 1722
Tau'u Island 1616
Tafahi 1616
Îles Wallis 1767
Caroline Island 1606
Rangiroa 1616
Makatea 1722
Ahe 1616
Marquesas Islands 1774
Raroia and Takume Islands 1606
Tuamotu Archipelago 1521
Hao 1606
Tahiti 1767
Vairaatea 1606
Actaeon Islands 1606
Pitcairn Island 1767
Ducie Island 1606
Henderson Island 1606
Easter Island 1722
Callao
Juan Fernández Islands 1616
Más Afuera 1767
Roebuck Bay 1699
to Spain
Bustard Bay 1770
New Caledonia 1774
Tonga Islands 1773
Niue 1774
Society Islands 1769
Norfolk Island 1774
Port Jackson 1770
Botany Bay 1770
Oct 1773
Three Kings Islands 1643
Murderers' Bay 1642
Cloudy Bay 1642
Van Diemen's Land (Tasmania)
Adventure Bay 1777
New Zealand
from England via Cape of Good Hope 1777
from Mauritius
Jun 1773
Nov 1774
PACIFIC OCEAN
Nov 1773: Cook sails nearly to Antarctic Circle in search of southern continent
from Antarctic Circle Mar 1773
to England
from Europe
Feb 1774: Cook returns from exploration of Southern Ocean
1000 km
1000 miles

European voyages of discovery

In the 16th century the Spanish sailed into the Pacific out of curiosity and greed, seeking routes to the riches of China and the 'Spice Islands'. At first they did not intrude too greatly on the life of the islands, using them as stopovers to pick up food and water. In Australasia the Dutch led the way, but, seeing no potential profit in Australia or New Zealand, left them alone. Things changed in the 18th century when the French and the British were competing for domination of the globe. The three voyages of Captain James Cook transformed Europe's understanding of Oceania and it was in part the popularity of accounts of Cook's voyages that spurred European and American exploitation and colonization of the region in the 19th century.

European exploration of the Pacific

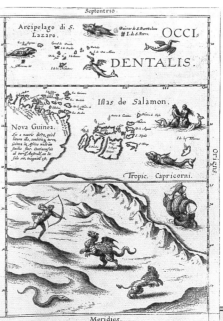

- **1520:** Magellan enters the Pacific
- **1526:** Jorge de Meneses first European to sight New Guinea
- **1567–69:** Alvaro de Mendaña explores Solomon Islands
- **1606:** Torres sails through strait that now bears his name and proves New Guinea is an island
- **1642:** Tasman, searching for a southern continent, finds Tasmania and New Zealand
- **1688:** William Dampier first Englishman to visit Australia
- **1699:** Dampier surveys west coast of Australia, but is unimpressed
- **1721–22:** Jacob Roggeveen visits many Polynesian islands
- **1768:** Cook's first voyage
- **1779:** Cook killed in Hawaii on third voyage
- **1788:** La Pérouse sunk off Vanikoro

1500 1550 1600 1650 1700 1750 1800

Dutch mariners provided the data for this 1593 map. It gives a reasonably accurate picture of the Solomon Islands and part of the north coast of New Guinea, but the shape and extent of Australia are still a mystery. Here, it is at least divided from New Guinea by a strait – many later maps show the two islands attached.

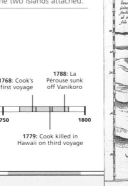

Septentrio
Arcipelago di S. Lazaro
OCCIDENTALIS
Islas de Salamon
Nova Guinea
Tropic. Capricorni
Meridies

The *Resolution*, James Cook's ship on his epic second voyage of 1772–75, was originally built to carry coal.

Burke and Wills set off in 1860 to cross Australia from south to north in a fanfare of publicity. Their confidence was misplaced; Aboriginals they encountered helped them find food and water, but eventually they died of hunger.

❷ Exploration in Australia and New Guinea 1798–1928

- George Bass and Matthew Flinders 1798–99
- Matthew Flinders 1802–03
- Charles Sturt 1828–46
- Thomas Mitchell 1836–46
- Edward Eyre 1839–41
- Ludwig Leichhardt 1844–45
- Edmund Kennedy 1848
- Robert Burke and William Wills 1860–61
- John Stuart 1861–62
- Peter Warburton 1872–73
- John Forrest 1874
- Ernest Giles 1875–76
- Luigi Maria d'Albertis 1876
- Alexander Forrest 1879
- Charles Karius 1927–28

1871–72: Telegraph line parallels Stuart's route

Burke and Wills fail to sight Gulf for coastal swamps

1861: On their return to Adelaide, Burke and Wills die here

Exploring Australia and New Guinea

- 1802–03: Flinders circumnavigates Australia
- 1813: Route found across Blue Mountains
- 1829–30: Sturt's journeys pave way for founding of colony of South Australia in 1836
- 1841: Eyre is first European to cross Nullarbor Plain
- 1875: D'Albertis makes first of three trips up Fly River
- 1879: Forrest explores from Port Hedland across Kimberley Plateau
- 1927–28: Karius expedition crosses New Guinea from south to north

Australia and New Guinea: explorers of the interior

Australia never aroused the curiosity of the Dutch who knew only the hostile west coast. The British, who settled in the more temperate southeast, were gradually drawn to the interior, first by the lure of gold and the search for grazing land, later by curiosity about the vast deserts of the interior. Expeditions such as those of Burke and Leichhardt used imported camels. New Guinea was even more unwelcoming to intruders with its mountains and dense rainforest. Most 19th-century explorers of the island followed the courses of rivers, while parts of the highlands remained inaccessible until the age of the aeroplane.

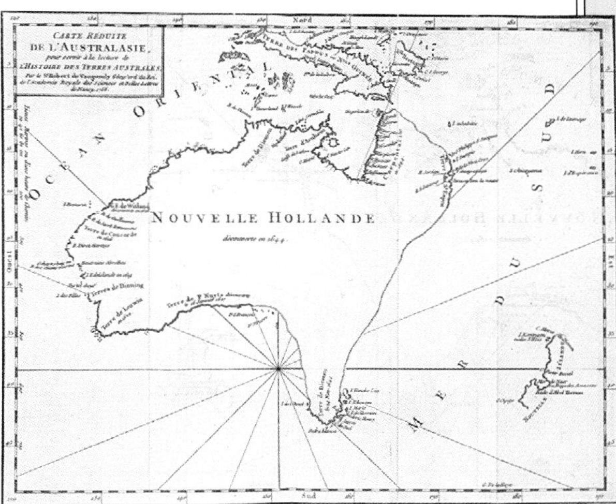

James Cook took a copy of this French map of 1756 with him on his voyage of 1768–71. The west coast of Australia is well charted because Dutch ships bound for the East Indies were often blown ashore there. The east was unexplored until Cook himself charted it and the fact that Tasmania was an island was established by Flinders and Bass in 1798–99.

Sealers, whalers, and traders

The first outsiders to have a significant impact in the Pacific were American sealers in the late 18th century. Traders soon followed to supply their sailing ships, establishing stations throughout the Pacific. By the 1820s, with Atlantic whale stocks depleted, whalers were also starting to arrive in large numbers, with calamitous results: introduced diseases caused the destruction of entire island societies. In the 1860s came a further threat – 'blackbirders', slave raiders operating initially out of Peru, later carrying off the young males of many islands to work in the canefields of Queensland, Australia.

Sperm whales were the chief quarry of Pacific whalers, due to the growing market for their oil, used in industrialized Europe and the US for lubricating machinery.

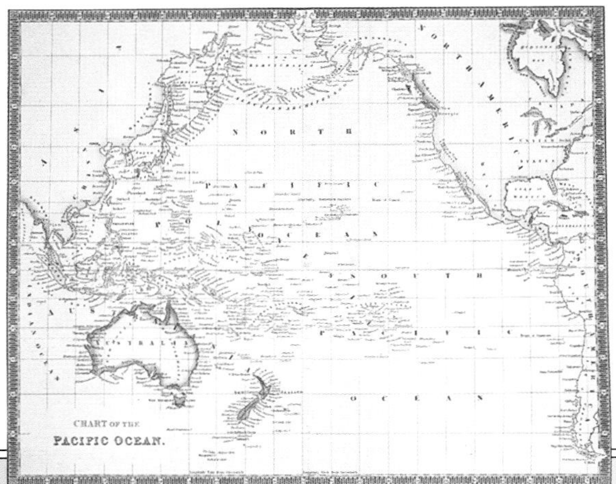

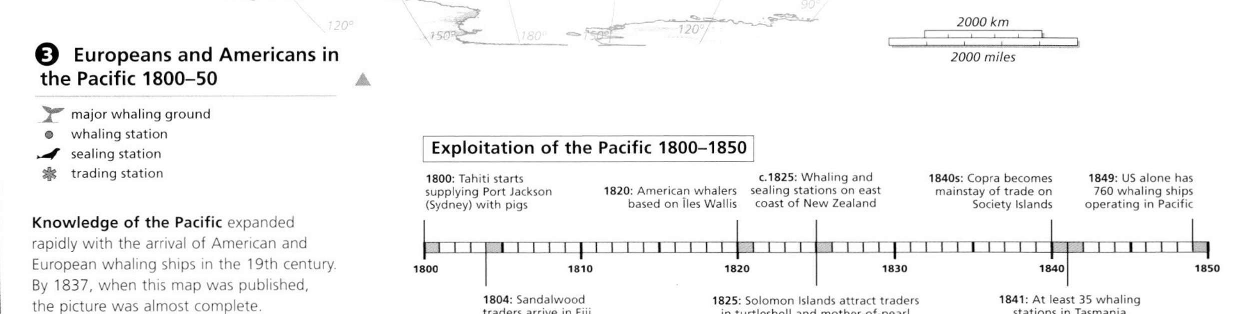

Knowledge of the Pacific expanded rapidly with the arrival of American and European whaling ships in the 19th century. By 1837, when this map was published, the picture was almost complete.

PREHISTORIC OCEANIA

This fine carving from Rurutu in the Austral Islands shows the local god A'a.

DURING THE ICE AGES, Australia, New Guinea, and Tasmania were linked by land bridges to form the continent of Sahul. The first people to inhabit the region were Australoids, ancestors of today's Papuans and Australia's Aborigines, who may have reached Sahul as early as 60,000 years ago. The next significant wave of immigrants did not come until 6000 BCE, when Austronesian people fanned out through the Philippines and the East Indies. They mixed with the resident Australoids to produce the heterogeneous population of Melanesia. Around 1500 BCE the Austronesians, the greatest seafarers of prehistory, reached Fiji, and soon after that Samoa, starting point for later Polynesian expansion to the eastern Pacific and the eventual settlement of islands as far apart as Hawaii and New Zealand.

THE DREAMTIME

Australian Aboriginal cultures vary greatly; however, nearly all share the concept of 'dreamtime' – the time of creation. Aboriginal lore maintains that, before creation, basic matter existed, but then the spirits of dreaming imbued the world with physical features and spiritual substance. The landscape can be read as a complex system of signs revealing the truth of these ancestral spirits.

The spirit figure in this rock painting in Kakadu National Park is Barrginj, wife of Lightning Man.

PACIFIC OCEAN
Sunda
Sahul
Huon Peninsula 38,000 BCE
Klowa 8300 BCE
Yuku 8000 BCE
New Guinea
New Ireland
Matenkupkum 31,000 BCE
New Britain
Buka 24,000 BCE
Bougainville
Solomon Islands
Timor
Kafiavana 9000 BCE
Nawamoyn and Malangangerr 21,000 BCE
Kosipe 26,000 BCE
Misisil 10,000 BCE
Early Man Shelter 11,000 BCE
8000–6000 BCE: New Guinea land bridge lost
Miriwun 16,000 BCE
Walkunder Arch 17,500 BCE
Colless Creek 16,000 BCE
Coral Sea
Talgai 14,000 BCE
Kenniff Cave 17,000 BCE
Mount Newman 18,000 BCE
Puntutjarba 8000 BCE
Menindee Lake 24,000 BCE
Upper Swan 37,000 BCE
Allen's Cave 23,000 BCE
Bass Point 15,000 BCE
Willandra Lakes 33,000 BCE
Mammoth Cave 35,000 BCE
Roonka 16,000 BCE
Kings Table 20,000 BCE
Kalgan Hall 17,000 BCE
Cohuna and Kow Swamp 60,000 BCE
Keilor 43,000 BCE
Clogg's Cave 15,000 BCE
Cave Bay Cave 21,000 BCE
10,000–8000 BCE: Tasmanian land bridge lost
Fraser Cave 18,000 BCE
500 km
500 miles

The settlement of Australia, Tasmania, and New Guinea

No one knows exactly when or by what route the first settlers reached Australia and New Guinea. What is certain is that they would have had to cross a stretch of open sea. In the case of Australia, this was probably from the island of Timor, 70 km from the mainland when sea level was at its lowest. Although Australia enjoyed a better climate with higher rainfall than today, settlement would have been largely near the coast. Valuable archaeological evidence was lost when sea levels rose again at the end of the last Ice Age. At this point the Tasmanians, who may have been an early wave of immigrants, were cut off from the mainland.

◄ **1 The settlement of Australia, Tasmania, and New Guinea**

Archaeological sites with approximate date of earliest human presence
- ◇ pre 20,000 BCE
- ◆ post 20,000 BCE
- probable migration routes
- possible migration routes
- maximum extent of Sahul landmass c.16,000 BCE
- maximum extent of Sunda landmass c.16,000 BCE

Within their home range, most Aborigines led a largely nomadic life, following the food supply according to the seasons. The men were armed with spears for hunting, as in this rock painting; the women carried digging sticks and baskets.

The settlement of Australia and New Guinea

- **60,000:** Possible date of partial male skeleton found at Kow Swamp on Murray River
- **40,000:** Australoids start voyaging out towards Solomon Islands
- **38,000:** Campfire site on New Guinea's Huon Peninsula
- **30,000:** Careful burial of male body near Lake Mungo, one of the Willandra Lakes sites
- **18,000:** Fraser Cave on southern tip of Tasmania occupied
- **10,000:** First human-like figures in Australian rock art
- **c.10,000:** Land bridge connecting Australia and Tasmania starts to disappear
- **c.8000–6000:** Rising sea level covers New Guinea land bridge

60,000 BCE | 50,000 | 40,000 | 30,000 | 20,000 | 10,000 | 1 CE

Prehistoric agricultural development on New Guinea

The Australoids of Sahul were hunter-gatherers. However, as early as 6000 BCE, New Guineans began clearing dense forests, placing them among the world's first crop gardeners. Remains of pigs and dogs dating from 4000–3000 BCE suggest these were brought to New Guinea by Austronesian immigrants, who also introduced techniques of taro cultivation and swamp drainage and management. These soon spread from coastal regions to the Western Highlands. The inhabitants of the Eastern Highlands, however, grew a different staple rootcrop, *Pueraria lobata*, while continuing to hunt and gather.

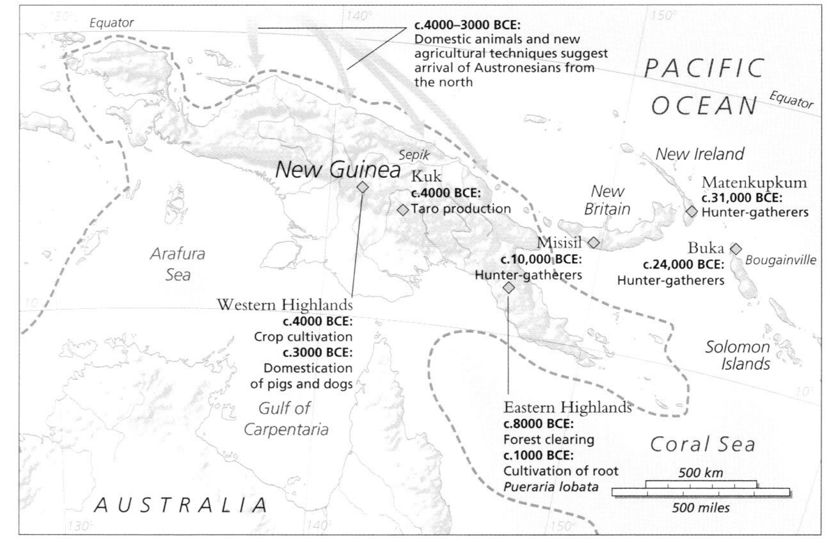

▲ **2 Prehistoric New Guinea**
- possible routes of Austronesians
- maximum extent of Sahul landmass c.16,000 BCE
- ◇ archaeological site

Horticulture in New Guinea has changed little over 8000 years. Yams, introduced from Asia by Austronesian peoples in about 4000 BCE, became a staple throughout the Pacific.

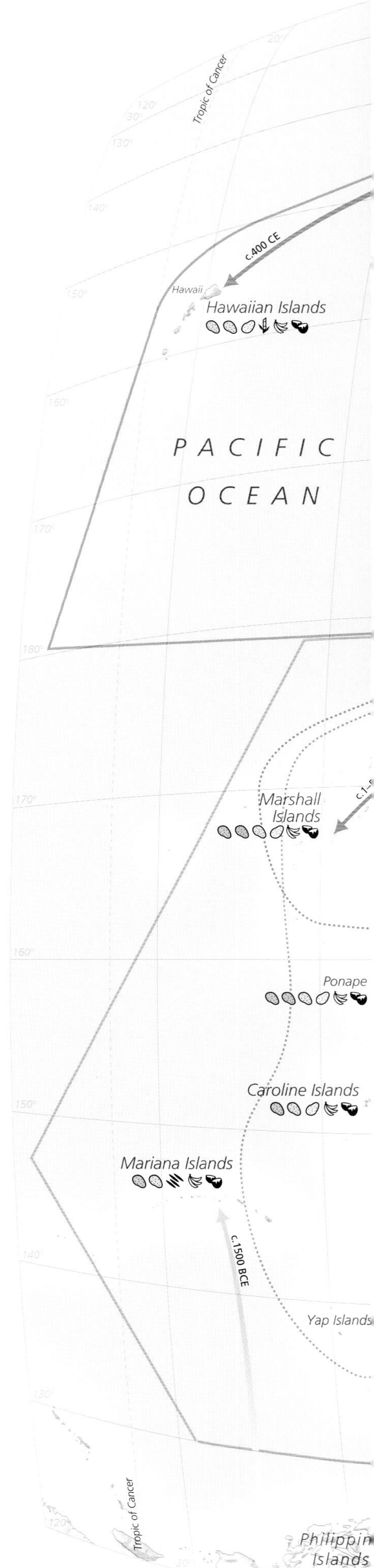

The peopling of the Pacific

Settlement of the Pacific was accomplished in two epic series of migrations. From about 2000 BCE Austronesian peoples settled Melanesia, sailing from the Philippines, the Bismarck Archipelago, the Solomons, and ultimately Fiji. Their spread can be charted by their distinctive Lapita pottery. The Fiji-Tonga-Samoa crescent was the cradle of a new, equally dynamic culture: the Polynesians. A major migration, probably from Samoa, to the Marquesas, was the springboard that launched the Polynesians to the remaining far-flung islands of the Pacific, from New Zealand in the south to Hawaii in the north and Rapa Nui (Easter Island) in the east.

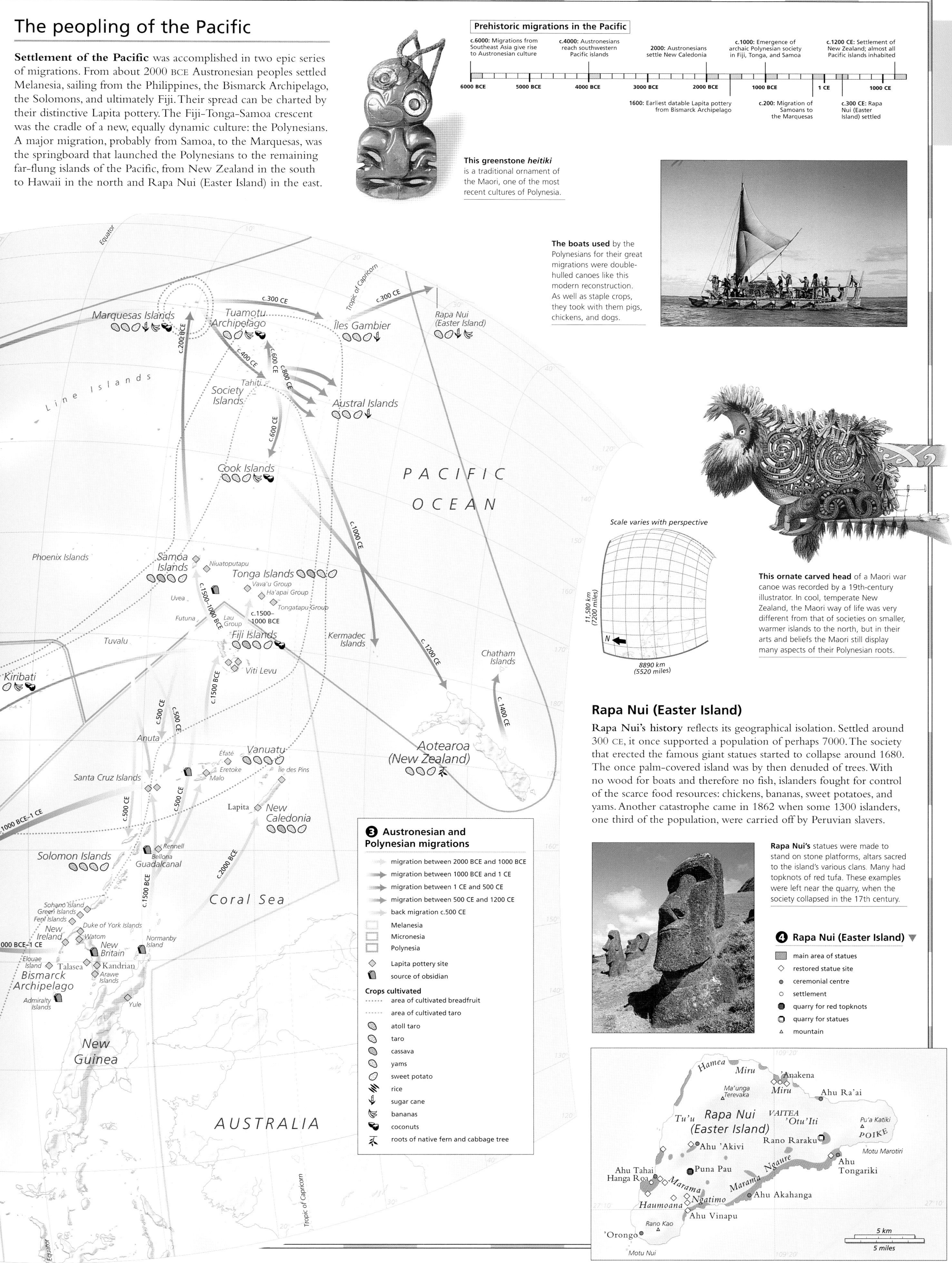

This greenstone *heitiki* is a traditional ornament of the Maori, one of the most recent cultures of Polynesia.

The boats used by the Polynesians for their great migrations were double-hulled canoes like this modern reconstruction. As well as staple crops, they took with them pigs, chickens, and dogs.

This ornate carved head of a Maori war canoe was recorded by a 19th-century illustrator. In cool, temperate New Zealand, the Maori way of life was very different from that of societies on smaller, warmer islands to the north, but in their arts and beliefs the Maori still display many aspects of their Polynesian roots.

Rapa Nui (Easter Island)

Rapa Nui's history reflects its geographical isolation. Settled around 300 CE, it once supported a population of perhaps 7000. The society that erected the famous giant statues started to collapse around 1680. The once palm-covered island was by then denuded of trees. With no wood for boats and therefore no fish, islanders fought for control of the scarce food resources: chickens, bananas, sweet potatoes, and yams. Another catastrophe came in 1862 when some 1300 islanders, one third of the population, were carried off by Peruvian slavers.

Rapa Nui's statues were made to stand on stone platforms, altars sacred to the island's various clans. Many had topknots of red tufa. These examples were left near the quarry, when the society collapsed in the 17th century.

THE COLONIZATION OF AUSTRALASIA

Australian convicts working in road gangs wore distinctive dress and were chained.

THE BRITISH COLONIES in Australia and New Zealand rank with the US as the most successful transplantations of European culture to another continent. Neither colony had auspicious beginnings: Australia was where Britain transported its unwanted criminals; New Zealand was a convenient base for sealers and whalers in search of quick profits. In time, both started to attract emigrants from Europe in their tens of thousands. As in the US, the colonists simply drove out the native peoples by any means available. The Aborigines of Australia and the Maori of New Zealand were treated as obstacles to the progress of settlers who wanted to raise familiar European crops and livestock on their lands. In Tasmania, settlers wiped out the entire population in the space of 70 years.

THE FIRST FLEET AND BOTANY BAY

In January 1788, to the astonishment of the local Aborigines, a fleet of 11 British ships sailed into Botany Bay. On board were 778 convicts and their jailers. After his visit in 1770, Captain Cook had described Botany Bay as well-watered and fertile, but this proved untrue and the convicts were moved to Port Jackson, a natural harbour to the north. The penal settlement at Port Jackson grew to become Australia's largest city – Sydney. However, it was the name Botany Bay that stuck in the British imagination as the time-honoured destination for transported convicts.

A detachment of ships from the First Fleet sails to join the others anchored in Botany Bay.

European impact in Australia

Britain's decision to colonize New South Wales was in part a result of the loss of its North American colonies, where convicted criminals had been transported in the past. The impact of the first convict settlement at Port Jackson (Sydney) indicated the course Australia's history would take. Aborigines living nearby were nearly wiped out by introduced disease, then driven off by force of arms. Further penal colonies were established, the most notorious being on Tasmania (Van Diemen's Land), where convicts were first landed in 1803. In 1821 over half the island's population consisted of convicts. Free immigrants came to New South Wales as early as 1793 and free colonies were established in Western Australia in 1829 and South Australia in 1836. The former suffered from a labour shortage, so convicts were shipped there in the 1850s. As the immigrant population grew, both with freed convicts and new settlers, pressure for new land for grazing resulted in frequent clashes between drovers and Aborigines.

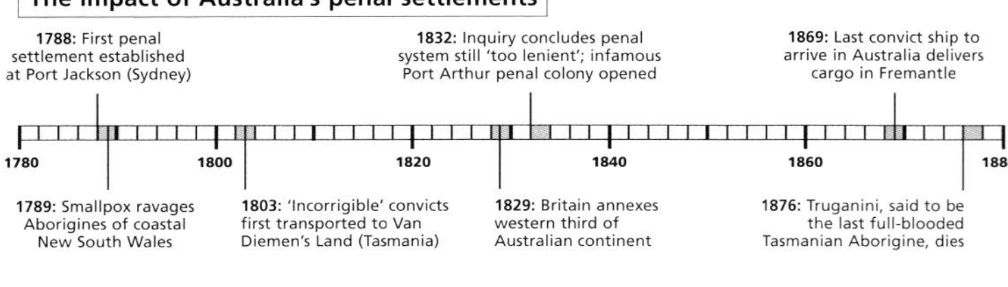

The lure of gold

The event that accelerated the growth of the Australian colonies was the discovery of gold in New South Wales and Victoria in 1851. The richest finds were at Bendigo and Ballarat, and in the 1850s more than 1000 tonnes of gold were dug up in Victoria. In a gold rush to rival that of California in 1849, the population of Australia trebled in less than a decade. A later gold rush occurred in the 1890s when gold was discovered at Kalgoorlie in the remote deserts of Western Australia.

Gold rushes in Australia 1851–1900

1851: First gold strike at Bathurst, New South Wales

1861: At Lambing Flat, white miners burn camps of 3000 Chinese miners

c.1890: Gold discovered at Kalgoorlie, Western Australia

1850 · 1860 · 1870 · 1880 · 1890 · 1900

1854–55: Eureka uprising by Ballarat miners; police kill 45. In following year New South Wales and Victoria granted parliaments

1890: Western Australia last state to be granted self-government

1,100,000 · 1 million · 900,000 · 800,000 · 700,000 · 600,000 · 500,000 · 400,000 · 300,000 · 200,000 · 100,000 · 0

1851 · 1861 · 1871 · 1881 · 1891

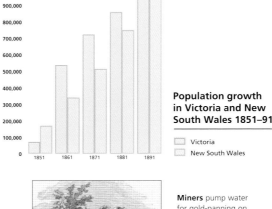

Population growth in Victoria and New South Wales 1851–91

Victoria

New South Wales

Miners pump water for gold-panning on a claim near Bathurst. Many who arrived in Australia in the 1850s were experienced prospectors from the California gold rush.

2 Australian goldfields 1850–90

Discovery of goldfields: 1850–60 · 1860–70 · 1870–90

QUEENSLAND · SOUTH AUSTRALIA · NEW SOUTH WALES · VICTORIA · TASMANIA · INDIAN OCEAN · Tasman Sea · Bass Strait · Great Dividing Range · Tropic of Capricorn · Darling · Murray · 250 km · 250 miles

Gympie · Brisbane · Hillgrove · Cobar · Gulgong · Hargraves · Newcastle · Forbes · Bathurst · Grenfell · Lambing Flat · Sydney · Adelaide · Echunga · Adelong · Araluen · Bendigo · Ovens · Ararat · Omeo · Clunes · Walhalla · Ballarat · Hill End · Castlemaine · Melbourne · Beaconsfield · Launceston · Mount Lyell · Lefroy · Hobart

Federation Australia

The Commonwealth of Australia was established in 1901 after referendums in the six states had voted for a federation. Throughout the 20th century, traditional agriculture and stock-rearing met problems through lack of water, and disasters such as a plague of introduced rabbits. After the Second World War, however, the country enjoyed a period of prosperity with the discovery of valuable mineral reserves and immigration was encouraged. In the late 1980s the Aboriginal population found a new political consciousness and began to lodge claims to traditional tribal lands.

Aboriginal protesters at the Australian bicentennial celebrations of 1988 display the Aboriginal flag to draw attention to two centuries of neglect and marginalization.

Federation Australia from 1901

- **1901:** Australia becomes self-governing federation within British Empire
- **1914–18:** Over 60,000 Australian troops lose lives in First World War
- **1930s:** Australia hit hard by global depression
- **1942:** Australia under threat of invasion as Japanese bomb Darwin
- **1948:** White immigration, especially from UK, becomes post-war policy
- **1972:** Labour government of Gough Whitlam challenges paternalistic attitude of UK to Australia
- **1975:** Restrictions imposed on immigration
- **1988:** Aboriginal protests at Bicentennial celebrations
- **1993:** Native Title Act recognizes Aborigine rights to land
- **2001:** 'Pacific Solution' of farming out asylum seekers to other countries adopted

3 Federal Australia from 1901

Land use: arable land; rough grazing; forest and woodland; desert; mountain region; major areas subject to Aboriginal title claims 1997; state boundary; state capital

Mineral resources: coal; oil; gas; iron; lead and zinc; bauxite/aluminium; uranium; gold; precious stones

Europe encounters New Zealand

The first European settlements in New Zealand were sealing and whaling stations, set up around 1800. At first they enjoyed good relations with the local Maori, who were keen to trade so they could get hold of metal axes and muskets. The results were disastrous: inter-tribal warfare took on a totally new character, tribes with muskets being able to massacre those without, and migrations spread the conflict throughout both islands. It was against this background that the New Zealand Company was set up to encourage British immigrants with assisted passages.

In this portrait drawn on Captain Cook's first voyage in 1769, the artist captures the pride and composure of a tattooed Maori warrior.

4 New Zealand 1800–40

main areas of Maori settlement 1800; European settlement established by 1850; Maori intertribal battle 1820–36; whaling station before 1840; sealing station before 1840; Maori migration; Maori raid on other Maoris in area

New Zealand 1800–40

- **1802:** First British and American sealing stations operating on east coast
- **1814:** Samuel Marsden establishes mission in the Bay of Islands
- **1818:** Start of Maori 'Musket Wars'
- **1825:** Musket Wars at their peak; Christian missionaries attempt to mediate
- **1830:** A mere 200 foreigners, mostly British, permanently resident in New Zealand
- **1833:** British Resident appointed in Kororareka to challenge attempted French colonization
- **1837:** New Zealand Company founded

New Zealand becomes British

The Treaty of Waitangi, signed in 1840 by over 500 Maori chiefs, gave sovereignty over New Zealand to Britain, while guaranteeing Maori ownership of the land. In practice, the Crown – and later private individuals – purchased the land for trifling sums. In response to this, the Maori fought long, bloody wars against the intruders. Unlike Australia's Aborigines, who used hit-and-run tactics, the Maori waged sustained battles from fortified stockades and earthworks. After their defeat, they were reduced to marginal existence. Only in the 1990s did the Maori, some 15% of the population, start to receive substantial compensation for the wrongs of Waitangi.

New Zealand 1840–70

- **1840:** Treaty of Waitangi
- **1841:** New Zealand becomes a separate Crown Colony
- **1845–46:** Northern War, started by Ngapuhi chiefs deprived of trade when capital moved from Russell to Auckland
- **1852:** Constitution Act divides New Zealand into six provinces
- **1858:** King Movement demands Maori state and opposes further land sales
- **1860:** Settler population over 100,000; Europeans outnumber Maori
- **1861:** Gold discovered in Otago province
- **1862:** Second Maori War
- **c.1865:** Some 14,000 British troops deployed in New Zealand
- **1870:** Maori resistance effectively crushed

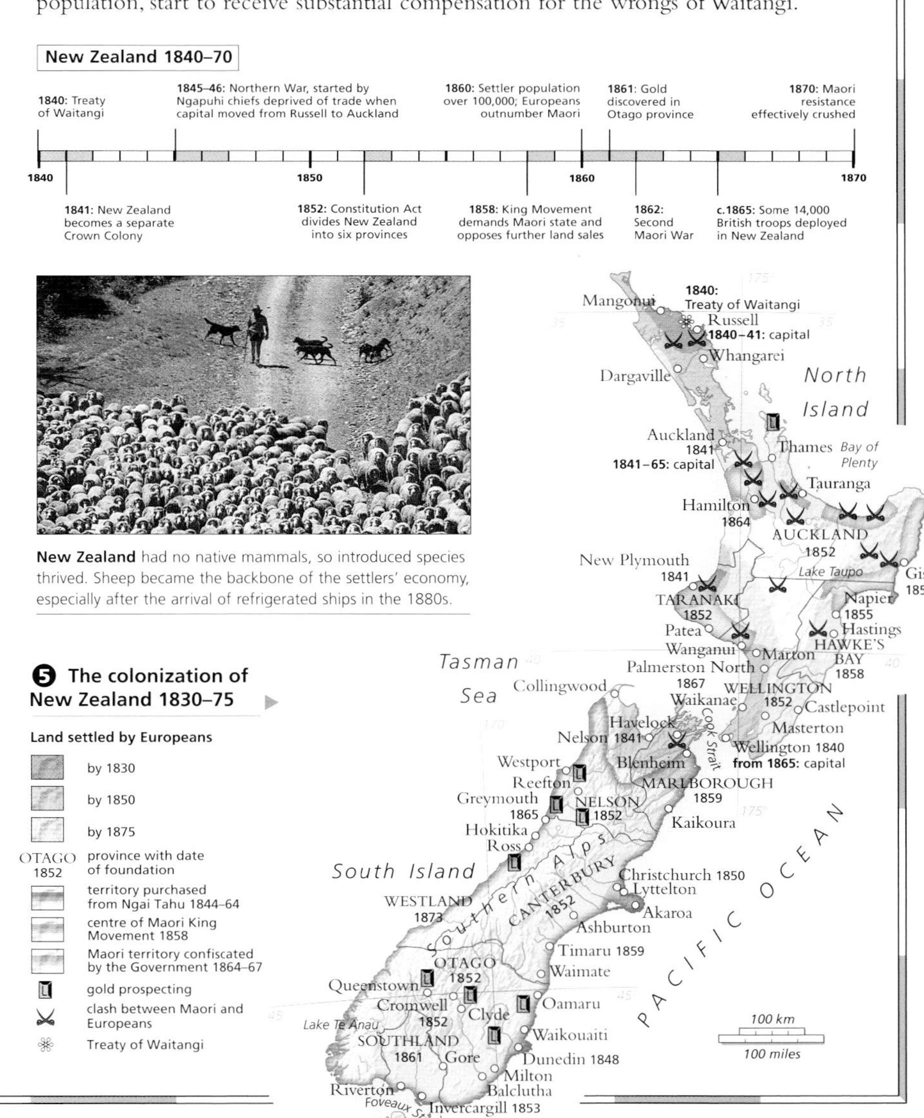

New Zealand had no native mammals, so introduced species thrived. Sheep became the backbone of the settlers' economy, especially after the arrival of refrigerated ships in the 1880s.

5 The colonization of New Zealand 1830–75

Land settled by Europeans: by 1830; by 1850; by 1875

OTAGO 1852: province with date of foundation; territory purchased from Ngai Tahu 1844–64; centre of Maori King Movement 1858; Maori territory confiscated by the Government 1864–67; gold prospecting; clash between Maori and Europeans; Treaty of Waitangi

THE COLONIZATION OF THE PACIFIC

A Hawaiian surfer typifies the modern image of the Pacific as a vast playground for leisure pursuits.

THE 19TH CENTURY WITNESSED the near annihilation of many Pacific island societies. Firearms made intertribal warfare more lethal, but many more deaths were caused by alien diseases, especially measles and influenza. Killings by colonial powers as they asserted their authority, and 'blackbirding' (slave-raiding for labourers in the sugar-cane fields of Queensland and elsewhere) also contributed to the rapid depopulation of the islands. Many demoralized communities experienced an alarming fall in birth rate. However, subsequent repopulation by immigrant Europeans, Indians, Chinese, Japanese, North and South Americans rebuilt many island societies with new forms of trade, culture, and administration. European and American governments put in place political structures that, over time, enabled remnant Pacific peoples to survive as a host of new nations, territories and federations. Many of these now seek a wider forum. In the 1990s governments started to make calls for a 'United States of the Pacific'.

MISSIONARIES IN THE SOUTH SEAS

Throughout most of the Pacific, a region that had hitherto known only nature and ancestor worship, ancient values and practices were swept away by the arrival of Christianity. In the 17th century the Spanish founded missions in Micronesia, but by the mid-19th century Roman Catholic, Anglican, and Wesleyan missions were operating across Polynesia. Often the islanders' first contact with European customs, the missions paved the way for the wholesale Europeanization of Pacific cultures. Today a conservative, communal Christianity is the dominant feature of many Pacific island communities.

The high priest of Tahitian ruler Pomare II kneels before representatives of the London Missionary Society. The conversion of Pomare, who took control of Tahiti in 1815, was seen as a triumph for the society.

Imperialism in the Pacific

The expense of administering far-flung islands in the Pacific did not always appeal to the great 19th-century colonial powers. As a rule, they preferred to promise friendly rulers the status of protectorate. Towards the end of the century, however, colonial rivalry, especially between the French, Germans, and British led to the formal annexation of many territories. In larger territories, such as Fiji and Hawaii, where there was the possibility of establishing plantations, annexation was followed by the importation of large numbers of migrant workers.

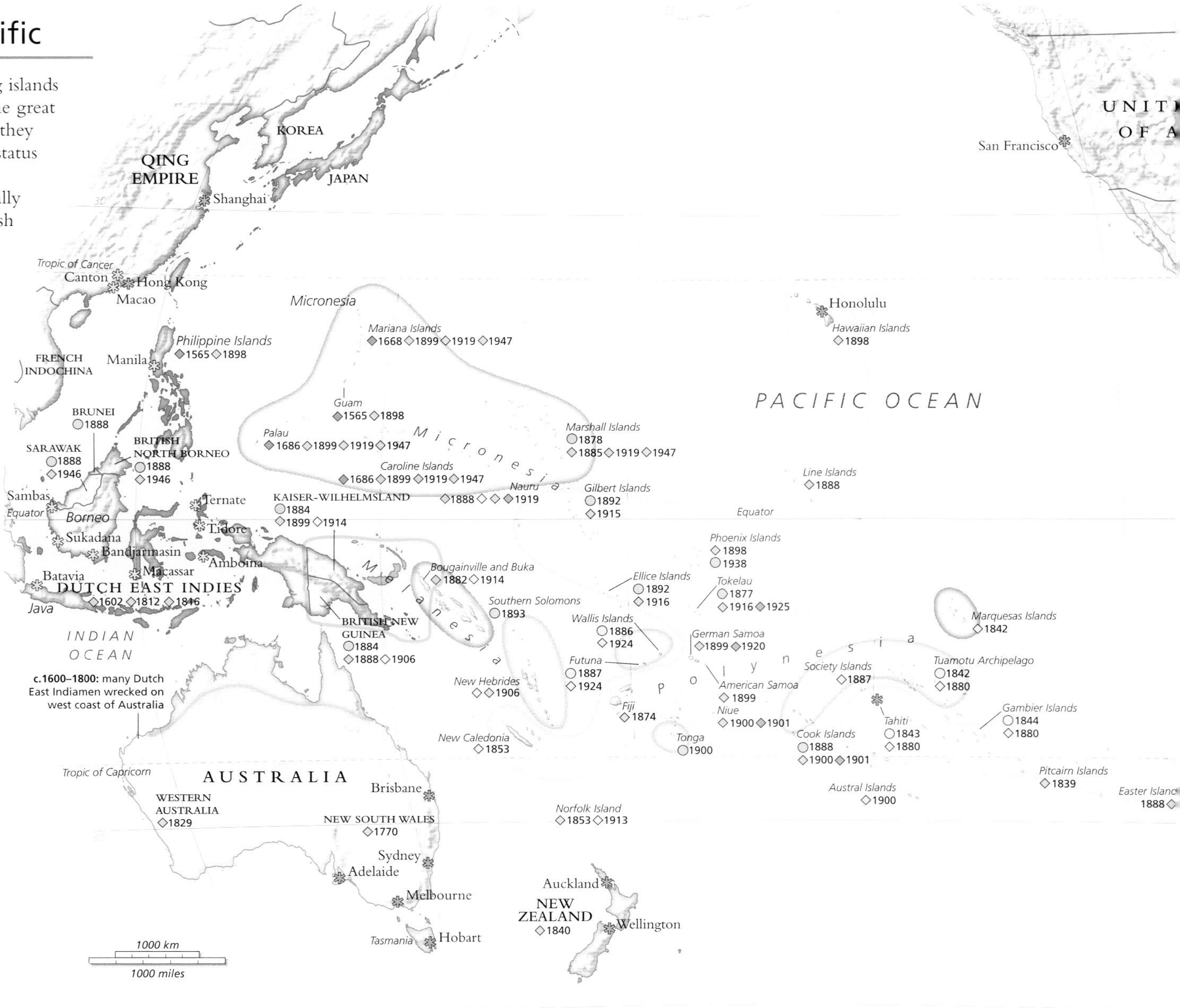

1 Imperialism in the Pacific

Period of first European contact
- 16th century
- 17th century
- 18th century

European and US trading posts
- by 1700
- by 1850

Protectorates and colonies
- ○ protectorate with date established
- ◇ colony with date established
- ◇ Australian
- ○◇ British
- ◇ Chilean
- ◇ Dutch
- ○◇ French
- ○◇ German
- ◇ Japanese
- ◇ NZ
- ◆ Spanish
- ○◇ US
- Australian mandate 1920
- frontiers 1900

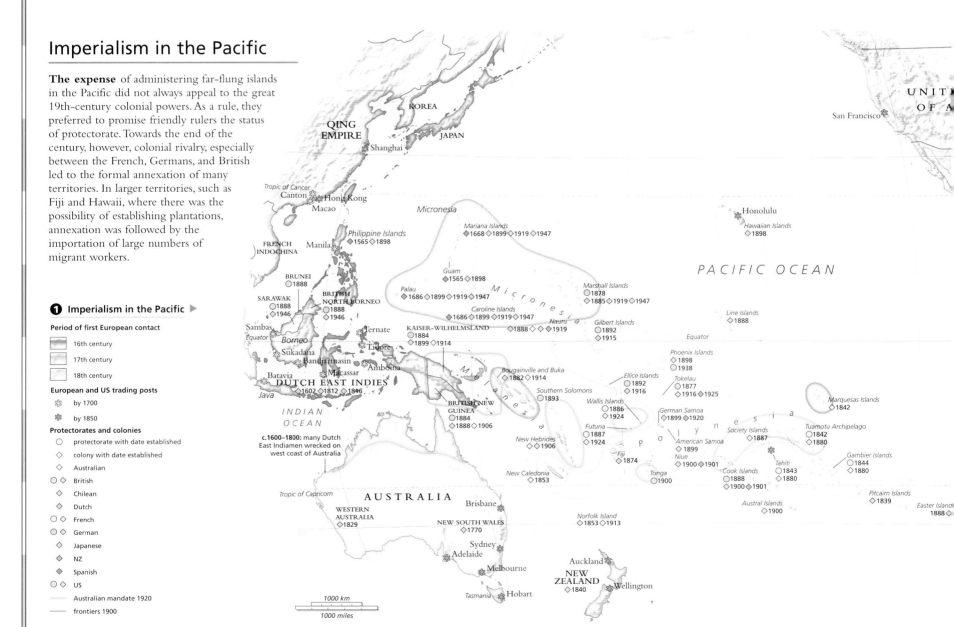

QING EMPIRE · KOREA · JAPAN · Shanghai · Tropic of Cancer · Canton · Hong Kong · Macao · FRENCH INDOCHINA · Manila · Philippine Islands ◆1565 ◇1898 · Micronesia · Mariana Islands ◆1668 ◇1899 ◇1919 ◇1947 · Guam ◆1565 ◇1898 · Palau ◆1686 ◇1899 ◇1919 ◇1947 · Caroline Islands ◆1686 ◇1899 ◇1919 ◇1947 · Marshall Islands ○1878 ◇1885 ◇1919 ◇1947 · Nauru ◇1888 ◇ ◇ ◇1919 · Gilbert Islands ○1892 ◇1915 · BRUNEI ○1888 · SARAWAK ○1888 ◇1946 · BRITISH NORTH BORNEO ○1888 ◇1946 · Sambas · Equator · Borneo · Ternate · Tidore · Sukadana · Bandjarmasin · Amboina · Macassar · Batavia · Java · DUTCH EAST INDIES ◇1602 ◇1812 ◇1846 · KAISER-WILHELMSLAND ○1884 ◇1899 ◇1914 · BRITISH NEW GUINEA ○1884 ◇1888 ◇1906 · Bougainville and Buka ◇1882 ◇1914 · Southern Solomons ○1893 · Melanesia · INDIAN OCEAN · c.1600–1800: many Dutch East Indiamen wrecked on west coast of Australia · Tropic of Capricorn · AUSTRALIA · WESTERN AUSTRALIA ◇1829 · Brisbane · NEW SOUTH WALES ◇1770 · Sydney · Adelaide · Melbourne · Tasmania · Hobart · New Hebrides ◇◇1906 · New Caledonia ◇1853 · Norfolk Island ◇1853 ◇1913 · Auckland · NEW ZEALAND ◇1840 · Wellington · Ellice Islands ○1892 ◇1916 · Wallis Islands ○1886 ◇1924 · Futuna ○1887 ◇1924 · Fiji ◇1874 · Tonga ○1900 · Tokelau ○1877 ◇1916 ◇1925 · Phoenix Islands ◇1898 ○1938 · German Samoa ◇1899 ◇1920 · American Samoa ◇1899 · Niue ◇1900 ◇1901 · Cook Islands ○1888 ◇1900 ◇1901 · Society Islands ◇1887 · Tahiti ○1843 ◇1880 · Austral Islands ○1900 · Polynesia · Line Islands ◇1888 · Honolulu · Hawaiian Islands ◇1898 · PACIFIC OCEAN · Equator · Marquesas Islands ◇1842 · Tuamotu Archipelago ○1842 ◇1880 · Gambier Islands ○1844 ◇1880 · Pitcairn Islands ◇1839 · Easter Island 1888 ◇ · San Francisco · UNITED STATES OF AMERICA

1000 km / 1000 miles

This pictorial proclamation, issued in Australia in 1829, aimed to show the fairness of British justice. If an Aborigine killed a European, he would be hanged; if a European killed an Aborigine, he would suffer the same fate. In practice, this ideal was very rarely implemented in any of the European colonies in the Pacific.

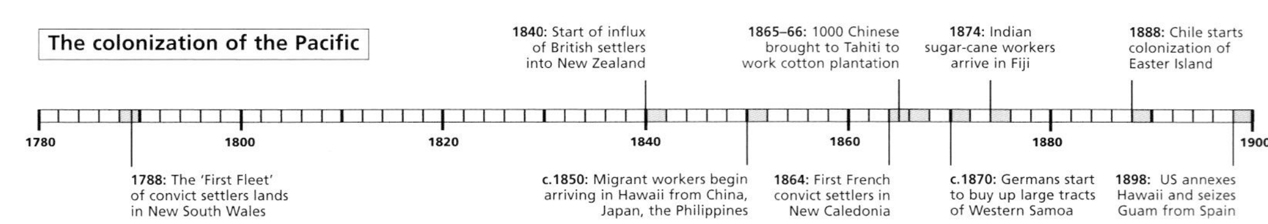

The colonization of the Pacific
1780
1800
1820
1840
1860
1880
1900
1788: The 'First Fleet' of convict settlers lands in New South Wales
1840: Start of influx of British settlers into New Zealand
c.1850: Migrant workers begin arriving in Hawaii from China, Japan, the Philippines
1864: First French convict settlers in New Caledonia
1865–66: 1000 Chinese brought to Tahiti to work cotton plantation
c.1870: Germans start to buy up large tracts of Western Samoa
1874: Indian sugar-cane workers arrive in Fiji
1888: Chile starts colonization of Easter Island
1898: US annexes Hawaii and seizes Guam from Spain

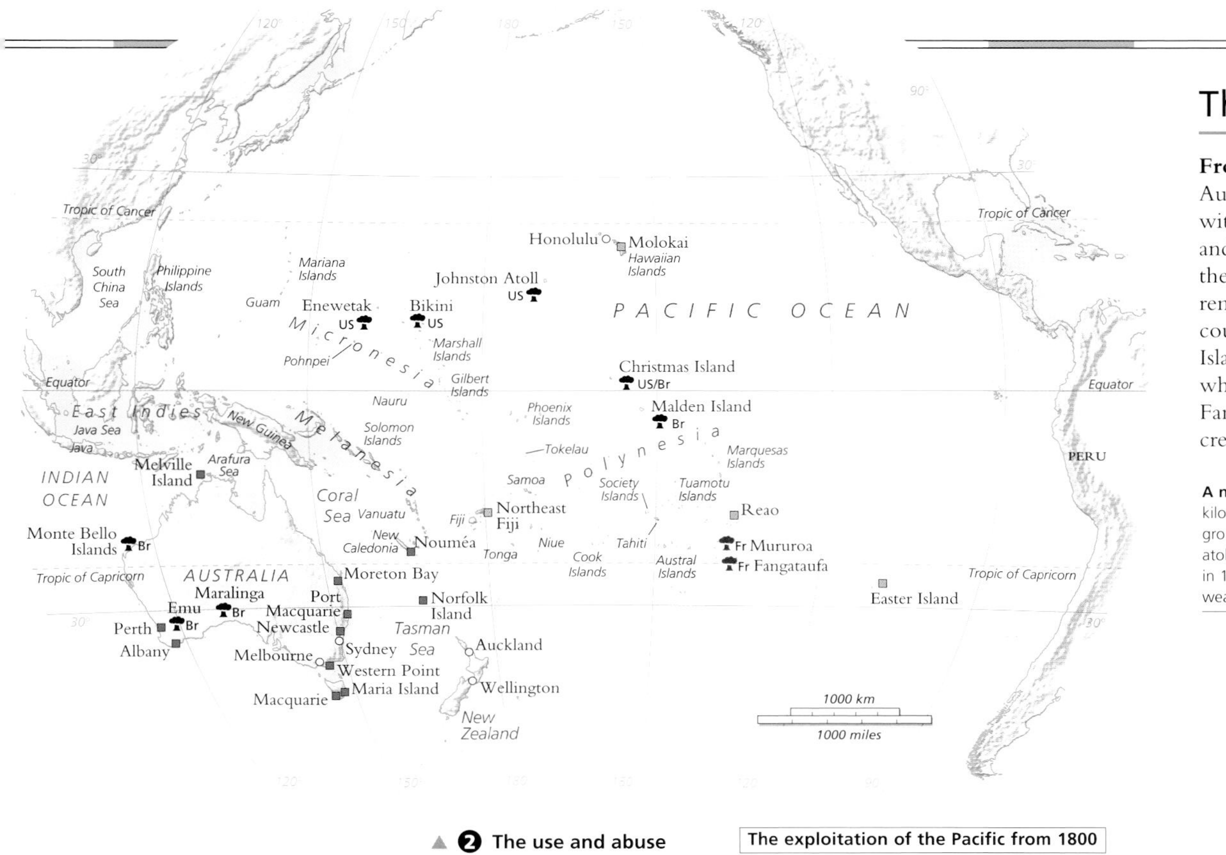

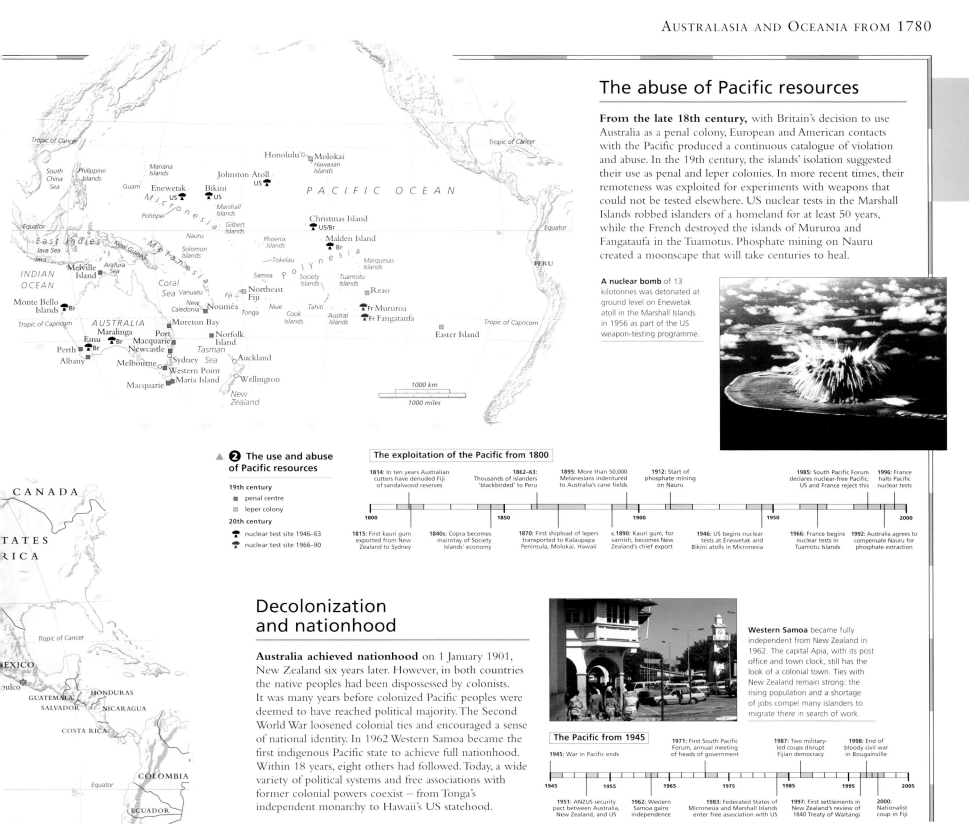

The abuse of Pacific resources

From the late 18th century, with Britain's decision to use Australia as a penal colony, European and American contacts with the Pacific produced a continuous catalogue of violation and abuse. In the 19th century, the islands' isolation suggested their use as penal and leper colonies. In more recent times, their remoteness was exploited for experiments with weapons that could not be tested elsewhere. US nuclear tests in the Marshall Islands robbed islanders of a homeland for at least 50 years, while the French destroyed the islands of Mururoa and Fangataufa in the Tuamotus. Phosphate mining on Nauru created a moonscape that will take centuries to heal.

A nuclear bomb of 13 kilotonnes was detonated at ground level on Enewetak atoll in the Marshall Islands in 1956 as part of the US weapon-testing programme.

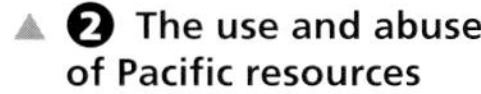

▲ **2 The use and abuse of Pacific resources**

19th century
- penal centre
- leper colony

20th century
- nuclear test site 1946–63
- nuclear test site 1966–90

The exploitation of the Pacific from 1800

- **1814:** In ten years Australian cutters have denuded Fiji of sandalwood reserves
- **1815:** First kauri gum exported from New Zealand to Sydney
- **1840s:** Copra becomes mainstay of Society Islands' economy
- **1862–63:** Thousands of islanders 'blackbirded' to Peru
- **1870:** First shipload of lepers transported to Kalaupapa Peninsula, Molokai, Hawaii
- **1895:** More than 50,000 Melanesians indentured to Australia's cane fields
- **c.1890:** Kauri gum, for varnish, becomes New Zealand's chief export
- **1912:** Start of phosphate mining on Nauru
- **1946:** US begins nuclear tests at Enewetak and Bikini atolls in Micronesia
- **1966:** France begins nuclear tests in Tuamotu Islands
- **1985:** South Pacific Forum declares nuclear-free Pacific; US and France reject this
- **1992:** Australia agrees to compensate Nauru for phosphate extraction
- **1996:** France halts Pacific nuclear tests

1800 1850 1900 1950 2000

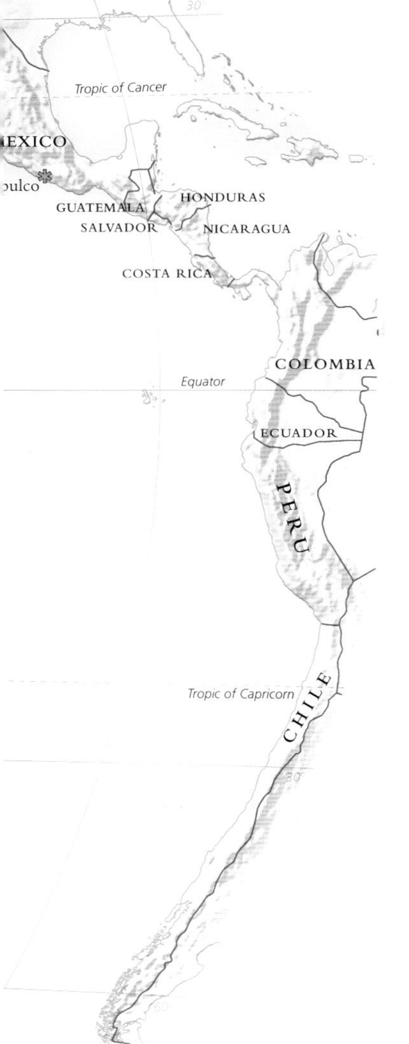

Decolonization and nationhood

Australia achieved nationhood on 1 January 1901, New Zealand six years later. However, in both countries the native peoples had been dispossessed by colonists. It was many years before colonized Pacific peoples were deemed to have reached political majority. The Second World War loosened colonial ties and encouraged a sense of national identity. In 1962 Western Samoa became the first indigenous Pacific state to achieve full nationhood. Within 18 years, eight others had followed. Today, a wide variety of political systems and free associations with former colonial powers coexist – from Tonga's independent monarchy to Hawaii's US statehood.

Western Samoa became fully independent from New Zealand in 1962. The capital Apia, with its post office and town clock, still has the look of a colonial town. Ties with New Zealand remain strong: the rising population and a shortage of jobs compel many islanders to migrate there in search of work.

The Pacific from 1945

- **1945:** War in Pacific ends
- **1951:** ANZUS security pact between Australia, New Zealand, and US
- **1962:** Western Samoa gains independence
- **1971:** First South Pacific Forum, annual meeting of heads of government
- **1983:** Federated States of Micronesia and Marshall Islands enter free association with US
- **1987:** Two military-led coups disrupt Fijian democracy
- **1997:** First settlements in New Zealand's review of 1840 Treaty of Waitangi
- **1998:** End of bloody civil war in Bougainville
- **2000:** Nationalist coup in Fiji

1945 1955 1965 1975 1985 1995 2005

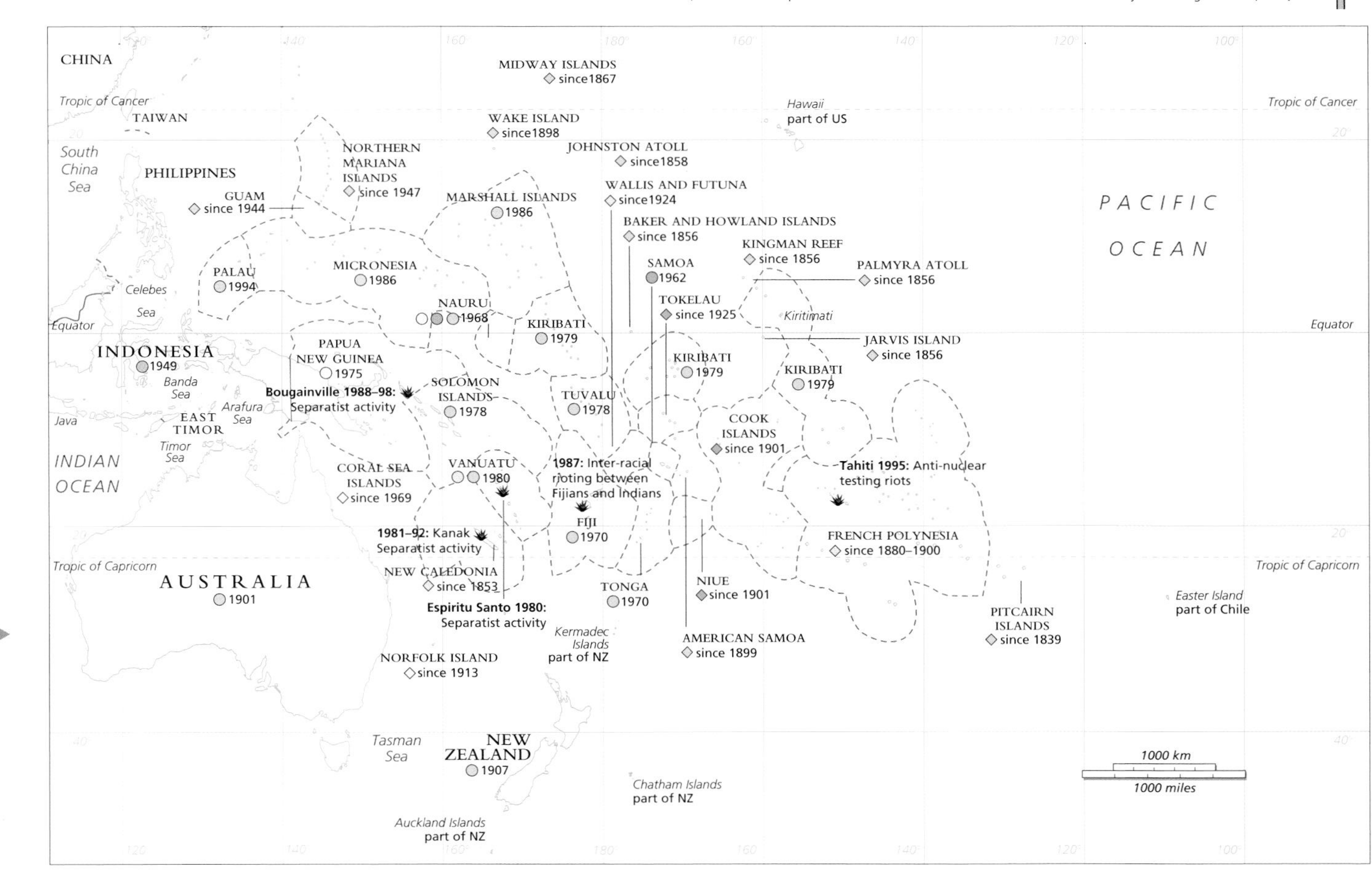

3 Decolonization and nationhood ▶

- independent from (with date)
- dependency of
- Australia
- France
- Netherlands
- New Zealand
- UK
- US
- conflict since 1980

THE ARCTIC AND ANTARCTICA

EXPLORATION AND MAPPING

The Norwegian Roald Amundsen led expeditions to the Arctic and Antarctica.

THE FROZEN LIMITS OF THE GLOBE – the Arctic an icy ocean, the Antarctic an ice-capped mountainous continent – were not fully explored until the 20th century. Their hostile environment still provides a challenge for explorers. Viking sailors travelled to Iceland and Greenland in the 9th and 10th centuries, establishing settlements on both islands. Not until the 16th century were serious attempts made to forge a passage around the Arctic Ocean. Despite the efforts of those who braved the turbulent southern waters in search of a new continent, the Antarctic remained mysterious until the 20th century, when it was confirmed that it was indeed a continent rather than an ice mass linking a series of islands. Further knowledge of both the Arctic and the Antarctic was gained by air exploration and of the Arctic by the use of submarines.

The search for northern routes to Asia

Aiming to circumvent Iberian control of the central Atlantic, Dutch and British sailors sought northern routes to Asia and the Pacific during the 16th century. Early attempts to find a northeast route were sponsored by the Muscovy Company, and Richard Chancellor was able to set up a trading partnership with Russia. Willem Barents, experienced in Arctic conditions, reached Novaya Zemlya in 1596. Martin Frobisher's 1576 journey was the first to attempt a western passage. In 1585–87, John Davis travelled between Greenland and Baffin Island, reaching 72°N. Henry Hudson bore west, to enter the vast bay that bears his name in 1610, and William Baffin, piloting Hudson's ship, *Discovery*, traced the northern reaches of Baffin Bay, although all attempts to find a viable northern passage to the Pacific were unsuccessful until the 19th century.

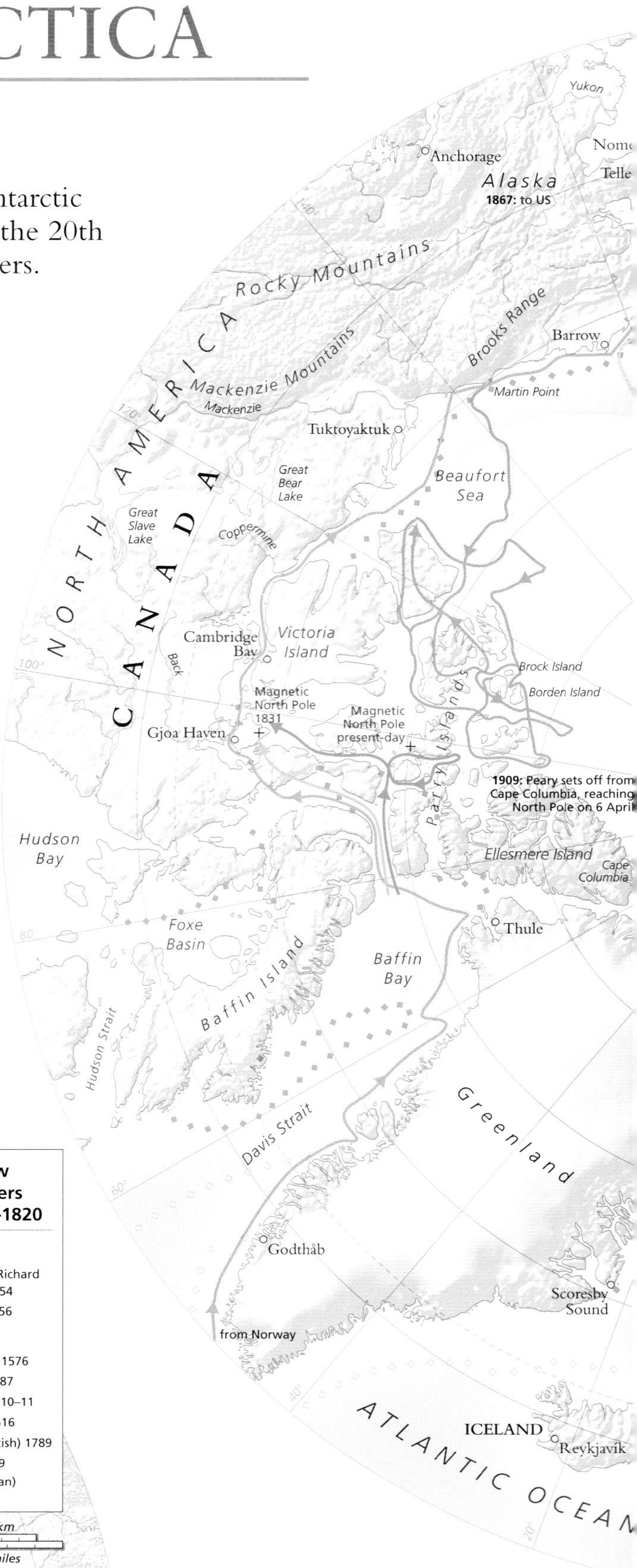

1 The search for new routes to Asia: explorers of the far north 1550–1820

Northeast passage
- Sir Hugh Willoughby and Richard Chancellor (English) 1553–54
- Willem Barents (Dutch) 1556

Northwest passage
- Martin Frobisher (English) 1576
- John Davis (English) 1585–87
- Henry Hudson (English) 1610–11
- William Baffin (English) 1616
- Alexander Mackenzie (British) 1789
- John Franklin (British) 1819
- Vitus Bering (Danish-Russian) 1728–30

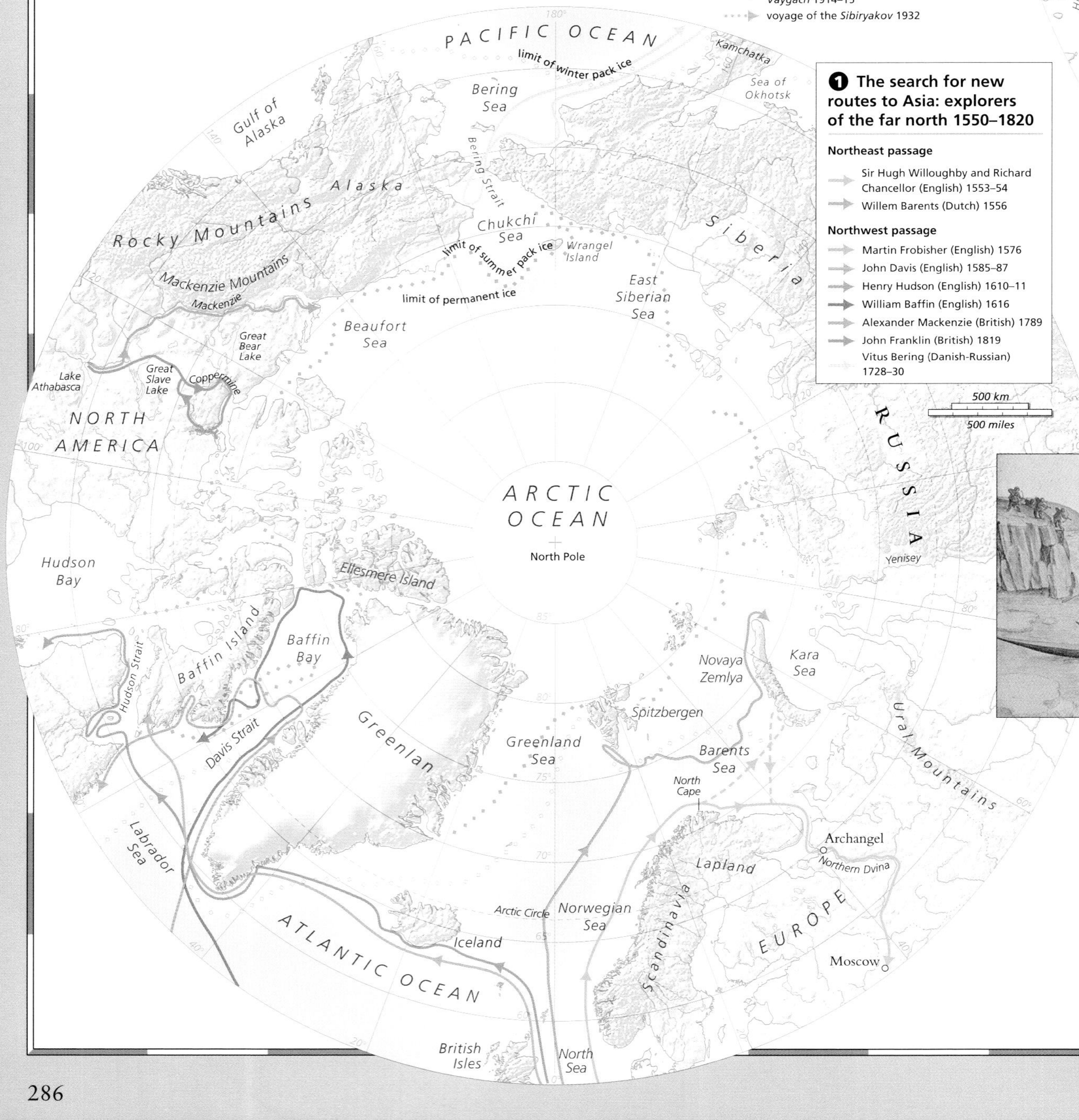

500 km / 500 miles

2 Charting the Arctic coast and the race to the North Pole

The western Arctic
- James Clark Ross (British) 1829–33
- John Franklin (British) 1845–47
- Roald Amundsen (Norwegian) 1903–06
- Vilhjalmur Stefansson (Canadian) 1913–18

The eastern Arctic
- Edward Parry (British) 1827
- Nils Nordenskjöld (Swedish) 1878–79
- Fridtjof Nansen (Norwegian) 1893–96

Exploring the North Pole
- Robert Peary (American) 1909
- Richard Evelyn Byrd (American) 1926
- Umberto Nobile (Italian) 1926

Russian icebreakers
- voyages of the *Taymyr* and *Vaygach* 1914–15
- voyage of the *Sibiryakov* 1932

1909: Peary sets off from Cape Columbia, reaching North Pole on 6 April

1867: to US

In 1576, Martin Frobisher took three ships from England to Labrador and then to Baffin Bay in search of the Northwest Passage. Several of his crew were killed in an encounter with hostile Inuit *(left)*.

The Dutchman Willem Barents travelled via Spitzbergen to Novaya Zemlya in 1596, where he and his crew were forced to spend the winter. They built a wooden shelter and hunted walrus *(below)* and polar bears.

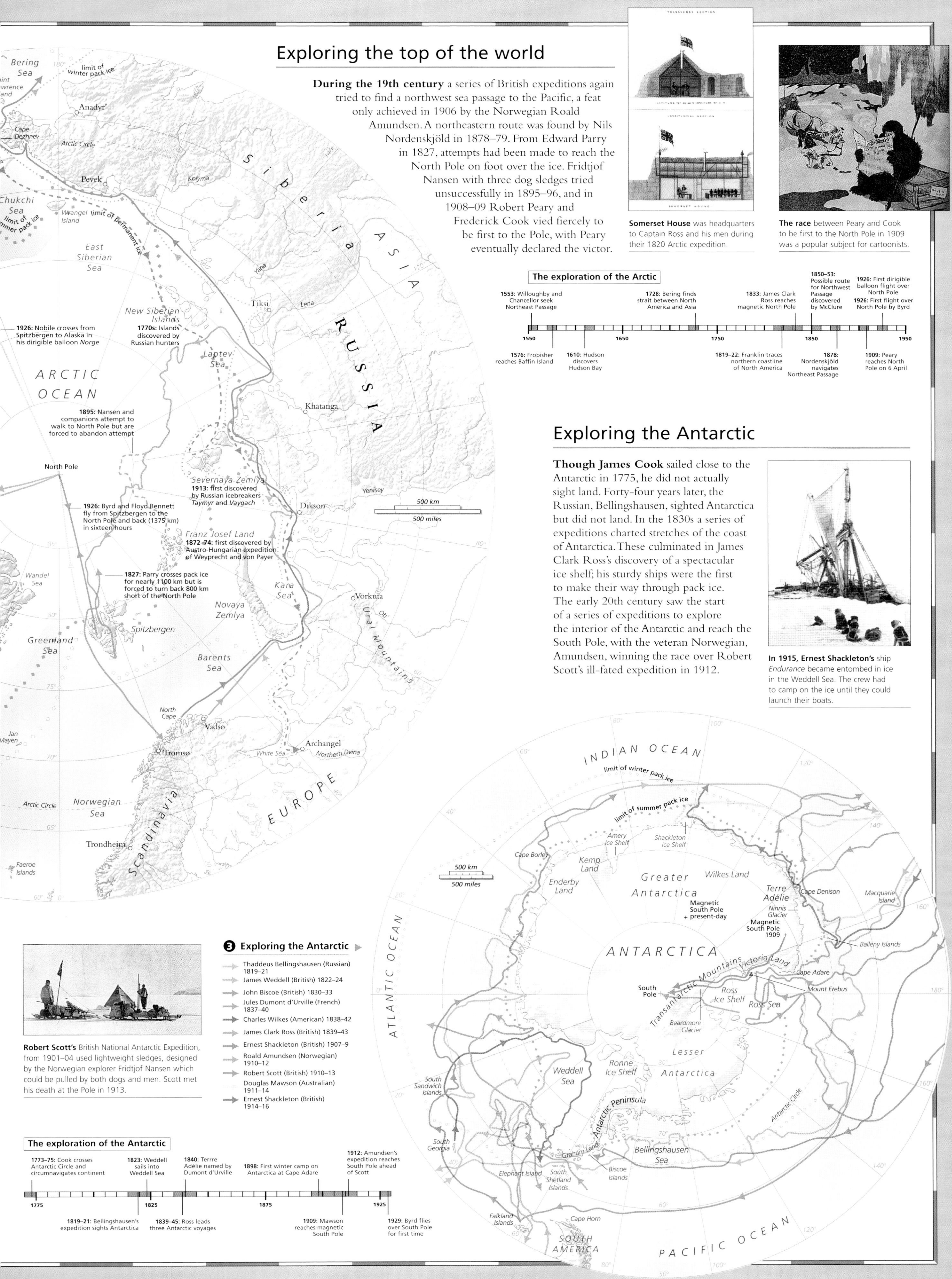

Exploring the top of the world

During the 19th century a series of British expeditions again tried to find a northwest sea passage to the Pacific, a feat only achieved in 1906 by the Norwegian Roald Amundsen. A northeastern route was found by Nils Nordenskjöld in 1878–79. From Edward Parry in 1827, attempts had been made to reach the North Pole on foot over the ice. Fridtjof Nansen with three dog sledges tried unsuccessfully in 1895–96, and in 1908–09 Robert Peary and Frederick Cook vied fiercely to be first to the Pole, with Peary eventually declared the victor.

Somerset House was headquarters to Captain Ross and his men during their 1820 Arctic expedition.

The race between Peary and Cook to be first to the North Pole in 1909 was a popular subject for cartoonists.

The exploration of the Arctic

- 1553: Willoughby and Chancellor seek Northeast Passage
- 1576: Frobisher reaches Baffin Island
- 1610: Hudson discovers Hudson Bay
- 1728: Bering finds strait between North America and Asia
- 1819–22: Franklin traces northern coastline of North America
- 1833: James Clark Ross reaches magnetic North Pole
- 1850–53: Possible route for Northwest Passage discovered by McClure
- 1878: Nordenskjöld navigates Northeast Passage
- 1909: Peary reaches North Pole on 6 April
- 1926: First dirigible balloon flight over North Pole
- 1926: First flight over North Pole by Byrd

1550 · 1650 · 1750 · 1850 · 1950

Exploring the Antarctic

Though James Cook sailed close to the Antarctic in 1775, he did not actually sight land. Forty-four years later, the Russian, Bellingshausen, sighted Antarctica but did not land. In the 1830s a series of expeditions charted stretches of the coast of Antarctica. These culminated in James Clark Ross's discovery of a spectacular ice shelf; his sturdy ships were the first to make their way through pack ice. The early 20th century saw the start of a series of expeditions to explore the interior of the Antarctic and reach the South Pole, with the veteran Norwegian, Amundsen, winning the race over Robert Scott's ill-fated expedition in 1912.

In 1915, Ernest Shackleton's ship *Endurance* became entombed in ice in the Weddell Sea. The crew had to camp on the ice until they could launch their boats.

Robert Scott's British National Antarctic Expedition, from 1901–04 used lightweight sledges, designed by the Norwegian explorer Fridtjof Nansen which could be pulled by both dogs and men. Scott met his death at the Pole in 1913.

❸ Exploring the Antarctic

- Thaddeus Bellingshausen (Russian) 1819–21
- James Weddell (British) 1822–24
- John Biscoe (British) 1830–33
- Jules Dumont d'Urville (French) 1837–40
- Charles Wilkes (American) 1838–42
- James Clark Ross (British) 1839–43
- Ernest Shackleton (British) 1907–9
- Roald Amundsen (Norwegian) 1910–12
- Robert Scott (British) 1910–13
- Douglas Mawson (Australian) 1911–14
- Ernest Shackleton (British) 1914–16

The exploration of the Antarctic

- 1773–75: Cook crosses Antarctic Circle and circumnavigates continent
- 1819–21: Bellingshausen's expedition sights Antarctica
- 1823: Weddell sails into Weddell Sea
- 1839–45: Ross leads three Antarctic voyages
- 1840: Terrre Adélie named by Dumont d'Urville
- 1898: First winter camp on Antarctica at Cape Adare
- 1909: Mawson reaches magnetic South Pole
- 1912: Amundsen's expedition reaches South Pole ahead of Scott
- 1929: Byrd flies over South Pole for first time

1775 · 1825 · 1875 · 1925

KEY TO MAP FEATURES

PHYSICAL FEATURES

- coastline
- ancient coastline
- major river
- minor river
- major seasonal river
- ancient river course
- canal
- aqueduct
- dam
- spring / well / waterhole / oasis
- perennial lake
- seasonal lake
- perennial salt lake
- ancient lake
- marsh / salt marsh
- ice cap / sheet
- ice shelf
- glacier
- summer pack ice limit
- winter pack ice limit
- elevation above sea level (mountain height)
- volcano
- pass

GRATICULE FEATURES

- Equator
- lines of latitude / longitude
- tropics / polar circles
- degrees of longitude / latitude

BORDERS

- international border
- undefined border
- vassal state border
- disputed border
- maritime border
- internal border

COMMUNICATIONS

- major road
- minor road
- major railway
- railway under construction

SETTLEMENT / POSSESSION

- settlement symbol
- colonial possession

TYPOGRAPHIC KEY

REGIONS

state / political region...LAOS

administrative region within a state.... HENAN

cultural / undefined region / group...............*FERGHANA*

SETTLEMENTS

settlement / symbol location / definition...........Farnham

PHYSICAL FEATURES

continent / ocean.............*AFRICA*

INDIAN OCEAN

landscape features........*Mekong*

Lake Rudolf

Tien Shan

Sahara

MISCELLANEOUS

tropics / polar circles.................... *Antarctic Circle*

people / cultural group.. *Samoyeds*

annotation...................... **1914**: British protectorate

POLITICAL COLOUR GUIDE

- China
- Persia / Iran
- Rome
- Japan
- Norway
- USA
- Italy
- Ottoman / Turkey
- England / Britain / UK
- France
- Denmark
- Spain (Castile)
- Spain (Aragon)
- Portugal
- Netherlands
- Germany
- Russia
- India
- New Zealand
- Australia
- Belgium
- other state / cultural region

(NB. the colours which identify political regions have, as far as possible, been used consistently throughout the atlas. Any variations are clearly identified in the individual map keys)

RELIGION COLOUR GUIDE

- Buddhism
- Islam
- Hinduism
- Confucianism / Taoism
- Christianity
- Roman Catholic
- Judaism
- other religion

GUIDE TO MAP INTERPRETATION

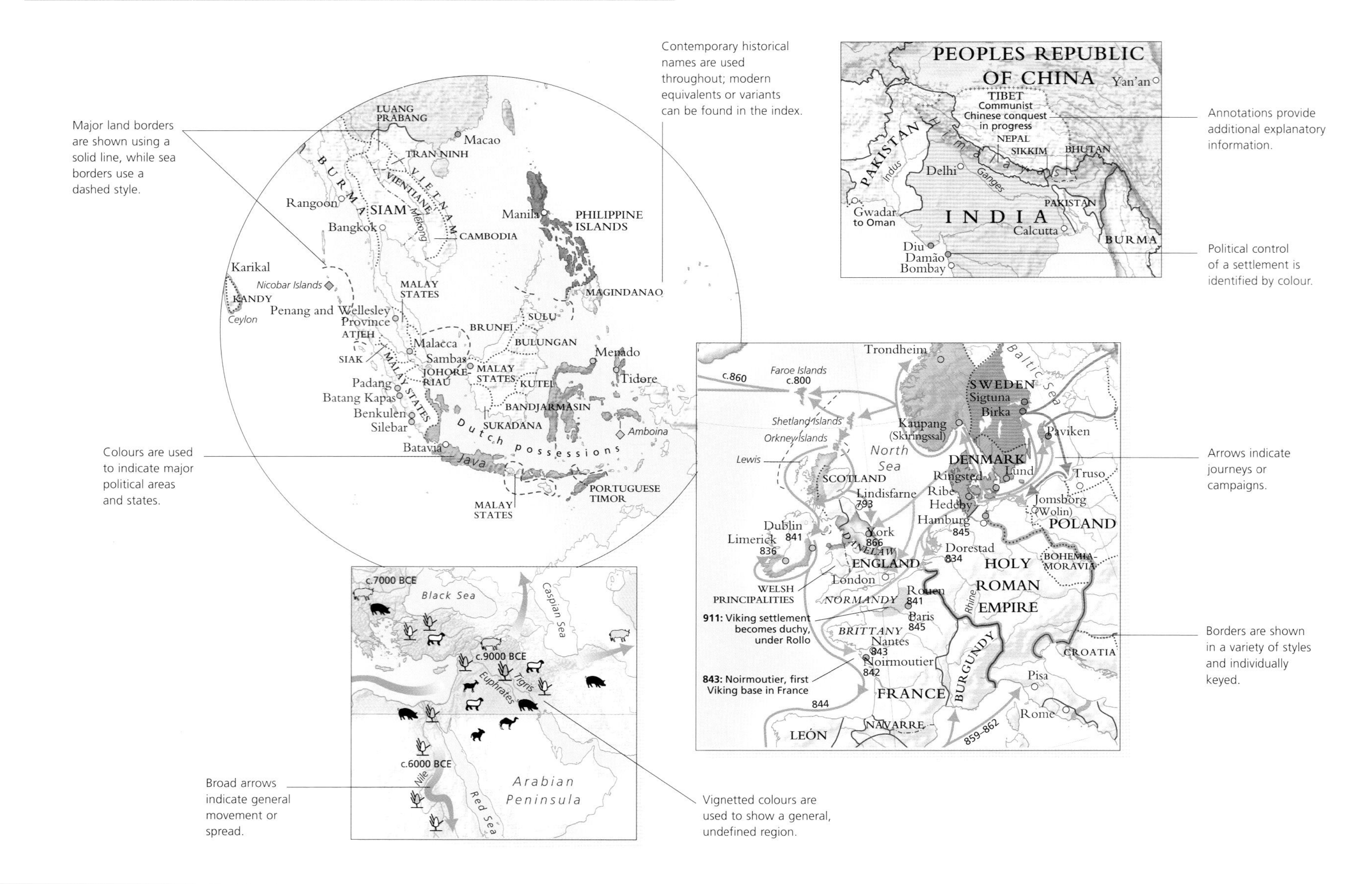

Major land borders are shown using a solid line, while sea borders use a dashed style.
Contemporary historical names are used throughout; modern equivalents or variants can be found in the index.
Annotations provide additional explanatory information.
Political control of a settlement is identified by colour.
Colours are used to indicate major political areas and states.
Arrows indicate journeys or campaigns.
Borders are shown in a variety of styles and individually keyed.
Broad arrows indicate general movement or spread.
Vignetted colours are used to show a general, undefined region.
PEOPLES REPUBLIC OF CHINA
TIBET Communist Chinese conquest in progress
INDIA
SIAM
PHILIPPINE ISLANDS
Dutch possessions
SWEDEN
DENMARK
POLAND
HOLY ROMAN EMPIRE
ENGLAND
FRANCE
North Sea
911: Viking settlement becomes duchy, under Rollo
843: Noirmoutier, first Viking base in France
Black Sea
Caspian Sea
c.7000 BCE
c.9000 BCE
c.6000 BCE
Arabian Peninsula
Red Sea

SUBJECT INDEX AND GLOSSARY

In addition to acting as a page reference guide to the people, events and themes referred to in the Atlas, the Subject Index and Glossary is intended to provide supplementary information and explanation of those features which appear in the Atlas.

Page references are indicated using the following symbols:

✤ text reference ● timeline reference

◆ map reference, indicating page number and map number;

❑ picture/caption reference.

Dates in the Atlas are expressed in the following way:

BP Before Present. Generally used for dates more than 10,000 years ago.

BCE Before Common Era (indicating number of years before the supposed year of Christ's birth).

CE Common Era (indicating number of years since the supposed year of Christ's birth).

A

Abbas I (*aka* Abbas the Great) (c.1571–1629) Safavid shah of Persia (r.1588–1629). Crushed the Uzbek rebellions, and recovered Persian territories from the Ottomans, expelling them from Mesopotamia. In 1598 he established the Persian capital at Isfahan. ✤79, ✤219●, ✤231, ✤231●, ❑238
Abbasid Caliphate (c.750–1258). The second great Islamic dynasty, replacing the Umayyads in 750 CE. The Abbasid capital from 762 was Baghdad, from where they exercised control over the Islamic world until the 10th century. The last Abbasid Caliph was killed by the Mongols in 1258. ✤56, ✤227, ◆57 (2), ◆58–9, ◆227 (4)
  dynasty founded (750) ✤59, ✤61
  fragmentation (800–1055) ✤227, ◆227 (6)
  overthrown by Mongols (1258) ✤67●
  rulers of Baghdad ✤228
Abd al-Qadir (1830s). Algerian resistance leader ✤90, ✤91●
Abd al-Rahman ibn Umar al-Sufi 10th-century astronomer ✤59
Abdul Hamid II (1842–1918) Ottoman sultan (r.1876–1909). An autocratic ruler, noted for suppression of revolts in the Balkans, which led to wars with Russia (1877–78), and for the Armenian massacres (1894–96). His failure to modernize his empire led to his deposition in 1909, following a revolt by the Young Turks. ❑232
Abdul Majid I (1823–61) Ottoman sultan (r.1839–61). Urged by Western Powers, Abdul Majid I issued a series of liberal decrees, known as the Tanzimat (1839–61) to reform the judiciary and administration of the Ottoman Empire. ✤232●
ABM *see* Anti-Ballistic Missile
Aborigines Native people of Australia, who probably first settled the continent c.60,000 years ago. From c.8000 BCE, when the land bridge to New Guinea was severed by rising sea levels, they lived in more or less complete isolation until the 18th century CE. In the north, there was occasional contact with sailors from the islands of the Torres Strait and Indonesia. ◆280 (1), ✤282
  armed for hunting ❑280
  bicentennial celebrations ❑283
  British justice ❑284
  civilization destroyed ✤91
  dreamtime ✤280
  resistance to colonization ◆282 (1)
  rock carving ❑15
  spirit figure rock painting ❑280
Abreu, António de 16th-century Portuguese explorer. Embarked on a voyage to India in 1508. He set out for the Spice Islands in 1511, exploring Amboina, Sumatra, Java and parts of New Guinea. He was appointed governor of Malacca in 1526. ◆239 (1)
Abydos Royal tombs ✤25
Abyssinia (*var.* Ethiopia). Italian defeat at ⚔ of Adowa (1896) ✤95●
Academy Award first Oscar ceremony (1929) ✤135●
Acadia Founded (1604–08) ✤82●
Achaean League Confederation of Greek city-states of the northern Peloponnese, dating back to the 4th-century BCE. The league's traditional enemy was Sparta. It was after the league attacked Sparta in 150 BCE, that the Romans destroyed Corinth, the leading city of the league, and made Achaea a Roman province. ✤179
Achaemenes *see* Achaemenid Empire
Achaemenid Empire (c.550–330 BCE). Greek name for the Persian royal dynasty named after Achaemenes (Hakhamani), an ancestor of Cyrus II 'the Great'. From c.550 BCE, Cyrus presided over the expansion of the Persian empire, conquering Lydia, Phrygia, Ionia, and Babylonia. The empire lasted until 330 BCE, when Darius III was killed after his defeat by Alexander at ⚔ Gaugamela. ✤35, ◆34–5, ✤39●, ✤223, ✤223●, ◆223 (4)
Achin (*var.* Atjeh). The Indonesian island of Sumatra became, from the 7th century CE, the centre of a powerful Hindu kingdom, established by Indian emigrants. In the 13th century CE, Arabs invaded the Sumatran kingdom of Achin, which converted to Islam. At the end of 16th century, the Dutch attempted to gain supremacy in Achin, a struggle which was to last for the next three centuries. ◆245 (1) (2) ◆248 (1)
Acolhua, Aztec civilization ✤125
Acre Crusader loss (1291) ✤64●, ✤65, ◆64–5 (1) (2)
Acropolis Ancient Greek fortified hilltop citadel, the best-known being that of Athens, rebuilt by Pericles after the Persian invasion in the second half of the 5th century BCE. It comprised a complex of buildings including the national treasury and many shrines, mostly devoted to Athene, the city's patron goddess. ✤177
Act of Supremacy (1534). Parliamentary Act which recognized King Henry VIII, and every British sovereign thereafter, as supreme head of the Church of England. ✤78●
Adelaide Founded 1835–36 ✤91, ◆279 (2)
Adena culture (c.1000–100 BCE). A series of North American communities, based around what is now southern Ohio, formed the Adena culture. Principally hunter-gatherers, they built circular houses with conical roofs constructed of willow and bark, used stone tools and produced simple pottery. Finds of copper and shell ornaments indicate long-distance trade.
  BCE culture ✤30●, ✤34, ◆36 (1), ✤38●, ✤42●
  moundbuilders ◆121 (4)
Adowa ⚔ of Italian invasion of Abyssinia (1896). Serious Italian defeat put an end to Italian colonial ambitions in Ethiopia. A settlement after the battle acknowledged the full sovereignty and independence of Ethiopia, but preserved Italian rights to Eritrea. 95●, ✤97, ◆97 (4)
Adrianopolis ⚔ (378). Visigothic victory over Romans. ◆52–3 (1)
Aegospotami ⚔ of Peloponnesian Wars (405 BCE). Spartan victory over Athens. ◆177 (3)
Aelfred *see* Alfred the Great
Aelius Gallus Roman general of the 1st century BCE, who led his troops on an exploratory expedition into Arabia. ◆218 (1)
Aetolian League Federal state of Aetolia, in ancient Greece, which by c.340 BCE became a leading military power. Having successfully resisted invasions by Macedonia in 322 BCE and 314–311 BCE, the league rapidly grew in strength expanding into Delphi and allying with Boeotia c.300 BCE. ✤179
Afghanistan
  British protectorate ◆248 (2)
  founded (1747) ✤87●
  emergence of Taliban ◆235 (4)
  Mahmud of Ghazni's kingdom ✤59, ✤63, ◆227 (6)
  Marathas defeated at Panipat (1761) ✤87
  Persian subjugation (1722–36) ✤87●
  Second Afghan War (1878–79) ✤95●
  Soviet invasion (1979–89) ✤111●, ✤138
Africa 154–169
  BCE ✤14, 15●, ✤16, ✤19, ✤30, ✤34
  (c.1300) ◆68 (2)
  diaspora ✤112
  exploration and mapping
    14th–15th century ✤156 (3)
    Niger Basin ◆156 (1) (2)
    African interior (19th century) ◆157 (4)
    Boer (Afrikaner) treks ✤90, ◆166 (2)
  history
    colonization ✤39●, ✤42, ✤62, ✤66–7, ✤95 ✤169, ◆166–67 (1) (2) (4)
    complex societies ✤160–1, ◆160 (1)
    early history ✤158–9
    early modern ✤164–5
    historical landscape ✤154–5, ❑154, ◆154–5
    Islam and new states ✤162–3, ✤163●
    Muslim empire (1863) ✤95●
    post-colonial ✤168–9
    Roman province ✤43●, ✤46
  home affairs
    agriculture ✤82
    conflict and crisis ✤169, ◆169 (4)
    independence ✤107, ✤168, ◆168 (1)
    tribal conflict ✤90
    Zulu War (1879) ✤95
  innovations
    Nok sculpture (BCE) ❑38
  Northeast Africa
    rise and fall of kingdoms ◆161 (4) (5)
    trade ◆161 (3)
    political development ✤164, ✤166, ◆166 (1) ✤168●, ✤169●,
  religion
    Donatist schism (311) ✤50●
  struggle for the Horn (1500–1700) ◆165 (3)
  trade and industry
    economy in 1999 ✤168, ◆168 (2) (3)
    Arab coastal settlements ✤58
    commerce (19th century) ✤166, ◆166 (1)
    Eurasian and African ◆44–5
    gold ✤66, ✤70
    Indian Ocean network (13th century) ✤66
    iron-working ✤38
    links with Morocco ✤78
    links with Portugal ✤78, ✤79●
    and the spread of Islam ◆162 (1)
  see also Boers; individual countries; slavery; trans-Saharan trade
Africa Nova Roman province (146 BCE) ◆161 (2)
African Association Club formed in London in 1788 'for promoting the discovery of the interior parts of Africa'. ✤157●
African National Congress (ANC). Organization founded in S Africa in 1912 to promote equality for Africans. It was banned by the South African government in 1961, and although its leaders were jailed or forced into exile, became the focus for resistance to the apartheid regime. The ANC signed an agreement with the ruling Nationalists in 1990 and came to power under Nelson Mandela at the election of 1994. ✤111, 169●
Afrikaner South African of European descent whose first language is Afrikaans, a development of Dutch. *See* Boers
Aghlabids (*var.* Banu Al-aghlab). Arab Muslim dynasty that ruled Ifriqiyah in present-day Tunisia and eastern Algeria from 800 to 909 CE. The Aghlabids were nominally subject to the Abbasid caliphs of Baghdad but were in fact independent. ◆227 (4)
  dynasty founded (800) ✤58●
  expelled by Fatimids (909) ✤58●
Agincourt ⚔ of Hundred Years' War (1415). French defeat by English. ✤75●
agriculture
  advent and spread of ✤20–1, ◆18–19, ◆21 (2), ◆22–3, ✤34
  African ◆158 (1), ◆166 (1)
  Andean ✤147, ❑147
  Australian (1845–1900) ◆22 (1)
  development of technology ◆158 (1)
  diffusion of staple crops ✤73, ◆73 (3)
  domestication ✤21, ✤21●
  early settlements ✤120, ◆121 (1), ❑171
  E Asian revolution (6000–2000 BCE) ◆258 (1)
  Europe ✤62, ✤198, ◆198 (1)
  grindstones ✤16
  Maya civilization ✤50
  mechanized ✤90
  Pacific ◆281 (3)
  prehistoric New Guinea ✤280, ❑280, ◆280 (2)
  source of Egypt's wealth (BCE) ❑27
  S America ◆144 (1), ◆153 (3)
  See also farming; irrigation
Ahmad ibn Fadi Allan Al-'umari *see* al 'Umari
Ahmad Khan Abdali (*var.* Ahmad Shah) (1724–73)
  founds Afghanistan (1747) ✤87●
Ahmad Shah *see* Ahmad Khan Abdali
Ahuitzotl Aztec ruler (1486–1502) ◆124 (1)
Ahura Mazda Zoroastrian god ❑36
Ai Khanoum Hellenistic city. ✤21
  Silver disc ❑21
Ain Jalut ⚔ of Mongol invasions (1260). Mongol defeat ✤67●, ✤69, ✤229
Aistulf (d.756) Lombard king, who captured Ravenna from the Byzantines and threatened to take Rome. The pope summoned the Frankish King Pepin to defeat him. 183●
Ajanta Buddhist centre ❑43
Akbar (*aka* Akbar the Great) (1542–1605) Mughal emperor (r.1556–1605). Became emperor at the age of 14. For the first seven years of his reign, Akbar was engaged in permanent conflict, which left him the undisputed ruler of an empire which stretched from Bengal to Sind, and Kashmir to the Godavari river. He evolved a standardized tax system, incorporated the rulers of conquered territory into his own army, and introduced a policy of marriage alliances between the Mughal nobles and the Rajput princely families. He was tolerant towards the Hindu religion, and encouraged a great florescence in the arts, particularly in miniature painting and architecture, which was remarkable for its synthesis of western and Islamic styles. ✤79●, ✤246, ❑246, ◆78–9, ◆246 (1)
Akhenaten (*var.* Akhenaton, Ikhnaton, Amenhotep, Amenophis IV) 18th Dynasty pharaoh of Egypt (r.1352–1333 BCE). A religious and cultural revolutionary who replaced the existing Egyptian pantheon with a monotheistic cult of the solar disc – Aten. He changed his name to reflect his beliefs, replaced the capital at Thebes with his own, El-Amarna (*var.* Akhetaten), and persecuted the older gods, expunging Amon's name from monuments across the country. A significant change in artistic style is representative of his rule, with both royals and commoners portrayed in a naturalistic rather than a formalized way. His unpopular religious reforms, and this artistic tradition, were reversed by Tutankhamun.
  Egyptian pharaoh ✤26, ✤27●, ❑28
  founds the city of El-Amarna ✤29, ◆29 (5)
  Great Palace fragment ❑29
Akkad *see* Sargon I of Akkad
Aksum (*var.* Axum) ◆161 (3) (4) (5)
  converts to Christianity (c.330) ✤50●
  incense trade ✤46
  kingdom emerges (c.50) ✤47●
  major trading power ✤161
  Meroë kingdom invasion (c.350) ✤50●
  Roman-Indian trading link ✤50
  stone stelae ❑161
Al-Azhar University established (970s) ✤58●
Al-Hajj Umar Ibn Said Tal *see* 'Umar Tal, Al-Hajj
Al-Idrisi *see* Idrisi
Al-Istakhri 10th-century Islamic geographer. ❑55
Al-Mu'tasim (794–842) Abbasid caliph (r.833–842). A son of Harun al-Rashid, al-Mu'tasim moved the Abbasid capital from Baghdad to Samarra. He waged war successfully against the Byzantines in Asia Minor and employed large numbers of Turkish slave soldiers, who subsequently became a powerful force in the Caliphate. (c.836) ✤59●
al-Rashid, Harun (*var.* Harun Ar-rashid, Ibn Muhammad al-Mahdi, Ibn al-mansur al-'Abbasi) (766/763–809). The fifth caliph of the Abbasid dynasty (786–809), who ruled Islam at the zenith of its empire. ✤58●, ✤227, ✤227●, ❑56, ❑227, ✤58–9
al 'Umari (*var.* Shihab Ad-din, Ahmad Ibn Fadl Allah Al-'umari) (1301–1349). Scholar and writer descended from 'Umar, the second Islamic caliph. His works on the administration of the Mamluk dominions of Egypt and Syria became standard sources for Mamluk history. ✤156
Alamo, The ⚔ of Texas Revolution (1836). Mexican victory. ◆129 (2)
Alans People who migrated to Europe from the steppes near the Caspian Sea. They joined the Vandals and Sueves in the Great Migration of 406 from Germany to the Iberian Peninsula. They briefly established a kingdom there, but were ousted by the Visigoths.
  migrations and invasions (300–500 CE) ✤50●, ✤182●, ◆52–3 (1)
Alaric (c.370–410). Chief of the Visigoths from 395 and leader of the army that sacked Rome in 410, an event that came to symbolize the fall of the Western Roman Empire. ✤50●, ✤53
Alaska
  Bering's first reconnaissance (1728) ✤86●
  discovery of gold (1880) ✤93
  Eskimos' Thule culture (c.900) ✤58●
  Russian expeditions ✤257, ◆119 (3) ✤128, ◆128–9(2)
Alaska Purchase (*aka* Seward's Folly). In 1867, US Secretary of State William H. Seward organized the purchase of Alaska from Russia for $7,200,000. ✤128–9
Alaung Phra *see* Alaungpaya
Alaungpaya (*var.* Alaung Phra, Alompra, Aungzeya) (1714–1760). King (r.1752–60) who unified Burma, and founded the Alaungpaya dynasty which held power in Burma until the British annexed the northern part of the region in 1886.
  founds Rangoon (1755) ✤87●
Albanel, Father Charles (1616–96). French Jesuit, who travelled in E Canada, reaching Hudson Bay and travelling along the Saguenay River, in search of fur-trading routes. ◆119 (2)
Albert, Prince of Saxe-Coburg-Gotha *see* Victoria
Albertis, Luigi Maria d' (1841–1901) Italian explorer of New Guinea. ◆279 (2)
Albigensians (*aka* Cathars). Heretical sect which flourished in southern France in the 12th century. It had little to do with Christianity; its most extreme followers believed in the evil of matter and aspired to reach the state of the 'perfect', those who had forsaken the material world. The Albigensian Crusade (1210–26) not only stamped out the heretics but also placed Toulouse and much of southern France under the control of the French crown.
  Albigensian Crusade ✤186●, ◆186 (1)
Aleut
  Arctic nomadic hunters ✤123
  sites ◆123 (3)
Alexander I (1777–1825) Tsar of Russia (r.1801–25). The early years of his reign were marked by attempts to reform Russia, but he failed to abolish serfdom. Initially a member of the coalition against Napoleon, but defeats at Austerlitz and Friedland led to Alexander concluding the Treaty of Tilsit (1807) with France. When Napoleon's invasion of Russia (1812) broke the treaty, Russia joined the Allied pursuit of the French to Paris. ❑201
Alexander the Great (*aka* Alexander III) (356–323 BCE) Greek emperor (r.336–323 BCE). Son of Philip II of Macedon, Alexander led one of the most rapid and dramatic military expansions in history, extended Hellenistic culture and conquest as far as India, founding cities and vassal states throughout West Asia.
  bust ❑40
  conquests ✤38, ✤40, ✤223
  empire ◆38–9, ◆40–1 (1)
  expeditions ◆218 (1)
  legacy ✤41, ✤41l
  oracle worship ✤37
  Pompeii mosaic ❑39, ❑40
  sarcophagus ❑40
  successors ✤224, ✤224●, ◆224 (1)
  death ✤38l, ✤39
Alexandria City founded by and named after Alexander the Great, on the delta of the River Nile. From the 3rd century BCE, for over a thousand years, the city of Alexandria became the commercial, cultural and scientific hub of all Eurasia, boasting the world's greatest library, and generating important schools of literature, poetry, drama, medicine, philosophy and cosmology.
  founded (332 BCE) ✤39●, ✤40●
  Christian centre (100 CE) ✤47●
  Classical scholarship ✤55
  Muslims at prayer ❑113
Alexius IV (d.1204) Byzantine emperor (r.1203–1204). He ascended the throne with the help of the Fourth Crusade but was deposed a year later by a national revolt. ✤187
Alfonso VI (*aka* Alfonso the Brave, *Sp.* Alfonso El Bravo) (1040–1109). King of León (r.1065–1109) and king of reunited Castile and León (1072–1109), who by 1077 had proclaimed himself 'emperor of all Spain'. His oppression of his Muslim vassals led to the invasion of Spain by an Almoravid army from North Africa in 1086.
  takes Toledo (1085) ✤64●
Alfred the Great (*var.* Aelfred) King of Wessex (r.871–899). Ruler of a Saxon kingdom in SW England. He prevented England from falling to the Danes and promoted learning and literacy. Compilation of the Anglo-Saxon Chronicle began during his reign, c. 890.
  reconquers London (885) ✤58●
Algeria
  French invasion (1830) ✤90, ✤232
  industrial growth ✤168, ◆168 (2)
  Islamic fundamentalism ✤235●
  uprising against France (1954) ✤107●
Algonquin N American sub-Arctic nomadic hunters ✤123
  war with Iroquois (1609) ✤126●
Alhambra Moorish palace in Granada, S Spain ❑192
Allegheny River Survey (1729) ✤119●
Allies (*aka* Allied Powers). General term applied to the victorious Great Powers at the end of WW I (after the US joined the Entente Powers – Britain, France, Russia – in 1917). More generally used to describe the alliance ranged against the Axis powers during WW II headed by Britain, France, Poland, and the USSR and US (from 1941). ✤104–5●, ✤◆206–211●
Allied Powers *see* Allies
Allouez, Father Claude (1622–89). French Jesuit missionary who explored the Great Lakes region of N America as well as the St. Lawrence River, setting up missions in present-day Wisconsin.
  expedition (1665–67) ◆119 (2)
Almagro, Diego de (1475–1538) Spanish *conquistador*. Companion of Pizarro in the conquest of Peru in 1532. In 1535 he set off southward in an attempt to conquer Chile. He later quarrelled with Pizarro and civil war broke out between their followers. ◆142 (1)
Almohad dynasty (1130–1269). Muslim dynasty. Founded by a revival Muslim revival movement, the Almohads eventually commanded North Africa as far east as Tripoli, as well as controlling most of the Iberian peninsula. ◆186 (1), 192●, ◆192 (3)
  defeated by Marinids (1269) ✤67●
  empire collapses (1228) ✤67●
  in Morocco and Spain (1147) ✤63●
  takeover of Almoravids (1128) ✤63●
Almoravid Empire Confederation of Berbers whose religious zeal and military enterprise built an empire in NW Africa and Muslim Iberia in the 11th and 12th centuries. ◆192 (3)
  12th century ◆62–3
  invasion of Ghana ✤163
  in N Africa and Iberia (c.1050) ✤63

Key to index: ✤ text ● timeline ❑ picture ◆ map *var.* variant name *aka* also known as *f/n* full name *prev.* previously known as r. ruled ⚔ battle WW I First World War WW II Second World War

reconquest of Spain ✤192, ✤192●, ◆192 (3)
takeover by Almohads (1128) ✤63●
Alodia Coptic Christianity ✤58
Alompra *see* Alaungpaya
alphabet *see* writing
Altai Mountains
burial sites (BCE) ✤39
wooden carving (BCE) ❑39
Alvarado, Pedro de (c.1485–1541) Spanish *conquistador*. Took part in the expeditions of Juan de Grijalva and Hernán Cortés in Mexico and Central America, later gaining control over highland Guatemala and El Salvador, and becoming governor of Honduras and Guatemala. ✤125
Alvare (d.1614) King of Kongo who was restored to his throne with the help of Portuguese troops after his country had been invaded in 1568.
as slave trader ❑85
Alvarez de Peneda, Alonso 16th-century Spanish explorer of the Yucatan Peninsula (1517–23). ✤125
Amadu Lobbo (1775–1844). Fulani leader who established a Muslim state in Masina, western Africa in the 19th century. ✤167●
Amazon River
mouth discovered (1500) ✤142●
sailed by Orellana (1542) ✤142●
Amazonia
development and deforestation ✤153●, ◆153 (4)
early settlements ◆145 (2)
amber Eurasian and African trade (c.1 CE) ◆44–5
Amde Sion Ruler of Ethiopia (d.1344) ✤71●
Amenhotep *see* Akhenaten
Amenhotep III *see* Amenophis III
Amenophis III (*var.* Amenhotep) (c.1390–1353 BCE) Egyptian pharaoh. His reign saw peaceful progress at home and effective diplomacy abroad. ✤27●
Amenophis IV *see* Akhenaten
America 116–153
historical landscape ✤117–18, ❑117, ◆116
BCE ✤18, ✤30, ✤34, ✤38
Committees of Correspondence (1772) ✤127●
Declaration of Independence adopted (1776) ✤82, ✤90
killer epidemics ❑81
Revolution of 1775 ✤86, ✤126–7, ◆127 (3)
road to independence ✤127●
Southwest, cultures, ✤58, ✤123, ◆123 (4)
Stamp Act (1765) ✤127●, ❑88
Sugar Act (1764) ✤127●
Townshend Acts (1767) ✤127●
See also Central America; N America; S America; slavery; USA; other individual countries
American Civil War (1861–65). Civil war between the northern states (the Union) and the southern Confederate states over the extension of slavery and the rights of individual states to make their own laws. Broke out in Apr 1861 following the secession of seven Confederate states from the Union. The war was won by the Union and slavery became illegal throughout the US. ✤◆130–31●
Amphipolis ⚔ of Peloponnesian War (422 BCE). Spartan victory over Athens. ◆177 (3)
amphitheatres Arenas of Etruscan origin, developed for a variety of open air entertainment. They consisted of tiered seats around a central round or oval performance space. The best known and largest is Rome's Colosseum, built 72–80 CE. ✤181, ❑181
amphora Two-handled ceramic jar with pointed base, commonly used to transport olive oil and wine. They are often stamped with a maker's mark, indicating their origin and compliance with size regulations. ❑48, ❑181, ✤181
Amritsar massacre (13 Apr 1919) India. Followed riots on the streets of Amritsar in the Punjab, protesting against the Rowlatt legislation (anti-sedition laws). British troops fired at the demonstrators, killing nearly 400 people, and wounding over 1000. The massacre caused widespread outrage. ✤99●
Amundsen, Roald (1872–1928) Norwegian explorer. Explored both the N and S Poles, tracing the Northwest Passage in 1903–06 and discovering the magnetic North Pole. Led first expedition to reach the S Pole in 1911. Explored the Arctic by air in the 1920s.
Antarctic exploration (1910–12) ◆287 (3)
Arctic explorer ✤286–7 (2)
Amur basin Russia withdraws (1689) ✤83●
An Lushan (703–757). Chinese general, who assembled an army of 160,000 and rebelled against the Tang. He captured Chang'an in 756, but was murdered the following year. ✤59●
Anasazi culture (200–1500 CE). Ancient culture of the southwestern US. The later period saw the development of complex adobe-built settlements known as pueblos.
✤58, ◆123 (4)
defensive pueblos (1050) ✤123●
fortified cliff dwellings (c.1100) ✤62●
pottery ❑62
Anatolia The Asian part of Turkey. A plateau, largely mountainous, which occupies the peninsula between the Black Sea, the Mediterranean, and the Aegean.
Arab forces annihilated (863) ✤59●
BCE villages ✤19
Europe's first cultures ❑171
seized by Ottomans ✤71
See also Asia Minor
ancestor worship ✤31, ✤36
Andersson, Charles (1827–67). Swedish explorer of southwest Africa (1853–59). ◆157 (4)
Andes
autonomous states ✤66
ceremonial vase ❑144
coastal empires (250–1375) ✤146, ◆146 (1)
early agricultural development ❑140
northern chiefdoms ✤146, ❑146
plant domestication (BCE) ✤18●, ✤144
temple complexes (2600 BCE) ✤22●
vertical economy ✤147, ❑147
see also Chavin; Inca; Moche; Nazca
Andronovo steppe cultures (1250 BCE) ◆26–7
Angevins Kings of Hungary between 1308 and 1387.
Baltic States (1100–1400) ✤144●, ◆187 (4), ◆189 (3)
Angevin dynasty (*aka* Plantagenets). English ruling dynasty established by Henry II, Count of Anjou in 1154. ✤186
Angkor Capital of the Khmer Empire (Kambujadesha), located in central Cambodia. Angkor was an extensive city, covering over 25 sq km, of stone temples dedicated to the Khmer god kings. The most impressive temples are Angkor Wat (12th century) and Angkor Thom (13th century).
Angkor Thom, temple complex ❑245
Angkor Wat, temple complex ✤59●, ✤63●, ❑63, ❑243
Angkorian dynasty Founded (802) ✤59●
See also Kambujadesha
Angles Germanic people who invaded England in the 5th century along with the Jutes and Saxons.
migrations and invasions ✤183, ◆52–3 (1)
Anglo-Burmese Wars (1824–26, 1852, 1885). In 1824, after Burmese encroachments on their territory, the British declared war on Burma. After two years of intermittent conflict the king of Ava signed the treaty of Yandabo, abandoning all claim to Assam and ceding the provinces of Arakan and Tenasserim. Further conflict in 1852 led to the annexation of the Irrawaddy valley. A third clash in 1885 led to the annexation of Upper Burma and (in 1890) the Shan states. ✤248●
Anglo-Gurkha War (1814–15). Conflict between the Gurkhas of Nepal and Britain in Sikkim and the Ganges plain. By the terms in the Treaty of Segauli, the Nepalis were obliged to withdraw from Sikkim and the lower ranges of the western Himalayas. ✤248●
Anglo-Japanese alliance (1902–23) ✤269
Anglo-Maratha Wars (1775–82, 1803–05, 1817–18). The first Maratha war began when Britain became involved in struggles between Maratha leaders. Though the British were crushed at Wadgaon in 1778, they conquered Gujarat and stormed Gwalior, to end the war, which concluded with the Treaty of Salabai (1782). During the Second Maratha war, Maratha artillery was particularly effective at the battles of Assaye and Argaon (1803). British conquest of the three great Maratha powers in the third war in 1818, allowed Britain to incorporate Maratha territory into her growing domains ✤248●
Anglo-Persian Oil Company founded ✤234●
Anglo-Tibetan Convention *see* Anglo-Tibetan Treaty
Anglo-Tibetan Treaty (*var.* Anglo-Tibetan Convention) (6 Sep 1904). Agreement of mutual support between Britain and Tibet following the opening of commercial relations and establishment of boundaries under the Sikkim Convention (1890, 1893). ✤257●
Angola
capture by Dutch (1641) ✤83●
civil war ✤109, ◆109 (5)
colonized (1570) ✤79●, ✤82
independence (1975) ✤107●, ✤111●, ✤168
animals
biological exchanges ◆81 (2)
biological origin and movement ◆81 (2)
domestication (BCE) ✤18, ✤21, ✤23 (2), ✤39, ❑120, ◆120 (1), ◆144 (1), ✤258●
Eurasian and African trade (c.1 CE) ◆44–5
exotic animal combat ❑44
used for draft ◆76–7 (1)
An Nafud Arabian Peninsula crossed by Palgrave (1862–63) ✤219●
Annam Historic state of mainland Southeast Asia, in area of modern North Vietnam; under Chinese suzerainty at various times from the 2nd century CE to independence (1428), part of French Indo-China from 1880s. ◆43, ✤43●, ✤59, ◆61 (3), ✤63, ✤67, ✤67●, ◆69 (1), ✤71, ✤75, ✤75●, ✤79, ✤83, ✤83●, ◆243 (5), ◆263 (7)
See also Dai-Viet, Vietnam
Anne of Bohemia (1366–94). First wife of Richard II of England. She died of plague without producing an heir. ❑72
Anpu *see* Anubis
Anschluss (1938). Nazi Germany's annexation of Austria, despite an express prohibition of such a union under the terms of the 1919 Versailles Treaty. ✤209●
Antarctic exploration ✤287●, ◆287 (3)
anthropomorphism The attribution of human characteristics to gods, animals or objects.
Anti-Ballistic Missile (ABM). Defence systems, developed by the US in the late 1960s. ✤109●
antibiotics Discovered and used in WW II. ✤102
Anti-Comintern Pact (25 Nov 1936). Joint declaration by Germany and Japan of opposition to Soviet Communism and Communist International; acceded to by Italy (Oct 1937). ✤103●
Antietam ⚔ of American Civil War (17 Sep 1862) Union victory. ◆131 (6)
Antigonid dynasty (c.306–168 BCE). Dynasty of Macedonian monarchs established by one of Alexander's generals Antigonus Cyclops – so called because he had lost an eye – after the death of Alexander. They established dominance over the Greek regions of Alexander's Empire. ◆41, ✤224, ✤224●, ◆224 (1)
Antigua, slave plantation (1823) ❑84
Antioch
captured by Khosrau I (628) ✤55
Crusader state ✤63, ✤65, ❑63
floor mosaic of Orpheus ❑181
reconquered by Byzantium (969) ✤59
Antiochus III (d.187 BCE) Seleucid emperor (r.223–187 BCE). Ruled over Syria and much of Asia Minor. His interference in Greek affairs brought him into conflict with Rome and he was defeated at Thermopylae in 191. ✤224, ✤224●
Anubis (*var.* Anpu). Ancient Egyptian god of the dead, represented by a jackal or the figure of a man with the head of a jackal. ❑37
Anxi Silk Road ✤45
Anyang Shang capital (1400 BCE) ✤27●
Anzio (*var.* Anzio Beach) ⚔ of WW II (Jan–May 1944). Allied landings in central Italy established a bridgehead north of German defensive lines. ◆211 (4)
Anzio Beach *see* Anzio
Anzus Pact (*var.* Anzus Treaty) (1951). Formerly known as the Pacific Security Treaty, and signed by the US, Australia and New Zealand, it aimed to protect the countries of the Pacific from armed attack. ◆138 (1)
Anzus Treaty *see* Anzus Pact
Aornos ⚔ of Alexander the Great's expansionist campaigns (327 BCE). ◆40–1 (3)
Aotearoa *see* New Zealand
Apache American Indian people of the US southwest. Their remote location meant that they suffered less initial disruption from European expansion. Led by Geronimo, they fought a series of wars (the Apache Wars) against the US army during the mid-19th century before they were eventually forced into reservations in 1887. ◆125 (4), ◆126 (1), ✤129●, ◆129 (2)
apartheid (apartness). Policy in South Africa from the 1960s to 1990, that sanctioned racial segregation and social, political and economic discrimination against the black majority.
See South Africa
Appalachia Migration (1917–20) ✤134, ◆134 (3)
Appalachians Occaneechee Path explored (1673) ✤119●
Appomattox (1865) Confederate surrender in American Civil War. ✤131●
aqueducts Artificial water channels, built by classical Roman engineers to supply their towns. Many were carried on vast arched bridges, some of which still survive. ❑180
Aquileia Sacked by the Huns ✤53
Aquinas, St. Thomas (*var.* Aquinas, Doctor Angelicus, *It.* San Tommaso D'Aquino) (c.1224–74). Italian scholar and Dominican theologian whose doctrinal system became known as Thomism. ✤187
Aquitaine
captured by Franks (507) ✤53●, ✤182●
Visigoth kingdom (418) ✤53, ✤182, ✤183
Ara Pacis (*var.* Altar of Peace) ❑42
Arab-Israeli Wars (1948–9, 1956, 1967, 1973, 1982). Series of five wars between Israel and the Arab states over the territorial and strategic consequences of the creation of a Jewish state. *See also* Six-Day War, Suez Crisis, Yom Kippur War, Lebanon, Invasion of. ✤234●
Arab League Association of Arab states founded in 1945 with the aim of encouraging Arab unity. The original members were Egypt, Syria, Lebanon, Transjordan, Iraq, Saudi Arabia and Yemen. By 1994 the League had 22 member states, including Palestine, represented by the Palestine Liberation Organization (PLO).
founded (1945) ✤103
Arab Revolt, the (1915–18). Uprising against Turkish rule during WW I by several Arab tribes. Centred on the Hejaz, the revolt subsequently helped the British to capture Palestine. ✤232–3●, ◆233 (2)
See also Lawrence, T.E. and Faisal, Emir.
Arabia
aromatic gum trade (1st century CE) ✤225, ❑225, ◆225 (3)
desert explored by Aelius Gallus (BCE) ◆218 (1)
European travellers ◆219 (4)
See also Saudi Arabia
Arabian American Oil Company (ARAMCO). Founded in 1936 by Standard Oil of California and Texaco to exploit petroleum concessions in Saudi Arabia, it is now among the most powerful oil groups in the world. In 1979 the Saudi Arabian government took complete control of the company. ✤234●
Arabs Semitic people originally of the Arabian Peninsula, but now widespread throughout the SW Asia and N Africa.
Classical world maps ❑55
coastal trading settlements ✤58
era of expansion from c.632 CE ✤61●
Indian Ocean trade (to c.1000 CE) ✤61, ◆61 (3)
lose control of Mediterranean (11th century) ✤62
mapping Niger Basin ◆156 (1)
skilled astronomers ❑59
tribal conflicts ❑59
Arafat, Yasser (1929–2004). Palestinian resistance leader, co-founder in 1959 of the Palestine Liberation Organization (PLO), and its chairman from 1969. In 1988 he persuaded the majority of his colleagues in the PLO to acknowledge the right of Israel to co-exist with an independent state of Palestine. In 1993, together with the Prime Minister of Israel, Yitzhak Rabin, he negotiated a peace agreement by which Israel agreed to withdraw from Jericho and the Gaza Strip. ❑234
Aragon
control of Sicily ✤66●
and possessions ◆66–7, ◆70–1
ARAMCO *see* Arabian American Oil Company
Araucanians People of central Chile. The Araucanians resisted European conquest for over 300 years. They quickly learnt to ride the horses introduced by the Spanish and proved formidable opponents in war. They were finally subdued by the Chilean army in the 1870s. ◆151 (3)
Arbela ⚔ of Wars between Parthia and Rome (216 BCE). ◆224 (2)
Archangel Reached by Willoughby (1553) ✤80●
Archimedes (c.287–212 BCE). Greek scientist and mathematician, who made many valuable contributions to theories of mechanics and hydrostatics; among them Archimedes' Principle which states that the volume of a body can be found by measuring the volume of the fluid it displaces. ✤38
Archimedean screw ❑38
Arcole ⚔ of (1796) Napoleonic Wars, Italian campaign. French victory. ◆200–1
Arctic Ocean
charting the coast ✤286, ◆286–7 (2)
exploration ✤287●
new routes to Asia ✤286, ◆286 (1)
Northeast Passage navigated, ◆257 (2)
Ardashir I (d.241 CE) Persian king (r.208–241 CE). In c.224 Ardashir overcame the Parthian, Artabanus V, and invaded Syria, establishing the Sassanian dynasty and empire. He made Ctesiphon on the River Tigris his capital (near modern Baghdad) and revived Zoroastrianism.
✤47, ✤225, ✤225●, ◆225 (6)
Ardennes ⚔ of WW II (Dec 1944–Feb 1945). Final and unsuccessful German counter-offensive in western Europe. ◆211 (4)
Ardipithecus ramidus Early hominid, dating from 4.4 million years ago. ◆12 (1), 12●
Ares (*var.* Mars) Greek god of war. ❑37 (3)
Argentina 148–153
Falklands war (1982) ✤110●
governed by Perón (1946–55) ✤102●, ✤106●
independence ✤90, ✤150, ◆150 (1)
Paraguayan War (1864–70) ✤94●
Arianism Christian doctrine developed by Arius (c.318) which regarded Jesus Christ as a demigod, less divine than God; widely observed by successor states to W Roman Empire (Visigoths, Vandals), but declared heretical at Council of Nicaea (325). ◆49 (4)
Arica ⚔ of War of the Pacific (1880). Chilean victory. ◆151 (4)
Armenia
annexed by Rome ✤47●, ✤51
kingdom ◆65 (3)
occupied by Sassanians ✤51●
solar system bronze (BCE), ❑31
Urartu kingdom ✤31
Arms Race General term for the technical development and stockpiling of weapons of mass destruction by the Western and Eastern blocs during the Cold War. ✤109●
Arnhem ⚔ of WW II (*var. Operation Market Garden*, Sep 1944). Unsuccessful Allied airborne operation intended to secure bridges across the Rhine in advance of land forces. ◆211 (4)
Arras, Congress of (1435) ✤192●
Arsaces I (d.211 BCE). Founder of the Parthian Empire, which he ruled (c.250–211 BCE), by leading a rebellion against the Seleucids. ✤43●, ◆224 (1)
Arsur ⚔ of crusades in the Holy Land (1191). Crusader victory. ◆65 (3)
Arthur, Gabriel 17th-century explorer of North America. In 1673, Arthur accompanied James Needham southwest across the Blue Ridge Mountains of North America, and into territory occupied by the Cherokee. During his travels he was captured by Indians. ◆119 (2)
Aryans Nomadic Indo-European-speaking people who migrated into northwest India some time after c.1500 BCE. Originally cattle pastoralists, they became sedentary farmers, and gradually spread eastwards. They were divided into various tribes, often warring amongst themselves. The early Aryan settlers of northern India coalesced, by c.600 BCE, into sixteen distinct political units (*see* Magadha), which dominated the Ganges plain.
religious practices ✤36
settle N India ✤35, ✤36●
Asante (*var.* Ashanti).
annexed by Britain (1900–01) ✤167●
court insignia ❑87
rise to prominence begins (1701) ✤164●
slave trade ✤82
well-armed warrior ❑164
W African dominance ✤86
ASEAN *see* Association of South-East Asian Nations
Ascalon ⚔ of crusades in the Holy Land (1099), city captured by crusaders (1153) ◆64 (2) (3)
Ashanti *see* Asante
Ashikaga Shogunate (1336–1573) Line of military governors of Japan.
founded (1336) ✤71●
Ashoka (*var.* Asoka) (d.227 BCE) Mauryan emperor (r.264–227 BCE). The grandson of Chandragupta Maurya, Ashoka established his rule over most of the Indian subcontinent. After his victory in Kalinga by the Bay of Bengal, he became an enthusiastic convert to Buddhism, and published the fundamental principles of the faith on pillars or rock-carved edicts, found throughout India. ✤38–9, ✤241, ✤242●, ✤243
promulgator of Buddhism ✤36●, ◆36 (2)
Ashur City-state ✤27
Ashurbanipal Last of the great kings of Assyria (r.668–627 BCE), who assembled the first systematically organized library in the ancient Middle East in Nineveh. ✤222, ◆34–5, ◆222 (2)
Asia Minor (*var.* Anatolia) (BCE) ✤39●
city states (BCE) ✤31
Asia
See East Asia, South and Southeast Asia, West Asia.
Asiento Slave Agreement Contract in use from the 16th to the mid-18th century, with the Spanish crown, which for an agreed sum of money granted a contractor (*asentista*), a monopoly in supplying African slaves for the Spanish colonies in the Americas. 86●
Asoka *see* Ashoka
Assassins Ismaili Shi'ite sect ✤229
Association of South-East Asian Nations (ASEAN), established in 1967 to promote economic, social and cultural cooperation. ◆253 (5)
Assyrian Empire (*var.* Neo-Assyrian Empire) (c.950–612 BCE). State based in Assur on the Tigris in upper Mesopotamia, which conquered its neighbours to establish a vast empire. At its height between the 9th and 8th centuries BCE, Assyria reached from the Mediterranean in the west to Persia in the east, and from the Persian Gulf northwards to the eastern Anatolian mountains. Overthrown by the Medes and Babylonians in 612 BCE.
(BCE) ✤31, ✤222, ✤222●, ✤34–5, ◆222 (2)
invade Egypt (667 BCE) ✤35●
ivory sphinx, ❑31
legend of flood ✤222, ❑223
astronomy
astrolabe ✤238, ❑218
Babylonian ❑31
Babylonian Venus tablet ❑33
Islamic knowledge ❑77
Jaipur observatory ❑238
mapping fixed stars ✤39
Maya civilization ✤54
Rigel (star) ✤59
stone alignment at Newgrange ❑33
Asunción Conflict with Jesuits (1640s) ✤143●
Atacama Desert ⚔ of War of Pacific (1879–83). ✤94●
Atahualpa (1502–1533). Last emperor of the Inca, who was victorious in a civil war with his half brother. He was later captured, held for ransom, and then executed by Francisco Pizarro. ❑148
Atatürk, Mustafa Kemal (*prev.* Mustafa Kemal Pasha) (1881–1938). Founder and first president of the republic of Turkey. Participated in the revolt of the Young Turks (1908). Served with distinction in WW I. In 1919 he broke away from the authority of the Istanbul government and established a provisional government in Ankara. As leader of the Turkish Nationalists he drove the Greeks from western Anatolia (1919–22). In 1922 the Ottoman Sultanate was formally abolished and Turkey became a secular republic, with Kemal as president. He launched a programme of social and political reform intended to transform Turkey into a westernized modern republic. In 1934 he took the name Atatürk, 'Father of the Turks'. ❑99, ✤233●
Aten (*var.* Aton). Originally the Egyptian sun disc, subsequently the sun god with which Pharaoh Akhenaten replaced the existing Middle Kingdom pantheon. ✤26, ✤28
Athabascan (*var.* Athapaskan, Athapascan). N American peoples, sub-Arctic nomadic hunters, mainly of western Canada, and the name given to the language group linking a number of peoples from this area. ✤123, ◆123 (3)
Athaulf Visigothic leader (*fl.*414) ✤53●
Athenian Empire (454–428 BCE) ✤177, ◆177 (2)
Athens The most celebrated of the city-states of Ancient Greece, both for its unrivalled cultural achievements and for its position under Pericles in the 5th century BCE as the most powerful Greek city-state. In 431 BCE Athens' role as leader of the Delian League provoked the hostility of Sparta, leading to the Peloponnesian War, in which Athens was completely defeated. Under the Romans (from 146 BCE) Athens was more important culturally than politically. In modern times it was chosen as capital of the new kingdom of Greece in 1834.
Athene patroness ❑177
city-state ✤179
conflict with Sparta ✤38
democracy established (505 BCE) ✤34●
Olympic Games revived (1896) ✤94●
plan showing BCE remains ◆177 (4)
Atjeh *see* Achin
athletics Pan-Hellenic festival (776 BCE) ✤31●
Atlanta ⚔ of American Civil War (20 Jul–2 Sep 1864). Union victory ✤131●
Atlanta race riots (1966) ✤137●

Key to index: ✤ text ❑ picture *var.* variant name *f/n* full name r. ruled WW I First World War
● timeline ◆ map *aka* also known as *prev.* previously known as ⚔ battle WW II Second World War

Atlantic, Battle of the Naval and air ⚔ of WW II. Protracted German campaign (1939–45) to disrupt Allied shipping and transatlantic convoys, largely through use of U-Boats, gradually defeated by Allied use of air cover and the convoy system. ❖210●, ◆211 (2)
Atlantic Ocean
coastal expeditions ❖118
convoy system (1564) ❖81●
shipping routes (1870–1910) ◆92 (1)
Atlas Contractus (Visscher) ❑119
Atlas Major (Blaeu) ❖83
Atlas (Ortelius) ❖173●
Atlas sive cosmographicae meditationes (Mercator) ❖173●
Aton *see* Aten
Atsugashi-yama ⚔ (1189). Defeat of Fujiwari clan. ◆265 (5)
Attalid Dynasty (282–133 BCE). Line of rulers, founded by Philetaerus, of a kingdom of Pergamum, in northwest Asia Minor, in the 3rd and 2nd centuries BCE. ❖40
Attila the Hun (c.400–453). Ruler of the Huns from c.445. Attila devastated much of the East Roman Empire and forced the emperor to pay tribute and grant his people lands in the Balkans. In 451 he invaded Gaul, but was defeated by a Roman and Gothic army at the battle of the Catalaunian Fields. After one more raid – into northern Italy in 452, when the Huns destroyed Aquileia – he died and his empire rapidly disintegrated. ❖50●, ❖53, ❖50–1. *See also* Huns.
Augusta ⚔ of American Revolutionary War (29 Jan 1779). British victory. ◆127 (3)
Augustine of Hippo, St. (354–430). Christian bishop and theologian, author of *The City of God.* ◆52 (1)
Augustine, St. (St. Augustine of Canterbury) (d.604). Christian missionary, who travelled to Britain in 597. His mission led to the conversion of many of the southern Anglo-Saxon kingdoms of Britain.
Papal missionary (597) ❖54●, ◆183●
Augustus Caesar (*var.* Octavian) (63 BCE–14 CE) First Roman emperor (27 BCE–14 CE). Octavian was the great nephew and adopted heir of Julius Caesar. On Caesar's death, he gradually won control of the Roman Empire, completing the task with his defeat of Mark Antony and Cleopatra. The Roman senate then granted him the title Augustus and guaranteed his authority for life. ❖42, ❖46●, ❖180
Aungzeya *see* Alaungpaya
Aurangzeb (1618–1707) Mughal emperor (r.1658–1707). The first Mughal emperor to conquer the sultans of the Delhi Sultanate and to extend his authority to the extreme south, Aurangzeb fought hard to maintain Mughal supremacy in the face of opposition from the Maratha Confederacy. His long reign was harsh and repressive, leading ultimately to the revolt and secession of many provinces. ❖83●, ❖87●, ❑246
Aurelius, Marcus *see* Marcus Aurelius
Aurignacian tool technology Technology which evolved in the Middle East about 45,000 years ago. Small flint tools were set into wooden or bone handles and spread rapidly throughout S Europe. ❖15●
Austerlitz ⚔ of Napoleonic Wars (1805). Russian/Austrian defeat by French forces. The victory that gave Napoleon virtual control of mainland Europe. ❖90●, ◆200–1 (1)
Australia 276–285
colonization ❖282–3
Botany Bay settled (1788) ❖87●
British (1829) ❖91
Federation (from 1901) ❖99●, ❖283, ❖283●, ◆281 (3)
Pacific imperialism ◆284 (1)
Pacific nationhood ❖285, ◆285 (3)
desert landscape ❑276
exploration and mapping ❖279, ❑279, ◆279 (2)
foreign affairs
possessions
1925 ◆98–9
1950 ◆102–3
1975 ◆106–7
home affairs
British justice ❑284
dingo introduced (c.2500 BCE) ❖27●
early European impact ◆282 (1)
gold fields ❖282, ❑282, ◆292 (2)
mineral finds (late 19th century) ◆93 (2)
penal settlements ❖91, ❖282●, ❖285, ❑282, ◆282 (1)
population growth (1851–91) ❑282
settlement ❖280, ❖280●, ◆280 (1)
whaling ❖279●
rock engravings ❖17, ◆17 (5)
rock painting ❑280
WW II, mobilization and casualty figures ❖105
Australoids People who colonized Australia and New Guinea some 60,000 years ago: the ancestors of the Australian Aboriginals and the Papuans. ❖280
Australopithecines (meaning 'southern ape'). The genus of ape-like, bipedal hominids which evolved in eastern Africa over 4.5 million years ago. Several species of *Australopithecus* have been identified, based on variations in skulls and teeth. It is still uncertain whether these early hominids are the precursors of fully modern humans, or represent a separate evolutionary line. ❖12, ◆12 (1)
Australopithecus afarensis Present from c.4 to 3.2 million years ago, *A. afarensis* is represented by the virtually complete 3.4-million year-old skeleton of an adult female, known as 'Lucy' found in the Hadar region of Ethiopia. *A. afarensis*, with its ape-like body and small brain, is seen as crossing the line from ape to human. ❖12, ❖154
Australopithecus africanus (c.3 to 2 million years ago). Found in cave sites of southern Africa, *A. africanus* is distinguished by higher, rounder braincase than *A. afarensis*, more powerful teeth and long powerful arms. ❖12
Australopithecus anamensis Represented by 4.2-million-year-old fossils found near the shores of Lake Rudolf in Kenya. The oldest known member of the Australopithecine genus. ❖12
Australopithecus boisei (c.2.7 to 1.7 million years ago). A robust species found in eastern Africa, distinguished by a powerful upper body, long upper jaw and the largest molars of any hominid. ❖12
Australopithecus robustus (c.2 to 1 million years ago). Found in southern Africa, and distinguished by heavy jaws, a brow ridge , a bony crest along the top of the skull, and a larger brain capacity than any other Australopithecine. ❖12
Austria 188–9, 193–203, 207–214
alliances opposing France (1792–1815) ❖201, ◆201 (3)
consolidation and resistance (17th century) ❖196, ❖196●, ◆196 (2)
Empire, 1850 ◆90–1
European power ❖197
Habsburg possessions
1200–1400 ◆189 (4)
1400 ◆70–1
1500 ◆74–5, ◆193 (4)
1600 ◆78–9
1700 ◆82–3
1795 ❖199 (3)
1800 ◆86–7
Napoleonic Wars (1805) ❖90●
partition ❖212, ◆212 (1)
rise of Brandenburg Prussia ❖199, ◆199 (3)
Treaty of Westphalia, ◆196 (1)
unification of Germany ❖203, ◆203 (2)
See also Habsburg Empire
Austria-Hungary
dual monarchy (1867) ❖94●
First World War *see* Wars, First World
rivalry with Germany ❖98
Austrian Succession, War of the (1740–48) On the succession of Maria Theresa to the Austrian throne, Frederick II of Prussia seized Silesia. France allied with Prussia, while Britain formed an alliance with Austria. In Italy, Austria confronted a Bourbon alliance of France and Spain. The war involved conflict in Silesia, Austria, the Austrian Netherlands, southern Germany, Italy, India and North America. At the end of the war Prussia's seizure of Silesia was recognized. ❖199●
Austronesians People who spread southeast from Asia through Indonesia c.6000 BCE, reaching New Guinea and the Bismarck Archipelago, from where they set out into the Pacific on voyages of colonization. The Austronesian language group includes most of the languages of Indonesia, all the Polynesian languages, and the language of Madagascar.
migrations ◆282 (3)
settlement of Pacific ❖281
automobiles *see* transport
Avar Empire *see* Avars
Avars Steppe nomads who migrated westwards in the 6th century. In the 7th century they settled on the Danube Plain where they ruled the local Slavic population. Their empire was totally crushed by Charlemagne in 796. ❖54●, ◆54–5, ❖184, ◆184 (1) *See also* Ruanruan
Averroes (b.1126) Muslim philosopher. ❖187●
Avidius Cassius Gaius (d.175 CE). Roman military commander. The son of one of Hadrian's civil servants, Avidius Cassius directed Rome's wars with the Parthians (161–65), and became commander of all the military forces in the eastern provinces. He usurped the throne for three months in 175 on hearing a false rumour of Marcus Aurelius' death, but was assassinated by one of his soldiers before Aurelius could arrive to confront him. ❖47
Avignon Papal residence (1309) ❖70●
Avila, Pedro Arias *see* Dávila, Pedrarias
Axayacatl Aztec ruler (1469–81) ◆124 (1)
Axis (*var.* Axis Powers). General term for Germany, Japan and Italy during WW II. Originating with the Pact of Steel (*var.* Axis Pact) between Germany and Italy (May 1939), consolidated by Tripartite Pact between Germany, Italy and Japan (Sep 1940) assuring mutual military, political and economic assistance in the event of war spreading beyond Europe. ◆104–105, ❖210–211
Sep 1939–Dec 1941 ◆104 (1)
Dec 1941–Jul 1943 ◆104 (2)
Jul 1943–Aug 1945 ◆104 (3)
global warfare ◆104 (4)
WW II nationalist states ❖104
Axis Powers *see* Axis
Axum *see* Aksum
Ayacucho ⚔ of wars of S American liberation (Dec 1824). Victory by Sucre liberated upper Peru (Bolivia). ◆150 (1)
Ayuthia *see* Ayutthaya
Ayutthaya (*var.* Ayuthia). Capital of Siam founded c.1350. ❖71●
Ayyubid dynasty (1171–1250). Sunni Muslim dynasty founded by Saladin. The Ayyubids ruled most of the Middle East and Egypt until 1250, when they were defeated by the Mamluks.
founded (1174) ❖63●
Aztec Empire (mid-14th century–1521). Dominant state in Mexico before the Spanish conquest of the 16th century. Centred on the valley of Mexico, the empire grew to include most of central and southern Mexico and was the focus of a sophisticated civilization. ❖66, ❖74, ❖78, ❖124, ◆76 (2), ◆124 (1) (2) (3), ◆125 (4) (5)
conquered by Hernán Cortés (1519–22) ❖78, ❖81●, ❖125, ◆125 (5)
cosmology ❑124
entry into valley of Mexico ❖122●
expansion ◆124 (1)
human sacrifice ❑74
rise and fall ❖124●
rulers ❖74●, ❖78●, ❖124
triple alliance (1434) ❖74●

B

Babur (*var.* Babar, Baber) (1483–1530) Founder of the Mughal dynasty (r.1526–30). At the battle of Panipat (1525) Babur confronted the forces of the Afghan Lodi sultans, and occupied Delhi and Agra. By 1530 his empire stretched from the Oxus to the frontier of Bengal and from the Himalayas to Gwalior. ❖79, ❖246, ❖246●, ◆246 (1)
Babylonian Empires (c.1795–1538 BCE) (612–539 BCE). Ancient empires of southern Mesopotamia. The first Babylonian empire was created by Hammurabi (c.1795–1750 BCE), with Babylon on the Euphrates as its capital. Following a Hittite attack in c.1595, Babylonia was ruled by the Kassites for 400 years. The second empire was established following the overthrow of Assyria in 612 BCE. Under its greatest ruler, Nebuchadnezzar II (605–562 BCE) it extended into Mesopotamia, Egypt and Palestine. It was brought to an end by the Persian conquest of 539–538 BCE.
astronomy ❑31, ❖39
city-state ❖27
conquest of Egypt (BCE) ❖34
Empire (612–539 BCE) ❖34–5, ❖222, ◆222 (2)
mapping ❑34
rebuilt by Nebuchadnezzar II (604 BCE) ❖35●
Bacon's Rebellion (1676). N America. Attempt by Nathaniel Bacon, a Virginia planter, to expand into Indian territory. It was denounced by Governor William Berkeley as a rebellion, and Bacon, in response, turned his forces against Berkeley and for a while had control over most of Virginia. ◆126 (1)
Bactria
classical world trade ◆44–5
coin showing King Demetrios ❑41
invaded by Kushans ❖47
plaque ❑261
secession ❖43
Baecula ⚔ of Punic Wars (208 BCE). Roman victory over Carthage. ◆179 (3)
Baffin, William (1584–1622) English navigator who searched for a Northwest Passage to Asia. He discovered Baffin Bay and used the position of the moon to determine longitude at sea. ❖239●, ◆286 (1)
Baghdad
Abbasid capital ❖59●, ❖227, ❑227, ◆227 (5)
arts and learning centre (786) ❖59●
Black Death (1347) ❖71●
captured by Buwayhids (945) ❖59●
Egypt's independence (969) ❖58
sacked by Mongols (1258) ❖67, ❖69●, ❖229, ❑229
sacked by Timur (1393) ❖71●
slave trade (9th–10th century) ❖85
Turkish control (936) ❖59●
Bahamas Columbus lands (1492) ❖80●, ❖118●, ❖125●
Bahia (*var.* Salvador). Capital of Brazil (1549–1763)
royal rule imposed (1549) ❖149●
Bahmani Kingdom (1347–1583). The earliest Muslim dynasty in the Deccan, founded by Alauddin in 1347, with its capital at Gulbarga. The Bahmani kingdom disintegrated into five independent Deccani kingdoms towards the end of the 14th century. ❖245, ◆74–5, ◆245 (4)
Bahram V (d.439) Sassanian king (421–439) ❑51
Bajazet *see* Bayezid
Baker, Samuel (1821–93). English explorer who, with John Hanning Speke, helped to locate the source of the Nile (1861–65). ◆157 (4)
Baku Azerbaijan, oil production (c.1900) ❖234●
Balaton ⚔ of WW II (Mar 1945). Battle in W Hungary in which a Soviet counter-offensive destroyed German military strength in SE Europe. ◆211 (4)
Balboa, Vasco Núñez de (c.1475–1519). Spanish conquistador and explorer. On an expedition across the Isthmus of Panama in 1513, he and his men were the first Spaniards to sight the Pacific Ocean. ❖125
Baldaya, Alfonso 15th-century Portuguese navigator, who explored the coast of West Africa on behalf of Prince Henry of Portugal (Henry the Navigator). ◆156 (3)
Baldwin I (*var.* Baldwin of Boulogne, *Fre.* Baudouin) (1058–1118). One of the leaders of the First Crusade, Baldwin captured Edessa in 1098, making the County of Edessa the first Crusader state. He was chosen to be King of Jerusalem and crowned in 1100. ◆64–5 (2)
Baldwin of Boulogne *see* Baldwin I
Balfour Declaration (1917). Contained in a letter from Britain's Foreign Secretary, Arthur Balfour, to Lord Rothschild, a prominent Zionist, the declaration stated the British government's support for the establishment of a national home for the Jewish people in Palestine. ❖99●
Bali Conquered by Majapahit (1343) ❖71●
Balkan Wars (1912–1913). Two short wars fought for possession of the Ottoman Empire's European territories. In the first, Montenegro, Bulgaria, Greece and Serbia attacked and defeated Turkey, which was forced to surrender most of her territories in Europe on condition that a new state of Albania was created. The second war was precipitated by disputes among the victors over the division of Macedonia. Romania joined Greece and Serbia against Bulgaria, which was heavily defeated and lost territory to all its enemies. ❖202●, ◆202 (5)
Balkans
bronze ritual axe ❑175
cartoon of Ottoman sultan (1908) ❑203
Crimean War (1854) ❖94
and WW I (1914) ❖98●
First World War *see* Wars, First World
invaded by Bulgars (680) ❖54●
nationalism ❖203, ◆203 (4)
Ottoman control ❖189●
religious map of Europe (1590) ◆194 (2)
separatism ❖112
slave trade (9th–10th century) ❖85
Wars against Ottomans (1912–13) ❖99●
Baltic states
conflict ❖195, ❖195●, ❖197, ◆195 (3), ◆197 (3)
Crusades ◆186 (1)
eastward expansion ❖189
states (1100–1400) ❖189●, ◆189 (3)
Bandkeramik pottery Pottery decorated with incised linear decorations by the earliest farming cultures of C Europe (c.5600 BCE), who are named after their pottery style. ❖20●, ❖174●
Bangladesh (*prev.* East Pakistan) founded (1971) ❖107●, ❖252, ◆252 (3)
banking *see* coins; economy
Banks, Sir Joseph (1743–1820). British explorer and naturalist. He was a long-time president of the Royal Society and was notable for his promotion of science.
African Association (1778) ❖157●
Bannockburn ⚔ (1314). Victory by Scots, led by Robert Bruce, over English forces. ◆188 (2)
Banpo
China, BCE farming village ❖19
wattle-and-daub house ❑21
Banshan culture (*var.* Panshan). Chinese Neolithic culture named after the site of Ban-shan in Gansu province, and known for its distinctive painted pottery, mostly large urns, produced between c.2500–2000 BCE. ❖23●
banteng Wild ox of SE Asia. ◆21 (2), ❖258
Bantu Linguistic group occupying much of the southern part of the African continent. From their homeland in present-day Nigeria, the Bantu migrated southward along eastern and western routes during the 2nd millennium BCE. They had reached present-day Zimbabwe by the 8th century CE.
at war with Boers (1779–80) ❖87●
colonize Africa (c.500 BCE) ❖39●, ❖42, ❖160, ◆160 (1)
farming village ❑160
Banu Al-aghlab *see* Aghlabids
Barbarossa Code name for the German invasion of the USSR during WW II (summer–autumn 1941). ❖104●, ❖210●, ◆210 (1)
Barents, Willem (c.1550–97). Dutch navigator who searched for a Northeast Passage to Asia. He discovered Bear Island and Spitzbergen and travelled beyond Novaya Zemlya, where he and his crew were the first recorded Europeans to winter in the Arctic.
search for Northeast passage (1556) ❑286, ◆257 (2), ◆286 (1)
barley Early domestication ❖19
barrow (*var.* tumulus, cairn). Neolithic and Bronze Age burial traditions included raising an earth mound over single or communal graves (where made of stone, known as a cairn) a practice characteristic of European and central and south Asian communities of the 3rd and 2nd millennia BCE. Barrows marked either inhumation or cremation burials, and sometimes also covered burial structures of wood, stone or megalithic chambers. They vary in shape, but are most commonly round or elongated ovals. ❖175, ◆175 (3)
Barth, Heinrich (1821–65) German geographer and explorer of Africa. He travelled the Mediterranean coastal areas that are now part of Tunisia and Libya (1845–47) and published his observations in 1849. ◆157 (4)
Basil II (958–1025) Byzantine emperor. Sole ruler of the empire (976–1025). He extended Byzantine rule to the Balkans, Georgia, Armenia and Mesopotamia. His 15-year war with Bulgaria culminated in victory and earned him the nickname 'Bulgar Slayer'. ❖58●, ❖63●
Bass, George (1771–1803). English surgeon and sailor who surveyed coastal Australia. ◆279 (2)
Bataan ⚔ of WW II in the Pacific (Jan–Apr 1941). Japanese victory over Allied forces. ◆272 (1)
Batavia (*mod.* Jakarta). Administrative and commercial centre of Dutch East Indies. ◆247 (4)
founded (1619) ❖83
trading centre ❖83
Bates, Henry (1825–92). English naturalist and scientific explorer, who spent 11 years in S America. On his travels in Brazil, he studied forms of mimicry, in which a defenseless organism bears a close resemblance to a noxious and conspicuous one. This form is called Batesian, in honour of its discoverer. ❖143●
Baton Rouge ⚔ of American Revolutionary War (21 Sep 1779). Victory by Spanish forces led to Spain controlling the area for the next 20 years. ◆127 (3)
Batts, Thomas (d.1698) Explorer of N America. Searched for South Sea with Robert Fallam, in 1671, reaching the edge of the Mississippi watershed. ◆119 (2)
Batu (d.1255). Mongol leader, a grandson of Genghis Khan, who led the invasion of Europe (1236–42).
campaigns in Europe ❖69●, ◆68–9 (1)
Bayeux Tapestry ❑186
See also William I
Bayezid I (*var.* Bayezit, Bajazet) (c.1360–1403) Ottoman Sultan (r.1389–1403). Known as 'the Thunderbolt', he conquered much of Anatolia and the Balkans, besieged Constantinople and invaded Hungary. He was defeated by Timur at the ⚔ of Ankara (1402). ❖230●
Bayezit *see* Bayezid
Bayinnaung (d.1581) Ruler of the Toungoo Kingdom in Burma (r.1551–81). Captured the Siamese capital of Ayutthaya, subdued the Shan states, and ruled over the whole of Burma, except Arakan. His constant warfare, however, reduced his own province to desolation and his son, Nandabayin, completed the ruin of the Toungoo kingdom. ❖79●
Baykonur Soviet space centre ❑275
Beaker culture Neolithic culture which may have originated in the lower Rhine region, and spread through western Europe around 2600–2200 BCE. It is named for its distinctive geometrically decorated pottery; one variety, so called Bell Beaker pottery, being shaped like an inverted bell. These pots are often found deposited with weapons as grave goods, and are seen as signalling a move away from earlier traditions of communal burial towards ostentatious statements of individual status and wealth. The burials of this period are frequently single graves covered with an earthen mound or barrow. ❖174
beans Early domestication ❖18, ◆120 (1), ◆144 (1)
Becan Maya fortified site (c.250 BCE) 121●
Beck, Harry Designer of London Underground map ❑102
Behaim, Martin Geographer. Martin Behaim's globe (1490–92) ❖75, ❑75, ◆76 (9)
Beijing (*var.* Peking)
captured by Manchu army ❖83
courtyards of the Forbidden City ❑75
founded by Kublai Khan (1266) ❖68●
occupation ❖95●
Song capital (1005) ❖63●
Tiananmen Square demonstration (1989) ❖111●
See also Khanbaliq
Belgium
devolution ❖112
expansion in Africa ❖96, ❖167●, ◆96 (1), ◆167 (4), ◆168 (1)
independence ❖90●, ❖202, ◆202 (1)
possessions
1925 ◆98–9
1975 ◆106–7
World Wars *see* Wars, First World; Second World
Bell, Alexander Graham (1847–1922) US inventor. Patented his design for the telephone in 1876. Later invented the photophone and the gramophone and founded the journal *Science* in 1883. He later concentrated on aeronautical design. ❖92●, ❖95, ❖135
Bell beaker *see* Beaker culture
Belle Isle, Strait of explored by Cartier (1532) ◆80
Bellingshausen, Thaddeus (*var.* Faddey Faddeyvich Bellingsgauzen) (1778–1852) Russian naval officer. Made circumnavigation of Antarctica 1820–21 and is credited with the first sighting of the continent. He discovered Peter I and Alexander I islands. ◆287 (3)
Bemis Heights ⚔ of American Revolutionary War (7 Oct 1777). British victories. ◆127 (3)
Benalcázar, Sebastián (c.1495–1551) Spanish *conquistador*. A member of Francisco Pizarro's expedition to Peru, he conquered the northern Inca capital, Quito, in 1533. ◆142 (1)
Benedict, St. (c.480–c.547) Italian founder of Western monasticism. Established the monastery on Monte Cassino near Naples, Italy. The Benedictine Rule served as the basis of Christian monastic organization.
regulates monasteries (529) ❖49●
Bengal
partition and reunification ❖99●, ❖250, ◆250 (2)
survey of India ❑239
under British control (1765) ❑87
Benin State established (c.1500) ❖79●, ❖163●
bronze statue ❑75
sculpture of horse ❑78
Bennington ⚔ of American Revolutionary War, 15 Oct 1777, American victory. ◆127 (3)
Benz, Karl Friedrich (1844–1929). German mechanical engineer who

designed and in 1885 built the world's first practical automobile to be powered by an internal-combustion engine. 92●
Beothuk Native American peoples of eastern Canada.
Indians enslaved (1501) ✣118●
sub-Arctic nomadic hunters ✣123, ◆123 (3)
Berber Pre-Arab inhabitants of North Africa. The Berbers were scattered in tribes across Morocco, Algeria, Tunisia, Libya, and Egypt and tended to be concentrated in the mountain and desert regions. They spoke various languages belonging to the Afro-Asiatic language family.
campaigns ✣46, ✣57, ◆57 (2)
states in North Africa ✣161, ◆161 (2)
trans-Saharan trade ✣50
Bering Strait Route to Alaska ✣257
Bering, Vitus (1681–1741). Danish-Russian navigator in the service of Tsar Peter the Great. Ordered in 1724 to find whether Asia and North America were connected by land or whether there was water between them. He set sail in 1728 and passed through the strait which bears his name into the Pacific, but bad weather prevented him seeing North America. Given command in 1733 of the Great Northern Expedition during which much of Siberia's Arctic coast was mapped. Died of scurvy on Bering Island. The Bering Sea is also named after him. ✣86●, ◆257 (2), ◆286 (1)
Beringia Name given to the land bridge which linked Asia to N America during the last Ice Age. ✣14, ◆116
Berlin Airlift (Jun 1948–Sep 1949). Maintenance, under siege conditions, of Western sector of occupied Berlin during Soviet blockade and formal partition of occupied Germany into E and W Germany. ❑108, ✣212, ◆212 (1) *See also* Berlin Blockade
Berlin ⚔ of WW II (May 1945). Scene of final German resistance to invading Soviet forces. ✣105, ◆211 (4)
Berlin Blockade (1948–49). International crisis where Soviet forces in eastern Germany began a blockade of transport and communications between Berlin and the West in an attempt to force the Western Allies to abandon their post-WW II jurisdictions in the city. ✣102●, ❑108, ◆212 (1)
Berlin Congress (13 Jun–13 Jul, 1878). Diplomatic meeting of the major European powers at which the Treaty of San Stefano which concluded the Russo-Turkish War (1877–78) was replaced by the Treaty of Berlin. Officially convened by the Austrian foreign minister, Count Gyula Andrassy, the congress met in Berlin on June 13. ✣203, ✣232●
Berlin Conference on Africa (Nov 1884–Feb 1885). Negotiations at Berlin whereby the major European nations met to discuss European involvement in Central Africa. ✣96, ✣167●
Berlin Wall (*var. Ger.* Berliner Mauer). Barrier that surrounded West Berlin and prevented access to East Berlin and adjacent areas of East Germany from 1961–89. In the years between 1949 and 1961, about 2.5 million East Germans had fled from East to West Germany. ✣106●, ✣108, ✣212, ✣214, ❑110, ❑212
Bernard of Clairvaux, St. (1090–1153) French Cistercian monk and religious reformer. Became first abbot of new monastery of Clairvaux, in Champagne, and later founded more than 70 monasteries. Drew up the statutes of the Knights Templars in 1128, and secured recognition from Pope Innocent II for the Cistercian order. He was canonized in 1174. ✣187●
Bessemer, Sir Henry (1813–98). British inventor and engineer, knighted in 1879, who developed the first process for manufacturing steel inexpensively (1856), leading to the development of the Bessemer converter. ✣92●
Bhimbetka rock shelter paintings ❑15
Biafra (1967–70) ✣107●, ◆106–7, ◆169 (4)
'Big Three' The three major Allied leaders during WW II: Roosevelt (US), Churchill (UK), and Stalin (USSR). ❑105
bin Laden, Osama (1957–) Leader of Islamist terrorist organization al-Qaeda, founded c.1988. The shadowy organization has been implicated in a number of major acts of terrorism, notably the destruction of the World Trade Center, New York, using hijacked passenger planes as suicide weapons in 2001. ✣235❑
Birmingham Civil Rights protest. Alabama (1963) ❑137
Birth of a Nation, The (film, 1915) ✣135●
Biscoe, John Antarctic exploration (1830–33) ◆287 (3)
Bismarck Archipelago Lapita pottery (c.1600 BCE) ✣27●, ◆281 (3)
Bismarck, Otto von (1815–98). German statesman, chief minister of Prussia (1862–90) and architect of the German Empire. Prussia's domination of mainland Europe was achieved by means of three wars: with Denmark (1864) over Schleswig-Holstein; with Austria and other German states (1866); and the Franco-Prussian War (1870–71). With the formation of the German Empire in 1871, he became its first Chancellor. During his years in power, he ruled autocratically (known as the 'Iron Chancellor'), reforming the Prussian army and carrying out extensive administrative reforms for the new empire. ✣94●, ✣203●, ❑202
Black Death Familiar name given to epidemic of bubonic plague that swept across Eurasia in the 14th century, which is estimated to have killed between one-third and one-half of the population of Europe. The name was first used during the 19th century. ✣72–3, ◆72–3 (1), ✣188 *See also* bubonic plague, plagues
Black Huns *see* Huns.
Black Prince *see* Edward, Prince of Wales
blackbirding Euphemism for slave-raiding in the Pacific in the 19th century. Gangs of Europeans would land on Pacific islands and forcibly 'recruit' labourers for the sugar-cane plantations of Queensland.
Blackburn English textile town ✣93
Blackstock ⚔ of American Revolutionary War (20 Nov 1780). American victory. ◆127 (3)
Blaeu, Willem and Joan, 17th-century Dutch cartographers ✣83, ❑83
Blitz, the Strategic bombing campaign of WW II launched by Germany against London and other industrial centres in Britain, 1940. ❑210
Blitzkrieg (*var.* Lightning War) Term used to describe German military strategy during WW II, involving combined operations of fast-moving armoured thrusts supported by tactical air power and reinforced by infantry. ✣210
Blombos Cave Site in S Africa of earliest known human art. ◆17 (2), 17●
Blue Nile Source discovered 1772 ✣157
Blunt, Wilfred Scawen (1840–1922). British author, poet, diplomat and explorer. In 1879, accompanied by his wife Anne, he travelled across the Arabian Peninsula. ◆219 (4)
boats *see* transport
Boer (*var. Dut.* Husbandman, or farmer). South African of Dutch or Huguenot descent, especially one of the early settlers of the Transvaal and the Orange Free State.
Bantu war (1779–80) ✣87●
Boer War (1899–1902) ✣95●, ✣96●, ◆96 (2)
Cape Colony land ✣95●, ✣166
'Great trek' in ox wagons ❑166
Natal annexed by British (1843) ✣166●
Orange Free State founded (1854) ✣166●
Republic (c.1880) ◆167 (4)
treks ✣90, ✣91●, ◆166 (2)
Vootrekkers' independence (1852) ✣166●
Zulu attacks (1838) ✣91●
Zulu War (1879) ✣95●
See also Afrikaner
Bohemia
civil war ❑193
under Ottokar II ✣189●, ◆189 (4)
under Charles IV ✣189●
forging of new state ✣193
Bojador, Cape Rounded by Portuguese explorer (1434) ✣156●
Bolivar, Simón (1783–1830). The most celebrated of the liberators of Spanish S America. Having liberated Venezuela in 1813, Bolivar had to fight against an army sent from Spain under General Morillo. He fled the country, but returned to liberate Venezuela again in 1818. ❑90, ❑150, ✣150, ◆150 (1)
Bolivia
Chaco War (1932–35) ✣102●, ✣152●, ❑152, ◆152 (2)
foundation (1825) ✣90
War of Pacific (1879–83) ✣94●, ✣151, ◆151 (4)
Bologna University founded (1119) ✣62●
Bolsheviks Members of the more radical wing of the Russian Social Democratic Workers' Party who seized power in Russia in the revolution of 1917. In 1918 they adopted the name 'Communists'. ✣98●, ✣99●, ✣208, ❑208, ◆208 (2)
Bombay (*var.* Mumbai)
railway station (1887) ❑95
urbanization ✣253
Bonpland, Aimé (1773–1858). French botanist who travelled in South America (1799–1804), discovering 6000 new species of plants. ✣143
Book of the Dead, The ❑30
Book of the Fixed Stars, The ❑59
Boone, Daniel (1735–1820) US frontiersman. Travelled to Kentucky through the Cumberland Gap in the Appalachian Mountains in 1767. Later traced the Wilderness Road and founded the town of Boonesboro on the Kentucky River. His explorations were instrumental in encouraging settlement west of the eastern mountains of the US. ❑119, ◆119 (2)
Booneville ⚔ of American Civil War (17 Jun 1861). Union victory. ◆131 (6)
Bornu Empire Kingdom and emirate of north eastern Nigeria. Originally a province of the Kanem Empire until the latter's territory was reduced to that of Bornu by c.1380. By the early 16th century Bornu had recaptured Kanem and made it a protectorate. The re-amalgamated Kanem-Bornu reached its height in the reign of Mai Idris Alawma (r.1571–1603). ✣87●, ◆165 (4), ◆167 (3)
Borobudur Buddhist temple (c.800) ✣49●, ✣59●
Borodino ⚔ of Napoleonic Wars (7 Sep 1812). Defeated Russians lost 50,000 troops. ◆200 (1)
Boshin War (1868–69). Restored the Meiji ('enlightened rule') emperor of Japan inaugurating a period of political and social reform. ✣270, ◆270 (1)
Bosnia
conflict (1992) ✣110●, ✣215, ❑215, ◆215 (3)
and Herzegovina, annexed by Austria-Hungary ✣232●
Boston
birth of American Revolution (1775) ✣127
European and native conflict (1676) ✣126
Massacre (1770) ✣127●
'Tea Party' (1773) ✣127●
Boston Massacre (5 Mar 1770). The culmination of a series of confrontations between British troops and American colonists in Boston, Massachusetts: five people were killed when troops opened fire on a crowd. The incident became a focus for British unpopularity and was depicted by the propagandist, Samuel Adams as a battle for American liberty. ✣127●
Botany Bay British settlement (1788) ✣87●, ✣282, ❑282
Bottego, Vittorio 19th-century Italian explorer of Ethiopia (1892–97). ◆157 (4)
Bougainville, Louis Antoine de (1729–1811). French soldier and explorer. Bougainville's scientific expedition of 1776–79 was the first French circumnavigation of the globe. His most important discoveries were in the Pacific and his glowing descriptions of Tahiti inspired French (and other European) interest in this Polynesian 'Garden of Eden'. ◆278 (1)
Boulton, Matthew (1728–1809). English manufacturer and engineer who financed and introduced James Watt's steam engine. ❑204
Bourbons (1589–1830). French royal dynasty which began with the accession of Henry of Bourbon, king of Navarre and a Calvinist. In the face of opposition by French Catholics, he renounced Calvinism in 1593, and became King Henry IV. The Bourbon dynasty reached its zenith with Louis XIV (1638–1715), who reigned for over fifty years as the personification of absolute power. The Bourbons continued to hold the throne of France until the French Revolution (1791) and again from 1814–48. ✣197●, ◆197 (5), ❑197
Boxer Rebellion (1900–01). Chinese popular uprising aimed at driving out all foreign traders, diplomats and missionaries. ✣95, ◆97 (4), ❑97, ◆268 (2)
Boyacá ⚔ of wars of S American liberation. Colombia liberated by Bolivar. ◆150 (1)
Braddock, General Edward (1675–1755). Led British attack against France in French Indian Wars in America. He was mortally wounded in 1755 on the way to Fort Duquesne (Pittsburgh) and his force was later decimated. ✣127, ◆127 (2)
Braganza, House of (*var.* House of Bragança). Ruling dynasty of Portugal (1640–1910) and of the empire of Brazil (1822–89).
nationalist revolt ✣196
Brahmans Hindus of the higher caste, traditionally assigned to the priesthood. ✣242
Brahmavarta, Home of Vedic Hinduism ✣36
Brandenburg Prussia In medieval times, Brandenburg was a margravate (border county) of the Holy Roman Empire. The margraves of Brandenburg became electors in 1415. Their territory expanded over the centuries to include Prussia. In 1701, the Elector of Brandenburg was granted the title king of Prussia.
growth (1648–1803) ✣199, ◆199 (3)
possessions ◆82–3
Treaty of Westphalia, ◆196 (1)
Brandywine ⚔ of American Revolutionary War (11 Sep 1777). British victory. ◆127 (3)
Brazil 149–153
foreign affairs, Paraguayan War (1864–70) ✣94
home affairs
black population ✣112, ◆112 (1)
borders with Spanish S America ◆148 (2)
colonized by Portugal ✣78●, ✣142●, ✣149, ◆149 (3)
Dutch conquest (1630–54) ✣82●, ✣149, ◆149 (4)
first Jesuit missions (1550) ✣143●
independence (1822) ✣90, ✣150, ◆150 (1)
Indians decimated (1562–63) ✣149●
Jesuits expelled (1759) ✣143●
military revolution (1930) ✣102●
Philip II of Spain becomes king (1580) ✣78●
viceroyalty (1663) ✣149●
trade and industry
rainforest development ✣153●, ❑153, ◆153 (4)
gold discovered (1695) ✣82●
gold rivalry (18th century) ✣86
slave trade ✣84, ✣85●, ❑149
sugar producer (c.1575) ✣78●
Yanomami tribe ❑110
Brazza, Pierre Savorgnan de (1852–1905). Italian-born French explorer and colonial administrator who founded the French Congo, and explored Gabon. He also founded the city of Brazzaville. ◆157 (4)
BRD *see* West Germany
Breda ⚔ of Dutch Revolt (1590). Dutch victory over Spain. ◆195 (5)
Breitenfeld ⚔ of Thirty Years War (1631). Swedish protestant forces defeat of Habsburg emperor Frederick II and the Catholic League. ◆196 (1)
Brest Litovsk, Treaty of (Mar 1918). The peace treaty which ended conflict between Russia and the Central Powers after WW I. The independence of Poland, Finland, Georgia, the Baltic states and Ukraine was recognized by Russia. The treaty was voided by the Armistice later that year. ◆207 (4)
Brétigny, Treaty of (1360). Treaty signed by England and France at Brétigny which concluded the first phase of the Hundred Years' War. Territory, including Aquitaine, was granted to Edward III of England, with the understanding that he renounced his claim to the French throne. ✣192●
Briar Creek ⚔ of American Revolutionary War (3 Mar 1779). British victory. ◆127 (3)
Bridgewater Treatise on Mineralogy and Geology (illustration) ❑91
Britain, Battle of Air ⚔ of WW II (Jul–Oct 1940). Prolonged struggle for air superiority over English Channel and southern England in which the RAF averted a planned German invasion of Britain. ✣210●, ❑210, ◆210 (1)
Britain
foreign affairs
voyages of expansion (1492–1597) ◆80–1 (1)
English possessions
1000–1200 ◆62–3
1154–89 ✣187●
1180 ◆187 (4)
1300 ◆66–7
1400 ◆70–1
1500 ◆74–5
1600 ◆78–9
1700 ◆82–3
British possessions
1800 ◆86–7
1850 ◆90–1
1900 ◆94–5
1925 ◆98–9
See also United Kingdom
Afghanistan, invasion (1878–79) ✣95●
Africa
Afrikaner treks and Mfecane wars ◆166 (2)
colonization ✣87●, ✣95, ✣166, ◆166 (1) (3) (4)
decolonization ✣168, ◆168 (1)
exploration of interior (19th century) ✣157, ◆157 (4) (5)
Ghana achieves independence (1957) ✣107●
imperialism (1880–1920) ✣96, ◆96 (1)
Natal annexed ✣91●
South Africa leaves Commonwealth ✣107●
struggle for South Africa ✣92, ✣92●, ◆92 (2)
America
Anglo-French conflict (1754–60) ✣126–7, ◆127 (2)
colonies declare independence (1776) ✣86●
colonies' cartoon (1776) ❑127
colonization of North America (to 1750) ◆126 (1)
exploration of North America (15th–17th century) ◆118–19 (1) (2)
gains Canada from France (1763) ✣86
Revolutionary War (1775–83) ◆127 (3)
S America exploration ◆142–3 (1) (2)
Argentina, Falklands war (1982) ✣110●
Asia, imperialism ✣97, ✣97●, ◆97 (3)
Australia
Botany Bay settled (1788) ✣87●
British colony (1829) ✣91
Commonwealth proclaimed (1901) ✣99●
Burma, annexation (1885–86) ✣95●
Ceylon, coastal area conquered (1796) ✣87●
China, Beijing occupied ✣95●
Egypt, invasion and occupation (1882) ✣95
First World War *see* Wars, First World
France, opposition alliances (1792–1815) ✣201, ◆201 (3)
Guiana, colony (c.1640) ✣149, ◆149 (4)
Hong Kong ceded (1842) ✣91
India, expansionism ✣87●, ✣248, ✣248●, ◆248 (1) (2)
Jamaica seized from Spain (1654) ✣82●
Middle East
Gulf War (1990–91) ◆235 (5)
Suez crisis (1956) ✣234●
New Zealand annexed (1840) ✣91●
Ottoman Empire partition ✣233
Pacific, decolonization and nationhood ✣285, ◆285 (3)
Pacific imperialism ◆284 (1)
Second World War *see* Wars, Second World
Tibet, first mission ✣257●
home affairs
accession of Canute (1016) ✣62●
Anglo-Saxon kingdoms ✣183●, ◆183 (3)
black population ✣112, ◆112 (1)
British Isles (1200–1400) ◆188 (2)
Civil War ✣196●, ❑196
defeat of Spanish Armada (1588) ✣78●
end of Danish rule (1042) ✣60●
Norwegian settlements (c.900 CE) ✣60●
Peasants' Revolt (1381) ✣70●, ◆188 (2)
population growth (1650–1800) ❑198
Viking raids ✣58, ✣60
trade and industry
industrial revolution ✣90, ✣204, ✣204●, ◆204 (1)
iron metallurgy (BCE) ✣31
slave trade ✣84, ✣85●, ✣165●
British Columbia Panning for gold ❑93
British South Africa Company Mercantile company, based in London, that was incorporated in 1889 under a royal charter at the instigation of Cecil Rhodes, with the object of acquiring and exercising commercial and administrative rights in south-central Africa. 96●
Bronze Age Following the Palaeolithic and Neolithic ages the Bronze Age was the third phase in the development of material culture among the ancient peoples of Europe, Asia, and the Middle East. The term also denotes the first period in which metal was used. The date at which the age began varied with regions; in Greece and China, for example, the Bronze Age began before 3000 BCE, whereas in Britain it did not start until about 1900 BCE. ✣26, ✣240, ✣240●, ❑240, ◆26–7, ◆175 (3), ◆240 (3)
bronze
balance scales ❑33
Benin sculpture of horse ❑78
Benin statue of Portuguese soldier ❑75
Celtic lunisolar calendar ❑33
ceramic moulds used for casting (BCE) ✣27●
of Charlemagne ❑184
Chinese casting ✣22●, ✣31●, ❑27
Chinese coins (BCE) ❑34, ❑259
Chola dynasty Shiva ❑59
development of metallurgy ✣26
Dong Son drum ❑240
Dotaku ceremonial bells (c.100 BCE) ❑264
E Asian (BCE) 258
European (2300 BCE) ✣27●
ibis (11th century) ❑163
major regions (c.1250 BCE) ◆26–7
model of solar system (BCE) ❑31
Mycenaean dagger blade ❑26
ornaments ✣31
ritual axe ❑175
ritual vessel (BCE) ❑31
Shang dynasty ❑259
slashing swords ✣175
weapon technology ✣31
working in SE Asia (1500 BCE) ✣27●
Broz, Josip *see* Tito, Marshal
Bruce, James (1730–94). Scottish explorer who whilst travelling in Ethiopia, reached the headstream of the Blue Nile in 1772, which was then thought to be the source of the Nile. ◆157 (4)
Bruges Medieval trading city ✣190
Brunel, Isambard Kingdom (1806–59). British civil and mechanical engineer who designed the 'the Great Western', the first transatlantic steamer in 1838 ✣204●
Brusilov offensive (Jun–Aug 1916). Major Russian offensive against Austria-Hungary during WW I, led by General Aleksey Alekseyevich Brusilov (1853–1926). ◆207 (4)
Brutus, Lucius Junius Legendary figure of the 6th century BCE, believed to have ousted the despotic Etruscan king Lucius Tarquinius Superbus from Rome in 509 and then to have founded the Roman Republic. ❑178
bubonic plague Bacterial disease spread to humans via rat fleas, and still endemic in parts of Asia. Infection results in delirium, fever and the formation of large buboes There were several major plague epidemics during the Middle Ages; the most devastating was the Black Death of the mid-14th century. *See also* Black Death. ◆72–73, ✣72–73
Bucephala ⚔ of Alexander's campaigns (326 BCE). Alexander's troops refused to go any further east. ◆40–1 (1)
Buckland, Revd William (1784–1856). English geologist and clergyman who attempted to relate geology to the biblical description of the creation. In 1845 he became Dean of Westminster. ✣91, ❑91
Buddha (*aka* Siddhartha Gautama, 'The Enlightened One') (c.566–c.483 BCE). Founder of the world religion of Buddhism. Born the son of a nobleman of the Hindu Kshatriya caste. When aged about 30, he abandoned earthly ambitions to pursue self-enlightenment. Traditionally, he attained this as he sat under a tree at Bodh Gaya. He spent the next 40 years teaching and gaining disciples and followers. Died at Kushinagara. *See* Buddhism. ✣36●, ◆36 (2), ✣49●, ◆49 (3), ❑49, ✣242, ◆242 (3)
Buddhism Major religion of S and E Asia founded by Siddhartha Gautama. Maintains that sorrow and suffering are inherent in life and one can be released from them by ridding oneself of desire and self-delusion.
✣35, ✣36, ✣43, ✣238, ✣242, ✣242●, ◆242 (3)
Borobudur temple ✣59●, ❑243
in Ceylon ✣51
in China ✣260–1
decline in S Asia ✣63●, ✣243, ✣243●, ◆243 (4)
depictions
Ashoka's edicts ❑39
bronze Buddha from Nara ❑265
Buddha in Gandhara style ❑242
cave-temple ❑51, ❑244
lotus flower ❑238
paintings of Buddha ❑43
rock-cut Buddha (c.460 CE) ❑49
Sanchi monuments ❑242
Tang wall painting ❑59
The Diamond Sutra ❑59
foundation of Zen (1191) ✣63●
in Japan ✣49●, ✣55, ✣264–5
Mahayana ◆49 (4)
spread ✣48, ✣49●, ✣243, ◆49 (3), ◆243 (5)
Tantric ◆49 (4)
in Tibet ✣49●, ✣55●
warrior priests ✣265, ◆265 (4)
Buena Vista ⚔ of US-Mexican War (1847). US victory. ◆129 (2)
Buenos Aires Satellite image ❑110
Buganda Occupied by Britain (1894) ✣167●
Bulgaria
1230 ◆189 (4)
Byzantine war ✣58●, ✣185●
copper mines (c.4000 BCE) ✣174
end of Communism (1989) ✣110●
granted independence ✣232
leading Balkan state ✣94●
WW II, mobilization and casualty

Key to index: ✣ text ● timeline ❑ picture ◆ map *var.* variant name *aka* also known as *f/n* full name *prev.* previously known as r. ruled ⚔ battle WW I First World War WW II Second World War

figures ✤105
See also Balkans, nationalism
Bulgarians *see* Bulgars
Bulgars (*var.* Bulgarians). People known in eastern European history during the Middle Ages. One branch of this people was ancestral to the modern Bulgarians. The Bulgars may have originated as a Turkic tribe of Central Asia and arrived in the European steppe west of the Volga River with the Huns about 370 CE; retreating with the Huns, they resettled about 460 CE in an arc of country north and east of the Sea of Azov.
crushed by Byzantium (1018) ✤185, ✤185●
invade Balkans (680) ✤54●
bull cults ❑37●
Bull Run (*aka* Manassas) ⚔ of American Civil War (two battles) (21 Jul and 29–30 Aug 1862). Confederate victories. ◆131 (6)
Bunker Hill (Boston) ⚔ of American Revolutionary War (17 Jun 1775). British victory. ✤127, ◆127 (3)
Buquer Servant's account of African river (1456) ✤156
Burckhardt, Johann Ludwig (1784–1817). Swiss explorer of the Middle East. He was the first European to visit Petra in Jordan and the Egyptian temple of Abu Simbel on the Nile. In 1814 he crossed the Red Sea from the Sudan and visited Mecca disguised as a Muslim. ◆219 (4)
Burebista Ruler of Dacia, a kingdom in the Carpathian Mountains and Transylvania, in present north-central and western Romania. The Roman province of Dacia eventually included wider territories both to the north and east. In about 60–50 BCE King Burebista unified and extended the kingdom, which, however, split into four parts after his death (45 BCE) ◆42–3
Burgundians Germanic tribes who occupied the lands of western Switzerland from the 5th century onward. Although they retained political control, they lost contact with their former homelands and were assimilated into the Roman Celtic population. ◆52–3 (1)
Burgundy
Frankish kingdom (531) ✤54●
and 14th-century possessions ◆70–1
in 15th century ◆192 (1) (2)
territories of Charles the Bold (1477) ◆193 (4)
burials
Adena culture (BCE) ✤30, ✤34, ✤38
African (BCE) ✤15●
Altai Mountain sites ✤39
E Asian (BCE) ✤258
Egyptian funerary equipment ❑26
Mehrgarh (BCE) ✤19
Neanderthal ❑12
Qafzeh Cave ✤15●
ritual ✤21, ✤22–3
Shang dynasty (BCE) ✤27
Urnfield (1200 BCE) ✤31●
See also grave goods; pyramids
Burke, Robert O'Hara (1821–61). Irish-born explorer of Australia. In 1853 he emigrated to Melbourne, where he joined the police. In 1860 he was chosen to lead an expedition crossing Australia from south to north. Coastal swamps prevented his party reaching the sea at the Gulf of Carpentaria. The journey ended in tragedy. Burke died of starvation with two of his companions; one of the party survived thanks to the assistance of local Aborigines.
❑279, ◆279 (2)
Burma ◆248 (1), ◆249 (4), ◆250 (1), ◆251 (4)
annexed by Britain (1885–86) ✤95●
areas under control (1575) ◆78–9
first state established (1044) ✤63●
invaded by China (1765–69) ✤87
Konbaung dynasty founded (1752) ✤87●
reunited (1755) ✤87●
Bursa Becomes Ottoman capital (1326) ✤71●
Burton, Sir Richard Francis (1821–90). British linguist, diplomat, writer and explorer. His extensive knowledge of Far Eastern customs and languages enabled him in 1853 to travel, disguised as a Muslim, to Medina and Mecca. Exploring E Africa with John Speke, in 1858 he explored Lake Tanganyika. The author of over 50 books, he is best known for his translation of *The Thousand Nights and a Night* (*The Arabian Nights*). ◆157 (4), ❑219, ◆219 (4)
Bush, George (1924–) 41st President of the US (Republican, 1988–92). Led US in Gulf War (1990–91) and signed arms limitation treaties with USSR and later, Russian Federation. Established NAFTA (North American Free Trade Agreement) with Canada and Mexico (1992). ✤139●
Bush, George W (1946–) 43rd President of the US (Republican, 2000–). Son of former president George Bush, George W. has involved his country in two large-scale military actions overseas. His reaction to the terrorist attacks on New York and Washington in 2001 was to form a US-led coalition to invade Afghanistan where the Taliban regime was sheltering the al-Qaeda terrorist organization. He received far less international support for his second venture, the invasion of Iraq on the grounds that Saddam Hussein's regime was concealing weapons of mass destruction. Saddam was quickly overthrown, but no such weapons were found. Attempts to rebuild the Iraqi state have met with determined, violent opposition. ✤139❑, ◆139 (4)
Bushi *see* Bushido
Bushido (*Jap.* Way of the warrior). Of or pertaining to *bushi, bushidan*, Japanese chivalric code based on feudal loyalty to lord or emperor, associated with samurai caste. ✤265
Buwayhid dynasty (945–1055). Islamic dynasty of Iranian and Shi'a character that provided native rule in western Iran and Iraq in the period between the Arab and Turkish conquests. ✤59●, ✤227, ◆227 (6)
Byblos Founded (c.3100) ✤24●
Byrd, Richard Evelyn (1888–1957). US naval officer. He made the first flight over N Pole in 1926, and in 1929 flew over the S Pole. Later explored Antarctica on foot, leading expeditions in 1933–34, 1939–41 and 1955–56). ◆287 (3)
Byzantine Empire (*var.* Eastern Roman Empire (395–1453). The Roman Empire in the West fell in 476, but the eastern empire with its capital at Constantinople (Byzantium) survived until it was conquered by the Ottoman Turks in 1453. Although Roman institutions survived, the empire was essentially Greek Orthodox and Christianity was the state religion. The empire expanded under emperors such as Justinian I and Basil II, but for most of its history was on the defensive, losing much territory to the Arabs in the 7th century, and for the first half of the 13th century being ousted from Constantinople by the Venetians and crusading knights from western Europe.
◆54–5, ◆58–9, ◆62–3, ◆64–5 (2) (3), ◆66–7, ◆70–1, ◆185 (3), ◆189 (4)
advance of Islam (750) ◆184 (2)
Bursa captured by Ottomans (1326) ✤71●
declines ✤62, ✤71, ✤75
on eve of Fourth Crusade ◆187 (5)
Macedonian rulers (867–1081) ✤59
Muslim advance stemmed (863) ✤59●
reconquests ✤182●, ◆182 (1)
regains Constantinople ✤66●
resurgence under Basil II ✤63
and Seljuk Turks ✤63●, ✤228, ◆228 (1)
struggle for Italy ✤184, ✤184●, ◆183 (4)
threatens Jerusalem (976) ✤59●
war with Bulgaria (996) ✤58●

C

Cabeza de Vaca, Álvar Núñez (c.1490–1560). Ill-fated Spanish explorer of N and S America. On an expedition of 1528 to colonize lands on the north coast of the Gulf of Mexico, he was one of only four survivors, who wandered the region for eight years. He later explored S America, and was appointed governor of the Río de la Plata province, but was replaced in 1545, after his men mutinied. ◆118 (1), ◆142 (1)
Cabot, John (c.1450–1499). Navigator, born in Genoa. In 1497, sponsored by Henry VII of England, he led the first recorded European expedition to the coast of N America since the Norwegian voyages of the 10th century, although he believed he had discovered China. ◆118 (1)
Cabot, Sebastian (1474–1557). Son of John Cabot, he was a cartographer, navigator and explorer who first travelled to N America in 1508, possibly reaching Hudson Bay and travelling down the eastern coast. In 1526, under the auspices of Spain, he led an expedition to S America to find a western route to the Pacific Ocean. He made a number of later voyages to find the Northeast Passage to China. ◆142 (1)
Cabral, Gonçalo Velho Early 15th-century Portuguese navigator, among the first Portuguese to sail to the Azores. ◆156 (3)
Cabral, Pedro Álvares (1467–1520). Portuguese navigator, discoverer of Brazil. After Vasco da Gama's successful voyage to India in 1498, King Manuel of Portugal sponsored a second expedition, captained by Cabral. In 1500, while following da Gama's course, sailing out into the Atlantic to use the prevailing winds, Cabral made an accidental landfall in S America, which he claimed for Portugal.
✤80●, ✤142●, ◆156 (3), ✤156●
Cacaxtla Fortified hilltop city in Central America. ✤122
Cadamosto, Alvise (*var.* Ca'da Mosto) (1432–88). Venetian explorer and trader retained by Henry the Navigator, believed to be the first European to reach the Cape Verde Islands in 1456. ◆156 (3)
Caesar, Gaius Julius (102–44 BCE). Roman statesman and general. Caesar's conquest of Gaul (58–51 BCE) and his victory in a civil war against his rival Pompey (48) raised Caesar to a position of complete dominance of the Roman world. In 46 he was named dictator for 10 years, but was assassinated by enemies, who feared his power would bring the Roman republic to an end.
✤42●, ✤180●
Cahokia
cultural site (1050) ✤123●
Mississippian site declines (c.1250) ✤66●
Caillé, René (1799–1839). French traveller who was the first European to reach the legendary city of Timbuktu and to survive and tell the tale of his experiences there. ◆157 (4), ❑157
cairn *see* barrow
Cairo
Al-Azhar university established (970s) ✤58●
Fatimid capital (969) ✤58●, ◆227 (6)
Ibn Tulun mosque ❑227
Cajamarca Inca site ✤148
Calabozo ⚔ of wars of S American liberation (Feb 1818) in Venezuela. ◆150 (1)
Calama ⚔ of War of the Pacific (1879). Chilean victory. ◆151 (4)
Calcutta Independence celebrations ❑251
Çaldiran (*var.* Chaldiron, Chaldiran) ⚔ between the Ottomans and the Safavids (1514). Ottoman victory enabled them to gain control of most of eastern Anatolia.
✤79●, ◆231 (4)
calendrical systems
core developmental regions ❑33
evolution ✤33, ◆33 (3)
hieroglyphic notations (BCE) ✤34
Islamic ✤226, ◆226 (2)
Maya civilization ✤54
California
ceded to US (1849) ✤90●, ◆129 (1) (2)
migration (1917–20) ✤134
Gold Rush ✤90●, ✤93●, ✤100●
Caliphate The caliph, seen as the successor to the Prophet Muhammad, was the leader of the Islamic world. Early caliphates were based at Medina and Damascus. Under the Abbasid dynasty (756–1258), the caliphate was based at the new city of Baghdad (founded 766), which was to become a potent symbol of Arab power. ✤227●, ◆227 (4)
caliphs, loss of power ✤59
See also Baghdad, Abbasid Caliphate, Umayyads
calligraphy *see* writing
Calvin, John (1509–64). French theologian. A leader of the Protestant Reformation in France and Switzerland, he established the first presbyterian government in Geneva. His *Institutes of the Christian Religion* (1546) presented the basis of what came to be known as Calvinism.
✤194●, ✤195, ✤195●, ◆195 (5)
Cambaluc (*var.* Khanbaliq, *later* Beijing, Peking), Kublai Khan's capital ❑69
Cambodia
becomes independent (1954) ✤107●
Khmer Rouge social programme ✤253
South, organized into Annam provinces (1691) ✤83●
USA university war protest (1970) ✤137●
Vietnam invasion (1979) ✤111●
Cambyses II (r.529–522 BCE). Achaemenid king of Persia, son of Cyrus the Great.
conquest of Egypt (525 BCE) ◆223, 223●
Camden ⚔ of American Revolutionary War (16 Jan 1781). British victory. ◆127 (3)
camels
introduced to Sahara (c.100 BCE) ✤43
used as transport ✤50, ✤58
W African slave trade (13th century) ✤66
Camp David Accords (1978). Named after the official country house of the US President, Camp David, in Maryland, the accords were a framework for a settlement to end the Middle East conflict. Brokered in 1978 by US President Jimmy Carter between President Sadat of Egypt and Prime Minister Begin of Israel, the Accords laid the foundation for the 1979 peace treaty between the two nations. ✤234●
Campbell's Station Tennessee, American Civil War campaign map ❑94
Cana Fortified entrepôt. ❑45
Canaanites Canaan was the ancient name for Palestine around 2000 BCE, and its people occupied the area between the Mediterranean coast eastwards possibly to the River Jordan and the Dead Sea. After the exodus of the Israelites from Egypt in the 13th century BCE they were confined to the coastal strip, and were condemned by the Hebrews for their worship of local deities, and their tradition of sacrifice and sacred prostitution. They developed the first truly alphabetic script.
27●, ✤32 (1), ◆223 (3)
Canada
British dominion (1867) ✤94
European settlement ✤128, ◆128 (2)
exploration and mapping ✤119, ◆119 (3)
gained from France (1763) ✤86
immigration ◆132 (1)
industrialization, urbanization ◆132 (1)
mineral finds (late 19th century) ◆93 (2)
regional inequality ✤136
Treaty of Paris (1763) ✤86
WW II, mobilization and casualty figures ✤105
Canadian Yukon Exploring Expedition (1887–89) ◆119 (3)
Candra Gupta *see* Chandragupta Maurya
Cannae ⚔ of Second Punic War (216 BCE). Hannibal's greatest victory over the Romans. ◆178 (3)
cannon Used in warfare 14th century ❑71
canoe *see* transport
Cantino, Alberto Agent of the Duke of Ferrara in Lisbon, who in 1502 obtained a Portuguese world map, showing the latest discoveries of Portuguese sailors, including the coast of Brazil and Madagascar. The famous map is known as the *Cantino Planisphere.*
map of India (1502) ✤239●
planisphere (1502) ❑142
Canton *see* Guangzhou
Canute (*var.* Canute the Great, Knut, Knud, Knut den Mektige). Danish king of England (r.1016–35), of Denmark (as Canute II; r.1019–35), and of Norway (r.1028–35), who was a power in the politics of Europe in the 11th century.
possessions (1028–35) ◆62–3
unifying accession (1016) ✤62●
Cão, Diogo (*fl.*1480–86). Portuguese navigator who in 1482, became the first European to discover the mouth of the Congo.
✤156●, ◆156 (3)
Cape Colony
Boers' 'Great Trek' (1830s) ✤90, ✤95●, ✤166
mining (1872) ❑95
Cape Town
founded by Dutch (1652) ✤164
captured by British (1795) ✤164●
Cape Verde, reached by Portuguese (1446) ✤156●, ◆156 (3)
Capetian Dynasty (987–1328). Ruling dynasty of France founded by Hugh Capet who replaced the previous Carolingian line. ✤191
Carabobo ⚔ of wars of S American independence. Last battle on Venezuelan soil won by Bolívar. ◆150 (1)
caravel Light sailing ship of the 15–17th centuries in Europe, developed by the Portuguese for exploring the coast of Africa. ✤78, ❑78
cardial pottery (*var.* cardium). Pottery decorated with impressions of cockle shells (cardium), made by the earliest communities to adopt farming along the shores of the Mediterranean (c.6200–5000 BCE). ✤174
Caribbean
Code Noir restricts slavery (1685) ✤85●
colonized by Spain (16th century) ✤78, ✤118
piracy (16th–17th century) ✤85, ◆65 (2)
plantation systems ✤82, ✤84
population of African descent ✤112, ◆112 (1)
Carlist Wars (1834–49) Regional opposition to the liberal Spanish regime led to war in support of the claims of Don Carlos (1788–1855) and his descendants to the throne of Spain.
✤202, ◆202 (1)
Carlowitz, Peace of *see* Karlowitz, Peace of
Carlsbad Decrees (1819) ✤90●
Carnac Stone avenues ✤23
carnelian Semi-precious stone; a variety of chalcedony. Translucent, with a reddish brown colour, it was highly valued by the Greeks and Romans, especially for rings. ✤25, ◆25 (2)
Carolina Stono slave rebellion (1799) ✤85●
Carolingian Dynasty (751–987). Frankish dynasty, named after Charlemagne (Carolus Magnus). The first Carolingian ruler of France was Pepin, father of Charlemagne, who was crowned in 751. ◆184 (1)
dynasty founded ✤184●
fragmentation of empire ✤185
raided by Vikings ✤58
Treaty of Verdun (843) ✤58●, ✤184●
Carpini, John of Plano (c.1182–1252). Italian Franciscan monk and traveller sent by Pope Innocent IV to meet the emperor of the Mongols. ◆256 (1)
Carranza, Venustiano (1859–1920). Mexican political leader. In 1910 led revolution against the government of Porfirio Diaz, and in 1913 led the overthrow of General Victoriano Huerta. He became president in 1915 following a power struggle. Carranza tried to establish a progressive constitution approved in 1917 but was overthrown in 1920, forced to flee and assassinated. ✤133, ◆133 (3)
Carrhae ⚔ (53 BCE). Stopped the Roman invasion of Parthian Mesopotamia.
✤43, 224●, ◆224 (1)
cars *see* transport
Carter, James Earl (Jimmy) (1924–) 39th President of the US (Democrat 1977–81). During Carter's presidency the Panama Canal Treaty and Camp David Accords were signed. The greatest crisis of his presidency was the seizure of the US embassy in Iran in 1979 following the overthrow of the shah. ✤139●
Carthage North African city founded by Phoenician merchants, possibly in 814 BCE. It began as a convenient harbour on the Phoenicians' route to the valuable tin and silver mines of southern Iberia. Between 550 BCE and c.500 BCE, Carthaginian soldiers conquered most of eastern Sicily, defeated the Phoenicians and Massaliotes on the coast of Corsica, and subdued Sardinia and the Balearic islands. However, conflict with the Roman Empire during the Punic Wars ended with the defeat and destruction of the empire in 146 BCE.
Carthage and Rome: the Punic Wars (264–201 BCE) ✤179, ◆179 (3)
captured by Arabs (698) ✤55●
Carthaginian Empire ✤42, ✤43●, ✤177●, ◆30–1, ◆34–5, ◆39, ◆179 (3)
falls to Vandals (439) ✤50●, ✤53●
N African state ◆161 (2)
peoples of Italy (500 BCE) ✤178, ◆178 (2)
Phoenician city ✤31●, ✤38, ✤177
Roman colony (46 BCE) ✤43●
Cartier, Jaques (1491–1557). French explorer and navigator. Sent to America by Francis I in 1534 in search of gold, he explored the Gulf of St. Lawrence, returning in 1535 to reach the site of the future city of Montreal, and again in 1541. His explorations were to prove important in the establishment of French claims on N America. ✤80, ✤126, ◆118 (1)
cartography
modern ◆173, ✤173●, ❑173
See also exploration and mapping; names of explorers and travellers
Casablanca Conference (12–14 Jan 1943). Allied summit conference of WW II between US President Roosevelt and UK Premier Churchill which agreed basis for Allied landings in Europe, the anti-U-Boat offensive, the Combined Bombing Offensive and supply of Soviet Union.
104●
Casimir III (*var.* Casimir the Great) (1309–70) Ruler of Poland (1333–70). Casimir restored Polish power in the region, strengthened administrative institutions, and founded a university at Cracow. In 1386, his daughter married the Lithuanian ruler Jagiello, uniting the two crowns. ✤189●, ◆189 (4)
Casiquiare River Mapped by Humboldt ✤143, ◆143 (3)
Caspian Sea Oil fields discovered (1990s) ✤234
Cassander Kingdom (301 BCE) ✤224, ◆224 (1)
Cassini, César François (1714–84). French astronomer and cartographer. Succeeded his father Jacques Cassini as director of the Paris observatory and began a detailed topographical map of France using the triangulation method. ❑173
Cassini, Jacques Dominique, Comte de (1748–1845). French astronomer and cartographer. Son of C.F. Cassini and his successor as director of the Paris observatory. Completed the topographical map of France begun by his father. ❑173
Cassino (*var.* Monte Cassino) ⚔ of WW II (Jan–May 1943). Site of major German resistance to Allied advance in central Italy. ◆211 (4)
caste system Form of social hierarchy unique to Hinduism, which is based on ideas of spiritual purity, and influences all social and physical contact. In this system, people are 'ordered' according to their religious purity, lineage and occupational group, the Brahmin or priest caste being the highest. Contact between castes is thought to be polluting and is avoided. ✤242
Castile, Council of Spanish bureaucratic body established in the late 15th century, for the execution of royal policy. The Catholic monarchs set up a Council of Finance in 1480, the Council of the Hermandad in 1476, the Council of the Inquisition 1483, and the Council of the Orders of Knighthood and they reorganized the Council of Aragon. Charles I and Philip II were later to continue this work adding further councils, notably those of the Indies (1524) and of Italy (1558). ✤81
Castro, Fidel (1926–). Leader of a guerrilla campaign (1954–58) waged against the repressive government of Fulgencio Batista in Cuba. In 1958 Castro's army captured Havana and Castro became prime minister the following year. Under Castro's rule the Communist Party of Cuba became the sole legal party and a new constitution was introduced (1976). Castro has continued to reject any moves towards economic liberalization, leading to increasing international isolation. ✤106●, ✤108
Catalan Atlas (c.1375) ❑70, ❑71, ❑68
Çatal Hüyük
founded (7000 BCE) ✤19●, ✤20●
BCE wall painting ❑18
bull worshipping ✤37
copper smelting (6500 BCE) ✤20●
earliest textile (6500 BCE) ✤20
female deities ✤21
plagued by malaria ✤20
terracotta figurines ❑19
Catalaunian Fields ⚔ (451). Attila the Hun defeated by Roman and Goth forces. ◆52 (1)
Cathars *see* Albigensians
Cathay Medieval European name for China.
Catherine II (*aka* Catherine the Great) (1729–96) Tsarina of Russia (1762–96). Born a German princess, she was an intelligent and enlightened monarch, but her attempts at reform achieved little for the Russian people. Pursuing an active foreign policy, her reign was marked by territorial expansion south to the Black Sea, and territorial gains in the partition of Poland. ❑198
Catholicism (*var.* Roman Catholicism)
95 Theses (Luther) ✤78●, ✤194●
12th-century renaissance ✤187, ◆187 (3)
Council of Trent ✤78●, ✤194, ✤194●
exploration of S America ✤143●
Great Schism (1378–1417) ✤70●, ✤75●
Protestant Reformation ✤78, ✤82, ✤194, ✤194●
religious map of Europe (1590) ◆194 (2)
St Benedict regulates monastries (529) ✤49●
See also Jesuits, Papacy, individual popes
Catholic Reformation *see* Counter-Reformation
Catholic Revival *see* Counter-Reformation
Caucasus Ottoman and Safavid clashes ✤79, ◆231 (4)
Cavour, Camillo Benso, Count (1810–61) Piedmontese statesman who masterminded the unification of all of northern Italy (the *Risorgimento*) under Victor Emmanuel II in 1859, and secretly encouraged the 1860 expedition of Garibaldi to Sicily and Naples which brought the south into a united Italy. ✤203, ◆203 (3)
Celts Identified by their common language and cultural features, the Celts probably originated in France and S Germany in the Bronze Age, and identifiably Celtic artefacts first appear in the upper Danube in the 13th century BCE. They

expanded around 800 BCE, sacked Rome in 390 BCE and Delphi a century later, eventually covering Asia Minor, Gaul (France), Italy, Galicia, Spain, and Britain. The Celts were gifted craftsmen and warriors, but their lack of political stability led to their demise in the 1st century BCE when the Romans and Germanic tribes marginalized them. Celtic dialects survive in several parts of Europe; including Wales, Brittany, and Ireland.
Anglo-Saxon Britain (600–800) ✣183, ✣183●
invade British Isles ✣38●
Iron Age (800 BCE) ✣31●
lunisolar calendar ❑33
sack Rome ✣38●
tribal societies ✣34
censorship Carlsbad Decrees (6–31 Aug 1819) ✣90●
CENTO Pact *see* Central Treaty Organization
Central Africa
inter-ethnic warfare ✣111
Rwandan crisis ✣169, ◆169 (5)
Central America
Communist subversion ✣139
cotton growing (BCE) ✣22●
cultures
Kaminaljuyú, (c.500 BCE) ✣121
Maya ✣46●, ✣50, ✣54, ❑58, ◆36 (1), ◆121 (2)
Olmec ✣30●, ✣34, 30, ◆36 (1), ◆121 (2) (3)
Toltec Empire ✣58, ✣62, ◆58–9
Zapotec ✣34, ◆121 (2)
early civilizations ✣120●, ✣121●, ✣122
moves towards democracy (1970s) ✣110
plant domestication (BCE) ✣18
revolt against rural elites ✣98
Spanish colonization (16th century) ✣78, ✣82, ✣118, ◆81 (3)
United Provinces 1823–38 ◆90–1
US intervention ✣139
See also individual countries
Central Asia
classical world trade ◆44–5●
Islam and nationalism ✣275, ◆275 (5)
Islamic states (16th century) ✣267
steppe kingdoms ✣261, ✣261●, ◆261 (6)
Central Intelligence Agency (CIA). Established in 1947 in the US to gather intelligence information abroad and report to the President and National Security Council. ✣113
Central Powers Term used for the members of the Triple Alliance in WW I: Germany and Austria-Hungary, together with their allies Turkey and Bulgaria. ✣206–7, ◆206–7
Central Treaty Organization (CENTO Pact) (1955). Defence alliance originally known as Baghdad Pact, between Iran, Iraq, Pakistan, Turkey and the United Kingdom. ◆108–9 (1)
ceramics
Chinese (650 BCE) ✣35●
hunter attacked by lion ❑51
moulds used for casting bronze (BCE) ✣27●
Tang Ferghana horse ❑55
Ceuta Captured by Portuguese (1415) ✣75●
Ceylon
British conquest (1796) ✣87●
Buddhism dominant faith ✣51
Chola conquests ✣59
economy (1857) ✣249, ◆249 (4)
Portuguese expelled by Dutch (1663) ✣83●
Chacabuco ⚔ of wars of S American independence (Feb 1817). Spanish forces defeated by San Martin. ◆150 (1)
Chaco Canyon
cliff dwellings (c.1100) ✣62●
peak importance (1200) ✣123●
Chaco War (1932–35). Conflict between Bolivia and Paraguay over the Chaco Boreal, a wilderness region that forms part of the Gran Chaco. A peace treaty was arranged by the Chaco Peace Conference and was signed in Buenos Aires on 21 Jul, 1938. Paraguay gained clear title to most of the disputed region, but Bolivia was given a corridor to the Paraguay River. ✣152●, ◆152 (2), ❑152
Chad, Lake Reached by Denham and Clapperton (1823) ✣157●
Chaeronea ⚔ of Alexander's campaigns in Europe (338 BCE). Decisive confrontation which left the Macedonians in effective control of all Greece. ✣40●
Chagatai (*var.* Jagatai) (d.1241) Mongol ruler, the second son of Genghis Khan. On the death of Genghis in 1227, Chagatai was granted a large vassal khanate in Central Asia, centred on Transoxiana. Despite its eclipse by Timur at the end of the 14th century, the Chagatai Khanate survived into the 16th century. ✣79
Chaka Zulu *see* Shaka Zulu
Chalcas Aztec civilization ✣125
Chaldean tribe ✣31
Chaldean dynasty (626–539 BCE). Originating in the area at the head of the Persian Gulf, the Chaldeans established a Babylonian dynasty in 626 BCE. After their overthrow in 539 BCE the Babylonian and Chaldean dynasties became synonymous.✣222, ◆222 (2)
Chaldiran *see* Çaldiran
Chaldiron *see* Çaldiran
Chalukya Dynasty (550–750 BCE). Deccan-based dynasty, founded in about 550 CE. The Chalukyas were eventually superseded by the Rashtrakutas in 750. The Rashtrakutas were overthrown in 973 CE by Taila II, a scion of the Chalukyas dynasty, who founded a second dynasty known as the Chalukyas of Kalyani, which went into decline during the 11th century. ✣59, ✣244
chamber tombs (*var.* dolmens). Megalithic monuments constructed of upright stones (orthostats) and capstones, beneath an earth mound. Often used for collective burials they comprise a series of chambers which can contain collections of different skeletal parts. Evidence suggests they were used over successive generations, during the Neolithic period in Europe, from c.5000 BCE. ✣23●
Champa South Vietnamese Hindu-Buddhist kingdom with its capital at Vijaya (modern Binh Dinh). The capital was annexed by the expanding north Vietnamese kingdom of Dai-Viet in 1471. ✣67●, ✣75●, ✣245●, ❑245, ◆245 (5) (6)
Champagne fairs ✣190●
Champlain, Lake French abandon forts (1757) ✣127●, ◆127 (2)
Champlain, Samuel de (1567–1635). French explorer of N America. Founded the colony of New France, later to become Canada. Explored the St. Lawrence River, establishing a colony at Port Royal in 1604, founding Quebec in 1608, and discovering Lake Champlain in 1609. ❑82, ✣118, ✣126●, ◆118–19 (1) (2)
Chan Chan Chimú capital (11th century) ✣62, ◆146 (1)
Chancellor, Richard (d.1556). British navigator and pioneer of Anglo-Russian trade. Appointed pilot-general in 1553 to Sir Hugh Willoughby's expedition seeking a Northeast passage to China. Separated from them by bad weather, he continued into the White Sea and went overland to Moscow. The Muscovy Company was founded in London to carry out the trade. ◆257 (2), ◆286 (1)
Chancellorsville ⚔ of American Civil War (1–4 May 1863). Confederate victory. ◆131 (6)
Chandragupta II (380–415) Gupta dynasty king (r.c.375–415). Famous for the long campaign he waged against the invading Shakas (Scythians), from 388 to 409. He extended the Gupta domains, both by military conquest and marriage alliance. ✣244
Chandragupta Maurya (*var.* Candra Gupta) Founder of the Mauryan dynasty (r.c.321–297 BCE) and the first emperor to unify most of India under one administration. Having seized the Magadhan throne in 327 BCE, Chandragupta Maurya annexed all the lands east of the Indus, occupied much of north-central India and captured much of Afghanistan from Seleucus Nicator, the successor of Alexander the Great. ✣36●, ✣39, ✣240
Chang'an
captured by An Lushan (756) ✣59●
nomad sacking (316) ❑51
plan of city ❑262
Chang Ch'ien *see* Zhang Qian
Chang Zhun (Ch'iu Ch'ang-ch'un) (1148–1227). Chinese Taoist sage summoned to attend the court of Genghis Khan and sent on a mission from Beijing, via the Altai Mountains, Samarkand and the Tien Shan to just south of Kabul. ✣256, ◆256 (1)
Chao Ju-kua *see* Zhao Rugua
Chaplin, Charlie (Sir Charles Spencer Chaplin) (1889–1977). English film actor and director, who won international fame in American-made silent comedy films.
first full-length film (1921) ✣135●
Charlemagne (*var. Lat.* Carolus Magnus) (c.742–814). King of the Franks and Holy Roman Emperor. Charlemagne's kingdom comprised France, much of Germany, and northern Italy, and became the first medieval Holy Roman Empire. The pope crowned him emperor in 800.
empire ✣184●, ◆184 (2)
bronze statue ❑184
Frankish king ✣58●
throne ❑184
Charles I (1600–49) King of England, Scotland and Ireland (r.1625–49). His marriage to the Catholic Henrietta Maria aroused public hostility. He dissolved three parliaments in the first four years of his reign, and then ruled without one for 11 years until rebellion in Scotland forced him to recall it. Conflict with the Long Parliaments led to the Civil War (1642–46). He was defeated at ⚔ Naseby in 1645 by Parliamentarian forces. He escaped briefly, but was recaptured, tried for treason and beheaded. ✣82●, ✣196
Charles IV (1316–78) Holy Roman Emperor (r.1347–78) and King of Bohemia (as Charles I). The greatest of the Luxembourg rulers of Bohemia. He briefly made Prague centre of the Empire. ✣189, ❑189
Charles Martel (c.688–741). Frankish leader, Mayor of the Palace to the late Merovingian kings (r.719–741). He was the effective ruler of the Frankish kingdoms and defeated Muslim invaders at Poitiers in 732. ✣54●, ✣184
Charles the Bold (1433–77) Last reigning duke of Burgundy (r.1467–77). Continually at war with Louis XI, he almost succeeded in creating a kingdom independent of France. His death while fighting the Swiss ended Burgundy's resistance to France. ✣193●, ◆193 (4)
Charles V (1500–58) Holy Roman Emperor. Charles inherited the Netherlands from his father, Spain (which he ruled as Charles I) from his mother, and the German Habsburg territories from his grandfather, all before he was 20. Elected Emperor in 1520, to protect his lands he had to fight numerous wars against France and the Ottoman Turks, while his reign also saw Germany torn apart by the wars of the Reformation. He abdicated in 1555, leaving his Spanish posessions and the Netherlands to his son Philip II and his Austrian and German lands to his brother Ferdinand. ✣78●, ✣142●, ✣192, ✣192●, ✣194
Charles VII (1403–61) King of France (r.1422–61). Not actually crowned until 1429 when Joan of Arc raised the siege of Orléans. By 1453 he had expelled the English from all France except Calais, thus ending the Hundred Years' War. ◆192 (2), ◆194 (1)
Charles VIII (1470–1498). King of France (r.1483–1498), remembered for beginning the French expeditions into Italy that lasted until the middle of the 16th century. ✣75●
Charles X (1622–60) King of Sweden (r.1654–60). Invaded Poland in 1655. In a successful war with Denmark (1657–58), Sweden reached the limit of her territorial expansion. ✣177●
Charleston ⚔ of American Revolutionary War (28 Jun 1776). British victory. ◆127 (3)
Chartres Construction of cathedral begins (1154) ❑62
Chateau-Thierry ⚔ of Napoleon's defence of France (12 Feb 1814). ◆200 (1)
Chattanooga ⚔ of American Civil War (23–25 Nov 1863). Union victory. ◆131 (7)
Chavín culture (1000–200 BCE). From its birth around 1000 BCE this culture united around 800 sq km of Peruvian coast from its base at Chavín de Huántar in the eastern Andes. This unity was religious rather than political, and was at its height around 400–200 BCE. Noted for their stone carvings of deities with jaguar fangs, the Chavín also made improvement in maize cultivation, metallurgy and weaving.
decorative motif (900 BCE) ❑30
influential Peruvian culture ✣145, ◆145 (3)
state religion (BCE) ✣38, ◆36 (1)
water vessel ❑144
Chavín de Huántar (c.850–200 BCE). The earliest urban civilization in the Andes, which flourished in the central highlands. The site of Chavín de Huántar, was dominated by a central temple complex adorned by a 4.5-m-high carving of a deity, the Oculate Being, with projecting fangs and a snarling mouth. Elements of this iconography spread throughout the Andean region and permeated the art and religion of later Andean cultures. ✣30, ✣145, ◆145 (3)
chemical warfare
used against Kurds ✣235
WW I gas masks ❑98
Cheng Ho *see* Zheng He.
Ch'eng Tsu *see* Chengzu
Chengzu (*aka* Yonglo) (1360–1424) (r.1402–24). Son of Zhu Yuanzhang, the founder of the Ming dynasty in China. Ruled China in the early 15th century. ✣266, ❑266
Cherokee Native people of N America. Formerly ranged across much of the southern US. Removed to reservations in Oklahoma and N Carolina in the late 19th century. ◆125 (4), ◆126 (1)
Chesapeake Bay
painted map (16th century) ❑118
plate from *Atlas Contractus* ❑119
Chester ⚔ (616). Britons defeated by Northumbrians. ◆183 (3)
Chiang Kai-shek *see* Jiang Jieshi.
Chibcha *see* Muisca
Chicago
in the 1860s ❑130
Democrat rally riots (1968) ✣137●
growth of the suburbs (1850–1950) ✣137, ◆137 (4)
race riots (1940s) ✣135●
Chichén Itzá Toltec altar ❑58
Chichimec People of NW Mexico (c.12th century CE). They created small city states and were in constant conflict with each other. In the 1170s, as their homeland became increasingly desiccated and famine-struck, they sacked the Toltec city of Tula. ✣62●
Chickamauga ⚔ of American Civil War (19–20 Sep 1863). Confederate victory. ◆131 (7)
Children's Crusade ✣186, ◆186 (1)
Chile 148–153
colonization, Rapa Nui (Easter Island) ✣284●
environmental survival strategies (BCE) 16
foreign affairs, War of Pacific (1879–83) ✣94●, ✣151, ◆151 (4)
home affairs
coup against Marxists (1973) ✣106●, ✣138●
democracy restored (1989) ✣110●
liberated (1817) ✣90●, ✣150, ◆150 (1)
Chimú culture (c.700–1476). Civilization of N Peru. Flourished for over 700 years until its defeat by the Incas in 1476. The Chimú empire was built around military conquest, efficient communications, and social control. Chimú craftsmen were noted for their metalwork, pottery and textiles.
11th century ✣62
conquered by Incas (1470) ✣74●
empire ✣146, ◆146 (1)
expansion (1200) ✣66●
funerary mask ❑66
gold dove ❑146
gold knife ❑146
Ch'i Dynasty *see* Qi Dynasty
Ch'in Dynasty *see* Qin Dynasty
Chin Dynasty *see* Jin Dynasty
China
conflicts, revolution (1911) ✣271, ✣271●, ◆271 (5)
conflicts
Boxer Rebellion (1900) ✣95, ❑96
Civil War (1920–26) ✣103●, ✣271, ◆271 (6)
Communist revolution (1927–49) ✣274, ✣274●, ◆274 (1)
Cultural Revolution (1966–70) ✣107●
famine (1877–79) ✣95●
fragmentation (220–589) ✣261, ◆261 (2) (3) (4) (5)
'Great Leap Forward' ✣107●, ❑274
'Long March' ✣103●, ❑274
peasant uprisings (870s) ✣59●
rebellions against Mongols (1335) ✣71●
cultures
Banshan ✣23●
Longshan ✣23●
dynasties, *see* Han ; Hongshan; Jin; Ming; Qi; Qin; Qing; Shang; Song; Sui; Tang
exploration and mapping
cartographers' map grids ❑256●
geography recorded (c.1000 BCE) ✣256●
travellers in Central Asia ◆256 (1)
Zhou sponsored (c.1000 BCE) ✣256●
foreign affairs
closer links with West ✣111
control of Korea (108 BCE) ✣43●
expansionism from 1949 ✣275, ✣275●, ◆275 (3)
influence on Japan ✣55, ✣256, ✣265
Japanese diplomatic mission (607) ✣256●
Taiwan annexed (1894–95) ✣95
Treaty of Nerchinsk with Russia (1689) ✣83●, ✣257●
war with Japan (1937) ✣103
home affairs
agriculture (BCE) ✣19, ✣21
empire collapses ✣99
empire expanded and unified ◆259 (5)
Hong Kong returned (1997) ✣111●
Mongol conquest begins (1211) ✣67●
Nationalists (Kuomintang/Guomindang) ✣271, ◆271 (7)
Republic declared (1911) ✣99●
reunification by Chiang Kai-Shek (Jiang Jieshi) ✣103●
Sixteen Kingdoms (c.400) ◆261 (3)
Three Kingdoms (c.250) ◆261 (2)
Tiananmen Square massacre (1989) ✣111
Toba Wei (c.440–500) ◆261 (4)
innovations
boxed compass (13th century) ❑67
bronze casting ✣22, ✣31●, ❑27
bronze coins ❑34, ❑259
crossbow ✣39
gunpowder weapons ✣71
introduced by 16th-century Jesuit missionary ✣80
lodestone compass (c.250) ✣256●
metal stirrups ❑51
movable type printing invented (c.1045) ✣63●
neolithic ◆258 (2)
paper money ✣59●, ✣263
planned villages (c.4000 BCE) ✣23●
pottery wheel (c.3000) ✣22
printing ❑59
silk (BCE) ✣23, ✣34
timber and brushwood dyke ❑83
wind power ✣63
writing paper ❑46
population
(1790) ✣87
first census (2 CE) ✣256●
Song period ◆263 (6)
religion
Buddhist cave temple ❑51
state (BCE) ✣36 (1)
Second World War
human cost of global war ✣105
mobilization and casualty figures ✣105
trade and industry
economic development (1950) ✣274, ◆274 (2)
with Arab world (c.800–907 CE) ✣61
exports to Russia and the West (18th century) ✣87
Han dynasty and the wider world ◆44–5
industrial expansion (late 1970s) ✣111
iron technology ✣35●, ✣43●
silk trade (BCE) ✣34
toy factory near Guangzhou ❑111
trade with Europe (BCE) ✣39
See also Silk Road
chinampas Artificial islands, used by peoples of Central America (e.g. the Aztecs) for raising crops. ✣124, ◆124 (2)
Chinese script *see* calligraphy
Ch'in dynasty *see* Qin dynasty
Ching dynasty *see* Qing dynasty
Ching Empire *see* Qing dynasty
Ching-Ghis Khan *see* Genghis Khan
Chingis Khan *see* Genghis Khan
Chiquito *Reducción* founded (1690) ✣143●
Choga Mami Irrigation system (5500 BCE) ✣20●
Chola dynasty (*var.* Cola dynasty) (c.860–1279). The Chola kingdom, mentioned in the inscriptions of Ashoka, came into prominence in southern India in c.860 CE. Under Rajaraja the Great, who came to the throne in 985, Chola control extended to Ceylon and parts of the Malay Peninsula. Chola power gradually declined after the 11th century.
conquers Ceylon (1018) ✣63●
dominates southeastern India ✣63
in India ✣59●, ✣63, ✣244, ✣224●, ◆244 (2)
sends embassy to China ✣63●
Shiva bronze ❑59
Chou dynasty *see* Zhou dynasty
Chou En-lai *see* Zhou Enlai
Christ, Jesus *see* Jesus of Nazareth
Christianity One of the world's great religions, an offshoot of Judaism that emerged in Palestine in the 1st century CE, based on the life and teachings of Jesus of Nazareth. The early Christian faith diverged into many sects, but by the 8th century there were two main branches: the Eastern Orthodox and the Roman Catholic Churches. In 16th-century Europe, a reaction to the Roman Church, known as the Reformation, led to the foundation of many breakaway Protestant churches which refused to recognize the authority of the pope in Rome.
origins ✣37, ✣46, ✣225
spread (600 CE) ◆48 (1), ✣226, ✣226●, ◆226 (1)
early growth (to 500 CE) ✣48●
Augustine converts Britain (597) ✣54●
in Africa ✣47●, ✣50, ✣67●, ◆161 (5)
Byzantine Empire ◆54–5
11th–12th-century Europe ✣62●
Roman Empire state religion ✣50●, ✣182
12th-century renaissance in Europe ◆187 (3)
the Crusades (1096–1270) ✣64–5, ◆64–5 (1) (2) (3), ◆186 (1)
in Anglo-Saxon England ✣183●
crucifixion of Christ (c.32 CE) ✣48●
depictions
amphora with two versions of the cross ❑48
carved sarcophagus ❑50, ❑225
Coptic weaving ❑58
Corpus Christi procession ❑148
and Islam (c.1090) ◆65 (1)
missionaries
in Africa (c.1880) ◆167 (4)
Chinese missions attacked (1850) ✣95●
journeys of St Paul ◆48 (1)
in the South Seas ✣284, ❑284
to pagans of Europe ✣186
persecutions, Diocletian (304 CE) ✣48●
Protestant Reformation ✣78, ✣82, ✣194, ✣194●
religious map of Europe (1590) ◆194 (2)
Roman-Orthodox schism (1054) ✣62●
See also Catholicism
Chu-ssu-pen *see* Zhu Siben
Chu Yuan-chang *see* Zhu Yuanzhang
Chucuito culture South American people of the Andes.
13th century ✣66
Churchill, Sir Winston Leonard Spencer (1874–1965) British statesman. Service in Omdurman campaign (1897–98) and as a journalist during the Boer War (1899–1900) preceded his entry to Parliament (1900). Became Home Secretary (1910) and First Lord of the Admiralty (1911–15), bearing responsibility for the Dardanelles campaign, thereafter serving in the trenches and entering political 'wilderness'. Formed coalition government (1940) and oversaw Britain's policy and strategy during WW II. Lost election upon Allied victory (1945), but returned as Prime Minister (1951–55).
Casablanca conference (1943) ✣104●
Tehran conference ✣105●
Yalta 'Big Three' conference (1945) ❑105
CIA *see* Central Intelligence Agency
cinema Major Hollwood studios (1919) ✣135, ◆135 (4)
Cipangu *see* Japan
CIS *see* Commonwealth of Independent States
Cistercians Roman Catholic monastic order that was founded in 1098 and named after the original establishment at Cîteaux, France. The order's founding fathers, led by St. Robert of Molesmes, were a group of Benedictine monks who wished to a live a solitary life under the strictest interpretation of the Rule of St. Benedict. ✣187, ✣187●, ◆187 (3)
cities
BCE growth ✣28–9, ◆28–9 (2) (3) (4) (5)
Central American civilization ✣122, ❑122
development ✣24, ✣28●
first Chinese ✣28, ✣258●
first on Deccan plateau (c.200) ✣47●
growth in Europe (18th century) ✣198, ◆198 (1)
medieval ✣190–1
Mongol warfare ✣69
Toltec ✣58, ✣122
and trade (BCE) ✣24●
urbanism ✣28, ◆28–9 (1)
city-state A single urban centre and its hinterland. Although politically autonomous, they frequently shared cultural traits – such as language and religion – with neighbouring city-states.
African (800–1500) ✣163, ✣163●
Greek ✣31, ✣34, ✣176, ✣179
Italian ✣75
Maya ✣50, ✣58●, ✣122, ◆122 (2)
Mesopotamia ✣23–4, ✣27
Mexican ✣66, ✣122●, ◆122 (1)
Swahili ✣66, ✣67●, ✣75
Civil Rights Movement US mass movement to combat segregation and discriminatory practices against Black people. Arose in the US in the 1950s and 1960s. The movement began with the Montgomery bus boycott of 1956, following the arrest of a black woman, Rosa Parks, for refusing to move to the 'Negro' section of the bus. The movement gained momentum with the involvement of Martin Luther King who advocated the principle of non-violent protest, culminating in the 1963 March on Washington by more than a million people. The Civil Rights Act of 1964 and the Voting Rights Act of 1965 were legal responses to the pressure generated by the movement. ✣137, ✣137●, ◆137 (6)
Cixi, Dowager Empress (*var.* Tz'u-Hsi) (1835–1908) Manchu empress (r.1861–1908). Became regent in China and opposed all modernization. Helped foment the Boxer Rebellion in 1900 and organized the murder of her

Key to index: ✣ text ● timeline ❑ picture ◆ map *var.* variant name *aka* also known as *f/n* full name *prev.* previously known as r. ruled ⚔ battle WW I First World War WW II Second World War

successor, the emperor Guangxu, in 1908. ❑271
Clapperton, Hugh (1788–1827). The first European explorer in W Africa to return with a first-hand account of the region around present-day N Nigeria. He journeyed with explorers Dixon Denham and Walter Oudney (1821–25). ◆157 (4)
Clark, William (1770–1838). US explorer. With Meriwether Lewis he was sent by President Thomas Jefferson to explore the lands acquired in the Louisiana Purchase of 1803, and to find a land route to the Pacific Ocean. ◆119 (3)
Classical Age Greece (5th–3rd centuries BCE). An era of city-states characterized by stone or marble monumental architecture – the zenith of architecture, art and sculpture, which set the standards of beauty and proportion for figurative art for the next 2500 years. This era also saw the flowering of literature, philosophy and science.
✣34, ✣37, ✣38, ◆44–5
Claudius Ptolemaeus *see* Ptolemy
Clavus 15th-century Danish mapmaker. Added detail of northern Europe to the Ptolemaic map of the world (1425). ✣173
Cleopatra VII (*var.* Thea Philopator) (69–30 BCE) Queen of Egypt (r.51–30 BCE). The last of the Ptolemaic dynasty which ruled Egypt after Alexander the Great's death. Cleopatra was a Macedonian, and ruled alongside her brothers, Ptolemy XIII, Ptolemy XIV, and subsequently, her son Ptolemy XV Caesar, and alone amongst her dynasty learned to speak Egyptian. She used her famed charm and beauty to delay Egypt's annexation by Rome, bearing children by two of its statesmen, Julius Caesar and Mark Antony. The latter restored much of the old Ptolemaic empire to her, and awarded areas of Rome's eastern provinces to their children, a policy which led to their defeat by Octavian at Actium in 31 BCE. Soon after, both she and Antony committed suicide.
✣42–43●
Clermont Urban II initiates First Crusade (1095) ✣63, ✣64
Clinton, William Jefferson (Bill) (1946–) 42nd President of the US. (Democrat, 1992–). The youngest-ever governor of Arkansas, in 1992 he defeated George Bush to become the first Democrat president since Jimmy Carter. Despite a number of scandals, remained enormously popular at home due to the buoyant US economy, and was re-elected in 1996. Became first 20th-century president to undergo an impeachment trial in 1999. ✣139●
Clive, Sir Robert (1725–74). Originally a clerk in the British East India Company, Clive commanded British troops at the defence of Arcot (1751), and defeated a combined French and Mughal force at the battle of Plassey (1757), which laid the foundations of the British empire in India. He became the Governor of the Company's settlements in Bengal (1757–60, 1765–67), and instituted major reforms of the Company's administration.
✣87●, ✣248
Clovis I (c.465–511). King of the Franks, responsible for creating the kingdom of France from the old Roman province of Gaul. He defeated the Visigoths in Aquitaine.
✣53, ✣54, ✣183●, ◆183 (5)
Clovis point Heavy projectile point, usually in the shape of a leaf, dating from the 10th millennium BCE, specifically in eastern New Mexico. They are often found close to finds of mammoth bones.
❑14●
cobalt *see* metallurgy
cocaine White crystalline alkaloid obtained from the leaves of the coca plant, cultivated in Africa, northern S America, SE Asia, and Taiwan. An increasingly popular recreational drug.
◆113 (4), ◆153, ◆153 (5), ❑153
Codomannus *see* Darius III
coins
Athenian tetradrachma ❑33
Bactrian King Demetrios ❑41
BCE Chinese ❑34, ❑259
Berber (c.118 BCE) ❑161
Carthage African elephant ❑179
dinar showing Abd al-Malik ❑226
Diocletian and Maximian ❑181
evolution ✣33
first issued by Lydia (BCE)
✣33, ✣35
gold ducats ✣191●
grosso introduced (c.1200)
✣190●
honouring Jan Hus ❑193
N African ❑162
Seleucus I ❑224
silver pfennig ❑188
Theban ❑33
Venetian ❑191
Viking (9th century) ❑60
Coke, Thomas William (1752–1842) (created Earl of Leicester in 1837). English agriculturalist who developed new and more robust strains of cattle, pigs and sheep, on his experimental farm. He also helped to initiate the switch from rye to wheat-growing in NW Norfolk. ❑198
Cola dynasty *see* Chola dynasty
Cold Harbor ⚔ of American Civil War (3 Jun 1864). Inconclusive result.
◆131 (7)
Cold War (c.1947–1991). Period of ideological, political, economic and military confrontation between Communist bloc, dominated by Soviet Union and China, and Western free market economy nations bound to US by NATO. Effectively ended by the dissolution of the Soviet Union in 1991.
politics of ✣106–7, ✣108–9
alliances ◆108–9 (1)
Angolan Civil War ◆109 (5)
arms race ✣109
Cuban Missile Crisis (1961–62)
✣106, ◆109 (2)
in Europe ◆108 (2)
ideological indoctrination
❑109
Korean War (1950–53)
✣106, ✣107●, ◆109 (4)
NATO and the Warsaw Pact ✣108
strategic balance ✣109
Vietnam War (1954–75)
✣106, ✣107●
Colônia do Sacramento
founded (1680s) ✣149●
Portuguese renounce claim (1750) ✣149●
Columbus, Christopher (*var. It.* Cristoforo Colombo) (c.1451–1506) Genoese explorer. In 1492, having been financed by Ferdinand and Isabella of Spain, Columbus crossed the Atlantic in search of China and Japan, but made a landfall, probably in the Bahamas, sailed on to Cuba, and then founded a colony on Hispaniola. He made three more voyages which greatly increased European knowledge of the Caribbean, but his governorship of the expanding colonies was never successful and once, in 1500, he was arrested and sent back to Spain in chains.
anchors near Trinidad (1498)
✣74●
expands Spanish empire (1493)
✣81●
N American expeditions (1492–93) (1502–04)
✣125●, ◆80 (1), ◆118 (1)
reaches Cuba and Hispaniola (1492) ◆74●, ✣76, ✣80●
ships used in exploration ✣78
sights S America ✣142●
Combined Bombing Offensive Joint strategic bombing campaign by US and RAF against Nazi-occupied Europe during WW II; inaugurated in 1942, reached a climax with the destruction of Dresden 13–15 Feb 1945. ✣211, ◆211 (4)
COMECON *see* Council for Economic Assistance
Comintern (*aka* Communist International). International socialist organization established 1919, promulgated by the leadership of Bolshevik Russia, envisioning export of Soviet Communism worldwide. Split the world socialist movement and led to uprisings in Europe and elsewhere. Dissolved in 1943.
✣271●
Committee of Correspondence Set up by legislatures in Britain's 13 American colonies to provide leadership to the Colonial cause and aid cooperation. The first group was organized by Samuel Adams at Boston in Nov 1772.
✣127●
Commodus, Caesar Marcus Aurelius (161–92 CE) Commodus' tenure as Roman emperor between 180–92 CE ended 84 years of stability and prosperity in Rome. As he lapsed into insanity, he renamed Rome 'Colonia Commodiana', and believed himself to be the god Hercules. When he took to appearing in gladiatorial garb his advisors in desperation had him strangled by a champion wrestler.
✣46●
Common Market *see* European Union.
Commonwealth of Independent States (CIS) (*var. Rus.* Sodruzhestvo Nezavisimykh Gosudarstv). Free association of sovereign states formed in 1991, and comprising Russia and 11 other republics that were formerly part of the Soviet Union. ✣215
See also Russian Federation
communications
improvements (1870–1910)
◆92 (1)
and organized crime ✣113, ◆113 (4)
Communism Political and social ideology developed by Karl Marx (1818–83) and Friedrich Engels (1820–95) whereby all property and goods are owned communally and distributed according to need. Implemented under socialist revolutionary conditions with escalating degrees of failure by Lenin and Stalin in Russia, and by Mao Zedong in China.
Bolshevik ✣98, ✣271●, ❑271
China under Communist rule
✣274●
Chinese ✣103, ✣107, ✣271, ✣271●, ◆271 (7)
Czechoslovakian ✣102●
Eisenhower Doctrine (1958)
✣138●
European collapse (1989–90)
✣109●, ✣110●
Hungarian ✣102●, ✣213
Khmer Rouge ❑253
in Middle East ✣138●
movements against (1950–70)
✣213, ◆213 (4)
Red Flag over Asia ✣251●, ✣271, ✣271●, ◆271 (8)
revolution in China (1927–49)
✣274, ◆274 (1)
Soviet
✣106, ✣213, ✣215●, ◆213 (4)
US fear the 'Red Scare' ✣135, ✣138–9
Communist Bloc (*var.* Eastern Bloc, the East). General geo-political term for the group of socialist (Communist states in military and economic alliance following WW II, led by USSR and China. Soviet hegemony was formalized by COMECON (1949) and the Warsaw Pact (1955) binding the Soviet-dominated nations of central and eastern Europe into a military grouping, although the Communist bloc was weakened by the Sino-Soviet dispute (1960). The Soviet alliance collapsed in 1989–90, and was partly replaced by the Commonwealth of Independent States (CIS, 1991).
✣213, ✣214
compass *see* navigation
computer technology
❑111
microprocessor chip ❑107
World Wide Web ❑113
Comstoke Lode Nevada, gold find (1849–50) ✣93●
Concepción ⚔ of wars of S American independence in Chile (May 1817).
◆150 (1)
Concord ⚔ of American Revolutionary War (19 Apr 1775). American victory. ◆127 (3)
Confederacy (Confederate states) The 11 Southern states which seceded from the United States in 1860–61 to form a separate government, so leading to Civil War. The states were Alabama, Arkansas, Florida, Georgia, Louisiana, Mississippi, N Carolina, South Carolina, Tennessee, Texas and Virginia. These were reincorporated into the Union in 1865 following the Confederate surrender.
✣130–131, ◆130–131
Confucius (*var.* K'ung-fu-tzu, Kongzi) 551–479 BCE). Chinese accountant, administrator, and philosopher whose teachings and writings (*Analects*) espoused the inherent common good in correct conduct, morality, ethics, education and respect, which codified the Chinese social and political system, acquiring the status of a religion.
BCE Chinese philosopher ✣35, ✣38, ✣39●, ✣259, ◆37 (4)
principles used in Han China
✣260–1
teachings ❑37
Congo
abandoned by Belgium (1960)
✣168●
Free State, formed (1882) ✣167●
river mouth discovered (1482)
✣156●
See also Zaire
conquistador (conqueror). Leaders in the Spanish conquest of America, especially of Mexico and Peru, in the 16th century. ❑78
See also individual entries on explorers of N and S America.
Conrad III (1093–1152). German king (r.1138–1152) who was the first sovereign of the Hohenstaufen family. ◆64–5 (2)
Constantine I (Constantine the Great) (c.280–337) Roman emperor (r.307–337). Constantine eliminated various rivals and co-emperors to emerge as sole ruler in 324. His reign was remarkable for his conversion to Christianity and the Edict of Milan (313), which granted toleration of Christianity throughout the empire. His creation of a new capital at Constantinople in 330 also had momentous consequences for the Roman Empire.
Christian Roman Emperor (280–337) ✣50●, ✣180, ❑180
assembles Council of Nicaea (325)
✣48●
division of Roman Empire
◆181 (4)
Edict of Milan (313 CE) ✣48●
Constantinople (*var.* Bysantion, Byzantium, *mod.* Istanbul).
besieged by Arabs (674–78)
✣54●, ✣55●, ✣184
Black Death (1347) ◆71●
Byzantine capital ✣54
captured by Latin crusaders (1204) ✣64●, ✣66●, ✣187, ❑187, ◆187 (5)
European tourists (1900) ❑232
regained by Byzantium ✣66●
Roman capital (324) ✣50
Swedish trading monopoly ✣60
taken by Ottomans (1453)
✣195●, ✣230, ❑75
Topkapi palace ❑231
Conti, Niccolò dei (c.1395–1469). Venetian merchant who embarked on journeys through Arabia, Persia, India, Burma and the East Indies. He was forced to convert to Islam on his travels, but on his return to Europe embraced Christianity.
✣239●, ◆239 (1)
Contras Nicaraguan counter-revolutionaries, supported by the US in the 1980s. From bases in Honduras, they mounted guerrilla actions against the ruling left-wing Sandinistas. ✣110●
Cook, Captain James (1728–79). English explorer of the Pacific. Cook's three epic voyages to the Pacific added immeasurably to European knowledge of the region. The ostensible purpose of the first (1768–71) was to observe the transit of Venus across the face of the sun from Tahiti, but Cook also mapped the whole of New Zealand and the uncharted east coast of Australia. The second (1772–75) included the circumnavigation of Antarctica, and the third (1776–79) took him north to the Bering Strait. On the way, he discovered the Hawaiian Islands. Returning there, he was killed in an argument between islanders and his crew.
18th-century navigator and explorer ✣86
explores Pacific (1768)
✣87●, ✣278●
map of New Zealand ❑87
Oceania voyages ◆278 (1)
second voyage ship ❑278
Cook, Frederick Arctic explorer (20th century) ❑287
Coolidge, (John) Calvin (1872–1933) 30th President of the US (Republican,1923–28). Became president on death of Warren Harding. His *laissez faire* policies, including tax cuts and business deregulation were later thought to have been responsible for the stock market crash of 1929. His administration presided over the Dawes Plan, reducing German reparations, and the Kellogg-Briand Pact. ✣134●
Copper Age Name given to the period in European history – the 5th and 4th millennia BCE – before the Bronze Age, when many societies started to work metal first by hammering, then by smelting. The metals used were chiefly copper and gold, the object made were generally ornamental rather than practical. ✣174, ✣174●, ◆174 (2)
copper
African trade (1868)
✣166●, ◆166 (1)
in the Balkans (5000 BCE)
✣20●
finds in 19th century ◆96 (2)
first use
✣18–19, ✣20●, ✣24●, ✣258
smelting at Çatal Hüyük (6500 BCE) ✣20●
trade ✣25
Copts Members of the Coptic Church, an ancient Monophysite branch of Christianity founded in Egypt in the 5th century which has survived to the present day.
altar cloth ❑58
missions (by 350 CE)
✣49●, ◆49 (4)
Coral Sea Naval ⚔ of WW II (May 1942). US forces halted Japanese advance in southwest Pacific.
◆272 (1)
Córdoba, Hernández de 16th-century Spanish explorer of N America (1517–24).
✣125, ◆125 (4)
Cordova, Caliphate of (756–1031). After the Umayyad Caliphate fell to the Abbasids in 749, one branch of the Umayyad dynasty won control of the Muslim territories in the Iberian Peninsula. In 929 Abd al-Rahman proclaimed himself Caliph. The rule of the Umayyads ended in the 10th century, as the Caliphate splintered into many small kingdoms. ◆57 (2), ◆227 (4)
Christian reconquest ✣66●
cord scoring Method of decoration created by imprinting unfired ceramic objects with a length of cord. ❑19
Corinth
Roman rule (146 BCE) ✣42●
ruins of the later Roman city
❑179
Cornwallis, General, Charles Cornwallis, 1st Marquis (1738–1805). English soldier. Despite opposing the taxation of American colonists, he led British forces against the Americans in the American Revolution, winning at Camden (1780) but was forced to surrender after the siege of Yorktown (1781) paving the way for British defeat in the war. He later held senior government and military posts in France, Ireland and India where he twice held the post of Governor-General. ✣127, ◆127 (3)
Coronado, Francisco Vázquez de (1510–54) Spanish explorer of N America. Appointed governor of New Galicia province in Mexico. In 1540 he set out to find the 'seven treasure cities of the north' on the orders of the viceroy. In 1541 he travelled north of the Arkansas River.
◆118 (1), ✣125, ◆125 (4)
Corregidor ⚔ of WW II (May 1942). Took place on island in Manila Bay, marking last defeat of US forces in Philippines by Japan. ◆104 (2)
Corsica Devolution ✣112
Cortenuova ⚔ (1237). Italian communes defeated by Frederick II.
◆189 (1)
Corte-Real, Gaspar and **Miguel** (d.1501 and 1502) Portuguese explorers. Gaspar travelled down the N American coast from Greenland c.1500 but his ship was lost on a subsequent expedition. On a later expedition in 1502, Miguel's ship was also lost. Spanish recognition of the lands they discovered allowed Portuguese exploitation of the rich fisheries in the Newfoundland banks. ◆118 (1)
Cortés, Hernán (*var.* Cortez) (1485–1547). Spanish *conquistador* who overthrew the Aztec empire (1519–21) and won Mexico for the Spanish crown.
colonizing expeditions (1519, 1522, 1532–42) ✣125, ◆125 (4) (5)
conquers Aztec Empire (1519–22)
✣78, ✣81, ✣124, ◆81 (3)
Indian allies ❑125
invasion and conquest of Mexico (1519–21) ◆125 (5)
mosaic serpent pendant ❑124
N American expedition (1519–21)
◆118 (1)
Cortéz, Hernán *see* Cortés, Hernán
Corupedium ⚔ of (281 BCE). Lysimachus defeated by Seleucus.
◆224 (1)
Cosa, Juan de la (d.1509) Spanish cartographer and navigator who accompanied Columbus on his second expedition in 1493. In 1500 he compiled a world map which records Columbus's discoveries.
❑219
Cosa Nostra *see* Mafia
cosmology ✣22, ❑22, ❑124, ❑238
Cossacks Inhabitants of the northern hinterlands of the Black and Caspian seas. They had a tradition of independence and finally received privileges from the Russian government in return for military services. ✣82
Cotopaxi Scaled by Wilhelm Reiss (1872) ✣143●
cotton
beneficiary of Industrial Revolution ✣93
British, Indian and American politics ✣93, ◆93 (5)
in central Andes (3000 BCE)
✣144●
collapse of cotton-growing ✣139, ◆139 (3)
commercial Africa (19th century)
◆166 (1)
market trading in India ❑93
plantation economy ❑90
production in Lancashire ◆93 (4)
Council for Economic Assistance (COMECON). Communist organization, established (1949), under auspices of Soviet Union, to create sphere of economic and trade links within Eastern Bloc countries. *See also* Communist bloc.
✣213●, ◆138 (1)
Counter-Reformation (*var.* Catholic Reformation, Catholic Revival). Efforts directed, in the 16th and early 17th centuries, both against the Protestant Reformation and toward internal renewal of the Catholic Church.
✣78●, ✣194, ◆194 (2)
Courland (*var.* Courland Pocket) ⚔ of WW II (Feb–May 1945). Led to reduction of German troops and military resistance by Soviet forces in Baltic region. ◆211 (4)
Courland Pocket *see* Courland
Covilhã, Pêro da (*var.* Pedro de Covilham, Covilhão) (c.1460–1526). Portuguese explorer. In 1487 he went in search of the mythical 'Prester John', sailing down the Red Sea and exploring the west coast of India and E Africa. Established relations between Portugal and Ethiopia. ◆156 (3), ◆239 (1)
Covilham, Pedro de *see* Covilhã, Pêro da
Cowpens ⚔ of American Revolutionary War (17 Jan 1781). American victory. ◆127 (3)
Crécy ⚔ of Hundred Years' War (1346). English defeat French.
✣70●, ❑192
Cree Native peoples of northwest N America.
✣123●, ◆123 (3), ◆126 (1)
cremation First known (26,000 BP)
✣16●
Creole Name given to descendants of European settlers in Central and S America and the Caribbean. Also language which is a mixture of a European and another, especially African language.
Cresques, Abraham 14th-century Majorcan cartographer to King Peter IV of Aragon, creator of the so-called 'Catalan Atlas'. ✣70
Crete
Linear A script (1650 BCE)
✣27●
Minoan civilization established (2000 BCE) ✣27●, ✣175, ◆175 (4)
Minos bull cult ✣37
occupied by Saracens (827) ✣58●
palace-based societies (c.2000)
✣175
potter's wheel introduced (c.1900) ✣175
crime Global organization of
✣113, ◆113 (4)
Crimea Conquered and annexed by Russia (1783) ✣86●
Crimean War (1853–56). War fought by France, Britain and Turkey against Russia. The origins of the war lay in Russia's claim to be the protector of all Greek Christians in the Turkish Empire and from British and French distrust of Russia's ambitions in the Black Sea area which posed a threat to their overland routes to India. Following a series of battles fought in the Crimean peninsula and a prolonged siege of the Russian fortress at Sebastapol, the Russians withdrew their forces from the peninsula. Peace negotiations at Paris checked Russian influence in southeast Europe. ✣203●, ◆203 (5)
Cristoforo Colombo *see* Christopher Columbus
Cromford Textile town ✣93, ◆93 (5)
cromlechs *see* megaliths
Cromwell, Oliver (1599–1658) English soldier and statesman.
A sincere Puritan, he was an effective leader of the anti-royalist forces in the English Civil War. After the battle of Naseby (1645) he led the demand for the execution of Charles I. After the king's execution, he quelled the Royalists in Scotland and Ireland. In 1653 he dissolved the 'Rump' Parliament and established the Protectorate, which he ruled as Lord Protector (1653–58).
❑196
Crusades Series of campaigns by western European armies to recapture the Holy Land from the Muslims. The success of the First Crusade in 1099 led to the foundation of the Kingdom of Jerusalem and other 'Latin' (i.e. western European, not Greek) states. Subsequent expeditions to defend these territories or reconquer land lost to the Muslims were less successful. The name crusade was given to campaigns in other parts of Europe, notably Spain and the Baltic.
the age of the Crusades
✣64–5, ◆64–5 (2)
major Crusades ✣64
capture of Antioch (1098) ❑63
Constantinople captured (1204)
✣66●
crusading ideal in Europe (1100–1300)
✣186, ✣186●, ◆186 (1)
Islam and Christianity (c.1090)
◆65 (1)
Latin states in the Holy Land
◆65 (3)
Lisbon taken from Moors
✣62●
medieval mapping ◆219 (3)
Saladin recaptures Jerusalem (1187) ✣63●, ✣64●, ✣228●
states in the Levant
✣63, ◆187 (5)
Venice and the Latin Empire
✣187, ✣187●
Ctesiphon
Parthian capital (90 BCE)
✣43●, ✣224
sacked by Romans (c.114) ✣47
Sassanian capital (637)
✣55●, ✣225, ✣225●
Cuba
Columbus lands (1492)
✣74●, ✣80●
Fidel Castro leader (1959) ✣106●
last slave ship (1867) ✣85●
preferential trade ends (1991–92)
✣110●
Revolution ◆89 (3), ✣152
role in Angolan civil war
✣109, ◆109 (5)
Spanish-American War (1898)
✣94●, ✣133, ◆133 (5)
US tightens blockade (1991–92)
✣110●
Cuban Missile Crisis (1961–62). Major Cold War confrontation between

the US and the Soviet Union over the siting of Soviet ballistic missile launching sites in Cuba.
✤106●, ✤108, ✤138●, ✤139, ◆108 (2), ◆139 (5)

Cúcuta ⚔ of wars of S American independence in Colombia (Feb 1813). ◆150 (1)

Cucuteni-Tripolye Villages (c.4000 BCE) ✤174

cults
- bull ❑37
- Chavin (850 BCE) ✤30
- origins of religion ✤37

Cultural Revolution (*aka* 'Great Proletarian Cultural Revolution). Movement to reaffirm core ideological values of Chinese Communism launched by Mao Zedong in 1966. It was fervently implemented by student groups organized into the Red Guard,. They revived extreme collectivism and attacked revisionists, intellectuals and any suspected of ideological weakness. This resulted in thousands of executions, and the purge of many of Mao's original coterie. After losing control of the movement, Mao disbanded the Red Guard in 1968, but depredations continued under, initially, the military control of Lin Biao, and then under the 'Gang of Four' (led by Mao's wife, Jiang Qing) until Mao's death in 1976.
✤274–5●

culture, US popular
- baseball star 'Babe' Ruth ❑135
- growth of US popular culture ✤135, ✤135●
- movie-going (1929–45) ❑135
- radio sets in the US (1921–35) ❑135
- sale of records (US 1921–25) ❑135
- Walt Disney's Mickey Mouse ❑135

Cumberland Gap Strategic route through the Cumberland Mountains close to the borders of Virginia, Kentucky and Tennessee in the eastern US. Daniel Boone's Wilderness Road ran through the Gap, which had been named in 1750 by Thomas Walker.
- Daniel Boone and settlers ❑119
- explored by John Finley (1752) ✤119●

cuneiform Form of writing developed by the Sumerians and used in southwest Asia for over 3000 years from the end of the 4th millennium BCE. It originally used pictographs which became stylized to represent words, syllables and phonetic elements. The earliest cuneiform was written from top to bottom.
✤25, ❑25, ✤32●, ◆32 (1), ✤220●, ✤224●,

Cush *see* Kush

Cuzco
- captured by Pizarro (1533) ✤78●, ✤148, ◆148 (1)
- Corpus Christi procession ❑148
- Inca settlement (c.1200) ✤62●

Cybele BCE cult ◆37 (3)

Cyclades Marble figurine (c.2600 BCE) ❑174

Cynoscephalae ⚔ (197 BCE). Roman victory over Greece. ◆179 (4)

Cyprus Occupied by British (1878) ✤232●

Cyril, St. (826–69) Christian missionary, originally called Constantine, who, with his brother Methodius (825–884), took the Orthodox faith from Constantinople to the Slavs of Moravia. Cyril invented an alphabet, based on Greek characters, to translate the Bible into Slavonic languages. A later version of the alphabet, called Cyrillic, is used in modern Russian and Bulgarian.
185●

Cyrus II (*aka* Cyrus the Great) (c.580/590 BCE–529 BCE). Cyrus created the Persian Achaemenid Empire, named after his ancestor Achaemenes, by defeating the Medes, Lydians and Babylonians. His empire extended from the Mediterranean to the Hindu Kush, and he was known for his enlightened and tolerant policies of religious conciliation. ✤35, ✤223, ✤223●, ❑223, ◆223 (4)

Czechoslovakia State of central Europe established (1918) following WW I, comprising ethnic former regions of Austria-Hungary (Bohemia, Moravia, Slovakia, Trans-Carpathia); occupied and partitioned by Germany during WW II, entering the Eastern Bloc following Soviet liberation; liberalism suppressed (1968); dissolved into separate states of Czech Republic and Slovakia (1993) following 'Velvet Revolution' and free elections (1990).
- end of Communism (1989) ✤110●, ◆214 (2)
- home affairs
  - Communist takeover (1948) ✤102●, ✤213
  - invaded by Germany (1938) ✤102●, ✤209, ❑209, ◆209 (5)
  - national church established ✤193
  - 'Prague Spring' (1968) ✤106●
  - Soviets crush reforms (1968) ✤108●, ❑213
- Soviet-sponsored regime (1948) ✤108●
- *See also* Wars, First World; Second World

D

D-Day *see* Normandy Landings

Dagobert I (r.623–638). Merovingian king of the Franks, who briefly reunited the Frankish Empire and made Paris his capital. ✤183●, ❑183

Dahomey
- captures Whydah (1727) ✤164●
- conquered by French (1893) ✤95●
- defeated by Oyo (1747) ✤87●
- slave trade ✤82

Dai-Viet Northern Vietnam won independence from China, which had dominated it for ten centuries, in 946. The newly independent kingdom was re-named Dai-Viet ('Greater Viet') in 1009. Dai-Viet repelled a Chinese invasion in 1076. When the Ming invaded in 1406, their oppressive rule led to a Vietnamese national resistance movement, and the Chinese armies were routed in 1426. Vietnamese independence was recognized in 1427, and a new capital was established at Hanoi. ◆245 (1) (2)

Daimler, Gottlieb Wilhelm (1834–1900). Developed early automobile. 92●

Daimyo (10th–19th centuries CE). Medieval Japanese provincial feudal lordships. ◆265 (4) (5)

Dakota Gold find (1876–78) ✤93●

Dakota *see* Sioux

Dalai Lama (*var.* Tenzin Gyatso) (1935–). Spiritual and titular leader of Tibet, regarded as reincarnation of Compassionate Buddha. Designated 14th Dalai Lama in 1937, installed in 1940 but ruled under regency until 1950, and negotiated autonomy agreement after Communist Chinese invasion of Tibet (1950). Following suppression of Tibetan uprising (1959) has lived in exile.
- Nobel Peace Prize 1989. ❑275

Damascus
- Crusade siege abandoned (1148) ✤64●
- Islamic centre (661) ✤55●

Dampier, William (c.1651–1715) English adventurer and explorer. Dampier gained notoriety as a buccaneer, raiding Spanish colonies in the Caribbean and S America. The first Englishman to land in Australia in 1688, he was later sent by the Admiralty on an official voyage of exploration around Australia and New Guinea (1699–1701). ✤278●

Darius I (*aka* Darius the Great) (550–486 BCE). King of Persia (522–486 BCE). Noted for his administrative reforms and religious toleration. Darius's military conquests consolidated the frontiers of the Achaemenid Empire, and his division of land into administrative provinces, or satrapies, outlasted the empire itself. His famed building projects included a renowned road system and a palace at Persepolis.
✤35, ✤39, ◆40 (1), ✤223●, ◆223 (4)

Darius III (*var.* Codomannus) (381–331 BCE) Persian king (r.336–331 BCE). Distant relative of Artaxerxes III who successfully fought against the Cadusians and ascended to the Persian throne in 336 BCE. He was defeated by Alexander at the battles of Issus and Gaugamela (331 BCE), and was subsequently murdered by the Bactrian satrap Bessus.
- Persian Emperor ✤39
- at the battle of Issus ❑40

Darwin, Charles Robert (1809–82). The first scientist to put forward the theory of evolution through natural selection following observations made in the Galapagos Islands.
✤143, ✤143●, ◆143 (3)

David (r.c.1000–966 BCE). The second king of Israel, David was the first of the dynasty that ruled Judaea and Israel together, uniting the Jewish tribes into a settled nation. He moved the capital from Hebron to Jerusalem (Zion, the 'City of David'), where he brought the Ark of the Covenant, said to contain the Ten Commandments. David defeated the Philistines when he slew their giant warrior Goliath.
✤222●, ◆222 (1)

Dávila, Pedrarias (*var.* Pedro Arias Avila) (c.1440–1531). Spanish soldier and colonial administrator who led the first Spanish expedition to found permanent colonies in the New World.
- colonizing expedition (1514–19) ✤125, ◆125 (4)

Davis, John (c.1550–1605). English navigator. Explored Davis Strait, Baffin Island and the Cumberland Sound in Canada in search of Northwest Passage to India between 1585 and 1587. In 1591 he travelled as far south as the Falkland Islands. He also published works on navigation and developed navigational instruments including the double quadrant. ◆118 (1), ◆286 (1)

Dawes Plan The report which outlined German reparations as compensation for WW I. Starting at 1,000,000,000 gold marks in 1924, payments were to rise to 2,500,000,000 by 1928, but no total amount was fixed. An initial loan of 800,000,000 marks was given to Germany.
✤208●

Dawson's City Gold rush settlement ✤93

DDR *see* East Germany

De Beers Consolidated Mines ✤167

Deccan First cities (c.200) ✤47●

Declaration of Independence Document drawn up by the Congressional representatives of the original 13 states of the US, declaring independence from Britain. It was signed on 4 Jul 1776.
✤127●

Deerfield European and native conflict (1676) ✤126

Delagoa Bay Dutch occupy Portuguese settlement (1720–30) ✤164●

Del Cano, Juan Sebastián (c.1476–1526). Basque navigator who sailed with Magellan. Captain of the one ship that completed the circumnavigation of the world on Magellan's voyage of 1519–21. After Magellan was killed in the Philippine Islands in 1521, del Cano sailed the *Victoria* back to Spain with a valuable cargo of cloves from the East Indies, so becoming the first man to complete the circumnavigation of the globe.
◆80–1 (1)

Delhi ◆244 (3)
- British occupation ✤246●
- Ibn Battuta serves as judge (1334–41) ✤68●
- mausoleum of ibn Tughluq (1321) ❑71
- Qutb Minar minaret ❑67
- Quwwat-al-Islam mosque (1199) ✤67
- route map to Kandahar ❑238

Delhi Sultanate (1206 to 1398) Turkish-Afghan dynasty, based at Delhi. Its control over northern India fluctuated along with its various rulers' fortunes; in 1294, under Alauddin Khalji, conquering armies invaded Gujarat, Rajputana and the southernmost tip of the subcontinent. Under the Sultanate, Muslims were appointed to high office, and Hindus became vassals. ✤67, ✤71, ✤79, ✤244, ◆244 (3)

Delian League Confederacy of ancient Greek states under the leadership of Athens, with headquarters at Delos, founded in 478 BCE during the Graeco-Persian wars. ✤177, ◆177 (2)

Delphi Site of Pythian Games ❑38

democracy From the Greek, meaning rule by the people, although in the Greek city-states suffrage was far from universal. The ideal of democracy was revived in Europe the 18th century, notably in the French Revolution. Since then, in most of the world's states, the granting of the vote to all members of society has led to the widely accepted modern ideal of democratic government ✤90

Democratic Party Major US political party. Originally founded by Thomas Jefferson as the Democratic Republican party, the modern name was first used c.1828. Until the 1930s, support for the Democrats was drawn mainly from the southern US, but the New Deal policies of Franklin D. Roosevelt in the 1930s, and the passage of social reform and civil rights legislation in the 1960s has drawn a wider base of support.
✤139, ◆135 (5), ◆139 (4)

Denham, Dixon (1786–1828). English soldier who became one of the early explorers of western Africa. He accompanied Walter Oudney and Hugh Clapperton on an expedition across the Sahara to the Lake Chad basin (1821–1825).
◆157 (4)

Denmark
- 800–1000 ◆185 (3)
- Baltic conflict (16th century) ✤195, ✤195●, ◆195 (3)
- Baltic states (1100–1400) ◆189 (3)
- Danes besiege Paris (896) ✤58●
- foreign affairs
  - accession of Canute (1016) ✤62●
  - end of rule in England (1042) ✤60●
  - possessions
    - 1000 ◆58–9
    - 1600 ◆78–9
    - 1700 ◆82–3
    - 1800 ◆86–7
    - 1900 ◆94–5
    - 1925 ◆98–9
    - 1950 ◆102–3
    - 1975 ◆106–7
- WW II, mobilization and casualty figures ✤105
- Treaty of Westphalia, ◆196 (1)
- Union of Kalmar (1397) ✤70●

Desert Storm (1991) Allied campaign against Iraqi forces which ended Gulf War.
✤235●, ◆235 (5)
See also Gulf War

Detroit Race riots (1940s) ✤137●, ◆137 (6)

Deventer, Jacob van 16th-century Dutch cartographer. ✤173●

Diamond Sutra, the Earliest documented printed work. ❑59

diamonds
- commercial Africa (19th century) ❑95, ◆166 (1)
- finds ✤148, ◆93 (2)

Dias, Bartolomeu (1450–1500). Portuguese navigator and explorer who led the first European expedition round the Cape of Good Hope in 1488, opening the sea route to Asia via the Atlantic and Indian oceans.
- exploration of Africa (1487) ✤76, ◆156 (3)

Dias, Diogo Portuguese navigator, a member of Cabral's expedition to India in 1500. On the outward journey he became separated from the main fleet and discovered Madagascar.
✤156●, ◆156 (3)

diaspora General term for migration or wide dispersion of a people.
✤47●, ✤48●, ✤225, ◆225 (5)
See also Jewish Diaspora.

Díaz de Solís, Juan (c.1470–1516). Spanish explorer of the Atlantic coast of S America. He sailed with Vicente Yáñez Pinzón and Amerigo Vespucci. He was killed by indigenous people while exploring the Plate river in search of a route to the Pacific. ◆142 (1)

Díaz, Porfirio (1830–1915). Mexican statesman and soldier. A hero of the war of the Reform (1857–60) and the French intervention (1861–67). Became president in 1876, after rebelling against the fourth re-election of Benito Juárez. Elected again in 1884, he ruled uninterrupted until he was deposed in 1911 at the start of the Mexican Revolution. ✤133

Diderot, Denis (1713–84) French philosopher and writer. Chief editor of the *Encyclopédie* (1751–72) which attempted to encompass the full breadth of Enlightenment thought. ✤198

Dien Bien Phu ⚔ (3 Feb–7 May 1954). Attempting to regain control in Vietnam, the French were surrounded by Viet-Minh. Subsequently they withdrew from Vietnam. ◆151 (5)

Difaqane *see* Mfecane

Dilmun (Bahrain), trading links (BCE) ✤24–5

Diocletian (245–316) Roman emperor (r.284–305). Responsible for reorganizing the administration of the Roman Empire, dividing it into four regions to be ruled by two senior and two junior emperors. His reign also saw widespread persecution of Christians.
✤50, ✤180, ❑181
- persecution of Christians (304 CE) ✤48●
- Tetrarchy ✤181, ◆181 (4)

Directoire *see* Directory

Directory (*var. Fr.* Directoire). Name given to the revolutionary executive power in France between Nov 1795 and Nov 1799. It came to an end when Napoleon staged a *coup d'état* and made himself First Consul. ✤199, ✤200●

diseases
- cholera (1832) ✤204●, ◆204 (3)
- diphtheria ✤81
- European colonial settlement ✤126, ✤282●
- influenza ✤81, ✤284
- measles ✤81, ✤126, ✤284
- origin and movement ✤81 (2)
- smallpox ✤81
- Spanish colonization ✤125, ✤142, ✤148
- syphilis, 16th-century death toll ✤81
- tuberculosis ✤102
- whooping cough ✤81

Disney, Walter Elias (Walt) (1901–69). US animator and film producer. Set up a studio producing animated cartoons in the 1920s. Creator of Mickey Mouse, and producer of some of the most technically advanced animated films, his company grew to become a huge entertainment empire. ❑135

Diu
- Portuguese colony in India.
- Portuguese victory over Ottoman fleet (1507) ✤79●, ◆247 (3)

Djet, King Egyptian ivory label ❑24

Djoser *see* Zoser

Doge Title of the elected ruler of Venice, from the Latin *dux*, from c.697 to the end of the Venetian Republic in 1797. ✤191, ◆191 (3), ❑191

dolmens *see* chamber tombs

Domesday Book *see* William I

Dominic, St. (c.1170–1221) Spanish founder of the Dominicans, the Order of Friars Preachers. He was canonized in 1234. ✤187, ✤187●

Dominican Republic US invasion ✤133●

Domino effect (*aka* Domino theory). Theory that, in the event of a Communist victory in the Vietnam War (1954–75), the adjacent states of SE Asia would fall successively under Communist control. ✤251

Domino theory *see* Domino effect

Dong Son Prehistoric Indo-Chinese culture named after the northern Vietnamese village where many remains have been found. The Dong Son used iron and built stone monuments, but are best known for their highly skilled bronze-working, especially the ritual kettle drums found at the site. ✤240, ◆240 (3), ❑240

Dorylaeum ⚔ of crusades (1147). Turkish victory over emperor Conrad. ✤64●, ◆64 (1)

Dougga *see* Thugga

Doughty, Charles Montagu (1843–1926). British explorer, writer and poet. From 1876–78 he travelled from Damascus to Mecca, recording his journey in his acclaimed *Travels in Arabia Deserta*, published in 1888.
◆219 (4)

Dr Strangelove (film 1964) ✤108●

Drake, Francis (c.1540–1596) English privateer. Regarded in Spain as a dangerous pirate, Drake made a career of attacking Spanish ships and ports in search of bullion. He played an important role in the defeat of the Spanish Armada in 1588. His greatest feat of navigation was his round-the world voyage of 1577–80 in the *Golden Hind*. ✤80, ✤85
- N American expedition (1579) ◆118 (1)
- privateer route (16th century) ◆85 (2)

Dred Scott decision (6 Mar 1857). Landmark decision about the spread of slavery in the US. Scott, a slave who had been taken by his master into the West argued that he should be free as slavery was not legal in the new territory. The Supreme Court ruled that Congress had no power to exclude slavery from the territories, thus making slavery legal in all US territories.
✤130, ◆130 (4)

Dubček, Alexander (1921–92). First secretary of the Communist Party of Czechoslovakia (5 Jan 1968–17 Apr 1969) whose liberal reforms led to the Soviet invasion and occupation of Czechoslovakia in Aug 1968. ✤213

Dublin Viking settlement ✤185●

Dumont d'Urville, Jules Sébastien-César (1790–1842). French naval officer. Acted as naturalist on a series of expeditions to the Pacific in 1826–29. In 1837–40 he travelled to Antarctica where he discovered Terre Adélie and Joinville Island.
◆286–287

Dunhuang Chinese Buddha ❑59

Dušan, Stefan (c.1308–55). Ruler of Serbia. Through his successful campaigns in the Balkans, Stefan carved out a large Serbian Empire.
✤189, ◆189 (4)

Dust Bowl Name given to the prairie states of the US (Oklahoma, Kansas etc.) which suffered from serious soil erosion during the 1930s following a prolonged period of drought. Thousands of farmers were forced to abandon their ruined land. ✤134, ◆134

Dutch East India Company (*var.* United East India Company; *Dut.* Vereenigde Oost-Indische Compagnie). Company founded by the Dutch in 1602 to protect their trade in the Indian Ocean and to assist in their war of independence from Spain. It was dissolved in 1799.
- 17th-century official cartographers ✤83
- founds Cape Town colony (1652) ✤164
- Java headquarters ✤83, ❑243
- Moluccas spice trade ✤83
- trade monopoly abolished (1834) ✤91●

Dutch East Indies General historic term for Dutch colonial holdings in SE Asia, 17th–20th centuries. ◆80, 86, 90, 94, ◆97 (3), ◆247 (4), ◆251 (4)
- decolonization ◆97 (3)
- Japanese colonizing occupations ◆250–51 (3)

dyke Chinese timber and brushwood ❑83

Dzungaria Invaded by China (1751) ✤87● *See also* Xiankiang

E

Eanes, Gil 15th-century Portuguese explorer credited with rounding Cape Bojador, Africa, in 1434.
- exploration of Africa (1433–35) ✤156●, ◆156 (3)

earth Babylonian depiction ❑34
- Jain depiction of universe ❑238

East, the *see* Communist Bloc

East Africa
- Arab coastal trading (c.900) ✤61
- inter-ethnic warfare ✤111
- Portuguese map (1558) ❑156
- Portuguese possessions ✤78, ✤82, ◆164 (1)

East Asia General geographic term for traditional regions of China, Mongolia, Manchuria, Korea and the Japanese archipelago.
- BCE ✤15, ✤15●, ✤19, ✤31●, ✤35, ✤39
- agrarian unrest (1850) ✤95
- agricultural revolution (BCE) ◆258 (1)
- c.1500 ✤77, ◆77 (4)
- Communism and capitalism ✤274–5
- early medieval (618–c.1300) ✤262–3
- economic growth ✤275●
- era of the Qing Empire ✤268, ◆268 (1) (2)
- first civilizations ✤258–9
- first states in Japan and Korea ✤264–5
- foreign imperialism ✤269, ◆269 (4)
- the Han and the great migrations ✤260–1
- historical landscape ✤254–5, ◆254–5
- internal rebellion (8th century) ✤59
- Ming dynasty ✤266–7
- modernization of the East ✤270–1
- Russian expansion ✤269, ◆269 (3)
- *See also* individual countries

East Germany (*var.* German Democratic Republic, DDR). Communist state formed (1949) by Soviet Union following post-war occupation of Germany, dissolved upon German reunification (1990).
✤212–3●, ◆212–3 (1) (3) (4) (5), ✤214●, ◆214 (1) (2)

East Indies General geographic term for the archipelagos of Maritime SE Asia.
- Arab trading ✤61, ◆61 (3)
- colonization and trade with Europeans ◆247 (4)
- decolonization ✤97●, ◆97 (3), ◆247 (5)
- development of states and empires ✤245●, ◆245 (5) (6)
- Dutch surrender to Japan (1942) ✤104●
- establishment of Islam ✤61, ◆243 (6)

East Pakistan *see* Bangladesh.

East Timor
- independence (1975) ✤251, ◆251 (4)
- occupied by Indonesia (1975) ✤111●
- troops looting rice ❑253

Easter Island *see* Rapa Nui

Eastern Bloc *see* Communist Bloc

Eastern Front The eastern theatre of war during WW I, including eastern Germany, Austria-Hungary, Poland, Romania and Russia.
✤207●, ◆207 (4)

Eastern Han *see* Han dynasty.

Eastern Zhou *see* Zhou dynasty.

East, the *see* Communist Bloc

EC *see* European Union.

economy
- BCE tax levy ✤35
- 18th-century Europe ✤198–9, ◆198 (1)
- 19th-century growth of USA ✤94
- inventions and the economic revolution (1835–95) ✤92●
- medieval Europe ✤191, ❑191
- plantation ✤82, ❑84, ❑90, ❑149
- and political entities ◆163 (2)
- S American ✤152, ◆152 (3)
- 'Tiger' economies from 1960 ◆275 (4)
- world market domination ✤90, ✤112
- *See also* Industrial Revolution; trade

ECSC *see* European Coal and Steel Community

Ecuador
- BCE ✤42●
- cultural region ◆145 (4)
- achieves independence ✤150, ◆150 (1)
- decolonization ◆153 (4)

Edessa
- Crusader state ✤63, ✤65
- falls to Muslims (1144) ✤63●
- political and economic development ◆151 (3)
- Valerian defeated (260) ✤51●

Edo Imperial capital of Tokugawa Japan ✤267

Edward I (1239–1307) King of England (r.1272–1307). Eldest son of Henry III. He supported Simon de Montfort in the Barons' War (1264–67), later joining his father

Key to index: ✤ text ● timeline ❑ picture ◆ map *var.* variant name *aka* also known as *f/n* full name *prev.* previously known as r. ruled ⚔ battle WW I First World War WW II Second World War

to defeat de Montfort at the battle of Evesham (1265). Constant campaigning led to the annexation of north and west Wales, and much of the rest of his reign was spent attempting to unite England and Scotland against fierce Scottish opposition. Though he defeated William Wallace's armies at Falkirk in 1298, he was unable to control Scotland and died at Carlisle on the way to confront the newly-crowned Robert the Bruce. His reorganization of both local and central government and judicial reforms won him comparisons with the emperor Justinian.
  campaigns ✤188, ◆188 (2)

Edward III (1312–77) King of England (r.1327–77). Son of Edward II, in 1330 he overthrew his French mother Isabella who had governed during his minority. In the early years of his reign he became involved in wars with Scotland. In 1337 his claim to the French throne provoked the Hundred Years' War, during which he fought in the battle of Crécy and at the siege of Calais.
  campaigns ✤192, ◆192 (1)

Edward, Prince of Wales (*aka* the Black Prince) (1330–76). The son of Edward III, he was an outstanding English military commander in the Hundred Years' War, fighting with distinction at Crécy and winning a great victory at Poitiers (1356). Said to have gained his title because he appeared in battle wearing black armour. ◆192 (1)

Edward the Confessor (c.1003–66). King of England (r.1042–66). Edward is remembered for his piety – he was canonized in 1611 – and as founder of Westminster Abbey in London. His reign, however, was marked by feuds that would erupt on his death into a battle for succession to the throne between Harold, son of Earl Godwin of Wessex and William of Normandy. ✤186●

EEC European Economic Community
  created (1957) ✤106●
  See also European Union

Egypt
  ancient Egypt
    ✤159●, ◆159 (1) (2) (3)
    BCE ✤30, ✤31●, ✤34–5
    See also Fatimid dynasty; Pharaonic Egypt; Ptolemaic dynasty; Saite dynasty
  foreign affairs
    Camp David Summit (1978) ✤169●
    invades Sudan (1820) ✤90
    Six Day War (1967) ✤107●
  growth, early history (c.5000–3000) ✤159, ✤159●, ◆159 (2) (3) (4) (5)
  home affairs
    agricultural wealth (BCE) ✤27●, ✤158
    cult centres (BCE) ◆37 (3)
    Hittite and Mitanni conflict (1500) ✤27●
    invasions (BCE) ✤35●, ✤38
    Mamluk takeover (1250) ✤67●
    Mamluks conquered by Ottomans (1517) ✤79●
    New Kingdom ✤26, ◆26–7
    occupied by British ✤95●, ✤167●, ✤232
    occupied by Napoleon Bonaparte (1798) ✤87●
    Roman province ✤42, ✤46
    ruled by Hyksos (1633 BCE) ✤27●
  innovations
    mummification ❏31
    papyrus ❏30
    pyramids ❏22
    Roman mummy case ❏47
  religion
    BCE state religion ◆36 (1)
    Christian converts ✤46, ✤50
    Islamic fundamentalism ✤235
    Jewish exodus (c.1200 BCE) ✤31
    sun worship (1350 BCE) ✤27●
  trade and industry
    factories and refineries (1816) ✤166●
    Nile–Red Sea canal (500 BCE) ✤35●

Egyptian-Israeli peace treaty (*var.* Camp David Agreement) (1979). Egypt became the first Arab state to recognize Israel. The lands in the Sinai occupied by Israel since 1967 were returned to Egypt. ✤138●, ✤169●, ✤234

einkorn Wheat (ancestor of modern wheat) ❏21

Einsatzgruppen German or Axis security police, controlled by SS, operating as extermination squads in eastern Europe in the wake of conventional armed forces. ✤211●

Eisenhower, Dwight David (1890–1969) US general and 34th President of the US (Republican 1952–60). During WW II he commanded US forces in N Africa and Operation Overlord. In 1944 he became Supreme Commander of the Allied forces. After the war he was Supreme Commander of NATO land forces until his election as US President in 1952. He oversaw the end of the Korean War (1953) and the setting up of SEATO, and his presidency witnessed the emergence of the Civil Rights Movement. He was re-elected in 1956. ✤139●

Eisenhower Doctrine (1957). US foreign-policy declaration by President Eisenhower which promised aid to any Middle Eastern country in combating aggression from Communist countries. Like the Truman Doctrine, it aimed at total resistance to any extension of Soviet influence. ✤138●

El Alamein ⚔ of WW II (Oct–Nov 1942). Marked the beginning of the Allied conquest of N Africa by British and Commonwealth forces. ◆210 (1)

El-Amarna (*var.* Akhetaten).
  plan of city ✤29, ◆29 (5)
  plaster fragment from Great Palace ❏29
  See also Akhenaten

El Dorado Myth among Spanish *conquistadores* in S America of a golden man or a golden country.
  search for ✤146, ❏149

El Mirador Maya city complex ✤46, ✤121●

El Salvador, civil war (1979–1991). Civil war between the US-backed right-wing government and left-wing FMLN guerrillas (named after Farabundo Marti, the leader of a popular insurrection in 1932). The war ended with a UN-brokered peace agreement.
  civil war ends (1991) ✤110●
  US intervention ◆139 (5)

Elam State of SW Mesopotamia. The Elamites made Susa their capital and flourished in the 13th century BCE, when their empire stretched from Babylon to Persepolis. They gained control of the great Sumerian city of Ur c.2000 BCE. ◆26–7, ◆222 (2)
  Assyrian siege of Elamite city ❏222

Eleanor of Aquitaine (c.1122–1204). Married first to Louis VII of France, Eleanor became the wife of Henry II of England, when that marriage was annulled. Active in the management of her own lands in political life, Eleanor supported her sons, Richard and John, in a rebellion against their father and was imprisoned for 15 years. Later she acted as regent for Richard I while he was crusading abroad, and led an army to crush a rebellion in Anjou against her son John in 1200. ❏187

electrostatics Development of ✤80

electrum Early use of ✤35

Elizabeth I (1533–1603) Queen of England (1558–1603). Daughter of Henry VIII and Anne Boleyn, she ascended the throne on the death of her half-sister Mary I. She established the Church of England and put an end to Catholic plots, notably by executing Mary, Queen of Scots (1587) and defeating the Spanish Armada (1588). An intelligent and industrious monarch, under her rule the nation achieved prestige, stability and prosperity, and a great flourishing of the arts.

Elmina (*var.* São Jorge da Mina)
  founded by Portuguese (1482) ✤75●, ✤156●
  taken by Dutch (1637) ✤164●
  trading post ✤78

Elvas Relief of siege ❏196

Emancipation Proclamation US President Abraham Lincoln's announcement of 22 Sep 1862, that all slaves in rebellion against the Confederate states were free from the start of 1863. The Civil War thus became a fight against slavery, and the Union was able to recruit thousands of black troops to its cause. ✤130–131

Emory, Lt. William 19th-century explorer of the western US.
  expedition (1846) ◆119 (3)

Empire of the Khwarizm Shah *see* Khwarizm Empire

Empty Quarter *see* Rub' al Khali.

Encyclopédie *see* Diderot

Endara, Guillermo President of Panama ✤139

Endeavour Captain Cook's ship ✤87

Endlösing *see* Final Solution.

England
  Scotland and Wales (1284–1337) ✤188●
  See also Britain

English Civil War (*aka* the Great Rebellion) (1640–51). Fighting in the British Isles between Parliamentarians and supporters of the monarchy. It was precipitated by the Bishops' War (1639, 1640) with Scotland. The civil wars caused comparatively little loss of life or destruction of property, but led to the execution of King Charles I and his replacement by the Protectorate of Oliver Cromwell.
  ✤196●, ◆196 (2)

English East India Company The 'Governor and Company of Merchants of London trading into the East Indies' was founded in 1600 by Queen Elizabeth I. Initially, British expeditions to the East were confronted by the Portuguese, but the building of a factory at Surat (1612) began the British settlement of India. The Company gained concessions under the Mughals, and won control of Bengal in 1757. But its political activities were gradually curtailed and, after the Mutiny of 1857, it ceased to be the British government's agency in India. It was dissolved in 1873.
  ✤79●, ✤91●, ✤95, ✤248, ❏239, ◆247 (3), ❏247
  coastal trading posts (17th century) ✤83●
  military campaigns (17th century) ✤87

Enigma Code name for German telecommunications encryption during WW II. *See also* Ultra. ❏210

Enlil Chief deity of the Sumerian pantheon, Enlil embodied energy and force. His Akkadian counterpart, Bel, was the Mesopotamian god of the atmosphere. ✤28

ensete African relative of the banana. ◆21 (2), ◆158 (1)

Entente forces Collective name given to the European nations in alliance against Germany, Austria-Hungary and their allies (the Central Powers) during WW I. Also used to denote the foreign powers in alliance against the Bolsheviks during the Russian Civil War. *See also* Allied forces. ✤206–7, ◆206–7 (1)–(6), ◆208 (2)

entrepôt A port to which goods are brought for import, export and distribution. ✤45

environment
  different ways of life (BCE) ✤16, ◆16 (1)
  survival strategies (BCE) ✤16

Eratosthenes of Cyrene (c.276–194 BCE). Greek geographer, astronomer, and mathematician. Among a range of achievements he measured the circumference of the earth and invented a system for identifying prime numbers, as well as writing on geography, literary criticism and chronology. ✤172

Erik the Red 10th-century Norwegian navigator and explorer. Having sighted Greenland in about 983, he returned to Iceland to persuade Viking settlers to follow him. He set out in 986 with 25 ships and founded two settlements. The early settlers of Greenland followed an Icelandic model of government; Erik the Red acted as the 'Law Speaker'. At its peak, the Norse population of Greenland numbered c.4000. ✤60●

Eriksson, Leif ('the Lucky') (b.c.970) Viking explorer. He may have been first European to land in N America. In search of grazing and timber he founded settlements in Greenland, and was later based at l'Anse-aux-Meadows in present-day Newfoundland.
  ✤62●, ◆118 (1)

Eriksson, Thorvald Viking explorer of N America (1003) and brother of Leif Eriksson. ◆118 (1)

Eritrea
  civil war (1984–85) ✤168●
  Italian colony (1889) ✤167●

Erlitou Founded (1900 BCE) ✤27●

Eskimo *see* Aleut; Inuit

Esperey, General d' lands in Istanbul ❏233

Esquival, Juan de 16th-century Spanish explorer of N America. ✤125, ◆125 (4)

Essequibo First Dutch settlements ✤149●

Estado Novo *see* New State

Ethelbald Anglo-Saxon Mercian king ✤183●

Ethiopia (*var.* Abyssinia)
  Arab trading in Highlands (c.1000) ✤61●
  aromatic gum trade (1st century CE) ✤225, ◆225 (3)
  Christian kingdom expands ✤67●
  death of Amde Sion (1344) ✤71●
  decline of ✤165●
  famine (1987) ✤111●
  Italian invasion (1935) ✤103●
  Jesuits expelled (1632) ✤165●
  Ogaden region conflict (1960) ✤168●
  revival of Red Sea trade ✤62
  Soviet anti-Western support ✤109
  struggle for the Horn of Africa ✤165, ◆165 (3)
  toured by James Bruce (1768–73) ✤157
  Zagwe dynasty church ❏62

Etowah Mississippian cultural site ✤123

Etruscans Ancient people who flourished in west and central Italy from the 8th century BCE. At their height they ruled in Rome. The last Etruscan king, Tarquin II, was overthrown in 509 BCE, and in 283 BCE they succumbed completely to the Romans, but their cultural influence endured; skilled engineers and urban planners, they were also accomplished metal workers and traded with Greece.
  1000 BCE–1 CE ✤176●
  city-states (BCE) ✤31●
  Mediterranean world (700–300 BCE) ◆176 (1)
  peoples of Italy (500 BCE) ✤178, ◆178 (2)
  Rome expels overlords (510 BCE) 34●
  sarcophagus ❏178
  state religion (BCE) ◆36 (1)
  tomb frescoes ❏34, ❏176

Etymologiae (Isidore of Seville) ✤173●

EU *see* European Union

Eudoxus of Cyzicus (b.c.135 BCE). Greek explorer, who twice made trading journeys to India on behalf of the Ptolemaic kings of Egypt.
  sails from Black Sea to W Africa (c.146 BCE) ✤218●
  sails from India to Egypt (120 BCE) ✤218●

Eugénie, Empress (1826–1920) Empress of France. Born in Spain, she was consort of the French emperor, Napoleon III. After his deposition in 1871, she fled to England, where he joined her after a period of imprisonment in Germany. ❏232

eunuchs in China ✤47

Euphrates Babylonian map ❏34

Eurasia Geopolitical term for combined continents of Europe and Asia, historically often including Egypt and Graeco-Roman tracts of N Africa.
  ✤16●, ✤30–1, ◆44–5 (c.1300) ◆68 (2)
  map by Ptolemy ❏44

Euripides (484–406 BCE). Athenian tragic dramatist, originally an artist, who took up literature and wrote 80 dramas, 19 of which survive. ✤177

Europe 170–215
  800–1000 ◆185 (3)
  Ages
    Crusades ✤186–7, ◆186–7 (1) (2) (3) (4) (5)
    Enlightenment ✤198–9
    Reformation ✤194–5, ✤194●
  BCE
    ✤15, ✤15●, ✤18, ✤31●, ✤38
    introduction of farming (7000–5000 BCE) ✤174, 174●, ◆174 (1)
    Copper Age (4500–2500 BCE) ✤174, ✤174●, ◆174 (2)
    Bronze Age (2300–2500 BCE) ✤175, ✤175●, ◆175 (3)
    historical landscape ✤171, ◆170–1
    prehistoric ✤174–5
    Central and southeastern (1200–1400) ✤189, ✤189●, ◆189 (4)
  conflict
    1743–63 ✤88●
    caused by land settlement (1250 BCE) ✤27
    Congress of Vienna (1815) ✤202, ✤202●, ◆202 (1)
    in crisis ✤188–9
    devolution ✤112, ❏112, ◆112 (2)
    division of postwar Europe ✤212–13, ◆212 (1) (2)
    empires ✤88, ◆88 (1)
    Europe between the wars ✤208–9, ◆208 (1) (2) (4)
    Hundred Years' War ✤70●, ✤75●, ✤187, ✤191, ✤192, ✤192●, ◆192 (1) (2)
    political consolidation and resistance in the 17th-century ✤196, ✤196●, ◆196 (2)
    revolutionary period (1830–48) ✤90
    Thirty Years' War (1618–48) ✤82, ✤196, ✤196●, ❏196, ◆196 (1)
    World Wars *see* Wars, First World; Second World
  expansion
    colonizing voyages (1492–1597) ◆80–1 (1)
    in S and SE Asia ✤248–9, ◆248 (1) (2)
    new era of prosperity ✤62, ✤62●
    territorial ◆77 (5)
    the Mediterranean world c.500 BCE ✤176–7
    migrations and invasions (350–500 CE) ◆53 (2)
  nation states
    ✤192–3
    evolution of state system (17th century) ✤196–7
    growth of nationalism ✤202–3, ✤209, ✤209●, ❏214
    struggle for supremacy ✤194, ◆194 (1)
  population ✤94, ✤198
  religion, Protestant Reformation ✤78, ✤82
  renaissance
    (12th century) ✤187, ✤187●, ◆187 (3)
    (15th century) ✤75, ✤192
  Roman Empire ✤182–3, ◆182 (1)
  trade and industry
    Asian commercial contacts ✤247, ✤247●, ◆247 (3) (4)
    development (1850–1914) ✤205, ✤205●, ❏205, ◆205 (4)
    medieval ◆190–1, ◆190–1 (1)
  See also individual countries

European Atomic Energy Community (EURATOM). International organization founded in 1957 by the Treaty of Rome to promote and develop the peaceful use of atomic energy in Europe. ✤214

European Coal and Steel Community (ECSC). Body established in 1952 to co-ordinate the production of coal and steel in France, Italy, W Germany, and the Benelux countries. ✤214

European Economic Community (EEC) *see* European Union

European Recovery Program *see* Marshall Plan

European Union (EU) Organization formed (1993) to integrate the economies of its member states and promote cooperation and coordination of policies. It originated in Treaty of Rome (1957) and the formation of the EEC (France, Germany, Italy, Belgium, Netherlands and Luxembourg). The UK, Irish Republic and Denmark were admitted in 1972 (EC). By 1995 the EU had 15 member states. In the 1990s the organization moved towards fuller integration. Membership expanded in 2004 to 25 with the admission of 10 new states, including several former members of the Communist bloc.
  ✤108, ✤214, ◆214 (1)
  EEC created (1957) ✤106●, ✤214, ❏214

European Union Treaty *see* Maastricht Treaty

EURATOM *see* European Atomic Energy Community

Eutaw Springs ⚔ of American Revolutionary War (8 Sep 1781). British victory. ◆127 (3)

Everest, Sir George (1790–1866). Army officer with the British East India Company, who instituted the great Trigonometrical Survey of India. From 1823 he was responsible for triangulating the entire subcontinent, and was renowned for his efficiency. Mount Everest was named after him. ✤239, ✤239●, ❏239

evolution
  development of modern humans ✤14–15, ◆14–15, ❏14–15
  Scopes 'Monkey Trial' (1925) ✤135

exploration and mapping
  Africa 156–7
    14th- and 15th-century exploration ✤156●, ◆156 (3)
    19th-century exploration ✤157●, ◆157 (4), ❏157
    Catalan Atlas ❏70, ❏71
    medieval accounts of W Africa ✤156●, ◆156 (1) (2)
    source of the Nile ✤157, ◆157 (5), ❏157
  Antarctica 286–7
    exploration ✤287●, ◆287 (3)
  Arctic 286–7
    charting the coast ✤286–7●, ◆286–7 (2)
    new routes to Asia ✤286, ◆286 (1)
    race to the N Pole ✤286–7●, ◆286–7 (2)
  Australasia and Oceania 278–9
    European voyages in the Pacific ✤278●, ◆278 (1), ❏279
    exploration of Australia ✤279●, ◆279 (2), ❏279
    known world 1500 ◆77 (7)
    Marshall Islands stick chart ❏278
    New Zealand, Captain Cook's map ❏87
    Polynesian migrations ✤60●, ◆60 (2), ❏60, ✤280–1●, ◆280–1 (3), ❏281
    Solomon Islands (1593) ❏278
  Europe ✤172–3
    cartography ✤173, ❏173
    Catalan Atlas ❏70
    Classical era ✤172●, ◆172 (1), ❏172
    geological maps (19th century) ❏91
    Greek world (500 BCE) ❏218
    Iceland, Viking voyages ✤172●, ◆172 (2)
    medieval mapping ✤173●, ❏173
    Peutinger Table ❏172
    printing ✤94
    road maps ❏99
    schematic maps ❏102
  North America 118–9
    Atlas Contractus ❏119
    Central America and the Caribbean (16th century) ❏79
    charting the West ✤119●, ◆119 (3)
    Civil War map ❏94
    early European explorers ✤118●, ◆118 (1)
    exploring the eastern interior ✤119●, ◆119 (2)
    Spanish exploration and colonization ✤125●, ◆125 (4)
  North and East Asia ✤256–7
    European exploration ✤257●, ◆257 (2), ❏257
    exploring Asia's great mountains ✤257●, ◆257 (3), ❏257
    Gyogi-style map of Honshu (1305) ❏256
    travellers in Central Asia (140 BCE–1295 CE) ✤256●, ◆256 (1), ❏256
  South America ✤142–3
    Beagle, voyage of (1832–35) ✤143, ◆143 (3), ❏143
    Cantino planisphere (1502) ❏142
    first European explorers ✤142●, ◆142 (1)
    Humboldt, Alexander von ✤143, ◆143 (3), ❏143
    Jesuit missions ✤143●, ◆143 (2), ❏143
    scientific explorers ✤143●, ◆143 (3)
  South and Southeast Asia 238–9
    indigenous mapping ✤238●, ❏238
    scientific exploration of SE Asia ✤239●, ◆239 (2), ❏239
    Survey of India ✤239●, ❏239
    travellers in S and SE Asia ✤239●, ◆239 (1), ❏239, ❏247
  West Asia 218–19
    al-Idrisi map (c.1154) ❏218
    Europeans in Arabia ✤219●, ◆219 (4), ❏219
    Babylonian map (c.600 BCE) ❏34
    Catalan Atlas ❏68
    Greek and Roman expeditions ✤218●, ◆218 (2), ❏218
    Indian Ocean ◆61 (3)
    Islamic travellers ✤218●, ◆218 (2), ❏218
    medieval and Renaissance travellers ✤219●, ◆219 (3), ❏219
    Nippur, map (1500 BCE) ❏28
    Jerusalem, mosaic map (6th century CE) ❏51
  world 80–1
    eastern hemisphere by Joan Blaeu (1662) ❏83
    Eurasia (Ptolemy) ❏44
    European voyages ✤80–1●, ◆80–1 (1), ❏80
    globes ❏55, ❏62, ❏75, ❏238
    Magellan's circumnavigation ❏80
    medieval *mappamundi* ❏66
    New World by Ortelius ✤79, ❏79
    remote-sensed mapping ❏110
    Viking world (c.1000) ◆60–1 (1)
  See also cartography; names of explorers and travellers

Eylau ⚔ of Napoleonic Wars – the War of the 3rd Coalition (1807). French victory. ◆200 (1), ❏200

Eyre, Edward (1815–1901). British-born explorer of Australia. Eyre's journeys were inspired by the search for new pasturelands for cattle. His greatest journey was his crossing of the Nullarbor Plain in 1840–41. It would have failed without the local Aborigines who helped the expedition find water. ◆279 (2)

Ezana Aksumite king (c.350) ✤50●

F

Faeroe Islands
  Settled by Vikings ✤172

Fa Hsien *see* Fa Xian

Faisal I (*var.* Feisal) (1885–1933). Joined T.E. Lawrence in Arab Revolt (1916–18) against Turkey during WW I. Became King of Iraq (1921–33). In 1930 he negotiated a treaty with the British, who held mandate in Iraq, that gave Iraq independence. ❏232
  See also Lawrence, T.E.

Falklands War Conflict (1982) between Argentina and the UK. ✤110●, ◆152 (1)

Fallam, Robert 17th-century explorer of eastern N America. Accompanied Thomas Batts in 1671 in search of a mythical South Sea. ◆119 (2)

Fallen Timbers ⚔ (20 Aug 1794). US victory over the Northwest Indian Confederation which enabled the extension of white settlement of their former territory, particularly in Ohio. ◆128–129 (2)

farming
  18th-century Europe ✤198
  Cucuteni-Tripolye villages (c.4000 BCE) ✤174
  development of communities (BCE) ✤22
  early N American ✤120, ◆121 (1)
  early S American ✤144, ◆147 (2)
  early spread of (7000–5000 BCE) ✤174●
  early village plan ❏18
  horticulture villages (BCE) ✤34●
  introduction to Europe (7000–5000 BCE) ✤174, ◆174 (1)
  major cash crops (1870–1910) ◆92 (1)
  permanent shelter ❏21
  refrigerated shipping (1880s) ✤92●
  societies (c.1350) ◆162 (1)
  technology opens markets (1870–1910) ◆92 (1)
  timber longhouse ❏174
  tools (BCE) ✤16●, ✤22, ✤34, ✤258●
  See also agriculture; animal and plant domestication

Fashoda ⚔ (1898). British and French clash in N Africa ✣95
Fasiladas, King (d.1667) Ethiopian emperor (r.1632–67). Severed links between his country and Europe, instigating a policy of isolation that lasted for more than two centuries. ✣❑165
Fatimid dynasty (909–1171). A Muslim dynasty, founded in Tunisia, N Africa, the Fatimids claimed descent from Fatima, Muhammad's daughter. In 969 the fourth Fatimid Caliph, Muizz, conquered Egypt and established his capital at Cairo, from where the Fatimids ruled until the 12th century. ✣58, ✣227, ◆227 (6)
  Caliphate (1144) ◆65 (3)
  control Egypt (969–1171) ✣58●, ✣58●, ✣63●, ✣162●
  expel Aghlabids (909) ✣58●
  lose control of Ifriqiya (1048) ✣63●
Fa Xian (*var.* Fa Hsien) (*fl.* c.400 CE). Chinese Buddhist monk and traveller. Made the first recorded journey overland from China to India and back by sea between 399 and 414 CE. The purpose of his travels was the gathering of religious texts, but his experiences greatly enriched Chinese geography. ✣49●, ◆256 (1)
Fazzan *see* Garamantes
Federal Bureau of Investigation (FBI). US government agency first established in 1908. Deals with matters of internal security, counter-intelligence and federal law-enforcement. ✣135●
Federal Republic of Germany *see* West Germany
Federmann, Nikolaus (d.1542) German explorer of S America. Federmann was a representative of the Welsers, Charles V's bankers, who were granted lands in present-day Venezuela. Federmann led expeditions into the interior in 1530 and 1537. On the second, he scaled the Cordillera Oriental of the Andes to reach Bogotá in 1539. He was recalled to Spain, accused of misappropriation of royal funds. ◆142 (1)
Feisal I *see* Faisal I
Ferdinand II (1578–1637) Holy Roman Emperor (1619–37). A devout Catholic, his deposition as king of Bohemia by Bohemian Protestants led to the Thirty Years' War. After his victory at White Mountain (1620) he reimposed Catholicism on Bohemia. ✣196●
Ferdinand of Aragon (1452–1516). The first monarch of all Spain, Ferdinand ruled as Ferdinand V of Castile (from 1474), Ferdinand II of Aragon and Sicily (from 1479) and Ferdinand III of Naples (from 1503). His marriage to Isabella of Castile (1451–1504) in 1469 led to the union of Aragon and Castile. His reconquest of Granada from the Moors (1492) completed the unification of Spain. He expelled the Jews from Spain and financed Columbus's voyage to the New World. ✣75●, ✣192●, ◆192 (3)
Ferghana Cavalry horse ❑44, ❑55
fertility cult Set of beliefs and practices associated with promulgating the fertility of the land. Finds of apparently pregnant female figures are often thought to have been associated with these kinds of beliefs. ❑19
Fezzan *see* Garamantes
Field of Blood ⚔ (1119) of crusades. Muslim victory. ◆65 (3)
Fiji
  immigration labour (1874) ✣284●
  Polynesian culture ✣55, ✣60
Final Solution (*var. Ger.* Endlösung). Nazi policy to exterminate European Jewry, implicit in Nazi anti-semitism from the 1930s, but formalized by Hitler in July 1941. The first death camp at Chełmno was opened in Dec 1941, detailed plans for implementation of the policy agreed at the Wannsee conference, Jan 1942. The policy was in operation until liberation of death camps in 1945. ✣211, ◆211 (3) (4), ❑211
Finland
  gains independence ◆208 (1)
  WW II, mobilization and casualty figures ✣105
Finley, John 18th-century explorer of the eastern US.
  explores Cumberland Gap (1752) ✣119●
First Emperor *see* Qin dynasty, Shi Huangdi.
First Fleet The name given to the convict ships that landed at Botany Bay in 1788 to found the first British colony in Australia. The fleet consisted of eleven ships under the command of Captain Arthur Phillip, the first governor of New South Wales. ✣282, ❑282
First Intermediate Period Period of almost 100 years in Egypt from c.2134 BCE, where the balance of power and governmental responsibility shifted from the court to the provinces. ✣158●
First World War (*var.* World War I, the Great War) (1914–18). Major conflict in which expansionist aggression by Germany, Austria-Hungary and the Ottoman Empire, in Europe and their colonial holdings (the Central Powers), was countered by an Allied coalition led by France, Britain, Russia, Italy and (from 1917) US. The first war to be fought on a truly industrial scale, involving mass mobilization of population and industry, and the innovative use of airplanes, gas and tanks on the battlefield, it was also a war of attrition on a massive scale. It heralded the end of European imperialism, the Communist (Bolshevik) Revolution in Russia, the redrafting of the map of Europe, and the dismemberment of the Ottoman Empire. ✣206–207●, ◆206–207 (2)–(6), ✣232
Fitch, Ralph (c.1550–1611). British merchant who was among the first Englishmen to travel through India and Southeast Asia. ◆239 (1)
Five Dynasties and Ten Kingdoms (907–960) Period of Chinese history that followed the Tang dynasty when China fragmented into as many as ten regional states. ✣263
Flanders
  as part of Spanish Empire ✣81
  Dutch Revolt ◆195 (5)
Fleurus ⚔ of Napoleonic Wars – the War of the 1st Coalition (1794). French victory ◆200 (1)
Flinders, Matthew (1774–1814) English naval officer. In 1798–99, with George Bass, he circumnavigated Tasmania, proving it was an island. He was then appointed Commander of HMS Investigator, the British ship that undertook a thorough survey of the entire coastline of Australia. ◆279 (2)
Florida
  exploration ◆125 (4)
  Jesuit missions established (1560s) ✣125●
  painted map (16th century) ❑118
  Seminole wars (1816–50) ◆129 (2)
  Spanish area conquered (1820) ✣90●
  Spanish settlements founded (16th century) ✣118
Flying Fortress Nickname for US B17 heavy bomber used for high-level daylight raids on Nazi Germany in WW II. ❑105
FNLA *see* National Front for the Liberation of Angola.
Ford, Gerald Rudolf (1913–) 38th President of the US (Republican,1974–76). Became President following the resignation of Richard Nixon in 1974, but failed to retain the Presidency at the next election. ✣139●
Ford, Henry (1863–1947). US engineer and car manufacturer. Founded the Ford Motor Company in 1903 where he pioneered the assembly-line method of mass production for his Model-T Ford automobile. ❑134
Ford, John (1895–1973). US film director who became identified with the Western genre.
  Director of *The Grapes of Wrath* (film 1939) ❑135
Former Han *see* Han dynasty
Formosa (*var.* Taiwan)
  conquered by Kangxi (1683) ✣83●
Forrest, Alexander 19th-century explorer of Australia. ◆279 (2)
Forrest, John (1847–1918). Australian explorer and politician. Forrest's first expedition in 1869 was in search of the lost party of Ludwig Leichhardt. He made several more journeys into the interior of Western Australia. His brother Alexander was also an explorer. In 1883 John Forrest became the colony's surveyor-general, and later Western Australia's first state premier. ◆279 (2)
Fort Donelson ⚔ of American Civil War (16 Feb 1862). Union victory. ◆131 (6)
Fort Henry ⚔ of American Civil War (6 Feb 1862). Union victory. ◆131 (6)
Fort Jesus
  founded by Portugal (1593) ❑83
  Mombasa, protected Portuguese trading (1593–1698) ❑164
  taken by Omani Arabs (1698) ✣83
Fort St. George (*var.* Madras) ❑247
Fort Sumter Attack starts Civil War (1861) ✣131 (6)
Fortress Europe General term for Nazi-occupied Europe during WW II, after the Soviet Union's entry to the war and the first Allied blockade was enforced. ✣210
Fountains Abbey ❑187
France
  foreign affairs
    voyages of expansion (1492–1597) ◆80–1 (1)
    possessions
      1500 ◆74–5
      1600 ◆78–9
      1700 ◆82–3
      1800 ◆86–7
      1850 ◆90–1
      1900 ◆94–5
      1925 ◆98–9
      1950 ◆102–3
      1975 ◆106–7
    colonies lost in 18th century ◆86–7
    Africa
      colonization (19th century) ◆166 (1) (3) (4)
      conquers Dahomey (1893) ✣95●
      decolonization ✣168, ◆168 (1)
      exploration of African interior (19th century) ◆157 (4) (5)
      imperialism (1880–1920) ✣96, ◆96 (1)
      Algeria, invasion (1830) ✣90, ✣232
    America
      colonization of N. America ✣126–7, ◆126–7 (1) (2)
      Revolutionary War (1775–83) ◆127 (3)
    Asia, imperialism in Southeast ✣97, ✣97●, ◆97 (3)
    Austria, defeated with Russian aid (1805) ✣90●
    Beijing, occupation ✣95●
    First World War *see* Wars, First World
    Germany, declares war on (1939) ✣102●
    Guiana, colony (c.1640) ✣149, ◆149 (4)
    India, power destroyed (1761) ✣87●
    Italy, invasion (1494) ✣75●
    N. American exploration (16th–17th century) ◆118 (1)
    Ottoman Empire partition ✣233
    Pacific
      decolonization and nationhood ✣285, ◆285 (3)
      imperialism ◆284 (1)
    Réunions (1679–84) ✣197
    Second World War *see* Wars, Second World
    South American colonization (16th–17th century) ◆142 (2)
    Suez crisis ✣234●
    Tunisia ✣232
    USA
      sells N. American territory (1803) ✣90●
      trading posts in N. America ✣82
  home affairs
    Agincourt defeat (1415) ✣75●
    battle of Crécy (1346) ✣70●, ❑192
    consolidation and resistance (17th century) ✣196, ✣196●, ◆196 (2)
    coup by Napoleon (1799) ✣86●
    Hundred Years' War (1337–1453) ✣70●, ✣75●, ✣192, ✣192●, ◆192 (1) (2)
    innovations, Eiffel Tower (1889) ❑92
    Jacquerie uprising (1358) ✣70●, ✣192●, ◆192 (1)
    King John's losses (1214) ✣66●
    population growth (1650–1800) ❑198
    Revolution ✣82, ✣86, ✣90, ✣199, ❑199, ◆199 (4)
    rivalry with Habsburgs ✣194, ✣194●, ◆194 (1)
    Second Empire collapses (1870) ✣94
    siege of Orléans (1429) ✣75●, ✣192●
    under Louis XIV (1660–1715) ✣197, ◆197 (5)
France Antarctique (*var.* Ilha de Villegagnon). Island off south eastern Brazil which was colonized by French Huguenots under Nicolas Durand de Villegaignon in 1555. A Portuguese invasion in 1560 forced the Huguenots to abandon the island. ✣149●
Francis I (*var.* François I) 1491–1547) King of France (r.1515–47). His reign was dominated by his rivalry with Emperor Charles V for the control of Italy. He was a notable patron of the Renaissance and created the Palace of Fontainebleau. ✣194, ✣194●, ◆194 (1)
Francis of Assisi, St. (c.1181–1226). Italian founder of the Franciscan Order, and later the 'Poor Clares', a Franciscan order for women. He was canonized in 1228. The members of the order strove to cultivate the ideals of the order's founder who insisted on 'holy poverty' as his guiding principle. ✣187, ✣187●
  exploration of S America ✣143●
Francis Xavier St. 16th-century Spanish missionary to China. ✣80
Franco, General Francisco (*f/n* Francisco Paulino Hermenegildo Teódulo Franco Bahamonde) (1892–1975). Spanish general and dictator and leader of the Spanish rebel forced in the Civil War (1936–1939). He seized power at the end of the war and in 1947 he announced that Spain was to become a monarchy again. This occurred, but only after Franco's death in 1975. ✣110●, ✣209
Franco-British-Turkish alliance (1854–56) ✣94●
Franco-Prussian War (1870–71) Prussian support for the accession of a Hohenzollern prince to the Spanish throne prompted Napoleon III of France, alarmed at the growth of Prussian power, to declare war on Prussia. The defeat of the French at Sedan (1 Sep 1870) and the Prussian annexation of Alsace-Lorraine, persuaded the southern German states to join the new German Reich. On 18 Jan 1871, King William I of Prussia was declared German emperor at Versailles. ✣203, ◆203 (3)
Frankish Empire A Germanic people based in the area of present-day France and western Germany, the Franks came to dominate the region after the collapse of the Western Roman Empire, c.493. Under Clovis I (481–511) and his successors the Franks became the most important successors to the Roman Empire, dominating much of western Europe for the next three centuries. Under Charlemagne, their realm extended to cover most of Germany. 182–3, ◆182 (1) (2), ❑183, ◆185 (5) (6), 184–5, ◆184 (2)
  conversion to Christianity (497 CE) ✣49●
  expansion (500 CE) ◆182 (1)
  kingdoms ✣183●, ◆183 (5) (6)
  migrations and invasions (300–500 CE) ◆52–3 (1)
  tribute taken by Vikings (845 CE) ✣60●
  See also Charlemagne
Franklin ⚔ of American Civil War (30 Nov 1864). Inconclusive result. ◆131 (7)
Franklin, Sir John (1786–1847). British naval officer and explorer. Made first expedition to Arctic in 1818. Later led two overland expeditions to chart the Arctic coast of N America, in 1819–22 and 1825–27. In 1845 he sailed in search of a Northwest Passage. The entire crew of 129 men perished, and a number of subsequent voyages were made in search of the lost Franklin party.
  Arctic explorer (1845–47) ◆286–7 (1) (2)
  exploration in N Canada (1820–21, 1825–27) ◆119 (3)
Franz Ferdinand, Archduke (*var.* Archduke of Austria-este Francis Ferdinand, Erzherzog von Österreich-Este Franz Ferdinand) (1863–1914). Austrian archduke whose assassination in Sarajevo, Bosnia and Herzegovina, was a catalyst for WW I. ✣98●, ✣206
Fraser River Gold finds ✣93●
Frederick I (*var.* Frederick Barbarossa) (1123–90) Holy Roman Emperor (r.1152–90) and King of Germany and Italy. Of the Hohenstaufen family. Established German predominance over much of western Europe. Gained authority over Italy, Poland, Hungary, Denmark and Burgundy. Led the Third Crusade in 1189, achieving victory at Philomelium and Iconium, but drowned before reaching the Holy Land.
  Crusade route (1189–92) ◆64–5 (2)
  in Crusader dress ❑186
  Italian commune liberties ✣190●
  protects University of Bologna ✣187●
Frederick II (*var. Lat.* Stupor Mundi) (1194–1250) Holy Roman Emperor (r.1220–1250) and King of Germany. Grandson of Frederick I, Barbarossa and the last great Hohenstaufen ruler.
  Empire ◆188 (1)
  laid claim to Italy ✣188
  regains control of Jerusalem (1229) ✣64●, ✣65●
Frederick II (*var.* Frederick the Great) (1712–86) King of Prussia (r.1740–86). An able administrator and a brilliant soldier, he ruled Prussia as an enlightened despot, introducing religious toleration, and reforming the army and agriculture. In 1740 he occupied Silesia, fighting to retain it in the War of the Austrian Succession (1740–48) and the Seven Years' War (1756–63). In the first partition of Poland (1772) he gained W Prussia. Under him, Prussia became a leading European power. ✣199
Frederick Barbarossa *see* Frederick I
Frederick William (*var.* the Great Elector) 1620–88 Elector of Brandenburg (r.1640–88). Under his rule, the state of Brandenburg gained full sovereignty in Prussia, and Brandenburg-Prussia became a powerful state with a large standing army. ✣199, ◆199 (3)
Fredericksburg ⚔ of American Civil War (13 Dec 1862). Confederate victory. ◆131 (6)
Freeman's Farm ⚔ of American Revolutionary War (19 Sep 1777). American victory. ◆127 (3)
Freetown British freed slave settlement (1787) ✣87●
Fremont, Lt. John Charles (1813–90). American explorer. During the early 1840s he explored much of the southwestern US and the map he produced as part of his report helped to popularize westward migration across the continent. He travelled to California and took part in the Bear Flag Revolt, after which he was court-marshalled and forced to resign his commission. Having made a fortune in the California Gold Rush of 1848 he ran as an unsuccessful presidential candidate in 1856.
  Memoirs illustration ❑119
  US expedition (1842–44) ◆119 (3)
French Revolution (1789). Political uprising which ended in the downfall of the monarchy and profoundly affected every aspect of government and society in France. In spring 1789, with the state heavily in debt and the peasantry crippled by taxes, Louis XVI was forced to convene the Estates-General. From it emerged the National Assembly which responded to public unrest, such as the storming of the Bastille (14 Jul), with sweeping political, economic and social reforms. These included the abolition of feudal and aristocratic privileges; the nationalization of church lands; and a Declaration of the Rights of Man. The royal family was removed from Versailles to Paris. In 1792, following an attempt to flee the country, they were imprisoned and executed, the monarchy abolished and France declared a republic. *See also* Bourbons, Directory, Jacobins, Robespierre, the Terror. ✣86●, ❑86, ✣88–9●, ◆88–9 (2), ✣199●, ◆199 (4), ❑199
French West Africa Federation created (1904) ✣167●
frescoes
  Etruscan tomb ❑34
  Kassapa's two heavenly maidens ❑51
  zodiac tomb ❑39
FRG *see* West Germany
Friedland ⚔ of Napoleonic Wars – the War of the 3rd Coalition (1807). French victory. ◆200 (1)
Frisius, Gemma 16th century Flemish theoretical mathematician, physician and astronomer who served as a mentor to Flemish cartographer Gerardus Mercator. ✣173●
Fritz, Samuel (c.1659–1725) German Jesuit missionary. Fritz served in the Jesuit mission to the Omagua people on the upper Amazon from 1686. He opposed interference in the region by the Portuguese and made great contributions to the mapping of the area.
  map of Amazon ❑143
Frobisher, Sir Martin (c.1535–94) English navigator who travelled in search of the Northwest Passage in 1576, discovering Frobisher Bay in Canada.
  ✣80, ✣80●
  explores Northwest passage ❑286, ◆286 (1)
  N American expedition (1576–77) ◆118 (1)
Fujiwara family Dynastic family that, by shrewd intermarriage and diplomacy, dominated the Japanese imperial government from the 9th to the 12th century. ✣63, ✣265●, ◆265 (4)
Fulani *see* Fulbe
Fulbe (*var.* Peul, Fulani). Primarily Muslim people who inhabit many parts of W Africa, from Lake Chad, in the east, to the Atlantic coast. (c.1730) ✣164●
  engraving of a town (1730) ❑164
fur trappers N and E Asian routes ◆257 (2)
Futa Jallon Fulbe confederation (Africa) (c.1730) ✣164●

Gadsden Purchase (1853). Purchase by US from Mexico of 77,700 sq km (30,000 sq miles) of land in New Mexico and Arizona by James Gadsden, in order to establish a southern railroad to the Pacific. ✣129, ◆129 (2)
Gai-Long (*var.* Nguyen Phuc Anh) (1762–1820). Emperor and founder of the last dynasty of Vietnam before conquest by France. ✣91
Gaiseric (*var.* Genseric) (d. 477). King of the Vandals and the Alani (r.428–477) who conquered a large part of Roman Africa and in 455 sacked Rome. ✣52●, ◆52 (1)
Galapagos Islands
  finches collected by Darwin ❑143
  map drawn by Beagle officers ❑143
Galerius (*var.* Gaius Galerius Valerius Maximianus) (d. 311). Roman emperor (305–311), notorious for his persecution of Christians. ✣51●
Galilee, Lake Harvesting of wild cereals (19,000 BP) ✣16●
Galileo (*var.* Galileo Galilei) (1564–1642). Italian natural philosopher, astronomer, and mathematician who made fundamental contributions to the sciences of motion, astronomy, and strength of materials and to the development of the scientific method. ✣83
galleon Full-rigged sailing ship that was built primarily for war, and which developed in the 15th and 16th centuries. The largest galleons were built by the Spanish and the Portuguese for their profitable overseas trade.
  Manila galleon ◆81 (3)
  See also transport
Gallipoli Campaign of WW I (Feb 1915–Dec 1916) between Allied forces and Turkey. Attempt by Allies to force a passage through the Dardanelles channel and occupy Constantinople. ✣99●, ◆207 (6), ◆233 (2), ❑233
Gama, Vasco da (c.1460–1524). A Portuguese navigator who, in 1497, was commissioned by the Portuguese king to establish trading links with the East Indies. Rounding the Cape of Good Hope, he stopped at coastal trading centres of eastern Africa, sailing northeast across the Indian Ocean, and reaching Calicut on 20 May 1498. He made a second voyage to India in 1502. ✣80●, ❑80, ◆80 (1), ◆239 (1)
  exploration of Africa (1497–99) ✣239●, ◆156 (3), ◆239 (1)
  voyage to India ✣75, ✣80, ✣156●
Gambia, River Engraving of a Fulbe town (1730) ❑164
Gandhara (*var.* Kandahar). Indo-Greek state of S Central Asia (3rd century BCE–5th century CE). Located in the Punjab, Gandhara was one of several Indo-Greek kingdoms which were the successors of the Greek colony of Bactria, founded by Alexander the Great. With the decline of the Mauryan empire, the Bactrian Greeks crossed into the Kabul valley and Punjab and founded independent kingdoms there. The Buddhist art of Gandhara is famous for its eclectic mixture of western and Indian styles. Gandhara, with its capital at Taxila, fell to invading Asian nomads (the Scythians) in c.90 BCE. ◆224 (1), ✣241●
  falls to Scythians (90 BCE) ✣43
  Persian satrapy (533 BCE) ✣35●
Gandhi, Indira (1917–84). Daughter of Nehru, Indian prime minister 1966–77. Confronted by a growing anti-government protest movement, she declared a national Emergency in 1975, and returned to power as leader of Congress I party, in 1980. She was assassinated by Sikh extremists. ✣111●, ❑252
Gandhi, Mohandas K. (*aka* Mahatma Gandhi) (1869–1948). Indian independence leader. Worked as a lawyer in South Africa, and became the leader of a movement for Indian civil rights there. On his return to India in 1915 he transformed the Indian National Congress into a powerful force, utilizing the techniques of passive resistance (*satyagraha*) and mass non-cooperation. His attacks on the Salt Tax and March to the Sea (1930) and major civil disobedience campaigns (1920–22, 1930–34, 1940–42) were important catalysts in India's progress towards independence. He was assassinated by a Hindu fanatic.
  hero of India's independence movement ✣99●, ❑103, ❑250
Gandhi, Rajiv (*var.* Rajiv Ratna Gandhi) (1944–1991). Leading general secretary of India's Congress Party from 1981, Gandhi became prime minister of India (1984–89) after the assassination of his mother, Indira Gandhi. He was himself assassinated by Tamil separatists. ❑252
Gang of Four *see* Cultural Revolution
Ganges
  BCE farming development ✣19
  valley, urban culture ✣36●
Gao Zu (*var.* Kao Tsu, *aka* Liu Chi, Liu Pang) (256–195 BCE). Founder and first emperor of the Han dynasty in 206 BCE, after emerging victorious from the civil war following the death of Shi Huangdi. Although often violent, he was a pragmatic and flexible ruler. ✣43
Garamantes (*var.* Fezzan, Fazzan, *Lat.* Phazania). Saharan kingdom, now the SW part of Libya. It was annexed by Rome in 19 BCE who called it Phazania. ✣38–39
Garay, Francisco de 16th-century Spanish explorer of N America.

Key to index: ✣ text ● timeline ❑ picture ◆ map *var.* variant name *aka* also known as *f/n* full name *prev.* previously known as r. ruled ⚔ battle WW I First World War WW II Second World War

colonizing expedition (1517–23) ✣125, ◆125 (4)
Garibaldi, Giuseppe (1807–82). Italian revolutionary, soldier and the greatest figure of the *Risorgimento*. When Italy's war of liberation broke out in 1859, he and his thousand 'Redshirts' captured Sicily and Naples, handing them over to Victor Emmanuel II.
meets Victor Emmanuel II ❑203
unification of Italy ✣203, ✣203●, ◆203 (3)
gas masks *see* chemical warfare
gas Reserves held in Saudi Arabia ✣234
Gaugamela ⚔ of Alexander's campaigns (331 BCE). Decisive battle against the Persians. ✣39●, ◆39 (1)
Gaul (*var.* Gallia)
Gallic empire of Postumus (260–74 CE) ◆181 (3)
invaded by Huns (451 CE) ✣53●
overrun (406) ✣50●
Roman control ✣42
Roman province ◆180 (1)
Gaulle, Charles de (*var.* Charles-André-Marie-Joseph de Gaulle) (1890–1970). French soldier, writer and statesman who orchestrated France's Fifth Republic. He played an active role in the French Resistance during WW II and became French president in 1947, relinquishing leadership in 1953. In 1958 he took office as the first president of the Fifth Republic. During the period 1959–60 he granted self-government to French African colonies. ✣106●
Gaza Taken by Israel in Six Day War (1967) ✣234●
Gedymin (c.1275–1341) Grand Duke of Lithuania (c.1315–42). His conquests laid the foundations of the great Lithuanian state (in personal union with Poland) of the late Middle Ages. ✣189●, ◆189 (3)
Geheime Staatspolizei *see* Gestapo
Genghis Khan (*var.* Ching-Gis, Chingis, Jenghiz, or Jinghis) (d.1227). Mongolian warrior-ruler, who unified tribes and then extended his empire across Asia to the Adriatic Sea through military conquest.
invades northern China (1211) ✣67
unites Mongols (1208) ✣67●
Jin Empire invasion (1211) ✣67●
'universal ruler' ✣69, ❑68
attacks Khwarizm (1219) ✣69●
empire at his death (1227) ◆66–7, ◆68–9 (1)
first known as Temujin ✣67●
homage from Mongol tribe leaders ❑67
leads a cavalry charge ❑68
Genoa
11th-century prosperity ✣62
and possessions 14th century ◆70–1
trade routes (c.1300) ✣190, ◆190–1 (1)
Genseric *see* Gaiseric
Geography (Ptolemy) ✣44, ✣55, ✣173●, ✣218●
Geography (Strabo) ✣44, ✣218●
Geological Survey, US Kanab Desert sketch (1880) ◆119 (3)
Georgia Former republic of the USSR, which became independent in 1991.
break-up of Soviet Union ◆215 (4)
Civil war ✣110
German Confederation (1815–66). Alliance of German sovereign states. At the Congress of Vienna the 39 states formed a loose grouping to protect themselves against French ambitions following Napoleon's destruction of the Holy Roman Empire (1806). ✣203●, ◆203 (3), ❑203
German Democratic Republic *see* East Germany
German Federal Republic *see* West Germany
Germanic tribes Roman Empire incursions 44●, ✣46, ✣50
Germantown ⚔ of American Revolutionary War (4 Oct 1777). British victory. ◆127 (3)
Germany 185–214
in 1925 ◆98–9
East, end of Communism (1989) ✣110●
Empire and possessions, 1900 ◆94–5
First World War *see* Wars, First World
foreign affairs
Africa
expansion (c.1880) ◆167 (4)
exploration of African interior (19th century) ◆157 (4) (5)
imperialism (1880–1920) ✣96, ◆96 (1)
Asia, imperialism in SE ✣97, ✣97●, ◆97 (3)
Baltic settlements (1100–1400) ◆189 (3)
Czechoslovakia invasion (1938) ✣102●
Empire in 1942 ◆102–3
Japanese anti-Comintern pact (1936) ✣103●
Pacific
colonies (1914) ✣99●
imperialism ◆284 (1)
Poland invasion (1939) ✣102●
Roman Empire incursions ✣44●
S American exploration ◆142 (1)
home affairs
in Cold War Europe ✣212●
postwar occupation ✣212, ◆212 (1)
revival of nationalism ✣102●
Thirty Years' War (1618–48) ✣82
unification ✣110, ✣203, ✣203●, ◆203 (2)
religion, Protestant Reformation ✣78
Second World War *see* Wars, Second World
Versailles Treaty ✣102
See also Holy Roman Empire; East Germany; West Germany
Gestapo (*var. Ger.* Geheime Staatspolizei). The secret police of Nazi Germany, originally part of the Prussian State Police, moulded by Goering and Himmler. ✣211
Gettysburg ⚔ of American Civil War (1–3 Jul 1863). Union victory. Often considered to be the turning point in the Civil War. ❑131, ◆131 (6)
Gettysburg Address (19 Nov 1863) Speech made by US President Abraham Lincoln at the dedication of the National Cemetery at Gettysburg. It ends with the hope that: *this nation, under God, shall have a new birth of freedom – and that government of the people, by the people, for the people, shall not perish from the earth.* ✣131●
Ghana
achieves independence (1957) ✣107●, ❑168
Almoravid invasion (1076) ✣63●
kingdom displaced by Mali Empire (13th century) ✣66
W African kingdom ✣58, ✣163●
Ghaznavid dynasty *see* Mahmud of Ghazni ✣59●, ✣63, ✣227, ◆227 (6)
Ghiyas al-Din *see* Muhammad of Ghur
Gildo Berber chief (c.397) ✣50●
Giles, Ernest (1835–97). British-born Australian who explored western Australia between 1872 and 1876. ◆279 (2)
Gilgamesh Legendary Sumerian king (c.3rd millennium BCE) ❑222
Gist, Christopher (c.1705–59). American explorer. Explored and surveyed the Ohio River Valley in 1750–51, and was part of George Washington's expedition to remove the French from the Ohio valley in 1753–54. ◆119 (2)
Giza Pyramids built (2530–2470 BCE) ✣23●, ❑22
glaciers, BCE retreat ✣18–19
Glendalough Irish monastery with look-out towers ❑58
Gnosticism System of religious beliefs, especially of cults of late pre-Christian and early Christian centuries, characterized by the belief that matter is evil and that emancipation comes through gnosis (knowledge).
spread (200–400 CE) ◆49 (4)
Goa ✣79●, ✣247, ❑247, ◆247 (3)
Godfrey of Bouillon (c.1060–1100) First king of Jerusalem (r.1099–1100). ✣65●
leads attack on Jerusalem ❑65
Crusade route (1096–99) ◆64–5 (2)
Golan Heights Taken by Israel in Six Day War (1967) ✣234●
gold
Asante court insignia ❑87
Australian gold fields ✣282, ❑282, ◆282 (2)
Californian Gold Rush (1849) ✣90●, ✣93●, ✣100●
Chimú ceremonial objects ❑146
commercial Africa (19th century) ◆166 (1)
discovered in Brazil (1695) ✣82●, ✣149●
Egyptian funerary equipment ❑26
Eurasian and African trade (c.1 CE) ◆44–5
figurine of Hittite king (c.1400 BCE) ❑27
first use ✣18
horned bull ❑18
Inca llama ❑148
Klondike and Yukon gold rushes ✣93, ◆93 (3)
major finds (late 19th century) ◆93 (2)
N African coins ❑162
Nubian deposits (BCE) ✣26
panning in British Columbia ❑93
slaves used for mining 149
sub-Saharan ✣58
W African trade (13th century) ✣66
Golden Bull (1356). Imperial edict of Charles IV, which established clear rules as to which rulers qualified as Electors with the right to choose the Holy Roman Emperor. ✣189●
Golden Horde Mongol Khanate of central Asia, with its capital at Saray. The khanate flourished from the 13th to the 15th century, exacting tribute from the Russian principalities to the northwest. ✣67, ✣69●, ✣70, ✣229, ◆229 (4)
founded by Batu (1242) ✣69●
vassals (1200–1400) ◆189 (4)
Golden Triangle Name given to the border areas between Thailand, Burma, Vietnam and Laos which is a major centre for the production and distribution of narcotics, primarily heroin. ◆113 (4)
Gomes, Diogo (1440–84). Portuguese explorer sent by Henry the Navigator to investigate the W African coast in about 1458.
account of African river (1456) ✣156
exploration of Africa (1458–60) ◆156 (3)
Gomez, Estaban (*var.* Estevão Gomes) (c.1484–1538). Portuguese pilot in the service of Spain. Refused to explore the southern part of the Strait of Magellan in 1520 and deserted, but in 1524–25 he traced the N American coast from Nova Scotia to Florida, charting the coast in great detail. He was killed by Indians while accompanying Pedro de Mendoza's expedition to the Plate river. ✣125, ◆125 (4),
Gone with the Wind (film, 1939) ✣135●
González Dávila, Gil 16th-century Spanish conquistador who explored the Lake Nicaraguan region and made the first, but failed attempt to conquer what is now Nicaragua in 1522. ✣125, ◆125 (4)
Good Hope, Cape of
Dutch colony established (1652) ✣83●, ✣164●
navigated by Dias (1488) ✣156●
seized by Britain (1795) ✣87●
Gorbachev, Mikhail Sergeyevich (1931–). Soviet official, the general secretary of the Communist Party of the Soviet Union (CPSU) from 1985 to 1991 and president of the Soviet Union in 1990–91. During his time in office he was responsible for introducing the policy of *glasnost* which encouraged more friendly relations between the Soviet Union and the West and for brokering reductions in the number of nuclear weapons held.
Soviet leader (1985) ✣110●, ✣214–15
Gordillo, Francisco 16th-century Spanish navigator who in 1522 made land fall near Cape Fear, initiating thorough exploration of the area. ✣125
Gorlice-Tarnow ⚔ of WW I (May 1915). Russian forces were driven back by the Central Powers (Austria-Hungary and Germany). ◆207 (4)
Goths General term for Germanic peoples whose incursions into the Roman Empire during the 4th century CE hastened its decline. *See also* Avars, Ostrogoths, Visigoths. ✣53, ✣53●
defeat of Attila the Hun (451) ✣50●
migrations and invasions (300–500 CE) ◆52–3 (1)
Ostrogoths
eastern Goths, ✣53
Empire ◆50–1
expansion (500 CE) ◆182 (1)
migrations and invasions (300–500 CE) ◆52–3 (1)
Visigoths
western Goths
conquests (600 CE) ◆182 (2)
cross dating from 6th century ❑182
defeat emperor Valens (378) ✣50●, ✣53●
kingdom of Aquitaine (418) ✣53, ✣182
migrations and invasions (300–500 CE) ◆52–3 (1)
sack Rome (410) ✣49●, ✣50●, ✣53●
Gotland Carving of Viking ship ❑185
Grañ, Ahmad *Jihad* against Ethiopia ◆167 (3)
Granada The last Moorish kingdom on the Iberian Peninsula, Granada fell to Spain in 1492. ✣192●, ◆192 (3)
controlled by Moors ✣66
regained by Spain (1492) ✣75●
Gran Colombia *see* Greater Colombia
Granicus ⚔ of (334 BCE). Alexander the Great's first major engagement with the Persians occurred at a river-crossing formerly known as the 'Gates of Asia', where he launched a famously audacious attack at dusk, tricking, surprising and overwhelming the various enemy forces ranged against him. ◆223 (4)
Grant, James, tracking the Nile ❑157, ◆157 (4)
Grant, Ulysses Simpson (*prev.* Hiram Ulysses Grant) (1822–85) US general and 18th President of the US (Republican,1869–77). Appointed supreme commander of the Union forces in 1864 during the American Civil War, his strategy of operating several armies at once against the less numerous Confederate forces headed by Robert E. Lee, led to the Confederacy's complete surrender in Apr 1865.
portrait ❑131
role in Civil War ✣131
Grapes of Wrath, The (film, 1939) ❑135
grave goods
E Asian ✣258
gold horned bull ❑18
Han ❑47, ❑260
Hopewell mica hand ❑120
limestone beads ❑19
Mehrgarh ✣19●
Mexican dog vessel ❑122
Mycenaean dagger blade ❑26
necklace from Mugharet el-Kebara ❑15
N American ✣34
Royal Graves at Ur ✣23●, ✣24
terracotta ❑259
wheeled chariots ✣24●
See also burials
Great Depression (c.1929–34). World-wide economic crisis sparked off by the Wall Street Crash of 1929. It resulted in the collapse of banking confidence and the calling-in of European loans, creating massive unemployment in America and Europe, and other industrialized areas of the world until the start of WW II. ✣102●, ✣134–5, ✣206, ✣209, ◆134 (2), ◆209 (3)
Greater Colombia (var. Gran Colombia, Republic of Colombia) (1822–30). Republic comprising the modern nations of Ecuador, Colombia, Panama and Venezuela (formerly the Viceroyalty of New Granada), set up as a result of the independence campaigns led by Simón Bolívar. The secession of Venezuela and Ecuador, and the death of Bolívar in 1830, led to the collapse of the Republic.
Greater East Asia Co-Prosperity Sphere Term used by Japan to describe the empire they established in E Asia from the 1930s onward. It collapsed in 1945 with the defeat of Japan. ✣272
Greater German Reich (*var. Ger.* Grossdeutschland). Core German state proclaimed by Nazis in 1939 following the acquisition of Saarland, Austria, Bohemia-Moravia, and Memelland, divided into Gaus. ✣211●, ◆211 (2) (3)
Greater Vehicle *see* Mahayana Buddhism
Great Lakes Exploration (17th century) ✣119●
Great Leap Forward (1958). Attempt to increase production in China by the creation of huge rural communes and urban associations. Resulted in famine and 30 million deaths and was abandoned in 1961. ✣272●, ❑272
Great Migration Name given to the many movements of peoples across Europe in the 5th century CE. The Vandals, Alans, and Sueves crossed the Rhine into the Roman Empire, then moved through Gaul to Iberia, the Vandals later continuing to N Africa. ✣52–53●, ❑52–53, ◆53 (1)
Great Northern Expedition (1733–42) Russian expedition commissioned by Tsar Peter the Great, commanded by Vitus Bering, to explore and map the Siberian coast and Kurile Islands. ◆257 (2)
Great Northern War (1700–21). Long drawn out struggle between Sweden and Russia for control of the Baltic region. After initial successes under Charles XII, Russia under Peter the Great emerged the dominant power in the region. ✣197, ◆193 (3)
Great Rebellion, the *see* English Civil War
Great Schism (1378–1417). Following the Avignon Papacy (1309–77), when the papacy was under French control, a Roman pope, Urban VI, was elected, only to be deposed by the cardinals. They elected a new pope, Clement VII, who returned the papacy to Avignon. The Great Schism (1378–1417) divided western Christendom until the Council of Constance (1414–18) when a new pope, Martin V was elected and universally recognized. ✣88●
Great Seljuk Empire *see* Seljuk Turks ◆62–3
Great Trek (*var. Af.* Groot Trek). The emigration of over 12,000 Afrikaner from Cape Colony, in South Africa, between 1835 and the early 1840s, in protest against the policies of the British government and in search of fresh pasturelands. ✣166●, ◆166 (2), ❑166
Great Wall of China General name for defensive barrier system across northern China, stretching from the Pacific coast to the Takla Makan Desert, erected to protect the Chinese heartland from the Xiongnu and other northern and Central Asian peoples. First conceived as a system during the Qin period (c.220 BCE), which linked earlier defensive barriers together, and extended far to the west under the Han, it reached its final form during the Ming period when a continuous masonry wall was created, punctuated by watchtowers from which warning beacon signals could be transmitted. ✣43●, ✣51●, ◆259 (1), ◆262 (1)
rebuilt ✣75●, ✣260, ❑266, ◆266 (1)
Great War *see* First World War
Great Zimbabwe Complex of stone enclosures in southern Africa, built by the Shona people from the 3rd century CE to the 15th century. The name is also applied to the kingdom centred on the site, which flourished in the 13th and 14th centuries.
Islamic kingdom ✣66
kingdom falls to Mutapa empire (c.1450) ✣75●
royal enclosure ✣163, ❑67
ruins ◆163 (3)
1819–30 ◆90–1
dissolution ✣150, ◆150 (2)
Greece
Ancient Greece
city states ✣27, ✣31, ✣176, ✣179, ◆34–5, ◆38–9
cultural
Classical Age (BCE) ✣34, ✣37, ✣38
exchanges with the Orient ✣41
mythological pantheon ❑41, ◆37 (3)
exploration and mapping ◆218 (1)
Africa (c.150) ◆156 (3)
Greek world (500 BCE) ❑281
foreign affairs
colonization (BCE) ✣176, ❑178
home affairs
cult centres (BCE) ◆37 (3)
independence ✣90, ✣232
major powers of the Greek world (200 BCE) ◆179 (4)
Roman control ✣42
state religion (BCE) ◆36 (1)
inventions
alphabet ✣34●
Archimedean screw ❑38
war elephant's tower ❑41
Mediterranean world (700–300 BCE) ✣176, ◆176 (1)
Mycenaean (c.1500–1150 BCE) ✣175, ✣175●, ◆175 (4)
Mycenaean goblet (c.1300 BCE) ❑174
Mycenaean pot ❑31
Rosetta stone ❑42
Modern Greece
partition of Ottoman Empire ✣233
First World War ✣207●, ◆207 (6)
growth in 19th century ✣203, ◆204 (4)
independence ✣202, ◆202 (1)
Second World War, mobilization and casualty figures ✣105
Greek Independence, War of (1821–30). The revolt by Greek subjects against Turkish domination. Greece fought alone until 1825, but thereafter her cause was taken up by Britain, Russia and later France. Following the destruction of Turkey's fleet at Navarino (1827) and the Treaty of Adrianople (1829), in 1830 Greek independence was confirmed by her allies. ✣90, ✣202, ✣232
Greenland
Bishop Eirik goes to N America (1121) ✣62●
Leif Eriksson sails to N America (c.1000) ✣60●, ✣62●
settled by Eric the Red (986 CE) ✣60●
Vikings in the N Atlantic ✣172
Gregory VII, St. (c.1020–1085). Great reform pope of the Middle Ages (r.1073-85). He criticised various abuses in the church. From 1075 onward he was engrossed in a contest with Emperor Henry IV over lay investiture. ✣62●
Grenada US intervention (1983) ✣138●, ✣139
Griffith, D.W. (David Llewelyn Wark) (1875–1948). Pioneering US film-maker and director of *Birth of a Nation* ✣135●
Grijalva, Juan de (c.1480–1527) Spanish *conquistador*. Took part in conquest of Cuba in 1508. In 1518 while reconnoitring Yucatan, became first European to receive information about the existence of the Aztec Empire. Later served in Central America under Pedrarias Dávila. ✣125, ◆125 (4)
grindstones Shaped sandstone containing abrasive quartz grains, used in many manufacturing and finishing processes, for example grinding flour or polishing surfaces. Initially worked by hand, grindstones were later incorporated into mechanized processes. ✣16●, ✣18●, ❑20
Groot Trek *see* Great Trek
Grossdeutschland *see* Greater German Reich
Groseilliers, Medart Chouart des 17th-century French explorer of N America (1659–60). ◆119 (2)
Guadalcanal Series of naval and land ⚔ during WW II (Aug 1942–Feb 1943). Fought on and around Guadalcanal in the Solomon Islands, the battles marked the halt by Allied forces of Japanese advance in the southwest Pacific. ✣104, ❑250
Guam Seized by US ✣284●
Guangala Coastal culture of western S America (c.250 BCE). ✣42●
Guangzhou (*var.* Canton),
sea route found by Arabs (8th century) ✣61
Chinese port ❑269
Guaraní Tupian-speaking South American people. The aboriginal Guaraní inhabited eastern Paraguay and adjacent areas in Brazil and Argentina. In the 14th and 15th centuries some Tupian speakers migrated inland to the Rio de la Plata, where they became the Guaraní of Paraguay.
protest at Madrid Treaty terms (1754–55) ✣143●
S American tribe ✣143, ◆147 (2)
Guarmani, Carlo 19th-century Italian explorer of the Arabian Peninsula. He was an enterprising Italian horse dealer who made an extensive journey from Jerusalem to the heart of Arabia to buy Arab stallions for the French government and for the King of Italy. ◆219 (4)
Guatemala
government downfall (1954) ✣139
Maya city-states ✣122
Guerra de 1847 *see* Mexican-American War
Guiana
colonization ◆149 (4)●
region explored by Schomburgk (1835–44) ✣143●
sugar plantations founded ✣82
Guilford Court House ⚔ of American Revolutionary War (5 Mar 1781). Inconclusive result. ◆125 (3)
Guinea-Bissau, rebel troops take refuge ❑169
Gulf Coast, emergence of Olmec civilization (1150 BCE) ✣121
Gulf
conflict ◆235 (5)
oil production ◆234 (1)
Operation Desert Storm ✣235●
Gulf War (1990–91). War precipitated by Iraq's invasion of Kuwait (Aug 1990). The UN condemned the invasion and demanded Iraq's withdrawal. When Iraq, led by President Saddam Hussein, refused to comply, a US-led coalition of 29 states launched Operation Desert Storm. Saddam's forces surrendered in Feb 1991. Kuwait was liberated and harsh economic sanctions imposed on Iraq by the UN. ◆235 (5), 111●
Guomindang *see* Kuomintang
Gupta dynasty (320–480 CE). During this period, India was ruled by five great monarchs from the city of Pataliputra, and subsequently Ayodhya. At its greatest extent, Gupta rule extended from the Punjab in the west to northern Bengal. Gupta administration was enlightened and tolerant, and arts, music, sculpture, and painting flourished. Trade extended in all directions. Buddhism was the state religion, but reviving Hinduism absorbed many Buddhist tenets. The invasions of the Huns in the 5th and 6th centuries brought about the political collapse of the empire. ✣48, ✣51, ✣244, ◆244 (1)
Gupta Empire *see* Gupta dynasty
Gurjara-Pratiharas (8th–11th century). Indian kingdom which originated in Rajasthan and, from 836 CE, controlled the area between eastern Punjab and northern Bengal, before disintegrating into smaller warring kingdoms in the 10th century. ✣59●, ✣224●, ◆224 (2)
Gustavus II (Gustavus Adolphus) (1594–1632). King of Sweden (r.1611–32). Recovered the Baltic provinces from Denmark, and ended the wars with Russia (1617) and Poland (1629). He championed the Protestant cause in the Thirty Years' War, winning a series of victories while campaigning in Germany. During his reign, Sweden became the strongest power in Europe. ✣82●, ✣197●
Gustavus Adolphus *see* Gustavus II
Gutenberg, Johannes (*var.* Johann Gensfleisch zur Laden zum Gutenberg) (d. 1468). German craftsman and inventor who originated a method of printing from movable type that was used without important change until the 20th century.
bible ❑74
use of metal movable type ✣74
Güyük (1206–1248) Grandson of Ghengis Khan (r.1246–48). ◆68–9 (1)

Guzmán, Nuño de 16th-century Spanish *conquistador*, who took part in the conquest of Mexico. ✤125, ◆125 (4)
Gyogi 8th-century Japanese Buddhist priest who began to compile maps of Japan's provinces. ✤256

H

Haarlem ⚔ of Dutch Revolt (1572–73). Spanish victory over Dutch. ◆195 (4)
Habsburg dynasty (*var.* Hapsburg). Major European royal and imperial family. From 1438 to 1806 all Holy Roman Emperors but one belonged to Habsburg house. Reached its peak as a world power under Charles V who brought Spain into the Habsburg dominions. After Charles' death, the house split into the Spanish line, which died out in 1700, and the Austrian line, which remained in power until 1918. *See also* Charles V, Holy Roman Empire.
  breaks up ✤98
  defeat of France ❑194
  expansion ✤193, ◆193 (4)
  Ottoman conflict (1663–171) ✤197, ◆197 (4)
  possessions, *see* Austria
  rise of Brandenburg Prussia ✤199, ◆199 (3)
  struggle for supremacy ✤194, ✤194●, ◆194 (1)
  See also Austria
Habuba Kabira Trading post (c.3100 BCE) ✤24●
Habyarimana Juvénal (1937–94) President of Rwanda (r.1973–94) ✤169
Hadrian (*var.* Publius Aelius Hadrianus) (76–138). Roman Emperor (r.117–138), under whom the Roman Empire consolidated its defences and enjoyed a period of peace and prosperity. Hadrian travelled extensively round the empire, not as a soldier, but as an administrator and connoisseur of the arts. He commissioned many new buildings, notably in Athens and Rome, and new cities, such as Aelia Capitolina, built on the ruins of Jerusalem.
  ✤180●, ◆180 (1)
Hadrian's Wall 117-km-long wall built by emperor Hadrian (r.117–38 CE) to consolidate the northern frontier of the Roman Empire. Constructed between 122–28 CE, it straddles northern England from the Solway Firth to the River Tyne, and was defended by 16 forts, 80 milecastles, and numerous signal turrets and stretches of ditch. Despite attacks by northern tribes it survived until c.400 CE.
  46●, ✤180●, ◆180 (1)
Hafsid dynasty Berber dynasty of the 13th–16th century in Ifriqiyah (Tunisia and eastern Algeria), founded by the Almohad governor Abu Zakriyya' Yahya about 1229. ✤163●, ◆162–3 (1)
Hagia Sofia *see* Santa Sofia.
Haile Selassie I (1892–1975) (r.1930–74) Emperor of Ethiopia, formerly Prince Ras Tafari. Driven out of Ethiopia by the Italian occupation of 1936–41, but led the reconquest, helped by Britain, and began to modernize Ethiopia. A revolution provoked by famine in 1974 deposed him and he died under house arrest. He is still revered by certain groups, notably the Rastafarians. ✤169●
Haiti
  independent state (1804) ✤85●
  slave revolt (1791) ✤85●, ✤89, ◆89 (3)
  US invasion ✤133●
Haj (*var.* Hajj). Pilgrimage to Mecca. Every adult Muslim is required to make the journey to the Islamic holy city of Mecca in Saudi Arabia at least once in his or her lifetime. The object of the pilgrimage is the Kaaba, the sacred shrine of Islam containing the 'black stone' in the middle of the great mosque.
  pilgrim routes to Mecca ◆218 (2)
Hajj *see* Haj
Hakataya culture *see* Patayan culture
Haldingham and Lafford 13th-century English mapmakers. ✤173●
Hallstatt, Iron Age (800 BCE) ✤31
Hamah, Syria, water wheel ❑57
Hammurabi, Babylonian king (1790–1750 BCE) ❑32
Han dynasty Ruling dynasty of China, successors to the Qin. The Former or Western Han (206 BCE–9 CE), with their capital at Chang'an, greatly expanded Chinese realms under emperor Wudi (140–87 BCE) The Later, or Eastern Han (25–220 CE), made their capital at Luoyang, during which Buddhism was introduced, and extended their domains into Central Asia, but their empire eventually collapsed under pressure from northern peoples. ✤46, ✤260, ◆42–3, ◆260 (1)
  architecture ✤260
  bronze bridle ❑260
  collapses ✤47, ✤261
  commanderies ✤260
  dynasty ✤260●
  tomb pottery ❑260
  trade links ◆44–5
Han Empire *see* Han dynasty.
Hangzhou, Song capital (1130) ✤63●
Hannibal (247–183 BCE). Carthaginian general who, in 218, invaded Roman Italy by marching his army (including elephants and cavalry) over the Alps. His initial campaigns were all successful, but he became pinned down in the south of Italy. He was eventually summoned to return to Africa, where he was defeated at Zama in 202. Hannibal fled to the court of Antiochus III, the Seleucid king of Syria. ❑179, ✤179●
Hanseatic League Trading association of north German and Baltic towns, which flourished between the13th and 15th centuries. Important members of the league included Lübeck, Cologne, Danzig, and Brunswick.
  trade routes (c.1300) ✤190, ◆190–1 (1) ◆189, ◆189 (3)
Hapsburg dynasty *see* Habsburg dynasty
Harald Hardrada (*var.* Haardraade) (1015–66) King of Norway. After fleeing Norway as a young man, he commanded the Varangian Guard in Constantinople, where he won a reputation as a fearsome warrior (Hardrada meant ruthless). On his return home, he first shared the kingdom with his nephew, then became sole ruler in 1048. In 1066, he claimed the throne of England but was defeated by Harold Godwinson, and killed at the battle of Stamford Bridge.
  ✤186, ◆186 (2)
Harappan culture The first urban communities of the Indian subcontinent developed c.2500 BCE in the Indus plain, with two major cities at Harappa and Mohenjo-Daro. Over 100 urban settlements are known, most of them major towns of baked brick buildings, dominated by citadels containing religious and ceremonial buildings. The Harappan cities had extensive trade links, reaching as far as southern Mesopotamia. The urban civilization ended c.2000 BCE; the reasons for its demise could be connected to Aryan invasion, or to changed environmental conditions disrupting Indus agriculture.
  BCE burials ✤19
  culture ✤23, ✤240, ✤240●, ❑240, ◆240 (1) (2)
  irrigation techniques (BCE) ✤23●
  pictograph writing ❑23
  trade (c.2500 BCE) ✤24●
  trading links (BCE) ✤24●, ✤25
  two-wheeled bullock cart ❑22
  urban civilization ✤23
Harding, Warren Gamaliel (1865–1923) 29th President of the US (Republican, 1921–23). On his election, Harding promised a return to normal life after WW I. His administration oversaw the completion of peace treaties with Germany, Austria and Hungary. However, the exposure of serious corruption by his Cabinet colleagues in 1923 (which became the so-called 'Teapot Dome' scandal) is thought to have contributed to his death. ✤134●
Hargreaves, James (c.1720–78). English inventor of the spinning jenny (c. 1764), the first practical application of multiple spinning by a machine, one of the major innovations of the Industrial Revolution. ✤204●
Harlem, race riots (1940s) ✤135●
Harold II (*var.* Harold Godwinson) (c.1022–66). *See* William I
Harris, Richard T. 19th-century explorer of Alaska.
  first gold strike in Alaska (1880) ✤93
Harrison, John (1693–1776). British clockmaker who made a clock accurate and reliable enough to be used to calculate longitude. ✤86
Hastings ⚔ of Norman invasion of England (1066). Victory of William, Duke of Normandy, over Harold, King of England.
  ✤62●, ◆186 (2)
Hastings, Warren (1732–1818). First Governor-General of India (1774–85). He instituted reforms in the system of revenue collection and civil courts. He was impeached on corruption charges, but finally acquitted in 1795. ❑248
Hatshepsut (*aka* Hatshopitu) (r.1472–1458 BCE). Pharaoh of Egypt.
  Deir el-Bahri temple ❑159
  Egyptian ruler ❑158
Hattin ⚔ of the Crusades (1187). Saladin defeats Christians of the Crusader States. ✤64●
Hattushash
  Hittite fortified citadel ✤27
  plan of city ✤28, ◆28 (3)
Hausa, city-states ✤163●
Hausaland, Usman dan Fodio's *jihad* (1804) ◆167
Havana, destruction of the *USS Maine* ❑133
Hawaii
  annexed by USA ✤284●
  settled by Polynesians ✤55, ✤60
  surfing ❑284
  united by Kamehameha I (1810) ✤91
Hawkins, Sir John (1532–95). English admiral who made three voyages to the New World (1562, 1564 and 1567), during which he made piratical attacks on Portuguese slavers, and forced the Spanish colonies to trade with him. From 1573 he became the principal administrative officer of the English navy. In 1588 he served as rear-admiral against the Spanish Armada and was knighted. He died, on an expedition with Sir Francis Drake, off the coast of Puerto Rico in 1595. ◆85 (2)
Hebrews ✤31
  See also Jews
Hedeby, Viking coin (9th century) ❑60
Hedin, Sven Anders von (1865–1952). Swedish explorer and geographer of uncharted regions of Central Asia, Tibet and China. ◆257 (3)
hegemony Leadership, or more specifically dominance, of one social group over another.
Hegira (*var.* Hijra). Muhammad's flight from Mecca to Medina (622) ✤55●
Heian Period (794–1185) Period of Japanese history that began with the transfer of the capital to Heian-kyo. ✤265●
Heijn, Piet *see* Heyn, Piet
Hejaz Mountainous plateau in western Saudi Arabia covering an area of some 388,500 sq km. It contains the holy cities of Islam, Mecca and Medina. ◆227 (4)
Hellenic age
  cities of W Asia ✤40
  culture ✤37
  empires and kingdoms ✤41●, ◆41 (2)
  outpost in the East ✤41, ❑41
henge Ritual monument, normally a circular space defined by an earthen bank with one or more entrances, with an internal ditch providing a symbolic separation between activities inside and outside the henge. Henges are sometimes further defined by arrangements of standing stones or menhirs, often precisely located along astronomical alignments. ✤22, ❑22, ✤174●
Hennepin, Father Louis (1640–c.1701) Belgian explorer. Sailed to Canada in 1675 as a Franciscan missionary. Explored the upper course of the Mississippi River with the Frenchman La Salle, but did not, as he claimed in a memoir of his travels, discover the river's mouth. ◆119 (2)
Henry II (1133–89) King of England (r.1154–89). French-born, he inherited the Duchy of Normandy from his mother and became Duke of Anjou on the death of his father, gaining Poitou and Guyenne on his marriage to Eleanor of Aquitaine. When he succeeded Stephen in 1154, he added England to his possessions. He extended the judicial and administrative power of the crown, but clashed with Thomas á Becket over his attempts to restrict church authority, and later with members of his own family. ✤187, ❑187, ◆187 (4)
  See also Angevin Empire
Henry V (1387–1422) King of England (r.1413–22). A skilful military leader, in 1415 he invaded France and defeated the French at Agincourt. By 1419 he had conquered Normandy, and was recognized as heir to the French throne. ◆192 (2)
Henry VIII (1491–1547) King of England (r.1509–1547). The Pope's refusal to annul his marriage to his first wife, Catherine of Aragon, because of her failure to produce male heirs, led to England's break with the Roman Catholic Church, and to Henry becoming supreme head of the Church in England. The dissolution of the monasteries followed. In 1536 he executed his second wife, Anne Boleyn for infidelity. Successive marriages were to Jane Seymour (died), Anne of Cleves (divorced), Catherine Howard (beheaded) and Catherine Parr (survived after Henry's death).
  Act of Supremacy (1534) ✤78●
  breaks with Rome (1534) ✤78●
  embraced Protestant religion ✤194
Henry II (1519–59) King of France (r.1547–59). His marriage to Catherine de Médicis produced three future kings of France. Dominated by his mistresses, Diane de Poitiers and Anne de Montmorency. Through the influence of the de Guise family he formed an alliance with Scotland, and declared war on England, which ended with the seizure of Calais in 1558. Continued wars against Emperor Charles V and Spain.
  ✤194, ✤194●
Henry IV (1050–1106). German Emperor (son of Henry III), who inherited the kingdoms of Germany, Italy, and Burgundy in 1056 under his mother's regency. His conflict with Pope Gregory VII over the investiture question led to his excommunication in 1075; in 1077, his public abasement at Canossa restored him to the Church. He appointed Clement III as anti-Pope in 1084 and was crowned emperor. Repeated conflict with the German nobles, eventually led by his younger son (Henry V), led to his forced abdication in 1105. ✤62●
Henry I (*aka* Henry the Fowler) King of Saxony (r.919–936). Henry was elected King of Germany, which he transformed into a viable state. His imperial ambitions were realized by his son Otto.
  ✤58, ✤185●
Henry the Navigator (*aka* Henry of Portugal) Founded school of navigation (1416). ✤156●
Hepthalites *see* Huns
Heracles (*var. Lat.* Hercules). Most popular demi-god of Greek pantheon, noted for his immense strength. ✤37, ❑37
Heraclius (c.572–642) East Roman Emperor. Proclaimed emperor in 610, He defeated the Persian armies that were threatening his empire and victory in the Tigris plain in 627 forced the Persians to make peace. In 629 Arab armies made their first incursion into Syria and, by 637, they had occupied Syria, Palestine and Egypt. Heraclius was ill and did little to confront the new threat. ✤55●
Herbert, Sir Thomas (1602–82) English traveller and author. In 1627 he embarked on a voyage to the Cape, Madagascar, Goa, and Surat, and made extensive journeys throughout Persia. He returned via Sri Lanka, the Coromandel coast and St. Helena. His service to the king in the Civil War was rewarded with a baronetcy at the Restoration (1660). He described his journeys, which included an account of the ruins of Persepolis, in his *Description of the Persian Monarchy* (1634). ◆219 (3)
Hercules *see* Heracles
Hereford 'T-in-O map' ❑173
Herjólfsson, Bjarni 10th-century Viking explorer, the first European to sight the New World. Icelandic sagas relate how, in c.985, Herjolfsson was blown off course from Greenland and sighted land to the west, the coast of Labrador. Some 15 years later, Leif Eriksson set sail from Greenland to investigate Herjolfsson's sightings. ◆118 (1)
Herod the Great (c.73–4 BCE). Herod's father served under Caesar in Egypt and appointed him ruler of Galilee. In 40 BCE Herod led the Roman army's expulsion of the Parthians from Jerusalem, became King of a Judaea loyal to Rome. ✤43●
Herodotus (c.484–420 BCE) Greek historian, writer and geographer, known as the 'Father of History'. He claimed to have made extensive journeys throughout the ancient world, but is best known for his history of the Persian Wars.
  African report (600 BCE) ✤156
heroin (*var.* Diacetylmorphine). Morphine derivative that makes up a large portion of the illicit traffic in narcotics. Morphine is an alkaloid found in opium, which is the dried milky exudate obtained from the unripe seedpods of the poppy plant. ◆113 (4)
Heyn, Piet (*var.* Heijn) (1577–1629) Dutch naval commander. As vice-admiral of the Dutch East India Company in 1624, he defeated the Spanish near San Salvador, Brazil and in 1626 off Bahia. His 1626 capture of the Spanish silver fleet let to his appointment as Admiral of Holland in 1629. ◆85 (2)
Hezbollah (*var.* Hizbullah, Hizbollah, 'Party of God'). The largest of the Shi'ite Islamic political groups in Lebanon. Under Iranian sponsorship, they have been associated with the kidnapping of Westerners and terrorist attacks to further their political aims, and have been in conflict with Israeli forces since Israel's invasion of Lebanon in 1982. ◆235 (4)
Hezhou, siege (1258–59) ❑69
Hidalgo, Father Miguel y Costilla (1753–1811). Mexican priest, celebrated as beginning the revolution against Spain which resulted in Mexican independence. He led a force of 80,000 against the Spanish before turning back at Mexico City in 1811. He was later executed. ❑89
Hieraconpolis, founded (c.3300) ✤24●, ◆159 (2)
hieratic writing ❑32
  See also writing
hieroglyphic Ancient system of writing using symbols or hieroglyphs, named from the Greek 'sacred carving'. They were originally pictographs, usually written right to left and giving three kinds of information: an object or concept in the real world; a consonant or sequence of consonants; or an explanation of an otherwise ambiguous associated symbol. The first evidence for hieroglyphs comes from c.3250 BCE and they continue in use into the late 3rd century CE. They mainly appear in religious and monumental contexts.
  Central American glyph ❑32
  Cretan ✤32●
  Egyptian ✤23●, ✤32, ✤32●, ◆32 (1), ◆223 (3)
  Harappa pictographs ❑23
  inscriptions ✤34
  Maya calendar ❑54
  Maya system ✤122
  pictographs (BCE) ✤23, ✤24●, ✤25, ✤32, ✤223, ❑25
  Rosetta stone ❑42
  tomb paintings ❑37
Hijra *see* Hegira
hillforts Earthwork monuments located on hilltops or high ground and comprising a central occupation area accessed through often complex 'gates' through the surrounding series of one or more banks and ditches. Built by Iron Age populations across western Europe, they acted as defensive centres when communities were under threat, and the scale of the earthworks was a declaration of the power and prestige of their builders. ✤174●
Himeji, Japanese fortified castle ❑267
Hind, Henry, 19th-century surveyor of the western US.
  US surveys (1857–58) ◆119 (3)
Hindenburg Line (*var.* the Siegfried Line). German fortified line of defence (named for Field Marshal Hindenburg) on the Western Front during WW I, to which German forces retreated following their initial thrust into France. The line remained unbroken until 1918. ◆206 (2) (3)
Hinduism The dominant religion in India that involves belief in destiny (Karma) and cycles of reincarnation (Samsara) and adheres to a particular moral law (Sharma). It is associated with a class system of social organization (caste) and includes ritual ceremonies, mystical contemplation and self-denying practices. All-embracing in its forms, capable of including extreme polytheism and high monotheism, animal sacrifice and refusal to take any form of life. Unique among world religions in having no single founder, but has grown over a period of 4000 years. The Vedas are accepted as the most sacred scriptures. ✤36, ✤43
  bronze deities ❑59, ❑241, ❑242
  establishment of cosmology ✤238, ❑48
  Puranic India ✤242, ◆242 (2)
  resurgence ✤243, ✤243●, ◆243 (4)
  spread (to 600 CE) ✤48●, ◆49 (4)
  statue of Surya ❑35
  trimurti ❑36
Hippalus 1st century CE Greek merchant who was the first westerner to recognize the regularity of the monsoon winds, harnessing them for his voyage through the Red Sea to the Indus from 14–37 CE.
  ◆218 (1)
Hipparchus (*var.* Hipparchos) (c.180–125 BCE). Greek astronomer and mathematician. He was the first to use latitude and longitude to define the position of places on the earth. ✤172
Hiroshima, atom bombs dropped (1945) ✤103●, ✤105●
Hispaniola
  Columbus lands (1492) ✤74●
  slave revolt (1522) ✤85●
History, The (Herodotus) ✤218
  See Herodotus
Hitler, Adolf (1889–1945). German dictator. Following service in the trenches in WW I, he became a political agitator during the Weimar period, building support for his National Socialist (Nazi) party, based on extreme nationalism, anti-Communism and racism. He became Chancellor in 1933, rapidly disposing of parliamentary constraints, and establishing dictatorship (as *Führer*, through the Enabling Law of 1933). Hitler transformed the German economy, by placing it on a war footing, and recovered pre-WW I territories, annexing Austria, and invading Poland (1939), to precipitate WW II. He adopted personal responsibility for the conduct of the war, and inaugurated the Final Solution against the Jews. He committed suicide as Soviet forces entered Berlin.
  annexation of Austria and Czechoslovakia, ◆209 (5)
  becomes Chancellor (1933) ✤102●, ✤209
  begins mass extermination of Jews (1942) ✤102●
  Nuremberg rally ❑102
  portrait ❑104
  Second World War, ◆210–11 (1)–(4)
Hittite Empire (*fl.*1450–1200 BCE). Indo-Europeans, who probably came from north of the Black Sea to settle in Anatolia and northern Syria, establishing their capital Hattushash near modern Boğazköy. After the indecisive battle of Kadesh against the Egyptians (c.1285 BCE) they established peace, but were overthrown c.1200.
  (1200 BCE) ✤31●
  (1250 BCE) ◆26–7
  conflict with Egypt ✤27
  gold figurine of a king (c.1400 BCE) ✤27●
Hizbollah *see* Hezbollah
Hizbullah *see* Hezbollah
Ho Chi Minh (1890–1969). Vietnamese statesman. In 1930 Ho Chi Minh founded the Indochina Communist Party. He became the leader of the Viet Minh guerrillas and at the end of WW II established a government in Hanoi. When the French tried to regain control of their former colony, he led the resistance that forced them to withdraw from the north. President of North Vietnam from 1954, he successfully countered American intervention in Vietnam in the 1960s. When the Vietnam War ended with the fall of Saigon in 1975, it was renamed Ho Chi Minh city in his honour.
  proclaims independent Vietnam (1945) ✤103●
Hobkirk's Hill ⚔ of American Revolutionary War (25 Apr 1781). American victory. ◆127 (3)
Hohenlinden ⚔ of Napoleonic Wars – the War of the 2nd Coalition (1800). French victory forced Austrians to sue for peace.◆200 (1)
Hohenstaufen dynasty (*var.* Staufer dynasty). German dynasty that ruled the Holy Roman Empire from 1138 to 1208 and from 1212 to 1254.
  dynasty ✤188, ◆188 (1)
  and the papacy ✤188●
Hohokam Native-American people of the US southwest.
  ✤58, ✤123, ◆123 (4)
Hojo Japanese family of warrior regents which dominated Japan in the 13th century, especially during the Mongol invasions of Japan in 1274 and 1281. ◆265 (5)
Hollywood
  annual consumer expenditure (1919–45) ❑135
  film industry (1919) ✤135, ❑135, ◆135 (4)
Holocaust Name given to persecution of the Europe's Jews by Nazi Germany from 1933–45, which led ultimately to the deaths of about six million Jews.
  cause of Jewish migration ✤234
Holy Land Latin states (1099–1229) ✤65, ◆65 (3)
Holy Roman Empire Complex of European territories under the rule of the Frankish or German king who bore the title of Roman emperor, founded by Charlemagne in 800. After Charlemagne, imperial power was at its greatest under the Hohenstaufens in the 12th–13th centuries. It was dissolved by Napoleon in 1806.
  800–1000 ◆185 (3)
  1100–1400 ◆189 (3), ◆189 (4)
  1200 ◆62–3, ◆187 (3)
  1300 ◆66–7
  1400 ◆70–1
  1500 ◆74–5
  1600 ◆78–9
  1700 ◆82–3
  1800 ◆86–7
  ✤184–5, ◆185 (3)
  abolished (1806) ✤202●
  Baltic conflict (16th century) ✤195, ✤195●, ◆195 (3)
  conflict in Bohemia ✤192, ◆193 (4)
  Crusades (1096–1270) ◆64–5 (2), ◆186 (1)
  Dutch revolt (1568–1609) ✤195, ✤195●, ◆195 (5)
  population growth (1650–1800) ❑198
  Treaty of Westphalia, ◆196 (1)
Homer (*var. Gk.* Homeros). 9th century BCE Greek poet, credited with writing the greatest early Greek poems, including *The Iliad* and *The Odyssey*. His work formalized the long oral traditions of recounting the stories and legends of ancient Greece. ✤37

Key to index: ✤ text ● timeline ❑ picture ◆ map *var.* variant name *aka* also known as *f/n* full name *prev.* previously known as r. ruled ⚔ battle WW I First World War WW II Second World War

Homo Term used for creatures belonging to the same group as modern humans. The earliest known homo is *Homo habilis*, which evolved about 2.5 million years ago.
❖12–13, ❑13, ◆13 (2)
Homo erectus ('upright man', c.1.6 million to 300,000 years ago and in some regions perhaps to 50,000 years ago). Species found in many regions of Asia, thought to have evolved there from *Homo ergaster*. By 500,000 years ago they had mastered the use of fire. ❖12–13, ◆13 (2)
Homo ergaster (c.1.8 million ago to perhaps 200,000 years ago). Species that appeared in Africa, distinguished by large brain size, tall, long-legged physique, and tool-making skills, including the invention of the hand-axe. ❖12–13, ❑13, ◆13 (2)
Homo habilis ('handy man', c.2.5 to 1.6 million years ago), so called because of its stone tool-making abilities. *H. habilis* was the earliest member of the genus *Homo*, with a brain capacity about half the size of modern humans', but about 50% larger than any Australopithecine. ❖12–13, ❑13, ◆13 (2)
Homo heidelbergensis (c.800,000 to c.200,000 years ago). Species probably descended from *Homo ergaster*, the first human inhabitants of Europe, formerly confusingly known as archaic *Homo sapiens*. The earliest fossils, found at Atapuerca in Spain, are sometimes attributed to a separate species, *Homo antecessor*. ◆13 (2)
Homo sapiens sapiens (c.150,000 years ago). First appearing in Africa, the earliest anatomically modern humans used their hunting skills, adaptability and innovative tool-making abilities to colonize the rest of the globe, reaching the southern tip of S America by c.12,000 BCE. They demonstrate the capacity for abstract thought, revealed in evidence of rituals and finds of rock art, dating back 45,000 years. ❖12–13, ❑13, ◆13 (2)
Honduras Contra guerrillas ❑139
honey Commercial Africa (19th century) ◆166 (1)
Hong Kong
ceded to British (1842) ❖91
returned to Chinese rule (1997) ❖111●
Hong Xiuquan (*var.* Hung Hsui-ch'uan, 1814–64) *see* Taiping Rebellion
Honshu Gyogi-style map ❑256
Hoover, Herbert Clark (1874–1964) 31st President of the US (Republican, 1929–33). Rose to prominence during WW I for his successful administration of relief activities. His Presidency was immediately struck by the Wall Street Crash and the subsequent Great Depression. Though he did institute some relief efforts, he lacked a 'common touch' and rapidly lost public support, resulting in his defeat by Franklin D. Roosevelt in his 1933 re-election bid. ❖134●, ❖135
Hopewell culture Based in the Scioto River Valley in present-day Ohio, between c.500 BCE and 400 CE. The Hopewell had a rich burial tradition and are known for their conical burial mounds and associated geometric ceremonial earthworks which include the largest burial mound in the US. The best known is the Great Serpent Mound in Ohio, which is 213 m long. The Hopewell are also renowned for their sculptures, often of animals and birds. ❖38●, ❖46●, ◆36 (1)
grave offering ❑120
moundbuilders ◆121–4
platform effigy pipe ❑121
trading empire ❖123
trading resources ◆121 (4)
Hormuz, Marco Polo visit (1292) ❖68●
horses
BCE domestication ❖258●
Chinese cavalry horse ❑44, ❑55
Eurasian and African trade (c.1 CE) ◆44–5
horse and trap, Han grave goods ❑47
invention of stirrup ❖51
lion attacks hunter ❑51
Mongol cavalryman ❑69
steppe warriors' skills ❑261
Hospital of St. John of Jerusalem *see* Knights Hospitallers
housing
BCE mud-brick ❖19
first Chinese cities ❖258●
Hsia dynasty *see* Xia dynasty
Hsin dynasty *see* Xin dynasty.
Hsuan-tsang *see* Xuan Zang
Hsiung-nu *see* Xiongnu
Huancavelica Mercury mine ❖148
Huari (c.500–800). Andean state, based in the Ayacucho basin. Militaristic expansion was facilitated by the construction of major trunk roads, interspersed with military barracks. The general populace laboured on public works as a form of taxation.
emergence (c.600) ❖54●, ❖145
empire ◆146 (1)
hand mirror ❑146
Huayna Capac (r.1493–1525). Sapa Inca who ascended to the royal throne in 1493 after a dynastic struggle for succession. He extended the northern boundary of the Inca Empire to the Ancasmayo River, before dying in an epidemic (which may have been spread by Spanish colonists). His death was followed by another struggle for succession, which was still unresolved when the Spanish arrived in 1532; within three years the Inca empire was lost. ❖74●, ❖78● ◆147 (3) ❖147●
Hudson, Henry (c.1565–1611). English navigator. Appointed by Muscovy Company to find Northwest Passage to Asia, in 1608 he sailed along the coast of Greenland as far as Spitzbergen. In 1609, sponsored by the Dutch East India Company, he attempted to find an eastern route but changed course and sailed to N America where he explored Chesapeake and Delaware Bays. On his last expedition, in 1610, he sailed into the great bay which bears his name and south into James Bay. ◆118 (1), ◆286 (1)
Hudson's Bay Company Set up in 1670 to occupy the land around Hudson Bay, and engage in trade, primarily the fur trade. Controlled the fur trade in Canada for nearly two centuries until it lost its charter in 1869. ❑126
Huerta, Victoriano (1854–1916). Mexican dictator. A general in the Mexican army, Huerta was allied with the liberal president Francisco Madero at the start of the Mexican Revolution in 1910, successfully suppressing armed dissent by Zapata and others. In 1913 he overthrew Madero's regime, violently suppressing dissent. He was forced into exile when the US government withdrew its support. ❖133, ◆133
Huitzilopochtli
Aztec temple ❑124
inauguration of pyramid temple (1487) ❖74●
sun god receives human sacrifice ❑74
Hülegü (c.1217–65). Mongol leader. Founder of the Il-Khanate after the sack of Baghdad in 1258.
death ❖67●
fall of Abbasid Caliphate (1258) ❖67●, ❖69
founds Il-Khanate (1258) ❖67●, ❖229, ◆229 (3)
invades Syria (1260) ❖69●
sacks Baghdad (1258) ❖67, ❖69●, ❖229, ❑229
human beings
emergence of modern humans ❖13, ◆13 (2)
hominid ancestors ❖12, ❖12●, ◆12 (1)
sacrifice
Aztec ❑74
Shang dynasty ❖29, ❖259
Tula (Mexico) (987) ❖58●
settlement (BCE) ❖14–15, ◆14–15
Humboldt, Alexander von (1769–1859). Prussian natural scientist, who made a notable journey to S America in 1799–1804. ❑143, ❖143, ◆143 (3)
Huna *see* Huns
Hundred Years' War (1337–1453). Struggle between England and France in the 14th–15th centuries over a series of disputes, stemming from Edward III's claim to the French throne. Notable English victories at Crécy (1346), Poitiers (1356) and Agincourt (1415) in the end mounted to nothing and the by 1455 the English crown had lost all its French possessions except Calais. ❖192●, ◆192 (1) (2), ❑192
Hungarian Revolt (1956). Demands by students for the withdrawal of Soviet troops led to mass demonstrations. When the deposed Imre Nagy was reinstated as premier, he announced that Hungary was leaving the Warsaw Pact. Soviet forces moved in to crush the revolt, killing 25,000 people. Nagy was executed following a show trial in 1958. ❖108●
Hungary 185–215
800–1000 ◆185 (3)
end of Communism (1989) ❖110●
foreign affairs, Magyar expansion ❖58●, ❖185●
home affairs
assimilated into Europe (11th century) ❖62
Avars establish state (c.500) ❖54●
Christian state (c.1000) ❖62●
Communist takeover (1948) ❖102●
growth ❖193, ◆209 (5)
Mongol invasion ❖69, ❖193
Soviet-sponsored regime (1948) ❖108●
Soviets crush uprising (1956) ❖108●
Warsaw Pact crushes revolt (1956) ❖106●
WW II, mobilization and casualty figures ❖105
Hung Hsui-ch'uan *see* Hong Xiuquan
Hung-wu *see* Zhu Yuanzhang
Huns (*var.* Huna, Hephthalites, White Huns) Coalition of steppe cavalry who moved east across C Asia in the late 4th century CE. The Black Huns under Attila invaded the Roman Empire in mid-5th century, but were defeated at the Catalaunian Fields in Gaul (451), thereafter breaking up. The Huna (White Huns or Hephthalites) invaded Gupta India (480 CE) and Sassanian Persia (484 CE). *See also* Xiongnu.
Empire (450) ◆50–1
enter Europe ❖44●
migrations and invasions (300–500 CE) ◆52–3 (1)
hunter-gatherers (*aka* foragers or band societies). Communities living on a combination of hunting animals and gathering food. At the start of the Mesolithic period the global population lived this way; amongst the tiny percentage of the world's population who do so today, men hunt exclusively and women gather. ❖18–20, ❖30, ❖258, ◆22–3, ◆26–7
African ◆158 (1), ◆162 (1)
cave images ❑120
N American ❖120
N and E Asia ❖254
S America 144–5
hunting
BCE big-game ❖18
Clovis-pointed spearheads ❑14, ❖15●, ❖120
mythical combat (BCE) ❑39
Hunyadi, János (c.1387–1456). Hungarian national hero. Won a series of victories against the Turks, but was defeated at Varna (1444). Regent of Hungary (1446–52). Victory at Belgrade (1456) checked Turkish invasion of Hungary for 70 years. ❖193, ◆193 (4)
Huron North American Indian people from the St. Lawrence River region, who gave French expeditions, led by Cartier and Champlain (1543, 1603), a friendly reception. At the end of the 16th century, the Iroquois drove many Huron westward into Ontario, where they formed a confederacy with a number of other tribes. In 1648–50 Iroquois invasions broke up the confederacy, leading to the death of many thousands of Hurons. ❖126●, ◆126 (1)
Hus, Jan (*var.* John Huss) (c.1369–1415). Bohemian religious reformer. His preaching against clerical privilege led to his excommunication (1411). In 1413 he published his main work, *De Ecclesia*. Tried and condemned for heresy. His death by burning provoked the Hussite Wars. ❖192, ❖192●
Husaynid dynasty Ruling dynasty of Tunisia from 1705 until the foundation of the Republic of Tunisia in 1957. ❖87●
Husky Code name for the Allied invasion of Sicily in Jul 1943 during WW II. ◆211 (4)
Huss, John *see* Hus, Jan
Hussein, Saddam (1937–) Iraqi dictator. Joined the Arab Ba'ath Socialist Party in 1957. He played a leading role in the 1968 revolution which ousted the civilian government and established a Revolutionary Command Council (RCC). In 1979 he became President of Iraq. His attack on Iran in 1980 led to a war of attrition which lasted eight years. His invasion of Kuwait in Aug 1990 plunged Iraq into another full-scale war. Iraq lost the war, was forced to retreat from Kuwait and suffered from heavy economic sanctions imposed by the UN. In 2003 an American-led coalition invaded Iraq on the pretext that Saddam was harbouring weapons of mass destruction. Saddam was deposed, captured and imprisoned.
See Iran-Iraq War; Gulf War.
campaign against Kurds ❖235
conflict in the Gulf ◆235 (5)
depicted in posters ❑235
Iraq War ◆235 (5)
Hussites Followers of the Bohemian religious reformer Jan Hus.
Bohemian civil war ❑192
Hutu (*var.* Bahutu, Wahutu). Bantu-speaking people of Rwanda and Burundi.
massacre in Rwanda (1994) ❖111●, ❖169, ◆169 (5)
Hyksos After the Middle Kingdom in Egypt the Hyksos, or 'Shepherd Kings', founded the 15th Dynasty, c.1670 BCE. They were nomads from the deserts of Palestine, who ruled Lower and parts of Upper Egypt until c.1550 BCE. Although credited with the introduction of the horse and chariot, in most other areas they appear to have deferred to native Egyptian culture.
rulers of Egypt (1633 BCE) ❖27●, ◆159 (4)

I

I dynasty *see* Yi dynasty
Ibarro, Francisco de 16th-century Spanish governor of the Mexican province of Nuevo Viscaya. The city of Durango, founded under his direction in 1563, was named after a city in his native province of Spain. ❖125, ◆125 (4)
Iberia
❖42
bust of Lady of Elche ❑177
captured by Visigoths ❖53, ❖182
Christian kingdoms regained from Muslims ❖65
Sueves establish kingdom (c.411) ❖52●
Ibn Al-mansur Al-'Abbas *see* Harun al-Rashid
Ibn Battuta (*var.* Muhammad Ibn Abdullah) (1304–68). Muslim traveller and writer. Leaving Tangier in 1325 he travelled along the north coast of Africa to Egypt, then north to Damascus. After a pilgrimage to Mecca, he undertook several journeys in Africa and W Asia, then travelled east along the Silk Road to Delhi, and from there to Sumatra and China.
14th century Islamic explorer ◆218 (2), ◆239 (1)
first pilgrimage to Mecca (1325) ❖68●
route (1325–1345) ◆68 (2)
serves as judge in Delhi (1334–41) ❖68●
travels in Africa ❖71●, ◆156 (3)
visits SE Asia and China (1335–46) ❖68●
voyage to E Africa (1331) ❖71●
Ibn Muhammad al-Mahdi *see* Harun al-Rashid
Ibn Saud *see* Saud, Abd al-Aziz ibn
Ibn Tughluq, Muhammad
Empire (1335) ❖244, ◆70–1, ◆244 (3)
mausoleum (1321) ❑71
Sultanate of Delhi (1320) ❖71●
See also Tughluqs
Ibn Tulun, Ahmad (r.868–883). The stepson of a Turkish general, who was given the fiefdom of Egypt in 868, he was sent to Egypt by his stepfather as lieutenant. Between 868 and 875 he built up a substantial power base in Egypt, founding a new city outside Cairo, embarking on a massive building programme and, in 875, refusing to send tribute to Baghdad. In 878 Ibn Tulun obtained the submission of the chief cities of Syria, leading to open rupture with the Caliph of Baghdad and the founding of the Tulunid dynasty. ❖58●
ICBM *see* Intercontinental Ballistic Missile
Ice Age Period of extreme cold in the earth's history. Effects of the last Ice Age include falls in sea levels, which occurred when water was locked in glaciers and the creation of land bridges, which helped humans and animals to colonize new parts of the globe. The last Ice Age reached its peak about 20,000 years ago, and ended about 10,000 years ago. ◆114–5, ◆140–1, ◆154–5, ◆170–1, ◆216–7, ◆236–7, ◆254–5, ◆276–7
Australian rock art ❖17, ◆17 (5)
cave paintings ❑17
coldest phase (27,000 BP) ❖16●
effect on N America ◆116–17
in Europe ❑171, ❖170
hand paintings ❑17
ice sheets ❖14, ❖18●, ❖120●
painted caves and rock art ❖17, ◆17 (3)
palaeolithic art ❖17, ◆17 (2)
portable art ❑17
rock engravings (petroglyphs) ❑17
Venus figurines in Europe ❖17, ◆17 (4)
Iceland
settled by Vikings (960 CE) ❖60●
Viking discovery ❖172, ◆172 (2)
I-ching *see* Yijing
Idrisi, ash Sharif al- (*var.* Abu Abd Allah Muhammad al) (c.1099–1165). Arab geographer born in Spain. After travelling in Spain, N Africa and Asia Minor, in c.1148 he joined the court of Roger II of Sicily. There he collated surveys of the known world, incorporating them into *The Book of Roger*, completed in 1154. He also compiled a seventy-part world map.
Moroccan geographer ❖156, ❖218
W Asian map (c.1154) ❑218
world map ❑62
Ieyasu *see* Tokugawa Ieyasu
Ifriqiya (*var.* Libya). Fatimids lose control (1048) ❖63●
Igbo Ukwu A small kingdom in the forests of southern Nigeria (8th–9th centuries CE). Evidence from burials indicate that the peoples of Igbo Ukwu were connected with the long-distance trade networks of the Sahara and Sahel. Carnelian, found in the burial of a dignitary, may even have come from Persia or India. Bronzes, believed to be the burial objects of a religious leader or ruler, indicate that metal-working had developed to a fine art. ❖58●
Ignatius Loyola, St. Founder of Jesuits ❑194
See also Jesuits
Il-Khanate (1256–1353) Mongol dynasty founded by Hülegü, who seized Persia in 1258 and captured Baghdad. Contact with the Mongol rulers of China was lost after the Il-Khan Ghazan (1255–1304) converted to Sunni Islam; conflict between Sunnis and Shi'a fatally weakened the dynasty.
founded by Hülegü ❖67●, ❖229, ◆229 (3)
converts to Islam (1295) ❖67●
Mamluk Sultanate ◆229 (4)
Ikhnaton *see* Akhenaten
Illinois River Explored by Jolliet and Marquette (1673) ❖119●
Imhotep (*fl.* 2680 BCE) Egyptian chancellor, architect, writer, physician, and high priest of the sun god in Heliopolis during the reign of Zoser (3rd Dynasty). He was the architect of the Step pyramid at Saqqara; his innovative genius was to translate building techniques which had hitherto only been used on wooden structures into quarried stone. He was deified during Ptolemaic times. ❑25
imperialism
cartoon, Germany preying on Africa (1890) ❑96
in Africa (1880–1920) ❖96, ❖96●, ❑96, ◆96 (1)
movements against colonial rule ❖97, ◆97 (4)
Pacific ◆284 (1)
in SE Asia ❖97, ❖97●, ◆97 (3)
the struggle for South Africa ❖96, ❖96●, ❑96, ◆96 (2)
Western (1879–1920) ❖96–7
Inca Empire (c.1470–1532). Empire which became the preeminent state in S America from c.1470, when it began to conquer neighbouring peoples, to 1532 when it fell into the hands of Spanish *conquistadores*. Following Andean tradition, the Inca Empire was expanded by military conquest, ruled by the Sapa Inca (believed to descend from the Sun God). It was a strictly hierarchical society, dependent on the mass organization of labour, for the construction of roads, towns, mining and agriculture. It had no writing system, and its administration was entirely dependent on an arithmetic system. ❖147●, ◆76 (2), ◆147 (3)
Andean valley settled ❖62
calculating device ❑147
conquered by Pizarro ❖78, ❖81●, ❖148, ◆148 (1)
gold llama ❑148
imperial expansion ❖74
Machu Picchu sacred shrine ❑74
settlements ❖62●, ❑74
statuettes ❑147
Inca Yupanqui *see* Topa
India
BCE plant domestication ❖19
conflict
Amritsar massacre (1919) ❖99●
Anglo-Maratha war (1775) ❖87●
British control ❖94, ❖103●
Chola domination ❖59●, ❖244, ◆244 (2)
domination by Gurjara-Pratiharas (c.900) ❖59●
independence struggle ❖250, ❖250●, ◆250 (1)
Kashmir sovereignty (1965) 107●
Mahmud of Ghazni (997) ❖59●
nationalist agitation (1904, 1919) ❖99●
partition (1947) ❖103●, ❖252, ◆252 (2)
Persian raids (18th century) ❖87
Revolt (Indian Mutiny) ❖95●, ❖249, ❖249●, ❑249, ◆249 (3)
settled by Aryans (BCE) ❖35
home affairs
All-India Muslim League founded (1906) ❖99●
city poverty ❑253
first Indian general election (1952) ❖107●
medieval states ❖244, ❖244●, ◆244 (2)
survey ❖239, ❖239●, ❑239
See also Indian National Congress
religion
❖242–3, ❖242●, ❖243●, ◆36 (1), ◆242 (1) (2) (3)
See also Buddhism; Hinduism; Jainism
trade and industry
politics of cotton ❖93, ❑93, ❑249, ◆93 (5)
economy (1857) ❖249, ◆249 (4)
Victoria, Empress of India (1876) ❖95●
Second World War *see* Wars, Second World
Indian Mutiny *see* **Indian Revolt**
Indian National Congress Founded in 1885, the party was transformed into a mass movement for Indian independence by Mohandas K. (Mahatma) Gandhi who instituted mass non-cooperation movements during the 1930s.
founded (1885) ❖95●, ❖250
controlled by Gandhi (1920) ❖99●
leaders arrested (1942) ❖103●
wins general election (1952) ❖107●
Indian Ocean
Arab traders c.1000 CE ❖61, ◆61 (3)
trade (15th–16th centuries) ❖230, ◆230 (2)
trade network (13th century) ❖66
trade route (c.1 CE) ◆44–5
Zheng He's voyages begin (1405) ❖75●, ◆167 (3)
Indian Removal Act (28 May, 1830). Act authorizing the granting of western territory to Indian tribes of E and SE USA in exchange for their lands which fell within state borders, in order to provide new lands for white settlers. Though a number of northern tribes relocated peacefully, a number of the SE groups put up substantial resistance to their removal from their settled farms to unknown western territory. ❖128●, ◆128–9 (2)
Indian Revolt (*var.* the Indian Mutiny) (1857–59). The revolt of 1857–59 was the result of disaffection within the ranks of the Bengal army, combined with an attempt by nobles and great landowners to throw off the imperial yoke. The Mutiny started with the seizure of Delhi by rebels (May 1857). The city was subsequently recaptured in September. The massacre of British evacuees at Cawnpore (27 Jun 1857) raised a storm of anger. The British re-taking of Lucknow (22 Mar 1858) after a protracted siege was a decisive turning-point. A campaign in central India (Feb–Jun 1858) effectively put an end to the Mutiny, although it continued to smoulder for many months. In 1858, the government of India was transferred from the East India Company to the British crown. ❖249, ◆249 (3)
Indies, Council of (*var.* Consejo de Indias). Supreme governing body of Spain's territories in America (1524–1834) which was responsible for all legislation governing the colonies in the king's name. ❖81
See also Council of Castile
Indo-China
decolonization ◆251 (4)
foreign imperialism ◆269 (4)
French control ❖97
seized by Japan (1942) ❖103●
Vietnam War ◆251 (5)
Indo-Greek culture *see* Gandhara
Indo-Pakistan Wars In 1948, war broke out between India and Pakistan over the Muslim-majority state of Kashmir, whose Hindu ruler had ceded to India. In 1949 the UN negotiated a ceasefire which effectively divided Kashmir between the two countries, but left the issue unresolved. In Aug 1965 war once again broke out, when the Indian army repelled Pakistan's forces and launched a counterattack. Soviet mediation led to the conclusion of a peace treaty at Tashkent (Jan 1966). Kashmir remains a major flashpoint between India and Pakistan. ❖252●, ◆252 (2)
Indonesia
economic crisis (1998) ❖111●
Independence (1949) ❖103●, ❖251●
occupies Timor (1975) ❖111●, ❑253
secessionist movements ◆253 (4)
seized by Japan (1942) ❖103●
urbanization ◆253 (5)
Indravarman I Khmer king ❖59●
Indus Valley civilization *see* Harappan culture
Industrial Revolution The transition from a primarily agricultural to an industrial economy, which had begun in Great Britain by 1750, with the striking expansion and greater efficiency of certain key industries: textiles and mining. In the late 18th century, a series of inventions and innovations, notably the steam engine, greatly increased output, and small workshops began to be replaced by large factories. Industrialization soon spread to other parts of

Europe, especially areas, such as northern France and the Ruhr valley, with extensive coal deposits, and to the US, which by 1890, thanks to rich natural resources, a growing population, and technological innovations had become the world's leading industrial nation. 204–5
economic boom ✣90
factors leading to ✣86
impact (1870–1914) ✣92
in Britain (1770–1870) ✣204–5, ❑205, ◆204 (1)
in Europe ◆205 (4)
location of manufacturing industry ◆92 (1)
steam power ❑204
technological advances ✣204●
trade unionism ✣205
US most powerful nation (1925) ✣98

Innocent III (*prev. It.* Lotario de'Conti di Segni) (1160–1216). Pope (r.1198–1216). His pontificate saw the apogee of medieval papal power, the Latin conquest of Constantinople in the Fourth Crusade, and the legitimization of itinerant preaching and apostolic poverty. ❑188

Intercontinental Ballistic Missile (ICBM). Key land and/or submarine-launched deterrent weapon initially developed by the Western Allies (early 1960s) during the Cold War, but built in proliferation by both Western and Eastern bloc superpowers by 1970s. ✣109

Internet International computer network. Initially set up to link universities and other educational institutions, in the 1980s it became a world-wide information network, used increasingly in business as both a sales and a communications channel. ✣113

Inuit Inupiaq-speaking peoples native to the far north of Canada, with an ancient hunting and gathering culture stretching back to perhaps 30,000 years ago. ✣123●
migration routes (1000–1500) ◆123 (3)
walrus ivory knife ❑123

inventions
Archimedean screw ❑38
astrolabe, Greek navigational aid ✣238, ❑218
and the economic revolution ✣92●
boxed compass (13th century) ❑67
bronze casting ✣22, ✣31●, ❑27
bronze coins ❑34, ❑259
horizontal loom ❑190
industrial revolution ✣204●
introduced by missionaries (16th century) ✣80
lodestone compass (c.250) ✣256●
metal stirrups ❑51
Marconi's radio technology (1894) ❑98
movable type printing (c.1045) ✣63●
mummification ❑31
paper (105 CE) ✣46
paper money ✣59●, ✣263
papyrus ❑30
potter's wheel (c.3000) ✣22
ship's chronometer (1762) ✣86
telephone (1876) ✣95
timber and brushwood dyke ❑83
wind power ✣63
writing paper ❑46
See also optical instruments, telecommunications

Ipsus ⚔ (301 BCE). Antigonus defeated by Seleucus and Lysimachus. ◆224 (1)

Iran-Iraq War (1980–88). Conflict between Iran and Iraq caused by a dispute over territory, and Iraq's fear of Iranian provocation of its own Shi'ite population following Iran's Islamic Revolution in 1979. In 1980, Iraq invaded Iran. By the time the war reached an inconclusive end, an estimated half a million lives had been lost on both sides. ✣111●, ◆235 (5)

Iran
Anglo-Persian Oil Company founded ✣234●
fundamentalism ✣111
hostage crisis ✣138●
Islamic revolution (1979) ✣111●
proclamation of Islamic republic ✣235●
resurgence of Shi'ite faith ✣235
trading links (BCE) ✣25
US intervention (1955) ✣138●

Iraq
British mandate ✣233
Gulf War ◆235 (5), ✣235●
Iran-Iraq War (1980–88) ✣111●, ◆235 (5), ✣235●
Iraq War (2003–) ◆235 (5)
Kuwait invasion (1990) ✣111●, ◆235 (5)
oil discovered ✣234●
Six Day War (1967) ✣107●

Ireland
c.1100–1300 ◆188 (2)
famine and emigration (1845) ✣90●, ✣100●
invaded by Edward Bruce ◆188 (2)
migrations and invasions (300–500 CE) ◆52–3 (1)
Viking raids ✣58, ✣60●

Irish famine (1845–51) Period of famine and unrest in Ireland caused by the failure in 1845 of the potato crop, Ireland's staple food. An estimated one million people died of starvation and another million emigrated to America and elsewhere.
famine and emigration (1845) ✣90●, ✣100●

Irish Free State From 1921, when Ireland was partitioned and the south gained dominion status, it was known as the Irish Free State. In 1937 it became a sovereign state as Eire and gained full independence in 1949 as the Republic of Ireland. ◆208 (1)

iron
BCE ✣30–1, ✣34, ✣35●, ✣38, ✣39●
development of African ✣160●
Nielsen hot blast process (1824) ❑90
Nok culture ✣160, ◆160 (1)

Iron Age The final prehistoric period in the Old World, used to denote (from c.1000 BCE) societies which used iron. In general, the Iron Age followed the Bronze Age, but in some parts of the Old World, for example, Africa, the transition was made from Stone Age to Iron Age, without the intervening Copper and Bronze Ages. ✣31●, ✣158●
in Africa ◆158 (1)

Iron Curtain Political, military, and ideological barrier, of the post World War II period, between the Soviet Union and its eastern European allies; and the West and other non-Communist areas. ✣108●, ✣213●, ◆213 (1) (2)

Iroquois In 1570, five nations of Native American peoples, the Mohawk, Oneida, Seneca, Onondaga, Cayuga, joined to form a confederacy know as the Iroquois. They were later joined by the Tuscarora. The Iroquois were an important influence in early colonial America, and the French, in particular, made alliances with them. The confederacy was split after the American Revolutionary War, when those groups which had supported the loyalist cause (the Cayugas, Senecas and Mohawks) migrated to Canada. ◆126 (1)
alliance with British (1690) ✣126●
de Champlain's exploration of the St. Lawrence ✣119
destroy Huron (1648–51) ✣126●
fortress attacked by de Champlain ❑82
war with Algonquin (1609) ✣126●

irrigation
Archimedean screw ❑38
BCE crop yields ✣18–19
earliest system (5500 BCE) ✣20●
global technologies (c.1500) ◆76–7 (1)
Indus Valley techniques (BCE) ✣23●
N American (c.800) ✣58
water wheel at Hamah, Syria ❑57

Isabella of Castile (1451–1504). *See* Ferdinand of Aragon
marries Ferdinand of Aragon (1469) ✣75●, ✣192●

Isandhlwana ⚔ of Zulu wars (1879). Zulus inflicted severe defeat on British.◆96 (2), ◆166 (1)

Isfahan Safavid capital (1587) ✣79●, ✣231●

Isfahani, Sadiq Encyclopedic work ❑238

Isidore of Seville (c.570–636) Spanish historian and encylopedist. He became archbishop of Seville in 609. Confronted by barbarian invasions, he dedicated himself to the preservation of Greek and Roman culture. His great work, the *Originum sive etymologiarum libri* (622–633) is a tribute to his extensive scholarship in the liberal arts, theology, the sciences and political theory. ✣173●

Islam The religion of the Muslims, founded by the prophet Muhammad (c.570–632). It teaches that there is only one God (Allah), and that Muhammad is his prophet. The Koran (Qu'ran) is the sacred book of Islam, believed to be the words of God dictated to Muhammad, through the medium of the angel Gabriel. 56–7, 226–7
800–1000 ◆185 (3)
era begins ✣54, ✣55●, ✣226, ◆226 (2)
Africa
new states ✣162–3, ✣162●, ◆162 (1)
reform in W Africa (19th century) ✣167
W African *jihad* ✣167●, ◆167 (3)
Asia
nationalism ✣275, ◆275 (5)
in SE Asia ✣243, ✣243●, ◆243 (6)
in W Asia ✣218
campaigns
invasion of Spain (711) ✣54●, ✣55●
victories against Crusaders ◆64–5 (2)
and Christianity (c.1090) ◆65 (1)
conversions
Il-Khan Ghazan (1295) ✣67●
Malacca (1445) ✣75●
Mongol Golden Horde ✣67
defeats, fall of Edessa (1144) ✣63●
Dome of the Rock shrine built in Jerusalem (692) ❑55
exploration and mapping
journeys of Ibn Battuta (1325–46) ◆218 (2)
Africa ✣42, ✣47, ◆218 (1)
fundamentalism ✣111, ✣235●
jihads ✣167●, ✣226, ◆167 (3)
resurgence of Shi'ite faith ✣235
growth
7th century ✣56–7, ✣57●, ◆184 (2)
impact ✣56–7, ✣57●
imprint (1000–1200) ✣57, ◆57 (2)
of Islamic world ❑57, ◆56–7 (1)
in the modern world ◆235 (4)
Muslim world (c.1500) ◆76 (3)
pan-Islamic world ✣113, ◆113 (3)
spread of Islam ✣56, ✣56●, ✣59●, ✣226, ✣226●, ◆226 (3)
the *Hegira* (622) ✣226, ◆226 (2)
religious map of Europe (1590) ◆194 (2)
trade ✣61, ✣66
See also Fatimids; Mongol Empire; Ottoman Empire

Ismail I (c.1487–1524) Shah of Persia and founder of the Shi'ite Safavid dynasty (1499). A revered national figure, regarded as both saint and Shah, he was a formidable warrior. In 1510, he defeated the Uzbeks who had been making regular incursions into Khurasan. In 1514, he was confronted by the forces of the Turkish sultan, Selim, who annexed Tabriz. ✣234, ◆235 (3)

Isonzo ⚔ of WW I (1915–17) Series of 12 battles which took place between Austria and Italy along the Isonzo River on the eastern Italian Front. The final battle, in October 1917, saw the Italians defeated after a heavy Austro-German bombardment. ✣206●, ◆206 (6)

Israel 234
foundation of state (1948) ✣103, ✣234, ◆234 (2)
(c.10,000–500 BCE) ✣222, ✣222●, ◆222 (1)
early shelter ✣15, ✣16
foreign affairs
Camp David Summit (1978) ✣169●
Egyptian-Israeli peace deal (1978) ✣138●, ✣169●, ✣234●
immigration ✣234, ◆234 (3)
invades Lebanon (1982) ✣234●
Oslo Accord signed by PLO (1993) ✣234
PLO agreement (1995) ✣111●
Suez crisis (1956) ✣234●
transport for Egyptian prisoners ❑234
Six Day War (1967) ✣107●, ✣234●, ◆234 (2)
Yom Kippur War (1973), ✣107●, ✣234●, ◆234 (2)
home affairs
Balfour Declaration (1917) ✣99
refugees swim ashore at Haifa (1948), ❑103
Jewish migration (1948–96) ◆234 (3)

Issus ⚔ (333 BCE). Major battle in Alexander the Great's invasion of Asia. ✣39, ✣223, ◆218 (1)

Italy 178–214
First World War *see* Wars, First World
foreign affairs
Empire in 1942 ◆102–3
possessions
1900 ◆94–5
1925 ◆98–9
1975 ◆106–7
Africa
decolonization ✣168, ◆168 (1)
imperialism (1880–1920) ✣96, ◆96 (1)
conquers Libya ✣232
defeated at Adowa (1896) ✣95●, ✣97
Eritrea colony established (1889) ✣167●
Ethiopia invaded (1935) ✣103●
expansion in Africa ◆167 (4)
home affairs
bubonic plague (1347) ✣70●
Byzantine and Lombard ✣183, ◆183 (4)
communal movement ✣190
cultural leaders of Europe ✣75, ✣190
Etruscan fortifications (BCE) ✣31
farming established ✣18●
invasions
E Roman Empire (533 CE) ✣53●
France (1494) ✣75●
Goths ✣53, ✣182–3
Justinian ✣54
peoples of the peninsula (500 BCE) ✣178, ◆178 (2)
politics
devolution ✣112
unification (1850–70) ✣203, ◆203 (3)
population growth (1650–1800) ❑198
Second World War *see* Wars, Second
trade and industry
12th and 13th century prosperity ✣62, ✣66
Medieval trade ✣190
trade links (BCE) ✣31
See also Rome

Itzcoatl Ruler of Aztec Empire (1427–40) ✣74●, ◆124 (1)

Ivan III (*var.* Ivan Vasilyevich, *aka* Ivan the Great) (1440–1505). Grand Prince of Moscow (r.1462–1505), he freed the city from the Tatars and extended the territories of Muscovite Russia. In 1472 he assumed the title 'Sovereign of all Russia'. ✣75

Ivan IV (*aka* Ivan the Terrible) (1530–84). First Tsar of Russia (r.1533–84). He created a centrally administered Russian state and began the eastward expansion of Russia into non-Slavic lands. He gave Russia its first national assembly in 1549. Unbalanced during his later years, he killed his son Ivan, and embarked on a reign of terror against the Boyars. ❑195, ◆195 (3)

ivory
African commercial trade ◆166 (1)
chesspieces (12th century) ❑60
Eurasian and African trade (c.1 CE) ◆44–5
horn (16th century) ❑162
Inuit knife ❑123
Kushan plaque ❑47
Megiddo plaque ❑222

Iwo Jima ⚔ of WW II (Feb–Mar 1945). Prolonged US amphibious assault in the Pacific which, with Okinawa, secured island base for sustained strategic bombing of Japanese Home Islands. ✣273●, ◆273 (3)

Izumo People of southwest Honshu, Japan. ✣264

J

Jackson, Andrew (*aka* 'Old Hickory') (1767–1845) 7th President of the US (Democrat, 1828–36). A hero of the war of 1812 following his defeat of the British at New Orleans. As President he was resolute in his defence of the Union, and encouraged Indian removals to free new lands for settlement on the frontier. ✣129

Jacobins Members of the most famous of the political clubs of the French Revolution, exercising great influence in the National Assembly. Became increasingly radical and, under Robespierre, instituted the Reign of Terror. ✣199●
See also French Revolution, Robespierre, the Terror.

Jacobite Church Christian church of Syria, Iraq and India, founded in the 6th century as a Monophysite church in Syria. Regarded as heretical by Roman Catholics and the Eastern Orthodox Church. ◆49 (4)

Jacquerie Peasant rebellion against the nobility in NE France in 1358, during the Hundred Years' War. ✣70●, ✣192, ◆192 (1)

jade This semi-precious stone is commonly green or white and occurs as jadeite (a green pyroxene) or nephrite (a variety of amphibole). Nephrite was being used for the manufacture of ritual objects in China by the 4rd millennium BCE, and jadeite for axes in the 4th–3rd millennia in Europe.
✣19●, ✣30, ✣258●, ❑121

Jagatai *see* Chagatai

Jagiello (c.1351–1434). Grand duke of Lithuania (r.1377–1401) and king of Poland (r.1386–1434) who founded Poland's Jagiellon dynasty (1386–1572).
possessions (1500) ✣193, ◆193 (4)

Jahan *see* Shah Jahan

Jahangir (r.1605–27). Mughal emperor. The son of Akbar, Jahangir moved the capital to Lahore. He was strongly influenced by his favourite wife, Nur Jahan, and the currency was struck in her name. During his reign, the English established themselves at Surat and sent an embassy to the Mughal court. ✣246●, ❑246

Jainism A sect of Hindu dissenters which, according to Jain tradition, was founded as early as the 7th century BCE. Jain theology centres on the quest for liberation from the transmigration of souls, through monastic discipline, abstinence, and chastity. Great stress is placed on the vow to preserve all living things.
✣35, ✣36, ✣36●, ✣48–9, ✣242, ✣242●, ◆242 (2)
diagram of the universe ❑238
growth and decline ✣243, ◆49 (4), ◆243 (4)
ornate and contemplative art ❑49, ❑243

Jamaica Seized by English (1654) ✣82●, ◆126 (1), ◆129 (2)
piracy in the Caribbean ✣85 (2)

Jamestown ⚔ of American Revolutionary War (6 Jul 1781). British victory. ◆127 (3)

Jamestown
English colony founded (1607) ✣82●, ✣126●
European and native conflict (1622, 1644) ✣126
receives slaves (1619) ✣83●

Jammu and Kashmir Muslim majority province contested between India and Pakistan since 1947, when control was left unresolved following the partition of India. Two wars have been fought over the province (1947–48 and 1965). ✣252, ◆252 (2)

Janapadas Series of states or realms, formed by Aryan settlers in India during the first millennium BCE. ✣242, ◆242 (1)
See also Magadha.

Janissary corps Military force which constituted the standing army of the Ottoman Empire. From 1330, a number of Christian boys were taken from their parents in the Ottoman provinces, apprenticed and enrolled into the new corps. By 1582, this strict mode of admission had been relaxed and the privileges of membership of the Corps were much sought after. In 1591 the whole corps numbered 48,688 men. Janissaries were not allowed to marry or leave their barracks, but were to spend their time practising the arts of war. The first recorded revolt of the Janissaries in 1443; repeated revolts and disorder culminated in the disbanding of the corps in 1826. ✣71●

Japan 258, 264–5, 269-275
dynasties
Ashikaga shogunate founded (1336) ✣71●, ✣267
Fujiwara family ✣63
Kamakura shogunate ✣71, ✣265, ✣267
Kyoho era begins (1716) ✣87●
Minamoto clan ✣63, ✣265, ◆265 (5)
Tokugawa founded (1603) ✣83●
Yamato state emerges ✣51, ✣264–5, ◆264 (1)
exploration and mapping
provinces first mapped (c.900) ✣256●
foreign affairs
possessions
1900 ◆94–5
1925 ◆98–9
1950 ◆102–3
annexes Korea (1910) ✣99●
Empire in 1942 ◆102–3
expansionism (1930s) ✣103
first recorded diplomatic mission to China (607) ✣256●
gains territory in Pacific (1914) ✣99●
German anti-Comintern pact (1936) ✣103●
neutrality pact with Russia (1939) ✣103●
occupies part of Manchuria (1918–20) ✣99●
occupies part of Siberia (1918–20) ✣99●
Pacific imperialism ◆284 (1)
Pacific naval power limited (1922) ✣99●
Russian commercial talks (1804) ✣91●
Taiwan annexed (1894–95) ✣95●
war with China (1937) ✣103
home affairs
the age of the Shoguns, ✣265, ◆265 (5)
arrival of Portuguese merchants (16th century) ❑80
Chinese influence ✣55, ✣256, ✣265
closure by Tokugawa shoguns ✣83●
Edo period ✣267, ◆267 (5)
expansionism ✣99, ✣270, ◆270 (2)
feudalism abolished (1871) ✣95●
Kamakura Shogunate ✣265
modernization ✣270, ✣270●, ❑95, ❑270, ◆270 (1)
Mongol invasions ✣67●, ✣69●
reunification ✣267, ◆267 (4)
rice cultivation ✣258, ✣264
rise of the warrior lords ✣265●, ◆265 (4)
state formation (100 BCE–650 CE) ✣264, ◆264 (1) (2) (3) (4)
in transition ✣267
under the Nara Ritsuryo state ◆265 (3)
US aid rebuilds economy ✣107
hunter-gatherer sites ◆258 (1)
inventions, earliest pottery ✣20●, ◆258 (1)
martial qualities ❑264, ❑265
religion, ✣49●, ✣55, ✣264–5, ◆49 (4)
Second World War
atom bomb ✣103●, ✣273, ◆273 (3)
attack on Pearl Harbor (1941) ✣103, ✣138, ✣272
campaign in Asia ❑104, ❑272
Japanese offensive ✣272, ✣272●, ◆272 (1)
kamikaze pilots ❑273
war in the Pacific ✣272–3, ✣273●
See also Wars, Second World
trade and industry
modernization (1868–1918) ◆270 (1)
rapid economic growth ❑275, ◆275 (4)

Java
Buddhist temple constructed (c.800) ✣59●
failed Mongol invasion (1293) ✣67●
Majapahit empire ✣71, ❑244
rebellion against Dutch rule (1926–27) ✣103●
sacred map (16th century) ❑238
spice trade tax ✣71

Jayavarman II (r.802–869). Founder of the Angkorian dynasty, which ruled the Khmer state in Cambodia (9th–12th centuries). He was worshipped as a deity. During his rule the Khmer capital was at Roulos; his great nephew, Yasovarman, began the construction of the magnificent temple of Angkor Thom c.900. ✣59●

Jazz Singer, The (first film with sound, 1927) ✣135●

Jeanne d'Arc *see* Joan of Arc

Jebe
Mongol commander ❑68
Russian raid (1222) ✣68

Jefferson, Thomas (1743–1826) 3rd President of the US (Republican Democrat, 1801–09). Drafted the Declaration of Independence and helped to form the Virginia state constitution acting as governor from 1779–81. In 1789, appointed Secretary of State by George Washington. Became Vice-President under John Adams (1797–1801). Presided over the war with Tripoli, and the Louisiana Purchase of 1803 which opened up much of the West to American expansion and the Embargo Act of 1807. ✣119, ❑128

Jena Auerstädt ⚔ of Napoleonic Wars – the War of the 3rd Coalition (1806). French victory. ◆200 (1)

Jenghiz Khan *see* Genghis Khan

Jenkinson, Anthony (d.1611). English merchant who travelled from Moscow down the Volga to Astrakhan and crossed the Caspian Sea into Persia, to the Mongol city of Bukhara. He wrote the first account of the Tatars in the English language. ◆219 (3)

Jenne Settlement founded (c.250 BCE) ✣39●

Jericho, veneration of ancestors (BCE) ✣21

Jerusalem
Byzantine threats (976) ✣59●
4th-century centre of pilgrimage ✣51
capital city (c.1000 BCE) ✣31
captured by Crusaders ✣63, ✣63●, ✣64
captured by Saladin (1187) ✣228
destroyed and rebuilt (BCE) ✣35●, ✣222, ✣222●
Dome of the Rock built (692) ❑55
medieval mapping ❑219
mosaic map ❑51
Romans destroy temple (70 CE) ✣47, ✣225, ❑225
Six Day War (1967) ✣234●

Jesuits Religious order founded by St. Ignatius Loyola in 1534, properly known as the Society of Jesus. The most vigorous defenders of the Catholic faith in the Counter-Reformation, the Jesuits specialized in education and missionary work. Dedicated Jesuit missionaries even carried Catholicism to China and Japan. In S America, their missions among the Indians became virtually autonomous states within the Spanish Empire. Their political power became so great that they were expelled from Portugal and its territories in 1759 and suppressed by the pope in 1773, though they were restored in 1814.
East and West links ✣80
expelled from Ethiopia (1632) ✣165●
Florida missions established (1560s) ✣125
founded by St. Ignatius Loyola ❑194
in S America ✣143●, ❑143, ◆143 (2), ◆148 (2)
missionaries in Tibet ✣257
See also Catholicism

Jesus of Nazareth (*aka* Jesus Christ) (c.4 BCE–32 CE). The inspiration of the Christian religion, believed by

his followers to be the Son of God, Jesus was crucified as a troublemaker in Jerusalem c.32 CE. The Greek *Khristos* means anointed one, a translation of the Hebrew Messiah. His life, preaching, and miracles are recounted in the New Testament. ✣46
See also Christianity

Jewish diaspora Term used today to describe the Jewish communities living outside the Holy Land. Originally used to designate the dispersal of the Jews outside Palestine after the Babylonian exile in 586 BCE, and following the Jewish revolts of 66–74 CE and 132–35 CE. ✣47●, ✣48●, ✣225, ◆225 (5), ✣226, ◆226 (1)

Jewish revolts Series of rebellions in Judaea following its conquest by the Romans in 63 CE. The first revolt began in 66 CE, was put down by Vespasian and his son Titus, and led to the legendary Jewish martyrdom at Masada in 74 CE. The second revolt of 132–135 led by Simon Bar Cochba. Suppression led to dispersal of Jews (diaspora) throughout southwest Asia and Roman Empire. ✣47, ✣225, ◆225 (4)

Jews People of southwest Asia, originally descendants of Judah, the fourth son of Jacob. Later came to designate followers of the religion of Judaism.
Arab revolt against immigration (1936) ✣103●
communities in 600 CE, ✣226, ◆226 (1)
Crusade massacres ✣186, ◆186 (1)
exodus from Egypt (c.1200 BCE) ✣31●
formal expulsion from St. Petersburg ❑100
human cost of global war ✣105
mass extermination under the Nazis ✣102●, ✣211, ◆211 (3)
migration (1880–1914) ✣101, ✣101●, ◆101 (2)
migration to Israel ◆234 (3)
settlement in New York ❑100

Jiang Jieshi (*var.* Chiang Kai-shek) (1887–1975). Chinese general and political leader. Leader of the Kuomintang from 1926, president of the republic 1928–31. Opposed the Chinese Communist Party until defeated in 1949 when he withdrew to Taiwan. ✣103●, ❑270–1

Jiang Qing *see* Cultural Revolution

jihad Holy war ✣56, ✣167, ◆235 (4)

Jin dynasty Chinese dynasty of the Sixteen Kingdoms period. ◆261 (3)
dynasty unifies China (280) ✣51●
Eastern dynasty moves to Nanjing ✣51

Jin dynasty (*var.* Chin dynasty) (r.1115–1234). Dynasty of northern China.
founded by the Jurchen ✣263
alliance with Song China ✣63 (c.1206) ◆68–9 (1)
capital city ✣69
conquered by Mongols ✣263, ◆263 (7)
first Mongol invasion (1211) ✣69●

Jin Empire *see* Jin dynasty

Jinghis Khan *see* Genghis Khan

Joan of Arc (*var. Fr.* Jeanne d'Arc, *aka* the Maid of Orleans, *Fr.* La Pucelle) (c.1412–31). French national heroine. Claiming to hear voices urging her to rid France of English domination, she led an army which raised the siege of Orleans (1429), enabling the dauphin to be crowned Charles VII at Rheims. Captured and sold to the English, she was convicted of heresy and burnt at the stake. She was canonized in 1920. ❑192
campaigns ◆192 (2)
saves Orléans (1429) ✣75●, ✣192, ✣192●

João III (1502–57) King of Portugal (r.1521–57). His kingdom suffered, both socially and economically, because of his subservience to the clerical party. He tried to stimulate the colonization of the new Portuguese territory in Brazil by granting captaincies. ✣148

João V (1689–1750) King of Portugal (1707–50). A supporter of the Triple Alliance (between Britain, Austria, and the Netherlands), he embarked on a series of unsuccessful campaigns in Castile during the War of the Spanish Succession. Though his treasury benefited from the recent discovery of gold in Brazil, João V was entirely under the influence of the clergy and the administration suffered from his neglect. ❑88

John (1167–1216) King of England (r.1199–1216). His reign saw the renewal of war with Philip II Augustus of France, to whom he had lost several continental possessions. Tensions between John and Pope Innocent III led to the imposition of an interdict over England in 1208 and the king's excommunication in 1212. He was also forced to grant the Magna Carta at Runnymede. ✣66●

Johnson, Lyndon Baines (1908–73) 36th President of the US (Democrat, 1963–68). Became President following the assassination of John F. Kennedy in 1963. His administration passed the Civil Rights Act (1964), the Voting Rights Act (1965) aimed at improving the position of African Americans, and introduced a series of economic and social reforms under the slogan the 'Great Society', but his personal standing was severely weakened by public protests against the escalation of the Vietnam War.
Democrat President ✣139
Civil Rights legislation ✣139

Jolliet, Father Louis (1645–1700). Explorer of N America. Born in Canada, Jolliet discovered the source of the Mississippi River with Jacques Marquette. In 1672–73 they travelled along the river to within 640 km of the Gulf of Mexico. ◆119 (2)

Jolson, Al (*prev.* Asa Yoelson) (1886–1950) Russian-born American actor and singer. He toured with various stage and minstrel shows, making his Broadway debut in 1911. In 1928, he made screen history when he starred in the first full-length 'talkie', *The Jazz Singer*. In 1927, his first big record hit 'Sonny boy/there's a rainbow round my shoulder' sold over three million copies. ✣135●

Jomon culture Hunters, fishers and gatherers who lived in Japan from c.7500 to 250 BCE. They fully exploited an abundance of fish, animal and plant resources and, in the densely populated east, lived in permanent villages, but there is no evidence of plant cultivation. Jomon pottery dates back to c.10,000 BCE, the earliest known anywhere in the world. The culture is named from the cord-decorated pottery found at the Omori shell mounds near Tokyo. ✣19

Jordan Six Day War (1967) ✣107●

Juan Carlos I (1938–) King of Spain (r.1978–). The grandson of Alfonso XIII (who abdicated in 1931), he was named successor to the dictator, General Franco in 1969, and proclaimed king in 1975. Juan Carlos presided over a rapid, and peaceful, transition to democracy; by 1978 Spain was declared a parliamentary monarchy. In 1981 King Juan Carlos foiled a Francoist military coup by taking preventative action and winning pledges of loyalty from military commanders. ✣110●

Juan-juan *see* Ruanruan

Juárez, Benito (Pablo) (1806–72) Mexican statesman (r.1861–72). As part of the Liberal government which replaced the Conservative Santa Anna, Juárez helped pass the anti-clerical and liberal constitution of 1857. In 1861 he assumed the role of president of Mexico, a post he held until his death. A French invasion under Maximilian forced him to retreat to the north, but after the French were defeated in 1867 he was able to restore Republican rule. ◆128–129 (2), ✣129

Judaism Religion of the Jewish people, developed among the ancient Hebrews and characterized by a belief in one God, its ethical system and its ritual practices, based on the Pentateuch as interpreted by the rabbis of the Talmudic period in the first five centuries CE and their successors up to the present day.
candelabra ❑37
origins ✣36–7
spread of (600 BCE) ◆48 (1)

Jugurtha (160–104 BCE) King of Numidia (r.118–105 BCE). Struggled to free his N African kingdom from Roman rule. ✣43●

Julio-Claudian dynasty The four successors of the Roman Emperor Augustus (r.31 BCE–14 CE), all indirectly descended from Julius Caesar. The Emperor Augustus, who had extended the frontiers of the empire and introduced stable and efficient government, was succeeded by Tiberius (14–37 CE), the most able of the dynasty. Caligula (37–41 CE) was famous for his excesses and capricious behaviour. He was succeeded by Claudius (41–54 CE), who devoted himself to public works and administrative reforms, although he never gained the respect of his subjects. The tyrannical Nero (54–68) was notorious for his ruthless murders, and the revenge he took on the Christians for the great fire of Rome (64 CE) which, it was rumoured, he had started himself. ✣46●

Julius Caesar *see* Caesar, Gaius Julius

Juneau, Joe 19th-century French explorer of Alaska. Founded town of Juneau. finds gold in Alaska (1880) ✣93, ◆93 (3)

Jupiter (*var. Gr.* Zeus). Most powerful god in the Greco-Roman pantheon. ✣37

Jurchen People originating in the mountains of eastern Manchuria, Central Asia. Established the Jin state and seized northern China 1126, restricting Song rule to the south of China. ✣263, ◆263 (5)
See also Jin dynasty

Justinian I (483–565) Byzantine Emperor. Born in what is now Yugoslavia, he was adopted by his uncle Justin I, who ascended the throne in 518, and succeeded him in 527. He is famous for his reforms of the Roman law codes and imperial constitutions, and the publication of the Codex Justinianus (534). His programme of costly public works included the building of the church of Hagia Sophia in Constantinople. He engaged in major campaigns against the Vandals in Spain and North Africa and the Goths in Italy, but his victories proved fragile. ❑54
reconquests ✣182, ◆182 (1)

Jutes Germanic people who, with the Angles and Saxons, invaded Britain in the 5th century CE. ✣183, ◆52–3 (1)

Jutland Naval ⚔ of WW I (31 May 1916) between the British and German fleets in the North Sea. Though the result was inconclusive, the Allies thereafter retained control of the North Sea. ✣206●

K

K'ang-hsi *see* Kangxi

Kabul, captured by Taliban (1996) ✣111●

Kadesh ⚔ between the Egyptians and Hittites (c.1285 BCE). First recorded battle in world history. ✣27●, ✣221, ◆221 (5)

Kadphises I (*var.* Kujula Kadphises, Chiu-Chiu-Chueh) Kushan ruler who achieved political unity of the Yuezhi tribes in the 1st century CE, and ruled over northern India, Afghanistan and parts of central Asia. ✣47

Kaifeng
captured by Mongols (1233) ✣67●, ◆68–9 (1)
scroll depicting 12th-century street life ❑63
Song capital ✣263, ◆263 (7)

Kairouan Great Mosque ❑56

Kalahari Desert, environmental survival strategies (BCE) 16

Kalewa ⚔ of WW II (May 1942). Marked furthest point of Japanese advance in Burma. ◆104 (2)

Kalhotia Mesolithic painting ❑14

Kali Important goddess in Hinduism, associated with death, disease and destruction. ❑48

Kalidasa 4th-century Indian poet and playwright. ✣51●

Kalmar, Union of (Jun 1397). Scandinavian union that brought the kingdoms of Norway, Sweden, and Denmark together under a single monarch until 1523. ✣70●, ✣195, ◆70–1, ◆74–5, ◆195 (3)

Kalmyks Buddhist Mongolian people of Central Asia who came under pressure from Qing China 1758–59. ✣268●, ◆268 (2)

Kamakura Shogunate (1185–1333) Military rulers of Japan. ✣71, ✣265, ✣265●

Kambujadesha The Khmer state of Kambujadesha, founded by Devaraya II in 802, controlled most of SE Asia for the next four centuries from the magnificent city of Angkor in southern Cambodia. Although Hinduism was the state religion, it combined many elements of Buddhism, as can be seen in the magnificent monumental architecture of Angkor, which reached its zenith under the rule of Jayavarman VII (c.1200). ✣245●, ◆245 (5)

Kamehameha I (1782–1819). The king of one of the four kingdoms of Hawaii who, with superior vessels and firearms, as well as foreign aid, succeeded in conquering all the islands, with the exception of Kauai and Niihau, by 1795. He reorganized government, encouraged industry, while withstanding foreign cultural influence and adhering to traditional Hawaiian religious practices (abolished after his death by his favourite queen, Kaahumanu). ✣91●

kami The combined forces of nature and ancestral spirits, central to Shinto religious observance. ❑264

kamikaze Japanese term for 'divine wind', a typhoon which halted second Mongol invasion attempt (1281); adopted as name by Japanese suicide fighter-bomber squadrons during final campaigns of WW II. ✣273, ❑273

Kaminalijuyú (*fl.* 500 BCE) Central American civilization ✣121

Kanab Desert US Geological Survey sketch (1880) ❑119

Kandahar *see* Gandhara

Kanem-Bornu W African kingdom ✣58
See also Bornu

Kangxi (*var.* K'ang-hsi) (1654–1722) Emperor of the Manchu (Qing) dynasty of China (r.1661–1722). ✣83●, ❑268

Kanishka (*var.* Kaniska) (r.c.78–96 CE). Ruler of the Kushan, or Kushana, Empire of south central Asia whose adoption of (Mahayana) Buddhism was instrumental in the spread of the faith to Central Asia and along the Silk Road to China. ✣47●, ✣48

Kansas Nebraska Act (1854). The third of the critical decisions regarding the extension of slavery in the US, the Kansas-Nebraska Act applied the principle of popular sovereignty to the territorial organization of Kansas and Nebraska. The passage of the act led to the formation of the Republican Party to oppose the expansion of slavery into new territories. ✣130, ◆130 (3)

Kao Tsu *see* Gao Zhu

Kara Khitai Muslim empire in central Asia which rose to prominence in the 12th century. In 1141 the Kara Khitai defeated the Seljuk Turks at Samarkand. ◆68–9 (1)

Karakorum ◆68–9 (1) (2)
Mongol capital built (1235) ✣68●
slave trade centre (13th century) ✣85

Karius, Charles 20th-century British explorer of New Guinea (1927–28). ◆279 (2)

Karlowitz, Peace of (*var.* Carlowitz) (1699). Peace settlement that ended hostilities (1683–99) between the Ottoman Empire and the Holy League (Austria, Poland, Venice, and Russia) which significantly diminished Turkish influence in east-central Europe, making Austria the dominant power there. ✣197●, ◆197 (4)

Kashmir
Indian-Pakistan war (1965) 107●
and Jammu ✣252, ◆252 (2)
refugees ❑252

Kassapa (447–495). Ruler of Sigiriya in Sri Lanka, who usurped power and believed he was a god-king.
god-king of Sigiriya ✣51●
palace, two heavenly maidens (5th century) ❑51

Katanga Secedes from Congo (1960) ✣107●

Kay, John Inventor of flying shuttle (1733) ✣204●

Kazakhs People of Central Asia. Traditionally pastoral nomads; incorporated into the Russian Empire in the mid-19th century, now mainly settled in Kazakhstan. ◆89 (2), ◆267 (3)

Kebara Neanderthal burial site ❑12

Kemal Pasha, Mustafa *see* Atatürk

Kennedy, Edmund (1818–48). Born in the Channel Islands, he migrated to New South Wales in 1840. Trained as a surveyor, he joined Sir Thomas Mitchell's expedition into central Queensland in 1847. In 1848 he led an expedition up the eastern coast of Queensland to Cape York. During the course of the arduous journey all his party perished – Kennedy was speared by Aborigines while within sight of his supply ship. ◆279 (2)

Kennedy, John Fitzgerald (1917–1963) 35th President of the US (Democrat, 1960–63). Following service in US navy during WW II, became the youngest elected US president at the age of 43. He aimed to introduce legislation for the improvement of civil rights and for the extension of funding for healthcare and education. Foreign policy issues included the unsuccessful invasion of the Bay of Pigs in Cuba, the division of Europe, the Cuban Missile Crisis which brought the world to the brink of nuclear war, and the continuing involvement of the US in Vietnam. He was assassinated in Dallas, Texas on 22 Nov 1963. ✣139●, ❑108

Kennesaw Mountain ⚔ of American Civil War (27 Jun 1864). Confederate victory. ◆131 (7)

Kent King converted to Christianity (597) ✣54●

Kenya 167–169
British penetration in 19th century ◆167 (3)
independence ◆168 (1)
terrorist bombing (1998) ✣235●

Kermario Stone alignments (c.3000 BCE). ❑174

Khanbaliq (*var.* Beijing, Cambaluc). founded by Kublai Khan (1266) ✣68●
Italian map (15th century) ❑69

Khedive of Egypt The title, granted by the Sultan of Turkey in 1867, to his viceroy in Egypt, Ismail. 'Khedive' is a Persian word meaning prince, or sovereign. The title was abandoned in 1914 when the title 'Sultan' was adopted. ✣232

Khitans (*var.* Liao) (907–1125). People of Mongolia who established the Liao Empire in Manchuria in the 10th century. ✣263, ◆263 (3) (4)

Khmer Rouge A Marxist party in Cambodia, led by Pol Pot, organized to oppose the right-wing government of Lon Nol, 1970–75. They overthrew the government in 1975 and instituted a reign of terror which led to the death of over two million Cambodians. They were overthrown in 1979 following a Vietnamese invasion. ✣253●, ◆253 (4), ❑253

Khmer state ✣245, ✣245●, ◆245 (5)
temple carvings ❑63
See also Kambujadesha

Khomeini, Ayatollah Ruhollah (1900–1989). Iranian religious and political leader. A Shi'ite Muslim whose bitter opposition to the pro-Western regime of Muhammad Reza Shah Pahlavi led to his exile from Iran in 1964. Following a popular revolution and the overthrow of the Shah's government in 1979, he returned to Iran and was proclaimed religious leader of the Islamic Revolution. Islamic law was once more imposed, and a return to strict fundamentalist Islamic tradition enforced. ❑235

Khosrau I (*var.* Khosrow I, *aka* Khosrau the Just) (r.531–579). Sassanian Persian Shah who quelled the Mazdakite rebellion and successfully resisted the Byzantines. ✣55, ✣225

Khosrau II (*var.* Khosrow II, *aka* Khosrau the Victorious) (r.591–628). Persian Shah at the apogee of the Sassanian era. In 601 he attacked Byzantium, capturing Antioch, Jerusalem and Alexandria. ✣225

Khrushchev, Nikita Sergeyevich (1894–1971) Soviet statesman and successor to Stalin. First Secretary of the Communist Party (1953–64). Deposed in a coup and replaced by Leonid Brezhnev. ❑108

Khufu (c.2575–2465 BCE) Egyptian pharaoh of the 4th dynasty who initiated the building of the largest pyramid at Giza: 147 m high, consisting of c.2.3 million blocks, each weighing c.2.5 tonnes. ✣23●

Khwarizm Empire (*aka* Empire of the Khwarizm Shah, Uzbek Empire) State of Turkic origin, broadly corresponding with ancient Chorasmia, N Persia, based around Samarkand from the 12th century. Overrun by Mongols, then forming part of Khanate of the Golden Horde, and subsequently conquered by Timur (1378), the state fragmented into a number of Muslim khanates based around Bukhara and Samarkand which were finally absorbed into the Russian Empire during the 19th century.
(1219) ◆66–7
(c.1206–19) ◆68–9 (1)
invaded by Mongols (1219) ✣67●, ✣69●

Kibi Ancient people of southern Honshu, Japan. ✣264

Kiev ⚔ of WW II (Sep–Nov 1943) Soviet forces defeat German counter-offensive in Ukraine. ◆105 (3), ◆211 (4)

Kiev
captured by Vikings ✣185
Russian capital ✣58●

Kievan Rus State established in 840 by Vikings from Sweden who were trading along the rivers between the Baltic and the Black seas. Kiev became a flourishing capital; through trading links with Byzantium the Christian faith became established there at the end of the 10th century. Repeated sackings by nomads from the east reduced Kiev to a number of independent and warring principalities from the middle of the 11th century. ✣185, ◆185 (3), ◆189 (3)
possessions ◆58–9
founded by Varangians ✣60

Kilwa
building programme ✣163●
coastal trading colony (c.800) ✣58

Kimberley South Africa, gold finds (1867) ✣93●

King, Clarence (1842–1901). American explorer and geologist. In 1867, as director in charge of the United States Geological Exploration of the Fortieth Parallel he began extensive ten-year survey of a 160–km-wide strip of land running from Cheyenne, Wyoming to the eastern Sierra Nevada. ◆119 (3)

King, Martin Luther (1929–1968) US civil rights leader. A baptist minister in Alabama, Martin Luther King founded the Southern Christian Leadership Conference in 1957 to organize activities for the promotion of black civil rights throughout the US. He advocated a policy of non-violence and passive resistance, an effective strategy which undoubtedly helped the passage of the Civil Rights Act of 1964 and the Voting Rights Act of 1965. He was awarded the Kennedy Peace Prize and the Nobel Prize. In 1968 he was assassinated in Memphis, Tennessee. The third Monday in January is now celebrated as Martin Luther King Day in the US.
assassination (1968) ✣137●
heads protest movement (1957) ✣137●
portrait ❑136
Washington march (1963) ✣137●

King Movement A Maori movement of the late 1850s that opposed land sales to European settlers and demanded a Maori state. It was led by chief 'King' Te Wherowhero. ✣283●

King Philip's War (1675–76) Conflict between English colonists and Indians in New England following the rapid expansion of European settlement into Indian territory from 1640 onwards. The conflict involved most of the tribes of New England including the Wapanoag and the Narragansett, and may have led to the loss of perhaps 600 settlers and 3000 Indians. The Indians thereafter fled north and west. ✣126, ◆126 (1)

King's Mountain ⚔ of American Revolutionary War, 7 Oct 1780, American victory. ◆127 (3)

Kingsley, Mary (1862–1900). English traveller who journeyed through western and equatorial Africa and became the first European to enter parts of present-day Gabon. ◆157 (4)

Kisesse Decorated caves (29,000 BP) ✣17●

Klerk, F.W. de (*f/n* Frederik Willem de Klerk) (1936–). Politician who as president of South Africa (1989–94), brought the apartheid system of racial segregation to an end. Both he and Nelson Mandela jointly received the Nobel Peace Prize in 1993, in recognition of their efforts to establish non-racial democracy in South Africa.
begins dismantling of apartheid (1990) ✣169●

Klondike Gold rush ✣93, ◆93 (3)

Knights Hospitaller (*var.* Knights of St. John). Military/religious order established at Jerusalem in the early 12th century following the success of the First Crusade. Its purpose was to care for pilgrims to the Holy Land, but the Knights also played an important role in the defence of the Crusader states. In 1310, the Hospitallers took Rhodes, which remained their base until 1522, when it was taken by the Ottomans. They were then granted the island of Malta by Charles V. ✣186, ◆189 (3)
conquer Rhodes (1306–10) ✣186●
fall of Rhodes to Ottomans ◆231 (3)
military order (c.1130) ✣64●, ✣186●

Knights of St. John *see* Knights Hospitallers

Knights Templar Military/religious order founded c.1118 to protect pilgrim routes to Jerusalem. In the 12th and 13th centuries, knights of the order fought in all the major campaigns against Islam. They acquired estates all over Christian Europe, but their wealth and influence made them enemies. In 1307, Philip IV of France had the order accused of heresy and other crimes and it was suppressed in 1312.
Order founded (c.118) ✣64●, ✣186●
European political force ❑186
Order suppressed (1312) ✣70●
Templar houses, ◆186 (1)

Knossos Bronze Age city on Crete, a focus of the Minoan civilization, and known for the artistic and architectural brilliance of its palace, built c.2000 BCE, which dominated the city's mansions, houses and paved roads. Knossos flourished for some 1500 years, despite its palace being destroyed several times (once by the erupton of Thera), and invasion by the Mycenaeans c.1450. It was finally destroyed by the Romans 68–67 BCE. *See* Minoan civilization.

Knut *see* Canute

Koguryo North Korean ruling clan destroyed by the Tang in 668. *See also* Korea.
controls Korea (c.220) ✣47●
establishes Pohai empire ✣264

Kök Türk (Blue Turk) Empire (551–72). ◆54–5

Konbaung dynasty Founded (1752) in Burma. ✣87●

Kongo
Kingdom formed (c.1390) ✣71●, ✣163●

outbreak of civil war (1665) ✤164●
Portuguese attempt colonization ✤82
Kongzi *see* Confucius
Königsberg ⚔ of WW II (Feb–Apr 1945) Prolonged siege of German forces by Soviet troops. ✤105, ◆211 (4)
Koran (*var.* Qu'ran). The holy book of Islam. ✤226, ❑56, ❑67, ❑167
See also Islam.
Korea Peninsula of E Asia, frequently under Chinese and Japanese influence and control; early states included Koguryo (c.150–668 CE), Paekche (c.250–663 CE) and Silla (from 313 CE). Silla Period (676–935). Koryo Period (936–1392). I (or Li) dynasty, capital at Kyongsang, ruled often as Ming or Qing vassals (1392–1910). Annexed to Japan 1910–1945. Partitioned into independent states of N and S Korea (1948).
agriculture (BCE) ✤23●, ✤31, ✤258
dynasties
Buddhist ✤59
Yi (1392) ✤71●
home affairs
annexed by Japan (1910) ✤99●
BCE subsistence ✤19●
controlled by native states (c.200) ✤47●
first empires ◆264 (2)
Koryo kingdom founded (935) ✤59●
peninsula united by Silla ✤55●
Silla's struggle for power ✤264●
state formation (100 BCE–650 CE) ✤264, ◆264 (1) (2) (3) (4)
innovations
bronze technology ✤31
earliest pottery ◆258 (1)
iron-working introduced (400 BCE) ✤39●
Korean War Conflict (1950–53) between newly created (1948) states of N and S Korea, precipitated when the Communist north invaded the south, escalating to involve Chinese, UN and US troops.
Korean War (1950–53) ✤106, ✤107●, ◆109 (4), ✤275, ◆275 (3)
partition ✤109, ❑109
South, industrial growth ✤111
Koryo Kingdom founded (935) ✤59●
Köse Dagh ⚔ (1243). Seljuks of Rum defeated by Mongols. ◆228 (1)
Kosovo (*var.* Kosovo Polje, 'Field of the Blackbirds') ⚔ (1389). Defeat of the Christian Serbs and Bosnians by the Muslim Ottomans under Murad I, who was killed in the battle. ◆189 (4)
Kosovo Province within the republic of Yugoslavia with ethnic Albanian majority population. Serb ethnic cleansing directed at Albanians led to NATO intervention in 1999.
conflict ✤214, ◆215 (3)
refugees ❑112
Krak des Chevaliers Fortified Crusader castle ❑65
Kristallnacht (*var. Eng.* 'The night of the broken glass') (9 Nov 1938). 91 Jews were killed and many synagogues burned down in coordinated attacks by Nazis against Jews and Jewish property in Germany and Austria. ✤211
K'ung-fu-tzu *see* Confucius
Ku Klux Klan Extreme right-wing organization, founded in the southern US after the American Civil War to oppose the new rights granted to Blacks. Though the original Klan was outlawed in 1871, a new version appeared in about 1915, reaching the height of its membership during the 1920s and carrying out acts of terrorism and murder against other minority groups including Jews, Catholics and other immigrants. ✤135, ❑135, ◆135 (6)
Kublai Khan (*var.* Kubilai Khan) (1215–94) Great Khan of the Mongols from 1260. Founder of the Yuan dynasty which united China, and first foreigner ever to rule a united China.
(d.1294) ✤67●, ✤69●
defeated by Japanese (1274) ❑263
elected Great Khan (1264) ✤67●
ends civil war (1264) ✤68●
founds Khanbaliq (Beijing) (1266) ✤68●, ❑69
Mongol campaigns (1260–94) ◆68–9 (1)
Song Empire campaign (1260–79) ✤67
Kuomintang (*var.* Guomindang). Chinese Nationalist Party. Political party that ruled China from 1928 until the Communist victory in 1949. ✤271
Kurds Sunni Muslim people, numbering some 9–10 million, who occupy a mountainous region divided between Turkey, Iran, Iraq and Syria which the Kurds themselves call Kurdistan. They are politically oppressed in Turkey, and subject to religious persecution in Iraq. In 1988 the support given by Kurdish insurgents to Iran during the Iran-Iraq war led to the use of chemical weapons against them by Saddam Hussein. When Iraq was defeated in the Gulf War, the Kurds staged a revolt in northern Iraq. ✤235, ◆235 (5)
Kursk ⚔ of WW II (Jul–Aug 1943). Major tank engagement in which Soviet forces destroyed much of Germany's armoured capacity in Russia; largest tank battle in history. ◆211 (4)
Kush (*var.* Cush) Nubian kingdom (BCE) ✤30, ✤31●, ✤34, ◆159 (4) (5), ◆161 (3) (4)
Kushan Empire (*var.* Kushana). State of south Central Asia created in 1st century CE, capital Peshawar, which grew to straddle the Hindu Kush and the Pamirs, incorporating Punjab, Afghanistan, and Sogdiana. The founder of the second Kushana dynasty, Kanishka (r.c.78–96 CE), adopted Buddhism, and aided its dissemination along the Silk Road to China. ◆44–5, ◆46–7, ✤47●
Kushana *see* Kushan Empire
Kutuzov, Mikhail Ilarionovich (1745–1813) Russian soldier. Commander-in-Chief of the Russian forces which defeated Napoleon at Borodino (1812) and pursued the French army during its retreat from Moscow. ◆200 (1)
Kyoho Era begins in Japan (1716) ✤87●
Kyoto Japanese capital (794) ✤59●, ◆265 (4)

L

La Florida Ceremonial centre built (c.1800 BCE) ✤26
La Pérouse, J.F. Galaup de *see* Pérouse, J.F. Galaup de
La Rochelle Siege (1628–29) ✤196●
La Salle, Rene-Robert Cavelier Sieur de (1643–87) French explorer of N America. Between 1679 and 1681 he explored the Great Lakes before travelling the length of the Mississippi and reaching its mouth in 1682. He took over the Mississippi Valley for France, naming the region Louisiana. ◆119 (2)
La Venta Olmec centre (BCE) ✤30, ✤34
lacquerwork An ancient Chinese invention, this is a hard waterproof substance made from the resin of the *rhus vernicifera* tree. It can be coloured, polished and carved and is used for many decorative purposes. ✤35●, ✤44
Laden, Osama bin *see* bin Laden, Osama
Lake Regillus ⚔ of (496 BCE). Roman victory over an alliance of surrounding Latin cities. The battle ensured Rome's dominance over neighbouring cities. ✤178●, ◆178 (1 inset)
Lalibela St. George's church ❑62
Lambton, William Survey of India ✤239, ✤239●, ❑239
Lancashire Cotton towns ◆93 (4)
land drainage *see* irrigation
Lander, Richard (1804–34). British explorer of W Africa who traced the course of the lower Niger River to its delta. ◆157 (4)
Langobardi *see* Lombards
Lao Tzu *see* Laozi
Laos
Burmese invasion ✤79
independence (1954) ✤107●, ◆251 (4)
Vietnam War ◆251 (5)
Laozi (*var.* Lao Tzu). 6th-century BCE Chinese philosopher and sage. Regarded as the inspiration for Taoism and for one of its principal works, the Tao-te Ching, compiled c.300 years after his death. This teaches self-sufficiency, simplicity, respect for nature and ancestors. ✤35●, ✤37, ✤259●
lapis lazuli Deep blue stone, a silicate of sodium and aluminium. Found in metamorphosed limestones, in ancient times it was used as the source of a blue pigment.
royal standard of Ur ❑23
trade (c.2500 BCE) ✤24●, ✤25, ◆24–5 (2)
Lapita Austronesian speakers, ancestors of modern Polynesians. Their distinctive style of pottery provides evidence for their migrations in the western Pacific. Remains of their pottery have been found in the Bismarck Archipelago, Fiji, Samoa, and New Caledonia, all dating from the first millennium BCE. ◆281 (3), ✤281●
colonizers of Pacific Ocean (c.1500 BCE) ✤27, ✤60●
pottery ❑27
Lascaux Cave paintings (17,000 BP) ✤17●, ◆17 (3)
Lashio ⚔ of WW II (Apr 1942) marking Japanese control of central Burma. ✤104, ◆104 (2)
Las Navas de Tolosa ⚔ of Reconquest of Spain (1212). Defeat of Almohads. ◆186 (1)
Later Han *see* Han dynasty.
Latin colony Dependency of ancient Rome in Italy, where inhabitants had limited rights compared to full Roman citizens. ✤178, ◆178 (1)
Latin League Confederacy of small city-states established in the 5th century BCE. The supremacy of Rome gradually made the principles of the league obsolete and it was formally abandoned in 338. ✤178
Latins People of central Italy whose lands were annexed by Rome in the 4th century BCE. Their language was carried by the Romans throughout their empire. ✤178●
Lausanne, Treaty of (1922–23). Peace treaty between WW I Allies and Turkey resolving problems caused by Treaty of Sèvres, which had been rejected by the new Turkish government led by Atatürk. Turkey recovered eastern Thrace, and the Dardanelles were opened to all shipping. ◆233 (3)
See also Sèvres, Treaty of
Lawrence, Thomas Edward (*aka* 'Lawrence of Arabia') (1888–1935) British scholar, soldier and author. In 1916 he joined the Arab Revolt against the Turks led by Emir Faisal, and participated in the capture of Damascus (1918). He was an adviser to Faisal at the Paris Peace Conference, but later withdrew from public life. His account of the Arab Revolt, *Seven Pillars of Wisdom* (1926), has become one of the classics of English literature. ✤❑232, ◆233 (2)
Le Maire, Jacob (d.1616) Dutch explorer. Commander of voyage round Cape Horn and across the Pacific in 1615–16 with Willem Schouten as pilot. The expedition failed in its aim of finding a practicable route to the Indies in order to break the Dutch East India Company's monopoly of the spice trade. Le Maire died in the Indian Ocean on the homeward journey. ◆278 (1)
lead First use ✤18–19
League of Nations Established by the Allied Powers in 1920 after the Paris Peace Conference (1919) after WW I, the League aimed, by arms reduction, international arbitration and diplomacy, to reduce the threat of further conflict. The League was weakened from the outset by the refusal of US Congress to ratify the Treaty of Versailles, and during the 1930s it proved unable to contain the expansionism of Germany, Japan and Italy. It was replaced in 1946 by the United Nations.
created (1920) ✤98●
proved ineffective ✤102
Lebanon Israel invades (1982) ✤234●, ◆234 (2)
Lechfeld ⚔ (955). Magyars defeated by Otto I. ◆185 (3)
Leeuwenhoek, Anton van Maker of optical instruments ✤83
Legnano ⚔ (1176). Defeat of Frederick Barbarossa by Lombard League. ◆188 (1)
Leichhardt, Ludwig (1813–48) Prussian-born explorer of the Australian interior. His party vanished without trace on his attempt to cross Australia from east to west in 1848. ◆279 (2)
Leipzig ⚔ of Napoleonic Wars (14–16 Oct 1813). Allies won great victory over Napoleon but he was able to escape with a remnant of his army. ◆200 (1)
Lenin, Vladimir Ilyich (*prev.* Ulyanov) (1870–1924) Russian revolutionary leader. The architect of the Bolshevik revolution in Russia, Lenin advocated the creation of a core of professional activists to spearhead a Marxist revolution. In Oct 1917, following the deposing of Tsar Nicholas II, Lenin's Bolsheviks overthrew the provisional government to inaugurate the 'dictatorship of the proletariat'. ❑208, ✤208
Leningrad (*hist.* and *mod.* St. Petersburg, *temp.* Petrograd, 1914–23, *var. Rus.* Sankt-Peterburg). City and port of western Russia, founded by Peter the Great; ⚔ of WW II, Soviets besieged by Germans 1941–44. ◆210 (1), ✤211●
Leo I, Pope (*aka* St. Leo I, Leo the Great) (d.461) (r.460–61).
saves Rome from Huns ✤53
Leo III, Pope (r.795–816). Leo called on Charlemagne to secure his papal throne and in return created him Holy Roman Emperor, thus beginning the medieval interdependence and rivalry between popes and emperors. ❑184
Leopold II (1835–1909). The second king of the Belgians (r.1865–1909). He was the prime mover behind the establishment of the Congo Free State, which gradually became his own private African business venture. The administration of the state was severely criticized for the brutal methods used to force native people to pick rubber. In 1908 Leopold handed the Congo over to the Belgian government and it was then administered as a colony. ✤167●, ◆195 (4)
Lepanto ⚔ of (1571) Decisive naval engagement at which the Ottoman fleet was destroyed by the Venetian-led Holy League. ✤79, ✤195●
Lepenski Vir Important early European settlement c.6000 BCE. ❑18
Léry, Chaussegros de 18th-century French explorer of North America. In his capacity as Chief Engineer of Canada, de Léry conducted a thorough survey of the upper Ohio river in 1729 ◆119 (2)
Lesotho Kingdom (1824) ◆166 (2)
Lesseps, Ferdinand, Vicomte de (1805–94) French diplomat and engineer. In 1854 he began to plan the Suez Canal, supervising its construction until its opening in 1869. In 1881 work began on his scheme for a Panama Canal, but this had to be abandoned in 1888 and was not completed until 1914. *See also* Suez Canal. ✤232
Levant Name formerly given to the countries bordering the eastern Mediterranean from Egypt to Turkey, and later more particularly to Lebanon and Syria.
Crusader states ✤65, ◆65 (3)
trade links (BCE) ✤31
Lewis, Meriwether (1774–1809) US explorer. With Clark, led the famous expedition (1804–06) sponsored by President Jefferson to explore the land acquired in the Louisiana Purchase and find a land route to the Pacific.
Columbia River map ❑119
portrait ❑118
US expedition (1804–06) ◆119 (3)
Lewis Outer Hebrides, chesspieces (12th century) ❑60
Lexington ⚔ of American Revolutionary War (19 Apr 1775). British victory. ◆127 (3)
Leyte Gulf Naval ⚔ of WW II (Oct 1944). Major US victory over Japan, facilitating US invasion of Philippines. ✤105, ◆273 (2)
Lhasa
Dalai Lama's Potala palace ❑257
first Jesuit mission (1661) ✤257●
visit by French monks (1846) ✤257●
Li dynasty *see* Yi dynasty
Li Tzu-cheng *see* Li Zicheng.
Li Zicheng (*var.* Li Tzu-cheng) (c.1605–45) Chinese rebel leader whose entry in 1644 into Beijing precipitated the suicide of the last Ming emperor. ✤266●
Liao *see* Khitans
Liao Empire Extensive state established by the nomadic Khitan people in Manchuria, Mongolia, and northeastern China in the early 10th century. The empire coexisted with the Chinese Song dynasty, but, in 1125, fell to the Jurchen people, who founded the Jin dynasty of northern China. ◆263 (3) (4)
founded by Khitans ✤263
defeated by Manchurian Jin (1125) ✤63●
Song China subject state (1005) ✤63●
Liberia Founded by freed slaves (1822) ✤91●
Libya 168–9
bombed by US (1986) ✤111●
conquered by Italy ✤232
industrial growth ✤168, ◆168 (2)
modern political development ◆169 (4)
Liegnitz ⚔ (1241). Polish army defeated by Mongols. ◆189 (3)
Liguria Lombard conquest (600 CE) ◆182 (2)
Lima
founded (1535) ✤148●
centre of Spanish Empire in S America ✤81
cultural region ◆145 (4)
limes Defensive lines built by the Romans to protect the borders of their empire. The *limes* could consist of a continuous wall, as in northern Britain and parts of the German frontier, or a string of isolated forts, as in Syria. ◆180 (1)
Limited War Doctrine Strategic policy of limited military commitment and geographic containment, developed by the Western Allies during Korean War, in an attempt to contain spread of Cold War confrontations into intercontinental conflict. ✤109
Lincoln, Abraham (1809–65) 16th President of the US (Republican, 1861–65). The setting up of the Republican party in 1856, to oppose the extension of slavery in the US, brought Abraham Lincoln, a self-educated lawyer, who had sat in Congress since 1846, to national prominence. In 1860 he won a comfortable majority in the presidential election but was unable to prevent the secession of seven of the southern states from the Union, and the resultant Civil War between the Union and Confederate states. While defining the preservation of the Union as the primary issue of the war, most famously in the Gettysburg Address of 1863, his Emancipation Proclamation of the same year freed the slaves in the southern states. Re-elected for a second term in 1865, he was assassinated barely a month after his inaugural address.
assassination ✤131●
Emancipation Proclamation ✤130, ✤131●
portrait ❑130
Linear A *see* Minoans
Linschoten, J. H. Van Late 16th-century Dutch cartographer. ✤239●, ❑239
Lisbon
expedition sent to Brazil (1502) ✤149●
Moors lose to Crusaders (1147) ✤62●, ◆64 (1)
in Spanish Empire ✤81
Lithuania
expansion ✤189, ◆189 (4)
joined with Poland (1386) ✤189●
Little Bighorn ⚔ (1876). American forces led by General Custer destroyed by Sioux and Cheyenne. ◆128–9 (2)
Livingstone, David (1813–73). Scottish missionary who, during his three visits to Africa in the period 1841–73, undertook journeys of exploration throughout the southern half of the continent. He was the first European to reach Lake Ngami in 1849 and the first to see the Victoria Falls in 1855. Appalled by the treatment of African slaves, he dedicated much of his life to fighting the trade, clashing frequently with the Boers and Portuguese. Between 1866 and 1871 no news was heard of Livingstone until he was tracked down by Henry Morton Stanley, who had been sent by a New York newspaper to find him.
explorer of Africa ◆157 (4)
Livonian Order *see* Sword Brothers. ✤189
Llanos de Mojos Drainage earthworks ✤145
Lübeck Seal ❑190
Lodi ⚔ of Napoleon's Italian campaign (1896). French victory. ◆200 (1)
Lodi, Peace of (1454) Ended wars in Italy between Milan, Venice, Florence and the Papal States. ✤75●
Lodz ⚔ of WW I (11–25 Nov 1914). German occupation followed Russian defeat ✤206●, ◆206 (4)
Lollards Reforming religious group, influential in Europe during the 14th–15th centuries, famous for their attacks on church corruption and emphasis on the biblical scriptures. ✤70
l'Olonnois, François 17th-century French privateer in the Caribbean. ◆85 (2)
Lombard League Alliance of cities of northern Italy formed in 1167, to oppose the German Emperor Frederick I (Barbarossa). 188●, ◆188 (1), ✤190●
Lombards (*var.* Langobardi). Germanic people settled along the Danube in the 5th century. In 568 they invaded northern Italy, swiftly overrunning the region now known as Lombardy, and establishing two southern duchies, Benevento and Spoleto. They never controlled the whole of Italy and conflict with the Byzantine Empire and the Papacy continued for 200 years, until their defeat by Charlemagne in 774.
capture Ravenna (752) ✤58●
defeated by Charlemagne (774) ✤58●
gem-studded gold buckle ❑183
glass drinking horn ❑182
kingdom and duchies (600 CE) ◆182 (2)
struggle for Italy ✤184, ✤184●, ◆183 (4)
London
reconquered by Alfred the Great (885) ✤58●
Underground ✤92●, ❑102
Long Island ⚔ of American Revolutionary War (27 Aug 1776). British victory. ◆127 (3)
Long, Major Stephen H. (1784–1864) US army engineer and explorer. Led expeditions along the Missouri (1819–20) and the Platte and South Platte Rivers in the Rocky Mountains, south to the Red River (1821). Produced a map which named the region as the Great American Desert. Later explored the 49th parallel. ◆119 (3)
Long March (Oct 1934–Oct 1935). Withdrawal of the Communist forces during the Chinese Civil War from their bases in southern China to the northwest, led by Mao Zedong. ✤274●, ❑274, ◆274 (1)
Longmen nr Luoyang, Chinese Buddhist cave-temple ❑51
Longshan culture Named after Long Shan (Dragon Mountain) in northeast China's Shandong province. This Neolithic culture developed from the Yangshao culture as bronze was coming into use, and flourished between c.3000–1700 BCE in the Yellow River valley. Their economy was based on millet, pigs, cows and goats, and is characterized by polished stone tools and distinctive pottery, the first in the Far East made on a fast wheel, and kiln – fired to a uniform black colour. ✤258●, ❑23, ◆258 (2)
López de Cárdenas, García 16th-century Spanish explorer of the Americas, a member of Coronado's expedition north from Mexico in 1540–42. ◆118 (1)
Lord Curzon (*f/n* George Nathanial Curzon, Marquis of Kedleston) (1898–1905) Viceroy of India (1898–1905). An energetic reformer of the civil service, education system and police force, he created the new Northwest Frontier Province (1898) and partitioned the province of Bengal (1905). ✤250
Los Angeles
ethnic distribution (1960–90) ✤137, ◆137 (6)
Hollywood film studios (1919) ✤135, ❑135
race riots (1940s) ✤135●
Watts Riots (1965) ✤137●
Louis I (*aka* Louis the Great) (1326–82). King of Hungary. A member of the Anjou dynasty that became kings of Naples in the 13th century, Louis frequently intervened in Neapolitan politics after the murder of his brother, the Queen's consort, in 1345. He also fought three wars with Venice for control of the Dalmatian coast. In 1370 he inherited the crown of Poland, but could not really impose his authority there. ✤189, ◆189 (4)
Louis the Pious (778–840) Frankish king, son of Charlemagne. Crowned by his father in 813, Louis attempted to hold the Carolingian Empire together, but the last decade of his reign was marked by civil wars between him and his four sons. ✤184, ✤184●
Louis VII (1120–80) King of France. In 1152 Louis divorced Eleanor of Aquitaine, who then married Henry of Anjou, who became king of England as Henry II in 1154. This weakened the position of the French crown, as large tracts of France came under English control. ✤187
Crusade route (1147–49) ◆64–5 (2)
trade monopoly ✤191●
Louis IX (*aka* St. Louis) (1214–70).King of France. Famed for his piety, for which he was canonized in 1297, Louis was also an enthusiastic crusader and organized and led two crusades. On the first in 1248, he was captured and ransomed in Egypt. On the second in 1270, he died while besieging Tunis. ✤64, ✤66●, ◆64–5 (2)
initiated W Asia exploration ✤219
coffin returned to France ❑64
Louis XIV (*aka* 'the Sun King') (1638–1715) King of France (r.1643–1715). Effective ruler after 1661, he established an absolute monarchy. For the next 50 years he was the most powerful monarch in Europe, but his ambition to establish French supremacy in Europe led to numerous wars, especially with Spain, Holland and England. His attempt to forge a union between France and Spain led to the War of the Spanish Succession (1701–14), which left France virtually bankrupt. His long reign was marked by a flourishing of the French arts, symbolized by the Palace of Versailles.
France under Louis XIV ✤197, ✤197●, ◆197 (5)
king of France (1643–1715) ✤86●, ✤196
portrait ❑82, ❑197
Louis XVI (1754–93) King of France. In 1788 Louis' financial problems forced him to summon the Estates-General (the French parliament that had not met since 1614). This became the National Assembly and precipitated the French Revolution. Louis became virtually a prisoner of the state. His unsuccessful attempt to flee France in 1791 led to his trial the following year and in 1793 he was guillotined for treason.
French Revolution ✤82, ✤86, ✤90, ✤199, ❑199, ◆199 (4)
guillotined (1793) ❑86

Key to index: ✤ text ● timeline ❑ picture ◆ map *var.* variant name *aka* also known as *f/n* full name *prev.* previously known as r. ruled ⚔ battle WW I First World War WW II Second World War

Louis-Napoleon *see* Napoleon III
Louis Philippe (1773–1850) King of France (r.1830–48). Son of the Duke of Orléans, cousin of Louis XVI, Louis Philippe, like his father, who was known as Philippe Egalité, at first supported the Revolution. But after Louis-Philippe fled the country, his father was executed in 1793. Louis Philippe was invited to become king in 1830 after the July Revolution of that year, but abdicated during the 1848 Revolution and died in exile in England. ✤90
Louisiana Purchase French territory added to the US in 1803 following its purchase from France for less than 3 cents an acre by Thomas Jefferson. It more than doubled the area of the US at the time, adding more than 2,144,520 sq km (828,000 sq miles) of territory. ◆129 (1), ✤128
 exploration by Lewis and Clarke (1805–06) ✤119●
 sale of French territory (1803) ✤90●
Lovelock Cave Duck decoys (c.1500 BCE) ❑26
Lower Moesia Visigoth settlement area ✤53
Lucius Tarquinius Priscus *see* Tarquin I
Lucius Tarquinius Superbus *see* Tarquin II
Luddite riots Protests by English textile workers, chiefly in the Midlands, alarmed at the introduction of industrial machinery and fearful for their jobs. The first such riots, accompanied by widespread machine-wrecking, occurred in 1811 ✤204●
Ludwig, Daniel Keith (1897–1992). American entrepreneur who began a billion-dollar development of the Jari River valley in Brazil, but in 1982 he abandoned the costly project, which had led to the destruction of large tracts of tropical rain forest. ✤153●
Luoyang
 conquered by Qin (256 BCE) ✤39
 northern Wei capital (c.490) ✤51●
Luther, Martin (1483–1546). German scholar and priest whose questioning of certain church practices led to the Protestant Reformation. He first clashed with the Catholic authorities in 1517 after his *95 Theses* attacking the sale of indulgences denied that the pope and clergy could forgive sins. He inspired a movement that revolutionized religious thought, incidentally provoking much social and political upheaval in northern Europe. ✤78●, ✤194, ✤194●
Luxembourg dynasty The counts of Luxembourg were a powerful dynasty in the late Middle Ages. They were also kings of Bohemia and four of their number were elected emperor, the most famous being Charles IV.
 possessions ◆70–1, ✤189 ◆189 (4), ◆194 (2)
 creation of modern duchy , ✤202, ◆202 (1 inset)
Luxor *see* Thebes ❑29
Lyasu I Ethiopian king ✤165●
Lydia
 (BCE) ✤35, ✤223, ◆34–5, ◆223 (4)
 issues first coins (BCE) ✤35
Lysimachus (*var. Gre.* Lysimachos) (360–281 BCE) General of Alexander the Great. Following Alexander's death in 323, Lysimachus became ruler of Thrace. He extended his territories in the wars between Alexander's successors, but was killed in battle against Seleucus, with whom he had formerly been allied. ✤224●, ◆224 (1)

M

Maastricht Treaty (*var.* European Union Treaty) (Dec 1991). International agreement between the states of the European Community (EC) in Maastricht, Netherlands which established the European Union (EU), with Union citizenship for every person holding the nationality of a member state. It provided for the establishment of a central banking system and the implementation of a common foreign and security policy. ✤214
Macao Portuguese colony in China.
 16th-century voyages by Portuguese ✤80
 returned to China (1999) ◆111
Macedonia
 Antigonid dynasty ✤41, ✤224, ✤224●, ◆224 (1)
 (BCE) ◆34–5, ◆38–9
 Byzantine rulers (867–1081) ✤59
 growth of power ✤40●
Machu Picchu Inca sacred shrine ❑74
MacKenzie, Colin (c.1753–1821) Officer in the British East India Company's army, whose accurate mapping led to his appointment as Surveyor-general of India in 1819. ✤239, ✤239●, ❑239
Mackenzie, Sir Alexander (c.1755–1820) Explorer and fur-trader. In 1789, on behalf of the Northwestern Company, he ventured to Great Slave Lake and down what was to become the Mackenzie River to the Arctic Ocean. His next expedition, starting from Lake Athabasca in 1792, eventually reached the Pacific Ocean, making him the first white man to cross N America north of Mexico. ◆286 (1)
MAD *see* Mutually Assured Destruction
Madaba 6th-century mosaic ❑51
Madagascar
 Arab trading settlements ✤58, ✤61, ◆61 (3)
 colonized by Malays ✤61
 French conquest (1883–96) ✤167●, ◆167
 Portuguese map (1558) ❑156
Madero, Francisco Indalecio (1873–1913) Mexican revolutionary and statesman. In 1908, Madero launched a presidential campaign against the dictator, Porfirio Díaz. Imprisoned by Díaz, he then fled to the US and launched a military campaign, capturing Ciudad Juárez, which he made his capital in May 1911. He made moderate reforms as President, but was increasingly faced by revolts demanding land reform. He was murdered in Feb 1913 following a military coup by Victoriano Huerta, assisted by the US ambassador. ✤133, ◆133 (3)
Mafia (*aka* Cosa Nostra). International criminal organization, originally based in Sicily and dating from the 13th century. In the US, the Mafia became one of the major forces in the development of organized crime, especially during the Prohibition era. ✤113, ◆113 (4)
Magadha One of the 16 mahajanapadas (great realms) which dominated the Ganges plain from c.600 BCE. Gradually all the other kingdoms were absorbed into Magadha, with its capital at Pataliputra (Patna), which dominated the lucrative Ganges trade routes. Magadha became the nucleus of the first Indian empire, the Mauryan Empire, when its throne was seized by Chandragupta Maurya in 327 BCE. Magadha was the scene of many of the incidents in the life of Gautama Buddha. Later the centre of the Gupta dynasty. ✤36, ✤39, ✤241, ◆241 (4)
Magellan, Ferdinand (c.1480–1521). Portuguese navigator, who undertook his most famous voyage in the service of the Spanish crown. In 1519 he sailed with five ships to discover a westward route to the Indies. This he achieved, sailing through the Strait of Magellan, then crossing the Pacific to the Philippines. There, Magellan was killed after intervening in a local war. One of his ships, captained by Sebastián del Cano, made the journey back to Spain, thus completing the first circumnavigation of the globe.
 16th-century Portuguese navigator ✤78, ◆239 (1)
 global circumnavigation ✤76, ❑80
 Oceania voyages ◆278 (1)
 reaches the Pacific (1520) ✤142
Magnesia, ⚔ (190 BCE). Roman victory over Seleucid king Antiochus III. ◆179 (4)
Magyars People of the steppes, the ancestors of today's Hungarians, who migrated into present-day Hungary in the late 9th century. Their raids at first struck fear into western European states, but following their defeat by Otto I at Lechfeld in 955, the Magyars started to lead a more settled existence and in the 11th century Hungary became a Christian kingdom.
 defeated by Otto I ✤58, ✤58●
 raids (c.800–1000) ◆185 (3)
 settle in Danube basin ✤185●
Mahabharata Sanskrit epic which, along with the *Ramayana*, was composed c.450 BCE. It tells the story of an epic struggle for supremacy between two groups of cousins, the Kauravas and the Pandavas. The battle was fought in northwestern India, and is probably an account of Mauryan expansion. ✤241, ❑241, ❑244, ◆241 (5)
Mahavira (c.540–468 BCE) Brought up as a pious Jain near Patna, Mahavira became a monk, who instructed 11 disciples, and became the foremost preceptor of the Jain religion. ✤242●, ◆242 (3)
Mahayana Buddhism (*aka* Greater Vehicle). Interpretation of Buddhism developed from 1st century CE which spread from NW India into China, Korea, Japan and Tibet; focusing on the concept of the Bodhisattva, who would postpone entry into *nirvana* until all others are similarly enlightened, Mahayana regards the historical Buddha as a temporary manifestation of the eternal and innate nature of the Buddha. *See also* Buddhism.
Mahmud of Ghazni (*var.* Muhammad of Ghazni) (r.971–1030). Ruler of an empire, consisting of Afghanistan, northeastern Persia, and northwest India (r.998–1030). Mahmud was the son of a Turkish ruler of Khurasan, a vassal of the Samanids. His reign was notable for the frequent raids he made on northern India. The Ghaznavid dynasty continued to rule until the late 12th century when they were overthrown by the Ghurids. ✤59●, ✤63, ◆227 (6)
Mainz First use of movable metal type ✤74
Majapahit Empire Javanese empire from the late 13th to the 16th century. Although Majapahit probably exercised direct rule only over Java and nearby small islands, in its heyday in the 14th century, its powerful fleets controlled trade over a far wider area, including the Moluccan Spice Islands. ✤71●, ✤245●, ❑244, ◆245 (6)
Makuria
 Arab invasion ✤162●
 Coptic Christianity ✤58
Malacca
 founded (c.1400) ✤75●
 captured by Dutch (1641) ✤83●
 captured by Portuguese (1510) ✤79●, ◆247 (4)
 converts to Islam (1445) ✤75●
 trading centre ✤75
Malay Peninsula
 Chola conquests ✤59
 rubber plantations ❑97
Malaya (now Malaysia)
 Independence (1957) ✤251, ◆251 (4)
 rebellion (1947–48) ❑251
 seized by Japan (1942) ✤103●
Mali Empire West African state at its most powerful in the 13th and 14th centuries. The empire was founded by Sundiata c.1235, though a small state had existed there for some two centuries before. ◆162 (1)–(7)
 founded ✤67●, ✤163●
 collapses (c.1660) ✤164●
 conquered by Songhay (1546) ✤79●
 conquered by Sunni Ali ✤75
 control of caravan trade ✤70, ✤163
 Ibn Battuta's visit (1352) ✤71●
 Jenne mosque ❑162
 Mansa Musa 14th-century ruler ❑71
 usurps Kingdom of Ghana (13th century) ✤66
Malinke West African people, the most influential of the Mali Empire, famous as travelling merchants. ✤163
Mamluks (*var.* Mamelukes). Slave soldiers in many medieval Islamic states, frequently of Turkish origin, noted for their skill and bravery. Mamluks often rose to occupy positions of great power. In Egypt they ruled the country from 1250 until 1517, when it was conquered by the Ottomans.
 and Mongols in W Asia ✤67●, ✤69, ✤229, ✤229●, ◆229 (3)
 conquered by Ottomans (1517) ✤79●
 superbly trained warriors ❑229
 takeover of Egypt (1250) ✤67●
Manassas *see* Bull Run
Manaus Founded (1674) ✤149●
Manchester
 expansion in 19th century ◆204 (2)
 market for finished cloth ✤93
Manchuria
 army topples Ming dynasty (1644) ✤83
 invasion of Burma (1765–69) ✤87●
 Mekong Delta settlement (1679) ✤83●
 rulers of the Qing dynasty ✤268
 occupied by Japan (1918–20) ✤99●
 Song–Jin alliance ✤63
 trade
 BCE jade imports ✤19●
 bronze technology ✤31
Manchu dynasty *see* Qing dynasty
Manda Coastal trading colony (c.800) ✤58
Mandela, Nelson (*f/n* Nelson Rolihlahla Mandela) (1918–). South African Black nationalist and statesman, who was imprisoned for 28 years (1962–90) but was subsequently elected to the presidency in 1994.
 imprisoned (1964–90) ✤107●, ✤111, ✤169●
 portrait ❑111
 wins presidency (1994) ✤111●, ✤168
Mandinka Merchants' topographic reports ✤156
Manichaeism Dualist religion founded in Persia in the 3rd century CE by Mani, who tried to integrate the messages of Zoroaster, Jesus and Buddha into one universal creed. Often regarded as a Christian heresy. ◆49 (4)
Manila galleon Every year, from the late 16th century, the Spanish sent a galleon laden with silver from Acapulco to Manila in the Philippines to pay for silk and other luxury goods from China. The galleon returned to Mexico, laden with silks and oriental luxury goods that were then shipped on to Spain. ✤81, ◆81 (3)
Mansa Musa Ruler of Mali Empire (r.c.1312–1337). Under Mansa Musa, the Mali Empire reached the height of its power, largely through its control of the West African gold trade. He demonstrated his country's great wealth on his pilgrimage to Mecca in 1324.
 pilgrimage to Mecca (1324) ✤70
 ruler of Mali (14th century) ❑71
Mansurah ⚔ of the Crusades (1250). Defeat of the crusader army of Louis IX as it advanced into Egypt. ✤64●, ◆65 (3)
Mansvelt, Edward 17th-century Dutch sailor, who raided Spanish colonies in the Caribbean. ◆85 (2)
Manzikert ⚔ of 1071. Decisive victory of the Seljuk Turks over the Byzantines which resulted in the collapse of Byzantine power in Asia Minor. ✤228●, ◆228 (1)
Mao Tse-tung *see* Mao Zedong
Mao Zedong (*var.* Mao Tse-tung) (1893–1976). Chinese Communist leader and first Chairman of the People's Republic of China (1949).
 Chinese Communists win civil war (1949) ✤103●, ✤274, ◆274 (1)
 'Great Leap Forward' begins (1958) ✤107●, ✤274, ❑274
 imposes Cultural Revolution (1966–70) ✤107●
 'Little Red Book' ✤107
 portrait ❑107
Maori Indigenous people of New Zealand of Polynesian origin. They reached New Zealand (Aotearoa) c.700 BCE, making it one of the last Pacific island groups to be colonized. ✤283
 carved canoe head ❑281
 resistance to colonization ✤283●
 Maori 'Musket Wars' ◆283 (4) (5)
 migration ◆283 (4)
mappamundi ✤173●, ❑66
maquilladora Name given to foreign-owned (often US) assembly plants in Mexico which are used for the import and assembly of duty-free items. ◆136 (1)
Maranhão
 established as separate colony from Brazil (1621) ✤149●, ◆149 (3)
 occupied by France (1568) ✤149●
 Portuguese expelled by Dutch (1625) ✤149●
Maratha Confederacy Hindu state, based in the rock forts of the Western Ghats, the Maratha Confederacy was founded by Sivaji. Although the Mughal emperor Aurangzeb checked the advance of the Marathas during his lifetime, after his death in 1707 the Confederacy gained control over much of India. In 1761 the Marathas confronted invading Afghans and were routed at ⚔ Panipat. Yet the Marathas continued to present a formidable military obstacle to the growing power of the British. The three Anglo-Maratha wars, which took place from 1775–1818 ultimately led to Maratha defeat. ✤87●, ✤246, ✤246●, ◆246 (2)
Marathon ⚔ (490 BCE). Athenian defeat of Persians. ◆223 (4)
Marchand, Jean-Baptiste (1863–1934). French soldier and explorer who in 1898 occupied Fashoda in the Sudan. ◆157 (4)
Marconi, Guglielmo Marchese (1874–1937) Italian physicist and inventor of wireless telegraphy (1895). ✤92●
Marcos, Ferdinand (1917–89). US-sponsored President of the Philippines (r.1965–86), accused of repression, fraud and corruption. Died in exile in Hawaii following electoral defeat. ✤252●
Marcus Antonius *see* Mark Antony
Marcus Aurelius (121–180 CE) Roman emperor, adopted son of Antoninus Pius. As emperor, he worked conscientiously for what he considered the public good, but his reign (161–180) was marked by warfare and disaster. War with the Parthians was followed by a highly infectious 'plague'. The emperor then fought a long campaign to secure the Danube frontier against incursions by Germanic tribes. While on campaign, he wrote his reflections on Stoic philosophy, the *Meditations*. ❑46
Marcus Ulpius Traianus *see* Trajan
Mari Ancient Mari was the most important city on the middle Euphrates in the 3rd and 2nd millennia BCE, until its destruction by the Babylonians in 1759 BCE. Its importance as the centre of a vast trading network covering northwest Mesopotamia is evidenced by around 20,000 cuneiform tablets which were found there. ✤27
Mariana Islands ⚔ of WW II (Jun–Aug 1944). Scene of a series of major US amphibious assaults during the'island-hopping' campaign in central Pacific. ◆105 (3), ◆272 (1), ✤273, ◆273 (2)
Marie Antoinette (1755–93) Queen of France. The daughter of Maria Theresa of Austria, she married the future Louis XVI of France in 1770. As an Austrian, she was never popular with the French. Her reputation sank even lower with the Revolution and she was tried and executed in 1793. ✤86
Marienburg Teutonic Knights headquarters ❑189
Marignano ⚔ (1515). Swiss defeated by Francis I of France. ◆194 (1)
Marin, Luis 16th-century Spanish colonizer of Mexico. ✤125
Marinids Berber dynasty that ruled Morocco from the 13th to the 15th century.
 defeat Almohads (1269) ✤67●
 take Tunis (1347) ✤71●
Marius, Gaius (157–86 BCE). Roman general and politician, who married into the aristocracy and achieved high position due to his military talents, including his role in suppressing the rebellious Numidian king, Jugurtha. Ruthlessly ambitious, he held an unprecedented seven consulships, and reformed the army by recruiting men of no property to create a professional fighting force, with the legions divided for the first time into cohorts and centuries. ✤43●
Mark Antony (*var.* Marcus Antonius) (83 BCE–30 BCE). A relative and staunch supporter of Julius Caesar. After Caesar's death in 44 BCE, he almost assumed absolute power in Rome, laying the foundations of future power struggles with Caesar's heir Octavian. While reorganizing the government of the eastern provinces he met Cleopatra, by whom he had several children. When he started giving large areas of Rome's eastern territories to his children, declaring Cleopatra's son by Julius Caesar heir in Octavian's place, Octavian rallied Rome against him. Antony was defeated at Actium in 31 BCE, and committed suicide soon after. ✤180
Market Garden, Operation *see* Arnhem
Marne ⚔ of WW I (Sep 1914). Saw the Allied halting of the German advance on Paris. ◆206 (2)
Marne ⚔ of WW I (Jul 1918). Ended the German offensive on the Western Front. ◆206 (3)
Marquesas Islands Settled by Polynesians ✤60
Marquette, Father Jacques (1637–75) French Jesuit missionary, who accompanied Louis Jolliet down the Mississippi River in 1673, coming to within 640 km of its mouth. ◆119 (2)
Marshall Plan (*aka* European Recovery Program) (Apr 1948–Dec 1951). US-sponsored programme designed to rehabilitate the economies of 17 European nations in order to create stable conditions in which democratic institutions could survive. ✤102●, ✤108●, ✤138, ✤213, ❑213, ◆213 (5)
Martínez de Irala, Domingo (c.1512–56) Commander of the precarious Spanish colony at Asunción in the 1540s and 1550s. He explored the Gran Chaco region and discovered a route across the continent to Peru. ◆142 (1)
Masada Mass suicide of Zealots ✤225
Masina Amadu Lobbo's *jihad* (1816) ✤167●
Masinissa (c.240–148 BCE). Masaeyli ruler of the N African kingdom of Numidia who assisted Rome conquer Carthaginian territory. ✤161●, ◆161 (2)
Massachusetts Bay English colony founded (1630) ✤82●
Massalia (*var. Lat.* Massilia, *mod.* Marseille). Greek colony in the south of France that was a significant political and economic power in the 3rd and 2nd centuries BCE. Gradually absorbed by Rome. ✤34●, ◆38–9
 possessions in 3rd century BCE ◆179 (3)
 possessions in 120 BCE ◆179 (4)
mastodon relative of the elephant, hunted to extinction c.10,000 years ago. ✤18
Mataram Sultanate of Java
 expansion in 17th century ✤83●, ◆245 (5), ◆247 (4)
mathematics
 Babylonian text ❑33
 16th-century revival of Chinese ✤80
 calculating device ❑147
 Egyptian counting stick ❑33
 evolution of numerical systems ✤33, ◆33 (2)
 Maya civilization ✤54
 Rhind mathematical papyrus ❑33
Matthias Corvinus *see* Matthias I Hunyadi
Matthias I Hunyadi (*aka* Matthias Corvinus) (1443–90) King of Hungary (r.1458–90). During his reign, Hungary was almost continually at war against Bohemia and the Turks. In 1477 his armies invaded Austria, besieging and capturing Vienna. Patron of learning and science and founder of the Corvina Library at Buda. ❑193, ◆193 (4)
Mauretania
 Christian converts (c.150 CE) ✤47●
 Roman control ✤46
Mauri Berber inhabitants of the Roman province of Mauretania. ◆161 (2)
Maurits of Nassau (1604–79). Sent by his cousin, the stadholder, Frederick Henry, to govern the colony in Brazil which the Dutch had taken from the Portuguese. After his successful governorship (1836–44) he returned to Europe and fought in wars against Britain and France. ✤149
Mauryan dynasty (321–180 BCE). Ancient Indian dynasty and the first to establish control over all India. Founded by Chandragupta Maurya in 321 BCE and extended by his son Bindusara and his grandson Ashoka. The dynasty's power declined under Ashoka's successors and finally ended in c.180 BCE. ✤43, ✤241, ✤241●, ◆38–9, ◆241 (4)
Mauryan Empire *see* Mauryan dynasty.
Mawson, Sir Douglas (1882–1958) Australian explorer and geologist. Accompanied Shackleton to the Antarctic in 1907–09 and reached the Magnetic S Pole. Led the Australasian Antarctic Expedition 1911–14, and a joint British, Australasian and New Zealand Antarctic expedition in 1929–31. ◆287 (3)
Maya People of Central American and the dominant culture of Central America, between 250 and 900 CE, in present-day southern Mexico, Guatemala, northern Belize and western Honduras. The Maya are famed for their skills in astronomy, including developing solar and sacred calendars, hieroglyphic writing and ceremonial architecture. An elite of priests and nobles ruled the agricultural population from political centres, characterized by plazas and vast palaces and pyramid temples.
 (200–790 CE) ◆122 (2)
 Arch of Labna ❑122
 calendar ✤54
 Classic Age (c.300–600) ✤50, ✤54●
 collapse in southern lowlands (850) ✤58●
 controlled by Aztecs (1519) ✤124
 early Central America ◆121 (2)
 El Mirador complex (1 CE) ✤46●
 Mayapán founded (1283) ✤66●
 in post-Classic period ◆124 (1)
 state religion ◆36 (1)
 Temple of the Jaguars ❑58
 vase ❑50
Meadowcroft Rock Shelter (15,000 BCE) ✤14●, ✤120●, ◆120 (1)
Mecca Capital of the Hejaz region of western Saudi Arabia. The birthplace of the Prophet Muhammad, it is Islam's holiest city and the centre of pilgrimage.
 annual Muslim pilgrimage ❑218
 captured by Wahhabis (1806) ✤233
 Ibn Battuta's first pilgrimage (1325) ✤68●
 Islamic religious centre ✤226, ✤56, ❑226, ◆226 (2) (3)
 pilgrimage by Mansa Musa (1324) ✤70
 See also Haj
Medes Ancient people who lived to the southwest of the Caspian Sea. They were at their peak during the 7th century BCE when, alongside the Babylonians, they conquered the Assyrians and extended their power westwards to central Anatolia and eastwards through most of Persia. Their empire was overwhelmed by the Persians in the mid-6th century BCE. ✤31, ◆34–35
Medina Muhammad's capital (622) ✤55●, ✤56, ✤226
Mediterranean
 700–300 BCE ◆176–7, ◆177 (1)
 colonization ✤176
 religions (BCE) ◆37 (3)

megaliths (*var.* cromlechs, *Gr.* mega lithas: large stones). – European prehistoric structures, often tombs, were constructed of massive, roughly dressed stone slabs and were built across Europe during the Neolithic period, from c.5000 BCE. They are comparable, although unrelated, to megalithic monuments found in S India, Tibet, and SE Asia. ◆22
Megiddo ⚔ of WWI (18–23 Sep 1918). Final battle of the Palestine campaign fought by British and Commonwealth troops against Turkey. A British and Commonwealth victory, it also marked the last use of massed cavalry in warfare. ✣232●, ◆233 (2)
Mehmet II 'the Conqueror' (1432–1481) Ottoman Sultan (r.1451–81) who in 1453 captured Constantinople (Istanbul) and pursued the rapid expansion of the empire into Greece, the Balkans, and Hungary.
  fall of Constantinople (1453) ✣75, ✣230
  Topkapi palace ❑231
Mehmet VI (1861–1926) Ottoman Sultan (r.1918–22). His failure to suppress the Turkish Nationalists, led by Mustafa Kemal (Atatürk), resulted in the abolition of the sultanate, and his subsequent exile. ✣233
Mehmet Ali *see* Muhammad Ali
Mehrgarh Early pottery discovered ✣19, ✣20●, ✣23●
Meiji Japanese term meaning 'enlightened rule'. The restoration of the Meiji emperor in 1868 ended Japan's two centuries of isolationism under the Tokugawa Shogunate and initiated a period of political and economic reform.
  modernization of Japan ◆270 (1)
Melanesia One of three broad geographical divisions of the Pacific, the others being Micronesia and Polynesia. Melanesia includes New Guinea, New Caledonia, the Solomons and Vanuatu. ✣276
Melbourne Founded (1835–36) ✣91
Memphis ⚔ of American Civil War (5 Jun 1862). Union victory. ◆131 (6)
Memphis (Egypt)
  founded (3100 BCE) ✣23●
  BCE invasions ✣34, ✣35●
Mena *see* Narmer
Mencius (*var.* Meng-tzu) (c.371–c.289 BCE) Chinese philosopher who continued the teachings of Confucius. Developed a school to promote Confucian ideas, and from the age of 40 travelled China for 20 years searching for a ruler to implement Confucian morals and ideals. Believed that man was by nature good, but required the proper conditions for moral growth. ✣37
Mendaña, Álvaro de (c.1542–95) Spanish explorer of the Pacific. On Mendaña's first Pacific voyage in 1568, he discovered the Solomon Islands. He was attempting to return there and establish a colony in 1595, but he could not find the islands. He died on Santa Cruz Island. ✣278●
Mendoza, Hurtado de 16th-century Spanish explorer of Lower California. ✣125, ◆125 (4)
Menéndez de Avilés, Pedro 16th-century Spanish *conquistador* and explorer of N America. Founded San Agustín in Florida (1565). ✣125, ◆125 (4)
Menes *see* Narmer
Meneses, Jorge de 16th-century Portuguese traveller in the East Indies. Sighted New Guinea (1526) ✣278●
Meng-tzu *see* Mencius
Meni *see* Narmer
Mercator, Gerardus (*prev.* Gerhard Kremer) (1512–94) Flemish cartographer. Originator of the Mercator projection and publisher of the first book to use the world 'Atlas' to describe a set of maps. ✣79, ✣173, ✣173●, ❑173
Meroë
  BCE–CE capital of Egypt ✣34–5, ✣42
  Cushite temple relic ❑35
  invaded by Axumites (c.350) ✣50●
Merovingians (c.448–751) The first dynasty of Frankish kings of Gaul, named after Merovech, grandfather of Clovis I. ✣183, ◆183 (5) (6)
Mesa Verde cliff dwellings (c.1100) ✣62●, ✣123●
Mesolithic Literally the 'middle stone age', this is a term applied to the transitional period between the Palaeolithic (old stone age) and Neolithic (new stone age) in western Europe. The Mesolithic covers the period from the end of the last Ice Age, c.10,000 BCE, to the adoption of farming, c.7000–6000 years ago. It is characterized in the archaeological record by chipped stone tools, in particular microliths, very small stone tools intended for mounting on a shaft. These, as well as tools made of bone, antler and wood, were used by hunter-gatherer communities, roughly contemporary with Neolithic farming groups further east. ✣14, ❑14, ✣18●
Mesopotamia The area between the Tigris and Euphrates, literally 'land between the rivers'. Lower Mesopotamia covered Baghdad to the Persian Gulf, and was home to the world's first urban civilizations in the 4th millennium BCE. Upper Mesopotamia extended from Baghdad northwest to the foothills of eastern Anatolia. ◆222 (1)
  BCE ✣19, ✣35, ✣43, ◆36 (1)
  city-states ✣27
  history and legends ✣222, ❑222
  Ottoman and Safavid clashes ✣79
  pictograph writing (c.3250) ✣23
  Seleucid Empire ✣41, ✣224, ◆38–9, ◆224 (1)
  trading links ✣25
  urban expansion and revolution (BCE) ✣23, ✣24●, ✣28, ◆28 (1)
metallurgy The range of techniques associated with metal-working: extracting metals from their ores, converting them into useful forms such as alloys, and fabricating objects.
  BCE use ✣18–19, ✣23●, ✣30–1, ✣34, ✣174–5
  development ✣26●
  Eurasian and African tin trade (c.1 CE) ◆44–5
  gold rushes ✣90●, ✣93
  See also bronze; copper; gold; silver
Metaurus River ⚔ of Punic Wars (207 BCE). Roman victory. ◆179 (3)
Metternich, Clemens Fürst von (1773–1859) Austrian statesman. In 1809 he became Austrian foreign minister and was instrumental in the fall of Napoleon. He was the architect of the 'Vienna system' in 1814–15, and the major force in European politics from 1814 until he was forced from office by the Viennese revolution of 1848. ❑202
Mexican Civil War (1858–67). Broke out between conservatives and liberals in 1858. The liberal leader Benito Juárez became president. His defeat of the conservative forces in 1860 was dependent on loans from western powers. France, Spain and Britain invaded Mexico to enforce loan repayments; in 1863 a French army occupied Mexico city. The French appointed Archduke Maximilian of Austria as Mexican emperor. He was ousted in 1867 by Juárez' forces, and Juárez was re-elected as president (1867–72). ✣94●, ✣128–9●
Mexican Revolution (1910–20). Beginning in 1910 with a revolt against the incumbent dictator, Porfirio Díaz, and the entrenched interests of landowners and industrialists, the Mexican Revolution drew in a range of different factions in a protracted struggle which eventually led to the creation of Mexico as a constitutional republic. ✣133, ◆133 (3)
  See also Victoriano Huerta, Francisco Madero, Pancho Villa, Emiliano Zapata
Mexican-American War (*var. Sp.* Guerra de 1847, Guerra de Estados Unidos) (Apr 1846–Feb 1848). The result of the US annexation of Texas in 1845 and a subsequent dispute over the territorial extent of Texas. A series of battles on land and sea resulted in US victory, and the military phase of the war ended with the fall of Mexico City. Via the Treaty of Guadalupe Hidalgo, the US gained the territory that would become the states of New Mexico, Utah, Nevada, Arizona, California, Texas, and western Colorado for $15,000,000. ✣129●, ◆128–9 (2)
Mexico 118–129,133,136–139
  cultures
    Aztec ✣66, ✣124●, ◆124 (2), ❑124
    city-states ✣66, ✣122
    major civilizations ◆122 (1)
    Maya ✣50●, ❑50, ✣122●
    Mexica ✣66
    Olmec (1200 BCE) ✣30
    Teotihuacán ✣50●, ✣122●, ❑122
    Toltec ✣58, ◆122 (1)
  foreign affairs
    Texan rebellion (1836) ✣90●
    US war (1846–48) ✣90●, ✣128, ✣129●, ◆128–9 (2)
  home affairs
    centre of Spanish Empire in N. America (1521) ✣81
    Civil War (1858) ✣94●, ✣129●
    Federalist-Centralist wars ✣129●
    gains independence (1821) ✣90●
    regional inequality ✣136
    revolution (1910) ✣98●, ✣128, ✣129●, ✣132–3, ◆133 (3), ❑133
  Spanish colonization ✣125●, ◆125 (4), ❑125
    church of St. Francis at Tlaxcala ❑125
    Cortés' invasion and conquest (1519–21) ◆125 (5)
Mfecane (*var.* Difaqane, 'the Crushing'). A series of Zulu and other Nguni wars and forced migrations in southern Africa during the first half of the 19th century which were set in motion by the rise of the Zulu military kingdom under Shaka. ✣166●, ◆166 (2)
Michael Palaeologus (c.1277–1320). Byzantine co-emperor with his father, Andronicus II, from 1295, who failed to stem the decline of the empire, despite his efforts in fighting the Turks and in resisting the invasions of Catalan mercenaries. ✣187●
Mickey Mouse First appearance (1928) ❑135
microliths Tool technology which developed in Africa c.30,000 years ago, and some time after the peak of the last Ice Age, c.16,000 years ago, in Europe. Small (microlithic) flints were mounted in a range of bone or wooden hafts, to make 'composite' tools, which could be used to exploit the much wider range of food resources becoming available as the last Ice Age ended. ✣16●
Micronesia Region of the western Pacific, dotted with tiny archipelagos, including the Marianas and the Marshall Islands. The peoples of Micronesia are of more mixed ancestry than those of Polynesia to the east, having had more frequent contact with mainland E Asia. ✣276, ◆281 (3)
microscopes *see* optical instruments
Middendorff, Alexander von 19th-century Russian explorer of Siberia. ◆257 (2)
Middleburg ⚔ of Dutch Revolt (1574). Dutch victory over Spain. ◆195 (5)
Middle East
  Arab-Israeli wars ✣234●, ◆234 (2) (3)
  peace process begins (1977) ✣111●
  spread of Communism (1958) ✣138●
  territorial crisis ✣98
  See also individual countries, West Asia
Middle Kingdom Division of ancient Egyptian history, c.2134–1640 BCE, which saw some expansion into Palestine, and fortification of the Nubian frontier. ✣27●, ✣159●, ◆159 (4)
Midway Naval ⚔ of WW II (Jun 1942). Defeat of Japanese by US forces in mid-Pacific Ocean, marking turning point in Pacific War. ✣103●, ◆104 (2), ◆272 (1)
migration
  aims ✣52
  of peoples (300–500 CE) ✣92–3●, ◆92–3 (1) (2) (3)
  19th century ✣100
  depictions
    Chinese construction workers ❑101
    hardship and overcrowding on ships ❑100
    settlers populate western USA ❑94
    to the US ❑100
    US Indians 'Trail of Tears' ✣129, ❑129
  from Ireland (1845) ✣90●
  German-led ✣189
  global ✣100–1
  indentured labour ✣101, ✣151, ◆101 (3)
  inheritors of western Europe (526 CE) ✣53, ◆53 (2)
  and invasions ✣52–3
  Jewish (1880–1914) ✣101, ✣101●, ◆101 (2)
  Jewish and Palestinian (1947–96) ◆234 (3)
  Magyar ◆185 (3)
  mass ✣90
  Polynesian ✣60, ◆60 (2)
  steppe kingdoms of Central Asia ✣261, ◆261 (6)
  to the New World ✣100●
  in the USA ✣134–5, ✣134●, ◆134 (3)
  world (c.1860–1920) ◆100 (1)
Milan, Edict of (313 CE). Proclamation that permanently established religious toleration for Christianity within the Roman Empire. It was the outcome of a political agreement concluded in Milan between the Roman emperors Constantine I and Licinius in Feb 313 CE. ✣48●
Milne Bay ⚔ of WW II (Aug 1942). Defeat of Japanese landing force in southeastern New Guinea. ✣104, ◆104 (2)
Milošević, Slobodan (1941–). Politician and administrator who, as leader of the League of Communists of Serbia (from 1987) and president (1989–97), pursued Serb nationalist policies that led to the breakup of Yugoslavia. ✣215
Milvian Bridge ⚔ (312). Constantine defeated his rival Maxentius just north of Rome to become master of the western half of the Roman Empire. He attributed his victory to a vision of the cross of Christ he had seen on the eve of the battle. ✣181●
Min *see* Narmer
Minamoto Yoritomo (1147–99). Founder of the Kamakura Shogunate in Japan, who crushed the Taira clan. ✣63●, ❑265
Minas Gerais The rich gold-mining area of Brazil, which helped prop up the Portuguese economy in the 18th century. Gold was first discovered there in 1695.
  gold discovered (1695) ✣149●
  Jesuits banned from region (1711) ✣143●, ◆143 (3), ✣149 (3)
minerals
  deposits in Africa ◆96 (2)
  early Central American resources ◆121 (2)
  late 19th-century finds ◆93 (2) (3)
  S American resources ◆153 (3)
Mines Act (1842) Act passed by British parliament, forbidding employment of women and children underground. ✣204●
Ming dynasty (1368–1644) Ruling dynasty of China.
  rulers of China ✣266–7, ✣70–1, ◆78–9, ◆266–7 (1)
  bowl (16th century) ❑162
  campaign against Mongols ✣75●, ✣266
  guardian of the spirit world ❑71
  and the outside world ✣267●, ◆267 (3)
  restores Chinese values ✣71
  revolts ✣22, ◆266 (2)
  self-sufficiency policy ✣75●
  toppled by Manchus (1644) ✣83
  Zhu Yuanzhang founder of dynasty ✣71, ✣266
Ming Empire *see* Ming dynasty
Minoan civilization Named after the legendary King Minos of Crete, the Minoans were the first great European civilization, c.2000 BCE, whose main cities were Knossos and Phaestus. They had strong trade links with Egypt, and flourished due to their control of sea routes c.2200–1450 BCE. Evidence from their complex palaces attests their high standards of art, metal-working and jewellery-making. Early Minoan pictorial writing has been found, dating to around 1880 BCE, which was superseded by the still undeciphered Linear A and then early Greek writing known as Linear B.
  civilization (2000 BCE) ✣27●, ✣175●, ◆175 (4)
  frescoes of bull-leaping game ❑27
  palace built (2000 BCE) ✣27●
  snake goddess (c.1500 BCE) ❑175
Minos The first king of Crete, according to legend, the son of Zeus and Europa, and husband of Pasiphae. Knossos was said to have been his capital from where he ruled a powerful seafaring empire. The ancient civilization of Crete, Minoan civilization, is named after him. His palace at Knossos was built c.2000 BCE.
  bull cult ✣37
Minsk ⚔ of WW II (Jun–Aug 1943). Encirclement of German forces by Soviets in Belorussia. ◆211 (3) (4)
MIRV *see* Multiple Independently Targeted Warhead Re-entry Vehicle.
Mississippian culture (c.1000–1500 CE). Based in the river valleys of the present-day states of Mississippi, Alabama, Georgia, Arkansas, Missouri, Kentucky, Illinois, Indiana, and Ohio, with scattered populations in Wisconsin and Minnesota and on the Great Plains. A settled agricultural culture, they are distinctive for the oval earthworks which dominated most settlements. ✣66●, ◆123 (5)
  first towns (c.750) ✣58●
  true towns (c.1050) ✣62●
Mississippi River
  earth mounds ✣66, ✣74
  explored by Jolliet and Marquette (1673) ✣119●
  explored by La Salle (1682) ✣119●
Missouri Compromise (1820). The measure which allowed for the admission of Missouri as the 24th US state in 1821. James Tallmadge's attempt to add an anti-slavery amendment legislation for the admission of new states to the US led to a major debate over the right of the government to restrict slavery in new states. The issue remained unresolved in Dec 1819 when the northern state of Maine applied for statehood. The Senate passed a bill allowing Maine to enter the Union as a free state and Missouri to be admitted with no restriction on slavery. A further amendment was then added that allowed Missouri to become a slave state but banned slavery in the rest of the Louisiana Purchase north of latitude 36°30'. ✣130, ◆130 (1)
Mitanni Indo-Persian people whose empire in northern Mesopotamia flourished between c.1500–1360 BCE. Their capital, Wahshukanni, was probably in the Khabur River region, and at their height they ruled over lands from the Zagros Mountains west to the Mediterranean.
  conflict with Egyptians and Hittites (1250 BCE) ✣27●, ✣26–7
Mitchell, Thomas (1792–1855) Scottish-born soldier and explorer. Surveyor-General of New South Wales from 1827, he led several important expeditions into the Australian interior. ◆279 (2)
Mithradates II (d.88 BCE). After recovering the eastern provinces that had been overrun during his father's reign, Mithradates was one of the most successful Parthian kings, concluding the first treaty between Parthia and Rome in 92 BCE. ◆42–3
Mithraism Worship of Mithras, an ancient Indian and Persian god of justice and law. Spread as a mystery cult in the Roman Empire, with Mithras as a divine saviour. Ousted by Christianity in the 4th century CE.
  BCE cult ❑37 (3)
  portrayal of Mithras ❑48
  spread of (600 BCE) ✣48, ◆48 (1)
Mithras *see* Mithraism
Mobile (⚔ of Mobile Bay). ⚔ of American Civil War (5 Aug 1864). Union victory. ◆131 (7)
Mobuto, Sese Seko Koko Ngbendu wa za Banga (Joseph-Désiré) (1930–97). President of Zaire. Mobutu staged a coup to become president in 1965 and held on to power for over 30 years despite the flagrant corruption of his regime. He finally lost control of Zaire, while in Europe for medical treatment in 1997 and never returned.
  overthrown (1997) ✣111
  portrait ❑107
moccasin BCE antelope hide ❑18
Moche culture (*var.* Mochica). The earliest major civilization on the north coast of Peru, based in the ancient city of Moche around 200 BCE–550 CE. It is best known for the twin brick pyramids of the Sun and Moon, Huaca del Sol and Huaca de la Luna, which were richly decorated with multi-coloured murals. The Moche people also carried out extensive irrigation, fortified their ceremonial centres, and produced cast, alloyed and gilded metalwork. ✣42●, ✣145, ◆145 (4), ◆146 (1)
  fanged deity pot ❑46
  stirrup-spouted vessel ❑54, ❑145
Mochica *see* Moche culture
Mogollon Native American culture of the US Southwest. ✣58, ◆123 (4)
  defensive pueblos (1050) ✣123●
  Mimbres pottery ❑123
Mogul dynasty *see* Mughal dynasty
Mohács ⚔ of (1526). Ottomans crush Hungarian army. ✣79●, ◆195 (2)
Mohammed *see* Muhammed
Mohenjo-Daro ✣23, ❑240, ◆240 (1)
Moluccas (Spice Islands) ✣79, ✣80, ❑239, ❑247
money *see* coins; economy
Möngke (d.1259) Mongol leader, a grandson of Genghis Khan, elected Great Khan in 1251. Möngke's rule saw the start of the so-called 'Mongol Peace', when travel and trade across Central Asia flourished. ✣68
  See also Mongols
Mongols Pastoralist, nomadic people of Central Asia. Their conquests from the 13th century onwards were the last assault by nomadic armies inflicted upon the settled peoples of western Asia. ◆68–9 (1) (2)
  age of the Mongols ✣68–9
  campaigns ✣69, ✣75●, ◆68–9 (1), ◆189 (4), ◆263 (7), ◆265 (5)
  capital of Karakorum founded (1235) ✣68●
  cavalryman ❑69
  Chinese rebellions (1335) ✣71●
  conquests
    13th century ✣69●
    Central Asia (1206) ✣256●
    Chinese (1449) ✣75●
    Kaifeng captured (1233) ✣67●
    Khwarizm Empire (1219) ✣67●
    northern China (1211) ✣67●
    Russian ✣66●, ✣69, ✣75, ✣189●
    sacking of Baghdad (1258) ✣67, ✣69●, ✣229, ❑229
    Song resistance crushed (1279) ✣69●
    converts to Islam ✣67
  defeats
    Ain Jalut (1260) ✣67●, ✣69●
    Annam and Pagan forays ✣67
    invasions of Japan (1274, 1281) ✣67●, ✣69●
    Java (1293) ✣67
    Mamluk ✣67●, ✣69, ✣229, ✣229●, ◆229 (3)
  periods of peace ✣68, ✣68●, ✣267
  Yuan period (c.1300) ✣263, ◆263 (7)
Monmouth Court House ⚔ of American Revolutionary War (28 Jun 1778). Inconclusive result. ◆127 (3)
monotheism ✣37, ◆36 (1)
monsoon Wind system involving seasonal reversal of prevailing wind direction. Occurs mainly in the Indian Ocean, the western Pacific, and off the W African coast. The term also applies to the rainy seasons of much of southern and eastern Asia, and of E and W Africa.
Montagnais Native American peoples of northeastern N America. ✣119, ◆126 (1)
Montcalm, Louis Joseph, Marquis de (1712–59). Commander of the French troops in Canada in the Seven Years' War. He was mortally wounded defending Quebec. ✣127, ◆127 (2)
Monte Albán
  influential Mexican city ❑122, ◆122 (1)
  Los Danzantes ❑34
  Zapotec culture ✣38●, ✣121
Monte Cassino *see* Cassino
Monte Verde
  early settlements ✣144●, ◆144 (1)
  environmental survival strategies (BCE) ✣14● 16
  stone tools ❑144
Montejos, the 16th-century Spanish explorers of N America (1527, 1545). ✣125, ◆125 (4)
Montenegro ✣203, ◆203 (4), ◆232 (1), ✣232
  See also Balkans, nationalism
Montezuma II *see* Motecuzoma Xocoyotl
Montgomery, Alabama Boycott against segregation (1955) ✣137●, ◆137 (2)
Montmirail ⚔ of Napoleon's defence of France (11 Feb 1814). French victory. ◆200 (1)
Montoya, Father Ruiz de 17th-century Jesuit missionary in South America. ✣143●
Montreal
  captured by British (1760) ✣127●, ◆127 (2)
  European and native conflict (1689) ✣126
  French settlement map (1642) ❑126
Morgan, Sir Henry (c.1635–88) Welsh buccaneer who operated in the West Indies, preying primarily on Spanish ships and territories including Panama, which he captured in 1671. Though arrested and transported to London to placate the Spanish, he returned to the West Indies and became a wealthy planter. ❑85, ◆85 (2)
Morgarten ⚔ (1315). Austrian Habsburg forces defeated by Swiss peasant army. ◆193 (5)
Morocco 165–169
  Almohad sect established (1147) ✣63●
  Almohads defeated by Marinids (1269) ✣67●
  Ceuta captured by Portuguese (1415) ✣75●
  French occupation ◆167 (4)
  independence ◆168 (1)
  Muhammad III becomes Sultan (1757) ✣87●
  Portuguese invasion crushed (1578) ✣79●
  Songhay Empire captured (1591) ✣79●
Morse Code Code consisting of dots and dashes devised for use with the electric telegraph he had designed by American painter and inventor Samuel Morse (1791–1872). ✣98
mosaics
  Aztec serpant pendant ❑124
  castle, ships and harbour of Ravenna (6th century) ❑182
  Darius III at ⚔ Issus ❑40
  floor mosaic of Orpheus ❑181
  Macedonian lion hunt ❑179
  map of Jerusalem ❑51
  Roman ❑47
  The Nile in flood ❑47
  Vandal landowner ❑52
Moscow ⚔ of WW II (Dec 1941). Soviet forces halted German advance during *Operation Barbarossa*. ◆210 (1)
Moscow Napoleon's retreat (1812) ✣90●
Moshoeshoe Lesotho kingdom (1824) ◆166 (2)
Moslem *see* Muslim
Motecuzoma I Aztec ruler (1440–68) ✣74●, ✣124 (1)
Motecuzoma Xocoyotl (*aka* Montezuma II) (1466–1520) 9th emperor of the Aztec Empire (1502–20). During the Spanish conquest of Mexico by Hernán

Key to index: ✣ text ● timeline ❑ picture ◆ map *var.* variant name *aka* also known as *f/n* full name *prev.* previously known as r. ruled ⚔ battle WW I First World War WW II Second World War

Cortés and his conquistadors, he was deposed as ruler and imprisoned.
  Aztec ruler (1502) ✣78●, ✣124, ◆124 (1)
  last Aztec emperor ✣78●
moundbuilders *see* earthworks
Moundville Mississippian cultural site ✣123, ◆123 (5)
Mount Olympus, cult centre ✣37
Mozambique independence (1975) ✣107●, ✣111●, ✣168, ◆168 (1)
  post-independence ◆169 (4)
MPLA *see* People's Movement for the Liberation of Angola
MRV *see* Multiple Re-entry Vehicle
Msiri 19th-century trader who settled with his Nyamwezi followers in southern Katanga, central Africa in 1856. Msiri dominated the region by about 1870. ✣166
Mughal dynasty (*var.* Mogul dynasty) (1526–1857). The victory of Babur, an Afghan Muslim, at Panipat in 1525, was the beginning of the Mughal Empire, which was to dominate India until 1739. The empire reached its peak during the reign of Akbar, when it extended from Bengal to Sind and Gujarat, and from Kashmir to the Godavari river. From the 1670s, confrontation with the Marathas, a new Hindu power, depleted the power of the Mughals and decline soon set in. In 1739 Nadir Shah of Persia swept into India, and sacked Delhi, and from this point the Mughals were merely puppet emperors. ✣79, ✣246, ✣246●, ◆78–9, ◆246 (1)
  Persian incursions ✣87
  powers declines (1707) ✣87
  route map ❑238
  troops raiding sheep herds ❑267
Mughal Empire *see* Mughal dynasty.
Muhammad (*var.* Mohammed) (c.570–632). Founder of Islamic religion, born in Mecca (Saudi Arabia). In 610 a vision of the Angel Gabriel revealed messages from God. These messages, written down as the Koran (meaning 'Reading' or 'Recitation'), are revered as the Holy Book of Islam. In 622 Muhammad and his followers were forced to move to Medina, a migration (*Hegira*) which marks the beginning of the Islamic calendar. As a religious leader, he conquered Mecca in 630, destroyed the pagan idols and unified much of Arabia. His legacy passed to his father-in-law, Abu Bakr, the first caliph. ✣55, ✣56, ✣66, ✣61●, ✣218, ✣226
  Hegira ◆226 (2)
Muhammad III Sultan of Morocco (r.1757–90), who introduced administrative reforms and reopened trade with Europe after a long embargo. ✣87●
Muhammad al Ghur *see* Muhammad of Ghur
Muhammad Ali (c.1769–1849) (*var.* Mehmet Ali, Mohammed Ali). Viceroy of Egypt (1805–48), who made Egypt the leading power in the eastern Mediterranean. An Albanian military officer, he went to Egypt (1801) in command of an Ottoman army sent to face Napoleon. After many successful military campaigns, he turned against the Ottomans, defeating them in Asia Minor (1839), but European intervention prevented the overthrow of the sultan. ✣232
  possessions 1840 ◆90–1
  Viceroy of Egypt (1804) ✣90
Muhammad Ibn Adullah *see* Ibn Battuta
Muhammad of Ghazni *see* Mahmud of Ghazni
Muhammad of Ghur (*var.* Ghiyas al-Din) (d.1202) (r.1173–1202). Leader of an Afghan army, in 1191 he defeated the Rajput clans of northern India, and in 1206 his general, Qutb al-Din Aybak, established the first Turko-Afghan dynasty in Delhi, ruling it as sultan.
  defeats Rajput clans (1191) ✣63●
  Ghurid dynasty ◆244 (2)
Muisca (*var.* Chibcha). Native people of the highlands around Bogotá. It was in Muisca lands that the legend of El Dorado caught the imagination of Spanish *conquistadores*. ❑147
Mujahedin (*var.* Mujahideen). Islamic nationalist forces during Afghan civil war (from 1973) who spearheaded resistance to Soviet invasion (1979–89) with Pakistani backing, forming a government (1983), but opposed by Taliban from 1995. ◆235 (4)
Mujahideen *see* Mujahedin
Multiple Re-entry Vehicle (MRV) ICBM developed by US in the early 1960s that could deliver a 'footprint' of warheads in a selected area, greatly increasing US nuclear potential during the Cold War. ✣109
Multiple Independently Targeted Warhead Re-entry Vehicle (MIRV) ICBM developed by US in late 1960s, that could select several targets, greatly escalating US nuclear potential during the Cold War. ✣109
Mumbai *see* Bombay
mummification Preservation of human and animal bodies by embalming and wrapping in lengths of cloth, after removal of the internal organs. Mummification is associated with belief in life after death, and was practised by the ancient Egyptians amongst others.
  ancestor cults ✣147
  Chimú funerary mask ❑66
  Egyptian ❑31
  goddess Anubis ❑37
  Paracas region ❑145
  Roman mummy case ❑47
Mungo, Lake Site of first known cremation (26,000 BP) ✣16●
Murad I (c.1326–89) Third Ottoman Sultan, who pursued the expansion of the empire in the Balkans, annexing Bulgaria and much of Serbia. He was killed at the battle of Kosovo Polje. ✣230, ◆230 (1)
Muret ⚔ of Albigensian Crusade (1213). Peter II of Aragon killed by crusading army. ◆186 (2)
Murfreesboro (⚔ of Stones River). ⚔ of American Civil War (31 Dec 1862–2 Jan 1863). Union victory. ◆131 (6)
Muscovy State created by the Grand Princes of Moscow in the 13th century. Though isolated, Muscovy became increasingly powerful through the annexation of Novgorod and the proclamation of independence from the Mongols in 1480. By 1556 Muscovy had annexed the Khanate of Astrakhan, controlling the Volga down to the Caspian Sea. In 1571 Moscow was sacked by Crimean Tatars.
  14th century ◆70–1
  throws off Mongol yoke (1480) ✣75●
Muscovy Company Formed in 1555 by the navigator and explorer Sebastian Cabot and various London merchants in order to trade with Russia, the company was granted a monopoly of Anglo-Russian trade.
  sponsors of Arctic exploration ✣286
Musket Wars A series of conflicts between Maori tribes in the 1820s, sparked by the introduction of European firearms into New Zealand. ✣283●, ◆283 (4)
Muslim (*var.* Moslem, Mussulman) Of or pertaining to the Islamic faith. *See* Islam
Muslim League Formed in 1906, as a result of the conflicts created within Bengal by Lord Curzon's 1905 partition of the province. The League's original aim was to promote separate electorates for Muslim minorities within Hindu majority areas, but by the 1940s it had started to demand a separate Muslim state. It was pressure from the League that led to the creation of Pakistan in 1947. ✣250●
Mussolini, Benito Amilcare Andrea (1883–1945) Italian dictator (1925–43). Expelled from the socialist party for pressing for support of the Allies during WW I; after the war Mussolini founded the *Fasci di Combattimento* (Fascist movement). Aided by Blackshirt supporters, he attacked Communism, and in 1922 marched on Rome. He was appointed Prime Minister by King Victor Emmanuel III, and by 1925 had declared himself *Il Duce* (the leader) and swiftly established a totalitarian regime within Italy. In 1935 he invaded Ethiopia as part of a plan to form an Italian empire, and by 1936 had formed the Rome-Berlin axis with Hitler, declaring war on the Allies in 1940. Dependence on Hitler broke support for Mussolini and he was deposed in 1943 and executed by partisans in 1945. ✣207, ✣209, ◆209 (3)
Mustafa Kemal Pasha *see* Atatürk
Mutapa Empire (var. Muwenutapa). Kingdom of southern Africa that flourished between the 15th and 18th centuries. ✣164
  absorbs Great Zimbabwe (c.1450) ✣75●
Mutually Assured Destruction (MAD). Term coined by US Secretary of State John Foster Dulles (1953–59) to describe Cold War intercontinental arms stalemate between US and Soviet Union. ✣108●
Mwenemutapa *see* Mutapa Empire
Mycale (*var.* Gre. Mykale) ⚔ (479 BCE) Defeat of the Persian navy by the Greeks off the coast of Asia Minor. ✣39, ◆176 (1)
Mycenaean Greece Named after its capital Mycenae, Bronze Age Greek culture which dominated mainland Greece between 1580–1120 BCE. The Mycenaeans appear to have conquered Knossos in Crete around 1450 BCE, and they traded widely in Asia Minor, Cyprus and Syria. Their sacking of Troy c.1200 BCE was later mythologized in Homer's *Iliad*. Archaeological evidence points to great wealth and skill, with palaces at Mycenae, Tiryns and Pylos at the centre of a system of government by a distinct warrior class overseeing a redistributive economy. The final destruction or abandonment of these palaces is now thought to be due to internal unrest rather than external conquest. 175●, ◆175 (4)
  bronze dagger blade ❑26
  civilization (1250 BCE) ◆26–7
  dominant power on Greek mainland (1550 BCE) ✣27●
  mythology ✣37
  pot ❑31
  ritual sprinkler ❑37
Mysore Conquered by Britain (1799) ✣87●
mythology Origins of religion ✣36–7
Mzilikazi Ndebele kingdom (1826) ◆166 (2)

N

Naddod 9th-century Viking explorer who visited Iceland (c.870). ◆172 (2)
Nadir Shah (1688–1747). A bandit chieftain of Turkish origin, in 1736 he seized the Safavid throne of Persia, immediately embarking on campaigns against neighbouring states. In 1739 he attacked Delhi, capital of Mughul India, slaughtered its citizens and stole the Koh-i-noor diamond. Cruel and ruthless, he was eventually assassinated by his own troops. ✣87, ✣246, ✣246●, ❑246
NAFTA *see* North American Free Trade Agreement
Nagasaki Atom bombs dropped (1945) ✣103●, ✣105●, ✣273●, ◆273 (3)
Nain Singh 19th-century Indian surveyor, who made an epic journey in disguise through Tibet on behalf of the Survey of India. ✣257●, ◆257 (3)
Nanda Empire ✣241, ◆241 (4)
Nanjing
  centre of Jin dynasty ✣51
  rebellion (1853) ✣95●
  Treaty (1842) ✣91●
Nanjing, Treaty of *see* Opium War
Nansen, Fridtjof (1861–1930). Norwegian scientist, explorer and statesman. Crossed Greenland icecap in 1888 on foot. In his specially-designed ship, the *Fram*, he explored the Arctic from 1893–96, stopping to take part in a bid for the North Pole. In 1918 he became a commissioner to the League of Nations and was awarded the Nobel Peace Prize in 1923 for his work in assisting famine-struck regions of the Soviet Union. ◆286–7 (2)
Nantes, Edict of (1598). Order signed by Henry IV of France granting Huguenots the right to practise their own religion. It was revoked in 1685 by Louis XIV, and as a result many non-Catholics fled the country. ✣78●
Napoleon I, Bonaparte (1769–1821) French military and political leader, and Emperor of France (1804–1815). Following successful Italian campaign (1796–7) and invasion of Egypt (1798), he assumed power as First Consul in 1799. A brilliant general, he defeated every European coalition which fought against him. Decline set in with failure of Peninsular War in Spain and disastrous invasion of Russia (1812). Defeated at Leipzig (1813) by a new European alliance, he went into exile but escaped and ruled as emperor during the Hundred Days. Finally defeated at Waterloo (1815) and exiled to St. Helena. As an administrator, his achievements were of lasting significance and include the *Code Napoléon*, which remains the basis for French law. ◆200–1 (1) (2)
  abdicates (1814) ✣202●
  aftermath of wars ✣90
  campaigns ✣200–1, ✣200●, ❑200, ◆200–1 (1)
  Code Napoléon ❑200
  coup brings power in France ✣86●
  defeated at Waterloo (1815) ✣200, ✣202●
  Emperor of France ❑201
  French Empire 1812 ◆90–1, ◆201 (2)
  occupies Egypt (1798) ✣87●, ✣200, ❑201
  opposition alliances ✣201, ◆201 (3)
  retreats from Moscow (1812) ✣90●, ✣200
  rise and fall ✣200
  Tilsit peace talks ❑201
Napoleon III (*var.* Charles Louis Napoléon Bonaparte) (1808–1873). Nephew of Napoleon I, Emperor of the French (1852–71). Involved France in the Crimean War (1853–6) and allowed Bismarck to provoke him into the Franco-Prussian War (1870–1), which ended in France's defeat and Napoleon's exile to Britain. *See also* Crimean War, Franco-Prussian War.
  president of Second Republic (1848) ✣202●
  revolts against his rule ✣202 (1)
  surrenders to Wilhelm I ❑203
Naqa Cushite temple relic ❑35
Naqada Founded (c.3300) ✣24●
Nara period (710–784). Period of Japanese history that began with the establishment of a capital at Heijo-kyo (to the west of the modern city of Nara). ✣55● ✣265●, ✣265, ◆265 (3)
Narbo (Narbonne), Visigothic state (414) ✣53●
Narmer, King (*var.* Menes, Mena, Meni, Min). The first pharaoh of the Old Kingdom in Egypt. Narmer unified the formerly discrete fortified towns of Upper and Lower Egypt into a powerful state, and is credited with founding the capital at Memphis near Cairo. According to the 3rd century BCE historian Manetho, Narmer ruled for 62 years and was killed by a hippo. ✣22
Narváez, Panfilo de (c.1478–1528) Spanish *conquistador*. Took part in conquest of Cuba and Cortés's conquest of Mexico. Commissioned to conquer Florida in 1526. The journey took ten months and decimated the crew, and Narváez himself who died on the Texas coast, although survivors of the party did go on to complete the map of the northern Gulf coast. ✣125, ◆118 (1), ◆125 (4)
NASA *see* National Aeronautics and Space Administration
Nashville ⚔ of American Civil War (15–16 Dec 1864). Union victory. ◆131 (7)
Nassau, William I, Prince of Orange (*aka* William of Nassau,1533–84) Dutch statesman who martialled resistance to Spanish Catholic rule in the Netherlands.
  Dutch revolt (1568–1609) ✣195, ✣195●, ◆195 (5)
Natal ◆96 (2), ◆166 (2)
  annexed by Britain ✣91●
  annexed by Britain (1843) ✣166●
National Aeronautics and Space Administration (NASA)
  space programme (1969) ✣106●
National Front for the Liberation of Angola (FNLA). Political party of Angola. ◆109 (5)
National Recovery Administration (NRA). US government agency set up as part of Roosevelt's New Deal programme. The National Industrial Recovery Act authorized the introduction of industry-wide codes to reduce unfair trade practices and cut down unemployment, establish minimum wages and maximum hours, and guarantee right of collective bargaining. The NRA ended when it was invalidated by the Supreme Court in 1935, but many of its provisions were included in subsequent legislation. ❑134
nationalism
  European growth ✣202–3, ✣214
  movements ✣90, ✣94, ✣99
  Serb ✣215
NATO *see* North Atlantic Treaty Organization
Natufian peoples Levantine people, named after the site of Wadi en-Natuf in Israel. From c.13,000 BCE, Natufian peoples intensively harvested wild cereals, using grindstones to crush the grains. They were the precursors of the first farmers. ✣15●
navigation
  Arab traders in the Indian Ocean ◆61 (3)
  harnessing winds ✣61, ✣75, ✣78, ✣218
  instruments
    astrolabe ❑77, ❑218
    Chinese magnetized needle (13th century) ❑67
    Harrison's chronometer ❑86
    lodestone compass used in China (c.250) ✣256●
    measuring longitude ✣86
    Magellan's global circumnavigation ❑80
  mapping
    latitude scales (16th century) ✣173●
    medieval ✣173
    Portolan charts ✣70, ✣173, ❑173
    stick chart ❑278
    Northeast Passage ◆257 (2)
    Polynesian ✣55, ✣60
  technology
    global (c.1500) ◆76–7 (1)
    and mariners ✣77
    satellite imagery ❑106
    trading network ✣78
Nazca culture Coastal culture of southern Peru which flourished between c.200 BCE and 500 CE. The Nazca are noted for their ceramic human and animal figures but are best known for the 'Nazca lines' large abstract designs and animal shapes which they laid out on a huge scale by clearing and aligning stones, and which can be best seen from the air. ✣38●, ❑42, ◆145 (4), ◆146 (1)
  desert figures (c.450) ✣51●, ❑145
  empire ◆146 (1)
  pottery figure ❑42
Nazi Party (*var.* National-Sozialistische Deutsche Arbeiterpartei) *see* Nazism
Nazi-Soviet Non-Aggression Pact Treaty signed Aug 1939 arranging for division of Poland. Paved way for outbreak of WW II in Europe. ✣209●
Nazism Political creed developed by Adolf Hitler in the 1920s and implemented by his National Socialist (Nazi) party after Hitler became Chancellor of Germany in 1933. Based on extreme nationalism, anti-Communism and racism (especially anti-semitism), Nazi policies of social and economic mobilization led to the dramatic recovery of Germany in the 1930s, but also led the nation into a programme of territorial aggression which plunged Europe into WW II. ✣209●, ◆209 (3)
  Nationalist Socialist ✣102, ✣104
  concentration camps ✣138, ❑211
  impact on Europe ✣211●
  Yalta 'Big Three' conference (1945) ❑105
Ndebele African Kingdom (1826) ◆166 (2)
Ndongo Portuguese seize territory (1663) ✣82
Neanderthals (c.120,000 to 28,000 years ago). Species of human, *Homo neanderthalensis*, contemporary with *Homo sapiens*. Named after the Neander Valley in Germany, where the first skull cap of their type was recognized, the Neanderthals lived in Europe and the Middle East. Distinguished by their strong, heavy skeleton, projecting face, broad nose and large teeth, their brain capacity was at least the size of modern humans. They were accomplished tool-makers, and were the first type of human known to bury their dead. They demonstrated, in their cultural behaviour and social organization, many of the characteristics of modern humans. ✣12, ❑12, ✣15●, ◆13 (2)
Nearchus (d.312 BCE) Admiral of Alexander the Great's fleet. In 325 BCE he was instructed to sail west along the coast from the mouth of the Indus to the mouth of the Euphrates. His voyage opened a coastal trading route to India for Greek merchants. ◆218 (1)
Nebuchadnezzar II (c.630–562 BCE). Babylon's most famous king and founder of the new Babylonian empire, (r.605–562 BCE) during which time the Babylonian civilization reached its peak. Nebuchadnezzar instituted many major building projects including the Hanging Gardens, one of the Seven Wonders of the ancient world. He led his father's army to victory over the Egyptians at Carchemish, and famously exiled the Jews after capturing Jerusalem in 586 BCE. ✣35●, ✣222, ❑222
Needham, James (d.1673) 17th-century explorer of N America. Gained experience of the frontier with Henry Woodward and then accompanied Gabriel Arthur on the journey to find a route to the 'South Sea'. ◆119 (2)
Nehru, Jawaharlal (1889–1964) First prime minister of independent India (r.1947–64). He joined the nationalist movement in 1920, and was President of the Indian National Congress Party 1920–30, 1936–7, 1946, 1951–4. ❑252
Nekhen Confederacy (BCE) ◆159 (2)
Nelson, Horatio, Viscount (1758–1805) British admiral. On the outbreak of war with France in 1793, he achieved a series of brilliant and decisive victories at the Nile (1798) and at Copenhagen (1801). His defeat of a united Spanish and French fleet at Trafalgar (1805) saved Britain from the threat of invasion by Napoleon. He was mortally wounded in the battle. ◆200 (1), , ✣200●
Nemausus (*var.* Nîmes), Pont du Gard ❑180
Neo-Assyrian Empire *see* Assyrian Empire
Neolithic The last subdivision of the Stone Age, the period when crops and animals were domesticated, pottery was manufactured, and stone tools were made by grinding and polishing.
  Africa ◆160 (1)
  China ◆258 (2)
Nepal Mapping and exploration ◆257 (3)
Nerchinsk, Treaty of (1689). Peace agreement between Russia and China, in which Russia withdrew from the area north of the Amur river. First treaty between China and a European power. ✣83, ✣275●
Nero (37–68 CE) Roman Emperor. The last of the family of Augustus Caesar to rule Rome (r.54–68). Palace intrigues and murders (including that of his mother) gave Nero's reign a notoriety unmatched by that of any previous emperor. He committed suicide as provincial governors joined in revolt against him. ✣48●
Nestorian Church Followers of Nestorius, whose Christian teachings, condemned by the councils of Ephesus (431) and Chalcedon (451), emphasized the independence of the divine and human natures of Christ. Represented today by the Syrian Orthodox Church. ✣226, ✣226●, ◆49 (4)
Netherlands
  foreign affairs
    voyages of expansion (1492–1597) ◆80–1 (1)
    possessions
      1600 ◆78–9
      1700 ◆164 (1)
    Africa
      Angola captured (1641) ✣83●
      British seize Cape colony (1795) ✣87●
      Cape of Good Hope colony established (1652) ✣83●
      Central Africa (1625) ◆164 (2)
      Orange River settled (1720) ✣87●
      S and E Africa (c.1700) ◆164 (1)
    America
      colonization and settlement of N America ✣126, ◆126 (1)
      New Amsterdam colony seized (1664) ✣82●
      S American exploration ◆142–3 (1) (2)
      trading posts in north ✣82
    Asia
      Indonesia gains independence (1949) ✣103●
      Malacca captured (1641) ✣83●
      rebellion against Dutch rule (1926–27) ✣103●
      Southeast trading ✣83●, ❑247
    Brazil, colonization (1630–54) ✣82●, ✣149, ◆149 (4)
    Guiana, colony (c.1640) ✣149, ◆149 (4)
    Pacific imperialism ◆284 (1)
  home affairs
    Dutch revolt (1568–1609) ✣195, ✣195●, ◆195 (5)
    population growth (1650–1800) ❑198
    Second World War *see* Wars, Second World War
Netjerykhet *see* Zoser
New Amsterdam
  colonized ◆126 (1)
  Dutch colony in America ✣82●
  seized by English; renamed New York (1664) ✣82●
New Caledonia Settled by French (1864) ✣284●, ◆284 (1), ✣285 (2)
New Deal *see* Roosevelt, Franklin
New England Settlement begins (1620) ✣126●, ◆126 (1)
New Granada
  Viceroyalty established (1739) ✣148●
  independence secured ✣90●
New Guinea
  BCE drainage and cultivation ✣19●
  Dutch annex west (1825) ✣91
  exploration and mapping ✣279, ◆279 (2)
  prehistoric agricultural development ✣280, ❑280, ◆280 (2)
  seized by Japan (1942) ✣103●
  settlement ✣280, ✣280●, ◆280 (1)
New Haven European and native conflict (1637) ✣126, ◆126 (1)
New Holland Established by Dutch (1630) ✣149●
New Kingdom (c.1530–1070 BCE). Period of ancient Egyptian history marked by strong central government control in ancient Egypt, and one which saw the height of Egyptian power. Punctuated by the El-Amarna period of Akhenaten. ✣26●, ✣26, ✣159●
New Spain (*var. Sp.* Virreinato de Nueva España). Spanish Viceroyalty established in 1535 to govern Spain's conquered lands north of the Isthmus of Panama and regions in present-day Lower California. ◆126 (1), ◆148 (2)
New State (*var. Port.* Estado Novo). Dictatorship (1937–45) of President Getúlio Vargas of Brazil, initiated by a new constitution issued in Nov 1937. Vargas himself wrote it with the assistance of his minister of justice, Francisco Campos. ✣82●, ◆152 (1)

New York
English colony (1664) ✣82●
See also New Amsterdam
New Zealand
Captain Cook's map ❏87
colonization
British
✣91, ✣283, ✣284●, ◆283 (5)
European (1800–40)
✣283, ◆283 (4)
Pacific decolonization and nationhood ✣285, ◆285 (3)
Pacific imperialism ◆284 (1)
Polynesian colonization
✣55●, ✣60, ◆60 (2), ✣281, ◆280–1 (2)
Maori carved canoe head ❏281
possessions
1925 ◆98–9
1975 ◆106–7
Second World War, mobilization and casualty figures ✣105
trade and industry
refrigerated shipping
✣92●, ✣283
sheep farming ❏283
whaling ✣279●, ◆283 (4)
Newbery, John 16th-century English explorer and merchant. Travelling to Hormuz in 1581–83 to survey its commercial prospects, he became the first Englishman to sail down the Euphrates and visit Hormuz, Shiraz and Isfahan. He returned overland through Persia to Constantinople. ◆219 (3)
Newfoundland Reached by Vikings (c.1000 CE) ✣60
Newton, Sir Isaac (1642–1727). English mathematician and physicist. His work on calculus, the laws of motion, gravity, and light made him the most celebrated scientist of his age. ❏83
Nez Percé War (1877) War which broke out between the Nez Percé Indians of the NW plains and the US army. It was the result of a long-running dispute over the drastic reduction of the Nez Percé reservation in 1863 after gold was discovered on their lands, and incursions by European settlers. Led by Chief Joseph, a band of 250 Nez Percé kept US forces at bay for more than five months. They were subsequently forced to relocate to Oklahoma.
◆128–9 (2)
Ngami, Lake Reached by Livingstone (1849) ✣157●
Nguni
dispersal of clans (1816) ✣166●
Mfecane wars ◆166 (2)
wars with Dutch begin (1779)
✣164●
Nguyen Anh Emperor of Vietnam (1774) ✣87●
Nguyen Puc Anh *see* Gai Long
Nian Rebellion (*var.* Nien) (1853–68) Chinese peasant rebellion of the mid-19th century. ◆268 (2)
Nicaea Council assembled by Constantine (325) ✣48●
Nicaragua, civil war (1978–89). After 40 years of dictatorship, a revolution in 1978 by the left-wing Sandinistas, who drew on the support of a rural peasant base, began 11 years of civil war. Despite losing the first free elections of 1990, the Sandinistas remain a potent force in the country, increasingly threatening the stability of the government.
civil war (1979)
✣110●
US intervention
✣139●, ◆139 (5)
Niebuhr, Carsten (1733–1815). German-born surveyor who took part in an international scientific expedition in 1761, financed by the King of Denmark, to explore the Arabian Peninsula. Niebuhr was the only survivor. His systematic accounts of the expedition, containing maps and illustrations, were published in 1772 and 1774. ◆219 (4)
Nielsen hot blast process (1824) ❏90
Nieuwpoort ⚔ of Dutch Revolt (1600). Dutch victory over Spain. ◆195 (5)
Niger Basin, Arabic and Portuguese views ◆156 (1) (2)
Niger Delta
Nok culture (BCE) ✣38
Oyo main tribe (1747)
✣87●
Nigeria
independence ◆169 (1)
industrial growth
✣168, ◆168 (2)
secession of Biafra and civil war (1967–70) ✣107●, ◆169 (4), ✣169●
Nimrud
(BCE) ✣31, ✣35●
Phoenician carved plaque ❏176
Ninety-five Theses (1517). Document demanding ecclesiastical reforms, especially with regard to the sale of indulgences, nailed to a church door in Wittenberg by Martin Luther. ✣95●
See also Martin Luther
Nineveh (BCE) ✣31, ✣35●
Niño, Andreas 16th-century Spanish explorer of Central America. ✣125, ◆125 (4)
Nippur Plan of city (BCE) ✣28, ❏28, ◆28 (2)
Nirvana *see* Buddhism.
Nisa Parthian capital ✣43
Nixon, Richard Milhous (1913–94) 37th President of the US. (Republican, 1969–74). Came to political prominence as a member of HUAC (the House Committee on Un-American Activities) investigating the Alger Hiss case. He served as Vice-President under Dwight D. Eisenhower from 1952–59, but lost the 1960 Presidential election to John F. Kennedy. He was eventually elected President in 1968 and won a second term in 1972 by a narrow margin. Nixon's term of office saw the invasion of Cambodia in 1970, the ending of the Vietnam War, the initiation of arms limitation talks with the Soviet Union and the reestablishment of US relations with China. His involvement in the Watergate scandal led to his resignation in 1974, although he was granted a full pardon by his successor Gerald Ford. ✣139●
Njinga Queen of the Ndongo kingdom in southwest Africa (r.1624–63). She resisted Portuguese attempts to expand their control of the Angola region. ❏164
Nkrumah, Dr. Kwame (1909–72). Ghanaian nationalist leader who led the Gold Goast's drive for independence from Britain and presided over its emergence as the new nation of Ghana. He headed the country from independence in 1957 until he was overthrown by a coup in 1966. ✣168
Nobile, Umberto (1885–1978) Italian aviator. Crossed the N Pole in his dirigible balloon in 1926, along with Amundsen and 14 others. A second expedition ended in disaster with the loss of seven lives. ◆286–7 (2)
Noin Ula Burial site (BCE) ✣39●
Nok culture *var.* Nok figurine culture. Ancient Iron Age culture that existed on the Benue plateau of Nigeria between about 500 BCE and 200 CE. They produced the earliest known iron-working south of the Sahara, and distinctive terracotta figurines. ✣160, ❏38, ◆160 (1)
Nok figurine culture *see* Nok culture
Norden's county maps ✣173
Nordenskjöld, Baron Nils Adolf Erik (1832–1901) Swedish explorer and scientist. Made several expeditions to Spitzbergen. In 1870 led expedition to explore Greenland ice cap. In 1878–79, he sailed through the Northeast Passage on the ship *Vega*. ◆286–7 (2)
Noriega, General Manuel Antonio Morena (1940–) Panamanian politician and soldier. As Commander of the National Guard and *de facto* ruler of Panama (1982–89), Noriega enjoyed US support until 1987. In 1988 he was indicted by a US grand jury on charges of drug trafficking, and in 1989 he was arrested during a US military operation in Panama, and deported to the US. ❏139
Normans Name given to the Vikings, chiefly of Danish origin, who, under their leader Rollo, settled in northern France from the early 10th century. Originally the word meant Northmen or Norsemen. The Viking settlers of Normandy soon became French speakers, well integrated with the local population, but their adventurous spirit showed itself in the 11th century in their conquests of England and of Southern Italy and Sicily.
conquest of England (1066)
✣62●, ✣186, ✣186●, ❏186, ◆186 (2)
of Sicily (1091) ✣62●
Normandy Landings (*var.* D-Day, *Operation Overlord*) ⚔ of WW II (Jun–Jul 1944). Allied combined operation, the largest amphibious landing in history, which initiated the Allied invasion of Nazi Europe. ✣105, ✣105●, ◆105 (3), ◆211 (4)
Normandy
Duchy founded by Vikings (911)
✣185●, ◆185 (3)
Norsemen *see* Vikings
North Africa 158–169
Berber states ✣161, ◆161 (2)
colonized by Vandals
✣52–3, ◆52 (1) (2)
Fatimid rulers ✣58
reconquered by Justinian ✣54
Roman amphitheatre ❏161
Roman Empire ◆42
spread of Islam ◆56 (1), ✣86, ✣111
North America 116–139
1865–1920 ✣132–3
Anglo-French conflict
✣126–7, ◆127 (2)
big game hunting (BCE) ✣18
boom and bust (1914–41) ✣134–5
Californian Gold Rush (1849)
✣90●, ✣93
cemetery (BCE) ✣18●
cities and empires
✣122–3
colonization ✣86, ◆126 (1)
cultures
Adena (1000 BCE) ✣30
Anasazi ✣58, ✣62●
Aztec, ✣66, ✣74, ✣78, ◆124 (1) (2) (3)
Hopewell (BCE) ✣38●, ✣46●, ✣120, ✣123, ◆36 (1)
Maya ✣46●, ✣50, ✣54, ✣58●, ✣66●, ✣124
Mogollon ✣58
Olmec (BCE) ✣30●, ✣34
decline of the Democratic South
✣139
early peoples ✣120–1, ◆121 (4)
early subsistence and agriculture
✣26, ✣90, ◆120 (1)
eastern interior ✣119, ◆119 (2)
expansion
✣82, ✣90, ✣128, ◆128 (2)
exploration and mapping ✣60●, ✣118, ◆118–19 (1) (2) (3)
historical landscape ✣116–17
indigenous people
✣90, ✣118, ✣123, ✣126, ✣128–9
population changes ✣126
seizing of the West
✣128, ✣128●, ◆128–9 (2)
settlement and conflict ✣126–7, ✣128–9, ✣136–7, ◆128 (2)
settlers populate the west
❏94, ❏128
societies in transition ✣136–7
Spanish exploration and colonization ✣125●, ◆125 (4)
struggle for Nationhood
✣128, ✣128●, ◆128–9 (2)
wagon trails ◆128 (2)
wildlife ❏118
North American Free Trade Agreement (NAFTA). Agreement between the US, Canada and Mexico to remove trade barriers between the three nations for a ten-year period. It came into force in Jan 1994.
✣136●
See also USA, Canada
North Atlantic Treaty Organization (NATO). Established in 1949 as security coalition among Western Allies, dominated by US. Frequently deployed troops from member states as peace-keeping forces, but played a large role in Gulf War (1991) and Yugoslav conflict (1999).
created 1949
✣108, ✣109●, ✣213
Cold War alliances
✣109, ✣138, ◆108–9 (1)
conventional arms limitation (1990) ✣109●
US collective defence treaties (1983) ◆138 (1)
Warsaw Pact (1955)
✣106●, ✣108, ◆108 (3)
North Korea *see* Korea
North Vietnam *see* Vietnam
Northeast Passage Maritime route along the northern coast of Europe and Asia between the Atlantic and Pacific oceans, not fully navigated until 20th century.
◆257 (2)
search for routes to Asia (1550–1820) ✣80●, ✣257●, ✣286, ◆286 (1)
Northern Chou *see* Northern Zhou
Northern Expedition (1926–28) An attempt by the Kuomintang (Guomindang) to unify China, led by Jiang Jieshi (Chiang Kai-shek).
✣271●
Northern Song *see* Song dynasty
Northern Wei *see* Toba Wei
Northern Zhou (var. Northern Chou) Ruling dynasty of northern China (557–581) who overthrew the Northern Qi.
✣261●, ◆261 (5)
Norway
800–1000 ◆185 (3)
accession of Canute (1016) ✣62●
foreign affairs
possessions
1925 ◆98–9
1950 ◆102–3
1975 ◆106–7
Norwegians settle in Scotland (c.900 CE) ✣60●
WW II, mobilization and casualty figures ✣105
Union of Kalmar (1397) ✣70●
Novgorod
founded by Rurik the Viking (862 CE) ✣60●, ✣185
granted independence (1136)
✣62●
NRA *see* National Recovery Administration
Nubia The name given by the Egyptians to the area extending from the First Cataract of the Nile south to the Sudan. Its capital was first at Napata then at Meroë. In the 2nd millennium BCE the Nubians were under Egyptian rule, but themselves ruled Egypt in the 1st millennium, making Napata briefly the centre of the ancient world. Egypt's 25th dynasty, 751–668 BCE, came from Cush and 300 of their pyramids remain.
BCE ✣30, ✣31●, ✣34
confederacy of chiefdoms
◆159 (3)
Coptic Christianity ✣58
gold deposits (BCE) ✣26
Nubt Confederacy (BCE) ◆159 (2)
Nuclear Age General term for the period since the end of WW II when nuclear fission technology, used for power generation and weapons of mass destruction, was developed by a coterie of powerful nations.
bombing of Japan
✣104, ✣273, ◆273 (3)
Pacific test sites ❏285, ◆285 (2)
numerical systems
evolution ✣33, ◆33 (2)
See also mathematics
Numidia Roman province north of the Sahara in N Africa.
Berber state ◆161 (2)
Christian converts (c.150 CE)
✣47●
Roman control ✣46
under Masinissa (c.210 BCE)
◆42–3
Nur al-Din (d.1174). Turkish leader of Muslim resistance to the crusader states from his territories in Syria. He sent his general Saladin to Egypt, where he brought the Fatimid Caliphate to an end in 1169. ✣65●
Nyasa, Lake Reached by Livingstone (1859) ✣157●, ◆168 (1)
Nyasaland (now Malawi). Granted independence (1963) ✣168●
Nyerere, Julius (1922–1999) The first prime minister of independent Tanganyika (1961), who became the first president of the new state of Tanzania (1964). Nyerere was also the major force behind the Organization of African Unity (OAU). ❏168

Oaxaca Region of southern Mexico which was the site for the some of the earliest civilizations of Central America including the Olmec.
◆36 (1), ✣121
Ocampo, Sebastián de Early 16th-century Spanish conquistador, leader of expedition from Hispaniola to Cuba. ✣125, ◆125 (4)
Occaneechee Path Exploration (1673)
✣119●
Oceania General geographic term for the island groups of the Pacific Ocean, sometimes including Australia and New Zealand.
276–285
✣55, ✣91
Austronesian and Polynesian migrations ◆280–1 (3)
and Australasia, historical landscape ✣276–7, ◆276–7
exploration and mapping
✣278–9, ◆278–9 (1) (3)
peopling the Pacific ◆280–1 (3)
prehistoric ✣15, ✣280–1
Octavian *see* Augustus Caesar.
Oda Nobunaga (1534–82) Provincial leader who initiated the unification of Japan (r.1568–82).
✣266, ◆266 (4)
Odoacer 5th-century Barbarian chieftain, who in 476 deposed the last Roman emperor, Romulus Augustulus, to become ruler of Italy with his capital at Ravenna. He was killed in 493 after surrendering to Theodoric.
rules Italy (476) ✣182●
defeated by Ostrogoths (492)
✣53●
Offa (r.757–96). King of Mercia, which during Offa's reign became the most powerful of the Anglo-Saxon kingdoms of Britain. 183●
Offa's Dyke Rampart and ditch built c.785 by Offa of Mercia to define the border between the English and the Welsh. ◆183 (3)
Ogedei *see* Ögödei
Ogilvie's road maps ✣173
Ögödei (var. Ogedei) (d.1241). Mongol leader, son of Genghis Khan, who led successful campaigns against the Khwarizm Shah and the Jin of northern China. He was elected Great Khan in 1229.
elected Great Khan (1229) ✣69●
Mongol campaigns (1229–41)
◆68–9 (1)
O'Higgins, Bernardo (1778–1842) Liberator of Chile. Son of an Irish-born soldier who emigrated to Chile, O'Higgins rose to be leader of the patriotic forces that fought for liberation from Spain from 1810. Defeated and driven from Chile in 1814, he received support from the newly-independent Republic of Río de la Plata, crossed the Andes with José de San Martin and won the decisive battle of Chacabuco in 1817. He became the first president of Chile, but his authoritarian rule was unpopular and he was driven from office in 1823. He died in exile in Peru.
◆150 (1)
Ohio
Kent State University protest (1970) ✣137●, ◆137 (7)
migration (1917–20) ✣134
Ohio River
Adena culture (1000 BCE) ✣30
first proper survey (1729) ✣119●
oil
crisis causes inflation (1973)
✣106●
exploitation ✣107, ✣138
OPEC founded ✣107●
pollution ❏235
production in Gulf region
◆234 (1)
Oirats Nomad raids on China ✣75
Okinawa ⚔ of WW II (Mar–Jun 1945). Major US amphibious assault which, with Iwo Jima, secured an island base for strategic bombing campaign against Japan. ◆272 (1), ◆273 (2)
Old Kingdom (2795–2180 BCE). Period of Egyptian history encompassing the 4th to the 8th Dynasties which was especially notable for the building of the pyramids. ◆36 (1), ✣159●, ◆159 (3)
Old World General geo-historic term for Africa and Eurasia, prior to European discovery of Americas and Australasia.
Olid, Cristóbal de Early 16th-century Spanish *conquistador*, leader of expedition from Mexico to Honduras. ✣125, ◆125 (4)
oligarchy In the ancient Greek city-states an oligarchy was in place when power was in the hands of a minority of male citizens, as contrasted with democracy when power was held by the majority.
✣176
Olmec culture Elaborate Central American Indian culture based on the Mexican Gulf coast, which flourished between 1200 and 600 BCE. The Olmecs influenced the rise and development of other great civilizations and are credited with having the first planned religious centres, with monumental sculptures and temples, and with devising the 260-day Mesoamerican calendar.
civilization (1200 BCE)
✣30●, ✣34, ❏30, ◆121 (2)
heartlands ◆121 (3)
jade ceremonial adze ❏121
state religion (BCE) ◆36 (1)
Olustee ⚔ of American Civil War (20 Feb 1864). Union victory. ◆131 (7)
Olympia Athletics festival (776 BCE)
✣31●
Olympic Games Revived (1896) ✣94●
Omagua People of the Upper Amazon region of S America.
✣147, ◆147 (2)
Omani Arabs
attack Portuguese in E Africa (1729) ✣164●
capture Mombasa (1698) ✣83●
Oñate, Cristóbal de 16th-century Spanish explorer, leader of an expedition from Mexico to New Mexico and Arizona. ✣125, ◆125 (4)
Oñate, Juan de (c.1550–1630) Spanish *conquistador*. Led colonizing expedition into New Mexico in 1598 establishing settlements north of the Rio Grande. Reached mouth of Colorado River in 1605. Governor of New Mexico from 1605–08. ✣125, ◆125 (4)
Onin War (1467–77). Struggle between Japanese warlords.
✣267●, ◆267 (4)
OPEC *see* Organization of Petroleum Exporting Countries
Operation Market Garden *see* Arnhem
Operation Overlord *see* D-Day, Normandy Landings
Opium Wars Confrontations (1839–42) (1850–60) arising from Chinese (Qing) attempts to limit the profitable British opium trade in south and east China. British naval forces attacked or blockaded several Chinese ports (Guangzhou, Xiamen, Fuzhou, Ningbo, Tianjin, Shanghai) wresting the first of many territorial trading cessions (Treaty Ports) in the peace settlement, the Treaty of Nanjing (1842). ✣91●, ✣269●, ◆269 (4)
optical instruments Newton's reflecting telescope ❏83
oracles
bones for divination ✣27●
Shang dynasty interpretations
❏32
Orange Free State founded (1854)
✣166●
Orange River, reached by Dutch settlers (1720) ✣87●
Orbigny, Alcide Dessalines d' (1802–57). French palaeontologist, who spent eight years (1826–34) travelling in South America, producing a 10-volume account of his travels and the first detailed map of the whole continent. His observations on fossils in sedimentary rocks gave rise to the science of micropalaeontology.
✣143
Orellana, Francisco de (c.1490–1546) Spanish *conquistador*. Orellana was a member of an expedition to the eastern slopes of the Andes led by Gonzalo Pizarro, brother of Francisco. He and companions became separated from the main party and travelled the length of the Amazon. ✣142●, ◆142 (1)
Organization of African Unity (OAU). Founded (1963). ✣169●
Organization of Petroleum Exporting Countries (OPEC). International organization seeking to regulate the price of oil. Founded in 1960, it consists of thirteen oil-producing countries which include Saudi Arabia, Iran, Iraq, Kuwait, Venezuela, Libya and Algeria.
founded ✣107●, ✣234
restricts supplies (1973) ✣107●
Orinoco Raleigh's expeditions ✣149
Oriskany ⚔ of American Revolutionary War (6 Aug 1777). American victory. ◆127 (3)
Orléans Siege (1429). Turning point in Hundred Years' War. The city, under siege from the English, was relieved by the French, inspired by Joan of Arc.
✣75●, ✣192, ✣192●
Oromo People of East Africa who migrated north into Ethiopia in large numbers in the 16th and 17th centuries. ✣165, ◆165 (3)
Orozco, Francisco 16th-century Spanish explorer of N America.
colonizing expedition (1521)
✣125, ◆125 (4)
Orozco, Pascual Mexican revolutionary leader ✣133
Ortelius, Abraham (1527–98) Dutch cartographer and publisher. Publisher of the first 'modern' atlas, the *Theatrum Orbis Terrarum* in 1570. ✣79, ✣173●
Osaka Emergence of Yamato state (c.300) ✣51●
Osei Tutu (d. 1712). Founder and first ruler of the Asante nation. ✣164●
Osman I (c.1258–1326) Founder of the Ottoman dynasty, which grew powerful in the regions of northwest Anatolia bordering Byzantium. By the time of his death the Ottomans controlled most of Bithynia.
✣67●, ❏230
Ostrogoths The 'Eastern Goths' first emerged as a threat to Rome in 453, after the death of Attila and the dispersal of the Huns. Under their leader Theodoric the Great, they conquered Italy in 493, establishing a kingdom that lasted until 553. ✣182
See also Goths
Otto I (*aka* Otto the Great) (912–73). He was elected King of the Germans in 936 and crowned Emperor in 962. His defeat of the Magyars at Lechfeld in 955 put an end to their raids on western Europe. Made Germany the most powerful political entity in western Europe.
defeats Magyars (955)
✣58●, ✣185
Holy Roman emperor
✣58, ✣185, ✣185●
Otto II (955–83) Holy Roman Emperor. Joint emperor with his father Otto I from 967.
Italian campaign ✣185●
portrait ❏185
Ottokar II (1230–78). King of Bohemia, who extended Bohemian rule almost to the Adriatic. He was defeated by the Emperor Rudolf of Habsburg at the battle of Marchfeld.
✣189●, ◆189 (4)
Ottoman Empire Islamic empire established in Anatolia in the late 13th century by Turkish tribes. It rapidly spread into Europe, reaching its peak in the 16th century when it stretched from the Persian Gulf to Morocco in the south, and from the Crimea to the gates of Vienna in the north. After the unsuccessful siege of Vienna (1683), the empire began a protracted decline, collapsing altogether when Turkey was defeated in WW I. 230–233
1200–1400 ◆189 (4)
1300–1500 ◆230 (1)
1400 ◆70–1, ◆229 (4)
1500 ◆74–5, ◆193 (4)
1512–1639 ◆231 (3)
1600 ◆78–9
1700 ◆82–3
1800 ◆86–7
1800–1913 ✣232, ✣232●, ◆167 (4), ◆232–3 (1)
1850 ◆90–1
1900 ◆94–5, ◆166 (1)
founded (1299) ✣67●, ✣230
Bursa becomes capital (1326)
✣71●
decline and collapse
✣86●, ✣98, 232
partition (1918–23) ✣233
defeats
by Timur (1402) ✣95●
European lands lost (1912–13)
✣99●
⚔ Lepanto (1571) ✣79, ✣231●
Safavid Persia (1501–1736)
✣231, ◆231 (4)
siege of Vienna (1683)
✣82●, ✣195
expansion
rise of the empire
✣230, ✣230●, ◆230 (1)
consolidation and resistance (17th century)
✣196, ✣196●, ◆196 (2)
frontier (16th century) ◆195 (4)
height of power (1512–1639)
✣231, ✣231●, ◆231 (3)

Key to index: ✣ text ● timeline ❏ picture ◆ map *var.* variant name *aka* also known as *f/n* full name *prev.* previously known as r. ruled ⚔ battle WW I First World War WW II Second World War

Mamluks conquered in Egypt (1517) ✤79●
naval campaigns (15th–16th century) ◆230 (2)
of power (1453–1571) ✤194, ✤194●
seizes Anatolia ✤71
southeastern Europe (1354) ✤71●
Trebizond (1461) ✤75●
WW I ✤99●
Habsburg conflict (1663–171) ✤197, ◆197 (4)
Indian Ocean trade ✤230, ◆230 (2)
Janissary corps (c.1380) ✤71●, ❑230
sultan deposed (1908) ✤99●
See also Balkans; Turkey

Ottonian dynasty Saxon dynasty, named after Otto I, Holy Roman Emperors in the 10th and 11th centuries. ✤185, ✤185●

Oudney, Walter (d.1824) British naval officer and explorer. He accompanied Denham and Clapperton across the Sahara to Lake Chad in 1822, but died during the journey. ◆157 (4)

Oyo West African state that dominated the region between the Volta and the Niger in the 18th century.
main power in Niger Delta (1747) ✤87●
slave trade ✤82
state established (c.1500) ✤79●

P

Pachacuti Inca (*var.* Pachacutec). The ruler in whose reign (1438–71) the Inca Empire expanded from its heartlands around Cuzco to dominate the Andean region as far north as Quito. ✤74●, ◆147 (3)

Pacific Ocean
colonization
(19th century) ✤284–5, ✤284●
c.1500 ✤27, ◆26–7
decolonization and nationhood ✤285, ◆285 (3)
imperialism ◆284 (1)
Japan takes German colonies (1914) ✤99
Japanese naval power limited (1922) ✤99●
missionaries in the South Seas ✤284, ❑284
Polynesian ✤55●, ✤60●, ◆60 (2), ✤280–1●, ◆280–1 (3)
reached by Russians (1649) ✤257●
use and abuse of resources ◆185 (2)
migrations
Austronesian and Polynesian ✤281, ◆280–1 (3)
importation of migrant workers ✤284
prehistoric ✤281●
Panama Canal opened (1914) ✤98●
trade
European and American ✤279, ◆279 (3)
exploitation ✤279●, ✤285, ✤285●
playground for wealthy tourists ❑284
volcanic landscape ❑276

Pacific Rim Geopolitical term for those countries of E Asia, Australasia and the Americas with Pacific shorelines, used in relation to trans-Pacific trade agreements and associated with the region's economic boom during the 1980s and 1990s. ◆275 (4)
See also Tiger Economies.

Pacific War (1937–45). General term for the war in the eastern theatre of operations during WW II. ✤272–273●, ◆272–273, ❑272–273

Pacific, War of the (1879–83). War between Chile, Peru, and Bolivia, fought over the valuable nitrate deposits in the Atacama Desert. Chile made substantial territorial gains from both Bolivia and Peru; Bolivia lost its access to the Pacific coast for ever. ✤151, ◆151 (4)

padrão Mariner's milestone placed by Portuguese navigators along the coast of Africa during the 14th–15th centuries. ❑156

Paekche Ancient kingdom of the Korean Peninsula. ✤264
See also Korea

Páez, José Antonio (1790–1873) Venezuelan revolutionary who fought against the Spanish with Simón Bolívar, and Venezuela's first president. In 1829 he led the movement to separate Venezuela from Gran Colombia and controlled the new country from his election as president in 1831 until 1846 when he was forced into exile. Returned as dictator 1861–63 and died in exile in New York. ❑150

Pagan (c.1050–1287) Burmese empire. The capital was at the predominantly Buddhist temple-city of Pagan (founded 847) on the banks of the Irrawaddy River. The empire was sacked by Mongol invaders in the 1287. ✤63, ✤245, ◆245 (5)
first Burmese state (1044) ✤63●
Mongol raids (13th century) ✤67

Pakistan 252–3
conflict zones ◆252 (2)
divided (1971) ✤107●
Independence (1947) ✤103●, ✤252, ✤251, ◆251 (4)
Islamic Republic (1956) ✤107●
See also India

Palaeolithic Period of human history from 2.5 million years ago (Lower Palaeolithic), to the Middle Palaeolithic (c.200,000 BCE), and ending with the Upper Palaeolithic (c.35,000–10,000 BCE). The Upper Palaeolithic in Europe is associated with evidence of technological innovation and the florescence of rock art and carving. ✤17, ◆17 (2), ❑17

Palas Late 8th-century Indian dynasty which maintained power in NE India, with strong Buddhist ties with Tibet.
✤59, ◆244 (2)

Pale of Settlement (*var. Rus.* Cherta Osedlosti) Area within the Russian Empire where Jews were permitted to live. Arose following the partitions of Poland in the late 18th century. Between 1783 and 1794, Catherine the Great issued a series of decrees restricting the rights of Jews to operate commercially within the newly-annexed areas. By the 19th century, the Pale included Russian Poland, Lithuania, Belorussia, most of Ukraine, the Crimea and Bessarabia, and with few exceptions, Jews were increasingly restricted to this area with further restriction occurring towards the end of the 19th century, when a census revealed a population of nearly 5 million Jews within the Pale, with about 200,000 elsewhere in Russia. ✤101●, ◆101 (2)

Palenque, Maya city built (c.300) ✤50●

Palestine
at the time of David (c.1006–966 BCE) ✤222, ◆222 (1)
Balfour Declaration (1917) ✤99●
British mandate ✤233
conquered by Rome (63 BCE) ✤225, ✤225●
emigration (1947–48) ◆234 (3)
immigration (c.1930–40s) ✤103●, ✤234
Jewish diaspora (66–135 CE) ✤48●, ✤225, ◆225 (5)
Jewish revolts ✤225, ◆225 (4)
Jewish settlement (c.1200 BCE) ✤31
united with Syria (c.1100 BCE) ✤31
See also Holy Land, Israel

Palestine Liberation Organizaton (PLO). Organization led by Yasser Arafat to restore the Palestinian people to their homeland. In 1974 it was recognized by the Arab nations as the 'sole legitimate representative of the Palestinian people'. In 1993 the PLO signed an agreement with Israel formally recognizing the state of Palestine and Israel. chairman Yasser Arafat ❑234
Israel agreement extends self-rule (1995) ✤111●
Palestinian problem (1947–82) ◆234 (2)
signs Oslo Accord with Israel (1993) ✤234
West Bank self-rule extended (1995) ✤111●
See also Arafat, Yasser

Palgrave, William Gifford (1826–88) British Jesuit explorer. Working as a spy for Napoleon III of France, he was the first European to make the west-east crossing of the Arabian Peninsula in 1862–63. ◆219 (4)

Palliser, Lt. John 19th-century Irish explorer of Canada, who conducted a major survey of the prairies and the Rocky Mountains in the 1850s. ◆119 (3)

Panama Canal Shipping canal across the Isthmus of Panama (64.85 km wide), linking the Atlantic and Pacific Oceans. In 1903 a strip of territory was granted to the US by Panama; construction of the canal began early in 1904. It was opened to traffic on 15 Aug, 1914. Further work to deepen and widen the canal was begun in 1959.
opened (1914), ◆96 (1) ✤98●
Zone ceded to US (1903) ✤98●, ✤133●, ◆133 (4)

Panaramittee, rock engravings (petroglyphs) ❑17

Panda Zulu king (r.1840–72). ❑91

Panipat ⚔ of (20 Apr 1526). A victory by the Mughal leader, Babur, who confronted the forces of the Afghan Lodi Sultanate. Babur's use of artillery was decisive, the Sultan was routed, and control of the entire Ganges valley passed to the Mughals. ✤87

Pannonia Roman province including territory now mostly in Hungary and Yugoslavia.
✤53, ◆180 (1), ◆184 (2)

Pantheon Temple to all the gods built in Rome c.27 BCE, well preserved to the present day. ❑43

Paoli ⚔ of American Revolutionary War (20 Sep 1777). British victory. ◆127 (3)

Papacy *see* Catholicism

Papal States (*var.* Patrimony of St. Peter). ◆188 (1), ◆193 (4)

paper
Chinese writing material ❑46
invention (105 CE) ✤46
money introduced by Chinese ✤59●, ✤263
papyrus ❑30
printed banknotes (c.1287) ❑263

Paracas culture Centred on a barren Peruvian peninsula, and renowned for its ornate prehistoric pottery and colourful textiles. Many artefacts have been found in mummified burials dating from about 600–100 BCE. ✤34●, ✤38●, ✤145, ❑147, ◆145 (4)

Paraguay
mission founded by Jesuits (1607) ✤143●, ✤148●
Chaco War (1932–35) ✤102●, ◆152 (2)
defeats Bolivia in Chaco War (1932–35) ✤102●
freed from Spanish control ✤150, ◆150 (1)

Paraguayan War (1864–70) Boundary disputes led Paraguay to go to war with Brazil in 1864, resulting in an invasion of Paraguay by an alliance of Argentina, Brazil and Uruguay early in 1865. An intense five-year struggle followed, involving every able-bodied citizen and only ending with the complete defeat of the Paraguayan forces. The total population of 1,337,439 was reduced to less than 250,000. ✤94●

Parhae *see* Pohai Empire

Paris, Matthew (c.1200–1259) Benedictine monk and chronicler. Produced the *Chronica Majora*, generally acknowledged to be the finest chronicle of the 13th century. ✤173

Paris
besieged by Danes ✤58●
entered by German troops (1940) ✤104●
liberated by Allies (1944) ✤105●
medieval (c.1400) ✤191, ✤191●, ◆191 (2)
medieval map (1576) ❑173
sacked by Vikings (845 CE) ✤60●
siege (1870) ✤203●
trade along the Seine ❑191

Park, Mungo (1771–1806) Scottish explorer and author of *Travels in the Interior of Africa*. He worked as chief medical officer with East India Company before carrying out two explorations of the Niger River system.
exploration of African interior (1795–96, 1805–06) ◆157 (4)
sponsored by African Associaton ✤157

Parry, Sir William Edward (1790–1855) British navigator and explorer. Travelled to Arctic on behalf of Royal Navy to protect whales from over-hunting. Led four expeditions to the Arctic between 1818 and 1827, navigating more than half of the Northeast Passage, and attempting to reach the N Pole on foot from Spitzbergen. ✤286–7 (2)

Parthenon The greatest temple of Athens, situated on the summit of the Acropolis, replacing an earlier Temple of Athena destroyed by the Persians in 480 BCE. Constructed during the rule of Pericles, it is built entirely from marble and decorated with a remarkable frieze, part of which is to be found in the British Museum in London (the Elgin Marbles). It was finally completed in 432 BCE. ✤177

Parthians Scythian people from Central Asia who in c.240 BCE rebelled against Seleucid rule, formed their own state, and came to dominate Asia Minor and Persia from about 140 BCE. In 53 BCE they defeated the Romans at the battle of Carrhae, and in 40 BCE they captured Jerusalem. The Parthians were attacked by the Romans in 216 CE, and finally crushed by the Sassanians in 224 CE.
Empire ✤43●, ✤45, ✤47
drinking cup ❑43
skilled mounted bowmen ❑224
wars with Rome ✤224, ◆224 (2)

pastoralism The practice of herding animals, such as cattle, sheep, camels, which is common in climates which are too dry, mountainous or too cold for agriculture. Pastoralists tend to be nomadic to varying degrees, and as a result may be important long-distance traders.

Patayán (Hakataya) culture of southwestern N America. ◆123 (4)

Patna ⚔ (1759). Challenge by Mughal crown prince repulsed by British army under Clive. ◆88 (1)

Paul, St. Jewish convert to Christianity who became the leading missionary and theologian of the early Church, undertaking great journeys to Greece and Asia Minor. Probably martyred in Rome between 62 and 68 CE.
journeys ✤48●, ◆48 (1)
martyrdom (64 CE) ✤48●

Paulistas In the 17th and 18th centuries, lawless bands of adventurers from São Paulo, who went on raids into the jungles of Brazil in search of Indians to enslave. In the 17th century they came into conflict with the Jesuits of Paraguay. ✤143
See also São Paulo.

Pazyryk Burial site (BCE) ✤39●

Pearl Harbor (1941) Japanese air attack on the US naval base in Hawaii which led to US entry into WW II. ✤102●, ✤104●, ◆104 (4)✤134●, ✤138, ✤272, ❑272, ◆272 (1)

Peary, Robert Edwin (1856–1920) US explorer of the Arctic. Reputedly the first man to reach the N Pole (6 Apr 1909). ❑286, ◆286–7 (2)

Peasants' Revolt (1381). Uprising in England led by Wat Tyler to protest against the Poll Tax. ✤70●

Pedro I, Emperor of Brazil (also Pedro IV, King of Portugal) (1798–1834) (r.1822–31 in Brazil). When Brazil and Portugal split in 1822, Pedro, son of King João VI, remained in Brazil as its first emperor. His father returned to Portugal, but died in 1826. This made Pedro king of Portugal, but he abdicated in favour of his daughter, Maria. In 1831 Pedro had to return to Portugal to fight his brother Miguel, who was trying to usurp the throne. ❑150, ◆150 (1)

Peipus, Lake ⚔ (1142). Russians defeat of Teutonic Knights. ◆186 (1)

Peking *see* Beijing

Peloponnesian Wars (431–404 BCE). Series of land and sea battles between Athens and Sparta. Caused by the threat of Athenian imperialism, the conflict only ended when the Persians intervened on the Spartans' side, leading to the dismantling of the Athenian Empire. ✤177, ◆177 (3)

penicillin ✤102

Peninsular War (1808–14). Campaign during the Napoleon Wars fought out in the Iberian Peninsula between France and an alliance of Britain, Spain and Portugal. Napoleon's invasion of Portugal (1807) and installation of his brother Joseph on the Spanish throne, sparked off a long guerrilla struggle. The initial British intervention ended in retreat. When Napoleon withdrew French troops to Russia, the future Duke of Wellington, Arthur Wellesley, invaded Spain from Portugal, winning a decisive battle at Vitoria in 1813.
✤200●, ◆200 (1)

People's Movement for the Liberation of Angola (MPLA). Political party of Angola founded in 1956 and backed during the civil war (1975–91) by Cuba and the Soviet Union. ✤109, ◆109 (5)

Pepin (*var.* Pepin the Short, *var. Fre.* Pépin le Bref) (c.714–68). Frankish king. Mayor of the Palace of the last Merovingian king of the Franks, Childeric III. He forced Childeric to abdicate and was crowned in his place. In 753 he won Ravenna from the Lombards for the Papacy.
campaigns (751–68) ◆184 (1) (2)
founder of Carolingian dynasty ✤184●

Pequot War (1637) Indian uprising against European encroachment in New England (N America). ✤126●, ◆126 (1)

Pergamum (*var. Gr.* Pergamon).
Asian kingdom ✤41, ✤179, ◆179 (4)
capital of the Attalid dynasty ✤40
statue of 'The Dying Gaul' ❑40

Pericles (c.495–429 BCE) Athenian general who became the uncrowned king of Athens' Golden Age (r.443–429). A political radical, he was responsible for establishing full democracy in Athens, and his opposition to Sparta was instrumental in provoking the Peloponnesian Wars. ✤38●

Periplus of the Erythraean Sea Greek trading manual of the 1st century CE. ✤45

Perón, Eva Wife of Juan Perón. ❑102

Perón, Juan (1895–1974) (*f/n* Juan Domingo Perón). Army colonel who became president of Argentina (1946–55, 1973–74), founder and leader of the Peronist movement. ✤102●

Pérouse, Jean François Galaup de la (1741–88) French explorer of the Pacific. His voyage of 1785–88 was financed by King Louis XVI. It was the most far-ranging voyage to the Pacific yet attempted, although it failed in its prime aim: to find the Northwest Passage. La Pérouse and his two ships were last seen by members of the First Fleet at Botany Bay in Mar 1788. It was later established that they sank off Vanikoro in the Santa Cruz Islands. ◆278 (1) (2)

Perry, Commodore Matthew (1794–1858) US naval commander. Led the expedition to Japan 1853–54 which forced Japan to end its isolation of two centuries and open trade and diplomatic relations with the world.
✤270, ❑270, ◆270 (1)

Perryville ⚔ of American Civil War (8 Oct 1862). Union victory. ◆131 (6)

Persepolis Capital of Achaemenid Persia, founded by Darius I c.151 BCE.
palace decoration (BCE) ❑35, ❑223

Persia 223–235
dynasties
Achaemenid ✤223●, ◆223 (4)
Parthian ✤43●, ✤45, ✤47
Safavid (1501–1736) ✤79, ✤231, ◆231 (4)
Sassanian ✤44●, ✤47, ✤51, ✤55, ✤225, ✤225●, ◆225 (6)
Seleucid ✤41, ✤224, ◆38–9, ◆224 (1)
foreign affairs
clashes with Ottomans ✤79, ✤231
conquest of Egypt (BCE) ✤34
on death of Nadir Shah (1747) ◆86–7
Hephthalite incursions ✤51
possessions ◆86–7
subjugation of Afghans (1722–36) ✤87●
home affairs
BCE empire ✤39, ✤223, ✤223●, ◆34–5, ◆223 (4)
conquered by Alexander the Great ✤38
overrun by Arabians (656) ✤55●
state religion (BCE) ◆36 (1)
innovations
decorated tile (13th century) ❑67
wind power ✤63
See also Achaemenid Empire, Parthian Empire, Safavid Empire, Sassanian Empire, Seleucid Empire, Iran

Persian Gulf, BCE farm settlements ✤19

Persian Royal Road *see* Royal Road

Perth Founded ✤91

Peru 142–3, 148, 150–3
cultures
✤30, ✤38●, ✤42, ✤46, ✤145, ✤145●, ◆145 (4)
early farming ✤26●
liberated by San Martin ✤90, ✤150, ◆150 (1)
metal-working ✤26●
Pizarro's conquest ✤148, ◆148 (1)
revolts against Spanish ✤86
revolutionary movement ❑152
slave trade ✤279, ✤281
Spanish Viceroyalty (16th century) ✤81, ✤148
War of Pacific (1879–83) ✤94●, ✤151, ◆151 (4)

Peruzzi Powerful banking family of Florence with branches across Europe from c.1275. The Peruzzi went bankrupt in the 1340s after Edward III of England had defaulted on repayment of large loans. ✤190–1, ◆190–1 (1)

Peshawar Kushan capital ✤47

Peter the Great (Peter I) (1672–1725) Tsar of Russia. He succeeded to the throne in 1682, taking full control in 1689. Following an extensive tour of Europe (1697–8), he set about the westernization of Russia. He fought major wars with the Ottoman Empire, Persia and Sweden, defeating the latter in the Great Northern War (1700–1721) which gained for Russia the Baltic coast where Peter founded his new capital, St. Petersburg.
founds St Petersburg (1703) ✤86●
Tsar of Russia, accession (1682) ✤82●
See also Great Northern War

Petra Capital of the Nabataeans from 4th century BCE–2nd century CE, it derived its prosperity from its position on the caravan trade route from southern Arabia, especially during the height of the frankincense trade. Petra was annexed by the Romans in 106 CE. The remains of the city include temples and tombs carved into the pink rock of the surrounding hills.
annexed by Rome (106) ✤47
discovered by Burckhardt (1812) ✤219●
rock-cut tombs ❑47

petroglyph Prehistoric rock carving, often taken to be some of the earliest examples of writing.
❑17, ✤118

Petrograd *see* Leningrad

Peul *see* Fulbe

Peutinger Table Copy (1265) of a Roman map showing road systems and routes within the Roman Empire. The map drastically reduces north-south distances, concentrating instead on routes from west to east. ❑172

Pharaonic Egypt During the New Kingdom from c.1500 BCE onwards Egypt was ruled by the Pharaohs or god-kings, who wielded immense religious, military and civil power and were believed to the sons of the god Osiris ruling on earth. They were the mediators between their mortal subjects and the gods and under their rule Egypt's power and territory greatly increased. The term was only used by the Egyptians themselves from 950 BCE onwards.
✤22●, ✤159● ◆159 (2)–(5)

Phidias (*var.* Pheidias) (c.490–430 BCE). Greece's greatest sculptor, was commissioned by Pericles to carry out Athens' major works and ultimately became superintendent of public works. His legacy includes the Parthenon, where he carried out the gold and ivory work. When accused of stealing the gold from his statue of Zeus at Olympia, Phidias fled from Athens. ✤177

Philby, Harry St. John (1885–1960) English explorer and Arabist. In 1932 he crossed the Rub' al Khali, or 'Empty Quarter', of Arabia. *See also* Rub' al Khali. ❑219, ◆219 (4)

Philip II of France (*var.* Augustus, Philip Augustus, *Fr.* Philippe Auguste) (1165– 1223). The first great Capetian king of medieval France (r.1179–1223), who gradually reclaimed French territories held by the kings of England and also extended the royal sphere into Flanders and Languedoc. He was a major figure in the Third Crusade to the Holy Land in 1191.
◆64–5 (2), ✤187

Philip II (c.382–336 BCE) King of Macedon. Rose to the Macedonian throne in 359 BCE and proceeded to recruit a formidable army. After the battle of Chaeronea (338 BCE), he assumed control of the Greek forces and planned an expedition to reverse the expansion of the Persian Empire, but was murdered in Aegeae before he could fulfil it. Father of Alexander the Great. ✤38●

Philip II (1527–98) King of Spain (r.1556–98), and king of Portugal as Philip I (r.1580–98) who championed the Roman Catholic Counter-Reformation. His reign saw the apogee of the Spanish Empire, though he failed to suppress the revolt of the Netherlands which began in 1566, and lost the Armada in the attempted invasion of England in 1588.
Dutch revolt (1568–1609) ✤195, ✤195●, ◆195 (5)
empire ✤81, ◆81 (3)
portrait ❑81
seizes Portuguese crown (1580) ✤78●

Philippines
colonized by Spain (16th century) ✤78, ✤79●, ✤81
gain independence (1946) ✤103●, ✤251
seized by Japan (1942) ✤103●
Spanish-American War (1898) ✤94●, ✤133, ◆133 (4)

Philistines An ancient people of the southeast coastal Mediterranean; originally a seafaring people who settled in south Palestine in the 12th century BCE. They gained powerful control of land and sea routes and were long-standing enemies of the Israelites until their defeat by King David. ✤31

Phoenicians Decendents of the Canaanites, the Phoenicians dominated the coastal strip of the eastern Mediterranean in the 1st millennium BCE. They made this area their base for expansion across the whole of the Mediterranean, establishing trading posts in the western Mediterranean and N Africa. The Phoenicians are noted for developing one of the first alphabets, which consisted purely of consonants.
✤30–1, ✤176–7, ✤177●
carved ivory plaque ❑177
Mediterranean world (700–300 BCE) ◆176 (1)
state religion (BCE) ◆36 (1)

phosphate mining On Nauru ✤285, ◆285 (2)

Phrygians Originating in Europe around 1200 BCE, the Phrygians occupied the central plateau and western edge of Asia Minor, reaching their widest extent at the start of the 1st millennium BCE. Their power declined in the 6th century BCE with the occupation by the Lydians. ✤31, ◆221 (5)

Piankhi (r.c.741–715 BCE) King of ancient Nubia (Cush). Subdued Upper Egypt c.721 BCE and defeated Tefnakhte of Lower Egypt, but returned to Nubian capital at Napata c.718 BCE. ✤34

pictograph (*var.* pictogram). The earliest forms of writing were based on these stylized outline

representations of objects. The earliest examples come from c.3000 BCE Egypt, but they occur across the world; because they represent objects rather than linguistic elements, pictograms cross conventional language boundaries. ✣32●, ✣32 (1), ✣223
See also hieroglyphics

Picts Group of tribes who occupied N Scotland in early Christian times, known for their fierce raiding. Connections between the kings of the Picts and the Scots of SW Scotland grew closer in the 9th century, leading to the creation of the medieval kingdom of Scotland. ◆52–3 (1)

Pike, Lt. Zebulon Montgomery (1779–1813) US soldier and explorer. In 1805–06, he led an expedition in search of the source of the Mississippi. In 1806–07, he travelled up the Arkansas River to the Colorado Mountains where he attempted to climb Pike's Peak. His party was captured by the Spanish, but later released. ◆119 (3)

pilgrimages
- Andean sites ✣54●
- 13th-century map of Jerusalem ❑219
- Marco Polo's travels ❑219
- to Mecca ✣70, ◆218 (2)

Pincevent Ancient shelter ❑16

Pinochet, General Augusto Ugarte (1915–). Leader of the military junta that overthrew the Marxist government of President Salvador Allende of Chile on 11 Sep, 1973. He subsequently headed Chile's military government (1974–90). ✣110●, ❑152

Pinzón, Vicente Yáñez (*fl.* 1492–1509). Spanish navigator who sailed with Columbus. Discovered the mouth of the Amazon (1500) and was made governor of Puerto Rico. Also explored (1508–09) the coasts of Honduras and Venezuela with Juan Díaz de Solís. ✣142●

piracy
- in the Caribbean (16th–17th centuries) ◆85 (2)

Pisa 11th-century prosperity ✣62

Pittsburgh First commercial radio station in the US. ✣98

Pizarro, Francisco (c.1475–1541) Spanish *conquistador*. Pizarro first sailed to the New World in 1502. He took part in several expeditions around the Caribbean, before turning his attention to Peru. In 1531 he set off from Panama with 185 men and 27 horses. By exploiting a recent civil war among the Incas, and treacherously killing their leader Atahualpa, Pizarro was able to conquer the great Inca empire and seize large quantities of gold ornaments that were melted down to be shipped to Spain. The early years of the colony were marked by rivalry between the *conquistadores* and Pizarro was killed by supporters of one of his lieutenants, Diego de Almagro, in 1541.
- conquers Inca Empire ✣78, ✣81●, ✣142●, ✣148, ◆148 (1)
- portrait ❑148

plagues
- agent of transmisssion ❑72
- agents of Black Death ❑72
- Black Death ✣71–2, ✣190●, ✣191, ❑70
- black rat ❑72
- bubonic ✣70●, ◆72 (1)
- cause of depopulation ✣74
- deathbed of Queen Anne of Bohemia ❑72
- effect on population levels ✣73, ◆73 (2)
- origin and movement ◆81 (2)
- spread ✣71●, ✣72, ✣72●, ◆72 (1)

plantain 'Englishman's foot' ❑81

plantation system System for the farming of cash crops such as rubber and cotton on a large scale in European colonies. This system was often reliant on slave labour. ✣84, ❑84

Plantagenets *see* Angevin Empire

plants
- African indigenous crops ◆158 (1)
- biological origin and movement ◆81 (2)
- domestication, BCE ✣16●, ✣21, ✣26, ✣34, ✣145, ✣258 (1), ◆18–19, ✣120●, ◆120 (1)
- maize and squash ❑121
- origin and movement of ◆81 (2)

Plassey, ⚔ of Anglo-French war in India (23 Jun 1757). The defeat of a large Indian army under the command of the Nawab of Bengal by British forces under the command of Robert Clive, at the village of Plassey on the Hooghly River. ✣87●, ◆87 (1)

Plataea ⚔ of the Persian Wars (480 BCE). The decisive defeat of the Persians by the Greeks. ✣39

Plato (c.427–347 BCE). An Athenian aristocrat and disciple of the philosopher Socrates, Plato travelled widely before founding his own academy of philosophy in Athens. His 35 dialogues, many of which feature Socrates, are concerned with defining moral concepts, and developing Plato's own doctrines and self criticisms. Plato distinguished between the transient and finite objects experienced by the senses and that of the timeless universal forms which he called the true objects of knowledge. His ideas influenced the Romans and shaped Christian theology and Western philosophy. ✣177

PLO *see* Palestine Liberation Organization

pogrom An organized massacre or riot. Originally used with reference to the murder of Russian Jews in the late 19th and early 20th centuries. ❑100

Pohai Empire (*var.* Parhae) Empire of Manchuria formed by Koguryo refugees in 696. Destroyed by Khitans in 926. ✣264●, ◆264 (2)

Poland 185–198, 208–215
- foreign affairs
  - assimilated into Europe (11th century) ✣62
  - Baltic conflict (16th century) ✣195, ✣195●, ◆195 (3)
  - joined with Lithuania (1386) ✣189●, ✣193●, ◆193 (4)
  - Mongol invasion ✣69
- home affairs
  - decline (1550–1795) ✣198●
  - end of Communism (1989) ✣110●
  - joins Catholic church (1000) ✣185●
  - Lublin Committee ✣213●
  - partition (1772–95) ✣198, ◆198 (2)
  - Soviets crush uprising (1956) ✣108●
  - states (1200–1400) ◆189 (4)
- Second World War *see* Wars, Second World

polis The Greek city-state, that of Athens being one of several which characterize the Classical Age. ✣34

pollution
- ecological damage ❑235
- oil ✣235

Polo, Marco (1254–1324) Venetian merchant and traveller. In 1271 he accompanied his father, Nicolò, and his uncle, Maffeo, on their second journey to the court of Kublai Khan, the Mongol ruler of China. He spent almost 17 years in the Khan's service, travelling extensively in China before returning to Venice in 1295. His account of his travels has remained a bestseller ever since, although its veracity has been questioned by some scholars.
- departs for China (1271) ❑66
- employed by Kublai Khan ✣68
- escorts Mongol princess to Hormuz (1292) ✣68●
- explorer of Central Asia ◆256 (1)
- explorer of W Asia ❑219, ◆219 (3)
- leaves China (1292) ✣67●
- reaches Kublai's summer palace (1275) ✣68●
- route (1271–1295) ◆68 (2), ◆76 (9)

Pol Pot (*aka* Saloth Sar) (1926–1998). Cambodian Communist leader. He led the pro-Chinese Communist Khmer Rouge guerrillas from the 1960s and seized power in 1975. He attempted to create a self-sufficient socialist state using brutal methods, resulting in a death toll of over 2 million, one-fifth of the population of Cambodia. Once overthrown in 1979 by the Vietnamese, he remained in the Khmer Rouge during a renewed guerrilla campaign. ✣111●

Polynesians People of the Pacific, who share close genetic and linguistic heritage with the peoples of the Philippines and central and eastern Indonesia. Early Lapita colonists (identified by their pottery), spread from the eastern islands of SE Asia as far east as Tonga and Samoa. Polynesian culture had its origins in the Fiji-Samoa region, c.1000 BCE. From c.200 BCE, Polynesian colonists settled all of the islands of the Pacific, reaching New Zealand by 1200 CE. Chiefdom societies developed throughout the region from c.1200 CE. ✣276
- culture, ✣55, ✣60●
- migrations (1500 BCE–1000 CE) ✣60, ◆60 (2)
- prehistoric migrations ◆280–1 (3)
- twin-hulled canoe ❑60, ❑281
- wooden carving of Ku ❑281

Pomare II Tahitian convert to Christianity ❑284

Pompeii
- destroyed (79 CE) ✣46●
- mosaic of Alexander the Great ❑39

Ponce de León, Juan (1460–1521). Spanish explorer who discovered Florida in 1513 and was made governor. Failing to subdue his new subjects, he retired to Cuba.
- colonizing expedition (1508, 1512) ✣125, ◆125 (4)
- N American expedition (1513) ◆118 (1)

Pondicherry Seized by British (1761) ✣87●

Pontus Empire under Mithridates Eupator (c.100 BCE) ◆42–3

Poor Men of Lyons *see* Waldensians

poppy Flower from which morphine, heroin, codeine, and papaverine are derived. Comes from the milky fluid in the unripe seed capsule of the opium poppy (*Papaver somniferum*), which is native to Turkey. ◆153 (5)

Popular Front International alliance of left-wing (socialist, Communist and other radicals) elements which gained some prominence during the 1930s, especially in Spain, where the Popular Front governed from 1936–39, and opposed General Franco and his supporters during the Spanish Civil War. ◆208 (4)

population
- Chinese ✣260, ✣266, ◆263 (6)
- cities and economic life (c.1750) ✣198, ◆198 (1)
- distribution (c.1400) ◆73 (2)
- early peoples ✣16●
- emergence of urban civilizations (BCE) ✣22–3
- Europe ✣94, ✣190, ✣198
- France (1650–1800) ❑198
- greater African nation ✣112, ◆112 (1)
- pan-Islamic world ✣113, ◆113 (3)
- settlements (BCE) ◆18–19
- South and SE Asia ◆253 (5)
- Swedish growth (1650–1800) ❑198
- USA (1900) ✣94

Port Hudson ⚔ of American Civil War (9 Jul 1863). Inconclusive result. ◆131 (6)

Port Jackson (Sydney). Penal colony ✣91, ✣282●, ◆282 (1)

portolan chart Navigational charts produced from c.1300–1500, mainly in Italy and Spain. They used a series of rhumb lines radiating out from a central point in the direction of the wind or the compass points. They were used primarily to enable pilots to find their way from harbour to harbour. ✣70, ✣173, ❑173

Portugal 186, 190, 192, 194–214
- 16th-century ships ✣78
- foreign affairs
  - voyages of expansion (1492–1597) ◆80–1 (1)
  - possessions
    - 1500 ◆74–5
    - 1600 ◆78–9, ◆164 (2)
    - 1700 ◆82–3, ◆164 (1)
    - 1800 ◆86–7
    - 1850 ◆90–1
    - 1900 ◆94–5
    - 1925 ◆98–9
    - 1950 ◆102–3
    - 1975 ◆106–7
  - Africa
    - aids Ethiopia (1540) ✣165●
    - Angola colony established (1570) ✣79●, ✣82
    - colonization (19th century) ◆166 (1) (3) (4)
    - decolonization ✣168, ◆168 (1)
    - exploration (1416–1500) ✣156, ✣156●
    - imperialism (1880–1920) ✣96, ◆96 (1)
    - leave E Africa (1729) ✣164●
    - mapping Niger Basin ◆156 (2)
    - stone cross marking territorial claim ❑156
  - America
    - Brazil colonized (1530s) ✣78, ✣86, ✣148 (2), ◆149 (3)
    - Brazil surrendered (1822) ✣90
    - N American exploration (15th–17th century) ◆118 (1)
    - South American exploration ◆142 (1) (2), ◆149 (3)
  - Asia
    - imperialism in Southeast ✣97, ◆97 (3)
    - Malacca captured (1511) ✣79●
    - India, Goa trading capital ✣79●, ✣247, ❑247, ◆247 (3)
    - Japan, arrival of merchants (16th century) ❑80
    - N Africa, Ceuta, Morocco, captured (1415) ✣75●
- home affairs
  - black population ✣112, ◆112 (1)
  - monarchy overthrown (1910) ✣98
  - union with Spain (1580) ✣78●, ✣81, ✣81●, ✣149●, ❑196
- trade and industry
  - E African trading posts (1505) ✣79●
  - slavery ✣75●, ✣84, ✣85●

postal system developed ✣204●

Potosí
- natives working the silver mine ❑148
- silver mine opened ✣78●, ✣81●, ✣148●

Potsdam Conference (17 Jul–2 Aug 1945). Allied conference of World War II held at Potsdam, Berlin. The conferees, including US President Harry Truman, British Prime Minister Winston Churchill or Clement Attlee, who became prime minister during the conference and Soviet Premier Joseph Stalin, discussed the substance and procedures of the peace settlements. The chief concerns of the three powers were the immediate administration of defeated Germany, the demarcation of the boundaries of Poland, the occupation of Austria, the definition of the Soviet Union's role in eastern Europe, the determination of reparations, and the further prosecution of the war against Japan. ✣212●

pottery
- development (BCE) ✣14, ✣20, ◆20 (1)
- early examples ❑20
- settlement and innovation (BCE) ✣20●
- America
  - Amazon Basin (4000 BCE) ✣22●
  - Anasazi culture ❑62
  - Chavín (BCE) ✣30
  - Chorrera-style (c.900 BCE) ✣30●
  - earliest Central American (2300 BCE) ✣120●
  - Maya vase ❑50
  - Mexican dog ❑122
  - Moche deity pot ❑46
  - Moche stirrup-spouted vessel ❑54, ❑145
  - Nazca figure, ❑42
- Asia
  - cord-scored amphora ❑19
  - earliest Chinese ✣20●, ◆258 (1)
  - East Asia (6000–2000 BCE) ◆258 (1)
  - Han period ❑260
  - Incipient Jomon ✣15, ❑14
  - Longshan Kui pitcher ❑23
  - Mehrgarh (BCE) ✣19, ✣20●, ✣23●
  - neolithic China ◆258 (2)
  - Shang dynasty ✣259
  - Song dynasty ❑262
  - Christian amphora with two crosses ❑48
- Europe
  - Bandkeramik (5200 BCE) ✣20●, ✣174●
  - Beaker ✣174
  - Cardial ✣174
  - Corded Ware ✣174●, ✣23●
  - Mycenaean goblet (c.1300 BCE) ❑174
  - stylized human figures ❑174
- grave goods ✣19●, ✣22–3, ✣259
- Lapita ✣60●, ❑27, ✣218, ◆281 (3)
- Mimbres ❑123
- Ottoman Iznik ❑230
- Saharan wavy-line ✣19●, ✣20●

Powhatan Native people of northeastern N America
- war with English and French (1609–14) ✣126●, ◆126 (1)

pozzolana Roman building material ✣43

Praeneste Roman mosaic ❑47

Prague ⚔ of WW II (May 1945). Final reduction of German troops by Soviet forces in Central Europe. ✣105, ◆211 (4)

Prague Defenestration (1419) ✣193●

'Prague Spring' Czechoslovakian reforms crushed (1968) ✣106●
See also Dubček, Alexander

precious stones Eurasian and African trade (c.1 CE) ◆44–5

Preveza, ⚔ of 1538. Defeat by the Ottomans of a combined Venetian and Spanish papal fleet. ✣231●, ◆231 (3)

Princeton ⚔ of American Revolutionary War (3 Jan 1777). British victory. ◆127 (3)

printing
- Chinese invention ❑59
- movable type invented (c.1045) ✣63●
- use of movable metal type ✣74

Prohibition Era The prohibition of the sale or manufacture of alcohol in the US, from 1919–33. It was added to the US Constitution as the 18th Amendment, and enforced by the Volstead Act of 1919, and repealed via the 33rd Amendment in 1933. ❑98, ✣133●
See also USA, home affairs

Protestantism The form of western Christianity which grew up following Martin Luther and his supporters' split from the Roman Catholic church in 1529. Protestants rejected the authority of the pope, and used the Bible (in a vernacular translation) as their principal source of spiritual authority.
- Reformation ✣78, ✣82, ✣194, ✣194●
- religious map of Europe (1590) ◆194 (2)

Prussia 193–203
- 18th-century growth ✣199●
- cavalry officers ❑199
- conquest by Teutonic Knights (1283) ✣186●, ✣189●
- foreign affairs
  - 1800 ◆86–7
  - 1850 ◆90–1
  - rise of Brandenburg Protestant state ✣199, ◆199 (3)
  - war of Austrian Succession (1740) ✣86●, ✣203
- *See also* Brandenburg, Franco-Prussian War

Przhevalsky, Nikolai Mikhailovich (1839–88) Russian soldier and explorer of Central Asia. Collected large number of botanical and zoological specimens, including *Equus przevalskii*, the last breed of wild horse known to exist. ◆257 (3)

Ptolemaic dynasty Dynasty of Macedonian kings founded by Alexander the Great's general Ptolemy I. After Alexander's death in 323 BCE the Ptolemies emerged as rulers of Egypt and the Hellenistic maritime empire in the Aegean and eastern Mediterranean. ✣41, ✣42, ✣43●, ✣224, ◆38–9, ◆161 (2), ◆224 (1)

Ptolemy (*var. Lat.* Claudius Ptolemaeus) (c.90–168 CE). Greek astronomer and geographer of Alexandria, Egypt. Author of the *Geography*, and considered the earth the centre of the universe.
- influence of ✣55, ✣62, ✣79, ✣218●
- astronomy ✣59
- classical Eurasia map ✣156, ✣173, ❑44
- points of reference ✣172

Ptolemy I (*var.* Soter 'Saviour') (c.366–283 BCE). Ptolemy was one of Alexander the Great's generals who ruled Egypt when the Macedonian Empire was dismantled after Alexander's death. In 304 he adopted a royal title and founded the Ptolemaic dynasty. An able military and administrative leader, he secured Palestine, Cyprus and parts of Asia Minor. ✣39●, ◆224 (1)

Ptolemy V (*r.*205–180 BCE) King of ancient Egypt of the Macedonian dynasty. Under his rule Egypt lost all of Palestine and Egyptian possessions in Asia Minor. Peace was gained by his marriage to Cleopatra, daughter of Antiochus III of Syria. ✣42

Publius Cornelius Scipio *see* Scipio Africanus

pueblo American Indians living in New Mexico and Arizona who are descended from the Anasazi culture (*see* Anasazi). The term is also used to describe the settlements they built.
- apartment villages ✣58
- culture ✣54●, ✣74, ✣123, ◆123 (4)

pundits Indian secret agent surveyors ✣257, ◆257 (3)

Punic Wars Three wars between between Rome and Carthage. The first (264–241 BCE) saw Rome build a navy powerful enough to compete with Carthage, but unable to conquer the Carthaginian homeland. In the second (218–201) Rome was threatened by the invasion of Italy by Hannibal, but fought back to impose a humiliating peace settlement on Carthage. The third (149–146) ended in the complete destruction of Carthage. ✣179●, ◆179 (3)

Puranas Collection of encyclopedic works, rich in geographic content, belonging to the sacred texts of Hinduism, which record the Creation and the early history of humanity. The Puranas relate to the expansion of the Aryan tribes and their formation into small kingdoms and republics during the first millennium BCE. ✣242, ◆242 (3)

Pusyamitra Founds Shunga dynasty (185–73 BCE) ✣43●

Pydna ⚔ of(168 BCE). Roman victory over Greece. ◆179 (4)

pyramid
- basalt figures at Tula ❑122
- Cushite ✣34
- Giza (2530–2470 BCE) ✣23●, ❑22
- Old Kingdom Egypt ✣159 (3)
- Pyramid of the Sun (Teotihuacán) ✣46
- temple to Huitzilopochtli inaugurated (1487) ✣74●
- Zoser ✣23●, ❑159
- *See also* burials

Pyramid Lake Great Basin survey team ❑119

Pyramid of the Sun Teotihuacán ✣46

Pytheas of Massalia (b.c.300 BCE) Greek navigator and geographer. Probably travelled around coast of Britain and northern Europe. He was one of the first people to fix the position of places using latitudes. ◆172 (1)

Pythian games Pan-Hellenic festival held every four years in the Sanctuary of Apollo at Delphi. The name Pythios meaning 'python slayer', was the name by which Apollo was known there. ✣38

Q

Qapaw tribe North American Indian village map ❑118

Qi dynasty (*var.* Ch'i). One of the Southern Dynasties of China (r.420–589).
- rules southern China (479) ✣51●

Qin dynasty (*var.* Ch'in dynasty) Ruling dynasty of China (221–206 BCE), founded by King Zheng, later the self-styled First Emperor (Shi Huangdi, 259–210 BCE, r.247–210 BCE) who ruled from Xianyang and from 230 unified China, imposing territorial reorganization, central bureaucracy, built first Great Wall, proscribed books and introduced universal weights and measures. ✣39, ✣43, ✣44, ◆259 (5)

Qin Empire *see* Qin dynasty

Qing dynasty (*var.* Ching, *aka* Manchu dynasty) (1644–1911) Ruling dynasty of China established by the Manchus. By the 19th century China was the most populous empire of the world, controlling vast territories in inner Asia, and treating as tributary states Korea, Indochina, Siam, Burma and Nepal. 268–269
- founded (1644) ✣83
- 1800 ◆86–7
- 1850 ◆90–1
- archery contest on silk ❑87
- China (1644–1911) ✣268, ◆268 (1)
- conquest of Xiankiang (1760) ✣87
- decline ✣94, ✣268
- expansion ✣268●
- foreign incursions ✣269●
- Nerchinsk Treaty (1689) ✣83●, ✣270●
- overthrown by Sun Yat Sen (1911) ✣99●, ✣278, ◆271 (5)
- produce specifically for the West ❑268
- protectorate of Tibet (18th century) ✣87
- revolts ✣268●, ◆268 (2)

Qing Empire *see* Qing dynasty.

Quebec ⚔ of American Revolutionary War (30–31 Dec 1775), French victory. ◆127 (3).

Quebec ⚔ of Seven Years' War in N America (1759). British victory over France. Britain subsequently gained control over much of N America. ✣88 (1), ◆127 (2), ✣127●

Quebec
- captured by British (1759) ✣127●
- colonized by Champlain (1608) ✣126●

Quetzalcoatl The serpent god of both the Toltec and Aztec civilizations. The symbol of death and resurrection, he was also known as the patron of priests, inventor of books and calendars. ❑124

Quexos, Pedro de 16th-century Spanish explorer of N America (1521). ✣125, ◆125 (4)

Quirós, Pedro Fernández de (c.1560–1614) Spanish explorer of the Pacific. After serving on several trans-Pacific sailings, in 1605 he realized his ambition of mounting an expedition of his own to find the mythical 'Great South Land'. He discovered a number of small islands, including Espiritu Santo, the principal island of Vanuatu, which he announced was the east coast of the *Terra Australis Incognita*. ◆278 (1)

Quito Expedition to test Earth's sphericity (1735) ✣143●

Qutb al-Din Aybak (*var.* Aybeg) *see* Muhammad of Ghur

Qutb al-din Founds Delhi Sultanate ✣67, ✣244

Qutb Minar minaret ❑67, ❑244

Quwwat-al-Islam mosque (1199) ✣67, ❑244

R

Ra In ancient Egyptian religion, the sun god, one of the most important gods of ancient Egypt. Early Egyptian kings alleged descent from Ra. Ra had several manifestations, the most common being the hawk and the lion. ✣26

radio
- technology invented by Marconi (1894) ❑98
- in the USA (1924) ✣135

Radisson, Pierre-Esprit (c.1636–1710). Fur-trader and explorer. Established Fort Nelson in Hudson Bay, (his brother-in-law, Groseilliers had previously established Fort Rupert). Their efforts led effectively to the founding of the Hudson's Bay Company in 1670. ◆119 (2)

Raffles, Sir Thomas Stamford (1760–1841). The founder of Singapore. In 1819, in his capacity as Lieutenant-Governor of Benkulen (the East India Company's principal station in Sumatra) he persuaded the sultan of Johore to cede the uninhabited island to him. It was incorporated into the British colony of the Straits Settlement in 1826. ✣91●, ❑248

Railroad Act (1866). Act passed by US Congress which allowed Railroad Companies to take over Indian lands in the west. ✣128–9●

railways
- Amazonian ◆153 (4)
- Central Pacific Railroad completed (1869) ✣92●
- European network (1900s) ✣94–5
- high-speed train in Japan ❑274
- Indian network ✣95, ❑249
- London Underground ✣92●, ❑102
- major networks (c.1914) ◆92 (1)
- Pacific coast terminal ❑151
- steam locomotion ✣90
- Stockton-Darlington line (1825) ✣204●
- Trans-Siberian ❑269
- US network ✣94–5, ✣132, ❑92, ❑128, ❑129, ◆128 (2), ◆132 (1)

rainforest
- Amazon ❑140
- Brazilian Yanomami tribe ❑110
- development of Brazilian ✣153●, ◆153 (4)
- equitorial ◆160 (1)
- Maya cities ✣50

Rajaraja the Great (r.985–1014). Chola king who extended Chola control into the eastern Deccan, Ceylon and the Malay Peninsula. By the time he died, he was the paramount ruler of southern India. ✣244, ◆244 (2)

Rajendra I (r.1014–44). King of the Chola dynasty of southern India. Under his rule the Chola navy took control of the eastern sea route between Arabia and China. He ruled from the city of Tanjore.
- Chola ruler (1014) ✣63●
- conquers Ceylon (1018) ✣63●

Rajput clans People of Rajputana, N India. Defeated in 1191 by the Afghan leader Muhammad of Ghur. ✣63●, ◆244 (3)

Raleigh, Sir Walter (c.1554–1618). English adventurer. He found favour under Elizabeth I and named the colony he founded at Roanoke Island in 1584 Virginia after the 'virgin queen'. Fell out of favour with Elizabeth and under James I was imprisoned. Released in 1616 to undertake a voyage to Guiana in search of El Dorado. This ended in disaster and Raleigh was executed on his return to England. ✣149

Ramayana Classical Sanskrit epic of India relating the adventures of Rama, probably composed in the 3rd century BCE. Based on numerous legends, the epic was revised and set down in its best known form by the poet Tulsi Das (1532–1623). ✣241, ◆36 (2)

Rameses III (*var.* Ramesses) (r.c.1184–53 BCE) Second king of the 20th dynasty of Egypt. Went to war with the Philistines and the 'Sea Peoples'. ✣31●

Ramesses *see* Rameses III

Rangoon Founded (1755) ✣87●

Rapa Nui (*var.* Easter Island)
- colonized by Chile ✣284●
- settled by Polynesians ✣55●, ✣60, ✣281, ◆281 (4)
- temple platforms ✣60●, ❑281

Rashtrakutas A powerful kingdom established in 753 CE in the northern Deccan. At its peak, Rashtrakuta control extended from southern Gujarat to Tanjore. ✣244●, ◆244 (2)

Ravenna Capital of Italy under the Ostrogoths and Byzantines.
- captured by Lombards (752) ✣58●
- captured by Ostrogoths (492) ✣53, ✣182
- detail from mosaic (6th century) ❑182
- sarcophagus ❑182

Raymond of Toulouse Crusade route (1096–99) ◆64–5 (2)

Reagan, Ronald Wilson (1911–2004). 40th president of the United States (Republican, 1981–89). A former movie actor, as president of the Screen Actors' Guild, Reagan cooperated with efforts to combat alleged Communist influences in the American film industry. He was governor of California from 1967–74. In 1980 he won the Presidential elections in a landslide victory. During his tenure he greatly increased military spending while reducing taxes and cutting back on general government expenditure. He introduced the controversial SDI (Strategic Defense Initiative) and signed the INF treaty with the Soviet Union which limited intermediate range missiles. His administration was damaged by revelations that profits from arms deals with Iran had been used to support the Contra rebels against the Sandinista government of Nicaragua. ✣139, ✣139●

Recife Taken by Portuguese (1654) ✣149●

Reconquest of Spain (*var. Sp.* Reconquista). The reconquest of Muslim Spain by the Christian states, from the 11th to the 15th century. ✣192, ✣192●, ◆186 (1), ◆192 (3)

Reconquista *see* Reconquest of Spain

Reconstruction (1865–77). Period following the US Civil War in which the southern states were controlled by a Federal government and social legislation, including the granting of new rights to Blacks was introduced. The return of a new Republican government returned power to white leaders who reintroduced segregation in the South. ✣132

Recuay Cultural region ◆145 (4)

Red River Indian War (1874–75). Major uprising by members of the Arapaho, Cheyenne, Comanche, Kiowa and Kataka tribes from reservations in Oklahoma and Texas against white settlers in the area. US forces led by General William Sherman were forced to fight 14 battles against the Indians in the Red River Valley, before their eventual surrender. ✣128–9●, ◆128–9

Red Scare Name given to the fear of Communist subversion in the US which arose in the late 1940s, leading to the setting up of schemes such as the Federal Employee Loyalty Program, and Senator Joseph McCarthy's list of government employees whom he claimed had Soviet sympathies. The scare led to a significant degree of persecution of those suspected of Communist sympathies, and many people – especially in the government, schools, universities, and the mass media – found themselves unable to work because of their suspected beliefs. ✣135●

Red Sea trade (1st century CE) ✣225, ◆225 (3)

reducciones Jesuit frontier settlements in Spanish S America ✣143, ◆143 (2)

Reformation Religious revolution of the 16th century which took place in the Roman Catholic church, led by Martin Luther and John Calvin. The Reformation had long-term political, economic, and social effects, and laid the groundwork for the foundation of Protestantism. ✣194–5, ✣195●

refrigeration First commercial units (1856) ✣92●

refugees and resettlement ✣212, ◆212 (3)

Reiss, Wilhelm 19th-century German explorer of S America, who scaled the volcano Cotopaxi in 1872. ✣143●

religion
- Buddhism (to 400 CE) ◆49 (3)
- characteristics ◆36 (1)
- development of organized ✣36–7
- global ✣48–9
- Mediterranean cults ◆37 (3)
- Mithraism, Judaism, and Christianity (to 600 CE) ◆48 (1)
- old world ✣49, ◆49 (4)
- South Asian ◆36 (2)
- state ◆36 (1)
- Taoism and Confucianism ◆37 (4)

Remojadas Early Mexican civilization (c.600–900 CE) ◆122 (1)

Renaissance (*var.* Renascence, c.1300–1550). Period of cultural, economic and political efflorescence in medieval Europe, characterized by the rediscovery of classical Greek and Roman culture, which found expression, initially in Italy, in the growth of Humanist studies and writing, and in a revitalization of architecture, painting, sculpture and the arts in general.
- comes into being ✣75
- in Europe (12th century) ✣187, ✣187●, ◆187 (3)
- travellers in W Asia ◆219 (3)

Renascence *see* Renaissance

Rennell, James (1742–1830). British naval officer who became the Surveyor-General of Bengal in 1764. He was responsible for the first consistent mapping of the Indian subcontinent, the Survey of India. ✣239●, ❑239

Republican Party One of the two major political parties of the US. Formed in 1854 to support anti-slavery policies prior to the Civil War, Abraham Lincoln was its first president. Today, it contains fewer limited government and interventionist foreign policy and is generally considered to be more right-wing than the Democratic Party. ✣130–1, ◆135 (5), ◆139 (4)

Réunions Lands occupied by France during the reign of Louis XIV following the decisions of a special court convened for the purpose, the Chambre des Réunions. Important annexations included Luxembourg (1679) and Strasbourg (1684). Most of the territories had to be returned by the Treaty of Ryswijk (1697). ✣197●, ◆197 (5)

revolts
- against rule of Louis-Napoleon ✣202, ✣202●
- Boxer rebellion (1898) ✣95, ✣97, ❑97, ◆268 (2)
- Dutch (1568–1609) ✣195, ✣195●, ◆195 (5)
- English Peasants' (1381) ✣70●, ◆188 (2)
- European students (1968) ✣106●
- following Black Death ✣70
- fragmentation of China (220–589) ✣261
- Hungarian Hunyadi ✣193●
- Indian Mutiny ✣95●, ✣249, ✣249●, ◆249 (3)
- movements against colonial rule (1880–1920) ✣97, ◆97 (4)
- Taiping rebellion (1850–64) ✣95●, ❑268
- Warsaw Pact crushes Hungarian (1956) ✣106●
- Yellow Turbans (147 CE) ✣47●

revolutions
- American (1775) ✣86, ✣126–7, ◆127 (3)
- Chinese (1911) ✣271, ◆271 (5)
- Cuban ✣152
- economic ✣92–3
- era of revolution 1768–1868 ✣89, ✣89●, ◆88–9 (2)
- in Europe ✣90●, ✣202●, ✣209
- factors leading to industrial ✣86
- French ✣82, ✣86, ✣90, ✣199, ❑199, ◆199 (4)
- impact of industrial ✣92, ◆92 (1)
- inventions and world economy (1835–95) ✣92●
- Liberty on the Barricades (painting) ❑89
- political crackdowns ✣100●
- Russian (1905, 1917) ✣98●, ✣99●, ✣208, ◆208 (2)
- *See also* industrial revolution

Rhodes Greek island
- Hospitallers headquarters (1310) ✣64●

Rhodes, Cecil (1853–1902). Financier, statesman, and empire builder of British South Africa. He was prime minister of Cape Colony (1890–96) and founder of the diamond mining company De Beers Consolidated Mines Limited (1888).
- De Beers Consolidated Mines ✣167
- portrait ❑166

Rhodesia ◆168 (1)
- Northern Rhodesia granted independence (1963) ✣168●
- *See also* Zimbabwe

Ri dynasty *see* Yi dynasty

Ricci, Matteo (1552–1610) Italian Jesuit missionary and cartographer. Joined Jesuit mission in Macao in 1582, and then established mission on Chinese territory, eventually settling in Beijing in 1601. His maps and other data, gave the Western world unprecedented access to information about China. ✣80

Richard I of England (*aka* Richard the Lion-Heart, Lion-Hearted, *Fr.* Richard Coeur de Lion) (1157–1199). Duke of Aquitaine from 1168 and of Poitiers from 1172 and king of England, Duke of Normandy, and Count of Anjou (r.1189–99). His prowess in the Third Crusade (1189–92) made him a popular king in his own time.
- Crusade route (1189–92) ◆64–5 (2)
- jousts with Saladin ❑64
- succession (1189) ✣187●

Richard II (1367–1400) King of England (r.1377–99). Son of Edward the Black Prince. Deposed in 1399 by his cousin, Henry of Lancaster, later crowned Henry IV. He died in prison, possibly murdered. ✣192●

Richelieu, Cardinal Chief minister of Louis XIII with whom he collaborated to make France a leading European power. ❑196

Riel Rebellions (1869) (1885). Rebellions by the Metis (mixed blood descendants of Cree Indians and French fur traders) and their Indian allies against incursions of European settlers into their lands. ◆129 (2)

Rig Veda Completed c.900 BCE, this is the great literary monument of Aryan settlers of the Punjab. A collection of sacred hymns, it traces the religious development of Aryan India and depicts the Aryan settlers as chariot-driving warriors who gradually adapt to a more sedentary life. It is rich in geographical references. ✣36, ✣242, 242●, ◆242 (1)

Rio de Janeiro
- Brazilian capital (1763) ✣149●
- Carnival dancers ❑112
- France Antarctique colony (1555) ✣149●

Río de la Plata Viceroyalty established (1776) ✣148●

Ripon Falls Source of Nile ✣157

roads
- maps ❑99
- Ogilvie's maps ✣173
- Peutinger Table ❑172
- Roman (by c.120 CE) ◆172 (1)

Robert I 'the Bruce' (1274–1329) King of Scotland (r.1306–29). Crowned in 1306 in defiance of King Edward I of England. Decisively defeated the English at the battle of Bannockburn (1314). English acknowledgement of Scottish independence and Robert's right to the throne came in 1328.
- victor at Bannockburn ✣188●, ❑188, ◆188 (2)

Robert of Normandy (c.1054–1134) Duke of Normandy (r.1087–1106). Eldest son of King William I of England. Inherited Normandy upon the death of his father, whilst his brother William inherited the throne of England. Took part in the First Crusade (1096–1100).
- Crusade route (1096–99) ◆64–5 (2)

Robespierre, Maximilien François Marie-Isidore de (1758–94). French revolutionary and Jacobin leader, who played a key role in the overthrow of the moderate Girondins. A member of the Committee for Public Safety which instituted the Reign of Terror (1793–4). Overthrown by the Convention, he was tried and guillotined. ✣199●
See also French Revolution, Jacobins, Terror, Reign of

rock art The oldest known art form, dating back to c.30,000 BCE in Western Europe, usually depicting hunting scenes, and found in caves or, commonly in African examples, rock shelters and exposed rock faces. The images are either painted or etched into the rock surface, and are not purely decorative: some occur in recesses so difficult to access that they are thought to have played a part in ritual activities. Rock art is more abundant in the Saharan region than anywhere else in the world. ✣17●, ◆17 (3) (5)

Roerich, Nicolas (1874–1947) Russian traveller and painter in Central Asia. ◆257 (3)

Roger II of Sicily (1095–1154) (r.1101–54) First Norman king of Sicily whose court at Palermo was one of the most magnificent in Europe, a meeting place for Christian and Arab scholars. Commissioned the *Book of Roger*, a medieval book of maps. ✣62, ✣218

Roggeveen, Jacob (1659–1729). Dutch explorer. His voyage across the Pacific in 1722 established the first European contact with a number of islands, including Rapa Nui (Easter Island) and Samoa. ✣278●

Roman Catholicism *see* Catholicism

Roman Empire The largest empire ever established in Europe, stretching from northern Britain to Egypt. From its apogee in the 2nd century CE, the empire became increasingly difficult to govern and in 395, it was divided into two. The Western Empire fell in 476, but the Eastern Roman (or Byzantine) Empire, with its capital at Constantinople, survived until 1453. ◆42–3, ◆46–7, ◆50–1, ◆52–3, ◆54–5
- 51 BCE to 138 CE ✣180●
- c.117 CE at the death of Trajan ◆161 (2)
- c.120 CE under Hadrian ◆180 (1)
- 240–395 CE ✣181, ◆181 (4)
- 250–400 CE ✣180●
- 476 CE end of the Empire ✣182
- Attila the Hun defeated (451) ✣50●
- and Carthage: the Punic Wars ✣42, ✣179, ◆179 (3)
- conflict with Sassanian ✣50
- conquests (to 120 BCE) ✣179, ◆179 (5)
- depictions
  - exotic animal combat ❑44
  - maritime trade ❑44
  - mummy case ❑47
  - The Nile in Flood mosaic ✣47, ❑47
- Europe after the fall ✣182, ◆182 (1)
- expansion programme ✣42, ✣179●, ✣224–5, ◆224 (2)
- exploration and mapping ✣42, ✣47, ◆218 (1)
  - Africa (c.150) ◆156 (3)
  - boundaries of ancient Europe ◆172 (1)
- Hadrian's defensive strategy ✣180
- Italian confederacy (264 BCE) ✣38●
- mythological pantheon ✣37
- overseas provinces (120 BCE) ✣179
- Palatine Hill village (BCE) ✣31●
- subjugation of Greece ✣179, ◆179 (4)
- territory (240 BCE) ◆178 (1)
- Tetrarchy of Diocletian ✣50, ✣181, ❑181, ◆181 (4)
- trade, classical world ◆44–5
- Western Empire collapses (476) ✣50●
- *See also* Rome

Romania
- end of Communism (1989) ✣110●
- granted independence ✣232
- *See also* Balkans, nationalism; Wars, First World; Second World

Rome Rome began as a small city-state which, through military might combined with skilful use of threats and alliances, conquered first the Italian Peninsula, then, by the 1st century BCE, the entire Mediterranean world. The city of Rome's importance declined from the 4th century CE. From the 7th century, it regained prestige as the seat of the pope and headquarters of the Roman Catholic Church. It was ruled by the Papacy until it became the capital of the newly-united kingdom of Italy in 1871.
- earthenware amphora ❑181
- Imperial Rome (c.300 CE) ✣181, ◆181 (2)
- legionary ❑178
- politics
  - capital of united Italy (1871) ✣94●
  - and the Italian Confederacy ✣178
  - and Latin allies (c.495 BCE) ◆178
  - ruins of Colosseum ❑181
  - sacked by Vandals (455) ✣52●
  - sacked by Visigoths (410) ✣53●, ✣182●
  - saved from Huns ✣53
  - saved from Lombards ✣183●
  - supply routes ✣181, ◆181 (3)
  - *See also* Roman Empire.

Rome, Treaty of *see* European Union

Romulus Augustus Last Roman emperor in the West, deposed (476) ✣50●

Roosevelt, Franklin Delano (*aka* FDR) (1882–1945) 32nd President of the US (Democrat, 1932–45). Roosevelt became president in 1932, on the cusp of the worst years of the Great Depression. He immediately launched a series of reforms collectively known as the 'New Deal' to combat the depression; these included the abandonment of the gold standard and agricultural price support, as well as programmes such as the Works Progress Administration, aimed at providing work for the unemployed and the creation of a Social Security Act. His 'common touch' and immense personal popularity saw him elected for an unprecedented four terms. Though initially opposed to involvement in conflict in Europe, by the outbreak of WW II, he broke with neutrality to support the Allied position, bringing the US fully into the war following the bombing of Pearl Harbor in Dec 1941.
- American President (1932–45) ✣134, ✣139
- New Deal ✣102, ✣134, ✣134●, ✣135
  - FDR effect ✣135
  - NRA recovery programme ❑134
  - WPA (Works Progress Administration) ❑134
  - portrait ❑135
- Second World War
  - Casablanca conference (1943) ✣104●
  - Tehran conference ✣105●
  - Yalta 'Big Three' conference (1945) ❑105

Roosevelt, Theodore (Teddy) (1858–1919) 26th President of the US. Republican. (1901–09). After commanding the 'Roughriders' in the Spanish-American War (1898), Roosevelt returned as Governor of New York from 1898–1900, and was subsequently elected Vice-President. He became president following the assassination of William McKinley. He initiated the building of the Panama Canal, strengthened the US navy, and won the Nobel Peace Prize in 1906 for his part in ending the Russo-Japanese war. He formed a 'progressive' movement in the Republican party but was defeated on the Progressive ticket in the elections of 1910.
- US President 1901–09 ✣132
- era of economic boom ❑132

Rosas, Juan Manuel de (1793–1877) Argentinian dictator. Although his official title was only Governor of Buenos Aires province, Rosas was the effective ruler of Argentina from 1829–52. He owed his position to his loyal force of gauchos, and his wars of conquest against the Patagonian Indians. ❑151

Rosebloom, Johannes 17th-century explorer in N America. Employed by Governor Thomas Dongan to discover new routes for the fur trade. Reached Michilimackinac between Lakes Huron and Michigan in 1685 after travelling for three months. ◆119 (2)

Rosenberg, Ethel and Julius (1915–53), (1918–53). American Communists and part of a transatlantic spy ring. Convicted of passing on atomic secrets to the Soviet Union and executed. They were the first US citizens to be executed for espionage. ❑108

Rosetta stone Basalt slab inscribed by priests of Ptolemy V of Egypt in hieroglyphic, demotic and Greek. Found near the city of Rosetta in Egypt in 1799 and taken by the British in 1801; now in the British Museum in London. Served as the key to understanding Egyptian hieroglyphic. ❑42

Ross, Sir James Clark (1800–62) British naval officer and explorer of the Poles. Accompanied both Edward Parry and his uncle John Ross on expeditions in the Arctic. In 1839–43 he led the navy's first major Antarctic expedition. He discovered the Ross Sea, the Ross Ice Shelf, Ross Island and Victoria Land.
- Antarctic exploration (1839–43) ◆287 (3)
- Arctic explorer (1829–33) ❑287, ◆286–7 (2)

Rotz, John Early map of S America (1542) ❑142

Rousseau, Jean Jacques (1712–78) French philosopher and writer. Believed in the original goodness of human nature and that it was society that created inequality and misery. His most famous work, *Du Contrat Social* (1762), profoundly influenced French revolutionary thought. ✣198

Royal Road Road constructed under the Persian Achaemenid Empire in the 6th century BCE from Susa, the ancient capital of Persia, to Sardis, on the Aegean Sea.
- construction ✣35, ✣223●, ◆223 (4)

Rozwi Empire Empire of southern Africa (c.1684–early 19th-century)
- challenges Portuguese (17th century) ✣164
- replaces Mwenemutapa ✣164

Ruanruan (*var.* Juan-juan, Avars). Nomadic steppe peoples whose expulsion from Mongolia by the Blue (Celestial) Turks in the 4th century CE impelled them westwards, entering Europe in the mid-6th century. *See also* Avars. ✣261●, ◆261 (4)

Rub' al Khali (*var.* the 'Empty Quarter'). Area of waterless desert covering some 650,000 sq km (250,000 sq miles) of the southern Arabian Peninsula.
- 19th- and 20th-century explorers ✣219●

Rudolf I (1218–91) Count of Habsburg and Holy Roman Emperor. The first Habsburg to be elected Emperor, Rudolf secured Austria as the centre of the Habsburg domains through his defeat of Ottokar II of Bohemia in 1278. ✣189●

Rukh (1377–1447). Mongol shah, son of Timur ✣75

Rum Seljuk Sultanate in Anatolia in the 12th and 13th centuries, with its capital at Konya (Iconium). Its name is derived from Rome, because its lands had been captured from the Byzantine (East Roman) Empire. ◆65 (1) (2), ✣228

Rurik the Viking (r.c.862–79). Semi-legendary Swedish ruler of the merchant town of Novgorod, seen as the founder of the Russian state (named after 'Rus', the Finnish word for Swede). ✣60●

Russia State originating in rise of Muscovy in 16th century under Ivan IV, who defeated the Tatars and united neighbouring principalities, proclaiming himself Tsar. Consolidated power in eastern Europe and expanded beyond Urals in 17th century (notably under Peter the Great), to dominate northern and central Asia by 18th century. Tsarist rule toppled by Bolshevik (Communist) revolution in 1917. 194–215, 257–273
- *See also* USSR
- foreign affairs
  - Alaskan expeditions (1816–65) ◆119 (3)
  - Balkan nationalism ✣203, ◆203 (4)
  - Baltic states, conflict ✣195, ✣195●, ✣197, ◆195 (3), ◆197 (3)
  - Bering Strait-Alaska exploration (16th–17th century) ✣257
  - claim on N America (1821) ◆128 (2)
  - conquers and annexes Crimea (1783) ✣86●
  - Crimean War (1854) ✣94, ✣203
  - Empire *see below*
  - First World War *see* Wars, First World
  - France, opposition alliances (1792–1815) ✣90●, ✣201, ◆201 (3)
  - neutrality pact with Japan (1939) ✣103●
  - Second World War see Wars, Second World
  - Treaty of Nerchinsk with China (1689) ✣83●, ✣257●
  - Turkey and the Black Sea ✣203, ✣232, ◆203 (4)
  - withdraws from Amur basin (1689) ✣83●

Golden Horde vassals (1200–1400) ◆189 (4)
home affairs
Bolshevik Revolution (1917) ✣98●
Mongol conquest begins (1237) ✣66●
Mongol raids (1222) ✣68
population growth (1650–1800) ❑198
revolutions (1905, 1917) ✣98●, ✣99●, ✣208, ◆208 (2)
serfdom abolished (1861) ✣94●, ✣269
trade and industry, Japanese commercial talks (1804) ✣91●
Russian Empire ✣195, ✣208
1800 ◆86–7
1850 ◆90–1
1900 ◆94–5
expansion ✣78, ✣82, ✣257, ✣269, ✣269●, ◆269 (3)
European, consolidation and resistance (17th century) ✣196, ✣196●, ◆196 (2)

Russian Revolution (1917). Revolution which saw the overthrow of the provisional government which had replaced the regime of Tsar Nicholas II by the Communist Bolsheviks, who took over the Winter Palace and swiftly established strongholds in towns throughout European Russia. In 1918, a new constitution was declared, which established the Union of Soviet Socialist Republics (USSR or Soviet Union). ✣208●, ◆208 (2)

Russo-Japanese War (1904–05) War caused by territorial disputes between Japan and Russia. Culminated in Japanese victory over the Russian Baltic Fleet in the Tsushima Strait. ✣99, ✣270, ◆270 (4)

Ruth, Babe (*aka* George Herman Ruth) (1895–1948) US baseball player. Played for Boston Red Sox, New York Yankees and Boston Braves. Famous for his 714 home runs and 10 World Series, he is still considered to be baseball's greatest all-rounder. ❑135

Rwanda
crisis ✣169, ❑169, ◆169 (5)
inter-ethnic warfare ✣111, ✣111●
Hutu massacre (1994) ✣111●

S

Sadat, Anwar (1918–81) President of Egypt (r.1970–81). Launched the unsuccessful invasion of Israel (1973). In 1979 he signed the Camp David Accord with Israel, but in revenge for his 'betrayal' was assassinated in 1981. ✣169●, ◆235 (4)

Saddam Hussein *see* Hussein, Saddam

Sadleir, George 19th-century British army officer and explorer of the Arabian Peninsula. On a diplomatic mission to the Egyptian forces operating against the Wahhabi tribesmen in Arabia, he was the first European to cross the Arabian peninsula from east to west. ✣219●

Safavid dynasty Persian dynasty which arose around 1500 under Shah Ismail I, who united the country and converted it from Sunni to Shi'ite Islam. The Safavids brought a halt to the Ottomans' eastward expansion.
clashes with Ottomans ✣79
Persian dynasty ✣231, ◆231 (4)
rise to power (1499) ✣75, ✣231

Sahara
BCE hunter-gatherers ✣19
desertification ✣19
introduction of camels (c.100 BCE) ✣43
rock art ✣19●, ✣20●, ❑21, ❑158
wavy-line pottery ✣19●, ✣20●

Sahel
(BCE) ✣34
onset of desiccation (c.1110) ✣63●

Saite dynasty The 26th dynasty of ancient Egypt which ruled from Sais (662–525 BCE). Pharaoh Samtik I asserted independence from the retreating Nubian Cushites and by gaining the trust of other princes was able to keep Egypt under a firm rule which allowed it to recover its material and cultural prosperity. ✣34, ✣35●

Saladin (1138–93). Kurdish Muslim general in the army of Nur al-Din who defeated the European Crusaders at Aleppo, Hattin and Acre, and in 1187 drove them from Jerusalem. A widely respected leader, he became ruler of Egypt, founded the Ayyubid dynasty, and restored Jerusalem's Muslim shrine the Dome of the Rock.
captured lands ◆65 (3)
Egyptian military leader ✣62
founder of Ayyubid dynasty (1174) ✣63●, ✣228, ✣228●, ❑228, ◆228 (2)
jousts with Richard I ❑64
recaptures Jerusalem (1187) ✣63●, ✣64●, ✣228●
reduces Crusader states (1188) ✣63●, ✣228

Salamis ⚔ of Graeco-Persian Wars (480 BCE). Greek victory. ✣39●, ✣223●, ◆223 (4)

SALT *see* Strategic Arms Limitation Treaty

Salvador *see* Bahia

Samanid dynasty (819–1005) Muslim dynasty of Persia. ✣227, ❑227, ◆44–5, ◆227 (6)

Samarkand
Silk Road ✣45
Timur's capital ✣71, ✣229

Samarra Islamic city 57, ✣57 (3)
capital founded by al-Mu'tasim (c.836) ✣59●
Jawsak wall painting ❑227
spiral minaret of Great Mosque ❑57

Samnites People of south central Italy. They were the most powerful of the tribes that opposed Rome's expansion in Italy in the 4th and 3rd centuries BCE. It took three wars (the last ending in 290 BCE) to defeat them. ✣178●, ◆178 (1)

Samoa
Lapita culture (BCE) ✣27
settled by Polynesians ✣60, ◆60 (2)

samurai Knightly warrior or retainer of Japanese feudal lord or emperor. ✣265, ◆265 (5)
samurai sword ❑265

San Agustín (*var.* St. Augustine).
founded (1565) ✣125
coastal fort, Castillo de San Marcos ❑125, ◆125 (4)

San Francisco, Treaty of (1952) Peace treaty between Japan and most of its WW II adversaries (excluding Soviet Union), by which Japan regained its independence. ✣148●

San Ildefonso, Treaty of (1777). Treaty between Spain and Portugal that defined boundaries between their respective colonies in S America, especially in the Uruguay region. ✣148●

San Juan Puerto Rico, founded (1509) ✣125●, ◆125 (4)

San Lorenzo
development ✣26, ◆121 (2) (3)
Olmec sculptures ❑30

San Martín, José de (1778–1850) Argentinian general and liberator of Chile and Peru from Spanish rule. Resigned as Protector of Peru in 1822 after differences with Simón Bolívar. Died in exile in France.
liberation campaign ✣90, ✣150, ◆150 (1)

Sanchi Great Stupa ❑39

Sandinistas Members of the Sandinist National Liberation Front (FSLN), founded in 1962 in Nicaragua as a left-wing, anti-US guerrilla group. The guerrilla campaign ended in full-scale civil war, resulting in the overthrow of the pro-US Somoza regime (1979).
civil war in Nicaragua ✣110●
Contra guerrillas in Honduras ❑139, ◆139 (5)

Sandoval, Gonzalo de 16th-century Spanish explorer of N America (1521) ✣125, ◆125 (4)

Santa Fe Founded (1609) ✣125

Santa Sofia (*var.* Hagia Sofia). Originally a Christian church at Constantinople (Istanbul) and later (1453) a mosque. Its present structure was built in 532–37 by the emperor Justinian. ✣49●

Santo Domingo Founded (1496) ✣125●, ◆125 (4)

São Jorge da Mina *see* Elmina

São Paulo
shanty town ❑106
slave raiders (Paulistas) ✣143

Saqqara
designed by Imhotep ✣25
Zoser step pyramid (2650 BCE) ✣23●

Saracens Greek and Roman term for the Arabs, hence used in medieval Europe for all Muslims.
occupy Crete and Sicily (827) ✣58●

Sarajevo Assassination of Franz Ferdinand ✣98

Saratoga ⚔ of American Revolutionary War (17 Oct 1777). American victory. ◆127 (3)

Sardis Royal Road constructed (BCE) ✣35

Sargon I of Akkad (*r.* c.2334–2279 BCE). Ruler of the Akkad area of central Mesopotamia, who founded the city of Agade in c.2340 BCE. In the south he conquered the Sumerians and expanded his lands to Syria and eastern Asia Minor. He ruled for 56 years, and despite revolts toward the end of his reign his conquests ensured Akkadian supremacy for the next hundred years. Although Akkad subsequently became simply the name of a region, Akkadian remained the major spoken language in Mesopotamia. ◆221 (4)
unites Mesopotamian city-states (2300 BCE) ✣27●

Sassanian Empire Persian ruling dynasty founded in 224 CE by Ardashir I (r.208–241). At its peak in the 6th century under Khosrau I, the Sassanian empire stretched from Roman Anatolia in the west to Taxila (now Pakistan) in the east. The empire fell to Muslim Arabs with their capture in 637 of the Sassanian capital Ctesiphon and their victory in 642 at the Battle of Nehavend. ✣44●, ✣51, ✣225, ✣225●, ◆225 (6)
defeated by Heraclius (628) ✣55●
dynasty founded ✣47
expansion ✣224, ✣224●, ◆182 (1), ◆224 (2)
occupy Armenia ✣51●
Shahanshah ❑51

Satavahanas dynasty of central India from the 1st to the 2nd century CE. Displaced by the Vakataka dynasty. ✣47

satellite
first manned space flight (1961) ✣108●
imagery ❑106, ❑110
Sputnik II launched (1957) ✣106●, ✣108●

satrapy BCE Persian province ✣35, ✣223, ◆223 (4)

Saud, Abd al-Aziz ibn (*var.* Ibn Saud) (1880–1953). The founder of the kingdom of Saudi Arabia. Born at Riyadh, his father was the youngest son of the Sultan of Nejd. Following civil wars (1875–91) between the sultan's successors, Ibn Saud recaptured Riyadh and was once again proclaimed ruler of Nejd in 1901. He laid the foundations of a non-tribal, nationalist Arab state, underpinned by an agricultural economy, and ruled by Sharia Islamic law. From 1918, Ibn Saud began to extend his kingdom and by 1926 had captured the Hejaz and the ultimate prize, Mecca. ❑233, ✣233

Saudi Arabia
founded (1932) ✣103●
emergence (1800–1932) ✣233, ◆233 (4)
gas reserves ✣234
oil production ❑234, ◆234 (1)

Savannah ⚔ of American Revolutionary War (29 Dec 1778). British victory. ◆127 (3)

Savorgnan de Brazza, Pierre *see* Brazza, Pierre Savorgnan de

Sawahili *see* Swahili

Saxons Germanic people who, upon the decline of the Roman Empire, began a series of campaigns of colonization around the North Sea, notably in England in the 5th century CE.
migrations and invasions ✣183, ◆52–3 (1)

Saxton's county map of England and Wales ❑173

Scandinavia
assimilated into Europe (11th century) ✣62
Protestant Reformation ✣78
Trundholm sun chariot ❑26

Schomburgk, Sir Robert Hermann (1804–65) Prussian-born British traveller and official. Sent by the Royal Geographical Society to explore British Guiana (1831–35) and employed to draw the controversial 'Schomburgk Line' as a provisional boundary with Venezuela and Brazil. ✣143●

Schouten, Willem (c.1567–1625) Dutch navigator and explorer. Completed circumnavigation of the world in 1616, rounding Cape Horn, which he named after his home town of Hoorn in Holland. ◆278 (1)

Schutzstaffel (SS). Elite troops of the Nazi Party, established 1925, and from 1929 developed by Heinrich Himmler into a security squad. Combat troops (Waffen SS) operated on the front line, while other formations were involved in implementing the Final Solution against the Jews. ✣211

Scipio Africanus (*var.* Publius Cornelius Scipio) (236–183 BCE) Roman general. His campaigns in the Iberian Peninsula against the Carthaginians (210–206 BCE) were the key to Rome's victory in the Second Punic War. In 204 he sailed to N Africa to confront the Carthaginians in their homeland. Carthage's greatest general, Hannibal, was recalled from Italy to counter the threat, but was defeated by Scipio at Zama in 202. On his triumphal return to Rome, Scipio received the honorary surname Africanus. ✣179●, ◆179 (3)

Scopes 'Monkey Trial' (Jul 10–21, 1925). Trial of John T. Scopes, a teacher in Dayton, Tennessee, for teaching pupils the theory of evolution. This was in violation of a state law which prohibited the teaching of any theory which denied the Biblical story of creation. ✣135●

Scotland
conflict with England (1296–1328) ✣188●, ◆188 (2)
devolution ❑112
Protestant Reformation ✣78
raided by Vikings (c.795 CE) ✣60●
settled by Norwegians (c.900 CE) ✣60●

Scott, Robert Falcon (1868–1912) British naval officer and polar explorer. In 1900, led expedition to the Antarctic on behalf of the Royal Geographical Society with Edmund Wilson and Ernest Shackleton. In 1910 he led a second expedition, reaching the South Pole on 17 Jan 1912, one month after the Norwegian, Roald Amundsen. The whole party later perished before reaching their base camp. ❑287, ◆287 (3)

scribes
Egyptian ❑25, ❑32
See also hieroglyphics; writing

script *see* writing

sculpture
Babylonian king carrying building materials ❑28
Bahia clay figure ❑145
Benin horse ❑78
bust of Lady of Elche ❑177
Hellenistic statue of a lion ❑41
late Roman sarcophagus ❑50
Lion Gate, Hattushash ❑28
marble figurine (c.2600 BCE) ❑174
Nok (BCE) ❑38, ❑160
Olmec sites ◆121 (3)
portable objects ❑15, ❑17
soapstone pipe ❑123

Scylax of Caryander 6th-century BCE Greek navigator who reached the Indus Valley, sailed down the river, then back along the Persian and Arabian coast to the Red Sea. ✣218●

Scythians An Indo-European, nomadic people of the Russian steppes, who migrated in the 8th century BCE to the area north of the Black Sea. They traded corn with the Greeks for luxury goods, and were driven out by the Medes. (700 BCE) ✣34●, ✣35●
leather loop stirrup ✣51
overrun Indo-Greek kingdoms (c.30 BCE) ✣43●
trade route (c.1 CE) ◆44–5

SDI *see* Strategic Defense Initiative

seal
cylinder ❑24, ❑223
of Lübeck ❑190

Second Republic (1848–52). Republican government of France from the deposition of Louis Philippe (1848) until the Second Empire (1852). ✣90●

Second World War (*var.* World War II). Major conflict (1939–45) arising from territorial expansion and aggressive racist policies of Germany, Italy and Japan (the Axis), who were countered by an Allied coalition led by Britain and the Commonwealth, forces from Axis-occupied nations, USSR and US (from 1941). Mass mobilization of the population and industry by all belligerents, the gradual involvement of most countries in the world, the prosecution of the war on land, sea and air, the widespread involvement of partisans, technological innovation, and the impact of the war on civilian populations led to its characterization as a 'Total War'. The insistence by the Allies on unconditional surrender, and their deployment of nuclear weapons over Japan proved decisive. The final stages saw the destruction and partition of Europe, the occupation of Japan and the emergence of USSR and US as ideologically opposed superpowers during the Cold War. ✣104–5●, ◆104–5, ◆210–11●, ◆210–11, ✣272–3●, ◆272–3 (1) (2)

segregation Civil Rights and protest movements ✣137, ◆137 (6)

Segu Conquered by al-Hajj Umar Tal (1861) ✣167●

Sekigahara ⚔ (1600) whereby Japanese Tokugawa Shogunate decisively established hegemony over rival warlord clans. ✣43●, ◆267 (5)

Seleucia-on-the-Tigris
captured by Parthians (141 BCE) ✣43●
sacked by Romans (c.114) ✣47

Seleucid Empire The dynasty of Macedonian kings, founded by one of Alexander's generals Seleucus, which after Alexander's death in 323 BCE ruled Persia, Syria, and Asia Minor until 64 BCE. Under Antiochus III (242–187 BCE), the Seleucid Empire extended from Bactria in the east to Egypt and Greece in the west. ✣41, ✣224, ◆224 (1) ◆38–9

Seleucus I (c.358–281 BCE). One of Alexander's generals, who after Alexander's death in 323 BCE, ruled Babylonia, founding a dynasty and an empire. ✣224, ◆224 (1)

Selim I (1470–1520) Ottoman Sultan (r.1512–1520). Massacred the followers of the Safavid Shah Ismail, and occupied Tabriz. In 1516–17 he overcame the Mamluks in Egypt and Syria, and by his death had established Ottoman rule in Jerusalem, Mecca and Medina. ✣231

Selim II (1524–74) Ottoman emperor of Turkey (r.1566–74). Defeated at the battle of Lepanto (1571) by Don John of Austria. ✣79●

Selimiye Mosque ❑231

Selinus Ruins of Greek colony ❑176

Seljuk Turks Nomadic Turkish people from Central Asia north of the River Oxus who in the 11th century began to spread southwards. They took Baghdad in 1055, conquered Armenia, expelled the Byzantines from Asia Minor, and seized Syria and Palestine from the Fatimids. By the 12th century they had reunited all of the old Abbasid territories, but in 1243 were routed by the Mongols at Köse Dagh. The Seljuks established a heritage of magnificent architecture.
growth of Empire ✣228, ✣228●, ◆228 (1)
and Byzantine Empire (from c.1025) ✣228, ◆228 (1)
campaigns (c.800–1200) ✣57, ◆57 (2)
capture Baghdad (1055) ✣63●
capture Manzikert (1071) ✣63●
establish regional states ✣67
Isfahan's Friday Mosque ❑228
Osman founds Ottoman state (1299) ✣67●
threat to Christianity ✣65

Seminole American Indian groups of the Creek Confederacy, originally based in Florida and the far South of the US. Fought a fierce series of wars against forced relocation from 1816–58. ✣129, ◆128–129 (2)

Semites Speakers of the Semitic group of languages, of which Arabic, Hebrew and Amharic are the main languages still current. ✣30

Sendero Luminoso, Partido Comunista de Peru *see* Shining Path

Senegal
conquered by al-Hajj Umar Tal (1852) ✣167●
Muslim empire (1863) ✣95●
Senegalese Rifles ❑167

Senegal River
Abd al-Kadir leads holy war (1776) ✣164●
reached by Portuguese (1445–46) ✣156●

Septimius Severus (*var.* Lucius Septimius Severus) (146–211 CE) Emperor of Rome (r.193–211 CE). A professional soldier who was proclaimed emperor by his troops, upon which he founded the Severan dynasty and adopted a militaristic style of government. He disbanded the elite Praetorian Guard, whose support was essential to achieving high office, and replaced them with his own men. He died at Eburacum (York, in England). ✣47●

Sera Metropolis *see* Chang'an

Serapis-Hercules *see* Heracles.
statuette (1st–4th century) ✣45

Serbia
granted independence ✣232
persecution of ethnic Albanians ✣215, ❑112
See also Balkans, nationalism; World Wars, First World; Second

serfs Peasant class with no personal property or freedom of movement, obligated to the lord on whose land they worked and to whom they contributed part of their own produce.
serfdom abolished in Russia (1861) ✣94●

Serpa Pinto, Alexandre (1846–1900). Portuguese explorer and colonial administrator who crossed southern and central Africa and mapped the interior of the continent. In 1887 he was named consul-general to Zanzibar and, in 1889, governor-general of Mozambique. ◆157 (4)

Serrão, Francisco (d.c.1516) Portuguese explorer. He accompanied de Abreu on his exploration of the East Indies, was captured by pirates and taken to Ternate – the first Portuguese to reach the Spice Islands. ✣239●, ◆239 (1)

Sevan Solar system bronze (BCE) ❑31

Seven Days ⚔ of American Civil War (25 Jun–1 Jul 1862). Confederate victory. ◆131 (6)

Seven Years' War (1756–63). Wide-ranging conflict between Prussia and Britain, and a coalition of Russia, Austria and France. It was both a struggle for maritime and colonial supremacy between Britain and France, and an attempt by Austria to regain Silesia which it had lost to Prussia in 1748. Prussia retained Silesia while, overseas, Britain destroyed French power in N America, the Caribbean and India. ✣88●, ◆88 (1), ❑88, ✣127●, ◆127 (2), ❑127, ✣199●

Seville Reconquered by Christians ✣66

Sèvres, Treaty of (1920). Part of the Versailles Peace Settlement, signed between the Allies and Turkey, which forced Turkey to give up all her non-Turkish lands. Syria became a French mandate, and Britain accepted the mandate for Iraq, Palestine and Transjordan. The treaty was rejected by Atatürk, who obtained a redefinition of Turkey's borders in the Treaty of Lausanne (1923). ✣223●
See also Atatürk, and Lausanne, Treaty of

Seward's Folly *see* Alaska Purchase

Shackleton, Sir Ernest Henry (1874–1922) British merchant naval officer and Antarctic explorer. After accompanying the Scott expedition of 1901–04, Shackleton explored the Antarctic on the ship *Nimrod* from 1907–09, reaching to within 150 km of the Pole. In 1914–17 he took the ship *Endurance* to the Weddell Sea, but the ship was crushed by ice. ❑287, ◆287 (3)

Shah Jahan (1592–1666) Mughal emperor (r.1627–58). The grandson of Akbar, Shah Jahan presided over the most magnificent period of the Mughal empire. He founded the city of Delhi, and created the Taj Mahal at Agra, the mausoleum of his favourite wife, Mumtaz. He had four sons; his third son, Aurangzeb, overthrew his brothers, proclaiming himself emperor while his father was still alive. ✣83, ✣246, ❑246, ◆246 (1)

Shahanshah *see* Sassanian Empire

Shaka Zulu (*var.* Chaka, Tshaka) (c.1787–1828). Zulu chief (r.1816–28) who founded southern Africa's Zulu Empire and created a fighting force that dominated the entire region.
Zulu leader (1816) ✣90, ✣116●, ❑91
organizes expansion ✣166
Zulu kingdom (1817) ◆166 (2)

Shang dynasty (19th–11th centuries BCE). The first Chinese dynasty identified from both archaeological and documentary evidence. Shang kings consulted diviners and the culture is named after Anyang where oracle bones were found, incised with the earliest known Chinese characters. The Shang were hunters and warriors of the north China plain, and their rule gradually extended over the Yellow River valley where they developed complex agriculture and the beginnings of bronze casting. The latter part of this dynasty is also known as the Yin dynasty, which was succeeded by the Zhou dynasty.
◆259 (3)
(1250 BCE) ◆26–7
ancestor worship ✣31
cities (BCE) ✣28, ❑29
earliest Chinese script ❑258
oracle bones ✣32●, ❑32
Zhengzhou city ✣28, ◆29 (4)

Shangdu (*var.* Xanadu). Kublai Khan's summer palace ✣68

Shapur I (c.242–272). Son of Ardashir, founder of the Sassanian Empire, Shapur inflicted a series of major defeats on the Romans, including the victory at Edessa in 260, and completed the conquest of Kushan. ✣51●

Shapur II (*aka* Shapur the Great) (309–79) Declared king of Persia at birth. Campaigned against the Romans, forcing them to cede five provinces (363), and established Persian control over Armenia. ✣51●

Sharia The Holy Law of Islam, which was compiled and codified by the great Muslim jurists of the 8th and 9th centuries. It describes in minute detail the Islamic way of life, and prescribes the way for a Muslim to fulfil the commands of God and reach heaven.
See also Islam

Shaybanids *see* Uzbeks.
descendants of Genghis Khan ✣75

shell midden Large heap consisting mainly of the discarded shells of edible shellfish, representing many years of accumulation. Shell middens can reveal the role played by marine resources in the prehistoric diet and often contain evidence of feasting and burials. ◆16 (1), ◆144 (1) (2)

Shepenmut Priestess of Thebes ❑31

Sherley, Sir Robert (c.1581–1628). With his brother, Anthony, travelled through Syria and Persia in 1598, and reached Isfahan, the Persian capital. Both brothers were sent by the Persian ruler, Shah Abbas 'the Great', as ambassadors to Europe. ◆219 (3)

Sherman, William Tecumseh (1820–91) Union soldier in the American Civil War, promoted to general after the first Battle of Bull Run. He destroyed the Confederate forces on his famous march

Key to index: ✣ text ● timeline ❑ picture ◆ map *var.* variant name *aka* also known as *f/n* full name *prev.* previously known as r. ruled ⚔ battle WW I First World War WW II Second World War

through Georgia (1864). Appointed head of the army in 1869 by President Grant. ✤131
Shetlands Settled by Vikings ✤172
Shiah i-Ali *see* Shi'ites
Shi Huangdi (*var.* Shi Huang-ti, King Zheng, First Emperor) *See also* Qin dynasty.
first Qin Emperor ✤43, ✤45, ✤259●
buried terracotta items ❑43, ❑259
Shi Huang-ti *see* Shi Huangdi
Shi'ites (*var. Ar.* Shiah i-Ali, 'the partisans of Ali'). Shi'ites comprise the largest minority group of Muslims. Although they developed different devotions and religious practices from the Sunni Muslims, there is no difference in the essentials of the faith in the two traditions. *See also* Sunnis.
early history ✤56
Fatimids ✤57, ✤58●
pan-Islamic world ✤113, ◆113 (3)
resurgence of faith ◆235 (4)
Shiloh ⚔ of American Civil War, Tennessee (6–7 Apr 1862). Union victory. ✤131●, ◆131 (6)
Shining Path (*var. Sp.* Sendero Luminoso, Partido Comunista de Peru). Revolutionary movement founded in 1970 which employed guerrilla tactics and violent terrorism in the name of Maoism. ✤152●, ◆152 (1)
Shinto Ancient religion of Japan characterized by ancestor worship, devotion to the gods of natural forces, and belief in the divinity of the Emperor. ◆49 (4)
formalized as a state religion ✤265
shrine at Hakata ❑264
ships *see* navigation, transport
Shiva Hindu god combining apparently contradictory qualities of destruction and restoration, revenge and benevolence, asceticism and sensuality.
Chola dynasty bronze ❑59
Temple of ✤36
Shogun Japanese military governor or warlord prior to the Meiji Restoration (1868).
age of the ✤265, ◆265 (5)
Shortughai Trade with Harappa (c.2500 BCE) ✤24●
Shotoku, Prince Japanese imperial structure ✤265
Shu, Wu and Wei Kingdoms When the Han dynasty ended, several of its generals fought for supremacy in China. The period 220–280 CE saw the country divided into three kingdoms, a period known as 'San-kuo': in the west the Shu kingdom controlled what is now Sichuan, the Wei controlled the north, while the Wu kingdom comprised present-day Nanjing, south of the Yangtze River. ✤47, ✤261●, ◆261 (2)
Shunga dynasty ✤43
Siam *see* Thailand
Siberia
BCE jade imports ✤19●
conquest (1580–1932) ✤257●
Cossack forts ✤82
occupied by Japan (1918–20) ✤99●
Russian expansion ✤269
sleigh travel for traders and colonists ❑257
Sibiryakov Voyages of the Russian icebreaker ◆257 (2), ◆286 (2)
Sicilian Vespers (1282). Popular uprising in Sicily against rule of Charles of Anjou. The Sicilian crown was then given to Peter III of Aragon. ✤66
Sicily 174–203
Allied forces landings (1943) ✤105●
controlled by Aragon ✤66●
farming established ✤18●
French driven off (1282) ✤66●
given to Charles of Anjou ✤188
Norman conquest (1091) ✤62●
occupied by Saracens (827) ✤58●
in Spanish Empire ✤81
sugar mill (c.600 CE) ❑73
Siddhartha Gautama *see* Buddha
Siege of Petersburg ⚔ of American Civil War (20 Jun 1864–2 Apr 1865). Union victory. ◆131 (7)
Siegfried Line *see* Hindenburg Line
Sierra Leone Established for freed slaves (1787) ✤165●
Sigirya Palace fortress built by Kassapa (447–495) in Sri Lanka. This impregnable rock citadel was surmounted by the royal palace, while other residences and courts were arranged on descending levels. The palace was reached by a walkway which clung precariously to the side of the rock. ✤51
Sikhism Indian religious order founded by Guru Nanak (1469–1539), who preached a devotion to God that was neither Hindu nor Muslim. Sikhs emerged as a militant movement in the Punjab in the 18th and 19th centuries, especially under the leadership of Ranjit Singh. They confronted and were defeated by the British in the Anglo-Sikh Wars. ✤242, ✤248●, ❑252
Sikh Wars In 1845, a Sikh army numbering 60,000 men invaded British territory. Four pitched battles were fought at Mudki, Frerozeshah, Aliwal and Sobraon, and the Sikhs were driven back across the Sutlej River and surrendered to the British, who annexed the tract between the Sutlej and Ravi rivers. In 1848, a general Sikh uprising broke out. After disastrous losses at Chillianwalla, the British destroyed the Sikh army at Gujarat, and annexed the Punjab. ✤248●
Silesia Acquired by Prussia ✤199
Silicon Valley High-tech industry (1980) ✤136, ❑136, ◆136 (3)
silk
weaving, neolithic China ✤23, ✤258
Eurasian and African trade (c.1 CE) ◆44–5
Han exports ✤44
painting, Chinese (650 BCE) ✤35●
Qing archery contest ❑89
Silk Road System of trade routes across Central Asia linking Southwest Asia and the Mediterranean with China. It developed during the Han period (from c.200 BCE). Split into seasonal routes running north and south of the Takla Makan Desert (summer and winter respectively) the system operated at the mercy of Central Asian tribes. A major conduit not only for east–west trade, it also provided passage for ideas such as Buddhism and Islam, and was revived during the 'Mongol Peace' c.1250–1350. ✤43, ✤55, ◆44–5, ◆256 (1)
merchants on the caravan route ❑68
Persian painting ❑256
Tang period art ❑262
Silla Ancient state of Korea established in the 3rd century CE. *See also* Korea. ✤55●
control of Korea (c.220) ✤47●
expansion ◆264 (1)
silver
Eurasian and African trade (c.1 CE) ◆44–5
major finds (late 19th century) ✤93 (2)
Potosí mine ✤78●, ✤81●, ❑148
revenue for Spain ✤148
South American trade ✤81
trade in Europe (c.1300) ◆190–1 (1)
Sima Yan Unites China (280) ✤51●
Simpson, Lt. James Survey of western US (1849–51) ◆119 (3)
Sinae *see* China
Sinai Taken by Israel in Six Day War (1967) ✤234●
Singapore ⚔ of WW II (Feb 1942). Defeat of British garrison by Japanese. ◆272 (1)
Singapore
founded by Raffles (1819) ✤91
industrial growth ✤111
modern financial centre ❑253
seized by Japan (1942) ✤103●, ✤104●
Sino- Of or pertaining to China, as in Sino-Japanese war or Sino-Soviet relations.
Sino-Indian War Conflict (1962) between India and China over border territory of Arunachal Pradesh; Chinese victory resulted in withdrawal of both factions troops, and Chinese occupation of various other border territories including Aksai Chin. ◆252 (1)
Sino-Japanese War (1894–95) War between China and Japan arising from disputes in Korea. The Treaty of Shimonoseki in 1895 granted Taiwan to Japan. ✤270●, ◆270 (3)
Sioux (*var.* Dakota). American Indian groups of the upper Mississippi and Missouri basins. Nomadic warrior people with a livelihood based on hunting buffalo, the Sioux offered major resistance to European attempts to remove them from their lands, especially at ⚔ Little Bighorn, where, led by Sitting Bull and Crazy Horse, they destroyed General Custer's forces. The Sioux were among the last of the American Indian peoples to be forced onto reservations, their resistance ending following ⚔ Wounded Knee in 1890 when more than 200 Sioux were killed by the US army. ✤94●, ✤125●, ◆125 (4), ◆126 (1), ◆128 (2), ✤129●
Sirens *see* Odysseus
Sistine Chapel Commissioned by Sixtus IV ✤75
Sitgreaves, Capt. Lorenzo 19th-century survey of the western US. ◆119 (3)
Sitting Bull (*var.* Tatanka Iyotake) (c.1834–90). Chief of the Teton Dakota Sioux, he was a determined opponent of the displacement of Indian peoples from their ancestral lands. He led the massacre of Custer and his troops at ⚔ Little Bighorn (1881), but was subsequently forced to live on the Sioux reservation at Standing Rock. ❑129
Sivaji (1627–80). The charismatic founder of the Maratha kingdom, Sivaji operated from his heavily fortified base in the Western Ghats. Leading a force of highly mobile, armoured horsemen, he relentlessly harried Mughal forces, carving out a kingdom which was ultimately to emasculate Mughal power. ✤246
Six Day War (5–10 June 1967). Arab-Israeli War caused by Egypt's closure of the Gulf of Aqaba to Israeli shipping. Israel defeated the combined forces of Egypt, Jordan and Syria, and occupied the Gaza Strip, the Sinai, Jerusalem, the West Bank of the Jordan and the Golan Heights. ✤234●, ❑234, ◆234 (2)
Sixteen Kingdoms, the Period of Chinese history (304–439 CE) when northern China was partitioned among Chinese, Xiongnu and Tibetan rulers. ✤261●, ◆261 (3)
Sixtus IV, Pope (*prev.* Francesco della Rovere) (1414–84). Pope from 1471 and a famous Franciscan preacher. He built the Sistine Chapel and was a patron of artists, but lowered the moral authority of the papacy. ❑75
Skara Brae Stone Age village ❑23
slavery
trading in human lives ✤84–5, ✤85●, ◆84–5 (1)
abolition movement
Emancipation Proclamation ✤130, ✤131●
Freetown settlement (1787) ✤87●
leads to indentured labour ✤101, ◆101 (3)
Africa
and Eurasian trade (c.1 CE) ◆44–5
growth of internal trade (19th century) ✤166, ✤166●
NE ◆161 (3)
W African trade ✤66, ✤84, ❑165
America
Brazilian trade ✤166●, ✤151, ❑151, ◆151 (3)
Dred Scott decision ✤130, ◆130 (4)
first shipment (1510) ✤78●
mining in Brazil 149
Paulista raids ✤143, ◆143 (2)
'slave' states ✤130, ◆130 (1)–(5)
voting rights refused (1789) ✤86
Asiento agreement (1713) 86●
auction sales ❑85
Australia, 'blackbirding' ✤279, ✤284, ✤285●
Europe
colonial settlement ✤126
influence (18th century) ✤86, ✤165●
Portuguese shipments ✤75●, ✤164●
iron headcollar ❑65
plantation economy ✤82, ❑84, ❑90, ❑149
trade routes
America (1861) ✤130, ◆130 (5)
Atlantic ✤78●, ✤82, ✤84, ✤126, ✤164
decline of Atlantic (c.1850) ✤166
English shipping (1592) ✤165●
Indian Ocean (15th–16th century) ◆230 (2)
Middle Passage transport ❑85
principal slave routes ◆165 (4)
world (1400–1860) ✤165, ✤165●, ◆84–5 (1), ◆165 (4)
Slavs Largest ethnic group of Europe, linguistically derived from the Indo-European family. Traditionally divided into West Slavs (*aka* Lusatians, including Poles, Czechs, Slovaks and Wends), the South Slavs (including Slovenes, Serbs, Croats, Montenegrins, Macedonians, Bosnians and Bulgars) and the largest subgroup, the East Slavs (comprising Russians, Belorussians (White Russians) and Ukrainians). ✤50, ❑75
expansion (600 CE) ◆182 (2)
Sluis ⚔ of Dutch Revolt (1604). Dutch victory over Spain. ◆195 (5)
smelting Process of extracting a metal from its ore by heating, using a fuel which will remove the ore's other components (e.g. the oxygen from oxides), and a flux to remove impurities. Copper was probably the first metal to be extracted in this way, and charcoal was universally used as fuel until the 18th century CE. ✤19, ◆204 (1)
Smith, John (c.1580–1631) British soldier, colonist and explorer in N America. First travelled to Virginia in 1605, hoping to find a river route to the Pacific. In 1608 he was elected leader of the Virginia colony. ◆119 (2)
Smoot–Hawley Tariff (17 Jun 1930). Protective tariff imposed on imports to the US following the 1929 Wall Street Crash which set an average level of duty of 50% against a previous average of 26%, causing serious disruption to US–European trade. ✤134●
Snell, Willebrod van Roijen (*var. Lat.* Snellius) (1580–1626) Dutch mathematician who discovered the law of refraction known as Snell's law. He was also instrumental in the development of triangulation in surveying. ✤173
Snellius *see* Snell, Willebrod van Roijen
Sobhuza Swazi kingdom (1820) ◆166 (2)
Sofala Arab trading centre (c.1000) ✤61●
Sogdiana Secedes from Seleucid rule ✤43
Sokoto Fulani kingdom Africa, established (1820) ✤167●, ◆167 (3)
Solomon (c.1015–977 BCE) King of Israel and second son of David and Bathsheba. The kingdom under Solomon attained its widest limit, and splendid temples and palaces were constructed. He was credited with transcendent wisdom and in Jewish and Muslim literature was believed to control the spirits of the invisible world. ✤31, ✤222●, ◆222 (1)
Somalia
inter-ethnic warfare ✤111
Ogaden region conflict (1960) ✤168●
Somme ⚔ of WW I (Jul–Nov 1916). Major battle on the Western Front, incurring massive casualties for both Britain and Germany; over one million men were killed or wounded over the course of four months. ✤206●, ◆206 (3)
Sonetti, Bartolommeo dalli Author of an *Isolario*, a book of maps of islands. ✤173●
Song dynasty (*var.* Sung dynasty) (960–1279). Dynasty of China, divided into Northern Song (960–1126), destroyed by the Jin, and Southern Song (1127–1279), overrun by the Mongol (Yuan) dynasty. ✤263, ✤263●, ◆58–9, ◆263 (3) (4) (5)
capital cities ✤63●, ✤263
establishes power in China (979) ✤59●
Five Dynasties, ✤263, ◆263 (3)
Kublai Khan campaign (1260–79) ✤67●, ✤69●
porcelain production techniques ❑263
scroll depicting Kaifeng (12th century) ❑63
Southern Song ✤263, ◆68–9 (1), ◆263 (5)
subject state of Liao ✤63●, ✤263
trade routes ✤163
Songgye *see* Yi dynasty
Songhay 15th–16th century empire of W Africa. 162–164
controls trans-Saharan trade route ✤78
destruction of Mali Empire (1546) ✤79●
expansion (1464) ✤75●
falls to Morocco (1591) ✤79●, ✤164●
to 1590 ◆78–9
Sorbonne Founded (1257) ✤191●
sorghum Cereal which resembles maize but has small dense heads of grain. It remains a staple food in much of Africa and parts of Asia. ◆20–21 (1), ◆73 (3)
Soter *see* Ptolemy I
Soto, Hernando de (c.1499–1542) Spanish *conquistador* and explorer. Fought in Panama and Nicaragua before joining the conquest of Peru. In 1535 he received a commission from Spain for the conquest of Florida. His expedition reached Tampa Bay in May 1539 but then became lost for three years. ✤125, ◆118 (1), ◆125 (4)
South Africa 168–169
See also Africa
Boer War (1899–1902) ✤95●
foreign affairs, Angolan civil war ✤109, ◆109 (5)
home affairs
Union founded (1910) ✤96●, ✤99●
leaves Commonwealth (1960) ✤107●
mineral finds (late 19th century) ◆93 (2)
multi-racial elections (1994) ✤111●, ✤168●
National Party commits to apartheid (1948–49) ✤103●
Second World War, mobilization and casualty figures ✤105
struggle for control (1854–1914) ✤76, ✤76●, ❑96, ◆96 (2)
struggle for majority rule ✤168
South America 140–153
colonization
colonial regimes ✤90, ✤148–9, ◆148–9 (1) (2) (3) (4)
rivalry between Spain and Portugal (18th century) ✤86, ◆148 (2)
Spanish ✤78, ✤148, ✤148●, ✤150, ◆148 (2)
cultures
early ✤144–5, ◆144–5 (1) (2) (3) (4)
indigenous ✤147, ◆147 (2)
See also Chavin; Huari; Incas; Moche; Nazca; Pueblo; Tiahuanaco
empires
✤146–7
See also Chimú; Huari; Tiahuanaco
exploration and mapping ✤142–3, ◆142 (1) (2) (3)
historical landscape ❑140, ◆140–1
home affairs
age of independence (1810–30) ◆150 (1)
Chaco War ✤152, ◆152 (2)
Confederacy formed (1861) ✤94
development of communities (BCE) ✤22
immigrant labour ✤151
liberation campaigns ✤150, ✤150●, ◆150 (1)
moves against segregation (1955–75) ✤137
political development ✤110, ✤151, ✤151●, ◆151 (3), ◆152 (1)
revolts against rural elites ✤98
religion, Jesuit missions ✤143, ◆143 (2)
trade and industry
economic development, ✤94, ❑151, ◆151 (3), ◆153 (3)
plantation economy ✤82, ✤139, ❑90, ❑151
BCE ✤22●
cotton growing ✤139, ◆139 (3)
narcotics trade ◆153 (5)
See also individual countries; slavery
South and Southeast Asia 236–253
exploration and mapping 238–9, ◆239 (1) (2)
colonial expansion ✤248–9, ◆248 (1) (2)
first civilizations ✤240–1, ✤241●, ◆240 (1) (2) (3), ◆241 (5) (6)
Mughals, Marathas, Europeans ✤246–7, ◆246 (1) (2) (3)
states and empires ✤244–5, ◆244–5 (1)–6
BCE ✤15, ✤19, ✤27, ✤39, ✤43
(c.1500) ◆76 (6)
conflict
imperialism ✤97, ◆97 (3)
Jammu and Kashmir ✤252, ◆252 (2)
secessionism and cooperation ✤253, ◆253 (4)
Second World War II *see* Wars, Second World
territorial changes ✤252, ✤252●
historical landscape ✤236, ◆236–7
influences
colonial apogee and demise ✤250–1
contemporary formation ◆252 (1)
decolonization ✤251, ◆251 (4)
Indian ✤241, ◆241 (6)
modern ✤252–3
political changes ✤251●
religions ✤242–3, 242●, 243●
urbanization ✤253, ◆253 (5)
See also Afghanistan; Burma; India
Southern Song *see* Song dynasty.
Soviet Union *see* Union of Soviet Socialist Republics
space technology Satellite imagery ❑106, ❑110
Spain 192–215
16th century ships ✤78
consolidation and resistance (17th century) ✤196, ✤196●, ◆196 (2)
foreign affairs
voyages of expansion (1492–1597) ◆80–1 (1)
Empire in 1600 ◆81 (3)
possessions
1500 ◆74–5
1600 ◆78–9
1700 ◆82–3
1800 ◆86–7
1850 ◆90–1
1900 ◆94–5
1925 ◆98–9
1950 ◆102–3
1975 ◆106–7
Africa
colonization (19th century) ◆166 (1) (4)
decolonization ✤168, ◆168 (1)
imperialism (1880–1920) ✤96, ◆96 (1)
America
colonization of Mexico and N America ✤125●, ✤148
colonizing expeditions in the New World ✤125, ✤126, ◆125 (4), ◆126 (1)
conquistador riding a llama ❑78
N American exploration (15th–17th century) ◆118 (1)
South American colonization ✤78, ✤79●, ✤86, ✤142–3, ◆143 (2), ◆148 (2)
South American exploration ✤142●, ✤143●, ◆142 (1)
Spanish–American war ✤133, ◆133 (4)
Council of the Indies ✤81
Dutch revolt (1568–1609) ✤195, ✤195●, ◆195 (5)
Dutch Wars of Independence ✤78●, ❑78
Pacific imperialism ◆284 (1)
West Indies, Jamaica seized by English (1654) ✤82●
home affairs
Almohads established in South (1147) ✤63●
Christian reconquest begins (1031) ✤62●
Civil War (1936–39) ✤102●, ✤209, ◆209 (4)
Council of Castile ✤81
defeat of Spanish Armada (1588) ✤78●
devolution ✤112
diamond finds (1867, 1869) ✤93●
Muslim invasions ✤54●, ✤55●, ✤62
population growth (1650–1800) ❑198
Reconquest ✤192, ✤192●, ◆186 (1), ◆192 (3)
trade and industry, 16th century ◆81 (3)
Treaty of Westphalia, ◆196 (1)
union with Portugal ✤81●, ✤149●, ❑196
Spanish–American War (1898) US intervention in a Cuban insurrection led to war with Spain. The Spanish fleet in the Far East was defeated by Admiral Dewey, although resistance to the invasion was sustained by Filipino partisans.The Spanish garrison at Santiago de Cuba surrendered after a fortnight's resistance. By the peace agreement of 9 Aug 1898, Spain renounced her rights of sovereignty over Cuba and Puerto Rico and ceded the Philippines and the island of Guam to the US. ✤133●, ◆133 (4)
Spanish Civil War (1936–39). Civil war between the elected Republican government of Spain and the conservative Nationalist opposition, supported by the military and receiving aid from Italy and Germany (both under fascist control at the time). The Republicans also received support from around 60,000 volunteer International Brigades from other European nations and the US, and from the Soviet Union. From the end of 1936, the Civil War became a war of attrition, with the Nationalists gradually gaining ground at the expense of the Republicans who eventually surrendered in March 1939. The Spanish Civil war is thought to have claimed at least 500,000 casualties. ✤209, ◆209 (4)
Spanish Succession, War of the (1701–14). In 1701, Leopold of Austria, supported by England and the Dutch Republic, invaded Italy in opposition to the will of Carlos II of Spain, which bequeathed Spain's possessions in Europe and overseas to Philip, grandson of Louis XIV of France. Portugal, Savoy and the Holy Roman Empire also declared war on France. A compromise was eventually reached at the Peace of Utrecht (1714); Philip retained Spain but the Spanish Netherlands and Italian territories went to the Austrian Habsburgs and Savoy. ✤94●, ✤197, ◆197 (5)
Sparta One of the leading Greek city-states, Sparta was forced to institute a series of military and social reforms in response to territorial revolts. As a result it remained inward-looking and militaristic in contrast to Athens' developing democracy and imperial acquisitions. ❑177, ✤179, ◆179 (4)
Special Economic Zones Regions of eastern and southern China (Beijing, Shanghai, Xiamen, Shantou, Shenzhen, Guangzhou, and since 1997, Hong Kong) established after 1978, under Deng Xiaoping, designed to attract foreign investment and develop Chinese economic strengths and relations with free market economies. ◆274 (2)
Speke, John Hanning (1827–94). English soldier and explorer of Africa. Accompanied Richard Burton on a voyage to Somaliland in 1854; three years later they were sent by the Royal Geographical Society to search for the great African lakes. Speke, exploring alone, came across the headwaters of the Nile, later confirming the location with James Grant in 1860.
discovers source of Nile (1862) ✤157
portrait ❑157
tracking the Nile ◆157 (4)
Spice Islands *see* Moluccas
spice trade
✤44–5, ✤71
commercial Africa (19th century) ◆166 (1)
Eurasian and African (c.1 CE) ◆44–5
pepper being harvested ❑79

Spion Kop ⚔ of 2nd Boer War (1900). Boer victoryover British. ◆96 (2)
Spiro mound site Soapstone pipe ❑123
Spotsylvania Court House ⚔ of American Civil War (8–19 May 1864). Inconclusive result. ◆131 (7)
Sputnik First artificial space satellite, launched in Oct 1957 by the Soviet Union. ✣106●
Sri Lanka (*var.* Taprobane, Ceylon)
 secessionist war ✣253
Srivijaya Maritime empire which emerged in western Indonesia in the 7th century CE, with a capital at Palembang in southern Sumatra. For seven centuries, Srivijaya controlled the lucrative trade passing through the straits of Malacca and Sunda Strait and across the Isthmus of Kra. ◆245 (5)
SS *see* Schutzstaffel
St. George's church Lalibela ❑62
St. Lawrence
 colonial settlement (to 1750) ✣126, ◆126 (1)
 explored by Cartier (1532, 1534) ✣80, ✣118●
St. Louis *see* Louis IX of France
St. Mark's Basilica ❑191
St. Petersburg, founded (1703) ✣86●, ❑197
Stalin, Josef (*var.* Iosif Vissarionovich Stalin, *Georg.* Ioseb Dzhugashvili) (1879–1953). Secretary-general of the Communist Party of the Soviet Union (1922–53) and premier of the Soviet state (1941–53), who for a quarter of a century dictatorially ruled the Soviet Union and transformed it into a major world power.
 comes to power (1925) ✣102
 Soviet expansion ✣213, ◆213 (4)
 Tehran conference ✣105●
 Yalta 'Big Three' conference (1945) ❑105
Stalingrad ⚔ of WW II (Sep 1942–Feb 1943) marking the halt by Soviet forces of the German advance into Russia; following a prolonged siege, Soviet forces secured the first surrender of German troops in the war. ✣104● ◆104 (2)
Stamford Bridge ⚔ (25 Sep 1066). English king, Harold Godwinson, defeated invading army of Norwegian king, Harald Hardrada. ◆186 (2)
Stamp Act (1765). Act, passed by British government, imposing direct taxes on all printed papers in the American colonies, including legal documents, newspapers and pamphlets, in order to raise revenue for the defence of the colonies. It was met by vigorous protest from the colonists who refused to use the stamps, as well as refusing to import British goods. They defended their right to be taxed only by their own consent. Though the Act was quickly repealed, the Declaratory Act, issued at the same time, asserted the British government's right to tax directly anywhere within its empire. ❑88, ✣127●
Standard Oil of California Extracts oil in Saudi Arabia (1933) ✣234●
Stanley, Henry Morton (*prev.* John Rowlands) (1841–1904). British-American explorer of central Africa, famous for his rescue of the Scottish missionary and explorer David Livingstone and for his discoveries in and development of the Congo region. He was knighted in 1899. ◆157 (4), ❑157
START *see* Strategic Arms Reduction Talks
Star Wars *see* Strategic Defense Initiative
Staufer dynasty *see* Hohenstaufen dynasty
Staunton ⚔ of American Civil War (8–9 Jun 1862). Confederate victory. ◆131 (6)
steel process for mass production invented (1856) ✣92●
Stefansson, Vilhjalmur (1879–1962). Explorer of the Canadian Arctic. From 1906–12 he studied the culture of the Inuit people of the Arctic. From 1913–18 he explored huge areas of the Arctic north of Canada and Alaska. ◆286–7 (2)
Stephen I (977–1038). King of Hungary. Stephen founded the kingdom of Hungary along western European lines and helped establish the Roman church in his country. In recognition of this, he was made a saint in 1083. ❑185
Stephenson, Robert (1803–59). English engineer, son of George Stephenson (1781–1848). They worked together on the Stockton to Darlington Railway (1825) and the Liverpool–Manchester Railway (1829), for which they built the famous steam engine *Rocket*. ✣90
steppe nomads General term for the various groups of pastoral nomads of the Eurasian Steppes, historically extending from S Ukraine to Manchuria. Often referred to by Greek and Roman writers as Scythians. *See also* Huns, Kazakhs, Uzbeks, Turks, Xiongnu. ✣39, ✣51, ✣54●
 Bactrian plaque ❑261
 bronze cauldron ❑53
 cultures (1250 BCE) ◆26–7
 horsemanship skills ❑261
 kingdoms of Central Asia ✣261, ✣261●, ◆261 (6)
Stilicho, Flavius (365–408) (r.394–408). Half-Vandal general who acted as regent to the Roman emperor Honorius. ❑52
stirrup *see* horses
Stockport Textile town ✣93
Stockton to Darlington railway, first passenger service (1825) ✣90
Stoicism A philosophical movement which flourished in Greece and Rome between 300 BCE and 180 CE, named after the Stoa Poikile, the painted colonnade in Athens where its founder Zeno of Citium taught. Its central premise was that reason is the governing principle of nature, thus an ideal life would see individuals living in harmony with nature and valuing equanimity in the face of life's uncertainties. ✣46
Stone Age The first known period of prehistoric human culture, characterized by the use of stone tools and conventionally divided into Palaeolithic, Mesolithic and Neolithic. ◆14–15 (1) (2), ◆160 (1)
Stonehenge Group of standing stones near Salisbury in England, originally in two concentric circles enclosing two horseshoes of smaller stones. Construction is thought to have begun c.2950 BCE. Its exact origin and purpose remain a mystery, but may have been connected with rituals of consecration and possibly some kind of sacrifice. On midsummer day the rising sun aligns with the axis of Stonehenge. ✣23, ❑22
Stono slave rebellion (1799) ✣85●
Strabo (c.63 BCE–23 CE) Roman historian and geographer. He travelled widely in Greece and Egypt, collecting material for his *Historical Studies* (47 vols), most of which have been lost, but his *Geographica* (17 vols) survived almost intact and contained valuable information on countries in Europe, Asia and Africa. ✣44, ✣218●
Strategic Arms Limitation Talks (SALT). SALT I (signed 1972) was the outcome of tentative negotiations between US and Soviet Union to reduce their nuclear arsenals, begun in 1969; SALT II (signed 1979) remained unratified by the US. ✣109●
Strategic Arms Reduction Talks (START). Initiated in 1982 in an attempt to control arms proliferation in US and Soviet Union during Cold War.
 START arms treaty signed (1991) ✣109●
Strategic Defense Initiative (SDI) (*aka* Star Wars). Satellite-based defence system initiated by US in mid-1980s in response to increased Soviet arms budget. ✣109
Stuart, John McDouall (1815–66) English-born explorer of Australia. In 1861–62 he crossed the continent from south to north, reaching the Indian Ocean just to the east of Darwin. ◆279 (2)
Sturt, Charles (1795–1869) British soldier and explorer of the Australian interior. He completed a survey of the Murray-Darling river system in 1830. Sturt's expedition of 1844–46 to the centre of Australia failed to find the inland sea he believed lay there. ◆279 (2)
Sübedei Mongol general, one of Genghis Khan's most trusted commanders.
 leads Mongol raid into Russia (1222) ✣68
Sucre, Antonio José de (1790–1830). Colleague of Simón Bolívar, general of armies of liberation in Colombia, Ecuador, Peru, and Bolivia. ◆150 (1)
SUDAM (*f/n* Superintendancy for the Development of the Amazon Region, *Port.* Superintendencia para o Desenvolvimento de Amazonia). A Brazilian agency founded in 1953 to funnel federal funds into development projects in Amazonia, and oversee tax incentives which were intended to stimulate investments of private capital, especially in manufacturing and rural enterprises. ✣153●
Sudan
 BCE ✣34
 colonization ◆167 (4)
 Egyptian invasion (1820) ✣91●
 fundamentalists seize power (1989) ✣235
 industry ◆168 (2)
 inter-ethnic warfare ✣111
 Islamic law imposed (1983) ✣235●
 political change ◆163 (4)–(7)
Suebi *see* Sueves
Sueves (*var.* Suevi, Suebi, Swabians). Roman name for group of German tribes. One group took part in the Great Migration of 406, eventually founding a kingdom in Galicia and northern Portugal.
 migrations and invasions (300–500 CE) ✣182●, ◆52–3 (1)
 ravage Gaul (406) ✣50●
Suevi *see* Sueves
Suez Canal Shipping canal 170 km long linking the Mediterranean to the Red Sea. Built to a plan by Ferdinand de Lesseps, who supervised its construction, it opened in 1869 and soon became one of the world's most heavily used waterways. In 1875 Britain paid the bankrupt Khedive of Egypt four million pounds for a substantial shareholding in the Canal. In 1956 Egypt nationalized the Suez Canal Company, precipitating the Suez War which temporarily closed the Canal. *See also* Lesseps, Ferdinand de.
 opened (1869) ✣95●, ✣232, ❑92, ❑232, ◆96 (1)
 nationalized by Egypt (1956) 107●
Suez Crisis (1956) Military conflict involving British, French, Israeli and Egyptian forces. Caused by Egypt nationalizing the Suez Canal. In a combined operation, Israel invaded Sinai and French and British troops occupied the Canal area. Under US pressure, invading forces withdrew and were replaced by a UN peace-keeping force. ✣234●
Sugar Act (1764). Act passed by British government, designed via strict customs enforcement to end the smuggling of sugar and molasses from the French and Dutch West Indies into the American colonies, and give additional funding for British military responsibilities in America. It was deeply unpopular in the American colonies. ✣127●
Sui dynasty (581–617) Ruling Chinese dynasty which united China in 589 after three centuries of disorder following the collapse of the Han dynasty. Replaced by the Tang dynasty in 618. ✣55
Sukarno, Ahmed (*aka* Bung Karno) (1902–70). Indonesian statesman, responsible for forming the Indonesian National Party in 1927. After suffering imprisonment by the Dutch authorities, he cooperated with the occupying Japanese authorities (1942–45). In Aug 1945 he declared independence from the Netherlands. In 1949, after four years of nationalist guerrilla war with the Dutch, Indonesia became independent under President Sukarno. In 1959, he assumed dictatorial powers, but was deposed by a military coup in 1965. ✣253●
Sukhothai Medieval Thai kingdom. ✣71●, ✣245●, ◆245 (6)
Suleyman I (*aka* Suleyman the Magnificent) (c.1495–1566). The son of Selim I, Suleyman became Ottoman Sultan in 1520 and presided over the period of the empire's greatest expansion and consolidation. In 1521 the Ottomans captured Belgrade and in 1526 defeated the Hungarians at Mohács. Suleyman was celebrated for his lawmaking and was an enthusiastic patron of architecture and the arts.
 Christian vassals pay homage ❑79
 Ottoman expansion ✣195, ◆195 (4)
 Selimiye mosque ❑231
Sumatra Rebellion against Dutch rule (1926–27). ✣103●
Sumer Term used to designate the southern part of ancient Mesopotamia, and area of Sumerian civilization. Sumerians are credited with the creation of the first cities and the invention of cuneiform writing. Excavations show a flourishing civilization by 3000 BCE.
 BCE state religion ✣36
 priestly statue ❑36
Sun Yat-sen *see* Sun Zhongshan
Sun Zhongshan (*var.* Sun Yat-sen) (1866–1925). Elected provisional head of state in China in 1911 during the anti-Qing revolution, but resigned a few months later. Gained full control of the country in 1923 and reorganized the Kuomintang (Guomindang) to resemble the Soviet Communist Party. Inspired both Nationalists and Communists. His efforts to unify China were continued by Jiang Jieshi. ✣99●, ✣271●.
Sundiata (d.1255) West African monarch who founded the empire of Mali. ✣67●
Sung dynasty *see* Song dynasty
Sunna *see* Sunni
Sunni (*var. Ar.* Sunna 'the way'). The Sunna is the way of the Prophet Muhammad and includes everything he did, said, caused, ordered or allowed to happen. A Sunni is a Muslim who follows this way. The word is most commonly used to distinguish the majority of Muslims from the Shi'ite minority. ✣56, ✣113, ✣231
 See also Islam, Shi'ites.
Sunni Ali (r.1464–92) Emperor of Songhay in W Africa. He reduced many former Mali provinces to Songhay dependencies, created a professional army and river-navy and introduced many administrative reforms. ✣75
Survey of India The appointment of James Rennell as Surveyor-General to Bengal was the beginning of Britain's systematic mapping of the Indian subcontinent. From the late 18th century, army officers such as Colin Mackenzie and William Lambton, pioneered trigonometrical surveys from 1800, and their work was continued, from 1823, by George Everest. ✣239, ✣239●, ❑239
surveying
 Roman milestone ❑42
 Royal Engineers (19th century) ❑173
 theodolite ✣173, ❑172
Surya Hindu deity ❑35
Suryavarman II Khmer warrior king (r.c.1113–50) ✣63●
Susa Royal Road constructed (BCE) ✣35
suspension bridge Development of ✣80
Sutter's Mill Start of California gold rush (1848) ✣93●
Sutton Hoo Gilt bronze helmet (7th century) ❑183
Svavarsson, Gardar 9th-century Viking explorer (c.860). ◆172 (2)
Swabians *see* Sueves
Swahili (*var. Ar.* Sawahili). Bantu language which dates from contacts between Arabian traders and the inhabitants of the east coast of Africa over many centuries.
 city-state mosques (c.1250) ✣66, ✣67●
 east coast *lingua franca* ✣162
 Ibn Battuta's journeys (1331) ✣71●
 Swahili city-states ✣162–3 (3), ◆162 (1), ◆163 (2)
 trading networks (13th century) ✣66
Swazi African kingdom (1820) ◆166 (2)
Sweden 186–215
 800–1000 ◆185 (3)
 Baltic states (1100–1400) ◆189 (3)
 conflict (16th century) ✣195, ✣195●, ◆195 (3)
 Empire (1560–1721) ◆197 (3)
 Thirty Years' War ✣196, ◆196 (1)
 Treaty of Westphalia, ✣197●, ◆196 (1)
 expansion
 consolidation and resistance (17th century) ✣196, ✣196●, ◆196 (2)
 imperial power (1560–1721) ◆197 (3)
 possessions (1700) ◆82–3
 trading explorers ✣60
 Union of Kalmar (1397) ✣70●
 home affairs, population growth (1650–1800) ❑198
Switzerland 196–215
 formation ✣193, ✣193●, ◆193 (5)
 battle of Morgarten ❑193
Sword Brothers (*var.* Livonian Order). Crusading order, which conquered Livonia in the Baltic region in the early 13th century. After their defeat by Lithuanians in 1236, their activities were taken over by the Teutonic Knights. ◆186 (1), ✣189
Syr Darya Colonized by Shaybanids ✣75
Syria 233–235
 ✣39, ✣99
 French mandate ✣233
 Parthian rule (BCE) ✣43
 Six Day War (1967) ✣107●
 vase of moulded glass (1st century CE) ❑224

T

Tahiti
 Chinese workers for cotton decolonization ◆284 (1)
 plantations ✣284●
 conversion of Pomare II ❑284
 riots against nuclear testing ✣285 (3)
Taika Reform Social and political reform of Japan initiated in 645. ✣264
Taiping Rebellion (1850–64) Major peasant uprising during late Qing dynasty China, led by quasi-Christian charismatic and ascetic, Hong Xiuquan. Originating in S China, around Guangxi, Hong proclaimed Taiping (the Heavenly Kingdom of Great Peace), and identified the Qing as satanic oppressors. By the mid-1850s the rebellion had gained massive support and their armies moved north to Wuchang and Nanjing where they established a separate government (and where over 40,000 defenders were slaughtered). They failed to take Shanghai (1860, 1862) and were finally defeated by Qing forces with enormous loss of life. ✣95●, ❑268, ◆261 (2)
Taira Clan Japanese warrior family ascendant in the 12th century. ◆265 (4)
Taiwan (*var. Port.* Formosa). Island lying between the East and South China seas. Part of China from the 17th century, Dutch trading post (Zeelandia 1624–62), ceded to Japan 1895, returned to China 1945, seat of Nationalist government of China since their mainland defeat in the civil war, 1949; mutual security pact with US, 1955, but lost seat in UN at People's Republic of China's insistence, 1971. One of the Pacific Rim 'Tiger Economies'.
 Dutch trade ◆267 (3)
 formation of independent republic of China ◆274 (1)
 industrial growth ✣111
 Japanese imperialism ◆269 (4)
 pro-Ming rebellion ◆268 (2)
 Qing China ◆268 (1)
Taizu *see* Zhu Yuanzhang.
Takla Makan Desert Silk Road ✣45
Takrur W African kingdom ✣58
Talas River ⚔ (751). Between victorious Arab (Muslim) and Tang armies in Central Asia, marking for a time the furthest expansion of each empire east and west respectively. ◆56 (1), ✣59●
Taleban *see* Taliban.
Taliban (*var.* Talibaan, Taleban). Extreme Sunni Muslim fundamentalist militia group which emerged in Afghanistan in the wake of the 1979–89 war. They took effective control of the capital and southern areas of the country from 1995. Under the Taliban, Afghanistan was used as a base by terrorist groups such as al-Qaeda. Following the attacks of 11 September 2001 on New York and Washington, a US-led coalition invaded Afghanistan and drove the Taliban from power.
 emergence ◆235 (4)
 capture Kabul (1996) ✣111●
 fall ◆235 (4)
Tamerlane *see* Timur
Tamil Eelam The aspiration of the minority Tamils in Sri Lanka is to break away from the majority Sinhalese and form an independent state (Tamil Eelam) in the north and east of the country. Civil war broke out in 1984 and the Sri Lankan government has always refused to to countenance federalism.
 Tamil, Tamil Tigers ❑253, ◆253 (4)
 Tamils assert power ✣47
Tang dynasty (618–907). Chinese ruling dynasty, which unified China after a long period of instability. The Tang Empire extended into Central Asia, with a population of c.60 million people. It established extensive trade links, both maritime and overland, with the West.
 (750) ◆54–5
 and its neighbours (c.750) ✣262, ❑262, ◆262 (1)
 Chinese Buddha ❑59
 collapse of dynasty (907) ✣59●, ✣61, ✣262
 defeated by Arabs (751) ✣256●
 emperor presented with a map ❑256
 invaded by Tibet (763) ✣59●
 peasant uprisings (870s) ✣59●
 printing invention (8th century) ✣59
 rise of dynasty (618 CE) ✣49●
 support for Silla state ✣264
Tang Empire *see* Tang dynasty.
Tanganyika Reached by Burton and Speke (1858) ✣157●
Tanguts People of southern Mongolia. Established a state in northwest China, the Xixia Empire (1038). ✣263●, ◆263 (3)
Tannenburg ⚔ of WW I (26–30 Aug, 1914). German victory over Russia which sustained the loss of almost an entire army, and massive quantities of weapons. The early Russian invasion of East Prussia meant that the Germans had to divert troops from their attack on France at a crucial moment of that campaign. ◆207 (4)
Tantric Buddhism (*var.* Tibetan Buddhism) School of Buddhism developed in Tibet from 8th century CE, and also practised in Mongolia, centred on monasticism and headed by the Dalai Lama as the reincarnation of the Compassionate Buddha and titular head of the Tibetan state. ✣242●
 See also Buddhism, Dalai Lama
Taoism Major Chinese religion, founded by Laozi, based on the Way, living in selfless accord with nature and natural forces, and respecting the example of ancestors. *See also* Laozi. ◆37 (4)
 BCE philosophy ✣35, ◆37 (4)
 founded by Lao-tzu ✣259●
 growth in China ✣261
Tapajós A chiefdom centred on Santarém in Brazil, which dominated the region in the 16th and 17th centuries. These warlike people dominated the surrounding area, extracting tribute and labour from those they controlled. ✣147, ◆145 (2), ◆147 (2)
Taprobane *see* Sri Lanka
Tarim Basin Invaded by China (1751) ✣87●
Tarquin I (*var. Lat.* Lucius Tarquinius Priscus) (r.616–578 BCE). The first Etruscan king of Rome. ✣176●
Tarquin II (*var. Lat.* Lucius Tarquinus Superbus) (*poss.* 534–509 BCE). Tyrannical Etruscan king of Rome, traditionally the seventh and last of his line whose expulsion in 509 BCE is seen as marking the start of the Republic. There is some debate over whether he is a historical or legendary figure. ✣176●
Tasman, Abel Janszoon (c.1603–59). Dutch explorer, employed by the Dutch East India Company. He made two voyages of exploration to New Holland (Australia). On the first (1642–43), he sailed from Mauritius, missed the Australian mainland altogether, but made a landfall on Tasmania, which he named Van Diemen's Land after the governor-general of Batavia. He also visited New Zealand, Tonga, and Fiji. The aim of his second, less successful, journey (1644) was to determine whether New Guinea and Australia were separate islands or parts of the same land mass. This he failed to do. ❑278, ◆278 (1)
Tasmania Settlement ✣280, ✣282●, ◆280 (1)
Tatanka Iyotake *see* Sitting Bull
Tavernier, Jean Baptiste (1605–89) French traveller and explorer in Asia. ◆239 (1)
Taymyr Russian icebreaker ◆257 (2), ◆286 (2)
technology
 British advances (from 1733) ✣204●
 development of agricultural ◆158 (1)
 global (c.1500) ✣76–7, ◆76–7 (1)
 impact on world trading systems ◆92 (1)
 prehistoric ✣12, ❑12
teff A cereal, almost exclusive to Ethiopia, mainly used for flour. ◆158 (1)
Tehran
 American embassy hostages (1979–81) ✣235●
Tehran Conference (Nov 1943–Jan 1944). Meeting at which the Allied leaders (Roosevelt, Churchill and Stalin) drew up plans for the Anglo-American invasion of France and a Russian offensive against eastern Germany. ✣105●
telecommunications
 first electric telegraph ✣92●, ✣204●
 satellite imagery ❑106
 telephone invented (1876) ✣95
 wireless telegraphy invented (1895) ✣92●
telescopes *see* optical instruments
Tell Agrab Two-wheeled chariot ❑24
Tell Brak Pictograph writing (c.3250) ✣23●, ✣24●
Temujin *see* Genghis Khan
Tenochtitlán
 founded 1325 ✣124
 capital of Aztec Empire (1428) ✣124
 conquered by Cortés ✣78●, ✣124●, ✣125●, ◆81 (3), ◆125 (5)
 Great Temple ❑124
 Huitzilopochtli's temple inaugurated (1487) ✣74●
 renamed México ✣78●, ✣81
 and satellite towns ◆124 (3)
Tenzin Gyatzo *see* Dalai Lama
Teotihuacán
 city continues expansion (400) ✣50●
 devasted by fire (750) ✣54●
 expands in grid pattern (100) ✣46●
 influential Mexican city ✣122, ◆122 (1)
 largest city of Americas (c.50) ✣42●, ✣46
 major trading centre (c.500) ✣54●
Tepanecs Overthrown by Aztecs (1428) ✣124
Terror, Reign of (1793–94). Final phase of the French Revolution. The Committee of Public Safety, led by Robespierre, carried out a ruthless elimination of political opponents of the Jacobins and anyone considered sympathetic to the counter-revolutionaries. Some 40,000 are thought to have been executed in France. ✣199●
 See also French Revolution, Jacobins, Robespierre
Tetrarchy Literally 'government of four'. The name was given to the

Key to index: ✣ text ● timeline ❑ picture ◆ map *var.* variant name *aka* also known as *f/n* full name *prev.* previously known as r. ruled ⚔ battle WW I First World War WW II Second World War

system of rule by two emperors (*Augusti*), assisted by two Caesars, introduced by Diocletian to govern the Roman Empire in the late 3rd century.
✣181●, ❏181, ◆181 (4)
Teutonic Knights Crusading order of knights, established during the Siege of Acre in 1190. The Knights subsequently subdued the pagan peoples of the Baltic in the 13th and 14th centuries, establishing their own state in Prussia, Livonia, and Estonia.
✣186●, ✣189, ✣193, ◆186 (1), ◆189 (3)
Baltic conflict (16th century) ✣195, ✣195●, ◆195 (3)
Texas Revolution (1835–36). Texas was originally part of Mexico. In 1836 it declared independence, becoming (briefly) a republic. In 1845 it became the 28th state of the US. ✣90●, ◆128–9 (2)
Texcoco, Lake Tenochtitlan established (1325) ✣124, ◆124 (2) (3)
textiles
earliest Old World ✣19●
Paracas ❏38
Thailand
bronze artefacts
✣27, ❏240, ❏241, ❏245
as Siam
absorbs Sukhothai (1378) ✣71●
capital founded (c.1350) ✣71●
invaded by Bayinnaung, king of Burma, (1563) ✣79●
Thea Philopator *see* Cleopatra VII
Theatrum Orbis Terrarum (Ortelius) ✣79, ✣173●
Thebes capital of New Kingdom Egypt ✣27●, ✣159
BCE invasions ✣34, ✣35●
theodolite Surveying instrument ❏172
Theodoric (c.445–526) Ostrogothic leader and king of Italy. After various wars against the East Roman Empire, Theodoric invaded Italy in 489 and defeated Odoacer. In 492 he took Ravenna, making it his capital. He preserved many of the traditions of Roman rule. ✣53, ✣182
Theodosius I (*aka* Theodosius the Great) (c.346–395) (r.379–95) Roman emperor. Appointed to rule the Eastern Empire upon the death of Valens, and administered the Western Empire after the death of Maximus in 388. He established Christianity as the official Roman religion in 380. After his death the Empire was finally divided into two halves. ✣182
Theravada Buddhism (*aka* Lesser Vehicle) Traditional interpretation of Buddhism, based on the personal experience and teachings of the Buddha, Siddhartha Gautama, and practised widely in Sri Lanka, Burma and SE Asia. *See* Buddhism.
Thermopylae ⚔ of (191 BCE). Roman victory over Seleucid king Antiochus III. ✣179●
Thesiger, Wilfred (1910–2003) British soldier, explorer and writer. Having explored in Ethiopia and the Sudan, in 1946–47 and 1947–49 he twice crossed the Rub' al Khali ('Empty Quarter') of Arabia, recording his journeys in the classic travel book *Arabian Sands* (1959). ◆219 (4)
See also Rub' al Khali
Thinis Confederacy (BCE) ◆159 (2)
Thirty Years' War (1618–48). Conflict between rival dynastic and religious interests in the Holy Roman Empire. The struggle began with a Protestant revolt in Bohemia against the Counter-Reformation policies of the imperial government at Prague. The war was divided into four periods: the Bohemian Period (1618–25), the Danish Period (1625–29), the Swedish Period (1630–35), and the Swedish-French Period (1635–48).
✣196●, ❏196, ◆196 (1)
Thomas, Bertram (1892–1950). A British political officer in the service of the Sultan of Muscat and Oman, he was the first European to cross the Rub' al Khali (the 'Empty Quarter') of southern Arabia, and the first to systematically record the topography of the region.◆219 (4)
See also Rub' al Khali
Thrace Zodiac fresco (BCE) ❏39
Three Feudatories Rebellion (1674–83) Pro-Ming rebellion in China eventually crushed by the Qing. ◆268 (2)
Three Hard Years Period of modern Chinese history (1959–62) following the failure of the Great Leap Forward initiative when agrarian decline, drought and crop failure resulted in widespread famine and up to 30 million deaths. ✣274●
Three Kingdoms *see* Shu, Wei, and Wu
Thugga (*var.* Dougga) Ruins of theatre ❏180
Thule culture Inuit (Eskimo) culture of the Canadian Arctic and Greenland. Partially sedentary, they hunted the rich wildlife of the Arctic.They expanded westwards between from c.1000 CE to become the dominant culture of the region.
✣58●, ✣123 (3)
Thutmosis III (*var.* Thutmose, Tuthmosis). (r.c.1479–c.1425) Egyptian pharaoh of the 18th dynasty, and one of the greatest rulers. He extended Egyptian territories and built and restored many temples. He erected the obelisk 'Cleopatra's Needle' which was brought to London in 1878 by Sir Erasmus Wilson. ◆159 (5)
Tiahuanaco culture Culture of the Andes established c.500–1000 CE. Its outstanding stone architecture included temple complexes, and large-scale land reclamation schemes were undertaken to feed its citizens.
✣54●, ✣145, ◆146 (1)
empire ✣146●, ◆146 (1)
Maya city ✣51●, ❏146
Tiananmen Square massacre (1989). Pro-democracy protests in Beijing in May and June by thousands of Chinese finally ended in the massacre of many demonstrators by the army. Between 400 and 800 are thought to have been killed. ✣111
Tibbu Tib (*var.* Tippu Tip) (1837–1905). 19th-century Arab trader in central and eastern Africa who in the 1860s built a state in central Africa based on the ivory trade. ❏166
Tibet Himalayan nation of south central Asia, unified by introduction of Buddhism in 7th century CE, centre of empire 7th–9th centuries CE, under Chinese (Qing) control from c.1720; closed to foreign visitors until late 19th century; entered British sphere of influence with Anglo-Tibetan Treaty (1904); invaded by Communist China 1950, and uprising crushed (1959) when titular head of state, Dalai Lama, forced into exile. Became nominally a Chinese Autonomous Region, 1965.
Buddhism ✣55●, ◆49 (4)
(c.800) ◆58–9
expansion and collapse of empire 650–840 ◆262 (1)
invaded by China ❏275
mapping and exploration ✣257, ❏257
Mongol control ◆263 (7)
population growth ◆274 (2)
Qing China ◆268 (1)
Qing protectorate (18th century) ✣87
unified with Qiang and Dian c.600 ◆261 (6)
See also Tantric Buddhism, Dalai Lama.
Tibetan Buddhism *see* Tantric Buddhism.
Tien Shan range Silk Road ✣45
Tiger economies Name given to the states in Southeast Asia, such as Singapore, Indonesia, Malaysia, that enjoyed an export-led boom and spectacular growth in the 1980s and early 1990s. ◆275 (4)
Tikal
built by Maya (c.300) ✣50●
invades Uaxactun (c.378) ✣50●
Timbuktu
captured by French ◆167 (4)
falls to al-Hajj Umar Tal (1863) ✣167●, ◆167 (3)
impact of Islam ◆162 (1)
regained from Mali ✣163
sketched by René Caillié (1828) ❏157
Timur (*aka* Timur the Lame, *var.* Tamerlane) (1336–1405). The Mongol (though ethnically Turkish) leader who in the 14th century embarked from his capital Samarkand upon a whirlwind of campaigns against the Persians, the Khanate of the Golden Horde, the Sultanate of Delhi, the Mamluks and the Ottomans.
Mongol conqueror (1336–1405) ✣71●, ✣229
burial site ❏229
campaigns (1379–1405) ✣229●, ◆229 (4)
conquests begin (1370) ✣71●
defeats Ottomans at Ankara (1402) ✣75●
empire ◆229 (4)
sacks Baghdad (1393) ✣71●
sacks Delhi ✣71, ✣244●
Turkish warrior chieftain ❏71, ❏228
tin *see* metallurgy
Tippu Tip *see* Tibbu Tib
Titicaca Chucuito culture ✣66
Tito, Marshal (*prev.* Josip Broz) (1892–1980) Yugoslav president. Tito led the Communist partisans who waged a successful guerrilla war against the occupying German forces in the Second World War. In 1945 he became head of a Communist government, but refused to take orders from the Soviet bloc and in 1948 split with Stalin and turned Yugoslavia into a non-aligned Communist state, which traded more with the West than the USSR. He was first elected president in 1953 and remained in power till his death. ✣215
Titus Flavius Sabinus Vespasianus *see* Vespasian
Tlaloc
Aztec god of rain ❏124
mosaic serpent pendant ❏124
Tlalteuctli Aztec earth god ❏124
Tlaxcala
church of St Francis ❏125
Cortés' retreat (1520) ◆125 (5)
Tlaxcaltecs Native American peoples of Central Mexico. During Cortés's conquest of the Aztec Empire (1519–21), they acted as allies to the Spanish conquistadors. ✣125, ◆125 (4) (5)
Toba Wei (*var.* Northern Wei) Ruling dynasty of northern China (c.380–524).
unify northern China (386) ✣51●
tobacco Plantation economy ❏90
Tokugawa Ieyasu (1543–1616) Shogun (military ruler) (r.1603–05) who won ⚔ Sekigahara in 1600 in the war to unify Japan. Ruler of the Tokugawa Shogunate. ✣267●, ❏267, ◆267 (5)
Tokugawa Shogunate (1603–1868) Dynasty of hereditary shoguns or military dictators ruling Japan, founded by Tokugawa Ieyasu. ✣91, ✣95
closure of Japan (1633) ✣83●
founded by Ieyasu ✣83●, ❏267, ◆267 (5)
Toltec Empire The dominant culture in central Mexico from c.900–1200 CE. They founded the city of Tula (*var.* Tikal) c.968, and destroyed the city of Teotihuacán, but the later years of the empire were marked by famine and drought, combined with increasing fragmentation of the surrounding city-states.
✣58, ◆58–9, ◆122 (1)
altar at Chichén Itzá ❏58
rise to power (900 CE) ✣122●
Tonga
Lapita culture (BCE) ✣27
settled by Polynesians ✣60
Tonghak Revolt (1894). Populist nationalist, quasi-religious rebellion in Korea which proved the catalyst for the Sino-Japanese War. ✣270●
tools
iron (BCE) ✣35●
stone ✣18
Topa (*var.* Inca Yupanqui) (r.1471–93). Inca ruler who extended the territory of the empire to its southernmost point, in present-day central Chile, and eliminated the last vestiges of resistance to Inca rule in southern Peru. ✣74●
Topiltzin Toltec religious leader (c.900) ✣58●
Tordesillas, Treaty of Papal decree of 1494, which divided new discoveries of the world between the two Catholic kingdoms of Spain and Portugal.
✣81, ◆81 (3), ❏142
Torii Sacred gateway to a Shinto shrine. ❏264
Torres, Luís Váez de 17th-century Spanish navigator on the Quirós expedition of 1605–07. In 1606 he found himself on the Pacific island of Espiritu Santo, separated from the leader of the expedition and in command of two ships. These he sailed west between Australia and New Guinea, through the strait that now bears his name. However, the Torres Strait did not appear on any map before the 18th century, because his surveys remained unpublished for nearly 100 years. ◆278 (1)
tortoiseshell Eurasian and African trade (c.1 CE) ◆44–5
Totonacs Native American peoples of Central Mexico. During Cortés's conquest of the Aztec Empire (1519–21), they acted as allies to the Spanish conquistadors. ✣125, ◆125 (4)
Toulouse
Inquistion established (1233) ✣186●
Viking raids (844) ✣185●
Touré, Samore Proclaims Islamic theocracy (1884) ✣167●
Toussaint l'Ouverture, Pierre Dominique (1743–1803). Leader of independence movement in Haiti. A former slave, Toussaint rose to prominence in the slave revolt in the French colony of St. Domingue in 1791. He then sided with the French Revolutionary authorities, becoming commander of the French forces on the island. However, when Napoleon came to power, he was determined to crush the slave revolt. Toussaint invaded Spanish Santo Domingo in 1801, but the following year was defeated and captured by French troops and taken to France, where he died in prison.
✣89, ◆89 (3), ❏89
Townshend Acts (15 Jun–2 Jul, 1767). Four acts passed by Britain in order to assert colonial authority via the suspension of the uncooperative colonial assembly, and the imposition of strict new taxes, and methods for their collection. The Acts were met with hostility, and on 5 Mar, 1770, most of the Acts' provisions were lifted. ✣127●
Toyotomi Hideyoshi (1536–98) (r.1585–98) Unifier of 16th-century Japan who carried on the struggle initiated by Oda Nobunaga. ✣267, ◆267 (4)
trade
archaeological sites ◆25 (3)
BCE ✣18–19, ✣30–1, ✣34–5, ✣240
and biological diffusion ◆72–3
blockades, Continental System ✣201
commodities
narcotics ◆153 (5)
opium ✣269, ❏112
Eurasian and African trade (c.1 CE) ◆44–5
and the first cities ✣24–5
frankincense ✣42
mother-of-pearl ✣44
Olmec ✣30
places
Africa
early Egyptian ◆159 (3) (4)
N (BCE) ◆161 (2)
NE ◆161 (3)
spread of Islam ◆162 (1)
America, South ✣94, ✣153 (3)
Asia
Japan ✣270
Ming China ✣267●, ◆267 (3)
South ✣247, ✣247●, ◆247 (3)
West ◆226 (2)
Classical World ◆44–5
Europe, Medieval ✣190, ◆190–1 (1)
India ✣249, ◆249 (4)
Mediterranean, Greek colonies ✣34
Oceans, Indian (15th century–16th century) ✣230, ◆230 (2)
routes
maritime ✣190
Persian Royal Road ◆218 (1)
Silk Road ✣43, ◆44–5, ◆256 (1)
trans-Alpine passes ✣190
trans-Asian ✣44–5, ✣260–1, ✣262–3
urban centres ◆25 (2)
See also Trans-Saharan route
seals ❏25, ❏190
technology, impact on trading systems (1870–1910) ◆92 (1)
Trafalgar ⚔ of Napoleonic Wars (21 Oct 1805). Victory of British fleet under Nelson over combined French and Spanish fleets. ◆200 (1)
Trail of Tears (1838–39). The forcible removal of the Cherokee people from their lands in Georgia, despite the finding of the Supreme Court that the Treaty of New Echota of 1835 which ceded Cherokee lands east of the Mississippi to the US, was not binding. Forced into camps, their homes destroyed, more than 15,000 Cherokee were sent west to NE Oklahoma, accompanied by 7000 US troops. More than 4000 Indians died en route. ◆128–9 (2)
Trajan (*var.* Marcus Ulpius Traianus) (53–117). Spanish-born Roman emperor. Trajan was adopted by the Emperor Nerva and, in turn, adopted his successor, Hadrian. Trajan's reign (98–117) was the last period of significant Roman expansion. He added Dacia to the empire, his campaigns there being immortalized on the column he had erected in Rome. His victories against the Parthians were less conclusive and many of his gains were given up on his death.
Roman emperor ✣46●, ✣47●, ✣180
annexes Armenia ✣47●
receives Indian embassy ✣47●
takes Seleucia ✣47●
Trans-Amazon Highway 5470 km (3400 mile) highway running from the Atlantic port of Recife in Brazil to Cruzeiro do Sul on the Peruvian border. ✣153●, ◆153 (4)
Trans-Saharan trade route ◆156 (1), ◆162 (1)
(c.1 CE) ✣50, ◆44–5
camel caravans ✣50, ✣58, ✣66
controlled by Songhay ✣78
Mali Empire ✣70, ✣75
Phoenicians ✣38
Sunni Ali (1460s–90s) ✣75●
Trans-Siberian Railway Major transportation link spanning the Russian Empire from Moscow to Vladivostok – 9198 km – (5778 miles). Built between 1891 and 1917. ◆208 (2)
Transjordan ✣99, ✣233
Transoxiana ✣227, ◆44–5, ◆227 (6)
transport
boats and ships
16th-century ships ✣78
cylinder seal showing reed boat ❏24
Egyptian sailing vessel ❏24
Indian ship ❏61
introduction of steam to shipping ❏92
Polynesian twin-hulled canoe ❏60
Portuguese caravel ❏156
reed boat ❏24
refrigerated shipping (1880s) ✣92●
Spanish caravel ❏78
trading junk ❏267
Viking longship ❏60
global (c.1500) ◆76–7 (1)
long-distance trading networks (BCE) ✣24
sleighs used in Siberia ❏257
wheeled
African chariot ❏160
ceramic bullock cart ❏22
chariots, Chinese ❏35, 259●
first automobile developed (1885) ✣92●
Ford Model-T production line ❏134
Tell Agrab two-wheeled chariot ❏24
vehicles in Copper Age ✣174
wheeled vehicles, ceramic bullock cart ❏22
See also railways
Transvaal
◆166 (2), ◆167 (4)
annexed by Britain (1877) ✣96
independence granted to Voortrekkers (1852) ✣166●
Transylvania Ottoman gain ✣195●, ✣197
Trasimenus, Lake (*var. Lat.* Lacus Trasimenus) ⚔ of Punic Wars (217 BCE). Victory of Hannibal and invading Carthaginian army over Romans. ◆179 (3)
Treaties
Alcaçovas (1479) ✣85
Anglo-Tibetan (1904) ✣257
Arras (1579) ✣195●, ◆195 (5)
Brétigny (1360) ✣192●, ◆192 (1)
Cateau-Cambrésis (1559) ✣194●
Egyptian-Israeli (1979) ✣234
Hubertusburg (1763) ✣199●
Kuchuk Kainarji (1774) ✣86●
Lausanne (1923) ✣233
London (1913) ✣203●
Maastricht (1991) ✣214
Madrid (1750) ✣143●, ✣148●, ◆148 (2)
Nanjing (1842) ✣91●
NATO from 1983 ◆138 (1)
Nerchinsk (1689) ✣83, 275●
Nystad (1721) ✣197●, ◆197 (3)
Paris (1763) ✣86, ❏88
Paris (1783) ✣127
Paris (1920) ✣98●
Peace of Augsburg (1555) ✣194●
Peace of Breda (1667) ✣149●
Peace of Karlowitz (1699) ✣179●
Peace of Lodi (1454) ✣75●
Peace of Roskilde (1658) ✣197●
Peace of Vereeniging ✣96
Peace of Westphalia (1648) ✣82, ✣199
Rio (1975) ◆138 (1)
Rome (1957) ✣108●
San Ildefonso (1777) ✣148●, ◆148 (2)
San Stefano (1878) ✣203●
Saragossa (1529) ✣81
Sèvres (1920) ✣233
South-East Asia Collective Defence (1954) ◆138 (1)
Stockholm (1720) ✣199●
Teusina (1595) ✣195●
Tordesillas (1494) ✣81, ❏142
Torun (1466) ✣193●
Troyes (1420) ✣192●
US bilateral defence ◆138 (1)
Utrecht (1713) ✣199●
Verdun (843) ✣58●, ✣184●
Versailles (1919) ✣102
Waitangi ✣91, ✣283, ✣285●
Westphalia (1648) ✣196, ✣197●, ◆196 (1)
Trebia ⚔ of Punic Wars (218 BCE). Carthaginian victory. ◆179 (3)
Trebizond Falls to Ottomans (1461) ✣75●
Trent, Council of Nineteenth ecumenical council of the Roman Catholic church (1545–63), which played a vital role in revitalizing the Roman Catholic church. ✣78●, ✣194, ✣194●
Trenton ⚔ of American Revolutionary War (25 Dec 1776). American victory. ◆127 (3)
Tri-Partite Pact Agreement signed on 27 Sept 1940 between Italy, Germany and Japan to support one another in the event of a spread of WW II to the Far East. ✣210
Trident Long range nuclear ballistic missile system, designed for delivery from submarines, developed by US during 1980s. ✣109
Tripoli Crusader state ✣63, ✣65
Truman, Harry S. (1884–1972) 33rd President of the US (Democrat, 1945–52). Born in Missouri, Truman served on the judiciary of the state from 1922–34 when he was elected to the US Senate. He became Vice-President in 1944 and President following the death of Roosevelt in 1945, and was re-elected in a surprise vote in 1948. During his Presidency, he authorized the dropping of the atom bombs, the Marshall Plan, the Truman Doctrine, the Berlin Airlift (1948–49) the establishment of NATO (1949), the deployment of US troops to combat Communism in South Korea and the setting up of the CIA, as well as the introduction of the 'Fair Deal' programme of economic reform.
✣109●, ✣213●, ❏139
Truman Doctrine (12 Mar 1947) US foreign policy promulgated by President Harry S. Truman (1945–52), guaranteeing US support for peoples and nations threatened by international Communism. ✣109●
Trundholm Sun chariot ❏26
Tshaka Zulu *see* Shaka Zulu
Tsybikov, Gombozhab (1873–1930) Russian scholar and traveller in Tibet. ◆257 (3)
Tuamotu Islands Polynesian colony (c.600) ✣55●
Tughluqs Dynasty of the Delhi Sultanate headed by Muhammad ibn Tughluq (1325–51). Under his rule, the Sultanate reached its greatest extent, incorporating 23 provinces and all the southern kingdoms. But administrative inefficiency, high taxation and an ill-advised attempt to move the capital to Daulatabad hastened the decline of the Sultanate, which, by 1398, had split into many warring kingdoms.
✣71●, ✣244
Tukulor Empire Muslim theocracy that flourished in the 19th century in western Africa from Senegal eastward to Timbuktu.
founded (1863) ✣167●, ◆167 (3)
destroyed by France (1892) ✣167●
Tula
founded by Topiltzin (c.900) ✣58●
sacked by Chichimec (c.1175) ✣62●
Toltec capital ✣122, ❏122
Tunis ⚔ of WW II (Apr–May 1943). Marked the surrender of the German Afrika Korps and final conquest of northern Africa by Allied forces. ◆211 (4)
Tunis
Aghlabid dynasty ✣58●
captured by Marinids (1347) ✣71●
Husaynid dynasty founded (1705) ✣87●
seized by France ✣232
tumulus *see* barrow
Tupac Yupanqui Inca Empire ◆147 (3)
Tupamaros (*var. Sp.* Movimiento De Liberación Nacional). Uruguayan leftist urban guerrilla organization founded c.1963. ◆152 (1)
Turkestan Conquered by Qing China (1750s) 257
Turkey 233–235
in 1925 ◆98–9
Kurdish refugees (1991) ✣235
Ottoman Empire partition ✣203, ✣233, ◆233 (3)
new republic founded (1923) ✣99
post WW I ✣233
See also Asia Minor; Byzantine Empire; Seljuk Turks; Ottoman Empire; Wars, First World War
Turkish Nationalists *see* Atatürk.
Turks General name for Central Asian peoples of nomadic pastoral origin who came to dominate the Steppes during the 1st millennium CE. ✣227, ✣228●,
Tuscarora War (1711). War between the Tuscarora Indians of N Carolina and European colonists, following the seizure of Tuscarora lands and the kidnapping of their people by colonists. The Tuscarora thereafter moved north, becoming the 6th nation of the Iroquois confederacy, and settling in New York state and SE Canada. ◆126 (1)
Tutankhamun (r.1333–1323 BCE). 18th Dynasty Egyptian pharaoh. Known mostly because the riches of his tomb survived undisturbed until their discovery by Howard Carter. A successor and son-in-law of the monotheist Akhenaten, he became pharaoh as a young boy and reinstated the pantheon of gods his predecessor had replaced. Unlike Akhenaten however, he did not persecute followers of the previous religion, but simply changed his name from Tutankhaten to reflect his beliefs, and moved his capital from El-Amarna to Memphis. ✣29
Tutsi (*var.* Batusi, Tussi, Watusi). Ethnic group whose members live within Rwanda and Burundi.
Hutu massacre in Rwanda (1994) ✣111●
Tyre Captured by Crusaders ✣65●
Tz'u-Hsi *see* Cixi, Dowager Empress.

U

U-Boat (*var. Ger.* Unterseeboot). German naval submarine of WW I and WW II. ✣210
Uaxactún Invaded by Tikal (c.378) ✣50●

Ubaid culture These first settlers of Sumer, who arrived between 4500–4000 BCE, were non-Semitic peoples, now called proto-Euphrateans or Ubaidians after the village al-Ubaid where their remains were first found. They began to develop trade and industry in the area; the progenitors of the Sumerian civilization although they were not Sumerian speakers.
✣19, ✣220 (2)

Uganda Rwanda invasion (1990) ✣169

Uighur Empire *see* Uighurs.

Uighurs Turkic people of Central Asia. Established empire on the steppe northwest of China. Latterly formed the largest Muslim ethnic group in China.
❑262, ◆262 (1)

Ukraine Environmental survival strategies (BCE) 16

Ulloa, Francisco de (d.c.1540) Spanish explorer sent by Hernán Cortés to explore the Gulf of California. He sailed to the head of the Gulf, thus proving that lower California was a peninsula. ✣125, ◆118 (1)

Ultra Code name for Allied decryptions of German Enigma intelligence during WW II. ✣210●, ❑210

'Umar Tal, Al-Hajj (*var.* Al-Hajj Umar Ibn Said Tal) (c.1797–1864). West African Tukulor leader who launched a *jihad* in 1854 which led to the foundation of the Muslim Tukulor Empire, between the upper Senegal and Niger rivers. ✣167●, ◆167 (3)
- conquers Segu (1861) ✣167●
- conquers Senegal valley (1852) ✣167●
- creates Muslim empire ✣95●
- founds Tukolor Empire (1863) ✣167●
- *jihad* route ◆167 (3)

Umayyad Caliphate Muslim dynasty of caliphs founded in 661. They were deposed in 750 by the Abbasids, but a branch continued to rule Muslim Spain (756–1031). ✣56–7, ✣59●, ✣54–5, ◆184 (2), ◆192 (3)

UN *see* United Nations

Union of Soviet Socialist Republics (USSR). Centralized Bolshevik (Communist) regime in Russia, formally organized in 1922, substantially expanded during World War II, and the principal Communist state, dominating Eastern Europe, during the Cold War. Dissolved under pressure for *glasnost* (openness), *perestroika* (reform) and devolution in 1991; the rump state formed the Russian Federation, the Union was replaced by a Commonwealth of Independent States (CIS). 208–213
- formation ✣208, ◆208 (2)
- foreign affairs
  - Angolan Civil War ✣109, ◆109 (5)
  - arms race ✣109
  - blockade of Berlin (1948–49) ✣102●
  - 'Cold War' ✣106–7, ✣108–9, ✣138, ✣212, ✣214, ◆212 (4)
  - criticizes colonialism ✣99
  - Cuban missile crisis ✣108, ◆108 (2)
  - Czechoslovakian reforms crushed (1968) ✣106●
  - ends Cuba trade agreement (1991–92) ✣110●
  - Korean War (1950–53) ✣109
  - Soviet-bloc creates Warsaw Pact (1955) ✣106●
- home affairs
  - in 1925 ◆98–9
  - Bolshevik Revolution (1917) ✣98●
  - disintegration ✣110●, ✣214–15, ◆214–15 (4)
  - expansionism and repression under Stalin ✣102●, ✣213, ◆213 (4)
  - Great Terror (1936) ✣102●
  - May Day parade ❑106
  - innovations, Sputnik II satellite (1957) ✣106●
  - politics, Soviet propaganda poster ❑99
- Second World War
  - Sep 1939–Dec 1941 ◆104 (1)
  - Dec 1941–July 1943 ◆104 (2)
  - Jul 1943–Aug 1945 ◆104 (3)
  - global warfare ◆104 (4)
  - causes and consequences ✣102–3
  - human cost of global war ✣105
  - major battles ✣104–5
  - mobilization and casualty figures ✣105
  - *See also* Russia

UNITA (National Union for the Total Independence of Angola). Backed by South Africa in the civil war (1975–91) against the MPLA. ✣109, ◆109 (5)

United Arab Emirates Oil strikes (1959) ✣234●

United East India Company *see* Dutch East India Company

United Kingdom
- possessions
  - 1950 ◆102–3
  - 1975 ◆106–7
  - *See also* Britain

United Nations (UN). Established in 1945 aiming to maintain international peace and security and to promote cooperation over economic, social, cultural and humanitarian problems. In 1999, there were 184 members, with the Security Council consisting of China, France, Russia, UK and US.
- Cold War ✣108–9, ◆108–9 (1)
- conflict in the Gulf ✣235
- ends civil war in El Salvador ✣110●
- established (1945) ✣102●
- Partition Plan (1947) ◆234 (2)

United Nations Conference on the Environment (*aka* Earth Summit). Conference held at Rio de Janeiro, Brazil (3–14 Jun, 1992), to reconcile worldwide economic development with protection of the environment.
✣153●

United Provinces Fighting for independence from Spain ◆78–9, ◆195 (5)
See also Netherlands

United States of America (USA). 128–139
- established 1783, *See also* America; Central, N, S America growth of a Superpower (1941–98) ✣138–9
- imperialism (1860–1920) ✣133, ◆133 (4)
- foreign affairs
  - possessions
    - 1900 ◆94–5
    - 1925 ◆98–9
    - 1975 ◆106–7
  - Asia, imperialism in Southeast ✣97, ◆97 (3)
  - Camp David Summit (1978) ✣169●
  - Central America intervention ✣138●, ✣139
  - Chile, coup against Marxists (1973) ✣106●, ✣138●
  - Cold War ✣106–7, ✣108–9, ✣138–9
  - Cuba
    - intervention ◆133 (5)
    - missile crisis (1961–62) ✣108, ✣138●, ✣139, ◆108 (2), ◆139 (5)
    - tightens blockade (1991–92) ✣110●
  - Europe
    - League of Nations rejected (1919) ✣98●
    - refuses to ratify Paris treaties (1920) ✣98●
  - First World War (1917) ✣98●
  - Guatemalan government downfall (1954) ✣139
  - Iran
    - hostage crisis (1979) ✣186●
    - intervention (1955) ✣136●
  - Japan, trading treaties (1853) ✣270
  - Korean war ✣107, ✣136●
  - Mexican war (1846–48) ✣90●
  - Middle East
    - Egyptian-Israeli peace deal (1978) ✣138●, ✣234●
    - Eisenhower Doctrine (1958) ✣138●
    - Gulf War (1990–91) ✣138●, ✣235 (5)
    - retaliation bombing of Sudan (1998) ✣235●
    - Tehran embassy hostages (1979–81) ◆257 (2)
  - Pacific
    - decolonization and nationhood ✣285, ◆285 (3)
    - imperialism ◆133 (4), ◆284 (1)
  - policies
    - collective defence treaties (1948–89) ✣138, ◆138 (1)
    - criticizes colonialism ✣99
    - investment overseas (1920) ✣138, ◆138 (2)
    - Military Air Transit Rights ◆138 (1)
    - Paris treaties (1920) ✣98●
  - Second World War
    - Sept 1939–Dec 1941 ◆104 (1)
    - amphibious operations ❑273
    - 'Flying Fortress' bomber ❑105
    - Pearl Harbor (1941) ✣102●, ✣104●, ✣134●, ✣138
    - war in the Pacific ✣272–3, ✣273●, ❑102, ❑273
    - women aviation engineers ❑105
  - Spanish-American war (1898) ✣94●
  - Vietnam War, *see* Vietnam World Wars, *see* Wars, First World; Second
- home affairs
  - founded 1783 ✣127, ✣128, ◆127 (3)
  - growth (1783–1896) ✣128, ✣128●, ❑128, ◆129 (1)
  - black population ✣112, ◆112 (1)
  - changes in urban life ✣137, ◆137 (4) (5)
  - Civil War *see* American Civil War
  - the Depression (1929) ✣102●, ✣134–5, ◆134 (2)
  - era of boom and bust (1914–41) ✣134–5
  - gold finds ✣90●, ✣93, ◆93 (2)
  - growth of the suburbs (1950–60s) ❑137
  - incidents of intolerance (1914–41) ✣135●
  - Indians' and settlers' conflicts ✣128–9, ◆128 (2)
  - Manhattan's ethnic neighbourhoods (c.1920) ◆132 (2)
  - migration ✣129, ✣129●, ✣134, ✣139, ❑132, ◆132 (1)
  - popular culture ✣135
  - population (1900) ✣94
  - postwar prosperity ✣136, ◆136 (2)
  - Prohibition (1919–33) ✣98, ✣135●, ❑98, ❑135
  - protest movements and urban unrest (1960s) ✣137, ◆137 (6)
  - racial intolerance (1914–41) ✣135, ◆135 (6)
  - regional inequality ✣136
  - slaves freed (1863) ✣85●
  - societies in transition ✣136–7
  - urbanization ✣132, ◆132 (1)
  - Wall Street Crash ✣102, ✣134
  - War of 1812 ✣128, ✣129●
  - westward expansion and territorial conflict ✣129, ✣129●
- politics
  - Civil Rights ✣137●, ✣139
  - Constitution ratified (1789) ❑86
  - Democratic Party ✣139
  - election results (1944–96) ✣139●
  - idealized family unit ❑136
  - immigration restricted (1921–29) ✣98●, ✣135
  - key elections (1948–96) ✣139, ◆139 (4)
  - New Deal (1933) ✣102, ✣134–5, ❑134
  - presidential elections ✣135, ✣139, ◆135 (5), ◆139 (4)
  - Voting Rights Act (1965) ✣137●
  - Works Progress Administration (WPA) ❑134
- territorial expansion ✣90●, ✣94●, ✣98●, ✣133, ◆129 (1), ◆133 (4)
- trade and industry
  - cotton growing ✣93, ✣139, ◆93 (5), ◆139 (3)
  - industrialization, ✣132, ❑132, ◆132 (1)
  - average family income by region (1949) ◆136 (1)
  - consumerism ❑136
  - high-tech at Silicon Valley ❑136
  - impact of industrial revolution ✣90, ◆92 (1)
  - major industries (c.1925) ✣134, ◆134 (1)
  - most powerful industrial nation ✣98
  - NRA regulates wages and labour (1933) ✣134●

Unterseeboot *see* U-boat

Upanishads Series of prose and verse reflections which, with the Vedas, form the central corpus of Hindu sacred literature. They were composed between 800 BCE and 300 CE. ✣36

Ur
- ram caught in a thicket ❑25
- Royal Graves ✣23●, ✣24
- royal standard ❑23
- trading city ◆24 (1)

Ur-Nammu Founder of the 3rd Dynasty of Sumeria, who made Ur the capital of a new Sumerian empire c.2150 BCE. He constructed the ziggurat at Nippur to confirm his position as earthly representative of Enlil. ✣24

Urartu Ancient kingdom of the Near East around Lake Van (c.1270–612 BCE), repeatedly attacked by Assyrian kings and invaded by the Scythians and Medes.
✣31●, ◆222 (2)

Urban II (c.1035–99) (r.1088–99). Pope who believed in the freedom of the Church from state interference. He preached the First Crusade in 1095. ✣63, ✣64

urbanization
- Britain ✣204, ◆204 (1)
- and public health ✣204, ◆204 (3)
- S America ◆152 (1)
- USA ✣132, ◆132 (1)

Urnfield cultures (1200 BCE) ✣31

Uruguay Paraguayan War (1864–70) ✣94●

Uruk
- city-state (c.3500 BCE) ✣23–4
- cylinder seal ❑24

Urville, Jules Dumont d' 19th-century French naval officer and explorer of the Antarctic.
◆287 (3)

Usman dan Fodio (*var.* Uthman, *Ar.* Uthman ibn Fudi) (1754–1817). Fulani philosopher, and revolutionary reformer who, in a *jihad* between 1804 and 1808, created a new Muslim state, the Fulani empire, in present-day Nigeria.
- conquers Hausa city-states (1804) ✣91●
- establishes Sokoto Fulani kingdom (1820) ✣167●, ◆167 (3)
- W African *jihad* (1804) ✣167●, ◆167 (3)

USSR *see* Union of Soviet Socialist Republics

Uthman *see* Usman dan Fodio

Uthman ibn Fodio *see* Usman dan Fodio

Utrecht, Union of (1579) During the Dutch Revolt (1565–1609) ten southern Catholic provinces were promised their liberty from Spain; in reply, seven Calvinist northern provinces formed the Union of Utrecht. Their independence was conceded by Spain in 1609.
✣195, ◆195 (5)

Uzbek Empire *see* Khwarizm Empire

V

Valdivia Ceramic figures (c.3000 BCE) ✣22, ❑22

Valdivia, Pedro de (1497–1554). Spanish *conquistador*, leader of a series of expeditions south from Peru to Chile (1548–53). His campaigns were successful until the Spanish were confronted by the warlike Araucanians. It was in a battle against them that Valdivia was killed.
- crosses Atacama Desert (1540) ✣142●, ◆142 (1)
- founds Santiago (1541) ✣148●

Valens (c.328–378) Eastern Roman emperor (r.364–378), appointed co-emperor by his brother Valentinian. Defeated and killed by the Visigoths at ⚔ Adrianopolis.
- Roman emperor ✣50●, ✣53●
- killed by Goths (378 CE) ✣53●

Valerian (c.190–260). Roman emperor (r.253–260) who led campaigns against the Goths and the Persians. Defeated at Edessa by the Persians and died in captivity.
- emperor depicted on a cameo ❑225
- Roman emperor, defeated at Edessa (259) ✣51●

Vandals Germanic people, who played a prominent role in the affairs of the later Roman Empire. After migrating through Gaul and Iberia, in 429 they crossed into N Africa, where they founded a kingdom that lasted until they were conquered by the Byzantines in 534. The Vandals gained their reputation for destructiveness after they sacked Rome in 455.
- capture Carthage (439) ✣50●
- invade N Africa (429) ✣50●, ✣53
- migrations and invasions (300–500 CE) ✣182●, ◆52–3 (1)
- mosaic of landowner ❑52
- ravage Gaul (406) ✣50●

Varangians Name given to the Vikings of Sweden famous for their navigation of the rivers of Russia. They reached Constantinople where the Byzantine emperors employed them as an elite fighting force, the Varangian Guard.
See Vikings

Vardhamana *see* Mahavira

Vargas, Getúlio Dornelles (1883–1954). President of Brazil (r.1930–45, 1951–54), who brought social and economic changes that helped modernize the country. In 1937 he introduced the corporate-style dictatorship of New State.
✣152, ◆152 (1)

Varna Gold horned bull ❑18

Varthema, Ludovico di (c.1468–1517) Italian adventurer. From 1502–07 he travelled widely in the Middle East and Asia, and was the first Christian to make the pilgrimage to Mecca, disguised as a Muslim.
✣219●, ◆219 (4)

Vasa Swedish and Polish dynasty founded by Gustav Eriksson Vasa, who became regent of Sweden in 1521 and King Gustavus I Vasa in 1523. His descendants reigned until 1818. ◆197 (3)

Vasilievich, Ivan *see* Ivan IV

Vauban, Sébastien le Prestre de (1633–1707). French military engineer who revolutionized the art of siege craft and defensive fortifications. ❑197, ◆197 (5)

Vavasore, Giovanni Andrea di 16th-century Italian mapmaker.
✣173●

Vaygach navigates Northeast Passage (1914–15) ◆257 (2)

Vázquez de Ayllón, Luis (d.c.1528) Spanish *conquistador*. Accompanied Narváez in his pursuit of Cortés and in 1523 obtained a contract to search for a strait to the Pacific Ocean. He reached the coast of Georgia/ S Carolina, but died of disease or wounds sustained fighting Indians.
✣125, ◆125 (4)

Vedas Collection of ancient Hindu hymns and sacred verses composed from 1800 BCE onwards. ✣36

Veii Etruscan city taken by Rome (396 CE) ✣176●, ✣178

Velasquez, Diego 16th-century Spanish explorer of N America.
✣125, ◆125 (4)

Venetian Republic
- possessions
  - 1200 ◆62–3
  - 1200–1400 ◆189 (4)
  - 1214 ◆187–5
  - 1300 ◆66–7, ◆188 (1)
  - 1400 ◆70–1
  - 1500 ◆74–5, ◆193 (4)
  - 1600 ◆78–9
  - 1700 ◆82–3
  - *See also* Venice

Venezuela
- independence secured (1821) ✣90●, ✣150, ◆150 (1)
- llanero lancers ❑150

Venice 184–215
- 11th-century prosperity ✣62
- and the Latin Empire (1204–1300) ✣186, ✣187●
- Marco Polo departs for China (1271) ❑66
- medieval ✣191, ✣191●, ◆191 (3)
- St. Mark's Basilica ❑191
- trade routes (c.1300) ✣190, ◆190–1 (1)
- *See also* Venetian Republic

Venus figurines Form of portable art, dating to c.25,000 BCE, found in Europe and Russia. These stylized carvings of female figures, with exaggerated breasts and buttocks, may have been representations of the mother goddess, or were perhaps associated with fertility rituals. ❑17

Veracruz
- influential Mexican city ◆122 (1)
- landing site of Cortés (1519) ✣125, ◆125 (5)

Verdun ⚔ of WW I (1916). French forces eventually repulsed a sustained German attack on the town of Verdun in northeastern France. ✣98●, ◆206 (2)

Verdun, Treaty of (843). Treaty that divided the Frankish realms between three sons of Louis the Pious: Charles the Bald, who took France, Louis the German who took lands east of the Rhine, and the Emperor Lothar, who took a broad strip of land between the other two kingdoms, as well as northern Italy.
✣58, ✣184●

Vereenigde Oost-Indische Compagnie *see* Dutch East India Company

Vereeniging, Peace of (31 May 1902). Treaty signed in Pretoria that ended the Boer War after initial Boer approval in Vereeniging, between representatives of the British and ex-republican Boer governments. Transvaal and the Orange Free State came under British military administration.
✣96●

Verrazano, Giovanni da (c.1480–1527) Italian navigator and explorer. Travelled to N America on behalf of Francis I of France in 1524, exploring the coast from Cape Fear to Cape Breton, and later travelling to Brazil and the West Indies. ◆118 (1)

Versailles, Treaty of (28 Jun 1919) Agreement signed between Germany and the Allies at the end of WW I. Germany lost territory to France, Belgium, Denmark, Poland and Japan; the Rhineland became a demilitarized zone and Danzig became a free city under the control of the newly-formed League of Nations. In addition Germany agreed to pay heavy war reparations. ✣98, ✣208, ◆208 (1)
See also Dawes Plan, League of Nations.

Vesconte, Pietro (*fl.*1311–27) Italian cartographer who drew portolan charts 1311–27, his *Carta Nautica* (1311) being the oldest extant example, and his *Mappamundi* the most famous. ✣173●

Vespasian (*var. Lat.* Titus Flavius Sabinus Vespasianus) (9–79 CE). Roman emperor and founder of the Flavian dynasty (69–79 CE). The civil wars which erupted after Nero's overthrow came to an end when Vespasian was declared emperor by his troops and they invaded Italy. He restored Rome to a sound financial footing, re-established army discipline and embarked on a lavish building programme which included the construction of Rome's Colosseum.
✣46●

Vespucci, Amerigo (1451–1512). Italian-born Spanish explorer after whom the American continent is named. He provisioned one or two of Christopher Columbus' expeditions. He discovered and explored the mouths of the Amazon and sailed as far south as the Rio de la Plata. He evolved a system for computing longitude accurately, and accepted South America as a new continent, not part of Asia. ❑142, ◆142 (1)

Vesuvius Destroys Pompeii (79 CE) ✣46●

Vichy France Sector of unoccupied southern France administered by French government in collaboration with Germany during WW II, 1940–42. Also administered French overseas territories. ✣210●, ◆210 (1), ◆211 (2) (3) (4)

Vicksburg ⚔ of American Civil War, (19 May–4 Jul 1863). Union victory. ✣130–1, ◆130–1 (6)

Victor Emmanuel II (1820–78) (r.1861–78) The first king of a united Italy. ❑203

Victoria Falls
- map annotated by Livingstone ❑157
- named by Livingstone (1853) ✣157●

Victoria (1819–1901). Queen of Great Britain and Ireland (r.1837–1901) and Empress of India (from 1876), she succeeded her uncle, William IV. Married (1840) to Prince Albert of Saxe-Coburg-Gotha (1819–61, *aka* the Prince Consort), her long reign was marked by an active British foreign policy, notably in the development of the British Empire, by the growth of Britain as a global industrial and military power, and by an assertion of middle-class family values. Her Diamond Jubilee (1897), marked a high point in British aspirations as a world power.
- Empress of India (1876) ✣95●

Viele, Arnout (1640–c.1704) Dutch explorer and interpreter in N America. From 1692–94 he led an expedition north of the Great Lakes into Canada and then down to the upper Ohio river and present-day Indiana. ◆119 (2)

Vienna ⚔ of WW II (Apr 1945). Soviet reduction of final German resistance in Austria. ◆211 (4)

Vienna
- Ottoman siege (1683) ✣82●, ✣197, ✣197●, ❑197, ◆197 (4)

Vienna, Congress of (1814–15). International peace conference that settled the affairs of Europe after the defeat of Napoleon.The dominant powers were Austria, Britain, Prussia and Russia. Its guiding principle was the restoration of legitimate rulers. ✣90●, ✣202, ✣202●, ◆202 (1)

Vietnam (*aka* Annam, *to Chinese*, Dai-Viet) 251–255
- divided into provinces (1679) ✣83●
- falls to Han Empire (111 BCE) ✣43
- first Mongol expedition (1258) ✣67●
- Gia-Long becomes emperor (1802) ✣91
- invaded by Champa (1471) ✣75●
- Cambodia invasion (1979) ✣111●
- gains independence (1945) ✣103●, ✣251●
- greeting governer of French Indo-China ❑97
- Nguyen Anh becomes emperor (1774) ✣87●
- French colonization ✣97●, ◆97 (3)
- N and South become independent (1954) ✣107●

Vietnam War The First and Second Indo-China Wars (1946–54) ended with French defeat at Dien Bien Phu, and the division of Vietnam at 17°N. From the late 1950s, conflict developed between north and south, supported by the USSR and USA respectively. US military involvement began in 1965. In 1973 the Paris Peace Accords were signed, but fighting continued until 1975 when Saigon fell to the north Vietnamese and the Americans were evacuated. In 1976 Vietnam was reunited as the Socialist Republic of Vietnam.
- impact of the Cold War, ✣251, ◆251 (5)
- USA
  - advisors help the South (1962) ✣107●
  - involvement in war ✣106●, ✣108●, ✣138●, ❑251
  - N Vietnam bombed (1965) ✣106●
  - protests (1967) ✣106●
  - soldiers with Viet Cong suspect ❑138
  - supported regime falls (1975) ✣107●
  - Washington protest march (1969) ✣137●
  - withdraws troops (1973) ✣138●

Vijayanagara A powerful Hindu kingdom (1345–1570), based on the Krishna valley. It exercised an ill-defined sovereignty over the whole of southern India from the 14th to 16th centuries, and was based at the magnificent city of Vijayanagara (modern Hampi). In 1565 the Muslim Sultanates of the Deccan (the successors of the Bahmani kingdom) united against the Hindu raja of Vijayanagara, who was defeated and slain in the battle of Talikota, which decisively ended Hindu supremacy in the south.
✣245, ❑254, ◆245 (4)

Key to index: ✣ text ● timeline ❑ picture ◆ map *var.* variant name *aka* also known as *f/n* full name *prev.* previously known as r. ruled ⚔ battle WW I First World War WW II Second World War

Vikings (*var.* Norsemen, Northmen, Varangians). Term used to describe Scandinavian voyagers and warriors of the 8th–12th centuries. Norwegian, Danish, and Swedish raiders, traders, and settlers mounted expeditions that eventually took them as far as the Caspian Sea and N America. They colonized Iceland and Greenland, were established as Dukes of Normandy, and ruled England under Canute.
- carving of ship ❑185
- coin (9th century) ❑60
- N American exploration discovery of Iceland ◆172 (2)
- expansionist exploration (8th–10th centuries CE) ◆172 (1) (10th–11th centuries) ◆118 (1)
- longship ❑60
- in N America ✣172●
- raid British Isles ✣58
- of Scandinavia ✣185
- settlements (c.800–1000) ◆123 (3), ◆185 (3)
- their world (c.1000 CE) ✣60, ◆60–1 (1)
- tiller and weather vane ❑172
- Varangians (eastern) ✣60
- voyages ✣60●, ✣172
- Western Europe raids ✣185●

Vilgerdarsson, Floki Viking navigator of the 9th century whose ice-locked overwintering in the western bays of Iceland encouraged Viking colonization of the island. He coined the name Iceland. ◆172 (2)

Villa, Francisco (Pancho) (*var.* Doroteo Arangol) (1877–1923) Mexican revolutionary leader. Originally allied with Venustiano Carranza against the dictatorship of Victoriano Huerta, Villa and Zapata were defeated by Carranza in 1915 in a struggle for control of the military. He withdrew to northern Mexico where he continued guerrilla activity both in Mexico and along the US border. His attacks on towns in the southern US led to punitive US intervention. ✣133, ◆133 (3)

Virginia Capes ⚔ of American Revolutionary War (5 Sep 1781). French victory. ◆127 (3)

Virginia Colonization expedition (1607–08) ✣119●, ◆119 (2)

Vishnu Hindu god and the object of special or exclusive worship to Vaishnavas, a major Hindu sect. Traditionally Vishnu manifested himself in nine incarnations (including Buddha) to save men from evil. His tenth and final incarnation is yet to come. ❑36, ❑241, ❑242, ✣242

Visigoths (*aka* Western Goths). The name was first used to describe the Goths who settled in Moesia in the late 4th century. Under their ruler Alaric, they raided the Balkans, then Italy, where they sacked Rome in 410. They came to an agreement with the Romans and settled in southwest France, their kingdom also extending south into Iberia. Pushed southwards by the Franks, they made Toledo their capital, controlling most of the Iberian Peninsula until the Muslim invasion of 711. *See* Goths.

Visscher's *Atlas Contractus* ❑119

Vittorio Veneto ⚔ of WW I (Oct 1918). Final battle of the Italian Front, resulted in victory for the Italians against Austrian forces, who obtained an armistice in Nov 1918. ✣207●, ◆207 (6)

Vizcaíno, Sebastián 16th–17th century Spanish navigator. Sailed regularly on the Manila treasure galleon from 1586. In the early 17th century made expeditions to trace the Pacific coast of N America, identifying a useful harbour at Monterey and making a detailed survey of the coast. Later commissioned to search the north Pacific for the islands of Rica de Oro and Rica de Plata and to establish diplomatic relations with Japan. ✣125, ◆118 (1)

Volga Slave trade centre (13th century) ✣85, ◆84 (1)

Volstead Act (28 Oct 1919). Law to enforce the 18th Amendment, which prohibited the sale and manufacture of alcoholic drinks in the US. ✣135●, ❑98

Voltaire Pseudonym of François-Marie Arouet (1694–1778). Wit, poet, dramatist. His outspoken belief in political, social and religious freedom made him the embodiment of the 18th-century Enlightenment. His major works include *Lettres Philosophiques* (1734) and his satire *Candide* (1759). ❑198

Voortrekker *see* Boers

Voting Rights Act (1965) ✣137●

voting rights Slave ✣86

votive mirror Han decorated ❑44

Vouillé ⚔ (517). Visigoths defeated by Clovis I. ◆183 (5)

Vulgate Latin version of bible completed (404) ✣48●

W

Wahhabis Followers of Muhammad ibn 'Abd al-Wahhab (1703–92), who founded an ultra-orthodox sect in Nejd, to preserve the 'purity of Islam'. An alliance between the Wahhabis and the Saud family led in the 18th century to the unification of most of the Arabian Peninsula under the Saudi banner. In 1902 Abd al-Aziz ibn Saud began to reform and expand the modern kingdom of Saudi Arabia. The Wahhabi form of Islam remains Saudi Arabia's official faith. ✣233
See also Abd al-Aziz ibn Saud.

Waitangi, Treaty of (6 Feb 1840) Treaty drawn up to facilitate British annexation of New Zealand. The Maori acknowledged British sovereignty in return for ownership of their lands, which could only be purchased from them by crown agents. The initial ceremony at Waitangi was followed by further signings at sites all over N Island and the treaty was eventually signed by over 500 Maori chiefs. The Maori translation of the English text led them to believe that they would retain authority over their lands and peoples. ❑91

Waldenses *see* Waldensians

Waldensians (*var.* Waldenses, *aka* Poor Men of Lyons) Reformist Christian sect founded c.1170, based on teachings of Peter Waldo/Valdez (c.1140–1217), based on simplicity, poverty and evangelical zeal. Highly critical of clerical behaviour, Waldo was condemned by the Council of Verona (1184), and his followers were subject to persecution during the period of the Albigensian Crusade (1209) ◆186 (1)

Waldseemüller, Martin (1470–1521) Cartographer from Lorraine. Famous as the man who coined the word 'America' after the Italian explorer Amerigo Vespucci for his world map of 1507. He also published an edition of Ptolemy's *Geography* in 1513. ✣142●, ✣239●

Wales, England and Scotland (1284–1337) ✣188●

Walker, J & C 19th-century British cartographers.
- Indian Atlas ❑239

Walker, Thomas (1715–94) American land speculator and public official. Rediscovered the Cumberland Gap in 1748. ◆119 (2)

Wall Street Crash (1929) Collapse in the price of stocks and shares on the New York stock exchange which created panic in financial markets across the world and was a major contributory factor in the Great Depression of the 1930s. ✣102, ✣134

Wallace, Alfred Russel (1823–1913) English naturalist who travelled to the Amazon (1848–52) and Malay archipelago (1854–62). He developed theories of natural selection which had a profound influence on Charles Darwin. The Wallace Line, which divides the different types of fauna found to the east and west of the archipelago, was named after him. ✣239, ❑239, ◆239 (2)

Wallace, William (c.1270–1305). Scottish national hero who led Scottish resistance forces during the first years of the long struggle against English rule. ◆188 (2)

Wandiwash ⚔ of Seven Years' War in India (1760). French defeated by British. ◆88 (1)

Wang Mang *see* Xin dynasty.
- founds Xin dynasty ✣47●

Wang Yangming (*var.* Wang Yang-ming) (1472–1529). Chinese Neo-Confucian philosopher of Ming dynasty, who taught that Confucian ethics of correct behaviour and morality were innate, and could be discovered and promoted through contemplation and self-awareness rather than the study of classical texts and ancestral tradition. His teachings are frequently compared to tenets of Zen Buddhism. ✣75

Wang Yang-min *see* Wang Yangming

Warburton, Peter (1813–89) English-born explorer of Australia. After emigrating in 1853, he set out north from Adelaide, exploring the Simpson Desert and S Queensland; in 1872 he travelled west from Alice Springs across the Great Sandy Desert to the west coast. ◆279 (2)

warfare
- amphibious invasion (1281) ❑263
- the cannon ❑71
- Chinese weapons (BCE) ✣35●, ✣39●
- crossbow ✣39
- defensive fortresses ❑197
- global technologies (c.1500) ◆76–7 (1)
- gunpowder weapons ✣71
- Mongol ✣69
- portable scaling ladder ❑222, ❑263
- prehistoric technology ❑12
- two-wheeled chariot ❑24
- USSR May Day parade ❑106

Warring States period (403–221 BCE) A time of civil war in China when the Zhou confederation collapsed into rival factions: the Qi in the northeast, Chu in the south, and Qin in the northwest. Brought to an end by the Qin dynasty. ✣37, ✣39●, ✣259●

warrior clans Rise of Japanese ✣265●, ◆259 (4), ◆265 (4)

wars
- Achaean ✣179
- American Civil War (1861–65) , ✣130–1, ❑94, ◆130–1 (1–7
- Anglo-Maratha (1775) ✣87●
- Arab-Israeli ✣234●
- Austrian Succession (1740) ✣86●, ✣199●
- Austro-Prussian (1866) ✣203●
- Balkan ✣99●, ✣203, 203●, ✣232●
- Belgian War of Independence (1830–31) ✣202●
- Boer (1899–1902) ✣95●, ✣96, ✣96●, ◆96 (2)
- Boer-Bantu (1779–80) ✣87●
- Boshin (1868–69) ✣270, ◆270 (1)
- Chaco (1932–35) ✣102●, ◆152 (2)
- Chinese Civil War (1920–26) ✣271, ◆271 (6)
- 'Cold War' ✣106–7, ✣108–9, ✣138, ✣212, ✣214, ✣212 (4), ◆251 (5)
- Crimean (1854) ✣94, ✣203, ✣232●
- Dutch War (1672–79) ✣197●
- Dutch Wars of Independence ❑78
- English Civil War ✣196●, ❑196
- Falklands (1982) ✣110●
- First World War
  - casualties ❑207
  - causes ✣98, 206, ◆206 (1)
  - Eastern Front ✣207, ✣207●, ❑207, ◆207 (4)
  - Italian Front ✣207, ✣207●, ❑207, ◆207 (5)
  - Southeast Europe and Balkans ✣207, ✣207●, ❑207, ◆207 (6)
  - in Southwest Asia ✣232●, ◆233 (2)
  - Western Front ✣206, ✣206●, ❑98, ❑206, ◆206 (2) (3)
- Franco-Prussian (1870) ✣94●, ✣203
- German-Danish (1864) ✣203●
- Great Northern (1700) ✣197●, ✣199●
- Great Turkish ✣197●
- Greek War of Independence (1821) ✣202●, ✣232●
- Gulf War (1990–91) ✣111●, ✣138●, ◆235 (5)
- Hundred Years' War ✣70●, ✣75●, ✣187, ✣191, ✣192, ◆192 (1) (2)
- Indian-Pakistan (1965) ✣107●
- Iran-Iraq (1980–88) ◆235 (5)
- Kieft's (1643–46) ✣126
- King Philip's (1675–76) ✣126
- Korean (1950–53) ✣106, ✣107●, ✣138●, ◆109 (4)
- Macedonian ✣179●
- Mexico Civil (1858) ✣94●
- Mexico-US (1846–48) ✣90●, ✣128, ✣129●, ◆128–9 (2)
- Napoleonic (1794–1815) ✣90, ✣200–1, ◆200–1 (1) (3)
- Nine Years' (1688–97) ✣197●
- Onin (1467–77) ✣267
- Opium (1839–42) ✣91●, ◆269 (4)
- Pacific (1879–83) ✣94●, ✣151, ◆151 (4)
- Paraguayan (1864–70) ✣94●
- Parthian ✣224, ◆224 (2)
- Peloponnesian (431–404) ✣38●, ✣177, ◆177 (3)
- Peninsular (1808–14) ✣200
- Pequot (1636–37) ✣126
- Punic ✣42●, ✣177●, ✣179, ◆179 (3)
- Revolutionary (1775–83) ✣127, ◆127 (3)
- Riel Rebellion (1869–85) ◆128–9 (2)
- Russian-Ottoman (1768) ✣86●
- Russo-Japanese (1904–05) ✣269, ✣270, ◆270 (4)
- Russo-Turkish (1877–78) ✣203
- Second Afghan (1878–79) ✣95●
- Second World War
  - Sept 1939–Dec 1941 ◆104 (1)
  - Dec 1941–July 1943 ◆104 (2)
  - July 1943–Aug 1945 ◆105 (3)
  - global warfare ◆105 (4)
  - battle of the Atlantic ✣210
  - Greater German Reich (1942) ✣211, ◆211 (2)
  - Allied invasion (1943–45) ✣211, ◆211 (4)
  - Allied counter-offensive ✣273, ◆273 (2)
  - bombardment of Japan ✣273, ◆273 (3)
  - causes and consequences ✣102–3
  - human cost of global war ✣105
  - impact on South and SE Asia ✣250–1, ◆250–1 (3)
  - Japanese offensive ✣272, ✣272●, ◆272 (1)
  - liberation of PoWs ❑138
  - major battles ✣104–5
  - mobilization and casualty figures ✣105
  - Pacific ✣272–3, ✣273●
- Seven Years' (1756–63) ✣86●, ✣88, ✣199●
- Sino-Japanese (1894–95) ✣270, ◆270 (3)
- Six Day War (1967) ✣107●, ✣234●
- of South American liberation (1808–30) ✣150●
- Spanish Carlist (1833–39) ✣202●
- Spanish Civil War (1936–39) ✣102●, ✣2–9, ◆209 (4)
- Spanish Succession (1701–14) ✣197●
- Spanish-American War ✣94●
- Texas Revolution (1835–36) ◆128–9 (2)
- Thirty Years' (1618–48) ✣82, ✣196, ✣196●, ❑196, ◆196 (1)
- Tuscarora (1711–13) ✣126
- US Indians' and settlers' conflicts ✣128, ✣129●, ◆128 (2)
- US international conflicts ✣128, ✣129●, ◆128 (2)
- Vietnam, ✣106●, ✣107●, ✣108●, ✣137●, ✣138●, ✣251, ❑138, ◆251 (5)
- War of 1812, ✣128, ✣129●, ◆128–9 (2)
- Yamasee (1715–28) ✣126
- Yom Kippur (1973) ✣107●, ✣234●
- Zulu ✣95, ✣96●

Warsaw Pact (*var.* Warsaw Treaty Organization) (1955). Cold War political and military alliance, dominated by USSR, including Poland, E Germany, Czechoslovakia, Hungary, Romania, Bulgaria, Albania (to1968).
- created by Soviet bloc (1955) ✣106●, ✣109●, ✣213, ◆213 (5)
- conventional arms limitation (1990) ✣109●
- crushes revolts ✣106●, ✣213
- and NATO ◆108 (3)

Warsaw Treaty Organization *see* Warsaw Pact

Washington, George (1732–99) 1st President of the US. (1789–97). Born in Virginia, Washington served with distinction on the British side during the Seven Years' War against France (1754–61). He later represented Virginia in the House of Burgesses, and in the Continental Congresses of 1774 and 1775. When war broke out between Britain and the American colonists, Washington was the first choice to lead the colonial army. Important successes included the battles of Trenton and Princeton, and the key battle of Yorktown in 1781 which virtually ended the American Revolution. From 1783, Washington sought to establish a constitutional government for the new nation. In 1789 the first government under the new constitution was assembled, with Washington at its President. He was elected to a second term, retiring in 1797 in the face of increasing disputes between the Democratic Republicans of Thomas Jefferson and the Federalists, led by Alexander Hamilton.
- first US president (1789) ✣86●
- forces Cornwallis to surrender (1781) ✣127

Washington Naval Agreement (1922) After the concession of various Pacific territories to Japan at the Treaty of Versailles, this agreement was designed to limit and balance the level of naval power in the region, assuring predominance to the Western Powers. ✣99●

WASP (White Anglo-Saxon Protestants) ✣135

Watergate (*aka* Watergate Affair). Scandal sparked off by involvement of US Republican President Richard M. Nixon's administration in a break-in at the Democratic Party national headquarters (the Watergate building, Washington) during the presidential elections (June 1972). The televised hearings of a special Senate committee revealed escalating degrees of White House involvement and attempted cover-up. This ultimately led to a House Judiciary Committee investigation, the release and publication of sensitive tapes, and the erosion of confidence in Nixon's administration (and Washington practices in general). The imprisonment of three of Nixon's senior aides preceded the adoption of three articles of impeachment against the president, resulting in Nixon's resignation (9 Aug 1974), although he was pardoned by his successor, Gerald R Ford. ✣106●

Waterloo ⚔ of Napoleonic Wars (18 Jun 1815). Final defeat of Napoleonic forces. ◆200 (1)

wattle and daub Mixture of clay plastered over a framework of interlaced wooden rods and twigs, used for the walls of huts or houses. It can last for several hundred years if adequately protected from the elements by overhanging eaves. ❑21

Watt, James Improves steam engine (1765) ✣204●

wavy line pottery The first pottery to be made in Africa (c.7000 BCE) by the hunters and fishers of the southern Sahara, who lived in a broad swathe stretching from Mali to the Nile Valley. The pottery was decorated by parallel wavy-lines; these could be made by dragging the spine of a fish across the clay while it was still wet, or using bone or wooden points. ✣19●

Weddell, James (1787–1834). English navigator whose claim to have sailed into the vast bay in W Antarctica (1823), bounded by the Antarctic Peninsula, Coats Land and the Ronne Ice Shelf, led to it being named after him. ◆287 (3)

Wei Kingdom *see* Shu

weights and measures ✣33, ❑33

Wellington, Arthur Wellesley, 1st Duke of (1769–1852) British general and statesman; Prime Minister (1828–30). Campaigned in India, then commanded the British forces in the Peninsular War (1808–14), driving the French out of Portugal and Spain. After Napoleon's escape from Elba, he defeated the French at Waterloo. ◆200 (1)

West, the Geopolitical term relating to the free market economies and countries of US/NATO alliance during the Cold War.

West Africa 156–169
- BCE development ✣34
- exploration and mapping, medieval interior ✣156
- Islamic reform (19th century) ✣167
- Islamic wars (1806–70) ✣167●, ◆167 (3)
- native kingdoms ✣58
- political change ◆163 (4) (5) (6) (7)

West Asia 216–235
- Arsacid (Parthian) dynasty founded (247 BCE) ✣43●
- BCE ✣14, ✣14●, ✣31●, ✣35●, ✣39
- collapse of Ottoman Empire (1918) ✣99●
- development of writing ✣223, ❑223, ◆223 (3)
- early empires ✣222–3
- historical landscape ❑216, ✣216–17
- modern history ✣234–5
- oil production ◆234 (1)
- overrun by Islam ✣55
- plant domestication (BCE) ✣19
- religions (c.600) ✣226, ✣226●
- Sassanian Empire, ✣44●, ✣51, ✣55

West Bank Taken by Israel in Six Day War (1967) ✣234●

West Germany (*var.* Federal Republic of Germany, FRG, Bundesrepublik Deutschland, BRD) Established 1949 following Soviet partition of post-war occupied Germany. Joined NATO (1955), and founder member of EEC enjoying huge economic growth until dissolution upon German reunification (1990).
- 1950 ◆102–3
- 1975 ◆106–7
- entry into NATO (1955) ✣108
- post-war recovery (1961) ✣106 ✣212, ✣214

West Indies
- colonization by Spain (16th century) ✣78, ✣125, ◆125 (4)
- colonization by other European powers ◆126 (1)
- piracy ✣85, ◆85 (3)
- US intervention ✣139, ◆139 (5)

Western Allies' Limited War doctrine ✣109
See also Limited War Doctrine

Western Front The western theatre of war during WW I, based primarily in northeast France and western Belgium. ✣206●, ◆206 (2) (3)

Western Goths *see* Visigoths

Western Han *see* Han dynasty.

Western Jin Ruling dynasty of China (265–304 CE) who overthrew the Wei and briefly established Chinese unity. ◆260 (3)

Western Railroad Surveys of US (1853–55) ◆119 (3)

Western Samoa Achieves independence (1962) ✣285, ✣285●
See also Samoa

Western Union Telegraph Surveys of US (1865–67) ◆119 (3)

Western Zhou *see* Zhou dynasty.

Westphalia, Peace of (1648) General name for the 11 separate treaties, negotiated 1643–48, between the Habsburgs and their adversaries, bringing to an end the Thirty Years' War, which recognized religious tolerance and secularization of Church lands in much of Germany, and the independence of the United Provinces and the Swiss Confederation. ✣82, ✣199

wheat
- agricultural mechanization ✣90
- commercial Africa (19th century) ◆166 (1)
- domestication ✣19●

Wheeler, George Montague (1842–1905) US army officer and explorer. After completing a survey for the military of the area east of the Sierras in 1869, he set up his own organization: the United States Geographical Surveys West of the One-Hundredth Meridian, and surveyed thousands of miles of the West. ◆119 (3)

Whitby, Synod of (663). Ecclesiastical council which led to Britain's Christian communities adopting the practices and doctrines of Rome rather than those of Celtic Christianity. 183●

White Cloud Indian Iowa chief, portrait ❑129

White Huns (*var.* Hephthalites) *see* Huns

White Mountain ⚔ of Thirty Years's War (1620). Bohemians defeated by Habsburg armies. ◆196 (1)

White Plains ⚔ of American Revolutionary War (28 Oct 1776). British victory. ✣127 (3)

Whitney, Eli (1765–1825). US inventor, whose development of the cotton gin, to separate cotton fibre from cotton seed in 1793, transformed the efficiency of the Southern cotton industry and the conditions of its slave work force. Never properly patented, his invention was widely copied. He later manufactured firearms using a prototype production line system. ✣93, ❑130

Whydah Captured by Dahomey (1727) ✣164●

Wilderness, The ⚔ of American Civil War (5–7 May 1864). Inconclusive result. ◆131 (7)

Wilhelm I (1797–1888) King of Prussia (r.1861–88) and first German Emperor (r.1871–88). Dominated by chancellor Bismarck, whose policies led to creation of German Empire. ✣94●

Wilhelm II (1859–1941) German emperor and king of Prussia (r.1888–1918). He dismissed Bismarck (1890) and in a long period of personal rule, asserted Germany's claim to world leadership. Forced to abdicate at the end of WW I. ❑94

Wilkes, Charles (1798–1877) US explorer of Antarctica. After appointment as head of Depot of Charts and Instruments (1834) he commanded the US Exploring Expedition (1838–42) in the Southern Ocean, surveying the part of Antarctica now named after him, Wilkes Land. Court-martialled for cruelty, he served during the American Civil War, retiring as rear-admiral. ◆287 (3)

William I (*aka* William, Duke of Normandy, William the Conqueror) (c.1028–87). First Norman king of England (r.1066–87), who inherited dukedom of Normandy in 1035, annexing Maine (1063) and invading England, defeating Harold Godwinson at the battle of Hastings (1066), ending the era of Saxon rule. His victory was recorded, and claims to the English throne justified, in the Bayeux Tapestry. He introduced religious, political and social reform, and began the process of English unification. Although largely based in Normandy, he commissioned the first systematic survey of English property, the Domesday Book (1085), the foundation of the English feudal system. ✣186●, ◆186 (2)

William, Duke of Normandy *see* William I

William of Nassau *see* Nassau

William the Conqueror *see* William I

William of Rubruck (c.1215–1295). A Franciscan friar, in 1253 he was sent on a religious mission to the Mongols by Louis IX of France. His description of his travels and his meeting with the Great Khan Möngke were contained in his Itinerary, one of the best-known works of travel of the medieval period.
- explorer of Central Asia (1253–54) ◆256 (1)
  - W Asia (1253–55) ◆219 (3)

Willoughby, Sir Hugh (d.1554) British military officer and explorer. Appointed captain-general of a fleet of three ships sent by London merchants to seek a Northeast Passage. One of the ships, commanded by Richard Chancellor, reached the White Sea. ✣80●, ◆257 (2), ◆286 (1)

Wills, William (1834–61) English explorer of Australia, who accompanied Robert Burke on his journey across Australia from south to north. Died of starvation at base camp, Cooper's Creek, after reaching swamps at the Gulf of Carpentaria. ❑279, ◆279 (2)
See also Burke, Robert O'Hara.

Wilson (Thomas) Woodrow (1856–1924) 28th President of the US. (Democrat, 1912–21). Under Wilson's administration, women's right to vote was added to the

Constitution, along with the prohibition of the sale of alcohol. Wilson took the US into WW I in 1917 and intervened in the Mexican Revolution following Pancho Villa's attacks on US territory and citizens. He laid out the 'fourteen point' plan for peace which led to the Armistice in Nov 1918, and gave vigorous support to the League of Nations. His health was broken by the Senate's refusal to ratify the Treaty of Versailles. ✣98

Wilson's Creek ⚔ of American Civil War (10 Aug 1861). Confederate victory. ◆131 (6)

windmills ✣63, ❑63

Witwatersrand
 gold finds (1886) ✣93●

Wolfe, General James (1727–59) English general. Led British forces during the Seven Years' War against France in N America. He was instrumental in the capture of Louisburg in 1758, but was killed during the Battle of Quebec in 1759 which resulted in British victory. ❑127

Woodstock (1969) Huge rock festival in upstate New York, often seen as the culmination of the so-called 'Summer of Love'. ❑137

Woodward, Dr Henry (d.c.1686) 17th-century explorer of N America. From 1668 he explored much of the Carolinas, including the Savannah river. ◆119 (2)

Works Progress Administration (WPA) (*var.* from 1939–43, Work Projects Administration). Set up in 1935, as part of the Roosevelt administration's New Deal, the WPA aimed to provide work for the unemployed on a series of government projects, including the building of new roads, public buildings, bridges, parks and airports, as well as the employment of writers, artists and actors in community arts and theatre projects. ❑134

World Trade Organization (WTO). Organization for the regulation and liberalization of world trade, set up in January 1995 as a successor to GATT (the General Agreement on Tariffs and Trade) which had been in existence since 1947. 104 countries were founding members of the WTO, which is responsible for making sure that GATT agreements are adhered to, as well as the setting up of new trade agreements.

World War I *see* First World War.

World War II *see* Second World War.

World Wide Web International computer network offering a huge interface for the storage, retrieval and exchange of information. ✣113
 See also Internet.

Wounded Knee, Massacre at (1890). More than 200 Sioux were killed by US army troops in what was to be the last major confrontation between Indians and the US army. ◆128 (2)

Wrangel, Baron Ferdinand von (1797–1870) Russian vice-admiral and explorer of Arctic waters and coasts of Siberia. ◆257 (2)

writing 32, 223
 evolution ✣32●, ✣223, ✣223●, ◆32 (1), ◆223 (3)
 alphabet ✣31, ✣34●, ◆223 (3)
 Canaanite script (1600 BCE) ✣27●
 Chinese ✣259●, ❑258, ◆32 (1)
 counting and calendars ✣32–3
 cuneiform ✣24●, ✣25, ✣32●, ✣223, ❑25, ❑34, ◆32 (1), ◆223 (3)
 Etruscan script (c.690) ✣176●
 first alphabetic script (1600 BCE) ✣27●
 first texts ✣25, ❑25
 Indus script ◆32 (1)
 Linear A script (1650 BCE) ✣27●
 Mesoamerican script ◆32 (1)
 Olmec syllabary writing system ✣121
 Phoenician ✣27●, ✣31, ✣32●, ❑32, ◆32 (1)
 recording of knowledge ◆76–7 (1)
 Roman lapidary inscription ❑32
 Runic script ◆32 (1)
 Zapotec ✣32
 See also hieroglyphics

Wu Kingdom *see* Shu, Wu and Wei Kingdoms

Wu-ti *see* Wudi.

Wudi (*var.* Wu-ti) (156–87 BCE). Most powerful of Former Han rulers (r.140–87 BCE), whose campaigns in south and southwest China, Vietnam and against the Xiongnu of Central Asia greatly extended Chinese realms. He established the role of emperor and Confucianism as state religion, and revived a central bureaucracy. ✣44●, ✣45

X

Xanadu *see* Shangdu

Xenophon (c.431–350 BCE). Greek historian and disciple of Socrates. A skilled soldier, he fought with 10,000 Greek mercenaries under the Persian prince, Cyrus, in the 401 BCE campaign against Cyrus' brother, the King of Persia. Cyrus' death left the Greeks stranded 1500 km from home. Elected leader, Xenophon led them safely to the Black Sea. ✣218●

Xerxes I (*var.* Xerxes the Great) (519–465 BCE). The son of Darius I, Achaemenid King of Persia, Xerxes (r.486–465 BCE) is known mainly for his massive and unsuccessful invasion of Greece from the Hellespont in 480 BCE. ✣39●, ✣223, ✣223●

Xhosa Bantu-speaking people of southern Africa, inhabitants of South African homeland of Transkei during late 20th century
 resist European colonists ✣86

Xia dynasty (*var.* Hsia, c.2000–1800 BCE) Ruling dynasty of first Chinese proto-state, forerunners of the Shang. ✣259●

Xiankiang (*var.* Dzungaria), conquered by Qing (1760) ✣87

Xin dynasty (*var.* Hsin dynasty) Ruling dynasty of China (9–23 CE) under sole emperor Wang Mang (former Han regent 1–8 CE) who introduced major reforms, including taxation, money lending, nationalization of estates and government monopolies on main industries (salt, coinage, iron, wine) during his brief interregnum before accession of Later Han. ✣47●

Xiongnu (*var.* Hsiung-nu). Chinese name for federation of largely nomadic steppe peoples that dominated Central Asia from c.3rd century BCE to the 4th century CE, constantly threatening China's northern borders. Disrupted by campaigns of Former Han, they split into eastern and western hordes; after decline of Han dynasty, Xiongnu generals established dynastic kingdoms in N China during the Sixteen Kingdoms period. Sometimes associated with the Huns.
 confederacy breaks up (55 BCE) ✣43●
 nomadic steppe people ✣259
 steppe cavalry tactics ❑261

Xixia Empire (*var.* Hsihsia) *See also* Tanguts.
 founded by the Tangut ✣263

Xochicalco Influential fortified city ❑122, ◆122 (1)

Xuan Zang (*var.* Hsuan-tsang, 596–664) Chinese pilgrim and traveller whose search for original Buddhist texts took him across the Gobi and Takla Makan deserts, to Bactria and the Punjab to the Gangetic Plain, returning overland. His account of his 16-year journey, and its geographical descriptions, were published by imperial command. ◆256 (1)

Y

yak Early domestication ❑258

Yalta Conference (4–11 Feb 1945) Meeting of Allied war leaders led by Roosevelt, Churchill and Stalin. Reaffirmed the decision to demand unconditional Axis surrender and planned a four-power occupation of Germany. Also discussed the plans for the United Nations.
 'Big Three' conference (1945) ✣105, ✣109●

Yamasee War (1715–16). Conflict between British colonists and the Yamasee Indians and their allies in SE South Carolina, a result of European incursions into Indian lands and the fur trade. ◆126 (1)

Yamato state Ancient Japanese state and clan on the island of Honshu.
 Chinese influence ✣264
 emergence (c.300) ✣51
 expansion ◆264 (1)

Yan'an (*var.* Yenan). End of Chinese Communists 'Long March' ✣103●

Yangshao culture (c.5000–3000 BCE) Early agricultural culture of China centred around the Yellow River basin, later replaced by Longshan culture. The Yangshao is characterized by square and round timber and thatch houses and handmade red burnished pottery, finished on a slow wheel. Yangshao communities grew millet, had domesticated pigs and dogs, and lived across much of the Yellow River valley in the 4th and early 3rd millennium BCE.
 geometrical decorated pot ❑258
 neolithic China ◆258 (2)

Yangtze
 delta rice cultivation ✣19
 first agricultural communities ✣258
 siege of Hezhou (1258–59) ❑69

Yanomani Hunter-gatherer tribal people of Amazonian rainforest, whose traditional lifestyle was threatened by commercial concerns developing in the region in the late 20th century. ❑110

Yayoi culture (c.300 BCE–300 CE). Period in Japanese history when rice, pottery and metals were introduced. ✣264, ◆264 (1)

Year of the Four Emperors (68–69 CE) When the Roman emperor Nero was overthrown in 68 CE the struggle for succession plunged the empire into civil war. The following twelve months saw Galba proclaimed as emperor in Spain but murdered on his return to Rome. His successor Otho committed suicide when Vitellius was proclaimed emperor in Germany. Finally Vespasian was declared emperor by his troops, invaded Italy and successfully claimed the throne. ✣46●

Yellow River
 BCE agricultural revolution ◆258 (1)
 massive floodings (1351) ✣71●

Yellow Turbans (*var.* Zhang Yue). Religious sectarian revolt of Later Han (184 CE), whose communal lifestyle and vision of a forthcoming age of 'Great Wellbeing' made them the most significant of the peasant revolts which attended Han decline. ✣47●, ◆260 (1)

Yellowknife River Expedition by Franklin (1821) ✣119●, ◆119 (3)

Yeltsin, Boris Nikolayevich (1931–) First president of Russia after the break-up of the Soviet Union in 1991. He oversaw the transformation of the Russian economy to a free market. In increasingly poor health and faced with the threat of impeachment, he resigned at the end of 1999. ✣214

Yenan *see* Yan'an

Yermak, Timofeyevich (d.1585) Russian Cossack whose campaign against the Tartar khanate across the centrals Urals (1581) led to the first Russian settlement of Siberia. Killed in a counter-offensive, his achievement initiated the systematic Russian exploration, occupation and settlement of Siberia. ✣257●, ◆257 (2)

Yi dynasty (*var.* I, Li, Ri, 1392–1910). Ruling dynasty of Korea, founded by Yi Songgye with Ming support. ✣71●

Yijing (*var.* I-ching). Chinese Buddhist pilgrim of late 7th century CE who visited the hearth of Buddhism by sea (685–695). ◆256 (1)

Yi Songgye *see* Yi dynasty

Yom Kippur War (6 Oct 1973). War in which Egypt and Syria launched a joint surprise attack on Israel on the Jewish festival of Yom Kippur. The war ended three weeks later when Israel had repulsed Syria, and crossed the Suez Canal, encircling an Egyptian army. Following UN cease-fire, Israel withdrew from Egyptian side of Canal and, after 1979 treaty, from Sinai. ✣234, ◆234 (2)

York Viking stronghold ✣60●, ✣185●

Yorkshire Cotton towns ◆93 (4)

Yorktown, Siege of ⚔ of American Revolutionary War (28 Sep–19 Oct 1781). American victory. ◆127 (3)

Yoruba People of W Africa, noted for urban cultures on lower reaches of Niger, whose kingdom of Oyo emerged as one of the most powerful in the region until the early 18th century. ✣86, ◆164 (2), ◆165 (4), ◆166 (1), ◆167 (3) (4)

Young Turks The failure of the Ottoman sultan, Abdul Hamid II, to modernize the empire led in 1908 to a revolution by the Young Turks, an association of army officers and reformers. The sultan was forced to restore the suspended constitution before his deposition in 1909. The Young Turks subsequently became the empire's dominant political party. ✣232
 See also Atatürk.

Younghusband, Francis (1863–1942) British explorer of Central Asia. In 1902 led the expedition which opened up Tibet to the western world, leading to Anglo-Tibetan Treaty (1904). ◆257 (3)

Yuan dynasty (1206–1367) Ruling Mongol dynasty of China. ✣67●, ✣263, ✣263●, ✣266, ◆263 (7)

Yuan Shih-k'ai *see* Yuan Shikai

Yuan Shikai (*var.* Yuan Shih-k'ai) (1859–1916). First president of the Republic of China in 1912 after the 1911 revolution. Precipitated civil war in 1913 by murdering the revolutionary party chairman and trying to create a new imperial dynasty. ✣271●

Yucatan
 Maya city-states ✣122, ◆122 (2)
 Maya civilization (1000 BCE) ✣121, ✣122●, ◆122 (2)
 Olmec civilization (1200 BCE) ✣30, ◆121 (4)
 ◆124 (1)

Yuezhi Tribal people of SC Asia who were unified under the Kushanas (c.60 CE) ✣47

Yugoslavia 208–215
 civil war (1991) ✣110●
 conflict ✣215, ✣215●, ◆215 (3)
 copper mines (c.4000 BCE) ✣174
 creation ◆208 (1)
 Second World War *see* Wars, Second World

Yukon
 Bluefish Cave settlement (13,000 BCE) ✣14●
 gold rush ✣93, ❑93, ◆93 (3)

Yungang Caves Datong, north central China, site of first colossal Buddhist rock-carvings, c.460 CE ❑49

Z

Zagwe dynasty (1137–1270). Ruling dynasty of Ethiopia, whose interregnum in the Solomonian line was marked by fragmentation and a move away from the ancient capital of Axum.
 church ❑62
 established in Ethiopia (1150) ✣63●

Zaire
 as Congo, Katanga secedes from Republic ✣107●
 President Mobutu overthrown (1997) ✣111●
 See also Congo

Zama ⚔ of Punic Wars (202 BCE). Decisive Roman victory. ◆179 (3)

Zangi (*aka* Imad al-Din Zangi, 1084–1146). Seljuk governor of Mosul (1126), who carved out an independent state around Aleppo, and whose capture of Edessa from the Franks (1144) caused the Second Crusade. Assassinated by associates whilst campaigning to capture Damascus. Succeeded by his son, Nur al-Din (1144) ✣65●

Zanzibar Arab trading settlements ✣58, ✣61, ◆162 (1)

Zapata, Emiliano (1879–1919) Mexican revolutionary. Following the outbreak of the Mexican Revolution (1910–17), Zapata organized the occupation of large estates, demanding the return of land to the people. His forces were mainly responsible for bringing down the dictatorship of Porfirio Diaz, and he later opposed the government of Venustiano Carranza. He continued agrarian reform in the south, setting up the Rural Loan Bank. ✣133, ◆133 (3)

Zapotec culture Pre-Columbian Middle American Indians whose culture flourished in southern Mexico between 300 BCE–300 CE. They were centred on Monte Albán and produced the earliest hieroglyphic inscriptions in the Americas.
 ✣34, ✣38●, ✣121, ◆121 (2)

Zen Buddhism Sectarian form of Buddhism developed and practised in China, Korea and Japan, based on intense meditation, austere discipline, and monasticism, seeking to achieve enlightenment through non-rational forms of thought. Frequently associated with martial arts and intense aestheticism. ✣49●, ✣63●

Zeus Greek god ❑37
 Sanctuary of (776 BCE), ✣31●
 See also Jupiter

Zhang Qian (*var.*Chang Ch'ien) (d.c.114 BCE). Han diplomat and ambassador whose travels in Central Asia seeking Han allies against the Xiongnu make him the earliest recorded explorer. Imprisoned by the Xiongnu for ten years (139–129 BCE), he escaped and travelled to Ferghana and Bactria, returning to China in 126 BCE. Reports of his journeys, which marked out the Silk Road, including a second trip to Parthia (115), encouraged Han expansion in Central Asia.
 explorer of Central Asia (138–126 BCE)
 ✣256, ◆256 (1), ✣260

Zhang Yue *see* Yellow Turbans

Zhao Rugua (*var.* Chao Ju-kua) 13th-century Chinese traveller, contemporary of Marco Polo, who recorded his journeys in Southeast Asia. ✣256●

Zheng He (var. Cheng Ho) (1371–1435) Chinese admiral and emissary of the emperor Chengzu. Undertook expeditions to SE Asia, India, Arabia and Africa.
 exploration of Africa ◆156 (3)
 Indian Ocean voyages ✣75●, ✣77
 silk painting of a giraffe ❑266, ✣267, ◆267 (3)

Zhengzhou
 plan of city ✣29, ◆29 (4)
 Shang capital ✣27●

Zhongdu Jin capital ✣69

Zhou dynasty (*var.* Chou). (1111–256 BCE). Chinese dynasty that overthrew the Shang dynasty in 1027 BCE. The Western Zhou developed political unity until 770 BCE, when the Eastern Zhou established a new capital at Luoyang and rivalry and dissent between the states eroded centralized power. The Zhou confederation collapsed into civil war (the Warring States period, 403–221 BCE) and was brought to an end by the Qin dynasty. ✣35, ✣30–1, ◆259 (4)
 bronze ritual vessel ❑31
 exploration of BCE China ✣256●
 Taoism ◆37 (4)

Zhou Enlai (*var.* Chou en-lai) (1898–1976) Chinese statesman, founder member of the Chinese Communist Party, and loyal supporter of Mao Zedong. Active during Japanese and Civil wars, became prime minister upon Communist victory (1949) until his death, also serving as foreign minister (1949–58). Generally moderate, in favour of detente, he established the Four Modernizations programme (1975). ✣270–271●

Zhu Siben (*var.* Chu-ssu-pen) (1273–1337). Chinese map-maker of Yuan (Mongol) dynasty, whose Atlas comprised a single-scale map of China and its neighbours, with details extending to the Indian Ocean, and most of the African coastline. ❑77, ❑256

Zhu Yuanzhang (*var.* Taizu, Hung-wu [mightily martial] emperor, Chu Yuan-chang) (1328–98). Founder and first emperor of Chinese Ming dynasty (r.1366–98). Born into poverty, he became a monk in 1344, before joining a bandit gang. Rose to become leader of a rebel army which seized Nanjing (1356) and over the next 12 years overthrew the Mongol (Yuan) rulers, proclaiming the Ming imperial dynasty in 1366. ✣71, ✣266, ❑266

ziggurat Built in Sumeria and adjacent Elam, these are temples constructed on a high pyramidal mound with a series of external stairways on all sides leading to a surmounting shrine. ✣220

Zimbabwe
 decolonizaton ◆168 (1)
 struggle for majority rule ✣168
 See also Great Zimbabwe, Rhodesia

Zimri-Lim Palace constructed (2300 BCE) ✣27●

Zirids Muslim dynasty ◆57 (2)

zodiac Thracian fresco (BCE) ❑39

Zollverein The customs union of German states organized in 1834 under Prussian auspices. It marked an important step towards German unification ✣203, ◆203 (3)

Zoroastrianism A monotheistic religion dating back to the Achaemenid era founded by Zoroaster (Zarathustra, Zardushi), a Persian or Bactrian prophet who lived from about 628–551 BCE. The roots of Zoroastrianism lay in the ancient polytheistic folk-myths of India, from which Zoroaster abstracted a single Wise God, Ahura Mazda, opposed by the Evil Spirit Angra Mainyu. After the Greek and Roman eras, the Sassanians restored Zoroastrianism as Persia's state religion. Its modern adherents are the Parsees. ✣51, ✣226, ❑36, ◆49 (4), ◆226 (1)

Zoser, King (*var.* Djoser, Netjerykhet) (c.2650–c.2575 BCE) Egyptian ruler of the 3rd dynasty. His reign was a period of technical innovation and cultural flowering, including the construction of Egypt's first stone buildings; formerly they were made of bricks and mud. He initiated the building of the first step pyramid, at Saqqara, the first structure of its size in the world. ✣23●, ❑159

Zulu kingdom Kingdom in southern Africa which arose under Zulu leader Shaka (r.1816–28), who with a well-disciplined and efficient fighting force, conquered most of present-day Natal.
 expansion ✣166●
 struggle for South Africa ✣92●, ◆92 (1), ◆166 (2)

Key to index: ✣ text ● timeline ❑ picture ◆ map *var.* variant name *aka* also known as *f/n* full name *prev.* previously known as r. ruled ⚔ battle WW I First World War WW II Second World War

INDEX-GAZETTEER

Glossary of Abbreviations

This glossary provides a comprehensive guide to the abbreviations used in this Atlas, in the Subject Index and Glossary and in the Index-Gazetteer.

A
abbrev. abbreviated
Afr. Afrikaans
aka also known as
Alb. Albanian
Amh. Amharic
anc. ancient
approx. approximately
Ar. Arabic
Arm. Armenian
ASEAN Association of South East Asian Nations
ASSR Autonomous Soviet Socialist Republic
Aust. Australian
Az. Azerbaijani
Azerb. Azerbaijan

B
Basq. Basque
BCE before Common Era
Bel. Belorussian
Ben. Bengali
Ber. Berber
B-H Bosnia-Herzegovina
Bibl. Biblical
bn billion (one thousand million)
BP British Petroleum
Bret. Breton
Brit. British
Bul. Bulgarian
Bur. Burmese

C
C central
C. Cape
Cam. Cambodian
Cant. Cantonese
CAR Central African Republic
Cast. Castilian
Cat. Catalan
Chin. Chinese
CIS Commonwealth of Independent States
Cro. Croat
Cz. Czech
Czech Rep. Czech Republic

D
Dan. Danish
Div. Divehi
Dom. Rep. Dominican Republic
Dut. Dutch

E
E east
EC see EU
EEC see EU
ECU European Currency Unit
EMS European Monetary System
Eng. English
est estimated
Est. Estonian
EU European Union (previously European Community [EC], European Economic Community [EEC])

F
Faer. Faeroese
Fij. Fijian
Fin. Finnish
Flem. Flemish
fl. Floruit
Fln. full name
Fr. French
Fris. Frisian
ft foot/feet
FYROM Former Yugoslav Republic of Macedonia

G
Gael. Gaelic
Gal. Galician
GDP Gross Domestic Product (the total value of goods and services produced by a country excluding income from foreign countries)
Geor. Georgian
Ger. German
Gk Greek
GNP Gross National Product (the total value of goods and services produced by a country)

H
Heb. Hebrew
HEP hydro-electric power
Hind. Hindi
hist. historical
Hung. Hungarian

I
I. Island
Icel. Icelandic
In. Inuit (Eskimo)
Ind. Indonesian
Intl International
Ir. Irish
Is Islands
It. Italian

J
Jap. Japanese

K
Kaz. Kazakh
Kir. Kirghiz
km kilometre(s)
km² square kilometre (singular)
Kor. Korean
Kurd. Kurdish

L
L. Lake
Lao. Laotian
Lapp. Lappish
Lat. Latin
Latv. Latvian
Liech. Liechtenstein
Lith. Lithuanian
Lux. Luxembourg

M
m million/metre(s)
Mac. Macedonian
Maced. Macedonia
Mal. Malay
Malg. Malagasy
Malt. Maltese
mi. mile(s)
mod. modern
Mong. Mongolian
Mt. Mountain
Mts Mountains

N
N north
NAFTA North American Free Trade Agreement
Nep. Nepali
Neth. Netherlands
Nic. Nicaraguan
Nor. Norwegian
NZ New Zealand

O
off. officially/ official name

P
Pash. Pashtu
Pers. Persian
PNG Papua New Guinea
Pol. Polish
Poly. Polynesian
Port. Portuguese
prev. previously known as

R
r. ruled
Rep. Republic
Res. Reservoir
Rmsch Romansch
Rom. Romanian
Rus. Russian
Russ. Fed. Russian Federation

S
S south
SCr. Serbo-Croatian
Sinh. Sinhala
Slvk. Slovak
Slvn. Slovene
Som. Somali
Sp. Spanish
St., St Saint
Strs Straits
Swa. Swahili
Swe. Swedish
Switz. Switzerland

T
Taj. Tajik
Th. Thai
Thai. Thailand
Tib. Tibetan
Turk. Turkish
Turkm. Turkmenistan

U
UAE United Arab Emirates
Uigh. Uighur
UK United Kingdom
Ukr. Ukrainian
UN United Nations
Urd. Urdu
US/USA United States of America
USSR Union of Soviet Socialist Republics
Uzb. Uzbek

V
var. variant
Vtn. Vietnamese

W
W west
Wel. Welsh
WWI First World War
WWII Second World War

Y
Yugo. Yugoslavia

This index lists all the place names and features shown on the maps in this Atlas.

Place name spelling

The policy followed throughout the Atlas is to use the contemporary historical name or spelling appropriate for the period or theme of the map. English conventional names, where they exist, have been used for international features e.g. oceans and country names.

All European language spellings use full diacritics, but no diacritics have been used for transliterated spellings (e.g. from Chinese or Cyrillic).

In translating Chinese names, the Pinyin system has been used throughout the Atlas, although alternative spelling systems have been cross referred.

In spelling pre-Columbian Central and South American names, the later addition of Spanish accents has been avoided.

The index also contains commonly-found alternative names and variant spellings, which are fully cross-referenced.

Index structure

All main entry names are those of settlements unless otherwise indicated by the use of italicized definitions.

In order to avoid unnecessary repetition, the names of frequently recurring states on the World Era Overview maps have been omitted. Those places which *only* appear on the World Era Overview maps have been included.

A

Aachen *anc.* Aquae Grani, Aquisgranum; *Dut.* Aken, *Fr.* Aix-la-Chapelle Central Europe (Germany) early modern states *193* (4) economy *190* (1) Franks *184* (2) medieval states *188* (1), (2) Reformation *195* (5) WWI *206* (3)
Aarhus *var.* Århus Scandinavia (Denmark) medieval states *185* (3)
Abadan *oil terminal* Southwest Asia (Iran) economy *234* (1)
Abai *see* Blue Nile
Abaj Takalik Central America (Mexico) first civilizations *121* (2)
Abancay South America (Peru) Incas *147* (3)
Abay Wenz *see* Blue Nile
Abbasid Caliphate *state* Southwest Asia early Islam *57* (2) medieval states *185* (3) Mongols *68–69* (1)
Abbeville France medieval states *192* (2)
Abdera Greece ancient Greece *177* (1), (2), (3)
Abéché *see* Abeshr
Abenaki *people* North America colonization *126* (1)
Abensberg *battle* Central Europe (Germany) Napoleon *200–201* (1)
Aberbrothock *see* Arbroath
Aberdeen *anc.* Devana British Isles (United Kingdom) medieval states *188* (2)
Abergwaun *see* Fishguard
Abertawe *see* Swansea
Aberteifi *see* Cardigan
Aberystwyth British Isles (Wales) medieval states *188* (2)
Abeshr *mod.* Abéché Central Africa (Chad) Islam *163* (1)
Abhiras *dynasty* South Asia first empires *241* (5) world religions *242* (2)
Abhisara *state* South Asia first empires *241* (5)
Abidjan West Africa (Ivory Coast) economy *168* (2)
Abina South Asia (India) medieval voyages *61* (3)
Abitibi *people* North America cultural groups *123* (3)
Abkhazia *region* Southwest Asia Soviet Union *214–215* (4)
Åbo Scandinavia (Finland) early modern states *195* (3) medieval states *189* (3)
Åbo *see* Surabaya
Abodrites *people* Central Europe Franks *184* (2)
Aboriginal Hunter-Gatherers of Australia *people* Australia the world in 2500 BCE *22–23 see also* Australian Aborigines
Abu Dhabi *var.* Abū Zabī; *Ar.* Abū Zaby Southwest Asia (United Arab Emirates) 20th-century politics *233* (4) economy *234* (1) exploration *219* (4)
Abu Dulaf Southwest Asia (Iraq) early Islam *57* (3)
Abu Hurayrah *see* Abu Hureyra
Abu Hureyra *var.* Abu Hurayrah Southwest Asia (Syria) the world in 5000 BCE *18–19*
Abuja *state* West Africa the world in 1850 *90–91*
Abu Rawash Egypt ancient Egypt *159* (3)
Abu Salabikh Southwest Asia (Iraq) first cities *220* (2)
Abu Simbel *early food production site* Egypt early agriculture *158* (1)
Abusir Egypt ancient Egypt *159* (2), (3)
Abū Zabī *see* Abu Dhabi
Abū Zaby *see* Abu Dhabi
Abydos *var.* Abydus Egypt ancient Egypt *159* (2), (3), (4), (5) first cities *28–29* (1) first civilizations *24* (2)
Abydos *var.* Abydus *settlement/state* Southwest Asia (Turkey) ancient Greece *177* (2) first civilizations *177* (1)
Abydus *see* Abydos
Abyssinia *mod.* Ethiopia *state* East Africa 20th-century politics *233* (4) European imperialism *96* (1), *97* (4) trade *165* (3), *167* (1) WWII *104* (2) *see also* Ethiopia
Acachinamco Central America (Mexico) Aztecs *124* (3)
Acadia *mod.* Nova Scotia *region* North America the world in 1700 *82–83 see also* Nova Scotia
Acalbixca Central America (Mexico) Aztecs *124* (2)
Acancéh Central America (Mexico) first civilizations *123* (2)
Acanthus *settlement/state* Greece ancient Greece *177* (2), (3)
Acapulco *var.* Acapulco de Juárez Central America (Mexico) European expansion *80–81* (1), *81* (3), *84–85* (1) exploration *143* (3) first civilizations *122* (1) US economy *136* (2)
Acapulco de Juárez *see* Acapulco
Acarí South America (Peru) Incas *147* (3)
Acarnania *state* Greece ancient Greece *179* (4)
Acatitla Central America (Mexico) Aztecs *124* (3)
Acatlan Central America (Mexico) first civilizations *122* (1)
Acayocan Central America (Mexico) Aztecs *124* (3)
Accho *see* Acco, Acre
Acco *mod.* 'Akko; *Bibl.* Accho, Ptolemaïs; *Eng.* Acre, *Fr.* Saint-Jean-d'Acre Southwest Asia (Israel) ancient Egypt *159* (5) *see also* Acre
Accra *var.* Fort James West Africa (Ghana) colonization *167* (4) economy *168* (2) empire and revolution *88* (1) slave trade *165* (4) trade *164* (2)
Aceh *see* Achin
Acemhüyük Southwest Asia (Turkey) first cities *28–29* (1)
Achaea *see* Achaia
Achaean League *var.* Principality of Achaia *state* Greece the world in 250 BCE *38–39 see also* Achaia
Achaia *var.* Achaea Greece ancient Greece *177* (3)
Achaia, Principality of *see* Achaean League
Achalapura South Asia (India) early medieval states *244* (2)
Acheh *see* Achin
Achin *var.* Acheh, Atchin, Atjeh; *mod.* Aceh Maritime Southeast Asia (Indonesia) colonialism *247* (4) early medieval states *245* European imperialism *97* (3) post-war politics *253* (4) trade *267* (3)
Acolapissa *people* North America colonization *126* (1)
Acolhuacan *state* Central America Aztecs *124* (1)
Acoma *people* North America colonization *126* (1)
Açores *see* Azores
Açores, Arquipélago dos *see* Azores
Açores, Ilhas dos *see* Azores
Acragas Italy first civilizations *177* (1)
Acre *mod.* 'Akko; *prev.* Acco; *Bibl.* Accho, Ptolemaïs; *Fr.* Saint-Jean-d'Acre Southwest Asia (Israel) crusades *228* (2), *65* (3) economy *190* (1) exploration *219* (3) medieval states *187* (5) Mongols *229* (3), *68* (2) Napoleon *200–201* (1) *see also* Acco
Acre *state* South America empire and revolution *151* (3)
Acropolis *temple* Greece ancient Greece *177* (4)
Acrothooi *state* Greece ancient Greece *177* (2)
Actaeon Islands *island group* Pacific Ocean exploration *278* (1)
Actium *Gk.* Aktion Greece the world in 1 CE *42–43*
Acton *battle* North America (USA) the growth of the US *129* (2)
Adab Southwest Asia (Iraq) first cities *220* (2) first civilizations *24* (3)
Adal *state* East Africa Islam *163* (1) trade *165* (3)
Adalia *mod.* Antalya; *prev.* Attalia; *anc.* Attaleia Southwest Asia (Turkey) 20th-century politics *233* (3) crusades *65* (3), *64–65* (2) *see also* Attalia
Adamawa *region* West Africa Islam *167* (3)
Adamawa Highlands *Mountain range* West Africa economy *163* (2)
Adamello *mountain* Italy WWI *207* (5)
'Adan *see* Aden, Eudaemon Arabia
Adana *var.* Seyhan Southwest Asia (Turkey) 20th-century politics *233* (3) early Islam *56–57* (1) Ottomans *230* (1)
Adare, Cape *headland* Antarctica Antarctic Exploration *287* (3)
Ad Dawḩah *see* Doha
Addis Ababa *Amh.* Ādīs Ābeba East Africa (Ethiopia) colonization *167* (4) economy *168* (2)
Adelaide Australia colonization *282* (1), (2), *283* (3), *284–285* (1) exploration *279* (2), (3) imperial global economy *92* (1)
Adélie, Terre *physical region* Antarctica Antarctic Exploration *287* (3)
Adelong *goldfield* Australia colonization *282* (2)
Aden *var.* Eudaemon Arabia; *Ar.* 'Adan, *Chin.* A-tan Southwest Asia (Yemen) ancient trade *44–45* (1) biological diffusion *72–73* (1) early Islam *56–57* (1), *57* (2) European expansion *84–85* (1) exploration *156* (3), *219* (4) imperial global economy *92* (1) Islam *163* (1), *226* (2), *227* (4) medieval voyages *61* (3) Mongols *68* (2) Ottomans *231* (3) trade *230* (2), *267* (3) 20th-century politics *233* (4) *see also* Eudaemon Arabia
Adena North America (USA) first religions *36* (1)
Adena *burial mound* North America (USA) first civilizations *121* (4)
Adena/Hopewell Culture *people* North America the world in 250 BCE *38–39* the world in 1 CE *42–43*
Adena Park *burial mound* North America (USA) first civilizations *121* (4)
Aden, Gulf of *var.* Badyarada 'Adméd *gulf* Southwest Asia early agriculture *158* (1) early cultures *161* (3), (4), (5) early trade *225* (3) economy *163* (2), (3) exploration *218* (2) Islam *163* (1) Ottomans *231* (3) slave trade *165* (4) Timur *229* (4) trade *165* (3), *230* (2) 20th-century politics *233* (4)
Aden Protectorate *colonial possession/state* Southwest Asia 20th-century politics *233* (4) Cold War *109* (1) WWII *104* (1)
Adige *Ger.* Etsch *river* Italy WWI *207* (5)
Ādīs Ābeba *see* Addis Ababa
Admiralty Islands *island group* Pacific Ocean early cultures *280–281* (3) medieval voyages *60* (2) WWII *272* (1), *273* (2)
Adobe Walls *battle* North America (USA) the growth of the US *129* (2)
Adrar Bous West Africa (Niger) early agriculture *158* (1)
Adrar Tioueïne North Africa (Algeria) early agriculture *158* (1)
Adria *see* Hadria
Adrianople *mod.* Edirne; *anc.* Adrianopolis, Hadrianopolis *Christian archbishopric/settlement* Southwest Asia (Turkey) Roman empire *182* (1) crusades *64–65* (2) medieval states *187* (5), *189* (4) Ottomans *195* (4), *230* (1), *231* (3) Reformation *194* (2) world religions *48* (1) WWI *207* (6) *see also* Adrianopolis, Edirne, Hadrianopolis
Adrianopolis *battle* Southwest Asia (Turkey) great migrations *52–53* (1)
Adriatic Sea *sea* Southeast Europe Roman empire *179* (3) Bronze Age *175* (3) Copper Age *174* (2) early agriculture *174* (1) early modern states *193* (4) early states *178* (1), (2) economy *190* (1) empire and revolution *202* (3) first civilizations *177* (1) civil war *209* (3), (5) medieval states *183* (4), *187* (5), *188* (1), *189* (4) Ottomans *230* (1) post-war economy *213* (5), *214* (2), *215* (3) post-war politics *212* (3) Reformation *194* (2) WWI *207* (5), (6)
Adulis *settlement/state* East Africa (Eritrea) ancient trade *44* (2), *44–45* (1) early cultures *160* (1), *161* (3), (4), (5) early trade *225* (3)
Adventure Bay *bay* Australia exploration *278* (1)
Adwuku West Africa (Ghana) early agriculture *158* (1)
Adygeya *region* Eastern Europe Soviet Union *214–215* (4)
Aegae Greece Hellenistic world *40–41* (1)
Aegates *mod.* Isole Egadi *island group* Italy Roman empire *179* (3)
Aegean Sea *Gk.* Aigaíon Pélagos, Aigaío Pélagos, *Turk.* Ege Denizi *sea* Greece/Turkey ancient Greece *177* (2), (3), *179* (4) Bronze Age *175* (3) early agriculture *174* (1) economy *190* (1) first civilizations *175* (4), *177* (1) medieval states *187* (5), *189* (4) Ottomans *197* (4), *230* (1) Reformation *194* (2) WWI *207* (6) WWII *210* (1), *211* (4) 20th-century politics *233* (3)
Aegina *var.* Aiyina, Egina *settlement/state* Greece ancient Greece *177* (2) first civilizations *175* (4)
Aegospotami *battle* Southwest Asia (Turkey) ancient Greece *177* (3)
Aegyptus *province* North Africa Roman empire *180–181* (1) ancient trade *44* (2)
Aelana Southwest Asia (Jordan) early cultures *161* (2), (3), (4), (5)
Aelaniticus, Sinus *see* Aqaba, Gulf of
Aelia Capitolina *see* Jerusalem
Aemona *see* Ljubljana
Aenea Greece ancient Greece *177* (2)
Aenus Greece first civilizations *177* (1), (2)
Aequi *people* Italy early states *178* (1), (2)
Aesernia *mod.* Isernia Italy early states *178* (1)
Aethiopia *region* East Africa ancient trade *44* (2)
Aetolia *region* Greece Hellenistic world *40–41* (1)
Afalou Bou Rhummel North Africa (Algeria) the world in 10,000 BCE *14–15*
Afars and Issas, French Territory of the *mod.* Djibouti; *prev.* French Somaliland *state* East Africa the world in 1975 *106–107* *see also* Djibouti, French Somaliland
Afghanistan *region/state* Central Asia Cold War *109* (1) colonialism *248* (1), (2), *269* (3), (4) Communism *271* (8) decolonization *250* (1), *251* (4) economy *249* (4) empire and revolution *249* (3) historical geography *275* (5) Islam *227* (4) medieval Persia *231* (4) Ottomans *232–233* (1) post-war economy *253* (5) post-war politics *252* (1), *253* (4) Soviet Union *208* (2), *213* (4) the world in 1950 *102–103* the modern world *113* (3), (4) US superpower *138* (1) world religions *226* (1), *243* (4) WWII *251* (3) 20th century *234* (2)
Afikpo *early food production site* West Africa (Nigeria) early agriculture *158* (1)
Africa *continent* *154-169*
Africa, Exarchate of *state* North Africa medieval states *183* (4)
Africa, Horn of *physical region* East Africa European expansion *84–85* (1) slave trade *165* (4) trade *165* (3)
Africa Nova *province* North Africa early cultures *161* (2)
Afuddo *mod.* Nimule East Africa (Sudan) exploration *157* (4), (5)
Afyeh *early food production site* Egypt early agriculture *158* (1)
Agadès *see* Agadez
Agadez *Fr.* Agadès West Africa (Niger) colonization *167* (4) early agriculture *158* (1) economy *163* (2) exploration *157* (4) Islam *163* (1)
Agadir North Africa (Morocco) exploration *157* (4)
Agartala South Asia (India) post-war politics *252* (1), (3)
Agatha *see* Agathe
Agathe *var.* Agatha; *mod.* Agde France first civilizations *177* (1)
Agde *see* Agathe
Agendicum *see* Sens
Aggassiz, Lake *lake* North America the world in 10,000 BCE *14–15*
Aghlabids *dynasty* North Africa early Islam *57* (2) Islam *227* (4)
Agincourt *battle* France medieval states *192* (2)
Aginsky Buryat AD *autonomous region* Siberia (Russian Federation) Soviet Union *214–215* (4)
Agordat *early food site* East Africa (Eritrea) early agriculture *158* (1)
Agra South Asia (India) colonialism *248* (1) early medieval states *244–245* (3) economy *249* (4) Mughal Empire *246* (1) post-war economy *253* (5) trade *267* (3)
Agra *state* South Asia Mughal Empire *246* (1)
Agra and Oudh, United Provinces of *see* Uttar Pradesh
Agram *see* Zagreb, Zágráb
Agri Decumates *region* Central Europe Roman empire *181* (4)
Agrigento *see* Agrigentum
Agrigentum *mod.* Agrigento Italy Roman empire *179* (3), *180–181* (1) first religions *37* (3)
Aguascalientes Central America (Mexico) Mexican Revolution *133* (3)
Agulhas, Cape *Afr.* Kaap Agulhas *headland* South Africa European imperialism *96* (2)
Agulhas, Kaap *see* Agulhas, Cape
Ahaggar *mountain range* North Africa ancient trade *44–45* (1) early cultures *160* (1) economy *163* (2) first humans *13* (2) historical geography *154–155* (1)
Ahe *island* Pacific Ocean exploration *278* (1)
Ah Kin Chel *state* Central America Aztecs *124* (1)
Ahmad *oil terminal* Southwest Asia (Kuwait) economy *234* (1)
Ahmadābād *see* Ahmadabad
Ahmadnagar *var.* Ahmednagar South Asia (India) Mughal Empire *246* (1)
Ahmadnagar *state* South Asia early medieval states *245* (4) Mughal Empire *246* (1)
Ahmedabad *var.* Ahmadābād South Asia (India) colonialism *247* (3), *248* (1) decolonization *250* (1) economy *249* (4) imperial global economy *93* (5) post-war economy *253* (5)
Ahmednagar *see* Ahmadnagar
Ahoms *dynasty* South Asia early medieval states *244–245* (3) Mughal Empire *246* (1)
Ahtena *people* North America cultural groups *123* (3)
Ahteut North America (USA) cultural groups *123* (3)
Ahu Akahanga *archaeological site* Pacific Ocean (Easter Island) early cultures *281* (4)
Ahu 'Akivi *archaeological site* Pacific Ocean (Easter Island) early cultures *281* (4)
Ahuehuetlan Central America (Mexico) Aztecs *124* (3)
Ahuilizapan Central America (Mexico) colonization *125* (5)
Ahu Ra'ai *archaeological site* Pacific Ocean (Easter Island) early cultures *281* (4)
Ahu Tongariki *archaeological site* Pacific Ocean (Easter Island) early cultures *281* (4)
Ahu Vinapu *archaeological site* Pacific Ocean (Easter Island) early cultures *281* (4)
Aichi *var.* Aiti *prefecture* Japan economy *270* (1)
Aigaíon Pélagos *see* Aegean Sea
Aigaío Pélagos *see* Aegean Sea
Aigues-Mortes France crusades *64–65* (2)
Aigun *see* Aihun
Aihun *var.* Aigun East Asia (China) colonialism *269* (4)
Ai Khanoum *see* Alexandria ad Oxum
Aikudi South Asia (India) early medieval states *244* (1)
Aila *var.* Elath; *mod.* Eilat, Elat Southwest Asia (Israel) medieval voyages *61* (3) *see also* Eilat, Elath
Ailah Southwest Asia (Israel) crusades *65* (3)
Ain Jalut *battle* Southwest Asia (Israel) Mongols *229* (3), *68–69* (1)
Ainu *people* Japan early modern states *265* (5) medieval states *262–263* (1), (2), *265* (3) trade *267* (3)
Air *state* West Africa slave trade *165* (4)
Airgialla *state* British Isles medieval states *188* (2)
Ais *people* North America colonization *125* (4), *126* (1)
Aisne *river* France WWI *206* (2), (3)
Aiti *see* Aichi
Aix-en-Provence France early modern states *197* (5)
Aix-la-Chapelle *see* Aachen
Aíyina *see* Aegina
Aizawl South Asia (India) post-war politics *252* (1)
Aizu Japan early modern states *267* (4)
Ajanta *Buddhist centre/settlement* South Asia (India) first religions *36* (2) world religions *49* (3)
Ajayameru *var.* Ajmer, Ajmere South Asia (India) early medieval states *244* (2) world religions *243* (4) *see also* Ajmer
Ajdabiya North Africa (Libya) early Islam *56–57* (1)
Ajman Southwest Asia (United Arab Emirates) first civilizations *24* (3)
Ajmer *var.* Ajayameru, Ajmere South Asia (India) colonialism *247* (3) Mughal Empire *246* (1) *see also* Ajayameru
Ajmer *var.* Ajmere *state* South Asia colonialism *248* (2) Mughal Empire *246* (1)
Ajmere *see* Ajmer, Ajayameru
Ajnadain Southwest Asia (Israel) Islam *226* (2)
Ajnadain *battle* Southwest Asia (Israel) early Islam *56–57* (1)
Akaba *see* Aelana, Aqaba
Akamagaseki *see* Shimonoseki
Akan States *state* West Africa Islam *163* (1) trade *164* (2)
Akaroa New Zealand colonization *283* (5)
Akbarpur South Asia (India) colonialism *247* (3)
Aken *see* Aachen
Akermanceaster *see* Bath
Akhaura South Asia (Bangladesh) post-war politics *252* (3)
Akhenaten Egypt ancient Egypt *159* (5)
Akhetaten *var.* Tell el-Amarna Egypt ancient Egypt *159* (5)
Akhisar *see* Thyatira
Akhmim *var.* Ipu Egypt ancient Egypt *159* (5)
Akira *early food production site* East Africa (Kenya) early agriculture *158* (1)
Akita Japan economy *270* (1) medieval states *264* (2), *265* (3), (4)
Akita *prefecture* Japan economy *270* (1)
Akjoujt *prev.* Fort-Repoux West Africa (Mauritania) early agriculture *158* (1)
Akkad Southwest Asia (Iraq) the world in 1250 BCE *26–27*
Akkad *state* Southwest Asia first civilizations *221* (4)
Akkerman Eastern Europe (Ukraine) Ottomans *195* (4)
'Akko *see* Acco, Acre
Ak Koyunlu *var.* Akkoyunlu, Aq Qoyunlu *state* Southwest Asia Islam *163* (1)
Akmola Central Asia (Kazakhstan) Soviet Union *214–215* (4)
Akmolinsk *region* Central Asia/Siberia colonialism *269* (3)
Akron North America (USA) US politics *135* (6)
Akrotiri Southwest Asia (Cyprus) first civilizations *175* (4)
Aksai Chin *Chin.* Aksayqin *region* South Asia post-war economy *275* (3) post-war politics *252* (1), (2)
Aksayqin *see* Aksai Chin
Aksha Egypt ancient Egypt *159* (5)
Aksu *var.* Aqsu East Asia (China) ancient trade *44–45* (1) early modern states *268* (1) empire and revolution *268* (2) medieval states *262–263* (1) world religions *49* (3)

Aksum East Africa (Ethiopia) ancient trade 44–45 (1) early cultures 160 (1), 161 (3), (4), (5) early trade 225 (3) world religions 49 (4)
Aktion see Actium
Akwamu state West Africa the world in 1700 82–83
Akwe Shavante people South America early cultures 147 (2)
Akyab Mainland Southeast Asia (Burma) trade 230 (2) WWII 272 (1), 273 (2)
Ala Italy WWI 207 (5)
Alabama state North America imperial global economy 93 (5) the growth of the US 129 (1) US Civil War 130 (2), (3), (4), (5), 131 (6), (7) US economy 134 (2), 139 (3) US society 137 (6) US superpower 139 (5)
Alabama people North America colonization 125 (4), 126 (1)
Alabama river North America US Civil War 131 (6)
Al-'Abbasa Egypt Mamluks 229 (3)
al Abyaḍ, Al Baḥr see White Nile
al Abyaḍ, An Nīl see White Nile
Alaca Hüyük Southwest Asia (Turkey) first cities 28–29 (1) first civilizations 221 (5)
Alacant see Alicante
Alaka people South America early cultures 145 (2)
Alalakh Greece ancient Egypt 159 (5)
Alalia mod. Aleria France first civilizations 177 (1) see also Aleria
Alamanni see Alemanni
Al 'Amārah see Amara
Alamgirpur archaeological site South Asia (India) first cities 240 (2)
Alamo, The battle North America (USA) the growth of the US 129 (2)
Alamut assassins site/settlement Southwest Asia (Iran) Mongols 229 (3), 68–69 (1) Seljuks 228 (1)
Alans people Eastern Europe Roman empire 181 (4) great migrations 52–53 , (1)
Al 'Arabīyah as Su'ūdīyah see Saudi Arabia
Alarcos Iberian Peninsula (Spain) Islam 192 (3)
Al 'Aṣab see Asab
Alasca, Golfo de see Alaska, Gulf of
Alashiya see Cyprus
Alaska prev. Russian America colonial possession/state North America Cold War 109 (1) colonialism 269 (3) Communism 273 (3) empire and revolution 88–89 (2) exploration 257 (2) imperial global economy 93 (3) the growth of the US 129 (2), 132 (1) US economy 136 (2) WWII 104 (1), 273 (2)
Alaska, Gulf of var. Golfo de Alasca gulf North America cultural groups 123 (3) exploration 118 (1), 119 (2), (3), 286 (1) the growth of the US 129 (2)
Alaska Range mountain range North America the growth of the US 129 (2)
Alavi South Asia (India) world religions 242 (3)
Albacete Iberian Peninsula (Spain) Civil War 209 (4)
Alba Fucens Italy early states 178 (1)
Al Baḥrayn see Bahrain
Albania Alb. Shqipëria state Southeast Europe Cold War 108 (3), 109 (1) early 20th century 206 (1) economy 205 (4) civil war 209 (3), (5) Ottomans 202 (4), 230 (1) post-war economy 213 (5), 214 (1), (2), 215 (3) post-war politics 212 (3) Soviet Union 213 (4) the modern world 112 (2), 113 (3), (4) WWI 208 (1) WWII 104 (1), 211 (2), (4)
Albanians people Southeast Europe the modern world 112 (2)
Albanus, Lacus lake Italy early states 178 (1)
Albanus, Mons mountain Italy early states 178 (1)
Albany penal colony/settlement Australia colonization 282 (1), 283 (3) environmentalism 285 (2) exploration 279 (2)
Albany North America (USA) colonization 126 (1) empire and revolution 127 (2), (3) exploration 119 (2) the growth of the US 129 (2), 132 (1) US politics 135 (6) US society 137 (6)
Alba Regia see Székesfehérvár
Al Başrah see Basra
Albert France WWI 206 (2), (3)
Alberta province North America the growth of the US 129 (2), 132 (1) US economy 136 (2)
Albert Edward Nyanza see Edward, Lake
Albert, Lake var. Albert Nyanza, Lac Mobutu Sese Seko lake East Africa early agriculture 158 (1) exploration 157 (4), (5) historical geography 154–155 (1) Islam 163 (1) slave trade 165 (4)
Albert Nyanza see Albert, Lake
Albi anc. Albiga France economy 190 (1)
Albiga see Albi
Albigensian crusade France crusades 186 (1)
Albion region British Isles ancient trade 44 (2)
Albis see Elbe
Alborz, Reshteh-ye Kūhhā-ye see Elburz Mountains
Albreda West Africa (Gambia) the world in 1700 82–83 empire and revolution 88 (1)
Albury Australia colonization 282 (1)
Alcacer Iberian Peninsula (Portugal) Islam 192 (3)
Alcántara Iberian Peninsula (Spain) crusades 186 (1) Islam 192 (3)
Alcobaça cistercian house Iberian peninsula (Spain) medieval states 187 (3)
Alcudia Iberian Peninsula (Spain) economy 190 (1)
Aldan river Eastern Europe early modern states 268 (1) Soviet Union 214–215 (4)
Aleksandrovka archaeological site Siberia (Russian Federation) early agriculture 258 (1)
Alemanni var. Alamanni people Central Europe Roman empire 181 (4), 182 (1) Franks 183 (5), (6) great migrations 53 (2) medieval states 182 (2)
Alemannia region Central Europe Franks 184 (2)
Alençon France early modern states 197 (5)
Alep see Aleppo
Aleppo var. Yamkhad; anc. Beroea; Ar. Ḥalab, Fr. Alep Southwest Asia (Syria) ancient Persia 223 (4) trade 72–73 (1) crusades 228 (2), 65 (1), (3) economy 190 (1) exploration 219 (3) first cities 28–29 (1) first civilizations 221 (4), (5) Islam 184 (1) Mongols 229 (3), 68–69 (1) Napoleon 200–201 (1) Ottomans 230 (1), 231 (3), 232–233 (1) Seljuks 228 (1) Timur 229 (4) trade 230 (2) world religions 226 (1) WWI 233 (2) 20th-century politics 233 (3)
Aleria France Roman empire 179 (3), 180–181 (1) early states 178 (2)
Alessandria Fr. Alexandrie Italy economy 190 (1), 190–191 medieval states 188 (1)
Aleut people North America cultural groups 123 (3)
Aleutian Islands island group North America cultural groups 123 (3) exploration 257 (2) the growth of the US 129 (2) US superpower 138 (1) WWII 272 (1), 273 (2)
Alexander, Empire of state Southwest Asia Hellenistic world 224 (1)
Alexandretta Turk. İskenderun Southwest Asia (Turkey) crusades 65 (3) WWI 233 (2)
Alexandria North America (USA) empire and revolution 127 (2)
Alexandria Ar. Al Iskandarīyah Egypt ancient Persia 225 (6) Roman empire 179 (5), 180–181 (1), 181 (3), (4), 182 (1), 224 (2), 225 (5) ancient trade 44 (2), 44–45 (1) plague 72–73 (1) colonization 167 (4) crusades 228 (2), 65 (3) early cultures 160 (1), 161 (2), (3) early Islam 57 (2) early trade 225 (3) economy 163 (2), 190 (1) exploration 156 (3), 157 (4), 218 (1), (2) first cities 240 (2) first empires 241 (4) Hellenistic world 224 (1), 41 (2) Islam 163 (1), 226 (2), 227 (4), (5) medieval states 185 (3) Mongols 229 (3) Napoleon 200–201 (1) Ottomans 232–233 (1) slave trade 165 (4) world religions 226 (1), 49 (4) WWI 233 (2) WWII 210 (1), 211 (4) 20th-century politics 233 (3)
Alexandria battle Egypt early Islam 56–57 (1) Islam 226 (2)
Alexandria ad Oxum var. Ai Khanoum Central Asia (Afghanistan) Hellenistic world 40–41 (1)
Alexandria Arachoton Central Asia (Afghanistan) Hellenistic world 40–41 (1)
Alexandria Areion var. Aria; mod. Herat Central Asia (Afghanistan) ancient trade 44–45 (1) exploration 218 (1), 219 (3) Hellenistic world 40–41 (1), 41 (2) see also Herat
Alexandria Eschate var. Kokand Central Asia (Uzbekistan) Hellenistic world 40–41 (1)
Alexandria Margiana mod. Merv Central Asia (Turkmenistan) Hellenistic world 41 (2)
Alexandrie see Alessandria
Alexandroupolis see Dedeagach
Al Fāshir see El Fasher
Al Faw var. Fao Southwest Asia (Iraq) economy 234 (1) see also Fao
Al Fujayrah see Fujairah
Al Furāt see Euphrates
Al Fustat Egypt early Islam 56–57 (1)
Algarve region Iberian Peninsula (Portugal) Islam 192 (3)
Alger see Algiers
Algeria prev. Algiers; anc. Icosium colonial possession/state North Africa early Islam 57 (2) economy 168 (2), (3) European imperialism 96 (1), 97 (4) Civil War 209 (4) Islam 235 (4) Ottomans 232–233 (1) the modern world 112 (1), 113 (3), (4) WWII 104 (1), 211 (4) Cold War 109 (1) colonization 167 (4) decolonization 168 (1) early 20th century 206 (1) see also Algiers
Algiers var. Al Jazair; Fr. Alger North Africa (Algeria) trade 72–73 (1) colonization 167 (4) crusades 186 (1) economy 168 (2), 190 (1) European expansion 84–85 (1) exploration 157 (4) Islam 184 (1) medieval states 185 (3) Napoleon 200–201 (1), 201 (2) Ottomans 231 (3), 232–233 (1) slave trade 165 (4) US superpower 138 (1) WWII 211 (4)
Algiers mod. Algeria; anc. Icosium state North Africa Napoleon 200–201 (1) slave trade 165 (4) trade 167 (1) see also Algeria
Algoa Bay bay South America exploration 156 (3)
Algonquin people North America colonization 126 (1) cultural groups 123 (3)
Al Hadhar see Hatra
Al Ḥaḍr see Hatra
Al-Hajj Umar Ahmadu Sefu state West Africa colonization 167 (4)
Al Hamad see Syrian Desert
Al Ḥijāz see Hejaz
Al Hira Southwest Asia (Iraq) early Islam 56–57 (1)
Al Hufūf see Hasa
Alicante Lat. Lucentum; Cat. Alacant Iberian Peninsula (Spain) economy 190 (1), 205 (4) Franks 184 (2) Civil War 209 (4) Islam 192 (3)
Alice Boër archaeological site South America (Brazil) early cultures 145 (2)
Alice Springs Australia colonization 283 (3) exploration 279 (2)
Alids dynasty Southwest Asia Islam 227 (4)
Aligarh South Asia (India) economy 249 (4)
Ali Kosh Southwest Asia (Iraq) early agriculture 220 (1)
Al Iskandarīyah see Alexandria
Al Jawf see Jauf
Al Jīzah see Giza
Al Kūfah see Kufa
Al-Kuwait see Kuwait
Al Kuwayt see Kuwait
Allada state West Africa the world in 1700 82–83
Allahabad South Asia (India) colonialism 247 (3), 248 (1) decolonization 250 (1) economy 249 (4) Mughal Empire 246 (1) post-war economy 253 (5)
Allahabad state South Asia Mughal Empire 246 (1)
'Allaqi, Wadi el- river Egypt ancient Egypt 159 (4)
Allen's Cave Australia exploration 280 (1)
Allia Bay archaeological site East Africa (Kenya) first humans 12 (1)
Allobroges people France Roman empire 179 (5)
Al Lubnān see Lebanon
Alma battle Eastern Europe (Ukraine) Ottomans 202 (4)
Alma-Ata Central Asia (Russian Federation) Soviet Union 213 (4)
Al Madain Southwest Asia (Iraq) early Islam 56–57 (1)
Al Madīnah see Medina
Al Mahdīyah see Mahdia
Almalyk var. Almalyq East Asia (China) biological diffusion 72–73 (1) Mongols 68–69 (1)
Al Manāmah see Manama
Al-Mariyya see Almeria
Almaty Central Asia (Kazakhstan) Soviet Union 214–215 (4)
Al Mawşil see Mosul
Almería anc. Unci; Lat. Portus Magnus; Ar. Al-Mariyya Iberian Peninsula (Spain) economy 190 (1) Civil War 209 (4) Islam 192 (3)
Almohad Empire state North Africa crusades 64–65 (2), 186 (1)
Almohads dynasty North Africa crusades 186 (1) early Islam 57 (2)
Almoravid Empire state Iberian Peninsula/North Africa crusades 64–65 (2) early Islam 57 (2)
Al Mukalla Southwest Asia (Yemen) exploration 219 (4)
Al Mukallā see Al Mukalla
Alodia state East Africa the world in 750 CE 54–55 the world in 1000 58–59
Alor South Asia (Pakistan) early medieval states 244 (2) world religions 243 (4)
Alpes Cottiae province France Roman empire 180–181 (1)
Alpes Graiae et Poeninae var. Alpes Penninae province France Roman empire 180–181 (1)
Alpes Maritimae province France Roman empire 180–181 (1)
Alpes Penninae see Alpes Graiae et Poeninae
Alpi see Alps
Alpi Giulie see Julian Alps
Alps Fr. Alpes, Ger. Alpen, It. Alpi mountain range Central Europe Roman empire 179 (3), 180–181 (1), 181 (3) Bronze Age 175 (3) Copper Age 174 (2) crusades 186 (1), 64–65 (2) early agriculture 174 (1) early Islam 56–57 (1), 57 (2) early modern states 193 (4), (5) economy 190 (1) European expansion 84–85 (1) exploration 172 (1) first religions 37 (3) Franks 183 (5), (6), 184 (2) great migrations 52–53 (1) medieval states 185 (3), 192 (1), (2) Napoleon 200–201 (1) Ottomans 232–233 (1) prehistoric culture 17 (3), (4) world religions 48 (1), 49 (4) WWI 207 (5) WWII 210 (1), 211 (4)
Al Qadisiya Southwest Asia (Iraq) ancient Persia 225 (6)
Al Qadisiya battle Southwest Asia (Iraq) Islam 226 (2)
Al Qāhirah see Cairo, Fustat
Al Qatif Southwest Asia (Saudi Arabia) exploration 219 (4)
Al Qayrawān see Kairouan
Al Quds see Jerusalem
Al Quds ash Sharīf see Jerusalem
Al Raydaniyya Egypt Ottomans 231 (3)
Alsace-Lorraine region France empire and revolution 202 (1i), (2) WWI 208 (1)
Alsium Italy early states 178 (1)
Alt see Olt
Altai region Siberia Soviet Union 214–215 (4)
Altai see Altai Mountains
Altaic Peoples people East Asia the world in 750 BCE 30–31
Al Ṭa'īf see Taif
Altai Mountains var. Altai; Chin. Altay Shan, Rus. Altay mountain range East Asia/Siberia ancient trade 44–45 (1) colonialism 269 (3), (4) early agriculture 258 (1) exploration 256 (1), 257 (3) first humans 13 (2) first states 260 (1) Hellenistic world 40 (1) medieval states 261 (6) Mongols 68–69 (1) trade 267 (3) world religions 49 (3), (4)
Altamira Central America (Mexico) first civilizations 121 (2)
Altamira archaeological site/settlement Iberian Peninsula (Spain) prehistoric culture 17 (3)
Altar de Sacrificios Central America (Mexico) first civilizations 121 (2)
Altar, Desierto de see Sonoran Desert
Altay see Altai Mountains
Altay Shan see Altai Mountains
Altepetlac Central America (Mexico) Aztecs 124 (3)
Altiplano physical region South America early cultures 145 (2), (4) politics 152 (2)
Alto Paraná see Paraná
Alto Ramírez South America (Chile) early cultures 146 (1)
Altun Shan mountain range East Asia early agriculture 258 (1) first states 260 (1)
Altxerri archaeological site Iberian Peninsula (Spain) prehistoric culture 17 (3)
Al Urdunn see Jordan
Alvastra monastery Scandinavia (Sweden) medieval states 187 (3)
Alwa state East Africa early cultures 160 (1), 161 (5) economy 163 (2)
Al Wajh see Wejh
Alwar South Asia (India) colonialism 247 (3)
Amabato South America (Ecuador) Incas 147 (3)
Amadzimba Southern Africa (South Africa) the world in 5000 BCE 18–19
Amakusa Japan early modern states 267 (4)
Amalfi Italy Franks 184 (2) medieval states 182 (2), 183 (4), 185 (3), 187 (5), 188 (1)
Amantlan Central America (Mexico) Aztecs 124 (3)
Amaquemecan Central America (Mexico) colonization 125 (5)
Amara var. Al 'Amārah Southwest Asia (Iraq) WWI 233 (2)
Amaravati Buddhist centre/settlement South Asia (India) early medieval states 244 (1) world religions 49 (3)
Amasia mod. Amasya Christian archbishopric Southwest Asia (Turkey) world religions 48 (1) see also Amasya
Amasya anc. Amasia Southwest Asia (Turkey) Ottomans 231 (3) see also Amasia
Amathus Southwest Asia (Cyprus) first civilizations 177 (1)
Amazon Port/Sp. Amazonas river South America colonization 148 (2), 149 (3), (4) early agriculture 20–21 (2) early cultures 144 (1), 145 (2), 146 (1), 147 (2) economy 153 (3) empire and revolution 150 (1), (2), 151 (3), 88 (1), 88–89 (2) environment 153 (4) European expansion 84–85 (1) exploration 142 (1), 143 (2), (3) global immigration 100 (1) global knowledge 76–77 imperial global economy 92 (1) Incas 147 (3), 148 (1) narcotics 153 (5) prehistoric culture 16 (1)
Amazonas see Amazon
Amazon Basin basin South America colonization 149 (3) early agriculture 20–21 (2) early cultures 145 (4), 147 (2) environment 153 (4) Incas 148 (1)
Ambala see Umballa
Ambianum see Amiens
Amboina prev. Ambon, Amboyna Maritime Southeast Asia (Indonesia) colonization 284–285 (1) empire and revolution 88 (1) WWII 272 (1), 273 (2)
Amboina var. Ambon; mod. Pulau Ambon island Maritime Southeast Asia colonialism 247 (4) Islam 243 (6) post-war politics 253 (4)
Ambon see Amboina
Ambon, Pulau see Amboina
Amboyna see Amboina
Ambracia Greece ancient Greece 177 (3), 179 (4)
Ameca Central America (Mexico) first civilizations 122 (1)
Amekni West Africa (Algeria) early agriculture 158 (1)
America see United States of America, North America, South America
American Samoa prev. Pago Pago colonial possession Pacific Ocean colonization 284–285 (1) decolonization 285 (3) exploration 279 (3) the growth of the US 133 (4) US superpower 138 (1) WWII 273 (2)
American Virgin Islands var. Virgin Islands of the United States; prev. Danish West Indies colonial possession West Indies Cold War 108 (2)
Amery Ice Shelf ice feature Antarctica Antarctic Exploration 287 (3)
Amida mod. Diyarbakir Christian archbishopric Southwest Asia (Turkey) world religions 48 (1) see also Diyarbakir
Amiens anc. Ambianum, Samarobriva France early modern states 197 (5) economy 190 (1) Franks 184 (2) medieval states 192 (2) Reformation 195 (5) WWI 206 (2), (3)
Amirante Islands var. Amirantes Group island group Indian Ocean the world in 1850 90–91 the world in 1900 94–95 the world in 1925 98–99
Amirantes Group see Amirante Islands
Amisus mod. Samsun Christian archbishopric/settlement Southwest Asia (Turkey) early cultures 161 (2) Hellenistic world 40–41 (1) world religions 48 (1)
Amjhera state South Asia empire and revolution 249 (3)
Amman var. 'Ammān; anc. Philadelphia, Bibl. Rabbah Ammon, Rabbath Ammon Southwest Asia (Jordan) early Islam 56–57 (1) Ottomans 232–233 (1) WWI 233 (2) 20th century 234 (2) 20th-century politics 233 (3), (4), 235 (5)
Ammon state Southwest Asia first civilizations 222 (1)
Amnok-kang see Yalu
Amol var. Amul Southwest Asia (Iran) Hellenistic world 40–41 (1) Mongols 68–69 (1)
Amoy see Xiamen
Amphipolis battle/settlement/state Greece ancient Greece 177 (2), (3)
Ampurias see Emporiae
Amri archaeological site South Asia (Pakistan) first cities 240 (2)
Amritsar South Asia (India) colonialism 247 (3), 248 (1) decolonization 250 (1) economy 249 (4) post-war politics 252 (1)
Amsa-dong archaeological site East Asia (South Korea) early agriculture 258 (1)
Amsterdam Low Countries (Netherlands) Cold War 108 (3) early modern states 193 (4) economy 198 (1), 205 (4) empire and revolution 202 (1), (1i), (2) European expansion 84–85 (1) global immigration 100 (1) Reformation 195 (5), 196 (1)
Amud archaeological site Southwest Asia (Israel) first humans 13 (2)
Amu Darya anc. Oxus; Rus. Amudar'ya, Taj. Dar"yoi Amu, Turkm. Amyderya, Uzb. Amudaryo river Central Asia ancient trade 44–45 (1) colonialism 248 (1), 269 (3) early Islam 56–57 (1), 57 (2) exploration 257 (3) first civilizations 24 (2), 25 (3) first humans 13 (2) Islam 226 (2), 227 (4), (5) medieval Persia 231 (4) Mongols 68 (2), 68–69 (1) Ottomans 232–233 (1) world religions 226 (1) see also Oxus
Amudaryo see Amu Darya
Amur region/state Siberia colonialism 269 (3), (4) early modern states 268 (1)
Amur Chin. Heilong Jiang river Siberia/East Asia ancient trade 44–45 (1) biological diffusion 72–73 (1) Chinese revolution 271 (5) colonialism 269 (3), (4) Communism 271 (8) early agriculture 20–21 (2), 258 (1) early modern states 265 (5) empire and revolution 268 (2) exploration 256 (1), 257 (2), (3) first states 260 (1) imperialism 270 (2) medieval states 261 (6), 262–263 (1), 263 (6), 264 (1), (2) Mongols 68–69 (1) post-war economy 275 (3) post-war politics 274 (2) Soviet Union 214–215 (4) trade 267 (3) world religions 49 (4)
Amyderya see Amu Darya
Ana Southwest Asia (Iraq) early Islam 56–57 (1)
Anadolu see Anatolia
Anadyr' Siberia (Russian Federation) exploration 287 (2)
Anadyr' see Anadyrsk
Anadyrsk var. Novomarinsk; mod. Anadyr' Siberia (Russian Federation) exploration 257 (2)
Anadyrskiy Khrebet see Chukot Range
Anahilapataka South Asia (India) the world in 750 CE 54–55
'Anakena Easter Island early cultures 281 (4)
Ananatuba archaeological site South America (Brazil) early cultures 144 (1), 145 (2)
Anartta state South Asia first empires 241 (5)
Anasazi Culture state North America the world in 1200 62–63
Anatolia physical region Southwest Asia plague 72–73 (1) Bronze Age 175 (3) crusades 64–65 (2) early agriculture 174 (1) early cultures 161 (2) early Islam 56–57 (1), 57 (2) economy 190 (1) exploration 218 (2), 219 (3) first cities 220 (2) first civilizations 175 (4), (5), 222 (2) first humans 13 (2) first religions 37 (3) global knowledge 76–77 (1) Hellenistic world 224 (1) historical geography 154–155 (1) Islam 227 (4) Mongols 68 (2), 68–69 (1) Ottomans 202 (4), 230 (1) Seljuks 228 (1) trade 230 (2) 20th-century politics 233 (3)
Anazarbus Christian archbishopric Southwest Asia (Turkey) world religions 48 (1)
Anbiya state West Africa trade 163 (4)
An Canul state Central America Aztecs 124 (1)
Anchorage North America (USA) exploration 287 (2)
Ancón archaeological site/settlement South America (Peru) early cultures 145 (3), 146 (1)
Ancona Italy Roman empire 180–181 (1), 181 (3) early cultures 161 (2) early modern states 193 (4) early states 178 (1) economy 190 (1), 205 (4) medieval states 188 (1)
Ancud see San Carlos de Ancud
Ancylus, Lake lake Scandinavia historical geography 170–171 (1)
Ancyra mod. Ankara, Eng. Angora Southwest Asia (Turkey) Roman empire 180–181 (1) Hellenistic world 40–41 (1) world religions 48 (1) see also Angora, Ankara
Andahuaylas South America (Peru) Incas 147 (3)
Åndalsnes Scandinavia (Norway) WWII 210 (1)
Andalucia region Iberian Peninsula (Spain) Islam 192 (3)
Andaman Islands island group South Asia ancient trade 44–45 (1) biological diffusion 72–73 (1) colonialism 248 (1), (2), 269 (4) decolonization 251 (4) European imperialism 97 (3) exploration 239 (1) historical geography 236–237 (1) medieval voyages 61 (3) post-war politics 253 (4) trade 230 (2), 267 (3) WWII 251 (3), 272 (1)
Andaman Sea sea Indian Ocean Bronze Age 240 (3) colonialism 247 (4), 248 (1), (2) decolonization 251 (4) early medieval states 245 (5), (6) European imperialism 97 (3) exploration 239 (1) medieval voyages 61 (3) Mongols 68–69 (1) post-war economy 253 (5) post-war politics 253 (4) world religions 243 (5) WWII 251 (3)
Andean Chiefdoms state South America the world in 500 CE 50–51 the world in 750 CE 54–55 the world in 1300 66–67
Andes mountain range South America colonization 148 (2) early agriculture 20–21 (2) early cultures 144 (1), 145 (2), (3), (4), 146 (1), 147 (2) empire and revolution 150 (1), (2), 151 (3) environment 153 (4) European expansion 84–85 (1) exploration 142 (1), 143 (2), (3) global knowledge 76–77 (1) imperial global economy 92 (1) Incas 147 (3), 148 (1) narcotics 153 (5) politics 151 (4) prehistoric culture 16 (1)
Andha state South Asia first empires 241 (5)
Andhapura South Asia (India) first empires 241 (4)
Andhra region/state South Asia first empires 241 (5) medieval states 261 (6) world religions 242 (2), 243 (4), 49 (3)
Andhra Pradesh region South Asia post-war politics 252 (1)
Anding province East Asia first states 260 (1)
Andong var. Antung; mod. Dandong; Jap. Antō East Asia (South Korea) colonialism 269 (4) Sino-Japanese War 270 (3) the growth of the US 133 (4) see also Dandong
Andorra Cat. Valls d'Andorra, Fr. Vallée d'Andorre state Iberian Peninsula empire and revolution 199 (4), 202 (1) Islam 192 (3) medieval states 192 (1), (2) Napoleon 200–201 (1) the modern world 112 (2)
Andravida Greece medieval states 189 (4)
Andronovo archaeological site/settlement Siberia (Russian Federation) early agriculture 258 (1)
Andros Greece ancient Greece 177 (3)
Andros island/state Greece ancient Greece 177 (2) Ottomans 230 (1)
Androsovo see Andrusovo
Andrusovo mod. Androsovo Eastern Europe (Russian Federation) empire and revolution 198 (2)
Anga region/state South Asia ancient India 242 (1) first religions 36 (2) world religions 242 (3)
Angara river Eastern Europe early agriculture 258 (1) first states 260 (1)
Angel North America (USA) cultural groups 122 (5)
Angers anc. Juliomagus settlement/university France crusades 186 (1) empire and revolution 199 (4) Franks 184 (2) medieval states 187 (3) see also Juliomagus
Angevin Empire state British Isles/France the World in 1300 66–67 (1)
Angkor Mainland Southeast Asia (Cambodia) biological diffusion 72–73 (1) early medieval states 245 (6) medieval states 262–263 (1) Mongols 68 (2) world religions 243 (5), 49 (4)
Angkor Borei see Naravaranagara
Angles people Central Europe Roman empire 181 (4) great migrations 53 (2)
Angles-sur-l'Anglin archaeological site France prehistoric culture 17 (3), (4)
Anglia see England
Anglo-Egyptian Sudan mod. Sudan state East Africa 20th-century politics 233 (4) European imperialism 96 (1), 97 (4) WWII 104 (1) see also Sudan
Anglo-Saxon Kingdoms state British Isles medieval states 182 (2)
Angola prev. People's Republic of Angola, Portuguese West Africa state Southern Africa Cold War 109 (1), (5) decolonization 168 (1) economy 168 (2), (3) European expansion 84–85 (1) European imperialism 96 (1), 97 (4) slave trade 165 (4) the modern world 112 (1), 113 (4) trade 164 (2), 167 (1)
Angora mod. Ankara; anc. Ancyra Southwest Asia (Turkey) 20th-century politics 233 (3) Ottomans 232–233 (1) WWI 233 (2) see also Ancyra, Ankara
Ango-Saxons people British Isles Roman empire 182 (1) medieval states 182 (2)
Angostura mod. Ciudad Bolívar South America (Venezuela) empire and revolution 150 (1), (2) exploration 143 (3) see also Ciudad Bolivar
Angoulême anc. Iculisma France Franks 184 (2)
Anguilla colonial possession West Indies Cold War 108 (2)
An-hsi see Anxi
Anhui var. Anhwei, Wan province East Asia Chinese revolution 271 (5) early modern states 268 (1) empire and revolution 268 (2) post-war politics 271 (7), 274 (2)
Anhui Clique movement East Asia Chinese Civil War 271 (6)
Anhwei see Anhui
Aniba var. Miam Egypt ancient Egypt 159 (4)
Anio river Italy early states 178 (1)
Anjengo South Asia (India) colonialism 247 (3)
Anjidiv Island South Asia (India) colonialism 247 (3)
Anjou France medieval states 187 (4)
Anjou region France medieval states 187 (4)
Anju East Asia (North Korea) Sino-Japanese War 270 (3)
Ankara prev. Angora, anc. Ancyra Southwest Asia (Turkey) early Islam 56–57 (1) first civilizations 221 (4) Napoleon 200–201 (1), 201 (3) Ottomans 230 (1) Timur 229 (4) WWI 233 (2) WWII 210 (1), 211 (4) Cold War 108 (3) see also Angora, Ancyra
Ankole state East Africa colonization 167 (4)
An Loc battle Mainland Southeast Asia (Vietnam) post-war politics 251 (5)
Annaba prev. Bône North Africa (Algeria) economy 168 (2) see also Bône
Annam mod. Trung Phân state Mainland Southeast Asia biological diffusion 72–73 (1) colonialism 269 (4) early modern states 266 (1), (2), 268 (1) European expansion 80–81 (1) European imperialism 97 (3), (4) medieval states 262–263 (1), 263 (3), (6) Mongols 68–69 (1) trade 267 (3)
Annanduhufu East Asia (China) medieval states 262–263 (1)
Annapolis North America (USA) the growth of the US 129 (2)
Anniston North America (USA) US society 137 (6)
Annomadu West Africa (Ghana) empire and revolution 88 (1)
Anping East Asia (China) first states 260 (1)
Anshan Southwest Asia (Iran) first cities 28–29 (1) first civilizations 24 (2), 25 (3)
Antakya see Antioch
Antalya see Adalia, Attalia
Antananarivo Madagascar economy 168 (2) politics 169 (4)
Antandros see Antandrus
Antandrus var. Antandros state Greece ancient Greece 177 (2)
Antarctica continent 286-287
Antarctic Peninsula coastal feature Antarctica Antarctic exploration 287 (3)
Antequera see Oaxaca
Antietam North America (USA) US Civil War 131 (6)
Antigua island West Indies empire and revolution 88 (1) WWII 104 (2)
Antigua river South America colonization 125 (5)
Antigua and Barbuda state West Indies the modern world 112 (1) US economy 136 (2) US politics 139 (4)
Antioch mod. Antakya; anc. Antiochia Southwest Asia (Turkey) ancient Persia 225 (6) Roman empire 180–181 (1), 181 (3), (4), 224 (2), 225 (5) ancient trade 44–45 (1) crusades 228 (2), 65 (3) early cultures 161 (2) early trade 225 (3) economy 190 (1) first religions 37 (3) Hellenistic world 224 (1), 41 (2) Islam 184 (1), 226 (2), 227 (5) medieval states 185 (3), 187 (5) Mongols 229 (3), 68 (2) Seljuks 228 (1) world religions 226 (1)
Antiochia var. Antiochia Pisidiae, Eng. Antioch in Pisidia Southwest Asia (Turkey) Roman empire 180–181 (1)
Antiochia Pisidiae see Antiochia
Antioch in Pisidia see Antiochia
Antioch, Principality of state Southwest Asia crusades 228 (2), 65 (3) medieval states 187 (5)
Antioquia South America (Colombia) empire and revolution 150 (2)
Antissa state Greece ancient Greece 177 (2)
Antium mod. Anzio Italy early states 178 (1) see Anzio
Antō see Andong, Dandong
Antofagasta South America (Chile) empire and revolution 151 (3) environment 153 (4) politics 151 (4)
Antonine Wall Lat. Vallum Antonini wall British Isles Roman empire 180–181 (1)
Antoniniana, Aqua aqueduct Italy Roman empire 181 (2)
Antoninianae, Thermae see Caracalla, Baths of
Antonini, Vallum see Antonine Wall
Antonio Plaza archaeological site Central America (Mexico) first civilizations 121 (3)
An tSionainn see Shannon
Antung see Andong, Dandong
Antwerp Fr. Anvers Low Countries (Belgium) early modern states 193 (4) economy 190 (1), 205 (4) empire and revolution 202 (1i) global immigration 100 (1) medieval states 188 (1), 192 (2) Reformation 195 (5) WWI 206 (2), (3)
Anupa region/state South Asia first empires 241 (5) world religions 242 (2)
Anuradhapura South Asia (Sri Lanka) early medieval states 244 (1), (2) exploration 256 (1) first empires 241 (4) world religions 49 (3)
Anuta var. Cherry Island island Pacific Ocean early cultures 280–281 (3) medieval voyages 60 (2)
Anu Ziggurat building Southwest Asia (Iraq) first cities 220 (3)
Anvers see Antwerp
Anxi var. An-hsi East Asia (China) ancient trade 44–45 (1) biological diffusion 72–73 (1) exploration 256 (1) medieval states 262–263 (1)
Anyang archaeological site/settlement East Asia (China) early agriculture 258 (2) early systems 32 (1), 33 (2), (3) first cities 259 (3), (4), 28–29 (1)
Anyi East Asia (China) first cities 259 (3), (5) first religions 37 (4)
Anyi vassal state East Asia first cities 259 (3)
Anzio battle/settlement Italy WWII 105 (3), 211 (4)
Aomen see Macao
Aomori Japan Communism 273 (3) economy 270 (1)
Aomori prefecture Japan economy 270 (1)
Aóos see Vjosë
Aornos battle Central Asia (Tajikistan) Hellenistic world 40–41 (1)
Aotearoa mod. New Zealand state New Zealand early cultures 280–281 (3) medieval voyages 60 (2)
Ao Thai see Siam, Gulf of; Thailand, Gulf of
Apache people North America colonization 126 (1)
Apalachee people North America colonization 125 (4), 126 (1)
Apamea Southwest Asia (Turkey) Hellenistic world 40–41 (1), 41 (2) world religions 48 (1)
Aparanta region South Asia first empires 241 (4)
Aparanta/Pascad-Desa region South Asia early religions 48 (2)
Apatzingán Central America (Mexico) first civilizations 122 (1)
Apennines mountain range Central Europe Roman empire 179 (3) early states 178 (1), (2) economy 190 (1) medieval states 183 (4) Napoleon 200–201 (1)
Aphrodisias Southwest Asia (Turkey) Hellenistic world 40–41 (1)
Aphytis settlement/state Greece ancient Greece 177 (2)
Apollo religious site Southwest Asia (Turkey) first religions 37 (3)
Apollo II Cave archaeological site Southern Africa (Namibia) prehistoric culture 17 (2)
Apollonia mod. Sozopol; prev. Sizebolu Southeast Europe (Bulgaria) ancient Greece 179 (4) first civilizations 177 (1) Hellenistic world 40–41 (1)
Apollonis Southwest Asia (Turkey) Hellenistic world 41 (2)
Apologos Southwest Asia (Kuwait) early trade 225 (3)
Appalachian Mountains mountain range North America colonization 126 (1) cultural groups 122 (5) early agriculture 120 (1), 20–21 (2) exploration 118 (1), 119 (2), (3) first civilizations 121 (4) the growth of the US 129 (2)
Appia, Aqua aqueduct Italy Roman empire 181 (2)
Appian Way see Via Appia
Appia, Via Eng. Appian Way road Italy Roman empire 181 (2) early states 178 (1)
Appomattox North America (USA) US Civil War 131 (7)
Apuli people Italy early states 178 (1), (2)
Apulia region Italy medieval states 183 (4)
Apulum prev. Bălgrad, Karlsburg, Károly-Fehérvár; Ger. Karlsburg, Weissenburg Hung. Gyulafehérvár, Rom. Alba Iulia Southeast Europe (Romania) Roman empire 180–181 (1) world religions 48 (1) see also Gyulafehérvár
Apure river South America empire and revolution 150 (1) exploration 143 (3) politics 152 (1)
Aqaba var. Akaba, 'Aqabah; anc. Aelana, Elath Southwest Asia (Jordan) 20th century 234 (2) 20th-century politics 233 (4) WWI 233 (2)
Aqaba, Gulf of var. Gulf of Elat; anc. Sinus Aelaniticus; Ar. Khalīj al 'Aqabah gulf Southwest Asia crusades 65 (3) 20th century 234 (2)
'Aqabah, Khalīj al see Aqaba, Gulf of
Aq Qoyunlu see Ak Koyunlu
Aqsu see Aksu
Aqua Antoniniana aqueduct Italy Roman empire 181 (2)
Aqua Appia aqueduct Italy Roman empire 180–181 (1)
Aqua Claudia aqueduct Italy Roman empire 181 (2)
Aquae Calidae see Bath
Aquae Grani see Aachen
Aquae Solis see Bath
Aqua Marcia aqueduct Italy Roman empire 181 (2)
Aqua Traiana aqueduct Italy Roman empire 181 (2)
Aqua Virgo aqueduct Italy Roman empire 181 (2)
Aquila Italy medieval states 189 (4)
Aquileia Italy Roman empire 179 (5), 180–181 (1), 181 (3) ancient trade 44–45 (1) great migrations 52–53 (1) medieval states 182 (2), 185 (3) world religions 48 (1)
Aquiles Serdán Central America (Mexico) first civilizations 121 (2)
Aquincum mod. Budapest legion headquarters Central Europe (Hungary) Roman empire 180–181 (1) see also Buda, Budapest
Aquisgranum see Aachen
Aquitaine mod. Guyenne; anc. Aquitania region France Franks 183 (6), 184 (2) medieval states 187 (4) see also Aquitania, Guyenne
Aquitania province France Roman empire 180–181 (1)
Arabia region Southwest Asia ancient Persia 223 (4) Roman empire 180–181 (1) ancient trade 44 (2) crusades 65 (1) exploration 156 (3), 157 (4), 218 (1), (2), 219 (3), (4), 239 (1) Islam 226 (2), 227 (4), (5) medieval voyages 61 (3) Mongols 68 (2) the modern world 113 (4) world religions 226 (1)
Arabian Desert var. Aş Şaírā' ash Sharqiyah; Eng. Eastern Desert desert Egypt ancient Egypt 159 (2), (3), (5) early agriculture 220 (1) early trade 225 (3) first cities 220 (2) first civilizations 221 (4) see also Eastern Desert
Arabian Peninsula physical region Southwest Asia ancient Egypt 159 (5) ancient Persia 223 (4) plague 72–73 (1) early agriculture 20–21 (2) early cultures 160 (1), 161 (3) early Islam 57 (2) early systems 223 (3) economy 163 (2) first civilizations 222 (2) Hellenistic world 41 (2) imperial global economy 92 (1) Islam 163 (1) medieval Persia 231 (4) medieval states 261 (6) Ottomans 231 (3), 232–233 (1) prehistoric culture 16 (1) slave trade 165 (4) trade 165 (3), 230 (2), 267 (3) world religions 49 (4) WWI 233 (2)
Arabian Sea var. Sinus Arabicus sea Indian Ocean ancient Persia 225 (6)

ancient trade 44–45 (1) trade 72–73 (1) colonialism 247 (3), 248 (1), (2) decolonization 251 (4) early agriculture 20–21 (2) early Islam 57 (2) early medieval states 244 (1), 244–245 (3) early religions 48 (2) early trade 225 (3) economy 249 (4) empire and revolution 249 (3), 88–89 (2) exploration 156 (3), 218 (1), (2), 219 (4), 239 (1) first cities 28–29 (1) first civilizations 24 (2), 25 (3) first religions 36 (2) Hellenistic world 224 (1) historical geography 236–237 (1), 275 (5) Islam 227 (4) Marathas 246 (2) medieval states 261 (6) medieval voyages 61 (3) Mongols 229 (3), 68–69 (1) post-war economy 253 (5) post-war politics 252 (1) Timur 229 (4) trade 230 (2) world religions 243 (4), 49 (3) WWII 251 (3) see also Arabicus, Sinus

Arabicus, Sinus sea Indian Ocean ancient trade 44 (2)

'Arab, Khalīj al see Persian Gulf

Arabs people Southwest Asia Roman empire 181 (4), 182 (1) ancient trade 44–45 (1) historical geography 275 (5) medieval states 182 (2) Ottomans 232–233 (1)

Aracaju South America (Brazil) politics 152 (1)

Arachosia region South Asia ancient Persia 223 (4) first empires 241 (4) Hellenistic world 224 (1)

Aradus Fr. Rouad; Bibl. Arvad; later Arwad Southwest Asia (Lebanon) first civilizations 177 (1) Hellenistic world 40–41 (1)

Arafura Sea Ind. Laut Arafuru sea Southeast Asia Bronze Age 240 (3) colonization 282 (1), 283 (3) European imperialism 97 (3) exploration 279 (2) Islam 243 (6) world religions 243 (5) WWII 272 (1), 273 (2)

Arafuru, Laut see Arafura Sea

Arago archaeological site Iberian Peninsula (France) first humans 13 (2)

Aragon Sp. Aragón state Iberian Peninsula crusades 186 (1), 64–65 (2) early modern states 194 (1) Islam 192 (3) medieval states 187 (3), (4), 192 (1), (2) Reformation 196 (2)

Araguaia var. Araguaya, Rio Araguaia river South America colonization 149 (3) early cultures 144 (1), 145 (2) environment 153 (4)

Araguaia, Río see Araguaia

Araguaya see Araguaia

Arakan prev. Candra state Mainland Southeast Asia colonialism 269 (4) early medieval states 245 (6) Mughal Empire 246 (1) see also Candra

Araks var. Aras Nehri river Southwest Asia first civilizations 24 (2), 25 (3)

Aral Sea Kaz. Aral Tengizi, Rus. Aral'skoye More, Uzb. Orol Dengizi inland sea Central Asia ancient Persia 225 (6) ancient trade 44–45 (1) colonialism 269 (3) Communism 271 (8) early Islam 56–57 (1), 57 (2) exploration 172 (1), 218 (2), 219 (3), 256 (1) first humans 13 (2) global knowledge 76–77 (1) Hellenistic world 224 (1) historical geography 275 (5) Islam 226 (2), 227 (4) medieval states 261 (6), 262–263 (1) Mongols 68 (2), 68–69 (1) Ottomans 232–233 (1) Seljuks 228 (1) Soviet Union 208 (2), 213 (4) Timur 229 (4) trade 230 (2), 267 (3) world religions 226 (1), 49 (3), (4)

Aral'skoye More see Aral Sea

Aral Tengizi see Aral Sea

Araluen goldfield Australia colonization 282 (2)

Aram var. Syria state Southwest Asia first civilizations 222 (1) see also Syria

Aramaeans people Southwest Asia first civilizations 221 (5)

Aram-Damascus state Southwest Asia first civilizations 222 (1)

Aramis hominid site Central Africa (Chad) first humans 12 (1)

Aram-Zobah state Southwest Asia first civilizations 222 (1)

Araouane Lake lake West Africa historical geography 154–155 (1)

Ara Pacis building Italy Roman empire 181 (2)

Arapaho people North America colonization 126 (1)

Araquinoid people South America the world in 500 CE 50–51 the world in 1000 58–59 the world in 1300 66–67

Ararat goldfield Australia colonization 282 (2)

Arash battle Southwest Asia (Azerbaijan) medieval Persia 231 (4)

Aras Nehri see Araks

Araucanians people South America early cultures 147 (2)

Arausio mod. Orange church council France world religions 48 (1) see also Orange

Aravali Range mountain range South Asia colonialism 247 (3), 248 (1) early medieval states 244 (1), 244–245 (3) first cities 240 (2) Mughal Empire 246 (1) world religions 243 (4)

Arawak people West Indies colonization 125 (4)

Arawe Islands island group New Guinea early cultures 280–281 (3) medieval voyages 60 (2)

Araxes river Southwest Asia Hellenistic world 40–41 (1)

Arbela var. Erbil, Irbīl, mod. Arbīl, Kurd. Hawlēr Christian archbishopric/settlement Southwest Asia (Iraq) exploration 218 (1) Hellenistic world 40–41 (1) world religions 48 (1) see also Arbil

Arbela battle Southwest Asia (Turkey) Roman empire 224 (2)

Arbil Southwest Asia (Iraq) 20th-century politics 235 (5)

Arbroath anc. Aberbrothock British Isles (United Kingdom) medieval states 188 (2)

Archangel Rus. Arkhangel'sk Eastern Europe (Russian Federation) economy 205 (4) European expansion 80–81 (1) exploration 257 (2), 286 (1), 287 (2) Soviet Union 208 (2), 213 (4) WWII 210 (1), 211 (4) see also Arkhangel'sk

Arcole battle Italy Napoleon 200–201 (1)

Arcot South Asia (India) colonialism 248 (1)

Arctic region North America early agriculture 120 (1) exploration 286-287

Arctic hunter-gatherers people Eastern Europe/Siberia/North America the world in 1250 BCE 26–27

Arctic Ocean ocean cultural groups 123 (3) early agriculture 120 (1) empire and revolution 88 (1), 88–89 (2) European expansion 80–81 (1), 81 (2) exploration 257 (2), 286 (1), 287 (2) first humans 13 (2) global immigration 100 (1) medieval states 185 (3), 262–263 (1) Soviet Union 208 (2), 213 (4) the growth of the US 129 (2), 132 (1), 133 (4) US superpower 138 (1) WWII 104 (1), (2), 105 (3), 211 (4) Cold War 109 (1) colonialism 269 (3)

Arcy-sur-Cure archaeological site France prehistoric culture 17 (3)

Ardabil Southwest Asia (Iran) early Islam 56–57 (1) Islam 226 (2), 227 (4) medieval Persia 231 (4) medieval states 185 (3)

Ardea Italy early states 178 (1)

Ardeal see Transylvania

Ardennes battle Low Countries (Belgium) WWII 105 (3)

Ardennes physical region Low Countries (Belgium) WWI 206 (2), (3) WWII 211 (4)

Ardwick British Isles economy 204 (2)

Arelas see Arelate, Arles

Arelate mod. Arles Christian archbishopric/settlement France Roman empire 180–181 (1) world religions 48 (1) see also Arles

Arene Candide Italy early agriculture 174 (1)

Areopagus building Greece ancient Greece 177 (4)

Arequipa South America (Peru) colonization 148 (2) empire and revolution 151 (3) environment 153 (4) politics 151 (4)

Ares, Temple of temple Greece ancient Greece 177 (4)

Arezzo anc. Arretium settlement/university Italy economy 190 (1) medieval states 187 (3) see also Arretium

Argentina prev. Argentine Confederation state South America empire and revolution 151 (3) global immigration 100 (1), 101 (2) imperial global economy 92 (1) narcotics 153 (5) politics 151 (4), 152 (1), (2) the growth of the US 133 (4) the modern world 112 (1), 113 (4) US superpower 138 (1) WWII 105 (3) Cold War 109 (1) economy 153 (3) see also Argentine Confederation

Argentine Confederation mod. Argentina state South America the world in 1850 90–91 see also Argentina

Argentoratum mod. Strasbourg legion headquarters/mithraic site France Roman empire 180–181 (1) world religions 48 (1) see also Strasbourg, Strassburg

Argeş battle Southeast Europe (Romania) WWI 207 (6)

Argesh Southeast Europe (Romania) Ottomans 230 (1)

Argilus state Greece ancient Greece 177 (2)

Arginusae Insulae see Arginusae Islands

Arginusae Islands Lat. Arginusae Insulae battle Greece ancient Greece 177 (3)

Argissa Greece early agriculture 174 (1)

Argonne France WWI 206 (2), (3)

Argos Greece ancient Greece 177 (3), 179 (4) first civilizations 175 (4), 177 (1)

Arguin West Africa (Mauritania) European expansion 84–85 (1)

Arguin Island island West Indies the world in 1500 74–75 the world in 1600 78–79 the world in 1700 82–83 the world in 1800 86–87 the world in 1850 90–91

Århus see Aarhus

Aria province/region Central Asia ancient Persia 223 (4) ancient trade 44 (2) Hellenistic world 40–41 (1)

Aria see Alexandria Areion, Herat

Arica prev. San Marcos de Arica South America (Chile) colonization 148 (2) empire and revolution 150 (1), 151 (3) environment 153 (4) European expansion 81 (3) politics 151 (4)

Arica battle South America (Chile) politics 151 (4)

Aricara battle North America (USA) the growth of the US 129 (2)

Aricia Italy early states 178 (1)

Arīḥā see Jericho

Arikara people North America colonization 126 (1)

Ariminum mod. Rimini Italy Roman empire 179 (3), 180–181 (1) early states 178 (1), (2) world religions 48 (1) see also Rimini

Arisbe settlement/state Southwest Asia (Turkey) ancient Greece 177 (2)

Aristé people South America the world in 1300 66–67

Arizona region/state North America Mexican Revolution 133 (3) the growth of the US 129 (1) US economy 134 (2)

Arizpe fort Central America (Mexico) colonization 125 (4)

Arkansas region North America imperial global economy 93 (5) the growth of the US 129 (1) US Civil War 130 (2), 130 (3), (4), (5), 131 (6), (7) US economy 134 (2), 139 (3) US society 137 (6) US superpower 139 (5)

Arkansas river North America colonization 125 (4), 126 (1) cultural groups 122 (5) exploration 118 (1), 119 (2) first civilizations 121 (4) the growth of the US 129 (2) US Civil War 131 (6)

Arkat mod. Arcot South Asia (India) Mughal Empire 246 (1) see also Arcot

Arkhangel'sk Eng. Archangel Eastern Europe (Russian Federation) Cold War 108 (3) Soviet Union 214–215 (4) see also Archangel

Arles var. Arles-sur-Rhône; anc. Arelas, Arelate France economy 190 (1) Franks 183 (5), (6), 184 (2) medieval states 188 (1) see also Arelate

Arles, Kingdom of state Central Europe/France medieval states 188 (1)

Arles-sur-Rhône see Arelate, Arles

Arlit West Africa (Niger) early agriculture 158 (1)

Armagaon South Asia (India) colonialism 247 (3)

Armagnac region France medieval states 192 (2)

Armant anc. Hermonthis Egypt ancient Egypt 159 (2), (4), (5)

Armenia prev. Armenian Soviet Socialist Republic; anc. Urartu; Arm. Hayastan region/state Southwest Asia ancient Persia 223 (4), 225 (6) Roman empire 180–181 (1), 181 (3), (4), 224 (2), 225 (5) ancient trade 44 (2), 44–45 (1) crusades 65 (3) early Islam 56–57 (1) economy 234 (1) Hellenistic world 224 (1) Islam 226 (2), 227 (4), (5), 235 (4) medieval Persia 231 (4) medieval states 185 (3), 187 (5) Ottomans 232–233 (1) post-war economy 214 (2) Soviet Union 208 (2), 214–215 (4) world religions 226 (1) WWI 233 (2) 20th-century politics 233 (3) see also Armenian Soviet Socialist republic, Urartu

Armenian Rulers state Southwest Asia Seljuks 228 (1)

Armenians people Southwest Asia Ottomans 232–233 (1)

Armenian Soviet Socialist Republic state Southwest Asia 20th-century politics 233 (3)

Armstrong region North America first civilizations 121 (4)

Arnhem Low Countries (Netherlands) WWII 211 (4)

Arno see Arnus

Arnus mod. Arno river Italy early states 178 (1)

Aromata East Africa (Somalia) ancient trade 44–45 (1)

Arpi Italy early states 178 (1)

Arras anc. Nemetocenna France early modern states 197 (5) economy 190 (1) empire and revolution 199 (4) medieval states 192 (2) Reformation 195 (5) WWI 206 (2), (3)

Arretium mod. Arezzo Italy Roman empire 180–181 (1) early states 178 (1), (2) first civilizations 177 (1) see also Arezzo

Arriaca see Guadalajara

Ar Riyāḍ see Riyadh

Arroyo Sonso archaeological site Central America (Mexico) first civilizations 121 (3)

Ar Rub 'al Khali Eng. Empty Quarter, Great Sandy Desert desert southwest Asia exploration 219 (4) historical geography 170–171 (1) 20th-century politics 233 (4)

Ar Rutbah var. Rutba Southwest Asia (Iraq) 20th-century politics 235 (5)

Arsenal var. Darsena building Italy economy 191 (3)

Arsur battle Southwest Asia (Israel) crusades 65 (3)

Arta anc. Ambracia Greece medieval states 189 (4) see also Ambracia

Artacoana Central Asia (Afghanistan) Hellenistic world 40–41 (1)

Artashat Christian patriarchate Southwest Asia (Armenia) world religions 48 (1)

Artemita Southwest Asia (Iraq) Hellenistic world 41 (2)

Artois region France medieval states 192 (2) Reformation 195 (5)

Arua people South America the world in 1400 70–71

Aruaki people South America early cultures 147 (2)

Aruba island West Indies the world in 1800 86–87 the world in 1850 90–91 the modern world 110–111

Aru Islands island group Maritime Southeast Asia exploration 239 (2)

Arumvale Australia the World in 10,000 BCE 14–15

Arunachal Pradesh prev. North East Frontier Agency region South Asia post-war economy 275 (3) post-war politics 252 (1)

Arvac people South America the world in 1500 74–75 the world in 1600 78–79 the world in 1700 82–83

Arvad see Aradus

Arvand Rūd see Shatt al 'Arab Waterway

Arverni people France Roman empire 179 (5)

Arwad see Aradus

Aryan people South Asia ancient India 242 (1)

Asab Ar. Al 'Aṣab oil field Southwest Asia economy 234 (1)

Asabon Southwest Asia (Oman) ancient trade 44–45 (1)

Asahikawa Japan economy 270 (1)

Asaku Japan medieval states 264 (1)

Asante var. Ashanti state West Africa colonization 167 (4) slave trade 165 (4) trade 167 (1)

Ascalon mod. Ashqelon Southwest Asia (Israel) ancient Egypt 159 (5) crusades 64–65 (2), 65 (3)

Ascension island Atlantic Ocean exploration 156 (3)

Ascensión Central America (Mexico) Mexican Revolution 133 (3)

Ascension Island see Pohnpei, Ponape

Ascoli Satriano see Asculum

Asculum mod. Ascoli Satriano Italy early states 178 (1)

Asejire West Africa (Nigeria) early agriculture 158 (1)

Ashanti see Asante

A Shau battle Mainland Southeast Asia (Vietnam) post-war politics 251 (5)

Ashburton New Zealand colonization 283 (5)

Ashburton River river Australia prehistoric culture 17 (5) colonization 282 (1) exploration 279 (2)

Ashgabat prev. Poltoratsk, earlier Ashkhabad Central Asia (Turkmenistan) Soviet Union 214–215 (4) see also shkhabad

Ashkhabad mod. Ashgabat; prev. Poltoratsk Central Asia (Turkmenistan) colonialism 269 (3) see also Ashgabat

Ashmaka region South Asia ancient India 242 (1) world religions 242 (2)

Ashmore and Cartier Islands colonial possession Indian Ocean global immigration 100 (1)

Ashqelon see Ascalon

Ash Shām see Damascus

Ash Shāriqah see Sharjah

ash Sharqīyah, Aş Şaḥrā' see Arabian Desert, Eastern Desert

Ashur Southwest Asia (Iraq) early systems 223 (3) first cities 220 (2) first civilizations 221 (4), 222 (2), 25 (3)

Asia continent 216-255 ancient trade 44–45 (1) plague 73 (3) crusades 65 (1) early agriculture 20–21 (2) early Islam 56–57 (1), 57 (2) early systems 32 (1), 33 (2), (3) empire and revolution 88 (1) European expansion 80–81 (1), 81 (2), (3) European imperialism 96 (1) exploration 156 (3), 172 (1), (2), 219 (3), 287 (2) first humans 13 (2) first religions 36 (1) global immigration 100 (1), 101 (3) historical geography 154–155 (1) imperial global economy 93 (2) Ottomans 232–233 (1) trade 230 (2), 267 (3) world religions 49 (4)

Asia province Southwest Asia Roman empire 179 (5), 180–181 (1)

Asiago Italy WWI 207 (5)

Asia Minor region Southwest Asia Roman empire 224 (2) ancient trade 44–45 (1) plague 72–73 (1) crusades 65 (1) early systems 223 (3) exploration 172 (1) Islam 226 (2), 227 (5) Ottomans 231 (3) world religions 226 (1), 49 (4)

Asiana province Southwest Asia Roman empire 181 (4)

Asir state Southwest Asia the world in 1925 98–99

Asir Ar. 'Asīr mountain range Southwest Asia 20th-century politics 233 (4) exploration 219 (4)

Asmaka region/state South Asia first empires 241 (5) first religions 36 (2)

Asmara East Africa (Eritrea) economy 168 (2) politics 169 (4)

Aspadana see Isfahan

Aspern-Essling battle Central Europe (Germany) Napoleon 200–201 (1)

Aspero early ceremonial centre/settlement South America (Peru) early cultures 144 (1)

Asphaltites, Lacus see Dead Sea

Aspinwall see Colón

Assam region/state South Asia colonialism 248 (2), 269 (4) decolonization 250 (2) early modern states 266 (1) economy 249 (4) Mughal Empire 246 (1) post-war politics 252 (1), (3), 253 (4)

Assamese States state South Asia the world in 1500 74–75 the world in 1600 78–79

Assassins people Southwest Asia crusades 65 (3)

Assiniboin people North America colonization 126 (1)

Assinie West Africa (Ivory Coast) the world in 1700 82–83

Assiout see Asyut

Assisi Italy medieval states 187 (3)

Assiut see Asyut

Asslou see Bir Aslu

Assos settlement/state Southwest Asia (Turkey) ancient Greece 177 (2)

Assouan see Aswân, Qus, Syene

Assuan see Aswân, Qus, Syene

Assus Southwest Asia (Turkey) first civilizations 177 (1)

As Suways see Suez

Assyria province Southwest Asia ancient Persia 223 (4)

Asta Colonia see Asti

Astacus settlement/state Southwest Asia (Turkey) ancient Greece 177 (2)

Astana Buddhist centre East Asia (China) world religions 49 (3)

Asta Pompeia see Asti

Asti anc. Asta Colonia, Asta Pompeia, Hasta Colonia, Hasta Pompeia Italy economy 190 (1), 190–191

Astrakhan Eastern Europe (Russian Federation) colonialism 269 (3) exploration 219 (3) Ottomans 231 (3) Soviet Union 208 (2), 213 (4) Timur 229 (4) trade 267 (3)

Astrakhan, Khanate of state Central Asia/Eastern Europe Islam 163 (1) trade 267 (3)

Astures people Iberian Peninsula Roman empire 179 (5)

Asturias state Iberian Peninsula Franks 184 (2) Islam 184 (1)

Asturias see Oviedo

Asturica Iberian Peninsula (Spain) Roman empire 180–181 (1)

Astypalaea settlement/state Greece ancient Greece 177 (2)

Asuka Japan medieval states 264 (2)

Asuka region Japan medieval states 265 (3)

Asunción South America (Paraguay) colonization 148 (2) empire and revolution 150 (1) environment 153 (4) exploration 143 (2) politics 152 (1), (2)

Asunción Mita Central America (Mexico) first civilizations 122 (2)

Asuristan state Southwest Asia ancient Persia 225 (6)

Aswân var. Assouan, Assuan, Qus; anc. Syene Egypt crusades 228 (2) early Islam 56–57 (1) economy 168 (2) Mongols 229 (3) see also Qus, Syene

Asyut var. Assiout, Assiut, Sauty, Siut; anc. Lycopolis Egypt ancient Egypt 159 (3), (4), (5) exploration 157 (5) first cities 28–29 (1) Islam 235 (4) see also Sauty

Atacama region/state South America politics 151 (4) the world in 250 BCE 38–39

Atacama people South America early cultures 147 (2)

Atacama Desert Eng. Desierto de Atacama desert South America early cultures 144 (1), 145 (2) empire and revolution 150 (1), 151 (3) Incas 147 (3) politics 151 (4)

Atacama, Desierto de see Atacama Desert

Atacama, San Pedro de South America (Chile) early cultures 146 (1)

Atakapa people Central America colonization 125 (4), 126 (1)

A-tan see Aden, Eudaemon Arabia

Atapuerca archaeological site Iberian Peninsula (Spain) first humans 13 (2)

Atarco South America (Peru) early cultures 146 (1)

Atazta Central America (Mexico) first civilizations 122 (1)

'Aṭbarah, Nahr see Atbara

Atchin see Achin

Aten Temple var. Aton building Egypt first cities 29 (5)

Atepehuacán Central America (Mexico) Aztecs 124 (3)

Atepetla Central America (Mexico) Aztecs 124 (3)

Atgram South Asia (Bangladesh) post-war politics 252 (3)

Athabasca var. Athabaska river North America the growth of the US 129 (2)

Athabasca, Lake lake North America colonization 126 (1) early agriculture 120 (1) exploration 119 (3), 286 (1) the growth of the US 129 (2)

Athabaska see Athabasca

Athenae see Athens

Athena, Temple of temple Greece ancient Greece 177 (4)

Athens prev. Athínai, anc. Athenae; Gk. Athína Greece ancient Greece 177 (3), 179 (4) ancient Persia 223 (4) Roman empire 179 (5), 180–181 (1), 181 (3), (4), 182 (1) biological diffusion 72–73 (1) Cold War 108 (3) early systems 32 (1), 33 (2), (3) economy 205 (4) empire and revolution 202 (1) exploration 172 (1) first cities 28–29 (1) first civilizations 175 (4), 177 (1) first religions 36 (1) great migrations 52–53 (1) Hellenistic world 224 (1) civil war 209 (3) Islam 226 (2) medieval states 182 (2), 185 (3), 187 (5), 189 (4) Napoleon 200–201 (1), 201 (2), (3) Ottomans 202 (4), 230 (1) post-war politics 212 (3) world religions 48 (1) WWII 210 (1), 211 (2), (4)

Athens state Greece medieval states 187 (5), 189 (4)

Athesis river Italy early states 178 (2)

Athína see Athens

Athínai see Athens

Athr Southwest Asia (Saudi Arabia) early Islam 56–57 (1) medieval voyages 61 (3)

Athribis Egypt first cities 28–29 (1)

Atico South America (Peru) Incas 147 (3)

Atitlán, Lago de lake Central America first civilizations 122 (2)

Atjeh see Achin

Atlacomulco Central America (Mexico) first civilizations 122 (1)

Atlacuihuayan Central America (Mexico) Aztecs 124 (3)

Atlan state Central America Aztecs 124 (1)

Atlanta North America (USA) the growth of the US 129 (2), 132 (1) US Civil War 130 (5), 131 (7) US economy 134 (1) US politics 135 (6) US society 137 (6)

Atlanta battle North America (USA) US Civil War 131 (7)

Atlantic and Pacific Railroad railway North America the growth of the US 129 (2)

Atlantic Ocean Port. Oceano Atlântico ocean ancient trade 44–45 (1) trade 72–73 (1), 73 (2), (3) colonization 125 (4), 126 (1), 148 (2), 149 (3), (4) empire and revolution 127 (2), (3), 150 (1), 151 (3), 202 (1), 88–89 (2) environment 153 (4) European expansion 80–81 (1), 81 (2), (3), 84–85 (1), 85 (2) European imperialism 96 (1), (2), 97 (4) exploration 118 (1), 119 (2), (3), 142 (1), 143 (2), (3), 156 (1), (2), (3), 172 (1), (2), 286 (1), 287 (2) global immigration 100 (1), 101 (2), (3) global knowledge 76 (1), (2), 76–77 (1), 77 (5) great migrations 52–53 (1), 53 (2) imperial global economy 92 (1), 93 (2) civil war 209 (3) medieval voyages 60–61 (1) politics 152 (1) post-war economy 213 (5) post-war politics 212 (3) slave trade 165 (4) the growth of the US 129 (2), 132 (1), 133 (4) the world in 1300 66–67 trade 163 (4), (5), (6), (7), 164 (2), 167 (1) US Civil War 131 (6), (7) US economy 138 (2) US superpower 138 (1) WWI 208 (1) WWII 104 (1), (2), 105 (3), (4), 210 (1), 211 (2), (4) see also Occidental, Oceanus

Atlapulco Central America (Mexico) Aztecs 124 (2)

Atlas Mountains mountain range North Africa Roman empire 180–181 (1) ancient trade 44–45 (1) trade 72–73 (1) Bronze Age 175 (3) crusades 64–65 (2) early agriculture 174 (1) early cultures 160 (1), 161 (2) early Islam 56–57 (1), 57 (2) economy 163 (2) global knowledge 76–77 (1) Islam 163 (1) medieval states 182 (2) Ottomans 232–233 (1) slave trade 165 (4) WWII 210 (1), 211 (4)

Atlatonco Central America (Mexico) Aztecs 124 (2)

Atlazolpa Central America (Mexico) Aztecs 124 (3)

Atlixco Central America (Mexico) colonization 125 (5)

Atomata major port/settlement East Africa (Somalia) early trade 225 (3)

Aton see Aten Temple

Atontonilco state Central America Aztecs 124 (1)

Atoyac Central America (Mexico) Aztecs 124 (3)

Atoyac river North America colonization 125 (5)

Atsugashi-yama battle Japan early modern states 265 (5)

Attaleia see Adalia, Attalia

Attalia later Adalia; mod. Antalya; anc. Attaleia Southwest Asia (Turkey) Roman empire 180–181 (1) Hellenistic world 41 (2) see also Adalia

Attica region Greece ancient Greece 177 (2)

Attigny France Franks 184 (2)

Attikamek people North America colonization 126 (1)

Attu island North America WWII 272 (1), 273 (2)

Atwetwebooso archaeological site West Africa (Ghana) early cultures 160 (1)

Atzacualco Central America (Mexico) Aztecs 124 (3)

Atzalan North America (USA) cultural groups 122 (5)

Atzcapotzalco see Azcapotzalco

Auberoche France medieval states 192 (1)

Auch France early modern states 197 (5)

Auckland New Zealand colonization 283 (4), (5), 284–285 (1) environmentalism 285 (2) exploration 279 (3)

Auckland region New Zealand colonization 283 (5)

Auckland Islands island group New Zealand decolonization 285 (3) exploration 276–277 (1)

Auerstedt see Jena Auerstädt

Augila var. Awjilah North Africa (Libya) Islam 163 (1)

Augsbourg see Augsburg

Augsburg anc. Augusta Vindelicorum; Fr. Augsbourg Central Europe (Germany) biological diffusion 72–73 (1) crusades 186 (1) economy 190 (1) Franks 184 (2) medieval states 188 (1) Reformation 194 (2) see also Augusta Vindelicorum

Augusta North America (USA) empire and revolution 127 (3) the growth of the US 129 (2) US Civil War 131 (7)

Augusta battle North America (USA) empire and revolution 127 (3)

Augusta see London, Londinium

Augusta Suessionum see Soissons

Augusta Taurinorum mod. Torino; Eng. Turin Italy great migrations 52–53 (1)

Augusta Treverorum mod. Trier, Eng. Treves, Fr. Trèves Central Europe (Germany) Roman empire 180–181 (1), 181 (3), (4) ancient trade 44 (2), 44–45 (1) great migrations 52–53 (1) world religions 48 (1) see also Trier

Augusta Vangionum see Worms

Augusta Vindelicorum mod. Augsburg Central Europe (Germany) Roman empire 180–181 (1) see also Augsburg

Augustobona Tricassium see Troyes

Augustodunum mod. Autun France Roman empire 180–181 (1)

Augustodurum see Bayeux

Augustoritum Lemovicensium see Limoges

Augustus, Mausoleum of building Italy Roman empire 181 (2)

Aupaga region South Asia world religions 242 (2)

Auraitis cultural region Southwest Asia Roman empire 225 (4)

Aurelianum see Orléans

Aurelia, Via road Italy Roman empire 181 (2) early states 178 (1)

Aurunci people Italy early states 178 (2)

Auschwitz-Birkenau concentration camp Central Europe WWII 211 (3)

Ausculum Italy early states 178 (1)

Aussa state East Africa the world in 1600 78–79

Austerlitz Central Europe (Austria) Napolean 200-201 the world in 1850 90–91

Austin North America (USA) the growth of the US 129 (2), 132 (1)

Australia prev. Australian Colonies, New Holland state Australia early agriculture 20–21 (2) early cultures 280–281 (3) environmentalism 285 (2) European expansion 80–81 (1) exploration 276–277 (1), 279 (2), (3) first humans 13 (2) global immigration 100 (1), 101 (3) historical geography 254–255 (1) imperial global economy 92 (1), 93 (2) medieval voyages 60 (2) the growth of the US 133 (4) US economy 138 (2) US superpower 138 (1) WWII 104 (1), 105 (4), 251 (3), 272 (1), 273 (2) Cold War 109 (1) colonization 282 (1) decolonization 251 (4), 285 (3) see also Australian Colonies

Australian Aborigines people Australia the world in 750 BCE 30–31

Australian Colonies mod. Australia; prev. New Holland colonial possession Australia the world in 1850 90–91 the world in 1900 94–95 see also Australia

Austral Islands island group Pacific Ocean colonization 284–285 (1) early cultures 280–281 (3) environmentalism 285 (2) exploration 279 (3) medieval voyages 60 (2)

Austrasia region Central Europe Franks 183 (6), 184 (2)

Austria Ger. Österreich region/state Central Europe early modern states 193 (4), (5), 194 (1) empire and revolution 198 (2), 199 (3), 202 (2) civil war 209 (3), (5) medieval states 183 (4), 188 (1), 189 (4) Napoleon 200–201 (1) post-war economy 213 (5), 214 (1), (2), 215 (3) post-war politics 212 (1), (3) Reformation 196 (1), (2) Soviet Union 213 (4) the modern world 112 (2), 113 (3) WWI 208 (1) WWII 210 (1), 211 (2), (3), (4) Cold War 108 (3)

Austria-Hungary state Central Europe economy 205 (4) global immigration 100 (1) imperial global economy 92 (1) WWI 207 (6)

Austrian Empire state Central Europe/Eastern Europe empire and revolution 202 (1) Napoleon 201 (2) Ottomans 232–233 (1)

Austrian Habsburg Possessions state Central Europe Reformation 194 (2)

Austrian Netherlands vassal state Low Countries empire and revolution 199 (3), (4)

Austro-Hungarian Empire state Central Europe empire and revolution 202 (3) Ottomans 202 (4) WWI 207 (4), (5) early 20th century 206 (1)

Autun see Augustodunum

Auvergne region France Franks 183 (6) medieval states 192 (1)

Ava Mainland Southeast Asia (Burma) colonialism 247 (4), 248 (1) early medieval states 245 (6) world religions 243 (5)

Ava region/state Mainland Southeast Asia Mughal Empire 246 (1) trade 267 (3)

Avalites East Africa (Djibouti) ancient trade 44–45 (1) early cultures 161 (3), (4), (5) early trade 225 (3)

Avanti South Asia (India) early religions 48 (2)

Avanti region/state South Asia ancient India 242 (1) early religions 48 (2) first religions 36 (2) world religions 242 (2)

Avar Empire state Central Europe early Islam 56–57 (1) medieval states 182 (2)

Avaricum see Bourges

Avaris Egypt ancient Egypt 159 (4)

Avars people Eastern Europe Franks 184 (2) medieval states 182 (2)

Avebury archaeological site British Isles (United Kingdom) Copper Age 174 (2)

Avenio see Avignon

Aventine Hill Lat. Mons Aventinus hill Italy Roman empire 181 (2)

Aventinus, Mons see Aventine Hill

Aversa Italy economy 190 (1)

Avignon anc. Avenio settlement/university France crusades 186 (1) early modern states 193 (4), 197 (5) economy 190 (1) Franks 183 (5), 184 (2) medieval states 187 (3), (4), 88 (1), (2) Reformation 194 (2)

Avignon anc. Avenio state France empire and revolution 199 (4)

Awadh state South Asia Mughal Empire 246 (1)

Awazu battle Japan early modern states 265 (5)

Awdaghost West Africa (Mauritania) Islam 163 (1) trade 163 (4), (5), (6), (7)

Awjilah see Augila

Axim West Africa (Ghana) exploration 156 (3) slave trade 165 (4) trade 164 (2)

Axiós see Vardar

Axocopan state Central America Aztecs 124 (1)

Axotla Central America (Mexico) Aztecs 124 (3)

Axum see Aksum

Ayacucho South America (Peru) Incas 148 (1) narcotics 153 (5)

Ayacucho battle South America (Peru) empire and revolution 150 (1), 88–89 (2)

Ayas see Laias

Ayaviri South America (Peru) Incas 147 (3)

Aydhab Egypt biological diffusion 72–73 (1) Islam 163 (1)

Ayeyarwady see Irrawaddy

Ayodhya South Asia (India) early medieval states 244 (1) early religions 48 (2) first religions 36 (2) Mughal Empire 246 (1)

Ayotzinco Central America (Mexico) colonization 125 (5)

Ayr British Isles (United Kingdom) economy 204 (1)

Ayuthia see Ayutthaya

Ayutla Central America (Mexico) Aztecs 124 (1)

Ayutthaya var. Ayuthia, Phra Nakhon Si Ayutthaya settlement/temple Mainland Southeast Asia (Thailand) early medieval states 245 (6) Marathas 246 (2) trade 267 (3) world religions 243 (5)

Ayyubid Sultanate state Egypt/North Africa/Southwest Asia crusades 65 (3) medieval states 187 (5) Mongols 68–69 (1)

Azad Kashmir region South Asia post-war politics 252 (1), (2)

Azak see Azov

Azärbaycan see Azerbaijan

Azcapotzalco var. Atzcapotzalco Central America (Mexico) Aztecs 124 (3)

Azerbaijan Az. Azärbaycan region Central Asia economy 234 (1) Islam 227 (4) medieval Persia 231 (4) post-war economy 214 (2) Soviet Union 208 (2), 213 (4) the modern world 113 (3) WWI 233 (2)

Azerbaijani Republic see Azerbaijan

Azeri people Southwest Asia Islam 275 (5)

Azimabad see Patna

Azores Port. Açores, Ilhas dos Açores, Arquipélago dos Açores island group Atlantic Ocean Cold War 109 (1) European expansion 80–81 (1) US superpower 138 (1) WWII 104 (2)

Azov Turk. Azak Eastern Europe (Ukraine) Ottomans 197 (4), 231 (3)

Azov, Sea of sea Eastern Europe Ottomans 202 (4), 230 (1), 231 (3) WWI 207 (4)

Azraq, Bahr El/ al Azraq, An Nīl see Blue Nile

Aztec Empire state Central America the world in 1500 74–75, 76 (2), 124-125

Aztecs people Central America colonization 126 (1)

'Azza see Gaza

Az Zāb al Kabīr see Great Zab

Aẓ Ẓahran see Dhahran

B

Ba var. Pa province/region East Asia first religions 37 (4) first states 260 (1)

Ba people East Asia first cities 259 (4)

Ba see Pegu

Baalbek var. Ba'labakk; anc. Heliopolis Lebanon Southwest Asia (Lebanon) crusades 65 (3) first religions 37 (3) see also Heliopolis

Bab-i Sin East Asia (China) trade 230 (2)

Babi Yar massacre Eastern Europe WWII 211 (3)

Babylon Southwest Asia (Iraq) ancient Persia 223 (4), 225 (6) Roman empire 224 (2), 225 (5) ancient trade 44 (2), 44–45 (1) early cultures 161 (3), (4), (5) early medieval states 244 (1) early systems 223 (3) early trade 225 (3) exploration 218 (1), (2) first civilizations 221 (4), (5), 222 (2) Hellenistic world 40–41 (1), 41 (2)

Babylonia province Southwest Asia ancient Persia 223 (4) first civilizations 221 (5), 222 (2) Hellenistic world 40–41 (1), 41 (2)

Bachíniva Central America (Mexico) Mexican Revolution 133 (3)

Back river North America exploration 287 (2)

Bactra var. Valhika, Zariaspa; mod. Balkh Buddhist centre/settlement Central Asia (Afghanistan) ancient Persia 223 (4) ancient trade 44 (2), 44–45 (1) exploration 256 (1) first empires 241 (4) Hellenistic world 224 (1) medieval states 262–263 (1) world religions 49 (3), (4) see also Balkh, Valhika

Bactria region/state Central Asia ancient Persia 223 (4), 225 (6) Roman empire 224 (2) ancient trade 44 (2), 44–45 (1) first empires 241 (4) Hellenistic world 224 (1)

Badajoz anc. Pax Augusta Iberian Peninsula (Spain) economy 190 (1) civil war 209 (4) Islam 192 (3) Napoleon 200–201 (1)

Badakhshan state Central Asia the world in 1800 86–87 the world in 1850 90–91

Badari Egypt ancient Egypt 159 (2)

Badarika South Asia (India) world religions 243 (4)

Baden state Central Europe early modern states 193 (5) empire and revolution 202 (1), (2) the world in 1850 90–91

Badr Southwest Asia (Saudi Arabia) early Islam 56–57 (1) Islam 226 (2), (3)

Badr battle Southwest Asia (Saudi Arabia) Islam 226 (2)

Badyarada 'Adméd see Aden, Gulf of

Baecula battle Iberian Peninsula (Spain) Roman empire 179 (3)

Baeterrae see Béziers

Baeterrae Septimanorum see Béziers

Baetica province Iberian peninsula Roman empire 180–181 (1)

Baffin Bay bay North America exploration 286 (1), 287 (2) the growth of the US 129 (2)

Baffin Island island North America cultural groups 123 (3) European expansion 80–81 (1) exploration 286 (1), 287 (2) the growth of the US 129 (2)

Baffinland Inuit people North America cultural groups 123 (3)

Bagacum France Roman empire 180–181 (1)

Bagamoyo East Africa (Tanzania) exploration 157 (4), (5)

Bagh Buddhist centre South Asia (India) world religions 49 (3)

Baghdad Ar. Baghdād Southwest Asia (Iraq) biological diffusion 72–73 (1) crusades 228 (2), 65 (1) early Islam 57 (2), (3) economy 234 (1) exploration 218 (2), 219 (3), (4) Islam 163 (1), 227 (4), (5) medieval Persia 231 (4) medieval states 185 (3) medieval voyages 61 (3) Mongols 229 (3), 68 (2), 68–69 (1) Ottomans 231 (3), 232–233 (1) Seljuks 228 (1) Timur 229 (4) trade 267 (3) world religions 226 (1) WWI 233 (2) 20th-century politics 233 (3), (4), 235 (5)

Baghirmi see Bagirmi

Baghouz Southwest Asia (Syria) early agriculture 220 (1)

Bagirmi var. Baghirmi; Fr. Baguirmi state West Africa colonization 167 (4) trade 167 (1)
Bago see Pegu
Bagradas North Africa (Tunisia) early cultures 161 (2)
Baguirmi see Bagirmi
Bahadurgarh state South Asia empire and revolution 249 (3)
Bahama Islands colonial possession/island group West Indies European expansion 84–85 (1), 85 (2)
Bahamas var. Bahama Islands colonial possession/island group/state West Indies colonization 125 (4), 126 (1) empire and revolution 88 (1) European expansion 84–85 (1), 85 (2) exploration 118 (1) historical geography 117 (1) the modern world 110–111 , 112 (1) US economy 136 (2) US politics 139 (4) US superpower 138 (1) WWII 104 (2) Cold War 108 (2)
Bahariya var. Wāhat el Bahariya oasis Egypt ancient Egypt 159 (2), (3), (4), (5)
Bahariya, Wāhat el see Bahariya Oasis
Bahawalpur state South Asia colonialism 248 (2)
Bahia mod. Salvador; prev. São Salvador South America (Brazil) colonization 149 (3), (4) empire and revolution 151 (3) exploration 142 (1), 143 (2), (3) see also Salvador
Bahia region South America colonization 149 (3) early cultures 145 (4)
Bahía Blanca South America (Argentina) empire and revolution 151 (3) environment 153 (4) exploration 143 (3)
Bahía Grande Gulf South America/Atlantic Ocean colonization 148 (2)
Bahía Honda West Indies (Cuba) US imperialism 133 (5)
Bahía Negra fort South America (Paraguay) politics 152 (2)
Bahlika state Central Asia first empires 241 (5)
Bahmani Kingdom state South Asia the world in 1400 70–71 the world in 1500 74–75
Bahrain Southwest Asia (Bahrain) exploration 156 (3) medieval Persia 231 (4) trade 230 (2)
Bahrain prev. Bahrein; anc. Tylos, Tyros Ar. Al Baḩrayn island/state Southwest Asia ancient Persia 225 (6) Cold War 109 (1) early Islam 56–57 (1) early systems 223 (3) economy 234 (1) Islam 227 (4) the modern world 110–111 , 113 (3) US economy 138 (2) WWII 104 (1) 20th-century politics 235 (5)
Bahrein see Bahrain
Bahr el Ghazal hominid site Africa first humans 12 (1)
Baiji Southwest Asia (Iraq) 20th-century politics 235 (5)
Baikal, Lake Rus. Ozero Baykal lake Central Asia ancient trade 44–45 (1) colonialism 269 (3), (4) early agriculture 258 (1) empire and revolution 268 (2) exploration 257 (2), (3) first humans 13 (2) first states 260 (1) historical geography 254–255 (1), 275 (5) medieval states 261 (6), 262–263 (1), 263 (6) Mongols 68 (2), 68–69 (1) Soviet Union 208 (2), 214–215 (4) trade 267 (3) world religions 49 (4) WWII 272 (1), 273 (2)
Baikunthpur South Asia (India) colonialism 247 (3)
Baile Átha Cliath see Dublin
Bailén var. Baylen Iberian Peninsula (Spain) Napoleon 200–201
Bailén var. Baylen battle Iberian Peninsula (Spain) Napoleon 200–201 (1)
Baipu people East Asia first cities 259 (4)
Baja California state Central America Mexican Revolution 133 (3) the growth of the US 129 (2)
Bajwara South Asia (India) colonialism 247 (3)
Bakan see Shimonoseki
Baker and Howland Islands US overseas possession Pacific Ocean the modern world 110–111
Bakı see Baku
Baku Az. Bakı Southwest Asia (Azerbaijan) economy 205 (4) global immigration 100 (1) medieval Persia 231 (4) Ottomans 231 (3) Soviet Union 208 (2), 214–215 (4) trade 267 (3) WWI 233 (2) 20th-century politics 233 (3) colonialism 269 (3) Communism 271 (8)
Ba'labakk see Baalbek, Heliopolis
Balaclava see Balaklava
Balaklava var. Balaclava battle Eastern Europe (Ukraine) Ottomans 202 (4)
Balancán Central America (Mexico) first civilizations 121 (2)
Balankanché Central America (Mexico) first civilizations 122 (1)
Balasaghun Central Asia (Kazahkstan) biological diffusion 72–73 (1) Mongols 68–69 (1)
Balasore var. Bāleshwar South Asia (India) colonialism 247 (3)
Balboa Central America (Panama) US economy 136 (2)
Balclutha New Zealand colonization 283 (5)
Bâle see Basle
Baleares Eng. Balearic Islands island group/region Mediterranean Sea Roman empire 179 (3), (5), 180–181 (1), 181 (4) see also Balearic Islands
Baleares, Islas see Balearic Islands
Baleares Major see Majorca
Balearic Islands var. Baleares island group Mediterranean Sea Roman empire 181 (3), 182 (1) crusades 186 (1), 64–65 (2) early Islam 56–57 (1) early modern states 194 (1) economy 190 (1) empire and revolution 202 (1) exploration 172 (1) first civilizations 177 (1) Islam 184 (1), 192 (3) medieval states 182 (2), 185 (3) medieval voyages 60–61 (1) Napoleon 201 (2) post-war economy 213 (5) post-war politics 212 (3) Reformation 194 (2) world religions 48 (1) WWII 210 (1) see also Baleares
Balearis Minor see Minorca
Bāleshwar see Balasore
Bălgrad see Apulum, Gyulafehérvár
Balhika region South Asia world religions 242 (2)
Bali island/region/state Maritime Southeast Asia ancient India 241 (6) colonialism 247 (4) early medieval states 245 (5), (6) European expansion 84–85 (1) exploration 239 (2) global knowledge 76–77 (1) historical geography 236–237 (1) Islam 243 (6) world religions 243 (5)
Balikpapan military campaign Maritime Southeast Asia WWII 273 (2)
Balkan Mountains Bul./SCr. Stara Planina mountain range Southeast Europe crusades 64–65 (2) early Islam 56–57 (1) WWI 207 (6)
Balkans physical region/state Southeast Europe Bronze Age 175 (3) early agriculture 174 (1) WWII 211 (3)
Balkh anc. Bactra, Valhika, Zariaspa Central Asia (Afghanistan) ancient Persia 225 (6) trade 72–73 (1) colonialism 248 (1) early Islam 56–57 (1) Islam 227 (4) medieval Persia 231 (4) Mongols 229 (3), 68–69 (1) Mughal Empire 246 (1) Timur 229 (4) trade 267 (3) see also Bactra, Valhika
Balkh anc. Bactra, Zariaspa state Central Asia colonialism 248 (1)
Balkhash, Lake Kaz. Balqash lake Central Asia ancient trade 44–45 (1) colonialism 269 (3), (4) Communism 271 (8) early agriculture 258 (1) early Islam 56–57 (1) empire and revolution 268 (2) exploration 256 (1), 257 (3) first cities 259 (5) first humans 13 (2) first states 260 (1) medieval states 261 (6), 262–263 (1) Mongols 68 (2), 68–69 (1) Soviet Union 208 (2), 214–215 (4) Timur 229 (4) trade 267 (3) world religions 49 (4)
Balkuwara cantonment Southwest Asia (Iraq) early Islam 57 (3)
Ballabgarh state South Asia empire and revolution 249 (3)
Ballarat goldfield Australia colonization 282 (2)
Balleny Islands island group Antarctica Antarctic Exploration 287 (3)
Balqash see Balkhash, Lake
Balsas river Central America early agriculture 121 (2) first civilizations 122 (1)
Baltic Peoples people Eastern Europe ancient trade 44–45 (1) Mongols 68–69 (1)
Baltic Sea Ger. Ostee, Rus. Baltiskoye More sea Northern Europe ancient trade 44–45 (1) trade 72–73 (1) Bronze Age 175 (3) Cold War 108 (3) Copper Age 174 (2) crusades 186 (1) early 20th century 206 (1) early agriculture 174 (1) early modern states 193 (4), 195 (3) economy 190 (1) empire and revolution 198 (2), 199 (3), 202 (1) exploration 172 (1) Franks 184 (2) great migrations 52–53 (1) civil war 209 (3), (5) medieval states 185 (3), 188 (1), 189 (3), (4) medieval voyages 60–61 (1) Mongols 68–69 (1) post-war economy 213 (5), 214 (1), (2) Soviet Union 208 (2) WWI 207 (4), 208 (1) WWII 210 (1), 211 (2), (3), (4)
Baltic States region Eastern Europe WWII 211 (3)
Baltimore North America (USA) empire and revolution 127 (2) the growth of the US 129 (2), 132 (1) US economy 134 (1), (3)
Baltiskoye More see Baltic Sea
Baltistan Agency region South Asia post-war politics 252 (2)
Baltkrievija see Belorussia
Baluchis people South Asia historical geography 275 (5)
Baluchistan region/state South Asia colonialism 247 (3), 248 (2) economy 249 (4) empire and revolution 249 (3) medieval Persia 231 (4) post-war politics 252 (1), 253 (4) world religions 243 (4)
Balurghat South Asia (Bangladesh) post-war politics 252 (3)
Balzi Rossi archaeological site Italy prehistoric culture 17 (4)
Bamako West Africa (Mali) colonization 167 (4) economy 168 (2)
Bamangwato state Southern Africa colonization 167 (4)
Bamberg Central Europe (Germany) crusades 186 (1) economy 190 (1)
Bamborough see Bamburgh
Bamburgh var. Bamborough British Isles (United Kingdom) medieval states 183 (3)
Bamiyan Buddhist centre Central Asia (Afghanistan) first religions 36 (2) world religions 49 (3)
Bampur Southwest Asia (Iran) first civilizations 24 (3)
Bampur archaeological site Southwest Asia (Iran) first cities 240 (2)
Banakat Central Asia (Tajikistan) Mongols 68–69 (1)
Banaras South Asia (India) early medieval states 244–245 (3)
Banat vassal state Southeast Asia Ottomans 197 (4)
Ban Chiang archaeological site/settlement Mainland Southeast Asia (Thailand) Bronze Age 240 (3)
Ban Chiang Miang Mainland Southeast Asia (Thailand) the world in 2500 BCE 22–23
Banda state West Africa the world in 1700 82–83
Banda Islands island group Maritime Southeast Asia colonialism 247 (4)
Banda, Laut see Banda Sea
Bandaneira island Maritime Southeast Asia Islam 243 (6)
Bandar Abbas mod. Bandar-e 'Abbās; prev. Gombroon, Gombrun Southwest Asia (Iran) economy 234 (1) medieval Persia 231 (4) see also Gombrun
Bandar-e 'Abbās see Bandar Abbas, Gombrun
Bandar-e Būshehr see Bushire
Bandar Seri Begawan prev. Brunei Town Maritime Southeast Asia (Brunei) post-war economy 253 (5)
Banda Sea var. Laut Banda sea Maritime Southeast Asia colonialism 247 (4) decolonization 251 (4), 285 (3) early medieval states 245 (6) European imperialism 97 (3) exploration 239 (1), (2) Islam 243 (6) post-war economy 253 (5) post-war politics 253 (4) world religions 243 (5)
Bandjarmasin Maritime Southeast Asia (Indonesia) colonialism 247 (4) colonization 284–285 (1) WWII 272 (1), 273 (2)
Bandjarmasin var. Banjermasin region Maritime Southeast Asia colonialism 247 (4)
Bangala mod. Bengal region/state South Asia early medieval states 244–245 (3) Mughal Empire 246 (1) see also Bengal
Bangalore South Asia (India) decolonization 250 (1) economy 249 (4) post-war economy 253 (5) post-war politics 252 (1)
Bangkok Thai. Krung Thep Mainland Southeast Asia (Thailand) colonialism 247 (4), 248 (1), 269 (4) European expansion 84–85 (1) European imperialism 97 (3) exploration 239 (1) Islam 275 (4) post-war economy 253 (5) the modern world 113 (4) trade 230 (2) US superpower 138 (1) world religions 243 (5) WWII 251 (3)
Bangladesh prev. East Pakistan state South Asia post-war economy 253 (5), 275 (3) post-war politics 252 (1), (3), 253 (4), 274 (2), 275 (5) the modern world 110–111 , 113 (3) US superpower 138 (1) see also East Pakistan
Bangor British Isles (United Kingdom) economy 204 (1)
Bangui Central Africa (Central African Republic) economy 168 (2)
Bangweulu, Lake var. Lake Bengweulu lake Southern Africa exploration 157 (4) first humans 12 (1)
Banja Luka Southeast Europe (Bosnia and Herzegovina) post-war economy 215 (3)
Banjermasin see Bandjarmasin
Banjul prev. Bathurst West Africa (Gambia) economy 168 (2) see also Bathurst
Ban Kao archaeological site/settlement Mainland Southeast Asia (Thailand) Bronze Age 240 (3)
Banks Island island North America the growth of the US 129 (2)
Ban Me Thuot battle Mainland Southeast Asia (Vietnam) post-war politics 251 (5)
Bannock people North America colonization 126 (1)
Bannockburn battle British Isles (United Kingdom) medieval states 188 (2)
Banpo archaeological site East Asia early agriculture 258 (1), (2)
Banshan archaeological site East Asia early agriculture 258 (1)
Bantam region/settlement Maritime Southeast Asia (Indonesia) colonialism 247 (4) early medieval states 245 (6) exploration 239 (1) trade 267 (3)
Bantam prev. Banten state Maritime Southeast Asia the world in 1600 78–79
Banten see Bantam
Bantry Bay British Isles (Ireland) Napoleon 200–201 (1)
Bantu people Southern Africa economy 163 (2) Islam 163 (1)
Banwari Trace archaeological site West Indies (Trinidad) early cultures 145 (2)
Banzart see Bizerta
Baoji archaeological site East Asia early agriculture 258 (2)
Baozitou archaeological site East Asia early agriculture 258 (1)
Bapaume France WWI 206 (3)
Bar France economy 190 (1)
Baraawe see Brava
Barabina archaeological site South America (Venezuela) early cultures 144 (1), 145 (2)
Baracoa West Indies (Cuba) colonization 125 (4)
Baranasi var. Banaras, Varanasi; Eng. Benares. South Asia (India) world religions 242 (3) see also Banaras, Benares, Varanasi
Baranovichi Eastern Europe (Belorussia) WWI 207 (4)
Barar mod. Berar state South Asia early medieval states 245 (4) Mughal Empire 246 (1) see also Berar
Barbados island/colonial possession/state West Indies Cold War 108 (2) colonization 126 (1) empire and revolution 150 (1) European expansion 84–85 (1) the growth of the US 129 (2) the modern world 110–111, 112 (1) US economy 136 (2) US politics 139 (4)
Barbalissus Southwest Asia (Syria) ancient Persia 225 (6)
Barbara region South Asia first empires 241 (5) world religions 242 (2)
Barbaria region East Africa ancient trade 44 (2)
Barbaricon var. Barbaricum South Asia (Pakistan) ancient trade 44–45 (1)
Barbaricum see Barbaricon
Barbuda island West Indies the world in 1700 82–83 the world in 1800 86–87 the world in 1850 90–91
Barca North Africa (Libya) Bronze Age 175 (3) cultural groups 122 (5) early Islam 56–57 (1) economy 163 (2) first civilizations 177 (1) Islam 163 (1)
Barca state North Africa early Islam 56–57 (1)
Barca battle North Africa (Libya) ancient Persia 223 (4)
Barcelona South America (Venezuela) exploration 143 (3)
Barcelona anc. Barcino, Barcinona Iberian Peninsula (Spain) crusades 186 (1) early Islam 57 (2) early modern states 194 (1) economy 190 (1), 205 (4) empire and revolution 202 (1) European expansion 84–85 (1) Franks 184 (2) civil war 209 (4) Islam 163 (1), 192 (3) medieval states 185 (3) Napoleon 200–201 (1), 201 (2), (3)
Barcelore see Coondapoor
Barcino see Barcelona
Barcinona see Barcelona
Barcoo river Australia exploration 279 (2)
Bardoli Taluka South Asia (India) decolonization 250 (1)
Bar, Duchy of state France early modern states 197 (5)
Barduli see Barletta
Bareilly var. Bareli South Asia (India) economy 249 (4)
Bareilly battle South Asia empire and revolution 249 (3)
Bareli see Bareilly
Barents Sea sea Artic Ocean exploration 256 (1), 287 (2) first humans 13 (2) medieval states 185 (3) Soviet Union 208 (2), 214–215 (4)
Barguzin see Barguzinsk
Barguzinsk mod. Barguzin Siberia (Russian Federation) exploration 257 (2)
Bari var. Bari delle Puglie; anc. Barium Italy crusades 186 (1), 64–65 (2) economy 190 (1) medieval states 185 (3), 187 (5), 188 (1) see also Barium
Bari delle Puglie see Bari
Baringo archaeological site East Africa (Kenya) first humans 12 (1)
Barium mod. Bari (Italy) early states 178 (1) see also Bari
Barka see Barca
Bar-le-Duc (France) WWI 206 (2)
Barletta anc. Barduli (Italy) crusades 186 (1) economy 190 (1)
Barnaul archaeological site/settlement Siberia early agriculture 258 (1)
Baroda var. Vadodara South Asia (India) colonialism 248 (1) decolonization 250 (1) economy 249 (4) Marathas 246 (2) see also Vadodara
Baropilas mine Central America (Mexico) colonization 125 (4)
Barotse state Southern Africa colonization 167 (4)
Barotseland-Northwestern Rhodesia colonial possession Southern Africa the world in 1900 94–95
Barqah see Cyrenaica
Barquisimeto South America (Venezuela) empire and revolution 150 (1), 151 (3) environment 153 (4)
Barrackpore rebellion South Asia (India) empire and revolution 249 (3)
Barrancabermeja South America (Colombia) narcotics 153 (5)
Barrancas archaeological site South America (Venezuela) early cultures 144 (1), 145 (2)
Barrancoid people South America early cultures 145 (2)
Barrancos people South America the world in 1200 62–63 the world in 1400 70–71
Barranquilla South America (Colombia) empire and revolution 151 (3) environment 153 (4)
Barrow North America (USA) exploration 287 (2)
Barrow-in-Furness British Isles (United Kingdom) economy 204 (1)
Barton Ramie Central America (Belize) first civilizations 121 (2)
Barumini fort Italy Bronze Age 175 (3)
Barus Maritime Southeast Asia (Indonesia) medieval voyages 61 (3)
Barygaza var. Bharukachha, Broach South Asia (India) ancient trade 44 (2) exploration 256 (1) medieval states 261 (6) see also Bharukachha, Broach
Basel see Basle, Uri
Bashkirs people Southwest Asia historical geography 275 (5)
Bashkortostan state Eastern Europe Soviet Union 214–215 (4)
Basketmaker Culture cultural region North America the world in 250 CE 46–47 the world in 500 CE 50–51
Basle Fr. Bâle, Ger. Basel Central Europe (Switzerland) early modern states 193 (4), (5) empire and revolution 202 (1), (2) Franks 184 (2) medieval states 188 (1), 192 (2) Reformation 194 (2) WWI 206 (2), (3)
Basque Republic state Iberian Peninsula Civil War 209 (4)
Basques people Iberian Peninsula Roman empire 182 (1) Franks 183 (5), (6), 184 (2) great migrations 53 (2) medieval states 182 (2)
Basra Southwest Asia (Iraq) early Islam 56–57 (1) Islam 226 (2)
Bassano battle Italy Napoleon 200–201 (1)
Bassano Italy WWI 207 (5)
Bassein var. Pathein Mainland Southeast Asia (Burma) colonialism 247 (3), (4), 248 (1)
Bass Point Australia exploration 280 (1)
Bass Strait sea waterway Australia colonization 282 (1), (2), 283 (3) exploration 279 (2) prehistoric culture 17 (5)
Bastia France (Corsica) economy 190–191
Bastille building (France) economy 191 (2)
Basuto state Southern Africa colonization 167 (4)
Basutoland mod. Lesotho colonial possession/state Southern Africa European imperialism 96 (1), (2) trade 167 (1) see also Lesotho
Bataan battle Philippines WWII 272 (1)
Batae Coritanorum see Leicester
Batanaea state Southwest Asia Roman empire 225 (4)
Batang Kapas Maritime Southeast Asia (Indonesia) the world in 1800 86–87
Batavia mod. Jakarta military base/settlement Maritime Southeast Asia (Indonesia) colonialism 247 (4) colonization 284–285 (1) European imperialism 97 (3) exploration 239 (1), (2) global immigration 100 (1) trade 267 (3) WWII 251 (3), 272 (1) see also Jakarta
Batavian Republic mod. Netherlands state Low Countries Napoleon 200–201 (1) see also Netherlands, United Provinces
Bat Cave archaeological site/settlement North America (USA) cultural groups 123 (4)
Bath prev. Akermanceaster, anc. Aquae Calidae, Aquae Solis British Isles (United Kingdom) economy 204 (1)
Bathurst mod. Banjul West Africa (Gambia) the world in 1850 90–91 see also Banjul
Bathurst Australia colonization 282 (1), (2) exploration 279 (2)
Baton Rouge North America (USA) US society 137 (6)
Baton Rouge battle North America (USA) the growth of the US 129 (2) US Civil War 131 (6)
Batticaloa South Asia (Sri Lanka) colonialism 247 (3)
Batu Buruk Mainland Southeast Asia (Malaysia) the world in 2500 BCE 22–23
Batum Southwest Asia (Georgia) Soviet Union 208 (2)
Bauchi West Africa (Nigeria) Islam 167 (3)
Bautzen battle Central Europe (Germany) Napoleon 200–201 (1)
Bauzanum see Bozen
Bavaria Ger. Bayern region/state Central Europe crusades 64–65 (2) early modern states 193 (5) empire and revolution 199 (3), 202 (1), (2) Franks 184 (2) medieval states 185 (3), 188 (1) Napoleon 200–201 (1) Ottomans 197 (4) Reformation 194 (2), 196 (1)
Bavarians people Central Europe Franks 183 (6)
Bayamo West Indies (Cuba) colonization 125 (4)
Bayana South Asia (India) colonialism 247 (3)
Bayern see Bavaria
Bayeux anc. Augustodurum France Franks 184 (2) medieval states 186 (2)
Bayji Southwest Asia (Iraq) 20th-century politics 235 (5)
Baykal, Ozero see Baikal, Lake
Baylen see Bailén
Bay of Islands whaling station New Zealand colonization 283 (4)
Bayonne anc. Lapurdum France early modern states 197 (5) medieval states 187 (4), 192 (1)
Bayrūt see Beirut
Baysān see Scythopolis
Bayt Laḩm see Bethlehem
Bayuda Desert desert Egypt ancient Egypt 159 (4)
Beaconsfield goldfield Australia colonization 282 (2)
Beagle Channel sea waterway South America exploration 143 (3)
Beaker Burials cultural region British Isles/France the World in 2500 BCE 22–23
Béal Feirste see Belfast
Beardmore Glacier glacier Antarctica Antarctic Exploration 287 (3)
Béarn France Franks 184 (2)
Béarn state France early modern states 194 (1) Islam 192 (3) medieval states 192 (1), (2) Reformation 194 (2)
Bear Paw Mountains battle North America (USA) the growth of the US 129 (2)
Bear River battle North America (USA) the growth of the US 129 (2)
Beas river South Asia early medieval states 244 (1) Mughal Empire 246 (1)
Beaufort Sea sea Arctic Ocean cultural groups 123 (3) exploration 118 (1), 119 (2), (3), 286 (1), 287 (2) imperial global economy 93 (3) the growth of the US 129 (2)
Beauvais anc. Bellovacum, Caesaromagus France economy 190 (1)
Beaver people North America cultural groups 123 (3)
Bec France medieval states 186 (2), 187 (3)
Becan Central America (Mexico) first civilizations 123 (2)
Bechuanaland mod. Botswana colonial possession/state Southern Africa Cold War 109 (1) European imperialism 96 (1), (2), 97 (4) WWII 104 (1) see also Botswana
Bechuanaland Protectorate state Southern Africa the world in 1950 102–103
Bécs see Vienna
Bedford burial mound/settlement North America (USA) empire and revolution 127 (3) first civilizations 121 (4)
Beduins people Southwest Asia economy 163 (2) Islam 163 (1) Mongols 68–69 (1)
Beer Alston British Isles (United Kingdom) economy 190 (1)
Beersheba Ar. Bir es Saba, Heb. Be'ér Sheva' Southwest Asia (Israel) 20th century 234 (2) first civilizations 222 (1)
Be'ér Sheva' see Beersheba
Beginner's Luck Cave (Australia) the world in 10,000 BCE 14–15
Begram see Kapisa
Beidha Southwest Asia (Jordan) the world in 5000 BCE 18–19
Beidi province East Asia (China) first states 260 (1)
Beihai var. Pakhoi East Asia (China) colonialism 269 (4) post-war politics 274 (2)
Beijing var. Pei-ching; prev. Khanbalik, Pei-p'ing, Beiping; Eng. Peking East Asia (China) plague 72–73 (1) Chinese revolution 271 (5) colonialism 269 (3), (4) Communism 271 (8) early modern states 266 (1), (2), 268 (1) empire and revolution 268 (2) exploration 257 (3) first religions 37 (4) global immigration 100 (1), 101 (3) global knowledge 76 (9) imperial global economy 92 (1) imperialism 270 (2) Islam 275 (4) post-war economy 275 (3) post-war politics 271 (7), 274 (2), 275 (4) Russo-Japanese War 270 (4) Sino-Japanese War 270 (3) the growth of the US 133 (4) trade 267 (3) see also Khanbalik, Peking
Beijing province East Asia post-war economy 275 (3) post-war politics 274 (2)
Beijing Eng. Peking battle East Asia (China) 274 (1)
Beiping Nationalist name for Beijing/Peking East Asia (China) civil war 271 (7)
Beira Southern Africa (Mozambique) colonization 167 (4) economy 168 (2)
Beirut var. Bayrūt; anc. Berytus Southwest Asia (Lebanon) 20th century 234 (2) 20th-century politics 233 (3), (4), 235 (5) crusades 65 (3) economy 190 (1) Islam 235 (4) Napoleon 200–201 (1) WWI 233 (2)
Beisān see Scythopolis
Beishouling var. Pei-shou-ling East Asia (China) the world in 5000 BCE 18–19
Beit el-Wali Egypt ancient Egypt 159 (5)
Bei Zhili province East Asia early modern states 266 (1), (2)
Belarus see Belorussia
Belcher North America (USA) cultural groups 122 (5)
Belchite Iberian Peninsula (Spain) Civil War 209 (4)
Belém var. Pará South America (Brazil) colonization 149 (3), (4) economy 153 (3) environment 153 (4) exploration 143 (2) politics 152 (1)
Belém do Pará South America (Brazil) colonization 149 (3), (4)
Belfast Southern Africa (South Africa) European imperialism 96 (2)
Belfast Ir. Béal Feirste British Isles (United Kingdom) economy 205 (4) civil war 209 (3) WWII 210 (1)
Belfast battle Southern Africa (South Africa) European imperialism 96 (2)
Belfort France WWI 206 (2), (3)
Belgard mod. Białogard Central Europe (Poland) medieval states 189 (3)
Belgian Congo mod. Congo (Zaire); prev. Congo Free State state Central Africa European imperialism 96 (1), 97 (4) WWII 104 (1) see also Congo Free State
Belgica province France Roman empire 180–181 (1)
België see Belgium
Belgique see Belgium
Belgium Dut. België, Fr. Belgique; prev. Spanish Netherlands, Southern Netherlands state Low Countries Cold War 108 (3), 109 (1) early 20th century 206 (1) economy 205 (4) empire and revolution 202 (1i), (2) civil war 209 (3), (5) post-war economy 213 (5), 214 (1), (2) post-war politics 212 (1), (3) Soviet Union 214–215 (4) US superpower 138 (1) WWI 206 (2), (3), 208 (1) WWII 104 (1), 211 (2), (3), (4) see also Spanish Netherlands
Belgrade anc. Singidunum; SCr. Beograd Southeast Europe (Yugoslavia) Cold War 108 (3) crusades 64–65 (2) early modern states 193 (4) economy 198 (1) empire and revolution 202 (1) civil war 209 (3) medieval states 185 (3), 189 (4) Napoleon 200–201 (1), 201 (2), (3) Ottomans 195 (4), 230 (1), 231 (3) post-war economy 215 (3) post-war politics 212 (3) Reformation 194 (2) WWI 207 (4), (6) WWII 210 (1), 211 (2), (3) see also Singidunum
Belice see Belize
Belize var. Belize City; Sp. Belice Central America (Belize) the world in 1700 82–83 the world in 1800 86–87
Belize prev. British Honduras; Sp. Belice state Central America colonization 126 (1) empire and revolution 88 (1) US economy 136 (2) US politics 139 (4) see also British Honduras
Belize City see Belize
Bell North America (Canada) cultural groups 123 (3)
Belleau Wood battle France WWI 206 (3)
Bellingshausen Sea sea Antarctica Antarctic Exploration 287 (3)
Bello Horizonte see Belo Horizonte
Bellona island Pacific Ocean early cultures 280–281 (3) medieval voyages 60 (2)
Bellote Central America (Mexico) first civilizations 123 (2)
Bellovacum see Beauvais
Belluno Italy WWI 207 (5)
Belo Horizonte prev. Bello Horizonte South America (Brazil) empire and revolution 151 (3) environment 153 (4) politics 152 (1)
Belonia South Asia (India) post-war politics 252 (3)
Belorussia var. Belarus, White Russia; Latv. Baltkrievija state Southeast Europe post-war economy 214 (1), (2) Soviet Union 214–215 (4) the modern world 112 (2), 113 (3) see also White Russia
Beloye More see White Sea
Belsen see Bergen-Belsen
Beluga Point North America (USA) cultural groups 123 (3)
Belvoir fort Southwest Asia (Israel) crusades 65 (3)
Belzec concentration camp Central Europe WWII 211 (3)
Bemba state Southern Africa colonization 167 (4)
Bemis Heights battle North America (USA) empire and revolution 127 (3)
Benaco see Garda, Lake
Benares mod. Vārānasi, anc. Kasi, Kashi South Asia (India) colonialism 247 (3), 248 (1) economy 249 (4) empire and revolution 249 (3) first religions 36 (2)
Bender mod. Tighina; Rus. Bendery Southeast Europe (Moldavia) Ottomans 231 (3)
Bendery see Bender
Bendigo goldfield/settlement (Australia) colonization 282 (1), (2)
Beneški Zaliv see Venice, Gulf of
Benevento anc. Beneventum, Malventum Italy Franks 184 (2) medieval states 183 (4) see also Beneventum
Benevento battle Italy medieval states 188 (1)
Benevento, Duchy of state Italy Franks 184 (2) medieval states 182 (2), 183 (4)
Benevento, Principality of state Italy medieval states 185 (3)
Beneventum mod. Benevento Italy early states 178 (1) see also Benevento
Bengal region/state South Asia colonialism 247 (3), 248 (1), (2) decolonization 250 (2) empire and revolution 249 (3)
Bengal, Bay of bay Indian Ocean ancient trade 44–45 (1) trade 72–73 (1) colonialism 247 (3), 248 (1), (2), 269 (4) decolonization 250 (2), 251 (4) early agriculture 258 (1) early medieval states 244 (1), (2), 244–245 (3) early modern states 268 (1) early religions 48 (2) economy 249 (4) empire and revolution 88–89 (2) European expansion 84–85 (1) exploration 239 (1) first humans 13 (2) historical geography 275 (5) Islam 275 (4) Marathas 246 (2) medieval voyages 61 (3) Mongols 68 (2), 68–69 (1) Mughal Empire 246 (1) post-war economy 253 (5), 275 (3) post-war politics 252 (1), (3), 253 (4) Timur 229 (4) trade 230 (2), 267 (3) world religions 242 (3), 243 (4), (5), 49 (3) WWII 251 (3)
Bengasi see Benghazi
Bengazi see Benghazi
Bengdoushan var. Peng-tou-shan East Asia (China) the world in 5000 BCE 18–19
Benghazi var. Bengazi; It. Bengasi North Africa (Libya) colonization 167 (4) economy 168 (2) Ottomans 232–233 (1) WWII 210 (1), 211 (4)
Bengkoeloe see Benkulen
Bengkulu Maritime Southeast Asia (Indonesia) colonialism 247 (4)
Bengkulu see Benkulen
Benguela var. Benguella Southern Africa (Angola) Cold War 109 (5) colonization 167 (4) European expansion 84–85 (1) European imperialism 96 (1) exploration 157 (4) slave trade 165 (4) trade 164 (2)
Benguela state Southern Africa Islam 163 (1)
Benguella see Benguela
Bengweulu, Lake see Bangweulu, Lake
Beni river South America early cultures 146 (1) Incas 147 (3) narcotics 153 (5)
Beni Hasan Egypt ancient Egypt 159 (3), (4)
Benin West Africa (Nigeria) Islam 163 (1)
Benin prev. Dahomey state West Africa decolonization 168 (1) economy 163 (2), (3) Islam 163 (1), 235 (4) slave trade 165 (4) the modern world 112 (1), 113 (3) trade 164 (2), 167 (1) see also Dahomey
Benin, Bight of gulf West Africa exploration 156 (3)
Benkoelen see Benkulen
Benkulen prev. Bengkoeloe, Benkoelen, Bengkulu Maritime Southeast Asia (Indonesia) empire and revolution 88 (1)
Bennington battle North America (USA) empire and revolution 127 (3), 88–89 (2)
Bennington North America (USA) empire and revolution 127 (3)
Bénoué see Benue
Bentenville North America (USA) US Civil War 131 (6)
Benue Fr. Bénoué river West Africa ancient trade 44–45 (1) early agriculture 158 (1) early cultures 160 (1) economy 163 (2) Islam 163 (1), 167 (3) trade 163 (4), (5), (6), (7), 164 (2)
Beograd see Belgrade, Singidunum
Beothuk people North America colonization 126 (1) cultural groups 123 (3)
Berar state South Asia colonialism 248 (2) the world in 1500 74–75
Berau state Maritime Southeast Asia (Indonesia) colonialism 248 (1)
Berber East Africa (Sudan) exploration 157 (5)
Berbera East Africa (Somalia) European expansion 80–81 (1) exploration 156 (3) Islam 163 (1)
Berbers people North Africa Roman empire 181 (4) ancient trade 44–45 (1) early cultures 160 (1) economy 163 (2) Islam 163 (1) trade 164 (2)
Berber States state North Africa Roman empire 182 (1) early cultures 160 (1) medieval states 182 (2)
Berbice state South America the world in 1700 82–83
Berenice East Africa (Sudan) ancient trade 44–45 (1) early cultures 161 (3), (4), (5) early trade 225 (3)
Berezina var. Byerezino river Eastern Europe Napoleon 200–201 (1) WWI 207 (4)
Berezov mod. Berezovo Eastern Europe (Russian Federation) exploration 257 (2)
Berezovo see Berezov
Berg state Central Europe (Germany) Napoleon 201 (2)
Bergama see Pergamum
Bergamo anc. Bergomum Italy economy 190–191 medieval states 188 (1)
Bergen Scandinavia (Norway) economy 190 (1)
Bergen-Belsen concentration camp Central Europe WWII 211 (3)
Bergerac France medieval states 192 (1) Reformation 194 (2)
Bergomum see Bergamo
Beringia physical region Egypt historical geography 117 (1)
Bering Sea sea Pacific Ocean cultural groups 123 (3) exploration 118 (1), 119 (2), (3), 286 (1), 287 (2) medieval states 262–263 (1) the growth of the US 129 (2), 133 (4)
Bering Strait sea waterway Arctic/Pacific Ocean early agriculture 120 (1) exploration 257 (2), 286 (1), 287 (2) imperial global economy 93 (3) the growth of the US 129 (2) WWII 272 (1), 273 (2)
Berlin Central Europe (Germany) Cold War 108 (3), 109 (1) early modern states 193 (4) economy 205 (4) empire and revolution 199 (3), 202 (1), (2) global immigration 101 (2) imperial global economy 92 (1) civil war 209 (5) medieval states 189 (3), (4) Napoleon 200–201 (1), 201 (2), (3) post-war politics 212 (1), (3) Reformation 194 (2), 196 (1) WWII 105 (3), 210 (1), 211 (2), (3), (4)
Bermuda var. Bermuda Islands, Bermudas; prev. Somers Islands colonial possession/island North Atlantic empire and revolution 88 (1) historical geography 117 (1) WWII 104 (2)
Bermuda Islands see Bermuda
Bermudas see Bermuda
Bern see Berne
Berne Ger. Bern Central Europe (Switzerland) Cold War 108 (3) early modern states 193 (5) Reformation 196 (1)
Bernicia region British Isles medieval states 183 (3)
Beroea see Aleppo
Berry region France crusades 64–65 (2)
Berwick British Isles (United Kingdom) economy 204 (1) medieval states 187 (4), 188 (2)
Berytus see Beirut
Besançon anc. Besontium, Vesontio France early modern states 197 (5) economy 190 (1) empire and revolution 199 (4) Franks 184 (2) medieval states 188 (1) see also Vesontio
Besarh see Vaisali
Beshbagowa archaeological site North America (USA) cultural groups 123 (4)
Beshbalik East Asia (China) biological diffusion 72–73 (1) medieval states 262–263 (1)
Besigheim Mithraic site Central Europe (Germany) world religions 48 (1)
Besontium see Besançon, Vesontio
Bessarabia region/state Southeast Europe Ottomans 232–233 (1) WWI 207 (4), 208 (1) WWII 210 (1), 211 (2), (4)
Beswick British Isles (United Kingdom) economy 204 (2)
Beszterce mod. Bistriţa; prev. Nösen; Ger. Bistritz Southeast Europe (Romania) medieval states 189 (4)
Betancí South America (Colombia) early cultures 146 (1)
Betatakin archaeological site North America (USA) cultural groups 123 (4)
Beth-Horon Southwest Asia (West Bank) Roman empire 225 (4)
Bethlehem Ar. Bayt Laḩm, Heb. Bet Leśem Southwest Asia (West Bank) world religions 226 (1)
Beth-Shean Southwest Asia (Israel) ancient Egypt 159 (5)
Bet Leśem see Bethlehem
Beycesultan Southwest Asia (Turkey) early agriculture 174 (1) first cities 28–29 (1)
Béziers anc. Baeterrae, Baeterrae Septimanorum, Julia Beterrae France crusades 186 (1) economy 190 (1) medieval states 187 (3), 192 (1)
Bezwada see Vijayawada
Bhaddiya South Asia (India) world religions 242 (3)
Bhagalpur South Asia (India) economy 249 (4)
Bhagatrav archaeological site South Asia (India) first cities 240 (2)
Bharadvaja region South Asia world religions 242 (2)
Bhārat see India
Bharata-Varsha region South Asia (India) first religions 36 (2)
Bharukaccha var. Barygaza; mod. Broach South Asia (India) ancient India 242 (1) early medieval states 244 (1) first empires 241 (4) world religions 48 (2) see also Barygaza, Broach
Bharukacchra South Asia (India) early religions 48 (2) world religions 49 (3)
Bhatkal South Asia (India) the world in 1600 78–79 the world in 1700 82–83
Bhaumas dynasty South Asia the world in 1000 58–59

Bhimbetka South Asia (India) the world in 10,000 BCE 14–15 (2)
Bhoganagara South Asia (India) world religions 242 (3)
Bhoja *region/state* South Asia first empires 241 (5) world religions 242 (2)
Bhojakata South Asia (India) early medieval states 244 (1)
Bhonsle *region* South Asia Marathas 246 (2)
Bhopal South Asia (India) colonialism 248 (1) post-war economy 253 (5) post-war politics 252 (1)
Bhopal *state* South Asia colonialism 248 (1), (2)
Bhota *see* Tibet
Bhubaneshwar *see* Bhubaneswar
Bhubaneswar *mod.* Bhubaneshwar South Asia (India) post-war politics 252 (1)
Bhuket *see* Phuket
Bhutan *var.* Druk-yul *colonial possession/state* South Asia colonialism 248 (1), (2), 269 (4) Communism 271 (8) decolonization 250 (1), (2), 251 (4) early modern states 268 (1) economy 249 (4) empire and revolution 249 (3) exploration 257 (3) historical geography 275 (5) post-war economy 253 (5), 275 (3) post-war politics 252 (1), 253 (4), 274 (2) the modern world 113 (3) WWII 251 (3)
Biache *archaeological site* France first humans 13 (2)
Biafra *region* West Africa politics 169 (4)
Biafra, Bight of *var.* Bight of Bonny *bay* West Africa exploration 156 (3)
Białogard *see* Belgard
Białystok *ghetto* Central Europe (Poland) WWII 211 (3)
Bian East Asia (China) medieval states 263 (5)
Biangliang East Asia (China) medieval states 263 (6)
Bianliang East Asia (China) medieval states 263 (6)
Bianzhou *var.* Pienchou East Asia (China) medieval states 262–263 (1)
Bibi Hakimeh *oil field* Southwest Asia (Iran) economy 234 (1)
Bida West Africa (Nigeria) Islam 167 (3)
Bidai *people* Central America colonization 125 (4)
Bidar South Asia (India) colonialism 247 (3) early medieval states 245 (4) Mughal Empire 246 (1)
Bidar *state* South Asia early medieval states 245 (4) Mughal Empire 246 (1)
Bié *see* Bihe
Biel *Fr.* Bienne Central Europe (Switzerland) early modern states 193 (5)
Biên Đông *see* South China Sea
Bien Hoa *battle* Mainland Southeast Asia (Vietnam) post-war politics 251 (5)
Bien Long Mainland Southeast Asia (Vietnam) exploration 256 (1)
Bienne *see* Biel
Big Cypress Swamp *battle* North America (USA) the growth of the US 129 (2)
Big Hole *battle* North America (USA) the growth of the US 129 (2)
Big Meadows *battle* North America (USA) the growth of the US 129 (2)
Big Mound *battle* North America (USA) the growth of the US 129 (2)
Bihać Southeast Europe (Bosnia and Herzegovina) post-war economy 215 (3)
Bihar *region/state* South Asia colonialism 248 (1), (2) decolonization 250 (2) Mughal Empire 246 (1) post-war politics 252 (1), (3)
Bihar-Bengal *state* South Asia world religions 243 (4)
Bihe *mod.* Bié *settlement/state* Southern Africa exploration 157 (4)
Bijagos, Archipelago *see* Bissagos Islands
Bijagós, Arquipélago dos *see* Bissagos Islands
Bijai-Raghogarh *state* South Asia empire and revolution 249 (3)
Bijapur South Asia (India) early medieval states 244–245 (3), 245 (4)
Bijapur *state* South Asia early medieval states 245 (4) Mughal Empire 246 (1)
Bikini *nuclear test* Pacific Ocean (Marshall Islands) environmentalism 285 (2)
Bilbao *Basq.* Bilbo Iberian Peninsula (Spain) economy 205 (4) civil war 209 (3), (4)
Bilbo *see* Bilbao
Bilma West Africa (Niger) colonization 167 (4) Islam 163 (1)
Biloxi *people* Central America colonization 125 (4)
Bilzingsleben *archaeological site* Central Europe (Germany) first humans 13 (2)
Bima Maritime Southeast Asia (Indonesia) colonialism 247 (4)
Bimlipatam South Asia (India) colonialism 247 (3)
Bingen *see* Bingium
Bingium *mod.* Bingen *mithraic site* Central Europe (Germany) world religions 48 (1)
Binh Đinh *see* Vijaya
Binxian *archaeological site* East Asia early agriculture 258 (2)
Bioco, Isla de *see* Bioko
Bioko *see* Fernando Po
Bir Aslu *var.* Asslou North Africa (Algeria) Islam 163 (1)
Birch Creek *battle* North America (USA) the growth of the US 129 (2)
Bird Creek *battle* North America (USA) the growth of the US 129 (2)
Bir es Saba *see* Beersheba
Birka Scandinavia (Sweden) medieval states 185 (3) medieval voyages 60–61 (1)
Birkenhead British Isles (United Kingdom) economy 204 (1)
Birmingham North America (USA) the growth of the US 132 (1) US economy 134 (1) US society 137 (6)
Birmingham British Isles (United Kingdom) economy 204 (1) civil war 209 (3) post-war politics 212 (3) WWII 210 (1)
Birnick North America (USA) cultural groups 123 (3)
Bir Sahara *archaeological site* North Africa (Libya) first humans 13 (2)
Bir Tarfawi *archaeological site* North Africa (Libya) first humans 13 (2)
Bisa *people* Southern Africa trade 167 (1)
Biscay, Bay of *bay* Atlantic Ocean economy 190 (1) empire and revolution 199 (4), 202 (1) Franks 183 (5), (6) medieval states 187 (4), 192 (1), (2)
Biscoe Islands *island group* Antarctica Antarctic Exploration 287 (3)
Bishkek *var.* Pishpek; *prev.* Frunze Central Asia (Kyrgyzstan) Soviet Union 214–215 (4)
Bishop's Lynn *see* King's Lynn
Bismarck North America (USA) the growth of the US 129 (2)
Bismarck Archipelago *island group* New Guinea European imperialism 97 (3) WWII 272 (1), 273 (2)
Bissagos Islands *var.* Archipelago Bijagos, Arquipélago dos Bijagós *island group* West Africa exploration 156 (3)
Bissau West Africa (Guinea-Bissau) the world in 1850 90–91
Bistriţa *see* Beszterce
Bistritz *see* Beszterce
Bit-Akitu *building* Southwest Asia (Iraq) first cities 220 (3)
Bithur *battle* South Asia empire and revolution 249 (3)
Bithynia *province/region/state* Southwest Asia Roman empire 179 (5) Hellenistic world 40–41 (1) world religions 48 (1)
Bithynia et Pontus *province* Southwest Asia Roman empire 180–181 (1)
Bitola *prev.* Bitolj; *Turk.* Monastir Southeast Europe (FYR Macedonia) post-war economy 215 (3) *see also* Bitolj, Monastir
Bitolj *mod.* Bitola; *Turk.* Monastir *battle* Southeast Europe (FYR Macedonia) WWI 207 (6) *see also* Bitola
Bitonto *anc.* Butuntum Italy economy 190 (1)
Bitorri Cave Central Africa (Congo) early agriculture 158 (1)
Bit-Resh *building* Southwest Asia (Iraq) first cities 220 (3)
Bituricae *Christian archbishopric* France world religions 48 (1)
Biya *river* Siberia historical geography 254–255 (1)
Biysk *archaeological site* Siberia (Russian Federation) early agriculture 258 (1)
Bizerta *Ar.* Banzart, *Fr.* Bizerte North Africa (Tunisia) WWII 211 (4)
Bizerte *see* Bizerta
Blackburn British Isles (United Kingdom) economy 204 (1) imperial global economy 93 (4)
Blackfoot *people* North America colonization 126 (1)
Black Mesa *archaeological site* North America (USA) cultural groups 123 (4)
Black Patch British Isles (United Kingdom) Bronze Age 175 (3)
Blackpool British Isles (United Kingdom) economy 204 (1)
Black River *river* Mainland Southeast Asia post-war politics 251 (5)
Black Sea *var.* Euxine Sea, Euxinus Pontus; *Bul.* Cherno More, *Rom.* Marea Neagră, *Rus.* Chernoye More, *Turk.* Karadeniz, *Ukr.* Chorne More *sea* Asia/Europe ancient Greece 179 (4) ancient Persia 223 (4), 225 (6) Roman empire 179 (5), 180–181 (1), 181 (3), (4), 224 (2), 225 (5) ancient trade 44–45 (1) biological diffusion 72–73 (1), 73 (3) Bronze Age 175 (3) Copper Age 174 (2) crusades 64–65 (2) early agriculture 174 (1), 20–21 (2), 220 (1) early Islam 56–57 (1), 57 (2) early trade 225 (3) economy 190 (1) empire and revolution 202 (1) exploration 172 (1), (2), 219 (3) first cities 220 (2), 28–29 (1) first civilizations 177 (1), 221 (4), (5), 222 (2), 25 (3) first humans 13 (2) first religions 37 (3) great migrations 52–53 (1), 53 (2) Hellenistic world 224 (1), 41 (2) civil war 209 (3) Islam 163 (1), 226 (2), 227 (4) medieval Persia 231 (4) medieval states 182 (2), 185 (3), 187 (5), 189 (4), 261 (6) medieval voyages 60–61 (1) Mongols 229 (3), 68 (2), 68–69 (1) Napoleon 200–201 (1), 201 (3) Ottomans 195 (4), 230 (1), 231 (3), 232–233 (1) Seljuks 228 (1) Timur 229 (4) world religions 226 (1), 49 (4) WWI 207 (4), (6), 233 (2) 20th-century politics 233 (3)
Black Sea Lake *lake* Asia/Europe the world in 10,000 BCE 14–15
Blackstock *battle* North America (USA) empire and revolution 127 (3)
Black Volta *var.* Borongo, Mouhoun, Moun Hou; *Fr.* Volta Noire *river* West Africa early agriculture 158 (1) economy 163 (2) trade 164 (2)
Blagoveshchensk Siberia (Russian Federation) colonialism 269 (3) Communism 271 (8) Soviet Union 208 (2), 214–215 (4)
Blanc, Cape *headland* West Africa exploration 156 (3)
Blanco *river* South America colonization 125 (5)
Blantyre *var.* Blantyre-Limbe East Africa (Malawi) economy 168 (2) exploration 157 (4)
Blantyre-Limbe *see* Blantyre
Blaye France early modern states 197 (5)
Blenheim New Zealand colonization 283 (5)
Blgariya *see* Bulgaria
Bloemfontein *var.* Mangaung Southern Africa (South Africa) colonization 166 (2) European imperialism 96 (2)
Blois France medieval states 192 (2)
Blois *region* France crusades 64–65 (2)
Blombos Cave Southern Africa palaeolithic art 17 (2)
Blucina *fort* Central Europe (Czech Republic) Bronze Age 175 (3)
Bluefish Cave North America (USA) the world in 10,000 BCE 14–15
Blue Nile *var.* Abai, Bahr El Azraq, al Azraq *Amh.* Åbay Wenz, *Ar.* An Nil al Azraq *river* East Africa early agriculture 158 (1) economy 163 (2) exploration 157 (5) Islam 163 (1) slave trade 165 (4) trade 165 (3)
Bluff *whaling station* New Zealand colonization 283 (4)
Blythe Intaglios *archaeological site* North America (USA) cultural groups 123 (4)
Bobangi *people* Central Africa trade 167 (1)
Boca del Río Central America (Mexico) first civilizations 121 (2)
Bocalos *people* Central America colonization 125 (4)
Bodensee *see* Constance, Lake
Bodh Gaya *var.* Buddh Gaya *Buddhist centre/settlement* South Asia (India) early religions 48 (2) exploration 256 (1) first religions 36 (2) world religions 49 (3)
Boeotia *state* Greece ancient Greece 179 (4)
Boeroe *see* Buru
Boğazköy *see* Hattushash
Bogotá *prev.* Santa Fe, Santa Fé de Bogotá South America (Colombia) empire and revolution 150 (1), (2), 151 (3) environment 153 (4) exploration 143 (3) narcotics 153 (5) politics 152 (1) the growth of the US 133 (4) *see also* Santa Fé de Bogotá
Bogram Central Asia (Afghanistan) Hellenistic world 41 (2)
Bo Hai *var. Po Hai gulf* East Asia early agriculture 258 (1), (2) early modern states 265 (5), 266 (1), (2) first cities 259 (3), (4), (5) first states 260 (1) medieval states 262–263 (1), 263 (4), (6), 264 (1), (2) Russo-Japanese War 270 (4) Sino-Japanese War 270 (3)
Bohai *var. Po Hai state* East Asia (China) medieval states 262–263 (1)
Bohemia *region/state* Central Europe crusades 64–65 (2) early modern states 193 (4) empire and revolution 199 (3), 202 (2) medieval states 188 (1), 189 (4) Napoleon 200–201 (1) Ottomans 197 (4) Reformation 196 (1), (2)
Bohemia-Moravia *region /state* Central Europe medieval states 185 (3) WWII 210 (1), 211 (2), (4)
Bohemian Crown, Lands of the *state* Central Europe early modern states 194 (1)
Bohemians *people* Central Europe Franks 184 (2)
Bohuslän *region* Scandinavia early modern states 197 (3)
Boise North America (USA) the growth of the US 129 (2)
Bojador, Cape *headland* Southwest Asia exploration 156 (3)
Bojnurd Central Asia (Iran) Hellenistic world 40–41 (1)
Bokhara *see* Bukhara
Bolgar *see* Bulgar
Bolgary *see* Bulgar
Bolivia *state* South America Cold War 109 (1) economy 153 (3) empire and revolution 150 (1), 151 (3), 88–89 (2) environment 153 (4) narcotics 153 (5) politics 151 (4), 152 (1), (2) the growth of the US 133 (4) the modern world 112 (1), 113 (4) US superpower 138 (1) WWII 104 (2)
Bologna *anc.* Felsina, *later* Bononia Italy crusades 186 (1) economy 190 (1) empire and revolution 202 (3) Franks 184 (2) medieval states 183 (4), 187 (3), 188 (1) Napoleon 200–201 (1), 201 (2)
Bol'sheretsk Siberia (Russian Federation) exploration 257 (2)
Bolsheviks *political faction* Communism 271 (8)
Bolton British Isles (United Kingdom) imperial global economy 93 (4)
Bolzano *see* Bozen
Boma Central Africa (Congo (Zaire)) exploration 157 (4)
Bombay *Guj.* Mumbai South Asia (India) colonialism 247 (3), 248 (1), 269 (4) decolonization 250 (1) economy 249 (4) empire and revolution 88 (1) European expansion 84–85 (1) exploration 239 (1) global immigration 100 (1), 101 (3) imperial global economy 92 (1), 93 (5) Mughal Empire 246 (1) post-war economy 253 (5) post-war politics 252 (1) trade 230 (2)
Bombay *region/state* South Asia colonialism 248 (2) empire and revolution 249 (3) post-war politics 253 (4)
Bombo Kaburi *archaeological site* East Africa (Kenya) early cultures 160 (1)
Bomboná *battle* South America (Colombia) empire and revolution 150 (1)
Bom Jardim *archaeological site* South America (Brazil) early cultures 145 (2)
Bonaire *island* West Indies the world in 1800 86–87 the world in 1850 90–91
Bonampak Central America (Mexico) first civilizations 123 (2)
Bône *mod.* Annaba North Africa (Algeria) economy 190 (1) WWII 211 (4) *see also* Annaba
Bone Cave (Australia) the world in 10,000 BCE 14–15
Bonin Islands *Jap.* Ogasawara-guntō *island group* Japan imperialism 270 (2) US superpower 138 (1) WWII 272 (1), 273 (2)
Bonn Central Europe (Germany) Cold War 108 (3) early modern states 197 (5) post-war politics 212 (1), (3)
Bonna *legion headquarters* (France) Roman empire 180–181 (1)
Bonneville, Lake *lake* North America historical geography 117 (1)
Bonny, Bight of *see* Biafra, Bight of
Bono *state* West Africa the world in 1700 82–83
Bononia *mod.* Bologna Italy Roman empire 180–181 (1) *see also* Bologna, Felsina
Bononia *see* Boulogne, Vidin
Boomplaats *archaeological site* Southern Africa (South Africa) early cultures 160 (1)
Boomplaats *battle* Southern Africa (South Africa) colonization 166 (2)
Boone *burial mound* North America (USA) first civilizations 121 (4)
Boonesboro *see* Boonesborough
Boonesborough *mod.* Boonesboro North America (USA) empire and revolution 127 (3) exploration 119 (2)
Booneville North America (USA) US Civil War 131 (6)
Bora Bora *island* Pacific Ocean US superpower 138 (1)
Borbetomagus *mod.* Worms Central Europe (Germany) great migrations 52–53 (1) *see also* Worms
Borburata South America (Venezuela) European expansion 85 (2)
Bordeaux *anc.* Burdigala France Roman empire 182 (1) biological diffusion 72–73 (1) crusades 186 (1) early modern states 194 (1), 197 (5) economy 190 (1), 205 (4) empire and revolution 199 (4), 202 (1) Franks 183 (5), (6), 184 (2) medieval states 185 (3), 187 (4), 192 (1), (2) Napoleon 200–201 (1), 201 (2) Reformation 194 (2) WWII 104 (2), 210 (1), 211 (2), (4) *see also* Burdigala
Borden Island *island* Arctic Ocean exploration 287 (2)
Border Cave *archaeological site/settlement* Southern Africa (South Africa) first humans 13 (2)
Borg in-Nadur *fort* Mediterranean Sea (Malta) Bronze Age 175 (3)
Borgo *see* Burgen
Borgu *state* West Africa Islam 163 (1) slave trade 165 (4) trade 164 (2)
Borgu Kingdoms *state* West Africa the world in 1400 70–71 the world in 1500 74–75 the world in 1700 82–83 the world in 1800 86–87 the world in 1850 90–91
Borley, Cape *headland* Antarctica Antarctic Exploration 287 (3)
Borneo *region/island* Maritime Southeast Asia ancient India 241 (6) ancient trade 44–45 (1) biological diffusion 72–73 (1) Bronze Age 240 (3) colonialism 247 (4), 248 (1), 269 (4) decolonization 251 (4) early agriculture 20–21 (2), 258 (1) early medieval states 245 (5), (6) European expansion 80–81 (1) European imperialism 97 (3) exploration 239 (1), (2), 278 (1) first humans 13 (2) global immigration 101 (3) global knowledge 76–77 (1) Islam 243 (6) post-war economy 253 (5) post-war politics 253 (4) trade 230 (2), 267 (3) world religions 243 (5), 49 (4) WWII 251 (3), 272 (1), 273 (2)
Bornholm *island* Scandinavia early modern states 197 (3) empire and revolution 202 (1)
Bornu *state* West Africa colonization 167 (4) economy 163 (2) slave trade 165 (4) trade 167 (1)
Borobudur *temple* Maritime Southeast Asia (Indonesia) early medieval states 245 (5) world religions 243 (5), 49 (4)
Borodino *battle* Eastern Europe (Russian Federation) Napoleon 200–201 (1)
Borongo *see* Black Volta
Bororo *people* South America early cultures 147 (2)
Bosanski Novi Southeast Europe (Bosnia and Herzegovina) post-war economy 215 (3)
Bosna Saray *see* Sarajevo
Bosnia *state/vassal state* Eastern Europe medieval states 189 (4) Ottomans 230 (1)
Bosnia and Herzegovina *prev.* Bosnia-Herzegovina *region/state/vassal state* Southeast Europe Islam 235 (4) Ottomans 202 (4), 232–233 (1) post-war economy 214 (1), (2), 215 (3) Soviet Union 214–215 (4) the world in 1900 94–95 the modern world 110–111 , 112 (2), 113 (3) WWI 207 (6)
Bosporan Kingdom *state/vassal state* Eastern Europe Roman empire 179 (5), 180–181 (1), 225 (5) ancient trade 44–45 (1)
Boston *prev.* St Botolph's Town British Isles (United Kingdom) economy 190 (1)
Boston North America (USA) colonization 126 (1) empire and revolution 127 (2), (3) global immigration 100 (1) imperial global economy 93 (5) the growth of the US 129 (2), 132 (1) US Civil War 130 (5) US economy 134 (1), (3), 136 (2)
Boston *battle* North America (USA) empire and revolution 88–89 (2)
Bostra Southwest Asia (Syria) Roman empire 180–181 (1) world religions 48 (1)
Bosumpra *early food production site* West Africa (Ivory Coast) early agriculture 158 (1)
Botany Bay *inlet* Australia exploration 278 (1)
Bothnia, Gulf of *Fin.* Pohjanlahti, *Swe.* Bottniska Viken *gulf* Scandinavia early modern states 197 (3) economy 205 (4)
Botsu Japan medieval states 264 (2)
Botswana *prev.* Bechuanaland *state* Southern Africa Cold War 109 (5) decolonization 168 (1) economy 168 (2) the modern world 112 (1), 113 (3) *see also* Bechuanaland
Bottniska Viken *see* Bothnia, Gulf of
Bouar *early food production site* Central Africa (Cameroon) early agriculture 158 (1)
Boucher *burial mound* North America (USA) first civilizations 121 (4)
Bougainville *island* Pacific Ocean colonization 284–285 (1) early cultures 280 (2) European imperialism 97 (3) exploration 279 (3), 280 (1) WWII 251 (3)
Bougie North Africa (Algeria) economy 190 (1) WWII 211 (4)
Bouillon Low Countries (Belgium) crusades 64–65 (2)
Boulogne *var.* Boulogne-sur-Mer; *anc.* Bononia, Gesoriacum, Gessoriacum (France) Franks 184 (2) medieval states 186 (2) Napoleon 200–201 (1) WWI 206 (2), (3)
Boulogne-sur-Mer *see* Boulogne
Bourbon *island* Indian Ocean the world in 1700 82–83
Bourem West Africa (Mali) exploration 157 (4)
Bourges *anc.* Avaricum France early modern states 197 (5) economy 190 (1) empire and revolution 199 (4) Franks 183 (5), (6) medieval states 192 (1), (2)
Bourgogne *see* Burgundy
Bourke Australia colonization 282 (1)
Boussargues *archaeological site* France Copper Age 174 (2)
Bouvines France medieval states 187 (4)
Bovec *see* Flitsch
Bovianum Vetus Italy early states 178 (1)
Bovillae Italy early states 178 (1)
Bowmans Brook North America (USA) cultural groups 122 (5)
Boxgrove *archaeological site* British Isles (United Kingdom) first humans 13 (2)
Boyacá *battle* South America (Colombia) empire and revolution 150 (1), 88–89 (2)
Boyra South Asia (Bangladesh) post-war politics 252 (3)
Bozeman Trail *wagon train route* North America the growth of the US 129 (2)
Bozen *anc.* Bauzanum; *It.* Bolzano Italy economy 190 (1), 190–191 WWI 207 (5) WWII 211 (3)
Brabant *province/region* Low Countries medieval states 192 (2) Reformation 195 (5)
Brač *var.* Brach; *anc.* Brattia; *It.* Brazza *island* Southeast Europe post-war economy 215 (3)
Bracara *var.* Bracara Augusta; *mod.* Braga *Christian archbishopric/settlement* Iberian Peninsula (Portugal) Roman empire 180–181 (1) world religions 48 (1)
Bracara Augusta *see* Bracara
Brach *see* Brač
Bradford British Isles (United Kingdom) economy 204 (1), (2) imperial global economy 93 (4)
Braga *see* Bracara
Brahmanabad South Asia (Pakistan) early medieval states 244 (2)
Brahmaputra *var.* Padma, Tsangpo; *Ben.* Jamuna, *Chin.* Yarlung Zangbo Jiang, *Ind.* Bramaputra, Dihang, Siang *river* South Asia ancient India 242 (1) ancient trade 44–45 (1) biological diffusion 72–73 (1), 73 (3) colonialism 247 (3), 248 (1), (2), 269 (4) decolonization 250 (1), (2) early agriculture 258 (1) early medieval states 244 (1), 244–245 (3) early religions 48 (2) economy 249 (4) empire and revolution 249 (3), 268 (2) exploration 239 (1), 257 (3) first religions 36 (2) first states 260 (1) imperial global economy 92 (1) Marathas 246 (2) medieval states 261 (6), 262–263 (1) Mongols 68–69 (1) Mughal Empire 246 (1) post-war politics 252 (1), (3) world religions 49 (3), (4)
Brahmavarta *region* South Asia world religions 242 (2)
Bramaputra *see* Brahmaputra
Branco *river* South America colonization 149 (3) politics 152 (1)
Brandanus *river* Italy early states 178 (1)
Brandelier *archaeological site* North America (USA) cultural groups 123 (4)
Brandenburg *var.* Hohenzollern *region/settlement/state* Central Europe early modern states 193 (4), 195 (3) empire and revolution 199 (3), 202 (2) medieval states 188 (1), 189 (3), (4) Reformation 194 (2), 196 (1), (2)
Brandywine *battle* North America (USA) empire and revolution 127 (3)
Brasil *see* Brazil
Brasília South America (Brazil) economy 153 (3) environment 153 (4) politics 152 (1)
Braşov Southeast Europe (Romania) post-war politics 212 (3)
Brass West Africa (Nigeria) European expansion 84–85 (1)
Brassempouy *archaeological site* France prehistoric culture 17 (4)
Brassó *mod.* Braşov; *prev.* Oraşul Stalin; *Ger.* Kronstadt Southeast Europe (Romania) medieval states 189 (4) *see also* Braşov
Bratislava *Ger.* Pressburg, *Hung.* Pozsony *ghetto/settlement* Central Europe (Slovakia) WWII 210 (1), 211 (3), (4) *see also* Pozsony
Bratsk Siberia (Russian Federation) exploration 257 (2)
Brattahlid *mod.* Julianehåb North America (Greenland) medieval voyages 60–61 (1)
Brattia *see* Brač
Braunschweig *see* Brunswick
Brava *var.* Baraawe East Africa (Somalia) exploration 156 (3) Islam 163 (1) trade 165 (3)
Bravo del Norte Río *see* Grande, Rio
Bravo, Río *see* Grande, Rio
Brazil *prev.* Empire of Brazil, United States of Brazil; *Port.* Brasil *colonial possession/state* South America Cold War 109 (1) colonization 149 (4) economy 153 (3) empire and revolution 150 (1), (2), 151 (3), 88–89 (2) environment 153 (4) European expansion 81 (3), 84–85 (1) global immigration 100 (1), 101 (2) imperial global economy 92 (1) narcotics 153 (5) politics 152 (1), (2) the growth of the US 133 (4) the modern world 112 (1), 113 (4) US politics 139 (4) US superpower 138 (1) WWII 104 (2)
Brazilian Highlands *Port.* Planalto Central *mountain range* South America colonization 149 (3), (4) early cultures 145 (2) environment 153 (4) exploration 143 (2), (3)
Brazil, United States of *see* Brazil
Brazil, Viceroyalty of *state* South America colonization 149 (3)
Brazos *river* North America colonization 125 (4)
Brazza *see* Brač
Brazzaville Central Africa (Congo) colonization 167 (4) economy 168 (2)
Brčko Southeast Europe (Bosnia and Herzegovina) post-war economy 215 (3)
Breda *battle* Low Countries (Netherlands) Reformation 195 (5)
Bréifne *state* British Isles medieval states 188 (2)
Breisach France early modern states 197 (5)
Breitenfeld *battle* Central Europe (Germany) Reformation 196 (1)
Brême *see* Bremen
Bremen *Fr.* Brême Central Europe (Germany) early modern states 193 (4), 197 (3) economy 190 (1), 205 (4) empire and revolution 199 (3), 202 (2) Franks 184 (2) civil war 209 (3) medieval states 188 (1), 189 (3) Napoleon 200–201 (1), 201 (2) post-war politics 212 (3) Reformation 196 (1) WWII 211 (4)
Bremen *region* Central Europe early modern states 197 (3)
Brenner Col du *see* Brenner Pass
Brennero, Passo del *see* Brenner Pass
Brenner Pass *var.* Brenner Sattel; *Fr.* Col du Brenner, *Ger.* Brennerpass, *It.* Passo del Brennero *pass* Central Europe economy 190 (1)
Brenner Sattel *see* Brenner Pass
Brenta *river* Italy WWI 207 (5)
Brescia *anc.* Brixia (Italy) economy 190 (1), 190–191 medieval states 188 (1) WWI 207 (5)
Breslau *Pol.* Wrocław Central Europe (Poland) early modern states 193 (4) empire and revolution 202 (2) medieval states 189 (3), (4) WWI 207 (4) *see also* Wrocław
Brest France early modern states 193 (4), 197 (5) economy 205 (4) empire and revolution 199 (4) medieval states 187 (4), 192 (1), (2) Napoleon 200–201 (1) WWII 104 (2)
Brest *prev.* Brześć Litewski; *Pol.* Brześć nad Bugiem, *Rus.* Brest-Litovsk Eastern Europe (Belorussia) post-war politics 212 (3) *see also* Brest-Litovsk
Brest-Litovsk *mod.* Brest; *prev.* Brześć Litewski; *Pol.* Brześć nad Bugiem Eastern Europe (Belorussia) empire and revolution 202 (1) WWI 207 (4) *see also* Brest
Brétigny France medieval states 192 (1)
Breton March *second order region* France Franks 184 (2)
Bretons *people* France Roman empire 182 (1) Franks 183 (5), (6)
Briançon France early modern states 197 (5)
Briar Creek *battle* North America (USA) empire and revolution 127 (3)
Bricgstow *see* Bristol
Bricindarioi *settlement/state* Greece ancient Greece 177 (2)
Brielle *see* Brill
Brigantium Iberian Peninsula (Spain) Roman empire 180–181 (1)
Brigetio Central Europe (Hungary) Roman empire 180–181 (1) world religions 48 (1)
Brighton British Isles (United Kingdom) economy 204 (1)
Brigukacha South Asia (India) world religions 242 (2)
Brill *Fr.* Brielle Low Countries (Netherlands) Reformation 195 (5)
Brindisi Italy economy 190 (1) medieval states 183 (4)
Brisbane Australia colonization 282 (1), (2), 283 (3), 284–285 (1) exploration 279 (2), (3)
Bristol *anc.* Bricgstow *settlement/state* British Isles (United Kingdom) economy 190 (1), 205 (4) European expansion 84–85 (1) medieval states 187 (4), 188 (2) Napoleon 200–201 (1), 201 (2) WWII 210 (1)
Bristol Channel *inlet* British Isles economy 204 (1)
Britain *var.* Great Britain *state* British Isles ancient trade 44–45 (1) biological diffusion 72–73 (1) economy 205 (4) empire and revolution 202 (1), 88–89 (2) European expansion 84–85 (1) European imperialism 97 (4) exploration 172 (1), (2) global immigration 100 (1) imperial global economy 93 (5) civil war 209 (3), (5) world religions 48 (1), 49 (4) WWI 206 (2), (3), 208 (1) WWII 104 (1), 211 (2), (4)
Britannia *province* British Isles Roman empire 180–181 (1), 181 (4)
British Central Africa *state* Southern Africa European imperialism 97 (4)
British Civil Wars *war* British Isles Reformation 196 (2)
British Colonies *colonial possession* North America empire and revolution 88 (1)
British Columbia *Fr.* Colombie-Britannique *province/state* North America the growth of the US 129 (1), (2), 132 (1) US Civil War 131 (7) US economy 136 (2)
British East Africa *mod.* Kenya *colonial possession* East Africa European imperialism 96 (1), 97 (4) *see also* Kenya
British Guiana *mod.* Guyana *colonial possession/state* South America Cold War 109 (1) empire and revolution 150 (1), 151 (3) global immigration 101 (3) WWII 104 (1) *see also* Guyana
British Honduras *mod.* Belize *colonial possession* Central America Cold War 108 (2), 109 (1) the growth of the US 129 (2) *see also* Belize
British India *colonial possession* South Asia empire and revolution 88–89 (2) European imperialism 97 (3)
British Indian Ocean Territory *colonial possession* Indian Ocean the modern world 110–111
British Isles *island group* Europe Bronze Age 175 (3) early agriculture 174 (1), 20–21 (2) exploration 286 (1) global knowledge 76–77 (1)
British Malaya *state* Mainland southeast Asia (Malaysia) european imperialism 97 (3)
British Malaysia *colonial possession* Mainland Southeast Asia European imperialism 97 (3)
British New Guinea *colonial possession* Maritime Southeast Asia colonization 284–285 (1) exploration 279 (3)
British North Borneo *mod.* Sabah *colonial possession* Maritime Southeast Asia Cold War 109 (1) colonialism 269 (4) colonization 284–285 (1) decolonization 251 (4) European imperialism 97 (3) exploration 279 (3) WWII 251 (3), 272 (1), 273 (2) *see also* Sabah
British Somaliland *colonial possession* East Africa European imperialism 96 (1), 97 (4)
British Virgin Islands *colonial possession* West Indies the modern world 110–111
Britons *people* British Isles Roman empire 182 (1) medieval states 182 (2)
Brittany *region/state* France Franks 184 (2) medieval states 186 (2), 187 (4), 192 (1), (2) medieval voyages 60–61 (1)
Brixia *see* Brescia
Brno *Ger.* Brünn Central Europe (Czech Republic) early modern states 193 (4) medieval states 189 (4) prehistoric culture 17 (4)
Broach South Asia (India) colonialism 247 (3)
Brock Island *island* Arctic Ocean exploration 287 (2)
Brody Eastern Europe (Ukraine) WWI 207 (4)
Broederstroom *archaeological site* Southern Africa (South Africa) early cultures 160 (1)
Broken Hill Australia colonization 282 (1), 283 (3)
Bronocice *archaeological site* Central Europe (Poland) Copper Age 174 (2)
Brooklyn Heights North America (USA) empire and revolution 127 (3)
Brooklyn Heights *battle* North America (USA) empire and revolution 127 (3)
Brooks Range *mountain range* North America exploration 287 (2) the growth of the US 129 (2)
Broome Australia colonization 282 (1)
Broucsella *see* Brussels
Broughton British Isles (United Kingdom) economy 204 (2)
Brskovo Southeast Europe (Yugoslavia) economy 190 (1)
Bruges Low Countries (Belguim) biological diffusion 72–73 (1) economy 190 (1) Reformation 195 (5) WWI 206 (2), (3)
Brundisium *mod.* Brindisi Italy Roman empire 180–181 (1), 181 (3) early states 178 (1) *see also* Brindisi
Brunei Maritime Southeast Asia (Brunei) biological diffusion 72–73 (1) colonialism 247 (4) early medieval states 245 (6) European imperialism 97 (3) exploration 239 (2)
Brunei *colonial possession/state* Maritime Southeast Asia colonialism 247 (4) colonization 284–285 (1) decolonization 251 (4) exploration 278 (1) Islam 275 (4) post-war economy 253 (5), 275 (3) post-war politics 253 (4) the modern world 112 (1) WWII 251 (3), 272 (1), 273 (2)
Brunei Town *see* Bandar Seri Begawan
Brunete Iberian Peninsula (Spain) civil war 209 (4)
Brünn *see* Brno
Brunswick *Ger.* Braunschweig *rebellion/settlement* Central Europe (Germany) early modern states 193 (4) economy 190 (1) empire and revolution 199 (3) medieval states 189 (3) Reformation 196 (2)
Brusa *var.* Bursa; *mod.* Brussa, *anc.* Prusa Southwest Asia (Turkey) medieval states 189 (4) *see also* Bursa, Prusa
Brussa *see* Brusa, Bursa, Prusa
Brussel *see* Brussels
Brussels *var.* Bruxelles; *anc.* Broucsella; *Dut.* Brussel, *Ger.* Brüssel Low Countries (Belgium) Cold War 108 (3) early modern states 193 (4) economy 190 (1) empire and revolution 199 (4), 202 (1), (1i), (2) civil war 209 (3) Napoleon 200–201 (1), 201 (2), (3) Reformation 194 (2), 195 (5) WWI 206 (2), (3)
Bruttii *people* Italy early states 178 (1), (2)
Bruxelles *see* Brussels
Brześć Litewski *see* Brest, Brest-Litovsk
Brześć nad Bugiem *see* Brest, Brest-Litovsk
Buang Bep *archaeological site* Mainland Southeast Asia (Thailand) Bronze Age 240 (3)
Bubastis Egypt ancient Egypt 159 (4), (5) first cities 28–29 (1)
Bucephala *battle* South Asia (Pakistan) Hellenistic world 40–41 (1)
Bucharest *Rom.* Bucureşti, *Turk.* Bükreş Southeast Europe (Romania) Cold War 108 (3) economy 205 (4) empire and revolution 202 (1) civil war 209 (3) Napoleon 200–201 (1), 201 (3) Ottomans 197 (4), 230 (1) post-war politics 212 (3) WWI 207 (6) WWII 210 (1), 211 (2), (4)
Buchenwald *concentration camp* Central Europe WWII 211 (3)
Bucureşti *see* Bucharest
Buda *mod.* Budapest Central Europe (Hungary) biological diffusion 72–73 (1) early modern states 193 (4), 194 (1) economy 190 (1) empire and revolution 202 (1) medieval states 187 (5), 188 (1), 189 (4) Napoleon 200–201 (1), 201 (2) Ottomans 195 (4), 230 (1), 231 (3) Reformation 194 (2) *see also* Aquincum, Budapest
Budapest *prev.* Buda; *SCr.* Budimpešta Central Europe (Hungary) Cold War 108 (3), 109 (1) empire and revolution 202 (1i) civil war 209 (5) Ottomans 202 (4), 232–233 (1) WWI 207 (4) WWII 210 (1), 211 (2), (3), (4) *see also* Buda
Buddh Gaya *see* Bodh Gaya
Budimpešta *see* Budapest
Buenaventura South America (Colombia) empire and revolution 150 (1), 151 (3)
Buena Vista *battle* Central America (Mexico) the growth of the US 129 (2)
Buenos Aires *prev.* Santa Maria del Buen Aire South America (Argentina) colonization 148 (2) empire and revolution 150 (1), 151 (3) environment 153 (4) European expansion 84–85 (1) exploration 142 (1), 143 (2), (3) global immigration 100 (1), 101 (2) imperial global economy 92 (1) politics 152 (1)
Buenos Aires *state* South America empire and revolution 151 (3)
Buenos Aires, Audiencia of *region* South America colonization 148 (2)
Buffalo North America (USA) the growth of the US 129 (2), 132 (1) US Civil War 130 (5) US economy 134 (1), (3)
Bug *Bel.* Zakhodni Buh, *Eng.* Western Bug, *Rus.* Zapadnyy Bug, *Ukr.* Zakhidnyy Buh *river* Eastern Europe WWI 207 (4)
Buganda *state* East Africa colonization 167 (4) exploration 157 (5) slave trade 165 (4) trade 167 (1)
Bu Gia Map *battle* Mainland Southeast Asia (Vietnam) post-war politics 251 (5)
Bu Hasa *Ar.* Bū Ḩaşā' *oil field* Southwest Asia economy 234 (1)
Buhen Egypt ancient Egypt 159 (3), (4), (5)
Bujumbura *see* Usumbura
Buka New Guinea (Papua New Guinea) early cultures 280 (2) exploration 280 (1)
Buka *island* Pacific Ocean colonization 284–285 (1) European imperialism 97 (3) exploration 279 (3)
Bukavu *prev.* Costermansville Central Africa (Congo (Zaire)) economy 168 (2)
Bukhara *var.* Bokhara, Bukhoro Central Asia (Uzbekistan) trade 72–73 (1) colonialism 269 (3) Communism 271 (8) crusades 65 (1) early Islam 56–57 (1), 57 (2) Hellenistic world 40–41 (1) Islam 226 (2), 227 (4), (5) medieval Persia 231 (4) Mongols 68–69 (1) Soviet Union 208 (2), 214–215 (4) Timur 229 (4) trade 267 (3)
Bukhara *province/region/state* Central Asia colonialism 248 (1), 269 (3) medieval Persia 231 (4)
Bukhoro *see* Bukhara
Bukit Tengku Lembu *archaeological site* Mainland Southeast Asia (Thailand) Bronze Age 240 (3)
Bukoba Eastern Africa (Tanzania) exploration 157 (5)
Bükreş *see* Bucharest
Bulawayo *var.* Buluwayo Southern Africa (Zimbabwe) colonization 167 (4) economy 168 (2) European imperialism 96 (2)
Bulgar *var.* Bolgar; *mod.* Bolgary Eastern Europe (Russian Federation) medieval states 185 (3) medieval voyages 60–61 (1) Mongols 68 (2), 68–69 (1) the world in 1000 58–59
Bulgaria *var.* Blgariya, Bulgariya; *Bul.* Bŭlgariya *state* Southeast Europe economy 190 (1), 205 (4) civil war 209 (3) medieval states 185 (3), (5), 188 (1), 189 (4) medieval voyages 60–61 (1) Mongols 68–69 (1) Ottomans 202 (4), 230 (1) post-war economy 213 (5), 214 (1), (2), 215 (3) post-war politics 212 (3) Soviet Union 208 (2), 213 (4) the modern world 112 (2), 113 (3), (4) WWI 207 (6), 208 (1), 233 (2) WWII 104 (2), 210 (1), 211 (2), (4) 20th-century politics 233 (3) Cold War 108 (3), 109 (1) early 20th century 206 (1)
Bulgarians *people* Eastern Europe the world in 750 CE 54–55
Bŭlgariya *see* Bulgaria
Bulgars *people* Eastern Europe Roman empire 182 (1)
Bull Brook North America (USA) the world in 5000 BCE 18–19
Bull Run *var.* Manassas *battle* North America (USA) US Civil War 131 (6)

Bulungan state Maritime Southeast Asia the world in 1800 86–87
Buluwayo see Bulawayo
Bunbury Australia colonization 282 (1)
Bunce Island West Africa (Liberia) slave trade 165 (4)
Bundaberg archaeological site Australia prehistoric culture 17 (5)
Bundelas state South Asia Mongols 68–69 (1)
Bundelkhand state South Asia empire and revolution 249 (3)
Bunker Hill battle North America (USA) empire and revolution 127 (3)
Bunyoro state East Africa colonization 167 (4) slave trade 165 (4) trade 167 (1)
Buraida Ar. Buraydah Southwest Asia (Saudi Arabia) 20th-century politics 233 (4)
Buraydah see Buraida
Burdigala mod. Bordeaux France Roman empire 180–181 (1), 181 (3), (4) world religions 48 (1) see also Bordeaux
Burgen It. Borgo Italy WWI 207 (5)
Burgos Iberian Peninsula (Spain) Franks 184 (2) civil war 209 (4) Islam 192 (3)
Burgundian Kingdom state Central Europe/France Roman empire 182 (1) great migrations 52–53 , (1) the world in 500 CE 50–51
Burgundians people Central Europe/France Roman empire 180–181 (1), 181 (4) great migrations 52–53 (1)
Burgundy Fr. Bourgogne; var. County of Burgundy, Duchy of Burgundy, Kingdom of Burgundy state/region France early modern states 193 (4) Franks 183 (5), (6), 184 (2) medieval states 185 (3), 187 (4), 192 (1), (2)
Burhanpur South Asia (India) colonialism 247 (3) early medieval states 244–245 (3)
Buritaca South America (Colombia) early cultures 146 (1)
Burketown Australia colonization 282 (1)
Burkina var. Burkina Faso; prev. Upper Volta state West Africa decolonization 168 (1) economy 168 (2), (3) the modern world 112 (1), 113 (3) see also Upper Volta
Burkina Faso see Burkina, Upper Volta
Burlag region Siberia Soviet Union 213 (4)
Burma var. Myanmar colonial possession/state Mainland Southeast Asia biological diffusion 72–73 (1) Bronze Age 240 (3) colonialism 248 (1), (2), 269 (4) Communism 271 (8) decolonization 250 (1), (2), 251 (4) early modern states 266 (1), (2), 268 (1) economy 249 (4) empire and revolution 249 (3) European imperialism 97 (4) exploration 257 (3) global immigration 100 (1), 101 (3) imperial global economy 92 (1) Islam 275 (4) medieval states 263 (6) post-war economy 253 (5), 275 (3) post-war politics 252 (1), (3), 253 (4), 271 (7), 274 (2) the modern world 113 (3), (4) trade 267 (3) world religions 243 (5), 49 (3) WWII 104 (1), 251 (3), 272 (1), 273 (2)
Burma Road road East Asia/Mainland Southeast Asia WWII 251 (3)
Burnt Corn Creek battle North America (USA) the growth of the US 129 (2)
Bursa var. Brussa; prev. Brusa, anc. Prusa Southwest Asia (Turkey) Ottomans 202 (4), 230 (1) see also Brusa, Prusa
Būr Sa'īd see Port Said
Buru Du. Boeroe island Maritime Southeast Asia colonialism 247 (4) European imperialism 97 (3) exploration 278 (1) Islam 243 (6)
Burundi prev. Urundi state Central Africa colonization 167 (4) decolonization 168 (1) economy 168 (2), (3) the modern world 112 (1), 113 (3) trade 167 (1) see also Ruanda-Urundi
Buryatia region Eastern Europe Soviet Union 214–215 (4)
Buryats people Siberia Mongols 68–69 (1) trade 267 (3)
Busan see Pusan
Bush Barrow burial mound British Isles (United Kingdom) Bronze Age 175 (3)
Būshehr see Bushire
Bushire var. Būshehr, Rus. Bandar-e Būshehr oil terminal/settlement Southwest Asia (Iran) 20th-century politics 235 (5) economy 234 (1) exploration 219 (4) trade 230 (2)
Busoga state East Africa the world in 1700 82–83 the world in 1800 86–87 the world in 1850 90–91
Busra see Basra
Busselton Australia colonization 282 (1)
Bussora see Basra
Bustard Bay bay Australia exploration 278 (1)
Buto Egypt ancient Egypt 159 (2) first cities 28–29 (1)
Butua state Southern Africa the world in 1600 78–79 the world in 1800 86–87
Butuntum see Bitonto
Buwayhids var. Buyids state Southwest Asia early Islam 57 (2) see also Buyids
Buyids people Southwest Asia Islam 227 (5)
Büyük Kaya hill Southwest Asia (Turkey) first cities 28 (3)
Büyükzap Suyu see Great Zab
Byblos var. Jebeil, Jubayl, Jubeil; Bibl. Gebal Southwest Asia (Lebanon) ancient Egypt 159 (4), (5) early agriculture 220 (1) early systems 223 (3) first cities 28–29 (1) first civilizations 177 (1), 221 (4), 222 (2) Hellenistic world 40–41 (1)
Byerezino see Berezina
Byker British Isles (United Kingdom) economy 204 (3)
Bylany Central Europe (Poland) early agriculture 174 (1)
Bynum burial mound North America (USA) first civilizations 121 (4)
Byzantine Empire var. East Roman Empire state Southeast Europe/Southwest Asia crusades 186 (1), 228 (2), 65 (3) early Islam 56–57 (1), 57 (2) economy 190 (1) Islam 184 (1), 226 (2), 227 (4), (5) medieval states 185 (3), 189 (4) medieval voyages 60–61 (1) Mongols 229 (3) Seljuks 228 (1) Timur 229 (4) see also East Roman Empire
Byzantium mod. Istanbul; Eng. Constantinople settlement/state Southwest Asia (Turkey) ancient Greece 177 (2), (3), 179 (4) ancient Persia 223 (4), 225 (6) Roman empire 179 (5), 180–181 (1), 181 (3), (4), 224 (2), 225 (5) ancient trade 44 (2), 44–45 (1) exploration 218 (1) first civilizations 177 (1) Hellenistic world 224 (1) see also Constantinople, Istanbul

C

Cabango Southern Africa (Angola) exploration 157 (4)
Cabillonum see Chalon-sur-Saône
Cabinda var. Kabinda Southern Africa (Angola) Cold War 109 (5) European imperialism 96 (1)
Cabinda var. Kabinda colonial possession Southern Africa Cold War 109 (5)
Cabo Verde see Cape Verde
Cabo Verde, Ilhas do see Cape Verde
Cacalco Central America (Mexico) Aztecs 124 (3)
Cacaxtla Central America (Mexico) first civilizations 122 (1)
Cáceres Ar. Qazris Iberian Peninsula (Spain) civil war 209 (4)
Cachar state South Asia the world in 1800 86–87
Cacheo see Cacheu
Cacheu var. Cacheo West Africa (Guinea-Bissau) European expansion 84–85 (1) Islam 163 (1) slave trade 165 (4) trade 164 (2)
Caddo people North America colonization 125 (4), 126 (1)
Cádiz anc. Gades, Gadier, Gadir, Gadire Iberian Peninsula (Spain) economy 190 (1), 205 (4) European expansion 81 (3) Franks 184 (2) civil war 209 (4) Islam 192 (3) Napoleon 200–201 (1) see also Gades
Cadurcum see Cahors
Caelian Hill Lat. Mons Caelius hill Italy Roman empire 181 (2)
Caelius, Mons see Caelian Hill
Caen France early modern states 197 (5) empire and revolution 199 (4) medieval states 186 (2), 192 (1)
Caerdydd see Cardiff
Caere mod. Cerveteri Italy early states 178 (1), (2) first civilizations 177 (1) first religions 36 (1)
Caer Glou see Gloucester
Caer Gybi see Holyhead
Caerleon see Chester, Deva, Isca Silurum
Caer Luel see Carlisle
Caesaraugusta var. Salduba; mod. Zaragoza; Eng. Saragossa Iberian peninsula (Spain) Roman empire 180–181 (1) see also Saragossa, Zaragoza
Caesarea Southwest Asia (Israel) Roman empire 225 (4), (5) crusades 65 (3) early cultures 161 (2)
Caesarea prev. Shershel; mod. Cherchell North Africa (Algeria) Roman empire 181 (4) ancient trade 44–45 (1) early cultures 161 (2)
Caesarea Cappadociae var. Eusebia, Mazaca; mod. Kayseri Southwest Asia (Turkey) Roman empire 180–181 (1) world religions 48 (1) see also Kayseri
Caesarea Maritima Southwest Asia (Israel) Roman empire 180–181 (1), 181 (3), (4)
Caesarodunum later Turoni; mod. Tours France Roman empire 180–181 (1) see also Tours, Turoni
Caesaromagus see Beauvais
Cafunfo Southern Africa (Angola) Cold War 109 (5)
Cagliari anc. Carales Italy economy 190 (1) see also Carales
Cahokia North America (USA) 62 (1) cultural groups 122 (5) empire and revolution 127 (3) first religions 36 (1)
Cahors anc. Cadurcum France empire and revolution 199 (4) Franks 184 (2) medieval states 187 (3)
Cahuachi South America (Peru) early cultures 145 (4)
Caiambé state South America the world in 750 CE 54–55 the world in 1000 58–59 the world in 1200 62–63
Caiffa see Haifa
Caiphas see Haifa
Cairns Australia colonization 282 (1), 283 (3)
Cairo North America (USA) US Civil War 131 (6)
Cairo prev. Fustat, Al Fustat; Ar. Al Qāhirah; var. El Qâhira Egypt biological diffusion 72–73 (1) colonization 167 (4) crusades 228 (2), 65 (1), (3) early Islam 57 (2) economy 168 (2), 190 (1) exploration 156 (3), 157 (4), (5), 218 (2), 219 (4) Islam 235 (4) medieval states 187 (5) Mongols 229 (3), 68 (2) Napoleon 200–201 (1) Ottomans 231 (3), 232–233 (1) Seljuks 228 (1) the world in 1800 86–87 Timur 229 (4) trade 230 (2) US superpower 138 (1) WWI 233 (2) WWII 210 (1), 211 (4) 20th-century politics 233 (3), (4) see also Al Fustat, Fustat
Cajamarca prev. Caxamarca South America (Peru) colonization 148 (2) Incas 147 (3), 148 (1)
Cajamarquilla South America (Peru) early cultures 146 (1)
Calabar var. Kalabar state West Africa trade 164 (2)
Calabozo battle South America (Venezuela) empire and revolution 150 (1)
Calais France early modern states 193 (4), 194 (1), 197 (5) economy 205 (4) medieval states 192 (1), (2) WWI 206 (2), (3)
Calais, Pas de see Dover, Strait of
Calama South America (Chile) politics 151 (4)
Calama battle South America (Chile) politics 151 (4)
Calatafimi battle Italy empire and revolution 202 (3)
Calatrava Iberian Peninsula (Spain) crusades 186 (1) Islam 192 (3)
Calcutta var. Kolkata South Asia (India) colonialism 247 (3), 248 (1), 269 (4) decolonization 250 (1), (2) economy 249 (4) European imperialism 97 (3) exploration 239 (1) global immigration 100 (1), 101 (3) Mughal Empire 246 (1) post-war economy 253 (5) post-war politics 252 (1) US superpower 138 (1) WWII 104 (2), 251 (3), 272 (1), 273 (2)
Caldera South America (Chile) empire and revolution 151 (3)
Çaldiran var. Chaldiran, Chaldiron battle Southwest Asia (Turkey) Ottomans 195 (4)
Çaldiran var. Chaldiran, Chaldiron Southwest Asia (Turkey) medieval Persia 231 (4) Ottomans 231 (3)
Caledonia region British Isles Roman empire 180–181 (1)
Calf Creek archaeological site North America (USA) cultural groups 123 (4)
Calgary North America (Canada) 129 (2), 132 (1), 136 (2)
Cali South America (Colombia) empire and revolution 150 (2), 151 (3) environment 153 (4) Incas 148 (1) narcotics 153 (5) politics 152 (1)
Calico Hills archaeological site North America (USA) The World in 10,000 BCE 14–15
Calicut var. Kozhikode, prev. Kalikod, Qalqut South Asia (India) trade 72–73 (1) colonialism 247 (3), 248 (1) economy 249 (4) European expansion 80–81 (1) exploration 239 (1) imperial global economy 93 (5) Mongols 68 (2) Mughal Empire 246 (1) trade 230 (2), 267 (3) see also Kalikod, Qalqut
California state North America early agriculture 120 (1) the growth of the US 129 (1) US Civil War 130 (2), (3), (4), (5) US economy 134 (2)
California, Gulf of prev. Sea of Cortez gulf North America colonization 125 (4) cultural groups 123 (4) Mexican Revolution 133 (3) the growth of the US 129 (2)
Calima state South America the world in 1200 62–63
Calisia see Kalisch, Kalish
Calixtlahuaca Central America (Mexico) first civilizations 122 (1)
Callao South America (Peru) colonization 148 (2) empire and revolution 150 (1), 151 (3) European expansion 81 (3), 84–85 (1) exploration 143 (3) Incas 148 (1) politics 152 (1)
Callatis mod. Mangalia Southeast Europe (Romania) first civilizations 177 (1)
Calpan Central America (Mexico) colonization 125 (5)
Calpotitlan Central America (Mexico) Aztecs 124 (3)
Calusa people North America colonization 125 (4), 126 (1)
Calydnioi settlement/state Greece ancient Greece 177 (2)
Calynda settlement/state Greece ancient Greece 177 (2)
Camagüey see Puerto Príncipe
Camani people South America (Colombia) The World in 250 CE 46–47
Camarina Italy first civilizations 177 (1)
Ca Mau battle Mainland Southeast Asia (Vietnam) post-war politics 251 (5)
Cambay South Asia (India) biological diffusion 72–73 (1) colonialism 247 (3)
Cambay, Gulf of see Khambhat, Gulf of
Camberia see Chambéry
Cambodia prev. Chenla, Funan, Kambujadesha, Khmer; Cam. Kampuchea state Mainland Southeast Asia Bronze Age 240 (3) Cold War 109 (1) colonialism 269 (4) decolonization 251 (4) European imperialism 97 (3) Islam 275 (4) post-war economy 253 (5), 275 (3) post-war politics 251 (5), 253 (4) trade 267 (3) US superpower 138 (1) see also Chenla, Funan, Kambujadesha, Khmer
Cambrai prev. Cambray, anc. Cameracum; Flem. Kambryk France early modern states 197 (5) Franks 184 (2) Reformation 195 (5) WWI 206 (3)
Cambray see Cambrai
Cambridge North America (USA) empire and revolution 127 (3)
Cambridge Lat. Cantabrigia British Isles (United Kingdom) economy 204 (1) medieval states 187 (3)
Cambridge Bay North America (Canada) exploration 287 (2)
Camden North America (USA) empire and revolution 127 (3)
Camden battle North America (USA) empire and revolution 127 (3), 88–89 (2)
Cameirus see Camirus
Cameracum see Cambrai
Cameroon var. Kamerun; prev. Cameroons, Cameroon Trusteeship; Fr. Cameroun state West Africa decolonization 168 (1) economy 168 (2) European imperialism 96 (1), 97 (4) Islam 235 (4) the modern world 112 (1), 113 (3), (4) WWII 104 (1) see also Kamerun
Cameroons see Cameroon
Cameroun see Cameroon
Camiri oil field South America politics 152 (2)
Camirus var. Cameirus state Greece ancient Greece 177 (2)
Camp Low Countries (Belgium) medieval states 187 (3)
Campa South Asia (India) first religions 36 (2) world religions 242 (3)
Campani people Italy early states 178 (2)
Campbell North America (USA) 136 (3)
Campbell Mound burial mound North America (USA) first civilizations 121 (4)
Campeche city/state Central America Aztecs 124 (1) Mexican Revolution 133 (3)
Campeche, Bahía de see Campeche, Bay of
Campeche, Gulf of Sp. Bahía de Campeche gulf Central America Aztecs 124 (1) Mexican Revolution 133 (3)
Camperdown Dut. Kamperduin battle Low Countries (Netherlands) Napoleon 200–201 (1)
Campo de la Alianza battle South America (Peru) politics 151 (4)
Campo Formio Italy Napoleon 200–201 (1)
Camp of the Praetorian Guard Lat. Castra Praetoria building Italy Roman empire 181 (2)
Campo Grande South America (Brazil) politics 152 (1)
Campus Stellae see Santiago de Compostela
Camranh Bay military base Mainland Southeast Asia (Vietnam) WWII 251 (3), 272 (1), 273 (2)
Camulodunum mod. Colchester; hist. Colneceaste British Isles (United Kingdom) Roman empire 180–181 (1) see also Colchester
Cana Southwest Asia (Yemen) ancient trade 44–45 (1) early cultures 161 (3), (5) early trade 225 (3)
Canada colonial possession/state North America Cold War 109 (1) empire and revolution 127 (3) European expansion 84–85 (1) exploration 287 (2) global immigration 100 (1), 101 (2), (3) imperial global economy 92 (1), 93 (3) the growth of the US 129 (2), 132 (1), 133 (4) the modern world 112 (1), 113 (4) (3), (2) US superpower 138 (1) WWII 104 (1), 105 (4), 272 (1)
Canadian Pacific Railway railway North America global immigration 100 (1), 129 (2)
Canadian River river North America exploration 119 (3)
Canadian Shield physical region North America historical geography 117 (1)
Çanakkale Boğazi see Dardanelles, Hellespont
Canal Zone region/canal Central America the world in 1925 98–99 the world in 1950 102–103 the world in 1975 106–107
Canareggio Italy economy 191 (3)
Canarias, Islas see Canary Islands
Canary Islands Sp. Islas Canarias island group Atlantic Ocean empire and revolution 88 (1) European expansion 80–81 (1) European imperialism 96 (1) exploration 156 (3) historical geography 154–155 (1) medieval voyages 60–61 (1) slave trade 165 (4) US superpower 138 (1) see also Fortunatae Insulae
Canberra Australia colonization 283 (3)
Cancha Rayada battle South America (Chile) empire and revolution 150 (1)
Candamo archaeological site Iberian Peninsula (Spain) prehistoric culture 17 (3)
Candelaria South America (Argentina) exploration 143 (2)
Candelaria river South America first civilizations 123 (2)
Candellas state South Asia Mongols 68–69 (1)
Candia mod. Crete; anc Creta; Gr. Kriti island Greece medieval states 187 (5) see also Creta, Crete
Candra later Arakan state Mainland Southeast Asia the world in 500 CE 50–51 see also Arakan
Cane Southwest Asia (Yemen) ancient trade 44 (2)
Cangwu province East Asia first states 260 (1)
Cangzhou var. Tsangchou East Asia (China) medieval states 262–263 (1)
Canhasan Southwest Asia (Turkey) early agriculture 174 (1)
Çankiri see Gangra
Cannae battle Italy Roman empire 179 (3)
Cannanore var. Kananur, Kannur South Asia (India) colonialism 247 (3)
Cannes France Napoleon 200–201 (1)
Canosa di Puglia see Canusium
Cantabri people Iberian Peninsula Roman empire 179 (5)
Cantabrian Mountains mountain range Iberian Peninsula prehistoric culture 17 (3)
Cantabrigia see Cambridge
Canterbury prev. Cantwaraburh, anc. Durovernum, Lat. Cantuaria British Isles (United Kingdom) crusades 65 (1) medieval states 183 (3), 186 (2), 187 (3), (4), 188 (2) Reformation 194 (2)
Canterbury region New Zealand colonization 283 (5)
Can Tho battle Mainland Southeast Asia (Vietnam) post-war politics 251 (5)
Cantigny France WWI 206 (3)
Canton Chin. Guangzhou; var. Kuang-chou, Kwangchow, Nanhai East Asia (China) colonization 284–285 (1) early medieval states 245 (6) empire and revolution 88–89 (2) European imperialism 97 (3) world religions 243 (5) see also Guangzhou, Nanhai
Cantor West Africa (Gambia) exploration 156 (3)
Cantuaria see Canterbury
Cantwaraburh see Canterbury
Canusium mod. Canosa di Puglia Italy early states 178 (1)
Canyon de Chelly archaeological site North America (USA) cultural groups 123 (4)
Canyon de Chelly battle North America (USA) the growth of the US 129 (2)
Cao Bang fort Mainland Southeast Asia post-war politics 251 (5)
Caoreng state East Asia first cities 259 (3)
Capacha Central America (Mexico) first civilizations 121 (2)
Capernaum Southwest Asia (Israel) Roman empire 180–181 (1)
Cap-Breton, Île du see Cape Breton Island
Cape Artemisium battle Greece ancient Persia 223 (4)
Cape Breton Island Fr. Île du Cap-Breton island North America colonization 126 (1)
Cape Coast prev. Cape Coast Castle West Africa (Ghana) European expansion 84–85 (1) see also Cape Coast Castle
Cape Coast Castle mod. Cape Coast West Africa (Ghana) slave trade 165 (4) see also Cape Coast
Cape Colony state Southern Africa European imperialism 96 (2) global immigration 101 (3)
Cape Denbigh North America (USA) cultural groups 123 (3)
Cape Fear river North America empire and revolution 127 (3)
Cape Krusenstern North America (USA) cultural groups 123 (3)
Capelletti North Africa (Algeria) early agriculture 158 (1)
Capena Italy early states 178 (1)
Cape Nome North America (USA) cultural groups 123 (3)
Capernaum Southwest Asia (Israel) Roman empire 225 (4), (5)
Cape Town var. Ekapa, Afr. Kaapstad, Kapstad Southern Africa (South Africa) colonization 167 (4) economy 168 (2) European expansion 84–85 (1) European imperialism 96 (1), (2) global immigration 100 (1), 101 (2) imperial global economy 92 (1) slave trade 165 (4) trade 164 (1) WWII 104 (2)
Cape Verde Port. Cabo Verde state West Africa decolonization 168 (1) economy 168 (2) the modern world 112 (1)
Cape Verde Islands Port. Ilhas do Cabo Verde colonial possession/island group Atlantic Ocean European expansion 84–85 (1) European imperialism 96 (1) exploration 142 (1), 143 (3) historical geography 154–155 (1) US superpower 138 (1)
Cape York Australia exploration 279 (2)
Cap-Haïtien see Le Cap
Capitoline Hill hill Italy Roman empire 181 (2)
Caporetto Ger. Karfreit Central Europe (Slovenia) WWI 207 (5)
Cappadocia region/state Southwest Asia ancient Persia 223 (4) Roman empire 179 (5), 180–181 (1), 225 (5) early cultures 161 (2) first civilizations 221 (4), 222 (2) Hellenistic world 224 (1) world religions 48 (1)
Capreae mod. Capri island Italy early states 178 (1)
Capri see Capreae
Caprivi Concession see Caprivi Strip
Caprivi Strip prev. Caprivi Concession; Ger. Caprivizipfel physical region Southern Africa Cold War 109 (5)
Caprivizipfel see Caprivi Strip
Capua Italy Roman empire 180–181 (1) early states 178 (1) economy 190 (1) Franks 184 (2) medieval states 188 (1) world religions 48 (1)
Caquetá region South America narcotics 153 (5)
Caquetá var. Rio Japurá, Yapurá river South America early cultures 145 (4) empire and revolution 150 (2)
Caquetá, Rio see Japurá
CAR see Central African Republic
Carabobo battle South America (Venezuela) empire and revolution 150 (1), 88–89 (2)
Caracalla, Baths of Lat. Thermae Antoninianae building (Italy) Roman empire 181 (2)
Caracas South America (Venezuela) Cold War 108 (2) colonization 126 (1), 148 (2) empire and revolution 150 (1), (2), 151 (3) European expansion 85 (2) exploration 143 (2), (3) politics 152 (1), 133 (4), 139 (4)
Caracas, Captaincy General and Presidencia of region South America colonization 148 (2)
Caracol Central America (Mexico) first civilizations 123 (2)
Carajás South America (Brazil) economy 153 (3)
Caral South America ceremonial centre 144 (1)
Carales var. Caralis; mod. Cagliari Italy Roman empire 179 (3), 180–181 (1) early states 178 (2) world religions 48 (1) see also Cagliari
Caralis see Cagliari, Carales
Carcaso see Carcassonne
Carcassonne anc. Carcaso France crusades 186 (1) Franks 184 (2) Islam 192 (3) medieval states 187 (4), 192 (1)
Carchemish Southwest Asia (Turkey) ancient Egypt 159 (5) early systems 223 (3) first cities 220 (2), 28–29 (1) first civilizations 221 (4), (5), 222 (2)
Cardiff Wel. Caerdydd British Isles (United Kingdom) economy 204 (1), 205 (4)
Cardigan Wel. Aberteifi British Isles (United Kingdom) medieval states 188 (2)
Caria region Southwest Asia ancient Greece 177 (2), (3) first civilizations 177 (1) Hellenistic world 40–41 (1)
Caribana people South America the world in 1700 82–83
Carib and Arawak people West Indies colonization 125 (4)
Caribbean region North America US economy 138 (2)
Caribbean Sea sea Atlantic Ocean Cold War 108 (2) colonization 125 (4), 126 (1), 148 (2) early agriculture 120 (1), 20–21 (2) early cultures 144 (1), 145 (2) economy 153 (3) empire and revolution 150 (1), 151 (3) European expansion 84–85 (1), 85 (2) exploration 118 (1), 119 (2), (3), 142 (1), 143 (2), (3) first civilizations 122 (1), 123 (2) Incas 148 (1) narcotics 153 (5) politics 152 (1) the growth of the US 129 (2) US economy 136 (2) US imperialism 133 (5)
Caribou Inuit people North America cultural groups 123 (3)
Caribs people West Indies colonization 125 (4)
Carinthia region Central Europe early modern states 193 (4), 194 (1) medieval states 185 (3), 188 (1), 189 (4)
Carinthian March region Central Europe Franks 184 (2)
Carlisle anc. Caer Luel, Luguvallium, Luguballium British Isles (United Kingdom) economy 204 (1) medieval states 186 (2)
Carlsbad Central Europe (Germany) the world in 1850 90–91
Carlsruhe see Karlsruhe
Carmania region Southwest Asia Hellenistic world 40–41 (1)
Carmen de Patagones South America (Argentina) colonization 148 (2)
Carmona see Uige
Carnac archaeological site France Copper Age 174 (2)
Carnarvon Australia colonization 282 (1)
Carnatic region/state South Asia colonialism 247 (3), 248 (1)
Carniola region/state Central Europe early modern states 193 (4), 194 (1) Franks 184 (2) medieval states 188 (1), 189 (4)
Carnuntum legion headquarters/mithraic site Central Europe (Austria) Roman empire 180–181 (1) world religions 48 (1)
Caroline Island prev. Thornton Island island Pacific Ocean exploration 278 (1)
Caroline Islands var. Carolines island group Pacific Ocean colonization 284–285 (1) early cultures 280–281 (3) exploration 279 (3) imperialism 270 (2) medieval voyages 60 (2) WWII 104 (1), 251 (3), 272 (1), 273 (2)
Carolingian Empire see Frankish Kingdom
Carpathian Mountains mountain range Eastern Europe Bronze Age 175 (3) crusades 186 (1), 64–65 (2) early agriculture 174 (1) economy 190 (1), 205 (4) great migrations 52–53 (1) medieval states 185 (3), 189 (4) Napoleon 200–201 (1)
Carpentaria, Gulf of gulf Australia colonization 282 (1), 283 (3) exploration 279 (2) prehistoric culture 17 (5)
Carpentaria, Lake lake Australia exploration 276–277 (1) historical geography 254–255 (1)
Carraig Fhearghais see Carrickfergus
Carrhae Southwest Asia (Iran) Hellenistic world 40–41 (1)
Carrhae battle Southwest Asia (Iran) Roman empire 224 (2)
Carrickfergus Ir. Carraig Fhearghais British Isles (United Kingdom) medieval states 187 (4)
Carrier people North America colonization 126 (1) cultural groups 123 (3)
Carrizal Central America (Mexico) Mexican Revolution 133 (3)
Carsedi see Carsioli
Carsioli var. Carsedi Italy early states 178 (1)
Carso see Karst
Carson City North America (USA) the growth of the US 129 (2)
Cartagena Iberian Peninsula (Spain) Roman empire 182 (1) economy 190 (1) civil war 209 (4) medieval states 182 (2) Napoleon 200–201 (1)
Cartagena var. Cartagena de Indias South America (Colombia) colonization 126 (1), 148 (2) empire and revolution 150 (1), (2), 151 (3) environment 153 (4) European expansion 84–85 (1), 85 (2) exploration 143 (2) narcotics 153 (5) see also Carthago Nova
Cartagena de Indias see Cartagena
Carteia Iberian Peninsula (Spain) Roman empire 180–181 (1)
Cartenna var. Cartennae North Africa (Algeria) Roman empire 179 (3), 180–181 (1)
Carthage Lat. Carthago North Africa (Tunisia) Roman empire 179 (3), (5), 180–181 (1), 181 (3), (4), 182 (1), 225 (5) ancient trade 44 (2), 44–45 (1) early agriculture 158 (1) early cultures 160 (1), 161 (2) early Islam 56–57 (1) exploration 172 (1) first civilizations 177 (1) first religions 36 (1), 37 (3) great migrations 52–53 (1) Islam 184 (1), 226 (2) medieval states 182 (2) world religions 48 (1), 49 (4) see also Carthago
Carthage state North Africa early Islam 56–57 (1)
Carthago see Carthage
Carthago Nova mod. Cartagena Iberian Peninsula (Spain) Roman empire 179 (3), (5), 180–181 (1), 181 (3) great migrations 52–53 (1) world religions 48 (1) see also Cartagena
Cartwright North America (Canada) WWII 104 (2)
Carusbur see Cherbourg
Carystus state Greece ancient Greece 177 (2)
Casablanca Ar. Dar-el-Beida North Africa (Morocco) economy 168 (2) US superpower 138 (1) WWII 104 (2), 211 (4)
Casa de Cruces Central America (Panama) European expansion 85 (2)
Casa Grande archaeological site North America (USA) cultural groups 123 (4)
Casanare and Los Llanos region South America colonization 148 (2) exploration 143 (2)
Casas Grandes archaeological site Central America (Mexico) cultural groups 123 (4)
Cascades battle North America (USA) the growth of the US 129 (2)
Casco Bay bay North America WWII 104 (2)
Casiquiare river South America exploration 143 (3)
Casper North America (USA) the world in 5000 BCE 18–19
Caspian Gates pass Southwest Asia (Iran) Hellenistic world 40–41 (1)
Caspian Sea anc. Mare Caspium; Az. Xäzär Dänizi, Kaz. Kaspiy Tengizi, Per. Baḥr-e Khazar, Daryā-ye Khazar, Rus. Kaspiyskoye More inland sea Asia/Europe ancient Persia 223 (4), 225 (6) Roman empire 181 (3), (4), 224 (2), 225 (5) ancient trade 44–45 (1) 73 (3) colonialism 269 (3) early agriculture 174 (1), 20–21 (2), 220 (1) early Islam 56–57 (1), 57 (2) early systems 223 (3) economy 205 (4), 234 (1) European expansion 84–85 (1) exploration 172 (1), (2), 219 (3) first cities 220 (2) first civilizations 222 (2), 25 (3) first humans 13 (2) first religions 36 (1) great migrations 52–53 (1), 53 (2) Hellenistic world 224 (1), 41 (2) historical geography 275 (5) Islam 226 (2), 227 (4) medieval Persia 231 (4) medieval states 261 (6) medieval voyages 60–61 (1) Mongols 229 (3), 68 (2), 68–69 (1) Ottomans 231 (3), 232–233 (1) Seljuks 228 (1) Soviet Union 208 (2), 213 (4) Timur 229 (4) trade 267 (3) world religions 48 (1) WWI 233 (2) see also Caspium, Mare
Caspium, Mare var. Caspian Sea inland sea Asia/Europe ancient trade 44 (2) see also Caspian Sea
Cassai see Kasai
Cassander, Kingdom of state Greece Hellenistic world 224 (1)
Cassange Southern Africa (Angola) exploration 157 (4)
Cassel see Kassel
Cassinga Southern Africa (Angola) Cold War 109 (5)
Castello Italy economy 191 (3)
Castellón de la Plana Iberian Peninsula (Spain) civil war 209 (4)
Castelluccio archaeological site/settlement Italy Copper Age 174 (2)
Castelvetere see Caulonia
Castiglione var. Castiglione delle Stiviere battle Italy Napoleon 200–201 (1)
Castiglione delle Stiviere see Castiglione
Castile region/state Iberian Peninsula crusades 186 (1) early modern states 194 (1) economy 190 (1) Islam 192 (3) medieval states 185 (3), 192 (1), (2) medieval voyages 60–61 (1) Reformation 196 (2)
Castillon battle France medieval states 192 (2)
Castle Cavern archaeological site Southern Africa (South Africa) early cultures 160 (1)
Castle Leazes British Isles (United Kingdom) economy 204 (3)
Castlemaine goldfield Australia colonization 282 (2)
Castlepoint New Zealand colonization 283 (4), (5)
Castra Praetoria see Camp of the Praetorian Guard
Castra Regina mod. Regensburg; hist. Ratisbona; Eng. Ratisbon, Fr. Ratisbonne Central Europe (Germany) world religions 48 (1) see also Regensburg, Ratisbon
Castrum Novum Italy early states 178 (1)
Catalan Counties state Iberian Peninsula medieval states 185 (3)
Catalaunian Fields battle France great migrations 52–53 (1)
Çatalhöyük see Çatal Hüyük
Çatal Hüyük Southwest Asia (Turkey) early agriculture 220 (1) first cities 220 (2) first civilizations 221 (4)
Catalonia state/region Iberian Peninsula crusades 64–65 (2) civil war 209 (4) Islam 192 (3) Napoleon 201 (2)
Catalonian Revolt war Iberian Peninsula Reformation 196 (2)
Catamarca South America (Argentina) empire and revolution 151 (3)
Catambela see Katombela
Catania Italy economy 190 (1) medieval states 187 (5)
Catarpe South America (Chile) Incas 147 (3)
Catawba people North America colonization 125 (4), 126 (1)
Catemaco Central America (Mexico) first civilizations 122 (1)
Cathars people France crusades 186 (1)
Cathay var. China physical region East Asia global knowledge 76 (9) see also China
Cato burial mound North America (USA) first civilizations 121 (4)
Cattaro mod. Kotor vassal state Southeast Europe Ottomans 197 (4)
Cattigara East Asia (China) ancient trade 44 (2), 44–45 (1)
Caturmukha mod. Phnom Penh, Phnum Penh Mainland Southeast Asia (Cambodia) early medieval states 245 (6)
Cauca river South America colonization 148 (2) Incas 148 (1)
Caucasians people Eastern Europe/Southwest Asia the world in 750 BCE 30–31 the world in 250 BCE 38–39 the world in 1 CE 42–43 the world in 250 CE 46–47 the world in 500 CE 50–51
Caucasus Rus. Kavkaz mountain range Central Asia ancient Persia 223 (4), 225 (6) Roman empire 180–181 (1), 181 (4), 182 (1) ancient trade 44–45 (1) Bronze Age 175 (3) early agriculture 174 (1) early Islam 56–57 (1), 57 (2) economy 205 (4) exploration 172 (1), (2), 219 (3) first humans 13 (2) Hellenistic world 224 (1) Islam 163 (1), 227 (4) medieval Persia 231 (4) medieval states 182 (2), 185 (3), 261 (6) Mongols 229 (3), 68–69 (1) Ottomans 231 (3), 232–233 (1) Seljuks 228 (1) Soviet Union 208 (2) Timur 229 (4) WWI 233 (2) WWII 210 (1), 211 (2)
Caudium Italy early states 178 (1)
Caulonia Italy early states 178 (1) first civilizations 177 (1)
Cauvery see Kaveri
Cave Bay Cave Australia exploration 280 (1)
Cave of Hearths archaeological site Southern Africa (South Africa) first humans 13 (2)
Cawnpore var. Kānpur rebellion/settlement South Asia (India) decolonization 250 (1) economy 249 (4) empire and revolution 249 (3) imperial global economy 93 (5)
Caxamarca see Cajamarca
Cayenne South America (French Guiana) colonization 149 (4) empire and revolution 151 (3) environment 153 (4) politics 152 (1)
Cayes var. Les Cayes West Indies (Haiti) empire and revolution 89 (3)
Cayman Islands colonial possession/state West Indies the modern world 113 (4)
Çayönü Southwest Asia (Turkey) the world in 5000 BCE 18–19
Cazombo Southern Africa (Angola) Cold War 109 (5)
Ceará mod. Fortaleza; prev. Villa do Forte de Assumpeão South America (Brazil) colonization 149 (4) see also Fortaleza
Ceará region South America colonization 149 (3)
Cebu off. Cebu City Philippines colonialism 247 (4) WWII 272 (1), 273 (2)
Cebu City see Cebu
Ceduna Australia colonization 282 (1)
Ceh Pech state Central America Aztecs 124 (1)
Celaya Central America (Mexico) Mexican Revolution 133 (3)
Celebes Ind. Sulawesi Island Maritime Southeast Asia ancient India 241 (6) ancient trade 44–45 (1) Bronze Age 240 (3) colonialism 247 (4) decolonization 251 (4) early medieval states 245 (6) European imperialism 97 (3) exploration 239 (1), (2) Islam 243 (6) post-war economy 253 (5) post-war politics 253 (4) trade 267 (3) world religions 243 (5), 49 (4) WWII 251 (3), 272 (1), 273 (2)
Celebes Sea Ind. Laut Sulawesi sea Maritime Southeast Asia Bronze Age 240 (3) colonialism 247 (4) decolonization 251 (4) early medieval states 245 (6) European imperialism 97 (3) exploration 239 (1), (2) Islam 243 (6) post-war economy 253 (5) post-war politics 253 (4) world religions 243 (5)
Celenderis Southwest Asia (Turkey) first civilizations 177 (1)
Celestial Empire see China, Han Empire
Celtiberi see Celtiberians
Celtiberians Lat. Celtiberi people Iberian Peninsula Roman empire 179 (5)
Celtic peoples people British Isles/France/Germany the world in 250 BCE 38–39 the world in 500CE 50–51
Celts people Western Europe ancient trade 44–45 (1) early systems 33 (3) first civilizations 177 (1) great migrations 53 (2) the world in 500 BCE 34–35
Cemenelium see Cemenelum
Cemenelum var. Cemenelium Italy Roman empire 180–181 (1)
Cempoala Central America (Mexico) first civilizations 122 (1)
Cempohuallan Central America (Mexico) colonization 125 (5)
Central African Empire see Central African Republic
Central African Republic abbrev. CAR; prev. Central African Empire, Ubangi-Shari, Oubangui-Chari state Central Africa Cold War 109 (1) decolonization 168 (1) economy 168 (2), (3) Islam 235 (4) the modern world 112 (1), 113 (3) see also Ubangi-Shari
Central America region Central America first religions 36 (1), 120-121, 122-123, 124-125, 126 (1), 128-129, 133 (3) US economy 138 (2)
Central America, United Provinces of state Central America empire and revolution 88–89 (2)
Central Asia region South Asia biological diffusion 73 (2)
Central Bihar region South Asia decolonization 250 (1)

Central India Agency state South Asia colonialism 248 (2)
Central Makran Range mountain range South Asia first cities 240 (2)
Central Overland Route wagon train route North America the growth of the US 129 (2)
Central Pacific Railroad railway North America global immigration 100 (1) the growth of the US 129 (2)
Central Provinces state South Asia colonialism 248 (2)
Central Siberian Plain plain Siberia exploration 257 (2)
Central Western Queensland archaeological site Australia prehistoric culture 17 (5)
Cephalonia island Greece ancient Greece 177 (3), 179 (4) Ottomans 230 (1)
Cer battle Southeast Europe (Yugoslavia) WWI 207 (6)
Ceram var. Serang, Pulau Seram, Seram island Maritime Southeast Asia colonialism 247 (4) early medieval states 245 (6) exploration 239 (1), (2) Islam 243 (6)
Ceramicus Cemetery Gr. Kerameikos Cemetery cemetery Greece ancient Greece 177 (4)
Ceram Sea var. Seram Sea; Ind. Laut Seram sea Maritime Southeast Asia early medieval states 245 (6) exploration 239 (2)
Ceras state South Asia Mongols 68–69 (1)
Ceres Sea sea Indian Ocean Islam 243 (6)
Ceribon see Cheribon
Cerignola battle Italy early modern states 194 (1)
Cerrillos South America (Peru) early cultures 145 (4)
Cerro Iberian Peninsula (Spain) Bronze Age 175 (3)
Cerro de la Bomba Central America (Mexico) first civilizations 121 (2)
Cerro de las Mesas region/settlement Central America first civilizations 121 (2), 122 (1)
Cerro Gordo Central America (Mexico) the growth of the US 129 (2)
Cerros Central America (Mexico) first civilizations 123 (2)
Cerro Sechin early ceremonial centre South America (Peru) early cultures 144 (1), 145 (3)
Cerro Vicús South America (Peru) early cultures 145 (4)
Cerveteri see Caere
Cēsis see Wenden
Česká Republika see Czech Republic
Cetinje Southeast Europe (Yugoslavia) WWI 207 (6)
Ceuta var. Sebta North Africa (Spain/Morocco) trade 72–73 (1) economy 190 (1) Islam 192 (3)
Cévennes mountain range France early modern states 197 (5)
Ceylon var. Saylan, Sarandib; mod. Sri Lanka; Chin. Hsi-lan; anc. Taprobane, Simhala, Sinhala, Lambakannas, Lanka region/state/island South Asia colonialism 247 (3), 248 (1), (2) decolonization 250 (1), 251 (4) economy 249 (4) European expansion 84–85 (1) exploration 239 (1) global immigration 100 (1) Marathas 246 (2) Mongols 68 (2) Mughal Empire 246 (1) trade 230 (2), 267 (3) WWII 251 (3), 272 (1), 273 (2) see also Lambakannas, Lanka, Simhala, Sri Lanka, Taprobana
Ceyre to the Caribs see Marie Galante
Chacabuco battle South America (Chile) empire and revolution 150 (1), 88–89 (2)
Chachalacas Central America (Mexico) first civilizations 122 (1)
Chachas state South Asia early medieval states 244 (2)
Chaco region South America colonization 148 (2) exploration 143 (2)
Chaco Canyon archaeological site/settlement North America (USA) cultural groups 123 (4)
Chad Fr. Tchad state Central Africa decolonization 168 (1) economy 168 (2), (3) Islam 235 (4) the modern world 112 (1), 113 (3), (4)
Chadians people Central Africa/West Africa ancient trade 44–45 (1) early cultures 160 (1)
Chad, Lake Fr. Lac Tchad lake Central Africa ancient trade 44–45 (1) early cultures 160 (1) economy 163 (2) European imperialism 96 (1) exploration 157 (4) first humans 12 (1), 13 (2) historical geography 154–155 (1) Islam 163 (1), 167 (3) slave trade 165 (4)
Chagai Hills mountain range South Asia first cities 240 (2)
Chagar Bazar Southwest Asia (Syria) first civilizations 221 (4)
Chagatai Khanate var. Khanate of Kashgar, Chagatayids state/region Central Asia/East Asia biological diffusion 72–73 (1) Mongols 229 (3), 68 (2) Timur 229 (4)
Chagatais people South Asia early medieval states 244–245 (3)
Chagatayids see Chagatai Khanate
Chagos Archipelago var. Chagos Islands; mod. British Indian Ocean Territory island group Indian Ocean the world in 1850 90–91 the world in 1900 94–95 the world in 1925 98–99 the world in 1950 102–103 see also British Indian Ocean Territory
Chagos Islands see British Indian Ocean Territory, Chagos Archipelago
Chahamanas state South Asia early medieval states 244 (2)
Chahar region East Asia post-war politics 271 (7)
Chahar people East Asia trade 267 (3)
Chakan state Central America Aztecs 124 (1)
Chakchiuma people Central America colonization 125 (4)
Chalandriani archaeological site Greece Copper Age 174 (2)
Chalcatzinco Central America (Mexico) first civilizations 121 (2), 122 (1)
Chalcedon Southwest Asia (Turkey) first civilizations 177 (1) world religions 226 (1)
Chalcedon state Greece ancient Greece 177 (2)
Chalchuapa Central America (El Salvador) first civilizations 121 (2)
Chalcis Southwest Asia (Syria) Roman empire 225 (4)
Chalcis mod. Chalkida; var. Halkida; prev. Khalkis settlement/state Greece ancient Greece 177 (2), (3), 179 (4) first civilizations 177 (1)
Chalco Central America (Mexico) Aztecs 124 (2)
Chalco state Central America Aztecs 124 (1)
Chalco, Lake lake Central America Aztecs 124 (2)
Chaldiran see Çaldiran
Chaldiron see Çaldiran
Chalkida see Chalcis
Chalma Central America (Mexico) Aztecs 124 (3)
Chalna var. Pankhali South Asia (Bangladesh) post-war politics 252 (3)
Chalon France Franks 183 (5), (6), 184 (2)
Châlons France Franks 184 (2)
Châlons-sur-Marne France early modern states 197 (5) economy 190 (1) WWI 206 (3)
Chalon-sur-Saône anc. Cabillonum France economy 190 (1)
Chaluka North America (USA) cultural groups 123 (3)
Chalukyas people/state South Asia world religions 243 (4)
Chamá Central America (Mexico) first civilizations 122 (2)
Chambal river South Asia colonialism 247 (3), 248 (2) decolonization 250 (1) early medieval states 244 (2), 244–245 (3) economy 249 (4) Marathas 246 (2) post-war politics 252 (1) world religions 242 (2), 243 (4)
Chambéry anc. Camberia France economy 190 (1)
Champa South Asia (India) early religions 48 (2)
Champa region/state Mainland Southeast Asia ancient India 241 (6) biological diffusion 72–73 (1) early medieval states 245 (5) first states 260 (1) medieval states 261 (6), 262–263 (1), 263 (6) Mongols 68–69 (1) trade 67 (3) world religions 243 (5), 49 (4)
Champagne region France economy 190 (1) medieval states 187 (4)
Champaran region South Asia decolonization 250 (1)
Champaubert battle France Napoleon 200–201 (1)
Champlain, Lake lake North America colonization 126 (1) empire and revolution 127 (2) exploration 119 (2)
Champutun state Central America Aztecs 124 (1)
Chams people Mainland Southeast Asia ancient trade 44–45 (1)
Chanca people South America early cultures 147 (2)
Chancay South America (Peru) early cultures 146 (1)
Chance North America (USA) cultural groups 122 (5)
Chancellorsville North America (USA) US Civil War 131 (6)
Chan Chan South America (Peru) early cultures 146 (1) Incas 147 (3)
Chandannagar prev. Chandernagore South Asia (India) post-war politics 252 (1) see also Chandernagore
Chandellas state South Asia early medieval states 244 (2)
Chandernagore colonial possession/settlement South Asia colonialism 247 (3), 248 (2), 269 (4) decolonization 251 (4) empire and revolution 88 (1) WWII 251 (3)
Chandigarh South Asia (India) post-war politics 252 (1)
Chandra state Mainland Southeast Asia ancient India 241 (6)
Chandragupta, Empire of state South Asia Hellenistic world 224 (1)
Chang'an var. Ch'ang-an East Asia (China) ancient trade 44–45 (1) exploration 256 (1) first religions 37 (4) first states 260 (1), 261 (2), (3) medieval states 261 (5), (6), 262–263 (1) world religions 49 (3), (4) see also Xi'an
Changbai East Asia (China) Cold War 109 (4)
Changchou see Changzhou
Changchun var. Ch'ang-ch'un; prev. Hsinking East Asia (China) imperialism 270 (2) Russo-Japanese War 270 (4)
Changchun battle East Asia (China) economy 274 (1) post-war politics 274 (2)
Changde East Asia (China) medieval states 263 (6)
Chang Jiang see Yangtze
Changle East Asia (China) trade 267 (3)
Changsha var. Ch'angsha, Ch'ang-sha East Asia (China) biological diffusion 72–73 (1) colonialism 269 (4) early modern states 268 (1) economy 274 (1) imperialism 270 (2) post-war politics 271 (7), 274 (2) world religions 49 (3) WWII 251 (3)
Changsha province East Asia first states 260 (1)
Changwu archaeological site East Asia (China) first humans 13 (2)
Changyang archaeological site East Asia (China) first humans 13 (2)
Changzhou var. Changchou East Asia (China) medieval states 262–263 (1)
Chanhu-Daro archaeological site/settlement South Asia (Pakistan) first cities 240 (2) first civilizations 24 (2)
Channel Islands Fr. Îles Normandes island group English Channel medieval states 186 (2)
Chantilly France WWI 206 (2), (3)
Chao see Zhao
Ch'ao-an see Chaozhou
Chaochow see Chaozhou
Chaoge vassal state East Asia first cities 259 (3)
Chaozhou var. Ch'ao-an; prev. Chaochow East Asia (China) medieval states 263 (5)
Chaplina, Mys Eng. Cape Chaplino headland Siberia exploration 257 (2)
Chaplino, Cape see Chaplina, Mys
Chapultepec Central America (Mexico) Aztecs 124 (2), (3) colonization 125 (5) first civilizations 122 (1)
Charax Southwest Asia (Iraq) ancient trade 44–45 (1) early cultures 161 (3), (4), (5) early trade 225 (3) Hellenistic world 41 (2)
Charay North Africa (Libya) Roman empire 179 (3)
Charcas, Presidencia of region South America colonization 148 (2)
Charlemagne, Empire of state France Franks 184 (2)
Charleroi Low Countries (Belgium) WWI 206 (2), (3)
Charleston North America (USA) colonization 126 (1) empire and revolution 127 (3) European expansion 84–85 (1) imperial global economy 93 (5) the growth of the US 129 (2), 132 (1) US Civil War 130 (5), 131 (6), (7) US society 137 (6)
Charleston battle North America (USA) empire and revolution 127 (3)
Charleville Australia colonization 282 (1)
Charlotte North America (USA) empire and revolution 127 (3)
Charlottenburg Central Europe (Germany) post-war politics 212 (2)
Charlottesville North America (USA) empire and revolution 127 (3)
Charlottetown North America (Canada) 129 (2), 132 (1)
Charolais States state France early modern states 197 (5)
Charolles state France early modern states 194 (1)
Charsadda South Asia (Pakistan) first religions 36 (2) Hellenistic world 41 (2)
Chartres France medieval states 187 (3)
Chasniki Eastern Europe (Belorussia) early modern states 195 (3)
Château-Thierry France Napoleon 200–201 (1) WW1 206 (2), (3)
Chatgaon mod. Chittagong; var. Chāttagām South Asia (Bangladesh) early medieval states 244–245 (3) Mughal Empire 246 (1) see also Chittagong
Chatgaon state South Asia Mughal Empire 246 (1)
Chatham British Isles (United Kingdom) economy 204 (1)
Chatham Islands island group Pacific Ocean decolonization 285 (3) early cultures 280–281 (3) medieval voyages 60 (2)
Chāttagām see Chatgaon, Chittagong
Chattahoochee river North America cultural groups 122 (5) US Civil War 131 (6)
Chattanooga North America (USA) US Civil War 131 (6), (7)
Chaul South Asia (India) colonialism 247 (3) early medieval states 245 (4) world religions 243 (4)
Chaulukyas dynasty South Asia Mongols 68–69 (1)
Chauri Chaura South Asia (India) decolonization 250 (1)
Chauvet archaeological site France prehistoric culture 17 (2)
Chavin state South America first religions 36 (1)
Chavin de Huantar early ceremonial centre South America (Peru) early cultures 144 (1), 145 (3), (4) first religions 36 (1)
Cheb see Eger
Chechen people Southwest Asia Soviet Union 213 (4)
Che-chiang see Zhejiang
Chechnya region Eastern Europe Soviet Union 214–215 (4)
Chedi var. Cedi region/state South Asia first empires 241 (5) first religions 36 (2)
Cheetham British Isles (United Kingdom) economy 204 (2)
Chefoo see Zhifu
Cheju-do prev. Quelpart; Jap. Saishū island East Asia Cold War 109 (4) early modern states 265 (5), 267 (4) medieval states 264 (1), (2) see also Quelpart
Chekiang see Zhejiang
Chełmno concentration camp Central Europe WWII 211 (3)
Chelmno see Kulm
Chelyabinsk Eastern Europe (Russian Federation) Soviet Union 214–215 (4)
Chelyuskin, Cape see Chelyuskin, Mys
Chelyuskin, Mys Eng. Cape Chelyuskin headland Siberia exploration 257 (2)
Chemin des Dames France WWI 206 (2), (3)
Chemulpo see Inchon
Chen East Asia (China) first cities 259 (5) first religions 37 (4)
Chen state East Asia medieval states 261 (5)
Chenab river South Asia colonialism 248 (1) early medieval states 244 (1) first cities 240 (2) Mughal Empire 246 (1) post-war politics 252 (2)
Ch'eng-chou, Chengchow see Zhengzhou
Chengdu var. Chengtu, Ch'eng-tu; prev. Shu East Asia (China) ancient trade 44–45 (1) biological diffusion 72–73 (1) colonialism 269 (4) early modern states 266 (1), (2), 268 (1) first states 260 (1), 261 (2) Islam 275 (4) medieval states 262–263 (1), 263 (3), (4), (5), (6) Mongols 68–69 (1) post-war economy 275 (3) post-war politics 274 (2) world religions 49 (3) WWII 272 (1), 273 (2)
Chenggao East Asia (China) first cities 259 (5)
Chenghsien see Zhengzhou
Chengtian rebellion East Asia early modern states 266 (2)
Ch'eng-tu, Chengtu see Chengdu
Chengziya archaeological site/settlement East Asia (China) early agriculture 258 (2)
Chenkiang see Zhenjiang
Chenla mod. Cambodia; prev. Funan, later Khmer, Kambujadesha state Mainland Southeast Asia ancient India 241 (6) world religions 49 (4) see also Cambodia, Funan, Kambujadesha, Khmer
Chenla and Empire of Funan see Chenla
Chennai see Madras
Cheraw North America (USA) empire and revolution 127 (3)
Cherbourg anc. Carusbur France early modern states 197 (5) medieval states 187 (4), 192 (1), (2) WWII 210 (1)
Cherchell see Caesarea, Iol
Cherchen Chin. Qiemo East Asia (China) biological diffusion 72–73 (1) first states 260 (1)
Cheribon mod. Ceribon; Dut. Tjeribon state Maritime Southeast Asia the world in 1600 78–79
Cherkess see Circassians
Chernigov Ukr. Chernihiv Eastern Europe (Ukraine) Mongols 68–69 (1)
Chernihiv see Chernigov
Chernobyl Eastern Europe (Ukraine) Soviet Union 214–215 (4)
Chernomen var. Maritsa battle Greece medieval states 189 (4)
Cherno More see Black Sea
Chernovaya archaeological site/settlement Siberia (Russian Federation) early agriculture 258 (1)
Chernoye More see Black Sea
Cherokee people North America colonization 125 (4), 126 (1)
Cherry Island see Anuta
Cherry Valley North America (USA) empire and revolution 127 (3)
Chersonesus state Greece ancient Greece 177 (2)
Chesapeake Bay inlet North America empire and revolution 127 (2), (3)
Cheshire region British Isles imperial global economy 93 (4)
Chesowanja archaeological site East Africa (Kenya) first humans 12 (1)
Chester hist. Legaceaster, Lat. Deva, Devana Castra; Wel. Caerleon British Isles (United Kingdom) economy 190 (1) medieval states 183 (3), 188 (2) see also Deva
Chester battle British Isles (United Kingdom) medieval states 183 (3)
Chesterfield canal British Isles economy 204 (1)
Chetiya region South Asia ancient India 242 (1) world religions 242 (3)
Chetwai South Asia (India) colonialism 247 (3)
Chevdar Southeast Europe (Bulgaria) early agriculture 174 (1)
Cheyenne North America (USA) the growth of the US 129 (2)
Cheyenne people North America colonization 126 (1)
Ch'i see Qi, Qi Empire
Chiang-hsi see Jiangxi
Chiang-ling see Jiangling
Chiang Mai see Chiengmai
Chiangnan Hsitao see Jiangnan Xidao
Chiang-su see Jiangsu
Chian-ning see Nanjing
Chiapa de Corzo Central America (Mexico) first civilizations 121 (2), 122 (1), 123 (2)
Chiapas state Central America Mexican Revolution 133 (3) the growth of the US 129 (2)
Chiba var. Tiba prefecture Japan economy 270 (1)
Chibcha people/state South America early cultures 147 (2)
Chibcha (Muisca) Chiefdoms state South America early cultures 146 (1)
Chicago North America (USA) exploration 119 (3) imperial global economy 92 (1) the growth of the US 129 (2), 132 (1) the modern world 113 (4) US Civil War 130 (5) US economy 134 (1), (3), 136 (2) US politics 135 (6)
Chicama archaeological site South America (Peru) early cultures 145 (3)
Chichén Itzá Central America (Mexico) Aztecs 124 (1) first civilizations 123 (2) first religions 36 (1)
Chichou see Jizhou
Chickamauga North America (USA) US Civil War 131 (7)
Chickamauga var. Chickamauga Creek battle North America (USA) US Civil War 131 (7)
Chickasaw people North America colonization 125 (4), 126 (1)
Chiclayo South America (Peru) environment 153 (4) narcotics 153 (5)
Chiconauhtla Central America (Mexico) Aztecs 124 (2)
Chien-Chung see Jianzhong
Chiengmai var. Chiangmai, Kiangmai; mod. Chiang Mai Mainland Southeast Asia (Thailand) colonialism 247 (4), 248 (1) exploration 239 (1) world religions 243 (5)
Chiengmai var. Chiangmai, Kiangmai; mod. Chiang Mai state Mainland Southeast Asia the world in 1300 66–67 the world in 1400 70–71 the world in 1500 74–75 the world in 1700 82–83
Chien-k'ang see Jiankang
Chiennan see Jiannan
Chien-yeh see Jianye, Nanjing
Chihli see Zhili
Chihuahua Central America (Mexico) Mexican Revolution 133 (3)
Chihuahua state Central America Mexican Revolution 133 (3) the growth of the US 129 (2)
Chihuahua battle Central America (Mexico) the growth of the US 129 (2)
Chikinchel state Central America Aztecs 124 (1)
Chilca South America (Peru) the world in 2500 BCE 22–23
Chilcotin people North America cultural groups 123 (3)
Children's Crusade crusade Central Europe crusades 186 (1)
Chile state South America economy 153 (3) empire and revolution 150 (1), 151 (3), 88–89 (2) global immigration 100 (1), 101 (2) imperial global economy 92 (1) narcotics 153 (5) politics 151 (4), 152 (1) the growth of the US 133 (4) the modern world 112 (1), 113 (4) US superpower 138 (1) WWII 105 (3) Cold War 109 (1)
Chile, Captaincy-General and Presidencia of region South America colonization 148 (2)
Chilecito South America (Argentina) empire and revolution 151 (3) Incas 147 (3)
Chi-lin see Jilin, Kirin
Chillon river South America early cultures 145 (3)
Chiloé, Isla de var. Isla Grande de Chiloé island South America European expansion 80–81 (1) exploration 143 (3)
Chimalhuacán Central America (Mexico) Aztecs 124 (2)
Chimbote South America (Peru) environment 153 (4)
Chimú people/state South America early cultures 147 (2)
Chin state East Asia medieval states 263 (3)
China var. People's Republic of China; prev. Cathay, Sinae, Qing Empire region/state East Asia ancient trade 44–45 (1) plague 72–73 (1) Chinese revolution 271 (5) early medieval states 245 (5) early systems 32 (1), 33 (2), (3) economy 274 (1) empire and revolution 88 (1) European expansion 84–85 (1) exploration 257 (3) first humans 13 (2) first religions 36 (1), 37 (4) global immigration 100 (1), 101 (2), (3) global knowledge 77 (6) imperial global economy 92 (1) imperialism 270 (2) Islam 235 (4) medieval states 261 (6), 264 (2) medieval voyages 61 (3) Mongols 68 (2) post-war economy 253 (5), 275 (3) post-war politics 251 (5), 252 (1), 253 (4), 274 (2) Soviet Union 208 (2), 213 (4) the growth of the US 133 (4) the modern world 113 (3), (4) world religions 243 (5), 49 (3), (4) WWI 104 (2), 105 (4), 251 (3), 272 (1), 273 (2) Cold War 109 (1), (4) colonization 284–285 (1) Communism 271 (8) decolonization 250 (1), 251 (4), 285 (3) see also Cathay, Qing Empire, Sinae
Chi-nan see Jinan
China, People's Republic of see China
China, Republic of var. Formosa, Formo'sa; mod. Taiwan state East Asia the world in 1950 102–103 see also Taiwan
Chincha, Islas de island group South America empire and revolution 151 (3)
Chin-ch'ang see Jinchang
Chin-ch'uan see Jinchuan
Chindaka-Nagas dynasty South Asia Mongols 68–69 (1)
Chingchi see Jingji
Ch'ing Hai see Qinghai, Hu
Chinghai see Qinghai
Ching-nan state East Asia medieval states 263 (3)
Ch'ing-tao see Qingdao, Tsingtao
Chinkiang see Zhenjiang
Chinkultic Central America (Mexico) first civilizations 123 (2)
Chinmen Tao see Quemoy
Chinnereth see Galilee, Sea of
Chinon France medieval states 192 (2)
Chinsura prev. Chunchura South Asia (India) colonialism 247 (3)
Chin-t'ien see Jintian
Chinwangtao see Qinhuangdao
Chioggia anc. Fossa Claudia Italy economy 190 (1)
Chios var. Hios, Khíos; It. Scio, Turk. Sakiz-Adasi settlement/island Greece ancient Greece 177 (2), (3), 179 (4) first civilizations 175 (4), 177 (1)
Chipata Southern Africa (Malawi) early cultures 160 (1)
Chipewyan people North America colonization 126 (1) cultural groups 123 (3)
Chippewa, Lake lake North America the world in 10,000 BCE 14–15
Chiquihuitillo Central America (Mexico) first civilizations 122 (1)
Chiquito people South America early cultures 147 (2)
Chiquitos region South America colonization 148 (2) exploration 143 (2)
Chiquitoy South America (Peru) Incas 147 (3)
Chire see Shire
Chiricahua Apache people North America colonization 125 (4)
Chiripa archaeological site South America (Bolivia) early cultures 144 (1)
Chishima-rettō see Kurile Islands
Chisholm Trail wagon train route North America the growth of the US 129 (2)
Chişinău see Kishinev
Chita Siberia (Russian Federation) colonialism 269 (3) Communism 271 (8) Soviet Union 208 (2)
Chitambo East Africa (Zambia) exploration 157 (4)
Chitato Southern Africa (Angola) Cold War 109 (5)
Chitimacha people Central America/North America colonization 125 (4), 126 (1)
Chitor South Asia (India) early medieval states 244–245 (3) Mughal Empire 246 (1)
Chittagong prev. Chatgaon; Ben. Chāttagām South Asia (Bangladesh) trade 72–73 (1) colonialism 247 (3), 248 (1) decolonization 250 (1) exploration 239 (1) post-war economy 253 (5) post-war politics 252 (3) trade 230 (2), 267 (3) WWII 251 (3) see also Chatgaon
Chittagong Hills region South Asia post-war politics 253 (4)
Chiusi see Clusium
Chkalov see Orenburg
Chocolá Central America (Mexico) first civilizations 122 (2)
Choctaw people North America colonization 125 (4), 126 (1)
Chocuan state Central America Aztecs 124 (1)
Choga Mami Southwest Asia (Iraq) early agriculture 220 (1)
Choga Mish Southwest Asia (Iran) first cities 220 (2)
Chogwe East Africa (Tanzania) exploration 157 (4)
Chokai-zan mountain Japan medieval states 265 (3)
Chokwe var. Cokwe people/state Central Africa/Southern Africa colonization 167 (4) trade 167 (1)
Cholas region/state South Asia ancient trade 44–45 (1) early medieval states 244 (2) Mongols 68–69 (1) world religions 242 (2)
Cholm see Kholm
Chololan Central America (Mexico) colonization 125 (5)
Cholula Central America (Mexico) first civilizations 122 (1)
Chondwe archaeological site Southern Africa (Zambia) early cultures 160 (1)
Chongjin East Asia (North Korea) Cold War 109 (4)
Chongoyapa archaeological site South America (Peru) early cultures 145 (3)
Chongqing var. Ch'ung-ch'ing, Chungking, Pahsien, Yuzhou East Asia (China) biological diffusion 72–73 (1) colonialism 269 (4) early modern states 266 (2), 268 (1) economy 274 (1) Islam 275 (4) medieval states 263 (6) post-war politics 271 (7), 274 (2) WWII 251 (3), 272 (1), 273 (2)
Chonju region East Asia medieval states 264 (2)
Chonos Archipelago island group South America exploration 143 (3)
Chopani-Mando South Asia (India) the world in 5000 BCE 18–19
Chorasmia province Central Asia ancient Persia 223 (4)
Chorlton British Isles (United Kingdom) economy 204 (2)
Chorne More see Black Sea
Chorrera archaeological site/settlement South America (Ecuador) early cultures 144 (1)
Chosan East Asia (North Korea) Cold War 109 (4)
Chōsen see Choson, Korea, Koryo, Silla
Chōsen-kaikyō see Korea Strait
Choshi Jap. Chōshi bomb target Japan Communism 273 (3)
Choson var. Chosen; later Silla; mod. Korea; Koryo state East Asia the world in 250 BCE 38–39 see also Korea, Silla, Koryo
Chotuna South America (Peru) early cultures 146 (1)
Christchurch New Zealand colonization 283 (4), (5)
Christiania var. Kristiania, mod. Oslo Scandinavia (Norway) early modern states 197 (3) economy 205 (4) see also Oslo
Christmas Island colonial possession/state Indian Ocean the world in 1975 106–107 the modern world 110–111
Christmas Island mod. Kiritimati island/nuclear test Pacific Ocean environmentalism 285 (2) WWII 272 (1), 273 (2) see also Kiritimati
Chryse Chersonesus region Greece ancient trade 44 (2)
Chu region/state East Asia first cities 259 (4), (5) first religions 37 (4) medieval states 263 (3)
Chubut river South America empire and revolution 151 (3) environment 153 (4)
Chubut see Rawson
Chucalissa North America (USA) cultural groups 122 (5)
Chucuito South America (Peru) early cultures 146 (1) Incas 147 (3)
Chudskoye Ozero see Peipus, Lake
Chu-fu see Zhufu
Chugacha South Asia (Bangladesh) post-war politics 252 (3)
Chukchi people Siberia the world in 1700 82–83 the world in 1800 86–87
Chukchi Sea sea Arctic Ocean exploration 257 (2), 286 (1), 287 (2)
Chukotka region Siberia exploration 257 (2)
Chukumuk Central America (Mexico) first civilizations 123 (2)
Chu-lu see Zhulu
Chunchura see Chinsura
Ch'ung-ch'ing, Chungking see Chongqing
Chung nan Shan see Zhongnan Shan
Chung t'iao Shan see Zhongtiao Shan
Chupicuaro Central America (Mexico) first civilizations 122 (2)
Chuquiabo South America (Bolivia) Incas 147 (3)
Chuquibamba South America (Peru) early cultures 146 (1)
Chuquicamata South America (Chile) environment 153 (4)
Chuquisaca var. La Plata; mod. Sucre South America (Bolivia) empire and revolution 150 (1) see also Sucre
Chur anc. Curia, Curia Rhaetorum; Fr. Coire, It. Coira, Rmsch. Cuera, Quera Central Europe (Switzerland) early modern states 193 (5) see also Curia
Churchill River river North America colonization 126 (1) the growth of the US 129 (2)
Chustenahlah battle North America (USA) the growth of the US 129 (2)
Chuuk see Truk
Chu, Wall of wall East Asia (China) first cities 259 (5)
Ciboney people West Indies colonization 125 (4)
Ciénaga de Oro South America (Colombia) early cultures 146 (1)
Cihuatlan state Central America Aztecs 124 (1)
Cilicia region Southwest Asia Roman empire 180–181 (1) crusades 65 (3) first civilizations 222 (2) Hellenistic world 40–41 (1)
Cimmerians people Southwest Asia the world in 750 BCE 30–31
Cina Selatan, Laut see South China Sea
Cincinnati North America (USA) the growth of the US 129 (2), 132 (1) US Civil War 131 (6), (7) US economy 134 (1), (3) US politics 135 (6)
Cipangu var. Japan island group Japan global knowledge 76 (9) see also Japan
Circassia region Eastern Europe Ottomans 231 (3)
Circassians var. Cherkess people Eastern Europe Mongols 68–69 (1) Ottomans 232–233 (1)
Circei mod. San Felice Circco Italy early states 178 (1)
Circeo archaeological site Italy first humans 13 (2)
Circum-Caribbean region/physical region West Indies early agriculture 120 (1) early cultures 144 (1)
Circus Maximus building Italy Roman empire 181 (2)
Cirencester anc. Corinium, Corinium Dobunorum British Isles (United Kingdom) medieval states 183 (3)
Cirta North Africa (Algeria) Roman empire 180–181 (1) early cultures 161 (2)
Cisalpine Republic state Italy the world in 1800 86–87
Cishan archaeological site/settlement East Asia early agriculture 258 (1), (2)
Citeaux major cistercian house/settlement France medieval states 187 (3), 188 (1)
Citlaltepec Central America (Mexico) Aztecs 124 (2)
Ciudad Bolivar prev. Angostura South America (Venezuela) empire and revolution 151 (3) see also Angostura
Ciudad del Este prev. Presidente Stroessner, Puerto Presidente Stroessner South America (Paraguay) environment 153 (4)
Ciudad de México see Mexico, Mexico City, Tenochtitlan
Ciudad de Panamá see Panamá, Panama City
Ciudad Guayana South America (Venezuela) environment 153 (4)
Ciudad Juárez Central America (Mexico) Mexican Revolution 133 (3)
Ciudad Madero Central America (Mexico) Mexican Revolution 133 (3)
Ciudad Real South America (Paraguay) colonization 148 (2)
Ciudad Rodrigo battle Iberian Peninsula (Spain) Napoleon 200–201 (1)
Ciudad Trujillo see Santo Domingo
Cividale Italy WWI 207 (5)
Civitas Nemetum see Speyer
Clairvaux major cistercian house France medieval states 187 (3)
Clasons Point North America (USA) cultural groups 122 (5)
Claudia, Aqua aqueduct Italy Roman empire 181 (2)
Claudius, Temple of building Italy Roman empire 181 (2)
Clausentum see Southampton
Clazomenae settlement/state Southwest Asia (Turkey) ancient Greece 177 (2) first civilizations 177 (1)
Clearwater battle North America (USA) the growth of the US 129 (2)
Clemsons Island North America (USA) cultural groups 122 (5)
Clermont France crusades 64–65 (2) Franks 183 (5), (6), 184 (2)
Clermont-Ferrand France economy 205 (4)
Cleveland North America (USA) the growth of the US 129 (2), 132 (1) US economy 134 (1), (3)
Cleves Ger. Kleve region Central Europe empire and revolution 199 (3)
Clipperton Island colonial possession/state/island Pacific Ocean the world in 1950 102–103 the world in 1975 106–107 the modern world 110–111
Clodia, Via road Italy early states 178 (1)
Clogg's Cave Australia exploration 280 (1)
Cloncurry Australia colonization 282 (1)
Clontarf British Isles (Ireland) crusades 186 (1)
Cloudy Bay bay New Zealand exploration 278 (1)
Clovis North America (USA) the world in 10,000 BCE 14–15
Clunes goldfield Australia colonization 282 (2)
Clunia Iberian Peninsula (Spain) Roman empire 180–181 (1)
Cluny France empire and revolution 199 (4)
Clusium mod. Chiusi Italy early states 178 (1), (2) first civilizations 177 (1)
Clyde New Zealand colonization 283 (5)
Cnidus Southwest Asia (Turkey) ancient Greece 177 (3) Roman empire 180–181 (1) first civilizations 177 (1) Hellenistic world 40–41 (1), 41 (2)
Cnidus state Greece ancient Greece 177 (2)
Cnossus see Knossos
Coahuila state Central America Mexican Revolution 133 (3) the growth of the US 129 (2)
Coahuiltec people Central America/North America colonization 125 (4), 126 (1)
Coast Mountains Fr. Chaîne Côtière mountain range North America the growth of the US 129 (2)
Coatepec var. Cuatepec Central America (Mexico) Aztecs 124 (2)
Coatlayauhcan Central America (Mexico) Aztecs 124 (3)
Coatlinchán Central America (Mexico) Aztecs 124 (2)
Coatzacoalcos river Central America first civilizations 121 (3)
Cobá Central America (Mexico) first civilizations 122 (2)
Cobar goldfield Australia colonization 282 (2)
Coblenz Central Europe (Germany) WWI 206 (2), (3)
Cocanada South Asia (India) WWII 251 (3)
Cochabamba prev. Oropeza South America (Bolivia) Incas 147 (3)
Cochimi people Central America colonization 125 (4)
Cochin var. Kochi; early Chin. Ko-chih South Asia (India) colonialism 247 (3), 248 (1) Mughal Empire 246 (1) post-war economy 253 (5) trade 230 (2), 267 (3)
Cochin China colonial possession/state Mainland Southeast Asia colonialism 269 (4) European imperialism 97 (3)
Cochinos, Bahía de see Pigs, Bay of
Coco people Central America colonization 125 (4)
Cocopa people Central America colonization 125 (4), 126 (1)
Cocos Islands colonial possession/island group Indian Ocean the world in 1900 94–95 the world in 1925 98–99 the world in 1950 102–103 the world in 1975 106–107 the modern world 110–111
Cod, Cape headland North America empire and revolution 127 (2)
Cognac anc. Compniacum France Reformation 194 (2)
Cohuna and Kow Swamp Australia exploration 280 (1)
Coimbatore South Asia (India) post-war economy 253 (5)
Coimbra anc. Conimbria, Conimbriga settlement Iberian Peninsula (Portugal) Franks 184 (2) Islam 192 (3) medieval states 187 (3)
Coira see Chur, Curia
Coire see Chur, Curia
Coixtlahuacan state Central America Aztecs 124 (1)
Cojumatlán Central America (Mexico) first civilizations 122 (1)
Cokwe see Chokwe
Cola state South Asia first empires 241 (5)
Colas see Cholas
Colchester hist. Colneceaste; anc. Camulodunum British Isles (United Kingdom) economy 204 (1) medieval states 183 (3) see also Camulodunum
Colchi South Asia (India) ancient trade 44–45 (1)
Colchis region Eastern Europe Hellenistic world 40–41 (1)
Cold Harbor battle North America (USA) US Civil War 131 (7)
Colee Hammock battle North America (USA) the growth of the US 129 (2)
Colenso battle Southern Africa (South Africa) European imperialism 96 (2)
Colesberg Southern Africa (South Africa) colonization 166 (2) European imperialism 96 (2)
Coles Creek Culture region North America the world in 500 CE 50–51 the world in 750 CE 54–55 the world in 1000 58–59
Coligny Central Europe (France) early systems 33 (3)
Colima Central America (Mexico) first civilizations 122 (1)
Colima state Central America Mexican Revolution 133 (3) the growth of the US 129 (2)
Colless Creek Australia exploration 280 (1)
Collingwood New Zealand colonization 283 (4), (5)
Collo North Africa economy 190 (1)
Colmar Ger. Kolmar France empire and revolution 199 (4)
Colneceaste see Camulodunum, Colchester
Cologne anc. Colonia, Colonia Agrippina, Oppidum Ubiorum; Ger. Köln bomb target/massacre/settlement Central Europe (Germany) biological diffusion 72–73 (1) crusades 186 (1) early modern states 193 (4), 197 (5) economy 190 (1), 205 (4) empire and revolution 202 (2) Franks 183 (5), (6), 184 (2) medieval states 187 (3), 188 (1), (2) post-war politics 212 (1) Reformation 194 (2), 195 (5), 196 (1) WWI 206 (2), (3) WWII 211 (4) see also Colonia, Colonia Agrippina
Colombia prev. Viceroyalty of New Granada state South America economy 153 (3) empire and revolution 151 (3) environment 153 (4) narcotics 153 (5) politics 152 (1) the growth of the US 133 (4) the modern world 112 (1), 113 (4) US politics 139 (4) US superpower 138 (1) WWII 105 (3) Cold War 108 (2), 109 (1) see also New Granada
Colombian Chiefdoms state South America the world in 1000 58–59
Colombie-Britannique see British Columbia
Colombo South Asia (Sri Lanka) colonialism 247 (3), 248 (1) economy 249 (4) European expansion 81 (3) exploration 239 (1) post-war economy 253 (5) post-war politics 252 (1) trade 230 (2), 267 (3) WWII 104 (2), 251 (3), 272 (1)
Colón prev. Aspinwall Central America (Panama) empire and revolution 150 (2)
Colón, Archipiélago de see Galapagos Islands
Colonia Port. Colônia do Sacramento South America (Uruguay) empire and revolution 151 (3) see also Colônia do Sacramento
Colonia mod. Cologne; anc. Colonia, Colonia Agrippina, Oppidum Ubiorum; Ger. Köln Central Europe (Germany) world religions 48 (1) Roman empire 180–181 (1), 181 (3), (4) see also Cologne, Colonia

Colônia do Sacramento var. Colonia; Eng. Colonia del Sacramento South America (Uruguay) colonization 148 (2) exploration 143 (2) see also Colonia
Colonia Dublán Central America (Mexico) Mexican Revolution 133 (3)
Colorado state North America the growth of the US 129 (1) US economy 134 (2)
Colorado river North America colonization 125 (4), 126 (1) cultural groups 123 (4) exploration 118 (1), 119 (2), (3) the growth of the US 129 (2)
Colorado, Río river South America environment 153 (4)
Colosseum building Italy Roman empire 181 (2)
Coltonoco Central America (Mexico) Aztecs 124 (3)
Columbia North America (USA) the growth of the US 129 (2) US society 137 (6)
Columbia river North America early agriculture 120 (1)
Columbia, Cape coastal feature North America exploration 287 (2)
Columbia, District of region North America the growth of the US 132 (1)
Columbus North America (USA) Mexican Revolution 133 (3) the growth of the US 129 (2) US Civil War 131 (6) US economy 134 (1) US politics 135 (6)
Comalcalco Central America (Mexico) first civilizations 122 (1), 123 (2)
Comana religious site Southwest Asia (Turkey) first religions 37 (3)
Comanche people North America colonization 126 (1)
Comani people South America the world in 250 CE 46–47
Comilla Ben. Kumillā South Asia (Bangladesh) decolonization 250 (1) post-war politics 252 (3)
Commagene state Southwest Asia the world in 1 CE 42–43
Como anc. Comum Italy economy 190 (1) medieval states 188 (1)
Comodoro Rivadavia South America (Argentina) environment 153 (4)
Comoro Islands var. Comoros colonial possession/island group East Africa European imperialism 96 (1) see also Comoros
Comoros prev. Comoro Islands state East Africa decolonization 168 (1) economy 168 (2) the modern world 112 (1), 113 (3) see also Comoro Islands
Compiègne France Franks 184 (2) medieval states 192 (2) WWI 206 (2), (3)
Compniacum see Cognac
Compostela Central America (Mexico) colonization 125 (4)
Compostella see Santiago de Compostela
Comum see Como
Conakry West Africa (Guinea) economy 168 (2)
Concelho de Ribeira Grande see Ribeira Grande
Concepción var. Villa Concepción South America (Paraguay) exploration 143 (2)
Concepción South America (Chile) colonization 148 (2) empire and revolution 151 (3) environment 153 (4) exploration 143 (3)
Concepción battle South America (Chile) empire and revolution 150 (1)
Concho people Central America colonization 125 (4), 126 (1)
Concord North America (USA) empire and revolution 127 (3) the growth of the US 129 (2) US Civil War 130 (5)
Concord battle North America (USA) empire and revolution 127 (3)
Condate see Rennes
Condivincum see Nantes
Conestoga see Susquehanna
Confederate States of America state North America 130-131
Congo prev. French Congo, Middle Congo; Fr. Moyen-Congo state Central Africa Cold War 109 (5) economy 168 (2), (3) the modern world 113 (3) see also French Congo
Congo var. Kongo; Fr. Zaire river Central Africa ancient trade 44–45 (1) early agriculture 158 (1), 20–21 (2) early cultures 160 (1) early systems 33 (2) economy 163 (2) European expansion 84–85 (1) exploration 156 (3), 157 (4) first humans 12 (1), 13 (2) first religions 36 (1) global immigration 100 (1) Islam 163 (1) prehistoric culture 16 (1) slave trade 165 (4) trade 164 (2), 167 (1)
Congo (Zaire) free state/state Central Africa decolonization 168 (1) economy 168 (2), (3) the modern world 112 (1)
Congo Basin basin Central Africa first humans 12 (1), 13 (2) slave trade 165 (4)
Congo Free State var. Belgian Congo, Zaire; mod. Democratic Republic of Congo state Central Africa the world in 1900 94–95 see also Belgian Congo, Congo (Zaire), Zaire
Conimbria see Coimbra
Conimbriga see Coimbra
Conjeeveram see Kanchipuram
Connacht region British Isles medieval states 186 (2)
Connecticut state North America empire and revolution 127 (2), (3) the growth of the US 129 (1) US Civil War 130 (2), (3), (4), (5) US economy 134 (2)
Connecticut river North America empire and revolution 127 (3)
Consentia see Cosentia
Constance var. Constanz; hist. Kostnitz, anc. Constantia; Ger. Konstanz Central Europe (Germany) early modern states 193 (4) Franks 184 (2) medieval states 188 (1)
Constance, Lake Ger. Bodensee lake Central Europe early modern states 193 (5)
Constanța Southeast Europe (Romania) WWI 207 (6)
Constantia see Constance
Constantine, Baths of Lat. Thermae Constantini building Italy Roman empire 181 (2)
Constantini, Thermae see Constantine, Baths of
Constantinople anc. Byzantium; Bul. Tsarigrad, Eng. Istanbul, Turk. Istanbul, Norse. Mikligard settlement Southwest Asia (Turkey) Roman empire 182 (1) plague 72–73 (1) crusades 186 (1), 64–65 (2), 65 (1) early Islam 56–57 (1), 57 (2) economy 190 (1), 205 (4) empire and revolution 202 (1) European expansion 84–85 (1) exploration 172 (1), 218 (2), 219 (3) global immigration 100 (1) great migrations 52–53 (1) imperial global economy 92 (1) Islam 163 (1), 226 (2), 227 (4), (5) medieval states 182 (2), 185 (3), 187 (5), 189 (4) medieval voyages 60–61 (1) Mongols 229 (3), 68 (2) Napoleon 200–201 (1), 201 (3) Ottomans 195 (4), 230 (1), 231 (3), 232–233 (1) Seljuks 228 (1) Timur 229 (4) world religions 226 (1), 49 (4) WWI 207 (6), 233 (2) 20th-century politics 233 (3) see also Byzantium, Istanbul
Constantinople battle Southwest Asia (Turkey) early Islam 56–57 (1) Islam 226 (2)
Constanz see Constance
Con Thien battle Mainland Southeast Asia (Vietnam) post-war politics 251 (5)
Conway British Isles (United Kingdom) medieval states 188 (2)
Cooch Behar region South Asia decolonization 250 (2)
Cook County region North America
Cook Islands colonial possession Pacific Ocean colonization 284–285 (1) decolonization 285 (3) early cultures 280–281 (3) environmentalism 285 (2) exploration 279 (3) medieval voyages 60 (2)
Cook Strait var. Raukawa sea waterway New Zealand colonization 283 (5)
Cooktown Australia colonization 283 (3)
Coomassie see Kumasi
Coondapoor var. Barcelore South Asia (India) colonialism 247 (3)
Cooper region North America first civilizations 121 (4)
Cooper Creek var. Barcoo, Cooper's Creek river Austrailia colonization 282 (1) see also Barcoo, Cooper's Creek
Coorg state South Asia colonialism 248 (2)
Coosa people North America colonization 126 (1)
Copán Central America (Honduras) first civilizations 121 (2), 122 (2)
Copena region North America first civilizations 121 (4)
Copenhagen anc. Hafnia; Dan. København Scandinavia (Denmark) early modern states 193 (4), 195 (3) economy 190 (1), 205 (4) empire and revolution 202 (1), (2) medieval states 189 (3) Napoleon 200–201 (1), 201 (2), (3) post-war politics 212 (3) Reformation 194 (2) WWII 210 (1), 211 (2), (3), (4) Cold War 108 (3)
Copiapó prev. San Francisco de Selva South America (Chile) empire and revolution 151 (3) exploration 143 (3) Incas 147 (3) politics 151 (4)
Copper Inuit people North America cultural groups 123 (3)
Coppermine river North America exploration 286 (1), 287 (2)
Coquimbo South America (Chile) colonization 148 (2)
Coral Sea sea Australia colonization 282 (1) decolonization 251 (4), 285 (3) early cultures 280–281 (3) environmentalism 285 (2) exploration 280 (1) medieval voyages 60 (2) post-war economy 253 (5) WWII 104 (2), 251 (3), 272 (1), 273 (2)
Coral Sea Islands colonial possession Pacific Ocean the modern world 110–111
Corcaigh see Cork
Corcyra Southeast Europe (Croatia) first civilizations 177 (1)
Corcyra var. Kérkira; mod. Corfu island Greece ancient Greece 177 (3), 179 (4) see also Corfu
Corcyra Nigra see Korčula
Corded Ware Burials cultural region Northeast Europe The World in 2500 BCE 22–23
Cordillera Central mountain range South America early cultures 145 (2)
Cordilleran Ice Sheet ice feature North America historical geography 117 (1)
Cordillera Occidental mountain range South America early cultures 145 (2)
Cordillera Oriental mountain range South America early cultures 145 (2)
Córdoba anc. Corduba; Eng. Cordova Iberian Peninsula (Spain) economy 190 (1) civil war 209 (4) Napoleon 201 (2) see also Corduba, Cordova
Córdoba South America (Argentina) colonization 148 (2) empire and revolution 150 (1), 151 (3) environment 153 (4) exploration 143 (2) politics 152 (1)
Cordova state Iberian Peninsula Franks 184 (2) medieval states 185 (3) medieval voyages 60–61 (1) the world in 1000 58–59 Islam 226 (2), 227 (4)
Cordova settlement Iberian peninsula (Spain) Roman empire 182 (1) crusades 186 (1), 64–65 (2), 65 (1) early Islam 56–57 (1), 57 (2) Franks 184 (2) Islam 184 (1), 192 (3) medieval states 182 (2), 185 (3)
Cordova, Caliphate of state Iberian Peninsula medieval states 185 (3) medieval voyages 60–61 (1) the World in 1000 58–59 (1)
Corduba mod. Córdoba; Eng. Cordova Iberian Peninsula (Spain) Roman empire 181 (4) great migrations 52–53 (1) world religions 48 (1) see also Córdoba, Cordova
Corfinium Italy Roman empire 180–181 (1) early states 178 (1)
Corfu var. Kérkira; Eng. Corfu island Greece empire and revolution 202 (1) Napoleon 201 (2) Ottomans 230 (1), 231 (3) see also Corcyra
Corinium, **Corinium Dobunorum** see Cirencester
Corinth North America (USA) US Civil War 131 (7)
Corinth anc. Corinthus; Gr. Kórinthos Greece ancient Greece 177 (3), 179 (4) Roman empire 179 (5), 180–181 (1), 181 (3), 182 (1) exploration 172 (1) first civilizations 177 (1) great migrations 52–53 (1) Hellenistic world 40–41 (1) medieval states 182 (2) world religions 48 (1)
Corinth, Gulf of anc. Corinthiacus Sinus gulf Greece ancient Greece 177 (2), (3) first civilizations 175 (4)
Corinthiacus Sinus see Corinth, Gulf of
Corinthus see Corinth
Cork Ir. Corcaigh British Isles (Ireland) economy 205 (4) medieval states 186 (2), 187 (4)
Corneto see Tarquinii
Coro prev. Santa Ana de Coro South America (Venezuela) exploration 142 (1)
Coromandel Coast physical region South Asia colonialism 247 (3), 248 (1), (2) decolonization 250 (1) early medieval states 244 (1), (2), 244–245 (3), 245 (4) economy 249 (4) first empires 241 (4), (5) Marathas 246 (2) Mughal Empire 246 (1) post-war politics 252 (1) world religions 242 (2), 243 (4)
Coromandel Peninsula coastal feature New Zealand colonization 283 (4)
Coron Greece medieval states 187 (5)
Corozal people South America the world in 1 CE 42–43 the world in 250 CE 46–47
Corregidor battle Philippines WWII 104 (2)
Correntes, Cape headland Southern Africa exploration 156 (3)
Correo Mexicano battle Gulf of Mexico the growth of the US 129 (2)
Corrientes prev. San Juan de Vera South America (Argentina) empire and revolution 151 (3) environment 153 (4) exploration 143 (2)
Corse see Corsica
Corsica Fr. Corse island France Roman empire 179 (3), 180–181 (1), 181 (3), (4), 182 (1) Bronze Age 175 (3) crusades 186 (1), 64–65 (2) early cultures 161 (2) early Islam 56–57 (1) economy 190 (1), 205 (4) empire and revolution 199 (4), 202 (1), (3), 88–89 (2) first civilizations 177 (1) first religions 37 (3) Franks 184 (2) civil war 209 (5) Islam 226 (2), 227 (4) medieval states 183 (4), 185 (3), (5), 188 (1) Napoleon 201 (2) Ottomans 231 (3) post-war economy 213 (5), 214 (1) post-war politics 212 (3) Reformation 196 (1), (2) the modern world 112 (2) world religions 48 (1) WWII 210 (1), 211 (2), (4)
Corsica and Sardinia province Italy Roman empire 179 (5)
Corsicans people France early states 178 (2) the modern world 112 (2)
Cortaillod-Est France Bronze Age 175 (3)
Cortellazzo Italy WWI 207 (5)
Cortenuova battle Italy medieval states 188 (1)
Cortes de Navarra Iberian Peninsula (Spain) Bronze Age 175 (3)
Cortez, Sea of see California, Gulf of
Cortina see Hayden
Cortona Italy early states 178 (2) first civilizations 177 (1)
Corumbá South America (Brazil) colonization 148 (2) empire and revolution 151 (3)
Corunna Sp. La Coruña Iberian Peninsula (Spain) Napoleon 200–201 (1), 201 (2)
Corupedium battle Southwest Asia (Turkey) Hellenistic world 224 (1)
Corvo, Passo di Italy early agriculture 174 (1)
Cos settlement/state Greece ancient Greece 177 (2) first civilizations 177 (1)
Cosa Italy early states 178 (1)
Cosentia var. Consentia Italy early states 178 (1)
Cosquer archaeological site France prehistoric culture 17 (2)
Cossack Revolt war Eastern Europe Reformation 196 (2)
Cossimbazar South Asia (India) colonialism 247 (3)
Costa Rica state Central America Cold War 108 (2), 109 (1) the growth of the US 129 (2) the modern world 112 (1) US economy 136 (2), 139 (4) US superpower 138 (1)
Costermansville see Bukavu
Côte d'Ivoire see Ivory Coast
Côte Française des Somalis see Djibouti, French Somaliland
Côtière, Chaîne see Coast Mountains
Cotopachi South America (Bolivia) Incas 147 (3)
Cotrone see Croton
Courland Ger. Kurland state Eastern Europe/Scandinavia early modern states 195 (3) Reformation 194 (2)
Courtrai Low Countries (Belgium) WWI 206 (2), (3)
Cova Negra archaeological site Iberian Peninsula (Spain) first humans 13 (2)
Coventry British Isles (United Kingdom) economy 190 (1) WWII 210 (1)
Coveta de l'Or Iberian Peninsula (Spain) early agriculture 174 (1)
Cowpens battle North America (USA) empire and revolution 127 (3)
Coyoacán Central America (Mexico) Aztecs 124 (3) colonization 125 (5)
Coyolapan state Central America Aztecs 124 (1)
Coyotepec Central America (Mexico) Aztecs 124 (2)
Coyotera Apache people North America colonization 125 (4)
Cozumel, Isla island North America Aztecs 124 (1) first civilizations 123 (2)
Crab Orchard region/burial mound North America first civilizations 121 (4)
Cracovia see Cracow
Cracow Lat. Cracovia; Ger. Krakau, Pol. Kraków settlement Central Europe (Poland) biological diffusion 72–73 (1) early modern states 193 (4), 194 (1) economy 190 (1) empire and revolution 198 (2), 202 (1) civil war 209 (3) medieval states 188 (1), 189 (3), (4) Mongols 68–69 (1) Napoleon 200–201 (1), 201 (2) Ottomans 195 (4) post-war politics 212 (3) Reformation 194 (2) WWI 207 (4) WWII 210 (1), 211 (3), (4)
Craig Harbour North America (Canada) cultural groups 123 (3)
Cranganur South Asia (India) colonialism 247 (3)
Cravant battle France medieval states 192 (2)
Crécy battle France medieval states 192 (1)
Cree people North America colonization 126 (1) cultural groups 123 (3)
Creek people North America colonization 125 (4), 126 (1)
Crema Italy economy 190 (1)
Cremera river Italy early states 178 (1)
Cremona Italy Roman empire 180–181 (1) economy 190 (1) Franks 184 (2) medieval states 183 (4)
Crépy France Reformation 194 (2)
Crestaulta Central Europe (Switzerland) Bronze Age 175 (3)
Creta prev. Candia; Eng. Crete, Gr. Kríti island Greece Roman empire 180–181 (1), 181 (4) see also Candia, Crete
Crete region/island Greece ancient Egypt 159 (5) ancient Greece 177 (2), 179 (4) ancient Persia 223 (4) Roman empire 179 (5), 181 (3), 182 (1), 24 (2), 225 (5) ancient trade 44–45 (1) Bronze Age 175 (3) crusades 186 (1), 64–65 (2) early cultures 161 (2) early Islam 56–57 (1) early systems 223 (3) economy 190 (1), 205 (4) empire and revolution 202 (1) first civilizations 175 (4), 177 (1) first religions 37 (3) Hellenistic world 224 (1) Islam 184 (1), 226 (2), 227 (4), (5) medieval states 182 (2), 185 (3) Napoleon 200–201 (1), 201 (2) Ottomans 230 (1), 231 (3), 232–233 (1) post-war economy 213 (5), 214 (1) post-war politics 212 (3) Reformation 196 (2) Seljuks 228 (1) world religions 226 (1) WWI 233 (2) WWII 210 (1), 211 (2), (4) 20th-century politics 233 (3)
Crete, Sea of sea Greece ancient Greece 179 (4) first civilizations 175 (4)
Crewe British Isles (United Kingdom) economy 204 (1)
Criel Mound burial mound North America (USA) first civilizations 121 (4)
Crimea Rus. Krym region/coastal feature Eastern Europe exploration 219 (3) historical geography 170–171 (1) Ottomans 202 (4), 232–233 (1) the modern world 112 (2) WWI 207 (4)
Crimea, Khanate of state/vassal state Eastern Europe Islam 163 (1) Ottomans 195 (4), 230 (1), 231 (3)
Crimean Tartars people Eastern Europe Soviet Union 213 (4)
Crna Gora see Montenegro
Croatia Ger. Kroatien, SCr. Hrvatska region/state Southeast Europe medieval states 185 (3), 189 (4) Ottomans 197 (4), 230 (1) post-war economy 214 (1), (2), 215 (3) Soviet Union 214–215 (4) the modern world 112 (2), 113 (3) WWII 210 (1), 211 (2), (4)
Croats people Southeast Europe Franks 184 (2)
Crocodile see Limpopo
Cro-Magnon France the world in 10,000 BCE 14–15
Cromford British Isles (United Kingdom) imperial global economy 93 (4)
Cromwell New Zealand colonization 283 (5)
Crooked Creek battle North America (USA) the growth of the US 129 (2)
Croquants rebel faction France Reformation 196 (2)
Cross, Cape headland Southern Africa exploration 156 (3)
Croton var. Cotrone; mod. Crotone; anc. Crotona Italy Roman empire 179 (3) early cultures 161 (2) early states 178 (1), (2) first civilizations 177 (1)
Crotona see Croton
Crotone see Croton
Crow people North America colonization 126 (1)
Crown Point North America (USA) empire and revolution 127 (2), (3)
Crozet Islands island group Indian Ocean the world in 1800 86–87
Crusader States state Southwest Asia Mongols 68–69 (1)
Cruz del Milagro archaeological site Central America (Mexico) first civilizations 121 (3)
Cruzeiro do Sul South America (Brazil) environment 153 (4)
Crystal II North America (Canada) cultural groups 123 (3)
Ctesiphon var. Tayspun Southwest Asia (Iraq) ancient Persia 225 (6) Roman empire 180–181 (1), 224 (2) ancient trade 44–45 (1) Islam 227 (4), (5) medieval states 261 (6) world religions 226 (1), 49 (4)
Cuahtitlan state Central America Aztecs 124 (1)
Cuahuacan state Central America Aztecs 124 (1)
Cuando var. Kwando river Southern Africa exploration 157 (4)
Cuangar Southern Africa (Angola) Cold War 109 (5)
Cuango var. Kwango river Southern Africa trade 164 (2) see also Kwango
Cuanza var. Kwanza river Southern Africa Cold War 109 (5) exploration 157 (4) trade 164 (2)
Cuarte Iberian Peninsula (Spain) Islam 192 (3)
Cuatepec see Coatepec
Cuauhatitlan Central America (Mexico) colonization 125 (5)
Cuauhquecholan Central America (Mexico) colonization 125 (5)
Cuauhtepec Central America (Mexico) Aztecs 124 (3)
Cuauhtochco state Central America Aztecs 124 (1)
Cuautitlán Central America (Mexico) Aztecs 124 (2)
Cuautlapan Central America (Mexico) Aztecs 124 (3)
Cuba colonial possession/state/island West Indies colonization 125 (4), 126 (1) early agriculture 120 (1) empire and revolution 88 (1) European expansion 84–85 (1), 85 (2) exploration 143 (3) global immigration 100 (1), 101 (3) historical geography 117 (1) imperial global economy 92 (1) the growth of the US 129 (2), 133 (4) the modern world 112 (1) US economy 136 (2) US imperialism 133 (5) US politics 139 (4) US superpower 138 (1) WWII 104 (1) Cold War 108 (2), 109 (1)
Cubango var. Kuvango; Port. Vila Artur de Paiva, Vila da Ponte river Southern Africa Cold War 109 (5) exploration 157 (4)
Cuckadoo Australia the world in 10,000 BCE 14–15
Cúcuta var. San José de Cúcuta South America (Colombia) empire and revolution 150 (2)
Cúcuta battle South America (Venezuela) empire and revolution 150 (1)
Cuello Central America (Belize) first civilizations 121 (2)
Cuenca South America (Ecuador) colonization 148 (2) empire and revolution 151 (3)
Cuera see Chur, Curia
Cuernavaca Central America (Mexico) colonization 125 (5)
Cuetlachtlan Central America (Mexico) colonization 125 (5)
Cuetlaxtlan state Central America Aztecs 124 (1)
Cueva people South America early cultures 147 (2)
Cuiabá prev. Cuyabá South America (Brazil) environment 153 (4) politics 152 (1)
Cuicatlán Central America (Mexico) first civilizations 122 (1)
Cuicuilco Central America (Mexico) first civilizations 121 (2)
Cuihuacan Central America (Mexico) first civilizations 122 (1)
Cuiry-lès-Chaudardes France early agriculture 174 (1)
Cuitlahuac Central America (Mexico) Aztecs 124 (2) colonization 125 (5)
Cuitzeo, Lake lake Central America Aztecs 124 (1)
Cularo see Grenoble
Culhuacan Central America (Mexico) Aztecs 124 (2), (3)
Culiacán var. Culiacán Rosales, Culiacán-Rosales Central America (Mexico) Mexican Revolution 133 (3)
Culiacán Rosales see Culiacán
Cullalvera archaeological site Iberian Peninsula (Spain) prehistoric culture 17 (3)
Cullerson's Ranch North America (USA) Mexican Revolution 133 (3)
Culver City North America (USA) US economy 135 (4)
Cumae Italy early states 178 (1), (2) first civilizations 177 (1)
Cumaná South America (Venezuela) colonization 148 (2) empire and revolution 150 (1), (2)
Cumans var. Kipchaks; Rus. Polovtsy people Eastern Europe crusades 186 (1) Mongols 68–69 (1)
Cumberland River river North America the growth of the US 129 (2)
Cunaxa battle Southwest Asia (Iraq) ancient Persia 223 (4)
Cunjamba Southern Africa (Angola) Cold War 109 (5)
Cupertino North America (USA) 136 (3)
Cupisnique archaeological site South America (Peru) early cultures 145 (3)
Cupul state Central America Aztecs 124 (1)
Curaçao island West Indies European expansion 85 (2)
Curia mod. Chur; anc. Curia Rhaetorum; Fr. Coire, It. Coira, Quera Central Europe (Switzerland) Roman empire 180–181 (1)
Curia Rhaetorum see Chur, Curia
Curitiba South America (Brazil) environment 153 (4)
Curium Southwest Asia (Cyprus) first civilizations 177 (1)
Curpeutaria, Lake ancient lake Australia the world in 10,000 BCE 14–15
Currarong Australia the world in 5000 BCE 18–19
Curzola see Korčula
Cusco var. Cuzco South America (Peru) environment 153 (4) narcotics 153 (5) see also Cuzco
Cush see Kush
Cushites see Kushites
Cutch, Gulf of see Kachchh, Gulf of
Cuttack South Asia (India) colonialism 247 (3), 248 (1) economy 249 (4)
Cuyabá see Cuiabá
Cuyutec people Central America colonization 125 (4)
Cuzco mod. Cusco South America (Peru) colonization 148 (2) early cultures 146 (1) empire and revolution 151 (3) exploration 142 (1) Incas 147 (3), 148 (1) see also Cusco
Cuzco state South America the world in 250 CE 46–47 the world in 1000 58–59 the world in 1200 62–63
Cyclades var. Kikládhes; Eng. Cyclades island group Greece ancient Greece 177 (2), (3) first civilizations 175 (4)
Cyme state Greece ancient Greece 177 (2)
Cymru see Wales
Cynoscephalae battle Greece ancient Greece 179 (4)
Cynossema battle Southwest Asia (Turkey) ancient Greece 177 (3)
Cyprus Gk. Kypros, Turk. Kıbrıs state Southwest Asia ancient Egypt 159 (4), (5) ancient Persia 223 (4), 225 (6) Roman empire 179 (5), 180–181 (1), 181 (3), (4), 182 (1), 224 (2), 225 (5) ancient trade 44–45 (1) Bronze Age 175 (3) crusades 228 (2) early agriculture 220 (1) early cultures 161 (2) early Islam 56–57 (1) early trade 225 (3) economy 190 (1) empire and revolution 202 (1) exploration 172 (1) first cities 220 (2) first civilizations 177 (1), 221 (4), (5), 222 (1), (2) first religions 37 (3) Hellenistic world 224 (1) historical geography 170–171 (1) Islam 184 (1), 226 (2), 227 (4), (5) medieval states 182 (2), 185 (3), 187 (5) kingdom 229 (3), 68–69 (1) Napoleon 200–201 (1) Ottomans 202 (4), 230 (1), 231 (3), 232–233 (1) post-war politics 212 (3) Seljuks 228 (1) the modern world 112 (2), 113 (3), (4) world religions 226 (1) WWI 233 (2) WWII 210 (1), 211 (2), (4)20th-century politics 233 (3), (4), 235 (5)
Cyprus, Kingdom of state Southwest Asia crusades 65 (3)
Cyrenaica var. Barqah region/state North Africa Roman empire 225 (5) colonization 167 (4) early cultures 161 (2) first civilizations 177 (1) Islam 227 (4) Ottomans 232–233 (1) slave trade 165 (4)
Cyrene North Africa (Libya) ancient Persia 223 (4) Roman empire 179 (5), 180–181 (1), 181 (3), (4), 225 (5) ancient trade 44–45 (1) early cultures 160 (1), 161 (2) first civilizations 177 (1) Hellenistic world 40–41 (1) world religions 48 (1)
Cyrene et Creta province North Africa Roman empire 180–181 (1)
Cyrrhus legion headquarters Southwest Asia (Syria) Roman empire 180–181 (1)
Cyrus river Southwest Asia ancient Persia 223 (4)
Cytorus Southwest Asia (Turkey) first civilizations 177 (1)
Cyzicus state Southwest Asia (Turkey) ancient Greece 177 (2), 179 (4) Roman empire 180–181 (1)
Czechoslovakia state Central Europe civil war 209 (3), (5) post-war economy 213 (5) post-war politics 212 (1), (3) Soviet Union 213 (4) WWI 208 (1) WWII 211 (3) Cold War 108 (3), 109 (1)
Czech Republic Cz. Česká Republika state Southeast Europe post-war economy 214 (1), (2) Soviet Union 214–215 (4) the modern world 112 (2), 113 (4) see also Czechoslovakia
Czernowitz Eastern Europe (Ukraine) WWI 207 (4)
Czikador major cistercian house Central Europe medieval states 187 (3)

D

Daamat state East Africa the world in 500 BCE 34–35
Dabal South Asia (Pakistan) world religions 243 (4)
Dacca mod. Dhaka South Asia (Bangladesh) colonialism 247 (3) decolonization 250 (1), (2) economy 249 (4) imperial global economy 93 (5) see also Dhaka
Dachau concentration camp Central Europe WWII 211 (3)
Dacia province/state Southeast Europe Roman empire 180–181 (1), 181 (4) ancient trade 44–45 (1) world religions 48 (1)
Dacians people Southeast Europe the world in 1 CE 42–43
Dade's Battle battle North America (USA) the growth of the US 129 (2)
Dading East Asia (China) medieval states 263 (4)
Dadiwan archaeological site East Asia early agriculture 258 (1)
Dadra and Nagar Haveli region South Asia post-war politics 252 (1)
Dadri state South Asia empire and revolution 249 (3)
Dadu East Asia (China) medieval states 263 (6)
Dagden see Dagö
Dagestan state Eastern Europe Soviet Union 214–215 (4)
Daghestan mod. Dagestan state Eastern Europe/Southwest Asia Mongols 68–69 (1) see also Dagestan
Dagö Est. Hiiumaa; Ger. Dagden, island Southeast Europe early modern states 195 (3) WWI 207 (4)
Dagomba state West Africa the world in 1800 86–87 the world in 1850 90–91
Dagon see Rangoon
Dagushan var. Takushan East Asia (China) Russo-Japanese War 270 (4)
Dahecun archaeological site East Asia early agriculture 258 (1)
Dahlak island East Africa Islam 163 (1)
Dahomey mod. Benin state West Africa colonization 167 (4) European imperialism 96 (1) Islam 167 (3) slave trade 165 (4) trade 167 (1) see also Benin
Dahshur Egypt ancient Egypt 159 (3), (4)
Daibul var. Daybul South Asia (Pakistan) medieval voyages 61 (3) see also Daybul
Dai Do battle Mainland Southeast Asia (Vietnam) post-war politics 251 (5)
Daifang East Asia (Korea) medieval states 264 (2)
Daijun East Asia (China) first cities 259 (5)
Dai-la mod. Hanoi; prev. Thang Long Mainland Southeast Asia (Vietnam) early medieval states 245 (5), (6) see also Hanoi
Daima archaeological site/settlement West Africa (Nigeria) ancient trade 44–45 (1) early agriculture 158 (1) early cultures 160 (1)
Dainzú Central America (Mexico) first civilizations 121 (2)
Dairen var. Dalian, Dalien, Jay Dairen, Lüda, Ta-lien; Rus. Dalny East Asia (China) colonialism 269 (4) imperialism 270 (2) Russo-Japanese War 270 (4) Sino-Japanese War 270 (3) Soviet Union 213 (4)
Dai-sen mountain Japan medieval states 265 (3)
Dai Viet state Mainland Southeast Asia early medieval states 245 (5) world religions 243 (5)
Daju state Central Africa the world in 1200 62–63 the world in 1300 66–67 the world in 1400 70–71
Dakar West Africa (Senegal) economy 168 (2) European imperialism 96 (1) global immigration 100 (1) US superpower 138 (1) WWII 104 (2)
Dakhla Oasis var. Wāhat el Dākhla oasis Egypt ancient Egypt 159 (2), (3), (5)
Dākhla, Wāhat el see Dakhla Oasis
Dakota people North America colonization 126 (1)
Đakovica Southeast Europe (Yugoslavia) post-war economy 215 (3)
Dakshina Koshala region South Asia world religions 242 (2)
Daksinapatha region South Asia ancient India 242 (1) first empires 241 (4)
Daksinatya/Daksinapatha region South Asia early religions 48 (2)
Dak To battle Mainland Southeast Asia (Vietnam) post-war politics 251 (5)
Dalautabad South Asia (India) early medieval states 244–245 (3)
Dali var. Xiaguan East Asia (China) early humans 13 (2) early medieval states 245 (5) medieval states 263 (3), (4) (5) Mongols 68–69 (1)
Dalian East Asia (China) Islam 275 (4) post-war politics 274 (2)
Daliang East Asia (China) first cities 259 (5)
Dalien see Dairen, Dalian
Dallas North America (USA) Cold War 108 (2) imperial global economy 93 (5) US economy 134 (1), (3), 136 (2) US politics 135 (6)
Dalmatia region Southeast Europe Roman empire 180–181 (1), 225 (5) early cultures 161 (2) empire and revolution 202 (1) Ottomans 230 (1)
Dalny see Dairen, Dalian
Dalriada state British Isles medieval states 183 (3)
Dalstroi region Siberia Soviet Union 213 (4)
Daluo Mainland Southeast Asia (Vietnam) Mongols 68–69 (1)
Daman settlement/colonial possession South Asia (India) colonialism 247 (3) post-war politics 252 (1) trade 230 (2)
Damão mod. Daman colonial possession/settlement South Asia empire and revolution 88–89 (2) trade 267 (3) WWII 251 (3)
Damargam state West Africa the world in 1850 90–91
Damas see Damascus
Damasco see Damascus
Damascus var. Ash Shām, Esh Sham; Ar. Dimashq, Fr. Damas, It. Damasco Southwest Asia (Syria) ancient Egypt 159 (5) ancient Persia 223 (4), 225 (6) Roman empire 180–181 (1), 224 (2), 225 (4), (5) ancient trade 44–45 (1) plague 72–73 (1) crusades 228 (2), 65 (1), (3) early cultures 161 (2) early Islam 56–57 (1), 57 (2) early trade 225 (3) exploration 156 (3), 218 (2), 219 (4) first civilizations 221 (4), (5), 222 (1), (2) Hellenistic world 224 (1) Islam 184 (1), 227 (4), (5) medieval states 185 (3) Mongols 229 (3), 68–69 (1) Napoleon 200–201 (1) Ottomans 231 (3), 232–233 (1) Seljuks 228 (1) Timur 229 (4) trade 230 (2) world religions 226 (1) WWI 233 (2) 20th century 234 (2) 20th-century politics 233 (3), (4), 235 (5)
Damascus, Emirate of state Southwest Asia crusades 65 (3)
Damb Sadaat archaeological site South Asia (Pakistan) first cities 240 (2)
Dambwa archaeological site Southern Africa (Zimbabwe) early cultures 160 (1)
Damghan Southwest Asia (Iran) early Islam 56–57 (1)
Damietta Ar. Dumyât Egypt crusades 64–65 (2), 65 (3) economy 190 (1)
Daming var. Ta-ming East Asia (China) medieval states 262 (2), 263 (4) Mongols 68–69 (1)
Damot state East Africa the world in 1000 58–59 the world in 1200 62–63
Dampier Australia colonization 283 (3)
Dan Southwest Asia (Israel) first civilizations 222 (1)
Dana Eastern Europe (Russian Federation) biological diffusion 72–73 (1)
Da Nang battle Mainland Southeast Asia (Vietnam) post-war politics 251 (5)
Dandaka region South Asia world religions 242 (2)
Dandanqan Central Asia (Turkmenistan) Seljuks 228 (1)
Dandong var. Tan-tung; prev. Antung; Jap. Antō East Asia (China) Cold War 109 (4) see also Andong
Danelaw state British Isles medieval states 185 (3) medieval voyages 60–61 (1)
Danes people Scandinavia Roman empire 182 (1) Franks 184 (2) medieval states 185 (3) the modern world 112 (2)
Danger Cave North America (USA) the world in 5000 BCE 18–19
Dangerous Archipelago see Tuamotu Islands
Daning East Asia (China) medieval states 263 (6)
Danish March region Central Europe Franks 184 (2)
Danishmends state Southwest Asia crusades 64–65 (2)
Danish West Indies see American Virgin Islands
Danmark see Denmark
Danmarksstraedet see Denmark Strait
Dannoura battle (Japan) early modern states 265 (5)
Dantapura South Asia (India) ancient India 242 (1)
Danube Lat. Danubius, Danuvius, Ister; Bul. Dunav, Cz. Dunaj, Ger. Donau, Hung. Duna, Rom. Dunărea; river Southeast Europe ancient Persia 225 (6) Roman empire 180–181 (1), 181 (3), (4), 224 (2), 225 (5) ancient trade 44–45 (1) Bronze Age 175 (3) Copper Age 174 (2) crusades 186 (1), 64–65 (2) early agriculture 174 (1), 20–21 (2) early Islam 56–57 (1), 57 (2) early modern states 193 (4) economy 190 (1) empire and revolution 199 (3), 202 (1), (2) exploration 172 (1) first civilizations 177 (1) first humans 13 (2) first religions 36 (1), 37 (3) Franks 184 (2) great migrations 52–53 (1), 53 (2) Hellenistic world 224 (1) Islam 163 (1), 226 (2), 227 (4) medieval states 182 (2), 185 (3), 188 (1), 189 (4) Napoleon 200–201 (1), 201 (2), (3) Ottomans 197 (4), 230 (1), 231 (3), 232–233 (1) prehistoric culture 16 (1), 17 (4) Reformation 196 (1) Seljuks 228 (1) world religions 226 (1), 49 (4) WWI 207 (6) WWII 210 (1), 211 (4) civil war 209 (5) post-war economy 215 (3) see also Danuvius
Danubius see Danube
Danum see Doncaster
Danuvius var. Danube river Southest Europe ancient trade 44 (2)
Danyang East Asia (China) first cities 259 (5) first religions 37 (4)
Danyang province East Asia first states 260 (1)
Danzig mod. Gdańsk Central Europe (Poland) trade 72–73 (1) early modern states 193 (4), 195 (3) economy 190 (1), 205 (4) empire and revolution 198 (2), 199 (3), 202 (1), (2) civil war 209 (3), (5) medieval states 189 (3), (4) Napoleon 200–201 (1) WWI 207 (4) WWII 210 (1), 211 (4)
Dapenkeng archaeological site East Asia early agriculture 258 (1)
Darada state South Asia first empires 241 (5)
Daradus river West Africa (Senegal) ancient trade 44 (2)
Dar al Baida, al see Rabat
Darbelo South Asia (Pakistan) colonialism 247 (3)
Dardanelles var. Hellespont; Turk. Çanakkale Boğazı sea waterway Southwest Asia/Europe first civilizations 175 (4) WWI 207 (6), 233 (2)
Dar-el-Beida see Casablanca
Dar es Salaam East Africa (Tanzania) colonization 167 (4) economy 168 (2) exploration 156 (3), 157 (4), (5)
Dar es-Soltan archaeological site North Africa (Morocco) first humans 13 (2), 14 (1)
Darfur state East Africa colonization 167 (4) slave trade 165 (4) trade 167 (1)
Dargaville New Zealand colonization 283 (4), (5)
Dariabad South Asia (India) colonialism 247 (3)
Darién, Golfo del see Darien, Gulf of
Darien, Gulf of Sp. Golfo del Darién gulf South America colonization 148 (2) Incas 148 (1)
Darien, Isthmus of see Panama, Isthmus of
Dariorigum France Roman empire 180–181 (1)
Dar'īyah see Deraya
Darjeeling South Asia (India) exploration 257 (3)
Darling river Australia colonization 282 (1), (2), 283 (3) early agriculture 20–21 (2) exploration 279 (2) prehistoric culture 17 (5)
Darlington British Isles (United Kingdom) economy 204 (1)
Darsena see Arsenal
Dar Tichit West Africa (Mauritania) early agriculture 158 (1)
Darwin prev. Palmerston, Port Darwin Australia colonization 282 (1), 283 (3) exploration 279 (2) WWII 251 (3), 272 (1)
Dar"yoi Amu see Amu Darya
Dās island Southwest Asia economy 234 (1)
Dasapura South Asia (India) early religions 48 (2)
Dasharna region/state South Asia first empires 241 (5) world religions 242 (2)
Dashhowuz see Dashkhovuz
Dashiqiao var. Tashihkiao East Asia (China) Russo-Japanese War 270 (4)
Dashkhovuz prev. Tashauz; Turkm. Dashhowuz Central Asia (Turkmenistan) Soviet Union 214–215 (4)
Dasht river South Asia first cities 240 (2) first civilizations 24 (2), 25 (3) first empires 241 (4), (5) Mughal Empire 246 (1) world religions 242 (2)
Dating East Asia (China) medieval states 263 (5)
Datong East Asia (China) medieval states 263 (4)
Datong East Asia (China) early modern states 266 (1) medieval states 263 (5) world religions 49 (3)
Daugava see Western Dvina
Daugavpils see Dünaburg
Daulatabad South Asia (India) early medieval states 245 (4)
Dauni people Italy early states 178 (2)
Dauphiné region France medieval states 192 (1), (2)
Davao off. Davao City Philippines colonialism 247 (4)
Davao City see Davao
Davis Strait sea waterway North America exploration 286 (1), 287 (2) the growth of the US 129 (2)
Daw state West Africa trade 163 (4)
Dawaro state East Africa the world in 1200 62–63 the world in 1300 66–67
Dawenkou archaeological site East Asia early agriculture 258 (1), (2)
Dawson see Dawson City
Dawson City mod. Dawson North America (Canada) imperial global economy 93 (3)

Dawston see Degsastan
Daybul var. Daibol South Asia (India) medieval voyages 61 (3) trade 230 (2)
Daybul see Daibul
Dayi Shang vassal state East Asia first cities 259 (3)
Dayton North America (USA) US politics 135 (6)
Da Yunhe see Grand Canal
Dazaifu Japan early modern states 265 (5) medieval states 264 (2), 265 (3)
Dazhangheguo state East Asia medieval states 263 (3)
DDR see German Democratic Republic
Dead Sea var. Bahret Lut, Lacus Asphaltites; Ar. Al Baḥr al Mayyit, Baḥrat Lūṭ, Heb. Yam HaMelah salt lake Southwest Asia 20th century 234 (2) 20th-century politics 233 (3) Roman empire 225 (4) crusades 65 (3) first civilizations 221 (4), 222 (1)
De Blicquy North America (Canada) cultural groups 123 (3)
Debrecen prev. Debreczen; Ger. Debreczin, Rom. Debreţin Central Europe (Hungary) Reformation 194 (2)
Debreczen, Debreczin see Debrecen
Debreţin see Debrecen
Decapolis state Southwest Asia Roman empire 225 (4)
Deccan plateau/region South Asia colonialism 247 (3), 248 (1) early medieval states 244 (1), (2), 244–245 (3) economy 249 (4) first empires 241 (4), (5) first religions 36 (2) imperial global economy 93 (5) Marathas 246 (2) Mughal Empire 246 (1) post-war politics 252 (1) world religions 242 (2), 243 (4)
Deccan States state South Asia colonialism 248 (2)
Dedeagach mod. Alexandroupolis Greece WWI 207 (6)
Dego battle Italy Napoleon 200–201 (1)
Degsastan var. Dawston battle British Isles (United Kingdom) medieval states 183 (3)
Dehli see Delhi, Indraprastha
Dehra Dun South Asia (India) decolonization 250 (1) exploration 257 (3)
Deira region British Isles medieval states 183 (3)
Deir el-Bahri Egypt ancient Egypt 159 (4)
Deir el-Balah Southwest Asia (Israel) ancient Egypt 159 (5)
Deir el-Bersha Egypt ancient Egypt 159 (4)
Deir el-Gabrawi Egypt ancient Egypt 159 (3)
Delagoa Bay var. Baia de Lourenço Marques bay Southern Africa slave trade 165 (4)
Delaware state North America empire and revolution 127 (2), (3) the growth of the US 129 (1) US Civil War 130 (2), (3), (4), (5), 131 (6), (7) US economy 134 (2)
Delaware people North America colonization 126 (1)
Delgado, Cape headland Southern Africa exploration 156 (3)
Delhi var. Dehli, Hind. Dilli; prev. Indraprastha; hist. Shahjahanabad South Asia (India) trade 72–73 (1) colonialism 247 (3), 248 (1), 269 (4) Communism 271 (8) decolonization 250 (1) early medieval states 244–245 (3) economy 249 (4) empire and revolution 249 (3) exploration 239 (1), 257 (3) global immigration 101 (3) imperial global economy 92 (1), 93 (5) Mongols 68 (2) Mughal Empire 246 (1) post-war economy 253 (5) Timur 229 (4) trade 267 (3) US superpower 138 (1) WWII 251 (3) see also Indraprastha
Delhi region South Asia post-war politics 252 (1)
Delhi, Sultanate of state South Asia Mongols 68–69 (1) Mughal Empire 246 (1) Timur 229 (4)
Delhi United Provinces state South Asia colonialism 248 (2)
Delium battle Greece ancient Greece 177 (3)
Delos Greece ancient Greece 179 (4)
Delphi religious site/settlement Greece ancient Greece 177 (3), 179 (4) Roman empire 180–181 (1) first religions 36 (1), 37 (3)
Demchok var. Dêmqog region South Asia post-war politics 252 (1)
Demerara colonial possession South America colonization 149 (4)
Demetrias Greece Hellenistic world 41 (2)
Demnat North Africa (Morocco) exploration 157 (4)
Demotika state Southeast Europe WWII 211 (2)
Dêmqog see Demchok
Dendra Greece first civilizations 175 (4)
Deng state East Asia first cities 259 (4)
Dengchong East Asia (China) medieval states 263 (6)
Dengkil archaeological site Mainland Southeast Asia (Malaysia) Bronze Age 240 (3)
Dengyue var. Tengchung East Asia (China) colonialism 269 (4)
Dengzhou var. Teng-chou East Asia (China) early modern states 265 (5), 266 (1) medieval states 264 (2) Mongols 68–69 (1)
Denison, Cape headland Antarctica Antarctic Exploration 287 (3)
Denjong see Sikkim
Denkyera state West Africa the world in 1700 82–83
Denmark anc. Hafnia; Dan. Danmark; state Scandinavia crusades 186 (1), 64–65 (2) early modern states 193 (4), 197 (3) economy 190 (1), 205 (4) empire and revolution 199 (3), 202 (1), (2) European expansion 84–85 (1) civil war 209 (3), (5) medieval states 185 (3), 188 (1), 189 (3), (4) medieval voyages 60–61 (1) Mongols 68–69 (1) Napoleon 200–201 (1), 201 (2) post-war economy 213 (5), 214 (1), (2) post-war politics 212 (1), (3) Reformation 196 (1) Soviet Union 213 (4) the modern world 112 (2) US superpower 138 (1) WWII 210 (1), 211 (2), (4) Cold War 108 (3), 109 (1) early 20th century 206 (1)
Denmark-Norway state Scandinavia early modern states 195 (3) Reformation 194 (2)
Denmark Strait var. Danmarksstraedet sea waterway Atlantic Ocean exploration 172 (2)
Denver North America (USA) the growth of the US 129 (2), 132 (1) US economy 134 (1), 136 (2) US politics 135 (6)
Depford Culture people North America the world in 250 BCE 38–39
Deraya Ar. Dar'īyah Southwest Asia (Saudi Arabia) 20th-century politics 233 (4)
Derbend see Derbent
Derbent Eastern Europe (Russian Federation) Islam 226 (2), 227 (4), (5) medieval Persia 231 (4) Mongols 229 (3), 68–69 (1) Ottomans 231 (3) Timur 229 (4)
Derby British Isles (United Kingdom) economy 204 (1)
Derbyshire region British Isles imperial global economy 93 (4)
Dereivka archaeological site Eastern Europe (Ukraine) Copper Age 174 (2)
Derna North Africa (Libya) colonization 167 (4)
Dertosa mod. Tortosa Iberian Peninsula (Spain) Roman empire 179 (3), 180–181 (1) see also Tortosa
Derwent river British Isles economy 204 (1)
Desalpur archaeological site South Asia (India) first cities 240 (2)
Deseado river South America colonization 148 (2)
Desert Gatherers people North America the world in 250 CE 46–47 passim
Des Moines North America (USA) the growth of the US 129 (2)
Desmumu state British Isles medieval states 188 (2)
Desna river Eastern Europe WWI 207 (4)
Desterro mod. Florianópolis South America (Brazil) colonization 149 (3), (4)
Detroit prev. Fort Pontchartrain North America (USA) colonization 126 (1) the growth of the US 129 (2), 132 (1) US economy 134 (1), (3) US politics 135 (6)
Deutschland see Germany
Deutsch-Südwestafrika see Southwest Africa, German Southwest Africa
Deva var. Legaceaster, Devana Castra; mod. Chester; Wel. Caerleon; legion headquarters/mithraic site British Isles (United Kingdom) Roman empire 180–181 (1) world religions 48 (1) see also Chester
Devagiri South Asia (India) early religions 48 (2)
Devagiri region South Asia early medieval states 244–245 (3)
Devana see Aberdeen
Devana Castra see Chester, Deva
Devapattana South Asia (Nepal) early medieval states 244 (1) first empires 241 (4)
Deventer Low Countries (Netherlands) economy 190 (1)
Devils Lake burial mound North America (USA) first civilizations 121 (4)
Dez river Southwest Asia first cities 220 (2) first civilizations 221 (4)
Dezful Southwest Asia (Iran) 20th-century politics 235 (5)
Dezhnev, Cape headland Siberia exploration 287 (2)
Dhahran Ar. Aẓ Ẓahran Southwest Asia (Saudi Arabia) 20th-century politics 233 (4), 235 (5) economy 234 (1) US superpower 138 (1)
Dhaka prev. Dacca South Asia (Bangladesh) post-war economy 253 (5) post-war politics 252 (1), (3) see also Dacca
Dhanbad South Asia (India) post-war economy 253 (5)
Dharangaon South Asia (India) colonialism 247 (3)
Dharwar South Asia (India) economy 249 (4)
Dhlo Dhlo Southern Africa (Zimbabwe) trade 164 (1)
Dhodhekánisos see Dodecanese
Dhofar Southwest Asia (Yemen) trade 267 (3)
Dholavira archaeological site South Asia (Pakistan) first cities 240 (2)
Dhualdadr see Dulkadir
Dhu Qar Southwest Asia (Iraq) ancient Persia 225 (6)
Di people East Asia first cities 259 (4) first states 261 (2)
Diamantina South America (Brazil) colonization 149 (3) empire and revolution 151 (3)
Dian people/state East Asia/Mainland Southeast Asia first cities 259 (5) first states 260 (1) medieval states 261 (6)
Dias Point see Volta, Cape da
Dibio see Dijon
Dickson North America (USA) cultural groups 122 (5)
Dicle see Tigris
Didyma religious site Southwest Asia (Turkey) first religions 37 (3)
Diedenhofen var. Thionville France Franks 184 (2)
Diegueño people North America colonization 125 (4)
Die Kelders archaeological site Southern Africa (South Africa) early cultures 160 (1) first humans 13 (2)
Dien Bien Phu battle Mainland Southeast Asia (Vietnam) post-war politics 251 (5)
Dieppe France WWI 206 (2), (3)
Dieu, Hôtel building France economy 191 (2)
Dihang see Brahmaputra
Dijlah see Tigris
Dijon anc. Dibio France early modern states 193 (4), 197 (5) empire and revolution 199 (4) Franks 184 (2) medieval states 187 (4), 192 (2)
Dikbosch archaeological site Southern Africa (South Africa) early cultures 160 (1)
Dikson Siberia (Russian Federation) exploration 287 (2)
Dikwa West Africa (Nigeria) exploration 157 (4)
Dili var. Dilli, Dilly Maritime Southeast Asia (Indonesia) WWII 272 (1), 273 (2)
Dilli, Dilly see Dili
Dilli see Delhi, Indraprastha
Dilmun Arabian Peninsula first civilizations 24 (2), 25 (3)
Dimashq see Damascus
Dinajpur South Asia (Bangladesh) post-war politics 252 (3)
Dinant Low Countries (Belgium) WWI 206 (2), (3)
Dingcun archaeological site East Asia (China) first humans 13 (2)
Dingiray West Africa (Guinea) Islam 167 (3)
Dingliao military base /rebellion East Asia early modern states 266 (1), (2)
Dingzhou East Asia (China) medieval states 263 (7)
Diocaesarea Christian archbishopric Southwest Asia (Syria) world religions 48 (1)
Diocletian, Baths of Lat. Thermae Diocletiani building (Italy) Roman empire 181 (2)
Diocletiani, Thermae see Diocletian, Baths of
Dion state Greece ancient Greece 177 (2)
Dionysus, Theatre of building Greece ancient Greece 177 (4)
Dioscurias Southwest Asia (Georgia) early cultures 161 (2) first civilizations 177 (1)
Diospolis Magna see Thebes
Dipylon see Dipylum
Dipylum var. Dipylon building Greece ancient Greece 177 (4)
Dire Dawa archaeological site East Africa (Ethiopia) first humans 13 (2)
Dishasha Egypt ancient Egypt 159 (3)
Dispur South Asia (India) post-war politics 252 (1)
Diu South Asia (India) colonialism 247 (3), 248 (1), 269 (4) decolonization 251 (4) empire and revolution 88–89 (2) exploration 239 (1) post-war politics 252 (1) trade 230 (2), 67 (3) WWII 251 (3)
Divi mod. Diu South Asia (India) world religions 243 (4) see also Diu
Divodurum Mediomatricum see Metz
Divostin Southeast Europe (Yugoslavia) early agriculture 174 (1)
Dixmude Low Countries (Belgium) WWI 206 (2), (3)
Diyala var. Rudkhaneh-ye Sīrvān, Sīrwan, Diyālā, Nahr river Southwest Asia first cities 220 (2) first civilizations 221 (4), (5)
Diyarbakir Southwest Asia (Turkey) 20th-century politics 235 (5)
Djailolo see Halmahera
Djakarta see Batavia, Jakarta
Djambi see Jambi
Djawa see Java
Djenné see Jenne
Djerba island North Africa Ottomans 231 (3)
Djibouti East Africa (Djibouti) colonization 167 (4) European imperialism 96 (1)
Djibouti var. Jibuti; prev. French Somaliland, French Territory of the Afars and Issas; Fr. Côte Française des Somlis state East Africa decolonization 168 (1) economy 168 (2) Islam 235 (4) the modern world 112 (1), 113 (3) see also French Somaliland, French Territory of the Afars and Issas
Dmanisi archaeological site West Asia early humans 13 (2)
Dnepr see Dnieper
Dnepropetrovsk see Dnipropetrovs'k, Yekaterinoslav
Dnestr see Dniester
Dnieper Bel. Dnyapro, Rus. Dnepr, Ukr. Dnipro river Eastern Europe ancient trade 44–45 (1) biological diffusion 72–73 (1) crusades 64–65 (2) early Islam 56–57 (1) economy 190 (1) empire and revolution 198 (2), 202 (1) exploration 172 (1) first humans 13 (2) Islam 227 (4) medieval states 185 (3) medieval voyages 60–61 (1) Mongols 68–69 (1) Napoleon 200–201 (1) Ottomans 202 (4), 230 (1), 231 (3), 232–233 (1) prehistoric culture 17 (4) Timur 229 (4) WWI 207 (4) WWII 210 (1), 211 (4)
Dniester anc. Tyras; Rom. Nistru, Rus. Dnestr, Ukr. Dnister river Eastern Europe Bronze Age 175 (3) Copper Age 174 (2) crusades 64–65 (2) early agriculture 174 (1) economy 190 (1), 205 (4) empire and revolution 198 (2), 202 (1) exploration 172 (1) great migrations 52–53 (1), 53 (2) medieval states 189 (4) Mon gols 68–69 (1) Napoleon 200–201 (1) Ottomans 197 (4), 230 (1), 231 (3) WWI 207 (4) WWII 210 (1), 211 (4)
Dnipro see Dnieper
Dnipropetrovs'k var. Yekaterinoslav; Rus. Dnepropetrovsk Eastern Europe (Ukraine) Soviet Union 214–215 (4) see also Yekaterinoslav
Dnister see Dniester
Dnyapro see Dnieper
Doboj Southeast Europe (Bosnia and Herzegovina) post-war economy 215 (3)
Dobro Polje battle Southeast Europe (FYR Macedonia) WWI 207 (6)
Dobruja region/vassal state Southeast Europe Ottomans 202 (4), 230 (1)
Dodecanese var. Dodecanese Islands, Nóties Sporádes; prev. Dhodhekánisos state/island group Greece ancient Greece 177 (2), (3) first civilizations 175 (4) medieval states 187 (5) Ottomans 202 (4), 232–233 (1) WWII 210 (1), 233 (2) WWII 211 (2), (4) 20th-century politics 233 (3)
Dodecanese Islands see Dodecanese
Do Dimmi West Africa (Niger) early agriculture 158 (1)
Dodoma East Africa (Tanzania) economy 168 (2) exploration 157 (5)
Dodona religious site Greece first religions 37 (3)
Doge's Palace building Italy economy 191 (3)
Dogrib people North America cultural groups 123 (3)
Doha Southwest Asia (Qatar) economy 234 (1) exploration 219 (4)
Dojran battle Southeast Europe (FYR Macedonia) WWI 207 (6)
Dolní Věstonice archaeological site/settlement Central Europe (Poland) prehistoric culture 17 (4)
Dolomites var. Dolomiti; It. Dolomitiche, Alpi mountain range Italy WWI 207 (5)
Dolomiti, Dolomitiche, Alpi see Dolomites
Dominica colonial possession/state/island West Indies empire and revolution 150 (1) European expansion 85 (2) the growth of the US 129 (2) the modern world 112 (1) US economy 136 (2) US politics 139 (4)
Dominican Republic state West Indies Cold War 108 (2), 109 (1) the growth of the US 129 (2), 133 (4) the world in 1850 90–91 the world in 1900 94–95 the world in 1925 98–99 the world in 1950 102–103 the world in 1975 106–107 the modern world 110–111, 112 (1), 113 (4) US economy 136 (2) US politics 139 (4) US superpower 138 (1) WWII 104 (1)
Domitian, Stadium of building Italy Roman empire 181 (2)
Domrémy France medieval states 192 (2)
Don anc. Tanais river Eastern Europe ancient trade 44–45 (1) biological diffusion 72–73 (1) Bronze Age 175 (3) early agriculture 174 (1) early Islam 56–57 (1) economy 205 (4) first humans 13 (2) great migrations 52–53 (1) Islam 163 (1), 227 (4) medieval states 185 (3) Mongols 68–69 (1) Napoleon 200–201 (1) Ottomans 230 (1), 231 (3), 232–233 (1) prehistoric culture 17 (4) Timur 229 (4) WWI 207 (4) WWII 210 (1), 211 (4)
Donau see Danube
Donbas region Eastern Europe economy 205 (4)
Doncaster anc. Danum British Isles (United Kingdom) economy 204 (1)
Don Cossacks people Eastern Europe/Siberia Reformation 196 (2)
Donets river Eastern Europe WWI 207 (4)
Donets'k Eastern Europe (Ukraine) Soviet Union 214–215 (4)
Dong Ap Bia see Hamburger Hill
Dong Dau Mainland Southeast Asia (Vietnam) the world in 2500 BCE 22–23
Dong Duong Mainland Southeast Asia (Vietnam) world religions 243 (5), 49 (4)
Dong Hai see East China Sea
Donghu state East Asia first cities 259 (5)
Dong Khe fort Mainland Southeast Asia post-war politics 251 (5)
Dongola var. Donqola, Dunqulah East Africa (Sudan) ancient trade 44–45 (1) colonization 167 (4) early cultures 161 (3), (4), (5) Islam 163 (1)
Dong Son archaeological site/settlement Mainland Southeast Asia (Thailand) Bronze Age 240 (3)
Dongting Hu lake East Asia early modern states 266 (1) first cities 259 (4), (5) first states 260 (1)
Dongye state East Asia first cities 259 (3)
Dongzhen state East Asia (Manchuria) 263 (5)
Donja Slatina fort Southeast Europe (Yugoslavia) Bronze Age 175 (3)
Donqola see Dongola
Doornik see Tournai
Dorchester anc. Durnovaria British Isles (United Kingdom) economy 204 (1) medieval states 183 (3)
Dordogne river France first civilizations 177 (1)
Dordrecht var. Dordt, Dort Low Countries (Netherlands) economy 190 (1)
Dordt see Dordrecht
Dorestad Low Countries (Netherlands) medieval states 185 (3) medieval voyages 60–61 (1)
Dori West Africa (Burkina) exploration 157 (4)
Dornach battle Central Europe (Switzerland) early modern states 193 (5)
Dorpat Eastern Europe (Estonia) early modern states 195 (3) economy 190 (1) medieval states 189 (3)
Dorsoduro Italy economy 191 (3)
Dort see Dordrecht
Dortmund Central Europe (Germany) economy 190 (1) medieval states 188 (1)
Dorylaeum Southwest Asia (Turkey) Roman empire 180–181 (1)
Dorylaeum battle Southwest Asia (Turkey) crusades 64–65 (2)
Douai anc. Duacum; prev. Douay France economy 190 (1)
Douala var. Duala Central Africa (Cameroon) colonization 167 (4) economy 168 (2)
Douanas river Mainland Southeast Asia ancient trade 44 (2)
Douay see Douai
Doullens France WWI 206 (2)
Douro Sp. Duero river Iberian Peninsula Bronze Age 175 (3) Copper Age 174 (2) crusades 64–65 (2) early agriculture 174 (1) economy 190 (1) first civilizations 177 (1) great migrations 52–53 (1), 53 (2) see also Duero
Dove Creek battle North America (USA) the growth of the US 129 (2)
Dover British Isles (United Kingdom) economy 204 (1), 205 (4) WWI 206 (2), (3)
Dover North America (USA) the growth of the US 129 (2)
Dover, Strait of var. Straits of Dover; Fr. Pas de Calais sea waterway Western Europe WWI 206 (2), (3)
Dover, Straits of see Dover, Strait of
Downpatrick Ir. Dún Pádraig British Isles (United Kingdom) Bronze Age 175 (3)
Drać see Durazzo
Drаç see Durazzo
Drakensberg physical region Southern Africa economy 163 (2) first humans 12 (1) slave trade 165 (4) trade 164 (1)
Drancy ghetto France WWII 211 (3)
Drangiana region Central Asia Hellenistic world 40–41 (1)
Drapsaca Central Asia (Afghanistan) Hellenistic world 40–41 (1)
Drau var. Drava; Eng. Drave, Hung. Dráva river Southeast Europe WWI 207 (5), (6) see also Drava
Drava var. Drau; Eng. Drave, Hung. Dráva river Southeast Europe post-war economy 215 (3) see also Drau
Dráva, Drave see Drau, Drava
Dravida region/state South Asia early religions 48 (2) first empires 241 (5) world religions 242 (2)
Drenthe province Low Countries Reformation 195 (5)
Drepanum see Trapani
Dresden Central Europe (Germany) early modern states 193 (4) economy 205 (4) empire and revolution 199 (3) post-war politics 212 (1) Reformation 196 (1) WWII 211 (4)
Dresden battle Central Europe (Germany) Napoleon 200–201 (1)
Drina river Southeast Europe exploration 257 (2) post-war economy 215 (3) WWI 207 (6)
Drontheim see Trondheim
Druk-yul see Bhutan
Dry Creek archaeological site North America the world in 10,000 BCE 14–15
Duacum see Douai
Duala see Douala
Dubai Ar. Dubayy Southwest Asia (United Arab Emirates) economy 234 (1)
Dubayy see Dubai
Dublin British Isles (Ireland) biological diffusion 72–73 (1) economy 190 (1), 205 (4) empire and revolution 202 (1) civil war 209 (3) medieval states 185 (3), 186 (2), 187 (4), 188 (2) medieval voyages 60–61 (1) Napoleon 200–201 (1), 201 (2) post-war politics 212 (3) Reformation 194 (2) WWII 211 (2)
Dubrae var. Dubris; mod. Dover archaeological site British Isles (United Kingdom) Roman empire 180–181 (1) see also Dover
Dubris see Dover, Dubrae
Dubrovnik It. Ragusa Southeast Europe (Croatia) post-war economy 215 (3) see also Ragusa
Ducie Island island Pacific Ocean exploration 278 (1)
Duero Port. Douro river Iberian Peninsula crusades 186 (1) early Islam 56–57 (1) exploration 172 (1) Franks 184 (2) civil war 209 (4) Islam 192 (3) Napoleon 200–201 (1) prehistoric culture 17 (3) see also Douro
Duff Islands island group Pacific Ocean exploration 278 (1)
Dufile East Africa (Uganda) exploration 157 (4)
Duinekerke see Dunkirk
Duji var. Tuchi province East Asia medieval states 262–263 (1)
Dukang East Asia (China) first cities 259 (5)
Duke of York Islands island group Pacific Ocean early cultures 280–281 (3)
Dulkadir var. Dhualdadr state Southwest Asia the world in 1400 70–71 the world in 1500 74–75
Dumbarton British Isles (United Kingdom) medieval states 186 (2)
Dumyâṭ see Damietta
Duna see Danube
Düna see Western Dvina
Dünaburg Eastern Europe (Latvia) early modern states 195 (3) medieval states 189 (3)
Dunaj see Danube, Vienna
Dunărea, Dunav see Danube
Dundee British Isles (United Kingdom) economy 204 (1)
Dunedin settlement/whaling station New Zealand colonization 283 (4), (5)
Dunholme see Durham
Dunhuang settlement East Asia (China) ancient trade 44–45 (1) exploration 256 (1), 257 (3) first states 260 (1), 261 (3) medieval states 261 (6), 262–263 (1), 263 (6) world religions 49 (3), (4)
Dunhuang province East Asia first states 260 (1)
Dunkerque see Dunkirk
Dunkirk prev. Dunquerque; Flem. Duinekerke, Fr. Dunkerque, France Reformation 195 (5) WWI 206 (3)
Dún Pádraig see Downpatrick
Dunquerque see Dunkirk
Dunqul Egypt ancient Egypt 159 (4)
Dunqulah see Dongola
Dura Europos settlement Southwest Asia (Iraq) ancient Persia 225 (6) Roman empire 180–181 (1), 224 (2), 225 (5) early trade 225 (3) Hellenistic world 41 (2) world religions 226 (1)
Durango Central America (Mexico) colonization 125 (4) Mexican Revolution 133 (3)
Durango state Central America Mexican Revolution 133 (3) the growth of the US 129 (2)
Durazzo anc. Dyrrachium; mod. Durrës, Dursi; SCr. Drać, Turk. Draç Southeast Europe (Albania) crusades 64–65 (2) early modern states 193 (4) medieval states 185 (3), 187 (5), 188 (1), 189 (4) Ottomans 230 (1) WWI 207 (6) see also Dyrrachium
Durban var. Port Natal Southern Africa (South Africa) colonization 166 (2), 167 (4) economy 168 (2) European imperialism 96 (2)
Durham prev. Dunholme British Isles (United Kingdom) medieval states 186 (2)
Dürnkrut battle Central Europe (Austria) medieval states 189 (4)
Durnovaria see Dorchester
Durocortorum France Roman empire 180–181 (1), 181 (4)
Durostorum var. Silistria; mod. Silistra, legion headquarters Southeast Europe (Bulgaria) Roman empire 180–181 (1) see also Silistria
Durovernum see Canterbury
Durrës see Durazzo, Dyrrachium
Dursi see Durazzo
Dushanbe var. Dyushambe; prev. Stalinabad, Taj. Stalinobod Central Asia (Tajikistan) Soviet Union 214–215 (4)
Dusky Sound sealing station New Zealand colonization 283 (4)
Düsseldorf Central Europe (Germany) WWI 206 (2), (3) WWII 211 (4)
Dust Bowl drought North America US economy 134 (3)
Dutch Brazil colonial possession South America colonization 149 (4)
Dutch East Indies mod. Indonesia; prev. Netherlands East Indies colonial possession Maritime Southeast Asia colonialism 269 (4) colonization 284–285 (1) European imperialism 97 (3), (4) exploration 279 (3) empire and revolution 88–89 (2) global immigration 100 (1) the growth of the US 133 (4) WWII 104 (1), 251 (3), 272 (1), 273 (2) see also Indonesia
Dutch Guiana var. Netherlands Guiana; mod. Surinam, Suriname colonial possession/state South America Cold War 109 (1) WWII 104 (1) see also Surinam
Dutch Harbor military base North America (USA) WWII 104 (2), 272 (1), 273 (2)
Dutch Netherlands rebellion Low Countries empire and revolution 88–89 (2)
Dutch New Guinea colonial possession/state New Guinea Cold War 109 (1) European imperialism 97 (3)
Dutch Republic see Batavian Republic, Netherlands, United Provinces
Dutch South Africa colonial possession Southern Africa slave trade 165 (4) trade 164 (1)
Dutch West Indies see Netherlands Antilles
Dvaraka South Asia (India) world religions 242 (2)
Dvarasamudra South Asia (India) early medieval states 244 (2), 244–245 (3)
Dvaravati South Asia (India) ancient India 242 (1) early religions 48 (2)
Dvaravati region/state South Asia ancient India 241 (6) early medieval states 245 (5) world religions 243 (5), 49 (4)
Dvin Christian archbishopric Southwest Asia (Armenia) world religions 48 (1)
Dvina river Eastern Europe early modern states 197 (3) WWI 207 (4)
Dvinsk Eastern Europe (Latvia) WWI 207 (4)
Dvinsk see Dünaburg
Dwarka South Asia (India) early medieval states 244–245 (3) world religions 243 (4)
Dyfed region British Isles medieval states 183 (3)
Dyrrhachium mod. Durrës; It. Durazzo, SCr. Drać, Turk. Draç Southeast Europe (Albania) Roman empire 179 (5), 180–181 (1) see also Durazzo
Dyushambe see Dushanbe
Dza Chu see Mekong
Dzhruchula archaeological site Eastern Europe (Russian Federation) first humans 13 (2)
Dzibilchaltún Central America (Mexico) first civilizations 121 (2), 122 (2)
Dzungaria region Central Asia ancient trade 44–45 (1) medieval states 262–263 (1)
Dzungars people/rebellion Central Asia early modern states 268 (1) empire and revolution 268 (2)
Dzungars, Khanate of the state East Asia
Dzvina see Western Dvina

E

Eagle Pass North America (USA) Mexican Revolution 133 (3)
Eagle Rock North America (USA) US economy 135 (4)
Eanna building Southwest Asia (Iraq) first cities 220 (3)
Early Kalachuris dynasty South Asia early medieval states 244 (2)
Early Man Shelter Australia exploration 280 (1)
Early Mississippian Culture people North America the world in 1000 58–59
East Anglia state British Isles medieval states 183 (3)
East Antarctica see Greater Antarctica
East Asia region East Asia biological diffusion 73 (2)
East Bengal and Assam region South Asia decolonization 250 (2)
East Berlin Central Europe (Germany) post-war politics 212 (2)
East Cape headland Australia colonization 283 (4)
East China Sea Chin. Dong Hai sea East Asia ancient trade 44–45 (1) biological diffusion 72–73 (1) decolonization 251 (4) early agriculture 20–21 (2), 258 (1), (2) early modern states 266 (1) economy 274 (1) first cities 259 (3), (4), (5) first states 260 (1) Islam 275 (4) medieval states 262–263 (1), 263 (6) Mongols 68 (2), 68–69 (1) post-war politics 271 (7) world religions 49 (3) WWII 272 (1), 273 (2)
Easter Island var. Isla de Pascua, Rapa Nui island Pacific Ocean colonization 284–285 (1) decolonization 285 (3) environmentalism 285 (2) exploration 278 (1), 279 (3) see also Rapa Nui
Eastern Chalukyas dynasty South Asia the world in 1000 58–59
Eastern Desert var. Aṣ Ṣahrā' ash Sharqīyah; Eng. Arabian Desert desert Egypt ancient Egypt 159 (5) see also Arabian Desert
Eastern Europe region Eastern Europe US economy 138 (2)
Eastern Gangas dynasty South Asia early medieval states 244 (2), 244–245 (3) Mongols 68–69 (1)
Eastern Ghats mountain range South Asia early medieval states 244 (1), 244–245 (3) economy 249 (4) first empires 241 (4) first religions 36 (2) Mughal Empire 246 (1) colonialism 247 (3), 248 (1)
Eastern Jin state East Asia first states 261 (3)
Eastern March region Eastern Europe Franks 184 (2)
Eastern Pomerania region Central Europe empire and revolution 199 (3)
Eastern Rumelia region Southeast Europe Ottomans 202 (4), 232–233 (1)
Eastern Sierra Madre see Sierra Madre Oriental
Eastern Solomons battle Pacific Ocean (Solomon Islands) WWII 273 (2)
Eastern States state South Asia colonialism 248 (2)
Eastern Thrace region Southwest Asia 20th-century politics 233 (3)
Eastern Turkestan state East Asia medieval states 262–263 (1)
Eastern Woodland Culture people North America the world in 500 CE 50–51 the world in 750 CE 54–55
East Fjords fjords Atlantic Ocean (Iceland) exploration 172 (2)
East Florida colonial possession North America empire and revolution 127 (3)
East Friesland see East Frisia
East Frisia var. East Friesland region Central Europe empire and revolution 199 (3)
East Germany state Central Europe Cold War 109 (1) post-war economy 213 (5) post-war politics 212 (3) Soviet Union 213 (4)
East Greenland Inuit people North America cultural groups 123 (3)
East Indies island group Maritime Southeast Asia ancient trade 44–45 (1) global knowledge 76–77 (1) medieval voyages 61 (3)
East Java Kingdom state Maritime Southeast Asia the world in 1000 58–59
East London prev. Emonti; Afr. Oos-Londen, Port Rex Southern Africa (South Africa) economy 168 (2) European imperialism 96 (2)
Eastmain North America (Canada) colonization 126 (1)
East Pakistan mod. Bangladesh state South Asia Cold War 109 (1) decolonization 251 (4) see also Bangladesh
East Prussia region Central Europe empire and revolution 198 (2), 199 (3), 202 (2) civil war 209 (3), (5) Soviet Union 213 (4) WWI 207 (4), 208 (1) WWII 210 (1)
East River river North America the growth of the US 132 (2)
East Roman Empire var. Byzantine Empire state Southeast Europe/Southwest Asia Roman empire 182 (1) early cultures 160 (1), 161 (5) Franks 183 (6) medieval states 182 (2), 183 (4) see also Byzantine Empire
East Siberian Sea sea Arctic Ocean exploration 257 (2), 286 (1), 287 (2)
East Timor region/state Maritime Southeast Asia decolonization 251 (4), 253 (4)
East Ukraine region Eastern Europe empire and revolution 198 (2)
Ebbou archaeological site France prehistoric culture 17 (3)
Eberbach major cistercian house Central Europe medieval states 187 (3)
Ebla Southwest Asia (Syria) early systems 223 (3) first civilizations 221 (4), 24 (2)
Eblana see Dublin
Ebora see Évora
Eboracum see Eburacum, York
Ebrach major cistercian house Central Europe medieval states 187 (3)
Ebro Lat. Iberus river Iberian Peninsula Roman empire 180–181 (1) crusades 186 (1) early cultures 161 (2) early Islam 56–57 (1) exploration 172 (1) first civilizations 177 (1) Franks 184 (2) civil war 209 (4) Islam 192 (3) medieval states 182 (2) Napoleon 200–201 (1) prehistoric culture 17 (3) see also Iberus
Eburacum var. Eboracum; mod. York legion headquarters/mithraic site/settlement British Isles (United Kingdom) Roman empire 180–181 (1), 181 (4) world religions 48 (1) see also York
Ebusus see Ibiza
Ecab state Central America Aztecs 124 (1)
Ecatepec Central America (Mexico) Aztecs 124 (2)
Ecbatana mod. Hamadan Southwest Asia (Iran) ancient Persia 223 (4), 225 (6) Roman empire 224 (2), 225 (5) ancient trade 44–45 (1) early trade 225 (3) exploration 218 (1) first civilizations 222 (2) Hellenistic world 224 (1) world religions 226 (1) see also Hamadan
Echunga goldfield Australia colonization 282 (2)
Eckmühl Central Europe (Germany) Napoleon 200–201 (1)
Ecuador state South America economy 153 (3) empire and revolution 150 (2), 151 (3) environment 153 (4) imperial global economy 92 (1) politics 152 (1) the growth of the US 133 (4) the modern world 112 (1), 113 (4) US superpower 138 (1) WWII 105 (3) Cold War 109 (1)
Edendale North America (USA) US economy 135 (4)
Edessa mod. Şanlıurfa, Urfa Christian archbishopric/settlement Southwest Asia (Turkey) Roman empire 224 (2), 225 (5) crusades 228 (2), 65 (3) Hellenistic world 41 (2) Islam 227 (4) world religions 226 (1)ancient Persia 225 (6) crusades 64–65 (2)
Edessa, County of state Southwest Asia Crusades 65 (3)
Edfu var. Idfu Egypt ancient Egypt 159 (3) first cities 28–29 (1) first civilizations 24 (2)
Edinburgh British Isles (United Kingdom) biological diffusion 72–73 (1) economy 190 (1), 205 (4) empire and revolution 202 (1) medieval states 186 (2), 187 (4), 188 (1) Napoleon 200–201 (1), 201 (2) Reformation 194 (2)
Edirne Greece Ottomans 202 (4)
Edmonton North America (Canada) the growth of the US 129 (2), 132 (1) US economy 136 (2) US superpower 138 (1)
Edo mod. Tokyo, Tōkyō (Japan) early modern states 267 (4), 268 (1) economy 270 (1) trade 267 (3) see also Tokyo
Edom state Southwest Asia first civilizations 222 (1)
Edward, Lake var. Albert Edward Nyanza, Edward Nyanza, Lac Idi Amin, Lake Rutanzige lake East Africa exploration 157 (4) first humans 12 (1)
Edward Nyanza see Edward, Lake
Edznā Central America (Mexico) first civilizations 122 (2)
Eems see Ems
Eesti see Estonia
Éfaté settlement/island Pacific Ocean (Vanuatu) early cultures 280–281 (3) environmentalism 285 (2) medieval voyages 60 (2)
Efes see Ephesus
Eflâk see Wallachia
Egadi, Isole see Aegates
Egbaland state West Africa Islam 167 (3)
Ege Denizi see Aegean Sea
Eger mod. Cheb Central Europe (Czech Republic) medieval states 188 (1)
Egina see Aegina
Egmont, Cape headland New Zealand colonization 283 (4)
Egoli see Johannesburg
Egtved burial mound/settlement Scandinavia (Denmark) Bronze Age 175 (3)
Egypt prev. United Arab Republic; anc. Aegyptus region/state Egypt ancient Egypt 159 (4) ancient Persia 223 (4) Roman empire 181 (4), 224 (2), 225 (5) ancient trade 44–45 (1) plague 72–73 (1) colonization 167 (4) crusades 65 (1), 228 (2), 65 (3) decolonization 168 (1) early 20th century 206 (1) early agriculture 220 (1) early cultures 161 (2), (3), (4), (5) early Islam 57 (2) early systems 223 (3), 32 (1), 33 (2), (3) early trade 225 (3) economy 168 (2), (3) European expansion 84–85 (1) European imperialism 96 (1), 97 (4) exploration 157 (5), 218 (1), (2), 219 (3), (4) first cities 220 (2) first civilizations 177 (1), 221 (5), 222 (1), (2) first religions 36 (1), 37 (3) Hellenistic world 224 (1), 41 (2) imperial global economy 92 (1) Islam 163 (1), 226 (2), 227 (4), (5), 235 (4) medieval states 187 (5) medieval voyages 61 (3) Mamluks 229 (3), 68 (2) Napoleon 200–201 (1) Ottomans 231 (3), 232–233 (1) Seljuks 228 (1) slave trade 165 (4) the modern world 112 (1), 113 (3), (4) Timur 229 (4) trade 167 (1), 230 (2) US superpower 138 (1) world religions 226 (1), 49 (4) WWII 233 (2) WWII 104 (1), (2), 210 (1), 211 (4) 20th century 234 (2) 20th-century politics 233 (3), (4), 235 (5) see also Aegyptus
Egyptians people East Africa trade 167 (1)
Ehime prefecture Japan economy 270 (1)
Eichstätt Central Europe (Germany) Franks 184 (2)
Eight Trigrams Sect rebellion East Asia empire and revolution 268 (2)
Eilat var. Aila, Elat, Elath Southwest Asia (Israel) 20th century 234 (2) see also Aila, Elath
Éire see Hibernia, Ireland
Éireann, Muir see Irish Sea
Eivissa see Ibiza
Ekain archaeological site Iberian Peninsula (Spain) prehistoric culture 17 (3)
Ekapa see Cape Town
Ekven North America (USA) cultural groups 123 (3)
El Abra Cave archaeological site South America (Colombia) early cultures 144 (1)
El Agheila North Africa (Libya) WWII 210 (1), 211 (4)
Elaine incident North America (USA) US politics 135 (6)
El Alamein battle Egypt WWII 104 (2), 211 (4)
Elam var. Susiana, Uvja; mod. Khuzestān, Khuzistan state Southwest Asia first civilizations 221 (4), (5), 222 (2)
El-Amarna Egypt first cities 28–29 (1), 29 (5)
Eland's Bay archaeological site Southern Africa (South Africa) early cultures 160 (1)
Elandslaagte battle Southern Africa (South Africa) European imperialism 96 (2)
El Argar fort Iberian Peninsula (Spain) Bronze Age 175 (3)
Elat see Aila, Eilat, Elath
Elatea Greece first civilizations 177 (1)
Elat, Gulf of see Aqaba, Gulf of
Elath var. Aila, Eilat; mod. Elat Southwest Asia (Israel) early trade 225 (3) see also Aila, Eilat
Elath see Aelana, Aqaba
Elba island Italy Napoleon 200–201 (1)

El-Ballas Egypt ancient Egypt 159 (2)
Elbasan var. Elbasani Southeast Europe (Albania) WWI 207 (6)
Elbasani see Elbasan
El Baúl Central America (Mexico) first civilizations 122 (2)
Elbe Lat. Albis; Lat. Albis river Central Europe Roman empire 180–181 (1) ancient trade 44–45 (1) Bronze Age 175 (3) Copper Age 174 (2) crusades 186 (1), 64–65 (2) early agriculture 174 (1) early modern states 193 (4) economy 205 (4) empire and revolution 199 (3), 202 (1), (2) exploration 172 (1) Franks 184 (2) great migrations 52–53 (1), 53 (2) civil war 209 (5) medieval states 182 (2), 187 (3), 188 (1), 189 (3), (4) Mongols 68–69 (1) Napoleon 200–201 (1), 201 (2), (3) prehistoric culture 17 (4) Reformation 196 (1) WWII 210 (1)
Elbeuf France WWI 206 (2), (3)
Elbing Central Europe (Poland) early modern states 197 (3) economy 190 (1) medieval states 189 (3)
El Bosque Central America (Nicaragua) the world in 10,000 BCE 14–15
Elburz Mountains Per. Reshteh-ye Kūhhā-ye Alborz mountain range Southwest Asia ancient Persia 223 (4), 225 (6) early agriculture 220 (1) economy 234 (1) exploration 218 (1), (2), 219 (3) first cities 28–29 (1) first civilizations 221 (4), 222 (2) Hellenistic world 224 (1) Mongols 68–69 (1) WWI 233 (2)
El Carmen South America (Argentina) exploration 143 (3)
El Castillo archaeological site Iberian Peninsula (Spain) prehistoric culture 17 (3)
El-Derr Egypt ancient Egypt 159 (5)
El Djazaïr see Algiers
Elea Italy first civilizations 177 (1)
Elephanta Buddhist centre South Asia (India) world religions 49 (3)
Elephantine Egypt ancient Egypt 159 (2), (3), (4), (5) early cultures 160 (1) first cities 28–29 (1) first civilizations 24 (2)
Elephant Island island Antarctica Antarctic Exploration 287 (3)
El Fasher var. Al Fāshir East Africa (Sudan) Islam 163 (1)
El Ferrol Iberian Peninsula (Spain) civil war 209 (4)
Elgin British Isles (United Kingdom) medieval states 188 (2)
El Gîza see Giza
El Guettar archaeological site North Africa (Tunisia) first humans 13 (2)
El Inga South America (Colombia) the world in 10,000 BCE 14–15
Elis state Greece ancient Greece 179 (4)
Élisabethville see Lubumbashi
El-Jadida see Mazagan
El Jobo Central America (Mexico) first civilizations 123 (2)
El-Kab Egypt ancient Egypt 159 (5) first civilizations 24 (2)
El Khartûm see Karri, Khartoum
El Khril North Africa (Morocco) early agriculture 158 (1)
El-Lahun Egypt ancient Egypt 159 (4)
Ellás see Greece, Hellas
Ellesmere Island island North America cultural groups 123 (3) exploration 286 (1), 287 (2) the growth of the US 129 (2)
Ellice Islands mod. Tuvalu island group Pacific Ocean colonization 284–285 (1) exploration 279 (3) see also Tuvalu
El-Lisht Egypt ancient Egypt 159 (4) first cities 28–29 (1)
Ellora Buddhist centre South Asia (India) world religions 49 (3)
El Mesón archaeological site Central America (Mexico) first civilizations 121 (3)
Elmham British Isles (United Kingdom) medieval states 183 (3)
Elmina West Africa (Ghana) European expansion 84–85 (1) exploration 156 (3) Islam 163 (1) slave trade 165 (4) trade 164 (2)
El Mirador Central America (Mexico) first civilizations 123 (2)
El Morro archaeological site North America (USA) cultural groups 123 (4)
Elne see Illiberis
Eloaue Island island Melanesia medieval voyages 60 (2)
El Opeño Central America (Mexico) first civilizations 121 (2)
Elouae Islands island group Melanesia early cultures 280–281 (3)
Elp Low Countries (Netherlands) Bronze Age 175 (3)
El Paraíso early ceremonial centre/settlement South America (Peru) early cultures 144 (1)
El Paso North America (USA) Mexican Revolution 133 (3) US economy 136 (2)
El Paso battle North America (USA) the growth of the US 129 (2)
El Paso del Norte North America (USA) colonization 125 (4)
El Purgatório South America (Peru) early cultures 146 (1)
El Qâhira see Cairo, Fustat
El Salvador prev. Salvador state Central America the growth of the US 129 (2) US economy 136 (2) US politics 139 (4) US superpower 138 (1) Cold War 108 (2), 109 (1) see also Salvador
Elsloo Low Countries (Netherlands) early agriculture 174 (1)
El Suweis see Suez
Elswick British Isles (United Kingdom) economy 204 (3)
El Tajín Central America (Mexico) first civilizations 122 (1)
El Teul Central America (Mexico) first civilizations 122 (1)
El Trapiche Central America (Mexico) first civilizations 121 (2)
Elvas Iberian Peninsula (Portugal) Reformation 196 (2)
El Viejón Central America (Mexico) first civilizations 121 (2)
Ely British Isles (United Kingdom) economy 204 (1) medieval states 186 (2)
Elymais state Southwest Asia Roman empire 224 (2)
Elymi people Italy early states 178 (2)
Emden Central Europe (Germany) Reformation 195 (5)
Emerald Isle see Montserrat
Emerald Mound North America (USA) cultural groups 122 (5)
Emerita Augusta mod. Mérida Iberian Peninsula (Spain) Roman empire 180–181 (1), 181 (4) world religions 48 (1) see also Mérida
Emesa religious site/settlement Southwest Asia (Syria) first religions 37 (3) Hellenistic world 40–41 (1)
Emilia region Italy medieval states 183 (4)
Emin mod. Niger river West Africa exploration 156 (2) see also Niger
Emmaus Southwest Asia (Syria) Roman empire 225 (4)
Emona see Ljubljana
Emonti see East London
Emporiae mod. Ampurias Iberian Peninsula (Spain) Roman empire 179 (3) first civilizations 177 (1)
Emporion East Africa (Somalia) ancient trade 44–45 (1) early cultures 161 (3), (5)
Emporium building Italy Roman empire 181 (2)
Empty Quarter see Ar Rub 'al Khali
Ems Dut. Eems river Central Europe Reformation 195 (5)
Emu nuclear test Australia environmentalism 285 (2)
Emuckfaw battle North America (USA) the growth of the US 129 (2)
Encounter Bay inlet Australia exploration 279 (2)
Enderby Land physical region Antarctica Antarctic Exploration 287 (3)
Enewetak prev. Eniwetok nuclear test Pacific Ocean environmentalism 285 (2) see also Eniwetok
Engaruka archaeological site East Africa (Tanzania) early cultures 160 (1)
Engis Low Countries (Belgium) the world in 10,000 BCE 14–15
England Lat. Anglia state British Isles crusades 186 (1), 64–65 (2) early modern states 194 (1) economy 190 (1) empire and revolution 202 (1) European expansion 80–81 (1) medieval states 185 (3), 186 (2), 187 (3), (4), 188 (1), (2) medieval voyages 60–61 (1) Reformation 194 (2), 196 (1), (2)
Englewood North America (USA) cultural groups 122 (5)
English Channel sea waterway Western Europe early modern states 197 (5) economy 204 (1) empire and revolution 199 (4) medieval states 183 (3), 186 (2), 187 (4), 188 (2), 192 (1), (2) WWI 206 (2), (3)
Eniwetok island Pacific Ocean WWII 104 (1), 273 (2)
Enkomi Cyprus ancient Egypt 159 (5)
Enlil, Temple of building Southwest Asia (Iraq) first cities 28 (2)
En Nazira see Nazareth
Eno people North America colonization 125 (4)
Enotachopco Creek battle North America (USA) the growth of the US 129 (2)
Enryakuji Buddhist temple army Japan medieval states 265 (4)
Entebbe East Africa (Uganda) colonization 167 (4)
Entrevaux France early modern states 197 (5)
Épernay France WWI 206 (2), (3)
Ephesos see Ephesus
Ephesus Southwest Asia (Turkey) ancient Greece 177 (3), 179 (4) ancient Persia 223 (4) Roman empire 179 (5), 180–181 (1), 181 (3), (4), 182 (1), 225 (5) crusades 64–65 (2) early cultures 161 (2) economy 190 (1) first civilizations 177 (1) first religions 37 (3) Hellenistic world 40–41 (1) world religions 226 (1)
Ephesus state Greece ancient Greece 177 (2)
Ephthalites see Hephthalites, Empire of the
Epidamnus Southeast Europe (Albania) ancient Greece 179 (4) first civilizations 177 (1)
Epidaurus Greece ancient Greece 177 (3)
Épinal France WWI 206 (2), (3)
Epirus region Greece ancient Greece 177 (3), 179 (4) Roman empire 179 (5), 180–181 (1), 225 (5) first civilizations 177 (1) Hellenistic world 224 (1) medieval states 189 (4) Mongols 68–69 (1)
Epirus, Despotate of state Southeast Europe medieval states 187 (5), 188 (1)
Epitoli see Pretoria
Equatorial Guinea var. Rio Muni; prev. Spanish Guinea state Central Africa decolonization 168 (1) economy 168 (2) the modern world 112 (1) see also Spanish Guinea
Erautini see Johannesburg
Erbil see Arbela
Erdély see Transylvania
Erebus, Mount mountain Antarctica Antarctic Exploration 287 (3)
Erech see Uruk
Erechtheum temple Greece ancient Greece 177 (4)
Eressus state Greece ancient Greece 177 (2)
Eretoka island Pacific Ocean early cultures 280–281 (3) medieval voyages 60 (2)
Eretria Greece ancient Greece 177 (3) first civilizations 177 (1)
Eretria state Greece ancient Greece 177 (2)
Erevan see Erivan, Yerevan
Erfurt rebellion/settlement Central Europe (Germany) early agriculture 174 (1) Reformation 196 (2)
Eridanos see Eridanus
Eridanus var. Eridanos river Greece ancient Greece 177 (4)
Eridu settlement/temple Southwest Asia (Iraq) early agriculture 220 (1) first cities 220 (2), 28–29 (1) first civilizations 221 (4)
Erie people North America colonization 126 (1)
Erie, Lake lake North America colonization 126 (1) cultural groups 122 (5) early agriculture 120 (1) empire and revolution 127 (2), (3) exploration 118 (1), 119 (2), (3) first civilizations 121 (4) the growth of the US 129 (2) US Civil War 131 (6), (7)
Eritrea colonial possession/state East Africa decolonization 168 (1) economy 168 (2), (3) European imperialism 96 (1) Islam 235 (4) the modern world 112 (1), 113 (3) WWII 104 (1) 20th-century politics 233 (4)
Erivan Southwest Asia (Azerbaijan) medieval Persia 231 (4)
Erligang archaeological site East Asia early agriculture 258 (2)
Erlitou archaeological site/settlement East Asia early agriculture 258 (1), (2) first cities 259 (3), 28–29 (1)
Ermeland see Warmia
Ermes Eastern Europe (Latvia) early modern states 195 (3)
Ertis see Irtysh
Erythrae settlement/state Southwest Asia (Turkey) ancient Greece 177 (2) first civilizations 177 (1)
Erzerum see Erzurum
Erzincan see Erzinjan
Erzinjan mod. Erzincan Southwest Asia (Turkey) WWI 233 (2)
Erzurum var. Erzerum; anc. Theodosiopolis Southwest Asia (Turkey) early Islam 56–57 (1) Islam 226 (2), 227 (4), (5) Ottomans 230 (1), 231 (3) WWI 233 (2)
Escalón Central America (Mexico) Mexican Revolution 133 (3)
Escaut see Scheldt
Eşfahān see Isfahan
Eshnunna settlement/temple Southwest Asia (Iraq) first cities 220 (2), 28–29 (1) first civilizations 221 (4), 24 (2), 25 (3)
Esh Shaheinab East Africa (Sudan) the world in 5000 BCE 18–19
Esh Sham see Damascus
Eskimo see Inuit
Esna var. Isna Egypt ancient Egypt 159 (4)
España see Spain
Esperance Australia colonization 282 (1), 283 (3) exploration 279 (2)
Espiríto Santo region South America colonization 149 (3)
Espiritu Santo settlement/island Pacific Ocean (Vanuatu) environmentalism 285 (2) exploration 278 (1) WWII 104 (2)
Esquiline Hill Lat. Mons Esquilinus hill Italy Roman empire 181 (2)
Esquilinus, Mons see Esquiline Hill
Essaouira see Mogador
Esseg see Osijek
Essen var. Essen an der Ruhr Central Europe (Germany) economy 205 (4) WWII 210 (1), 211 (2), (3)
Essen an der Ruhr see Essen
Essequibo colonial possession South America colonization 149 (4)
Essex state British Isles medieval states 183 (3)
Es-Skhul archaeological site Southwest Asia (Israel) first humans 13 (2)
Estero Rabón archaeological site Central America (Mexico) first civilizations 121 (3)
Estland see Estonia
Estonia Est. Eesti, Ger. Estland, Latv. Igaunija region/state Eastern Europe early modern states 195 (3) civil war 209 (3) post-war economy 214 (1), (2) post-war politics 212 (3) Soviet Union 208 (2), 213 (4) the modern world 112 (2) WWI 207 (4), 208 (1) WWII 210 (1)
Estonians people Eastern Europe crusades 186 (1), 68–69 (1)
Eszék see Osijek
Esztergom anc. Strigonium; Ger. Gran battle/settlement Central Europe (Hungary) medieval states 185 (3), 188 (1), 189 (4) Mongols 68–69 (1) see also Gran
Étaples France WWI 206 (2), (3)
Etaules fort France Bronze Age 175 (3)
Etawah South Asia (India) colonialism 247 (3)
Ethiopia prev. Abyssinia state East Africa decolonization 168 (1) economy 163 (2), (3) European expansion 84–85 (1) exploration 157 (5) Islam 163 (1), 235 (4) medieval voyages 61 (3) slave trade 165 (4) the modern world 112 (1), 113 (3), (4) trade 230 (2) world religions 226 (1), 49 (4) 20th-century politics 233 (4) Cold War 109 (1) see also Abyssinia
Ethiopian Highlands var. Ethiopian Plateau plateau East Africa ancient trade 44–45 (1) early cultures 160 (1), 161 (3), (4), (5) early trade 225 (3) exploration 157 (5) first humans 12 (1), 13 (2) medieval voyages 61 (3) slave trade 165 (4) trade 165 (3)
Ethiopian Plateau see Ethiopian Highlands
Etowah North America (USA) cultural groups 122 (5)
Etowah battle North America (USA) the growth of the US 129 (2)
Etruscan Cities state Italy the world in 500 BCE 34–35
Etruscans people Italy early states 178 (1), (2) first religions 36 (1)
Etsch see Adige
Etzatlán Central America (Mexico) first civilizations 122 (1)
Euboea vassal state/island Greece ancient Greece 177 (2), (3), 179 (4) first civilizations 175 (4)
Eudaemon Arabia var. Aden; Ar. 'Adan, Chin. A-tan Southwest Asia (Yemen) early trade 225 (3) see also Aden
Euhesperides North Africa (Libya) first civilizations 177 (1)
Eupatoria Eastern Europe (Ukraine) Ottomans 202 (4)
Euphrates Ar. Al Furāt, Turk. Firat Nehri river Southwest Asia ancient Egypt 159 (5) ancient Persia 223 (4), 225 (6) Roman empire 180–181 (1), 224 (2), 225 (5) ancient trade 44–45 (1) plague 72–73 (1), 73 (3) Bronze Age 175 (3) crusades 228 (2), 65 (3) early agriculture 174 (1), 20–21 (2), 220 (1) early cultures 161 (2), (3), (4), (5) early Islam 56–57 (1), 57 (2), (3) early systems 223 (3) early trade 225 (3) economy 234 (1) exploration 172 (1), (2), 219 (3), (4) first cities 220 (2), 28–29 (1) first civilizations 221 (4), (5), 222 (2), 25 (3) first humans 13 (2) first religions 36 (1) great migrations 52–53 (1) Hellenistic world 224 (1), 41 (2) Islam 163 (1), 226 (2), 227 (4), (5) medieval Persia 231 (4) medieval states 185 (3), 261 (6) Mongols 229 (3), 68–69 (1) Ottomans 230 (1), 231 (3), 232–233 (1) Seljuks 228 (1) Timur 229 (4) trade 230 (2) world religions 226 (1), 49 (4) WWI 233 (2) WWII 211 (4) 20th-century politics 233 (3), 235 (5)
Europa var. Europe continent ancient trade 44 (2) see also Europe
European Russia region Eastern Europe global immigration 100 (1)
Eurymedon, River battle Southwest Asia (Turkey) ancient Persia 223 (4)
Eusebia see Caesaria Cappadociae, Kayseri
Eutaw Springs battle North America (USA) empire and revolution 127 (3)
Euxine Sea see Black Sea
Euxinus, Pontus sea Asia/Europe ancient trade 44 (2)
Even see Lamut
Everest, Mount mountain East Asia exploration 257 (3)
Évora anc. Ebora; Lat. Liberalitas Julia Iberian Peninsula (Portugal) Islam 192 (3)
Évreux France WWI 206 (2), (3)
Évros see Maritsa
Exeter anc. Isca Dumnoniorum British Isles (United Kingdom) economy 204 (1) medieval states 183 (3), 186 (2) see also Isca Dumnoniorum
Exloo archaeological site/settlement Low Countries (Belgium) Copper Age 174 (2)
Eylau battle Central Europe (Poland) Napoleon 200–201 (1)
Eyre, Lake salt lake Australia exploration 276–277 (1)
Eyu East Asia (China) first cities 259 (5)
Ezero fort Southeast Europe (Bulgaria) Bronze Age 175 (3)

F

Fadak Southwest Asia (Saudi Arabia) world religions 226 (1)
Faenza anc. Faventia Italy economy 190 (1) medieval states 188 (1)
Faeroe Islands Dan. Færøerne, Faer. Føroyar colonial possession/island group Atlantic Ocean exploration 172 (1), (2) historical geography 170–171 (1) medieval states 185 (3) medieval voyages 60–61 (1) the modern world 112 (2) WWII 210 (1), 211 (4)
Faesulae mod. Fiesole Italy early states 178 (1)
Failaka Southwest Asia (Iraq) first civilizations 24 (2), 25 (3)
Fairbanks North America (USA) US superpower 138 (1)
Faisalabad South Asia (Pakistan) post-war economy 253 (5)
Faiyum Egypt ancient Egypt 159 (2), (4) early agriculture 158 (1)
Faizābād, Faizabad see Fyzabad
Falaise France medieval states 186 (2)
Falisci people Italy early states 178 (1), (2)
Falkland Islands var. Falklands, Islas Malvinas colonial possession/state/island group South America Antarctic Exploration 287 (3) empire and revolution 151 (3) environment 153 (4) exploration 142 (1), 143 (3) historical geography 140–141 (1) war 152 (1) see also Malvinas, Islas
Falklands see Falkland Islands, Malvinas, Islas
Fallen Timbers battle North America (USA) the growth of the US 129 (2)
Famagusta Southwest Asia (Cyprus) crusades 64–65 (2), 65 (3) economy 190 (1)
Fang state East Asia first cities 259 (3)
Fante var. Fanti state West Africa trade 167 (1)
Fanti see Fante
Fao oil terminal/settlement Southwest Asia (Iraq) 20th-century politics 235 (5) economy 234 (1)
Farawiyyn state West Africa trade 163 (4)
Far Eastern Republic state Siberia Communism 271 (8)
Farewell, Cape headland New Zealand colonization 283 (4)
Faro Iberian Peninsula (Portugal) Islam 192 (3)
Farrukhabad South Asia (India) economy 249 (4)
Farrukhabad state South Asia empire and revolution 249 (3)
Farruknagar state South Asia empire and revolution 249 (3)
Fars region/state Southwest Asia ancient Persia 225 (6) early Islam 56–57 (1) medieval Persia 231 (4)
Fars, Khalīj-e see Persian Gulf
Fartak state Southwest Asia Islam 163 (1)
Fashoda East Africa (Sudan) colonization 167 (4)
Fatehgarh rebellion South Asia (India) empire and revolution 249 (3)
Fatehpur South Asia (India) colonialism 247 (3)
Fatimid Caliphate state Egypt crusades 64–65 (2), 65 (3) Seljuks 228 (1)
Fatimids dynasty Egypt/Southwest Asia early Islam 57 (2) Islam 227 (5) medieval states 185 (3)
Faventia see Faenza
Faxaflói fjords Iceland exploration 172 (2)
Fayetteville North America (USA) US Civil War 131 (7)
Fazzān see Fezzan
Færøerne see Faeroe Islands
Fehrbellin battle Central Europe (Germany) early modern states 197 (3)
Felicitas Julia see Lisbon, Olisipo
Fellin Est. Viljandi Eastern Europe (Estonia) early modern states 195 (3)
Fell's Cave archaeological site/settlement South America (Chile) early cultures 144 (1)
Felsina var. Bononia; mod. Bologna Italy early states 178 (2) see also Bononia, Bologna
Feltre Italy WWI 207 (5)
Feng East Asia (China) first cities 259 (4) Mongols 68–69 (1)
Fengtian region East Asia Chinese revolution 271 (5) imperialism 270 (2)
Fengtian Clique movement East Asia Chinese Civil War 271 (6)
Fengtien see Mukden, Shenyang
Fengyuan East Asia (China) medieval states 263 (6)
Fengzhou East Asia (China) medieval states 263 (5)
Feni Islands island group Pacific Ocean early cultures 280–281 (3) medieval voyages 60 (2)
Fenni see Fenny
Fenny var. Fenni South Asia (Bangladesh) post-war politics 252 (3)
Feodosiya see Kaffa, Theodosia
Fère France WWI 206 (2), (3)
Fergana see Ferghana
Fergana Valley physical region Central Asia biological diffusion 73 (1)
Ferghana region/state Central Asia/East Asia ancient trade 44–45 (1) colonialism 269 (3) early Islam 56–57 (1) first states 260 (1) medieval states 261 (6), 262–263 (1) world religions 49 (3)
Fernandia North America (USA) US Civil War 131 (6)
Fernando de Noronha island South America the modern world 110–111
Fernando Po var. Bioko; prev. Macías Nguema Biyogo; Sp. Fernando Póo; island West Africa exploration 156 (3) trade 164 (2)
Ferozepore rebellion South Asia (India) empire and revolution 249 (3)
Ferrara anc. Forum Alieni Italy early modern states 193 (4) economy 190 (1) medieval states 188 (1)
Fertile Crescent region Southwest Asia early agriculture 174 (1)
Fès see Fez
Fetegar state East Africa the world in 1200 62–63
Fetterman's Defeat battle North America (USA) the growth of the US 129 (2)
Feyzābād see Fyzabad
Fez var. Fès North Africa (Morocco) biological diffusion 72–73 (1) crusades 64–65 (2), 65 (1) early Islam 56–57 (1) exploration 156 (3) Islam 163 (1) medieval states 185 (3) exploration 68 (2) Ottomans 231 (3)
Fezzan mod. Fazzān; anc. Phazania region/state North Africa Ottomans 232–233 (1)
Field of Blood battle Southwest Asia (Syria) crusades 65 (3)
Fiesole see Faesulae
Fifth Cataract Waterfall Egypt ancient Egypt 159 (5)
Fiji state/island group Pacific Ocean colonization 284–285 (1) decolonization 285 (3) early cultures 280–281 (3) environmentalism 285 (2) exploration 276–277 (1), 279 (3) global immigration 101 (3) medieval voyages 60 (2) the modern world 113 (3)
Filitosa fort France Bronze Age 175 (3)
Finanj Mainland Southeast ASia (Malaysia) trade 230 (2)
Finca Arizona Central America (Mexico) first civilizations 123 (2)
Fingira Southern Africa (Malawi) early agriculture 158 (1)
Finland colonialpossession/region/state Scandinavia early modern states 197 (3) economy 205 (4) empire and revolution 202 (1) civil war 209 (3) medieval states 189 (3) post-war economy 213 (5), 214 (1) post-war politics 212 (3) Soviet Union 208 (2), 213 (4) the modern world 112 (2), 113 (4) WWI 207 (4), 208 (1) WWII 104 (1), (2), 210 (1), 211 (2), (3), (4) Cold War 108 (3) early 20th century 206 (1)
Finland, Gulf of Est. Soome Laht, Fin. Suomenlahti, Ger. Finnischer Meerbusen, Rus. Finskiy Zaliv, Swe. Finska Viken gulf Scandinavia early modern states 197 (3) WWI 207 (4)
Finnic Peoples people Eastern Europe/Scandinavia the world in 750 CE 54–55 the world in 1000 58–59
Finnischer Meerbusen see Finland, Gulf of
Finno-Ugrians people Eastern Europe/Scandinavia the world in 750 BCE 30–31 passim.
Finns people Scandinavia crusades 186 (1) Mongols 68–69 (1)
Finska Viken, Finskiy Zaliv see Finland, Gulf of
Firat Nehri see Euphrates
Firenze see Florence, Florentia
Firmum var. Firmum Picenum Italy early states 178 (1)
Firmum Picenum see Firmum
First Cataract waterfall Egypt ancient Egypt 159 (2), (3), (4), (5)
First Riel Rebellion North America (Canada) 129 (2)
Firuzukh South Asia (Afghanistan) early medieval states 244 (2)
Fisher North America (USA) cultural groups 122 (5)
Fishguard Wel. Abergwaun British Isles (United Kingdom) economy 204 (1)
Fitzroy river Australia colonization 282 (1) prehistoric culture 17 (5)
Fiume see Rijeka
Flagler Bay North America (Canada) cultural groups 123 (3)
Flaminia, Via road Italy Roman empire 181 (2) early states 178 (1)
Flaminia, Via road Italy early states 178 (1)
Flanders province/region Low Countries crusades 64–65 (2) early modern states 197 (5) economy 190 (1) medieval states 192 (1) Reformation 195 (5)
Flathead people North America colonization 126 (1)
Flensborg Ger. Flensburg Central Europe (Germany) empire and revolution 199 (3)
Flensburg see Flensborg
Fleurus battle Low Countries (Belgium) empire and revolution 199 (4)
Flinders river Australia colonization 282 (1) exploration 279 (2) prehistoric culture 17 (5)
Flint Run North America (USA) the world in 5000 BCE 18–19
Flitsch mod. Bovec; It. Plezzo Central Europe (Slovenia) WWI 207 (5)
Florence North America (USA) cultural groups 122 (5) US Civil War 131 (7)
Florence anc. Florentia; It. Firenze Italy early modern states 193 (4) economy 190 (1) Franks 184 (2) medieval states 188 (1) Napoleon 200–201 (1), 201 (2), (3) Reformation 194 (2)
Florence state Italy Reformation 194 (2)
Florentia mod. Florence, Firenze Italy Roman empire 180–181 (1) see also Florence
Flores island Maritime Southeast Asia colonialism 247 (4) decolonization 251 (4) early medieval states 245 (6) exploration 239 (1), (2) Islam 243 (6) post-war economy 253 (5) post-war politics 253 (4) world religions 243 (5) WWII 251 (3), 272 (1), 273 (2)
Flores Sea sea Maritime Southeast Asia colonialism 247 (4) early medieval states 245 (5), (6) European imperialism 97 (3) exploration 239 (1), (2) Islam 243 (6) world religions 243 (5)
Floreşti Southeast Europe (Moldova) early agriculture 174 (1)
Florianópolis see Desterro
Florida state North America the growth of the US 129 (1) US Civil War 130 (2), (3), (4), (5), 131 (6), (7) US economy 134 (2), 139 (3) US society 137 (6) US superpower 139 (5)
Florina battle Greece WWI 207 (6)
Florisbad archaeological site Southern Africa (South Africa) first humans 13 (2)
Flossenbürg concentration camp Central Europe WWII 211 (3)
Foča Southeast Europe (Bosnia and Herzegovina) post-war economy 215 (3)
Foix France crusades 186 (1)
Folkestone British Isles (United Kingdom) economy 204 (1)
Folsom North America (USA) the world in 5000 BCE 18–19
Fontbrégoua Italy early agriculture 174 (1)
Font-de-Gaume archaeological site France prehistoric culture 17 (3)
Foochow see Fuzhou
Forbes goldfield Australia colonization 282 (2)
Forbes Quarry archaeological site Iberian Peninsula (Spain) first humans 13 (2)
Forlì anc. Forum Livii Italy economy 190 (1)
Former Shu state East Asia medieval states 263 (3)
Formosa mod. Taiwan, Republic of China island/state East Asia biological diffusion 72–73 (1) colonialism 247 (4) the world in 1925 98–99 trade 267 (3) world religions 243 (5), 49 (3), (4) WWII 104 (1), (2), 272 (1), 273 (2) see also China, Republic of, Taiwan
Føroyar see Faeroe Islands
Fort Albany North America (Canada) colonization 126 (1)
Fortaleza prev. Ceará, Villa do Forte de Assuppeãs South America (Brazil) environment 153 (4) see also Ceará
Fort Ancient burial mound/settlement North America (USA) cultural groups 122 (5) first civilizations 121 (4)
Fort Augusta fort North America (USA) empire and revolution 127 (2)
Fort Beauséjour fort North America (USA) empire and revolution 127 (2)
Fort Chambly fort North America (USA) empire and revolution 127 (3)
Fort Churchill North America (Canada) colonization 126 (1)
Fort Dauphin see Fort Liberté
Fort Dearborn battle North America (USA) the growth of the US 129 (2)
Fort Detroit fort North America (USA) empire and revolution 127 (2), (3)
Fort Donelson fort North America (USA) US Civil War 131 (6)
Fort Duquesne fort North America (USA) empire and revolution 127 (2)
Fort Fisher fort North America US Civil War 131 (7)
Fort Frontenac fort North America (USA) empire and revolution 127 (2)
Fort Gaines battle North America (USA) US Civil War 131 (7)
Forth and Clyde canal British Isles economy 204 (1)
Fort Hatteras fort North America (USA) US Civil War 131 (6), (7)
Fort Henry battle North America (USA) empire and revolution 127 (3)
Fort Henry fort North America (USA) empire and revolution 127 (3) US Civil War 131 (6)
Fortín Balliván fort South America (Paraguay) politics 152 (2)
Fortín Boquerón fort South America (Paraguay) politics 152 (2)
Fortín Nanawa fort South America (Paraguay) politics 152 (2)
Fort Jackson fort North America (USA) US Civil War 131 (6)
Fort James see Accra
Fort James Island West Africa (Gambia) slave trade 165 (4)
Fort Kaministikwia North America (USA) colonization 126 (1)
Fort Kearney battle North America (USA) the growth of the US 129 (2)
Fort Kosmo North America (USA) imperial global economy 93 (3)
Fort Liberté var. Fort Dauphin West Indies (Haiti) empire and revolution 89 (3)
Fort Louis Central Europe (Germany) early modern states 197 (5)
Fort Macon fort North America (USA) US Civil War 131 (6), (7)
Fort Malden fort North America (USA) empire and revolution 127 (3)
Fort Maurits South America (Brazil) colonization 149 (3), (4)
Fort Mellon battle North America (USA) the growth of the US 129 (2)
Fort Mims battle North America (USA) the growth of the US 129 (2)
Fort Monroe fort North America (USA) US Civil War 131 (6), (7)
Fort Necessity fort North America (USA) empire and revolution 127 (2)
Fort Niagara fort North America (USA) empire and revolution 127 (2), (3)
Fort Ninety Six fort North America (USA) empire and revolution 127 (3)
Fort Orange North America (USA) colonization 126 (1)
Fort Oswego fort North America (USA) empire and revolution 127 (2), (3)
Fort Pickens fort North America (USA) US Civil War 131 (6), (7)
Fort Pitt var. Fort Pittsburgh North America (USA) empire and revolution 127 (3)
Fort Pittsburgh see Fort Pitt
Fort Pontchartrain see Detroit
Fort Pulaski fort North America (USA) US Civil War 131 (6), (7)
Fort-Repoux see Akjoujt
Fort St Andries see New Amsterdam
Fort St David South Asia (India) empire and revolution 88 (1)
Fort St John fort North America (USA) empire and revolution 127 (2)
Fort St John's fort North America (USA) empire and revolution 127 (3)
Fort St Phillip fort North America (USA) US Civil War 131 (6)
Fort Sedgewick battle North America (USA) the growth of the US 129 (2)
Fort Selkirk North America (Canada) imperial global economy 93 (3)
Fort Stanwix fort North America (USA) empire and revolution 127 (3)
Fort Sumter fort North America (USA) US Civil War 131 (6), (7)
Fort Ticonderoga battle North America (USA) empire and revolution 127 (3)
Fort Ticonderoga fort North America (USA) empire and revolution 127 (2), (3)
Fortunatae Insulae island group Atlantic Ocean ancient trade 44 (2)
Fort Walton North America (USA) cultural groups 122 (5)
Fort Willam Henry fort North America (USA) empire and revolution 127 (2)
Fort William North America (Canada) 129 (2)
Fort William H Seward North America (USA) imperial global economy 93 (3)
Fort Worth North America (USA) Cold War 108 (2) the growth of the US 132 (1)
Fort Wrangell mod. Wrangell North America (USA) imperial global economy 93 (3)
Fortymile North America (Canada) imperial global economy 93 (3)
Forum Alieni see Ferrara
Forum Julii var. Cividale Italy medieval states 183 (4) see also Cividale
Forum Julii mod. Fréjussee also Fréjus archaeological site France Roman empire 180–181 (1)
Forum Livii see Forli
Forum Romanum Italy Roman empire 181 (2)
Fossa Claudia see Chioggia
Fossoli ghetto Italy WWII 211 (3)
Fountains major cistercian house British Isles (United Kingdom) medieval states 187 (3)
Fourth Cataract waterfall Egypt ancient Egypt 159 (4), (5)
Fou-shan see Fushun
Fouta-Djallon see Futa Jallon, Serram Geley
Fouta-Toro see Futa Toro
Foveaux Strait sea waterway New Zealand colonization 283 (5)
Fowltown battle North America (USA) the growth of the US 129 (2)
Fox people North America colonization 126 (1)
Foxe Basin sea North America exploration 287 (2) the growth of the US 129 (2)
France anc. Gaul; Lat. Gallia; Fr. Gaule state France plague 72–73 (1) 109 (1) crusades 186 (1), 64–65 (2) early modern states 193 (4), (5), 194 (1), 197 (5) economy 190 (1), 205 (4) empire and revolution 199 (3), (4), 202 (1), (1i), (2), (3), 88 (1), 88–89 (2) European expansion 80–81 (1) European imperialism 97 (4) Franks 184 (2) Islam 192 (3) medieval states 185 (3), 186 (2), 187 (3), (4), 188 (1), (2) medieval voyages 60–61 (1) Napoleon 200–201 (1) Ottomans 231 (3) post-war economy 213 (5), 214 (1), (2) post-war politics 212 (1), (3) Reformation 194 (2), 195 (5), 196 (1), (2) Soviet Union 213 (4) the modern world 112 (1), (2), 113 (3), (4) imperial global economy 92 (1) civil war 209 (3), (4), (5) US superpower 138 (1) WWI 206 (2), (3), 208 (1) WWII 104 (1), 211 (2), (3), (4) Cold War 108 (3) early 20th century 206 (1) see also Gallia, Gaul, French Empire
Franche-Comté state Central Europe/France early modern states 193 (4), 194 (1), 197 (5) Reformation 194 (2), 196 (1)
Franchthi Greece early agriculture 174 (1)
Francia see Frankish Kingdom
Franciscans religious group South America exploration 143 (2)
Franconia region Central Europe medieval states 185 (3), 188 (1)
Frankfort North America (USA) the growth of the US 129 (2) US Civil War 131 (6)
Frankfurt var. Frankfurt am Main Central Europe (Germany) early modern states 193 (4) economy 190 (1), 205 (4) Franks 184 (2) medieval states 189 (3) Napoleon 201 (2) post-war politics 212 (1) Reformation 196 (1) WWII 211 (4)
Frankfurt am Main see Frankfurt
Frankfurt an der Oder Central Europe (Germany) empire and revolution 199 (3)
Frankhthi Greece the world in 5000 BCE 18–19
Frankish Empire state France early Islam 56–57 (1), 57 (2)
Frankish Kingdom var. Francia, Carolingian Empire, Frankish Empire, Kingdom of the Franks state France great migrations 53 (2) Islam 184 (1) see also Frankish Empire, Franks, Kingdom of the
Franklin battle North America (USA) US Civil War 131 (7)
Franks people Central Europe Roman empire 181 (4)
Franks, Kingdom of the state France Roman empire 182 (1) Franks 183 (6) medieval states 182 (2), 183 (4)
Franz Josef Land island group Arctic Ocean exploration 257 (2)
Fraser Cave Australia exploration 280 (1)
Fraxinetum France medieval states 185 (3) medieval voyages 60–61 (1)
Fredericksburg North America (USA) US Civil War 131 (6), (7)
Fredericton North America (Canada) the growth of the US 132 (1)
Frederiksnagar var. Frederiksnagore; later Serampore,Serampur; mod. Shrīrāmpur South Asia (India) the world in 1800 86–87 see also Serampore
Frederiksnagore see Frederiksnagar, Serampore
Freeman's Farm battle North America (USA) empire and revolution 127 (3)
Freetown West Africa (Sierra Leone) economy 168 (2) European imperialism 96 (1) WWII 104 (2)
Fregellae Italy early states 178 (1)
Fregenae Italy early states 178 (1)
Freiburg Central Europe (Germany) economy 190 (1) post-war politics 212 (1)
Freie und Hansestadt Hamburg see Brandenburg
Freising Central Europe (Germany) Franks 184 (2)
Fréjus anc. Forum Julii France Franks 184 (2) see also Forum Julii
Fremantle Australia colonization 282 (1), 283 (3)
Fremont region North America cultural groups 123 (4)
French Algeria colonial possession North Africa empire and revolution 88–89 (2)
French Congo colonial possession Central Africa European imperialism 96 (1)
French Empire state France Napoleon 201 (2)
French Equatorial Africa state Central Africa European imperialism 96 (1), 97 (4) WWII 104 (1), (2)
French Guiana var. Guiana, Guyane colonial possession South America empire and revolution 150 (1), 151 (3) environment 153 (4) politics 152 (1) the modern world 112 (1) WWII 104 (1), (2) Cold War 109 (1)
French Guinea see Guinea
French Indo-China colonial possession Mainland Southeast Asia Chinese revolution 271 (5) colonialism 269 (4) Communism 271 (8) economy 274 (1) European imperialism 97 (3), (4) imperialism 270 (2) post-war politics 271 (7) WWII 104 (1), 251 (3), 272 (1), 273 (2)
French North Africa colonial possession North Africa WWII 104 (2)
French Polynesia colonial possession Pacific Ocean decolonization 285 (3)
French Republic see France, French Empire, Gallia, Gaul
French Somaliland mod. Djibouti; Fr. Côte Française des Somalis; later French Territory of the Afars and Issas colonial possession/state East Africa European imperialism 96 (1) 20th-century politics 233 (4) Cold War 109 (1) see also Afars and Issas, French Territory of the, Djibouti
French Sudan see Mali
French Territory of the Afars and Issas see French Somaliland
French Togoland see Togo
French West Africa colonial possession West Africa European imperialism 96 (1), 97 (4) WWII 104 (1), (2)
Frentani people Italy early states 178 (1), (2)
Fribourg Ger. Freiburg Central Europe (Switzerland) early modern states 193 (5)
Friedland battle Central Europe (Poland) Napoleon 200–201 (1)
Friedrichshain Central Europe (Germany) post-war politics 212 (2)
Friendly Islands see Tonga
Friesland province Low Countries Reformation 195 (5)
Frisia region Low Countries Franks 184 (2) medieval states 185 (3), 188 (1)
Frisians people Low Countries Franks 183 (5), (6)
Friuli Italy Franks 184 (2)
Friuli region Italy medieval states 188 (1)
Friuli, Duchy of state Italy medieval states 183 (4)

Friuli, March of Central Europe Franks 184 (2)
Fronde war France Reformation 196 (2)
Frunze see Bishkek
Fu-chien see Fujian
Fu-chou see Fuzhou
Fucino, Lago see Fucinus, Lacus
Fucinus, Lacus mod. Lago Fucino lake Italy early states 178 (1)
Fudodo archaeological site Japan early agriculture 258 (1)
Fuga East Africa (Tanzania) exploration 157 (4)
Fujairah Ar. Al Fujayrah Southwest Asia (United Arab Emirates) economy 234 (1)
Fujian var. Fu-chien, Fuhkien, Fujian Sheng, Fukien, Min province East Asia early modern states 266 (1), (2), 268 (1) economy 274 (1) empire and revolution 268 (2) imperialism 270 (2) post-war economy 275 (3) post-war politics 271 (7), 274 (2) Chinese revolution 271 (5) see also Min
Fuji-san mountain Japan medieval states 265 (3)
Fujiwara Japan medieval states 265 (3) battle early modern states 265 (5)
Fukien see Fujian
Fukuhara Japan early modern states 265 (5)
Fukui var. Hukui Japan Communism 273 (3) economy 270 (1)
Fukui var. Hukui prefecture Japan economy 270 (1)
Fukui Cave archaeological site/settlement Japan early agriculture 20 (1)
Fukuoka var. Hukuoka; hist. Najima Japan Communism 273 (3) economy 270 (1)
Fukuoka var. Hukuoka prefecture Japan economy 270 (1)
Fukuoka-ken see Fukuoka
Fukushima var. Hukusima Japan economy 270 (1)
Fukushima var. Hukusima prefecture Japan economy 270 (1)
Fulani Empire see Fulbe Empire
Fulbe Empire var. Fulani Empire state West Africa colonization 167 (4)
Funan state Mainland Southeast Asia ancient India 241 (6) medieval states 261 (6)
Fundy, Bay of bay North America empire and revolution 127 (2)
Fünfkirchen see Pécs
Funing East Asia (China) Russo-Japanese War 270 (4)
Funj state East Africa Islam 163 (1)
Fur people East Africa early cultures 161 (5)
Fusan see Pusan
Fushimi battle Japan economy 270 (1)
Fushun var. Fou-shan, Fu-shun East Asia (China) Russo-Japanese War 270 (4)
Fustat var. Cairo, El Qâhira, Al Fustat; Ar. Al Qâhirah Egypt early Islam 56–57 (1) Islam 163 (1), 226 (2)
Futa Jallon Fr. Fouta-Djallon region/state West Africa Islam 167 (3) slave trade 165 (4) trade 167 (1) see also Serram Geley
Futa Toro Fr. Fouta-Toro region/state West Africa Islam 167 (3) slave trade 165 (4) the world in 1700 82–83 the world in 1800 86–87 the world in 1850 90–91 trade 167 (1)
Futuna island Pacific Ocean colonization 284–285 (1) early cultures 280–281 (3) exploration 279 (3) medieval voyages 60 (2)
Fuyō see Puyo
Fuyu people East Asia first states 260 (1)
Fuzhou var. Foochow, Fu-chou settlement/rebellion East Asia (China) ancient trade 44–45 (1) colonialism 269 (4) early modern states 266 (1), (2), 268 (1) economy 274 (1) empire and revolution 88–89 (2) imperialism 270 (2) medieval states 262–263 (1), 263 (4), (5) Mongols 68–69 (1) post-war politics 271 (7), 274 (2) trade 267 (3)
FYR Macedonia see Macedonia
Fyzabad var. Faizabad, Faizābād, Feyzābād rebellion/settlement South Asia (India) colonialism 248 (1) empire and revolution 249 (3)

G

Gabae Southwest Asia (Iran) Hellenistic world 40–41 (1)
Gabès var. Qābis North Africa (Tunisia) crusades 65 (1) economy 190 (1) WWII 211 (4)
Gabii Italy early states 178 (1)
Gabon prev. Gaboon state Central Africa decolonization 168 (1) economy 168 (2) the modern world 112 (1), 113 (3)
Gabonese Republic see Gabon
Gaboon see Gabon
Gachsaran oil field Southwest Asia economy 234 (1)
Gadara Southwest Asia (Jordan) Roman empire 225 (4)
Gades mod. Cádiz Iberian Peninsula (Spain) Roman empire 179 (3), 180–181 (1), 181 (3), (4) ancient trade 44–45 (1) early cultures 161 (2) exploration 172 (1) first civilizations 177 (1) world religions 48 (1) see also Cádiz
Gaeta Italy medieval states 188 (1)
Gaeta colonial possession Italy medieval states 185 (3)
Gahadavalas dynasty South Asia early medieval states 244 (2)
Gaikwar region South Asia Marathas 246 (2)
Gail river Central Europe WWI 207 (5)
Gaineis Battle battle North America (USA) the growth of the US 129 (2)
Gajapatis dynasty South Asia the world in 1500 74–75
Galam state West Africa trade 163 (4)
Galangi state Southern Africa the world in 1800 86–87 the world in 1850 90–91
Galapagos Islands var. Islas de los Galápagos, Tortoise Islands; Sp. Archipiélago de Colón island group South America exploration 142 (1), 143 (3) US superpower 138 (1)
Galápagos, Islas de los see Galapagos Islands
Galatia province/region/state Southwest Asia Roman empire 180–181 (1), 225 (5) Hellenistic world 40–41 (1) world religions 48 (1)
Galepsus Greece ancient Greece 177 (2)
Galič see Galich
Galich var. Galič, Pol. Halicz Eastern Europe (Russian Federation) Mongols 68–69 (1)
Galich see Galicia
Galicia Rus. Galich region/state Central Europe empire and revolution 198 (2), 202 (1) Islam 192 (3) Napoleon 200–201 (1) WWI 207 (4) WWII 211 (2)
Galicia-Volhynia var. Vladimir-Galich state Eastern Europe medieval states 189 (3)
Galilee province Southwest Asia Roman empire 225 (4)
Galilee, Sea of var. Sea of Chinnereth, Bahr Tabariya; Ar. Bahrat Tabariya, Heb. Yam Kinneret lake Southwest Asia Roman empire 225 (4) first civilizations 222 (1)
Galindo South America (Peru) early cultures 145 (4)
Gallaeci people Iberian Peninsula Roman empire 179 (5)
Galla, Lake lake East Africa the world in 10,000 BCE 14–15
Galle prev. Point de Galle South Asia (Sri Lanka) colonialism 247 (3) the world in 1600 78–79
Gallia province/region/state France Roman empire 180–181 (1), 181 (4), 225 (5) ancient trade 44 (2)
Gallia Cisalpina region Italy Roman empire 179 (5)
Gallic Empire of Postumus state France Roman empire 181 (4)
Gallicus, Sinus see Lions, Gulf of
Gallipoli Turk. Gelibolu Southwest Asia (Turkey) Ottomans 230 (1) WWI 233 (2)
Gallipoli Peninsula Turk. Gelibolu Yarımadası coastal feature Southwest Asia WWI 207 (6)
Galveston North America (USA) imperial global economy 93 (5) US Civil War 131 (6), (7)
Gamala Southwest Asia (Syria) Roman empire 225 (4)
Gamarra battle South America (Venezuela) empire and revolution 150 (1)
Gambia var. The Gambia colonial possession/state West Africa colonization 167 (4) decolonization 168 (1) economy 168 (2), (3) European imperialism 96 (1) Islam 235 (4) the modern world 112 (1), 113 (3) WWII 104 (1) Cold War 109 (1)
Gambia Fr. Gambie river West Africa exploration 156 (2), (3) trade 164 (2), 167 (1)
Gambie see Gambia
Gambier Islands island group Pacific Ocean colonization 284–285 (1) early cultures 280–281 (3) exploration 276–277 (1)
Gampala South Asia (Sri Lanka) early medieval states 245 (4)
Gan see Jiangxi
Ganaane see Juba
Gand see Ghent
Gandaki river South Asia first religions 36 (2)
Gandhara province/region Central Asia ancient India 242 (1) ancient Persia 223 (4) first religions 36 (2) world religions 242 (2), 49 (3)
Gandhinagar South Asia (India) post-war politics 252 (1)
Gangaikondacholapuram South Asia (India) early medieval states 244 (2)
Gangem region South Asia ancient trade 44 (2)
Ganges Ben. Padma river South Asia ancient India 242 (1) ancient trade 44 (2), 44–45 (1), colonialism 247 (3), 248 (1), (2), 269 (4) decolonization 250 (1), (2) early agriculture 20–21 (2), 258 (1) early medieval states 244 (1), (2), 244–245 (3) early religions 48 (2) economy 249 (4) empire and revolution 249 (3), 268 (2) European expansion 84–85 (1) exploration 239 (1), 257 (3) first empires 241 (4), (5) first humans 13 (2) first religions 36 (1), (2) imperial global economy 92 (1) Marathas 246 (2) medieval states 262–263 (1) Mongols 68 (2), 68–69 (1) Mughal Empire 246 (1) post-war economy 253 (5), 275 (3) post-war politics 252 (1), (3) prehistoric culture 16 (1) Timur 229 (4) trade 230 (2), 267 (3) world religions 242 (2), (3), 243 (4), 49 (3), (4) WWII 251 (3) see also Padma
Ganges/Northern Deccan region South Asia first cities 28–29 (1)
Gangeticus, Sinus sea South Asia ancient trade 44 (2)
Gangra Southwest Asia (Turkey) Roman empire 180–181 (1) world religions 48 (1)
Gangtok South Asia (India) post-war politics 252 (1)
Ganja Southwest Asia (Azerbaijan) medieval Persia 231 (4) Ottomans 231 (3)
Gansu var. Kansu province/state East Asia Chinese revolution 271 (5) early modern states 268 (1) empire and revolution 268 (2) medieval states 261 (6), 262–263 (1), 263 (6) post-war politics 271 (7), 274 (2)
Gantoli var. Kan-t'o-li state Maritime Southeast Asia the world in 500 CE 50–51
Ganuweriwala var. Ganweriwala archaeological site South Asia (Pakistan) first cities 240 (2)
Ganzhou military base/settlement East Asia (China) early modern states 266 (1) medieval states 262–263 (1), 263 (6)
Gao West Africa (Mali) ancient trade 44–45 (1) colonization 167 (4) early cultures 160 (1) exploration 156 (3) Islam 163 (1) trade 163 (5)
Gaocheng East Asia (China) first states 260 (1)
Gaoyang Buddhist centre East Asia (China) world religions 49 (3)
Garagum see Kara Kum
Garamantes people/state North Africa ancient trade 44–45 (1) early cultures 160 (1)
Garda, Lago di see Garda, Lake
Garda, Lake var. Benaco; Ger. Gardasee; It.Lago di Garda lake Italy WWI 207 (5)
Gardasee see Garda, Lake
Gareus, Temple of temple Southwest Asia (Iraq) first cities 220 (3)
Gargas archaeological site France prehistoric culture 17 (3)
Garhgaon South Asia (India) Mughal Empire 246 (1)
Garoga North America (USA) cultural groups 122 (5)
Garonne river France early Islam 56–57 (1) early modern states 197 (5) empire and revolution 199 (4) Franks 183 (5) medieval states 187 (4), 192 (1), (2) prehistoric culture 17 (3)
Garysburg North America (USA) US Civil War 131 (7)
Gasawe people Central America colonization 126 (1)
Gascogne see Gascony
Gascony region France Franks 184 (2) medieval states 187 (4), 192 (1), (2)
Gasus, Wadi river Egypt ancient Egypt 159 (4)
Gath Southwest Asia (Israel) first civilizations 222 (1)
Gatow airport Central Europe (Germany) post-war politics 212 (2)
Gatton archaeological site Australia prehistoric culture 17 (5)
Gaua island Pacific Ocean exploration 278 (1)
Gauda South Asia (Bangladesh) early medieval states 244 (2)
Gauda region South Asia first empires 241 (4)
Gauda-Desha region South Asia world religions 242 (2)
Gaugamela Southwest Asia (Iraq) the world in 250 BCE 38–39
Gaugamela battle Southwest Asia (Iraq) ancient Persia 223 (4) Hellenistic world 40–41 (1)
Gaul province/region/state France ancient trade 44–45 (1) exploration 172 (1) world religions 48 (1)
Gaulanitis state Southwest Asia Roman empire 225 (4)
Gaule see France, French Empire, Gallia, Gaul
Gauls people France Roman empire 179 (5)
Gaur South Asia (India) early medieval states 244–245 (3)
Gauteng see Johannesburg
Gawilgarh South Asia (India) early medieval states 245 (4)
Gaya South Asia (India) first empires 241 (4) first religions 36 (2) world religions 242 (2)
Gaza Ar. Ghazzah, Heb. 'Azza Southwest Asia (Gaza Strip) 20th century 234 (2) ancient Egypt 159 (5) Roman empire 181 (3), 225 (4) ancient trade 44–45 (1) early cultures 161 (3), (4), (5) early trade 225 (3) exploration 218 (1) first civilizations 222 (2) Hellenistic world 40–41 (1) Napoleon 200–201 (1) WWI 233 (2)
Gaza state Southern Africa the world in 1850 90–91
Gaza Strip Ar. Qita Ghazzah region Southwest Asia 20th century 234 (2)
Gdańsk prev. Danzig Central Europe (Poland) post-war politics 212 (3) see also Danzig
Gdov Eastern Europe (Russian Federation) early modern states 197 (3)
Gê people South America the world in 1500 74–75 the world in 1600 78–79 the world in 1700 82–83
Gebel Adda East Africa (Sudan) early cultures 161 (4), (5)
Gebel Barkal East Africa (Sudan) early cultures 160 (1)
Gebelein Egypt ancient Egypt 159 (2)
Gedrosia region Southwest Asia ancient Persia 223 (4) ancient trade 44 (2) Hellenistic world 224 (1) medieval states 261 (6)
Geelong Australia colonization 283 (3)
Gela prev. Terranova di Sicilia Italy first civilizations 177 (1) WWII 211 (4)
Gelderland province Low Countries Reformation 195 (5)
Geldria see Pulicat
Gelibolu see Gallipoli
Gelibolu Yarımadası see Gallipoli Peninsula
Gelnhausen Central Europe (Germany) medieval states 188 (1)
Gembloux battle Low Countries (Belgium) Reformation 195 (5)
Genalē Wenz see Juba
General Gouvernement province Central Europe WWII 211 (2)
Gênes see Genoa, Genua
Geneva Fr. Genève, Ger. Genf, It. Ginevra Central Europe (Switzerland) Cold War 108 (3) early modern states 193 (4), (5) economy 190 (1) empire and modern world 199 (4), 202 (1) Franks 184 (2) civil war 209 (3) medieval states 188 (1) Napoleon 200–201 (1), 201 (2), (3), (4) Reformation 194 (2)
Geneva, Lake Fr. Lac de Genève, Lac Léman, le Léman, Ger. Genfer See lake Central Europe early modern states 193 (5)
Genève see Geneva
Genève, Lac de see Geneva lake
Genf see Geneva
Genfer See see Geneva, Lake
Geng vassal state East Asia first cities 259 (3)
Genoa anc. Genua; Fr. Gênes, It. Genova Italy Roman empire 182 (1) biological diffusion 72–73 (1) crusades 186 (1), 64–65 (2) early modern states 193 (4) economy 190 (1), 205 (4) empire and revolution 202 (3) European expansion 84–85 (1) Franks 184 (2) global immigration 100 (1) medieval states 182 (2), 183 (4), 187 (3), (5), 188 (1) Reformation 194 (2), 196 (1) WWII 104 (2) see also Genua
Genoa state Italy early modern states 193 (4), 194 (1) empire and revolution 199 (4) Reformation 194 (2), 196 (1), (2)
Genova see Genoa, Genua
Genshū see Wonju
Gent see Ghent
Genua Eng. Genoa, Fr. Gênes, It. Genova Italy early states 178 (2) great migrations 52–53 (1) see also Genoa
Genusia Italy early states 178 (1)
George Sound sealing station New Zealand colonization 283 (4)
George Town Maritime Southeast Asia (Malaysia) WWII 272 (1), 273 (2)
Georgetown North America (USA) US Civil War 131 (7)
Georgetown South America (Guyana) empire and revolution 151 (3) environment 153 (4) politics 152 (1)
Georgia Russ. Gruziya, Georg. Sak'art'velo region/state/vassal state Southwest Asia Roman empire 224 (2) economy 234 (1) Islam 235 (4) medieval Persia 231 (4) medieval states 187 (5) Mongols 229 (3), 68–69 (1) post-war economy 214 (2) Soviet Union 208 (2), 214–215 (4) the modern world 113 (3) Timur 229 (4) WWI 233 (2) 20th-century politics 233 (3) see also Georgia States
Georgia region/state North America empire and revolution 127 (3) imperial global economy 93 (5) the growth of the US 129 (1) US Civil War 130 (2), (3), (4), (5), 131 (6), (7) US economy 134 (2), 139 (3) US society 137 (6) US superpower 139 (5)
Georgian Bay lake bay North America empire and revolution 127 (3)
Georgians people Southwest Asia Ottomans 232–233 (1)
Georgian States state Southwest Asia Islam 163 (1) medieval states 185 (3) Ottomans 231 (3) Seljuks 228 (1)
Gepidae people Eastern Europe Roman empire 181 (4)
Gepids, Kingdom of the state Eastern Europe/Southeast Europe Roman empire 182 (1)
Geraldton Australia colonization 282 (1), 283 (3) exploration 279 (2)
Gerf Hussein Egypt ancient Egypt 159 (5)
German Democratic Republic var. East Germany state Central Europe Cold War 108 (3) see also East Germany, Germany
German East Africa colonial possession East Africa European imperialism 96 (1), 97 (4)
German Empire Central Europe imperial global economy 92 (1)
Germania region/state Central Europe Roman empire 180–181 (1), 225 (5) ancient trade 44 (2)
Germania Inferior province Central Europe Roman empire 180–181 (1)
Germania Superior province Central Europe Roman empire 180–181 (1)
Germanic Peoples people Central Europe/Scandinavia the world in 750 BCE 30–31 passim.
Germanicum, Mare see North Sea
German New Guinea colonial possession New Guinea European imperialism 97 (3) exploration 279 (3) see also Kaiser Wilhelm's Land
German Ocean see North Sea
German Samoa colonial possession Pacific Ocean colonization 284–285 (1) exploration 279 (3)
German South West Africa colonial possession/state Southern Africa European imperialism 96 (1), (2), 97 (4)
Germantown battle North America (USA) empire and revolution 127 (3)
Germany Lat. Germania; prev. Germania; Ger. Deutschland; later split into Federal Republic of Germany and German Democratic Republic, East Germany, West Germany region/state Central Europe ancient trade 44–45 (1) plague 72–73 (1) economy 205 (4) European imperialism 97 (4) medieval states 189 (3) post-war economy 214 (2) post-war politics 212 (1) Soviet Union 214–215 (4) the modern world 112 (2), 113 (3), (4) world religions 48 (1), 49 (4) early 20th century 206 (1) global immigration 100 (1) WWI 206 (2), (3), 207 (4), 208 (1) civil war 209 (3), (5) WWII 104 (1), (2), 210 (1), 211 (3), (4) see also East Germany, Federal Republic of Germany, German Democratic Republic, Germania, Germany, Kingdom of, West Germany
Germany, Federal Republic of see Germany
Germany, Kingdom of state Central Europe crusades 186 (1) medieval states 185 (3), 188 (1)
Gerona var. Girona; anc. Gerunda Iberian Peninsula (Spain) economy 190 (1) Franks 184 (2) Islam 192 (3)
Gerrha Southwest Asia (Saudi Arabia) ancient trade 44 (2), 44–45 (1) early cultures 161 (3), (5) early trade 225 (3)
Gerunda see Gerona
Gerza Egypt ancient Egypt 159 (2)
Gesoriacum, Gessoriacum see Boulogne
Gettysburg North America (USA) US Civil War 131 (6)
Gezer Southwest Asia (Israel) ancient Egypt 159 (5)
Ghadamès North Africa (Libya) Islam 163 (1)
Ghaghara river South Asia colonialism 247 (3), 248 (1) early medieval states 244 (1), 244–245 (3) economy 249 (4) Marathas 246 (2) Mughal Empire 246 (1) world religions 242 (2), 243 (4)
Ghana prev. Gold Coast state West Africa decolonization 168 (1) economy 168 (2), (3) Islam 235 (4) the modern world 112 (1), 113 (3) trade 163 (4), (6) see also Gold Coast
Gharantal state West Africa trade 163 (4)
Ghassanids dynasty Southwest Asia the world in 500 CE 50–51
Ghat North Africa (Libya) colonization 167 (4) exploration 157 (4) Islam 163 (1)
Ghawar oil field Southwest Asia (Saudi Arabia) economy 234 (1)
Ghazna see Ghazni
Ghaznavids dynasty Central Asia/Southwest Asia early Islam 57 (2) early medieval states 244 (2) Islam 227 (5)
Ghazni var. Ghazna Central Asia (Afghanistan) early medieval states 244 (2), 244–245 (3) Islam 227 (4), (5) Mongols 68–69 (1) world religions 243 (4), 49 (3)
Ghazzah see Gaza
Ghent var. Gent; Fr. Gand Low Countries (Belgium) economy 190 (1) Franks 184 (2) Reformation 195 (5)
Ghilan state Southwest Asia Islam 163 (1)
Ghir Yu state West Africa the world in 1200 62–63
Ghoraghat South Asia (Bangladesh) colonialism 247 (3)
Ghurid Empire state Central Asia/South Asia early medieval states 244 (2) Mongols 68–69 (1)
Giau Pass pass Central Europe WWI 207 (5)
Gibraltar South America (Venezuela) European expansion 85 (2)
Gibraltar colonial possession/state/settlement Iberian Peninsula Cold War 109 (1) empire and revolution 202 (1) Napoleon 200–201 (1), 201 (2), (3) the modern world 112 (2) WWII 210 (1), 211 (4)
Gibraltar, Strait of Fr. Détroit de Gibraltar, Sp. Estrecho de Gibraltar sea waterway Africa/Europe economy 190 (1) exploration 156 (3)
Gibson Desert desert Australia exploration 279 (2) prehistoric culture 17 (5)
Gien France medieval states 192 (2)
Gifu var. Gihu Japan economy 270 (1)
Gifu var. Gihu prefecture Japan economy 270 (1)
Gihu see Gifu
Gijón Iberian Peninsula (Spain) economy 205 (4) civil war 209 (4)
Gila Cliff Dwellings archaeological site North America (USA) cultural groups 123 (4)
Gilbert Islands mod. Kiribati, Tungaru island group Pacific Ocean colonization 284–285 (1) environmentalism 285 (2) exploration 279 (3) WWII 272 (1), 273 (2) see also Kiribati
Gilgit South Asia (India) post-war politics 252 (2) world religions 49 (3)
Gilgit Agency state South Asia colonialism 248 (2)
Gilimanuk archaeological site Maritime Southeast Asia (Indonesia) Bronze Age 240 (3)
Gilolo see Halmahera
Gilroy North America (USA)
Ginevra see Geneva
Giornico battle Central Europe (Switzerland) early modern states 193 (5)
Gipeswic see Ipswich
Girin see Jilin, Kirin
Girinagara South Asia (India) early medieval states 244 (1) early religions 48 (2) first empires 241 (4)
Girona see Gerona
Girsu Southwest Asia (Iraq) first civilizations 24 (3)
Gisborne New Zealand colonization 283 (4), (5)
Giudecca Italy economy 191 (3)
Giudecca, Canale della canal Italy economy 191 (3)
Giurgiu battle Southeast Europe (Romania) Ottomans 195 (4)
Giza var. Al Jizah, El Giza, Gizeh Egypt ancient Egypt 159 (3), (5) first religions 36 (1)
Gizeh see Giza
Gjoa Haven North America (Canada) exploration 287 (2)
Gla Greece first cities 28–29 (1) first civilizations 175 (4)
Gladstone Australia colonization 282 (1), 283 (3)
Glasgow British Isles (United Kingdom) economy 204 (1), 205 (4) imperial global economy 93 (5) WWII 210 (1)
Glastonbury British Isles (United Kingdom) medieval states 183 (3)
Glavn'a Morava see Morava, Velika Morava
Glendale North America (USA)
Glen Elliott archaeological site/settlement Southern Africa (South Africa) early agriculture 158 (1) early cultures 160 (1)
Glevum see Gloucester
Gloucester hist. Caer Glou; Lat. Glevum British Isles (United Kingdom) economy 204 (1)
Gnesen Central Europe (Poland) economy 190 (1)
Gnezdovo Eastern Europe (Belorussia) medieval states 185 (3) medieval voyages 60–61 (1)
Gniezno Ger. Gnesen Central Europe (Poland) medieval states 188 (1) see also Gnesen
Goa prev. Gove, Old Goa, Vela Goa, Velha Goa South Asia (India) colonialism 247 (3), 248 (1), (2) 269 (2) decolonization 251 (4) European expansion 80–81 (1), 81 (3), 84–85 (1) exploration 239 (1) Mughal Empire 246 (1) empire and revolution 88–89 (2) post-war politics 252 (1), 253 (4) trade 230 (2), 267 (3) WWII 251 (3) see also Gove
Gobedra East Africa (Ethiopia) early agriculture 158 (1)
Gobi desert East Asia ancient trade 44–45 (1) plague 72–73 (1), 73 (3) colonialism 269 (4) early agriculture 20–21 (2), 258 (1), (2) early modern states 266 (1), (2) economy 274 (1) empire and revolution 268 (2) exploration 256 (1), 257 (3) first cities 259 (3), (4), (5), 28–29 (1) first humans 13 (2) first religions 37 (4) first states 260 (1) medieval states 261 (5), (6), 262–263 (1), 263 (4), (5), (6) Mongols 68 (2), 68–69 (1) post-war economy 275 (3) post-war politics 274 (2) trade 267 (3) world religions 49 (3), (4)
Gobir state West Africa slave trade 165 (4) trade 164 (2)
Godavari river South Asia ancient India 242 (1) colonialism 247 (3), 248 (1), (2) decolonization 250 (1) early medieval states 244 (1), (2), 244–245 (3) economy 249 (4) first empires 241 (4), (5) first religions 36 (2) Marathas 246 (2) Mughal Empire 246 (1) post-war politics 252 (1) world religions 242 (2), 243 (4)
Godin Tepe Southwest Asia (Iran) first cities 220 (2) first civilizations 24 (2)
Godthåb North America (Greenland) exploration 287 (2) medieval voyages 60–61 (1)
Goede Hoop, Kaap die/de see Good Hope, Cape of
Goettingen see Göttingen
Gogra see Ghaghara, Sarayu
Goiás South America (Brazil) colonization 149 (3)
Goiás region South America colonization 149 (3)
Gojjam state East Africa the world in 1200 62–63
Gokarna South Asia (India) world religions 242 (2)
Gokomere archaeological site Southern Africa (Zimbabwe) early cultures 160 (1)
Golan Heights Heb. HaGolan region Southwest Asia 20th century 234 (2)
Golconda var. Golkonda state South Asia the world in 1600 78–79 see also Golkonda
Gold Coast mod. Ghana state West Africa colonization 167 (4) European imperialism 96 (1), 97 (4) WWII 104 (1) see also Ghana
Gold Coast coastal feature West Africa Islam 163 (1) slave trade 165 (4)
Golden Horde, Khanate of the state/region Eastern Europe biological diffusion 72–73 (1) economy 190 (1) Islam 163 (1) medieval states 189 (4) Mongols 229 (3), 68 (2) Timur 229 (4)
Goldsboro North America (USA) US Civil War 131 (7)
Goliad Massacre battle North America (USA) the growth of the US 129 (2)
Golkonda South Asia (India) early medieval states 245 (4) Mughal Empire 246 (1)
Golkonda state South Asia early medieval states 245 (4) Mughal Empire 246 (1)
Gomati var. Gumti river South Asia first religions 36 (2)
Gombe West Africa (Nigeria) Islam 167 (3)
Gombe Point archaeological site Central Africa (Congo (Zaire)) early cultures 160 (1)
Gombroon see Bandar Abbas, Gombrun
Gombrun var. Gombroon; mod. Bandar Abbas, Bandar-e 'Abbās Southwest Asia (Iran) Ottomans 231 (3) see also Bandar Abbas
Gomel' Eastern Europe (Russian Federation) Soviet Union 208 (2) WWII 211 (4)
Gomolava Southeast Europe (Yugoslavia) Bronze Age 175 (3) early agriculture 174 (1)
Gonâve island West Indies empire and revolution 89 (3)
Gondar mod. Gonder East Africa (Ethiopia) trade 165 (3)
Gonder see Gondar
Gondeshapur Christian archbishopric Southwest Asia (Iran) world religions 48 (1)
Gondokoro East Africa (Sudan) exploration 157 (4), (5)
Gondwana region/state South Asia colonialism 247 (3) early medieval states 244–245 (3) Mughal Empire 246 (1)
Gonja state West Africa the world in 1700 82–83
Goodall burial mound/region North America (USA) first civilizations 121 (4)
Good Hope, Cape of Afr. Kaap de Goede Hoop, Kaap die Goeie Hoop headland Southern Africa European expansion 80–81 (1), 81 (2) European imperialism 96 (2) exploration 156 (3) slave trade 165 (4) trade 164 (1)
Goose Bay North America (Canada) US superpower 138 (1)
Gooty region South Asia Marathas 246 (2)
Goražde Southeast Europe (Bosnia and Herzegovina) civil war 215 (3)
Gordium Southwest Asia (Turkey) first cities 28–29 (1) first civilizations 221 (4), 222 (2) Hellenistic world 40–41 (1)
Gore New Zealand colonization 283 (5)
Goreé West Africa (Senegal) European expansion 84–85 (1) slave trade 165 (4) trade 164 (2)
Gorée island West Africa empire and revolution 88 (1)
Gorgan Southwest Asia (Iran) medieval voyages 60–61 (1)
Gorica see Görz
Gorlice Central Europe (Poland) WWI 207 (4)
Gornichevo Greece WWI 207 (6)
Gorton British Isles (United Kingdom) economy 204 (2)
Gortyna Christian archbishopric/settlement Greece Roman empire 180–181 (1) world religions 48 (1)
Goryōkaku battle Japan economy 270 (1)
Görz Slv. Gorica Italy WWI 207 (5)
Goslar Central Europe (Germany) economy 190 (1) medieval states 189 (3)
Gothenburg Swed. Göteborg Scandinavia (Sweden) early modern states 195 (3)
Gotland island Scandinavia early modern states 195 (3) medieval states 185 (3)
Göttingen var. Goettingen Central Europe (Germany) medieval states 189 (3)
Gough Island island Atlantic Ocean the modern world 110–111
Gough's Cave British Isles (United Kingdom) the world in 10,000 BCE 14–15
Goulburn Australia colonization 282 (1)
Gouwu state East Asia first cities 259 (4)
Govardhana South Asia (India) early medieval states 244 (1)
Gove mod. Goa; prev. Old Goa, Vela Goa, Velha Goa South Asia (India) early medieval states 244–245 (3) see also Goa
Goyaz mod. Goiás South America (Brazil) empire and revolution 151 (3) see also Goiás
Graaff-Reinet Southern Africa (South Africa) colonization 166 (2)
Grado Italy WWI 207 (5)
Graeco Bactria state Central Asia the world in 250 BCE 38–39
Grafton Australia colonization 282 (1)
Graham Land physical region Antarctica Antarctic Exploration 287 (3)
Grahamstad see Grahamstown
Grahamstown Afr. Grahamstad Southern Africa (South Africa) colonization 166 (2)
Gran anc. Strigonium; Hung. Esztergom Central Europe (Hungary) Ottomans 231 (3) see also Esztergom
Granada Iberian Peninsula (Spain) crusades 64–65 (2) early Islam 57 (2) economy 190 (1), 205 (4) European expansion 84–85 (1) exploration 156 (3) Franks 184 (2) civil war 209 (4) Islam 163 (1), 192 (3), 227 (4) exploration 68 (2)
Granada Central America (Nicaragua) European expansion 85 (2)
Granada, Kingdom of state Iberian Peninsula economy 190 (1) medieval states 187 (3)
Gran Chaco var. Chaco physical region South America colonization 148 (2) early cultures 144 (1), 145 (2) environment 153 (4) exploration 142 (1), 143 (2) politics 152 (1)
Gran Colombia see Great Colombia
Grand Canal canal British Isles economy 191 (3)
Grand Canal Chin. Da Yunhe canal East Asia early modern states 266 (1)
Grand Canyon valley North America colonization 125 (4) cultural groups 123 (4)
Grande, Bahia bay South America colonization 148 (2)
Grande de Chiloé, Isla see Chiloé, Isla de
Grande, Rio var. Río Bravo, Sp. Río Bravo del Norte, Bravo del Norte river North America colonization 125 (4), 126 (1) cultural groups 122 (5), 123 (4) early agriculture 120 (1), 20–21 (2) exploration 118 (1), 119 (2), (3) first religions 36 (1) historical geography 117 (1) Mexican Revolution 133 (3) the growth of the US 129 (2)
Grand Junction canal British Isles economy 204 (1)
Grand Lac de l'Ours see Great Bear Lake
Grand Lac des Esclaves see Great Slave Lake
Grandsee see Grandson
Grandson Ger. Grandsee battle Central Europe (Switzerland) early modern states 193 (5)
Grand Village North America (USA) cultural groups 122 (5)
Granicus Southwest Asia (Turkey) ancient Persia 223 (4)
Granicus, River battle Southwest Asia (Turkey) Hellenistic world 40–41 (1)
Gran Quivira archaeological site North America (USA) cultural groups 123 (4)
Gran Santiago see Santiago
Grasshopper archaeological site North America (USA) cultural groups 123 (4)
Gratianopolis see Grenoble
Grattanis Defeat battle North America (USA) the growth of the US 129 (2)
Gratz see Graz
Grave Creek battle North America (USA) the growth of the US 129 (2)
Grave Creek Mound burial mound North America (USA) first civilizations 121 (4)
Graz prev. Gratz Central Europe (Austria) early modern states 193 (4) medieval states 188 (1) Ottomans 197 (4) post-war politics 212 (1) Reformation 196 (1)
Great Australian Bight bight Indian Ocean colonization 282 (1) exploration 279 (2) prehistoric culture 17 (5)
Great Basin region North America early agriculture 120 (1)
Great Bear Lake Fr. Grand Lac de l'Ours lake North America (Canada) cultural groups 123 (3) early agriculture 120 (1) exploration 118 (1), 119 (2), (3), 286 (1), 287 (2), 129 (2)
Great Britain see Britain
Great Colombia Sp. Gran Colombia state South America empire and revolution 150 (1), 88–89 (2)
Great Depression historical period North America US economy 134 (2)
Great Dividing Range mountain range Australia colonization 282 (2), 283 (3) exploration 279 (2)
Greater Antarctica var. East Antarctica physical region Antarctica Antarctic Exploration 287 (3)
Greater Antilles island group West Indies exploration 118 (1), 119 (2), (3)
Greater German Reich 211–212
Greater Pallavas dynasty South Asia early medieval states 244 (2)
Great Fulo state West Africa trade 164 (2)
Great Grimsby mod. Grimsby British Isles (United Kingdom) economy 204 (1)
Great Indian Desert see Thar Desert
Great Khan, Empire of the var. Great Khanate state East Asia Mongols 68 (2)
Great Lake see Tonle Sap
Great Lakes lakes North America early agriculture 20–21 (2) first religions 36 (1)
Great Plain of China plain East Asia Mongols 68–69 (1)
Great Plains var. High Plains physical region North America early agriculture 120 (1), 20–21 (2) exploration 118 (1), 119 (2), (3)
Great Rift Valley var. Rift Valley depression East Africa first humans 12–15
Great Ruaha river East Africa exploration 157 (4)
Great Salt Desert desert Southwest Asia Hellenistic world 40–41 (1) historical geography 254–255 (1)
Great Salt Lake salt lake North America cultural groups 123 (4) the growth of the US 129 (2)
Great Sand Dunes archaeological site North America (USA) cultural groups 123 (4)
Great Sandy Desert desert Australia colonization 283 (3) exploration 279 (2)
Great Sandy Desert see Ar Rub 'al Khali
Great Seljuk Empire state Southwest Asia crusades 64–65 (2) Seljuks 228 (1)
Great Slave Lake Fr. Grand Lac des Esclaves lake North America (Canada) colonization 126 (1) cultural groups 123 (3) early agriculture 120 (1) exploration 119 (3), 286 (1), 287 (2)
Great Victoria Desert desert Australia exploration 279 (2) prehistoric culture 17 (5)
Great Yarmouth var. Yarmouth British Isles (United Kingdom) economy 190 (1) see also Yarmouth
Great Zab Ar. Az Zāb al Kabīr, Kurd. Zē-i Bādīnān, Turk. Büyükzap Suyu river Southwest Asia first cities 220 (2) first civilizations 221 (4), (5)
Great Zimbabwe settlement/archaeological site Southern Africa (Zimbabwe) early cultures 160 (1) economy 163 (2) the world in 1300 66–67
Great Zimbabwe state Southern Africa economy 163 (2)
Greece Gk. Ellás; anc. Hellas region/state Greece ancient trade 44–45 (1) plague 72–73 (1) early 20th century 206 (1) early systems 223 (3) economy 205 (4) empire and revolution 88–89 (2) exploration 172 (1) first religions 36 (1) imperial global economy 92 (1) civil war 209 (3) Ottomans 232–233 (1) post-war economy 213 (5), 214 (1), 215 (3) post-war politics 212 (3) Soviet Union 208 (2), 213 (4) US superpower 138 (1) world religions 48 (1) WWI 207 (6), 208 (1), 233 (2) WWII 104 (1), 211 (2), (4) 20th-century politics 233 (3) Cold War 108 (3), 109 (1) see also Hellas
Greek Pantheon religious building Greece first religions 37 (3)
Greeks people Greece Ottomans 232–233 (1) the modern world 112 (2)
Green Islands var. Nissan Islands island group Pacific Ocean early cultures 280–281 (3) exploration 278 (1) medieval voyages 60 (2)
Greenland colonial possession/island North America cultural groups 123 (3) early agriculture 120 (1), 20–21 (2) European expansion 80–81 (1) exploration 118 (1), 119 (2), (3), 172 (2), 286 (1), 287 (2) first humans 13 (2) global knowledge 76–77 (1) historical geography 117 (1) medieval voyages 60–61 (1) the growth of the US 129 (2), 132 (1) US superpower 138 (1) WWII 104 (1) Cold War 109 (1)
Greenland Ice Sheet ice feature North America the world in 10,000 BCE 14–15
Greenland Sea sea Atlantic Ocean exploration 172 (2), 286 (1), 287 (2)
Greenock British Isles (United Kingdom) economy 204 (1)
Greensboro North America (USA) US society 137 (6)
Greenwood North America (USA) US society 137 (6)
Grenada state/island West Indies colonization 126 (1) empire and revolution 88 (1) European expansion 84–85 (1) the modern world 112 (1) US politics 139 (4) US superpower 138 (1)
Grenfell goldfield Australia colonization 282 (2)
Grenoble anc. Cularo, Gratianopolis France early modern states 197 (5) Franks 184 (2) medieval states 187 (3)
Gresik prev. Grissee, Grisee Maritime Southeast Asia (Indonesia) colonialism 247 (4)
Greymouth New Zealand colonization 283 (5)
Grijalva river Central America first civilizations 123 (2)
Grimaldi France the world in 10,000 BCE 14–15
Grimsby see Great Grimsby
Griqua people/state Southern Africa trade 164 (1)
Griquatown Southern Africa (South Africa) exploration 157 (4)
Grisee see Gresik
Grissee see Gresik
Grobiņa Eastern Europe (Lithuania) medieval states 185 (3)

Grodno *Bel.* Hrodna Eastern Europe (Belorussia) empire and revolution 198 (2) WWI 207 (4)
Grol Low Countries (Netherlands) Reformation 195 (5)
Groningen Low Countries (Netherlands) economy 190 (1)
Groningen *province* Low Countries Reformation 195 (5)
Grosse Morava *see* Morava, Velika Morava
Grosser Wannsee *lake* Central Europe post-war politics 212 (2)
Gross-Rosen *concentration camp* Central Europe WWII 211 (3)
Grosswardein *see* Várad
Gros Ventres *people* North America colonization 126 (1)
Grotta dell'Uzzo Italy early agriculture 174 (1)
Grotte Arnaud *archaeological site* France Copper Age 174 (2)
Grotte Gazel France early agriculture 174 (1)
Grozny Eastern Europe (Russian Federation) Soviet Union 214–215 (4)
Grumentum Italy early states 178 (1)
Grunwald *see* Tannenberg
Gruziya *see* Georgia
Gua Bintong *archaeological site* Mainland Southeast Asia (Malaysia) Bronze Age 240 (3)
Gua Cha *archaeological site/settlement* Mainland Southeast Asia (Malaysia) Bronze Age 240 (3)
Guachichil *people* Central America colonization 125 (4), 126 (1)
Guadalajara *anc.* Arriaca; *Ar.* Wad Al-Hajarah Iberian Peninsula (Spain) civil war 209 (4)
Guadalajara Central America (Mexico) colonization 125 (4) Mexican Revolution 133 (3)
Guadalcanal *battle* Pacific Ocean (Solomon Islands) WWII 104 (2)
Guadalcanal *island* Pacific Ocean early cultures 280–281 (3) medieval voyages 60 (2) US superpower 138 (1) WWII 251 (3), 272 (1)
Guadalquivir *river* Iberian Peninsula economy 190 (1) first civilizations 177 (1) Franks 184 (2) Islam 192 (3) Napoleon 200–201 (1)
Guadeloupe *island/colonial possession* West Indies colonization 126 (1) empire and revolution 150 (1) European expansion 84–85 (1), 85 (2) global immigration 101 (3) the growth of the US 129 (2) the modern world 112 (1) Cold War 108 (2)
Guadeloupe, Isla *island* Pacific Ocean the modern world 110–111
Guadiana *river* Iberian Peninsula Franks 184 (2) Islam 192 (3)
Guaira *people* South America early cultures 147 (2)
Guairá *region* South America colonization 148 (2) exploration 143 (2)
Gua Kechil *archaeological site* Mainland Southeast Asia (Malaysia) Bronze Age 240 (3)
Gua Lawa Maritime Southeast Asia (Indonesia) the world in 5000 BCE 18–19
Gualupita Central America (Mexico) first civilizations 121 (2)
Guam *island/military base/colonial possession* Pacific Ocean colonization 284–285 (1) decolonization 285 (3) environmentalism 285 (2) exploration 278 (1), 279 (3) imperialism 270 (2) the growth of the US 133 (4) WWII 251 (3), 272 (1) Cold War 109 (1)
Guamares *people* Central America colonization 125 (4)
Gua Musang *archaeological site* Mainland Southeast Asia (Malaysia) Bronze Age 240 (3)
Guanajay *military base* West Indies (Cuba) Cold War 108 (2)
Guanajuato *province* Central America Mexican Revolution 133 (3) the growth of the US 129 (2)
Guang *vassal state* East Asia first cities 259 (3)
Guangala *region/state* South America (Peru) early cultures 145 (4)
Guangdong *var.* Kuang-tung, Kwangtung, Yue *province* East Asia early modern states 266 (1), (2), 268 (1) economy 274 (1) empire and revolution 268 (2) post-war politics 271 (7), 274 (2) Chinese revolution 271 (5)
Guanghan *province* East Asia first states 260 (1)
Guangju *see* Kongju, Kwangju
Guangling East Asia (China) first states 260 (1)
Guangu East Asia (China) first states 261 (3)
Guangxi *province/region* East Asia early modern states 266 (1), (2), 268 (1) empire and revolution 268 (2) post-war economy 275 (3) post-war politics 271 (7), 274 (2) Chinese revolution 271 (5)
Guangzhou *var.* Kuang-chou, Kwangchow, Nanhai; *Eng.* Canton East Asia (China) plague 72–73 (1) colonialism 248 (1), 269 (4) early modern states 266 (1) economy 274 (1) Islam 275 (4) medieval states 262–263 (1), 263 (3), (6) medieval voyages 61 (3) Mongols 68 (2), 68–69 (1) post-war economy 275 (3) post-war politics 274 (2) trade 267 (3) world religions 49 (3) WWII 251 (3) *see also* Canton, Nanhai
Guangzhouwan *var.* Kwangchowwan *colonial possession/settlement* East Asia (China) colonialism 269 (4)
Guanipa *archaeological site* South America (Venezuela) early cultures 145 (2)
Guannei *var.* Kuannei *province* Central Asia medieval states 262–263 (1)
Guantánamo West Indies (Cuba) US superpower 138 (1) WWII 104 (2)
Guantánamo Bay *military base* West Indies (Cuba) Cold War 108 (2) US imperialism 133 (5)
Guarani *people* South America colonization 148 (2) early cultures 147 (2) exploration 143 (2)
Guasave *people* Central America colonization 125 (4)
Guatavita South America (Colombia) early cultures 146 (1)
Guatemala *state* Central America the growth of the US 129 (2), 133 (4) the modern world 113 (4) US economy 136 (2) US politics 139 (4) US superpower 138 (1) WWII 104 (1) Cold War 108 (2), 109 (1)
Guatemala City Central America (Guatemala) the growth of the US 129 (2) US economy 136 (2)
Guaviare *region* South America narcotics 153 (5)
Guayanas, Macizo de las *see* Guiana Highlands
Guayaquil *var.* Santiago de Guayaquil South America (Ecuador) empire and revolution 150 (1), (2), 151 (3)
environment 153 (4) exploration 143 (3)
Guaymas Central America (Mexico) Mexican Revolution 133 (3)
Guazhou *var.* Kua-chou East Asia (China) medieval states 262–263 (1)
Gubbio *see* Iguvium
Guencame *mine* Central America (Mexico) colonization 125 (4)
Guernica Iberian Peninsula (Spain) civil war 209 (4)
Guerrero *region* Central America Mexican Revolution 133 (3)
Gui *state* East Asia first cities 259 (3)
Gui *people* East Asia medieval states 263 (3)
Guiana *state* South America European expansion 84–85 (1)
Guiana *see* French Guiana
Guiana Chiefdoms *region* South America the world in 750 CE 54–55 the world in 1200 62–63 the world in 1400 70–71
Guiana Highlands *Sp.* Macizo de las Guayanas *mountain range* South America colonization 148 (2), 149 (3), (4) early agriculture 20–21 (2) early cultures 145 (2) environment 153 (4) exploration 142 (1), 143 (2), (3)
Guiba *see* Juba
Guibray France economy 190 (1)
Guida Farm North America (USA) cultural groups 122 (5)
Guidriari Pass *pass* Central Europe WWI 207 (5)
Guienne *see* Guyenne
Guiji East Asia (China) first cities 259 (4), (5) first religions 37 (4)
Guilá Naquitz Central America (Mexico) the world in 5000 BCE 18–19
Guildford North America (USA) empire and revolution 127 (3)
Guildford Court House *battle* North America (USA) empire and revolution 127 (3)
Guilin *var.* Kuei-lin, Kweilin East Asia (China) early modern states 266 (1) economy 274 (1) post-war politics 271 (7)
Guimarães Iberian Peninsula (Portugal) economy 190 (1)
Guinea *var.* Guinée; *prev.* French Guinea *state* West Africa decolonization 168 (1) economy 168 (2) Islam 235 (4) the modern world 112 (1), 113 (3)
Guinea-Bissau *Fr.* Guinée-Bissau; *Port.* Guiné-Bissau; *prev.* Portuguese Guinea *state* West Africa decolonization 168 (1) economy 168 (2), (3) Islam 235 (4) the modern world 112 (1), 113 (3) *see also* Portuguese Guinea
Guinea, Gulf of *Fr.* Golfe de Guinée *gulf* Atlantic Ocean economy 168 (2), (3) exploration 156 (3) slave trade 165 (4) trade 164 (2)
Guinée *see* Guinea
Guiné-Bissau, Guinée-Bissau *see* Guinea-Bissau, Portuguese Guinea
Guinée, Golfe de *see* Guinea, Gulf of
Guitans *var.* Guti *people* Southwest Asia first civilizations 221 (4)
Guitarrero Cave *archaeological site/settlement* South America (Peru) early cultures 144 (1)
Guiyang *var.* Kuei-Yang, Kueyang, Kweiyang; *prev.* Kweichu East Asia (China) early modern states 266 (1) economy 274 (1)
Guiyang *province* East Asia first states 260 (1)
Guizhou *var.* Kuei-chou, Kweichow, Qian *province* East Asia Chinese revolution 271 (5) early modern states 266 (1), (2), 268 (1) empire and revolution 268 (2) post-war politics 271 (7), 274 (2)
Gujarat *region/state* South Asia colonialism 247 (3) early medieval states 244–245 (3) Mughal Empire 246 (1) post-war politics 252 (1), 253 (4) world religions 243 (4)
Gujarat States and Baroda *state* South Asia colonialism 248 (2)
Gujerat *see* Gujarat
Gujranwala South Asia (Pakistan) post-war economy 253 (5)
Gulbarga South Asia (India) decolonization 250 (1) early medieval states 244–245 (3), 245 (4) Mughal Empire 246 (1)
Gulf Coast Tradition *people* North America the world in 500 BCE 34–35
Gulf, The *var.* Persian Gulf; *Ar.* Khalīj al 'Arabī, *Per.* Khalīj-e Fars *gulf* Southwest Asia economy 234 (1) *see also* Persian Gulf
Gulgong *goldfield* Australia colonization 282 (2)
Gulja *see* Kuldja
Gumbinnen Eastern Europe (Lithuania) WWI 207 (4)
Gumla *archaeological site* South Asia (India) first cities 240 (2)
Gumma *see* Gunma
Gumti *see* Gomati
Gundu *archaeological site* Southern Africa (Zambia) early cultures 160 (1)
Gunma *var.* Gumma *prefecture* Japan economy 270 (1)
Güns *mod.* Kőszeg Central Europe (Hungary) Ottomans 231 (3)
Gupta Empire *var.* Magadha *state* South Asia the world in 500 CE 50–51 *see also* Magadha
Gur *people* West Africa early cultures 160 (1)
Gurgan *var.* Gorgan *fort* Southwest Asia (Iran) early Islam 56–57 (1) *see also* Gorgan
Gurjara-Pratiharas *dynasty* South Asia early medieval states 244 (2)
Gurkhaland *region* South Asia post-war politics 253 (4)
Gurma *state* West Africa trade 164 (2)
Guti *see* Guitans
Guyana *prev.* British Guiana *state* South America economy 153 (3) environment 153 (4) narcotics 153 (5) politics 152 (1) the modern world 112 (1), 113 (3) US politics 139 (4) *see also* British Guiana
Guyane *see* French Guiana, Guiana
Guyenne *var.* Guienne *region* France medieval states 192 (1), (2) *see also* Aquitaine, Aquitania
Gwadar *region/settlement* South Asia (Pakistan) Hellenistic world 40–41 (1) post-war politics 252 (1) trade 230 (2)
Gwādar, Gwador *see* Gwadar
Gwalior South Asia (India) colonialism 248 (1) economy 249 (4) *battle* early religions 48 (2) empire and revolution 249 (3)
Gwalior *state* South Asia colonialism 248 (2)
Gwandu West Africa (Niger) exploration 157 (4) Islam 167 (3)
Gwisho Southern Africa (Zambia) early agriculture 158 (1)
Gwy *see* Wye
Gwynedd *var.* Gwyneth *region* British Isles medieval states 183 (3)
Gwyneth *see* Gwynedd
Gyangtse *mod.* Gyangzê East Asia (China) exploration 257 (3)
Gyangzê *see* Gyangtse
Gympie *goldfield* Australia colonization 282 (2)
Gyulafehérvár *prev.* Apulum, Bălgrad, Karlsburg, Károly-Fehérvár; *Ger.* Karlsburg, Weissenburg *Hung.* Gyulafehérvár, *Rom.* Alba Iulia Southeast Europe (Romania) medieval states 189 (4) Ottomans 195 (4) Reformation 194 (2) *see also* Apulum

H

Ha'apai Group *island group* Pacific Ocean early cultures 280–281 (3) medieval voyages 60 (2)
Haapsalu *see* Hapsal
Haarlem *prev.* Harlem *battle* Low Countries (Netherlands) Reformation 195 (5)
Haarlem *prev.* Harlem Low Countries (Netherlands) crusades 186 (1)
Ḥabbānīyah, Buḥayrat al *see* Habbaniya, Lak
Habbānīyah, Hawr al *see* Habbaniya, Lake
Habsburg Empire *state* Central Europe empire and revolution 198 (2) Napoleon 200–201 (1)
Habuba Kabira Southwest Asia (Turkey) first cities 220 (2)
Ha-chia-pang *see* Majiabang
Hacilar Southwest Asia (Turkey) early agriculture 174 (1) first cities 220 (2) first civilizations 221 (4)
Hadar *archaeological site* East Africa (Ethiopia) first humans 12 (1)
Hadda *Buddhist centre* Central Asia (Afghanistan) world religions 49 (3)
Hadejia West Africa (Nigeria) Islam 167 (3)
Hadhramaut *state/region* Southwest Asia 20th-century politics 233 (4) exploration 219 (4) Islam 226 (2), 227 (5) world religions 226 (1)
Hadhramaut, Wadi *valley* Southwest Asia exploration 219 (4)
Ḥaḍramawt *see* Hadhramaut
Hadria *mod.* Adria Italy early states 178 (1)
Hadriani, Murus *see* Hadrian's Wall
Hadrian, Library of *building* Greece ancient Greece 177 (4)
Hadrian, Mausoleum of *building* Italy Roman empire 181 (2)
Hadrianopolis *var.* Adrianopolis; *mod.* Edirne; *Eng.* Adrianople Southwest Asia (Turkey) Roman empire 180–181 (1) *see also* Edirne, Adrianople, Adrianopolis
Hadrian's Wall *Lat.* Murus Hadriani *wall* British Isles Roman empire 180–181 (1)
Hadrian, Temple of *building* Italy Roman empire 181 (2)
Hadrumetum *mod.* Sousse North Africa (Tunisia) Roman empire 179 (3), 180–181 (1) first civilizations 177 (1) *see also* Sousse
Hadya *state* East Africa the world in 1300 66–67
Haerae *state* Greece ancient Greece 177 (2)
Haerbin, Haerhpin *see* Harbin
Ha-erh-pin *see* Harbin
Hafit Southwest Asia (Oman) first civilizations 24 (3)
Hafnia *see* Copenhagen, Denmark
Hafren *see* Severn
Hafsids *dynasty* North Africa economy 163 (2), 190 (1) Islam 163 (1)
HaGolan *see* Golan Heights
Haguenau *burial mound/settlement* France Bronze Age 175 (3) medieval states 188 (1)
Hague, The Low Countries (Netherlands) empire and revolution 202 (1i), (2) inter-war 209 (5) Reformation 195 (5)
Haguro-san *mountain* Japan medieval states 265 (3)
Haidarabad *see* Hyderabad
Haifa *anc.* Sycaminum; *hist.* Caiffa, Caiphas; *Heb.* Hefa Southwest Asia (Israel) 20th century 234 (2) crusades 65 (3)
Haihayas *dynasty* South Asia Mongols 68–69 (1)
Hainan *var.* Qiong *island* East Asia ancient India 241 (6) ancient trade 44–45 (1) colonialism 247 (4), 248 (1), 269 (4) decolonization 251 (4) early agriculture 258 (1) early medieval states 245 (5), (6) early modern states 266 (1), (2) economy 274 (1) European expansion 80–81 (1) European imperialism 97 (3) exploration 239 (1) first cities 259 (5) first states 260 (1), 261 (2), (3) medieval states 261 (4), (5), 262–263 (1), 263 (3), (4), (5), (6) Mongols 68–69 (1) post-war economy 253 (5) post-war politics 251 (5), 253 (4) world religions 243 (5), 49 (3), (4) WWII 104 (2), 251 (3), 272 (1), 273 (2)
Hainaut *province* France Reformation 195 (5)
Haiphong Mainland Southeast Asia (Vietnam) post-war economy 253 (5)
Haiphong *battle* Mainland Southeast Asia (Vietnam) post-war politics 251 (5)
Haiti *off.* Republic of Haiti *state* West Indies empire and revolution 150 (1), 88–89 (2) European expansion 84–85 (1) the growth of the US 129 (2), 133 (4) US economy 136 (2) US politics 139 (4) US superpower 138 (1) WWII 104 (1) Cold War 108 (2), 109 (1)
Haizhou East Asia (China) medieval states 263 (5)
Hajj Creiem *archaeological site* North Africa (Libya) first humans 13 (2)
Hakata Japan medieval states 264 (2), 265 (3) Mongols 68–69 (1)
Hakodate Japan economy 270 (1)
Haku *mountain* Japan medieval states 265 (3)
Ḥalab *see* Aleppo
Halicarnassus Southwest Asia (Turkey) first civilizations 177 (1) Hellenistic world 40–41 (1)
Halicz *var.* Galič; *Rus.* Galich Eastern Europe (Ukraine) medieval states 189 (3), (4) *see also* Galich
Halicz *state* Eastern Europe medieval states 189 (4)
Halifax British Isles (United Kingdom) economy 204 (1)
Halifax North America (Canada) colonization 126 (1) empire and revolution 127 (2) global immigration 100 (1) the growth of the US 129 (2), 132 (1) WWII 104 (2)
Halkida *see* Chalcis
Hallan Cemi Southwest Asia (Turkey) the world in 5000 BCE 18–19
Halland *region* Scandinavia early modern states 197 (3)
Halle *var.* Halle an der Saale Central Europe (Germany) medieval states 189 (3)
Halle an der Saale *see* Halle
Hallein *mine* Central Europe Bronze Age 175 (3)
Halls Creek Australia colonization 282 (1)
Hallstatt *mine* Central Europe Bronze Age 175 (3)
Hallunda Scandinavia (Sweden) Bronze Age 175 (3)
Halmahera *prev.* Djailolo, Gilolo, Jailolo *island* Maritime Southeast Asia colonialism 247 (4) early medieval states 245 (6) European imperialism 97 (3)
Halys *river* Southwest Asia ancient Persia 223 (4) first cities 220 (2), 28 (3) first civilizations 221 (4), (5), 222 (2) Hellenistic world 40–41 (1)
Hamadan *anc.* Ecbatana Southwest Asia (Iran) early Islam 56–57 (1) exploration 218 (2) first civilizations 221 (4), 24 (2) medieval Persia 231 (4) Mongols 229 (3), 68–69 (1) Ottomans 231 (3)20th-century politics 235 (5) *see also* Ecbatana
Hamah Southwest Asia (Syria) Islam 235 (4)
Hamamatsu *bomb target* Japan Communism 273 (3)
Hamath Southwest Asia (Syria) first civilizations 221 (5)
Hamburg Central Europe (Germany) early modern states 197 (3) economy 190 (1), 205 (4) empire and revolution 202 (1), (2) global immigration 100 (1) civil war 209 (3), (5) medieval states 189 (3) medieval voyages 60–61 (1) Napoleon 200–201 (1), 201 (2) post-war politics 212 (1) Reformation 194 (2), 196 (1) WWII 210 (1), 211 (2), (3), (4)
Hamburger Hill *Vtn.* Dong Ap Bia *battle* Mainland Southeast Asia (Vietnam) post-war politics 251 (5)
Hamdanids *dynasty* Southwest Asia early Islam 57 (2) Islam 227 (5) medieval states 185 (3)
Hamdullahi West Africa (Mali) Islam 167 (3)
Hamdullahi *state* West Africa trade 167 (1)
Hamea *people* Easter Island early cultures 281 (4)
HaMelah, Yam *see* Dead Sea
Hamelin *see* Hameln
Hameln *Eng.* Hamelin Central Europe (Germany) medieval states 189 (3)
Hamersley Range *mountain range* Australia colonization 283 (3)
Hami *var.* Ha-mi, *Uigh.* Kumul, Qomul East Asia (China) early modern states 268 (1) exploration 257 (3) trade 267 (3)
Hamilton New Zealand colonization 283 (5)
Hamilton North America (Canada) the growth of the US 132 (1)
Hammamiya Egypt ancient Egypt 159 (2)
Hamwih *see* Southampton
Han *state* East Asia first cities 259 (5)
Han *people* North America cultural groups 123 (3)
Han Caine *region* East Asia ancient trade 44–45 (1)
Hanchou *see* Hanzhou
Hanchu *region* East Asia medieval states 264 (2)
Han-chung *see* Hanzhong, Nanzheng
Handan *var.* Han-tan East Asia (China) first cities 259 (5) first religions 37 (4)
HaNegev *see* Negev
Han Empire *state* East Asia ancient trade 44–45 (1)
Hanga Roa Easter Island early cultures 281 (4)
Hang-chou *see* Hangzhou, Lin'an
Hangchow *see* Hangzhou, Lin'an
Hang Gon Mainland Southeast Asia (Vietnam) the world in 2500 BCE 22–23
Hangö Scandinavia (Finland) WWI 207 (4)
Hangzhou *var.* Hang-chou, Hangchow, Lin'an East Asia (China) ancient trade 44–45 (1) biological diffusion 72–73 (1) colonialism 269 (4) early modern states 266 (1) economy 274 (1) exploration 256 (1) imperialism 270 (2) medieval states 263 (3), (6) Mongols 68 (2), 68–69 (1) post-war politics 271 (7), 274 (2) *see also* Lin'an
Hanka, Lake *see* Khanka *lake*
Hankou *var.* Han-kou, Han-k'ou, Hanyang, Wuchang, Wuhan, Wu-han; *prev.* Hankow East Asia (China) ancient trade 44–45 (1) colonialism 269 (4) empire and revolution 268 (2) Mongols 68–69 (1) *see also* Wuhan
Hankow *see* Hankou, Wuhan
Hannover *see* Hanover
Hanoi *mod.* Ha Nôi; *prev.* Dai-La, Thang Long Mainland Southeast Asia (Vietnam) colonialism 247 (4), 248 (1), 269 (4) early modern states 268 (1) Islam 275 (4) medieval states 262–263 (1), 263 (6) post-war economy 253 (5) world religions 243 (5), 49 (4) WWII 251 (3), 272 (1), 273 (2) *battle* post-war politics 251 (5) *see also* Dai-La
Hanover *Ger.* Hannover Central Europe (Germany) empire and revolution 199 (3), 202 (1) medieval states 189 (3) Napoleon 200–201 (1), 201 (2) post-war politics 212 (1)
Hanover *Ger.* Hannover *state* Central Europe empire and revolution 202 (1), (2), 88 (1) Napoleon 200–201 (1)
Han-tan *see* Handan
Hanyang *see* Hankou, Wuhan
Hanzhong *var.* Han-Chung, Nanzheng *province/rebellion/settlement* East Asia (China) early modern states 266 (2) first religions 37 (4) first states 260 (1) Mongols 68–69 (1) *see also* Nanzheng
Hanzhou *var.* Hanchou East Asia (China) medieval states 262–263 (1)
Hao East Asia (China) first cities 259 (5)
Hao *island* East Asia exploration 278 (1)
Happo *var.* Masan Mainland Southeast Asia (South Korea) Mongols 68–69 (1)
Hapsal *Est.* Haapsalu Eastern Europe (Estonia) early modern states 195 (3)
Hara Japan early modern states 267 (4)
Haradvara South Asia (India) world religions 242 (2)
Haraga Egypt ancient Egypt 159 (2)
Hara-Huna *state* Central Asia first empires 241 (5)
Harappa *archaeological site/settlement* South Asia (India) first cities 240 (2) first civilizations 24 (2)
Harar East Africa (Ethiopia) trade 165 (3)
Harar *state* East Africa the world in 1200 62–63 the world in 1600 78–79 the world in 1700 82–83 the world in 1800 86–87 the world in 1850 90–91
Harare *prev.* Salisbury Southern Africa (Zimbabwe) economy 168 (2) *see also* Salisbury
Harbin *var.* Haerbin, Ha-erh-pin, Kharbin; *prev.* Haerhpin, Pingkiang, Pinkiang East Asia (China) colonialism 269 (4) Communism 271 (8) economy 274 (1) imperialism 270 (2) Islam 275 (4) post-war politics 274 (2) Russo-Japanese War 270 (4)
Hare *people* North America cultural groups 123 (3)
Harfleur France medieval states 192 (2)
Hargraves *goldfield* Australia colonization 282 (2)
Haripunjaya *region/state* Mainland Southeast Asia early medieval states 245 (5) Mongols 68–69 (1)
Harjedalen *region* Scandinavia early modern states 197 (3)
Harlem *incident* North America (USA) US politics 135 (6)
Harlem *see* Haarlem
Harmozia *mod.* Hormuz, Ormuz Southwest Asia (Iran) Hellenistic world 40–41 (1) *see also* Hormuz, Ormuz
Harness *burial mound* North America (USA) first civilizations 121 (4)
Harper's Ferry North America (USA) US Civil War 131 (6)
Harran Southwest Asia (Turkey) ancient Persia 223 (4) first civilizations 221 (4), (5), 222 (2)
Harrisburg North America (USA) the growth of the US 129 (2)
Harrodsborough *mod.* Harrodsburg North America (USA) empire and revolution 127 (3)
Harrodsburg *see* Harrodsborough
Hartford North America (USA) empire and revolution 127 (3) the growth of the US 129 (2)
Haryana *region* South Asia post-war politics 253 (4)
Hasa *mod.* Hofuf; *Ar.* Al Hufūf Southwest Asia (Saudi Arabia) early Islam 56–57 (1) medieval voyages 61 (3)
Hasa *region* Southwest Asia Ottomans 232–233 (1) WWI 233 (2)
Hasanlu Southwest Asia (Iran) first cities 220 (2) first civilizations 24 (2)
Hasinai *people* Central America colonization 125 (4)
Hassuna Southwest Asia (Iraq) the world in 5000 BCE 18–19
Hasta Colonia *see* Asti
Hasta Pompeia *see* Asti
Hastinapura South Asia ancient India 242 (1) first empires 241 (5) world religions 242 (3)
Hastings New Zealand colonization 283 (5)
Hastings *battle* British Isles (United Kingdom) medieval states 186 (2)
Hatra *var.* Al Hadhar; *mod.* Al Ḥaḍr Southwest Asia (Iraq) Roman empire 224 (2)
Hattin Southwest Asia (Israel) crusades 228 (2) *battle* crusades 65 (3)
Hattushash *mod.* Boğazkoy Southwest Asia (Turkey) early systems 223 (3) first cities 28 (3), 28–29 (1) first civilizations 221 (4), (5)
Hatuncolla South America (Peru) Incas 147 (3)
Haua Fteah *archaeological site/settlement* North Africa (Libya) early agriculture 158 (1) first humans 13 (2)
Haumoana *people* Easter Island early cultures 281 (4)
Hausaland *see* Hausa States
Hausa States *var.* Hausaland *state* West Africa Islam 163 (1)
Haute-Volta *see* Upper Volta
Havana *Sp.* La Habana West Indies (Cuba) colonization 126 (1) European expansion 81 (3), 84–85 (1), 85 (2) exploration 119 (2), (3) *battle* empire and revolution 88 (1) the growth of the US 129 (2) US economy 136 (2) US imperialism 133 (5) Cold War 108 (2)
Havana *burial mound* North America (USA) first civilizations 121 (4)
Havana *region* North America first civilizations 121 (4)
Havel *river* Central Europe post-war politics 212 (2)
Havelock New Zealand colonization 283 (5)
Havre *see* Le Havre
Hawaii *state* North America US economy 136 (2) WWII 104 (1)
Hawaiian Islands *mod.* Hawaii; *prev.* Sandwich Islands; *island group* Pacific Ocean early cultures 280–281 (3) environmentalism 285 (2) exploration 279 (3) medieval voyages 60 (2) the growth of the US 133 (4) WWII 272 (1), 273 (2) Cold War 109 (1) colonization 284–285 (1) decolonization 249 (3) *see also* Hawaii
Hawara Egypt ancient Egypt 159 (4)
Hawikuh *archaeological site* North America (USA) cultural groups 123 (4)
Hawke's Bay *region* New Zealand colonization 283 (5)
Hawlēr *see* Arbela
HaYarden *see* Jordan
Hayden *lt.* Cortina Italy WWI 207 (5)
Hazor Southwest Asia (Israel) ancient Egypt 159 (5) first cities 28–29 (1)
Heavenly Principle Sect *rebellion* East Asia empire and revolution 268 (2)
Hebei *var.* Hopei *province* East Asia medieval states 262–263 (1) post-war politics 274 (2)
Hebrides *island group* British Isles medieval states 185 (3)
Hebron Southwest Asia (Israel) 20th century 234 (2) first civilizations 222 (1)
Hebrus *see* Maritsa
Hecatompylos Southwest Asia (Iran) Roman empire 225 (5) ancient trade 44–45 (1) Hellenistic world 224 (1)
Hedeby Scandinavia (Denmark) medieval voyages 60–61 (1) medieval states 185 (3)
Hefa *see* Haifa
Hefei East Asia (China) first states 260 (1) post-war economy 275 (3)
Heian-kyo *mod.* Kyoto Japan early modern states 265 (5) medieval states 264 (2) *see also* Kyoto
Heijo-kyo *mod.* Nara Japan medieval states 264 (2), 265 (3)
Heiligenkreuz *major cistercian house* Central Europe medieval states 187 (3)
Heilong Jiang *see* Amur
Heilongjiang *province* East Asia post-war politics 274 (2)
Hejaz *var.* Hijaz; *Ar.* Al Ḥijāz *region/state* Southwest Asia 20th-century politics 233 (4) crusades 228 (2) early Islam 56–57 (1), 57 (2) exploration 219 (4) Islam 226 (2), 227 (4), (5) Mongols 229 (3) Ottomans 231 (3), 232–233 (1) Seljuks 228 (1) trade 230 (2) world religions 226 (1) WWI 233 (2)
Hejian *var.* Ho-chien *Buddhist centre/settlement* East Asia (China) Mongols 68–69 (1) world religions 49 (3)
Helena North America (USA) the growth of the US 129 (2)
Heliopolis Egypt ancient Egypt 159 (2), (4), (5) early Islam 56–57 (1) first cities 220 (2), 28–29 (1) first civilizations 24 (2) Hellenistic world 40–41 (1)
Heliopolis *battle* Egypt Islam 226 (2)
Heliopolis *mod.* Baalbek *settlement/religious site* Southwest Asia (Lebanon) Roman empire 180–181 (1) first religions 37 (3) *see also* Baalbek
Hellas *region* Greece Hellenistic world 40–41 (1)
Helles *battle* Southwest Asia (Turkey) WWI 207 (6)
Hellespont *region* Greece ancient Greece 177 (2)
Hellespont *var.* Dardanelles, Çanakkale, Bogazi *sea waterway* Southeast Europe/Southwest Asia exploration 218 (1) *see also* Dardanelles
Helluland *region* North America medieval voyages 60–61 (1)
Helmand *var.* Rūd-e Hīrmand *river* Central Asia first cities 240 (2)
Helmsdorf *burial mound* Central Europe (Germany) Bronze Age 175 (3)
Helsingfors *Fin.* Helsinki Scandinavia (Finland) early modern states 195 (3) empire and revolution 202 (1) WWI 207 (4) *see also* Helsinki
Helsinki *Swe.* Helsingfors Scandinavia (Finland) Cold War 108 (3) post-war politics 212 (3) Soviet Union 208 (2) WWII 210 (1), 211 (2), (4) *see also* Helsingfors
Helvetia *state* Switzerland Napoleon 201 (2)
Helvetian Republic *var.* Helvetic Republic; *mod.* Switzerland; *anc.* Helvetica; *Fr.* La Suisse, *Ger.* Schweiz, *It.* Svizzera *state* Central Europe the world in 1800 86–87 *see also* Helvetia, Swiss Confederation, Switzerland
Helvetic Republic *see* Helvetia, Helvetian Republic, Swiss Confederation, Switzerland
Hemeroscopium Iberian Peninsula (Spain) first civilizations 177 (1)
Hemudu *var.* Ho-mu-tu *archaeological site/settlement* East Asia (China) early agriculture 258 (1), (2)
Henan *var.* Yégainnyin East Asia (China) medieval states 263 (3), (4), (5)
Henan *var.* Honan *province/region* East Asia Chinese revolution 271 (5) early modern states 266 (1), (2), 268 (1) empire and revolution 268 (2) first cities 259 (3), (4), (5) medieval states 262–263 (1), 263 (6) post-war politics 271 (7), 274 (2)
Henderson Island *island* Pacific Ocean exploration 278 (1)
Hendū Kosh *see* Hindu Kush
Henegouwen *see* Holland
Henen-nesut Egypt ancient Egypt 159 (5)
Heng Shan *mountain* East Asia first religions 37 (4)
Hengzhen *archaeological site* East Asia early agriculture 258 (2)
Hengzhou East Asia (China) medieval states 263 (6)
Hephaestus, Temple of *var.* Temple of Hephaistus *temple* Greece ancient Greece 177 (4)
Hephthalites *var.* Hepthalites, Ephthalites, White Huns *people* Central Asia early medieval states 244 (1)
Hephthalites, Empire of the *var.* Ephthalites, White Huns *state* Central Asia the world in 500 CE 50–51 *see also* Ephthalites
Hepu *province* East Asia first states 260 (1)
Heraclea Italy early states 178 (1)
Heraclea Pontica Southwest Asia (Turkey) Roman empire 180–181 (1) first civilizations 177 (1) Hellenistic world 40–41 (1)
Heracleopolis Egypt ancient Egypt 159 (3) first cities 28–29 (1)
Herat Central Asia (Afghanistan) ancient Persia 223 (4) biological diffusion 72–73 (1) colonialism 248 (1) early Islam 56–57 (1) Islam 226 (2), 227 (4), (5) medieval Persia 231 (4) Mongols 229 (3), 68–69 (1) Mughal Empire 246 (1) Timur 229 (4) trade 267 (3) world religions 226 (1)
Herdoniae Italy early states 178 (1)
Hereford British Isles (United Kingdom) economy 204 (1) medieval states 186 (2)
Héristal *see* Herstal
Hermonthis *see* Armant
Hernici *people* Italy early states 178 (2)
Herrerias *archaeological site* Iberian Peninsula (Spain) prehistoric culture 17 (3)
Herstal *Fr.* Héristal Low Countries (Belgium) Franks 184 (2)
Hertenrits *archaeological site* South America (Surinam) early cultures 145 (2)
Heruli *people* Eastern Europe Roman empire 181 (4)
Herzegovina *vassal state* Southeast Europe Ottomans 230 (1) *see also* Bosnia and Herzegovina
Hestiaea *see* Histiaea Oreus
Hexham British Isles (United Kingdom) medieval states 183 (3)
Hezhou East Asia (China) Mongols 68–69 (1)
Hibernia *var.* Éire, *mod.* Ireland *island* British Isles Roman empire 180–181 (1), 181 (4) ancient trade 44 (2) *see also* Ireland
Hidalgo *province* Central America Mexican Revolution 133 (3)
Hidalgo del Paral *see* Parral
Hiei-zan *mountain* Japan medieval states 265 (3)
Hieraconpolis Egypt ancient Egypt 159 (2), (3) first cities 28–29 (1) first civilizations 24 (2)
Hierakonpolis *see* Hieraconpolis
Hierapolis *Christian archbishopric* Southwest Asia (Turkey) world religions 48 (1)
Hierosolyma *see* Jerusalem
High Cliff *burial mound* North America (USA) first civilizations 121 (4)
Highland Maya *region* Central America first civilizations 123 (2)
High Plains *see* Great Plains
Higo Japan early modern states 267 (4)
Hiiumaa *see* Dagö
Hijaz *see* Hejaz
Hijili South Asia (India) colonialism 247 (3)
Hiko-san *mountain* Japan medieval states 265 (3)
Hili Southwest Asia (Oman) first civilizations 24 (3)
Hill End *goldfield* Australia colonization 282 (2)
Hillgrove *goldfield* Australia colonization 282 (2)
Hilli *var.* Hili South Asia (Bangladesh) post-war politics 252 (3)
Hill Tippera *see* Tripura
Himachal Pradesh *region* South Asia post-war politics 252 (1), (2)
Himalaya *see* Himalayas
Himalayas *var.* Himalaya, *Chin.* Himalaya Shan *mountain range* South Asia ancient India 242 (1) ancient trade 44–45 (1), 72–73 (1), 73 (3) Chinese revolution 271 (5) colonialism 247 (3), 248 (1), 269 (3), (4) Communism 271 (8) early agriculture 20–21 (2), 258 (1) early medieval states 244 (1), 244–245 (3) early religions 48 (2) economy 249 (4) empire and revolution 268 (2), 88 (1) European expansion 84–85 (1) exploration 239 (1), 257 (3) first cities 240 (2), 259 (5) first empires 241 (4), (5) first humans 13 (2) first religions 36 (2) first states 260 (1) Hellenistic world 40–41 (1) historical geography 275 (5) imperial global economy 92 (1) Marathas 246 (2) medieval states 261 (6), 262–263 (1) medieval voyages 61 (3) Mongols 68–69 (1) Mughal Empire 246 (1) post-war politics 252 (1) prehistoric culture 16 (1) Timur 229 (4) trade 230 (2), 267 (3) world religions 242 (2), (3), 243 (4), 49 (3), (4)
Himalaya Shan *see* Himalayas
Himavat *region* South Asia world religions 242 (3)
Himera Italy first civilizations 177 (1)
Hims *see* Homs
Himyar Southwest Asia (Yemen) early cultures 161 (4), (5)
Himyarites *state* Southwest Asia early cultures 160 (1), 161 (3), (4), (5)
Hindu Kush *Per.* Hendū Kosh *mountain range* Central Asia ancient Persia 223 (4), 225 (6) Roman empire 224 (2) ancient trade 44–45 (1) trade 72–73 (1) colonialism 247 (3), 248 (1), 269 (3) early Islam 56–57 (1), 57 (2) early medieval states 244 (1), 244–245 (3) exploration 218 (2), 256 (1), 257 (3) first empires 241 (4) first cities 24 (2), 25 (3) first empires 241 (4) first states 260 (1) Hellenistic world 224 (1) Islam 227 (4) Marathas 246 (2) medieval states 261 (6) Mongols 229 (3), 68–69 (1) Mughal Empire 246 (1) Timur 229 (4) world religions 243 (4), 49 (3) Communism 271 (8)
Hindu Shahis *dynasty* South Asia early medieval states 244 (2)
Hios *see* Chios
Hippo Diarrhytus *var.* Hipp Zarytus North Africa (Tunisia) first civilizations 177 (1)
Hipponium *mod.* Vibo Valentia; *prev.* Monteleone di Calabria Italy first civilizations 177 (1)
Hippo Regius North Africa (Algeria) Roman empire 180–181 (1) first civilizations 177 (1)
Hippo Zarytus *see* Hippo Diarrhytus
Hirado Japan early modern states 267 (4)
Hiraizumi Japan medieval states 265 (5) medieval states 265 (4)
Hirmand, Rūd-e *see* Helmand
Hiroshima *var.* Hirosima Japan Communism 273 (3) economy 270 (1), 275 (4) Russo-Japanese War 270 (4) Sino-Japanese War 270 (3) WWII 104–105, 272–273
Hiroshima *var.* Hirosima *prefecture* Japan economy 270 (1)
Hirosima *see* Hiroshima
Hirpini *people* Italy early states 178 (1)
Hispalis *mod.* Seville, Sevilla *Christian archbishopric/settlement* Iberian Peninsula (Spain) Roman empire 180–181 (1) world religions 48 (1) *see also* Seville
Hispana *see* Hispania, Iberia, Spain
Hispania *province/region* Iberian Peninsula Roman empire 180–181 (1), 181 (4), 225 (5) ancient trade 44 (2) world religions 48 (1)
Hispania Citerior *province* Iberian Peninsula Roman empire 179 (5)
Hispania Ulterior *province* Iberian Peninsula Roman empire 179 (5)
Hispaniola *island* West Indies colonization 125 (4), 126 (1) early agriculture 120 (1) empire and revolution 150 (1), 89 (3) European expansion 84–85 (1), 85 (2) exploration 142 (1)
Hissar Southwest Asia (Iran) first cities 220 (2)
Histiaea Oreus *var.* Hestiaea *state* Greece ancient Greece 177 (2)
Histria *see* Istrus
Hitachi Japan economy 275 (4)
Hitichi *people* North America colonization 125 (4), 126 (1)
Hittite Empire *state* Southwest Asia first civilizations 221 (5)
Hiwassee Island North America (USA) cultural groups 122 (5)
Hoa Binh Mainland Southeast Asia (Vietnam) post-war politics 251 (5)
Hoa Binh *battle* Mainland Southeast Asia (Vietnam) post-war politics 251 (5)
Hobart *prev.* Hobarton, Hobart Town *penal colony/settlement* Australia colonization 282 (1), (2), 283 (3), 284–285 (1) exploration 279 (2), (3)
Hobarton *see* Hobart
Hobart Town *see* Hobart
Hobkirk's Hill *battle* North America (USA) empire and revolution 127 (3)
Hocaba *state* Central America Aztecs 124 (1)
Hochelaga *mod.* Montreal, Montréal North America (Canada) European expansion 80–81 (1) *see also* Montreal
Ho-chien *see* Hejian
Ho Chi Minh City *var.* Hô Chi Minh; *prev.* Saigon Mainland Southeast Asia (Vietnam) Islam 275 (4) post-war economy 253 (5) *see also* Saigon
Hodeida Southwest Asia (Yemen) biological diffusion 72–73 (1)
Hoeryong *Jap.* Kainei East Asia (North Korea) Russo-Japanese War 270 (4)
Hofei *see* Hefei
Hofuf *see* Hasa
Hogoley Islands *see* Chuuk, Truk
Hohenlinden *battle* Central Europe (Germany) Napoleon 200–201 (1)
Hohenzollern *state* Central Europe early modern states 193 (5)
Hohhot East Asia (China) post-war economy 275 (3) post-war politics 274 (2)
Hohlenstein *archaeological site* Central Europe (Germany) prehistoric culture 17 (2)
Hohnstein *region* Central Europe empire and revolution 199 (3)
Hohokam *region/state* Central America/North America cultural groups 123 (4)
Hojo *region* Japan early modern states 267 (4)
Hokitika New Zealand colonization 283 (5)
Hokkaido *Jap.* Hokkaidō *island* Japan Communism 273 (3) early modern

states 265 (5) economy 270 (1) exploration 257 (2) imperialism 270 (2) medieval states 263 (6), 264 (1), (2), 265 (3), (4)
Hokō see Pohang
Hokurikudo var. Hokurokudo region Japan medieval states 265 (3)
Hokurokudo see Hokurikudo
Holkar region South Asia Marathas 246 (2)
Holland Dut. Henegouwen province/region Low Countries Reformation 195 (5) see also Batvian Republic, Netherlands, United Provinces
Hollandia mod. Jayapura; prev. Sukarnapura New Guinea (Indonesia) european imperialism 97 (3) WWII 272 (1), 273 (2)
Hollywood North America (USA) cultural groups 122 (5) US economy 135 (4)
Holm see Kholm
Holmgard see Novgorod
Holmul Central America (Mexico) first civilizations 123 (2)
Holstein state Central Europe early modern states 193 (4), 195 (3)
Holyhead Wel. Caer Gybi British Isles (United Kingdom) economy 204 (1)
Holy Roman Empire state Central Europe crusades 186 (1) early modern states 193 (4), 194 (1), 195 (3), 197 (5) economy 190 (1) empire and revolution 199 (4) medieval states 185 (3), (4), 192 (1), (2) medieval voyages 60–61 (1) Mongols 68–69 (1) Ottomans 230 (1), 231 (3) Reformation 195 (5)
Homestead Air Force Base military base North America Cold War 108 (2)
Homs var. Hims; anc. Emesa Southwest Asia (Syria) crusades 65 (3) early Islam 56–57 (1) Mongols 229 (3), 68–69 (1) WWI 233 (2)
Ho-mu-tu see Hemudu
Honan see Henan, Luoyang
Honavar South Asia (India) colonialism 247 (3)
Hondschoote battle Low Countries (Belgium) empire and revolution 199 (4)
Honduras state Central America the growth of the US 129 (2), 133 (4) the modern world 112 (1) US economy 136 (2) US politics 139 (4) US superpower 138 (1) WWII 104 (1) Cold War 108 (2)
Honduras, Gulf of gulf Central America Aztecs 124 (1) colonization 126 (1)
Honein North Africa (Morocco) economy 190 (1)
Hong Kong var. Xianggang colonial possession/settlement East Asia (China) (1) colonialism 269 (4) Communism 271 (8) decolonization 251 (4) economy 274 (1) empire and revolution 88–89 (2) European imperialism 97 (3) global immigration 100 (1) imperial global economy 92 (1) Islam 275 (4) post-war economy 275 (3) post-war politics 274 (2) the growth of the US 133 (4) the world in 1975 106–107 the modern world 113 (4) WWII 251 (3), 272 (1), 273 (2) Cold War 109
Hongshan archaeological site East Asia early agriculture 258 (2)
Hongzhou var. Hungchou East Asia (China) medieval states 262–263 (1)
Honing var. Karakorum East Asia (Mongolia) medieval states 263 (5) see also Karakorum
Honolulu Hawaiian Islands environmentalism 285 (2)
Honshu Jap. Honshū island Japan early modern states 265 (5), 267 (4), (5) economy 270 (1) imperialism 270 (2) medieval states 264 (1), (2), 265 (4) Sino-Japanese War 270 (3) WWII 273 (3)
Hooghly South Asia (India) colonialism 247 (3)
Hooper Bay North America (USA) cultural groups 123 (3)
Hopei see Hebei
Hopewell burial mound/settlement North America (USA) first civilizations 121 (4) first religions 36 (1)
Hopewell Culture people North America the world in 250 CE 46–47
Hopi people North America colonization 125 (4), 126 (1)
Hora Hora region South Asia world religions 242 (2)
Hormoz, Tangeh-ye see Hormuz, Strait of
Hormuz var. Ormuz; anc. Harmozia Southwest Asia (Iran) biological diffusion 72–73 (1) early Islam 56–57 (1), 57 (2) Islam 227 (4), (5) Mongols 229 (3), 68 (2) Seljuks 228 (1) Timur 229 (4) trade 267 (3) see also Harmozia, Ormuz
Hormuz, Strait of var. Strait of Ormuz, Per. Tangeh-ye Hormoz sea waterway Southwest Asia economy 234 (1)
Horn, Cape Sp. Cabo de Hornos headland South America Antarctic Exploration 287 (3) colonization 148 (2) European expansion 80–81 (1), 81 (2) exploration 142 (1), 143 (3) global knowledge 76–77 (1)
Hornos, Cabo de see Horn, Cape
Hortus archaeological site France first humans 13 (2)
Hoshangabad South Asia (India) economy 249 (4)
Hoshino Japan the world in 10,000 BCE 14–15
Hososhima Japan early modern states 265 (5)
Ho-t'ien, Hotan see Khotan
Houdayue state East Asia medieval states 263 (4)
Hougang archaeological site East Asia early agriculture 258 (1), (2)
Houma people North America colonization 125 (4), 126 (1)
Houston North America (USA) Cold War 108 (2) the growth of the US 129 (2), 132 (1) US economy 134 (1), (3), 136 (2)
Howard Lake burial mound North America (USA) first civilizations 121 (4)
Howieson's Poort archaeological site Southern Africa (South Africa) first humans 13 (2)
Howrah South Asia (India) economy 249 (4)
Hoysalas dynasty South Asia early medieval states 244 (2), 244–245 (3) Mongols 68–69 (1)
Hrodna see Grodno
Hrvatska see Croatia
Hsia-men see Xiamen
Hsi-an see Chang'an, Xi'an
Hsiangchou see Xiangzhou
Hsiang-yang see Xiangyang
Hsi Chiang see Xi Jiang
Hsien-pi see Xianbi
Hsi-hsia see Xixia
Hsi-lan see Ceylon, Lambakannas, Lanka, Simhala, Sri Lanka, Taprobana
Hsing-k'ai Hu see Khanka, Lake
Hsinking see Changchun
Hsin-yeh see Xinye
Hsi-tsang see Tibet
Hsiung-nu see Xiongnu
Hsuanchou see Xuanzhou
Hsüan-hua see Xuanhua
Hu Egypt ancient Egypt 159 (2)
Huaca Colorada South America (Peru) early cultures 146 (1)
Huaca del Brujo South America (Peru) early cultures 145 (4)
Huaca de los Reyes archaeological site South America (Peru)
Huacalco Central America (Mexico) Aztecs 124 (3)
Huaca Prieta archaeological site/settlement South America (Peru) early cultures 144 (1)
Huacho South America (Peru) empire and revolution 150 (1)
Huai river East Asia early modern states 266 (1) first states 260 (1)
Huainan var. Huaninan province Central Asia medieval states 262–263 (1)
Huaitará var. Huaytará South America (Peru) Incas 147 (3)
Hualfín South America (Argentina) early cultures 146 (1)
Huallaga river South America early cultures 145 (3), (4) exploration 143 (2) narcotics 153 (5)
Hualla Tampu South America (Bolivia) Incas 147 (3)
Huamachuco South America (Peru) Incas 148 (1)
Huambo Port. Nova Lisboa Southern Africa (Angola) Cold War 109 (5)
Huamunga South America (Peru) Incas 147 (3)
Huancabamba South America (Peru) Incas 147 (3)
Huancayo South America (Peru) Incas 148 (1) narcotics 153 (5)
Huanggang East Asia (China) Mongols 68–69 (1)
Huang Hai see Yellow Sea
Huang He see Yellow River
Huaninan see Huainan
Huánuco South America (Peru) Incas 147 (3)
Huarás prev. Huaraz South America (Peru) Incas 147 (3) see also Huaraz
Huaraz var. Huarás South America (Peru) Incas 148 (1) see also Huarás
Huari South America (Peru) early cultures 146 (1)
Huari region/state South America the world in 750 CE 54–55
Huaricoto South America (Peru) the world in 2500 BCE 22–23
Huarmey river South America early cultures 145 (3)
Hua Shan mountain East Asia (China) first religions 37 (4)
Huating archaeological site East Asia (China) early agriculture 258 (2)
Huaura river South America early cultures 145 (3)
Huaxian archaeological site East Asia (China) early agriculture 258 (2)
Huayin archaeological site East Asia (China) early agriculture 258 (2)
Huaylas South America (Peru) Incas 147 (3)
Huaymil state Central America Aztecs 124 (1)
Huaytará see Huaitará
Hubei var. Hupeh, Hupei province/region East Asia Chinese revolution 271 (5) early modern states 266 (1), (2), 268 (1) economy 274 (1) empire and revolution 268 (2) post-war politics 271 (7), 274 (2)
Hubli South Asia (India) colonialism 247 (3)
Huddersfield British Isles (United Kingdom) economy 204 (1)
Hudson Bay bay North America (Canada) colonization 126 (1) cultural groups 123 (3) early agriculture 120 (1) European expansion 84–85 (1) exploration 118 (1), 119 (2), (3), 286 (1), 287 (2), 129 (2), 132 (1)
Hudson Bay Company colonial possession/state North America empire and revolution 88 (1)
Hudson, Détroit d' see Hudson Strait
Hudson River river North America empire and revolution 127 (3) the growth of the US 132 (2)
Hudson Strait Fr. Détroit d'Hudson sea waterway North America exploration 286 (1), 287 (2), 129 (2)
Hué mod. Huê Mainland Southeast Asia (Vietnam) colonialism 247 (4), 248 (1) European imperialism 97 (3) medieval states 262–263 (1)
Hué mod. Huê battle Mainland Southeast Asia (Vietnam) post-war politics 251 (5)
Huehuetoca Central America (Mexico) Aztecs 124 (2)
Hueiyi state East Asia first cities 259 (3)
Huelva anc. Onuba Iberian Peninsula (Spain) civil war 209 (4)
Huepochtlan state Central America Aztecs 124 (1)
Huesca anc. Osca Iberian Peninsula (Spain) Islam 192 (3)
Huétamo var. Huétamo de Núñez Central America (Mexico) first civilizations 122 (1)
Huétamo de Núñez see Huétamo
Huexotzinco Central America (Mexico) colonization 125 (5)
Huextepec state Central America Aztecs 124 (1)
Hueyotlipan Central America (Mexico) colonization 125 (5)
Hughenden Australia colonization 282 (1)
Huguang province East Asia early modern states 266 (1), (2) medieval states 263 (6)
Huguenots religious faction France Reformation 196 (2)
Hui rebellion East Asia empire and revolution 268 (2)
Huining East Asia (China) medieval states 263 (5)
Huipulco Central America (Mexico) Aztecs 124 (2)
Huitzilpochco Central America (Mexico) Aztecs 124 (3)
Huitzlan Central America (Mexico) Aztecs 124 (2)
Huitznahuac Central America (Mexico) Aztecs 124 (3)
Huixian East Asia (China) first cities 259 (3), 28–29 (1)
Hukui see Fukui
Hukuoka see Fukuoka
Hukusima see Fukushima
Hull var. Kingston upon Hull British Isles (United Kingdom) economy 204 (1) WWII 210 (1)
Hulme British Isles (United Kingdom) economy 204 (2)
Hulst battle Low Countries (Netherlands) Reformation 195 (5)
Humahuaca South America (Argentina) early cultures 146 (1)
Humaita archaeological site South America (Brazil) early cultures 145 (2)
Humber estuary British Isles medieval states 183 (3), 186 (2)
Huna region South Asia world religions 242 (2)
Húnaflói fjords Iceland exploration 172 (2)
Hunan var. Xiang province/region East Asia Chinese revolution 271 (5) early modern states 266 (1) empire and revolution 268 (2) post-war politics 271 (7), 274 (2)
Hunas var. Huns people South Asia early medieval states 244 (1)
Hunchun East Asia (China) colonialism 269 (4) imperialism 270 (2)
Hungarian Revolts rebellion Central Europe Reformation 196 (2)
Hungarians people Eastern Europe the modern world 112 (2)
Hungary Ger. Ungarn, Hung. Magyarország, Rom. Ungaria, SCr. Madarska, Ukr. Uhorshchyna state Central Europe crusades 186 (1), 64–65 (2) early modern states 193 (4), 194 (1) economy 190 (1) empire and revolution 202 (1), (2) civil war 209 (3), (5) Islam 163 (1) medieval states 185 (3), (5), 188 (1), 189 (3), (4) medieval voyages 60–61 (1) Mongols 68–69 (1) Napoleon 200–201 (1) Ottomans 195 (4), 230 (1), 231 (3) post-war economy 213 (5), 214 (1), (2), 215 (3) post-war politics 212 (1), (3) Reformation 194 (2), 196 (1), (2) Soviet Union 213 (4) the modern world 112 (2), 113 (4) WWI 208 (1) WWII 104 (2), 210 (1), 211 (2), (3), (4) Cold War 108 (3), 109 (1)
Hungchou see Hongzhou
Hungnam East Asia (North Korea) Cold War 109 (4)
Huns people Eastern Europe/Central Europe great migrations 52–53 (1)
Huns see Hunas, Xiongnu
Huns, Empire of the state Eastern Europe great migrations 52–53 (1)
Hunter-gatherers people Central Asia/Americas/Africa/Australia the world in 2500 BCE 22–23 the world in 1250 BCE 26–27
Hunter-gatherers of the Great Plains people North America the world in 2500 BCE 22–23
Hun tribal confederacy
Huo vassal state East Asia first cities 259 (3)
Huon Peninsula New Guinea (Papua New Guinea) exploration 280 (1)
Huo Shan mountain East Asia (China) first religions 37 (4)
Hupeh, Hupei see Hubei
Huron people North America colonization 126 (1)
Huron, Lake lake North America colonization 126 (1) cultural groups 122 (5) early agriculture 120 (1) empire and revolution 127 (2), (3) exploration 118 (1), 119 (2), (3) first civilizations 121 (4) the growth of the US 129 (2) US Civil War 131 (6)
Hurri state Southwest Asia first civilizations 221 (5)
Hurrians var. Hurri people Southwest Asia first civilizations 221 (4)
Hvar It. Lesina; anc. Pharus island Southeast Europe post-war economy 215 (3)
Hwang-hae see Yellow Sea
Hwicce people British Isles medieval states 183 (3)
Hydaspes mod. Jhelum river South Asia first cities 240 (2) Hellenistic world 40–41 (1) see also Jhelum
Hyderabad var. Haidarabad South Asia (India) colonialism 248 (1) economy 249 (4) imperial global economy 93 (5) post-war economy 253 (5) post-war politics 252 (1)
Hyderabad state South Asia colonialism 248 (2) empire and revolution 249 (3)
Hydraotes mod. Ravi river South Asia first cities 240 (2) Hellenistic world 40–41 (1) see also Ravi
Hyères France crusades 186 (1)
Hyesan East Asia (North Korea) Cold War 109 (4)
Hyogo Japan early modern states 267 (4)
Hyogo prefecture Japan economy 270 (1)
Hyphasis mod. Beas river South Asia first cities 240 (2) Hellenistic world 40–41 (1) see also Beas
Hyrax Hill archaeological site East Africa (Kenya) early cultures 160 (1)
Hyrcania region Central Asia Hellenistic world 40–41 (1)

I

Iader see Zadar, Zara
Ia Drang battle Mainland Southeast Asia (Vietnam) post-war politics 251 (5)
Ialysus Greece first civilizations 177 (1)
Ialysus state Greece ancient Greece 177 (2)
Iaşi Southeast Europe (Romania) post-war politics 212 (3)
Iazyges people Eastern Europe Roman empire 181 (4)
Ibadan Central Africa (Nigeria) economy 168 (2)
Ibar Alb. Ibër river Southeast Europe post-war economy 215 (3)
Ibaraki prefecture Japan economy 270 (1)
Ibër see Ibar
Iberia region Iberian Peninsula ancient trade 44–45 (1) early Islam 56–57 (1) exploration 172 (1) first civilizations 177 (1) first religions 37 (3)
Iberian Peninsula physical region Europe Bronze Age 175 (3) early agriculture 174 (1) early cultures 161 (2)
Iberians people Iberian Peninsula the world in 750 BCE 30–31 the world in 500 BCE 34–35 the world in 250 BCE 38–39
Iberus mod. Ebro river Iberian Peninsula Roman empire 179 (3) see also Ebro
Ibiza var. Iviza, Eivissa; anc. Ebusus island Iberian Peninsula civil war 209 (4)
Ica South America (Peru) Incas 147 (3) narcotics 153 (5)
Ica river South America early cultures 145 (4)
Içá, Rio see Putumayo
Iceland Dan. Island, Icel. Ísland state/island Atlantic Ocean 109 (1) early agriculture 20–21 (2) European expansion 80–81 (1) exploration 172 (1), (2), 286 (1), 287 (2) historical geography 117 (1) medieval states 185 (3) medieval voyages 60–61 (1) US superpower 138 (1) WWII 104 (1), 211 (4), Cold War 108 (3)
Ichang see Yichang
Ichigodani Japan early modern states 265 (5)
Ichinotani battle Japan early modern states 265 (5)
Iconium mod. Konya, Konia, Konieh Christian archbishopric/settlement Southwest Asia (Turkey) Roman empire 180–181 (1) world religions 48 (1) see also Konya
Icosium see Algeria, Algiers
Iculisma see Angoulême
Idaho state North America the growth of the US 129 (1) US economy 134 (2)
Idalium Southwest Asia (Cyprus) first civilizations 177 (1)
Idfu see Edfu
Idi Amin, Lac see Edward Lake
Idojiri archaeological site Japan early agriculture 258 (1)
Idrisids dynasty North Africa early Islam 57 (2) Islam 227 (4)
Ifat state East Africa economy 163 (2)
Ife West Africa (Nigeria) Islam 163 (1)
Ife state West Africa Islam 167 (3)
Ifni state North Africa the world in 1900 94–95 the world in 1925 98–99 the world in 1950 102–103
Ifriqiyah state North Africa Islam 226 (2)
Igala state West Africa Islam 163 (1) trade 164 (2), 167 (1)
Igaunija see Estonia
Igbo state West Africa colonization 167 (4)
Igbo States state West Africa trade 164 (2)
Iglau, Igława see Jihlava
Iglesias Italy economy 190 (1)
Igluligardjuk North America (Canada) cultural groups 123 (3)
Iglulik Inuit people North America cultural groups 123 (3)
Iguaçu river South America politics 152 (2)
Iguvium mod. Gubbio Italy early states 178 (1)
Ihnāsiyat al Madīnah see Ihnasya el-Medina
Ihnâsya el Madîna see Ihnasya el-Medina
Ihnasya el-Medina var. Ihnâsya el Madîna, Ihnāsiyat al Madīnah Egypt ancient Egypt 159 (4)
Ijebu state West Africa Islam 167 (3)
Ijebu Ode West Africa (Nigeria) Islam 167 (3)
Ijsselmeer see Zuider Zee
Ikkur Egypt ancient Egypt 159 (4)
Ikoruga Japan medieval states 264 (1)
Ile see Ili
Île de Ré fort France early modern states 197 (5)
Île d'Oléron fort France early modern states 197 (5)
Ileret archaeological site/settlement East Africa (Kenya) early agriculture 158 (1) early cultures 160 (1) first humans 12 (1)
Îles Saint-Pierre et Miquelon see St. Pierre and Miquelon
Île Ste-Marguerite fort France early modern states 197 (5)
Ilhéus hist. São Jorge dos Ilhéos South America (Brazil) colonization 149 (3), (4)
Ili region East Asia colonialism 269 (3), (4) early modern states 268 (1)
Ili Kaz. Ile, Rus. Reka Ili river Central Asia first states 260 (1) Mongols 68–69 (1)
Ilipa battle Iberian Peninsula (Spain) Roman empire 179 (3)
Ilissos river Greece ancient Greece 177 (4)
Il-Khanate state/region Central Asia biological diffusion 72–73 (1) early medieval states 244–245 (3) economy 163 (2), 190 (1) Mongols 229 (3)
Il-Khans, Khanate of the state Central Asia/Southwest Asia Mongols 68 (2)
Illiberis mod. Elne church council Iberian Peninsula (Spain) world religions 48 (1)
Illichpur South Asia (India) Mughal Empire 246 (1)
Illinois state North America the growth of the US 129 (1) US Civil War 130 (2), (3), (4), (5), 131 (6), (7) US economy 134 (2)
Illinois people North America colonization 126 (1)
Illinois Post, The North America (USA) colonization 126 (1)
Illummersuit North America (Greenland) cultural groups 123 (3)
Illutalik North America (Greenland) cultural groups 123 (3)
Illyria region Greece Hellenistic world 40–41 (1)
Illyrian Provinces state Southeast Europe Napoleon 201 (2)
Illyrians Lat. Illyrii people Southeast Europe Roman empire 179 (5)
Illyricum province/region Southeast Europe Roman empire 179 (5), 180–181 (1) world religions 48 (1)
Illyrii see Illyrians
Ilorin West Africa (Nigeria) Islam 167 (3)
Ilorin, Emirate of state West Africa Islam 167 (3)
Ilva mod. Elba island Italy early states 178 (1) see also Elba
Ilyas Shahis people South Asia early medieval states 244–245 (3)
Imagawa region Japan early modern states 267 (4)
Imola Italy medieval states 188 (1)
Imperial City East Asia (China) medieval states 262 (2)
Imperial Fora Italy Roman empire 181 (2)
Imphal South Asia (India) colonialism 248 (1) post-war politics 252 (1) WWII 251 (3), 272 (1), 273 (2)
Imuris people Central America colonization 126 (1)
Inanna Temple building Southwest Asia (Iraq) first cities 28 (2)
Inanna, Ziggurat of building Southwest Asia (Iraq) first cities 220 (3)
Inca people South America early cultures 147 (2) Incas 148 (1) global knowledge 76 (2)
Inca Empire state South America early cultures 147 (2) Incas 148 (1) global knowledge 76 (2)
Incahuasi see Incawasi
Incawasi var. Incahuasi South America (Peru) Incas 147 (3)
Inchon prev. Chemulpo; Jap. Jinsen East Asia (South Korea) Cold War 109 (4) Sino-Japanese War 270 (3) see also Inchon
Incirlik Southwest Asia (Iran) 20th-century politics 235 (5)
Incognita, Terra physical region ancient trade 44 (2)
Independence North America (USA) the growth of the US 129 (2)
India colonial possession/region/state South Asia ancient Persia 223 (4) ancient trade 44 (2), 44–45 (1) trade 72–73 (1) colonialism 269 (3), (4) Communism 271 (8) crusades 65 (1) decolonization 251 (4) early Islam 56–57 (1), 57 (2) early systems 32 (1), 33 (2), (3) economy 249 (4) empire and revolution 88 (1) European expansion 80–81 (1) European imperialism 97 (4) exploration 156 (3), 218 (2), 239 (1), 257 (3) first humans 13 (2) first religions 36 (1) first states 260 (1) global immigration 100 (1), 101 (2), (3) imperial global economy 92 (1), 93 (5) Islam 227 (4) medieval states 261 (6), 262–263 (1) medieval voyages 61 (3) Mongols 68 (2) post-war economy 253 (5), 275 (3) post-war politics 252 (1), (2), 253 (4), 274 (2) Soviet Union 213 (4) the growth of the US 133 (4) the modern world 112 (1), 113 (3), (4) trade 230 (2), 267 (3) US superpower 138 (1) world religions 49 (3) WWII 104 (1), 105 (4), 251 (3), 272 (1), 273 (2)
Indiana state North America the growth of the US 129 (1) US Civil War 130 (2), (3), (4), (5), 131 (6), (7) US economy 134 (2)
Indianapolis North America (USA) the growth of the US 129 (2), 132 (1) US Civil War 131 (6) US politics 135 (6)
Indian Desert see Thar Desert
Indian Ocean ocean ancient trade 44–45 (1), 72–73 (1), 73 (2), (3) Bronze Age 240 (3) colonialism 247 (3), (4), 248 (1), (2) decolonization 250 (1), 251 (4), 285 (3) economy 168 (2), (3), 249 (4) empire and revolution 88 (1), 88–89 (2) European expansion 80–81 (1), 81 (2), (3), 84–85 (1) European imperialism 97 (4) exploration 156 (3), 157 (4), 239 (1) first humans 13 (2) global immigration 100 (1), 101 (2), (3) global knowledge 76 (10), (3), (4), 76–77 (1), 77 (5), (6) imperial global economy 92 (1), 93 (2) Islam 163 (1), 243 (6) medieval voyages 61 (3) Mughal Empire 246 (1) post-war economy 275 (3) post-war politics 252 (1) prehistoric culture 16 (1), 17 (2) slave trade 165 (4) the modern world 113 (3) trade 230 (2), 267 (3) US superpower 138 (1) WWII 105 (4), 251 (3), 272 (1), 273 (2) Cold War 109 (1)
Indian Reserve region North America empire and revolution 127 (3)
Indian Union see India
Indicus, Oceanus mod. Indian Ocean ocean Indian Ocean ancient trade 44 (2) see also Indian Ocean
Indigirka river Siberia early agriculture 258 (1) exploration 257 (2)
Indo-China region Mainland Southeast Asia WWII 104 (2)
Indo-Greeks people South Asia early medieval states 244 (1)
Indonesia prev. Dutch East Indies, Netherlands East Indies state Maritime Southeast Asia decolonization 251 (4), 285 (3) Islam 275 (4) post-war economy 253 (5), 275 (3) post-war politics 253 (4) the modern world 113 (3), (4) see also Dutch East Indies
Indo-Parthian Empire var. Seistan, Sistan state South Asia Roman empire 224 (2) see also Seistan
Indore South Asia (India) colonialism 247 (3) economy 249 (4) post-war economy 253 (5)
Indraprastha mod. Delhi, Hind. Dilli South Asia (India) early religions 48 (2) first empires 241 (5) world religions 242 (2), (3) see also Dehli
Indrapura Mainland Southeast Asia (Vietnam) medieval states 261 (6)
Indus Chin. Yindu He river South Asia ancient India 242 (1) ancient Persia 223 (4), 225 (6) ancient trade 44 (2), 44–45 (1), 72–73 (1), 73 (3) colonialism 247 (3), 248 (1), (2), 269 (4) decolonization 250 (1) early agriculture 20–21 (2) early Islam 56–57 (1), 57 (2) early medieval states 244 (1), (2), 244–245 (3) early religions 48 (2) early systems 223 (3) economy 249 (4) empire and revolution 249 (3), 268 (2) exploration 218 (1), (2), 239 (1), 257 (3) first cities 240 (2) first civilizations 24 (2), 25 (3) first empires 241 (4), (5) first humans 13 (2) first religions 36 (1), (2) Hellenistic world 224 (1) imperial global economy 92 (1) Islam 226 (2), 227 (4) Marathas 246 (2) medieval Persia 231 (4) medieval states 261 (6), 262–263 (1) Mongols 229 (3), 68 (2), 68–69 (1) Mughal Empire 246 (1) post-war economy 253 (5) post-war politics 252 (1), (2) Timur 229 (4) trade 230 (2), 267 (3) world religions 242 (2), 243 (4), 49 (3), (4) WWII 251 (3)
Indus Valley region South Asia first civilizations 24 (2)
Ingaladdi Shelter Australia the world in 5000 BCE 18–19
Ingalik people North America cultural groups 123 (3)
Ingapirca South America (Equador) Incas 147 (3)
Ingelheim Central Europe (Germany) Franks 184 (2)
Ingria region Eastern Europe early modern states 197 (3)
Ingushetia region Eastern Europe Soviet Union 214-215 (4)
Inhambane Southern Africa (Mozambique) European expansion 84–85 (1) slave trade 165 (4) trade 164 (1)
Injaram South Asia (India) colonialism 247 (3)
Inkerman battle Eastern Europe (Ukraine (Crimea)) Ottomans 202 (4)
Inland Sea Jap. Seto-naikai inland sea Japan WWII 273 (3) early modern states 267 (4) economy 270 (1)
Inner Mongolia var. Nei Mongol, Inner Mongolian Autonomous Region; Chin. Nei Monggol Zizhiqu region East Asia Chinese revolution 271 (5) early modern states 268 (1) economy 274 (1) empire and revolution 268 (2) post-war economy 275 (3) post-war politics 271 (7), 274 (2) WWII 272 (1), 273 (2)
Innsbruch see Innsbruck
Innsbruck var. Innsbruch Central Europe (Austria) early modern states 193 (4)
Insubres people Italy early states 178 (2)
Insula see Lille
Interlacustrine States state East Africa Islam 163 (1)
Internum, Mare sea Europe/Asia/Africa ancient trade 44 (2)
Inuarfissuaq North America (Greenland) cultural groups 123 (3)
Inuit people North America 22–23, 30–31, 34–35, 38–39, 42–43, 46–47, 50–51, 54–55, 58–59, 62–63,66–67, 70–71, 74–75, 78–79, 82–83, 86–87
Inussuk North America (Greenland) cultural groups 123 (3)
Invercargill New Zealand colonization 283 (5)
Inverell Australia colonization 282 (1)
Iol var. Iol Caesarea; mod. Cherchell North Africa (Algeria) Roman empire 179 (3)
Iol Caesarea see Iol
Iolcus Greece first civilizations 175 (4)
Iona British Isles (United Kingdom) medieval states 183 (3)
Ionia region Greece ancient Greece 177 (2) ancient Persia 223 (4)
Ionian Islands Gr. Iónioi Nisoi island group Greece first civilizations 175 (4) Napoleon 201 (2) Ottomans 202 (4)
Ionian Republic state Greece the world in 1800 86–87
Ionian Sea sea Southeast Europe ancient Greece 179 (4) early states 178 (1) first civilizations 175 (4) Ottomans 202 (4) WWI 207 (6)
Iónioi Nísoi see Ionian Islands
Iowa state North America the growth of the US 129 (1) US Civil War 130 (2), (3), (4), (5) US economy 134 (2)
Iowa people North America colonization 126 (1)
Ipet-isut var. Karnak Egypt ancient Egypt 159 (4)
Ipsus battle Southwest Asia (Turkey) Hellenistic world 224 (1)
Ipswich hist. Gipeswic British Isles (United Kingdom) economy 190 (1)
Ipu see Akhmim
Iquique South America (Chile) empire and revolution 151 (3) environment 153 (4) exploration 143 (3) politics 151 (4)
Iquitos South America (Ecuador) empire and revolution 150 (2), 151 (3) narcotics 153 (5)
Iran prev. Persia Persian Empire, Sassanian Empire, Safavid Empire state Southwest Asia economy 234 (1) Islam 235 (4) Soviet Union 213 (4) the modern world 113 (3), (4) US economy 138 (2) 20th-century politics 235 (5) Cold War 109 (1) see also Persia, Persian Empire, Sassanian Empire, Safavid Empire
Iranian Plateau var. Plateau of Iran plateau Southwest Asia ancient Persia 223 (4) ancient trade 44–45 (1) early Islam 56–57 (1), 57 (2) first cities 220 (2), 28–29 (1) first civilizations 221 (4), 24 (2), 25 (3) Hellenistic world 40–41 (1) medieval states 261 (6) Mongols 229 (3) trade 267 (3)
Iranians people Central Asia ancient trade 44–45 (1)
Iran, Plateau of see Iranian Plateau
Iranshahr see Pura
Iraq Ar. 'Irāq state Southwest Asia 20th-century politics 233 (3), (4), 235 (5) Cold War 109 (1) economy 234 (1) exploration 219 (4) Islam 227 (4) Soviet Union 208 (2), 213 (4) the modern world 113 (3), (4) US economy 138 (2) WWII 104 (1), 211 (4)
Irbīl see Arbela
Irboska see Izborsk
Ireland anc. Hibernia; Ir. Éire state/island British Isles Bronze Age 175 (3) crusades 186 (1), 64–65 (2) early agriculture 174 (1) economy 190 (1), 205 (4) empire and revolution 202 (1), 88–89 (2) exploration 172 (1) global immigration 100 (1) civil war 209 (3) medieval states 186 (2), 187 (3), (4), 188 (2) post-war politics 212 (3) Reformation 194 (2) Soviet Union 213 (4) the modern world 112 (2), 113 (4) WWII 210 (1), 211 (2), (4) Cold War 108 (3) see also Hibernia
Ireland, Republic of state British Isles post-war economy 214 (1) Soviet Union 214–215 (4)
Ireland, War in British Isles Reformation 196 (2)
Irian see New Guinea
Irian Barat see Dutch New Guinea, Irian Jaya, Netherlands New Guinea
Irian Jaya var. Irian Barat, West Irian, West New Guinea; prev. Dutch New Guinea, Netherlands New Guinea region Maritime Southeast Asia decolonization 251 (4) post-war politics 253 (4) see also Dutch New Guinea, Netherlands New Guinea
Irigal building Southwest Asia (Iraq) first cities 220 (3)
Irish people British Isles Roman empire 182 (1) medieval states 182 (2)
Irish Free State state British Isles WWI 208 (1)
Irish Kingdoms state British Isles medieval states 185 (3) medieval voyages 60–61 (1)
Irish Revolt rebellion British Isles Reformation 196 (2)
Irish Sea Ir. Muir Éireann sea British Isles economy 204 (1) imperial global economy 93 (4) medieval states 183 (3), 186 (2), 187 (4), 188 (2)
Irkutsk settlement/archaeological site Siberia (Russian Federation) colonialism 269 (3), (4) Communism 271 (8) early agriculture 258 (1) exploration 257 (2), (3) Soviet Union 213 (4)
Irkutsk region Siberia colonialism 269 (3)
Ironbridge British Isles (United Kingdom) economy 204 (1)
Iroquois people North America colonization 126 (1)
Irrawaddy var. Ayeyarwady river Mainland Southeast Asia ancient India 241 (6) ancient trade 44–45 (1) biological diffusion 72–73 (1), 73 (3) Bronze Age 240 (3) colonialism 247 (3), (4), 248 (1), (2), 269 (4) early medieval states 245 (5), (6) exploration 256 (1) first states 260 (1) medieval states 262–263 (1), 263 (6) Mongols 68–69 (1) Mughal Empire 246 (1) post-war economy 275 (3) world religions 243 (5), 49 (3)
Irtish see Irtysh
Irtysh var. Irtish, Kaz. Ertis river Central Asia/Siberia 72–73 (1) colonialism 269 (3), (4) empire and revolution 268 (2) exploration 257 (3) first states 260 (1) medieval states 261 (6), 262–263 (1) Mongols 68–69 (1) trade 267 (3)
Iruñea see Pamplona
Irwell river British Isles economy 204 (1)
Isanapura Mainland Southeast Asia (Cambodia) ancient India 241 (6)
Isandhlwana battle Southern Africa (South Africa) colonization 166 (2) European imperialism 96 (2)
Isauria region Southwest Asia Hellenistic world 40–41 (1)
Isca Dumnoniorum mod. Exeter British Isles (United Kingdom) Roman empire 180–181 (1) see also Exeter
Isca Silurum mod. Caerleon mithraic site/legion headquarters British Isles (United Kingdom) Roman empire 180–181 (1) world religions 48 (1)
Ise Buddhist temple army/settlement Japan economy 270 (1) medieval states 265 (4)
Isernia see Aesernia
Isfahan var. Isphahan; anc. Aspadana; Ar. Eşfahān Southwest Asia (Iran) trade 72–73 (1) crusades 65 (1) early Islam 56–57 (1) economy 234 (1) exploration 218 (2) Islam 226 (2), 227 (4), (5) medieval Persia 231 (4) Ottomans 231 (3), 232–233 (1) Seljuks 228 (1) Timur 229 (4) trade 230 (2) world religions 226 (1)
Ishango Central Africa (Congo (Zaire)) the world in 5000 BCE 18–19
Ishibashi-yama battle Japan early modern states 265 (5)
Ishiguchi mountain Japan medieval states 265 (3)
Ishika region South Asia world religions 242 (2)
Ishikawa var. Isikawa prefecture Japan economy 270 (1)
Isikawa see Ishikawa
Isipatana var. Sarnath South Asia (India) world religions 242 (3)
İskenderun see Alexandretta
Isla de Tenaspi archaeological site Central America (Mexico) first civilizations 121 (3)
Islamabad South Asia (Pakistan) post-war economy 253 (5) post-war politics 252 (1), (2)
Island see Iceland
I-ning see Kuldja
Islands region Greece ancient Greece 177 (2)
Ismailis dynasty Southwest Asia early Islam 57 (2)
Isna see Esna
Isonzo var. Soča river Italy WWI 207 (5)
Ispahan see Isfahan
Israel Heb. Yisrael, Yisra'el state Southwest Asia first civilizations 222 (1), (2) Islam 235 (4) the modern world 113 (3), (4) US economy 138 (2) 20th century 234 (2), (3) 20th-century politics 235 (5) see also Palestine
Issedon Scythia Central Asia ancient trade 44 (2)
Issedon Serica Central Asia ancient trade 44 (2)
Issiq Köl see Issyk-Kul
Issus battle Southwest Asia (Turkey) ancient Persia 223 (4) Hellenistic world 40–41 (1)
Issyk-Kul var. Issiq Köl, Kir. Ysyk-Köl, Issyk-kul', Ozero lake East Asia exploration 257 (3) first states 260 (1) Mongols 68–69 (1)
Istabl Antar Egypt ancient Egypt 159 (5)
Istanbul prev. Constantinople; anc. Byzantium; Bul. Tsarigrad Southwest Asia (Turkey) Cold War 108 (3) post-war politics 212 (3) WWI 233 (2) WWII 210 (1), 211 (4) see also Byzantium, Constantinople
Ister see Danube
Istra see Istria
Istria var. Istra coastal feature Southeast Europe WWI 207 (5)
Istrus Southeast Europe (Romania) first civilizations 177 (1) Hellenistic world 40–41 (1)
Isyaslavl state Eastern Europe medieval states 189 (4)
Itacclhatl mountain range Central America Aztecs 124 (2)
Italia province/state Italy Roman empire 179 (5), 180–181 (1), 181 (4), 225 (5)
Italiae region Italy ancient trade 44 (2)
Italian East Africa colonial possession East Africa WWII 104 (1)
Italian Somaliland colonial possession East Africa European imperialism 96 (1), 97 (4) WWII 104 (2)
Italian States state Italy early modern states 193 (4)
Italica Iberian Peninsula (Spain) Roman empire 180–181 (1)
Italy prev. Kingdom of Italy, It. Italia, Republica Italiana region/state Italy plague 72–73 (1) early 20th century 206 (1) early cultures 161 (2) early systems 223 (3) economy 205 (4) empire and revolution 202 (2) European imperialism 97 (4) exploration 172 (1) first civilizations 177 (1) first religions 37 (3) global immigration 100 (1) imperial global economy 92 (1) fascism 209 (3), (5) medieval states 187 (5) post-war economy 213 (5), 214 (1), (2), 215 (3) post-war politics 212 (1), (3) Soviet Union 213 (4) the modern world 112 (2), 113 (4) US superpower 138 (1) world religions 48 (1) WWI 207 (5), (6), 208 (1) WWII 104 (1), (2), 210 (1), 211 (2), (3), (4) Cold War 108 (3), 109 (1)
Italy, Kingdom of state Italy crusades 186 (1) medieval states 185 (3), 188 (1) Napoleon 201 (2)
Itanagar South Asia (India) post-war politics 252 (1)
Itanos Crete first civilizations 177 (1)
Itatín region South America colonization 148 (2) exploration 143 (2)
Itil Eastern Europe (Russian Federation) medieval voyages 60–61 (1)
Ituraea state Southwest Asia Roman empire 225 (4)
Itza state Central America Aztecs 124 (1)
Itztepetl Central America (Mexico) first civilizations 122 (1)
Itzyocan Central America (Mexico) colonization 125 (5)
Iuliobona France Roman empire 180–181 (1)
Iuny see Armant
Iuthungi people Central Europe Roman empire 181 (4)
Iuvavum Central Europe (Austria) Roman empire 180–181 (1)
Ivangorod Eastern Europe (Russian Federation) early modern states 195 (3)
Ivanovo Eastern Europe (Russian Federation) Soviet Union 208 (2)
Iviza see Ibiza
Ivory Coast Fr. Côte d'Ivoire state West Africa colonization 167 (4) decolonization 168 (1) economy 168 (2) European imperialism 96 (1) Islam 235 (4) the modern world 112 (1), 113 (3)
Ivrea Italy Franks 184 (2)
Iwate prefecture Japan economy 270 (1)
Iwo Eleru West Africa (Nigeria) early agriculture 158 (1)
Iwo Jima battle/island/military base Japan Cold War 109 (1) WWII 105 (3), 272 (1)
Ixcaquiztla Central America (Mexico) first civilizations 122 (1)
Ixcatec people Central America colonization 125 (4)
Ixhuacan Central America (Mexico) colonization 125 (5)
Ixhuatepec Central America (Mexico) Aztecs 124 (3)
Ixtacala Central America (Mexico) Aztecs 124 (3)
Ixtacalco Central America (Mexico) Aztecs 124 (3)
Ixtaccíhuatal, Volcán var. Volcano Iztac-Cihuate volcano Central America colonization 125 (5)
Ixtahuacan Central America (Mexico) first civilizations 122 (1)
Ixtapalapa Central America (Mexico) Aztecs 124 (2), (3)
Ixtapalucan Central America (Mexico) Aztecs 124 (2)

Ixtlán var. Ixtlán del Río Central America (Mexico) first civilizations 122 (1)
Ixtlán del Río see Ixtlan
Ixtlapalapan Central America (Mexico) colonization 125 (5)
Iya Japan early modern states 265 (5)
Izamal Central America (Mexico) first civilizations 122 (1), 123 (2)
Izapa archaeological site/settlement Central America (Mexico) first civilizations 121 (2)
Izawa Japan medieval states 265 (4)
Izborsk Est. Irboska Eastern Europe (Russian Federation) early modern states 195 (3) medieval states 185 (3)
İzmir see Smyrna
Izmit see Nicomedia
Iznik var. Nicaea Southwest Asia (Turkey) Ottomans 230 (1) see also Nicaea
Iztac-Cihuate, Volcano see Ixtaccihuatal, Volcán
Iztac-Maxtitlán Central America (Mexico) colonization 125 (5)
Iztahuacán Central America (Mexico) Aztecs 124 (2)
Iztapalapan Central America (Mexico) Aztecs 124 (2)
Izumo state Japan medieval states 264 (1)

J

Jabalpur prev. Jubbulpore South Asia (India) post-war economy 253 (5)
Jabbaren North Africa (Algeria) early agriculture 158 (1)
Jablanica Southeast Europe (Bosnia and Herzegovina) post-war economy 215 (3)
Jackson North America (Canada) cultural groups 123 (3)
Jackson North America (USA) the growth of the US 129 (2) US society 137 (6)
Jackson Bay whaling station New Zealand colonization 283 (4)
Jackson, Lake North America (USA) cultural groups 122 (5)
Jacksonville North America (USA) Cold War 108 (2) the growth of the US 129 (2) US Civil War 131 (6), (7)
Jadar river Southeast Europe WWI 207 (6)
Jaén Iberian Peninsula (Spain) economy 190 (1) Islam 192 (3)
Jaffa Southwest Asia (Israel) 20th century 234 (2) crusades 65 (3)
Jaffna South Asia (Sri Lanka) colonialism 247 (3), 248 (1) Mughal Empire 246 (1)
Jagannathapuram South Asia (India) colonialism 247 (3)
Jago Maritime Southeast Asia (Indonesia) world religions 243 (5)
Jailolo see Halmahera
Jaipur prev. Jeypore South Asia (India) colonialism 247 (3) economy 249 (4) post-war economy 253 (5) post-war politics 252 (1)
Jajce battle Southeast Europe (Hungary) early modern states 193 (4)
Jajnagar South Asia (India) early medieval states 244 (2), 244–245 (3)
Jakarta prev. Djakarta; Dut. Batavia Maritime Southeast Asia (Indonesia) early medieval states 245 (6) Islam 275 (5) post-war economy 253 (5), 275 (4) trade 230 (2) see also Batavia
Jaketown burial mound North America (USA) first civilizations 121 (4)
Jakobstadt Eastern Europe (Latvia) WWI 207 (4)
Jalalpur South Asia (Pakistan) colonialism 247 (3)
Jalilpur South Asia (Pakistan) the world in 2500 BCE 22–23
Jalisco state Central America Mexican Revolution 133 (3) the growth of the US 129 (2)
Jalula Southwest Asia (Iran) ancient Persia 225 (6)
Jamaica colonial possession/state/island West Indies colonization 125 (4), 126 (1) empire and revolution 150 (1) European expansion 84–85 (1), 85 (2) global immigration 100 (1), 101 (3) the growth of the US 129 (2) the modern world 112 (1), 136 (2), 139 (4) US superpower 138 (1) Cold War 108 (2), 109 (1)
Jamapa river North America colonization 125 (5)
Jambi var. Telanaipura; prev. Djambi Maritime Southeast Asia (Indonesia) colonialism 247 (4) world religions 243 (5)
Jambi var. Djambi region Maritime Southeast Asia colonialism 247 (4)
Jambukolapattana South Asia (India) early medieval states 244 (1) first empires 241 (4)
James Bay bay North America (Canada) colonization 126 (1) empire and revolution 127 (2)
James Island island West Africa empire and revolution 88 (1)
Jamestown North America (USA) colonization 126 (1) exploration 118 (1), 119 (2), (3)
Jamestown battle North America (USA) empire and revolution 127 (3)
Jammu region South Asia post-war politics 252 (2), 253 (4)
Jammu and Kashmir var. Jammu-Kashmir, Kashmir region/state South Asia colonialism 248 (2) post-war politics 252 (1), (2) see also Kashmir
Jammu-Kashmir see Jammu and Kashmir, Kashmir
Jamshedpur South Asia (India) post-war economy 253 (5)
Jämtland region Scandinavia early modern states 197 (3)
Jamuna see Brahmaputra
Janchou see Runzhou
Jand var. Jend South Asia (Pakistan) Mongols 68–69 (1)
Jankau battle Central Europe (Czech Republic) Reformation 196 (1)
Jan Mayen colonial possession/island Atlantic Ocean exploration 287 (2)
Jano people Central America colonization 126 (1)
Japan island group/state East Asia ancient trade 44–45 (1) Chinese revolution 271 (5) decolonization 251 (4) early agriculture 20 (1), 20–21 (2), 258 (1) early modern states 265 (5), 267 (4) empire and revolution 88–89 (2) European expansion 80–81 (1) exploration 257 (2) first cities 259 (5) global immigration 100 (1) global knowledge 77 (6) Islam 275 (4) medieval states 261 (6), 262–263 (1), 263 (6), 264 (2) Mongols 68–69 (1) Russo-Japanese War 270 (4) Sino-Japanese War 270 (3) Soviet Union 208 (2), 213 (4) the growth of the US 133 (4) the modern world 113 (4) trade 267 (3) US economy 138 (2) US superpower 138 (1) world religions 49 (4) WWII 104 (1), (2), 105 (4), 251 (3), 272 (1), 273 (2) Cold War 109 (1), (4) colonialism 269 (3), (4) Communism 271 (8)
Japanese people the world in 750 BCE 30–31 the world in 500 BCE 34–35 the world in 250 BCE 38–39
Japanese Empire state Japan the world in 1925 98–99
Japan, Sea of Jap. Nihon-kai sea East Asia ancient trade 44–45 (1), 72–73 (1) early agriculture 258 (1) early modern states 265 (5), 267 (4), (5) economy 270 (1) empire and revolution 268 (2) first humans 13 (2) first states 260 (1) imperialism 270 (2) medieval states 262–263 (1), 263 (6), 264 (1), (2), 265 (3), (4) Mongols 68 (2), 68–69 (1) Russo-Japanese War 270 (4) Sino-Japanese War 270 (3) trade 267 (3) world religions 49 (4) WWII 272 (1), 273 (2) Chinese revolution 271 (5) Cold War 109 (4) colonialism 269 (3), (4) Communism 273 (3)
Japurá var. Río Caquetá, Yapurá river South America early cultures 145 (2), 146 (1) see also Caquetá
Japurá, Rio see Caquetá
Jarmo Southwest Asia (Iraq) early agriculture 220 (1)
Jaroslavl see Yaroslavl'
Jarrow British Isles (United Kingdom) civil war 209 (3) medieval states 183 (3)
Jarvis Island island Pacific Ocean the modern world 110–111
Jassy Southeast Europe (Romania) Napoleon 200–201 (1) Ottomans 195 (4), 231 (3)
Jauari archaeological site South America (Brazil) early cultures 145 (2)
Jauf Ar. Al Jawf Southwest Asia (Saudi Arabia) 20th-century politics 233 (4) exploration 219 (4)
Jauja South America (Peru) Incas 147 (3), 148 (1)
Jaunpur South Asia (India) colonialism 247 (3)
Java island Maritime Southeast Asia ancient India 241 (6) ancient trade 44–45 (1), 72–73 (1) Bronze Age 240 (3) colonialism 247 (4) decolonization 251 (4) early agriculture 20–21 (2) early medieval states 245 (5), (6) European expansion 80–81 (1) European imperialism 97 (3), (4) exploration 239 (1), (2) first humans 13 (2) global immigration 101 (3) Islam 243 (6) Mongols 68 (1) post-war economy 253 (5) post-war politics 253 (4) trade 230 (2), 267 (3) world religions 243 (5), 49 (4) WWII 251 (3), 272 (1), 273 (2)
Java Sea Ind. Laut Jawa sea Maritime Southeast Asia ancient India 241 (6) ancient trade 44–45 (1) Bronze Age 240 (3) colonialism 247 (3), 248 (1) decolonization 251 (4) early medieval states 245 (5), (6) European imperialism 97 (3) exploration 239 (1), (2) Islam 243 (6) post-war economy 253 (5) post-war politics 253 (4) world religions 243 (5) WWII 251 (3), 272 (1), 273 (2)
Jawa see Java
Jawa, Laut see Java Sea
Jaxartes var. Sai Hun, Sir Darya, Syrdarya, Kaz. Syrdariya, Rus. Syrdar'ya, Uzb. Sirdaryo; mod. Syr Darya river Central Asia ancient Persia 225 (6) Roman empire 224 (2) ancient trade 44 (2) exploration 256 (1) Hellenistic world 224 (1), 41 (2) medieval states 261 (6) world religions 49 (3), (4) see also Syr Darya
Jayapura see Hollandia
Jay Dairen see Dairen, Dalian
Jaydebpur South Asia (Bangladesh) post-war politics 252 (3)
Jebeil see Byblos
Jebel, Bahr el see White Nile
Jebel Irhoud archaeological site North Africa (Morocco) first humans 13 (2)
Jedda Ar. Jiddah Southwest Asia (Saudi Arabia) trade 72–73 (1) early Islam 56–57 (1) exploration 156 (3), 218 (2), 219 (4) Islam 163 (1) medieval voyages 61 (3) Ottomans 231 (3) trade 230 (2), 267 (3) 20th-century politics 233 (4)
Jedisan vassal state Eastern Europe Ottomans 197 (4)
Jędrzejów monastery Central Europe medieval states 187 (3)
Jefferson City North America (USA) the growth of the US 129 (2)
Jehol region /province East Asia Chinese revolution 271 (5) imperialism 270 (2) post-war politics 271 (7)
Jelgava see Mitau, Mitava
Jemappes battle France empire and revolution 199 (4)
Jemdet Nasr Southwest Asia (Iraq) first cities 220 (2)
Jena Central Europe (Germany) empire and revolution 199 (3)
Jena Auerstädt mod. Auerstedt battle Central Europe (Germany) Napoleon 200–201 (1)
Jend see Jand
Jenderam Hilir archaeological site Mainland Southeast Asia (Malaysia) Bronze Age 240 (3)
Jenne var. Jenné; Fr. Djenné archaeological site/settlement West Africa (Mali) ancient trade 44–45 (1) crusades 65 (1) early cultures 160 (1) economy 163 (2) Islam 163 (1), 167 (3) exploration 68 (2) trade 163 (5)
Jenne state West Africa trade 163 (6)
Jenne-jeno West Africa (Mali) the world in 250 BCE 38–39
Jérémie West Indies (Haiti) empire and revolution 89 (3)
Jerez Iberian Peninsula (Spain) economy 190 (1) Islam 192 (3)
Jerez de la Frontera battle Iberian Peninsula (Spain) Islam 226 (2)
Jericho Ar. Arīḥā, Heb. Yeriḥo Southwest Asia (Israel) Roman empire 225 (4) early agriculture 220 (1) first cities 220 (2) first civilizations 221 (5), 222 (1) Islam 226 (2) 20th century 234 (2)
Jerusalem Ar. Al Quds, Al Quds ash Sharif, Heb. Yerushalayim, anc. Hierosolyma Southwest Asia (Israel) politics 233 (3), (4), 235 (5) ancient Egypt 159 (4), (5) ancient Persia 223 (4), 225 (6) Roman empire 180–181 (1), 224 (2), 225 (4), (5) ancient trade 44–45 (1) crusades 228 (2), 65 (1), (3) early Islam 56–57 (1), 57 (2) early trade 225 (3) economy 190 (1) exploration 156 (3), 218 (2), 219 (3), (4) first civilizations 221 (5), 222 (1), (2) first religions 36 (1), 37 (3) Hellenistic world 224 (1) Islam 163 (1), 226 (2), 227 (5) medieval states 185 (3), 187 (5) Mamluks 229 (3), 68 (2), 68–69 (1) Napoleon 200–201 (1) Ottomans 232–233 (1) Seljuks 228 (1) the world in 1 CE 42–43 world religions 48 (1), 49 (4) WWI 233 (2) 20th century 234 (2) 20th-century
Jerusalem, Kingdom of state Southwest Asia crusades 228 (2), 65 (3) medieval states 187 (5)
Jervaulx major cistercian house British Isles (United Kingdom) medieval states 187 (3)
Jesmond British Isles (United Kingdom) economy 204 (3)
Jessore South Asia (Bangladesh) post-war politics 252 (3)
Jeypore see Jaipur
Jhajjar state South Asia empire and revolution 249 (3)
Jhansi battle South Asia empire and revolution 249 (3)
Jharkhand region/state South Asia early medieval states 244–245 (3) Mughal Empire 246 (1)
Jhelum river South Asia Mughal Empire 246 (1)
Ji East Asia (China) first cities 259 (4), (5) first religions 37 (4)
Ji see Jilin, Kirin
Ji'an East Asia (China) medieval states 263 (7)
Jianchang military base East Asia (China) early modern states 266 (1)
Jiangling East Asia (China) medieval states 263 (4) Mongols 68–69 (1) world religions 49 (3)
Jiangnan Xidao var. Chiangnan Hsitao province Central Asia medieval states 262–263 (1)
Jiangning East Asia (China) medieval states 263 (4), (5)
Jiangou archaeological site East Asia early agriculture 258 (2)
Jiangsu var. Chiang-su, Kiangsu, Su province/region East Asia Chinese revolution 271 (5) early modern states 266 (1) empire and revolution 268 (2) post-war politics 271 (7), 274 (2)
Jiangxi var. Chiang-hsi, Gan, Kiangsi province East Asia Chinese revolution 271 (5) early modern states 266 (1), (2), 268 (1) empire and revolution 268 (2) medieval states 263 (6) post-war politics 271 (7), 274 (2)
Jiangxia province East Asia first states 260 (1)
Jiangzhai archaeological site East Asia early agriculture 258 (1)
Jiangzhe province East Asia medieval states 263 (6)
Jiankang Wg. Chien-k'ang Buddhist centre/settlement East Asia (China) first states 261 (2), (3) medieval states 261 (4), (5) world religions 49 (3)
Jiannan var. Chien-nan province Central Asia medieval states 262–263 (1)
Jianning military base East Asia (China) early modern states 266 (1)
Jianwei province East Asia first states 260 (1)
Jianye var. Chien-yeh, Nan-ching, Nanking; mod. Nanjing; prev. Chianning, Chian-ning, Kiang-ning East Asia (China) the world in 250 CE 46–47 see also Nanjing
Jianzhong var. Chien-chung province Central Asia medieval states 262–263 (1)
Jiaohei East Asia (China) ancient trade 44–45 (1)
Jiaoli East Asia (China) first states 260 (1)
Jiaozhi province East Asia first states 260 (1)
Jiaozhou East Asia (China) early modern states 266 (1) the world in 1900 94–95
Jibannagar South Asia (Bangladesh) post-war politics 252 (3)
Jibuti see Djibouti
Jicarilla Apache people North America colonization 125 (4)
Jiddah see Jedda
Jih-k'a-tse see Shigatse
Jihlava Ger. Iglau, Pol. Igława Central Europe (Czech Republic) economy 190 (1)
Jilin var. Chi-lin, Girin, Kirin; prev. Yungki, Yunki East Asia (China) Russo-Japanese War 270 (4)
Jilin battle East Asia (China) economy 274 (1)
Jilin province East Asia post-war politics 274 (2)
Jiménez Central America (Mexico) Mexican Revolution 133 (3)
Jimo East Asia (China) first cities 259 (5)
Jin state East Asia first cities 259 (4) medieval states 263 (5) Mongols 68–69 (1)
Jinan var. Chinan, Chi-nan, Tsinan East Asia (China) early modern states 266 (1) economy 274 (1) Islam 275 (4) Mongols 68–69 (1) post-war politics 271 (7)
Jinchang var. Chin-ch'ang East Asia (China) exploration 256 (1)
Jincheng province East Asia first states 260 (1)
Jinchuan var. Chin-ch'uan rebellion East Asia empire and revolution 268 (2)
Jingji var. Ching-chi province East Asia medieval states 262–263 (1)
Jingyuan see Ningbo
Jingzhou rebellion/settlement East Asia (China) early modern states 266 (2) medieval states 263 (4)
Jinji South Asia (India) early medieval states 245 (4)
Jinmen Dao see Quemoy
Jinsen see Inchon
Jin Shui river East Asia first cities 29 (4)
Jintian var. Chin-t'ien East Asia (China) empire and revolution 268 (2)
Jinyang East Asia (China) first cities 259 (5) first religions 37 (4)
Jinzhou East Asia (China) economy 274 (1)
Jiuchuan province East Asia first states 260 (1)
Jiujiang var. Kiukiang East Asia (China) colonialism 269 (4)
Jiuzhang province East Asia first states 260 (1)
Jiuzhen province Mainland Southeast Asia first states 260 (1)
Jizan state Southwest Asia the world in 1500 74–75
Jizhou var. Chi-chou East Asia (China) medieval states 262–263 (1)
Joal mod. Joal-Fadiout West Africa (Senegal) the world in 1800 86–87
Joal-Fadiout see Joal
João Pessoa see Paraíba
Jo'burg see Johannesburg
Jocome people Central America colonization 126 (1)
Johannesburg var. Egoli, Erautini, Gauteng, abbrev. Jo'burg Southern Africa (South Africa) colonization 166 (2), 167 (4) economy 168 (2) European imperialism 96 (2) imperial global economy 92 (1)
Johnston Atoll colonial possession/island Pacific Ocean decolonization 285 (3) nuclear test 285 (2) WWII 104 (1)
Johor see Johore
Johore var. Johor, Johore, Sultanate of region/state Maritime Southeast Asia colonialism 247 (4)
Johore-Riau state Maritime Southeast Asia the world in 1800 86–87
Jolof state West Africa the world in 1000 58–59 the world in 1200 62–63
Jomsborg var. Julin, Jumneta, Jomsburg Central Europe (Poland) medieval voyages 60–61 (1)
Jomsburg see Jomsborg
Jonaz people Central America colonization 125 (4), 126 (1)
Jordan Ar. Al Urdunn; prev. Transjordan state Southwest Asia Islam 235 (4) the modern world 113 (3) US economy 138 (2) 20th century 234 (2) 20th-century politics 235 (5) see also Transjordan
Jordan Ar. Urdunn, Heb. HaYarden river Southwest Asia 20th century 234 (2) 20th-century politics 233 (3) Roman empire 225 (4) crusades 65 (3) early agriculture 220 (1) first civilizations 222 (1)
Jotapata Southwest Asia (Israel) Roman empire 225 (4)
Jova people Central America colonization 125 (4)
Ju East Asia (China) first cities 259 (5)
Juan Fernández Islands Sp. Islas Juan Fernández island group South America exploration 278 (1) the modern world 110–111
Juan-juan see Ruanruan, Kingdom of the
Juba var. Jūbā East Africa (Sudan) ancient trade 44–45 (1) exploration 157 (5) Islam 163 (1)
Juba Amh. Genalē Wenz, It. Giuba, Som. Ganaane, Webi Jubba river East Africa early cultures 160 (1)
Jubayl see Byblos
Jubba, Webi see Juba
Jubbulpore see Jabalpur
Jubeil see Byblos
Judaea var. Palaestina province/region/state Southwest Asia Roman empire 180–181 (1), 225 (4), (5) first religions 37 (3)
Judah region/state Southwest Asia first civilizations 222 (1), (2) first religions 36 (1)
Jujuy South America (Argentina) empire and revolution 151 (3) politics 151 (4)
Jukun state West Africa slave trade 165 (4) trade 164 (2)
Juli South America (Peru) Incas 147 (3)
Julia Beterrae see Béziers
Julian Alps Ger. Julische Alpen, It. Alpi Giulie, Slvn. Julijske Alpe mountain range Southeast Europe WWI 207 (5)
Julianehaab var. Qaqortoq, Brattahlid, Julianehåb North America (Greenland) WWII 104 (2) see also Brattahlid
Julianehåb see Brattahlid, Julianehaab
Julijske Alpe see Julian Alps
Julin see Jomsborg
Juliomagus mod. Angers France Roman empire 180–181 (1) see also Angers
Julische Alpen see Julian Alps
Jullundur South Asia (India) economy 249 (4)
Julu East Asia (China) first states 260 (1)
Jumano people Central America colonization 125 (4), 126 (1)
Jumbe state Southern Africa colonization 167 (4)
Jummoo see Jammu
Jumneta see Jomsborg
Junagadh var. Junagarh physical region South Asia post-war politics 252 (1)
Junagarh var. Jūnāgadh South Asia (India) colonialism 248 (1)
Juneau North America (USA) imperial global economy 93 (3) the growth of the US 129 (2), 132 (1)
Junejo-Daro archaeological site South Asia (Pakistan) first cities 240 (2)
Jungernhof concentration camp Eastern Europe (Latvia) WWII 211 (3)
Junín battle South America (Peru) empire and revolution 150 (1), 88–89 (2)
Junkseylon see Phuket
Junnar South Asia (India) Mughal Empire 246 (1)
Jupiter, Temple of building Italy Roman empire 181 (2)
Jurchen people Siberia medieval states 263 (5) trade 267 (3)
Juruá var. Río Yuruá river South America colonization 149 (3) early cultures 144 (1), 145 (2), (4), 146 (1) economy 153 (3) environment 153 (4) Incas 147 (3), 148 (1) politics 152 (1)
Jutes people British Isles/Scandinavia great migrations 53 (2)
Juvavum see Salzburg
Juxtlahuaca Cave Central America (Mexico) first civilizations 121 (2)
Juyan East Asia (China) first states 260 (1)
Juyang East Asia (China) first cities 259 (5) first religions 37 (4)
Južna Morava Ger. Südliche Morava river Central Europe post-war economy 215 (3)
Jysan state Southwest Asia Islam 163 (1)

Kaabu state West Africa slave trade 165 (4) trade 164 (2)
Kaapstad see Cape Town
Kaarta state West Africa slave trade 165 (4) trade 167 (1)
Kabáh Central America (Mexico) first civilizations 122 (2)
Kabamba state Central Africa economy 163 (2)
Kabaregas East Africa (Uganda) exploration 157 (5)
Kabi var. Kebbi state West Africa slave trade 165 (4) trade 164 (2)
Kabinda see Cabinda
Kabul Central Asia (Afghanistan) ancient India 242 (1) ancient Persia 225 (6) trade 72–73 (1) colonialism 248 (1), 269 (3), (4) early Islam 56–57 (1), 57 (2) early medieval states 244 (2), 244–245 (3) exploration 218 (2) Islam 226 (2), 227 (4), (5), 235 (4) Mongols 68–69 (1) Mughal Empire 246 (1) Ottomans 232–233 (1) post-war economy 253 (5) post-war politics 252 (1) Timur 229 (4) world religions 226 (1), 49 (3) WWII 251 (3) Communism 271 (8)
Kabul state Central Asia Mughal Empire 246 (1)
Kabul var. Daryā-ye Kābul river Central Asia colonialism 247 (3), 248 (1) early medieval states 244 (1), (2), 244–245 (3) first cities 240 (2) Mughal Empire 246 (1) world religions 242 (2), 243 (4)
Kābul, Daryā-ye see Kabul
Kabwe archaeological site East Africa eary humans 13 (2)
Kach var. Kutch state South Asia Mughal Empire 246 (1)
Kachchh, Gulf of var. Gulf of Cutch, Gulf of Kutch gulf South Asia first cities 240 (2)
Kachchh, Rann of see Kutch, Rann of
Kachiya region South Asia world religions 242 (2)
Kadambas dynasty South Asia Mongols 68–69 (1)
Kadaram Mainland Southeast Asia (Malaysia) ancient India 241 (6)
Kadero East Africa (Sudan) early agriculture 158 (1)
Kadesh Southwest Asia first civilizations 221 (5), 222 (1)
Kadesh battle Southwest Asia ancient Egypt 159 (5)
Kadiri Maritime Southeast Asia (Indonesia) early medieval states 245 (5)
Kadranj East Asia (China) medieval voyages 61 (3)
Kaduna Central Africa (Nigeria) economy 168 (2)
Kaédi West Africa (Mauritania) colonization 167 (4)
Kaekyong East Asia (Korea) medieval states 263 (6)
Kaesong East Asia (North Korea) early modern states 265 (5), 267 (4) Mongols 68–69 (1) world religions 49 (3)
Kaffa var. Kefe, Caffa; mod. Feodosiya; anc. Theodosia Eastern Europe (Ukraine) biological diffusion 72–73 (1) economy 190 (1) Ottomans 195 (4), 230 (1), 231 (3) Timur 229 (4) see also Theodosia
Kaffa state East Africa trade 167 (1)
Kafiavana New Guinea (Papua New Guinea) exploration 280 (1)
Kafue river West Africa exploration 157 (4)
Kagawa prefecture Japan economy 270 (1)
Kagoshima var. Kagosima Japan economy 270 (1)
Kagoshima var. Kagosima prefecture Japan economy 270 (1)
Kagosima see Kagoshima
Kaiapoi New Zealand colonization 283 (4)
Kaifeng var. Bian East Asia (China) ancient trade 44–45 (1), 72–73 (1) empire and revolution 268 (2) exploration 256 (1) first religions 37 (4) medieval states 263 (3), (4), (6) Mongols 68–69 (1) trade 267 (3) early modern states 266 (1) economy 274 (1) medieval states 263 (4)
Kai Islands island group Maritime Southeast Asia Islam 243 (6) post-war politics 253 (4)
Kai Kepulauan see Kai Islands
Kaikoura settlement/whaling station New Zealand colonization 283 (4), (5)
Kailasha East Asia (China) world religions 243 (4)
Kainei see Hoeryong
Kaira region South Asia decolonization 250 (1)
Kairouan var. Al Qayrawān North Africa (Tunisia) crusades 65 (1) early Islam 56–57 (1), 57 (2) economy 190 (1) Islam 226 (2), 227 (4) medieval states 185 (3)
Kaiser Wilhelm's Land colonial possession New Guinea the world in 1900 94–95, 284–285 (1) see also German New Guinea
Kajangala South Asia (India) world religions 242 (3)
Kakatiyas dynasty South Asia early medieval states 244 (2), 244–245 (3) Mongols 68–69 (1)
Kakimbon West Africa (Guinea) early agriculture 158 (1)
Kakonda state Southern Africa the world in 1800 86–87 the world in 1850 90–91
Kakongo state Central Africa Islam 163 (1) trade 164 (2)
Kalabar see Calabar
Kalabhras dynasty South Asia the world in 500 CE 50–51
Kalacuris dynasty South Asia the world in 1000 58–59
Kaladi South Asia (India) world religions 243 (4)
Kalahari Desert desert Southern Africa early agriculture 158 (1), 20–21 (2) early cultures 160 (1) economy 163 (2) European expansion 84–85 (1) first humans 12 (1) slave trade 165 (4)
Kalam state West Africa trade 164 (2)
Kalambo Falls archaeological site/settlement East Africa (Tanzania) early agriculture 158 (1) early cultures 160 (1)
Kalanjar South Asia (India) early medieval states 244 (2)
Kalat South Asia (Pakistan) colonialism 248 (1)
Kalewa battle Mainland Southeast Asia (Burma) WWII 104 (2)
Kalgan Hall Australia exploration 280 (1)
Kalgoorlie Australia colonization 282 (1), 283 (3)
Kalhat var. Qalhat Southwest Asia (Oman) trade 230 (2)
Kaliakra Southeast Europe (Bulgaria) medieval states 189 (4)
Kalibangan archaeological site/settlement South Asia (India) first cities 240 (2) first civilizations 24 (2)
Kalikod var. Qalqut; mod. Calicut, Kozhikode South Asia (India) early medieval states 245 (4) see also Calicut, Qalqut
Kalinga region/state South Asia early religions 48 (2) first empires 241 (4), (5) world religions 242 (2)
Kalinganagara South Asia (India) early medieval states 244 (1), (2)
Kalinin see Tver'
Kaliningrad Eastern Europe (Russian Federation) Soviet Union 213 (4)
Kalisch anc. Calisia; Pol. Kalisz, Rus. Kalish Central Europe (Poland) empire and revolution 199 (3) see also Kalish
Kalish anc. Calisia; Ger, Kalisch, Pol. Kalisz Central Europe (Poland) WWI 207 (4) see also Kalisch
Kalisz see Kalisch, Kalish
Kalka battle/settlement Eastern Europe (Ukraine) Mongols 68–69 (1)
Kalleh Nisar Southwest Asia (Iran) first civilizations 24 (3)
Kalmar Scandinavia (Sweden) medieval states 189 (3)
Kalmykia region/state Eastern Europe early modern states 268 (1) Soviet Union 214–215 (4)
Kalmyks people Central Asia early modern states 268 (1) Soviet Union 213 (4) trade 267 (3)
Kalocsa Central Europe (Hungary) medieval states 185 (3)
Kalonga state Southern Africa slave trade 165 (4) trade 164 (1)
Kalpi battle South Asia empire and revolution 249 (3)
Kaluga Eastern Europe (Russian Federation) Soviet Union 208 (2)
Kalunde state Central Africa the world in 1700 82–83 the world in 1800 86–87 the world in 1850 90–91
Kalundu archaeological site Southern Africa (Zambia) early cultures 160 (1)
Kalyani South Asia (India) early medieval states 244 (2)
Kalyani, Chalukyas of dynasty South Asia early medieval states 244 (2)
Kamabai West Africa (Sierra Leone) early agriculture 158 (1)
Kamaishi bomb target Japan WWII 273 (3)
Kamakatsu Japan medieval states 263 (6)
Kamakura Japan early modern states 267 (4) medieval states 265 (4)
Kamalpur South Asia (Bangladesh) post-war politics 252 (3)
Kamba people East Africa trade 167 (1)
Kamboja region South Asia ancient India 242 (1) first religions 36 (2) world religions 242 (2)
Kambryk see Cambrai
Kambujadesha mod. Cambodia; prev. Chenla, Funan; later Khmer state Mainland Southeast Asia early medieval states 245 (5) see also Cambodia, Chenla, Funan, Khmer
Kamchatka Russ. Kamchatka, Poluostrov region Siberia colonialism 269 (3) early agriculture 258 (1) exploration 257 (2) medieval states 262–263 (1) WWII 272 (1), 273 (2)
Kamenets var. Kamyanyets Eastern Europe (Russian Federation) Mongols 68–69 (1)
Kamerun colonial possession Central Africa the world in 1900 94–95
Kami-Kuroiwa archaeological site/settlement Japan early agriculture 20 (1)
Kaminaljuyú Central America (Guatemala) first civilizations 121 (2)
Kamnama archaeological site Southern Africa (Malawi) early cultures 160 (1)
Kampala East Africa (Uganda) colonization 167 (4) economy 168 (2) exploration 157 (4), (5)
Kampe state Maritime Southeast Asia ancient India 241 (6)
Kampen Low Countries (Netherlands) economy 190 (1)
Kamperduin see Camperdown
Kampilya South Asia (India) world religions 242 (3)
Kampoi hominid site Africa first humans 12 (1)
Kampuchea see Cambodia
Kamyanyets see Kamenets
Kanagawa prefecture Japan economy 270 (1)
Kanaky see New Caledonia
Kananga prev. Luluabourg Central Africa (Congo (Zaire)) economy 168 (2)
Kananur see Cannanore
Kanara var. Karnātaka, prev. Maisur, Mysore region South Asia colonialism 247 (3) see also Karnātaka, Mysore
Kanauj var. Karnnauj South Asia (India) early religions 48 (2) first religions 36 (2) world religions 49 (3)
Kanazawa Japan economy 270 (1)
Kanchi South Asia (India) world religions 242 (2)
Kanchipuram Buddhist centre/settlement South Asia (India) early medieval states 244 (1), (2) early religions 48 (2) exploration 256 (1) first empires 241 (4) world religions 49 (3)
Kan-chou state East Asia medieval states 263 (3)
Kanchou see Ganzhou
Kandahar South Asia (Pakistan) ancient trade 44–45 (1)
Kandahar var. Kandahār, Per. Qandahār, Qandhar Central Asia (Afghanistan) ancient Persia 223 (4) colonialism 247 (3), 248 (1) early Islam 56–57 (1) Islam 227 (4) medieval Persia 231 (4) Timur 229 (4) see also Qandhar
Kandana Southern Africa (Zambia) early agriculture 158 (1)
Kandiaro South Asia (Pakistan) colonialism 247 (3)
Kandrian island Pacific Ocean early cultures 280–281 (3) medieval voyages 60 (2)
Kandy South Asia (Sri Lanka) colonialism 248 (1) decolonization 250 (1) economy 249 (4) world religions 49 (3) WWII 251 (3)
Kandy, Kingdom of state South Asia colonialism 248 (1)
Kane County region North America
Kanem var. Kaneu state West Africa colonization 167 (4) economy 163 (2)
Kanem-Bornu state Central Africa Islam 163 (1)
Kanesh mod. Kültepe Southwest Asia (Turkey) early systems 223 (3) first cities 220 (2), 28–29 (1) first civilizations 221 (4), (5) see also Kultepe
Kaneu see Kanem
Kangeq North America (Greenland) cultural groups 123 (3)
Kanggye East Asia (North Korea) Cold War 109 (4)
Kangju region East Asia medieval states 264 (2)
Kangra state South Asia Mughal Empire 246 (1)
Kaniok state Central Africa the world in 1800 86–87 the world in 1850 90–91
Kanior state Central Africa the world in 1700 82–83
Kannanur var. Vikrampura South Asia (India) early medieval states 244 (2)
Kannauj see Kanauj
Kannur see Cannanore
Kano Central Africa (Nigeria) colonization 167 (4) economy 163 (2) exploration 157 (4) Islam 163 (1), 167 (3)
Kano state West Africa slave trade 165 (4) trade 164 (2)
Kānpur see Cawnpore
Kansa people North America colonization 126 (1)
Kansas state North America the growth of the US 129 (1) US Civil War 130 (5) US economy 134 (2)
Kansas river North America cultural groups 122 (5) first civilizations 121 (4)
Kansas City North America (USA) exploration 119 (3) first civilizations 121 (4) the growth of the US 132 (1) US economy 134 (1)
Kansas Territory region North America US Civil War 130 (3), (4), (5)
Kansu see Gansu
Kantipur see Kathmandu
Kantō see Kwantung
Kan-t'o-li see Gantoli
Kanyakubja South Asia (India) early medieval states 244 (1), (2) world religions 242 (2), (3)
Kanya Kumari South Asia (India) world religions 243 (4)
Kaolan see Lanzhou
Kao-li state East Asia medieval states 263 (3), (4)
Kapilavastu var. Kapilavatthu South Asia (India) early religions 48 (2) first empires 241 (4) first religions 36 (2) see also Kapilavatthu
Kapilavatthu var. Kapilavastu South Asia world religions 242 (3) see also Kapilavastu
Kapisa mod. Begram; var. Alexandria ad Caucasum Central Asia (Afghanistan) 45 (1) early medieval states 244 (1)
Kapishi South Asia (Pakistan) first empires 241 (4)
Kapiti Island whaling station New Zealand colonization 283 (4)
Kapstad see Cape Town
Kapwirimbwe archaeological site Southern Africa (Zambia) early cultures 160 (1)
Karabakh see Qarabagh
Kara Balgasun East Asia (China) the world in 750 CE 54–55
Karachay people Eastern Europe Soviet Union 213 (4)
Karachay-Cherkessia state Eastern Europe Soviet Union 214–215 (4)
Karachi var. Karāchi South Asia (Pakistan) decolonization 250 (1) economy 249 (4) exploration 239 (1) imperial global economy 93 (5) post-war economy 253 (5) post-war politics 252 (1) US superpower 138 (1)
Karadeniz see Black Sea
Karafuto colonial possession Siberia imperialism 270 (2)
Karaganda archaeological site/settlement Central Asia (Kazakhstan) early agriculture 258 (1) Soviet Union 214–215 (4)
Karagwe state East Africa colonization 167 (4)
Karahüyük Southwest Asia (Turkey) first cities 28–29 (1)
Kara-Indash Temple temple Southwest Asia (Iraq) first cities 220 (3)
Karakhanids var. Qarakhanids people/state Central Asia Islam 227 (5) Seljuks 228 (1) see also Qarakhanids
Kara Khitai Empire state Central Asia/East Asia the world in 1200 62–63
Karakol var. Przheval'sk Central Asia (Kyrgyzstan) exploration 257 (3)
Karakoram Range mountain range Central Asia first empires 241 (4)
Karakorum East Asia (Mongolia) trade 72–73 (1) exploration 257 (3) medieval states 262–263 (1), 263 (6) Mongols 68–69 (1) the world in 1300 66–67
Karakotas dynasty South Asia the world in 750 CE 54–55
Karakum desert Central Asia early Islam 56–57 (1)
Karaman Southwest Asia (Turkey) first civilizations 221 (4)
Karanbas South Asia (India) colonialism 247 (3)
Karankawa people North America colonization 125 (4), 126 (1)
Karanovo archaeological site/settlement Southeast Europe (Bulgaria) Copper Age 174 (2) early agriculture 174 (1)
Kara Sea sea Arctic Ocean exploration 257 (2), 286 (1), 287 (2)
Karaskara region South Asia world religions 242 (2)
Karasuk archaeological site/settlement Siberia (Russian Federation) early agriculture 258 (1)
Kara-Ukok archaeological site Central Asia (Kazakhstan) early agriculture 258 (1)
Karelia region/state Eastern Europe early modern states 197 (3) post-war politics 212 (3) Soviet Union 213 (4) WWII 211 (2)
Karenni state Mainland Southeast Asia colonialism 248 (2)
Karepuna people South America the world in 1500 74–75
Karfreit see Caporetto
Karg see Kharg Island
Kargil South Asia post-war politics 252 (2)
Kariba Southern Africa (Zimbabwe) exploration 157 (4)
Karikal colonial possession/settlement South Asia colonialism 247 (3), 269 (4) decolonization 251 (4) empire and revolution 88 (1), 88–89 (2) post-war politics 252 (1) WWII 251 (3)
Karimganj South Asia (India) post-war politics 252 (3)
Karipuna people South America early cultures 147 (2)
Karkarichinkat West Africa (Mali) early agriculture 158 (1)
Karkheh river Southwest Asia first cities 220 (2) first civilizations 221 (4)
Karkotas dynasty South Asia early medieval states 244 (2)
Karkūk see Kirkuk
Karlag region Siberia Soviet Union 213 (4)
Karle Buddhist centre South Asia (India) world religions 49 (3)
Karlovac Ger. Karlstadt, Hung. Károlyváros Southeast Europe (Croatia) post-war economy 215 (3)
Karlsburg see Apulum, Gyulafehérvár
Karlsruhe var. Carlsruhe Central Europe (Germany) empire and revolution 202 (2) WWI 206 (3)
Karlstadt see Karlovac
Karmana Central Asia (Uzbekistan) ancient trade 44 (2)
Karmi Cyprus ancient Egypt 159 (5)
Karnak part of Thebes var. Ipet-isut Egypt ancient Egypt 159 (4) see also Thebes, Luxor
Karnapravarana state South Asia first empires 241 (5)
Karnata region South Asia early religions 48 (2) world religions 242 (2)
Karnataka region/state South Asia post-war politics 252 (1), 253 (4) world religions 243 (4)
Károly-Fehérvár see Apulum, Gyulafehérvár
Károlyváros see Karlovac
Karpathos see Scarpanto
Karri var. El Khartûm, Khartoum, Khartum East Africa (Sudan) Islam 163 (1) see also Khartoum
Kars var. Qars Southwest Asia (Turkey) medieval Persia 231 (4) Ottomans 231 (3) Soviet Union 208 (2) WWI 233 (2) 20th-century politics 233 (3)
Karst var. Kras; It. Carso physical region Southeast Europe WWI 207 (5)
Karusha state South Asia first empires 241 (5)
Karwar South Asia (India) colonialism 247 (3)
Kasai var. Cassai, Kassai river Central Africa early cultures 160 (1) exploration 157 (4) trade 164 (2)
Kasanje state Southern Africa slave trade 165 (4) trade 167 (1)
Kaschau see Kassa
Kashgar Buddhist centre/settlement East Asia (China) ancient trade 44–45 (1) trade 72–73 (1) colonialism 248 (1) early modern states 268 (1) empire

and revolution 268 (2) exploration 256 (1) first states 260 (1) medieval states 261 (6), 262–263 (1) Mongols 68–69 (1) trade 267 (3) world religions 49 (3)
Kashgar, Khanate of state East Asia trade 267 (3)
Kashi *Chin.* Kaxgar, K'o-shih, Uigh see Varanasi region/settlement East Asia (China) early medieval states 244 (2) world religions 242 (2)
Kashir see Kashgar
Kashi/Varanasi *var.* Baranasi; *Eng.* Benares South Asia (India) world religions 243 (4)
Kashmir region/state South Asia decolonization 251 (4) early medieval states 244–245 (3) empire and revolution 249 (3) exploration 257 (3) Mongols 68–69 (1) Mughal Empire 246 (1) post-war politics 252 (2), 253 (4) Soviet Union 213 (4) trade 267 (3) world religions 243 (4), 49 (3)
Kashmira region South Asia world religions 242 (2)
Kasi *mod.* Vārānasi, *var.* Kashi South Asia (India) early religions 48 (2)
Kasi region/state South Asia first empires 241 (5) first religions 36 (2)
Kaska people North America cultural groups 123 (3)
Kaskaskia North America (USA) empire and revolution 127 (3)
Kaspiyskoye More see Caspian Sea
Kaspiy Tengizi see Caspian Sea
Kassa *var.* Kovsice; *Ger.* Kaschau; *mod.* Košice Central Europe (Slovakia) early modern states 193 (4)
Kassai see Kasai
Kassala East Africa (Sudan) early cultures 161 (4), (5)
Kassel *prev.* Cassel Central Europe (Germany) early modern states 193 (4)
Kassites people Southwest Asia first civilizations 221 (4)
Katagum Central Africa (Nigeria) Islam 167 (3)
Kataha East Asia (China) medieval voyages 61 (3)
Katak *mod.* Cuttack South Asia (India) Mughal Empire 246 (1) see also Cuttack
Kataka South Asia (India) early medieval states 244 (2), 244–245 (3)
Katanga region Central Africa Cold War 109 (1) politics 169 (4)
Katarpur South Asia (India) decolonization 250 (1)
Katehar region South Asia early medieval states 244–245 (3)
Katherine Australia colonization 282 (1)
Kathiawar state South Asia Mughal Empire 246 (1)
Kathio North America (USA) cultural groups 122 (5)
Kathmandu *prev.* Kantipur South Asia (Nepal) colonialism 248 (1) early medieval states 244–245 (3) early modern states 268 (1) exploration 257 (3) post-war economy 253 (5) post-war politics 252 (1) WWII 251 (3)
Katiki, Volcán mountain Pacific Ocean early cultures 281 (4)
Katima Mulilo Southern Africa (Namibia) exploration 157 (4)
Katombela *mod.* Catambela Southern Africa (Angola) exploration 157 (4)
Katpatuka see Cappadocia
Katsina Central Africa (Nigeria) economy 168 (2) exploration 157 (4) Islam 163 (1), 167 (3)
Katsina state West Africa slave trade 165 (4) trade 164 (2)
Kattegat *Dan.* Kattegatt sea waterway Scandinavia early modern states 197 (3)
Kattegatt see Kattegat
Kattura South Asia (India) early religions 48 (2)
Katuruka archaeological site East Africa (Tanzania) early cultures 160 (1)
Katyn massacre Eastern Europe WWII 211 (3)
Kauen see Kaunas, Kovno
Kaunas *prev. Rus.* Kovno; *Ger.* Kauen, *Pol.* Kowno Eastern Europe (Lithuania) early modern states 195 (3) WWII 211 (3) see also Kovno
Kaupang Scandinavia (Norway) medieval voyages 60–61 (1)
Kaushambi South Asia (India) first religions 36 (2) world religions 242 (3)
Kauthara Mainland Southeast Asia (Vietnam) ancient India 241 (6)
Kavalla Greece WWI 207 (6)
Kavat Central Asia (Turkmenistan) the world in 2500 BCE 22–23
Kaveri *var.* Cauvery river South Asia colonialism 247 (3) decolonization 250 (1) early medieval states 244 (2), 244–245 (3), 245 (4) economy 249 (4) first empires 241 (4), (5) first religions 36 (2) Marathas 246 (2) post-war politics 252 (1) world religions 242 (2), 243 (4)
Kavik North America (USA) cultural groups 123 (3)
Kavkaz see Caucasus
Kawa East Africa (Sudan) ancient Egypt 159 (5) early cultures 160 (1)
Kawasaki bomb target Japan WWII 273 (3)
Kawhia New Zealand colonization 283 (4)
Kawkau *mod.* Songhay state West Africa trade 163 (4)
Kawthule State see Kaya
Kaxgar see Kashgar, Kashi
Kaya *Jap.* Mimana East Asia (Korea) medieval states 264 (1)
Kaya *var.* Kawthule State, Kayin State state East Asia medieval states 264 (1)
Kayalapattinam *var.* Punneikayal, Kayalpatnam South Asia (India) colonialism 247 (3) world religions 243 (4)
Kayankulam South Asia (India) colonialism 247 (3)
Kayapo people South America early cultures 147 (2)
Kayenta archaeological site North America (USA) cultural groups 123 (4)
Kayes West Africa (Mali) colonization 167 (4)
Kayin State see Kaya
Kayor state West Africa trade 164 (2)
Kayseri *prev.* Eusebia, Mazacca; *anc.* Caesarea Cappadociae Southwest Asia (Turkey) first civilizations 221 (4) Mongols 68–69 (1) see also Caesarea Cappadociae
Kazakh Khanate state Central Asia trade 267 (3)
Kazakhs people Central Asia historical geography 275 (5)
Kazakhstan *var.* Kazakstan, *Kaz.* Qazaqstan; *Rus.* Kazakhskaya SSR state Southwest Asia economy 234 (1) historical geography 275 (5) Islam 235 (4) post-war economy 214 (2), 275 (3) post-war politics 274 (2) Soviet Union 214–215 (4) the modern world 110–111 , 113 (3), (4)
Kazakstan see Kazakhstan
Kazan' Eastern Europe (Russian Federation) colonialism 269 (3) Soviet Union 208 (2), 214–215 (4) trade 267 (3)
Kazan', Khanate of state Eastern Europe/Siberia the world in 1500 74–75
Kazeh see Tabora
Kazembe state Southern Africa trade 167 (1)
Kazvin *mod.* Qazvin Southwest Asia (Iran) exploration 219 (3) see also Qazvin
Kebara archaeological site East Africa first humans 12 (1), 13 (2)
Kebbi see Kabi
Kedah region/settlement Mainland Southeast Asia (Malaysia) colonialism 247 (4) early medieval states 245 (5)
Kedara South Asia (India) world religions 243 (4)
Kediri state Maritime Southeast Asia the world in 1200 62–63
Kedungbrubus archaeological site Maritime Southeast Asia (Indonesia) first humans 13 (2)
Kefe see Kaffa, Theodosia
Keijō see Seoul
Keilor Australia exploration 280 (1)
Keishū see Kumsong, Kyongju
Kelso North America (USA) cultural groups 122 (5)
Kemp Land physical region Antarctica Antarctic Exploration 287 (3)
Kendari Maritime Southeast Asia (Indonesia) WWII 272 (1), 273 (2)
Kenduli South Asia (India) world religions 243 (4)
Kénitra see Port Lyautey
Kennesaw Mountain battle North America (USA) US Civil War 131 (7)
Kennet and Avon canal British Isles economy 204 (1)
Kenniff Cave Australia exploration 280 (1)
Kent state British Isles medieval states 183 (3)
Kentucky state North America the growth of the US 129 (1) US Civil War 130 (2), (3), (4), (5), 131 (6), (7) US economy 134 (2), 139 (3) US superpower 139 (5)
Kentucky Frontier region North America empire and revolution 127 (3)
Kenya *prev.* British East Africa state East Africa decolonization 168 (1) economy 168 (2), (3) Islam 235 (4) the modern world 112 (1), 113 (3) WWII 104 (1) Cold War 109 (1) see also British East Africa
Kenya, Mount *mod.* Kirinyaga mountain East Africa exploration 157 (4)
Kenyérmező battle Southeast Europe early modern states 193 (4)
Keppel Island see Niuatoputapu
Kerala region/state South Asia early religions 48 (2) first empires 241 (5) post-war politics 252 (1), 253 (4) world religions 242 (2)
Kerameikos Cemetery see Ceramicus Cemetery
Kerbela battle Southwest Asia (Iraq) Islam 226 (2)
Kerch see Panticapaeum
Kerguelen island Indian Ocean the world in 1800 86–87
Kerikeri New Zealand colonization 283 (4)
Kérkira see Corcyra, Corfu
Kerkuk see Kirkuk
Kerma East Africa (Sudan) ancient Egypt 159 (4) early cultures 161 (4), (5)
Kermadec Islands island group New Zealand decolonization 285 (3) early cultures 280–281 (3) medieval voyages 60 (2)
Kerman Southwest Asia (Iran) 20th-century politics 235 (5) early Islam 56–57 (1) economy 234 (1) medieval Persia 231 (4) Ottomans 232–233 (1)
Kerman region/state Southwest Asia ancient Persia 225 (6) early Islam 56–57 (1) economy 234 (1) medieval Persia 231 (4)
Kermanshah Southwest Asia (Iran) first civilizations 221 (4), 24 (2) Islam 227 (5) Seljuks 228 (1)
Kernonen burial mound France Bronze Age 175 (3)
Kern River people North America colonization 125 (4)
Kerulen river East Asia exploration 256 (1) first states 260 (1)
Ketu state West Africa Islam 167 (3)
Kexholm Eastern Europe (Russian Federation) early modern states 195 (3)
Key Marco North America (USA) cultural groups 122 (5)
Key West Naval Air Station military base North America (USA) Cold War 108 (2)
Khabarovsk Siberia (Russian Federation) colonialism 269 (3) economy 275 (4) Soviet Union 208 (2)
Khafajah see Tutub
Khairabad South Asia (India) colonialism 247 (3)
Khairpur state South Asia colonialism 248 (2)
Khakasia region Eastern Europe Soviet Union 214–215 (4)
Khalandriani Greece the world in 2500 BCE 22–23
Khalkha people East Asia early modern states 266 (1) trade 267 (3)
Khalkís see Chalcis
Khambhat, Gulf of *Eng.* Gulf of Cambay gulf South Asia first cities 240 (2)
Khami Southern Africa (Zimbabwe) trade 164 (1)
Khanbalik *var.* Khanbaliq; *mod.* Beijing East Asia (China) exploration 256 (1) Mongols 68 (2) see also Beijing, Peking
Khandesh region/state South Asia early medieval states 244–245 (3) Mughal Empire 246 (1)
Khanka, Lake *var.* Hsing-k'ai Hu, Lake Hanka, *Chin.* Xingkai Hu, *Rus.* Ozero Khanka lake East Asia early modern states 265 (5) first states 260 (1) medieval states 264 (1), (2)
Khanka, Ozero see Khanka, Lake
Khanty-Mansi region Eastern Europe Soviet Union 214–215 (4)
Kharbin see Harbin
Kharga Egypt Islam 163 (1)
Kharga oasis Egypt ancient Egypt 159 (2), (3), (4), (5)
Kharg Island *var.* Karg; *Per.* Jazireh-ye Khārk island Southwest Asia 20th-century politics 235 (5) economy 234 (1)
Khārk, Jazīreh-ye see Kharg Island
Kharkov Eastern Europe (Ukraine) Soviet Union 208 (2) WWII 211 (3), (4)
Khartoum *var.* El Khartûm, Khartum East Africa (Sudan) colonization 167 (4) economy 168 (2) exploration 157 (5) see also Karri
Khasa region South Asia early religions 48 (2) world religions 242 (2)
Khasi States state South Asia colonialism 248 (2)
Khatanga Siberia (Russian Federation) exploration 287 (2)
Khazar, Daryā-ye see Caspian Sea
Khazar Empire region/state Central Asia/Eastern Europe early Islam 56–57 (1), 57 (2) Islam 226 (2)
Khe Sanh battle Mainland Southeast Asia (Vietnam) 251 (5)
Kheta river East Asia early modern states 268 (1)
Khíos see Chios
Khirokitia Southwest Asia (Cyprus) early agriculture 220 (1)
Khitan state East Asia medieval states 263 (3)
Khitan people East Asia medieval states 262–263 (1)
Khitan Empire *var.* Liao Empire state East Asia medieval states 263 (4) the world in 1000 58–59
Khiva *mod.* Khiwa Central Asia (Turkmenistan) colonialism 269 (3) Communism 271 (8) medieval Persia 231 (4) Soviet Union 208 (2) trade 267 (3)
Khiva *var.* Chorasmia, Khwarizm region/state Central Asia colonialism 269 (3) medieval Persia 231 (4) see also Khwarizm
Khiwa see Khiva
Khmer *mod.* Cambodia; *prev.* Chenla state Mainland Southeast Asia medieval states 262–263 (1), 263 (6) Mongols 68–69 (1) world religions 243 (5) see also Cambodia, Chenla, Funan, Kambujadesha
Khocho Buddhist centre East Asia (China) world religions 49 (3)
Khoisan peoples people Southern Africa early cultures 160 (1) economy 163 (2) Islam 163 (1)
Khokand Central Asia (Uzbekistan) trade 267 (3)
Khokand see Kokand
Kholm *var.* Cholm, Holm Eastern Europe (Russian Federation) early modern states 195 (3)
Khorasan see Khurasan
Khorat see Nakhon Ratchasima
Khor Bahan Egypt ancient Egypt 159 (2)
Khorramabad Southwest Asia (Iran) 20th-century politics 235 (5)
Khorramshahr *var.* Khurramshahr, Muhammerah; *prev.* Mohammerah Southwest Asia (Iran) 20th-century politics 235 (5)
Khorsabad Southwest Asia (Iraq) first civilizations 222 (2)
Khotan *var.* Hotan, Ho-t'ien East Asia (China) ancient trade 44–45 (1) trade 72–73 (1) early medieval states 244 (1) early modern states 268 (1) exploration 256 (1), 257 (3) first empires 241 (4) first states 260 (1) medieval states 262–263 (1) world religions 49 (3)
Khotin Southeast Europe (Moldavia) Ottomans 231 (3)
Khulna South Asia (Bangladesh) post-war politics 252 (3)
Khurasan region/state Central Asia ancient Persia 225 (6) early Islam 56–57 (1) Islam 227 (4) medieval Persia 231 (4) Seljuks 228 (1) Timur 229 (4)
Khurja South Asia (India) colonialism 247 (3)
Khurramshahr see Khorramshahr
Khūzestān see Elam, Susiana
Khwarizm physical region Central Asia medieval states 262–263 (1) see also Khiva
Khwarizm Shah, Empire of the state Southwest Asia early Islam 57 (2) Islam 227 (4) Mongols 68–69 (1) Seljuks 228 (1) the world in 1200 62–63
Kiaka state Southern Africa the world in 1800 86–87 the world in 1850 90–91
Kiangmai see Chiengmai
Kiang-ning see Jianye, Nanjing
Kiangsi see Jiangxi
Kiangsu see Jiangsu
Kiatuthlana archaeological site North America (USA) cultural groups 123 (4)
Kibi state Japan medieval states 264 (1)
Kibris see Cyprus
Kibyra state Southwest Asia Roman empire 179 (5)
Kichai people North America colonization 125 (4)
Kickapoo people North America colonization 126 (1)
Kiel Central Europe (Germany) empire and revolution 199 (3) medieval states 189 (3)
Kiet Siel archaeological site North America (USA) cultural groups 123 (4)
Kiev *Rus.* Kiyev, *Ukr.* Kyyiv battle Eastern Europe (Russian Federation) WWII 105 (3)
Kiev state Eastern Europe medieval states 189 (4)
Kievan Rus state Eastern Europe medieval states 185 (3) medieval voyages 60–61 (1)
Kifri Southwest Asia (Iraq) 20th-century politics 235 (5)
Kiik-Koba archaeological site Eastern Europe (Ukraine) first humans 13 (2)
Kikládhes see Cyclades
Kikonja state Central Africa the world in 1700 82–83 the world in 1800 86–87 the world in 1850 90–91
Kilimane see Quelimane
Kilimanjaro *var.* Uhuru Peak mountain East Africa exploration 157 (4), (5)
Killala Bay bay British Isles (Ireland) Napoleon 200–201 (1)
Killam South Asia (India) world religions 243 (4)
Kilmain see Quelimane
Kilwa *mod.* Kilwa Kivinje East Africa (Tanzania) economy 163 (2) European expansion 80–81 (1) exploration 156 (3) Islam 163 (1) exploration 68 (2) slave trade 165 (4) trade 230 (2)
Kilwa Kivinje see Kilwa
Kimberley Southern Africa (South Africa) colonization 167 (4) economy 168 (2) European imperialism 96 (2)
Kimberley Plateau plateau Australia colonization 283 (3) exploration 279 (2)
Kimchaek *prev.* Sŏngjin East Asia (North Korea) Cold War 109 (4)
Kimmswoci archaeological site North America the world in 10,000 BCE 14–15
Kinai state Japan medieval states 264 (1)
Kingisepp see Yam
Kingman Reef colonial possession Pacific Ocean the modern world 110–111
King's Lynn *var.* Bishop's Lynn, Lynn Regis British Isles (United Kingdom) economy 190 (1)
Kings Mounds North America (USA) cultural groups 122 (5)
King's Mountain battle North America (USA) empire and revolution 127 (3)
King's Table Australia exploration 280 (1)
Kingston West Indies (Jamaica) Cold War 108 (2), 129 (2), 136 (2)
Kingston upon Hull see Hull
Kinishba archaeological site North America (USA) cultural groups 123 (4)
Kinlichee archaeological site North America (USA) cultural groups 123 (4)
Kinneret, Yam see Galilee, Sea of
Kinshasa *prev.* Léopoldville Central Africa (Congo (Zaire)) economy 168 (2) see also Léopoldville
Kintampo West Africa (Ghana) early agriculture 158 (1)
Kioga, Lake see Kyoga, Lake
Kiowa people North America colonization 126 (1)
Kipchaks see Cumans
Kirata state South Asia first empires 241 (5)
Kirensk Siberia (Russian Federation) exploration 257 (2)
Kirghiz people Central Asia historical geography 275 (5) medieval states 262–263 (1) trade 267 (3)
Kirghizia see Kyrgyzstan
Kiribati state/island Pacific Ocean decolonization 285 (3) early cultures 280–281 (3)
Kirin *var.* Chi-lin, Girin, Ji, Jilin Sheng province East Asia Russo-Japanese War 270 (4) see also Jilin
Kirinyaga see Kenya, Mount
Kiritimati *prev.* Christmas Island island Pacific Ocean exploration 278 (1) see also Christmas Island
Kirkstall major cistercian house British isles (United Kingdom) medieval states 187 (3)
Kirkuk *var.* Karkūk, Kerkuk Southwest Asia (Iraq) 235 (5) economy 234 (1) WWI 233 (2) 20th-century politics 233 (3)
Kirman Southwest Asia (Iran) exploration 219 (3) medieval voyages 61 (3)
Kirov see Vologda, Vyatka
Kirte battle Southwest Asia (Turkey) WWI 207 (6)
Kisangani *prev.* Stanleyville Central Africa (Congo (Zaire)) economy 168 (2)
Kisese East Africa (Tanzania) prehistoric culture 17 (2)
Kish Southwest Asia (Iraq) early systems 33 (3) first cities 220 (2), 28–29 (1) first civilizations 221 (4), 24 (2), 25 (3)
Kishinev *var.* Chişinău Southeast Europe (Moldavia) post-war politics 212 (3) Soviet Union 208 (2) WWI 207 (4)
Kiska island North America WWII 272 (1), 273 (2)
Kiso Japan early modern states 265 (5)
Kistna see Krishna
Kisumu *prev.* Port Florence East Africa (Kenya) colonization 167 (4)
Kitagiri South Asia (India) world religions 242 (3)
Kitai East Asia (China) ancient trade 44–45 (1)
Kitanosho battle Japan early modern states 267 (4)
Kitava state South Asia first empires 41 (5)
Kition Cyprus ancient Egypt 159 (5) first civilizations 177 (1)
Kiukiang see Jiujiang
Kiungchow see Qiongzhou
Kivu, Lac see Kivu, Lake
Kivu, Lake *Fr.* Lac Kivu lake Central Africa exploration 157 (4), (5) first humans 12 (1)
Kiyev see Kiev
Kizil Irmak river Southwest Asia first civilizations 24 (2)
Klaipeda Eastern Europe (Lithuania) post-war politics 212 (3)
Klasies River Mouth archaeological site/settlement Southern Africa (South Africa) first humans 13 (2)
Kleve see Cleves
Klokotnitsa battle Greece medieval states 189 (4)
Klondike City North America (Canada) imperial global economy 93 (3)
Klowa New Guinea (Papua New Guinea) exploration 280 (1)
Knight burial mound North America (USA) first civilizations 121 (4)
Knights of St. John state Malta the world in 1700 82–83
Knights of St. John state Greece medieval states 189 (4) Ottomans 230 (1)
Knights of the Cross see Teutonic Order
Knin Southeast Europe (Croatia) post-war economy 215 (3)
Knosós see Knossos
Knossos archaeological site/palace/religious site/settlement Crete ancient Egypt 159 (5) Bronze Age 175 (3) Copper Age 174 (2) early agriculture 174 (1) early systems 223 (3) first cities 28–29 (1) first civilizations 175 (4), 177 (1) first religions 37 (3) Hellenistic world 40–41 (1)
Knoxville North America (USA) the growth of the US 129 (2) US Civil War 131 (6), (7) US society 137 (6)
Kobe *Jap.* Kōbe bomb target/settlement Japan WWII 273 (3) economy 270 (1), 275 (4)
København see Copenhagen
Koblenz Central Europe (Germany) early modern states 197 (5)
Kochi *var.* Kôti Japan early modern states 267 (4) economy 270 (1)
Kochi prefecture Japan economy 270 (1)
Kochi, Ko-chih see Cochin
Kodiak Island North America (USA) cultural groups 123 (3)
Kodiak Island island North America imperial global economy 93 (3)
Koepang see Kupang
Kofu *Jap.* Kōfu bomb target Japan WWII 273 (3)
Kofukuji Buddhist temple army Japan medieval states 265 (4)
Koguryo state East Asia medieval states 264 (1) world religions 49 (4)
Kohat South Asia (India) decolonization 250 (1)
Kohima South Asia (India) post-war politics 252 (1)
Koil South Asia (Estonia) colonialism 247 (3)
Kokala South Asia (Pakistan) Hellenistic world 40–41 (1)
Kokand *var.* Khokand, Qŭqon see Alexandria Eschate state Central Asia the world in 1800 86–87 the world in 1850 90–91 see also Khokand
Kokasati people North America colonization 125 (4)
Kokchetav *Kaz.* Kökshetaū archaeological site Siberia early agriculture 258 (1)
Kokenhausen *mod.* Koknese Eastern Europe (Latvia) medieval states 189 (3)
Koknese see Kokenhausen
Kokoli state West Africa trade 164 (2)
Koko Nor lake East Asia exploration 257 (3) see also Qinghai Hu
Kökshetaū see Kokchetav
Kola region Eastern Europe Soviet Union 214–215 (4)
Kolam see Quilon
Kola Peninsula Russ. Kol'skiy Poluostrov coastal feature Eastern Europe exploration 257 (2)
Kolberg *mod.* Kołobrzeg Central Europe (Poland) economy 190 (1) medieval states 189 (3)
Kolhapur South Asia (Maharashtra, India) Marathas 246 (2)
Kolkata see Calcutta
Kollam see Quilon
Kolmar see Colmar
Köln see Cologne, Colonia Agrippina
Köln-Lindenthal Central Europe (Germany) early agriculture 174 (1)
Ko-Lo state Mainland Southeast Asia ancient India 241 (6)
Ko-lo Mainland Southeast Asia (Malaysia) ancient India 241 (6)
Kołobrzeg see Kolberg
Kololo people Africa colonization 166 (2)
Kolomna Eastern Europe (Russian Federation) Mongols 68–69 (1)
Kolomoki North America (USA) cultural groups 122 (5)
Kolozsvár Southeast Europe (Romania) early modern states 193 (4)
Kol'skiy Poluostrov see Kola Peninsula
Kolubara battle Southeast Europe (Yugoslavia) WWI 207 (6)
Kolyma river Siberia exploration 257 (2)
Komandorski Islands island group Siberia WWII 272 (1), 273 (2)
Komatipoort Southern Africa (South Africa) European imperialism 96 (2)
Komatsu Japan early modern states 267 (4)
Kom el-Hisn Egypt first cities 28–29 (1)
Komi region Eastern Europe Soviet Union 214–215 (4)
Komi-Permyak region Eastern Europe Soviet Union 214–215 (4)
Kom Medinet Ghurab Egypt ancient Egypt 159 (5)
Kommos Crete ancient Egypt 159 (5)
Kompong Som Mainland Southeast Asia (Cambodia) post-war politics 251 (5)
Kompong Thom Mainland Southeast Asia (Cambodia) post-war politics 251 (5)
Kondavidu South Asia (India) early medieval states 244–245 (3)
Kondūz see Drapsaca, Kunduz
Kong state West Africa slave trade 165 (4) trade 167 (1)
Kongju *Jap.* Kōshū *var.* Kwangju East Asia (Korea) medieval states 264 (1) see also Kwangju
Kongo state Central Africa Islam 163 (1) slave trade 165 (4) trade 164 (2), 167 (1)
Kongo people Central Africa trade 167 (1)
Konia see Iconium, Konya
Konieh see Iconium, Konya
Königsberg battle/rebellion/settlement Eastern Europe (Russian Federation) crusades 186 (1) early modern states 193 (4), 195 (3) economy 190 (1) empire and revolution 202 (2) medieval states 189 (3), (4) post-war politics 212 (3) Reformation 194 (2) WWI 207 (4) WWII 105 (3), 210 (1), 211 (4)
Königshofen Mithraic site Central Europe (Germany) world religions 48 (1)
Konjic Mithraic site Southeast Europe (Bosnia and Herzegovina) world religions 48 (1)
Konkan region South Asia colonialism 247 (3)
Konkana region South Asia early religions 48 (2)
Konstanz see Constance
Kontum battle Mainland Southeast Asia (Vietnam) 251 (5)
Konya *var.* Konieh; *prev.* Konia, *anc.* Iconium Southwest Asia (Turkey) crusades 228 (2) early Islam 57 (2) first civilizations 221 (4) Mongols 229 (3) Seljuks 228 (1) Timur 229 (4) see also Iconium
Konya, Lake lake Southwest Asia historical geography 170–171 (1)
Koobi Fora archaeological site East Africa (Kenya) first humans 12 (1), 13 (2)
Koolan Australia the world in 10,000 BCE 14–15
Koolburra archaeological site Australia prehistoric culture 17 (5)
Koonalda Cave Australia prehistoric culture 17 (2)
Kopor'ye Eastern Europe (Russian Federation) early modern states 195 (3)
Korat see Nakhon Ratchasima
Korčula *It.* Curzola; *anc.* Corcyra Nigra island Southeast Europe post-war economy 215 (3)
Korea region East Asia ancient trade 44–45 (1) colonialism 269 (3), (4) Communism 271 (8), 273 (3) decolonization 251 (4) early modern states 266 (1), 267 (4), (5), 268 (1) economy 274 (1) empire and revolution 268 (2) first cities 259 (5) first religions 37 (4) first states 260 (1) imperialism 270 (2) medieval states 261 (6) post-war politics 271 (7) Russo-Japanese War 270 (4) Sino-Japanese War 270 (3) Soviet Union 208 (2) trade 267 (3) US superpower 138 (1) world religions 49 (3) WWII 104 (1), 251 (3), 272 (1), 273 (2) Chinese revolution 271 (5) Cold War 109 (1), (4)
Koreans people East Asia the world in 750 BCE 30–31 the world in 500 BCE 34–35
Korea Strait *Jap.* Chōsen-kaikyō, *Kor.* Taehan-haehyŏp sea waterway East Asia Cold War 109 (4)
Koriabo people South America the world in 1300 66–67
Kórinthos see Corinth
Koritsa Southeast Europe (Albania) WWI 207 (6)
Korkai South Asia (India) first empires 241 (4)
Kormarow battle Central Europe (Poland) WWI 207 (4)
Korone Greece medieval states 189 (4)
Kororareka *var.* Russell New Zealand colonization 283 (4)
Koroska Egypt exploration 157 (5)
Koryaks people Siberia the world in 1700 82–83
Koryo *mod.* Korea *prev.* Koryo; *anc.* Choson, Silla; *Jap.* Chōsen *var.* Chosen state East Asia early modern states 265 (5) medieval states 263 (5), (6) Mongols 68–69 (1) see also Choson, Korea, Silla
Köse Dagh battle Southwest Asia (Turkey) Seljuks 228 (1)
Koshala *var.* Kosala region/state South Asia ancient India 242 (1) first empires 241 (4), (5) first religions 36 (2) world religions 242 (2), (3)
K'o-shih see Kashgar, Kashi
Kōshū see Kongju, Kwangju
Kosi river South Asia first religions 36 (2)
Košice see Kassa
Kosipe New Guinea (Papua New Guinea) exploration 280 (1)
Kosovo *var.* Kosovo Polje province Southeast Europe Ottomans 230 (1) post-war economy 215 (3) the modern world 112 (2)
Kosovska Mitrovica see Mitrovica
Koster North America (USA) the world in 5000 BCE 18–19
Kostienki archaeological site/settlement Eastern Europe (Russian Federation) prehistoric culture 17 (4)
Kostnitz see Constance
Kostroma Eastern Europe (Russian Federation) Soviet Union 208 (2)
Kostromskaya Eastern Europe (Russian Federation) first religions 36 (1)
Kőszeg battle Central Europe (Hungary) Ottomans 195 (4)
Kőszeg see Güns
Kota Baharu see Kota Bharu
Kotabangun Maritime Southeast Asia (Indonesia) world religions 243 (5)
Kota Bharu *var.* Kota Baharu, Kota Bahru Mainland Southeast Asia (Malaysia) WWII 251 (3)
Kot Diji archaeological site South Asia (Pakistan) first cities 240 (2)
Kôti see Kochi
Kotor see Cattaro
Kotosh early ceremonial centre/settlement South America (Peru) early cultures 144 (1), 145 (3)
Kouklia Cyprus ancient Egypt 159 (5)
Kourou archaeological site South America (French Guiana) early cultures 145 (2)
Kourounkorokale West Africa (Mali) early agriculture 158 (1)
Kovno Eastern Europe (Lithuania) economy 190 (1) Napoleon 200–201 (1)
Koweit see Kuwait
Kowloon colonial possession East Asia (China) colonialism 269 (4)
Kowno see Kaunas, Kovno
Kow Swamp Australia the world in 10,000 BCE 14–15
Koyahan East Asia (South Korea) medieval states 264 (2)
Koya-san Buddhist temple army Japan medieval states 265 (4)
Koya-san mountain Japan medieval states 265 (3)
Koyukon people North America cultural groups 123 (3)
Kozhikode see Calicut, Kalikad, Qalqut
Kragujevac massacre/settlement Southeast Europe (Yugoslavia) post-war economy 215 (3) WWII 211 (3)
Kra, Isthmus of coastal feature Mainland Southeast Asia European imperialism 97 (3) post-war politics 253 (4)
Krakau see Cracow
Krak des Chevaliers settlement/fort Southwest Asia (Syria) crusades 228 (2), 65 (3)
Krak des Moabites fort Southwest Asia (Jordon) crusades 65 (3)
Kraków see Cracow
Kras see Karst
Krasnik battle Central Europe (Poland) WWI 207 (4)
Krasnoy Eastern Europe (Russian Federation) Napoleon 200–201 (1)
Krasnoyarsk Siberia (Russian Federation) colonialism 269 (3) exploration 257 (2) Soviet Union 208 (2), 213 (4), 214–215 (4)
Kremenets state Eastern Europe medieval states 189 (4)
Kreuzberg Central Europe (Germany) post-war politics 212 (2)
Krievija see Russia, Russian Empire, Russian Federation, Soviet Union, Union of Soviet Socialsist Republics
Krishna *prev.* Kistna river South Asia colonialism 247 (3), 248 (2) decolonization 250 (1) early medieval states 244 (1), (2), 244–245 (3), 245 (4) economy 249 (4) first empires 241 (4), (5) first religions 36 (2) Marathas 246 (2) Mughal Empire 246 (1) post-war politics 252 (1) world religions 242 (2), 243 (4)
Kristiania see Christiania, Oslo
Kríti see Candia, Creta, Crete, Crete
Krivoy Rog Eastern Europe (Ukraine) WWII 211 (4)
Kroatien see Croatia
Kromdraai archaeological site Southern Africa (South Africa) first humans 12 (1)
Kronstadt see Brasou, Brassó
Krung Thep see Bangkok
Kruševac Southeast Europe (Yugoslavia) post-war economy 215 (3)
Krym see Crimea
Kuachou see Guazhou
K'uai Chi Shan see Kuaiji Shan
Kuaiji Shan *var.* K'uai Chi Shan mountain East Asia first religions 37 (4)
Kuala Lumpur Mainland Southeast Asia (Malaysia) Islam 275 (4) post-war economy 253 (5) WWII 251 (3), 272 (1), 273 (2)
Kuang-chou see Canton, Guangzhou
Kuang-tung see Guangdong
Kuannei see Guannei
Kuaua archaeological site North America (USA) cultural groups 123 (4)
Kuba state Central Africa slave trade 165 (4) trade 167 (1)
Kubaniya Egypt ancient Egypt 159 (2)
Kucha *var.* Kuqa East Asia (China) first states 260 (1)
Kūchek, Rūdkhāneh-ye Zāb-e see Little Zab
Kuching *prev.* Sarawak Maritime Southeast Asia (Malaysia) exploration 239 (2) WWII 251 (3)
Kuei-chou see Guizhou
Kuei-lin see Guilin
Kuei-Yang see Guiyang
Kueyang see Guiyang
Kufa *var.* Al Kūfah Southwest Asia (Iraq) early Islam 56–57 (1)
Kugha state West Africa trade 163 (4)
Kuizhou East Asia (China) medieval states 263 (4)
Kuk New Guinea (Papua New Guinea) early cultures 280 (2)
Kuka West Africa (Nigeria) Islam 163 (1)
Kukawa West Africa (Nigeria) Islam 167 (3)
Ku Klux Klan movement North America US politics 135 (6)
Kukura state South Asia first empires 241 (5)
Kulam Mali South Asia (India) medieval voyages 61 (3)
Kuldja *var.* Gulja; *Chin.* Yining Buddhist centre/settlement East Asia (China) ancient trade 44–45 (1) early modern states 268 (1) world religions 49 (3)
Kulm *mod.* Chełmno Central Europe (Poland) medieval states 189 (3)
Kůlna Cave archaeological site Central Europe (Czech Republic) first humans 13 (2)
Kültepe *var.* Kanesh Southwest Asia (Turkey) first civilizations 24 (2) see also Kanesh
Kum see Qom, Qum
Kumamoto Japan economy 270 (1)
Kumano Buddhist temple army Japan medieval states 265 (4)
Kumanova see Kumanovo
Kumanovo *Turk.* Kumanova Southeast Europe (FYR Macedonia) post-war economy 215 (3) WWI 207 (6)
Kumari South Asia (India) world religions 242 (2)
Kumasi *prev.* Coomassie West Africa (Ghana) colonization 167 (4) economy 168 (2)
Kumaun state South Asia Mughal Empire 246 (1)
Kumillā see Comilla
Kumma Egypt ancient Egypt 159 (5)
Kumsong *var.* Kyongju *Jap.* Keishū East Asia (Korea) medieval states 264 (2) see also Kyongju
Kumul see Hami
Kundagrama South Asia (India) world religions 242 (3)
Kundivrsa state South Asia first empires 241 (5)
Kunduz *anc.* Drapsaca; *Per.* Kondūz state Central Asia the world in 1800 86–87 the world in 1850 90–91 see also Drapsaca
Kungitavik North America (USA) cultural groups 123 (3)
Kungnaesong East Asia (China) medieval states 264 (2)
Kunjakari South Asia (India) world religions 243 (4)
Kunjja North America (Canada) cultural groups 123 (3)
Kunlun Mountains *Chin.* Kunlun Shan mountain range Central Asia exploration 256 (1), 257 (3) first states 260 (1) medieval states 261 (6), 262–263 (1) Mongols 68–69 (1)
Kunlun Shan see Kunlun Mountains
Kunming *var.* K'un-ming; *prev.* Yunnan East Asia (China) ancient trade 44–45 (1) colonialism 269 (4) post-war economy 274–275 (2), (4) post-war politics 275 (3) WWII 272 (1), 275 (3) see also Yunan
Kunming people East Asia medieval states 263 (3)
Kuntala region/state South Asia first empires 241 (5) world religions 242 (2)
Kuntur Wasi archaeological site South America (Peru) early cultures 145 (3)
Kuocang Shan *var.* K'uo Ts'ang Shan mountain East Asia first religions 37 (4)
Kuomintang movement East Asia Chinese Civil War 271 (6)
K'uo Ts'ang Shan see Kuocang Shan
Kuowu state East Asia first cities 259 (4)
Kupang *prev.* Koepang Maritime Southeast Asia (Indonesia) colonialism 247 (4)
Kuqa see Kucha
Kür see Kura
Kura *Az.* Kür, *Geor.* Mtkvari, *Turk.* Kura Nehri river Southwest Asia Mongols 68–69 (1)
Kura Nehri see Kura
Kura-Panchala *var.* Kuru-Pancala region South Asia first religions 36 (2)
Kuratoy archaeological site Siberia (Russian Federation) early agriculture 258 (1)
Kurdistan region Southwest Asia 20th-century politics 233 (3)
Kurds people Southwest Asia historical geography 275 (5) medieval Persia 231 (4) Ottomans 232–233 (1)
Kure Japan WWII 273 (3) economy 270 (1)
Kurikara-tani battle Japan 265 (5)
Kurile Islands *var.* Kuril'skiye Ostrova; *Jap.* Chishima-rettō island group Siberia ancient trade 44–45 (1) colonialism 269 (3) early agriculture 258 (1) early modern states 265 (5) imperialism 270 (2) WWII 272 (1), 73 (2)
Kuril'skiye Ostrova see Kurile Islands
Kuriyagawa Japan early modern states 265 (5)
Kurkur Egypt ancient Egypt 159 (4)
Kurkur Oasis oasis Egypt ancient Egypt 159 (3), (5)
Kurland see Courland
Kursk battle Eastern Europe (Russian Federation) WWII 105 (3), 211 (4)
Kuru region South Asia ancient India 242 (1) early religions 48 (2) world religions 242 (2), (3)
Kurukshetra battle South Asia (India) first empires 241 (5)
Kuruman Southern Africa (South Africa) exploration 157 (4)
Kuru-Pancala see Kura-Panchala
Kush *var.* Meroe, Cush settlement/state East Africa (Sudan) ancient Egypt 159 (4), (5) ancient trade 44–45 (1) early cultures 161 (3), (4) see also Meroe
Kushana state Central Asia the world in 250 CE 46–47
Kushites *var.* Cushites people East Africa ancient trade 44–45 (1) early cultures 160 (1), 161 (5) economy 163 (2) Islam 163 (1)
Kushan Empire state South Asia ancient trade 44–45 (1) early religions 48 (2) medieval states 261 (6)
Kushinara South Asia world religions 242 (3)
Kusinagara South Asia (India) early religions 48 (2) first religions 36 (2)
Kut al Amara Southwest Asia (Iraq) WWI 233 (2)
Kutch see Kach
Kutch, Gulf of see Kachchh, Gulf of
Kutchin people North America cultural groups 123 (3)
Kutch, Rann of physical region South Asia economy 249 (4) post-war politics 252 (1)
Kutei state Maritime Southeast Asia the world in 1700 82–83 the world in 1800 86–87
Kutná Hora *Ger.* Kuttenberg Central Europe (Czech Republic) economy 190 (1)
Kuttenberg see Kutná Hora
Kuvango see Cubango
Kuwait *var.* Dawlat al Kuwait, Koweit, Kuweit colonial possession/state Southwest Asia economy 234 (1) European imperialism 97 (4) exploration 219 (4) Islam 235 (4) Ottomans 232–233 (1) the modern world 110–111 , 113 (3) US economy 138 (2) WWI 233 (2) 20th-century politics 233 (3), (4), 235 (5) Cold War 109 (1)
Kuweit see Kuwait
Kuybyshev see Samara
Kvarnby Scandinavia (Sweden) Bronze Age 175 (3)
Kwa people West Africa early cultures 160 (1)
Kwajalein island Pacific Ocean Cold War 109 (1) US superpower 138 (1) WWII 272 (1), 273 (2)
Kwale archaeological site East Africa (Kenya) early cultures 160 (1)
Kwando see Cuando
Kwangchow see Canton, Guangzhou
Kwangchowwan see Guangzhouwan
Kwangchu see Konju, Kwangju
Kwangju *var.* Guangju, Kongju, Kwangchu; *Jap.* Kōshū East Asia (South Korea) Cold War 109 (4) see also Kongju
Kwangtung see Guangdong,
Kwantung *Jap.* Kantō colonial possession East Asia imperialism 270 (2)

Kwanza see Cuanza
Kwararafa state West Africa Islam 163 (1)
Kwazulu/Natal see Natal
Kweichow see Guizhou
Kweichu see Guiyang
Kweilin see Guilin
Kweiyang see Guiyang
Kwekwe prev. Que Que Southern Africa (Zimbabwe) economy 168 (2)
Kyoga, Lake var. Lake Kioga lake East Africa exploration 157 (5) first humans 12 (1)
Kyongju var. Kumsong; Jap. Keishū East Asia (Korea) early modern states 265 (5) medieval states 264 (1), (2) see also Kumsong
Kyŏngsŏng see Seoul
Kyoto Jap. Kyōto prev. Heian-kyo Japan early modern states 267 (4), 268 (1) economy 270 (1) medieval states 262–263 (1), 263 (6), 265 (4) trade 267 (3) world religions 49 (4) see also Heiankyo
Kyoto prefecture Japan economy 270 (1)
Kypros see Cyprus
Kyrgyzstan var. Kirghizia state Central Asia historical geography 275 (5) Islam 235 (4) post-war economy 275 (3) post-war politics 274 (2), 275 (5) Soviet Union 214–215 (4) the modern world 113 (3)
Kythera island Greece ancient Greece 177 (2)
Kyushu Jap. Kyūshū island Japan WWII 273 (3) early modern states 265 (5), 267 (4), (5) economy 270 (1) imperialism 270 (2) medieval states 264 (1), (2), 265 (3), (4) Sino-Japanese War 270 (3)
Kyyiv see Kiev

L

Laatokka see Ladoga, Lake
La Banda Oriental see Uruguay
La Baume-Latrone archaeological site France prehistoric culture 17 (3)
Labe see Elbe
Labicana, Via road Italy ancient Rome 181 (2)
Labici var. Labicum Italy early states 178 (1)
Labicum see Labici
La Blanca Central America (Guatemala) first civilizations 121 (2)
Labná Central America (Mexico) first civilizations 123 (2)
Labrada Central America (Mexico) first civilizations 122 (1)
Labrador region North America colonization 126 (1) European expansion 80–81 (1) exploration 118 (1), 119 (2), (3), 129 (2)
Labrador Inuit people North America cultural groups 123 (3)
Labrador Sea sea North America cultural groups 123 (3) exploration 286 (1), 129 (2)
Labuan var. Pulau Labuan island Maritime Southeast Asia the world in 1850 90–91
Labuan, Pulau see Labuan
Laccadive Islands var. Lakshadweep island group South Asia Mongols 68 (2)
Lacedaemon see Sparta
La Chapelle-aux-Saints archaeological site France first humans 13 (2)
Lachish Southwest Asia (Israel) ancient Egypt 159 (5) first cities 28–29 (1)
Laconia state Greece ancient Greece 179 (4)
La Copa archaeological site South America (Peru) early cultures 145 (3)
La Coruña Iberian Peninsula (Spain) economy 205 (4) inter-war 209 (4)
La Couronne France the world in 2500 BCE 22–23
Ladaka mod. Ladakh state South Asia first empires 241 (5) see also Ladakh
Ladakh region South Asia early cultures 145 (3) exploration 257 (3) post-war politics 252 (2)
Ladha region South Asia world religions 242 (3)
Lado vassal state East Africa the world in 1900 94–95
Ladoga, Lake Fin. Laatokka; var. Ladozhskoye, Ozero lake Eastern Europe early modern states 195 (3) economy 205 (4) exploration 172 (1) medieval states 185 (3) Soviet Union 208 (2) WWI 207 (4)
Ladozhskoye, Ozero see Ladoga lake
Lady Franklin Point North America (Canada) cultural groups 123 (3)
Ladysmith Southern Africa (South Africa) European imperialism 96 (2)
Lae New Guinea (Papua New Guinea) WWII 272 (1), 273 (2)
Laetolil archaeological site East Africa (Tanzania) first humans 12 (1), 13 (2)
La Fère-Champenoise battle France Napoleon 200–201 (1)
La Ferrassie archaeological site France prehistoric culture 17 (2)
La Ferté major cistercian house France medieval states 187 (3)
La Florida South America (Peru) the world in 1250 BCE 26–27
La Galgada early ceremonial centre/settlement/archaeological site South America (Peru) early cultures 144 (1), 145 (3)
Lagash var. Shipurla Southwest Asia (Iraq) first cities 220 (2), 28–29 (1) first civilizations 221 (4), 24 (3)
Laghouat North Africa (Algeria) colonization 167 (4)
Lagny France economy 190 (1)
Lagoa Santa archaeological site South America (Brazil) early cultures 145 (2)
Lagos Central Africa (Nigeria) colonization 167 (4) economy 168 (2) European imperialism 96 (1) global immigration 100 (1) Islam 167 (3)
La Gruta archaeological site South America (Venezuela) early cultures 144 (1), 145 (2)
Laguna South America (Brazil) colonization 149 (3)
Laguna de los Cerros Central America (Mexico) first civilizations 121 (2), (3)
La Habana see Havana
La Hoguette France the world in 2500 BCE 22–23
La Honradez Central America (Mexico) first civilizations 123 (2)
Lahontan, Lake lake North America historical geography 117 (1)
Lahor mod. Lahore South Asia (Pakistan) early medieval states 244–245 (3) Mughal Empire 246 (1) see also Lahore, Lahur
Lahore var. Lahor South Asia (Pakistan) colonialism 247 (3), 248 (1) crusades 65 (1) decolonization 250 (1) early religions 48 (2) economy 249 (4) exploration 257 (3) imperial global economy 93 (5) post-war economy 253 (5) post-war politics 252 (1) see also Lahor
Lai East Asia (China) first cities 259 (5)
Laias var. Ayas Southwest Asia (Turkey) exploration 219 (3)
Laibach see Ljubljana
Lai-chou East Asia (China) exploration 256 (1)
Laighin region British Isles medieval states 188 (2)
Lake Mungo Australia the world in 10,000 BCE 14–15
Lake Naoich battle Eastern Europe (Belorussia) WWI 207 (4)
Lakhawar South Asia (India) colonialism 247 (3)
Lakhmids state Southwest Asia the world in 500 CE 50–51
Lakhnau see Lucknow
Lakshadweep see Laccadive Islands
Lalibela Cave East Africa (Ethiopia) early agriculture 158 (1) world religions 49 (4)
La Madeleine archaeological site/settlement France prehistoric culture 17 (4)
Lamanai Central America (Mexico) first civilizations 123 (2)
Lamar North America (USA) cultural groups 122 (5)
Lambaesis mod. Tazoult legion headquarters/mithraic site North Africa (Algeria) ancient Rome 180–181 (1) world religions 48 (1)
Lambakannas mod. Sri Lanka; Chin. Hsi-lan; anc. Taprobane state South Asia the world in 250 CE 46–47 the world in 500 CE 50–51 the world in 750 CE 54–55 the world in 1000 58–59 see also Ceylon, Lanka, Simhala, Sri Lanka, Taprobane
Lambayeque river South America early cultures 145 (3), (4)
Lambing Flat goldfield Australia colonization 282 (2)
Lamb Spring North America the world in 10,000 BCE 14–15
La Mosquitia see Mosquito Coast, Mosquito Prefecture
Lampsacus Southwest Asia (Turkey) ancient Greece 177 (3) first civilizations 177 (1)
Lampsacus state Greece ancient Greece 177 (2)
Lamut var. Even people Siberia trade 267 (3)
Lancang Jiang see Mekong
Lancashire admin. region British Isles imperial global economy 93 (4)
Lancaster British Isles (United Kingdom) economy 204 (1)
Lan Chang mod. Louanphabang, Louangphrabang, Luang, Prabang Mainland Southeast Asia (Laos) early medieval states 245 (6)
Lanchow, Lan-chou, Lan-chow see Lanzhou
Langebaan archaeological site Southern Africa (South Africa) first humans 13 (2)
Langkasuka Mainland Southeast Asia (Thailand) ancient India 241 (6)
Lang Son fort Mainland Southeast Asia (Vietnam) 251 (5)
Langtandong archaeological site East Asia (China) first humans 13 (2)
Languedoc region France medieval states 192 (1)
Langweiler Low Countries (Netherlands) early agriculture 174 (1)
Langye Buddhist centre East Asia (China) world religions 49 (3)
Langye var. Lang-Yeh region East Asia first religions 37 (4)
Lang-Yeh see Langye
Lanka var. Simhala; see also Ceylon island South Asia first religions 36 (2) world religions 48 (2) see also Lambakannas, Simhala, Sri Lanka, Taprobane
Lanka region South Asia early religions 48 (2)
Lan-Na region Mainland Southeast Asia early medieval states 245 (6)
L'Anse aux Meadows North America (Canada) medieval voyages 60–61 (1)
Lansing North America (USA) the growth of the US 129 (2)
Lantian archaeological site/settlement East Asia (China) first cities 259 (4) first humans 13 (2) first states 260 (1)
Lan-ts'ang Chiang see Mekong
Lanuvium Italy early states 178 (1)
Lanzhou var. Lan-chou, Lanchow, Lan-chow; prev. Kaolan archaeological site/settlement East Asia (China) plague 72–73 (1) early agriculture 258 (2) early modern states 266 (1) economy 274 (1) empire and revolution 268 (2) first states 260 (1) Islam 275 (4) medieval states 261 (6) post-war politics 271 (7), 274 (2)
Lao Cai fort Mainland Southeast Asia post-war politics 251 (5)
Laodicea Southwest Asia (Syria/Turkey) ancient Rome 180–181 (1) world religions 48 (1)
Laodicea ad Mare see Laodicea
Laodicea in Media mod. Nehavend Southwest Asia (Iran) Hellenistic world 41 (2)
Laon battle France Napoleon 200–201 (1)
Laos off. Lao People's Democratic Republic state/vassal state Mainland Southeast Asia Bronze Age 240 (3) Cold War 109 (1) colonialism 269 (4) decolonization 251 (4) early modern states 268 (1) economy 274 (1) European imperialism 97 (3) Islam 275 (4) post-war economy 253 (5), 275 (3) post-war politics 251 (5), 253 (4), 274 (2)
Laos people Mainland Southeast Asia the world in 1300 66–67
La Paz Central America (Mexico) colonization 125 (4)
La Paz var. La Paz de Ayacucho South America (Bolivia) colonization 148 (2) empire and revolution 150 (1), 151 (3) environment 153 (4) Incas 148 (1) narcotics 153 (5) politics 151 (4), 152 (1)
La Paz de Ayacucho see La Paz
La Perouse Strait Jap. Sōya-kaikyō sea waterway East Asia WWII 273 (3)
Lapita archaeological site Pacific Ocean (New Caledonia) early cultures 280–281 (3)
Lapland Fin. Lappi, Swe. Lappland physical region Scandinavia exploration 286 (1)
La Plata South America (Bolivia) colonization 148 (2) exploration 142 (1), 143 (2)
La Plata South America (Argentina) empire and revolution 151 (3)
La Plata see Chuquisaca
La Plata, United Provinces of state South America empire and revolution 150 (1), 88–89 (2)
La Playa South America (Argentina) Incas 147 (3)
Lappland, Lappi see Lapland
Lapps people Scandinavia the world in 1200 62–63 the world in 1300 66–67 the world in 1400 70–71 the world in 1500 74–75
Laptev Sea sea Arctic Ocean exploration 257 (2)
La Puerta battle South America (Venezuela) empire and revolution 150 (1)
Lapurdum see Bayonne
Larache see Lixus
Laredo North America (USA) Mexican Revolution 133 (3)
Larino see Larinum
Larinum mod. Larino Italy early states 178 (1)
La Rioja South America (Argentina) empire and revolution 151 (3)
Larissa Christian archbishopric Greece world religions 48 (1)
La Roche archaeological site France prehistoric culture 17 (4)
La Roche-aux-Moines France medieval states 187 (4)
La Rochelle anc. Rupella France crusades 186 (1) early modern states 197 (5) economy 198 (1) medieval states 192 (1) Reformation 196 (2)
Larsa Southwest Asia (Iraq) first cities 220 (2), 28–29 (1) first civilizations 221 (4)
La-sa see Lhasa
Las Bocas Central America (Mexico) early agriculture 120 (1)
Lascaux archaeological site/settlement France prehistoric culture 17 (3) the world in 10,000 BCE 14–15
La Serena South America (Chile) empire and revolution 151 (3) politics 151 (4)
Las Flores Central America (Mexico) first civilizations 122 (1)
Las Haldas archaeological site/settlement South America (Peru) early cultures 144 (1)
Lashio Mainland Southeast Asia (Burma) WWII 273 (2) WWII 104 (2)
Lashkari Bazar Central Asia (Afghanistan) early Islam 56–57 (1)
Las Limas archaeological site Central America (Mexico) first civilizations 121 (3)
Las Navas de Tolosa battle Iberian Peninsula (Spain) crusades 186 (1) Islam 192 (3)
Las Palomas Iberian Peninsula the world in 10,000 BCE 14–15
Lassa see Lhasa
La Suisse see Switzerland
Las Vegas archaeological site South America (Ecuador) early cultures 144 (1) the modern world 113 (4)
Las Victorias Central America (El Salvador) first civilizations 121 (2)
Latacunga South America (Equador) Incas 147 (3)
Latakia see Laodicea
Later Kalachuris dynasty South Asia early medieval states 244 (2)
Later Liang dynasty East Asia medieval states 263 (3)
Latina, Via road Italy early states 178 (1) ancient Rome 181 (2)
Latin Cities state Italy the world in 500 BCE 34–35
Latin Empire state Southeast Europe Mongols 68–69 (1)
Latini people Italy early states 178 (1), (2)
La Tolita South America (Colombia) the world in 250 BCE 38–39
Latome East Africa (Sudan) exploration 157 (4)
La Tranche France early agriculture 174 (1)
Lattaquié see Laodicea
Latvia Ger. Lettland, Latv. Latvija state Southeast Europe inter-war 209 (3), (5) post-war economy 214 (1), (2) post-war politics 212 (3) Soviet Union 208 (2), 213 (4) the modern world 112 (2), 113 (4) WWI 207 (4), 208 (1) WWII 210 (1)
Latvija see Latvia
Laugerie Basse archaeological site France prehistoric culture 17 (3)
Lau Group island group Pacific Ocean early cultures 280–281 (3) medieval voyages 60 (2)
Lauis see Lugano
Launceston Australia colonization 282 (1), (2), 283 (3) exploration 279 (2)
Laurentian Highlands var. Laurentian Mountains, Fr. Les Laurentides plateau North America 129 (2)
Laurentian Mountains see Laurentian Highlands
Laurentide Ice Sheet ice feature North America historical geography 117 (1)
Lausanne It. Losanna Central Europe (Switzerland) early modern states 193 (5)
Lavak island Southwest Asia 20th-century politics 235 (5)
Lavan oil terminal Southwest Asia (Iran) economy 234 (1)
Lāvān, Jazīreh-ye see Lavan
Lavapura mod. Lop Buri Mainland Southeast Asia (Thailand) ancient India 241 (6) see also Lopburi
La Venta Central America (Mexico) first civilizations 121 (2), (3) first religions 36 (1)
La Victoria Central America (Guatemala) first civilizations 121 (2)
Lavinium Italy early states 178 (1)
Lavo state Mainland Southeast Asia the world in 1300 66–67
Laz people Southwest Asia Ottomans 232–233 (1)
Lazica state Southwest Asia the world in 500 CE 50–51 the world in 750 CE 54–55
Lealui Southern Africa (Zambia) exploration 157 (4)
Lebanon Ar. Al Lubnān, Fr. Liban region/state Southwest Asia exploration 219 (4) Islam 235 (4) Ottomans 232–233 (1) the modern world 113 (3) US economy 138 (2) WWII 210 (1), 211 (4) 20th century 234 (2) 20th-century politics 235 (5) Cold War 109 (1)
Le Cap var. Cap-Haïtien West Indies (Haiti) empire and revolution 89 (3)
Lechfeld battle Central Europe (Austria) medieval states 185 (3)
L'Écluse see Sluis, Sluys
Le Creusot France economy 205 (4)
Ledo South Asia (India) WWII 251 (3)
Ledro Italy Bronze Age 175 (3)
Leeds British Isles (United Kingdom) economy 204 (1) imperial global economy 93 (4)
Leeds and Liverpool canal British Isles economy 204 (1)
Leer Central Europe (Germany) Reformation 195 (5)
Leeward Islands colonial possession West Indies the world in 1900 94–95 the world in 1925 98–99 the world in 1950 102–103
Lefkosía, Lefkoşa see Nicosia
Lefroy goldfield Australia colonization 282 (2)
Le Gabillou archaeological site France prehistoric culture 17 (3)
Legaceaster see Chester, Deva
Legio VII Gemina legion headquarters Iberian Peninsula (Spain) ancient Rome 180–181 (1)
Legnano battle Italy medieval states 188 (1)
Legnica Ger. Liegnitz Central Europe (Poland) Mongols 68–69 (1) see also Liegnitz
Leh South Asia (India) biological diffusion 72–73 (1) post-war politics 252 (2)
Le Havre prev. le Havre-de-Grâce; Eng. Havre France early modern states 197 (5) economy 205 (4) empire and revolution 199 (4) inter-war 209 (3)
le Havre-de-Grâce see Le Havre
Leicester Lat. Batae Coritanorum British Isles (United Kingdom) economy 204 (1)
Leiden Low Countries (Netherlands) Reformation 195 (5)
Leie see Lys
Leinster region British Isles medieval states 186 (2)
Leipsic see Leipzig
Leipzig anc. Lipsia; hist. Leipsic; Pol. Lipsk Central Europe (Germany) early modern states 193 (4) economy 190 (1), 205 (4) empire and revolution 202 (2) post-war politics 212 (1) Reformation 196 (1)
Leli see Tianlin
Léman, le, Lac see Geneva lake
Le Mas d'Azil archaeological site France prehistoric culture 17 (3)
Lemberg Pol. Lwów, Rus. L'vov, Ukr. L'viv Eastern Europe (Ukraine) empire and revolution 198 (2) WWI 207 (4) see also L'vov, Lwów
Lemnos island Greece ancient Greece 177 (2), (3), 179 (4) first civilizations 175 (4) WWI 207 (6)
Lemovices see Limoges
Lena river Siberia colonialism 269 (3) early agriculture 20–21 (2), 258 (1) early modern states 268 (1) exploration 257 (2) first humans 13 (2) first states 260 (1) Mongols 68–69 (1) prehistoric culture 16 (1) Soviet Union 208 (2) trade 267 (3)
Leningrad prev. and mod. Sankt-Peterburg, prev. Petrograd; Eng. Saint Petersburg, Fin. Pietari Eastern Europe (Russian Federation) Cold War 108 (3) post-war politics 212 (3) Soviet Union 213 (4) WWII 210 (1), 211 (2), (4) see also Petrograd, St Petersburg
Lens France WWI 206 (2), (3)
Lentia see Linz
Leoben Central Europe (Austria) Napoleon 200–201 (1)
León Iberian Peninsula (Spain) Franks 184 (2) inter-war 209 (4) Islam 192 (3) medieval states 185 (3)
León state/region Iberian Peninsula crusades 186 (1) Islam 192 (3) medieval states 185 (3) medieval voyages 60–61 (1)
León and Castile state Iberian Peninsula crusades 64–65 (2)
Leopard's Kopje archaeological site Southern Africa (Zimbabwe) early cultures 160 (1)
Leopoldville mod. Kinshasa; Fr. Léopoldville Central Africa (Congo (Zaire)) colonization 167 (4) exploration 157 (4) see also Kinshasa
Lepanto battle Greece Ottomans 231 (3)
Lepenski Vir Southeast Europe the world in 5000 BCE 18–19
Leptis var. Leptis Magna mithraic site/settlement North Africa (Libya) ancient Rome 179 (3), 180–181 (1) ancient trade 44–45 (1) early cultures 160 (1) first civilizations 177 (1) The World in 1975 106–107 world religions 48 (1)
Leptis Magna see Leptis
Lérida settlement/university Iberian Peninsula (Spain) Islam 192 (3) medieval states 187 (3)
Lerma river Central America first civilizations 121 (2)
Les Bolards mithraic site France world religions 48 (1)
Lesbos mod. Lésvos island Greece ancient Greece 177 (2), (3), 179 (4) first civilizations 175 (4)
Les Cayes see Cayes
Les Combarelles archaeological site France prehistoric culture 17 (3)
Les Halles building France economy 191 (2)
Lesina see Hvar
Les Laurentides see Laurentian Highlands
Lesotho prev. Basutoland state Southern Africa decolonization 168 (1) economy 168 (2), (3) the modern world 112 (1) see also Basutoland
Lespugue archaeological site France prehistoric culture 17 (4)
Lesser Antarctica var. West Antarctica physical region Antarctica Antarctic Exploration 287 (3)
Lesser Antilles island group West Indies colonization 125 (4) exploration 118 (1), 119 (2), (3)
Les Trois Frères archaeological site France prehistoric culture 17 (3)
Lésvos see Lesbos
Le Temple building France economy 191 (2)
Leticia South America (Colombia) politics 152 (1)
Lettland see Latvia
Le Tuc d'Audoubert archaeological site France prehistoric culture 17 (3)
Lëtzebuerg see Luxembourg
Leubingen burial mound/settlement Central Europe (Germany) Bronze Age 175 (3)
Leucas Greece ancient Greece 177 (3)
Leucas island Greece ancient Greece 179 (4)
Leucecome Southwest Asia (Saudi Arabia) ancient trade 44–45 (1) early cultures 161 (3), (4), (5) early trade 225 (3)
Levant region Southwest Asia Bronze Age 175 (3) first civilizations 24 (2)
Levoča see Locse
Lexington battle/settlement North America (USA) US Civil War 131 (6)
Lexington battle North America (USA) empire and revolution 127 (3)
Leyte Philippines WWII 251 (3), 273 (2)
Leyte Gulf battle Philippines WWII 105 (3), 273 (2)
Lezetxiki archaeological site Iberian Peninsula (Spain) first humans 13 (2)
Lhasa var. La-sa, Lassa East Asia (China) biological diffusion 72–73 (1) colonialism 248 (1), 269 (4) early medieval states 244–245 (3) early modern states 268 (1) exploration 257 (3) medieval states 262–263 (1), 263 (6) post-war economy 275 (3)
Li vassal state East Asia first cities 259 (3)
Liang state East Asia medieval states 261 (4)
Liangcheng archaeological site East Asia early agriculture 258 (2)
Liang-chou see Liangzhou
Liangzhou var. Liang-chou state East Asia (China) early modern states 266 (1) medieval states 262–263 see also Wuwei
Liangzhu archaeological site East Asia (China) early agriculture 258 (1), (2)
Lianyungang East Asia (China) post-war politics 274 (2)
Liao state East Asia early modern states 265 (5)
Liao people East Asia the world in 1200 62–63
Liaodong East Asia (China) early modern states 266 (1)
Liaodong Peninsula coastal feature East Asia Russo-Japanese War 270 (4) Sino-Japanese War 270 (3)
Liao Empire see Khitan Empire
Liaoning province East Asia post-war politics 274 (2)
Liaoxi province East Asia first states 260 (1)
Liaoyang battle East Asia (China) medieval states 263 (5) Russo-Japanese War 270 (4)
Liaoyang province East Asia early modern states 266 (1), (2) medieval states 263 (6)
Liban see Lebanon
Libau see Libava
Libava Ger. Libau Eastern Europe (Latvia) WWI 207 (4)
Liberalitas Julia see Evora
Liberia state West Africa colonization 167 (4) decolonization 168 (1) economy 168 (2) European imperialism 96 (1) Islam 235 (4) the modern world 112 (1), 113 (3) trade 167 (1) WWII 105 (3)
Libreville Central Africa (Gabon) colonization 167 (4) economy 168 (2) exploration 157 (4)
Libya region/state North Africa ancient trade 44 (2) decolonization 168 (1) early Islam 56–57 (1), 57 (2) economy 168 (2) European imperialism 96 (1), 97 (4) Islam 163 (1), 226 (2), 227 (4), (5), 235 (4) Napoleon 200–201 (1) Ottomans 232–233 (1) the modern world 112 (1), 113 (3), (4) world religions 48 (1) WWII 104 (1), (2), 210 (1), 211 (4) Cold War 109 (1)
Lichfield British Isles (United Kingdom) medieval states 183 (3)
Lichtenberg Central Europe (Germany) post-war politics 212 (2)
Lidice massacre Central Europe (Czech Republic) WWII 211 (3)
Liechtenstein state Central Europe early modern states 193 (5) the modern world 112 (2)
Liège Dut. Luik, Ger. Lüttich Low Countries (Belgium) economy 190 (1) Franks 184 (2) Reformation 195 (5) WWI 206 (2), (3)
Liegnitz battle Central Europe (Poland) medieval states 189 (3)
Lietuva see Lithuania
Liger see Loire
Ligny/Quatre-Bras var. Ligny Quatre-Bras battle Low Countries (Belgium) Napoleon 200–201 (1)
Ligure, Mar see Ligurian Sea
Ligures people Italy early states 178 (1), (2)
Ligurian Republic state Italy the world in 1800 86–87
Ligurians people France/Italy the world in 750 BCE 30–31 the world in 250 BCE 38–39
Ligurian Sea Fr. Mer Ligurienne, It. Mar Ligure sea Italy early states 178 (1)
Ligurienne, Mer see Ligurian Sea
Liivi Laht see Riga, Gulf of
Lille var. l'Isle; prev. Lisle, anc. Insula; Dut. Rijssel, Flem. Ryssel France early modern states 197 (5) economy 190 (1) inter-war 209 (3) Reformation 195 (5)
Lilybaeum mod. Marsala Italy ancient Rome 179 (3), 180–181 (1) early cultures 161 (2) first civilizations 177 (1)
Lim river Southeast Europe post-war economy 215 (3)
Lima South America (Peru) colonization 148 (2) early cultures 145 (4) empire and revolution 150 (1), 151 (3) economy 153 (3) European expansion 80–81 (1) exploration 142 (1), 143 (2), (3) global immigration 100 (1) Incas 148 (1) narcotics 153 (5) politics 152 (1)
Lima region South America early cultures 145 (4)
Lima, Audiencia of region South America colonization 148 (2)
Limassol Southwest Asia (Cyprus) crusades 65 (3)
Limburg province/state Low Countries empire and revolution 202 (1i) Reformation 195 (5)
Limerick Ir. Luimneach British Isles (Ireland) economy 205 (4) medieval states 185 (3) medieval voyages 60–61 (1)
Limin Vathéos see Samos
Limoges anc. Augustoritum Lemovicensium, Lemovices France early modern states 197 (5) medieval states 187 (4)
Limonum see Poitiers
Limpopo var. Crocodile river Southern Africa early cultures 160 (1) European imperialism 96 (2) first humans 12 (1) Islam 163 (1) slave trade 165 (4) trade 164 (1)
Limpurg region Central Europe empire and revolution 199 (3)
Lin East Asia (China) first cities 259 (5)
Lin'an var. Hangchou, Hangchow, Hangzhou East Asia (China) medieval states 263 (5) see also Hangzhou
Lincoln anc. Lindum, Lindum Colonia British Isles (United Kingdom) economy 190 (1) medieval states 183 (3) see also Lindum
Lincoln North America (USA) the growth of the US 129 (2)
Lincoln Sea sea Arctic Ocean exploration 287 (2)
Líndhos see Lindus
Lindisfarne religious building/settlement British Isles (United Kingdom) medieval states 183 (3) medieval voyages 60–61 (1)
Lindos see Lindus
Lindsey region British Isles medieval states 183 (3)
Lindum var. Lindum Colonia; mod. Lincoln British Isles (United Kingdom) ancient Rome 180–181 (1) see also Lincoln
Lindum Colonia see Lincoln, Lindum
Lindus var. Líndhos; mod. Lindos Greece ancient Greece 177 (3) first civilizations 177 (1)
Lindus state Greece ancient Greece 177 (2)
Line Islands island group Pacific Ocean colonization 284–285 (1) early cultures 280–281 (3) exploration 279 (3) medieval voyages 60 (2)
Lingen region Central Europe empire and revolution 199 (3)
Lingfang East Asia (China) first states 260 (1)
Lingling province East Asia first states 260 (1)
Lingnan province Central Asia medieval states 262–263 (1)
Lingzhi people East Asia first cities 259 (4)
Linhuai Buddhist centre East Asia (China) world religions 49 (3)
Linhuang East Asia (China) the world in 1000 58–59
Linny Egypt ancient Egypt 159 (3)
Lintao East Asia (China) first states 60 (1)
Linyanti Southern Africa (Nambia) exploration 157 (4)
Linz anc. Lentia Central Europe (Austria) economy 190 (1) WWII 210 (1), 211 (2), (3), (4)
Linzi East Asia (China) first cities 259 (4), (5) first religions 37 (4) first states 260 (1)
Lion Cave Southern Africa (Swaziland) prehistoric culture 17 (2)
Lion, Golfe du, Lion, Gulf of see Lions, Gulf of
Lions, Gulf of Fr. Golfe du Lion; var. Gulf of Lion; anc. Sinus Gallicus gulf France early modern states 197 (5)
Lipan people Central America colonization 126 (1)
Lipan Apache people Central America/North America colonization 125 (4)
Lipari archaeological site Italy Copper Age 174 (2)
Lipsk, Lipsia see Leipzig
Lisan, Lake lake Southwest Asia historical geography 216–217 (1)
Lisboa see Lisbon, Olisipo
Lisbon anc. Felicitas Julia, Olisipo; Port. Lisboa Iberian Peninsula (Portugal) trade 72–73 (1) crusades 186 (1), 64–65 (2) early Islam 56–57 (1) economy 190 (1), 205 (4) empire and revolution 202 (1) European expansion 81 (3), 84–85 (1) exploration 156 (3) Franks 184 (2) inter-war 209 (3), (4) Islam 192 (3), 226 (2) medieval states 185 (3) Napoleon 200–201 (1), 201 (2), (3) Ottomans 231 (3) Reformation 194 (2) WWII 210 (1), 211 (4) see also Olisipo
Lishi East Asia (China) first cities 259 (5)
Lisieux anc. Noviomagus France Franks 184 (2)
Lisle, l'Isle see Lille
Litauen see Lithuania
Lithuania Ger. Litauen, Lith. Lietuva, Pol. Litwa, Rus. Litva region/state Eastern Europe economy 190 (1) empire and revolution 198 (2) inter-war 209 (3), (5) Islam 163 (1) medieval states 189 (3), (4) Ottomans 230 (1) post-war economy 214 (1), (2) post-war politics 212 (3) Soviet Union 208 (2), 213 (4) the modern world 112 (2) WWI 207 (4), 208 (1) WWII 210 (1)
Lithuanians people Eastern Europe crusades 186 (1), 64–65 (2) medieval states 185 (3)
Little Armenia state Southwest Asia economy 190 (1) Mongols 229 (3), 68–69 (1)
Little Big Horn battle North America (USA) the growth of the US 129 (2)
Little Rock North America (USA) the growth of the US 129 (2), 132 (1) US society 137 (6)
Little Salt Spring North America (USA) the world in 10,000 BCE 14–15
Little Wallachia vassal state Eastern Europe Ottomans 197 (4)
Little Zab Ar. Nahraz Zāb aş Şaghīr, Kurd. Zē-i Kōya, Per. Rūdkhāneh-ye Zāb-e Kūchek river Southwest Asia first cities 220 (2) first civilizations 221 (4), (5)
Litva, Litwa see Lithuania
Liu Song state East Asia medieval states 261 (4)
Livenza river Italy WWI 207 (5)
Liverpool British Isles (United Kingdom) economy 204 (1), 205 (4) global immigration 100 (1) imperial global economy 93 (4), (5) inter-war 209 (3) WWII 210 (1)
Livingstone var. Maramba Southern Africa (Zambia) colonization 167 (4)
Livno Southeast Europe (Bosnia and Herzegovina) civil war 215 (3)
Livonia region Central Europe early modern states 195 (3) empire and revolution 198 (2)
Livonians people Eastern Europe medieval states 189 (3)
Lixus mod. Larache North Africa (Morocco) first civilizations 177 (1)
Lizard Mound burial mound North America (USA) first civilizations 121 (4)
Ljubljana anc. Aemona, Emona; Ger. Laibach, It. Lubiana Central Europe (Slovenia) post-war economy 215 (3)
Llano del Jicaro archaeological site Central America (Mexico) first civilizations 121 (3)
Llanos physical region South America early cultures 144 (1), 147 (2) empire and revolution 150 (1), (2) environment 153 (4)
Llanos de Mojos archaeological site South America (Bolivia) early cultures 145 (2)
Loanda see Luanda
Loango Central Africa (Congo) European expansion 84–85 (1) slave trade 165 (4) trade 164 (2)
Loango state Central Africa slave trade 165 (4) trade 164 (2), 167 (1)
Lobito Southern Africa (Angola) Cold War 109 (5) economy 168 (2)
Lob Nor see Lop Nor
Lobo, Cape see St. Mary, Cape
Loburi see Lop Buri
Loch Garman see Wexford
Loc Ninh battle Mainland Southeast Asia (Vietnam) 251 (5)
Locri Italy early states 178 (1), (2) first civilizations 177 (1)
Locri Epizephyrii see Locri
Locse mod. Levoča Central Europe (Slovakia) medieval states 189 (4)
Lodi battle Italy Napoleon 200–201 (1)
Lodi Sultanate of Delhi state South Asia the world in 1500 74–75
Lodz Central Europe (Poland) WWI 207 (4)
Lo Fu Shan see Luofu Shan
Loire var. Liger river France crusades 186 (1), 64–65 (2) early Islam 56–57 (1) early modern states 197 (5) economy 190 (1), 205 (4) empire and revolution 199 (4), 202 (1) exploration 172 (1) Franks 183 (5), (6), 184 (2) medieval states 185 (3), 187 (4), 192 (1), (2) Napoleon 200–201 (1), 201 (2), (3) prehistoric culture 17 (3), (4) WWI 206 (2), (3)
Lokoja West Africa (Nigeria) colonization 167 (4)
Loltun Cave Central America (Mexico) first civilizations 123 (2)
Lombardia see Lombardy
Lombards people Southeast Europe ancient Rome 181 (4), 182 (1) great migrations 53 (2)
Lombardy var. Kingdom of the Lombards; It. Lombardia region/state Italy crusades 64–65 (2) early Islam 56–57 (1) economy 190 (1) empire and revolution 202 (3) Franks 184 (2) Islam 184 (1) medieval states 182 (2), 183 (4), 188 (1)
Lombardy and Venetia, Kingdom of state Italy early modern states 193 (5)
Lombardy-Venetia see Venetia
Lombok island Maritime Southeast Asia early medieval states 245 (5), (6) European imperialism 97 (3) exploration 239 (2)
Lombok Strait battle Maritime Southeast Asia (Indonesia) WWII 272 (1)
Lomé West Africa (Togo) colonization 167 (4)
Lomekwi archaeological site East Africa (Kenya) first humans 12 (1)
Lonato battle Italy Napoleon 200–201 (1)
Londinium mod. London; anc. Augusta British Isles (United Kingdom) ancient Rome 180–181 (1), 181 (3) great migrations 52–53 (1) world religions 48 (1) see also London
London North America (Canada) 132 (1)
London anc. Londinium British Isles (United Kingdom) ancient Rome 182 (1) plague72–73 (1) crusades 186 (1) economy 190 (1), 205 (4) empire and revolution 202 (1) European expansion 84–85 (1) imperial global economy 92 (1), 93 (5) inter-war 209 (3) medieval states 182 (2), 183 (3), 186 (2), 187 (3), (4), 188 (2) medieval voyages 60–61 (1) Napoleon 200–201 (1), 201 (2), (3) post-war politics 212 (3) Reformation 194 (2) WWI 206 (2), (3) WWII 210 (1), 211 (2), (3), (4) Cold War 108 (3) see also Londinium
Longarone Italy WWI 207 (5)
Long Island island North America empire and revolution 127 (2)
Longjingcun var. Lungchingtsun East Asia (China) colonialism 269 (4) 270 (2)
Longkou var. Lungkow East Asia (China) colonialism 269 (4)
Longobucco Italy economy 190 (1)
Longreach Australia colonization 282 (1)
Long's Drift East Africa (Kenya) early agriculture 158 (1)
Longwy France early modern states 197 (5)
Longxi province East Asia first states 260 (1)
Longxing East Asia (China) medieval states 263 (4), (5), (6)
Longyu var. Lungyu province Central Asia medieval states 262–263 (1)
Longzhou var. Lungchow East Asia (China) colonialism 269 (4)
Loochoo Islands see Ryukyu Islands
Loos France WWI 206 (2), (3)
Lop Buri var. Loburi Mainland Southeast Asia (Thailand) world religions 243 (5) see also Lavapura
Lopera Iberian Peninsula (Spain) inter-war 209 (4)
Lop Nor var. Lob Nor, Lop Nur, Lo-pu Po lake East Asia early agriculture 258 (1) exploration 257 (3) first states 260 (1) Mongols 68–69 (1) world religions 49 (3)
Lop Nur, Lo-pu Po see Lop Nor
Lorca Iberian Peninsula (Spain) Islam 192 (3)
Lorient France early modern states 197 (5)
Lorna Negra South America (Peru) early cultures 145 (4)
Lorraine region France crusades 64–65 (2)
Lorraine, Duchy of state France early modern states 197 (5) Reformation 196 (1)
Los Altos North America (USA) 136 (3)
Los Angeles North America (USA) exploration 119 (3) global immigration 100 (1), 101 (3) the growth of the US 129 (2), 132 (1) the modern world 113 (4) US economy 134 (1), (3), 136 (2) US politics 135 (6)
Losanna see Lausanne
Los Gatos North America (USA) 136 (3)
Los Idolos archaeological site Central America (Mexico) first civilizations 121 (3)
Los Millares archaeological site Iberian Peninsula (Spain) Copper Age 174 (2)
Los Naranjos Central America (Honduras) first civilizations 121 (2)
Los Palmos South America (Peru) early cultures 145 (4)
Los Soldados archaeological site Central America (Mexico) first civilizations 121 (3)
Los Toldos archaeological site South America (Argentina) early cultures 144 (1)
Los Tuxtlas Central America (Mexico) first civilizations 122 (1)
Lot river France prehistoric culture 17 (3)
Lothagam archaeological site East Africa (Kenya) first humans 12 (1)
Lothal archaeological site/settlement South Asia (India) first cities 240 (2) first civilizations 24 (2), 25 (3)
Loualaba see Lualaba
Louangphrabang see Lan Chang, Luang Prabang
Louisbourg North America (Canada) empire and revolution 127 (2) empire and revolution 88 (1)
Louisiana colonial possession/state North America colonization 126 (1) empire and revolution 88 (1) imperial global economy 93 (5) the growth of the US 129 (1) US Civil War 130 (2), (3), (4), (5), 131 (6), (7) US economy 134 (2), 139 (3) US society 137 (6) cotton 139 (3)
Louisville North America (USA) the growth of the US 129 (2), 132 (1) US Civil War 131 (6)
Loulan Buddhist centre East Asia (China) world religions 49 (3)
Lourenço Marques mod. Maputo Southern Africa (Mozambique) colonization 166 (2), 167 (4) exploration 156 (3) see also Maputo
Lourenço Marques, Baía de see Delagoa Bay
Louvain Low Countries (Belgium) economy 190 (1)
Louvo region Mainland Southeast Asia early medieval states 245 (5)
Louvre building France economy 191 (2)

Lovat' river Eastern Europe exploration 172 (1)
Lovelock Cave archaeological site North America (USA) the world in 1250 BCE 26–27
Loviisa see Lovisa
Lovisa Fin. Loviisa Scandinavia (Finland) WWI 207 (4)
Low Countries var. Netherlands state Low Countries early modern states 193 (4), 194 (1) Reformation 194 (2)
Lower Bembe state Southern Africa trade 164 (2)
Lower Burma state Mainland Southeast Asia European imperialism 97 (3)
Lower California Sp. Baja California coastal feature North America exploration 118 (1), 119 (2), (3) see also Baja California
Lower Egypt state Egypt ancient Egypt 159 (5)
Lower Lorraine region Central Europe medieval states 185 (3), 188 (1)
Lower Palatinate state Central Europe early modern states 197 (5)
Lower Pima people Central America colonization 126 (1)
Lower Tunguska Russ. Nizhnyaya Tunguska river Siberia Soviet Union 214–215 (4)
Lowland Maya people Central America first civilizations 123 (2)
Lowry archaeological site North America (USA) cultural groups 123 (4)
Lo-yang see Luoyang
Lozi state Southern Africa slave trade 165 (4) trade 167 (1)
Loznica Southeast Europe (Yugoslavia) WWI 207 (6)
Lu region/state East Asia first cities 259 (4), (5) first religions 37 (4)
Lualaba Fr. Loualaba river Central Africa exploration 157 (4)
Luanda var. Loanda; hist. São Paulo de Loanda Southern Africa (Angola) Cold War 109 (5) colonization 167 (4) economy 168 (2) European expansion 81 (3), 84–85 (1) exploration 157 (4) slave trade 165 (4) trade 164 (2)
Luang Prabang var. Lan Chang, Louangphrabang, Louangphabang Mainland Southeast Asia (Laos) colonialism 247 (4), 248 (1) see also Lan Chang
Luang Prabang state Mainland Southeast Asia the world in 1800 86–87 the world in 1850 90–91
Luba state Central Africa slave trade 165 (4) trade 167 (1)
Lubaantun Central America (Belize) first civilizations 123 (2)
Lubango Port. Sá da Bandeira Southern Africa (Angola) Cold War 109 (5)
Lübeck Central Europe (Germany) trade 72–73 (1) early modern states 193 (4), 195 (3) economy 190 (1) empire and revolution 199 (3) medieval states 188 (1), 189 (3) Napoleon 200–201 (1), 201 (2)
Lubiana see Ljubljana
Lublin Central Europe (Poland) early modern states 193 (4) economy 190 (1) medieval states 189 (3) WWI 207 (4) WWII 211 (3)
Lubumbashi prev. Élisabethville Central Africa (Congo (Zaire)) economy 168 (2)
Lubusi archaeological site Southern Africa (Zambia) early cultures 160 (1)
Luca see Lucca
Lucani people Italy early states 178 (1), (2)
Lucayans people West Indies the world in 1500 74–75
Lucca anc. Luca Italy crusades 186 (1) economy 190 (1)
Lucca anc. Luca state Italy empire and revolution 202 (1) Napoleon 201 (2)
Lucentum see Alicante
Luceria Italy early states 178 (1)
Lucerna, Lucerne see Luzern
Luchow see Hefei
Lucknow settlement South Asia (India) colonialism 247 (3) decolonization 250 (1) economy 249 (4) empire and revolution 249 (3) imperial global economy 93 (5) post-war politics 252 (1)
Lucus Augusti Iberian Peninsula (Spain) ancient Rome 180–181 (1)
Lüda see Dairen, Dalian
Ludhiana South Asia (India) post-war economy 253 (5)
Luena var. Lwena; Port. Luso Southern Africa (Angola) Cold War 109 (5)
Lugano Ger. Lauis Central Europe (Switzerland) early modern states 193 (5)
Lugdunensis province France ancient Rome 180–181 (1)
Lugdunum mod. Lyon, Lyons settlement France ancient Rome 179 (5), 180–181 (1), 181 (3), (4) world religions 48 (1) see also Lyon, Lyons
Lugenda river Central Africa exploration 157 (4)
Luguvallium see Carlisle
Luguvallum see Carlisle
Luhun state East Asia first cities 259 (3)
Luik see Liège
Luimneach see Limerick
Lukenya archaeological site/settlement East Africa (Kenya) early agriculture 158 (1) early cultures 160 (1)
Luluabourg see Kananga
Lululampembele East Africa (Tanzania) early agriculture 158 (1)
Lumbini South Asia (Nepal) first empires 241 (4) first religions 36 (2) world religions 242 (3)
Lund Scandinavia (Sweden) medieval states 185 (3)
Lunda state Central Africa slave trade 165 (4) trade 167 (1)
Lundu state Southern Africa slave trade 165 (4) trade 164 (1)
Lüneburg Central Europe (Germany) economy 190 (1)
Lunéville France WWI 206 (2), (3)
Lungcheng East Asia (China) first states 261 (3)
Lungchingtsun see Longjingcun
Lungchow see Longzhou
Lungkow see Longkou
Lungyu see Longyu
Luni Italy Bronze Age 175 (3)
Luni river South Asia early medieval states 244 (1) first cities 240 (2) Mughal Empire 246 (1)
Luofu Shan var. Lo Fu Shan mountain East Asia first religions 37 (4)
Luolang var. P'yŏngyang-si, P'yŏngyang; mod. Pyongyang East Asia (North Korea) first states 260 (1), medieval states 261 (6), 264 (1), (2)
Luoling East Asia (China) first states 260 (1)
Luoyang var. Honan, Lo-yang East Asia (China) ancient trade 44–45 (1), 72–73 (1) early agriculture 258 (2) economy 274 (1) exploration 256 (1) first cities 28–29 (1), 259 (3), (4), (5), first religions 36 (1), 37 (4) first states 260 (1), 261 (2), (3) medieval states 261 (4), (6), 262–263 (1) Mongols 68–69 (1) world religions 49 (3)
Luoyi East Asia (China) first cities 259 (4)
Luristan region Southwest Asia medieval Persia 231 (4)
Lusaka Southern Africa (Zambia) colonization 167 (4) economy 168 (2)
Lusatia region Central Europe medieval states 188 (1)
Lu Shan mountain East Asia (China) first religions 37 (4)
Lü-shun see Port Arthur
Lusitani people Iberian Peninsula ancient Rome 179 (5)
Lusitania province Iberian Peninsula ancient Rome 180–181 (1)
Luso see Luena
Lustucru battle France Reformation 196 (2)
Lūt, Baḩrat see Dead Sea
Lut, Bahret see Dead Sea
Lutetia var. Lutetia Parisiorum, Parisii; mod. Paris France ancient Rome 180–181 (1) great migrations 52–53 (1) see also Paris
Lutetia Parisiorum see Lutetia, Paris
Lutsk Eastern Europe (Ukraine) WWI 207 (4)
Lutter battle Central Europe (Germany) Reformation 196 (1)
Lüttich see Liège
Lützel major cistercian house Central Europe medieval states 187 (3)
Lützen battle Central Europe (Germany) Napoleon 200–201 (1) Reformation 196 (1)
Luxembourg Low Countries (Luxembourg) early modern states 197 (5) empire and revolution 202 (1i), (2)
Luxembourg var. Lëtzebuerg, Luxemburg state Low Countries empire and revolution 202 (1i) inter-war 209 (3), (5) post-war economy 213 (5), 214 (1), (2) post-war politics 212 (1), (3) Soviet Union 214–215 (4) the modern world 112 (2), 113 (4) US superpower 138 (1) WWI 206 (2), (3), 208 (1) WWII 210 (1) Cold War 108 (3),109 (1)
Luxemburg Fr. Luxembourg Low Countries (Luxembourg) early modern states 193 (4) medieval states 192 (1) Reformation 195 (5) see also Luxembourg
Luxemburg province Low Countries Reformation 195 (5)
Luxor Egypt ancient Egypt 159 (5) Islam 235 (4) see also Karnak, Ipet-isut, Thebes
Luzern Fr. Lucerne, It. Lucerna Central Europe (Switzerland) early modern states 193 (5)
Luzhou East Asia (China) medieval states 263 (6)
Luzon island Maritime Southeast Asia ancient trade 44–45 (1) colonialism 247 (4) European imperialism 97 (3) exploration 239 (1) post-war economy 275 (3) post-war politics 253 (4) world religions 243 (5) WWII 272 (1)
L'viv see Lemberg, L'vov, Lwów
L'vov Ger. Lemberg, Pol. Lwów, Ukr. L'viv Eastern Europe (Ukraine) economy 190 (1) post-war politics 212 (3) WWII 211 (4) see also Lemberg, Lwów
Lwena see Luena
Lwów Eastern Europe (Ukraine) early modern states 193 (4) WWII 210 (1), 211 (3)
Lximché Central America (Guatemala) Aztecs 124 (1)
Lycaonia region Southwest Asia Hellenistic world 40–41 (1)
Lycia region/state Southwest Asia ancient Rome 179 (5), 180–181 (1) first civilizations 177 (1) Hellenistic world 40–41 (1) world religions 48 (1)
Lycopolis see Asyut
Lydenburg archaeological site Southern Africa (South Africa) early cultures 160 (1)
Lydia region/state Southwest Asia ancient Persia 223 (4) early systems 33 (2) first civilizations 222 (2) first religions 37 (3) Hellenistic world 40–41 (1)
Lydians people Southwest Asia first civilizations 221 (5)
Lynn see King's Lynn
Lynn Regis see King's Lynn
Lyon anc. Lugdunum; Eng. Lyons France crusades 186 (1) early modern states 193 (4), 197 (5) economy 190 (1), 205 (4) empire and revolution 199 (4), 202 (1) Franks 183 (5), (6), 184 (2) Islam 184 (1) medieval states 185 (3), 192 (1), (2) Napoleon 200–201 (1), 201 (2) Reformation 194 (2) WWII 210 (1), 211 (4)
Lyons see Lugdunum, Lyon
Lys battle France WWI 206 (3)
Lys var. Leie river France WWI 206 (2), (3)
Lysimachus, Kingdom of state Southwest Asia Hellenistic world 224 (1)
Lystra Southwest Asia (Turkey) Hellenistic world 40–41 (1)
Lyttelton settlement/whaling station New Zealand colonization 283 (4), (5)
Lyublin see Lublin

M

Maadi Egypt ancient Egypt 159 (2)
Maas river Low Countries empire and revolution 199 (4)
Maastricht var. Maestricht; anc. Traiectum ad Mosam, Traiectum Tungorum Low Countries (Netherlands) empire and revolution 202 (1i) WWI 206 (2), (3)
Maba archaeological site/settlement East Asia (China) first humans 13 (2)
Mabaruma people South America the world in 1300 66–67
Mabiyyat Southwest Asia (Saudi Arabia) early Islam 56–57 (1)
Mabveni archaeological site Southern Africa (Zimbabwe) early cultures 160 (1)
Macao East Asia (China) early modern states 266 (1)
Macao var. Macau, Mação, Chin. Aomen East Asia (China) colonialism 247 (4), 248 (1) colonization 284–285 (1) decolonization 251 (4) early modern states 268 (1) European expansion 80–81 (1) , 97 (3) post-war economy 275 (3) trade 267 (3) WWII 251 (3), 272 (1), 273 (2)
Macapá South America (Brazil) politics 152 (1)
Macassar region/settlement Maritime Southeast Asia colonialism 247 (4) colonization 284–285 (1) WWII 272 (1), 273 (2)
Macassar Strait Ind. Selat Makasar sea waterway Maritime Southeast Asia ancient India 241 (6) colonialism 247 (4) early medieval states 245 (6) Islam 243 (6) world religions 243 (5)
Macau see Macao
Maçayó see Maceió
Macbar region South Asia early medieval states 244–245 (3)
Machiwara South Asia (India) colonialism 247 (3)
Macdonnell Ranges mountain range Australia colonization 283 (3) exploration 279 (2)
Macedon var. Macedonia; mod. FYR Macedonia state Southeast Europe ancient Greece 179 (4)
Macedonia region/state Southeast Europe ancient Persia 223 (4) ancient Rome 179 (5), 180–181 (1), 225 (5) early agriculture 174 (1) early systems 223 (3) exploration 218 (1) first civilizations 177 (1) Hellenistic world 224 (1), 41 (2) Ottomans 202 (4), 232–233 (1) post-war economy 214 (1), (2), 215 (3) Soviet Union 214–215 (4) the modern world 112 (2), 113 (3), (4) US superpower 138 (1)
Maceió prev. Maçayó South America (Brazil) empire and revolution 151 (3) environment 153 (4)
Machaerus Southwest Asia (Jordan) ancient Rome 225 (4)
Machang archaeological site East Asia early agriculture 258 (2)
Machaquilá Central America (Mexico) first civilizations 123 (2)
Machu Picchu South America (Peru) Incas 147 (3)
Macina see Masina
Mackay Australia colonization 282 (1)
Mackenzie river North America cultural groups 123 (3) early agriculture 120 (1) early systems 32 (1), 33 (2) exploration 118 (1), 119 (2), 286 (1), 287 (2) prehistoric culture 16 (1), 129 (2)
Mackenzie, District of province North America the growth of the US 132 (1)
Mackenzie Inuit people North America cultural groups 123 (3)
Mackenzie Mountains mountain range North America exploration 286 (1), 287 (2), 129 (2)
Macon North America (USA) US Civil War 131 (7)
Macquarie penal centre Australia environmentalism 285 (2)
Macquarie Harbour penal colony Australia colonization 282 (1)
Macquarie Island island Pacific Ocean Antarctic Exploration 287 (3)
Macsó admin. region Southeast Europe medieval states 189 (4)
Madagascar Malg. Madagasikara; prev. Malagasy Republic colonial possession/state/island Indian Ocean early agriculture 158 (1), 20–21 (2) early cultures 160 (1) economy 163 (2) European expansion 80–81 (1) European imperialism 96 (1), 97 (4) exploration 157 (4) first humans 13 (2) global immigration 100 (1) historical geography 254–255 (1) imperial global economy 92 (1) Islam 163 (1) slave trade 165 decolonization 168 (1) the modern world 112 (1), 113 (3), (4) trade 164 (1), 230 (2) WWII 104 (1), (2)
Madagasikara see Madagascar
Madapallam see Narasapur
Mađarska see Hungary
Madasa state West Africa trade 163 (4)
Madeira var. Ilha de Madeira island Atlantic Ocean slave trade 165 (4)
Madeira Sp. Río Madera river South America colonization 149 (3) early cultures 144 (1), 145 (2), 146 (1), 147 (2) economy 153 (3) empire and revolution 151 (3) environment 153 (4) exploration 142 (1), 143 (2), 156 (3)
Madeira, Ilha de see Madeira
Madera, Río see Madeira
Madhya-Desa region South Asia early religions 48 (2)
Madhyama-Dish region South Asia ancient India 242 (1)
Madhyama Pava South Asia (India) world religions 242 (3)
Madhya Pradesh region South Asia post-war politics 252 (1)
Madira Bickel Mound North America (USA) cultural groups 122 (5)
Madison North America (USA) the growth of the US 129 (2)
Madras var. Chennai South Asia (India) colonialism 247 (3), 248 (1), (2), 269 (4) decolonization 250 (1) economy 249 (4) empire and revolution 88 (1) Mughal Empire 246 (1) post-war economy 253 (5) post-war politics 252 (1) trade 267 (3)
Madras region/state South Asia colonialism 248 (2) decolonization 250 (2) empire and revolution 249 (3) post-war politics 253 (4)
Madras States state South Asia colonialism 248 (2)
Madre de Dios river South America colonization 148 (2) early cultures 145 (4)
Madrid Iberian Peninsula (Spain) early modern states 194 (1) economy 198 (1), 205 (4) empire and revolution 202 (1) inter-war 209 (3), (4) Islam 192 (3) Napoleon 200–201 (1), 201 (2), (3) Ottomans 231 (3) post-war politics 212 (3) Reformation 194 (2) WWII 210 (1), 211 (4) Cold War 108 (3)
Madu Egypt ancient Egypt 159 (4)
Madura mod. Madurai; prev. Mathurai South Asia (India) colonialism 247 (3) early religions 48 (2) imperial global economy 93 (5) see also Madurai
Madurai prev. Madura, Mathurai South Asia (India) colonialism 248 (1) early medieval states 244 (1), (2), 244–245 (3), 245 (4) first empires 241 (4) Mughal Empire 246 (1) post-war economy 253 (5) see also Madura
Maebashi var. Maebasi, Mayebashi Japan economy 270 (1)
Maebasi see Maebashi
Mae Nam Khong see Mekong
Mae Nam Yom river Mainland Southeast Asia first states 260 (1)
Mae Nan Ping river Mainland Southeast Asia first states 260 (1)
Maeotis Palus inland sea Eastern Europe ancient trade 44 (2)
Maes Howe archaeological site British Isles (United Kingdom) Copper Age 174 (2)
Maestricht see Maastricht
Mafeking Southern Africa (South Africa) colonization 167 (4) European imperialism 96 (2)
Mafia island East Africa economy 163 (2)
Magadan Eastern Europe (Russian Federation) Soviet Union 214–215 (4)
Magadha South Asia (India) first religions 36 (1)
Magadha region/state South Asia ancient India 242 (1) ancient trade 44–45 (1) early religions 48 (2) first empires 241 (4), (5) first religions 36 (2) medieval states 261 (6) world religions 242 (2), (3)
Magaliesburg Southern Africa (South Africa) exploration 157 (4)
Magallanes see Punta Arenas
Magallanes, Estrecho de see Magellan, Strait of
Magdalena river South America colonization 148 (2) early cultures 145 (2), 146 (1) empire and revolution 150 (2), 151 (3) environment 153 (4) exploration 143 (3) Incas 148 (1) politics 152 (1)
Magdeburg Central Europe (Germany) economy 190 (1) empire and revolution 199 (3) Franks 184 (2) medieval states 185 (3), 188 (1), 189 (3) Reformation 196 (2)
Magdeburg region Central Europe empire and revolution 199 (3)
Magellan, Strait of Sp. Estrecho de Magallanes sea waterway South America colonization 148 (2) European expansion 80–81 (1) exploration 142 (1), 143 (3)
Magersfontein battle Southern Africa (South Africa) European imperialism 96 (2)
Maghreb physical region North Africa early Islam 56–57 (1)
Maghsharen Tuareg state West Africa trade 163 (6)
Magindanao state Philippines the world in 1800 86–87 the world in 1850 90–91
Magna Graecia region Italy first religions 37 (3)
Magnesia battle Southwest Asia (Turkey) ancient Greece 179 (4)
Magnus Sinus sea East Asia ancient trade 44 (2)
Magonsaetas people British Isles medieval states 183 (3)
Magyarország see Hungary
Magyars people Central Europe medieval states 185 (3)
Mahagama South Asia (Sri Lanka) early medieval states 244 (2)
Mahagara South Asia (India) the world in 2500 BCE 22–23
Maha-Meghavahanas state South Asia ancient trade 44–45 (1)
Mahanadi river South Asia colonialism 247 (3), 248 (1), (2) decolonization 250 (1) early medieval states 244 (1), (2), 244–245 (3), 245 (4) economy 249 (4) first empires 241 (4), (5) Marathas 246 (2) Mughal Empire 246 (1) world religions 242 (2), 243 (4)
Maharashtra region South Asia post-war politics 252 (1), 253 (4) world religions 242 (2), 49 (3)
Mahasna Egypt ancient Egypt 159 (2)
Mahdia var. Al Mahdīyah, Mehdia North Africa (Tunisia) early Islam 56–57 (1)
Mahe prev. Mayyali; Fr. Mahé colonial possession/settlement South Asia (India) colonialism 247 (3), 248 (2), 269 (4) decolonization 251 (4) empire and revolution 88 (1), 88–89 (2) post-war politics 252 (1) WWII 251 (3)
Maheshwar South Asia (India) Marathas 246 (2)
Maheya region South Asia world religions 242 (2)
Mahican var. Mohican people North America colonization 126 (1)
Mahisamandala region South Asia first empires 241 (4)
Mahishmati religious site/settlement South Asia (India) first religions 36 (2) world religions 243 (4)
Maidum Egypt ancient Egypt 159 (3)
Mailand see Mediolanum, Milan
Mailapura South Asia (India) world religions 243 (4)
Main river Central Europe empire and revolution 199 (3) WWI 206 (2), (3)
Maina Greece medieval states 187 (5)
Mainaca Iberian Peninsula (Spain) first civilizations 177 (1)
Maine region France medieval states 187 (4)
Maine colonial possession/state North America empire and revolution 127 (2) the growth of the US 129 (1) US Civil War 130 (2), (3), (4), (5) US economy 134 (2)
Maine, Gulf of gulf North America empire and revolution 127 (2)
Mainz settlement/state Central Europe (Germany) ancient Rome 182 (1) crusades 186 (1) early modern states 193 (4), 197 (5) economy 190 (1) empire and revolution 199 (3) Franks 184 (2) medieval states 182 (2), 185 (3) post-war politics 212 (1) Reformation 196 (1) WWI 206 (2), (3)
Maipú battle South America (Chile) empire and revolution 150 (1), 88–89 (2)
Maisur see Kanara, Karnataka, Mysore
Majapahit Maritime Southeast Asia (Indonesia) early medieval states 245 (6)
Majapahit state Maritime Southeast Asia the world in 1300 66–67 the world in 1400 70–71 the world in 1500 74–75
Majdanek concentration camp Central Europe (Poland) WWII 211 (3)
Maji East Africa (Ethiopia) ancient trade 44–45 (1)
Majiabang archaeological site/settlement East Asia (China) early agriculture 258 (1)
Majiayao archaeological site East Asia (China) early agriculture 258 (1)
Majorca state/island Iberian Peninsula crusades 186 (1) inter-war 209 (4) Islam 192 (3)
Makapansgat archaeological site Southern Africa (South Africa) first humans 12 (1)
Makasar see Macassar, Ujungpandang
Makasar, Selat see Makassar, Straits of
Makassar see Macassar, Ujungpandang
Makatea island Pacific Ocean exploration 278 (1)
Makgadikgadi, Lake lake Southern Africa historical geography 154–155 (1)
Makira see San Cristóbal
Makkah see Mecca
Makran province/state Southwest Asia ancient Persia 223 (4), 225 (6)
Makuria state East Africa Islam 163 (1)
Makwe Southern Africa (South Africa) the world in 5000 BCE 18–19
Malab East Africa (Somalia) early cultures 161 (3), (5) early trade 225 (3)
Malabar state South Asia world religions 243 (4)
Malabar Coast physical region South Asia colonialism 247 (3), 248 (1), (2) decolonization 250 (1) early medieval states 244 (1), (2), 244–245 (3), 245 (4) economy 249 (4) first empires 241 (4), (5) Marathas 246 (2) Mughal Empire 246 (1) post-war politics 252 (1) world religions 242 (2), 243 (4)
Malaca mod. Málaga Iberian Peninsula (Spain) ancient Rome 179 (3) great migrations 52–53 (1) see also Málaga
Malacca Mal. Melaka Mainland Southeast Asia (Malaysia) biological diffusion 72–73 (1) European expansion 80–81 (1), 81 (3) exploration 239 (1), (2) trade 230 (2), 267 (3)
Malacca state South Asia first empires 241 (5)
Malacca, Strait of Ind. Selat Melaka sea waterway Maritime Southeast Asia ancient India 241 (6) colonialism 247 (4) early medieval states 245 (5), (6) Islam 243 (6) medieval voyages 61 (3) world religions 243 (5)
Malacca, Sultanate of Mal. Melaka state Mainland Southeast Asia trade 267 (3)
Málaga Iberian Peninsula (Spain) ancient Rome 182 (1) economy 190 (1) inter-war 209 (4) Islam 192 (3) medieval states 182 (2)
Malagasy Republic see Madagascar
Malakula see Malekula
Malakunanja archaeological site Australia prehistoric culture 17 (2)
Malange see Malanje
Malanje var. Malange Southern Africa (Angola) Cold War 109 (5)
Malao East Africa (Somalia) ancient trade 44 (2)
Malapati archaeological site Southern Africa (Zimbabwe) early cultures 160 (1)
Malatya anc. Melitene Southwest Asia (Turkey) early Islam 56–57 (1) first cities 28–29 (1) first civilizations 221 (5) Ottomans 230 (1) see also Melitene
Malava region/state South Asia first empires 241 (5) Hellenistic world 40–41 (1)
Malawi prev. Nyasaland state Southern Africa decolonization 168 (1) economy 168 (2) the modern world 112 (1), 113 (3) see also Nyasaland
Malawi, Lake see Nyasa
Malaya colonial possession/region/state Mainland Southeast Asia colonialism 269 (4) global immigration 100 (1), 101 (3) WWII 104 (1), 272 (1), 273 (2)
Malay Peninsula region/coastal feature Mainland Southeast Asia ancient India 241 (6) colonialism 247 (4) early medieval states 245 (5), (6) exploration 239 (2) first humans 13 (2) Islam 243 (6) world religions 243 (5), 49 (3)
Malays people Maritime Southeast Asia/Philippines ancient trade 44–45 (1) economy 163 (2) Islam 163 (1)
Malaysia prev. the separate territories of Federation of Malaya, Sarawak and Sabah state Mainland Southeast Asia decolonization 251 (4) historical geography 275 (5) Islam 275 (4) post-war economy 253 (5), 275 (3) post-war politics 253 (4) the modern world 113 (3), (4)
Malay States state Maritime Southeast Asia colonialism 248 (1) WWII 251 (3)
Malayu Maritime Southeast Asia (Indonesia) ancient India 241 (6) early medieval states 245 (5), (6)
Malayu state Maritime Southeast Asia ancient India 241 (6)
Malazgirt Southwest Asia (Turkey) first civilizations 221 (4)
Malbork see Marienburg
Malden Island nuclear test Pacific Ocean environmentalism 285 (2)
Maldive Islands var. Maldives island group/colonial possession/state Indian Ocean colonialism 248 (2) decolonization 251 (4) exploration 239 (1) medieval voyages 61 (3) post-war economy 253 (5) post-war politics 253 (4) the modern world 113 (3) trade 230 (2), 267 (3) world religions 49 (4) WWII 251 (3)
Maldives see Maldive Islands
Malema archaeological site East Africa (Tanzania) first humans 12 (1)
Malemba Central Africa (Angola) slave trade 165 (4)
Malembo Central Africa (Congo (Zaire)) European expansion 84–85 (1)
Maleruakik North America (Canada) cultural groups 123 (3)
Malgal people Siberia medieval states 262–263 (1)
Mali prev. French Sudan, Sudanese Republic state West Africa decolonization 168 (1) economy 163 (2), (3) Islam 163 (1), 235 (4) exploration 68 (2) the modern world 112 (1), 113 (3), (4) trade 163 (4), (5), (6), (7), 164 (2)
Malinalco Central America (Mexico) first civilizations 122 (1)
Malinalco state Central America Aztecs 124 (1)
Malindi East Africa (Kenya) economy 163 (2) European expansion 80–81 (1) exploration 68 (2), 156 (3) Islam 163 (1) trade 164 (1), 230 (2), 267 (3)
Maliseet people North America colonization 126 (1)
Malla region/state South Asia ancient India 242 (1) first religions 36 (2)
Mallia Greece first cities 28–29 (1)
Mallicolo see Malekula
Mallorca see Majorca
Malmö Scandinavia (Sweden) early modern states 197 (3) economy 205 (4) medieval states 189 (3)
Malo island Pacific Ocean early cultures 280–281 (3) medieval voyages 60 (2)
Maloyaroslavets battle Eastern Europe (Russian Federation) Napoleon 200–201 (1)
Mal'ta Siberia (Russian Federation) the world in 10,000 BCE 14–15
Malta anc. Melita colonial possession/state/island Mediterranean Sea Bronze Age 175 (3) crusades 186 (1) empire and revolution 202 (1) first civilizations 177 (1) Islam 227 (4) medieval states 185 (3) Napoleon 200–201 (1), 201 (2) Ottomans 231 (3) the modern world 112 (2) WWII 104 (2), 210 (1), 211 (4) see also Melita
Maluku, Laut see Molucca Sea
Malventum see Benevento, Beneventum
Malvinas, Islas Eng. Falkland Islands island group South America colonization 148 (2) see also Falkland Islands
Malwa region/state South Asia colonialism 247 (3) early medieval states 244–245 (3) empire and revolution 249 (3) Mughal Empire 246 (1)
Malyy Trostinets concentration camp Eastern Europe (Belorussia) WWII 211 (3)
Mamluks state Africa/Southwest Asia economy 163 (2), 190 (1) Islam 163 (1) Mongols 229 (3) Timur 229 (4) trade 230 (2)
Mammoth Cave Australia exploration 280 (1)
Mamoré var. Río Mamoré river South America early cultures 144 (1) Incas 147 (3)
Mamoré, Río see Mamoré
Mampava var. Mempawah state Maritime Southeast Asia the world in 1700 82–83
Mamprusi state West Africa the world in 1700 82–83 the world in 1800 86–87 the world in 1850 90–91
Man state British Isles medieval states 186 (2), 187 (4), 188 (2)
Man people East Asia first cities 259 (4) medieval states 263 (3)
Manacapuru state South America the world in 500 CE 50–51 the world in 750 CE 54–55 the world in 1200 62–63
Manado see Menado
Managua Central America (Nicaragua) the growth of the US 129 (2)
Manama Ar. Al Manāmah Southwest Asia (Bahrain) economy 234 (1)
Manáos mod. Manaus; hist. São José do Rio Negro; later Villa da Barra South America (Brazil) colonization 149 (3) empire and revolution 151 (3) exploration 143 (2) see also Manaus
Manapadu South Asia (India) colonialism 247 (3)
Manar see Mannar
Manassas North America (USA) US Civil War 131 (6)
Manassas see Bull Run
Manaus prev. Manáos; hist. São José do Rio Negro; later Villa da Barra South America (Brazil) economy 153 (3) environment 153 (4) politics 152 (1) see also Manáos
Manchán South America (Peru) early cultures 146 (1)
Manchester British Isles (United Kingdom) economy 204 (1), (2), 205 (4) imperial global economy 93 (4), (5) inter-war 209 (3) WWII 210 (1)
Manchester Ship Canal canal British Isles economy 204 (2)
Man-chou-li see Manzhouli
Manchukuo var. Manchuria vassal state East Asia Communism 271 (8) post-war politics 271 (7) WWII 104 (1), (2)
Manchuria var. Manchukuo region East Asia trade 72–73 (1) Chinese revolution 271 (5) colonialism 269 (3), (4) early modern states 266 (2), 268 (1) economy 274 (1) empire and revolution 268 (2) exploration 256 (1), 257 (3) global immigration 101 (2) imperialism 270 (2) medieval states 264 (1), (2) Russo-Japanese War 270 (4) Sino-Japanese War 270 (3) Soviet Union 213 (4) WWII 272 (1), 273 (2)
Manchurian Plain plain East Asia first states 260 (1)
Manchus var. Qing, Ch'ing people East Asia early modern states 266 (1) trade 267 (3)
Mancunium see Manchester
Manda archaeological site/settlement East Africa (Tanzania) first cities 240 (2) medieval voyages 61 (3)
Mandagora South Asia (India) ancient trade 44–45 (1)
Mandalay Mainland Southeast Asia (Burma) colonialism 269 (4) economy 275 (4) world religions 243 (5) WWII 251 (3)
Mandasor battle South Asia (India) empire and revolution 249 (3)
Mande people West Africa early cultures 160 (1)
Mandeville North America (USA) first religions 36 (1)
Mandheera East Africa (Somalia)
Mandjarur South Asia (India) medieval voyages 61 (3)
Mandu Mandu Cave archaeological site Australia prehistoric culture 17 (2)
Mane state West Africa trade 164 (2)
Manfredonia Italy medieval states 189 (4)
Mangalia see Callatis
Mangalore South Asia (India) colonialism 247 (3) Marathas 246 (2)
Mangalur mod. Mangalore South Asia (India) early medieval states 245 (4) Mughal Empire 246 (1) see also Mangalore
Mangaung see Bloemfontein
Mangazeya Siberia (Russian Federation) exploration 257 (2)
Mangbetu state East Africa trade 167 (1)
Mangonui New Zealand colonization 283 (5)
Maní Central America (Mexico) first civilizations 121 (2)
Maní state Central America Aztecs 124 (1)
Maniago Italy WWI 207 (5)
Manila Philippines colonialism 247 (4) colonization 284–285 (1) European expansion 81 (3), 84–85 (1) European imperialism 97 (3) exploration 279 (3) global immigration 100 (1) imperial global economy 92 (1) Islam 275 (4) post-war economy 253 (5) trade 267 (3) US superpower 138 (1) WWII 251 (3), 272 (1), 273 (2)
Manipur region/state South Asia colonialism 248 (2) post-war politics 252 (1), 253 (4)
Man, Isle of island British Isles medieval states 185 (3)
Manitoba province North America (Canada) 129 (2), 132 (1), 136 (2)
Manitoba, Lake lake North America historical geography 117 (1)
Man Mound burial mound North America (USA) first civilizations 121 (4)
Mann burial mound North America (USA) first civilizations 121 (4)
Mannar var. Manar South Asia (Sri Lanka) colonialism 247 (3)
Mannea state Southwest Asia first civilizations 222 (2)
Mannheim Central Europe (Germany) WWI 206 (3) WWII 211 (4)
Manoa state South America the world in 1500 74–75
Manoa people South America early cultures 147 (2) the world in 1700 82–83
Manpo var. Manp'ojin East Asia (North Korea) Cold War 109 (4)
Manp'ojin see Manpo
Mansura South Asia (Pakistan) early Islam 56–57 (1) medieval voyages 61 (3) world religions 243 (4)
Mansurah battle Egypt crusades 65 (3)
Manta people South America the world in 1000 58–59 the world in 1200 62–63 the world in 1400 70–71
Mantes France medieval states 192 (2)
Mantinea battle Greece ancient Greece 177 (3)
Mantoue see Mantua
Mantova see Mantua
Mantua It. Mantova, Fr. Mantoue Italy economy 190 (1) Franks 184 (2) medieval states 188 (1) Napoleon 200–201 (1) WWI 207 (5)
Manus island Pacific Ocean WWII 251 (3)
Manyakheta South Asia (India) early medieval states 244 (2)
Manzhouli var. Man-chou-li East Asia (China) colonialism 269 (4)
Manzikert Southwest Asia (Turkey) crusades 65 (1) early Islam 57 (2) Seljuks 228 (1)
Mao Khe battle Mainland Southeast Asia (Vietnam) 251 (5)
Maoris people New Zealand the world in 1200 62–63 the world in 1300 66–67 the world in 1400 70–71 the world in 1500 74–75 the world in 1600 78–79 the world in 1700 82–83 the world in 1800 86–87
Mao Shan mountain East Asia first religions 37 (4)
Ma-pa see Maba
Mapungubwe state Southern Africa the world in 1200 62–63
Maputo prev. Lourenço Marques Southern Africa (Mozambique) economy 168 (2) see also Lourenço Marques
Maracaibo South America (Venezuela) colonization 148 (2) empire and revolution 150 (1), (2), 151 (3) environment 153 (4) European expansion 85 (2) Incas 148 (1) politics 152 (1)
Maracaibo, Gulf of see Venezuela, Gulf of
Maracaibo, Lago de see Maracaibo, Lake
Maracaibo, Lake Sp. Maracaibo, Lago de inlet South America colonization 148 (2) early cultures 145 (2), 146 (1) Incas 148 (1)
Maracanda var. Samarkand, Samarqand Central Asia (Uzbekistan) Hellenistic world 40–41 (1) see also Samarkand
Maradi West Africa (Niger) Islam 167 (3)
Maradi state West Africa the world in 1850 90–91
Maragheh Southwest Asia (Iran) Mongols 68–69 (1)
Marajó region/people South America the world in 1 CE 42–43 the world in 250 CE 46–47 the world in 500 CE 50–51 the world in 750 CE 54–55 the world in 1000 58–59 the world in 1200 62–63
Marajó archaeological site South America early cultures 145 (2)
Marajoara region South America early cultures 145 (2)
Marakanda Central Asia (Uzbekistan) ancient trade 44–45 (1)
Maralinga nuclear test Australia environmentalism 285 (2)
Marama people Easter Island early cultures 281 (4)
Maramba see Livingstone
Maranhão region South America colonization 149 (3)
Maranhão see São Luis, São Luiz do Maranhão
Marañón river South America colonization 148 (2) early cultures 144 (1), 145 (2), (3), (4), 146 (1) economy 153 (3) empire and revolution 150 (2) environment 153 (4) exploration 143 (2) Incas 147 (3), 148 (1) narcotics 153 (5) politics 152 (1)
Marash Southwest Asia (Turkey) Islam 227 (4)
Maratha Confederacy state South Asia the world in 1800 86–87
Marathas state South Asia colonialism 248 (1)
Marathon battle Greece ancient Persia 223 (4)
Maravi state Southern Africa Islam 163 (1)
Marburg see Maribor
Marcellus, Theatre of building Italy ancient Rome 181 (2)
March see Morava
Marcia, Aqua aqueduct Italy ancient Rome 181 (2)
Marcianopolis Christian archbishopric Southeast Europe (Bulgaria) world religions 48 (1)
Marcomanni people Central Europe ancient Rome 180–181 (1), 181 (4)
Marcus Island var. Minami-tori-shima island Pacific Ocean WWII 272 (1)
Mar del Plata South America (Argentina) empire and revolution 151 (3)
Mardi var. Mardoi region Southwest Asia Hellenistic world 40–41 (1)
Mardoi see Mardi
Margarita Island island West Indies European expansion 85 (2)
Mari Southwest Asia (Iraq) first cities 220 (2), 28–29 (1) first civilizations 221 (4), 24 (2), 25 (3)
Maria Island penal centre Australia colonization 282 (1) environmentalism 285 (2)
Mariana Islands var. Marianas island group Pacific Ocean colonization 284–285 (1) early cultures 280–281 (3) exploration 279 (3) imperialism 270 (2) medieval voyages 60 (2) US superpower 138 (1) WWII 104 (1), 105 (3), 272 (1), 273 (2)
Marianas see Mariana Islands
Maria-Theresiopel see Subotica
Ma'rib Southwest Asia (Yemen) early trade 225 (3)
Maribor Ger. Marburg Central Europe (Slovenia) post-war economy 215 (3)
Marica see Maritsa
Maricopa people North America colonization 125 (4)
Marie Galante var. Ceyre island West Indies the world in 1800 86–87
Mari El region Eastern Europe Soviet Union 214–215 (4)
Marienburg mod. Malbork Central Europe (Poland) early modern states 195 (3) medieval states 188 (1)
Marietta burial mound North America (USA) first civilizations 121 (4)
Marifa oil field Southwest Asia economy 234 (1)
Marignano mod. Melegnano battle Italy early modern states 194 (1)
Marinids dynasty North Africa economy 163 (2), 190 (1)
Marion North America (USA) US society 137 (6)
Mariqua battle Southern Africa (South Africa) colonization 166 (2)
Maritsa var. Marica; anc. Hebrus Gk. Évros, Turk. Meriç river Southeast Europe WWI 207 (6)
Maritsa see Chernomen
Maritzburg see Pietermaritzburg
Marj Dabik see Marj Dabiq
Marj Dabiq var. Marj Dabik Southwest Asia (Syria) Ottomans 231 (3)
Mark region Central Europe empire and revolution 199 (3)
Marka East Africa (Somalia) economy 163 (2)
Markland region North America medieval voyages 60–61 (1)
Marksville burial mound/region/settlement North America (USA) first civilizations 121 (4) first religions 36 (1)

Marksville Culture *people* North America the world in 250 CE *46–47* the world in 500 CE *50–51*
Marlborough *region* New Zealand colonization *283* (5)
Marlik Southwest Asia (Iran) first civilizations *24* (3)
Marmara Denizi *see* Marmara, Sea of
Marmara, Sea of *var.* Marmara Denizi *sea* Southwest Asia ancient Greece *177* (2), (3) first civilizations *175* (4), *177* (1) WWI *207* (6)
Marne *river/battle* France WWI *206* (3)
Maroc *see* Morocco
Maronea *state* Greece ancient Greece *177* (2)
Maroni Cyprus ancient Egypt *159* (5)
Marquesas Islands *Fr.* Îles Marquises *island group* Pacific Ocean colonization *284–285* (1) early cultures *280–281* (3) environmentalism *285* (2) exploration *278* (1), *279* (3) medieval voyages *60* (2)
Marquises, Îles *see* Marquesas Islands
Marrakech *see* Marrakesh
Marrakesh *prev.* Morocco; *Fr.* Marrakech North Africa (Morocco) trade *72–73* (1) economy *163* (2) exploration *156* (3), *157* (4) Islam *163* (1), Mongols *68* (2)
Marree Australia colonization *282* (1)
Marrucini *people* Italy early states *178* (1)
Marruecos *see* Morocco
Marsala *see* Lilybaeum
Marseille *anc.* Massalia, Massilia; *Eng.* Marseilles France ancient Rome *182* (1) biological diffusion *72–73* (1) crusades *186* (1), *64–65* (2) early modern states *197* (5) economy *190* (1), *205* (4) empire and revolution *199* (4), *202* (1) European expansion *84–85* (1) Franks *183* (5), (6), *184* (2) global immigration *100* (1) medieval states *182* (2), *185* (3) Napoleon *200–201* (1), *201* (2), (3) WWII *210* (1), *211* (2), (4) *see also* Massalia, Massilia
Marseilles *see* Marseille, Massalia, Massilia
Marshall Islands *island group/state* Pacific Ocean colonization *284–285* (1) decolonization *285* (3) early cultures *280–281* (3) environmentalism *285* (2) exploration *278* (1), *279* (3) imperialism *270* (2) medieval voyages *60* (2) WWII *273* (2)
Marsi *people* Italy early states *178* (1)
Martaban *var.* Moktama Mainland Southeast Asia (Burma) colonialism *247* (4) trade *230* (2)
Martinique *colonial possession/state/island* West Indies Cold War *108* (2) colonization *126* (1) empire and revolution *88* (1), *150* (1) European expansion *84–85* (1), *129* (2) the modern world *112* (1)
Martin Point *headland* North America exploration *287* (2)
Marton New Zealand colonization *283* (5)
Maru-Desa *region* South Asia world religions *242* (2)
Marwar *region* South Asia early medieval states *244–245* (3)
Mary *see* Alexandria Margiana, Merv
Maryborough Australia colonization *282* (1)
Maryland *state* North America empire and revolution *127* (2), (3) the growth of the US *129* (1) US Civil War *130* (2), (3), (4), (5), *131* (6), (7) US economy *134* (2)
Marzūq *see* Murzuk
Masada Southwest Asia (Israel) ancient Rome *225* (4)
Más Afuera *island* Pacific Ocean exploration *278* (1)
Masan *see* Happo
Masawa *see* Massawa
Mascat *see* Muscat
Mascouter *people* North America colonization *126* (1)
Masena West Africa (Chad) exploration *157* (4)
Masharrahet, al- *hunting palace* Southwest Asia (Iraq) early Islam *57* (3)
Masina *region/state* West Africa Islam *167* (3) trade *164* (2)
Masishaka *state* South Asia first empires *241* (5)
Masjed Southwest Asia (Iran) 20th-century politics *235* (5)
Masjed-e Soleymān *see* Masjed Soleymān
Masjed Soleyman *var.* Masjed-e Soleyman, Masjid-i Sulaiman Southwest Asia (Iran) economy *234* (1) 20th-century politics *235* (5)
Masjid-i Sulaiman *see* Masjed Soleymān
Maskat *see* Muscat
Masqat *see* Muscat
Massa and Carrara *state* Italy empire and revolution *202* (1)
Massachusetts *colonial possession/state* North America empire and revolution *127* (2), (3) the growth of the US *129* (1) US Civil War *130* (2), (3), (4), (5) US economy *134* (2)
Massacre Canyon *battle* North America (USA) the growth of the US *129* (2)
Massalia *mod.* Marseille, Marseilles; *Lat.* Massilia France first civilizations *177* (1) ancient Rome *179* (3) exploration *172* (1) *see also* Marseille, Massilia
Massangano Southern Africa (Angola) exploration *157* (4)
Massawa *var.* Masawa; *Amh.* Mits'iwa East Africa (Eritrea) colonization *167* (4) Ottomans *231* (3) trade *165* (3)
Massif Central *plateau* France *197* (5) prehistoric culture *17* (3)
Massilia *var.* Massalia; *mod.* Marseille, Marseilles France ancient Rome *179* (5), *180–181* (1), *181* (3) ancient trade *44* (2), *44–45* (1) early cultures *161* (2) great migrations *52–53* (1) world religions *48* (1) *see also* Marseille, Massalia
Massilia *mod.* Marseille *state* France ancient Rome *179* (5)
Masterton New Zealand colonization *283* (5)
Masulipatam South Asia (India) ancient trade *44–45* (1) colonialism *247* (3) early medieval states *245* (4) economy *249* (4) Mughal Empire *246* (1) trade *267* (3) WWII *272* (1)
Masurian Lakes *battle* Central Europe (Poland) WWI *207* (4)
Matabele *see* Ndebele
Matacanela Central America (Mexico) first civilizations *122* (1)
Matacapan Piedra Central America (Mexico) first civilizations *122* (1)
Matamba *state* Southern Africa slave trade *165* (4) trade *164* (2)
Matamorros *battle* Central America (Mexico) the growth of the US *129* (2)
Matanzas West Indies (Cuba) European expansion *85* (2)
Matara South Asia (Sri Lanka) colonialism *247* (3)
Matara East Africa (Eritrea) early cultures *160* (1)
Mataram *region/state* Maritime Southeast Asia colonialism *247* (4) early medieval states *245* (5)
Matenkupum New Guinea (New Ireland) early cultures *280* (2) exploration *280* (1)
Mathila South Asia (India) world religions *242* (2)
Mathura *Buddhist centre/settlement* South Asia (India) ancient trade *44–45* (1) early medieval states *244* (1) exploration *256* (1) first empires *241* (4) first religions *36* (2) world religions *242* (2), (3), *243* (4), *49* (3)
Mathurai *see* Madura, Madurai
Mathuru *see* Mathura, Muttra
Matianus *see* Urmia, Lake
Matjiesrivier Southern Africa (South Africa) early agriculture *158* (1)
Matmar Egypt ancient Egypt *159* (2)
Mato Grosso *region* South America colonization *149* (3)
Mato Grosso *see* Vila Bela
Mato Grosso, Planalto de *plateau* South America colonization *149* (3) early cultures *144* (1), *145* (2) empire and revolution *151* (3) environment *153* (4) exploration *142* (1), *143* (2), (3)
Matola *archaeological site* Southern Africa (Mozambique) early cultures *160* (1)
Matsu *island* China Cold War *109* (1) post-war economy *275* (3)
Matsubara *var.* Matubara Japan medieval states *264* (2), *265* (3)
Matsuura Japan early modern states *267* (4)
Matsuyama Japan WWII 273 (3) economy *270* (1)
Matsya *region/state* South Asia ancient India *242* (1) first empires *241* (5) first religions *36* (2) world religions *242* (2)
Matubara *see* Matsubara
Matupi Cave *settlement/archaeological site* Central Africa (Congo (Zaire)) early agriculture *158* (1) first humans *13* (2) prehistoric culture *17* (2)
Matuyama *see* Matsuyama
Mau *var.* Maunāth Bhanjan South Asia (India) colonialism *247* (3)
Maubeuge France WWI *206* (2), (3)
Mauer *archaeological site* Central Europe (Germany) first humans *13* (2)
Maule *river* South America Incas *147* (3)
Maulmain *see* Moulmein
Maunāth Bhanjan *see* Mau
Mauretania *province/region* North Africa ancient Rome *179* (5), *181* (4), *225* (5) ancient trade *44* (2), *44–45* (1) early cultures *161* (2) the modern world *113* (3) world religions *48* (1)
Mauretania Caesariensis *province* North Africa ancient Rome *180–181* (1)
Mauretania Tingitana *province* North Africa ancient Rome *180–181* (1)
Maurice *see* Mauritius
Mauritania *region/state* West Africa decolonization *168* (1) economy *168* (2), (3) European imperialism *96* (1) Islam *235* (4) the modern world *112* (1), *113* (4)
Mauritius *Fr.* Maurice *colonial possession/state/island* Indian Ocean decolonization *168* (1) economy *168* (2) European expansion *84–85* (1) European imperialism *96* (1) global immigration *100* (1), *101* (3) the modern world *112* (1), *113* (3)
Mauritsstad *see* Pernambuco, Recife
Mauryan Empire *state* South Asia the world in 250 BCE *38–39*
Mauthausen *concentration camp* Central Europe (Austria) WWII *211* (3)
Mawhai Point *whaling station* New Zealand colonization *283* (4)
Mawlamyine *see* Moulmein
Maw Shans *region* Mainland Southeast Asia early medieval states *245* (6)
Maxwell Bay North America (Canada) cultural groups *123* (3)
Maya South Asia (India) early religions *48* (2)
Maya *people* Central America colonization *125* (4), *126* (1) first religions *36* (1)
Maya City States *state* Central America the world in 500 CE *50–51* the world in 1000 *58–59* the world in 1200 *62–63* the world in 1300 *66–67* the world in 1400 *70–71* the world in 1500 *74–75*
Mayapán Central America (Mexico) Aztecs *124* (1) first civilizations *122* (1)
Maya-Toltec *region* Central America first civilizations *123* (2)
Mayebashi *see* Maebashi
Mayence *see* Mainz
Maykop Eastern Europe (Russian Federation) the world in 1250 BCE *26–27*
Maynas *region* South America colonization *148* (2) exploration *143* (2)
Mayotte *colonial possession* Indian Ocean the world in 1975 *106–107* the modern world *110–111*
Mayyafariqin Southwest Asia (Iraq) crusades *228* (2)
Mayyali *see* Mahe
Mayyit, Al Bahr al *see* Dead Sea
Mazaca *see* Caesarea, Cappadocia, Kayseri
Mazagan *mod.* El-Jadida North Africa (Morocco) the world in 1600 *78–79*
Mazantzintamalco Central America (Mexico) Aztecs *124* (3)
Mazapil *mine* Central America (Mexico) colonization *125* (4)
Mazar-i Sharif Central Asia (Afghanistan) world religions *243* (4)
Mazatec *people* Central America colonization *125* (4)
Mazatlán Central America (Mexico) Mexican Revolution *133* (3)
Mazouro Iberian Peninsula the world in 10,000 BCE *14–15*
Mazumbo A Kalunga *state* Southern Africa the world in 1700 *82–83*
Mazun *state* Southwest Asia ancient Persia *225* (6)
Mbailundu *state* Southern Africa slave trade *165* (4) trade *167* (1)
Mbakannas *state* South Asia early medieval states *244* (2)
Mbamba *state* Central Africa economy *163* (2)
Mbata *state* Central Africa economy *163* (2)
Mbwila *state* Southern Africa trade *164* (2)
McHenry County *region* North America
McLennan Creek *battle* North America (USA) the growth of the US *129* (2)
Meadowcroft North America (USA) the world in 10,000 BCE *14–15*
Meath *region* British Isles medieval states *186* (2)
Meaux France medieval states *192* (2) WWI *206* (2)
Mecca *Ar.* Makkah Southwest Asia (Saudi Arabia) biological diffusion *72–73* (1) crusades *65* (1) early cultures *161* (3), (4), (5) early Islam *56–57* (1), *57* (2) early trade *225* (3) European expansion *84–85* (1) exploration *156* (3), *218* (2), *219* (4) Islam *163* (1), *226* (2), (3), *227* (4), (5), *235* (4) medieval voyages *61* (3) Mongols *229* (3), *68* (2) Ottomans *231* (3) trade *230* (2), *267* (3) world religions *226* (1), *49* (4) 20th-century politics *233* (4)
Mecca, Sharifs of *state* Southwest Asia the world in 1400 *70–71*
Mecklenburg *state* Central Europe empire and revolution *202* (2)
Mecyberna *state* Greece ancient Greece *177* (2)
Medan Maritime Southeast Asia (Indonesia) post-war economy *253* (5) WWII *272* (1), *273* (2)
Medellín South America (Colombia) empire and revolution *150* (2), *151* (3) environment *153* (4) narcotics *153* (5) the modern world *113* (4)
Medeshamstede *see* Peterborough
Media *region/state* Southwest Asia ancient Persia *223* (4) ancient Rome *224* (2) ancient trade *44* (2) first civilizations *222* (2) Hellenistic world *224* (1)
Media Atropatene *state* Central Asia ancient Rome *224* (2) Hellenistic world *224* (1)
Medias Aguas *archaeological site* Central America (Mexico) first civilizations *121* (3)
Medina *var.* Yathrib, *Ar.* Al Madīnah Southwest Asia (Saudi Arabia) crusades *228* (2), *65* (1) early cultures *161* (3), (4), (5) early Islam *56–57* (1), *57* (2) early trade *225* (3) exploration *219* (4) Islam *163* (1), *227* (4) medieval voyages *61* (3) Mongols *229* (3) Ottomans *231* (3) WWI *233* (2) 20th-century politics *233* (4) *see also* Yathrib
Medina del Campo Iberian Peninsula (Spain) economy *190* (1)
Medina, Sharifs of *state* Southwest Asia the world in 1400 *70–71*
Mediolanum *mod.* Milan, Milano, *Ger.* Mailand *settlement* Italy ancient Rome *180–181* (1), *181* (4) great migrations *52–53* (1) world religions *48* (1) *see also* Milan
Mediomatrica *see* Metz
Mediterranean Sea *Fr.* Mer Méditerranée; *Lat.* Mare Internum *sea* Europe/Asia/Africa ancient Greece *179* (4) ancient Persia *223* (4), *225* (6) ancient Rome *179* (3), (5), *180–181* (1), *181* (3), (4), *224* (2), *225* (4), (5) ancient trade *44–45* (1) biological diffusion *73* (3) Bronze Age *175* (3) Copper Age *174* (2) crusades *186* (1), *228* (2) early 20th century *206* (1) early agriculture *174* (1), *20–21* (2), *220* (1) early cultures *160* (1), *161* (2), (3), (4), (5) early Islam *56–57* (1), *57* (2) early systems *223* (3) early trade *225* (3) economy *163* (2), (3), *190* (1), *205* (4) empire and revolution *202* (1) European expansion *84–85* (1) exploration *156* (3), *157* (4), (5), *172* (1), (2), *219* (3) first cities *220* (2), *28–29* (1) first civilizations *175* (4), *177* (1), *221* (4), (5), *222* (2) first humans *13* (2) first religions *36* (1), *37* (3) great migrations *52–53* (1), *53* (2) Hellenistic world *40–41* (1), *41* (2) inter-war *209* (3) Islam *184* (1), *226* (2), *227* (4) medieval states *182* (2), *183* (4), *185* (3), (5), *188* (1) medieval voyages *60–61* (1) Mongols *229* (3) Napoleon *200–201* (1) Ottomans *230* (1), *231* (3), *232–233* (1) post-war economy *213* (5) post-war politics *212* (3) Reformation *194* (2), *196* (1), (2) Seljuks *228* (1) slave trade *165* (4) the modern world *113* (4) trade *167* (1) world religions *226* (1), *49* (4) WWI *208* (1), *233* (2) WWII *104* (1), *105* (3) 20th century *234* (2) 20th-century politics *233* (3)
Méditerranée, Mer *see* Mediterranean Sea
Medja *state* Egypt ancient Egypt *159* (4)
Medlock *river* British Isles economy *204* (2)
Meeker Agency *battle* North America (USA) the growth of the US *129* (2)
Meerut South Asia (India) economy *249* (4) empire and revolution *249* (3) post-war economy *253* (5) world religions *49* (3)
Mega Chad *lake* Central Africa historical geography *154–155* (1)
Megáli Préspa, Límni *see* Prespa
Megalo-Vlachia *state* Greece medieval states *189* (4)
Megara Greece first civilizations *177* (1)
Megara-Hyblaea Italy first civilizations *177* (1)
Meghalaya *region* South Asia post-war politics *252* (1), (3)
Meghna *river* South Asia *252* (3)
Megiddo Southwest Asia (Israel) ancient Egypt *159* (4), (5) first cities *220* (2), *28–29* (1) first civilizations *221* (5), *222* (1) *battle* WWI *233* (2)
Mehadia Southeast Europe (Romania) WWI *207* (6)
Mehdia *see* Mahdia
Meherpur South Asia (Bangladesh) post-war politics *252* (3)
Mehran Southwest Asia (Iran) 20th-century politics *235* (5)
Mehrgarh *archaeological site/settlement* South Asia (Pakistan) first cities *240* (2)
Meir Egypt ancient Egypt *159* (4)
Meissen *region* Central Europe medieval states *188* (1)
Mekong *Cam.* Mékôngk, *Chin.* Lancang Jiang, Lan-ts'ang Chiang, *Lao.* Mènam Khong, *Thai.* Mae Nam Khong, *Tib.* Dza Chu, *Vtn.* Sông Tiên Giang *river* Mainland Southeast Asia ancient India *241* (6) ancient trade *44–45* (1) biological diffusion *72–73* (1), *73* (3) Bronze Age *240* (3) colonialism *247* (4), *248* (1), *269* (4) early agriculture *20–21* (2), *258* (1) early medieval states *245* (5), (6) early modern states *266* (1) first humans *13* (2) first religions *36* (1) first states *260* (1) global immigration *100* (1) medieval states *263* (6) Mongols *68–69* (1) post-war politics *251* (5) prehistoric culture *16* (1) the modern world *110–111* trade *230* (2) world religions *243* (5), *49* (3), (4)
Mékôngk *see* Mekong
Melaka Mainland Southeast Asia (Malaysia) early medieval states *245* (6)
Melaka, Selat *see* Malacca, Strait of
Melanesia *island group* Pacific Ocean WWII *272* (1), *273* (2)
Melbourne *penal colony/settlement* Australia colonization *282* (1), (2), *284–285* (1) environmentalism *285* (2) exploration *279* (2), (3) global immigration *100* (1) imperial global economy *92* (1) prehistoric culture *17* (5)
Melegnano *see* Marignano
Melilla *anc.* Rusaddir, Russadir North Africa trade *72–73* (1)
Melilla *see* Rusaddir
Melita *mod.* Malta *island* Mediterranean Sea ancient Rome *179* (3) *see also* Malta
Melitene *mod.* Malatya Southwest Asia (Turkey) ancient Rome *180–181* (1) Hellenistic world *40–41* (1) world religions *48* (1) *see also* Malatya
Melk Central Europe (Austria) medieval states *188* (1)
Melka Kunture East Africa (Ethiopia) the world in 5000 BCE *18–19*
Mellifont *major cistercian house* British Isles (United Kingdom) medieval states *187* (3)
Melos Greece first civilizations *177* (1)
Melos *island* Greece ancient Greece *177* (2) first civilizations *175* (4)
Melrose *major cistercian house* British Isles (United Kingdom) medieval states *183* (3)
Meltus *see* Miletus
Melun France medieval states *192* (2)
Melville Island *island/penal centre* Australia colonization *282* (1) environmentalism *285* (2)
Melville Koppies *archaeological site* Southern Africa (South Africa) early cultures *160* (1)
Mema *state* West Africa trade *163* (6)
Memel *Lith.* Klaipeda Eastern Europe (Lithuania) early modern states *197* (3) empire and revolution *199* (3) inter-war *209* (5) WWI *207* (4) *see also* Klaipeda
Memel *see* Neman
Memorana North America (Canada) cultural groups *123* (3)
Mempawah *see* Mampava
Memphis Egypt ancient Egypt *159* (3), (4), (5) ancient Persia *223* (4) ancient Rome *180–181* (1) early cultures *160* (1), *161* (2) early Islam *56–57* (1) early systems *32* (1), *33* (2), (3) first cities *220* (2), *28–29* (1) first civilizations *222* (2) first religions *37* (3), *48* (1) Hellenistic world *40–41* (1)
Memphis North America (USA) imperial global economy *93* (5) the growth of the US *129* (2), *132* (1) US Civil War *131* (7) US economy *136* (2) US politics *135* (6) US society *137* (6)
Menado *mod.* Manado Maritime Southeast Asia (Indonesia) colonialism *247* (4) European expansion *84–85* (1) US Civil War *131* (6)
Mènam Khong *see* Mekong
Menasha Mounds *burial mound* North America (USA) first civilizations *121* (4)
Mende *settlement/state* Greece ancient Greece *177* (2) first civilizations *177* (1)
Mendes Egypt ancient Egypt *159* (2), (3)
Mendota Mounds *burial mound* North America (USA) first civilizations *121* (4)
Mendoza South America (Argentina) colonization *148* (2) empire and revolution *150* (1), *151* (3) environment *153* (4)
Mendut Maritime Southeast Asia (Indonesia) world religions *243* (5)
Menelaion *palace* Greece first civilizations *175* (4)
Mengtsz *see* Mengzi
Mengzi *var.* Mengtsz East Asia (China) colonialism *269* (4)
Meniet North Africa (Algeria) early agriculture *158* (1)
Menindee Australia exploration *279* (2)
Menindee Lake Australia exploration *280* (1)
Menominee *people* North America colonization *126* (1)
Menongue *prev.* Vila Serpa Pinto, Serpa Pinto Southern Africa (Angola) civil war *109* (5)
Menorca *anc.* Balearis Minor, *Eng.* Minorca *island* Mediterranean Sea inter-war *209* (4) *see also* Minorca
Menzies Australia colonization *282* (1)
Meran *It.* Merano Italy WWI *207* (5)
Merano *see* Meran
Mercia *state* British Isles medieval states *183* (3)
Mergui Mainland Southeast Asia (Burma) colonialism *247* (4), *248* (1)
Meriç *see* Maritsa
Mérida South America (Venezuela) empire and revolution *150* (1)
Mérida *anc.* Emerita Augusta Iberian Peninsula (Spain) early Islam *56–57* (1) Franks *184* (2) inter-war *209* (4) *see also* Emerita Augusta
Mérida Central America (Mexico) colonization *125* (4), *126* (1) exploration *118* (1) Mexican Revolution *133* (3)
Merimda Egypt ancient Egypt *159* (2) early agriculture *158* (1)
Merina *see* Merina Kingdom
Merina Kingdom *var.* Merina *state* Madagascar the world in 1800 *86–87* the world in 1850 *90–91*
Merkits *people* East Asia/Siberia Mongols *68–69* (1)
Meroe *archaeological site/settlement* East Africa (Sudan) early agriculture *158* (1) early cultures *160* (1), *161* (3), (4), (5) early trade *225* (3) the world in 250 CE *46–47*
Mersa Gawasis *var.* Sawu Egypt ancient Egypt *159* (4)
Merseburg Central Europe (Germany) medieval states *188* (1), *189* (3)
Mersin Southwest Asia (Turkey) early agriculture *174* (1) first cities *220* (2) first civilizations *221* (4), (5)
Merthyr Tydfil British Isles (United Kingdom) economy *204* (1)
Merv *mod.* Mary; *anc.* Alexandria Margiana Southwest Asia (Turkmenistan) ancient Persia *223* (4), *225* (6) ancient Rome *224* (2) ancient trade *44–45* (1) biological diffusion *72–73* (1) Hellenistic world *224* (1) Islam *226* (2), *227* (4), (5) medieval Persia *231* (4) medieval states *261* (6) Seljuks *228* (1) world religions *226* (1) *see also* Alexandria Margiana
Mesa Grande *archaeological site* North America (USA) cultural groups *123* (4)
Mesa Verde North America (USA) the world in 1200 *62–63*
Mesa Verde National Park *archaeological site* North America (USA) cultural groups *123* (4)
Mescalero *people* North America colonization *126* (1)
Mescalero Apache *people* North America colonization *125* (4)
Mesembria Southeast Europe (Greece) first civilizations *177* (1)
Meshan *state* Southwest Asia ancient Persia *225* (6)
Meshed Southwest Asia (Iran) Hellenistic world *40–41* (1) medieval Persia *231* (4)
Meskhetians *people* Southwest Asia Soviet Union *213* (4)
Mesoamerica *region* Central America biological diffusion *73* (2) early agriculture *120* (1)
Mesopotamia *region* Southwest Asia 20th-century politics *233* (4) ancient Rome *180–181* (1), *224* (2), *225* (5) Bronze Age *175* (3) crusades *228* (2) early agriculture *220* (1) early Islam *56–57* (1), *57* (2), (3) early systems *223* (3), *32* (1), *33* (3) exploration *218* (1), (2), *219* (3) first cities *220* (2) first civilizations *221* (4), *222* (2) first religions *36* (1) Hellenistic world *40–41* (1) Islam *226* (2), *227* (5) medieval Persia *231* (4) medieval states *261* (6) Ottomans *231* (3) world religions *226* (1) WWI *233* (2)
Messana *mod.* Messina; *prev.* Zancle Italy ancient Rome *179* (3), *180–181* (1), *181* (3) *see also* Messina
Messapii *people* Italy early states *178* (2)
Messene Greece ancient Greece *179* (4)
Messene *see* Messina
Messenia *state* Greece ancient Greece *179* (4)
Messina Italy crusades *186* (1), *64–65* (2) economy *190* (1) Islam *227* (4) medieval states *188* (1), *189* (4) WWII *211* (4)
Messina, Strait of *sea waterway* Italy ancient Rome *179* (3)
Messines France WWI *206* (2), (3)
Meta *region* South America narcotics *153* (5)
Meta *river* South America early cultures *146* (1) exploration *143* (2) narcotics *153* (5)
Metapontum Italy early states *178* (1) first civilizations *177* (1)
Metaurus, River *battle* Italy ancient Rome *179* (3)
Methone Greece ancient Greece *177* (3)
Methymna *state* Greece ancient Greece *177* (2)
Metis *see* Metz
Metz *massacre/settlement* France crusades *186* (1) early modern states *193* (4), *197* (5) economy *190* (1) empire and revolution *199* (4) Franks *183* (5), (6), *184* (2) medieval states *188* (1)
Metztitlán *state* Central America Aztecs *124* (1)
Meung *academic centre/settlement* France medieval states *187* (3), *192* (2)
Meuniers, Pont aux *bridge* France economy *191* (2)
Meuse *river* Low Countries Bronze Age *175* (3) empire and revolution *202* (1), (2) Franks *183* (5) great migrations *52–53* (1), *53* (2) WWI *206* (2), (3)
Mexicaltzinco Central America (Mexico) Aztecs *124* (2), (3)
Mexico *state* Central America empire and revolution *88–89* (2) global immigration *100* (1), *101* (2) imperial global economy *92* (1) Mexican Revolution *133* (3) the growth of the US *129* (2), *132* (1), *133* (4) the modern world *112* (1), *113* (4) US economy *136* (2) US politics *139* (4) US superpower *138* (1) WWII *104* (2) Cold War *108* (2), *109* (1)
México *var.* Mexico City; *prev.* Tenochtitlan; *Sp.* Ciudad de México Central America (Mexico) colonization *125* (4) *see also* Mexico City, Tenochtitlan
Mexico City *var.* México; *prev.* Tenochtitlan; *Sp.* Ciudad de México Central America (Mexico) colonization *126* (1) European expansion *81* (3), *84–85* (1), *85* (2) exploration *119* (3) global immigration *100* (1) imperial global economy *92* (1) Mexican Revolution *133* (3) the growth of the US *129* (2) the modern world *113* (4) US economy *136* (2) Cold War *108* (2) *see also* México, Tenochtitlan
Mexico, Gulf of *gulf* North America Aztecs *124* (1) colonization *125* (4), (5), *126* (1) cultural groups *122* (5) early agriculture *120* (1), *20–21* (2) empire and revolution *88–89* (2) European expansion *84–85* (1), *85* (2) exploration *118* (1), *119* (2), (3) first civilizations *121* (2), (3), (4), *122* (1) global knowledge *76–77* (1) Mexican Revolution *133* (3) the growth of the US *129* (2), *132* (1) US Civil War *131* (6), (7) US economy *136* (2) Cold War *108* (2)
Mexiquito Central America (Mexico) first civilizations *122* (1)
Mezcala Central America (Mexico) first civilizations *121* (2)
Mezcalapa *river* Central America first civilizations *122* (1)
Mezhirich Eastern Europe the world in 10,000 BCE *14–15*
Mézières France WWI *206* (2), (3)
Mezőkeresztes *battle* Southeast Europe (Hungary) Ottomans *195* (4)
Mfengu *people* Southern Africa colonization *166* (2)
Mfolosi *river* Southern Africa colonization *166* (2)
Miam *see* Aniba
Miami North America (USA) the growth of the US *133* (4) the modern world *113* (4) US economy *134* (1), *136* (2) US society *137* (6) Cold War *108* (2)
Miami *people* North America colonization *126* (1)
Miamisburg *burial mound* North America (USA) first civilizations *121* (4)
Mian *state* Mainland Southeast Asia medieval states *263* (7)
Miao *rebellion* East Asia empire and revolution *268* (2)
Miaodigou *archaeological site* East Asia (China) early agriculture *258* (2)
Michigan *state* North America the growth of the US *129* (1) US Civil War *130* (2), (3), (4), (5) US economy *134* (2)
Michigan, Lake *lake* North America colonization *126* (1) cultural groups *122* (5) early agriculture *120* (1) empire and revolution *127* (3) exploration *118* (1), *119* (2), (3) first civilizations *121* (4) the growth of the US *129* (2), *132* (1) US Civil War *131* (6)
Michilimackinac North America (Canada) colonization *126* (1)
Michoacán *var.* Tarascan *state* Central America Aztecs *124* (1) Mexican Revolution *133* (3) the growth of the US *129* (2)
Micmac *people* North America colonization *126* (1)
Micronesia *island group* Pacific Ocean WWII *272* (1), *273* (2)
Micronesia, Federated States of *state* Pacific Ocean environmentalism *285* (2)
Middelburg Southern Africa (South Africa) European imperialism *96* (2)
Middelburg *battle* Low Countries (Netherlands) Reformation *195* (5)
Middle Angles *people* British Isles medieval states *183* (3)
Middle Congo *see* Congo
Middle East *region* Southwest Asia US economy *138* (2)
Middleport North America (USA) cultural groups *122* (5)
Middlesbrough British Isles (United Kingdom) economy *204* (1)
Midhe *mod.* Meath *state* British Isles medieval states *188* (2) *see also* Meath
Midway Islands *battle/colonial possession/island group* Pacific Ocean Cold War *109* (1) decolonization *285* (3) exploration *276–277* (1) the growth of the US *133* (4) US superpower *138* (1)
Mie *prefecture* Japan economy *270* (1)
Miguel de Aguayo *Jesuit mission* Central America (Mexico) colonization *125* (4)
Mihambo East Africa (Tanzania) exploration *157* (4)
Mikindani East Africa (Tanzania) exploration *157* (4)
Mikligard *see* Byzantium, Constantinople, Istanbul
Milan *anc.* Mediolanum; *Ger.* Mailan, *It.* Milano Italy crusades *186* (1) early modern states *193* (4), *194* (1) economy *190* (1), *205* (4) empire and revolution *202* (1), (3) Franks *184* (2) medieval states *188* (2), *183* (4), *185* (3), (5), *188* (1) Napoleon *200–201* (1), *201* (2), (3) post-war politics *212* (3) Reformation *194* (2), *196* (1) WWII *210* (1), *211* (2), (3), (4) Cold War *108* (3) *see also* Mediolanum
Milan *duchy* Italy early modern states *194* (1) Reformation *194* (2), *196* (1), (2)
Milano *see* Mediolanum, Milan
Miletos *see* Miletus
Miletus *settlement/state* Southwest Asia (Turkey) ancient Greece *177* (2), (3) ancient Persia *223* (4) ancient Rome *180–181* (1) exploration *172* (1) first civilizations *175* (4), *177* (1), *221* (5), *222* (2) Hellenistic world *40–41* (1)
Miller *burial mound* North America (USA) first civilizations *121* (4)
Miller *region* North America first civilizations *121* (4)
Millstream Australia the world in 5000 BCE *18–19*
Milne Bay *battle* New Guinea (Papua New Guinea) WWII *104* (2)
Milpitas North America (USA) *136* (3)
Milton New Zealand colonization *283* (5)
Milwaukee North America (USA) the growth of the US *132* (1) US economy *134* (1), (3)
Mimi *see* Kaya
Mimbres Valley *archaeological site* North America (USA) cultural groups *123* (4)
Min *state* East Asia medieval states *263* (3)
Mina *archaeological site* South America (Brazil) early cultures *144* (1), *145* (2)
Minab Southwest Asia (Iran) economy *234* (1)
Minā Baranis *see* Berenice
Minami-tori-shima *see* Marcus Island
Minangkabau *region* Maritime Southeast Asia early medieval states *245* (6)
Minas Gerais *region* South America colonization *149* (3)
Minas Novas South America (Brazil) colonization *149* (3) empire and revolution *151* (3)
Minca South America (Colombia) early cultures *146* (1)
Mindanao *island* Philippines colonialism *247* (4) European imperialism *97* (3) exploration *239* (1) historical geography *236–237* (1) Islam *243* (6) post-war politics *253* (4) world religions *243* (5) WWII *272* (1), *273* (2)
Minden *anc.* Minthun Central Europe (Germany) medieval states *189* (3)
Minden *region* Central Europe empire and revolution *199* (3)
Mindoro *island* Philippines European imperialism *97* (3) WWII *273* (2)
Mifeng *see* Niya
Ming Empire *state* East Asia early modern states *266* (1), (2), *267* (4) European expansion *80–81* (1) trade *230* (2), *267* (3) *see also* China
Minisink North America (USA) cultural groups *122* (5)
Minneapolis North America (USA) the growth of the US *132* (1) US economy *134* (1), (3)
Minnesota *state* North America the growth of the US *129* (1) US Civil War *130* (5) US economy *134* (2)
Minnesota Territory *region* North America US Civil War *130* (2), (3), (4)
Minong, Lake *lake* North America the world in 10,000 BCE *14–15*
Minorca *var.* Menorca; *anc.* Balearis Minor *island* Mediterranean Sea empire and revolution *88* (1) *see also* Menorca
Minshat Egypt ancient Egypt *159* (2)
Minsk Eastern Europe (Belorussia) empire and revolution *198* (2) post-war politics *212* (3) Soviet Union *208* (2), *214–215* (4) WWI *207* (4) WWII *211* (2), (3), (4)
Minthun *see* Minden
Minyue *province/state* East Asia first cities *259* (5) first states *260* (1)
Mirabib *archaeological site* Southern Africa (Namibia) early cultures *160* (1)
Miraflores South America (Colombia) narcotics *153* (5)
Miraflores South America (Chile) politics *151* (4)
Mirambo *state* East Africa colonization *167* (4)
Miran East Asia (China) world religions *49* (3)
Miriwun Australia exploration *280* (1)
Miru *people* Easter Island early cultures *281* (4)
Mirzapur South Asia (India) economy *249* (4)
Misasa Japan early modern states *265* (5)
Misenum *archaeological site* Italy ancient Rome *180–181* (1)
Misisil Melanesia (New Britain) early cultures *280* (2) exploration *280* (1)
Mississippi *state* North America imperial global economy *93* (5) the growth of the US *129* (1) US Civil War *130* (2), (3), (4), (5), *131* (6), (7) US economy *134* (2), *139* (3) US society *137* (6) US superpower *139* (5)
Mississippi *river* North America colonization *125* (4), *126* (1) cultural groups *122* (5) early agriculture *120* (1), *20–21* (2) empire and revolution *127* (3), *88* (1) European expansion *84–85* (1) exploration *118* (1), *119* (2), (3) first civilizations *121* (4) first religions *36* (1) imperial global economy *92* (1) prehistoric culture *16* (1) the growth of the US *129* (2), *132* (1) US Civil War *130* (5), *131* (6), (7)
Mississippian Cultures *people* North America the world in 1200 *62–63* the world in 1300 *66–67* the world in 1400 *70–71* the world in 1500 *74–75*
Missoula, Lake *lake* North America the world in 10,000 BCE *14–15*
Missouri *state* North America the growth of the US *129* (1) US Civil War *130* (2), (3), (4), (5), *131* (6), (7) US economy *134* (2)
Missouri *people* North America colonization *126* (1)
Missouri *river* North America colonization *126* (1) cultural groups *122* (5) early agriculture *120* (1), *20–21* (2) exploration *118* (1), *119* (2), (3) first civilizations *121* (4) first religions *36* (1) the growth of the US *129* (2) US Civil War *130* (5)
Mistra Greece medieval states *187* (5), *189* (4)
Miswar Southwest Asia (Yemen) early trade *225* (3)
Mitanni, Kingdom of *state* Southwest Asia first civilizations *221* (5)
Mitau *Latv.* Jelgava; *Rus.* Mitava Eastern Europe (Latvia) early modern states *195* (3) *see also* Mitava
Mitava *Latv.* Jelgava; *Rus.* Mitau Eastern Europe (Latvia) WWI *207* (4) *see also* Mitau
Mithila South Asia (India) ancient India *242* (1) world religions *242* (3)
Mithraeum *building* Southwest Asia (Iraq) first cities *220* (3)
Mitla Central America (Mexico) first civilizations *122* (1)
Mitrovica *var.* Kosovska Mitrovica Southeast Europe (Yugoslavia) civil war *215* (3)
Mits'iwa *see* Massawa
Mitte Central Europe (Germany) post-war politics *212* (2)
Mitte *region* Eastern Europe WWII *211* (2)
Mitterberg *mine* Central Europe Bronze Age *175* (3)
Mittimatalik North America (Canada) cultural groups *123* (3)
Mitylene *see* Mytilene
Miwa *mountain* Japan medieval states *265* (3)
Mixcoac Central America (Mexico) Aztecs *124* (2), (3)
Mixco Viejo Central America (Guatemala) Aztecs *124* (1)
Mixincan Central America (Mexico) Aztecs *124* (3)
Mixquic Central America (Mexico) Aztecs *124* (2)
Mixtlan Central America (Mexico) Aztecs *124* (1)
Miyagi *prefecture* Japan economy *270* (1)
Miyanouchi Japan early modern states *265* (5)
Miyazaki *prefecture* Japan economy *270* (1)
Mizda North Africa (Libya) exploration *157* (4)
Mizoram *region* South Asia post-war politics *252* (1), (3), *253* (4)
Mizquic Central America (Mexico) colonization *125* (5)
Mizu-shima *battle* Japan early modern states *265* (5)
Mladec *archaeological site* Central Europe (Czech Republic) the world in 10,000 BCE *14–15*
Mlozi *state* East Africa colonization *167* (4)
Mo *people* East Asia first cities *259* (4)
Moab *state* Southwest Asia first civilizations *222* (1)
Mobile North America (USA) Cold War *108* (2) European expansion *84–85* (1) the growth of the US *129* (2) US Civil War *131* (7) US society *137* (6)
Mobile *battle* North America (USA) US Civil War *131* (7)
Mobutu Sese Seko, Lac *see* Albert, Lake
Moçambique *see* Mozambique, Portuguese East Africa
Moçâmedes *see* Mossamedes, Namibe
Moccasin Bluff North America (USA) cultural groups *122* (5)
Moche South America (Peru) early cultures *145* (4)
Moche *region/state* South America early cultures *145* (4)
Moche *river* South America early cultures *145* (3), (4)
Moche/Chan Chan *state* South America the world in 1000 *58–59*
Moctezuma *river* Central America first civilizations *121* (2)
Modder River *Afr.* Modderrivier *battle* Southern Africa (South Africa) European imperialism *96* (2)
Modderrivier *see* Modder River
Modena *anc.* Mutina Italy economy *190* (1) Franks *184* (2) medieval states *188* (1) *see also* Mutina
Modena *state* Italy empire and revolution *202* (1), (3) Reformation *194* (2), *196* (1), (2)
Modon Greece economy *190* (1) medieval states *187* (5)
Moeraki *whaling station* New Zealand colonization *283* (4)
Moero, Lac *see* Mweru, Lake
Moers *see* Mors
Moesia *province/region* Southeast Europe ancient Rome *180–181* (1), *181* (4) ancient trade *44* (2) world religions *48* (1)
Moesia Inferior *province* Southeast Europe ancient Rome *180–181* (1)
Moesia Superior *province* Southeast Europe ancient Rome *180–181* (1)
Mogadishu early *Chin.* Mo-ku-ta-shu, *Som.* Muqdisho East Africa (Somalia) biological diffusion *72–73* (1) colonization *167* (4) economy *163* (2) European expansion *80–81* (1) exploration *156* (3) global immigration *100* (1) Islam *163* (1) medieval voyages *61* (3) Mongols *68* (2) trade *165* (3), *230* (2), *267* (3)
Mogador *mod.* Essaouira North Africa (Morocco) early cultures *160* (1) exploration *157* (4)
Mogilev Eastern Europe (Belorussia) economy *190* (1) Soviet Union *208* (2) WWI *207* (4) WWII *210* (1), *211* (4)
Mogollon *archaeological site* North America (USA) cultural groups *123* (4)
Mogollon Culture *region/state* North America/Central America cultural groups *123* (4)
Mogontiacum *mod.* Mainz *settlement* Central Europe (Germany) ancient Rome *180–181* (1), *181* (4) great migrations *52–53* (1) *see also* Mainz
Mogul Empire *see* Mughal Empire
Mohács Central Europe (Hungary) Ottomans *231* (3)
Mohács *battle* Southeast Europe Ottomans *195* (4)
Mohammerah *see* Khorramshahr
Mohelnice Central Europe (Czech Republic) early agriculture *174* (1)
Mohenjo-Daro *archaeological site/settlement* South Asia (Pakistan) early systems *223* (3) first cities *240* (2), *24* (2), *25* (3)

Mohican see Mahican
Mojave people North America colonization 125 (4), 126 (1)
Mojave Desert desert North America cultural groups 123 (4)
Moji Japan economy 270 (1)
Mojos people South America colonization 148 (2) exploration 143 (2)
Mokpo Jap. Moppo East Asia (South Korea) Cold War 109 (4) early modern states 267 (4) Russo-Japanese War 270 (4)
Moktama see Martaban
Mo-ku-ta-shu see Mogadishu
Moldavia var. Moldova region/state Southeast Europe early modern states 193 (4) empire and revolution 198 (2), 202 (1) medieval states 189 (3), (4) Napoleon 200–201 (1) Ottomans 195 (4), 231 (3) post-war economy 214 (1), (2) Reformation 194 (2) Soviet Union 213 (4) the modern world 112 (2) WWI 207 (4)
Moldova see Moldavia
Mollendo South America (Peru) empire and revolution 151 (3)
Mologa river Eastern Europe Mongols 68–69 (1)
Molokai leper colony Pacific Ocean environmentalism 285 (2)
Molopo river Southern Africa European imperialism 96 (2)
Molotov Eastern Europe (Russian Federation) Soviet Union 213 (4)
Moluccas prev. Spice Islands; Dut. Molukken, Eng. Moluccas island group Maritime Southeast Asia ancient trade 44–45 (1) trade 72–73 (1) Bronze Age 240 (3) European expansion 80–81 (1), 81 (3) exploration 239 (1), (2) Islam 243 (6) trade 230 (2), 267 (3)
Molucca Sea Ind. Laut Maluku sea Maritime Southeast Asia Bronze Age 240 (3) early medieval states 245 (6) Islam 243 (6)
Molukken see Moluccas
Mombasa East Africa (Kenya) colonization 167 (4) economy 163 (2) European expansion 81 (3), 84–85 (1) European imperialism 96 (1) exploration 156 (3), 157 (4), (5) global immigration 100 (1) Islam 163 (1) Mongols 68 (2) slave trade 165 (4) trade 164 (1), 230 (2), 267 (3)
Mon state Mainland Southeast Asia world religions 49 (4)
Monacan people North America colonization 125 (4), 126 (1)
Monaco var. Monaco-Ville; anc. Monoecus state France empire and revolution 202 (1), (3) the modern world 112 (2), 113 (4)
Monaco see Munich
Monaco-Ville see Monaco
Mon and Malay States state Mainland Southeast Asia the world in 250 CE 46–47 the world in 500 CE 50–51
Monastir var. Bitolj; mod. Bitola fort/settlement Southeast Europe (FYR Macedonia) early Islam 56–57 (1) WWI 207 (6) see also Bitola, Bitolj
Moncastro Eastern Europe (Ukraine) economy 190 (1) medieval states 189 (4)
Mondidier France WWI 206 (2), (3)
Mondovi battle Italy Napoleon 200–201 (1)
Monemvasia Greece medieval states 187 (5) Ottomans 230 (1), 231 (3)
Monfalcone Italy WWI 207 (5)
Monghyr var. Munger South Asia (India) economy 249 (4)
Mongol Empire state East Asia medieval states 263 (5)
Mongolia prev. Outer Mongolia; Mong. Mongol Uls region/state East Asia trade 72–73 (1) Chinese revolution 271 (5) colonialism 269 (4) early modern states 266 (2) economy 274 (1) exploration 257 (3) historical geography 275 (5) Islam 275 (4) post-war economy 275 (3) post-war politics 271 (7), 274 (2) Soviet Union 208 (2), 213 (4) the modern world 113 (3), (4) world religions 49 (4) WWII 104 (1), (2), 272 (1), 273 (2) Cold War 109 (1) Communism 271 (8) see also Oirats, Khanate of the, Outer Mongolia, Inner Mongolia
Mongolia, Plateau of plateau East Asia Mongols 68–69 (1)
Mongols people East Asia/Siberia early modern states 266 (1) Mongols 68–69 (1) trade 267 (3)
Mongol Uls see Mongolia, Oirats, Khanate of the, Outer Mongolia
Monkchester see Newcastle-upon-Tyne
Mon-Khmer Peoples people Mainland Southeast Asia ancient trade 44–45 (1)
Monkwearmouth religious building British Isles (United Kingdom) medieval states 183 (3)
Monmouth North America (USA) empire and revolution 127 (3)
Monmouth Court House battle North America (USA) empire and revolution 127 (3)
Monoecus see Monaco
Monopoli Italy economy 190 (1)
Monrovia West Africa (Liberia) economy 168 (2)
Mons Low Countries (Belgium) WWI 206 (2), (3)
Montagnais people North America colonization 126 (1) cultural groups 123 (3)
Montana state North America the growth of the US 129 (1) US economy 134 (2)
Montauban France early modern states 197 (5) Reformation 194 (2)
Mont-Dauphin France early modern states 197 (5)
Monte Albán region Central America first civilizations 122 (1)
Monte Albán Central America (Mexico) Aztecs 124 (1) first civilizations 121 (2), 122 (1) first religions 36 (1)
Monte Alegre archaeological site South America (Brazil) early cultures 144 (1)
Monte Alto Central America (Mexico) first civilizations 123 (2)
Monte Bello Islands nuclear test Australia environmentalism 285 (2)
Monte Cassino Italy Franks 184 (2) medieval states 183 (4) WWII 211 (4)
Montecristi West Indies (Dominican Republic) European expansion 85 (2)
Monteleone di Calabria see Hipponium
Montenegro SCr. Crna Gora state/vassal state Southeast Europe early modern states 193 (4) economy 205 (4) Napoleon 200–201 (1), 201 (2) Ottomans 195 (4), 232–233 (1) Reformation 194 (2) WWI 207 (6) WWII 211 (2), (4) early 20th century 206 (1), civil war 215 (3)
Montenotte battle Italy Napoleon 200–201 (1)
Montereau battle France Napoleon 200–201 (1)
Monterey North America (USA) the growth of the US 129 (2)
Monterey see Monterrey
Monterrey var. Monterey Central America (Mexico) exploration 119 (2), (3) Mexican Revolution 133 (3) the growth of the US 129 (2) US economy 136 (2) Cold War 108 (2)
Montespan archaeological site France prehistoric culture 17 (3)
Monte Verde archaeological site/settlement South America (Chile) early cultures 144 (1)
Montevideo South America (Uruguay) colonization 148 (2) empire and revolution 150 (1), 151 (3) environment 153 (4) exploration 143 (3) global immigration 100 (1) imperial global economy 92 (1) politics 152 (1)
Montezuma Castle archaeological site North America (USA) cultural groups 123 (4)
Montferrat state Italy Reformation 196 (1)
Montgaudier archaeological site France prehistoric culture 17 (3)
Montgomery British Isles (United Kingdom) medieval states 188 (2)
Montgomery North America (USA) the growth of the US 129 (2), 132 (1) US Civil War 131 (7) US society 137 (6)
Montmaurin archaeological site France first humans 13 (2)
Montmirail France WWI 206 (2), (3) battle 200–201 (1)
Montpelier North America (USA) the growth of the US 129 (2)
Montpellier settlement/university France early modern states 197 (5) economy 190 (1) empire and revolution 199 (4) medieval states 187 (3), 192 (1)
Montreal var. Hochelaga; Fr. Montréal North America (Canada) colonization 126 (1) empire and revolution 127 (2), (3), 88 (1) European expansion 84–85 (1) exploration 119 (2), (3) imperial global economy 92 (1) the growth of the US 129 (2), 132 (1) US economy 136 (2) see also Hochelaga
Montréal fort Southwest Asia (Jordan) crusades 65 (3)
Montreuil France WWI 206 (2)
Montserrat var. Emerald Isle colonial possession West Indies the world in 1975 106–107 the modern world 110–111
Monza Italy medieval states 183 (4)
Mook battle Low Countries (Netherlands) Reformation 195 (5)
Mooloya Estate rebellion South Asia (Sri Lanka) decolonization 250 (1)
Moose Factory North America (Canada) colonization 126 (1)
Mootwingee archaeological site Australia prehistoric culture 17 (5)
Moppo see Mokpo
Moquegua South America (Peru) politics 151 (4)
Moradabad South Asia (India) economy 249 (4)
Morat Ger. Murten battle Central Europe (Switzerland) early modern states 193 (5)
Morava var. Glavn'a Morava, March, Velika Morava; Ger. Grosse Moravavar river Central Europe WWI 207 (6) see also Velika Morava
Moravia region/state Central Europe early modern states 193 (4) empire and revolution 199 (3) medieval states 189 (4) Napoleon 200–201 (1) Ottomans 197 (4)
Moravians people Central Europe Franks 184 (2)
Mordovia region Eastern Europe Soviet Union 214–215 (4)
Morea vassal state Greece Ottomans 230 (1)
Morelos state Central America Mexican Revolution 133 (3)
Moreruela major cistercian house Iberian Peninsula medieval states 187 (3)
Moreton Bay penal centre Australia colonization 282 (1) environmentalism 285 (2)
Morgan Hill North America (USA) 136 (3)
Morgarten battle Central Europe (Switzerland) early modern states 193 (5)
Mori region Japan early modern states 267 (4)
Morimond major cistercian house France medieval states 187 (3)
Morioka Japan economy 270 (1)
Mormon Trail wagon train route North America (USA) the growth of the US 129 (2)
Morocco Fr. Maroc, Sp. Marruecos region/state North Africa colonization 167 (4) decolonization 168 (1)early Islam 57 (2) economy 168 (2), (3) European expansion 84–85 (1) European imperialism 96 (1), 97 (4) global immigration 101 (2) Islam 235 (4) Napoleon 200–201 (1) Ottomans 231 (3) slave trade 165 (4) the modern world 112 (1), 113 (3), (4) trade 164 (2), 167 (1) WWII 104 (1), 211 (4) early 20th century 206 (1) Cold War 109 (1)
Mörs var. Moers Central Europe (Germany) Reformation 195 (5)
Mörs region Central Europe empire and revolution 199 (3)
Moscow Rus. Moskva Eastern Europe (Russian Federation) biological diffusion 72–73 (1) colonialism 269 (3) economy 190 (1), 205 (4) empire and revolution 202 (1) exploration 257 (2), 286 (1) global immigration 100 (1), 101 (2) imperial global economy 92 (1) Mongols 68 (2), 68–69 (1) Napoleon 200–201 (1) post-war politics 212 (3) Reformation 196 (2) Soviet Union 208 (2), 213 (4) Timur 229 (4) WWII 104 (2), 210 (1), 211 (2), (3), (4) Cold War 108 (3)
Mosega battle Southern Africa (South Africa) colonization 166 (2)
Mosel Fr. Moselle river France Reformation 195 (5) see also Moselle
Moselle Ger. Mosel river France empire and revolution 199 (4), 202 (2) WWI 206 (2), (3) see also Mosel
Moskva see Moscow
Mosquito Coast colonial possession/state Central America colonization 126 (1) empire and revolution 88 (1)
Mosquito Protectorate state Central America the world in 1850 90–91
Mossamedes var. Namibe; mod. Moçâmedes Southern Africa (Angola) exploration 157 (4) see also Namibe
Mossel Bay bay Southern Africa exploration 156 (3)
Mossi state West Africa Islam 163 (1) trade 163 (4), (6), (7), 164 (2)
Mostagedda Egypt ancient Egypt 159 (2)
Mostar Southeast Europe (Bosnia and Herzegovina) Napoleon 200–201 (1) Ottomans 230 (1) civil war 215 (3)
Mosul Ar. Al Mawṣil Southwest Asia (Iraq) 20th-century politics 233 (3), 235 (5) crusades 228 (2) early Islam 56–57 (1), 57 (2), (3) economy 234 (1) exploration 219 (3) Islam 227 (5) Mongols 229 (3) Seljuks 228 (1) Timur 229 (4) WWI 233 (2)
Mosyllon East Africa (Somalia) early trade 225 (3)
Motagua river Central America first civilizations 123 (2)
Motecuzoma Central America (Mexico) Aztecs 124 (3)
Motuhora whaling station New Zealand colonization 283 (4)
Motul var. Motul de Felipe Carrillo Puerto Central America (Mexico) first civilizations 122 (1)
Motul de Felipe Carrillo Puerto see Motul
Motu Marotiri island Pacific Ocean early cultures 281 (4)
Motu Nui island Pacific Ocean early cultures 281 (4)
Motupalli South Asia (India) colonialism 247 (3)
Motya Italy ancient Rome 179 (3) early states 178 (2) first civilizations 177 (1)
Mouhoun see Black Volta
Mouila archaeological site Central Africa (Gabon) early cultures 160 (1)
Moukden see Mukden, Shenyang
Moulins France early modern states 197 (5)
Moulmein var. Maulmain, Mawlamyine Mainland Southeast Asia (Burma) WWII 251 (3)
Mound Bottom North America (USA) cultural groups 122 (5)
Mound Building Villages region North America the world in 500 BCE 34–35
Mound City burial mound North America (USA) first civilizations 121 (4)
Mounds State Park burial mound North America (USA) first civilizations 121 (4)
Moundville North America (USA) cultural groups 122 (5)
Moun Hou see Black Volta
Mount Acay South America (Argentina) Incas 147 (3)
Mountain people North America cultural groups 123 (3)
Mountain View North America (USA) 136 (3)
Mount Burr Australia the world in 5000 BCE 18–19
Mount Cameron West archaeological site Australia prehistoric culture 17 (5)
Mount Isa Australia colonization 282 (1), 283 (3)
Mount Lyell goldfield Australia colonization 282 (2)
Mount Magnet Australia colonization 282 (1)
Mount Newham Australia exploration 280 (1)
Mount Olympus religious site Greece first religions 36 (1), 37 (3)
Mount Royal North America (USA) cultural groups 122 (5)
Mourzouk see Murzuk
Moxeke early ceremonial centre South America (Peru) early cultures 144 (1), 145 (3)
Moyen-Congo see Congo
Mozambique Port. Moçambique Southern Africa (Mozambique) colonization 167 (4) European expansion 81 (3), 84–85 (1) exploration 156 (3) Islam 163 (1) slave trade 165 (4) trade 164 (1)
Mozambique prev. Portuguese East Africa, Moçambique state Southern Africa decolonization 168 (1) economy 168 (2), (3) European expansion 84–85 (1) European imperialism 96 (1), (2) the modern world 112 (1), 113 (3) trade 167 (1) Cold War 109 (1) see also Portuguese East Africa
Mozambique, Canal de see Mozambique Channel
Mozambique Channel Fr. Canal de Mozambique, Mal. Lakandranon' i Mozambika sea waterway Indian Ocean first humans 12 (1), 13 (2) slave trade 165 (4)
Mpangu state Central Africa economy 163 (2)
Mpondo see Pondo
Mrohaung var. Myohaung Mainland Southeast Asia (Burma) colonialism 248 (1) early medieval states 245 (6)
Msalala East Africa (Tanzania) exploration 157 (5)
Msiri state Central Africa colonization 167 (4)
Msiri people Central Africa trade 167 (1)
Msiris Southern Africa (Congo (Zaire)) exploration 157 (4)
Mtamvuna var. Orange River, Oranjerivier river Southern Africa colonization 166 (2) see also Orange River
Mtkvari see Kura
Mtskheta Southwest Asia (Georgia) world religions 48 (1)
Mubi West Africa (Nigeria) exploration 157 (4)
Muchiri South Asia (India) world religions 243 (4)
Mudgagiri South Asia (India) early medieval states 244 (2)
Muenchen see Munich
Muenster see Münster
Mughal Empire var. Mogul Empire state South Asia medieval Persia 231 (4)
Mughals state South Asia colonialism 248 (1)
Mugharet el-'Aliya archaeological site North Africa (Morocco) first humans 13 (2)
Mugi East Africa (Sudan) exploration 157 (5)
Muhammerah see Khorramshahr
Muhi battle Central Europe (Hungary) medieval states 189 (4)
Mühlberg Central Europe (Germany) Reformation 194 (2)
Mühlhausen var. Mühlhausen in Thüringen Central Europe (Germany) medieval states 189 (3)
Mühlhausen in Thüringen see Mühlhausen
Muju region East Asia medieval states 264 (2)
Mukalla Ar. Al Mukallā Southwest Asia (Yemen) 20th-century politics 233 (4)
Mukden prev. Fengtien; Chin. Shenyang, Shen-yang, Eng. Moukden East Asia (China) early modern states 266 (1) post-war politics 271 (7) Russo-Japanese War 270 (4) Sino-Japanese War 270 (3) Communism 271 (8) see also Shenyang
Mülhausen see Mulhouse
Mulhouse Ger. Mülhausen Central Europe (France) early modern states 193 (5)
Multan South Asia (Pakistan) trade 72–73 (1) colonialism 247 (3), 248 (1) decolonization 250 (1) early Islam 56–57 (1), 57 (2) early medieval states 244–245 (3) economy 249 (4) empire and revolution 249 (3) imperial global economy 93 (5) Mongols 68 (2), 68–69 (1) Mughal Empire 246 (1) world religions 243 (4), 49 (3)
Multan region/state South Asia early medieval states 244–245 (3)
Mumbai see Bombay
Mumhain region British Isles medieval states 188 (2)
München see Munich
Munda region/state South Asia first empires 241 (5) world religions 242 (2)
Mundigak archaeological site/settlement Central Asia (Afghanistan) first cities 240 (2) first civilizations 24 (2), 25 (3)
Mundus East Africa (Somalia) early cultures 161 (3), (5) early trade 225 (3)
Munger see Monghyr
Mu Nggava see Rennell
Munich Ger. München, Muenchen; It. Monaco Central Europe (Germany) early modern states 193 (4) economy 205 (4) empire and revolution 202 (1), (2) inter-war 209 (5) Napoleon 200–201 (1), 201 (2) post-war politics 212 (1), (3) Reformation 196 (1) WWII 210 (1), 211 (2), (3), (4)
Munster region British Isles medieval states 186 (2)
Münster var. Muenster, Münster in Westfalen rebellion/settlement Central Europe (Germany) early modern states 193 (4) Franks 184 (2) medieval states 189 (3) Reformation 194 (2)
Münster in Westfalen see Münster
Muqdisho see Mogadishu
Murchison River river Australia colonization 282 (1) exploration 279 (2) prehistoric culture 17 (5)
Murcia Iberian Peninsula (Spain) economy 190 (1) Islam 192 (3)
Murderer's Bay bay Australia exploration 278 (1)
Muret battle France crusades 186 (1)
Mureybat Southwest Asia (Turkey) early agriculture 220 (1)
Murfreesboro North America (USA) US Civil War 131 (6)
Mūrītānīyah see Mauritania
Murmansk Eastern Europe (Russian Federation) early modern states 197 (3) WWII 211 (4)
Muroran bomb target Japan WWII 273 (3)
Murray River river Australia colonization 282 (1), (2), 283 (3) exploration 279 (2) prehistoric culture 17 (5)
Murrumbidgee Australia exploration 279 (2)
Mursa Southeast Europe (Croatia) ancient Rome 180–181 (1)
Murshidabad South Asia (India) colonialism 248 (1) economy 249 (4) Mughal Empire 246 (1)
Murten see Morat
Murzuch see Murzuk
Murzuk var. Marzūq, Murzuq, It. Murzuch North Africa (Libya) ancient trade 44–45 (1) colonization 167 (4) exploration 157 (4) Islam 163 (1)
Murzuq see Murzuk
Musang Cave Philippines the world in 5000 BCE 18–19
Musawwarat es Sufra East Africa (Sudan) early cultures 160 (1)
Musay'id see Umm Said
Muscat var. Maskat, Mascat; Ar. Masqaṭ Southwest Asia (Oman) biological diffusion 72–73 (1) early Islam 56–57 (1), 57 (2) economy 234 (1) European expansion 81 (3), 84–85 (1) exploration 219 (4) Islam 226 (2), 227 (4) medieval voyages 61 (3) Seljuks 228 (1) trade 230 (2) world religions 226 (1) 20th-century politics 233 (4)
Muscat and Oman see Oman
Muscoda Mounds burial mound North America (USA) first civilizations 121 (4)
Muscovy region/state Eastern Europe biological diffusion 72–73 (1)
Muskogean see Tallahassee
Mutapa state Southern Africa Islam 163 (1)
Mutina mod. Modena mithraic site Italy world religions 48 (1) see also Modena
Muttra var. Mathura, Mathuru South Asia (India) economy 249 (4) see also Mathura
Mu Us Shamo see Ordos Desert
Muza Southwest Asia (Yemen) ancient trade 44 (2) early cultures 161 (3), (4), (5) early trade 225 (3)
Muzaffarabad South Asia (Pakistan) post-war politics 252 (2)
Muziris South Asia (India) ancient trade 44–45 (1)
Muzumbo a Kalunga state Southern Africa trade 164 (2)
Mwanza East Africa (Tanzania) exploration 157 (5)
Myanmar see Burma
Mycale battle Southwest Asia (Turkey) ancient Persia 223 (4)
Mycenae Greece Bronze Age 175 (3) first cities 28–29 (1) first civilizations 175 (4)
Myitkyina Mainland Southeast Asia (Burma) WWII 272 (1), 273 (2)
Mylae Italy ancient Rome 179 (3)
Myongju region East Asia medieval states 264 (2)
Myos Hormus var. Myus Hormus Egypt ancient trade 44–45 (1) early cultures 161 (3), (5) early trade 225 (3)
Myra Christian archbishopric/settlement Southwest Asia (Turkey) ancient Rome 180–181 (1) world religions 48 (1)
Myrina Greece first civilizations 177 (1)
Mysia region Southwest Asia first religions 37 (3) Hellenistic world 40–41 (1)
Mysore South Asia (India) economy 249 (4) imperial global economy 93 (5)
Mysore region/state South Asia colonialism 248 (1), (2) post-war politics 253 (4)
Mytilene Greece ancient Greece 179 (4)
Mytilene state Greece ancient Greece 177 (2)
Myus Hormus see Myos Hormos

N

Nabataea province/state Southwest Asia early cultures 161 (3), (5)
Nabataeans people Southwest Asia ancient Rome 225 (4)
Nabesna people North America cultural groups 123 (3)
Nabta Egypt the world in 5000 BCE 18–19
Nabta Playa Egypt early agriculture 158 (1)
Nachi-san mountain Japan medieval states 265 (3)
Nadikagama South Asia (India) world religions 242 (3)
Nad-i-Ali Central Asia (Afghanistan) Hellenistic world 40–41 (1)
Nafplio see Nauplia
Naga ed-Der Egypt ancient Egypt 159 (2)
Nagaland region South Asia post-war politics 252 (1), 253 (4)
Nagano prefecture Japan economy 270 (1)
Nagappattinam var. Negapatam Buddhist centre South Asia (India) world religions 49 (3) see also Negapatam
Nagara Sridharmaraj see Nakhon Si Thammarat
Nagarjunakonda settlement South Asia (India) exploration 256 (1) world religions 49 (3)
Nagasaki Japan trade 72–73 (1) WWII 273 (3) early modern states 267 (4), (5) economy 270 (1), 275 (4) European expansion 80–81 (1) trade 267 (3) WWII 272 (1), 273 (2)
Nagasaki prefecture Japan economy 270 (1)
Nagata Japan medieval states 265 (4)
Nagelwanze South Asia (India) colonialism 247 (3)
Nagidus Southwest Asia (Turkey) first civilizations 177 (1) Hellenistic world 40–41 (1)
Nagorno-Karabakh region Eastern Europe Soviet Union 214–215 (4)
Nagoya Japan early modern states 267 (4) economy 270 (1) Islam 275 (4) medieval states 262–263 (1) WWII 273 (3)
Nagpur South Asia (India) colonialism 248 (1) decolonization 250 (1) economy 249 (4) Marathas 246 (2) post-war economy 253 (5)
Nagur South Asia (India) world religions 243 (4)
Nagysalló battle Central Europe (Hungary) empire and revolution 88–89 (2)
Nagyszeben mod. Sibiu Southeast Europe (Romania) early modern states 193 (4)
Nahr see Diyala
Naimans people East Asia/Siberia Mongols 68–69 (1)
Na'in see Nayin
Nairobi East Africa (Kenya) colonization 167 (4) economy 168 (2)
Naishadha region South Asia world religions 242 (2)
Naissus see Niš, Nish
Najd see Nejd
Najima see Fukuoka
Najran Southwest Asia (Saudi Arabia) early cultures 161 (3), (4), (5) early Islam 56–57 (1) early trade 225 (3) Islam 226 (2) world religions 226 (1)
Nakambé see White Volta
Nakhichevan Southwest Asia (Azerbaijan) medieval Persia 231 (4) Ottomans 231 (3)
Nakhon Pathom settlement/temple Mainland Southeast Asia (Thailand) early medieval states 245 (5) world religions 243 (5)
Nakhon Ratchasima var. Khorat, Korat Mainland Southeast Asia (Thailand) colonialism 247 (4), 248 (1)
Nakhon Si Thammarat var. Nagara Sridharmaraj, Nakhon Sithamnaraj Mainland Southeast Asia (Thailand) colonialism 248 (2)
Nakhon Sithamnaraj see Nakhon Si Thammarat
Naknek North America (USA) cultural groups 123 (3)
Nakum Central America (Mexico) first civilizations 123 (2)
Nal archaeological site South Asia (Pakistan) first cities 240 (2)
Nalanda South Asia (India) ancient trade 44–45 (1) first religions 36 (2) world religions 242 (3)
Nama people Southern Africa trade 164 (1)
Namen see Namur
Namibe Port. Moçâmedes, Mossamedes Southern Africa (Angola) Cold War 109 (5) see also Mossamedes
Namibia prev. German Southwest Africa, Southwest Africa state Southern Africa decolonization 168 (1) economy 168 (2), (3) the modern world 112 (1), 113 (4) see also German Southwest Africa, Southwest Africa
Namiquipa Central America (Mexico) Mexican Revolution 133 (3)
Namnetes see Nantes
Nam Tun East Asia (China) the world in 5000 BCE 18–19
Namu island Pacific Ocean exploration 278 (1)
Namur Dut. Namen Low Countries (Belgium) early modern states 197 (5) WWI 206 (2), (3)
Namur province Low Countries Reformation 195 (5)
Nan province East Asia first states 260 (1)
Nanagunas river South Asia ancient trade 44 (2)
Nana Mode archaeological site Central Africa (Central African Republic) early cultures 160 (1)
Nanchang var. Nan-ch'ang, Nanch'ang-hsien rebellion/settlement East Asia (China) biological diffusion 72–73 (1) early modern states 266 (1), (2), 268 (1) economy 274 (1) post-war politics 271 (7)
Nanch'ang-hsien see Nanchang
Nanchao see Nanzhao, Yunnan
Nan-chao see Nanzhao, Yunnan
Nan-ching see Jianye, Nanjing
Nancy France empire and revolution 199 (4) medieval states 192 (1), (2) WWI 206 (2), (3) battle early modern states 193 (4), 197 (5)
Nandivardhana South Asia (India) early medieval states 244 (1)
Nan Hai see South China Sea
Nanhai var. Canton, Guangzhou East Asia (China) ancient trade 44–45 (1) exploration 256 (1) first states 260 (1) medieval states 261 (6) see also Canton, Guangzhou
Nanhai province East Asia first states 260 (1)
Nanhan state East Asia medieval states 263 (3)
Nanjing var. Nan-ching, Nanking; prev. Chianning, Chian-ning, Kiang-ning East Asia (China) colonialism 269 (4) early modern states 266 (1) economy 274 (1) empire and revolution 268 (1) first religions 37 (4) Islam 275 (4) medieval states 263 (5) Mongols 68–69 (1) post-war politics 271 (7), 274 (2) trade 267 (3) WWII 272 (1), 273 (2) Chinese revolution 271 (5)
Nanjing province East Asia early modern states 266 (1), (2)
Nankaido region Japan medieval states 265 (3)
Nanking see Jianye, Nanjing
Nanning var. Nan-ning; prev. Yung-ning East Asia (China) plague 72–73 (1) colonialism 269 (4) WWII 272 (1), 273 (2)
Nansei-shotō see Ryukyu Islands
Nan Shan mod. Qilian Shan mountain range East Asia exploration 257 (3) see also Qilian Shan
Nansha Qundao see Spratly Islands
Nantes anc. Condivincum, Namnetes; Bret. Naoned France crusades 186 (1) early modern states 197 (5) economy 205 (4) empire and revolution 199 (4) Franks 184 (2) medieval states 185 (3), 187 (4), 192 (1), (2) medieval voyages 60–61 (1) Reformation 194 (2)
Nantong East Asia (China) post-war politics 274 (2)
Nanyang Buddhist centre East Asia (China) world religions 49 (3)
Nanyue state East Asia first cities 259 (5)
Nanzhao var. Nan-chao; mod. Yunnan region/state East Asia early medieval states 245 (5), 261 (6) medieval states 262–263 (1) Mongols 68–69 (1) world religions 49 (3), (4) see also Yunnan
Nanzheng var. Hanzhong, Han-Chung East Asia (China) first cities 259 (5) see also Hanzhong
Naoned see Nantes
Napata var. Gebel Barkal East Africa (Sudan) ancient Egypt 159 (5) early cultures 160 (1) see also Gebel Barkal
Napier settlement/whaling station New Zealand colonization 283 (4), (5)
Naples anc. Neapolis; It. Napoli, Ger. Neapel Italy plague 72–73 (1) crusades 186 (1) early modern states 194 (1) economy 190 (1), 205 (4) empire and revolution 202 (1), (3) Franks 184 (2) global immigration 100 (1) medieval states 182 (2), 183 (4), 187 (3), (5), 188 (1), 189 (4) Napoleon 200–201 (1), 201 (2), (3) Ottomans 230 (1) post-war politics 212 (3) Reformation 194 (2) the modern world 113 (4) see also Neapolis
Naples colonial possession/state Italy early modern states 193 (4), 194 (1) medieval states 185 (3), 189 (4) Napoleon 201 (2) Ottomans 195 (4), 230 (1), 231 (3) Reformation 194 (2), 196 (1), (2)
Napo river South America early cultures 144 (1), 145 (4), 146 (1) empire and revolution 150 (2) exploration 142 (1) Incas 147 (3) politics 152 (1)
Napoli see Naples, Neapolis
Naqa East Africa (Sudan) the world in 500 BCE 34–35
Naqada Egypt ancient Egypt 159 (2), (3) first civilizations 24 (2)
Nara var. Heijo-kyo Japan early modern states 265 (5), 267 (4) medieval states 262–263 (1), 264 (2), 265 (4) world religions 49 (4)
Nara prefecture Japan economy 270 (1)
Naranjo Central America (Mexico) first civilizations 123 (2)
Narasapur var. Madapallam South Asia (India) colonialism 247 (3)
Naravaranagara mod. Angkor Borei Mainland Southeast Asia ancient India 241 (6)
Narbo mod. Narbonne settlement France ancient Rome 179 (3), 180–181 (1), 181 (3), (4) early cultures 161 (2) great migrations 52–53 (1) world religions 48 (1) see also Narbonne
Narbonensis province France ancient Rome 180–181 (1)
Narbonne anc. Narbo settlement France Franks 184 (2) Islam 184 (1) medieval states 182 (2), 187 (3), 192 (1) see also Narbo
Narbonne battle France early Islam 56–57 (1)
Narce Italy Bronze Age 175 (3)
Narev Pol. Narew river Central Europe WWI 207 (4)
Narew see Narev
Nargund state South Asia empire and revolution 249 (3)
Nariokotome archaeological site East Africa (Kenya) first humans 13 (2)
Narmada archaeological site South Asia (India) first humans 13 (2)
Narmada river South Asia colonialism 247 (3), 248 (1), (2) decolonization 250 (1) early medieval states 244 (1), (2), 244–245 (3), 245 (4) economy 249 (4) first cities 240 (2) first empires 241 (4), (5) first religions 36 (2) Marathas 246 (2) Mughal Empire 246 (1) post-war politics 252 (1) world religions 242 (2), 243 (4)
Narni see Narnia
Narnia mod. Narni Italy early states 178 (1)
Narosura archaeological site/settlement East Africa (Kenya) early agriculture 158 (1) early cultures 160 (1)
Narraganset people North America colonization 126 (1)
Narva Eastern Europe (Estonia) early modern states 195 (3)
Narvik Scandinavia (Norway) WWII 104 (2), 210 (1), 211 (4)
Narym Eastern Europe (Russian Federation) exploration 257 (2)
Nasarpur South Asia (Pakistan) colonialism 247 (3)
Nashika South Asia (India) world religions 242 (2)
Nashville battle/settlement North America (USA) the growth of the US 129 (2), 132 (1) US Civil War 131 (6), (7) US society 137 (6)
Nasik South Asia (India) decolonization 250 (1) exploration 256 (1)
Naskapi people North America cultural groups 123 (3)
Nassau West Indies (Bahamas) Cold War 108 (2)
Natal South America (Brazil) colonization 149 (3), (4) environment 153 (4) politics 152 (1)
Natal colonial possession/state Southern Africa colonization 167 (4) European imperialism 96 (2) global immigration 101 (3)
Natchez people Central America colonization 125 (4)
Natrun, Wadi el- river Egypt ancient Egypt 159 (2), (3)
Naucratis Egypt first civilizations 177 (1)
Naujan North America (Canada) cultural groups 123 (3)
Naumburg Central Europe (Germany) medieval states 189 (3)
Nauplia mod. Nafplio; prev. Navplion Greece medieval states 189 (4)
Nauru state/island Pacific Ocean colonization 284–285 (1) decolonization 285 (3) environmentalism 285 (2) exploration 279 (3)
Nautaca Central Asia (Uzbekistan) Hellenistic world 40–41 (1)
Navadvipa South Asia (Bangladesh) early medieval states 244 (2)
Navajo people North America colonization 125 (4), 126 (1)
Navarino battle Greece empire and revolution 88–89 (2)
Navarra see Navarre
Navarre Sp. Navarra state/region Iberian Peninsula crusades 64–65 (2) early modern states 194 (1) Franks 184 (2) Islam 192 (3) medieval states 185 (3), 192 (1), (2) medieval voyages 60–61 (1) Reformation 194 (2)
Navplion see Nauplia
Nawait, Lake lake Australia the world in 10,000 BCE 14–15
Nawamoyn and Malangangerr Australia exploration 280 (1)
Naxos state/island Greece ancient Greece 177 (2) first civilizations 175 (4) medieval states 187 (5), 189 (4) Ottomans 230 (1)
Naxos Greece first civilizations 177 (1)
Nayakas dynasty South Asia Mughal Empire 246 (1)
Nayarit state Central America Mexican Revolution 133 (3)
Nayin var. Na'in Southwest Asia (Iran) early Islam 56–57 (1)
Nazareth Southwest Asia (Israel) ancient Rome 225 (4) 20th century 234 (2)
Nazca South America (Peru) early cultures 145 (4) Incas 147 (3)
Nazca region South America early cultures 145 (4)
Nazca people South America the world in 250 BCE 38–39 the world in 1 CE 42–43 the world in 250 CE 46–47
Nazlet Khatir archaeological site/settlement East Africa (Sudan) first humans 13 (2)
Ncao Central America (Honduras) Aztecs 124 (1)
Ndebele var. Matabele state Southern Africa the world in 1850 90–91
Ndebele var. Matabele people Southern Africa colonization 166 (2)
N'Dhala Gorge archaeological site Australia prehistoric culture 17 (5)
Ndola Southern Africa (Zambia) economy 168 (2)
Ndongo state Southern Africa Islam 163 (1) trade 164 (2)
Ndulu state Southern Africa the world in 1800 86–87 the world in 1850 90–91
Neagrā, Marea see Black Sea
Neanderthal archaeological site Central Europe (Germany) first humans 13 (2)
Nea Nikomideia Greece early agriculture 174 (1)
Neapel see Naples, Neapolis
Neapolis Ger. Neapel; mod. Napoli; Eng. Naples Italy ancient Rome 180–181 (1) early states 178 (1), (2) first civilizations 177 (1) great migrations 52–53 (1) see also Naples
Nebas Central America (Mexico) first civilizations 123 (2)
Nebraska state North America the growth of the US 129 (1) US economy 134 (2)
Nebraska Territory region North America US Civil War 130 (3), (4), (5)
Nechtansmere battle British Isles (United Kingdom) medieval states 183 (3)
Nederland see Netherlands
Neerwinden battle Low Countries (Belgium) empire and revolution 199 (4)
Nefertare Southeast Europe (Bosnia and Herzegovina) world religions 48 (1)
Negapatam mod. Nāgappattinam South Asia (India) colonialism 247 (3) imperial global economy 93 (5) see also Nagappattinam
Negev Heb. HaNegev desert Southwest Asia 20th century 234 (2) crusades 65 (3)
Negombo South Asia (Sri Lanka) colonialism 247 (3)
Negoro Buddhist temple army Japan medieval states 265 (4)
Negotin Southeast Europe (Serbia) WWI 207 (6)
Negroponte Greece economy 190 (1)
Negroponte region Greece medieval states 187 (5)
Negro, Río river South America colonization 148 (2), 149 (3) early cultures 144 (1), 145 (2) economy 153 (3) empire and revolution 151 (3) environment 153 (4) exploration 143 (2), (3) Incas 148 (1)
Nehavend Southwest Asia (Iran) ancient Persia 225 (6) battle early Islam 56–57 (1) Islam 226 (2)
Nei Mongol see Inner Mongolia
Nejd region/state Southwest Asia early Islam 56–57 (1), 57 (2) European imperialism 97 (4) exploration 219 (4) Ottomans 232–233 (1) WWI 233 (2) 20th-century politics 233 (4)
Nekheb see El-Kab
Nelson New Zealand colonization 283 (4), (5)
Nelson region New Zealand colonization 283 (5)
Nelson river North America colonization 126 (1) the growth of the US 129 (2)
Nelson Bay archaeological site/settlement Southern Africa (South Africa) early cultures 160 (1)
Neman Bel. Nyoman, Ger. Memel, Lith. Nemunas, Pol. Niemen, river Eastern Europe early modern states 197 (3) Napoleon 200–201 (1)
Nemausus mod. Nîmes, Nismus France ancient Rome 180–181 (1) see also Nîmes
Nemetocenna see Arras
Nemorensis, Lacus lake Italy early states 178 (1)
Nemours France Reformation 194 (2)
Nemunas see Neman
Nen Jiang var. Nonni river East Asia first states 260 (1)
Nepal colonial possession/region/state South Asia colonialism 247 (3), 248 (1), (2), 269 (4) decolonization 250 (1), 251 (4) early modern states 268 (1) economy 249 (4) empire and revolution 249 (3) exploration 257 (3) historical geography 275 (5), 275 (3) post-war economy 253 (5), 275 (3) post-war politics 252 (1), (3), 253 (4), 274 (2) the modern world 113 (3) trade 267 (3) WWII 251 (3)
Nepala region South Asia early medieval states 244–245 (3)
Nepalese Principalities state South Asia the world in 1500 74–75 the world in 1600 78–79 the world in 1700 82–83
Nepeña river South America early cultures 145 (3)
Nerchinsk Siberia (Russian Federation) colonialism 269 (3) exploration 257 (2)
Nerja, Cueva de Iberian Peninsula (Spain) early agriculture 174 (1)
Nestepe archaeological site Central America (Mexico) first civilizations 121 (3)
Netherlands var. Holland; prev. Batavian Republic, Dutch Republic,

United Provinces; *Dut.* Nederland *state* Low Countries early 20th century 206 (1) economy 205 (4) empire and revolution 199 (3), 202 (1), (2) European expansion 80–81 (1) European imperialism 97 (4) inter-war 209 (3), (5) post-war economy 214 (1), (2) post-war politics 212 (1), (3) Soviet Union 213 (4) the modern world 112 (1), (2), 113 (3), (4) US superpower 138 (1) WWI 206 (2), (3), 208 (1) WWII 104 (1), 211 (2), (3), (4) Cold War 108 (3), 109 (1)
see also Batavian Republic, United Provinces
Netherlands Antilles *prev.* Dutch West Indies *colonial possession* West Indies Cold War 108 (2)
Netherlands East Indies *see* Dutch East Indies, Indonesia
Netherlands Guiana *see* Dutch Guiana, Surinam
Netherlands New Guinea *var.* Dutch New Guinea, Irian Barat, West Irian, West New Guinea; *mod.* Irian Jaya *state* Maritime Southeast Asia the world in 1950 102–103
see also Irian Jaya, Dutch New Guinea
Netsilik Inuit *people* North America cultural groups 123 (3)
Neuchâtel *Ger.* Neuenburg Central Europe (Switzerland) early modern states 193 (5)
Neuchâtel *region/state* Central Europe early modern states 193 (5) empire and revolution 199 (3), (4), 202 (1) Napoleon 200–201 (1)
Neuenburg *see* Neuchâtel
Neuenheim *mithraic site* Central Europe (Germany) world religions 48 (1)
Neukölln Central Europe (Germany) post-war politics 212 (2)
Neumark *region* Central Europe early modern states 195 (3)
Neuquén South America (Argentina) empire and revolution 151 (3) environment 153 (4)
Neusatz *see* Novi Sad
Neustria *region* France Franks 183 (6), 184 (2)
Neuve-Chapelle France WWI 206 (2)
Neva *battle* Eastern Europe (Russian Federation) medieval states 189 (3)
Nevada *state* North America the growth of the US 129 (1) US economy 134 (2)
Nevel' Eastern Europe (Russian Federation) early modern states 195 (3)
Nevers *anc.* Noviodunum France medieval states 192 (2)
Neville's Cross *battle* British Isles (United Kingdom) medieval states 188 (2)
Nevome *people* Central America colonization 126 (1)
New Amsterdam North America (USA) colonization 126 (1)
New Amsterdam *prev.* Fort St Andries South America (Guyana) colonization 149 (4)
Newark *burial mound* North America (USA) first civilizations 121 (4)
Newbattle *major cistercian house* British Isles (United Kingdom) medieval states 187 (3)
New Britain *island* Melanesia early cultures 280 (2), 280–281 (3) exploration 278 (1) medieval voyages 60 (2) WWII 251 (3)
New Brunswick *province* North America (Canada) 129 (2), 132 (1), 136 (2)
New Calabar West Africa (Nigeria) European expansion 84–85 (1) slave trade 165 (4)
New Caledonia *var.* Kanaky, *Fr.* Nouvelle-Calédonie *colonial possession/island* Pacific Ocean colonization 284–285 (1) decolonization 285 (3) early cultures 280–281 (3) environmentalism 285 (2) exploration 278 (1), 279 (3) medieval voyages 60 (2) WWII 272 (1), 273 (2) Cold War 109 (1)
Newcastle *penal centre/settlement* Australia colonization 282 (1), (2), 283 (3) environmentalism 285 (2)
Newcastle-upon-Tyne *var.* Newcastle; *hist.* Monkchester; *Lat.* Pons Aelii British Isles (United Kingdom) economy 190 (1) medieval states 186 (2)
Newchwang *see* Niuzhuang, Yingkou
New Delhi South Asia (India) post-war politics 252 (1)
New East Prussia *region* Central Europe empire and revolution 198 (2)
New England *region* North America colonization 126 (1) empire and revolution 127 (2)
Newfoundland *Fr.* Terre-Neuve *colonial possession/island/province* North America empire and revolution 88 (1) exploration 118 (1), 119 (2), (3) cultural groups 123 (3) colonization 126 (1), 129 (2),132 (1) US economy 136 (1), (2)
New France *colonial possession* North America colonization 126 (1) empire and revolution 127 (2), 88 (1)
New Goa *see* Panaji
New Granada, Viceroyalty of *mod.* Colombia *colonial possession* South America colonization 148 (2) empire and revolution 150 (1), (2), 88 (1) European expansion 84–85 (1)
see also Columbia
Newgrange *archaeological site/settlement* British Isles (Ireland) Copper Age 174 (2) early systems 33 (3)
New Guinea *island* New Guinea Bronze Age 240 (3) colonialism 247 (4) decolonization 251 (4) early agriculture 20–21 (2) early cultures 280 (2), 280–281 (3) European expansion 80–81 (1) European imperialism 97 (3) exploration 239 (1), (2), 276–277 (1) historical geography 236–237 (1) Islam 243 (6) medieval voyages 60 (2) post-war economy 253 (5) post-war politics 253 (4) the modern world 113 (4) world religions 243 (5) WWII 104 (1), 251 (3), 272 (1), 273 (2) Cold War 109 (1)
New Hampshire *state* North America empire and revolution 127 (2), (3) the growth of the US 129 (1) US Civil War 130 (2), (3), (4), (5) US economy 134 (2)
New Haven North America (USA) empire and revolution 127 (3)
Newhaven British Isles (United Kingdom) economy 204 (1)
New Hebrides *mod.* Vanuatu; *Fr.* Nouvelles Hébrides *colonial possession/island group* Pacific Ocean colonization 284–285 (1) exploration 278 (1), 279 (3) WWII 272 (1), 273 (2)
see also Vanuatu
New Holland *see* Australia, Australian Colonies
New Ireland *island* Melanesia early cultures 280 (2), 280–281 (3) exploration 278 (1) medieval voyages 60 (2)
New Jersey *state* North America empire and revolution 127 (2), (3) the growth of the US 129 (1) US Civil War 130 (2), (3), (4), (5), 131 (6), (7) US economy 134 (2)
New London North America (USA) empire and revolution 127 (3)
New Mexico *region/state* North America Mexican Revolution 133 (3) the growth of the US 129 (1) US economy 134 (2)
New Mexico Territory *region* North America US Civil War 130 (2), (3), (4), (5)
New Munster *mod.* South Island *island* New Zealand colonization 283 (4)
see also South Island
New Orleans North America (USA) colonization 126 (1) European expansion 84–85 (1) exploration 119 (2), (3) global immigration 100 (1) imperial global economy 92 (1), 93 (5) the growth of the US 129 (2), 132 (1), 133 (4) US Civil War 130 (5), 131 (6), (7) US economy 134 (1), 136 (2) US society 137 (6) Cold War 108 (2)
New Plymouth *settlement/whaling station* New Zealand colonization 283 (4), (5)
Newport North America (USA) colonization 126 (1) empire and revolution 127 (3)
New Sarai Eastern Europe (Russian Federation) trade 72–73 (1) Mongols 68 (2) Timur 229 (4)
New Sarum *see* Salisbury
New Siberian Islands *island group* Arctic Ocean exploration 257 (2)
New Silesia *region* Central Europe empire and revolution 199 (3)
New South Wales *state* Australia colonization 282 (1), (2), 283 (3) environmentalism 285 (2)
New Spain, Viceroyalty of *colonial possession* Central America/West Indies colonization 126 (1), 148 (2) empire and revolution 88 (1) European expansion 81 (3), 84–85 (1), 85 (2)
New Territories *colonial possession* East Asia colonialism 269 (4)
Newton British Isles (United Kingdom) economy 204 (2)
New Ulm *battle* North America (USA) the growth of the US 129 (2)
New Ulster *mod.* North Island *island* New Zealand colonization 283 (4)
see also North Island
New York North America (USA) colonization 126 (1) empire and revolution 127 (2), (3) European expansion 84–85 (1) exploration 119 (2), (3) global immigration 100 (1), 101 (2), (3) imperial global economy 92 (1) the growth of the US 129 (2), 132 (1) the modern world 113 (4) US Civil War 130 (5) US economy 134 (1), (3), 136 (2) US politics 135 (6) Cold War 108 (2)
New York *region/state* North America empire and revolution 127 (2), (3) first civilizations 121 (4) the growth of the US 129 (1) US Civil War 130 (2), (3), (4), (5) US economy 134 (2)
New Zealand *state/island group* Pacific Ocean colonization 284–285 (1) decolonization 285 (3) early agriculture 20–21 (2) environmentalism 285 (2) exploration 276–277 (1), 279 (3) global immigration 100 (1) imperial global economy 92 (1) the modern world 113 (4) US economy 138 (2) US superpower 138 (1) WWII 104 (1), 105 (4) Cold War 109 (1)
Nextitlan Central America (Mexico) Aztecs 124 (3)
Neyriz *see* Niriz
Neyshabur *see* Nishapur
Nezahualcoyotl, Dyke of *dam* Central America Aztecs 124 (2)
Ngatimo *people* Easter Island early cultures 281 (4)
Ngaure *people* Easter Island early cultures 281 (4)
Ngoni *state* Southern Africa the world in 1850 90–91
Ngoni *people* Southern Africa colonization 166 (2)
Ngoyo *state* Central Africa/Southern Africa Islam 163 (1) trade 164 (2)
Nguigmi *var.* N'Guigmi West Africa (Niger) exploration 157 (4)
Nguni *people* Southern Africa trade 164 (1)
Ngwane *people* Southern Africa colonization 166 (2)
Niagara North America (USA) colonization 126 (1)
Niah Cave Maritime Southeast Asia (Malaysia) the world in 10,000 BCE 14–15 the world in 5000 BCE 18–19
Niani West Africa (Guinea) Islam 163 (1) Mongols 68 (2)
Niaux *archaeological site/settlement* France prehistoric culture 17 (3)
Nicaea *mod.* Iznik Southwest Asia (Turkey) crusades 64–65 (2) Hellenistic world 41 (2) medieval states 187 (5) Seljuks 228 (1) world religions 226 (1)
see also Iznik
Nicaea *see* Nice
Nicaea, Empire of *state* Greece/Southwest Asia medieval states 187 (5) Mongols 68–69 (1)
Nicaragua *colonial possession/state* Central America the growth of the US 129 (2), 133 (4) the modern world 112 (1), 113 (4) US economy 136 (2) US politics 139 (4) WWII 104 (1) Cold War 108 (2), 109 (1)
Nice *It.* Nizza; *anc.* Nicaea France early modern states 193 (4), 197 (5) empire and revolution 199 (4) medieval states 188 (1) Napoleon 200–201 (1)
Nice *region/state* France empire and revolution 199 (4), 202 (3)
Nicephorium *mod.* Nikephorion Southwest Asia (Syria) Hellenistic world 40–41 (1)
Nicobar Islands *island group* Indian Ocean ancient trade 44–45 (1), 72–73 (1) colonialism 248 (1), (2), 269 (4) decolonization 251 (4) European imperialism 97 (3) exploration 239 (1) post-war politics 253 (4) trade 230 (2) WWII 251 (3), 272 (1), 273 (2)
Nicomedia Southwest Asia (Turkey) ancient Greece 179 (4) ancient Rome 180–181 (1), 181 (4) Hellenistic world 40–41 (1), 41 (2) medieval states 187 (5) world religions 48 (1)
Nicomedia *mod.* Izmit *battle* Southwest Asia (Turkey) crusades 64–65 (2)
Nicopolis Southwest Asia (Turkey) ancient Rome 180–181 (1)
Nicopolis *var.* Nikopolis; *mod.* Nikopol Southeast Europe (Bulgaria) ancient Rome 180–181 (1) Ottomans 230 (1) medieval states 189 (4)
Nicopolis Greece world religions 48 (1)
Nicopolis Egypt ancient Rome 180–181 (1)
Nicosia *Gk.* Lefkosia, *Turk.* Lefkoşa Southwest Asia (Cyprus) crusades 64–65 (2), 65 (3)
Nida Central Europe (Germany) world religions 48 (1)
Nidaros *see* Trondheim
Nie Japan early modern states 265 (5)
Niemen *see* Neman
Nieuw Guinea *see* New Guinea
Nieuwpoort *battle* Low Countries (Netherlands) Reformation 195 (5)
Nieveria South America (Peru) early cultures 145 (4)
Niger *state* West Africa decolonization 168 (1) economy 168 (2), (3) Islam 235 (4) the modern world 112 (1), 113 (3), (4)
Niger *river* West Africa ancient trade 44 (2), 44–45 (1) early agriculture 158 (1), 20–21 (2) early cultures 160 (1) economy 163 (2) exploration 156 (1), (3), 157 (4) first humans 13 (2) first religions 36 (1) global immigration 100 (1) Islam 163 (1), 167 (3) prehistoric culture 16 (1) slave trade 165 (4) trade 163 (4), (5), (6), (7), 164 (2), 167 (1)
Niger-Congo Peoples *people* West Africa the world in 750 BCE 30–31
Nigeria *state* West Africa decolonization 168 (1) economy 168 (2), (3) European imperialism 96 (1) Islam 235 (4) the modern world 112 (1), 113 (3), (4)
Nihon *see* Japan
Nihon-kai *see* Japan, Sea of
Niigata Japan economy 270 (1)
Niigata *prefecture* Japan economy 270 (1)
Nijmegen *anc.* Noviomagus; *Ger.* Nimwegen Low Countries (Netherlands) Franks 184 (2)
Nijmegen *battle* Low Countries (Netherlands) Reformation 195 (5)
Nikephorion *see* Nicephorium
Nikki West Africa (Benin) colonization 167 (4)
Nikolayev Eastern Europe (Ukraine) Soviet Union 208 (2) WWII 207 (4)
Nikopol *see* Nicopolis
Nikopolis *see* Nicopolis
Nile *Ar.* Nahr an Nil, *Lat.* Nilus *river* Africa ancient Egypt 159 (2), (3), (4), (5) ancient Persia 223 (4), 225 (6) ancient Rome 180–181 (1), 224 (2), 225 (5) ancient trade 44–45 (1) biological diffusion 72–73 (1), 73 (3) crusades 65 (3), 228 (2) early agriculture 158 (1), 20–21 (2), 220 (1) early cultures 160 (1), 161 (2), (3), (4), (5) early Islam 56–57 (1), 57 (2) early systems 223 (3), 32 (1), 33 (2), (3) early trade 225 (3) economy 163 (2), (3) empire and revolution 88 (1), 88–89 (2) European expansion 84–85 (1) exploration 156 (3), 157 (4), (5), 172 (1), (2), 219 (3), (4) first cities 220 (2), 28–29 (1) first civilizations 177 (1), 222 (2) first humans 12 (1), 13 (2) first religions 36 (1), 37 (3) global immigration 100 (1) great migrations 53 (2) Hellenistic world 224 (1), 41 (2) imperial global economy 92 (1) Islam 163 (1), 226 (2), 227 (4) Mongols 229 (3), 68 (2), 68–69 (1) Napoleon 200–201 (1) Ottomans 231 (3), 232–233 (1) prehistoric culture 16 (1) Seljuks 228 (1) slave trade 165 (4) Timur 229 (4) trade 167 (1), 230 (2) world religions 226 (1), 49 (4) WWI 233 (2) WWII 210 (1), 211 (4) 20th-century politics 233 (3)
see also Nilus
Nile Delta *delta* Egypt Bronze Age 175 (3)
Nile of the Blacks *river* West Africa exploration 156 (1)
Nile Valley *valley* Egypt early agriculture 20 (1)
Nil, Nahr an *see* Nile
Nilo-Saharan Peoples *people* Africa the world in 750 BCE 30–31 the world in 1600 78–79 the world in 1700 82–83 the world in 1800 86–87 the world in 1850 90–91
Nilotic Peoples *people* Central Africa/East Africa early cultures 160 (1)
Nil, Shatt al *river* Southwest Asia (Iraq) first cities 28 (2)
Nilus *var.* Nahr an Nil, Nile *river* Africa ancient trade 44 (2) *see also* Nile
Nîmes *anc.* Nemausus, Nismes France early modern states 197 (5) empire and revolution 199 (4) Franks 184 (2)
see also Nemausus
Nimrud Southwest Asia (Iraq) early systems 33 (2) first civilizations 222 (2)
Nimule *see* Afuddo
Nimwegen *see* Nijmegen
Nineveh Southwest Asia (Iraq) ancient Persia 223 (4) first cities 220 (2) first civilizations 221 (4), (5), 222 (2) Hellenistic world 40–41 (1) early Islam 56–57 (1)
Ningbo *var.* Ning-po, Ningpu, Ninghsien; *prev.* Jingyuan East Asia (China) ancient trade 44–45 (1) colonialism 269 (4) empire and revolution 88–89 (2) Mongols 68–69 (1) post-war politics 274 (2) trade 267 (3)
Ning-hsia *see* Ningxia
Ninghsien *see* Ningbo
Ningi *state* West Africa trade 164 (2)
Ning-po *see* Ningbo
Ningpu *see* Ningbo
Ningsia *see* Ningxia
Ningxia *var.* Ning-hsia, Ningsia East Asia (China) biological diffusion 72–73 (1) medieval states 263 (6) Mongols 68–69 (1) early modern states 266 (1) post-war economy 275 (3) post-war politics 274 (2)
Ninnis Glacier *glacier* Antarctica Antarctic Exploration 287 (3)
Nioro *var.* Nioro du Sahel West Africa (Mali) colonization 167 (4) Islam 167 (3)
Nioro du Sahel *see* Nioro
Nipissing *people* North America colonization 126 (1)
Nipissing, Lake *lake* North America exploration 119 (2)
Nippon *see* Japan
Nippur Southwest Asia (Iraq) ancient Persia 223 (4) early agriculture 220 (1) first cities 220 (2), 28–29 (1) first civilizations 221 (4), 24 (2), 25 (3)
Niriz *var.* Neyriz Southwest Asia (Iran) early Islam 56–57 (1)
Niš Southeast Europe (Yugoslavia) post-war economy 215 (3)
Nisa Southwest Asia (Iran) ancient Rome 224 (2)
Nisch *see* Niš, Nish
Nish *var.* Niš, Naissus, Nisch Southeast Europe (Yugoslavia) crusades 64–65 (2) early modern states 193 (4) medieval states 189 (4) WWI 207 (6) Ottomans 197 (4)
Nishada *state* South Asia first empires 241 (5)
Nishadha *state* South Asia first empires 241 (5)
Nishapur *Per.* Neyshabur Southwest Asia (Iran) ancient Persia 225 (6) early Islam 56–57 (1), 57 (2) Islam 226 (2), 227 (4), (5) medieval Persia 231 (4) Mongols 68–69 (1) Timur 229 (4)
Nisibis *Christian archbishopric/settlement* Southwest Asia (Turkey) ancient Rome 224 (2) Hellenistic world 40–41 (1), 41 (2) world religions 48 (1)
Nismes *see* Nemausus, Nîmes
Nissan Islands *see* Green Islands
Nistru *see* Dniester
Nitaro Cave Japan the world in 5000 BCE 18–19
Niuatobutabu *see* Niuatoputapu
Niuatoputapu *var.* Niuatobutabu; *prev.* Keppel Island *island* Pacific Ocean early cultures 280–281 (3) medieval voyages 60 (2)
Niuchwang *see* Niuzhuang, Yingkou
Niue *colonial possession/island* Pacific Ocean colonization 284–285 (1) decolonization 285 (3) environmentalism 285 (2) exploration 278 (1), 279 (3)
Niuzhuang *var.* Newchwang, Ying-k'ou, Yingkow East Asia (China) colonialism 269 (4) *see also* Yinkou
Niya *var.* Minfeng *Buddhist centre/settlement* Central Asia (China) world religions 49 (3)
Niya Syria ancient Egypt 159 (5)
Nizampatam *var.* Petapoli South Asia (India) colonialism 247 (3), 248 (1)
Nizam's Dominions *var.* Hyderabad *state* South Asia colonialism 248 (1)
see also Hyderabad
Nizhne-Kamchatsk Siberia (Russian Federation) exploration 257 (2)
Nizhne-Kolymsk Siberia (Russian Federation) exploration 257 (2)
Nizhniy Novgorod Eastern Europe (Russian Federation) biological diffusion 72–73 (1) Soviet Union 208 (2), 214–215 (4)
Nizhnyaya Tunguska *see* Lower Tunguska
Nizza *see* Nice
Njimbo a Kalunga *state* Southern Africa slave trade 165 (4)
Njoro River Cave *archaeological site* East Africa (Kenya) early cultures 160 (1)
Nkope *archaeological site* Southern Africa (Malawi) early cultures 160 (1)
Nkore *state* East Africa trade 167 (1)
Noakhali and Tippera *region* South Asia decolonization 250 (1)
Nobi *state* Japan medieval states 264 (1)
Nocera Inferiore *see* Nuceria
Nogales Central America (Mexico) Mexican Revolution 133 (3)
Noin Ula East Asia (Mongolia) the world in 250 BCE 38–39
Noirmoutier France medieval voyages 60–61 (1)
Nok *archaeological site/settlement* West Africa (Nigeria) ancient trade 44–45 (1) early cultures 160 (1)
Nok *people* West Africa the world in 500 BCE 34–35 the world in 250 BCE 38–39
Nola Italy early states 178 (1)
Nomadic Hunters *people* North America/South America the world in 750 BCE 30–31 the world in 500 BCE 34–35 the world in 250 BCE 38–39 the world in 500 CE 50–51 the world in 750 CE 54–55 the world in 1000 58–59 the world in 1200 62–63 the world in 1300 66–67 the world in 1400 70–71 the world in 1500 74–75 the world in 1600 78–79 the world in 1700 82–83
Nomadic Plains Cultures *state* North America the world in 1600 78–79 the world in 1700 82–83
Nombe New Guinea (Papua New Guinea) the world in 10,000 BCE 14–15
Nombre de Dios Central America (Panama) European expansion 85 (2)
Nome North America (USA) exploration 287 (2) imperial global economy 93 (3)
Nomentana, Via *road* Italy early states 178 (1) ancient Rome 181 (2)
Nomentum Italy early states 178 (1)
Nomuka *island* Pacific Ocean exploration 278 (1)
Nong Chae Sao *archaeological site* Mainland Southeast Asia (Thailand) Bronze Age 240 (3)
Nonni *see* Nen Jiang
Non Nok Tha *archaeological site/settlement* Mainland Southeast Asia (Thailand) Bronze Age 240 (3)
Nonoalco Central America (Mexico) Aztecs 124 (3)
Noordzee *see* North Sea
Nora Italy first civilizations 177 (1)
Nord *region* Eastern Europe WWII 211 (2)
Nördlingen Central Europe (Germany) economy 190 (1) Reformation 196 (1)
Nord, Mer du *see* North Sea
Nord-Ouest, Territoires du *see* Northwest Territories
Nordsee *see* North Sea
Nordsjøen *see* North Sea
Nordsøen *see* North Sea
Norfolk North America (USA) empire and revolution 127 (2), (3) US Civil War 131 (6), (7) US society 137 (6)
Norfolk Island *colonial possession/island* Pacific Ocean colonization 284–285 (1) decolonization 285 (3) exploration 278 (1), 279 (3)
Norge *see* Norway
Noricum *province* Central Europe ancient Rome 180–181 (1) world religions 48 (1)
Normanby Island *island* Pacific Ocean early cultures 280–281 (3) medieval voyages 60 (2)
Normandes, Îles *see* Channel Islands
Normandy *colonial possession/region* France crusades 64–65 (2) medieval states 185 (3), 186 (2), 187 (4), 192 (1), (2) medieval voyages 60–61 (1) WWII 105 (3), 211 (4)
Normanton Australia colonization 282 (1), 283 (3)
Norsemen *people* Scandinavia the world in 750 CE 54–55
Norske Havet *see* Norwegian Sea
North Alaskan Inuit *people* North America cultural groups 123 (3)
North America *continent* 116–139
Northampton British Isles (United Kingdom) economy 204 (1) medieval states 188 (2)
North Bay North America (Canada) the growth of the US 132 (1)
North Cape *headland* Scandinavia exploration 257 (2)
North Cape *headland* New Zealand colonization 283 (4)
North Carolina *state* North America empire and revolution 127 (2), (3) the growth of the US 129 (1) US Civil War 130 (2), (3), (4), (5), 131 (6), (7) US economy 134 (2), 139 (3) US society 137 (6) US superpower 139 (5)
North China Plain *region* East Asia first cities 28–29 (1)
North Dakota *state* North America the growth of the US 129 (1) US economy 134 (2)
Northeastern Rhodesia *colonial possession* Southern Africa the world in 1900 94–95
Northeast Fiji *leper colony* Pacific Ocean (Fiji) environmentalism 285 (2)
North East Frontier Agency *see* Arunachal Pradesh
North East Rhodesia *see* Northern Rhodesia
Northern Areas *region* South Asia post-war politics 252 (1), (2)
Northern Bukovina *state* Eastern Europe/Southeast Europe WWII 210 (1), 211 (2)
Northern Circars *state* South Asia colonialism 248 (1)
Northern Dvina *var.* Severnaya Dvina *river* Eastern Europe exploration 286 (1), 287 (2)
Northern Greece *region* Greece first cities 28–29 (1)
Northern Ireland *var.* The Six Counties *region* British Isles WWII 208 (1)
Northern Kyushu *state* Japan medieval states 264 (1)
Northern Liang *state* East Asia first states 261 (3)
Northern Long Wall *road* Greece ancient Greece 177 (4)
Northern Mariana Islands *colonial possession/island group* Pacific Ocean decolonization 285 (3) environmentalism 285 (2) WWII 251 (3)
Northern Pacific Railroad *railway* North America global immigration 100 (1) the growth of the US 129 (2)
Northern Qi *state* East Asia medieval states 261 (5)
Northern Rhodesia *mod.* Zambia; *prev.* North West Rhodesia and North East Rhodesia, Northeastern Rhodesia *state* Southern Africa European imperialism 96 (1), 97 (4) WWII 104 (1) *see also* Northeastern Rhodesia, Zambia
Northern Sarkars *var.* Northern Circars *state* South Asia the world in 1800 86–87 *see also* Northern Circars
Northern Shakas *people* South Asia first empires 241 (4)
Northern Shoshoni *people* North America colonization 126 (1)
Northern Ui Néill *state* British Isles medieval states 188 (2)
Northern Wei *see* Toba
Northern Woodland Cultures *people* North America the world in 1600 78–79
Northern Xiongnu *people* East Asia the world in 1 CE 42–43, 260 (1) *see also* Xiongnu
Northern Yan *state* East Asia first states 261 (3)
Northern Zhou *state* East Asia medieval states 261 (5)
North European Plain *plain* Europe crusades 64–65 (2) early agriculture 174 (1)
North Horr East Africa (Kenya) early agriculture 158 (1)
North Island *island* New Zealand colonization 283 (5)
North Korea *state* East Asia Soviet Union 213 (4) Islam 275 (4) post-war economy 275 (4) post-war politics 275 (3)
North Ossetia *region* Eastern Europe Soviet Union 214–215 (4)
North Sea *prev.* German Ocean; *Lat.* Mare Germanicum; *Dan.* Nordsøen, *Dut.* Noordzee, *Fr.* Mer du Nord, *Ger.* Nordsee, *Nor.* Nordsjøen *sea* Northwest Europe ancient Rome 180–181 (1), 181 (3), (4) ancient trade 44–45 (1), 72–73 (1) Bronze Age 175 (3) Copper Age 174 (2) crusades 186 (1), 64–65 (2) early 20th century 206 (1) early agriculture 174 (1) economy 190 (1), 205 (4) empire and revolution 199 (3) exploration 172 (1), (2) great migrations 52–53 (1), 53 (2) inter-war 209 (3) medieval states 182 (2), 183 (3), 186 (2), 187 (3), 188 (1), (2) medieval voyages 60–61 (1) post-war economy 213 (5) prehistoric culture 17 (4) Reformation 195 (5), 196 (1), (2) world religions 48 (1) WWII 210 (1), 211 (4)
Northumbria *state* British Isles medieval states 183 (3) the world in 750 CE 54–55
North Vietnam *state* Mainland Southeast Asia Cold War 109 (1) post-war politics 251 (5)
Northwest Coast Cultures *region* North America early agriculture 120 (1)
Northwest Frontier Province *region* South Asia colonialism 248 (2) post-war politics 252 (1), 253 (4)
North West Muslim Rising East Asia empire and revolution 88–89 (2)
Northwest Provinces *state* South Asia empire and revolution 249 (3)
North West Rhodesia *see* Northern Rhodesia
Northwest Territories *Fr.* Territoires du Nord-Ouest *province* North America (Canada) 129 (2), 132 (1), 136 (2)
North Yemen *see* Yemen
Norton *burial mound* North America (USA) first civilizations 121 (4)
Norway *Nor.* Norge *state* Scandinavia Cold War 108 (3), 109 (1) colonialism 269 (3) crusades 186 (1), 64–65 (2) early 20th century 206 (1) early modern states 197 (3) economy 190 (1), 205 (4) empire and revolution 202 (1) exploration 172 (2) imperial global economy 92 (1) inter-war 209 (3) medieval states 185 (3) medieval voyages 60–61 (1) Napoleon 200–201 (1), 201 (2) post-war economy 213 (5), 214 (1) post-war politics 212 (3) Soviet Union 208 (2), 213 (4) the world in 1400 70–71 the modern world 112 (2) US superpower 138 (1) WWI 207 (4), 208 (1) WWII 104 (1), 211 (2), (4)
Norwegians *people* Scandinavia medieval states 185 (3)
Norwegian Sea *Nor.* Norske Havet *sea* Atlantic Ocean exploration 172 (2), 286 (1), 287 (2)
Norwegian Settlers *migration* North America the world in 1000 58–59
Norwich British Isles (United Kingdom) economy 190 (1) medieval states 186 (2)
Noryllag *gulag/region* Siberia Soviet Union 213 (4)
Nösen *see* Beszterce
Nossa Senhora de Belém do Grão Pará *see* Belém do Pará
Nossi-Bé *var.* Nosy Be *island* Indian Ocean the world in 1850 90–91
Nosy Be *see* Nossi-Bé
Nóties Sporádes *see* Dodecanese
Notium *battle* Southwest Asia (Turkey) ancient Greece 177 (3)
Noto Japan medieval states 264 (2)
Nottingham British Isles (United Kingdom) economy 204 (1) medieval states 183 (3)
Nouméa New Caledonia environmentalism 285 (2) US superpower 138 (1)
Nouveau-Brunswick *see* New Brunswick
Nouvelle-Calédonie *see* New Caledonia
Nouvelle Écosse *see* Nova Scotia
Nouvelles Hébrides *see* New Hebrides, Vanuatu
Novae Southeast Europe (Bulgaria) ancient Rome 180–181 (1) world religions 48 (1)
Nova Lisboa *see* Huambo
Novara *anc.* Novaria Italy Franks 184 (2) *battle* early modern states 194 (1)
Novaria *see* Novara
Nova Scotia *var.* Nouvelle Écosse; *prev.* Acadia *province/state* North America colonization 126 (1) the growth of the US 129 (2), 132 (1) US economy 136 (2) *see also* Acadia
Novaya Zemlya *island group* Arctic Ocean European expansion 80–81 (1) exploration 257 (2), 286 (1), 287 (2)
Novgorod *Norse.* Holmgard Eastern Europe (Russian Federation) biological diffusion 72–73 (1) early modern states 195 (3) economy 190 (1) medieval states 185 (3) Mongols 68–69 (1) Soviet Union 208 (2)
Novgorod *state* Eastern Europe medieval states 189 (3)
Noviodunum *see* Nevers, Soissons
Noviomagus British Isles (United Kingdom) ancient Rome 180–181 (1)
Noviomagus *see* Lisieux, Nijmegen
Novi Sad *Ger.* Neusatz, *Hung.* Újvidék Southeast Europe (Yugoslavia) post-war economy 215 (3)
Novocherkassk Eastern Europe (Russian Federation) Soviet Union 208 (2)
Novomarinsk *see* Anadyrsk
Novorossiysk Eastern Europe (Russian Federation) Soviet Union 208 (2)
Novosibirsk Eastern Europe (Russian Federation) global immigration 100 (1) Soviet Union 213 (4)
Novo-Urgench *see* Urgench
Noyon France WWI 206 (2), (3)
Nsundi *state* Central Africa economy 163 (2)
Ntereso West Africa (Ghana) early agriculture 158 (1)
Nubia *state* NE Africa early cultures 159 (3), (4), (5), 160 (1), 161 (5)
Nubian Desert *desert* Egypt ancient Egypt 159 (4) exploration 157 (5)
Nuceria *var.* Nuceria Alfaterna; *mod.* Nocera Inferiore Italy early states 178 (1)
Nuceria Alfaterna *see* Nuceria
Nu Chiang *see* Salween
Nuevo León *state* Central America Mexican Revolution 133 (3) the growth of the US 129 (2)
Nu Jiang *see* Salween
Nulato North America (USA) imperial global economy 93 (3)
Nullarbor Plain *plateau* Australia colonization 283 (3) exploration 279 (2) prehistoric culture 17 (5)
Numantia Iberian Peninsula (Spain) ancient Rome 179 (3), (5)
Numazu Japan early modern states 265 (5)
Numidia *region/state* North Africa ancient Rome 179 (5), 180–181 (1), 225 (5) early cultures 161 (2) first civilizations 177 (1)
Nunguvik North America (Canada) cultural groups 123 (3)
Nunivak Island North America (USA) cultural groups 123 (3)
Nupe *state* West Africa Islam 163 (1) trade 164 (2)
Nu-Pieds *battle* France Reformation 196 (2)
Nuqui South America (Colombia) narcotics 153 (5)
Nur Central Asia (Uzbekistan) Mongols 68–69 (1)
Nuremberg *Ger.* Nürnberg Central Europe (Germany) early modern states 193 (4) economy 190 (1) empire and revolution 202 (2) medieval states 188 (1), 189 (3) post-war politics 212 (1), (3) Reformation 194 (2), 196 (1) WWII 211 (2)
Nuri East Africa (Sudan) early cultures 160 (1)
Nürnberg *see* Nuremberg
Nursia Italy early states 178 (1)
Nusaybin *see* Nisibis
Nuzi Southwest Asia (Iraq) first cities 220 (2) first civilizations 24 (2)
Nyamwezi *people* East Africa trade 167 (1)
Nyangwe Central Africa (Congo) exploration 157 (4)
Nyasa, Lake *var.* Lake Malawi; *Port.* Lago Nyassa *lake* East Africa early agriculture 158 (1) economy 163 (2), (3) European imperialism 96 (1) exploration 156 (3), 157 (4) first humans 12 (1), 13 (2) Islam 163 (1) slave trade 165 (4) trade 164 (1)
Nyasaland *mod.* Malawi *state* East Africa European imperialism 96 (1) WWII 104 (1) *see also* Malawi
Nyassa, Lago *see* Nyasa
Nylstroom Southern Africa (South Africa) colonization 166 (2)
Nyoman *see* Neman
Nysa Southwest Asia (Turkey) Hellenistic world 41 (2)
Nzabi *archaeological site* Central Africa (Congo) early cultures 160 (1)
Nziko *state* Central Africa trade 164 (2)

O

Oahu *island* Pacific Ocean WWII 272 (1), 273 (2)
Oakfield North America (USA) cultural groups 122 (5)
Oak Hill North America (USA) cultural groups 122 (5)
Oamaru New Zealand colonization 283 (5)
Oaxaca *var.* Oaxaca de Juárez; *prev.* Antequera *religious site/settlement* Central America (Mexico) first religions 36 (1) Mexican Revolution 133 (3) *see also* Antequera
Oaxaca *state* Central America Mexican Revolution 133 (3) the growth of the US 129 (2)
Oaxaca de Juárez *see* Oaxaca
Ob' *river* Siberia colonialism 269 (3) early agriculture 20–21 (2) early modern states 268 (1) exploration 257 (2) first humans 13 (2) first religions 36 (1) first states 260 (1) global immigration 100 (1) Mongols 68–69 (1) prehistoric culture 16 (1) Soviet Union 208 (2) trade 267 (3)
Obb East Africa (Sudan) exploration 157 (4)
Obdorsk *mod.* Salekhard Eastern Europe (Russian Federation) exploration 257 (2)
Obero Central America (Mexico) first civilizations 123 (2)
Obi *island* Maritime Southeast Asia colonialism 247 (4)
Occidentalis, Oceanus *mod.* Atlantic Ocean *ocean* Atlantic Ocean ancient trade 44 (2) *see also* Atlantic Ocean
Occupied France *region* France WWII 211 (2), (3)
Oceania *region* Pacific Ocean biological diffusion 73 (2) global knowledge 76–77 (1)
Oc Eo Mainland Southeast Asia (Cambodia) ancient trade 44–45 (1)
Ochrida, Lake *see* Ohrid *lake*
Očkov *fort* Central Europe (Slovakia) Bronze Age 175 (3)
Ocmulgee North America (USA) cultural groups 122 (5)
Octodurum Central Europe (Switzerland) ancient Rome 180–181 (1)
Ocucaje South America (Peru) early cultures 145 (4)
Oculián *state* Central America Aztecs 124 (1)
Oda *region* Japan early modern states 267 (4)
Odawara Japan early modern states 265 (5) early modern states 267 (4)
Oder *Cz./Pol.* Odra *river* Central Europe early modern states 193 (4) economy 190 (1), 205 (4) empire and revolution 198 (2), 199 (3), 202 (2) Franks 184 (2) inter-war 209 (5) medieval states 188 (1), 189 (3), (4) Mongols 68–69 (1) Napoleon 200–201 (1), 201 (2), (3) prehistoric culture 17 (4) Reformation 196 (1) WWI 207 (4) WWII 210 (1)
Odesa *Russ.* Odessa Eastern Europe (Ukraine) Soviet Union 214–215 (4) WWI 207 (4) *see also* Odessa
Odessa *Ukr.* Odesa Eastern Europe (Ukraine) economy 205 (4) empire and revolution 202 (1) global immigration 100 (1), 101 (2) Napoleon 200–201 (1) post-war politics 212 (3) Soviet Union 208 (2), 213 (4) *see also* Odesa
Odessus Southeast Europe (Bulgaria) first civilizations 177 (1) Hellenistic world 40–41 (1)
Odeum *building* Greece ancient Greece 177 (4)
Odra *see* Oder
Oea North Africa (Libya) ancient Rome 180–181 (1) first civilizations 177 (1)
Oescus Southeast Europe (Bulgaria) ancient Rome 180–181 (1)
Oesel *see* Ösel
Ofiral *see* Sharm el Sheikh
Ogachi Japan medieval states 265 (4)
Ogasawara-guntō *see* Bonin Islands
Ogooué *river* Central Africa trade 164 (2)
Ohio *state* North America the growth of the US 129 (1) US Civil War 130 (2), (3), (4), (5), 131 (6), (7) US economy 134 (2)
Ohio *river* North America colonization 126 (1) cultural groups 122 (5) early agriculture 120 (1) empire and revolution 127 (2), (3) exploration 118 (1), 119 (2) first civilizations 121 (4) the growth of the US 129 (2)
Ohrid, Lake *var.* Lake Ochrida; *Alb.* Liqeni i Ohrit, *Mac.* Ohridsko Ezero *lake* Southeast Europe post-war economy 215 (3) WWI 207 (6)
Ohridsko Ezero *see* Ohrid, Lake
Ohrit, Liqeni i *see* Ohrid, Lake
Oirats, Khanate of the *state* East Asia the world in 1400 70–71 the world in 1500 74–75
Oise *river* France WWI 206 (2), (3)
Oita *prefecture* Japan economy 270 (1)
Ojibwa *people* North America colonization 126 (1) cultural groups 123 (3)
Okayama *prefecture* Japan economy 270 (1)
Okayama *bomb target* Japan WWII 273 (3)
Okhotsk Siberia (Russian Federation) colonialism 269 (3) exploration 257 (2)
Okhotsk, Sea of *sea* Siberia ancient trade 44–45 (1) biological diffusion 72–73 (1) colonialism 269 (3) early agriculture 258 (1) early modern states 268 (1) exploration 257 (2), 286 (1) medieval states 262–263 (1) Soviet Union 208 (2) world religions 49 (4) WWII 272 (1), 273 (2)
Oki *island* Japan WWII 273 (3) early modern states 265 (5), 267 (4) medieval states 264 (1), (2), 265 (3), (4)
Okinawa *island* Japan WWII 251 (3), 272 (1) WWII 105 (3) Cold War 109 (1)
Oklahoma *state* North America the growth of the US 129 (1) US economy 134 (2), 139 (3) US superpower 139 (5)
Oklahoma City North America (USA) US economy 134 (1)
Okuma Japan early modern states 265 (5)
Okunev *archaeological site* Siberia early agriculture 258 (1)
Okvik Island North America (USA) cultural groups 123 (3)
Öland *island* Scandinavia early modern states 197 (3)
Olary *archaeological site* Australia prehistoric culture 17 (5)
Olbia *prev.* Terranova Pausania Italy ancient Rome 179 (3) first civilizations 177 (1) Hellenistic world 40–41 (1)
Old Crow *archaeological site* North America the world in 10,000 BCE 14–15
Oldenzaal Low Countries (Netherlands) Reformation 195 (5)
Old Fort North America (USA) cultural groups 122 (5)
Old Goa *see* Goa, Gove
Old Providence Island *island* Central America European expansion 85 (2)
Old Spanish Trail *wagon train route* North America the growth of the US 129 (2)
Olduvai Gorge *archaeological site* East Africa (Tanzania) first humans 12 (1), 13 (2)
Olekminsk Siberia (Russian Federation) exploration 257 (2)
Olieboompoort *archaeological site* Southern Africa (South Africa) early cultures 160 (1)
Olinda South America (Brazil) colonization 149 (3)
Olisipo *var.* Felicitas Julia; *mod.* Lisboa; *Eng.* Lisbon Iberian peninsula (Portugal) ancient Rome 180–181 (1), 181 (3) *see also* Lisbon
Ollantaytambo South America (Peru) Incas 147 (3), 148 (1)

Olmec *region/state* Central America first religions *36* (1)
Olmütz *see* Olomouc
Olomouc *Ger.* Olmütz, *Pol.* Ołomuniec Central Europe (Czech Republic) medieval states *189* (3)
Olomuniec *see* Olomouc
Olophyxus *state* Greece ancient Greece *177* (2)
Olot *rebellion* East Asia empire and revolution *268* (2)
Olszanica Central Europe (Poland) early agriculture *174* (1)
Olt *var.* Oltul, *Ger.* Alt *river* Southeast Europe WWI *207* (6)
Oltul *see* Olt
Olustee *battle* North America (USA) US Civil War *131* (7)
Olympia Greece the world in 750 BCE *30–31*
Olympia North America (USA) the growth of the US *129* (2)
Olympian Zeus, Temple of *temple* Greece ancient Greece *177* (4)
Olympus Greece first civilizations *175* (4)
Olynthus *state* Greece ancient Greece *177* (2)
Omagua *people* South America early cultures *147* (2)
Omaha North America (USA) US economy *134* (1)
Oman *prev.* Muscat and Oman; *Ar.* 'Umān *colonial possession/region/state* Southwest Asia early Islam *56–57* (1), *57* (2) economy *163* (2), *234* (1) exploration *219* (4) Islam *163* (1), *226* (2), *227* (4), (5), *235* (4) Mongols *68–69* (1) the modern world *112* (1), *113* (3), (4) trade *230* (2), *267* (3) US economy *138* (2) world religions *226* (1) 20th-century politics *233* (4), *235* (5)
Omana *see* Ommana
Oman, Gulf of *Ar.* Khalij 'Umān *gulf* Southwest Asia economy *234* (1) medieval Persia *231* (4) medieval voyages *61* (3) Timur *229* (4) 20th-century politics *233* (4)
Omani *state* East Africa trade *167* (1)
Omani-Swahili *people* East Africa trade *167* (1)
Omari Egypt ancient Egypt *159* (2)
Omdurman *var.* Umm Durmān East Africa (Sudan) colonization *167* (4)
Omeo *goldfield* Australia colonization *282* (2)
Ommana *var.* Omana Southwest Asia (United Arab Emirates) ancient trade *44–45* (1) early cultures *161* (3), (5) early trade *225* (3)
Omo *archaeological site* East Africa (Sudan) first humans *12* (1), *13* (2)
Omsk Siberia (Russian Federation) colonialism *269* (3) Communism *271* (8) exploration *257* (2) Soviet Union *208* (2), *213* (4)
Ona *people* South America early cultures *147* (2)
Onega, Lake *Russ.* Onezhskoye Ozero *lake* Eastern Europe economy *205* (4)
Onezhskoye Ozero *see* Onega, Lake
Oniguayál *people/state* South America early cultures *147* (2)
Onon Gol *river* Central Asia first states *260* (1)
Ontario *province* North America the growth of the US *129* (2), *132* (1) US economy *136* (2)
Ontario, Lake *lake* North America colonization *126* (1) cultural groups *122* (5) early agriculture *120* (1) empire and revolution *127* (2), (3) exploration *118* (1) first civilizations *121* (4) the growth of the US *129* (2) US Civil War *131* (6)
Onuba *see* Huelva
Oodnadatta Australia colonization *282* (1) exploration *279* (2)
Oos-Londen *see* East London
Opata *people* Central America colonization *125* (4)
Open Bay Islands *sealing station* New Zealand colonization *283* (4)
Openshaw British Isles (United Kingdom) economy *204* (2)
Opiana South Asia (Pakistan) Hellenistic world *40–41* (1)
Opochka Eastern Europe (Russian Federation) early modern states *195* (3)
Opone East Africa (Somalia) ancient trade *44* (2) early cultures *161* (3), (5) early trade *225* (3)
Oporto Iberian Peninsula (Portugal) economy *198* (1), *205* (4) Franks *184* (2) inter-war *209* (3) Islam *192* (3) Napoleon *200–201* (1)
Opotiki New Zealand colonization *283* (4)
Oppidum Ubiorum *see* Cologne, Colonia, Colonia Agrippina
Oradea *see* Várad
Orahovac *Alb.* Rahovec Southeast Europe (Yugoslavia) post-war economy *215* (3)
Orak *archaeological site* Siberia (Russian Federation) early agriculture *258* (1)
Oral *see* Ural'sk
Oran *var.* Ouahran, Wahran North Africa (Algeria) colonization *167* (4) economy *168* (2), *190* (1) Ottomans *231* (3) WWII *211* (4)
Orange *anc.* Arausio France empire and revolution *199* (4) *see also* Arausio
Orange *state* France early modern states *197* (5) medieval states *192* (1), (2)
Orange Free State *state* Southern Africa colonization *167* (4) European imperialism *96* (2)
Orange River *var.* Mtamvuna; *Afr.* Oranjerivier *river* Southern Africa early agriculture *158* (1), *20–21* (2) early cultures *160* (1) economy *163* (2) European imperialism *96* (2) exploration *156* (3), *157* (4) first humans *12* (1), *13* (2) Islam *163* (1) slave trade *165* (4) trade *164* (1) *see also* Mtamvuna
Oranjerivier *see* Mtamvuna, Orange River
Oraşul Stalin *see* Brasov, Brassó
Orchestra Shell Cave Australia the world in 5000 BCE *18–19*
Orchha *state* South Asia Mughal Empire *246* (1)
Orchomenos *see* Orchomenus
Orchomenus *var.* Orchomenos, Orkhómenos; *mod.* Orchomenos; *prev.* Skripón Greece first cities *28–29* (1) first civilizations *175* (4)
Ordos Desert *Chin.* Mu Us Shamo *desert* East Asia early agriculture *258* (1), (2) early modern states *266* (1) exploration *257* (3) first cities *259* (3), (4), (5) first states *260* (1)
Oregon *state* North America the growth of the US *129* (1) US Civil War *130* (5) US economy *134* (2)
Oregon Territory *region* North America US Civil War *130* (2), (3), (4), (5)
Oregon Trail *wagon train route* North America the growth of the US *129* (2)
Orel Eastern Europe (Russian Federation) Soviet Union *208* (2) WWII *210* (1), *211* (4)
Orenburg *prev.* Chkalov Siberia (Russian Federation) colonialism *269* (3) exploration *257* (2) Soviet Union *208* (2)
Oreshek Eastern Europe (Russian Federation) early modern states *195* (3)
Orhomenos *see* Orchomenus
Orhon *var.* Orkhon *river* Southwest Asia Mongols *68–69* (1)
Oriens *province* Southwest Asia ancient Rome *181* (4)
Oriente *region* South America politics *152* (1)
Orinoco *river* South America colonization *148* (2) early agriculture *20–21* (2) early cultures *144* (1), *145* (2) empire and revolution *150* (1), (2), *151* (3) environment *153* (4) exploration *142* (1), *143* (2), (3) first religions *36* (1)
Orinoqueponi *people* South America early cultures *147* (2)
Orisa *mod.* Orissa *state* South Asia Mughal Empire *246* (1) world religions *243* (4) *see also* Orissa
Oriskany *battle* North America (USA) empire and revolution *127* (3)
Orissa *region/state* South Asia colonialism *248* (2) post-war politics *252* (1), *253* (4)
Orkhómenos *see* Orchomenus
Orkhon *see* Orhon
Orkney, Earldom of *vassal state* British Isles medieval states *185* (3), *186* (2)
Orkney Islands *island group* British Isles exploration *172* (2) medieval states *185* (3), *188* (2) medieval voyages *60–61* (1)
Orléans *anc.* Aurelianum *settlement* France crusades *186* (1) early modern states *197* (5) empire and revolution *199* (4) Franks *183* (5), (6), *184* (2) medieval states *185* (3), *192* (1), (2) Napoleon *200–201* (1) Reformation *194* (2) WWII *210* (1), *211* (4)
Ormuz *var.* Hormuz; *anc.* Harmozia Southwest Asia (Iran) exploration *218* (2), *219* (3) medieval Persia *231* (4) Ottomans *231* (3) trade *230* (2) *see also* Hormuz, Harmozia
Ormuz, strait of *see* Hormuz, Strait of
Orol Dengizi *see* Aral Sea
Oromo *people* East Africa trade *165* (3)
Orongo *archaeological site* Easter Island early cultures *281* (4)
Oropeza *see* Cochabamba
Orşova Southeast Europe (Romania) WWI *207* (6)
Ortospana *see* Kabul
Orungallu South Asia (India) early medieval states *244* (2)
Orvieto *anc.* Velsuna Italy economy *190* (1)
Oryokko *see* Yalu
Osage *people* North America colonization *125* (4), *126* (1)
Osaka Japan WWII *273* (3) early modern states *265* (5) economy *270* (1), *275* (4) medieval states *264* (2) WWII *272* (1), *273* (2) *battle* early modern states *267* (5)
Osca *see* Huesca
Osceola's Capture *battle* North America (USA) the growth of the US *129* (2)
Oseberg Scandinavia (Norway) medieval states *185* (3)
Ösel *prev.* Saare; *Ger.* Oesel; *Est.* Saaremaa *island* Eastern Europe early modern states *195* (3) WWI *207* (4)
Osh Central Asia (Kyrgyzstan) Soviet Union *214–215* (4)
Oshima *mountain* Japan medieval states *265* (3)
Osiek *see* Osijek
Osijek *prev.* Osiek, Osjek; *Ger.* Esseg, *Hung.* Eszék Southeast Europe (Croatia) post-war economy *215* (3)
Osjek *see* Osijek
Oslo *prev.* Christiania, Kristiania Scandinavia (Norway) early modern states *195* (3) economy *190* (1) inter-war *209* (3) medieval states *185* (3) post-war politics *212* (3) WWII *210* (1), *211* (2), (4) *see also* Christiania Cold War *108* (3)
Osnabrück Central Europe (Germany) economy *190* (1) medieval states *189* (3) Reformation *196* (1)
Osrhoene *var.* Osroene *state* Southwest Asia the world in 1 CE *42–43*
Osroene *see* Osrhoene
Ostee *see* Baltic Sea
Ostend Low Countries (Belgium) crusades *186* (1) Reformation *195* (5) WWI *206* (2), (3)
Osterbucken Central Europe (Germany) world religions *48* (1)
Österreich *see* Austria
Ostia *settlement* Italy ancient Rome *179* (3) ancient trade *44–45* (1) early cultures *161* (2) early states *178* (1) world religions *48* (1)
Ostiensis, Via *road* Italy ancient Rome *181* (2) early states *178* (1)
Ostinoid *people* West Indies the world in 500 CE *50–51* the world in 1000 *58–59*
Ostmark *see* Austria
Ostrava-Petřkovice *archaeological site* Central Europe (Poland) prehistoric culture *17* (4)
Ostrogoths *people* Eastern Europe ancient Rome *181* (4) great migrations *52–53* (1)
Ostrogoths, Kingdom of the *state* Central Europe/Italy/Southeast Europe ancient Rome *182* (1) Franks *183* (5) great migrations *53* (2)
Ostrolenka *Pol.* Ostrołęka *battle* Central Europe (Poland) empire and revolution *88–89* (2)
Ostrov Eastern Europe (Russian Federation) early modern states *195* (3)
Ōsumi-kaikyō *see* Osumi Strait
Osumi Strait *Jap.* Ōsumi-kaikyō *sea waterway* Japan WWII *273* (3)
Otago *region* New Zealand colonization *283* (5)
Otago Peninsula *coastal feature* New Zealand colonization *283* (4)
Otaki New Zealand colonization *283* (4)
Otaru Japan economy *270* (1)
Oto *people* North America colonization *126* (1)
Otomi *people* Central America colonization *125* (4)
Otomo *region* Japan early modern states *267* (4)
Otoncalpulco Central America (Mexico) Aztecs *124* (2)
Otranto Italy medieval states *185* (3), *188* (1)
Otrar Central Asia (Kazakhstan) Mongols *68–69* (1) Timur *229* (4)
Ottawa North America (Canada) the growth of the US *129* (2), *132* (1) the world in 1925 *98–99* US economy *136* (2)
Ottawa *people* North America colonization *126* (1)
Ottawa *river* North America colonization *126* (1) empire and revolution *127* (3)
Ottio *region* North America first civilizations *121* (4)
Ottoman Empire *state* Africa/Asia/Europe early 20th century *206* (1) early modern states *194* (1) economy *205* (4) empire and revolution *202* (1), (3), *88–89* (2) European expansion *84–85* (1) European imperialism *97* (4) global immigration *100* (1), *101* (2) imperial global economy *92* (1) Islam *163* (1), *192* (3) medieval Persia *231* (4) Napoleon *200–201* (1), *201* (2), (3) Ottomans *195* (4), *230* (1), *231* (3), *232–233* (1) Reformation *194* (2) Timur *229* (4) trade *230* (2) WWI *207* (6), *233* (2) 20th-century politics *233* (4)
Otu'Iti *people* Easter Island early cultures *281* (4)
Otumba *var.* Otumba de Gómez Farías Central America (Mexico) colonization *125* (5)
Otumba de Gómez Farías *see* Otumba
Ouadaï *see* Wadai
Ouaddaï *see* Wadai
Ouahran *see* Oran
Ouan Muhaggiag North Africa (Niger/Algeria) early agriculture *158* (1)
Oubangui *see* Ubangi
Oubangui-Chari *see* Central African Republic, Ubangi-Shari
Oudh *region/state* South Asia colonialism *247* (3), *248* (1) empire and revolution *249* (3)
Ouidah West Africa (Benin) European expansion *84–85* (1)
Oundle British Isles (United Kingdom) medieval states *183* (3)
Ouro Prêto South America (Brazil) empire and revolution *151* (3)
Ouse *river* British Isles economy *204* (1) medieval states *186* (2)
Ouse Burn *river* British Isles economy *204* (3)
Outer Mongolia *region/state* East Asia colonialism *269* (3) early modern states *268* (1) empire and revolution *268* (2)
Ovens *goldfield* Australia colonization *282* (2)
Overijssel *province* Low Countries Reformation *195* (5)
Oviedo *anc.* Asturias Iberian Peninsula (Spain) Franks *184* (2) inter-war *209* (4) Islam *192* (3)
Ovimbundu *people* Southern Africa trade *167* (1)
Owasco North America (USA) cultural groups *122* (5)
Owl Creek North America (USA) cultural groups *122* (5)
Owyhee Forks *battle* North America (USA) the growth of the US *129* (2)
Oxford *Lat.* Oxonia *settlement* British Isles (United Kingdom) economy *190* (1) medieval states *187* (3), (4), *188* (2)
Oxford *canal* British Isles economy *204* (1)
Oxitipan *state* Central America Aztecs *124* (1)
Oxonia *see* Oxford
Oxtotitlán Cave Central America (Mexico) first civilizations *121* (2)
Oxus *anc.* Oxus; *Rus.* Amudar'ya, *Taj.* Dar"yoi Amu, *Turkm.* Amyderya, *Uzb.* Amudaryo *river* Central Asia ancient Persia *223* (4), *225* (6) ancient Rome *224* (2) ancient trade *44* (2) early systems *223* (3) exploration *218* (1), (2), *219* (3), *256* (1) Hellenistic world *224* (1), *41* (2) medieval states *261* (6) Mongols *229* (3) Seljuks *228* (1) Timur *229* (4) world religions *49* (3), (4) *see also* Amu Darya
Oxyrhynchus Egypt Hellenistic world *40–41* (1)
Oyo *state* West Africa economy *163* (2) slave trade *165* (4) trade *164* (2), *167* (1)
Ozaki Japan early modern states *267* (4)

P

Pa *see* Ba
Paardeberg *battle* Southern Africa (South Africa) European imperialism *96* (2)
Pacatnamú South America (Peru) early cultures *145* (4), *146* (1)
Pachacamac South America (Peru) early cultures *145* (4), *146* (1) Incas *147* (3)
Pachamachay South America (Peru) the world in 5000 BCE *18–19*
Pacheco South America (Peru) early cultures *146* (1)
Pacific Islands, Trust Territory of the *colonial possession* Pacific Ocean the world in 1950 *102–103*
Pacific Ocean *ocean* ancient trade *44–45* (1) Antarctic Exploration *287* (3) Aztecs *124* (1) biological diffusion *72–73* (1), *73* (2), (3) Bronze Age *240* (3) Cold War *109* (1) colonialism *247* (4), *269* (3), (4) colonization *125* (4), *148* (2), *283* (4), (5), *284–285* (1) WWII *273* (3) cultural groups *123* (4) decolonization *251* (4), *285* (3) early agriculture *120* (1), *20–21* (2), *258* (1) early cultures *145* (2), (3), (4), *146* (1), *147* (2), *280–281* (3) early modern states *267* (4), (5) empire and revolution *150* (1), *151* (3), *268* (2), *88* (1), *88–89* (2) environmentalism *285* (2) European expansion *80–81* (1), *81* (2), (3), *84–85* (1) European imperialism *97* (3), (4) exploration *118* (1), *119* (2), (3), *142* (1), *143* (2), (3), *239* (1), (2), *279* (3), *280* (1) first civilizations *121* (2), *122* (1) first humans *13* (2) global immigration *100* (1), *101* (2), (3) global knowledge *76* (1), (2), (3), (4), *76–77* (1), *77* (5), (6), (7) imperial global economy *92* (1), *93* (2), (3) imperialism *270* (2) Incas *147* (3), *148* (1) medieval states *264* (2) medieval voyages *60* (2) politics *151* (4) prehistoric culture *16* (1) the growth of the US *129* (2), *132* (1), *133* (4) the modern world *112* (1), *113* (3) trade *267* (3) US economy *136* (2) US superpower *138* (1) world religions *243* (5) WWII *104* (1), *105* (3), (4), *251* (3), *272* (1), *273* (2)
Padah-lin Mainland Southeast Asia (Burma) the world in 5000 BCE *18–19*
Padang Maritime Southeast Asia (Indonesia) colonialism *247* (4)
Paderborn Central Europe (Germany) Franks *184* (2)
Padilla Central America (Mexico) the growth of the US *129* (2)
Padma *var.* Ganges *river* South Asia post-war politics *252* (3) *see also* Ganges
Padma *see* Brahmaputra
Padova *see* Patavium, Padua
Padre Piedra Central America (Mexico) first civilizations *121* (2)
Padua Italy economy *190* (1) medieval states *182* (2), *183* (4), *187* (3) WWI *207* (5)
Padus *river* Italy early states *178* (2)
Paekche *region/state* East Asia medieval states *264* (1) early modern states *265* (5) world religions *49* (4)
Paestum *prev.* Posidonia Italy early states *178* (1) first religions *37* (3) *see also* Posidonia
Páfos *see* Paphos
Pagan Mainland Southeast Asia (Burma) biological diffusion *72–73* (1) medieval states *262–263* (1), *263* (6) Mongols *68* (2), *68–69* (1) world religions *243* (5), *49* (3), (4)
Pagan *state* Mainland Southeast Asia early medieval states *245* (5) Mongols *68–69* (1)
Pagani East Africa (Tanzania) economy *163* (2)
Pago Pago *see* American Samoa
Pahlavas *region/state* South Asia ancient trade *44–45* (1) first empires *241* (5) world religions *242* (2)
Pahlevi Dynasty *people* South Asia Communism *271* (8)
Pahsien *see* Chongqing
Paide *see* Weissenstein
Paisley British Isles (United Kingdom) imperial global economy *93* (5)
Paita South America (Peru) colonization *148* (2) Incas *148* (1)
Paithan South Asia (India) early religions *48* (2)
Paiute *people* North America colonization *126* (1)
Pajajaran *state* Maritime Southeast Asia the world in 1400 *70–71*
Pakhoi *see* Beihai
Pakhtunistan *region* South Asia post-war politics *252* (1)
Pakistan *state* South Asia Cold War *109* (1) historical geography *275* (5) Islam *235* (4) post-war economy *253* (5) post-war politics *252* (1), (2), *253* (4) Soviet Union *213* (4) the modern world *113* (3), (4) US superpower *138* (1)
Palaeosiberians *people* Siberia the world in 750 BCE *30–31* the world in 500 BCE *34–35* the world in 250 BCE *38–39* the world in 1 CE *42–43* the world in 250 CE *46–47* the world in 500 CE *50–51* the world in 750 CE *54–55* the world in 1000 *58–59* the world in 1200 *62–63* the world in 1300 *66–67* the world in 1400 *70–71* the world in 1500 *74–75* the world in 1600 *78–79*
Palaestina *state* Southwest Asia ancient Rome *224* (2)
Palaestina *see* Judaea, Palestine
Palas *state* South Asia early medieval states *244* (2) Medieval voyages *61* (3)
Palatine Hill *Lat.* Mons Palatinus *hill* Italy ancient Rome *181* (2)
Palatinus, Mons *see* Palatine Hill
Palau *military base/state/island group* Pacific Ocean colonization *284–285* (1) decolonization *285* (3) exploration *279* (3) the modern world *110–111* WWII *251* (3), *272* (1), *273* (2)
Palau *see* Palau Islands
Palawan *island* Maritime Southeast Asia European imperialism *97* (3) exploration *278* (1) Islam *243* (6)
Pale Southeast Europe (Bosnia and Herzegovina) civil war *215* (3)
Palembang Maritime Southeast Asia (Indonesia) biological diffusion *72–73* (1) colonialism *247* (4) European imperialism *97* (3) exploration *256* (1) post-war economy *253* (5) world religions *243* (5), (4) WWII *251* (3), *272* (1), *273* (2)
Palembang *region* Maritime Southeast Asia colonialism *247* (4)
Palenque Central America (Mexico) first civilizations *123* (2)
Palerme *see* Palermo, Panormus
Palermo *anc.* Panhormus, Panormus; *Fr.* Palerme *academic centre/settlement* Italy biological diffusion *72–73* (1) crusades *186* (1) economy *190* (1) Islam *227* (4) medieval states *185* (3), (5), *188* (1) Napoleon *200–201* (1), *201* (2), (3) Ottomans *230* (1) WWII *211* (4) *see also* Panormus
Palestine *Lat.* Palaestina *state* Southwest Asia 20th-century politics *233* (3), (4) early agriculture *220* (1) exploration *219* (4) first religions *37* (3) global immigration *101* (2) Hellenistic world *40–41* (1) Ottomans *232–233* (1) world religions *48* (1) WWII *233* (2) WWII *210* (1), *211* (4) *see also* Israel
Pālghāt *see* Pulicat
Palibothra South Asia (India) ancient trade *44* (2)
Palk Strait *sea waterway* South Asia economy *249* (4) post-war politics *252* (1)
Pallipuram South Asia (India) colonialism *247* (3)
Palma *var.* Palma de Mallorca Iberian Peninsula (Spain) crusades *186* (1) economy *190* (1) inter-war *209* (4) Islam *192* (3)
Palma de Mallorca *see* Palma
Palmas, Cape *headland* West Africa exploration *156* (3)
Palmerston *see* Darwin
Palmerston North New Zealand colonization *283* (5)
Palmyra *var.* Tadmur, Tamar; *Bibl.* Tadmor Southwest Asia (Syria) ancient Rome *180–181* (1), *181* (4), *225* (5) early cultures *161* (3), (4), (5) early trade *225* (3) first civilizations *221* (4), (5) Hellenistic world *224* (1) *see also* Tadmor
Palmyra Atoll *colonial possession/island* Southwest Asia the modern world *110–111* WWII *104* (2)
Palmyra, Kingdom of *state* Southwest Asia ancient Rome *181* (4)
Palo Alto North America (USA) *136* (3)
Palo Duro Canyon *battle* North America (USA) the growth of the US *129* (2)
Pame *people* Central America colonization *125* (4), *126* (1)
Pamir *see* Pamirs
Pamirs *Rus.* Pamir *mountain range* Central Asia ancient trade *44–45* (1) biological diffusion *72–73* (1) colonialism *269* (3) exploration *218* (2), *256* (1), *257* (3) first empires *241* (4) first states *260* (1) medieval states *261* (6) Mongols *68–69* (1) Timur *229* (4) world religions *49* (3)
Pamlico *people* North America colonization *126* (1)
Pampa Aullagas, Lago *see* Poopó, Lago
Pampa Grande South America (Peru) early cultures *145* (4)
Pampahun Mainland Southeast Asia (Thailand) world religions *243* (5)
Pampa Ingenio South America (Peru) early cultures *145* (4)
Pampas *plain* South America colonization *148* (2) early cultures *144* (1), *147* (2) environment *153* (4) exploration *142* (1), *143* (2)
Pampeluna *see* Pamplona
Pamplona *prev.* Pampeluna, *anc.* Pompaelo; *Basq.* Iruñea; Iberian Peninsula (Spain) Franks *184* (2) Islam *192* (3) medieval states *187* (3), *192* (1), (2)
Pamsurastra *state* South Asia first empires *241* (5)
Pamwak Papua New Guinea (Admiralty Island) the world in 10,000 BCE *14–15*
Panaji *var.* Pangim, Panjim, New Goa South Asia (India) post-war politics *252* (1)
Panamá *var.* Ciudad de Panamá; *Eng.* Panama City Central America (Panama) colonization *126* (1), *148* (2) empire and revolution *150* (1), (2), *151* (3) European expansion *80–81* (1), *81* (3), *85* (2) exploration *142* (1) Incas *148* (1) the modern world *113* (4)
Panamá *state* Central America Cold War *108* (2), *109* (1) economy *153* (3) environment *153* (4) imperial global economy *92* (1) narcotics *153* (5) politics *152* (1) the growth of the US *133* (4) the modern world *112* (1) US economy *136* (2) US politics *139* (4) US superpower *138* (1) WWII *104* (2)
Panama Canal *canal* Central America empire and revolution *151* (3) global immigration *100* (1)
Panama Canal Zone *region* Central America (Panama) US superpower *138* (1)
Panama City *var.* Ciudad de Panamá, Panamá Central America (Panama) Cold War *108* (2) US economy *136* (2) *see also* Panamá
Panamá, Golfo de *see* Panama, Gulf of
Panama, Gulf of *Sp.* Golfo de Panamá *gulf* Central America colonization *148* (2) early cultures *144* (1), *145* (2), *146* (1)
Panama, Isthmus of *Sp.* Istmo de Panamá; *prev.* Isthmus of Darien *coastal feature* Central America early agriculture *120* (1) exploration *118* (1)
Panamá, Istmo de *see* Panama, Isthmus of
Pañamarca South America (Peru) early cultures *145* (4), *146* (1)
Panaramitee Australia the world in 10,000 BCE *14–15*
Panathenaic Way *road* Greece ancient Greece *177* (4)
Pancanada *region* South Asia early religions *48* (2)
Pančevo Southeast Europe (Yugoslavia) post-war economy *215* (3)
Panchagarh South Asia (Bangladesh) post-war politics *252* (3)
Panchala *region/state* South Asia ancient India *242* (1) early religions *48* (2) first empires *241* (5) first religions *36* (2) world religions *242* (2), (3)
Panchanada *region* South Asia world religions *242* (2)
Panduranga Mainland Southeast Asia (Vietnam) ancient India *241* (6) medieval voyages *61* (3)
Pandyas South Asia ancient trade *44–45* (1) early medieval states *244* (2), *244–245* (3) early religions *48* (2) first empires *241* (4) Mongols *68–69* (1) world religions *242* (2)
Pangim *see* Panaji
Panhormus *see* Palermo, Panormus
Panipat *battle* South Asia (India) the world in 1800 *86–87*
Panjab *mod.* Punjab *state* South Asia Mughal Empire *246* (1) *see also* Punjab
Panjim *see* Panaji
Pankhali *see* Chalna
Pankow Central Europe (Germany) post-war politics *212* (2)
Panlongcheng East Asia (China) first cities *259* (3)
Panmunjom East Asia (North Korea) Cold War *109* (4)
Pannonhalma Central Europe (Hungary) medieval states *189* (4)
Pannonia *province* Southeast Europe ancient Rome *180–181* (1), *181* (4) world religions *48* (1)
Pannonia Inferior *province* Southeast Europe ancient Rome *180–181* (1)
Pannonian March *region* Eastern Europe Franks *184* (2)
Pannonia Superior *province* Southeast Europe ancient Rome *180–181* (1)
Panormus *var.* Palerme, Panhormus; *mod.* Palermo Italy ancient Rome *179* (3), (5), *180–181* (1) early states *178* (2) first civilizations *177* (1) *see also* Palermo
Pantheon *building* Italy ancient Rome *181* (2)
Panther Intaglio *burial mound* North America (USA) first civilizations *121* (4)
Panticapaeum Eastern Europe (Ukraine) ancient Rome *181* (3), *225* (5) ancient trade *44–45* (1) first civilizations *177* (1) Hellenistic world *40–41* (1)
Pantlaco Central America (Mexico) Aztecs *124* (3)
Panuco *river* Central America first civilizations *122* (1)
Paoli *battle* North America (USA) empire and revolution *127* (3)
Papago *people* Central America colonization *125* (4), *126* (1)
Papal States *state* Italy *186* (1), *64–65* (2) early modern states *193* (4), *194* (1) empire and revolution *202* (1), (3) medieval states *187* (3), (5), *189* (4), *195* (4), (3), *230* (1), *231* (3) Napoleon *200–201* (1) Reformation *194* (2), *196* (1), (2)
Paphlagonia *region/state* Southwest Asia first civilizations *177* (1) Hellenistic world *40–41* (1) the world in 250 BCE *38–39*
Paphos Southwest Asia (Cyprus) first civilizations *177* (1) Hellenistic world *40–41* (1)
Paphus Southwest Asia (Cyprus) ancient Rome *180–181* (1)
Paplocan *river* Central America first civilizations *122* (1)
Papua *colonial possession* New Guinea the modern world *113* (4)
Papua New Guinea *state* New Guinea decolonization *251* (4), *285* (3) post-war economy *253* (5) US economy *138* (2)
Papuans *people* New Guinea *30–31*, *34–35*, *38–39*, *42–43*, *46–47*, *50–51*, *54–55*, *58–59*, *62–63*, *66–67*, *70–71*, *74–75*, *78–79*, *82–83*, *86–87*, *90–91*
Papua, Territory of *state* New Guinea European imperialism *97* (3)
Pará South America (Brazil) empire and revolution *151* (3)
Pará *region* South America colonization *149* (3)
Paracas South America (Peru) early cultures *145* (4)
Paracas *state* South America the world in 500 BCE *34–35* the world in 250 BCE *38–39*
Paracel Islands *island group* Maritime Southeast Asia post-war economy *275* (3)
Parada *region/state* South Asia first empires *241* (5) world religions *242* (2)
Paraetacene *region* Southwest Asia Hellenistic world *40–41* (1)
Paraetonium Egypt Hellenistic world *40–41* (1)
Paraguai *see* Paraguay
Paraguay *state* South America economy *153* (3) empire and revolution *150* (1), *151* (3), *88–89* (2) narcotics *153* (5) politics *152* (1), (2) the modern world *112* (1), *113* (4) US superpower *138* (1) WWII *105* (3) Cold War *109* (1)
Paraguay *var.* Río Paraguay; *Port.* Paraguai *river* South America colonization *148* (2), *149* (3) early cultures *144* (1), *145* (2) empire and revolution *150* (1), *151* (3) exploration *142* (1), *143* (2) politics *152* (2)
Paraguay, Río *see* Paraguay
Parahiba *see* Paraíba
Parahyba *see* Paraíba
Paraíba *mod.* João Pessoa South America (Brazil) colonization *149* (3), (4)
Paraíba *prev.* Parahiba, Parahyba *region* South America colonization *149* (3)
Paramaras *dynasty* South Asia early medieval states *244* (2) Mongols *68–69* (1)
Paramaribo South America (Surinam) colonization *149* (4) empire and revolution *151* (3) environment *153* (4) politics *152* (1)
Paramonga South America (Peru) early cultures *146* (1) Incas *147* (3)
Paraná *people* South America the world in 1 CE *42–43*
Paraná *var.* Alto Paraná *river* South America colonization *148* (2), *149* (3), (4) early agriculture *20–21* (2) early cultures *144* (1), *145* (2) economy *153* (3) empire and revolution *150* (1), *151* (3) environment *153* (4) exploration *142* (1), *143* (2), (3) politics *152* (2) prehistoric culture *16* (1)
Paranaíba *river* South America politics *152* (1)
Parapamisus *region* Central Asia Hellenistic world *40–41* (1)
Paraspur *see* Parihasapura
Para-Tangana *state* South Asia first empires *241* (5)
Parava *state* South Asia first empires *241* (5)
Paredão *state* South America the world in 1000 *58–59* the world in 1200 *62–63*
Parhae *state* East Asia (China) medieval states *262–263* (1)
Paria South America (Bolivia) Incas *147* (3)
Paricora *people* South America early cultures *147* (2)
Parihasapura *var.* Paraspur *Buddhist centre* South Asia (India) world religions *49* (3)
Paris *settlement* France ancient Rome *182* (1) biological diffusion *72–73* (1) crusades *186* (1), *64–65* (2), *65* (1) early modern states *194* (1), *197* (5) economy *190* (1), *205* (4) empire and revolution *199* (4), *202* (1) Franks *183* (5), (6), *184* (2) imperial global economy *92* (1) inter-war *209* (3) medieval states *182* (2), *185* (3), *186* (2), *187* (3), (4), *192* (1), (2) Napoleon *200–201* (1), *201* (2), (3) post-war politics *212* (3) Reformation *194* (2), *195* (5), *196* (2) WWI *206* (2), (3) WWII *210* (1), *211* (2), (3), (4) Cold War *108* (3)
Parisii *see* Lutetia, Paris
Parkersburg North America (USA) US Civil War *131* (6)
Parma Italy economy *190* (1) medieval states *183* (4), *188* (1)
Parma *state* Italy empire and revolution *202* (1), (3) Reformation *194* (2), *196* (1), (2)
Parmana *state* South America the world in 1200 *62–63*
Parmana *archaeological site* South America (Venezuela) early cultures *144* (1), *145* (2)
Parni *var.* Parnoi *people* Central Asia Hellenistic world *224* (1)
Parnoi *see* Parni
Pärnu *see* Pernau
Paros *island* Greece ancient Greece *179* (4) first civilizations *175* (4)
Parral *var.* Hidalgo del Parral Central America (Mexico) Mexican Revolution *133* (3)
Parras *var.* Parras de la Fuente *jesuit mission/settlement* Central America (Mexico) colonization *125* (4) Mexican Revolution *133* (3)
Parras de la Fuente *see* Parras
Parry Islands *mod.* Queen Elizabeth Islands *island group* North America exploration *287* (2)
Parsi *religious group* South Asia world religions *243* (4)
Parthenon *temple* Greece ancient Greece *177* (4)
Parthia *region/state* Southwest Asia ancient Persia *223* (4) ancient trade *44–45* (1) Hellenistic world *224* (1), *41* (2) medieval states *261* (6)
Parthian Empire *state* Southwest Asia ancient Rome *180–181* (1), *181* (3), *224* (2), *225* (5) early cultures *161* (3)
Parthian Ruins *ruin* Southwest Asia first cities *220* (3)
Parvan *var.* Parwan Central Asia (Afghanistan) Mongols *68–69* (1)
Parvat Asreya *region* South Asia early religions *48* (2)
Parwan *see* Parvan
Pasadena North America (USA)
Pasargadae Southwest Asia (Iran) ancient Persia *223* (4) first religions *36* (1) Hellenistic world *40–41* (1)
Pascua, Isla de *see* Easter Island, Rapa Nui
Pashash South America (Peru) early cultures *145* (4)
Pashupathinatha South Asia (India) world religions *243* (4)
Passamaquoddy *people* North America colonization *126* (1)
Passau Central Europe (Germany) early modern states *193* (4) Franks *184* (2) medieval states *189* (4)
Passchendaele France WWI *206* (2), (3)
Pasto South America (Colombia) empire and revolution *150* (2)
Pataccara *state* South Asia first empires *241* (5)
Patagonia *physical region* South America colonization *148* (2) early agriculture *20–21* (2) early cultures *144* (1), *147* (2) empire and revolution *150* (1), *151* (3), *88–89* (2) environment *153* (4) exploration *142* (1), *143* (3)
Patala South Asia (Pakistan) early medieval states *244* (1) first empires *241* (4)
Pataliputra *mod.* Patna; *var.* Azimabad *settlement* South Asia (India) ancient India *242* (1) ancient trade *44–45* (1) early medieval states *244* (1) early religions *48* (2) early systems *32* (1), *33* (2), (3) exploration *256* (1) first empires *241* (4) first religions *36* (2) medieval states *261* (6), *262–263* (1) world religions *242* (3), (4) *see also* Patna
Patalla *see* Pattala
Patan-Somnath South Asia (India) colonialism *247* (3)
Patara Southwest Asia (Turkey) first civilizations *177* (1)
Patavium *Eng.* Padua, *It.* Padova Italy great migrations *52–53* (1) *see also* Padua
Patay *battle* France medieval states *192* (2)
Patayan *region* North America cultural groups *123* (4)
Patea New Zealand colonization *283* (5)
Pathein *see* Bassein
Patmadoer *see* Vembar
Patna *prev.* Pataliputra; *var.* Azimabad South Asia (India) trade *72–73* (1) colonialism *247* (3), *248* (1) decolonization *250* (2) early medieval states *244–245* (3) economy *249* (4) imperial global economy *93* (5) Mughal Empire *246* (1) post-war economy *253* (5) post-war politics *252* (1) empire and revolution *88* (1) *see also* Pataliputra
Patne South Asia (India) prehistoric culture *17* (2)
Patos, Paso de los *pass* South America empire and revolution *150* (1)
Pattala *mod.* Patalla South Asia (Pakistan) Hellenistic world *40–41* (1)
Patura South Asia (India) ancient trade *44* (2)
Pau France early modern states *197* (5)
Paulistas *military group* South America exploration *143* (2)
Pava South Asia (India) world religions *242* (3)
Pavia Italy Franks *184* (2) medieval states *182* (2), *185* (3)
Paviken Scandinavia (Sweden) medieval voyages *60–61* (1)
Pavón Central America (Mexico) first civilizations *121* (2)
Pawnee *people* North America colonization *126* (1)
Pax Augusta *see* Badajoz
Pax Julia Iberian Peninsula (Portugal) ancient Rome *180–181* (1)
Pays D'En Haut *state* North America colonization *126* (1)
Pazyryk Siberia (Russian Federation) first religions *36* (1)
Peace *river* North America the growth of the US *129* (2)
Pearl *river* East Asia Bronze Age *240* (3)
Pearl Harbor *military base/settlement* Hawaii (USA) US superpower *138* (1) WWII *104* (2), *272* (1), *273* (2)
Peć Southeast Europe (Yugoslavia) post-war economy *215* (3)
Pechenegs *people* Southeast Europe crusades *64–65* (2)
Pechenga *see* Petsamo
Pech-Merle *archaeological site* France prehistoric culture *17* (3)
Pecos *archaeological site* North America (USA) cultural groups *123* (4)
Pecos *people* North America colonization *125* (4), *126* (1)
Pecos *river* North America colonization *125* (4) cultural groups *123* (4)
Pécs *Ger.* Fünfkirchen; *Lat.* Sopianae Central Europe (Hungary) early modern states *193* (4) medieval states *188* (1), *189* (4)
Pedra Furada *archaeological site/settlement* South America (Brazil) early cultures *145* (2)
Pedra Pintada *archaeological site* South America (Brazil) early cultures *145* (2)
Pee Dee *river* North America empire and revolution *127* (3)
Pegu *var.* Bago Mainland Southeast Asia (Burma) trade *72–73* (1) colonialism *247* (4), *248* (1) early medieval states *245* (5), (6) early modern states *268* (1) exploration *239* (1) medieval states *262–263* (1), *263* (6) world religions *243* (5), *49* (4)
Pegu *colonial possession/state* East Asia/Mainland Southeast Asia colonialism *269* (4) medieval states *263* (6)
Pei-ching *see* Beijing, Khanbalik, Peking
Peikthanomyo Mainland Southeast Asia (Burma) ancient India *241* (6)
Peikthanomyo *state* Mainland Southeast Asia ancient India *241* (6)
Peiligang *var.* P'ei-li-kang *archaeological site/settlement* East Asia (China) early agriculture *258* (1)
P'ei-li-kang *see* Peiligang
Pei-p'ing *see* Beijing, Khanbalik, Peking
Peipsi Järv *see* Peipus, Lake
Peipus, Lake *Est.* Peipsi Järv, *Ger.* Peipus, *Rus.* Chudskoye Ozero *lake* Eastern Europe early modern states *197* (3) battle *186* (1) medieval states *189* (3)
Peipus-See *see* Peipus, Lake
Pei-shou-ling *see* Beishouling
Pekarna *archaeological site* Central Europe (Czech Republic) prehistoric culture *17* (4)
Peking *var.* Beijing, Khanbalik, Pei-ching; *prev.* Pei-p'ing East Asia (China) plague *72–73* (1) world religions *49* (3) WWII *272* (1), *273* (2) *see also* Beijing, Khanbalik
Pella Greece ancient Greece *179* (4) ancient Persia *223* (4) early Islam *56–57* (1) Hellenistic world *40–41* (1), *41* (2)
Peloponnese *region* Greece Bronze Age *175* (3) first civilizations *175* (4) first religions *37* (3)
Peloponnesus *see* Peloponnese, Morea
Pelopónnisos *see* Peloponnese, Morea
Pelusium Egypt Hellenistic world *40–41* (1)
Pemba *island* East Africa ancient trade *44–45* (1) economy *163* (2) exploration *157* (5) Islam *163* (1) trade *164* (1), *230* (2)
Pembroke British Isles (United Kingdom) economy *204* (1)
Pembroke Clark North America (Canada) cultural groups *123* (3)
Penang Mainland Southeast Asia (Malaysia) colonialism *247* (4)
Penang *colonial possession* Mainland Southeast Asia (Malaysia) colonialism *248* (1)
Penas, Golfo de *gulf* South America colonization *148* (2)
Peng *state* East Asia first cities *259* (3)
Pengli East Asia (China) first cities *259* (5)

Pengli Lake mod. Poyang Hu lake East Asia first cities 259 (4), (5) see also Poyang Hu
Peng-tou-shan see Bengdoushan
Peninj archaeological site East Africa (Tanzania) first humans 12 (1)
Peninsular Malaysia see Malaya
Pennine Chain see Pennines
Pennines var. Pennine Chain mountain range British Isles imperial global economy 93 (4)
Pennsylvania state North America empire and revolution 127 (2), (3) the growth of the US 129 (1) US Civil War 130 (2), (3), (4), (5), 131 (6), (7) US economy 134 (2)
Pensacola North America (USA) the growth of the US 129 (2), 132 (1) US Civil War 131 (6), (7)
Pensacola people Central America colonization 125 (4)
Pentapolis region Italy medieval states 183 (4)
Pentun people North America colonization 126 (1)
Penugonda South Asia (India) early medieval states 244–245 (3), 245 (4)
Penza Eastern Europe (Russian Federation) Soviet Union 208 (2)
Penzance British Isles (United Kingdom) economy 204 (1)
Pepper Coast physical region West Africa Islam 163 (1)
Pequot people North America colonization 126 (1)
Pera Southeast Europe (Turkey) economy 190 (1)
Perak region Maritime Southeast Asia colonialism 247 (4)
Perath Southwest Asia (Iraq) world religions 48 (1)
Pereira South America (Colombia) narcotics 153 (5)
Pereyaslav Eastern Europe (Ukraine) Mongols 68–69 (1)
Pereyaslavl' Eastern Europe (Russian Federation) Mongols 68–69 (1)
Pergamon see Pergamum
Pergamum Gk. Pergamon; Turk. Bergama Southwest Asia (Turkey) ancient Rome 179 (5), 180–181 (1), 224 (2) first religions 37 (3) Hellenistic world 224 (1), 41 (2) world religions 226 (1)
Pergamum Gk. Pergamon; Turk. Bergama state Southwest Asia ancient Greece 179 (4)
Perge Southwest Asia (Turkey) Hellenistic world 40–41 (1) world religions 48 (1)
Périgueux anc. Vesuna France medieval states 187 (4)
Perinthus state Greece ancient Greece 177 (2)
Perleberg Central Europe (Germany) Bronze Age 175 (3)
Perm' Eastern Europe (Russian Federation) colonialism 269 (3) economy 205 (4) Soviet Union 208 (2), 214–215 (4)
Pernambuco var. Mauritsstad; mod. Recife South America (Brazil) empire and revolution 151 (3) European expansion 84–85 (1) see also Recife
Pernambuco region South America colonization 149 (3)
Pernau var. Pernov; mod. Pärnu Eastern Europe (Estonia) early modern states 195 (3) medieval states 189 (3)
Pernov see Pernau
Péronne France WWI 206 (2), (3)
Perote Central America (Mexico) first civilizations 122 (1)
Pérouse see Perugia, Perusia
Peroz-Shapur battle Southwest Asia (Iraq) ancient Persia 225 (6)
Perpignan France early modern states 197 (5) economy 190 (1)
Perryville North America (USA) US Civil War 131 (6)
Persepolis Southwest Asia (Iran) ancient Persia 223 (4), 225 (6) ancient Rome 224 (2), 225 (5) ancient trade 44 (2), 44–45 (1) early systems 223 (3), 32 (1), 33 (2), (3) early trade 225 (3) exploration 218 (1), (2), 219 (3) Hellenistic world 224 (1) medieval states 261 (6)
Persia region/state Southwest Asia ancient Rome 181 (4), 224 (2) ancient trade 44–45 (1), 72–73 (1) colonialism 248 (1), 269 (3) Communism 271 (8) crusades 65 (1) early 20th century 206 (1) early Islam 56–57 (1), 57 (2) early systems 223 (3) economy 205 (4) empire and revolution 88–89 (2) European expansion 84–85 (1) European imperialism 97 (4) exploration 218 (1), (2), 219 (3) first cities 220 (2) first religions 36 (1) Islam 226 (2), 227 (4), (5) medieval states 261 (6) medieval voyages 61 (3) Mongols 229 (3) Ottomans 232–233 (1) Seljuks 228 (1) Soviet Union 208 (2) Timur 229 (4) trade 230 (2), 267 (3) world religions 226 (1) WWI 233 (2) WWII 104 (1) 20th-century politics 233 (3), (4)
Persian Empire state Southwest Asia ancient Persia 223 (4) first civilizations 177 (1)
Persian Gates pass Southwest Asia Hellenistic world 40–41 (1)
Persian Gulf Ar. Khalīj al 'Arabī, Per. Khalīj-e Fars gulf Southwest Asia ancient Persia 223 (4), 225 (6) ancient Rome 224 (2), 225 (5) ancient trade 44–45 (1) biological diffusion 72–73 (1) early agriculture 220 (1) early cultures 161 (3), (4), (5) early Islam 56–57 (1), 57 (2) early systems 223 (3) early trade 225 (3) economy 163 (2), 234 (1) exploration 157 (4), 218 (1), (2), 219 (3), (4), 239 (1) first cities 220 (2), 28–29 (1) first civilizations 221 (4), 222 (2), 25 (3) first humans 13 (2) Hellenistic world 224 (1), 41 (2) Islam 163 (1), 226 (2), 227 (4) medieval Persia 231 (4) medieval voyages 61 (3) Mongols 229 (3), 68 (2), 68–69 (1) Ottomans 231 (3), 232–233 (1) Seljuks 228 (1) Timur 229 (4) trade 230 (2), 267 (3) world religions 226 (1), 49 (4) WWI 233 (2) 20th-century politics 233 (3), (4), 235 (5) see also Gulf, The
Persians people Southwest Asia first civilizations 222 (2) historical geography 275 (5)
Persicus, Sinus sea Southwest Asia ancient trade 44 (2)
Persis province Southwest Asia ancient Persia 223 (4) ancient trade 44 (2) Hellenistic world 224 (1)
Perth British Isles (United Kingdom) medieval states 186 (2)
Perth Australia prehistoric culture 17 (5) colonization 282 (1), 283 (3) environmentalism 285 (2) European imperialism 96 (1) exploration 279 (2)
Peru state South America economy 153 (3) empire and revolution 150 (1), (2), 151 (3), 88–89 (2) environment 153 (4) global immigration 101 (2), (3) narcotics 153 (5) politics 151 (4), 152 (1) the growth of the US 133 (4) the modern world 112 (1), 113 (4) US superpower 138 (1) WWII 105 (3) Cold War 109 (1)
Perugia settlement Italy early modern states 193 (4) economy 190 (1) Franks 184 (2) medieval states 183 (4), 187 (3), 188 (1)
Perugia, Lake of see Lacus Trasimenus lake
Perusia mod. Perugia; Fr. Pérouse Italy ancient Rome 179 (3), 180–181 (1) early states 178 (1), (2) see also Pérouse, Perugia
Peru, Viceroyalty of colonial possession South America colonization 148 (2) empire and revolution 150 (1) European expansion 81 (3), 84–85 (1)
Perwali Central Asia (Afghanistan) exploration 256 (1)
Pescadores Islands military base/island group Japan (East Asia) colonialism 247 (4) WWII 272 (1), 273 (2)
Peshawar settlement South Asia (Pakistan) decolonization 250 (1) economy 249 (4) exploration 256 (1) post-war economy 253 (5) post-war politics 252 (1) world religions 49 (3)
Peshwa region South Asia Marathas 246 (2)
Pessinus religious site Southwest Asia (Turkey) first religions 37 (3)
Pest Central Europe (Hungary) economy 198 (1) empire and revolution 202 (1) medieval states 185 (3) Mongols 68–69 (1) Napoleon 200–201 (1), 201 (2) Ottomans 197 (4)
Petapoli see Nizampatam
Petatlán Central America (Mexico) first civilizations 122 (1)
Peten physical region Central America first civilizations 123 (2)
Peterborough prev. Medeshamstede British Isles (United Kingdom) economy 204 (1)
Petersburg North America (USA) empire and revolution 127 (3) US Civil War 131 (7)
Petersburg, Siege of battle North America (USA) US Civil War 131 (7)
Petlacalco state Central America Aztecs 124 (1)
Petra settlement Southwest Asia (Jordan) ancient Rome 180–181 (1) ancient trade 44–45 (1) early cultures 161 (3), (4), (5) early systems 223 (3) early trade 225 (3) exploration 219 (4) world religions 226 (1)
Petralona archaeological site Greece first humans 13 (2)
Petroglyph Canyons archaeological site North America (USA) cultural groups 123 (4)
Petrograd var. St. Petersburg; Eng. Saint Petersburg, Fin. Pietari; prev. and mod. Sankt-Peterburg, prev. Petrograd Eastern Europe (Russian Federation) Soviet Union 208 (2) see also Leningrad, St Petersburg
Petropavlovsk mod. Petropavlovsk-Kamchatskiy settlement Siberia (Russian Federation) colonialism 269 (3) early agriculture 258 (1) exploration 257 (2)
Petropavlovsk-Kamchatskiy see Petropavlovsk
Petroskoi see Petrozavodsk
Petrovaradin battle Southeast Europe (Yugoslavia) Ottomans 197 (4)
Petrozavodsk Fin. Petroskoi Eastern Europe (Russian Federation) Soviet Union 208 (2)
Petsamo mod. Pechenga Eastern Europe (Russian Federation) WWII 210 (1), 211 (4)
Pettau see Poetovio
Peucetii people Italy early states 178 (1), (2)
Pevek Siberia (Russian Federation) exploration 287 (2)
Pevensey British Isles (United Kingdom) medieval states 186 (2)
Phaestus see Phaistos
Phaistos Lat. Phaestus Crete Bronze Age 175 (3) first cities 28–29 (1) first civilizations 175 (4)
Phalaborwa archaeological site Southern Africa (South Africa) early cultures 160 (1)
Phaleric Long Wall road Greece ancient Greece 177 (4)
Phanagoria Eastern Europe (Russian Federation) first civilizations 177 (1)
Phan Thiet battle Mainland Southeast Asia (Vietnam) post-war politics 251 (5)
Pharus see Hvar
Phaselis Southwest Asia (Turkey) first civilizations 177 (1)
Phaselis state Greece ancient Greece 177 (2)
Phasis Eastern Europe (Greece) first civilizations 177 (1) Hellenistic world 40–41 (1)
Phayao state Mainland Southeast Asia the world in 1300 66–67
Phazania see Fezzan
Philadelphia North America (USA) colonization 126 (1) empire and revolution 127 (2), (3) exploration 119 (2), (3) imperial global economy 93 (5) the growth of the US 129 (2), 132 (1) US Civil War 130 (5), 131 (6), (7) US economy 134 (1), (3) US politics 135 (6) US society 137 (6) Cold War 108 (2)
Philadelphia Southwest Asia (Syria/Turkey) Hellenistic world 41 (2) medieval states 189 (4) world religions 48 (1)
Philippine Islands see Philippines
Philippines var. Philippine Islands colonial possession/state/island group Philippines ancient trade 44–45 (1) Bronze Age 240 (3) colonialism 269 (4) colonization 284–285 (1) decolonization 251 (4), 285 (3) early agriculture 20–21 (2), 258 (1) early cultures 280–281 (3) economy 274 (1) empire and revolution 88 (1), 88–89 (2) environmentalism 285 (2) European expansion 80–81 (1), 81 (3), 84–85 (1) European imperialism 97 (3), (4) exploration 239 (1), (2), 276–277 (1), 279 (3) global immigration 101 (3) historical geography 236–237 (1) imperialism 270 (2) Islam 243 (6), 275 (4) post-war economy 253 (5), 275 (3) post-war politics 253 (4) the growth of the US 133 (4) the modern world 113 (3), (4) trade 267 (3) world religions 243 (5), 49 (4) WWII 104 (1), 251 (3), 272 (1), 273 (2) Cold War 109 (1)
Philippine Sea battle Pacific Ocean WWII 273 (2)
Philippopolis mod. Plovdiv Southeast Europe (Bulgaria) ancient Rome 180–181 (1) great migrations 52–53 (1) Hellenistic world 40–41 (1), 41 (2) medieval states 182 (2)
Philippsbourg Central Europe (Germany) early modern states 197 (5)
Philistia state Southwest Asia first civilizations 222 (1)
Phnom Penh prev. Caturmukha; var. Phnum Penh Mainland Southeast Asia (Cambodia) colonialism 247 (4), 248 (1), 269 (4) European imperialism 97 (3) post-war economy 253 (5) post-war politics 251 (5) WWII 251 (3) see also Caturmukha
Phnum Penh see Caturmukha, Phnom Penh
Phocaea Southwest Asia (Turkey) ancient Greece 177 (3) economy 190 (1) first civilizations 177 (1)
Phoenicia province/state Southwest Asia ancient Rome 225 (4) first civilizations 222 (1) first religions 36 (1) Hellenistic world 40–41 (1)
Phoenix North America (USA) the growth of the US 129 (2)
Phoenix Islands island group Pacific Ocean colonization 284–285 (1) early cultures 280–281 (3) environmentalism 285 (2) exploration 279 (3)
Phongsali see Phong Saly
Phong Saly mod. Phongsali region Mainland Southeast Asia post-war politics 251 (5)
Phopo Hills archaeological site Southern Africa (Malawi) early cultures 160 (1)
Phra Nakhon Si Ayutthaya see Ayutthaya
Phrygia state/region Southwest Asia ancient Greece 177 (3) first civilizations 177 (1), 222 (2) Hellenistic world 224 (1)
Phrygians people Southwest Asia first civilizations 221 (5)
Phuket var. Bhuket, Puket; prev. Junkseylon, Salang; Mal. Ujung Salang; Mainland Southeast Asia (Thailand) colonialism 247 (4), 248 (1)
Phuoc Long battle Mainland Southeast Asia (Vietnam) 251 (5)
Phylakopi Greece first civilizations 175 (4)
Pi province East Asia first cities 259 (3)
Piacenza settlement Italy economy 190 (1) medieval states 187 (3), 188 (1)
Piauí region South America colonization 149 (3)
Piave river Italy WWI 207 (5)
Picentes people Italy early states 178 (1), (2)
Pichincha battle South America (Equador) empire and revolution 88–89 (2)
Pictish Kingdoms state British Isles medieval states 183 (3)
Picts people British Isles ancient Rome 181 (4), 182 (1) medieval states 182 (2)
Piedmont It. Piemonte region/state Italy empire and revolution 199 (4), 202 (3)
Piedras Negras var. Porfirio Díaz Central America (Mexico) first civilizations 123 (2) see also Porfirio Díaz
Piemonte see Piedmont
Pienchou see Bianzhou
Pierre North America (USA) the growth of the US 129 (2)
Pietari see Leningrad, Petrograd, St Petersburg
Pietermaritzburg Southern Africa (South Africa) colonization 166 (2) European imperialism 96 (2)
Pietersburg Southern Africa (South Africa) colonization 166 (2)
Pieve di Cadore Italy WWI 207 (5)
Pigs, Bay of Sp. Bahía de Cochinos bay West Indies Cold War 108 (2)
Pijijiapan Central America (Mexico) first civilizations 121 (2)
Pikes Peak burial mound North America (USA) first civilizations 121 (4)
Pikilacta South America (Peru) early cultures 146 (1)
Pikimachay South America (Peru) the world in 10,000 BCE 14–15
Pilcomayo river South America colonization 148 (2) environment 153 (4) politics 152 (2)
Pilica see Pilitsa
Pilitsa Pol. Pilica river Central Europe WWI 207 (4)
Pima people Central America/North America colonization 125 (4)
Pima Bajo people Central America colonization 125 (4)
Pinciacum see Poissy
Ping East Asia (China) first cities 259 (5)
Pingcheng East Asia (China) first states 261 (3) medieval states 261 (4)
Pingkiang see Harbin
Pingliangtai East Asia (China) the world in 2500 BCE 22–23
Pingyang East Asia (China) first cities 259 (5)
Pinkiang see Harbin
Pins, Île des island Pacific Ocean early cultures 280–281 (3) medieval voyages 60 (2)
Pinsk Eastern Europe (Belorussia) WWI 207 (4)
Pinson burial mound North America (USA) first civilizations 121 (4)
Pinyang East Asia (China) first religions 37 (4)
Piombino state Italy Napoleon 201 (2)
Pipli South Asia (India) colonialism 247 (3)
Pi-Ramesse Egypt ancient Egypt 159 (5) first cities 28–29 (1)
Pirapora South America (Brazil) empire and revolution 151 (3)
Pirincay people South America the world in 500 BCE 34–35 the world in 250 BCE 38–39
Pirineos see Pyrenees
Pirot Southeast Europe (Serbia) WWI 207 (6)
Pisa var. Pisae Italy early modern states 193 (4) economy 190 (1) Franks 184 (2) medieval states 185 (3), (5), 188 (1) the world in 1200 62–63 see also Pisae
Pisa state Italy crusades 186 (1)
Pisae mod. Pisa Italy ancient Rome 179 (3), 180–181 (1) early states 178 (1), (2) see also Pisa
Pisagua South America (Chile) politics 151 (4)
Pisagua South America (Chile) empire and revolution 151 (3)
Pisco South America (Peru) empire and revolution 151 (3)
Pishpek see Bishkek
Pisidia region/state Southwest Asia ancient Rome 179 (5) Hellenistic world 40–41 (1)
Pistoia anc. Pistoria, Pistoriæ Italy economy 190 (1)
Pistoria see Pistoia
Pistoriæ see Pistoia
Pitcairn Island island Pacific Ocean exploration 278 (1)
Pitcairn Islands colonial possession/island group Pacific Ocean colonization 284–285 (1) decolonization 285 (3)
Pithecusa Italy first civilizations 177 (1)
Pithecusae island Italy early states 178 (1)
Pit River battle North America (USA) the growth of the US 129 (2)
Pitsane var. Pitsani Southern Africa (Botswana) European imperialism 96 (2)
Pitsani see Pitsane
Pittsburgh North America (USA) US economy 134 (1), (3) US politics 135 (6)
Pittsburg Landing var. Shiloh battle North America (USA) US Civil War 131 (6) see also Shiloh
Pityusae var. Pityussae island group Iberian Peninsula ancient Rome 179 (3)
Pityussae see Pityusae
Pitzuwo see Piziwo
Piura South America (Peru) Incas 147 (3) narcotics 153 (5)
Piura river South America early cultures 145 (4), 146 (1)
Piziwo var. Pitzuwo East Asia (China) Russo-Japanese War 270 (4)
Placentia mod. Piacenza Italy ancient Rome 179 (3), 180–181 (1) see also Piacenza
Placentia Bay North America (Canada) WWII 104 (2)
Plains Hunters and Gatherers people North America the world in 250 CE 46–47
Plains Villages region North America the world in 1400 70–71 the world in 1500 74–75
Planalto Central see Brazilian Highlands
Planina, Stara see Balkan Mountains
Plassey South Asia (India) the world in 1800 86–87
Plassey battle South Asia (India) empire and revolution 88 (1)
Plataea battle Greece ancient Persia 223 (4)
Plata, Río de la see Plate, River
Plateau region North America early agriculture 120 (1)
Plate, River Sp. Río de la Plata inlet South America colonization 148 (2) European expansion 80–81 (1) exploration 142 (1), 143 (2)
Platte Bridge battle North America (USA) the growth of the US 129 (2)
Platte River river North America cultural groups 122 (5)
Playa de los Muertos Central America (Honduras) first civilizations 121 (2)
Pleiku battle Mainland Southeast Asia (Vietnam) 251 (5)
Plenty, Bay of bay New Zealand colonization 283 (5)
Plesetsk Eastern Europe (Russian Federation) Soviet Union 214–215 (4)
Pleskau see Pskov
Pleskava see Pskov
Pleven see Plevna
Plevna mod. Pleven Southeast Europe (Bulgaria) WWI 207 (6)
Plezzo see Flitsch
Plock Central Europe (Poland) medieval states 189 (4)
Ploeşti Southeast Europe (Romania) WWII 210 (1), 211 (4)
Plovdiv see Philippopolis
Plymouth British Isles (United Kingdom) economy 204 (1) WWII 210 (1)
Po river Italy Bronze Age 175 (3) Copper Age 174 (2) crusades 64–65 (2) early agriculture 174 (1) early modern states 193 (4) early states 178 (1) economy 190 (1) exploration 172 (1) first civilizations 177 (1) first religions 37 (3) Franks 184 (2) great migrations 52–53 (1) medieval states 183 (4), 188 (1) Napoleon 200–201 (1), 201 (2), (3) WWI 207 (5)
Podgorica prev. Titograd Southeast Europe (Yugoslavia) post-war economy 215 (3)
Podolia region/vassal state Central Europe/Eastern Europe empire and revolution 198 (2) Ottomans 197 (4)
Poduca South Asia (India) ancient trade 44–45 (1)
Poetovio mod. Ptuj; Ger. Pettau Central Europe (Slovenia) world religions 48 (1)
Pohai var. Parhae state East Asia/Mainland Southeast Asia medieval states 262–263 (1), 263 (3), 264 (2)
Pohang Jap. Hokō East Asia (South Korea) Cold War 109 (4)
Pohjanlahti see Bothnia, Gulf of
Pohnpei prev. Ponape, Ponape Ascension Island; see also Ponape island Pacific Ocean environmentalism 285 (2)
Poictiers see Poitiers
Poike physical region Easter Island early cultures 281 (4)
Point Barrow North America (USA) cultural groups 123 (3)
Point de Galle see Galle
Pointe-Noire Central Africa (Congo) economy 168 (2)
Point of Pines archaeological site North America (USA) cultural groups 123 (4)
Poissy anc. Pinciacum France medieval states 192 (1)
Poitiers battle France early Islam 56–57 (1) Islam 226 (2) medieval states 192 (1)
Polada Italy Bronze Age 175 (3)
Poland Pol. Polska region/state Central Europe biological diffusion 72–73 (1) crusades 64–65 (2) early 20th century 206 (1) early modern states 194 (1) empire and revolution 199 (3), 202 (1), (2) inter-war 209 (3), (5) medieval states 185 (3), (4) medieval voyages 60–61 (1) Ottomans 195 (4), 230 (1) post-war economy 213 (5), 214 (1), (2) post-war politics 212 (1), (3) Reformation 196 (1), (2) Soviet Union 208 (2), 213 (4) the modern world 112 (2), 113 (4) WWI 207 (4), 208 (1) WWII 104 (1), 211 (3) Cold War 108 (3), 109 (1)
Poland-Lithuania state Central Europe/Eastern Europe early modern states 193 (4), 195 (3) Ottomans 231 (3) Reformation 194 (2)
Polar Inuit people North America cultural groups 123 (3)
Po-Li state Maritime Southeast Asia ancient India 241 (6)
Polish Principalites state Central Europe medieval states 188 (1)
Polish States state Central Europe crusades 186 (1) economy 190 (1) Mongols 68–69 (1)
Polonnaruwa Buddhist centre/settlement South Asia (Sri Lanka) early medieval states 244–245 (3) world religions 49 (3)
Polotsk Eastern Europe (Belorussia) medieval states 189 (3)
Polovtsy see Cumans
Polska see Poland
Poltava Eastern Europe (Ukraine) Soviet Union 208 (2)
Poltoratsk see Ashgabat, Ashkhabad
Polyanitsa archaeological site Southeast Europe (Bulgaria) Copper Age 174 (2)
Polychrome region South America early cultures 145 (2)
Polygar Kingdoms var. Poygars state South Asia the world in 1600 78–79 the world in 1700 82–83
Polynesia island group Pacific Ocean the world in 750 CE 54–55
Pomata South America (Bolivia) Incas 147 (3)
Pomerania region/state Central Europe crusades 186 (1) empire and revolution 202 (2) medieval states 188 (1), 189 (3)
Pomeranians people Central Europe crusades 64–65 (2)
Pompaelo see Pamplona
Pompeii Italy the world in 250 CE 46–47
Pompeiopolis Southwest Asia (Turkey) ancient Rome 180–181 (1)
Ponape mod. Pohnpei; prev. Ascension Island island Pacific Ocean early cultures 280–281 (3) medieval voyages 60 (2) see also Pohnpei
Pondicherry colonial possession/settlement South Asia (India) colonialism 247 (3), 248 (1), (2), 269 (4) decolonization 250 (1), 251 (4) empire and revolution 88 (1), 88–89 (2) post-war politics 252 (1) WWII 251 (3)
Pondichéry see Pondicherry
Pondo var. Mpondo people Southern Africa the world in 1850 90–91
Pons Aelii see Newcastle-upon-Tyne
Pons Saravi mithraic site France world religions 48 (1)
Pontebba Italy WWI 207 (5)
Ponthieu region France medieval states 192 (1)
Ponthion France Franks 184 (2)
Pontiae island Italy early states 178 (1)
Pontianuntum Italy world religions 48 (1)
Pontigny major cistercian house France medieval states 187 (3)
Pontnewydd archaeological site British Isles (United Kingdom) first humans 13 (2)
Pontus province Southwest Asia ancient Rome 179 (5), 181 (4), 225 (5) Hellenistic world 224 (1) world religions 48 (1)
Pony Express Trail wagon train route North America the growth of the US 129 (2)
Poona mod. Pune South Asia (India) colonialism 248 (1) decolonization 250 (1) economy 249 (4) imperial global economy 93 (5) Marathas 246 (2) see also Pune
Poopó, Lago see Poopó Lake
Poopó, Lake var. Lago Pampa Aullagas, Lago Poopó lake South America colonization 148 (2) early cultures 146 (1) Incas 147 (3) war of the Pacific 151 (4)
Popacatépetl, Volcán volcano Central America colonization 125 (5)
Popayán South America (Colombia) empire and revolution 150 (2) narcotics 153 (5)
Popayán state South America the world in 1200 62–63
Popo state West Africa trade 164 (2)
Popotlan Central America (Mexico) Aztecs 124 (2), (3)
Populonia Italy early states 178 (1), (2) first civilizations 177 (1)
Porakad South Asia (India) colonialism 247 (3)
Porfirio Díaz prev. Piedras Negras Central America (Mexico) Mexican Revolution 133 (3) see also Piedras Negras
Porirua New Zealand colonization 283 (4)
Porkhov Eastern Europe (Russian Federation) early modern states 195 (3)
Port Arthur Chin. Lü-shun; Jap. Ryojun colonial possession/settlement East Asia (China) colonialism 269 (3), (4) imperialism 270 (2) Russo-Japanese War 270 (4) Sino-Japanese War 270 (3) WWII 272 (1), 273 (2)
Port Arthur penal colony Australia colonization 282 (1)
Port Augusta Australia colonization 282 (1) exploration 279 (2)
Port-au-Prince West Indies (Haiti) empire and revolution 89 (3) US economy 136 (2)
Port Dalrymple penal colony Australia colonization 282 (1)
Port Darwin see Darwin
Port-de-Paix West Indies (Haiti) empire and revolution 89 (3)
Port Desire mod. Puerto Deseado South America (Argentina) exploration 143 (3)
Port Elizabeth Southern Africa (South Africa) colonization 166 (2), 167 (4) economy 168 (2) European imperialism 96 (2)
Porter burial mound North America (USA) first civilizations 121 (4)
Porter region North America first civilizations 121 (4)
Port Essington Australia exploration 279 (2)
Port Florence see Kisumu
Port-Gentil Central Africa (Gabon) economy 168 (2)
Port Harcourt Central Africa (Nigeria) economy 168 (2)
Port Hedland Australia colonization 282 (1), 283 (3) exploration 279 (2)
Port Hudson fort/settlement North America (USA) US Civil War 131 (6), (7)
Port Hudson battle North America (USA) US Civil War 131 (7)
Port Jackson harbour Australia exploration 278 (1)
Port Láirge see Waterford
Portland North America (USA) the growth of the US 132 (1) US politics 135 (6)
Portland Bay bay Australia exploration 279 (2)
Port Lincoln Australia colonization 282 (1) exploration 279 (2)
Port Lyautey mod. Kénitra North Africa (Morocco) US superpower 138 (1)
Port Macquarie penal centre/settlement Australia colonization 282 (1) environmentalism 285 (2) exploration 279 (2)
Port Moller North America (USA) cultural groups 123 (3)
Port Molyneux whaling station New Zealand colonization 283 (4)
Port Moresby military base/settlement New Guinea (Papua New Guinea) European imperialism 97 (3) WWII 104 (2), 251 (3), 272 (1), 273 (2)
Port Natal see Durban
Pôrto Alegre var. Porto Alegre South America (Brazil) colonization 148 (2), 149 (3) empire and revolution 151 (3) environment 153 (4) politics 152 (1)
Porto Bello see Portobelo, Puerto Bello
Portobelo Central America (Panama) European expansion 84–85 (1), 85 (2)
Port of Spain West Indies (Trinidad and Tobago) WWII 104 (2)
Porto Novo South Asia (India) colonialism 247 (3) economy 249 (4)
Porto Rico see Puerto Rico
Porto Seguro South America (Brazil) colonization 149 (4)
Porto Seguro region South America colonization 149 (3)
Porto Velho var. Velho South America (Brazil) economy 153 (3) environment 153 (4) politics 152 (1)
Port Pegasus sealing station New Zealand colonization 283 (4)
Port Phillip penal colony Australia colonization 282 (1)
Port Pirie Australia colonization 282 (1)
Port Rex see East London
Port Royal North America (USA) European expansion 85 (2) US Civil War 131 (6), (7)
Port Said Ar. Būr Sa'īd Egypt 20th century 234 (2) economy 168 (2) Ottomans 232–233 (1)
Portsmouth British Isles (United Kingdom) economy 204 (1)
Portsmouth burial mound North America (USA) first civilizations 121 (4)
Port Stephens penal centre Australia colonization 282 (1)
Port Sudan East Africa (Sudan) economy 168 (2) exploration 157 (5)
Portudal West Africa (Senegal) Islam 163 (1) trade 164 (2)
Portuensis, Via road Italy ancient Rome 181 (2)
Portugal anc. Lusitania state Iberian Peninsula crusades 186 (1) early 20th century 206 (1) economy 190 (1), 205 (4) empire and revolution 202 (1), 88–89 (2) European expansion 80–81 (1) European imperialism 97 (4) global immigration 100 (1) inter-war 209 (3), (4) Islam 192 (3) medieval states 187 (3), 231 (3) Napoleon 200–201 (1), 201 (2) post-war economy 213 (5), 214 (1) post-war politics 212 (3) Reformation 194 (2) Soviet Union 214–215 (4) the modern world 112 (1), (2), 113 (4) US superpower 138 (1) WWI 208 (1) WWII 104 (1), 211 (4) Cold War 108 (3), 109 (1) see also Lusitania
Portuguese East Africa mod. Mozambique; prev. Moçambique colonial possession/state Southern Africa European imperialism 97 (4) see also Mozambique
Portuguese Guinea mod. Guinea-Bissau; Fr. Guinée-Bissau; Port. Guiné-Bissau state West Africa colonization 167 (4) European imperialism 96 (1) Cold War 109 (1) see also Guinea-Bissau
Portuguese Timor colonial possession/state Maritime Southeast Asia European imperialism 97 (3) WWII 272 (1), 273 (2)
Portuguese West Africa see Angola
Portus Itius France ancient Rome 180–181 (1)
Portus Magnus archaeological site North Africa (Algeria) ancient Rome 180–181 (1)
Portus Magnus see Almería
Portus Namnetum France ancient Rome 180–181 (1)
Port William whaling station New Zealand colonization 283 (4)
Posen Pol. Poznań Central Europe (Poland) economy 190 (1) empire and revolution 198 (2), 199 (3), 202 (1), (2) see also Poznań
Posen Pol. Poznań region Central Europe empire and revolution 202 (2)
Posidonia Italy first civilizations 177 (1)
Potano people North America colonization 126 (1)
Potchefstroom Southern Africa (South Africa) colonization 166 (2)
Potidaea var. Potidea settlement/state Greece ancient Greece 177 (2), (3) first civilizations 177 (1)
Potidea see Potidaea
Potomac river North America colonization 126 (1) empire and revolution 127 (3)
Potosí South America (Bolivia) colonization 148 (2) empire and revolution 150 (1), 151 (3) exploration 143 (2) politics 151 (4)
Potrero Nuevo archaeological site Central America (Mexico) first civilizations 121 (3)
Potsdam Central Europe (Germany) empire and revolution 199 (3)
Poverty Point Central America (Mexico) the world in 1250 BCE 26–27
Powder River battle North America (USA) the growth of the US 129 (2)
Powhatan people North America colonization 126 (1)
Powys region British Isles medieval states 183 (3)
Poyang Hu lake East Asia early modern states 266 (1)
Poygars see Polygar Kingdoms
Poznań Ger. Posen Central Europe (Poland) early modern states 193 (4) medieval states 188 (1), 189 (3), (4) see also Posen
Pozo Almonte South America (Chile) politics 151 (4)
Pozsony mod. Bratislava; Ger. Pressburg Central Europe (Slovakia) early modern states 193 (4) medieval states 188 (1), 189 (4) see also Bratislava
Pozsony battle Southeast Europe medieval states 185 (3)
Prabang see Lan Chang
Prabhasa South Asia (India) world religions 242 (2)
Prachya region South Asia ancient India 242 (1) first empires 241 (4)
Pracya/Purva-Desa region South Asia early religions 48 (2)
Praeneste Italy early states 178 (1)
Praenestina, Via road Italy ancient Rome 181 (2)
Prag see Prague
Praga see Prague
Pragjyotisapura South Asia (India) early medieval states 244 (1) first empires 241 (4)
Pragjyotisha region South Asia world religions 242 (2)
Prague Cz. Praha, Ger. Prag, Pol. Praga Central Europe (Czech Republic) crusades 186 (1) early modern states 193 (4) economy 190 (1), 205 (4) empire and revolution 199 (3), 202 (1), (2) inter-war 209 (5) medieval states 185 (3), 188 (1), 189 (3), (4) Napoleon 200–201 (1), 201 (2), (3) post-war politics 212 (3) Reformation 194 (2), 196 (1) WWII 105 (3), 210 (1), 211 (4) Cold War 109 (1)
Prague, Defenestration of riot Central Europe Reformation 196 (2)
Praha see Prague
Prambanan Maritime Southeast Asia (Indonesia) world religions 243 (5)
Prasodes Mare sea Indian Ocean ancient trade 44 (2)
Prasum Promontorium headland East Africa ancient trade 44 (2)
Prathet Thai see Siam, Thailand
Pratichya region South Asia ancient India 242 (1)
Pratisthana South Asia (India) early medieval states 244 (1) first empires 241 (4) world religions 242 (2)
Pravarapura South Asia (India) early medieval states 244 (1)
Prayaga South Asia (India) early medieval states 244 (1) early religions 48 (2) first empires 241 (4) first religions 36 (2) world religions 242 (2), (3), 243 (4)
Predmostí Central Europe (Slovakia) the world in 10,000 BCE 14–15
Prenzlauer Berg Central Europe (Germany) post-war politics 212 (2)
Preservation Bay sealing station New Zealand colonization 283 (4)
Presidente Stroessner see Ciudad del Este
Presidi, Stato Dei state Italy Reformation 194 (2)
Prespa battle Southeast Europe (Serbia) WWI 207 (6)
Prespa, Limni see Prespa
Prespës, Liqeni i see Prespa, Lake
Pressburg see Bratislava, Pozsony
Preston British Isles (United Kingdom) economy 204 (1) imperial global economy 93 (4)
Pretoria var. Epitoli, Tshwane Southern Africa (South Africa) colonization 166 (2) economy 168 (2) European imperialism 96 (2)
Preussen see Prussia
Preveza Greece Ottomans 231 (3)
Priene Southwest Asia (Turkey) first civilizations 177 (1) Hellenistic world 40–41 (1)
Primorskiy Kray see Maritime Territory
Prince-Edouard, Île-du see Prince Edward Island
Prince Edward Island Fr. Île-du Prince-Edouard; prev. Ile St Jean, Eng. Isle St John province North America (Canada) 129 (2), 132 (1), 136 (2)
Prince's Island see Principe
Princeton battle North America (USA) empire and revolution 127 (3), 88–89 (2)
Príncipe var. Príncipe Island, Eng. Prince's Island island West Africa exploration 156 (3)
Príncipe Island see Príncipe
Pripet Bel. Prypyats', Ukr. Pryp"yat' river Eastern Europe WWI 207 (4)
Pripet Marshes wetland Eastern Europe early agriculture 174 (1) Napoleon 200–201 (1) WWI 207 (4)
Priština settlement/battle Southeast Europe (Yugoslavia) Ottomans 197 (4) post-war economy 215 (3) WWI 207 (6)
Prizren Alb. Prizreni Southeast Europe (Yugoslavia) post-war economy 215 (3), WWI 207 (6)
Prizreni see Prizren
Progreso Central America (Mexico) Mexican Revolution 133 (3)
Prome Mainland Southeast Asia (Burma) world religions 243 (5), 49 (4)
Prospect Farm archaeological site East Africa (Kenya) early cultures 160 (1)
Provence region France early modern states 193 (4) Franks 183 (6), 184 (2) medieval states 192 (2)
Providence North America (USA) empire and revolution 127 (3) the growth of the US 129 (2), 132 (1)
Providence, Cape headland New Zealand colonization 283 (4)
Provins France crusades 186 (1) economy 190 (1)
Prusa later Brusa, Brussa; mod. Bursa Southwest Asia (Turkey) ancient Rome 180–181 (1) see also Brusa, Bursa
Prussia state Central Europe/Eastern Europe early modern states 195 (3) empire and revolution 198 (2), 202 (1), (2) Napoleon 200–201 (1), 201 (2) Reformation 194 (2), 196 (1), (2)
Prussians people Central Europe crusades 186 (1), 64–65 (2) medieval states 185 (3)
Prut see Pruth
Pruth var. Prut river Eastern Europe WWI 207 (4)
Pryp"yat' see Pripet
Prypyats' see Pripet
Przemyśl Central Europe (Poland) post-war politics 212 (3) WWI 207 (4)
Przheval'sk see Karakol
Pskov Ger. Pleskau; Latv. Pleskava Eastern Europe (Russian Federation) early modern states 195 (3) economy 190 (1) medieval states 189 (3) post-war politics 212 (3) Soviet Union 208 (2) WWI 207 (4)
Pskov Ger. Pleskau; Latv. Pleskava state Eastern Europe medieval states 189 (3)
Ptolemaic Empire state Egypt/Southwest Asia ancient Rome 179 (5) Hellenistic world 224 (1)
Ptolemais Southwest Asia (Syria) ancient Rome 225 (4)
Ptolemais North Africa (Libya) ancient Rome 180–181 (1)
Ptolemaïs var. Acco, Acre Southwest Asia (Israel) world religions 48 (1) see also Acco, Acre
Ptuj see Poetovio
Pucará South America (Peru) early cultures 146 (1)
Pucará de Andalgalá South America (Argentina) Incas 147 (3)
Pu-chou see Puzhou
Puduchcheri see Pondicherry
Puebla var. Puebla de Zaragoza Central America (Mexico) colonization 125 (4) Mexican Revolution 133 (3)
Puebla state Central America Mexican Revolution 133 (3) the growth of the US 129 (2)
Puebla de Zaragoza see Puebla
Pueblo Grande archaeological site North America (USA) cultural groups 123 (4)
Pueblos region North America the world in 750 CE 54–55
Puelche people South America early cultures 147 (2)
Puerto Bello var. Porto Bello; mod. Portobelo Central America (Panama) empire and revolution 150 (2) see also Portobelo
Puerto Cabello South America (Venezuela) empire and revolution 150 (1), (2)
Puerto Casado fort South America (Paraguay) politics 152 (2)
Puerto Deseado see Port Desire
Puerto Hormiga archaeological site South America (Colombia) early cultures 144 (1)
Puerto Montt South America (Chile) empire and revolution 151 (3)
Puerto Plata West Indies (Dominican Republic) European expansion 85 (2)
Puerto Presidente Stroessner see Ciudad del Este
Puerto Príncipe mod. Camagüey West Indies (Cuba) European expansion 85 (2)
Puerto Rico colonial possession/island West Indies colonization 125 (4),

126 (1) empire and revolution 150 (1) European expansion 85 (2) global immigration 100 (1) historical geography 140–141 (1) the growth of the US 133 (4) the modern world 113 (4) US politics 139 (4) Cold War 108 (2), 109 (1)
Puerto San Julián var. San Julián South America (Argentina) European expansion 80–81 (1)
Puket see Phuket
Pulicat var. Pālghāt, Geldria South Asia (India) colonialism 247 (3)
Pulinda region/state South Asia first empires 241 (5) world religions 242 (2)
Pumpo South America (Peru) Incas 147 (3)
Punakha South Asia (Bhutan) colonialism 248 (1)
Puna Pau archaeological site Easter Island early cultures 281 (4)
Pundra South Asia (Bangladesh) first empires 241 (4)
Pundra region/state South Asia (Bangladesh) early religions 48 (2) first empires 241 (5) world religions 242 (2)
Pundravardhana South Asia (Bangladesh) early medieval states 244 (1) world religions 242 (2)
Pune prev. Poona South Asia (India) post-war economy 253 (5) see also Poona
Punjab region/state South Asia colonialism 247 (3), 248 (2) economy 249 (4) empire and revolution 249 (3) post-war politics 252 (2), 253 (4) world religions 243 (4)
Punjab, (East) region South Asia post-war politics 252 (1)
Punjab, (West) region South Asia post-war politics 252 (1)
Punjab States state South Asia colonialism 248 (2)
Punkuri archaeological site South America (Peru) early cultures 145 (3)
Punneikayal see Kayalapattinam
Puno South America (Peru) empire and revolution 150 (1) politics 151 (4)
Punt region/state NE Africa 159 (5)
Punta Arenas prev. Magallanes South America (Chile) empire and revolution 151 (3) environment 153 (4)
Punta de Angamos battle South America (Chile) politics 151 (4)
Puntutjarpa Australia exploration 280 (1)
Pura mod. Iranshahr Southwest Asia (Iran) Hellenistic world 40–41 (1)
Puranadhisthana var. Shrinagara South Asia (India) first empires 241 (4)
Puri South Asia (India) biological diffusion 72–73 (1)
Puritjarra Australia the world in 10,000 BCE 14–15
Purosottama-Puri South Asia (India) world religions 243 (4)
Purus Sp. Río Purús river South America colonization 149 (3) early cultures 144 (1), 145 (2), (4), 146 (1) environment 153 (4)
Purusapura mod. Peshwar South Asia (Pakistan) Hellenistic world 224 (1)
Purush Khaddum Southwest Asia (Turkey) first civilizations 221 (4)
Purús, Río see Purus
Pusan var. Busan; Jap. Fusan East Asia (South Korea) early modern states 267 (4) Islam 275 (4) Russo-Japanese War 270 (4) Sino-Japanese War 270 (3) trade 267 (3) Cold War 109 (4)
Pushkar see Puskara
Pushkari archaeological site Eastern Europe (Russian Federation) the world in 10,000 BCE 14–15
Pusilha Central America (Mexico) first civilizations 123 (2)
Puskalavati South Asia (Pakistan) world religions 242 (2)
Puskara mod. Pushkar South Asia (India) early medieval states 244 (1) world religions 243 (4)
Pusyabhutis state South Asia early medieval states 244 (2)
Putan Maya state Central America Aztecs 124 (1)
Puteoli Italy ancient Rome 180–181 (1), 181 (3)
Puttalam South Asia (Sri Lanka) colonialism 247 (3)
Putumayo region South America narcotics 153 (5)
Putumayo var. Rio Içá river South America colonization 148 (2) early cultures 145 (4), 146 (1) empire and revolution 150 (2), 151 (3) environment 153 (4) Incas 148 (1)
Puyang East Asia (China) first religions 37 (4)
Puye archaeological site North America (USA) cultural groups 123 (4)
Puyo East Asia (Korea) medieval states 264 (1), (2)
Puzhou var. Pu-chou East Asia (China) Mongols 68–69 (1)
Pydna battle Greece ancient Greece 179 (4)
Pygela state Greece ancient Greece 177 (2)
Pylos Greece ancient Greece 177 (3), 179 (4) Bronze Age 175 (3) early systems 223 (3) first cities 28–29 (1) first civilizations 175 (4)
Pyongyang prev. Luolang; var. P'yŏngyang-si, P'yŏngyang East Asia (North Korea) Cold War 109 (4) early modern states 267 (4) Islam 275 (4) Sino-Japanese War 270 (3) world religions 49 (3) see also Luolang
P'yŏngyang-si see Luolang, Pyongyang
Pyramid Lake battle North America (USA) the growth of the US 129 (2)
Pyrenaei Montes see Pyrenees
Pyrenees Fr. Pyrénées, Sp. Pirineos; anc. Pyrenaei Montes mountain range France/Iberian Peninsula ancient Rome 179 (3), 180–181 (1), 181 (3) Bronze Age 175 (3) crusades 186 (1), 64–65 (2) early agriculture 174 (1) early Islam 56–57 (1), 57 (2) early modern states 197 (5) economy 190 (1), 205 (4) exploration 172 (1) Franks 183 (5), (6), 184 (2) great migrations 52–53 (1) historical geography 170–171 (1) Islam 192 (3) medieval states 185 (3), 192 (1), (2) Napoleon 200–201 (1) prehistoric culture 17 (3), (4) world religions 48 (1) WWII 210 (1), 211 (4)
Pyrrha state Greece ancient Greece 177 (2)
Pyu region/state Mainland Southeast Asia medieval states 262–263 (1) the world in 750 CE 54–55 world religions 49 (3), (4)

Q

Qābis see Gabès
Qadesh Southwest Asia (Lebanon) first cities 28–29 (1)
Qadisiya battle Southwest Asia (Iraq) early Islam 56–57 (1)
Qafzeh archaeological site Southwest Asia (Israel) first humans 13 (2), 15 (1)
Qaidam Pendi see Tsaidam Basin
Qalat mod. Kalat South Asia (Pakistan) Mughal Empire 246 (1) see also Kalat
Qalat state South Asia Mughal Empire 246 (1)
Qalhat see Kalhat
Qalqut var. Kalikod; mod. Calicut, Kozhikode South Asia (India) early medieval states 244–245 (3) see also Calicut, Kalikod
Qânâq see Thule
Qandahar mod. Kandahar South Asia (Pakistan) early medieval states 244–245 (3) Mughal Empire 246 (1) see also Kandahar
Qandahar state South Asia Mughal Empire 246 (1)
Qandahâr see Kandahar, Qandahar
Qannauj South Asia (India) early medieval states 244–245 (3)
Qaqortoq see Julianehaab
Qarabagh mod. Karabakh region Southwest Asia medieval Persia 231 (4)
Qaraghandy see Karaganda
Qarakhanids var. Karakhanids state Central Asia early Islam 57 (2) see also Karakhanids
Qarmatians dynasty Southwest Asia early Islam 57 (2) Islam 227 (4), (5)
Qarmatis dynasty South Asia the world in 1000 58–59
Qars see Kars
Qatar colonial possession/state Southwest Asia economy 234 (1) Islam 235 (4) the modern world 113 (3) US economy 138 (2) 20th-century politics 233 (4), 235 (5) Cold War 109 (1)
Qatna Southwest Asia (Syria) ancient Egypt 159 (4), (5)
Qaw Egypt ancient Egypt 159 (2)
Qaw el-Kebir Egypt ancient Egypt 159 (4)
Qazaqstan see Kazakhstan
Qazris see Cáceres
Qazvin var. Kazvin Southwest Asia (Iran) early Islam 56–57 (1) Mongols 229 (3), 68–69 (1) 20th-century politics 235 (5) see also Kazvin
Qeshm Southwest Asia (Iran) economy 234 (1)
Qeshm var. Jazīreh-ye Qeshm, Qeshm Island island Southwest Asia economy 234 (1)
Qeshm Island see Qeshm
Qeshm, Jazīreh-ye see Qeshm
Qi var. Ch'i region/state East Asia first cities 259 (4), (5) first religions 37 (4)
Qiang East Asia (China) first cities 259 (4)
Qiang state East Asia first cities 259 (3)
Qiang people East Asia first cities 259 (4) first states 260 (1), 261 (2) medieval states 261 (4), (6), 262–263 (1)
Qiantang East Asia (China) first states 260 (1)
Qiemo see Cherchen
Qi Empire var. Ch'i state East Asia the world in 500 CE 50–51 see also China
Qift Egypt ancient Egypt 159 (4)
Qilian Shan mountain range East Asia early agriculture 258 (1) early modern states 266 (1) first cities 259 (5) first religions 37 (4) first states 260 (1) trade 267 (3)
Qin state East Asia first cities 259 (4), (5) first religions 37 (4)
Qin Empire state East Asia the world in 250 BCE 38–39 see also China
Qing see Qinghai
Qingdao var. Ching-Tao, Ch'ing-tao, Tsingtao, Tsintao; Ger. Tsingtau East Asia (China) economy 274 (1) imperialism 270 (2) Islam 275 (4) post-war politics 274 (2) Russo-Japanese War 270 (4)
Qingdao var. Tsingtao colonial possession East Asia colonialism 269 (4)
Qing Empire mod. China; var. Manchuria, Ch'ing state East Asia colonialism 248 (1), (2), 269 (3), (4) decolonization 250 (2) economy 249 (4) empire and revolution 249 (3), 88–89 (2) European imperialism 97 (3), (4) Russo-Japanese War 270 (4) Sino-Japanese War 270 (3) see also China
Qinghai var. Chinghai, Qing, Tsinghai province/state East Asia Chinese revolution 271 (5) early modern states 266 (1), (2), 268 (1) empire and revolution 268 (2) post-war economy 274 (2), 275 (3)
Qinghai Hu var. Ch'ing Hai, Tsing Hai, Mong. Koko Nor lake East Asia early modern states 266 (1) first states 260 (1)
Qingjiang East Asia (China) medieval states 263 (6)
Qingliangang archaeological site East Asia (China) early agriculture 258 (2)
Qingtang Xiang state East Asia medieval states 263 (3)
Qingyang rebellion East Asia early modern states 266 (2)
Qingzhou prev. Yidu rebellion/settlement East Asia (China) early modern states 266 (2) medieval states 263 (4)
Qinhuangdao var. Chinwangtao East Asia (China) colonialism 269 (4) post-war politics 274 (2)
Qiong see Hainan
Qiongzhou var. Kiungchow East Asia (China) colonialism 269 (4)
Qita Ghazzah see Gaza Strip
Qizhou military base East Asia early modern states 266 (1)
Qom var. Kum, Qum Southwest Asia (Iran) economy 234 (1) see also Qum
Qomul see Hami
Quadi people Eastern Europe ancient Rome 180–181 (1), 181 (4)
Quang Tri battle Mainland Southeast Asia (Vietnam) 251 (5)
Quanrong state East Asia first cities 259 (3)
Quanzhou East Asia (China) ancient trade 44–45 (1) medieval states 263 (5) Mongols 68 (2), 68–69 (1) trade 267 (3)
Quapaw people North America colonization 126 (1)
Quarai archaeological site North America (USA) cultural groups 123 (4)
Quban Egypt ancient Egypt 159 (4), (5)
Quebec var. Québec North America (Canada) colonization 126 (1) empire and revolution 127 (2), (3) empire and revolution 88 (1)European expansion 84–85 (1) exploration 118 (1), 119 (2), (3) global immigration 100 (1), 101 (3) 129 (2), 132 (1) the world in 1800 86–87, 136 (2)
Quebec colonial possession/province North America empire and revolution 127 (3), 129 (2), 132 (1), 136 (2)
Queen Elizabeth Islands see Parry Islands
Queensland region Australia colonization 282 (1), (2), 283 (3)
Queenstown New Zealand colonization 283 (5)
Quelimane var. Kilimane, Kilmain, Quilimane Southern Africa (Mozambique) exploration 157 (4) Islam 163 (1) trade 164 (1)
Quelpart Jap. Saishū; Kor. Cheju-do island East Asia Sino-Japanese War 270 (3) see also Cheju-do
Quemoy var. Chinmen Tao, Jinmen Dao island East Asia Cold War 109 (1) post-war economy 275 (3)
Quentovic France medieval states 185 (3)
Que Que see Kwekwe
Quera see Chur, Curia
Querero South America the world in 10,000 BCE 14–15
Queres people North America colonization 126 (1)
Querétaro state Central America Mexican Revolution 133 (3) the growth of the US 129 (2)
Quetta South Asia (Pakistan) Hellenistic world 40–41 (1) post-war politics 252 (1)
Quetzaltepec Central America (Mexico) Aztecs 124 (1)
Qufu East Asia (China) first cities 259 (5) first religions 37 (4)
Quiahuac Central America (Mexico) Aztecs 124 (1)
Quiahuitztlan Central America (Mexico) colonization 125 (5)
Quiauhteopan state Central America Aztecs 124 (1)
Quiberon Bay battle France empire and revolution 88 (1)
Quierzy France Franks 184 (2)
Quilimane see Quelimane
Quilon var. Kolam, Kollam South Asia (India) biological diffusion 72–73 (1) colonialism 247 (3)
Quimbaya state South America the world in 1200 62–63
Quimbaya Chiefdoms state South America early cultures 146 (1)
Quimper anc. Quimper Corentin France Franks 184 (2)
Quimper Corentin see Quimper
Qui Nhon battle Mainland Southeast Asia (Vietnam) post-war politics 251 (5)
Quintana Roo state Central America Mexican Revolution 133 (3)
Quiriguá Central America (Guatemala) first civilizations 122 (1), 122 (2)
Quirinal Hill Lat. Collis Quirinalis hill Italy ancient Rome 181 (2)
Quirinalis Collis see Quirinal Hill
Quito South America (Ecuador) colonization 148 (2) empire and revolution 150 (1), (2), 151 (3) environment 153 (4) exploration 142 (1), 143 (2), (3) Incas 147 (3), 148 (1) politics 152 (1)
Quito, Presidencia of region South America colonization 148 (2)
Qujialing archaeological site East Asia (China) early agriculture 258 (2)
Qum mod. Qom Southwest Asia (Iran) medieval Persia 231 (4) Mongols 229 (3), 68–69 (1) see also Qom
Qumis Southwest Asia (Iran) early Islam 56–57 (1)
Quonset North America (USA) WWII 104 (2)
Qûqon see Kokand
Qurein see Kuwait
Qus var. Assouan, Assuan, Aswân; anc. Syene Egypt crusades 228 (2) see also Aswân, Syene

R

Rabat var. al Dar al Baida North Africa (Morocco) early Islam 56–57 (1) economy 168 (2)
Rabaul military base/settlement New Guinea (Papua New Guinea) WWII 104 (2), 251 (3), 272 (1), 273 (2)
Rabbah Ammon see Amman
Rabbath Ammon see Amman
Rabeh people Central Africa trade 167 (1)
Racibórz see Ratibor
Radom Central Europe (Poland) empire and revolution 198 (2)
Rae Bareli region South Asia decolonization 250 (1)
Raeti people Italy early states 178 (2)
Raetia var. Rhaetia province Central Europe ancient Rome 180–181 (1) Franks 184 (2) see also Rhaetia
Rafa see Rafah
Rafah var. Rafa, Rafaḥ; Heb. Rafiaḥ, Raphiah Southwest Asia (Gaza Strip) 20th century 234 (2)
Rafiah see Rafah
Ragusa mod. Dubrovnik Southeast Europe (Croatia) early modern states 193 (4) economy 190 (1) medieval states 188 (1), 189 (4) Ottomans 195 (4) Reformation 196 (2) see also Dubrovnik
Ragusa state Southeast Europe early modern states 193 (4), 194 (1) Ottomans 195 (4), 230 (1), 231 (3) Reformation 194 (2)
Rahanagar South Asia (Bangladesh) post-war politics 252 (3)
Rahovec see Orahovac
Rai see Rayy
Rajagriha South Asia (India) first empires 241 (4) first religions 36 (1), (2),36 (2) world religions 242 (3)
Rajamahendri South Asia (India) early medieval states 244–245 (3), 245 (4)
Rajarattha region South Asia first empires 241 (4)
Rajasthan region/state South Asia post-war politics 252 (1) world religions 243 (4)
Rajgir religious site South Asia (India) first religions 36 (2)
Rajputana region/state South Asia colonialism 247 (3), 248 (1), (2)
Rajputs people South Asia early medieval states 244–245 (3)
Rajput States state South Asia the world in 1500 74–75
Rakhigarhi West India early city 240 (2)
Rakka see Raqqa
Rakvere see Wesenberg
Raleigh North America (USA) the growth of the US 129 (2), 132 (1) US Civil War 131 (7) US society 137 (6)
Ramagama South Asia (India) world religions 242 (3)
Ramazan state Southwest Asia the world in 1400 70–71 the world in 1500 74–75
Rameshwaram South Asia (India) world religions 243 (4)
Ramhormoz Southwest Asia (Iran) 20th-century politics 235 (5)
Rampur South Asia (India) colonialism 248 (1) economy 249 (4)
Rampur state South Asia colonialism 248 (2)
Ramsay's Mill North America (USA) empire and revolution 127 (3)
Ramsgate British Isles (United Kingdom) WWI 206 (2), (3)
Rana Ghundai archaeological site South Asia (India) first cities 240 (2)
Ranas Central America (Mexico) first civilizations 122 (1)
Ranchillos South America (Argentina) Incas 147 (3)
Rancho la Chua North America (USA) colonization 125 (4)
Rancho Peludo archaeological site South America (Venezuela) early cultures 144 (1), 145 (2)
Rangiroa island Pacific Ocean exploration 278 (1)
Rangoon var. Yangon; anc. Dagon Mainland Southeast Asia (Burma) colonialism 247 (4), 248 (1), 269 (4) economy 249 (4) European expansion 84–85 (1) European imperialism 97 (3) Islam 275 (4) post-war economy 253 (5) US superpower 138 (1) world religions 243 (5) WWII 251 (3), 272 (1), 273 (2)
Rangpur archaeological site/settlement South Asia (Bangladesh) colonialism 247 (3) first cities 240 (2) post-war politics 252 (3)
Rano Kao see Rano Kau
Rano Kau var. Rano Kao volcano Pacific Ocean early cultures 281 (4)
Rano Raraku archaeological site Easter Island early cultures 281 (4)
Rapa Nui var. Isla de Pascua, Easter Island island Pacific Ocean early cultures 280–281 (3), 281 (4) medieval voyages 60 (2) see also Easter Island
Raphiah see Rafah
Raqqa var. Rakka Southwest Asia (Syria) early Islam 56–57 (1)
Raroia island Pacific Ocean exploration 278 (1)
Ra's al Junayz Southwest Asia (Oman) first civilizations 25 (3)
Ras al Khaimah Ar. Ra's al Khaymah Southwest Asia (United Arab Emirates) economy 234 (1)
Ra's al Khaymah see Ras al Khaimah
Ras Dashen mountain East Africa (Ethiopia) exploration 157 (5)
Rashtrakutas dynasty South Asia early medieval states 244 (2) the world in 750 CE 54–55
Ra's Shamrah see Ugarit
Ras Tannura oil terminal Southwest Asia (Saudi Arabia) economy 234 (1)
Rasulids dynasty Southwest Asia economy 163 (2)
Ratiaria Christian archbishopric Southeast Europe (Bulgaria) world religions 48 (1)
Ratibor mod. Racibórz Central Europe (Poland) medieval states 189 (3)
Ratisbon anc. Castra Regina, Reginum; hist. Ratisbona; Fr. Ratisbonne, Ger. Regensburg massacre/settlement Central Europe (Germany) crusades 186 (1) early modern states 193 (4) Franks 184 (2) medieval states 188 (1), 189 (3), (4) Napoleon 200–201 (1) see also Castra Regina, Regensburg
Ratisbona see Castra Regina, Ratisbon, Regensburg
Ratisbonne see Castra Regina, Ratisbon, Regensburg
Ratnagiri South Asia (India) exploration 256 (1)
Ratomagus see Rotomagus
Raukawa see Cook Strait
Ravenna Italy ancient Rome 180–181 (1), 181 (4), 182 (1) economy 190 (1) Franks 184 (2) great migrations 52–53 (1) medieval states 182 (2), 183 (4) Ottomans 230 (1) world religions 48 (1) early modern states 194 (1)
Ravenna, Exarchate of state Italy medieval states 183 (4)
Ravensberg region Central Europe empire and revolution 199 (3)
Ravensbrück concentration camp Central Europe WWII 211 (3)
Ravi river South Asia colonialism 247 (3) early medieval states 244 (1), (2), 244–245 (3) economy 249 (4) Marathas 246 (2) Mughal Empire 246 (1)
Rawak Buddhist centre East Asia (China) world religions 49 (3)
Rawalpindi South Asia (Pakistan) post-war economy 253 (5)
Rawson South America (Argentina) empire and revolution 151 (3)
Ray see Rayy
Rayigama South Asia (Sri Lanka) early medieval states 244–245 (3)
Raysut Southwest Asia (Oman) early Islam 56–57 (1) medieval voyages 61 (3)
Rayy var. Rai, Ray, Rey; anc. Rhagae Southwest Asia (Iran) biological diffusion 72–73 (1) Islam 227 (5) Mongols 229 (3), 68–69 (1)
Real Alto archaeological site/settlement South America (Ecuador) early cultures 144 (1)
Reao leper colony Pacific Ocean environmentalism 285 (2)
Reate Italy early states 178 (1)
Recife var. Pernambuco; Dut. Mauritsstad South America (Brazil) colonization 149 (3), (4) economy 153 (3) environment 153 (4) exploration 142 (1), 143 (2) politics 152 (1) see also Pernambuco
Recuay South America (Peru) early cultures 145 (4)
Recuay region South America early cultures 145 (4)
Reddis dynasty South Asia the world in 1400 70–71
Red River river North America colonization 125 (4) cultural groups 122 (5) early agriculture 120 (1) exploration 118 (1), 119 (2) first civilizations 121 (4) the growth of the US 129 (2) US Civil War 131 (6), (7)
Red River var. Yuan, Chin. Yuan Jiang, Vtn. Sông Hông Hà river East Asia ancient India 241 (6) Bronze Age 240 (3) colonialism 247 (4), 248 (1) early medieval states 245 (5), (6) post-war politics 251 (5) world religions 243 (5)
Redruth British Isles (United Kingdom) economy 204 (1)
Red Sea anc. Sinus Arabicus sea Africa/Asia ancient Egypt 159 (2), (3), (4), (5) ancient Persia 223 (4) ancient Rome 180–181 (1), 181 (4), 224 (2), 225 (5) ancient trade 44–45 (1), 72–73 (1) crusades 65 (3) early agriculture 158 (1) early cultures 160 (1), 161 (2), (3), (4), (5) early Islam 56–57 (1), 57 (2) early trade 223 (3), 225 (3) economy 163 (2), (3) exploration 156 (3), 157 (5), 172 (1), (2), 219 (3), (4) first cities 220 (2), 28–29 (1) first civilizations 222 (2) first humans 12 (1), 13 (2) Hellenistic world 224 (1), 41 (2) Islam 163 (1), 226 (2), (3), 227 (4) medieval voyages 61 (3) Mongols 229 (3) Ottomans 231 (3), 232–233 (1) Seljuks 228 (1) slave trade 165 (4) Timur 229 (4) trade 165 (3), 167 (1), 230 (2) WWII 233 (2) 20th century 234 (2) 20th-century politics 233 (4)
Redstone Fort North America (USA) empire and revolution 127 (3)
Reefton see Reef Town
Reef Town mod. Reefton New Zealand colonization 283 (5)
Reged region British Isles medieval states 183 (3)
Regensburg anc. Castra Regina, Reginum; Eng. Ratisbon; hist. Ratisbona; Fr. Ratisbonne Central Europe (Germany) crusades 64–65 (2), 65 (1) economy 190 (1) see also Castra Regina, Ratisbon
Reggio var. Reggio di Calabria; anc Rhegium Italy economy 190 (1) medieval states 188 (1) Ottomans 231 (3) see also Rhegium
Regillus Lacus lake Italy early states 178 (1)
Regina North America (Canada) the growth of the US 129 (2)
Reginum see Castra Regina, Ratisbon, Regensburg
Reichenau Central Europe (Poland) Franks 184 (2)
Reichskommissariat-Ostland region Eastern Europe WWII 211 (2)
Reichskommissariat-Ukraine region Eastern Europe WWII 211 (2)
Reims see Durocortorum, Rheims
Reindeer Lake lake North America the growth of the US 129 (2)
Reine-Élisabeth, Îles de la see Queen Elizabeth Islands
Reinickendorf Central Europe (Germany) post-war politics 212 (2)
Reka see Rijeka
Reka Ili see Ili
Remedello archaeological site Italy Copper Age 174 (2)
Remedios military base West Indies (Cuba) Cold War 108 (2)
Remi see Rheims
Remojadas Central America (Mexico) first civilizations 121 (2), 122 (1)
Remojadas region Central America first civilizations 122 (1)
Ren state East Asia first cities 259 (3)
Rennell var. Mu Nggava island Pacific Ocean early cultures 280–281 (3) medieval voyages 60 (2)
Renner burial mound North America (USA) first civilizations 121 (4)
Rennes anc. Condate; Bret. Roazon France empire and revolution 199 (4) Franks 184 (2) medieval states 187 (4)
Resolute North America (Canada) cultural groups 123 (3)
Réunion prev. Bourbon colonial possession/island/state Indian Ocean Europe expansion 84–85 (1) European imperialism 96 (1) global immigration 101 (3) see also Bourbon
Reval Rus. Revel; mod. Tallinn Eastern Europe (Estonia) crusades 186 (1) early modern states 195 (3) economy 190 (1) medieval states 189 (3) see also Revel, Tallin
Revel Eastern Europe (Estonia) early modern states 197 (3) Soviet Union 208 (2)
Revillagigedo Islands see Revillagigedo, Islas
Revillagigedo, Islas Eng. Revillagigedo Islands island group North America the modern world 110–111
Rewardashur Christian archbishopric Southwest Asia (Iran) world religions 48 (1)
Rey see Rayy
Reykjavík Europe (Iceland) exploration 287 (2) medieval voyages 60–61 (1) WWII 104 (2)
Reẓā'īyeh, Daryācheh-ye see Urmia, Lake
Rha river Eastern Europe ancient trade 44 (2)
Rhaetia var. Raetia province/region Central Europe Franks 183 (6) world religions 48 (1) see also Raetia
Rhagae Southwest Asia (Iran) Hellenistic world 40–41 (1)
Rhapta East Africa (Ethiopia) ancient trade 44 (2)
Rhegium var. Reggio; mod. Reggio di Calabria Italy ancient Rome 179 (3), 180–181 (1) early states 178 (1) first civilizations 177 (1) see also Reggio
Rheims France ancient Rome 182 (1) economy 190 (1) Franks 183 (5), (6), 184 (2) medieval states 185 (3), 188 (1), (2) Napoleon 200–201 (1) WWI 206 (2), (3)
Rhein see Rhine
Rhenus see Rhine
Rhin see Rhine
Rhine Dut. Rijn, Fr. Rhin, Ger. Rhein; Lat. Rhenus river Central Europe, Low Countries ancient Rome 180–181 (1), 181 (3), (4) ancient trade 44–45 (1) biological diffusion 72–73 (1) Bronze Age 175 (3) Copper Age 174 (2) crusades 186 (1), 64–65 (2) early agriculture 174 (1), 20–21 (2) early Islam 56–57 (1) early modern states 193 (4), (5) economy 190 (1) empire and revolution 199 (3), (4), 202 (1), (1i), (2) exploration 172 (1) first humans 13 (2) Franks 183 (5), (6), 184 (2) great migrations 52–53 (1), 53 (2) medieval states 182 (2), 185 (3), 188 (1), (2) Napoleon 200–201 (1), 201 (2) prehistoric culture 16 (1) Reformation 195 (5), 196 (1) world religions 48 (1) WWI 206 (2), (3) WWII 210 (1), 211 (4)
Rhine, Confederation of the state Central Europe Napoleon 201 (2)
Rhodanus see Rhône
Rhode Iberian Peninsula (Spain) ancient Rome 179 (3)
Rhode Island colonial possession/state North America empire and revolution 127 (2), (3) the growth of the US 129 (1) US Civil War 130 (2), (5) US economy 134 (2)
Rhodes Greece (Rhodes) ancient Greece 177 (3), 179 (4) early Islam 56–57 (1) economy 190 (1) Hellenistic world 40–41 (1) medieval states 187 (5) Ottomans 231 (3) world religions 48 (1) Islam 226 (2)s
Rhodes var. Ródhos; Gr. Ródos; Lat. Rhodus, It. Rodi state/island Greece ancient Greece 177 (2), (3), 179 (4) ancient Persia 223 (4) ancient Rome 179 (5) crusades 64–65 (2) first civilizations 175 (4), 177 (1), 221 (5) Islam 226 (2) medieval states 187 (5) Ottomans 230 (1) post-war politics 212 (3)
Rhodesia mod. Zimbabwe; prev. Southern Rhodesia state Southern Africa the world in 1975 106–107 see also Southern Rhodesia, Zimbabwe
Rhodos see Rhodes
Rhodus Greece ancient Rome 180–181 (1)
Rhône Lat. Rhodanus river France ancient Rome 180–181 (1), 181 (3) ancient trade 44–45 (1) biological diffusion 72–73 (1) Bronze Age 175 (3) Copper Age 174 (2) crusades 186 (1), 64–65 (2) early agriculture 174 (1) early Islam 56–57 (1) early modern states 193 (4) economy 190 (1), 205 (4) first civilizations 177 (1) Franks 183 (5), (6), 184 (2) great migrations 52–53 (1), 53 (2) medieval states 185 (3), 187 (4), 188 (1) prehistoric culture 17 (3) world religions 48 (1)
Rialto Bridge bridge Italy economy 191 (3)
Ribe Scandinavia (Denmark) medieval voyages 60–61 (1)
Ribeira Grande var. Concelho de Ribeira Grande island Atlantic Ocean the world in 1500 74–75
Richmond North America (USA) colonization 126 (1) empire and revolution 127 (3) European expansion 84–85 (1) the growth of the US 129 (2), 132 (1) US Civil War 130 (5), 131 (6), (7) US society 137 (6)
Rievaulx major cistercian house British Isles (United Kingdom) medieval states 187 (3)
Rift Valley see Great Rift Valley
Riga Latv. Rīga settlement Eastern Europe (Latvia) biological diffusion 72–73 (1) crusades 186 (1) early modern states 193 (4), 195 (3) economy 190 (1) empire and revolution 198 (2), 202 (1) medieval states 189 (3) Napoleon 200–201 (1), 201 (2) post-war politics 212 (3) Reformation 194 (2) Soviet Union 214–215 (4) WWI 207 (4) WWII 211 (2), (3), (4) Cold War 108 (3)
Rigaer Bucht see Riga, Gulf of
Riga, Gulf of Est. Liivi Laht, Ger. Rigaer Bucht, Latv. Rīgas Jūras Līcis, Rus. Rizhskiy Zaliv; prev. Est. Riia Laht gulf Eastern Europe WWI 207 (4)
Rīgas Jūras Līcis see Riga, Gulf of
Riia Laht see Riga, Gulf of
Rijeka anc. Tarsatica; Ger. Sankt Veit am Flaum; It. Fiume; Slvn. Reka Southeast Europe (Croatia) post-war economy 215 (3)
Rijn see Rhine
Rijssel see Lille
Rim archaeological site/settlement West Africa (Burkina) early agriculture 158 (1) early cultures 160 (1)
Rimini anc. Ariminum Italy economy 190 (1) medieval states 183 (4), 188 (1) see also Ariminum
Rinaldone Italy the world in 2500 BCE 22–23
Rinan province Mainland Southeast Asia first states 260 (1)
Ringsted Scandinavia (Sweden) medieval voyages 60–61 (1)
Rio see Rio de Janeiro
Riobamba South America (Equador) Incas 147 (3)
Rio Barbate battle Iberian Peninsula (Spain) early Islam 56–57 (1)
Rio Bec Central America (Mexico) first civilizations 123 (2)
Rio Branco South America (Brazil) politics 152 (1)
Rio de Janeiro var. Rio; hist. São Sebastião de Rio de Janeiro South America (Brazil) colonization 149 (3), (4) economy 153 (3) empire and revolution 151 (3) environment 153 (4) European expansion 84–85 (1) exploration 143 (2), (3) global immigration 100 (1) imperial global economy 92 (1) politics 152 (1)
Rio de Janeiro region South America colonization 149 (3)
Rio de la Hacha South America (Columbia) European expansion 85 (2)
Rio de la Plata, Viceroyalty of colonial possession South America colonization 148 (2) empire and revolution 150 (1) European expansion 84–85 (1)
Rio de Oro later Spanish Sahara; mod. Western Sahara state North Africa the world in 1900 94–95 the world in 1925 98–99 see also Spanish Sahara, Western Sahara
Rio Grande var. Rio Grande do Sul; hist. São Pedro do Rio Grande do Sul South America (Brazil) colonization 149 (3) empire and revolution 151 (3) environment 153 (4)
Rio Grande do Sul region South America colonization 149 (3)
Riom France early modern states 197 (5)
Rio Muni state Central Africa European imperialism 96 (1)
Ripuarian Franks people Central Europe Franks 183 (5)
Riverton settlement/whaling station New Zealand colonization 283 (4), (5)
Rivière au Vase North America (USA) cultural groups 122 (5)
Rivoli var. Rivoli Veronese battle Italy Napoleon 200–201 (1)
Rivoli Veronese see Rivoli
Riyadh Ar. Ar Riyāḍ Southwest Asia (Saudi Arabia) economy 234 (1) exploration 219 (4) 20th-century politics 233 (4), 235 (5)
Rizhskiy Zaliv see Riga, Gulf of
Roanoke river North America empire and revolution 127 (3)
Roazon see Rennes
Roccastrada Italy economy 190 (1)
Roc de Sers archaeological site France prehistoric culture 17 (3)
Rochdale Canal canal British Isles economy 204 (2)
Rochefort France early modern states 197 (5)
Rock Eagle North America (USA) cultural groups 122 (5)
Rockhampton Australia colonization 282 (1), 283 (3)
Rocks Point sealing station New Zealand colonization 283 (4)
Rocky Mountains mountain range North America colonization 125 (4), 126 (1) early agriculture 120 (1), 20–21 (2) exploration 118 (1), 119 (2), (3), 286 (1), 287 (2) prehistoric culture 16 (1) the growth of the US 129 (2)
Ródhos see Rhodes
Rodi see Rhodes
Ródos see Rhodes
Rodrigues var. Rodriquez island Indian Ocean the modern world 110–111
Rodriquez see Rodrigues
Roebourne Australia colonization 279 (2)
Roebuck North America (USA) cultural groups 122 (5)
Rohilkhand region/state South Asia colonialism 247 (3), 248 (1) empire and revolution 249 (3)
Rojadi South Asia (India) first civilizations 24 (2)
Roma var. Rome. Italy ancient trade 44 (2)
Romagna state Italy empire and revolution 202 (3)
Romanelli Southern Europe (Italy)
Roman Empire state Europe/Africa ancient Persia 225 (6) ancient Rome 181 (4), 224 (2), 225 (5) ancient trade 44–45 (1) early cultures 161 (3), (4) early trade 225 (3) great migrations 53 (2) world religions 226 (1), 49 (4)
Romania Bul. Rumŭniya, Ger. Rumänien, Hung. Románia, Rom. România, SCr. Rumunjska, Ukr. Rumuniya; prev. Roumania, Rumania, Rominia state/vassal state Southeast Europe early 20th century 206 (1) economy 205 (4) inter-war 209 (3), (5) medieval states 187 (5) Ottomans 202 (4), 232–233 (1) post-war economy 213 (5), 214 (1), (2), 215 (3) post-war politics 212 (3) Soviet Union 208 (2), 213 (4) the modern world 112 (2) WWI 207 (4), (6), 208 (1) WWII 104 (2), 210 (1), 211 (2), (3), (4) Cold War 108 (3), 109 (1)
Rome var. Roma. Italy ancient Rome 179 (3), (5), 180–181 (1), 181 (3), (4), 182 (1), 225 (5) ancient trade 44–45 (1) crusades 186 (1), 64–65 (2), 65 (1) early cultures 161 (2) early Islam 56–57 (1), 57 (2) early modern states 193 (4), 194 (1) early states 178 (1), (2) early systems 32 (1), 33 (2), (3) economy 190 (1), 205 (4) empire and revolution 202 (1), (3) European expansion 84–85 (1) exploration 172 (1) first religions 36 (1), 37 (3) Franks 184 (2) great migrations 52–53 (1) inter-war 209 (5), 227 (4) medieval states 182 (2), 183 (4), 184 (1), 185 (3), (5), 188 (1) medieval voyages 60–61 (1) Napoleon 200–201 (1), 201 (2), (3) Ottomans 195 (4) post-war politics 212 (3) Reformation 194 (2) world religions 48 (1), 49 (4) WWII 210 (1), 211 (2), (4) Cold War 108 (3) see also Roma
Rome state Italy the world in 250 BCE 38–39
Rome, Duchy of state Italy medieval states 183 (4)
Rominia see Romania
Roncesvalles battle Iberian Peninsula (Spain) Franks 184 (2)
Rong state East Asia first cities 259 (3)
Rong people East Asia first cities 259 (4)
Ronne Ice Shelf ice feature Antarctica Antarctic Exploration 287 (3)
Roonka Australia exploration 280 (1)
Roque River battle North America (USA) the growth of the US 129 (2)
Rorke's Drift battle Southern Africa (South Africa) European imperialism 96 (2)
Rosario South America (Argentina) empire and revolution 151 (3) environment 153 (4)
Rosario var. Rosario de Tezopaco mine/settlement Central America (Mexico) colonization 125 (4) Mexican Revolution 133 (3)
Rosario de Tezopaco see Rosario
Rosenkrans burial mound North America (USA) first civilizations 121 (4)
Roskilde Scandinavia (Denmark) early modern states 197 (3) medieval states 185 (3)
Ross New Zealand colonization 283 (5)
Ross Ice Shelf ice feature Antarctica Antarctic Exploration 287 (3)
Rossiyskaya Federatsiya see Russia, Russian Empire, Russian Federation, Soviet Union, Union of Socialist Republics
Ross Sea sea Antarctica Antarctic Exploration 287 (3)
Rostock Central Europe (Germany) economy 190 (1), 205 (4) empire and revolution 202 (2) medieval states 189 (3)
Rostov var. Rostov-on-Don Eastern Europe (Russian Federation) biological diffusion 72–73 (1) medieval states 185 (3) Soviet Union 208 (2), 214–215 (4) WWI 207 (4) WWII 210 (1), 211 (4)
Rostov-on-Don see Rostov
Rotomagus var. Ratomagus; mod Rouen Christian archbishopric/settlement France ancient Rome 180–181 (1) world religions 48 (1) see also Rouen
Rotterdam air raid Low Countries WWII 210 (1)
Rottweil Central Europe (Germany) early modern states 193 (5)
Rouad see Aradus
Rouen anc. Ratomagus, Rotomagus France crusades 65 (1) early modern states 197 (5) economy 190 (1) empire and revolution 199 (4) Franks 184 (2) medieval states 185 (3), 186 (2), 187 (4), 192 (1), (2) medieval voyages 60–61 (1) Napoleon 200–201 (1), 201 (2) WWI 206 (2), (3) see also Rotomagus
Roumania see Romania
Roussillon region/state France/Iberian Peninsula early modern states 197 (5) medieval states 192 (2)
Rovereto see Rovreit
Rovine battle Southeast Europe (Romania) medieval states 189 (4)
Rovreit It. Rovereto Italy WWI 207 (5)
Rovuma see Ruvuma
Roxolani people Southeast Europe ancient Rome 180–181 (1)
Royal Military Canal canal British Isles economy 204 (1)
Royal Palace building France economy 191 (2)
Royal Prussia region Central Europe early modern states 193 (4), 195 (3)
Rozwi state Southern Africa slave trade 165 (4) trade 164 (1)
Ruanda see Rwanda
Ruanda-Urundi mod. Burundi, Rwanda state East Africa WWII 104 (1)
Ruanruan var. Avars people East Asia medieval states 261 (4), (6) see also Avars
Ruanruan, Empire of the var. Juan-juan state East Asia the world in 500 CE 50–51
Ruapuke Island whaling station New Zealand colonization 283 (4)
Rubuga East Africa (Tanzania) exploration 157 (4)
Rudolf, Lake var. Lake Turkana lake East Africa early agriculture 158 (1) economy 163 (2) exploration 157 (4), (5) first humans 12 (1) Islam 163 (1) slave trade 165 (4) trade 165 (3)
Rufiji river East Africa exploration 157 (5)
Ruhr region Central Europe economy 205 (4) WWI 208 (1)
Rum state Southwest Asia economy 190 (1)
Rumania see Romania

Rumänien *see* Romania
Rummelsburger See *lake* Central Europe post-war politics 212 (2)
Rum, Seljuks of *state* Southwest Asia crusades 228 (2) Mongols 229 (3) Timur 229 (4)
Rumŭniya *see* Romania
Rumunjska *see* Romania
Runan *province* East Asia first states 260 (1)
Runzhou *var.* Janchou East Asia (China) medieval states 262–263 (1)
Ruo *see* Yanying
Rupar *archaeological site* South Asia (India) first cities 240 (2)
Rupella *see* La Rochelle
Rupert House North America (Canada) colonization 126 (1)
Rupert's Land *var.* Hudson Bay Company *state* North America colonization 126 (1) *see also* Hudson Bay Company
Rusaddir North Africa (Spain) ancient Rome 179 (3), 180–181 (1) early cultures 161 (2)
Ruschuk *mod.* Ruse Southeast Europe (Romania) WWI 207 (6)
Ruse *see* Ruschuk
Rusellae Italy early states 178 (2)
Ruseştii-Noui *archaeological site* Southeast Europe (Romania) Copper Age 174 (2)
Rush Creek *battle* North America (USA) the growth of the US 129 (2)
Ruspina *see* Monastir
Russadir *see* Melilla, Rusaddir
Russell New Zealand colonization 283 (5)
Russell *see* Kororareka
Russia *region/state* Eastern Europe/Siberia Chinese revolution 271 (5) crusades 65 (1) early modern states 195 (3) empire and revolution 202 (2), 88 (1) exploration 257 (3), 286 (1), 287 (2) imperialism 270 (2) Ottomans 195 (4) Reformation 194 (2) Russo-Japanese War 270 (4) the growth of the US 129 (2), 132 (1), 133 (4) *see also* Russian Empire, Russian Federation, Russian Principalities
Russian America *see* Alaska
Russian Empire *state* Eastern Europe/Southwest Asia colonialism 269 (3), (4) early 20th century 206 (1) economy 205 (4) empire and revolution 198 (2), 202 (1), 88–89 (2) European expansion 84–85 (1) European imperialism 97 (4) global immigration 100 (1), 101 (2) imperial global economy 92 (1) Napoleon 200–201 (1), 201 (3) Ottomans 202 (4), 231 (3), 232–233 (1) WWI 207 (4), (6), 233 (2) *see also* Russia, Russian Federation, Russian Principalities
Russian Federation *var.* Russia; *prev.* Russian Empire, Soviet Union, Union of Soviet Republics; *Latv.* Krievija, *Rus.* Rossiyskaya Federatsiya *state* Eastern Europe/Southwest Asia economy 190 (1) historical geography 275 (5) Islam 235 (4) post-war economy 214 (1), (2), 275 (3) post-war politics 274 (2) Soviet Union 214–215 (4) the modern world 112 (2), 113 (4) *see also* Russia, Russian Empire, Soviet Union, Union of Soviet Republics
Russian Principalities *state* Eastern Europe crusades 186 (1), 64–65 (2) medieval states 187 (3) Mongols 68–69 (1) *see also* Russia, Russian Empire, Russian Federation
Russian steppes *region* Siberia first cities 28–29 (1)
Rustenburg Southern Africa (South Africa) colonization 166 (2)
Rutanzige, Lake *see* Edward *Lake*
Ruvuma *Port.* Rovuma *river* East Africa exploration 157 (4) trade 164 (1)
Rwanda *prev.* Ruanda *state* Central Africa colonization 167 (4) decolonization 168 (1) economy 168 (2), (3) the modern world 112 (1) trade 167 (1) Cold War 109 (1) *see also* Ruanda-Urundi
Ryazan' Eastern Europe (Russian Federation) Mongols 68–69 (1) Soviet Union 214–215 (4)
Ryazan' *state* Eastern Europe the world in 1400 70–71 the world in 1500 74–75
Ryojun *see* Port Arthur
Ryssel *see* Lille
Ryukyu Islands *prev.* Loochoo Islands; *Jap.* Nansei-shotō *island group* East Asia colonialism 269 (4) imperialism 270 (2) trade 267 (3) WWII 272 (1), 273 (2)
Ryzan *state* Russia Islam 163 (1)

S

Saami Hunter-Gatherers *people* Eastern Europe the world in 2500 BCE 22–23
Saar *region* Central Europe post-war politics 212 (1) WWI 208 (1)
Saare *see* Ösel
Saaremaa *see* Ösel
Saarlouis Central Europe (Germany) early modern states 197 (5)
Saba East Africa (Eritrea) early cultures 161 (4)
Saba *var.* Sheba *state* East Africa/Southwest Asia the world in 500 BCE 34–35
Šabac Southeast Europe (Serbia) WWI 207 (6)
Sabah *prev.* British North Borneo, North Borneo *region* Maritime Southeast Asia post-war economy 275 (3) *see also* British North Borneo
Sabarmati *river* South Asia first cities 240 (2) Mughal Empire 246 (1)
Sabatinus, Lacus *lake* Italy early states 178 (1)
Sabe *state* West Africa trade 164 (2)
Sabine North America (USA) US Civil War 131 (6), (7)
Sabini *people* Italy early states 178 (1), (2)
Sabotiers *battle* France Reformation 196 (2)
Sabrata North Africa (Libya) ancient Rome 180–181 (1) first civilizations 177 (1)
Saccopastore *archaeological site* Italy first humans 13 (2)
Sachsen *see* Saxony
Sachsenhausen *concentration camp* Central Europe WWII 211 (3)
Sacramento North America (USA) the growth of the US 129 (2)
Sá da Bandeira *see* Lubango
Sado *var.* Sadoga-shima *island* Japan Communism 273 (3) early modern states 265 (5), 267 (4) economy 270 (1) medieval states 264 (1), (2), 265 (3), (4)
Sadoga-shima *see* Sado
Sadowa *battle* Central Europe (Czech Republic) empire and revolution 202 (2)
Sadras South Asia (India) colonialism 247 (3)
Saena Julia *see* Siena, Sena Iulia
Safad *see* Safed
Safavid Empire *state* Southwest Asia Islam 163 (1) medieval Persia 231 (4) Mughal Empire 246 (1) Ottomans 231 (3)
Safed *Ar.* Safad, *Heb.* Zefat Southwest Asia (Israel) crusades 65 (1)
Safety Harbor North America (USA) cultural groups 122 (5)
Saffarids *dynasty* Southwest Asia early Islam 57 (2) Islam 227 (4)
Safi North Africa (Morocco) exploration 157 (4)
Safinaya *oil field* Southwest Asia economy 234 (1)
Saga *prefecture* Japan economy 270 (1)
Sagartia *province* Southwest Asia ancient Persia 223 (4)
Sagrajas Iberian Peninsula (Portugal) Islam 192 (3)
Sagua la Grande *military base* West Indies (Cuba) Cold War 108 (2)
Sagunto *see* Saguntum
Saguntum *var.* Sagunto Iberian Peninsula (Spain) ancient Rome 179 (3), 180–181 (1)
Sahagún Iberian Peninsula (Spain) Napoleon 200–201 (1)
Sahajati South Asia (India) world religions 242 (3)
Sahara *desert* North Africa ancient Persia 223 (4) ancient trade 44–45 (1) biological diffusion 72–73 (1), 73 (3) Bronze Age 175 (3) early agriculture 158 (1), 20–21 (2) early cultures 160 (1), 161 (2), (3), (4), (5) early Islam 56–57 (1), 57 (2) economy 163 (2) European expansion 84–85 (1) European imperialism 96 (1) exploration 156 (1), (2), (3), 157 (4) first humans 12 (1), 13 (2) imperial global economy 92 (1) Islam 163 (1) prehistoric culture 16 (1) slave trade 165 (4) trade 164 (2)
Sahara el Gharbîya *see* Western Desert
Saharan Peoples *people* Central Africa/West Africa the world in 500 BCE 34–35 the world in 250 BCE 38–39 the world in 1 CE 42–43 the world in 250 CE 46–47 the world in 500 CE 50–51 the world in 750 CE 54–55 the world in 1000 58–59 the world in 1200 62–63
Sahel *physical region* West Africa ancient trade 44–45 (1) slave trade 165 (4) trade 164 (2)
Sahul *var.* Sahul Shelf *physical region* Australia exploration 276–277 (1) historical geography 254–255 (1)
Sahul Shelf *see* Sahul
Saidpur *var.* Syedpur South Asia (Bangladesh) post-war politics 252 (3)
Saigon *var.* Hô Chi Minh, Ho Chi Minh City, Mainland Southeast Asia (Vietnam) colonialism 247 (4), 248 (1), 269 (4) European imperialism 97 (3) exploration 239 (1) trade 230 (2) US superpower 138 (1) WWII 251 (3) post-war politics 251 (5) *see also* Ho Chi Minh City
Saigon-Cholon *military base* Mainland Southeast Asia (Vietnam) WWII 272 (1), 273 (2)
Sai Hun *see* Jaxartes, Syr Darya
Saikaido *region* Japan medieval states 265 (3)
St Agostin *see* St Augustine, San Agostin, San Austin
St Augustine *prev.* San Agostin, St Agostin, San Agustín North America (USA) colonization 126 (1) European expansion 85 (2) US Civil War 131 (6) *see also* San Agostín, San Agustín
Saint Augustine North America (USA) colonization 126 (1)
St Botolph's Town *see* Boston
St. Catherine, Cape *headland* Central Africa exploration 156 (3)
St. Césaire *archaeological site* France first humans 13 (2)
Saint Christopher-Nevis *see* St. Kitts and Nevis
St Clairís Defeat *battle* North America (USA) the growth of the US 129 (2)
St. Denis France economy 190 (1)
Saint Domingue *colonial possession* West Indies empire and revolution 89 (3) *state* West Indies colonization 126 (1)
St Francis North America (USA) empire and revolution 127 (2)
St Gall Central Europe (Switzerland) Franks 184 (2)
St. Gallen Central Europe (Switzerland) early modern states 193 (5)
St. Gilles France crusades 186 (1) economy 190 (1)
St Gotthard *battle* Southeast Europe (Austria) Ottomans 197 (4)
St. Gotthard Pass *pass* Central Europe economy 190 (1)
Saint Helena *colonial possession/island* Atlantic Ocean exploration 156 (3)
St. Helena Bay *bay* Southern Africa exploration 156 (3)
St Jago de Vega West Indies (Jamaica) colonization 125 (4)
St James River *burial mound* North America (USA) first civilizations 121 (4)
Saint-Jean-d'Acre *see* Acco, Acre
St Jean, Ile *see* Prince Edward Island
St John, Isle *see* Prince Edward Island
St John's North America (Canada) the growth of the US 132 (1)
St. Kitts and Nevis *var.* Saint Christopher-Nevis *state* North America the modern world 112 (1) US economy 136 (2) US politics 139 (4)
St. Lawrence *river* North America colonization 126 (1) early agriculture 20–21 (2) empire and revolution 127 (2), (3) European expansion 80–81 (1) exploration 118 (1), 119 (2) first religions 36 (1) medieval voyages 60–61 (1) the growth of the US 129 (2)
St. Lawrence, Gulf of *gulf* North America colonization 126 (1) empire and revolution 127 (2) the growth of the US 129 (2)
Saint Lawrence Island *island* North America exploration 287 (2)
Saint Lawrence Island Inuit *people* North America cultural groups 123 (3)
Saint-Louis *settlement/island* West Africa (Senegal) empire and revolution 88 (1) European expansion 84–85 (1) slave trade 165 (4)
St Louis North America (USA) empire and revolution 127 (3) exploration 119 (2), (3) the growth of the US 129 (2), 132 (1) US Civil War 130 (5), 131 (6), (7) US economy 134 (1), (3), 136 (2) US politics 135 (6) Cold War 108 (2)
St Lucia *island/state* West Indies empire and revolution 88 (1) European expansion 84–85 (1) US economy 136 (2) US politics 139 (4) WWII 104 (2) Cold War 108 (2)
St-Malo France early modern states 197 (5)
St. Marks *battle* North America (USA) the growth of the US 129 (2)
St Martin *Dut.* Sint Maarten *island* West Indies the world in 1700 82–83 the world in 1800 86–87 the world in 1850 90–91 the world in 1900 94–95 the world in 1925 98–99 the world in 1950 102–103
St. Mary, Cape *var.* Cape Lobo *headland* West Africa exploration 156 (3)
St Michael North America (USA) imperial global economy 93 (3)
St Mihiel France WWI 206 (2), (3)
St Nazaire France WWII 104 (2)
St. Omer France economy 190 (1)
St. Paul North America (USA) the growth of the US 129 (2)
St. Peter, Patrimony of *state* Italy Franks 184 (2)
St Petersburg *prev.* Leningrad, Petrograd; *Russ.* Sankt-Peterburg, *Fin.* Pietari; Eastern Europe (Russian Federation) colonialism 269 (3) colonization 126 (1) early modern states 197 (3) economy 205 (4) empire and revolution 202 (1) exploration 257 (2) global immigration 100 (1) Napoleon 200–201 (1) Soviet Union 214–215 (4) WWI 207 (4) *see also* Leningrad, Petrograd
St. Pierre and Miquelon *colonial possession/island group* North America empire and revolution 88 (1) the growth of the US 129 (2)
St-Pierre et Miquelon, Îles *see* St Pierre and Miquelon
St Pol France WWI 206 (2), (3)
St Quentin France WWI 206 (2), (3)
Saint Thomas *see* São Tomé
St. Thomé South Asia (India) colonialism 247 (3)
St. Valéry France medieval states 186 (2)
St Vincent *island* West Indies empire and revolution 88 (1) European expansion 84–85 (1)
Saint Vincent *see* São Vicente
St. Vincent and the Grenadines *state* North America US economy 136 (2) US politics 139 (4)
Saipan *island/military base* Pacific Ocean WWII 104 (2), 251 (3), 272 (1), 273 (2)
Sais Egypt first cities 28–29 (1)
Saishū *see* Cheju-do, Quelpart Island
Saitama *prefecture* Japan economy 270 (1)
Saitobaru *state* Japan medieval states 264 (1)
Sai Yok *archaeological site* Mainland Southeast Asia (Thailand) Bronze Age 240 (3)
Saka *state* Central Asia first empires 241 (5)
Sak'art'velo *see* Georgia
Sakata Japan economy 270 (1)
Sakchu *region* East Asia medieval states 264 (2)
Saketa South Asia (India) world religions 242 (3)
Sakhalin *island* East Asia colonialism 269 (3), (4) exploration 257 (2) first states 260 (1) imperialism 270 (2) medieval states 263 (6) WWII 272 (1), 273 (2)
Sakiz-Adasi *see* Chios
Salado *river* South America colonization 148 (2) early cultures 146 (1) Incas 147 (3) politics 152 (1)
Saladoid *people* South America early cultures 145 (2)
Salaga West Africa (Ghana) Islam 163 (1)
Salala Southwest Asia (Oman) 20th-century politics 233 (4) exploration 219 (4)
Salamanca Iberian Peninsula (Spain) inter-war 209 (4) Islam 192 (3) medieval states 187 (3) Napoleon 200–201 (1)
Salamantica *mod.* Salamanca Iberian Peninsula (Spain) ancient Rome 180–181 (1) *see also* Salamanca
Salamaua *air raid* New Guinea (Papua New Guinea) WWII 272 (1)
Salamis Southwest Asia (Cyprus) ancient Rome 180–181 (1) first civilizations 177 (1) Hellenistic world 40–41 (1) world religions 48 (1)
Salamis *battle* Greece ancient Persia 223 (4)
Salang *see* Phuket
Salaria vetus, Via *road* Italy ancient Rome 181 (2) early states 178 (1), ancient Rome 181 (2),
Saldae *mod.* Bougie North Africa (Algeria) ancient Rome 179 (3) *see also* Bougie
Salduba *see* Saragossa, Zaragoza
Salekhard *see* Obdorsk
Salem South Asia (India) colonialism 247 (3)
Salem North America (USA) the growth of the US 129 (2)
Salerno Italy Franks 184 (2) medieval states 183 (4), 187 (3)
Salerno, Principality of *state* Italy medieval states 185 (3)
Salford British Isles (United Kingdom) economy 204 (2)
Salghurids *dynasty* Southwest Asia Mongols 68–69 (1)
Salian Franks *people* France Franks 183 (5)
Salina Cruz Central America (Mexico) Mexican Revolution 133 (3)
Salinas la Blanca Central America (Mexico) first civilizations 123 (2)
Salisbury Southern Africa (Zimbabwe) colonization 167 (4)
Salisbury *var.* New Sarum British Isles (United Kingdom) economy 190 (1)
Sallentini *people* Italy early states 178 (1)
Salmon *archaeological site* North America (USA) cultural groups 123 (4)
Salonae *mod.* Solin *settlement* Southeast Europe (Croatia) ancient Rome 180–181 (1), 181 (3) early cultures 161 (2) world religions 48 (1)
Salonica *var.* Salonika; *mod.* Thessaloníki; *prev.* Thessalonica; *SCr.* Solun, *Turk.* Selânik Greece economy 198 (1) empire and revolution 202 (1) medieval states 187 (5), 189 (4) Napoleon 200–201 (1) Ottomans 195 (4), 230 (1) Reformation 194 (2) WWI 207 (6) *see also* Thessalonica
Salonica *state/region* Greece medieval states 187 (5) WWI 207 (6) WWII 211 (2)
Salonika *see* Salonica, Thessalonica
Salsette Island South Asia (India) colonialism 247 (3)
Salta South America (Argentina) empire and revolution 150 (1), 151 (3) politics 151 (4) empire and revolution 88–89 (2)
Salţanat 'Umān *see* Oman
Saltillo Central America (Mexico) Mexican Revolution 133 (3)
Salt Lake City North America (USA) the growth of the US 129 (2), 132 (1) US economy 136 (2)
Salt River *river* North America cultural groups 123 (4)
Saluum *state* West Africa the world in 1400 70–71 trade 163 (6)
Salva *state* South Asia first empires 241 (5)
Salvador *prev.* Bahia, São Salvador South America (Brazil) environment 153 (4) European expansion 84–85 (1) politics 152 (1) *see also* Bahia
Salvador *mod.* El Salvador Central America, *state* the world in 1900 94–95 WWII 104 (1) *see also* El Salvador
Salvador *see* Bahia
Salween *Bur.* Thanlwin, *Chin.* Nu Chiang, Nu Jiang *river* Mainland Southeast Asia ancient India 241 (6) Bronze Age 240 (3) colonialism 247 (4) early medieval states 245 (5), (6) first states 260 (1) Mongols 68–69 (1) world religions 243 (5)
Salzburg *anc.* Juvavum Central Europe (Austria) early modern states 193 (4) Franks 184 (2) medieval states 185 (3), 188 (1), 189 (4) post-war politics 212 (1) Reformation 196 (1)
Salzkammergut *mine* Central Europe Bronze Age 175 (3)
Sama *state* West Africa the world in 1200 62–63
Samana South Asia (India) colonialism 247 (3)
Samanids *dynasty* Central Asia/Southwest Asia early Islam 57 (2) Islam 227 (4), (5)
Samapa South Asia (India) first empires 241 (4)
Samar *island* Maritime Southeast Asia exploration 278 (1)
Samara *prev.* Kuybyshev Eastern Europe (Russian Federation) colonialism 269 (3) Soviet Union 208 (2), 214–215 (4)
Samara Egypt ancient Egypt 159 (2)
Samarang *see* Semarang
Samaria Southwest Asia (Israel) Hellenistic world 40–41 (1)
Samaria *province* Southwest Asia ancient Rome 225 (4)
Samarkand *anc.* Maracanda; *Uzb.* Samarqand Central Asia (Uzbekistan) trade 72–73 (1) colonialism 269 (3) crusades 65 (1) early Islam 56–57 (1), 57 (2) exploration 218 (2), 256 (1) Islam 226 (2), 227 (4), (5) medieval Persia 231 (4) medieval states 261 (6) Mongols 229 (3), 68–69 (1) Ottomans 232–233 (1) Soviet Union 214–215 (4) Timur 229 (4) trade 267 (3) world religions 49 (3), (4) *see also* Maracanda
Samarkand *province* Central Asia medieval states 269 (4)
Samarobriva *see* Amiens
Samarqand *see* Maracanda, Samarkand
Samarra Southwest Asia (Iraq) early Islam 56–57 (1), 57 (2), (3) Islam 227 (4) WWI 233 (2)
Sambas Maritime Southeast Asia (Indonesia) colonialism 247 (4)
Samhar Southwest Asia (Oman) early cultures 161 (3), (5) early trade 225 (3)
Samkashya South Asia (India) first religions 36 (2) world religions 242 (3)
Sam Neua *mod.* Xam Nua *region* Mainland Southeast Asia post-war politics 251 (5)
Samnites *people* Italy early states 178 (1), (2)
Samoa *state/island group* Pacific Ocean the modern world 110–111, early cultures 280–281 (3) exploration 278 (1) medieval voyages 60 (2)
Sāmoa-i-Sisifo *see* Western Samoa
Samori *state* West Africa colonization 167 (4)
Samos *prev.* Limín Vathéos Greece first civilizations 177 (1)
Samos *state* Greece ancient Greece 177 (2)
Samosata *mod.* Samsat *settlement* Southwest Asia (Turkey) ancient Rome 180–181 (1) first cities 220 (2)
Samothrace *island/state* Greece ancient Greece 177 (2), 179 (4)
Samoyeds *people* Eastern Europe/Siberia trade 267 (3)
Samsat *see* Samosata
Samsun *see* Amisus
Samun Dukiya *archaeological site* West Africa (Nigeria) early cultures 160 (1)
San *river* Eastern Europe WWI 207 (4)
Sana *var.* Şan'ā', San'a Southwest Asia (Yemen) ancient trade 44–45 (1) early Islam 56–57 (1) early trade 225 (3) exploration 156 (3) medieval voyages 61 (3) 20th-century politics 233 (4)
San Agostín *fort* North America (USA) colonization 125 (4)
San Agustín North America (USA) European expansion 85 (2) exploration 119 (2)
San Agustín *state* South America the world in 1 CE 42–43 the world in 250 CE 46–47
San Ambrosio *island* South America the world in 1950 102–103 the modern world 110–111
Sanandita *oil field* South America politics 152 (2)
San Antonio North America (USA) Cold War 108 (2) Mexican Revolution 133 (3) the growth of the US 129 (2)
San Antonio *fort* North America (USA) colonization 125 (4)
San Carlos de Ancud *mod.* Ancud South America (Chile) colonization 148 (2)
San Casciano Italy medieval states 188 (1)
Sanchi *Buddhist centre/settlement* South Asia (India) early religions 48 (2) world religions 242 (3)
San Cristóbal South America (Venezuela) empire and revolution 150 (1), (2) politics 152 (1)
San Cristóbal *var.* San Cristóbal de la Barranca Central America (Mexico) Mexican Revolution 133 (3)
San Cristóbal *var.* Makira *island* Pacific Ocean exploration 278 (1)
San Cristóbal *military base* West Indies (Cuba) Cold War 108 (2)
San Cristóbal de Havana West Indies (Cuba) colonization 125 (4)
San Cristóbal de la Barranca *see* San Cristóbal
Sancti Spíritus West Indies (Cuba) European expansion 85 (2)
Sanctuary of Ammon *var.* Siwa Oasis Egypt Hellenistic world 40–41 (1)
Sand Creek *battle* North America (USA) the growth of the US 129 (2)
San Diego North America (USA) exploration 119 (2), (3) the growth of the US 129 (2) US economy 136 (2)
Sandomierz Russ. Sandomir Central Europe (Poland) medieval states 189 (3) Mongols 68–69 (1)
Sandomir *see* Sandomierz
Sandu'ao *var.* Santuao East Asia (China) colonialism 269 (4)
Sandwich Islands *see* Hawaii, Hawaiian Islands
Sandy Creek *archaeological site* Australia prehistoric culture 17 (2)
Sandy Hill *burial mound* North America (USA) first civilizations 121 (4)
San Felice Circco *see* Circei
San Felipe Central America (Mexico) first civilizations 123 (2)
San Félix, Isla *island* Pacific Ocean the modern world 110–111 the world in 1950 102–103
San Fernando *see* San Fernando de Apure
San Fernando de Apure *var.* San Fernando South America (Venezuela) empire and revolution 150 (1), (2)
San Francisco *prev.* San Francisco de Asís North America (USA) exploration 119 (2), (3) global immigration 100 (1), 101 (3) imperial global economy 92 (1) the growth of the US 129 (2), 132 (1) US economy 134 (1), (3), 136 (2)
San Francisco de Asís *see* San Francisco
San Francisco de Macorís West Indies (Dominican Republic) empire and revolution 89 (3)
San Francisco de Selva *see* Copiapó
Sanga *archaeological site* Central Africa (Congo (Zaire)) early cultures 160 (1)
Sangamas *dynasty* South Asia early medieval states 244–245 (3)
Sangela South Asia (India) Hellenistic world 40–41 (1)
Sangiran *archaeological site* Maritime Southeast Asia (Indonesia) first humans 13 (2)
Sangju *region* East Asia medieval states 264 (2)
San Ignacio de Ostimuri *mine* Central America (Mexico) colonization 125 (4)
Sanindo *region* Japan medieval states 265 (3)
San Isidoro *archaeological site* South America (Ecuador) the world in 5000 BCE 18–19
San Isidro Piedra Parada Central America (Guatemala) first civilizations 121 (2)
Sanjayani South Asia (India) world religions 243 (4)
San Jerónimo Central America (Mexico) first civilizations 121 (2)
San Jorge, Golfo de *var.* Gulf of San Jorge *gulf* South America colonization 148 (2)
San Jorge, Gulf of *see* San Jorge, Golfo de
San Jose North America (USA) 136 (3)
San José Central America (Mexico) first civilizations 122 (2)
San José Central America (Costa Rica) the growth of the US 129 (2)
San José de Cúcuta *see* Cúcuta
San José Mogote Central America (Mexico) first civilizations 121 (2)
San Juan West Indies (Puerto Rico) Cold War 108 (2) colonization 125 (4), 126 (1) US economy 136 (2) WWII 104 (2)
San Juan Central America (Mexico) exploration 118 (1)
San Juan Bautista *mod.* Villahermosa Central America (Mexico) colonization 125 (4)
San Juan Bautista Tuxtepec *see* Tuxtepec
San Juan del Río Central America (Mexico) first civilizations 122 (1)
San Juan de Ulna Central America (Mexico) colonization 125 (5)
San Juan de Vera *see* Corrientes
San Julián *see* Puerto San Julián
Sankt-Peterburg *see* Leningrad, St Petersburg, Petrograd
Sankt Veit am Flaum *see* Rijeka
Sanliqiao *archaeological site* East Asia (China) early agriculture 258 (2)
Sanli Urfa *see* Edessa
San Lorenzo Central America (Mexico) first civilizations 121 (2), (3), 122 (1) first religions 36 (1)
San Luis South America (Argentina) empire and revolution 151 (3)
San Luis Potosí *mine/settlement* Central America (Mexico) colonization 125 (4) the growth of the US 129 (2)
San Luis Potosí *state* Central America Mexican Revolution 133 (3) the growth of the US 129 (2)
San Marco Italy economy 191 (3)
San Marco, Canale di *canal* Italy economy 191 (3)
San Marcos de Arica *see* Arica
San Marino *state* Italy empire and revolution 202 (3)
San Martín Pajapán *archaeological site* Central America (Mexico) first civilizations 121 (3)
San Miguel South America (Peru) Incas 148 (1)
San Miguel Central America (Mexico) first civilizations 123 (2)
San Miguel Allende Central America (Mexico) first civilizations 122 (1)
San Miguel de Culiacán Central America (Mexico) colonization 125 (4)
San Miguel de Tucumán *var.* Tucumán South America (Argentina) environment 153 (4) exploration 143 (2) *see also* Tucumán
Sannār *see* Sennar
San Pedro *jesuit mission* North America (USA) colonization 125 (4)
San Pedro de Lagunas *jesuit mission* Central America (Mexico) colonization 125 (4)
San Salvador Central America (El Salvador) the growth of the US 129 (2)
San Salvador De Jujuy *see* Jujuy
San Sebastián Iberian Peninsula (Spain) inter-war 209 (4)
Sanshui East Asia (China) first states 260 (1)
Santa Ana de Coro *see* Coro
Santa Barbara North America (USA) exploration 119 (3)
Santa Catarina *region* South America colonization 149 (3)
Santa Clara North America (USA) 136 (3)
Santa Clara *jesuit mission* North America (USA) colonization 125 (4)
Santa Clara *military base* West Indies (Cuba) Cold War 108 (2)
Santa Croce Italy economy 191 (3)
Santa Cruz Central America (Mexico) first civilizations 121 (2)
Santa Cruz *mod.* Santa Cruz Cabrália South America (Brazil) colonization 149 (4) empire and revolution 151 (3)
Santa Cruz *var.* Santa Cruz de la Sierra South America (Bolivia) empire and revolution 151 (3) economy 153 (3) narcotics 153 (5)
Santa Cruz Cabrália, Santa Cruz de la Sierra *see* Santa Cruz
Santa Cruz Islands *island group* Pacific Ocean early cultures 280–281 (3) medieval voyages 60 (2) the world in 1900 94–95 WWII 272 (1), 273 (2)
Santa Cruz Valley *region* North America US economy 136 (3)
Santa Elena *fort* North America (USA) colonization 125 (4)
Santa Fe South America (Argentina) environment 153 (4) exploration 143 (2), (3)
Santa Fe North America (USA) colonization 125 (4), 126 (1) exploration 118 (1), 119 (2), (3) the growth of the US 129 (2)
Santa Fé, Audiencia of *region* South America colonization 148 (2)
Santa Fé de Bogotá *mod.* Bogotá South America (Colombia) colonization 148 (2) exploration 142 (1), 143 (2) Incas 148 (1) *see also* Bogotá
Santa Fe Trail *wagon train route* North America the growth of the US 129 (2)
Santa Lucia *fort* North America (USA) colonization 125 (4)
Santa Maria de Belém *see* Belém do Pará
Santa Maria del Buen Aire *see* Buenos Aires
Santa Marta South America (Colombia) colonization 148 (2) empire and revolution 150 (1), (2), 151 (3) exploration 142 (1) Incas 148 (1)
Santa Monica North America (USA)
Santana de Riacho *archaeological site* South America (Brazil) early cultures 145 (2)
Santander Iberian Peninsula (Spain) economy 205 (4) inter-war 209 (4)
Santarém Iberian Peninsula (Portugal) Islam 192 (3)
Santarém South America (Brazil) economy 153 (3) empire and revolution 151 (3)
Santarém *state* South America the world in 1000 58–59 the world in 1200 62–63 the world in 1400 70–71
Santarém *see* Tapajoso
Santa Rita Central America (Mexico) first civilizations 122 (1), 123 (2)
Santa Rosa Central America (Mexico) first civilizations 123 (2)
Santee *people* North America colonization 126 (1)
Santiago West Indies (Dominican Republic) empire and revolution 89 (3)
Santiago Central America (Cuba) exploration 119 (2), (3)
Santiago *var.* Gran Santiago South America (Chile) colonization 148 (2) empire and revolution 150 (1), 151 (3) environment 153 (4) exploration 142 (1), 143 (2), (3) imperial global economy 92 (1) Incas 147 (3) politics 152 (1)
Santiago *see* Santiago de Compostela
Santiago de Compostela *var.* Santiago, *Eng.* Compostella; *anc.* Campus Stellae Iberian Peninsula (Spain) crusades 186 (1) inter-war 209 (4) Islam 192 (3) medieval states 185 (3)
Santiago de Cuba *var.* Santiago West Indies (Cuba) colonization 125 (4) exploration 118 (1) US imperialism 133 (5) Cold War 108 (2) *see also* Santiago
Santiago de Guayaquil *see* Guayaquil
Santiago del Estero South America (Argentina) empire and revolution 151 (3)
Santiago de Saltillo Central America (Mexico) colonization 125 (4)
Santo *see* Espiritu Santo
Santo Domingo West Indies (Dominican Republic) colonization 125 (4), 126 (1) empire and revolution 89 (3) European expansion 85 (2) exploration 118 (1) the growth of the US 129 (2) Cold War 108 (2)
Santo Domingo *colonial possession* West Indies empire and revolution 89 (3)
Santo Domingo *jesuit mission* North America (USA) colonization 125 (4)
Santo Domingo Tehuantepec *see* Tehuantepec
Santorini *see* Thera
Santos South America (Brazil) colonization 149 (3) empire and revolution 151 (3)
Santuao *see* Sandu'ao
Sanussi *people* North Africa trade 167 (1)
San Vicente del Caguán South America (Colombia) narcotics 153 (5)
Sanyodo *region* Japan medieval states 265 (3)
Saochou *see* Shaozhou
São Francisco *river* South America colonization 149 (3), (4) early agriculture 20–21 (2) early cultures 144 (1), 145 (2) economy 153 (3) environment 153 (4) exploration 142 (1), 143 (2)
São Jorge da Mina *see* Elmina
São Jorge dos Ilhéos *see* Ilhéus
São José do Rio Negro *see* Manáos, Manaus
São Luís South America (Brazil) colonization 149 (3), (4)
São Luiz do Maranhão *var.* Maranhão, *mod.* São Luís South America (Brazil) empire and revolution 151 (3)
Saône *river* France Bronze Age 175 (3) Copper Age 174 (2) early agriculture 174 (1) great migrations 52–53 (1) WWI 206 (2), (3)
São Paulo South America (Brazil) colonization 149 (3), (4) empire and revolution 151 (3) environment 153 (4) European expansion 84–85 (1) exploration 143 (2) politics 152 (1)
São Paulo *region* South America colonization 149 (3)
São Paulo de Loanda *see* Luanda
São Pedro do Rio Grande do Sul *see* Rio Grande
São Salvador *see* Bahia, Salvador
São Sebastião de Rio de Janeiro *see* Rio de Janeiro
São Tomé *island* Atlantic Ocean European expansion 84–85 (1) European imperialism 96 (1) trade 164 (2)
Sao Tome and Principe *var.* São Tomé and Príncipe *island group/state* Atlantic Ocean the modern world 112 (1)
São Vicente *Eng.* Saint Vincent South America (Brazil) colonization 149 (3)
Saponi *people* North America colonization 125 (4)
Sapporo Japan economy 275 (4)
Saqqara Egypt the world in 2500 BCE 22–23 ancient Egypt 159 (3), (5) first religions 36 (1)
Saracens *people* North Africa medieval states 185 (3)
Saragossa *var.* Zaragoza; *anc.* Caesaraugusta, Salduba Iberian Peninsula (Spain) early Islam 56–57 (1) economy 190 (1) inter-war 209 (4) Islam 192 (3) Napoleon 200–201 (1) *see also* Caesaraugusta, Zaragoza
Saraguro South America (Equador) Incas 147 (3)
Sarai Khola *archaeological site* South Asia (Pakistan) first cities 240 (2)
Sarajevo Southeast Europe (Bosnia and Herzogovina) economy 205 (4) Ottomans 197 (4), 232–233 (1) post-war economy 215 (3) civil war 212 (3) WWI 207 (6) WWII 210 (1), 211 (4)
Sarandib *see* Ceylon, Lambakannas, Lanka, Simhala, Sri Lanka, Taprobane
Sarapion East Africa (Somalia) ancient trade 44–45 (1)
Saratoga North America (USA) empire and revolution 127 (3) empire and revolution 127 (3), 88–89 (2)
Saratov Eastern Europe (Russian Federation) Soviet Union 208 (2)
Sarawak Maritime Southeast Asia (Indonesia) European imperialism 97 (3)
Sarawak *colonial possession/region* Maritime Southeast Asia colonialism 269 (4) colonization 284–285 (1) decolonization 251 (4) European imperialism 97 (3) post-war economy 275 (3) WWII 251 (3), 272 (1), 273 (2)
Sarayu *mod.* Ghaghara, Gogra *river* South Asia first religions 36 (2) *see also* Ghaghara
Sardegna *see* Sardinia
Sardes *see* Sardis
Sardinia *state* Italy early modern states 193 (4), (5), 194 (1) economy 205 (4) empire and revolution 202 (1i), (3) Napoleon 200–201 (1), 201 (2) Reformation 194 (2)
Sardinia *island* Italy ancient Rome 179 (3), 180–181 (1), 181 (3), (4), 182 (1), 225 (5) Bronze Age 175 (3) crusades 186 (1), 64–65 (2) early cultures 161 (2) early Islam 56–57 (1) economy 190 (1) empire and revolution 88–89 (2) exploration 172 (1) first civilizations 177 (1) first religions 37 (3) historical geography 170–171 (1) inter-war 209 (5) Islam 184 (1), 226 (2), 227 (4) medieval states 182 (2), 183 (4), 185 (3), (5) Ottomans 231 (3) post-war economy 213 (5), 214 (1) post-war politics 212 (3) world religions 48 (1) WWII 210 (1), 211 (2), (4)
Sardinia et Corsica *province* France/Italy ancient Rome 180–181 (1)
Sardinians *people* Italy early states 178 (2)
Sardis *var.* Sardes Southwest Asia (Turkey) ancient Persia 223 (4) exploration 218 (1) first civilizations 222 (2) Hellenistic world 40–41 (1) world religions 226 (1)
Sarkel Eastern Europe (Russian Federation) medieval voyages 60–61 (1)
Sarkhej South Asia (India) colonialism 247 (3)
Sarmatia *region* Eastern Europe ancient trade 44 (2)
Sarmatians *people* Central Europe/Eastern Europe ancient Rome 180–181 (1), 181 (4) ancient trade 44–45 (1)
Sarmizegethusa *var.* Sarmizegetusa Central Europe (Romania) ancient Rome 180–181 (1) world religions 48 (1)
Sarmizegetusa *see* Sarmizegethusa
Sarnath *Buddhist centre/settlement* South Asia (India) exploration 256 (1) first religions 36 (2) world religions 49 (3)
Sarnath *see* Isipatana
Saschutkenne *people* North America cultural groups 123 (3)
Sasebo Japan Communism 273 (3) economy 270 (1) Sino-Japanese War 270 (3)
Saskatchewan *province* North America the growth of the US 129 (2), 132 (1) US economy 136 (2)
Saskatchewan *river* North America colonization 126 (1) the growth of the US 129 (2)
Saskatoon North America (Canada) the growth of the US 129 (2)
Sassanian Empire *var.* Iran, Persia, Persian Empire, Safavid Empire *state* Central Asia/Southwest Asia ancient Persia 225 (6) ancient Rome 181 (4), 182 (1) early cultures 161 (4), (5) early religions 48 (2) medieval states 182 (2) world religions 226 (1), 49 (4) *see also* Iran, Persia, Persian Empire, Safavid Empire
Satala *legion headquarters* Southwest Asia (Turkey) ancient Rome 180–181 (1)
Satara South Asia (India) Marathas 246 (2)
Satavahanas *dynasty* South Asia (Turkey) ancient trade 44–45 (1)
Satpura Range *mountain range* South Asia colonialism 247 (3), 248 (1) early medieval states 244 (1), 244–245 (3) first empires 241 (4) Mughal Empire 246 (1) world religions 243 (4)
Saturnia Italy early states 178 (1)
Saturn, Temple of *building* Italy ancient Rome 181 (2)
Sau *see* Sava
Saudi Arabia *Ar.* Al 'Arabīyah as Su'ūdīyah state Southwest Asia economy 234 (1) Islam 235 (4) the modern world 112 (1), 113 (3), (4) US economy 138 (2) US superpower 138 (1) WWII 105 (3), 210 (1), 211 (4) 20th century 234 (2) 20th-century politics 233 (3), (4), 235 (5) Cold War 109 (1)
Sauk *people* North America colonization 126 (1)
Saulteaux *people* North America cultural groups 123 (3)
Sault Ste Marie North America (Canada) the growth of the US 129 (2)
Saurimo *Port.* Henrique de Carvalho, Vila Henrique de Carvalho Southern Africa (Angola) Cold War 109 (5)
Sauty *var.* Assiout, Assiut, Asyut, Siut; *anc.* Lycopolis Egypt ancient Egypt 159 (2) *see also* Asyut
Sauvira *region/state* South Asia first empires 241 (5) world religions 242 (2)
Sava *Eng.* Save, *Ger.* Sau, *Hung.* Száva *river* Southeast Europe post-war economy 215 (3)
Savannah North America (USA) colonization 126 (1) empire and revolution 127 (3) imperial global economy 93 (5) the growth of the US 129 (2), 132 (1) US Civil War 131 (7) US society 137 (6)
Savannah *river* North America colonization 125 (4) US Civil War 131 (6)
Savanur *region* South Asia Marathas 246 (2)
Savaria Central Europe (Hungary) ancient Rome 180–181 (1)
Save *see* Sava
Savoia, Savoie *see* Savoy
Savoy *var.* Savoia, Savoie *region/state* France/Italy early modern states 194 (1), 197 (5) empire and revolution 199 (4), 202 (3) Reformation 194 (2), 196 (1), (2)
Savulus *state* South Asia Mughal Empire 246 (1)
Savu, Pulau *see* Savu
Savu Sea *Ind.* Laut Sawu *sea* Maritime Southeast Asia early medieval states 245 (6)
Sawakin *see* Suakin
Sawaris Egypt ancient Egypt 159 (3)
Sawu *see* Mersa Gawasis, Savu
Sawu, Laut *see* Savu Sea
Saxe *see* Saxony

Saxons *people* Central Europe ancient Rome *181* (4) Franks *183* (5), (6) great migrations *53* (2)
Saxony *region/state* Central Europe crusades *64–65* (2) economy *205* (4) empire and revolution *199* (3), *202* (1), (2) Franks *184* (2) medieval states *185* (3), *188* (1) Napoleon *200–201* (1) Reformation *194* (2), *196* (1), (2) the world in 1850 *90–91*
Say West Africa (Niger) colonization *167* (4) exploration *157* (4)
Şaydā, Sayida *see* Sidon
Sayil Central America (Mexico) first civilizations *123* (2)
Saylac *see* Zeila
Saylan *see* Ceylon, Lambakannas, Lanka, Simhala, Sri Lanka, Taprobane
Sayn *region* Central Europe empire and revolution *199* (3)
Sayultec *people* Central America colonization *125* (4)
Scalabis *see* Scallabis
Scallabis *var.* Scalabis Iberian Peninsula (Portugal) ancient Rome *180–181* (1)
Scandia *region* Scandinavia ancient trade *44* (2)
Scandinavia *region* Europe biological diffusion *72–73* (1) Bronze Age *175* (3) crusades *65* (1) early agriculture *174* (1), *20–21* (2) exploration *172* (1), *287* (2) first humans *13* (2) global immigration *100* (1) historical geography *170–171* (1) medieval states *185* (3) WWII *211* (3)
Scania *Swe.* Skåne *region* Scandinavia early modern states *197* (3)
Scapa Flow *sea waterway* British Isles WWII *104* (2)
Scarpanto *mod.* Karpathos *island* Greece medieval states *187* (5)
Scebeli *see* Shebeli
Schaffhausen *Fr.* Schaffhouse Central Europe (Switzerland) early modern states *193* (5)
Schaffhouse *see* Schaffhausen
Schelde *see* Scheldt
Scheldt *Dut.* Schelde, *Fr.* Escaut *river* Low Countries Bronze Age *175* (3) empire and revolution *202* (1i) great migrations *52–53* (1) WWI *206* (2), (3)
Schemnitz Central Europe (Hungary) economy *190* (1)
Schleswig *see* Slesvig
Schleswig-Holstein *state* Central Europe/Scandinavia empire and revolution *202* (1i), (2)
Schmalkalden Central Europe (Germany) Reformation *194* (2)
Schöneberg Central Europe (Germany) post-war politics *212* (2)
Schönefeld *airport* Central Europe (Germany) post-war politics *212* (2)
Schweiz *see* Helvetia, Helvetian Republic, Swiss Confederation, Switzerland
Schwiebus *region* Central Europe empire and revolution *199* (3)
Schwyz *region* Central Europe early modern states *193* (5)
Scilly, Isles of *island group* British Isles exploration *172* (1)
Scio *see* Chios
Scione *state* Greece ancient Greece *177* (2)
Scodra *mod.* Shkodër Southeast Europe (Albania) world religions *48* (1)
Scoglio del Tonno Italy Bronze Age *175* (3)
Scone British Isles (United Kingdom) medieval states *186* (2), *187* (4)
Scoresby Sound North America (Greenland) exploration *287* (2)
Scotland *anc.* Caledonia *state* British Isles crusades *186* (1), *64–65* (2) economy *190* (1) empire and revolution *202* (1) medieval states *185* (3), *186* (2), *187* (3), (4), *188* (1) medieval voyages *60–61* (1) Reformation *196* (2) the modern world *112* (2) *see also* Caledonia
Scots *people* British Isles ancient Rome *181* (4) medieval states *182* (2)
Scottish Covenanters *war* British Isles Reformation *196* (2)
Scottish Kingdoms *state* British Isles the world in 750 CE *54–55*
Scott River *archaeological site* Australia prehistoric culture *17* (5)
Scotts Lake North America (USA) cultural groups *122* (5)
Scrobesbyrig' *see* Shrewsbury
Scupi *mod.* Skopje, Skoplje, Üsküb, Üsküp Southeast Europe (FYR Macedonia) world religions *48* (1)
Scutari Southeast Europe (Albania) WWI *207* (6)
Scythia *region* Central Asia ancient trade *44* (2), *44–45* (1) first civilizations *177* (1) first religions *36* (1) Hellenistic world *40–41* (1)
Scythians *people* Central Asia/Eastern Europe/South Asia first empires *241* (4)
Scythopolis *Ar.* Baysān, Beisān Southwest Asia (Israel) ancient Rome *225* (5)
Sea Territories *province* Southwest Asia ancient Persia *223* (4)
Seattle North America (USA) the growth of the US *129* (2) the growth of the US *132* (1) US economy *136* (2)
Sebastia *see* Sivas
Sebastopol *Russ.* Sevastopol Eastern Europe (Ukraine) economy *205* (4) empire and revolution *202* (1) Napoleon *200–201* (1) Ottomans *232–233* (1) *see also* Sevastopol
Sebezh Eastern Europe (Russian Federation) early modern states *195* (3)
Sebka d'Idjil West Africa (Mauritania) Islam *163* (1)
Sebonac North America (USA) cultural groups *122* (5)
Sebta *see* Ceuta
Secheles Southern Africa (Botswana) exploration *157* (4)
Sechin Alto *early ceremonial centre* South America (Peru) early cultures *144* (1)
Sechura Desert *desert* South America early cultures *145* (4), *146* (1)
Second Cataract *waterfall* Egypt ancient Egypt *159* (4), (5)
Second Riel Rebellion *rebellion* North America (Canada) the growth of the US *129* (2)
Sedan France early modern states *197* (5) empire and revolution *202* (2) WWI *206* (2), (3) WWII *210* (1), *211* (4)
Sedeinga Egypt ancient Egypt *159* (5)
Sedunum *see* Sion
Segestica *see* Sisak
Seghedin *see* Szeged
Segni *see* Signia
Segontium British Isles (United Kingdom) world religions *48* (1)
Ségou *see* Segu
Segovia *settlement* Iberian Peninsula (Spain) crusades *186* (1) medieval states *187* (3)
Segu *Fr.* Ségou West Africa (Mali) Islam *167* (3)
Segu *Fr.* Ségou *state* West Africa slave trade *165* (4) trade *167* (1)
Segusio France ancient Rome *180–181* (1)
Sehwan South Asia (Pakistan) colonialism *247* (3)
Seibal Central America (Guatemala) first civilizations *121* (2)
Seila Egypt ancient Egypt *159* (3)
Seine *river* France Bronze Age *175* (3) Copper Age *174* (2) crusades *64–65* (2) early agriculture *174* (1) early modern states *197* (5) economy *190* (1), *191* (2), *205* (4) empire and revolution *199* (4), *202* (1) Franks *183* (5), (6) great migrations *52–53* (1), *53* (2) medieval states *185* (3), *186* (2), *187* (4), *192* (1), (2) Napoleon *200–201* (1), *201* (2) prehistoric culture *17* (3) Reformation *195* (5) WWI *206* (2), (3)
Seip *burial mound* North America (USA) first civilizations *121* (4)
Seistan *region/state* Southwest Asia early Islam *56–57* (1) Islam *227* (4) medieval Persia *231* (4) Timur *229* (4)
Sekani *people* North America cultural groups *123* (3)
Sekigahara *battle* Japan early modern states *267* (5)
Sekomis Southern Africa (Botswana) exploration *157* (4)
Sekondi *see* Sekondi-Takoradi
Sekondi-Takoradi *var.* Sekondi West Africa (Ghana) economy *168* (2)
Selânik *see* Salonica, Thessalonica
Selenga *Mong.* Selenge Mörön *river* East Asia/Siberia first states *260* (1) Mongols *68–69* (1)
Selenge Mörön *see* Selenga
Seleucia *mod.* Silifke Southwest Asia (Turkey) ancient Rome *180–181* (1) Hellenistic world *41* (2) world religions *48* (1)
Seleucia-on-the-Tigris Southwest Asia (Iraq) Hellenistic world *224* (1)
Seleucia Pieria Southwest Asia (Turkey) Hellenistic world *41* (2)
Seleucia Sidera Southwest Asia (Turkey) Hellenistic world *41* (2)
Seleucid Empire *var.* Empire of Seleucus *state* Southwest Asia ancient Greece *179* (4) ancient Rome *179* (5) Hellenistic world *224* (1)
Selima *oasis* East Africa ancient Egypt *159* (4)
Selinus Italy first civilizations *177* (1)
Seljuk Empire *state* Southwest Asia Mongols *68–69* (1)
Seljuks of Rum *state* Southwest Asia crusades *64–65* (2), *65* (3) medieval states *187* (5) Seljuks *228* (1)
Seljuk States *state* Southwest Asia economy *190* (1) medieval states *189* (4)
Selma North America (USA) US Civil War *131* (7) US society *137* (6)
Selymbria *state* Greece ancient Greece *177* (2)
Semarang *var.* Samarang Maritime Southeast Asia (Indonesia) post-war economy *253* (5)
Semey *see* Semipalatinsk
Seminole *people* North America colonization *125* (4)
Semipalatinsk *Kaz.* Semey Siberia (Kazakhstan) colonialism *269* (3) exploration *257* (2)
Semipalatinsk *Kaz.* Semey Oblysy *region* Central Asia colonialism *269* (3)
Semirech'ye *region* Central Asia colonialism *269* (3), (4)
Semites *people* East Africa/East Asia/Southwest Asia the world in 750 BCE *30–31* the world in 500 BCE *34–35* the world in 250 BCE *38–39* the world in 1 CE *42–43* the world in 250 CE *46–47*
Semna West Egypt ancient Egypt *159* (5)
Sempach *battle* Central Europe (Switzerland) early modern states *193* (5)
Sena Southern Africa (Mozambique) exploration *157* (4) Islam *163* (1)
Sena Gallica *mod.* Senigallia Italy early states *178* (1)
Sena Iulia *var.* Saena Julia, *mod.* Siena, Sienne Italy early states *178* (1) *see also* Siena
Senas *dynasty* South Asia early medieval states *244* (2) Mongols *68–69* (1)
Sendai Japan Communism *273* (3) economy *270* (1)
Senegal *Fr.* Sénégal *state* West Africa colonization *167* (4) decolonization *168* (1) economy *168* (2), (3) European imperialism *96* (1) Islam *235* (4) the modern world *112* (1), *113* (3)
Senegal *Fr.* Sénégal *river* West Africa early agriculture *158* (1) early cultures *160* (1) economy *163* (2) exploration *156* (1), (2), (3) Islam *163* (1) slave trade *165* (4) trade *163* (4), (5), (6), (7), *164* (2), *167* (1)
Senigallia *see* Sena Gallica
Senna *see* Sofala
Sennar *var.* Sannār East Africa (Sudan) ancient trade *44–45* (1) early cultures *160* (1), *161* (3), (5) Islam *163* (1) trade *165* (3)
Sennar *state* East Africa slave trade *165* (4)
Senones *see* Sens
Senpoku Japan early modern states *267* (4)
Senpukuji *archaeological site* Japan early agriculture *258* (1)
Sens *anc.* Agendicum, Senones France Franks *184* (2)
Senta *Hung.* Zenta Southeast Europe (Yugoslavia) post-war economy *215* (3) *see also* Zenta
Sentinum Italy early states *178* (1)
Seoul *prev.* Kyŏngsŏng; *Kor.* Sŏul, Sŏul-t'ŭkpyŏlsi *Jap.* Keijō East Asia (South Korea) Cold War *109* (4) early modern states *267* (4) Islam *275* (4) Russo-Japanese War *270* (4) Sino-Japanese War *270* (3)
Septimania *region/state* France Franks *183* (5), (6), *184* (2)
Serabit el-Khadim Egypt ancient Egypt *159* (5)
Sera Metropolis East Asia (China) ancient trade *44* (2)
Seram, Laut *see* Ceram Sea
Serampore *var.* Shrirāmpur, Frederiksnagore, Frederiksnagar; *prev.* Serampur South Asia (India) colonialism *247* (3) *see also* Frederiksnagar
Seram, Pulau *see* Ceram
Serampur *see* Frederiksnagar, Serampore
Serang *see* Ceram
Serapis, Temple of *building* Italy ancient Rome *181* (2)
Serbia *var.* Serbien *state* Southeast Europe early 20th century *206* (1) economy *190* (1), *205* (4) medieval states *187* (3), (5), *188* (1), *189* (4) Mongols *68–69* (1) Ottomans *197* (4), *230* (1) post-war economy *215* (3) WWI *207* (4), (6), *233* (2) WWII *211* (2), (4)
Serbia and Montenegro *state* Southeast Europe *112* (2), *214* (1)
Serbien *see* Serbia
Serdica *mod.* Sofia, Sofija, Sophia *settlement* Southeast Europe (Bulgaria) ancient Rome *180–181* (1) world religions *48* (1) *see also* Sofia
Seres *mod.* Serrai Greece medieval states *189* (4) WWI *207* (6)
Sergipe *region* South America colonization *149* (3)
Sergipe *see* Sergipe del Rey
Sergipe del Rey *mod.* Sergipe South America (Brazil) colonization *149* (4)
Serica *physical region* Central Asia ancient trade *44* (2)
Seringapatam South Asia (India) colonialism *248* (1)
Sermermiut North America (Greenland) cultural groups *123* (3)
Sermylia Greece ancient Greece *177* (2)
Serpa Pinto *see* Menongue
Serpent Mound *burial mound/settlement* North America (USA) first religions *36* (1)
Serrai *see* Seres
Serram Geley *mod.* Futa Jallon, Fouta-Djallon *mountain range* West Africa exploration *156* (2) *see also* Futa Jallon
Serrano *people* North America colonization *125* (4)
Serranopolis *archaeological site* South America (Brazil) early cultures *145* (2)
Serrey *region* Eastern Europe empire and revolution *199* (3)
Servia *see* Serbia
Sesamus Southwest Europe (Turkey) first civilizations *177* (1)
Sesebi Egypt ancient Egypt *159* (5)
Sesheke *var.* Sesheko Southern Africa (Zambia) exploration *157* (4)
Sesheko *see* Sesheke
Sestus Southeast Europe (Turkey) first civilizations *177* (1)
Setavya South Asia (India) world religions *242* (3)
Setia *mod.* Sezze Italy early states *178* (1)
Seto-naikai *see* Inland Sea
Sevastopol' *var.* Sebastopol Eastern Europe (Ukraine) Ottomans *202* (4) Soviet Union *208* (2) WWI *207* (4) *see also* Sebastopol
Seven Days' Battle *battle* North America (USA) US Civil War *131* (6)
Severin *region* Southeast Europe medieval states *189* (4)
Severn *Wel.* Hafren *river* British Isles economy *204* (1) medieval states *183* (3)
Severnaya Dvina *see* Northern Dvina
Severnaya Zemlya *island group* Arctic Ocean exploration *257* (2)
Severn Factory North America (Canada) colonization *126* (1)
Sevilla *see* Hispalis, Seville
Sevilla la Nueva West Indies (Jamaica) colonization *125* (4)
Seville *Sp.* Sevilla; *anc.* Hispalis *settlement/university* Iberian Peninsula (Spain) crusades *186* (1) early Islam *57* (2) economy *190* (1) European expansion *84–85* (1) Franks *184* (2) inter-war *209* (4) Islam *192* (3), *227* (4) medieval states *185* (3) medieval voyages *60–61* (1) Reformation *194* (2) *see also* Hispalis
Seychelle Islands *see* Seychelles
Seychelles *var.* Seychelle Islands *colonial possession/state/island group* Indian Ocean decolonization *168* (1) economy *168* (2) the modern world *112* (1), *113* (3) trade *230* (2)
Seyhan *see* Adana
Sezze *see* Setia
Shaan *see* Shaanxi
Shaanxi *var.* Shaan, Shan-hsi, Shenshi, Shensi *province* East Asia early modern states *266* (1), (2), *268* (1) empire and revolution *268* (2) post-war politics *274* (2) Chinese revolution *271* (5)
Shaat Egypt ancient Egypt *159* (3), (4)
Shaba *see* Katanga
Shabara *state* South Asia first empires *241* (5)
Shabeelle, Webi *see* Shebeli
Shabwah Southwest Asia (Yemen) early trade *225* (3)
Shache *see* Yarkand
Shachou *see* Shazhou
Shackleton Ice Shelf *ice feature* Antarctica Antarctic Exploration *287* (3)
Shagarh *state* South Asia empire and revolution *249* (3)
Shahdad Southwest Asia (Iran) first civilizations *24* (3)
Shaheinab East Africa (Sudan) early agriculture *158* (1)
Sha Hi *see* Urmia, Lake
Shahi-tump *archaeological site* South Asia (Pakistan) first cities *240* (2)
Shahjahanabad *see* Delhi, Indraprastha
Shahjahanpur South Asia (India) economy *249* (4)
Shahr-i Sokhta *settlement/archaeological site* Southwest Asia (Iran) early systems *223* (3) first cities *240* (2), *28–29* (1) first civilizations *24* (2)
Shah Tepe Southwest Asia (Iran) first civilizations *24* (3)
Shakala South Asia (India) early medieval states *244* (1)
Shakambhari South Asia (India) early medieval states *244* (2)
Shakas *dynasty* South Asia ancient trade *44–45* (1) first empires *241* (4)
Shaksgam *region* East Asia/South Asia post-war politics *252* (2)
Shalagrama South Asia (Nepal) world religions *243* (4)
Shalva *region* South Asia world religions *242* (2)
Shām, Bādiyat ash *see* Syrian Desert
Shandong *var.* Lu, Shantung *province/region* East Asia early modern states *266* (1), (2), *268* (1) empire and revolution *268* (2) first cities *259* (3), (4), (5) imperialism *270* (2) post-war politics *271* (5), *274* (2)
Shandong Bandao *see* Shandong Peninsula
Shandong Peninsula *var.* Shandong Bandao, Shantung Peninsula *peninsula* East Asia early modern states *265* (5) medieval states *264* (1), (2) Sino-Japanese War *270* (3)
Shangdu East Asia (China) trade *72–73* (1) Mongols *68* (2), *263* (7)
Shanggu East Asia (China) first cities *259* (5)
Shanghai *var.* Shang-hai East Asia (China) colonialism *269* (4) economy *274* (1) empire and revolution *268* (2) global immigration *100* (1), *101* (3) imperial global economy *92* (1) Islam *275* (4) post-war economy *275* (3) post-war politics *271* (7), *274* (2) WWII *272* (1), *273* (2) Communism *271* (8)
Shangqiu *var.* Zhuji East Asia (China) first cities *259* (4), (5) first religions *37* (4)
Shangyong East Asia (China) first cities *259* (5)
Shan-hsi *see* Jin, Shanxi, Shaanxi
Shanidar *archaeological site* Southwest Asia (Iraq) first humans *13* (2)
Shannan Dongdao *var.* Shannan Tungtao *province* Central Asia medieval states *262–263* (1)
Shannan Hsitao *see* Shannan Xidao
Shannan Tungtao *see* Shannan Dongdao
Shannan Xidao *var.* Shannan Hsitao *province* Central Asia medieval states *262–263* (1)
Shannon *Ir.* An tSionainn *river* British Isles medieval states *186* (2)
Shansi *see* Jin, Shanxi
Shan States *state* Mainland Southeast Asia colonialism *248* (2) medieval states *263* (6)
Shantou *var.* Shan-t'ou, Swatow East Asia (China) colonialism *269* (4) post-war politics *271* (7), *274* (2)
Shantung *see* Shandong
Shantung Peninsula *see* Shandong Peninsula
Shanxi *var.* Jin, Shan-hsi, Shansi *province* East Asia early modern states *266* (1), (2), *268* (1) empire and revolution *268* (2) post-war politics *274* (2) Chinese revolution *271* (5)
Shaoxing *rebellion* East Asia early modern states *266* (2)
Shaozhou *var.* Shaochou East Asia (China) medieval states *262–263* (1)
Sharada South Asia (Pakistan) world religions *243* (4)
Sharjah *Ar.* Ash Shāriqah Southwest Asia (United Arab Emirates) economy *234* (1)
Sharkara South Asia (Pakistan) world religions *243* (4)
Shark Bay *bay* Australia exploration *278* (1)
Sharm ash Shaykh *see* Sharm el Sheikh
Sharm el Sheikh *var.* Ofiral, Sharm ash Shaykh Egypt 20th century *234* (2)
Sharpsburg *battle* North America (USA) US Civil War *131* (6)
Sharqis *state* South Asia the world in 1400 *70–71*
Shaṭṭ al 'Arab *see* Shatt al 'Arab Waterway
Shatt al 'Arab Waterway *Ar.* Shaṭṭ al 'Arab, *Per.* Arvand Rūd *river* Southwest Asia 20th-century politics *235* (5)
Shavli Eastern Europe (Lithuania) WWI *207* (4)
Shawnee *people* North America colonization *126* (1)
Shaybanids *dynasty* Central Asia the world in 1500 *74–75*
Shazhou *var.* Shachou East Asia (China) medieval states *263* (3)
Sheba *see* Saba
Shebelē Wenz, Wabē *see* Shebeli
Shebeli *Amh.* Wabē Shebelē Wenz, *It.* Scebeli, *Som.* Webi Shabeelle *river* East Africa early cultures *160* (1) trade *165* (3)
Shechem Southwest Asia (Israel) ancient Egypt *159* (4) first civilizations *222* (1)
Sheffield British Isles (United Kingdom) economy *204* (1) imperial global economy *93* (4)
Shengle East Asia (China) medieval states *261* (4)
Shenshi, Shensi *see* Shaanxi
Shenyang *prev.* Fengtien; *Chin.* Shen-yang, *Eng.* Moukden, Mukden East Asia (China) economy *274* (1) Islam *275* (4) post-war politics *274* (2) Cold War *109* (4) *see also* Mukden
Shenzhen East Asia (China) post-war politics *274* (2)
Sherman North America (USA) US economy *135* (4)
Sherpur South Asia (Bangladesh) colonialism *247* (3)
Shershell *see* Caesarea
Shetland Islands *island group* British Isles exploration *172* (1), (2) medieval states *185* (3) medieval voyages *60–61* (1) WWII *210* (1), *211* (4)
Shibam Southwest Asia (Yemen) early Islam *56–57* (1)
Shibushi Japan early modern states *265* (5)
Shiga *var.* Siga *prefecture* Japan economy *270* (1)
Shigatse *var.* Jih-k'a-tse, Xigaze, Xigazê East Asia (China) exploration *257* (3)
Shihr Southwest Asia (Yemen) European expansion *84–85* (1)
Shikarpur South Asia (Bangladesh) post-war politics *252* (3)
Shikoku *island* Japan early modern states *265* (5), *267* (4), (5) economy *270* (1) imperialism *270* (2) medieval states *264* (1), (2), *265* (3), (4) Communism *273* (3)
Shillacoto *settlement/archaeological site* South America (Peru) early cultures *145* (3) the world in 2500 BCE *22–23*
Shillong South Asia (India) decolonization *250* (2) post-war politics *252* (1)
Shilluk *state* East Africa slave trade *165* (4) trade *167* (1)
Shiloh North America (USA) US Civil War *131* (6), (7)
Shimabara *var.* Simabara Japan early modern states *267* (5)
Shimane *var.* Simane *prefecture* Japan economy *270* (1)
Shimazu *region* Japan early modern states *267* (4)
Shimla *see* Simla
Shimonoseki *var.* Simonoseki; *hist.* Akamagaseki, Bakan Japan economy *270* (1) Russo-Japanese War *270* (4) Sino-Japanese War *270* (3)
Shimonoseki *island* Japan Communism *273* (3)
Shinohara *var.* Shinowara *battle* Japan early modern states *265* (5)
Shinowara *see* Shinohara
Ship Island North America (USA) US Civil War *131* (6)
Shipurla *see* Lagash
Shira *state* West Africa trade *164* (2)
Shiraz *var.* Shīrāz Southwest Asia (Iran) trade *72–73* (1) early Islam *56–57* (1) economy *234* (1) exploration *218* (2), *219* (3) medieval Persia *231* (4) medieval voyages *61* (3) Seljuks *228* (1) Timur *229* (4) 20th-century politics *235* (5)
Shire *var.* Chire *river* Southern Africa exploration *157* (4)
Shirvan Southwest Asia (Iran) medieval Persia *231* (4)
Shirwan *var.* Shirvan *region* Southwest Asia medieval Persia *231* (4)
Shiwei *people* East Asia medieval states *262–263* (1)
Shizugatake *battle* Japan early modern states *267* (4)
Shizuoka *var.* Sizuoka Japan economy *270* (1)
Shizuoka *var.* Sizuoka *prefecture* Japan economy *270* (1)
Shkodër *see* Scodra
Shoa *state* East Africa the world in 1000 *58–59* the world in 1200 *62–63*
Sholapur South Asia (India) economy *249* (4) imperial global economy *93* (5)
Shonai Japan early modern states *267* (4)
Shongweni *archaeological site* Southern Africa (South Africa) early cultures *160* (1)
Shorapur *state* South Asia empire and revolution *249* (3)
Shortughai Central Asia (Tajikistan) first civilizations *24* (2)
Shouchun East Asia (China) first cities *259* (5) first religions *37* (4)
Shoufang *province* East Asia first states *260* (1)
Shqipëria *see* Albania
Shravana Belgola South Asia (India) first empires *241* (4)
Shravasti South Asia (India) world religions *242* (3)
Shreveport North America (USA) the growth of the US *129* (2) US society *137* (6)
Shrewsbury *hist.* Scrobesbyrig' British Isles (United Kingdom) economy *190* (1) medieval states *186* (2)
Shriksetra *var.* Shrikshetra; *mod.* Prome Mainland Southeast Asia (Burma) early medieval states *245* (5) *see also* Prome, Shrikshetra
Shrikshetra *var.* Shriksetra; *mod.* Prome Mainland Southeast Asia (Burma) ancient India *241* (6) *see also* Prome, Shriksetra
Shrinagara *var.* Srinagar; South Asia (India) early medieval states *244* (1), (2), *244–245* (3) world religions *243* (4)
Shriperambudur South Asia (India) world religions *243* (4)
Shripurushottama South Asia (India) world religions *242* (2)
Shrirāmpur *see* Frederiksnagar, Serampore
Shrirangam South Asia (India) early medieval states *244–245* (3) world religions *243* (4)
Shrirangapattanam *var.* Srirangapattanam; *mod.* Seringapattam South Asia (India) early medieval states *245* (4) *see also* Seringapatam, Srirangapattanam
Shriver North America (USA) the world in 10,000 BCE *14–15*
Shu *var.* Chengdu East Asia (China) first cities *259* (5) first religions *37* (4) *see also* Chengdu
Shu *province/region/state* East Asia first cities *259* (5) first religions *37* (4) first states *260* (1), *261* (2)
Shu *people* East Asia first cities *259* (4)
Shuar *people* South America the world in 1700 *82–83*
Shu Han *state* East Asia the world in 250 CE *46–47*
Shuidonggou *archaeological site* East Asia early humans *15* (1)
Shuruppak Southwest Asia (Iraq) first civilizations *24* (3)
Shūsh, Shushan *see* Susa
Siak *state* Maritime Southeast Asia the world in 1800 *86–87*
Sialk Southwest Asia (Iran) first cities *220* (2) first civilizations *24* (2)
Sialkot South Asia (Pakistan) colonialism *247* (3)
Siam *mod.* Thailand, Prathet Thai *state/region* Mainland Southeast Asia biological diffusion *72–73* (1) colonialism *248* (1), *269* (4) early modern states *266* (1), (2), *268* (1) global immigration *100* (1), *101* (3) trade *267* (3) WWII *251* (3), *272* (1), *273* (2) Communism *271* (8) *see also* Thailand
Siam, Gulf of *var.* Gulf of Thailand, *Thai.* Ao Thai, *Vtn.* Vinh Thai Lan *gulf* Mainland Southeast Asia decolonization *251* (4) Mongols *68–69* (1) WWII *251* (3) *see also* Thailand, Gulf of
Siam, Kingdom of *state* Mainland Southeast Asia European imperialism *97* (3), (4)
Sian *see* Chang'an Xi'an
Siang *see* Brahmaputra
Siberia *Russ.* Sibir' *physical region* Asia ancient trade *44–45* (1) biological diffusion *72–73* (1) colonialism *269* (3) crusades *65* (1) early agriculture *20–21* (2), *258* (1) empire and revolution *88–89* (2) exploration *257* (2), *286* (1), *287* (2) first humans *13* (2) global immigration *100* (1) medieval states *261* (6), *262–263* (1) prehistoric culture *16* (1) world religions *49* (4) Communism *271* (8)
Siberia, Khanate of *state* Siberia trade *267* (3)
Siberian Inuit *people* Siberia cultural groups *123* (3)
Siberian Tatars *people* Siberia trade *267* (3)
Sibi *state* South Asia first empires *241* (5)
Sibir' *see* Siberia
Sibiu *see* Nagyszeben
Siblag *gulag/region* Siberia Soviet Union *213* (4)
Sicani *people* Italy early states *178* (2)
Sichuan *province/region* East Asia early modern states *266* (1), (2), *268* (1) economy *274* (1) empire and revolution *268* (2) first religions *37* (4) medieval states *263* (6) post-war economy *275* (3) post-war politics *274* (2) Chinese revolution *271* (5)
Sichuan Basin *basin* East Asia early modern states *266* (1)
Sicilia *province* Italy ancient Rome *179* (5)
Sicilian Revolt *war* Italy Reformation *196* (2)
Sicily *var.* It. Sicilia *island/state* Italy ancient Rome *180–181* (1), *181* (3), (4), *182* (1), *225* (5) biological diffusion *72–73* (1) Bronze Age *175* (3) crusades *186* (1), *64–65* (2) early cultures *161* (2) early Islam *56–57* (1) early modern states *194* (1) economy *190* (1), *205* (4) empire and revolution *88–89* (2) exploration *172* (1) first civilizations *177* (1) first religions *37* (3) inter-war *209* (5) Islam *184* (1), *226* (2), *227* (4) medieval states *182* (2), *183* (4), *185* (3), (5), *188* (1), *189* (4) medieval voyages *60–61* (1) Napoleon *201* (2) Ottomans *195* (4), *230* (1), *231* (3) post-war economy *213* (5), *214* (1) post-war politics *212* (3) Reformation *194* (2) the modern world *113* (4) world religions *48* (1) WWII *210* (1), *211* (2), (4)
Siculi *people* Italy early states *178* (2)
Sidama States *state* East Africa the world in 1400 *70–71*
Side Southwest Asia (Turkey) first civilizations *177* (1) Hellenistic world *40–41* (1)
Sidhu *region* South Asia first empires *241* (4)
Sidi Abderrahman *archaeological site* North Africa (Morocco) first humans *13* (2)
Sidi Barrani Egypt WWII *210* (1)
Sidon *var.* Şaydā, Sayida *settlement* Southwest Asia (Lebanon) ancient Persia *223* (4) ancient Rome *225* (4) crusades *65* (3) early trade *225* (3) first civilizations *177* (1), *221* (5), *222* (1), (2) Hellenistic world *40–41* (1) world religions *226* (1)
Sidra *see* Sirt
Siebenbürgen *see* Transylvania
Siena *anc.* Saena Julia, Sena Iulia; *Fr.* Sienne Italy economy *190* (1) medieval states *183* (4), *187* (3), *188* (1) *see also* Sena Iulia
Sienne *see* Siena
Sienpi *see* Xianbi
Sierra Leone *state* West Africa colonization *167* (4) decolonization *168* (1) economy *168* (2) European imperialism *96* (1) Islam *235* (4) the modern world *112* (1), *113* (3) trade *167* (1) WWII *104* (1) Cold War *109* (1)
Sierra Leone, Cape *headland* West Africa European expansion *80–81* (1)
Sierra Madre *var.* Sierra de Soconusco *mountain range* North America cultural groups *123* (4)
Sierra Madre del Sur *mountain range* North America exploration *118* (1), *119* (2), (3) first civilizations *121* (2), *122* (1)
Sierra Madre Occidental *var.* Western Sierra Madre *mountain range* Central America exploration *118* (1), *119* (2), (3) Mexican Revolution *133* (3) the growth of the US *129* (2)
Sierra Madre Oriental *var.* Eastern Sierra Madre *mountain range* Central America exploration *118* (1), *119* (2), (3) first civilizations *121* (2) Mexican Revolution *133* (3) the growth of the US *129* (2)
Siga *see* Shiga
Sigiriya *Buddhist centre/settlement* South Asia (Sri Lanka) world religions *49* (3)
Signak Central Asia (Kazakhstan) Mongols *68–69* (1)
Signan *see* Chang'an Xi'an
Signia *mod.* Segni Italy early states *178* (1)
Sigtuna Scandinavia (Sweden) medieval states *185* (3) medieval voyages *60–61* (1)
Siine *state* West Africa Islam *163* (1) trade *163* (6), (7), *164* (2)
Sijilmassa North Africa (Morocco) ancient trade *44–45* (1) Islam *163* (1)
Sikh States *state* South Asia the world in 1800 *86–87*
Siking *see* Chang'an, Xi'an
Sikkim *state* South Asia colonialism *248* (2), *269* (4) decolonization *250* (2) economy *249* (4) empire and revolution *249* (3) post-war politics *252* (1)
Silaharas *dynasty* South Asia Mongols *68–69* (1)
Silebar Maritime Southeast Asia (Indonesia) the world in 1700 *82–83* the world in 1800 *86–87*
Silesia *region/state/vassal state* Central Europe early modern states *193* (4) economy *205* (4) empire and revolution *198* (2), *199* (3), *202* (2) medieval states *189* (3) Ottomans *197* (4) WWII *211* (2)
Silesian Principalities *state* Central Europe medieval states *189* (4)
Silifke *see* Seleucia
Silistra *see* Durostorum, Silistria
Silistria *mod.* Silistra; *anc.* Durostorum Southeast Europe (Romania) Ottomans *202* (4) *see also* Durostorum
Silla *region/state* East Asia medieval states *262* (1), *264* (1), (2) world religions *49* (4)
Silla *region/state* West Africa trade *163* (4)
Silumiut North America (Canada) cultural groups *123* (3)
Silver Leaves *archaeological site* Southern Africa (South Africa) early cultures *160* (1)
Silves Iberian peninsula (Portugal) Franks *184* (2) Islam *192* (3)
Simabara *see* Shimabara
Simane *see* Shimane
Simao *var.* Szemao East Asia (China) colonialism *269* (4)
Simferopol' Eastern Europe (Ukraine) Soviet Union *208* (2)
Simhala *var.* Ceylon, Saylan, Sarandib; *mod.* Sri Lanka; *Chin.* Hsi-lan; *anc.* Simhala, Sinhala, Lambakannas, Lanka, Taprobane *region/state/island* South Asia early medieval states *244–245* (3) early religions *48* (2) world religions *49* (4) world religions *242* (2) *see also* Ceylon, Lambakannas, Lanka, Simhala, Sri Lanka, Taprobana
Simhala States *state* South Asia Mongols *68–69* (1)
Simla *mod.* Shimla South Asia (India) post-war politics *252* (1)
Simonoseki *see* Shimonoseki
Simpson Desert *desert* Australia exploration *279* (2) prehistoric culture *17* (5)
Simylla South Asia (India) ancient trade *44* (2)
Simyra Southwest Asia (Syria) ancient Egypt *159* (5)
Sinā' *see* Sinai
Sinae *region* Mainland Southeast Asia ancient trade *44* (2)
Sinae *physical region* East Asia ancient trade *44* (2) global knowledge *76* (8) *see also* China
Sinai *var.* Sinai Peninsula, *Ar.* Shibh Jazirat Sīnā', Sinā' *region* Egypt ancient Egypt *159* (2), (3), (4), (5) ancient Persia *223* (4) crusades *64–65* (2), *65* (3) first cities *220* (2) first civilizations *222* (1), (2) Islam *163* (1) WWI *233* (2) 20th century *234* (2)
Sinai Peninsula *see* Sinai
Sinaloa *state* Central America Mexican Revolution *133* (3) the growth of the US *129* (2)
Sind *var.* Sindh *region/state* South Asia colonialism *248* (2) early medieval states *244–245* (3) Mughal Empire *246* (1) post-war politics *252* (1), *253* (4) world religions *243* (4)
Sindae Insulae *island* Indian Ocean ancient trade *44* (2)
Sindh *see* Sind
Sindhia *region* South Asia Marathas *246* (2)
Sindhu *region* South Asia world religions *242* (2)
Singa *archaeological site* East Africa (Sudan) first humans *13* (2)
Singan *see* Chang'an, Xi'an
Singapore *prev.* Singapura *military base/settlement/state* Mainland Southeast Asia (Singapore) Cold War *109* (1) colonialism *269* (4) decolonization *251* (4) European imperialism *97* (3) exploration *239* (1), (2) global immigration *100* (1) imperial global economy *92* (1) Islam *275* (4) post-war economy *253* (5) post-war politics *253* (4) the modern world *113* (3) trade *267* (3) WWII *104* (2), *251* (3), *272* (1), *273* (2) *see also* Singapura
Singapura *mod.* Singapore Mainland Southeast Asia (Singapore) early medieval states *245* (6) *see also* Singapore
Singhalese *see* Sinhalese
Singhasari Maritime Southeast Asia (Indonesia) early medieval states *245* (6) world religions *243* (5)
Singhasari *region* Maritime Southeast Asia early medieval states *245* (5)
Singhbhum *state* South Asia empire and revolution *249* (3)
Singidunum *mod.* Beograd; *Eng* Belgrade *legion headquarters* Southeast Europe (Yugoslavia) ancient Rome *180–181* (1) *see also* Belgrade
Singkiang *see* Xinjiang
Singora *see* Songkhla
Singos *see* Singus
Singus *var.* Singos *state* Greece ancient Greece *177* (2)
Sinhala *var.* Ceylon, Saylan, Sarandib; *mod.* Sri Lanka; *Chin.* Hsi-lan; *anc.* Taprobane, Simhala, Lambakannas, Lanka *island* South Asia *see also* Ceylon, Lambakannas, Lanka, Simhala, Sri Lanka, Taprobana
Sinhalese *var.* Singhalese *people* South Asia world religions *243* (5)
Sinitic Peoples *people* East Asia the world in 750 BCE *30–31* the world in 500 BCE *34–35* the world in 250 BCE *38–39*
Sin-Kashid, Palace of *palace* Southwest Asia (Iraq) first cities *220* (3)
Sinkiang *var.* Xinjiang, Sinking Uighur Autonomous Region; *Chin.* Xinjiang, Xin Xinjiang *region* East Asia early medieval states *261* (6) *see also* Turkestan
Sinkiang Uighur Autonomous Region *see* Sinkiang, Turkestan, Xinjiang
Sinope *Class.* Sinope Southwest Asia (Turkey) ancient Persia *223* (4) ancient Rome *180–181* (1) crusades *64–65* (2) early cultures *161* (2) early Islam *56–57* (1) first civilizations *177* (1) Hellenistic world *40–41* (1) Ottomans *195* (4), *232–233* (1) Seljuks *228* (1) world religions *226* (1)
Sinope *battle* Southwest Asia (Turkey) Ottomans *202* (4)
Sint Maarten *see* St Martin
Sinú Chiefdoms *state* South America early cultures *146* (1)
Sinuessa Italy early states *178* (1)
Sinuiju East Asia (North Korea) Cold War *109* (4)
Sion *anc.* Sedunum; *Ger.* Sitten Central Europe (Switzerland) early modern states *193* (5)
Sioux *people* North America the world in 1600 *78–79* the world in 1700 *82–83*
Sioux City North America (USA) US economy *134* (1)
Šipka *archaeological site* Central Europe (Czech Republic) first humans *13* (2)
Sippar Southwest Asia (Iraq) first civilizations *24* (2), *25* (3)
Sira South Asia (India) Mughal Empire *246* (1)
Sira *state* South Asia Mughal Empire *246* (1)
Siracusa *see* Syracuse
Siraf Southwest Asia (Iran) early Islam *56–57* (1) medieval voyages *61* (3)
Sir Darya *see* Jaxartes, Syr Darya
Sirdaryo *see* Jaxartes, Syr Darya
Şiria *see* Világos
Siria *see* Syria
Sirmium *settlement* Southeast Europe (Yugoslavia) ancient Rome *180–181* (1), *181* (4) world religions *48* (1)
Sironj South Asia (India) colonialism *247* (3)
Sirt *var.* Sidra, Sirte, Surt North Africa (Libya) early Islam *56–57* (1)
Sirvān, Rudkhaneh-ye, Sirwan *see* Diyala
Sirwa Pass *battle* South Asia empire and revolution *249* (3)
Sisak *var.* Siscia; *anc.* Segestica; *Ger.* Sissek, *Hung.* Sziszek Southeast Europe (Croatia) post-war economy *215* (3)
Siscia Southeast Europe (Croatia) ancient Rome *180–181* (1)
Siscia, Sissek *see* Sisak
Sistan *see* Indo-Parthian Empire
Sitagroi Greece early agriculture *174* (1)
Sitifis North Africa (Algeria) Roman empire *180–181* (1)
Sitka North America (USA) imperial global economy *93* (3) the growth of the US *129* (2)
Sitten *see* Sion
Siut *see* Asyut
Siuyen *see* Xiuyan
Sivas *anc.* Sebastia Southwest Asia (Turkey) Mongols *68–69* (1) Timur *229* (4)
Siwa *var.* Sīwah Egypt Islam *163* (1)
Sīwah *see* Siwa
Siwa Oasis *see* Sanctuary of Ammon
Six Counties, The *see* Northern Ireland
Sizebolu *see* Apollonia
Sizuoka *see* Shizuoka
Skaka *region* South Asia world religions *242* (2)
Skåne *see* Scania
Skanör Scandinavia (Sweden) economy *190* (1)
Skardu South Asia (Pakistan) post-war politics *252* (2)
Skopje *var.* Üsküb; *anc.* Scupi; *Turk.* Üsküp, Üsküb Southeast Europe (FYR Macedonia) post-war economy *215* (3) post-war politics *212* (3) *see also* Skoplje, Scupi
Skoplje *var.* Üsküb; *mod.* Skopje; *anc.* Scupi; *Turk.* Üsküp, Üsküb Southeast Europe (FYR Macedonia) medieval states *189* (4) WWI *207* (6)
Skripón *see* Orchomenus
Skull Cave *battle* North America (USA) the growth of the US *129* (2)
Slagtersnek Southern Africa (South Africa) colonization *166* (2)
Slankamen *battle* Southeast Europe (Yugoslavia) Ottomans *197* (4)
Slave *people* North America cultural groups *123* (3)
Slave *river* North America the growth of the US *129* (2)
Slave Coast *physical region* West Africa Islam *163* (1) slave trade *165* (4)
Slavonia *vassal state* Southeast Europe medieval states *189* (4) Ottomans *230* (1)
Slavs *people* Eastern Europe ancient Rome *182* (1) medieval states *182* (2)
Slesvig *Ger.* Schleswig Central Europe (Denmark) empire and revolution *199* (3)

Sloan *archaeological site* North America the world in 5000 BCE *18–19*

Slovakia *Ger.* Slowakei, *Hung.* Szlovákia, *Slvk.* Slovensko *state* Central Europe post-war economy *214* (1), (2) Soviet Union *214–215* (4) the modern world *112* (2), *113* (4) WWII *104* (2), *210* (1), *211* (2), (4) *see also* Czechoslovakia

Slovaks *people* Eastern Europe Franks *184* (2)

Slovenia *Ger.* Slowenien, *Slvn.* Slovenija *state* Southeast Europe post-war economy *214* (1), (2), *215* (3) Soviet Union *214–215* (4) the modern world *110–111* , *112* (2), *113* (3)

Slovenija *see* Slovenia

Slovensko *see* Slovakia

Slowakei *see* Slovakia

Slowenien *see* Slovenia

Sluis *var.* Sluys; *Fr.* L'Écluse *battle* Low Countries (Netherlands) Reformation *195* (5) *see also* Sluys

Sluys *var.* Sluis; *Fr.* L'Écluse *battle* Low Countries (Netherlands) medieval states *192* (1) *see also* Sluis

Smolensk Eastern Europe (Russian Federation) early modern states *195* (3) economy *190* (1) empire and revolution *198* (2) medieval states *189* (3), (4) Napoleon *200–201* (1) post-war politics *212* (3) Soviet Union *208* (2) WWI *207* (4)

Smolensk *state* Eastern Europe medieval states *189* (3), (4)

Smorgon' *Pol.* Smorgonie Eastern Europe (Belorussia) Napoleon *200–201* (1)

Smorgonie *see* Smorgon'

Smyrna *mod.* İzmir *settlement* Southwest Asia (Turkey) 20th-century politics *233* (3) empire and revolution *202* (1) first civilizations *221* (5) Hellenistic world *40–41* (1) medieval states *185* (3), *189* (4) Napoleon *200–201* (1) Ottomans *202* (4), *230* (1) Timur *229* (4) world religions *48* (1) WWI *233* (2)

Snaketown *archaeological site* North America (USA) cultural groups *123* (4)

Soasiu *see* Tidore

Soba East Africa (Sudan) early cultures *161* (4), (5)

Sobibor *concentration camp* Eastern Europe WWII *211* (3)

Soča *see* Isonzo

Soccorra *mod.* Socorro North America (USA) colonization *125* (4)

Société, Archipel de la *see* Society Islands

Société, Îles de la *see* Society Islands

Society Islands *Fr.* Archipel de la Société, Îles de la Société *island group* Pacific Ocean colonization *284–285* (1) early cultures *280–281* (3) environmentalism *285* (2) exploration *276–277* (1), *279* (3) medieval voyages *60* (2)

Sockna, **Socna** *see* Sokna

Soconusco *state* Central America the growth of the US *129* (2)

Soconusco, Sierra de *see* Sierra Madre

Socorro *see* Soccorra

Socotra *var.* Sokotra, Suqutra *island* Indian Ocean ancient trade *44–45* (1) biological diffusion *72–73* (1) early cultures *161* (3), (4), (5) early Islam *56–57* (1) early trade *225* (3) Islam *163* (1) Ottomans *231* (3) trade *165* (3), *230* (2), *267* (3) 20th-century politics *233* (4)

Soemba *see* Sumba

Soembawa *see* Sumbawa

Soerabaja *see* Surabaya

Sofala *var.* Senna Southern Africa (Mozambique) economy *163* (2) European expansion *80–81* (1) exploration *156* (3) Islam *163* (1) slave trade *165* (4) trade *164* (1)

Sofia *var.* Sofija, Sophia; *Lat.* Serdica Southeast Europe (Bulgaria) crusades *64–65* (2) early modern states *193* (4) economy *198* (1) Napoleon *200–201* (1), *201* (2), (3) Ottomans *197* (4), *230* (1), *231* (3), *232–233* (1) post-war politics *212* (3) WWI *207* (6) WWII *211* (2) *see also* Serdica

Sofija *see* Serdica, Sofia

Sogabe *region* Japan early modern states *267* (4)

Sogamoso South America (Colombia) early cultures *146* (1)

Sogdiana *province* Central Asia ancient Persia *223* (4) ancient trade *44* (2), *44–45* (1) early Islam *56–57* (1) first empires *241* (4) Hellenistic world *224* (1) medieval states *262–263* (1)

Sogdian Rock Central Asia (Kazakhstan) Hellenistic world *40–41* (1)

Sohano Islands *island group* Pacific Ocean early cultures *280–281* (3) medieval voyages *60* (2)

Sohar *see* Suhar

Soissons *anc.* Augusta Suessionum, Noviodunum France crusades *64–65* (2) early modern states *197* (5) Franks *183* (5), (6) WWI *206* (2), (3)

Sokna *var.* Sockna; *It.* Socna North Africa (Libya) exploration *157* (4) Islam *163* (1)

Sokol Eastern Europe (Russian Federation) early modern states *195* (3)

Sokoto West Africa (Nigeria) colonization *167* (4) exploration *157* (4) Islam *167* (3)

Sokoto *state* West Africa trade *167* (1)

Sokotra *see* Socotra

Solander Island *sealing station* New Zealand colonization *283* (4)

Solankis *var.* Chaulukyas *dynasty* South Asia early medieval states *244* (2)

Soldaia Eastern Europe (Ukraine) Mongols *68–69* (1)

Soldier Spring *battle* North America (USA) the growth of the US *129* (2)

Soleb Egypt ancient Egypt *159* (5)

Soleure *see* Solothurn

Soli Southwest Asia (Turkey) first civilizations *177* (1)

Solikamsk Eastern Europe (Russian Federation) economy *205* (4)

Solin *see* Salonae

Solomon Islands *island group/state* Pacific Ocean decolonization *285* (3) early cultures *280* (2), *280–281* (3) environmentalism *285* (2) European imperialism *97* (3) exploration *280* (1) medieval voyages *60* (2) WWII *251* (3), *272* (1), *273* (2)

Solothurn *Fr.* Soleure Central Europe (Switzerland) early modern states *193* (5)

Solun *see* Salonica, Thessalonica

Somalia *prev.* Italian Somaliland, *Som.* Soomaaliya; Somaliland Protectorate *state* East Africa decolonization *168* (1) economy *168* (2) Islam *235* (4) trusteeship *102-103* the modern world *112* (1), *113* (3), (4) US superpower *138* (1) *see also* Italian Somaliland

Somaliland Protectorate *see* Italian Somaliland, Somalia

Somalis *people* East Africa trade *165* (3)

Sombor *Hung.* Zombor Southeast Europe (Yugoslavia) post-war economy *215* (3)

Somers Islands *see* Bermuda

Somme *battle* France WWI *206* (2)

Somme *river* France WWI *206* (2), (3)

Somnath *archaeological site/settlement* South Asia (India) early medieval states *244–245* (3) first cities *240* (2)

Son *var.* Sone *river* South Asia first religions *36* (2) first states *260* (1) world religions *242* (3)

Sone *see* Son

Song *state* East Asia first cities *259* (4), (5) medieval states *263* (5)

Songdo *see* Kaesong

Song Empire *var.* Sung, China *state* East Asia the world in 1000 *58–59* *see also* China

Songhai *see* Kawkav, Songhay

Songhay *var.* Songhai, Kawkav *state* West Africa economy *163* (2) Islam *163* (1) the world in 1400 *70–71* trade *163* (5), (6), (7), *164* (2) *see also* Kawkav

Sông Hông Hà *see* Red River

Songhua *river* East Asia medieval states *264* (1), (2)

Sŏngjin *see* Kimchaek

Songkhla *var.* Songkla, *Mal.* Singora East Asia (China) colonialism *248* (1)

Songkla *see* Songkhla

Songo *state* Southern Africa trade *164* (2)

Song Shan *var.* Sung Shan *mountain* East Asia first religions *37* (4)

Sông Tiên Giang *see* Mekong

Songze *var.* Sung-tse East Asia (China) the world in 5000 BCE *18–19*

Sonoma *battle* North America (USA) the growth of the US *129* (2)

Sonora *state* Central America Mexican Revolution *133* (3) the growth of the US *129* (2)

Sonoran Desert *var.* Desierto de Altar *desert* Central America cultural groups *123* (4)

Sonpur South Asia (India) early religions *48* (2)

Soochow *see* Suzhou

Soomaaliya *see* Italian Somaliland, Somalia

Soome Laht *see* Finland, Gulf of

Sophia *see* Serdica, Sofia

Sopianae *see* Pécs

Sora Italy early states *178* (1)

Sorbonne *university* France economy *191* (2)

Sorbs *people* Eastern Europe Franks *184* (2)

Soreyya South Asia (India) world religions *242* (3)

Soshangane *people* Southern Africa colonization *166* (2)

Sotho *people* Southern Africa trade *164* (1) refugees *166* (2)

Sotho Refugees *people* Southern Africa colonization *166* (2)

Sotuta *state* Central America Aztecs *124* (1)

Sŏul-t'ŭkpyŏlsi *see* Seoul

Sousse *fort* North Africa (Tunisia) early Islam *56–57* (1)

South Africa *prev.* South African Republic, Union of South Africa, *Afr.* Suid-Afrika *state* Southern Africa decolonization *168* (1) economy *168* (2), (3) global immigration *100* (1), *101* (2) trade *167* (1) US economy *138* (2) WWII *105* (4) *see also* South African Republic, Union of South Africa

South African Republic *var.* Union of South Africa, *Afr.* Suid-Afrika *state* Southern Africa colonization *167* (4) European imperialism *96* (2) *see also* South Africa, South Africa, Union of

South Africa, Union of *prev.* South African Republic; *mod.* South Africa, Suid-Afrika *state* Southern Africa European imperialism *96* (1), (2), *97* (4) imperial global economy *92* (1) WWII *104* (1) *see also* South Africa, South African Republic

South Alaskan Inuit *people* North America cultural groups *123* (3)

South America *continent* 140–153

Southampton *hist.* Hamwih, *Lat.* Clausentum *bomb target/settlement* British Isles (United Kingdom) economy *190* (1) global immigration *100* (1) WWII *210* (1)

Southampton Inuit *people* North America cultural groups *123* (3)

Southampton Island *island* North America the growth of the US *129* (2)

South Arabia, Protectorate of *see* Aden Protectorate, South Yemen

South Asia *region* Asia biological diffusion *73* (2)

South Australia *region* Australia colonization *282* (1), (2), *283* (3)

South Cape *headland* New Zealand colonization *283* (4)

South Carolina *state* North America empire and revolution *127* (2), (3) imperial global economy *93* (5) the growth of the US *129* (1) US Civil War *130* (2), (3), (4), (5), *131* (6), (7) US economy *134* (2), *139* (3) US society *137* (6) US superpower *139* (5)

South China Sea *Chin.* Nan Hai, *Ind.* Laut Cina Selatan, *Vtn.* Biên Đông *sea* East Asia ancient India *241* (6) ancient trade *44–45* (1) trade *72–73* (1) Bronze Age *240* (3) colonialism *247* (4), *248* (1), *269* (4) decolonization *251* (4) early agriculture *20–21* (2), *258* (1) early medieval states *245* (5), (6) early modern states *266* (1), (2) economy *274* (1) empire and revolution *268* (2) European expansion *84–85* (1) European imperialism *97* (3) exploration *239* (1), (2) first cities *259* (5) first humans *13* (2) first religions *37* (4) first states *260* (1) historical geography *275* (5) Islam *243* (6), *275* (4) medieval states *262–263* (1), *263* (6) medieval voyages *61* (3) Mongols *68* (2), *68–69* (1) post-war economy *253* (5), *275* (3) post-war politics *251* (5), *253* (4), *274* (2) trade *230* (2), *267* (3) world religions *49* (3) WWII *251* (3), *272* (1), *273* (2)

South Dakota *state* North America the growth of the US *129* (1) US economy *134* (2)

Southeast Asia *region* Asia biological diffusion *73* (2)

Southeast Chiefdoms and Confederacies *state* North America the world in 1600 *78–79*

Southern Alps *mountain range* New Zealand colonization *283* (5)

Southern Capital East Asia (China) medieval states *263* (4)

Southern Liang *state* East Asia first states *261* (3)

Southern Long Wall *road* Greece ancient Greece *177* (4)

Southern Netherlands *see* Belgium

Southern Ocean *ocean* European expansion *80–81* (1) global knowledge *76–77* (1)

Southern Overland Trail *wagon train route* North America the growth of the US *129* (2)

Southern Pacific Railroad *railway* North America the growth of the US *129* (2)

Southern Qi *state* East Asia medieval states *261* (4)

Southern Rhodesia *later* Rhodesia; *mod.* Zimbabwe *colonial possession/state* Southern Africa European imperialism *96* (1), (2), *97* (4) WWII *104* (1) *see also* Rhodesia, Zimbabwe

Southern Shoshoni *people* North America colonization *126* (1)

Southern Solomons *island group* Pacific Ocean colonization *284–285* (1) exploration *279* (3)

Southern Song Empire *var.* Sung *state* East Asia Mongols *68–69* (1) the world in 1200 *62–63*

Southern Xiongnu *people* East Asia the world in 1 CE *42–43*, *260* (1) *see also* Xiongnu

Southern Yan *state* East Asia first states *261* (3)

South Georgia *island* Atlantic Ocean Antarctic Exploration *287* (3) exploration *142* (1), *143* (3)

South Georgia and the South Sandwich Islands *colonial possession* Atlantic Ocean the modern world *110–111*

South Glendale North America (USA) US economy *135* (4)

South Island *island* New Zealand colonization *283* (5)

South Korea *Kor.* Taehan Min'guk *state* East Asia Cold War *109* (1) Islam *275* (4) post-war economy *275* (4), *275* (3) Soviet Union *213* (4) the modern world *113* (4) US superpower *138* (1)

Southland *region* New Zealand colonization *283* (5)

South Prussia *region* Central Europe empire and revolution *198* (2)

South Sandwich Islands *island group* Atlantic Ocean Antarctic Exploration *287* (3)

South Shetland Islands *island group* Antarctica Antarctic Exploration *287* (3)

South Tyrol *region* Central Europe WWI *208* (1)

South Vietnam *var.* Republic of Vietnam *state* Mainland Southeast Asia Cold War *109* (1) post-war politics *251* (5)

Southwest *region* Central America/North America early agriculture *120* (1)

Southwest Africa *prev.* German Southwest Africa; *mod.* Namibia; *Afr.* Suidwes-Afrika, *Ger.* Deutsch-Südwestafrika; *state* Southern Africa Cold War *109* (5) WWII *104* (1) *see also* German Southwest Africa, Namibia

South Yemen *prev.* Federation of South Arabia, Protectorate of South Arabia, Aden Protectorate *state* Southwest Asia the world in 1975 *106–107* *see also* Aden Protectorate

Soviet Union *state* Eastern Europe, Siberia US economy *138* (2) US superpower *138* (1) *see also* Russia, Russian Empire, Russian Federation, Russian Principalities

Sōya-kaikyō *see* La Perouse Strait

Soyo Southern Africa (Angola) civil war *109* (5)

Soyo *state* Central Africa economy *163* (2)

Sozopol *see* Apollonia

Spain *anc.* Hispania, Iberia; *Lat.* Hispana; *Sp.* España *region/state/vassal state* Iberian Peninsula biological diffusion *72–73* (1) Cold War *108* (3), *109* (1) early 20th century *206* (1) early modern states *194* (1), *197* (5) economy *205* (4) empire and revolution *199* (4), *202* (1), *88–89* (2) European expansion *80–81* (1) European imperialism *97* (4) global immigration *100* (1) imperial global economy *92* (1) inter-war *209* (3), (4) Islam *226* (2), *227* (4) Napoleon *200–201* (1), *201* (2) Ottomans *231* (3) post-war economy *213* (5), *214* (1) post-war politics *212* (3) Reformation *194* (2) Soviet Union *214–215* (4) the modern world *112* (2), *113* (4) US superpower *138* (1) WWI *208* (1) WWII *104* (1), *211* (2), (4) *see also* Hispania, Iberia

Spalato Southeast Europe (Croatia) medieval states *187* (5)

Spandau Central Europe (Germany) post-war politics *212* (2)

Spanish Guinea *mod.* Equatorial Guinea; *prev.* Rio Muni *state* Central Africa the world in 1925 *98–99* the world in 1950 *102–103* *see also* Equatorial Guinea

Spanish March *region* Iberian Peninsula Franks *184* (2)

Spanish Morocco *region/colonial possession* North Africa European imperialism *96* (1) inter-war *209* (4) WWII *210* (1), *211* (4)

Spanish Netherlands *state* Low Countries early modern states *197* (5) Reformation *196* (1), (2)

Spanish Sahara *mod.* Western Sahara; *prev.* Rio de Oro *state* North Africa the world in 1950 *102–103* the world in 1975 *106–107* *see also* Rio de Oro, Western Sahara

Sparta *var.* Lacedaemon Greece ancient Greece *177* (3), *179* (4) ancient Persia *223* (4) ancient Rome *180–181* (1) exploration *172* (1) Hellenistic world *40–41* (1)

Spartolos *see* Spartolus

Spartolus *state* Greece ancient Greece *177* (2) battle *177* (3)

Speyer *anc.* Civitas Nemetum, Spira; *Eng.* Spires *massacre/settlement* Central Europe (Germany) crusades *186* (1) Franks *184* (2) Reformation *194* (2)

Sphacteria *battle* Greece ancient Greece *177* (3)

Spice Islands *see* Moluccas

Spion Kop *battle* Southern Africa (South Africa) European imperialism *96* (2)

Spira, **Spires** *see* Speyer

Spirit Cave Mainland Southeast Asia (Burma) the world in 5000 BCE *18–19*

Spiro North America (USA) cultural groups *122* (5)

Spišsky Štvrtok *fort* Central Europe (Slovakia) Bronze Age *175* (3)

Spitsbergen *see* Spitzbergen

Spitzbergen *var.* Spitsbergen, Svalbard *colonial possession/island group* Scandinavia European expansion *80–81* (1) exploration *257* (2) WWII *104* (1) Cold War *109* (1) *see also* Svalbard

Split *It.* Spalato Southeast Europe (Croatia) post-war economy *215* (3) *see also* Spalato

Spokane Plain *battle* North America (USA) the growth of the US *129* (2)

Spoletium *mod.* Spoleto Italy early states *178* (1) *see also* Spoleto

Spoleto Italy Franks *184* (2) medieval states *183* (4)

Spoleto, Duchy of *state* Italy Franks *184* (2) medieval states *183* (4)

Sporades *island group* Greece first civilizations *175* (4)

Spotsylvania Court House *battle* North America (USA) US Civil War *131* (7)

Spratly Islands *Chin.* Nansha Qundao *island group* Maritime Southeast Asia the modern world *110–111*

Spree *river* Central Europe post-war politics *212* (2)

Springfield North America (USA) the growth of the US *129* (2), *132* (1)

Springfield North America (USA) US Civil War *131* (6)

Springfontein Southern Africa (South Africa) European imperialism *96* (2)

Spy *archaeological site* France first humans *13* (2)

Squawkie Hill *burial mound* North America (USA) first civilizations *121* (4)

Sravasti *religious site/settlement* South Asia (India) early religions *48* (2) first religions *36* (2)

Srbica Southeast Europe (Yugoslavia) post-war economy *215* (3)

Srbija *see* Serbia

Srebrenica Southeast Europe (Bosnia and Herzegovina) civil war *215* (3)

Sredne-Kolymsk Siberia (Russian Federation) exploration *257* (2)

Sresthapura Mainland Southeast Asia (Cambodia) ancient India *241* (6)

Sriksetra *state* Mainland Southeast Asia ancient India *241* (6)

Sri Lanka *prev.* Ceylon; *var.* Sri Lanka, Sinhala, Taprobane; *var.* Saylan, Sarandib; *mod.* Sri Lanka; *Chin.* Hsi-lan; *anc.* Taprobane, Simhala, Sinhala, Lambakannas, Lanka *state* South Asia post-war economy *253* (5) post-war politics *252* (1), *253* (4) the modern world *113* (3) world religions *243* (4) *see also* Ceylon, Lambakannas, Lanka, Simhala, Taprobane

Srinagar *settlement* South Asia (India) colonialism *247* (3), *248* (1) decolonization *250* (1) economy *249* (4) Mughal Empire *246* (1) post-war politics *252* (1), (2) trade *267* (3) world religions *49* (3)

Shrirangapattanam *var.* Seringapatam South Asia (India) Mughal Empire *246* (1) *see also* Seringapatam, Shrirangapattanam

Srivijaya Maritime Southeast Asia (Indonesia) the world in 750 CE *54–55*

Srivijaya *state* Maritime Southeast Asia ancient India *241* (6) early medieval states *245* (5) Mongols *68–69* (1) world religions *243* (5), *49* (4)

Ssu-ch'uan *see* Sichuan

Stabroek *var.* Stabrok; *mod.* Georgetown South America (Guyana) colonization *149* (4) *see also* Georgetown

Stabrok *see* Georgetown, Stabroek

Stagirus *state* Greece ancient Greece *177* (2)

Stalin *see* Odessus, Varna

Stalinabad *see* Dushanbe

Stalingrad *mod.* Volgograd; *prev.* Tsaritsyn Eastern Europe (Russian Federation) WWII *104* (2) WWII *210* (1), *211* (2), (4) *see also* Tsaritsyn, Volgograd

Stalinobod *see* Dushanbe

Stamford Bridge *battle* British Isles (United Kingdom) medieval states *186* (2)

Stanislau Eastern Europe (Ukraine) WWI *207* (4)

Stanley Falls *waterfall* Central Africa exploration *157* (4)

Stanleyville *see* Kisangani

Staraya Ladoga Eastern Europe (Russian Federation) medieval states *185* (3) medieval voyages *60–61* (1)

Staraya Russa Eastern Europe (Russian Federation) early modern states *195* (3)

Stargard Central Europe (Poland) medieval states *189* (3)

Staroselye *archaeological site* Eastern Europe (Ukraine) first humans *13* (2)

States, The *see* United States of America

Staunton North America (USA) US Civil War *131* (6)

Stavanger *air raid* Scandinavia (Norway) WWII *210* (1)

Steen Mountains *battle* North America (USA) the growth of the US *129* (2)

Steglitz Central Europe (Germany) post-war politics *212* (2)

Steinheim *archaeological site* Central Europe (Germany) first humans *13* (2)

Stelvio Pass *pass* Italy WWI *207* (5)

Stentinello Italy early agriculture *174* (1)

Steppes *physical region* Siberia crusades *65* (1) early agriculture *258* (1) first states *260* (1) global knowledge *76–77* (1) medieval states *261* (6) trade *267* (3)

Steptoe Butte *battle* North America (USA) the growth of the US *129* (2)

Sterkfontein *archaeological site* Southern Africa (South Africa) first humans *12* (1), *13* (2)

Stettin *Pol.* Szczecin Central Europe (Poland) early modern states *193* (4), *195* (3) medieval states *188* (1), *189* (3) post-war politics *212* (3) Reformation *196* (1)

Stewart Island *island* New Zealand colonization *283* (4), (5)

Sthanika South Asia (India) world religions *243* (4)

Sthanvishvara South Asia (India) early medieval states *244* (2)

Stillman's Defeat *battle* North America (USA) the growth of the US *129* (2)

Stirling British Isles (United Kingdom) medieval states *188* (2)

Stobi *settlement* Greece ancient Rome *180–181* (1) world religions *48* (1)

Stockholm Scandinavia (Sweden) biological diffusion *72–73* (1) early modern states *195* (3) economy *190* (1) empire and revolution *198* (2), *202* (1) medieval states *189* (3) Napoleon *200–201* (1), *201* (2), (3) post-war politics *212* (3) Reformation *194* (2) Soviet Union *208* (2) WWII *210* (1), *211* (2), (4) Cold War *108* (3)

Stockport British Isles (United Kingdom) imperial global economy *93* (4)

Stockstadt Central Europe (Germany) world religions *48* (1)

Stockton *var.* Stockton on Tees, Stockton-on-Tees British Isles (United Kingdom) economy *204* (1)

Stockton on Tees *see* Stockton

Stoke *var.* Stoke-on-Trent British Isles (United Kingdom) economy *204* (1)

Stoke-on-Trent *see* Stoke

Stolos *state* Greece ancient Greece *177* (2)

Stonehenge *archaeological site* British Isles (United Kingdom) Copper Age *174* (2) early systems *33* (3) first religions *36* (1)

Stony Lake *battle* North America (USA) the growth of the US *129* (2)

Stora Köpinge *archaeological site* Scandinavia (Sweden) Copper Age *174* (2)

Stormberg *battle* Southern Africa (South Africa) European imperialism *96* (2)

Stralsund Central Europe (Germany) early modern states *197* (3) economy *190* (1) medieval states *189* (3)

Stranraer British Isles (United Kingdom) economy *204* (1)

Strasbourg *anc.* Argentoratum; *Ger.* Strassburg France early modern states *197* (5) empire and revolution *199* (4) Franks *183* (5), (6) Napoleon *200–201* (1) *see also* Argentoratum, Strassburg

Strassburg *anc.* Argentoratum; *Fr.* Strasbourg France early modern states *193* (4) economy *190* (1) empire and revolution *202* (2) Franks *184* (2) WWI *206* (2), (3) *see also* Argentoratum, Strasbourg

Strathclyde *county* British Isles medieval states *183* (3)

Strathcona Sound North America (Canada) cultural groups *123* (3)

Strepsa *state* Greece ancient Greece *177* (2)

Stretford British Isles (United Kingdom) economy *204* (2)

Strigonium *see* Esztergom, Gran

Struma *Gk.* Strymónas *river* Southeast Europe WWI *207* (6)

Strymónas *see* Struma

Studyanka Eastern Europe (Russian Federation) Napoleon *200–201* (1)

Stuhlweissenberg *see* Székesfehérvár

Sturts Meadows *archaeological site* Australia prehistoric culture *17* (5)

Stuttgart Central Europe (Germany) early modern states *193* (4) empire and revolution *202* (2) post-war politics *212* (1) WWII *211* (4)

Styria *region/state* Central Europe early modern states *193* (4), *194* (1) medieval states *188* (1), *189* (4)

Su *see* Jiangsu

Suakin *var.* Sawakin East Africa (Sudan) exploration *156* (3) Islam *163* (1) Ottomans *231* (3) trade *230* (2)

Süanhua *see* Xuanhua

Subotica *Ger.* Maria-Theresiopel, *Hung.* Szabadka Southeast Europe (Yugoslavia) post-war economy *215* (3)

Sub-Saharan pastoralists *people* Africa the world in 1250 BCE *26–27*

Suceava Southeast Europe (Romania) Ottomans *230* (1)

Su-chou, Suchow *see* Suzhou

Sucre *hist.* Chuquisaca, La Plata South America (Bolivia) empire and revolution *151* (3) environment *153* (4) politics *151* (4), *152* (1) *see also* Chuquisaca, La Plata

Sudan *prev.* Anglo-Egyptian Sudan *state* East Africa biological diffusion *72–73* (1) colonization *167* (4) decolonization *168* (1) economy *168* (2), (3) exploration *157* (5) Islam *235* (4) the modern world *112* (1), *113* (3), (4) 20th-century politics *235* (5) *see also* Anglo-Egyptian Sudan

Sudan *physical region* East Africa economy *163* (2) Islam *163* (1)

Sudanese Republic *see* Mali

Sudbury North America (Canada) the growth of the US *129* (2)

Sudd *wetland* East Africa first humans *12* (1)

Suddhammavati Mainland Southeast Asia (Burma) ancient India *241* (6)

Sudetenland *region* Central Europe WWII *211* (2)

Südliche Morava *see* Južna Morava

Sueves *people* Iberian Peninsula great migrations *52–53* (1), *53* (2)

Sueves, Kingdom of the *state* Iberian Peninsula ancient Rome *182* (1)

Suez *Ar.* As Suways, El Suweis Egypt exploration *156* (3), *157* (5) Ottomans *231* (3), *232–233* (1) trade *230* (2) 20th century *234* (2) 20th-century politics *233* (4)

Suez Canal *Ar.* Qanát as Suways *canal* Southwest Asia exploration *219* (4) Ottomans *232–233* (1) 20th century *234* (2) 20th-century politics *233* (3), (4)

Suez, Gulf of *Ar.* Khalīj as Suways *gulf* Egypt 20th century *234* (2)

Suhar *var.* Sohar Southwest Asia (Oman) early Islam *56–57* (1) Islam *226* (2) medieval voyages *61* (3)

Suid-Afrika *see* South Africa, South African Republic, South Africa, Union of

Suidwes-Afrika *see* Namibia

Sukadana Maritime Southeast Asia (Indonesia) colonization *284–285* (1)

Sukadana *region/state* Maritime Southeast Asia colonialism *247* (4)

Sukarnapura *see* Hollandia

Sukhothai *var.* Sukotai Mainland Southeast Asia (Thailand) early medieval states *245* (6) medieval states *263* (6) world religions *243* (5), *49* (4)

Sukhothai *state* Mainland Southeast Asia the world in 1300 *66–67* the world in 1400 *70–71*

Sukhoye Ozero *archaeological site* Siberia (Russian Federation) early agriculture *258* (1)

Sukkur South Asia (Pakistan) colonialism *247* (3)

Sukotai *see* Sukhothai

Sulaiman Range *mountain range* South Asia colonialism *247* (3), *248* (1) early medieval states *244* (1), *244–245* (3) economy *249* (4) first cities *240* (2) Mughal Empire *246* (1) world religions *243* (4)

Sulawesi *see* Celebes

Sulawesi, Laut *see* Celebes Sea

Sulci *see* Sulcis

Sulcis *var.* Sulci Italy first civilizations *177* (1)

Suleyman Southwest Asia (Iran) early Islam *56–57* (1)

Sullana South America (Peru) Incas *147* (3), *148* (1)

Sultanabad Southwest Asia (Iran) WWI *233* (2)

Sulu *state* Maritime Southeast Asia the world in 1600 *78–79* the world in 1700 *82–83* the world in 1800 *86–87* the world in 1850 *90–91*

Sulu, Laut *see* Sulu Sea

Sulu Sea *Ind.* Laut Sulu *sea* Maritime Southeast Asia ancient India *241* (6) Bronze Age *240* (3) decolonization *251* (4) exploration *239* (1), (2) Islam *243* (6) post-war economy *253* (5) post-war politics *253* (4) world religions *243* (5)

Suma *people* Central America colonization *125* (4), *126* (1)

Suma-misquito *people* Central America the world in 1500 *74–75*

Sumatera *see* Sumatra

Sumatra *Ind.* Sumatera *island* Maritime Southeast Asia ancient India *241* (6) ancient trade *44–45* (1) Biological diffusion *72–73* (1) Bronze Age *240* (3) colonialism *247* (4), *248* (1), *269* (4) decolonization *251* (4) early agriculture *20–21* (2), *258* (1) early medieval states *245* (5), (6) European expansion *80–81* (1) European imperialism *97* (3), (4) exploration *239* (1), (2) first humans *13* (2) global immigration *101* (3) historical geography *236–237* (1) Islam *243* (6) post-war economy *253* (5) post-war politics *253* (4) trade *230* (2), *267* (3) world religions *243* (5), *49* (4) WWII *251* (3), *272* (1), *273* (2)

Sumba *Dut.* Soemba *island* Maritime Southeast Asia colonialism *247* (4) decolonization *251* (4) early medieval states *245* (6) European imperialism *97* (3) exploration *239* (1), (2) post-war economy *253* (5) post-war politics *253* (4) WWII *251* (3), *272* (1), *273* (2)

Sumbawa *Dut.* Soembawa *island* Maritime Southeast Asia colonialism *247* (4) early medieval states *245* (5), (6) European imperialism *97* (3) exploration *239* (1), (2) Islam *243* (6) world religions *243* (5)

Sumer Southwest Asia (Iraq) first religions *36* (1)

Sumer *state* Southwest Asia first cities *220* (2) first civilizations *221* (4)

Sumha *region* South Asia world religions *242* (2)

Sunchon East Asia (South Korea) early modern states *267* (4)

Sunda *physical region* Maritime Southeast Asia exploration *276–277* (1) historical geography *254–255* (1)

Sunda Strait *battle* Maritime Southeast Asia (Indonesia) WWII *272* (1)

Sunderland *var.* Wearmouth British Isles (United Kingdom) economy *204* (1)

Sundown Point *archaeological site* Australia prehistoric culture *17* (5)

Sung *see* Song Empire, Southern Song Empire

Sungari *river* East Asia early agriculture *258* (1)

Sungaria *see* Dzungaria

Sunghir *archaeological site* Eastern Europe (Russian Federation) the world in 10,000 BCE *14–15*

Sung Shan *see* Song Shan

Sung-tse *see* Songze

Sunnyvale North America (USA) *136* (3)

Sunomata *battle* Japan early modern states *265* (5)

Süntel *battle* Central Europe (Germany) Franks *184* (2)

Suomenlahti *see* Finland, Gulf of

Suomen Tasavalta *see* Finland

Suomi *see* Finland

Suomussalmi Scandinavia (Finland) WWII *210* (1)

Supara South Asia (India) medieval voyages *61* (3)

Superior, Lake *lake* North America colonization *126* (1) cultural groups *123* (3) early agriculture *120* (1) exploration *118* (1), *119* (2), (3) first civilizations *121* (4) the growth of the US *129* (2), *132* (1) US Civil War *131* (6)

Suqutra *see* Socotra

Sūr *see* Syria

Surabaja *see* Surabaya

Surabaya *prev.* Soerabaja, Surabaja *military base/settlement* Maritime Southeast Asia (Indonesia) exploration *239* (2) Islam *275* (4) post-war economy *253* (5) trade *267* (3) WWII *272* (1)

Surasena *region/state* South Asia ancient India *242* (1) first empires *241* (5) first religions *36* (2) world religions *242* (3)

Surashtra *region/state* South Asia first empires *241* (4), (5) world religions *242* (2)

Surat South Asia (India) colonialism *247* (3) decolonization *250* (1) early medieval states *244–245* (3) economy *249* (4) empire and revolution *88* (1) trade *230* (2)

Surgut Eastern Europe (Russian Federation) colonialism *269* (3) exploration *257* (2)

Surinam *var.* Suriname; *prev.* Dutch Guiana, Netherlands Guiana *state* South America colonization *149* (4) economy *153* (3) empire and revolution *150* (1), *151* (3) environment *153* (4) global immigration *101* (3) politics *152* (1) the modern world *112* (1), *113* (3) *see also* Dutch Guiana

Suriname *see* Dutch Guiana, Surinam

Sūrīya *see* Syria

Surkotada *archaeological site* South Asia (India) first cities *240* (2)

Surparaka South Asia (India) early religions *48* (2) first empires *241* (4)

Surt *see* Sirt

Susa *mod.* Shūsh; *Bibl.* Shushan Southwest Asia (Iran) ancient Persia *223* (4), *225* (6) ancient Rome *224* (2), *225* (5) early Islam *56–57* (1) early systems *223* (3) early trade *225* (3) exploration *218* (1) first cities *220* (2), *28–29* (1) first civilizations *221* (4), *24* (2), *25* (3) Hellenistic world *224* (1) Islam *227* (4), (5)

Susia Central Asia (Turkmenistan) Hellenistic world *40–41* (1)

Susiana *province/region* Southwest Asia ancient Persia *223* (4) Hellenistic world *40–41* (1)

Susquehanna *var.* Conestoga *people* North America colonization *126* (1)

Susquehanna *river* North America empire and revolution *127* (3)

Sussex *state* British Isles medieval states *183* (3)

Sutkagen Dor *archaeological site* South Asia (Pakistan) first cities *240* (2)

Sutlej *river* South Asia ancient India *242* (1) colonialism *247* (3), *248* (1), (2) decolonization *250* (1) early medieval states *244* (1), (2), *244–245* (3) economy *249* (4) Marathas *246* (2) Mughal Empire *246* (1) world religions *242* (2), *243* (4)

Sutrium Italy early states *178* (1)

Sutton Hoo British Isles (United Kingdom) medieval states *183* (3)

Suva (Fiji) WWII *104* (2)

Suvarnagiri South Asia (India) first empires *241* (4)

Suvla Bay *battle* Southwest Asia (Turkey) WWI *207* (6)

Suways, Khalīj as *see* Suez, Gulf of

Suways, Qanāt as *see* Suez Canal

Suzdal Eastern Europe (Russian Federation) Mongols *68–69* (1)

Suzhou *var.* Soochow, Su-chou, Suchow; *prev.* Wuhsien East Asia (China) colonialism *269* (4) early modern states *266* (1) imperialism *270* (2) medieval states *263* (6)

Svalbard *var.* Spitsbergen, Spitzbergen *colonial possession/island group* Arctic Ocean exploration *286* (1), *287* (2) *see also* Spitsbergen

Sverdlovsk Eastern Europe (Russian Federation) Soviet Union *213* (4)

Sverige *see* Sweden

Svizhden *state* Eastern Europe medieval states *189* (4)

Svizzera *see* Helvetia, Helvetian Republic, Swiss Confederation, Switzerland

Svobodnyy Eastern Europe (Russian Federation) Soviet Union *214–215* (4)

Swabia *region* Central Europe crusades *64–65* (2) medieval states *185* (3), *188* (1)

Swahili City-States *region/state* East Africa/Southern Africa economy *163* (2)

Swanscombe *archaeological site* British Isles (United Kingdom) first humans *13* (2)

Swansea *Wel.* Abertawe British Isles (United Kingdom) economy *204* (1)

Swartkrans *archaeological site* Southern Africa (South Africa) first humans *12* (1)

Swatow *see* Shantou

Swazi *people* Southern Africa the world in 1850 *90–91*

Swazi *see* Swaziland

Swaziland *prev.* Swazi *state* Southern Africa decolonization *168* (1) economy *168* (2), (3) European imperialism *96* (1) trade *167* (1)

Sweden *Swe.* Sverige *state* Scandinavia colonialism *269* (3) crusades *186* (1), *64–65* (2) early 20th century *206* (1) early modern states *193* (4), *195* (3) economy *190* (1), *205* (4) empire and revolution *198* (2), *199* (3), *202* (1), (2) imperial global economy *92* (1) inter-war *209* (3), (5) medieval states *185* (3) medieval voyages *60–61* (1) Mongols *68–69* (1) Napoleon *200–201* (1), *201* (2) post-war economy *213* (5), *214* (1), (2) post-war politics *212* (3) Reformation *194* (2), *196* (1), (2) Soviet Union *208* (2), *213* (4) the modern world *112* (2) WWI *207* (4), *208* (1) WWII *104* (1), *211* (2), (4) Cold War *108* (3)

Swedes *people* Scandinavia medieval states *185* (3) the modern world *112* (2)

Swedish Pomerania *colonial possession* Central Europe empire and revolution *199* (3) Napoleon *200–201* (1)

Swiss Confederation *var.* Switzerland; *Fr.* La Suisse, *Ger.* Schweiz, *It.* Svizzera; *prev.* Helvetia, Helvetian Republic; *anc.* Helvetia *state* Central Europe early modern states *193* (4), *197* (5) empire and revolution *199* (3), (4) Napoleon *200–201* (1) Reformation *194* (2), *196* (1), (2) *see also* Helvetia, Helvetian Republic, Switzerland

Switzerland *var.* Swiss Confederation, *Fr.* La Suisse, *Ger.* Schweiz, *It.* Svizzera; *prev.* Helvetia, Helvetian Republic; *state* Central Europe early 20th century *206* (1) economy *205* (4) empire and revolution *202* (1), (2), (3) inter-war *209* (3), (5) post-war economy *213* (5), *214* (1), (2) post-war politics *212* (1), (3) Soviet Union *213* (4) the modern world *112* (2), *113* (3), (4) WWI *206* (2), (3), *207* (5), *208* (1) WWII *104* (1), *211* (2), (3), (4) Cold War *108* (3) *see also* Helvetia, Helvetian Republic, Swiss Confederation

Sword Brothers *crusade* Eastern Europe crusades *186* (1)

Syagrius, Kingdom of *state* France Franks *183* (5)

Sybaris Italy first civilizations *177* (1)

Sycaminum *see* Haifa

Sydney *settlement* Australia colonization *282* (1), (2), *283* (3), *284–285* (1) environmentalism *285* (2) exploration *279* (2), (3) global immigration *100* (1) imperial global economy *92* (1) prehistoric culture *17* (5)

Syedpur *see* Saidpur

Syene *var.* Assouan, Assuan, Qus; *Ar.* Aswân Egypt Hellenistic world *40–41* (1) *see also* Aswân, Qus

Sylhet South Asia (Bangladesh) post-war politics *252* (3)

Synnada Southwest Asia (Turkey) world religions *48* (1)

Syracusa, **Syracusae** *see* Syracuse

Syracuse *mod.* Siracusa; *Lat.* Syracusae; *It.* Syracusa *settlement* Italy ancient Rome *179* (3), (5), *180–181* (1), *181* (3), (4) crusades *186* (1) early cultures *161* (2) early states *178* (2) economy *190* (1) first civilizations *177* (1) first religions *37* (3) Islam *184* (1), *227* (4) medieval states *183* (4), *188* (1)

Syr Darya *region* Central Asia colonialism *269* (3)

Syr Darya *var.* Sai Hun, Sir Darya, Syrdarya, *Kaz.* Syrdariya, *Rus.* Syrdar'ya, *Uzb.* Sirdaryo *river* Central Asia ancient trade *44–45* (1) biological diffusion *72–73* (1) colonialism *269* (3) early Islam *56–57* (1) exploration *257* (3) first humans *13* (2) Mongols *68–69* (1) the world in 1500 *74–75* *see also* Jaxartes

Syrdar'ya *see* Jaxartes, Syr Darya

Syria *var.* Siria, Syrie, Sūrīya *region/state* Southwest Asia ancient Persia *225* (6) ancient Rome *180–181* (1), *224* (2), *225* (4), (5) ancient trade *44–45* (1) crusades *65* (3), *228* (2) early cultures *161* (3), (5) early Islam *56–57* (1), *57* (2) early trade *225* (3) economy *234* (1) exploration *218* (2), *219* (4) first religions *37* (3) Hellenistic world *224* (1), *41* (2) Islam *226* (2), *227* (4), (5), *235* (4) medieval states *187* (5) Mongols *229* (3) Napoleon *200–201* (1) Ottomans *231* (3), *232–233* (1) Seljuks *228* (1) Soviet Union *208* (2), *214–215* (4) the modern world *113* (3) Timur *229* (4) US economy *138* (2) world religions *226* (1), *49* (4) WWI *233* (2) WWII *104* (1), (2), *210* (1), *211* (2), (4) 20th century *234* (2) 20th-century politics *233* (3), (4), *235* (5) Cold War *109* (1) *see also* Aram

Syrian Desert *Ar.* Al Hamad, Bādiyat ash Shām *desert* Southwest Asia ancient Persia *223* (4) ancient Rome *180–181* (1), *181* (4) early agriculture *220* (1) economy *234* (1) exploration *219* (4) first cities *220* (2), *28–29* (1) first civilizations *221* (4), *222* (1), (2), *25* (3) Hellenistic world *40–41* (1)

Syrie *see* Syria

Szabadka *see* Subotica

Száva *see* Sava

Szczecin *see* Stettin

Szechuan, **Szechwan** *see* Sichuan

Szeged Ger. Szegedin, Rom. Seghedin Central Europe (Hungary) early modern states 193 (4) medieval states 189 (4)
Szegedin see Szeged
Székesfehérvár anc. Alba Regia; Ger. Stuhlweissenberg Central Europe (Hungary) medieval states 188 (1)
Szemao see Simao
Szigetvár Central Europe (Hungary) Ottomans 231 (3)
Sziszek see Sisak
Szlovákia see Slovakia

T

Tabaristan state Central Asia early Islam 56–57 (1)
Tabariya, Bahr, **Tabariya, Bahrat** see Galilee, Sea of
Tabasco state Central America Mexican Revolution 133 (3) the growth of the US 129 (2)
Tabon Cave Philippines (Philippines) the world in 10,000 BCE 14–15
Tábor Central Europe (Czech Republic) early modern states 193 (4)
Tabora var. Unyanyembe, Kazeh East Africa (Tanzania) exploration 157 (4), (5)
Tabriz Southwest Asia (Iran) biological diffusion 72–73 (1) exploration 218 (2), 219 (3) Islam 226 (2), 227 (4), (5) medieval Persia 231 (4) Mongols 68 (2), 68–69 (1) Ottomans 231 (3) Seljuks 228 (1) Soviet Union 208 (2) Timur 229 (4) world religions 226 (1) WWI 233 (2) 20th-century politics 233 (3), 235 (5)
Tabuk Philippines early Islam 56–57 (1)
Tabun archaeological site Southwest Asia (Israel) first humans 13 (2)
Tacna South America (Peru) empire and revolution 150 (1), 151 (3) politics 151 (4)
Tacna region South America politics 151 (4)
Tacuba Central America (Mexico) Aztecs 124 (2) colonization 125 (5)
Tacubaya Central America (Mexico) Aztecs 124 (2)
Tadmor var. Tamar Southwest Asia (Syria) first civilizations 222 (1) see also Palmyra
Tadmur see Palmyra
Tadzhikistan see Tajikistan
Taegu East Asia (South Korea) Cold War 109 (4)
Taehan-haehyŏp see Korea Strait
Taehan Min'guk see South Korea
Taejon Jap. Taiden East Asia (South Korea) Cold War 109 (4)
Tafahi island Pacific Ocean exploration 278 (1)
Taforalt archaeological site North Africa (Algeria) first humans 13 (2)
Taga Japan early modern states 265 (5) medieval states 264 (2), 265 (3), (4)
Taghaza West Africa (Mauritania) exploration 156 (3) Islam 163 (1)
Tagish people North America cultural groups 123 (3)
Tagliacozzo battle Italy medieval states 188 (1)
Tagliamento river Italy WWI 207 (5)
Tagus Port. Rio Tejo, Sp. Río Tajo river Iberian Peninsula ancient Rome 180–181 (1) Bronze Age 175 (3) Copper Age 174 (2) crusades 64–65 (2) early agriculture 174 (1) economy 190 (1), 205 (4) first civilizations 177 (1) Franks 184 (2) great migrations 52–53 (1), 53 (2) inter-war 209 (4) Islam 192 (3) Napoleon 200–201 (1), 201 (2) prehistoric culture 17 (3)
Tahert North Africa (Algeria) early Islam 56–57 (1) Islam 163 (1)
Tahirids dynasty Central Asia Islam 227 (4)
Tahiti island Pacific Ocean colonization 284–285 (1) early cultures 280–281 (3) environmentalism 285 (2) exploration 278 (1), 279 (3) medieval voyages 60 (2)
Tahltan people North America cultural groups 123 (3)
Ta'if Ar. Al Ṭa'if Southwest Asia (Saudi Arabia) early Islam 56–57 (1) Islam 226 (3) world religions 226 (1) 20th-century politics 233 (4)
Tai Hu lake East Asia early modern states 266 (1) first states 260 (1)
Taiji var. Imperial Palace palace East Asia (China) medieval states 262 (2)
Taima Taima archaeological site/settlement South America (Venezuela) early cultures 144 (1)
Taimyr Peninsula see Taymyr, Poluostrov
Taipei East Asia (Taiwan) Islam 275 (4)
Taiping military campaign East Asia empire and revolution 88–89 (2)
Taira Japan economy 270 (1)
Tairona state South America the world in 1200 62–63
Tairona Chiefdoms state South America early cultures 146 (1)
Tai Shan var. T'ai Shan mountain East Asia first religions 37 (4)
Taiwan var. Formosa prev. China, Republic of island/state East Asia ancient trade 44–45 (1) colonialism 269 (4) decolonization 251 (4), 285 (3) early agriculture 258 (1) early modern states 266 (2), 268 (1) empire and revolution 268 (2) European imperialism 97 (3) first cities 259 (4), (5) first religions 37 (4) first states 260 (1), 261 (2), (3) historical geography 236–237 (1) imperialism 270 (2) Islam 275 (4) medieval states 261 (4), (5), 262–263 (1), 263 (3), (4), (5), (6) Mongols 68–69 (1) post-war economy 253 (5), 275 (3) post-war politics 271 (7) the growth of the US 133 (4) the modern world 113 (4) WWII 251 (3) Communist revolution 274 (1) Cold War 109 (1) see also China, Republic of, Formosa
Taiwanese rebellion East Asia empire and revolution 268 (2)
Taixicun East Asia (China) first cities 259 (3)
Taiyuan prev. T'ai-yuan, T'ai-yüan, Yangku East Asia (China) biological diffusion 72–73 (1) early modern states 266 (1) economy 274 (1) Islam 275 (4) medieval states 262–263 (1), 263 (4), (5) post-war politics 271 (7), 274 (2)
Tajikistan Rus. Tadzhikistan, Taj. Tojikiston state Central Asia Islam 235 (4) post-war economy 275 (3) Soviet Union 214–215 (4) the modern world 113 (3)
Tajiks people Central Asia historical geography 275 (5)
Tajo, Río see Tagus
Takamatsu battle Japan early modern states 267 (4)
Takaoka Japan economy 270 (1)
Takeda region Japan early modern states 267 (4)
Takedda West Africa (Mali/Niger) exploration 156 (3)
Ta Kieu Mainland Southeast Asia (Vietnam) ancient India 241 (6)
Takkola Mainland Southeast Asia (Thailand) ancient India 241 (6)
Takla Makan Desert Chin. Taklimakan Shamo desert East Asia ancient trade 44–45 (1) biological diffusion 72–73 (1) colonialism 269 (4) early agriculture 258 (1) empire and revolution 268 (1), (2) exploration 256 (1), 257 (3) first cities 259 (5) first states 260 (1) medieval states 261 (6), 262–263 (1) Mongols 68–69 (1) trade 267 (3) world religions 49 (3), (4)
Taklimakan Shamo see Takla Makan Desert
Takoradi West Africa (Ghana) colonization 167 (4)
Takrur var. Toucouleur state West Africa Islam 163 (1) trade 163 (4), (6), (7)
Taksashila var. Taxila South Asia (Pakistan) early medieval states 244 (1) first empires 241 (4) see also Taxila
Takume island Pacific Ocean exploration 278 (1)
Takushan see Dagushan
Talasea island Pacific Ocean early cultures 280–281 (3) medieval voyages 60 (2)
Talas River battle Central Asia (Kazakhstan) early Islam 56–57 (1) Islam 226 (2)
Talavera var. Talavera de la Reina Iberian Peninsula (Spain) Napoleon 200–201 (1)
Talavera de la Reina see Talavera
Talca South America (Chile) empire and revolution 150 (1), 151 (3) environment 153 (4) Incas 147 (3)
Talcahuano battle South America (Chile) empire and revolution 150 (1)
Talgai Australia exploration 280 (1)
Ta-lien see Dairen, Dalian
Tal-i Ghazir Southwest Asia (Iran) first cities 220 (2)
Tal-i Iblis Southwest Asia (Iran) first civilizations 24 (2)
Tal-i Malyan Southwest Asia (Iran) first cities 220 (2)
Tallahassee prev. Muskogean North America (USA) the growth of the US 129 (2) US Civil War 131 (6), (7) US society 137 (6)
Tallasahatchee battle North America (USA) the growth of the US 129 (2)
Tallin see Reval, Revel, Tallinn
Tallinn Ger. Reval, Rus. Tallin, Revel Eastern Europe (Estonia) post-war politics 212 (3) Soviet Union 214–215 (4) see also Reval, Revel
Tall-i Qaleh Southwest Asia (Iran) first civilizations 25 (3)
Taltal South America (Chile) politics 151 (4)
Tamanrasset var. Tamenghest North Africa (Algeria) colonization 167 (4)
Tamar see Palmyra, Tadmor
Tamar Hat archaeological site North Africa (Algeria) prehistoric culture 17 (2)
Tamatsukuri Japan early modern states 265 (5)
Tamaulipas state Central America Mexican Revolution 133 (3) the growth of the US 129 (2)
Tamazultec people Central America colonization 125 (4)
Tambo Colorado South America (Peru) Incas 147 (3)
Tambora island Maritime Southeast Asia European expansion 84–85 (1)
Tambov Eastern Europe (Russian Federation) Soviet Union 208 (2)
Tambo Viejo South America (Peru) early cultures 145 (4)
Tambralinga Mainland Southeast Asia (Thailand) ancient India 241 (6) early medieval states 245 (5)
Tambralinga region Mainland Southeast Asia early medieval states 245 (5)
Tame South America (Colombia) empire and revolution 150 (1)
Tamenghest see Tamanrasset
Tamil Nadu region/state South Asia post-war politics 252 (1) world religions 243 (4)
Tamils people South Asia the world in 250 CE 46–47
Ta-ming see Daming
Tamluk religious site/settlement South Asia (India) ancient trade 44–45 (1) first religions 36 (2)
Tammaulipeco people Central America colonization 126 (1)
Tampa North America (USA) Cold War 108 (2)
Tampico Central America (Mexico) colonization 125 (4), 126 (1) exploration 118 (1) Mexican Revolution 133 (3) the growth of the US 129 (2) Cold War 108 (2)
Tamralipti South Asia early medieval states 244 (1) early religions 48 (2) first empires 241 (4) world religions 242 (2), (3)
Tamuín Central America (Mexico) first civilizations 122 (1)
Tamworth British Isles (United Kingdom) medieval states 183 (3)
Tana Eastern Europe (Russian Federation) economy 190 (1) Ottomans 195 (4)
T'ana Häyk' see Tana, Lake
Tanais see Don
Tana, Lake var. T'ana Häyk' lake East Africa early cultures 161 (3), (4), (5) early trade 225 (3) exploration 157 (5) first humans 12 (1), 13 (2) trade 165 (3)
Tanana people North America cultural groups 123 (3)
Tanana river North America imperial global economy 93 (3)
Tanasari Mainland Southeast Asia (Burma) trade 230 (2)
Tancáh Central America (Mexico) first civilizations 123 (2)
Tanchon East Asia (North Korea) Cold War 109 (4)
Tanchou see Tanzhou
Tanegashima island Japan early modern states 265 (5) Communism 273 (3)
Tang vassal state East Asia first cities 259 (3)
Tangana state South Asia first empires 241 (5)
Tanganhuato Central America (Mexico) first civilizations 122 (1)
Tanganyika mod. Tanzania; prev. German East Africa colonial possession East Africa WWII 104 (1) Cold War 109 (1) see also German East Africa, Tanzania
Tanganyika, Lake lake East Africa early agriculture 158 (1) early cultures 160 (1) economy 163 (2) European imperialism 96 (1) exploration 156 (3), 157 (4), (5) first humans 12 (1), 13 (2) Islam 163 (1) slave trade 165 (4)
Tang Empire state East Asia medieval states 262–263 (1) world religions 49 (4)
Tanger, **Tánger** see Tangier, Tingis
Tanggula Shan see Tanglha Range
Tangier var. Tangiers; anc. Tingis; Fr./Ger. Tanger, Sp. Tánger North Africa (Morocco) early Islam 57 (2) economy 163 (2) European imperialism 96 (1) exploration 156 (3), 157 (4) inter-war 209 (4) Islam 163 (1), 192 (3) Mongols 68 (2) Napoleon 200–201 (1), 201 (2) slave trade 165 (4) see also Tingis
Tangiers see Tangier, Tingis
Tangjin battle East Asia (South Korea) Sino-Japanese War 270 (3)
Tanglha Range Chin. Tanggula Shan mountain range East Asia exploration 257 (3)
Tang Protectorate see Ferghana
Tanguts people East Asia early modern states 266 (1) medieval states 263 (3) trade 267 (3)
Tangxiang state East Asia medieval states 263 (3)
Tanis var. Avaris Egypt ancient Egypt 159 (5) first civilizations 221 (5) see also Avaris
Tanjavur South Asia (India) early medieval states 244–245 (3)
Tanjore var. Thanjāvūr South Asia (India) colonialism 248 (1) economy 249 (4) Mughal Empire 246 (1)
Tanjore region/state South Asia (India) colonialism 248 (1) Marathas 246 (2) Mughal Empire 246 (1)
Tanjungpura Maritime Southeast Asia (Indonesia) early medieval states 245 (6) exploration 239 (1) world religions 243 (5)
Tannenberg var. Grunwald battle Central Europe (Poland) early modern states 193 (4) WWI 207 (4)
Tannu Tuva var. Uriankhai, Uryankhai region/state Siberia colonialism 269 (4) Communism 271 (8) Soviet Union 208 (2), 213 (4) WWII 104 (1)
Tan-Tan state Maritime Southeast Asia ancient India 241 (6)
Tan-tung see Andong, Dandong
Tanzania prev. German East Africa, Tanganyika and Zanzibar, state East Africa decolonization 168 (1) economy 168 (2), (3) the modern world 112 (1), 113 (3), (4) see also German East Africa, Tanganyika, Zanzibar
Tanzhou var. Tanchou East Asia (China) medieval states 262–263 (1), 263 (3)
Taodeni Fr. Taoudenni, Taoudenit West Africa (Mali) Islam 163 (1)
Taos North America (USA) colonization 126 (1) exploration 119 (3)
Taos people North America colonization 126 (1)
Taoudenit see Taodeni, Taoudenni
Taoudenni var. Taoudenit, Taodeni West Africa (Mali) colonization 167 (4) see also Taodeni
Taourirt North Africa (Morocco) Islam 163 (1)
Tapajojó people South America early cultures 147 (2)
Tapajós state South America the world in 1500 74–75
Tapajós var. Tapajóz river South America colonization 149 (3) early cultures 144 (1), 145 (2) empire and revolution 151 (3) environment 153 (4) exploration 142 (1), 143 (2)
Tapajoso var. Santarém region South America early cultures 145 (2)
Tapajóz see Tapajós
Tapasha region South Asia world religions 242 (2)
Taprobane var. Sarandib, Saylan, Sri Lanka island South Asia ancient trade 44 (2) world religions 49 (3) see also Ceylon, Lambakannas, Lanka, Simhala, Sri Lanka
Taquira Tradition people South America the world in 1000 58–59
Tara Eastern Europe (Russian Federation) exploration 257 (2)
Tarābulus see Tripoli, Tripolis
Ṭarābulus al Gharb see Oea, Tripoli
Ṭarābulus ash Shām see Tripoli, Tripolis
Taradavadi South Asia (India) early medieval states 244 (2)
Tarahumara people Central America colonization 125 (4)
Tarakan military campaign Maritime Southeast Asia WWII 273 (2)
Taranaki region New Zealand colonization 283 (5)
Tarangambādi see Tranquebar
Taranto var. Tarantum, Tarentum Italy crusades 186 (1), 64–65 (2) economy 190 (1) medieval states 187 (5) see also Tarantum, Tarentum
Tarantum var. Tarentum; mod. Taranto Italy ancient Rome 180–181 (1), 181 (4) see also Taranto, Tarentum
Tarapacá region South America politics 151 (4)
Tarawa military campaign Gilbert Islands WWII 273 (2)
Tarazona Iberian Peninsula (Spain) medieval states 187 (3)
Tardanizats rebel faction France Reformation 196 (2)
Tarentaise France Franks 184 (2)
Tarentum var. Tarantum; mod. Taranto Italy ancient Rome 179 (3), (5) early states 178 (1), (2) first civilizations 177 (1) see also Taranto, Tarantum
Târgovişte see Tûrgovişte
Târgu-Jiu battle Southeast Europe (Romania) WWI 207 (6)
Târguşor prev. Tîrguşor Southeast Europe (Romania) world religions 48 (1) see also Tîrguşor
Tari East Asia (China) first cities 259 (5)
Tarifa Iberian Peninsula (Spain) Islam 192 (3)
Tarim river East Asia exploration 257 (3) first states 260 (1) medieval states 262–263 (1) Mongols 68–69 (1)
Tarka Southern Africa (South Africa) colonization 166 (2)
Tarkhan Egypt ancient Egypt 159 (2)
Tarma South America (Peru) Incas 147 (3)
Tarnow Central Europe (Poland) WWI 207 (4)
Taroudannt var. Taroudant North Africa (Morocco) Islam 163 (1)
Taroudant see Taroudannt
Tarquinia see Tarquinii
Tarquinii mod. Tarquinia; hist. Corneto Italy early states 178 (1), (2) first civilizations 177 (1)
Tarraco mod. Tarragona settlement Iberian Peninsula (Spain) ancient Rome 179 (3), 180–181 (1), 181 (3), (4), 225 (5) early cultures 161 (2) great migrations 52–53 (1) world religions 48 (1) see also Tarragona
Tarraconensis province Iberian peninsula ancient Rome 180–181 (1)
Tarragona Iberian Peninsula (Spain) ancient Rome 182 (1) inter-war 209 (4) Islam 192 (3) medieval states 182 (2)
Tarsatica see Rijeka
Tarsus settlement Southwest Asia (Turkey) ancient Rome 180–181 (1) crusades 228 (2), 65 (3) early Islam 56–57 (1) first civilizations 221 (4), 24 (2) Hellenistic world 40–41 (1) Islam 226 (2), 227 (4) medieval states 185 (3) Mongols 229 (3) world religions 48 (1)
Tartars see Tatars
Tartu see Dorpat
Taruga archaeological site/settlement West Africa (Nigeria) ancient trade 44–45 (1) early agriculture 158 (1) early cultures 160 (1)
Taruma state Maritime Southeast Asia ancient India 241 (6)
Tarut Southwest Asia (Saudi Arabia) first civilizations 24 (3)
Tarvisium see Treviso
Tarxien (Malta) the world in 2500 BCE 22–23
Tases state Central America Aztecs 124 (1)
Tashauz see Dashkhovuz
Tashi Chho Dzong see Thimphu
Tashihkiao see Dashiqiao
Tashi Lhunpo East Asia (China) exploration 257 (3)
Tashkent Uzb. Toshkent Central Asia (Uzbekistan) biological diffusion 72–73 (1) colonialism 269 (3), (4) Communism 271 (8) exploration 256 (1), 257 (3) global immigration 100 (1) Hellenistic world 40–41 (1) medieval Persia 231 (4) medieval states 261 (6) Mongols 68–69 (1) Ottomans 232–233 (1) Soviet Union 208 (2), 214–215 (4) trade 267 (3)
Tasmania prev. Van Diemen's Land region/island Australia colonization 282 (1), (2), 283 (3) exploration 276–277 (1), 279 (2), (3) medieval voyages 60 (2)
Tasman Sea sea Pacific Ocean colonization 282 (1), 283 (4), (5) environmentalism 285 (2) medieval voyages 60 (2) prehistoric culture 17 (5)
Tatars var. Tartars people East Asia/Siberia historical geography 275 (5) Mongols 68–69 (1)
Tatarstan state Eastern Europe Soviet Union 214–215 (4)
Tatta South Asia (Pakistan) colonialism 248 (1)
Tatta see Thatta
Ta-t'ung, **Tatung** see Datong
Tauchira North Africa (Libya) first civilizations 177 (1)
Taung archaeological site Southern Africa (South Africa) first humans 12 (1)
Taunton British Isles (United Kingdom) economy 204 (1)
Taunum Central Europe (Germany) world religions 48 (1)
Taupo, Lake lake New Zealand colonization 283 (5)
Tauranga New Zealand colonization 283 (5)
Tauroggen region Eastern Europe empire and revolution 199 (3)
Taurus Mountains var. Toros Dağları mountain range Southwest Asia ancient Persia 223 (4), 225 (6) crusades 64–65 (2) early agriculture 220 (1) exploration 218 (1), (2), 219 (3) first cities 220 (2), 28–29 (1) first civilizations 221 (4), (5), 222 (2) Hellenistic world 224 (1) Ottomans 231 (3), 232–233 (1) Seljuks 228 (1) WWI 233 (2)
Tau'u Island island Pacific Ocean exploration 278 (1)
Tavascan see Michoacan
Tawahi Mainland Southeast Asia (Burma) trade 230 (2)
Tawakoni people North America colonization 125 (4)
Taxila Buddhist centre/religious site/settlement South Asia (India) ancient Persia 225 (6) ancient Rome 224 (2) ancient trade 44 (2), 44–45 (1) exploration 256 (1) first religions 36 (2) Hellenistic world 224 (1), 41 (2) medieval states 262–263 (1) world religions 49 (3), (4)
Taxla Central America (Mexico) first civilizations 121 (2)
Tayasal Central America (Guatemala) Aztecs 124 (1)
Tayloris Battle battle North America (USA) the growth of the US 129 (2)
Taymyr, Poluostrov Eng. Taimyr Peninsula headland Siberia exploration 257 (2)
Tayspun see Ctesiphon
Taz river Eastern Europe exploration 257 (2)
Tazoult see Lambaesis
Tazumal Central America (Mexico) first civilizations 123 (2)
T'bilisi Eng. Tiflis Southwest Asia (Georgia) Soviet Union 214–215 (4) see also Tiflis
Tchad see Chad
Tchefuncte Culture people North America the world in 250 BCE 38–39
Tchongking see Chongqing
Te Anau, Lake lake New Zealand colonization 283 (5)
Teano see Teanum
Teanum var. Teanum Sidicinum; mod. Teano Italy early states 178 (1)
Teanum Apulum Italy early states 178 (1)
Teanum Sidicinum see Teanum
Tebuk Southwest Asia (Saudi Arabia) 20th-century politics 233 (4)
Tecama Central America (Mexico) Aztecs 124 (2)
Tecklenburg region Central Europe empire and revolution 199 (3)
Tecoac Central America (Mexico) colonization 125 (5)
Tédèllis North Africa (Algeria) economy 190 (1)
Tegasta fort North America (USA) colonization 125 (4)
Tegel airport Central Europe (Germany) post-war politics 212 (2)
Tegeler See lake Central Europe post-war politics 212 (2)
Tegucigalpa Central America (Honduras) the growth of the US 129 (2)
Teheran see Tehran
Tehran var. Teheran; Pers. Tehrān Southwest Asia (Iran) colonialism 269 (3) economy 234 (1) Islam 235 (4) medieval Persia 231 (4) Ottomans 231 (3), 232–233 (1) 20th-century politics 235 (5) Communism 271 (8)
Tehri Garhwal state South Asia colonialism 248 (2)
Tehuacán Central America (Mexico) first civilizations 122 (1) Mexican Revolution 133 (3)
Tehuacán Valley valley Central America early agriculture 20 (1)
Tehuantepec var. Santo Domingo Tehuantepec Central America (Mexico) first civilizations 122 (1) Mexican Revolution 133 (3)
Tehuantepec, Golfo de see Tehuantepec, Gulf of
Tehuantepec, Gulf of var. Tehuantepec, Golfo de gulf Central America Aztecs 124 (1) Mexican Revolution 133 (3)
Tehuantepec, Isthmus of var. Istmo de Tehuantepec coastal feature Central America Aztecs 124 (1)
Tehuantepec, Istmo de see Tehuantepec, Isthmus of
Tehuelche people South America early cultures 147 (2)
Tejo, Rio see Tagus
Teke state Central Africa the world in 1700 82–83 the world in 1800 86–87 the world in 1850 90–91
Tekesta people North America colonization 125 (4), 126 (1)
Telanaipura see Jambi
Tel Aviv Southwest Asia (Israel) 20th-century politics 235 (5)
Tel Aviv-Yafo Southwest Asia (Israel) 20th century 234 (2)
Telingana region/state South Asia early medieval states 244–245 (3)
Tell Agrab var. Tell Ajrab settlement/temple Southwest Asia (Iraq) first cities 220 (2) first civilizations 25 (3)
Tell 'Asmar, **Tell Asmar** see Eshnunna
Tell Aswad Southwest Asia (Iraq) first cities 220 (2)
Tell Brak Southwest Asia (Syria) early systems 223 (3), 32 (1) first cities 28–29 (1) first civilizations 24 (2)
Tell el-Ajjul Southwest Asia (Israel) ancient Egypt 159 (4)
Tell el-Amarna see Akhetaten
Tell el 'Ubaid Southwest Asia (Iraq) early agriculture 220 (1) first cities 220 (2)
Teller North America (USA) exploration 287 (2)
Tell es Sawwan Southwest Asia (Iraq) early agriculture 220 (1)
Tell Halaf Southwest Asia (Syria) early agriculture 220 (1)
Tell Ibrahim Awad Egypt ancient Egypt 159 (2)
Tellicherry var. Thalassery South Asia (India) colonialism 247 (3)
Telloh Southwest Asia (Iraq) first cities 220 (2)
Tell Sleimeh var. Tell as-Suleimeh, Awal Southwest Asia (Iran) first civilizations 24 (3)
Tell 'Uqair settlement/temple Southwest Asia (Iraq) first cities 220 (2) first civilizations 221 (4)
Teloapan Central America (Mexico) Aztecs 124 (1)
Telo Martius see Toulon
Telugucodas state South Asia Mongols 68–69 (1)
Temazcalpan Central America (Mexico) Aztecs 124 (2)
Temesvár battle Southeast Europe (Romania) Ottomans 197 (4)
Tempelhof Central Europe (Germany) crusades 186 (1)
Tempelhof airport Central Europe (Germany) post-war politics 212 (2)
Tenango Central America (Mexico) first civilizations 122 (1)
Tenanitla Central America (Mexico) Aztecs 124 (3)
Tenasserim state/colonial possession Mainland Southeast Asia colonialism 269 (4) European imperialism 97 (3)
Tenayuca Central America (Mexico) Aztecs 124 (3)
Tenerife battle South America (Colombia) empire and revolution 150 (1)
Ténès North Africa (Algeria) economy 190 (1)
Teng East Asia (China) first cities 259 (5)
Teng state East Asia first cities 259 (5)
Tenganapatam var. Ft. St. David South Asia (India) colonialism 247 (3)
Tengasseri South Asia (India) colonialism 247 (3)
Teng-chou see Dengzhou
Tengchung see Dengyue
Tennant Creek Australia colonization 282 (1), 283 (3) exploration 279 (2)
Tennessee state North America the growth of the US 129 (1) US Civil War 130 (2), (3), (4), (5), 131 (6), (7) US economy 134 (2), 139 (3) US society 137 (6) US superpower 139 (5)
Tennessee river North America cultural groups 122 (5) first civilizations 121 (4) the growth of the US 129 (2) US Civil War 131 (6)
Tenochtitlán mod. Ciudad de Mexico, México, Mexico City archaeological site/settlement Central America (Mexico) Aztecs 124 (1), (2), (3) colonization 125 (5) exploration 118 (1) first civilizations 121 (3) see also México, Mexico City
Tenos mod. Tínos island Greece Ottomans 230 (1)
Teodomiro state Iberian Peninsula the world in 750 CE 54–55
Teos settlement/state Greece ancient Greece 177 (2) first civilizations 177 (1)
Teotihuacán Central America (Mexico) Aztecs 124 (2) first civilizations 122 (1)
Teotihuacán region Central America first civilizations 122 (1)
Teotitlán Central America (Mexico) first civilizations 122 (1)
Teotitlán del Camino state Central America Aztecs 124 (1)
Tepeacac Central America (Mexico) first civilizations 122 (1)
Tepeacac state Central America Aztecs 124 (1)
Tepecano people Central America colonization 125 (4)
Tepecuacuilco state Central America Aztecs 124 (1)
Tepe Gawra settlement/temple Southwest Asia (Iraq) early agriculture 220 (1) first cities 220 (2)
Tepe Giyan Southwest Asia (Iran) early agriculture 220 (1) first civilizations 24 (2)
Tepe Guran Southwest Asia (Iran) early agriculture 220 (1)
Tepe Hissar Southwest Asia (Iran) first civilizations 24 (3)
Tepehuan people Central America colonization 125 (4), 126 (1)
Tepe Sabz Southwest Asia (Iraq) early agriculture 220 (1)
Tepetlacalco Central America (Mexico) Aztecs 124 (3)
Tepetlatzinco Central America (Mexico) Aztecs 124 (3)
Tepetzinco Central America (Mexico) Aztecs 124 (2)
Tepexic Central America (Mexico) first civilizations 122 (1)
Tepexpan Central America (Mexico) Aztecs 124 (2)
Tepeyacac Central America (Mexico) Aztecs 124 (2), (3) colonization 125 (5)
Tepe Yahya Southwest Asia (Iran) first civilizations 24 (3)
Tepic Central America (Mexico) Mexican Revolution 133 (3)
Tepoatlan Central America (Mexico) first civilizations 122 (1)
Tepotzotlán Central America (Mexico) Aztecs 124 (2)
Tequexquinahuac Central America (Mexico) Aztecs 124 (3)
Tequisistlan Central America (Mexico) Aztecs 124 (2)
Terevaka, Cerro mountain Pacific Ocean early cultures 281 (4)
Ternate Maritime Southeast Asia (Indonesia) colonialism 247 (4) colonization 284–285 (1) trade 267 (3)
Ternate island Maritime Southeast Asia colonialism 247 (4) early medieval states 245 (6) exploration 239 (2) Islam 243 (6) world religions 243 (5)
Ternopol' Eastern Europe (Ukraine) WWII 211 (4)
Terranova di Sicilia see Gela
Terranova Pausania see Olbia
Terre-Neuve see Newfoundland
Teruel anc. Turba Iberian Peninsula (Spain) inter-war 209 (4) Islam 192 (3)
Tešetice-Kyjovice Central Europe (Czech Republic) early agriculture 174 (1)
Teshik Tash archaeological site Central Asia (Uzbekistan) first humans 13 (2)
Tete Southern Africa (Mozambique) colonization 167 (4) exploration 157 (4) Islam 163 (1) trade 164 (1)
Tetecpilco Central America (Mexico) Aztecs 124 (3)
Tetelco Central America (Mexico) Aztecs 124 (2)
Teton people North America colonization 126 (1)
Tetzcoco Central America (Mexico) colonization 125 (5)
Teul people Central America colonization 125 (4)
Teurnia Central Europe (Austria) ancient Rome 180–181 (1)
Teutonic Knights crusade/state Eastern Europe crusades 186 (1) Mongols 68–69 (1)
Teutonic Order var. Knights of the Cross state Eastern Europe early modern states 193 (4) economy 190 (1) medieval states 188 (1), 189 (3), (4)
Teutonic Peoples people Central Europe/Eastern Europe/Scandinavia the world in 250 CE 46–47
Tevere see Tiber, Tiberis
Texas region/state North America imperial global economy 93 (5) Mexican Revolution 133 (3) the growth of the US 129 (1) US Civil War 130 (2), (3), (4), (5), 131 (6), (7) US economy 134 (2), 139 (3) US superpower 139 (5)
Texcoco Central America (Mexico) Aztecs 124 (1), (2)
Texcoco, Lake lake Central America Aztecs 124 (1), (2), (3) colonization 125 (5) first civilizations 122 (1)
Texcotzinco Central America (Mexico) Aztecs 124 (2)
Tezampa Central America (Mexico) Aztecs 124 (2)
Tezoyuca Central America (Mexico) Aztecs 124 (2)
Thaba Bosiu Southern Africa (South Africa) colonization 166 (2)
Thaba Nchu Southern Africa (South Africa) colonization 166 (2)
Thailand prev. Siam; Thai Prathet Thai state Mainland Southeast Asia Bronze Age 240 (3) decolonization 251 (4) historical geography 275 (5) Islam 275 (4) post-war economy 253 (5), 275 (3) post-war politics 251 (5), 253 (4) the modern world 113 (3), (4) US superpower 138 (1) WWII 104 (1), (2) Cold War 109 (1) see also Siam
Thailand, Gulf of var. Gulf of Siam, Thai Ao Thai, Vtn. Vinh Thai Lan gulf Mainland Southeast Asia ancient India 241 (6) colonialism 247 (4), 248 (1) early medieval states 245 (5), (6) exploration 239 (1) Islam 243 (6) post-war economy 253 (5) post-war politics 253 (4) world religions 243 (5) see also Siam, Gulf of
Thais people Mainland Southeast Asia the world in 750 CE 54–55 the world in 1000 58–59 the world in 1200 62–63
Thalassery see Tellicherry
Thalcozauhtitlan state Central America Aztecs 124 (1)
Thalner South Asia (China) early medieval states 244–245 (3)
Thames New Zealand colonization 283 (5)
Thames river British Isles Bronze Age 175 (3) Copper Age 174 (2) early agriculture 174 (1) economy 204 (1) great migrations 52–53 (1) medieval states 186 (2), 187 (4), 188 (2)
Thames and Severn canal British Isles economy 204 (1)
Tham Khuyen archaeological site Mainland Southeast Asia (Vietnam) first humans 13 (2)
Thamugadi North Africa (Algeria) ancient Rome 180–181 (1)
Thana mod. Thāne South Asia (India) economy 249 (4)
Thāne see Thana
Thang Long see Hanoi
Thang Phong battle Mainland Southeast Asia (Vietnam) 251 (5)
Thanh Hoa Mainland Southeast Asia (Vietnam) early medieval states 245 (6) Mongols 68–69 (1)
Thanjāvūr see Tanjore
Thanlwin see Salween
Thapsacus Southwest Asia (Syria) Hellenistic world 40–41 (1)
Thapsus North Africa (Tunisia) ancient Rome 180–181 (1) first civilizations 177 (1)
Thara Southwest Asia (Iran) medieval voyages 61 (3)
Thar Desert var. Great Indian Desert, Indian Desert desert South Asia ancient India 242 (1) ancient trade 44–45 (1) biological diffusion 72–73 (1) colonialism 247 (3), 248 (1) early Islam 56–57 (1) early medieval states 244 (1), (2), 244–245 (3) early religions 48 (2) economy 249 (4) first cities 240 (2) first empires 241 (5) first humans 13 (2) first religions 36 (2) Marathas 246 (2) medieval Persia 231 (4) Mughal Empire 246 (1) post-war politics 252 (1) world religions 242 (2), 243 (4), 49 (3)
Tharrus Italy first civilizations 177 (1)
Thasos Greece ancient Greece 177 (3) first civilizations 177 (1)
Thasos state/island Greece ancient Greece 177 (2), (3)
That Khe fort Mainland Southeast Asia (Vietnam) 251 (5)
Thaton Mainland Southeast Asia (Burma) ancient trade 44–45 (1) medieval states 262–263 (1)
Thaton state Mainland Southeast Asia the world in 750 CE 54–55 the world in 1000 58–59
Thatta var. Tatta South Asia (Pakistan) early medieval states 244–245 (3) Mughal Empire 246 (1) world religions 243 (4)
Thebae see Thebes
Thebes Egypt ancient Egypt 159 (3), (4), (5) ancient Persia 223 (4) early cultures 160 (1), 161 (3), (4), (5) Hellenistic world 40–41 (1)
Thebes settlement Greece ancient Greece 177 (3), (4), (5) first cities 28–29 (1) first civilizations 175 (4), 222 (2) first religions 37 (3) Hellenistic world 40–41 (1) see also Karnak, Ipet-isut, Luxor
Theiss see Tisza
Thenae North Africa (Tunisia) first civilizations 177 (1)
Theodosia var. Caffa, Kefe; mod. Feodosiya; It. Kaffa Eastern Europe (Ukraine) first civilizations 177 (1) Hellenistic world 40–41 (1) see also Kaffa
Theodosiopolis see Erzurum
Thera Greece first civilizations 177 (1)
Thera var. Santorini island Greece first civilizations 175 (4)
Theresienstadt concentration camp Central Europe WWII 211 (3)
Thermopylae Greece great migrations 52–53 (1) ancient Greece 179 (4) ancient Persia 223 (4)
Thessalonica mod. Thessaloníki; Eng. Salonica, Salonika, SCr. Solun, Turk. Selânik Greece ancient Greece 179 (4) ancient Rome 179 (5), 180–181 (1), 181 (4), 182 (1) crusades 64–65 (2) early cultures 161 (2) Hellenistic world 41 (2) world religions 48 (1) see also Salonica
Thessaloníki see Salonica, Thessalonica
Thessaly region Greece ancient Greece 177 (3), 179 (4) first civilizations 175 (4) first religions 37 (3) Ottomans 202 (4) WWI 207 (6)
Thimbu see Thimphu
Thimphu var. Thimbu; prev. Tashi Chho Dzong South Asia (Bhutan) post-war economy 253 (5)
Thinis Egypt ancient Egypt 159 (3)
Thionville see Diedenhofen
Third Cataract waterfall Egypt ancient Egypt 159 (4), (5)
Thirteen Colonies colonial possession North America empire and revolution 127 (3)
Thiruvanathapuram see Trivandrum
Thíva see Thebes
Thon Buri Mainland Southeast Asia (Thailand) biological diffusion 72–73 (1)
Thorn Pol. Toruń Central Europe (Poland) economy 190 (1) medieval states 188 (1) WWI 207 (4) see also Toruń
Thornton Island see Caroline Island
Thospitis see Van, Lake
Thovela state Southern Africa the world in 1700 82–83
Thrace anc. Thracia region Greece/Southeast Europe ancient Greece 177 (2), 179 (4) ancient Persia 223 (4) ancient Rome 225 (5) ancient trade 44–45 (1) exploration 218 (1) first civilizations 175 (4), 177 (1) first religions 37 (3) Hellenistic world 224 (1) Ottomans 202 (4), 230 (1) world religions 48 (1) see also Thracia
Thracia var. Thrace province Southeast Europe ancient Rome 180–181 (1), 181 (4) see also Thrace
Thracians people Southeast Europe ancient Rome 179 (5)
Three Kings Islands island group Pacific Ocean exploration 278 (1)
Thugga North Africa (Tunisia) ancient Rome 180–181 (1)
Thule var. Qânâq North America (Greenland) cultural groups 123 (3) exploration 287 (2) the growth of the US 129 (2)
Thule island Atlantic Ocean ancient trade 44 (2)
Thuna South Asia (India) world religions 242 (3)
Thurii Italy ancient Rome 179 (3) early states 178 (1)
Thüringen see Thuringia
Thuringia Fr. Thuringe; Ger.Thüringen region/state Central Europe empire and revolution 202 (2) Franks 184 (2) medieval states 185 (3), 188 (1)
Thuringian March region Central Europe Franks 184 (2)
Thuringians people Central Europe ancient Rome 182 (1) Franks 183 (5), (6) great migrations 53 (2) medieval states 182 (2)
Thyatira mod. Akhisar seven churches of asia Southwest Asia world religions 48 (1)
Thyssus state Greece ancient Greece 177 (2)
Tiahuanaco South America (Bolivia) early cultures 146 (1) Incas 147 (3)
Tiahuanaco state South America the world in 250 BCE 38–39 the world in 1 CE 42–43 the world in 1000 58–59 the world in 1200 62–63
Tianjin var. Tientsin East Asia (China) colonialism 269 (4) empire and revolution 268 (2) Islam 275 (4) post-war politics 274 (2)
Tianjin province East Asia post-war politics 274 (2)
Tianjin battle East Asia (China) economy 274 (1)
Tianlin prev. Leli East Asia (China) medieval states 263 (6)
Tian Shan see Tien Shan
Tianshui province East Asia first states 260 (1)
Tianshui var. T'ien-shui Buddhist centre/sacred mountain East Asia (China) world religions 49 (3)
Tiayo Central America (Mexico) first civilizations 122 (1)
Tiba see Chiba
Tibbu Tib people East Africa/Central Africa trade 167 (1)
Tiber river Italy medieval states 183 (4)
Tiberias Southwest Asia (Israel) ancient Rome 225 (4)
Tiberias, Lake lake Southwest Asia crusades 65 (3)
Tiberis mod. Tevere; Eng. Tiber river Italy ancient Rome 181 (2) early states 178 (1), (2) see also Tevere, Tiber
Tibesti var. Tibesti Massif, Ar. Tībistī mountain range North Africa ancient trade 44–45 (1) early cultures 160 (1) economy 163 (2) first humans 13 (2) Islam 163 (1)
Tibesti Massif see Tibesti
Tibet var. Hsi-tsang; anc. Xizang; Chin. prev. Tufan, Bhota province/region/state East Asia colonialism 248 (1), (2), 269 (3), (4) early modern states 266 (1), (2), 268 (1) empire and revolution 249 (3), 268 (2) exploration 257 (3) first states 260 (1) medieval states 261 (6), 262–263 (1), 263 (3), (4), (5), (6) Mongols 68 (2), 68–69 (1) post-

war economy 275 (3) post-war politics 252 (1), (2), 271 (7), 274 (2) trade 267 (3) world religions 243 (4), 49 (3), (4) WWII 272 (1), 273 (2) Chinese revolution 271 (5) Cold War 109 (1) Communism 271 (8)
Tibetans people East Asia ancient trade 44–45 (1) empire and revolution 268 (2)
Tibet, Plateau of var. Xizang Gaoyuan, Qingzang Gaoyuan plateau East Asia ancient trade 44–45 (1) biological diffusion 72–73 (1) colonialism 247 (3) early agriculture 258 (1) early religions 48 (2) exploration 256 (1), 257 (3) first humans 13 (2) first religions 37 (4) first states 260 (1) global knowledge 76–77 (1) Marathas 246 (2) medieval states 262–263 (1), 263 (3), (4), (5), (6) Mughal Empire 246 (1) trade 267 (3) world religions 49 (3), (4)
Tibisti see Tibesti
Tibur Italy early states 178 (1)
Tiburón, Cabo headland South America European expansion 80–81 (1)
Tiburtina vetus, Via road Italy ancient Rome 181 (2)
Tiburtina, Via road Italy ancient Rome 181 (2) early states 178 (1)
Tichitt West Africa (Mauritania) the world in 2500 BCE 22–23
Ticoman Central America (Mexico) Aztecs 124 (3)
Tidore var. Soasiu Maritime Southeast Asia (Indonesia) colonialism 247 (4) colonization 284–285 (1)
Tidore region Maritime Southeast Asia colonialism 247 (4) early medieval states 245 (6)
Tien Shan Chin. Tian Shan, Rus. Tyan'-Shan'; var. T'ien Shan mountain range East Asia ancient trade 44–45 (1) biological diffusion 72–73 (1) colonialism 269 (4) early agriculture 258 (1) empire and revolution 268 (2) exploration 256 (1), 257 (3) first cities 259 (5) first humans 13 (2) first states 260 (1) historical geography 275 (5) medieval states 261 (6), 262–263 (1) Mongols 68–69 (1) trade 267 (3) world religions 49 (3)
T'ien-shui see Tianshui
Tientsin see Tianjin
Tieoman Central America (Mexico) Aztecs 124 (3)
Tiergarten Central Europe (Germany) post-war politics 212 (2)
Tierra del Fuego island South America empire and revolution 151 (3) exploration 142 (1)
Tieum Southwest Asia (Turkey) first civilizations 177 (1)
Tiflis var. T'bilisi Southwest Asia (Georgia) early Islam 56–57 (1), 57 (2) Islam 226 (2), 227 (4) medieval Persia 231 (4) Mongols 68–69 (1) Ottomans 195 (4), 231 (3), 232–233 (1) Seljuks 228 (1) Timur 229 (4) world religions 226 (1)
see also T'bilisi
Tighina see Bender
Tigris Ar. Dijlah, Turk. Dicle river Southwest Asia ancient Persia 223 (4), 225 (6) ancient Rome 180–181 (1), 224 (2), 225 (5) ancient trade 44–45 (1), 72–73 (1), 73 (3) crusades 228 (2) early agriculture 174 (1), 20–21 (2), 220 (1) early cultures 161 (3), (4), (5) early Islam 56–57 (1), 57 (2), (3) early systems 223 (3) early trade 225 (3) economy 234 (1) exploration 172 (1), (2), 219 (3), (4) first cities 220 (2), 28–29 (1) first civilizations 221 (4), (5), 222 (2), 25 (3) first religions 36 (1) great migrations 52–53 (1) Hellenistic world 224 (1), 41 (2) Islam 163 (1), 226 (2), 227 (4), (5) medieval Persia 231 (4) medieval states 185 (3) Mongols 229 (3), 68–69 (1) Ottomans 230 (1), 231 (3), 232–233 (1) Seljuks 228 (1) Timur 229 (4) trade 230 (2) world religions 226 (1), 49 (4) WWI 233 (2) 20th-century politics 233 (3), (4), 235 (5)
Ti-hua, Tihwa see Urumchi, Ürümqi
Tikal Central America (Guatemala) early systems 32 (1), 33 (2), (3) first civilizations 121 (2)
Tikopia island Pacific Ocean exploration 278 (1)
Tiksi Siberia (Russian Federation) exploration 287 (2)
Tilanga region South Asia world religions 242 (2)
Tilantango Central America (Mexico) first civilizations 122 (1)
Tilcara South America (Argentina) Incas 147 (3)
Tilimsen see Tlemcen
Tilio Martius see Toulon
Tilsit Eastern Europe (Russian Federation) Napoleon 200–201 (1), 201 (2)
Timaru settlement/whaling station New Zealand colonization 283 (4), (5)
Timbuktu Fr. Tombouctou West Africa (Mali) ancient trade 44–45 (1) biological diffusion 72–73 (1) colonization 167 (4) crusades 65 (1) economy 163 (2) European expansion 84–85 (1) exploration 156 (3), 157 (4) Islam 163 (1), 167 (3) Mongols 68 (2) trade 163 (5)
Timna Southwest Asia (Jordan) ancient Egypt 159 (5)
Timna Southwest Asia (Yemen) 159 (5) early cultures 161 (3), (5) early trade 225 (3)
Timor island Maritime Southeast Asia (Indonesia) colonialism 247 (4) decolonization 251 (4) early medieval states 245 (6) European expansion 81 (3), 84–85 (1) European imperialism 97 (3) exploration 239 (1), (2) Islam 243 (6) post-war economy 253 (5) post-war politics 253 (4) trade 267 (3) world religions 243 (5) WWII 251 (3), 272 (1), 273 (2)
Timor Sea sea Maritime Southeast Asia Bronze Age 240 (3) colonialism 247 (4) decolonization 251 (4) early medieval states 245 (6) exploration 239 (1), (2) WWII 272 (1), 273 (2)
Timucua people North America colonization 125 (4)
Timur, Empire of state Southwest Asia Timur 229 (4)
Timurids state South Asia/Southwest Asia the world in 1500 74–75
Tingis var. Tangiers; Eng. Tangier, Fr./Ger. Tanger, Sp. Tánger North Africa (Morocco) ancient Rome 179 (3), 180–181 (1), 181 (3), (4) ancient trade 44–45 (1)
see also Tangier
Tingo María South America (Peru) narcotics 153 (5)
Tinian island Pacific Ocean WWII 251 (3), 272 (1)
Tinos see Tenos
Tin Tellust West Africa (Niger) exploration 157 (4)
Tio state Central Africa Islam 163 (1) slave trade 165 (4) trade 167 (1)
Tipecanoe battle North America (USA) the growth of the US 129 (2)
Tirana Southeast Europe (Albania) Cold War 108 (3) Ottomans 232–233 (1) post-war politics 212 (3) WWI 207 (6) WWII 210 (1), 211 (2), (4)
Tirangole East Africa (Sudan) exploration 157 (4)
Tîrgovişte mod. Targovişte battle Southeast Europe (Bulgaria) Ottomans 195 (4)
Tirguşor var. Târguşor Southeast Europe (Romania) world religions 226 (1)
see also Târguşor
Tirnovo mod. Veliko Tŭrnovo Southeast Europe (Bulgaria) medieval states 189 (4)
Tiruchchirappalli see Trichinopoly
Tiryns palace/settlement Greece first cities 28–29 (1) first civilizations 175 (4)
Tisza Ger. Theiss river Southeast Europe Mongols 68–69 (1) post-war economy 215 (3)
Tiszapolgár archaeological site Central Europe (Hungary) Copper Age 174 (2)
Titicaca, Lake lake South America colonization 148 (2) early cultures 145 (2), (4), 146 (1), 147 (2) empire and revolution 150 (1) Incas 147 (3), 148 (1)
Titograd see Podgorica
Tiwa people North America colonization 125 (4)
Tizapán Central America (Mexico) Aztecs 124 (2)
Tizapantzinco Central America (Mexico) colonization 125 (5)
Tizayucan Central America (Mexico) Aztecs 124 (2)
Tjeribon see Cheribon
Tlaceteco Central America (Mexico) Aztecs 124 (3)
Tlacho state Central America Aztecs 124 (1)
Tlachquiaucho state Central America Aztecs 124 (1)
Tlacopan Central America (Mexico) Aztecs 124 (1), (2), (3) colonization 125 (5)
Tlacopaque Central America (Mexico) Aztecs 124 (3)
Tlacoquemecan Central America (Mexico) Aztecs 124 (3)
Tlalnepantla Central America (Mexico) Aztecs 124 (2), (3)
Tlaloc, Cerro mountain range Central America Aztecs 124 (2)
Tlalpan Central America (Mexico) Aztecs 124 (2)
Tlaltenango Central America (Mexico) Aztecs 124 (3)
Tlapacoya Central America (Mexico) Aztecs 124 (2) first civilizations 121 (2)
Tlapacoyan state Central America Aztecs 124 (1)
Tlapan state Central America Aztecs 124 (1)
Tlatayan Central America (Mexico) first civilizations 122 (1)
Tlateloco Central America (Mexico) Aztecs 124 (2), (3)
Tlatilco Central America (Mexico) first civilizations 121 (2)
Tlatlauhquitepec state Central America Aztecs 124 (1)
Tlaxcala Central America (Mexico) Aztecs 124 (1)
Tlaxcala state Central America Mexican Revolution 133 (3) the growth of the US 129 (2)
Tlaxcalan Central America (Mexico) colonization 125 (5)
Tlaxcalan state Central America Aztecs 124 (1)
Tlaxcalan people Central America colonization 125 (4)
Tlaxialtemalco Central America (Mexico) Aztecs 124 (3)
Tlemcen var. Tilimsen, Tlemsen North Africa (Algeria) Islam 163 (1)
Tlemsen see Tlemcen
Tlilhuacan Central America (Mexico) Aztecs 124 (3)
Tlingit region North America the world in 1700 82–83 the world in 1800 86–87
Tmutarakan Eastern Europe (Russian Federation) medieval states 185 (3)
Toala Island archaeological site Central Africa (Chad) early cultures 160 (1)
Toba var. Northern Wei; Chin. T'o-pa state East Asia medieval states 261 (4) the world in 500 CE 50–51
Tobago island West Indies empire and revolution 88 (1) European expansion 84–85 (1)
Tobol'sk var. Tobolsk Siberia (Russian Federation) colonialism 269 (3) exploration 257 (2) Soviet Union 208 (2)
Tobol'sk region Eastern Europe colonialism 269 (3)
Toboso people Central America colonization 125 (4), 126 (1)
Tobruk North Africa (Libya) WWII 210 (1), 211 (4)
Tocabaga fort North America (USA) colonization 125 (4)
Tocantins river South America colonization 149 (3), (4) early cultures 144 (1), 145 (2) environment 153 (4) exploration 142 (1), 143 (2) politics 152 (1)
Tochari var. Tocharians people East Asia the world in 500 BCE 34–35 ancient trade 44–45 (1)
Tocharian Principalities state Central Asia the world in 1 CE 42–43
Tochigi var. Totigi prefecture Japan economy 270 (1)
Tochpan state Central America Aztecs 124 (1)
Tochtepec state Central America Aztecs 124 (1)
Tocobaga jesuit mission North America (USA) colonization 125 (4)
Tocopilla South America (Chile) empire and revolution 151 (3)
Tocuyanoid region South America early cultures 145 (2)
Todaiji Japan medieval states 265 (3)
Todmorden British Isles (United Kingdom) empire global economy 93 (4)
Toeban see Tuban
Togariishi archaeological site Japan early agriculture 258 (1)
Togiak North America (USA) cultural groups 123 (3)
Togo prev. French Togoland, Togoland colonial possession/state West Africa decolonization 168 (1) economy 168 (2) European imperialism 96 (1) Islam 235 (4) the modern world 112 (1), 113 (3) WWII 104 (1)
Togoland see Togo
Tohome people Central America colonization 125 (4)
Tojikiston see Tajikistan
Tokaido region Japan medieval states 265 (3)
Tokelau island group/state Pacific Ocean colonization 284–285 (1) decolonization 285 (3)
environmentalism 285 (2) exploration 279 (3) the modern world 110–111
Tokio see Edo, Tokyo
Tokushima Japan early modern states 265 (5)
Tokushima var. Tokusima prefecture Japan economy 270 (1)
Tokyo Jap. Tōkyō; prev. Edo Japan Communism 271 (8), 273 (3) imperial global economy 92 (1) imperialism 270 (2) Islam 275 (4) WWII 272 (1), 273 (2)
see also Edo
Tolan Central America (Mexico) Aztecs 124 (3)
Toledo anc. Toletum settlement Iberian Peninsula (Spain) ancient Rome 182 (1) crusades 186 (1), 64–65 (2), 65 (1) early Islam 56–57 (1) economy 190 (1) Franks 184 (2) inter-war 209 (3), (4) Islam 192 (3), 226 (2), 227 (4) medieval states 182 (2), 185 (3)
see also Toletum
Toletum mod. Toledo Christian archbishopric/settlement Iberian peninsula (Spain) ancient Rome 180–181 (1) great migrations 52–53 (1) world religions 48 (1)
see also Toledo
Tolimán Central America (Mexico) first civilizations 122 (1)
Tollantzinco Central America (Mexico) first civilizations 122 (1)
Tolmezzo Italy WWI 207 (5)
Tolosa mod. Toulouse France ancient Rome 179 (3), (5), 180–181 (1) ancient trade 44 (2) great migrations 52–53 (1)
see also Toulouse
Toltec Empire state Central America the world in 1000 58–59
Tomar Iberian Peninsula (Portugal) crusades 186 (1)
Tombouctou see Timbuktu
Tomebamba South America (Ecuador) Incas 147 (3)
Tomi mod. Constanţa Southeast Europe (Romania) ancient Rome 180–181 (1), 181 (3)
see also Constanţa
Tomóchic Central America (Mexico) Mexican Revolution 133 (3)
Tomsk region/archaeological site/settlement Siberia (Russian Federation) colonialism 269 (3), (4) Communism 271 (8) early agriculture 258 (1) exploration 257 (2) Soviet Union 208 (2), 214–215 (4)
Tonalá Central America (Mexico) first civilizations 122 (1), (2)
Tonga var. Friendly Islands colonial possession/island group/state Pacific Ocean colonization 284–285 (1) decolonization 285 (3) early cultures 280–281 (3) environmentalism 285 (2) exploration 276–277 (1), 279 (3) medieval voyages 60 (2)
Tongatapu island Pacific Ocean exploration 278 (1)
Tongatapu Group island group Pacific Ocean early cultures 280–281 (3) medieval voyages 60 (2)
Tongchuan East Asia (China) medieval states 263 (4)
Tonggou mod. Ji'an East Asia (China) medieval states 264 (1) see also Ji'an
Tongguan var. T'ung-kuan East Asia Mongols 68–69 (1)
Tonghua East Asia (China) Cold War 109 (4)
Tongking var. Tonkin state Mainland Southeast Asia colonialism 269 (4) European imperialism 97 (3)
Tongking, Gulf of gulf Mainland Southeast Asia colonialism 247 (4), 248 (1) decolonization 251 (4) early medieval states 245 (5), (6) early modern states 266 (1) exploration 239 (1) medieval voyages 61 (3) post-war politics 251 (5), 253 (4) WWII 251 (3)
Tongnae East Asia (South Korea) early modern states 267 (4)
Tongzi archaeological site East Asia (China) first humans 13 (2)
Tonkawa people North America colonization 125 (4), 126 (1)
Tonkin see Tongking
Tonle Sap Eng. Great Lake lake Mainland Southeast Asia post-war politics 251 (5) world religions 243 (5)
Tonto archaeological site North America (USA) cultural groups 123 (4)
Toolesboro Mounds burial mound North America (USA) first civilizations 121 (4)
Toowoomba Australia colonization 282 (1)
T'o-pa see Toba
Topeka North America (USA) the growth of the US 129 (2)
Topoc Maze archaeological site North America (USA) cultural groups 123 (4)
Toprakkale Southwest Asia (Turkey) first civilizations 222 (2)
Torgut people East Asia early modern states 266 (1)
Torino see Augusta, Taurinorum, Turin
Tornacum see Tournai
Tornaval South America (Peru) early cultures 145 (4)
Toro Egypt exploration 156 (3)
Toro state East Africa the world in 1700 82–83 the world in 1800 86–87 the world in 1850 90–91
Torone Greece first civilizations 177 (1)
Torone state Greece ancient Greece 177 (2)
Toronto North America (Canada) the growth of the US 129 (2), 132 (1) US economy 136 (2)
Toropets Eastern Europe (Russian Federation) early modern states 195 (3)
Toros Dağları see Taurus Mountains
Torrance North America (USA)
Torreón Central America (Mexico) Mexican Revolution 133 (3)
Torres Strait sea waterway Australia exploration 276–277 (1), 279 (2)
Tortoise Islands see Galapagos Islands
Tortosa anc. Dertosa Iberian Peninsula (Spain) crusades 186 (1) Franks 184 (2) Islam 192 (3)
see also Dertosa
Tortuga var.Tortuga Island; mod. Île de la Tortue island West Indies empire and revolution 89 (3) European expansion 85 (2)
Toruń Ger. Thorn Central Europe (Poland) early modern states 193 (4) medieval states 189 (3) see also Thorn
Torwa state Southern Africa Islam 163 (1)
Torzhok var. Toržok Eastern Europe (Russian Federation) Mongols 68–69 (1)
Toržok see Torzhok
Tosando region Japan medieval states 265 (3)
Toscana see Tuscany
Toshka Egypt ancient Egypt 159 (3)
Toshkent see Tashkent
Tószeg Southeast Europe (Hungary) Bronze Age 175 (3)
Toterfout burial mound Low Countries (Netherlands) Bronze Age 175 (3)
Totigi see Tochigi
Totopec state Central America Aztecs 124 (1)
Tottori prefecture Japan economy 270 (1)
Toucouleur see Takrur
Toulon anc. Telo Martius, Tilio Martius France early modern states 197 (5) economy 205 (4) empire and revolution 199 (4) European expansion 84–85 (1) Napoleon 200–201 (1) WWII 211 (2)
Toulouse anc. Tolosa settlement France ancient Rome 182 (1) crusades 186 (1), 64–65 (2) early modern states 197 (5) economy 190 (1), 205 (4) empire and revolution 199 (4) Franks 183 (5), (6), 184 (2) inter-war 209 (3) Islam 184 (1), 192 (3), 226 (2) medieval states 182 (2), 185 (3), (4), 192 (1), (2) Napoleon 200–201 (1), 201 (2), 17 (3) Reformation 194 (2)
see also Tolosa
Toulouse region France crusades 64–65 (2) medieval states 187 (4)
Toulouse battle France early Islam 56–57 (1)
Toungoo Mainland Southeast Asia (Burma) early medieval states 245 (6) WWII 251 (3)
Toungoo state Mainland Southeast Asia the world in 1400 70–71 the world in 1500 74–75
Tournai var. Tournay; anc. Tornacum; Dut. Doornik Low Countries (Belgium) early modern states 197 (5) economy 190 (1) Franks 183 (5), (6), 184 (2) WWI 206 (2), (3)
Tournay see Tournai
Tours anc. Caesarodunum, Turoni settlement France early modern states 197 (5) Franks 183 (5), 184 (2) medieval states 187 (3), 192 (1), (2)
see also Caesarodunum, Turoni
Town Creek North America (USA) cultural groups 122 (5)
Townsville Australia colonization 282 (1), 283 (3)
Towosahgy North America (USA) cultural groups 122 (5)
Toyama prefecture Japan economy 270 (1)
Toyohashi var. Toyohasi Japan economy 270 (1), 275 (4)
Toyohasi see Toyohashi
Trâblous see Tripoli, Tripolis
Trabzon see Trapezus, Trebizond
Trachonitis state Southwest Asia ancient Rome 225 (4)
Trafalgar battle Iberian Peninsula (Spain) Napoleon 200–201 (1)
Traiana, Aqua aqueduct Italy ancient Rome 181 (2)
Traiani, Thermae see Trajan, Baths of
Traiectum ad Mosam, Traiectum Tungorum see Maastricht
Trajan, Baths of Lat. Thermae Traiani building Italy ancient Rome 181 (2)
Trajan, Temple of building Italy ancient Rome 181 (2)
Trajectum ad Rhenum see Utrecht
Trang Mainland Southeast Asia (Thailand) ancient trade 44–45 (1)
Trani anc. Turenum Italy economy 190 (1)
Tran Ninh state Mainland Southeast Asia the world in 1600 78–79 the world in 1700 82–83 the world in 1800 86–87
Tranquebar mod. Tarangambādi South Asia (India) colonialism 247 (3)
Trans-Amazon Highway road South America 153 (4)
Transantarctic Mountains mountain range Antarctica Antarctic Exploration 287 (3)
Transbaikal region Siberia colonialism 269 (3)
Transcaspian region Central Asia colonialism 269 (3)
Trans-Gangem region South Asia ancient trade 44 (2)
Transilvania see Transylvania
Transjordan mod. Jordan region/state Southwest Asia exploration 219 (4) WWII 104 (1), 211 (4) 20th century 234 (2) 20th-century politics 233 (3), (4)
see also Jordan
Transnistria state Eastern Europe WWII 211 (2)
Transoxiana region/state Central Asia ancient trade 44–45 (1) early Islam 56–57 (1), 57 (2) Islam 227 (4) medieval Persia 231 (4) medieval states 261 (6), 262–263 (1) Timur 229 (4) world religions 49 (3)
Trans-Siberian Railway railway Siberia global immigration 100 (1)
Transvaal state Southern Africa European imperialism 96 (2)
Transylvania Eng. Ardeal, Transilvania, Ger. Siebenbürgen, Hung. Erdély region/state Southeast Europe medieval states 189 (4) Napoleon 200–201 (1) Ottomans 195 (4), 230 (1) Reformation 194 (2) WWI 208 (1)
Trapani anc. Drepanum Italy economy 190 (1)
Trapezus Eng. Trebizond, Turk. Trabzon archaeological site/settlement Southwest Asia (Turkey) ancient Rome 180–181 (1), 181 (3), (4) ancient trade 44–45 (1) early cultures 161 (2) first civilizations 177 (1) Hellenistic world 40–41 (1) world religions 226 (1)
see also Trebizond
Trasimene, Lake see Trasimenus, Lacus
Trasimeno, Lago see Trasimenus, Lacus
Trasimenus, Lacus Eng. Lake Trasimene, Lago Trasimeno battle Italy ancient Rome 179 (3)
Trau see Trogir
Travancore state South Asia colonialism 248 (1)
Trebia battle Italy ancient Rome 179 (3)
Trebinje Southeast Europe (Bosnia and Herzegovina) post-war economy 215 (3)
Trebizond anc. Trapezus; Turk. Trabzon Southwest Asia (Turkey) biological diffusion 72–73 (1) crusades 64–65 (2) early Islam 56–57 (1) exploration 219 (3) medieval states 185 (3), 261 (6) Ottomans 195 (4), 230 (1) Seljuks 228 (1) WWI 233 (2) 20th-century politics 233 (3)
see also Trapezus
Trebizond, Empire of state Southwest Asia economy 190 (1) Mongols 229 (3), 68–69 (1) Timur 229 (4)
Treblinka concentration camp Central Europe (Poland) WWII 211 (3)
Trempealeau burial mound North America (USA) first civilizations 121 (4)
Tremper burial mound North America (USA) first civilizations 121 (4)
Trent It. Trento Italy WWI 207 (5)
Trent and Mersey canal British Isles economy 204 (1)
Trento see Trent
Trenton North America (USA) empire and revolution 127 (3) the growth of the US 129 (2)
Trenton battle North America (USA) empire and revolution 127 (3), 88–89 (2)
Treptow Central Europe (Germany) post-war politics 212 (2)
Tres Zapotes Central America (Mexico) first civilizations 121 (2), (3), 122 (1)
Treves see Augusta Taurinorum, Augusta Treverorum, Trier
Treviso anc. Tarvisium Italy economy 190 (1) WWI 207 (5)
Trévoux France early modern states 197 (5)
Trichinopoly mod. Tiruchchirappalli South Asia (India) economy 249 (4)
Trier anc. Augusta Taurinorum, Augusta Treverorum; Eng. Treves, Fr. Trèves massacre/settlement Central Europe (Germany) ancient Rome 182 (1) crusades 186 (1) Franks 184 (2) medieval states 182 (2), 188 (1) WWI 206 (2), (3)
Trieste Slvn. Trst Italy economy 205 (4) medieval states 189 (4) post-war politics 212 (3) WWI 207 (5) WWII 211 (2), (3)
Trieste, Free Territory of state Italy the world in 1950 102–103
Trigarta region South Asia world religions 242 (2)
Trinacria see Sicily
Trincomalee var. Trinkomali air raid/settlement South Asia (Sri Lanka) colonialism 247 (3) WWII 251 (3), 272 (1)
Trindade island Atlantic Ocean the modern world 110–111
Trinidad colonial possession/island West Indies colonization 125 (4) empire and revolution 150 (1) European expansion 85 (2) global immigration 101 (3)
Trinidad and Tobago colonial possession/state West Indies Cold War 108 (2) environment 153 (4) politics 152 (1) the modern world 112 (1) US economy 136 (2) US politics 139 (4) US superpower 138 (1)
Trinil archaeological site Maritime Southeast Asia (Indonesia) first humans 13 (2)
Trinkomali see Trincomalee
Tripoli var. Tarābulus, Ţarābulus ash Shām, Trâblous; anc. Tripolis Southwest Asia (Lebanon) crusades 65 (3) medieval states 187 (5) 20th-century politics 233 (3)
see also Tripolis
Tripoli var. Ţarābulus al Gharb, Oea; Ar. Ţarābulus North Africa (Libya) biological diffusion 72 (1) colonization 166 (4) early Islam 56 (1) economy 162 (2), 168 (2), 190 (1) European Expansion 84 (1) exploration 156 (2) Islam 162 (1), 226 (2), (4) Napolean 200 (1) Ottomans 230 (3), 232 (1) US superpower 138 (1) WWII 210 (1), (4)
see also Oea
Tripoli region/state North Africa early Islam 56–57 (1) slave trade 165 (4) trade 167 (1)
Tripoli var. County of Tripoli, Kingdom of Tripoli state Southwest Asia crusades 228 (2), 65 (3) medieval states 187 (5)
Tripolis Southwest Asia (Lebanon) ancient Rome 180–181
Tripolitania region/state North Africa colonization 167 (4) first civilizations 177 (1) Ottomans 232–233 (1)
Tripura var. Hill Tippera region/state South Asia colonialism 248 (2) post-war politics 252 (1), 253 (4)
Tripuri South Asia (India) early medieval states 244 (2)
Tristan da Cunha colonial possession/island Atlantic Ocean the modern world 110–111
Trivandrum var. Thiruvanathapuram South Asia (India) colonialism 248 (1) economy 249 (4) post-war economy 253 (5) post-war politics 252 (1)
Troesmis archaeological site/legion headquarters Southeast Europe (Romania) ancient Rome 180–181 (1)
Trogir It. Trau Southeast Europe (Croatia) medieval states 189 (4)
Troia Italy crusades 186 (1)
Tromelin, Île island Indian Ocean the modern world 110–111
Tromsø Scandinavia (Norway) exploration 287 (2)
Trondheim prev. Nidaros, Trondhjem; Ger. Drontheim Scandinavia (Norway) early modern states 197 (3) exploration 287 (2) medieval states 185 (3) medieval voyages 60–61 (1) WWII 104 (2)
Trondheim region Scandinavia early modern states 197 (3)
Trondhjem see Trondheim
Troy archaeological site/religious site/settlement Southwest Asia (Turkey) Bronze Age 175 (3) Copper Age 174 (2) first cities 220 (2) first civilizations 175 (4), 221 (5) first religions 37 (3)
Troyes anc. Augustobona Tricassium France crusades 186 (1) early modern states 193 (4) economy 190 (1) medieval states 188 (1), (2) Reformation 194 (2) WWI 206 (2), (3)
Trst see Trieste
Trucial Coast see Trucial Oman, United Arab Emirates
Trucial Oman mod. United Arab Emirates; prev. Trucial Coast; later Trucial States colonial possession/state Southwest Asia 20th-century politics 233 (4)
see also United Arab Emirates
Trucial States see Trucial Oman, United Arab Emirates
Truckee battle North America (USA) the growth of the US 129 (2)
Trujillo South America (Venezuela) empire and revolution 150 (1)
Trujillo South America (Peru) colonization 126 (1), 148 (2) empire and revolution 150 (1), 151 (3) exploration 143 (3) politics 152 (1)
Truk var. Hogoley Islands, Chuuk island group Pacific Ocean WWII 104 (2), 251 (3), 272 (1), 273 (2)
Trundholm Scandinavia (Denmark) the world in 1250 BCE 26–27
Trung Phân see Annam
Truso Central Europe (Poland) medieval states 185 (3) medieval voyages 60–61 (1)
Tsaidam Basin Chin. Qaidam Pendi basin East Asia exploration 257 (3)
Tsangchou see Cangzhou
Tsangpo see Brahmaputra
Tsarigrad see Byzantium, Constantinople, Istanbul
Tsaritsyn mod. Volgograd; prev. Stalingrad see Stalingrad, Volograd Eastern Europe (Russian Federation) Soviet Union 208 (2)
Tsetsaut people North America cultural groups 123 (3)
Tshwane see Pretoria
Tsinan see Jinan
Tsing Hai, Tsinghai see Koko Nor, Qinghai Hu
Tsingtao, Tsingtau, Tsintao see Qingdao
Tsou see Zou
Tsugaru-kaikyō see Tsugaru Strait
Tsugaru Strait Jap. Tsugaru-kaikyō sea waterway Japan Communism 273 (3)
Tsushima battle Japan Russo-Japanese War 270 (4)
Tsushima var. Tsushima-tō, Tusima island group Japan Cold War 109 (4) early modern states 265 (5), 267 (4) medieval states 264 (2), 265 (3), (4)
Tsushima-kaikyō see Tsushima Strait
Tsushima Strait var. Tsushima-kaikyō sea waterway Japan early modern states 267 (4) economy 270 (1) Sino-Japanese War 270 (3)
Tsushima-tō see Tsushima
Tu state East Asia first cities 259 (3)
Tuadmumu state British Isles medieval states 188 (2)
Tuamotu, Archipel des see Tuamotu Islands
Tuamotu, Îles see Tuamotu Islands
Tuamotu Islands Fr. Îles Tuamotu; var. Archipel des Tuamotu, Dangerous Archipelago, Tuamotu Archipelago island group Pacific Ocean colonization 284–285 (1) early cultures 280–281 (3) exploration 279 (3) medieval voyages 60 (2)
Tuareg state West Africa trade 163 (4)
Tuaregs people North Africa/West Africa economy 163 (2) Islam 163 (1)
Tuban prev. Toeban Maritime Southeast Asia (Indonesia) trade 230 (2)
Tubar people Central America colonization 126 (1)
Tubuai, Îles, Tubuai Islands see Australes, Îles
Tuchi see Duji
Tucson North America (USA) the growth of the US 129 (2), 132 (1)
Tucumán var. San Miguel de Tucumán South America (Argentina) empire and revolution 150 (1), 151 (3) politics 151 (4)
see also San Miguel de Tucumán
Tucumán battle South America (Argentina) empire and revolution 88–89 (2)
Tufan see Tibet
Tughluq's Empire state South Asia the world in 1400 70–71
Tugur see Tugursk
Tugursk mod. Tugur Siberia (Russian Federation) exploration 257 (2)
Tukela River river Southern Africa colonization 166 (2)
Tuktoyaktuk North America (Canada) exploration 287 (2)
Tula Eastern Europe (Russian Federation) Soviet Union 208 (2), 214–215 (4)
Tula var. Tula de Allende Central America (Mexico) first civilizations 122 (1)
Tula de Allende see Tula
Tulpetlac Central America (Mexico) Aztecs 124 (2)
Tulsa settlement North America (USA) US economy 134 (1) US politics 135 (6)
Tulucan state Central America Aztecs 124 (1)
Tulunids dynasty Egypt/Southwest Asia early Islam 57 (2) Islam 227 (4)
Tulyehualco Central America (Mexico) Aztecs 124 (2)
Tumaco South America (Colombia) Incas 148 (1)
Tumbes South America (Peru) colonization 148 (2) empire and revolution 150 (2), 151 (3) Incas 147 (3), 148 (1)
Tumbos East Africa (Sudan) ancient Egypt 159 (5)
Tumet people East Asia early modern states 266 (1), (2) trade 267 (3)
Tunes see Tunis, Tunisia
Tung-kuan see Tongguan
Tungus people Siberia trade 267 (3)
see also Xianbei, Xianbi
Tunica people North America colonization 125 (4), 126 (1)
Tunis var. Tūnis; anc. Tunes North Africa (Tunisia) biological diffusion 72–73 (1) colonization 167 (4) crusades 186 (1), 64–65 (2) early Islam 57 (2) economy 163 (2), 190 (1) European expansion 84–85 (1) exploration 156 (3), 157 (4) Islam 163 (1), 227 (4) medieval states 185 (3) Napoleon 200–201 (1), 201 (2) Ottomans 231 (3), 232–233 (1) WWII 210 (1), 211 (4)
Tunis var. Tūnis; mod. Tunisia; anc. Tunes region/state North Africa colonization 167 (4) Napoleon 200–201 (1) slave trade 165 (4) trade 167 (1)
see also Tunisia
Tunis battle North Africa (Tunisia) WWII 104 (2)
Tunisia prev. Tunis, anc. Tunes state North Africa decolonization 168 (1) early 20th century 206 (1) early Islam 57 (2) economy 168 (2), (3) European imperialism 96 (1), 97 (4) Islam 235 (4) Ottomans 232–233 (1) the modern world 112 (1), 113 (3) WWII 210 (1), 211 (4)
see also Tunis
Tunja South America (Colombia) early cultures 146 (1) empire and revolution 150 (1)
Tunjur state Central Africa Islam 163 (1)
Tun-Sun state Mainland Southeast Asia ancient India 241 (6)
Tupi people South America the world in 250 CE 46–47 the world in 500 CE 50–51 the world in 750 CE 54–55 the world in 1500 74–75
Tupi-Guarani people South America early cultures 145 (2)
Tupinambá people South America early cultures 147 (2)
Tupiza South America (Bolivia) Incas 147 (3)
Turba see Teruel
Turenum see Trani
Turfan Buddhist centre/settlement East Asia (China) ancient trade 44–45 (1) early modern states 268 (1) first states 260 (1) medieval states 261 (6), 262–263 (1) trade 267 (3) world religions 49 (3)
Turgay region Central Asia colonialism 269 (3)
Turin It. Torino; anc. Augusta, Taurinorum Italy ancient Rome 182 (1) early modern states 193 (4) economy 205 (4) empire and revolution 202 (3) Franks 184 (2) medieval states 182 (2), 183 (4) Napoleon 200–201 (1)
Turkana, Lake see Rudolf, Lake
Turkestan var. Sinkiang; Sinkiang Uighur Autonomous Region; Chin. Xin, Xinjiang region/state East Asia colonialism 269 (3) early modern states 268 (1) exploration 257 (3) medieval states 261 (6) trade 267 (3) world religions 49 (3), (4)
see also Sinkiang, Xinjiang
Turkey Turk. Türkiye state Southwest Asia economy 234 (1) inter-war 209 (3) Islam 235 (4) post-war economy 213 (5), 214 (1), (2) post-war politics 212 (3) Soviet Union 208 (2), 213 (4) the modern world 113 (3), (4) US superpower 138 (1) WWI 208 (1) WWII 105 (3), 210 (1), 211 (2), (4) 20th-century politics 233 (3), 235 (5) Cold War 108 (3), 109 (1)
Turkic Peoples people Eastern Europe/Siberia the world in 500 CE 50–51 the world in 750 CE 54–55 the world in 1000 58–59 the world in 1200 62–63 the world in 1500 74–75 the world in 1600 78–79
Türkiye see Turkey
Turkmenistan state Central Asia ancient Rome 224 (2) economy 234 (1) historical geography 275 (5) Islam 235 (4) Soviet Union 214–215 (4) the modern world 113 (3) 20th-century politics 235 (5)
Turkmens people Central Asia historical geography 275 (5)
Turks people East Asia/Siberia/Southwest Asia medieval states 263 (3) Ottomans 232–233 (1) the modern world 112 (2)
Turks and Caicos Islands colonial possession/island group West Indies the world in 1925 98–99 the world in 1950 102–103 the world in 1975 106–107 the modern world 110–111
Turner burial mound North America (USA) first civilizations 121 (4)
Turoni mod. Tours France world religions 48 (1)
see also Caesarodunum, Tours
Turpan see Turfan
Turtle Mound North America (USA) cultural groups 122 (5)
Turukhansk Siberia (Russian Federation) exploration 257 (2)
Tus Central Asia (Turkmenistan) early Islam 56–57 (1)
Tusayan archaeological site North America (USA) cultural groups 123 (4)
Tuscany It. Toscana region/state Italy empire and revolution 202 (1), (3) medieval states 188 (1) Napoleon 200–201 (1) Reformation 196 (1), (2)
Tuscarora people North America colonization 126 (1)
Tuscia region Italy medieval states 183 (4)
Tusculana, Via road Italy ancient Rome 181 (2)
Tusculum Italy early states 178 (1)
Tushara state Central Asia/South Asia first empires 241 (5) world religions 242 (2)
Tushki Egypt colonization 167 (4)
Tushpa Southwest Asia (Turkey) first civilizations 222 (2)
Tusima see Tsushima
Tuskegee people North America colonization 125 (4)
Tutchone people North America cultural groups 123 (3)
Tutelo people North America colonization 125 (4), 126 (1)
Tuticorin South Asia (India) colonialism 247 (3)
Tutishcainyo archaeological site South America (Peru) early cultures 144 (1), 145 (2)
Tutub mod. Khafajah settlement/temple Southwest Asia (Iraq) first cities 220 (2) first civilizations 221 (4), 24 (3)
Tututepec Central America (Mexico) first civilizations 122 (1)
Tu'u people Easter Island early cultures 281 (4)
Tuvalu state/island group Pacific Ocean decolonization 285 (3) early cultures 280–281 (3) exploration 276–277 (1) Islam 192 (3) medieval voyages 60 (2)
Tuvu region Eastern Europe Soviet Union 214–215 (4)
Tuxtepec var. San Juan Bautista Tuxtepec Central America (Mexico) first civilizations 122 (1)
Tuyuhun var. Tu-yu-hun state East Asia the world in 500 CE 50–51
Tuyuhun people East Asia medieval states 261 (4)
Tuzigoot archaeological site North America (USA) cultural groups 123 (4)
Tuzla Southeast Europe (Bosnia and Herzegovina) post-war economy 215 (3)
Tuz, Lake lake Southwest Asia WWI 233 (2) 20th-century politics 233 (3)
Tver' prev. Kalinin Eastern Europe (Russian Federation) Mongols 68–69 (1) Soviet Union 208 (2)
Two Sicilies, Kingdom of the state Italy (Mediterrananean Sea) empire and revolution 202 (1), (3)
Tyana Southwest Asia (Turkey) Hellenistic world 40–41 (1)
Tyan'-Shan' see Tien Shan
Tylisian Kingdom state Southeast Europe the world in 250 BCE 38–39
Tylos see Bahrain
Tyne river British Isles economy 204 (3) medieval states 186 (2)
Tyras Southeast Europe (Ukraine) Hellenistic world 40–41 (1)
Tyras see Dniester
Tyre var. Şūr; anc. Tyre var. Tyrus settlement Southwest Asia (Lebanon) ancient Egypt 159 (5) ancient Persia 223 (4) ancient Rome 225 (4), (5) crusades 64–65 (2), 65 (3) early cultures 161 (3), (4), (5) early trade 225 (3) exploration 172 (1) first civilizations 177 (1), 221 (5), 222 (1), (2) Hellenistic world 40–41 (1) medieval states 185 (3) world religions 48 (1)
see also Tyrus
Tyrol region/state Central Europe early modern states 193 (4), 194 (1) medieval states 188 (1) WWI 207 (5)
Tyrrhenian Sea sea Italy ancient Rome 179 (3) crusades 64–65 (2) early states 178 (1), (2) economy 190 (1) empire and revolution 202 (3) medieval states 183 (4)
Tyrus var. Tyrus; anc. Tyre; Eng. Tyre Southwest Asia (Lebanon) ancient Rome 180–181 (1), 181 (3) ancient trade 44–45 (1)
see also Tyre
Tyumen' Eastern Europe (Russian Federation) Soviet Union 214–215 (4)
Tzauhtlan Central America (Mexico) colonization 125 (5)
Tziccoac state Central America Aztecs 124 (1)
Tzilcayoapan Central America (Mexico) first civilizations 122 (1)
Tzinapecuaro Central America (Mexico) first civilizations 122 (1)
Tzintzuntzan Central America (Mexico) Aztecs 124 (1) first civilizations 122 (1)
Tzompantzinco Central America (Mexico) colonization 125 (5)
Tz'u-shan see Cishan

U

UAE see United Arab Emirates
Uaxactún Central America (Guatemala) first civilizations 121 (2)
Ubangi Fr. Oubangui river Central Africa early agriculture 158 (1) economy 163 (2) Islam 163 (1) slave trade 165 (4)
Ubangi Shari region Central Africa European imperialism 96 (1)
Ubangi-Shari see Central African Republic
Ucayali river South America colonization 148 (2) early cultures 145 (2), (4), 146 (1) environment 153 (4) exploration 143 (2) Incas 147 (3), 148 (1) narcotics 153 (5) politics 152 (1)
Udabhanda South Asia (Pakistan) early medieval states 244 (2)
Udaiyars state South Asia Mughal Empire 246 (1)
Udichya region South Asia ancient India 242 (1)
Udicya/Uttarapatha region South Asia early religions 48 (2)
Udine Italy WWI 207 (5)
Udmurtia region Eastern Europe Soviet Union 214–215 (4)
Uelen North America (USA) cultural groups 123 (3)
Uesugi region Japan early modern states 267 (4)
Ufa Eastern Europe (Russian Federation) Soviet Union 208 (2), 214–215 (4) trade 267 (3)
Uganda state East Africa Cold War 109 (1) decolonization 168 (1) economy 168 (2), (3) European imperialism 96 (1), 97 (4) the modern world 112 (1), 113 (3) WWII 104 (1)
Ugarit Ar. Ra's Shamrah religious site/settlement Southwest Asia (Syria) ancient Egypt 159 (4), (5) early agriculture 220 (1) first cities 28–29 (1) first civilizations 221 (4), (5) first religions 37 (3)
Ugogi East Africa (Tanzania) exploration 157 (5)
Ugrians people Eastern Europe/Siberia the world in 750 CE 54–55
Uhorshchyna see Hungary
Uhuru Peak see Kilimanjaro
Uige prev. Carmona, Vila Marechal Carmona Southern Africa (Angola) Cold War 109 (5)
Uighur City States var. Uygur state East Asia the world in 1200 62–63
Uighur Empire state East Asia the world in 750 CE 54–55
Uighurs people East Asia historical geography 275 (5) medieval states 262–263 (1), 263 (3), (5) trade 267 (3)
Uitenhage Southern Africa (South Africa) colonization 166 (2)
Ujain see Ujjain, Ujjayini
Uji-gawa battle Japan early modern states 265 (5)
Ujiji East Africa (Tanzania) exploration 157 (4), (5)
Ujjain prev. Ujain, Ujjayini South Asia (India) colonialism 248 (1) Marathas 246 (2) see also Ujjayini
Ujjayani see Ujjayini
Ujjayini var. Ujain, Ujjain, Ujjayani settlement South Asia (India) early medieval states 244 (1), (2), 244–245 (3) early religions 48 (2) first empires 241 (4) first religions 36 (2) world religions 242 (2) see also Ujjain
Ujungpandang var. Macassar, Makassar; prev. Makasar Maritime Southeast Asia (Indonesia) post-war economy 253 (5) see also Macassar
Ujung Salang see Phuket
Újvidék see Novi Sad
UK see United Kingdom
Ukraina see Ukraine
Ukraine Rus. Ukraina, Ukr. Ukrayina region/state Eastern Europe post-war economy 214 (1), (2) Soviet Union 208 (2), 214–215 (4) the modern world 112 (2) WWI 207 (4) WWII 210 (1)
Ukrayina see Ukraine
Ulaanbaatar see Ulan Bator, Urga
Ulaidh mod. Ulster state British Isles medieval states 188 (2) see also Ulster
Ulan Bator prev. Urga; Mong. Ulaanbaatar East Asia (Mongolia) Communism 271 (8) Islam 275 (4) see also Urga
Ulan-Ude see Verkhneudinsk
Ulenje people Southern Africa trade 164 (1)
Uliassutai East Asia (Mongolia) exploration 256 (1)
Ulithi island Pacific Ocean WWII 251 (3), 272 (1)
Ullung-do island East Asia Cold War 109 (4)
Ulm Central Europe (Germany) early modern states 193 (4) medieval states 188 (1)
Ulsan East Asia (South Korea) early modern states 267 (4)
Ulster region British Isles medieval states 186 (2)
Ulundi battle Southern Africa (South Africa) European imperialism 96 (2)
'Umān, Khalīj see Oman, Gulf of
Umataka archaeological site Japan early agriculture 258 (1)
Umayyad Caliphate state Iberian Peninsula/North Africa/Southwest Asia Islam 184 (1)
Umayyads dynasty Iberian Peninsula/North Africa early Islam 57 (2) Islam 227 (4)
Umballa var. Ambala battle South Asia empire and revolution 249 (3)
Umbri people Italy early states 178 (2)
Umbu archaeological site South America (Brazil) early cultures 145 (2)
Umma Southwest Asia (Iraq) first civilizations 24 (3)
Umm an Nar Southwest Asia (United Arab Emirites) first civilizations 24 (2), 25 (3)
Umm Durmān see Omdurman
Umm Saïd var. Musay'īd Southwest Asia (Qatar) economy 234 (1)
Unci see Almería
Undi state Southern Africa slave trade 165 (4) trade 164 (1)
Ungaria, **Ungarn** see Hungary
Ungava, District of province North America the growth of the US 132 (1)
Ungava, Péninsule d' coastal feature North America the growth of the US 129 (2)
Ungju region East Asia medieval states 264 (2)
Ungro-Vlachia see Wallachia
Unguja see Zanzibar
Union of Soviet Socialist Republics state Eastern Europe economy 274 (1) inter-war 209 (3), (5) Islam 275 (4) post-war economy 213 (5) post-war politics 212 (3), 271 (7) Soviet Union 208 (2), 213 (4) WWI 208 (1) WWII 104 (1), 105 (4), 210 (1), 211 (2), (3), (4), 272 (1), 273 (2) 20th-century politics 233 (3) Cold War 109 (1), (4) Communism 271 (8)
Union Pacific Railroad railway North America the growth of the US 129 (2)
United Arab Emirates abbrev. UAE; prev. Trucial Coast, Trucial States, Trucial Oman state Southwest Asia economy 234 (1) Islam 235 (4) the modern world 113 (3) US economy 138 (2) 20th-century politics 235 (5) see also Trucial Oman
United Arab Republic see Egypt
United Kingdom abbrev. UK state British Isles early 20th century 206 (1) imperial global economy 92 (1) Napoleon 200–201 (1), 201 (2) post-war economy 213 (5), 214 (1) post-war politics 212 (3) Soviet Union 214–215 (4) the modern world 112 (2), 113 (4) Cold War 108 (3), 109 (1) US superpower 138 (1) see also Britain
United Mexican States see Mexico
United Netherlands state Low Countries empire and revolution 202 (1)
United Provinces var. Holland, prev. Batavian Republic, Dutch Republic, United Provinces; Dut. Nederland state Low Countries early modern states 197 (5) Reformation 196 (1), (2) see also Batavian Republic, Netherlands
United Provinces see Uttar Pradesh
United States see United States of America
United States of America var. America, The States, prev. United States of North America; abbrev. U.S., USA state North America empire and revolution 127 (3), 88–89 (2) European expansion 84–85 (1) global immigration 101 (2), (3) imperial global economy 92 (1), 93 (5) Mexican Revolution 133 (3) the growth of the US 129 (2), 132 (1), 133 (4) the modern world 112 (1), 113 (4) US economy 138 (2) US politics 139 (4) US superpower 138 (1) WWII 104 (1), 105 (4), 272 (1), 273 (2) Cold War 108 (2), 109 (1)
United States of North America see United States of America
University burial mound North America (USA) first civilizations 121 (4)
Unorganized territory region North America the growth of the US 130 (1) US Civil War 130 (2), (3), (4), (5)
Unterwalden region Central Europe early modern states 193 (5)
Unyanyembe see Tabora
Upper Bembe state Southern Africa trade 164 (2)
Upper Burma state Mainland Southeast Asia European imperialism 97 (3)
Upper Egypt state Egypt ancient Egypt 159 (5)
Upper Gelderland var. Upper Gelders province/region Central Europe empire and revolution 199 (3) Reformation 195 (5)
Upper Gelders see Upper Gelderland
Upper Lorraine region Central Europe medieval states 185 (3), 188 (1)
Upper Ohio Frontier region North America empire and revolution 127 (3)
Upper Silesia region Central Europe WWI 208 (1)
Upper Swan Australia exploration 280 (1)
Upper Volta state West Africa European imperialism 96 (1)
Uppsala Scandinavia (Sweden) early modern states 197 (3) medieval states 189 (3)
Ur Southwest Asia (Iraq) early systems 223 (3) first cities 28–29 (1) first civilizations 221 (4), (5), 222 (2), 25 (3) first religions 36 (1) first cities 220 (2)
Uraiyur South Asia (India) early medieval states 244 (1) first empires 241 (4) world religions 243 (4)
Ural Kaz. Zayyq river Central Asia/Eastern Europe biological diffusion 72–73 (1) colonialism 269 (3) medieval states 261 (6), 262–263 (1) Mongols 68–69 (1) Ottomans 231 (3)
Ural Mountains Rus. Ural'skiy Khrebet, Ural'skiye Gory mountain range Eastern Europe ancient trade 44–45 (1) biological diffusion 72–73 (1) colonialism 269 (3) early agriculture 174 (1) exploration 172 (1), 257 (2), 286 (1), 287 (2) first humans 13 (2) medieval states 185 (3) Mongols 68–69 (1) Soviet Union 208 (2)
Ural'sk Kaz. Oral Central Asia (Kazakhstan) Soviet Union 214–215 (4)
Ural'sk region Central Asia colonialism 269 (3)
Ural'skiye Gory, **Ural'skiy Khrebet** see Ural Mountains
Urartu mod. Armenia state Southwest Asia first civilizations 222 (2) see also Armenia
Urbino Italy early modern states 193 (4)
Urbino state Italy Ottomans 195 (4) Reformation 194 (2)
Urdunn see Jordan
Uren North America (USA) cultural groups 122 (5)
Ures Central America (Mexico) colonization 125 (4)
Urewe archaeological site East Africa (Kenya) early cultures 160 (1)
Urfa see Edessa
Urga mod. Ulan Bator; Mong. Ulaanbaatar East Asia (Mongolia) colonialism 269 (3) early modern states 268 (1) exploration 256 (1), 257 (3) Soviet Union 208 (2) see also Ulan Bator
Urganch see Urgench
Urgench var. Urganch; prev. Novo-Urgench Central Asia (Uzbekistan) Mongols 68–69 (1)
Uri Ger. Basel region Central Europe early modern states 193 (5)
Uriankhai var. Tannu Tuva, Uryankhai region East Asia imperialism 268 (1), 269 (4)
Uribe South America (Colombia) narcotics 153 (5)
Urmia, Lake var. Matianus, Sha Hi, Urumi Yeh; prev. Daryācheh-ye Reṣā'īyeh lake Southwest Asia ancient Persia 223 (4), 225 (6) early agriculture 220 (1) economy 234 (1) first cities 220 (2) first civilizations 221 (4), (5), 222 (2), 25 (3) Hellenistic world 224 (1) medieval Persia 231 (4) medieval states 185 (3) Mongols 229 (3) Seljuks 228 (1) Timur 229 (4) 20th-century politics 233 (3)
Uruguai, Rio see Uruguay
Uruguay prev. La Banda Oriental state South America Cold War 109 (1) empire and revolution 150 (1), 151 (3), 88–89 (2) environment 153 (4) global immigration 100 (1), 101 (2) imperial global economy 92 (1) politics 152 (1) the modern world 112 (1), 113 (4) US superpower 138 (1) WWII 105 (3)
Uruguay var. Rio Uruguai river South America colonization 148 (2) empire and revolution 151 (3) environment 153 (4) exploration 143 (2) politics 152 (1)
Uruk var. Erech settlement/temple Southwest Asia (Iraq) early agriculture 220 (1) early systems 223 (3) first cities 28–29 (1) first civilizations 221 (4), 222 (2), 25 (3)
Uruk IV Buildings building Southwest Asia (Iraq) first cities 220 (3)
Urumchi var. Tihwa, Urumqi, Urumtsi, Wu-lu-k'o-mu-shi, Wu-lu-mu-ch'i; prev. Ti-hua; mod. Ürümqi East Asia (China) early modern states 268 (1) exploration 256 (1), 257 (3) see also Ürümqi
Urumi Yeh see Urmia, Lake
Urumqi see Urumchi, Ürümqi
Ürümqi var. Urumchi, Urumqi, Urumtsi, Tihwa, Wu-lu-k'o-mu-shi, Wu-lu-mu-ch'i; prev. Ti-hua East Asia (China) post-war economy 275 (3) see also Urumchi
Urumtsi see Urumchi, Ürümqi
Urundi see Burundi
Uruvela South Asia (India) world religions 242 (3)
Uryankhai var. Tannu Tuva, Uriankhai region East Asia colonialism 269 (3) see also Tannu Tuva, Uriankhai
U.S. see United States of America
U.S.A. see United States of America
Ushinara region South Asia world religions 242 (3)
Üsküb, **Üsküp** see Scupi, Skopje, Skoplje
Uspanapa river Central America first civilizations 121 (3)
Ussuri region/state Siberia colonialism 269 (3), (4) early modern states 268 (1) post-war economy 275 (3)
Ussuri var. Usuri, Wusuri, Chin. Wusuli Jiang river East Asia first states 260 (1)
Usui East Africa (Tanzania) exploration 157 (4)
Usumacinta river Central America first civilizations 122 (1)
Usumbura mod. Bujumbura East Africa (Burundi) exploration 157 (5)
Usuri see Ussuri
Utah var. Utah Territory state/region North America the growth of the US 129 (1) US Civil War 130 (2), (3), (4), (5) US economy 134 (2)
Utatlán Central America (Guatemala) Aztecs 124 (1) first civilizations 122 (2)
Ute people North America colonization 125 (4), 126 (1)
U Thong Mainland Southeast Asia (Thailand) ancient India 241 (6)
Utica North Africa (Tunisia) ancient Rome 179 (3), 180–181 (1) first civilizations 177 (1)
Utkala region South Asia world religions 242 (2)
Utqiagvik North America (USA) cultural groups 123 (3)
Utrecht Lat. Trajectum ad Rhenum Low Countries (Netherlands) economy 190 (1) empire and revolution 202 (1i) Franks 184 (2) medieval states 188 (1) Reformation 194 (2), 195 (5)
Utrecht province Low Countries Reformation 195 (5)
Utsunomiya Japan early modern states 265 (5)
Uttara Parvat-Asreya region South Asia early religions 48 (2)
Uttarapatha region South Asia first empires 241 (4)
Uttar Pradesh prev. United Provinces, United Provinces of Agra and Oudh region South Asia post-war politics 252 (1)
Utz North America (USA) cultural groups 122 (5)
Uvea island Pacific Ocean early cultures 280–281 (3) medieval voyages 60 (2)
Uvira Central Africa (Congo) exploration 157 (4)
Uvja see Elam
Uxmal Central America (Mexico) first civilizations 123 (2)
Uygur see Uighur City States
Uzbegs see Uzbeks
Uzbek Empire state Central Asia trade 267 (3)
Uzbekistan state Central Asia historical geography 275 (5) Islam 235 (4) Soviet Union 214–215 (4) the modern world 113 (3)
Uzbeks var. Uzbegs dynasty South Asia Mughal Empire 246 (1)
Uzbeks people Central Asia historical geography 275 (5) medieval Persia 231 (4)
Uzhgorod Eastern Europe (Ukraine) post-war politics 212 (3)

V

Vaccaei people Iberian Peninsula ancient Rome 179 (5)
Vadodara prev. Baroda South Asia (India) post-war economy 253 (5) see also Baroda
Vadsø Scandinavia (Norway) exploration 287 (2)
Vagarshapat Christian archbishopric Southwest Asia (Armenia) world religions 48 (1)
Vahavasi South Asia (India) first empires 241 (4)
Vaidisha region South Asia world religions 242 (2)
Vaikam South Asia (India) decolonization 250 (1)
Vairaatea island Pacific Ocean exploration 278 (1)
Vaishali mod. Besarh religious site/settlement South Asia (India) early religions 48 (2) first religions 36 (2)
Vaitea physical region Easter Island early cultures 281 (4)
Vajji region South Asia ancient India 242 (1)
Vajji Confederation state South Asia the world in 500 BCE 34–35
Vakatakas dynasty South Asia the world in 500 CE 50–51
Valabhi religious site South Asia (India) first religions 36 (2)
Valachia see Wallachia
Valdivia South America (Chile) colonization 148 (2) empire and revolution 151 (3) environment 153 (4) exploration 143 (3)
Valdivia archaeological site South America (Ecuador) early cultures 144 (1)
Valence anc. Valentia, Valentia Julia, Ventia France medieval states 192 (1)
Valencia South America (Venezuela) empire and revolution 150 (1), 151 (3) environment 153 (4)
Valencia Iberian Peninsula (Spain) economy 190 (1) Franks 184 (2) inter-war 209 (4) Islam 192 (3) Napoleon 200–201 (1), 201 (2)
Valenciennes France early modern states 197 (5)
Valentia mod. Valencia Iberian Peninsula (Spain) ancient Rome 180–181 (1) see also Valencia
Valentia Julia see Valence
Valeria, Via road Italy early states 178 (1)
Valhika var. Bactra; mod. Balkh Central Asia (Afghanistan) early medieval states 244 (1) see also Bactria, Balkh
Valladolid Iberian Peninsula (Spain) economy 190 (1) inter-war 209 (4) Islam 192 (3)
Valle de Bravo Central America (Mexico) first civilizations 122 (1)
Vallée d'Andorre see Andorra
Valle San Bartolomé Central America (Mexico) colonization 125 (4)
Valley Forge North America (USA) empire and revolution 127 (3)
Valls d'Andorra see Andorra
Valmiera see Wolmar
Valmy battle France empire and revolution 199 (4)
Valona mod. Vlorë; prev. Vlonë; It. Vlora Southeast Europe (Albania) medieval states 189 (4) WWI 207 (6)
Valparaíso South America (Chile) colonization 148 (2) empire and revolution 150 (1), 151 (3) environment 153 (4) exploration 143 (2), (3) global immigration 100 (1) imperial global economy 92 (1) politics 152 (1)
Valsequillo Central America (Mexico) the world in 10,000 BCE 14–15
Vamsha region South Asia ancient India 242 (1) world religions 242 (3)
Vanavashika region South Asia world religions 242 (2)
Vanavasi South Asia (India) early medieval states 244 (1) world religions 242 (2)
Vanchi South Asia (India) early medieval states 244 (1) first empires 241 (4)
Vancouver North America (Canada) global immigration 100 (1) the growth of the US 129 (2), 132 (1) US economy 136 (2)
Vandals people Eastern Europe ancient Rome 181 (4) great migrations 52–53 (1)
Vandals, Kingdom of the state Italy/North Africa ancient Rome 182 (1) early cultures 160 (1) great migrations 53 (2)
Van Diemen's Land mod. Tasmania island Australia exploration 278 (1) see also Tasmania
Vanga region South Asia early religions 48 (2) first empires 241 (4) world religions 242 (2)
Van, Lake anc. Thospitis salt lake Southwest Asia ancient Persia 223 (4) crusades 228 (2) early agriculture 220 (1) first cities 220 (2) first civilizations 221 (4), (5), 222 (2), 25 (3) great migrations 52–53 (1) Hellenistic world 224 (1) medieval Persia 231 (4) Mongols 229 (3) Ottomans 231 (3) Seljuks 228 (1) Timur 229 (4) WWI 233 (2) 20th-century politics 233 (3)
Vannes anc. Dariorigum France Franks 184 (2) see also Dariorigum
Vanuatu prev. New Hebrides island group/state Pacific Ocean decolonization 285 (3) early cultures 280–281 (3) environmentalism 285 (2) medieval voyages 60 (2)
Vapheio Greece first civilizations 175 (4)
Várad Ger. Grosswardein, Rom. Oradea Southeast Europe (Romania) medieval states 189 (4) Ottomans 195 (4)
Varanasi prev. Banaras, Benares, Baranasi; hist. Kashi South Asia (India) early medieval states 244 (1) post-war economy 253 (5) see also Banaras, Baranasi, Benares
Varaždin Southeast Europe (Croatia) post-war economy 215 (3)
Vardar Gk. Axiós river Southeast Europe post-war economy 215 (3) WWI 207 (6)
Varmans state South Asia early medieval states 244 (2)
Varna prev. Stalin; anc. Odessus archaeological site/settlement Southeast Europe (Bulgaria) Copper Age 174 (2) economy 190 (1) Napoleon 200–201 (1) Ottomans 202 (4), 230 (1) WWI 207 (6) see also Odessus
Varshava see Warsaw
Varunadvipa state Maritime Southeast Asia world religions 243 (5)
Vasa Scandinavia (Finland) economy 205 (4)
Vasati state South Asia first empires 241 (5)
Vatapi South Asia (India) early medieval states 244 (1), (2)
Vatapi, Chalukyas of state South Asia early medieval states 244 (2)
Vatican City state Italy the modern world 112 (2)
Vatnajökull glacier Iceland exploration 172 (2)
Vatsa region/state South Asia first empires 241 (5) first religions 36 (2)
Vatsagulma South Asia (India) early medieval states 244 (1)
Vattina Southeast Europe (Romania) Bronze Age 175 (3)
Vauchamps battle France Napoleon 200–201 (1)
Vava'u Group island group Pacific Ocean early cultures 280–281 (3) medieval voyages 60 (2)
Vegkop battle Southern Africa (South Africa) colonization 166 (2)
Veii Italy early states 178 (1), (2) first civilizations 177 (1)
Vela Goa, **Velha Goa** see Goa, Gove
Velho see Porto Velho
Velia var. Elea Italy early states 178 (1)
Velika Morava var. Glavn'a Morava, March, Morava, Ger. Grosse Morava river Central Europe post-war economy 215 (3) see also Morava
Velikiye Luki Eastern Europe (Russian Federation) early modern states 195 (3)
Veliko Tŭrnovo see Tirnovo
Velitrae Italy early states 178 (1)
Velizh Eastern Europe (Russian Federation) early modern states 195 (3)
Velsuna see Orvieto
Vembar var. Patmadoer South Asia (India) colonialism 247 (3)
Venaissin state France early modern states 197 (5) medieval states 192 (1), (2)
Vendée region France empire and revolution 199 (4)
Venedig see Venice
Veneti people Italy early states 178 (1), (2)
Venetia var. Lombardy-Venetia state Italy empire and revolution 202 (1), (3)
Venetia see Venice
Venetian Republic state Italy/Southwest Europe crusades 186 (1), 64–65 (2) early modern states 193 (4), 194 (1) medieval states 185 (3), 188 (1), 189 (4) Ottomans 195 (4), 231 (3) Reformation 194 (2), 196 (1)
Venezia see Venice
Venezia, Golfo di see Venice, Gulf of
Venezuela state South America economy 153 (3) empire and revolution 150 (2), 151 (3) environment 153 (4) narcotics 153 (5) politics 152 (1) the growth of the US 133 (4) the modern world 112 (1), 113 (4) US politics 139 (4) US superpower 138 (1) WWII 105 (3) Cold War 108 (2), 109 (1)
Venezuela, Golfo de see Venezuela, Gulf of
Venezuela, Gulf of var. Gulf of Maracaibo, Sp. Golfo de Venezuela gulf South America colonization 148 (2) Incas 148 (1)
Vengi South Asia (India) early medieval states 244 (1)
Vengipura South Asia (India) early religions 48 (2)
Vengurla South Asia (India) colonialism 247 (3)
Venice anc.Venetia; Fr. Venise, Ger. Venedig, It. Venezia settlement Italy biological diffusion 72–73 (1) crusades 186 (1), 64–65 (2) early modern states 193 (4) economy 190 (1) empire and revolution 202 (1), (3) European expansion 84–85 (1) Franks 184 (2) Islam 163 (1) medieval states 185 (3), (5), 188 (1) Mongols 68 (2) Napoleon 200–201 (1), 201 (2), (3) Ottomans 230 (1), 231 (3) Reformation 194 (2), 196 (1) WWI 207 (5)
Venice state Italy Reformation 196 (2)
Venice, Gulf of It. Golfo di Venezia, Slvn. Beneški Zaliv gulf Southeast Europe WWI 207 (5)
Venice, Lagoon of lagoon Italy economy 191 (3)
Venise see Venice
Venosa see Venusia
Venta Belgarum see Winchester
Ventia see Valence
Ventspils see Vindava, Windau
Venus and Rome, Temple of building Italy ancient Rome 181 (2)
Venusia mod. Venosa Italy early states 178 (1)
Vera Cruz see Veracruz
Veracruz mod. Vera Cruz settlement/battle/region/state Central America (Mexico) first civilizations 122 (1) colonization 125 (4), (5), 126 (1) Mexican Revolution 133 (3) European expansion 84–85 (1) battle 85 (2) exploration 118 (1) Mexican Revolution 133 (3) the growth of the US 129 (2) Cold War 108 (2)
Veracruz Llave see Veracruz
Veranja South Asia (India) world religions 242 (3)
Vercellae see Vercelli
Vercelli anc. Vercellae Italy economy 190 (1) medieval states 188 (1)
Verde, Cape headland West Africa exploration 156 (3)
Verden region Central Europe early modern states 197 (3)
Verdun var. Verdun-sur-Meuse; anc. Verodunum France early modern states 197 (5) Franks 184 (2) medieval states 188 (1) WWI 206 (2), (3)
Verdun-sur-Meuse see Verdun
Verkhneudinsk mod. Ulan-Ude Siberia (Russian Federation) exploration 257 (3)
Vermont state North America the growth of the US 129 (1) US Civil War 130 (2), (3), (4), (5) US economy 134 (2)
Vernon North America (USA) US economy 135 (4)
Verny mod. Alma-Ata; Kaz. Almaty Central Asia (Kazakhstan) exploration 257 (3) see also Alma-Ata
Verodunum see Verdun
Verona Italy crusades 186 (1) early modern states 193 (4) economy 190 (1) Franks 184 (2) great migrations 52–53 (1) medieval states 182 (2), 183 (4) WWI 207 (5)
Verona region Italy medieval states 188 (1)
Versailles France early modern states 197 (5) WWI 206 (2), (3)
Verulamium mod St. Albans British Isles (United Kingdom) ancient Rome 180–181 (1)
Vesali South Asia early medieval states 244 (1) world religions 242 (3)
Vesontio var. Besontium; mod. Besançon France ancient Rome 180–181 (1) world religions 48 (1) see also Besançon
Vesta, Temple of building Italy ancient Rome 181 (2)
Vestini people Italy early states 178 (1), (2)
Vesuna see Périgueux
Vetera legion headquarters Central Europe (Germany)ancient Rome 180–181 (1)
Vetulonia Italy early states 178 (1), (2) first civilizations 177 (1)
Vézeronce battle France Franks 183 (5)
Viborg Eastern Europe (Russian Federation) early modern states 197 (3)
Viborg Scandinavia (Denmark) medieval states 185 (3)
Vibo Valentia see Hipponium
Vicentia see Vicenza
Vicenza var. Vicentia settlement Italy economy 190 (1) medieval states 187 (3) WWI 207 (5)
Viceroyalty of New Granada see Colombia, New Granada
Vichy France WWII 210 (1), 211 (2), (3), (4)
Vichy France region France WWII 210 (1), 211 (2), (3), (4)
Vicksburg North America (USA) the growth of the US 129 (2) US Civil War 131 (6), (7)
Victoria mod. Vitória South America (Brazil) empire and revolution 151 (3) see also Vitória
Victoria North America (Canada) the growth of the US 129 (2), 132 (1)
Victoria region Australia colonization 282 (1), (2), 283 (3)
Victoria Falls waterfall Southern Africa exploration 157 (4)
Victoria Island island North America cultural groups 123 (3) exploration 287 (2) the growth of the US 129 (2)
Victoria, Lake var. Victoria Nyanza lake East Africa ancient trade 44–45 (1) early agriculture 158 (1) early cultures 160 (1) economy 163 (2), (3) European imperialism 96 (1) exploration 156 (3), 157 (4), (5) first humans 12 (1), 13 (2) Islam 163 (1) slave trade 165 (4)
Victoria Land physical region Antarctica Antarctic Exploration 287 (3)
Victoria Nyanza see Victoria, Lake
Victoria River river Australia prehistoric culture 17 (5)
Vicus Elbii see Viterbo
Vidarbha region/state South Asia first empires 241 (5) world religions 242 (2)
Videha region/state South Asia first empires 241 (5) world religions 242 (2), (3)
Vídeň see Vienna, Vindo Bona
Vidin Southeast Europe (Bulgaria) medieval states 189 (4) Ottomans 230 (1) WWI 207 (6)
Vidisha var. Bhilsa religious site/settlement South Asia (India) early medieval states 244 (1) first empires 241 (4) first religions 36 (2) world religions 242 (2), (3)
Vienna mod. Vienne Christian archbishopric/settlement France ancient Rome 181 (4) world religions 48 (1)
Vienna mod. Wien; anc. Vindobona; Hung. Bécs, Slvk. Vídeň, Slvn. Dunaj battle/settlement Central Europe (Austria) ancient Rome 193 180–181 (1) early modern states 193 (4), 194 (1) economy 198 (1), 205 (4) empire and revolution 198 (2), 202 (1), (2) inter-war 209 (5) medieval states 185 (3), 188 (1), 189 (3), (4) Mongols 68–69 (1) Napoleon 200–201 (1), 201 (2), (3) Ottomans 195 (4), 231 (3) post-war politics 212 (1), (3) Reformation 194 (2), 196 (1), (2) WWII 210 (1), 211 (2), (3), (4) Cold War 108 (3) see also Vindobona
Vienne see Vienna
Viennensis province France ancient Rome 181 (4)
Vientiane Mainland Southeast Asia (Laos) colonialism 247 (4), 248 (1) post-war economy 253 (5) post-war politics 251 (5) world religions 243 (5)
Vientiane state Mainland Southeast Asia the world in 1800 86–87
Vierzon France medieval states 192 (1)
Vietnam state Mainland Southeast Asia Bronze Age 240 (3) colonialism 248 (1) decolonization 251 (4) economy 274 (1) Islam 275 (4) post-war economy 253 (5) post-war politics 251 (5), 253 (4), 274 (2) the modern world 113 (4) US superpower 138 (1) Cold War 109 (1)
Vigo Iberian Peninsula (Spain) Napoleon 200–201 (1)
Viipuri see Viborg, Vyborg
Vijaya mod. Binh Đinh Mainland Southeast Asia (Vietnam) ancient India 241 (6) early medieval states 245 (5), (6)
Vijayanagar state South Asia the world in 1400 70–71 the world in 1500 74–75
Vijayanagara region/settlement South Asia colonialism 247 (3) early medieval states 244–245 (3), 245 (4)
Vijayans dynasty South Asia the world in 1 CE 42–43
Vijayapura South Asia (India) early medieval states 244 (2)
Vijayapura state Maritime Southeast Asia ancient India 241 (6)
Vijayawada prev. Bezwada South Asia (India) post-war economy 253 (5)
Vijosa, **Vijosë** see Vjosë
Vikings people Scandinavia medieval states 185 (3)
Vila Artur de Paiva see Cubango
Vila Bela var. Mato Grosso South America (Brazil) colonization 149 (3)
Vila da Ponte see Cubango
Vila do Zumbo see Zumbo
Világos mod. Şiria battle Central Europe (Hungary) empire and revolution 88–89 (2)
Vila Henrique de Carvalho see Saurimo
Vila Marechal Carmona see Uige
Vila Serpa Pinto see Menongue
Vilcas South America (Peru) Incas 147 (3)
Vilcas Huamán South America (Peru) Incas 148 (1)
Viljandi see Fellin
Villa Alta var. S.I. Villa Alta Central America (Mexico) first civilizations 122 (1)
Villach Central Europe (Austria) WWI 207 (5)
Villa Concepción see Concepción
Villa da Barra see Manáos, Manaus
Villa de la Veracruz Central America (Mexico) colonization 125 (5)
Villa do Forte de Assumpeão see Ceará, Fortaleza
Villahermosa see San Juan Bautista
Villa Montes South America (Bolivia) politics 152 (2)
Villa San Luis Central America (Mexico) colonization 125 (4)
Villefranche-de-Conflent France early modern states 197 (5)
Vilna mod. Vilnius; Ger. Wilna, Pol. Wilno Eastern Europe (Lithuania) early modern states 193 (4), 195 (3) empire and revolution 198 (2) medieval states 189 (3), (4) Napoleon 200–201 (1) WWI 207 (4) see also Vilnius, Wilno
Vilnius prev. Vilna; Ger. Wilna, Pol. Wilno Eastern Europe (Lithuania) post-war politics 212 (3) Soviet Union 214–215 (4) see also Vilna, Wilno
Vilno see Vilna
Vimeiro Iberian Peninsula (Portugal) Napoleon 200–201 (1)
Viminacium legion headquarters Southeast Europe (Yugoslavia) ancient Rome 180–181 (1)
Viminal Hill Lat. Collis Viminalis hill Italy ancient Rome 181 (2)
Viminalis Collis see Viminal Hill
Viña del Mar South America (Chile) empire and revolution 151 (3)
Viňca Southeast Europe (Yugoslavia) early agriculture 174 (1)
Vincennes fort North America (USA) empire and revolution 127 (3)
Vindava Ger. Windau, Lat. Ventspils Eastern Europe (Latvia) WWI 207 (4) see also Windau
Vindhya Mountains see Vindhya Range
Vindhya-Prstha region South Asia early religions 48 (2)
Vindhya Range var. Vindhya Mountains mountain range South Asia colonialism 247 (3), 248 (1) early medieval states 244 (1), 244–245 (3) first empires 241 (4) Mughal Empire 246 (1) world religions 243 (4)
Vindobona mod. Wien; Eng. Vienna, Hung. Bécs, Slvk. Vídeň, Slvn. Dunaj legion headquarters Central Europe (Austria) ancient Rome 180–181 (1) see also Vienna
Vine Mound burial mound North America (USA) first civilizations 121 (4)
Vinh Thai Lan see Siam, Gulf of; Thailand, Gulf of
Vinh Yen battle Mainland Southeast Asia (Vietnam) post-war politics 251 (5)
Vinjha region South Asia world religions 242 (3)
Vinland region North America medieval voyages 60–61 (1)
Vinot South Asia (Pakistan) world religions 243 (4)
Virginia colonial possession/state North America empire and revolution 127 (2), (3) the growth of the US 129 (1) US Civil War 130 (2), (3), (4), (5), 131 (6), (7) US economy 134 (2), 139 (3) US society 137 (6) US superpower 139 (5)
Virginia Capes battle North America (USA) empire and revolution 127 (3)
Virgin Islands island group West Indies Cold War 108 (2) empire and revolution 88 (1) the growth of the US 133 (4)
Virgin Islands of the United States see American Virgin Islands
Virgo, Aqua aqueduct Italy ancient Rome 181 (2)
Virú river South America early cultures 145 (3)
Virunum Central Europe (Austria) ancient Rome 180–181 (1)
Visakhapatnam South Asia (India) post-war economy 253 (5)
Visby Ger. Wisby Scandinavia (Sweden) economy 190 (1) see also Wisby
Višegrad Southeast Europe (Bosnia and Herzogovina) WWI 207 (6)
Visigoths people Southeast Europe/Southwest Asia ancient Rome 181 (4) great migrations 52–53 (1)
Visigoths, Kingdom of the state France/Iberian Peninsula ancient Rome 182 (1) early Islam 56–57 (1) Franks 183 (5), (6) great migrations 52–53 (1), 53 (2) medieval states 182 (2)
Vistula Pol. Wisła, Ger. Weichsel river Central Europe Bronze Age 175 (3) Copper Age 174 (2) crusades 64–65 (2) early agriculture 174 (1) early modern states 193 (4) economy 205 (4) empire and revolution 198 (2), 199 (3), 202 (2) exploration 172 (1) great migrations 52–53 (1) medieval states 189 (3), (4) Mongols 68–69 (1) Napoleon 200–201 (1), 201 (2), (3) prehistoric culture 17 (4) WWI 207 (4)
Vitcos South America (Peru) Incas 147 (3)
Vitebsk var. Vitsyebsk Eastern Europe (Belorussia) early modern states 195 (3) economy 190 (1) Soviet Union 208 (2)
Viterbo anc. Vicus Elbii Italy economy 190 (1) medieval states 188 (1)
Vitez Southeast Europe (Bosnia and Herzegovina) post-war economy 215 (3)
Viti Levu island Pacific Ocean early cultures 280–281 (3) medieval voyages 60 (2) US superpower 138 (1)
Vitim river Eastern Europe early modern states 268 (1) first states 260 (1)
Vitoria Iberian Peninsula (Spain) Napoleon 200–201 (1)
Vitória prev. Victoria South America (Brazil) colonization 149 (3) see also Victoria
Vitsyebsk see Vitebsk
Vittorio Veneto Italy WWI 207 (5)
Viye state Southern Africa slave trade 165 (4) trade 167 (1)
Vizagapatam settlement South Asia (India) colonialism 247 (3) decolonization 250 (1) WWII 251 (3), 272 (1)
Vizcaíno, Desierto de desert Central America cultural groups 123 (4)
Vjosë var. Vijosa; Vijosë, Gk. Aóos river Southeast Europe WWI 207 (6)
Vladimir var. Volodymyr-Volyns'kyy; Pol. Włodzimierz Eastern Europe (Russian Federation) medieval states 189 (4) Mongols 68–69 (1) see also Włodzimierz
Vladimir state Eastern Europe medieval states 189 (4)
Vladimir-Galich see Galicia-Volhynia
Vladivostok Siberia (Russian Federation) colonialism 269 (3), (4) Communism 271 (8) exploration 257 (2) global immigration 100 (1) imperialism 270 (2) Islam 275 (4) Russo-Japanese War 270 (4) Soviet Union 208 (2), 214–215 (4) Cold War 109 (4)
Vlonë, **Vlora**, **Vlorë** see Valona
Vogelherd archaeological site Central Europe (Germany) prehistoric culture 17 (2)
Vojvodina Ger. Wojwodina province Southeast Europe post-war economy 215 (3)
Volaterrae Italy early states 178 (1), (2) first civilizations 177 (1)
Volcae people France ancient Rome 179 (5)
Volci var. Vulci Italy first civilizations 177 (1) see also Vulci
Voldtofte Scandinavia (Denmark) Bronze Age 175 (3)
Volga river Eastern Europe ancient trade 44–45 (1), 72–73 (1) early agriculture 20–21 (2) early Islam 56–57 (1) early modern states 197 (3) economy 205 (4) empire and revolution 202 (1) exploration 172 (1), 218 (2), 219 (3) first humans 13 (2) global immigration 100 (1) great migrations 52–53 (1), 53 (2) Islam 163 (1) medieval states 185 (3), 261 (6) medieval voyages 60–61 (1) Mongols 68–69 (1) Ottomans 231 (3), 232–233 (1) prehistoric culture 16 (1), 17 (4) Soviet Union 208 (2) Timur 229 (4) WWII 210 (1), 211 (4)
Volga Bulgaria state Eastern Europe medieval states 185 (3)
Volga Bulgars var. Bulgars, White Bulgars people Eastern Europe Mongols 68–69 (1)
Volga Germans people Eastern Europe Soviet Union 213 (4)
Volgograd prev. Stalingrad, Tsaritsyn Eastern Europe (Russian Federation) Soviet Union 214–215 (4) see also Stalingrad, Tsaritsyn
Vol'mar see Wolmar
Volodymyr-Volyns'kyy see Vladimir, Włodzimierz
Vologda mod. Kirov Eastern Europe (Russian Federation) Soviet Union 208 (2)
Volsci people Italy early states 178 (2)
Volsiniensis, Lacus lake Italy early states 178 (1)
Volsinii Italy early states 178 (1), (2) first civilizations 177 (1)
Volta river West Africa Islam 163 (1)
Volta Blanche see White Volta
Volta, Cape da var. Dias Point headland West Africa exploration 156 (3)
Volta, Lake reservoir West Africa economy 168 (2), (3)
Volta Noire see Black Volta
Volterra see Volaterrae

Volturno see Volturnus
Volturnus mod. Volturno river Italy early states 178 (1)
Volubilis mithraic site North Africa (Morocco) world religions 48 (1)
Vorkuta Eastern Europe (Russian Federation) exploration 287 (2)
Voronezh Eastern Europe (Russian Federation) Soviet Union 208 (2), 214–215 (4)
Vorskla river Eastern Europe WWI 207 (4)
Vosges mountain range France early modern states 197 (5) WWI 206 (2), (3)
Vouillé battle France Franks 183 (5)
Vrijji see Vrji
Vrjji var. Vrijji region South Asia first religions 36 (2)
Vrshni state South Asia first empires 241 (5)
Vryburg Southern Africa (South Africa) European imperialism 96 (2)
Vukovar Hung. Vukovár Southeast Europe (Croatia) civil war 215 (3)
Vulci Italy early states 178 (1), (2)
Vungu state Central Africa economy 163 (2)
Vyadhapura Mainland Southeast Asia (Cambodia) ancient India 241 (6)
Vyatka mod. Kirov Eastern Europe (Russian Federation) Soviet Union 208 (2)
Vyborg Eastern Europe (Russian Federation) early modern states 195 (3) WWI 207 (4) WWII 211 (4)

W

Waalo state West Africa trade 167 (1)
Wabash river North America US Civil War 131 (6), (7)
Wadai var. Ouadaï, Ouaddai state Central Africa colonization 167 (4) slave trade 165 (4) trade 167 (1)
Wad Al-Hajarah see Guadalajara
Wadan West Africa (Mauritania) biological diffusion 72–73 (1)
Wadi Halfa var. Wādī Ḥalfā' Egypt colonization 167 (4)
Wadi Maghara Southwest Asia (Saudi Arabia) ancient Egypt 159 (5)
Wagadugu state West Africa trade 167 (1)
Wagram Central Europe (Czech Republic) Napoleon 200–201 (1)
Wągrowiec monastery Central Europe medieval states 187 (3)
Wahabites Rising rebellion Southwest Asia empire and revolution 88–89 (2)
Wahhabi Expansion historical episode 20th-century politics 233 (4)
Wahhabi Territory region Southwest Asia 20th-century politics 233 (4)
Wahran see Oran
Waicuri people Central America colonization 125 (4)
Waikanae New Zealand colonization 283 (5)
Waikawa whaling station New Zealand colonization 283 (4)
Waikouaiti settlement/whaling station New Zealand colonization 283 (4), (5)
Waimate New Zealand colonization 283 (5)
Wairagarh South Asia (India) colonialism 247 (3)
Wakayama Japan economy 270 (1)
Wakayama off. Wakayama-ken prefecture Japan economy 270 (1)
Wake Island colonial possession/ island Pacific Ocean exploration 276–277 (1) imperialism 270 (2) the growth of the US 133 (4) US superpower 138 (1) WWII 272 (1) Cold War 109 (1)
Walachei, Walachia see Wallachia
Walata West Africa (Mauritania) exploration 156 (3)
Waldensians people Italy crusades 186 (1)
Wales Wel. Cymru state British Isles empire and revolution 202 (1) medieval states 188 (2) the modern world 112 (2)
Walhalla goldfield Australia colonization 282 (2)
Walkunder Arch Australia exploration 280 (1)
Wallachia var. Walachia; Ger. Walachei, Rom. Valachia, Turk. Eflâk region Southeast Europe early modern states 193 (4) empire and revolution 202 (1) medieval states 189 (4) Napoleon 200–201 (1), 201 (2) Ottomans 195 (4), 230 (1), 231 (3) Reformation 194 (2)
Walla Walla battle North America (USA) the growth of the US 129 (2)
Wallis and Futuna colonial possession/island group Pacific Ocean decolonization 285 (3)
Wallis, Îles var. Wallis Islands island group Pacific Ocean colonization 284–285 (1) exploration 278 (1), 279 (3)
Walnut Canyon archaeological site North America (USA) cultural groups 123 (4)
Walo state West Africa slave trade 165 (4)
Walvisbaai see Walvis Bay
Walvis Bay Afr. Walvisbaai Southern Africa (Namibia) colonization 167 (4) economy 168 (2) European imperialism 96 (1), (2)
Walvis Bay Afr. Walvisbaai state Southern Africa the world in 1900 94–95 the world in 1925 98–99
Walvis Bay bay Southern Africa exploration 156 (3)
Wambu state Southern Africa slave trade 165 (4) trade 167 (1)
Wan var. Nanyang East Asia (China) first cities 259 (5) first states 260 (1) see also Nanyang
Wan see Anhui
Wandel Sea sea Arctic Ocean exploration 287 (2)
Wandiwash battle South Asia (India) empire and revolution 88 (1)
Wandu state Southern Africa slave trade 165 (4)
Wang vassal state East Asia first cities 259 (3)
Wanganui New Zealand colonization 283 (4), (5)
Wangchenggang archaeological site East Asia early agriculture 258 (1)
Wanhsien see Wanxian
Wankarani state South America the world in 500 BCE 34–35
Wanxian var. Wanhsien East Asia (China) colonialism 269 (4)
Warangal South Asia (India) colonialism 247 (3) early medieval states 244–245 (3), 245 (4)
Warash Southwest Asia (Turkey) early Islam 56–57 (1)
Warka Southwest Asia (Iraq) the world in 5000 BCE 18–19
Warmia Ger. Ermeland region Central Europe early modern states 195 (3)
Warrnambool Australia colonization 282 (1), 283 (3)
Warsaw Central Europe (Poland) economy 205 (4) empire and revolution 198 (2), 199 (3), 202 (1), (1i) global immigration 101 (2) medieval states 189 (3), (4) Napoleon 200–201 (1), 201 (2), (3) post-war politics 212 (3) Reformation 194 (2) Soviet Union 208 (2) WWI 207 (4) WWII 210 (1), 211 (2), (3), (4) Cold War 108 (3)
Warsaw, Grand Duchy of state Central Europe Napoleon 201 (2)
Warschau, Warszawa see Warsaw
Warwick British Isles (United Kingdom) medieval states 187 (4)
Washington var. Washington Territory state North America (USA) US Civil War 130 (3), (5) US economy 134-135, 136 (2)
Washington DC North America (USA) empire and revolution 127 (3) the growth of the US 129 (1), (2), 132 (1) US Civil War 131 (6), (7) Cold War 108 (2) the growth of the US 132 (1) the modern world 113 (4) US economy 134 (1), (3), 136 (2)
Washita battle North America (USA) the growth of the US 129 (2)
Washshukanni Southwest Asia (Iraq) first civilizations 221 (5)
Wasserburg mod. Wasserburg am Inn Central Europe (Germany) Bronze Age 175 (3)
Wasserburg am Inn see Wasserburg
Wateree people North America colonization 125 (4)
Waterford Ir. Port Láirge British Isles (Ireland) medieval states 185 (3), 187 (4)
Waterloo battle France Napoleon 200–201 (1)
Watom island Pacific Ocean early cultures 280–281 (3) medieval voyages 60 (2)
Wattasids dynasty North Africa Islam 163 (1), 192 (3)
Wattignies battle France empire and revolution 199 (4)
Waverley major Cistercian house British Isles (United Kingdom) medieval states 187 (3)
Wawat state Egypt ancient Egypt 159 (4), (5)
Wearmouth see Sunderland
Weddell Sea sea Antactica Antarctic Exploration 287 (3)
Wedding Central Europe (Germany) post-war politics 212 (2)
Weeden Island settlement North America (USA) cultural groups 123 (5)
Weeden Island Culture North America the world in 500 CE 50–51
Weenen Southern Africa (South Africa) colonization 166 (2)
Wei province/state East Asia first cities 259 (3), (4), (5) first states 261 (2), (3)
Weichou see Weizhou
Weichsel see Vistula
Weihaiwei East Asia (China) Russo-Japanese War 270 (4)
Weihaiwei battle East Asia (China) Sino-Japanese War 270 (3)
Weihaiwei colonial possession East Asia (China) colonialism 269 (4)
Wei, Long Wall of wall East Asia (China) first cities 259 (5)
Weissenburg see Apulum, Gyulafehérvár
Weissensee Central Europe (Germany) post-war politics 212 (2)
Weissenstein Est. Paide Scandinavia (Sweden) early modern states 195 (3)
Weizhou var. Weichou East Asia (China) medieval states 262–263 (1)
Wejh Ar. Al Wajh Southwest Asia (Saudi Arabia) 20th-century politics 233 (4)
Welle see Uele
Wellington New Zealand colonization 283 (4), (5), 284–285 (1) environmentalism 285 (2) exploration 279 (3)
Wellington region New Zealand colonization 283 (5)
Wellington penal colony Australia colonization 282 (1)
Welsh Principalities state British Isles crusades 64–65 (2) medieval states 183 (3), 186 (2)
Welsh States state British Isles medieval states 187 (4)
Wen-chou, Wenchow see Wenzhou
Wenden mod. Cēsis; Latv. Cēsis Eastern Europe (Latvia) early modern states 195 (3) medieval states 189 (3)
Wends people Central Europe crusades 64–65 (2)
Wenzhou var. Wen-chou, Wenchow East Asia (China) colonialism 269 (4) medieval states 263 (5) post-war politics 274 (2)
Wesenberg Est. Rakvere Eastern Europe (Estonia) early modern states 195 (3)
Weser river Central Europe empire and revolution 199 (3) Franks 184 (2)
Wessex state British Isles medieval states 183 (3)
West Alaskan Inuit people North America cultural groups 123 (3)
West and Central Punjab region South Asia decolonization 250 (1)
West Antarctica see Lesser Antarctica
West Asia region Asia biological diffusion 73 (2)
West Atlantic Peoples people West Africa early cultures 160 (1)
West Bank region Southwest Asia 20th century 234 (2)
West Bengal region South Asia post-war politics 252 (1), (3), 253 (4)
West Berlin Central Europe (Germany) post-war politics 212 (2)
West Bihar region South Asia decolonization 250 (1)
West Coast physical region South America early cultures 144 (1)
West Coast see Westland
West Dawson North America (Canada) imperial global economy 93 (3)
Westeregeln Central Europe (Germany) early agriculture 174 (1)
Western Australia region Australia colonization 282 (1), 283 (3)
Western Bug see Bug
Western Cree people North America cultural groups 123 (3)
Western Desert var. Aş Şaḥrā' al Gharbīyah, Sahara el Gharbîya desert North Africa ancient Egypt 159 (2), (3), (5)
Western Dvina Bel. Dzvina, Ger. Düna, Latv. Daugava, Rus. Zapadnaya Dvina river Eastern Europe economy 190 (1) medieval states 185 (3) Timur 229 (4)
Western Europe region Europe US economy 138 (2)
Western Ghats mountain range South Asia colonialism 247 (3), 248 (1) early medieval states 244 (1), 244–245 (3) economy 249 (4) first empires 241 (4) first religions 36 (2) Mughal Empire 246 (1)
Western Liang state East Asia first states 261 (3)
Western Pomerania region Central Europe empire and revolution 199 (3)
Western Port penal centre Australia colonization 282 (1) environmentalism 285 (2)
Western Regions region Central Asia first states 260 (1)
Western Sahara region/state North Africa decolonization 168 (1) economy 168 (2), (3) Islam 235 (4) the modern world 113 (3)
Western Samoa var. Sāmoa-i-Sisifo; prev. German Samoa; mod. Samoa state Pacific Ocean decolonization 285 (3) environmentalism 285 (2) see also German Samoa, Samoa
Western Shoshoni people North America colonization 126 (1)
Western Sierra Madre see Madre Occidental, Sierra
Western Tarahumara people North America colonization 126 (1)
Western Turkestan region Central Asia medieval states 262–263 (1)
Western Turks people Central Asia medieval states 261 (4), (5), 262–263 (1)
Western Ukrainian Republic see West Ukraine
West Fjords fjords Iceland exploration 172 (2)
West Florida colonial possession North America empire and revolution 127 (3)
West Galicia region Central Europe empire and revolution 198 (2)
Westgate British Isles (United Kingdom) economy 204 (3)
West Germany state Central Europe Cold War 108 (3), 109 (1) post-war economy 213 (5), 214 (1) post-war politics 212 (3) Soviet Union 213 (4) US superpower 138 (1)
West Greenland Inuit people North America cultural groups 123 (3)
West India States state South Asia colonialism 248 (2)
West Indies island group North America colonization 126 (1) early agriculture 20–21 (2)
West Irian see Dutch New Guinea, Irian Jaya, Netherlands New Guinea
Westland mod. West Coast region New Zealand colonization 283 (5)
West Malaysia see Malaya
West New Guinea see Dutch New Guinea, Irian Jaya, Netherlands New Guinea
West Pakistan state South Asia decolonization 251 (4) post-war politics 252 (1)
Westphalia region Central Europe empire and revolution 202 (2)
West Point North America (USA) empire and revolution 127 (3)
West Pomerania region Central Europe early modern states 197 (3)
Westport New Zealand colonization 283 (5)
West Prussia region Central Europe empire and revolution 198 (2), 199 (3), 202 (2) WWI 207 (4)
West River burial mound North America (USA) first civilizations 121 (4)
West River see Xi Jiang
West Roman Empire state Europe/Africa great migrations 52–53 (1)
West Siberian Plain plain Siberia exploration 257 (2)
West Turkana archaeological site East Africa (Kenya) first humans 12 (1)
West Ukraine var. Western Ukrainian Republic region Eastern Europe empire and revolution 198 (2)
West Virginia state North America the growth of the US 129 (1) US Civil War 130 (5), 131 (6), (7) US economy 134 (2), 139 (3) US superpower 139 (5)
West Wales var. Wessex state British Isles medieval states 183 (3) see also Wessex
Wexford Ir. Loch Garman British Isles (Ireland) medieval states 185 (3), 187 (4)
Wey and Arun canal British Isles economy 204 (1)
Whakatane New Zealand colonization 283 (4)
Whangarei New Zealand colonization 283 (4), (5)
Whitby religious building British Isles (United Kingdom) medieval states 183 (3)
Whitebird Creek battle North America (USA) the growth of the US 129 (2)
White Bulgars see Volga Bulgars
Whitehorse North America (Canada) the growth of the US 129 (2) US superpower 138 (1)
White Huns see Ephthalites; Hephthalites, Empire of the
White Lotus rebellion East Asia empire and revolution 268 (2)
White Mountain battle Central Europe (Czech Republic) Reformation 196 (1)
White Nile Ar. Al Baḩr al Abyaḑ, An Nīl al Abyaḑ, Bahr el Jebel river East Africa early agriculture 158 (1) economy 163 (2) exploration 157 (5) Islam 163 (1) slave trade 165 (4) trade 165 (3)
White Plains battle North America (USA) empire and revolution 127 (3)
White Russia state Eastern Europe Soviet Union 208 (2)
White Sea Rus. Beloye More sea Arctic Ocean exploration 257 (2) historical geography 170–171 (1)
Whitestone Hill battle North America (USA) the growth of the US 129 (2)
White Temple temple Southwest Asia (Iraq) first cities 220 (3)
White Volta var. Nakambé, Fr. Volta Blanche river West Africa Islam 163 (1) trade 163 (4), (5), (6), (7), 164 (2)
Whittier North America (USA)
Whydah mod. Ouidah; Eng. Wida West Africa empire and revolution 88 (1) slave trade 165 (4) see also Ouidah
Wichita people North America colonization 125 (4), 126 (1)
Wichita Village battle North America (USA) the growth of the US 129 (2)
Wida see Ouidah, Whydah
Wien see Vienna, Vindobona
Wigan British Isles (United Kingdom) economy 204 (1)
Wight, Isle of island British Isles medieval states 186 (2)
Wigorna Ceaster see Worcester
Wila state Southern Africa trade 164 (2)
Wilderness, The battle North America (USA) US Civil War 131 (7)
Wilkes-Barre North America (USA) empire and revolution 127 (3)
Wilkes Land physical region Antarctica Antarctic Exploration 287 (3)
Willandra Lakes Australia exploration 280 (1)
Willendorf archaeological site Central Europe (Switzerland) prehistoric culture 17 (4)
Williamsburg North America (USA) empire and revolution 127 (2), (3)
Willkawain South America (Peru) early cultures 146 (1)
Wilmersdorf Central Europe (Germany) post-war politics 212 (2)
Wilmington North America (USA) empire and revolution 127 (2), (3) US Civil War 131 (6), (7)
Wilna see Vilna, Vilnius, Wilno
Wilno Eastern Europe (Lithuania) WWII 210 (1), 211 (4)
Wilson Butte Cave North America (USA) the world in 10,000 BCE 14–15
Wilson's Creek battle North America (USA) US Civil War 131 (6)
Wilson's Promontory Australia the world in 5000 BCE 18–19
Wilton archaeological site/settlement Southern Africa (South Africa) early agriculture 158 (1) early cultures 160 (1)
Wiluna Australia colonization 282 (1)
Wilzi people Central Europe Franks 184 (2)
Winburg Southern Africa (South Africa) colonization 166 (2)
Winburg-Potchefstroom, Republic of state Southern Africa the world in 1850 90–91
Winchester hist. Wintanceaster, Lat. Venta Belgarum British Isles (United Kingdom) economy 190 (1) medieval states 183 (3), 186 (2), 187 (4)
Windau var. Vindava, mod. Ventspils; Eastern Europe (Latvia) medieval states 189 (3) see also Vindava
Windhoek Ger. Windhuk Southern Africa (Namibia) colonization 167 (4) economy 168 (2) European imperialism 96 (2)
Windhuk see Windhoek
Windward Coast physical region West Africa slave trade 165 (4)
Windward Islands colonial possession/state West Indies the world in 1900 94–95 the world in 1925 98–99 the world in 1950 102–103
Winneba West Africa (Ghana) empire and revolution 88 (1)
Winnebago people North America colonization 126 (1)
Winnipeg North America (Canada) the growth of the US 129 (2), 132 (1) US economy 136 (2)
Winnipeg, Lake lake North America colonization 126 (1) cultural groups 123 (3) exploration 118 (1), 119 (2), (3) the growth of the US 129 (2)
Wintanceaster see Winchester
Winterville North America (USA) cultural groups 122 (5)
Winwaed battle British Isles (United Kingdom) medieval states 183 (3)
Wisby mod. Visby Scandinavia (Sweden) medieval states 189 (3) see also Visby
Wisconsin state North America the growth of the US 129 (1) US Civil War 130 (2), (3), (4), (5) US economy 134 (2)
Wisła see Vistula
Wismar Central Europe (Germany) economy 190 (1) medieval states 189 (3)
Wismar region Central Europe early modern states 197 (3)
Wittenberg Central Europe (Germany) Reformation 194 (2)
Wittstock battle Central Europe (Germany) Reformation 196 (1)
Włodzimierz var. Volodymyr-Volyns'kyy; Rus. Vladimir Eastern Europe (Russian Federation) medieval states 189 (3) see also Vladimir
Woju people East Asia first states 260 (1)
Wojwodina see Vojvodina
Wollongong Australia colonization 283 (3)
Wolmar Latv. Valmiera; Rus. Vol'mar Eastern Europe (Latvia) early modern states 195 (3)
Wolof state West Africa Islam 163 (1) trade 163 (4), (6), (7)
Wolverhampton British Isles (United Kingdom) economy 204 (1)
Wonju Jap. Genshū East Asia (South Korea) Cold War 109 (4)
Wonsan East Asia (North Korea) early modern states 267 (4) Russo-Japanese War 270 (4) Sino-Japanese War 270 (3) Cold War 109 (4)
Wood Lake battle North America (USA) the growth of the US 129 (2)
Woodland Culture people North America/South America the world in 1000 58–59 the world in 1200 62–63 the world in 1300 66–67 the world in 1400 70–71 the world in 1500 74–75 the world in 1700 82–83
Worcester anc. Wigorna Ceaster British Isles (United Kingdom) medieval states 183 (3)
Workington British Isles (United Kingdom) economy 204 (1)
Wormatia see Worms
Worms anc. Augusta Vangionum, Borbetomagus, Wormatia settlement Central Europe (Germany) ancient Rome 182 (1) crusades 186 (1) economy 190 (1) Franks 184 (2) medieval states 182 (2), 187 (3) Reformation 194 (2) see also Borbetomagus
Wounded Knee battle North America (USA) the growth of the US 129 (2)
Wrangel Island island Arctic Ocean colonialism 269 (3) exploration 257 (2)
Wrangell see Fort Wrangell
Wrocław Ger. Breslau Central Europe (Poland) economy 190 (1) medieval states 188 (1) see also Breslau
Wu East Asia (China) first cities 259 (4), (5) first religions 37 (4)
Wu region/state East Asia first religions 37 (4) first states 261 (2) medieval states 263 (3)
Wubei East Asia (China) first states 260 (1)
Wuchang var. Wu-ch'ang settlement East Asia (China) biological diffusion 72–73 (1) early modern states 266 (1), (2) medieval states 263 (6) world religions 49 (3)
Wuchang see Hankou, Wuhan
Wucheng East Asia (China) first cities 259 (3)
Wu-chou, Wuchow see Wuzhou
Wuci East Asia (China) first states 260 (1)
Wudahai East Asia (China) Mongols 68–69 (1)
Wudang Shan var. Wu Tang Shan mountain East Asia first religions 37 (4)
Wudu province East Asia first states 260 (1)
Wuhan var. Hankou, Han-kou, Han-k'ou, Hanyang, Wuchang, Wu-han; prev. Hankow East Asia (China) Chinese revolution 271 (5) Communism 271 (8) economy 274 (1) Islam 275 (4) post-war economy 275 (3) post-war politics 271 (7), 274 (2) see also Hankou
Wuhsien see Suzhou
Wu-hsing see Wuxing
Wuhu var. Wu-na-mu East Asia (China) colonialism 269 (4)
Wuhuan people East Asia first states 260 (1), 261 (2)
Wuling province East Asia first states 260 (1)
Wulu East Asia (China) first states 260 (1)
Wu-lu-k'o-mu-shi, Wu-lu-mu-ch'i see Urumchi, Ürümqi
Wu-na-mu see Wuhu
Wupatki archaeological site North America (USA) cultural groups 123 (4)
Wuqie Mainland Southeast Asia (Vietnam) first states 260 (1)
Württemberg state Central Europe early modern states 193 (5) empire and revolution 202 (1), (2)
Würzburg Central Europe (Germany) medieval states 189 (3)
Wusuli Jiang, Wusuri see Ussuri
Wu Tang Shan see Wudang Shan
Wuwei Buddhist centre/settlement East Asia (China) ancient trade 44–45 (1) first states 260 (1), 261 (3) world religions 49 (3)
Wuwei province East Asia first states 260 (1)
Wuxing var. Wu-hsing Buddhist centre East Asia (China) world religions 49 (3)
Wuyi Buddhist centre East Asia (China) world religions 49 (3)
Wuyi Shan mountain range East Asia historical geography 254–255 (1)
Wuyuan East Asia (China) first states 260 (1)
Wuyue state East Asia medieval states 263 (3)
Wuzhong people East Asia first cities 259 (4)
Wuzhou var. Wu-chou, Wuchow East Asia (China) colonialism 269 (4) medieval states 262–263 (1)
Wye Wel. Gwy river British Isles economy 204 (1)
Wyndham Australia colonization 282 (1), 283 (3)
Wyoming state North America the growth of the US 129 (1) US economy 134 (2)
Wyoming battle North America (USA) empire and revolution 127 (3)

Xacalta Central America (Mexico) first civilizations 122 (1)
Xalpan Central America (Mexico) Aztecs 124 (3)
Xaltenco Central America (Mexico) Aztecs 124 (3)
Xaltocán Central America (Mexico) Aztecs 124 (2) colonization 125 (5)
Xaltocán, Lake lake Central America Aztecs 124 (2) colonization 125 (5)
Xam Nua see Sam Neua
Xanthus Southwest Asia (Turkey) first civilizations 177 (1) Hellenistic world 40–41 (1)
Xäzär Dänizi see Caspian Sea
Xeloc Central America (Mexico) Aztecs 124 (2)
Xhosa people Southern Africa the world in 1800 86–87
Xia state East Asia first states 261 (3)
Xiachuan archaeological site East Asia early humans 15 (1)
Xiaguan see Dali
Xiamen var. Hsia-men; prev. Amoy East Asia (China) colonialism 269 (4) economy 274 (1) empire and revolution 88–89 (2) imperialism 270 (2) post-war politics 274 (2) trade 267 (3) WWII 251 (3)
Xi'an var. Changan, Ch'ang-an, Hsi-an, Sian, Signan, Siking, Singan, Xian East Asia biological diffusion 72–73 (1) early agriculture 258 (2) early modern states 266 (1), (2), 268 (1) economy 274 (1) Islam 275 (4) Mongols 68–69 (1) post-war economy 275 (3) post-war politics 271 (7), 274 (2) trade 267 (3) see also Chang'an
Xianbei people East Asia first states 260 (1), 261 (2) medieval states 261 (6) see also Xianbi
Xianbi var. Xianbei, Hsien-pi, Sienpi, Tungus people East Asia the world in 250 CE 46–47
Xiang vassal state East Asia first cities 259 (3)
Xianggang see Hong Kong
Xiangping East Asia (China) first cities 259 (5)
Xiangyang var. Hsiang-yang settlement East Asia (China) early modern states 266 (2) medieval states 263 (4), (5) Mongols 68–69 (1) world religions 49 (3)
Xiangzhou var. Hsiangchou East Asia (China) medieval states 262–263 (1)
Xianrendong archaeological site East Asia early agriculture 258 (1)
Xianyang East Asia (China) first cities 259 (5)
Xianyun people East Asia first cities 259 (4)
Xiapi East Asia (China) first states 260 (1)
Xico Central America (Mexico) Aztecs 124 (2) first civilizations 122 (1)
Xicochimalco Central America (Mexico) colonization 125 (5)
Xie East Asia (China) first cities 259 (5) first religions 37 (4)
Xie state East Asia first cities 259 (5)
Xigazê see Shigatse
Xiiqtepec state Central America Aztecs 124 (1)
Xi Jiang var. Hsi Chiang, Eng. West River river East Asia early modern states 266 (1), (2) first cities 28–29 (1) first religions 37 (4) first states 260 (1) medieval states 261 (6), 262–263 (1), 263 (4), (6) Mongols 68–69 (1) post-war politics 274 (2)
Xi Jiang Delta region East Asia first cities 28–29 (1)
Xin see Sinkiang, Turkestan, Xinjiang
Xing vassal state East Asia first cities 259 (3)
Xingan East Asia (China) first states 260 (1)
Xingkai Hu see Khanka, Lake
Xingqing var. Xingqingfu East Asia (China) medieval states 263 (5)
Xingqing Palace palace East Asia (China) medieval states 262 (2)
Xingqingfu var. Xingqing East Asia (China) medieval states 263 (5)
Xingtai East Asia (China) first cities 259 (3)
Xingu river South America colonization 149 (3) early cultures 144 (1), 145 (2) economy 153 (3) empire and revolution 151 (3) environment 153 (4) exploration 142 (1), 143 (2)
Xingyuan East Asia (China) medieval states 263 (4)
Xingzhong East Asia (China) medieval states 263 (5)
Xining East Asia (China) economy 274 (1)
Xinje state Southern Africa trade 164 (2)
Xinjiang var. Sinkiang, Sinkiang Uighur Autonomous Region, Xin, Turkestan province/state East Asia ancient trade 44–45 (1) colonialism 269 (3), (4) revolution 271 (5) Communism 271 (8) early modern states 268 (1) empire and revolution 268 (2) exploration 257 (3) post-war economy 274 (2), 275 (3) post-war politics 252 (2), 275 (3)
Xinjiang see Sinkiang, Turkestan
Xinye var. Hsin-yeh Buddhist centre East Asia (China) world religions 49 (3)
Xinzheng East Asia (China) first cities 259 (4), (5) first religions 37 (4)
Xiong'er Jiang river East Asia first cities 29 (4)
Xiongnu var. Hsiung-nu, Huns people East Asia ancient trade 44–45 (1) first cities 259 (5) first states 260 (1), 261 (2) medieval states 261 (6)
Xiongnu, Empire of the var. Hsiung-nu, Hun tribal confederacy state East Asia the world in 250 BCE 38–39
Xi Shan mountain East Asia first religions 37 (4)
Xiuhquilpan Central America (Mexico) first civilizations 122 (1)
Xiuhtetelco Central America (Mexico) first civilizations 122 (1)
Xiuyan var. Siuyen East Asia (China) Sino-Japanese War 270 (3)
Xixia var. Hsi-hsia state East Asia medieval states 263 (4), (5) Mongols 68–69 (1)
Xizang see Tibet
Xizang Gaoyuan see Tibet, Plateau of
Xoc Central America (Mexico) first civilizations 121 (2)
Xochicalco Central America (Mexico) first civilizations 122 (1)
Xochicalco region Central America first civilizations 122 (1)
Xochimanca Central America (Mexico) Aztecs 124 (3)
Xochimilco, Lake lake Central America Aztecs 124 (2), (3)
Xochinuac Central America (Mexico) Aztecs 124 (3)
Xochmilco Central America (Mexico) Aztecs 124 (2)
Xoconocho Central America (Mexico) Aztecs 124 (1)
Xoconocho state Central America Aztecs 124 (1)
Xocotitlán Central America (Mexico) Aztecs 124 (1), (3) first civilizations 122 (1)
Xocotitlán state Central America Aztecs 124 (1)
Xocoyahualco Central America (Mexico) Aztecs 124 (3)
Xola-Xalac Central America (Mexico) Aztecs 124 (3)
Xpuhil Central America (Mexico) first civilizations 123 (2)
Xtampak Central America (Mexico) first civilizations 123 (2)
Xuanfu military base East Asia (China) early modern states 266 (1)
Xuanhua var. Hsüan-hua, Süanhua East Asia (China) Mongols 68–69 (1)
Xuan Loc battle Mainland Southeast Asia (Vietnam) post-war politics 251 (5)
Xuanzhou var. Hsuanchou East Asia (China) medieval states 262–263 (1)
Xuchou rebellion East Asia early modern states 266 (2)
Xujiayao archaeological site East Asia (China) first humans 13 (2)
Xunantunich Central America (Belize) first civilizations 121 (2)
Xuyi state East Asia first cities 259 (3)
Xuzhou battle East Asia (China) economy 274 (1)

Y

Yadavagiri South Asia (India) world religions 243 (4)
Yadavas dynasty South Asia early medieval states 244 (2) Mongols 68–69 (1)
Yadufu East Asia (Korea) medieval states 263 (3)
Yagala West Africa (Sierra Leone) early agriculture 158 (1)
Yagul Central America (Mexico) first civilizations 122 (1)
Yahata see Yawata
Yaka state Central Africa slave trade 165 (4) trade 167 (1)
Yakuts people Siberia the world in 1600 78–79
Yakutsk Siberia (Russian Federation) colonialism 269 (3) exploration 257 (2) Soviet Union 213 (4)
Yakutsk region Siberia colonialism 269 (3)
Yala Alego archaeological site East Africa (Kenya) early cultures 160 (1)
Yalu Chin. Yalu Jiang, Jap. Oryokko, Kor. Amnok-kang river East Asia Cold War 109 (4) early modern states 265 (5), 267 (4) first states 260 (1) medieval states 264 (1), (2)
Yalu Jiang see Yalu
Yalu River battle East Asia (China/North Korea) Sino-Japanese War 270 (3)
Yam var. Yamburg; mod. Kingisepp NE Europe (Russia) early modern states 195 (3)
Yamagata Japan economy 270 (1)
Yamagata prefecture Japan economy 270 (1)
Yamagawa Japan early modern states 267 (4)
Yamaguchi var. Yamaguti prefecture Japan economy 270 (1)
Yamaguti see Yamaguchi
Yamalo-Nenets region Eastern Europe Soviet Union 214–215 (4)
Yamal Peninsula see Yamal, Poluostrov
Yamal, Poluostrov Eng. Yamal Peninsula headland Eastern Europe exploration 257 (2)
Yamama Southwest Asia (Saudi Arabia) early Islam 56–57 (1)
Yamamoto Buddhist temple army Japan medieval states 265 (4)
Yamanashi var. Yamanasi prefecture Japan economy 270 (1)
Yamanasi see Yamanashi
Yamasee people North America colonization 125 (4), 126 (1)
Yamato state Japan medieval states 264 (1)
Yamazaki battle Japan early modern states 267 (4)
Yamburg see Yam
Yambuya Central Africa (Congo (Zaire)) exploration 157 (4)
Yamkhad see Aleppo
Yamuna river South Asia colonialism 247 (3), 248 (1), (2) decolonization 250 (1) early medieval states 244 (1), (2), 244–245 (3) economy 249 (4) first empires 241 (4), (5) first religions 36 (2) first states 260 (1) Marathas 246 (2) Mughal Empire 246 (1) world religions 242 (2), (3), 243 (4)
Yan East Asia (China) first states 260 (1)
Yan var. Yen region/state East Asia first cities 259 (4), (5) first religions 37 (4) see also Yen
Yana river Siberia exploration 287 (2)
Yanam var. Yanaon colonial possession/settlement South Asia (India) colonialism 247 (3), 248 (2), 269 (4) decolonization 251 (4) empire and revolution 88 (1), 88–89 (2) post-war politics 252 (1) WWII 251 (3)
Yan'an var. Yanan East Asia (China) the world in 1950 102–103
Yanaon see Yanam
Yanbu', Yanbu'al Baḩr see Yenbo
Yang East Asia (China) medieval states 261 (4)
Yangchou see Yongzhou
Yang-chou, Yangchow see Yangzhou
Yang He river East Asia early agriculture 258 (1)
Yangju region East Asia medieval states 264 (2)
Yangku see Taiyuan
Yangon see Rangoon
Yangshao archaeological site/settlement East Asia (China) early agriculture 258 (2)
Yangshaocun archaeological site East Asia (China) early agriculture 258 (1)
Yangtze var. Yangtze Kiang; Chin. Chang Jiang river East Asia ancient trade 44–45 (1), 72–73 (1) colonialism 269 (4) early agriculture 20–21 (2), 258 (1), (2) early modern states 266 (1), (2) economy 274 (1) empire and revolution 268 (2) exploration 256 (1), 257 (3) first cities 259 (3), (4), (5), 28–29 (1) first humans 13 (2) first religions 36 (1) first states 260 (1), 261 (2), (3) global immigration 100 (1) Islam 275 (4) medieval states 261 (4), (5), (6), 262–263 (1), 263 (3), (4), (5), (6) Mongols 68 (2), 68–69 (1) post-war economy 275 (3) prehistoric culture 16 (1) trade 230 (2), 267 (3) world religions 49 (3) Chinese revolution 271 (5)
Yangtze Kiang see Yangtze
Yangzhou var. Yang-chou, Yangchow East Asia (China) early modern states 266 (1) medieval states 263 (4), (5) Mongols 68–69 (1)
Yanikant Central Asia (Kazakhstan) Mongols 68–69 (1)
Yanjing East Asia (China) the world in 1200 62–63
Yanjing Rong state East Asia first cities 259 (3)
Yankton people North America colonization 126 (1)
Yanktonai people North America colonization 126 (1)
Yan, Long Wall of wall East Asia (China) first cities 259 (5)
Yanmen East Asia (China) first cities 259 (5)
Yantai East Asia (China) post-war politics 274 (2)
Yanying East Asia (China) first cities 259 (5) first religions 37 (4)
Yao people East Africa trade 164 (1)
Yao rebellion East Asia empire and revolution 268 (2)
Yao Chiefs state East Africa colonization 167 (4)
Yaoyang East Asia (China) first states 260 (1)
Yap island Pacific Ocean medieval voyages 60 (2) WWII 272 (1), 273 (2)
Yapanskoye More see Japan, Sea of
Yapapatuna mod. Jaffna South Asia (Sri Lanka) early medieval states 245 (4)
Yap Islands island group Pacific Ocean early cultures 280–281 (3)
Yapurá see Caquetá, Japurá
Yaresna state West Africa trade 163 (4)
Yarim Tepe Southwest Asia (Turkey) the world in 5000 BCE 18–19
Yarkand var. Yarkant; Chin. Shache Buddhist centre/settlement East Asia (China) ancient trade 44–45 (1) colonialism 248 (1) early modern states 268 (1) first states 260 (1) medieval states 261 (6), 262–263 (1) world religions 49 (3)
Yarkant see Yarkand
Yarlung Zangbo Jiang see Brahmaputra
Yarmouth var. Great Yarmouth British Isles (United Kingdom) economy 204 (1) see also Great Yarmouth
Yarmuk battle Southwest Asia (Jordan) early Islam 56–57 (1) Islam 226 (2)
Yaroslavl var. Jaroslavl Eastern Europe (Russian Federation) Mongols 68–69 (1) Soviet Union 208 (2)
Yarumela Central America (Honduras) first civilizations 121 (2)
Yashima battle Japan early modern states 265 (5)
Yatenga state West Africa trade 167 (1)
Yathrib var. Al Madinah, Medina Southwest Asia (Saudi Arabia) Islam 226 (2), (3), 227 (5) world religions 226 (1) see also Medina
Yawata var. Yahata Japan Communism 273 (3) economy 270 (1)
Yaxchilán Central America (Guatemala) the world in 750 CE 54–55
Yaxha Central America (Mexico) first civilizations 123 (2)
Yaxuná Central America (Mexico) first civilizations 122 (2)
Yazd var. Yezd Southwest Asia (Iran) early Islam 56–57 (1)
Yazilikaya Southwest Asia (Turkey) first cities 28 (3) first civilizations 221 (5)
Ye East Asia (China) first cities 259 (5) medieval states 261 (5)
Ye Buddhist centre East Asia (China) world religions 49 (3)
Yeha East Africa (Eritrea) early cultures 160 (1)
Yeh-Po-Ti state Maritime Southeast Asia ancient India 241 (6)
Yekaterinburg prev. Sverdlovsk Eastern Europe (Russian Federation) colonialism 269 (3) Soviet Union 208 (2), 214–215 (4)
Yekaterinoslav Eastern Europe (Ukraine) Soviet Union 208 (2) WWI 207 (4)
Yelang East Asia (China) first states 260 (1)
Yelets Eastern Europe (Russian Federation) Timur 229 (4)
Yeliseyevichi archaeological site Eastern Europe (Belorussia) prehistoric culture 17 (4)
Yellowknife North America (Canada) the growth of the US 129 (2), 132 (1)
Yellowknife people North America cultural groups 123 (3)

Yellow River *var.* Huang He *river* East Asia ancient trade 44–45 (1), 72–73 (1) colonialism 269 (4) early agriculture 20–21 (2), 258 (1), (2) early modern states 266 (1), (2) early systems 32 (1), 33 (2), (3) economy 274 (1) empire and revolution 268 (2) exploration 256 (1), 257 (3) first cities 259 (3), (4), (5), 28–29 (1) first humans 13 (2) first religions 36 (1), 37 (4) first states 260 (1), 261 (2), (3) global immigration 100 (1) historical geography 236–237 (1) Islam 275 (4) medieval states 261 (4), (5), (6), 262–263 (1), 263 (3), (4), (5), (6) Mongols 68 (2), 68–69 (1) post-war economy 275 (3) prehistoric culture 16 (1) trade230 (2), 267 (3) world religions 49 (3), (4) Chinese revolution 271 (5)
Yellow Sea *Chin.* Huang Hai, *Kor.* Hwang-hae *sea* East Asia ancient trade 44–45 (1) decolonization 251 (4) early agriculture 258 (1), (2) early modern states 265 (5), 266 (1), (2) empire and revolution 268 (2) first cities 259 (3), (4), (5), 28–29 (1) first states 260 (1), 261 (2), (3) Islam 275 (4) medieval states 261 (4), (5), (6), 262–263 (1), (2) Mongols 68–69 (1) post-war economy 275 (3) post-war politics 271 (7) Russo-Japanese War 270 (4) Sino-Japanese War 270 (3) trade 267 (3) Cold War 109 (4)
Yellowstone *battle* North America (USA) the growth of the US 129 (2)
Yelwa *archaeological site* West Africa (Nigeria) early cultures 160 (1)
Yemen *prev.* North Yemen *region/state* Southwest Asia ancient trade 44–45 (1) early Islam 56–57 (1), 57 (2) exploration 219 (4) Islam 163 (1), 226 (2), 227 (4), (5), 235 (4) Ottomans 232–233 (1) the modern world 112 (1), 113 (3), (4) trade 230 (2) US economy 138 (2) world religions 226 (1) WWII 104 (1) 20th-century politics 233 (4) Cold War 109 (1)
Yen *state* East Asia medieval states 263 (3)
Yenan East Asia (China) economy 274 (1)
Yenbo *mod.* Yanbu'; *Ar.* Yanbu' al Baīr, Yanbur Southwest Asia (Saudi Arabia) crusades 228 (2) Islam 226 (3) Mongols 229 (3) WWI 233 (2) 20th-century politics 233 (4)
Yenisey *river* Siberia colonialism 269 (3) early agriculture 20–21 (2), 258 (1) early modern states 268 (1) empire and revolution 268 (2) exploration 257 (2), (3), 286 (1) first humans 13 (2) first states 260 (1) global immigration 100 (1) medieval states 261 (6), 262–263 (1) Mongols 68–69 (1) prehistoric culture 16 (1) Soviet Union 208 (2)
Yeniseysk Siberia (Russian Federation) colonialism 269 (3) exploration 257 (2)
Yeniseysk *region* Siberia colonialism 269 (3)
Yerevan *var.* Erevan; *Eng.* Erivan Southwest Asia (Armenia) Soviet Union 214–215 (4)
see also Erivan
Yeriho *see* Jericho
Yerushalayim *see* Jerusalem
Yezd *see* Yazd
Yichang *var.* Ichang East Asia (China) colonialism 269 (4)
Yidu *see* Qingzhou
Yiling East Asia (China) first states 260 (1)
Yindu He *see* Indus
Ying East Asia (China) first cities 259 (4), (5) first religions 37 (4)
Yingkou *var.* Ying-k'ou, Yingkow; *prev.* Newchwang, Niuchwang, Niuzhuang East Asia (China) Russo-Japanese War 270 (4) Sino-Japanese War 270 (3)
see also Niuzhuang
Yingkow *see* Niuzhuang, Yingkou
Yingtian East Asia (China) medieval states 263 (4)
Yin-hsien *see* Ningbo
Yining *see* Kuldja
Yisra'el, **Yisrael** *see* Israel
Yiyang East Asia (China) first cities 259 (5)
Yizhou *province* East Asia first states 260 (1)
Yoaltepec *state* Central America Aztecs 124 (1)
Yochow *see* Yuezhou
Yohualinchan Central America (Mexico) first civilizations 122 (1)
Yojoa Central America (Honduras) first civilizations 121 (2)
Yojoa, Lago de *lake* Central America first civilizations 123 (2)
Yokohama Japan WWII 273 (3) economy 270 (1) global immigration 100 (1)
Yokokurayama Japan early modern states 265 (5)
Yokotagawahara *battle* Japan early modern states 265 (5)
Yola West Africa (Nigeria) exploration 157 (4) Islam 167 (3)
Yong East Asia (China) first cities 259 (4), (5)
Yongchang *rebellion* East Asia early modern states 266 (2)
Yongzhou *var.* Yang-chou East Asia (China) medieval states 263 (4), (5)
Yonne *river* France WWI 206 (2), (3)
Yopitzinco *state* Central America Aztecs 124 (1)
York *anc.* Eboracum, Eburacum British Isles (United Kingdom) crusades 65 (1) economy 190 (1) exploration 172 (1) medieval states 182 (2), 183 (3), 186 (2), 187 (4), 188 (2) medieval voyages 60–61 (1) Reformation 194 (2)
see also Eburacum
York, Cape *headland* Australia exploration 278 (1)
York Factory North America (Canada) colonization 126 (1)
Yorkshire *region* British Isles imperial global economy 93 (4)
Yorktown North America (USA) empire and revolution 127 (3) US Civil War 131 (7)
Yoro *state* East Africa trade 167 (1)
Yoruba States *state* West Africa colonization 167 (4)
Yoshino-yama *mountain* Japan medieval states 265 (3)
Yoshkar Ola Eastern Europe (Russian Federation) Soviet Union 214–215 (4)
Youngstown North America (USA) US politics 135 (6)
Ypres Low Countries (Belgium) economy 190 (1) WWI 206 (2), (3)
Ysyk-Köl *see* Issyk-Kul
Yu *see* Henan
Yuan, **Yuan Jiang** *see* Red River
Yucatán *state* Central America Mexican Revolution 133 (3) the growth of the US 129 (2)
Yucatan Maya *people* Central America colonization 125 (4)
Yucatan Peninsula *coastal feature* Central America Aztecs 124 (1) colonization 125 (4), 126 (1) first civilizations 121 (2), 122 (1), 123 (2)
Yuchi *people* North America colonization 125 (4), 126 (1)
Yucunudahui Central America (Mexico) first civilizations 122 (1)
Yue *state* East Asia first cities 259 (4), (5)
Yue *people* East Asia first cities 259 (4), (5) first states 260 (1)
Yue *see* Guangdong
Yuesui *province* East Asia first states 260 (1)
Yuezhou *var.* Yochow East Asia (China) colonialism 269 (4)
Yufu East Asia (China) first states 260 (1)
Yugoslavia *state* Southeast Europe Cold War 108 (3), 109 (1) inter-war 209 (3), (5) post-war economy 213 (5), 215 (3) post-war politics 212 (3) Soviet Union 213 (4) the world in 1950 102–103 the modern world 113 (3), (4) WWI 208 (1) WWII 104 (1), 211 (2), (4) 20th-century politics 233 (3)
Yukon *river* North America cultural groups 123 (3) exploration 287 (2) imperial global economy 93 (3) the growth of the US 129 (2)
Yukon Territory *var.* Yukon *province* North America the growth of the US 129 (2), 132 (1) US economy 136 (2)
Yuku New Guinea (Papua New Guinea) exploration 280 (1)
Yule *island* Pacific Ocean early cultures 280–281 (3) medieval voyages 60 (2)
Yulian *military base* East Asia early modern states 266 (1)
Yulin *province* East Asia first states 260 (1)
Yuma *people* North America colonization 125 (4)
Yun *see* Nanzhao, Yunnan
Yungay South America (Peru) empire and revolution 151 (3)
Yungki *see* Jilin
Yung-ning *see* Nanning
Yunki *see* Jilin
Yunnan *var.* K'un-ming; *mod.* Kunming; *prev.* Yunnan East Asia trade 72–73 (1) early modern states 266 (1), (2) empire and revolution 268 (2)
see also Kunming
Yunnan *var.* Nanzhao, Yun, Yünnan, Yun-nan *province* East Asia Chinese revolution 271 (5) early modern states 266 (1), (2), 268 (1) empire and revolution 268 (2) post-war politics 274 (2)
see also Nanzhao
Yunnan Muslim Rising *rebellion* East Asia empire and revolution 88–89 (2)
Yunxian *archaeological site* East Asia (China) first humans 13 (2)
Yunyang *military base/rebellion* East Asia early modern states 266 (1), (2)
Yuruá, Río *see* Juruá
Yur'yev *see* Dorpat
Yusef, Bahr *river* Egypt ancient Egypt 159 (2), (3), (5)
Yushien East Asia (China) Mongols 68–69 (1)
Yuwan Rong *state* East Asia first cities 259 (3)
Yuzhou *see* Chongqing
Yuzhsiblag *gulag* Siberia Soviet Union 213 (4)

Zaayfontein *archaeological site* Southern Africa (South Africa) early cultures 160 (1)
Zāb aş Şaghīr, Nahraz *see* Little Zab
Zabid Southwest Asia (Yemen) early Islam 56–57 (1) medieval voyages 61 (3)
Zabulistan *state* Central Asia early Islam 56–57 (1)
Zacaleu Central America (Guatemala) Aztecs/Maya 124 (1)
Zacapú Central America (Mexico) first civilizations 122 (1)
Zacatec *people* Central America colonization 125 (4), 126 (1)
Zacatecas *state* Central America Mexican Revolution 133 (3) the growth of the US 129 (2)
Zacatenco Central America (Mexico) Aztecs 124 (3)
Zacatlalmanco Central America (Mexico) Aztecs 124 (3)
Zacatollan Central America (Mexico) first civilizations 122 (1)
Zacualpa Central America (Guatemala) first civilizations 122 (2)
Zacynthus Greece first civilizations 176 (1)
Zacynthus *island* Greece ancient Greece 177 (3), 179 (4)
Zadar *anc.* Iader; *It.* Zara Southeast Europe (Croatia) 215 (3)
see also Zara
Zafar Southwest Asia (Yemen) early cultures 161 (3), (4), (5) early trade 225 (3)
Zafarwal South Asia (Pakistan) colonialism 247 (3)
Zafunu *state* West Africa trade 163 (4), (6)
Zaghawa *state* Central Africa the world in 750 CE 54–55 the world in 1000 58–59
Zágráb *Croat.* Zagreb; *Ger.* Agram Southeast Europe (Croatia) early modern states 193 (4) medieval states 188 (1), 189 (4)
see also Zagreb
Zagreb *Ger.* Agram, *Hung.* Zágráb Southeast Europe (Croatia) inter-war 209 (3) Ottomans 230 (1) post-war economy 215 (3) post-war politics 212 (3) WWII 210 (1), 211 (2), (3), (4)
see also Zágráb
Zāgros, Kūhhā-ye *see* Zagros Mountains
Zagros Mountains *Pers.* Zāgros, Kūhhā-ye *mountain range* Southwest Asia ancient Persia 223 (4) ancient trade 44–45 (1) early agriculture 220 (1) early Islam 56–57 (1) economy 234 (1) exploration 218 (1), (2), 219 (3) first cities 220 (2), 28–29 (1) first civilizations 221 (4), 222 (2), 25 (3) first humans 13 (2) Hellenistic world 224 (1) Islam 227 (4) medieval Persia 231 (4) Mongols 229 (3) Seljuks 228 (1) Timur 229 (4) WWI 233 (2)
Zahuatlán Central America (Mexico) Aztecs 124 (3)
Zaidi Imams *state* Southwest Asia early Islam 57 (2)
Zaire *state* Central Africa Cold War 109 (5)
Zaire *see also* Congo, Belgian Congo, Congo Free State
Zaitun East Asia (China) trade 72–73 (1)
Zajsan *see* Zaysan
Zakhidnyy Buh, **Zakhodni Buh** *see* Bug
Zákinthos *see* Zante
Zakro *var.* Zakros Greece ancient Egypt 159 (5) first cities 28–29 (1) first civilizations 175 (4)
Zakros *see* Zakro
Zákynthos *see* Zante
Zama North Africa (Tunisia) early cultures 161 (2) ancient Rome 179 (3)
Zambesi, **Zambeze** *see* Zambezi
Zambezi *var.* Zambesi, *Port.* Zambeze *river* Southern Africa early agriculture 158 (1), 20–21 (2) economy 163 (2), (3) exploration 156 (3), 157 (4) first humans 12 (1), 13 (2) Islam 163 (1) slave trade 165 (4) trade 164 (1)
Zambia *prev.* Northern Rhodesia *state* Southern Africa decolonization 168 (1) economy 168 (2), (3) the modern world 112 (1), 113 (3), (4) Cold War 109 (5)
see also Northern Rhodesia
Zambujal *archaeological site* Iberian Peninsula (Portugal) Copper Age 174 (2)
Zamfara *state* West Africa trade 164 (2)
Zamorin *state* South Asia Mughal Empire 246 (1)
Zancle *see* Messana, Messina
Zande *state* Central Africa trade 167 (1)
Zangke *province* East Asia first states 260 (1)
Zanja Central America (Mexico) first civilizations 121 (2)
Zante *Gr.* Zákynthos; *var.* Zákinthos *island* Greece Ottomans 230 (1)
Zanzibar *Swa.* Unguja East Africa (Tanzania) *colonial possession/state/island* East Africa ancient trade 44–45 (1) economy 168 (2) exploration 157 (4) Islam 163 (1) medieval voyages 61 (3), 157 (5) slave trade 165 (4) trade 164 (1), 230 (2)
Zapadnaya Dvina *see* Western Dvina
Zapadnyy Bug *see* Bug
Zaporogian Cossacks *people/state* Eastern Europe Reformation 196 (2)
Zapotec *state* Central America the world in 500 BCE 34–35
Zapotitlán Central America (Mexico) Aztecs 124 (2)
Zara *mod.* Zadar; *anc.* Iader Southeast Europe (Croatia) early modern states 193 (4) medieval states 187 (5), 188 (1), 189 (4)
see also Zadar
Zaradros *mod.* Sutlej *river* South Asia first cities 240 (2) Hellenistic world 40–41 (1) *see also* Sutlej
Zaragoza *anc.* Caesaraugusta, Salduba; *Eng.* Saragossa Iberian Peninsula (Spain) crusades 65 (1) Franks 184 (2) *see also* Caesaraugusta, Saragossa
Zaria West Africa (Nigeria) Islam 167 (3)
Zaria *state* West Africa slave trade 165 (4)
Zariaspa *see* Balkh, Bactra, Valhika
Zarnuq Central Asia (Uzbekistan) Mongols 68–69 (1)
Zasaragi *archaeological site* Japan early humans 15 (1)
Zauzau West Africa economy 163 (2)
Zavoloch'ye Eastern Europe (Russian Federation) early modern states 195 (3)
Zawila North Africa (Libya) early Islam 56–57 (1)
Zawty *see* Asyut
Zawyet el-Amwat Egypt ancient Egypt 159 (3)
Zawyet el-'Aryan Egypt ancient Egypt 159 (3)
Zawyet Umm el-Rakham North Africa (Egypt) ancient Egypt 159 (5)
Zaysan *var.* Zajsan Siberia (Kazakhstan) exploration 257 (3)
Zaysan Köl *see* Zaysan, Lake; Zaysan, Ozero
Zaysan, Lake *Rus.* Ozero Zaysan; *Kaz.* Zaysan Köl *lake* Central Asia Mongols 68–69 (1) *see also* Zaysan, Ozero
Zaysan, Ozero *var.* Lake Zaysan, *Kaz.* Zaysan Köl *lake* Central Asia first states 260 (1) *see also* Zaysan, Lake
Zayyanids *dynasty* North Africa economy 163 (2), 190 (1) Islam 163 (1), 192 (3)
Zayyq *see* Ural
Zeebrugge Low Countries (Belgium) WWI 206 (2), (3)
Zeeland *province* Low Countries Reformation 195 (5)
Zeelandia East Asia (Taiwan) trade 267 (3)
Zefat *see* Safed
Zehlendorf Central Europe (Germany) post-war politics 212 (2)
Zeila *var.* Saylac East Africa (Somalia) 72–73 (1) exploration 156 (3) Islam 163 (1) trade 165 (3)
Zē-i Bādīnān *see* Great Zab
Zē-i Kōya *see* Little Zab
Zela Southwest Asia (Turkey) Roman empire 180–181 (1)
Zenebi West Africa (Nigeria) early agriculture 158 (1)
Zengpiyan *archaeological site* East Asia early agriculture 258 (1)
Zenica Southeast Europe (Bosnia and Herzegovina) civil war 215 (3)
Zenobia Southwest Asia (Oman) ancient trade 44–45 (1)
Zenta *battle* Southeast Europe (Yugoslavia) Ottomans 197 (4)
Žepa Southeast Europe (Bosnia and Herzegovina) civil war 215 (3)
Zeugma Southwest Asia (Turkey) Roman empire 180–181 (1) early trade 225 (3) Hellenistic world 41 (2)
Zhangye East Asia (China) first states 261 (3)
Zhangyi *province* East Asia first states 260 (1)
Zhanjiang East Asia (China) post-war politics 274 (2)
Zhao *var.* Chao *region* East Asia first religions 37 (4)
Zhao, Long Wall of *wall* East Asia (China) first cities 259 (5)
Zhaoqing East Asia early modern states 266 (2)
Zhe *see* Zhejiang
Zhejiang *var.* Che-chiang, Chekiang, Zhe *province* East Asia Chinese revolution 271 (5) early modern states 266 (1), (2), 268 (1) empire and revolution 268 (2)
Zhending East Asia (China) medieval states 263 (4), (5), (6)
Zheng *state* East Asia first cities 259 (4)
Zhengzhou *var.* Ch'eng-chou, Chengchow; *prev.* Chenghsien *archaeological site/settlement* East Asia early agriculture 258 (2) first cities 259 (3), 28–29 (1), 29 (4) Islam 275 (4) post-war politics 271 (7), 274 (2)
Zhenjiang *var.* Chinkiang, Chenkiang East Asia (China) colonialism 269 (4)
Zhifu *var.* Chefoo East Asia (China) colonialism 269 (4)
Zhigalovo *archaeological site* Siberia early agriculture 258 (1)
Zhigansk Siberia (Russian Federation) exploration 257 (2)
Zhili *var.* Chihli *region* East Asia Chinese revolution 271 (5) early modern states 268 (1) empire and revolution 268 (2)
Zhili Clique *political faction* East Asia Chinese Civil War 271 (6)
Zhitomir Eastern Europe (Ukraine) Soviet Union 208 (2)
Zhongdu *var.* Dadu East Asia (China) medieval states 263 (5) Mongols 68–69 (1) *see also* Dadu
Zhongdu *battle* East Asia (China) Mongols 68–69 (1)
Zhongmou East Asia (China) first cities 259 (5) first religions 37 (4)
Zhongnan Shan *var.* Chung Nan Shan *mountain* East Asia first religions 37 (4)
Zhongshan *state* East Asia first cities 259 (5)
Zhongshu *province* East Asia medieval states 263 (6)
Zhongtiao Shan *var.* Chung t'iao Shan *mountain* East Asia first religions 37 (4)
Zhongxing East Asia (China) medieval states 263 (6)
Zhou *state* East Asia first cities 259 (3), (4), (5)
Zhou China *state* East Asia the world in 500 BCE 34–35
Zhoukoudian *archaeological site* East Asia (China) first humans 13 (2)
Zhufu *var.* Chu-Fu East Asia (China) first religions 37 (4)
Zhuhai East Asia (China) post-war politics 274 (2)
Zhuji *see* Shangqiu
Zhulu *var.* Chu-Lu *region* East Asia first religions 37 (4)
Zimapan Central America (Mexico) Aztecs 124 (1)
Zimbabwe *var.* Great Zimbabwe Southern Africa (Zimbabwe) Islam 163 (1) trade 164 (1)
Zimbabwe *prev.* Rhodesia, Southern Rhodesia *state* Southern Africa decolonization 168 (1) economy 168 (2), (3) the modern world 112 (1), 113 (3), (4)
see also Rhodesia, Southern Rhodesia
Zinder West Africa (Niger) colonization 167 (4) exploration 157 (4) Islam 167 (3)
Zirids *dynasty* North Africa crusades 64–65 (2) early Islam 57 (2) medieval states 185 (3)
Ziwa *archaeological site* Southern Africa (Zimbabwe) early cultures 160 (1)
Zomba East Africa (Malawi) exploration 157 (4)
Zombor *see* Sombor
Zou *var.* Tsou East Asia (China) first religions 37 (4)
Zoug *see* Zug
Zug *Fr.* Zoug Central Europe (Switzerland) early modern states 193 (5)
Zuider Zee *var.* IJsselmeer *lake* Low Countries Reformation 195 (5)
Zulu *var.* Zululand *state* Southern Africa trade 167 (1) colonization 167 (4)
Zulu *people* Southern Africa the world in 1850 90–91
Zuluf Safinaya *oil field* Persian Gulf economy 234 (1)
Zululand *see* Zulu
Zumbo *var.* Vila do Zumbo Southern Africa (Mozambique) trade 164 (1)
Zumpango Central America (Mexico) Aztecs 124 (2) colonization 125 (5)
Zungaria *see* Dzungaria
Zungomero East Africa (Tanzania) exploration 157 (4)
Zuni *people* North America colonization 125 (4), 126 (1)
Zurich *Ger.* Zürich, *It.* Zurigo Central Europe (Switzerland) early modern states 193 (4), (5) medieval states 188 (1) Napoleon 200–201 (1), 201 (2), (3) Reformation 194 (2)
Zurigo *see* Zurich
Zutphen *province* Low Countries Reformation 195 (5)
Zuttiyen *archaeological site* Southwest Asia (Israel) first humans 13 (2)

BIBLIOGRAPHY

World history

Atlases:

Atlante Storico De Agostini Novara, 1995

Atlante Storico del Cristianesimo Andrea Dué, Juan Maria Laboa, Milan, 1997

Atlas Historico Universal y de Espagna Santillana Madrid, 1995

Atlas of Ancient Archaeology Jacquetta Hawkes (ed.), London, 1974

Atlas of Atlases: The Map Makers Vision of the World Phillip Allen, New York, 1992

Atlas of Disease Distributions: Analytical Approaches to Epidemiological Data Andrew D. Cliff and Peter Haggett, Oxford, 1988

Atlas of Food Crops J. Bertin (et al.), Paris, 1971

Atlas of Islamic History H.W. Hazard, Princeton, 1952

Atlas of Jewish History Dan Cohen-Sherbok, London and New York, 1996

Atlas of Modern Jewish History (revised from the Hebrew edn.) Evyatar Friesel, Oxford, New York,1990

Atlas of the Christian Church Henry Chadwick and G.R. Evans (eds.), Oxford, 1987

Atlas of the Jewish World Nicholas de Lange, Oxford, 1995

Atlas zur Geschichte V.E.B. Hermann Haack, GDR, 1988

Atlas zur Kirchengeschichte H. Jedin, K.S. Latourette, J. Martin, Freiburg, 1970

Cambridge Illustrated Atlas: Warfare, Renaissance to Revolution 1492–1792 Jeremy Black,Cambridge, 1996

Cambridge Illustrated Atlas: Warfare, The Middle Ages 768–1487 Nicholas Hooper and Matthew Bennett, Cambridge, 1996

Cassell Atlas of World History John Haywood, Brian Catchpole, Simon Hall, Edward Barratt, Oxford, 1997

Chambers Atlas of World History, Edinburgh, 1975

Collins Atlas of Twentieth Century World History Michael Dockrill, 1991

Grand Atlas Historique Georges Duby, Paris,1996

Grosser Atlas zur Weltgeschichte, Braunschweig, 1997

Grosser Historischer Weltatlas (3 vols.) Bayerischer Schulbuch-Verlag, Munich, 1981

Hammond Atlas of World History, Maplewood, New Jersey, 1997

Historical Atlas of Islam William C. Brice (ed.), Leiden, 1981

Historical Atlas of the Muslim Peoples R. Roolvink, London, 1957

Historical Atlas of World Mythology Vol. I: The Way of the Animal Powers J. Campbell, New York, 1984

Historical Atlas of World Mythology Vol. II: The Way of the Seeded Earth, Part I: The Sacrifice Joseph Campbell, New York, 1988

Historical Atlas of the World's Religions, Isma'il Ragi al Faruqi, New York, 1974

New Cambridge Modern History Atlas, H.C. Darby, Harold Fullard (eds.), 1970

Past Worlds: The Times Atlas of Archaeology C. Scarre (ed.) London, 1988

Philip's Atlas of Exploration, London, 1996

Putzger Historische Weltatlas, Berlin, 1997

Rand McNally Atlas of World History 1993 (published in England as **Philip's Atlas of World History**, London, 1992)

Review and Atlas of Palaeovegetation: Preliminary Land Ecosystem Maps of the World Since the last Glacial Maximum J.M. Adams and H. Faure (eds.), Quaternary Environments Network, www.soton.ac.uk/~tjms/adams4.html

Soguatlas, Stockholm, 1992

Társadalom – És Művelődéstörtèneti Atlasz Budapest, 1991

The World...its History in Maps W.H. McNeill, M.R. Buske, A.W. Roehm, Chicago, 1969

Times Atlas of Exploration Felipe Fernandez-Armesto (ed.), London, 1991

Times Atlas of the 20th Century Richard Overy (ed.), London, 1996

Times Atlas of the Second World War J. Keegan (ed.), London, 1989

Times Atlas of World History Geoffrey Barraclough (ed.), London, 1993

Times Concise Atlas of World History Geoffrey Barraclough (ed.), London, 1994

Tortenelmi Vilagatlasz, Budapest, 1991

WDTV Atlas zur Weltgeschichte (2 vols.) H. Kinder & W. Hilgemann, Stuttgart, 1964 (Published in English as **The Penguin Atlas of World History** London, 1974 and 1978)

WWF Atlas of the Environment Geoffrey Lean and Don Hinrischsen, Oxford, 1992

West Point Atlas of American Wars: Volume II, 1900-1953 Vincent J. Esposito (chief ed.), New York, 1959

West Point Military History Series: Atlas for the Arab-Israeli War and the Korean War Thomas E. Greiss (series ed.), Wayne, New Jersey,1986

West Point Military History Series: Atlas for the Great War Thomas E. Greiss (series ed.), Wayne New Jersey, 1986

West Point Military History Series: Atlas for the Second World War (vols. I–III) Thomas E. Greiss (series ed.), Wayne, New Jersey,1985

Other works:

A History of Discovery and Exploration: The Search Begins London,1973

A History of Islamic Societies I.M. Lapidus, Cambridge, 1988

A History of World Societies John P. McKay, Bennett D. Hill, John Buckler, Boston, 1997

A Study of History Arnold Toynbee, Oxford, 1972

Asia Before Europe: Economy and Civilization of the Indian Ocean from the Rise of Islam to 1750 K.N. Chauduri, Cambridge, 1991

Before European Hegemony: The World System AD 1250-1350 J.L. Abu-Lughod, Oxford, 1991

Claudius Ptolemy: The Geography Translated and edited by Edward Luther Stevenson, London, 1991

Columbia Lippincott Gazetteer of the World Saul B. Cohen (ed.), New York, 1999

Cross-cultural Trade in World History P.D. Curtin, Cambridge, 1984

Encyclopedia of World History, revised edn. W.L. Langer (ed.), London, 1987

Heck's Pictorial Archive of Military Science, Geography and History J.G. Heck, New York, 1994

Into the Unknown National Geographic Society: Washington, 1987

Maps and History J. Black, New Haven, 1997

Maps and Politics J. Black, London,1997

Maps from the Age of Discovery, Columbus to Mercator Kenneth Nebenzahl, London, 1990

Navies and Nations: Warships, Navies and State Building in Europe and America 1500-1860 J. Glete, Stockholm, 1993

Peoples and Places of the Past National Geographic Society: Washington, 1983

Plagues and Peoples W.H. McNeill, New York, 1992

Portugaliae Monumenta Cartographica Lisbon, 1960

The Atlantic Slave Trade P.D. Curtin, Madison, 1972

The Atlantic Slave Trade: Effects on Economy, Society and Population in Africa, America and Europe J.E. Inikori, S.L. Engerman, Durham, NC 1992

The Discoverers: An Encyclopedia of Explorers and Exploration Helen Delpar (ed.), New York, 1980

The Distribution of Wild Wheats and Barleys J.R. Harlan, D. Zohary, Science, 1966

The Earth and its Peoples: a Global History Richard W. Bulliet, Pamela Kyle, Crossley, Daniel R. Headrick, Steven W. Hirsch, Lyman L. Johnson, David Northrup, Boston, New York, 1997

The Evolution of International Business G. Jones, London, 1996

The First Imperial Age: European Overseas Expansion c. 1400–1715 G.V. Scammel London, 1992

The Geography behind History W.G. East, London, 1965

The History of Cartography (various vols.) J.B. Harley, D. Woodward, Chicago, 1987–

The Hutchinson History of the World, revised edn. J.M. Roberts, London, 1987

The Mapmaker's Art: A History of Cartography John Goss, London, 1993

The Osprey Companion to Military History Robert Cowley and Geoffrey Parker, London, 1996

The Oxford History of the British Empire II, the Eighteenth Century P.J. Marshall (ed.), Oxford, 1998

The Oxford History of the British Empire: The Origins of Empire Nicholas Canny (ed.), Oxford, 1998

The Oxford Illustrated History of Modern War C. Townshend (ed.), Oxford, 1999

The Plants and Animals that Nourish Man J.R. Harlan, Scientific American, 1976

The Revolutionary Age 1760–1791 H. Quebec Neaty, London, 1966

The Rise of Christianity: A Sociologist Reconsiders History R. Stark, Princeton, 1996

The Rise of the West: A History of the Human Community W.H, McNeill, Chicago, 1991

The Rise of Western Christendom: Triumph and Diversity 200–1000 P. Brown, Oxford, 1996

The Story of Archaeology Paul G. Bahn (ed.), London, 1996

The Wealth and Property of Nations D. Landes, London, 1998

The World since 1500: A Global History, 6th edn L.S. Stavrianos, Englewood Cliffs NJ, 1991

The World to 1500: A Global History, 5th edn L.S. Stavrianos, Englewood Cliffs NJ, 1991

The World: an Illustrated History Geoffrey Parker (ed.), London, 1986

The World's Religions Ninian Smart, Cambridge, 1992

War and the World: Military Power and the Fate of Continents 1450–2000 J Black, New York, 1998

War in the Early Modern World 1450–1815 J. Black (ed.), London, 1999

Why Wars Happen J. Black, London, 1998

North America

Atlases:

Atlas of American Indian Affairs Francis Paul Prucha, Lincoln, Nebraska, 1990

Atlas of Ancient America Michael Coe, Dean Snow, Elizabeth Benson, Oxford and New York, 1993

Atlas of Early American History L. Cappon (et al), Chicago, 1976

Atlas of Great Lakes Indian History Helen Tanner, Norman, Oklahoma, 1987

Atlas of North American Exploration: from Norse Voyages to the Race to the Pole William H. Goetzmann, Glyndwr Williams, New York, 1992

Atlas of the Civil War James M. McPherson, New York, 1994

Atlas of the North American Indian C. Waldman, M. Braun, New York, 1995

Atlas of Westward Expansion Alan Wexler, Molly Braun, New York, 1995

Civil War Newspaper Maps, a Historical Atlas David Bosse, Baltimore and London, 1993

Historical Atlas of Canada Donald Kerr and Deryck W. Holdsworth (eds.), Toronto, 1990

Historical Atlas of the American West Warren A. Beck and Ynez D. Haase, Norman, Oklahoma, 1989

Historical Atlas of New York E. Homberger, A. Hudson, New York, 1994

Historical Atlas of the United States: Centennial Edition National Geographic Society: Washington, 1988

Mapping America's Past: a Historical Atlas M.C. Carnes, P. Williams, J. A. Garraty, New York, 1997

Our United States...its History in Maps E.B. Wesley, Chicago, 1977

Penguin Historical Atlas of North America Eric Homberger, London,1995

The Settling of North America: the Atlas of the Great Migrations into North America from the Ice Age to the Present Helen Hornbeck Tanner (ed.), New York, 1995)

Other works:

A Guide to the Historical Geography of New Spain Peter Gerhard, Norman, Oklahoma, 1993

America in 1492: the World of the Indian Peoples before the Arrival of Columbus Alvin M. Josephy, New York, 1992

An Introduction to American Archaeology (vols. 1 & 2) Englewood Cliffs, NJ, 1970

Battle Cry of Freedom: the Civil War Era James McPherson, Oxford, 1988

Documents of American History Henry Steele Commager, 1973

European and Native American Warfare 1675–1815 A. Starkey, London, 1998

Encyclopedia of North America Indians Frederick E. Hoxie, Boston, 1996

Handbook of Middle American Indians Austin, Texas, 1964-76

Handbook of North American Indians Smithsonian Institution, Washington, D.C., 1978- (20 volumes projected)

Hispaniola; Caribbean Chiefdoms in the Age of Columbus S. M.Wilson, Tuscaloosa,1990

Native American Time: a Historical Time Line of Native America Lee Francis, New York, 1996

Oxford History of the American West Clyde A. Milner et al., Oxford and New York, 1994

Prehistory of North America, 3rd edn. J.D. Jennings, Mountain View, Calif., 1989

The American Century: the Rise and Decline of the United States as a World Power Donald W. White, New Haven, 1996

The Americans: Their Archaeology and Prehistory D. Snow London, 1976

The Fur Trader and the Indian L.O. Saum London, 1965

The Limits of Liberty Maldwyn A. Jones, Oxford/New York, 1983

The Market Revolution America: Social, Political and Religious Expressions, 1800–1880 M. Stokes, S. Conway, Charlottesville, 1996

The Northern Frontier of New Spain Peter Gerhard, Norman, Oklahoma, 1993

The Slave Trade Hugh Thomas, London/New York, 1997

The Southeast Frontier of New Spain Peter Gerhard, Norman, Oklahoma, 1993

The Spanish Frontier in North America D.J. Weber, New Haven, 1992

The Maya Michael D. Coe, London, 1993

South America

Atlases:

Atlas of Ancient America Michael Coe, Dean Snow, Elizabeth Benson, Oxford and New York, 1993

Latin American History: a Teaching Atlas Cathryn L. Lombardi, John V. Lombardi, Kym L. Stoner, Madison, Wisconsin, 1983

Other works:

A History of Latin America: Empires and Sequels, 1450–1930 Peter John Bakewell, Gainesville, 1998

Anthropological Perspectives A. C. Roosevelt (ed.), Tucson and London, 1994

Ancient Mexico in the British Museum Colin McEwan, London, 1995

Ancient South America K. Bruhns, Cambridge 1994

Archaeology in the Lowland American Tropics P. W. Stahl (ed.), Cambridge, 1994

Cambridge History of Latin America Leslie Bethel (ed.), Cambridge, 1985

Chavin and the Origins of Andean Civilization R. L. Burger, London, 1992

Chiefdoms and Chieftaincy in the Americas E. M. Redmond (ed.), Malden Mass, 1997

Chieftains, Power and Trade: Regional Interaction in the Intermediate Area of the Americas C. H. Langebaek & F. C-Arroyo (eds.), Departamento de Antropologia, Universidad de los Andes: Bogota, Colombia, 1996

Moundbuilders of the Amazon. Geophysical Archaeology on Marajo Island, Brazil A. C. Roosevelt, New York, 1991

Parmana: Prehistoric Maize and Manioc Subsistence along the Amazon and Orinoco A. C. Roosevelt, New York, 1980

Prehistory of the Americas S. J. Fiedel, Cambridge, 1987

The Conquest of the Incas John Hemming, London, 1970

The Discoverie of the Large, Rich and Bewtiful Empire of Guiana by Sir Walter Ralegh N. L. Whitehead (ed.), Exploring Travel Series Vol. 1, Manchester University Press: Manchester, American Exploration and Travel Series Vol. 71, Oklahoma University Press: Norman, 1998

The Incas and Their Ancestors: The Archaeology of Peru M. E. Moseley, New York, 1992

The Meeting of Two Worlds: Europe and the Americas, 1492–1650 W. Bray (ed.), Proceedings of the British Academy 81, Oxford, 1993

The Penguin History of Latin America Edwin Williamson, London, 1992

Africa

Atlases:

An Atlas of African History J.D. Fage London, 1958

Atlas of African Affairs Ieuan LL. Griffiths, London and New York, 1994

Atlas of Ancient Egypt John Baines and Jaromir Malek, Oxford, 1996

Cultural Atlas of Africa Jocelyn Murray (ed.), Oxford, 1993

New Atlas of African History G.S.P. Freeman-Grenville, London, 1991

Penguin Historical Atlas of Ancient Egypt Bill Manley, London, 1996

Other works:

A History of West Africa (2 vols.) 3rd edn. J.F.A. Ajaya, M. Crowder, 1985

A Survey of West African History B.A. Ogot (ed.), London, 1974–1976

Africa and Africans in the Formation of the Atlantic World 1400–1680 John Thornton, Cambridge and New York, 1992

Africa and Asia: Mapping Two Continents Natalie Ettinger, Elspeth Huxley, Paul Hamilton, London, 1973

Africa in the Iron Age c.500 BC–AD 1400 R. Oliver, B. Fagan, Cambridge, 1975

Africa since 1800, 3rd edn. R. Oliver, A. Atmore, Cambridge, 1981

African Archaeology, 2nd edn. David W. Phillipson, Cambridge, 1993

An Economic History of Africa From Earliest Times to Partition P.L. Wickins, New York, 1981

Arab Seafaring in the Indian Ocean in Ancient and Medieval Times G.F. Hourani and J.Carswell, Princeton, 1995

Cambridge History of Africa J.D. Fage, R. Oliver (eds.), Cambridge, 1975–

Early Egypt: The Rise of Civilisation in the Nile Valley A.J. Spencer, London, 1993

Economic History of West Africa A.G. Hopkins, London, 1973

General History of Africa II: Ancient Civilizations of Africa G. Mokhtar (ed.), Paris and London, 1981

General History of Africa III: Africa from the Seventh to the Eleventh Century M. Elfasi (ed.), I. Hrbek (asst. ed.), Paris and London, 1981

General History of Africa VII: Africa under Colonial Domination 1880–1935 A.A. Boahen (ed.), Paris and London, 1981

Oxford History of South Africa (vols. 1 & 2) Oxford, 1969, 1971

The African Inheritance Ieuan L.L. Griffiths, London and New York, 1995

The Art and Architecture of Ancient Egypt, revised edn. W.S. Smith, London, 1981

The Changing Geography of Africa and the Middle East Graham P. Chapman and Kathleen M. Baker, London and New York, 1992

Wars and Imperial Conquest in Africa 1830–1914 B. Vandervort, London, 1998

West Africa under Colonial Rule M. Crowder, London, 1968

Europe

Atlases:

Atlas of Medieval Europe Angus Mackay, David Ditchburn (eds.), London, 1997

Atlas of the Classical World A.M. Van der Heydon, H.H. Scullard, London, 1959

Atlas of the Crusades Jonathon Riley-Smith, New York and Oxford, 1991

Atlas of the Greek World Peter Levi, Oxford, 1997

Atlas of the Roman World Tim Cornell, John Matthews, New York, 1982

Atlas Historyczny Polski Warsaw, 1967

Cultural Atlas of France John Ardagh and Colin Jones, Oxford, 1991

Cultural Atlas of Spain and Portugal Mary Vincent and R.A. Stradling, Oxford, 1994

Cultural Atlas of the Viking World J.Graham-Campbell (ed.), Oxford, 1994

Historical Atlas of East Central Europe: Volume I Paul Robert Magosci, Seattle and London, 1993

Penguin Historical Atlas of Ancient Greece Robert Morkot, London, 1996

Penguin Historical Atlas of Ancient Rome Chris Scarre, London, 1995

Penguin Historical Atlas of Russia John Channon with Robert Hudson, London, 1995

Penguin Historical Atlas of the Third Reich Richard Overy, London, 1996

Penguin Historical Atlas of the Vikings John Haywood, London, 1995

Russian History Atlas M. Gilbert, London, 1972

Times Atlas of European History London, 1994

Other works:

A History of Ancient Greece N. Demand, New York, 1996

A History of Business in Medieval Europe 1200–1550 E.H. Hunt and J. Murray, Cambridge, 1999

A Russian Economic History A. Kahan, Chicago, 1991

An Historical Geography of Western Europe before 1800, revised edn. C.T. Smith, London and New York

As the Romans Did: a Sourcebook in Roman Social History, 2nd ed. Jo-Ann Shelton, Oxford, 1997

Britain and Industrial Europe 1750–1870 W.O. Henderson, Liverpool, 1965

Britain as a Military Power 1688–1815 J. Black, London, 1999

Cambridge Economic History of Europe II: Trade and Industry in the Middle Ages, 2nd edn. A. Miller (ed.), Cambridge, 1987

Capetian France 987–1328 E. Hallam, London, 1980

Eighteenth Century Europe 2nd edn. J. Black, London, 1999

Eighteenth Century Europe: Tradition and Progress I. Woloch, London and New York, 1982

Enlightened Absolutism H.M. Scott (ed.), London, 1990

Europe in the Eighteenth Century, 2nd edn J. Black, London, 1999

Europe in the Fourteenth and Fifteenth Centuries D.Hay, London, 1966

Europe under Napoleon, 1799–1815 M.G. Broers, London, 1997

European Warfare 1453–1815 J. Black (ed.), London, 1999

Frederick II. A Medieval Emperor D.Abulafia, London, 1988

From Louis XIV to Napoleon: The Fate of a Great Power J. Black, London, 1999

From Tsar to Soviets C. Read, 1996

Gainful Pursuits: The Making of Industrial Europe 1600–1914 J. Goodman, K. Honeyman, London, 1988

Geography of the Soviet Union J.P. Cole, London, 1984

Germany and the Germans, after Unification John Ardagh, London, 1991

Germany in the Middle Ages 800–1056 T. Reuter, London, 1991

History of the Byzantine State G. Ostrogorsky, Oxford, 1969

History of the National Economy of Russia to the 1917 Revolution P.I. Lyaschenko, New York, 1949

Information USSR Oxford and New York, 1962

Ireland 1912–85 J.J. Lee, 1989

Louis XIV and the French Monarchy A. Lossky, London, 1995

Medieval England: Towns, Commerce and Crafts 1086–1348 E. Miller, J. Hatcher London, 1995

Medieval Trade in the Mediterranean World: Illustrative Documents R.S. Lopez and I.W. Raymond, reprinted New York, 1990

Money and its Use in Medieval Europe P. Spufford, Cambridge, 1988

Moorish Spain R. Fletcher, Phoenix, 1994

Napoleon and the Legacy of the French Revolution M. Lyons, London, 1994

Napoleon's Integration of Europe S.J. Woolf, London, 1991

National States and National Minorities C.A. Macartney, 1968

New Cambridge Medieval History, vol. V, c.1198–c.1300 David Abulafia (ed.), Cambridge, 1999

New Cambridge Medieval History, vol. VI, c.1300–c.1415 Michael Jones (ed.), Cambridge, 1999

New Cambridge Medieval History, vol. VII, c.1415–c.1500 Christopher Allmand Jones (ed.), Cambridge, 1998

Northern Europe in the Early Modern Period: the Baltic World 1492–1772 D. Kirby, London, 1990

Oxford Classical Dictionary, 3rd ed. Simon Hornblower and Antony Spawforth (eds.), Oxford, 1996

Oxford History of the Classical World J. Boardman (ed.), Oxford, 1989

Oxford Illustrated History of the Crusades J. Riley-Smith (ed.), Oxford, 1997

Oxford Illustrated History of the Vikings P. Sawyer (ed.) Oxford, 1997

Oxford Illustrated Prehistory of Europe B. Cunliffe, Oxford, 1994

Poverty and Capitalism in Pre-Industrial Europe C. Lis and H. Soly, Brighton, 1982

Roman Civilization (2 vols) 3rd ed. Naphtali Lewis and Meyer Reinhold (eds.), New York, 1990

Seventeenth-century Europe 1598–1700 T. Munck, London, 1990

Seventeenth–century Europe, 2nd ed. D.H. Pennington, London, 1989

Spain in the Middle Ages: from Frontier to Empire Angus Mackay, London, 1977

Textiles, Towns and Trade J.H. Munro, Aldershot, 1994

The British Revolution: British Politics 1880–1939 Robert Rhodes, London, 1978

The Cambridge Ancient History J.B. Bury, S.A. Cook, F.E. Adcock (eds.), Cambridge, 1923–; 2nd edn 1982–

The Civilization of Europe in the Renaissance J.R.Hale, London, 1993

The Creation of the Roman Frontier S.L. Dyson, Princeton, 1985

The Crusades: a Short History J.Riley -Smith, 1990

The Emergence of the Rus J. Shepherd, S. Franklin, 1996

The European Dynastic States 1494–1660 R. Bonney, Oxford, 1991

The German Hansa P.J. Dollinger, trans. D.S. Ault, S.H. Steinberg, London, 1970

The Habsburg Monarchy, 1618–1815 C. Ingrao, Cambridge, 1994

The Hundred Years War. England and France at War c.1300–c.1450 C.T. Allmand, Cambridge, 1988

The Huns E.A. Thompson, 1996

The Industrialization of Soviet Russia (3 vols.) R.W. Davis, Cambridge, 1989

The Italian City Republics, 3rd edn. D.Waley, London and New York, 1988

The Later Crusades 1274–1580: from Lyons to Alcazar N.Housley, Oxford, 1992

The Legacy of Rome: A New Appraisal Richard Jenkins (ed.) Oxford, 1992

The Making of Europe. Conquest, Colonization and Cultural Change 950–1350 R.Bartlett, London, 1993

The Making of Roman Italy Edward Togo Salmon, Ithaca, NY, 1982

The Mediterranean World in Late Antiquity AD 395–600 A.M. Cameron, London, 1993

The Merovingian Kingdoms 450–758 I.N. Wood, London, 1994

The Old European Order 1660–1800, 2nd ed. W. Doyle, Oxford, 1992

The Origins of the Second World War in Europe P.M.H. Bell, 1986

The Roman Empire, 27 BC–AD 476: A Study in Survival Chester G. Starr, New York, 1982

The State in Early Modern France J.B. Collins, Cambridge, 1995

The Struggle for Mastery in Germany, 1779–1850 B. Simms, London, 1998

The Thirty Years War Geoffrey Parker, London, 1984

The Transformation of the Roman World 400–900 L. Webster, M. Brown, London, 1997

The Two Cities. Medieval Europe 1050–1320 M.Barber, London and New York, 1992

The Wars of Napoleon C.J. Esdaile, London, 1995

The World in Depression 1929–1939 C. Kindleberger, 1973

Venice: A Maritime Republic F.C. Lane, Baltimore, 1973

War and Imperialism in Republican Rome 327–70 BC William V. Harris, Oxford, 1979

War in the Middle Ages P. Contamine, Oxford, 1984

West Asia:

Atlases:

Atlas of the Jewish World Nicholas de Lange, Oxford, 1984

Cultural Atlas of Mesopotamia and the Ancient Near East Michael Roaf, New York and Oxford, 1996

Historical Atlas of Islam William C. Brice (ed.), Leiden, 1981

Historical Atlas of the Middle East G.S.P. Freeman-Grenville, New York, 1993

Times Concise Atlas of the Bible James B. Pritchard (ed.), London, 1991

Other works:

A History of the Arab People A. Hourani, Harvard, 1991

A History of the Ottoman Empire to 1730 M.A. Cook (ed.), Cambridge, 1976

A Popular Dictionary of Islam Ian Richard Netton, Richmond, 1997

An Introduction to Islam David Waites, Cambridge, 1996

Arabia Without Sultans Fred Halliday, London, 1979

Cambridge Encyclopedia of The Middle East and North Africa Cambridge, 1988

Encyclopaedia of Islam (10 vols.) new edn. H.A.R. Gibb et al. (eds.), Leiden, 1960

Histoire de l'Empire Ottoman R. Mantran, Paris, 1989

History of the First World War B.H. Liddell Hart, London, 1979

Lords of Horizons: A History of the Ottoman Empire Jason Goodwin, Henry Hoh and Company, 1999

Middle East Sources: A MELCOM Guide to Middle Eastern and Islamic Books and Materials in the United Kingdom and Irish Libraries Ian Richard Netton, Richmond, 1998

Muhammed, Prophet and Statesman W. Montgomery Watt, London, 1961, 1967

Ottoman Warfare 1500–1600 R Murphy, London, 1999

Palestine and the Arab Israeli conflict C.D. Smith, 1994

The Age of the Crusades. The Near East from the Eleventh Century to 1517 P. M. Holt, London and New York

The Ancient Near East c. 3000–300 BC A.T.L. Kuhrt, London, 1995

The Arabs Peter Mansfield, London , 1997

The Birth of the Palestinian Refugee Problem 1947–1949 Benny Morris, Cambridge, 1988

The Cambridge History of Iran (vol. 3) E Yarshater (ed.) Cambridge, 1983

The Fifty Years War: Israel and the Arabs Ahron Bregman and Jihan el-Jahri, Penguin, London, 1996

The Lessons of Modern War: The Iran-Iraq War Anthony H. Cordesman and Abraham R. Wagner, Boulder and San Francisco, 1990

The Neolithic of the Near East J. Mellaart, London, 1975

The Ottoman Empire: The Classical Age 1300–1600 Halil Inalcik, London, 1973

The Ottoman Turks: an Introductory History to 1923 J. McCarthy, London, 1994

The Prophet and the Age of Caliphates: The Islamic Near East from the Sixth to the Eleventh Century Hugh Kennedy, London and New York, 1986

The Travels of Ibn Battuta AD 1325–1354 (4 vols.) Ibn Battuta trans. by H.A.R. Gibb and C.F. Beckingham, Cambridge, 1958–1984

The Venture of Islam (3 vols.) Marshall G.S. Hodgson, Chicago, 1974

The World of Islam Ernst J. Grube, London, 1966

The World of Islam Bernard Lewis, London, 1976

South and Southeast Asia

Atlases:

Historical Atlas of South Asia, 2nd edn. Joseph E. Schwartzberg, Oxford and New York, 1992

Historical Atlas of South-East Asia Jan M. Pluvier, Leiden, 1995

Historical Atlas of the Indian Peninsula C.C. Davies, London, 1959

Historical Atlas of the Vietnam War Harry G. Summers Jr., Boston and New York, 1995

Macmillan's Atlas of South-East Asia London, 1988

Other works:

A History of India M.A. Edwardes, London, 1961

A History of India Burton Stein, Oxford, 1998

A History of India Romila Thapar, London, 1967

A History of Malaya 1400–1959 J. Kennedy, London, 1967

A History of South-East Asia, 4th edn. D.G.E. Hall London, 1981

A History of Vedic India Z.A. Ragozin, Delhi, 1980

A New History of India S. Wolpert, Oxford, 1993

Cambridge Economic History of India, Vol. 1, c.1200–c.1750 Tapan Raycgaudhuri and Irfan Habib (eds.), Cambridge, 1981

Cambridge Economic History of India, Vol. 2, c.1757–c.1970 Dharma Kumar and Meghnad Desai (eds.), Cambridge, 1983

Early India and Pakistan to Ashoka M. Wheeler, London, 1968

In Search of Southeast Asia, revised edn. David Joel Steinberg, Honolulu, 1987

In Search of the Indo-Europeans: Language, Archaeology and Myth J.P. Mallory, London, 1994

India: A Modern History, new edn. Percival Spear, Ann Arbor, Michigan, 1972

New Cambridge History of India G. Johnson (ed.), Cambridge, 1989

Prehistoric India to 1000 BC S. Piggott, London, 1992

Prehistoric Thailand from Early Settlement to Sukhothai C.F.W. Higham, R. Thosarat, Bangkok, 1999

Prehistory of the Indo-Malay Archipelago P. Bellwood, Ryde, NSW, 1985

South-East Asia C.A. Fisher, London, 1964

Southeast Asia: An Introductory History, 2nd edn. M.E. Osborne

Southeast Asia: History, Culture, People, 5th revised edn. E. Graff, H.E. Hammond, Cambridge, 1980

Thailand: A Short History David Wyatt, New Haven, 1984

The Archaeology of Mainland Southeast Asia Charles Higham, Cambridge, 1989

The Archaeology of Mainland Southeast Asia from 1000 BC to the Fall of Angkor C.F.W. Higham, Cambridge, 1989

The Birth of Indian Civilisation B. and R. Allchin, London, 1968

The History of Post-War Southeast Asia: Independence Problems John F. Cady, Athens, Ohio, 1972

The Indianized states of Southeast Asia Georges Coedes, Honolulu, 1968

The Making of South-East Asia D.J.M. Tate, Kuala Lumpur, 1971

The Stone Age of Indonesia, revised edn. H.R. Van Heekeren, The Hague, 1972

The Traditional Trade of Asia C.F. Simkin, Oxford, 1968

The Vedic Age R.C. Majumdar, Bombay, 1951

The Wonder That Was India (2 vols.) 3rd revised edn. A.L. Basham, London, 1987

Trade and Civilization in the Indian Ocean: An Economic History of the rise of Islam to 1750 K.N. Chauduri, Cambridge, 1985

Vietnam S.C Tucker, London, 1999

War, Culture and Economy in Java 1677–1721 M.C. Ricklefs, The Hague, 1990

North and East Asia

Atlases:

Ajiarekishi chizu Matsui and Mori, Tokyo, 1965

Atlas of China Chiao-min Hsieh, USA, 1973

Cultural Atlas of China, C. Blunden and M. Elvin, Oxford, 1991

Historical and Commercial Atlas of China A. Herrmann, Harvard, 1935

Historical Atlas of China A. Herrmann, Edinburgh, 1966

Cultural Atlas of Japan, M. Collcutt, M. Jansen, Isao Kumakura Oxford, 1991

Nihon rekishi jiten Atlas Tokyo, 1959

Times Atlas of China P.J.M. Geelan D.C. Twitchett (eds.), London, 1974

Tubinger Atlas der Orients (various vols.) Wiesbaden, 1972-

Other works:

A Historical Geography of Russia H.Parker (ed.), London, 1968

A History of the Peoples of Siberia J. Forsyth, Cambridge, 1992

Cambridge Illustrated History of China P. B. Ebrey, Cambridge, 1996

Cambridge History of China D. Twitchett, M. Loewe (eds.), Cambridge, 1979–

China, Korea and Japan: The Rise of Civilization in East Asia, Gina L. Barnes London, 1993

The Early Civilization of China Yong Yap and A. Cotterel, London, 1975

Histoire du Parti Communiste Chinois J. Guillermaz, Paris, 1968, English translation 1972

Inner Asian Frontiers of China O. Lattimore, New York, 1951

An Introduction to Chinese History, B. Wiethoff London, 1975

Le Monde Chinois J. Gernet, Paris, 1969; English translation 1982

The Archaeology of Ancient China, 4th edn. K.C. Chang, New Haven, 1986

The Empire of the Steppes: A History of Central Asia R. Grousset, New Brunswick, NJ, 1970

World Prehistory, G. Clarke, Cambridge, 1977

Australasia and Oceania

Atlases:

Aboriginal Languages and Clans: An Historical Atlas of Western and Central Victoria J.D. Clark, Clayton, South Australia, 1988

Cultural Atlas of Australia New Zealand and the South Pacific Richard Nile and Christian Clerk, Oxford, 1996

Other works:

A Prehistory of Australia, New Guinea, and Sahul J.P. White and J.F. O'Connell, Sydney, 1982

Aboriginal Australians: Black Responses to White Dominance Richard Broome, Sydney, 1982

Australia Unveiled Günter Schilder, Amsterdam, 1976

Australian Civilisation Richard Nile (ed.), Melbourne, 1994

Blood on the Banner: Nationalist Struggles in the South Pacific D.Robie, London, 1989

Convict Workers: Reinterpreting Australian History Stephen Nicholas, Cambridge (UK), 1988

Culture and Democracy in the South Pacific Ron Crocombe et al. (eds.), Suva, Fiji, 1992

Dispossession: Black Australians and White Invaders Henry Reynolds (ed.), Sydney, 1989

Easter Island Studies Steven Roger Fischer (ed.), Oxford, 1993

Ethnicity, Class and Gender in Australia Gill Bottomley and Marie de Lepervanche (eds.), Sydney, 1991

European Vision and the South Pacific Bernard Smith, New Haven, Conn., 1992

Fatal Necessity: British Intervention in New Zealand Peter Adams, Auckland, 1977

Frontier: Aborigines, Settlers and the Land Henry Reynolds, Sydney, 1987

Historical Charts and Maps of New Zealand Peter B. Maling, Auckland, 1996

History of Australia John Malony, Ringwood, Victoria (Australia), 1987

History of New Zealand Keith A. Sinclair, Auckland, 1988

History of the Pacific Islands I.C.Campbell, Berkeley, 1989

Man's Conquest of the Pacific Peter Bellwood, Auckland, 1978

Native Lands: Prehistory and Environmental Usage in Australia and the South-West Pacific J. Dodson (ed.), Melbourne, 1992

New History of Australia Frank Crowley, Melbourne, 1974

New Zealand Politics in Perspective H. Gold, Auckland, 1985

Oxford History of Australia Geoffrey Bolton (ed.), Melbourne, 1994

Oxford History of New Zealand W.H. Oliver and B.R. Williams, Wellington, 1981

Oxford Illustrated History of New Zealand Keith Sinclair (ed.), Auckland, 1990

Pacific Navigation and Voyaging Ben F. Finney (ed.), Wellington, 1976

Social Change in the Pacific Islands A.D. Robillard (ed.), London, 1992

Sunda and Sahul: Prehistoric Studies in Southeast Asia, Melanesia and Australia J. Allen, J. Golson and R. Jones (eds.), London, 1977

The Australian Colonists K.S. Inglis, Melbourne, 1974

The Discovery of the Pacific Islands Andrew Sharp, Oxford, 1960

The Evolution of Highland Papua New Guinea Societies D.K. Feil, Cambridge, 1987

The Exploration of the Pacific J.C. Beaglehole, Stanford, 1966

The Journals of Captain James Cook on his Voyages of Discovery (4 vols.) Beaglehole, J.C. (ed.), Cambridge, 1955–1974

The Maori Population of New Zealand 1769–1971 Ian Pool, Auckland, 1977

The Pacific Islands: Politics, Economics and International Relations Te'o I.J. Fairburn et al., Honolulu, 1991

The Pacific Since Magellan O.H.K. Spate, Canberra, 1988

The People's History of Australia since 1788 Verity Burgman and Jenney Lee (eds.), Melbourne, 1988

The Polynesians Peter Bellwood, London, 1987

The Prehistoric Exploration and Colonisation of the Pacific Geoffrey Irwin, Cambridge, 1992

The Prehistory of Australia D.J. Mulvaney, Ringwood, Victoria (Australia), 1975

The Prehistory of Polynesia Jesse D. Jennings (ed.), Cambridge (USA), 1979

The Quiet Revolution: Turbulence and Transition in Contemporary New Zealand Colin James, Wellington, 1986

The South Pacific: An Introduction Ron Crocombe, Suva, Fiji, 1989 (revised edition)

The World of the First Australians: Aboriginal Traditional Life – Past and Present R.M. and C.H Berndt, Canberra, 1988

We, the Navigators: The Ancient Art of Land-finding in the Pacific David Lewis, Canberra, 1972

Chronologies

Chronology of the Ancient World E.J. Bickermann, London, 1968

Chronology of the Expanding World N. Williams, London, 1969

Chronology of the Modern World N. Williams, London, 1961

Encyclopedia of Dates and Events L.C. Pascoe (ed.), London, 1991

ACKNOWLEDGMENTS

The publisher would like to thank the following for their kind permission to reproduce the photographs.

A = Above, b = below, B = Bottom, C = Centre, L = Left, R = Right, T = Top.

1 **© 1996 Visual Language**.

2/3 **© 1996 Visual Language**.

5 **E.T. Archive**: British Library, London TC

10/11 **© Michael Holford**: British Museum, London.

12 **The Natural History Museum, London**: TRb, CA, BRA, CR, CB; **Science Photo Library**: John Reader TL.

13 **The Natural History Museum, London**: TCL, TR; **Science Photo Library**: John Reader TCR.

14 **DK Picture Library**: CL, BCL; **Professor Joseph E. Schwartzberg**: TRb; **Dr David Price Williams**: BRA.

15 **DK Picture Library**: CRA; Ashmolean Museum, Oxford TR; University Museum of Archaeology and Anthropology, Cambridge TL; **Eye Ubiquitous**: John Miles CRb.

16 **CM Dixon**: CR; **DK Picture Library**: CLL, BL, BCR; University Museum of Archaeology and Anthropology, Cambridge TL; **Dr David Price Williams**: CL.

17 **Ancient Art & Architecture Collection**: Ronald Sheridan TCR; **Coo-ee Historical Picture Library**: Ron Ryan BR; **DK Picture Library**: University Museum of Archaeology and Anthropology, Cambridge CL, CR; **© Michael Holford**: TCL.

18 **Ancient Art & Architecture Collection**: Ronald Sheridan TRb; **James Mellaant**: BR; **Scala, Florence**: Archaeological Museum, Belgrade CL; **The Utah Museum of Natural History, University of Utah**: BL.

19 **British Museum, London**: TCRb; **Robert Harding Picture Library**: Bildagentur Schuster / Schenk BR; **© Michael Holford**: Ankara Museum TCL; **Catherine Jarrige**: Centre de Recherches Archéologiques Indus-Baluchistan, Musée Guimet, Paris CRb.

20 **DK Picture Library**: CL(round-based shape); British Museum, London TL, CL(flat-based beaker); Museum of London CLA.

21 **Bridgeman Art Library, London / New York**: Photograph: Mrs Sally Greene TL; **DK Picture Library**: TR, BCL; British Museum, London BC.

22 **DK Picture Library**: TR; **Robert Harding Picture Library**: John G Ross BRA; Karachi Museum, Pakistan / Photograph: R Harding CL; **Smithsonian Institute**: Presented by Mrs Alice K Bache, Purchased from James Judge and Eugenia Rodriquez / Photograph: David Heald BL.

23 **James Davis Travel Photography**: TC; **Robert Harding Picture Library**: TRb, CR; **© Michael Holford**: British Museum, London CRb.

24 **British Museum, London**: CLb; **DK Picture Library**: British Museum, London BL; **Werner Forman Archive**: Ashmolean Museum, Oxford TL; **Hirmer Verlag München**: Iraq Museum, Baghdad CbL.

25 **Bridgeman Art Library, London / New York**: Ashmolean Museum, Oxford BRA; British Museum, London TRb; **DK Picture Library**: British Museum, London C, CR, BR; University Museum of Archaeology and Anthropology, Cambridge BCRA.

26 **AKG London / Erich Lessing**: BL; **Bridgeman Art Library, London / New York**: National Archaeological Museum, Athens BL(insert); **E.T. Archive**: National Museum, Copenhagen TRb; **National Museum of the American Indian**: Smithsonian Institute / Collected by MR Harrington / Photograph: David Heald CL.

27 **AKG London**: Archaeological Museum, Heraklion TL; **AKG London/ Erich Lessing**: BCL; **© Michael Holford**: Musée Cernuschi CRA; **DK Picture Library**: British Museum, London TR; **The University of Auckland**: Department of Anthropology / Excavated by Prof. R.C. Green CRb.

28 **Bridgeman Art Library, London / New York**: Musée du Louvre, Paris TL; **DK Picture Library**: British Museum, London CAL; **Friedrich-Schiller-Universität Jena / Hilprecht Collection of Near Eastern Antiquities**: Prof. Dr. Manfred Krebernik CbL; **Turkish Information Office, London**: BLA.

29 **© Michael Holford**: BRA; Ashmolean Museum, Oxford BR; **The Institute of Archaeology, Beijing**: Professor Zheng Zhen Xiang CRA.

30 **Werner Forman Archive**: Anthropology Museum, Veragruz University, Jalapa TR; **Robert Harding Picture Library**: BCL; **South American Pictures**: Kathy Jarvis CL.

31 **Bridgeman Art Library, London / New York**: Royal Albert Memorial Museum, Exeter BCL; **DK Picture Library**: British Museum, London TCL; **E.T. Archive**: British Museum, London CRA; Historical Museum of Armenia, Erevn TCRb; **Robert Harding Picture Library**: CRb.

32 **Bridgeman Art Library, London / New York**: Musée du Louvre, Paris / Photograph: Peter Willi CLL; **DK Picture Library**: British Library, London C; British Museum, London TL, TCR, BL, BCL; **© Michael Holford:** British Museum, London CL; Musée du Louvre, Paris CR.

33 **Bridgeman Art Library, London / New York**: Ashmolean Museum, Oxford CR(Athenian coin); British Museum, London TL, TCR; **DK Picture Library**: Ashmolean Museum, Oxford CRb; British Museum, London CL, C, CR(counting stick); **Robert Harding Picture Library**: Adam Woolfitt CbR; **© Michael Holford**: British Museum, London CR(Heracles); **Ch. Thioc, Musée de la Civilisation Gallo-Romaine, Lyon**: CLb.

34 **British Museum, London**: CL; **E.T. Archive**: TCR; **N.J. Saunders**: CLb.

35 **DK Picture Library**: Ashmolean Museum, Oxford CRb; British Museum, London TLb, CRA; **© Michael Holford:** British Museum, London TCLb; **Robert Harding Picture Library**: BCL; ACI TR.

36 **AKG London / Erich Lessing**: Iraq Museum, Baghdad TL; **Ancient Art & Architecture Collection**: Brian Wilson TCR; **Werner Forman Archive**: BL.

37 **AKG London**: BR; The Israel Museum, Jerusalem CRA; **AKG London / Erich Lessing**: National Museum of Archaeology, Naples CLA; **DK Picture Library**: British Museum, London CbR; **E.T. Archive**: Olympia Museum, Greece TC; **Werner Forman Archive**: Musées Royaux du Cinquantenaire, Brussels CbL.

38 **E.T. Archive**: British Museum, London CL; **Werner Forman Archive**: David Bernstein Collection, New York BL; **© Michael Holford:** British Museum, London BCR; **Tony Stone Images**: Robert Everts TCR.

39 **E.T. Archive**: TL; The Hermitage, Leningrad CRA; National Archaeological Museum, Naples TR; **The Art Archive** CRb.

40 **E.T. Archive**: National Archaeological Museum, Naples CL; **Robert Harding Picture Library**: Archaeological Museum, Istanbul / Photograph: Christina Gascoigne TL; R Ashworth TCR; **Scala, Florence**: Museo Capitolini, Rome BL.

41 **British Museum, London**: CRb; **Robert Harding Picture Library**: CRA; **Réunion des Musées Nationaux Agence Photographique**: Musée des Arts Asiatique-Guimet, Paris C; **Scala, Florence**: Museo di Villa Giulia, Rome TCR; Museo Gregoriano Egizio, Vatican TCb.

42 **Axiom**: Guy Marks TC; **Bridgeman Art Library, London / New York**: British Museum, London BRA; **E.T. Archive**: Archaeological Museum, Lima CL; **Scala, Florence**: Museo della Civilta' Romana, Rome BCL.

43 **Axiom**: James Morris CR; **Robert Harding Picture Library**: TCRb; Richard Ashworth CRb; **Novosti (London)**: TCL.

44 **Bridgeman Art Library, London / New York**: British Museum, London TR; **CM Dixon**: CLb; **E.T. Archive**: Archaeological Museum of Merida CL; **Robert Harding Picture Library**: TL, CA.

45 **Ancient Art & Architecture Collection**: B Crip TR; J Powell: CRA; **Chris Scarre**: BC.

46 **Ancient Art & Architecture Collection**: Ronald Sheridan BL; **Bridgeman Art Library, London / New York**: British Museum, London CL; Fitzwilliam Museum, University of Cambridge TC.

47 **Bruce Coleman Ltd**: Fred Bruemmer TL; **Robert Harding Picture Library**: TC; **© Michael Holford:** British Museum, London BCL; Museo Prenestino CR; **Réunion des Musées Nationaux Agence Photographique**: Musée des Arts Asiatiques-Guimet, Paris / Photograph: Richard Lambert BR.

48 **Bridgeman Art Library, London / New York**: British Museum, London TCb; Galleria e Museo Estense, Modena CRb; National Museum of India, New Delhi BCA; **British Museum, London**: TL.

49 **CM Dixon**: Victoria & Albert Museum, London BR; **Werner Forman Archive**: TCR.

50 **AKG London / Erich Lessing**: Musée Lapidaire, Arles TC; **Werner Forman Archive**: Private Collection, New York CLb; **© Michael Holford:** British Museum, London CRb.

51 **DK Picture Library**: British Museum, London TR; **Werner Forman Archive**: CRb; **Sonia Halliday Photographs**: CR; **Robert Harding Picture Library**: CbL; Chinese Exhibition TCL.

52 **Ancient Art & Architecture Collection**: Ronald Sheridan TL; **Bridgeman Art Library, London / New York**: Private Collection TC; **© Michael Holford**: British Museum, London BR.

53 **AKG London / Erich Lessing**: National Museum, Budapest CRb; **Ancient Art & Architecture Collection**: Ronald Sheridan TC; **E.T. Archive**: Archaeological Museum, Madrid BL.

54 **Bridgeman Art Library, London / New York**: San Vitale, Ravenna TC; **Werner Forman Archive**: National Museum of Anthropology, Mexico BR; **© Michael Holford:** Museum of Mankind, London CbL.

55 **Werner Forman Archive**: Idemitsu Museum of Arts, Tokyo CRA; **Robert Harding Picture Library**: Bildagentur Schuster / Krauskopf TL; **Bridgeman Art Library, London / New York:** British Museum, London BR; **Leiden University Library, The Netherlands**: (Or. 3101) TCR.

56 **Ancient Art & Architecture Collection**: Ronald Sheridan TL; **Bridgeman Art Library, London / New York**: British Library, London (Or.6810 f.27v) CL; **Werner Forman Archive**: TC.

57 **AKG London**: Bibliothèque Nationale de France, Paris (Arabe 5847, fol.84) TL; **Robert Harding Picture Library**: BC; D Kraus TCL.

58 **DK Picture Library**: British Museum, London CRb; **Robert Harding Picture Library**: Gavin Hellier TC; **Tony Stone Images**: Robert Frerck CLb.

59 **Bodleian Library**: (Ms. Marsh 144 P.167) CR; **Bridgeman Art Library, London / New York**: British Library, London TL; **British Library, London**: TC; **DK Picture Library**: British Museum, London CLb; **E.T. Archive**: British Museum, London CRb.

60 **Bridgeman Art Library, London / New York**: Science Museum, London C; **Coo-ee Historical Picture Library**: BL; **Werner Forman Archive**: State Historiska Museum, Stockholm TL; **© Trustees of the National Museums of Scotland**: TCR.

61 **AKG London**: Bibliothèque Nationale, Paris (Arabe 5847, fol.119) BL.

62 **Axiom**: Chris Bradley CRb; **Bodleian Library**: Pocoche (Ms. fol. 3v-4r) CL; **Werner Forman Archive**: Maxwell Museum of Anthropology, Albuquerque, New Mexico BL; **Robert Harding Picture Library**: TC.

63 **Bridgeman Art Library, London / New York**: Bibliothèque Nationale de France, Paris (Fr 2630 f.111v) TC; **E.T. Archive**: National Palace Museum, Taiwan CR; **Robert Harding Picture Library**: CRb; **Hulton Getty:** (Ms. Bodleian 264) TL.

64 **Bridgeman Art Library, London / New York**: Château Roux, France TR; British Library, London (Roy 2A XX11 f.220) TL, (Add 42130 f.82) BC.

65 **E.T. Archive**: Bibliothèque Nationale de France, Paris TLb; **Robert Harding Picture Library**: C.

66 **DK Picture Library**: British Library, London BL; Museum of Mankind, London CL; **Robert Harding Picture Library**: Bodleian Library, Oxford TCR.

67 **Bridgeman Art Library, London / New York**: Bibliothèque Nationale de France, Paris CR; **DK Picture Library**: National Maritime Museum, London TR; **Robert Harding Picture Library**: BR; I Van Der Harst BCL; **© Michael Holford:** British Museum, London TL.

68 **Bridgeman Art Library, London / New York**: National Palace Museum, Taipei TL; Private Collection TR; **DK Picture Library**: British Library, London CL.

69 **Bridgeman Art Library, London / New York**: British Museum, London CR; Victoria & Albert Museum, London BR; **Werner Forman Archive**: Formerly Gulistan Imperial Library, Teheran CLA.

70 **Bridgeman Art Library, London / New York**: British Museum, London BL; **Werner Forman Archive**: University Library, Prague TC.

71 **Bridgeman Art Library, London / New York**: British Museum, London BL; **British Library, London**: (Harl.4379, fol.83v) TL; **Robert Harding Picture Library**: TR; MPH CR; Adam Woolfitt BR.

72 **Bridgeman Art Library, London / New York**: British Library, London (Harl 4380, f.22) BC; **Jean-Loup Charmet**: Musée d'Histoire de la Médecine, Lyon CLA; **DK Picture Library**: National Maritime Museum, London TL; **Scala, Florence**: State Archive, Lucca BL; **Science Photo Library**: John Burbridge BL(insert).

73 **Collections**: Liz Stares CA; **Katz Pictures**: The Mansell Collection / Time Inc. BLA; **Scala, Florence**: Galleria Sabauda, Torino TR.

74 **AKG London**: BC; **E.T. Archive**: TR; **Tony Stone Images**: Jerry Alexander CLb.

75 **AKG London**: TC; Pinacoteca Vaticana, Rome TL; **Ancient Art & Architecture Collection**: Ronald Sheridan BLA; **E.T. Archive**: CRb; **Sonia Halliday Photographs**: CAR.

76 **E.T. Archive**: Bibliothèque Nationale de France, Paris TL

77 **Bridgeman Art Library, London / New York**: Bibliothèque Nationale d France, Paris (Fr 2810 f.188) BCL; **E.T. Archive**: University Library, Istanbul BL; **Library of Congress, Washington, D.C.**: (GA 1124 1555 F.8 G&M RR Plate 43) BCR.

78 **Bridgeman Art Library, London / New York**: Kunsthistorisches Museum, Vienna TCR; **DK Picture Library**: BCL; **© Michael Holford:** British Museum, London BCR; **Peter Newark's Pictures**: CL.

79 **Bridgeman Art Library, London / New York**: Bibliothèque Nationale de France, Paris (Fr 2810, f.84) CRb; **DK Picture Library**: British Library, London TRb; **Sonia Halliday Photographs**: Topkapi Palace Museum, Istanbul TL.

80 **AKG London**: BL; **Bridgeman Art Library, London / New York**: British Library, London (Sloane 197 f.18) TL; **Werner Forman Archive**: Art Institute, Chicago BR.

81 **Bridgeman Art Library, London / New York**: Prado, Madrid / Index BC; **British Library, London**: C; Institut Amatller D'Art Hispànic, Barcelona: CR.

82 **Bridgeman Art Library, London / New York**: Château de Versailles, France / Giraudon TC; **Peter Newark's Pictures**: CLb.

83 **E.T. Archive**: Musée Guimet Paris TC; **Robert Harding Picture Library**: BCL; M Robertson CRb; **© Michael Holford:** Science Museum, London TCLb; **Royal Geographical Society Picture Library**: CR.

84 **Bridgeman Art Library, London / New York**: British Library, London BC; **DK Picture Library**: TL; **E.T. Archive:** National Maritime Museum, London CAR.

85 **AKG London**: CR; **DK Picture Library**: BL; **E.T. Archive**: Bibliothèque Nationale de France, Paris TCR; **Mary Evans Picture Library:** Cb; **Peter Newark's Pictures:** TL.

86 **DK Picture Library**: National Maritime Museum, London BCL; **Peter Newark's Pictures:** TC, CL.

87 **Bridgeman Art Library, London / New York**: Victoria & Albert Museum, London CRb; **British Library, London:** TC; **Werner Forman Archive:** British Museum, London BC; **National Maritime Museum, London:** TL.

88 **Bridgeman Art Library, London / New York:** Private Collection CA; **Hulton Getty**: TL; **Peter Newark's Pictures:** CR.

89 **The Granger Collection, New York:** TCR; **Hulton Getty:** BR; **Peter Newark's Pictures:** BL.

90 **Bridgeman Art Library, London / New York:** Private Collection CLb; **Image Select:** Ann Ronan TC; **Public Record Office Picture Library:** BCL; **Peter Newark's Pictures:** CL.

91 **Bridgeman Art Library, London / New York:** National Maritime Museum, London TL; Alexander Turnbull Library, National Library of New Zealand, Te Puna Mātauranga o Aotearoa CR; The Stapleton Collection BC; **DK Picture Library:** TCR.

92 **Mary Evans Picture Library:** TCR, CL; **Hulton Getty:** TL; **Library of Congress, Washington, D.C.:** C.

93 **Corbis:** Bettmann CA, CRA; **Mary Evans Picture Library:** CLb.

94 **Bridgeman Art Library, London / New York:** Historisches Museum der Stadt, Vienna TC; **Public Record Office Picture Library:** BC; **William L. Clements Library, University of Michigan** CL.

95 **AKG London:** BC; **British Library, London:** (Shelfmark No. 2443) TC; **Werner Forman Archive:** CD Wertheim Collection TL; **Peter Newark's Pictures:** CR.

96 **Jean-Loup Charmet:** CLb; **Mary Evans Picture Library:** TL, TCR, TR; **Hulton Getty:** BRA.

97 **Corbis:** BL; **Mary Evans Picture Library:** TCRb, TRb.

98 **Advertising Archives:** CL; **E.T. Archive:** BC; **Frank Spooner Pictures:** Roger Viollet TCR.

99 **AKG London:** TC; **Jean-Loup Charmet:** BC; **Corbis:** Bettmann / Underwood TL; **National Motor Museum, Beaulieu:** CR.

100 **Corbis:** Bettmann BCL; **DK Picture Library:** National Maritime Museum, London TL; **Mary Evans Picture Library:** CLA, BL.

101 **Corbis:** Bettmann CAL; **Peter Newark's Pictures:** CRb.

102 **Corbis:** Burs Can TCR; Hulton-Deutsch Collection BR; **Hulton Getty:** Keystone / Oscar Kersenbaum BC; **London Transport Museum:** CL.

103 **Hulton Getty:** TL, TR, BC.

104 **Rex Features:** TL.

105 - **Corbis:** UPI / Bettmann BL; **Topham Picturepoint:** C; Associated Press TLb.

106 **Robert Harding Picture Library:** David Lomax BC; **Hulton Getty:** TCR; **Tony Stone Images:** Earth Imaging CL.

107 **DK Picture Library:** TC, CR; **Hulton Getty:** TL; **Frank Spooner Pictures:** Cilo BC.

108 **Corbis:** Bettmann / UPI TL; **Hulton Getty:** BL; **Topham Picturepoint:** CA.

109 **Rex Features:** TC; Sipa-Press BL; **Topham Picturepoint:** A Young-Joon C.

110 **Robert Harding Picture Library:** R. Hanbury-Tenison BC; **Rex Features:** Sipa-Press TR; **Science Photo Library:** CNES, 1986 Distribution Spot Image CLA.

111 **Corbis:** Philippe Wojazer / Reuter BC; **Rex Features:** Setboun / Sipa-Press TL; **Corbis:** Jagadeesh Nv / Reuters TCb; **Tony Stone Images:** Robert Mort CR.

112 **Rex Features:** TL; Alexandra Boulat BR; **Frank Spooner Pictures:** Gamma / Tom Kidd CLB; **Still Pictures:** Jorgen Shytte CLA.

113 **Corbis:** Reuters TC; **Panos Pictures:** Chris Stowers CbR; **Rex Features:** Sipa Press BR.

114/115 **© 1996 Visual Language**.

117 **Robert Harding Picture Library:** Robert Frerck / Odyssey / Chicago BC; **Tony Stone Images:** Tom Bean Cb; Jake Rajas CRb.

118 **Bibliothèque Nationale de France, Paris:** BC; **Bridgeman Art Library, London / New York:** British Library, London BR; **Robert Harding Picture Library:** New York Historical Society TL; **Musée de L'Homme, Paris:** D Ponsard TCR.

119 **DK Picture Library:** C, BL, CRb; **Robert Harding Picture Library:** TCb; **Peter Newark's Pictures:** TLb.

120 **DK Picture Library:** CL; **E.T. Archive:** BL; **Werner Forman Archive:** Field Museum of Natural History, Chicago TL; **Robert Harding Picture Library:** Robert Frerck / Odyssey / Chicago TCR.

121 **Werner Forman Archive:** British Museum, London TC; Ohio State Museum BR.

122 **Bridgeman Art Library, London / New York:** British Museum, London TL; **James Davis Travel Photography:** Cb; **E.T. Archive:** CLb; **Robert Harding Picture Library:** Robert Frerck / Odyssey / Chicago BR; **© Michael Holford:** CAR; **Hutchison Library:** Edward Parker TCR.

123 **DK Picture Library:** Museum of Mankind, London TL; **Werner Forman Archive:** Arizona State Museum C; Museum of the American Indian, Heye Foundation, New York CR.

124 **Ancient Art & Architecture Collection:** Ronald Sheridan TR; **E.T. Archive:** Antochiw Collection Cb; National Library, Mexico TL; **Werner Forman Archive:** British Museum, London CA.

125 **Ancient Art & Architecture Collection:** G Tortoli TL; **Robert Harding Picture Library:** Mexican Museum of Natural History BR; **Peter Newark's Pictures:** CRA.

126 **E.T. Archive:** TC; **Peter Newark's Pictures:** TL, CR.

127 **Bridgeman Art Library, London / New York:** Trinity College, Cambridge BR; **Peter Newark's Pictures:** CLA, BC.

128 **Bridgeman Art Library, London / New York:** City of Bristol Museum and Art Gallery TL; **Corbis:** Bettmann TCR; **Peter Newark's Pictures:** BCL.

129 **Bridgeman Art Library, London / New York:** Photograph: D.F. Barry, Dakota TRb; **Mary Evans Picture Library:** BR; **Robert Harding Picture Library:** National Gallery of Art, Washington CR.

130 **Corbis:** Bettmann TR, C; **Mary Evans Picture Library:** TL.

131 **Corbis:** Bettmann BL; **Peter Newark's Pictures:** CRb; Alexander Gardener TC.

132 **Bridgeman Art Library, London / New York:** Liberty Island, New York TL; **Corbis:** Bettmann / UPI TCR; **Peter Newark's Pictures:** TRb, BR.

133 **AKG London:** Photograph: Agust n Victor Casasola, (1874-1938) TLb; **Peter Newark's Pictures:** CL.

134 **Corbis:** CAL, Cb, BL; Bettmann TL, **Hulton Getty:** TCR.

135 **Corbis:** TR; **Mary Evans Picture Library:** CRb; **Ronald Grant Archive:** CA, © Disney CRA; **Peter Newark's Pictures:** CbL.

136 **Corbis:** Grant Smith TCR; **Robert Harding Picture Library:** D Lomax BR; **Peter Newark's Pictures:** CRb; **Frank Spooner Pictures:** Hulton Getty Liaison TL.

137 **Corbis:** CLA; UPI TC, BL; **Redferns**: Elliot Landy CRb.

138 **Corbis:** Bettmann / UPI CL; Najlah Feanny C; **Rex Features:** JFK Library TL.

139 **Corbis:** Bettmann / UPI TCR; Reuters CR; Sygma TCRb; **Rex Features:** Sipa-Press C.

140 **Robert Harding Picture Library:** Christopher Rennie CLb; **N.H.P.A.:** M Wendler Cb; **South American Pictures:** Tony Morrison BC.

142 **E.T. Archive:** Biblioteca Estense, Modena CL; **Mary Evans Picture Library:** TL; **Robert Harding Picture Library:** Cartes et Plans, Bibliothèque Nationale de France, Paris TC.

143 **Bridgeman Art Library, London / New York:** Royal Geographical Society, London BCR; **DK Picture Library:** BR; **Robert Harding Picture Library:** National Gallery, East Berlin CbR; **Royal Geographical Society Picture Library:** TLb.

144 **Bridgeman Art Library, London / New York:** British Museum, London BR; **E.T. Archive:** University Museum, Cuzco BL; **Robert Harding Picture Library:** Robert Frerck / Odyssey / Chicago TRb; **South American Pictures:** Tony Morrison TL.

145 **Ancient Art & Architecture Collection:** Mike Andrews BR; **Bridgeman Art Library, London / New York:** British Museum, London BC; **Werner Forman Archive:** David Bernstein Fine Art, New York CL.

146 **Bridgeman Art Library, London / New York:** British Museum, London BR; **Dumbarton Oaks Research Library and Collections, Washington, D.C.:** BC; **© Michael Holford:** Collection of Señor Mujica Gallo, Lima TL, BL; **South American Pictures:** Kimball Morrison CbL.

147 **Ancient Art & Architecture Collection:** Museo Oro del Peru, Lima / Photograph: R Sheridan CbR; **E.T. Archive:** Museo del Oro, Bogota CL; **Werner Forman Archive:** Museum fur Volkerkunde, Berlin BCA; **Robert Harding Picture Library:** BLA; **South American Pictures:** Tony Morrison TC.

148 **Jean-Loup Charmet:** TR; **E.T. Archive:** Archbishop Palace Museum Cuzco TL; **Mary Evans Picture Library:** BL; **Robert Harding Picture Library:** British Museum, London Cb; **South American Pictures:** CL.

149 **Bridgeman Art Library, London / New York:** Harold Samuel Collection, Corporation of London BC; **Jean-Loup Charmet:** Bibliothèque des Arts Decoratifs CL; **E.T. Archive:** BL; **Royal Geographical Society Picture Library:** CLA.

150 **AKG London:** TL, CL; **DK Picture Library:** TCR.

151 **Bridgeman Art Library, London / New York:** British Library, London CL; **DK Picture Library:** BRA; **Mary Evans Picture Library:** CR.

152 **Rex Features:** Sipa-Press / Arias TL; **Sygma:** A Balaguer TC; **Topham Picturepoint:** CR.

153 **Panos Pictures:** Michael Harvey Cb; **Rex Features:** Sipa-Press CRb; Sipa-Press / Poveda TR.

154 **Bruce Coleman Ltd:** Christer Fredriksson CLb; **Tony Stone Images:** Hugh Sitton CRb; **World Pictures:** BC.

156 **DK Picture Library:** TL; **E.T. Archive:** British Library, London BR; **Katz Pictures:** The Mansell Collection / Time Inc. CL.

157 **AKG London:** TR; **Bridgeman Art Library, London / New York:** Royal Geographical Society, London CbL; **Royal Geographical Society Picture Library:** TC, BL; **Topham Picturepoint:** BR.

158 **AKG London / Erich Lessing:** Egyptian Museum, Berlin, SMPK TL; **Robert Estall Photo Library:** David Coulson CRA; **Dr David Price Williams:** TCR.

159 **Axiom:** James Morris CR; **Robert Harding Picture Library:** Gavin Hellier CLb.

160 **Werner Forman Archive:** Courtesy Entwistle Gallery, London TL; **Sonia Halliday Photographs:** James Wellard CAR; **Dr David Price Williams:** CAL.

161 **AKG London / Jean-Louis Nou:** TR; **Ancient Art & Architecture Collection:** Ronald Sheridan TC; **Werner Forman Archive:** Cb.

162 **Ashmolean Museum, Oxford:** Hebreden Coin Room TL; **Werner Forman Archive:** TC; Tanzania National Museum, Dar Es Salaam TCb; **© Michael Holford:** British Museum, London TRB.

163 **Musée de L'Homme, Paris:** BCL.

164 **Bridgeman Art Library, London / New York:** British Library, London (Sloane 197 f.225v-6) TCb; **British Library, London:** TL, BC; **DK Picture Library:** CL.

165 **Axiom:** Chris Bradley TR; **Jean-Loup Charmet:** Bibliothèque de L'Arsenal, Paris BLA.

166 **Mary Evans Picture Library:** TL, CL, CRb; **Sonia Halliday Photographs:** Africana Library, Durban / Photograph: Jane Taylor BC.

167 **Chester Beatty Library, Dublin:** (Ms 1599 fols 1v-2r) TCb; **Corbis:** Bettmann BR.

168 **Corbis:** Bettmann CAL; UPI Photo TL.

169 **PA News Photo Library**: EPA Photo / Lusa / Joao Relvas CL; **Panos Pictures:** Betty Press BR.

171 **The J. Allan Cash Photolibrary:** BCR; **Bruce Coleman Ltd**: Dr Eckart Pott Cb; **World Pictures:** CRb.

172 **AKG London:** Postmuseum, Berlin BR; **DK Picture Library:** Danish National Museum CLb(Insert); Statens Historika Museum, Stockholm CLb; **© Michael Holford:** Science Museum, London TL.

173 **Bridgeman Art Library, London / New York:** British Library, London C; Hereford Cathedral TC; **British Library, London:** BL, BC; **DK Picture Library:** National Maritime Museum, London TR; **E.T. Archive:** Musée Carnavalet CR; **Ordnance Survey © Crown Copyright:** BR; **Royal Geographical Society Picture Library:** CLb.

174 **DK Picture Library:** CL; British Museum, London TC, CRb; **© Michael Holford:** British Museum, London TL; **Images Colour Library:** The Charles Walker Collection BR.

175 **Bridgeman Art Library, London / New York:** Archaeological Museum, Iraklion / Lauros-Giraudon BCL; **DK Picture Library:** Museum of London CR; **E.T. Archive:** Historical Museum, Sofia TC.

176 **Ancient Art & Architecture Collection:** Mike Andrews CLb; Dr S Coyne BC; **Bridgeman Art Library, London / New York:** British Museum, London TCR; **© Michael Holford:** British Museum, London TL.

177 **Ancient Art & Architecture Collection:** Ronald Sheridan BL; **DK Picture Library:** British Museum, London C; **Scala, Florence:** National Archaeological Museum, Madrid TL.

178 **Robert Harding Picture Library:** Robert Frerck / Odyssey / Chicago BC; **© Michael Holford:** British Museum, London TL; **Scala, Florence:** Musei Capitolini, Roma TC; Museo di Villa Giulia, Roma Cb.

179 **E.T. Archive:** CLA(Insert); **Robert Harding Picture Library:** Gascoigne BL; **© Michael Holford:** CbR; British Museum CLA.

180 **Werner Forman Archive:** TL; **Sonia Halliday Photographs:** BL; **© Michael Holford:** TCRb.

181 **Ancient Art & Architecture Collection:** Ronald Sheridan BR; **DK Picture Library:** TL; **Sonia Halliday Photographs:** The Hatay Museum, Antioch, Turkey BL; **© Michael Holford:** TC, CRb.

182 **Ancient Art & Architecture Collection:** Ronald Sheridan CbR; **DK Picture Library:** British Museum, London TL; **E.T. Archive:** San Apollinare Nuovo, Ravenna CLA; **Sonia Halliday Photographs:** TR.

183 **Bibliothèque Nationale de France, Paris:** BC; **E.T. Archive:** Medieval Museum, Rome TC; **© Michael Holford:** British Museum, London TLb.

184 **AKG London / Erich Lessing:** Musée du Louvre, Paris TL; **Bridgeman Art Library, London / New York:** Musée Goya, Castres (PF 2826, f.106r) / Photograph: Giraudon C; **E.T. Archive:** Palatine Chapel, Aachen CL.

185 **Ancient Art & Architecture Collection:** Ronald Sheridan BL; **Bridgeman Art Library, London / New York:** Musée Condé, Chantilly (PE 7887, Ms. 14) TLb; **© Michael Holford:** Statens Historiska Museum, Stockholm TC.

186 **AKG London:** Biblioteca Apostolica Vaticana, Rome TL; **E.T. Archive:** Templar Chapel, Cressac CL; **© Michael Holford:** Musée de Bayeaux C.

187 **Bridgeman Art Library, London / New York:** Private Collection BLA; **E.T. Archive:** Bibliothèque de L'Arsenal, Paris CbR; **Robert Harding Picture Library:** TRb.

188 **AKG London:** San Benedetto Monastery, Subiaco (Sacro Speco) TCRb; **Ancient Art & Architecture Collection:** Ronald Sheridan TL; **Bridgeman Art Library, London / New York:** British Library, London CL.

189 **AKG London:** CRb; **Robert Harding Picture Library:** K Gillham TC.

190 **Archiv der Hansestadt Lübeck:** TL; **Bridgeman Art Library, London / New York:** Bibliothèque Nationale de France, Paris (Fr 12420 f.71) BL.

191 **AKG London / Cameraphoto:** CRb; **E.T. Archive:** Bibliothèque Nationale de France, Paris TCRb; **Scala, Florence:** Museo Correr, Venezia TCLb; Santa Francesco, Prato TC.

192 **Bridgeman Art Library, London / New York:** Archives Nationales, Paris / Giraudon TL; Bibliothèque Nationale de France, Paris (Fr 2643 f.165v) TCb; **Robert Harding Picture Library:** Simon Harris BR.

193 **AKG London:** Burgerbibliothek, Bern (Mss hist.helv I, 1, fol.70) BL; **DK Picture Library:** Wallace Collection, London CL; **E.T. Archive:** TLb; National Gallery of Art, Budapest BR.

194 **AKG London:** National Museum, Stockholm TL; **Bridgeman Art Library, London / New York:** Musée de Sibiu, Rumania / Giraudon CLb; **E.T. Archive:** Capodimonte, Naples C.

195 **Bridgeman Art Library, London / New York:** British Library, London (Add 33733 f.9) C; Nationalmuseet, Copenhagen TL; **Mary Evans Picture Library:** CR.

196 **AKG London:** CL; Musée du Louvre, Paris TL; **Bridgeman Art Library, London / New York:** Private Collection BCR; **DK Picture Library:** BRA.

197 **AKG London:** Historische Museum der Stadt Wien, Vienna TR; Musée des Beaux-Arts, Arras BL; **Mary Evans Picture Library:** BCL; **Scala, Florence:** Museo Statale Russo, Leningrad C.

198 **Bridgeman Art Library, London / New York:** Private Collection / Giraudon BRA; The Stapleton Collection BR; Tretyakov Gallery, Moscow TL; By kind permission of the **Earl of Leicester and the Trustees of the Holkham Estate:** CLA.

199 **Bildarchiv Preußischer Kulturbesitz:** Kunstbibliothek Preußischer Kulturbesitz, Berlin CR; **Bridgeman Art Library, London / New York:** Musée Carnavalet, Paris BL.

200 **Bridgeman Art Library, London / New York:** Bibliothèque Nationale de France, Paris / Lauros-Giraudon TL; Musée du Louvre, Paris / Giraudon CLA; **Mary Evans Picture Library:** CLb.

201 **Bridgeman Art Library, London / New York:** Musée du Louvre, Paris / Giraudon TCR; **E.T. Archive:** Musée de Versailles CRb; **Mary Evans Picture Library:** BL.

202 **AKG London:** TR; Slg. E. Werner, Berlin TL.

203 **AKG London:** TCLb; **E.T. Archive:** Palazzo Pubblico, Siena BL; **Mary Evans Picture Library:** TLb, C.

204 **AKG London:** TCR; **Corbis:** Bettmann CLA; **DK Picture Library:** TL; **E.T. Archive:** BR.

205 **AKG London:** BL, BR; **DK Picture Library:** The Science Museum, London TR.

206 By kind permission of **The Trustees of The Imperial War Museum, London:** CLA, CR, CRb; **Topham Picturepoint:** TL.

207 **Corbis:** Bettmann TCb; **Hulton Getty:** CL; **Topham Picturepoint:** BR.

208 **Corbis:** Bettmann BR; **Hulton Getty:** CL; **Rex Features:** Sipa-Press TL.

209 **Hulton Getty:** CRA; **Topham Picturepoint:** CLb, BC.

210 **Bridgeman Art Library, London / New York:** The Stapleton Collection TL; **Corbis:** CLA; **Robert Hunt Library:** BC.

211 **Corbis:** UPI / Bettmann CLb; **Rex Features:** BL.

212 **AKG London**: TL; **Corbis:** Jerry Cooke CLb; **Hulton Getty:** Keystone Munich CLA.

213 **Corbis:** Bettmann BLA; **David King Collection:** TRb; **Topham Picturepoint:** CR.

214 **Corbis:** Jean-Marc Loos/Reuters CA; **Panos Pictures:** Jeremy Hartley Cb; **Rex Features:** TL; Darryn Lyons BL.

215 **Rex Features:** Sipa-Press / Alexandra Boulat CLA.

216 **James Davis Travel Photography:** CLb; **Robert Harding Picture Library:** CRb, BC.

218 **Bibliothèque Nationale de France, Paris:** (Ms Arabe 5847.f.19) BL; **Bridgeman Art Library, London / New York:** Bibliothèque Nationale de Cartes et Plans, Paris TL; **British Library, London:** (Maps 856.(6.)) BR.

219 **Bridgeman Art Library, London / New York:** Bibliothèque Nationale de France, Paris TR; **E.T. Archive:** Naval Museum, Genoa TCb; Richmond Borough Council BC; **Koninklijke Bibliotheek, The Hague:** (76 F 5: fol. 1r) CR; **Royal Geographical Society Picture Library:** CRb, BL.

220 **Bridgeman Art Library, London / New York:** Ashmolean Museum, Oxford TCRb; British Museum, London C; Reconstruction by **Mrs James Mellaant:** CL; **Scala, Florence:** The Iraq Museum, Baghdad TL.

221 **Caroline Chapman:** TRb; **Robert Harding Picture Library:** CRb; **© Michael Holford:** British Museum, London CLb.

222 **AKG London / Erich Lessing:** British Museum, London BR; Musée du Louvre, Paris TCR; **Caroline Chapman:** CL; **Topham Picturepoint:** TL.

223 **British Museum, London:** TCb; **Robert Harding Picture Library:** CL, CR; **© Michael Holford:** British Museum, London TRb.

224 **Bridgeman Art Library, London / New York:** British Museum, London TCR; Private Collection / Ancient Art and Architecture Collection Ltd BL; **© Michael Holford:** British Museum, London TL.

225 **Ancient Art & Architecture Collection:** Ronald Sheridan CR; **Bibliothèque Nationale de France, Paris:** BR; **DK Picture Library:** British Museum, London CLb; **Werner Forman Archive:** Coptic Museum, Cairo TCb.

226 **Ancient Art & Architecture Collection:** Ronald Sheridan TC; **Bridgeman Art Library, London / New York:** Institute of Oriental Studies, St Petersburg (Ms.E-4/322a) / Giraudon CL; **British Library, London:** (Add 27261 f.363) CbL; **DK Picture Library:** British Museum, London TL.

227 **Bildarchiv Preußischer Kulturbesitz:** C; **Werner Forman Archive:** BR; **Robert Harding Picture Library:** Ellen Rooney BL.

228 **E.T. Archive:** Forrester / Wilkinson TL; Victoria & Albert Museum, London BC; **Robert Harding Picture Library:** TCR; **Peter Newark's Pictures:** BL.

229 **AKG London:** Bibliothèque Nationale de France, Paris (Add. 18866, fol.140) CLA; **Bildarchiv Preußischer Kulturbesitz:** Staatsbibliothek zu Berlin Preußischer Kulturbesitz Orientabteilung (Ms. Diez A.Fol.70) C; **Robert Harding Picture Library:** CLb.

230 **Bridgeman Art Library, London / New York:** Victoria & Albert Museum, London BR; **Sonia Halliday Photographs:** Topkapi Palace Museum, Istanbul (Ms. 3109) TL, (Ms. H1523 p.165A) CL.

231 **Werner Forman Archive:** CLb; **Sonia Halliday Photographs:** TL; Topkapi Palace Museum, Istanbul (Ms. H.1523 p.19A) C.

232 **AKG London:** TL; **Bridgeman Art Library, London / New York:** Château de Compiegne, Oise / Lauros-Giraudon BC; **Jean-Loup Charmet:** TCR; By kind permission of **The Trustees of The Imperial War Museum, London:** BR.

233 **Corbis:** Bettmann / UPI TR; **Hulton Getty:** BLA, BCL; **Royal Geographical Society Picture Library:** Capt. W.I. Shakespear CR.

234 **Rex Features:** Keystone USA BC; Sipa-Press TL; **Reuters:** Ali Jasim C.

235 **Corbis:** Reuters CR; **Rex Features:** Sipa C, CRB; **Frank Spooner Pictures:** Eslami Rad TLB.

Frank Spooner Pictures: Eslami Rad TRb; **Rex Features:** Sipa-Press C, BR; **Reuters:** CR.

236 **Eye Ubiquitous:** David Cumming BC; **Robert Harding Picture Library:** Thomas Laird Cb; **Tony Stone Images:** Hugh Sitton CLb.

238 **British Library, London:** CRA, BR; (Egerton 1018 fol.335) BL; **E.T. Archive:** British Library, London TCR; **Robert Harding Picture Library:** C; © Free Gallery of Art Washington BC; **The History of Cartography, University of Wisconsin:** Bharat Kala Bhavan, Varanasi TL; **Professor Joseph E. Schwartzberg:** CLb.

239 **British Library, London:** TRb; (Sloane 197, fol.395v-396) CA; **DK Picture Library:** CR, BRA; **Robert Harding Picture Library:** Jim Thompson Collection CRA; **Royal Geographical Society Picture Library:** CbL, BL, BC.

240 **British Museum, London:** BR; **Robert Harding Picture Library:** CLb; HRH Princess Chumbhot Collection BRA; Karachi Museum, Pakistan TL, TC; **Scala, Florence:** New Delhi Museum, India Cb.

241 **Bridgeman Art Library, London / New York:** Oriental Museum, Durham University CL; **Robert Harding Picture Library:** BR; Adam Woolfitt TCR.

242 **DK Picture Library:** Ashmolean Museum, Oxford BL; **Robert Harding Picture Library:** TL; Adam Woolfitt CbR; **© Michael Holford:** Musée Guimet, Paris CAL.

243 **British Library, London:** CbL; **Werner Forman Archive:** Private Collection TRb; **Robert Harding Picture Library:** BR; Gavin Hellier CR.

244 **Robert Harding Picture Library:** TL; Nigel Cameron CL; A Kennet TC, C; Adam Woolfitt BC; **Hutchison Library:** Christine Pemberton BCR.

245 **Robert Harding Picture Library:** TR, CA; Bangkok National Museum, Thailand BCL; Rolf Richardson BC.

246 **Ancient Art & Architecture Collection:** Chebel Sotun Palace, Isfahan / Photograph: Ronald Sheridan BCL; **Bridgeman Art Library, London / New York:** Metropolitan Museum of Art, New York TL; Private Collection / The Stapleton Collection CLb; **Robert Harding Picture Library:** TCR; Gavin Hellier CLA.

247 **Bridgeman Art Library, London / New York:** Private Collection / The Stapleton Collection CR, CLb; **British Library, London:** TR, BR.

248 **Bridgeman Art Library, London / New York:** Victoria & Albert Museum, London BC; **DK Picture Library:** British Library, London TCRb; **E.T. Archive:** India Office Library BR; Zoological Society of London TL.

249 **Bridgeman Art Library, London / New York:** British Library, London TLb, (As10 Vol.52 ff.3 4896.cat.201 i-iv) CR; **Mary Evans Picture Library:** BR.

250 **Corbis:** UPI BC; **Robert Harding Picture Library:** Alain Evrard TL; **Hulton Getty:** CLA.

251 **Hulton Getty:** CL; **Rex Features:** Tim Page TCR; **Topham Picturepoint:** CRA.

252 **Hulton Getty:** BC; Bert Hardy TL; **Frank Spooner Pictures:** Gamma CL.

253 **Robert Harding Picture Library:** J Bright BL; **Pictor International:** BCL; **Frank Spooner Pictures:** Olivier Duffau / Gamma TR; Gamma CRA; Xinhua-Chine / Gamma TC.

254 **Robert Harding Picture Library:** Cb, BC; Nigel Blythe CLb.

256 **British Library, London:** TL, CR, BR; **Werner Forman Archive:** Archaeological Museum, Teheran CRb; **Ninnaji Temple, Kyoto:** TRb.

257 **Fotomas Index:** CR; **Réunion des Musées Nationaux Agence Photographique:** Musée des Arts Asiatiques-Guimet, Paris / Photograph: Arnaudet CLb; **Royal Geographical Society Picture Library:** Compiled by T.G. Montgomerie from the work of Nain Singh BL.

258 **Corbis:** Royal Ontario Museum TL; **Werner Forman Archive:** Art and History Museum, Shanghai BL; **Robert Harding Picture Library:** Gavin Hellier TCR.

259 **Bridgeman Art Library, London / New York:** Tomb of Qin Shi Huang Di, Xianyang, China BL; **DK Picture Library:** British Museum, London C; **E.T. Archive:** British Museum, London TR.

260 **Bridgeman Art Library, London / New York:** Private Collection BR; **DK Picture Library:** British Museum, London TL; **E.T. Archive:** British Museum, London TC.

261 **Bridgeman Art Library, London / New York:** Bonhams, London CR; **Werner Forman Archive:** TCR; **The Art Archive:** Musée Cernuschi Paris C.

262 **Ancient Art & Architecture Collection:** Ronald Sheridan TL; **Werner Forman Archive:** Christian Deydier, London BCL; **Collection of the National Palace Museum, Taiwan, Republic of China:** BL.

263 **Ancient Art & Architecture Collection:** Kadokawa TLb; Ronald Sheridan CAR, BCR; **Fotomas Index:** BRA.

264 **DK Picture Library:** National Museum of Scotland, Edinburgh TL; **E.T. Archive:** National Museum of Tokyo CL; **Robert Harding Picture Library:** Nigel Blythe BR.

265 **AKG London:** National Museum of Tokyo BL; **Ancient Art & Architecture Collection:** Ronald Sheridan TR; **E.T. Archive:** Forrester / Wilkinson CRb.

266 **Robert Harding Picture Library:** Michael J Howell TC; **Collection of the National Palace Museum, Taiwan, Republic of China:** TL; **Philadelphia Museum of Art, Pennsylvania:** Given by John T. Dorrance CR.

267 **Bridgeman Art Library, London / New York:** National Museum of India, New Delhi CLA; Private Collection CRb; **DK Picture Library:** National Maritime Museum, London CA; **Robert Harding Picture Library:** Gavin Hellier BL.

268 **Christie's Images:** TL; **E.T. Archive:** School of Oriental and African Studies, London Cb; **Peter Newark's Pictures:** TC.

269 **Bridgeman Art Library, London / New York:** Taylor Gallery, London BR; **Topham Picturepoint:** CLA.

270 **AKG London:** TL; **Bridgeman Art Library, London / New York:** British Museum, London CL; **E.T. Archive:** Postal Museum, Frankfurt Cb; **© Michael Holford:** Print by Kokyo BC.

271 **David King Collection:** CLb; **Smithsonian Institute:** Freer Gallery of Art / Arthur M Sackler Gallery Archive / Photograph: Hsun-Ling TC.

272 **Robert Hunt Library:** TL; **Rex Features:** Sipa-Press CL; **Topham Picturepoint:** Associated Press Photos TCR.

273 **Robert Hunt Library:** BR; **Topham Picturepoint:** TR.

274 **Corbis:** Bettmann / UPI BR; **E.T. Archive:** TC; **David King Collection:** CL; **Tony Stone Images:** TL.

275 **Rex Features:** Sipa-Press / Photograph: East News BL; Sipa-Press / Photograph: Ben Simmons CbR; **Frank Spooner Pictures:** Gamma / Photograph: Xinhua TR.

276 **Bruce Coleman Ltd:** Nicholas de Vore BC; **Robert Harding Picture Library:** Nick Servian CLb; **Planet Earth Pictures:** Frank Krahmer Cb.

278 **Bridgeman Art Library, London / New York:** Mitchell Library, State Library of New South Wales BR; **DK Picture Library:** Museum of Mankind, London TR; **E.T. Archive:** National Library, Canberra, Australia TL; **Maritiem Museum 'Prins Hendrik', Rotterdam, The Netherlands:** BCR.

279 **British Library, London:** CRA; **Coo-ee Historical Picture Library:** CLb, BL; **Mary Evans Picture Library:** TL.

280 **Bridgeman Art Library, London / New York:** British Museum, London TL; **Robert Harding Picture Library:** Richard Ashworth C; Robert Francis TR; David Holdsworth BL.

281 **© Michael Holford:** British Museum, London TC; Royal Geographical Society, London CR; **Peter Crawford:** TRb; **Robert Harding Picture Library:** Geoff Renner BRA.

282 **Coo-ee Historical Picture Library:** TL; **Corbis:** Gleason's Pictorial Drawing-Room Companion BC; **State Library of New South Wales:** TRb.

283 **Panos Pictures:** Penny Tweedie TL; **Tony Stone Images:** Paul Chesley CRb; **Topham Picturepoint:** CL.

284 **Bridgeman Art Library, London / New York:** National Library of Australia, Canberra BL; **Hulton Getty:** TCRb; **Tony Stone Images:** Warren Bolster TL.

285 **Hutchison Library:** CR; **Science Photo Library:** US Department of Energy TRb.

286 **Corbis:** Bettmann TL; **E.T. Archive:** BR; British Museum, London CbR.

287 **Corbis:** Underwood & Underwood CR; **Mary Evans Picture Library:** TR, BL; **Hulton Getty:** TCR;

Endpapers **© 1996 Visual Language**.

All other images © Dorling Kindersley.

For further information see **www.dkimages.com**

Dorling Kindersley Photography:

David Ashby, Geoff Brighting, Tina Chambers, Andy Crawford, Geoff Dann, Mike Dunning, Lynton Gardiner, Steve Gorton, Peter Hayman, Chas Howson, Ivor Kerslake, Dave King, Andrew McRobb, Gillie Newman, Nick Nicholls, Laurence Pordes, James Stevenson, Linda Whitwam, Peter Wilson, John Woodcock.

Dorling Kindersley would like to thank:

Alice Whitehead at Bridgeman Art Library, Ute Krebs at AKG London, Caroline Haywood and all staff at E.T. Archive, Themis Halvantzi at Werner Forman Archive, Michael Holford, all at Robert Harding Picture Library and Mark Vivian at Mary Evans Picture Library for all their assistance with picture research.

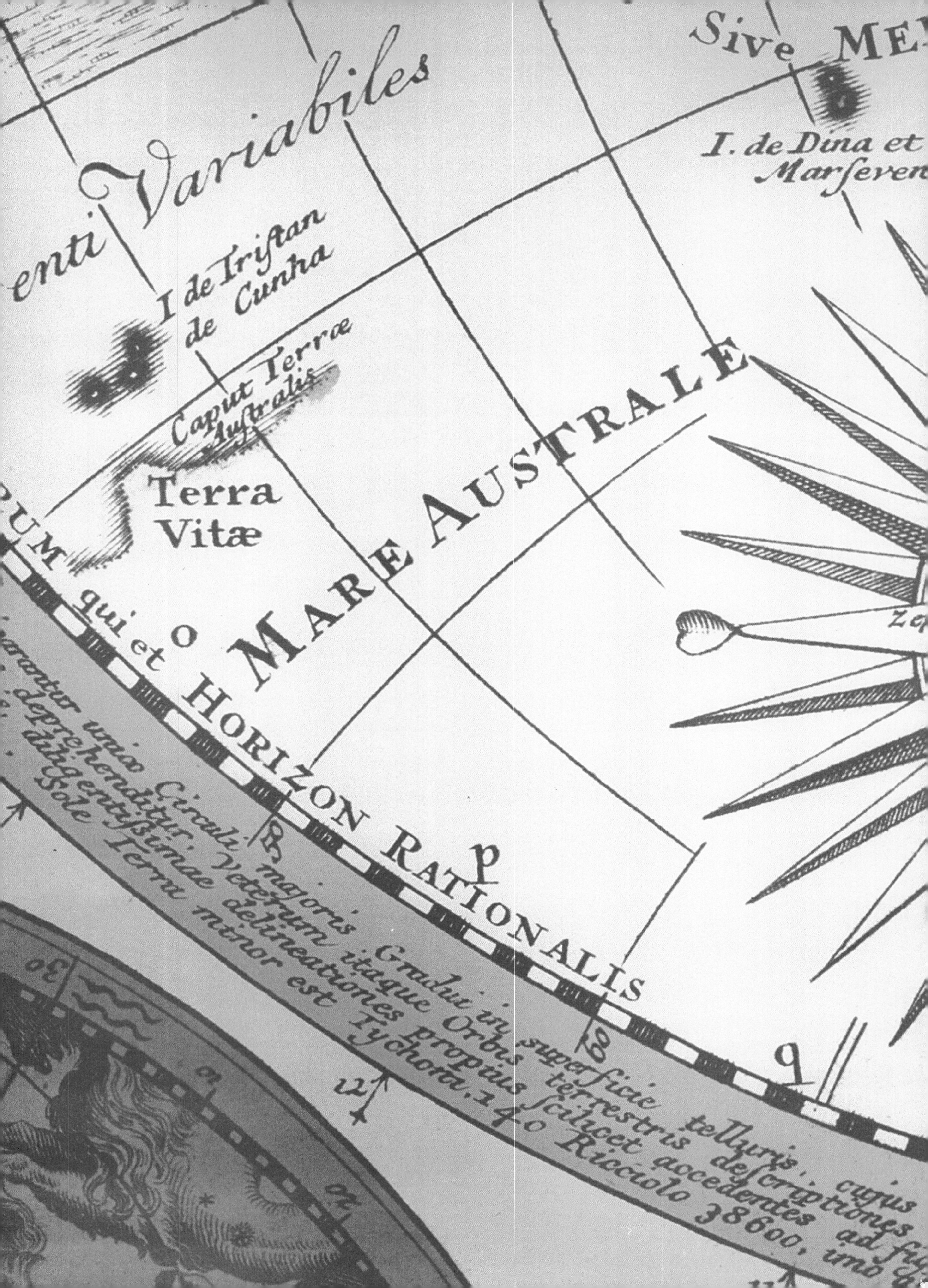

Sive ME

enti Variabiles

I. de Dina et
Marseven

I de Tristan
de Cunha

Caput Terræ
Australis

Terra
Vitæ

MARE AUSTRALE

RUM qui et HORIZON RATIONALIS

o

p

q

parantur unius Circuli majoris Gradui in superficie telluris, cujus
deprehenditur. Veterum itaque Orbis terrestris descriptiones
diligentissimae delineationes propius scilicet accedentes ad fig
Sole Terra minor est Tychoni, 140 Ricciolo 38600, imo